T0295899

Occupational Outlook Handbook

2022–2032 Edition

U.S. Department of Labor
Julie Su, Acting Secretary of Labor

U.S. Bureau of Labor Statistics
William J. Wiatrowski, Acting Commissioner

Suggested citation: Bureau of Labor Statistics, U.S. Department of Labor, *Occupational Outlook Handbook*, 2022–2032 Edition.

Published by Bernan Press
An imprint of The Rowman & Littlefield Publishing Group, Inc.
4501 Forbes Boulevard, Suite 200, Lanham, Maryland 20706
www.rowman.com

86-90 Paul Street, London, EC2A 4NE

ISBN 978-1-63671-429-5 (hardback)
ISBN 978-1-63671-430-1 (paperback)

∞™ The paper used in this publication meets the minimum requirements of American National Standard for Information Sciences—Permanence of Paper for Printed Library Materials, ANSI/NISO Z39.48-1992.

Acknowledgments

The U.S. Bureau of Labor Statistics (BLS) produces the *Occupational Outlook Handbook* (*OOH*) under the general guidance and direction of Kirk Mueller, Assistant Commissioner for Occupational Statistics and Employment Projections, and Michael Wolf, Division Chief of Employment Projections. Kathleen Green, Branch Chief of Outreach and Publications, and Francisco Velez, Jr., Branch Chief of Projections Research and Analysis, provided planning and day-to-day direction.

Staff responsible for research and preparation of material in the *OOH* included Domingo Angeles, Javier Colato, Nicholas Dezarn, Ryan Farrell, Lindsey Ice, Stanislava Ilic-Godfrey, William Lawhorn, Christine Machovec, Sarah Mattson, Michael J. Rieley, Dustin Riles, Victoria Roderick, Emily Rolen, Patricia Tate, and Elka Torpey.

Other projections data produced for the *OOH* were provided by Satya Datla, Kevin Dubina, Daniel Elmore, Nicholas Hale, Maria Hussain, Youyang Li, Nicholas Orsini, and Samuel Rinde under the direction of Kathryn Laurence, Branch Chief of Macro and Input-Output. Data-processing and technical support were provided by Cal Hockemeyer, Janie-Lynn Kim, Alan Lacey, Curtisjames Miller, Eraj Mohiuddin, and William O'Brien under the supervision of Andrew O'Bar, Branch Chief of Employment Systems and Processing. Project management support was provided by Amy Hopson, Meredith Miller, and An Nguyen under the supervision of Emily Krutsch, Branch Chief of Special Projects.

Editorial support was provided by staff in the Office of Publications: Richard Hernandez, Lisa Huynh, Harry Nitzberg, John C. Roach, and Jonathan Yoe under the supervision of Maureen Soyars Hicks, Branch Chief of Special Publications, and Karen Ransom, Division Chief of Publishing Services. Technical and computer-programming support was provided by the Office of Technology and Survey Processing: Aju Cherian, Robbin Galloway, Janiece Johnson, Jerie Refugia, Roopa Sengupta, Connie Sielaff, Sabrina Washington, and Cindy Zhao under the supervision of Thao Do, Branch Chief, and Jo-Ann Yu, Division Chief of Enterprise Web Systems.

Most of the photographs used in the *OOH* are stock photographs; however, BLS wishes to express its appreciation to the organizations that contributed photographs. Situations portrayed in the photographs may not be free of every possible safety or health hazard. The depiction of a company or trade name in no way constitutes endorsement by the U.S. Department of Labor.

Contents

Special Features

Occupational Coverage

Installation, Maintenance, and Repair

Legal

Life, Physical, and Social Science

Management

Projections Data

Fastest Growing Occupations, 2022–2032

(Twenty occupations with the highest percent change of employment between 2022–2032.)

Occupation	Growth Rate, 2022–2032	2022 Median Pay
Wind turbine service technicians	45%	$57,320
Nurse practitioners	45%	$121,610
Data scientists	35%	$103,500
Statisticians	32%	$98,920
Information security analysts	32%	$112,000
Medical and health services managers	28%	$104,830
Epidemiologists	27%	$78,520
Physician assistants	27%	$126,010
Physical therapist assistants	26%	$62,770
Software developers	26%	$127,260
Occupational therapy assistants	24%	$64,250
Actuaries	23%	$113,990
Computer and information research scientists	23%	$136,620
Operations research analysts	23%	$85,720
Solar photovoltaic installers	22%	$45,230
Home health and personal care aides	22%	$30,180
Taxi drivers	21%	$30,670
Personal care and service workers, all other	21%	$34,670
Veterinary technologists and technicians	21%	$38,240
Veterinary assistants and laboratory animal caretakers	20%	$34,740

Number of New Jobs, Projected, 2022–2032

(Twenty occupations with the highest projected numeric change in employment.)

Occupation	Number of New Jobs (Projected), 2022–2032	2022 Median Pay
Home health and personal care aides	804,600	$30,180
Software developers	410,400	$127,260
Cooks, restaurant	277,600	$34,110
Stockers and order fillers	178,600	$34,220
Registered nurses	177,400	$81,220
Laborers and freight, stock, and material movers, hand	158,800	$36,110
General and operations managers	147,300	$98,100
Medical and health services managers	144,700	$104,830
Light truck drivers	133,800	$40,410
Financial managers	126,600	$139,790
Nurse practitioners	118,600	$121,610
Market research analysts and marketing specialists	116,600	$68,230
Medical assistants	105,900	$38,270
Management analysts	95,700	$95,290
Heavy and tractor-trailer truck drivers	89,300	$49,920
Computer and information systems managers	86,000	$164,070
Substance abuse, behavioral disorder, and mental health counselors	71,500	$49,710
Accountants and auditors	67,400	$78,000
Lawyers	62,400	$135,740
Construction laborers	61,900	$40,750

Highest Paying Occupations, 2022

(Twenty occupations with the highest median annual pay.)

Occupation	2022 Median Pay
Oral and maxillofacial surgeons	This wage is equal to or greater than $239,200 per year
Surgeons, all other	This wage is equal to or greater than $239,200 per year
Pediatric surgeons	This wage is equal to or greater than $239,200 per year
Orthopedic surgeons, except pediatric	This wage is equal to or greater than $239,200 per year
Radiologists	This wage is equal to or greater than $239,200 per year
Physicians, pathologists	This wage is equal to or greater than $239,200 per year
Obstetricians and gynecologists	This wage is equal to or greater than $239,200 per year
Emergency medicine physicians	This wage is equal to or greater than $239,200 per year
Dermatologists	This wage is equal to or greater than $239,200 per year

Occupation	2022 Median Pay
Cardiologists	This wage is equal to or greater than $239,200 per year
Anesthesiologists	This wage is equal to or greater than $239,200 per year
Psychiatrists	$226,880 per year
Neurologists	$224,260 per year
Physicians, all other	$223,410 per year
Ophthalmologists, except pediatric	$219,810 per year
General internal medicine physicians	$214,460 per year
Dentists, all other specialists	$212,740 per year
Airline pilots, copilots, and flight engineers	$211,790 per year
Family medicine physicians	$211,300 per year
Nurse anesthetists	$203,090 per year

Occupational Information Included in the *OOH*

The *Occupational Outlook Handbook* (*OOH*) is a career resource offering information on the hundreds of occupations that provide the majority of jobs in the United States. Each occupational profile describes the typical duties performed by the occupation, the work environment of that occupation, the typical education and training needed to enter the occupation, the median pay for workers in the occupation, and the job outlook over the coming decade for that occupation. Each profile is in a standard format that makes it easy to compare occupations, such as by projected employment change.

Sections of Occupational Profiles

- Summary
- What They Do
- Work Environment
- How to Become One
- Pay
- Job Outlook
- More Information

Summary

All profiles have a "Quick Facts" table that gives information on the following topics:

Median Pay: The wage at which half of the workers in the occupation earned more than that amount and half earned less. Median wage data are from the Bureau of Labor Statistics (BLS) Occupational Employment Statistics (OES) survey.

Typical Entry-Level Education: The level of education that most workers need to enter an occupation.

Work Experience in a Related Occupation: The skills and know-how that a worker receives in another occupation which is usually considered necessary by employers or is a commonly accepted substitute for more formal types of training or education.

On-the-job Training: Postemployment training necessary to attain competency in the skills needed in the occupation. The training is occupation specific rather than job specific; the skills learned can be transferred to another job in the same occupation.

Number of Jobs: The employment, or size, of the occupation in the base year of the employment projections.

Job Outlook: The projected percent change in employment over the projections decade.

Employment Change: The projected numeric change in employment over the projections decade.

The summary section briefly describes all of the sections included in each occupational profile.

What They Do

This section describes the main work of people in the occupation.

All occupations have a list of duties or typical tasks performed by these workers. The list includes daily responsibilities, such as answering phone calls or taking a patient's medical history.

This section also may describe the equipment, tools, software, or other items that people in the occupation typically use. For example, medical records and health information technicians frequently use electronic health records to document a patient's medical information. The section also may describe those with whom workers in the occupation interact, such as clients, patients, and coworkers.

Some profiles discuss specialties, alternate job titles, or types of occupations within a given occupation. This subsection includes a brief explanation of each specialty's job duties and how specialties differ from one another. For example, the profile on dentists includes several specialties, such as orthodontists, oral and maxillofacial surgeons, and pediatric dentists.

Work Environment

Jobseekers and career planners should learn an occupation's working conditions, including the typical workplace, the expected level of physical activity, and typical working hours.

The section typically begins by noting the employment size of the occupation in the base year and includes a table of the industries which employed the most workers in the occupation that year. The section also notes whether employees sometimes need to travel, and if so, how frequently. The section describes the workplace and discusses whether employees work in a safe work environment (such as an office) or a potentially hazardous one (such as a commercial fishing boat). If the workplace is hazardous, the section typically lists the type of equipment an employee must wear, such as a hardhat or protective goggles, to guard against accidents or exposure to harmful conditions. A subsection on Injuries and Illnesses may appear if this information is notable.

Work Schedules

Information on the typical schedule for workers in an occupation is included in this section, noting whether the majority of workers are employed full time or part time. Full-time workers typically work 35 or more hours in a week, whereas part-time employees work less than 35 hours. For some occupations, the profile also may include the time of day an employee is expected to begin work and for how long. Registered nurses, for example, may work all hours of the day and on weekends because medical facilities are open 24 hours. A discussion of work schedules for occupations in which work may be seasonal, such as agricultural workers, also is in this section.

How to Become One

Knowing how to prepare to enter an occupation gives jobseekers and students an idea of how to become a doctor, flight attendant, or wind turbine technician, for example. All profiles have subsections on education and important qualities of workers in the occupation. Optional subsections include information on work experience; training; other experience, such as volunteering or internships; licenses, certifications, and registrations; and advancement.

Education

This subsection describes the education that most workers typically need to enter an occupation. Some occupations require no formal education, whereas others may require, for example, a doctoral or professional degree. In some occupations, such as computer support specialists, workers can enter with different educational backgrounds. In these cases, the profile discusses all of the typical paths for entry into the occupation.

This subsection also may include information on the college majors and subjects that people usually study in preparation for the occupation, as well as a list of typical courses that may aid a high school student in preparing for an occupation. For example, high school students interested in applying to respiratory therapy programs should take courses in health, biology, math, chemistry, and physics.

Work Experience in a Related Occupation

This subsection describes whether employers require work experience in a related occupation. Many managerial occupations rely on work experience in a related occupation. For example, architectural and engineering managers typically have previous work experience as an architect or engineer.

Training

This subsection describes the typical on-the-job training necessary to attain competency in an occupation, including both practical and classroom training that workers receive after being hired. For example, firefighters must complete training at a fire academy or at an institution with a similar program before they are considered prepared to combat fires.

Apprenticeships, internships, and residency programs also are discussed in this subsection. For example, the profile on physicians and surgeons includes information on residency programs and the profile for brickmasons, blockmasons, and stonemasons has information on the apprenticeships that they typically complete as part of a training program.

Other Experience

Other types of experience may be helpful or essential in getting a job in the occupation, such as experience gained through volunteering or student internships completed while one is in school. Students and jobseekers may find this section helpful as it may provide additional content for their résumés.

Licenses, Certifications, and Registrations

This subsection describes whether credentials such as licenses, certifications, and registrations typically are needed for an occupation and, if so, how workers can earn the credentials.

States issue licenses to workers to signify that they have met specific legal requirements to practice in certain occupations. To become licensed, workers usually need to pass an exam and comply with eligibility requirements, such as possessing a minimum level of education, work experience, or training; or completing an internship, a residency, or an apprenticeship. States have their own regulatory boards that set standards for practicing a licensed occupation, so rules and eligibility criteria, including recertification requirements, may vary by state, even for the same occupation.

Some occupations have certifications available that typically are voluntary. For example, fitness trainers and instructors may obtain certification on their own before entering the occupation. Certification requires demonstrated competency in a skill or a set of skills and commonly requires passing an exam or having a certain amount and type of work experience or training. For some certification programs, the candidate must have a certain level of education before becoming eligible for certification.

This subsection explains any prerequisites for certification, licensure, or registration, as well as how a person would complete them—such as by passing an exam, performing a certain type of work, or receiving certain training or education. If states require workers to be certified before they can be licensed, this section also notes that information.

Certification should not be confused with certificates from an educational institution. A certificate awarded by a postsecondary educational institution is a postsecondary nondegree award and is discussed in the subsection on education.

Registrations typically are required and issued by state or local governments. Workers seeking registration may need to be licensed or certified. In most cases, workers must pay fees to receive or maintain their registration.

Important Qualities

What does it take to be an engineer or teacher? This subsection describes important characteristics of workers in the occupation and includes an explanation of why those characteristics are useful.

The qualities may include skills, aptitudes, and personal characteristics. For example, an emergency medical technician (EMT) must be physically fit, and a web developer needs creativity and customer-service skills.

Advancement

This subsection explains the requirements for advancement, such as certification or additional formal education.

Opportunities for advancement can come from within the occupation, such as a promotion to a supervisory or managerial level; from advancement into another occupation, such as moving from a computer support specialist to a network and computer systems administrator; or by becoming self-employed, such as a dentist opening up his or her own practice.

Pay

Almost all occupational profiles in the *OOH* show median wage data for wage and salary workers in the occupation. The median wage is the wage at which half of the workers in an occupation earned more and half earned less. The data are from the Bureau of Labor Statistics (BLS) Occupational Employment Statistics (OES) program. A chart that compares the median wage of workers in the occupation to the median wage of workers across all occupations accompanies the wage data.

Profiles typically include median wages and the wages earned by the top 10 percent and bottom 10 percent of workers in the occupation. Profiles also may include wages earned by workers in selected industries—those in which most of an occupation's workers are employed. The wage data by industry also are from the OES survey.

Some occupational profiles may cite wage data from sources other than the BLS. For example, the Medical Group Management Association provides wage data for physicians and surgeons. Unless otherwise noted, the source of pay data for occupations in the *OOH* is the OES survey.

The Pay section provides work schedule information, also found in the Work Environment section. When noteworthy, the section may include information about union membership.

Job Outlook

Is employment projected to grow or decline over the projections decade? This section has a chart that compares the rate of growth or decline for the occupation(s) covered in the profile to the rate for all occupations. The section also discusses the major factors expected to affect the outlook for employment in the occupation. Some of the factors are changes in technology, in business practices, and in demographics.

The outlook section sometimes includes a Job Prospects subsection, which provides a qualitative discussion of the relative ease or difficulty experienced by those who seek to enter the occupation.

More Information

This section includes external links to associations, organizations, and other institutions that provide readers with additional information.

Architecture and Engineering

Aerospace Engineering and Operations Technologists and Technicians

Summary

Quick Facts: Aerospace Engineering and Operations Technologists and Technicians	
2022 Median Pay	$74,410 per year $35.78 per hour
Typical Entry-Level Education	Associate's degree
Work Experience in a Related Occupation	None
On-the-job Training	None
Number of Jobs, 2022	10,200
Job Outlook, 2022-32	8% (Faster than average)
Employment Change, 2022-32	800

What Aerospace Engineering and Operations Technologists and Technicians Do

Aerospace engineering and operations technologists and technicians run and maintain equipment used to develop, test, produce, and sustain aircraft and spacecraft.

Work Environment

Aerospace engineering and operations technologists and technicians usually work in manufacturing plants, laboratories, and offices. Most work full time.

How to Become an Aerospace Engineering and Operations Technologist or Technician

Aerospace engineering and operations technologists and technicians typically need an associate's degree in engineering technology or a related field. Some employers consider candidates who have a high school diploma or have completed a certificate program.

Pay

The median annual wage for aerospace engineering and operations technologists and technicians was $74,410 in May 2022.

Job Outlook

Employment of aerospace engineering and operations technologists and technicians is projected to grow 8 percent from 2022 to 2032, faster than the average for all occupations.

About 1,000 openings for aerospace engineering and operations technologists and technicians are projected each year, on average, over the decade. Many of those openings are expected to result from the need to replace workers who transfer to different occupations or exit the labor force, such as to retire.

Aerospace engineering and operations technicians operate and calibrate computer systems so that they comply with test requirements.

What Aerospace Engineering and Operations Technologists and Technicians Do

Aerospace engineering and operations technologists and technicians install, run, and maintain equipment used to develop,

Aerospace engineering and operations technologists and technicians work to make sure that testing goes smoothly.

test, produce, and sustain aircraft and spacecraft. Their work is critical to ensuring the safety and precision of key parts of these vehicles and systems.

Duties

Aerospace engineering and operations technologists and technicians typically do the following:

- Meet with aerospace engineers to discuss details and implications of test procedures
- Build and maintain test facilities for aircraft systems
- Make and install parts and systems to be tested in test equipment
- Operate and calibrate computer systems so that they comply with test and manufacturing requirements
- Make sure that test procedures are performed smoothly and safely
- Record data from test parts and assemblies
- Install instruments in aircraft and spacecraft
- Monitor and ensure quality in producing systems that go into the aircraft

New aircraft designs undergo years of testing before they are put into service. As part of the job, technologists and technicians often calibrate test equipment, such as wind tunnels, and determine the causes of equipment malfunctions. They also may program and run computer simulations that test the new designs.

Work Environment

Aerospace engineering and operations technologists and technicians held about 10,200 jobs in 2022. The largest employers of aerospace engineering and operations technologists and technicians were as follows:

Aerospace product and parts manufacturing	36%
Engineering services	28
Scientific research and development services	8
Computer and electronic product manufacturing	7

Aerospace engineering and operations technologists and technicians who work in manufacturing or industrial plants are frequently involved in assembly.

Work Schedules

Most aerospace engineering and operations technologists and technicians work full time. Depending on the employer or project, they may work in shifts or be required to work overtime.

How to Become an Aerospace Engineering and Operations Technologist or Technician

Aerospace engineering and operations technologists and technicians typically need an associate's degree in engineering technology or a related field. Some employers consider candidates

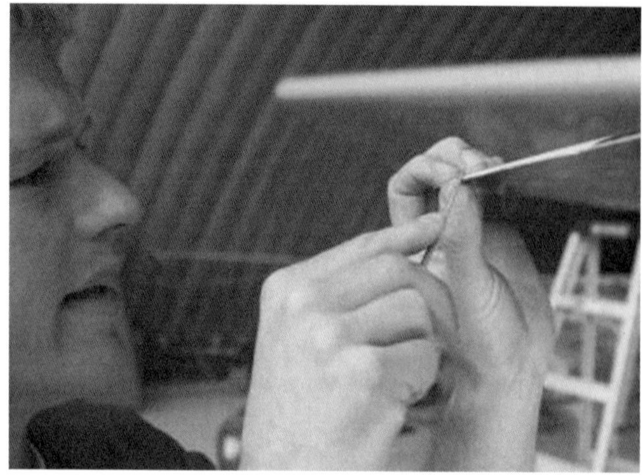

Aerospace engineering and operations technologists and technicians install instruments in aircraft and spacecraft.

who have a high school diploma or have completed a certificate program. Some aerospace engineering and operations technologists and technicians must have security clearances to work on projects related to national defense. U.S. citizenship may be required for certain types and levels of clearance.

Education

High school students interested in becoming an aerospace engineering and operations technologist or technician should take classes in math, science, and, if available, drafting and information technology.

Aerospace engineering and operations technologists and technicians typically need an associate's degree in engineering technology or a related field. Some employers consider candidates who have a high school diploma or have completed a certificate program. Associate's degree and certificate programs are available at community colleges or vocational–technical schools.

Aerospace engineering and operations technologists and technicians work to prevent the failure of key parts of new aircraft, spacecraft, or missiles.

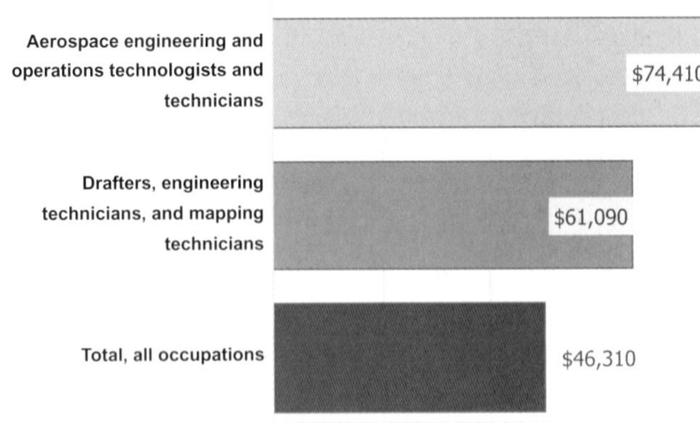

Note: All Occupations includes all occupations in the U.S. Economy.
Source: U.S. Bureau of Labor Statistics, Occupational Employment and Wage Statistics.

Important Qualities

Communication skills. Aerospace engineering and operations technologists and technicians must be able to follow instructions from aerospace engineers. They also need to clearly convey problems to their supervisors.

Detail oriented. Aerospace engineering and operations technologists and technicians take precise measurements needed by aerospace engineers. In addition, they must keep accurate records of these measurements.

Interpersonal skills. Aerospace engineering and operations technologists and technicians must be able to work well with others. They interact with people from other divisions, businesses, and governments.

Math skills. Aerospace engineering and operations technologists and technicians use mathematics for measurement, analysis, design, and troubleshooting tasks.

Mechanical skills. Aerospace engineering and operations technologists and technicians assist aerospace engineers by building what the engineers design. They need technical skills to guide processes from design to production.

Problem-solving skills. Aerospace engineering and operations technologists and technicians help aerospace engineers troubleshoot design issues. They must be able to help evaluate system capabilities, formulate questions, and then find the answers.

Licenses, Certifications, and Registrations

Although not required for the job, SpaceTEC, the National Science Foundation's Center for Aerospace Technical Education, offers the Certified Aerospace Technician Core Certification. Recertification is required every 3 years.

Pay

The median annual wage for aerospace engineering and operations technologists and technicians was $74,410 in May 2022.

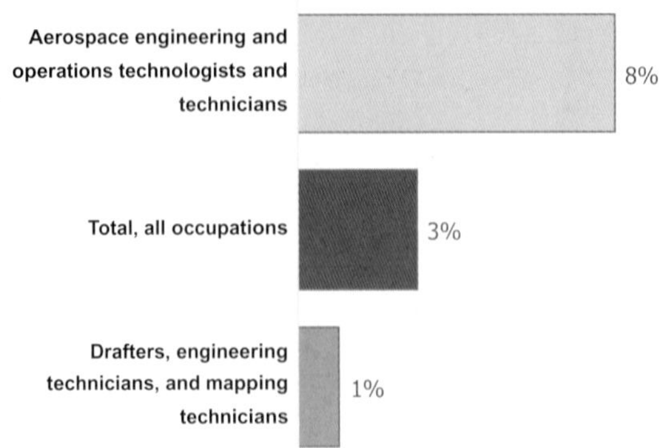

Note: All Occupations includes all occupations in the U.S. Economy.
Source: U.S. Bureau of Labor Statistics, Employment Projections program.

The median wage is the wage at which half the workers in an occupation earned more than that amount and half earned less. The lowest 10 percent earned less than $47,950, and the highest 10 percent earned more than $109,610.

In May 2022, the median annual wages for aerospace engineering and operations technologists and technicians in the top industries in which they worked were as follows:

Computer and electronic product manufacturing	$80,020
Aerospace product and parts manufacturing	78,050
Scientific research and development services	72,980
Engineering services	66,360

Most aerospace engineering and operations technologists and technicians work full time. Depending on the employer or project, they may work in shifts or be required to work overtime.

Job Outlook

Employment of aerospace engineering and operations technologists and technicians is projected to grow 8 percent from 2022 to 2032, faster than the average for all occupations.

About 1,000 openings for aerospace engineering and operations technologists and technicians are projected each year, on average, over the decade. Many of those openings are expected to result from the need to replace workers who transfer to different occupations or exit the labor force, such as to retire.

Employment

Technological advances have reduced the cost of launching satellites. Demand for aerospace engineering and operations technologists and technicians is expected to increase as space becomes more accessible, especially with innovations that make small satellites commercially viable. New developments in types of aircrafts, such as electric hybrids, also are expected to drive an increase in employment. In addition, continued interest in drones is expected to support employment growth for these workers.

Occupational Title	SOC Code	Employment, 2022	Projected Employment, 2032	Change, 2022-32	
				Percent	Numeric
Aerospace engineering and operations technologists and technicians	17-3021	10,200	11,000	8	800

Contacts for More Information

For more information about accredited aeronautics and engineering programs, visit

- ABET

For more information about careers in engineering, visit

- Technology Student Association
- For more information about certification, visit
- SpaceTEC

Aerospace Engineers

Summary

Quick Facts: Aerospace Engineers	
2022 Median Pay	$126,880 per year $61.00 per hour
Typical Entry-Level Education	Bachelor's degree
Work Experience in a Related Occupation	None
On-the-job Training	None
Number of Jobs, 2022	63,800
Job Outlook, 2022-32	6% (Faster than average)
Employment Change, 2022-32	3,900

What Aerospace Engineers Do

Aerospace engineers design, develop, and test aircraft, spacecraft, satellites, and missiles.

Work Environment

Aerospace engineers typically work in an office setting, often using a computer. Most work full time, and some work more than 40 hours per week.

How to Become an Aerospace Engineer

Aerospace engineers must have a bachelor's degree in aerospace engineering or a related field to enter the occupation. Aerospace engineers who work on projects that are related to national defense may need a security clearance.

Pay

The median annual wage for aerospace engineers was $126,880 in May 2022.

Job Outlook

Employment of aerospace engineers is projected to grow 6 percent from 2022 to 2032, faster than the average for all occupations.

About 3,800 openings for aerospace engineers are projected each year, on average, over the decade. Many of those openings are expected to result from the need to replace workers who transfer to different occupations or exit the labor force, such as to retire.

What Aerospace Engineers Do

Aerospace engineers design, develop, and test aircraft, spacecraft, satellites, and missiles. In addition, they create and test prototypes to make sure that they function according to design.

Aerospace engineers design aircraft and propulsion systems, and study the aerodynamic performance of aircraft.

Aerospace engineers evaluate designs to see that the products meet engineering principles.

Duties

Aerospace engineers typically do the following:

- Coordinate and direct the design, manufacture, and testing of aircraft and aerospace products
- Assess project proposals to determine whether they are technically and financially feasible
- Determine whether proposed projects will be safe and meet defined goals
- Evaluate designs to ensure that products meet engineering principles, customer requirements, and environmental regulations
- Develop criteria for design, quality, completion, and sustainment after delivery
- Ensure that projects meet required standards
- Inspect malfunctioning or damaged products to identify sources of problems and possible solutions

Aerospace engineers develop technologies for use in aviation, defense systems, and spacecraft. They may focus on areas such as aerodynamic fluid flow; structural design; guidance, navigation, and control; instrumentation and communication; robotics; or propulsion and combustion.

Aerospace engineers may design specific aerospace products, such as commercial and military airplanes and helicopters; remotely piloted aircraft and rotorcraft; spacecraft, including launch vehicles and satellites; and military missiles and rockets.

The following are the two common types of aerospace engineers:

Aeronautical engineers work with aircraft. They are involved primarily in designing aircraft and propulsion systems and in studying the aerodynamic performance of aircraft and construction materials. They work with the theory, technology, and practice of flight within the Earth's atmosphere.

Astronautical engineers work with the science and technology of spacecraft and how they perform inside and outside the Earth's atmosphere. This includes work on small satellites such as cubesats, and traditional large satellites.

Aerospace engineers evaluate designs to see that the products meet engineering principles.

Work Environment

Aerospace engineers held about 63,800 jobs in 2022. The largest employers of aerospace engineers were as follows:

Aerospace product and parts manufacturing	34%
Engineering services	16
Federal government, excluding postal service	16
Research and development in the physical, engineering, and life sciences	10
Navigational, measuring, electromedical, and control instruments manufacturing	6

Aerospace engineers typically work in an office setting, often using a computer. They also may travel to meet with clients.

Work Schedules

Most aerospace engineers work full time, and some work more than 40 hours per week. Engineers may need to work extra hours to monitor progress and troubleshoot when problems arise.

How to Become an Aerospace Engineer

Aerospace engineers typically need a bachelor's degree in aerospace engineering or a related field to enter the occupation. Aerospace engineers who work on projects that are related to national defense may need a security clearance. Some types and levels of clearance require U.S. citizenship.

Education

Aerospace engineers typically need a bachelor's degree in engineering or a related field. High school students interested in studying aerospace engineering should take classes in chemistry, physics, and math.

Bachelor's degree programs in engineering usually include classroom, laboratory, and field courses in subjects such as stability and control, structures, and mechanics.

College students may have an opportunity to participate in cooperative education programs or internships. Through partnership with local businesses, these programs allow students to gain practical experience while they complete their education.

Some colleges and universities offer a 5-year program that leads to both a bachelor's degree and a master's degree. A graduate degree may allow an engineer to work as an instructor at a university or to do research and development.

Employers may prefer to hire graduates of aerospace engineering programs accredited by a professional association such as ABET. A degree from an accredited program is usually required to become licensed.

Licenses, Certifications, and Registrations

Licensure is not required for entry-level aerospace engineer positions. Experienced engineers may obtain a Professional Engineering (PE) license, which allows them to oversee the

Aerospace engineers use the principles of calculus, trigonometry, and other advanced topics in mathematics for analysis, design, and troubleshooting in their work.

work of other engineers, sign off on projects, and provide services directly to the public.

State licensure generally requires a bachelor's or higher degree from an ABET-accredited engineering program, a passing score on the Fundamentals of Engineering (FE) exam, several years of relevant work experience, and a passing score on the PE exam.

Each state issues its own license. Most states recognize licensure from other states, as long as the licensing state's requirements meet or exceed their own licensure requirements. Several states require continuing education for engineers to keep their licenses.

Advancement

Aerospace engineers who gain experience or who have additional education or credentials may advance into technical or supervisory positions. Those with leadership skills also may become engineering managers or project management specialists.

Important Qualities

Analytical skills. Aerospace engineers must be able to evaluate project design elements and propose improvements, if necessary.

Business skills. Meeting federal standards in aerospace engineering requires business knowledge, including commercial law. Project management or systems engineering skills also may be useful.

Communication skills. Aerospace engineers must be able to explain, both orally and in writing, the details of their designs. They may need to convey information to a variety of audiences, including nontechnical ones.

Interpersonal skills. Aerospace engineers often work on teams and must be able to interact with other types of engineers and with nontechnical team members.

Math skills. Aerospace engineers use calculus, trigonometry, and other math in their analysis, design, and troubleshooting work.

Problem-solving skills. Aerospace engineers upgrade designs and troubleshoot problems to improve aircraft, such as for increased fuel efficiency or safety.

Pay

The median annual wage for aerospace engineers was $126,880 in May 2022. The median wage is the wage at which half the workers in an occupation earned more than that amount and half earned less. The lowest 10 percent earned less than $78,170, and the highest 10 percent earned more than $176,280.

In May 2022, the median annual wages for aerospace engineers in the top industries in which they worked were as follows:

Research and development in the physical, engineering, and life sciences	$141,730
Navigational, measuring, electromedical, and control instruments manufacturing	129,890
Aerospace product and parts manufacturing	128,550
Federal government, excluding postal service	127,150
Engineering services	122,480

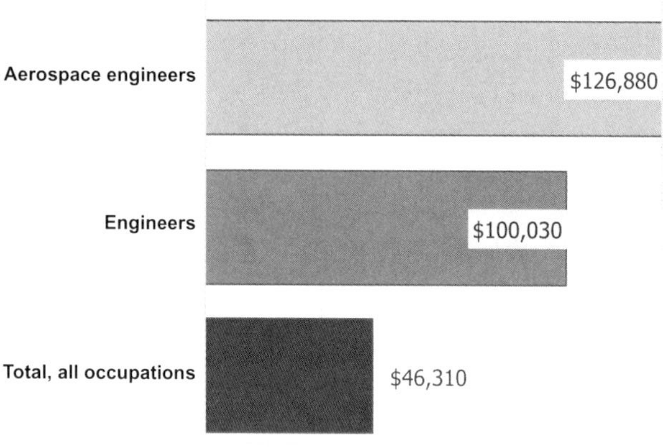

Note: All Occupations includes all occupations in the U.S. Economy.
Source: U.S. Bureau of Labor Statistics, Occupational Employment and Wage Statistics.

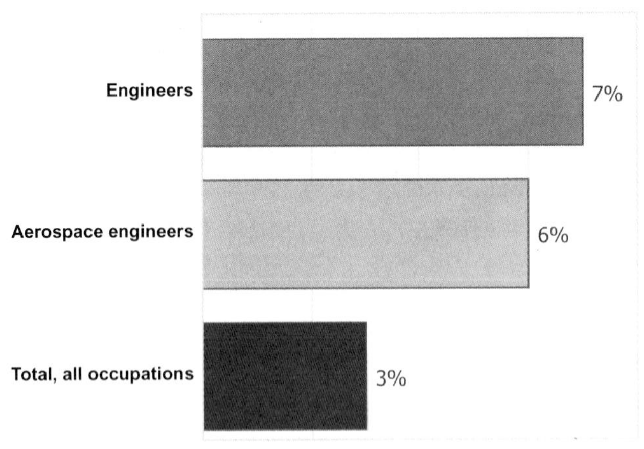

Note: All Occupations includes all occupations in the U.S. Economy.
Source: U.S. Bureau of Labor Statistics, Employment Projections program.

Most aerospace engineers work full time, and some work more than 40 hours per week. Engineers may need to work extra hours to monitor progress and to troubleshoot when problems arise.

Job Outlook

Employment of aerospace engineers is projected to grow 6 percent from 2022 to 2032, faster than the average for all occupations.

About 3,800 openings for aerospace engineers are projected each year, on average, over the decade. Many of those openings are expected to result from the need to replace workers who transfer to different occupations or exit the labor force, such as to retire.

Employment

Aircraft are being redesigned for less noise pollution and better fuel efficiency, which should help drive demand for aerospace engineers.

Technological advancements have reduced the cost of launching satellites. Demand for aerospace engineers is expected to increase as space becomes more accessible, especially with developments in small satellites that have greater commercial viability. In addition, continued interest in drones for certain uses, such as forest fire detection, may help to drive employment growth for these engineers.

Occupational Title	SOC Code	Employment, 2022	Projected Employment, 2032	Change, 2022-32	
				Percent	Numeric
Aerospace engineers	17-2011	63,800	67,700	6	3,900

Contacts for More Information

For more information, visit

- American Society for Engineering Education (ASEE)
- Technology Student Association (TSA)
- National Council of Examiners for Engineering and Surveying (NCEES)
- National Society of Professional Engineers (NSPE)
- ABET
- The American Institute of Aeronautics and Astronautics (AIAA)

Agricultural Engineers

Summary

Quick Facts: Agricultural Engineers	
2022 Median Pay	$83,260 per year $40.03 per hour
Typical Entry-Level Education	Bachelor's degree
Work Experience in a Related Occupation	None
On-the-job Training	None
Number of Jobs, 2022	1,600
Job Outlook, 2022-32	6% (Faster than average)
Employment Change, 2022-32	100

What Agricultural Engineers Do

Agricultural engineers solve problems concerning power supplies, machine efficiency, the use of structures and facilities, pollution and environmental issues, and the storage and processing of agricultural products.

Work Environment

Agricultural engineers work mostly in offices, but may spend time traveling to agricultural settings. Agricultural engineers typically work full time.

How to Become an Agricultural Engineer

Agricultural engineers typically need a bachelor's degree in an engineering field, such as agricultural or biological engineering.

Pay

The median annual wage for agricultural engineers was $83,260 in May 2022.

Job Outlook

Employment of agricultural engineers is projected to grow 6 percent from 2022 to 2032, faster than the average for all occupations.

About 100 openings for agricultural engineers are projected each year, on average, over the decade. Many of those openings are expected to result from the need to replace workers who

Agricultural engineers sometimes travel to farms to oversee the installation of new systems.

transfer to different occupations or exit the labor force, such as to retire.

What Agricultural Engineers Do

Agricultural engineers attempt to solve agricultural problems concerning power supplies, the efficiency of machinery, the use of structures and facilities, pollution and environmental issues, and the storage and processing of agricultural products.

Duties

Agricultural engineers typically do the following:

- Use computer software to design equipment, systems, or structures
- Modify environmental factors that affect animal or crop production, such as airflow in a barn or runoff patterns on a field
- Test equipment to ensure its safety and reliability
- Oversee construction and production operations
- Plan and work together with clients, contractors, consultants, and other engineers to ensure effective and desirable outcomes

Agricultural engineers often have to observe the results of their work where the crops are actually grown.

Agricultural engineers work in farming, including aquaculture (farming of seafood), forestry, and food processing. They work on a wide variety of projects. For example, some agricultural engineers work to develop climate control systems that increase the comfort and productivity of livestock whereas others work to increase the storage capacity and efficiency of refrigeration. Many agricultural engineers attempt to develop better solutions for animal waste disposal. Those with computer programming skills work to integrate artificial intelligence and geospatial systems into agriculture. For example, they work to improve efficiency in fertilizer application or to automate harvesting systems.

Work Environment

Agricultural engineers held about 1,600 jobs in 2022. The largest employers of agricultural engineers were as follows:

Federal government, excluding postal service	25%
Engineering services	14
Manufacturing	12
State government, excluding education and hospitals	11
Colleges, universities, and professional schools; state	5

Agricultural engineers may test the effects that specific growing conditions have on plants, in a laboratory setting.

Agricultural engineers typically work in offices, but may spend time at a variety of worksites, both indoors and outdoors. They may travel to agricultural settings to see that equipment and machinery are functioning according to both the manufacturers' specifications and federal and state regulations. Some agricultural engineers occasionally work in laboratories to test the quality of processing equipment. They may work onsite when they supervise livestock facility upgrades or water resource management projects.

Agricultural engineers work with others in designing solutions to problems or applying technological advances. They work with people from a variety of backgrounds, such as business, agronomy, animal sciences, and public policy.

Injuries and Illnesses

Agricultural engineers have one of the highest rates of injuries and illnesses of all occupations.

Work Schedules

Agricultural engineers typically work full time. Schedules may vary because of weather conditions or other complications. When working on outdoor projects, agricultural engineers may work more hours to take advantage of good weather or fewer hours in case of bad weather.

In addition, agricultural engineers may need to be available outside of normal work hours to address unexpected problems that come up in manufacturing operations or rural construction projects.

How to Become an Agricultural Engineer

Agricultural engineers typically need a bachelor's degree in an engineering field, such as agricultural or biological engineering.

Education

High school students who are interested in studying agricultural engineering should take classes in math and science. College students take courses in calculus, physics, biology, and chemistry. They also may take courses in business, public policy, and economics.

Entry-level jobs in agricultural engineering typically require a bachelor's degree in engineering, including agricultural engineering or biological engineering. College students may gain practical experience through internships or from working on projects for engineering competitions, in which teams of students design equipment and attempt to solve real problems.

Employers may prefer to hire candidates who have graduated from programs accredited by a professional association, such as ABET.

Important Qualities

Analytical skills. Agricultural engineers must analyze the needs of complex systems that involve workers, crops, animals, machinery and equipment, and the environment.

Bachelor's degree programs in biological and agricultural engineering typically include significant hands-on components in areas such as science.

Communication skills. Agricultural engineers must understand the needs of clients, workers, and others working on a project. Furthermore, they must communicate their thoughts about systems and about solutions to any problems they have been working on.

Math skills. Agricultural engineers use calculus, trigonometry, and other advanced mathematical disciplines for analysis, design, and troubleshooting.

Problem-solving skills. Agricultural engineers' main role is to solve problems found in agricultural production. Goals may include designing safer equipment for food processing or reducing erosion. To solve these problems, agricultural engineers must creatively apply the principles of engineering.

Licenses, Certifications, and Registrations

Licensure is not required for entry-level positions as an agricultural engineer. A Professional Engineering (PE) license, which allows for higher levels of leadership and independence, can be acquired later in one's career. Licensed engineers are called professional engineers (PEs). A PE can oversee the work of other engineers, sign off on projects, and provide services directly to the public. State licensure generally requires

- A degree from an ABET-accredited engineering program
- A passing score on the Fundamentals of Engineering (FE) exam
- Relevant work experience, typically at least 4 years
- A passing score on the Professional Engineering (PE) exam

The initial FE exam can be taken after one earns a bachelor's degree. Engineers who pass this exam are commonly called engineers in training (EITs) or engineer interns (EIs). After meeting work experience requirements, EITs and EIs can take the second exam, called the Principles and Practice of Engineering (PE).

Each state issues its own licenses. Most states recognize licensure from other states, as long as the licensing state's requirements meet or exceed their own licensure requirements. Several states require engineers to take continuing education to keep their licenses. For licensing requirements, check with your state's licensing board.

Advancement

New engineers usually work under the supervision of experienced engineers. As they gain knowledge and experience, beginning engineers move to more difficult projects and increase their independence in developing designs, solving problems, and making decisions.

With experience, agricultural engineers may advance to supervise a team of engineers and technicians. Some advance to become engineering managers. Agricultural engineers who become sales engineers use their engineering background to discuss a product's technical aspects with potential buyers and to help in product planning, installation, and use.

Engineers who have a master's degree or a Ph.D. are more likely to be involved in research and development activities, and may become postsecondary teachers.

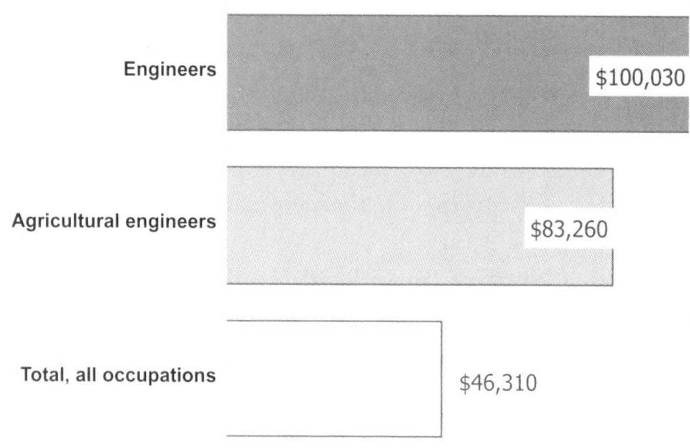

Note: All Occupations includes all occupations in the U.S. Economy.
Source: U.S. Bureau of Labor Statistics, Occupational Employment and Wage Statistics.

Pay

The median annual wage for agricultural engineers was $83,260 in May 2022. The median wage is the wage at which half the workers in an occupation earned more than that amount and half earned less. The lowest 10 percent earned less than $50,480, and the highest 10 percent earned more than $146,350.

In May 2022, the median annual wages for agricultural engineers in the top industries in which they worked were as follows:

Federal government, excluding postal service	$87,300
Engineering services	85,830
Manufacturing	81,760
Colleges, universities, and professional schools; state	74,850
State government, excluding education and hospitals	61,230

Agricultural engineers typically work full time. Schedules may vary because of weather conditions or other complications. When working on outdoor projects, agricultural engineers may work more hours to take advantage of good weather or fewer hours in case of bad weather.

In addition, agricultural engineers may need to be available outside of normal work hours to address unexpected problems that come up in manufacturing operations or rural construction projects.

Job Outlook

Employment of agricultural engineers is projected to grow 6 percent from 2022 to 2032, faster than the average for all occupations.

About 100 openings for agricultural engineers are projected each year, on average, over the decade. Many of those openings are expected to result from the need to replace workers who transfer to different occupations or exit the labor force, such as to retire.

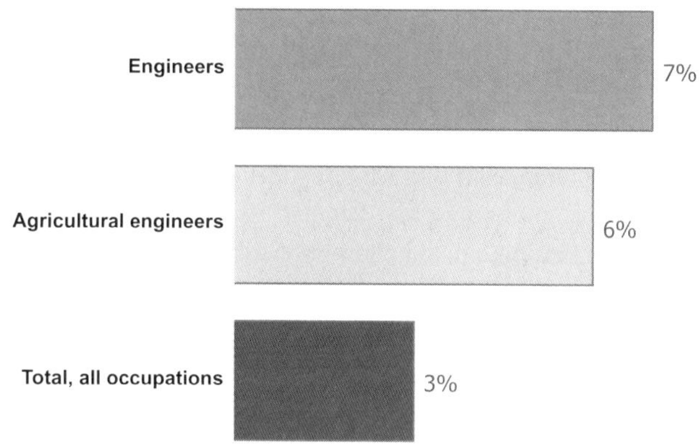

Note: All Occupations includes all occupations in the U.S. Economy.
Source: U.S. Bureau of Labor Statistics, Employment Projections program.

Employment

Farms will continue to need agricultural engineers to design more efficient machinery, equipment, and buildings and to help reduce environmental damage.

Agricultural engineers are expected to continue working on projects such as alternative energies and biofuels; precision and automated farming technologies for irrigation, spraying, and harvesting; and worker safety systems.

In addition, strong global competition should further support demand for these workers as farmers seek ways to reduce costs and increase production.

Occupational Title	SOC Code	Employment, 2022	Projected Employment, 2032	Change, 2022-32	
				Percent	Numeric
Agricultural engineers	17-2021	1,600	1,700	6	100

Contacts for More Information

For more information about agricultural engineers, visit

- American Society of Agricultural and Biological Engineers
- American Society for Engineering Education
- Technology Student Association
- National Council of Examiners for Engineering and Surveying
- National Society of Professional Engineers
- National Institute for Certification in Engineering Technologies
- ABET
- Future Farmers of America
- National Institute of Food and Agriculture, U.S. Department of Agriculture
- U.S. Food and Drug Administration

Architects

Summary

Quick Facts: Architects	
2022 Median Pay	$82,840 per year $39.83 per hour
Typical Entry-Level Education	Bachelor's degree
Work Experience in a Related Occupation	None
On-the-job Training	Internship/residency
Number of Jobs, 2022	123,700
Job Outlook, 2022-32	5% (Faster than average)
Employment Change, 2022-32	6,000

Architects plan and design many different structures.

What Architects Do

Architects plan and design houses, factories, office buildings, and other structures.

Work Environment

Architects spend much of their time in offices, where they develop plans, meet with clients, and consult with engineers and other architects. They also visit construction sites to prepare initial drawings and review the progress of projects to ensure that clients' objectives are met.

How to Become an Architect

There are typically three main steps to becoming a licensed architect: completing a bachelor's degree in architecture, gaining relevant experience through a paid internship, and passing the Architect Registration Examination.

Pay

The median annual wage for architects was $82,840 in May 2022.

Job Outlook

Employment of architects is projected to grow 5 percent from 2022 to 2032, faster than the average for all occupations.

About 8,200 openings for architects are projected each year, on average, over the decade. Many of those openings are expected to result from the need to replace workers who transfer to different occupations or exit the labor force, such as to retire.

What Architects Do

Architects plan and design houses, factories, office buildings, and other structures.

Architects use CADD during the design process.

Duties

Architects typically do the following:

- Meet with clients to determine objectives and requirements for structures
- Give preliminary estimates on cost and construction time
- Prepare structure specifications
- Direct workers who prepare drawings and documents
- Prepare scaled drawings, either with computer software or by hand
- Prepare contract documents for building contractors
- Manage construction contracts
- Visit worksites to ensure that construction adheres to architectural plans
- Seek new work by marketing and giving presentations

People need places to live, work, play, learn, shop, and eat. Architects are responsible for designing these places. They work on public or private projects and design both indoor and outdoor spaces. Architects can be commissioned to design anything from a single room to an entire complex of buildings.

Architects discuss with clients the objectives, requirements, and budget of a project. In some cases, architects provide pre-design services, such as feasibility and environmental impact studies, site selection, cost analyses, and design requirements.

Architects develop final construction plans on the initial proposal after discussing with clients. The architects' plans show the building's appearance and details of its construction. These plans include drawings of the structural system; air-conditioning, heating, and ventilating systems; electrical systems; communications systems; and plumbing. Sometimes, landscape plans are included as well. In developing designs, architects must follow state and local building codes, zoning laws, fire regulations, and other ordinances, such as those requiring reasonable access for people with disabilities.

Architects use computer-aided design and drafting (CADD) and building information modeling (BIM) for creating designs and construction drawings. However, hand-drawing skills are still required, especially during the conceptual stages of a project and when an architect is at a construction site.

As construction continues, architects may visit building sites to ensure that contractors follow the design, adhere to the schedule, use the specified materials, and meet work-quality standards. The job is not complete until all construction is finished, required tests are conducted, and construction costs are paid.

Architects may also help clients get construction bids, select contractors, and negotiate construction contracts.

Architects often collaborate with workers in related occupations, such as civil engineers, urban and regional planners, drafters, interior designers, and landscape architects.

Work Environment

Architects held about 123,700 jobs in 2022. The largest employers of architects were as follows:

Architectural, engineering, and related services	76%
Self-employed workers	13
Construction	4
Government	3

Although architects usually work in an office, they must also travel to construction sites.

Architects spend much of their time in offices, where they meet with clients, develop reports and drawings, and work with other architects and engineers. They also visit construction sites to ensure that clients' objectives are met and to review the progress of projects. Some architects work from home offices.

Work Schedules

Most architects work full time and many work additional hours, especially when facing deadlines. Self-employed architects may have more flexible work schedules.

How to Become an Architect

There are typically three main steps to becoming a licensed architect: completing a bachelor's degree in architecture, gaining relevant experience through a paid internship, and passing the Architect Registration Examination.

Education

Architects typically need a bachelor's degree in architecture. Most architects earn their degree through a 5-year Bachelor of Architecture degree program. Many earn a master's degree in architecture, which can take 1 to 5 additional years. The time required depends on the extent of the student's previous education and training in architecture.

Architects need internships to gain practical experience.

A typical bachelor's degree program includes courses in architectural history and theory, building design with an emphasis on computer-aided design and drafting (CADD), structures, construction methods, professional practices, math, physical sciences, and liberal arts.

About two-thirds of states require that architects hold a degree in architecture from one of more than 120 schools of architecture accredited by the National Architectural Accrediting Board (NAAB). State licensing requirements can be found at the National Council of Architectural Registration Boards (NCARB).

Training

All state architectural registration boards require architecture graduates to complete a lengthy paid internship—generally lasting 3 years—before they may sit for the Architect Registration Examination. Most new graduates complete their training period by working at architectural firms through the Architectural Experience Program (AXP), a program run by NCARB that guides students through the internship process. Some states allow a portion of the training to occur in the offices of employers in related careers, such as engineers and general contractors. Architecture students who complete internships while still in school can count some of that time toward the 3-year training period.

Interns in architectural firms may help design part of a project. They may help prepare architectural documents and drawings, build models, and prepare construction drawings on CADD. Interns may also research building codes and write specifications for building materials, installation criteria, the quality of finishes, and other related details. Licensed architects take the documents that interns produce, make edits to them, finalize plans, and then sign and seal the documents.

Licenses, Certifications, and Registrations

All states and the District of Columbia require architects to be licensed. Licensing requirements typically include completing a degree program in architecture, gaining relevant experience through a paid internship, and passing the Architect Registration Examination.

Most states also require some form of continuing education to keep a license. Continuing education requirements vary by state but usually involve additional education through workshops, university classes, conferences, self-study courses, or other sources.

Advancement

After many years of work experience, some architects advance to become architectural and engineering managers. These managers typically coordinate the activities of employees and may work on larger construction projects.

Architects

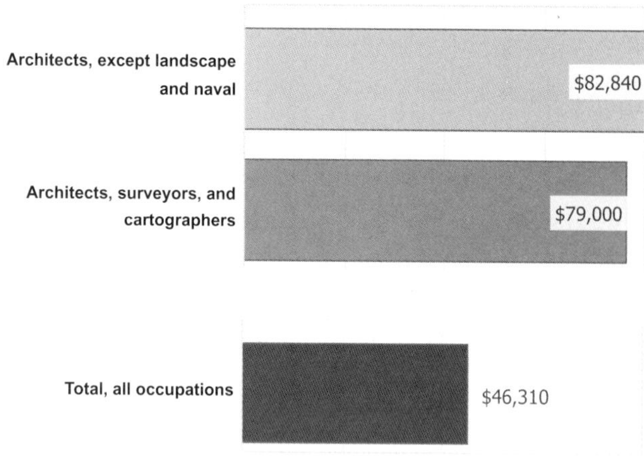

Note: All Occupations includes all occupations in the U.S. Economy.
Source: U.S. Bureau of Labor Statistics, Employment Projections program.

Architects

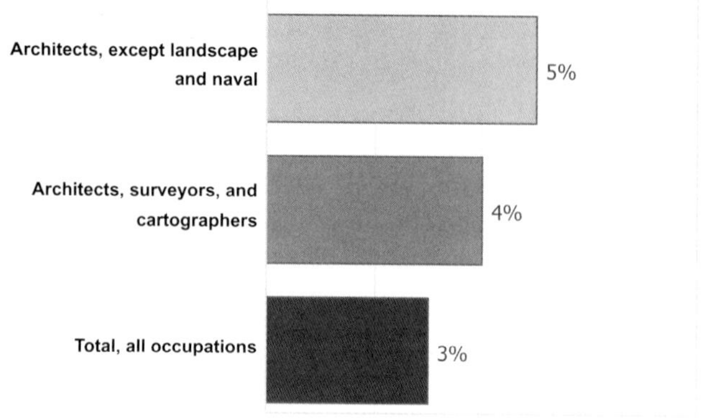

Note: All Occupations includes all occupations in the U.S. Economy.
Source: U.S. Bureau of Labor Statistics, Occupational Employment and Wage Statistics.

Important Qualities

Analytical skills. Architects must understand the content of designs and the context in which they were created. For example, architects must understand the locations of mechanical systems and how those systems affect building operations.

Communication skills. Architects share their ideas, both in oral presentations and in writing, with clients, other architects, and workers who help prepare drawings. Many also give presentations to explain their ideas and designs.

Creativity. Architects design the overall look of houses, buildings, and other structures. They must ensure that the final product is both attractive and functional.

Organizational skills. Architects often manage contracts. Therefore, they must keep records related to the details of a project, including total cost, materials used, and progress.

Technical skills. Architects need to use CADD technology to create plans as part of building information modeling (BIM).

Visualization skills. Architects must be able to envision how the parts of a structure relate to each other. They also must be able to visualize how the overall building will look once completed.

Pay

The median annual wage for architects was $82,840 in May 2022. The median wage is the wage at which half the workers in an occupation earned more than that amount and half earned less. The lowest 10 percent earned less than $51,310, and the highest 10 percent earned more than $136,400.

In May 2022, the median annual wages for architects in the top industries in which they worked were as follows:

Government	$103,170
Architectural, engineering, and related services	82,170
Construction	80,480

Most architects work full time and many work additional hours, especially when facing deadlines. Self-employed architects may have more flexible work hours.

Job Outlook

Employment of architects is projected to grow 5 percent from 2022 to 2032, faster than the average for all occupations.

About 8,200 openings for architects are projected each year, on average, over the decade. Many of those openings are expected to result from the need to replace workers who transfer to different occupations or exit the labor force, such as to retire.

Employment

Architects are expected to be needed to make plans and designs, particularly in sustainable design, for the construction and renovation of homes, schools, healthcare facilities, and other structures. Improved building information modeling (BIM) software and measuring technology are expected to allow architects to take on activities once performed by other workers, such as architectural and civil drafters, interior designers, and engineers.

Occupational Title	SOC Code	Employment, 2022	Projected Employment, 2032	Change, 2022-32	
				Percent	Numeric
Architects, except landscape and naval	17-1011	123,700	129,700	5	6,000

Contacts for More Information

For information about careers in architecture, visit

- American Institute of Architects
- National Architectural Accrediting Board
- National Council of Architectural Registration Boards

Bioengineers and Biomedical Engineers

Summary

Quick Facts: Bioengineers and Biomedical Engineers	
2022 Median Pay	$99,550 per year $47.86 per hour
Typical Entry-Level Education	Bachelor's degree
Work Experience in a Related Occupation	None
On-the-job Training	None
Number of Jobs, 2022	19,700
Job Outlook, 2022-32	5% (Faster than average)
Employment Change, 2022-32	1,000

What Bioengineers and Biomedical Engineers Do

Bioengineers and biomedical engineers combine engineering principles with sciences to design and create equipment, devices, computer systems, and software.

Work Environment

Bioengineers and biomedical engineers work in manufacturing, in research facilities, and for a variety of other employers. Most work full time, and some work more than 40 hours per week.

How to Become a Bioengineer or Biomedical Engineer

Bioengineers and biomedical engineers typically need a bachelor's degree in bioengineering or biomedical engineering or in a related engineering field. Some positions require a graduate degree.

Pay

The median annual wage for bioengineers and biomedical engineers was $99,550 in May 2022.

Job Outlook

Employment of bioengineers and biomedical engineers is projected to grow 5 percent from 2022 to 2032, faster than the average for all occupations.

About 1,200 openings for bioengineers and biomedical engineers are projected each year, on average, over the decade. Many of those openings are expected to result from the need to replace workers who transfer to different occupations or exit the labor force, such as to retire.

What Bioengineers and Biomedical Engineers Do

Bioengineers and biomedical engineers combine engineering principles with sciences to design and create equipment, devices, computer systems, and software.

Duties

Bioengineers and biomedical engineers typically do the following:

- Design equipment and devices, such as artificial internal organs, replacements for body parts, and machines for diagnosing medical problems
- Install, maintain, or provide technical support for biomedical equipment
- Collaborate with manufacturing staff on the safety and effectiveness of biomedical equipment
- Train clinicians and others on the proper use of biomedical equipment
- Work with scientists to research how engineering principles apply to biological systems
- Develop statistical models or simulations using statistical or modeling software
- Prepare procedures and write technical reports and research papers
- Present research findings to a variety of audiences, including scientists, clinicians, managers, other engineers, and the public
- Design or conduct followup experiments as needed

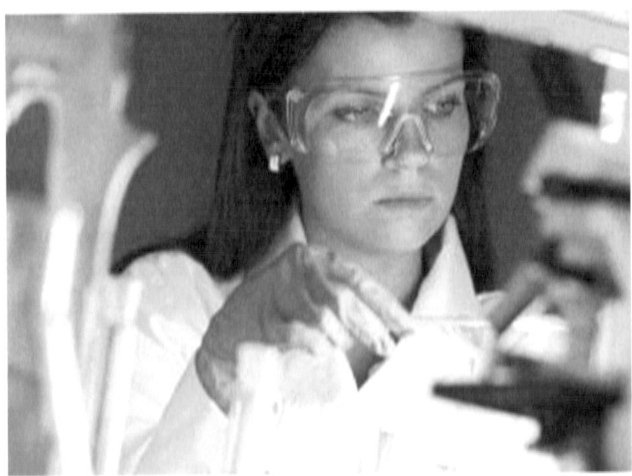

Bioengineers and biomedical engineers design and create equipment and devices used in healthcare.

Bioengineers and biomedical engineers install, maintain, or provide technical support for biomedical equipment.

Bioengineers and biomedical engineers frequently work in research and development or quality assurance.

The work of bioengineers spans many fields. For example, although their expertise is in engineering and biology, they often design computer software to run complicated instruments, such as three-dimensional x-ray machines. Others use their knowledge of chemistry and biology to develop new drug therapies. Still others draw on math and statistics to understand signals transmitted by the brain or heart. Some are involved in sales.

Biomedical engineers focus on advances in technology and medicine to develop new devices and equipment for improving human health. For example, they might design software to run medical equipment or computer simulations to test new drug therapies. In addition, they design and build artificial body parts, such as hip and knee joints, or develop materials to make replacement parts. They also design rehabilitative exercise equipment.

The following are examples of types of bioengineers and biomedical engineers:

Biochemical engineers focus on cell structures and microscopic systems to create products for bioremediation, biological waste treatment, and other uses.

Bioinstrumentation engineers use electronics, computer science, and measurement principles to develop tools for diagnosing and treating medical problems.

Biomaterials engineers study naturally occurring or laboratory-designed substances for use in medical devices or implants.

Biomechanics engineers study thermodynamics and other systems to solve biological or medical problems.

Clinical engineers apply medical technology to improve healthcare.

Genetic engineers alter the genetic makeup of organism using recombinant deoxyribonucleic acid (rDNA) technology, such as in developing vitamin-fortified food crops to prevent disease in humans.

Rehabilitation engineers develop devices that aid people who are recovering from or adapting to physical or cognitive impairments.

Systems physiologists use engineering tools to understand how biological systems function and respond to changes in their environment.

Other bioengineering occupations are described in separate profiles; see, for example, chemical engineers and agricultural engineers. Some people with training in biomedical engineering become postsecondary teachers.

Work Environment

Bioengineers and biomedical engineers held about 19,700 jobs in 2022. The largest employers of bioengineers and biomedical engineers were as follows:

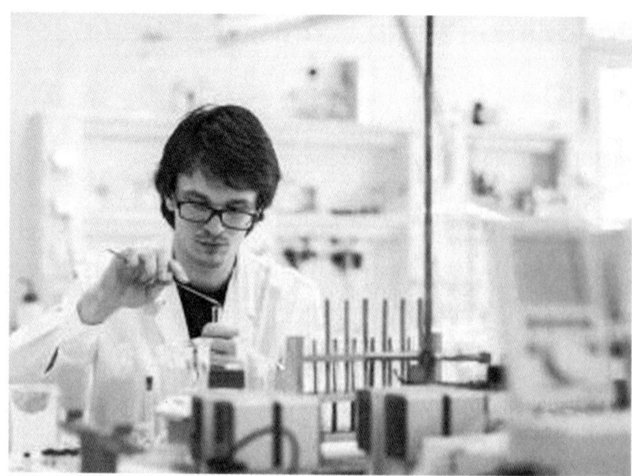

Bioengineers and biomedical engineers work in laboratory and clinical settings.

Research and development in the physical, engineering, and life sciences	23%
Medical equipment and supplies manufacturing	13
Professional and commercial equipment and supplies merchant wholesalers	11
Engineering services	9
Healthcare and social assistance	8

Bioengineers and biomedical engineers work on teams with scientists, healthcare workers, or other engineers. Where and how they work depends on the project. For example, a biomedical engineer who has developed a new device might spend hours in a hospital to ensure that the device works as planned. If the device needs adjusting, the engineer might need to suggest alterations in the manufacturing process.

Work Schedules

Most bioengineers and biomedical engineers work full time, and some work more than 40 hours per week.

How to Become a Bioengineer or Biomedical Engineer

Bioengineers and biomedical engineers typically need a bachelor's degree in bioengineering, biomedical engineering, or a related engineering field. Some positions require a graduate degree.

Education

In high school, students interested in becoming bioengineers or biomedical engineers should take classes in sciences such as chemistry, physics, and biology. They should also study math, including algebra, geometry, trigonometry, and calculus. If available, classes in drafting, mechanical drawing, and computer programming are also useful.

At the bachelor's degree level, prospective bioengineers should study bioengineering, biomedical, or other engineering fields. Students who pursue other engineering degrees, such as

Bioengineers and biomedical engineers frequently work in research and development or in quality assurance.

mechanical or electrical, may benefit from taking biological science courses.

Bachelor's degree programs in bioengineering and biomedical engineering focus on engineering and biological sciences. These programs typically include laboratory- and classroom-based courses in biological sciences and subjects such as fluid and solid mechanics, circuit design, and biomaterials.

These programs also include substantial training in engineering design. As part of their study, students may have an opportunity to participate in co-ops or internships with hospitals and medical device and pharmaceutical manufacturing companies. Bioengineering and biomedical engineering programs are accredited by ABET.

Important Qualities

Analytical skills. Bioengineers and biomedical engineers must assess the needs of patients and customers prior to designing products.

Communication skills. Because bioengineers and biomedical engineers sometimes work with patients and customers and frequently work on teams, they must be able to express themselves clearly in discussions. They also write reports and research papers.

Creativity. Bioengineers and biomedical engineers must be creative to come up with innovations in healthcare equipment and devices.

Math skills. Bioengineers and biomedical engineers use calculus and other advanced math and statistics for analysis, design, and troubleshooting in their work.

Problem-solving skills. Bioengineers and biomedical engineers typically deal with intricate biological systems. They must be able to work independently and with others to incorporate ideas into the complex problem-solving process.

Advancement

Bioengineers and biomedical engineers may increase their responsibilities as they gain experience or advanced degrees. To lead a research team, a bioengineer or biomedical engineer typically needs a graduate degree. Those who are interested in basic research may become medical scientists.

Some bioengineers attend medical or dental school to specialize in techniques such as using electric impulses in new ways to get muscles moving again. Others earn law degrees and work as patent attorneys. Still others pursue a master's degree in business administration (MBA) and move into managerial positions. For more information, see the profiles on lawyers and architectural and engineering managers.

Pay

The median annual wage for bioengineers and biomedical engineers was $99,550 in May 2022. The median wage is the wage at which half the workers in an occupation earned more than that amount and half earned less. The lowest 10 percent earned less than $63,420, and the highest 10 percent earned more than $159,130.

In May 2022, the median annual wages for bioengineers and biomedical engineers in the top industries in which they worked were as follows:

Engineering services	$146,540
Professional and commercial equipment and supplies merchant wholesalers	100,440
Research and development in the physical, engineering, and life sciences	99,240
Medical equipment and supplies manufacturing	99,010
Healthcare and social assistance	84,970

Most bioengineers and biomedical engineers work full time, and some work more than 40 hours per week.

Job Outlook

Employment of bioengineers and biomedical engineers is projected to grow 5 percent from 2022 to 2032, faster than the average for all occupations.

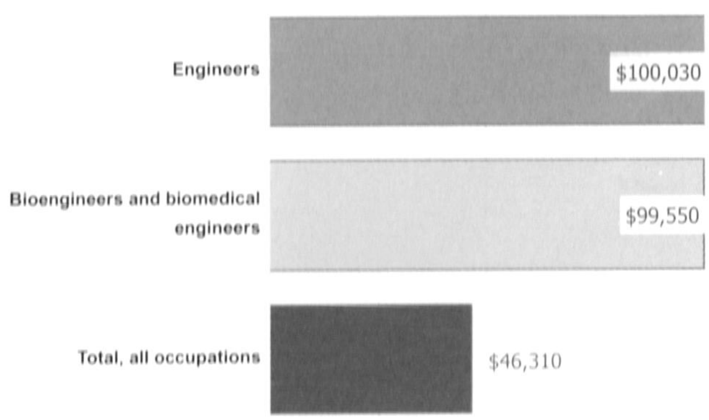

Note: All Occupations includes all occupations in the U.S. Economy.
Source: U.S. Bureau of Labor Statistics, Occupational Employment and Wage Statistics.

Bioengineers and Biomedical Engineers

Percent change in employment, projected 2022-32

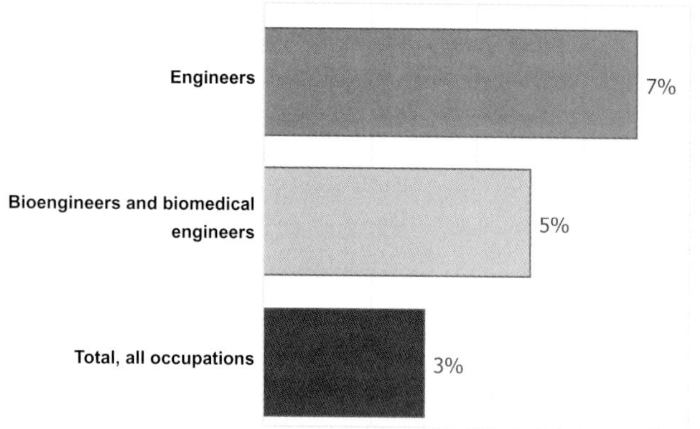

Note: All Occupations includes all occupations in the U.S. Economy.
Source: U.S. Bureau of Labor Statistics, Employment Projections program.

About 1,200 openings for bioengineers and biomedical engineers are projected each year, on average, over the decade. Many of those openings are expected to result from the need to replace workers who transfer to different occupations or exit the labor force, such as to retire.

Employment

Bioengineers and biomedical engineers are expected to see employment growth as demand for biomedical devices and procedures, such as hip and knee replacements, continues to increase. In addition, with continued public awareness of medical advances, increasing numbers of people will seek biomedical solutions to their health problems.

Bioengineers and biomedical engineers continue to collaborate with scientists, other medical researchers, and manufacturers to address a range of injuries and physical disabilities. Their work in healthcare, manufacturing, agriculture, and other fields is expanding the possibilities for biomedical engineering products and services.

Occupational Title	SOC Code	Employment, 2022	Projected Employment, 2032	Change, 2022-32	
				Percent	Numeric
Bioengineers and biomedical engineers	17-2031	19,700	20,700	5	1,000

Contacts for More Information

For information about education and career resources for bioengineering, biomedical engineering, and general engineering, visit

- American Institute for Medical and Biological Engineering
- American Society for Engineering Education
- Biomedical Engineering Society
- IEEE Engineering in Medicine and Biology Society
- Technology Student Association
- ABET

Cartographers and Photogrammetrists

Summary

Quick Facts: Cartographers and Photogrammetrists	
2022 Median Pay	$71,890 per year $34.56 per hour
Typical Entry-Level Education	Bachelor's degree
Work Experience in a Related Occupation	None
On-the-job Training	None
Number of Jobs, 2022	14,000
Job Outlook, 2022-32	5% (Faster than average)
Employment Change, 2022-32	700

What Cartographers and Photogrammetrists Do

Cartographers and photogrammetrists collect, measure, and interpret geographic information in order to create and update maps and charts for regional planning, education, and other purposes.

Work Environment

Although cartographers and photogrammetrists spend much of their time in offices, certain jobs require extensive travel to locations that are being mapped.

How to Become a Cartographer or Photogrammetrist

Cartographers and photogrammetrists typically need a bachelor's degree in cartography, geography, geomatics, or surveying.

Pay

The median annual wage for cartographers and photogrammetrists was $71,890 in May 2022.

Cartographers and photogrammetrists measure, map, and chart the earth's surface.

Job Outlook

Employment of cartographers and photogrammetrists is projected to grow 5 percent from 2022 to 2032, faster than the average for all occupations.

About 1,000 openings for cartographers and photogrammetrists are projected each year, on average, over the decade. Many of those openings are expected to result from the need to replace workers who transfer to different occupations or exit the labor force, such as to retire.

What Cartographers and Photogrammetrists Do

Cartographers and photogrammetrists collect, measure, and interpret geographic information in order to create and update maps and charts for regional planning, education, and other purposes.

Duties

Cartographers typically do the following:

- Collect geographic data
- Create visual representations of data, such as annual precipitation patterns
- Examine and compile data from ground surveys, reports, aerial photographs, and satellite images

Cartographers and photogrammetrists typically collect and verify data used in creating maps.

- Prepare maps in digital or graphic form for environmental and educational purposes
- Update and revise existing maps and charts

Photogrammetrists typically do the following:

- Plan aerial and satellite surveys to ensure complete coverage of the area in question
- Collect and analyze spatial data, such as elevation and distance
- Develop base maps that allow Geographic Information System (GIS) data to be layered on top

Cartographers are mapmakers who design user-friendly maps. Photogrammetrists are specialized mapmakers who use various technologies to build models of the Earth's surface and its features for the purpose of creating maps.

Cartographers and photogrammetrists use information from geodetic surveys (land surveys that account for the curvature of the Earth's surface) and remote-sensing systems, including aerial cameras and satellites. Some also use light-imaging detection and ranging (LIDAR) technology. LIDAR systems use lasers attached to planes or cars to digitally map the topography of the Earth. Because LIDAR is often more accurate than traditional surveying methods, it can also be used to collect other forms of data, such as the location and density of forests.

Cartographers and photogrammetrists often develop online and mobile maps. Interactive maps are popular, and cartographers and photogrammetrists collect data and design these maps for mobile phones and navigation systems.

Cartographers and photogrammetrists also create maps and perform aerial surveys for governments, to aid in urban and regional planning. Such maps may include information on population density and demographic characteristics. Some cartographers and photogrammetrists help build maps for government agencies for work involving national security and public safety. Accurate maps help emergency responders provide assistance as quickly as possible.

Cartographers and photogrammetrists who use GIS technology to create maps are often known as *geographic information specialists*. GIS technology is typically used to assemble, integrate, analyze, and present spatial information in a digital format. Maps created with GIS technology combine spatial graphic features with data. These maps are used to provide support for decisions involving environmental studies, geology, engineering, land-use planning, and business marketing.

Work Environment

Cartographers and photogrammetrists held about 14,000 jobs in 2022. The largest employers of cartographers and photogrammetrists were as follows:

Local government, excluding education and hospitals	33%
Architectural, engineering, and related services	20

Cartographers may travel to the physical locations that they are mapping to better understand the topography of the region.

Management, scientific, and technical consulting services	7
Federal government	4
State government, excluding education and hospitals	4

Although cartographers and photogrammetrists spend much of their time in offices, certain jobs require extensive fieldwork to collect data and verify results. For example, cartographers may travel to the physical locations they are mapping to better understand the topography of the region. Similarly, photogrammetrists may conduct fieldwork to plan for aerial surveys and to validate interpretations.

Work Schedules

Most cartographers and photogrammetrists work full time. They may have longer workdays during fieldwork.

How to Become a Cartographer or Photogrammetrist

Cartographers and photogrammetrists typically need a bachelor's degree in cartography, geography, geomatics, or surveying. Some states require cartographers and photogrammetrists to be licensed as surveyors, and some states have specific licenses for photogrammetrists.

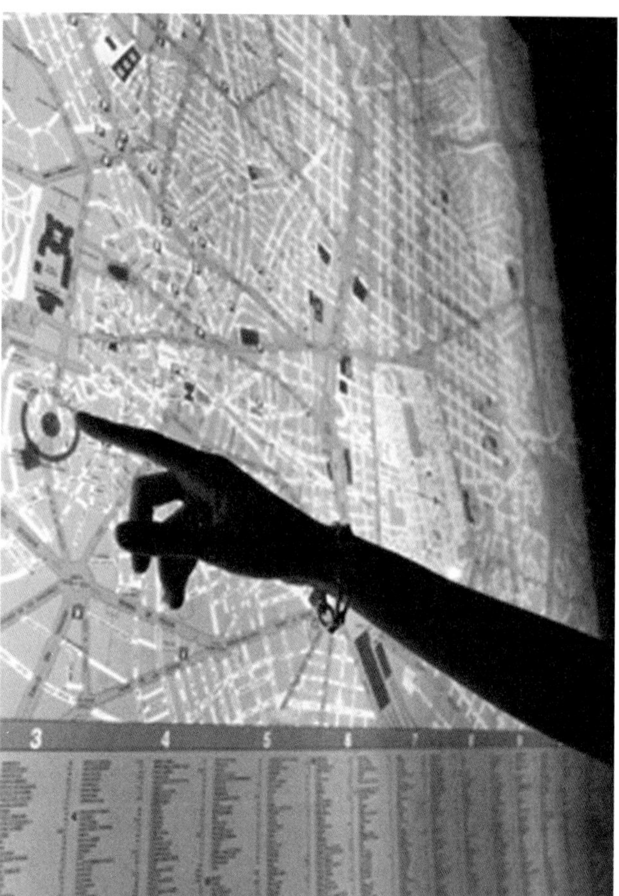

Cartographers and photogrammetrists usually learn to create maps through degrees in cartography, geography, geomatics, or surveying.

Education

Cartographers and photogrammetrists typically need a bachelor's degree in cartography, geography, geomatics, or surveying. (Geomatics combines a variety of disciplines, such as engineering, natural resources, and mathematics.)

The growing use of Geographic Information System (GIS) technology has resulted in cartographers and photogrammetrists requiring more courses in computer programming, engineering, math, GIS technology, surveying, and geography.

Cartographers must also be familiar with Web-based mapping technologies, including newer modes of compiling data that incorporate the positioning capabilities of mobile phones and in-car navigation systems.

Photogrammetrists must be familiar with remote sensing, image processing, and light-imaging detection and ranging (LIDAR) technology, and they must be knowledgeable about using the software that is necessary with these tools.

Many aspiring cartographers and photogrammetrists benefit from internships while in school.

Licenses, Certifications, and Registrations

Licensing requirements for cartographers and photogrammetrists vary by state. Some states require cartographers and photogrammetrists to be licensed as surveyors, and some states have specific licenses for photogrammetry and remote sensing. Although licensing requirements vary by state, candidates must meet educational requirements and pass a test.

Cartographers and photogrammetrists may also receive certification from the American Society for Photogrammetry and Remote Sensing (ASPRS). The United States Geospatial Intelligence Foundation offers certifications for GIS professionals. Candidates must meet experience and education requirements and must pass an exam. Although certifications are not required, they can demonstrate competence and may help candidates get a job.

Important Qualities

Computer skills. Both cartographers and photogrammetrists must have experience working with computer data and coding. Maps are created digitally, so knowing how to edit them on a computer is essential.

Critical-thinking skills. Cartographers may work from existing maps, surveys, and other records, and they must be able to determine the accuracy of each feature being mapped.

Decision-making skills. Both cartographers and photogrammetrists must make decisions about the accuracy and readability of a map. They must decide what information they require in order to meet the client's needs.

Detail oriented. Cartographers must focus on details when conceiving a map and deciding what features to include. Photogrammetrists must pay close attention to detail when interpreting aerial photographs and remotely sensed data.

Problem-solving skills. Cartographers and photogrammetrists must be able to reconcile differences between aerial photographs, land surveys, and satellite images.

Pay

The median annual wage for cartographers and photogrammetrists was $71,890 in May 2022. The median wage is the wage at which half the workers in an occupation earned more than that amount and half earned less. The lowest 10 percent earned less than $47,550, and the highest 10 percent earned more than $107,600.

In May 2022, the median annual wages for cartographers and photogrammetrists in the top industries in which they worked were as follows:

Federal government	$97,490
Local government, excluding education and hospitals	72,570
State government, excluding education and hospitals	65,640
Architectural, engineering, and related services	63,960
Management, scientific, and technical consulting services	61,850

Most cartographers and photogrammetrists work full time. They may have longer workdays during fieldwork.

Job Outlook

Employment of cartographers and photogrammetrists is projected to grow 5 percent from 2022 to 2032, faster than the average for all occupations.

About 1,000 openings for cartographers and photogrammetrists are projected each year, on average, over the decade. Many of those openings are expected to result from the need to replace workers who transfer to different occupations or exit the labor force, such as to retire.

Employment

The use of maps for government planning should lead to some employment growth. Cartographers and photogrammetrists also will be needed to map and locate areas that require help during natural disasters, often using Geographic Information Systems (GIS).

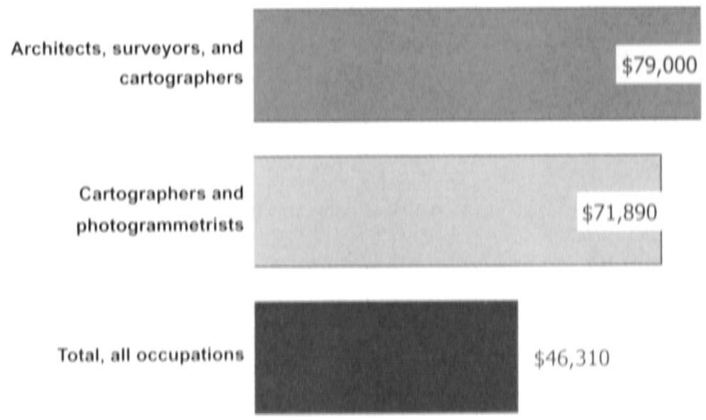

Note: All Occupations includes all occupations in the U.S. Economy.
Source: U.S. Bureau of Labor Statistics, Occupational Employment and Wage Statistics.

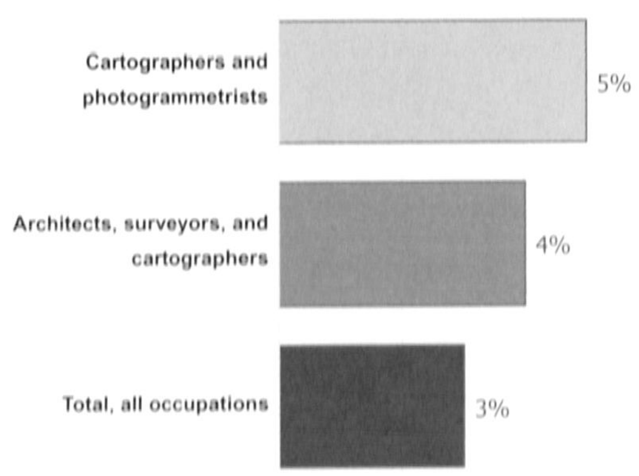

Note: All Occupations includes all occupations in the U.S. Economy.
Source: U.S. Bureau of Labor Statistics, Employment Projections program.

Occupational Title	SOC Code	Employment, 2022	Projected Employment, 2032	Change, 2022-32	
				Percent	Numeric
Cartographers and photogrammetrists	17-1021	14,000	14,700	5	700

Contacts for More Information

For more information visit

- Cartography and Geographic Information Society
- American Society for Photogrammetry and Remote Sensing
- Association of American Geographers
- United States Geospatial Intelligence Foundation

Chemical Engineers

Summary

Quick Facts: Chemical Engineers	
2022 Median Pay	$106,260 per year $51.09 per hour
Typical Entry-Level Education	Bachelor's degree
Work Experience in a Related Occupation	None
On-the-job Training	None
Number of Jobs, 2022	20,800
Job Outlook, 2022-32	8% (Faster than average)
Employment Change, 2022-32	1,700

What Chemical Engineers Do

Chemical engineers apply the principles of chemistry, physics, and engineering to design equipment and processes for manufacturing products such as gasoline, detergents, and paper.

Work Environment

Chemical engineers typically work in an office setting or in laboratories. Most chemical engineers work full time, and some work more than 40 hours per week.

Chemical engineers apply the principles of chemistry, biology, physics, and math to solve problems involving the production of chemicals, fuel, drugs, food, and many other products.

How to Become a Chemical Engineer

To enter the occupation, chemical engineers typically need a bachelor's degree in chemical engineering or a related field. Some employers prefer to hire candidates who have gained experience in an internship or a cooperative education program.

Pay

The median annual wage for chemical engineers was $106,260 in May 2022.

Job Outlook

Employment of chemical engineers is projected to grow 8 percent from 2022 to 2032, faster than the average for all occupations.

About 1,300 openings for chemical engineers are projected each year, on average, over the decade. Many of those openings are expected to result from the need to replace workers who transfer to different occupations or exit the labor force, such as to retire.

What Chemical Engineers Do

Chemical engineers apply the principles of chemistry, physics, and engineering to design equipment and processes for manufacturing products such as gasoline, detergents, and paper.

Chemical engineers develop and design chemical manufacturing processes.

Duties

Chemical engineers typically do the following:

- Conduct research to develop new and improved manufacturing processes
- Design and plan the layout of equipment
- Establish safety procedures for working with dangerous chemicals
- Conduct tests and monitor production processes
- Troubleshoot problems in manufacturing processes
- Evaluate equipment and processes to ensure compliance with safety and environmental regulations
- Estimate production costs for management

Chemical engineers work on producing a variety of chemicals and products, such as electronics, food, clothing, and paper. Along with designing and developing manufacturing processes, they ensure the safety of both work environments and consumers.

Chemical engineers commonly use computer-aided design (CAD) software in developing materials and products. Many engineers are generalists whose knowledge is transferable across industries.

Some chemical engineers specialize in a particular process, such as oxidation (a reaction of oxygen with chemicals to make other chemicals), or in developing specific products. Others specialize in a particular field, such as nanomaterials (extremely small substances).

Chemical engineers also may collaborate on research projects in a variety of other fields, including life sciences, biotechnology, and business services.

Work Environment

Chemical engineers held about 20,800 jobs in 2022. The largest employers of chemical engineers were as follows:

Chemical manufacturing	35%
Engineering services	13
Research and development in the physical, engineering, and life sciences	13
Federal government, excluding postal service	5

Chemical engineers typically work in an office setting or in laboratories. They also may visit industrial plants, refineries, and other locations to monitor operations. Chemical engineers also may collaborate with those who design other systems, such as in biotechnology, or work with the technicians and mechanics who put designs into practice.

Injuries and Illnesses

Chemical engineers may be exposed to health or safety hazards when handling certain chemicals and plant equipment. Workers reduce their risk of injury or illness by following safety procedures and wearing protective equipment, such as gloves, goggles, and hard hats.

Chemical engineers generally work in offices or laboratory settings, although sometimes they must work in an industrial setting to oversee production.

Work Schedules

Most chemical engineers work full time, and some work more than 40 hours per week. They may have to work additional hours to meet production targets or to troubleshoot problems with manufacturing processes.

How to Become a Chemical Engineer

To enter the occupation, chemical engineers typically need a bachelor's degree in chemical engineering or a related field. Some employers prefer to hire candidates who have gained practical experience in an internship or a cooperative education program.

Education

High school students interested in chemical engineering should take classes in sciences such as chemistry, physics, and biology. They also should take math courses, including algebra, calculus, and trigonometry.

Becoming a chemical engineer requires a bachelor's degree in chemical engineering or a related field.

Bachelor's degree programs in chemical engineering or a related field typically include classroom, laboratory, and field studies. These programs usually take 4 years, but some colleges and universities have 5-year engineering programs that lead to both a bachelor's and a master's degree.

Employers often prefer to hire graduates of ABET-accredited engineering programs. In chemical engineering, ABET-accredited programs include courses in chemistry, physics, and biology and the application of these sciences to process design and analysis.

Some colleges and universities offer internships or cooperative education programs. In these programs, students gain practical experience while completing their education.

Licenses, Certifications, and Registrations

Licensure is not required for entry-level chemical engineers.

Experienced engineers may obtain a Professional Engineer (PE) license, which allows them to oversee the work of other engineers, sign off on projects, and provide services directly to the public.

State licensure generally requires a bachelor's or higher degree from an ABET-accredited engineering program, a passing score on the Fundamentals of Engineering (FE) exam, several years of relevant work experience, and a passing score on the PE exam.

Each state issues its own license. Most states recognize licensure from other states if the licensing state's requirements meet or exceed their own licensure requirements. Some states require engineers to take continuing education to maintain licensure.

Advancement

Chemical engineers may advance to supervise a team of engineers and technicians or to become engineering managers. Advancing into supervisory or management positions usually requires several years of experience, often working under the guidance of a senior-level engineer.

Important Qualities

Analytical skills. Chemical engineers must be able to evaluate designs and processes and to propose improvements, if necessary.

Communication skills. Because chemical engineers frequently work on teams, they must be able to express themselves clearly in discussions and develop good relationships with colleagues.

Creativity. Chemical engineers explore new ways of applying engineering to invent new materials and advance manufacturing techniques in chemical engineering.

Math skills. Chemical engineers use calculus and other advanced math for analysis, design, and troubleshooting in their work.

Problem-solving skills. Chemical engineers must be able to anticipate and identify problems, such as those related to manufacturing processes, and to devise solutions.

Chemical Engineers

Median annual wages, May 2022

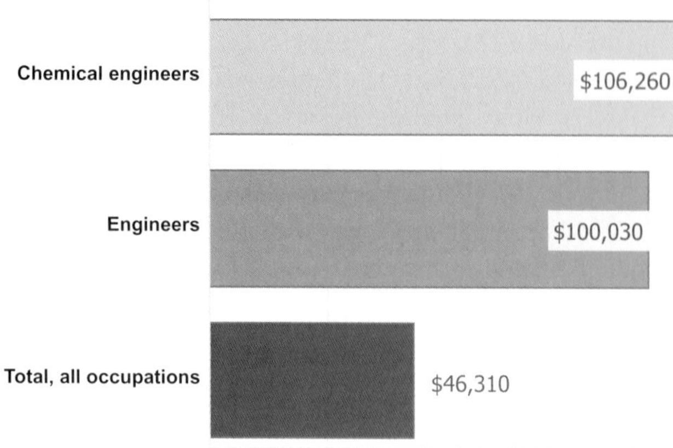

Note: All Occupations includes all occupations in the U.S. Economy.
Source: U.S. Bureau of Labor Statistics, Occupational Employment and Wage Statistics.

Pay

The median annual wage for chemical engineers was $106,260 in May 2022. The median wage is the wage at which half the workers in an occupation earned more than that amount and half earned less. The lowest 10 percent earned less than $72,490, and the highest 10 percent earned more than $171,400.

In May 2022, the median annual wages for chemical engineers in the top industries in which they worked were as follows:

Engineering services	$118,840
Federal government, excluding postal service	117,730
Research and development in the physical, engineering, and life sciences	109,290
Chemical manufacturing	104,950

Most chemical engineers work full time, and some work more than 40 hours per week. They may have to work additional hours to meet production targets or to troubleshoot problems with manufacturing processes.

Job Outlook

Employment of chemical engineers is projected to grow 8 percent from 2022 to 2032, faster than the average for all occupations.

About 1,300 openings for chemical engineers are projected each year, on average, over the decade. Many of those openings are expected to result from the need to replace workers who transfer to different occupations or exit the labor force, such as to retire.

Employment

Demand for chemical engineers' services depends largely on demand for the products that these workers help to develop. For example, environmental and sustainability concerns have

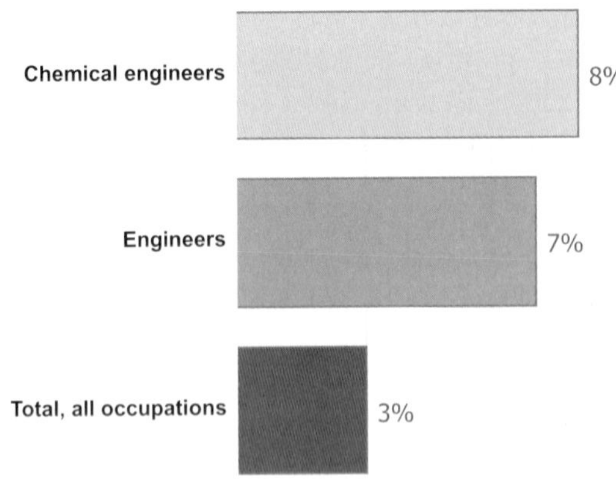

Note: All Occupations includes all occupations in the U.S. Economy.
Source: U.S. Bureau of Labor Statistics, Employment Projections program.

led chemistry and manufacturing firms to research alternative fertilizers, resulting in a need for chemical engineers.

In addition, demand for these workers will continue with chemical engineering's migration into nanotechnology, alternative energies, biotechnology, and other fields.

Occupational Title	SOC Code	Employment, 2022	Projected Employment, 2032	Change, 2022-32	
				Percent	Numeric
Chemical engineers	17-2041	20,800	22,500	8	1,700

Contacts for More Information

For more information, visit

- American Institute of Chemical Engineers (AIChE)
- American Society for Engineering Education (ASEE)
- Technology Student Association (TSA)
- ABET
- National Council of Examiners for Engineering and Surveying (NCEES)
- National Society of Professional Engineers (NSPE)

Civil Engineering Technologists and Technicians

Summary

Quick Facts: Civil Engineering Technologists and Technicians	
2022 Median Pay	$59,630 per year $28.67 per hour
Typical Entry-Level Education	Associate's degree
Work Experience in a Related Occupation	None
On-the-job Training	None
Number of Jobs, 2022	64,800
Job Outlook, 2022-32	1% (Little or no change)
Employment Change, 2022-32	600

What Civil Engineering Technologists and Technicians Do

Civil engineering technologists and technicians help civil engineers plan, design, and build infrastructure and development projects.

Work Environment

Civil engineering technologists and technicians work in offices, helping civil engineers plan and design projects. They also visit construction jobsites to collect or test materials or to observe activities as a project inspector.

How to Become a Civil Engineering Technologist or Technician

An associate's degree, preferably in civil engineering technology, is typically required to enter the occupation.

Pay

The median annual wage for civil engineering technologists and technicians was $59,630 in May 2022.

Job Outlook

Employment of civil engineering technologists and technicians is projected to show little or no change from 2022 to 2032.

Civil engineering technicians help with residential development, and work under civil engineers.

Despite limited employment growth, about 5,900 openings for civil engineering technologists and technicians are projected each year, on average, over the decade. Most of those openings are expected to result from the need to replace workers who transfer to different occupations or exit the labor force, such as to retire.

What Civil Engineering Technologists and Technicians Do

Civil engineering technologists and technicians help civil engineers plan, design, and build highways, bridges, utilities, and other infrastructure projects. They also help to plan, design, and build commercial, industrial, residential, and land development projects.

Duties

Civil engineering technologists and technicians typically do the following:

- Read and review project drawings and plans to determine the sizes of structures
- Confer with engineers to prepare plans
- Develop plans and estimate costs for constructing systems and operating facilities
- Use computer aided design (CAD) software to draft project drawings
- Conduct field surveys to collect data on site conditions and inspect structures
- Test appropriateness of construction materials and soil samples
- Observe project sites to ensure that construction conforms to design specifications and applicable codes
- Prepare reports and document project activities and data
- Set up and help maintain project files and records

Civil engineering technicians confer with project supervisors to determine details of a project.

Civil engineering technicians typically install, troubleshoot, and maintain designs created by engineers. They may work under the direction of engineers or engineering technologists.

Civil engineering technologists typically help licensed engineers improve designs or incorporate new technology. They may be team leaders, instructing civil engineering technicians on installing equipment, systems, or structures.

These technologists and technicians observe progress on a jobsite, collect data, and complete reports to document project activities. Because they are not licensed, civil engineering technologists and technicians cannot approve designs or supervise the overall project.

In addition, civil engineering technologists and technicians sometimes estimate construction costs, develop specifications, and prepare drawings. They also may set up and monitor various instruments for traffic studies. Their duties often require use of software to design projects, collect and analyze data, prepare reports, and manage files.

Work Environment

Civil engineering technologists and technicians held about 64,800 jobs in 2022. The largest employers of civil engineering technologists and technicians were as follows:

Engineering services	43%
State government, excluding education and hospitals	23

Civil engineering technicians work on-site to help civil engineers in implementing project plans correctly.

Local government, excluding education and hospitals 20
Construction 2

Civil engineering technologists and technicians work in offices, helping civil engineers plan and design projects. They also visit construction jobsites to collect or test materials or to observe activities as a project inspector. They may work at several sites, using cars or trucks as a mobile office.

Civil engineering technologists and technicians frequently work on teams with civil engineers, surveyors and surveying technicians, construction workers, and others involved with projects.

Work Schedules

Civil engineering technologists and technicians usually work full time. When working at construction sites, their schedules may be subject to factors that affect construction, such as weather. Their schedules also may be tied to those of the construction projects they are involved with.

How to Become a Civil Engineering Technologist or Technician

An associate's degree, preferably in civil engineering technology, is typically required to enter the occupation.

Education

Prospective civil engineering technologists and technicians should take courses in science and math, such as chemistry, physics, geometry, and trigonometry.

Employers may prefer to hire engineering technologists and technicians who have an associate's degree from a program accredited by ABET, although a degree is not always required. Engineering technology programs also are available at technical or vocational schools that award a postgraduate certificate or diploma.

Degree and nondegree programs may include coursework in subjects such as engineering, design, and sciences.

Some employers require a bachelor's degree in engineering technology for civil engineering technologists.

Other Experience

Some civil engineering technologists and technicians enter the occupation after gaining work experience in a related occupation, particularly as drafters or CAD operators. Drafters or CAD operators working for an engineering firm may advance to civil engineering technologist or technician positions as their knowledge of design and construction increases.

Licenses, Certifications, and Registrations

Certification is not required to enter this occupation, but it may help technologists and technicians develop in their careers. For example, the National Institute for Certification in Engineering

Civil engineering technicians prepare reports and document project activities and data.

Technologies (NICET) oversees certification for civil engineering technicians who pass an exam and provide supporting documentation. NICET requires technicians to update their skills and knowledge through a recertification process that encourages continuing professional development.

Advancement

Civil engineering technologists and technicians may advance in their careers by learning to design systems for a variety of projects, such as storm sewers, and to become skilled at reading graphical drawings of proposed projects.

Technicians who obtain appropriate education or certification may advance to become technologists.

Important Qualities

Critical-thinking skills. Civil engineering technologists and technicians carry out project plans and designs that engineers have approved. They must be able to understand and interpret the reports and documents describing these projects.

Decision-making skills. Civil engineering technologists and technicians must be able to discern which information is most important and which actions will help keep a project on schedule.

Math skills. Civil engineering technologists and technicians use math for analysis, design, and troubleshooting.

Civil Engineering Technologists and Technicians

Median annual wages, May 2022

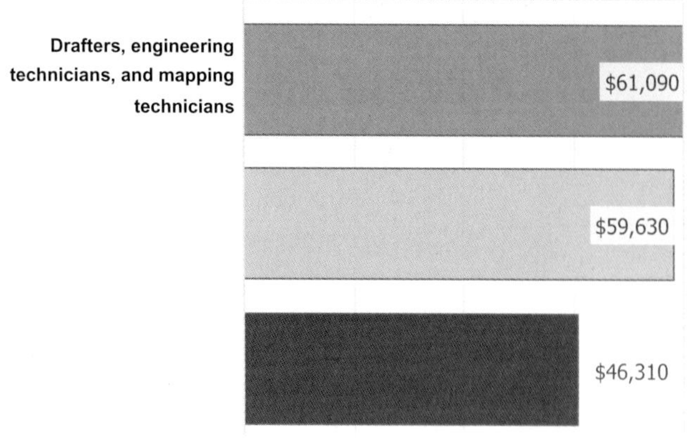

Note: All Occupations includes all occupations in the U.S. Economy.
Source: U.S. Bureau of Labor Statistics, Occupational Employment and Wage Statistics.

Observational skills. Civil engineering technologists and technicians sometimes visit jobsites to assess a project and report back to the engineer.

Problem-solving skills. As assistants to civil engineers, these technologists and technicians must be able to help engineers identify problems and design projects to solve them.

Writing skills. Civil engineering technologists and technicians must be able to prepare reports that are well organized and clearly convey information.

Pay

The median annual wage for civil engineering technologists and technicians was $59,630 in May 2022. The median wage is the wage at which half the workers in an occupation earned more than that amount and half earned less. The lowest 10 percent earned less than $37,430, and the highest 10 percent earned more than $85,740.

In May 2022, the median annual wages for civil engineering technologists and technicians in the top industries in which they worked were as follows:

Local government, excluding education and hospitals	$63,620
Construction	61,130
Engineering services	60,190
State government, excluding education and hospitals	50,160

Civil engineering technologists and technicians usually work full time. When working at construction sites, their schedules may be subject to factors that affect construction, such as weather. Their schedules also may be tied to those of the construction projects they are involved with.

Job Outlook

Employment of civil engineering technologists and technicians is projected to show little or no change from 2022 to 2032.

Despite limited employment growth, about 5,900 openings for civil engineering technologists and technicians are projected each year, on average, over the decade. Most of those openings are expected to result from the need to replace workers who transfer to different occupations or exit the labor force, such as to retire.

Civil Engineering Technologists and Technicians

Percent change in employment, projected 2022-32

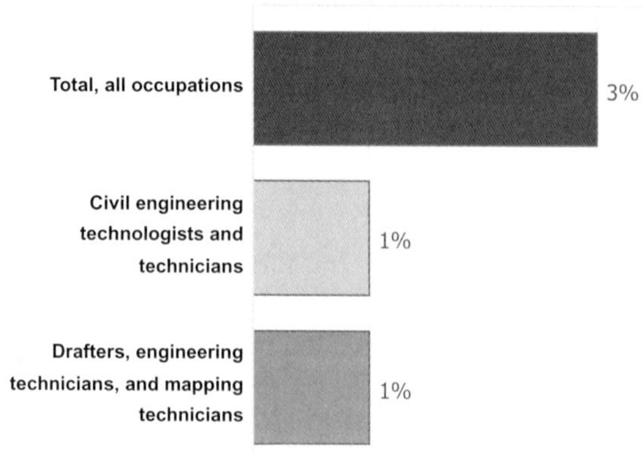

Note: All Occupations includes all occupations in the U.S. Economy.
Source: U.S. Bureau of Labor Statistics, Employment Projections program.

Employment

The need to preserve, repair, and upgrade the country's infrastructure continues to increase. Bridges, roads, levees, airports, and dams will need to be rebuilt, maintained, and enhanced. In addition, more waste treatment plants will be needed to help clean the nation's waterways, and water systems must be maintained to reduce or eliminate loss of potable water. Civil engineers plan, design, and oversee this work, and civil engineering technologists and technicians will be needed to assist the engineers in these projects.

Civil engineering technologists and technicians also will find work assisting civil engineers with renewable-energy projects. For example, these technologists and technicians may assist in developing a wind farm by helping engineers minimize project costs associated with the sizeable dimensions and weight of wind turbines.

However, employment in this occupation may be limited as improved drafting tools, such as computer-aided design (CAD) software, increase worker productivity.

Occupational Title	SOC Code	Employment, 2022	Projected Employment, 2032	Change, 2022-32	
				Percent	Numeric
Civil engineering technologists and technicians	17-3022	64,800	65,400	1	600

Contacts for More Information

For more information, visit

- Pathways to Science
- ABET
- National Institute for Certification in Engineering Technologies (NICET)

Civil Engineers

Summary

Quick Facts: Civil Engineers	
2022 Median Pay	$89,940 per year $43.24 per hour
Typical Entry-Level Education	Bachelor's degree
Work Experience in a Related Occupation	None
On-the-job Training	None
Number of Jobs, 2022	326,300
Job Outlook, 2022-32	5% (Faster than average)
Employment Change, 2022-32	16,200

What Civil Engineers Do

Civil engineers plan, design, and supervise the construction and maintenance of building and infrastructure projects.

Work Environment

Civil engineers work in a variety of locations and conditions, commonly splitting their time between an office setting and construction sites. Most civil engineers work full time, and some work more than 40 hours per week.

How to Become a Civil Engineer

Civil engineers typically need a bachelor's degree in civil engineering or a related field to enter the occupation. They typically need a state-issued license if they provide services directly to the public.

Pay

The median annual wage for civil engineers was $89,940 in May 2022.

Job Outlook

Employment of civil engineers is projected to grow 5 percent from 2022 to 2032, faster than the average for all occupations.

Civil engineers provide cost estimates for materials and labor to determine a project's economic feasibility.

About 21,200 openings for civil engineers are projected each year, on average, over the decade. Many of those openings are expected to result from the need to replace workers who transfer to different occupations or exit the labor force, such as to retire.

What Civil Engineers Do

Civil engineers plan, design, and supervise the construction and maintenance of building and infrastructure projects. These projects may include facilities, bridges, roads, tunnels, and water and sewage systems.

Duties

Civil engineers typically do the following:

- Analyze plans, survey reports, maps, and other data related to project design
- Consider regulations, site selection, and other factors relevant to a project
- Analyze the results of tests on soil and building materials to determine strength for foundations and other support
- Prepare cost estimates for equipment, materials, and labor to determine a project's economic feasibility
- Use design software to plan transportation systems, hydraulic systems, and structures

Civil engineers design major transportation projects.

- Submit permit applications to local, state, and federal agencies, as needed, and confirm that projects comply with regulations
- Perform or oversee surveying to establish building locations, site layouts, grades, and elevations to guide construction
- Manage the construction or repair, maintenance, and replacement of buildings and infrastructure

Civil engineers work in all aspects of planning, designing, and constructing or repairing a building or infrastructure project to ensure that structures and systems are assembled correctly. Depending on the job, civil engineers may be involved in a project from start to finish or for certain stages of it.

Civil engineers' responsibilities during the planning stage may include researching specific topics, such as building codes for a construction proposal or traffic patterns near an intended site. They also may conduct analyses, such as for estimating availability and costs of concrete and other building materials, to determine a project's timeline and feasibility.

During design and preconstruction stages, civil engineers may focus on specific elements such as site layout, grading (shaping) the land, and identifying appropriate stormwater and sewage systems for the project. Engineers use computer-aided design (CAD) software to create detailed project plans and may make presentations related to the final design, such as about its environmental impact. They often review project documents and secure required permits before work may begin.

Civil engineers also oversee the building of structures or systems throughout a project's construction, and they help with signoff and other postconstruction activities. They ensure that work complies with safety regulations and adheres to design specifications, helping to resolve problems that may arise. At the conclusion of a project, they may finalize billing, inspection, and other completion details.

Civil engineers may collaborate on projects with other workers, such as architects, construction managers, and urban planners. They may be assisted by civil engineering technicians.

Civil engineers often work as generalists on a variety of projects, gaining skills in different areas that are widely applicable. Some specialize in one of several areas. The following are examples of types of civil engineers:

Construction engineers manage construction projects, ensuring that they are scheduled and built according to plans and specifications. They typically are responsible for the design and safety of any temporary structures used during construction. They also may oversee a project's budget and communications.

Geotechnical engineers ensure the safety and sturdiness of foundations for streets, buildings, and other structures and systems. They focus on how these manmade objects interact with the earth, including soil and rock. In this way, their work relates to that of environmental engineers.

Structural engineers design and assess major projects, such as buildings, bridges, and dams, to ensure their strength and durability.

Although civil engineers work in an office setting to produce plans, they also spend time onsite to oversee construction.

Transportation engineers plan, design, and maintain streets and highways, airports, mass transit systems, harbors, and related systems.

Work Environment

Civil engineers held about 326,300 jobs in 2022. The largest employers of civil engineers were as follows:

Employer	Percent
Engineering services	48%
State government, excluding education and hospitals	12
Local government, excluding education and hospitals	10
Nonresidential building construction	6
Federal government, excluding postal service	3

Civil engineers work in a variety of locations and conditions, including indoors in office settings and outdoors at construction sites. Some construction jobs require setting up a temporary office, such as in a trailer, to work onsite.

Work Schedules

Most civil engineers work full time, and some work more than 40 hours per week. Engineers who direct projects sometimes work extra hours to ensure that designs meet requirements and that the projects are on track to meet deadlines.

Civil engineers typically need a bachelor's degree in civil engineering or a related field.

How to Become a Civil Engineer

Civil engineers typically need a bachelor's degree in civil engineering or a related field. Although licensure requirements vary by state, civil engineers usually must be licensed if they provide services directly to the public.

Education

Civil engineers typically need a bachelor's degree in civil engineering or a related field. Civil engineering programs include coursework in math, physics, engineering mechanics, and construction systems. Courses may include a mix of academic learning and laboratory work.

Employers usually prefer to hire graduates of civil engineering programs accredited by ABET. Some students attend schools that have cooperative-education programs (also known as co-ops); others participate in internships. Co-ops and internships provide students with an opportunity to gain practical experience while pursuing a degree.

Licenses, Certifications, and Registrations

Licensure is not required for entry-level civil engineers. However, civil engineers typically must be licensed if they provide services directly to the public. Engineers who have a Professional Engineer (PE) license are called professional engineers (PEs).

A PE may oversee the work of other engineers, approve design plans, sign off on projects, and provide services directly to the public. State licensure generally requires a bachelor's or higher degree from an ABET-accredited engineering program, a passing score on the Fundamentals of Engineering (FE) exam, several years of relevant work experience, and a passing score on the PE exam.

Each state issues its own licenses. Most states recognize licensure from other states, as long as the licensing state's requirements meet or exceed their own licensure requirements. Some states require continuing education for engineers to keep their licenses.

Certifications, such as in coastal engineering or geotechnical engineering from the American Society of Civil Engineers, also are available. Optional certification may demonstrate a level of competence and experience that make candidates attractive to prospective employers.

Advancement

With experience, some PEs advance to supervisory or administrative positions. Their responsibilities may focus on a specific project, such as a construction site, or encompass broad oversight, such as in working as a city engineer, public works director, or city manager.

Graduate-level education, along with a PE license and experience, may be helpful for advancing into supervisory positions, such as engineering managers.

PEs who have certification that demonstrates expertise in a civil engineering specialty also may be able to advance into senior technical or managerial positions.

Important Qualities

Communication skills. Civil engineers must be able to explain, both orally and in writing, the details of their projects. They may need to convey information to a variety of audiences, including nontechnical ones.

Decision-making skills. Civil engineers must be able to balance a variety of objectives, such as the feasibility of plans against cost and safety.

Interpersonal skills. Civil engineers often manage projects and the teams that work on them. They must be able to lead urban planners, surveyors, civil engineering technicians, and others.

Math skills. Civil engineers use calculus, trigonometry, and other mathematics for analysis, design, and troubleshooting.

Organizational skills. Civil engineers often oversee several projects at the same time and must be able to allocate resources effectively.

Problem-solving skills. Civil engineers may encounter problems during each stage of their work. They must be able to evaluate issues that arise and troubleshoot to find solutions.

Pay

The median annual wage for civil engineers was $89,940 in May 2022. The median wage is the wage at which half the workers in an occupation earned more than that amount and half earned less. The lowest 10 percent earned less than $61,040, and the highest 10 percent earned more than $138,690.

In May 2022, the median annual wages for civil engineers in the top industries in which they worked were as follows:

Federal government, excluding postal service	$103,170
Local government, excluding education and hospitals	101,460
State government, excluding education and hospitals	87,010

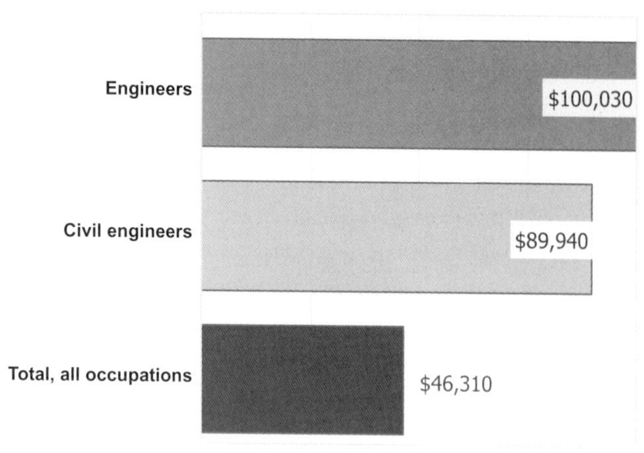

Note: All Occupations includes all occupations in the U.S. Economy.
Source: U.S. Bureau of Labor Statistics, Occupational Employment and Wage Statistics.

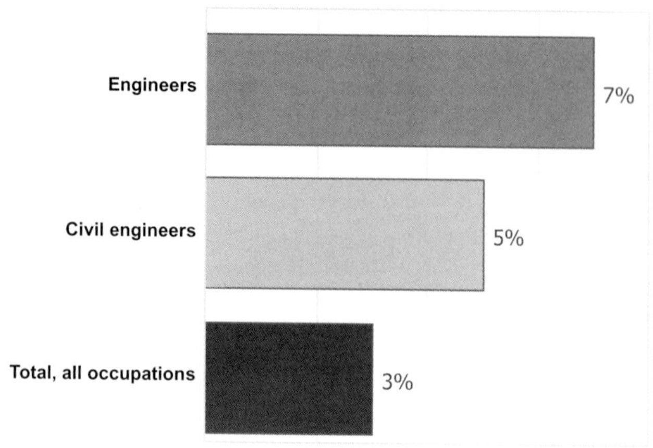

Note: All Occupations includes all occupations in the U.S. Economy.
Source: U.S. Bureau of Labor Statistics, Employment Projections program.

Engineering services	86,440
Nonresidential building construction	78,420

Most civil engineers work full time, and some work more than 40 hours per week. Engineers who direct projects sometimes work extra hours to ensure that designs meet requirements and that projects are on track to meet deadlines.

Job Outlook

Employment of civil engineers is projected to grow 5 percent from 2022 to 2032, faster than the average for all occupations.

About 21,200 openings for civil engineers are projected each year, on average, over the decade. Many of those openings are expected to result from the need to replace workers who transfer to different occupations or exit the labor force, such as to retire.

Employment

With continued investment in U.S. infrastructure, civil engineers will be needed to manage projects that meet society's need for upgrading bridges, roads, water systems, buildings, and other structures.

Civil engineers also will be needed to oversee renewable-energy projects, such as construction of wind farms and solar arrays, as these projects gain approval.

Public projects may depend on funding from state and local governments. Employment of civil engineers may fluctuate with the availability of project funds.

Occupational Title	SOC Code	Employment, 2022	Projected Employment, 2032	Change, 2022-32	
				Percent	Numeric
Civil engineers	17-2051	326,300	342,500	5	16,200

Contacts for More Information

For information about general engineering education and career resources, visit

- American Society for Engineering Education (ASEE)
- Technology Student Association (TSA)
- National Council of Examiners for Engineering and Surveying (NCEES)
- National Society of Professional Engineers (NSPE)
- ABET
- American Society of Civil Engineers (ASCE)

Computer Hardware Engineers

Summary

Quick Facts: Computer Hardware Engineers	
2022 Median Pay	$132,360 per year $63.64 per hour
Typical Entry-Level Education	Bachelor's degree
Work Experience in a Related Occupation	None
On-the-job Training	None
Number of Jobs, 2022	78,100
Job Outlook, 2022-32	5% (Faster than average)
Employment Change, 2022-32	3,600

What Computer Hardware Engineers Do

Computer hardware engineers research, design, develop, and test computer systems and components.

Work Environment

Computer hardware engineers usually work in research laboratories that build and test various types of computer models. Most work in computer systems design services and in manufacturing.

How to Become a Computer Hardware Engineer

Computer hardware engineers typically need a bachelor's degree from an accredited program.

Pay

The median annual wage for computer hardware engineers was $132,360 in May 2022.

Job Outlook

Employment of computer hardware engineers is projected to grow 5 percent from 2022 to 2032, faster than the average for all occupations.

About 4,600 openings for computer hardware engineers are projected each year, on average, over the decade. Many of those openings are expected to result from the need to replace workers who transfer to different occupations or exit the labor force, such as to retire.

What Computer Hardware Engineers Do

Computer hardware engineers research, design, develop, and test computer systems and components such as processors, circuit boards, memory devices, networks, and routers.

Duties

Computer hardware engineers typically do the following:

- Design new computer hardware, creating schematics of computer equipment to be built
- Test the computer hardware they design
- Analyze the test results and modify the design as needed
- Update existing computer equipment so that it will work with new software
- Oversee the manufacturing process for computer hardware

Many hardware engineers design devices used in manufactured products that incorporate processors and other computer components and that connect to the Internet. For example, many new cars, home appliances, and medical devices have Internet-ready computer systems built into them.

Computer hardware engineers ensure that computer hardware components work together with the latest software. Therefore, hardware engineers often work with software developers. For example, the hardware and software for mobile phones and other devices frequently are developed at the same time.

Work Environment

Computer hardware engineers held about 78,100 jobs in 2022. The largest employers of computer hardware engineers were as follows:

Computer hardware engineers solve problems that arise in computer hardware.

Computer hardware engineers research, design, develop, and test computer systems and components such as circuit boards.

Research and development in the physical, engineering, and life sciences	20%
Semiconductor and other electronic component manufacturing	16
Computer systems design and related services	15
Computer and peripheral equipment manufacturing	8
Federal government	7

Work Schedules

Most computer hardware engineers work full time.

How to Become a Computer Hardware Engineer

Computer hardware engineers typically need a bachelor's degree from an accredited program.

Education

Entry-level computer hardware engineers typically need a bachelor's degree in computer engineering or a related field, such as computer and information technology. Employers may prefer to hire candidates who have graduated from an engineering program accredited by a professional association, such as ABET. To prepare for a major in computer or electrical engineering, students should have a solid background in math and science.

Because hardware engineers commonly work with computer software systems, a familiarity with computer programming is usually expected. This background may be obtained through computer science courses.

Some large firms or specialized jobs may require a master's degree in computer engineering. Some experienced engineers obtain a master's degree in business administration (MBA). All engineers must continue their learning over the course of their careers in order to keep up with rapid advances in technology.

Other Experience

Some students participate in internships while in school so that they can gain practical experience.

Advancement

Some computer hardware engineers can advance to become computer and information systems managers.

Important Qualities

Analytical skills. Computer hardware engineers use computer programming tools to analyze the digital circuits in hardware to determine the best design.

Critical-thinking skills. These engineers use logic and reasoning to clarify goals, examine assumptions, and identify the strengths and weaknesses of alternative solutions.

Problem-solving skills. Computer hardware engineers identify complex problems in computer hardware, develop and evaluate possible solutions, and figure out the best way to implement them.

Communication skills. Engineers often work on teams and must be able to communicate with other types of engineers, software developers and programmers, as well as with nontechnical team members.

Pay

The median annual wage for computer hardware engineers was $132,360 in May 2022. The median wage is the wage at which half the workers in an occupation earned more than that amount and half earned less. The lowest 10 percent earned less than $78,380, and the highest 10 percent earned more than $208,200.

In May 2022, the median annual wages for computer hardware engineers in the top industries in which they worked were as follows:

Research and development in the physical, engineering, and life sciences	$163,150
Computer and peripheral equipment manufacturing	143,640

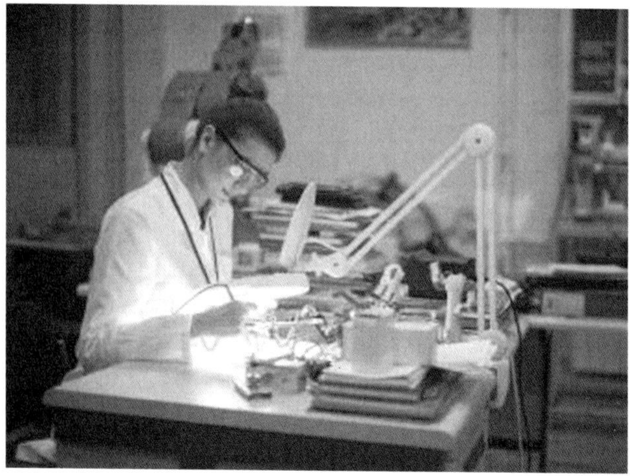

Most hardware engineers work in labs where they test different types of computer models.

Entry-level computer hardware engineers typically need a bachelor's degree in computer engineering or a related field, such as computer and information technology.

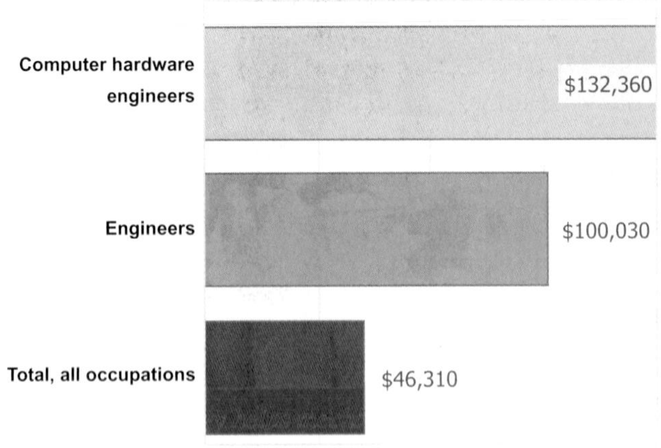

Note: All Occupations includes all occupations in the U.S. Economy. Source: U.S. Bureau of Labor Statistics, Occupational Employment and Wage Statistics.

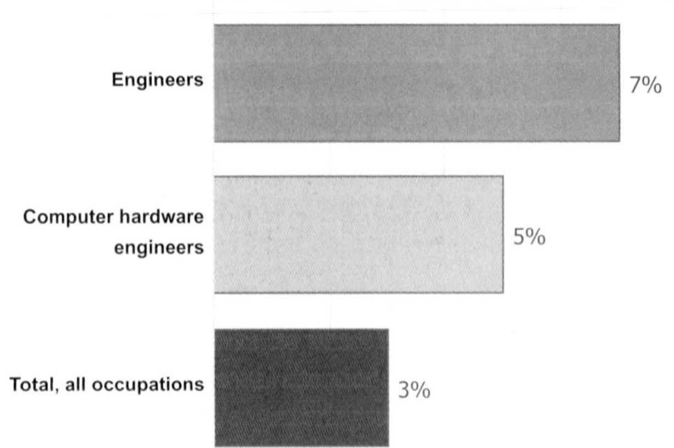

Note: All Occupations includes all occupations in the U.S. Economy. Source: U.S. Bureau of Labor Statistics, Employment Projections program.

Semiconductor and other electronic component manufacturing	131,950
Computer systems design and related services	129,460
Federal government	122,680

Most computer hardware engineers work full time.

Job Outlook

Employment of computer hardware engineers is projected to grow 5 percent from 2022 to 2032, faster than the average for all occupations.

About 4,600 openings for computer hardware engineers are projected each year, on average, over the decade. Many of those openings are expected to result from the need to replace workers who transfer to different occupations or exit the labor force, such as to retire.

Employment

Demand for computer hardware engineers is expected to grow, as these workers are needed to design parts for manufactured products that use processors and other components, such as household appliances, medical devices, and automobiles. As new technologies expand, however, an expected uptick in focus on software innovation compared with hardware may temper demand for these engineers.

Occupational Title	SOC Code	Employment, 2022	Projected Employment, 2032	Change, 2022-32	
				Percent	Numeric
Computer hardware engineers	17-2061	78,100	81,600	5	3,600

Contacts for More Information

For more information about computer hardware engineers, visit

- Association for Computing Machinery
- IEEE Computer Society
- ABET

Drafters

Summary

Quick Facts: Drafters	
2022 Median Pay	$60,400 per year $29.04 per hour
Typical Entry-Level Education	Associate's degree
Work Experience in a Related Occupation	None
On-the-job Training	None
Number of Jobs, 2022	197,300
Job Outlook, 2022-32	-2% (Decline)
Employment Change, 2022-32	-4,300

What Drafters Do
Drafters use software to convert the designs of engineers and architects into technical drawings.

Work Environment
Although drafters spend much of their time working on computers in an office, some may visit jobsites in order to collaborate with architects and engineers. Most drafters work full time.

How to Become a Drafter
Drafters typically complete education after high school, often through a program at a community college or technical school. Some programs lead to an associate of applied science in drafting or a related degree. Others result in a certificate or diploma.

Pay
The median annual wage for drafters was $60,400 in May 2022.

Job Outlook
Overall employment of drafters is projected to decline 2 percent from 2022 to 2032.

Despite declining employment, about 16,600 openings for drafters are projected each year, on average, over the decade. All of those openings are expected to result from the need to replace workers who transfer to other occupations or exit the labor force, such as to retire.

What Drafters Do
Drafters use software to convert the designs of architects and engineers into technical drawings. Most workers specialize in architectural, civil, electrical, or mechanical drafting and use technical drawings to help design everything from microchips to skyscrapers.

Duties
Drafters typically do the following:

- Design plans using computer-aided design (CAD) software
- Work from rough sketches and specifications created by engineers and architects
- Design products with engineering and manufacturing techniques
- Add details to architectural plans from their knowledge of building techniques
- Specify dimensions, materials, and procedures for new products
- Work under the supervision of engineers or architects

Some drafters are referred to as *CAD operators*. Using CAD systems, drafters create and store technical drawings digitally. These drawings contain information on how to build a structure or machine, the dimensions of the project, and what materials are needed to complete the project.

Drafters work with CAD to create schematics that can be viewed, printed, or programmed directly into building information modeling (BIM) systems. These systems allow drafters, architects, construction managers, and engineers to create and collaborate on digital models of physical buildings and machines. Through three-dimensional rendering, BIM software allows designers and engineers to see how different elements in their projects work together.

Drafters take designs from engineers and architects and convert them into plans needed for construction.

Drafters prepare technical drawings and plans.

The following are examples of types of drafters:

Architectural drafters draw structural features and details for buildings and other construction projects. These workers may specialize in a type of building, such as residential or commercial. They may also specialize by the materials used, such as steel, wood, or reinforced concrete.

Civil drafters prepare topographical maps used in construction and civil engineering projects, such as highways, bridges, and dams.

Electrical drafters prepare wiring diagrams that construction workers use to install and repair electrical equipment and wiring in power plants, electrical distribution systems, and residential and commercial buildings.

Electronics drafters produce wiring diagrams, assembly diagrams for circuit boards, and layout drawings used in manufacturing and in installing and repairing electronic devices and components.

Mechanical drafters prepare layouts that show the details for a variety of machinery and mechanical tools and devices, such as medical equipment. These layouts indicate dimensions, fastening methods, and other requirements for assembly. Mechanical drafters sometimes create production molds.

Work Environment

Drafters held about 197,300 jobs in 2022. Employment in the detailed occupations that make up drafters was distributed as follows:

Architectural and civil drafters	107,100
Mechanical drafters	49,600
Electrical and electronics drafters	21,800
Drafters, all other	18,700

The largest employers of drafters were as follows:

Architectural, engineering, and related services	49%
Manufacturing	23
Construction	11
Administrative and support and waste management and remediation services	3

Although drafters spend much of their time working on computers in an office, some may visit jobsites to collaborate with architects and engineers.

Work Schedules

Most drafters work full time. Some work more than 40 hours a week.

How to Become a Drafter

Drafters typically complete education after high school, often through a program at a community college or technical school. Some programs lead to an associate of applied science in drafting or a related degree. Others result in a certificate or diploma.

Education

Drafters typically need an associate of applied science in drafting or a related degree from a community college or technical school. Some drafters prepare for the occupation by earning a certificate or diploma.

Programs in drafting may include instruction in design fundamentals, sketching, and computer-aided design (CAD) software. It generally takes about 2 years of full-time education to earn an associate's degree. Certificate and diploma programs vary in length but usually may be completed in less time.

Students frequently specialize in a particular type of drafting, such as mechanical or architectural drafting.

High school students may begin preparing by taking classes in mathematics, science, computer technology, design, computer graphics, and, where available, drafting.

Licenses, Certifications, and Registrations

The American Design Drafting Association (ADDA) offers certification for drafters. Although not mandatory, certification

Drafters spend much of their time working on computers using specialized software in an office.

Drafters generally need to complete postsecondary education in drafting.

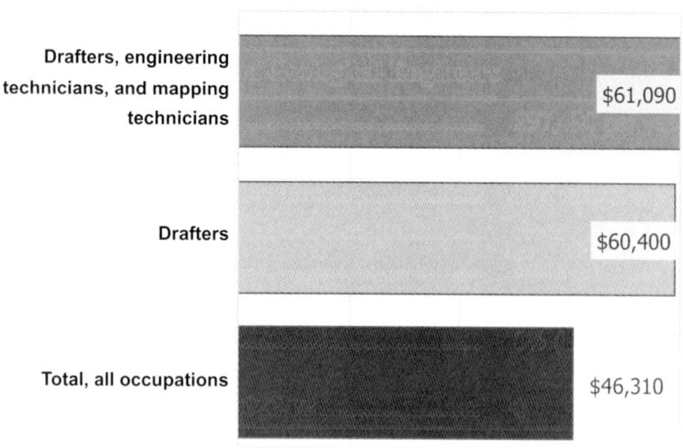

Note: All Occupations includes all occupations in the U.S. Economy.
Source: U.S. Bureau of Labor Statistics, Occupational Employment and Wage Statistics.

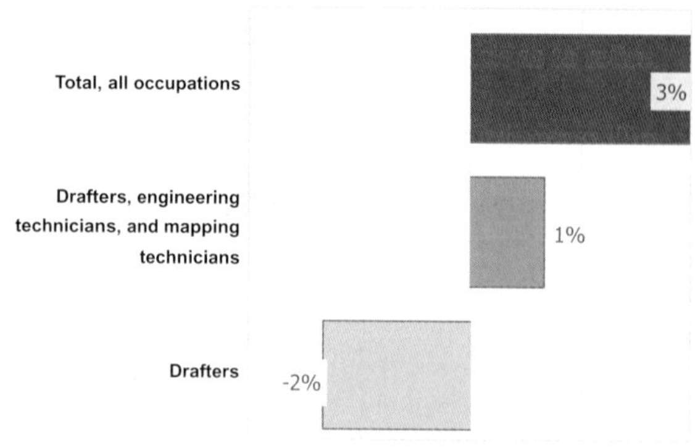

Note: All Occupations includes all occupations in the U.S. Economy.
Source: U.S. Bureau of Labor Statistics, Employment Projections program.

demonstrates competence and knowledge of nationally recognized practices. Certifications are offered for several specialties, including architectural, civil, and mechanical drafting.

Important Qualities

Creativity. Drafters must be able to turn plans and ideas into technical drawings of buildings, tools, and systems.

Detail oriented. Drafters must take care that the plans they convert are technically accurate according to the outlined specifications.

Interpersonal skills. Drafters work closely with architects, engineers, and other designers to make sure that final plans are accurate. This requires the ability to communicate effectively and work well with others.

Math skills. Drafters work on technical drawings. They may be required to calculate angles, weights, costs, and other values.

Technical skills. Drafters in all specialties must be able to use computer software, such as CAD, and work with database tools, such as building information modeling (BIM).

Time-management skills. Drafters often work under deadline. As a result, they must work efficiently to produce the required output according to set schedules.

Pay

The median annual wage for drafters was $60,400 in May 2022. The median wage is the wage at which half the workers in an occupation earned more than that amount and half earned less. The lowest 10 percent earned less than $38,360, and the highest 10 percent earned more than $93,570.

Median annual wages for drafters in May 2022 were as follows:

Electrical and electronics drafters	$64,240
Mechanical drafters	61,310
Architectural and civil drafters	59,820
Drafters, all other	57,640

In May 2022, the median annual wages for drafters in the top industries in which they worked were as follows:

Construction	$62,140
Architectural, engineering, and related services	60,170
Manufacturing	58,900
Administrative and support and waste management and remediation services	58,850

Most drafters work full time. Some work more than 40 hours a week.

Job Outlook

Overall employment of drafters is projected to decline 2 percent from 2022 to 2032.

Despite declining employment, about 16,600 openings for drafters are projected each year, on average, over the decade. All of those openings are expected to result from the need to replace workers who transfer to other occupations or exit the labor force, such as to retire.

Employment

Expected employment decreases will be driven by the use of computer-aided design (CAD) and building information modeling (BIM) technologies. These technologies increase drafter productivity and allow engineers and architects to perform many tasks that used to be done by drafters.

Occupational Title	SOC Code	Employment, 2022	Projected Employment, 2032	Change, 2022-32	
				Percent	Numeric
Drafters	17-3010	197,300	193,000	-2	-4,300
Architectural and civil drafters	17-3011	107,100	107,700	1	600
Electrical and electronics drafters	17-3012	21,800	22,000	1	200

Occupational Title	SOC Code	Employment, 2022	Projected Employment, 2032	Change, 2022-32	
				Percent	Numeric
Mechanical drafters	17-3013	49,600	46,000	-7	-3,600
Drafters, all other	17-3019	18,700	17,300	-8	-1,500

Contacts for More Information

For more information, visit

- Accrediting Commission of Career Schools and Colleges
- American Design Drafting Association

Electrical and Electronic Engineering Technologists and Technicians

Summary

Quick Facts: Electrical and Electronic Engineering Technologists and Technicians	
2022 Median Pay	$66,390 per year $31.92 per hour
Typical Entry-Level Education	Associate's degree
Work Experience in a Related Occupation	None
On-the-job Training	None
Number of Jobs, 2022	102,500
Job Outlook, 2022-32	1% (Little or no change)
Employment Change, 2022-32	800

What Electrical and Electronic Engineering Technologists and Technicians Do

Electrical and electronic engineering technologists and technicians help engineers design and develop equipment that is powered by electricity or electric current.

Work Environment

Electrical and electronic engineering technologists and technicians work on teams with electrical engineers. They may work in offices, laboratories, or factories. Most work full time.

Electrical and electronics engineering technicians use diagnostic devices to adjust, test, and repair equipment.

How to Become an Electrical or Electronic Engineering Technologist or Technician

Electrical and electronic engineering technologists and technicians typically need an associate's degree.

Pay

The median annual wage for electrical and electronic engineering technologists and technicians was $66,390 in May 2022.

Job Outlook

Employment of electrical and electronic engineering technologists and technicians is projected to show little or no change from 2022 to 2032.

Despite limited employment growth, about 9,900 openings for electrical and electronic engineering technologists and technicians are projected each year, on average, over the decade. Most of those openings are expected to result from the need to replace workers who transfer to different occupations or exit the labor force, such as to retire.

What Electrical and Electronic Engineering Technologists and Technicians Do

Electrical and electronic engineering technologists and technicians help electrical and electronics engineers plan and develop communications equipment, computers, medical monitoring devices, or other equipment that is powered by other electricity or electric current. They often work in product evaluation and

Electrical and electronic engineering technologists and technicians help engineers design and develop computers and other electrical and electronic equipment.

testing, using measuring and diagnostic devices to test, adjust, and repair equipment. They are also involved in assembling equipment for automation.

Duties

Electrical engineering technologists and technicians typically do the following:

- Assemble electrical and electronic systems and prototypes
- Build, calibrate, and repair electrical instruments or testing equipment
- Visit sites where systems are made to observe conditions affecting design
- Identify solutions to technical design problems that arise in making electrical systems
- Inspect designs for quality control, report findings, and recommend changes, if necessary
- Draw diagrams and write specifications about design details of experimental electronics units

Electrical engineering technologists and technicians install and maintain electrical control systems and equipment and adjust electrical prototypes, parts, and assemblies to correct problems. When testing systems, they set up equipment and evaluate how the parts, assemblies, or systems perform under simulated conditions. They also analyze test information to resolve design problems.

Electronic engineering technologists and technicians typically do the following:

- Create basic circuitry and draft sketches to clarify details of design, under engineers' direction
- Build prototypes from plans or sketches
- Assemble, test, and maintain circuitry or electronic components according to engineering instructions, knowledge of electronics, and technical manuals
- Adjust and replace defective circuitry and electronic components
- Make parts, such as coils and terminal boards, using bench lathes, drills, or other machine tools

Electronic engineering technologists and technicians identify and repair equipment malfunctions. They also calibrate and perform preventive maintenance on equipment and systems.

These workers often need to read blueprints, diagrams, and engineering instructions for assembling electronic units. They also write reports and record data on testing techniques, laboratory equipment, and specifications.

Work Environment

Electrical and electronic engineering technologists and technicians held about 102,500 jobs in 2022. The largest employers of electrical and electronic engineering technologists and technicians were as follows:

Electrical and electronic engineering technologists and technicians build, calibrate, and repair electrical instruments or testing equipment.

Engineering services	13%
Federal government	12
Semiconductor and other electronic component manufacturing	12
Navigational, measuring, electromedical, and control instruments manufacturing	7
Utilities	6

Electrical and electronic engineering technologists and technicians work on teams with electrical and electronics engineers. They work in offices, laboratories, and factories because their job tasks involve both engineering theory and assembly-line production.

Electrical and electronic engineering technologists and technicians may be exposed to hazards from equipment or toxic materials, but incidents are rare if procedures are followed.

Work Schedules

Most electrical and electronic engineering technologists and technicians work full time. Some work day or night shifts, depending on production schedules. In the federal government, their schedules usually follow a standard workweek.

How to Become an Electrical or Electronic Engineering Technologist or Technician

Electrical and electronic engineering technologists and technicians typically need an associate's degree. However, requirements may vary by employer.

Education

Associate's degree programs in electrical or electronic engineering technology are available at community colleges and vocational–technical schools. Programs accredited by ABET or other organizations typically include courses such as algebra, programming languages, physics, and circuitry.

Depending on the job tasks or the industry, employers may prefer to hire candidates who have a bachelor's degree. Candidates for other jobs may qualify with a high school diploma.

Licenses, Certifications, and Registrations

Certifications in a variety of fields are available for electrical and electronic engineering technologists and technicians. While optional, these credentials show that the designee has advanced knowledge. Among the organizations that offer certification are the National Institute for Certification in Engineering Technologies (NICET), ETA International, and the International Society of Automation.

Important Qualities

Communication skills. Electrical and electronic engineering technologists and technicians must be able to follow instructions from engineers and others. They also need to clearly convey problems to engineers.

Detail oriented. Electrical engineering technologists and technicians must pay attention to detail when assembling, troubleshooting, and repairing electronic and electrical mechanical systems.

Math skills. Electrical and electronic engineering technologists and technicians use mathematics for analysis, design, and troubleshooting tasks.

Mechanical skills. Electronic engineering technologists and technicians must use hand tools and soldering irons on small circuitry and electronic parts to build components by hand.

Problem-solving skills. Electrical and electronic engineering technologists and technicians must be able to identify and fix problems that arise in assembling and inspecting electrical engineers' designs and prototypes.

Writing skills. Electrical and electronic engineering technologists and technicians write reports about onsite construction, design problems, or testing results. Their writing must be clear and well organized to convey the information in the reports.

Pay

The median annual wage for electrical and electronic engineering technologists and technicians was $66,390 in May 2022.

Electrical and electronic engineering technologists and technicians typically need an associate's degree.

The median wage is the wage at which half the workers in an occupation earned more than that amount and half earned less. The lowest 10 percent earned less than $43,930, and the highest 10 percent earned more than $101,480.

In May 2022, the median annual wages for electrical and electronic engineering technologists and technicians in the top industries in which they worked were as follows:

Utilities	$84,190
Federal government	79,440
Navigational, measuring, electromedical, and control instruments manufacturing	64,170
Engineering services	64,000
Semiconductor and other electronic component manufacturing	61,610

Most electrical and electronic engineering technologists and technicians work full time. Some work day or night shifts, depending on production schedules. In the federal government, their schedules usually follow a standard workweek.

Job Outlook

Employment of electrical and electronic engineering technologists and technicians is projected to show little or no change from 2022 to 2032.

Despite limited employment growth, about 9,900 openings for electrical and electronic engineering technologists and technicians are projected each year, on average, over the decade. Most of those openings are expected to result from the need to replace workers who transfer to different occupations or exit the labor force, such as to retire.

Employment

Electrical and electronics engineering technologists and technicians work closely with electrical and electronics engineers and computer hardware engineers. These workers are needed to support the continuing integration of computer and

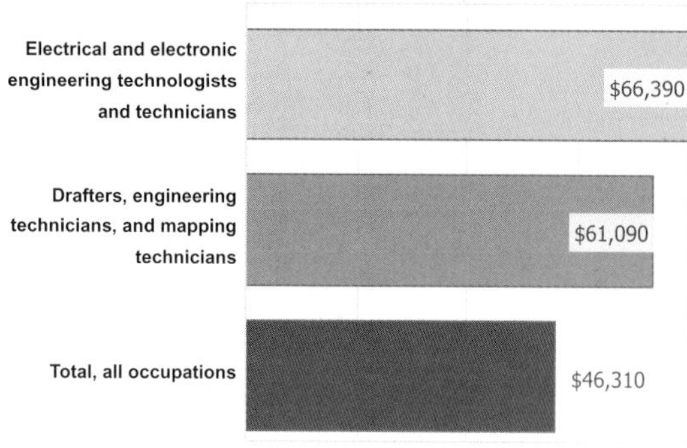

Note: All Occupations includes all occupations in the U.S. Economy.
Source: U.S. Bureau of Labor Statistics, Occupational Employment and Wage Statistics.

electronics systems, such as those found in automobiles and in various portable and household products. However, as more manual tasks performed by these technologists and technicians are automated, growth in this occupation could be limited.

Occupational Title	SOC Code	Employment, 2022	Projected Employment, 2032	Change, 2022-32	
				Percent	Numeric
Electrical and electronic engineering technologists and technicians	17-3023	102,500	103,300	1	800

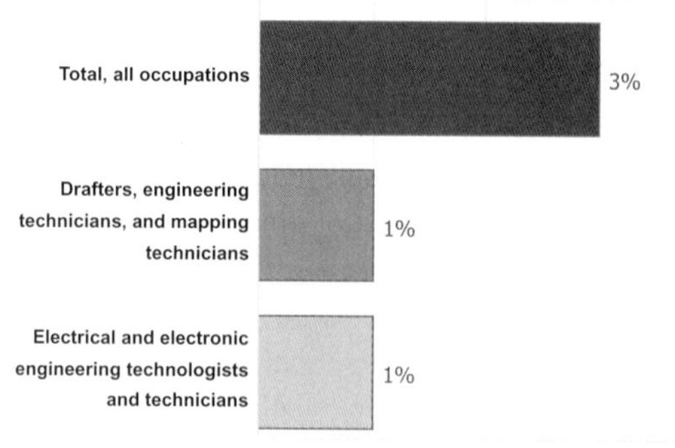

Note: All Occupations includes all occupations in the U.S. Economy.
Source: U.S. Bureau of Labor Statistics, Employment Projections program.

Contacts for More Information

For more information, visit

- American Society for Engineering Education (ASEE)
- Technology Student Association (TSA)
- ABET
- ETA International
- International Society of Automation (ISA)
- National Institute for Certification in Engineering Technologies (NICET)
- Automation Federation

Electrical and Electronics Engineers

Summary

Quick Facts: Electrical and Electronics Engineers	
2022 Median Pay	$104,610 per year $50.29 per hour
Typical Entry-Level Education	Bachelor's degree
Work Experience in a Related Occupation	None
On-the-job Training	None
Number of Jobs, 2022	299,700
Job Outlook, 2022-32	5% (Faster than average)
Employment Change, 2022-32	15,800

What Electrical and Electronics Engineers Do

Electrical engineers design, develop, test, and supervise the manufacture of electrical equipment.

Work Environment

Electrical and electronics engineers work in industries including research and development, engineering services, manufacturing, telecommunications, and the federal government. Electrical and electronics engineers generally work indoors in offices. However, they may have to visit sites to observe a problem or a piece of complex equipment.

How to Become an Electrical or Electronics Engineer

Electrical and electronics engineers must have a bachelor's degree. Employers also value practical experience, such as

Electronics engineers design electronic components and systems for commercial, industrial, or scientific applications.

internships or participation in cooperative engineering programs.

Pay

The median annual wage for electrical engineers was $103,320 in May 2022.

The median annual wage for electronics engineers, except computer was $108,170 in May 2022.

Job Outlook

Overall employment of electrical and electronics engineers is projected to grow 5 percent from 2022 to 2032, faster than the average for all occupations.

About 17,800 openings for electrical and electronics engineers are projected each year, on average, over the decade. Many of those openings are expected to result from the need to replace workers who transfer to different occupations or exit the labor force, such as to retire.

What Electrical and Electronics Engineers Do

Electrical engineers design, develop, test, and supervise the manufacture of electrical equipment, such as electric motors, radar and navigation systems, communications systems, or power generation equipment. Electrical engineers also design the electrical systems of automobiles and aircraft.

Electronics engineers design and develop electronic equipment, including broadcast and communications systems, such as portable music players and Global Positioning System (GPS) devices. Many also work in areas closely related to computer hardware.

Duties

Electrical engineers typically do the following:

- Design new ways to use electrical power to develop or improve products
- Perform detailed calculations to develop manufacturing, construction, and installation standards and specifications
- Direct the manufacture, installation, and testing of electrical equipment to ensure that products meet specifications and codes
- Investigate complaints from customers or the public, evaluate problems, and recommend solutions
- Work with project managers on production efforts to ensure that projects are completed satisfactorily, on time, and within budget

Electronics engineers analyze the requirements and costs of electrical systems.

Electronics engineers typically do the following:

- Design electronic components, software, products, or systems for commercial, industrial, medical, military, or scientific applications
- Analyze customer needs and determine the requirements, capacity, and cost for developing an electrical system plan
- Develop maintenance and testing procedures for electronic components and equipment
- Evaluate systems and recommend design modifications or equipment repair
- Inspect electronic equipment, instruments, and systems to make sure they meet safety standards and applicable regulations
- Plan and develop applications and modifications for electronic properties used in parts and systems in order to improve technical performance

Electronics engineers who work for the federal government research, develop, and evaluate electronic devices used in a variety of areas, such as aviation, computing, transportation, and manufacturing. They work on federal electronic devices and systems, including satellites, flight systems, radar and sonar systems, and communications systems.

The work of electrical engineers and electronics engineers is often similar. Both use engineering and design software and equipment to do engineering tasks. Both types of engineers also must work with other engineers to discuss existing products and possibilities for engineering projects.

Engineers whose work is related exclusively to computer hardware are considered computer hardware engineers.

Work Environment

Electrical engineers held about 188,800 jobs in 2022. The largest employers of electrical engineers were as follows:

Engineering services	19%
Electric power generation, transmission and distribution	9
Navigational, measuring, electromedical, and control instruments manufacturing	7
Research and development in the physical, engineering, and life sciences	5
Semiconductor and other electronic component manufacturing	4

Electrical and electronic engineers work in various industries, including engineering services, research and development, and manufacturing.

Electronics engineers, except computer held about 110,900 jobs in 2022. The largest employers of electronics engineers, except computer were as follows:

Telecommunications	18%
Federal government, excluding postal service	14
Semiconductor and other electronic component manufacturing	11
Engineering services	7
Navigational, measuring, electromedical, and control instruments manufacturing	6

Electrical and electronics engineers generally work indoors in offices. However, they may visit sites to observe a problem or a piece of complex equipment.

Work Schedules

Most electrical and electronics engineers work full time.

How to Become an Electrical or Electronics Engineer

Electrical and electronics engineers must have a bachelor's degree. Employers also value practical experience, such as internships or participation in cooperative engineering programs, in which students earn academic credit for structured work experience.

Becoming an electrical or electronics engineer involves the study of math and engineering.

Education

High school students interested in studying electrical or electronics engineering benefit from taking courses in physics and math, including algebra, trigonometry, and calculus. Courses in drafting are also helpful, because electrical and electronics engineers often are required to prepare technical drawings.

Electrical and electronics engineers typically need a bachelor's degree in electrical engineering, electronics engineering, or a related engineering field. Programs include classroom, laboratory, and field studies. Courses include digital systems design, differential equations, and electrical circuit theory. Programs in electrical engineering, electronics engineering, or electrical engineering technology should be accredited by ABET.

Some colleges and universities offer cooperative programs in which students gain practical experience while completing their education. Cooperative programs combine classroom study with practical work. Internships provide similar experience and are growing in number.

At some universities, students can enroll in a 5-year program that leads to both a bachelor's degree and a master's degree. A graduate degree allows an engineer to work as an instructor at some universities, or in research and development.

Important Qualities

Concentration. Electrical and electronics engineers design and develop complex electrical systems and electronic components and products. They must keep track of multiple design elements and technical characteristics when performing these tasks.

Initiative. Electrical and electronics engineers must apply their knowledge to new tasks in every project they undertake. In addition, they must engage in continuing education to keep up with changes in technology.

Interpersonal skills. Electrical and electronics engineers must work with others during the manufacturing process to ensure that their plans are implemented correctly. This collaboration includes monitoring technicians and devising remedies to problems as they arise.

Math skills. Electrical and electronics engineers must use the principles of calculus and other advanced math in order to analyze, design, and troubleshoot equipment.

Speaking skills. Electrical and electronics engineers work closely with other engineers and technicians. They must be able to explain their designs and reasoning clearly and to relay instructions during product development and production. They also may need to explain complex issues to customers who have little or no technical expertise.

Writing skills. Electrical and electronics engineers develop technical publications related to equipment they develop, including maintenance manuals, operation manuals, parts lists, product proposals, and design methods documents.

Licenses, Certifications, and Registrations

Licensure is not required for entry-level positions as electrical and electronics engineers. A Professional Engineering (PE) license, which allows for higher levels of leadership and independence, can be acquired later in one's career. Licensed engineers are called professional engineers (PEs). A PE can oversee the work of other engineers, sign off on projects, and provide services directly to the public. State licensure generally requires

- A degree from an ABET-accredited engineering program
- A passing score on the Fundamentals of Engineering (FE) exam
- Relevant work experience, typically at least 4 years
- A passing score on the Professional Engineering (PE) exam

The initial FE exam can be taken after earning a bachelor's degree. Engineers who pass this exam commonly are called engineers in training (EITs) or engineer interns (EIs). After meeting work experience requirements, EITs and EIs can take the second exam, called the Principles and Practice of Engineering (PE).

Each state issues its own licenses. Most states recognize licensure from other states, as long as the licensing state's requirements meet or exceed their own licensure requirements. Several states require continuing education for engineers to keep their licenses.

Advancement

Electrical and electronic engineers may advance to supervisory positions in which they lead a team of engineers and technicians. Some may move to management positions, working as engineering or program managers. Preparation for managerial positions usually requires working under the guidance of a more experienced engineer. For more information, see the profile on architectural and engineering managers.

For sales work, an engineering background enables engineers to discuss a product's technical aspects and assist in product planning and use. For more information, see the profile on sales engineers.

Pay

The median annual wage for electrical engineers was $103,320 in May 2022. The median wage is the wage at which half the workers in an occupation earned more than that amount and half earned less. The lowest 10 percent earned less than $65,480, and the highest 10 percent earned more than $166,970.

The median annual wage for electronics engineers, except computer was $108,170 in May 2022. The lowest 10 percent earned less than $74,880, and the highest 10 percent earned more than $171,430.

In May 2022, the median annual wages for electrical engineers in the top industries in which they worked were as follows:

Research and development in the physical, engineering, and life sciences	$128,520
Semiconductor and other electronic component manufacturing	123,390
Navigational, measuring, electromedical, and control instruments manufacturing	108,080
Electric power generation, transmission and distribution	104,990
Engineering services	99,470

In May 2022, the median annual wages for electronics engineers, except computer in the top industries in which they worked were as follows:

Electrical and Electronics Engineers

Median annual wages, May 2022

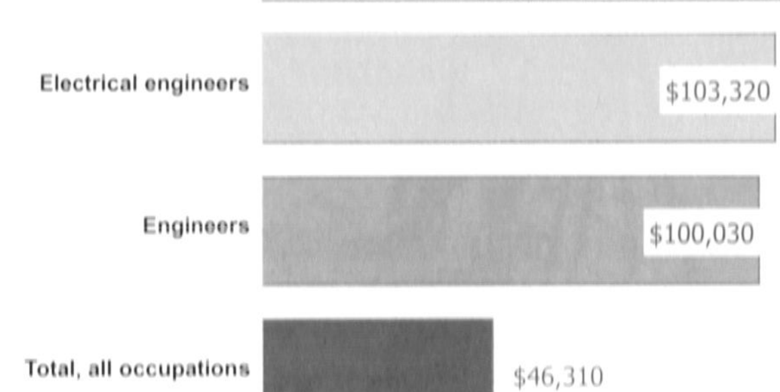

Note: All Occupations includes all occupations in the U.S. Economy.
Source: U.S. Bureau of Labor Statistics, Occupational Employment and Wage Statistics.

Navigational, measuring, electromedical, and control instruments manufacturing	$128,270
Semiconductor and other electronic component manufacturing	127,650
Federal government, excluding postal service	120,640
Engineering services	107,920
Telecommunications	101,900

Most electrical and electronics engineers work full time.

Job Outlook

Overall employment of electrical and electronics engineers is projected to grow 5 percent from 2022 to 2032, faster than the average for all occupations.

About 17,800 openings for electrical and electronics engineers are projected each year, on average, over the decade. Many of those openings are expected to result from the need to replace workers who transfer to different occupations or exit the labor force, such as to retire.

Employment

Projected employment of electrical and electronics engineers varies by occupation (see table).

Some employment growth is expected as companies continue to utilize the expertise of engineers for projects involving electronic devices and systems. These engineers are expected to have key roles in developing sophisticated consumer electronics, solar arrays, semiconductors, and communications technologies.

Occupational Title	SOC Code	Employment, 2022	Projected Employment, 2032	Change, 2022-32	
				Percent	Numeric
Electrical and electronics engineers	17-2070	299,700	315,500	5	15,800
Electrical engineers	17-2071	188,800	196,600	4	7,900
Electronics engineers, except computer	17-2072	110,900	118,900	7	7,900

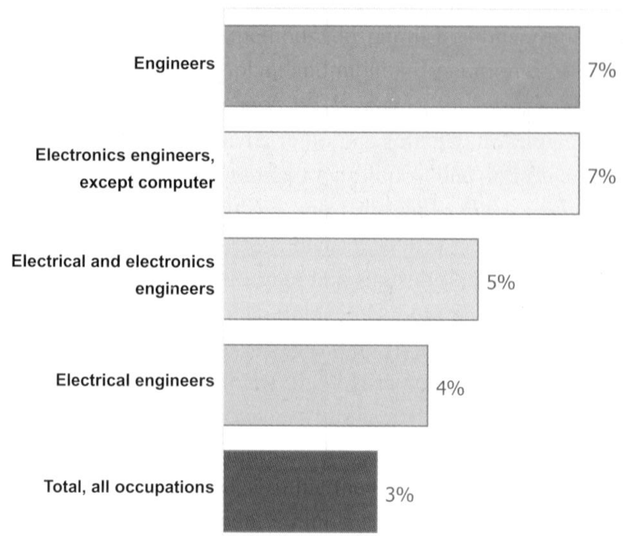

Note: All Occupations includes all occupations in the U.S. Economy.
Source: U.S. Bureau of Labor Statistics, Employment Projections program.

Contacts for More Information

For more information about general engineering education and career resources, visit

- American Society for Engineering Education
- Technology Student Association
- National Council of Examiners for Engineering and Surveying
- National Society of Professional Engineers
- International Society of Automation
- ABET

Electro-mechanical and Mechatronics Technologists and Technicians

Summary

Quick Facts: Electro-mechanical and Mechatronics Technologists and Technicians

2022 Median Pay	$60,570 per year $29.12 per hour
Typical Entry-Level Education	Associate's degree
Work Experience in a Related Occupation	None
On-the-job Training	None
Number of Jobs, 2022	15,200
Job Outlook, 2022-32	-3% (Decline)
Employment Change, 2022-32	-400

What Electro-mechanical and Mechatronics Technologists and Technicians Do

Electro-mechanical and mechatronics technologists and technicians operate, test, and maintain electromechanical or robotic equipment.

Work Environment

Electro-mechanical and mechatronics technologists and technicians work with electrical and mechanical engineers. Most work full time, and some work more than 40 hours per week.

How to Become an Electro-mechanical or Mechatronic Technologist or Technician

Electro-mechanical and mechatronics technologists and technicians typically need either an associate's degree or a postsecondary certificate.

Electro-mechanical technicians verify dimensions of parts, by using precision measuring instruments, to ensure that specifications are met.

Pay

The median annual wage for electro-mechanical and mechatronics technologists and technicians was $60,570 in May 2022.

Job Outlook

Employment of electro-mechanical and mechatronics technologists and technicians is projected to decline 3 percent from 2022 to 2032.

Despite declining employment, about 1,300 openings for electro-mechanical and mechatronics technologists and technicians are projected each year, on average, over the decade. All of those openings are expected to result from the need to replace workers who transfer to other occupations or exit the labor force, such as to retire.

What Electro-mechanical and Mechatronics Technologists and Technicians Do

Electro-mechanical and mechatronics technologists and technicians combine knowledge of mechanical technology with knowledge of electrical and electronic circuitry. They operate, test, and maintain unmanned, automated, robotic, or electromechanical equipment.

Duties

Electro-mechanical and mechatronics technologists and technicians typically do the following:

- Read blueprints, schematics, and diagrams to determine the method and sequence of assembly of a machine or a piece of equipment
- Verify dimensions of parts, using precision measuring instruments
- Operate metalworking machines to make housings, fittings, and fixtures

Electro-mechanical and mechatronics technologists and technicians install, repair, upgrade, and test electronic and computer-controlled mechanical systems.

- Inspect parts for surface defects
- Repair and calibrate hydraulic and pneumatic assemblies
- Use instruments to test the performance of electromechanical assemblies
- Use soldering equipment and handtools to install electronic parts and hardware
- Operate, test, or maintain robotic equipment
- Analyze and record test results

Electro-mechanical and mechatronics technologists and technicians test and operate machines in factories and at other worksites. They also document the tests they performed and analyze and record the results of those tests.

Electro-mechanical and mechatronics technologists and technicians install, maintain, and repair automated machinery and computer-controlled mechanical systems in industrial settings.

They also test, operate, or maintain robotic equipment at worksites. This equipment may include unmanned submarines, aircraft, or similar types of equipment for uses that include oil drilling, deep-ocean exploration, or hazardous-waste removal.

Work Environment

Electro-mechanical and mechatronics technologists and technicians held about 15,200 jobs in 2022. The largest employers of electro-mechanical and mechatronics technologists and technicians were as follows:

Scientific research and development services	14%
Engineering services	13
Navigational, measuring, electromedical, and control instruments manufacturing	8
Machinery manufacturing	8
Transportation equipment manufacturing	4

Electro-mechanical and mechatronics technologists and technicians work with electrical engineers and mechanical engineers.

Electro-mechanical and mechatronics technologists and technicians test the performance of electro-mechanical assemblies, using test instruments.

They work primarily in manufacturing industries, including those of computer and electronic products and of machinery, and in professional, scientific, and technical services. They often work both at production sites and in offices.

Electro-mechanical and mechatronics technologists and technicians are sometimes exposed to hazards from equipment or toxic materials. However, incidents are rare as long as workers follow safety procedures.

Work Schedules

Most electro-mechanical and mechatronics technologists and technicians work full time, and some work more than 40 hours per week.

How to Become an Electro-mechanical or Mechatronic Technologist or Technician

Electro-mechanical and mechatronics technologists and technicians typically need either an associate's degree or a postsecondary certificate.

Education

Associate's degree programs and postsecondary certificates for electro-mechanical and mechatronics technologists and technicians are offered at vocational–technical schools and community colleges.

Employers may prefer to hire graduates of programs accredited by an organization such as ABET. Associate's degree programs usually include courses in subjects such as algebra, trigonometry, and sciences. Depending on the program, students may have the option of concentrating in a field such as electromechanics, mechatronics, or industrial maintenance.

Electro-mechanical and mechatronics technologists and technicians typically need either an associate's degree or a postsecondary certificate.

Important Qualities

Communication skills. Electro-mechanical and mechatronics technologists and technicians must be able to follow instructions from engineers. They also need to clearly convey problems to engineers.

Detail oriented. Electro-mechanical and mechatronics technologists and technicians must take and record the precise measurements that engineers need.

Dexterity. Electro-mechanical and mechatronics technologists and technicians must be adept in using handtools and soldering irons on small circuitry and electronic parts to create electronic components.

Logical-thinking skills. To carry out engineers' designs, inspect designs for quality control, and assemble prototypes, electro-mechanical and mechatronics technologists and technicians must follow a specific sequence or a set of rules.

Math skills. Electro-mechanical and mechatronics technologists and technicians use mathematics for analysis, design, and troubleshooting in their tasks.

Mechanical skills. Electro-mechanical and mechatronics technologists and technicians must create components for industrial machinery or equipment. They must be able to operate equipment such as drill presses, grinders, and engine lathes.

Problem-solving skills. Electro-mechanical and mechatronics technologists and technicians must be able to identify and fix problems that arise with engineering designs and prototypes.

Writing skills. Electro-mechanical and mechatronics technologists and technicians must write clear, well-organized reports that describe onsite construction, testing results, and problems they found in carrying out designs.

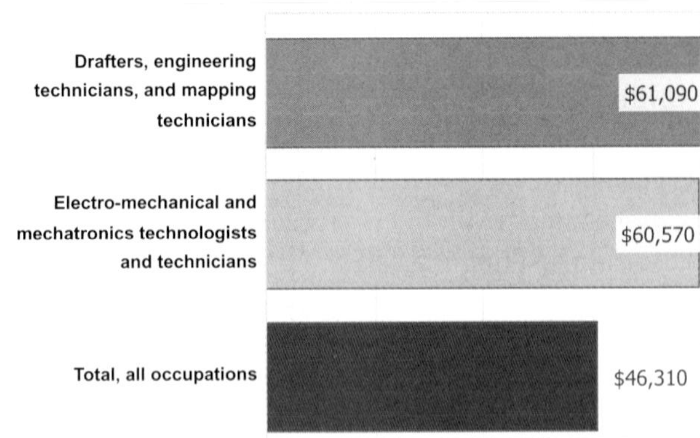

Note: All Occupations includes all occupations in the U.S. Economy.
Source: U.S. Bureau of Labor Statistics, Occupational Employment and Wage Statistics.

Licenses, Certifications, and Registrations

Electro-mechanical and mechatronics technologists and technicians may earn optional certification to demonstrate professional competence.

The International Society of Automation offers the Certified Control Systems Technician (CCST) and Certified Automation Professional (CAP) designations. Both require a written exam, and recertification is required after a specified number of years.

The National Institute for Certification in Engineering Technologies (NICET) offers certification in electrical power testing and other specialties. The technologist certification requires a 4-year engineering technology degree.

Pay

The median annual wage for electro-mechanical and mechatronics technologists and technicians was $60,570 in May 2022. The median wage is the wage at which half the workers in an occupation earned more than that amount and half earned less. The lowest 10 percent earned less than $40,300, and the highest 10 percent earned more than $99,390.

In May 2022, the median annual wages for electro-mechanical and mechatronics technologists and technicians in the top industries in which they worked were as follows:

Scientific research and development services	$70,540
Transportation equipment manufacturing	64,100
Engineering services	61,670
Machinery manufacturing	56,110
Navigational, measuring, electromedical, and control instruments manufacturing	50,330

Most electro-mechanical and mechatronics technologists and technicians work full time, and some work more than 40 hours per week.

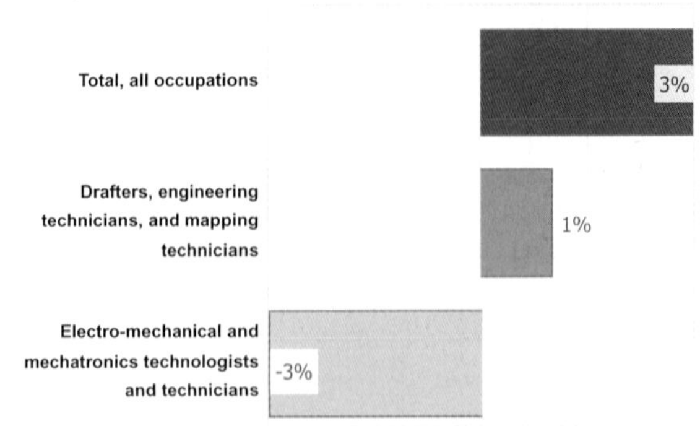

Note: All Occupations includes all occupations in the U.S. Economy.
Source: U.S. Bureau of Labor Statistics, Employment Projections program.

Job Outlook

Employment of electro-mechanical and mechatronics technologists and technicians is projected to decline 3 percent from 2022 to 2032.

Despite declining employment, about 1,300 openings for electro-mechanical and mechatronics technologists and technicians are projected each year, on average, over the decade. All of those openings are expected to result from the need to replace workers who transfer to other occupations or exit the labor force, such as to retire.

Employment

Many of these technologists and technicians are employed in manufacturing industries, for which employment projections vary. Automation in manufacturing could affect this occupation in both positive and negative ways. While automation may replace certain responsibilities, electro-mechanical and mechatronics technologists and technicians will still be needed to operate and maintain the robotic equipment.

Occupational Title	SOC Code	Employment, 2022	Projected Employment, 2032	Change, 2022-32	
				Percent	Numeric
Electro-mechanical and mechatronics technologists and technicians	17-3024	15,200	14,800	-3	-400

Contacts for More Information

For more information, visit

- American Society for Engineering Education (ASEE)
- IEEE
- Technology Student Association (TSA)
- ABET
- International Society of Automation (ISA)
- National Institute for Certification in Engineering Technologies (NICET)
- Automation Federation

Environmental Engineering Technologists and Technicians

Summary

Quick Facts: Environmental Engineering Technologists and Technicians	
2022 Median Pay	$50,980 per year $24.51 per hour
Typical Entry-Level Education	Associate's degree
Work Experience in a Related Occupation	None
On-the-job Training	None
Number of Jobs, 2022	13,900
Job Outlook, 2022-32	1% (Little or no change)
Employment Change, 2022-32	200

What Environmental Engineering Technologists and Technicians Do

Environmental engineering technologists and technicians implement the plans that environmental engineers develop.

Work Environment

Most environmental engineering technologists and technicians work full time. They may work both indoors and outside and often have regular working hours.

How to Become an Environmental Engineering Technologist or Technician

Environmental engineering technologists and technicians typically need an associate's degree in environmental engineering technology or a related field.

Pay

The median annual wage for environmental engineering technologists and technicians was $50,980 in May 2022.

Environmental engineering technologists and technicians conduct pollution surveys, for which they collect and analyze samples such as air and ground water.

Job Outlook

Employment of environmental engineering technologists and technicians is projected to show little or no change from 2022 to 2032.

Despite limited employment growth, about 1,300 openings for environmental engineering technologists and technicians are projected each year, on average, over the decade. Most of those openings are expected to result from the need to replace workers who transfer to different occupations or exit the labor force, such as to retire.

What Environmental Engineering Technologists and Technicians Do

Environmental engineering technologists and technicians carry out the plans that environmental engineers develop.

Duties

Environmental engineering technologists and technicians typically do the following:

- Set up, test, operate, and modify equipment used to prevent or clean up environmental pollution
- Maintain project records and computer program files
- Collect and analyze samples, such as of ground water, for monitoring pollution or treatment
- Review documents to ensure that they are complete and conform to reporting requirements
- Review work plans to schedule activities
- Arrange for the disposal of asbestos, lead, and other hazardous materials

Environmental engineering technologists and technicians work both indoors and outdoors help to ensure environmental quality. Their tasks aid environmental engineers in developing solutions to control, prevent, and mitigate damage caused by pollution and other environmental problems.

In laboratories, environmental engineering technologists and technicians record observations and test results and document

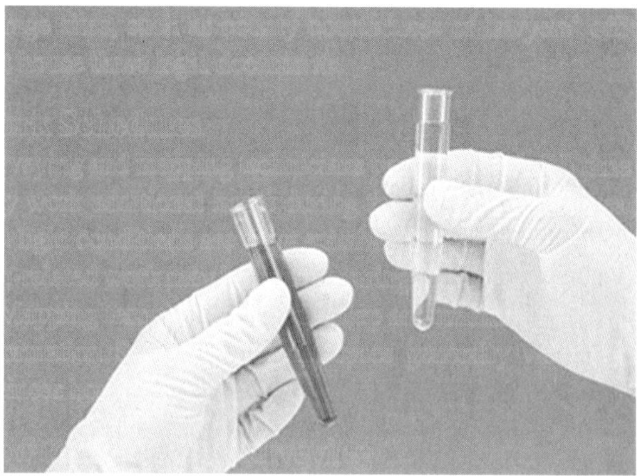

Environmental engineering technologists and technicians collect water samples.

photographs. To keep laboratories supplied, they also may gather product information, identify vendors and suppliers, and order materials and equipment.

In the field, environmental engineering technologists and technicians may collect air, soil, or ground and surface water samples of an area. They also prepare and clean equipment, operate field sampling pumps, and monitor instruments.

They also may inspect facilities for compliance with regulations governing substances such as asbestos, lead, and wastewater.

Work Environment

Environmental engineering technologists and technicians held about 13,900 jobs in 2022. The largest employers of environmental engineering technologists and technicians were as follows:

Engineering services	30%
Management, scientific, and technical consulting services	17
Government	15
Waste management and remediation services	10
Manufacturing	7

Environmental engineering technologists and technicians work under the direction of environmental engineers and as part of a team with other technicians. Environmental engineering technologists and technicians may work indoors, often in laboratories. They also work outdoors, sometimes in remote locations.

Because environmental engineering technologists and technicians help with environmental cleanup, they may be exposed to hazards from equipment, chemicals, or toxic materials. For this reason, they must follow proper safety procedures, such as wearing hazmat suits and respirators as needed. When they work in wet areas, environmental engineering technologists and technicians wear rubber boots to keep their legs and feet dry.

Environmental engineering technologists and technicians must wear protective gear when they are working outdoors on environmental remediation.

Work Schedules

Most environmental engineering technologists and technicians work full time and typically have regular hours. However, they may work irregular hours in order to monitor operations or contain a major environmental threat.

How to Become an Environmental Engineering Technologist or Technician

Environmental engineering technologists and technicians typically need an associate's degree in environmental engineering technology or a related field.

Education

Prospective environmental engineering technologists and technicians should take science and math courses in high school to prepare for postsecondary programs in engineering technology.

Employers usually prefer to hire candidates who have completed ABET-accredited postsecondary programs. Although some candidates may be hired with a high school diploma and postsecondary coursework, environmental engineering technologists and technicians typically need an associate's degree in environmental engineering technology or a related field to enter the occupation.

Environmental engineering technologists and technicians perform indoor and outdoor environmental quality work.

Associate degree programs in environmental engineering technology are available in community colleges and vocational–technical schools. These programs generally include courses in chemistry, environmental assessment, hazardous-waste management, and mathematics. Some environmental engineering technologists and technicians enter the occupation with a bachelor's degree.

Licenses, Certifications, and Registrations

Some states require environmental technologists and technicians to have permits or licenses to remove hazardous waste. Workers also may be required to have Occupational Safety & Health Administration (OSHA) Hazardous Waste Operations and Emergency Response Standard (HAZWOPER) certification. HAZWOPER certification includes training in health hazards, personal protective equipment, site safety, recognizing and identifying hazards, and decontamination. Refresher training may be required to maintain certification.

Advancement

Environmental engineering technologists and technicians usually begin work as trainees in entry-level positions and are supervised by an environmental engineer or experienced technician. As they gain experience, technologists and technicians take on more responsibility. Some advance to become senior environmental technologists and technicians or lead environmental technologists and technicians, functioning as supervisors onsite.

Technicians with a bachelor's degree may advance to become environmental engineers.

Important Qualities

Communication skills. When working on teams, environmental engineering technologists and technicians must listen attentively and convey information to others.

Critical-thinking skills. Environmental engineers rely on technologists and technicians to help identify problems and solutions and to implement the engineers' plans.

Observational skills. Environmental engineering technologists and technicians must be able to evaluate situations, recognize problems, and inform environmental engineers as quickly as possible.

Problem-solving skills. Environmental engineering technologists and technicians implement plans designed by environmental engineers. They must be able to resolve issues that arise, such as unexpected findings during fieldwork.

Reading skills. Environmental engineering technologists and technicians must be able to understand legal and technical documents in order to ensure that regulations are being met.

Pay

The median annual wage for environmental engineering technologists and technicians was $50,980 in May 2022. The median wage is the wage at which half the workers in an

Environmental Engineering Technologists and Technicians

Median annual wages, May 2022

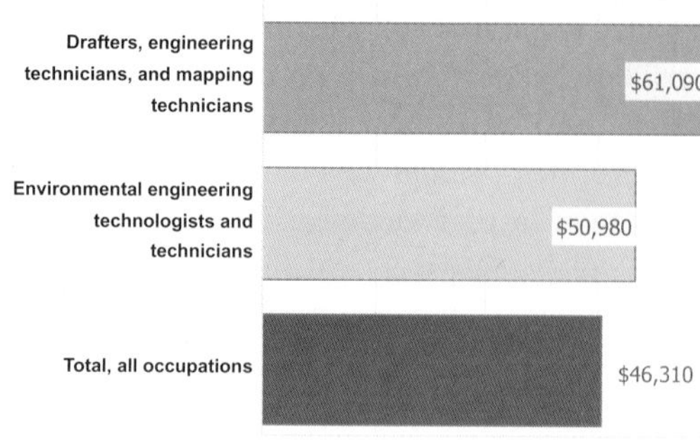

Note: All Occupations includes all occupations in the U.S. Economy.
Source: U.S. Bureau of Labor Statistics, Occupational Employment and Wage Statistics.

occupation earned more than that amount and half earned less. The lowest 10 percent earned less than $35,810, and the highest 10 percent earned more than $84,430.

In May 2022, the median annual wages for environmental engineering technologists and technicians in the top industries in which they worked were as follows:

Manufacturing	$64,310
Government	60,230
Management, scientific, and technical consulting services	56,010
Engineering services	50,250
Waste management and remediation services	42,980

Most environmental engineering technologists and technicians work full time and typically have regular hours. However, they must sometimes work irregular hours in order to monitor operations or contain a major environmental threat.

Job Outlook

Employment of environmental engineering technologists and technicians is projected to show little or no change from 2022 to 2032.

Environmental Engineering Technologists and Technicians

Percent change in employment, projected 2022-32

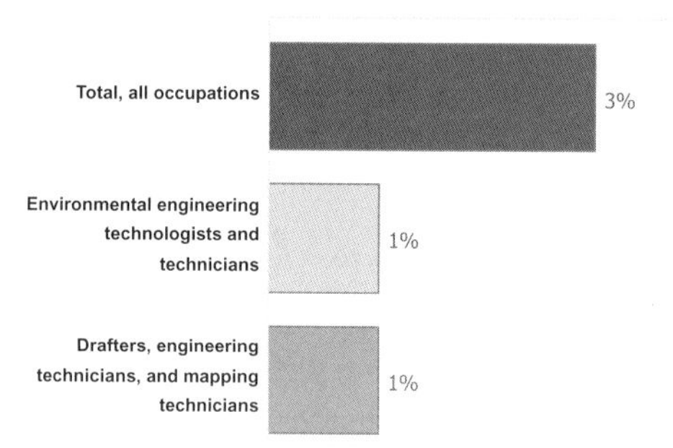

Note: All Occupations includes all occupations in the U.S. Economy.
Source: U.S. Bureau of Labor Statistics, Employment Projections program.

Despite limited employment growth, about 1,300 openings for environmental engineering technologists and technicians are projected each year, on average, over the decade. Most of those openings are expected to result from the need to replace workers who transfer to different occupations or exit the labor force, such as to retire.

Employment

Employment in this occupation is typically tied to projects created by environmental engineers. Some demand for environmental engineering technologists and technicians is expected over the decade as increasing concerns about pollution lead to water- and air-quality improvement efforts. However, employment growth may be limited as automated environmental testing increases productivity for these workers.

Occupational Title	SOC Code	Employment, 2022	Projected Employment, 2032	Change, 2022-32	
				Percent	Numeric
Environmental engineering technologists and technicians	17-3025	13,900	14,100	1	200

Contacts for More Information

For more information, visit

- ABET
- Technology Student Association
- U.S. Department of Labor, Occupational Safety & Health Administration

Environmental Engineers

Summary

Quick Facts: Environmental Engineers

2022 Median Pay	$96,530 per year $46.41 per hour
Typical Entry-Level Education	Bachelor's degree
Work Experience in a Related Occupation	None
On-the-job Training	None
Number of Jobs, 2022	47,300
Job Outlook, 2022-32	6% (Faster than average)
Employment Change, 2022-32	2,900

What Environmental Engineers Do

Environmental engineers use engineering disciplines in developing solutions to problems of planetary health.

Environmental engineers obtain, update, and maintain plans, permits, and standard operating procedures for environmental projects.

Work Environment

Environmental engineers work both in an office setting and in the field. Most work full time, and some work more than 40 hours per week.

How to Become an Environmental Engineer

Environmental engineers typically need a bachelor's degree in environmental engineering or a related field, such as civil, chemical, or general engineering. Some employers prefer to hire candidates who have gained practical experience in an internship or a cooperative education program.

Pay

The median annual wage for environmental engineers was $96,530 in May 2022.

Job Outlook

Employment of environmental engineers is projected to grow 6 percent from 2022 to 2032, faster than the average for all occupations.

About 3,400 openings for environmental engineers are projected each year, on average, over the decade. Many of those openings are expected to result from the need to replace workers who transfer to different occupations or exit the labor force, such as to retire.

What Environmental Engineers Do

Environmental engineers use engineering disciplines in developing solutions to problems of planetary health. Their work may involve concerns such as waste treatment, site remediation, and pollution control technology.

Duties

Environmental engineers typically do the following:

Environmental engineers design systems for managing and cleaning municipal water supplies.

- Prepare, review, update, and present reports on issues related to the environment
- Design systems that protect the environment, such as those to reclaim water or to control air pollution
- Obtain, update, and maintain plans, permits, and standard operating procedures
- Provide technical support for environmental remediation projects and for legal actions
- Analyze scientific data and do quality-control checks
- Monitor the progress of environmental improvement programs
- Inspect industrial and municipal facilities and programs to ensure compliance with environmental regulations
- Advise corporations, government agencies, and other interested parties about environmental issues, including procedures for cleaning up contaminated sites

Environmental engineers work on a variety of projects. For example, they may conduct hazardous-waste management studies in which they evaluate a hazard and advise on treating and containing it. They also design systems for municipal and industrial water supplies and wastewater treatment. In government, they may focus on prevention and compliance, such as researching the environmental impact of proposed construction projects or enforcing regulations for disposal of agricultural waste.

Some of these engineers study ways to minimize the effects of environmental threats such as acid rain, automobile emissions, and ozone depletion. They also collaborate with workers who focus on environmental sustainability and other issues, including environmental scientists and specialists, hazardous materials removal workers, lawyers, and urban and regional planners.

Work Environment

Environmental engineers held about 47,300 jobs in 2022. The largest employers of environmental engineers were as follows:

Engineering services	28%
Management, scientific, and technical consulting services	20
State government, excluding education and hospitals	13
Federal government, excluding postal service	6
Local government, excluding education and hospitals	6

Environmental engineers work with other engineers and with urban and regional planners.

Environmental engineers may work both indoors, such as in an office setting, and outdoors, such as at a construction site. They sometimes travel to attend meetings or present research.

Work Schedules

Most environmental engineers work full time. They may need to work more than 40 hours per week, such as to monitor a project's progress or to troubleshoot problems.

How to Become an Environmental Engineer

Environmental engineers typically need a bachelor's degree in environmental engineering or a related field, such as chemical, civil, or general engineering. Some employers prefer to hire candidates who have gained practical experience in an internship or cooperative education program.

A bachelor's degree is needed to become an environmental engineer.

Education

High school students interested in becoming an environmental engineer should take classes in chemistry, biology, physics, and math, including algebra, trigonometry, and calculus.

Entry-level environmental engineering jobs typically require a bachelor's degree in engineering. Programs usually include courses in subjects such as construction systems, engineering mechanics, and geochemistry and involve academic instruction, laboratory study, and fieldwork.

Some college and university programs offer cooperative education in which students gain practical experience while completing their studies. Students also may get relevant experience through internships or by volunteering in positions that focus on the environment.

Bachelor's degree programs usually take 4 years, but some colleges and universities have 5-year engineering programs that lead to both a bachelor's and a master's degree.

Employers often prefer to hire graduates of ABET-accredited engineering programs. A degree from an accredited program is usually necessary for engineers to become licensed.

Licenses, Certifications, and Registrations

Licensure is not required for entry-level environmental engineers.

Experienced engineers may obtain a Professional Engineer (PE) license, which allows them to oversee the work of other engineers, sign off on projects, and provide services directly to the public.

State licensure generally requires a bachelor's or higher degree from an ABET-accredited engineering program, a passing score on the Fundamentals of Engineering (FE) exam, several years of relevant work experience, and a passing score on the PE exam.

Each state issues its own license. Most states recognize licensure from other states if the licensing state's requirements meet or exceed their own licensure requirements. Several states require engineers to take continuing education to keep their licenses.

After licensing, environmental engineers can earn board certification from the American Academy of Environmental Engineers and Scientists. This certification shows that an environmental engineer has expertise in one or more areas of specialization.

Some states require environmental engineers to have Occupational Safety & Health Administration (OSHA) Hazardous Waste Operations and Emergency Response Standard (HAZWOPER) certification. HAZWOPER certification includes training in health hazards, personal protective equipment, site safety, recognizing and identifying hazards, and decontamination. Refresher training may be required to maintain certification.

Advancement

As engineers gain knowledge and experience, they take on more difficult projects and have greater independence to develop designs, solve problems, and make decisions.

Some environmental engineers advance to become technical specialists or to supervise a team of engineers and technicians. Others become engineering managers or project management specialists to direct and coordinate the activities of specific projects.

Important Qualities

Communication skills. Environmental engineers must explain plans, specifications, findings, and other information both orally and in writing to technical and nontechnical audiences.

Creativity. Environmental engineers must be able to design systems that interact with the machinery and equipment components of a larger system.

Interpersonal skills. Environmental engineers coordinate with a variety of workers, such as the engineers and scientists who design systems and the technicians and mechanics who put systems into practice.

Math skills. Environmental engineers use calculus, trigonometry, and other math in their analysis, design, and troubleshooting work.

Problem-solving skills. Environmental engineers must identify and anticipate problems to design systems that prevent or mitigate environmental damage.

Pay

The median annual wage for environmental engineers was $96,530 in May 2022. The median wage is the wage at which half the workers in an occupation earned more than that amount and half earned less. The lowest 10 percent earned less than $60,020, and the highest 10 percent earned more than $150,840.

In May 2022, the median annual wages for environmental engineers in the top industries in which they worked were as follows:

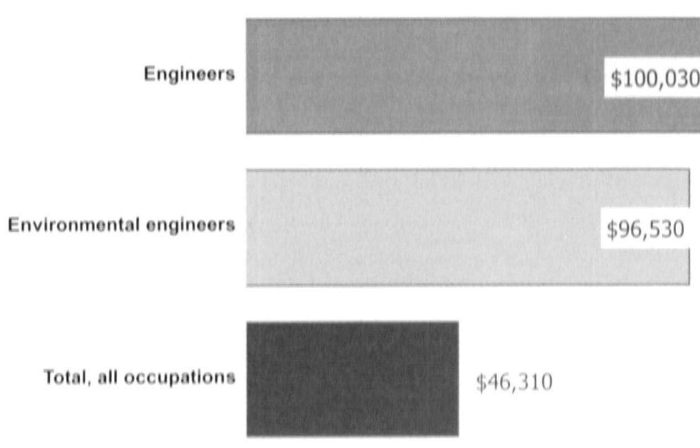

Note: All Occupations includes all occupations in the U.S. Economy.
Source: U.S. Bureau of Labor Statistics, Occupational Employment and Wage Statistics.

Federal government, excluding postal service	$111,590
Engineering services	97,740
Local government, excluding education and hospitals	95,360
State government, excluding education and hospitals	87,710
Management, scientific, and technical consulting services	80,560

Most environmental engineers work full time. They may need to work more than 40 hours per week, such as to monitor a project's progress or to troubleshoot problems.

Job Outlook

Employment of environmental engineers is projected to grow 6 percent from 2022 to 2032, faster than the average for all occupations.

About 3,400 openings for environmental engineers are projected each year, on average, over the decade. Many of those openings are expected to result from the need to replace workers who transfer to different occupations or exit the labor force, such as to retire.

Employment

Heightened public awareness of the hazards facing the environment is expected to support demand for environmental engineers. For example, these workers are expected to be needed to help design solutions to improve water and air quality amid growing concerns about pollution and the lack of access to clean drinking water across the country.

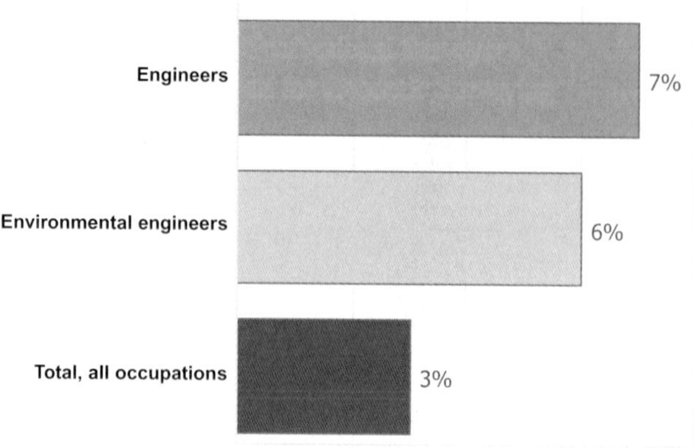

Note: All Occupations includes all occupations in the U.S. Economy.
Source: U.S. Bureau of Labor Statistics, Employment Projections program.

Occupational Title	SOC Code	Employment, 2022	Projected Employment, 2032	Change, 2022-32 Percent	Change, 2022-32 Numeric
Environmental engineers	17-2081	47,300	50,200	6	2,900

Contacts for More Information

For more information, visit

- American Academy of Environmental Engineers and Scientists (AAEES)
- American Society for Engineering Education (ASEE)
- ABET
- National Council of Examiners for Engineering and Surveying (NCEES)
- National Society of Professional Engineers (NSPE)

Health and Safety Engineers

Summary

Quick Facts: Health and Safety Engineers	
2022 Median Pay	$100,660 per year $48.40 per hour
Typical Entry-Level Education	Bachelor's degree
Work Experience in a Related Occupation	None
On-the-job Training	None
Number of Jobs, 2022	22,000
Job Outlook, 2022-32	4% (As fast as average)
Employment Change, 2022-32	800

What Health and Safety Engineers Do

Health and safety engineers combine knowledge of engineering and of health and safety to develop procedures and design systems to protect people from illness and injury and property from damage.

Work Environment

Health and safety engineers typically work in offices. However, they also must spend time at worksites when necessary, which sometimes requires travel.

How to Become a Health and Safety Engineer

Health and safety engineers typically need a bachelor's degree in an engineering discipline or in environmental health and safety. Some employers prefer to hire candidates who have practical experience, so cooperative-education programs may be valuable as well.

Pay

The median annual wage for health and safety engineers was $100,660 in May 2022.

Job Outlook

Employment of health and safety engineers is projected to grow 4 percent from 2022 to 2032, about as fast as the average for all occupations.

Health and safety engineers identify and correct potential hazards.

About 1,300 openings for health and safety engineers are projected each year, on average, over the decade. Many of those openings are expected to result from the need to replace workers who transfer to different occupations or exit the labor force, such as to retire.

What Health and Safety Engineers Do

Health and safety engineers develop procedures and design systems to protect people from illness and injury and property from damage. They combine knowledge of engineering and of health and safety to make sure that chemicals, machinery, software, furniture, and other products will not cause harm to people or damage to property.

Duties

Health and safety engineers typically do the following:

- Maintain and apply knowledge of current health and safety policies, regulations, and industrial processes
- Review plans and specifications for new machinery and equipment to make sure that they meet safety requirements

Health and safety in the workplace is a major concern of health and safety engineers.

- Identify and correct potential hazards by inspecting facilities, machinery, and safety equipment
- Evaluate the effectiveness of various industrial control mechanisms
- Ensure that buildings or products comply with health and safety regulations, especially after an inspection that required changes
- Install safety devices on machinery or direct the installation of these devices
- Review employee safety programs and recommend improvements

Health and safety engineers also investigate industrial accidents and injuries to determine their causes and to determine whether the incidents were avoidable or can be prevented in the future. They interview employers and employees to learn about work environments and incidents that lead to accidents or injuries. They also evaluate the corrections that were made to remedy violations found during health inspections.

Health and safety engineering is a broad field covering many activities. The following are examples of types of health and safety engineers:

Fire prevention and protection engineers conduct analyses and make recommendations regarding the potential fire hazards of buildings, materials, and transportation systems. They also design, install, and maintain fire prevention and suppression systems and inspect systems to ensure that they meet government safety regulations. Fire prevention and protection engineers must be licensed and must keep up with changes in fire codes and regulations.

Product safety engineers, sometimes called ***product compliance engineers***, develop and conduct tests to make sure that various products are safe and comply with industry or government safety regulations. These engineers work on a wide range of products, from nuclear submarine reactors and robotics to cell phones and computer systems.

Systems safety engineers identify and analyze risks and hazards associated with system designs in order to make them safe while ensuring that the systems remain operational and effective. They work in many fields, including aerospace, and are moving into new fields, such as software safety, medical safety, and environmental safety.

For information on health and safety engineers who work in mines, see the profile on mining and geological engineers.

Work Environment

Health and safety engineers held about 22,000 jobs in 2022. The largest employers of health and safety engineers were as follows:

Manufacturing	28%
Government	15
Construction	12

Health and safety engineers may need to spend time at worksites.

Engineering services	8
Management, scientific, and technical consulting services	6

Health and safety engineers typically work in offices. However, they also must spend time at worksites when necessary, which sometimes requires travel.

Work Schedules

Most health and safety engineers work full time.

How to Become a Health and Safety Engineer

Health and safety engineers typically need a bachelor's degree in an engineering discipline or in environmental health and safety. Some employers prefer to hire candidates who have practical experience, so cooperative-education programs may be valuable as well.

Education

Entry-level jobs for health and safety engineers typically require a bachelor's degree in an engineering discipline, such as chemical, mechanical, industrial, or systems engineering, or in environmental health and safety. Bachelor's degree programs typically include classroom, laboratory, and field studies in applied engineering. Engineering students interested in becoming health and safety engineers also should take courses in occupational safety and health, industrial hygiene, ergonomics, or environmental safety. Employers may prefer to hire graduates of engineering programs accredited by a professional association such as ABET.

Some colleges and universities offer cooperative-education programs that allow students to gain practical experience while completing their education. Students also may choose to participate in an internship.

A few colleges and universities offer 5-year accelerated programs through which students graduate with both a bachelor's and a master's degree. A master's degree allows engineers to

Health and safety engineers inspect facilities, machinery, and safety equipment to identify and correct potential hazards.

enter the occupation at a higher level, from which they can develop and implement safety systems.

Important Qualities

Communication skills. Health and safety engineers must be able to interpret federal and state regulations and their intent so that they can propose proper designs for specific work environments. Health and safety engineers also prepare and present training materials to workers and must be able to describe new regulations and procedures to a variety of audiences.

Creativity. Health and safety engineers produce designs showing potential problems and remedies for them. They must be creative, in order to deal with situations that are unique to a project.

Critical-thinking skills. Health and safety engineers must be able to identify hazards to humans and property in the workplace or in the home before those hazards cause material damage or become a health threat.

Observational skills. Health and safety engineers must observe and learn how operations function so that they can identify risks to people and property. This requires the ability to think in terms of overall processes within an organization. Health and safety engineers can then recommend systemic changes to minimize risks.

Problem-solving skills. In designing solutions for entire organizational operations, health and safety engineers must take into account processes from more than one system at the same time. In addition, they must try to anticipate a range of human reactions to the changes they recommend.

Licenses, Certifications, and Registrations

Licensure is not required for entry-level positions as a health and safety engineer. A Professional Engineering (PE) license, which allows for higher levels of leadership and independence, can be acquired later in one's career. Licensed engineers are called professional engineers (PEs). A PE can oversee the work of other engineers, sign off on projects, and provide services directly to the public. State licensure generally requires

- A degree from an ABET-accredited engineering program
- A passing score on the Fundamentals of Engineering (FE) exam
- Relevant work experience, typically at least 4 years
- A passing score on the Professional Engineering (PE) exam

The initial FE exam can be taken after one earns a bachelor's degree. Engineers who pass this exam are commonly called engineers in training (EITs) or engineer interns (EIs). After meeting work experience requirements, EITs and EIs can take the second exam, called the Principles and Practice of Engineering (PE).

Each state issues its own licenses. Most states recognize licensure from other states, as long as the licensing state's requirements meet or exceed their own licensure requirements. Several states require continuing education for engineers to keep their licenses.

Health and safety engineers can earn professional certifications, including the following:

- The Board of Certified Safety Professionals offers the Certified Safety Professional (CSP) certification, the Occupational Health and Safety Technologist (OHST) certification, and the new Associate Safety Professional (ASP) certification
- The American Board of Industrial Hygiene awards the Certified Industrial Hygienist (CIH) certification
- The American Society of Safety Professionals offers a Certificate in Safety Management (CSM)
- The International Council on Systems Engineering offers a program leading to designation as a Certified Systems Engineering Professional (CSEP)

Pay

The median annual wage for health and safety engineers was $100,660 in May 2022. The median wage is the wage at which half the workers in an occupation earned more than that amount and half earned less. The lowest 10 percent earned less than $59,090, and the highest 10 percent earned more than $152,550.

In May 2022, the median annual wages for health and safety engineers in the top industries in which they worked were as follows:

Engineering services	$105,130
Manufacturing	101,600
Management, scientific, and technical consulting services	98,920
Government	97,780
Construction	89,980

Most health and safety engineers work full time.

Job Outlook

Employment of health and safety engineers is projected to grow 4 percent from 2022 to 2032, about as fast as the average for all occupations.

About 1,300 openings for health and safety engineers are projected each year, on average, over the decade. Many of those openings are expected to result from the need to replace workers who transfer to different occupations or exit the labor force, such as to retire.

Employment

Health and safety engineers will be needed to help protect people from potential hazards. As new regulations are created, organizations are expected to rely on these engineers for help in complying with requirements that safeguard people from illness and injury and property from damage.

Health and Safety Engineers

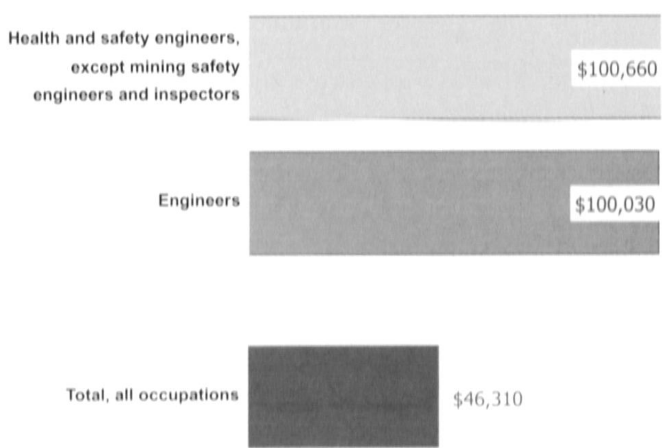

Note: All Occupations includes all occupations in the U.S. Economy. Source: U.S. Bureau of Labor Statistics, Occupational Employment and Wage Statistics.

Health and Safety Engineers

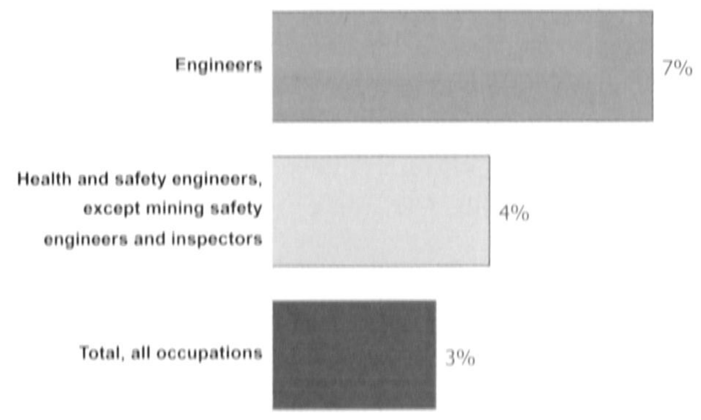

Note: All Occupations includes all occupations in the U.S. Economy. Source: U.S. Bureau of Labor Statistics, Employment Projections program.

Occupational Title	SOC Code	Employment, 2022	Projected Employment, 2032	Change, 2022-32	
				Percent	Numeric
Health and safety engineers, except mining safety engineers and inspectors	17-2111	22,000	22,800	4	800

Contacts for More Information

For more information, visit

- American Society of Safety Professionals
- Technology Student Association
- ABET
- National Council of Examiners for Engineering and Surveying
- National Society of Professional Engineers
- American Industrial Hygiene Association
- American Board of Industrial Hygiene
- American Society of Safety Professionals
- Board of Certified Safety Professionals
- International Council on Systems Engineering

Industrial Engineering Technologists and Technicians

Summary

Quick Facts: Industrial Engineering Technologists and Technicians

2022 Median Pay	$61,210 per year $29.43 per hour
Typical Entry-Level Education	Associate's degree
Work Experience in a Related Occupation	None
On-the-job Training	None
Number of Jobs, 2022	69,100
Job Outlook, 2022-32	3% (As fast as average)
Employment Change, 2022-32	2,200

What Industrial Engineering Technologists and Technicians Do

Industrial engineering technologists and technicians help engineers solve problems affecting manufacturing layout or production.

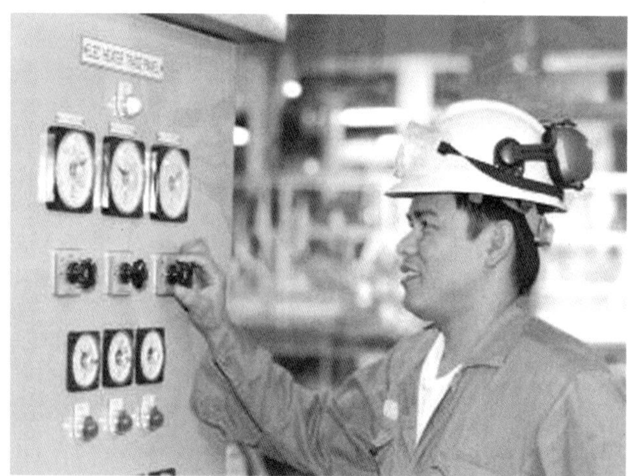

Industrial engineering technicians collect data to assist in process improvement activities.

Work Environment

Most industrial engineering technologists and technicians work in manufacturing industries. Most work full time.

How to Become an Industrial Engineering Technologist or Technician

Industrial engineering technologists and technicians typically need an associate's degree or a postsecondary certificate to enter the occupation. Community colleges or technical institutes typically offer associate's degree programs, and vocational–technical schools offer certificate programs.

Pay

The median annual wage for industrial engineering technologists and technicians was $61,210 in May 2022.

Job Outlook

Employment of industrial engineering technologists and technicians is projected to grow 3 percent from 2022 to 2032, about as fast as the average for all occupations.

About 6,500 openings for industrial engineering technologists and technicians are projected each year, on average, over the decade. Many of those openings are expected to result from the need to replace workers who transfer to different occupations or exit the labor force, such as to retire.

What Industrial Engineering Technologists and Technicians Do

Industrial engineering technologists and technicians help engineers solve problems affecting manufacturing layout or production. They prepare machinery and equipment plans, design workflows, conduct statistical production studies, and analyze production costs.

Duties

Industrial engineering technologists and technicians typically do the following:

- Suggest revisions to operation methods, material handling, or equipment layout

Industrial engineering technologists and technicians interpret schematic diagrams and formulas.

- Interpret engineering drawings, schematic diagrams, and formulas
- Confer with management or engineering staff on quality and reliability standards
- Help plan work assignments, considering factors such as machine capabilities and production schedules
- Prepare charts, diagrams, and other graphs to illustrate workflow, routing, floor layouts, how materials are handled, and how machines are used
- Collect data to assist in process improvement activities

Industrial engineering technologists and technicians study the time and steps workers take to do a task (time and motion studies). To set reasonable production rates, they analyze operations such as maintenance, production, and service.

The work of industrial engineering technologists and technicians is versatile and applicable to a variety of projects. For example, in supply chain management, they help businesses minimize inventory costs; in quality assurance, they help with customer satisfaction; and in project management, they help to control costs and maximize efficiencies.

Industrial engineering technologists and technicians generally work on teams under the supervision of industrial engineers.

Manufacturing engineering technologists and technicians work to raise production quality and profitability. By planning, testing, and custom making industrial products, they help engineers improve manufacturing processes and output. They may assess prototypes, analyze machinery performance, or try new production methods.

Work Environment

Industrial engineering technologists and technicians held about 69,100 jobs in 2022. The largest employers of industrial engineering technologists and technicians were as follows:

Computer and electronic product manufacturing	17%
Transportation equipment manufacturing	12
Professional, scientific, and technical services	11
Chemical manufacturing	8
Machinery manufacturing	8

Industrial engineering technologists and technicians help carry out studies and make observations to assist industrial engineers.

Industrial engineers usually ask industrial engineering technologists and technicians to help carry out studies and draw conclusions. Consequently, these technologists and technicians typically work at the location where products are manufactured or services are provided.

Work Schedules

Industrial engineering technologists and technicians usually work a standard schedule. Most work full time.

How to Become an Industrial Engineering Technologist or Technician

Industrial engineering technologists and technicians typically need an associate's degree or a postsecondary certificate to enter the occupation. Community colleges and technical institutes generally offer associate's degree programs, and vocational–technical schools offer certificate programs.

Education

High school students interested in becoming industrial engineering technologists and technicians should take courses in math, science, and drafting, where available.

Postsecondary programs in industrial engineering technology are offered at vocational–technical schools, technical institutes, and community colleges. Vocational–technical schools typically award a certificate. Community colleges programs usually lead to associate's degrees.

Employers may prefer to hire candidates who have completed an engineering or engineering technology program accredited by ABET.

Becoming an industrial engineering technologist or technician usually requires either an associate's degree or a postsecondary certificate to enter the occupation.

Industrial engineering technologists and technicians may choose to major in applied science, industrial technology, or industrial engineering technology. These programs may include instruction in computer-aided design/computer-aided manufacturing software, known as CAD/CAM.

Important Qualities

Analytical skills. Industrial engineering technologists and technicians assess changes in conditions, operations, and the environment to help industrial engineers figure out how systems should work.

Communication skills. Industrial engineering technologists and technicians must listen carefully to instructions from engineers and must clearly articulate problems to their supervisors.

Critical-thinking skills. Industrial engineering technologists and technicians must identify and correct weaknesses to help industrial engineers solve problems.

Detail oriented. Industrial engineering technologists and technicians must record precisely what they measure and observe.

Math skills. Industrial engineering technologists and technicians use mathematics and statistical techniques to analyze data collected from studies.

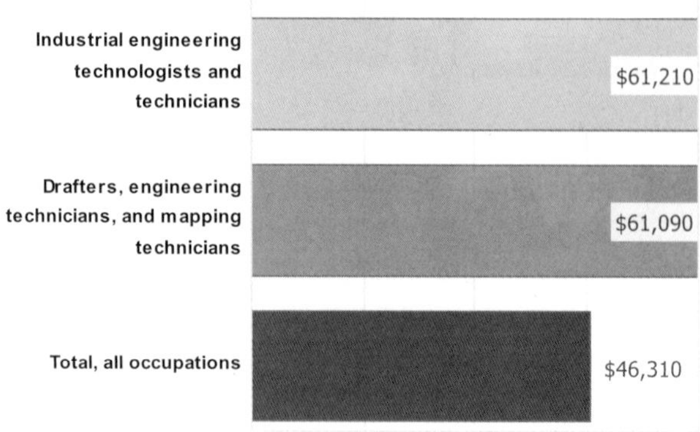

Note: All Occupations includes all occupations in the U.S. Economy.
Source: U.S. Bureau of Labor Statistics, Occupational Employment and Wage Statistics.

Observational skills. Industrial engineering technologists and technicians closely watch the performance of people or organizations so that they can suggest improvements.

Pay

The median annual wage for industrial engineering technologists and technicians was $61,210 in May 2022. The median wage is the wage at which half the workers in an occupation earned more than that amount and half earned less. The lowest 10 percent earned less than $40,710, and the highest 10 percent earned more than $90,430.

In May 2022, the median annual wages for industrial engineering technologists and technicians in the top industries in which they worked were as follows:

Professional, scientific, and technical services	$65,780
Chemical manufacturing	63,200
Computer and electronic product manufacturing	61,210
Transportation equipment manufacturing	61,200
Machinery manufacturing	60,840

Industrial engineering technologists and technicians usually work standard schedules. Most work full time.

Job Outlook

Employment of industrial engineering technologists and technicians is projected to grow 3 percent from 2022 to 2032, about as fast as the average for all occupations.

About 6,500 openings for industrial engineering technologists and technicians are projected each year, on average, over the decade. Many of those openings are expected to result from the need to replace workers who transfer to different occupations or exit the labor force, such as to retire.

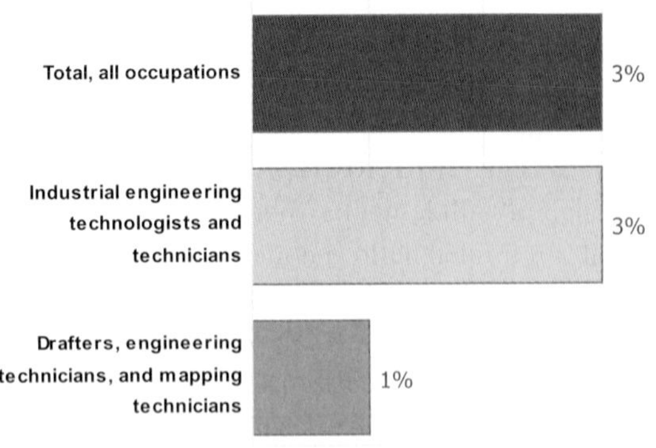

Note: All Occupations includes all occupations in the U.S. Economy.
Source: U.S. Bureau of Labor Statistics, Employment Projections program.

Employment

An emphasis on cost control through increased efficiency, along with industrial engineering technologists and technicians' role in assisting with automation, is expected to sustain demand for these workers.

Occupational Title	SOC Code	Employment, 2022	Projected Employment, 2032	Change, 2022-32	
				Percent	Numeric
Industrial engineering technologists and technicians	17-3026	69,100	71,300	3	2,200

Contacts for More Information

For more information, visit

- Institute of Industrial & Systems Engineers
- Society of Manufacturing Engineers
- American Society for Engineering Education
- ABET

Industrial Engineers

Summary

Quick Facts: Industrial Engineers	
2022 Median Pay	$96,350 per year $46.32 per hour
Typical Entry-Level Education	Bachelor's degree
Work Experience in a Related Occupation	None
On-the-job Training	None
Number of Jobs, 2022	327,300
Job Outlook, 2022-32	12% (Much faster than average)
Employment Change, 2022-32	38,400

Industrial engineers review production schedules, engineering specifications, and process flows to understand activities in manufacturing and services.

What Industrial Engineers Do

Industrial engineers devise efficient systems that integrate workers, machines, materials, information, and energy to make a product or provide a service.

Work Environment

Depending on their tasks, industrial engineers work either in offices or in the settings they are trying to improve. For example, when observing problems, they may watch workers assembling parts in a factory. When solving problems, they may be in an office at a computer, looking at data that they or others have collected.

How to Become an Industrial Engineer

Industrial engineers typically need a bachelor's degree in industrial engineering or a related field, such as mechanical or electrical engineering or industrial engineering technologies.

Pay

The median annual wage for industrial engineers was $96,350 in May 2022.

Job Outlook

Employment of industrial engineers is projected to grow 12 percent from 2022 to 2032, much faster than the average for all occupations.

About 22,800 openings for industrial engineers are projected each year, on average, over the decade. Many of those openings are expected to result from the need to replace workers who transfer to different occupations or exit the labor force, such as to retire.

Industrial engineers develop job evaluation programs, amongst other duties.

What Industrial Engineers Do

Industrial engineers find ways to eliminate wastefulness in production processes. They devise efficient systems that integrate workers, machines, materials, information, and energy to make a product or provide a service.

Duties

Industrial engineers typically do the following:

- Review production schedules, engineering specifications, process flows, and other information to understand methods that are applied and activities that take place in manufacturing and services
- Figure out how to manufacture parts or products, or deliver services, with maximum efficiency
- Develop management control systems to make financial planning and cost analysis more efficient
- Enact quality control procedures to resolve production problems or minimize costs
- Design control systems to coordinate activities and production planning in order to ensure that products meet quality standards
- Confer with clients about product specifications, vendors about purchases, management personnel about manufacturing capabilities, and staff about the status of projects

Industrial engineers apply their skills to many different situations, from manufacturing to healthcare systems to business administration. For example, they design systems for

- moving heavy parts within manufacturing plants
- delivering goods from a company to customers, including finding the most profitable places to locate manufacturing or processing plants
- evaluating job performance
- paying workers.

Some industrial engineers, called ***manufacturing engineers***, focus entirely on the automated aspects of manufacturing processes. They design manufacturing systems to optimize the use of computer networks, robots, and materials.

Industrial engineers focus on how to get the work done most efficiently, balancing many factors, such as time, number of workers needed, available technology, actions workers need to take, achieving the end product with no errors, workers' safety, environmental concerns, and cost.

The versatility of industrial engineers allows them to engage in activities that are useful to a variety of businesses, governments, and nonprofits. For example, industrial engineers engage in supply chain management to help businesses minimize inventory costs, conduct quality assurance activities to help businesses keep their customer bases satisfied, and work in the growing field of project management as industries across the economy seek to control costs and maximize efficiencies.

Work Environment

Industrial engineers held about 327,300 jobs in 2022. The largest employers of industrial engineers were as follows:

Transportation equipment manufacturing	16%
Professional, scientific, and technical services	13
Computer and electronic product manufacturing	12
Machinery manufacturing	9
Fabricated metal product manufacturing	6

Depending on their tasks, industrial engineers work either in offices or in the settings they are trying to improve. For example, when observing problems, they may watch workers assembling parts in a factory. When solving problems, industrial engineers may be in an office at a computer where they analyze data that they or others have collected.

Industrial engineers must work well on teams because they need help from others to collect information about problems and to implement solutions.

Industrial engineers may need to travel to observe processes and make assessments in various work settings.

Work Schedules

Most industrial engineers work full time. Depending upon the projects in which these engineers are engaged, and the

Industrial engineers figure out how to manufacture parts or products or deliver services with maximum efficiency.

industries in which the projects are taking place, hours may vary.

How to Become an Industrial Engineer

Industrial engineers typically need a bachelor's degree. Some employers prefer to hire candidates who have experience, so cooperative-education programs may be beneficial.

Education

High school students interested in industrial engineering should take classes in mathematics, such as algebra, trigonometry, and calculus; computer science; and sciences, such as chemistry and physics.

Industrial engineers typically need a bachelor's degree in industrial engineering or industrial engineering technologies. However, many industrial engineers have degrees in mechanical engineering, electrical engineering, manufacturing engineering, or general engineering.

Bachelor's degree programs include lectures in classrooms and practice in laboratories. Courses include statistics, production systems planning, and manufacturing systems design, among others. Many colleges and universities offer cooperative

To find ways to reduce waste and improve performance, industrial engineers carefully study product requirements.

education programs in which students gain practical experience while completing their education.

Several colleges and universities offer 5-year degree programs in industrial engineering that lead to a bachelor's and master's degree upon completion, and several more offer similar programs in mechanical engineering. A graduate degree allows an engineer to work as a professor at a college or university or to engage in research and development. Some 5-year or even 6-year cooperative education plans combine classroom study with practical work, permitting students to gain experience and to finance part of their education.

Programs in industrial engineering are accredited by ABET.

Important Qualities

Creativity. Industrial engineers use creativity and ingenuity to design new production processes in many kinds of settings in order to reduce the use of material resources, time, or labor while accomplishing the same goal.

Critical-thinking skills. Industrial engineers create new systems to solve problems related to waste and inefficiency. Solving these problems requires logic and reasoning to identify strengths and weaknesses of alternative solutions, conclusions, or approaches to the problems.

Listening skills. These engineers often operate in teams, but they also must solicit feedback from customers, vendors, and production staff. They must listen to customers and clients in order to fully grasp ideas and problems.

Math skills. Industrial engineers use the principles of calculus, trigonometry, and other advanced topics in mathematics for analysis, design, and troubleshooting in their work.

Problem-solving skills. In designing facilities for manufacturing and processes for providing services, these engineers deal with several issues at once, from workers' safety to quality assurance.

Speaking skills. Industrial engineers sometimes have to explain their instructions to production staff or technicians before they can make written instructions available. Being able to explain concepts clearly and quickly is crucial to preventing costly mistakes and loss of time.

Writing skills. Industrial engineers must prepare documentation for other engineers or scientists, or for future reference. The documentation must be coherent and explain their thinking clearly so that the others can understand the information.

Licenses, Certifications, and Registrations

Licensure is not required for entry-level positions as an industrial engineer. A Professional Engineering (PE) license, which allows for higher levels of leadership and independence, can be acquired later in one's career. Licensed engineers are called professional engineers (PEs). A PE can oversee the work of other engineers, sign off on projects, and provide services directly to the public. State licensure generally requires

- A degree from an ABET-accredited engineering program
- A passing score on the Fundamentals of Engineering (FE) exam
- Relevant work experience, typically at least 4 years
- A passing score on the Professional Engineering (PE) exam.

The initial FE exam can be taken after one earns a bachelor's degree. Engineers who pass this exam are commonly called engineers in training (EITs) or engineer interns (EIs). After meeting work experience requirements, EITs and EIs can take the second exam, called the Principles and Practice of Engineering.

Each state issues its own licenses. Most states recognize licensure from other states, as long as the licensing state's requirements meet or exceed their own licensure requirements. Several states require continuing education for engineers to keep their licenses.

The Society of Manufacturing Engineers offers certification, which requires a minimum of 8 years of a combination of education related to manufacturing and at least 4 years of work experience.

Advancement

Industrial engineers who are just starting out usually work under the supervision of experienced engineers. In large companies, new engineers also may receive formal training in classes or seminars. As beginning engineers gain knowledge and experience, they move on to more difficult projects with greater independence to develop designs, solve problems, and make decisions.

Eventually, industrial engineers may advance to become technical specialists, such as quality engineers or facility planners. In that role, they supervise a team of engineers and technicians. Earning a master's degree facilitates such specialization and thus advancement.

Many industrial engineers move into management positions because the work they do is closely related to the work of managers. For more information, see the profile on architectural and engineering managers.

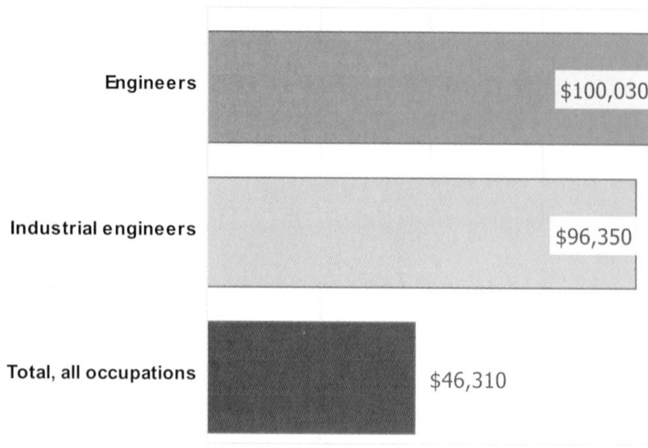

Note: All Occupations includes all occupations in the U.S. Economy.
Source: U.S. Bureau of Labor Statistics, Occupational Employment and Wage Statistics.

Pay

The median annual wage for industrial engineers was $96,350 in May 2022. The median wage is the wage at which half the workers in an occupation earned more than that amount and half earned less. The lowest 10 percent earned less than $62,730, and the highest 10 percent earned more than $134,990.

In May 2022, the median annual wages for industrial engineers in the top industries in which they worked were as follows:

Professional, scientific, and technical services	$99,950
Computer and electronic product manufacturing	99,920
Transportation equipment manufacturing	98,530
Machinery manufacturing	85,380
Fabricated metal product manufacturing	79,380

Most industrial engineers work full time. Depending upon the projects in which these engineers are engaged, and the industries in which the projects are taking place, hours may vary.

Job Outlook

Employment of industrial engineers is projected to grow 12 percent from 2022 to 2032, much faster than the average for all occupations.

About 22,800 openings for industrial engineers are projected each year, on average, over the decade. Many of those openings are expected to result from the need to replace workers who transfer to different occupations or exit the labor force, such as to retire.

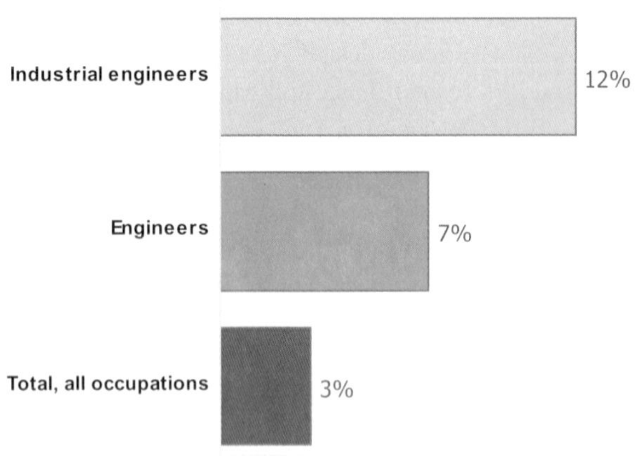

Note: All Occupations includes all occupations in the U.S. Economy.
Source: U.S. Bureau of Labor Statistics, Employment Projections program.

Employment

Industrial engineers focus on reducing internal costs, making their work valuable in manufacturing and other industries, such as consulting and engineering services and research and development firms. As more companies look to lower costs, demand is expected to increase for industrial engineers to optimize production processes, manage supply chains and logistics, and provide expertise on automation.

Occupational Title	SOC Code	Employment, 2022	Projected Employment, 2032	Change, 2022-32	
				Percent	Numeric
Industrial engineers	17-2112	327,300	365,700	12	38,400

Contacts for More Information

For more information, visit

- Institute of Industrial & Systems Engineers
- American Society for Engineering Education
- Technology Student Association
- National Council of Examiners for Engineering and Surveying
- National Society of Professional Engineers
- Society of Manufacturing Engineers
- ABET

Landscape Architects

Summary

Quick Facts: Landscape Architects	
2022 Median Pay	$73,210 per year $35.20 per hour
Typical Entry-Level Education	Bachelor's degree
Work Experience in a Related Occupation	None
On-the-job Training	Internship/residency
Number of Jobs, 2022	23,600
Job Outlook, 2022-32	1% (Little or no change)
Employment Change, 2022-32	200

What Landscape Architects Do

Landscape architects design parks and other outdoor spaces.

Work Environment

Landscape architects spend much of their time in offices, where they create designs, prepare models, and meet with clients. They spend the rest of their time at jobsites.

How to Become a Landscape Architect

All states require landscape architects to be licensed. Licensing requirements vary by state but usually include at least a bachelor's degree in landscape architecture from an accredited school, internship experience, and passing the Landscape Architect Registration Examination.

Pay

The median annual wage for landscape architects was $73,210 in May 2022.

Job Outlook

Employment of landscape architects is projected to show little or no change from 2022 to 2032.

Despite limited employment growth, about 1,800 openings for landscape architects are projected each year, on average, over the decade. Most of those openings are expected to result from the need to replace workers who transfer to different occupations or exit the labor force, such as to retire.

Landscape architects plan and design land areas for parks, recreational facilities, and other open spaces.

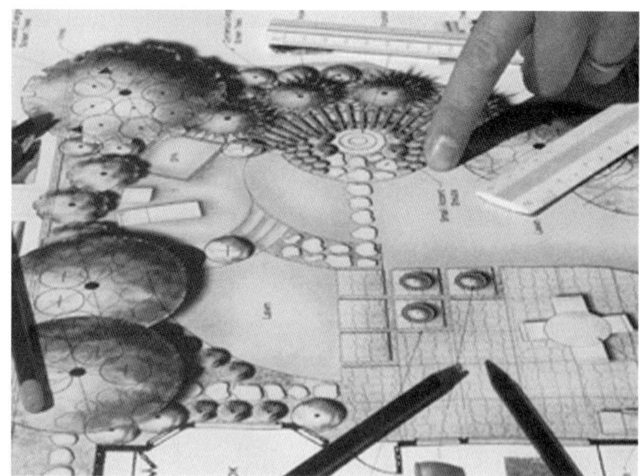

Landscape architects create graphic representations of plans.

What Landscape Architects Do

Landscape architects design parks and the outdoor spaces of campuses, recreational facilities, businesses, private homes, and other open spaces.

Duties

Landscape architects typically do the following:

- Meet with clients, engineers, and building architects to understand the requirements of a project
- Prepare site plans, specifications, and cost estimates
- Coordinate the arrangement of existing and proposed land features and structures
- Prepare graphic representations of plans using computer-aided design and drafting (CADD) software
- Select appropriate landscaping materials
- Analyze environmental reports on land conditions, such as drainage and energy usage
- Inspect landscape project progress to ensure that it adheres to plans
- Seek new work through marketing activities or by giving presentations

Landscape architects design attractive and functional public parks, gardens, playgrounds, residential areas, college campuses, and public spaces. They also plan the locations of buildings, roads, walkways, flowers, shrubs, and trees within these environments. Landscape architects design these areas so that they are not only easy to use but also harmonious with the natural environment.

Landscape architects use various technologies in their work. For example, using CADD software, landscape architects prepare models of their proposed work. They present these models to clients for feedback and then prepare the final look of the project. Many landscape architects also use Geographic Information Systems (GIS) which offer GPS coordinates of different geographical features. This helps landscape architects design different environments by providing clues on where to start planning and how to anticipate future effects of the landscape, such as rainfall running into a valley.

The goals of landscape architects are to enhance the natural beauty of a space and foster environmental benefits. Landscape architects may plan the restoration of natural places that were changed by humans or nature, such as wetlands, streams, and mined areas. They also may design green roofs (roofs that are covered in soil and plants) or rooftop gardens that can retain storm water, absorb air pollution, and cool buildings while also providing pleasant scenery.

Work Environment

Landscape architects held about 23,600 jobs in 2022. The largest employers of landscape architects were as follows:

Architectural, engineering, and related services	45%
Self-employed workers	23
Administrative and support and waste management and remediation services	18
Government	8
Construction	2

Landscape architects spend much of their time in offices, where they create plans and designs, prepare models and preliminary cost estimates, and meet with clients and workers involved in designing or planning a project. They spend the rest of their time at jobsites.

How to Become a Landscape Architect

Landscape architects usually need at least a bachelor's degree in landscape architecture and a state-issued license, which typically requires completion of an internship.

Education

Landscape architects typically need a bachelor's or master's degree in landscape architecture or a related field, such as architecture. There are two undergraduate landscape architect degrees: a Bachelor of Landscape Architecture (BLA) and a Bachelor of Science in Landscape Architecture (BSLA). These programs usually require 4 to 5 years of study.

Landscape architects may design gardens for resorts.

Interns are often supervised by more experienced landscape architects.

Accredited programs are approved by the Landscape Architectural Accreditation Board (LAAB). Prospective landscape architects whose undergraduate degree is in another field may enroll in a Master of Landscape Architecture (MLA) graduate degree program, which typically takes 3 years of full-time study.

Courses typically include landscape design and construction, landscape ecology, and site design. Other relevant coursework may include history of landscape architecture, plant and soil science, and professional practice.

The design studio is a key component of any curriculum. When possible, students are assigned projects that offer hands-on experience. These projects allow students to work with computer-aided design and drafting (CADD), model building, and other design software.

Training

To become licensed, candidates must meet experience requirements determined by each state. A list of training requirements is available from the Council of Landscape Architectural Registration Boards.

New hires awaiting licensure may be called intern landscape architects. Although duties vary with the type and size of the employing firm, interns typically must work under the supervision of a licensed landscape architect for the experience to count toward licensure. Potential landscape architects may benefit by completing an internship with a landscape architecture firm during educational studies. Interns may improve their technical skills and gain an understanding of the day-to-day operations of the business, including learning how to recruit clients, generate fees, and work within a budget.

Licenses, Certifications, and Registrations

All states require landscape architects to be licensed. Candidates for licensure must pass the Landscape Architect Registration Examination (LARE), which is sponsored by the Council of Landscape Architectural Registration Boards.

Candidates who are interested in taking the exam usually need a degree from an accredited school and experience working under the supervision of a licensed landscape architect, although standards vary by state. For candidates without a degree in landscape architecture, many states offer alternative paths—which usually require more work experience—to qualify to take the LARE.

In addition to the LARE, some states have their own registration exam to test for competency on state-specific issues, such as earthquakes in California or hurricanes in Florida. State-specific exams may focus on laws, environmental regulations, plants, soils, climate, and other characteristics unique to the state.

Licensed landscape architects also may obtain voluntary certification from the Council of Landscape Architectural Registration Boards, which might make it easier to get licensed in another state.

Important Qualities

Analytical skills. Landscape architects must understand how their designs will affect locations. When designing a building's drainage system, for example, landscape architects must understand the interaction between the building and the surrounding land.

Communication skills. Landscape architects share their ideas, both orally and in writing, with clients, other architects, and workers who help prepare drawings. Effective communication is essential to ensuring that the vision for a project gets translated into reality.

Creativity. Landscape architects create the overall look of gardens, parks, and other outdoor areas. Their designs should be both pleasing to the eye and functional.

Problem-solving skills. When designing outdoor spaces, landscape architects must be able to provide solutions to unanticipated challenges. These solutions often involve looking at challenges from different perspectives and providing the best recommendations.

Technical skills. Landscape architects use computer-aided design and drafting (CADD) programs to create representations of their projects. Some also must use Geographic Information Systems (GIS) for their designs.

Visualization skills. Landscape architects must be able to imagine how an overall outdoor space will look once completed.

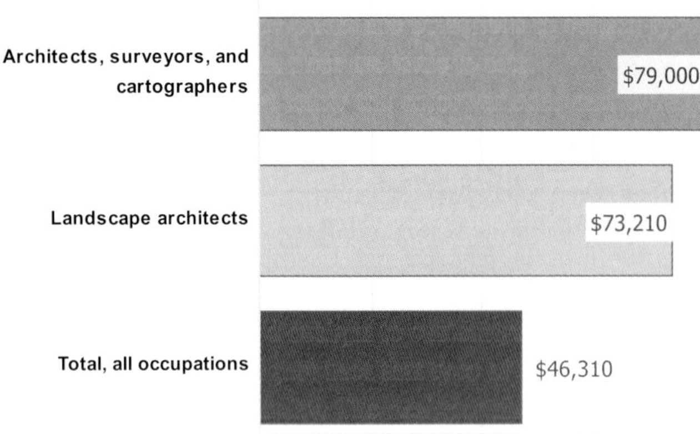

Note: All Occupations includes all occupations in the U.S. Economy.
Source: U.S. Bureau of Labor Statistics, Occupational Employment and Wage Statistics.

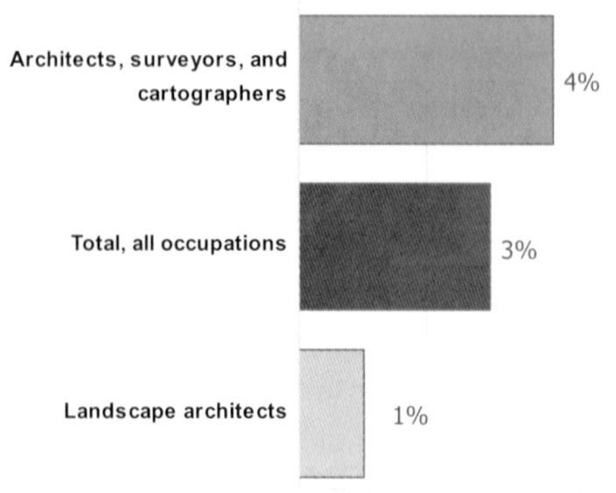

Note: All Occupations includes all occupations in the U.S. Economy.
Source: U.S. Bureau of Labor Statistics, Employment Projections program.

Pay

The median annual wage for landscape architects was $73,210 in May 2022. The median wage is the wage at which half the workers in an occupation earned more than that amount and half earned less. The lowest 10 percent earned less than $42,870, and the highest 10 percent earned more than $121,660.

In May 2022, the median annual wages for landscape architects in the top industries in which they worked were as follows:

Government	$92,660
Architectural, engineering, and related services	76,170
Construction	61,850
Administrative and support and waste management and remediation services	58,510

Job Outlook

Employment of landscape architects is projected to show little or no change from 2022 to 2032.

Despite limited employment growth, about 1,800 openings for landscape architects are projected each year, on average, over the decade. Most of those openings are expected to result from the need to replace workers who transfer to different occupations or exit the labor force, such as to retire.

Employment

Improving technologies are expected to increase landscape architects' productivity, which should reduce overall demand for the occupation over the decade.

However, there will continue to be some need for these workers to plan and develop landscapes for commercial, industrial, and residential projects. Environmental concerns and efforts to conserve water and prevent waterway pollution also may create some demand for landscape architects.

Occupational Title	SOC Code	Employment, 2022	Projected Employment, 2032	Change, 2022-32	
				Percent	Numeric
Landscape architects	17-1012	23,600	23,800	1	200

Contacts for More Information

For more information, visit

- American Society of Landscape Architects
- Council of Landscape Architectural Registration Boards

Marine Engineers and Naval Architects

Summary

Quick Facts: Marine Engineers and Naval Architects	
2022 Median Pay	$96,910 per year $46.59 per hour
Typical Entry-Level Education	Bachelor's degree
Work Experience in a Related Occupation	None
On-the-job Training	None
Number of Jobs, 2022	8,000
Job Outlook, 2022-32	1% (Little or no change)
Employment Change, 2022-32	100

What Marine Engineers and Naval Architects Do

Marine engineers and naval architects design, build, and maintain ships, from aircraft carriers to submarines and from sailboats to tankers.

Work Environment

Marine engineers and naval architects typically work in offices, where they have access to computer software and other tools necessary for analyzing projects and designing solutions. Sometimes, they must go to sea to test or maintain the ships that they have designed or built.

How to Become a Marine Engineer or Naval Architect

Marine engineers and naval architects typically need a bachelor's degree in marine engineering and naval architecture, respectively, or in a related field, such as engineering.

Pay

The median annual wage for marine engineers and naval architects was $96,910 in May 2022.

Marine engineers and naval architects design and build ships from sailboats to tankers.

Job Outlook

Employment of marine engineers and naval architects is projected to show little or no change from 2022 to 2032.

Despite limited employment growth, about 400 openings for marine engineers and naval architects are projected each year, on average, over the decade. Most of those openings are expected to result from the need to replace workers who transfer to different occupations or exit the labor force, such as to retire.

What Marine Engineers and Naval Architects Do

Marine engineers and naval architects design, build, and maintain ships, from aircraft carriers to submarines and from sailboats to tankers. Marine engineers are also known as *marine design engineers* or *marine mechanical engineers* and are responsible for the internal systems of a ship, such as the propulsion, electrical, refrigeration, and steering systems. Naval architects are responsible for the ship design, including the form, structure, and stability of hulls.

Duties

Marine engineers typically do the following:

- Prepare system layouts and detailed drawings and schematics
- Inspect marine equipment and machinery, and draw up work requests and job specifications

Marine engineers and naval architects may work directly on ships.

- Conduct environmental, operational, or performance tests on marine machinery and equipment
- Design and oversee the testing, installation, and repair of marine equipment
- Investigate and test machinery and equipment to ensure compliance with standards
- Coordinate activities with regulatory bodies to ensure that repairs and alterations are done safely and at minimal cost
- Prepare technical reports for use by engineers, managers, or sales personnel
- Prepare cost estimates, contract specifications, and design and construction schedules
- Maintain contact with contractors to make sure that the work is being done correctly, on schedule, and within budget

Naval architects typically do the following:

- Study design proposals and specifications to establish basic characteristics of a ship, such as its size, weight, and speed
- Develop sectional and waterline curves of the ship's hull to establish the center of gravity, the ideal hull form, and data on buoyancy and stability
- Design entire ship hulls and superstructures, following safety and regulatory standards
- Design the complete layout of ships' interiors, including spaces for machinery and auxiliary equipment, passenger compartments, cargo space, ladder wells, and elevators
- Confer with marine engineers to design the layout of boiler room equipment, heating and ventilation systems, refrigeration equipment, electrical distribution systems, safety systems, steering systems, and propulsion machinery
- Lead teams from a variety of specialties to oversee building and testing prototypes
- Evaluate how ships perform during trials, both in the dock and at sea, and change designs as needed to make sure that national and international standards are met

Marine engineers and naval architects apply knowledge from a range of engineering fields to the entire water vehicles' design and production processes. Marine engineers also design and maintain offshore oil rigs and may work on alternative energy projects, such as wind turbines located offshore and tidal power.

Marine engineers and naval architects who work for ship and boat building firms design large ships, such as passenger ships and cargo ships, as well as small craft, such as inflatable boats and rowboats. Those who work in the federal government may design or test the designs of ships or systems for the Army, Navy, or Coast Guard.

Marine engineers should not be confused with ship engineers, who operate or supervise the operation of the machinery on a ship. For more information on ship engineers, see the profile on water transportation workers.

Marine engineers and naval architects design and oversee testing, installation, and repair of marine apparatus and equipment.

Work Environment

Marine engineers and naval architects held about 8,000 jobs in 2022. The largest employers of marine engineers and naval architects were as follows:

Professional, scientific, and technical services	42%
Federal government, excluding postal service	15
Water transportation	3

Marine engineers and naval architects typically work in offices, where they have access to computer software and other tools necessary for analyzing projects and designing solutions. Sometimes, they must go to sea to test or maintain the ships that they have designed or built.

Marine engineers and naval architects who work on power generation projects, such as offshore wind turbines and tidal power, work along the coast—both offshore and on land. They also sometimes work on oil rigs, where they oversee the repair or maintenance of systems that they may have designed.

Naval architects often lead teams to create feasible designs, and they must effectively use the skills that each person brings to the design process.

Work Schedules

Most marine engineers and naval architects work full time and some work more than 40 hours per week. Marine engineers who work at sea will work a schedule tied to the operations of their particular ship. Those who work onshore will have somewhat more regular work schedules. Naval architects, and marine engineers who are engaged primarily in design, are much more likely to work a regular schedule in an office or at a shipyard.

How to Become a Marine Engineer or Naval Architect

Marine engineers and naval architects typically need a bachelor's degree in marine engineering and naval architecture,

Marine engineers and naval architects must give clear instructions and explain complex concepts when leading projects.

respectively, or a related field, such as engineering. Some marine engineering and naval architecture programs are offered at state maritime academies.

Education

High school students interested in becoming a marine engineer or naval architect should take classes in math, such as algebra, trigonometry, and calculus; and science, such as chemistry and physics. If available, drafting courses may be helpful for aspiring naval architects.

College students interested in this occupation typically pursue a degree in an engineering field. Programs in marine engineering and naval architecture usually include courses in computer-aided design, fluid mechanics, ship hull strength, and mechanics of materials. Most programs also include time at sea, during which students gain hands-on experience on a vessel.

Some marine engineering and naval architecture programs are offered at state maritime academies. Students studying at the maritime academies spend time at sea, usually during the summer, to gain onboard operating experience. For more information about state maritime academies, visit the Maritime Administration of the U.S. Department of Transportation.

Employers may prefer to hire candidates who graduate from a program accredited by a professional association such as ABET.

Important Qualities

Communication skills. Marine engineers and naval architects must give clear instructions and explain complex concepts when leading projects.

Ingenuity. Marine engineers and naval architects must use operations analysis to create a design to perform the ship's functions. They then employ critical-thinking skills to anticipate and correct any deficiencies before the ship is built or set to sea.

Interpersonal skills. Marine engineers and naval architects meet with clients to analyze their needs for ship systems. Engineers must discuss progress with clients to keep redesign options open before the project is too far along.

Math skills. Marine engineers and naval architects use the principles of calculus, trigonometry, and other advanced topics in math for analysis, design, and troubleshooting in their work.

Problem-solving skills. Marine engineers must design several systems that work well together in ships. Naval architects and marine engineers are expected to solve problems for their clients. They must draw on their knowledge and experience to make effective decisions.

Licenses, Certifications, and Registrations

Along with earning a bachelor's degree, students at states' maritime academies take exams for licensure from the U.S. Coast Guard.

Another type of engineering license is the Professional Engineering (PE) license, which allows for higher levels of leadership and independence and can be acquired later in one's career. Licensed engineers are called professional engineers (PEs). A PE can oversee the work of other engineers, sign off on projects, and provide services directly to the public. State licensure generally requires

- A degree from an ABET-accredited engineering program
- A passing score on the Fundamentals of Engineering (FE) exam
- Relevant work experience, typically at least 4 years
- A passing score on the Professional Engineering (PE) exam

The initial FE exam can be taken after earning a bachelor's degree. Engineers who pass this exam are commonly called engineers in training (EITs) or engineer interns (EIs). After meeting work experience requirements, EITs and EIs can take the second exam, called the Principles and Practice of Engineering (PE).

Other Experience

Employers also value practical experience, so cooperative education programs and internships, which provide college credit or structured job experience, can be helpful in getting a job in this occupation.

Advancement

Beginning marine engineers usually work under the supervision of experienced engineers. In larger companies, new engineers also may receive formal training in classrooms or seminars. As beginning engineers gain knowledge and experience, they move on to more difficult projects, on which they have greater independence to develop designs, solve problems, and make decisions.

Eventually, marine engineers may advance to become technical specialists or to supervise a team of engineers and

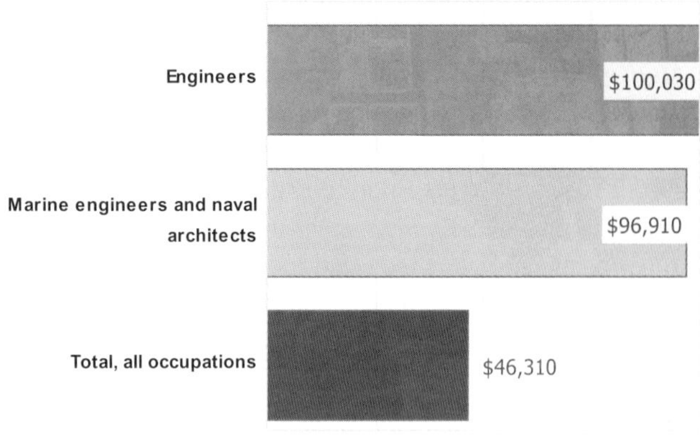

Note: All Occupations includes all occupations in the U.S. Economy.
Source: U.S. Bureau of Labor Statistics, Occupational Employment and Wage Statistics.

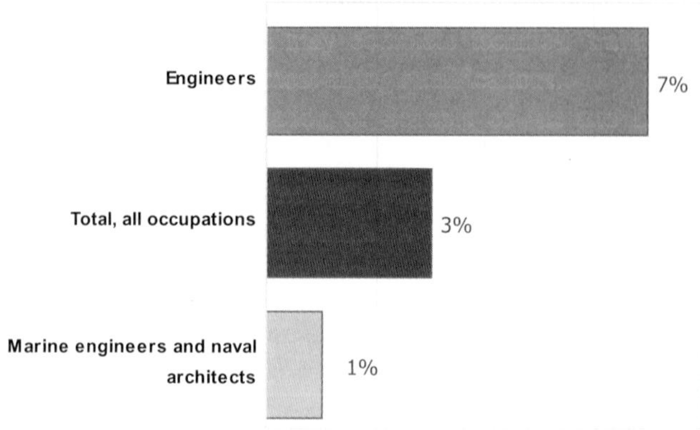

Note: All Occupations includes all occupations in the U.S. Economy.
Source: U.S. Bureau of Labor Statistics, Employment Projections program.

technicians. Some may even become engineering managers or move into other managerial positions or sales work. In sales, an engineering background enables them to discuss technical aspects of certain kinds of engineering projects. Such knowledge is also useful in assisting clients in project planning, installation, and use. For more information, see the profiles on architectural and engineering managers and sales managers.

Pay

The median annual wage for marine engineers and naval architects was $96,910 in May 2022. The median wage is the wage at which half the workers in an occupation earned more than that amount and half earned less. The lowest 10 percent earned less than $66,360, and the highest 10 percent earned more than $150,260.

In May 2022, the median annual wages for marine engineers and naval architects in the top industries in which they worked were as follows:

Water transportation	$124,810
Federal government, excluding postal service	107,850
Professional, scientific, and technical services	84,860

Most marine engineers and naval architects work full time and some work more than 40 hours per week. Marine engineers who work at sea will work a schedule tied to the operations of their particular ship. Those who work onshore will have somewhat more regular work schedules. Naval architects, and marine engineers who are engaged primarily in design, are much more likely to work a regular schedule in an office or at a shipyard.

Job Outlook

Employment of marine engineers and naval architects is projected to show little or no change from 2022 to 2032.

Despite limited employment growth, about 400 openings for marine engineers and naval architects are projected each year, on average, over the decade. Most of those openings are expected to result from the need to replace workers who transfer to different occupations or exit the labor force, such as to retire.

Employment

Marine engineers and naval architects are expected to be needed to help design ships and port facilities that meet increasingly strict international emissions standards. In addition, as offshore wind energy projects become more feasible, marine engineers and naval architects are expected to be needed to provide expertise for the construction of wind platforms.

Occupational Title	SOC Code	Employment, 2022	Projected Employment, 2032	Change, 2022-32	
				Percent	Numeric
Marine engineers and naval architects	17-2121	8,000	8,100	1	100

Contacts for More Information

For more information, visit

- Marine Engineers' Beneficial Association
- American Society of Naval Engineers
- American Society for Engineering Education
- Maritime Administration of the U.S. Department of Transportation
- Technology Student Association
- ABET

Materials Engineers

Summary

Quick Facts: Materials Engineers	
2022 Median Pay	$100,140 per year $48.15 per hour
Typical Entry-Level Education	Bachelor's degree
Work Experience in a Related Occupation	None
On-the-job Training	None
Number of Jobs, 2022	22,300
Job Outlook, 2022-32	5% (Faster than average)
Employment Change, 2022-32	1,100

What Materials Engineers Do
Materials engineers develop, process, and test materials used to create a wide range of products.

Work Environment
Materials engineers generally work in offices where they have access to computers and design equipment. Others work in factories or research and development laboratories. Materials engineers typically work full time and may work overtime hours when necessary.

How to Become a Materials Engineer
Materials engineers typically need a bachelor's degree in materials science and engineering or in a related engineering field. Completing internships and cooperative-engineering programs while in school may be helpful for gaining hands-on experience.

Pay
The median annual wage for materials engineers was $100,140 in May 2022.

Job Outlook
Employment of materials engineers is projected to grow 5 percent from 2022 to 2032, faster than the average for all occupations.

About 1,500 openings for materials engineers are projected each year, on average, over the decade. Many of those openings are expected to result from the need to replace workers who transfer to different occupations or exit the labor force, such as to retire.

What Materials Engineers Do
Materials engineers develop, process, and test materials used to create a range of products, from computer chips and aircraft wings to golf clubs and biomedical devices. They study the properties and structures of metals, ceramics, plastics, composites, nanomaterials (extremely small substances), and other substances in order to create new materials that meet certain mechanical, electrical, and chemical requirements. They also help select materials for specific products and develop new ways to use existing materials.

Duties
Materials engineers typically do the following:

- Plan and evaluate new projects, consulting with other engineers and managers as necessary
- Prepare proposals and budgets, analyze labor costs, write reports, and perform other managerial tasks
- Supervise the work of technologists, technicians, and other engineers and scientists
- Design and direct the testing of processing procedures
- Monitor how materials perform and evaluate how they deteriorate
- Determine causes of product failure and develop ways of overcoming such failure
- Evaluate technical specifications and economic factors relating to the design objectives of processes or products

Materials engineers develop, process, and test materials to create a wide range of products.

Materials engineers work with metals, ceramics, and plastics to create new materials.

- Evaluate the impact of materials processing on the environment

Materials engineers create and study materials at the atomic level. They use computers to understand and model the characteristics of materials and their components. They solve problems in several different engineering fields, such as mechanical, chemical, electrical, civil, nuclear, and aerospace.

Materials engineers may specialize in understanding specific types of materials. The following are examples of types of materials engineers:

Ceramic engineers develop ceramic materials and the processes for making them into useful products, from high-temperature rocket nozzles to glass for LCD flat-panel displays.

Composites engineers develop materials with special, engineered properties for applications in aircraft, automobiles, and related products.

Metallurgical engineers specialize in metals, such as steel and aluminum, usually in alloyed form with additions of other elements to provide specific properties.

Plastics engineers develop and test new plastics, known as polymers, for new applications.

Semiconductor processing engineers apply materials science and engineering principles to develop new microelectronic materials for computing, sensing, and related applications.

Work Environment

Materials engineers held about 22,300 jobs in 2022. The largest employers of materials engineers were as follows:

Transportation equipment manufacturing	14%
Computer and electronic product manufacturing	13
Engineering services	10
Research and development in the physical, engineering, and life sciences	6
Primary metal manufacturing	6

Materials engineers may work in laboratories or industrial settings to observe the results of their research and development.

Materials engineers often work in offices where they have access to computers and design equipment. Others work in factories or research and development laboratories. Materials engineers may work in teams with scientists and engineers from other backgrounds.

Work Schedules

Materials engineers generally work full time. Some materials engineers work more than 40 hours per week.

How to Become a Materials Engineer

Materials engineers typically need a bachelor's degree in materials science and engineering or in a related engineering field. Completing internships and cooperative-engineering programs while in school may be helpful for gaining hands-on experience.

Education

High school students interested in studying materials engineering should take classes in math, such as algebra, trigonometry, and calculus; science, such as biology, chemistry, and physics; and computer programming.

Entry-level jobs for materials engineers typically require a bachelor's degree in engineering. Programs typically last 4 years and include classroom and laboratory work focusing on engineering principles.

Some colleges and universities offer a 5-year program leading to both a bachelor's and master's degree. A graduate degree allows an engineer to work as a postsecondary teacher or to do research and development.

Many colleges and universities offer internships and cooperative programs in partnership with industry employers. In these programs, students gain practical experience while completing their education.

Employers may prefer to hire graduates of engineering programs accredited by a professional association such as ABET. A degree from an accredited program is usually necessary to become a licensed professional engineer.

Materials engineers plan and evaluate new projects, consulting with others as necessary.

Important Qualities

Analytical skills. Materials engineers often work on projects related to other fields of engineering. They must determine how materials will be used and how they must be structured to withstand different conditions.

Math skills. Materials engineers use the principles of calculus and other advanced topics in math for analysis, design, and troubleshooting in their work.

Problem-solving skills. Materials engineers must understand the relationship between materials' structures, their properties, how they are made, and how these factors affect the products they are used to make. They must also figure out why a product might have failed, design a solution, and then conduct tests to make sure that the product does not fail again. These skills involve being able to identify root causes when many factors could be at fault.

Speaking skills. While working with technicians, technologists, and other engineers, materials engineers must state concepts and directions clearly. When speaking with managers, these engineers must also communicate engineering concepts to people who may not have an engineering background.

Writing skills. Materials engineers must write plans and reports clearly so that people without a materials engineering background can understand the concepts.

Licenses, Certifications, and Registrations

Licensure for materials engineers is not as common as it is for other engineering occupations, nor it is required for entry-level positions. A Professional Engineering (PE) license, which allows for higher levels of leadership and independence, can be acquired later in one's career. Licensed engineers are called professional engineers (PEs). A PE can oversee the work of other engineers, sign off on projects, and provide services directly to the public. State licensure generally requires

- A degree from an ABET-accredited engineering program
- A passing score on the Fundamentals of Engineering (FE) exam
- Relevant work experience, typically at least 4 years
- A passing score on the Professional Engineering (PE) exam

The initial FE exam can be taken after earning a bachelor's degree. Engineers who pass this exam are commonly called engineers in training (EITs) or engineer interns (EIs). After meeting work experience requirements, EITs and EIs can take the second exam, called the Principles and Practice of Engineering (PE).

Each state issues its own licenses. Most states recognize licensure from other states, as long as the licensing state's requirements meet or exceed their own licensure requirements. Several states require continuing education for engineers to keep their licenses.

Certification in the field of metallography, the science and art of dealing with the structure of metals and alloys, is available through ASM International and other materials science organizations.

Additional training in fields directly related to metallurgy and materials' properties, such as corrosion or failure analysis, is available through ASM International.

Advancement

Junior materials engineers usually work under the supervision of experienced engineers. In large companies, new engineers may receive formal training in classrooms or seminars. As engineers gain knowledge and experience, they move on to more difficult projects where they have greater independence to develop designs, solve problems, and make decisions.

Eventually, materials engineers may advance to become technical specialists or to supervise a team of engineers and technicians. Many become engineering managers or move into other managerial positions or sales work. An engineering background is useful in sales because it enables sales engineers to discuss a product's technical aspects and assist in product planning, installation, and use. For more information, see the profiles on architectural and engineering managers and sales engineers.

Pay

The median annual wage for materials engineers was $100,140 in May 2022. The median wage is the wage at which half the workers in an occupation earned more than that amount and half earned less. The lowest 10 percent earned less than $60,700, and the highest 10 percent earned more than $162,300.

In May 2022, the median annual wages for materials engineers in the top industries in which they worked were as follows:

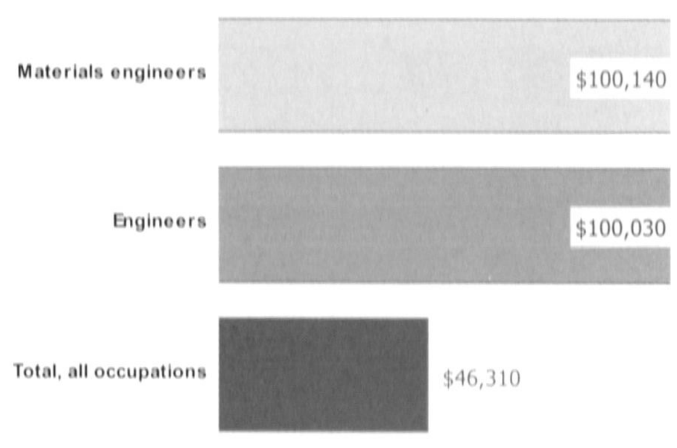

Note: All Occupations includes all occupations in the U.S. Economy.
Source: U.S. Bureau of Labor Statistics, Occupational Employment and Wage Statistics.

Research and development in the physical, engineering, and life sciences	$119,040
Computer and electronic product manufacturing	106,670
Transportation equipment manufacturing	105,030
Primary metal manufacturing	95,280
Engineering services	87,280

Most materials engineers work full time. Some materials engineers work more than 40 hours per week.

Job Outlook

Employment of materials engineers is projected to grow 5 percent from 2022 to 2032, faster than the average for all occupations.

About 1,500 openings for materials engineers are projected each year, on average, over the decade. Many of those openings are expected to result from the need to replace workers who transfer to different occupations or exit the labor force, such as to retire.

Employment

As demand for new materials and manufacturing processes continues to increase, more materials engineers are expected to be needed to help develop these products and systems. For example, new metal alloys are expected to be developed to make airplanes lighter and more fuel efficient. A greater focus on environmental sustainability also may create demand for materials engineers.

Occupational Title	SOC Code	Employment, 2022	Projected Employment, 2032	Change, 2022-32	
				Percent	Numeric
Materials engineers	17-2131	22,300	23,500	5	1,100

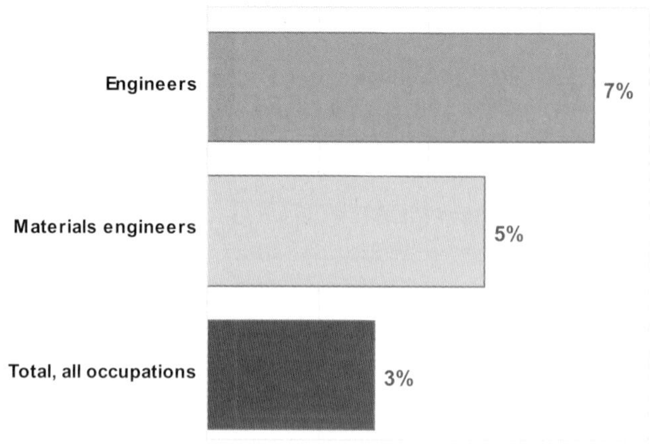

Note: All Occupations includes all occupations in the U.S. Economy.
Source: U.S. Bureau of Labor Statistics, Employment Projections program.

Contacts for More Information

For more information, visit

- The American Ceramic Society
- American Institute of Mining, Metallurgical, and Petroleum Engineers
- Materials Research Society
- The Minerals, Metals and Materials Society
- American Society for Engineering Education
- Technology Student Association
- National Council of Examiners for Engineering and Surveying
- National Society of Professional Engineers
- ASM International
- ABET

Mechanical Engineering Technologists and Technicians

Summary

Quick Facts: Mechanical Engineering Technologists and Technicians	
2022 Median Pay	$61,990 per year $29.80 per hour
Typical Entry-Level Education	Associate's degree
Work Experience in a Related Occupation	None
On-the-job Training	None
Number of Jobs, 2022	41,100
Job Outlook, 2022-32	1% (Little or no change)
Employment Change, 2022-32	300

What Mechanical Engineering Technologists and Technicians Do

Mechanical engineering technologists and technicians help mechanical engineers design, develop, test, and manufacture machines and other devices.

Work Environment

Mechanical engineering technologists and technicians work primarily in factories or in research and development labs. Most work full time.

How to Become a Mechanical Engineering Technologist or Technician

Mechanical engineering technologists and technicians typically need an associate's degree or other postsecondary training to enter the occupation.

Pay

The median annual wage for mechanical engineering technologists and technicians was $61,990 in May 2022.

Job Outlook

Employment of mechanical engineering technologists and technicians is projected to show little or no change from 2022 to 2032.

Despite limited employment growth, about 3,700 openings for mechanical engineering technologists and technicians are projected each year, on average, over the decade. Most of those openings are expected to result from the need to replace workers who transfer to different occupations or exit the labor force, such as to retire.

What Mechanical Engineering Technologists and Technicians Do

Mechanical engineering technologists and technicians help mechanical engineers design, develop, test, and manufacture tools, engines, machines, and other devices. They may make sketches and rough layouts, record and analyze data, and report their findings.

Duties

Mechanical engineering technologists and technicians typically do the following:

- Evaluate specifications in design drawings prior to adding or replacing tools
- Prepare layouts and drawings of the assembly process and parts to be made, usually using three-dimensional design software
- Recommend cost-effective changes in equipment design to improve reliability and safety

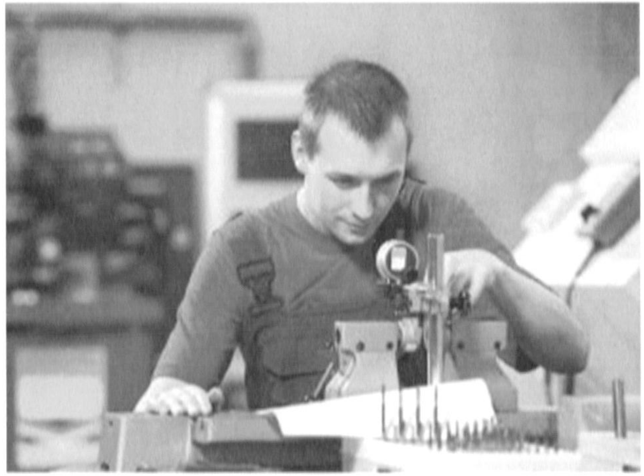

Mechanical engineering technicians plan, produce, and assemble new or changed mechanical parts for products, such as industrial machinery or equipment.

Mechanical engineering technicians plan the assembly process to be used in industrial settings.

- Review instructions and blueprints in order to ensure that project plans follow test specifications and procedures and meet objectives
- Plan, produce, and assemble mechanical parts for products, such as industrial equipment
- Set up and conduct tests of complete units and their components, and record results
- Compare test results with design specifications and with test objectives and recommend changes, if needed, in products or test methods
- Make calculations for business estimates, such as of labor costs and equipment lifespan

Mechanical engineering technicians typically install, troubleshoot, and maintain designs created by engineers. They may work under the direction of engineers or engineering technologists.

Mechanical engineering technologists typically help engineers improve designs or incorporate new technology. They may be team leaders, instructing mechanical engineering technicians on installing equipment, systems, or structures.

Some mechanical engineering technologists and technicians test and inspect machines and equipment or work with engineers to eliminate production problems. For example, they may help test products by setting up instruments for vehicle crash tests.

Work Environment

Mechanical engineering technologists and technicians held about 41,100 jobs in 2022. The largest employers of mechanical engineering technologists and technicians were as follows:

Industry	Percent
Architectural, engineering, and related services	21%
Machinery manufacturing	13
Scientific research and development services	11
Transportation equipment manufacturing	9
Computer and electronic product manufacturing	7

Because mechanical engineering technicians work with machines of all types, they must take safety precautions in their workspace.

Some mechanical engineering technologists and technicians, particularly those working in factories, are exposed to hazards from equipment, chemicals, or toxic materials. However, their risk of injury or illness is low if they follow procedures.

Work Schedules

Most mechanical engineering technologists and technicians work full time.

How to Become a Mechanical Engineering Technologist or Technician

Mechanical engineering technologists and technicians typically need an associate's degree or other postsecondary training to enter the occupation.

Education

High school students interested in becoming a mechanical engineering technologist or technician should take classes in math, science, and computer science.

Mechanical engineering technologists and technicians typically need an associate's degree or a certificate from a community college or vocational–technical school. Employers may prefer to hire candidates who have completed a bachelor's

Mechanical engineering technicians help mechanical engineers manufacture industrial machinery and other equipment.

degree or whose programs are accredited by an organization such as ABET.

Licenses, Certifications, and Registrations

The National Institute for Certification in Engineering Technologies (NICET) offers optional credentials through its technician certification programs. For example, mechanical engineering technologists and technicians who examine water-based fire protection systems may obtain certification in fire sprinkler layout or fire sprinkler inspection and testing. An engineering technologist's or technician's supervisor usually must verify the candidate's performance competency as part of the certification process.

Advancement

Technicians who obtain appropriate education or certification may advance to become technologists.

Important Qualities

Communication skills. Mechanical engineering technologists and technicians must be able to clearly explain, both orally and in writing, the need for changes in designs or test procedures.

Detail oriented. Mechanical engineering technologists and technicians must make precise measurements and keep accurate records for mechanical engineers.

Math skills. Mechanical engineering technologists and technicians use mathematics for analysis, design, and troubleshooting.

Mechanical skills. Mechanical engineering technologists and technicians must apply theory and instructions from engineers by making new components for industrial machinery or equipment. They may need to be able to operate machinery such as drill presses, grinders, and engine lathes.

Problem-solving skills. Mechanical engineering technologists and technicians help mechanical engineers bring their plans and designs to life. This may require helping the engineer overcome problems that emerge throughout development or manufacturing.

Pay

The median annual wage for mechanical engineering technologists and technicians was $61,990 in May 2022. The median wage is the wage at which half the workers in an occupation earned more than that amount and half earned less. The lowest 10 percent earned less than $39,890, and the highest 10 percent earned more than $94,720.

In May 2022, the median annual wages for mechanical engineering technologists and technicians in the top industries in which they worked were as follows:

Transportation equipment manufacturing	$63,270
Architectural, engineering, and related services	62,710
Computer and electronic product manufacturing	62,040
Scientific research and development services	61,750
Machinery manufacturing	59,910

Most mechanical engineering technologists and technicians work full time.

Job Outlook

Employment of mechanical engineering technologists and technicians is projected to show little or no change from 2022 to 2032.

Despite limited employment growth, about 3,700 openings for mechanical engineering technologists and technicians are projected each year, on average, over the decade. Most of those openings are expected to result from the need to replace workers who transfer to different occupations or exit the labor force, such as to retire.

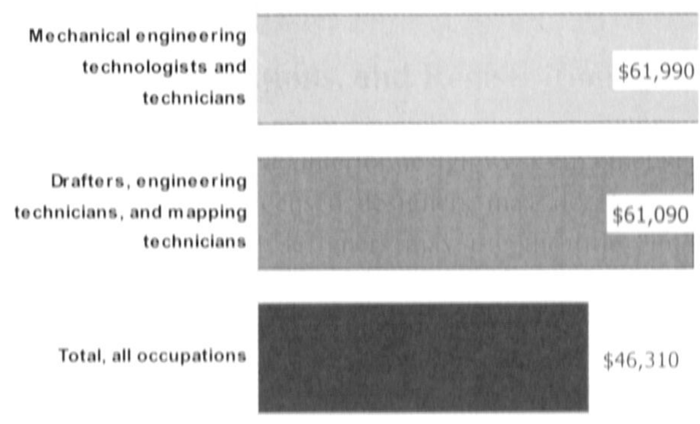

Note: All Occupations includes all occupations in the U.S. Economy.
Source: U.S. Bureau of Labor Statistics, Occupational Employment and Wage Statistics.

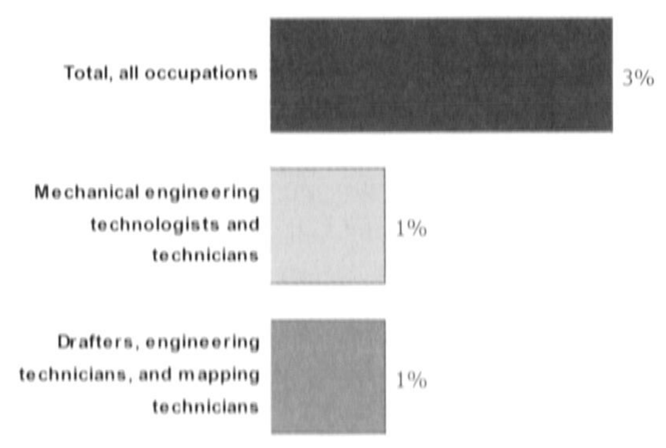

Note: All Occupations includes all occupations in the U.S. Economy.
Source: U.S. Bureau of Labor Statistics, Employment Projections program.

Employment

Mechanical engineering technologists and technicians will continue to be needed to help engineers plan for and design increasingly complex mechanical products, equipment, and systems. However, automation of routine engineering and design tasks also may reduce the need for workers in this occupation.

Occupational Title	SOC Code	Employment, 2022	Projected Employment, 2032	Change, 2022-32	
				Percent	Numeric
Mechanical engineering technologists and technicians	17-3027	41,100	41,400	1	300

Contacts for More Information

For more information, visit

- American Society for Engineering Education
- American Society of Mechanical Engineers
- Technology Student Association
- ABET
- The National Institute for Certification in Engineering Technologies (NICET)

Mechanical Engineers

Summary

Quick Facts: Mechanical Engineers

2022 Median Pay	$96,310 per year $46.31 per hour
Typical Entry-Level Education	Bachelor's degree
Work Experience in a Related Occupation	None
On-the-job Training	None
Number of Jobs, 2022	286,100
Job Outlook, 2022-32	10% (Much faster than average)
Employment Change, 2022-32	28,500

What Mechanical Engineers Do

Mechanical engineers design, develop, build, and test mechanical and thermal sensors and devices.

Work Environment

Mechanical engineers generally work in offices. They may occasionally visit worksites where a problem or piece of equipment needs their personal attention. Mechanical engineers work mostly in engineering services, research and development, and manufacturing.

Many mechanical engineers work in industries that manufacture machinery or automotive parts.

How to Become a Mechanical Engineer

Mechanical engineers typically need a bachelor's degree in mechanical engineering or mechanical engineering technology. All states and the District of Columbia require mechanical engineers who sell services to the public to be licensed.

Pay

The median annual wage for mechanical engineers was $96,310 in May 2022.

Job Outlook

Employment of mechanical engineers is projected to grow 10 percent from 2022 to 2032, much faster than the average for all occupations.

About 19,200 openings for mechanical engineers are projected each year, on average, over the decade. Many of those openings are expected to result from the need to replace workers who transfer to different occupations or exit the labor force, such as to retire.

What Mechanical Engineers Do

Mechanical engineers research, design, develop, build, and test mechanical and thermal sensors and devices, including tools, engines, and machines.

Duties

Mechanical engineers typically do the following:

- Analyze problems to see how mechanical and thermal devices might help solve a particular problem
- Design or redesign mechanical and thermal devices or subsystems, using analysis and computer-aided design
- Investigate equipment failures or difficulties to diagnose faulty operation and to recommend remedies

Computer technology helps mechanical engineers create and analyze designs.

- Develop and test prototypes of devices they design
- Analyze the test results and change the design or system as needed
- Oversee the manufacturing process for the device

Mechanical engineering is one of the broadest engineering fields. Mechanical engineers design and oversee the manufacture of many products ranging from medical devices to new batteries.

Mechanical engineers design power-producing machines, such as electric generators, internal combustion engines, and steam and gas turbines, as well as power-using machines, such as refrigeration and air-conditioning systems.

Mechanical engineers design other machines inside buildings, such as elevators and escalators. They also design material-handling systems, such as conveyor systems and automated transfer stations.

Like other engineers, mechanical engineers use computers extensively. Mechanical engineers are routinely responsible for the integration of sensors, controllers, and machinery. Computer technology helps mechanical engineers create and analyze designs, run simulations and test how a machine is likely to work, interact with connected systems, and generate specifications for parts.

The following are examples of types of mechanical engineers:

Auto research engineers seek to improve the performance of cars. These engineers work to improve traditional features of cars such as suspension, and they also work on aerodynamics and new possible fuels.

Heating and cooling systems engineers work to create and maintain environmental systems wherever temperatures and humidity must be kept within certain limits. They develop such systems for airplanes, trains, cars, schools, and even computer rooms.

Robotic engineers plan, build, and maintain robots. These engineers plan how robots will use sensors for detecting things based on light or smell, and they design how these sensors will fit into the designs of the robots.

Work Environment

Mechanical engineers held about 286,100 jobs in 2022. The largest employers of mechanical engineers were as follows:

Architectural, engineering, and related services	20%
Machinery manufacturing	15
Transportation equipment manufacturing	10
Scientific research and development services	8
Computer and electronic product manufacturing	7

Mechanical engineers generally work in offices. They may occasionally visit worksites where a problem or piece of equipment needs their personal attention. In most settings, they work with other engineers, engineering technicians, and other professionals as part of a team.

Work Schedules

Most mechanical engineers work full time and some work more than 40 hours a week.

How to Become a Mechanical Engineer

Mechanical engineers typically need a bachelor's degree in mechanical engineering or mechanical engineering technology.

Although they do most of their work in an office setting, mechanical engineers also visit worksites to gain firsthand knowledge of their designs.

Mechanical engineers who sell services publicly must be licensed in all states and the District of Columbia.

Education

Mechanical engineers typically need a bachelor's degree in mechanical engineering or mechanical engineering technologies. Mechanical engineering programs usually include courses in mathematics and life and physical sciences, as well as engineering and design. Mechanical engineering technology programs focus less on theory and more on the practical application of engineering principles. They may emphasize internships and co-ops to prepare students for work in industry.

Some colleges and universities offer 5-year programs that allow students to obtain both a bachelor's and a master's degree. Some 5-year or even 6-year cooperative plans combine classroom study with practical work, enabling students to gain valuable experience and earn money to finance part of their education.

ABET accredits programs in engineering and engineering technology. Most employers prefer to hire students from an accredited program. A degree from an ABET-accredited program is usually necessary to become a licensed professional engineer.

Important Qualities

Creativity. Mechanical engineers design and build complex pieces of equipment and machinery. A creative mind is essential for this kind of work.

Listening skills. Mechanical engineers often work on projects with others, such as architects and computer scientists. They must listen to and analyze different approaches made by other experts to complete the task at hand.

Math skills. Mechanical engineers use the principles of calculus, statistics, and other advanced subjects in math for analysis, design, and troubleshooting in their work.

Mechanical engineers analyze problems to see how a mechanical device might help to solve them.

Mechanical skills. Mechanical skills allow engineers to apply basic engineering concepts and mechanical processes to the design of new devices and systems.

Problem-solving skills. Mechanical engineers need good problem-solving skills to take scientific principles and discoveries and use them to design and build useful products.

Licenses, Certifications, and Registrations

Licensure is not required for entry-level positions as a mechanical engineer. A Professional Engineering (PE) license, which allows for higher levels of leadership and independence, can be acquired later in one's career. Licensed engineers are called professional engineers (PEs). A PE can oversee the work of other engineers, sign off on projects, and provide services directly to the public. State licensure generally requires

- A degree from an ABET-accredited engineering program
- A passing score on the Fundamentals of Engineering (FE) exam
- Relevant work experience typically at least 4 years
- A passing score on the Professional Engineering (PE) exam.

The initial FE exam can be taken after one earns a bachelor's degree. Engineers who pass this exam are commonly called engineers in training (EITs) or engineer interns (EIs). After meeting work experience requirements, EITs and EIs can take the second exam, called the Principles and Practice of Engineering.

Several states require engineers to take continuing education to renew their licenses every year. Most states recognize licensure from other states, as long as the other state's licensing requirements meet or exceed their own licensing requirements.

Several professional organizations offer a variety of certification programs for engineers to demonstrate competency in specific fields of mechanical engineering.

Advancement

A Ph.D. is essential for engineering faculty positions in higher education, as well as for some research and development programs. Mechanical engineers may earn graduate degrees in engineering or business administration to learn new technology, broaden their education, and enhance their project management skills. Mechanical engineers may become administrators or managers after gaining work experience.

Pay

The median annual wage for mechanical engineers was $96,310 in May 2022. The median wage is the wage at which half the workers in an occupation earned more than that amount and half earned less. The lowest 10 percent earned less than $61,990, and the highest 10 percent earned more than $151,260.

In May 2022, the median annual wages for mechanical engineers in the top industries in which they worked were as follows:

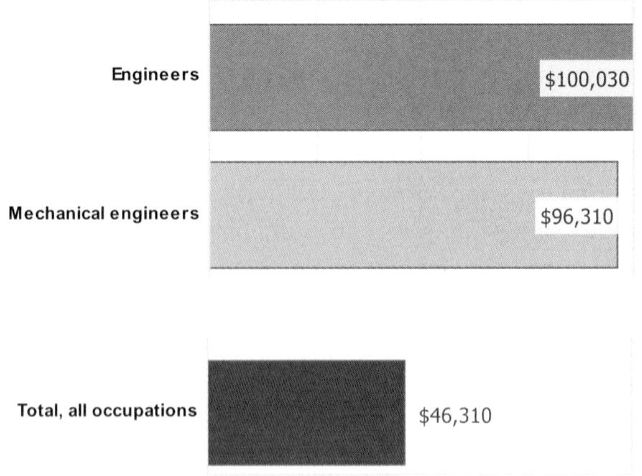

Note: All Occupations includes all occupations in the U.S. Economy.
Source: U.S. Bureau of Labor Statistics, Occupational Employment and Wage Statistics.

Scientific research and development services...	$125,850
Computer and electronic product manufacturing	101,100
Transportation equipment manufacturing	98,360
Architectural, engineering, and related services	98,280
Machinery manufacturing	82,280

Most mechanical engineers work full time and some work more than 40 hours a week.

Job Outlook

Employment of mechanical engineers is projected to grow 10 percent from 2022 to 2032, much faster than the average for all occupations.

About 19,200 openings for mechanical engineers are projected each year, on average, over the decade. Many of those openings are expected to result from the need to replace workers who transfer to different occupations or exit the labor force, such as to retire.

Employment

Mechanical engineers work in a range of industries and on many types of projects. As a result, employment growth for these workers varies by industry.

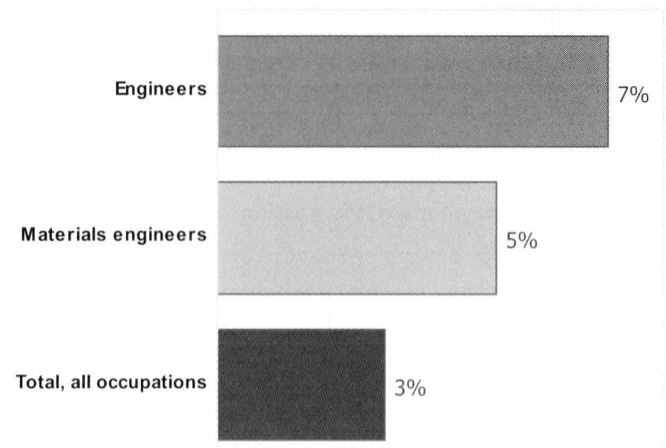

Note: All Occupations includes all occupations in the U.S. Economy.
Source: U.S. Bureau of Labor Statistics, Employment Projections program.

As manufacturing processes incorporate more complex automation machinery, mechanical engineers are expected to be needed to help plan for and design this equipment.

Occupational Title	SOC Code	Employment, 2022	Projected Employment, 2032	Change, 2022-32	
				Percent	Numeric
Mechanical engineers	17-2141	286,100	314,700	10	28,500

Contacts for More Information

For more information, visit

- American Society of Mechanical Engineers
- American Society for Engineering Education
- Technology Student Association
- ABET
- National Council of Examiners for Engineering and Surveying
- National Society of Professional Engineers

For information about certification, visit

- American Society of Mechanical Engineers

Mining and Geological Engineers

Summary

Quick Facts: Mining and Geological Engineers	
2022 Median Pay	$97,490 per year $46.87 per hour
Typical Entry-Level Education	Bachelor's degree
Work Experience in a Related Occupation	None
On-the-job Training	None
Number of Jobs, 2022	7,500
Job Outlook, 2022-32	0% (Little or no change)
Employment Change, 2022-32	0

What Mining and Geological Engineers Do
Mining and geological engineers design mines to safely and efficiently remove minerals for use in manufacturing and utilities.

Work Environment
Many mining and geological engineers work where mining operations are located, such as mineral mines or sand-and-gravel quarries, in remote areas or near cities and towns. Others work in offices or onsite for oil and gas extraction firms or engineering services firms.

How to Become a Mining or Geological Engineer
Mining and geological engineers typically need a bachelor's degree in engineering to enter the occupation.

Pay
The median annual wage for mining and geological engineers was $97,490 in May 2022.

Job Outlook
Employment of mining and geological engineers is projected to show little or no change from 2022 to 2032.

Mining engineers and geological engineers ensure that mines are operated in safe and environmentally sound ways.

Despite limited employment growth, about 400 openings for mining and geological engineers are projected each year, on average, over the decade. Most of those openings are expected to result from the need to replace workers who transfer to different occupations or exit the labor force, such as to retire.

What Mining and Geological Engineers Do
Mining and geological engineers design mines to safely and efficiently remove minerals such as coal and metals for use in manufacturing and utilities.

Duties
Mining and geological engineers typically do the following:

- Design open-pit and underground mines
- Supervise the construction of mine shafts and tunnels
- Devise methods for transporting minerals to processing plants
- Prepare technical reports for miners, engineers, and managers
- Monitor mine production to assess the effectiveness of operations
- Provide solutions to problems related to land reclamation, water and air pollution, and sustainability

Mining and geological engineers prepare technical reports for miners, engineers, and managers.

- Ensure that mines are operated in safe and environmentally sound ways

Geological engineers search for mineral deposits and evaluate possible sites. Once a site is identified, they plan how the metals or minerals will be extracted in efficient and environmentally sound ways.

Mining engineers often specialize in one particular mineral or metal, such as coal or gold. They typically design and develop mines and determine the best way to extract metal or minerals to get the most out of deposits.

Some mining engineers work with geoscientists and metallurgical engineers to find and evaluate ore deposits. Other mining engineers develop new equipment or direct mineral-processing operations to separate minerals from dirt, rock, and other materials.

Mining safety engineers use best practices and their knowledge of mine design to ensure workers' safety and to maintain compliance with state and federal safety regulations. They inspect the walls and roofs of mines, monitor the air quality, and examine mining equipment for possible hazards.

Engineers who hold a master's or a doctoral degree may teach engineering at colleges and universities. For more information, see the profile on postsecondary teachers.

Work Environment

Mining and geological engineers held about 7,500 jobs in 2022. The largest employers of mining and geological engineers were as follows:

Engineering services	35%
Metal ore mining	14
Coal mining	9
Government	6
Oil and gas extraction	3

Many work where mining operations are located, such as mineral mines or sand-and-gravel quarries, in remote areas or near cities and towns. Others work in offices or onsite for oil and gas extraction firms or engineering services firms.

Work Schedules

Most mining and geological engineers work full time and some work more than 40 hours a week. The remoteness of some mining locations gives rise to variable schedules and weeks during which they work more hours than usual.

How to Become a Mining or Geological Engineer

Mining and geological engineers, including a mining safety engineers, typically need a bachelor's degree in engineering to enter the occupation.

Mining and geological engineers must visit the worksite to keep close watch on the progression of their designs.

Education

High school students interested in studying mining or geological engineering should take classes in math and science.

College students typically get a degree in an engineering field. Because relatively few schools offer programs in mining engineering or geological engineering, a degree in civil or environmental engineering or geoscience is often acceptable. Bachelor's degree programs in mining engineering typically include courses in geology, thermodynamics, and mine design and safety. Bachelor's degree programs in geological engineering typically include courses in geology, chemistry, and fluid mechanics. Both types of programs also include laboratory and field work, along with academic study.

Employers may prefer to hire mining and geological engineering candidates who have graduated from a program accredited by a professional association such as ABET.

Master's degree programs in mining and geological engineering typically are 2-year programs and include coursework in specialized subjects, such as mineral resource development and mining regulations. Some programs require a written thesis for graduation.

A bachelor's degree from an accredited engineering program is required to become a mining or geological engineer.

Important Qualities

Analytical skills. Mining and geological engineers must take many factors into account when evaluating new mine locations and designing facilities. They must also plan for the restoration of the surrounding environment after operations end.

Decision-making skills. These engineers make decisions that influence many critical outcomes—from worker safety to mine production. The ability to anticipate problems and deal with them immediately is crucial.

Logical-thinking skills. In planning mines' operations, mineral processing, and environmental reclamation, these engineers have to put work plans into a coherent, logical sequence.

Math skills. Mining and geological engineers use the principles of calculus, trigonometry, and other advanced topics in math for analysis, design, and troubleshooting in their work.

Problem-solving skills. Mining and geological engineers must explore for potential mines, plan their operations and mineral processing, and design environmental reclamation projects. These are all complex projects requiring an ability to identify and work toward goals, while solving problems along the way.

Writing skills. Mining and geological engineers must prepare reports and instructions for other workers. Therefore, they must be able to write clearly so that others can easily understand their ideas and plans.

Licenses, Certifications, and Registrations

Licensure is not required for entry-level positions as a mining or geological engineer. A Professional Engineering (PE) license, which allows for higher levels of leadership and independence, can be acquired later in one's career. Licensed engineers are called professional engineers (PEs). A PE can oversee the work of other engineers, sign off on projects, and provide services directly to the public. State licensure generally requires

- A degree from an ABET-accredited engineering program
- A passing score on the Fundamentals of Engineering (FE) exam
- Relevant work experience, typically at least 4 years
- A passing score on the Professional Engineering (PE) exam

The initial FE exam can be taken after one earns a bachelor's degree. Engineers who pass this exam are commonly called engineers in training (EITs) or engineer interns (EIs). After meeting work experience requirements, EITs and EIs can take the second exam, called the Principles and Practice of Engineering.

In several states, engineers must earn continuing education credits to keep their licenses. Most states recognize licenses from other states, provided that licensure requirements in the other states meet or exceed the first state's own requirements.

Advancement

New mining and geological engineers usually work under the supervision of experienced engineers. In large companies, new engineers also may receive formal classroom or seminar-type training. As engineers gain knowledge and experience, they are assigned more difficult projects and they are given greater independence to develop designs, solve problems, and make decisions.

Engineers may advance to become technical specialists or supervise a staff or team of engineers and technicians. Some eventually become engineering managers or enter other managerial or sales jobs. In sales, an engineering background enables them to discuss a product's technical aspects and to assist in product planning, installation, and use. For more information, see the profiles on architectural and engineering managers and sales engineers.

Pay

The median annual wage for mining and geological engineers was $97,490 in May 2022. The median wage is the wage at which half the workers in an occupation earned more than that

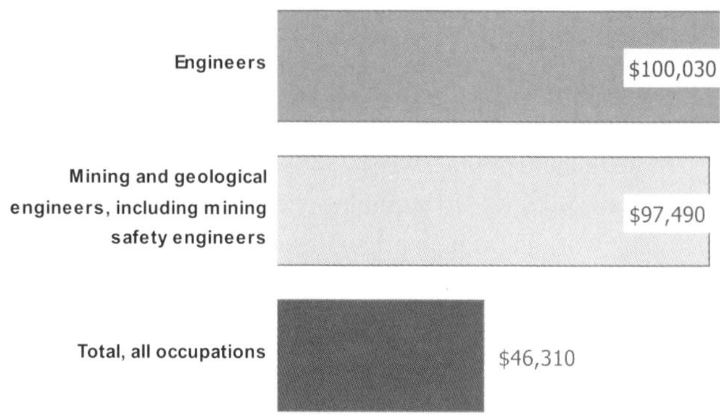

Note: All Occupations includes all occupations in the U.S. Economy.
Source: U.S. Bureau of Labor Statistics, Occupational Employment and Wage Statistics.

amount and half earned less. The lowest 10 percent earned less than $55,460, and the highest 10 percent earned more than $158,540.

In May 2022, the median annual wages for mining and geological engineers in the top industries in which they worked were as follows:

Oil and gas extraction	$164,320
Government	134,660
Coal mining	99,100
Metal ore mining	98,760
Engineering services	93,970

Most mining and geological engineers work full time and some work more than 40 hours a week. The remoteness of some mining locations gives rise to variable schedules and weeks during which they work more than usual.

Job Outlook

Employment of mining and geological engineers is projected to show little or no change from 2022 to 2032.

Despite limited employment growth, about 400 openings for mining and geological engineers are projected each year, on average, over the decade. Most of those openings are expected to result from the need to replace workers who transfer to different occupations or exit the labor force, such as to retire.

Employment

Employment growth for mining and geological engineers will depend on demand for coal, metals, and minerals. These resources are used in many products, including construction materials, electric vehicles, smartphones, and computers. Rising demand for these products may create some jobs for mining and geological engineers. However, decreased demand for coal and increased automation of mining activities are expected to offset some of this growth.

Occupational Title	SOC Code	Employment, 2022	Projected Employment, 2032	Change, 2022-32 Percent	Change, 2022-32 Numeric
Mining and geological engineers, including mining safety engineers	17-2151	7,500	7,600	0	0

Mining and Geological Engineers

Percent change in employment, projected 2022-32

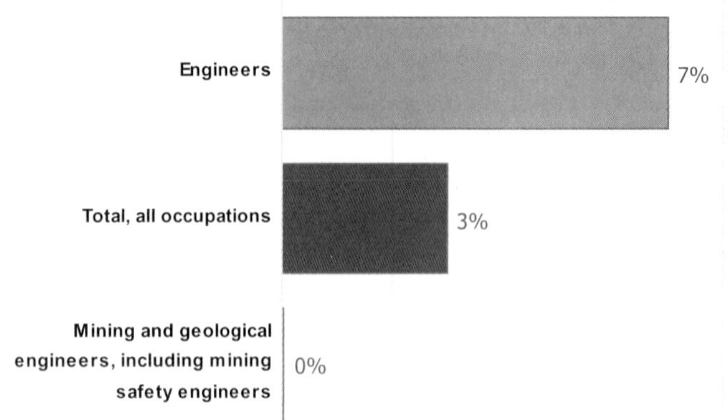

Note: All Occupations includes all occupations in the U.S. Economy.
Source: U.S. Bureau of Labor Statistics, Employment Projections program.

Contacts for More Information

For more information about mining and geological engineers, visit

- ➤ Society for Mining, Metallurgy, and Exploration

For information about general engineering education and career resources, visit

- ➤ American Society for Engineering Education
- ➤ Technology Student Association

For more information about licensure as a mining or geological engineer, visit

- ➤ National Council of Examiners for Engineering and Surveying
- ➤ National Society of Professional Engineers

For information about accredited engineering programs, visit

- ➤ ABET

Nuclear Engineers

Summary

Quick Facts: Nuclear Engineers	
2022 Median Pay	$122,480 per year $58.89 per hour
Typical Entry-Level Education	Bachelor's degree
Work Experience in a Related Occupation	None
On-the-job Training	None
Number of Jobs, 2022	13,800
Job Outlook, 2022-32	1% (Little or no change)
Employment Change, 2022-32	100

What Nuclear Engineers Do

Nuclear engineers research and develop projects or address problems concerning the release, control, and use of nuclear energy and nuclear waste disposal.

Work Environment

Nuclear engineers typically work in office settings, but it may vary by employer. Most nuclear engineers work full time.

How to Become a Nuclear Engineer

Nuclear engineers typically need at least a bachelor's degree in nuclear engineering or a related field. They typically do not need a license to enter the occupation.

Pay

The median annual wage for nuclear engineers was $122,480 in May 2022.

Job Outlook

Employment of nuclear engineers is projected to show little or no change from 2022 to 2032.

Despite limited employment growth, about 800 openings for nuclear engineers are projected each year, on average, over the decade. Most of those openings are expected to result from the need to replace workers who transfer to different occupations or exit the labor force, such as to retire.

What Nuclear Engineers Do

Nuclear engineers research and develop projects or address problems concerning the release, control, and use of nuclear energy and nuclear waste disposal. Some of these engineers research new reactor designs. Others may specialize in the development of safety regulations related to the handling of nuclear materials or operation of nuclear power.

Duties

Nuclear engineers typically do the following:

- Design or develop nuclear equipment—such as reactor cores, nuclear batteries, and radiation shielding—and its associated instruments
- Test whether methods of managing nuclear material or reclaiming nuclear fuel are acceptable
- Write instructions to be used in operating nuclear plants or other nuclear equipment or in managing nuclear materials
- Monitor nuclear facility design, construction, and operation practices to ensure compliance with state and federal regulations

Nuclear engineers may work in the following areas:

Defense. Nuclear engineers in the military work on nuclear propulsion systems for naval vessels. They may help design or evaluate these systems to ensure compliance with safety standards and system specifications. They also work aboard nuclear-powered vessels to monitor and maintain the nuclear systems. In addition, they may review and evaluate technical information related to nuclear weapons, such as readiness and safe storage.

Nuclear engineers direct maintenance activities at operational nuclear power plants to ensure that they meet safety standards.

Nuclear engineers monitor nuclear facility operations.

Medical. Nuclear engineers provide dose and shielding calculations for medical isotope production. They design and conduct irradiation experiments and then analyze and document the results of these experiments.

Research and regulation. Nuclear engineers research new uses and management of nuclear power or material. They examine nuclear accidents and analyze the data to aid in designing preventive measures. Some test whether methods of using and managing nuclear material or reclaiming nuclear fuel are acceptable. They may assist in drafting new regulations and standards based on research and experiments.

Space exploration. Nuclear engineers design nuclear batteries used in spacecraft, satellites, and space rovers. They also may design radiation shielding for spacecraft and calculate and analyze radiation in space.

Utility power generation. Nuclear engineers who work for utilities help design and operate nuclear power plants. They also may direct maintenance activities to ensure that these plants meet safety standards.

Work Environment

Nuclear engineers held about 13,800 jobs in 2022. The largest employers of nuclear engineers were as follows:

Nuclear electric power generation	28%
Federal government, excluding postal service	20
Scientific research and development services	16
Engineering services	7
Manufacturing	5

Nuclear engineers typically work in office settings. However, where their office is located varies with the industry in which they work. For example, those employed in power generation and supply work in power plants. Those working for the federal government may be in the military or employed by a regulatory agency or a national laboratory. Others may work for professional, scientific, and technical services, which include consulting firms.

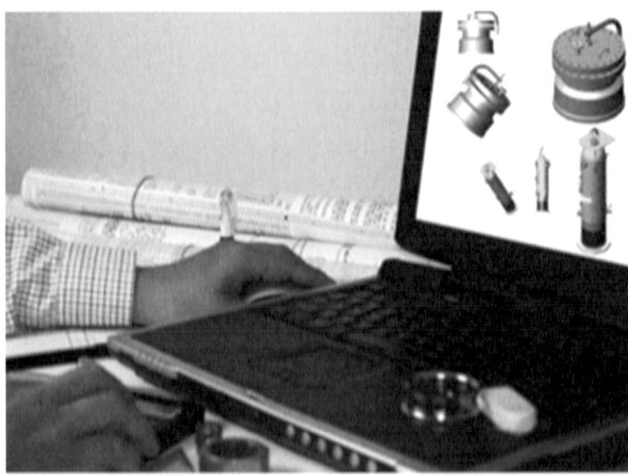

Nuclear engineers design equipment that may be used at nuclear power plants.

Nuclear engineers work with others, including mechanical engineers and electrical engineers, to incorporate other systems into their own designs.

Work Schedules

Most nuclear engineers work full time. Their schedules vary with the industries in which they work.

How to Become a Nuclear Engineer

Nuclear engineers typically need at least bachelor's degree in nuclear engineering or a related field of engineering.

Education

High school students interested in studying nuclear engineering should take classes in mathematics, such as algebra, trigonometry, and calculus; and science, such as biology, chemistry, and physics.

Entry-level nuclear engineering jobs commonly require a bachelor's degree in engineering, engineering technologies, or a physical science field. Some jobs, such as those in research and development, require a master's degree or Ph.D.

Nuclear engineers write operational instructions to be used in nuclear plant operations or in handling and disposing of nuclear waste.

Bachelor's degree engineering programs often consist of classroom, laboratory, and field studies. Courses include calculus, physics, and nuclear design. Colleges and universities may offer internship or cooperative-education programs with businesses, allowing students to gain work experience while completing their education.

Some colleges and universities offer 5-year programs that lead to both a bachelor's and a master's degree. Programs in nuclear engineering are accredited by ABET.

Training

At a nuclear power plant, new employees usually must complete onsite training in topics such as safety procedures, practices, and regulations. Length of training varies, depending on the employer and the power plant. In addition, nuclear engineers must undergo training every year to stay current on applicable laws, regulations, and safety procedures.

Licenses, Certifications, and Registrations

Licensure is not required for entry-level nuclear engineer positions. Experienced engineers may obtain a Professional Engineering (PE) license, which allows them to oversee the work of other engineers, sign off on projects, and provide services directly to the public.

State licensure typically requires a bachelor's or higher degree in engineering, a passing score on the Fundamentals of Engineering (FE) exam, several years of relevant work experience, and a passing score on the PE exam.

Each state issues its own license. Most states recognize licensure from other states, as long as the licensing state's requirements meet or exceed their own licensure requirements. Several states require continuing education for engineers to keep their licenses.

Nuclear engineers may be licensed as a Senior Reactor Operator, a credential granted by the Nuclear Regulatory Commission (NRC). Contact the NRC for more information.

Other Experience

Some nuclear engineers get their training in the military. Experience in a related military occupation may be beneficial for transferring to a civilian position.

Advancement

Nuclear engineers may advance to supervise a team of engineers and technicians. Some become engineering managers or move into sales work. For more information, see the profiles on architectural and engineering managers and sales engineers.

Important Qualities

Analytical skills. Nuclear engineers must evaluate technical information for safe use of nuclear energy and materials.

Communication skills. Nuclear engineers collaborate with other engineers and technicians. They must be able to convey information clearly, both in writing and in person.

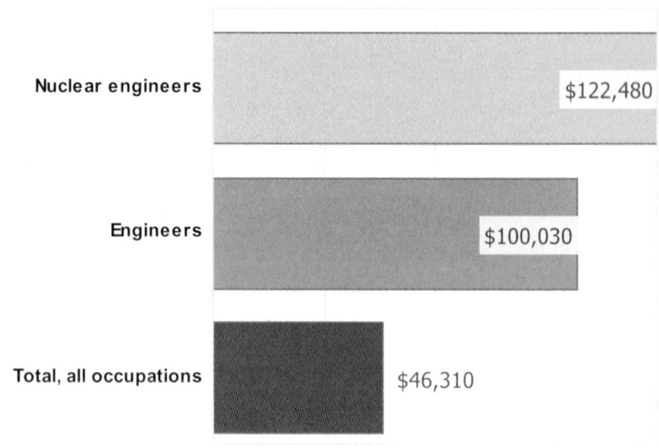

Note: All Occupations includes all occupations in the U.S. Economy.
Source: U.S. Bureau of Labor Statistics, Occupational Employment and Wage Statistics.

Computer skills. Nuclear engineers need a working knowledge of programming languages and computer systems.

Detail oriented. Nuclear engineers supervise nuclear facilities and must pay attention to ensure that they operate safely.

Logical-thinking skills. In designing complex systems, nuclear engineers must order information clearly and sequentially.

Math skills. Nuclear engineers use calculus, trigonometry, and other advanced math in their work.

Problem-solving skills. Nuclear engineers must be able to identify and fix problems that arise in designing and maintaining facilities.

Pay

The median annual wage for nuclear engineers was $122,480 in May 2022. The median wage is the wage at which half the workers in an occupation earned more than that amount and half earned less. The lowest 10 percent earned less than $79,440, and the highest 10 percent earned more than $169,580.

In May 2022, the median annual wages for nuclear engineers in the top industries in which they worked were as follows:

Scientific research and development services	$129,370
Engineering services	128,790
Nuclear electric power generation	121,380
Manufacturing	109,430
Federal government, excluding postal service	104,170

Most nuclear engineers work full time.

Job Outlook

Employment of nuclear engineers is projected to show little or no change from 2022 to 2032.

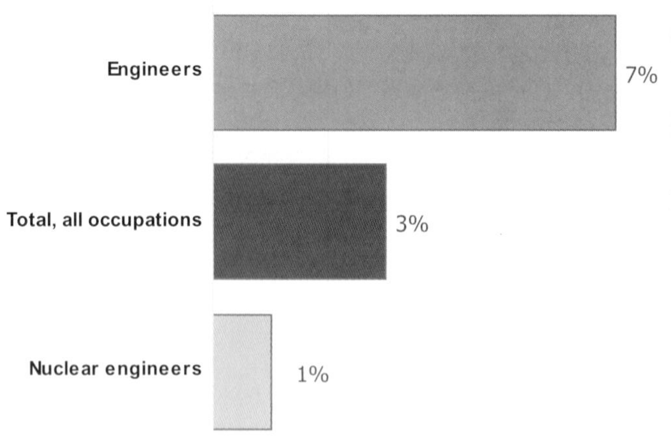

Note: All Occupations includes all occupations in the U.S. Economy.
Source: U.S. Bureau of Labor Statistics, Employment Projections program.

Despite limited employment growth, about 800 openings for nuclear engineers are projected each year, on average, over the decade. Most of those openings are expected to result from the need to replace workers who transfer to different occupations or exit the labor force, such as to retire.

Employment

Traditionally, utilities that own or build nuclear power plants have employed the greatest number of nuclear engineers. However, the increasing viability of renewable energy and limited construction of new nuclear power plants puts economic pressure on traditional nuclear power generation and reduces demand for these engineers.

Occupational Title	SOC Code	Employment, 2022	Projected Employment, 2032	Change, 2022-32	
				Percent	Numeric
Nuclear engineers	17-2161	13,800	13,900	1	100

Contacts for More Information

For more information, visit

- American Nuclear Society
- American Society for Engineering Education
- Health Physics Society
- Nuclear Energy Institute
- Society of Nuclear Medicine and Molecular Imaging
- Technology Student Association
- National Council of Examiners for Engineering and Surveying
- National Society of Professional Engineers
- ABET
- Engineering For Kids
- USAJOBS

Petroleum Engineers

Summary

Quick Facts: Petroleum Engineers

2022 Median Pay	$131,800 per year $63.37 per hour
Typical Entry-Level Education	Bachelor's degree
Work Experience in a Related Occupation	None
On-the-job Training	None
Number of Jobs, 2022	21,400
Job Outlook, 2022-32	2% (As fast as average)
Employment Change, 2022-32	500

What Petroleum Engineers Do

Petroleum engineers design and develop methods for extracting oil and gas from deposits below the Earth's surface.

Work Environment

Petroleum engineers generally work in offices or at drilling and well sites. Travel is frequently required to visit these sites or to meet with other engineers, oilfield workers, and customers.

How to Become a Petroleum Engineer

Petroleum engineers typically need a bachelor's degree in petroleum engineering or a related field, such as mechanical, civil, or chemical engineering. Cooperative-education programs, in which students gain practical experience while earning academic credit, may be beneficial.

Petroleum engineers design equipment to extract oil and gas in the most profitable way.

Pay

The median annual wage for petroleum engineers was $131,800 in May 2022.

Job Outlook

Employment of petroleum engineers is projected to grow 2 percent from 2022 to 2032, about as fast as the average for all occupations.

About 1,200 openings for petroleum engineers are projected each year, on average, over the decade. Many of those openings are expected to result from the need to replace workers who transfer to different occupations or exit the labor force, such as to retire.

What Petroleum Engineers Do

Petroleum engineers design and develop methods for extracting oil and gas from deposits below the Earth's surface. Petroleum engineers also find new ways to extract oil and gas from older wells.

Duties

Petroleum engineers typically do the following:

- Design equipment to extract oil and gas from onshore and offshore reserves deep underground
- Develop plans to drill in oil and gas fields, and then to recover the oil and gas
- Develop ways to inject water, chemicals, gases, or steam into an oil reserve to force out more oil or gas
- Make sure that oilfield equipment is installed, operated, and maintained properly
- Evaluate the production of wells through surveys, testing, and analysis

Oil and gas deposits, or reservoirs, are located deep in rock formations underground. These reservoirs can be accessed only by drilling wells, either on land, or at sea from offshore oil rigs.

Once oil and gas are discovered, petroleum engineers work with geoscientists and other specialists to understand the geologic formation of the rock containing the reservoir. They then determine the drilling methods, design the drilling equipment, implement the drilling plan, and monitor operations.

The best techniques currently being used recover only a portion of the oil and gas in a reservoir, so petroleum engineers also research and develop new ways to recover more of the oil and gas. This additional recovery helps to lower the cost of drilling and production.

The following are examples of types of petroleum engineers:

Completions engineers decide the best way to finish building wells so that oil or gas will flow up from underground. They oversee work to complete the building of wells—a project that might involve the use of tubing, hydraulic fracturing, or pressure-control techniques.

Drilling engineers determine the best way to drill oil or gas wells, taking into account a number of factors, including cost. They also ensure that the drilling process is safe, efficient, and minimally disruptive to the environment.

Production engineers take over wells after drilling is completed. They typically monitor wells' oil and gas production. If wells are not producing as much as expected, production engineers figure out ways to increase the amount being extracted.

Reservoir engineers estimate how much oil or gas can be recovered from underground deposits, known as reservoirs. They study reservoirs' characteristics and determine which methods will get the most oil or gas out of the reservoirs. They also monitor operations to ensure that optimal levels of these resources are being recovered.

Work Environment

Petroleum engineers held about 21,400 jobs in 2022. The largest employers of petroleum engineers were as follows:

Oil and gas extraction	29%
Support activities for mining	16

Petroleum engineers help find oil and gas for the country's energy needs.

Petroleum engineers generally work in an office setting, but must sometimes work on site to monitor operations.

Management of companies and enterprises	16
Engineering services	13
Petroleum and coal products manufacturing	7

Petroleum engineers generally work in offices or at drilling and well sites. Travel is frequently required to visit these sites or to meet with other engineers, oilfield workers, and customers.

Large oil and gas companies maintain operations around the world; therefore, petroleum engineers sometimes work in other countries. Petroleum engineers also must be able to work with people from a wide variety of backgrounds, including other types of engineers, scientists, and oil and gas field workers.

Work Schedules

Petroleum engineers typically work full time. Overtime may be necessary when traveling to and from drilling sites to help in their operation or respond to problems when they arise.

How to Become a Petroleum Engineer

Petroleum engineers typically need a bachelor's degree in petroleum engineering or a related field, such as mechanical, civil, or chemical engineering. Cooperative-education programs, in which students gain practical experience while earning academic credit, may be beneficial.

Petroleum engineers must have a bachelor's degree in engineering, preferably in petroleum engineering.

Education

High school students interested in studying petroleum engineering may benefit from taking classes in math, such as algebra, trigonometry, and calculus; and science, such as biology, chemistry, and physics.

College students typically pursue a bachelor's degree in engineering. Bachelor's degree engineering programs typically take 4 years and include academic, laboratory, and field work in areas such as engineering principles, geology, and thermodynamics. Some colleges and universities offer cooperative programs in which students gain practical experience while completing their education.

Colleges and universities may offer 5-year engineering programs that lead to both a bachelor's degree and a master's degree. Some employers prefer to hire candidates who have a master's degree. A graduate degree also allows an engineer to work as an instructor at some universities or in research and development.

Employers may prefer candidates who completed their studies in an engineering program accredited by a professional association such as ABET.

Important Qualities

Analytical skills. Petroleum engineers must be able to compile and make sense of large amounts of technical information and data in order to ensure that facilities operate safely and effectively.

Creativity. Because each new drill site is unique and therefore presents new challenges, petroleum engineers must be able to come up with creative designs to extract oil and gas.

Interpersonal skills. Petroleum engineers must work with others on projects that require highly complex machinery, equipment, and infrastructure. Communicating and working well with other engineers and oil and gas workers is crucial to ensuring that projects meet customer needs and run safely and efficiently.

Math skills. Petroleum engineers use the principles of calculus and other advanced topics in math for analysis, design, and troubleshooting in their work.

Problem-solving skills. Identifying problems in drilling plans is critical for petroleum engineers because these problems can be costly. Petroleum engineers must be careful not to overlook any potential issues and must quickly address those which do occur.

Licenses, Certifications, and Registrations

Licensure is not required for entry-level positions as a petroleum engineer. A Professional Engineering (PE) license, which allows for higher levels of leadership and independence, can be acquired later in one's career. Licensed engineers are called professional engineers (PEs). A PE can oversee the work of other engineers, sign off on projects, and provide services directly to the public. State licensure generally requires

- A degree from an ABET-accredited engineering program
- A passing score on the Fundamentals of Engineering (FE) exam
- Relevant work experience, typically at least 4 years
- A passing score on the Professional Engineering (PE) exam

The initial FE exam can be taken after one earns a bachelor's degree. Engineers who pass this exam are commonly called engineers in training (EITs) or engineer interns (EIs). After meeting work experience requirements, EITs and EIs can take the second exam, called the Principles and Practice of Engineering (PE).

Several states require engineers to take continuing education courses in order to keep their licenses. Most states recognize licensure from other states if the licensing state's requirements meet or exceed their own licensure requirements. The Society of Petroleum Engineers offers certification. To be certified, petroleum engineers must be members of the Society, pass an exam, and meet other qualifications.

Advancement

Entry-level engineers usually work under the supervision of experienced engineers. In large companies, new engineers also may receive formal training. As engineers gain knowledge and experience, they move to more difficult projects on which they have greater independence to develop designs, solve problems, and make decisions.

Eventually, petroleum engineers may advance to supervise a team of engineers and technicians. Some become engineering managers or move into other managerial positions. For more information, see the profile on architectural and engineering managers.

Petroleum engineers also may go into sales and use their engineering background to inform the discussion of a product's technical aspects with potential buyers and to help in product planning, installation, and use. For more information, see the profile on sales engineers.

Pay

The median annual wage for petroleum engineers was $131,800 in May 2022. The median wage is the wage at which half the workers in an occupation earned more than that amount and half earned less. The lowest 10 percent earned less than $76,960, and the highest 10 percent earned more than $220,040.

In May 2022, the median annual wages for petroleum engineers in the top industries in which they worked were as follows:

Management of companies and enterprises	$156,840
Oil and gas extraction	154,810
Petroleum and coal products manufacturing	134,370
Engineering services	130,790
Support activities for mining	108,030

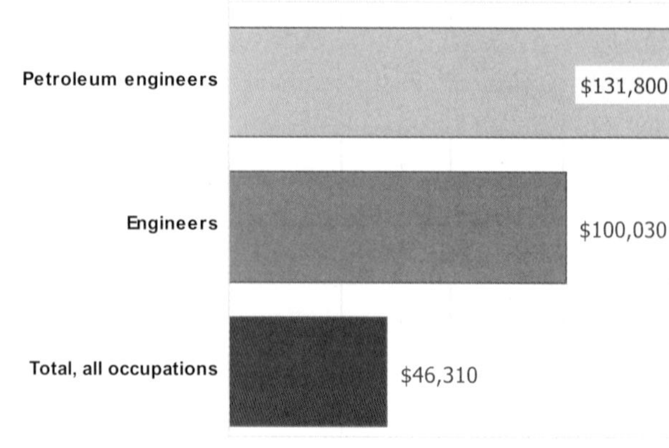

Note: All Occupations includes all occupations in the U.S. Economy.
Source: U.S. Bureau of Labor Statistics, Occupational Employment and Wage Statistics.

Petroleum engineers typically work full time. Overtime may be necessary when traveling to and from drilling and well sites to help in their operation or respond to problems when they arise.

Job Outlook

Employment of petroleum engineers is projected to grow 2 percent from 2022 to 2032, about as fast as the average for all occupations.

About 1,200 openings for petroleum engineers are projected each year, on average, over the decade. Many of those openings are expected to result from the need to replace workers who transfer to different occupations or exit the labor force, such as to retire.

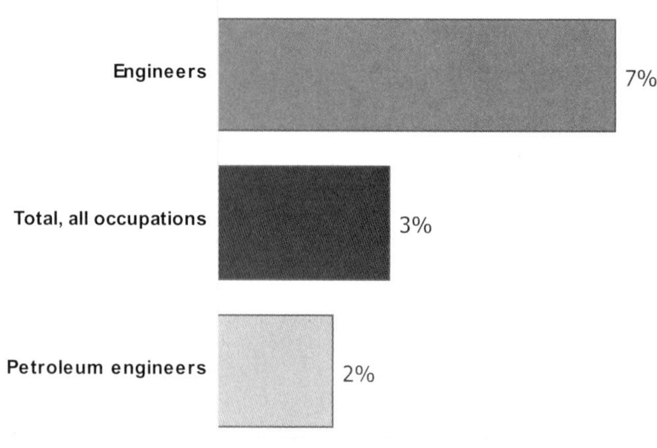

Note: All Occupations includes all occupations in the U.S. Economy.
Source: U.S. Bureau of Labor Statistics, Employment Projections program.

Employment

The need for petroleum engineers to help facilitate oil and gas extraction at existing operations is expected to create some demand for these workers. However, increased use of renewable energy and weaker investments in fossil fuel production may limit job growth over the projections decade.

Occupational Title	SOC Code	Employment, 2022	Projected Employment, 2032	Change, 2022-32	
				Percent	Numeric
Petroleum engineers	17-2171	21,400	21,900	2	500

Contacts for More Information

For more information, visit

- American Society for Engineering Education
- Technology Student Association
- National Council of Examiners for Engineering and Surveying
- National Society of Professional Engineers
- ABET
- Society of Petroleum Engineers

Surveying and Mapping Technicians

Summary

Quick Facts: Surveying and Mapping Technicians	
2022 Median Pay	$47,180 per year $22.68 per hour
Typical Entry-Level Education	High school diploma or equivalent
Work Experience in a Related Occupation	None
On-the-job Training	Moderate-term on-the-job training
Number of Jobs, 2022	64,200
Job Outlook, 2022-32	3% (As fast as average)
Employment Change, 2022-32	2,100

What Surveying and Mapping Technicians Do

Surveying and mapping technicians collect data and make maps of the Earth's surface.

Surveying and mapping technicians collect data and make maps of the Earth's surface.

Work Environment

Surveying technicians work outside extensively and can be exposed to all types of weather. Mapping technicians work primarily indoors on computers. Most surveying and mapping technicians work for firms that provide engineering, surveying, and mapping services on a contract basis. Local governments also employ these workers in highway and planning departments.

How to Become a Surveying or Mapping Technician

Surveying technicians usually need a high school diploma. However, mapping technicians often need formal education after high school to study technology applications, such as Geographic Information Systems (GIS).

Pay

The median annual wage for surveying and mapping technicians was $47,180 in May 2022.

Job Outlook

Employment of surveying and mapping technicians is projected to grow 3 percent from 2022 to 2032, about as fast as the average for all occupations.

About 7,800 openings for surveying and mapping technicians are projected each year, on average, over the decade. Many of those openings are expected to result from the need to replace workers who transfer to different occupations or exit the labor force, such as to retire.

What Surveying and Mapping Technicians Do

Surveying and mapping technicians collect data and make maps of the Earth's surface. Surveying technicians visit sites to take measurements of the land. Mapping technicians use geographic data to create maps. They both assist surveyors, and cartographers and photogrammetrists.

Duties

Surveying technicians typically do the following:

- Visit sites to record survey measurements and other descriptive data

Surveying technicians operate surveying instruments, such as electronic distance-measuring equipment.

- Operate surveying instruments, such as electronic distance-measuring equipment (robotic total stations), to collect data on a location
- Set out stakes and marks to conduct a survey
- Search for previous survey points, such as old stone markers
- Enter the data from surveying instruments into computers, either in the field or in an office

Surveying technicians help surveyors in the field on teams known as survey parties. A typical survey party has a party chief and one or more surveying technicians. The party chief, either a surveyor or a senior surveying technician, leads day-to-day work activities. After data is collected by the survey party, surveying technicians help process the data by entering the data into computers.

Mapping technicians typically do the following:

- Select needed information from databases to create maps
- Edit and process images that have been collected in the field
- Produce maps showing boundaries, water locations, elevation, and other features of the terrain
- Update maps to ensure accuracy
- Assist photogrammetrists by laying out aerial photographs in sequence to identify areas not captured by aerial photography

Mapping technicians help cartographers and photogrammetrists produce and update maps. They do this work on computers, combining data from different sources. Mapping technicians may use drones to take photos and collect other information required to complete maps or surveys.

Geographic Information System (GIS) technicians use GIS technology to assemble, integrate, and display data about a particular location in a digital format. GIS technicians also maintain and update databases for GIS devices.

Work Environment

Surveying and mapping technicians held about 64,200 jobs in 2022. The largest employers of surveying and mapping technicians were as follows:

Surveying technicians visit sites to take measurements of the land.

Architectural, engineering, and related services	57%
Self-employed workers	10
Local government, excluding education and hospitals	9
Utilities	4
Mining, quarrying, and oil and gas extraction	1

Most surveying and mapping technicians work for firms that provide engineering, surveying, and mapping services on a contractual basis. Local governments also employ these workers in highway and planning departments.

Surveying technicians work outside extensively and can be exposed to all types of weather. They often stand for long periods, walk considerable distances, and may have to climb hills with heavy packs of surveying instruments. Traveling is sometimes part of the job, and surveying technicians may commute long distances, stay away from home overnight, or temporarily relocate near a survey site.

Mapping technicians work primarily on computers in office environments. However, mapping technicians must sometimes conduct research by using resources such as survey maps and legal documents to verify property lines and to obtain information needed for mapping. This task may require traveling to storage sites, such as county courthouses or lawyers' offices, that house these legal documents.

Work Schedules

Surveying and mapping technicians typically work full time but may work additional hours during the summer, when weather and light conditions are most suitable for fieldwork. Construction-related work may be limited during times of harsh weather.

Mapping technicians who develop and maintain Geographic Information System (GIS) databases generally work normal business hours.

How to Become a Surveying or Mapping Technician

Surveying technicians usually need a high school diploma. However, mapping technicians often need formal education

Learning to master the equipment is a big part of the training for surveying and mapping technicians.

after high school to study technology applications, such as Geographic Information Systems (GIS).

Education

Surveying technicians generally need a high school diploma, but some have postsecondary training in survey technology. Postsecondary training is more common among mapping technicians where an associate's degree or bachelor's degree in a relevant field, such as geomatics, is beneficial.

High school students interested in working as a surveying or mapping technician should take courses in algebra, geometry, trigonometry, drafting, mechanical drawing, and computer science. Knowledge of these subjects may help in finding a job and in advancing.

Training

Surveying technicians learn their job duties under the supervision of a surveyor or a surveying party chief. Initially, surveying technicians handle simple tasks, such as placing markers on land and entering data into computers. With experience, they help decide where and how to measure the land.

Mapping technicians receive on-the-job training under the supervision of a lead mapper. During training, technicians learn how maps are created and stored in databases.

Licenses, Certifications, and Registrations

The growing need to make sure that data are useful to other professionals has caused certification to become more common. The American Society for Photogrammetry and Remote Sensing (ASPRS) offers certification for photogrammetry, remote-sensing, and Geographic Information/Land Information Systems (GIS/LIS). The National Society of Professional Surveyors offers the Certified Survey Technician credential, and the GIS Certification Institute offers a GIS Professional certification.

Advancement

Depending on state licensing requirements, surveying technicians with many years of experience and formal training in surveying may be able to become licensed surveyors.

Important Qualities

Decision-making skills. Surveying technicians must be able to exercise some independent judgment in the field because they may not always be able to communicate with team members.

Detail oriented. Surveying and mapping technicians must be precise and accurate in their work. Their results are often entered into legal records.

Listening skills. Surveying technicians work outdoors and must communicate with party chiefs and other team members across distances. Following spoken instructions from the party chief is crucial for saving time and preventing errors.

Physical stamina. Surveying technicians usually work outdoors, often in rugged terrain. Physical fitness is necessary to carry equipment and to stand most of the day.

Problem-solving skills. Surveying and mapping technicians must be able to identify and fix problems with their equipment. They must also note potential problems with the day's work plan.

Pay

The median annual wage for surveying and mapping technicians was $47,180 in May 2022. The median wage is the wage at which half the workers in an occupation earned more than that amount and half earned less. The lowest 10 percent earned less than $31,840, and the highest 10 percent earned more than $77,310.

In May 2022, the median annual wages for surveying and mapping technicians in the top industries in which they worked were as follows:

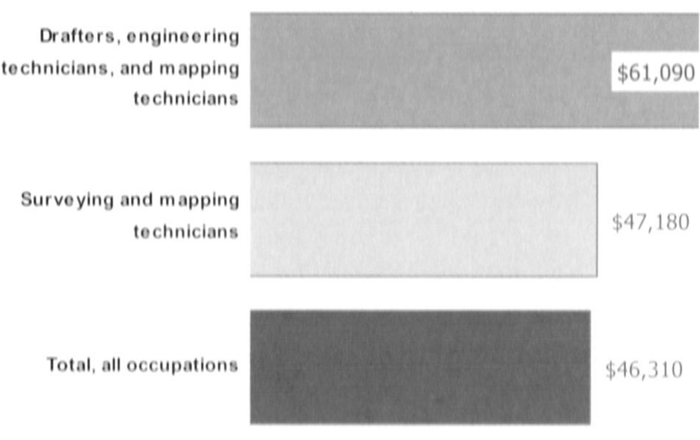

Note: All Occupations includes all occupations in the U.S. Economy.
Source: U.S. Bureau of Labor Statistics, Occupational Employment and Wage Statistics.

Utilities	$72,460
Local government, excluding education and hospitals	55,180
Mining, quarrying, and oil and gas extraction	54,730
Architectural, engineering, and related services	45,970

Surveying and mapping technicians typically work regular schedules but may work additional hours during the summer, when weather and light are most suitable for fieldwork. Construction-related work may be limited during times of harsh weather.

Mapping technicians who develop and maintain Geographic Information System (GIS) databases generally work normal business hours.

Job Outlook

Employment of surveying and mapping technicians is projected to grow 3 percent from 2022 to 2032, about as fast as the average for all occupations.

About 7,800 openings for surveying and mapping technicians are projected each year, on average, over the decade. Many of those openings are expected to result from the need to replace workers who transfer to different occupations or exit the labor force, such as to retire.

Employment

Increased demand for map information is expected to require surveying and mapping technicians to gather and prepare related data, even as drones and other advancements make workers more efficient and limit projected employment growth.

Surveying and Mapping Technicians

Percent change in employment, projected 2022-32

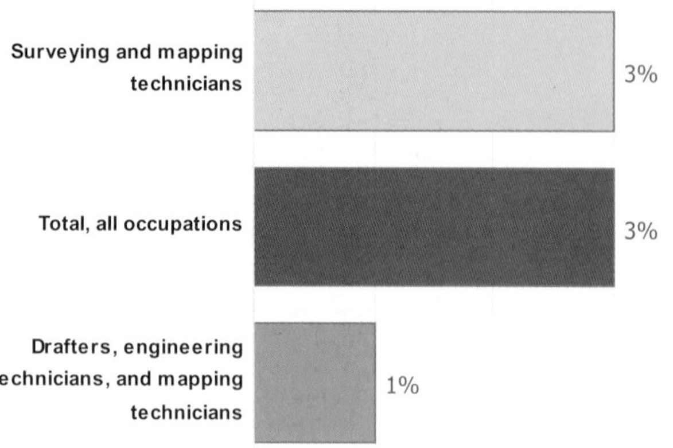

Note: All Occupations includes all occupations in the U.S. Economy.
Source: U.S. Bureau of Labor Statistics, Employment Projections program.

Employment projections data for surveying and mapping technicians, 2022-32

Occupational Title	SOC Code	Employment, 2022	Projected Employment, 2032	Change, 2022-32 Percent	Change, 2022-32 Numeric	Employment by Industry
SOURCE: U.S. Bureau of Labor Statistics, Employment Projections program						
Surveying and mapping technicians	17-3031	64,200	66,300	3	2,100	Get data

Contacts for More Information

For more information, visit

- ➤ GIS Certification Institute
- ➤ National Society of Professional Surveyors
- ➤ American Society for Photogrammetry and Remote Sensing

Surveyors

Summary

Quick Facts: Surveyors

2022 Median Pay	$63,080 per year $30.33 per hour
Typical Entry-Level Education	Bachelor's degree
Work Experience in a Related Occupation	None
On-the-job Training	Internship/residency
Number of Jobs, 2022	50,800
Job Outlook, 2022-32	5% (Faster than average)
Employment Change, 2022-32	2,300

What Surveyors Do

Surveyors make precise measurements to determine property boundaries.

Work Environment

Surveying involves both fieldwork and office work. When working outside, surveyors may stand for long periods and often walk long distances, sometimes in bad weather. Most work full time.

How to Become a Surveyor

Surveyors typically need a bachelor's degree. They must be licensed before they can certify legal documents and provide surveying services to the public.

Pay

The median annual wage for surveyors was $63,080 in May 2022.

Job Outlook

Employment of surveyors is projected to grow 5 percent from 2022 to 2032, faster than the average for all occupations.

Surveyors map out boundaries for construction.

About 3,500 openings for surveyors are projected each year, on average, over the decade. Many of those openings are expected to result from the need to replace workers who transfer to different occupations or exit the labor force, such as to retire.

What Surveyors Do

Surveyors make precise measurements to determine property boundaries. They provide data relevant to the shape and contour of the Earth's surface for engineering, mapmaking, and construction projects.

Duties

Surveyors typically do the following:

- Measure distances and angles between points on, above, and below the Earth's surface
- Travel to locations and use known reference points to determine the exact location of important features
- Research land records, survey records, and land titles
- Look for evidence of previous boundaries to determine where boundary lines are located
- Record the results of surveying and verify the accuracy of data
- Prepare plots, maps, and reports
- Present findings to clients and government agencies
- Establish official land and water boundaries for deeds, leases, and other legal documents and testify in court regarding survey work

Surveyors mark and document the location of legal property lines. For example, when a house or commercial building is bought or sold, surveyors may mark property boundaries to prevent or resolve disputes. They use a variety of measuring equipment depending upon the type of survey.

When taking measurements in the field, surveyors make use of the Global Positioning System (GPS), a system of satellites that locates reference points with a high degree of precision. Surveyors use handheld GPS units and automated systems known as robotic total stations to collect relevant information about the terrain they are surveying. Surveyors then interpret and verify the results on a computer.

Surveyors also use Geographic Information Systems (GIS)—technology that allows surveyors to present spatial information visually as maps, reports, and charts. For example, a surveyor can overlay aerial or satellite images with GIS data, such as tree density in a given region, and create digital maps. They then use the results to advise governments and businesses on where to plan homes, roads, and landfills.

Although advances in surveying technology now allow many jobs to be performed by just one surveyor, other jobs may be performed by a crew, consisting of a licensed surveyor and trained surveying technicians. The person in charge of the crew, known as the *party chief*, may be either a surveyor or a senior surveying technician. The party chief leads day-to-day work activities.

Surveyors also work with civil engineers, landscape architects, cartographers and photogrammetrists, and urban and regional planners to develop comprehensive design documents.

The following are examples of types of surveyors:

Boundary or land surveyors determine the legal property lines and help determine the exact locations of real estate and construction projects.

Surveyors update boundary lines and prepare sites for construction so that legal disputes are prevented.

Engineering or construction surveyors determine the precise location of roads or buildings and proper depths for building foundations. They show changes to the property line and indicate potential restrictions on the property, such as what can be built on it and how large the structure can be. They also may survey the grade and topography of roads.

Forensic surveyors survey and record accident scenes for potential landscape effects.

Geodetic surveyors use high-accuracy technology, including aerial and satellite observations, to measure large areas of the Earth's surface.

Marine or hydrographic surveyors survey harbors, rivers, and other bodies of water to determine shorelines, the topography of the floor, water depth, and other features.

Mine surveyors survey and map the tunnels in an underground mine. They survey surface mines to determine the volume of materials mined.

Work Environment

Surveyors held about 50,800 jobs in 2022. The largest employers of surveyors were as follows:

Architectural, engineering, and related services	70%
Government	8
Construction	7
Self-employed workers	4
Mining, quarrying, and oil and gas extraction	1

Depending on the specific job duties, surveying involves both fieldwork and office work. Fieldwork involves working outdoors in all types of weather, walking long distances, and standing for extended periods while taking measurements. Surveyors sometimes climb hills with heavy packs of surveying instruments. When working near hazards such as traffic, surveyors generally wear brightly colored or reflective vests so they may be seen more easily. When working in underground mines, surveyors work in enclosed spaces.

Traveling is often part of the job, and surveyors may commute long distances or stay at a project location for an extended period of time. Those who work on resource extraction projects may work in remote areas and spend long periods away from home.

Work Schedules

Surveyors usually work full time. When construction activity is high, they may work more hours than usual.

How to Become a Surveyor

Surveyors typically need a bachelor's degree. They must be licensed before they can certify legal documents and provide surveying services to the public.

Education

Surveyors typically need a bachelor's degree. Some colleges and universities offer programs that prepare students to become licensed surveyors. A bachelor's degree in a related field, such as engineering or natural resources, may be acceptable as well. Many states require individuals who want to become licensed surveyors to have a bachelor's degree from a school accredited by an organization such as ABET.

In some cases, employers may hire candidates who have an associate's degree and additional training.

Training

In order to become licensed, most states require approximately 4 years of work experience and training under a licensed surveyor after obtaining a bachelor's degree. Other states may allow substituting more years of work experience and supervised training under a licensed surveyor in place of education.

Work Experience in a Related Occupation

In some states, surveying technicians can become licensed surveyors after working for as many as 10 years under a licensed

Surveyors collect data outdoors.

Along with a degree, surveyors typically need to work with a licensed surveyor.

surveyor. The amount of work experience required varies by state. Check with your state for more information.

Licenses, Certifications, and Registrations

All 50 states and the District of Columbia require surveyors to be licensed before they can certify legal documents that show property lines or determine proper markings on construction projects. Candidates with a bachelor's degree usually must work for several years under the direction of a licensed surveyor in order to qualify for licensure.

Although the process of obtaining a license varies by state, the National Council of Examiners for Engineering and Surveying has a generalized process of four steps:

1. Complete the level of education required in your state
2. Pass the Fundamentals of Surveying (FS) exam
3. Gain sufficient work experience under a licensed surveyor
4. Pass the Principles and Practice of Surveying (PS) exam

Most states also have continuing education requirements for surveyors to maintain their license.

Important Qualities

Communication skills. Surveyors must provide clear instructions to team members, clients, and government officials. They also must be able to follow instructions from architects and construction managers, and explain the job's progress to developers, lawyers, financiers, and government authorities.

Detail oriented. Surveyors must work with precision and accuracy because they produce legally binding documents.

Physical stamina. Surveyors traditionally work outdoors, often in rugged terrain. They must be able to walk long distances and for long periods.

Problem-solving skills. Surveyors must figure out discrepancies between documents showing property lines and current conditions on the land. If there were changes in previous years, they must discover the reason behind them and reestablish property lines.

Time-management skills. Surveyors must be able to effectively plan their time and their team members' time on the job. This is critical when pressing deadlines exist or while working outside during winter months when daylight hours are short.

Visualization skills. Surveyors must be able to envision new buildings and altered terrain.

Pay

The median annual wage for surveyors was $63,080 in May 2022. The median wage is the wage at which half the workers in an occupation earned more than that amount and half earned less. The lowest 10 percent earned less than $39,060, and the highest 10 percent earned more than $106,880.

In May 2022, the median annual wages for surveyors in the top industries in which they worked were as follows:

Government	$80,990
Mining, quarrying, and oil and gas extraction	68,010
Construction	66,720
Architectural, engineering, and related services	62,170

Surveyors usually work full time. When construction activity is high, they may work more hours than usual.

Job Outlook

Employment of surveyors is projected to grow 5 percent from 2022 to 2032, faster than the average for all occupations.

About 3,500 openings for surveyors are projected each year, on average, over the decade. Many of those openings are expected to result from the need to replace workers who transfer to different occupations or exit the labor force, such as to retire.

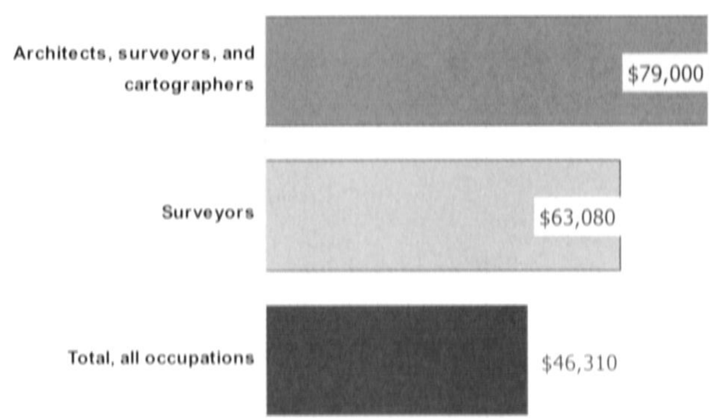

Note: All Occupations includes all occupations in the U.S. Economy.
Source: U.S. Bureau of Labor Statistics, Occupational Employment and Wage Statistics.

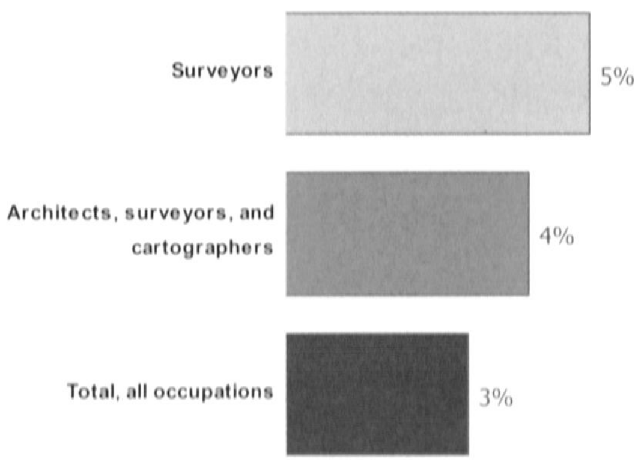

Note: All Occupations includes all occupations in the U.S. Economy.
Source: U.S. Bureau of Labor Statistics, Employment Projections program.

Employment

Surveyors will continue to be needed to certify boundary lines and review sites for construction. Employment demand also will be tied to projects such as road repair and mining activities, although the use of drones and other technologies may limit growth somewhat by increasing worker productivity.

Employment projections data for surveyors, 2022-32

Occupational Title	SOC Code	Employment, 2022	Projected Employment, 2032	Change, 2022-32		Employment by Industry
				Percent	Numeric	
SOURCE: U.S. Bureau of Labor Statistics, Employment Projections program						
Surveyors	17-1022	50,800	53,100	5	2,300	Get data

Contacts for More Information

For more information, visit

- National Council of Examiners for Engineering and Surveying
- National Society of Professional Surveyors
- American Association for Geodetic Surveying
- ABET

Arts and Design

Art Directors

Summary

Quick Facts: Art Directors	
2022 Median Pay	$105,180 per year $50.57 per hour
Typical Entry-Level Education	Bachelor's degree
Work Experience in a Related Occupation	5 years or more
On-the-job Training	None
Number of Jobs, 2022	135,100
Job Outlook, 2022-32	6% (Faster than average)
Employment Change, 2022-32	8,200

What Art Directors Do

Art directors are responsible for the visual style and images in magazines, newspapers, product packaging, and movie and television productions.

Work Environment

Most art directors are self-employed. Others work for advertising and public relations firms, newspaper and magazine publishers, motion picture and video industries, and specialized design services firms.

How to Become an Art Director

Art directors need at least a bachelor's degree in an art or design subject and previous work experience. Depending on the industry, art directors may have previously worked as graphic designers, illustrators, copy editors, or photographers, or in another art or design occupation.

Art directors oversee the work of other designers and artists who produce images for television, film, advertisements, or video games.

Pay

The median annual wage for art directors was $105,180 in May 2022.

Job Outlook

Employment of art directors is projected to grow 6 percent from 2022 to 2032, faster than the average for all occupations.

About 13,800 openings for art directors are projected each year, on average, over the decade. Many of those openings are expected to result from the need to replace workers who transfer to different occupations or exit the labor force, such as to retire.

What Art Directors Do

Art directors are responsible for the visual style and images in magazines, newspapers, product packaging, and movie and television productions. They create the overall design and direct others who develop artwork or layouts.

Art directors determine which photographs, art, or other design elements to use.

Duties

Art directors typically do the following:

- Determine how best to represent a concept visually
- Determine which photographs, art, or other design elements to use
- Develop the overall look or style of a publication, an advertising campaign, or a theater, television, or film set
- Manage graphic designers, set and exhibit designers, or other design staff
- Review and approve designs, artwork, photography, and graphics developed by other staff members
- Talk to clients to develop an artistic approach and style
- Coordinate activities with other artistic and creative departments
- Develop detailed budgets and timelines
- Present designs to clients for approval

Art directors typically oversee the work of other designers and artists who produce images for television, film, live performances, advertisements, or video games. They determine the overall style in which a message is communicated visually to its audience. For each project, they articulate their vision to artists. The artists then create images, such as illustrations, graphics, photographs, or charts and graphs, or design stage and movie sets, according to the art director's vision.

Art directors work with art and design staffs in advertising agencies, public relations firms, or book, magazine, or newspaper publishing to create designs and layouts. They also work with producers and directors of theater, television, or movie productions to oversee set designs. Their work requires them to understand the design elements of projects, inspire other creative workers, and keep projects on budget and on time. Sometimes they are responsible for developing budgets and timelines.

The following are some specifics of what art directors do in different industries:

In advertising and public relations, art directors ensure that their clients' desired message and image are conveyed to consumers. Art directors are responsible for the overall visual aspects of an advertising or media campaign and coordinate the work of other artistic or design staff, such as graphic designers.

In publishing, art directors typically oversee the page layout of catalogs, newspapers, or magazines. They also choose the cover art for books and periodicals. Often, this work includes publications for the Internet, so art directors oversee production of the websites used for publication.

In movie production, art directors collaborate with directors to determine what sets will be needed for the film and what style or look the sets should have. They hire and supervise a staff of assistant art directors or set designers to complete designs.

Work Environment

Art directors held about 135,100 jobs in 2022. The largest employers of art directors were as follows:

Art directors determine how best to represent a concept visually.

Self-employed workers	58%
Advertising, public relations, and related services	13
Motion picture and video industries	3
Specialized design services	3

Even though most art directors are self-employed, they must still collaborate with designers or other staff on visual effects or marketing teams. Art directors usually work in a fast-paced office environment, and they often work under pressure to meet strict deadlines.

How to Become an Art Director

Art directors need at least a bachelor's degree in an art or design subject and previous work experience. Depending on the industry, they may have worked as graphic designers, fine artists, editors, or photographers, or in another art or design occupation before becoming art directors.

Education

Art directors typically need a bachelor's degree in fine arts, a design subject, or a related field, such as communications technology.

Many art directors start out in another art-related occupation, such as fine artists or photographers. Work experience in art or design occupations develops an art director's ability to visually communicate to a specific audience creatively and effectively. Workers gain the appropriate education for that occupation, usually by earning a bachelor of arts or bachelor of fine arts degree.

Some art directors earn a master of fine arts (MFA) degree to supplement their work experience and show their creative or managerial ability.

Work Experience in a Related Occupation

Most art directors have 5 or more years of work experience in another occupation before becoming art directors. Depending on the industry in which they previously worked, art directors

Many art directors start out as graphic designers or in another art occupation, such as fine artists or photographers.

may have had jobs as graphic designers, fine artists, editors, photographers, or in another art or design occupation.

For many artists, including art directors, developing a portfolio—a collection of an artist's work that demonstrates his or her styles and abilities—is essential. Managers, clients, and others look at artists' portfolios when they are deciding whether to hire an employee or contract for an art project.

Important Qualities

Communication skills. Art directors must be able to listen to and speak with staff and clients to ensure that they understand employees' ideas and clients' desires for advertisements, publications, or movie sets.

Creativity. Art directors must be able to come up with interesting and innovative ideas to develop advertising campaigns, set designs, or layout options.

Leadership skills. Art directors must be able to organize, direct, and motivate other artists. They need to articulate their visions to artists and oversee the work as it progresses.

Resourcefulness. Art directors must be able to adapt their latest designs to the changing technology used in their industry.

Time-management skills. Balancing competing priorities and multiple projects while meeting strict deadlines is critical for art directors.

Art Directors

Median annual wages, May 2022

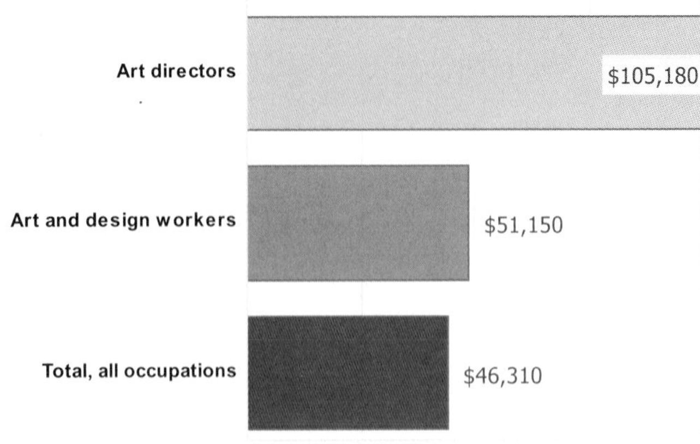

Note: All Occupations includes all occupations in the U.S. Economy.
Source: U.S. Bureau of Labor Statistics, Occupational Employment and Wage Statistics.

Pay

The median annual wage for art directors was $105,180 in May 2022. The median wage is the wage at which half the workers in an occupation earned more than that amount and half earned less. The lowest 10 percent earned less than $57,820, and the highest 10 percent earned more than $207,060.

In May 2022, the median annual wages for art directors in the top industries in which they worked were as follows:

Motion picture and video industries	$135,130
Advertising, public relations, and related services	113,670
Specialized design services	81,880

Art Directors

Percent change in employment, projected 2022-32

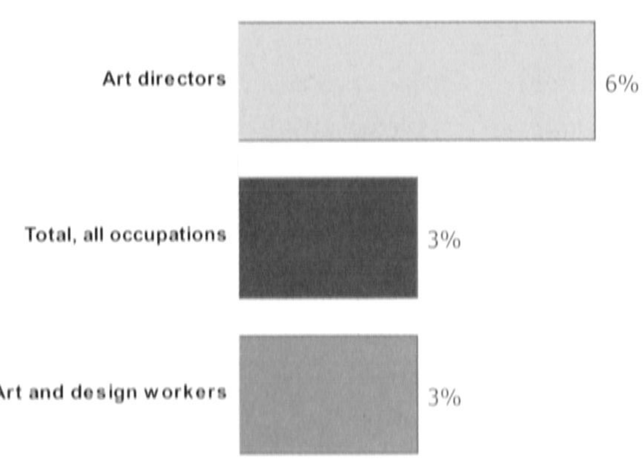

Note: All Occupations includes all occupations in the U.S. Economy.
Source: U.S. Bureau of Labor Statistics, Employment Projections program.

Job Outlook

Employment of art directors is projected to grow 6 percent from 2022 to 2032, faster than the average for all occupations.

About 13,800 openings for art directors are projected each year, on average, over the decade. Many of those openings are expected to result from the need to replace workers who transfer to different occupations or exit the labor force, such as to retire.

Employment

As traditional print publications lose ground to other media forms, art directors are shifting their focus to the design of websites and mobile platforms. This shift in focus is expected to increase demand for art directors.

Occupational Title	SOC Code	Employment, 2022	Projected Employment, 2032	Change, 2022-32	
				Percent	Numeric
Art directors	27-1011	135,100	143,200	6	8,200

Contacts for More Information

For more information, visit:

➤ Art Directors Guild

Craft and Fine Artists

Summary

Quick Facts: Craft and Fine Artists	
2022 Median Pay	$53,140 per year $25.55 per hour
Typical Entry-Level Education	See How to Become One
Work Experience in a Related Occupation	None
On-the-job Training	Long-term on-the-job training
Number of Jobs, 2022	54,600
Job Outlook, 2022-32	4% (As fast as average)
Employment Change, 2022-32	2,400

What Craft and Fine Artists Do

Craft and fine artists use a variety of materials and techniques to create art for sale and exhibition.

Fine art painters paint landscapes, portraits, and other subjects in a variety of styles, ranging from realistic to abstract.

Work Environment

Many artists work in fine- or commercial-art studios located in office buildings, warehouses, or lofts. Others work in private studios in their homes. Some artists share studio space, where they also may exhibit their work.

How to Become a Craft or Fine Artist

Craft and fine artists improve their skills through practice and repetition. A bachelor's degree is common for these artists.

Pay

The median annual wage for craft and fine artists was $53,140 in May 2022.

Job Outlook

Overall employment of craft and fine artists is projected to grow 4 percent from 2022 to 2032, about as fast as the average for all occupations.

About 5,500 openings for craft and fine artists are projected each year, on average, over the decade. Many of those openings are expected to result from the need to replace workers who transfer to different occupations or exit the labor force, such as to retire.

What Craft and Fine Artists Do

Craft and fine artists use a variety of materials and techniques to create original works of art for sale and exhibition. Craft artists create objects, such as pottery, glassware, and textiles, that are designed to be functional. Fine artists, including painters, sculptors, and illustrators, create pieces of art more for aesthetics than for function.

Duties

Craft and fine artists typically do the following:

- Use techniques such as knitting, weaving, glassblowing, painting, drawing, and sculpting
- Develop creative ideas or new methods for making art

Craft and fine artists use a variety of materials and techniques to create art for sale and exhibition.

- Create sketches, templates, or models to guide their work
- Select which materials to use on the basis of color, texture, strength, and other criteria
- Shape, join, or cut materials for a final product
- Use visual techniques, such as composition, color, space, and perspective, to produce desired artistic effects
- Develop portfolios highlighting their artistic styles and abilities to show to gallery owners and others interested in their work
- Display their work at auctions, craft fairs, galleries, museums, and online marketplaces
- Complete grant proposals and applications to obtain financial support for projects

Artists create objects that are beautiful, thought provoking, and sometimes shocking. They often strive to communicate ideas or feelings through their art.

Craft artists work with many different materials, including ceramics, glass, textiles, wood, metal, and paper. They use these materials to create unique pieces of art, such as pottery, quilts, stained glass, furniture, jewelry, and clothing. Many craft artists also use fine-art techniques—for example, painting, sketching, and printing—to add finishing touches to their products.

Fine artists typically display their work in museums, in commercial or nonprofit art galleries, at craft fairs, in corporate collections, on the Internet, and in private homes. Some of their artwork may be commissioned (requested by a client), but most is sold by the artist or through private art galleries or dealers. The artist, gallery, and dealer together decide in advance how much of the proceeds from the sale each will keep.

Most craft and fine artists spend their time and effort selling their artwork to potential customers and building a reputation. In addition to selling their artwork, many artists have at least one other job to support their craft or art careers.

Some artists work in museums or art galleries as art directors or as archivists, curators, or museum workers, planning and setting up exhibits. Others teach craft or art classes or conduct workshops in schools or in their own studios. For more information on workers who teach art classes, see the profiles on kindergarten and elementary school teachers, middle school teachers, high school teachers, career and technical education teachers, and postsecondary teachers.

Craft and fine artists specialize in one or more types of art. The following are examples of types of craft and fine artists:

Cartoonists create simplified or exaggerated drawings to visually convey political, advertising, comic, or sports concepts. Some cartoonists work with others who create the idea or story and write captions. Others create plots and write captions themselves. Most cartoonists have humorous, critical, or dramatic talent, in addition to drawing skills.

Ceramic artists shape, form, and mold artworks out of clay, often using a potter's wheel and other tools. They glaze and fire pieces in kilns, which are large, special furnaces that dry and harden the clay.

Digital artists use design and production software to create interactive art online. The digital imagery may then be transferred to paper or some other form of printmaking or made available directly on web-accessible devices.

Fiber artists use fabric, yarn, or other natural and synthetic materials to weave, knit, crochet, or sew textile art. They may use a loom to weave fabric, needles to knit or crochet yarn, or a sewing machine to join pieces of fabric for quilts or other handicrafts.

Fine-art painters paint landscapes, portraits, and other subjects in a variety of styles, ranging from realistic to abstract. They may work in a variety of media, such as watercolors, oil paints, and acrylics.

Furniture makers cut, sand, join, and finish wood and other materials to make handcrafted furnishings. For information about other workers who assemble wood furniture, see the profile on woodworkers.

Glass artists process glass in a variety of ways—such as by blowing, shaping, staining, or joining it—to create artistic pieces. Some processes require the use of kilns, ovens, and other equipment and tools that bend glass at high temperatures. These workers also decorate glass objects, such as by etching or painting.

Illustrators create pictures for books, magazines, and other publications and for commercial products, such as textiles, wrapping paper, stationery, greeting cards, and calendars. Illustrators increasingly use computers in their work. They might draw in pen or pencil and then scan the image, using software to add color, or they might use a special pen to draw images directly onto the computer.

Jewelry artists use metals, stones, beads, and other materials to make objects for personal adornment, such as earrings or necklaces. For more information about other workers who create jewelry, see the profile on jewelers and precious stone and metal workers.

Medical and scientific illustrators combine drawing skills with knowledge of biology or other sciences. Medical illustrators work with computers or with pen and paper to create images, three-dimensional models, and animations of human anatomy and surgical procedures. Scientific illustrators draw animal and plant life, atomic and molecular structures, and geologic and planetary formations. These illustrations are used in medical and scientific publications and in audiovisual presentations for teaching purposes. Some medical and scientific illustrators work for lawyers, producing exhibits for court cases.

Public artists create large paintings, sculptures, and displays called "installations" that are meant to be seen in open spaces. These works are typically displayed in parks, museum grounds, train stations, and other public areas.

Printmakers create images on a silk screen, woodblock, lithography stone, metal etching plate, or other types of matrices. A printing hand press then creates the final work of art, inking and transferring the matrix to a piece of paper.

Sculptors design and shape three-dimensional works of art, either by molding and joining materials such as clay, glass, plastic, and metal or by cutting and carving forms from a block of plaster, wood, or stone. Some sculptors combine various materials to create mixed-media installations, such as by incorporating light, sound, and motion into their work.

Sketch artists are a type of illustrator who often use pencil, charcoal, or pastels to create likenesses of subjects. Their sketches are used by law enforcement agencies to help identify suspects, by the news media to show courtroom scenes, and by individual customers for their own enjoyment.

Tattoo artists use stencils and draw by hand to create original images and text on skin. With specialized needles, these artists use a variety of styles and colors based on their clients' preferences.

Video artists record avant-garde, moving imagery that is typically shown in a loop in art galleries, museums, or performance spaces. These artists sometimes use multiple monitors or create unusual spaces for the video to be shown.

Work Environment

Craft and fine artists held about 54,600 jobs in 2022. Employment in the detailed occupations that make up craft and fine artists was distributed as follows:

Fine artists, including painters, sculptors, and illustrators	29,100
Artists and related workers, all other	14,000
Craft artists	11,500

The largest employers of craft and fine artists were as follows:

Self-employed workers	55%
Independent artists, writers, and performers	9
Federal government, excluding postal service	6
Motion picture and sound recording industries	4
Personal care services	3

Many artists work in fine art or commercial art studios located in office buildings, warehouses, or lofts.

Many artists work in fine- or commercial-art studios located in office buildings, warehouses, or lofts. Others work in private studios in their homes. Some artists share studio space, where they also may exhibit their work.

Studios are usually well lit and ventilated. However, artists may be exposed to fumes from glue, paint, ink, and other materials. They may also have to deal with dust or other residue from filings, splattered paint, or spilled cleaning and other fluids. Artists often wear protective gear, such as breathing masks and goggles, in order to remain safe from exposure to harmful materials. Ceramic and glass artists must use caution in working with materials that may break into sharp pieces and in using equipment that can get very hot, such as kilns.

Injuries and Illnesses

Artists and related workers, all other have one of the highest rates of injuries and illnesses of all occupations. ("All other" titles represent occupations with a wide range of characteristics that do not fit into any of the other detailed occupations.)

Work Schedules

Most craft and fine artists work full time, although part-time and variable schedules are also common. Many hold another job in addition to their work as an artist. During busy periods, artists may work additional hours to meet deadlines. Those who are self-employed usually determine their own schedules.

How to Become a Craft or Fine Artist

Craft and fine artists improve their skills through practice and repetition. Formal education is often helpful for these artists.

Education

Most fine artists pursue postsecondary education to improve their skills and job prospects. A formal educational credential is typically not needed to be a craft artist. However, it is difficult to gain adequate artistic skills without some formal education. For example, high school art classes can teach prospective craft artists the basic drawing skills they need.

A number of colleges and universities offer bachelor's and master's degrees in fields related to fine and performing arts. In addition to studio art and art history, postsecondary programs may include core subjects, such as English, marketing, social science, and natural science. Independent schools of art and design also offer postsecondary education programs, which can lead to a certificate in an art-related specialty or to an associate's, bachelor's, or master's degree in fine arts.

The National Association of Schools of Art and Design (NASAD) accredits more than 360 postsecondary institutions with programs in art and design. Most of these schools award a degree in art.

Medical illustrators must have artistic ability and a detailed knowledge of human or animal anatomy, living organisms, and surgical and medical procedures. They usually need a bachelor's degree that combines art and premedical courses.

Education gives artists an opportunity to develop their portfolio, which is a collection of an artist's work that demonstrates his or her styles and abilities.

Medical illustrators may choose to get a master's degree in medical illustration. Four accredited schools offer this degree in the United States.

Education gives artists an opportunity to develop their portfolio, which is a collection of an artist's work that demonstrates his or her styles and abilities. Portfolios are essential, because art directors, clients, and others look at them when deciding whether to hire an artist or to buy the artist's work. In addition to compiling a physical portfolio, many artists choose to create a portfolio online.

Those who want to teach fine arts at public elementary or secondary schools usually must have a teaching certificate in addition to a bachelor's degree. For more information on workers who teach art classes, see the profiles on kindergarten and elementary school teachers, middle school teachers, high school teachers, career and technical education teachers, and postsecondary teachers.

Training

Craft and fine artists improve their skills through practice and repetition. They can train in several ways other than, or in addition to, formal schooling. Craft and fine artists may train with simpler projects before attempting something more ambitious.

Some artists learn on the job from more experienced artists. Others attend noncredit classes or workshops or take private lessons, which may be offered in artists' studios or at community colleges, art centers, galleries, museums, or other art-related institutions.

Important Qualities

Artistic ability. Craft and fine artists create artwork and other objects that are visually appealing or thought provoking. This endeavor usually requires significant skill and attention to detail in one or more art forms.

Business skills. Craft and fine artists must promote themselves and their art to build a reputation and to sell their art. They often study the market for their crafts or artwork to increase their understanding of what prospective customers might want. Craft and fine artists also may sell their work on the internet, so developing an online presence is often an important part of their art sales.

Creativity. Artists must have active imaginations to develop new and original ideas for their work.

Customer-service skills. Craft and fine artists, especially those who sell their work themselves, must be good at dealing with customers and prospective buyers.

Dexterity. Artists must be good at manipulating tools and materials to create their art.

Interpersonal skills. Artists should be comfortable interacting with people, including customers, gallery owners, and the public.

Advancement

Craft and fine artists advance professionally as their work circulates and as they establish a reputation for their particular style. Successful artists continually develop new ideas, and their work often evolves over time.

Until they become established as professional artists, many artists create artwork while continuing to hold a full-time job. Others work as an artist part time while still in school to develop experience and to build a portfolio.

Self-employed and freelance artists try to establish a set of clients who regularly contract for work. Some of these artists are recognized for their skill in a specialty, such as cartooning or illustrating children's books. They may earn enough to choose the types of projects they undertake.

Pay

The median annual wage for craft and fine artists was $53,140 in May 2022. The median wage is the wage at which half the workers in an occupation earned more than that amount and half earned less. The lowest 10 percent earned less than $27,490, and the highest 10 percent earned more than $117,590.

Median annual wages for craft and fine artists in May 2022 were as follows:

Artists and related workers, all other	$69,760
Fine artists, including painters, sculptors, and illustrators	57,560
Craft artists	38,150

In May 2022, the median annual wages for craft and fine artists in the top industries in which they worked were as follows:

Federal government, excluding postal service	$100,580
Motion picture and sound recording industries	100,080
Personal care services	92,180
Independent artists, writers, and performers	46,430

Earnings for self-employed artists vary widely. Some charge only a nominal fee while they gain experience and build a reputation for their work. Artists who are well established may earn more than salaried artists.

Most craft and fine artists work full time, although part-time and variable schedules are also common. In addition to pursuing their work as an artist, many hold another job because it may be difficult to rely solely on income earned from selling paintings or other works of art. During busy periods, artists may have long workdays to meet deadlines.

Job Outlook

Overall employment of craft and fine artists is projected to grow 4 percent from 2022 to 2032, about as fast as the average for all occupations.

About 5,500 openings for craft and fine artists are projected each year, on average, over the decade. Many of those openings are expected to result from the need to replace workers who transfer to different occupations or exit the labor force, such as to retire.

Employment

Employment growth for artists depends largely on the overall state of the economy and whether people are willing to spend money on art, because people usually buy art when they can afford to do so. During good economic times, people and businesses are interested in buying more artwork; during economic downturns, they generally buy less. However, there is always some demand for art by private collectors and museums.

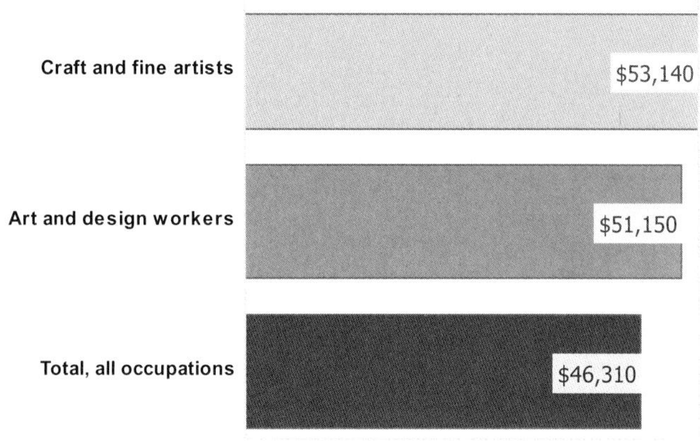

Note: All Occupations includes all occupations in the U.S. Economy.
Source: U.S. Bureau of Labor Statistics, Occupational Employment and Wage Statistics.

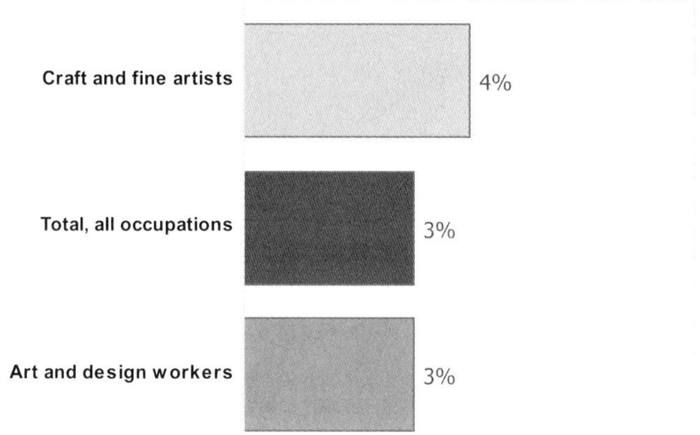

Note: All Occupations includes all occupations in the U.S. Economy.
Source: U.S. Bureau of Labor Statistics, Employment Projections program.

Job growth for craft and fine artists may be limited by the sale of inexpensive, machine-produced items designed to look like handmade crafts. A continued interest in locally made products and crafted goods will likely offset some of these employment losses.

Occupational Title	SOC Code	Employment, 2022	Projected Employment, 2032	Change, 2022-32	
				Percent	Numeric
Craft and fine artists	—	54,600	57,000	4	2,400
Craft artists	27-1012	11,500	12,000	4	400
Fine artists, including painters, sculptors, and illustrators	27-1013	29,100	30,600	5	1,500
Artists and related workers, all other	27-1019	14,000	14,500	3	500

Contacts for More Information

For more information, visit

- National Association of Schools of Art and Design
- American Craft Council
- New York Foundation for the Arts
- Association of Medical Illustrators
- National Endowment for the Arts

Fashion Designers

Summary

Quick Facts: Fashion Designers	
2022 Median Pay	$76,700 per year $36.87 per hour
Typical Entry-Level Education	Bachelor's degree
Work Experience in a Related Occupation	None
On-the-job Training	None
Number of Jobs, 2022	24,900
Job Outlook, 2022-32	3% (As fast as average)
Employment Change, 2022-32	800

What Fashion Designers Do

Fashion designers create clothing, accessories, and footwear.

Work Environment

Fashion designers work in wholesale or manufacturing establishments, apparel companies, retailers, theater or dance companies, and design firms. Most fashion designers work in New York and California.

Fashion designers decide on a theme for a collection.

How to Become a Fashion Designer

Fashion designers typically need a bachelor's degree to enter the occupation. Employers may prefer to hire creative candidates who have technical knowledge of the production processes for clothing, accessories, or footwear.

Pay

The median annual wage for fashion designers was $76,700 in May 2022.

Job Outlook

Employment of fashion designers is projected to grow 3 percent from 2022 to 2032, about as fast as the average for all occupations.

About 2,300 openings for fashion designers are projected each year, on average, over the decade. Many of those openings are expected to result from the need to replace workers who transfer to different occupations or exit the labor force, such as to retire.

What Fashion Designers Do

Fashion designers create original clothing, accessories, and footwear. They sketch designs, select fabrics and patterns, and give instructions on how to make the products they design.

Duties

Fashion designers typically do the following:

- Study fashion trends and anticipate designs that will appeal to consumers
- Decide on a theme for a collection
- Use computer-aided design (CAD) programs to create designs
- Visit manufacturers or trade shows to get samples of fabric

Fashion designers sketch designs of clothing, footwear, and accessories.

- Select fabrics, embellishments, colors, or a style for each garment or accessory
- Work with other designers or team members to create prototype designs
- Present design ideas to creative directors or showcase their ideas in fashion or trade shows
- Market designs to clothing retailers or to consumers
- Oversee the final production of their designs

Larger apparel companies typically employ a team of designers headed by a creative director. Some fashion designers specialize in clothing, footwear, or accessory design; others create designs in all three fashion categories.

For some fashion designers, the first step in creating a new design is researching current fashion and making predictions about future trends, such as by reading reports published by fashion industry trade groups. Other fashion designers create collections using a variety of inspirations, including art media, their surroundings, or cultures they have experienced and places they have visited.

After they have an initial idea, fashion designers try out various fabrics and produce a prototype, often with less expensive material than will be used in the final product. They work with models to see how the design will look and adjust the designs as needed.

Although most designers first sketch their designs by hand, many now also sketch their ideas digitally with computer-aided design (CAD) programs. CAD allows designers to see their work on virtual models. They can try different colors, designs, and shapes while making adjustments more easily than they can when working with real fabric on real people.

Designers produce samples with the actual materials that will be used in manufacturing. Samples that get good responses from fashion editors or trade and fashion shows are then manufactured and sold to consumers.

The design process may vary by specialty, but it generally takes 6 months, from initial design concept to final production, to release either the spring or fall collection. In addition to releasing designs during the spring and fall, some companies release new designs every month.

The Internet and e-commerce allow fashion designers to offer their products outside of traditional brick-and-mortar stores. These designers ship directly to the consumer, without having to invest in a physical shop to showcase their product lines of collections.

The following are examples of types of fashion designers:

Accessory designers design and produce items such as handbags, suitcases, belts, scarves, hats, hosiery, and eyewear.

Costume designers design costumes for the performing arts and for motion picture and television productions. They research the styles worn during the period in which the performance is set, or they work with directors to select and create appropriate attire. They also must stay within the production's costume budget.

Clothing designers create and help produce men's, women's, and children's apparel, including casual wear, suits, sportswear, evening wear, outerwear, maternity clothing, and intimate apparel.

Footwear designers create and help produce different styles of shoes and boots. As new materials, such as lightweight synthetic materials used in shoe soles, become available, footwear designers produce new designs that combine comfort, form, and function.

Work Environment

Fashion designers held about 24,900 jobs in 2022. The largest employers of fashion designers were as follows:

Employer	Percent
Apparel, piece goods, and notions merchant wholesalers	31%
Self-employed workers	17
Management of companies and enterprises	13
Apparel manufacturing	9
Motion picture and video industries	3

Many fashion designers work in-house for wholesalers or manufacturers. These wholesalers and manufacturers sell apparel and accessories to retailers or other marketers for distribution to individual stores, catalog companies, or online retailers.

Fashion designers select fabrics, colors, or styles for each garment or accessory.

Fashion designers occasionally work long hours to meet production deadlines or prepare for fashion shows.

Self-employed fashion designers typically create high-fashion garments and one-of-a-kind (custom) apparel. In some cases, a self-employed fashion designer may have a clothing line that bears his or her name.

Most designers travel several times a year to trade and fashion shows to learn about the latest trends. Designers also sometimes travel to other countries to meet suppliers of materials and manufacturers who make the final products.

Most fashion designers work in New York and California.

Work Schedules

Fashion designers occasionally work many hours to meet production deadlines or prepare for fashion shows. Generally, designers who freelance are under contract; these designers often have long workdays that require them to adjust to their clients' schedules and deadlines.

How to Become a Fashion Designer

Fashion designers typically need a bachelor's degree to enter the occupation. Employers may prefer to hire creative candidates who have technical knowledge of the production processes for clothing, accessories, or footwear.

Education

Fashion designers typically have a bachelor's degree in a fine arts or business field such as fashion design or fashion merchandising. These fashion-focused programs teach students about textiles and fabrics and how to use computer-aided design (CAD) technology. Students also work on projects they can add to their portfolio, which showcases their designs.

For many artists, including fashion designers, developing a portfolio—a collection of design ideas that demonstrates their styles and abilities—is essential. Students studying fashion design often have opportunities to develop their portfolios further by entering their designs in student or amateur contests. When making hiring decisions, employers rely on these portfolios to gauge talent and creativity.

The National Association of Schools of Art and Design accredits more than 360 postsecondary institutions with programs in art and design, and many of them award degrees in fashion design. These schools often require students to have completed basic art and design courses before entering a program. Applicants usually must submit sketches and other examples of their artistic ability.

Other Experience

Fashion designers often gain experience in the fashion industry through internships or by working as an assistant designer. Internships introduce aspiring fashion designers to the design process, building their knowledge of textiles and colors and of how the industry works.

Important Qualities

Artistic ability. Fashion designers sketch their initial design ideas, which are used to create prototypes. Designers must be able to express their vision for the design through illustration.

Communication skills. Throughout the design process, fashion designers must be able to communicate effectively. For example, they may need to instruct sewers about garment construction.

Computer skills. Fashion designers must be able to use computer-aided design (CAD) programs and be familiar with graphics editing software.

Creativity. Fashion designers work with a variety of fabrics, shapes, and colors. Their ideas must be unique, functional, and stylish.

Decision-making skills. When working on teams, fashion designers are exposed to many ideas. They must be able to decide which ideas to incorporate into their designs.

Detail oriented. Fashion designers must have a good eye for small differences in color and other details that can make a design successful.

Pay

The median annual wage for fashion designers was $76,700 in May 2022. The median wage is the wage at which half the workers in an occupation earned more than that amount and half earned less. The lowest 10 percent earned less than $34,660, and the highest 10 percent earned more than $139,920.

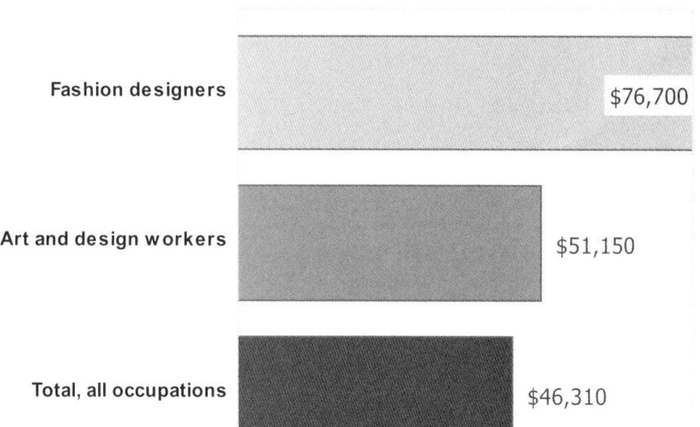

Note: All Occupations includes all occupations in the U.S. Economy.
Source: U.S. Bureau of Labor Statistics, Occupational Employment and Wage Statistics.

In May 2022, the median annual wages for fashion designers in the top industries in which they worked were as follows:

Motion picture and video industries	$109,890
Management of companies and enterprises	86,680
Apparel, piece goods, and notions merchant wholesalers	78,630
Apparel manufacturing	75,110

Fashion designers occasionally work many hours to meet production deadlines or prepare for fashion shows. Generally, designers who freelance are under contract; these designers often have long workdays that require them to adjust to their clients' schedules and deadlines.

Job Outlook

Employment of fashion designers is projected to grow 3 percent from 2022 to 2032, about as fast as the average for all occupations.

About 2,300 openings for fashion designers are projected each year, on average, over the decade. Many of those openings are expected to result from the need to replace workers who transfer to different occupations or exit the labor force, such as to retire.

Employment

The increased demand for a constant flow of new fashion designs has been accelerated by social media influencers and by retailers advertising and selling directly to consumers online. Growing consumer preference for sustainable options in the fashion industry also has created a desire for designs that use eco- and vegan-friendly materials. However, there will be fewer opportunities for self-employed fashion designers, who are unable to compete with large-scale clothing production, limiting overall employment growth of these workers.

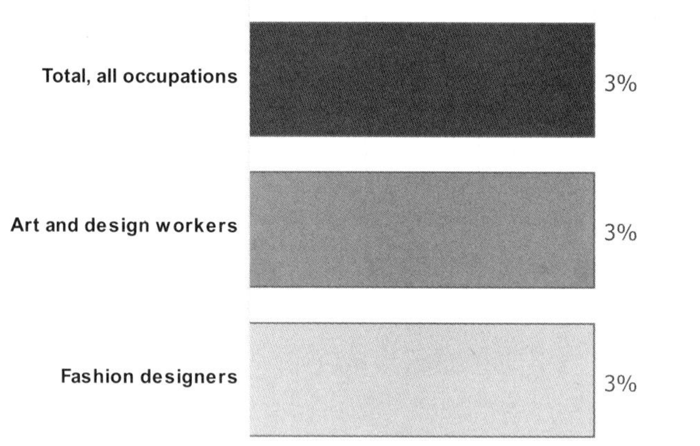

Note: All Occupations includes all occupations in the U.S. Economy.
Source: U.S. Bureau of Labor Statistics, Employment Projections program.

Occupational Title	SOC Code	Employment, 2022	Projected Employment, 2032	Change, 2022-32	
				Percent	Numeric
Fashion designers	27-1022	24,900	25,700	3	800

Contacts for More Information

For more information about careers in fashion design, visit

➤ Council of Fashion Designers of America

For more information about educational programs in fashion design, visit

➤ National Association of Schools of Art and Design

Floral Designers

Summary

Quick Facts: Floral Designers	
2022 Median Pay	$33,160 per year $15.94 per hour
Typical Entry-Level Education	High school diploma or equivalent
Work Experience in a Related Occupation	None
On-the-job Training	Moderate-term on-the-job training
Number of Jobs, 2022	54,500
Job Outlook, 2022-32	-18% (Decline)
Employment Change, 2022-32	-9,800

What Floral Designers Do

Floral designers arrange live, dried, and silk flowers and greenery to make decorative displays.

Work Environment

Most floral designers work in retail businesses, usually flower shops and grocery stores.

Floral designers use their sense of artistry and knowledge of different types of flowers to choose the appropriate flowers for each occasion.

How to Become a Floral Designer

Most floral designers have a high school diploma or the equivalent and learn their skills on the job in a few months.

Pay

The median annual wage for floral designers was $33,160 in May 2022.

Job Outlook

Employment of floral designers is projected to decline 18 percent from 2022 to 2032.

Despite declining employment, about 4,700 openings for floral designers are projected each year, on average, over the decade. All of those openings are expected to result from the need to replace workers who transfer to other occupations or exit the labor force, such as to retire.

What Floral Designers Do

Floral designers, also called florists, arrange live, dried, and silk flowers and greenery to make decorative displays. They also help customers select flowers and containers, ribbons, and other accessories.

Duties

Floral designers typically do the following:

- Buy flowers and other products from wholesalers and suppliers to ensure that an adequate supply meets customers' needs
- Determine the type of arrangement desired, the occasion, and the date, time, and location for delivery
- Recommend plants or flowers and greenery for each arrangement in accordance with the customer's budget
- Design floral displays that evoke a particular sentiment or style
- Answer telephones, take orders, and wrap arrangements

Floral designers may create a single arrangement for a specific purpose or multiple displays for special occasions, such as weddings or funerals. They use artistry and their knowledge of different types of blooms to choose appropriate flowers or plants for each occasion. Floral designers need to know when flowers and plants are in season and available.

Floral designers also need to know the properties of flowers and other plants. Some flowers, such as carnations, can last for many hours outside of water. Other flowers are delicate and wilt more quickly. Some plants are poisonous to certain types of animals. For example, lilies are toxic to cats.

Floral designers must know the color varieties and average size of each flower and plant they sell. They may need to calculate the number of flowers that will fit into a particular vase or how many rose petals cover a space, such as the length of a walkway for a wedding procession.

Floral designers use their knowledge to recommend plants or flowers, greenery, and designs to customers. If the customer selects flowers, the designer uses that type of flower to arrange a visually appealing display. The designer may include items, such as stuffed animals or balloons, or use a decorative basket or vase when creating an arrangement.

Plants typically are showcased in attractive containers and are available for immediate sale. Although more complex floral displays must be ordered in advance, floral designers often create small bouquets or arrangements while customers wait. When they are responsible for multiple arrangements for a special occasion, such as a wedding or funeral, floral designers usually create and set up these decorations just before the event, then remove them afterward. Some floral designers work with event planners on a contract basis when creating arrangements for these types of occasions.

Floral designers also give customers instructions on how to care for flowers and plants, including what the ideal temperature is and how often the water should be changed. For plants or cut flowers, floral designers often provide plant or flower food as part of the sale.

Floral designers also order new flowers, greenery, and plants from suppliers. They process newly arrived shipments by stripping leaves that would be below the water line. Floral designers cut new flowers, transplant plants, mix plant or flower food solutions, fill containers with the food solutions, and sanitize workspaces. They keep most flowers and plants in cool display cases so that the products stay fresh and live longer.

Some floral designers have formal agreements with the managers of hotels and restaurants or the owners of office buildings and private homes to replace old flowers or plants with new ones on a recurring schedule—usually daily, weekly, or monthly—to keep areas looking fresh and appealing. They may work with interior designers in creating displays.

Floral designers who are self-employed or have their own shop also must do business tasks, such as advertising, pricing, inventory, and taxes. Some designers hire and supervise staff to help with these tasks.

Work Environment

Floral designers held about 54,500 jobs in 2022. The largest employers of floral designers were as follows:

Floral designers perform customer-service duties, such as answering telephones and taking orders.

Florists	52%
Self-employed workers	20
Grocery and specialty food retailers	11
Wholesale trade	3
Lawn and garden equipment and supplies retailers	2

Floral designers in retail businesses serve walk-in customers as well as customers placing orders over the telephone, on the Internet, or through other florists. Some floral designers who work on a contract basis when creating arrangements for events, such as weddings, have to travel to event locations.

Work Schedules

Many floral designers work full time, although their hours may vary with the work setting.

Independent shops are typically open during regular business hours. Floral departments inside grocery stores or other stores may stay open longer.

Floral designers are busier at certain times of the year, such as holidays, than at other times. Because freshly cut flowers are perishable, most orders cannot be completed too far in advance. Therefore, designers often work additional hours just before and during holidays. In addition, many part-time and seasonal opportunities are available around certain holidays, such as Christmas, Valentine's Day, and Mother's Day.

How to Become a Floral Designer

Most floral designers have a high school diploma or the equivalent and learn their skills on the job in a few months.

Education

Most floral designers have a high school diploma or the equivalent. Postsecondary programs may be useful for florists who want to start their own business. Programs in floral design and caring techniques for flowers and plants are available through private floral schools, vocational schools, and community

Most floral designers learn their skills on the job over the course of a few months.

colleges. Most of these programs offer a certificate or diploma. Classes in flower and plant identification, floral design concepts, and advertising and other business courses, as well as experience working in a greenhouse, are part of many certificate and diploma programs. Some community colleges and universities offer certificates or associate's degrees in floriculture/floristry operations and management.

Training

New floral designers typically get hands-on experience working with an experienced floral designer. They may start by preparing simple flower arrangements and practicing the basics of tying bows and ribbons, cutting stems to appropriate lengths, and learning about the proper handling and care of flowers and plants. Floral designers also learn about the different types and growth properties of flowers and plants, how to use flowers in complex floral designs, and which flowers and plants complement each other.

Licenses, Certifications, and Registrations

The American Institute of Floral Designers offers the Certified Floral Designer credential. Although certification is voluntary, it indicates a measure of floral design knowledge and expertise gained through work experience or education.

Advancement

Formal training in floral design may be helpful for people who are interested in opening their own business or in becoming a chief floral designer or supervisor.

Important Qualities

Artistic ability. Floral designers use their sense of style to develop aesthetically pleasing designs.

Creativity. Floral designers must develop appropriate designs for different occasions. They must also be open to new ideas because trends in floral design change quickly.

Customer-service skills. Floral designers spend much of their day interacting with customers and suppliers. They must be able to understand what a customer is looking for, explain options, and provide high-quality products and service.

Organizational skills. Floral designers need to be well organized to keep the business operating smoothly and to ensure that orders are completed on time.

Pay

The median annual wage for floral designers was $33,160 in May 2022. The median wage is the wage at which half the workers in an occupation earned more than that amount and half earned less. The lowest 10 percent earned less than $23,540, and the highest 10 percent earned more than $46,560.

In May 2022, the median annual wages for floral designers in the top industries in which they worked were as follows:

Grocery and specialty food retailers	$34,570
Lawn and garden equipment and supplies retailers	34,120
Wholesale trade	33,450
Florists	31,770

Many floral designers work full time, although their hours may vary with the work setting.

Independent floral shops are typically open during regular business hours. Floral departments inside grocery stores or other stores may stay open longer.

Floral designers are busier at certain times of the year, such as holidays, than at other times. Because freshly cut flowers are perishable, most orders cannot be completed too far in advance. Therefore, designers often work additional hours just before and during holidays. In addition, many part-time and seasonal opportunities are available around holidays for which flowers

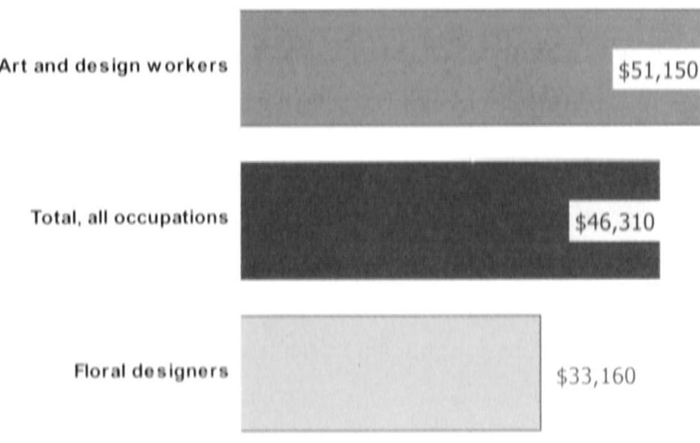

Note: All Occupations includes all occupations in the U.S. Economy.
Source: U.S. Bureau of Labor Statistics, Occupational Employment and Wage Statistics.

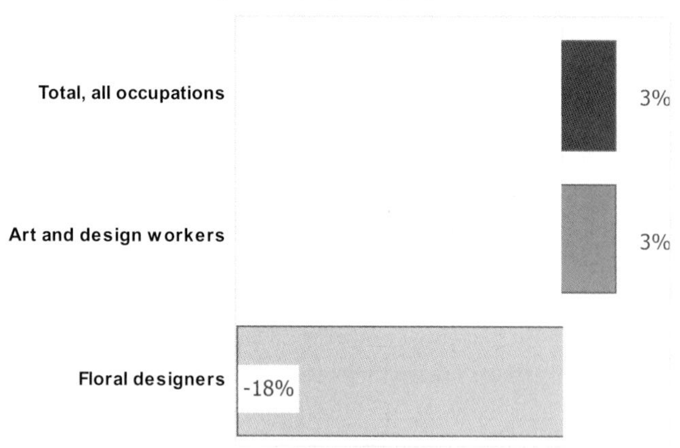

Note: All Occupations includes all occupations in the U.S. Economy.
Source: U.S. Bureau of Labor Statistics, Employment Projections program.

or plants are popular gifts, such as Christmas, Valentine's Day, and Mother's Day.

Job Outlook

Employment of floral designers is projected to decline 18 percent from 2022 to 2032.

Despite declining employment, about 4,700 openings for floral designers are projected each year, on average, over the decade. All of those openings are expected to result from the need to replace workers who transfer to other occupations or exit the labor force, such as to retire.

Employment

Although there will continue to be demand for floral arrangements at events such as weddings and funerals, the need for floral designers is projected to decline along with the number of florist shops. Local florist shops often fulfill online orders from flower delivery services. This practice may increase the number of orders florist shops receive, but it also may dampen the demand for additional shops as each existing shop widens its customer service area.

In addition, grocery stores offer floral decorations, cut flowers, and plants. Customers may find it more convenient to buy flowers or plants at these stores than to travel to florist shops.

Occupational Title	SOC Code	Employment, 2022	Projected Employment, 2032	Change, 2022-32	
				Percent	Numeric
Floral designers	27-1023	54,500	44,700	-18	-9,800

Contacts for More Information

For more information about becoming a Certified Floral Designer, visit

- American Institute of Floral Designers
- For more information about careers in floral design, visit
- Society of American Florists

Graphic Designers

Summary

Quick Facts: Graphic Designers

2022 Median Pay	$57,990 per year $27.88 per hour
Typical Entry-Level Education	Bachelor's degree
Work Experience in a Related Occupation	None
On-the-job Training	None
Number of Jobs, 2022	270,900
Job Outlook, 2022-32	3% (As fast as average)
Employment Change, 2022-32	8,900

What Graphic Designers Do

Graphic designers create visual concepts, using computer software or by hand, to communicate ideas that inspire, inform, and captivate consumers.

Work Environment

Many of these workers are employed in specialized design services, publishing, or advertising, public relations, and related services industries.

How to Become a Graphic Designer

Graphic designers usually need a bachelor's degree in graphic design or a related field. Candidates for graphic design positions should have a portfolio that demonstrates their creativity and originality.

Graphic designers combine art and technology to develop graphics for product illustrations, logos, and websites.

Pay

The median annual wage for graphic designers was $57,990 in May 2022.

Job Outlook

Employment of graphic designers is projected to grow 3 percent from 2022 to 2032, about as fast as the average for all occupations.

About 22,800 openings for graphic designers are projected each year, on average, over the decade. Many of those openings are expected to result from the need to replace workers who transfer to different occupations or exit the labor force, such as to retire.

What Graphic Designers Do

Graphic designers create visual concepts, using computer software or by hand, to communicate ideas that inspire, inform, and captivate consumers. They develop the overall layout and production design for applications such as advertisements, brochures, magazines, and reports.

Duties

Graphic designers typically do the following:

- Meet with clients or the art director to determine the scope of a project
- Use digital illustration, photo editing software, and layout software to create designs
- Create visual elements such as logos, original images, and illustrations to help deliver a message
- Design layouts, including selection of colors, images, and typefaces
- Present design concepts to clients or art directors
- Incorporate changes recommended by clients or art directors into final designs
- Review designs for errors before printing or publishing them

Graphic designers create designs either by hand or using computer software packages.

Graphic designers, also referred to as graphic artists or communication designers, combine art and technology to communicate ideas through images and the layout of websites and printed pages. They may use a variety of design elements to achieve artistic or decorative effects.

Graphic designers work with both text and images. They often select the type, font, size, color, and line length of headlines, headings, and text. Graphic designers also decide how images and text will go together in print or on a webpage, including how much space each will have. When using text in layouts, graphic designers collaborate with writers, who choose the words and decide whether the words will be put into paragraphs, lists, or tables. Through the use of images, text, and color, graphic designers may transform data into visual graphics and diagrams to make complex ideas more accessible.

Graphic design is important to market and sell products, and it is a critical component of brochures and logos. Therefore, graphic designers often work closely with people in advertising and promotions, public relations, and marketing.

Frequently, designers specialize in a particular category or type of client. For example, some designers create the graphics used on product packaging, and others may work on the visual designs used on book jackets.

Graphic designers need to keep up to date with software and computer technologies in order to remain competitive.

Some individuals with a background in graphic design become postsecondary teachers and teach in design schools, colleges, and universities.

Some graphic designers specialize in experiential graphic design. These designers work with architects, industrial designers, landscape architects, and interior designers to create interactive design environments, such as museum exhibitions, public arts exhibits, and retail spaces.

Work Environment

Graphic designers held about 270,900 jobs in 2022. The largest employers of graphic designers were as follows:

Self-employed workers	19%
Advertising, public relations, and related services	9
Specialized design services	9
Printing and related support activities	6
Publishing industries	6

Graphic designers generally work in studios, where they have access to equipment such as drafting tables, computers, and software. Although many graphic designers work independently, those who work for specialized graphic design firms are often part of a design team. Many graphic designers collaborate with colleagues or work with clients on projects.

Graphic designers generally work in a studio where they have access to drafting tables and computers.

Work Schedules

Graphic designers' schedules vary depending on workloads and deadlines.

Those who are self-employed may need to adjust their workday to meet with clients in the evenings or on weekends. In addition, they may spend some of their time looking for new projects or competing with other designers for contracts.

How to Become a Graphic Designer

Graphic designers usually need a bachelor's degree in graphic design or a related field. Candidates for graphic design positions should have a portfolio that demonstrates their creativity and originality.

Graphic designers should demonstrate their creativity and originality through a professional portfolio.

Education

Graphic designers typically need a bachelor's degree in graphic design or a related fine arts field. People who have a bachelor's degree in another field may complete technical training in graphic design to meet most hiring qualifications.

The National Association of Schools of Art and Design accredits more than 360 postsecondary colleges, universities, and independent institutes with programs in art and design. Most programs include courses in studio art, principles of design, computerized design, commercial graphics production, printing techniques, and website design. In addition, students should consider courses in writing, marketing, and business, all of which are useful in helping designers work effectively on project teams.

High school students interested in graphic design should take basic art and design courses, if available. Many bachelor's degree programs require students to complete a year of basic art and design courses before being admitted to a formal degree program. Some schools require applicants to submit sketches and other examples of their artistic ability.

Many programs provide students with the opportunity to build a portfolio—a collection of completed works that demonstrates an artist's styles and abilities. For many artists, including graphic designers, developing a portfolio is essential because employers rely on portfolios in making hiring decisions.

Graphic designers must keep up with new and updated computer graphics and design software, either on their own or through formal software training programs. Professional associations that specialize in graphic design, such as AIGA, offer courses intended to keep the skills of their members up to date.

Other Experience

Graphic designers often gain experience through internships, which they may undertake while enrolled in a design program. Internships allow aspiring graphic designers to work with designers and to experience the design process from concept to completion.

Licenses, Certifications, and Registrations

Certification programs are generally available through software product vendors. Certification in graphic design software demonstrates competence and may provide jobseekers with a competitive advantage.

Advancement

Experienced graphic designers may advance to chief designer, art director, or other supervisory positions.

Important Qualities

Analytical skills. Graphic designers must be able to perceive their work from their consumers' point of view to ensure that the designs convey the client's message.

Graphic Designers

Median annual wages, May 2022

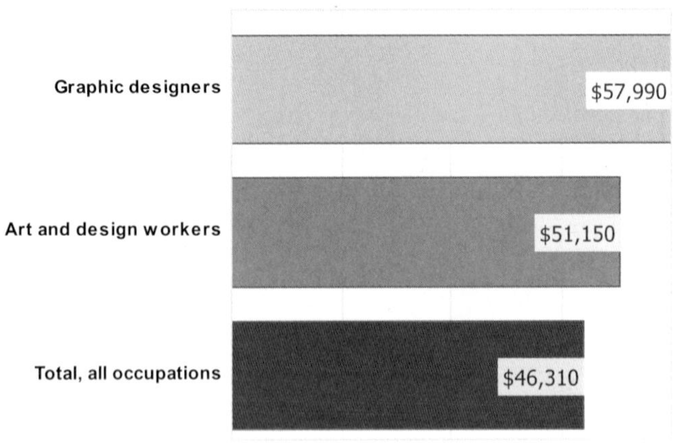

Note: All Occupations includes all occupations in the U.S. Economy.
Source: U.S. Bureau of Labor Statistics, Occupational Employment and Wage Statistics.

Graphic Designers

Percent change in employment, projected 2022-32

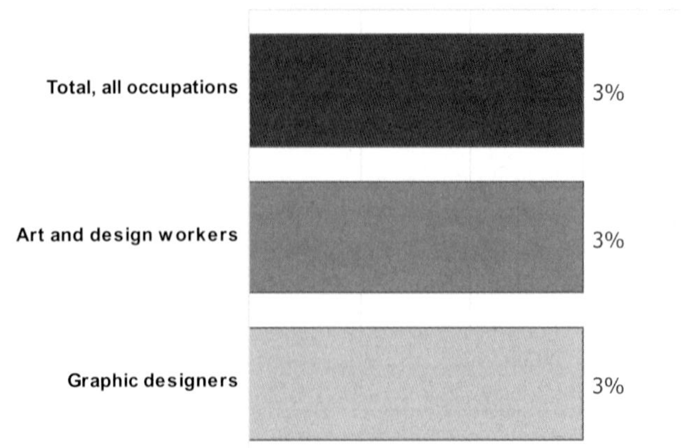

Note: All Occupations includes all occupations in the U.S. Economy.
Source: U.S. Bureau of Labor Statistics, Employment Projections program.

Artistic ability. Graphic designers must be able to create designs that are artistically interesting and appealing to clients and consumers. They produce rough illustrations of design ideas, either by hand sketching or by using computer programs.

Communication skills. Graphic designers must communicate with clients, customers, and other designers to ensure that their designs accurately and effectively convey information.

Computer skills. Most graphic designers use specialized graphic design software to prepare their designs.

Creativity. Graphic designers must be able to think of new approaches to communicating ideas to consumers. They develop unique designs that convey their client's message.

Time-management skills. Graphic designers often work simultaneously on multiple projects, each with a different deadline.

Pay

The median annual wage for graphic designers was $57,990 in May 2022. The median wage is the wage at which half the workers in an occupation earned more than that amount and half earned less. The lowest 10 percent earned less than $35,430, and the highest 10 percent earned more than $100,920.

In May 2022, the median annual wages for graphic designers in the top industries in which they worked were as follows:

Specialized design services	$61,510
Advertising, public relations, and related services	58,750
Publishing industries	51,660
Printing and related support activities	43,060

Graphic designers' schedules vary depending on workload and deadlines.

Those who are self-employed may need to adjust their workday to meet with clients in the evenings or on weekends. In addition, they may spend some of their time looking for new projects or competing with other designers for contracts.

Job Outlook

Employment of graphic designers is projected to grow 3 percent from 2022 to 2032, about as fast as the average for all occupations.

About 22,800 openings for graphic designers are projected each year, on average, over the decade. Many of those openings are expected to result from the need to replace workers who transfer to different occupations or exit the labor force, such as to retire.

Employment

As companies continue to increase their digital presence, graphic designers may be needed to help create visually appealing and effective layouts of websites and social media sites. However, a decrease in print newspapers and magazines may limit employment growth for graphic designers who create advertisements for companies and products.

Occupational Title	SOC Code	Employment, 2022	Projected Employment, 2032	Change, 2022-32	
				Percent	Numeric
Graphic designers	27-1024	270,900	279,800	3	8,900

Contacts for More Information

For more information about graphic design, visit

- AIGA
- Graphic Artists Guild
- Society for Experiential Graphic Design
- National Association of Schools of Art and Design

Industrial Designers

Summary

Quick Facts: Industrial Designers	
2022 Median Pay	$75,910 per year $36.50 per hour
Typical Entry-Level Education	Bachelor's degree
Work Experience in a Related Occupation	None
On-the-job Training	None
Number of Jobs, 2022	32,400
Job Outlook, 2022-32	2% (As fast as average)
Employment Change, 2022-32	700

What Industrial Designers Do
Industrial designers combine art, business, and engineering to develop the concepts for manufactured products.

Work Environment
Industrial designers work in a variety of industries. Although industrial designers work primarily in offices, they may travel to testing facilities, design centers, clients' exhibit sites, users' homes or workplaces, and places where the product is manufactured.

How to Become an Industrial Designer
Industrial designers typically need a bachelor's degree to enter the occupation. They also need an electronic portfolio with examples of their design projects.

Pay
The median annual wage for industrial designers was $75,910 in May 2022.

Job Outlook
Employment of industrial designers is projected to grow 2 percent from 2022 to 2032, about as fast as the average for all occupations.

About 2,200 openings for industrial designers are projected each year, on average, over the decade. Many of those openings are expected to result from the need to replace workers who transfer to different occupations or exit the labor force, such as to retire.

What Industrial Designers Do
Industrial designers develop the concepts for manufactured products, such as cars, home appliances, and toys. They combine art, business, and engineering to make products that people use every day. Industrial designers consider the function, aesthetics, production costs, and usability of products when developing new product concepts.

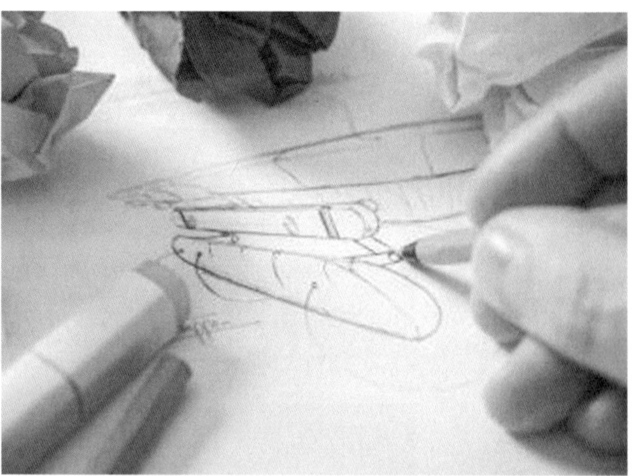

Industrial designers imagine how consumers might use a product when they create and test designs.

Duties
Industrial designers typically do the following:

- Consult with clients to determine requirements for designs
- Research the various ways a particular product might be used, and who will use it
- Sketch ideas or create renderings, which are images on paper or on a computer that provide a visual of design ideas
- Use computer software to develop virtual models of different designs
- Create physical prototypes of their designs
- Examine materials and manufacturing requirements to determine production costs
- Work with other specialists, such as mechanical engineers and manufacturers, to evaluate whether their design concepts will fill needs at a reasonable cost
- Evaluate product safety, appearance, and function to determine if a design is practical
- Present designs and demonstrate prototypes to clients for approval

Industrial designers work primarily in offices, but they may travel to the places where the products are manufactured.

Some industrial designers focus on a particular product category. For example, they may design medical equipment or work on consumer electronics products, such as computers and smart phones. Other designers develop ideas for products such as new bicycles, furniture, housewares, and snowboards.

Other designers, sometimes called *user interface designers* or *interaction designers*, focus on the usability of a product, such as an electronic device, and ensure that the product is both simple and enjoyable to use.

Industrial designers imagine how consumers might use a product and test different designs with consumers to see how each design looks and works. Industrial designers often work with engineers, production experts, and market research analysts to find out if their designs are feasible. They apply the input from their colleagues' professional expertise to further develop their designs. For example, industrial designers may work with market research analysts to develop plans to market new product designs to consumers.

Computers are a major tool for industrial designers. Industrial designers use two-dimensional computer-aided design and drafting (CADD) software to sketch ideas, because computers make it easy to make changes and show alternatives. Three-dimensional CAD software is increasingly being used by industrial designers as a tool to transform their two-dimensional designs into models with the help of three-dimensional printers. If they work for manufacturers, they also may use computer-aided industrial design (CAID) software to create specific machine-readable instructions that tell other machines exactly how to build the product.

Work Environment

Industrial designers held about 32,400 jobs in 2022. The largest employers of industrial designers were as follows:

Manufacturing	34%
Wholesale trade	15
Specialized design services	9
Architectural, engineering, and related services	9
Self-employed workers	5

Work spaces for industrial designers often include work tables for sketching designs, meeting rooms with whiteboards for brainstorming with colleagues, and computers and other office equipment for preparing designs and communicating with clients. Although industrial designers work primarily in offices, they may travel to testing facilities, design centers, clients' exhibit sites, users' homes or workplaces, and places where the product is manufactured.

Work Schedules

Industrial designers who are self-employed or work for firms that hire them out to other organizations may need to adjust their workdays frequently in order to meet with clients in the evenings or on weekends. In addition, they may spend some of their time looking for new projects or competing with other designers for contracts.

Work spaces for industrial designers often include drafting tables and meeting rooms for brainstorming with colleagues.

How to Become an Industrial Designer

Industrial designers typically need a bachelor's degree to enter the occupation. They also need an electronic portfolio with examples of their design projects.

Education

A bachelor's degree is usually required for entry-level industrial design jobs. Common fields of degree include fine arts, engineering, or architecture. Most industrial design programs include courses in drawing, computer-aided design and drafting (CADD), and three-dimensional modeling, as well as courses in business, industrial materials and processes, and manufacturing methods.

The National Association of Schools of Art and Design accredits more than 360 postsecondary colleges, universities, and independent institutes with programs in art and design. Many schools require successful completion of some basic art and design courses before granting entry into a bachelor's degree program. Applicants also may need to submit sketches and other examples of their artistic ability.

Many programs provide students with the opportunity to build a professional portfolio of their designs from classroom projects, internships, or other experiences. Students can use these examples of their work to demonstrate their design skills when applying for jobs and bidding on contracts for work.

Important Qualities

Analytical skills. Industrial designers use logic or reasoning skills to study consumers and recognize the need for new products.

Artistic ability. Industrial designers sketch their initial design ideas, which are used later to create prototypes. As such, designers must be able to express their design through illustration.

A bachelor's degree in industrial design, architecture, or engineering is usually required for entry-level industrial design jobs.

Computer skills. Industrial designers use computer-aided design software to develop their designs and create prototypes.

Creativity. Industrial designers must be innovative in their designs and the ways in which they integrate existing technologies into their new product.

Interpersonal skills. Industrial designers must develop cooperative working relationships with clients and colleagues who specialize in related disciplines.

Mechanical skills. Industrial designers must understand how products are engineered, at least for the types of products that they design.

Problem-solving skills. Industrial designers determine the need, size, and cost of a product; anticipate production issues; develop alternatives; evaluate options; and implement solutions.

Advancement

Experienced designers in large firms may advance to chief designer, design department head, or other supervisory positions. Some designers become teachers in design schools or in colleges and universities. Many teachers continue to consult privately or operate small design studios in addition to teaching. Some experienced designers open their own design firms.

Pay

The median annual wage for industrial designers was $75,910 in May 2022. The median wage is the wage at which half the workers in an occupation earned more than that amount and half earned less. The lowest 10 percent earned less than $43,680, and the highest 10 percent earned more than $125,780.

In May 2022, the median annual wages for industrial designers in the top industries in which they worked were as follows:

Architectural, engineering, and related services	$96,610
Specialized design services	75,510
Manufacturing	71,710
Wholesale trade	68,500

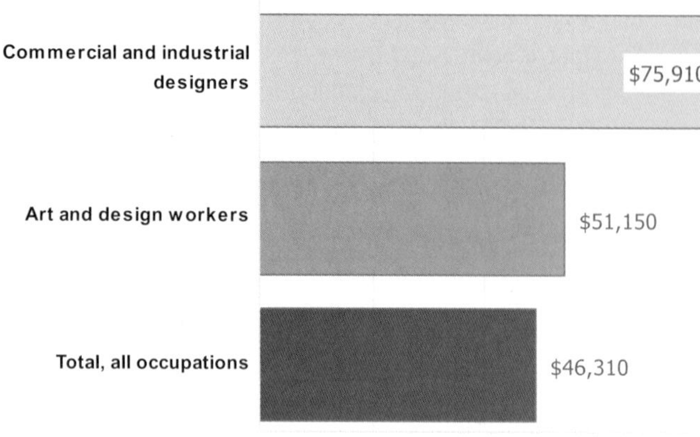

Note: All Occupations includes all occupations in the U.S. Economy.
Source: U.S. Bureau of Labor Statistics, Occupational Employment and Wage Statistics.

Industrial designers who are self-employed or work for firms that hire them out to other organizations may need to adjust their workdays frequently in order to meet with clients in the evenings or on weekends. In addition, they may spend some of their time looking for new projects or competing with other designers for contracts.

Job Outlook

Employment of industrial designers is projected to grow 2 percent from 2022 to 2032, about as fast as the average for all occupations.

About 2,200 openings for industrial designers are projected each year, on average, over the decade. Many of those openings are expected to result from the need to replace workers who transfer to different occupations or exit the labor force, such as to retire.

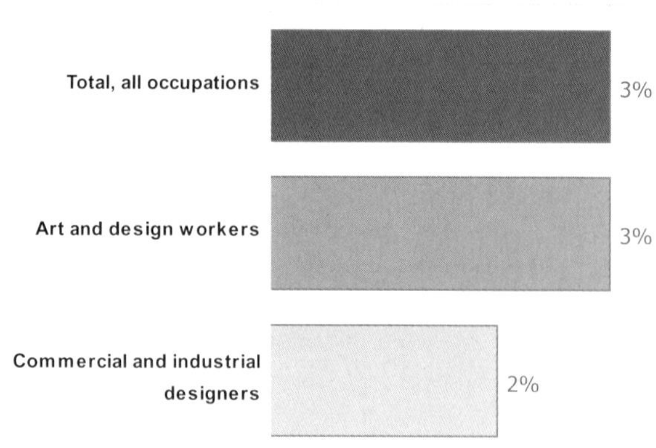

Note: All Occupations includes all occupations in the U.S. Economy.
Source: U.S. Bureau of Labor Statistics, Employment Projections program.

Employment

The need for new and innovative designs, especially for hi-tech products, is expected to support demand for industrial designers. However, projected employment declines in some manufacturing industries may offset this expected growth.

Occupational Title	SOC Code	Employment, 2022	Projected Employment, 2032	Change, 2022-32	
				Percent	Numeric
Commercial and industrial designers	27-1021	32,400	33,000	2	700

Contacts for More Information

For more information about industrial designers, visit

- Industrial Designers Society of America
- National Association of Schools of Art and Design

Interior Designers

Summary

Quick Facts: Interior Designers

2022 Median Pay	$61,590 per year $29.61 per hour
Typical Entry-Level Education	Bachelor's degree
Work Experience in a Related Occupation	None
On-the-job Training	None
Number of Jobs, 2022	94,900
Job Outlook, 2022-32	4% (As fast as average)
Employment Change, 2022-32	3,700

What Interior Designers Do

Interior designers make indoor spaces functional, safe, and beautiful by determining space requirements and selecting essential and decorative items.

Work Environment

Many interior designers work in specialized design services or in architectural, engineering, and related services.

Interior designers select and specify colors, furniture, and other materials to create useful and stylish interiors for buildings.

How to Become an Interior Designer

Interior designers typically need a bachelor's degree to enter the occupation.

Pay

The median annual wage for interior designers was $61,590 in May 2022.

Job Outlook

Employment of interior designers is projected to grow 4 percent from 2022 to 2032, about as fast as the average for all occupations.

About 9,000 openings for interior designers are projected each year, on average, over the decade. Many of those openings are expected to result from the need to replace workers who transfer to different occupations or exit the labor force, such as to retire.

What Interior Designers Do

Interior designers make indoor spaces functional, safe, and beautiful by determining space requirements and selecting essential and decorative items, such as colors, lighting, and materials. They must be able to draw, read, and edit blueprints.

Interior designers make interior spaces functional, safe, and beautiful for almost every type of building.

They also must be aware of building codes, inspection regulations, and other considerations, such as accessibility standards.

Duties

Interior designers typically do the following:

- Search for and bid on new projects
- Determine the client's goals and requirements for the project
- Consider how the space will be used and how people will move through the space
- Sketch preliminary design plans, including electrical and partition layouts
- Specify materials and furnishings, such as lighting, furniture, wall finishes, flooring, and plumbing fixtures
- Create a timeline for the interior design project and estimate project costs
- Place orders for materials and oversee the installation of the design elements
- Oversee construction and coordinate with general building contractors to implement the plans and specifications for the project
- Visit the site after the project is complete, to ensure that the client is satisfied

Interior designers work closely with architects, civil engineers, mechanical engineers, and construction laborers and helpers to determine how interior spaces will function, look, and be furnished. Interior designers read blueprints and must be aware of building codes and inspection regulations.

Although some sketches may be freehand, most interior designers use computer-aided design (CAD) software for most of their drawings. Throughout the design process, interior designers often use building information modeling (BIM) software to create three-dimensional visualizations that include construction elements such as walls or roofs.

Many designers specialize in particular types of buildings, such as homes, hospitals, or hotels; specific rooms, such as bathrooms or kitchens; or a specific style. Some designers work for home-furnishings stores, providing design services to help customers choose materials and furnishings.

Some interior designers produce designs, plans, and drawings for construction and installation. These products may include information for construction and demolition, electrical layouts, and building permits. Interior designers may draft the preliminary design into documents ranging from simple sketches to construction schedules and attachments.

The following are examples of types of interior designers:

Corporate designers create interior designs for professional workplaces in a variety of settings, from small offices to large buildings. They focus on creating spaces that are efficient, functional, and safe for employees. In their designs, they may incorporate elements of a company's brand.

Healthcare designers plan and renovate healthcare centers, clinics, doctors' offices, hospitals, and residential care facilities. They specialize in evidence-based design, which uses data and research in design decisionmaking to achieve positive results for patients, residents, and facilities.

Kitchen and bath designers specialize in kitchens and bathrooms and have expert knowledge of cabinet, fixture, appliance, plumbing, and electrical solutions for these rooms.

Sustainable designers suggest strategies to improve energy and water efficiencies and indoor air quality as well as environmentally sustainable products, such as bamboo and cork for floors. They may obtain certification in Leadership in Energy and Environmental Design (LEED) from the U.S. Green Building Council. Such certification indicates expertise in designing buildings and spaces with sustainable practices in mind.

Universal designers renovate spaces in order to make them more accessible. Often, these designs are used to renovate spaces for elderly people and people with special needs; however, universal designs benefit everyone. For example, an entryway without steps may be necessary for someone in a wheelchair, but it is also helpful for someone pushing a baby stroller.

Work Environment

Interior designers held about 94,900 jobs in 2022. The largest employers of interior designers were as follows:

Self-employed workers	32%
Specialized design services	27
Architectural, engineering, and related services	14
Wholesale trade	4

Most interior designers work in offices, but technology has changed the way many designers work. For example, interior designers now use software rather than drafting tables to create two- or three-dimensional images.

Interior designers also travel to clients' design sites.

Work Schedules

Interior designers may need to adjust their workday to suit their clients' schedules and deadlines, including meeting with clients in the evening and on weekends.

Interior designers travel to the clients' design sites.

Interior designers must be able to work closely with architects and builders to determine the design of the interior space.

How to Become an Interior Designer

Interior designers typically need a bachelor's degree to enter the occupation.

Education

Interior designers entering the occupation typically need a bachelor's degree in any field, with fine arts subjects being most common. Studies should include courses in interior design, drawing, and computer-aided design (CAD).

Programs in interior design are available at the associate's, bachelor's, and master's degree levels. Applicants to these programs may need to submit sketches and other examples of their artistic ability.

The National Association of Schools of Art and Design accredits more than 360 postsecondary colleges, universities, and independent institutes that have programs in art and design. The Council for Interior Design Accreditation accredits about 180 professional-level (bachelor's or master's degree) interior design programs.

Nearly 100 colleges and universities are affiliated with the National Kitchen & Bath Association. These schools offer programs on kitchen and bath design at the certificate, associate's degree, and bachelor's degree levels.

Licenses, Certifications, and Registrations

Licensure requirements vary by state. In some states, only licensed designers may do interior design work. In other states, both licensed and unlicensed designers may do such work; however, only licensed designers may use the title "interior designer." In still other states, both licensed and unlicensed designers may call themselves interior designers and do interior design work.

In states with laws restricting the use of the title "interior designer," only candidates who pass their state-approved exam, most commonly the National Council for Interior Design Qualification (NCIDQ) exam, may call themselves registered interior designers. Candidate eligibility for taking the NCIDQ exam includes having at least a bachelor's degree in interior design and 2 years of full-time work experience.

California requires a different exam, administered by the California Council for Interior Design Certification (CCIDC). To take this exam, eligible candidates must have a combination of education and experience.

Voluntary certification in an interior design specialty, such as environmental design, allows designers to demonstrate expertise in a particular area of the occupation. Interior designers often specialize to distinguish the type of design work they do and to promote their expertise. Certifications usually are available through professional and trade associations and are independent of the NCIDQ licensing examination.

Important Qualities

Artistic ability. Interior designers use their sense of style to develop aesthetically pleasing designs.

Creativity. Interior designers need to be imaginative in selecting furnishings and fabrics and in creating functional spaces that serve the client's needs and fit the client's lifestyle.

Detail oriented. Interior designers need to be precise in measuring interior spaces and creating drawings, so that their drawings can be used by workers such as engineers or other designers.

Interpersonal skills. Interior designers need to be able to communicate effectively with clients and others. They spend much of their time soliciting new clients and new work and collaborating with other designers, engineers, and general building contractors on ongoing projects.

Problem-solving skills. Interior designers must address challenges, such as construction delays or unavailability of certain materials, while keeping the project on time and within budget.

Visualization. Interior designers need a strong sense of proportion and visual awareness in order to understand how the pieces of a design will fit together to create the intended environment.

Pay

The median annual wage for interior designers was $61,590 in May 2022. The median wage is the wage at which half the workers in an occupation earned more than that amount and half earned less. The lowest 10 percent earned less than $36,610, and the highest 10 percent earned more than $101,550.

In May 2022, the median annual wages for interior designers in the top industries in which they worked were as follows:

Architectural, engineering, and related services	$71,360
Wholesale trade	66,770
Specialized design services	60,870

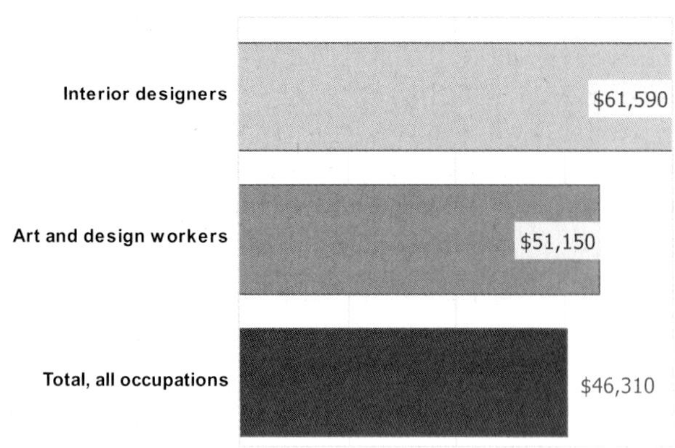

Note: All Occupations includes all occupations in the U.S. Economy.
Source: U.S. Bureau of Labor Statistics, Occupational Employment and Wage Statistics.

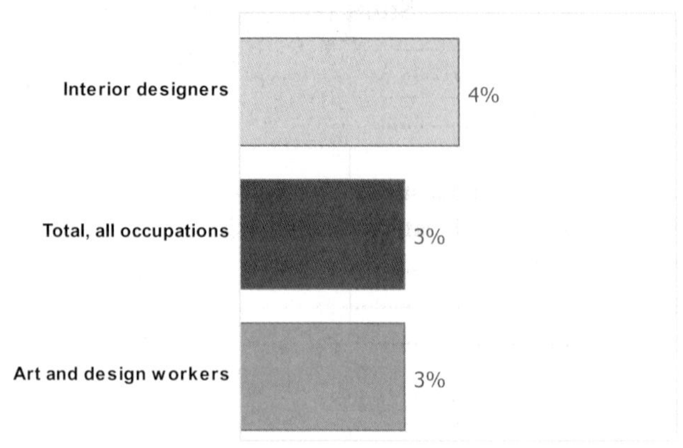

Note: All Occupations includes all occupations in the U.S. Economy.
Source: U.S. Bureau of Labor Statistics, Employment Projections program.

Interior designers may need to adjust their workday to suit their clients' schedules and deadlines, including meeting with clients in the evening and on weekends.

Job Outlook

Employment of interior designers is projected to grow 4 percent from 2022 to 2032, about as fast as the average for all occupations.

About 9,000 openings for interior designers are projected each year, on average, over the decade. Many of those openings are expected to result from the need to replace workers who transfer to different occupations or exit the labor force, such as to retire.

Employment

As the demand for renovation projects increases, homeowners and companies are expected to need services provided by interior designers to help create safe and functional spaces. A greater focus on building codes, as well as the need to design spaces that meet accessibility standards, may also help to create jobs for these workers.

However, there will be fewer opportunities for self-employed interior designers to renovate existing homes, commercial buildings, and other facilities.

Occupational Title	SOC Code	Employment, 2022	Projected Employment, 2032	Change, 2022-32	
				Percent	Numeric
Interior designers	27-1025	94,900	98,700	4	3,700

Contacts for More Information

For more information about interior designers, visit

- American Society of Interior Designers
- International Interior Design Association
- National Association of Schools of Art and Design
- Council for Interior Design Accreditation
- National Council for Interior Design Qualification
- California Council for Interior Design Certification
- National Kitchen & Bath Association

Special Effects Artists and Animators

Summary

Quick Facts: Special Effects Artists and Animators	
2022 Median Pay	$98,950 per year $47.57 per hour
Typical Entry-Level Education	Bachelor's degree
Work Experience in a Related Occupation	None
On-the-job Training	None
Number of Jobs, 2022	89,300
Job Outlook, 2022-32	8% (Faster than average)
Employment Change, 2022-32	7,400

What Special Effects Artists and Animators Do

Special effects artists and animators create images that appear to move and visual effects for various forms of media and entertainment.

Work Environment

Many artists and animators work in offices; others work from home.

How to Become a Special Effects Artist or Animator

Special effects artists and animators typically need a bachelor's degree in computer graphics, art, or a related field to develop both a portfolio of work and the technical skills that many employers prefer.

Pay

The median annual wage for special effects artists and animators was $98,950 in May 2022.

Job Outlook

Employment of special effects artists and animators is projected to grow 8 percent from 2022 to 2032, faster than the average for all occupations.

About 9,400 openings for special effects artists and animators are projected each year, on average, over the decade. Many of those openings are expected to result from the need to replace workers who transfer to different occupations or exit the labor force, such as to retire.

What Special Effects Artists and Animators Do

Special effects artists and animators create two- and three-dimensional models, images that appear to move, and visual effects for television, movies, video games, and other forms of media.

Duties

Special effects artists and animators typically do the following:

- Use computer programs and illustrations to create graphics and animation (images that appear to move)
- Work with a team of animators and artists to create a movie, game, or visual effect
- Research upcoming projects to help create realistic designs or animation
- Edit animation and effects on the basis of feedback from directors, other animators, game designers, or clients
- Meet with clients, other animators, games designers, directors, and other staff (which may include actors) to review deadlines and development timelines

Special effects artists and animators often work in a specific medium. Some focus on creating animated movies or video games. Others create visual effects for movies and television shows. Creating computer-generated images (known as CGI) may include taking images of an actor's movements and then animating them into three-dimensional characters. Other animators design scenery or backgrounds for locations.

Artists and animators can further specialize within these fields. Within animated movies and video games, artists often specialize in characters or in scenery and background design.

Multimedia artists and animators create animation and visual effects for television, movies, video games, and other media.

Special effects artists and animators create two- and three-dimensional models and animation.

Video game artists may focus on level design: creating the look, feel, and layout for the levels of a video game.

Animators work in teams to develop a movie, a visual effect, or an electronic game. Each animator works on a portion of the project, and then the pieces are put together to create one cohesive animation.

Some special effects artists and animators create their work primarily by using computer software or by writing their own computer code. Many animation companies have their own computer animation software that artists must learn to use. Video game designers also work in a variety of platforms, including mobile gaming and online social networks.

Other artists and animators prefer to work by drawing and painting by hand and then translating the resulting images into computer programs. Some special effects artists use storyboards or "animatics," which look like a comic strip, to help visualize the final product during the design process.

Many special effects artists and animators put their creative work on the Internet. If the images become popular, these artists can gain more recognition, which may lead to future employment or freelance work.

Work Environment

Special effects artists and animators held about 89,300 jobs in 2022. The largest employers of special effects artists and animators were as follows:

Self-employed workers	58%
Motion picture and video industries	19
Software publishers	6
Computer systems design and related services	5
Advertising, public relations, and related services	1

Many artists and animators work in offices; others work from home.

Special effects artists and animators frequently work in offices.

Work Schedules

Most special effects artists and animators work a regular schedule; however, when deadlines are approaching, they may need to work nights and weekends.

How to Become a Special Effects Artist or Animator

Special effects artists and animators typically need a bachelor's degree in computer graphics, art, or a related field to develop both a portfolio of work and the technical skills that many employers prefer.

Education

Special effects artists and animators typically need a bachelor's degree in computer graphics, animation, fine arts, or a related field.

Bachelor's degree programs in computer graphics often include courses in computer science in addition to art. Programs in animation often require classes in drawing, animation, and film. Programs in fine arts may include courses in painting, drawing, and sculpture. Schools also may have specialized degrees in topics such as interactive media or game design.

Employers look for workers who have a good portfolio of work and strong computer programming skills.

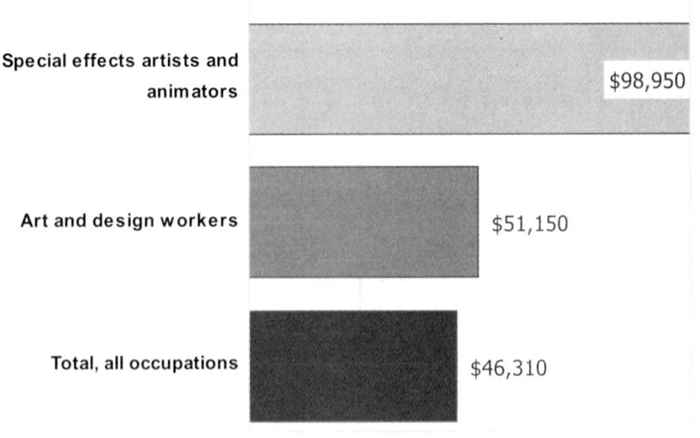

Note: All Occupations includes all occupations in the U.S. Economy.
Source: U.S. Bureau of Labor Statistics, Occupational Employment and Wage Statistics.

Employers usually prefer to hire candidates who have a good portfolio and strong technical skills, both of which students may develop while earning a degree.

Advancement

Special effects artists and animators who show strong teamwork and time-management skills can advance to supervisory positions, where they are responsible for one aspect of a visual effects team. Some artists might advance to leadership or directorial positions, such as an art director or producer or director.

Other Experience

Skills in graphics and animation can be honed through self-study. Special effects artists and animators can develop these skills to enhance their portfolios, which may make it easier to find job opportunities.

Important Qualities

Artistic talent. Animators and artists should have artistic ability and a good understanding of color, texture, and light. However, they may be able to compensate for artistic shortcomings with better technical skills.

Communication skills. Special effects artists and animators need to work as part of a team and respond well to criticism and feedback.

Computer skills. Many special effects artists and animators use computer programs or write programming code to do most of their work.

Creativity. Artists and animators must be able to think creatively to develop original ideas and make them come to life.

Time-management skills. The workdays required by most studio and game design companies can be long, particularly when there are tight deadlines. Artists and animators need to be able to manage their time effectively when a deadline approaches.

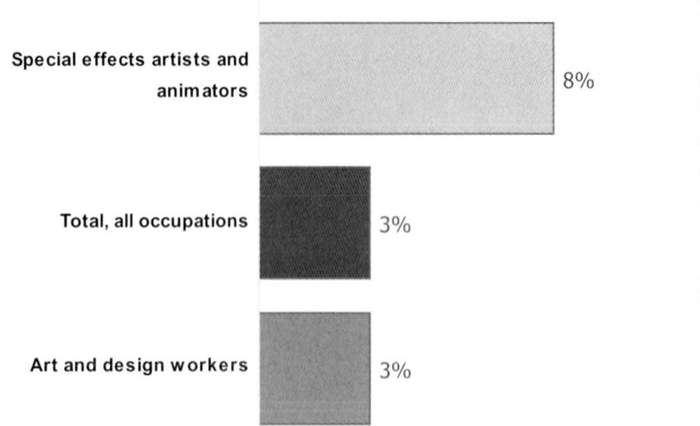

Note: All Occupations includes all occupations in the U.S. Economy.
Source: U.S. Bureau of Labor Statistics, Employment Projections program.

Pay

The median annual wage for special effects artists and animators was $98,950 in May 2022. The median wage is the wage at which half the workers in an occupation earned more than that amount and half earned less. The lowest 10 percent earned less than $52,660, and the highest 10 percent earned more than $174,140.

In May 2022, the median annual wages for special effects artists and animators in the top industries in which they worked were as follows:

Motion picture and video industries	$129,670
Software publishers	103,560
Advertising, public relations, and related services	81,870
Computer systems design and related services	79,210

Most special effects artists and animators work a regular full-time schedule; however, when deadlines are approaching, they may need to work nights and weekends.

Job Outlook

Employment of special effects artists and animators is projected to grow 8 percent from 2022 to 2032, faster than the average for all occupations.

About 9,400 openings for special effects artists and animators are projected each year, on average, over the decade. Many of those openings are expected to result from the need to replace workers who transfer to different occupations or exit the labor force, such as to retire.

Employment

Projected employment growth will be due to increased demand for animation and visual effects in video games, movies, and television. Consumer demand will continue for more realistic video games, movie and television special effects, and three-dimensional movies. Additional special effects artists and animators will be required to meet increased demand for these enhanced visual complexities.

Furthermore, continued demand for computer graphics for mobile devices, such as smart phones, will lead to more job opportunities. Special effects artists will be needed to create animation for games and for mobile applications.

Occupational Title	SOC Code	Employment, 2022	Projected Employment, 2032	Change, 2022-32	
				Percent	Numeric
Special effects artists and animators	27-1014	89,300	96,600	8	7,400

Contacts for More Information

For information, visit

- ➤ National Association of Schools of Art and Design
- ➤ Game Career Guide

Building and Grounds Cleaning

Grounds Maintenance Workers

Summary

Quick Facts: Grounds Maintenance Workers	
2022 Median Pay	$36,160 per year $17.39 per hour
Typical Entry-Level Education	See How to Become One
Work Experience in a Related Occupation	None
On-the-job Training	See How to Become One
Number of Jobs, 2022	1,281,600
Job Outlook, 2022-32	3% (As fast as average)
Employment Change, 2022-32	44,200

What Grounds Maintenance Workers Do

Grounds maintenance workers install and maintain landscapes, prune trees or shrubs, and do other tasks to ensure that vegetation is attractive, orderly, and safe.

Work Environment

Most grounds maintenance work is done outdoors in all weather conditions. Some work is seasonal, available mainly in the spring, summer, and fall. The work may be repetitive and physically demanding, requiring frequent bending, kneeling, lifting, or shoveling.

How to Become a Grounds Maintenance Worker

Grounds maintenance workers typically do not need a formal educational credential and are trained on the job. States may require licensing for workers who apply pesticides and fertilizers.

Grounds maintenance workers work outdoors in all kinds of weather.

Pay

The median hourly wage for grounds maintenance workers was $17.39 in May 2022.

Job Outlook

Overall employment of grounds maintenance workers is projected to grow 3 percent from 2022 to 2032, about as fast as the average for all occupations.

About 170,300 openings for grounds maintenance workers are projected each year, on average, over the decade. Many of those openings are expected to result from the need to replace workers who transfer to different occupations or exit the labor force, such as to retire.

What Grounds Maintenance Workers Do

Grounds maintenance workers install and maintain landscapes, prune trees or shrubs, and do other tasks to ensure that vegetation is attractive, orderly, and safe.

Duties

Grounds maintenance workers typically do the following:

- Mow, edge, and fertilize lawns
- Weed and mulch landscape beds
- Trim hedges, shrubs, and small trees
- Remove dead, damaged, or unwanted trees or branches
- Plant flowers, trees, shrubs, and other plants
- Apply pesticides, herbicides, or other treatments to plants or soil
- Water lawns, landscapes, and gardens
- Monitor and maintain plant health

Grounds maintenance workers mow, edge, and fertilize lawns.

Grounds maintenance workers do a variety of tasks to achieve pleasant and functional environments. They care for outdoor grounds of businesses, homes, parks, and other spaces and for indoor plants in hotels, malls, botanical gardens, and other commercial and public facilities. They generally work under the direction of a landscaping, lawn service, or groundskeeping supervisor.

Depending on their specific tasks, grounds maintenance workers may use a variety of handheld tools (such as such as garden shears, spray applicators, and shovels) and power equipment (including lawnmowers, chain saws, and backhoes).

The following are examples of types of grounds maintenance workers:

Landscaping workers plant flowers, shrubs, trees, and other vegetation to create new outdoor spaces or to upgrade existing ones. They also trim, fertilize, mulch, and water plants. Some grade and install lawns or construct hardscapes such as walkways, patios, and decks. Others help install lighting or sprinkler systems. Landscaping workers attend to a variety of commercial and residential settings, such as apartment buildings, homes, hotels and motels, office buildings, and shopping malls.

Groundskeeping workers, also called *groundskeepers*, focus on property upkeep. Their duties include maintaining plants and trees, raking and mulching leaves, and laying sod. They also care for ornamental features, such as fountains, planters, and benches; clear snow and debris from walkways and parking lots; and tend to groundskeeping equipment. They work on many of the same settings that landscaping workers do, as well as on athletic fields, cemeteries, and other lands that need maintenance.

Groundskeeping workers who care for athletic fields keep natural and artificial turf in top condition, mark boundaries, and may paint turf with team logos and names before events. They regularly mow, water, fertilize, and aerate natural fields and ensure that the underlying soil drains properly. They also vacuum and disinfect artificial turf to prevent growth of harmful bacteria and replace worn turf or cushioning periodically.

In parks and recreation facilities, groundskeepers care for lawns, trees, and shrubs. They also maintain playgrounds; clean buildings and inspect, repair, and paint them as needed; and keep parking lots, picnic areas, and other spaces free of litter. They may erect and dismantle snow fences and maintain swimming pools.

Some groundskeepers specialize in caring for cemeteries and memorial gardens. They dig graves to specified depths. They mow grass regularly, apply fertilizers and other chemicals, prune shrubs and trees, plant flowers, and remove debris from graves.

Greenskeepers maintain golf courses. Although similar overall to that of groundskeepers, their work on turf maintenance may be more complex. They also periodically relocate holes on putting greens and maintain canopies, benches, and tee markers along the course.

Pesticide handlers, sprayers, and applicators apply herbicides, fungicides, and insecticides to plants or soil to prevent or control weeds, insects, and diseases. They inspect lawns for problems and apply chemical or other treatments to stimulate growth and prevent or control threats to cultivated plants.

Tree trimmers and pruners, also called *arborists,* cut away dead or excess branches from trees or shrubs to clear utility lines, roads, sidewalks, and other areas. Some specialize in diagnosing and treating tree diseases. Others specialize in pruning, trimming, and shaping ornamental trees and shrubs.

Work Environment

Grounds maintenance workers held about 1.3 million jobs in 2022. Employment in the detailed occupations that make up grounds maintenance workers was distributed as follows:

Landscaping and groundskeeping workers	1,176,100
Tree trimmers and pruners	66,000
Pesticide handlers, sprayers, and applicators, vegetation	23,200
Grounds maintenance workers, all other	16,300

The largest employers of grounds maintenance workers were as follows:

Tree trimmers and pruners use chainsaws, chippers, and stump grinders while on the job.

Services to buildings and dwellings	47%
Self-employed workers	20
Amusement, gambling, and recreation industries	7
Government	7
Educational services; state, local, and private	3

Grounds maintenance work is usually done outdoors in all kinds of weather. The work may be repetitive and physically demanding, requiring frequent bending, kneeling, lifting, and shoveling.

Injuries and Illnesses

Grounds maintenance work may be dangerous. Workers who use equipment such as lawnmowers and chain saws must wear protective clothing, eyewear, and earplugs. Those who apply chemicals such as pesticides or fertilizers must wear protective gear, including appropriate clothing, gloves, goggles, and sometimes respirators.

Tree trimmers and pruners and grounds maintenance workers, all other, have some of the highest rates of injuries and illnesses of all occupations. ("All other" titles represent occupations with a wide range of characteristics that do not fit into any of the other detailed occupations.)

Although fatalities are uncommon, tree trimmers and pruners experience one of the highest rates of fatalities of all occupations. These workers are often at great heights and must use fall protection gear and wear hardhats and goggles for most activities.

Work Schedules

Most grounds maintenance workers are full time, and their work schedules may vary. These workers may be busier or work longer hours in the spring, summer, and fall, when planting, mowing, and trimming activities are most frequent.

Some jobs are seasonal. However, grounds maintenance workers sometimes provide other services during the winter months, such as snow removal.

How to Become a Grounds Maintenance Worker

Grounds maintenance workers typically do not need a formal educational credential and are trained on the job. States may require licensing for workers who apply pesticides or fertilizers.

Education

Entry-level grounds maintenance jobs typically have no formal education requirements, although employers may prefer to hire candidates who have a high school diploma or equivalent. Prospective grounds maintenance workers may benefit from studying topics such as landscape design, horticulture, or arboriculture.

Licenses, Certifications, and Registrations

Most states require licensing for workers who apply pesticides. Licensing for workers who handle fertilizers varies by state. Obtaining a license usually involves passing a test on the proper use and disposal of insecticides, herbicides, and fungicides. Check with your state's licensing official for more information.

Some workers study topics such as landscape design or horticulture.

Although professional certification is not required, it demonstrates competency and reliability for prospective clients and employers. For example, the National Association of Landscape Professionals (NALP) and the Professional Grounds Management Society (PGMS) offer credentials in landscaping and grounds maintenance for workers at various experience levels. The Tree Care Industry Association (TCIA) and the International Society of Arboriculture (ISA) offer certifications for tree care workers.

Training

Grounds maintenance workers typically need 1 month or less of on-the-job training to learn the skills they need, including how to plant and maintain areas and how to use mowers, trimmers, leaf blowers, small tractors, and other equipment. Pesticide sprayers, handlers, and applicators may need additional training that lasts up to 1 year. Large institutional employers such as golf courses, university campuses, and municipalities may supplement on-the-job training with instruction in horticulture, arboriculture, urban forestry, insect and disease diagnosis, tree climbing, or small-engine repair.

Advancement

Grounds maintenance workers who have other qualifications, such as formal education or several years of related experience, may become crew leaders or advance into other supervisory positions. Some workers use their experience to start their own business, such as a landscaping company.

Important Qualities

Ability to work at heights. Tree trimmers and pruners and other grounds maintenance workers must be comfortable working high off the ground when cutting tree limbs and branches.

Communication skills. Grounds maintenance workers must be able to convey information and instructions to clients, customers, and supervisors.

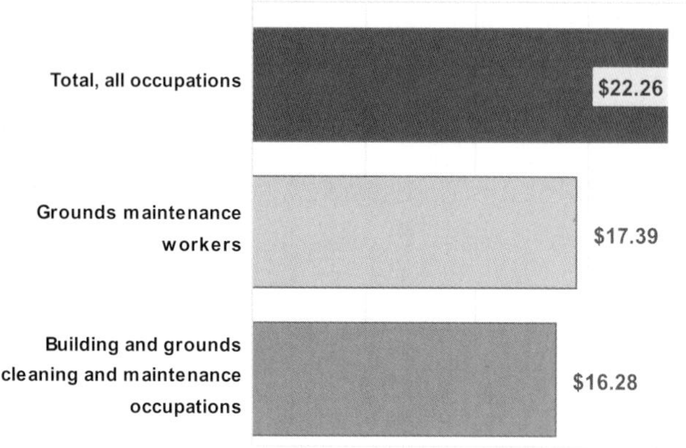

Note: All Occupations includes all occupations in the U.S. Economy. Source: U.S. Bureau of Labor Statistics, Occupational Employment and Wage Statistics.

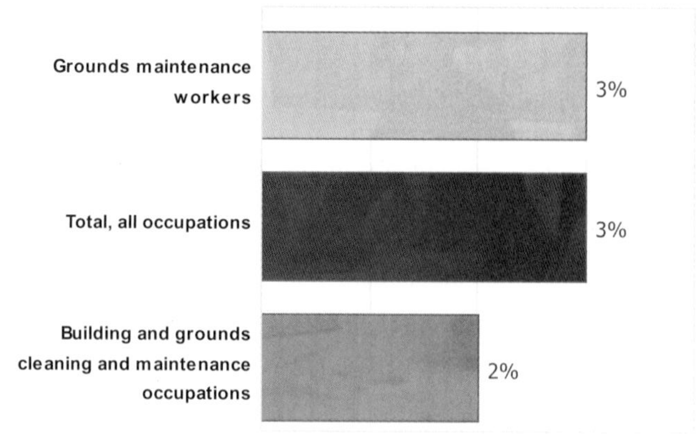

Note: All Occupations includes all occupations in the U.S. Economy. Source: U.S. Bureau of Labor Statistics, Employment Projections program.

Dexterity. Grounds maintenance workers must have good eye, foot, and hand coordination when using dangerous or heavy equipment such as backhoes, mowers, and tractors.

Physical stamina. Grounds maintenance workers must be able to do strenuous labor for long periods of time, occasionally in extreme heat or cold.

Physical strength. These workers may need to be able to lift heavy equipment or supplies.

Self-motivated. Because they often work with little supervision, grounds maintenance workers must be able to do their tasks independently.

Visualization. Grounds maintenance workers must be able to imagine how plants, shrubs, trees, and other landscaping will look before planting or trimming.

Pay

The median hourly wage for grounds maintenance workers was $17.39 in May 2022. The median wage is the wage at which half the workers in an occupation earned more than that amount and half earned less. The lowest 10 percent earned less than $13.32, and the highest 10 percent earned more than $24.20.

Median hourly wages for grounds maintenance workers in May 2022 were as follows:

Tree trimmers and pruners	$22.64
Pesticide handlers, sprayers, and applicators, vegetation	19.93
Grounds maintenance workers, all other	19.00
Landscaping and groundskeeping workers	17.26

In May 2022, the median hourly wages for grounds maintenance workers in the top industries in which they worked were as follows:

Educational services; state, local, and private	$18.72
Services to buildings and dwellings	17.62
Government	17.36
Amusement, gambling, and recreation industries	14.73

Most grounds maintenance workers are full time, and their work schedules may vary. These workers may be busier or work longer hours in the spring, summer, and fall, when planting, mowing, and trimming activities are most frequent.

Some jobs are seasonal. However, grounds maintenance workers sometimes provide other services during the winter months, such as snow removal.

Job Outlook

Overall employment of grounds maintenance workers is projected to grow 3 percent from 2022 to 2032, about as fast as the average for all occupations.

About 170,300 openings for grounds maintenance workers are projected each year, on average, over the decade. Many of those openings are expected to result from the need to replace workers who transfer to different occupations or exit the labor force, such as to retire.

Employment

Landscaping and groundskeeping workers will be needed to keep up with increasing demand for lawn care and landscaping services from homeowners and from large institutions, such as universities and corporate campuses. As communities invest resources in creating more green spaces in urban areas, the demand for ground maintenance workers to plant and maintain these landscapes will increase.

Occupational Title	SOC Code	Employment, 2022	Projected Employment, 2032	Change, 2022-32	
				Percent	Numeric
Grounds maintenance workers	—	1,281,600	1,325,800	3	44,200
Landscaping and groundskeeping workers	37-3011	1,176,100	1,217,900	4	41,700
Pesticide handlers, sprayers, and applicators, vegetation	37-3012	23,200	23,700	2	500
Tree trimmers and pruners	37-3013	66,000	67,600	3	1,700
Grounds maintenance workers, all other	37-3019	16,300	16,600	2	400

Contacts for More Information

For more information, visit

➤ International Society of Arboriculture
➤ Tree Care Industry Association
➤ National Association of Landscape Professionals
➤ Professional Grounds Management Society

Janitors and Building Cleaners

Summary

Quick Facts: Janitors and Building Cleaners	
2022 Median Pay	$31,990 per year $15.38 per hour
Typical Entry-Level Education	No formal educational credential
Work Experience in a Related Occupation	None
On-the-job Training	Short-term on-the-job training
Number of Jobs, 2022	2,382,900
Job Outlook, 2022-32	1% (Little or no change)
Employment Change, 2022-32	29,900

What Janitors and Building Cleaners Do

Janitors and building cleaners keep many types of buildings clean, sanitary, orderly, and in good condition.

Janitors need physical stamina because they spend much of their time on their feet.

Work Environment

Janitors and building cleaners usually work indoors, but they may also work outdoors on tasks such as sweeping walkways or removing snow. Most janitors and building cleaners work full time, although part-time work is common. Work schedules may vary to include evenings, nights, or weekends.

How to Become a Janitor or Building Cleaner

Janitors and building cleaners typically do not need formal education to enter the occupation. However, some employers may require or prefer that workers have a high school diploma or equivalent. Most janitors and building cleaners learn on the job.

Pay

The median hourly wage for janitors and building cleaners was $15.38 in May 2022.

Job Outlook

Employment of janitors and building cleaners is projected to show little or no change from 2022 to 2032.

Despite limited employment growth, about 336,700 openings for janitors and building cleaners are projected each year, on average, over the decade. Most of those openings are expected to result from the need to replace workers who transfer to different occupations or exit the labor force, such as to retire.

What Janitors and Building Cleaners Do

Janitors and building cleaners keep many types of buildings clean, sanitary, orderly, and in good condition.

Duties

Janitors and building cleaners typically do the following:

- Gather and empty trash
- Sweep, mop, or vacuum building floors
- Clean restrooms and stock them with supplies
- Clean spills and other hazards with appropriate equipment
- Wash windows, walls, and glass

Janitors and building cleaners wash windows and glass.

- Clean and disinfect surfaces that are touched frequently
- Order cleaning supplies
- Make minor building repairs
- Notify managers when a building needs major repairs
- Lock doors to secure buildings

Janitors and building cleaners keep office buildings, schools, hospitals, and other places clean, sanitary, and in good condition. Some clean only, while others have a wide range of duties.

In addition to keeping the inside of buildings clean and orderly, some janitors and building cleaners work outdoors. They may do tasks such as mowing lawns, sweeping walkways, and removing snow. Some also monitor the building's heating and cooling system, ensuring that it functions properly.

Janitors and building cleaners use many tools and types of equipment. Simple cleaning tools may include brooms, mops, and rakes. Other tools include sprayers, floor buffers, and snowblowers.

Some janitors are responsible for repairing minor electrical or plumbing problems, such as leaky faucets.

The following are examples of types of janitors and building cleaners:

Building superintendents are responsible for maintaining residential buildings, such as apartments and condominiums. Although their duties are like those of other janitors, some building superintendents also help collect rent and show vacancies to potential tenants.

Janitors and building cleaners usually work indoors, but they may work outdoors on some tasks such as sweeping walkways.

Custodians are janitors or cleaning workers who typically maintain institutional facilities, such as schools and hospitals.

For data on workers who maintain private homes or businesses, such as hotels, see maids and housekeeping cleaners.

Work Environment

Janitors and building cleaners held about 2.4 million jobs in 2022. The largest employers of janitors and building cleaners were as follows:

Services to buildings and dwellings	35%
Elementary and secondary schools; state, local, and private	13
Healthcare and social assistance	7
Self-employed workers	5
Government	5

Janitors and building cleaners usually work indoors, but they may work outdoors on tasks such as sweeping walkways, mowing lawns, and shoveling snow. They spend most of the day walking, standing, or bending while cleaning. They often move or lift heavy supplies and equipment. As a result, the work may be strenuous on the back, arms, and legs. Some tasks, such as cleaning restrooms and trash areas, are dirty or unpleasant.

Injuries and Illnesses

Janitors and building cleaners sometimes get injured on the job. For example, they may suffer sprains or strains from heavy lifting or pain and soreness from repetitive motion. Workers may receive safety and ergonomics training to help minimize these risks.

Work Schedules

Most janitors and building cleaners work full time, but part-time work is common. Work schedules may vary. Because

Most janitors and building cleaners learn on the job. They use many types of tools and equipment, including snowblowers.

office buildings are often cleaned while they are empty, many cleaners work evening hours. When there is a need for 24-hour maintenance, such as in hospitals, cleaners work in shifts that may include nights, weekends, or holidays.

How to Become a Janitor or Building Cleaner

Janitors and building cleaners typically do not need formal education to enter the occupation. However, some employers may require or prefer that workers have a high school diploma or equivalent. Most janitors and building cleaners learn on the job.

Education

Janitors and building cleaners typically do not need a formal educational credential to qualify for entry-level jobs. But for some positions, they may need to have a high school diploma or equivalent.

Elective high school courses, such as in industrial arts, may be helpful for occupations involving repair.

Training

Most janitors and building cleaners learn on the job. Beginners typically work with a more experienced janitor, learning how to use and maintain equipment such as vacuums, floor buffers, and other equipment and tools. They also may learn how to repair minor electrical and plumbing problems.

Licenses, Certifications, and Registrations

Although not required, certification is available through the Building Service Contractors Association International, the ISSA—The International Sanitary Supply Association, and IEHA, a division of ISSA. Certification demonstrates competence and may make applicants more appealing to employers.

Important Qualities

Interpersonal skills. Janitors and building cleaners must interact well other cleaners and the people who live or work in the buildings they service.

Janitors and Building Cleaners

Median hourly wages, May 2022

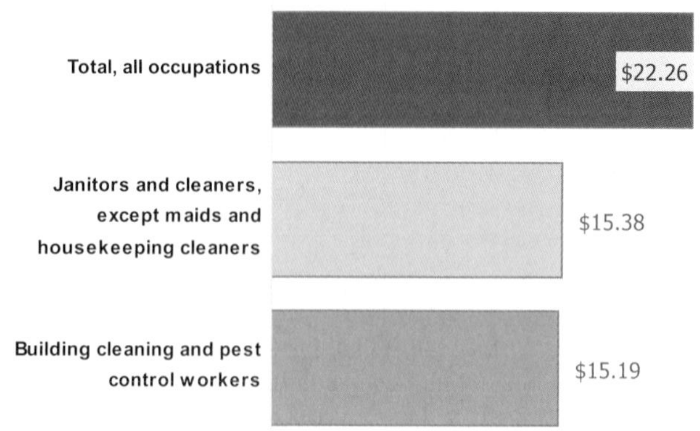

Note: All Occupations includes all occupations in the U.S. Economy.
Source: U.S. Bureau of Labor Statistics, Occupational Employment and Wage Statistics.

Mechanical skills. Janitors and building cleaners need to understand general building operations and should be able to make routine repairs, such as to leaky faucets.

Physical stamina. Janitors and building cleaners spend most of their workday standing to operate cleaning equipment.

Physical strength. Janitors and building cleaners often must lift and move heavy cleaning materials and equipment.

Time-management skills. Janitors and building cleaners must plan and complete tasks in a timely manner.

Pay

The median hourly wage for janitors and building cleaners was $15.38 in May 2022. The median wage is the wage at which half the workers in an occupation earned more than that amount and half earned less. The lowest 10 percent earned less than $11.13, and the highest 10 percent earned more than $22.31.

In May 2022, the median hourly wages for janitors and building cleaners in the top industries in which they worked were as follows:

Government	$19.06
Elementary and secondary schools; state, local, and private	16.85
Healthcare and social assistance	15.67
Services to buildings and dwellings	14.47

Most janitors and building cleaners work full time, although part-time work is common. Work schedules may vary. Because office buildings are often cleaned while they are empty, many cleaners work evening hours. When there is a need for 24-hour maintenance, such as in hospitals, cleaners work in shifts that may include nights, weekends, or holidays.

Job Outlook

Employment of janitors and building cleaners is projected to show little or no change from 2022 to 2032.

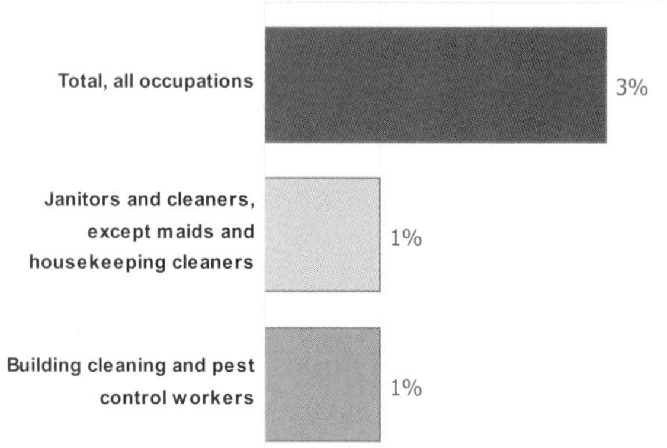

Note: All Occupations includes all occupations in the U.S. Economy.
Source: U.S. Bureau of Labor Statistics, Employment Projections program.

Despite limited employment growth, about 336,700 openings for janitors and building cleaners are projected each year, on average, over the decade. Most of those openings are expected to result from the need to replace workers who transfer to different occupations or exit the labor force, such as to retire.

Employment

The continued need for clean and healthy spaces will support demand for the services that janitors and building cleaners provide. However, this demand will be offset by the increase in remote and hybrid work environments, which will reduce the number of physical office spaces that require regular cleanings and maintenance. In addition, the continued use of hi-tech cleaning methods may limit employment growth for these workers.

Occupational Title	SOC Code	Employment, 2022	Projected Employment, 2032	Change, 2022-32	
				Percent	Numeric
Janitors and cleaners, except maids and housekeeping cleaners	37-2011	2,382,900	2,412,800	1	29,900

Contacts for More Information

For more information about janitors and building cleaners, visit

- ➤ Association of Residential Cleaning Services International (ARSCI)
- ➤ Building Service Contractors Association International (BSCAI)
- ➤ IEHA
- ➤ ISSA-The Worldwide Cleaning Industry Association

Pest Control Workers

Summary

Quick Facts: Pest Control Workers

2022 Median Pay	$38,310 per year $18.42 per hour
Typical Entry-Level Education	High school diploma or equivalent
Work Experience in a Related Occupation	None
On-the-job Training	Moderate-term on-the-job training
Number of Jobs, 2022	95,000
Job Outlook, 2022-32	3% (As fast as average)
Employment Change, 2022-32	3,000

What Pest Control Workers Do

Pest control workers remove insects, rodents, and other pests that infest buildings and surrounding areas.

Work Environment

Pest control workers often kneel, bend, and crawl in tight spaces to inspect sites. Because there are health risks associated with pesticide use, workers are trained in pesticide safety and typically wear protective gear, which may include gloves, goggles, and respirators. Most pest control workers are employed full time. Working evenings and weekends is common.

How to Become a Pest Control Worker

Pest control workers typically need a high school diploma and receive on-the-job training. State laws require pest control workers to be licensed.

Pest control workers determine the type of treatment needed to eliminate pests.

Pay

The median annual wage for pest control workers was $38,310 in May 2022.

Job Outlook

Employment of pest control workers is projected to grow 3 percent from 2022 to 2032, about as fast as the average for all occupations.

About 12,600 openings for pest control workers are projected each year, on average, over the decade. Many of those openings are expected to result from the need to replace workers who transfer to different occupations or exit the labor force, such as to retire.

What Pest Control Workers Do

Pest control workers remove unwanted pests, such as roaches, rodents, ants, and termites, that infest buildings and surrounding areas.

Duties

Pest control workers typically do the following:

- Inspect buildings and premises for signs of pests or infestation
- Determine the type of treatment needed to eliminate pests
- Measure the dimensions of the area needing treatment
- Estimate the cost of their services
- Use baits and set traps to remove, control, or eliminate pests
- Apply pesticides in and around buildings and other structures
- Design and carry out pest management plans
- Drive trucks equipped with power spraying equipment
- Create barriers to prevent pests from entering a building

Unwanted pests that infest buildings and surrounding areas are a nuisance and may pose health and safety risks to occupants. Pest control workers control, manage, and remove these creatures from apartments, homes, offices, and other structures in a way that does not harm inhabitants and maintains the structural integrity of buildings.

Pest control workers inspect a building and its premises for signs of pests.

To design and carry out integrated pest management plans, pest control workers must know the identity and biology of a wide range of pests. They also must know the best ways to control and remove the pests.

Although certain rodents and insects, such as mice and termites, are among the most common pests, some pest control workers also remove birds, squirrels, and other wildlife from homes and buildings.

Pest control workers' position titles and job duties often vary by state.

The following are examples of types of pest control workers:

Pest control technicians are usually entry-level workers who identify potential and actual pest problems, conduct inspections, and design control strategies. They work directly with customers and use a limited range of pesticides.

Applicators use a wide range of pesticides and may specialize in an area of pest control:

- Termite control workers may use chemicals or baiting techniques and modify structures to eliminate termites and prevent future infestations. Some also repair structural damage caused by termites and build barriers to separate pests from their food source.
- Fumigators use gases, called fumigants, to treat specific kinds of pests or large-scale infestations. Fumigators seal all or part of an infested building before using hoses to fill the structure with fumigants. They post warning signs to keep people from going into the fumigated area and monitor it closely to detect and stop leaks.

Work Environment

Pest control workers held about 95,000 jobs in 2022. The largest employers of pest control workers were as follows:

Exterminating and pest control services	91%
Self-employed workers	3

Pest control workers must travel to a client's home or business. They work both indoors and outdoors, in all types of weather.

Injuries and Illnesses

Pest control workers have one of the highest rates of injuries and illnesses of all occupations. These workers are susceptible to strains and sprains because they may need to kneel, bend, and crawl in tight spaces. In addition, some pesticides are toxic and may be harmful to humans, so workers must take precautions when using such chemicals.

All pesticide products are reviewed and approved by the Environmental Protection Agency (EPA) and workers must follow label directions. Pest control workers are trained and licensed for pesticide use and must wear protective equipment, including gloves, goggles, and respirators, to reduce the risk of harm.

Pest control workers must travel to a client's home or business.

Work Schedules

Most pest control workers are employed full time. Working evenings and weekends is common. Some work more than 40 hours per week.

How to Become a Pest Control Worker

Pest control workers typically need a high school diploma and receive on-the-job training. State laws require pest control workers to be licensed.

State laws require pest control workers to be licensed.

Many pest control companies require that employees have a driver's license and a good driving record.

Education

Pest control workers typically need high school diploma or equivalent to enter the occupation. Employers may consider experienced candidates for some pest control jobs.

Training

Most pest control workers begin as technicians, typically receiving on-the-job training. They often study specialties such as rodent control, termite control, and fumigation. Technicians also must complete general training in pesticide use and safety. Pest control training can usually be completed in less than 3 months.

After completing training, workers are qualified to provide pest control services. Because pest control methods change, workers often attend continuing education classes.

Licenses, Certifications, and Registrations

Most states require pest control workers to be licensed. Licensure requirements vary by state, but workers usually must complete training and pass an exam. Some states have additional requirements, such as having a high school diploma or equivalent. States may have additional requirements for applicators. Check with your state regulatory agency for more information.

Advancement

Pest control workers typically advance as they gain experience. For example, applicators who have several years of experience may become supervisors. Some workers start their own pest management business.

Important Qualities

Bookkeeping skills. Pest control workers must keep accurate records of the hours they work, chemicals they use, and payments they collect. Self-employed workers, in particular, need these skills in order to run their business.

Customer-service skills. Pest control workers should be friendly and polite when they interact with customers at their homes or businesses.

Detail oriented. Because pest control workers apply potentially toxic chemicals, they must be able to follow instructions precisely to prevent harm to residents, pets, the environment, and themselves.

Physical stamina. Pest control workers may spend hours standing, bending, kneeling, or crawling. They also must be able to withstand uncomfortable conditions, such as summer heat in attics and winter cold in crawl spaces.

Pay

The median annual wage for pest control workers was $38,310 in May 2022. The median wage is the wage at which half

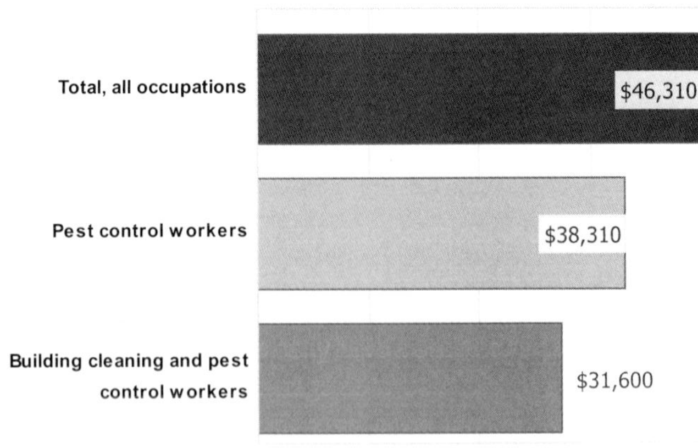

Note: All Occupations includes all occupations in the U.S. Economy.
Source: U.S. Bureau of Labor Statistics, Occupational Employment and Wage Statistics.

the workers in an occupation earned more than that amount and half earned less. The lowest 10 percent earned less than $29,250, and the highest 10 percent earned more than $58,970.

In May 2022, the median annual wages for pest control workers in the top industries in which they worked were as follows:

Exterminating and pest control services $38,160

Most pest control workers are employed full time. Working evenings and weekends is common. Some work more than 40 hours per week.

Job Outlook

Employment of pest control workers is projected to grow 3 percent from 2022 to 2032, about as fast as the average for all occupations.

About 12,600 openings for pest control workers are projected each year, on average, over the decade. Many of those openings are expected to result from the need to replace workers who

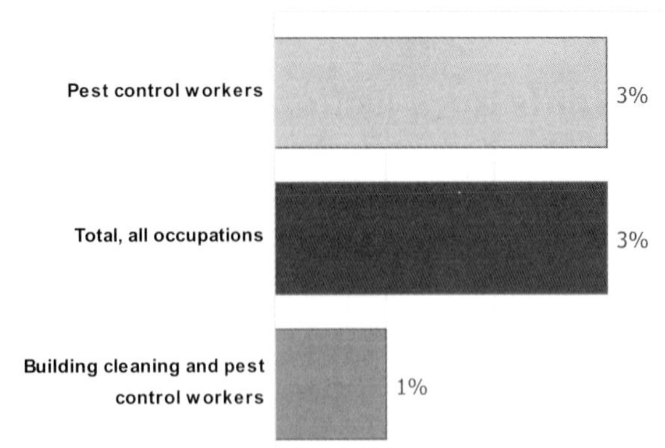

Note: All Occupations includes all occupations in the U.S. Economy.
Source: U.S. Bureau of Labor Statistics, Employment Projections program.

transfer to different occupations or exit the labor force, such as to retire.

Employment

The growing number of invasive insect species, such as stink bugs, is expected to create demand for pest control services. Although some people may choose to control pests themselves, many prefer to hire professional pest control services.

Occupational Title	SOC Code	Employment, 2022	Projected Employment, 2032	Change, 2022-32	
				Percent	Numeric
Pest control workers	37-2021	95,000	98,000	3	3,000

Contacts for More Information

For more information, visit

➤ National Pest Management Association (NPMA)

Business and Financial

Accountants and Auditors

Summary

Quick Facts: Accountants and Auditors	
2022 Median Pay	$78,000 per year $37.50 per hour
Typical Entry-Level Education	Bachelor's degree
Work Experience in a Related Occupation	None
On-the-job Training	None
Number of Jobs, 2022	1,538,400
Job Outlook, 2022-32	4% (As fast as average)
Employment Change, 2022-32	67,400

What Accountants and Auditors Do

Accountants and auditors prepare and examine financial records.

Work Environment

Most accountants and auditors work full time. Overtime hours are typical at certain periods of the year, such as for quarterly audits or during tax season.

How to Become an Accountant or Auditor

A bachelor's degree in accounting or a related field is typically required to become an accountant or auditor. Completing certification in a specific field of accounting, such as becoming a licensed Certified Public Accountant (CPA), may improve job prospects.

Pay

The median annual wage for accountants and auditors was $78,000 in May 2022.

Job Outlook

Employment of accountants and auditors is projected to grow 4 percent from 2022 to 2032, about as fast as the average for all occupations.

About 126,500 openings for accountants and auditors are projected each year, on average, over the decade. Many of those openings are expected to result from the need to replace workers who transfer to different occupations or exit the labor force, such as to retire.

What Accountants and Auditors Do

Accountants and auditors prepare and examine financial records, identify potential areas of opportunity and risk, and provide solutions for businesses and individuals. They ensure that financial records are accurate, that financial and data risks are evaluated, and that taxes are paid properly. They also assess financial operations and work to help ensure that organizations run efficiently.

Duties

Accountants and auditors typically do the following:

- Examine financial statements to ensure that they are accurate and comply with laws and regulations
- Compute taxes owed, prepare tax returns, and ensure that taxes are paid properly and on time

Accountants and auditors ensure that financial records are accurate and taxes are paid properly and on time.

Accountants and auditors examine financial statements for accuracy and conformance with laws.

- Inspect account books and accounting systems for efficiency and use of accepted accounting procedures and identify potential risks for fraud
- Organize, analyze, and maintain financial records
- Assess financial operations, identify risks and challenges, and make best-practices recommendations to management
- Suggest ways to reduce costs, enhance revenues, and improve profits

Accountants and auditors may use technology, such as artificial intelligence (AI) and robotics process automation, to increase their productivity. Automating some routine tasks makes these workers more efficient by allowing them to focus on analysis and other high-level responsibilities.

In addition to examining and preparing financial documents, accountants and auditors must explain their findings. This includes preparing written reports and meeting face-to-face with organization managers and individual clients.

Many accountants and auditors specialize, depending on their employer. Some work for organizations that specialize in assurance services (improving the quality or context of information for decision makers) or risk management (determining the probability of a misstatement on financial documents). Other organizations specialize in specific industries, such as finance, insurance, or healthcare.

The following are examples of types of accountants and auditors:

Government accountants maintain and examine the records of government agencies and audit private businesses and individuals whose activities are subject to government regulations or taxation. Accountants employed by federal, state, and local governments ensure that revenues are received and spent according to laws and regulations. Their responsibilities include auditing, financial reporting, and management accounting.

Management accountants are also called *cost, corporate, industrial, managerial*, or *private accountants*. They combine accounting and financial information to guide business decision making. They also understand financial and nonfinancial data and how to integrate information. The information that management accountants prepare is intended for internal use by business managers, not for the public.

Management accountants often prepare budgets and evaluate performance. They also may help organizations plan the cost of doing business. Some work with financial managers on asset management, which involves planning and selecting financial investments such as stocks, bonds, and real estate.

Public accountants have a broad range of accounting, auditing, tax, and consulting tasks. Their clients include corporations, governments, individuals, and nonprofits.

Public accountants work with financial documents that clients are required by law to disclose, such as tax forms and financial statements that corporations must provide to current and potential investors. Some public accountants concentrate on tax matters, advising corporations about the tax advantages of certain business decisions or preparing individual income tax returns.

Other public accountants specialize in forensic accounting, investigating financial crimes such as securities fraud and embezzlement, bankruptcies and contract disputes, and other complex and potentially criminal financial transactions. Forensic accountants combine their knowledge of accounting and finance with law and investigative techniques to determine if an activity is illegal. Many forensic accountants work closely with law enforcement personnel and lawyers during investigations and often appear as expert witnesses during trials.

Still others work with individuals, advising them on important personal financial matters. These public accountants combine their expertise in data management, economics, financial planning, and tax law to develop strategies for their clients. Advisory services cover topics including cash flow, insurance, investment, retirement, and wealth transfer planning to help clients meet financial goals, such as retirement, paying for a child's education, or buying a home.

Public accountants, many of whom are Certified Public Accountants (CPAs), generally have their own businesses or work for public accounting firms. Publicly traded companies are required to have CPAs sign documents they submit to the Securities and Exchange Commission (SEC), including annual and quarterly reports.

External auditors check for proper management of an organization's funds, sources of revenue, and internal controls, such as financial data preparation or managing risks to cybersecurity or the supply chain. They are employed by an outside organization, rather than the one they are auditing. They review clients' financial statements and inform authorities, investors, and regulators that the statements have been correctly prepared and reported with no material misstatements.

Information technology (IT) auditors review controls for their organization's IT systems to ensure that both financial and nonfinancial data come from a reliable source.

Internal auditors have duties that are similar to external auditors, but these workers are employed by the organization they are auditing. They identify ways to improve the processes for finding and eliminating waste, fraud, and other financial risks to the organization. The practice of internal auditing is not regulated, but the Institute of Internal Auditors (IIA) provides generally accepted standards.

Work Environment

Accountants and auditors held about 1.5 million jobs in 2022. The largest employers of accountants and auditors were as follows:

Accounting, tax preparation, bookkeeping, and payroll services	23%
Finance and insurance	8

Most accountants and auditors work full time.

Government	8
Management of companies and enterprises	6
Self-employed workers	4

Most accountants and auditors work in offices, but some work from home. Although accountants and auditors usually work in teams, some work alone. Accountants and auditors may travel to their clients' places of business.

Work Schedules

Most accountants and auditors work full time. Longer periods of work are typical at certain times of the year, such as for quarterly audits or during tax season.

How to Become an Accountant or Auditor

Accountants and auditors typically need at least a bachelor's degree in accounting or a related field to enter the occupation. Completing certification in a specific field of accounting, such as becoming a licensed Certified Public Accountant (CPA), may improve job prospects.

Most accountants and auditors need at least a bachelor's degree in accounting or a related field.

Education

Accountants and auditors typically need a bachelor's degree in accounting or a related field, such as business. Some employers prefer to hire applicants who have a master's degree, either in accounting or in business administration with a concentration in accounting.

Some universities and colleges offer specialized programs for a bachelor's or master's degree, such as in accounting, forensic accounting, internal auditing, or tax accounting. In some cases, those with an associate's degree, as well as bookkeepers, accounting, and auditing clerks who meet the education and experience requirements set by their employers, may get junior accounting positions and advance by showing their accounting skills on the job.

Students may gain practical experience through internships with public accounting or business firms.

Licenses, Certifications, and Registrations

Any accountant who files a report with the Securities and Exchange Commission (SEC) is required to be a licensed Certified Public Accountant (CPA). Other accountants choose to become a CPA to enhance their job prospects or to gain clients. Employers may pay the costs associated with the CPA exam.

CPAs are licensed by their state's Board of Accountancy. Becoming a CPA requires passing a national exam and meeting other state requirements. All states require CPA candidates to complete 150 semester hours of college coursework to be licensed, which is 30 hours more than the usual 4-year bachelor's degree. Many schools offer a 5-year combined bachelor's and master's degree to meet the 150-hour requirement, but a master's degree is not required.

A few states allow a number of years of public accounting experience to substitute for a college degree.

All states use the four-part Uniform CPA Examination from the American Institute of Certified Public Accountants (AICPA). Candidates do not have to pass all four parts at once, but most states require that candidates pass all four parts within 18 months of passing their first part.

All states require CPAs to take continuing education courses, including ethics, to maintain their license.

Certification provides an advantage in the job market because it shows professional competence in a specialized field of accounting and auditing. Accountants and auditors seek certifications from a variety of professional societies. Some of the most common certifications are listed below:

The AICPA offers several designations. For accountants with a CPA, the AICPA offers the Accredited in Business Valuation (ABV), Certified Financial Forensics (CFF), Certified Information Technology Professional (CITP), and Personal Financial Specialist (PFS) certifications. All of these credentials require experience in the related area, continuing education, and passing an exam.

AICPA and the Chartered Institute of Management Accountants (CIMA) developed the Chartered Global Management Accountant (CGMA) designation as an internationally recognized professional credential. Candidates must complete a program, pass an exam, and meet a requirement for work experience.

The Association of Government Accountants (AGA) offers the Certified Government Financial Manager (CGFM) credential to accountants or auditors working with federal, state, or local government. To earn this certification, candidates must have a bachelor's degree from an accredited college or university, pass examinations, and have professional-level experience in government financial management. To keep the certification, CGFMs must complete continuing professional education.

The Institute of Internal Auditors (IIA) offers the Certified Internal Auditor (CIA) credential to graduates from accredited colleges and universities who have work experience as internal auditors and have passed an exam. The IIA also offers the Certified in Control Self-Assessment (CCSA), Certified Government Auditing Professional (CGAP), Certified Financial Services Auditor (CFSA), and Certification in Risk Management Assurance (CRMA) to those who pass the exams and meet educational and experience requirements.

The Institute of Management Accountants (IMA) offers the Certified Management Accountant (CMA) to applicants who complete a bachelor's degree. Applicants must have work experience in management accounting, pass an exam, agree to meet continuing education requirements, and comply with standards of professional conduct.

ISACA offers the Certified Information Systems Auditor (CISA) to candidates who pass an exam and have work experience auditing information systems. Information systems experience, financial or operational auditing experience, or related college credit hours may be substituted for some of the experience required in information systems auditing, control, or security.

Advancement

Some top executives and financial managers have a background in accounting, internal auditing, or finance.

Entry-level public accountants may advance to senior positions as they gain experience and take on more responsibility. Those who excel may become supervisors, managers, or partners; open their own public accounting firm; or transfer to executive positions in management accounting or internal auditing in private firms.

Management accountants often start as cost accountants, junior internal auditors, or trainees for other accounting positions. As they rise through the organization, they may advance to become accounting managers, budget directors, chief cost accountants, or managers of internal auditing. Some become controllers, treasurers, financial vice presidents, chief financial officers, or corporation presidents.

Public accountants, management accountants, and internal auditors may move from one type of accounting and auditing to another. Public accountants often move into management accounting or internal auditing. Management accountants may become internal auditors, and internal auditors may become management accountants. However, it is less common for management accountants or internal auditors to move into public accounting.

Important Qualities

Analytical and critical-thinking skills. Accountants and auditors must be able to critically evaluate data, identify issues in documentation, and suggest solutions. For example, internal auditors might detect fraudulent use of funds, and public accountants may work to minimize tax liability.

Communication skills. Accountants and auditors must be able to listen to and discuss facts and concerns from clients, managers, and other stakeholders. They must also be able to discuss the results of their work both in meetings and in written reports.

Detail oriented. Accountants and auditors must pay attention to detail when compiling and examining documents.

Math skills. Accountants and auditors must be able to analyze, compare, and interpret facts and figures. They may use advanced math skills, such as calculus and statistical analysis, for these tasks.

Organizational skills. Strong organizational skills are important for accountants and auditors, who often work with a range of financial documents for a variety of clients.

Pay

The median annual wage for accountants and auditors was $78,000 in May 2022. The median wage is the wage at which half the workers in an occupation earned more than that

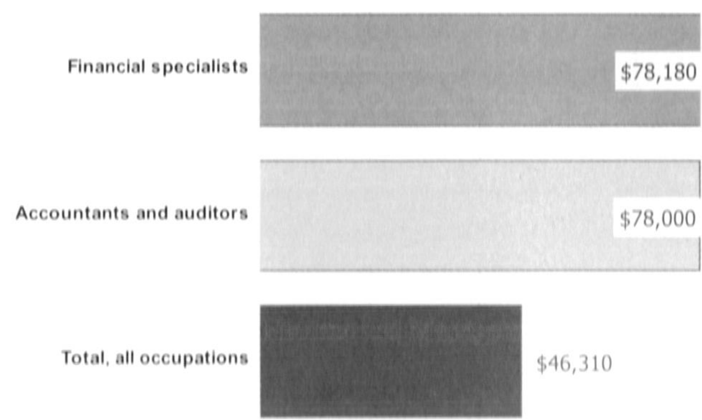

Note: All Occupations includes all occupations in the U.S. Economy.
Source: U.S. Bureau of Labor Statistics, Occupational Employment and Wage Statistics.

amount and half earned less. The lowest 10 percent earned less than $48,560, and the highest 10 percent earned more than $132,690.

In May 2022, the median annual wages for accountants and auditors in the top industries in which they worked were as follows:

Finance and insurance	$81,020
Management of companies and enterprises	80,260
Accounting, tax preparation, bookkeeping, and payroll services	78,320
Government	77,440

Most accountants and auditors work full time. Longer hours are typical at certain times of the year, such as for quarterly audits or during tax season.

Job Outlook

Employment of accountants and auditors is projected to grow 4 percent from 2022 to 2032, about as fast as the average for all occupations.

About 126,500 openings for accountants and auditors are projected each year, on average, over the decade. Many of those openings are expected to result from the need to replace workers who transfer to different occupations or exit the labor force, such as to retire.

Employment

Globalization, a growing economy, and a complex tax and regulatory environment are expected to continue leading the strong demand for accountants and auditors.

In general, employment growth of accountants and auditors is expected to be closely tied to the health of the overall economy. As the economy grows, these workers will continue being needed to prepare and examine financial records. In addition, as more companies go public, there will be greater need for public accountants to handle the legally required financial documentation.

The continued globalization of business may lead to increased demand for accounting expertise and services related to international trade and international mergers and acquisitions.

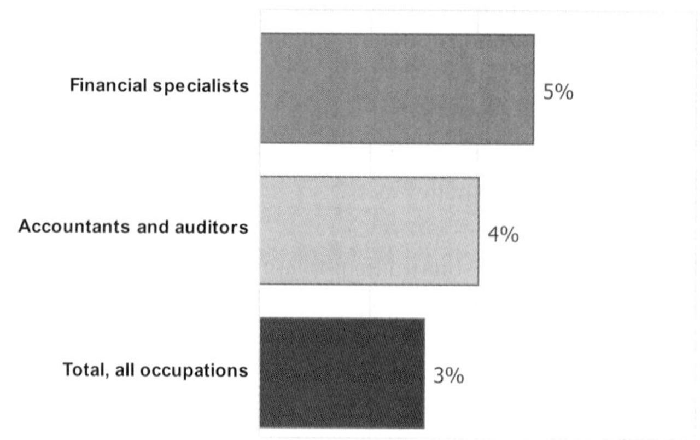

Note: All Occupations includes all occupations in the U.S. Economy.
Source: U.S. Bureau of Labor Statistics, Employment Projections program.

Technological change is expected to affect the role of accountants over the projections decade. Some routine accounting tasks may be automated as platforms such as cloud computing, artificial intelligence (AI), and blockchain become more widespread. Although it will increase accountants' efficiency, this change is not expected to reduce overall demand. The automation of routine tasks, such as data entry, will instead make accountants' advisory and analytical duties more prominent.

Occupational Title	SOC Code	Employment, 2022	Projected Employment, 2032	Change, 2022-32	
				Percent	Numeric
Accountants and auditors	13-2011	1,538,400	1,605,800	4	67,400

Contacts for More Information

For more information, visit

- AACSB
- American Institute of Certified Public Accountants (AICPA)
- Association of Government Accountants (AGA)
- Institute of Management Accountants
- The Institute of Internal Auditors
- ISACA
- Global Academy of Finance and Management

Appraisers and Assessors—Property

Summary

Quick Facts: Property Appraisers and Assessors	
2022 Median Pay	$61,560 per year $29.60 per hour
Typical Entry-Level Education	Bachelor's degree
Work Experience in a Related Occupation	None
On-the-job Training	Long-term on-the-job training
Number of Jobs, 2022	77,600
Job Outlook, 2022-32	5% (Faster than average)
Employment Change, 2022-32	3,600

What Property Appraisers and Assessors Do

Property appraisers and assessors provide a value estimate on real estate and on tangible personal and business property.

Work Environment

Although property appraisers and assessors work in offices, they may spend a large part of their time conducting site visits. Most work full time, and some work more than 40 hours per week.

How to Become a Property Appraiser or Assessor

Property appraisers and assessors typically need a bachelor's degree, although educational requirements vary. Appraisers of real estate must meet state licensure or certification requirements.

Pay

The median annual wage for property appraisers and assessors was $61,560 in May 2022.

Job Outlook

Employment of property appraisers and assessors is projected to grow 5 percent from 2022 to 2032, faster than the average for all occupations.

About 6,900 openings for property appraisers and assessors are projected each year, on average, over the decade. Many of those openings are expected to result from the need to replace workers who transfer to different occupations or exit the labor force, such as to retire.

Appraisers and assessors prepare current data before visiting properties.

What Property Appraisers and Assessors Do

Property appraisers and assessors provide a value estimate on real estate and tangible personal and business property.

Duties

Property appraisers and assessors typically do the following:

- Verify descriptions of property, such as by consulting public records
- Inspect property, noting its characteristics
- Photograph items or real estate
- Analyze "comparables," or similar items or properties, to help provide values
- Prepare written reports on property values
- Prepare and maintain current data on each real estate property or other tangible asset

Property appraisers and assessors work in localities or with items that they are familiar with so that they know any factors that may affect the property's value.

Appraisers of personal and business property estimate the value of items such as jewelry, art, antiques, collectibles, and equipment. They prepare reports for their clients of the fair market value, replacement cost, or liquidation at a given point for personal and business property.

When appraising personal and business property, these workers may use a variety of tools or resources to estimate its value. These include software, internet searches, or personal records of the actual cost to replace the item and estimates of the property income projected to be generated.

Appraisers of real estate estimate the value of land and buildings, usually before these assets are sold, mortgaged, taxed, insured, or developed. They typically value one property

Appraisers and assessors estimate the value of property.

at a time, and they often specialize in a certain type of real estate:

- Commercial appraisers specialize in income-producing properties, such as office buildings, hotels, and stores.
- Residential appraisers focus on appraising properties in which people live, such as single unit homes and condominiums. They appraise only properties that house one to four units.

When evaluating a property's value, appraisers note the characteristics of the property and surrounding area, such as its view or a noisy highway nearby. They also consider the overall condition of a building, including its foundation and roof or any renovations that may have been done. Appraisers photograph the outside of the building and some of the interior features to document its condition. After visiting the property, the appraiser analyzes the property relative to comparable home sales, including lease records, location, view, previous appraisals, and income potential. During the entire process, appraisers record their research, observations, and methods used in providing an estimate of the property's value.

Assessors of real estate value properties for property tax assessments. Most work for local governments. Unlike appraisers, who generally focus on one property at a time, assessors often value an entire neighborhood of homes at once by using mass appraisal techniques and computer-assisted appraisal systems.

Assessors must be up to date on tax assessment procedures. Taxpayers sometimes challenge the assessed value because they feel they are being charged too much for property tax. Assessors must be able to defend the accuracy of their property assessments, either to the owner directly or at a public hearing.

Assessors also keep a database of every property in their jurisdiction, identifying the property owner, assessment history, and characteristics of the property, as well as property maps detailing the property distribution of the jurisdiction.

Work Environment

Property appraisers and assessors held about 77,600 jobs in 2022. The largest employers of property appraisers and assessors were as follows:

Local government, excluding education and hospitals	36%
Real estate	23
Self-employed workers	20
Finance and insurance	8

Although property appraisers and assessors work in offices, they may spend a large part of their time conducting site visits. Time spent away from the office depends on the specialty. For example, residential appraisers work in offices less often than do commercial appraisers, who might spend several weeks analyzing information and writing reports about a single property. Appraisers employed by banks and mortgage companies generally work in an office, making site visits only when necessary.

Appraisers and assessors research data on property and write reports.

Work Schedules

Most property appraisers and assessors work full time, and some work more than 40 hours per week. Self-employed appraisers, often called *independent fee appraisers*, may work more than 40 hours per week.

How to Become a Property Appraiser or Assessor

The requirements to become a fully qualified property appraiser or assessor are complex and vary by state and, sometimes, by the value or type of property. These workers typically need a bachelor's degree, although some qualify with a high school diploma. Appraisers of real estate also must meet state licensure or certification requirements. Check with your state's licensing board for specific requirements.

Education

Although requirements vary, property appraisers and assessors typically need a bachelor's degree. Common fields of degree include business, social science, and psychology.

Assessors and appraisers tend to take the same courses for certification.

College courses in subjects such as computer science, finance, and business or real estate law may be useful for prospective appraisers and assessors.

Most states set education and experience requirements that assessors must meet in order to practice. A few states have no statewide requirements; instead, each locality sets the standards. In some localities, candidates may qualify with a high school diploma.

Training

Employers may require new workers to take basic appraisal courses and complete on-the-job training that lasts 12 months or more. Appraisers and assessors also may need to work enough hours to meet requirements for licensing or certification.

Licenses, Certifications, and Registrations

Federal law requires appraisers of real estate to have a state license or certification when working on federally related transactions, such as appraisals for loans made by federally insured banks and financial institutions. The Appraisal Foundation (TAF) offers information on appraisal licensing. There is no such federal requirement for appraisers of personal and business property or for assessors, although some states require certification. For state-specific requirements, applicants should contact their state licensing board.

Real estate appraisers usually value one property at a time, while assessors value many at once. However, both occupations use similar methods and techniques. As a result, assessors and appraisers often take the same courses for certification. In addition to passing a statewide examination, candidates must usually complete a set number of on-the-job hours.

The credential level determines what type of property a real estate appraiser may value. There are four federal appraiser classifications: Licensed Trainee Appraiser, Licensed Residential Appraiser, Certified Residential Appraiser, and Certified General Appraiser.

Each credential requires different education and training to complete. All of them except for the Trainee License also require that candidates receive instruction on the Uniform Standards of Professional Appraisal Practice and pass an exam.

The American Society of Appraisers (ASA) offers information on professional appraisers representing all disciplines: Appraisal Review and Management, Business Valuation, Gems and Jewelry, Machinery and Technical Specialties, Personal Property and Real Property.

Unlike appraisers of real estate, neither appraisers of personal and business property nor assessors have federal requirements for certification. In states that mandate certification for assessors, the requirements are usually similar to those for appraisers. For example, the International Association of Assessing Officers (IAAO) offers the Certified Assessment Evaluator (CAE) credential covering topics such as property valuation, assessment administration, and property tax policy.

In states that do not require certification for assessors, employers may require candidates to take basic appraisal courses, complete on-the-job training, and meet the work-hours requirements for appraisal licenses or certificates. Assessors also may get a state appraiser license or credential.

Both appraisers and assessors must take continuing education courses to keep their license or certification. Requirements vary by state and credential.

Important Qualities

Analytical skills. Property appraisers and assessors use many sources of data when estimating values. As a result, they must research and evaluate all factors before determining their estimate and producing a final report.

Customer-service skills. Because appraisers regularly interact with clients, being polite and friendly is important.

Math skills. Analyzing real estate data for valuation requires making calculations, such as square footage of land and building space, so workers must have good math skills.

Organizational skills. To successfully accomplish tasks related to appraising and assessing property, these workers need to keep good records and be methodical in completing their tasks.

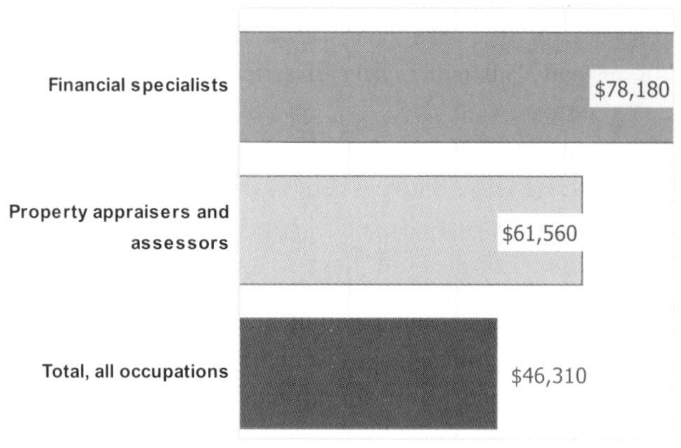

Note: All Occupations includes all occupations in the U.S. Economy. Source: U.S. Bureau of Labor Statistics, Occupational Employment and Wage Statistics.

Problem-solving skills. Appraising or assessing a property's value may involve unexpected problems. The ability to develop and apply alternative solutions is crucial to successfully completing the appraisal and report on time.

Time-management skills. Property appraisers and assessors often work under time constraints, sometimes appraising many properties in a single day. As a result, managing their workloads to meet deadlines is important.

Pay

The median annual wage for property appraisers and assessors was $61,560 in May 2022. The median wage is the wage at which half the workers in an occupation earned more than that amount and half earned less. The lowest 10 percent earned less than $35,700, and the highest 10 percent earned more than $117,600.

In May 2022, the median annual wages for property appraisers and assessors in the top industries in which they worked were as follows:

Finance and insurance	$77,850
Local government, excluding education and hospitals	59,880
Real estate	57,870

Earnings for independent fee appraisers can vary significantly because they are paid fees on the basis of each appraisal.

Most property appraisers and assessors work full time, and some work more than 40 hours per week. Self-employed appraisers, often called *independent fee appraisers*, may be especially likely to work more than 40 hours per week.

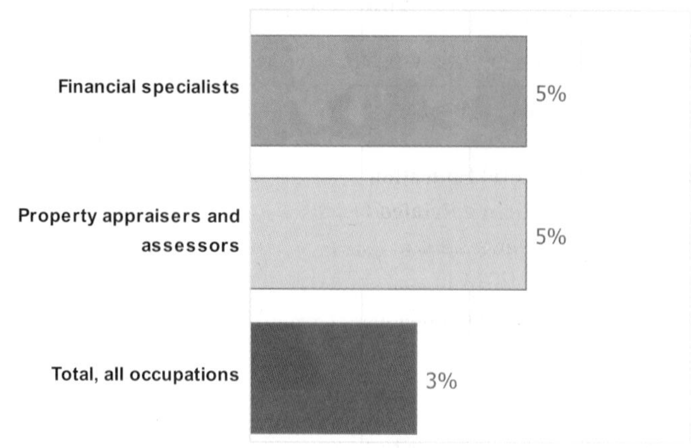

Note: All Occupations includes all occupations in the U.S. Economy. Source: U.S. Bureau of Labor Statistics, Employment Projections program.

Job Outlook

Employment of property appraisers and assessors is projected to grow 5 percent from 2022 to 2032, faster than the average for all occupations.

About 6,900 openings for property appraisers and assessors are projected each year, on average, over the decade. Many of those openings are expected to result from the need to replace workers who transfer to different occupations or exit the labor force, such as to retire.

Employment

Demand for appraisal services is linked to the real estate market, which may fluctuate in the short term. Over the projections decade, employment growth will be driven by economic expansion; the need for business valuations; and general demand for residential, personal, and other properties. Productivity may rise with greater use of mobile technology and automated valuation models, which enable workers to appraise and assess properties more efficiently.

Occupational Title	SOC Code	Employment, 2022	Projected Employment, 2032	Change, 2022-32	
				Percent	Numeric
Property appraisers and assessors	13-2020	77,600	81,100	5	3,600

Contacts for More Information

For more information about property appraisers, visit

- American Society of Appraisers
- Appraisal Institute
- International Association of Assessing Officers
- The Appraisal Foundation

Budget Analysts

Summary

Quick Facts: Budget Analysts	
2022 Median Pay	$82,260 per year $39.55 per hour
Typical Entry-Level Education	Bachelor's degree
Work Experience in a Related Occupation	None
On-the-job Training	None
Number of Jobs, 2022	51,600
Job Outlook, 2022-32	3% (As fast as average)
Employment Change, 2022-32	1,700

What Budget Analysts Do

Budget analysts help public and private organizations plan their finances.

Work Environment

Budget analysts work in government agencies, private companies, and universities. Most work full time.

How to Become a Budget Analyst

Budget analysts typically need a bachelor's degree to enter the occupation. Courses in accounting, economics, and statistics are helpful.

Pay

The median annual wage for budget analysts was $82,260 in May 2022.

Job Outlook

Employment of budget analysts is projected to grow 3 percent from 2022 to 2032, about as fast as the average for all occupations.

About 3,600 openings for budget analysts are projected each year, on average, over the decade. Many of those openings are expected to result from the need to replace workers who transfer to different occupations or exit the labor force, such as to retire.

Budget analysts help public and private institutions organize their finances.

What Budget Analysts Do

Budget analysts help public and private organizations plan their finances. They prepare budget reports and monitor organizational spending.

Duties

Budget analysts typically do the following:

- Work with program and project managers to develop the organization's budget
- Review managers' budget proposals and funding requests for completeness, accuracy, and compliance with laws and other regulations
- Combine program and department budgets into a consolidated organizational budget
- Explain funding requests to others in the organization, to legislators, and to the public
- Help top managers analyze proposed plans and find alternatives if the projected results are unsatisfactory
- Monitor organizational spending to ensure that it is within budget
- Inform program managers of the status and availability of funds
- Estimate future financial needs

Budget analysts advise organizations—including governments, private companies, and universities—about the details of their finances. They prepare annual and special reports and evaluate budget proposals. They analyze data to determine the costs and benefits of various programs, and they recommend funding levels based on their findings. Although government officials or top executives in a private company usually decide on an

Budget analysts prepare budget reports and monitor spending.

organization's budget, they rely on the work of budget analysts to prepare the information for that decision.

Sometimes, budget analysts use cost–benefit analyses to review financial requests, assess program tradeoffs, and explore alternative funding methods. Budget analysts also may examine past budgets and research economic and financial developments that affect the organization's income and expenditures. Budget analysts may recommend cutting spending on particular programs or redistributing funds.

Throughout the year, budget analysts oversee spending to ensure that organizations comply with the budget and to determine whether certain programs need changes in funding. Analysts also evaluate programs to determine whether they are producing desired results.

In addition to providing technical analysis, budget analysts must communicate their recommendations effectively within the organization. For example, if there is a difference between the approved budget and actual spending, budget analysts may write a report explaining those discrepancies and recommend changes to reconcile them.

Budget analysts working in government may attend committee hearings to explain their recommendations to legislators. Occasionally, budget analysts evaluate how well a program is doing, assess policy, and draft budget-related legislation.

Work Environment

Budget analysts held about 51,600 jobs in 2022. The largest employers of budget analysts were as follows:

Employer	Percent
Federal government	24%
Educational services; state, local, and private	14
State government, excluding education and hospitals	11
Local government, excluding education and hospitals	10
Professional, scientific, and technical services	9

Budget analysts work in a variety of settings including government agencies, universities, and companies.

Although budget analysts usually work in offices, they may travel to get budget details firsthand or to verify funding allocations.

Work Schedules

Most budget analysts work full time, and overtime is sometimes required during development, mid-year, and final reviews of budgets. The pressures of deadlines and tight work schedules may be stressful.

How to Become a Budget Analyst

Budget analysts typically need a bachelor's degree to enter the occupation. Some employers prefer to hire applicants who have a master's degree. Courses in accounting, economics, and statistics are helpful.

Education

Budget analysts typically need at least a bachelor's degree in fields such as business, social science, psychology, or mathematics. Because developing a budget requires numeracy and analytical skills, coursework in accounting, economics, and statistics is helpful.

Sometimes, budget- or finance-related work experience may be substituted for formal education.

Budget analysts must present technical information in writing that is understandable for the intended audience.

Licenses, Certifications, and Registrations

Budget analysts working in federal, state or local government may earn the optional Certified Government Financial Manager (CGFM) credential from the Association of Government Accountants (AGA). CGFM candidates must have at least a bachelor's degree, abide by the AGA's Code of Ethics, pass examinations, and complete a designated period of professional-level experience in governmental financial management. To maintain certification, CGFMs must complete continuing education.

Although the CGFM is not required, having a designation may help with career advancement.

Important Qualities

Analytical skills. Budget analysts must be able to process a variety of information, evaluate costs and benefits, and solve complex problems.

Communication skills. Budget analysts must be able to explain and defend their analyses and recommendations in meetings and legislative committee hearings.

Detail oriented. Creating an efficient budget requires careful analysis of each budget item.

Math skills. Budget analysts need math skills and the ability to use financial-management software and programs.

Writing skills. Budget analysts must present written technical information in a way that is understandable to the intended audience.

Pay

The median annual wage for budget analysts was $82,260 in May 2022. The median wage is the wage at which half the workers in an occupation earned more than that amount and half earned less. The lowest 10 percent earned less than $53,000, and the highest 10 percent earned more than $128,170.

In May 2022, the median annual wages for budget analysts in the top industries in which they worked were as follows:

Professional, scientific, and technical services	$98,360
Federal government	90,440
Local government, excluding education and hospitals	81,380
State government, excluding education and hospitals	74,980
Educational services; state, local, and private	68,440

Most budget analysts work full time, and overtime is sometimes required during development, mid-year, and final reviews of budgets. The pressures of deadlines and tight work schedules may be stressful.

Job Outlook

Employment of budget analysts is projected to grow 3 percent from 2022 to 2032, about as fast as the average for all occupations.

About 3,600 openings for budget analysts are projected each year, on average, over the decade. Many of those openings are expected to result from the need to replace workers who transfer to different occupations or exit the labor force, such as to retire.

Employment

Calls for efficient use of public funds will lead to continued demand for budget analysts to estimate program costs, develop budgets, and explain their findings to legislators and the public. Demand for these workers is somewhat tied to the government funding that is allocated for these positions. However, budget

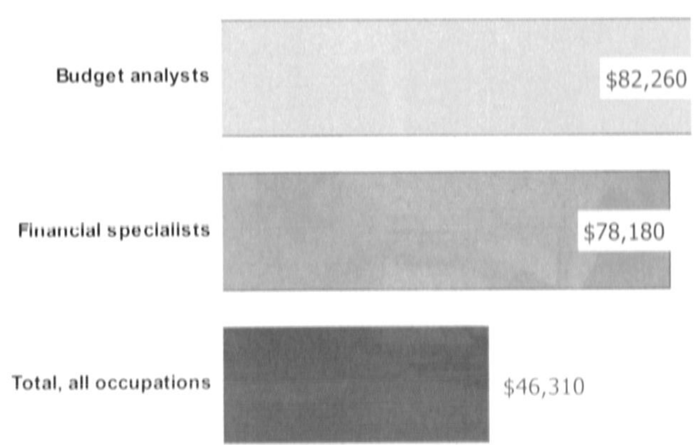

Note: All Occupations includes all occupations in the U.S. Economy.
Source: U.S. Bureau of Labor Statistics, Occupational Employment and Wage Statistics.

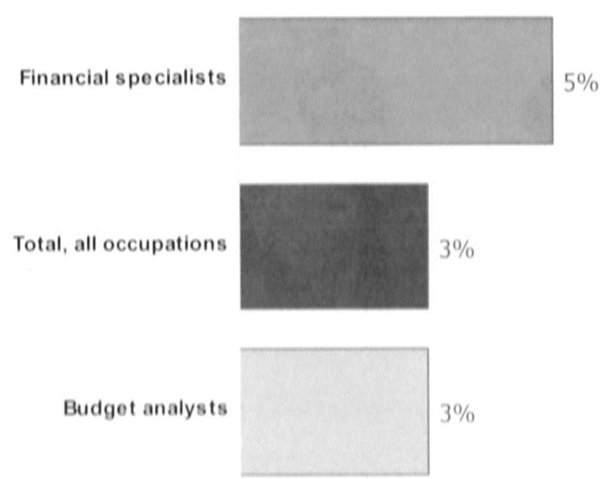

Note: All Occupations includes all occupations in the U.S. Economy.
Source: U.S. Bureau of Labor Statistics, Employment Projections program.

analysts manage resource allocation and will be needed even during times of tight budgets.

Occupational Title	SOC Code	Employment, 2022	Projected Employment, 2032	Change, 2022-32	
				Percent	Numeric
Budget analysts	13-2031	51,600	53,300	3	1,700

Contacts for More Information

For information about the Government Financial Manager certification, visit

➤ Association of Government Accountants

Claims Adjusters, Appraisers, Examiners, and Investigators

Summary

Quick Facts: Claims Adjusters, Appraisers, Examiners, and Investigators

2022 Median Pay	$72,040 per year $34.63 per hour
Typical Entry-Level Education	See How to Become One
Work Experience in a Related Occupation	None
On-the-job Training	See How to Become One
Number of Jobs, 2022	342,600
Job Outlook, 2022-32	-3% (Decline)
Employment Change, 2022-32	-10,700

What Claims Adjusters, Appraisers, Examiners, and Investigators Do

Claims adjusters, appraisers, examiners, and investigators evaluate insurance claims.

Work Environment

Most claims adjusters, appraisers, examiners, and investigators work full time. They often work outside the office, inspecting properties on which insurance claims have been made, such as damaged automobiles and buildings.

Claims adjusters, appraisers, examiners, and investigators evaluate insurance claims.

How to Become a Claims Adjuster, Appraiser, Examiner, or Investigator

A high school diploma or equivalent is typically required for a person to work as an entry-level claims adjuster, examiner, or investigator, although some positions need a bachelor's degree or insurance-related work experience. Auto damage appraisers typically have either a postsecondary nondegree award or work experience in identifying and estimating the cost of automotive repair.

Pay

The median annual wage for claims adjusters, examiners, and investigators was $72,230 in May 2022.

The median annual wage for insurance appraisers, auto damage was $69,380 in May 2022.

Job Outlook

Overall employment of claims adjusters, appraisers, examiners, and investigators is projected to decline 3 percent from 2022 to 2032.

Despite declining employment, about 21,500 openings for claims adjusters, appraisers, examiners, and investigators are projected each year, on average, over the decade. All of those openings are expected to result from the need to replace workers who transfer to other occupations or exit the labor force, such as to retire.

What Claims Adjusters, Appraisers, Examiners, and Investigators Do

Claims adjusters, appraisers, examiners, and investigators evaluate insurance claims. They decide whether an insurance company must pay a claim and if so, how much.

Duties

Claims adjusters, appraisers, examiners, and investigators typically do the following:

- Investigate, evaluate, and settle insurance claims
- Determine whether the insurance policy covers the loss claimed
- Decide the appropriate amount the insurance company should pay
- Ensure that claims are not fraudulent
- Contact claimants' doctors or employers to get additional information on questionable claims

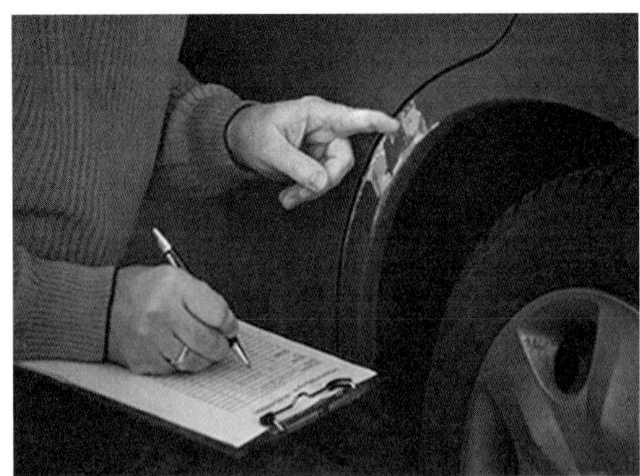

Claims adjusters inspect property damage to determine how much the company should pay for the loss.

- Talk with legal counsel about claims when needed
- Negotiate settlements
- Authorize payments

Claims adjusters, appraisers, examiners, and investigators have varying duties, depending on the type of insurance company they work for. They must know a lot about what their company insures. For example, workers in property and casualty insurance must know housing and construction costs so that they can properly evaluate damage from floods or fires. Workers in health insurance must be able to determine which types of treatments are medically necessary and which are questionable.

Adjusters inspect property damage or personal injury claims to determine how much the insurance company should pay for the loss. They might inspect a home, a business, or an automobile.

Adjusters interview the claimant and witnesses, inspect the property, and do additional research, such as look at police reports. They may consult with other workers, such as accountants, architects, construction workers, engineers, lawyers, and physicians, who can offer a more expert evaluation of a claim.

Adjusters gather information—including photographs and statements, either written or recorded on audio or video—and put together a report for claims examiners to review. When the examiner approves the claim, the adjuster negotiates with the policyholder and settles the claim.

If the claimant contests the outcome of the claim or the settlement, adjusters work with attorneys and expert witnesses to defend the insurer's position.

Some claims adjusters work as ***public adjusters***. Often, they are hired by claimants who prefer not to rely on the insurance company's adjuster. The goal of adjusters working for insurance companies is to save as much money for the company as possible. The goal of a public adjuster working for a claimant is to get the highest possible amount paid to the claimant. They are paid a percentage of the settled claim.

Appraisers estimate the cost or value of an insured item. Most appraisers who work for insurance companies and independent adjusting firms are ***auto damage appraisers***. They inspect damaged vehicles after an accident and estimate the cost of repairs. This information then goes to the adjuster, who puts the estimated cost of repairs into the settlement.

Claims examiners review claims after they are submitted to make sure claimants and adjusters followed proper guidelines. They may help adjusters with complicated claims or when, for example, a natural disaster occurs and the volume of claims increases.

Examiners who work for health insurance companies review health-related claims to see whether the costs are reasonable, given the diagnosis. After they review the claim, they authorize appropriate payment, deny the claim, or refer the claim to an investigator.

Examiners who work for life insurance companies review the causes of death and pay particular attention to accidents, because most life insurance companies pay additional benefits if a death is accidental. Examiners also may review new applications for life insurance policies to make sure that the applicants have no serious illnesses that would make them a high risk to insure.

Insurance investigators handle claims in which the company suspects fraudulent or criminal activity such as arson, staged accidents, or unnecessary medical treatments. The severity of insurance fraud cases varies, from overstated claims of vehicle damage to complicated fraud rings. Investigators often do surveillance work. For example, in the case of a fraudulent workers' compensation claim, an investigator may covertly watch the claimant to see if he or she does anything that would be suspicious based on injuries stated in the claim.

Work Environment

Claims adjusters, examiners, and investigators held about 329,000 jobs in 2022. The largest employers of claims adjusters, examiners, and investigators were as follows:

Direct insurance (except life, health, and medical) carriers	33%

Workers who inspect damaged buildings must be wary of potential hazards, such as collapsed roofs and floors, as well as weakened structures.

Agencies, brokerages, and other insurance related activities	28
Federal government	14
Direct health and medical insurance carriers	8
State government, excluding education and hospitals	3

Insurance appraisers, auto damage held about 13,600 jobs in 2022. The largest employers of insurance appraisers, auto damage were as follows:

Insurance carriers	68%
Agencies, brokerages, and other insurance related activities	25
Self-employed workers	1

Claims adjusters and examiners work in offices when reviewing documents and conducting research. They work outside when examining damaged property. Appraisers and investigators work outside more often, inspecting damaged automobiles and buildings and conducting surveillance. Auto damage appraisers spend much of their time at automotive body shops estimating vehicle damage costs.

Workers who inspect damaged buildings must be careful around potential hazards, such as collapsed roofs and floors, as well as weakened structures.

Work Schedules

Most claims adjusters, appraisers, examiners, and investigators work full time. However, their work schedules may vary.

Adjusters often arrange their work schedules to accommodate evening and weekend appointments with clients. This requirement sometimes results in adjusters working irregular schedules, especially when they have a lot of claims to review.

Insurance investigators often work irregular schedules because of the need to contact people who are not available during normal business hours. Early morning, evening, and weekend work is common.

In contrast, auto damage appraisers typically work regular hours and rarely work on weekends.

How to Become a Claims Adjuster, Appraiser, Examiner, or Investigator

A high school diploma or equivalent is typically required for a person to work as an entry-level claims adjuster, examiner, or investigator, although some positions require a bachelor's degree or insurance-related work experience. Auto damage appraisers typically have either a postsecondary nondegree award or work experience in identifying and estimating the cost of automotive repair.

Education

A high school diploma or equivalent is typically required for a person to work as an entry-level claims adjuster or examiner.

At the beginning of their careers, claims adjusters, appraisers, examiners, and investigators work on small claims, under the supervision of an experienced worker.

However, employers sometimes prefer to hire applicants who have a bachelor's degree or some insurance-related work experience.

For investigator jobs, a high school diploma or equivalent is the typical education requirement. Some insurance companies prefer to hire people trained as law enforcement officers or private investigators, because these workers have good interviewing and interrogation skills.

Auto damage appraisers typically have either a postsecondary nondegree award or experience working in an auto repair shop, identifying and estimating the cost of automotive repair. Many vocational schools and some community colleges offer programs in autobody repair that teach students how to estimate the cost of repairing damaged vehicles.

Training

Entry-level claims adjusters, examiners, and investigators work on small claims under the supervision of an experienced worker. As they learn more about claims investigation and settlement, they are assigned larger, more complex claims.

Auto damage appraisers typically get on-the-job training, which may last several months. This training usually involves working under the supervision of an experienced appraiser while estimating damage costs, until the employer decides that the trainee is ready to do estimates on their own.

Licenses, Certifications, and Registrations

Licensing requirements for claims adjusters, appraisers, examiners, and investigators vary by state. Some states have few requirements; others require either completing prelicensing education or receiving a satisfactory score on a licensing exam (or both). Jobseekers should verify the licensing laws with the state and locality in which they want to work.

In some states, claims adjusters employed by insurance companies do not have to become licensed themselves because they can work under the company license.

Public adjusters may need to meet separate or additional requirements.

Some states that require licensing also require a certain number of continuing education credits per year to renew the license. Federal and state laws and the outcomes of claim disputes adjudicated in court affect how the claims must be handled and what insurance policies can and must cover. Examiners working on life and health claims must stay up to date on new medical procedures and prescription drugs. Examiners working on auto claims must be familiar with the most recent car models and repair techniques. To fulfill their continuing education requirements, workers can attend classes or workshops, write articles for claims publications, or give lectures and presentations.

The National Insurance Producer Registry (NIPR) provides information about state licensing requirements.

Important Qualities

Analytical skills. Adjusters and examiners must each evaluate whether the insurance company is obligated to pay a claim and determine the amount to pay. Adjusters must consider various pieces of information to reach a decision.

Communication skills. Claims adjusters and investigators must get information from a range of people, including claimants, witnesses, and medical experts. They must know the right questions to ask in order to gather the information they need.

Detail oriented. Adjusters, appraisers, examiners, and investigators must carefully review documents and damaged property, because small details can have large financial consequences.

Interpersonal skills. Adjusters, examiners, and investigators often meet with claimants and others who may be upset by the situation that requires a claim or by the settlement the company is offering. These workers must be understanding, yet firm regarding their company's policies.

Pay

The median annual wage for claims adjusters, examiners, and investigators was $72,230 in May 2022. The median wage is the wage at which half the workers in an occupation earned more than that amount and half earned less. The lowest 10 percent earned less than $46,040, and the highest 10 percent earned more than $102,630.

The median annual wage for insurance appraisers, auto damage was $69,380 in May 2022. The lowest 10 percent earned less than $49,940, and the highest 10 percent earned more than $94,440.

In May 2022, the median annual wages for claims adjusters, examiners, and investigators in the top industries in which they worked were as follows:

Federal government	$83,870
Direct insurance (except life, health, and medical) carriers	75,740
State government, excluding education and hospitals	67,120
Agencies, brokerages, and other insurance related activities	65,650
Direct health and medical insurance carriers	51,300

Claims Adjusters, Appraisers, Examiners, and Investigators

Median annual wages, May 2022

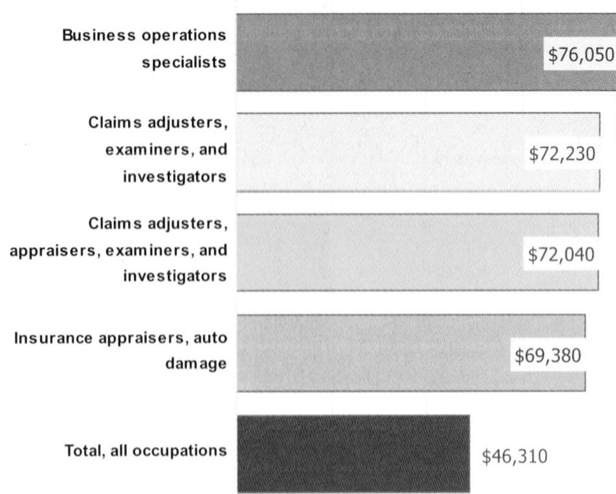

Note: All Occupations includes all occupations in the U.S. Economy.
Source: U.S. Bureau of Labor Statistics, Occupational Employment and Wage Statistics.

In May 2022, the median annual wages for insurance appraisers, auto damage in the top industries in which they worked were as follows:

Insurance carriers	$73,010
Agencies, brokerages, and other insurance related activities	67,620

Most claims adjusters, appraisers, examiners, and investigators work full time. However, their work schedules may vary.

Adjusters often arrange their work schedules to accommodate evening and weekend appointments with clients. This requirement sometimes results in adjusters working irregular schedules, especially when they have a lot of claims to review.

Insurance investigators often work irregular schedules because of the need to contact people who are not available during normal business hours. Early morning, evening, and weekend work is common.

In contrast, auto damage appraisers typically work regular hours and rarely work on weekends.

Job Outlook

Overall employment of claims adjusters, appraisers, examiners, and investigators is projected to decline 3 percent from 2022 to 2032.

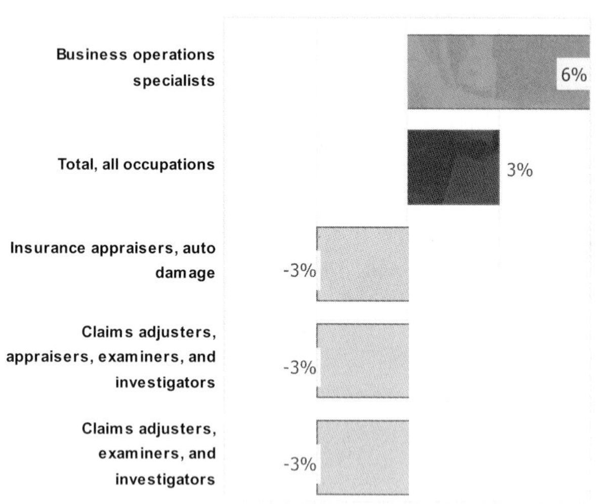

Note: All Occupations includes all occupations in the U.S. Economy.
Source: U.S. Bureau of Labor Statistics, Employment Projections program.

Despite declining employment, about 21,500 openings for claims adjusters, appraisers, examiners, and investigators are projected each year, on average, over the decade. All of those openings are expected to result from the need to replace workers who transfer to other occupations or exit the labor force, such as to retire.

Employment

Technology is expected to automate some of the tasks that these workers currently perform. For example, computer software can evaluate photographs of damaged property and calculate an estimated claim amount. In addition, data collection and processing speed will continue to increase, which will improve efficiency and make workers more productive.

The number of natural disasters, such as floods and fires, influences demand for claims adjusters in property and casualty insurance. Future increases in the number of natural disasters could result in some employment growth for claims adjusters in the field.

Occupational Title	SOC Code	Employment, 2022	Projected Employment, 2032	Change, 2022-32	
				Percent	Numeric
Claims adjusters, appraisers, examiners, and investigators	—	342,600	331,900	-3	-10,700
Claims adjusters, examiners, and investigators	13-1031	329,000	318,700	-3	-10,300
Insurance appraisers, auto damage	13-1032	13,600	13,300	-3	-400

Contacts for More Information

For more information about education and credentials for insurance-related occupations, visit

- The Institutes
- International Claim Association
- National Association of Public Insurance Adjusters
- National Insurance Producer Registry (NIPR)

Compensation, Benefits, and Job Analysis Specialists

Summary

Quick Facts: Compensation, Benefits, and Job Analysis Specialists

2022 Median Pay	$67,780 per year $32.59 per hour
Typical Entry-Level Education	Bachelor's degree
Work Experience in a Related Occupation	Less than 5 years
On-the-job Training	None
Number of Jobs, 2022	98,200
Job Outlook, 2022-32	7% (Faster than average)
Employment Change, 2022-32	6,900

What Compensation, Benefits, and Job Analysis Specialists Do

Compensation, benefits, and job analysis specialists oversee wage and nonwage programs that an organization provides to its employees in return for their work. They also evaluate position descriptions to determine details such as classification and salary.

Work Environment

Compensation, benefits, and job analysis specialists are employed in nearly every industry. They typically work in offices, and most are full time.

How to Become a Compensation, Benefits, and Job Analysis Specialist

Compensation, benefits, and job analysis specialists typically need a bachelor's degree and related work experience to enter the occupation.

Pay

The median annual wage for compensation, benefits, and job analysis specialists was $67,780 in May 2022.

Job Outlook

Employment of compensation, benefits, and job analysis specialists is projected to grow 7 percent from 2022 to 2032, faster than the average for all occupations.

Specialists may present their analysis and recommendations to management.

About 7,700 openings for compensation, benefits, and job analysis specialists are projected each year, on average, over the decade. Many of those openings are expected to result from the need to replace workers who transfer to different occupations or exit the labor force, such as to retire.

What Compensation, Benefits, and Job Analysis Specialists Do

Compensation, benefits, and job analysis specialists oversee wage and nonwage programs that an organization provides to its employees in return for their work. They also evaluate position descriptions to determine details such as classification and salary.

Duties

Compensation, benefits, and job analysis specialists typically do the following:

- Research compensation and benefits policies and plans
- Use data and cost analyses to compare compensation and benefits plans
- Evaluate position descriptions to determine classification and salary

Specialists research compensation and benefits policies and plans.

- Ensure that an organization complies with federal and state laws
- Design and prepare reports summarizing research and analysis
- Present recommendations to other human resources managers

Some specialists perform tasks within all areas of compensation, benefits, and job analysis. Others specialize in a specific area.

Compensation specialists assess an organization's pay structure for employees. They research compensation trends and review surveys to determine how their organization's pay compares with that of other organizations in a particular industry and region. They often perform complex data and cost analyses to evaluate compensation policies. They also ensure that the organization's pay practices comply with federal and state laws and regulations, such as equal pay laws, minimum wage, overtime, and workers' compensation.

Benefits specialists administer an organization's compensation programs that are supplemental to wages, including retirement plans, leave policies, wellness programs, and insurance plans. They research, analyze, and then recommend benefits plans, policies, and programs. They frequently monitor government regulations, legislation, and benefits trends to ensure that their programs are current, legal, and competitive. They also work closely with insurance brokers and benefits carriers and manage the enrollment, delivery of benefits, and renewal to the organization's employees.

Job analysis specialists, also known as *position classifiers*, evaluate an organization's positions by writing or assigning job descriptions, determining position classifications, and preparing salary scales. When the organization introduces a new job or reviews existing jobs, specialists must conduct research and make recommendations to managers on the classification, description, status, and salary of those jobs.

Work Environment

Compensation, benefits, and job analysis specialists held about 98,200 jobs in 2022. The largest employers of compensation, benefits, and job analysis specialists were as follows:

Insurance carriers and related activities	16%
Professional, scientific, and technical services	13
Management of companies and enterprises	12
Local government, excluding education and hospitals	8
Healthcare and social assistance	7

Compensation, benefits, and job analysis specialists work in nearly every industry.

They typically work in offices.

Specialists typically work in offices, briefing workers about benefits and overseeing the enrollment process.

Work Schedules

Most compensation, benefits, and job analysis specialists work full time.

How to Become a Compensation, Benefits, and Job Analysis Specialist

Compensation, benefits, and job analysis specialists typically need a bachelor's degree and related work experience to enter the occupation.

Education

Employers typically require that compensation, benefits, and job analysis specialists have a bachelor's degree. Common fields of degree include business, social science, psychology, and communications. Some employers accept additional related work experience in lieu of a degree.

Regardless of major, students interested in this occupation may find it useful to take courses in subjects such as human resources management, finance, and accounting.

Work Experience in a Related Occupation

Employers typically require that compensation, benefits, and job analysis specialists have experience that includes compensation analysis, benefits administration, or general human resources work. Experience in related fields, such as finance, insurance, or business administration, also may be helpful. Some candidates gain this experience through internships. However, others gain experience from working in human resources occupations, such as human resources specialists.

Licenses, Certifications, and Registrations

Although professional certification is not required, it demonstrates expertise. Some employers prefer to hire candidates who have certification, but other employers allow their employees to earn certification after they have begun working. Certification programs often require applicants to have several years of related work experience in order to qualify for the credential.

Specialists typically need previous work experience in human resources occupations.

Many associations for human resources workers offer classes to enhance the skills of their members. Some associations, including the International Foundation of Employee Benefit Plans and WorldatWork, offer certification programs that specialize in compensation and benefits. Others, including the HR Certification Institute and the Society for Human Resource Management, offer general human resources credentials.

Advancement

Compensation, benefits, and job analysis specialists may advance to become a compensation and benefits manager or a human resources manager. Specialists typically need several years of work experience to advance.

Important Qualities

Analytical skills. Compensation, benefits, and job analysis specialists perform data and cost analyses to evaluate their organization's policies. They also must be able to interpret the details of contracts and laws.

Business skills. Specialists must understand basic finance and accounting. They help set the wages and benefits packages for new employees.

Compensation, Benefits, and Job Analysis Specialists

Median annual wages, May 2022

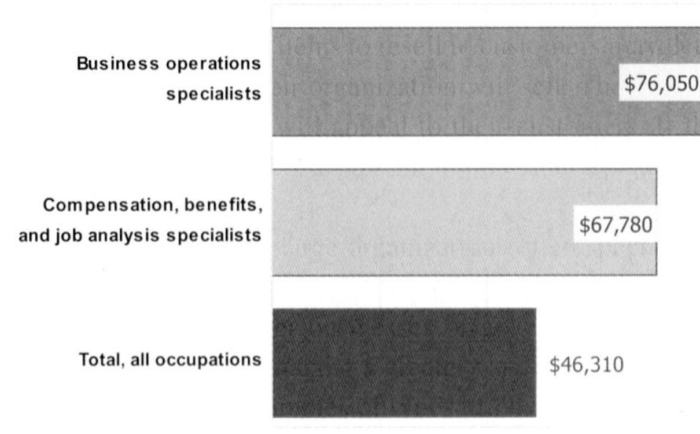

Note: All Occupations includes all occupations in the U.S. Economy.
Source: U.S. Bureau of Labor Statistics, Occupational Employment and Wage Statistics.

Compensation, Benefits, and Job Analysis Specialists

Percent change in employment, projected 2022-32

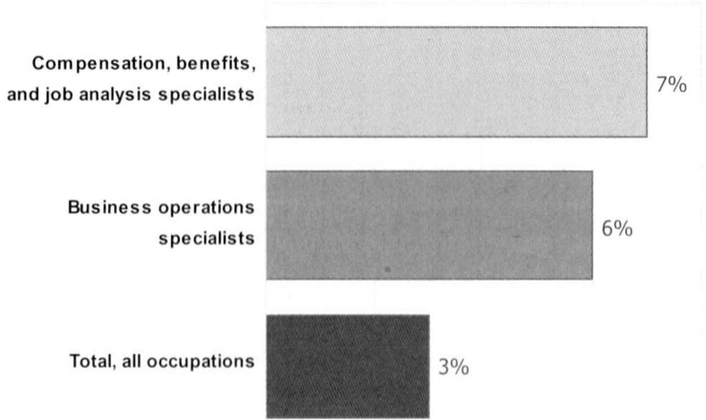

Note: All Occupations includes all occupations in the U.S. Economy.
Source: U.S. Bureau of Labor Statistics, Employment Projections program.

Communication skills. Specialists need to provide information about compensation and benefits in a way that is understandable to employees at all levels throughout their organization.

Critical-thinking skills. Specialists must be able to evaluate job positions, salary scales, promotion practices, and other compensation and benefits policies.

Pay

The median annual wage for compensation, benefits, and job analysis specialists was $67,780 in May 2022. The median wage is the wage at which half the workers in an occupation earned more than that amount and half earned less. The lowest 10 percent earned less than $42,250, and the highest 10 percent earned more than $117,060.

In May 2022, the median annual wages for compensation, benefits, and job analysis specialists in the top industries in which they worked were as follows:

Professional, scientific, and technical services ..	$77,730
Management of companies and enterprises	76,000
Local government, excluding education and hospitals	66,280
Insurance carriers and related activities	64,500
Healthcare and social assistance	62,300

Most compensation, benefits, and job analysis specialists work full time.

Job Outlook

Employment of compensation, benefits, and job analysis specialists is projected to grow 7 percent from 2022 to 2032, faster than the average for all occupations.

About 7,700 openings for compensation, benefits, and job analysis specialists are projected each year, on average, over the decade. Many of those openings are expected to result from the need to replace workers who transfer to different occupations or exit the labor force, such as to retire.

Employment

Organizations will continue to hire benefits specialists to analyze, select, and update their benefits policies. Employee wellness programs are a popular way to reduce healthcare costs. Organizations will need benefits specialists to design, evaluate, and administer these programs.

In addition, organizations must offer competitive compensation packages to attract and keep highly qualified workers. To allocate their compensation funds effectively, many organizations use strategies such as pay-for-performance plans, which may include bonuses, paid leave, or other incentives as part of the compensation package. Organizations will need specialists to analyze these compensation policies and plans and to ensure that they are both competitive and cost effective.

Occupational Title	SOC Code	Employment, 2022	Projected Employment, 2032	Change, 2022-32	
				Percent	Numeric
Compensation, benefits, and job analysis specialists	13-1141	98,200	105,100	7	6,900

Contacts for More Information

For more information, visit

- International Foundation of Employee Benefit Plans
- WorldatWork
- Society for Human Resource Management
- HR Certification Institute

Cost Estimators

Summary

Quick Facts: Cost Estimators	
2022 Median Pay	$71,200 per year $34.23 per hour
Typical Entry-Level Education	Bachelor's degree
Work Experience in a Related Occupation	None
On-the-job Training	Moderate-term on-the-job training
Number of Jobs, 2022	231,400
Job Outlook, 2022-32	-3% (Decline)
Employment Change, 2022-32	-6,500

What Cost Estimators Do

Cost estimators collect and analyze data in order to assess the time, money, materials, and labor required to make a product or provide a service.

Work Environment

Cost estimators work mostly in office settings, and some estimators also visit construction sites and factory assembly lines. Most cost estimators work full time, and some work more than 40 hours per week.

How to Become a Cost Estimator

Cost estimators typically need a bachelor's degree to enter the occupation, although workers with several years of experience in construction sometimes qualify in that industry without a degree.

Pay

The median annual wage for cost estimators was $71,200 in May 2022.

Job Outlook

Employment of cost estimators is projected to decline 3 percent from 2022 to 2032.

Despite declining employment, about 18,000 openings for cost estimators are projected each year, on average, over the decade. All of those openings are expected to result from the need to replace workers who transfer to other occupations or exit the labor force, such as to retire.

What Cost Estimators Do

Cost estimators collect and analyze data in order to assess the time, money, materials, and labor required to manufacture a product, construct a building, or provide a service. They generally specialize in a particular product or industry.

Duties

Cost estimators typically do the following:

Cost estimators often collaborate with engineers.

- Identify factors affecting costs, such as production time, materials, and labor
- Read blueprints and technical documents in order to prepare estimates
- Collaborate with engineers, architects, clients, and contractors
- Calculate, analyze, and adjust estimates
- Recommend ways to cut costs
- Work with sales teams to prepare estimates and bids for clients
- Maintain records of estimated and actual costs

Accurately estimating the costs of construction and manufacturing projects is vital to the survival of businesses. Cost estimators provide managers with the information they need in order to submit competitive contract bids or to price products appropriately.

Estimators analyze production processes to determine how much time, money, and labor a project needs. Their estimates account for many things, including allowances for wasted material, bad weather, shipping delays, and other variables that can increase costs and lower profits.

In building construction, cost estimators use software to simulate the construction process and evaluate the price of design choices. They often check databases and their own records to compare the costs of similar projects.

The following are examples of types of cost estimators:

Construction cost estimators prepare estimates for building, road, and other construction projects. They may calculate the total cost of constructing a bridge or commercial shopping center, or they may calculate the cost of just one part, such as the foundation. They identify costs of elements such as raw materials and labor, and they may set a timeline for how long they expect the project to take. Although many work directly for construction firms, some work for contractors and engineering firms.

Manufacturing cost estimators calculate the expense of developing, producing, or redesigning a company's goods or services.

For example, an estimator working for a home appliance manufacturer may determine a new dishwasher's production costs, aiding managers in making decisions about its assembly.

Other workers, such as operations research analysts and construction managers, also may estimate costs in the course of their usual duties.

Work Environment

Cost estimators held about 231,400 jobs in 2022. The largest employers of cost estimators were as follows:

Specialty trade contractors	35%
Construction of buildings	16
Manufacturing	12
Automotive repair and maintenance	8
Heavy and civil engineering construction	5

Cost estimators work mostly in office settings, and some estimators visit construction sites and factory assembly lines during the course of their work.

Work Schedules

Most cost estimators work full time, and some work more than 40 hours per week.

Cost estimators may visit construction sites to gather information.

How to Become a Cost Estimator

Cost estimators typically need a bachelor's degree to enter the occupation, although workers with several years of experience in construction sometimes qualify in that industry without a degree.

Education

Employers generally prefer to hire candidates who have a bachelor's degree.

Construction cost estimators typically need a bachelor's degree in a related field, such as construction or engineering. Manufacturing cost estimators typically need a degree in business or finance.

Training

Most cost estimators receive on-the-job training, which may include instruction in cost estimation techniques and software and in building information modeling (BIM), computer-aided design (CAD), or other industry-specific software.

Work Experience in a Related Occupation

Some employers prefer that construction cost estimators, particularly those without a bachelor's degree, have work experience in the construction industry. Some construction cost estimators become qualified solely through extensive work experience.

Important Qualities

Analytical skills. Cost estimators must review and evaluate different construction and manufacturing methods to find cost-effective options.

Detail oriented. Cost estimators must be precise, because minor changes may greatly affect the overall expense of a project or product.

Math skills. Cost estimators need excellent math skills to calculate labor, material, and equipment estimates for construction projects.

Cost estimators learn to use specialized cost estimating software.

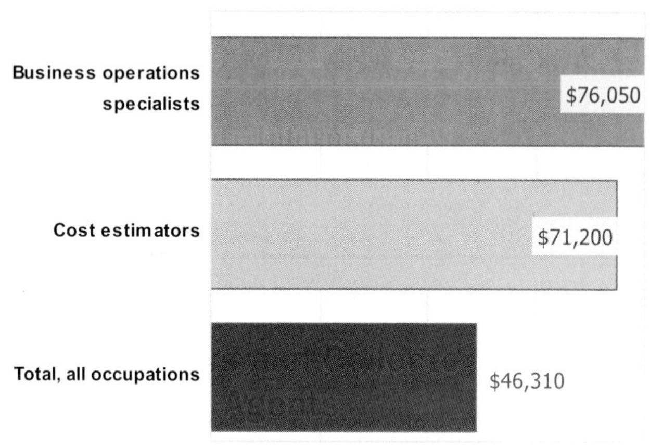

Note: All Occupations includes all occupations in the U.S. Economy. Source: U.S. Bureau of Labor Statistics, Occupational Employment and Wage Statistics.

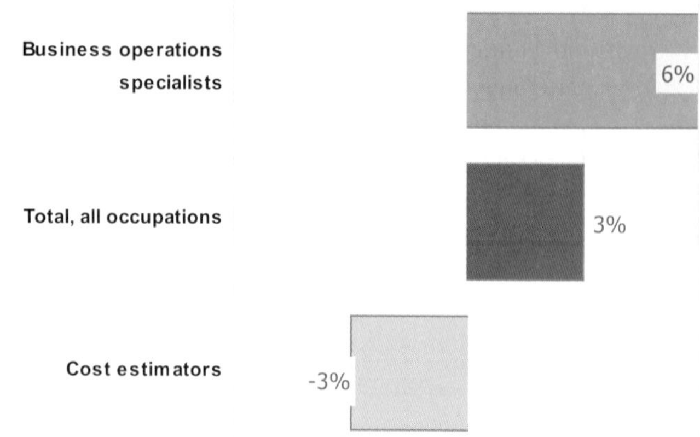

Note: All Occupations includes all occupations in the U.S. Economy. Source: U.S. Bureau of Labor Statistics, Employment Projections program.

Time-management skills. Cost estimators must plan in advance and work efficiently to meet their deadlines.

Writing skills. Cost estimators must have excellent writing skills to prepare comprehensive reports, which often help managers make production decisions.

Pay

The median annual wage for cost estimators was $71,200 in May 2022. The median wage is the wage at which half the workers in an occupation earned more than that amount and half earned less. The lowest 10 percent earned less than $42,110, and the highest 10 percent earned more than $120,600.

In May 2022, the median annual wages for cost estimators in the top industries in which they worked were as follows:

Heavy and civil engineering construction	$85,190
Construction of buildings	75,910
Specialty trade contractors	73,400
Manufacturing	66,180
Automotive repair and maintenance	60,410

Most cost estimators work full time, and some work more than 40 hours per week.

Job Outlook

Employment of cost estimators is projected to decline 3 percent from 2022 to 2032.

Despite declining employment, about 18,000 openings for cost estimators are projected each year, on average, over the decade. All of those openings are expected to result from the need to replace workers who transfer to other occupations or exit the labor force, such as to retire.

Employment

Cost estimation software is improving the productivity of these workers, requiring fewer estimators to do the same amount of work. This will limit employment growth of cost estimators.

However, there will continue to be some demand for these workers because companies need accurate cost projections to ensure that their products and services are profitable.

Occupational Title	SOC Code	Employment, 2022	Projected Employment, 2032	Change, 2022-32	
				Percent	Numeric
Cost estimators	13-1051	231,400	224,900	-3	-6,500

Contacts for More Information

For more information about cost estimators, visit

- American Society of Professional Estimators (ASPE)
- Association for the Advancement of Cost Engineering International (AACE International)
- International Cost Estimating and Analysis Association (ICEAA)

Financial Analysts

Summary

Quick Facts: Financial Analysts	
2022 Median Pay	$96,220 per year $46.26 per hour
Typical Entry-Level Education	Bachelor's degree
Work Experience in a Related Occupation	None
On-the-job Training	None
Number of Jobs, 2022	376,100
Job Outlook, 2022-32	8% (Faster than average)
Employment Change, 2022-32	29,000

What Financial Analysts Do

Financial analysts guide businesses and individuals in decisions about expending money to attain profit.

Work Environment

Financial analysts work in offices. Most work full time, and some work more than 40 hours per week.

How to Become a Financial Analyst

Financial analysts typically need a bachelor's degree to enter the occupation.

Pay

The median annual wage for financial and investment analysts was $95,080 in May 2022.

The median annual wage for financial risk specialists was $102,120 in May 2022.

Job Outlook

Overall employment of financial analysts is projected to grow 8 percent from 2022 to 2032, faster than the average for all occupations.

About 27,400 openings for financial analysts are projected each year, on average, over the decade. Many of those openings are expected to result from the need to replace workers who transfer to different occupations or exit the labor force, such as to retire.

What Financial Analysts Do

Financial analysts guide businesses and individuals in decisions about expending money to attain profit. They assess the performance of stocks, bonds, and other types of investments.

Duties

Financial analysts typically do the following:

- Recommend individual investments and collections of investments, known as portfolios
- Evaluate current and historical financial data
- Study economic and business trends
- Examine a company's financial statements to determine its value
- Meet with company officials to gain better insight into the company's prospects
- Assess the strength of the management team
- Prepare written reports

Financial analysts evaluate opportunities to commit money for the purpose of generating profit.

Financial analysts can be divided into two categories: buy-side analysts and sell-side analysts.

- Buy-side analysts develop investment strategies for companies that have a lot of money to invest. These companies, called institutional investors, include hedge funds, insurance companies, independent money managers, nonprofit organizations with large endowments, private equity firms, and pension funds.
- Sell-side analysts advise financial services sales agents who sell stocks, bonds, and other investments.

Financial analysts recommend individual investments and collections of investments, which are known as portfolios.

Financial analysts work in banks, pension funds, insurance companies, and other businesses.

Analysts may work for the business media or other research houses, which are independent from the buy and sell side.

Financial analysts generally focus on trends affecting a specific geographical region, industry, or type of product. For example, they may focus on a subject area or a foreign exchange market. They must understand how economic trends, new regulations, policies, and political situations may affect investments.

Investing has become more global, and some specialize in a particular country or world region. Companies want these specialists to understand the business environment, culture, language, and political conditions in the country or region that they cover.

The following are examples of types of financial analysts:

Financial risk specialists, also called *financial risk analysts*, evaluate threats to investment decisions and determine how to manage unpredictability and limit potential losses. They make investment decisions such as selecting dissimilar stocks or having a combination of stocks, bonds, and mutual funds in a portfolio. They also make recommendations to limit risk.

Fund managers work exclusively with hedge funds or mutual funds. Both fund managers and portfolio managers frequently make buy or sell decisions in reaction to quickly changing market conditions.

Investment analysts assess information involving investment programs or financial data of institutions, such as business valuation. They also respond to queries from clients and client advisors regarding asset allocation and alternative investment topics including hedge funds, real property, and venture capital.

Portfolio managers select the mix of products, industries, and regions for their company's investment portfolio. These managers are responsible for the overall performance of the portfolio. They are also expected to explain investment decisions and strategies in meetings with stakeholders.

Ratings analysts evaluate the ability of companies or governments to pay their debts, including bonds. Based on these evaluations, a management team rates the risk of a company or government not being able to repay its bonds.

Securities analysts evaluate securities markets and trends to identify high-yield assets for clients and companies. They may use resources such as bond performance reports, daily stock quotes, market and economic forecasts, and other financial statements and publications.

Work Environment

Financial and investment analysts held about 317,200 jobs in 2022. The largest employers of financial and investment analysts were as follows:

Securities, commodity contracts, and other financial investments and related activities	24%
Professional, scientific, and technical services	13
Management of companies and enterprises	11
Credit intermediation and related activities	11
Insurance carriers and related activities	7

Financial analysts may work at institutions that are based in large cities.

Financial risk specialists held about 58,900 jobs in 2022. The largest employers of financial risk specialists were as follows:

Credit intermediation and related activities	31%
Securities, commodity contracts, and other financial investments and related activities	15
Insurance carriers and related activities	15
Management of companies and enterprises	13
Professional, scientific, and technical services	8

Financial analysts work primarily in offices but may travel to visit companies or clients.

Work Schedules

Most financial analysts work full time and some work more than 40 hours per week.

How to Become a Financial Analyst

Financial analysts typically need a bachelor's degree to enter the occupation.

Financial analysts must process a range of information in finding profitable investments.

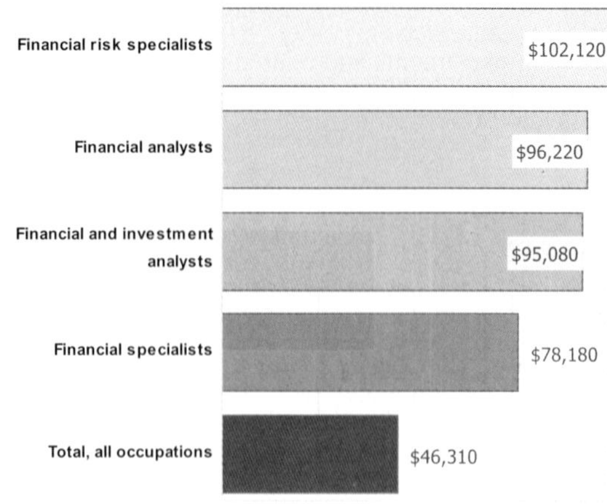

Note: All Occupations includes all occupations in the U.S. Economy.
Source: U.S. Bureau of Labor Statistics, Occupational Employment and Wage Statistics.

Education

Most entry-level positions for financial analysts require a bachelor's degree; a common field of degree is business. Some employers prefer to hire job candidates who have a master's degree.

Licenses, Certifications, and Registrations

The Financial Industry Regulatory Authority (FINRA) is the main licensing organization for the securities industry. A license is generally required to sell financial products, which may apply to some positions. Because most of the licenses require sponsorship by an employer, companies do not expect individuals to have these licenses before starting a job.

Employers often recommend certification, which may improve the chances for advancement. An example is the Chartered Financial Analyst (CFA) certification from the CFA Institute. Financial analysts can become CFA certified if they have a bachelor's degree and several years of work experience and pass multiple exams. They also may choose to become certified in their field of specialty.

Advancement

Financial analysts typically start by specializing in an investment field. As they gain experience, they may become portfolio managers and select the mix of investments for a company's portfolio. They also may become fund managers of large investment portfolios for individual investors. Having a master's degree in finance or business administration may improve an analyst's chances of advancing to one of these positions.

Important Qualities

Analytical skills. Financial analysts must evaluate a range of information in finding profitable investments.

Communication skills. Financial analysts must be able to clearly explain their recommendations to clients.

Computer skills. Financial analysts must be adept at using software to analyze financial data and trends, create portfolios, and make forecasts.

Decision-making skills. Financial analysts must reach conclusions so that they can recommend whether to buy, hold, or sell a security.

Detail oriented. Financial analysts must pay attention when reviewing a possible investment, as even small issues may have large implications for its health.

Math skills. Financial analysts use mathematics to estimate the value of financial securities.

Pay

The median annual wage for financial and investment analysts was $95,080 in May 2022. The median wage is the wage at which half the workers in an occupation earned more than that amount and half earned less. The lowest 10 percent earned less than $58,950, and the highest 10 percent earned more than $169,940.

The median annual wage for financial risk specialists was $102,120 in May 2022. The lowest 10 percent earned less than $59,510, and the highest 10 percent earned more than $175,720.

In May 2022, the median annual wages for financial and investment analysts in the top industries in which they worked were as follows:

Securities, commodity contracts, and other financial investments and related activities...	$106,390
Professional, scientific, and technical services .	95,200
Management of companies and enterprises	90,000
Credit intermediation and related activities	88,100
Insurance carriers and related activities	85,910

In May 2022, the median annual wages for financial risk specialists in the top industries in which they worked were as follows:

Securities, commodity contracts, and other financial investments and related activities..	$128,880
Professional, scientific, and technical services	104,260
Management of companies and enterprises.....	103,300
Credit intermediation and related activities.....	100,500
Insurance carriers and related activities..........	97,200

Fund managers are typically compensated by fees, usually structured as a percentage of assets under management and a percentage of the fund's annual return.

Most financial analysts work full time, and some work more than 40 hours per week.

Job Outlook

Overall employment of financial analysts is projected to grow 8 percent from 2022 to 2032, faster than the average for all occupations.

About 27,400 openings for financial analysts are projected each year, on average, over the decade. Many of those openings are expected to result from the need to replace workers who transfer to different occupations or exit the labor force, such as to retire.

Employment

Demand for financial analysts generally increases with overall economic activity. These workers will be needed to evaluate investment opportunities when new businesses are established or as existing businesses expand. In addition, emerging markets throughout the world are providing new investment opportunities, requiring expertise in geographic regions where those markets are located.

Demand also is projected to increase as big data and technological improvements allow financial analysts to conduct high-quality analysis. This analysis will help businesses manage their finances, identify investment trends, and deliver new products or services to clients.

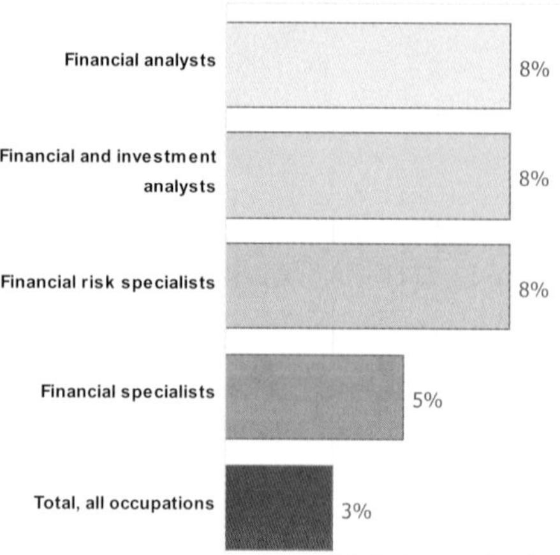

Note: All Occupations includes all occupations in the U.S. Economy.
Source: U.S. Bureau of Labor Statistics, Employment Projections program.

Occupational Title	SOC Code	Employment, 2022	Projected Employment, 2032	Change, 2022-32	
				Percent	Numeric
Financial analysts	—	376,100	405,100	8	29,000
Financial and investment analysts	13-2051	317,200	341,400	8	24,200
Financial risk specialists	13-2054	58,900	63,700	8	4,800

Contacts for More Information

For more information about licensure for financial analysts, visit

- Financial Industry Regulatory Authority (FINRA)
- CFA Institute
- Global Academy of Finance and Management

Financial Examiners

Summary

Quick Facts: Financial Examiners	
2022 Median Pay	$82,210 per year $39.52 per hour
Typical Entry-Level Education	Bachelor's degree
Work Experience in a Related Occupation	None
On-the-job Training	Long-term on-the-job training
Number of Jobs, 2022	65,600
Job Outlook, 2022-32	20% (Much faster than average)
Employment Change, 2022-32	12,800

What Financial Examiners Do

Financial examiners ensure compliance with laws that govern institutions handling monetary transactions.

Work Environment

Most financial examiners work for the finance and insurance industry, the federal government, or state governments. Most financial examiners work full time.

How to Become a Financial Examiner

Financial examiners typically need a bachelor's degree that includes some coursework in accounting. Entry-level examiners are trained on the job by senior examiners.

Pay

The median annual wage for financial examiners was $82,210 in May 2022.

Job Outlook

Employment of financial examiners is projected to grow 20 percent from 2022 to 2032, much faster than the average for all occupations.

About 6,300 openings for financial examiners are projected each year, on average, over the decade. Many of those openings are expected to result from the need to replace workers who transfer to different occupations or exit the labor force, such as to retire.

What Financial Examiners Do

Financial examiners ensure compliance with laws that govern institutions handling monetary transactions. They review balance sheets, evaluate the risk level of loans, and assess bank management.

Duties

Financial examiners typically do the following:

- Monitor the condition of banks and other financial institutions
- Review balance sheets, operating income and expense accounts, and loan documentation to confirm an institution's assets and liabilities
- Prepare reports that detail an institution's safety and soundness
- Examine the minutes of meetings of managers and directors
- Train other examiners in the financial examination process
- Review and analyze new regulations and policies to determine their impact on an institution
- Establish guidelines for procedures and policies that comply with new and revised regulations

Financial examiners typically work in one of two main areas: risk assessment or consumer compliance.

Those working in risk assessment evaluate the health of financial institutions. Their role is to ensure that banks and other financial institutions offer safe loans and that they have enough cash on hand to manage unexpected losses. These procedures help ensure that the financial system as a whole remains

Financial examiners ensure compliance with laws governing financial institutions and transactions.

Financial examiners working in consumer compliance monitor lending activity to ensure that borrowers are treated fairly.

stable. These examiners also evaluate the performance of bank managers.

Financial examiners working in consumer compliance monitor lending activity to ensure that borrowers are treated fairly. They ensure that banks extend loans that borrowers are likely to be able to pay back. They help borrowers avoid "predatory loans"—loans that may generate profit for banks through high interest payments but may be costly to borrowers and damage their credit scores. Examiners also ensure that banks do not discriminate against borrowers based on race, ethnicity, or other characteristics.

Work Environment

Financial examiners held about 65,600 jobs in 2022. The largest employers of financial examiners were as follows:

Credit intermediation and related activities	42%
Securities, commodity contracts, and other financial investments and related activities	15
Federal government	10
Management of companies and enterprises	9
State government, excluding education and hospitals	8

Financial examiners typically work in offices. They frequently have to travel to inspect a bank onsite.

Work Schedules

Most financial examiners work full time.

How to Become a Financial Examiner

Financial examiners typically need a bachelor's degree that includes some coursework in accounting. Entry-level examiners are trained on the job by senior examiners.

Education

Financial examiners typically need a bachelor's degree to enter the occupation. A degree in business or a related field is common. Coursework should include accounting, finance, or related subjects.

Licenses, Certifications, and Registrations

Although it is not required, professional certification indicates competencies for financial examiners who have it. The Society of Financial Examiners (SOFE) offers the Accredited Financial Examiner (AFE) and the Certified Financial Examiner (CFE) designations. Both may be earned after completing extensive requirements and passing a series of examinations. Continuing education is required to maintain these designations.

Some financial examiners become Certified Public Accountants (CPAs). CPAs are licensed by their state's Board of Accountancy. Becoming a CPA requires passing a national exam and meeting other state requirements.

Training

Once hired, financial examiners receive on-the-job training. Entry-level workers learn their job duties while supervised by senior examiners. The length of training varies but typically lasts more than 1 year.

Advancement

After a few years of experience, financial examiners may advance to a senior examiner position. Senior examiners handle more complex cases and may lead examination teams. Requirements for these positions vary, but employers often prefer candidates who have a master's degree in either accounting or business administration or who are Certified Public Accountants (CPAs).

Financial examiners typically work in offices. They frequently have to travel to inspect a bank onsite.

Professional certification, although not required, indicates competency for financial examiners who have it.

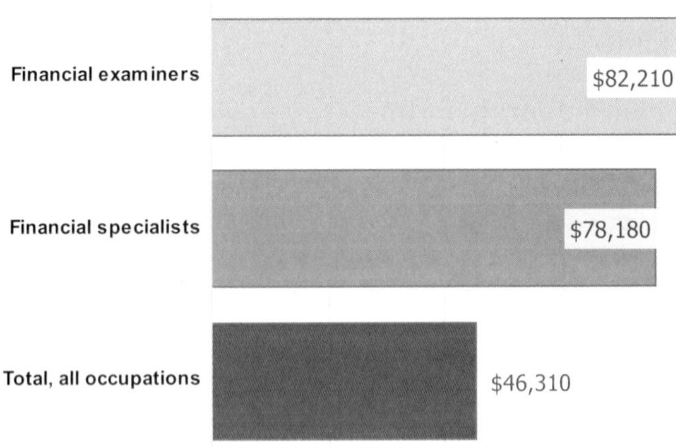

Note: All Occupations includes all occupations in the U.S. Economy.
Source: U.S. Bureau of Labor Statistics, Occupational Employment and Wage Statistics.

Important Qualities

Analytical skills. Financial examiners need to evaluate how well the managers of financial institutions are handling risk and whether the individual loans the institution makes are safe.

Detail oriented. Financial examiners must pay close attention to minutiae when reviewing balance sheets in order to identify risky assets.

Math skills. Financial examiners must do calculations and monitor balance sheets to ensure that a financial institution has available cash.

Writing skills. Financial examiners regularly write reports on the safety and soundness of financial institutions. They must be able to explain technical information clearly.

Pay

The median annual wage for financial examiners was $82,210 in May 2022. The median wage is the wage at which half the workers in an occupation earned more than that amount and half earned less. The lowest 10 percent earned less than $48,490, and the highest 10 percent earned more than $162,760.

In May 2022, the median annual wages for financial examiners in the top industries in which they worked were as follows:

Federal government	$128,910
Securities, commodity contracts, and other financial investments and related activities	101,070
Management of companies and enterprises	82,820
State government, excluding education and hospitals	79,970
Credit intermediation and related activities	75,220

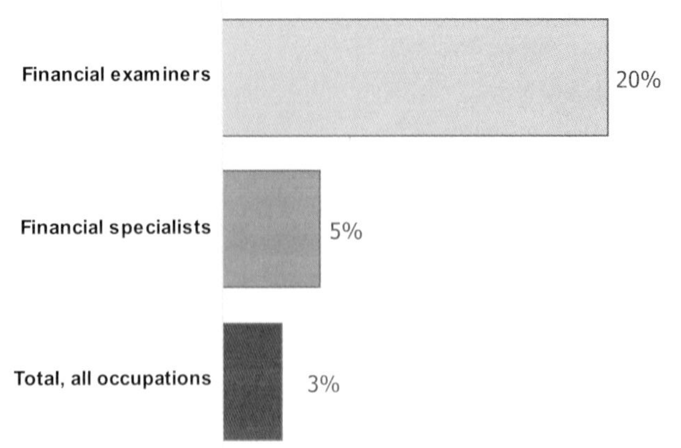

Note: All Occupations includes all occupations in the U.S. Economy.
Source: U.S. Bureau of Labor Statistics, Employment Projections program.

Most financial examiners work full time.

Job Outlook

Employment of financial examiners is projected to grow 20 percent from 2022 to 2032, much faster than the average for all occupations.

About 6,300 openings for financial examiners are projected each year, on average, over the decade. Many of those openings are expected to result from the need to replace workers who transfer to different occupations or exit the labor force, such as to retire.

Employment

Demand for these workers has risen, particularly in the financial industry, because of the need for banking institutions to comply with federal regulation. More of these institutions are hiring financial examiners to help navigate the regulatory environment and reduce the cost of compliance. Financial examiners also will continue to be needed at the federal level to enforce regulations.

Occupational Title	SOC Code	Employment, 2022	Projected Employment, 2032	Change, 2022-32	
				Percent	Numeric
Financial examiners	13-2061	65,600	78,500	20	12,800

Contacts for More Information

For more information about financial examiners, visit

- Federal Deposit Insurance Corporation
- Consumer Financial Protection Bureau
- Society of Financial Examiners
- American Institute of Certified Public Accountants (AICPA)

Fundraisers

Summary

Quick Facts: Fundraisers	
2022 Median Pay	$61,190 per year $29.42 per hour
Typical Entry-Level Education	Bachelor's degree
Work Experience in a Related Occupation	None
On-the-job Training	None
Number of Jobs, 2022	124,000
Job Outlook, 2022-32	5% (Faster than average)
Employment Change, 2022-32	6,500

What Fundraisers Do

Fundraisers organize events and campaigns to raise money and other kinds of donations for an organization.

Work Environment

Fundraisers work primarily for nonprofit organizations, including educational institutions, religious organizations, health research foundations, social services organizations, and political campaigns. Most work full time.

How to Become a Fundraiser

Fundraisers typically need a bachelor's degree and strong communication and organizational skills. Employers may prefer candidates who have studied public relations, communications, English, or business.

Pay

The median annual wage for fundraisers was $61,190 in May 2022.

Job Outlook

Employment of fundraisers is projected to grow 5 percent from 2022 to 2032, faster than the average for all occupations.

About 9,900 openings for fundraisers are projected each year, on average, over the decade. Many of those openings are expected to result from the need to replace workers who transfer to different occupations or exit the labor force, such as to retire.

What Fundraisers Do

Fundraisers organize events and campaigns to raise money and other kinds of donations for an organization. They also may design promotional materials and increase awareness of an organization's work, goals, and financial needs.

Duties

Fundraisers typically do the following:

- Research prospective donors
- Create a strong fundraising message that appeals to potential donors
- Identify and contact potential donors
- Use online platforms to raise donations
- Organize campaigns or events to solicit donations
- Maintain records of donor information
- Evaluate the success of previous fundraising events
- Train volunteers in fundraising procedures and practices
- Ensure that all legal reporting requirements are satisfied

Fundraisers plan and oversee campaigns and events to raise money and other kinds of donations for an organization. They ensure that campaigns are effective by researching potential donors and examining records of those who have given in the past.

Fundraisers who work for political campaigns must be knowledgeable about campaign finance laws, such as the contribution limits of an individual giving to a specific candidate.

The following are examples of types of fundraisers:

Annual campaign fundraisers solicit donations once a year for their organization. Many nonprofit organizations have annual giving campaigns.

Fundraisers plan and oversee campaigns and events to raise money and other donations for an organization.

Fundraisers must create a strong fundraising message that appeals to potential donors.

Capital campaign fundraisers raise money for a specific project, such as the construction of a new building at a university. Capital campaigns also raise money for renovations and the creation or expansion of an endowment.

Major-gifts fundraisers specialize in face-to-face interaction with donors who can give large amounts.

Planned-giving fundraisers solicit donations from those who are looking to pledge money at a future date or in installments over time. These fundraisers must have specialized training in taxes regarding gifts of stocks, bonds, charitable annuities, and real estate bequests in a will.

Work Environment

Fundraisers held about 124,000 jobs in 2022. The largest employers of fundraisers were as follows:

Religious, grantmaking, civic, professional, and similar organizations	42%
Educational services; state, local, and private	22
Healthcare and social assistance	16
Arts, entertainment, and recreation	6

Fundraisers spend much of their time communicating with potential donors.

Most fundraisers raise funds for an organization which employs them directly, although some fundraisers work for consulting firms that have many clients.

Fundraisers spend much of their time communicating with other employees and potential donors, either in person, on the phone, or through email.

Some fundraisers may need to travel to locations where fundraising events are held. Events may include charity runs, walks, galas, and dinners.

Work Schedules

Most fundraisers work full time. Some attend fundraising events on nights and weekends, possibly requiring additional hours.

How to Become a Fundraiser

Fundraisers typically need a bachelor's degree and strong communication and organizational skills. Employers may prefer candidates who have studied public relations, communications, English, or business.

Education

Although fundraisers have a variety of academic backgrounds, common bachelor's degree fields include communications, business, and social science. Degrees in other subjects also are acceptable.

Other Experience

Internships and previous work experience are important in obtaining a paid position as a fundraiser. Many fundraising campaigns rely on volunteers having face-to-face or over-the-phone interaction with potential donors. It is important for the fundraiser who organizes the campaign to have experience with this type of work.

Licenses, Certifications, and Registrations

Laws vary by state, but many states require some types of fundraisers to register with a state authority. Check with your state for more information.

Fundraisers typically need a bachelor's degree and strong communication skills.

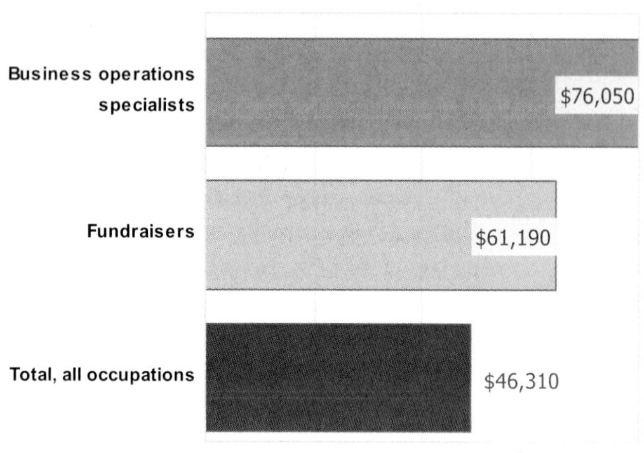

Note: All Occupations includes all occupations in the U.S. Economy.
Source: U.S. Bureau of Labor Statistics, Occupational Employment and Wage Statistics.

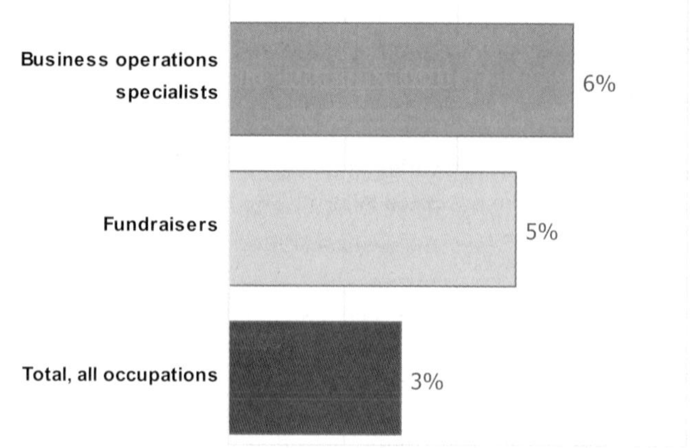

Note: All Occupations includes all occupations in the U.S. Economy.
Source: U.S. Bureau of Labor Statistics, Employment Projections program.

Advancement

Fundraisers can advance to fundraising manager positions. However, some manager positions may also require a master's degree, in addition to years of work experience as a fundraiser.

Important Qualities

Communication skills. Fundraisers need strong communication skills to clearly explain the message and goals of their organization so that people will make donations.

Detail oriented. Fundraisers must be detail oriented because they deal with large volumes of data, including lists of people's names and phone numbers, and must comply with state and federal regulations. Failing to do so may result in penalties.

Interpersonal skills. Fundraisers need strong interpersonal skills to develop and maintain relationships with donors.

Organizational skills. Fundraisers manage large campaigns and events. They must have strong planning and organizational skills in order to succeed.

Pay

The median annual wage for fundraisers was $61,190 in May 2022. The median wage is the wage at which half the workers in an occupation earned more than that amount and half earned less. The lowest 10 percent earned less than $37,700, and the highest 10 percent earned more than $102,740.

In May 2022, the median annual wages for fundraisers in the top industries in which they worked were as follows:

Educational services; state, local, and private	$64,690
Religious, grantmaking, civic, professional, and similar organizations	62,480
Arts, entertainment, and recreation	56,650
Healthcare and social assistance	54,120

Most fundraisers work full time. Some attend fundraising events on nights and weekends, possibly requiring additional hours.

Job Outlook

Employment of fundraisers is projected to grow 5 percent from 2022 to 2032, faster than the average for all occupations.

About 9,900 openings for fundraisers are projected each year, on average, over the decade. Many of those openings are expected to result from the need to replace workers who transfer to different occupations or exit the labor force, such as to retire.

Employment

Employment growth will be driven by the continued need of nonprofit organizations to collect donations in order to run their operations.

Many nonprofit organizations are focusing on cultivating an online presence and are increasingly using social media for fundraising activities. As a result, social media platforms have created new avenues for fundraisers to connect with potential donors and to spread their organization's message.

Occupational Title	SOC Code	Employment, 2022	Projected Employment, 2032	Change, 2022-32	
				Percent	Numeric
Fundraisers	13-1131	124,000	130,500	5	6,500

Contacts for More Information

The *Handbook* does not have contacts for more information for this occupation

Human Resources Specialists

Summary

Quick Facts: Human Resources Specialists	
2022 Median Pay	$64,240 per year $30.88 per hour
Typical Entry-Level Education	Bachelor's degree
Work Experience in a Related Occupation	None
On-the-job Training	None
Number of Jobs, 2022	874,500
Job Outlook, 2022-32	6% (Faster than average)
Employment Change, 2022-32	51,400

What Human Resources Specialists Do

Human resources specialists recruit, screen, and interview job applicants and place newly hired workers in jobs. They also may handle compensation and benefits, training, and employee relations.

Work Environment

Human resources specialists generally work in office settings. Some, particularly recruitment specialists, travel to attend job fairs, visit college campuses, and meet with applicants. Most human resources specialists work full time during regular business hours. Some work more than 40 hours per week.

How to Become a Human Resources Specialist

To enter the occupation, human resources specialists typically need a bachelor's degree in human resources, business, or a related field.

Pay

The median annual wage for human resources specialists was $64,240 in May 2022.

Job Outlook

Employment of human resources specialists is projected to grow 6 percent from 2022 to 2032, faster than the average for all occupations.

About 78,700 openings for human resources specialists are projected each year, on average, over the decade. Many of those openings are expected to result from the need to replace workers who transfer to different occupations or exit the labor force, such as to retire.

What Human Resources Specialists Do

Human resources specialists recruit, screen, and interview job applicants and place newly hired workers in jobs. They also may handle compensation and benefits, training, and employee relations.

Duties

Human resources specialists typically do the following:

- Consult with employers to identify hiring needs
- Interview job applicants about their relevant experience, education, and skills
- Check applicants' references and backgrounds
- Inform applicants about job details, such as duties, benefits, and working conditions
- Hire or refer qualified applicants
- Run or help with new employee orientation
- Keep employment records and process paperwork

Human resources specialists often are trained in tasks for all disciplines of a human resources department. In addition to recruiting applicants and placing workers, human resources specialists help guide employees through human resources procedures and answer questions about an organization's policies. They sometimes administer benefits, process payroll, and handle associated questions or problems. Some specialists focus more on strategic planning and hiring than on administrative

Many human resources specialists interview applicants and help place workers.

Recruitment specialists may distribute information at job fairs or online.

duties. They also ensure that all human resources functions comply with federal, state, and local regulations.

The following are examples of types of human resources specialists:

Human resources generalists handle all aspects of human resources work. Their duties include recruitment, compensation, benefits, training, and employee relations, as well as administering human resources policies, procedures, and programs.

Recruitment specialists, sometimes known as ***recruiters*** or ***"talent acquisition specialists,"*** find, screen, and interview applicants for job openings in an organization. They search for applicants by posting listings, attending job fairs, and visiting college campuses. They also may test applicants, contact references, and extend job offers.

Some specialists focus on a certain area of human resources, such as retirement or training. For information about those who focus on an organization's wage and nonwage programs for workers, see the profile on compensation, benefits, and job analysis specialists. For information about those who plan and administer programs that improve workers' skills and knowledge, see the profile on training and development specialists.

Work Environment

Human resources specialists held about 874,500 jobs in 2022. The largest employers of human resources specialists were as follows:

Employment services	18%
Professional, scientific, and technical services	13
Healthcare and social assistance	10
Government	9
Manufacturing	7

Some organizations contract recruitment and placement work to outside firms, such as those in the employment services industry or the professional, scientific, and technical industry.

Work Schedules

Human resources specialists generally work in office settings. Some, particularly recruitment specialists, travel to attend job fairs, visit college campuses, and meet with applicants.

Most specialists work full time during regular business hours. Some work more than 40 hours per week.

How to Become a Human Resources Specialist

Human resources specialists typically need a bachelor's degree to enter the occupation.

Education

Human resources specialists typically need a bachelor's degree in human resources, business, communications, or a related field.

By working in an internship during college, students gain relevant experience that may be helpful in competing for human resources specialist jobs. Internships in human resources departments may help prospective specialists to increase their understanding of the occupation and to network in an industry.

Other Experience

Some positions require human resources specialists to have relevant work experience. Candidates may gain experience as human resources assistants (information clerks), customer service representatives, or in related occupations.

Employers also may prefer to hire candidates who have experience in areas such as personnel recruitment, staff training and development, employee relations, and compensation and benefits. Candidates sometimes get this experience while in college, either through courses or by volunteering.

Licenses, Certifications, and Registrations

Professional associations that specialize in human resources offer courses to enhance the skills of their members, and some offer certification programs. For example, the Society for Human

Employment interviewers speak with applicants and ask them questions before referring them to appropriate jobs.

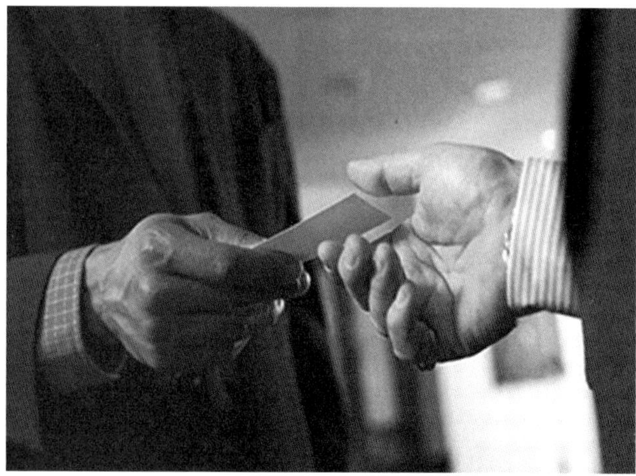

Human resources specialists must usually have a bachelor's degree in human resources, business, or a related field.

Resource Management (SHRM) offers the SHRM Certified Professional (SHRM-CP) and SHRM Senior Certified Professional (SHRM-SCP), and the HR Certification Institute (HRCI) offers a range of certifications for varying levels of expertise.

Certification usually requires that candidates pass an exam that covers human resources knowledge and asks candidates to apply their knowledge to different situations. Candidates for certification also typically need to meet minimum education and experience requirements.

Although certification is usually voluntary, some employers prefer or require it. Human resources generalists, in particular, may benefit from certification because it shows knowledge and professional competence across all human resources areas.

Advancement

Human resources specialists who have a thorough knowledge of their organization and its personnel regulations may advance to become human resources managers. Specialists may increase their chance of advancement by taking on new responsibilities or completing voluntary certification programs.

Important Qualities

Communication skills. Listening and speaking skills are essential for human resources specialists. They must convey information effectively and respond to questions and concerns from employers, job applicants, and employees.

Decision-making skills. Human resources specialists must use sound judgment when reviewing applicants' qualifications or when working to resolve disputes.

Detail oriented. Specialists must pay attention to detail when evaluating applicants' qualifications, doing background checks, maintaining records of an employee grievance, and ensuring that a workplace complies with labor standards.

Interpersonal skills. Specialists continually interact with others and must be able to converse and connect with people from varied backgrounds.

Pay

The median annual wage for human resources specialists was $64,240 in May 2022. The median wage is the wage at which half the workers in an occupation earned more than that amount and half earned less. The lowest 10 percent earned less than $39,340, and the highest 10 percent earned more than $116,060.

In May 2022, the median annual wages for human resources specialists in the top industries in which they worked were as follows:

Professional, scientific, and technical services	$77,460
Government	75,030
Manufacturing	73,710
Healthcare and social assistance	58,920
Employment services	50,190

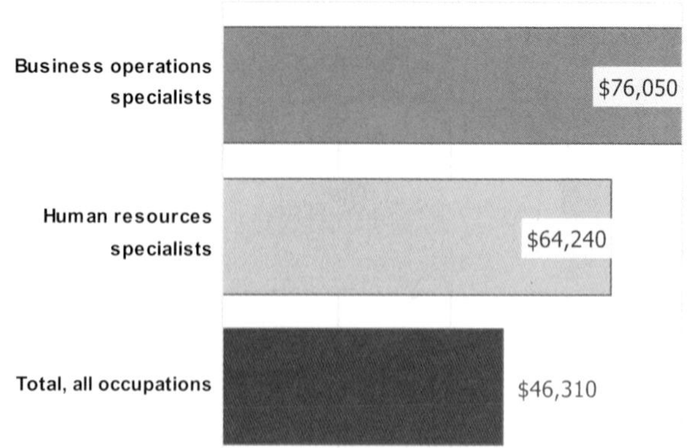

Note: All Occupations includes all occupations in the U.S. Economy.
Source: U.S. Bureau of Labor Statistics, Occupational Employment and Wage Statistics.

Some human resources specialists, particularly recruitment specialists, travel to attend job fairs, visit college campuses, and meet with applicants.

Most specialists work full time during regular business hours. Some work more than 40 hours per week.

Job Outlook

Employment of human resources specialists is projected to grow 6 percent from 2022 to 2032, faster than the average for all occupations.

About 78,700 openings for human resources specialists are projected each year, on average, over the decade. Many of those openings are expected to result from the need to replace workers who transfer to different occupations or exit the labor force, such as to retire.

Employment

Employment growth is expected as human resources specialists are needed to explain increasingly complex employment

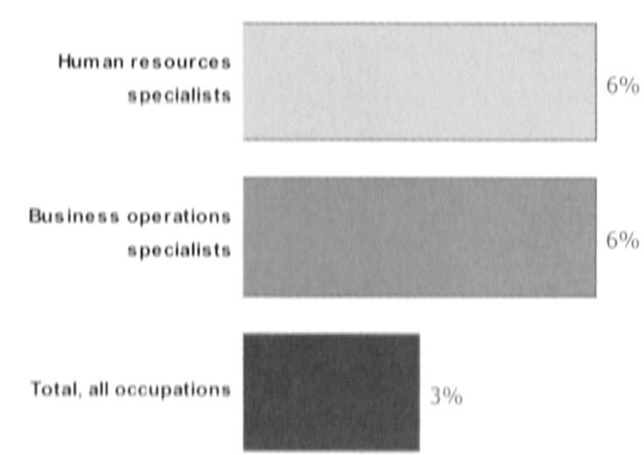

Note: All Occupations includes all occupations in the U.S. Economy.
Source: U.S. Bureau of Labor Statistics, Employment Projections program.

laws and benefit options. At the same time, some companies may outsource human resources functions to organizations that provide these services, rather than directly employing human resources specialists.

Occupational Title	SOC Code	Employment, 2022	Projected Employment, 2032	Change, 2022-32	
				Percent	Numeric
Human resources specialists	13-1071	874,500	925,900	6	51,400

Contacts for More Information

For more information about human resources careers and certification, visit

- HR Certification Institute
- International Public Management Association for Human Resources
- Society for Human Resource Management
- WorldatWork

Insurance Underwriters

Summary

Quick Facts: Insurance Underwriters

2022 Median Pay	$76,230 per year $36.65 per hour
Typical Entry-Level Education	Bachelor's degree
Work Experience in a Related Occupation	None
On-the-job Training	Moderate-term on-the-job training
Number of Jobs, 2022	125,500
Job Outlook, 2022-32	-2% (Decline)
Employment Change, 2022-32	-3,000

What Insurance Underwriters Do

Insurance underwriters evaluate insurance applications and decide whether to approve them.

Work Environment

Insurance underwriters work in an office setting during regular business hours. Most work full time.

How to Become an Insurance Underwriter

Insurance underwriters typically need a bachelor's degree to enter the occupation. Certification may be beneficial.

Insurance underwriters determine the risk of insuring a client.

Pay

The median annual wage for insurance underwriters was $76,230 in May 2022.

Job Outlook

Employment of insurance underwriters is projected to decline 2 percent from 2022 to 2032.

Despite declining employment, about 8,200 openings for insurance underwriters are projected each year, on average, over the decade. All of those openings are expected to result from the need to replace workers who transfer to other occupations or exit the labor force, such as to retire.

What Insurance Underwriters Do

Insurance underwriters evaluate insurance applications and decide whether to approve them. For approved applications, underwriters determine coverage amounts and premiums.

Duties

Insurance underwriters typically do the following:

- Analyze information stated on insurance applications
- Determine the risk involved in insuring a client
- Screen applicants based on set criteria
- Use automated software to determine the risk of insuring applicants

Most insurance underwriters specialize in one of three broad fields: health, life, and property and casualty.

- Review recommendations from underwriting software
- Contact field representatives, medical personnel, and others to obtain additional information
- Decide whether to offer insurance
- Determine appropriate premiums and amounts of coverage

Underwriters are the main link between an insurance company and an insurance sales agent. Insurance underwriters use computer software to analyze risk for determining whether to approve an applicant. They take specific information about an applicant and enter it into a program. The program then provides recommendations on coverage and premiums. Underwriters evaluate these recommendations and decide whether to approve or reject the application. If a decision is difficult, they may consult additional sources, such as medical documents and credit scores.

For simple and common types of insurance, such as automobile insurance, underwriters typically rely on automated recommendations. For specific and complex insurance types, such as workers' compensation, underwriters need to rely more on analytical insight.

Underwriters analyze the risk factors appearing on an application. For example, if an applicant reports a previous bankruptcy, the underwriter must determine whether that information is relevant to the policy being applied for. If relevant, the underwriter would then consider how far in the past the bankruptcy occurred and how the applicant's financial situation has changed since the bankruptcy filing.

Insurance underwriters must achieve a balance between risky and cautious decisions. If underwriters allow too much risk, the insurance company will pay out too many claims. But if they don't approve enough applications, the company will not make enough money from premiums.

Most insurance underwriters specialize in one of three broad fields: health, life, and property and casualty. Although the job duties in each field are similar, the criteria that underwriters use vary. For example, for someone seeking life insurance, underwriters consider the person's age and financial history. For someone applying for car insurance (a form of property and casualty insurance), underwriters consider the person's driving record.

Within the broad field of property and casualty, underwriters may specialize in commercial (business) insurance or personal insurance. They also may specialize by the type of policy, such as for insuring automobiles, homes, or pets.

Work Environment

Insurance underwriters held about 125,500 jobs in 2022. The largest employers of insurance underwriters were as follows:

Direct insurance (except life, health, and medical) carriers	46%
Insurance agencies and brokerages	26
Other insurance related activities	5
Direct health and medical insurance carriers	4
Credit intermediation and related activities	3

Most underwriters work full time.

Underwriters work in an office setting during regular business hours. They spend much of their time alone at a computer, most often working on applications but sometimes handling customer inquiries.

Some property and casualty underwriters travel to assess properties in person.

Work Schedules

Most underwriters work full time.

How to Become an Insurance Underwriter

Insurance underwriters typically need a bachelor's degree to enter the occupation. However, candidates who have an associate's degree or a high school diploma and insurance-related work experience sometimes qualify for positions. Certification may be beneficial.

Education

Employers usually prefer to hire candidates who have a bachelor's degree. A common field of degree is business. Coursework in finance, economics, and mathematics is helpful.

Some colleges and universities partner with local businesses to offer internships. These opportunities allow students to gain knowledge or practical experience through assisting in a variety of tasks, such as underwriting.

Most firms prefer to hire applicants with a bachelor's degree.

Training

Beginning underwriters typically work under the supervision of senior underwriters for up to 12 months. Trainees work on basic applications and learn the most common risk factors. Some companies offer training programs that include classroom instruction on the basics of underwriting.

As new underwriters gain experience, they may work independently and handle more complex applications.

Licenses, Certifications, and Registrations

Employers may expect underwriters to become certified through coursework. These courses are important for keeping current with new insurance policies and changes in state and federal regulations.

Many options are available for certification or insurance specialty designations. Examples include the Life Underwriter Training Council Fellow (LUTCF) designation, the Chartered Property and Casualty Underwriter (CPCU) designation, and the Chartered Life Underwriter (CLU) certification.

Requirements for certification or designation vary and often include coursework or exams or both. Some credentials are available to new underwriters, but others require candidates to have a specified number of years of experience.

Advancement

Experienced underwriters may advance to become senior underwriters or underwriter managers. Underwriters may need certification to progress into these positions.

Important Qualities

Analytical skills. Underwriters must evaluate information from a variety of sources to balance risk against caution.

Decision-making skills. Underwriters determine whether to approve applicants for insurance coverage and, if approved, at what level to set premiums.

Detail oriented. Underwriters must stay focused when reviewing insurance applications because each item may affect the coverage decision.

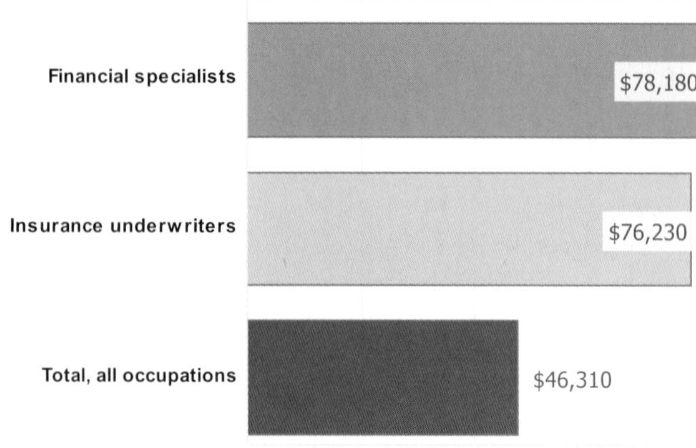

Note: All Occupations includes all occupations in the U.S. Economy.
Source: U.S. Bureau of Labor Statistics, Occupational Employment and Wage Statistics.

Interpersonal skills. Underwriters need to communicate and relate well with people because much of their work involves dealing with clients or others, such as insurance sales agents.

Math skills. Underwriters need math knowledge to ensure accuracy in determining the probability of losses and calculating appropriate premiums on an insurance policy.

Pay

The median annual wage for insurance underwriters was $76,230 in May 2022. The median wage is the wage at which half the workers in an occupation earned more than that amount and half earned less. The lowest 10 percent earned less than $47,340, and the highest 10 percent earned more than $130,210.

In May 2022, the median annual wages for insurance underwriters in the top industries in which they worked were as follows:

Credit intermediation and related activities	$83,000
Direct insurance (except life, health, and medical) carriers	76,860
Other insurance related activities	74,780
Insurance agencies and brokerages	74,310
Direct health and medical insurance carriers	74,000

Most underwriters work full time.

Job Outlook

Employment of insurance underwriters is projected to decline 2 percent from 2022 to 2032.

Despite declining employment, about 8,200 openings for insurance underwriters are projected each year, on average, over the decade. All of those openings are expected to result from the need to replace workers who transfer to other occupations or exit the labor force, such as to retire.

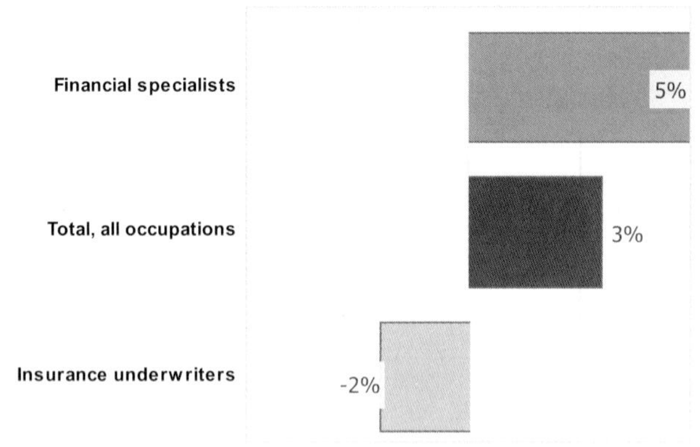

Note: All Occupations includes all occupations in the U.S. Economy.
Source: U.S. Bureau of Labor Statistics, Employment Projections program.

Employment

Automated underwriting software allows workers to process applications quickly, reducing the need for underwriters. As this technology continues to improve and become more widely adopted in the insurance industry, more underwriting decisions are expected to be made automatically.

However, there still will be a need for underwriters to review and update the criteria that run the automation. In addition, their analytical insight will be needed in specific fields, such as workers' compensation, marine insurance, and health insurance.

Occupational Title	SOC Code	Employment, 2022	Projected Employment, 2032	Change, 2022-32	
				Percent	Numeric
Insurance underwriters	13-2053	125,500	122,400	-2	-3,000

Contacts for More Information

For more information about property and casualty insurance, visit

- Insurance Information Institute (III)
- The Institutes
- The American College of Financial Services
- National Association of Insurance and Financial Advisors (NAIFA)

Labor Relations Specialists

Summary

Quick Facts: Labor Relations Specialists	
2022 Median Pay	$82,010 per year $39.43 per hour
Typical Entry-Level Education	Bachelor's degree
Work Experience in a Related Occupation	Less than 5 years
On-the-job Training	None
Number of Jobs, 2022	64,600
Job Outlook, 2022-32	-1% (Little or no change)
Employment Change, 2022-32	-500

What Labor Relations Specialists Do

Labor relations specialists interpret and administer labor contracts.

Work Environment

Labor relations specialists generally work in offices. Most work full time during regular business hours.

How to Become a Labor Relations Specialist

To enter the occupation, these specialists typically need a bachelor's degree in labor relations, human resources, industrial relations, business, or a related field. However, the level of education and experience required varies by position and employer.

Pay

The median annual wage for labor relations specialists was $82,010 in May 2022.

Job Outlook

Employment of labor relations specialists is projected to show little or no change from 2022 to 2032.

Despite limited employment growth, about 5,200 openings for labor relations specialists are projected each year, on average, over the decade. Most of those openings are expected to

Labor relations specialists interpret and administer labor contracts regarding issues such as employee welfare, healthcare, and pensions.

result from the need to replace workers who transfer to different occupations or exit the labor force, such as to retire.

What Labor Relations Specialists Do

Labor relations specialists interpret and administer labor contracts regarding issues such as wages and salaries, healthcare, pensions, and union and management practices.

Duties

Labor relations specialists typically do the following:

- Advise management on contracts, worker grievances, and disciplinary procedures
- Lead meetings between management and labor
- Meet with union representatives
- Draft proposals and rules or regulations
- Ensure that human resources policies are consistent with union agreements
- Interpret formal communications between management and labor
- Investigate validity of labor grievances
- Train management on labor relations

Labor relations specialists work with representatives from a labor union and a company's management. In addition to leading meetings between the two groups, these specialists draft formal language as part of the collective bargaining process. These contracts are called collective bargaining agreements (CBAs), and they serve as a legal and procedural guide for employee/management relations.

Labor relations specialists also address specific grievances workers might have, and ensure that all labor and management solutions comply within the relevant CBA.

Work Environment

Labor relations specialists held about 64,600 jobs in 2022. The largest employers of labor relations specialists were as follows:

Labor relations specialists draft proposals and rules or regulations in order to help facilitate collective bargaining.

Labor relations specialists generally work in offices.

Labor unions and similar labor organizations	74%
Government	4
Management of companies and enterprises	2

Labor relations specialists generally work in offices. Some may travel for arbitration meetings or to discuss contracts with employees or management. The work of labor relations specialists can be stressful because negotiating contracts and resolving labor grievances can be tense.

Work Schedules

Most labor relations specialists work full time during regular business hours. Some specialists work longer periods when preparing for meetings or settling disputes.

How to Become a Labor Relations Specialist

To enter the occupation, these specialists typically need a bachelor's degree in labor relations, human resources, industrial relations, business, or a related field. However, the level of education and experience required to become a labor relations specialist varies by position and employer.

Education

Labor relations specialists typically need a bachelor's degree. Some schools offer a bachelor's degree in labor or employment relations. These programs focus on labor-specific topics such as employment law and contract negotiation.

Candidates also may qualify for labor relations specialist positions with a bachelor's degree in human resources, industrial relations, business, or a related field. Coursework typically includes business, professional writing, human resource management, and accounting.

Work Experience in a Related Occupation

Many positions require previous work experience. Candidates can gain experience as human resources specialists, compensation, benefits, and job analysis specialists, or human resources generalists before specializing in labor relations.

Labor relations specialists usually have a bachelor's degree in labor relations, human resources, industrial relations, business, or a related field.

Licenses, Certifications, and Registrations

Some colleges and universities offer labor relations certificates to specialists who prefer greater specialization in certain topics, such as mediation. Earning these certificates give participants a better understanding of labor law, the collective bargaining process, and worker grievance procedures.

Advancement

Labor relations specialists who seek further expertise in contract negotiation, labor law, and similar topics may become lawyers. They will need to earn a law degree and pass their state's bar exam.

Important Qualities

Decision-making skills. Labor relations specialists use decisionmaking skills to help management and labor agree on decisions when resolving grievances or other disputes.

Detail oriented. Specialists must be detail oriented when evaluating labor laws and maintaining records of an employee grievance.

Interpersonal skills. Interpersonal skills are essential for labor relations specialists. When mediating between labor and management, specialists must be able to converse and connect with people from different backgrounds.

Listening skills. Listening skills are essential for labor relations specialists. When evaluating grievances, for example, they must pay careful attention to workers' responses, understand the points they are making, and ask relevant follow-up questions.

Writing skills. All labor relations specialists need strong writing skills to be effective at their job. They often draft proposals, and these proposals must be able to convey complex information to both workers and management.

Pay

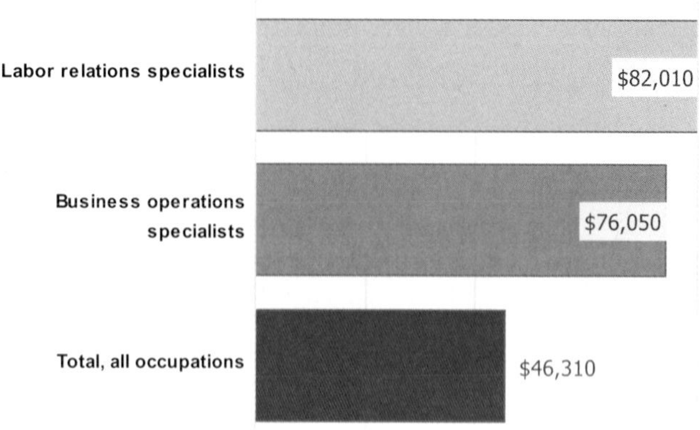

Note: All Occupations includes all occupations in the U.S. Economy.
Source: U.S. Bureau of Labor Statistics, Occupational Employment and Wage Statistics.

The median annual wage for labor relations specialists was $82,010 in May 2022. The median wage is the wage at which half the workers in an occupation earned more than that amount and half earned less. The lowest 10 percent earned less than $38,900, and the highest 10 percent earned more than $131,660.

In May 2022, the median annual wages for labor relations specialists in the top industries in which they worked were as follows:

Management of companies and enterprises	$101,030
Government	81,500
Labor unions and similar labor organizations	80,880

Most labor relations specialists work full time during regular business hours. Some specialists work longer periods when preparing for meetings or settling disputes.

Job Outlook

Employment of labor relations specialists is projected to show little or no change from 2022 to 2032.

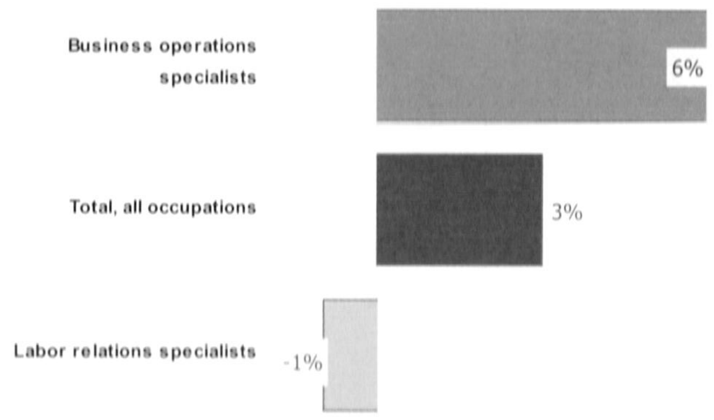

Note: All Occupations includes all occupations in the U.S. Economy.
Source: U.S. Bureau of Labor Statistics, Employment Projections program.

Despite limited employment growth, about 5,200 openings for labor relations specialists are projected each year, on average, over the decade. Most of those openings are expected to result from the need to replace workers who transfer to different occupations or exit the labor force, such as to retire.

Employment

If union membership rates decline, overall demand for these specialists will be limited. However, there will still be some need for labor relations specialists' expertise as union negotiations and contract disputes continue.

Employment projections data for labor relations specialists, 2022-32

Occupational Title	SOC Code	Employment, 2022	Projected Employment, 2032	Change, 2022-32		Employment by Industry
				Percent	Numeric	
SOURCE: U.S. Bureau of Labor Statistics, Employment Projections program						
Labor relations specialists	13-1075	64,600	64,000	-1	-500	Get data

Contacts for More Information

For more information about labor relations careers and certification, visit

➤ Society for Human Resource Management

➤ Federal Labor Relations Authority

Loan Officers

Summary

Quick Facts: Loan Officers

2022 Median Pay	$65,740 per year $31.60 per hour
Typical Entry-Level Education	Bachelor's degree
Work Experience in a Related Occupation	Less than 5 years
On-the-job Training	Moderate-term on-the-job training
Number of Jobs, 2022	354,800
Job Outlook, 2022-32	3% (As fast as average)
Employment Change, 2022-32	10,400

What Loan Officers Do

Loan officers evaluate, authorize, or recommend approval of loan applications.

Loan officers meet with potential borrowers and approve loans.

Work Environment

Most loan officers are employed by commercial banks, credit unions, mortgage companies, and other financial institutions. Most loan officers work full time, and some work more than 40 hours per week. Except for consumer loan officers, who spend most of their time in offices, these workers may travel to visit clients.

How to Become a Loan Officer

Loan officers typically need a bachelor's degree and on-the-job training. Mortgage loan officers must be licensed.

Pay

The median annual wage for loan officers was $65,740 in May 2022.

Job Outlook

Employment of loan officers is projected to grow 3 percent from 2022 to 2032, about as fast as the average for all occupations.

About 25,300 openings for loan officers are projected each year, on average, over the decade. Many of those openings are expected to result from the need to replace workers who transfer to different occupations or exit the labor force, such as to retire.

What Loan Officers Do

Loan officers evaluate, authorize, or recommend approval of applications for personal and business loans.

Duties

Loan officers typically do the following:

- Contact businesses or people to ask if they need a loan
- Talk with loan applicants to gather information and answer questions
- Explain to applicants the different types of loans and the terms of each type
- Obtain, verify, and analyze applicants' financial information, such as credit rating and income

Consumer loan officers specialize in loans to people, such as loans for buying cars or paying for college tuition.

- Review loan agreements to ensure that they comply with federal and state regulations
- Approve loan applications or refer them to management for a decision

Loan officers use a process called underwriting to assess whether applicants qualify for loans. After collecting and verifying all the required financial documents, loan officers evaluate the information to determine an applicant's need for a loan and ability to repay it. Most firms use underwriting software, which produces a loan recommendation based on the applicant's financial status. Loan officers review the software output together with the evaluation of an applicant's financial information to make a final decision.

The work of loan officers has customer-service and sales components. For example, loan officers often answer questions and guide customers through the application process. In addition, many loan officers market the products and services of their lending institution and actively solicit new business.

The following are common types of loan officers:

Commercial loan officers specialize in loans to businesses, which often use the loans to buy supplies and to upgrade or expand operations. Commercial loans frequently are larger and more complicated than other types of loans. Some commercial loans are so large and complex that no single bank will provide the entire amount requested. In such cases, loan officers may have to work with multiple banks to put together a package of loans.

Consumer loan officers specialize in loans to people for a variety of uses, such as buying a car or paying college tuition. For simple consumer loans, the underwriting process may be fully automated. However, the loan officer still guides applicants through the process. Some institutions—usually small banks and credit unions—rely on loan officers to complete the underwriting process instead of using underwriting software.

Mortgage loan officers specialize in loans that are used to buy real estate (property and buildings). Mortgage loan officers work on loans for both business and residential purchases. Often, these officers seek out clients, which requires them to develop relationships with real estate companies and other sources that can refer prospective borrowers.

Within these three fields, some loan officers specialize in a particular part of the loan process:

Loan collection officers contact borrowers who fail to make payments. They work with borrowers to help them find a way to keep paying off the loan. If the borrower continues to miss payments on secured loans—those involving collateral, such as a home or a car, that the borrower uses to secure the loan—these officers start the process of taking away the asset and selling it to repay the loan.

Loan underwriters specialize in evaluating whether a client is creditworthy. Underwriters collect, verify, and evaluate the financial information that clients provide on their loan applications and then use loan underwriting software to produce recommendations.

Work Environment

Loan officers held about 354,800 jobs in 2022. The largest employers of loan officers were as follows:

Employer	Percent
Credit intermediation and related activities	82%
Management of companies and enterprises	4
Automobile dealers	3

Most loan officers work full time.

The credit intermediation industry includes commercial banks, savings institutions, and mortgage companies.

Loan officers who specialize in consumer loans usually work in offices. Mortgage and commercial loan officers may work outside the office and meet with clients at their homes or businesses.

Work Schedules

Most loan officers work full time, and some work more than 40 hours per week.

How to Become a Loan Officer

Loan officers typically need a bachelor's degree and on-the-job training. Mortgage loan officers must be licensed.

Education

Loan officers typically need a bachelor's degree, usually in a field such as business or finance. Because commercial loan officers analyze the finances of businesses applying for credit, they need to understand general business accounting, including how to read financial statements.

Some jobseekers may be able to enter the occupation without a bachelor's degree if they have related work experience, such as in banking, customer service, or sales. Organizations that specialize in certain fields typically prefer to hire candidates who have some experience in those areas. For example, mortgage companies may prefer to hire candidates with residential mortgage or real estate experience.

Training

Once hired, loan officers typically receive some on-the-job training. This may be a combination of formal, company-sponsored training and informal training during the first few months on the job.

Loan officers must pay attention to detail, as each piece of information on an application can have a major effect on the profitability of a loan.

Licenses, Certifications, and Registrations

Mortgage loan officers must have a Mortgage Loan Originator (MLO) license. To become licensed, they must complete prelicensing courses, pass a national exam, and submit to background and credit checks. Licenses must be renewed annually, and individual states may have additional requirements. Check your state licensing agency website for more information.

Several banking associations, including the American Bankers Association and the Mortgage Bankers Association, as well as a number of schools, offer courses, training programs, or certifications for loan officers. Although not required, certification shows dedication and expertise and thus may enhance a candidate's employment opportunities.

Important Qualities

Decision-making skills. Loan officers must assess an applicant's financial information and decide whether to approve the loan.

Detail oriented. Information on an application affects the potential profitability of a loan, so loan officers must pay attention to details.

Initiative. Loan officers may act as salespeople in promoting their lending institution, so they must contact people and businesses to determine their need for a loan.

Interpersonal skills. Loan officers must be able to guide customers through the application process and answer their questions.

Pay

The median annual wage for loan officers was $65,740 in May 2022. The median wage is the wage at which half the workers in an occupation earned more than that amount and half earned less. The lowest 10 percent earned less than $34,920, and the highest 10 percent earned more than $138,580.

In May 2022, the median annual wages for loan officers in the top industries in which they worked were as follows:

Automobile dealers	$92,230
Management of companies and enterprises	76,870
Credit intermediation and related activities	64,390

Compensation varies widely by employer. Some loan officers are paid a flat salary; others are paid on commission. Those on commission usually are paid a base salary plus a commission for the loans they originate. Loan officers also may receive extra commission or bonuses based on the number of loans they originate or how well the loans perform.

Most loan officers work full time, and some work more than 40 hours per week.

Job Outlook

Employment of loan officers is projected to grow 3 percent from 2022 to 2032, about as fast as the average for all occupations.

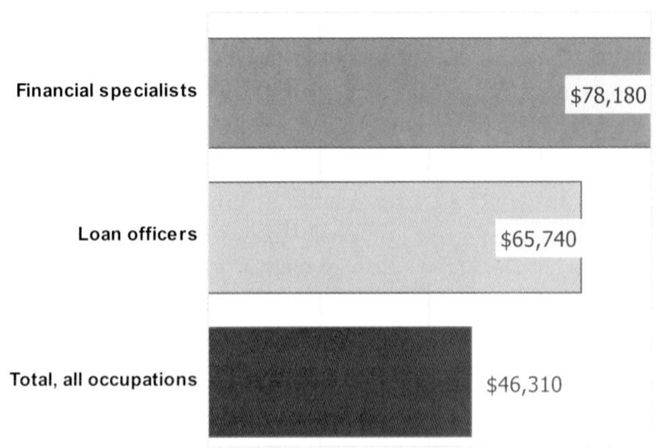

Note: All Occupations includes all occupations in the U.S. Economy. Source: U.S. Bureau of Labor Statistics, Occupational Employment and Wage Statistics.

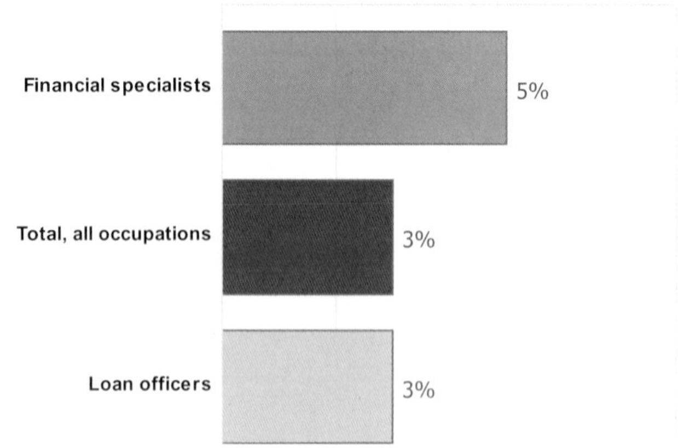

Note: All Occupations includes all occupations in the U.S. Economy. Source: U.S. Bureau of Labor Statistics, Employment Projections program.

About 25,300 openings for loan officers are projected each year, on average, over the decade. Many of those openings are expected to result from the need to replace workers who transfer to different occupations or exit the labor force, such as to retire.

Employment

Increased demand for loan officers is expected as both businesses and individuals seek credit to finance commercial investments and personal spending. Loan officers will be needed to evaluate the creditworthiness of applicants and determine the likelihood that loans will be paid back in full and on time.

However, the decline of bank branches and the increased use of productivity-enhancing technology in loan processing are expected to slow employment growth.

Occupational Title	SOC Code	Employment, 2022	Projected Employment, 2032	Change, 2022-32	
				Percent	Numeric
Loan officers	13-2072	354,800	365,300	3	10,400

Contacts for More Information

For more information about certification and training for loan officers, visit

- American Bankers Association (ABA)
- Mortgage Bankers Association (MBA)
- Nationwide Multistate Licensing System (NMLS)

Logisticians

Summary

Quick Facts: Logisticians	
2022 Median Pay	$77,520 per year $37.27 per hour
Typical Entry-Level Education	Bachelor's degree
Work Experience in a Related Occupation	None
On-the-job Training	None
Number of Jobs, 2022	208,700
Job Outlook, 2022-32	18% (Much faster than average)
Employment Change, 2022-32	38,300

What Logisticians Do

Logisticians analyze and coordinate an organization's supply chain.

Work Environment

Logisticians work in nearly every industry. The job can be stressful because logistical work is fast-paced. Most logisticians work full time during regular business hours.

How to Become a Logistician

A bachelor's degree is typically required to enter the occupation, although an associate's degree may be sufficient for some logistician jobs.

Pay

The median annual wage for logisticians was $77,520 in May 2022.

Job Outlook

Employment of logisticians is projected to grow 18 percent from 2022 to 2032, much faster than the average for all occupations.

Logisticians work to understand customers' needs and how to meet them.

About 21,800 openings for logisticians are projected each year, on average, over the decade. Many of those openings are expected to result from the need to replace workers who transfer to different occupations or exit the labor force, such as to retire.

What Logisticians Do

Logisticians analyze and coordinate an organization's supply chain—the system that moves a product from supplier to consumer. They manage the entire life cycle of a product, which includes how a product is acquired, allocated, and delivered.

Duties

Logisticians typically do the following:

- Manage a product's life cycle from design to disposal
- Direct the allocation of materials, supplies, and products
- Develop business relationships with suppliers and clients
- Understand clients' needs and how to meet them
- Review logistical functions and identify areas for improvement
- Propose strategies to minimize the cost or time required to transport goods

Logisticians oversee activities that include purchasing, transportation, inventory, and warehousing. They may direct the movement of a range of goods, people, or supplies, from common consumer goods to military supplies and personnel.

Logisticians use software systems to plan and track the movement of products. They operate software programs designed specifically to manage logistical functions, such as procurement, inventory management, and other supply chain planning and management systems.

Work Environment

Logisticians held about 208,700 jobs in 2022. The largest employers of logisticians were as follows:

Manufacturing	24%
Federal government	17
Professional, scientific, and technical services	16
Management of companies and enterprises	10
Wholesale trade	10

Logisticians work in almost every industry. Some logisticians work in the logistical department of a company, and others work for firms that specialize in logistical work, such as freight-shipping companies.

The job can be stressful because logistical work is fast-paced. Logisticians must ensure that operations stay on schedule, and they must work quickly to solve any problems that arise. Some logisticians travel to manufacturing plants or distribution centers.

Work Schedules

The majority of logisticians work full time and they sometimes work overtime to ensure that operations stay on schedule.

Logisticians manage the life cycle of a product, which includes how a product is distributed and delivered.

When problems arise, logisticians must respond quickly and devise solutions.

How to Become a Logistician

A bachelor's degree is typically required for most positions, although an associate's degree may be sufficient for some logistician jobs. In some cases, related work experience may substitute for education. Industry certification is helpful for jobseekers.

Education

Logisticians may qualify for some positions with an associate's degree. However, due to complex logistics and supply chains, companies prefer to hire workers who have at least a bachelor's degree. Logisticians typically have a bachelor's degree in logistics and supply chain management, business, or a related field.

Bachelor's degree programs often include coursework in operations and database management, and system dynamics. In addition, most programs offer courses that train students on software and technologies commonly used by logisticians, such as radio-frequency identification (RFID).

Licenses, Certifications, and Registrations

Although not required, certification can demonstrate professional competence and a broad knowledge of logistics. Logisticians can obtain certification through the Association for Supply Chain Management or the International Society of Logistics (SOLE). To become certified, a logistician typically needs to meet education and work experience requirements and pass an exam.

A bachelor's degree is typically required for most positions, although an associate's degree may be sufficient for some logistician jobs.

There are several certifications available from the Defense Acquisition University (DAU). These certifications are required for Department of Defense acquisitions.

Work Experience in a Related Occupation

Some employers allow applicants to substitute work experience in place of a specific degree. Previous work experience in a field related to logistics, supply chains, or business can be beneficial. Some gain work experience while working in a logistical support role, such as dispatchers and clerks or while serving in the military. Experience allows a worker to learn about production and supply chain processes.

Important Qualities

Communication skills. Logisticians need strong communication skills to collaborate with colleagues and do business with suppliers and customers.

Critical-thinking skills. Logisticians must develop, adjust, and carry out logistical plans. They often must find ways to reduce costs and improve efficiency.

Customer service skills. Logisticians must know the needs of their customers in order to coordinate the movement of materials between suppliers and customers. They gain this knowledge through listening to the customer and applying their knowledge of the products and systems to provide what is required.

Organizational skills. Logisticians must be able to keep detailed records and simultaneously manage several projects in a fast-paced environment.

Problem-solving skills. Logisticians must handle unforeseen issues, such as delivery problems, and adjust plans as needed to resolve the issues.

Pay

The median annual wage for logisticians was $77,520 in May 2022. The median wage is the wage at which half the workers in an occupation earned more than that amount and half earned less. The lowest 10 percent earned less than $46,260, and the highest 10 percent earned more than $124,050.

In May 2022, the median annual wages for logisticians in the top industries in which they worked were as follows:

Federal government	$91,330
Manufacturing	80,550
Management of companies and enterprises	80,200
Professional, scientific, and technical services	73,760
Wholesale trade	67,130

The majority of logisticians work full time and they sometimes work overtime to ensure that operations stay on schedule.

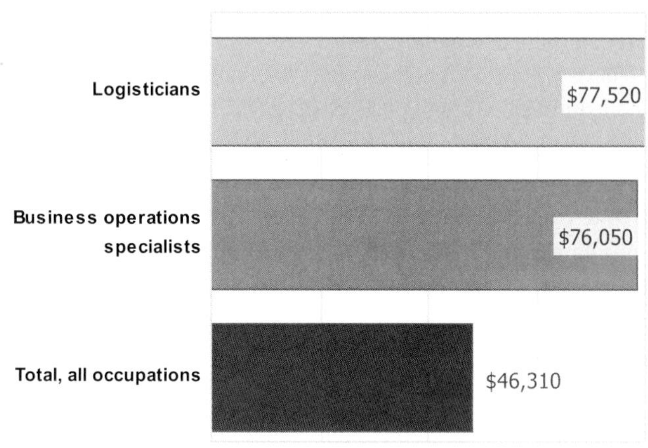

Note: All Occupations includes all occupations in the U.S. Economy.
Source: U.S. Bureau of Labor Statistics, Occupational Employment and Wage Statistics.

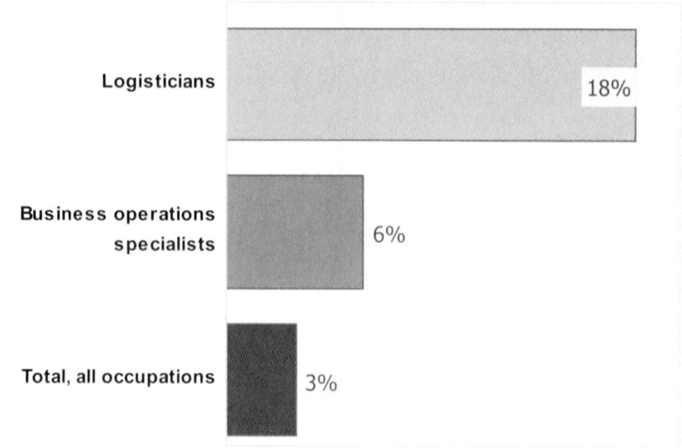

Note: All Occupations includes all occupations in the U.S. Economy.
Source: U.S. Bureau of Labor Statistics, Employment Projections program.

Job Outlook

Employment of logisticians is projected to grow 18 percent from 2022 to 2032, much faster than the average for all occupations.

About 21,800 openings for logisticians are projected each year, on average, over the decade. Many of those openings are expected to result from the need to replace workers who transfer to different occupations or exit the labor force, such as to retire.

Employment

As the growth of e-commerce makes logistics more dynamic and complex, logisticians will be in demand to move products more efficiently, solve problems, and identify areas for improvement. The increased volume of inventory and need to manage multiple supply chains have made logisticians' work critical. In addition, as more goods are purchased online, timeliness of delivery remains a priority for companies, further increasing demand for these workers.

Occupational Title	SOC Code	Employment, 2022	Projected Employment, 2032	Change, 2022-32	
				Percent	Numeric
Logisticians	13-1081	208,700	246,900	18	38,300

Contacts for More Information

For more information, visit

- Association for Supply Chain Management
- Defense Acquisition University
- International Society of Logistics

Management Analysts

Summary

Quick Facts: Management Analysts	
2022 Median Pay	$95,290 per year $45.81 per hour
Typical Entry-Level Education	Bachelor's degree
Work Experience in a Related Occupation	Less than 5 years
On-the-job Training	None
Number of Jobs, 2022	987,600
Job Outlook, 2022-32	10% (Much faster than average)
Employment Change, 2022-32	95,700

What Management Analysts Do

Management analysts recommend ways to improve an organization's efficiency.

Work Environment

Management analysts may travel frequently to meet with clients. Some work more than 40 hours per week.

How to Become a Management Analyst

Management analysts typically need at least a bachelor's degree and several years of related work experience.

Pay

The median annual wage for management analysts was $95,290 in May 2022.

Job Outlook

Employment of management analysts is projected to grow 10 percent from 2022 to 2032, much faster than the average for all occupations.

About 92,900 openings for management analysts are projected each year, on average, over the decade. Many of those

Management analysts propose ways to improve an organization's efficiency.

openings are expected to result from the need to replace workers who transfer to different occupations or exit the labor force, such as to retire.

What Management Analysts Do

Management analysts, often called *management consultants*, recommend ways to improve an organization's efficiency. They advise managers on how to make organizations more profitable through reduced costs and increased revenues.

Duties

Management analysts typically do the following:

- Gather and organize information about the problems to be solved or the procedures to be improved
- Interview personnel and conduct onsite observations to determine the methods, equipment, and personnel that will be needed
- Analyze financial and other data, including revenue, expenditure, and employment reports

Although some management analysts work for the company that they are analyzing, most work as consultants on a contractual basis.

- Develop solutions or alternative practices
- Recommend new systems, procedures, or organizational changes
- Make recommendations to management through presentations or written reports
- Confer with managers to ensure changes are working

Although some management analysts work for the organization that they analyze, many work as consultants on a contractual basis.

The work of management analysts may vary from project to project. Some projects require a team of analysts, each specializing in one area. On other projects, analysts work independently with the client organization's managers.

Management analysts often specialize in certain areas, such as inventory control or reorganizing corporate structures for efficiency. Some focus on a specific industry, such as healthcare or telecommunications. In government, management analysts usually specialize by type of agency.

Organizations hire management analysts to develop strategies for entering and remaining competitive in the market.

Management analysts who work on contract may write proposals and bid for jobs. Typically, an organization that needs the help of a management analyst requests proposals from a number of consultants and consulting companies that specialize in the needed work. Interested companies then submit a proposal that explains details such as how the work will be completed, what the schedule will be, and how much it will cost. The organization selects the proposal that best meets its needs and budget.

Work Environment

Management analysts held about 987,600 jobs in 2022. The largest employers of management analysts were as follows:

Professional, scientific, and technical services	35%
Government	17
Self-employed workers	14
Finance and insurance	12
Management of companies and enterprises	4

Management analysts usually divide their time between their offices and the client's site. Because they must spend a significant amount of time with clients, analysts travel frequently. Analysts may experience stress, especially when trying to meet a client's demands on a tight schedule.

Work Schedules

Analysts often work many hours under tight deadlines. Some work more than 40 hours per week.

How to Become a Management Analyst

Management analysts typically need at least a bachelor's degree and several years of related work experience.

Because they must spend a significant portion of their time with clients, analysts travel frequently.

Education

A bachelor's degree is the typical entry-level requirement for management analysts. However, some employers prefer to hire candidates who have a master's degree in business administration (MBA).

Management analysts address a range of topics, and many fields of study provide a suitable educational background.

A bachelor's degree is the typical entry-level requirement for obtaining a management analyst position.

Fields of bachelor's degree study may include business, social science, and engineering.

Licenses, Certifications, and Registrations

The Institute of Management Consultants USA (IMC USA) offers the Certified Management Consultant (CMC) designation to those who meet minimum levels of education and experience and who complete other requirements. Management analysts are not required to get certification, but having the credential may give jobseekers a competitive advantage.

Work Experience in a Related Occupation

Many analysts enter the occupation with several years of work experience. Organizations that specialize in certain fields typically try to hire candidates who have experience in those areas. For example, tax preparation firms may prefer candidates who have worked as an accountant or auditor, and software companies might seek those with experience as a computer systems analyst.

Advancement

As management analysts gain experience, they often take on more responsibility. Senior-level analysts may supervise teams working on complex projects and may become involved in seeking out new business. Those with exceptional skills may eventually become partners in their organization and focus on attracting new clients and bringing in revenue. Senior analysts may leave consulting and move to management positions at non-consulting organizations.

Important Qualities

Analytical skills. Management analysts must be able to interpret information and use their findings to make proposals.

Communication skills. Management analysts must be able to convey information clearly in both writing and speaking. Analysts also need good listening skills to understand an organization's problems and recommend appropriate solutions.

Interpersonal skills. Management analysts work with managers and other employees of the organizations for which they provide consulting services. They should be able to work as a team toward achieving the organization's goals.

Problem-solving skills. Management analysts must be able to think creatively to solve clients' problems. Although some aspects of clients' problems may be similar, each situation is likely to present unique challenges for the analyst to solve.

Time-management skills. Management analysts often work under tight deadlines and must use their time efficiently to complete projects on schedule.

Pay

The median annual wage for management analysts was $95,290 in May 2022. The median wage is the wage at which half the

Management Analysts

Median annual wages, May 2022

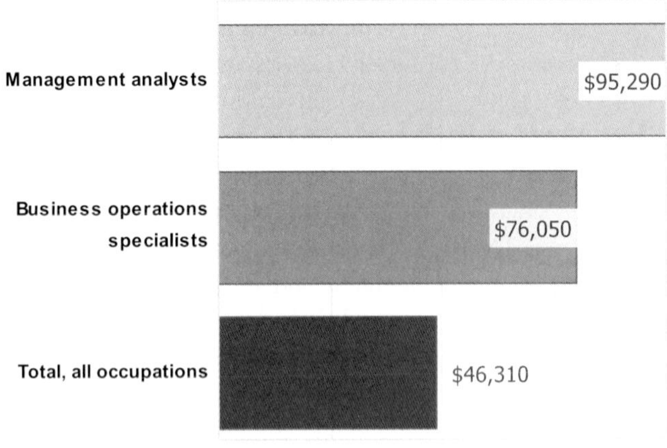

Note: All Occupations includes all occupations in the U.S. Economy.
Source: U.S. Bureau of Labor Statistics, Occupational Employment and Wage Statistics.

workers in an occupation earned more than that amount and half earned less. The lowest 10 percent earned less than $55,590, and the highest 10 percent earned more than $167,650.

In May 2022, the median annual wages for management analysts in the top industries in which they worked were as follows:

Professional, scientific, and technical services..	$101,900
Management of companies and enterprises.......	96,810
Finance and insurance..	93,650
Government..	85,280

Management analysts working for consulting firms are usually paid a base salary in addition to a year-end bonus. Self-employed analysts are paid directly by their clients, typically by either the hour or the project.

Analysts often work many hours under tight deadlines. Some work more than 40 hours per week.

Job Outlook

Employment of management analysts is projected to grow 10 percent from 2022 to 2032, much faster than the average for all occupations.

About 92,900 openings for management analysts are projected each year, on average, over the decade. Many of those openings are expected to result from the need to replace workers who transfer to different occupations or exit the labor force, such as to retire.

Management Analysts

Percent change in employment, projected 2022-32

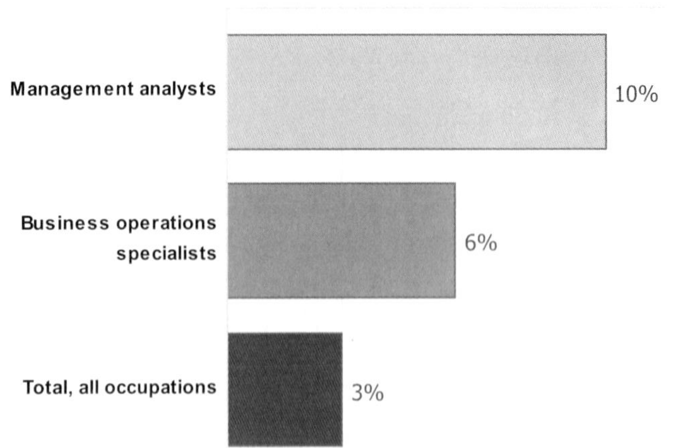

Note: All Occupations includes all occupations in the U.S. Economy.
Source: U.S. Bureau of Labor Statistics, Employment Projections program.

Employment

Demand for consulting services is expected to increase as organizations seek ways to improve efficiency and control costs. As markets become more competitive, firms will need to use resources more efficiently.

Information technology (IT) consultants are expected to see high demand. Businesses will seek out consulting firms to help them attain a high level of cybersecurity and make sure their IT systems are efficient and up to date.

Growth is expected to be particularly strong in smaller consulting companies that specialize in specific industries or types of business function, such as information technology or human resources. Government agencies also are expected to seek the services of management analysts as they look for ways to reduce spending and improve efficiency.

Occupational Title	SOC Code	Employment, 2022	Projected Employment, 2032	Change, 2022-32	
				Percent	Numeric
Management analysts	13-1111	987,600	1,083,300	10	95,700

Contacts for More Information

For more information about the Certified Management Consultant designation, visit

➤ Institute of Management Consultants USA

For more information about other certifications in management consulting, visit

➤ Global Academy of Finance and Management

Market Research Analysts

Summary

Quick Facts: Market Research Analysts	
2022 Median Pay	$68,230 per year $32.80 per hour
Typical Entry-Level Education	Bachelor's degree
Work Experience in a Related Occupation	None
On-the-job Training	None
Number of Jobs, 2022	868,600
Job Outlook, 2022-32	13% (Much faster than average)
Employment Change, 2022-32	116,600

What Market Research Analysts Do

Market research analysts study consumer preferences, business conditions, and other factors to assess potential sales of a product or service.

Work Environment

Because most industries use market research, these analysts are employed throughout the economy. Most analysts work full time during regular business hours.

How to Become a Market Research Analyst

Market research analysts typically need a bachelor's degree. Some employers require or prefer that job candidates have a master's degree.

Pay

The median annual wage for market research analysts was $68,230 in May 2022.

Job Outlook

Employment of market research analysts is projected to grow 13 percent from 2022 to 2032, much faster than the average for all occupations.

About 94,600 openings for market research analysts are projected each year, on average, over the decade. Many of those openings are expected to result from the need to replace workers who transfer to different occupations or exit the labor force, such as to retire.

What Market Research Analysts Do

Market research analysts study consumer preferences, business conditions, and other factors to assess potential sales of a product or service. They help companies understand what products people want, who will buy them, and at what price.

Duties

Market research analysts typically do the following:

- Monitor and forecast marketing and sales trends
- Measure the effectiveness of marketing programs and strategies
- Devise and evaluate methods for collecting data, such as surveys, questionnaires, and opinion polls
- Gather data on consumers, competitors, and market conditions
- Analyze data using statistical software
- Convert data and findings into tables, graphs, and written reports
- Prepare reports and present results to clients and management

Market research analysts gather data and study other information to help a company promote its products or services. They gather data on consumer buying habits, demographics, needs, and preferences. They collect data and information using a variety of methods, such as focus groups, interviews, literature reviews, market analysis surveys, public opinion polls, and questionnaires.

Analysts help determine a company's position in the marketplace by researching their competitors and studying their marketing methods, prices, and sales. Using this information, analysts may determine potential markets, product demand,

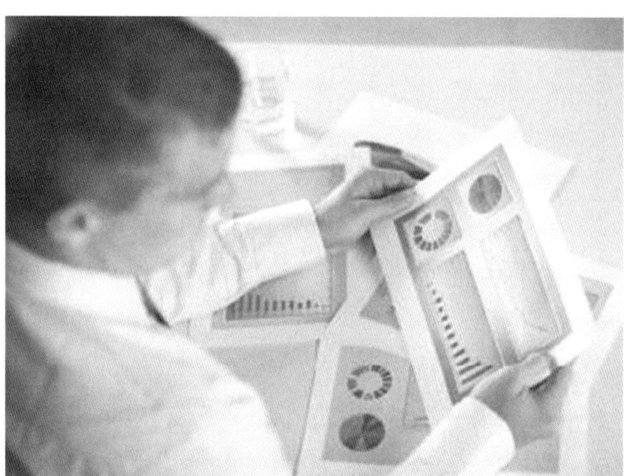

Market research analysts perform research and gather data to help a company market its products or services.

Market research analysts gather and analyze data on consumers and competitors.

and pricing. Their knowledge of the targeted consumer enables analysts to develop advertising brochures and commercials, product promotions, and sales plans.

Market research analysts evaluate data using statistical techniques and software. They must interpret what the data mean for their client, and they may forecast future trends. They often make charts, graphs, infographics, and other visual aids to present the results of their research.

Workers who design and conduct surveys that market research analysts use are survey researchers.

Work Environment

Market research analysts held about 868,600 jobs in 2022. The largest employers of market research analysts were as follows:

Management, scientific, and technical consulting services	11%
Finance and insurance	9
Information	8
Wholesale trade	7
Management of companies and enterprises	7

Because most industries use market research, these analysts are employed throughout the economy.

Market research analysts work individually or as part of a team, collecting, analyzing, and presenting data. For example, some analysts work with graphic designers and artists to create charts, graphs, and infographics summarizing their research and findings.

Market research analysts may give presentations to clients.

Work Schedules

Most market research analysts work full time during regular business hours.

How to Become a Market Research Analyst

Market research analysts typically need a bachelor's degree. Some employers require or prefer that job candidates have a master's degree. Strong research and analytical skills are essential.

Education

Market research analysts typically need a bachelor's degree in market research or a related business, communications, or social science field.

Courses in statistics, research methods, and marketing are important for prospective analysts. Courses in communications and social sciences, such as economics or consumer behavior, are also helpful.

Some employers of market research analysts require or prefer a master's degree. Several schools offer graduate programs in marketing research, but analysts may choose to complete a bachelor's degree in another field, such as statistics and marketing, and earn a master's degree in business administration (MBA). A master's degree is often required for leadership positions or positions that perform more technical research.

Licenses, Certifications, and Registrations

Analysts may pursue certification, which is voluntary, to demonstrate a level of professional competency. The Insights Association offers several certifications for market research analysts, including the IPC Principal and the IPC Masters. Candidates qualify based on industry experience and passing an exam.

Other Experience

Completing an internship while in school may be helpful. Prospective analysts also may gain experience by volunteering

Market research analysts measure the effectiveness of marketing strategies.

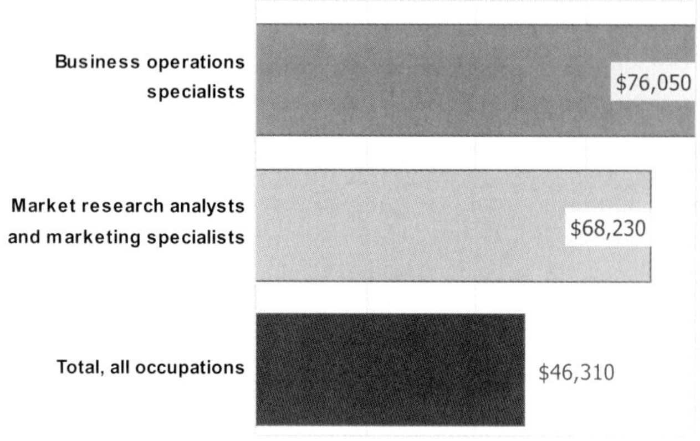

Note: All Occupations includes all occupations in the U.S. Economy.
Source: U.S. Bureau of Labor Statistics, Occupational Employment and Wage Statistics.

for an organization and helping with market research or related projects.

Employers may prefer to hire candidates who have experience in other positions that require collecting and analyzing data or writing reports to summarize research.

Important Qualities

Analytical skills. Market research analysts must evaluate large amounts of data and information related to market conditions.

Communication skills. Market research analysts must be able to clearly convey information when gathering material, interpreting data, and presenting results to clients.

Critical-thinking skills. To determine which marketing strategies would work best for a company, market research analysts must assess all available information.

Detail oriented. Market research analysts must pay attention to minutiae to evaluate data.

Pay

The median annual wage for market research analysts was $68,230 in May 2022. The median wage is the wage at which half the workers in an occupation earned more than that amount and half earned less. The lowest 10 percent earned less than $38,280, and the highest 10 percent earned more than $131,850.

In May 2022, the median annual wages for market research analysts in the top industries in which they worked were as follows:

Management of companies and enterprises	$82,740
Information	82,380
Finance and insurance	78,920
Wholesale trade	67,560
Management, scientific, and technical consulting services	64,900

Most market research analysts work full time during regular business hours.

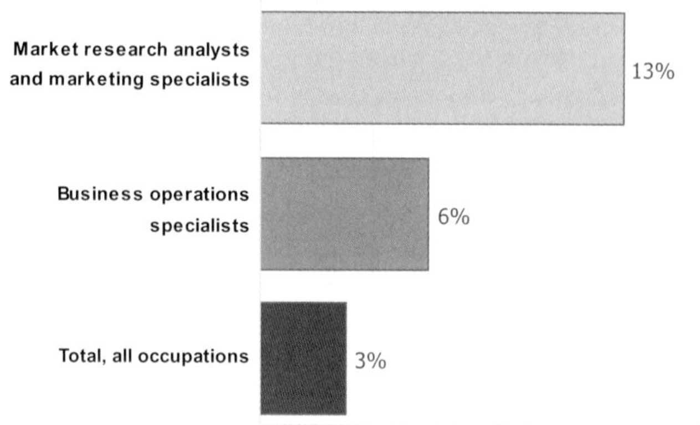

Note: All Occupations includes all occupations in the U.S. Economy.
Source: U.S. Bureau of Labor Statistics, Employment Projections program.

Job Outlook

Employment of market research analysts is projected to grow 13 percent from 2022 to 2032, much faster than the average for all occupations.

About 94,600 openings for market research analysts are projected each year, on average, over the decade. Many of those openings are expected to result from the need to replace workers who transfer to different occupations or exit the labor force, such as to retire.

Employment

Employment growth will be driven by an increasing use of data and market research across many industries. These workers will be needed to help understand the needs and wants of customers, measure the effectiveness of marketing and business strategies, and identify the factors affecting product demand.

The increase in the collection and analyses of big data—extremely large sets of information, such as social media comments or online product reviews—can provide insight on consumer behaviors and preferences. Businesses will need market research analysts to conduct analyses of the data and information.

Occupational Title	SOC Code	Employment, 2022	Projected Employment, 2032	Change, 2022-32	
				Percent	Numeric
Market research analysts and marketing specialists	13-1161	868,600	985,200	13	116,600

Contacts for More Information

For more information, visit

➤ Insights Association

For resources and information about qualitative research, visit

➤ Qualitative Research Consultants Association (QRCA)

Meeting, Convention, and Event Planners

Summary

Quick Facts: Meeting, Convention, and Event Planners	
2022 Median Pay	$52,560 per year $25.27 per hour
Typical Entry-Level Education	Bachelor's degree
Work Experience in a Related Occupation	None
On-the-job Training	None
Number of Jobs, 2022	132,000
Job Outlook, 2022-32	8% (Faster than average)
Employment Change, 2022-32	9,900

What Meeting, Convention, and Event Planners Do

Meeting, convention, and event planners arrange all aspects of events and professional gatherings.

Work Environment

Meeting, convention, and event planners work in their offices and onsite at hotels or conference centers. They often travel to attend events and visit meeting sites. During meetings or conventions, planners may work many more hours than usual.

How to Become a Meeting, Convention, or Event Planner

Meeting, convention, and event planners typically need a bachelor's degree. Some experience related to event planning may be helpful.

Pay

The median annual wage for meeting, convention, and event planners was $52,560 in May 2022.

Meeting, convention, and event planners coordinate all aspects of events and professional meetings. They arrange meeting locations, transportation, and other details.

Job Outlook

Employment of meeting, convention, and event planners is projected to grow 8 percent from 2022 to 2032, faster than the average for all occupations.

About 15,200 openings for meeting, convention, and event planners are projected each year, on average, over the decade. Many of those openings are expected to result from the need to replace workers who transfer to different occupations or exit the labor force, such as to retire.

What Meeting, Convention, and Event Planners Do

Meeting, convention, and event planners arrange all aspects of events and professional gatherings. They arrange meeting locations, transportation, and other details.

Duties

Meeting, convention, and event planners typically do the following:

- Meet with clients to understand the purpose of the event
- Plan the scope of the event, including its time, location, and cost
- Solicit bids from venues and service providers

Meeting, convention, and event planners meet with clients to understand the purpose of their meeting or event.

- Inspect venues to ensure that they meet the client's requirements
- Coordinate event services such as rooms, transportation, and food
- Monitor event activities to ensure that the client and the attendees are satisfied
- Review event bills and approve payments

Meeting, convention, and event planners organize a variety of social and professional events, including weddings, educational conferences, and business conventions. They coordinate every detail of these events, including finances. Before planning a meeting, for example, planners meet with clients to estimate attendance and determine the meeting's purpose. During the event, they handle logistics, such as registering guests and organizing audiovisual equipment. After the meeting, they make sure that all vendors are paid, and they may survey attendees to obtain feedback on the event.

Meeting, convention, and event planners search for potential meeting sites, such as hotels and convention centers. They consider the lodging and services that the facility can provide, how easy it will be for people to get there, and the attractions that the surrounding area has to offer.

Once a location is selected, planners arrange the meeting space and support services, such as catering and interpreters. They negotiate contracts with suppliers and coordinate plans with the venue's staff. They may also organize speakers, entertainment, and activities.

The following are examples of types of meeting, convention, and event planners:

Meeting planners plan large meetings for organizations. *Healthcare meeting planners* specialize in organizing meetings and conferences for healthcare professionals. *Corporate planners* organize internal business meetings and meetings between businesses. These events may be in person or online and held either within corporate facilities or offsite to include more people.

Convention planners plan conventions and conferences for organizations. *Association planners* organize annual conferences and trade shows for professional associations. *Convention service managers* work for hotels and convention centers. They act as liaisons between the meeting facility and the planners who work for associations, businesses, and governments. They present food service options to outside planners, coordinate special requests, and suggest hotel services that work within a planner's budget.

Event planners arrange the details of a variety of events. *Wedding planners* are the most well known, but event planners also coordinate celebrations such as anniversaries, reunions, and other large social events, as well as corporate events, including product launches, galas, and award ceremonies. *Nonprofit event planners* plan large events with the goal of raising donations for a charity or advocacy organization. Events may include banquets, charity races, and food drives.

Meeting, convention, and event planners regularly collaborate with clients, hospitality workers, and meeting attendees.

Exhibition organizers are responsible for all aspects of planning, promoting, and producing a display. They are also called exhibit managers, show managers, or show organizer.

Work Environment

Meeting, convention, and event planners held about 132,000 jobs in 2022. The largest employers of meeting, convention, and event planners were as follows:

Industry	Percent
Religious, grantmaking, civic, professional, and similar organizations	17%
Arts, entertainment, and recreation	12
Accommodation and food services	12
Administrative and support services	9
Self-employed workers	4

Meeting, convention, and event planners spend time in their offices and at event locations, such as hotels and convention centers. They may travel regularly to attend the events they organize and to visit meeting sites.

The work of meeting, convention, and event planners can be fast paced and demanding. Planners oversee many aspects of an event at the same time and face numerous deadlines, and they may coordinate multiple meetings or events at the same time.

Work Schedules

Most meeting, convention, and event planners work full time, and many work more than 40 hours per week. They often work additional hours to finalize preparations as major events approach. During meetings or conventions, planners may work on weekends.

How to Become a Meeting, Convention, or Event Planner

Meeting, convention, and event planners typically need a bachelor's degree. Some experience related to event planning may be helpful.

Meeting, convention, and event planners typically need a bachelor's degree.

Education

Meeting, convention, and event planners typically need a bachelor's degree. Although some colleges offer programs in meeting and event management, other common fields of degree include business, communications, and social science.

Planners who have studied meeting and event management or hospitality management may start out with greater responsibilities than do those from other academic disciplines. Some colleges offer continuing education courses in meeting and event planning.

Licenses, Certifications, and Registrations

A number of voluntary certifications are available for meeting and convention planners. Although not required, these certifications demonstrate specific knowledge or professional expertise.

The Events Industry Council offers the Certified Meeting Professional (CMP) credential, which is widely recognized in the industry and may help in career advancement. To qualify for the CMP, candidates' applications must include proof of experience and education. Those who qualify must then pass an exam that covers topics such as strategic planning, financial and risk management, facility operations and services, and logistics.

The Society of Government Meeting Professionals offers the Certified Government Meeting Professional (CGMP) designation for meeting planners who work for, or contract with, federal, state, or local government. This certification is helpful for candidates who want to show that they know government purchasing policies and travel regulations. To qualify, candidates must have worked as a meeting planner for at least 1 year and have been a member of SGMP for 6 months. To become a certified planner, members must take a 3-day course and pass an exam.

The International Association of Exhibitions and Events offers the Certified in Exhibition Management (CEM) designation, which demonstrates meeting professional standards for exhibitions and events management. Candidates obtain this credential by completing nine courses.

Some organizations, including the American Association of Certified Wedding Planners, offer certifications in wedding planning that may be helpful for attracting clients.

Other Experience

Meeting, convention, and event planners may benefit from having some experience in meeting and event planning. Working in a variety of positions at hotels, convention centers, and convention bureaus provides knowledge of how the hospitality industry operates. Other beneficial work experiences include coordinating university or volunteer events and shadowing professionals.

Important Qualities

Communication skills. Meeting, convention, and event planners exchange information with clients, suppliers, and event staff. They must have excellent written and oral communication skills to express the needs of their clients.

Interpersonal skills. Meeting, convention, and event planners must establish and maintain positive relationships with clients and suppliers.

Negotiation skills. Meeting, convention, and event planners must be able to secure quality products and services at reasonable prices for their clients.

Organizational skills. Meeting, convention, and event planners must multitask, pay attention to details, and meet tight deadlines.

Problem-solving skills. Meeting, convention, and event planners must be able to anticipate potential issues and prepare creative solutions that satisfy clients.

Pay

The median annual wage for meeting, convention, and event planners was $52,560 in May 2022. The median wage is the

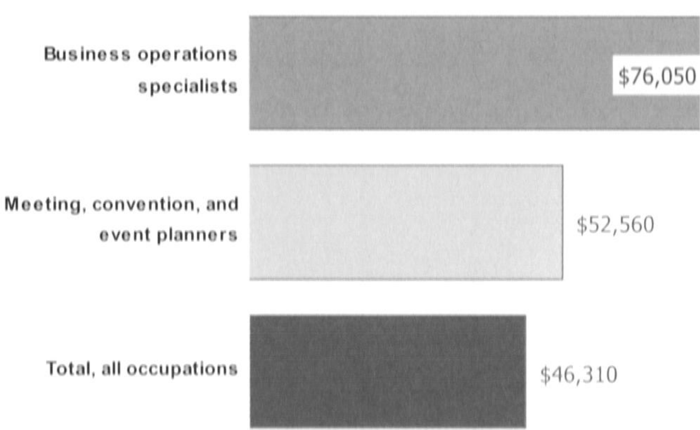

Note: All Occupations includes all occupations in the U.S. Economy.
Source: U.S. Bureau of Labor Statistics, Occupational Employment and Wage Statistics.

wage at which half the workers in an occupation earned more than that amount and half earned less. The lowest 10 percent earned less than $32,050, and the highest 10 percent earned more than $92,880.

In May 2022, the median annual wages for meeting, convention, and event planners in the top industries in which they worked were as follows:

Administrative and support services	$57,630
Religious, grantmaking, civic, professional, and similar organizations	55,940
Accommodation and food services	48,270
Arts, entertainment, and recreation	47,160

Most meeting, convention, and event planners work full time, and many work more than 40 hours per week. They often work additional hours to finalize preparations as major events approach. During meetings or conventions, planners may work on weekends.

Job Outlook

Employment of meeting, convention, and event planners is projected to grow 8 percent from 2022 to 2032, faster than the average for all occupations.

About 15,200 openings for meeting, convention, and event planners are projected each year, on average, over the decade. Many of those openings are expected to result from the need to replace workers who transfer to different occupations or exit the labor force, such as to retire.

Employment

Event planners' services are expected to be in demand by people who want help organizing personal events, such as weddings. In addition, demand for professionally planned meetings and events will stem from businesses and organizations that host events. However, virtual meeting technology may dampen employment growth as virtual meetings continue to replace some in-person events.

Meeting, Convention, and Event Planners

Percent change in employment, projected 2022-32

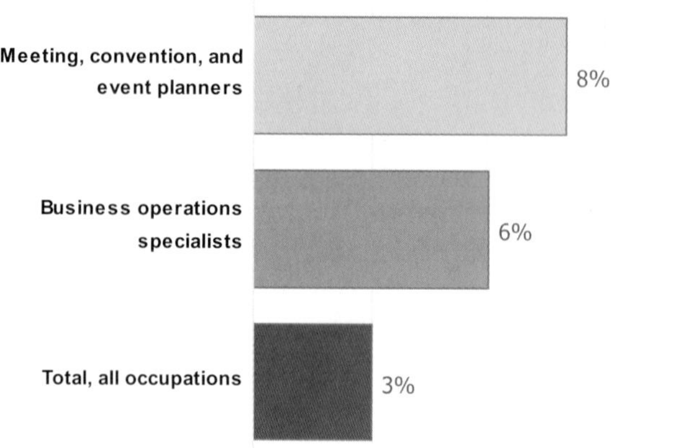

Note: All Occupations includes all occupations in the U.S. Economy.
Source: U.S. Bureau of Labor Statistics, Employment Projections program.

Occupational Title	SOC Code	Employment, 2022	Projected Employment, 2032	Change, 2022-32	
				Percent	Numeric
Meeting, convention, and event planners	13-1121	132,000	141,900	8	9,900

Contacts for More Information

For more information, visit

- Events Industry Council
- International Association of Exhibitions and Events
- Society of Government Meeting Professionals
- American Association of Certified Wedding Planners
- Association of Bridal Consultants

Personal Financial Advisors

Summary

Quick Facts: Personal Financial Advisors	
2022 Median Pay	$95,390 per year $45.86 per hour
Typical Entry-Level Education	Bachelor's degree
Work Experience in a Related Occupation	None
On-the-job Training	Long-term on-the-job training
Number of Jobs, 2022	327,600
Job Outlook, 2022-32	13% (Much faster than average)
Employment Change, 2022-32	42,000

What Personal Financial Advisors Do

Personal financial advisors provide advice to help individuals manage their money and plan for their financial future.

Work Environment

Most personal financial advisors work in the finance and insurance industry or are self-employed. They typically work full time, and some work more than 40 hours per week. They also may meet with clients in the evenings or on weekends.

How to Become a Personal Financial Advisor

Personal financial advisors typically need a bachelor's degree to enter the occupation. A master's degree and certification may improve chances for advancement.

Pay

The median annual wage for personal financial advisors was $95,390 in May 2022.

Job Outlook

Employment of personal financial advisors is projected to grow 13 percent from 2022 to 2032, much faster than the average for all occupations.

About 25,600 openings for personal financial advisors are projected each year, on average, over the decade. Many of those openings are expected to result from the need to replace workers who transfer to different occupations or exit the labor force, such as to retire.

What Personal Financial Advisors Do

Personal financial advisors provide advice on investments, insurance, mortgages, estate planning, taxes, and retirement to help individuals manage their finances.

Duties

Personal financial advisors typically do the following:

- Meet with clients to discuss their financial goals
- Explain to potential clients the types of financial services they provide
- Educate clients and answer questions about investment options and potential risks
- Recommend investments to clients or select investments on their behalf
- Help clients plan for specific circumstances, such as education or retirement
- Monitor clients' accounts and determine if changes are needed to improve financial performance or to accommodate life changes, such as getting married or having children
- Research investment opportunities

Personal financial advisors assess the financial needs of individuals and help them with decisions on investments (such as stocks and bonds), tax laws, and insurance. Advisors help clients plan for short- and long-term goals, such as budgeting for education expenses and saving for retirement through investments.

Personal financial advisors help people with investments, taxes, and insurance decisions.

Personal financial advisors meet with clients to discuss their financial goals.

They invest clients' money based on the clients' decisions. Many advisors also provide tax advice or sell insurance.

Although most planners offer advice on a wide range of topics, some specialize in areas such as retirement or risk management (evaluating the investor's willingness to take chances and adjusting investments accordingly).

Many personal financial advisors spend a lot of time marketing their services, and they meet potential clients by giving seminars or participating in business and social networking.

After financial advisors have invested funds for a client, they and the client receive regular investment reports. Advisors monitor the client's investments and usually meet with each client at least once a year to update the client on potential investments and to adjust the financial plan based on the client's circumstances or because investment options may have changed.

Many personal financial advisors are licensed to directly buy and sell financial products, such as stocks, bonds, annuities, and insurance. Depending on the agreement they have with their clients, personal financial advisors may have the client's permission to make decisions about buying and selling stocks and bonds.

Work Environment

Personal financial advisors held about 327,600 jobs in 2022. The largest employers of personal financial advisors were as follows:

Securities, commodity contracts, and other financial investments and related activities	63%
Credit intermediation and related activities	17
Self-employed workers	12
Insurance carriers and related activities	3
Management of companies and enterprises	1

Personal financial advisors typically work in offices. Some also travel to attend conferences, teach finance seminars in the evening, and attend networking events to bring in more clients.

Many personal financial advisors travel to attend conferences or teach finance classes in the evening to bring in more clients.

Work Schedules

Most personal financial advisors work full time and some work more than 40 hours per week. They also may go to meetings on evenings and weekends to meet with prospective or existing clients.

How to Become a Personal Financial Advisor

Personal financial advisors typically need a bachelor's degree to enter the occupation. A master's degree and certification may improve chances for advancement.

Education

Personal financial advisors typically need a bachelor's degree, although employers usually do not require a specific course of study. However, common fields of degree include business, social science, or mathematics. Courses in investments, taxes, estate planning, and risk management may be helpful.

Training

After they are hired, personal financial advisors typically need on-the-job training to attain competency. During this time, new advisors work under the supervision of senior advisors and learn how to build a client network, develop investment portfolios, and perform other duties. This training usually lasts for more than a year.

Licenses, Certifications, and Registrations

Personal financial advisors who directly buy or sell stocks, bonds, or insurance policies, or who provide specific investment advice, may need a combination of licenses that varies with the products they sell. In addition to being required to have those licenses, advisors in small firms that manage clients' investments must be registered with state regulators, and those in large firms must be registered with the U.S. Securities and Exchange Commission (SEC). Personal financial advisors who choose to sell insurance need licenses issued by state boards.

Personal financial advisors must establish trust with clients and respond to their questions and concerns.

Information on state licensing board requirements for registered investment advisors is available from the North American Securities Administrators Association (NASAA).

Certifications may enhance a personal financial advisor's reputation and help bring in new clients. The Certified Financial Planner Board of Standards offers the Certified Financial Planner (CFP) designation. For this certification, advisors must have a bachelor's degree, complete coursework on financial planning through a CFP Board Registered Program, have relevant work experience, pass an exam, and agree to adhere to a code of ethics.

Advancement

A master's degree in a field such as finance or business administration may improve a personal financial advisor's chances of becoming a financial manager and of attracting new clients.

Important Qualities

Analytical skills. In determining an investment portfolio for a client, personal financial advisors must be able to assess a range of information, including economic trends, regulatory changes, and the client's comfort with risky decisions.

Interpersonal skills. A major part of a personal financial advisor's job is making clients feel comfortable. Advisors must establish trust with clients and respond well to their questions and concerns.

Math skills. Personal financial advisors must be adept at working with numbers to determine the amount invested, how that amount has grown or decreased over time, and how a portfolio is distributed among different investments.

Sales skills. To expand their base of clients, personal financial advisors must be convincing and persistent in selling their services.

Speaking skills. Personal financial advisors interact with clients every day. They must explain complex financial concepts in a way that clients understand.

Pay

The median annual wage for personal financial advisors was $95,390 in May 2022. The median wage is the wage at which half the workers in an occupation earned more than that amount and half earned less. The lowest 10 percent earned less than $46,700, and the highest 10 percent earned more than $239,200.

In May 2022, the median annual wages for personal financial advisors in the top industries in which they worked were as follows:

Securities, commodity contracts, and other financial investments and related activities	$102,140
Management of companies and enterprises	93,690
Credit intermediation and related activities	77,500
Insurance carriers and related activities	74,980

Personal Financial Advisors

Median annual wages, May 2022

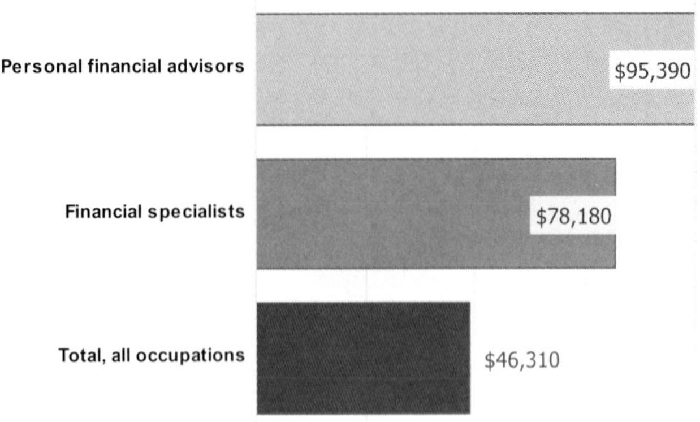

Note: All Occupations includes all occupations in the U.S. Economy.
Source: U.S. Bureau of Labor Statistics, Occupational Employment and Wage Statistics.

Personal financial advisors who work for financial services firms are often paid a salary plus bonuses. Commissions, incentive pay, and production bonuses are included in the wage data here; nonproduction bonuses are not included.

Advisors who work for financial investment firms or financial planning firms or who are self-employed earn money for their services in one of two ways. They either charge a flat fee or earn commissions for the financial products that they sell.

Most personal financial advisors work full time, and some work more than 40 hours per week. They also may go to meetings on evenings and weekends to meet with existing clients or to try to bring in new ones.

Job Outlook

Employment of personal financial advisors is projected to grow 13 percent from 2022 to 2032, much faster than the average for all occupations.

About 25,600 openings for personal financial advisors are projected each year, on average, over the decade. Many of those openings are expected to result from the need to replace workers who transfer to different occupations or exit the labor force, such as to retire.

Employment

The primary driver of employment growth will be the aging population. As large numbers of baby boomers continue to retire, they are likely to seek planning advice from personal financial advisors. Also, longer lifespans will lead to longer retirement periods, further increasing demand for financial planning services.

In addition, the replacement of traditional pension plans with individual retirement accounts is expected to continue. Many people used to receive defined pension payments in retirement, but most companies no longer offer these plans. Therefore,

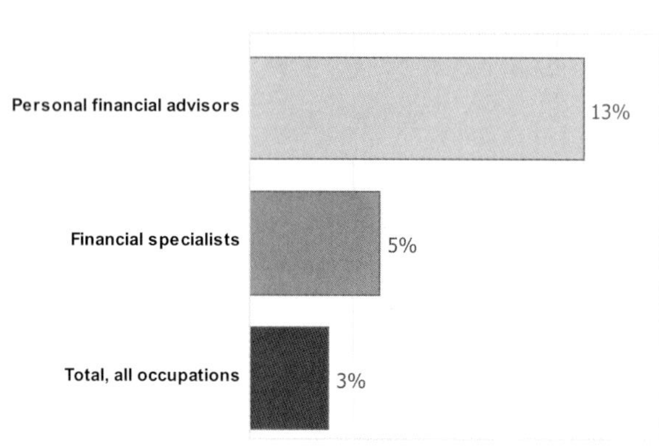

Note: All Occupations includes all occupations in the U.S. Economy.
Source: U.S. Bureau of Labor Statistics, Employment Projections program.

individuals must save and invest for their own retirement, increasing the demand for personal financial advisors.

The availability of "robo-advisors," computer programs that provide automated investment advice based on user inputs, may partially temper demand for personal financial advisors. However, the impact of this technology should be limited as consumers continue turning to human advisors for more complex and specialized investment advice over the projections decade.

Occupational Title	SOC Code	Employment, 2022	Projected Employment, 2032	Change, 2022-32	
				Percent	Numeric
Personal financial advisors	13-2052	327,600	369,600	13	42,000

Contacts for More Information

For more information about personal financial advisors, visit

- Financial Industry Regulatory Authority (FINRA)
- North American Securities Administrators Association
- U.S. Securities and Exchange Commission (SEC)
- Certified Financial Planner Board of Standards
- Global Academy of Finance and Management

Project Management Specialists

Summary

Quick Facts: Project Management Specialists	
2022 Median Pay	$95,370 per year $45.85 per hour
Typical Entry-Level Education	Bachelor's degree
Work Experience in a Related Occupation	None
On-the-job Training	None
Number of Jobs, 2022	881,300
Job Outlook, 2022-32	6% (Faster than average)
Employment Change, 2022-32	54,700

Project management specialists organize, plan, and oversee all aspects of a project from beginning to end.

What Project Management Specialists Do

Project management specialists coordinate the budget, schedule, staffing, and other details of a project.

Work Environment

Project management specialists usually work in an office setting, but they occasionally travel to visit clients. Most work full time, and some work more than 40 hours per week.

How to Become a Project Management Specialist

Project management specialists typically need a bachelor's degree that may be in a variety of fields, including business or project management. Although not always required, certification may be beneficial.

Pay

The median annual wage for project management specialists was $95,370 in May 2022.

Job Outlook

Employment of project management specialists is projected to grow 6 percent from 2022 to 2032, faster than the average for all occupations.

About 68,100 openings for project management specialists are projected each year, on average, over the decade. Many of those openings are expected to result from the need to replace workers who transfer to different occupations or exit the labor force, such as to retire.

What Project Management Specialists Do

Project management specialists coordinate the budget, schedule, and other details of a project. They lead and guide the work of technical staff. Project management specialists also may serve as a point of contact for the client or customer.

Duties

Project management specialists typically do the following:

- Communicate with clients to determine project requirements and objectives
- Develop project plans to include information such as objectives, funding, schedules, and staff
- Identify, review, and select vendors or consultants to meet project needs
- Assign duties or responsibilities to project staff
- Confer with project staff to identify and resolve problems
- Monitor project costs to stay within budget
- Monitor project milestones and deliverables
- Propose, review, and approve modifications to project plans
- Produce and distribute project documents

Project management specialists may begin a project by defining its scope or goals, using input from the client. They then create a plan that itemizes the individual activities, data, and resources needed to complete the project. Project management specialists ensure that the plan estimates costs, identifies potential risks, and specifies a timeline for completion.

Once a project is underway, project management specialists direct the team in carrying out the work. They monitor progress by tracking milestones and troubleshooting problems that may arise, including adjusting the project to address changes requested by the client. Finally, they close out the project by reviewing and organizing financial statements, contracts, and other documents.

These specialists may oversee a variety of projects, such as building a new commercial center, improving business processes, or expanding sales into additional markets. In coordinating a project, they may work closely with those whose expertise is in a particular field. For example, a project management specialist may collaborate with an emergency management director in disaster relief efforts or a construction manager in building a facility.

Work Environment

Project management specialists held about 881,300 jobs in 2022. The largest employers of project management specialists were as follows:

Professional, scientific, and technical services	28%
Construction	20
Manufacturing	7
Administrative and support services	7
Finance and insurance	5

Project management specialists usually work in an office setting. Although project management specialists may collaborate on teams, some work independently. Project management specialists also may travel to their clients' places of business.

Work Schedules

Project management specialists generally work during normal business hours. However, their schedules may require flexibility, such as when working across time zones or during off-peak hours. Most work full time, and some may work more than 40 hours per week.

How to Become a Project Management Specialist

Project management specialists typically need a bachelor's degree that may be in a variety of fields, including business or project management. Although not always required, certification may be beneficial.

Once a project is underway, project management specialists direct the team in carrying out the work.

Project management specialists may work on teams of other specialists, or they may work independently.

Project management specialists typically need a bachelor's degree to enter the occupation.

Education

To enter the occupation, project management specialists typically need a bachelor's degree in business, project management, or a related field. Some employers prefer to hire candidates who have a degree in a technical field related to the industry in which they will work, such as computer and information technology or engineering.

Licenses, Certifications, and Registrations

Although not always required, professional certification demonstrates competency to prospective clients and employers. For example, the Project Management Institute (PMI) offers several certifications in project management for workers at various experience levels, including the Project Management Professional (PMP).

Other Experience

Some positions require project management specialists to have relevant work experience. Candidates may gain experience as business analysts, information security analysts, training and development specialists, or in other related occupations.

Employers also may prefer to hire candidates who have experience in areas such as personnel recruitment, employee relations, or compensation and benefits. Candidates sometimes get this experience by volunteering or while in college, either through courses or internships.

Advancement

Project management specialists may advance to more senior positions as they gain experience and take on more responsibility. For example, they may begin as trainees working on small projects and progress to large, complex projects.

Important Qualities

Analytical skills. Project management specialists must be able to understand large amounts of information and data.

Communication skills. Project management specialists need to convey information to staff and must get input from and present results to clients.

Critical-thinking skills. To determine which strategy would work best for a particular project, these specialists must assess its goals and impact.

Interpersonal skills. Project management specialists must establish trust with clients and respond well to their questions and concerns.

Organizational skills. Project management specialists' work involves balancing a variety of responsibilities, and they may oversee more than one project at one time.

Problem-solving skills. Project management specialists must be able to handle difficult or unexpected situations and find effective solutions.

Time-management skills. Project management specialists often work under tight deadlines and must use their time efficiently to complete projects on schedule.

Pay

The median annual wage for project management specialists was $95,370 in May 2022. The median wage is the wage at which half the workers in an occupation earned more than that amount and half earned less. The lowest 10 percent earned less than $52,500, and the highest 10 percent earned more than $159,150.

In May 2022, the median annual wages for project management specialists in the top industries in which they worked were as follows:

Finance and insurance	$104,930
Professional, scientific, and technical services	100,390
Manufacturing	97,350
Administrative and support services	90,120
Construction	84,310

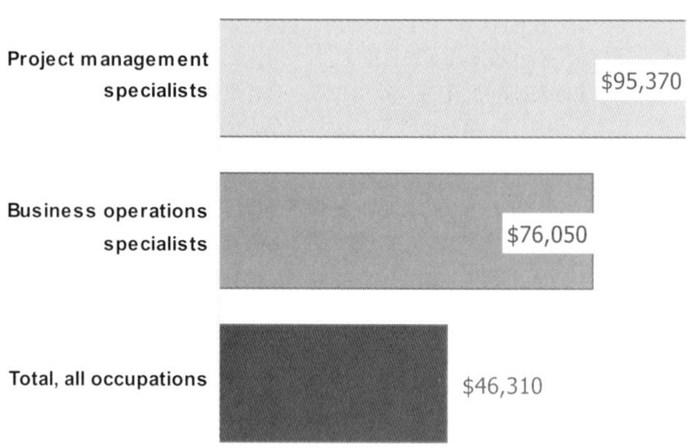

Note: All Occupations includes all occupations in the U.S. Economy.
Source: U.S. Bureau of Labor Statistics, Occupational Employment and Wage Statistics.

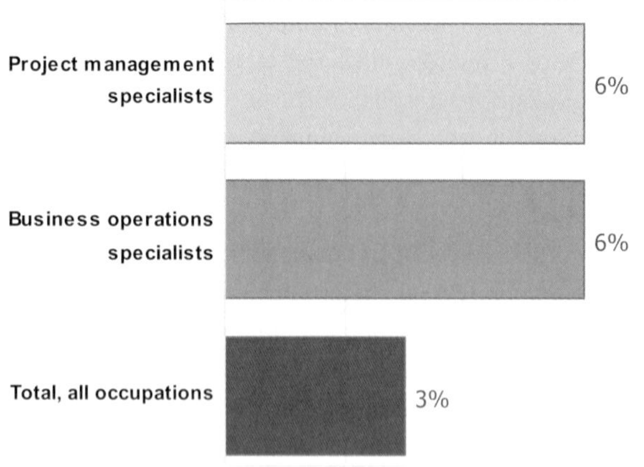

Note: All Occupations includes all occupations in the U.S. Economy.
Source: U.S. Bureau of Labor Statistics, Employment Projections program.

Most project management specialists work full time, and some work more than 40 hours per week.

Job Outlook

Employment of project management specialists is projected to grow 6 percent from 2022 to 2032, faster than the average for all occupations.

About 68,100 openings for project management specialists are projected each year, on average, over the decade. Many of those openings are expected to result from the need to replace workers who transfer to different occupations or exit the labor force, such as to retire.

Employment

As organizations seek ways to maintain and improve productivity, employment of project management specialists is expected to increase. These specialists will be needed to help manage various business operations, ensuring that projects meet their goals and are completed on time and within budget.

Demand for project management specialists is expected to be strong in computer systems design services. More project management specialists will be needed to manage the growing volume and complexity of information technology (IT) projects required to support expanded telework.

Occupational Title	SOC Code	Employment, 2022	Projected Employment, 2032	Change, 2022-32	
				Percent	Numeric
Project management specialists	13-1082	881,300	936,000	6	54,700

Contacts for More Information

For more information about project management specialists, including details about certification, visit

➤ Project Management Institute (PMI)

Purchasing Managers, Buyers, and Purchasing Agents

Summary

Quick Facts: Purchasing Managers, Buyers, and Purchasing Agents

2022 Median Pay	$75,120 per year $36.12 per hour
Typical Entry-Level Education	Bachelor's degree
Work Experience in a Related Occupation	See How to Become One
On-the-job Training	See How to Become One
Number of Jobs, 2022	571,900
Job Outlook, 2022-32	-6% (Decline)
Employment Change, 2022-32	-34,600

What Purchasing Managers, Buyers, and Purchasing Agents Do

Buyers and purchasing agents buy products and services for organizations. Purchasing managers oversee the work of buyers and purchasing agents.

Work Environment

Most purchasing managers and buyers and purchasing agents work full time. Some work more than 40 hours per week.

How to Become a Purchasing Manager, Buyer, or Purchasing Agent

Buyers and purchasing agents typically have a bachelor's degree. Purchasing managers must also have a few years of work experience.

Pay

The median annual wage for buyers and purchasing agents was $67,620 in May 2022.

The median annual wage for purchasing managers was $131,350 in May 2022.

Job Outlook

Overall employment of purchasing managers, buyers, and purchasing agents is projected to decline 6 percent from 2022 to 2032.

Despite declining employment, about 45,000 openings for purchasing managers, buyers, and purchasing agents are

Purchasing managers, buyers, and purchasing agents evaluate suppliers, negotiate contracts, and review product quality.

projected each year, on average, over the decade. All of those openings are expected to result from the need to replace workers who transfer to other occupations or exit the labor force, such as to retire.

What Purchasing Managers, Buyers, and Purchasing Agents Do

Buyers and purchasing agents buy products and services for organizations to use or resell. They evaluate suppliers, negotiate contracts, and review the quality of products. Purchasing managers oversee the work of buyers and purchasing agents and typically handle more complex procurement tasks.

Duties

Purchasing managers and buyers and purchasing agents typically do the following:

- Evaluate suppliers on the basis of the price, quality, and speed of delivery of their products and services

Purchasing agents and buyers consider price, quality, availability, reliability, and technical support when choosing suppliers and merchandise.

- Interview vendors and visit suppliers' plants and distribution centers to examine and learn about products, services, and prices
- Attend meetings, trade shows, and conferences to learn about new industry trends and make contacts with suppliers
- Analyze price proposals, financial reports, and other information to determine reasonable prices
- Negotiate contracts on behalf of their organization
- Work out agreements with suppliers, such as when products will be delivered
- Meet with staff and vendors to discuss defective or unacceptable goods or services and determine corrective action
- Evaluate and monitor contracts to be sure that vendors and suppliers comply with the terms and conditions of the contract and to determine the need for changes
- Maintain and review records of items bought, costs, deliveries, product performance, and inventories

In addition to these tasks, purchasing managers also plan and coordinate the work of buyers and purchasing agents and hire and train new staff.

Purchasing managers are also responsible for developing their organization's procurement policies and procedures. These policies help ensure that procurement professionals are meeting ethical standards to avoid potential conflicts of interest or inappropriate supplier and customer relations.

Buyers and purchasing agents buy farm products, durable and nondurable goods, and services for organizations and institutions. They try to get the best deal for their organization: the highest quality goods and services at the lowest cost. They do this by studying sales records and inventory levels of current stock, identifying foreign and domestic suppliers, and keeping up to date with changes affecting both the supply of, and demand for, products and materials.

Purchasing agents and buyers consider price, quality, availability, reliability, and technical support when choosing suppliers and merchandise. To be effective, purchasing agents and buyers must have a working technical knowledge of the goods or services they are purchasing.

Evaluating suppliers is one of the most critical functions of a buyer or purchasing agent. They ensure the supplies are ordered in time so that any delays in the supply chain does not shut down production and cause the organization to lose customers.

Buyers and purchasing agents use many resources to find out all they can about potential suppliers. They attend meetings, trade shows, and conferences to learn about new industry trends and make contacts with suppliers.

They often interview prospective suppliers and visit their plants and distribution centers to assess their capabilities. For example, they may discuss the design of products with design engineers, quality concerns with production supervisors, or shipping issues with managers in the receiving department.

Buyers and purchasing agents must make certain that the supplier can deliver the desired goods or services on time, in the correct quantities, and without sacrificing quality. Once they have gathered information on suppliers, they sign contracts with suppliers who meet the organization's needs and they place orders.

Buyers who purchase items to resell to customers may determine which products their organization will sell. They need to be able to predict what will appeal to their customers. If they are wrong, they could jeopardize the profits and reputation of their organization.

Buyers who work for large organizations often specialize in purchasing one or two categories of products or services. Buyers who work for smaller businesses or government agencies may be responsible for making a greater variety of purchases.

The following are examples of types of buyers and purchasing agents:

Purchasing agents and buyers of farm products buy agricultural products for further processing or resale. Examples of these products are grain, cotton, and tobacco.

Purchasing agents, except wholesale, retail, and farm products buy items for the operation of an organization. Examples of these items are chemicals and industrial equipment needed for a manufacturing establishment, and office supplies.

Wholesale and retail buyers purchase goods for resale to consumers. Examples of these goods are clothing and electronics. Purchasing specialists who buy finished goods for resale are commonly known as *buyers* or *merchandise managers*.

Work Environment

Buyers and purchasing agents held about 494,400 jobs in 2022. The largest employers of buyers and purchasing agents were as follows:

Manufacturing	23%
Wholesale trade	14
Government	12
Management of companies and enterprises	9
Retail trade	8

Purchasing managers plan and coordinate the work of buyers and purchasing agents.

Purchasing managers held about 77,500 jobs in 2022. The largest employers of purchasing managers were as follows:

Manufacturing	26%
Management of companies and enterprises	18
Government	12
Wholesale trade	10
Professional, scientific, and technical services	9

Most purchasing managers and buyers and purchasing agents work in offices. Travel is sometimes necessary to visit suppliers or review products.

Work Schedules

Most purchasing managers and buyers and purchasing agents work full time. Overtime is common in these occupations.

How to Become a Purchasing Manager, Buyer, or Purchasing Agent

Buyers and purchasing agents typically have a bachelor's degree. A bachelor's degree and a few years of work experience in procurement is required for purchasing manager positions.

Educational requirements vary for buyers and purchasing agents, who also receive on-the-job training.

Education

Purchasing managers, buyers, and purchasing agents typically need a bachelor's degree. Programs vary but may include fields of study such as military technologies. Purchasing managers also need 5 or more years of work experience in procurement.

Educational requirements for buyers and purchasing agents usually vary with the size of the organization. Although a high school diploma may be enough at some organizations, many businesses require applicants to have a bachelor's degree. For many positions, a degree in business, finance, or supply management is sufficient. For positions as a buyer or purchasing agent of farm products, a degree in agriculture, agriculture production, or animal science may be beneficial.

Training

Buyers and purchasing agents typically get on-the-job training for a few months. During this time, they learn how to perform their basic duties, including monitoring inventory levels and negotiating with suppliers.

Licenses, Certifications, and Registrations

There are several certifications available for buyers and purchasing agents. Although some employers may require certification, many do not.

Most of these certifications involve oral or written exams and have education and work experience requirements.

The American Purchasing Society offers the Certified Purchasing Professional (CPP) certification. The CPP certification is valid for 5 years. Candidates must earn a certain number of professional development "points" to renew their certification. Candidates initially become eligible and can renew their certification through a combination of purchasing-related experience, education, and professional contributions (such as published articles or delivered speeches).

The Association for Supply Chain Management offers the Certified Supply Chain Professional (CSCP) credential. Applicants must have 3 years of relevant business experience or a bachelor's degree in order to be eligible for the CSCP credential. The credential is valid for 5 years. Candidates must also earn a certain number of professional development points to renew their certification.

The Next Level Purchasing Association offers the Senior Professional in Supply Management (SPSM) certification. Although there are no education or work experience requirements, applicants must complete six online courses and pass an SPSM exam. Certification is valid for 4 years. Candidates must complete 32 continuing education hours in procurement-related topics to recertify for an additional 4-year period.

The Universal Public Procurement Certification Council (UPPCC) offers two certifications for workers in federal, state, and local government. The Certified Professional Public Buyer (CPPB) credential requires applicants to have earned at least an associate's degree, possess at least 3 years of public procurement experience, and complete relevant training courses. The Certified Public Purchasing Officer (CPPO) requires applicants to have earned a bachelor's degree, possess at least 5 years of public procurement experience, and complete additional training courses.

Those with the CPPB or the CPPO designation must renew their certification every 5 years by completing continuing education courses or attending procurement-related conferences or events.

The National Institute of Government Purchasing (NIGP) and the National Association of State Procurement Officials (NASPO) offer preparation courses for the UPPCC certification exams.

Work Experience in a Related Occupation

Purchasing managers typically must have at least 5 years of experience as a buyer or purchasing agent. At the top levels, purchasing manager duties may overlap with other management functions, such as production, planning, logistics, and marketing.

Advancement

An experienced purchasing agent or buyer may become an assistant purchasing manager before advancing to purchasing manager, supply manager, or director of materials management.

Purchasing managers and buyers and purchasing agents with extensive work experience can also advance to become the Chief Procurement Officer (CPO) for an organization.

Important Qualities

Analytical skills. When evaluating suppliers, purchasing managers and buyers and purchasing agents must analyze their options and choose a supplier with the best combination of price, quality, delivery, or service.

Decision-making skills. Purchasing managers and buyers and purchasing agents must have the ability to make informed and timely decisions, choosing products that they think will sell.

Math skills. Purchasing managers and buyers and purchasing agents must possess math skills. They must be able to compare prices from different suppliers to ensure that their organization is getting the best deal.

Negotiating skills. Purchasing managers and buyers and purchasing agents often must negotiate the terms of a contract with a supplier. Interpersonal skills and self-confidence, in addition to knowledge of the product, can help lead to successful negotiations.

Pay

The median annual wage for buyers and purchasing agents was $67,620 in May 2022. The median wage is the wage at which half the workers in an occupation earned more than that amount and half earned less. The lowest 10 percent earned less than $41,060, and the highest 10 percent earned more than $116,370.

Purchasing Managers, Buyers, and Purchasing Agents

Median annual wages, May 2022

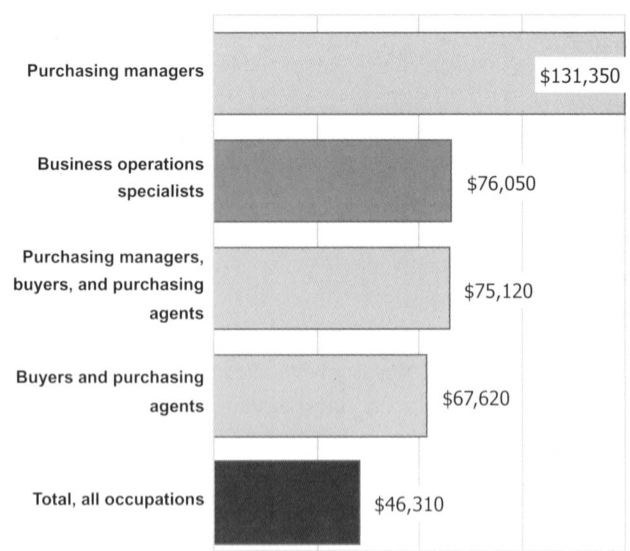

Note: All Occupations includes all occupations in the U.S. Economy.
Source: U.S. Bureau of Labor Statistics, Occupational Employment and Wage Statistics.

The median annual wage for purchasing managers was $131,350 in May 2022. The lowest 10 percent earned less than $80,000, and the highest 10 percent earned more than $210,000.

In May 2022, the median annual wages for buyers and purchasing agents in the top industries in which they worked were as follows:

Government	$84,640
Management of companies and enterprises	79,660
Manufacturing	69,060
Wholesale trade	62,770
Retail trade	49,660

In May 2022, the median annual wages for purchasing managers in the top industries in which they worked were as follows:

Professional, scientific, and technical services	$158,250
Management of companies and enterprises	151,980
Government	134,950
Manufacturing	126,940
Wholesale trade	122,360

Most purchasing managers and buyers and purchasing agents work full time. Overtime is common in these occupations.

Job Outlook

Overall employment of purchasing managers, buyers, and purchasing agents is projected to decline 6 percent from 2022 to 2032.

Purchasing Managers, Buyers, and Purchasing Agents

Percent change in employment, projected 2022-32

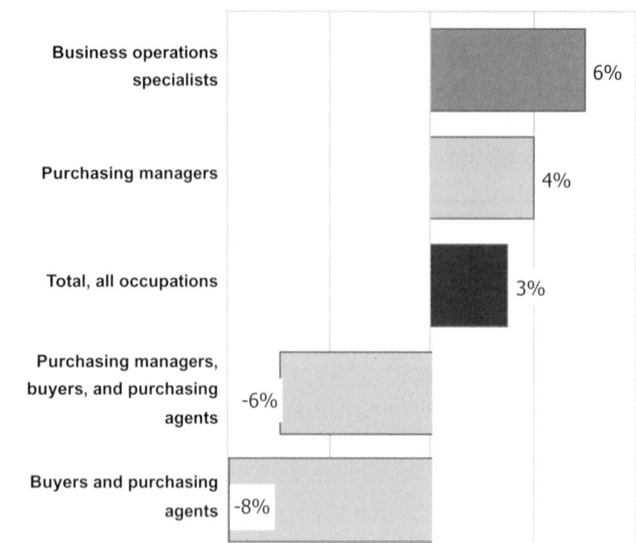

Note: All Occupations includes all occupations in the U.S. Economy.
Source: U.S. Bureau of Labor Statistics, Employment Projections program.

Despite declining employment, about 45,000 openings for purchasing managers, buyers, and purchasing agents are projected each year, on average, over the decade. All of those openings are expected to result from the need to replace workers who transfer to other occupations or exit the labor force, such as to retire.

Employment

Projected employment of purchasing managers, buyers, and purchasing agents varies by occupation (see table).

Purchasing managers will continue to be needed to help procure goods and services for business operations or for resale to customers.

Employment of buyers and purchasing agents is projected to decline due to increased automation of some procurement tasks. Organizations will likely adopt automation for simple procurement functions, such as finding suppliers or processing purchase orders.

In the public sector, employment demand may be impacted by the increasing use of cooperative purchasing agreements. These agreements allow state and local governments to share resources to buy supplies, which may limit the need for procurement officers.

Occupational Title	SOC Code	Employment, 2022	Projected Employment, 2032	Change, 2022-32	
				Percent	Numeric
Purchasing managers, buyers, and purchasing agents	—	571,900	537,300	-6	-34,600

Occupational Title	SOC Code	Employment, 2022	Projected Employment, 2032	Change, 2022-32	
				Percent	Numeric
Purchasing managers	11-3061	77,500	80,900	4	3,400
Buyers and purchasing agents	13-1020	494,400	456,300	-8	-38,000

Contacts for More Information

For more information, visit

- American Purchasing Society
- Association for Supply Chain Management
- Next Level Purchasing Association
- The National Institute of Government Purchasing (NIGP), Institute for Public Procurement
- Universal Public Procurement Certification Council
- National Association of State Procurement Officials

Tax Examiners and Collectors, and Revenue Agents

Summary

Quick Facts: Tax Examiners and Collectors, and Revenue Agents	
2022 Median Pay	$57,950 per year $27.86 per hour
Typical Entry-Level Education	Bachelor's degree
Work Experience in a Related Occupation	None
On-the-job Training	Moderate-term on-the-job training
Number of Jobs, 2022	55,000
Job Outlook, 2022-32	1% (Little or no change)
Employment Change, 2022-32	300

What Tax Examiners and Collectors, and Revenue Agents Do

Tax examiners and collectors, and revenue agents determine how much is owed in taxes and collect tax from individuals and businesses on behalf of the government.

Tax examiners and collectors, and revenue agents review tax returns, conduct audits, identify taxes owed, and collect overdue tax payments.

Work Environment

Tax examiners and collectors, and revenue agents work for federal, state, and local governments. Many work primarily in an office setting; others spend most of their time doing field audits in taxpayers' homes or places of business. Most tax examiners and collectors, and revenue agents work full time.

How to Become a Tax Examiner or Collector, or Revenue Agent

Tax examiners and collectors, and revenue agents typically need a bachelor's degree in accounting or a related field. However, the level of education and experience required varies with the position and employer.

Pay

The median annual wage for tax examiners and collectors, and revenue agents was $57,950 in May 2022.

Job Outlook

Employment of tax examiners and collectors, and revenue agents is projected to show little or no change from 2022 to 2032.

Despite limited employment growth, about 4,100 openings for tax examiners and collectors, and revenue agents are projected each year, on average, over the decade. Most of those openings are expected to result from the need to replace workers who transfer to different occupations or exit the labor force, such as to retire.

What Tax Examiners and Collectors, and Revenue Agents Do

Tax examiners and collectors, and revenue agents determine how much is owed in taxes and collect tax from individuals and businesses on behalf of federal, state, and local governments. They review tax returns, conduct audits, identify taxes owed, and collect overdue tax payments.

Duties

Tax examiners and collectors, and revenue agents typically do the following:

- Review filed tax returns to determine whether credits and deductions claimed are allowed by law

Tax examiners and collectors, and revenue agents are responsible for ensuring that individuals and businesses pay the taxes they owe.

- Contact taxpayers to address problems and to request supporting documentation
- Conduct field audits and investigations of income tax returns to verify information or to update tax liabilities
- Evaluate financial information, using their understanding of accounting procedures and knowledge of changes to tax laws and regulations
- Keep records on each active case including telephone numbers and actions taken
- Notify taxpayers of overpayment or underpayment and issue a refund or request additional payment

Tax examiners and collectors, and revenue agents ensure that individuals and businesses pay the appropriate amount of taxes owed, as prescribed by laws and regulations. In addition to verifying that tax returns are filed correctly, they follow up with taxpayers whose returns are questionable or who owe more money.

Different levels of government collect different types of taxes. The federal government's Internal Revenue Service (IRS) deals primarily with business and personal income taxes. State governments collect income and sales taxes. Local governments collect property and sales taxes.

Because some states base income taxes on taxpayers' reported federal income, tax examiners working for the federal government report to the states any adjustments or corrections they make. State tax examiners then determine whether the adjustments affect the state taxpayer liability.

Tax examiners and collectors, and revenue agents have different duties and responsibilities:

Tax examiners typically deal with simple tax returns filed by individual taxpayers who claim few deductions and by small businesses. Tax examiners also may contact individual taxpayers in order to resolve outstanding problems with their returns.

Much of a tax examiner's job involves making sure that tax credits and deductions claimed by taxpayers are lawful. If a taxpayer owes additional taxes, tax examiners adjust the total amount by assessing fees, interest, and penalties and then notify the taxpayer of the total amount owed.

Revenue agents, called *internal revenue agents* in the IRS, specialize in tax-related accounting. Like tax examiners, they review returns for accuracy. However, revenue agents handle the complex tax returns of large businesses and corporations.

Some experienced revenue agents focus exclusively on a particular area, such as multinational business. Regardless of their specialty, revenue agents must keep up to date with changes in tax laws and regulations.

Tax collectors, also called *internal revenue officers* in the IRS, deal with overdue accounts. The process of collecting an overdue payment starts with the revenue agent or tax examiner sending a report to the taxpayer. If the taxpayer makes no effort to pay, the case is assigned to a tax collector.

When a tax collector takes a case, he or she first sends a notice to the taxpayer. The tax collector then works with the taxpayer to settle the debt. Settlement may involve setting up a plan in which the amount owed is paid back in small amounts over time.

When delinquent taxpayers claim that they cannot pay their taxes, collectors investigate and verify the claims. Tax collectors research information on taxpayer financial statements or mortgages and locate taxpayer-owned items of value through third parties, such as local departments of motor vehicles. Ultimately, they must decide whether the IRS should place a lien—a claim on an asset such as a bank account, real estate, or an automobile—to settle a debt. Tax collectors also have the authority to garnish wages—that is, take a portion of earned wages—to collect taxes owed.

Work Environment

Tax examiners and collectors, and revenue agents held about 55,000 jobs in 2022. The largest employers of tax examiners and collectors, and revenue agents were as follows:

Tax examiners and collectors, and revenue agents work for federal, state, and local governments.

Federal government	44%
State government, excluding education and hospitals	36
Local government, excluding education and hospitals	18

Tax examiners and collectors, and revenue agents work primarily in an office setting; others spend most of their time conducting field audits in taxpayers' homes or places of business.

Work Schedules

Most tax examiners and collectors, and revenue agents work full time.

How to Become a Tax Examiner or Collector, or Revenue Agent

Tax examiners and collectors, and revenue agents typically need a bachelor's degree in accounting or a related field. However, the required level of education and experience varies with the position and employer.

Education

Tax examiners and collectors, and revenue agents typically need a bachelor's degree in accounting or a related field, such as business. For some jobs, work experience may substitute for a degree.

Candidates for tax examiner and collector positions at the Internal Revenue Service (IRS) may qualify with a bachelor's degree in any field of study or with specialized experience, or with a combination of education and experience. Internal revenue agents at the IRS generally need a bachelor's degree in accounting; a combination of education and experience equivalent to a major in accounting; or a Certified Public Accountant (CPA) certificate.

Training

Newly hired tax examiners and collectors, and revenue agents typically receive on-the-job training that lasts between 1 month and 1 year. These workers also must keep current with changes to the tax code and in enforcement and collection procedures.

Most tax examiners and collectors, and revenue agents need a bachelor's degree in accounting or a related field.

Work Experience in a Related Occupation

Some employers accept work experience as a substitute for education. For example, employers may hire tax examiners and revenue agents who have experience as accountants or bookkeepers, or they may hire tax collectors who have experience working as bill and account collectors, customer service representatives, or credit checkers.

Advancement

Tax examiners who review individual tax returns may advance to revenue agent positions, working on more complex business returns.

Tax examiners and collectors, and revenue agents who demonstrate leadership skills and a thorough knowledge of tax collection activities may advance to supervisory or managerial positions.

Important Qualities

Analytical skills. Tax examiners and revenue agents must be able to identify questionable claims for credits and deductions and determine if claims are lawful.

Communication skills. Tax collectors must be able to clearly explain complex details, especially about sensitive information, in their work with the public.

Detail oriented. Tax examiners and revenue agents verify the accuracy of each entry on the tax returns they review. Therefore, it is important that they pay attention to detail.

Interpersonal skills. Tax collectors must be comfortable interacting with people. When pursuing overdue accounts, tax collectors should be firm and composed.

Math skills. Tax collectors and revenue agents deal with numbers daily and must be comfortable with arithmetic. They also need to analyze, compare, and interpret facts and figures.

Organizational skills. Tax examiners and revenue agents may work with multiple returns and a variety of financial documents. Keeping the various pieces of information organized is essential.

Pay

The median annual wage for tax examiners and collectors, and revenue agents was $57,950 in May 2022. The median wage is the wage at which half the workers in an occupation earned more than that amount and half earned less. The lowest 10 percent earned less than $36,570, and the highest 10 percent earned more than $107,120.

In May 2022, the median annual wages for tax examiners and collectors, and revenue agents in the top industries in which they worked were as follows:

Federal government	$59,780
State government, excluding education and hospitals	57,890

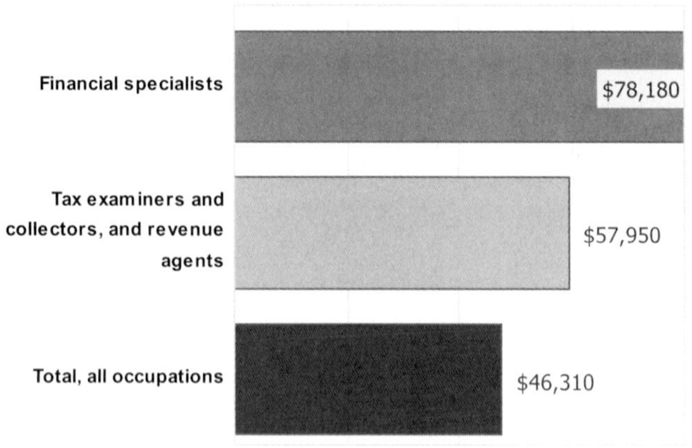

Note: All Occupations includes all occupations in the U.S. Economy.
Source: U.S. Bureau of Labor Statistics, Occupational Employment and Wage Statistics.

Local government, excluding education and hospitals 48,920

Most tax examiners and collectors, and revenue agents work full time.

Job Outlook

Employment of tax examiners and collectors, and revenue agents is projected to show little or no change from 2022 to 2032.

Despite limited employment growth, about 4,100 openings for tax examiners and collectors, and revenue agents are projected each year, on average, over the decade. Most of those openings are expected to result from the need to replace workers who transfer to different occupations or exit the labor force, such as to retire.

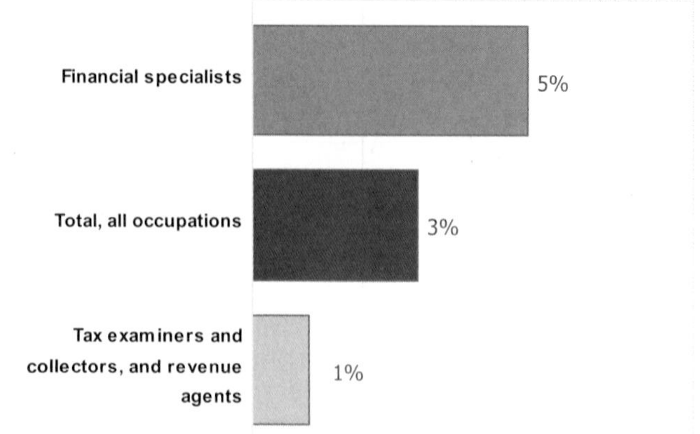

Note: All Occupations includes all occupations in the U.S. Economy.
Source: U.S. Bureau of Labor Statistics, Employment Projections program.

Employment

Employment of these workers will depend primarily on future changes to federal, state, and local government budgets. Because the salaries of tax examiners and collectors, and revenue agents are paid with public funds, budgetary constraints may directly impact governments' ability to hire these workers and, in turn, affect employment growth.

Occupational Title	SOC Code	Employment, 2022	Projected Employment, 2032	Change, 2022-32	
				Percent	Numeric
Tax examiners and collectors, and revenue agents	13-2081	55,000	55,400	1	300

Contacts for More Information

For more information, visit

- IRS Careers
- U.S. Office of Personnel Management (OPM)

Training and Development Specialists

Summary

Quick Facts: Training and Development Specialists	
2022 Median Pay	$63,080 per year $30.33 per hour
Typical Entry-Level Education	Bachelor's degree
Work Experience in a Related Occupation	Less than 5 years
On-the-job Training	None
Number of Jobs, 2022	385,800
Job Outlook, 2022-32	6% (Faster than average)
Employment Change, 2022-32	24,200

What Training and Development Specialists Do
Training and development specialists plan and administer programs that improve the skills and knowledge of their employees.

Work Environment
Training and development specialists work in nearly every industry. They spend much of their time working with people, giving presentations, and leading training activities.

How to Become a Training and Development Specialist
In addition to a bachelor's degree, training and development specialists also need work experience and strong communication skills.

Pay
The median annual wage for training and development specialists was $63,080 in May 2022.

Job Outlook
Employment of training and development specialists is projected to grow 6 percent from 2022 to 2032, faster than the average for all occupations.

About 35,400 openings for training and development specialists are projected each year, on average, over the decade. Many of those openings are expected to result from the need to replace workers who transfer to different occupations or exit the labor force, such as to retire.

Training and development specialists often lead educational sessions.

What Training and Development Specialists Do
Training and development specialists plan and administer programs that train employees and improve their skills and knowledge.

Duties
Training and development specialists typically do the following:

- Assess training needs through surveys, interviews with employees, or consultations with managers or instructors
- Design and create training manuals, online learning modules, and course materials
- Review training materials from multiple sources and choose appropriate materials
- Deliver training to employees using a variety of instructional techniques
- Assist in evaluating training programs
- Perform administrative tasks such as monitoring costs, scheduling classes, setting up systems and equipment, and coordinating enrollment

Training and development specialists help create, plan, and run training programs for businesses and organizations. To do this, they must first assess the needs of an organization. They then develop custom training programs that may take place online, in classrooms, or in training facilities.

Training and development specialists organize or run training sessions using lectures, team exercises and other formats. Training also may be in the form of a video, a self-guided instructional manual, or an online application. Training may be collaborative, allowing employees to connect informally with colleagues, experts, and mentors.

Work Environment
Training and development specialists held about 385,800 jobs in 2022. The largest employers of training and development specialists were as follows:

Training and development specialists guide employees through exercises.

Educational services; state, local, and private	12%
Professional, scientific, and technical services	11
Healthcare and social assistance	11
Finance and insurance	9
Administrative and support services	8

Training and development specialists spend much of their time working with people, giving presentations, and leading training activities. They also may need to travel to training sites.

Work Schedules

Most training and development specialists work full time during regular business hours.

How to Become a Training and Development Specialist

Training and development specialists typically need a bachelor's degree and related work experience. However, candidates who do not have a bachelor's degree sometimes qualify for jobs if they have relevant experience.

Education

Training and development specialists typically need a bachelor's degree, often in a business field such as organizational development or human resources. Other fields of degree include education, social science, psychology, and communications.

Candidates who do not have a bachelor's degree sometimes qualify for jobs if they have experience developing and delivering training. The experience may need to be extensive and specific to the employer's industry.

Work Experience in a Related Occupation

Related work experience is important for most training and development specialists. Positions may require work experience in areas such as staff development or instructional design or in related occupations, such as human resources specialists or teachers.

Employers also may prefer to hire candidates who have work experience in a relevant industry or with virtual learning, mobile training, and technology-based tools. However, employers may hire candidates who have a master's degree instead of work experience.

They spend much of their time working with people, giving presentations, and leading training activities.

Training and development specialists must have strong instructional skills to meet the learning needs of a particular group.

Licenses, Certifications, and Registrations

Although not usually required, certification shows professional expertise and credibility. However, some employers prefer to hire certified candidates, and some positions require certification. The Association for Talent Development (ATD) and International Society for Performance Improvement (ISPI) are among the organizations that offer certification programs in training and development.

Advancement

Training and development specialists may advance to training and development manager or human resources manager positions. Workers typically need several years of experience to advance.

Important Qualities

Analytical skills. Training and development specialists must evaluate training programs, methods, and materials and choose those that best fit each situation.

Collaboration skills. Specialists need strong interpersonal skills because delivering training programs requires coordinating with instructors, subject-matter experts, and trainees. Specialists accomplish much of their work through teams.

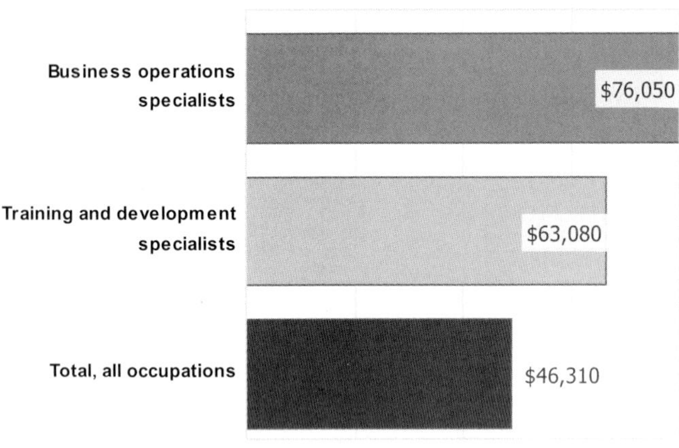

Note: All Occupations includes all occupations in the U.S. Economy.
Source: U.S. Bureau of Labor Statistics, Occupational Employment and Wage Statistics.

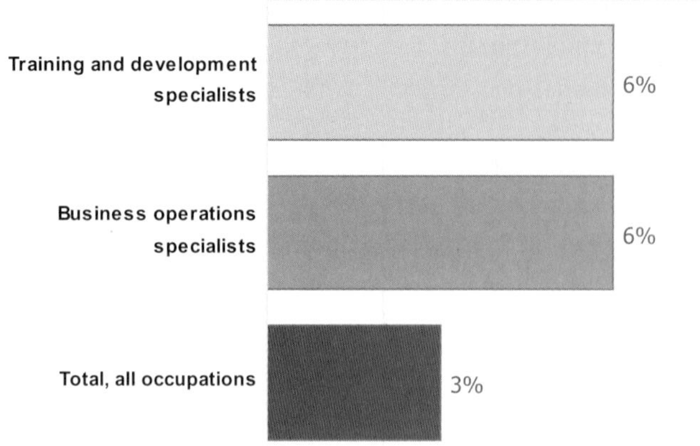

Note: All Occupations includes all occupations in the U.S. Economy.
Source: U.S. Bureau of Labor Statistics, Employment Projections program.

Communication skills. Training and development specialists must convey information clearly and facilitate learning to diverse audiences.

Creativity. Specialists should be resourceful when developing training materials. They may need to think of and implement new approaches when considering training methods.

Instructional skills. Training and development specialists deliver employee training programs. They must have strong training skills to meet the learning needs of a particular group.

Pay

The median annual wage for training and development specialists was $63,080 in May 2022. The median wage is the wage at which half the workers in an occupation earned more than that amount and half earned less. The lowest 10 percent earned less than $34,950, and the highest 10 percent earned more than $108,530.

In May 2022, the median annual wages for training and development specialists in the top industries in which they worked were as follows:

Professional, scientific, and technical services	$79,040
Finance and insurance	70,580
Educational services; state, local, and private	67,860
Healthcare and social assistance	60,920
Administrative and support services	50,770

Most training and development specialists work full time during regular business hours.

Job Outlook

Employment of training and development specialists is projected to grow 6 percent from 2022 to 2032, faster than the average for all occupations.

About 35,400 openings for training and development specialists are projected each year, on average, over the decade. Many of those openings are expected to result from the need to replace workers who transfer to different occupations or exit the labor force, such as to retire.

Employment

Employees in many occupations are required to take continuing education and skill development courses throughout their careers, creating demand for workers who lead training activities.

Employment of training and development specialists is projected to grow in many industries as companies develop and introduce new media and technology into their training programs. Innovations in training methods and learning technology should continue throughout the next decade.

In addition, some organizations meet their employees' needs by outsourcing instruction to firms that specialize in training and development.

Employment projections data for training and development specialists, 2022-32

Occupational Title	SOC Code	Employment, 2022	Projected Employment, 2032	Change, 2022-32		Employment by Industry
				Percent	Numeric	
SOURCE: U.S. Bureau of Labor Statistics, Employment Projections program						
Training and development specialists	13-1151	385,800	409,900	6	24,200	Get data

Contacts for More Information

For more information about training and development specialists, visit

- ➤ Association for Talent Development (ATD)
- ➤ International Society for Performance Improvement (ISPI)

Community and Social Service

Community Health Workers

Summary

Quick Facts: Community Health Workers	
2022 Median Pay	$46,190 per year $22.21 per hour
Typical Entry-Level Education	High school diploma or equivalent
Work Experience in a Related Occupation	None
On-the-job Training	Short-term on-the-job training
Number of Jobs, 2022	67,200
Job Outlook, 2022-32	14% (Much faster than average)
Employment Change, 2022-32	9,400

What Community Health Workers Do

Community health workers promote wellness by helping people adopt healthy behaviors. They implement programs and advocate for people who may have limited access to health resources and social services.

Work Environment

Community health workers are employed in a variety of settings, including hospitals, public health departments, and community-based organizations. Most work full time.

How to Become a Community Health Worker

To enter the occupation, community health workers typically need at least a high school diploma; some employers prefer to hire candidates who have postsecondary education. To attain competency, they typically complete a brief period of on-the-job training, and some states require certification.

Pay

The median annual wage for community health workers was $46,190 in May 2022.

Job Outlook

Employment of community health workers is projected to grow 14 percent from 2022 to 2032, much faster than the average for all occupations.

About 8,000 openings for community health workers are projected each year, on average, over the decade. Many of those openings are expected to result from the need to replace workers who transfer to different occupations or exit the labor force, such as to retire.

What Community Health Workers Do

Community health workers promote wellness by helping people adopt healthy behaviors. They implement programs and advocate for people who may have limited access to health resources and social services.

Duties

Community health workers typically do the following:

- Coordinate care among individuals, communities, and health and social service systems
- Conduct outreach, such as through home visits
- Provide culturally appropriate health and informational resources
- Oversee case management and resource access
- Advocate for individuals and communities regarding housing, food security, and other needs
- Provide coaching and social support, such as nutrition training, recovery services for mental health and substance use disorders, and chronic disease management and prevention
- Provide services, such as basic health screenings and first aid
- Increase individual and community participation in assessments and education to improve health and well-being

Community health workers act as intermediaries between their clients and providers of healthcare and social services. They identify health-related issues, collect data, and discuss clients' health concerns within the community. For example, community health workers might identify barriers preventing clients from access to transportation and provide referrals to resources that provide it.

Ideally, these workers have close ties to the communities they serve so that they understand their clients' unique needs. They share that information with providers of healthcare and social

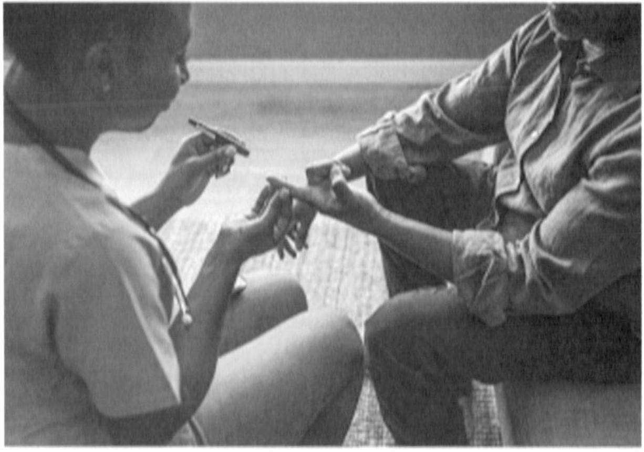

Community health workers provide services such as basic health screenings.

services for determining appropriate programs and care. They also advocate for community wellness needs and conduct outreach to engage clients, assist with navigating healthcare, and improve coordination of care.

Community health workers may have different titles, depending on the population they serve. For example, *community health representatives* increase health knowledge and access to care for Tribal communities. *Promotores de la salud* reduce barriers to healthcare and social services in Spanish-speaking communities. *Peer support specialists* have experienced a mental health or substance use disorder and are in recovery while providing support to others experiencing similar challenges.

Community health workers work closely with other healthcare and social service providers, including registered nurses, social workers, and substance abuse, behavioral disorder, and mental health counselors.

Work Environment

Community health workers held about 67,200 jobs in 2022. The largest employers of community health workers were as follows:

Social assistance	20%
Ambulatory healthcare services	17
Local government, excluding education and hospitals	15
Hospitals; state, local, and private	10
Religious, grantmaking, civic, professional, and similar organizations	10

community health workers may spend part of their day in an office for activities such as recordkeeping and writing reports. However, they spend much of their time in the field to interact with community members, hold events, and collect data. They may travel to a variety of settings, including homes or medical facilities, to meet with clients.

To interact with community members, community health workers may travel to a variety of settings.

Community health workers often collaborate with healthcare and social service providers as part of an interdisciplinary team.

Work Schedules

Most community health workers are employed full time. They may need to work evenings and weekends to attend community events, programs, or meetings.

How to Become a Community Health Worker

To enter the occupation, community health workers typically need at least a high school diploma; some employers prefer to hire candidates who have postsecondary education. To attain competency, they typically complete a brief period of on-the-job training, and some states require certification.

Education

Community health workers typically need at least a high school diploma, although some jobs require postsecondary education. Postsecondary community health worker programs may lead to a 1-year certificate or a 2-year associate's degree. These programs cover topics such as wellness, ethics, and cultural awareness.

Training

Community health workers typically complete on-the-job training. They learn about topics useful in their work, including communication styles, outreach and advocacy methods, and legal and ethical issues.

Some workers participate in apprenticeships or other programs that provide opportunities for hands-on experience.

Other Experience

Community health workers usually benefit from understanding the specific community, culture, medical condition, or disability with which they work. They may have personal experience in these areas, or they may gain experience by working in

Community health workers need instructional skills to lead programs.

activities such as community development, public health, or social outreach.

The ability to speak another language is helpful for working in some communities.

Licenses, Certifications, and Registrations

Some states require certification for community health workers, which may include completing an approved training program. For more information, contact your state's board of health, nursing, or human services.

Advancement

Experienced community health workers may move into supervisory positions.

With additional education, community health workers may be able to transition to occupations such as health education specialists; registered nurses; social workers; or substance abuse, behavioral disorder, and mental health counselors.

Important Qualities

Communication skills. Community health workers must be able to clearly convey information in health-related materials to those they serve and in written proposals for programs and funding.

Cultural sensitivity. Community health workers must be respectful of the communities they serve and be understanding of their concerns.

Instructional skills. Community health workers lead programs and facilitate discussions with clients.

Interpersonal skills. Community health workers interact with people from a variety of backgrounds. They must be good listeners and be empathetic in responding to the needs of the communities they serve.

Problem-solving skills. Community health workers must think creatively about the best ways to serve their clients. For example, they may need to adapt program planning because of budget constraints or when encountering resistance from community members.

Pay

The median annual wage for community health workers was $46,190 in May 2022. The median wage is the wage at which half the workers in an occupation earned more than that amount and half earned less. The lowest 10 percent earned less than $32,180, and the highest 10 percent earned more than $73,730.

In May 2022, the median annual wages for community health workers in the top industries in which they worked were as follows:

Hospitals; state, local, and private	$54,390
Local government, excluding education and hospitals	47,770
Religious, grantmaking, civic, professional, and similar organizations	46,150
Ambulatory healthcare services	44,230
Social assistance	40,910

Most community health workers are employed full time. They may need to work evenings and weekends to attend community events, programs or meetings.

Job Outlook

About 8,000 openings for community health workers are projected each year, on average, over the decade. Many of those

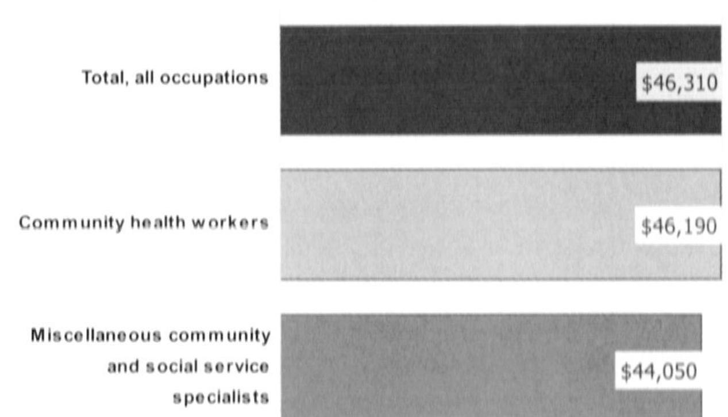

Note: All Occupations includes all occupations in the U.S. Economy.
Source: U.S. Bureau of Labor Statistics, Occupational Employment and Wage Statistics.

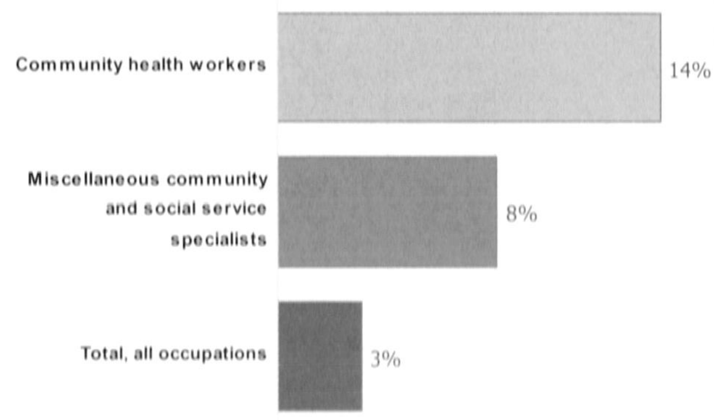

Note: All Occupations includes all occupations in the U.S. Economy.
Source: U.S. Bureau of Labor Statistics, Employment Projections program.

openings are expected to result from the need to replace workers who transfer to different occupations or exit the labor force, such as to retire.

Employment

Community health workers will continue to be needed to help organizations and government agencies provide people with health-related information, such as how to access medical services. Demand for these workers will also stem from their role in implementing public health initiatives, including preventive measures to reduce the spread of disease.

Occupational Title	SOC Code	Employment, 2022	Projected Employment, 2032	Change, 2022-32	
				Percent	Numeric
Community health workers	21-1094	67,200	76,600	14	9,400

Contacts for More Information

For more information about community health workers, visit

- American Public Health Association
- Association of State and Territorial Health Officials
- National Association of Community Health Representatives
- National Association of Community Health Workers
- National Association of Peer Supporters
- Visión y Compromiso

Health Education Specialists

Summary

Quick Facts: Health Education Specialists

2022 Median Pay	$59,990 per year $28.84 per hour
Typical Entry-Level Education	Bachelor's degree
Work Experience in a Related Occupation	None
On-the-job Training	None
Number of Jobs, 2022	60,400
Job Outlook, 2022-32	7% (Faster than average)
Employment Change, 2022-32	4,400

What Health Education Specialists Do

Health education specialists develop programs to teach people about conditions affecting well-being.

Work Environment

Health education specialists are employed in a variety of settings, including hospitals, nonprofit organizations, and government agencies. Most work full time.

Health educators and community health workers teach people about behaviors that promote wellness.

How to Become a Health Education Specialist

Health education specialists typically need at least a bachelor's degree. Certification may be required or preferred for some health education specialists.

Pay

The median annual wage for health education specialists was $59,990 in May 2022.

Job Outlook

Employment of health education specialists is projected to grow 7 percent from 2022 to 2032, faster than the average for all occupations.

About 6,600 openings for health education specialists are projected each year, on average, over the decade. Many of those openings are expected to result from the need to replace workers who transfer to different occupations or exit the labor force, such as to retire.

What Health Education Specialists Do

Health education specialists teach people about behaviors that promote wellness. They develop strategies to improve the well-being of individuals and communities.

Duties

Health education specialists typically do the following:

- Assess the health needs of individuals and communities
- Develop programs, materials, and events to teach people about health topics, such as managing existing conditions
- Evaluate the effectiveness of programs and educational materials
- Help people find health services or information
- Provide training programs for community health workers or other healthcare providers
- Supervise staff who implement health education programs
- Collect and analyze data to learn about a particular community and improve programs and services

Health educators and community health workers educate people about the availability of healthcare services.

- Advocate for improved health resources and policies that promote health

Health education specialists have different duties depending on where they work. The following are descriptions of duties for health education specialists, by work setting:

- In *healthcare facilities*, health education specialists may work one-on-one with patients or their families. They teach patients about their diagnoses and treatment options. They also lead efforts to develop and administer surveys for identifying health concerns in the community and to develop programs that meet those needs. For example, they may help to organize blood-pressure screenings or classes on proper installation of car seats. Health education specialists also create programs to train medical staff to interact more effectively with patients.
- In *nonprofits*, health education specialists create programs and materials about health issues in the community they serve. They help organizations obtain funding, such as through grants for promoting health and disease awareness. They also educate policymakers about ways to improve public health. In nonprofits that focus on a particular disease or audience, health education specialists tailor programs to meet those needs.
- In *public health departments*, health education specialists develop public health campaigns on topics such as emergency preparedness, immunizations, or proper nutrition. They also develop materials for use in the community and by public health officials. Some health education specialists collaborate with other workers, such as on statewide or local committees, to create public policies on health and wellness topics. They may also oversee grants and grant-funded programs to improve the public health.

Health education specialists create workplace programs or suggest modifications that focus on wellness. For example, they may develop incentives for employees to adopt healthy behaviors, such as controlling cholesterol, or recommend changes in the workplace to improve employee health, such as creating smoke-free areas.

For information about workers who promote wellness and coordinate care for different populations, see the profile on community health workers. For information about workers who teach health classes in middle and high schools, see the profiles on middle school teachers and high school teachers.

Work Environment

Health education specialists held about 60,400 jobs in 2022. The largest employers of health education specialists were as follows:

Government	26%
Ambulatory healthcare services	17
Hospitals; state, local, and private	17
Social assistance	9
Educational services; state, local, and private	6

Although most health education specialists work in offices, they may spend a lot of time away from their desks to carry out programs or attend meetings.

Work Schedules

Most health education specialists are employed full time. They may need to work nights and weekends to attend programs or meetings.

How to Become a Health Education Specialist

Health education specialists typically need at least bachelor's degree. Some employers require or prefer that health education specialists be certified.

Education

Health education specialists typically need at least a bachelor's degree in health education or health promotion. Employers

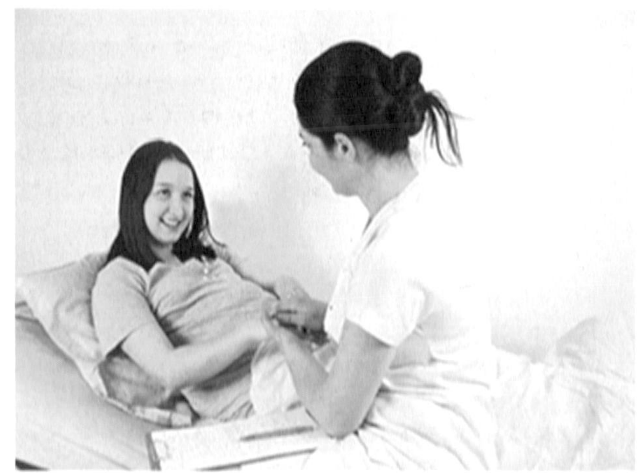

Health educators often work in hospitals, where they help patients understand and adjust to their diagnosis.

may accept a variety of other majors, including business, social science, and healthcare and related fields. Students may gain additional knowledge and skills through an internship.

Some health education specialist positions require candidates to have a master's or doctoral degree. Graduate program fields of degree may include community health education, school health education, public health education, or health promotion. Applicants to these master's degree programs generally do not need a specific undergraduate major.

Licenses, Certifications, and Registrations

Employers may require or prefer that health education specialists obtain certification, such as the Certified Health Education Specialist (CHES) credential offered by the National Commission for Health Education Credentialing, Inc. or the Certified Diabetes Care and Education Specialist (CDCES) credential offered by the Certification Board for Diabetes Care and Education.

Important Qualities

Analytical skills. Health education specialists collect and evaluate data to determine the needs of the people they serve.

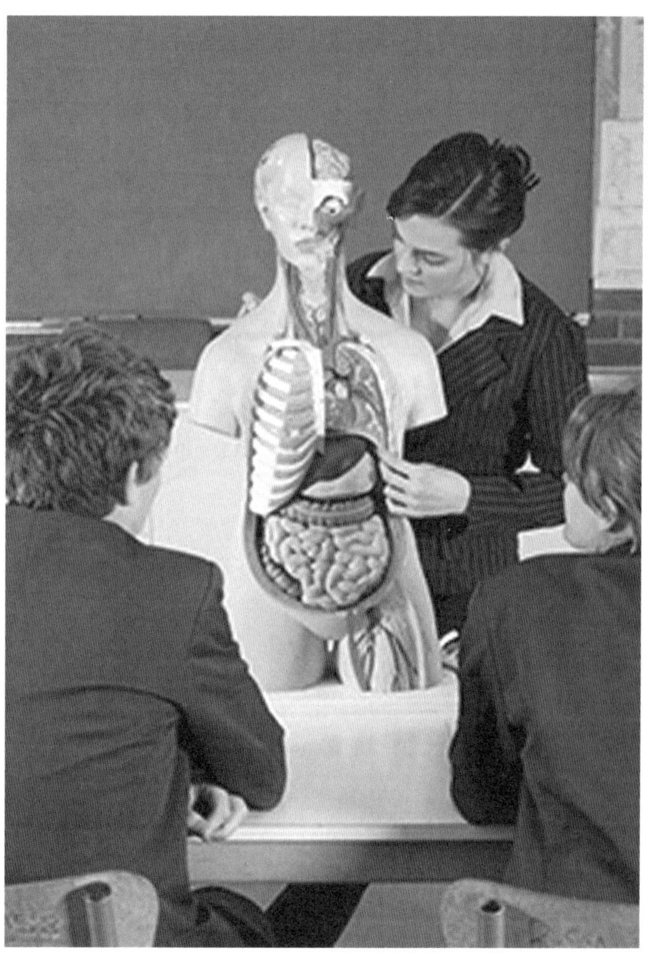

Health educators need at least a bachelor's degree.

Communication skills. Health education specialists must be able to clearly convey information in health-related materials and in written proposals for programs and funding.

Instructional skills. Health education specialists lead programs, teach classes, and facilitate discussion with clients and families.

Interpersonal skills. Health education specialists interact with many people from a variety of backgrounds. They must be good listeners and be empathetic in responding to the needs of the people they serve.

Problem-solving skills. Health education specialists must think creatively about improving the health of the community. In addition, they may need to solve problems that arise in planning programs, such as budget constraints or resistance from the community they are serving.

Pay

The median annual wage for health education specialists was $59,990 in May 2022. The median wage is the wage at which half the workers in an occupation earned more than that amount and half earned less. The lowest 10 percent earned less than $37,140, and the highest 10 percent earned more than $106,210.

In May 2022, the median annual wages for health education specialists in the top industries in which they worked were as follows:

Hospitals; state, local, and private	$77,740
Government	61,650
Educational services; state, local, and private	57,390
Ambulatory healthcare services	56,910
Social assistance	43,790

Most health education specialists are employed full time. They may need to work nights and weekends to attend programs or meetings.

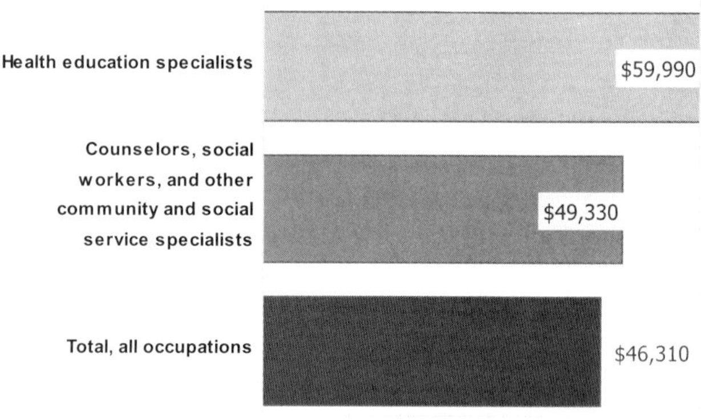

Note: All Occupations includes all occupations in the U.S. Economy.
Source: U.S. Bureau of Labor Statistics, Occupational Employment and Wage Statistics.

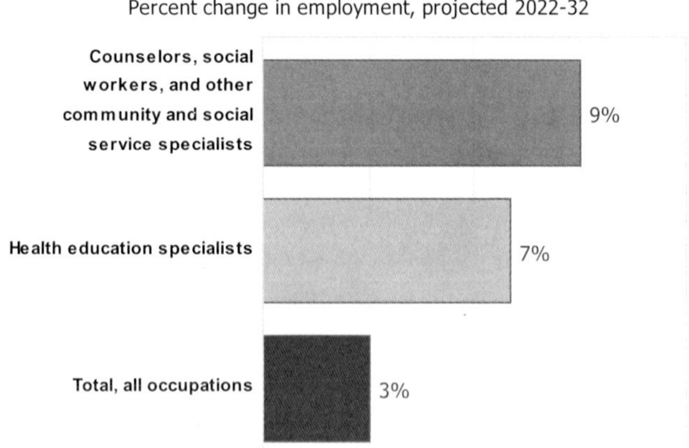

Note: All Occupations includes all occupations in the U.S. Economy.
Source: U.S. Bureau of Labor Statistics, Employment Projections program.

Job Outlook

Employment of health education specialists is projected to grow 7 percent from 2022 to 2032, faster than the average for all occupations.

About 6,600 openings for health education specialists are projected each year, on average, over the decade. Many of those openings are expected to result from the need to replace workers who transfer to different occupations or exit the labor force, such as to retire.

Employment

An emphasis on promoting healthy behaviors is expected to increase demand for these specialists over the decade.

Governments, healthcare providers, and social services providers want to find ways to improve the quality of care and health outcomes while reducing costs. This objective should increase demand for health education specialists to teach people about health and wellness, which in turn helps to prevent costly diseases and medical procedures.

Occupational Title	SOC Code	Employment, 2022	Projected Employment, 2032	Change, 2022-32	
				Percent	Numeric
Health education specialists	21-1091	60,400	64,800	7	4,400

Contacts for More Information

For more information about health education specialists, visit

- Society for Public Health Education
- American Public Health Association
- Certification Board for Diabetes Care and Education
- National Commission for Health Education Credentialing, Inc.

Marriage and Family Therapists

Summary

Quick Facts: Marriage and Family Therapists

2022 Median Pay	$56,570 per year $27.20 per hour
Typical Entry-Level Education	Master's degree
Work Experience in a Related Occupation	None
On-the-job Training	Internship/residency
Number of Jobs, 2022	71,200
Job Outlook, 2022-32	15% (Much faster than average)
Employment Change, 2022-32	10,600

What Marriage and Family Therapists Do

Marriage and family therapists help people manage and overcome problems with family and other relationships.

Work Environment

Marriage and family therapists work in a variety of settings, such as private practice and mental health centers. Most work full time.

How to Become a Marriage and Family Therapist

Marriage and family therapists typically need a master's degree and a license to practice.

Marriage and family therapists help people manage problems with their family and relationships.

Pay

The median annual wage for marriage and family therapists was $56,570 in May 2022.

Job Outlook

Employment of marriage and family therapists is projected to grow 15 percent from 2022 to 2032, much faster than the average for all occupations.

About 5,900 openings for marriage and family therapists are projected each year, on average, over the decade. Many of those openings are expected to result from the need to replace workers who transfer to different occupations or exit the labor force, such as to retire.

What Marriage and Family Therapists Do

Marriage and family therapists help people manage problems with their family and other relationships.

Duties

Marriage and family therapists typically do the following:

- Encourage clients to discuss their emotions and experiences
- Help clients process their reactions and adjust to difficult changes in their life, such as divorce and layoffs
- Guide clients through the process of making decisions about their future
- Help clients develop strategies and skills to change their behavior and to cope with difficult situations
- Refer clients to other resources or services in the community, such as support groups or inpatient treatment facilities
- Complete and maintain confidential files and mandated records

Marriage and family therapists use a variety of techniques and tools to help their clients. Many apply cognitive behavioral therapy, a goal-oriented approach that helps clients understand harmful thoughts, feelings, and beliefs and teaches how to replace them with positive, life-enhancing ones.

Many marriage and family therapists work in private practice. They must market their practice to prospective clients and work with insurance companies and clients to get payment for their services.

Marriage and family therapists work with individuals, couples, and families. They bring a family-centered perspective to treatment, even when treating individuals. They evaluate family roles and development, to understand how clients' families affect their mental health. They treat the clients' relationships, not just the clients themselves. They address issues, such as low self-esteem, stress, addiction, and substance abuse.

Marriage and family therapists coordinate patient treatment with other professionals, such as psychologists and social workers.

Work Environment

Marriage and family therapists held about 71,200 jobs in 2022. The largest employers of marriage and family therapists were as follows:

Individual and family services	29%
Offices of other health practitioners	28
Outpatient care centers	13
Self-employed workers	11
State government, excluding education and hospitals	6

Marriage and family therapists work in a variety of settings, such as mental health centers, substance abuse treatment centers, and hospitals. They also work in private practice and in Employee Assistance Programs (EAPs), which are mental health programs that some employers provide to help employees deal with personal problems.

Work Schedules

Marriage and family therapists generally work full time. Some therapists work evenings and weekends to accommodate their clients' schedules.

Marriage and family therapists encourage clients to discuss their emotions and experiences.

Many marriage and family therapists work in private practice.

Master's programs in marriage and family therapy prepare students to provide counseling to couples, individuals, and groups.

How to Become a Marriage and Family Therapist

Marriage and family therapists typically need a master's degree and a license to practice.

Education

To become a marriage and family therapist, applicants need a master's degree in psychology, marriage and family therapy, or a related mental health field. Although a bachelor's degree in psychology is common, most undergraduate fields are acceptable for entering a master's degree program.

Marriage and family therapy programs teach students about how marriages, families, and relationships function and how these relationships can affect mental and emotional disorders.

There are several organizations that accredit counseling programs, including the Council for Accreditation of Counseling & Related Educational Programs (CACREP), the Commission on Accreditation for Marriage and Family Therapy Education (COAMFTE), and the Masters in Psychology and Counseling Accreditation Council (MPCAC).

Training

Candidates gain hands-on experience through postdegree supervised clinical work, sometimes referred to as an internship or residency. In training, they learn to provide family therapy, group therapy, psychotherapy, and other therapeutic interventions, under the supervision of a licensed counselor.

Licenses, Certifications, and Registrations

All states require marriage and family therapists to be licensed. Licensure requires a master's degree and 2,000 to 4,000 hours of postdegree supervised clinical experience, sometimes referred to as an internship or residency. In addition, therapists must pass a state-recognized exam and complete annual continuing education classes.

Contact and licensing information for marriage and family therapists is available through the Association of Marital and Family Therapy Regulatory Boards.

Important Qualities

Compassion. Marriage and family therapists often work with people who are dealing with stressful and difficult situations, so they must be compassionate and empathize with their clients.

Interpersonal skills. Marriage and family therapists work with different types of people. They spend most of their time working directly with clients and other professionals and must be able to encourage good relationships.

Listening skills. Marriage and family therapists need to give their full attention to their clients to understand their problems, values, and goals.

Organizational skills. Marriage and family therapists in private practice must keep track of payments and work with insurance companies.

Speaking skills. Marriage and family therapists need to be able to communicate with clients effectively. They must express information in a way that clients can understand easily.

Pay

The median annual wage for marriage and family therapists was $56,570 in May 2022. The median wage is the wage at which half the workers in an occupation earned more than that amount and half earned less. The lowest 10 percent earned less than $36,840, and the highest 10 percent earned more than $98,700.

In May 2022, the median annual wages for marriage and family therapists in the top industries in which they worked were as follows:

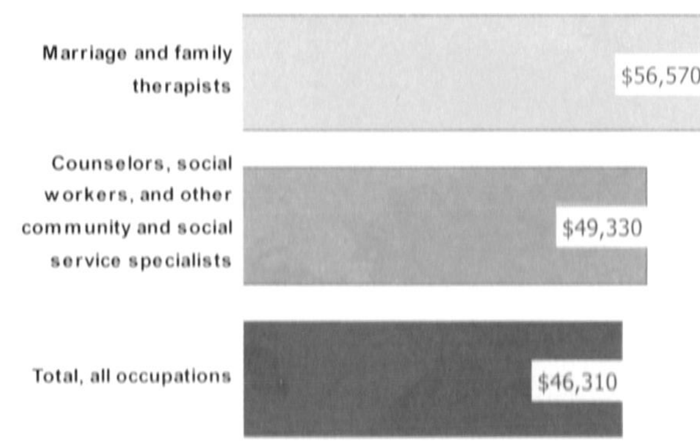

Note: All Occupations includes all occupations in the U.S. Economy.
Source: U.S. Bureau of Labor Statistics, Occupational Employment and Wage Statistics.

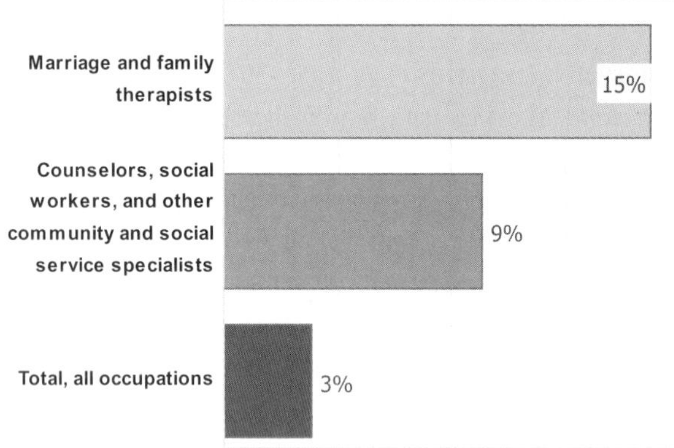

Note: All Occupations includes all occupations in the U.S. Economy.
Source: U.S. Bureau of Labor Statistics, Employment Projections program.

State government, excluding education and hospitals	$77,000
Outpatient care centers	59,870
Offices of other health practitioners	50,920
Individual and family services	50,370

Marriage and family therapists generally work full time. Some therapists work evenings and weekends to accommodate their clients' schedules.

Job Outlook

Employment of marriage and family therapists is projected to grow 15 percent from 2022 to 2032, much faster than the average for all occupations.

About 5,900 openings for marriage and family therapists are projected each year, on average, over the decade. Many of those openings are expected to result from the need to replace workers who transfer to different occupations or exit the labor force, such as to retire.

Employment

Growth is expected due to the increasing use of integrated care, which is a treatment of multiple problems at one time by a group of specialists. In providing integrated care, marriage and family therapists are working with counselors such as substance abuse, behavior disorder, and mental health counselors to address patients' issues as a team.

Occupational Title	SOC Code	Employment, 2022	Projected Employment, 2032	Change, 2022-32	
				Percent	Numeric
Marriage and family therapists	21-1013	71,200	81,800	15	10,600

Contacts for More Information

For more information about accredited programs, visit

- Commission on Accreditation for Marriage and Family Therapy Education
- Council for Accreditation of Counseling & Related Educational Programs
- Masters in Psychology and Counseling Accreditation Council
- American Association for Marriage and Family Therapy
- Association of Marital and Family Therapy Regulatory Boards
- American Counseling Association
- National Board for Certified Counselors

Probation Officers and Correctional Treatment Specialists

Summary

Quick Facts: Probation Officers and Correctional Treatment Specialists	
2022 Median Pay	$59,860 per year $28.78 per hour
Typical Entry-Level Education	Bachelor's degree
Work Experience in a Related Occupation	None
On-the-job Training	Moderate-term on-the-job training
Number of Jobs, 2022	93,900
Job Outlook, 2022-32	3% (As fast as average)
Employment Change, 2022-32	2,400

What Probation Officers and Correctional Treatment Specialists Do

Probation officers and correctional treatment specialists assist in rehabilitating law offenders in custody or on probation or parole.

Work Environment

Most probation officers and correctional treatment specialists work full time. Their jobs may involve traveling to meet with probationers and parolees. Working in high-crime areas or in institutions may be stressful and dangerous.

How to Become a Probation Officer or Correctional Treatment Specialist

Probation officers and correctional treatment specialists typically need a bachelor's degree. In addition, candidates may be required to pass oral, written, and psychological exams.

Pay

The median annual wage for probation officers and correctional treatment specialists was $59,860 in May 2022.

Job Outlook

Employment of probation officers and correctional treatment specialists is projected to grow 3 percent from 2022 to 2032, about as fast as the average for all occupations.

About 7,400 openings for probation officers and correctional treatment specialists are projected each year, on average, over the decade. Many of those openings are expected to result from the need to replace workers who transfer to different occupations or exit the labor force, such as to retire.

What Probation Officers and Correctional Treatment Specialists Do

Probation officers and correctional treatment specialists assist in rehabilitating law offenders in custody or on probation or parole.

Duties

Probation officers and correctional treatment specialists typically do the following:

- Interview probationers and parolees, their friends, and their relatives in an office or at a residence to assess progress
- Evaluate probationers and parolees to determine the best course of rehabilitation
- Connect probationers and parolees with resources, such as job training
- Test clients for drugs and, if necessary, offer substance abuse counseling
- Complete prehearing investigations and testify in court or before parole boards regarding clients' backgrounds and progress
- Write reports and maintain case files on clients

Probation officers and correctional treatment specialists work with and monitor law offenders to prevent them from committing new crimes.

Correctional treatment specialists counsel law offenders and create rehabilitation plans for them to follow when they are no longer in prison.

Probation officers and correctional treatment specialists supervise and counsel probationers or parolees, overseeing their clients' actions in a variety of ways. For example, they may use electronic monitoring to track a client's movement in the community.

The number of cases a probation officer or correctional treatment specialist handles at one time depends on each individual's needs and associated risks. Higher risk clients usually command more of an officer's time and resources. Caseload also varies by agency.

The following are examples of types of probation officers and correctional treatment specialists:

Probation officers supervise people who have been placed on probation instead of sent to prison. These workers ensure that probationers are not a danger to the community and help in their rehabilitation by visiting frequently. Probation officers write reports that detail each probationer's treatment plan and progress since being put on probation. Most work exclusively with either adults or juveniles.

Parole officers work with people who have been released from prison and are serving parole, helping them re-enter society. Parole officers monitor postrelease parolees and provide them with information on various resources, such as substance abuse counseling or job training, to aid in their rehabilitation. By doing so, the officers try to change the parolee's behavior and thus reduce the risk of that person committing another crime and having to return to prison.

Both probation and parole officers supervise probationers and parolees through personal contact with them and their families (also known as community supervision). These officers require parolees and probationers to keep in contact regularly by scheduling either telephone calls or office visits. They also check on them at their homes or places of work, taking into account the safety of the neighborhood. Probation and parole officers note mental health considerations and oversee drug testing and electronic monitoring of those under supervision. In some states, workers perform the duties of both probation and parole officers.

Pretrial services officers investigate a defendant's background to determine whether they can be safely allowed back into the community before their trial date. Officers must assess the risk and make a recommendation to a judge, who decides on the appropriate sentencing (in settled cases with no trial) or bond amount. When pretrial defendants are allowed back into the community, pretrial officers supervise them to make sure that they stay within the terms of their release and appear at their trials.

Correctional treatment specialists, also known as *case managers* or *correctional counselors*, advise probationers and parolees and develop rehabilitation plans for them to follow. They may evaluate inmates using questionnaires and psychological tests. They also work with inmates, parole officers, and staff of other agencies to develop parole and release plans. For example, they may plan education and training programs to improve probationers' job skills.

Correctional treatment specialists write case reports that cover the inmate's history and the likelihood that he or she will commit another crime. When inmates are eligible for release, the case reports are given to the appropriate parole board. The specialist may help set up counseling for the parolees and their families, find substance abuse or mental health treatment options, aid in job placement, and find housing. Correctional treatment specialists also explain the terms and conditions of the inmate's release and keep detailed written accounts of each parolee's progress.

Work Environment

Probation officers and correctional treatment specialists held about 93,900 jobs in 2022. The largest employers of probation officers and correctional treatment specialists were as follows:

State government, excluding education and hospitals	51%
Local government, excluding education and hospitals	46
Social assistance	1

Most probation officers and correctional treatment specialists work full time. Their jobs may involve frequent travel, either to perform home and employment checks or property searches or to attend court hearings.

Probation officers and correctional treatment specialists may have court-imposed deadlines, adding pressure to complete time-sensitive tasks. Dealing with probationers and parolees who violate the terms of their supervision can be frustrating. Working in high-crime areas or in institutions may be stressful. Because of the hostile environments they may encounter, some officers and specialists carry a firearm or pepper spray for protection.

Despite the job's challenges, however, the work also may be rewarding. Probation officers and correctional treatment specialists may receive personal satisfaction from counseling

Extensive travel and paperwork can also contribute to more hours of work.

members of their community and helping them become productive citizens.

Work Schedules

Most probation officers and correctional treatment specialists work full time. Some workers may be on call and must respond to any issues with probationers, parolees, or law enforcement 24 hours a day.

Meeting with clients often requires travel and working during nonstandard hours.

How to Become a Probation Officer or Correctional Treatment Specialist

Probation officers and correctional treatment specialists typically need a bachelor's degree. In addition, candidates may be required to pass competency exams, drug testing, and a criminal background check.

A valid driver's license may be required, and some agencies require applicants to be at least 21 years old.

Education

Probation officers and correctional treatment specialists typically need a bachelor's degree. Common fields of degree include criminal justice or a related security and protective service field, social science, or psychology. Requirements vary by jurisdiction.

Training

Most probation officers and correctional treatment specialists must complete a training program sponsored by their state or local government or the federal government, after which they may have to pass a certification test. In addition, they may be required to work as trainees for up to 1 year before being offered a permanent position.

Some probation officers and correctional treatment specialists focus on a certain type of casework. For example, an officer may deal only with domestic violence probationers or with substance abuse cases; others work only on cases involving juvenile offenders. Officers and specialists receive training to prepare them to work with the type of client their casework involves.

Probation officers may go on to specialize in a certain type of casework, such as working with juvenile law offenders.

Other Experience

Although job requirements vary, volunteer or paid work experience in the criminal justice field may be helpful for some positions.

Advancement

Advancement to supervisory positions is based primarily on experience and performance. A master's degree in criminal justice, social work, or psychology may be helpful for advancing.

Important Qualities

Communication skills. Probation officers and correctional treatment specialists must be able to effectively convey information to different types of people, including clients and their families, lawyers, judges, and treatment providers.

Critical-thinking skills. Probation officers and correctional treatment specialists must be able to assess clients' needs to determine the best resources for helping them.

Decision-making skills. Probation officers and correctional treatment specialists must consider the best rehabilitation plan for clients.

Interpersonal skills. Probation officers and correctional treatment specialists must be able to develop relationships with different types of people, including those who may be hostile or challenging.

Organizational skills. Probation officers and correctional treatment specialists must be able to manage multiple cases at the same time.

Pay

The median annual wage for probation officers and correctional treatment specialists was $59,860 in May 2022. The median wage is the wage at which half the workers in an occupation earned more than that amount and half earned less. The lowest 10 percent earned less than $38,550, and the highest 10 percent earned more than $101,080.

In May 2022, the median annual wages for probation officers and correctional treatment specialists in the top industries in which they worked were as follows:

Local government, excluding education and hospitals	$63,380
State government, excluding education and hospitals	55,760
Social assistance	36,710

Most probation officers and correctional treatment specialists work full time. Some workers may be on call and must respond

Probation Officers and Correctional Treatment Specialists

Median annual wages, May 2022

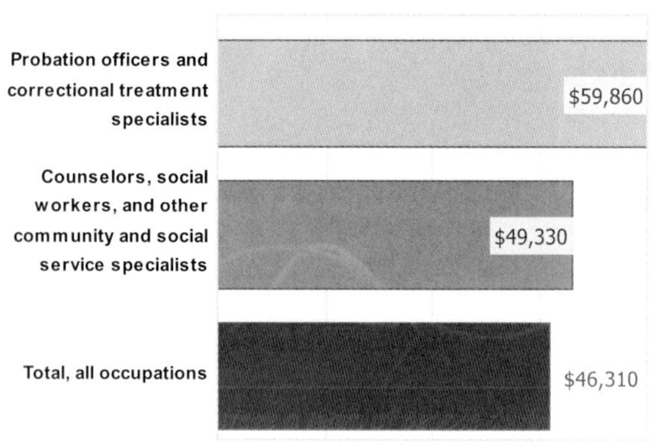

Note: All Occupations includes all occupations in the U.S. Economy.
Source: U.S. Bureau of Labor Statistics, Occupational Employment and Wage Statistics.

Probation Officers and Correctional Treatment Specialists

Percent change in employment, projected 2022-32

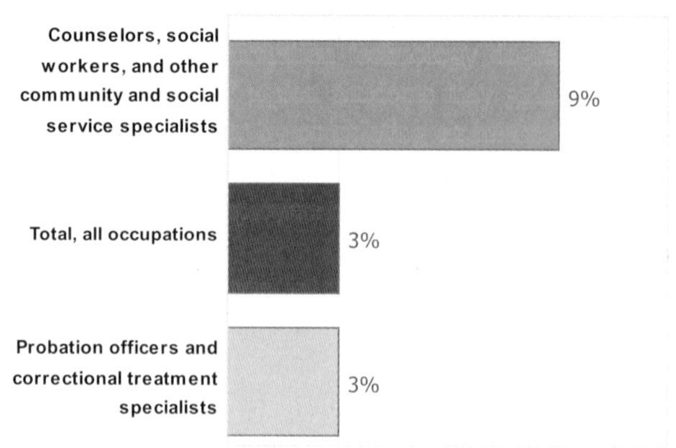

Note: All Occupations includes all occupations in the U.S. Economy.
Source: U.S. Bureau of Labor Statistics, Employment Projections program.

to any issues with probationers or law enforcement 24 hours a day.

Job Outlook

Employment of probation officers and correctional treatment specialists is projected to grow 3 percent from 2022 to 2032, about as fast as the average for all occupations.

About 7,400 openings for probation officers and correctional treatment specialists are projected each year, on average, over the decade. Many of those openings are expected to result from the need to replace workers who transfer to different occupations or exit the labor force, such as to retire.

Employment

Employment growth depends primarily on the amount of state and local government funding for corrections, especially the amount allocated to probation and parole systems.

Demand for probation officers and correctional treatment specialists should be strong as governments continue to recognize the advantages of community corrections over incarceration in certain situations. Parole officers will continue to be needed to supervise individuals who will be released from prison in the future.

Occupational Title	SOC Code	Employment, 2022	Projected Employment, 2032	Change, 2022-32	
				Percent	Numeric
Probation officers and correctional treatment specialists	21-1092	93,900	96,200	3	2,400

Contacts for More Information

For more information about probation officers and correctional treatment specialists, visit

➤ American Probation and Parole Association

Rehabilitation Counselors

Summary

Quick Facts: Rehabilitation Counselors	
2022 Median Pay	$39,990 per year $19.23 per hour
Typical Entry-Level Education	Master's degree
Work Experience in a Related Occupation	None
On-the-job Training	None
Number of Jobs, 2022	84,800
Job Outlook, 2022-32	2% (As fast as average)
Employment Change, 2022-32	1,600

What Rehabilitation Counselors Do

Rehabilitation counselors help people with physical, mental, developmental, or emotional disabilities live independently.

Work Environment

Rehabilitation counselors work in a variety of settings, such as community rehabilitation centers, senior citizen centers, and youth guidance organizations.

How to Become a Rehabilitation Counselor

Rehabilitation counselors typically need a master's degree in rehabilitation counseling or a related field. Some positions require certification or a license.

Pay

The median annual wage for rehabilitation counselors was $39,990 in May 2022.

Job Outlook

Employment of rehabilitation counselors is projected to grow 2 percent from 2022 to 2032, about as fast as the average for all occupations.

Rehabilitation counselors help people with physical, mental, developmental, and emotional disabilities live independently.

About 6,700 openings for rehabilitation counselors are projected each year, on average, over the decade. Many of those openings are expected to result from the need to replace workers who transfer to different occupations or exit the labor force, such as to retire.

What Rehabilitation Counselors Do

Rehabilitation counselors help people with physical, mental, developmental, or emotional disabilities live independently. They work with clients to overcome or manage the personal, social, or psychological effects of disabilities on employment or independent living.

Duties

Rehabilitation counselors typically do the following:

- Provide individual and group counseling to help clients adjust to their disability
- Evaluate clients' abilities, interests, experiences, skills, health, and education
- Develop a treatment plan for clients, in consultation with other professionals, such as doctors, therapists, and psychologists
- Arrange for clients to obtain services, such as medical care or career training
- Help employers understand the needs and abilities of people with disabilities, as well as laws and resources that affect people with disabilities
- Help clients develop their strengths and adjust to their limitations
- Locate resources, such as wheelchairs or computer programs, that help clients live and work more independently
- Maintain client records and monitor clients' progress, adjusting the rehabilitation or treatment plan as necessary
- Advocate for the rights of people with disabilities to live in a community and work in the job of their choice

Rehabilitation counselors help people with disabilities develop strategies to live with their disability and transition to employment.

Rehabilitation counselors help people with disabilities at various stages in their lives. Some work with students, to develop strategies to live with their disability and transition from school to work. Others help veterans cope with the mental or physical effects of their military service. Still others help elderly people adapt to disabilities developed later in life from illness or injury. Some may provide expert testimony or assessments during personal-injury or workers' compensation cases.

Some rehabilitation counselors deal specifically with employment issues. These counselors, sometimes called ***vocational rehabilitation counselors***, typically work with older students and adults.

Work Environment

Rehabilitation counselors held about 84,800 jobs in 2022. The largest employers of rehabilitation counselors were as follows:

Community and vocational rehabilitation services	34%
State government, excluding education and hospitals	17
Nursing and residential care facilities	14
Individual and family services	14
Self-employed workers	1

Rehabilitation counselors work in a variety of settings, such as community rehabilitation centers, senior citizen centers, and youth guidance organizations.

Rehabilitation counselors work in a variety of settings, such as community rehabilitation centers, senior citizen centers, and youth guidance organizations.

Work Schedules

Depending on where they work, some rehabilitation counselors may work evenings or weekends.

How to Become a Rehabilitation Counselor

Rehabilitation counselors typically need a master's degree in rehabilitation counseling or a related field. Some positions require certification or a license.

Education

Most employers require a master's degree in rehabilitation counseling or a related field. Master's degree programs teach students to evaluate clients' needs, formulate and implement job placement strategies, and understand the medical and psychological aspects of disabilities. These programs typically include a period of supervised clinical experience, such as an internship.

Although some employers hire workers with a bachelor's degree in rehabilitation and disability studies, these workers typically cannot offer the full range of services that a rehabilitation counselor with a master's degree can provide. Students in bachelor's degree programs learn about issues faced by people

Rehabilitation counselors may need to complete a period of supervised clinical experience as part of a master's degree.

with disabilities and about the process of providing rehabilitation services. Some universities offer dual-degree programs in rehabilitation counseling, in which students can earn a bachelor's and master's degree in 5 years.

Licenses, Certifications, and Registrations

Licensing requirements for rehabilitation counselors differ by state and by type of services provided. Rehabilitation counselors who provide counseling services to clients and patients must attain a counselor license through their state licensing board. Rehabilitation counselors who provide other services, however, may be exempt from state licensing requirements. For example, rehabilitation counselors who provide only vocational rehabilitation services or job placement assistance may not need a license.

Licensure typically requires a master's degree and 2,000 to 4,000 hours of supervised clinical experience. In addition, counselors must pass a state-recognized exam. To maintain their license, counselors must complete annual continuing education credits.

Applicants should contact their state licensing board for information on which services or counseling positions require licensure. Contact information for these state licensing boards can be found through the Commission on Rehabilitation Counselor Certification.

Some employers prefer or require rehabilitation counselors to be certified. The Commission on Rehabilitation Counselor Certification offers the Certified Rehabilitation Counselor (CRC) certification. Applicants must meet advanced education, work experience, and clinical supervision requirements and pass a test. Certification must be renewed every 5 years. Counselors must complete continuing education requirements or pass a reexamination to renew their certification.

Important Qualities

Communication skills. Rehabilitation counselors need to be able to communicate effectively with clients. They must express ideas and information in a way that is easy to understand.

Compassion. Rehabilitation counselors often work with people who are dealing with stressful and difficult situations. They must be compassionate and empathize with their clients.

Critical-thinking skills. Rehabilitation counselors must be able to develop a treatment plan to help clients reach their goals by considering each client's abilities and interests.

Interpersonal skills. Rehabilitation counselors must be able to work with different types of people. They spend most of their time working directly with clients, families, employers, or other professionals. They must be able to develop and maintain good working relationships.

Listening skills. Good listening skills are essential for rehabilitation counselors. They need to give their full attention in sessions in order to understand clients' problems, concerns, and values.

Rehabilitation Counselors

Median annual wages, May 2022

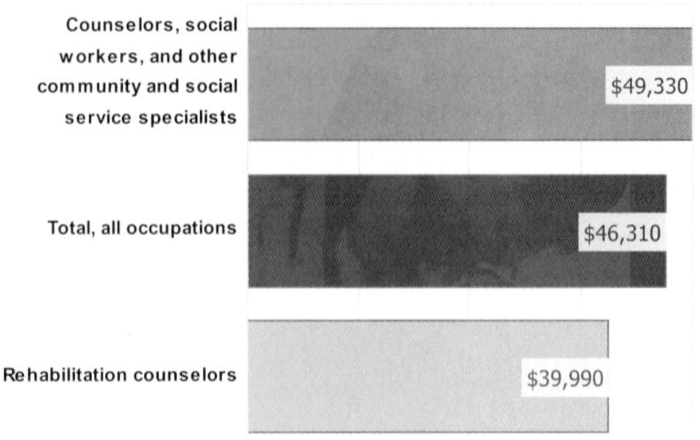

Note: All Occupations includes all occupations in the U.S. Economy.
Source: U.S. Bureau of Labor Statistics, Occupational Employment and Wage Statistics.

Patience. Rehabilitation counselors must have patience to help clients learn new skills and strategies to address their disabilities.

Pay

The median annual wage for rehabilitation counselors was $39,990 in May 2022. The median wage is the wage at which half the workers in an occupation earned more than that amount and half earned less. The lowest 10 percent earned less than $29,120, and the highest 10 percent earned more than $71,270.

In May 2022, the median annual wages for rehabilitation counselors in the top industries in which they worked were as follows:

State government, excluding education and hospitals	$54,790
Individual and family services	40,260
Community and vocational rehabilitation services	36,400
Nursing and residential care facilities	35,730

Depending on where they work, some rehabilitation counselors may work evenings or weekends.

Job Outlook

Employment of rehabilitation counselors is projected to grow 2 percent from 2022 to 2032, about as fast as the average for all occupations.

About 6,700 openings for rehabilitation counselors are projected each year, on average, over the decade. Many of those openings are expected to result from the need to replace workers who transfer to different occupations or exit the labor force, such as to retire.

Employment

Demand for rehabilitation counselors is expected to grow with the increase in the elderly population and with the continued

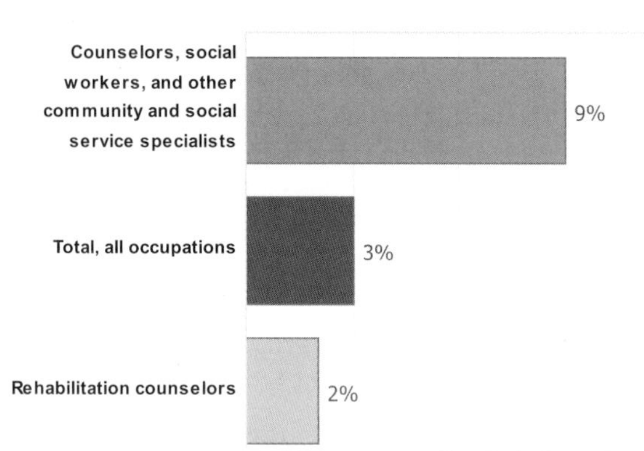

Note: All Occupations includes all occupations in the U.S. Economy.
Source: U.S. Bureau of Labor Statistics, Employment Projections program.

rehabilitation needs of other groups, such as veterans and people with disabilities.

Older adults are more likely than other age groups to become disabled or injured. Rehabilitation counselors will be needed to help the elderly learn to adapt to any new limitations and learn strategies to live independently.

In addition, there will be a continued need for rehabilitation counselors to work with veterans who were disabled during their military service. They will also be needed to work with other groups, such as people who have learning disabilities, autism spectrum disorders, or substance abuse problems.

Occupational Title	SOC Code	Employment, 2022	Projected Employment, 2032	Change, 2022-32	
				Percent	Numeric
Rehabilitation counselors	21-1015	84,800	86,400	2	1,600

Contacts for More Information

For more information about counseling and information about counseling specialties, visit

- American Counseling Association
- American Rehabilitation Counseling Association
- Council for Accreditation of Counseling & Related Educational Programs
- Commission on Rehabilitation Counselor Certification

School and Career Counselors and Advisors

Summary

Quick Facts: School and Career Counselors and Advisors

2022 Median Pay	$60,140 per year $28.92 per hour
Typical Entry-Level Education	Master's degree
Work Experience in a Related Occupation	None
On-the-job Training	None
Number of Jobs, 2022	342,400
Job Outlook, 2022-32	5% (Faster than average)
Employment Change, 2022-32	18,400

What School and Career Counselors and Advisors Do

School counselors help students develop academic and social skills. Career counselors and advisors help people choose a path to employment.

Work Environment

School counselors work in public and private schools. Career counselors and advisors are employed primarily in colleges and universities but also work in career centers and private practice. Both types of counselors usually work full time.

How to Become a School or Career Counselor or Advisor

Most school counselors need a master's degree in school counseling or a related field and have a state-issued credential. Some states require licensure for career counselors and advisors.

Pay

The median annual wage for school and career counselors and advisors was $60,140 in May 2022.

School counselors help students develop academic and social skills.

Job Outlook

Employment of school and career counselors and advisors is projected to grow 5 percent from 2022 to 2032, faster than the average for all occupations.

About 26,600 openings for school and career counselors and advisors are projected each year, on average, over the decade. Many of those openings are expected to result from the need to replace workers who transfer to different occupations or exit the labor force, such as to retire.

What School and Career Counselors and Advisors Do

School counselors help students develop academic and social skills and plans for after graduation. Career counselors and advisors help students and other clients develop skills, explore an occupation, or choose an educational program that will lead to a career.

Duties

School counselors typically do the following:

- Help students understand and overcome social or behavioral challenges
- Analyze data to identify factors, such as poor attendance, that negatively affect academic performance
- Advise individuals and small groups based on their needs
- Work with students to develop skills that support learning, such as effective time management and study habits
- Evaluate students' abilities and interests through aptitude assessments and interviews
- Collaborate with teachers and families to help students plan academic, career, and social goals
- Teach students and school staff about specific topics such as bullying and drug use
- Present options to students for educational or vocational plans after graduation
- Maintain records as required

Career counselors assist people with the process of making career decisions.

- Report cases of possible neglect or abuse and refer students and parents to resources for additional support

The specific duties of school counselors vary with their students' ages.

Elementary school counselors visit classrooms or meet with students individually or in groups to help them develop their social and academic skills. They also meet with parents or guardians to discuss the child's strengths and weaknesses, challenges, or special needs. School counselors work with teachers and administrators to ensure that the curriculum addresses students' developmental and academic needs.

Middle school counselors work with school staff and families to help students improve their decision-making, study, and social skills. These counselors support students going through challenges in school or at home and offer one-on-one meetings to discuss these challenges. Middle school counselors also assist students in their transition to high school, preparing them for the next level of academic and social development.

High school counselors advise students in making academic and career plans. Many help students overcome personal issues that interfere with their academic development. They help students choose classes and plan for their lives after graduation. Counselors provide information about choosing and applying for colleges, training programs, financial aid, and internships and apprenticeships. They may present career lessons to help students learn how to search and apply for jobs.

Career counselors and advisors typically do the following:

- Use aptitude and achievement assessments to help students or clients evaluate their interests, skills, and abilities
- Evaluate students' or clients' background, education, and training, to help them develop realistic goals
- Guide students in making decisions about careers, such as choosing an occupation and the type of degree to pursue
- Help students select and apply for educational programs to obtain the necessary degrees, credentials, and skills
- Teach students or clients job-search skills, such as interviewing and networking
- Assist clients in locating and applying for jobs, by teaching them strategies that will be helpful in finding openings and writing a résumé

The specific duties of career counselors and advisors vary by student or client.

Career coaches work with people who have already entered the workforce. These counselors develop plans with customized objectives and activities to improve their clients' careers. They motivate their clients and support them to achieve the goals they set together. Career coaches also provide advice about entering a new occupation or helping to resolve workplace issues.

College advisors help students choose a major or determine the jobs they are qualified for with their degrees. These advisors also help people find and get jobs by teaching them job search,

School counselors work in private and public schools where they have private offices.

résumé writing, and interviewing techniques. College advisors often specialize in counseling students in one area of the college experience, such as admissions or financial aid.

Some career counselors work in outplacement firms and assist laid-off workers with transitioning into new jobs or careers.

Work Environment

School and career counselors and advisors held about 342,400 jobs in 2022. The largest employers of school and career counselors and advisors were as follows:

Elementary and secondary schools; state, local, and private	46%
Junior colleges, colleges, universities, and professional schools; state, local, and private	38
Healthcare and social assistance	6
Other educational services; state, local, and private	4
Self-employed workers	1

Work Schedules

Both types of counselors and advisors usually work full time. Most counselors and advisors who work in schools and colleges may not work when school is not in session, such as during the summer.

How to Become a School or Career Counselor or Advisor

School counselors typically must have a master's degree in school counseling or a related field and have a state-issued credential. Some states require licensure for career counselors and advisors.

Education

Nearly all states and the District of Columbia require school counselors to have a master's degree, which is typically in a field such as counseling or psychology. Degree programs teach counselors the essential skills of the job, such as how to foster development; conduct group and individual counseling; work with support systems, such as parents, school staff, and community organizations; and use data to develop, implement, and evaluate comprehensive counseling programs. These programs often require counselors to complete an internship.

Career counselors who work in private practices may also need a license.

Some employers prefer that career counselors have a master's degree in counseling with a focus on career development. Career counseling programs prepare students to assess clients' skills and interests and to teach career development techniques. For career or academic advisors, employers may prefer candidates who have a bachelor's degree and work experience.

Master's degree programs in counseling usually require students to have a period of supervised experience, such as an internship.

Licenses, Certifications, and Registrations

Public school counselors must have a state-issued credential to practice. Depending on the state, this credential may be called a certification, a license, or an endorsement. Obtaining this credential typically requires a master's degree in school counseling, an internship or practicum completed under the supervision of a licensed professional school counselor, and successful completion of a test.

Some employers prefer or require candidates to have classroom teaching experience, or to hold a teaching license, prior to being certified. Most states require a criminal background check as part of the credentialing process. Information about requirements for each state is available from the American School Counselor Association.

Some states require licensure for career counselors; check with your state for more information. Contact information for state regulating boards is available from the National Board for Certified Counselors.

Optional certifications for career and academic advisors are available from some professional associations.

Important Qualities

Analytical skills. School and career counselors and advisors interpret student records, schoolwide data, and assessments to match interests and abilities with potential careers.

Compassion. School and career counselors and advisors often work with people who are dealing with stressful and difficult situations, so they must be able to empathize with their clients and students.

Interpersonal skills. School and career counselors and advisors must be able to work with people of all backgrounds and personalities. They need to form and maintain collaborative relationships with clients, students, or other professionals.

Listening skills. School and career counselors and advisors need to give full attention to students and clients in order to understand their problems.

Speaking skills. School and career counselors and advisors must communicate effectively with clients and students. They should express ideas and information in a way that their clients and students understand.

Pay

The median annual wage for school and career counselors and advisors was $60,140 in May 2022. The median wage is the wage at which half the workers in an occupation earned more than that amount and half earned less. The lowest 10 percent earned less than $38,280, and the highest 10 percent earned more than $98,530.

In May 2022, the median annual wages for school and career counselors and advisors in the top industries in which they worked were as follows:

Elementary and secondary schools; state, local, and private	$65,930
Other educational services; state, local, and private	52,390
Junior colleges, colleges, universities, and professional schools; state, local, and private	50,370
Healthcare and social assistance	39,650

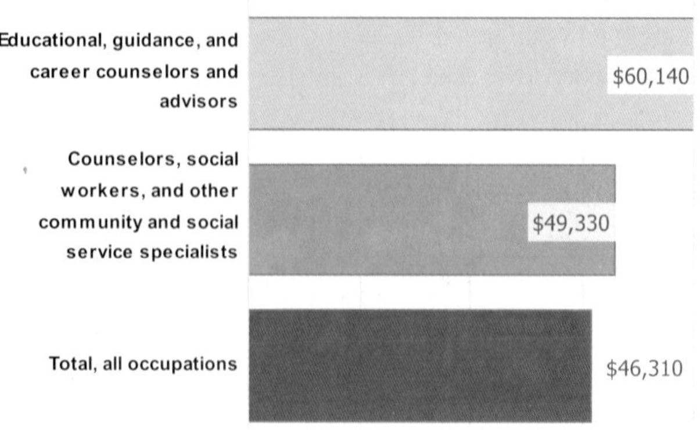

Note: All Occupations includes all occupations in the U.S. Economy.
Source: U.S. Bureau of Labor Statistics, Occupational Employment and Wage Statistics.

Both types of counselors and advisors usually work full time. Most counselors and advisors who work in schools and colleges may not work when school is not in session, such as during the summer.

Job Outlook

Employment of school and career counselors and advisors is projected to grow 5 percent from 2022 to 2032, faster than the average for all occupations.

About 26,600 openings for school and career counselors and advisors are projected each year, on average, over the decade. Many of those openings are expected to result from the need to replace workers who transfer to different occupations or exit the labor force, such as to retire.

Employment

Schools are expected to hire more counselors and advisors to respond to the developmental, academic, and career-planning

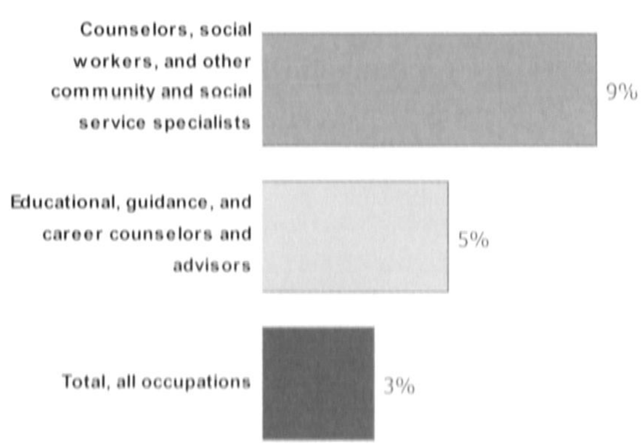

Note: All Occupations includes all occupations in the U.S. Economy.
Source: U.S. Bureau of Labor Statistics, Employment Projections program.

needs of their students. Demand for career counselors is projected to increase as a growing number of colleges and universities open career centers that focus on helping students prepare to enter the workforce.

Career counselors and advisors also will be needed to assist jobseekers, such as those changing careers, laid-off workers looking for jobs, and military veterans transitioning into the civilian labor market.

Occupational Title	SOC Code	Employment, 2022	Projected Employment, 2032	Change, 2022-32	
				Percent	Numeric
Educational, guidance, and career counselors and advisors	21-1012	342,400	360,800	5	18,400

Contacts for More Information

For more information about counseling and information about counseling specialties, visit

- American Counseling Association
- American School Counselor Association
- National Career Development Association

For more information about state credentialing, visit

- National Board for Certified Counselors

Social and Human Service Assistants

Summary

Quick Facts: Social and Human Service Assistants	
2022 Median Pay	$38,520 per year $18.52 per hour
Typical Entry-Level Education	High school diploma or equivalent
Work Experience in a Related Occupation	None
On-the-job Training	Short-term on-the-job training
Number of Jobs, 2022	415,100
Job Outlook, 2022-32	9% (Much faster than average)
Employment Change, 2022-32	35,600

What Social and Human Service Assistants Do

Social and human service assistants provide client services in a variety of fields, such as psychology, rehabilitation, and social work.

Social and human service assistants help clients identify and obtain benefits and services.

Work Environment

Many social and human service assistants work for nonprofit organizations, for-profit social service agencies, and state and local governments. They generally work full time, and some work nights and weekends.

How to Become a Social and Human Service Assistant

Requirements for social and human service assistants vary, although they typically have at least a high school diploma and must complete a brief period of on-the-job training.

Pay

The median annual wage for social and human service assistants was $38,520 in May 2022.

Job Outlook

Employment of social and human service assistants is projected to grow 9 percent from 2022 to 2032, much faster than the average for all occupations.

About 47,400 openings for social and human service assistants are projected each year, on average, over the decade. Many of those openings are expected to result from the need to replace workers who transfer to different occupations or exit the labor force, such as to retire.

What Social and Human Service Assistants Do

Social and human service assistants provide client services, including support for families, in a wide variety of fields, such as psychology, rehabilitation, and social work. They assist other workers, such as social workers, and they help clients find benefits or community services.

Duties

Social and human service assistants typically do the following:

Social and human service assistants help the elderly stay in their own homes and live under their own care whenever possible.

- Help determine what type of aid their clients need
- Work with clients and other professionals, such as social workers, to develop a treatment plan
- Help clients find assistance with daily activities, such as eating and bathing
- Research services, such as food stamps and Medicaid, that are available to clients
- Coordinate services provided to clients
- Help clients complete paperwork to apply for assistance programs
- Check in with clients to ensure that services are provided appropriately

Social and human service assistants have many job titles, including *case work aide*, *clinical social work aide*, *family service assistant*, *social work assistant*, *addictions counselor assistant*, and *human service worker*.

Social and human service assistants help clients identify and obtain benefits and services. In addition to initially connecting clients with benefits or services, social and human service assistants may follow up with clients to ensure that they are receiving the intended services and that the services are meeting their needs. They work under the direction of social workers, psychologists, or other community and social service workers.

With ***children and families***, social and human service assistants ensure that the children live in safe homes. They help parents get needed resources for their children, such as food stamps or childcare.

With the ***elderly***, these workers help clients stay in their own homes and live under their own care whenever possible. Social and human service assistants may coordinate meal deliveries or find personal care aides to help with the clients' day-to-day needs, such as running errands and bathing. In some cases, human service assistants help look for residential care facilities, such as nursing homes.

For ***people with disabilities***, social and human service assistants help find rehabilitation services that aid their clients. They may work with employers to make a job more accessible to people with disabilities. Some workers find personal care services to help clients with daily living activities, such as bathing and making meals.

For ***people with addictions***, human service assistants find rehabilitation centers that meet their clients' needs. They also may find support groups for people who are dependent on alcohol, drugs, gambling, or other substances or behaviors.

With ***veterans***, assistants help people who have been discharged from the military adjust to civilian life. They help with practical needs, such as locating housing and finding ways to apply skills gained in the military to civilian jobs. They may also help their clients navigate the services available to veterans.

For ***people with mental illnesses***, social and human service assistants help clients find the appropriate resources to help them cope with their illness. They find self-help and support groups to provide their clients with an assistance network. In addition, they may find personal care services or group housing to help those with more severe mental illnesses care for themselves.

With ***immigrants***, workers help clients adjust to living in a new country. They help the clients locate jobs and housing. They may also help them find programs that teach English, or they may find legal assistance to help immigrants get administrative paperwork in order.

With ***former prison inmates***, human service assistants find job training or placement programs to help clients reenter society. Human service assistants help former inmates find housing and connect with programs that help them start a new life for themselves.

With ***homeless people***, assistants help clients meet their basic needs. They find temporary or permanent housing for their clients and locate places, such as soup kitchens, that provide meals. Human service assistants also help homeless people find resources to address other problems they may have, such as joblessness.

Work Environment

Social and human service assistants held about 415,100 jobs in 2022. The largest employers of social and human service assistants were as follows:

Social and human service assistants sometimes travel around their community to see clients.

Industry	Percent
Individual and family services	29%
Local government, excluding education and hospitals	13
Nursing and residential care facilities	11
Community and vocational rehabilitation services	10
State government, excluding education and hospitals	8

Social and human service assistants work in offices, clinics, hospitals, group homes, and shelters. Some travel around their communities to see clients.

Work Schedules

Most social and human service assistants work full time. Some work nights and weekends.

How to Become a Social and Human Service Assistant

Requirements for social and human service assistants vary, although they typically have at least a high school diploma and must complete a brief period of on-the-job training.

The duties of social and human service assistants are often determined by their level of education.

Some employers require a criminal background check. Social and human service assistants also may need a valid driver's license.

Education

Although a high school diploma is typically required, some employers prefer to hire workers who have relevant work experience or education beyond high school. A certificate or an associate's degree in a subject such as human services, gerontology (working with older adults), or social or behavioral science is becoming more common for workers entering this occupation. Although not required, a bachelor's degree in fields such as social science, psychology, or public policy and social services may provide useful background knowledge.

Human service degree programs train students to observe and interview patients, carry out treatment plans, and handle people who are undergoing a crisis. Many programs include fieldwork to give students hands-on experience.

The level of education that social and human service assistants have completed often determines the responsibilities they are given. Those with a high school diploma are likely to do lower level work, such as helping clients fill out paperwork. Assistants with some college education may coordinate program activities or manage a group home.

Training

Many social and human service assistants, particularly those without any postsecondary education, undergo a short period of on-the-job training. Because such workers often are dealing with multiple clients from a wide variety of backgrounds, on-the-job training in case management helps prepare them to respond appropriately to the different needs and situations of their clients.

Advancement

For social and human service assistants, additional education is almost always necessary for advancement. In general, advancement to case management or social work jobs requires a bachelor's or master's degree in human services, counseling, rehabilitation, social work, or a related field.

Important Qualities

Communication skills. Social and human service assistants talk with clients about the challenges in their lives and assist them in getting help. These workers must be able to listen to their clients and to communicate the clients' needs to organizations that can help them.

Compassion. Social and human service assistants often work with people who are in stressful and difficult situations. To develop strong relationships, they must have compassion and empathy for their clients.

Interpersonal skills. Social and human service assistants must make their clients feel comfortable discussing sensitive

Social and Human Service Assistants

Median annual wages, May 2022

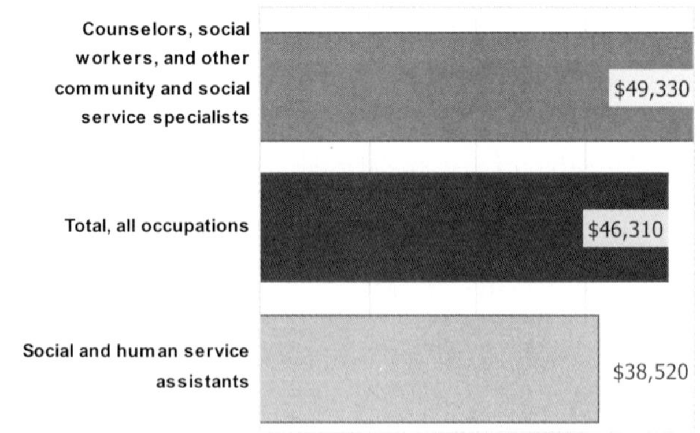

Note: All Occupations includes all occupations in the U.S. Economy.
Source: U.S. Bureau of Labor Statistics, Occupational Employment and Wage Statistics.

Social and Human Service Assistants

Percent change in employment, projected 2022-32

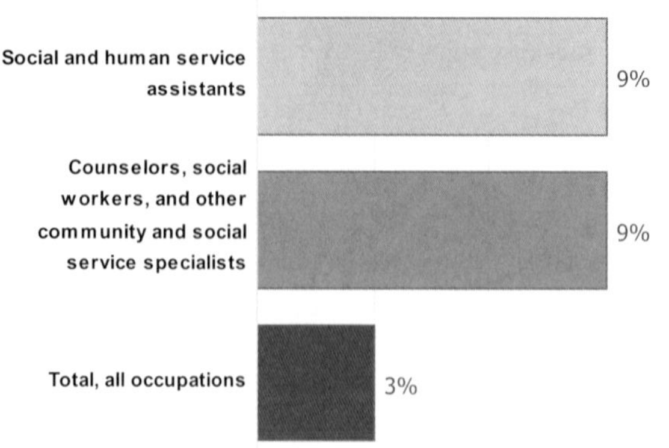

Note: All Occupations includes all occupations in the U.S. Economy.
Source: U.S. Bureau of Labor Statistics, Employment Projections program.

issues. Assistants also build relationships with other service providers to become familiar with all of the resources that are available in their communities.

Organizational skills. Social and human service assistants must often complete lots of paperwork and work with many different clients. They must be organized in order to ensure that the paperwork is filed properly and that clients are getting the help they need.

Problem-solving skills. Social and human service assistants help clients find solutions to their problems. They must be able to listen carefully to their clients' needs and offer practical solutions.

Time-management skills. Social and human service assistants often work with many clients. They must manage their time effectively to ensure that their clients are getting the attention they need.

Pay

The median annual wage for social and human service assistants was $38,520 in May 2022. The median wage is the wage at which half the workers in an occupation earned more than that amount and half earned less. The lowest 10 percent earned less than $28,610, and the highest 10 percent earned more than $58,770.

In May 2022, the median annual wages for social and human service assistants in the top industries in which they worked were as follows:

Local government, excluding education and hospitals	$46,790
State government, excluding education and hospitals	41,520
Individual and family services	38,210
Community and vocational rehabilitation services	36,170
Nursing and residential care facilities	35,020

Most social and human service assistants work full time. Some work nights and weekends.

Job Outlook

Employment of social and human service assistants is projected to grow 9 percent from 2022 to 2032, much faster than the average for all occupations.

About 47,400 openings for social and human service assistants are projected each year, on average, over the decade. Many of those openings are expected to result from the need to replace workers who transfer to different occupations or exit the labor force, such as to retire.

Employment

A growing population of older people and rising demand for social services are expected to drive demand for these workers.

An increase in the number of older adults is expected to result in growing demand for the social services they use, including home-delivered meals and community center activities. Because social and human service assistants often arrange and provide these services, more of these workers will be needed to meet the increased demand.

In addition, employment growth is expected as more people with substance use disorders enroll in treatment programs rather than being sent to jail. As a result, demand should increase for social and human service assistants who work in treatment programs or who work with people with addictions.

Employment projections data for social and human service assistants, 2022-32

Occupational Title	SOC Code	Employment, 2022	Projected Employment, 2032	Change, 2022-32 Percent	Change, 2022-32 Numeric	Employment by Industry
SOURCE: U.S. Bureau of Labor Statistics, Employment Projections program						
Social and human service assistants	21-1093	415,100	450,600	9	35,600	Get data

Social Workers

Summary

Quick Facts: Social Workers	
2022 Median Pay	$55,350 per year $26.61 per hour
Typical Entry-Level Education	See How to Become One
Work Experience in a Related Occupation	None
On-the-job Training	See How to Become One
Number of Jobs, 2022	728,600
Job Outlook, 2022-32	7% (Faster than average)
Employment Change, 2022-32	53,800

What Social Workers Do
Social workers help people prevent and cope with problems in their everyday lives.

Work Environment
Social workers are employed in a variety of settings, including child welfare and human service agencies, healthcare providers, and schools. Most work full time, and some work evenings, weekends, and holidays.

How to Become a Social Worker
Social workers typically need a bachelor's or master's degree in social work from a program accredited by the Council on Social Work Education. They also may need a license; specific requirements vary by state.

Clinical social workers need a master's degree, supervised clinical experience, and a license from the state in which they practice.

Pay
The median annual wage for social workers was $55,350 in May 2022.

Social workers help people solve and cope with problems.

Job Outlook
Overall employment of social workers is projected to grow 7 percent from 2022 to 2032, faster than the average for all occupations.

About 63,800 openings for social workers are projected each year, on average, over the decade. Many of those openings are expected to result from the need to replace workers who transfer to different occupations or exit the labor force, such as to retire.

What Social Workers Do
Social workers help individuals, groups, and families prevent and cope with problems in their everyday lives. Clinical social workers diagnose and treat mental, behavioral, and emotional problems.

Duties
Social workers typically do the following:

- Identify people and communities in need of help
- Assess clients' needs, situations, strengths, and support networks to determine their goals
- Help clients adjust to changes and challenges in their lives, such as illness, divorce, or unemployment
- Research, refer, and advocate for community resources, such as food stamps, childcare, and healthcare, to assist and improve a client's well-being
- Respond to crisis situations such as child abuse and mental health emergencies
- Monitor clients' situations, and follow up to ensure that they have improved
- Maintain case files and records
- Provide psychotherapy services

Social workers help people cope with challenges in their lives. They help with a wide range of situations, such as adopting a child, being diagnosed with a terminal illness, or preventing and treating substance abuse.

Child and family social workers protect vulnerable children and support families in need of assistance.

Some social workers get involved at a broad level to help community organizations and policymakers develop or improve social programs, services, and conditions. This is sometimes referred to as macro social work.

Advocacy is an important aspect of social work. Social workers advocate or raise awareness with and on behalf of their clients and constituents. Additionally, they may advocate for the social work occupation on local, state, and national levels.

Social workers who are licensed to diagnose and treat mental, behavioral, and emotional disorders are called ***clinical social workers*** (CSW), ***licensed clinical social workers*** (LCSW), or have a similar title; specific titles vary by state. They provide individual, group, family, and couples therapy; work with clients to develop strategies to change behavior or cope with difficult situations; and refer clients to other resources or services, such as support groups or other mental health workers. Clinical social workers may develop treatment plans with the client, doctors, and other healthcare workers and may adjust the treatment plan if necessary based on their client's progress. They may work in a variety of specialties.

The following are examples of types of social workers:

Child and family social workers protect vulnerable children and help families in need of assistance. They help families find housing or services, such as childcare, or apply for benefits, such as food stamps. They intervene when children are in danger of neglect or abuse. Some help arrange adoptions, locate foster families, or work to reunite families.

School social workers work with teachers, parents, and school administrators to develop plans and strategies to improve students' academic performance and social development. They help students with problems such as aggressive behavior or bullying. Additionally, school social workers meet with families to discuss issues such as access to special education resources or frequent student absences.

Healthcare social workers help clients understand their diagnosis and adjust their lifestyle, housing, or healthcare. For example, they may help people transition from the hospital to their homes and communities. In addition, they may provide information about services, such as home healthcare or support groups, to help clients manage their illness or disease. Social workers help doctors and other healthcare workers understand the effects that diseases and illnesses have on clients' mental and emotional health. Some healthcare social workers specialize in geriatric social work, hospice and palliative care, or medical social work.

Mental health and substance abuse social workers help clients with mental illnesses or addictions. They provide information on services, such as support groups and 12-step programs, to help clients cope with their illness. These workers often are licensed clinical social workers.

Work Environment

Social workers held about 728,600 jobs in 2022. Employment in the detailed occupations that make up social workers was distributed as follows:

Although most social workers work in an office, they may spend a lot of time away from the office visiting clients.

Child, family, and school social workers	355,300
Healthcare social workers	191,400
Mental health and substance abuse social workers	113,500
Social workers, all other	68,400

The largest employers of social workers were as follows:

Employer	Percent
Individual and family services	17%
Ambulatory healthcare services	14
Local government, excluding education and hospitals	14
State government, excluding education and hospitals	13
Hospitals; state, local, and private	10

Most social workers work in an office setting. They may spend time visiting clients and meeting with colleagues and community specialists or other support workers. School social workers may be assigned to multiple schools and travel around the school district to see students. Understaffing and large caseloads may cause the work to be stressful.

Injuries and Illnesses

Social workers, all other have one of the highest rates of injuries and illnesses of all occupations. ("Social workers, all other" includes criminal justice social workers, adult protective service social workers, and forensic social workers, among other titles.)

Work Schedules

Most social workers are employed full time. They sometimes work evenings, weekends, and holidays to see clients or attend meetings, and they may be on call.

How to Become a Social Worker

Social workers typically need a bachelor's or master's degree in social work from a program accredited by the Council on

Clinical social workers need a master's degree, supervised experience, and a license to provide mental health or counseling services.

Social Work Education. They also may need a license; specific requirements vary by state.

Clinical social workers need a master's degree, supervised clinical experience, and a license from the state in which they practice.

Education and Training

Most social workers need either a bachelor's or a master's degree from a program accredited by the Council on Social Work Education.

A bachelor's degree in social work (BSW) is the most common requirement for entry-level nonclinical social worker positions. BSW programs teach students about diverse populations, human behavior, social welfare policy, and ethics in social work. All programs require students to complete supervised fieldwork or an internship.

Clinical social workers typically need a master's degree in social work (MSW). These programs prepare students for work in their chosen specialty by developing clinical assessment and diagnostic skills. Some nonclinical social workers also may complete master's-level programs. MSW programs generally take 2 years to complete and include a supervised practicum or internship.

A bachelor's degree in social work is not required in order to enter a master's degree program in social work. Although a bachelor's degree in almost any field is acceptable, common majors include public policy and social services, psychology, or social science. Recommended coursework includes sociology, economics, and political science. Some programs allow graduates with a bachelor's degree in social work to earn their master's degree in under 2 years.

After obtaining an MSW degree, clinical social workers must complete supervised training and experience. The length of clinical training varies by state but may take several years.

Licenses, Certifications, and Registrations

All states require clinical social workers to be licensed. Some states also require nonclinical social workers to have a license or credential.

Becoming a licensed clinical social worker requires a master's degree in social work from an accredited program and supervised clinical experience after graduation. After completing their supervised experience, clinical social workers must pass a clinical exam to be licensed.

Because licensing requirements vary by state, those interested should contact their state licensure board. For more information about regulatory licensure boards by state, visit the Association of Social Work Boards.

Important Qualities

Communication skills. Clients talk to social workers about challenges in their lives. To provide effective help, social workers must be able to listen to and understand their clients' needs.

Compassion. Social workers often work with people who are in stressful and difficult situations. To develop strong relationships, they must have patience and empathy for their clients.

Interpersonal skills. Social workers must be able to work with different groups of people. They need to foster healthy and productive relationships with their clients, colleagues, and other support specialists.

Organizational skills. Social workers must help and manage multiple clients, often assisting with their paperwork or documenting their treatment.

Problem-solving skills. Social workers must analyze their clients' complex situations and develop practical solutions.

Pay

The median annual wage for social workers was $55,350 in May 2022. The median wage is the wage at which half the workers in an occupation earned more than that amount and half earned less. The lowest 10 percent earned less than $36,600, and the highest 10 percent earned more than $87,300.

Social Workers

Median annual wages, May 2022

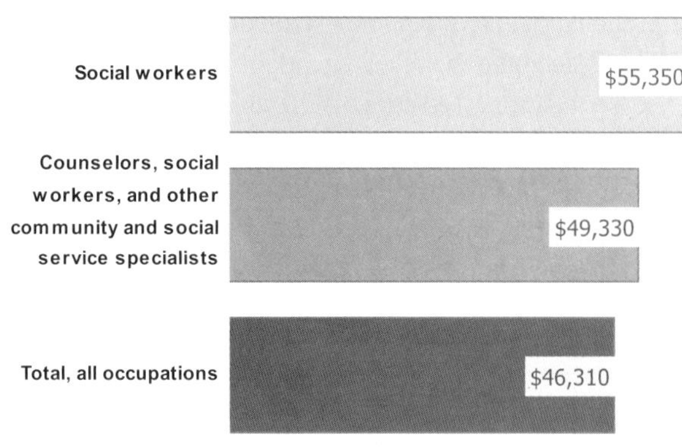

Note: All Occupations includes all occupations in the U.S. Economy.
Source: U.S. Bureau of Labor Statistics, Occupational Employment and Wage Statistics.

Median annual wages for social workers in May 2022 were as follows:

Social workers, all other	$61,420
Healthcare social workers	60,280
Mental health and substance abuse social workers	51,240
Child, family, and school social workers	50,820

In May 2022, the median annual wages for social workers in the top industries in which they worked were as follows:

Hospitals; state, local, and private	$66,300
Local government, excluding education and hospitals	62,390
Ambulatory healthcare services	58,690
State government, excluding education and hospitals	52,640
Individual and family services	46,670

Most social workers are employed full time. They sometimes work evenings, weekends, and holidays to see clients or attend meetings, and they may be on call.

Job Outlook

Overall employment of social workers is projected to grow 7 percent from 2022 to 2032, faster than the average for all occupations.

About 63,800 openings for social workers are projected each year, on average, over the decade. Many of those openings are expected to result from the need to replace workers who transfer to different occupations or exit the labor force, such as to retire.

Employment

Projected employment of social workers varies by occupation (see table).

Child, family, and school social workers will be needed to help strengthen parenting skills, prevent child abuse, and identify alternative homes for children who are unable to live with their biological families. However, employment growth for these social workers may be limited by federal, state, and local budget constraints.

Healthcare social workers will continue to be needed to help aging populations and their families adjust to new treatments, medications, and lifestyles.

Employment of mental health and substance abuse social workers will grow as more people seek treatment for mental illness and for substance abuse, especially recovery from opioid use disorder. In addition, drug offenders are increasingly being directed to treatment programs, which are staffed by these social workers, as a supplement or occasionally an alternative to incarceration.

Social Workers

Percent change in employment, projected 2022-32

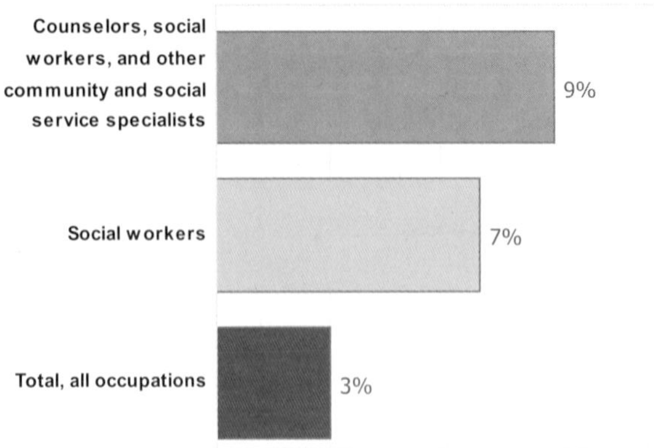

Note: All Occupations includes all occupations in the U.S. Economy.
Source: U.S. Bureau of Labor Statistics, Employment Projections program.

Occupational Title	SOC Code	Employment, 2022	Projected Employment, 2032	Change, 2022-32	
				Percent	Numeric
Social workers	21-1020	728,600	782,500	7	53,800
Child, family, and school social workers	21-1021	355,300	374,300	5	18,900
Healthcare social workers	21-1022	191,400	209,800	10	18,400
Mental health and substance abuse social workers	21-1023	113,500	125,500	11	12,000
Social workers, all other	21-1029	68,400	72,900	7	4,500

Contacts for More Information

For more information about social workers and clinical social workers, visit

- Association for Community Organization and Social Action
- National Association of Social Workers
- School Social Work Association of America
- Council on Social Work Education
- Association of Social Work Boards

Occupational Requirements Survey

For a profile highlighting selected BLS data on occupational requirements, see

- Mental health and substance abuse social workers (PDF)

Substance Abuse, Behavioral Disorder, and Mental Health Counselors

Summary

Quick Facts: Substance Abuse, Behavioral Disorder, and Mental Health Counselors	
2022 Median Pay	$49,710 per year $23.90 per hour
Typical Entry-Level Education	Bachelor's degree
Work Experience in a Related Occupation	None
On-the-job Training	None
Number of Jobs, 2022	388,200
Job Outlook, 2022-32	18% (Much faster than average)
Employment Change, 2022-32	71,500

What Substance Abuse, Behavioral Disorder, and Mental Health Counselors Do

Substance abuse, behavioral disorder, and mental health counselors advise people on a range of issues, such as those relating to alcoholism, addictions, or depression.

Work Environment

Substance abuse, behavioral disorder, and mental health counselors work in a variety of settings, such as mental health centers, community health centers, and private practice. Most work full time, although part-time work is common.

How to Become a Substance Abuse, Behavioral Disorder, or Mental Health Counselor

Education and training requirements vary for entering these occupations. Substance abuse and behavioral disorder counselors typically need at least a bachelor's degree, whereas mental health counselors typically need a master's degree and an internship. Some counselors need a state-issued license.

Substance abuse, behavioral disorder, and mental health counselors help clients recover from addiction or mental health issues, or modify problem behaviors.

Pay

The median annual wage for substance abuse, behavioral disorder, and mental health counselors was $49,710 in May 2022.

Job Outlook

Employment of substance abuse, behavioral disorder, and mental health counselors is projected to grow 18 percent from 2022 to 2032, much faster than the average for all occupations.

About 42,000 openings for substance abuse, behavioral disorder, and mental health counselors are projected each year, on average, over the decade. Many of those openings are expected to result from the need to replace workers who transfer to different occupations or exit the labor force, such as to retire.

What Substance Abuse, Behavioral Disorder, and Mental Health Counselors Do

Substance abuse, behavioral disorder, and mental health counselors advise people on a range of issues, such as those relating to alcoholism, addictions, or depression. They provide support, including for prevention, to help clients recover from addiction, modify problem behaviors, or improve mental health.

Substance abuse, behavioral disorder, and mental health counselors provide treatment and support.

Duties

Substance abuse, behavioral disorder, and mental health counselors typically do the following:

- Evaluate clients' mental and physical health, addiction, or problematic behavior and assess their readiness for treatment
- Develop, recommend, and review treatment goals and plans with clients and their families
- Assist clients in developing skills and behaviors necessary to recover from their addiction or modify their behavior
- Work with clients to identify behaviors or situations that interfere with their recovery
- Document and maintain records of clients' progress
- Teach clients' family members about addiction or behavior disorders and help them develop strategies to support clients in recovery
- Refer clients to other resources and services, such as job placement services and support groups
- Prepare clients for transition out of counseling through discharge planning
- Conduct outreach programs to help people identify the signs of addiction and other destructive behavior, as well as steps to take to avoid such behavior

Substance abuse counselors and ***behavioral disorder counselors***, also called *addiction counselors*, work with clients individually and in group sessions. They teach clients how to cope with stress and life's problems in ways that help them recover. Furthermore, they help clients rebuild professional relationships and, if necessary, reestablish their career. They also help clients improve their personal relationships and find ways to discuss their addiction or other problems with family and friends.

Some addiction counselors work in facilities that employ many types of healthcare and mental health professionals. Addiction counselors may work with psychologists, psychiatrists, social workers, physicians, and registered nurses to develop treatment plans and coordinate care for patients.

Some counselors work with clients who have been ordered by a judge or referred by other people, such as a parole officer, to receive treatment for addiction. Others work with specific populations, such as teenagers, veterans, or people with disabilities. Counselors may have to intervene in crises by stepping in when someone is endangering his or her own life or the lives of others. They also intervene in noncrisis situations by encouraging a person with addictions or other issues, such as difficulty processing emotions, to get help. Noncrisis interventions often are requested by friends and family.

Mental health counselors advise individuals, families, couples, and groups. Some work with specific populations, such as children or older adults. Mental health counselors treat clients who have a variety of conditions, including anxiety, depression, grief, and stress. They also help with emotional health and relationship problems.

Substance abuse, behavioral disorder, and mental health counselors work in a wide variety of settings, including mental health centers, prisons, probation or parole agencies, and juvenile detention facilities.

Work Environment

Substance abuse, behavioral disorder, and mental health counselors held about 388,200 jobs in 2022. The largest employers of substance abuse, behavioral disorder, and mental health counselors were as follows:

Outpatient mental health and substance abuse centers	18%
Individual and family services	15
Offices of other health practitioners	12
Hospitals; state, local, and private	9
Residential mental health and substance abuse facilities	9

Substance abuse, behavioral disorder, and mental health counselors work in a variety of settings, including inpatient and outpatient treatment centers, correctional facilities, and hospitals. Some addiction counselors work in residential treatment centers, where clients live in the facility during their recovery.

Although rewarding, the work of substance abuse, behavioral disorder, and mental health counselors is often stressful. Many counselors have large workloads and do not always have enough resources to meet the demand for their services. In addition, counselors may have to intervene in crisis situations or work with agitated clients.

Work Schedules

Most substance abuse, behavioral disorder, and mental health counselors work full time, although part-time work is common. In some settings, such as inpatient or residential facilities, they may need to work evenings, nights, or weekends.

How to Become a Substance Abuse, Behavioral Disorder, or Mental Health Counselor

Education and training requirements vary for entering these occupations. Substance abuse and behavioral disorder

Substance abuse, behavioral disorder, and mental health counselors need a license in private practice.

counselors typically need at least a bachelor's degree, although some positions require a high school diploma and others require a master's degree. Mental health counselors typically need a master's degree and an internship. In addition, some counselors must be licensed.

Education

Substance abuse, behavioral disorder, and mental health counselors typically need at least a bachelor's degree, although the education required or preferred may vary by position, state, or employer. For example, substance abuse and behavioral disorder counselors typically need a bachelor's degree to enter the occupation, but requirements may vary from a high school diploma to a master's degree.

Mental health counselors typically need a master's degree. Common fields of undergraduate study include psychology, public policy and social services, and social science. Master's degree programs often include an internship that is clinically supervised.

Licenses, Certifications, and Registrations

Substance abuse and behavioral disorder counselors in private practice must be licensed. Licensing requirements vary by state, but all states require these counselors to have a master's degree and complete a specified number of hours of supervised clinical experience. In addition, counselors must pass an examination and complete continuing education every year. Contact information for your state's regulating board is available through the National Board for Certified Counselors.

Licensure requirements for substance abuse and behavioral disorder counselors outside of private practice vary by state. For example, not all states require applicants to have a specific degree, but some require them to pass an exam. Contact information for individual states' licensing boards is available through the Addiction Technology Transfer Center Network.

All states require mental health counselors to be licensed. Licensure requires successfully completing a national examination and supervised clinical work under the supervision of a licensed counselor.

Some jobs require counselors to have certification in basic life support (BLS) or cardiopulmonary resuscitation (CPR).

Advancement

Substance abuse and behavioral disorder counselors who earn a master's degree and complete a specified number of hours of supervised clinical experience are eligible to get a state license. This allows them to go into private practice or start their own business.

Other Experience

Counselors who have personal experience overcoming alcohol or drug addictions are sometimes viewed as especially helpful and insightful to those seeking treatment.

Important Qualities

Communication skills. Substance abuse, behavioral disorder, and mental health counselors need to effectively convey ideas and information to clients. They must also write concise but detailed reports documenting clients' progress.

Compassion. Substance abuse, behavioral disorder, and mental health counselors often work with people who are dealing with stressful and difficult situations, so they must empathize with their clients.

Interpersonal skills. Substance abuse, behavioral disorder, and mental health counselors must be able to develop and nurture good relationships with different types of people.

Listening skills. Substance abuse, behavioral disorder, and mental health counselors must give clients their full attention to be able to understand each client's problems and values.

Patience. Substance abuse, behavioral disorder, and mental health counselors must be able to remain calm when working with all types of clients, including those who may be distressed or angry.

Pay

The median annual wage for substance abuse, behavioral disorder, and mental health counselors was $49,710 in May 2022. The median wage is the wage at which half the workers in an occupation earned more than that amount and half earned less. The lowest 10 percent earned less than $34,580, and the highest 10 percent earned more than $82,710.

In May 2022, the median annual wages for substance abuse, behavioral disorder, and mental health counselors in the top industries in which they worked were as follows:

Hospitals; state, local, and private	$54,740
Offices of other health practitioners	50,260
Individual and family services	49,210
Outpatient mental health and substance abuse centers	48,640
Residential mental health and substance abuse facilities	44,150

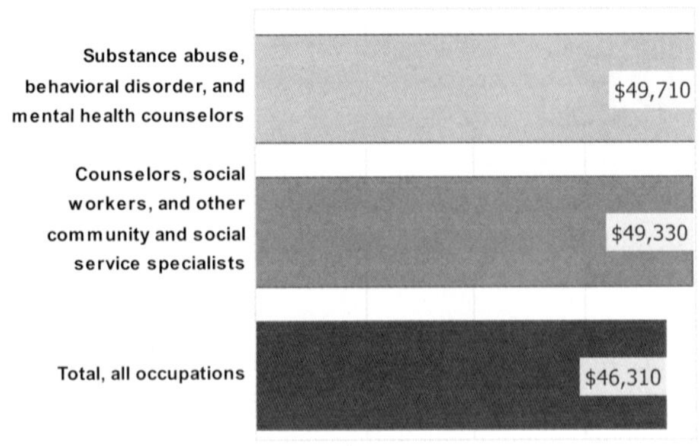

Note: All Occupations includes all occupations in the U.S. Economy.
Source: U.S. Bureau of Labor Statistics, Occupational Employment and Wage Statistics.

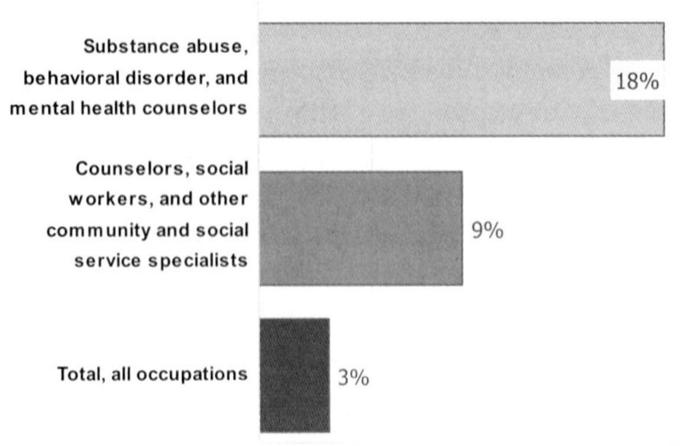

Note: All Occupations includes all occupations in the U.S. Economy.
Source: U.S. Bureau of Labor Statistics, Employment Projections program.

Most substance abuse, behavioral disorder, and mental health counselors work full time, although part-time work is common. In some settings, such as inpatient or residential facilities, they may need to work evenings, nights, or weekends.

Job Outlook

Employment of substance abuse, behavioral disorder, and mental health counselors is projected to grow 18 percent from 2022 to 2032, much faster than the average for all occupations.

About 42,000 openings for substance abuse, behavioral disorder, and mental health counselors are projected each year, on average, over the decade. Many of those openings are expected to result from the need to replace workers who transfer to different occupations or exit the labor force, such as to retire.

Employment

Employment growth is expected for substance abuse, behavioral disorder, and mental health counselors as people continue to seek treatment for addiction and mental health issues.

Increased demand for these workers is expected because of a growth in the number of people, including youths, who have mental health and behavioral disorders. Additionally, there will be continued need for services to assist the large number of people with addictions, especially those who have opioid use disorder.

Occupational Title	SOC Code	Employment, 2022	Projected Employment, 2032	Change, 2022-32	
				Percent	Numeric
Substance abuse, behavioral disorder, and mental health counselors	21-1018	388,200	459,600	18	71,500

Contacts for More Information

For more information about addiction counselors, visit

- Addiction Technology Transfer Center Network
- NAADAC, The Association for Addiction Professionals
- American Counseling Association
- National Board for Certified Counselors

Computer and Information Technology

Computer and Information Research Scientists

Summary

Quick Facts: Computer and Information Research Scientists	
2022 Median Pay	$136,620 per year $65.69 per hour
Typical Entry-Level Education	Master's degree
Work Experience in a Related Occupation	None
On-the-job Training	None
Number of Jobs, 2022	36,500
Job Outlook, 2022-32	23% (Much faster than average)
Employment Change, 2022-32	8,300

What Computer and Information Research Scientists Do

Computer and information research scientists design innovative uses for new and existing computing technology.

Work Environment

Most computer and information research scientists work full time.

How to Become a Computer and Information Research Scientist

Computer and information research scientists typically need at least a master's degree in computer science or a related field. In the federal government, a bachelor's degree may be sufficient for some jobs.

Pay

The median annual wage for computer and information research scientists was $136,620 in May 2022.

Job Outlook

Employment of computer and information research scientists is projected to grow 23 percent from 2022 to 2032, much faster than the average for all occupations.

About 3,400 openings for computer and information research scientists are projected each year, on average, over the decade. Many of those openings are expected to result from the need to replace workers who transfer to different occupations or exit the labor force, such as to retire.

Computer and information research scientists study and solve complex problems in computing.

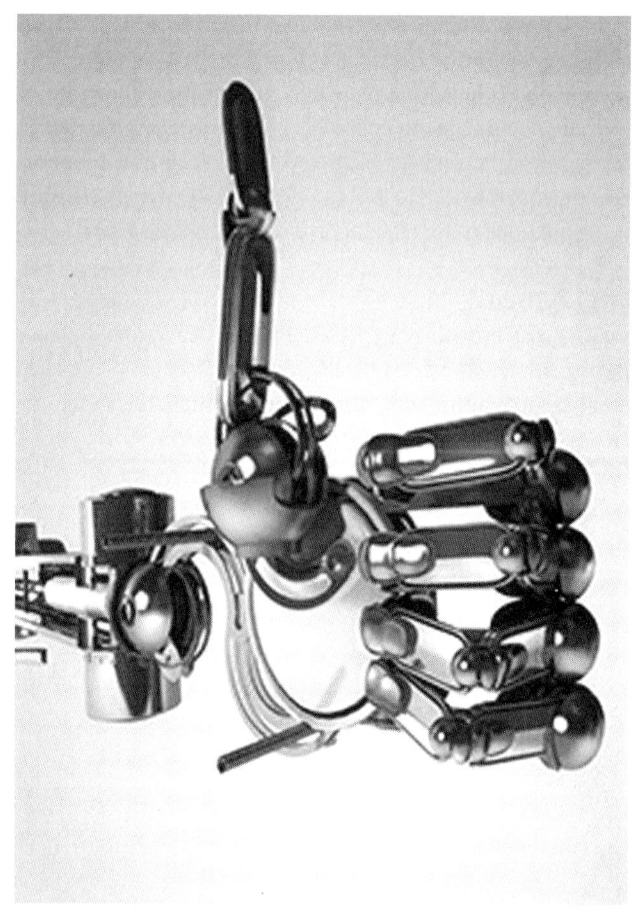

Some computer scientists create programs to control robots.

What Computer and Information Research Scientists Do

Computer and information research scientists design innovative uses for new and existing technology. They study and solve complex problems in computing for business, science, medicine, and other fields.

Duties

Computer and information research scientists typically do the following:

- Explore problems in computing and develop theories and models to address those problems
- Collaborate with scientists and engineers to solve complex computing problems
- Determine computing needs and system requirements
- Develop new computing languages, software systems, and other tools to improve how people work with computers
- Design and conduct experiments to test the operation of software systems, frequently using techniques from data science and machine learning
- Analyze the results of their experiments
- Write papers for publication and present research findings at conferences

Computer and information research scientists create and improve computer software and hardware.

To create and improve software, computer and information research scientists work with algorithms: sets of instructions that tell a computer what to do. Some difficult computing tasks require complex algorithms, which these scientists simplify to make computer systems as efficient as possible. These simplified algorithms may lead to advancements in many types of technology, such as machine learning systems and cloud computing.

To improve computer hardware, these scientists design computer architecture. Their work may result in increased efficiencies, such as better networking technology, faster computing speeds, and improved information security.

The following are examples of specialties for computer and information research scientists:

Programming. Some computer and information research scientists study and design new programming languages that are used to write software. New languages make software writing efficient by improving an existing language, such as Java, or by simplifying a specific aspect of programming, such as image processing.

Robotics. These scientists study the development and application of robots. They explore how a machine can interact with the physical world. For example, they may create systems that control the robots or design robots to have features such as information processing or sensory feedback.

Some computer and information research scientists work on multidisciplinary projects with electrical engineers, computer hardware engineers, and other specialists. For example, robotics specialists and engineers who design robots' hardware may team up to test whether the robots complete tasks as intended.

Work Environment

Computer and information research scientists held about 36,500 jobs in 2022. The largest employers of computer and information research scientists were as follows:

Employer	Percent
Federal government, excluding postal service	28%
Computer systems design and related services	28
Research and development in the physical, engineering, and life sciences	17
Colleges, universities, and professional schools; state, local, and private	5
Software publishers	3

Some scientists collaborate with engineers or other specialists or research scientists in different locations and do much of their work online.

Work Schedules

Most computer and information research scientists work full time.

How to Become a Computer and Information Research Scientist

Computer and information research scientists typically need at least a master's degree in computer science or a related field. In the federal government, a bachelor's degree may be sufficient for some jobs.

Education

Computer and information research scientists typically need a master's or higher degree in computer science or a related field, such as computer engineering. A master's degree usually requires 2 to 3 years of study after earning a bachelor's degree in a computer-related field, such as computer science or

Computer and information research scientists improve ways to sort, manage, and display data.

Some computer scientists specialize in computer languages.

information systems. Some employers prefer to hire candidates who have a Ph.D. Others, such as the federal government, may hire candidates who have a bachelor's degree in computer and information technology.

Computer and information research scientists who work in a specialized field may need knowledge of that field. For example, those working on biomedical applications may need to have studied biology.

Advancement

Some computer and information research scientists advance to become computer and information systems managers.

Important Qualities

Analytical skills. Computer and information research scientists must be organized in their thinking to evaluate the results of their research.

Communication skills. Computer and information research scientists must be able to clearly explain their research, including to a nontechnical audience. They write papers for publication and present their research at conferences.

Detail oriented. Computer and information research scientists must pay close attention to their work, such as when testing the systems they design. Small programming errors could affect an entire project.

Interpersonal skills. Computer and information research scientists must work effectively with programmers and managers. They also may be on teams with engineers or other specialists.

Logical thinking. Computer and information research scientists must use sound reasoning when working on algorithms.

Math skills. Computer and information research scientists need a solid grasp of advanced math and other technical subjects critical to computing.

Problem-solving skills. Computer and information research scientists must think creatively to find innovative solutions in their research.

Pay

The median annual wage for computer and information research scientists was $136,620 in May 2022. The median wage is the

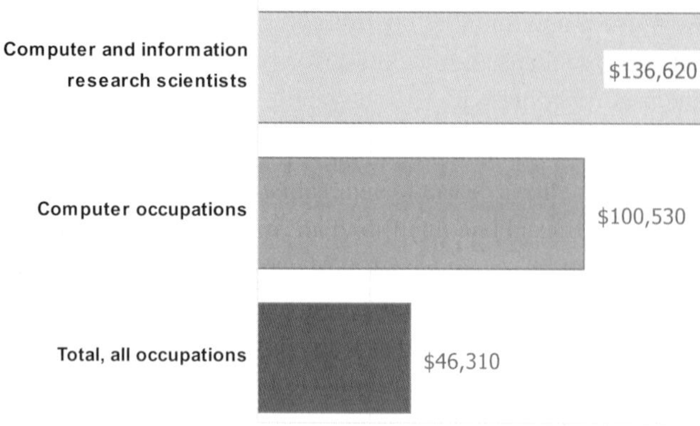

Note: All Occupations includes all occupations in the U.S. Economy.
Source: U.S. Bureau of Labor Statistics, Occupational Employment and Wage Statistics.

wage at which half the workers in an occupation earned more than that amount and half earned less. The lowest 10 percent earned less than $78,190, and the highest 10 percent earned more than $232,010.

In May 2022, the median annual wages for computer and information research scientists in the top industries in which they worked were as follows:

Software publishers	$186,280
Research and development in the physical, engineering, and life sciences	160,310
Computer systems design and related services	142,430
Federal government, excluding postal service	115,400
Colleges, universities, and professional schools; state, local, and private	84,440

Most computer and information research scientists work full time.

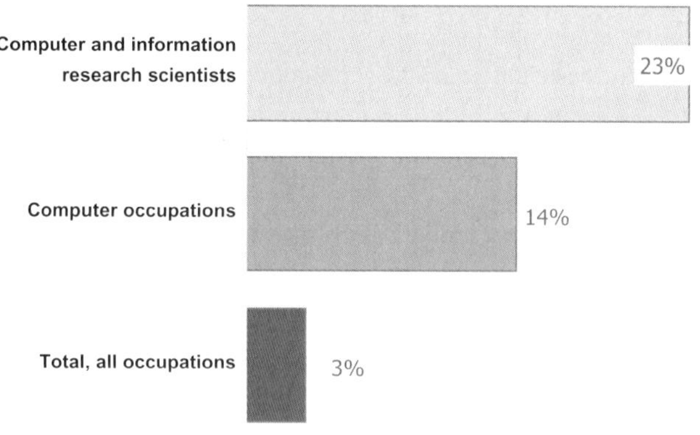

Note: All Occupations includes all occupations in the U.S. Economy.
Source: U.S. Bureau of Labor Statistics, Employment Projections program.

Job Outlook

Employment of computer and information research scientists is projected to grow 23 percent from 2022 to 2032, much faster than the average for all occupations.

About 3,400 openings for computer and information research scientists are projected each year, on average, over the decade. Many of those openings are expected to result from the need to replace workers who transfer to different occupations or exit the labor force, such as to retire.

Employment

The research and development conducted by computer and information research scientists turn ideas into technology. As demand for new and better technology grows, demand for computer and information research scientists will grow as well.

Rapid growth in data collection by businesses will lead to an increased need for data-mining services. Computer and information research scientists will be needed to write algorithms that help businesses make sense of very large amounts of data.

A growing emphasis on cybersecurity also should lead to new jobs because computer and information research scientists will be needed to find innovative ways to prevent potential cyberattacks. In addition, an increase in demand for software may increase the need for computer and information research scientists who create new programming languages to make software writing more efficient.

Occupational Title	SOC Code	Employment, 2022	Projected Employment, 2032	Change, 2022-32	
				Percent	Numeric
Computer and information research scientists	15-1221	36,500	44,800	23	8,300

Contacts for More Information

For more information about computer and information research scientists, visit

- Association for Computing Machinery
- Computing Research Association
- IEEE Computer Society
- National Center for Women & Information Technology
- USAJOBS

Computer Network Architects

Summary

Quick Facts: Computer Network Architects	
2022 Median Pay	$126,900 per year $61.01 per hour
Typical Entry-Level Education	Bachelor's degree
Work Experience in a Related Occupation	5 years or more
On-the-job Training	None
Number of Jobs, 2022	180,200
Job Outlook, 2022-32	4% (As fast as average)
Employment Change, 2022-32	6,300

What Computer Network Architects Do

Computer network architects design and build data communication networks, including local area networks (LANs), wide area networks (WANs), and Intranets.

Work Environment

Most computer network architects work full time. Some work more than 40 hours per week.

How to Become a Computer Network Architect

Computer network architects typically need a bachelor's degree in a computer-related field and experience in a related occupation, such as network and computer systems administrators.

Pay

The median annual wage for computer network architects was $126,900 in May 2022.

Job Outlook

Employment of computer network architects is projected to grow 4 percent from 2022 to 2032, about as fast as the average for all occupations.

Computer network architects plan and lay out the internal computer networks used by workers in an organization.

About 10,200 openings for computer network architects are projected each year, on average, over the decade. Many of those openings are expected to result from the need to replace workers who transfer to different occupations or exit the labor force, such as to retire.

What Computer Network Architects Do

Computer network architects design and build data communication networks, including local area networks (LANs), wide area networks (WANs), and Intranets. These networks range from small connections between two offices to next-generation networking capabilities such as a cloud infrastructure that serves multiple customers. Network architects must have extensive knowledge of an organization's business plan to design a network that can help the organization achieve its goals.

Duties

Computer network architects typically do the following:

- Create plans and layouts for data communication networks
- Present plans to management and explain why they are in the organization's best interest to pursue them
- Consider information security when designing networks
- Upgrade hardware, such as routers or adaptors, and software, such as network drivers, as needed to support computer networks
- Research new networking technologies to determine what would best support their organization in the future

Computer network architects, or *network engineers*, design and deploy computer and information networks. After deployment, they also may manage the networks and troubleshoot any issues as they arise. Network architects also predict future network needs by analyzing current data traffic and estimating how growth will affect the network.

Some computer network architects work with other IT workers, such as network and computer system administrators and computer and information systems managers to ensure workers' and clients' networking needs are being met. They also must work with equipment and software vendors to manage upgrades and support the networks.

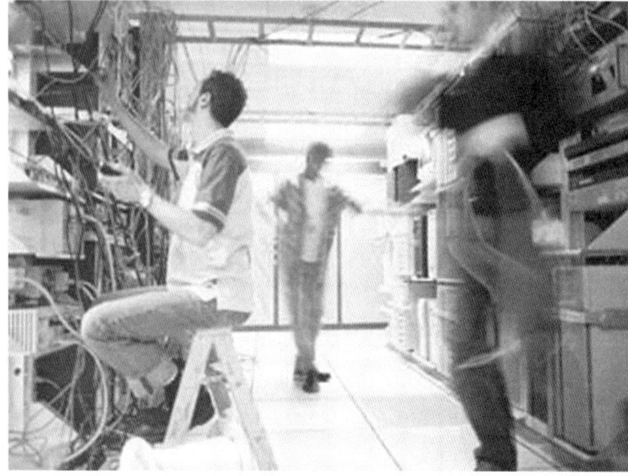

Network architects design LANs, WANs, and intranets.

Work Environment

Computer network architects held about 180,200 jobs in 2022. The largest employers of computer network architects were as follows:

Computer systems design and related services	26%
Telecommunications	10
Management of companies and enterprises	8
Educational services; state, local, and private	5
Temporary help services	5

Computer network architects spend most of their time in offices, but occasionally work in server rooms where they have access to the hardware that make up an organization's computer and information network.

Work Schedules

Most computer network architects work full time. Some work more than 40 hours per week.

Most network architects work full time.

How to Become a Computer Network Architect

Computer network architects typically need a bachelor's degree in a computer-related field and experience in a related occupation, such as network and computer systems administrators.

Education

Computer network architects typically need at least a bachelor's degree in computer and information technology, engineering, or a related field. Degree programs in a computer-related field give prospective network architects hands-on experience in classes such as network security or database design. These programs prepare network architects to be able to work with the wide array of technologies used in networks.

Employers of network architects sometimes prefer applicants to have a master's of business administration (MBA) in information systems. MBA programs generally require 2 years of study beyond the undergraduate level and include both business and computer-related courses.

Work Experience in a Related Occupation

Network architects generally need to have at least 5 to 10 years of experience working with information technology (IT) systems. They often have experience as a network and computer system administrator but also may come from other computer-related occupations such as database administrator or computer systems analyst.

Licenses, Certifications, and Registrations

Certification programs are generally offered by product vendors or software firms. Vendor-specific certification verifies a set of skills to ensure network architects are able to work in specific networking environments. Companies may require their network architects to be certified in the products they use.

Advancement

Some network architects advance to become computer and information systems managers.

Network architects often have several years of experience in a related occupation, such as a network administrator.

Important Qualities

Analytical skills. Computer network architects have to examine data networks and decide how to best connect the networks based on the needs and resources of the organization.

Detail oriented. Computer network architects create comprehensive plans of the networks they are creating with precise information describing how the network parts will work together.

Interpersonal skills. These workers must work with different types of employees to successfully design and implement computer and information networks.

Leadership skills. Many computer network architects direct teams of engineers, such as computer hardware engineers, who build the networks they have designed.

Organizational skills. Computer network architects who work for large firms must coordinate many different types of communication networks and make sure they work well together.

Pay

The median annual wage for computer network architects was $126,900 in May 2022. The median wage is the wage at which half the workers in an occupation earned more than that amount and half earned less. The lowest 10 percent earned less than $73,490, and the highest 10 percent earned more than $185,170.

In May 2022, the median annual wages for computer network architects in the top industries in which they worked were as follows:

Computer systems design and related services..	$129,230
Management of companies and enterprises	128,720
Temporary help services	128,610
Telecommunications	108,150
Educational services; state, local, and private....	92,470

Most computer network architects work full time. Some work more than 40 hours per week.

Computer Network Architects

Median annual wages, May 2022

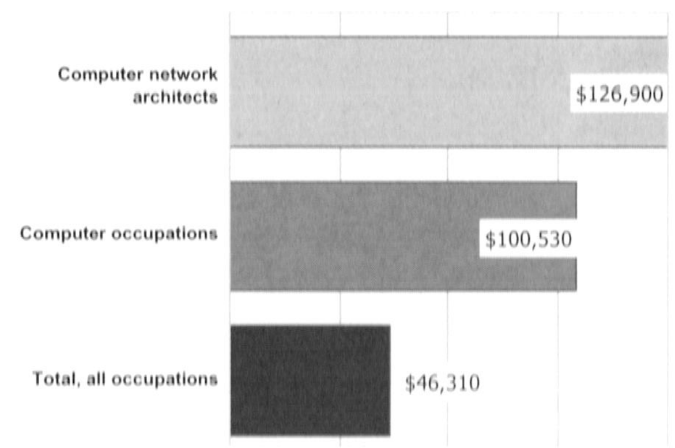

Note: All Occupations includes all occupations in the U.S. Economy.
Source: U.S. Bureau of Labor Statistics, Occupational Employment and Wage Statistics.

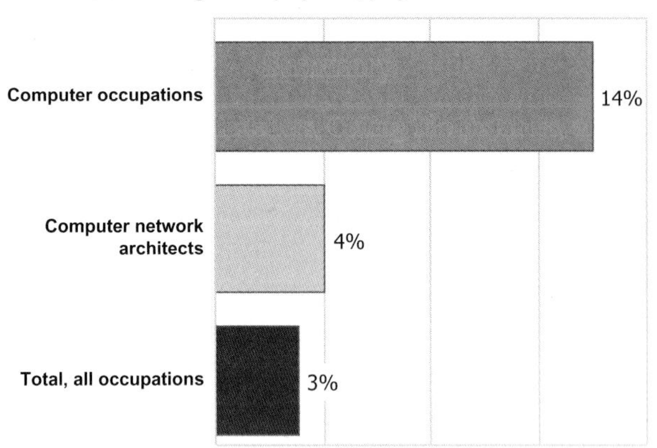

Note: All Occupations includes all occupations in the U.S. Economy.
Source: U.S. Bureau of Labor Statistics, Employment Projections program.

Job Outlook

Employment of computer network architects is projected to grow 4 percent from 2022 to 2032, about as fast as the average for all occupations.

About 10,200 openings for computer network architects are projected each year, on average, over the decade. Many of those openings are expected to result from the need to replace workers who transfer to different occupations or exit the labor force, such as to retire.

Employment

Demand for computer network architects will grow as firms continue to design and build new information technology (IT) networks and upgrade existing ones. Continued expansion of cloud computing will increase demand for these workers to ensure that networks are properly designed and that transition to the new network proceeds smoothly.

However, demand for computer network architects is expected to be limited over the projections decade. Some computer network tasks, such as monitoring systems and troubleshooting network problems, continue to be automated and consolidated. In addition, some businesses, especially smaller ones with minimal IT requirements, find it more cost effective to contract with outside firms for these services rather than to hire computer network architects directly.

Occupational Title	SOC Code	Employment, 2022	Projected Employment, 2032	Change, 2022-32	
				Percent	Numeric
Computer network architects	15-1241	180,200	186,600	4	6,300

Contacts for More Information

For more information, visit

- Association for Computing Machinery
- IEEE Computer Society
- Computing Research Association
- CompTIA
- National Center for Women & Information Technology

Computer Programmers

Summary

Quick Facts: Computer Programmers	
2022 Median Pay	$97,800 per year $47.02 per hour
Typical Entry-Level Education	Bachelor's degree
Work Experience in a Related Occupation	None
On-the-job Training	None
Number of Jobs, 2022	147,400
Job Outlook, 2022-32	-11% (Decline)
Employment Change, 2022-32	-16,600

What Computer Programmers Do

Computer programmers write, modify, and test code and scripts that allow computer software and applications to function properly.

Work Environment

Programmers usually work in office settings, most commonly in the computer systems design and related services industry. Most computer programmers work full time.

How to Become a Computer Programmer

Computer programmers typically need a bachelor's degree to enter the occupation. Most programmers specialize in several programming languages.

Programmers spend most of their time writing and testing computer code.

Pay

The median annual wage for computer programmers was $97,800 in May 2022.

Job Outlook

Employment of computer programmers is projected to decline 11 percent from 2022 to 2032.

Despite declining employment, about 6,700 openings for computer programmers are projected each year, on average, over the decade. All of those openings are expected to result from the need to replace workers who transfer to other occupations or exit the labor force, such as to retire.

What Computer Programmers Do

Computer programmers write, modify, and test code and scripts that allow computer software and applications to function properly. They turn the designs created by software developers and engineers into instructions that a computer can follow. In addition, programmers run tests to ensure that newly created applications and software produce the expected results. If the products do not work correctly, programmers check the code or scripts for mistakes and modify them.

Duties

Computer programmers typically do the following:

- Write programs in a variety of computer languages, such as C++ and Java
- Update and expand existing programs
- Test programs for errors and fix the faulty lines of computer code
- Create, modify, and test code or scripts in software that simplifies development

Programmers work closely with software developers, and in some businesses their duties overlap. When such overlap occurs, programmers may be required to take on some of the tasks that are typically assigned to developers, such as designing programs.

Computer programmers write programs in a variety of computer languages, such as C++ and Java.

Programmers use code libraries, which are collections of independent lines of code, to simplify their writing and improve their efficiency. They may create their own code libraries or make use of existing ones.

In addition, programmers may write or use software-as-a-service (SaaS) applications that are centrally hosted online. Although programmers typically need to rewrite their programs to work on different system platforms, such as Windows or OS X, applications created with SaaS work on all platforms. Accordingly, programmers writing SaaS applications may not have to rewrite as much code as other programmers do and can instead spend more time writing new programs.

Work Environment

Computer programmers held about 147,400 jobs in 2022. The largest employers of computer programmers were as follows:

Computer systems design and related services	32%
Self-employed workers	7
Manufacturing	6
Finance and insurance	6
Software publishers	6

Programmers usually work in office settings, which may be in their homes.

Work Schedules

Most computer programmers work full time.

How to Become a Computer Programmer

Computer programmers typically need a bachelor's degree in computer science or a related subject. Most programmers specialize in several programming languages.

Education

Computer programmers typically need a bachelor's degree in computer and information technology or a related field, such

Most programmers work independently in offices.

Most programmers have a degree in computer science or a related field.

as mathematics. However, some employers hire workers who have other degrees or experience in specific programming languages. Programmers who work in specific fields, such as healthcare or accounting, may take classes in that field to supplement their computer-related degree. In addition, employers may prefer to hire candidates who have experience gained through internships.

Most programmers learn computer languages while in school. However, a computer science degree gives students the skills they need to learn new computer languages easily. Students get experience writing code, testing programs, fixing errors, and doing many other tasks that they will perform on the job.

To keep up with changing technology, computer programmers may take continuing education classes and attend professional development seminars to learn new programming languages or about upgrades to programming languages they already know.

Licenses, Certifications, and Registrations

Programmers may become certified in specific programming languages or for vendor-specific programming products. Some companies require their computer programmers to be certified in the products they use.

Advancement

Programmers who have general business experience may become computer systems analysts. With experience, some programmers may become software developers. They may also be promoted to managerial positions. For more information, see the profiles on computer systems analysts, software developers, and computer and information systems managers.

Important Qualities

Analytical skills. Computer programmers must understand complex instructions in order to create computer code.

Communication skills. Although computer programmers work alone to write code, they must have effective communication skills to coordinate work on large projects with team members and managers.

Detail oriented. Computer programmers must closely examine the code that they write, modify, or test, because a small mistake may affect the entire computer program.

Problem-solving skills. Programmers check the code for errors and fix any they find.

Pay

The median annual wage for computer programmers was $97,800 in May 2022. The median wage is the wage at which half the workers in an occupation earned more than that amount and half earned less. The lowest 10 percent earned less than $54,310, and the highest 10 percent earned more than $157,690.

In May 2022, the median annual wages for computer programmers in the top industries in which they worked were as follows:

Software publishers	$106,120
Finance and insurance	103,340
Manufacturing	101,250
Computer systems design and related services	93,270

Most computer programmers work full time.

Job Outlook

Employment of computer programmers is projected to decline 11 percent from 2022 to 2032.

Despite declining employment, about 6,700 openings for computer programmers are projected each year, on average, over the decade. All of those openings are expected to result

Computer Programmers

Median annual wages, May 2022

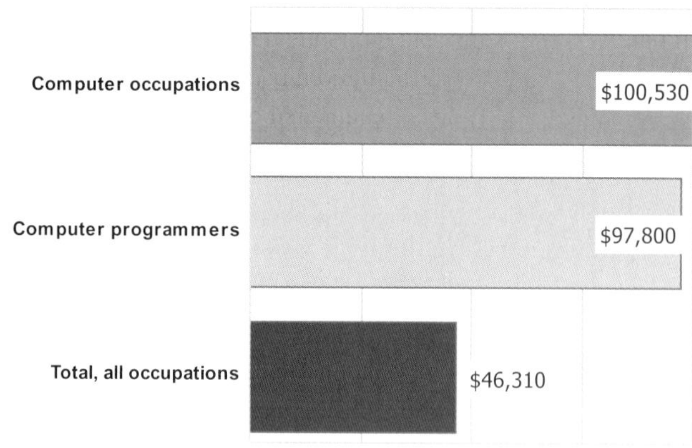

Note: All Occupations includes all occupations in the U.S. Economy.
Source: U.S. Bureau of Labor Statistics, Occupational Employment and Wage Statistics.

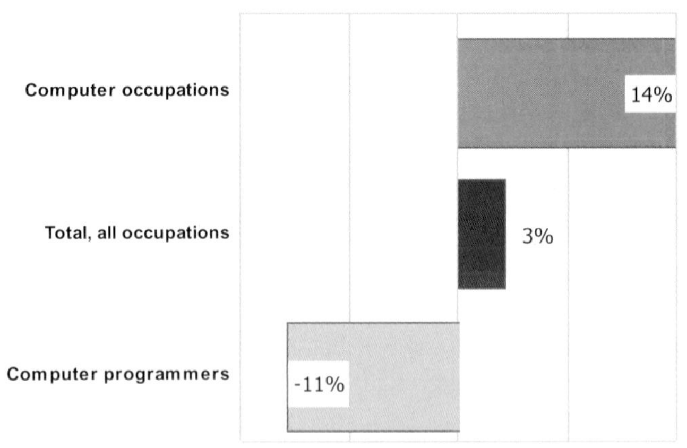

Note: All Occupations includes all occupations in the U.S. Economy.
Source: U.S. Bureau of Labor Statistics, Employment Projections program.

from the need to replace workers who transfer to other occupations or exit the labor force, such as to retire.

Employment

Computer programming work continues to be automated, helping computer programmers to become more efficient in some of their tasks. Many companies are leveraging technologies to automate repetitive tasks, such as code formatting, to save time and money. Automation of this routine work could allow computer programmers to focus on other tasks, such as strategic planning activities, that cannot be automated. In addition, some computer programming tasks are more commonly done by other computer occupations, such as developers or analysts.

Occupational Title	SOC Code	Employment, 2022	Projected Employment, 2032	Change, 2022-32	
				Percent	Numeric
Computer programmers	15-1251	147,400	130,800	-11	-16,600

Contacts for More Information

For more information about computer programmers, visit

- ➤ Association for Computing Machinery
- ➤ CompTIA
- ➤ IEEE Computer Society
- ➤ National Center for Women & Information Technology

Computer Support Specialists

Summary

Quick Facts: Computer Support Specialists	
2022 Median Pay	$59,660 per year $28.68 per hour
Typical Entry-Level Education	See How to Become One
Work Experience in a Related Occupation	None
On-the-job Training	Moderate-term on-the-job training
Number of Jobs, 2022	914,100
Job Outlook, 2022-32	5% (Faster than average)
Employment Change, 2022-32	49,200

What Computer Support Specialists Do

Computer support specialists maintain computer networks and provide technical help to computer users.

Work Environment

Most computer support specialists work full time. Because computer support services may need to be available 24 hours a day, some specialists work nights or weekends.

How to Become a Computer Support Specialist

Entry requirements vary for computer support specialists. Network support specialists typically need an associate's degree, and user support specialists typically need to complete some college courses. However, candidates may qualify with a high school diploma plus relevant information technology (IT) certifications.

Pay

The median annual wage for computer network support specialists was $68,050 in May 2022.

The median annual wage for computer user support specialists was $57,890 in May 2022.

Some computer support specialists, called help-desk technicians, assist non-IT users who are having computer problems.

Job Outlook

Overall employment of computer support specialists is projected to grow 5 percent from 2022 to 2032, faster than the average for all occupations.

About 66,500 openings for computer support specialists are projected each year, on average, over the decade. Many of those openings are expected to result from the need to replace workers who transfer to different occupations or exit the labor force, such as to retire.

What Computer Support Specialists Do

Computer support specialists assist computer users and organizations. These specialists either maintain computer networks or provide technical help directly to computer users.

Duties

Computer network support specialists typically do the following:

- Test and evaluate existing network systems
- Perform regular maintenance to ensure that networks operate correctly
- Troubleshoot local area networks (LANs), wide area networks (WANs), and Internet systems

Computer network support specialists analyze and troubleshoot computer network problems. They have an important role in the daily, weekly, or monthly maintenance of their organization's networks. This maintenance may be routine or part of the organization's disaster recovery efforts. Network support specialists also may assist computer users through phone, email, or in-person visits. They often work under the direction of network and computer systems administrators, who handle more complex tasks.

Computer user support specialists typically do the following:

- Analyze customers' computer problem to diagnose it and determine the cause
- Document customers' descriptions of their computer problems
- Guide customers through the recommended problem-solving steps
- Set up or repair computer equipment and related devices
- Install and train users on new hardware or software
- Inform team members and managers of major problems or of customers' recurring concerns

Computer user support specialists, also called *help-desk technicians*, usually provide technical help to non-IT computer users. They respond to requests for help in a number of ways, such as in person or by phone, online chat, or email.

Help-desk technicians solve a range of problems that vary with the industry and the particular firm. Some technicians work for large software companies or for support service firms and instruct business customers in the use of business-specific programs, such as an electronic health records program used in hospitals or physicians' offices.

Other help-desk technicians work in call centers and take customers through a problem step by step, such as to reestablish an Internet connection or to troubleshoot Wi-Fi routers or other household IT products.

Work Environment

Computer network support specialists held about 177,900 jobs in 2022. The largest employers of computer network support specialists were as follows:

Computer systems design and related services	19%
Educational services; state, local, and private	12
Telecommunications	10
Government	7
Finance and insurance	6

Computer user support specialists held about 736,200 jobs in 2022. The largest employers of computer user support specialists were as follows:

Network support specialists analyze, troubleshoot, and maintain computer networks.

Computer support specialists work for a variety of industries.

Computer systems design and related services	22%
Educational services; state, local, and private	11
Wholesale trade	6
Finance and insurance	6
Government	6

Some computer support specialists are able to telework. Others must be onsite or may need to travel to clients' locations.

Work Schedules

Most computer support specialists work full time. Because computer support services may need to be available 24 hours a day, some specialists work nights or weekends.

How to Become a Computer Support Specialist

Entry requirements vary for computer support specialists. Network support specialists typically need an associate's degree, and user support specialists typically need to complete some college courses. However, candidates for either type of position may qualify with a high school diploma plus relevant information technology (IT) certifications.

Education

Education requirements for computer support specialists vary. Computer user support specialist jobs require some computer knowledge but not necessarily a college degree. Applicants who have taken courses in areas such as networking, server administration, and information security may qualify for these jobs. For computer network support specialists, employers may accept applicants who have an associate's degree, although some prefer that applicants have a bachelor's degree.

Large software companies that provide support to business users who buy their products or services may require applicants to have a bachelor's degree. Positions that are more technical are likely to require a degree in a field such as computer and information technology or engineering. For others, the applicant's field of degree is less important.

Communication skills are important for computer support specialists.

To keep up with changes in technology, computer support specialists may need to continue their education throughout their careers.

Licenses, Certifications, and Registrations

Certification programs are generally offered by vendors or from vendor-neutral certification providers. Certification validates the knowledge of and best practices required by computer support specialists. Companies may require their computer support specialists to hold certifications in the products the companies use. Other types of certifications, such as CompTIA A+, may be a helpful starting point for workers seeking entry into the occupation.

Advancement

Many computer support specialists advance to other information technology positions, such as information security analysts, network and computer systems administrators and software developers. Some become managers in the computer support services department. Some organizations provide paths for support specialists to move into other parts of the organization, such as sales.

Important Qualities

Communication skills. Computer support specialists must clearly convey information, both orally and in writing. They must describe solutions to computer problems in way that nontechnical users can understand.

Customer-service skills. Computer support specialists must be patient and sympathetic. They often help people who are frustrated trying to use software or hardware.

Listening skills. Support workers must be able to understand the problems that their customers are describing and know when to ask questions for clarification.

Problem-solving skills. Support workers must identify both simple and complex computer problems and then analyze and solve them.

Pay

The median annual wage for computer network support specialists was \$68,050 in May 2022. The median wage is the wage at which half the workers in an occupation earned more than that amount and half earned less. The lowest 10 percent earned less than \$42,440, and the highest 10 percent earned more than \$115,220.

The median annual wage for computer user support specialists was \$57,890 in May 2022. The lowest 10 percent earned less than \$36,580, and the highest 10 percent earned more than \$94,920.

In May 2022, the median annual wages for computer network support specialists in the top industries in which they worked were as follows:

Telecommunications	\$78,930
Computer systems design and related services	68,010
Finance and insurance	67,550

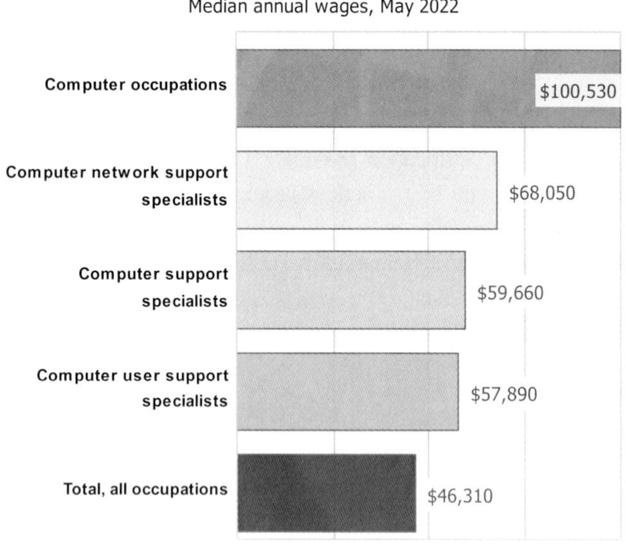

Note: All Occupations includes all occupations in the U.S. Economy.
Source: U.S. Bureau of Labor Statistics, Occupational Employment and Wage Statistics.

Government	67,220
Educational services; state, local, and private	62,670

In May 2022, the median annual wages for computer user support specialists in the top industries in which they worked were as follows:

Government	$66,850
Finance and insurance	60,570
Wholesale trade	58,550
Computer systems design and related services	56,620
Educational services; state, local, and private	52,050

Most computer support specialists work full time. Because computer support services may need to be available 24 hours a day, some specialists work nights or weekends.

Job Outlook

Overall employment of computer support specialists is projected to grow 5 percent from 2022 to 2032, faster than the average for all occupations.

About 66,500 openings for computer support specialists are projected each year, on average, over the decade. Many of those openings are expected to result from the need to replace workers who transfer to different occupations or exit the labor force, such as to retire.

Employment

Computer support specialists will be needed to provide technical help and training to users with new hardware or software.

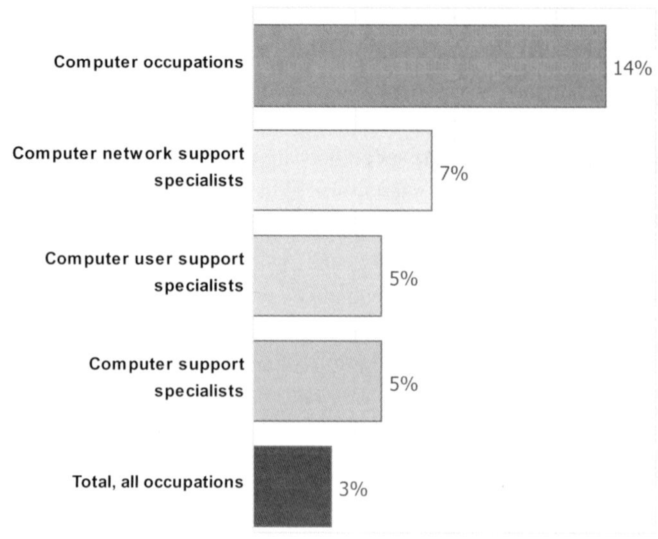

Note: All Occupations includes all occupations in the U.S. Economy.
Source: U.S. Bureau of Labor Statistics, Employment Projections program.

However, this demand may be offset somewhat as organizations continue to implement automated tools, such as chatbots, for troubleshooting. This use of automation may free up some computer support specialists to handle more complex cases and troubleshooting that require attention. Some businesses, especially smaller ones with minimal information technology (IT) requirements, may find it more cost effective to contract with outside firms for these services rather than to hire computer support specialists directly.

Occupational Title	SOC Code	Employment, 2022	Projected Employment, 2032	Change, 2022-32	
				Percent	Numeric
Computer support specialists	15-1230	914,100	963,300	5	49,200
Computer network support specialists	15-1231	177,900	190,400	7	12,500
Computer user support specialists	15-1232	736,200	772,900	5	36,800

Contacts for More Information

For more information about computer support specialists, visit

- Association of Support Professionals
- Help Desk Institute (HDI)
- Technology Services Industry Association
- Association for Computing Machinery
- Computing Research Association
- Computing Technology Industry Association (CompTIA)
- IEEE Computer Society
- National Center for Women & Information Technology

Computer Systems Analysts

Summary

Quick Facts: Computer Systems Analysts	
2022 Median Pay	$102,240 per year $49.15 per hour
Typical Entry-Level Education	Bachelor's degree
Work Experience in a Related Occupation	None
On-the-job Training	None
Number of Jobs, 2022	531,400
Job Outlook, 2022-32	10% (Much faster than average)
Employment Change, 2022-32	51,100

What Computer Systems Analysts Do
Computer systems analysts study an organization's current computer systems and design ways to improve efficiency.

Work Environment
Most computer systems analysts work full time.

How to Become a Computer Systems Analyst
Computer systems analysts typically need a bachelor's degree to enter the occupation. Studying a computer science or information systems field is common, although not always a requirement. Some firms hire job candidates who have a degree in business or liberal arts along with relevant skills.

Pay
The median annual wage for computer systems analysts was $102,240 in May 2022.

Job Outlook
Employment of computer systems analysts is projected to grow 10 percent from 2022 to 2032, much faster than the average for all occupations.

Analysts create diagrams to help programmers and architects build computer systems.

About 37,600 openings for computer systems analysts are projected each year, on average, over the decade. Many of those openings are expected to result from the need to replace workers who transfer to different occupations or exit the labor force, such as to retire.

What Computer Systems Analysts Do
Computer systems analysts, sometimes called *systems architects*, study an organization's current computer systems and procedures and design improvements to them. In doing so, these analysts help the organization operate more efficiently.

Duties
Computer systems analysts typically do the following:

- Consult with managers to determine the role of information technology (IT) systems in an organization
- Research different technologies to decide if they would increase the organization's efficiency
- Analyze costs and benefits of IT systems and upgrades to help managers decide which, if any, to install
- Devise ways to add functionality to existing computer systems
- Design new systems by configuring hardware and software

Analysts create diagrams to help programmers and architects build computer systems.

- Oversee the installation and configuration of new systems and customize them for the organization
- Test systems to ensure that they work as expected
- Write instruction manuals and train the systems' end users

Most computer systems analysts specialize in computer systems that are specific to their organization type. For example, an analyst might work with financial computer systems or with engineering computer systems. Computer systems analysts work with other IT team members to help an organization's business leaders understand how computer systems best serve the organization.

Computer systems analysts use a variety of techniques, such as data modeling, to design computer systems. Data modeling allows analysts to view processes and data flows. Analysts conduct indepth tests and analyze information and trends in the data to increase a system's efficiency.

Analysts calculate requirements for how much memory, storage, and computing power the computer system needs. They prepare diagrams for programmers or engineers to use when building the system. Analysts also work with these people to solve problems that arise after the initial system setup. Most analysts do some programming in the course of their work.

Analysts who focus on coding and debugging, in addition to their other tasks, may be referred to as *programmer analysts.* They also may design and update their system's software and create applications tailored to their organization's needs. For information about other occupations that do programming or testing, see the profiles on computer programmers and software developers, quality assurance analysts, and testers.

In some cases, analysts who supervise the installation or upgrade of IT systems from start to finish may be called *IT project managers*. They monitor a project's progress to ensure that deadlines, standards, and cost targets are met. IT project managers who also plan and direct an organization's IT department or IT policies are included in the profile on computer and information systems managers.

Work Environment

Computer systems analysts held about 531,400 jobs in 2022. The largest employers of computer systems analysts were as follows:

Computer systems design and related services	24%
Finance and insurance	13
Management of companies and enterprises	10
Information	8
Government	7

Computer systems analysts may work directly for an organization or as contractors, often for an information technology firm. The projects that computer systems analysts work on usually require them to collaborate with others.

Some systems analysts work as consultants.

Work Schedules

Most computer systems analysts work full time.

How to Become a Computer Systems Analyst

Computer systems analysts typically need a bachelor's degree to enter the occupation. Studying a computer science or information systems field is common, although not always a requirement. Some firms hire job candidates who have a degree in business or liberal arts along with relevant skills.

Education

Computer systems analysts typically need a bachelor's degree in computer and information technology or a related field, such as mathematics. Because these analysts are involved in the business side of an organization, taking business courses or majoring in management information systems may be helpful. Some employers hire job candidates who have liberal arts degrees and have gained programming or technical expertise elsewhere.

Some employers prefer applicants who have a master's degree in business administration (MBA) with a concentration in information systems. For technically complex jobs, a master's degree in computer science may be more appropriate.

Most computer systems analysts have a bachelor's degree.

Systems analysts may take continuing education courses throughout their careers to stay abreast of new technology. Technological advances are common in the computer field, and continual study is necessary to remain competitive.

Systems analysts also must understand the industry they are working in. For example, an analyst working in a hospital may need a thorough understanding of healthcare plans and programs such as Medicare and Medicaid, and an analyst working for a bank may need to understand finance. Having industry-specific knowledge helps systems analysts communicate with managers to determine the role of the information technology (IT) systems in an organization.

Advancement

With experience, systems analysts may advance to become project managers and lead a team of analysts. Some eventually become IT directors or chief technology officers. For more information, see the profile on computer and information systems managers.

Important Qualities

Analytical skills. Analysts must interpret complex information from various sources and decide the best way to move forward on a project. They must also figure out how changes may affect the project.

Business skills. Analysts design and implement computer systems or upgrade existing systems to meet an organization's business goals. Analysts must have a thorough understanding of their organization's business objectives in order to meet its needs.

Communication skills. Analysts work as a liaison between management and the IT department and must explain complex issues in a way that both understand.

Creativity. Because analysts are tasked with finding innovative solutions to computer problems, they must be resourceful and use ingenuity in their work.

Detail oriented. Analysts study an organization's computer systems and must pay attention to the minutiae to find areas of inefficiency or error.

Organizational skills. Analysts may coordinate work with different areas of an organization and must keep track of many tasks and deadlines to ensure that projects proceed according to plan.

Pay

The median annual wage for computer systems analysts was $102,240 in May 2022. The median wage is the wage at which half the workers in an occupation earned more than that amount and half earned less. The lowest 10 percent earned less than $61,390, and the highest 10 percent earned more than $161,980.

In May 2022, the median annual wages for computer systems analysts in the top industries in which they worked were as follows:

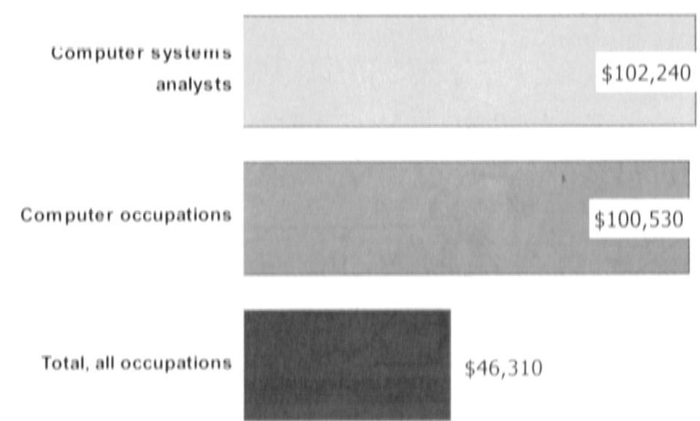

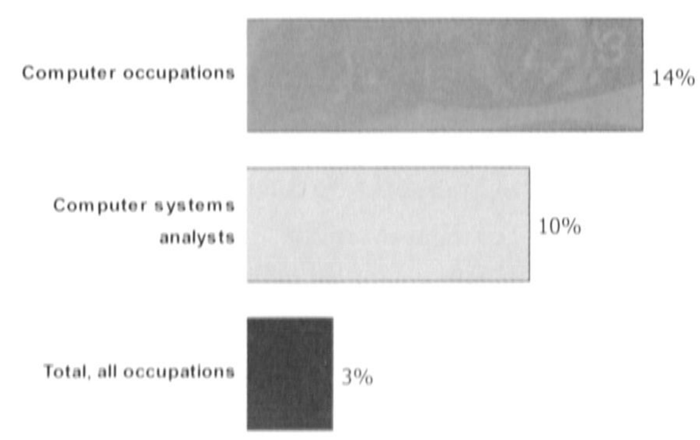

Management of companies and enterprises	$105,300
Finance and insurance	103,710
Computer systems design and related services	103,640
Information	102,960
Government	86,010

Most computer systems analysts work full time.

Job Outlook

Employment of computer systems analysts is projected to grow 10 percent from 2022 to 2032, much faster than the average for all occupations.

About 37,600 openings for computer systems analysts are projected each year, on average, over the decade. Many of those openings are expected to result from the need to replace workers who transfer to different occupations or exit the labor force, such as to retire.

Employment

As organizations across the economy continue to rely on information technology (IT), computer systems analysts will be hired to design and install new computer systems. Small firms with minimal IT requirements will find it more cost effective to contract with outside firms for these services rather than to hire computer systems analysts directly.

Occupational Title	SOC Code	Employment, 2022	Projected Employment, 2032	Change, 2022-32	
				Percent	Numeric
Computer systems analysts	15-1211	531,400	582,600	10	51,100

Contacts for More Information

For more information about computer systems analysts, visit

- Association for Computing Machinery
- Computing Research Association
- IEEE Computer Society
- National Center for Women & Information Technology

Database Administrators and Architects

Summary

Quick Facts: Database Administrators and Architects	
2022 Median Pay	$112,120 per year $53.91 per hour
Typical Entry-Level Education	Bachelor's degree
Work Experience in a Related Occupation	See How to Become One
On-the-job Training	None
Number of Jobs, 2022	149,300
Job Outlook, 2022-32	8% (Faster than average)
Employment Change, 2022-32	12,300

What Database Administrators and Architects Do

Database administrators and architects create or organize systems to store and secure data.

Work Environment

Many database administrators and architects work in firms that provide computer design services or in industries that have large databases, such educational institutions and insurance companies. Most database administrators and architects work full time.

How to Become a Database Administrator or Architect

Database administrators and architects typically need a bachelor's degree in computer and information technology or a related field.

Pay

The median annual wage for database administrators was $99,890 in May 2022.

The median annual wage for database architects was $134,870 in May 2022.

Job Outlook

Overall employment of database administrators and architects is projected to grow 8 percent from 2022 to 2032, faster than the average for all occupations.

About 10,200 openings for database administrators and architects are projected each year, on average, over the decade. Many of those openings are expected to result from the need to replace workers who transfer to different occupations or exit the labor force, such as to retire.

Database administrators ensure that data are available to many different users.

Database administrators ensure databases run efficiently.

What Database Administrators and Architects Do

Database administrators and architects create or organize systems to store and secure a variety of data, such as financial information and customer shipping records. They also make sure that the data are available to authorized users.

Duties

Database administrators and architects typically do the following:

- Identify user needs to create and administer databases
- Design and build new databases
- Ensure that organizational data are secure
- Back up and restore data to prevent data loss
- Ensure that databases operate efficiently and without error
- Make and test modifications to database structure when needed
- Maintain databases and update permissions

Database administrators, often called DBAs, make sure that data analysts and other users can easily use databases to find the information they need. They also ensure that systems perform as they should by monitoring database operation and providing support.

Many databases contain personal, proprietary, or financial information. Database administrators often are responsible for planning security measures to protect this important information.

Database architects design and build new databases for systems and applications. They research the technical requirements of an organization during the design phase and then create models for building the database. Finally, they code new data architecture, integrating existing databases or infrastructure, and check for errors or inefficiencies.

The duties of database administrators and database architects may overlap. For example, administrators and architects may be generalists who work on both systems and applications. However, some DBAs specialize in certain tasks, such as maintenance, that vary with an organization and its needs. Two common specialties are as follows:

System DBAs are responsible for the physical and technical aspects of a database, such as installing upgrades and patches to fix program bugs. They ensure that the firm's database management systems work properly.

Application DBAs do all the tasks of a general DBA focusing solely on a database for a specific application or set of applications, such as customer-service software. They may write or debug programs and must be able to manage the applications that work with the database.

Work Environment

Database administrators held about 85,200 jobs in 2022. The largest employers of database administrators were as follows:

Computer systems design and related services	14%
Finance and insurance	13
Information	10
Educational services; state, local, and private	9
Management of companies and enterprises	8

Database architects held about 64,000 jobs in 2022. The largest employers of database architects were as follows:

Computer systems design and related services	36%
Finance and insurance	13
Management of companies and enterprises	7
Administrative and support services	6
Computing infrastructure providers, data processing, web hosting, and related services	6

Database administrators and architects work in nearly all industries. For example, in retail they may design databases that track buyers' shipping information; in healthcare, they may manage databases that secure patients' medical records.

Database administrators are often referred to as DBAs.

Database administrators usually have a bachelor's degree in an information- or computer-related subject such as computer science.

Work Schedules

Most database administrators and architects work full time.

How to Become a Database Administrator or Architect

Database administrators (DBAs) and architects typically need a bachelor's degree in computer and information technology or a related field.

Education

Database administrators and architects typically need a bachelor's degree in computer and information technology or a related field, such as engineering; some DBAs study business. Employers may prefer to hire applicants who have a master's degree focusing on data or database management, typically either in computer science, information systems, or information technology.

Database administrators and architects need an understanding of database languages, such as Structured Query Language, or SQL. DBAs will need to become familiar with whichever programming language their firm uses.

Licenses, Certifications, and Registrations

Certification is typically offered directly from software vendors or vendor-neutral certification providers. Employers may require their database administrators and architects to be certified in the products they use.

Advancement

Database administrators and architects may advance to become computer and information systems managers. Experienced database administrators may advance to become database architects.

Important Qualities

Analytical skills. DBAs monitor a database system's performance to determine when action is needed. They must evaluate information from a variety of sources to decide on an approach.

Communication skills. Most database administrators and architects work on teams and need to convey information effectively to developers, managers, and other workers.

Detail oriented. Working with databases requires an understanding of complex systems, in which a minor error can cause major problems.

Problem-solving skills. When database problems arise, administrators and architects must troubleshoot and correct the problems.

Pay

The median annual wage for database administrators was $99,890 in May 2022. The median wage is the wage at which half the workers in an occupation earned more than that amount and half earned less. The lowest 10 percent earned less than $53,010, and the highest 10 percent earned more than $153,870.

The median annual wage for database architects was $134,870 in May 2022. The lowest 10 percent earned less than $74,980, and the highest 10 percent earned more than $197,350.

In May 2022, the median annual wages for database administrators in the top industries in which they worked were as follows:

Computer systems design and related services.	$113,200
Finance and insurance	109,040
Information	106,540
Management of companies and enterprises	105,780
Educational services; state, local, and private	80,650

In May 2022, the median annual wages for database architects in the top industries in which they worked were as follows:

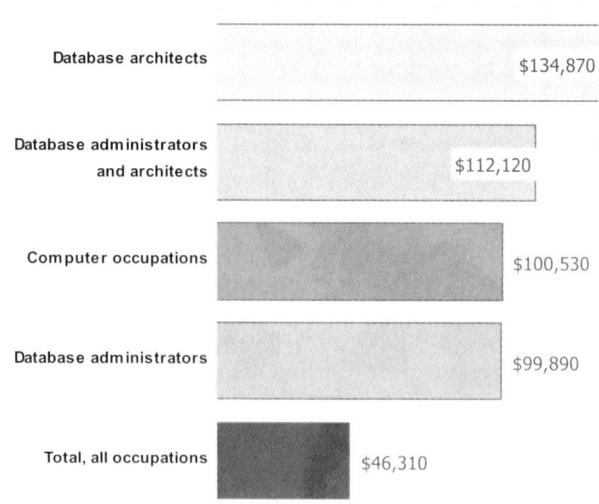

Note: All Occupations includes all occupations in the U.S. Economy.
Source: U.S. Bureau of Labor Statistics, Occupational Employment and Wage Statistics.

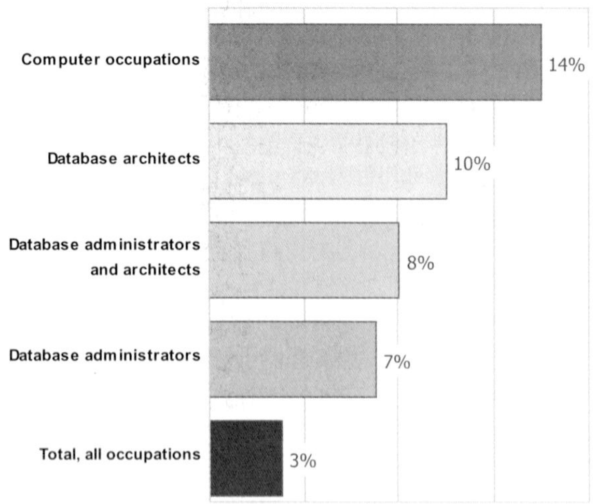

Note: All Occupations includes all occupations in the U.S. Economy.
Source: U.S. Bureau of Labor Statistics, Employment Projections program.

Computer systems design and related services...	$156,000
Computing infrastructure providers, data processing, web hosting, and related services....	136,480
Administrative and support services................	133,690
Finance and insurance......................................	131,250
Management of companies and enterprises......	128,190

Most database administrators and architects work full time.

Job Outlook

Overall employment of database administrators and architects is projected to grow 8 percent from 2022 to 2032, faster than the average for all occupations.

About 10,200 openings for database administrators and architects are projected each year, on average, over the decade. Many of those openings are expected to result from the need to replace workers who transfer to different occupations or exit the labor force, such as to retire.

Employment

Employment growth will be driven by the continued data needs of companies in nearly all sectors of the economy. Database administrators and database architects will be needed to organize and present information to stakeholders in a user-friendly format. As organizations continue to migrate to cloud environments, these administrators and architects will be critical to ensuring proper database design, transition, backup, and security and to ensuring that connections to legacy systems remain intact.

Occupational Title	SOC Code	Employment, 2022	Projected Employment, 2032	Change, 2022-32	
				Percent	Numeric
Database administrators and architects	—	149,300	161,600	8	12,300
Database administrators	15-1242	85,200	91,200	7	6,000
Database architects	15-1243	64,000	70,400	10	6,400

Contacts for More Information

For more information about database administrators and architects, visit

- Association for Computing Machinery
- Computing Research Association
- IEEE Computer Society
- National Center for Women & Information Technology

Information Security Analysts

Summary

Quick Facts: Information Security Analysts

2022 Median Pay	$112,000 per year $53.85 per hour
Typical Entry-Level Education	Bachelor's degree
Work Experience in a Related Occupation	Less than 5 years
On-the-job Training	None
Number of Jobs, 2022	168,900
Job Outlook, 2022-32	32% (Much faster than average)
Employment Change, 2022-32	53,200

What Information Security Analysts Do

Information security analysts plan and carry out security measures to protect an organization's computer networks and systems.

Work Environment

Most information security analysts work for computer companies, consulting firms, or business and financial companies.

How to Become an Information Security Analyst

Information security analysts typically need a bachelor's degree in a computer science field, along with related work experience. Employers may prefer to hire analysts who have professional certification.

Information security analysts work to protect a company's computer systems.

Pay

The median annual wage for information security analysts was $112,000 in May 2022.

Job Outlook

Employment of information security analysts is projected to grow 32 percent from 2022 to 2032, much faster than the average for all occupations.

About 16,800 openings for information security analysts are projected each year, on average, over the decade. Many of those openings are expected to result from the need to replace workers who transfer to different occupations or exit the labor force, such as to retire.

What Information Security Analysts Do

Information security analysts plan and carry out security measures to protect an organization's computer networks and systems.

Information security analysts install software, such as firewalls, to protect computer networks.

Duties

Information security analysts typically do the following:

- Monitor their organization's networks for security breaches and investigate when one occurs
- Use and maintain software, such as firewalls and data encryption programs, to protect sensitive information
- Check for vulnerabilities in computer and network systems
- Research the latest information technology (IT) security trends
- Prepare reports that document general metrics, attempted attacks, and security breaches
- Develop security standards and best practices for their organization
- Recommend security enhancements to management or senior IT staff
- Help computer users when they need to install or learn about new security products and procedures

Information security analysts are heavily involved with creating their organization's disaster recovery plan, a procedure that IT employees follow in case of emergency. These plans allow for the continued operation of an organization's IT department. The recovery plan includes preventive measures such as regularly copying and transferring data to an offsite location. It also involves plans to restore proper IT functioning after a disaster. Analysts continually test the steps in their recovery plans.

Information security analysts must stay up to date on IT security and on the latest methods attackers are using to infiltrate computer systems. Analysts need to research new security technology to decide what will most effectively protect their organization.

Work Environment

Information security analysts held about 168,900 jobs in 2022. The largest employers of information security analysts were as follows:

Many analysts work in IT departments and manage the security of their companies computer networks.

Computer systems design and related services	25%
Finance and insurance	16
Information	10
Management of companies and enterprises	9
Management, scientific, and technical consulting services	6

Many information security analysts work with other members of an information technology department, such as network administrators or computer systems analysts.

Work Schedules

Most information security analysts work full time, and some work more than 40 hours per week. Information security analysts sometimes have to be on call outside of normal business hours in case of an emergency.

How to Become an Information Security Analyst

Information security analysts typically need a bachelor's degree in a computer science field, along with related work experience.

There are a number of information security certifications available, and many employers prefer candidates to have certification.

Employers may prefer to hire analysts who have professional certification.

Education

Information security analysts typically need a bachelor's degree in computer and information technology or a related field, such as engineering or math. However, some workers enter the occupation with a high school diploma and relevant industry training and certifications.

Work Experience in a Related Occupation

Information security analysts may need to have work experience in a related occupation. Many analysts have experience in an information technology department, often as a network and computer systems administrator.

Licenses, Certifications, and Registrations

Many employers prefer to hire candidates who have information security certification. Some of these certifications, such as Security+, are for workers at the entry level; others, such as the Certified Information Systems Security Professional (CISSP), are designed for experienced information security workers. Certification in specialized areas, such as systems auditing, also is available.

Advancement

Information security analysts may advance to become chief security officers or another type of computer and information systems manager. Information security analysts also may advance within the occupation as they gain experience. For example, they may lead a team of other information security analysts or become an expert in a particular area of information security.

Important Qualities

Analytical skills. Information security analysts study computer systems and networks and assess risks to determine improvements for security policies and protocols.

Communication skills. Information security analysts must be able to explain information security needs and potential threats to technical and nontechnical audiences within their organizations.

Creative skills. Information security analysts must anticipate information security risks and implement new ways to protect their organizations' computer systems and networks.

Detail oriented. Because cyberattacks may be difficult to detect, information security analysts must pay careful attention to computer systems and watch for minor changes in performance.

Problem-solving skills. Information security analysts must respond to security alerts and uncover and fix flaws in computer systems and networks.

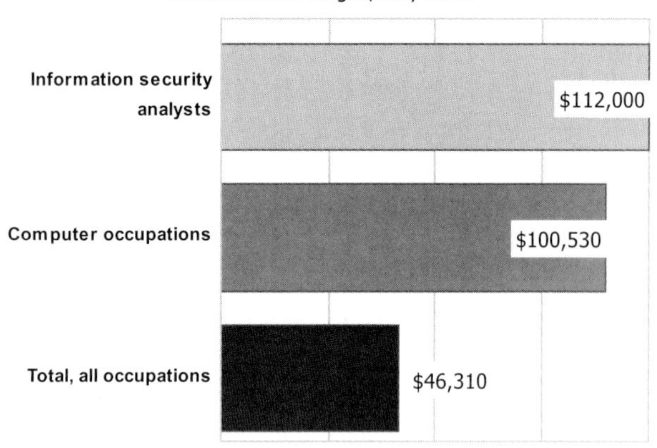

Note: All Occupations includes all occupations in the U.S. Economy.
Source: U.S. Bureau of Labor Statistics, Occupational Employment and Wage Statistics.

Pay

The median annual wage for information security analysts was $112,000 in May 2022. The median wage is the wage at which half the workers in an occupation earned more than that amount and half earned less. The lowest 10 percent earned less than $66,010, and the highest 10 percent earned more than $174,540.

In May 2022, the median annual wages for information security analysts in the top industries in which they worked were as follows:

Information	$131,910
Finance and insurance	122,810
Computer systems design and related services	119,270
Management of companies and enterprises	110,490
Management, scientific, and technical consulting services	108,440

Most information security analysts work full time, and some work more than 40 hours per week. Information security analysts sometimes have to be on call outside of normal business hours in case of an emergency.

Job Outlook

Employment of information security analysts is projected to grow 32 percent from 2022 to 2032, much faster than the average for all occupations.

About 16,800 openings for information security analysts are projected each year, on average, over the decade. Many of those openings are expected to result from the need to replace workers who transfer to different occupations or exit the labor force, such as to retire.

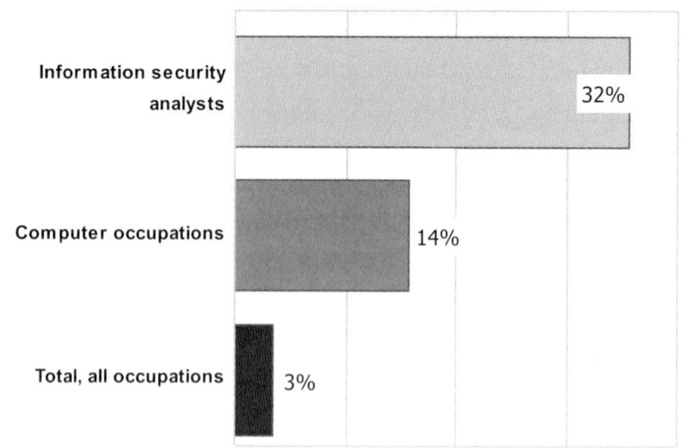

Note: All Occupations includes all occupations in the U.S. Economy.
Source: U.S. Bureau of Labor Statistics, Employment Projections program.

Employment

High demand is expected for information security analysts. Cyberattacks have grown in frequency, and these analysts will be needed to create innovative solutions to prevent hackers from stealing critical information or creating problems for computer networks.

As businesses focus on enhancing cybersecurity, they will need information security analysts to secure new technologies from outside threats or hacks. A shift to remote work and the rise of e-commerce have increased the need for enhanced security, contributing to the projected employment growth of these workers over the decade.

Strong growth in digital health services and telehealth will also increase data security risks for healthcare providers. More of these analysts are likely to be needed to safeguard patients' personal information and data.

Occupational Title	SOC Code	Employment, 2022	Projected Employment, 2032	Change, 2022-32	
				Percent	Numeric
Information security analysts	15-1212	168,900	222,200	32	53,200

Contacts for More Information

For more information about computer careers, visit

- Association for Computing Machinery
- Computing Research Association
- IEEE Computer Society
- National Center for Women & Information Technology

Network and Computer Systems Administrators

Summary

Quick Facts: Network and Computer Systems Administrators	
2022 Median Pay	$90,520 per year $43.52 per hour
Typical Entry-Level Education	Bachelor's degree
Work Experience in a Related Occupation	None
On-the-job Training	None
Number of Jobs, 2022	339,900
Job Outlook, 2022-32	2% (As fast as average)
Employment Change, 2022-32	8,300

What Network and Computer Systems Administrators Do

Network and computer systems administrators install, configure, and maintain organizations' computer networks and systems.

Work Environment

Network and computer systems administrators work for a variety of organizations, including computer systems design firms, schools, and financial institutions. Most work full time, and some work more than 40 hours per week. Administrators may work evenings, nights, and weekends to monitor, maintain, or update networks and systems.

How to Become a Network and Computer Systems Administrator

To enter the occupation, network and computer systems administrators typically need a bachelor's degree in a field related to computer or information science.

Administrators maintain network LANs, WANs, and intranets.

Pay

The median annual wage for network and computer systems administrators was $90,520 in May 2022.

Job Outlook

Employment of network and computer systems administrators is projected to grow 2 percent from 2022 to 2032, about as fast as the average for all occupations.

About 19,800 openings for network and computer systems administrators are projected each year, on average, over the decade. Many of those openings are expected to result from the need to replace workers who transfer to different occupations or exit the labor force, such as to retire.

What Network and Computer Systems Administrators Do

Network and computer systems administrators install, configure, and maintain organizations' local area networks (LANs), wide area networks (WANs), data communication networks, operating systems, and servers.

Duties

Network and computer systems administrators typically do the following:

Administrators fix computer server problems.

- Determine an organization's network and system needs and install operating and application hardware and software
- Provide input on hardware or software for an organization's purchasing decisions
- Make needed upgrades and repairs to networks and ensure that systems are operating correctly
- Maintain network and computer system security
- Evaluate and optimize network and system performance
- Add users to a network and assign security permissions
- Train users on the organization's network and systems
- Diagnose and resolve problems when alerted by a user or an automated monitoring system

Network and computer systems administrators may oversee both networks and systems, but they often specialize in one or the other. Network administrators typically focus on setting up and maintaining the infrastructure that connects an organization's computers. Systems administrators set up and maintain organizations' software and enable user access.

Network administrators install, configure, and manage computer infrastructure, such as routers, switches, and cables, that support an organization's computer networks. These networks include Local Area Networks (LANs), which connect devices in a single location, and Wide Area Networks (WANs), which connect multiple LANs or locations. They may help computer network architects design and analyze network models. Some administrators manage telecommunication networks.

Systems administrators manage an organization's servers and desktop and mobile equipment and software. They ensure that email and data storage networks within an organization's computer system work properly. They install and configure software and system updates and monitor system performance to ensure that employees' workstations are efficient.

Some administrators provide technical support to users, such as when computer support specialists are unable to resolve a problem.

Work Environment

Network and computer systems administrators held about 339,900 jobs in 2022. The largest employers of network and computer systems administrators were as follows:

Computer systems design and related services	17%
Educational services; state, local, and private	11
Finance and insurance	9
Information	9
Management of companies and enterprises	7

Network and computer systems administrators are employed by a variety of organizations and work in a variety of settings. In addition to those shown in the table, top employers also include manufacturing industries, healthcare providers, and government agencies.

Network and computer systems administrators collaborate with other IT workers

Network and computer systems administrators often collaborate with many types of information technology (IT) workers, such as computer support specialists, database administrators, computer network architects, and computer and information systems managers.

Work Schedules

Most network and computer systems administrators work full time, and some work more than 40 hours per week. Administrators may need to work evenings, nights, or weekends to monitor, maintain, or update networks and systems.

How to Become a Network and Computer Systems Administrator

To enter the occupation, network and computer systems administrators typically need a bachelor's degree in a field related to computer or information science. Others may require a postsecondary certificate or an associate's degree.

Education

Some employers require a postsecondary certificate or an associate's degree. However, network and computer systems administrators typically need a bachelor's degree in computer and information technology or a related field, such as engineering. These programs usually include courses in computer programming, networking, and systems design.

Network and computer systems administrators need to keep up with developments in the constantly changing field of information technology (IT). They may continue to take courses throughout their careers and attend IT conferences to keep up with the latest technology.

Licenses, Certifications, and Registrations

Employers may require their network and computer systems administrators to be certified in the products they use. Certification programs usually are offered directly from vendors or from vendor-neutral certification providers. Certification

Administrators need analytical skills to ensure that networks and systems perform reliably

validates the knowledge and the use of best practices that are required of network and computer systems administrators.

Advancement

Network administrators may advance to become computer network architects. They also may advance to managerial jobs in IT departments, such as computer and information systems managers.

Important Qualities

Analytical skills. Administrators need to evaluate networks and systems to make sure that they perform reliably and to anticipate new requirements as organizations' needs change.

Communication skills. Administrators should be able to explain technical concepts and processes to non-IT workers.

Creative skills. Administrators may need to take an innovative approach to make networks or systems work, such as when integrating new products with existing hardware or software.

Multitasking skills. Administrators may have to work on many tasks at the same time, whether setup, monitoring, or troubleshooting.

Problem-solving skills. Administrators must be able to resolve problems that arise with computer networks and systems.

Technical skills. Administrators need programming skills and the ability to work with a variety of computer hardware and software.

Pay

The median annual wage for network and computer systems administrators was $90,520 in May 2022. The median wage is the wage at which half the workers in an occupation earned more than that amount and half earned less. The lowest 10 percent earned less than $56,260, and the highest 10 percent earned more than $140,430.

In May 2022, the median annual wages for network and computer systems administrators in the top industries in which they worked were as follows:

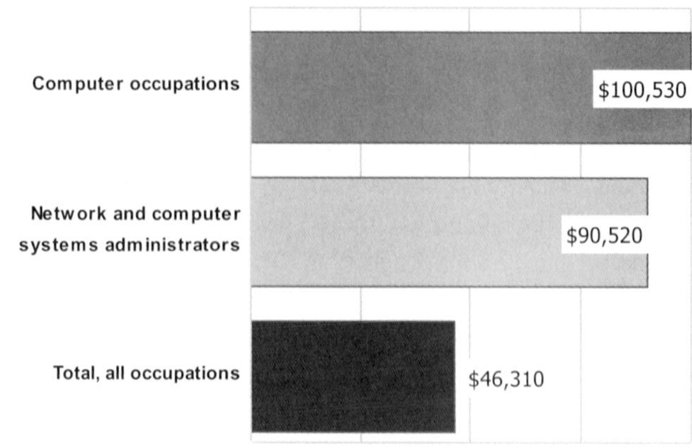

Note: All Occupations includes all occupations in the U.S. Economy.
Source: U.S. Bureau of Labor Statistics, Occupational Employment and Wage Statistics.

Information	$100,880
Management of companies and enterprises	100,400
Finance and insurance	98,770
Computer systems design and related services	92,230
Educational services; state, local, and private	80,620

Most network and computer systems administrators work full time, and some work more than 40 hours per week. Administrators may need to work evenings, nights, or weekends to monitor, maintain, or update networks and systems.

Job Outlook

Employment of network and computer systems administrators is projected to grow 2 percent from 2022 to 2032, about as fast as the average for all occupations.

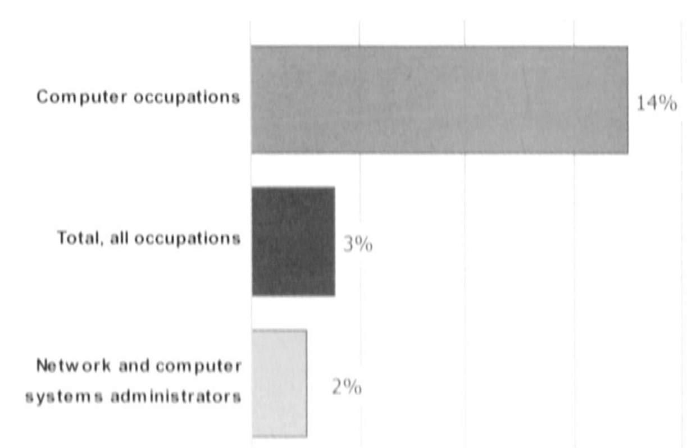

Note: All Occupations includes all occupations in the U.S. Economy.
Source: U.S. Bureau of Labor Statistics, Employment Projections program.

About 19,800 openings for network and computer systems administrators are projected each year, on average, over the decade. Many of those openings are expected to result from the need to replace workers who transfer to different occupations or exit the labor force, such as to retire.

Employment

Demand for network and computer systems administrators should continue, along with firms' investment in newer, faster technology and mobile networks. The continued expansion of cloud computing and the demand for upgraded computer equipment and software will support a need for network and computer systems administrators to maintain these systems.

Occupational Title	SOC Code	Employment, 2022	Projected Employment, 2032	Change, 2022-32	
				Percent	Numeric
Network and computer systems administrators	15-1244	339,900	348,200	2	8,300

Contacts for More Information

For more information about computer careers, visit

- Association for Computing Machinery
- CompTIA
- IEEE Computer Society
- National Center for Women & Information Technology

Software Developers, Quality Assurance Analysts, and Testers

Summary

Quick Facts: Software Developers, Quality Assurance Analysts, and Testers

2022 Median Pay	$124,200 per year $59.71 per hour
Typical Entry-Level Education	Bachelor's degree
Work Experience in a Related Occupation	None
On-the-job Training	None
Number of Jobs, 2022	1,795,300
Job Outlook, 2022-32	25% (Much faster than average)
Employment Change, 2022-32	451,200

What Software Developers, Quality Assurance Analysts, and Testers Do

Software developers design computer applications or programs. Software quality assurance analysts and testers identify problems with applications or programs and report defects.

Software developers design computer programs.

Work Environment

Many software developers, quality assurance analysts, and testers work in computer systems design and related services, in manufacturing, or for software publishers. They often work in offices and on teams with other software developers or quality assurance analysts and testers.

How to Become a Software Developer, Quality Assurance Analyst, or Tester

Software developers, quality assurance analysts, and testers typically need a bachelor's degree in computer and information technology or a related field. Some employers prefer to hire developers who have a master's degree.

Pay

The median annual wage for software developers was $127,260 in May 2022.

The median annual wage for software quality assurance analysts and testers was $99,620 in May 2022.

Job Outlook

Overall employment of software developers, quality assurance analysts, and testers is projected to grow 25 percent from 2022 to 2032, much faster than the average for all occupations.

About 153,900 openings for software developers, quality assurance analysts, and testers are projected each year, on average, over the decade. Many of those openings are expected to result from the need to replace workers who transfer to different occupations or exit the labor force, such as to retire.

What Software Developers, Quality Assurance Analysts, and Testers Do

Software developers create the computer applications that allow users to do specific tasks and the underlying systems that run the devices or control networks. Software quality assurance analysts and testers design and execute software tests to identify problems and learn how the software works.

Developers create diagrams that help programmers write computer code.

Duties

Software developers typically do the following:

- Analyze users' needs and then design and develop software to meet those needs
- Recommend software upgrades for customers' existing programs and systems
- Design each piece of an application or system and plan how the pieces will work together
- Create a variety of models and diagrams showing programmers the software code needed for an application
- Ensure that a program continues to function normally through software maintenance and testing
- Document every aspect of an application or system as a reference for future maintenance and upgrades

Software quality assurance analysts and testers typically do the following:

- Create test plans, scenarios, and procedures for new software
- Identify project risks and recommend steps to minimize those risks
- Implement software testing, using either manual or automated programs and exploratory testing, and evaluate results
- Document and report defects or problems with software
- Provide feedback to software developers and stakeholders regarding usability and functionality

Software developers, quality assurance analysts, and testers are involved in the entire process of creating a software program. Developers may begin by asking how the customer plans to use the software so that they can identify the core functionality the user needs. Software developers also determine other requirements, such as security. They design the program and then work closely with programmers, who write computer code. However, some developers write code themselves instead of giving instructions to programmers.

Software quality assurance analysts and testers design and execute systems to check the software for problems. As part of their testing, these workers document and track the software's potential defects or risks. They also assess its usability and functionality to identify difficulties a user might have. After completing testing, they report the results to software or web developers and review ways to solve any problems they found.

After the program is released to the customer, a developer may perform upgrades and maintenance. Quality assurance analysts and testers run manual and automated checks to look for errors and usability problems once the software is released and after any upgrades or maintenance.

The following are examples of types of software developers:

Applications software developers design computer applications, such as games, for consumers. They may create custom software for a specific customer or commercial software to be sold to the general public. Some applications software developers create databases or programs for use internally or online.

Software engineers take a broad view of a project's system and software requirements, planning its scope and order of work. These workers may direct software developers, quality assurance analysts, and testers.

Systems software developers create the operating systems for the public or specifically for an organization. These operating systems keep computers functioning and control most of the consumer electronics in use today, including those in cell phones and cars. Often, systems software developers also build the interface that allows users to interact with the computer.

Developers who supervise a software project from the planning stages through implementation sometimes are called information technology (IT) project managers. These workers monitor the project's progress to ensure that it meets deadlines, standards, and cost targets. For information on IT project managers who plan and direct an organization's IT department or IT policies, see the profile on computer and information systems (CIS) managers.

Work Environment

Software developers held about 1.6 million jobs in 2022. The largest employers of software developers were as follows:

Computer systems design and related services	33%
Software publishers	11
Finance and insurance	10
Manufacturing	8
Management of companies and enterprises	5

Software quality assurance analysts and testers held about 200,800 jobs in 2022. The largest employers of software quality assurance analysts and testers were as follows:

Computer systems design and related services	32%

Developers may oversee a team of people during the software development process.

Finance and insurance	11
Software publishers	10
Manufacturing	7
Administrative and support services	7

Developing software is usually a collaborative process. As a result, developers, quality assurance analysts, and testers work on teams with others who also contribute to designing, developing, and programming successful software.

Work Schedules

Most software developers, quality assurance analysts, and testers work full time.

How to Become a Software Developer, Quality Assurance Analyst, or Tester

Software developers, quality assurance analysts, and testers typically need a bachelor's degree in computer and information technology or a related field. Some employers prefer to hire developers who have a master's degree.

Software developers, quality assurance analysts, and testers typically need a bachelor's degree.

Education

Software developers, quality assurance analysts, and testers typically need a bachelor's degree in computer and information technology or a related field, such as engineering or mathematics. Computer and information technology degree programs cover a broad range of topics. Students may gain experience in software development by completing an internship, such as at a software company, while in college. For some software developer positions, employers may prefer that applicants have a master's degree.

Although writing code is not their primary responsibility, developers must have a strong background in computer programming. They usually gain this experience in school. Throughout their career, developers must keep up to date on new tools and computer languages.

Advancement

Software developers can advance to become project management specialists or computer and information systems managers, positions in which they oversee the software development process.

Important Qualities

Analytical skills. Software developers, quality assurance analysts, and testers must evaluate users' needs and then design software to function properly and meet those needs.

Communication skills. These workers must be able to give clear instructions and explain problems that arise to other team members involved in development. They must also be able to explain to nontechnical users, such as customers, how the software works and answer any questions that arise.

Creativity. Software developers, quality assurance analysts, and testers must be innovative in their approaches to designing, identifying problems with, and improving computer software.

Detail oriented. These workers often need to concentrate on many parts of an application or system at the same time, and they must pay attention to detail when looking for potential areas of user error.

Interpersonal skills. Software developers, quality assurance analysts, and testers must be able to work well with others who contribute to designing, programming, and testing successful software.

Problem-solving skills. Because these workers produce software from beginning to end, they must be able to solve problems that arise throughout the design process.

Pay

The median annual wage for software developers was $127,260 in May 2022. The median wage is the wage at which half the workers in an occupation earned more than that amount and half earned less. The lowest 10 percent earned less than $71,280, and the highest 10 percent earned more than $198,100.

Software Developers, Quality Assurance Analysts, and Testers

Median annual wages, May 2022

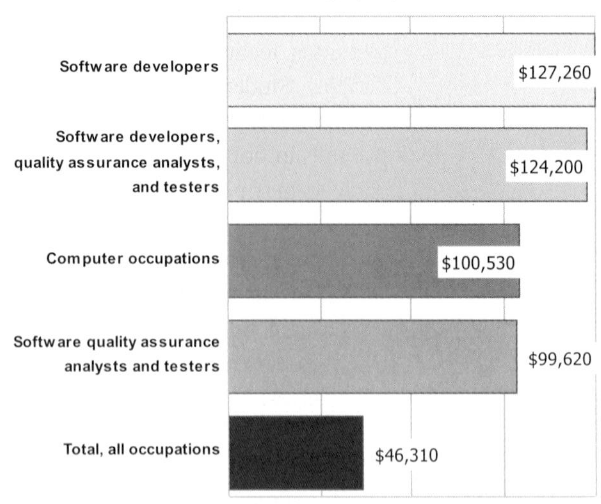

Note: All Occupations includes all occupations in the U.S. Economy.
Source: U.S. Bureau of Labor Statistics, Occupational Employment and Wage Statistics.

The median annual wage for software quality assurance analysts and testers was $99,620 in May 2022. The lowest 10 percent earned less than $55,510, and the highest 10 percent earned more than $159,740.

In May 2022, the median annual wages for software developers in the top industries in which they worked were as follows:

Software publishers	$134,430
Manufacturing	132,130
Finance and insurance	128,960
Management of companies and enterprises	127,880
Computer systems design and related services	112,510

In May 2022, the median annual wages for software quality assurance analysts and testers in the top industries in which they worked were as follows:

Manufacturing	$105,280
Software publishers	101,820
Finance and insurance	97,350
Computer systems design and related services	96,880
Administrative and support services	93,560

Most software developers, quality assurance analysts, and testers work full time.

Job Outlook

Overall employment of software developers, quality assurance analysts, and testers is projected to grow 25 percent from 2022 to 2032, much faster than the average for all occupations.

About 153,900 openings for software developers, quality assurance analysts, and testers are projected each year, on average, over the decade. Many of those openings are expected to result from the need to replace workers who transfer to different occupations or exit the labor force, such as to retire.

Software Developers, Quality Assurance Analysts, and Testers

Percent change in employment, projected 2022-32

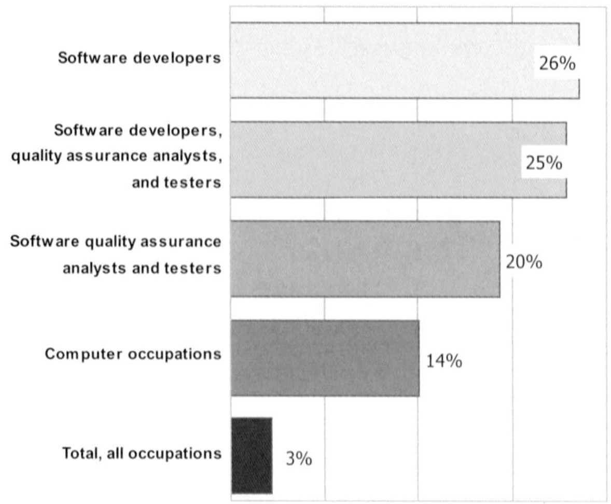

Note: All Occupations includes all occupations in the U.S. Economy.
Source: U.S. Bureau of Labor Statistics, Employment Projections program.

Employment

Increased demand for software developers, software quality assurance analysts, and testers will stem from the continued expansion of software development for artificial intelligence (AI), Internet of Things (IoT), robotics, and other automation applications.

In response to concerns over threats to computer security, organizations are expected to increase investment in software that protects their electronic networks and infrastructure. This investment could result in an increased demand for developers to create security software and for quality assurance analysts and testers to create and execute software tests.

Software developers, software quality assurance analysts, and testers are likely to see new opportunities because of the increasing number of products that use software. For example, software systems continue to be built for consumer electronics and other products, including IoT-connected devices and electric vehicles.

Occupational Title	SOC Code	Employment, 2022	Projected Employment, 2032	Change, 2022-32	
				Percent	Numeric
Software developers, quality assurance analysts, and testers	—	1,795,300	2,246,500	25	451,200
Software developers	15-1252	1,594,500	2,004,900	26	410,400
Software quality assurance analysts and testers	15-1253	200,800	241,600	20	40,800

Contacts for More Information

For more information about software developers, quality assurance analysts, and testers, visit

- Association for Computing Machinery
- Association for Software Testing
- IEEE Computer Society
- Computing Research Association
- CompTIA
- National Center for Women & Information Technology

Web Developers and Digital Designers

Summary

Quick Facts: Web Developers and Digital Designers	
2022 Median Pay	$80,730 per year $38.81 per hour
Typical Entry-Level Education	Bachelor's degree
Work Experience in a Related Occupation	None
On-the-job Training	None
Number of Jobs, 2022	216,700
Job Outlook, 2022-32	16% (Much faster than average)
Employment Change, 2022-32	34,700

What Web Developers and Digital Designers Do

Web developers create and maintain websites. Digital designers develop, create, and test website or interface layout, functions, and navigation for usability.

Work Environment

Some web developers and digital designers work in the computer systems design and related services industry. Others are self-employed. Still others work in industries including publishing, management consulting, and advertising.

How to Become a Web Developer or Digital Designer

Educational requirements for web developers and digital designers vary, ranging from a high school diploma to a bachelor's degree.

Pay

The median annual wage for web and digital interface designers was $83,240 in May 2022.

The median annual wage for web developers was $78,580 in May 2022.

Job Outlook

Overall employment of web developers and digital designers is projected to grow 16 percent from 2022 to 2032, much faster than the average for all occupations.

About 19,000 openings for web developers and digital designers are projected each year, on average, over the decade. Many of those openings are expected to result from the need to replace workers who transfer to different occupations or exit the labor force, such as to retire.

What Web Developers and Digital Designers Do

Web developers create and maintain websites. They are also responsible for the site's technical aspects, such as its performance and capacity, which are measures of a website's speed and how much traffic the site can handle. In addition, web developers may create content for the site. Digital designers develop, create, and test website or interface layout, functions, and navigation for usability. They are responsible for the look and functionality of the website or interface.

Duties

Web developers and digital designers typically do the following:

Web developers are responsible for both the look of a website and its technical aspects.

Some developers work with graphics and other designers to determine the website's layout.

- Meet with clients or management to discuss the needs, design, and functionality of a website or interface
- Create and test applications, interfaces, and navigation menus for a website
- Write code for the website, using programming languages such as HTML or XML
- Work with other team members to determine what information the site will contain
- Work with graphics and other designers to determine the website's layout
- Integrate graphics, audio, and video into the website
- Monitor website traffic
- Create prototypes and mockups of websites or applications
- Design and develop graphics

When creating a website, developers and designers have to make their client's vision a reality. They build particular types of websites, such as ecommerce, news, or gaming sites, to fit clients' needs. Different types of websites require different applications. For example, a gaming site should be able to handle advanced graphics, whereas an ecommerce site would need a payment-processing application. The developer decides which applications and designs will best fit the site, and the designer focuses on the look and usability of these elements across browsers or devices.

Some developers and designers handle all aspects of a website's construction, and others specialize in a certain aspect of it. The following are examples of types of specialized web developers or digital designers:

Back-end web developers are responsible for the overall technical construction of the website. They create the basic framework of the site and ensure that it functions as expected. Back-end web developers also establish procedures for allowing others to add new pages to the website and meet with management to discuss major changes to the site.

Front-end web developers create the technical features for a website's look. They develop the site's layout and integrate graphics, applications (such as a retail checkout tool), and other content. They also write webdesign programs in a variety of computer languages, such as HTML or JavaScript.

Web and digital interface designers are responsible for creating the look and feel of a website or interface with regard to photos, color, font type and size, graphics, and layout. They also are responsible for the functionality, usability, and compatibility of the website or interface.

Webmasters maintain and update websites. They ensure that websites operate correctly, and they test for errors such as broken links. Many webmasters respond to user comments as well.

Work Environment

Web and digital interface designers held about 117,900 jobs in 2022. The largest employers of web and digital interface designers were as follows:

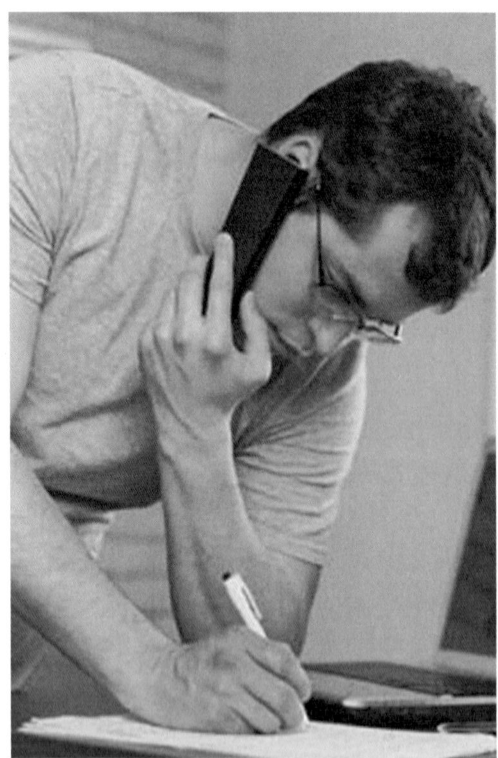

Developers build websites for all types of businesses.

Computer systems design and related services	17%
Self-employed workers	13
Retail trade	7
Finance and insurance	5
Advertising, public relations, and related services	4

Web developers held about 98,800 jobs in 2022. The largest employers of web developers were as follows:

Computer systems design and related services	21%
Educational services; state, local, and private	7
Self-employed workers	7
Management, scientific, and technical consulting services	6
Software publishers	6

Work Schedules

Most web developers and digital designers work full time.

How to Become a Web Developer or Digital Designer

Educational requirements vary for web developers and digital designers, based on work setting and other factors.

Education

Educational requirements for web developers and digital designers range from a high school diploma to a bachelor's degree.

Developers often have both programming and graphic design knowledge.

Some employers prefer to hire web developer candidates who have a bachelor's degree in a specific field, such as computer science or programming.

Web developers need to have a thorough understanding of HTML programming. Many employers also want developers to understand other programming languages, such as JavaScript or SQL, and have knowledge of multimedia publishing tools, such as Flash. Throughout their career, web developers must keep up to date on new tools and computer languages.

Employers of digital designers may prefer to hire candidates who have a bachelor's degree in a field such as web design, digital design, or graphic arts.

Web developers and digital designers may not need specific education credentials if they can demonstrate their abilities through prior work experience or projects.

Advancement

Web developers and digital designers who have a bachelor's degree may advance to become project managers. For more information, see the profile on computer and information systems managers.

Important Qualities

Communication skills. Web developers and digital designers need to communicate effectively with coworkers to coordinate work on projects.

Creativity. Web developers and digital designers often are involved in creating the appearance of a website and must make sure that it is appealing as well as functional.

Customer-service skills. Webmasters have to respond politely to user questions and requests.

Detail oriented. Web developers and digital designers must focus for long periods and write code precisely, because a minor error could cause an entire webpage to stop working.

Problem-solving skills. Web developers and digital designers must check for coding errors and fix any that they find.

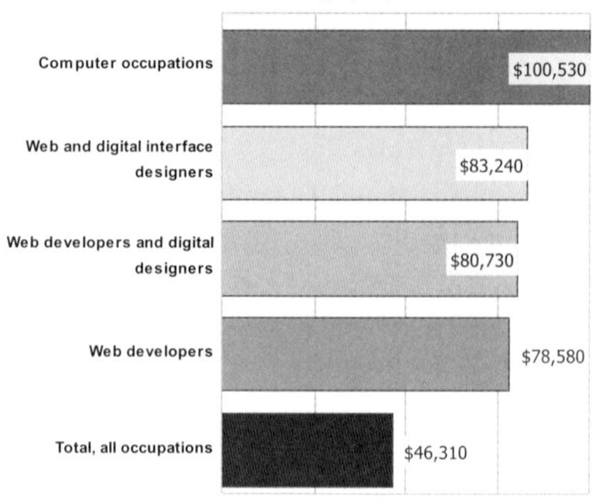

Note: All Occupations includes all occupations in the U.S. Economy.
Source: U.S. Bureau of Labor Statistics, Occupational Employment and Wage Statistics.

Pay

The median annual wage for web and digital interface designers was $83,240 in May 2022. The median wage is the wage at which half the workers in an occupation earned more than that amount and half earned less. The lowest 10 percent earned less than $43,100, and the highest 10 percent earned more than $166,180.

The median annual wage for web developers was $78,580 in May 2022. The lowest 10 percent earned less than $40,460, and the highest 10 percent earned more than $144,690.

In May 2022, the median annual wages for web and digital interface designers in the top industries in which they worked were as follows:

Finance and insurance	$105,360
Computer systems design and related services	85,040
Advertising, public relations, and related services	71,720
Retail trade	60,150

In May 2022, the median annual wages for web developers in the top industries in which they worked were as follows:

Software publishers	$138,010
Management, scientific, and technical consulting services	80,270
Computer systems design and related services	72,740
Educational services; state, local, and private	69,840

Most web developers and digital designers work full time.

Job Outlook

Overall employment of web developers and digital designers is projected to grow 16 percent from 2022 to 2032, much faster than the average for all occupations.

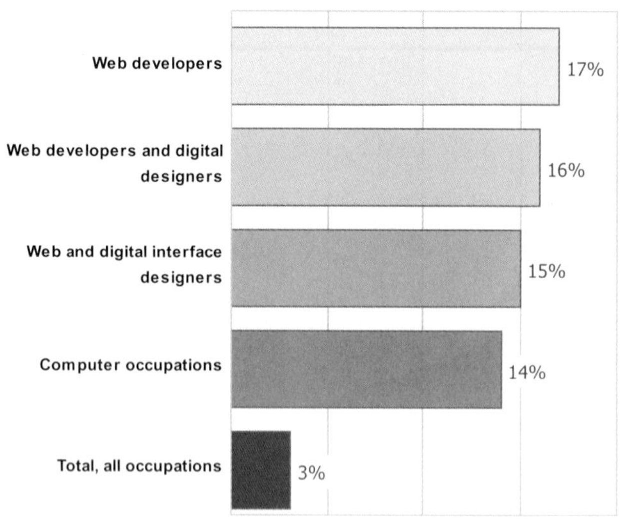

Note: All Occupations includes all occupations in the U.S. Economy.
Source: U.S. Bureau of Labor Statistics, Employment Projections program.

About 19,000 openings for web developers and digital designers are projected each year, on average, over the decade. Many of those openings are expected to result from the need to replace workers who transfer to different occupations or exit the labor force, such as to retire.

Employment

Employment of web developers and digital designers is projected to grow as e-commerce continues to expand. As retail firms keep increasing their online offerings, demand for these workers is expected to grow. In addition, the continued use of mobile devices to search the web is expected to generate demand for web developers and digital designers to create websites and interfaces that work on mobile devices with many different screen sizes.

Occupational Title	SOC Code	Employment, 2022	Projected Employment, 2032	Change, 2022-32	
				Percent	Numeric
Web developers and digital designers	—	216,700	251,300	16	34,700
Web developers	15-1254	98,800	115,500	17	16,700
Web and digital interface designers	15-1255	117,900	135,800	15	17,900

Contacts for More Information

For more information about web developers and digital designers, visit

- World Organization of Webmasters
- Association for Computing Machinery
- Computing Research Association
- IEEE Computer Society
- National Center for Women & Information Technology

Construction and Extraction

Boilermakers

Summary

Quick Facts: Boilermakers	
2022 Median Pay	$66,920 per year $32.17 per hour
Typical Entry-Level Education	High school diploma or equivalent
Work Experience in a Related Occupation	None
On-the-job Training	Apprenticeship
Number of Jobs, 2022	13,700
Job Outlook, 2022-32	-4% (Decline)
Employment Change, 2022-32	-500

What Boilermakers Do

Boilermakers assemble, install, maintain, and repair boilers, closed vats, and other large vessels or containers that hold liquids and gases.

Work Environment

Boilermakers do physically demanding work. They may travel to worksites and be away from home for extended periods.

How to Become a Boilermaker

Boilermakers typically learn their trade through an apprenticeship program.

Pay

The median annual wage for boilermakers was $66,920 in May 2022.

Boilermakers assemble and install containers that hold liquids and gases.

Job Outlook

Employment of boilermakers is projected to decline 4 percent from 2022 to 2032.

Despite declining employment, about 1,100 openings for boilermakers are projected each year, on average, over the decade. All of those openings are expected to result from the need to replace workers who transfer to other occupations or exit the labor force, such as to retire.

What Boilermakers Do

Boilermakers assemble, install, maintain, and repair boilers, closed vats, and other large vessels or containers that hold liquids and gases.

Duties

Boilermakers typically do the following:

- Read blueprints to determine locations, positions, and dimensions of boiler parts
- Install small, premade boilers in buildings and manufacturing facilities

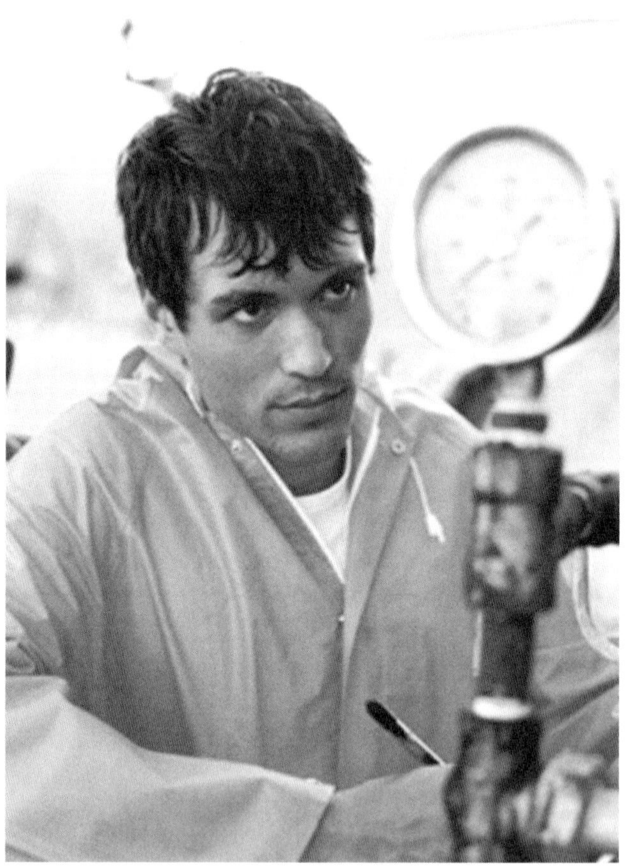

Boilermakers install and maintain boiler systems.

- Lay out prefabricated parts of large boilers before assembling them
- Assemble boiler tanks, often using robotic or automatic welders
- Test and inspect boiler systems for leaks or defects
- Clean vats with scrapers, wire brushes, and cleaning solvents
- Replace or repair broken valves, pipes, or joints, using hand and power tools, gas torches, and welding equipment

Boilers, tanks, and vats are used in many buildings, factories, and ships. Boilers heat water or other fluids under extreme pressure to generate electric power and to provide heat. Large tanks and vats are used to process and store chemicals, oil, beer, and hundreds of other products.

Boilers are made of steel, iron, copper, or stainless steel. Most manufacturers have automated the production of boilers for improved quality. However, boilermakers still assemble and maintain boilers manually. For example, they often use hand and power tools and flame-cutting torches to align, cut, and shape pieces for a boiler. Boilermakers also use plumb bobs, levels, wedges, and turnbuckles to align pieces.

During a boiler installation, boilermakers align boilerplates and boiler parts, using metalworking machinery and other tools to remove irregular edges so that the parts fit together properly. If the plate sections are very large, boilermakers signal crane operators to lift the plates into place. Boilermakers then join the plates and parts by bolting, welding, and riveting them together.

Boilermakers may help erect and repair air pollution abatement equipment, blast furnaces, water treatment plants, storage and process tanks, and smokestacks. Boilermakers also install refractory brick and other heat-resistant materials in fireboxes or pressure vessels. Some install and maintain the huge pipes used in dams to send water to and from hydroelectric power generation turbines.

During regular maintenance, boilermakers inspect systems and their components, including safety and check valves, water and pressure gauges, and boiler controls. They also clean boilers and boiler furnaces and repair and replace parts, as needed.

Work Environment

Boilermakers held about 13,700 jobs in 2022. The largest employers of boilermakers were as follows:

Utility system construction	18%
Nonresidential building construction	16
Plumbing, heating, and air-conditioning contractors	14
Fabricated metal product manufacturing	6
Other building equipment contractors	2

Boilermakers do physically demanding work in cramped spaces inside boilers, vats, or tanks that are often dark, damp, noisy, and poorly ventilated. They frequently work outdoors in all types of weather, including extreme heat and cold.

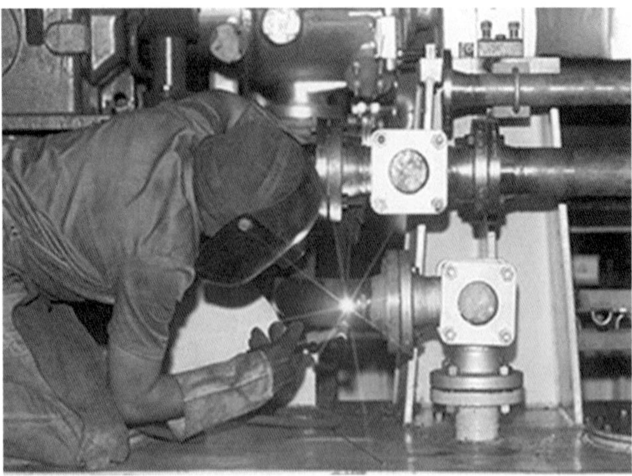

Boilermakers must wear protective gear to reduce injuries.

Because dams, boilers, storage tanks, and pressure vessels are large, boilermakers frequently work at great heights. For example, they may be hundreds of feet above the ground when working on a dam.

Injuries and Illnesses

The work that boilermakers do can be dangerous. Workers must follow specific safety procedures to avoid injuries and illnesses and must be mindful of potential dangers to themselves and their coworkers. To reduce the risk of injury, boilermakers wear hardhats, earplugs, safety glasses, and other protective equipment. When working in enclosed spaces, boilermakers often wear a respirator.

Work Schedules

Most boilermakers work full time, and work schedules may vary. Boilermakers may experience extended periods of overtime when equipment is shut down for maintenance or repair, or when necessary to meet construction or production deadlines. In contrast, because most field construction and repair is contract work, there may be periods of unemployment upon completion of a contract.

Boilermakers may travel to worksites and be away from home for extended periods.

How to Become a Boilermaker

Most boilermakers learn their trade through an apprenticeship program.

Education

A high school diploma or equivalent is generally required.

Training

Boilermakers typically learn their trade through an apprenticeship program. During training, workers learn how to use boilermaker tools and equipment on the job. They also learn about metals and installation techniques, blueprint reading and sketching, safety practices, and other topics.

Candidates have a better chance to be accepted into training programs if they have welding experience.

Apprenticeship programs typically last 4 years. When boilermakers finish an apprenticeship, they are considered to be journey-level workers. A few groups, including unions and contractor associations, sponsor apprenticeship programs.

Apprenticeship applicants who have previous welding or other related experience, such as through the military, may have priority over applicants without experience. In addition, those with experience or education may qualify for a shortened apprenticeship.

Some boilermakers enter apprenticeships after working as pipefitters, millwrights, sheet metal workers, or welders. The core training for these occupations is similar to the training for boilermakers.

Licenses, Certifications, and Registrations

Some states require boilermakers to have a license; check with your state for more information. Licensure requirements typically include work experience and passing an exam.

Employers may require or prefer that boilermakers hold certification from the National Center for Construction Education and Research (NCCER). Welding certifications may also be helpful.

Important Qualities

Mechanical skills. Boilermakers use and maintain a variety of equipment, such as hoists and welding machines.

Physical stamina. Boilermakers spend many hours on their feet while lifting heavy boiler components.

Physical strength. Boilermakers must be able to move heavy vat components into place.

Unafraid of confined spaces. Boilermakers often work inside boilers and vats.

Unafraid of heights. Some boilermakers work at great heights. While installing water storage tanks, for example, workers may need to weld tanks several stories above the ground.

Pay

The median annual wage for boilermakers was $66,920 in May 2022. The median wage is the wage at which half the workers in an occupation earned more than that amount and half earned less. The lowest 10 percent earned less than $46,560, and the highest 10 percent earned more than $95,700.

In May 2022, the median annual wages for boilermakers in the top industries in which they worked were as follows:

Nonresidential building construction	$77,020
Utility system construction	74,250
Other building equipment contractors	68,680
Plumbing, heating, and air-conditioning contractors	63,740
Fabricated metal product manufacturing	58,150

Apprentices receive less pay than fully trained boilermakers. They receive pay increases as they learn more skills.

Most boilermakers work full time, and work schedules may vary. Boilermakers may experience extended periods of

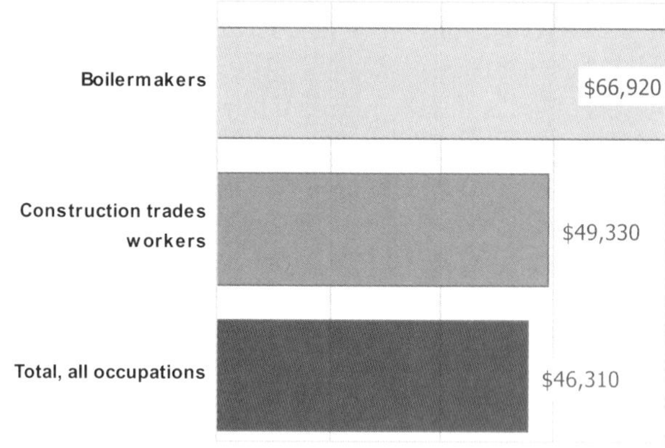

Note: All Occupations includes all occupations in the U.S. Economy.
Source: U.S. Bureau of Labor Statistics, Occupational Employment and Wage Statistics.

overtime when equipment is shut down for maintenance or repair, or when necessary to meet construction or production deadlines. In contrast, because most field construction and repair work is contract work, there may be periods of unemployment upon completion of a contract.

Boilermakers may travel to worksites and be away from home for extended periods.

Job Outlook

Employment of boilermakers is projected to decline 4 percent from 2022 to 2032.

Despite declining employment, about 1,100 openings for boilermakers are projected each year, on average, over the decade. All of those openings are expected to result from the need to replace workers who transfer to other occupations or exit the labor force, such as to retire.

Employment

Boilers typically last for decades, but there will be an ongoing need for boilermakers to replace and maintain parts, such as boiler tubes, heating elements, and ductwork. Boilermakers will also continue to be needed to install new equipment, including boilers, pressure vessels, air pollution abatement equipment, and storage and process tanks.

However, the shift away from coal-fired electricity generation will reduce the need for boilermakers. Renewable photovoltaic and wind generation systems do not have boilers, and natural gas plants require less ongoing boiler maintenance than coal plants.

Employment projections data for boilermakers, 2022-32

Occupational Title	SOC Code	Employment, 2022	Projected Employment, 2032	Change, 2022-32 Percent	Change, 2022-32 Numeric	Employment by Industry
SOURCE: U.S. Bureau of Labor Statistics, Employment Projections program						
Boilermakers	47-2011	13,700	13,100	-4	-500	Get data

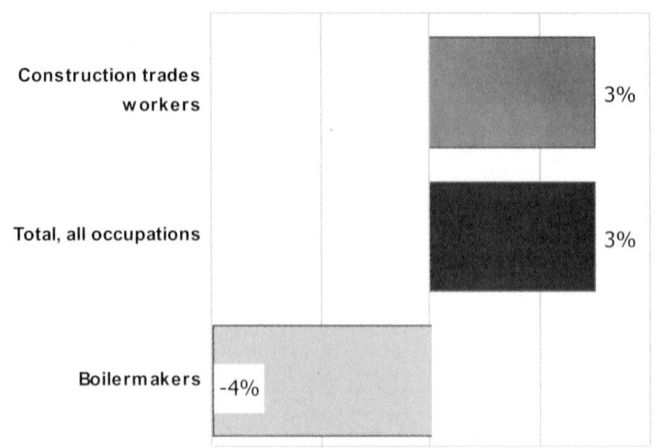

Note: All Occupations includes all occupations in the U.S. Economy.
Source: U.S. Bureau of Labor Statistics, Employment Projections program.

Contacts for More Information

Apprenticeship information is available from the U.S. Department of Labor's Apprenticeship program online, or by phone at 877-872-5627. Visit Apprenticeship.gov to search for apprenticeship opportunities.

For more information visit

- Boilermakers National Apprenticeship Program
- International Brotherhood of Boilermakers, Iron Ship Builders, Blacksmiths, Forgers and Helpers
- National Center for Construction Education and Research (NCCER)
- American Welding Society
- Helmet to Hardhats

Carpenters

Summary

Quick Facts: Carpenters

2022 Median Pay	$51,390 per year $24.71 per hour
Typical Entry-Level Education	High school diploma or equivalent
Work Experience in a Related Occupation	None
On-the-job Training	Apprenticeship
Number of Jobs, 2022	956,300
Job Outlook, 2022-32	1% (Little or no change)
Employment Change, 2022-32	8,600

What Carpenters Do
Carpenters construct, repair, and install building frameworks and structures made from wood and other materials.

Work Environment
Carpenters work indoors and outdoors on many types of construction projects, from installing kitchen cabinets to building highways and bridges.

How to Become a Carpenter
Carpenters typically learn on the job and through apprenticeships.

Pay
The median annual wage for carpenters was $51,390 in May 2022.

Job Outlook
Employment of carpenters is projected to show little or no change from 2022 to 2032.

Despite limited employment growth, about 79,500 openings for carpenters are projected each year, on average, over the decade. Most of those openings are expected to result from the need to replace workers who transfer to different occupations or exit the labor force, such as to retire.

Carpenters are involved in many different types of construction.

What Carpenters Do
Carpenters construct, repair, and install building frameworks and structures made from wood and other materials.

Duties
Carpenters typically do the following:

- Follow blueprints and building plans to meet the needs of clients
- Install structures and fixtures, such as windows and molding
- Measure, cut, and shape wood, plastic, and other materials
- Construct and install building frameworks, including walls, floors, and doorframes
- Inspect and replace damaged framework or other structures and fixtures
- Instruct and direct laborers and other construction helpers

Carpenters have many different tasks. Some carpenters insulate office buildings; others install drywall or kitchen cabinets in homes. Still others focus on production or commercial work

Carpenters work with different tools.

to help construct tall buildings or bridges, installing wooden concrete forms for cement footings or pillars. These carpenters also erect shoring and scaffolding for buildings.

Carpenters use many different tools to cut and shape wood, plastic, fiberglass, or drywall. They use handtools, including squares, levels, and chisels, as well as many power tools, such as sanders, circular saws, nail guns, and welding machines. On large projects, carpenters may use rigging hardware and cranes as part of the installation process. Carpenters may also use smart phones, tablets, and other personal electronic devices to assist with planning, drafting, or other calculations.

Carpenters fasten materials with nails, screws, staples, and adhesives and check their work to ensure that it is correct. They use tape measures or laser measures on nearly every project to quickly determine distances. Many employers require carpenters to supply their own tools on the job.

The following are examples of types of carpenters:

Construction carpenters construct, install, and repair structures and fixtures of wood, plywood, and wallboard, using carpenters' handtools and power tools.

Rough carpenters build rough wooden structures, such as concrete forms; scaffolds; tunnel, bridge, or sewer supports; and temporary frame shelters, according to sketches, blueprints, or oral instructions.

Wood flooring installers put in a variety of materials, including plank, strip, end-grain, and parquet flooring. These wood products may be nailed in place or glued down. Floor sanders and finishers may smooth the flooring onsite or it may be prefinished prior to installation.

Work Environment

Carpenters held about 956,300 jobs in 2022. The largest employers of carpenters were as follows:

Self-employed workers	27%
Residential building construction	23
Building finishing contractors	13
Nonresidential building construction	12
Foundation, structure, and building exterior contractors	10

Carpenters work indoors and outdoors on many types of construction projects, from installing kitchen cabinets to building highways and bridges. Carpenters may work in cramped spaces and frequently alternate between lifting, standing, and kneeling. Those who work outdoors are subject to variable weather, which may affect a project's schedule.

Injuries and Illnesses

Carpenters sometimes get injured on the job, such as from strains caused by overexertion due to lifting and moving materials. Other common injuries result from falls, slips, trips, and contact with objects or equipment. Workers often wear

Self-employed carpenters often work in residential construction.

equipment such as boots, hardhats, protective eyewear, and reflective vests as a safeguard against injuries.

Work Schedules

Most carpenters work full time, which may include evenings and weekends to meet clients' deadlines. Extreme temperatures or inclement weather may impact building construction timelines, which in turn may affect carpenters' work hours.

How to Become a Carpenter

Carpenters typically need a high school diploma and learn on the job or through apprenticeships.

Education

A high school diploma or equivalent is typically required to enter the occupation. Certain high school courses, such as mathematics and mechanical drawing, may be useful. Some vocational-technical schools offer associate's degrees in carpentry. The programs vary in length and teach basics and specialties in carpentry.

Training

Carpenters typically learn on the job or through apprenticeships. They often begin doing simple tasks, such as measuring and cutting wood, under the guidance of experienced

Apprentice carpenters learn by working with more experienced coworkers.

carpenters or other construction workers. They then progress to more complex tasks, such as reading blueprints and building wooden structures.

Several groups, such as unions and contractor associations, sponsor apprenticeship programs. For each year of a typical program, apprentices must complete a predetermined number of hours of technical training and paid on-the-job training. Apprenticeship program requirements differ based on the type of program and by region. Apprentices learn carpentry basics, blueprint reading, mathematics, building code requirements, and safety and first aid practices. They also may receive specialized training in creating and setting concrete forms, rigging, welding, scaffold building, and working within confined workspaces. All carpenters must pass the Occupational Safety and Health Administration (OSHA) 10-hour safety course.

Work Experience in a Related Occupation

Some carpenters work as construction laborers or helpers before becoming carpenters. Laborers and helpers learn tasks that are similar to those of carpenters.

Licenses, Certifications, and Registrations

Carpenters may need a driver's license to travel to jobsites.

Optional programs offer certification by specialty that may allow carpenters to find additional work opportunities or lead to career advancement. For example, the National Association of the Remodeling Industry offers various levels of certification for remodeling. The National Wood Flooring Association offers certification for installers, craftsman, and master craftsman.

Advancement

Carpenters are involved in many phases of construction and may have opportunities to become first-line supervisors, lead carpenters, independent contractors, or general construction supervisors.

Important Qualities

Business skills. Self-employed carpenters must conduct activities such as bidding on new jobs, tracking inventory, and directing workers.

Detail oriented. Carpenters must be able to precisely cut, measure, and modify the materials they work with.

Dexterity. Carpenters use many tools and need hand-eye coordination to avoid injuring themselves or damaging materials.

Interpersonal skills. Carpenters need to work as a member of a team, cooperating with and assisting others. They also may interact with customers.

Math skills. Carpenters frequently use math skills, including basic trigonometry, to calculate the area, size, and amount of material needed for the job.

Physical strength. Carpenters use heavy tools and materials that weigh up to 100 pounds. They also must be able to stand, climb, or bend for many hours.

Problem-solving skills. Carpenters may work independently with little guidance. They need to be able to modify building materials and make adjustments onsite to complete projects.

Reading comprehension skills. Carpenters need advanced reading ability to understand and follow complex instructions for installing certain products, such as doors.

Pay

The median annual wage for carpenters was $51,390 in May 2022. The median wage is the wage at which half the workers in an occupation earned more than that amount and half earned less. The lowest 10 percent earned less than $36,160, and the highest 10 percent earned more than $89,950.

In May 2022, the median annual wages for carpenters in the top industries in which they worked were as follows:

Nonresidential building construction	$59,850
Building finishing contractors	54,210
Foundation, structure, and building exterior contractors	50,550
Residential building construction	49,660

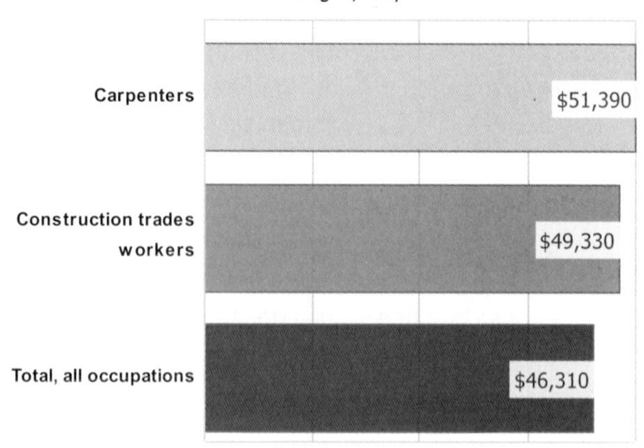

Note: All Occupations includes all occupations in the U.S. Economy.
Source: U.S. Bureau of Labor Statistics, Occupational Employment and Wage Statistics.

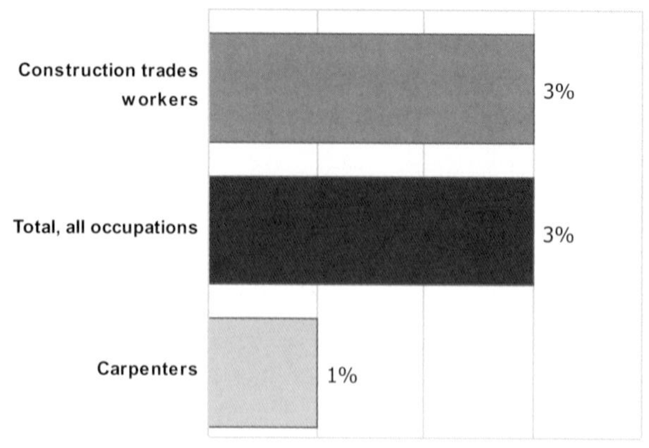

Note: All Occupations includes all occupations in the U.S. Economy.
Source: U.S. Bureau of Labor Statistics, Employment Projections program.

The starting pay for apprentices is less than what fully trained carpenters make. As apprentices gain experience, they receive more pay.

Most carpenters work full time, which may include evenings and weekends to meet clients' deadlines. Extreme temperatures or inclement weather may impact building construction timelines, which in turn may affect carpenters' hours.

Job Outlook

Employment of carpenters is projected to show little or no change from 2022 to 2032.

Despite limited employment growth, about 79,500 openings for carpenters are projected each year, on average, over the decade. Most of those openings are expected to result from the need to replace workers who transfer to different occupations or exit the labor force, such as to retire.

Employment

Population growth should result in more new-home construction—one of the largest segments employing carpenters—which will create some jobs for carpenters. Construction of factories and other nonresidential buildings also is projected to result in some new jobs over the decade.

However, the popularity of modular and prefabricated components for homes and businesses reduces the need for carpenters to build new structures. Roofs, insulation, walls, and other components, as well as entire buildings, may be manufactured in a separate facility and then assembled onsite.

Occupational Title	SOC Code	Employment, 2022	Projected Employment, 2032	Change, 2022-32	
				Percent	Numeric
Carpenters	47-2031	956,300	964,900	1	8,600

Contacts for More Information

Apprenticeship information is available from the U.S. Department of Labor's Apprenticeship program online or by phone at 877-872-5627. Visit Apprenticeship.gov to search for apprenticeship opportunities.

For more information, visit

- Associated Builders and Contractors
- Associated General Contractors of America
- Home Builders Institute
- National Association of the Remodeling Industry
- NCCER
- National Wood Flooring Association
- Occupational Safety and Health Administration
- United Brotherhood of Carpenters and Joiners of America, Carpenters Training Fund
- Home Builders Institute
- National Building Trades Union
- Helmets to Hardhats

Construction and Building Inspectors

Summary

Quick Facts: Construction and Building Inspectors	
2022 Median Pay	$64,480 per year $31.00 per hour
Typical Entry-Level Education	High school diploma or equivalent
Work Experience in a Related Occupation	5 years or more
On-the-job Training	Moderate-term on-the-job training
Number of Jobs, 2022	142,400
Job Outlook, 2022-32	-2% (Decline)
Employment Change, 2022-32	-2,200

What Construction and Building Inspectors Do

Construction and building inspectors ensure that construction meets building codes and ordinances, zoning regulations, and contract specifications.

Work Environment

Construction and building inspectors examine worksites, both alone and as part of a team. Some inspectors climb ladders or crawl in tight spaces. Most work full time during regular business hours.

How to Become a Construction or Building Inspector

Construction and building inspectors usually need a high school diploma and work experience in a construction trade to enter the occupation. They typically learn on the job to attain competency. Many states and localities require some type of license or certification.

Pay

The median annual wage for construction and building inspectors was $64,480 in May 2022.

Construction inspectors take detailed notes during inspections.

Job Outlook

Employment of construction and building inspectors is projected to decline 2 percent from 2022 to 2032.

Despite declining employment, about 15,700 openings for construction and building inspectors are projected each year, on average, over the decade. All of those openings are expected to result from the need to replace workers who transfer to other occupations or exit the labor force, such as to retire.

What Construction and Building Inspectors Do

Construction and building inspectors ensure that construction meets local and national building codes and ordinances, zoning regulations, and contract specifications.

Duties

Construction and building inspectors typically do the following:

- Review building plans and approve those that meet requirements
- Monitor construction sites periodically to ensure overall compliance
- Use equipment and testing devices, such as moisture meters to check for plumbing leaks or flooding damage and electrical testers to ensure that electrical components are functional
- Inspect plumbing, electrical, and other systems to ensure that they meet code

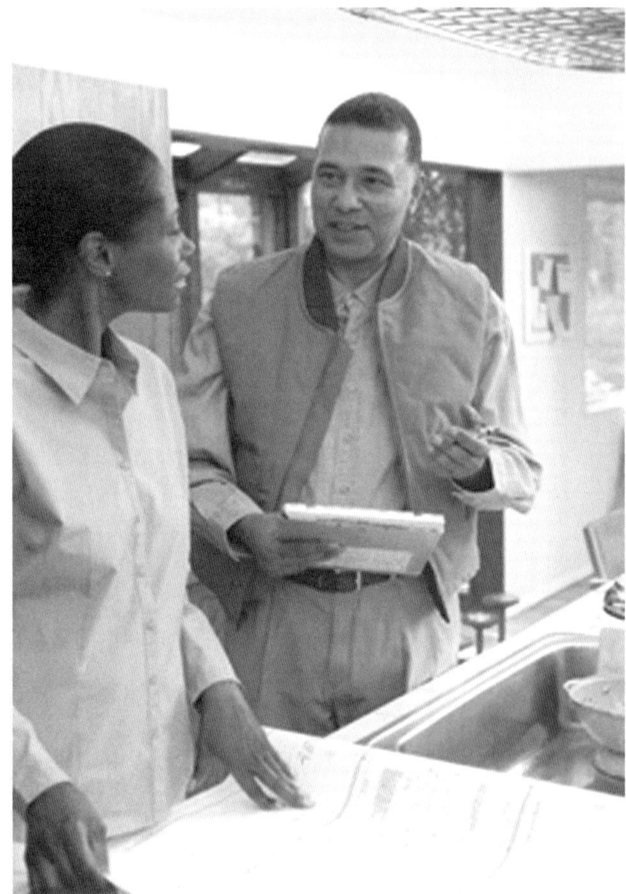

Home inspectors inform potential homebuyers of a home's deficiencies.

- Use survey equipment to verify alignment, level, and elevation of structures and ensure building meets specifications
- Issue violation notices and stop-work orders if building is not compliant
- Keep daily logs, which may include digital images from inspections
- Document findings in writing

Construction and building inspectors ensure safety compliance of buildings, dams, bridges, and other structures; highways and streets; and sewer and water systems. They also inspect electrical; heating, ventilation, air-conditioning, and refrigeration (HVACR); and plumbing systems. Inspectors typically check a project several times: for an initial check in the early construction phase, for followup inspections as the project progresses, and for a comprehensive examination after its completion. At each inspection, they may provide written or oral feedback about their findings.

The following are examples of types of construction and building inspectors:

Building inspectors check the structural quality, architectural requirements, and general safety of buildings. Some building inspectors focus on fire prevention and safety. Fire inspectors and investigators ensure that buildings meet fire codes.

Coating inspectors examine the exterior paint and coating on bridges, pipelines, and large holding tanks. In their checks throughout the painting process, inspectors ensure that protective layers are correctly applied.

Electrical inspectors examine a building's installed electrical systems to ensure compliance and proper functioning. These systems may include new and existing sound and security systems, lighting, photovoltaic systems, generating equipment, and wiring for HVACR systems and appliances.

Elevator inspectors examine lifting and conveying devices, such as elevators, escalators, moving sidewalks, lifts and hoists, inclined railways, ski lifts, and amusement rides. They inspect both the mechanical and electrical control systems.

Home inspectors typically examine houses, condominiums, townhomes, and other dwellings to report on their structure and overall condition. Home sellers or home buyers, or both, may seek inspectors' objective assessment of a dwelling before placing it on the market or submitting an offer.

In addition to checking structural quality, home inspectors examine home systems and features, including the roof, foundation, interior and exterior walls, and plumbing, electrical, and HVACR systems. They may identify violations of building codes but do not have the authority to enforce compliance.

Mechanical inspectors examine HVACR systems and equipment to ensure that they are installed and function properly. They also may inspect commercial kitchen equipment, gas-fired appliances, and boilers. Mechanical inspectors' work differs from that of quality control inspectors, who inspect goods at manufacturing plants.

Plans examiners determine whether the plans for a building or other structure comply with adopted building codes, regulations, and ordinances.

Plumbing inspectors examine the installation of systems that ensure the safety of drinking water and industrial piping and the sanitary disposal of waste.

Public works inspectors ensure that the construction of federal, state, and local government water and sewer systems; roads and bridges; and dams conforms to specifications. They may specialize in projects such as highways, structural steel, or dredging operations required for bridges, dams, or harbors.

Special inspectors ensure that critical construction work, such as high-strength concrete, steel fabrication, and welding, is installed and tested according to design specifications. Special inspectors represent the owner's interests, not those of the general public. Insurance companies and financial institutions also may use their services.

Work Environment

Construction and building inspectors held about 142,400 jobs in 2022. The largest employers of construction and building inspectors were as follows:

Local government, excluding education and hospitals	34%
Engineering services	18
Construction	8
Self-employed workers	7
State government, excluding education and hospitals	4

Although construction and building inspectors spend most of their time examining worksites, they also spend time in an office reviewing blueprints, writing reports, and scheduling inspections.

Some inspectors climb ladders or crawl in tight spaces as part of their work.

Building inspectors often work outdoors to check the exterior structure of a house.

Inspectors typically work alone. However, inspectors may work as part of a team on large, complex projects, particularly if they specialize in one area of construction.

Work Schedules

Most inspectors work full time during regular business hours. However, some work additional hours during periods of heavy construction. Also, if an accident occurs at a construction site, inspectors must respond immediately and may work additional hours to complete their report. Some inspectors—especially those who are self-employed—work evenings and weekends. This is particularly true of home inspectors, who typically inspect homes during the day and write reports in the evening.

How to Become a Construction or Building Inspector

Construction and building inspectors usually need a high school diploma and work experience in a construction trade to enter the occupation. They typically learn on the job to attain competency. Many states and localities require some type of license or certification.

Education

Most employers require inspectors to have at least a high school diploma, even for workers who have considerable experience.

Some employers may seek candidates who have a bachelor's degree in engineering or architecture or who have another postsecondary credential. Many community colleges offer a certificate or an associate's degree program in building inspection technology and have courses in building inspection, home inspection, construction technology, and drafting. Courses in blueprint reading, vocational subjects, algebra, geometry, and writing are also useful. Courses in business management are helpful for those who plan to run their own inspection business.

Some jurisdictions require that construction and building inspectors take continuing education courses to maintain their credentials.

Inspectors often have a combination of certifications and previous experience in various construction and maintenance trades.

Training

Training requirements vary by state, locality, and type of inspector. In general, construction and building inspectors receive much of their training on the job. Construction and building inspectors learn building codes and standards as a prerequisite to obtaining their license and through continuing education. Working with an experienced inspector, they learn about inspection techniques; codes, ordinances, and regulations; contract specifications; and recordkeeping and reporting duties. Training also may include supervised onsite inspections.

Work Experience in a Related Occupation

Employers may prefer to hire applicants who have both training and experience in a construction trade. For example, many inspectors have experience working as carpenters, electricians, or plumbers. Many home inspectors get experience in multiple specialties and enter the occupation with a combination of certifications and experience.

Licenses, Certifications, and Registrations

Most states and localities require construction and building inspectors to have a license or certification. Some states have individual licensing programs for construction and building inspectors. Others may require certification by associations such as the International Code Council, the International Association of Plumbing and Mechanical Officials, the International Association of Electrical Inspectors, and the International Association of Certified Home Inspectors.

Similarly, most states require home inspectors to follow defined trade practices or to get a state-issued license or certification.

Home inspector license or certification requirements vary by state but may require that inspectors have experience with inspections, maintain liability insurance, and pass an exam.

Many states use the National Home Inspector Examination as part of the licensing process. Most inspectors must renew their license periodically and take continuing education courses.

Inspectors must have a valid driver's license to travel to inspection sites.

Advancement

Construction and building inspectors may advance to become a plans examiner or building official. Advancement opportunities may require additional education, along with experience as a construction or building inspector.

Important Qualities

Communication skills. Inspectors must be able to explain problems they discover and to write a report that clearly describes their findings.

Detail oriented. Inspectors thoroughly examine many different construction activities. They must pay close attention so as not to overlook any details.

Construction and Building Inspectors

Median annual wages, May 2022

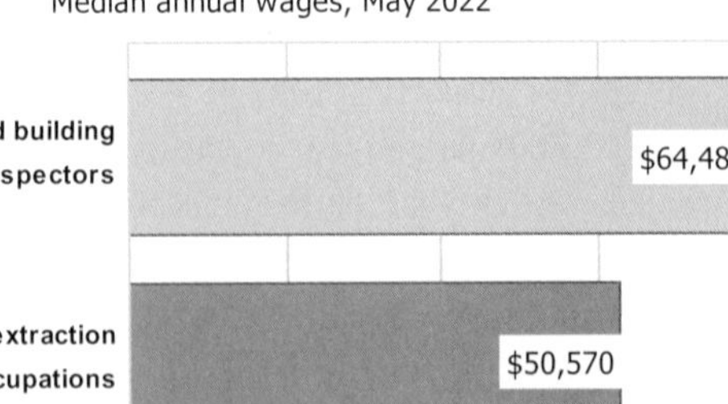

Note: All Occupations includes all occupations in the U.S. Economy.
Source: U.S. Bureau of Labor Statistics, Occupational Employment and Wage Statistics.

Construction and Building Inspectors

Percent change in employment, projected 2022-32

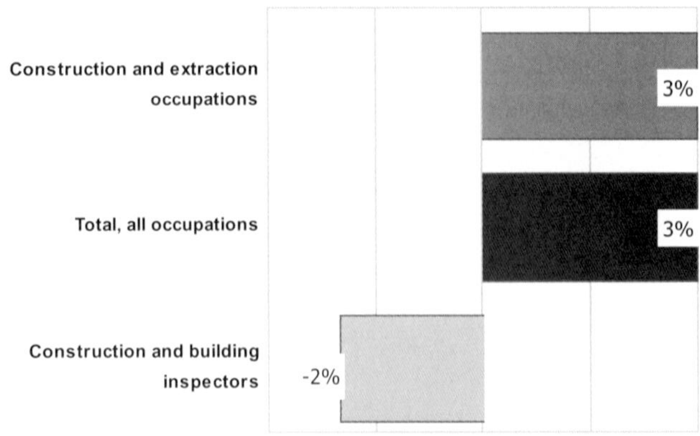

Note: All Occupations includes all occupations in the U.S. Economy.
Source: U.S. Bureau of Labor Statistics, Employment Projections program.

Mechanical knowledge. Inspectors use a variety of testing equipment to check complex systems and must therefore understand how the systems operate.

Physical stamina. Inspectors are frequently on their feet and often climb and crawl through attics and other tight spaces. As a result, they should be physically fit.

Pay

The median annual wage for construction and building inspectors was $64,480 in May 2022. The median wage is the wage at which half the workers in an occupation earned more than that amount and half earned less. The lowest 10 percent earned less than $40,370, and the highest 10 percent earned more than $104,110.

In May 2022, the median annual wages for construction and building inspectors in the top industries in which they worked were as follows:

Engineering services	$65,690
Local government, excluding education and hospitals	64,190
Construction	64,070
State government, excluding education and hospitals	61,450

Most inspectors work full time during regular business hours. However, some work additional hours during periods of heavy construction. Also, if an accident occurs at a construction site, inspectors must respond immediately and may work additional hours to complete their report. Some inspectors—especially those who are self-employed—work evenings and weekends. This is particularly true of home inspectors, who typically inspect homes during the day and write reports in the evening.

Job Outlook

Employment of construction and building inspectors is projected to decline 2 percent from 2022 to 2032.

Despite declining employment, about 15,700 openings for construction and building inspectors are projected each year, on average, over the decade. All of those openings are expected to result from the need to replace workers who transfer to other occupations or exit the labor force, such as to retire.

Employment

The increasing use of remote inspections will reduce the need for inspectors in state and local government. However, continued public interest in safety and the desire to improve the quality of construction are among the factors expected to create demand for inspectors.

Occupational Title	SOC Code	Employment, 2022	Projected Employment, 2032	Change, 2022-32	
				Percent	Numeric
Construction and building inspectors	47-4011	142,400	140,200	-2	-2,200

Contacts for More Information

For more information, visit

- International Code Council
- National Fire Protection Association
- The Association for Materials Protection and Performance (AMPP)
- Association of Construction Inspectors
- International Association of Electrical Inspectors
- National Association of Elevator Safety Authorities International
- International Association of Plumbing and Mechanical Officials
- American Society of Home Inspectors
- International Association of Certified Home Inspectors (InterNACHI)

Construction Equipment Operators

Summary

Quick Facts: Construction Equipment Operators	
2022 Median Pay	$51,050 per year $24.54 per hour
Typical Entry-Level Education	High school diploma or equivalent
Work Experience in a Related Occupation	None
On-the-job Training	Moderate-term on-the-job training
Number of Jobs, 2022	483,300
Job Outlook, 2022-32	3% (As fast as average)
Employment Change, 2022-32	13,300

What Construction Equipment Operators Do

Construction equipment operators drive, maneuver, or control the heavy machinery used to construct roads, buildings, and other structures.

Work Environment

Construction equipment operators may work even in unpleasant weather. Most operators work full time, and some have irregular work schedules that include nights.

How to Become a Construction Equipment Operator

Many workers learn how to operate construction equipment on the job after earning a high school diploma or equivalent; others learn through an apprenticeship or by attending vocational schools.

Pay

The median annual wage for construction equipment operators was $51,050 in May 2022.

Construction equipment operators may use excavators to prepare sites.

Job Outlook

Overall employment of construction equipment operators is projected to grow 3 percent from 2022 to 2032, about as fast as the average for all occupations.

About 42,300 openings for construction equipment operators are projected each year, on average, over the decade. Many of those openings are expected to result from the need to replace workers who transfer to different occupations or exit the labor force, such as to retire.

What Construction Equipment Operators Do

Construction equipment operators drive, maneuver, or control the heavy machinery used to construct roads, bridges, buildings, and other structures.

Duties

Construction equipment operators typically do the following:

- Clean and maintain equipment, making basic repairs as necessary
- Report malfunctioning equipment to supervisors
- Move levers, push pedals, or turn valves to drive and maneuver equipment
- Coordinate machine actions with crew members using hand or audio signals

Construction equipment operators use machinery to move building supplies, earth, and other heavy materials at construction sites and mines. They operate equipment that clears and grades land to prepare it for the construction of roads, bridges, buildings, aircraft runways, dams, and other structures.

The following are examples of types of construction equipment operators:

Operating engineers and other construction equipment operators work with one or several types of power construction equipment. They may operate excavation and loading machines equipped with scoops, shovels, or buckets that dig sand, gravel, earth, or similar materials. They also operate bulldozers, trench

Pile drivers drive piles to support structures such as piers.

excavators, road graders, and similar equipment. Sometimes, they drive and control industrial trucks or tractors equipped with forklifts or booms for lifting materials. They may also operate and maintain air compressors, pumps, and other power equipment at construction sites.

Paving and surfacing equipment operators control the machines that spread and level asphalt or spread and smooth concrete for roadways or other structures. ***Tamping equipment operators*** use machines that compact earth and other fill materials for roadbeds and other construction sites or that break up old pavement and drive guardrail posts into the ground.

Pile driver operators use large machines mounted on skids, barges, or cranes to hammer piles into the ground. Piles are long, heavy beams of concrete, wood, or steel driven into the ground to support retaining walls, bridges, piers, or building foundations. Some pile driver operators work on offshore oil rigs.

Workers who operate cranes are covered in the material moving machine operators profile.

Work Environment

Construction equipment operators held about 483,300 jobs in 2022. Employment in the detailed occupations that make up construction equipment operators was distributed as follows:

Operating engineers and other construction equipment operators	437,600
Paving, surfacing, and tamping equipment operators	42,300
Pile driver operators	3,300

The largest employers of construction equipment operators were as follows:

Employer	Percent
Specialty trade contractors	29%
Heavy and civil engineering construction	28
Local government, excluding education and hospitals	14
Mining, quarrying, and oil and gas extraction	5
Construction of buildings	5

Construction equipment operators work even in unpleasant weather, although rain or extreme cold can stop some types of construction. Workers often get dirty, greasy, muddy, or dusty. Some operators work in remote locations on large construction projects, such as highways and dams, or in factories or mines.

Injuries and Illnesses

Construction equipment operators risk injury from hazards such as falls, slips, and trips and transportation incidents. Workers can avoid injury by observing proper operating procedures and safety practices, such as wearing personal protective equipment. Bulldozers, scrapers, and pile drivers are noisy and shake or jolt the operator, which may lead to repetitive stress injuries.

Work Schedules

Construction equipment operators may have irregular schedules, such as continuing around the clock or late into the night. Most construction equipment operators work full time, and some work more than 40 hours per week. The work may be seasonal in areas of the country that experience extreme cold.

How to Become a Construction Equipment Operator

Workers may learn equipment operation on the job after earning a high school diploma or equivalent, through an apprenticeship, or by attending vocational schools.

Education

A high school diploma or equivalent is typically required to become a construction equipment operator. Vocational training and math courses are useful, and a course in automotive mechanics may be helpful because workers often maintain their equipment.

Construction equipment operators work in nearly all weather conditions.

Construction equipment operators should have steady hands and feet to guide and control heavy machinery precisely.

Learning at vocational schools may be beneficial in finding a job. Schools may specialize in a particular brand or type of construction equipment.

Some schools incorporate sophisticated simulator training into their courses, allowing beginners to familiarize themselves with the equipment in a virtual environment before operating real machines.

Training

Many workers learn their jobs by operating light equipment, such as a trench roller, under the guidance of an experienced operator. Later, they may operate heavier equipment, such as bulldozers. Operators of some equipment, such as machines with computerized controls, may need more training and some understanding of electronics.

Other workers learn their trade through a 3- or 4-year apprenticeship. For each year of a typical program, apprentices must complete a predetermined number of hours of technical instruction and paid on-the-job training. Apprenticeship program requirements differ based on the type of program and by region. During technical instruction, apprentices learn operating procedures for equipment as well as safety practices, first aid, and how to read grading plans. On the job, apprentices learn to maintain equipment, operate machinery, and use technology, such as Global Positioning System (GPS) devices.

After completing an apprenticeship program, apprentices are considered journey workers and perform tasks with less guidance.

Licenses, Certifications, and Registrations

Construction equipment operators often need a commercial driver's license (CDL) to haul their equipment to various jobsites. State laws governing CDLs vary.

A few states have special licenses for operators of backhoes, loaders, and bulldozers.

Some states and cities require pile driver operators to have a crane license, because similar operational concerns apply to both pile drivers and cranes. Requirements vary by state. For more information, contact your local or state licensing board.

Important Qualities

Ability to work at heights. Construction equipment operators may need to service pulleys or other devices located at the top of structures, which may be several stories tall.

Hand-eye-foot coordination. Construction equipment operators should have steady hands and feet to guide and control heavy machinery precisely, sometimes in tight spaces.

Mechanical skills. Construction equipment operators often perform basic maintenance on the equipment they operate. As a result, they should be familiar with hand and power tools and standard equipment care.

Physical stamina. Construction equipment operators may be required to frequently push, carry, or move heavy objects.

Physical strength. Construction equipment operators may be required to lift more than 50 pounds as part of their duties.

Pay

The median annual wage for construction equipment operators was $51,050 in May 2022. The median wage is the wage at which half the workers in an occupation earned more than that amount and half earned less. The lowest 10 percent earned less than $36,550, and the highest 10 percent earned more than $92,390.

Median annual wages for construction equipment operators in May 2022 were as follows:

Pile driver operators	$64,310
Operating engineers and other construction equipment operators	51,430
Paving, surfacing, and tamping equipment operators	47,270

In May 2022, the median annual wages for construction equipment operators in the top industries in which they worked were as follows:

Heavy and civil engineering construction	$58,970
Construction of buildings	58,270
Specialty trade contractors	51,360
Mining, quarrying, and oil and gas extraction	50,180
Local government, excluding education and hospitals	48,480

Apprentices receive less pay than fully trained construction equipment operators. They receive pay increases as they learn more skills.

Construction equipment operators may have irregular schedules, such as continuing around the clock or late into the night. Most construction equipment operators work full time, and some work more than 40 hours per week. The work may be seasonal in areas of the country that experience extreme cold.

Construction Equipment Operators

Median annual wages, May 2022

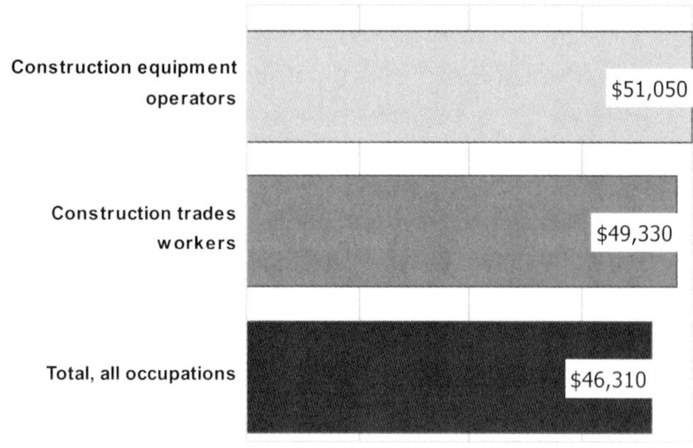

Note: All Occupations includes all occupations in the U.S. Economy.
Source: U.S. Bureau of Labor Statistics, Occupational Employment and Wage Statistics.

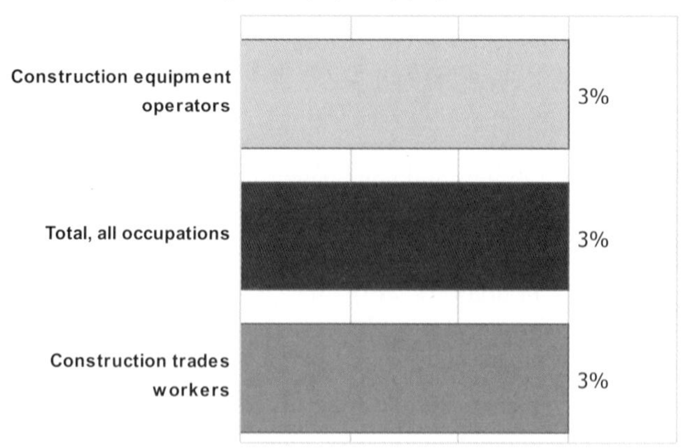

Note: All Occupations includes all occupations in the U.S. Economy.
Source: U.S. Bureau of Labor Statistics, Employment Projections program.

Job Outlook

Overall employment of construction equipment operators is projected to grow 3 percent from 2022 to 2032, about as fast as the average for all occupations.

About 42,300 openings for construction equipment operators are projected each year, on average, over the decade. Many of those openings are expected to result from the need to replace workers who transfer to different occupations or exit the labor force, such as to retire.

Employment

Projected employment of construction equipment operators varies by occupation (see table).

Spending on infrastructure is expected to increase, resulting in some new jobs over the decade. Across the country, many roads, bridges, and water and sewer systems are in need of repair. In addition, population growth will require new infrastructure, such as roads and sewer lines, the projects for which are expected to generate jobs.

Occupational Title	SOC Code	Employment, 2022	Projected Employment, 2032	Change, 2022-32	
				Percent	Numeric
Construction equipment operators	47-2070	483,300	496,600	3	13,300
Paving, surfacing, and tamping equipment operators	47-2071	42,300	43,900	4	1,600
Pile driver operators	47-2072	3,300	3,400	3	100
Operating engineers and other construction equipment operators	47-2073	437,600	449,200	3	11,600

Contacts for More Information

Apprenticeship information is available from the U.S. Department of Labor's Apprenticeship program online or by phone at 877-872-5627. Visit apprenticeship.gov to search for apprenticeship opportunities.

For more information, visit

- The Associated General Contractors of America
- Pile Driving Contractors Association
- International Union of Operating Engineers
- NCCER
- National Commission for the Certification of Crane Operators
- Helmets to Hardhats

Construction Laborers and Helpers

Summary

Quick Facts: Construction Laborers and Helpers	
2022 Median Pay	$39,520 per year $19.00 per hour
Typical Entry-Level Education	See How to Become One
Work Experience in a Related Occupation	None
On-the-job Training	Short-term on-the-job training
Number of Jobs, 2022	1,624,800
Job Outlook, 2022-32	4% (As fast as average)
Employment Change, 2022-32	57,900

What Construction Laborers and Helpers Do

Construction laborers and helpers perform many tasks that require physical labor on construction sites.

Work Environment

Most construction laborers and helpers typically work full time and do physically demanding work. Some work at great heights or outdoors in all weather conditions. Construction laborers have one of the highest rates of injuries and illnesses of all occupations.

How to Become a Construction Laborer or Helper

Construction laborers and helpers learn their trade through on-the-job training. Formal education is not typically required.

Pay

The median annual wage for construction laborers and helpers was $39,520 in May 2022.

Construction laborers and helpers perform physical labor on construction sites.

Job Outlook

Overall employment of construction laborers and helpers is projected to grow 4 percent from 2022 to 2032, about as fast as the average for all occupations.

About 151,400 openings for construction laborers and helpers are projected each year, on average, over the decade. Many of those openings are expected to result from the need to replace workers who transfer to different occupations or exit the labor force, such as to retire.

What Construction Laborers and Helpers Do

Construction laborers and helpers perform many tasks that require physical labor on construction sites.

Duties

Construction laborers and helpers typically do the following:

- Clean and prepare construction sites by removing debris and possible hazards
- Load or unload building materials to be used in construction
- Build or take apart bracing, scaffolding, and temporary structures

Construction laborers and helpers assist craftworkers.

- Dig trenches, backfill holes, or compact earth to prepare for construction
- Operate or tend equipment and machines used in construction
- Follow construction plans and instructions from supervisors or more experienced workers
- Assist craftworkers with their duties

Construction laborers and helpers work on almost all construction sites, performing a wide range of tasks varying in complexity from very easy to extremely difficult and hazardous.

Construction laborers, also referred to as *construction craft laborers*, perform a wide variety of construction-related activities during all phases of construction. Many laborers spend their time preparing and cleaning up construction sites, using tools such as shovels and brooms. Other workers, such as those on road crews, may specialize and learn to control traffic patterns and operate pavement breakers, jackhammers, earth tampers, or surveying equipment.

With special training, laborers may help transport and use explosives or run hydraulic boring machines to dig out tunnels. They may learn to use lasers to place pipes and to use computers to control robotic pipe cutters. They may become certified to remove asbestos, lead, or chemicals.

Helpers assist construction craftworkers, such as electricians and carpenters, with a variety of tasks. They may carry tools and materials or help set up equipment. For example, many helpers work with cement masons to move and set the forms that determine the shape of poured concrete. Many other helpers assist with taking apart equipment, cleaning up sites, and disposing of waste, as well as helping with any other needs of craftworkers.

Many construction trades have helpers who assist craftworkers. The following trades have associated helpers:

- Brickmasons, blockmasons, and stonemasons, and tile and marble setters
- Carpenters
- Electricians
- Painters, paperhangers, plasterers, and stucco masons
- Pipelayers, plumbers, pipefitters, and steamfitters
- Roofers

Work Environment

Construction laborers and helpers held about 1.6 million jobs in 2022. Employment in the detailed occupations that make up construction laborers and helpers was distributed as follows:

Construction laborers	1,418,600
Helpers--electricians	72,500
Helpers--pipelayers, plumbers, pipefitters, and steamfitters	47,800
Helpers, construction trades, all other	28,300
Helpers--carpenters	25,100
Helpers--brickmasons, blockmasons, stonemasons, and tile and marble setters	17,900

Construction laborers and helpers wear gloves, safety glasses, and other protective gear.

Helpers--painters, paperhangers, plasterers, and stucco masons	8,700
Helpers--roofers	5,900

The largest employers of construction laborers and helpers were as follows:

Specialty trade contractors	32%
Self-employed workers	25
Construction of buildings	17
Heavy and civil engineering construction	15
Temporary help services	3

Most construction laborers and helpers perform physically demanding work. Some work at great heights or outdoors in all weather conditions; others may be required to work in tunnels. They must use earplugs around loud equipment and wear gloves, safety glasses, and other protective gear.

Injuries and Illnesses

Construction laborers and helpers, construction trades, all other have some of the highest rates of injuries and illnesses of all occupations. ("All other" titles represent occupations with a wide range of characteristics that do not fit into any of the other detailed occupations.)

Workers may experience cuts from materials and tools, fatal and nonfatal falls from ladders and scaffolding, and burns from chemicals or equipment. Some jobs expose workers to harmful materials, fumes, or odors, or to dangerous machinery. Workers may also experience muscle fatigue and injuries related to lifting and carrying heavy materials.

Work Schedules

Like many construction workers, most laborers and helpers work full time. Although they must sometimes stop work because of bad weather, they may work overtime to meet deadlines. Laborers and helpers on highway and bridge projects may need to work overnight to avoid causing major traffic disruptions. In some parts of the country, construction laborers and helpers may work only during certain seasons. For example, in northern climates, cold weather frequently disrupts construction activity in the winter.

Some construction laborers are self-employed. In contrast, very few helpers are self-employed.

How to Become a Construction Laborer or Helper

Construction laborers and helpers learn their trade through on-the-job training (OJT). The length of training depends on the employer and the specialization. Formal education is not typically required.

Education

Although formal education is not typically required for most positions, helpers of electricians and helpers of pipelayers, plumbers, pipefitters, and steamfitters typically need a high school diploma. High school classes in mathematics, blueprint reading, welding, and other vocational subjects can be helpful.

Training

Construction laborers and helpers typically learn through OJT after being hired by a construction contractor. Workers usually learn by performing tasks under the guidance of experienced workers.

Although the majority of construction laborers and helpers learn by assisting experienced workers, some construction laborers may opt for apprenticeship programs. These programs generally include 2 to 4 years of technical instruction and OJT. The Laborers' International Union of North America (LIUNA) requires a combination of OJT and related classroom instruction in such areas as signaling, blueprint reading, using proper tools and equipment, and following health and safety

While formal education is not required to enter the occupation, some construction laborers take classes as part of an apprenticeship.

procedures. The remainder of the curriculum consists of specialized training in one of these eight areas:

- Building construction
- Demolition and deconstruction
- Environmental remediation
- Road and utility construction
- Tunneling
- Masonry
- Landscaping
- Pipeline construction

Licenses, Certifications, and Registrations

Laborers who remove hazardous materials (hazmat) must meet the federal and state requirements for hazardous materials removal workers.

Depending on the work they do, laborers may need specific certifications, which may be attained through LIUNA. Rigging and scaffold building are commonly attained certifications. Certification can help workers prove that they have the knowledge to perform more complex tasks.

Advancement

Through experience and training, construction laborers and helpers can advance into positions that involve more complex tasks. For example, laborers may earn certifications in welding, erecting scaffolding, or finishing concrete, and then spend more time performing those activities. Similarly, helpers sometimes move into construction craft occupations after gaining experience in the field. For example, experience as an electrician's helper may lead someone to becoming an apprentice electrician.

Important Qualities

Color vision. Construction laborers and helpers may need to be able to distinguish colors to do their job. For example, an electrician's helper must be able to distinguish different colors of wire to help the lead electrician.

Math skills. Construction laborers and some helpers need to perform basic math calculations while measuring on jobsites or assisting a surveying crew.

Mechanical skills. Construction laborers are frequently required to operate and maintain equipment, such as jackhammers.

Physical stamina. Construction laborers and helpers must have the endurance to perform strenuous tasks throughout the day. Highway laborers, for example, spend hours on their feet—often in hot temperatures—with few breaks.

Physical strength. Construction laborers and helpers must often lift heavy materials or equipment. For example, cement mason helpers must move cinder blocks, which typically weigh more than 40 pounds each.

Pay

The median annual wage for construction laborers and helpers was $39,520 in May 2022. The median wage is the wage

Construction Laborers and Helpers

Median annual wages, May 2022

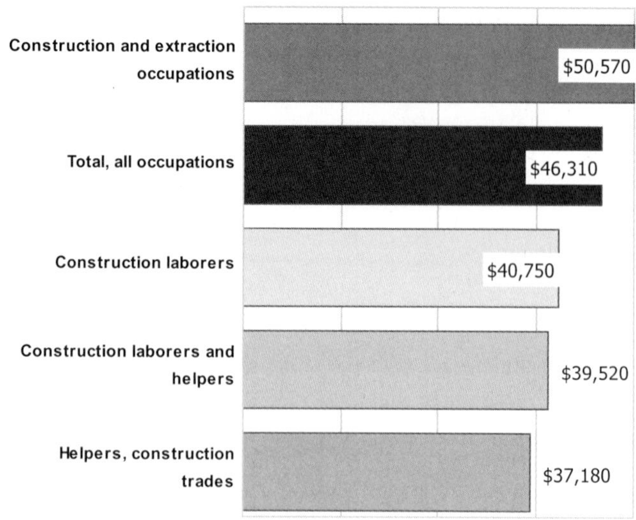

Note: All Occupations includes all occupations in the U.S. Economy.
Source: U.S. Bureau of Labor Statistics, Occupational Employment and Wage Statistics.

at which half the workers in an occupation earned more than that amount and half earned less. The lowest 10 percent earned less than $29,490, and the highest 10 percent earned more than $66,850.

Median annual wages for construction laborers and helpers in May 2022 were as follows:

Construction laborers	$40,750
Helpers--brickmasons, blockmasons, stonemasons, and tile and marble setters	39,430
Helpers, construction trades, all other	37,820
Helpers--carpenters	37,490
Helpers--electricians	37,070
Helpers--roofers	37,020
Helpers--pipelayers, plumbers, pipefitters, and steamfitters	36,340
Helpers--painters, paperhangers, plasterers, and stucco masons	36,080

In May 2022, the median annual wages for construction laborers and helpers in the top industries in which they worked were as follows:

Heavy and civil engineering construction	$44,850
Construction of buildings	42,470
Specialty trade contractors	38,790
Temporary help services	31,060

The starting pay for most apprentices is usually about 60 percent of what fully trained laborers make. Apprentices receive pay increases as they learn more skills.

Like many construction workers, most construction laborers and helpers work full time. Although they sometimes stop

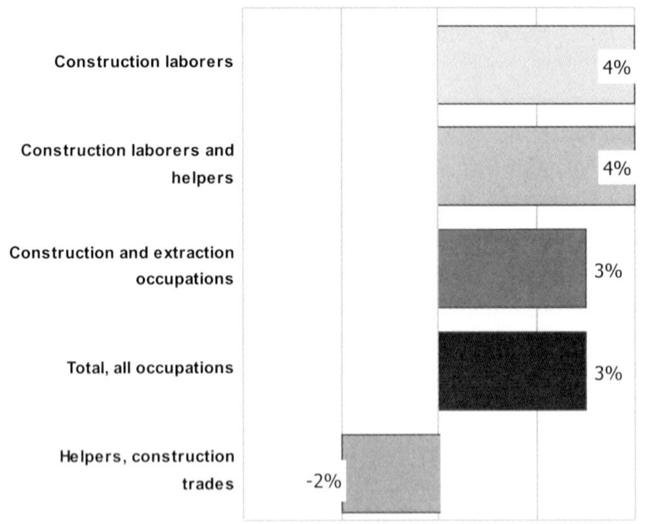

Note: All Occupations includes all occupations in the U.S. Economy.
Source: U.S. Bureau of Labor Statistics, Employment Projections program.

work because of bad weather, they may work overtime to meet deadlines. Laborers and helpers on highway and bridge projects may need to work overnight to avoid causing major traffic disruptions. In some parts of the country, construction laborers and helpers may work only during certain seasons. For example, in northern climates, cold weather frequently disrupts construction activity in the winter.

Some construction laborers are self-employed. In contrast, very few helpers are self-employed.

Job Outlook

Overall employment of construction laborers and helpers is projected to grow 4 percent from 2022 to 2032, about as fast as the average for all occupations.

About 151,400 openings for construction laborers and helpers are projected each year, on average, over the decade. Many of those openings are expected to result from the need to replace workers who transfer to different occupations or exit the labor force, such as to retire.

Employment

Projected employment of construction laborers and helpers varies by occupation (see table). Construction laborers work in all fields of construction, and demand for laborers should mirror the level of overall construction activity. Repairing and replacing the nation's infrastructure, such as roads and water lines, may result in steady demand for laborers.

Employment growth for specific types of construction helpers is expected to be driven by the construction and renovation of homes and nonresidential structures. However, shifts in preference for materials, such as prefabricated components, will continue to reduce demand for helpers of carpenters, of electricians, and of other construction workers.

Occupational Title	SOC Code	Employment, 2022	Projected Employment, 2032	Change, 2022-32	
				Percent	Numeric
Construction laborers and helpers	—	1,624,800	1,682,600	4	57,900
Construction laborers	47-2061	1,418,600	1,480,500	4	61,900
Helpers–brickmasons, blockmasons, stonemasons, and tile and marble setters	47-3011	17,900	15,900	-11	-2,000
Helpers–carpenters	47-3012	25,100	23,700	-5	-1,300
Helpers–electricians	47-3013	72,500	70,000	-3	-2,500
Helpers–painters, paperhangers, plasterers, and stucco masons	47-3014	8,700	8,900	2	100
Helpers–pipelayers, plumbers, pipefitters, and steamfitters	47-3015	47,800	48,900	2	1,100
Helpers–roofers	47-3016	5,900	6,000	2	100
Helpers, construction trades, all other	47-3019	28,300	28,800	2	400

Contacts for More Information

Apprenticeship information is available from the U.S. Department of Labor's Apprenticeship program online or by phone at 877-872-5627.

For more information, visit

- Laborers' International Union of North America
- NCCER

Drywall Installers, Ceiling Tile Installers, and Tapers

Summary

Quick Facts: Drywall Installers, Ceiling Tile Installers, and Tapers

2022 Median Pay	$51,160 per year $24.60 per hour
Typical Entry-Level Education	No formal educational credential
Work Experience in a Related Occupation	None
On-the-job Training	Moderate-term on-the-job training
Number of Jobs, 2022	134,500
Job Outlook, 2022-32	1% (Little or no change)
Employment Change, 2022-32	1,400

What Drywall Installers, Ceiling Tile Installers, and Tapers Do

Drywall and ceiling tile installers hang wallboard and install ceiling tile inside buildings. Tapers prepare the wallboard for painting.

Work Environment

Drywall installers, ceiling tile installers, and tapers work indoors. Workers spend most of the day standing, bending, or reaching, and they often must lift and maneuver heavy wallboard.

How to Become a Drywall Installer, Ceiling Tile Installer, or Taper

Most drywall installers, ceiling tile installers, and tapers learn their trade on the job. A formal educational credential is typically not required to enter the occupation.

Drywall and ceiling tile installers hang wallboard and install ceiling tile inside buildings.

Pay

The median annual wage for drywall and ceiling tile installers was $50,440 in May 2022.

The median annual wage for tapers was $62,360 in May 2022.

Job Outlook

Overall employment of drywall installers, ceiling tile installers, and tapers is projected to show little or no change from 2022 to 2032.

Despite limited employment growth, about 9,000 openings for drywall installers, ceiling tile installers, and tapers are projected each year, on average, over the decade. Most of those openings are expected to result from the need to replace workers who transfer to different occupations or exit the labor force, such as to retire.

What Drywall Installers, Ceiling Tile Installers, and Tapers Do

Drywall installers and ceiling tile installers hang wallboard and install ceiling tile inside buildings. Tapers prepare the wallboard for painting, using tape and other materials. Many workers both install and tape wallboard.

Drywall installers, ceiling tile installers, and tapers work with many different types of tools.

Duties

Drywall installers, ceiling tile installers, and tapers typically do the following:

- Measure, mark, and cut drywall panels according to design plans
- Fasten panels and tiles to support structures
- Patch, trim, and smooth rough spots and edges
- Apply tape and sealing compound to cover joints between wallboards
- Add coats of sealing compound to create an even surface
- Sand all joints and holes for a smooth, seamless finish

Drywall and ceiling tile installers place panels over the walls and ceilings of interior rooms in buildings. The panels cover insulation, electrical wires, and pipes; dampen sound; and provide fire resistance. Tapers prepare the drywall for finishing.

Workers may use mechanical lifts or stand on stilts, ladders, or scaffolds to hang and prepare ceilings. After hanging wallboards, workers use trowels to spread coats of sealing compound over cracks, indentations, and other imperfections. Some workers use a mechanical applicator, a tool that spreads sealing compound on the wall joint while dispensing and setting tape at the same time.

Drywall installers are also called *drywallers* or *hangers*. They cut and hang the panels of wallboard. The tools they use include tape measures, straightedges, utility knives, and power saws.

Ceiling tile installers hang ceiling tiles and create suspended ceilings. Tiles may be applied directly to the ceiling, attached to furring strips, or suspended on runners that are connected by wire to the ceiling. Workers are sometimes called *acoustical carpenters*, because they also install tiles that block sound.

Tapers, also called *finishers*, prepare the drywall for covering by paint and wallpaper. Tapers apply paper or fiberglass mesh tape to cover drywall seams. They also smooth the tape after affixing it and apply a finishing compound to the tape.

In addition to performing new installations, many installers and tapers make repairs such as fixing damaged drywall and replacing ceiling tiles. The wall coverings applied to the finished drywall are installed by painters, plasterers, and paperhangers.

Work Environment

Drywall and ceiling tile installers held about 116,400 jobs in 2022. The largest employers of drywall and ceiling tile installers were as follows:

Drywall and insulation contractors	60%
Self-employed workers	22
Nonresidential building construction	5

Tapers held about 18,100 jobs in 2022. The largest employers of tapers were as follows:

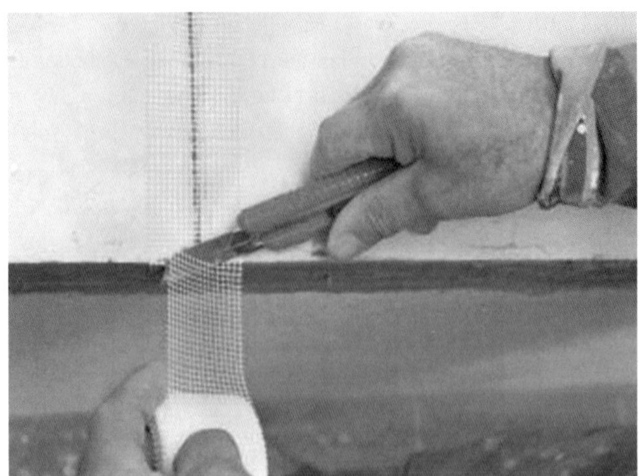

Tapers cover the seams where drywall edges meet.

Drywall and insulation contractors	66%
Self-employed workers	22
Nonresidential building construction	5
Painting and wall covering contractors	4

Drywall installers, ceiling tile installers, and tapers work indoors. The work is physically demanding. Workers spend most of the day standing, bending, or reaching, and they must often lift and maneuver heavy wallboard.

Work Schedules

Most drywall installers, ceiling tile installers, and tapers work full time.

How to Become a Drywall Installer, Ceiling Tile Installer, or Taper

Most drywall installers, ceiling tile installers, and tapers learn their trade on the job. A formal educational credential is typically not required to enter the occupation.

New drywall installers, ceiling tile installers, and tapers typically learn their job by working with more experienced workers.

Education

There are no educational credential requirements for becoming a drywall installer, ceiling tile installer, or taper, although some employers prefer to hire candidates who have a high school diploma or equivalent.

A high school diploma or equivalent is typically required for workers starting an apprenticeship.

Training

Most drywall installers, ceiling tile installers, and tapers learn their trade on the job by helping experienced workers and gradually taking on more duties. They start by carrying materials and cleaning up and then learn to use the tools of the trade. They learn to measure, cut, and install or apply materials. They may start out working on less visible areas, such as closets. Their on-the-job training typically lasts up to 12 months.

A few groups, including the United Brotherhood of Carpenters, International Union of Painters and Allied Trades, and contractor associations, sponsor apprenticeship programs for drywall installers, ceiling tile installers, and tapers. Apprenticeships combine on-the-job training with technical instruction and typically last 2 to 4 years.

During their apprenticeship training, drywall installers, ceiling tile installers, and tapers learn a number of safety rules, many of which are standardized through the Occupational Safety & Health Administration (OSHA).

Advancement

Drywall installers, ceiling tile installers, and tapers may advance to become supervisors, general superintendents, project managers, or estimators. Workers may also choose to start their own business after gaining experience in the occupation.

Workers who join a union may also find career advancement opportunities within their union, such as becoming the business manager for a local chapter or becoming an instructor for the apprenticeship program.

Important Qualities

Ability to work at heights. Drywall installers, ceiling tile installers, and tapers may be required to work on ladders, scaffolding, lifts, or stilts.

Attention to detail. Drywall installers, ceiling tile installers, and tapers must take precise measurements, follow specific instructions, and be meticulous in their work.

Balance. Drywall installers, ceiling tile installers, and tapers often wear stilts. They must be able to move around and use tools overhead without falling.

Dexterity. Drywall installers, ceiling tile installers, and tapers work with hand tools on every job.

Math skills. Drywall installers, ceiling tile installers, and tapers must be able to estimate the quantity of materials needed when cutting panels.

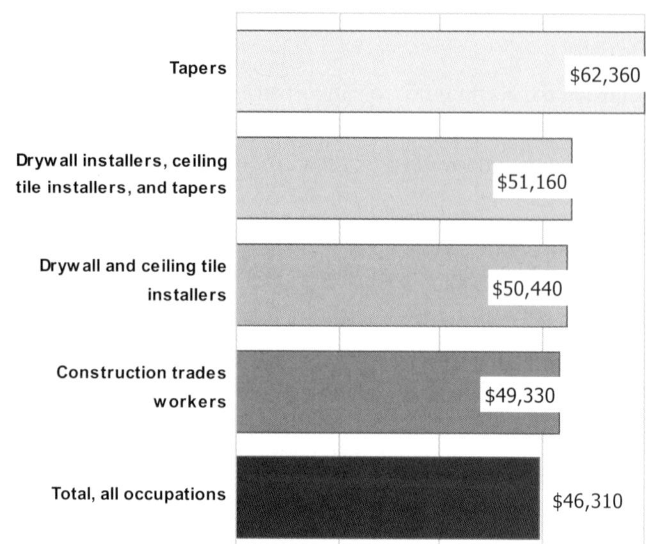

Note: All Occupations includes all occupations in the U.S. Economy.
Source: U.S. Bureau of Labor Statistics, Occupational Employment and Wage Statistics.

Physical stamina. Drywall installers, ceiling tile installers, and tapers routinely lift and move heavy materials into place, so workers should be physically fit.

Physical strength. Drywall and ceiling tile installers must often lift heavy panels over their heads to secure onto the ceiling and must carry heavy materials to work areas.

Pay

The median annual wage for drywall and ceiling tile installers was $50,440 in May 2022. The median wage is the wage at which half the workers in an occupation earned more than that amount and half earned less. The lowest 10 percent earned less than $35,250, and the highest 10 percent earned more than $96,160.

The median annual wage for tapers was $62,360 in May 2022. The lowest 10 percent earned less than $38,780, and the highest 10 percent earned more than $100,820.

In May 2022, the median annual wages for drywall and ceiling tile installers in the top industries in which they worked were as follows:

Nonresidential building construction	$56,360
Drywall and insulation contractors	50,430

In May 2022, the median annual wages for tapers in the top industries in which they worked were as follows:

Nonresidential building construction	$70,760
Drywall and insulation contractors	61,270
Painting and wall covering contractors	45,130

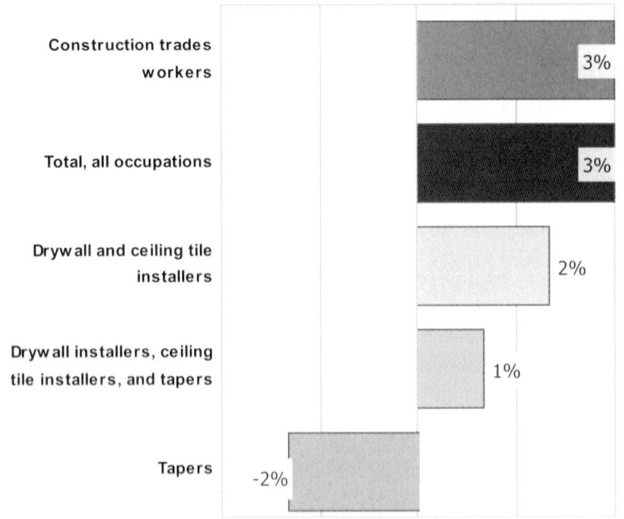

Note: All Occupations includes all occupations in the U.S. Economy.
Source: U.S. Bureau of Labor Statistics, Employment Projections program.

Most drywall installers, ceiling tile installers, and tapers work full time.

Job Outlook

Overall employment of drywall installers, ceiling tile installers, and tapers is projected to show little or no change from 2022 to 2032.

Despite limited employment growth, about 9,000 openings for drywall installers, ceiling tile installers, and tapers are projected each year, on average, over the decade. Most of those openings are expected to result from the need to replace workers who transfer to different occupations or exit the labor force, such as to retire.

Employment

Projected employment of drywall installers, ceiling tile installers, and tapers varies by occupation (see table).

Demand for drywall and ceiling tile installers, especially for work on construction of new buildings, is expected to continue. Home-remodeling projects also are expected to be a source of job growth. The continued use of new tools that allow workers to do more in less time will limit employment growth of tapers.

Occupational Title	SOC Code	Employment, 2022	Projected Employment, 2032	Change, 2022-32	
				Percent	Numeric
Drywall installers, ceiling tile installers, and tapers	47-2080	134,500	135,900	1	1,400
Drywall and ceiling tile installers	47-2081	116,400	118,200	2	1,900
Tapers	47-2082	18,100	17,700	-2	-400

Contacts for More Information

Apprenticeship information is available from the U.S. Department of Labor's Apprenticeship program online or by phone at 877-872-5627. Visit Apprenticeship.gov to search for apprenticeship opportunities.

For more information, visit

- Associated Builders and Contractors
- Association of the Wall and Ceiling Industry
- Finishing Trades Institute
- National Association of Home Builders
- NCCER
- United Brotherhood of Carpenters

Electricians

Summary

Quick Facts: Electricians	
2022 Median Pay	$60,240 per year $28.96 per hour
Typical Entry-Level Education	High school diploma or equivalent
Work Experience in a Related Occupation	None
On-the-job Training	Apprenticeship
Number of Jobs, 2022	762,600
Job Outlook, 2022-32	6% (Faster than average)
Employment Change, 2022-32	49,200

What Electricians Do
Electricians install, maintain, and repair electrical power, communications, lighting, and control systems.

Work Environment
Almost all electricians work full time. Work schedules may include evenings and weekends. Overtime is common.

How to Become an Electrician
Most electricians learn through an apprenticeship, but some start out by attending a technical school. Most states require electricians to be licensed.

Pay
The median annual wage for electricians was $60,240 in May 2022.

Job Outlook
Employment of electricians is projected to grow 6 percent from 2022 to 2032, faster than the average for all occupations.

Electricians connect a variety of fixtures to internal and external electricity sources.

About 73,500 openings for electricians are projected each year, on average, over the decade. Many of those openings are expected to result from the need to replace workers who transfer to different occupations or exit the labor force, such as to retire.

What Electricians Do
Electricians install, maintain, and repair electrical power, communications, lighting, and control systems in homes, businesses, and factories.

Duties
Electricians typically do the following:

- Read blueprints or technical diagrams
- Install and maintain wiring, control, and lighting systems
- Inspect electrical components, such as transformers and circuit breakers
- Identify electrical problems using a variety of testing devices
- Repair or replace wiring, equipment, or fixtures using handtools and power tools
- Follow state and local building regulations based on the National Electrical Code
- Direct and train workers to install, maintain, or repair electrical wiring or equipment

Electricians often cap wires before installing an outlet.

Almost every building has an electrical power, communications, lighting, and control system that is installed during construction and maintained after that. These systems power the lights, appliances, and equipment that make people's lives and jobs easier and more comfortable.

Installing electrical systems in newly constructed buildings is often less complicated than maintaining equipment in existing buildings because electrical wiring is more easily accessible during construction. Maintaining equipment and systems involves identifying problems and repairing broken equipment that is sometimes difficult to reach. Maintenance work may include fixing or replacing parts, light fixtures, control systems, motors, and other types of electrical equipment.

Electricians read blueprints, which include technical diagrams of electrical systems that show the location of circuits, outlets, and other equipment. They use different types of handtools and power tools, such as conduit benders, to run and protect wiring. Other commonly used tools include screwdrivers, wire strippers, drills, and saws. While troubleshooting, electricians also may use ammeters, voltmeters, thermal scanners, and cable testers to find problems and ensure that components are working properly.

Many electricians work alone, but sometimes they collaborate with others. For example, experienced electricians may work with building engineers and architects to help design electrical systems for new construction. Some electricians may also consult with other construction specialists, such as elevator installers and heating and air conditioning workers, to help install or maintain electrical or power systems. Electricians employed by large companies are likely to work as part of a crew; they may direct helpers and apprentices to complete jobs.

Lineman electricians install distribution and transmission lines to deliver electricity from its source to customers; this occupation is covered in the line installers and repairers profile.

Work Environment

Electricians held about 762,600 jobs in 2022. The largest employers of electricians were as follows:

Electrical contractors and other wiring installation contractors	65%
Self-employed workers	8
Manufacturing	6
Employment services	4
Government	3

Electricians work indoors and outdoors at homes, businesses, factories, and construction sites. Because electricians must travel to different worksites, local or long-distance commuting is often required.

On the jobsite, they occasionally work in cramped spaces. The long periods of standing and kneeling can be tiring. Electricians may be exposed to dirt, dust, debris, or fumes.

Electricians wear a variety of safety equipment to reduce their risk of injury.

Those working outside may be exposed to hot or cold temperatures and inclement weather. Those who work in factories are often subject to noisy machinery.

Electricians may be required to work at great heights, such as when working on construction sites, inside buildings, or on renewable energy projects.

Many electricians work alone, but sometimes they collaborate with others. Electricians employed by large companies are likely to work as part of a crew, directing helpers and apprentices to complete jobs.

Injuries and Illnesses

Working with electricity is dangerous. Electricians must take precautions to avoid getting hurt. Although accidents are potentially fatal, common injuries include electrical shocks, falls, burns, and other minor injuries.

To reduce these risks, workers must wear protective clothing and safety glasses. Electricians who are subject to loud noises, such as those in factories, must wear hearing protection.

Work Schedules

Almost all electricians work full time. Work schedules may include evenings and weekends. Overtime is common.

Self-employed electricians often work in residential construction and may be able to set their own schedule.

How to Become an Electrician

Most electricians learn through an apprenticeship, but some start out by attending a technical school. Most states require electricians to be licensed. For more information, contact your local or state electrical licensing board.

Education

A high school diploma or equivalent is required to become an electrician.

Some electricians start out by attending a technical school. Many technical schools offer programs related to circuitry, safety

Most electricians learn on the job through an apprenticeship.

practices, and basic electrical information. Graduates of these programs usually receive credit toward their apprenticeship.

Training

Most electricians learn their trade in a 4- or 5-year apprenticeship program. For each year of the program, apprentices typically receive 2,000 hours of paid on-the-job training as well as some technical instruction.

Workers who gained electrical experience in the military or in the construction industry may qualify for a shortened apprenticeship based on their experience and testing.

Technical instruction for apprentices includes electrical theory, blueprint reading, mathematics, electrical code requirements, and safety and first-aid practices. They may also receive specialized training related to soldering, communications, fire alarm systems, and elevators.

Several groups, including unions and contractor associations, sponsor apprenticeship programs. Apprenticeship requirements vary by state and locality.

Some electrical contractors have their own training programs, which are not recognized apprenticeship programs but include both technical and on-the-job training. Although most workers enter apprenticeships directly, some electricians enter apprenticeship programs after working as a helper. The Home Builders Institute offers a preapprenticeship certificate training (PACT) program for eight construction trades, including electricians.

After completing an apprenticeship program, electricians are considered to be journey workers and may perform duties on their own, subject to local or state licensing requirements.

Licenses, Certifications, and Registrations

Most states require electricians to pass a test and be licensed. Requirements vary by state. For more information, contact your local or state electrical licensing board. Many of the requirements can be found on the National Electrical Contractors Association's website.

The tests have questions related to the National Electrical Code and state and local electrical codes, all of which set standards for the safe installation of electrical wiring and equipment.

Electricians may be required to take continuing education courses in order to maintain their licenses. These courses are usually related to safety practices, changes to the electrical code, and training from manufacturers in specific products.

Electricians may obtain additional certifications, which demonstrate competency in areas such as solar photovoltaic, electrical generating, or lighting systems.

Electricians may be required to have a driver's license.

Advancement

After meeting additional requirements and working as a qualified electrician, journey workers may advance to become master electricians. Electricians may also find opportunities to advance to supervisor or to other roles in project management.

Important Qualities

Color vision. Electricians must identify electrical wires by color.

Critical-thinking skills. Electricians perform tests and use the results to diagnose problems. For example, when an outlet is not working, they may use a multimeter to check the voltage, amperage, or resistance in order to determine the best course of action.

Customer-service skills. Electricians work with people on a regular basis. They should be friendly and be able to address customers' questions.

Physical stamina. Electricians often need to move around all day while running wire and connecting fixtures to the wire.

Physical strength. Electricians need to be strong enough to move heavy components, which may weigh up to 50 pounds.

Troubleshooting skills. Electricians find, diagnose, and repair problems. For example, if a motor stops working, they perform tests to determine the cause of its failure and then, depending on the results, fix or replace the motor.

Pay

The median annual wage for electricians was $60,240 in May 2022. The median wage is the wage at which half the workers in an occupation earned more than that amount and half earned

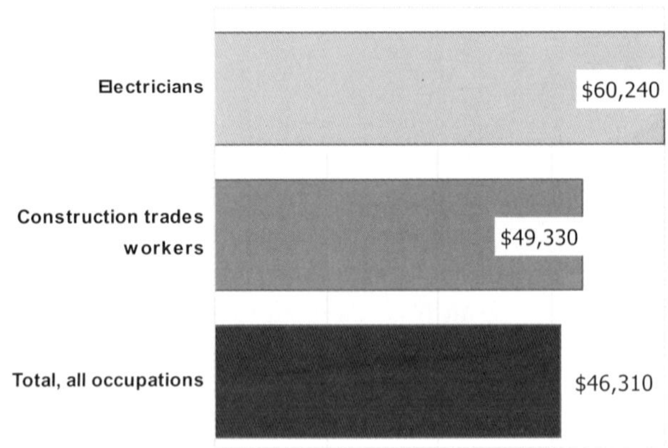

Note: All Occupations includes all occupations in the U.S. Economy.
Source: U.S. Bureau of Labor Statistics, Occupational Employment and Wage Statistics.

less. The lowest 10 percent earned less than $37,440, and the highest 10 percent earned more than $102,300.

In May 2022, the median annual wages for electricians in the top industries in which they worked were as follows:

Government	$68,140
Manufacturing	66,000
Electrical contractors and other wiring installation contractors	59,270
Employment services	49,790

Apprentices receive less pay than fully trained electricians, but their pay increases as they learn to do more.

Almost all electricians work full time. Work schedules may include evenings and weekends and may vary during times of inclement weather. During scheduled maintenance or on construction sites, electricians should expect to work overtime.

Self-employed electricians often work in residential construction and may be able to set their own schedule.

Job Outlook

Employment of electricians is projected to grow 6 percent from 2022 to 2032, faster than the average for all occupations.

About 73,500 openings for electricians are projected each year, on average, over the decade. Many of those openings are expected to result from the need to replace workers who transfer to different occupations or exit the labor force, such as to retire.

Employment

Nearly every building has electricity. Electricians are needed to install and replace these power systems. Alternative power generation, such as solar and wind, is a growing field that should require more electricians for installation. Electricians will continue to be needed to link these alternative systems to homes and power grids over the projections decade. However, employment growth stemming from these alternative sources may depend on government provisions—such as credits, net metering, and tax incentives—that spur consumer demand by lowering installation costs.

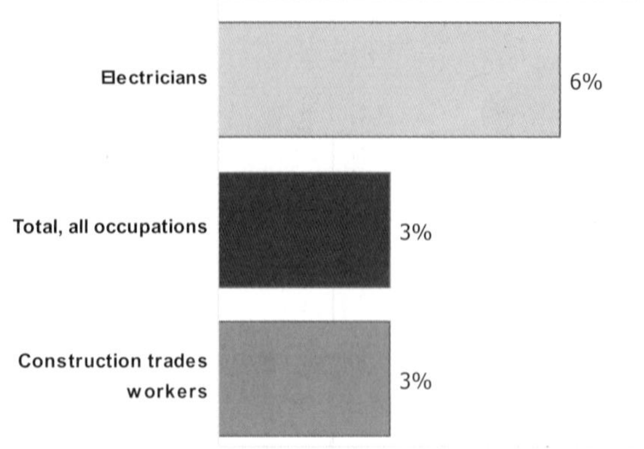

Note: All Occupations includes all occupations in the U.S. Economy.
Source: U.S. Bureau of Labor Statistics, Employment Projections program.

Occupational Title	SOC Code	Employment, 2022	Projected Employment, 2032	Change, 2022-32	
				Percent	Numeric
Electricians	47-2111	762,600	811,800	6	49,200

Contacts for More Information

For more details about apprenticeships or other work opportunities in this trade, contact the offices of the state employment service, the state apprenticeship agency, local electrical contractors, firms that employ maintenance electricians, or local union-management electrician apprenticeship committees. Apprenticeship information is available from the U.S. Department of Labor's Apprenticeship program online or by phone at 877-872-5627. Visit apprenticeship.gov to search for apprenticeship opportunities.

For more information about apprenticeship and training programs for electricians, visit

- Associated Builders and Contractors, Inc.
- Explore the Trades
- Home Builders Institute
- IBEW – NECA Electrical Training Alliance
- Independent Electrical Contractors, Inc.
- National Association of Home Builders
- National Electrical Contractors Association
- NCCER

Elevator and Escalator Installers and Repairers

Summary

Quick Facts: Elevator and Escalator Installers and Repairers

2022 Median Pay	$99,000 per year $47.60 per hour
Typical Entry-Level Education	High school diploma or equivalent
Work Experience in a Related Occupation	None
On-the-job Training	Apprenticeship
Number of Jobs, 2022	25,100
Job Outlook, 2022-32	1% (Little or no change)
Employment Change, 2022-32	400

What Elevator and Escalator Installers and Repairers Do

Elevator and escalator installers and repairers install, maintain, and fix elevators, escalators, moving walkways, and other lifts.

Work Environment

Elevator and escalator installers and repairers often work in cramped areas inside crawl spaces and machine rooms, and they may work at heights in elevator shafts. Most elevator and escalator installers and repairers work full time. Repairers may be on call 24 hours a day or may need to work overtime.

How to Become an Elevator or Escalator Installer and Repairer

Elevator and escalator installers and repairers typically need a high school diploma or equivalent. Nearly all learn how to do the work through an apprenticeship. Most states require workers to be licensed.

Pay

The median annual wage for elevator and escalator installers and repairers was $99,000 in May 2022.

Job Outlook

Employment of elevator and escalator installers and repairers is projected to show little or no change from 2022 to 2032.

Despite limited employment growth, about 2,100 openings for elevator and escalator installers and repairers are projected each year, on average, over the decade. Most of those openings are expected to result from the need to replace workers who transfer to different occupations or exit the labor force, such as to retire.

What Elevator and Escalator Installers and Repairers Do

Elevator and escalator installers and repairers install, maintain, and fix elevators, escalators, moving walkways, and other lifts.

Duties

Elevator and escalator installers and repairers typically do the following:

- Read and interpret blueprints to determine the layout of system components and to select the equipment needed for installation or repair
- Assemble elevator cars and components for similar systems
- Connect electrical wiring to control panels and motors
- Test newly installed equipment to ensure that it meets specifications
- Troubleshoot malfunctions in brakes, motors, switches, and control systems
- Dismantle elevator, escalator, or similar units to remove and replace defective parts, using hoists, ladders, and handtools or power tools
- Repair or replace faulty components in order to return elevator or escalator to fully operational status

Elevator mechanics often work in elevator machine rooms, which are at the top of some elevator hoistways.

Mechanics check many parts, including the rails of an escalator.

- Conduct preventive maintenance and inspections of elevators, escalators, and similar equipment to comply with safety regulations and building codes
- Keep service records of all maintenance and repair tasks

Elevator and escalator installers and repairers, also called *elevator and escalator constructors* or *mechanics*, assemble, install, maintain, and replace elevators, escalators, chairlifts, moving walkways, and similar equipment.

Elevator and escalator installers and repairers usually specialize in installation, maintenance, or repair work. Maintenance and repair workers generally need to know more about electronics, hydraulics, and electricity than do installers. Most elevators and similar mechanisms have computerized control systems, requiring maintenance and repair workers to do complex troubleshooting.

After an elevator, escalator, or other equipment is installed, workers must regularly maintain and repair it. Maintenance includes oiling and greasing moving parts, replacing worn parts, and adjusting equipment for optimal performance. Workers also troubleshoot and may be called for emergency repair.

A service crew usually handles major repairs—for example, replacing cables, doors and other components, or machine bearings. Service crews may need to use cutting torches or rigging equipment and also may need to do major modernization and alteration, such as replacing electric motors, hydraulic pumps, and control panels.

Work Environment

Elevator and escalator installers and repairers held about 25,100 jobs in 2022. The largest employers of elevator and escalator installers and repairers were as follows:

Building equipment contractors	85%
Government	3
Educational services; state, local, and private	1

Elevator mechanics also work on chair lifts.

Elevator and escalator installation and repair work is usually physically demanding. These workers may sit or stand for extensive periods, lift items that weigh up to 200 pounds, and work in cramped areas inside crawl spaces and machine rooms. They also may work at heights in elevator shafts, in dusty and dirty places with oily and greasy equipment, and in hot or cold environments.

Injuries and Illnesses

Elevator and escalator installers and repairers may suffer injuries from falls, burns from electrical shocks, and muscle strains from lifting and carrying heavy equipment. To reduce their risks and prevent injury, workers must wear protective equipment such as hardhats, harnesses, and safety glasses.

Work Schedules

Most elevator and escalator installers and repairers work full time. They may work overtime to make emergency repairs or to meet construction deadlines. They may be on call 24 hours a day.

How to Become an Elevator or Escalator Installer and Repairer

Elevator and escalator installers and repairers typically need a high school diploma or equivalent. Nearly all learn how to do

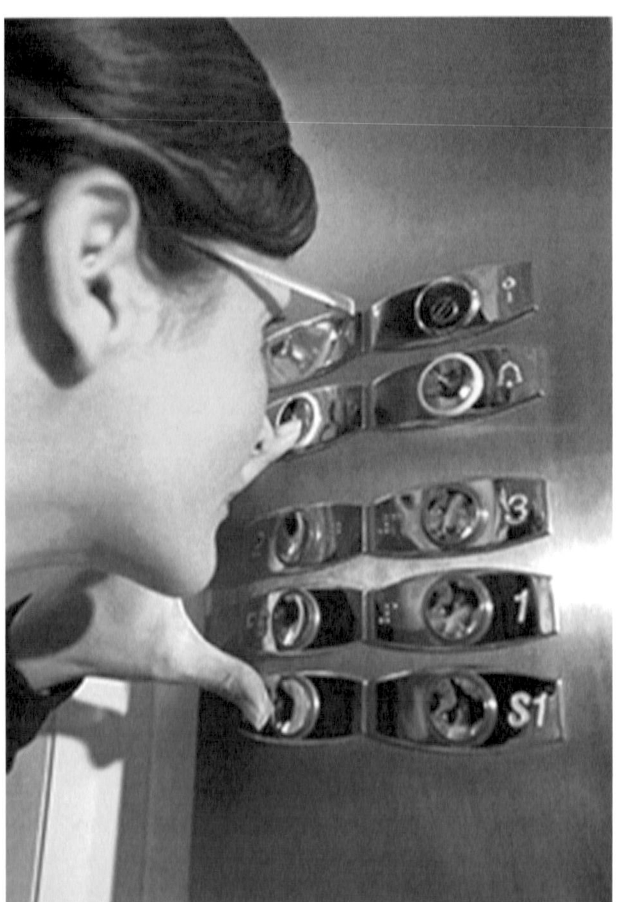

The fine tuning of an elevator is done by an adjustor.

the work through an apprenticeship. Most states require workers to be licensed.

Education

A high school diploma or equivalent is typically required. High school classes in math, mechanical drawing, and physics may be helpful.

Training

A career in elevator or escalator installation and repair typically begins with a 4-year apprenticeship program sponsored by a union, industry association, or employer. For each year of a typical program, apprentices must complete a predetermined number of hours of technical instruction and paid on-the-job training. During training, apprentices learn about safety, blueprint reading, mathematics, applied physics, elevator and escalator parts, electrical and digital theory, and electronics.

When they finish the apprenticeship program, fully trained elevator and escalator installers and repairers become mechanics or assistant mechanics. Elevator and escalator installers and repairers need ongoing training in order to keep up with technological developments.

Workers with relevant experience who can document it and demonstrate their skill may qualify for a shorter apprenticeship.

Licenses, Certifications, and Registrations

Most states require elevator and escalator installers and repairers to be licensed. Check with your state for more information.

Although not required, certification shows competence and proficiency in the field.

Elevator and escalator installers and repairers can become Certified Elevator Technicians (CET) or Certified Accessibility and Private Residence Lift Technicians (CAT) through the National Association of Elevator Contractors. They can also be certified as Qualified Elevator Inspectors (QEI) through the National Association of Elevator Safety Authorities International.

Employers may require elevator and escalator installers to have a driver's license or reliable transportation to travel to jobsites.

Advancement

Installers may receive additional training to specialize and advance to become a mechanic-in-charge, adjuster, or supervisor.

Important Qualities

Ability to work at heights. Some elevator and escalator installers may have to work atop ladders, mechanical lifts, or in elevator shafts.

Detail oriented. Elevator and escalator installers must keep accurate records of their service schedules. They need to carefully review complex blueprints and follow blueprint instructions exactly.

Mechanical skills. Elevator and escalator installers use a variety of power tools and handtools to install and repair lifts.

Physical stamina. Elevators and escalator installers must be able to do strenuous work, including in cramped and confined spaces, for long periods.

Physical strength. Elevator and escalator installers often lift heavy equipment and parts, including escalator steps, conduit, and metal tracks. They may be required to lift equipment weighing up to 200 pounds.

Troubleshooting skills. Elevator and escalator installers must be able to diagnose problems, especially when making repairs.

Pay

The median annual wage for elevator and escalator installers and repairers was $99,000 in May 2022. The median wage is the wage at which half the workers in an occupation earned more than that amount and half earned less. The lowest 10 percent earned less than $47,850, and the highest 10 percent earned more than $135,130.

In May 2022, the median annual wages for elevator and escalator installers and repairers in the top industries in which they worked were as follows:

Government	$103,610
Building equipment contractors	100,680
Educational services; state, local, and private	85,360

The starting pay for apprentices is usually about 50 percent of what fully trained elevator and escalator installers and repairers make. They earn pay increases as they progress in their apprenticeship. Apprentices who are also certified welders usually receive higher wages while welding.

Most elevator and escalator installers and repairers work full time. They may work overtime to make emergency repairs or to

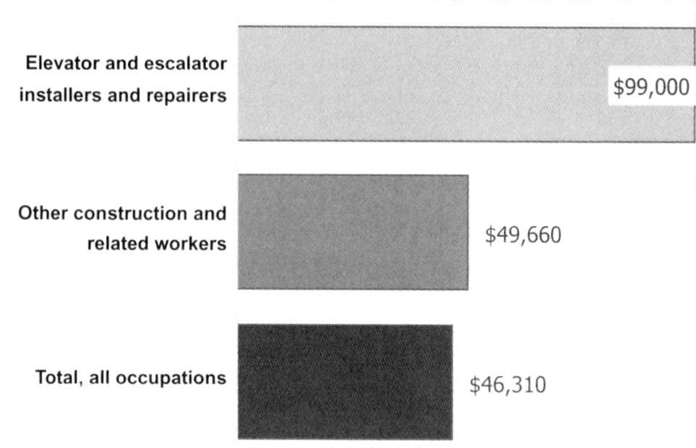

Note: All Occupations includes all occupations in the U.S. Economy.
Source: U.S. Bureau of Labor Statistics, Occupational Employment and Wage Statistics.

Elevator and Escalator Installers and Repairers

Percent change in employment, projected 2022-32

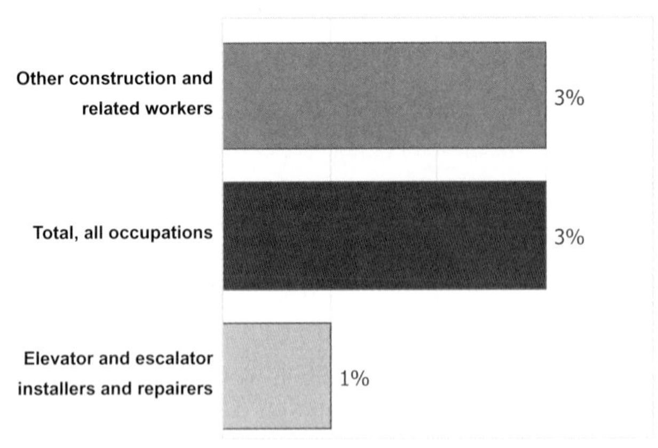

Note: All Occupations includes all occupations in the U.S. Economy.
Source: U.S. Bureau of Labor Statistics, Employment Projections program.

meet construction deadlines. Workers may be on call 24 hours a day.

Job Outlook

Employment of elevator and escalator installers and repairers is projected to show little or no change from 2022 to 2032.

Despite limited employment growth, about 2,100 openings for elevator and escalator installers and repairers are projected each year, on average, over the decade. Most of those openings are expected to result from the need to replace workers who transfer to different occupations or exit the labor force, such as to retire.

Employment

Demand for elevator and escalator installers and repairers is closely tied to the construction of office buildings and stores that have elevators and escalators, and this type of construction is expected to slow over the projections decade.

However, the need to regularly maintain, update, and repair old equipment; provide access for people with disabilities; and install increasingly sophisticated equipment and controls will sustain demand for elevator and escalator installers and repairers.

Occupational Title	SOC Code	Employment, 2022	Projected Employment, 2032	Change, 2022-32	
				Percent	Numeric
Elevator and escalator installers and repairers	47-4021	25,100	25,500	1	400

Contacts for More Information

For information about apprenticeships or job opportunities as an elevator and escalator installer or repairer, contact local elevator and escalator contractors, a local chapter of the International Union of Elevator Constructors, a local joint union–management apprenticeship committee, or the nearest office of your state employment service or apprenticeship agency. Apprenticeship information is available from the U.S. Department of Labor's Apprenticeship program online or by phone at 877-872-5627. Visit Apprenticeship.gov to search for apprenticeship opportunities.

For more information about elevator installers and repairers, visit

- International Union of Elevator Constructors
- National Elevator Industry Educational Program

For more information about the NAEC Apprenticeship Program, the Certified Elevator Technician program, or the Certified Accessibility and Private Residence Lift Technician program, visit

- National Association of Elevator Contractors

For more information about certification as a Qualified Elevator Inspector, visit

- National Association of Elevator Safety Authorities International

For information about opportunities for military veterans, visit:

- Helmets to Hardhats

Flooring Installers and Tile and Stone Setters

Summary

Quick Facts: Flooring Installers and Tile and Stone Setters	
2022 Median Pay	$47,890 per year $23.03 per hour
Typical Entry-Level Education	No formal educational credential
Work Experience in a Related Occupation	None
On-the-job Training	See How to Become One
Number of Jobs, 2022	120,900
Job Outlook, 2022-32	3% (As fast as average)
Employment Change, 2022-32	3,500

What Flooring Installers and Tile and Stone Setters Do

Flooring installers and tile and stone setters lay and finish carpet, wood, vinyl, tile, and other materials.

Work Environment

Installing flooring, tile, and stone is physically demanding, with workers spending much of their time reaching, bending, and kneeling. Most work full time, although schedules may vary.

How to Become a Flooring Installer or Tile and Stone Setter

Flooring installers and tile and stone setters typically need no formal educational credential. They learn their trade on the job, sometimes starting as a helper.

Pay

The median annual wage for flooring installers and tile and stone setters was $47,890 in May 2022.

Floor sanders and finishers must remove old stain before applying the new coats.

Job Outlook

Overall employment of flooring installers and tile and stone setters is projected to grow 3 percent from 2022 to 2032, about as fast as the average for all occupations.

About 9,800 openings for flooring installers and tile and stone setters are projected each year, on average, over the decade. Many of those openings are expected to result from the need to replace workers who transfer to different occupations or exit the labor force, such as to retire.

What Flooring Installers and Tile and Stone Setters Do

Flooring installers and tile and stone setters lay and finish carpet, wood, vinyl, and other materials, such as ceramic, glass, marble, and granite.

Duties

Flooring installers and tile and stone setters typically do the following:

- Remove existing materials from floors, walls, or other surfaces
- Clean and level the surface to be covered
- Measure the area and cut material to fit
- Arrange materials according to design plans
- Place materials and secure with adhesives, nails, or staples
- Fill joints with filler compound and remove excess compound
- Trim excess carpet or linoleum
- Apply finishes, such as sealants and stains

Flooring installers and tile and stone setters lay the materials that improve the look and feel of homes, offices, restaurants, and other buildings. Many of these workers install materials on floors. However, they also work on walls, ceilings, countertops, and showers.

Installing floors and tiles requires a smooth, even base of mortar or plywood. Flooring installers and tile and stone setters or other construction craftworkers lay this base. On remodeling

Some tile and stone setters create intricate designs.

jobs, workers may need to remove old flooring and smooth the surface before laying the base.

The following are examples of types of flooring installers and tile and stone setters:

Carpet installers lay carpet on new floors or over existing flooring. They use special tools, including "knee kickers" to position the carpet and power stretchers to pull the carpet snugly against walls. They also join carpet edges and seam edges by sewing or by using tape with glue and a heated carpet iron.

Carpet tile installers lay modular pieces of carpet that may be glued into place. Installing carpet tiles may be an option where standard carpet is impractical, such as in designing a pattern over an area.

Floor sanders and finishers scrape and smooth wood floors, often using power sanders. They then apply stains and sealants to preserve the wood. (For information on workers who install wood floors, see the profile on carpenters.)

Floor layers, except carpet, wood, and hard tiles, install a variety of resilient flooring materials. ***Linoleum installers*** lay washable flooring material of the same name, cutting the linoleum to size and gluing it into place. ***Vinyl installers*** lay plastic-based flooring that includes vinyl ester, vinyl sheeting, and vinyl tile. Installers of laminate, manufactured wood, and wood tile floors are included in this category.

Tile and stone setters install pieces of ceramic, marble, granite, glass, or other materials. ***Tile installers***, sometimes called ***tile setters,*** cut tiles using wet saws, tile scribes, or handheld tile cutters. They then use trowels of different sizes to spread mortar or a sticky paste, called mastic, evenly on the work surface before placing the tiles. ***Tile finishers*** apply grout between tiles after the tiles are set by using a rubber trowel, called a float, and then wipe the tiles clean after the grout dries. ***Stone setters*** may cut marble, granite, or other stone to a specified size with a wet saw. They use special adhesives to fasten the stone to the desired surface; in remodeling projects, they may first need to smooth the underlying surface after removing old materials.

Work Environment

Flooring installers and tile and stone setters held about 120,900 jobs in 2022. Employment in the detailed occupations that make up flooring installers and tile and stone setters was distributed as follows:

Tile and stone setters	59,400
Floor layers, except carpet, wood, and hard tiles	30,200
Carpet installers	25,100
Floor sanders and finishers	6,200

The largest employers of flooring installers and tile and stone setters were as follows:

Specialty trade contractors	49%
Self-employed workers	30
Manufacturing	5
Construction of buildings	5

Carpet installers spend a lot of time kneeling when stretching carpet.

Installing flooring, tile, and stone is physically demanding, requiring workers to spend much of their time reaching, bending, and kneeling. Workers typically wear kneepads while kneeling; safety goggles when using grinders, saws, and sanders; and dust masks or respirator systems to prevent inhaling work-generated dust in enclosed areas with poor ventilation.

Injuries and Illnesses

Carpet installers and floor sanders and finishers have some of the highest rates of injuries and illnesses of all occupations.

Work Schedules

Most flooring installers and tile and stone setters work full time, although schedules may vary. In commercial settings, they may need to work evenings and weekends to avoid disturbing regular business operations.

How to Become a Flooring Installer or Tile and Stone Setter

Flooring installers and tile and stone setters typically need no formal educational credential. They learn their trade on the

Most flooring installers and tile and stone setters learn on the job working with experienced installers.

job, sometimes starting as a helper. Some learn through an apprenticeship.

Education

There are typically no formal education requirements for becoming a flooring installer or tile and stone setter, although candidates entering an apprenticeship program may need a high school diploma or equivalent.

Certain high school courses, such as art and math, may be helpful for flooring installers and tile and stone setters.

Training

Flooring installers and tile and stone setters typically learn on the job, working with experienced installers or starting as helpers.

New workers usually do simple tasks, such as moving materials. As they gain experience, they take on more complex tasks, such as cutting carpet. Some helpers work as tile finishers before becoming tile installers.

Some flooring installers and tile and stone setters learn their trade through a 2- to 4-year apprenticeship. For each year of a typical program, apprentices must complete a predetermined number of hours of technical instruction and paid on-the-job training. Technical instruction in the apprenticeship may include mathematics, building code requirements, safety and first-aid practices, and blueprint reading. After completing an apprenticeship program, flooring installers and tile and stone setters are considered journey workers and may perform duties on their own.

Certification

Several organizations offer certification for floor and tile installers. Although certification is not required, it demonstrates that a flooring installer and tile and stone setter has a specific mastery of skills to do a job.

The Ceramic Tile Education Foundation (CTEF) offers the Certified Tile Installer (CTI) designation for workers with 2 or more years of experience as a tile installer. Applicants must pass a written test and a hands-on performance evaluation.

Several groups, including the Ceramic Tile Education Foundation, the International Masonry Institute (IMI), the International Union of Bricklayers & Allied Craftworkers (IUBAC), the National Tile Contractors Association (NTCA), the Tile Contractors' Association of America (TCAA), and the Tile Council of North America (TCNA) have created the Advanced Certifications for Tile Installers (ACT) program. To qualify for the program, applicants must have either completed a qualified apprenticeship program or earned the CTI certification. Requirements for certification include passing both an exam and a field test.

The National Wood Flooring Association (NWFA) offers optional certification for floor sanders and finishers. Sanders and finishers must have 2 years of experience and must have completed NWFA-approved training. Applicants are required to complete written and performance tests.

The International Certified Floorcovering Installers Association (CFI) offers certification for flooring and tile installers. Installers need 2 years of experience before they can take the written test and performance evaluation.

The International Standards & Training Alliance (INSTALL) offers a comprehensive flooring certification program for flooring and tile installers. INSTALL certification requires both classroom and hands-on training and covers all major types of flooring.

Important Qualities

Color vision. Flooring installers and tile and stone setters often determine small color variations and must be able to distinguish among colors in patterns for the best looking finish.

Customer-service skills. Flooring installers and tile and stone setters must be courteous with and considerate of customers, especially while completing tasks in customers' homes.

Detail oriented. Flooring installers and tile and stone setters need to be thorough and exacting to ensure that tile, wood, and carpet patterns are properly aligned.

Math skills. Flooring installers and tile and stone setters use math to measure an area to be covered and to calculate the amount of material needed to cover it.

Physical stamina. Flooring installers and tile and stone setters must be able to stand or kneel for many hours in order to spread adhesive quickly and place tiles before the adhesive hardens.

Physical strength. Flooring installers and tile and stone setters must be able to lift, carry, and set heavy pieces of flooring material into position.

Pay

The median annual wage for flooring installers and tile and stone setters was $47,890 in May 2022. The median wage is the wage at which half the workers in an occupation earned more than that amount and half earned less. The lowest 10 percent earned less than $31,620, and the highest 10 percent earned more than $79,950.

Median annual wages for flooring installers and tile and stone setters in May 2022 were as follows:

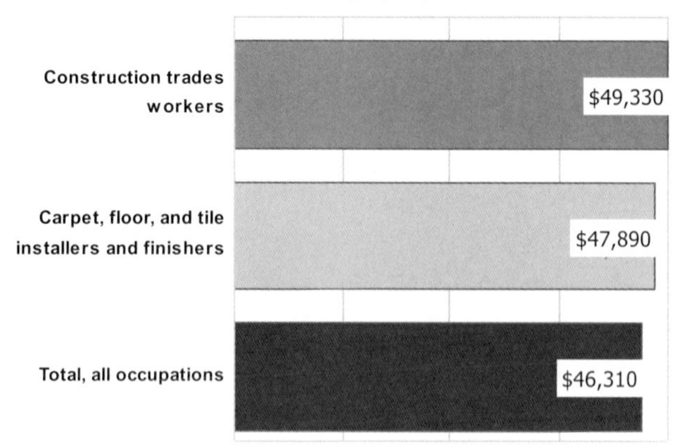

Note: All Occupations includes all occupations in the U.S. Economy.
Source: U.S. Bureau of Labor Statistics, Occupational Employment and Wage Statistics.

Floor layers, except carpet, wood, and hard tiles..	$48,870
Tile and stone setters	48,340
Floor sanders and finishers	46,060
Carpet installers	45,240

In May 2022, the median annual wages for flooring installers and tile and stone setters in the top industries in which they worked were as follows:

Specialty trade contractors	$49,110
Construction of buildings	46,330
Manufacturing	43,200

Most flooring installers and tile and stone setters work full time, although schedules may vary. In commercial settings, they may need to work evenings and weekends to avoid disturbing regular business operations.

Job Outlook

Overall employment of flooring installers and tile and stone setters is projected to grow 3 percent from 2022 to 2032, about as fast as the average for all occupations.

About 9,800 openings for flooring installers and tile and stone setters are projected each year, on average, over the decade. Many of those openings are expected to result from the need to replace workers who transfer to different occupations or exit the labor force, such as to retire.

Employment

Projected employment of flooring installers and tile and stone setters varies by occupation (see table). The construction of new homes and the renovation of existing units will be the primary source of flooring and tile and stone installation over the projections decade.

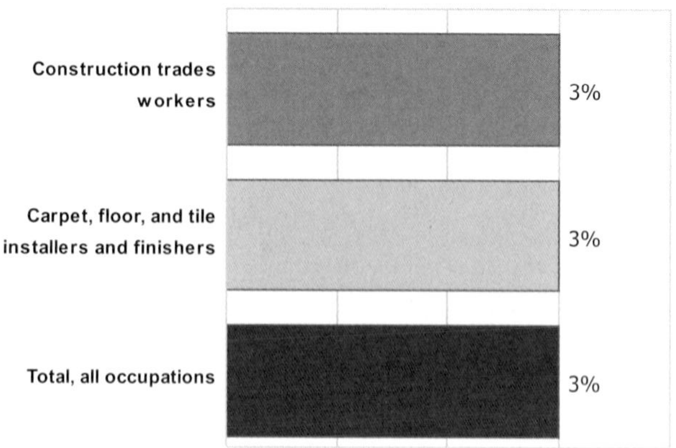

Note: All Occupations includes all occupations in the U.S. Economy.
Source: U.S. Bureau of Labor Statistics, Employment Projections program.

Vinyl and other resilient flooring products have become increasingly popular, especially in homes, which will lead to employment growth for floor layers. Tile and stone installation will continue to be common for bathrooms, restaurants, and other buildings, supporting demand for these workers.

Occupational Title	SOC Code	Employment, 2022	Projected Employment, 2032	Change, 2022-32	
				Percent	Numeric
Carpet, floor, and tile installers and finishers	47-2040	120,900	124,400	3	3,500
Carpet installers	47-2041	25,100	22,300	-11	-2,800
Floor layers, except carpet, wood, and hard tiles	47-2042	30,200	32,300	7	2,200
Floor sanders and finishers	47-2043	6,200	6,200	0	0
Tile and stone setters	47-2044	59,400	63,500	7	4,100

Contacts for More Information

Apprenticeship information is available from the U.S. Department of Labor's Apprenticeship program online or by phone at 877-872-5627. Visit Apprenticeship.gov to search for apprenticeship opportunities.

For more information about flooring installers and tile and stone setters, visit

- Ceramic Tile Education Foundation
- International Masonry Institute
- International Union of Bricklayers & Allied Craftworkers
- Tile Contractors' Association of America
- The Tile Council of North America, Inc.
- Home Builders Institute
- International Certified Floorcovering Installers Association
- Finishing Trades Institute International
- International Standards & Training Alliance (INSTALL)
- National Tile Contractors Association
- National Wood Flooring Association

Glaziers

Summary

Quick Facts: Glaziers	
2022 Median Pay	$48,720 per year $23.42 per hour
Typical Entry-Level Education	High school diploma or equivalent
Work Experience in a Related Occupation	None
On-the-job Training	Apprenticeship
Number of Jobs, 2022	54,500
Job Outlook, 2022-32	2% (As fast as average)
Employment Change, 2022-32	1,200

What Glaziers Do
Glaziers install glass in windows, skylights, and other fixtures in buildings.

Work Environment
As in many other construction trades, the work of glaziers is physically demanding. They may experience cuts from tools and glass, falls from ladders and scaffolding, and exposure to solvents. Most work full time.

How to Become a Glazier
Glaziers typically enter the occupation with a high school diploma and learn their trade through an apprenticeship or on-the-job training.

Pay
The median annual wage for glaziers was $48,720 in May 2022.

Job Outlook
Employment of glaziers is projected to grow 2 percent from 2022 to 2032, about as fast as the average for all occupations.

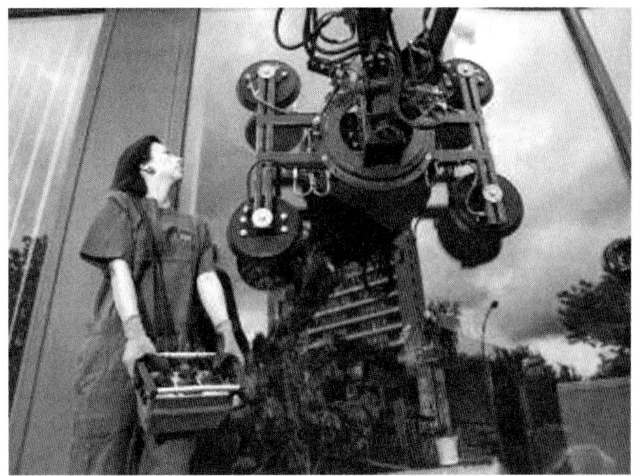

Glaziers may use specialized equipment to move windows into place.

About 5,500 openings for glaziers are projected each year, on average, over the decade. Many of those openings are expected to result from the need to replace workers who transfer to different occupations or exit the labor force, such as to retire.

What Glaziers Do
Glaziers install glass in windows, skylights, and other fixtures in buildings.

Duties
Glaziers typically do the following:

- Follow blueprints and specifications
- Remove any existing glass before installing replacement glass
- Cut glass to the specified size and shape
- Use measuring tape, plumb lines, and levels to ensure proper fitting
- Make or install sashes and moldings for installing glass
- Fasten glass into sashes or frames with clips, moldings, or other types of fasteners
- Add weather seal or putty around pane edges to seal joints

Glaziers specialize in installing different glass products, such as insulated glass that retains warm or cool air and tempered glass that is less prone to breaking.

In homes, glaziers install or replace glass items including windows, mirrors, shower doors, and bathtub enclosures. On commercial projects, glaziers install items such as room dividers, display cases, and security windows. For either residential or commercial exterior projects, glaziers may install items such as architectural glass systems (glass used for exterior walls or other building material) or storefront windows in businesses.

For most large construction projects, glass is precut and mounted into frames at a factory or shop. The finished glass arrives at the jobsite ready for glaziers to position and secure into place. Using cranes or hoists with suction cups, workers lift large, heavy pieces of glass for installation. If the glass is not secure inside the frame, glaziers may attach steel and aluminum

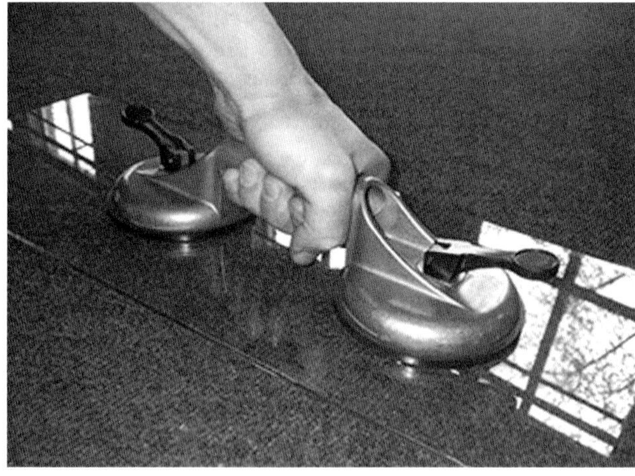

Suction handles are used to pick up and maneuver glass.

Glaziers may need to work at great heights

sashes or frames to the building and then secure the glass with clips, moldings, or other types of fasteners.

Workers who replace and repair glass in motor vehicles are described in the automotive body and glass repairers profile.

Work Environment

Glaziers held about 54,500 jobs in 2022. The largest employers of glaziers were as follows:

Foundation, structure, and building exterior contractors	68%
Self-employed workers	5
Building finishing contractors	5
Manufacturing	4

As in many other construction trades, the work of glaziers is physically demanding. Glaziers spend most of the day standing, bending, or reaching, and they often must lift and maneuver heavy, cumbersome materials, such as large glass plates. Glaziers are often exposed to the weather while installing glass. They may be required to travel to different jobsites for commercial or residential work.

Injuries and Illnesses

The work of glaziers can be dangerous, and workers risk injury. Injuries may include cuts from tools and glass, falls from ladders and scaffolding, and exposure to solvents. To minimize their risk of harm, workers may wear protective gear, such as safety glasses, harnesses, and gloves.

Work Schedules

Most glaziers work full time.

How to Become a Glazier

Glaziers typically enter the occupation with a high school diploma and learn their trade through an apprenticeship or on-the-job training.

Education

Glaziers typically need a high school diploma or equivalent to enter the occupation.

Glaziers typically learn their trade through a 4-year apprenticeship or on-the-job training.

Training

Glaziers typically learn their trade through a 3- or 4-year apprenticeship or on-the-job training. On the job, they learn to use the tools and equipment of the trade; handle, measure, cut, and install glass and metal framing; cut and fit moldings; and install and balance glass doors. Technical training includes learning different installation techniques, blueprint reading and sketching, general construction techniques, safety practices, and first aid.

A few groups sponsor apprenticeship programs, including several union and contractor associations. Most programs require apprentices to have a high school diploma or equivalent and be at least 18 years old. After completing an apprenticeship program, glaziers are considered to be journey workers who may do tasks on their own.

Licenses, Certifications, and Registrations

Some states may require glaziers to have a license; check with your state for more information. Licensure requirements typically include passing a test and having a combination of education and work experience.

Glaziers may choose to get optional certification, such the Architectural Glass and Metal Technician (AGMT),

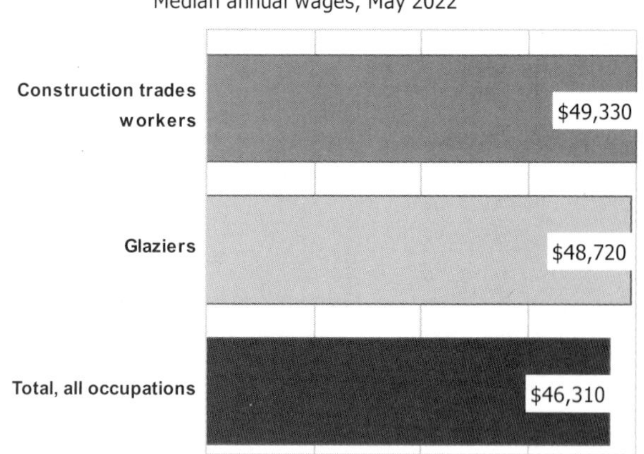

Note: All Occupations includes all occupations in the U.S. Economy.
Source: U.S. Bureau of Labor Statistics, Occupational Employment and Wage Statistics.

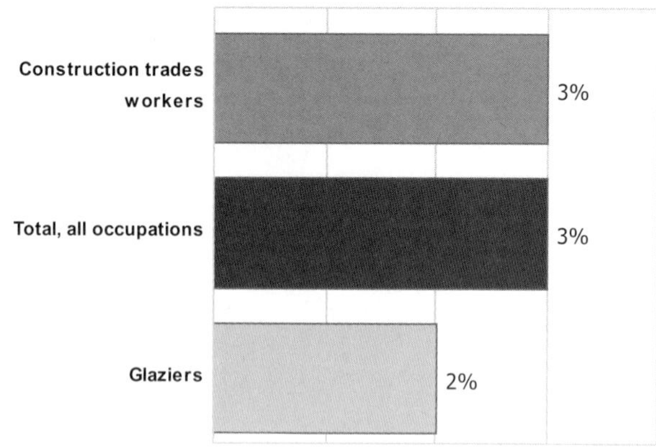

Note: All Occupations includes all occupations in the U.S. Economy.
Source: U.S. Bureau of Labor Statistics, Employment Projections program.

to demonstrate competency and to broaden employment opportunities.

Important Qualities

Ability to work at heights. Glaziers must not be afraid to work at great heights while installing glass windows in skyscrapers or other tall buildings.

Communication skills. Glaziers need to be able to convey information to other team members and customers to ensure that the work is done correctly.

Detail oriented. Glaziers must be precise in their measurements, cuts, and modifications to avoid making costly mistakes.

Physical stamina. Glaziers are on their feet most of the day moving heavy pieces of glass. They also need to be able to hold glass in place until it can be fully secured.

Physical strength. Glaziers often must lift heavy pieces of glass for hanging.

Reading comprehension skills. Glaziers must be able to understand and follow complex blueprints and instruction manuals.

Pay

The median annual wage for glaziers was $48,720 in May 2022. The median wage is the wage at which half the workers in an occupation earned more than that amount and half earned less. The lowest 10 percent earned less than $34,580, and the highest 10 percent earned more than $87,400.

In May 2022, the median annual wages for glaziers in the top industries in which they worked were as follows:

Foundation, structure, and building exterior contractors	$49,470
Building finishing contractors	45,970
Manufacturing	43,450

Pay for apprentices is less than what fully trained glaziers make. Apprentices receive more pay as they gain experience. Glaziers who work at heights may be eligible for hazard pay.

Most glaziers work full time.

Job Outlook

Employment of glaziers is projected to grow 2 percent from 2022 to 2032, about as fast as the average for all occupations.

About 5,500 openings for glaziers are projected each year, on average, over the decade. Many of those openings are expected to result from the need to replace workers who transfer to different occupations or exit the labor force, such as to retire.

Employment

An important component of buildings, glass improves access to natural light. Demand for glaziers stems both from new construction and from the need to repair and replace windows and other glass in existing buildings.

Occupational Title	SOC Code	Employment, 2022	Projected Employment, 2032	Change, 2022-32	
				Percent	Numeric
Glaziers	47-2121	54,500	55,700	2	1,200

Contacts for More Information

Apprenticeship information is available from the U.S. Department of Labor's Apprenticeship program online or by phone at 877-872-5627. Visit Apprenticeship.gov to search for apprenticeship opportunities.

For more information about glaziers, visit

- Associated Builders and Contractors, Inc.
- Finishing Trades Institute
- International Union of Painters and Allied Trades
- National Glass Association

For information about opportunities for military veterans, visit:

- Helmets to Hardhats

Hazardous Materials Removal Workers

Summary

Quick Facts: Hazardous Materials Removal Workers	
2022 Median Pay	$46,690 per year $22.45 per hour
Typical Entry-Level Education	High school diploma or equivalent
Work Experience in a Related Occupation	None
On-the-job Training	Moderate-term on-the-job training
Number of Jobs, 2022	48,700
Job Outlook, 2022-32	1% (Little or no change)
Employment Change, 2022-32	400

What Hazardous Materials Removal Workers Do

Hazardous materials removal workers identify and dispose of harmful substances such as asbestos, lead, and radioactive waste.

Work Environment

Work environments for hazmat removal workers vary. Completing projects may require night and weekend work. Overtime is common for some workers, particularly for those who respond to emergencies or disasters.

How to Become a Hazardous Materials Removal Worker

Hazmat removal workers typically need a high school diploma and are trained on the job. Workers may complete training that follows Occupational Safety and Health Administration (OSHA) standards. Some hazmat removal workers need federally or state-mandated training, licensing, or permits, depending on the type of waste remediation.

Pay

The median annual wage for hazardous materials removal workers was $46,690 in May 2022.

Job Outlook

Employment of hazardous materials removal workers is projected to show little or no change from 2022 to 2032.

Despite limited employment growth, about 5,200 openings for hazardous materials removal workers are projected each year, on average, over the decade. Most of those openings are expected to result from the need to replace workers who transfer to different occupations or exit the labor force, such as to retire.

What Hazardous Materials Removal Workers Do

Hazardous materials (hazmat) removal workers identify and dispose of harmful substances, such as asbestos, lead, mold, and radioactive waste. They also neutralize and clean up materials that are flammable, corrosive, or toxic.

Duties

Hazmat removal workers typically do the following:

- Follow safety procedures before, during, and after cleanup
- Comply with state and federal laws regarding waste disposal
- Test hazardous materials to determine the proper way to clean up
- Construct scaffolding or build containment areas before cleaning up
- Remove, neutralize, or clean up hazardous materials that are found or spilled
- Clean contaminated tools and equipment for reuse
- Package, transport, or store hazardous materials
- Keep records of cleanup activities

Hazmat removal workers clean up materials that are harmful to people and the environment. They usually work in teams and

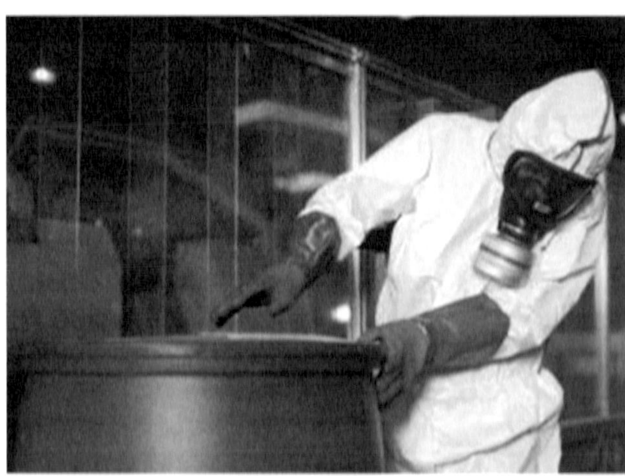

Workers dispose of hazardous materials.

Hazmat removal workers remove, neutralize, or clean up hazardous materials.

follow strict instructions and guidelines. The specific duties of hazmat removal workers depend on the substances that are targeted and the location of the cleanup. For example, some workers remove and treat radioactive materials generated by nuclear facilities and power plants. They break down contaminated items such as "glove boxes," which are used to process radioactive materials, and they clean and decontaminate facilities that are closed or decommissioned (taken out of service).

Hazmat removal workers may clean up hazardous materials in response to natural or human-made disasters and accidents, such as those involving trains, trucks, or other vehicles transporting hazardous materials.

Workers dealing with radiation may also measure, record, and report radiation levels; operate high-pressure cleaning equipment for decontamination; and package radioactive materials for removal or storage.

In addition, workers may prepare and transport hazardous materials for treatment, storage, or disposal following U.S. Environmental Protection Agency (EPA) or Occupational Safety and Health Administration (OSHA) regulations. Using equipment such as forklifts, earthmoving machinery, and trucks, workers move materials from contaminated sites to incinerators, landfills, or storage facilities. They also organize and track the locations of items in these facilities.

Asbestos abatement workers and ***lead abatement workers*** remove asbestos and lead, respectively, from buildings and structures, particularly those being renovated or demolished. Most of this work is in older buildings that were originally built with asbestos insulation and lead-based paints—both of which are now banned.

Asbestos and lead abatement workers apply chemicals to surfaces, such as walls and ceilings, in order to soften asbestos or remove lead-based paint. Once the chemicals are applied, workers remove asbestos from the surfaces or strip the walls. They package the residue or paint chips and place them in approved bags or containers for proper disposal. Asbestos abatement workers use scrapers or vacuums to remove asbestos from buildings. Lead abatement workers operate sandblasters, high-pressure water sprayers, and other tools to remove paint.

Work Environment

Hazardous materials removal workers held about 48,700 jobs in 2022. The largest employers of hazardous materials removal workers were as follows:

Remediation and other waste management services	62%
Waste treatment and disposal	10
Construction	6

Working conditions vary with the hazardous material being removed. For example, workers removing lead or asbestos often spend time in confined spaces or at great heights and must bend or stoop to remove the material. Workers responding to

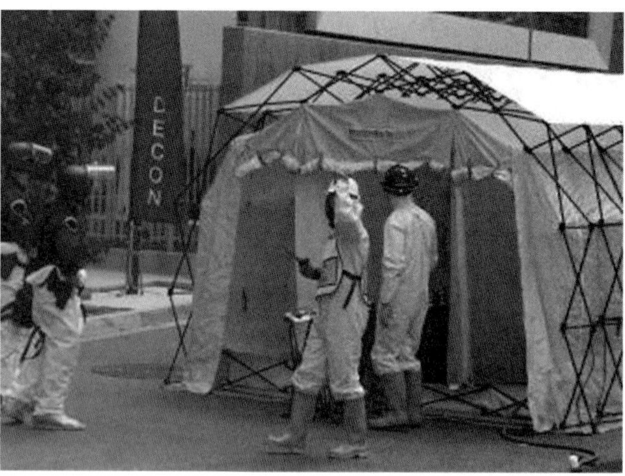

Hazmat removal workers wear protective clothing to reduce exposure to toxic materials.

emergency and disaster scenarios may be outside in all types of weather.

Asbestos and lead abatement workers typically are in buildings being renovated or torn down, or in confined spaces.

Hazmat removal work may be physically demanding and strenuous.

Injuries and Illnesses

Cleaning or removing hazardous materials is dangerous, and workers must follow specific safety procedures to avoid injuries and illnesses. They usually work in teams and follow instructions from a team leader or site supervisor.

Workers wear coveralls, gloves, shoe covers, and safety glasses or goggles to reduce their exposure to harmful materials. Some must wear fully closed protective suits for several hours at a time, which may be hot and uncomfortable. For extremely toxic cleanups, hazmat removal workers also are required to wear respirators to protect themselves from airborne particles or noxious gases. Lead abatement workers wear personal air monitors that measure the amount of lead exposure.

Work Schedules

Most hazmat removal workers are employed full time. Overtime is common for some workers, especially for those who respond to emergency and disaster scenarios.

Some hazmat removal workers travel to areas affected by a disaster. During a cleanup, workers may be away from home for several days or weeks until the project is completed.

How to Become a Hazardous Materials Removal Worker

Hazardous materials (hazmat) removal workers typically need a high school diploma and are trained on the job. They must complete training that follows federal, state, and local standards.

Education

Hazmat removal workers typically need a high school diploma.

Hazmat removal workers learn on the job.

Training

Hazmat removal workers receive training on the job. Training generally includes a combination of technical instruction and fieldwork. For technical training, they learn safety procedures and the proper use of personal protective equipment. Onsite, they learn about equipment and chemicals and are supervised by an experienced worker.

The length of training and the information covered in training varies, depending on regulatory requirements and type of hazardous material that a worker is being trained to remove or reduce.

Employers may require workers to have completed OSHA Hazardous Waste Operations and Emergency Response Standard (HAZWOPER) training. The training covers health hazards, personal protective equipment, site safety, recognizing and identifying hazards, and decontamination. Refresher training may be required periodically.

To work with a specific hazardous material, workers must complete training requirements and work requirements set by state or federal agencies on handling that material.

Workers who treat asbestos or lead, the most common contaminants, must complete an employer-sponsored training program that covers technical and safety subjects outlined by OSHA.

Workers at nuclear facilities receive extensive training. In addition to completing HAZWOPER training, workers must take courses on nuclear materials and radiation safety as mandated by the U.S. Nuclear Regulatory Commission.

Organizations and companies provide training through programs that are approved by the U.S. Environmental Protection Agency.

Apprenticeships, such as Construction Craft Laborer through the Laborers' International Union of North America (LIUNA), provide training, hands-on instruction, and certification tests for hazmat workers.

Licenses, Certifications, and Registrations

Some states require workers to have permits or licenses for each type of hazardous waste they remove, particularly asbestos and lead. Workers who transport hazardous materials may need a state or federal permit.

License requirements vary by state, but candidates typically must meet the following criteria:

- Be at least 18 years old
- Complete training mandated by a state or federal agency
- Pass a written exam

To maintain licensure, workers must take continuing education courses each year. For more information, check with the state's licensing agency.

Some certifications, such as for HAZWOPER training, may be required. Others, such as Department of Transportation (DOT) hazmat transportation certification, are optional but may lead to more employment opportunities.

Work Experience in a Related Occupation

Hazmat materials removal workers typically do not need related experience to enter the occupation. However, some employers prefer candidates who have experience in the construction trades—workers such as construction laborers and helpers—or in military careers.

Advancement

Hazmat removal workers may advance to become a supervisor after gaining experience and completing additional training, such as the OSHA HAZWOPER supervisor training. Workers also may advance to different positions within their industry, such as a radiation safety technician later becoming a supervisor in the nuclear power industry. After gaining experience, workers also may choose to start their own hazmat removal business.

Important Qualities

Decision-making skills. Hazmat removal workers identify materials in a spill or leak and choose the proper method for safe cleanup.

Detail oriented. Hazmat removal workers must follow safety procedures, understand laws and regulations, and keep records of their work.

Mechanical skills. Hazmat removal workers may operate heavy equipment to clean up contaminated sites and set up machinery needed for remediation.

Physical stamina. Workers may have to stand and scrub equipment or surfaces for hours at a time to remove toxic materials.

Physical strength. Some hazmat removal workers lift and move heavy pieces of materials they are removing from a site.

Pay

The median annual wage for hazardous materials removal workers was $46,690 in May 2022. The median wage is the wage at which half the workers in an occupation earned more

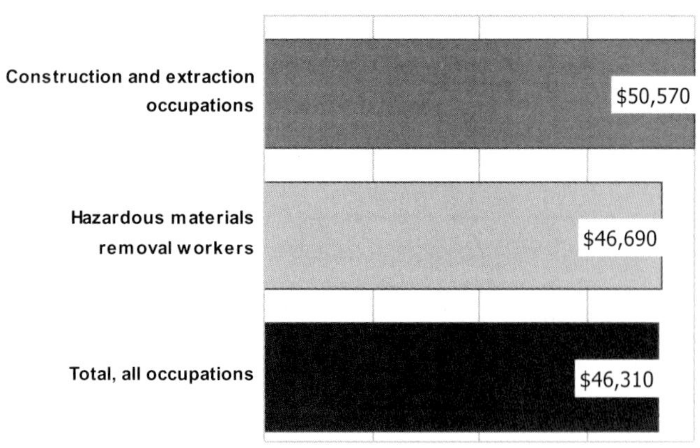

Note: All Occupations includes all occupations in the U.S. Economy.
Source: U.S. Bureau of Labor Statistics, Employment Projections program.

than that amount and half earned less. The lowest 10 percent earned less than $32,910, and the highest 10 percent earned more than $81,130.

In May 2022, the median annual wages for hazardous materials removal workers in the top industries in which they worked were as follows:

Construction	$54,480
Remediation and other waste management services	46,310
Waste treatment and disposal	40,910

Apprentices are paid less than fully trained hazmat removal workers. Apprentices receive pay increases as they advance through the apprenticeship program.

Most hazmat removal workers are employed full time. Overtime is common for some workers, especially for those who respond to emergency and disaster situations.

Some hazmat removal workers travel to areas affected by a disaster. During a cleanup, workers may be away from home for several days or weeks until the project is completed.

Job Outlook

Employment of hazardous materials removal workers is projected to show little or no change from 2022 to 2032.

Despite limited employment growth, about 5,200 openings for hazardous materials removal workers are projected each year, on average, over the decade. Most of those openings are expected to result from the need to replace workers who transfer to different occupations or exit the labor force, such as to retire.

Employment

Employment growth will be driven by the need to safely remove and clean up hazardous materials (hazmat) at sites recognized

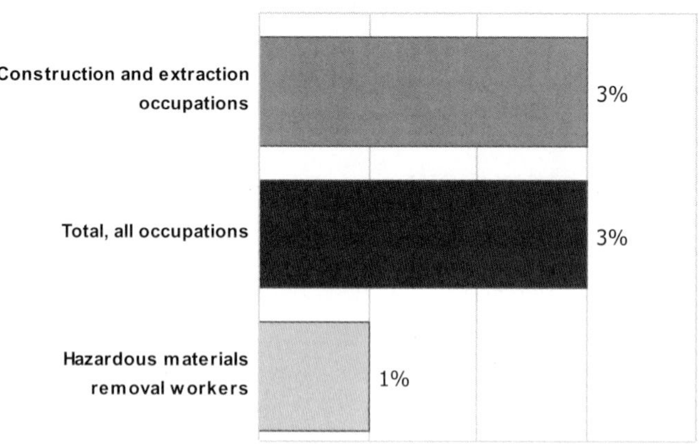

Note: All Occupations includes all occupations in the U.S. Economy.
Source: U.S. Bureau of Labor Statistics, Occupational Employment and Wage Statistics.

by the U.S. Environmental Protection Agency. However, funding for these activities may be sporadic; furthermore, construction laborers also perform some hazmat cleanup, offsetting demand for hazardous materials removal workers.

As nuclear plants are decommissioned, hazmat removal workers also will be needed to decontaminate equipment, store waste, and clean up these facilities for safe closure. However, some of the planned decommissioning activities have been delayed by the recent extension of site licenses.

Occupational Title	SOC Code	Employment, 2022	Projected Employment, 2032	Change, 2022-32	
				Percent	Numeric
Hazardous materials removal workers	47-4041	48,700	49,100	1	400

Contacts for More Information

For more information, visit

- Laborers' International Union of North America

For more information about working in the nuclear industry, visit

- Nuclear Energy Institute

For information about training and regulations mandated by federal agencies, visit

- Mine Safety and Health Administration
- Occupational Safety & Health Administration
- U.S. Department of Energy
- U.S. Department of Transportation
- U.S. Environmental Protection Agency
- U.S. Nuclear Regulatory Commission

Insulation Workers

Summary

Quick Facts: Insulation Workers	
2022 Median Pay	$47,980 per year $23.07 per hour
Typical Entry-Level Education	See How to Become One
Work Experience in a Related Occupation	None
On-the-job Training	See How to Become One
Number of Jobs, 2022	61,600
Job Outlook, 2022-32	2% (As fast as average)
Employment Change, 2022-32	1,000

What Insulation Workers Do

Insulation workers install and replace the materials used to insulate buildings or mechanical systems.

Work Environment

Insulators generally work indoors. Mechanical insulators work both indoors and outdoors, sometimes in extreme temperatures. They spend most of their workday standing, bending, or kneeling, often in confined spaces.

How to Become an Insulation Worker

Floor, ceiling, and wall insulators typically learn their trade on the job. Mechanical insulators may complete an apprenticeship program after earning a high school diploma or equivalent.

Pay

The median annual wage for insulation workers, floor, ceiling, and wall was $45,380 in May 2022.

The median annual wage for insulation workers, mechanical was $50,590 in May 2022.

Insulators must wear safety gear when working in confined spaces.

Job Outlook

Overall employment of insulation workers is projected to grow 2 percent from 2022 to 2032, about as fast as the average for all occupations.

About 4,800 openings for insulation workers are projected each year, on average, over the decade. Many of those openings are expected to result from the need to replace workers who transfer to different occupations or exit the labor force, such as to retire.

What Insulation Workers Do

Insulation workers, also called *insulators*, install and replace the materials used to insulate buildings or mechanical systems.

Duties

Insulators typically do the following:

- Remove and dispose of old insulation
- Review blueprints and specifications to determine the amount and type of insulation needed
- Measure and cut insulation to fit into walls and around pipes
- Secure insulation with staples, tape, or screws
- Use air compressors to spray foam insulation
- Install plastic barriers to protect insulation from moisture

Insulators install and replace the material that saves energy and helps reduce noise in buildings and around vats, vessels, boilers, steam pipes, and water pipes. Insulators also install firestopping materials to prevent the spread of a fire and smoke throughout a building.

Insulators often must remove old insulation when renovating buildings. In the past, asbestos—now known to cause cancer—was used extensively to insulate walls, ceilings, pipes, and industrial equipment. Because of the health risks associated with handling asbestos, hazardous materials removal workers or specially trained insulators must remove asbestos before workers begin installing new insulation.

Insulators use common handtools, such as knives, trowels, and scissors. They also may use a variety of power tools, such

Mechanical insulators install preformed insulation.

as welders to secure clamps, staple guns to fasten insulation to walls, and air compressors to spray insulation.

Insulators sometimes wrap a cover of aluminum, sheet metal, or plastic over the insulation. Doing so protects the insulation from contact damage and keeps moisture out.

Floor, ceiling, and wall insulators install insulation in attics, under floors, and behind walls in homes and other buildings. To fill the space between wall studs and ceiling joists, workers either unroll, cut, fit, and staple batts of insulation or spray foam insulation.

Mechanical insulators apply insulation to equipment, pipes, or ductwork in many types of buildings.

Work Environment

Insulation workers, floor, ceiling, and wall held about 34,400 jobs in 2022. The largest employers of insulation workers, floor, ceiling, and wall were as follows:

Drywall and insulation contractors	66%
Building equipment contractors	14
Self-employed workers	4
Nonresidential building construction	3
Foundation, structure, and building exterior contractors	2

Insulation workers, mechanical held about 27,200 jobs in 2022. The largest employers of insulation workers, mechanical were as follows:

Building equipment contractors	70%
Drywall and insulation contractors	14
Self-employed workers	4
Other specialty trade contractors	1

Insulators generally work indoors. Mechanical insulators work both indoors and outdoors, sometimes in extreme temperatures. They spend most of their workday standing, bending, or kneeling in confined spaces. Insulators may work at great heights on scaffolding, work platforms, or ladders.

Injuries and Illnesses

Common hazards for insulation workers include falls from ladders and cuts from knives. In addition, small particles from insulation materials can irritate the eyes, skin, and lungs. To protect themselves, insulators must keep the work area well-ventilated and follow product and employer safety recommendations. They also may wear personal protective equipment (PPE), including suits, masks, and respirators, to protect against hazardous fumes or materials.

Mechanical insulators may get burns from insulating pipes that are in service.

Work Schedules

Most insulators work full time, and more than 40 hours a week may be required to meet construction deadlines. Those who insulate outdoors may not be able to work in bad weather, such as during a storm or in extreme heat or cold.

How to Become an Insulation Worker

Most floor, ceiling, and wall insulators learn their trade on the job. Many mechanical insulators complete an apprenticeship program after earning a high school diploma or equivalent.

Education

There are no specific education requirements for floor, ceiling, and wall insulators. Apprenticeships for mechanical insulators typically require a high school diploma or equivalent. High school courses in subjects such as math, mechanical drawing, and science are helpful for all types of insulators.

Training

Most floor, ceiling, and wall insulators learn their trade on the job. New workers learn about installation and get mandatory Occupational Safety and Health Administration (OSHA)

Mechanical insulators often work in large industrial buildings.

Many insulators are trained on the job.

safety training on insulation handling and asbestos abatement. Beginning insulators work alongside more experienced ones to learn how to use equipment for installing spray insulation.

Many mechanical insulators learn their trade through a 4- to 5-year apprenticeship, which includes both technical instruction and paid on-the-job training.

Unions and individual contractors offer apprenticeships. Although most insulators start out by entering apprenticeships directly, others begin by working as helpers. The International Association of Heat and Frost Insulators and Allied Workers, an affiliate of the North American Building Trades Union, provides contact information on local union chapters.

Licenses, Certifications, and Registrations

Insulation workers who remove and handle asbestos must be trained through programs accredited by the U.S. Environmental Protection Agency. Some states require a license for asbestos abatement. Check with your state for more information. Mechanical insulators who complete an apprenticeship through the International Association of Heat and Frost Insulators and Allied Workers may receive this license as part of their apprenticeship.

The National Insulation Association offers a certification for mechanical insulators who conduct energy appraisals to determine if and how insulation can benefit industrial customers. Mechanical insulators also may receive certification in other job duties, such as fire stopping

Advancement

After completing an apprenticeship, mechanical insulators reach journey-level status. After becoming journey workers, mechanical insulators may advance to supervisor or superintendent positions, or they may choose to start their own business offering mechanical insulation services.

Important Qualities

Ability to work at heights. Insulators may be required to work high on ladders or scaffolds to install or remove insulation.

Dexterity. To install insulation, insulators often must reach overhead, sometimes while confined in spaces where maneuvering is difficult.

Math skills. Insulators need to measure the equipment or areas they are insulating and to calculate the amount and dimensions of insulation needed.

Mechanical skills. Insulators must be adept at using a variety of handtools and power tools to install insulation.

Physical stamina. Insulators spend much of the workday standing, kneeling, and bending in uncomfortable positions.

Physical strength. Insulators may be required to lift or carry up to 50 pounds of tools or materials.

Pay

The median annual wage for insulation workers, floor, ceiling, and wall was $45,380 in May 2022. The median wage is the wage at which half the workers in an occupation earned more than that amount and half earned less. The lowest 10 percent earned less than $29,830, and the highest 10 percent earned more than $76,960.

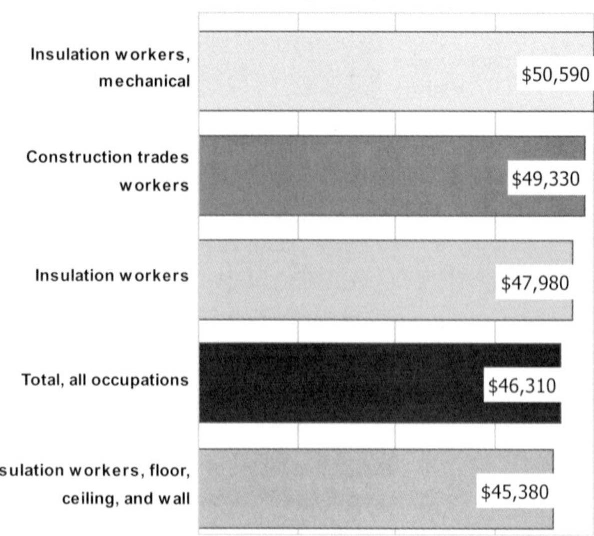

Note: All Occupations includes all occupations in the U.S. Economy.
Source: U.S. Bureau of Labor Statistics, Occupational Employment and Wage Statistics.

The median annual wage for insulation workers, mechanical was $50,590 in May 2022. The lowest 10 percent earned less than $37,460, and the highest 10 percent earned more than $93,710.

In May 2022, the median annual wages for insulation workers, floor, ceiling, and wall in the top industries in which they worked were as follows:

Nonresidential building construction	$77,200
Building equipment contractors	49,270
Foundation, structure, and building exterior contractors	45,070
Drywall and insulation contractors	43,630

In May 2022, the median annual wages for insulation workers, mechanical in the top industries in which they worked were as follows:

Building equipment contractors	$50,590
Drywall and insulation contractors	48,930
Other specialty trade contractors	48,380

The starting pay for apprentices is less than that of a fully trained insulator. Apprentices earn more pay as they acquire skills.

Most insulators work full time, and they sometimes need to work more than 40 hours a week to meet construction deadlines. Those who insulate outdoors may not be able to work in bad weather, such as during a storm or in extreme heat or cold.

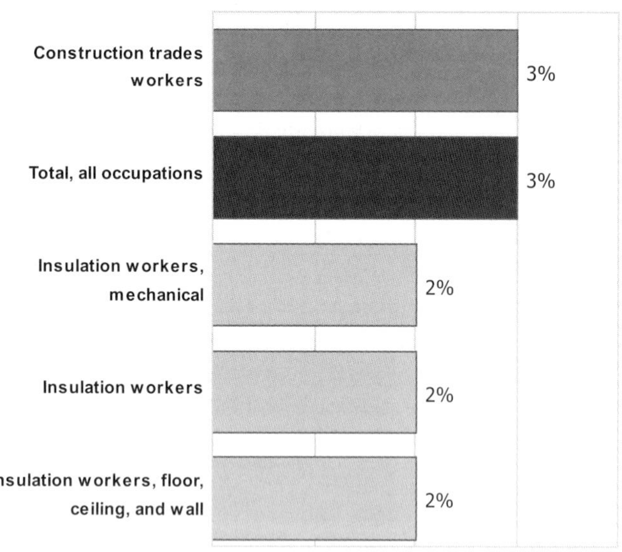

Note: All Occupations includes all occupations in the U.S. Economy.
Source: U.S. Bureau of Labor Statistics, Employment Projections program.

Job Outlook

Overall employment of insulation workers is projected to grow 2 percent from 2022 to 2032, about as fast as the average for all occupations.

About 4,800 openings for insulation workers are projected each year, on average, over the decade. Many of those openings are expected to result from the need to replace workers who transfer to different occupations or exit the labor force, such as to retire.

Employment

The continuing need to make new and existing buildings and systems more energy efficient will drive the demand for mechanical insulation workers.

The amount of new home building and retrofitting of existing insulation will continue to be linked to the employment of floor, ceiling, and wall insulation workers over the projections decade.

Occupational Title	SOC Code	Employment, 2022	Projected Employment, 2032	Change, 2022-32	
				Percent	Numeric
Insulation workers	47-2130	61,600	62,600	2	1,000
Insulation workers, floor, ceiling, and wall	47-2131	34,400	35,000	2	600
Insulation workers, mechanical	47-2132	27,200	27,600	2	500

Contacts for More Information

Apprenticeship program online or by phone at 877-872-5627. Visit Apprenticeship.gov to search for apprenticeship opportunities.

For more information, visit

- National Insulation Association
- NCCER
- International Association of Heat and Frost Insulators and Allied Workers
- North American Building Trades Union
- U.S. Environmental Protection Agency

Ironworkers

Summary

Quick Facts: Ironworkers

2022 Median Pay	$58,330 per year $28.04 per hour
Typical Entry-Level Education	High school diploma or equivalent
Work Experience in a Related Occupation	None
On-the-job Training	Apprenticeship
Number of Jobs, 2022	94,400
Job Outlook, 2022-32	2% (As fast as average)
Employment Change, 2022-32	1,600

What Ironworkers Do

Ironworkers install structural and reinforcing iron and steel to form and support buildings, bridges, and roads.

Work Environment

Ironworkers perform physically demanding and dangerous work, often at great heights. Workers must wear safety equipment to reduce the risk of falls or other injuries.

How to Become an Ironworker

Most ironworkers learn through an apprenticeship or on-the-job training.

Pay

The median annual wage for reinforcing iron and rebar workers was $51,070 in May 2022.

The median annual wage for structural iron and steel workers was $60,500 in May 2022.

Job Outlook

Overall employment of ironworkers is projected to grow 2 percent from 2022 to 2032, about as fast as the average for all occupations.

Ironworkers connect iron and steel with bolts, wire, or welds.

About 8,100 openings for ironworkers are projected each year, on average, over the decade. Many of those openings are expected to result from the need to replace workers who transfer to different occupations or exit the labor force, such as to retire.

What Ironworkers Do

Ironworkers install structural and reinforcing iron and steel to form and support bridges, roads, and other structures.

Reinforcing ironworkers install rebar to strengthen concrete walls.

Duties

Ironworkers typically do the following:

- Read and follow blueprints, sketches, and other instructions
- Unload and stack prefabricated iron and steel so that it can be lifted with slings
- Signal crane operators who lift and position structural and reinforcing iron and steel
- Use shears, rod-bending machines, torches, handtools, and welding equipment to cut, bend, and weld the structural and reinforcing iron and steel
- Align structural and reinforcing iron and steel vertically and horizontally, using tag lines, plumb bobs, lasers, and levels
- Connect iron and steel with bolts, wire, or welds
- Install metal decking used in building construction

Structural and reinforcing iron and steel are important components of buildings, bridges, roads, and other structures. Even though the primary metal involved in this work is steel, workers often are known as ironworkers or *erectors*. Most of the work involves erecting new structures, but some ironworkers also help in the demolition, decommissioning, and rehabilitation of older buildings and bridges.

Structural iron and steel workers erect, place, and join steel girders, columns, and other pieces to form structural frameworks. They also may assemble precut metal buildings and the cranes and derricks that move materials and equipment around the construction site. Some ironworkers install precast walls or work with wood or composite materials.

Reinforcing iron and rebar workers position and secure steel bars or mesh in concrete forms for purposes of reinforcement. Those who work with reinforcing steel (rebar) are sometimes called *rod busters*, in reference to rods of rebar.

Structural metal fabricators and fitters manufacture metal products in shops that are usually located away from construction sites.

Work Environment

Reinforcing iron and rebar workers held about 22,800 jobs in 2022. The largest employers of reinforcing iron and rebar workers were as follows:

Foundation, structure, and building exterior contractors	49%
Self-employed workers	24
Heavy and civil engineering construction	6
Nonresidential building construction	5
Other specialty trade contractors	3

Structural iron and steel workers held about 71,600 jobs in 2022. The largest employers of structural iron and steel workers were as follows:

Foundation, structure, and building exterior contractors	45%

Ironworkers wear safety harnesses when they work at heights.

Nonresidential building construction	20
Manufacturing	8
Heavy and civil engineering construction	6
Building equipment contractors	4

Ironworkers usually work outside in many types of weather. Some work at great heights. Their tasks are physically demanding, as they spend much of their time moving and stooping to carry, bend, cut, and connect iron or steel at a steady pace so projects stay on schedule.

Injuries and Illnesses

The work of ironworkers can be dangerous. Common injuries include cuts, sprains, overexertion, and falls; from great heights, falls can be deadly. To reduce these risks, ironworkers must wear safety equipment such as harnesses, hard hats, boots, gloves, and safety glasses.

Work Schedules

Most ironworkers work full time. They may have to travel to jobsites.

Structural ironworkers who work at great heights do not work when conditions are wet, icy, or extremely windy. Reinforcing ironworkers may be limited by precipitation.

How to Become an Ironworker

Most ironworkers learn through an apprenticeship or on-the-job training.

Education

A high school diploma or equivalent is generally required to enter an apprenticeship. Workers learning through on-the-job training may not need a high school diploma or equivalent. Courses in math, as well as training in vocational subjects such as blueprint reading and welding, are useful.

Training

Many ironworkers learn their trade through a 3- or 4-year apprenticeship. Sponsors of apprenticeship programs, nearly all of which teach both reinforcing and structural ironworking, include unions and contractor associations. For each year of the program, apprentices must have at least 144 hours of related technical instruction and 2,000 hours of paid on-the-job training. Ironworkers who complete an apprenticeship program are considered journey-level workers and may perform tasks without direct supervision.

Other ironworkers receive on-the-job training that varies in length and is provided by their employer.

On the job, apprentices and trainees learn to use the tools and equipment of the trade; handle, measure, cut, and lay rebar; and construct metal frameworks. They also learn about topics such as blueprint reading and sketching, general construction techniques, safety practices, and first aid.

Licenses, Certifications, and Registrations

Certifications in welding, rigging, and crane signaling may make ironworkers more attractive to prospective employers. Several organizations provide certifications for different aspects of the work. For example, the American Welding Society offers welding certification, and several organizations offer rigging certifications, including the National Commission for the Certification of Crane Operators, and the National Center for Construction Education and Research.

Many ironworkers learn their trade through a 3- or 4-year apprenticeship.

Advancement

After gaining experience, ironworkers may advance to become a supervisor or a manager, a position in which they have more responsibilities and are tasked with directing other ironworkers.

Important Qualities

Ability to work at heights. Ironworkers must not be afraid to work at great heights. For example, workers connecting girders during skyscraper construction may have to walk on narrow beams that are 50 stories or higher.

Balance. Ironworkers often walk on narrow beams, so a good sense of balance is important to keep them from falling.

Critical thinking. Ironworkers need to identify problems, monitor and assess potential risks, and evaluate the best courses of action. They must use logic and reasoning when finding alternatives so that they safely accomplish their tasks

Depth perception. Ironworkers often signal crane operators who move beams and bundles of rebar, so they must be able to judge the distance between objects.

Hand-eye coordination. Ironworkers must be able to tie rebar together quickly and precisely.

Physical stamina. Ironworkers must have physical endurance because they spend many hours each day performing physically demanding tasks, such as moving rebar.

Physical strength. Ironworkers must be strong enough to guide heavy beams into place and tighten bolts.

Pay

The median annual wage for reinforcing iron and rebar workers was $51,070 in May 2022. The median wage is the wage at which half the workers in an occupation earned more than that amount and half earned less. The lowest 10 percent earned less than $38,310, and the highest 10 percent earned more than $89,880.

The median annual wage for structural iron and steel workers was $60,500 in May 2022. The lowest 10 percent earned less than $37,890, and the highest 10 percent earned more than $100,930.

In May 2022, the median annual wages for reinforcing iron and rebar workers in the top industries in which they worked were as follows:

Heavy and civil engineering construction	$61,630
Nonresidential building construction	51,660
Foundation, structure, and building exterior contractors	51,070
Other specialty trade contractors	47,560

In May 2022, the median annual wages for structural iron and steel workers in the top industries in which they worked were as follows:

Building equipment contractors	$69,160
Heavy and civil engineering construction	68,970
Foundation, structure, and building exterior contractors	60,150
Nonresidential building construction	59,600
Manufacturing	51,320

The starting pay for apprentices is usually about 50 percent of what journey-level ironworkers make. They receive pay increases as they learn to do more.

Most ironworkers work full time. Structural ironworkers who work at great heights do not work when conditions are

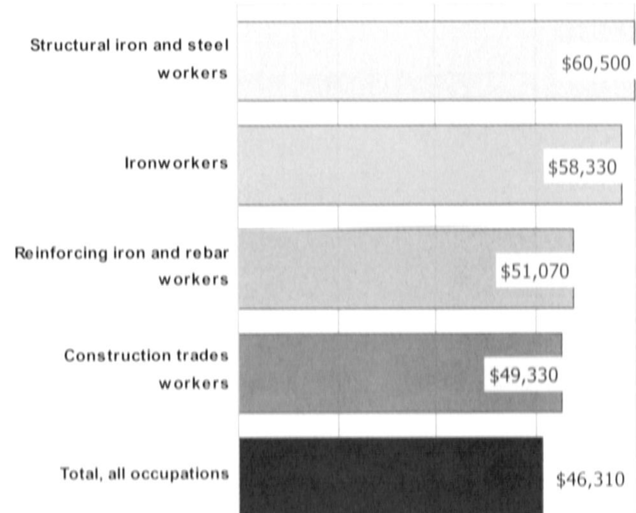

Note: All Occupations includes all occupations in the U.S. Economy.
Source: U.S. Bureau of Labor Statistics, Occupational Employment and Wage Statistics.

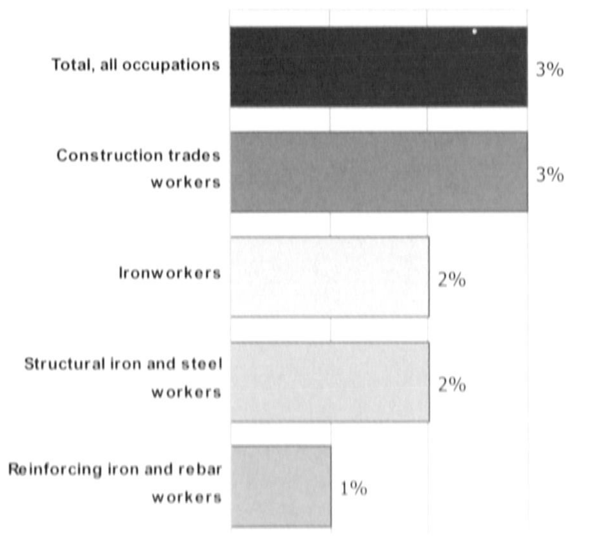

Note: All Occupations includes all occupations in the U.S. Economy.
Source: U.S. Bureau of Labor Statistics, Employment Projections program.

wet, icy, or extremely windy. Reinforcing ironworkers may be limited by precipitation.

Job Outlook

Overall employment of ironworkers is projected to grow 2 percent from 2022 to 2032, about as fast as the average for all occupations.

About 8,100 openings for ironworkers are projected each year, on average, over the decade. Many of those openings are expected to result from the need to replace workers who transfer to different occupations or exit the labor force, such as to retire.

Employment

Steel and reinforced concrete are important parts of commercial and industrial buildings. Future construction of these structures is expected to require ironworkers. The need to fix, maintain, or replace an increasing number of older highways and bridges also is expected to lead to some employment growth.

Occupational Title	SOC Code	Employment, 2022	Projected Employment, 2032	Change, 2022-32	
				Percent	Numeric
Ironworkers	—	94,400	95,900	2	1,600
Reinforcing iron and rebar workers	47-2171	22,800	23,100	1	300
Structural iron and steel workers	47-2221	71,600	72,900	2	1,300

Contacts for More Information

Apprenticeship information is available from the U.S. Department of Labor's Apprenticeship program online or by phone at 877-872-5627. Visit Apprenticeship.gov to search for apprenticeship opportunities.

For ironworker and apprenticeship information, visit

- International Association of Bridge, Structural, Ornamental and Reinforcing Iron Workers

For more information about ironworkers, visit

- Associated Builders and Contractors
- Associated General Contractors of America
- National Center for Construction Education and Research

For more information about certification, visit

- National Commission for the Certification of Crane Operators
- American Welding Society

Masonry Workers

Summary

Quick Facts: Masonry Workers

2022 Median Pay	$49,490 per year $23.79 per hour
Typical Entry-Level Education	See How to Become One
Work Experience in a Related Occupation	None
On-the-job Training	See How to Become One
Number of Jobs, 2022	294,200
Job Outlook, 2022-32	-3% (Decline)
Employment Change, 2022-32	-8,900

What Masonry Workers Do

Masonry workers use bricks, concrete and concrete blocks, and natural and manmade stones to build structures.

Work Environment

Masonry work is physically demanding, requiring heavy lifting and long periods of standing, kneeling, and bending. Most masons work full time.

How to Become a Masonry Worker

Masons typically need a high school diploma or equivalent and learn the trade either through an apprenticeship or on the job.

Pay

The median annual wage for masonry workers was $49,490 in May 2022.

Masons construct walls using bricks, blocks, and stones.

Masons clean excess mortar with trowels and other hand tools.

Job Outlook

Overall employment of masonry workers is projected to decline 3 percent from 2022 to 2032.

Despite declining employment, about 21,200 openings for masonry workers are projected each year, on average, over the decade. All of those openings are expected to result from the need to replace workers who transfer to other occupations or exit the labor force, such as to retire.

What Masonry Workers Do

Masonry workers, also known as *masons*, use bricks, concrete and concrete blocks, and natural and manmade stones to build walkways, walls, and other structures.

Duties

Masons typically do the following:

- Read blueprints or drawings to calculate materials needed
- Lay out patterns, forms, or foundations according to plans
- Break or cut materials to required size
- Mix mortar or grout and spread it onto a slab or foundation
- Clean excess mortar with trowels and other handtools
- Construct masonry walls
- Align structures, using levels and plumbs
- Clean and polish surfaces with handtools or power tools
- Fill expansion joints with caulking materials
- Lay out and install rainscreen water systems

Masons build structures with brick, block, and stone, some of the most common and durable materials used in construction. They also use concrete—a mixture of cement, sand, gravel, and water—as the foundation for everything from patios and floors to dams and roads.

The following are examples of types of masons:

Brickmasons and ***blockmasons***—often called *bricklayers*—build and repair walls, fireplaces, and other structures with brick, terra cotta, precast masonry panels, concrete block, and other masonry materials. *Pointing, cleaning, and caulking workers* are brickmasons who repair brickwork, particularly on older structures. *Refractory masons* are brickmasons who specialize in installing heat- and fire-resistant masonry materials in high-temperature areas such as boilers, furnaces, and soaking pits in industrial buildings.

Cement masonsandconcrete finishers place and finish concrete. They may color concrete surfaces, expose small stones in walls and sidewalks, or make concrete beams, columns, and panels. Throughout the process of pouring, leveling, and finishing concrete, cement masons use their knowledge of how conditions may affect concrete and take steps to prevent defects. On small jobs, such as constructing sidewalks, cement masons may use a supportive wire mesh called a lath. On large jobs, such as constructing building foundations, reinforcing iron and rebar workers install the reinforcing mesh.

Stonemasons build stone walls and set stone exteriors and floors. They work with two types of stone: natural-cut stone, such as marble, granite, and limestone; and artificial stone, made from concrete, marble chips, or other masonry materials. Using a special hammer or a diamond-blade saw, workers cut stone into various shapes and sizes. Some stonemasons specialize in setting marble, which is similar to setting large pieces of stone.

Terrazzo workers and finishers, also known as *terrazzo masons*, create decorative walkways, floors, patios, and panels. Much of the preliminary work of pouring, leveling, and finishing concrete for terrazzo is similar to that of cement masons. Terrazzo workers create decorative finishes by blending fine marble chips into the epoxy, resin, or cement, which is often colored. Once the terrazzo is thoroughly set, workers correct imperfections with a grinder. Terrazzo workers also install decorative microtoppings or polishing compounds to new or existing concrete.

Work Environment

Masonry workers held about 294,200 jobs in 2022. Employment in the detailed occupations that make up masonry workers was distributed as follows:

Masons typically work outdoors.

Occupation	Employment
Cement masons and concrete finishers	206,200
Brickmasons and blockmasons	73,000
Stonemasons	13,500
Terrazzo workers and finishers	1,600

The largest employers of masonry workers were as follows:

Employer	Percent
Poured concrete foundation and structure contractors	30%
Masonry contractors	20
Self-employed workers	10
Construction of buildings	10
Heavy and civil engineering construction	7

As with many other construction occupations, masonry work is strenuous. Masons often lift heavy materials and stand, kneel, and bend for long periods. The work may be either indoors or outdoors in areas that are dusty, dirty, or muddy. Inclement weather may affect outdoor masonry work.

Injuries and Illnesses

Brickmasons and blockmasons risk injury on the job. Cuts are common, as are injuries occurring from falls and being struck by objects. To avoid injury, workers wear protective gear such as hardhats, safety glasses, high-visibility vests, and harnesses and other apparel to prevent falls.

Apprentices learn by working with experienced masons.

Work Schedules

Most masons work full time, and some work overtime to meet construction deadlines. Masons work mostly outdoors, so inclement weather may affect their schedules. Terrazzo masons may need to work hours that differ from a regular business schedule, to avoid disrupting normal operations.

How to Become a Masonry Worker

Masons typically need a high school diploma or equivalent and learn the trade either through an apprenticeship or on the job.

Education

A high school diploma or equivalent is typically required to enter the occupation.

Many technical schools offer programs in masonry. These programs operate both independently and in conjunction with apprenticeship training.

Training

Masons typically learn the trade through apprenticeships and on the job, working with experienced masons.

Several groups, including unions and contractor associations, sponsor apprenticeship programs. Apprentices learn construction basics, such as blueprint reading; mathematics for measurement; building code requirements; and safety and first-aid practices. After completing an apprenticeship program, masons are considered journey workers and are able to do tasks on their own.

The Home Builders Institute and the International Masonry Institute offer pre-apprenticeship training programs for eight construction trades, including masonry.

Work Experience in a Related Occupation

Some workers start out as construction laborers and helpers before becoming masons.

Advancement

After becoming a journey worker, masonry workers may find opportunities to advance to supervisor, superintendent, or other construction management positions. Experienced masonry workers may choose to become independent contractors. Masonry workers in a union may also find opportunities for advancement within their union.

Important Qualities

Ability to work at heights. Masonry workers often use scaffolding, so they should be comfortable working at heights.

Color vision. Masonry workers need to be able to distinguish between small variations in color when setting terrazzo patterns in order to produce the best looking finish.

Dexterity. Masonry workers must be able to place bricks, stones, and other materials with precision.

Hand–eye coordination. Masonry workers need to apply smooth, even layers of mortar; set bricks; and remove any excess before the mortar hardens.

Physical stamina. Masonry workers must keep up a steady pace while setting bricks, and the constant lifting can be tiring.

Physical strength. Masonry workers should be able to lift more than 50 pounds. They carry heavy tools, equipment, and other materials, such as bags of mortar and grout.

Pay

The median annual wage for masonry workers was $49,490 in May 2022. The median wage is the wage at which half the workers in an occupation earned more than that amount and half earned less. The lowest 10 percent earned less than $36,180, and the highest 10 percent earned more than $82,780.

Median annual wages for masonry workers in May 2022 were as follows:

Brickmasons and blockmasons	$59,000
Terrazzo workers and finishers	52,330
Stonemasons	50,210
Cement masons and concrete finishers	48,300

In May 2022, the median annual wages for masonry workers in the top industries in which they worked were as follows:

Masonry contractors	$58,380
Construction of buildings	53,180
Heavy and civil engineering construction	50,030
Poured concrete foundation and structure contractors	47,800

Most masons work full time, and some work overtime to meet construction deadlines. Masons work mostly outdoors, so inclement weather may affect schedules. Terrazzo masons may need to work hours that differ from a regular business schedule, to avoid disrupting normal operations.

Job Outlook

Overall employment of masonry workers is projected to decline 3 percent from 2022 to 2032.

Despite declining employment, about 21,200 openings for masonry workers are projected each year, on average, over the decade. All of those openings are expected to result from the need to replace workers who transfer to other occupations or exit the labor force, such as to retire.

Employment

Projected employment of masonry workers varies by occupation (see table).

The employment of masons is linked to the overall demand for new building and road construction. Masonry, such as brick and stone, is still popular in both interior and exterior applications, but changes in products and installation practices are expected to decrease the need for masons. For example, fewer

Note: All Occupations includes all occupations in the U.S. Economy.
Source: U.S. Bureau of Labor Statistics, Occupational Employment and Wage Statistics.

Note: All Occupations includes all occupations in the U.S. Economy.
Source: U.S. Bureau of Labor Statistics, Employment Projections program.

workers are needed to install innovations such as thin bricks, which allow buildings to have the look of brick construction at a lower cost. Additionally, the increased use of prefabricated panels will reduce the demand for most masonry workers. These panels are created offsite by either contractors or manufacturers in climate-protected environments, but fewer masons are needed to install the panels at the construction site.

Employment of terrazzo workers and finishers is expected to decline due to the increased installation of polished concrete, which will shift some work from terrazzo workers to cement masons and concrete finishers.

Occupational Title	SOC Code	Employment, 2022	Projected Employment, 2032	Change, 2022-32	
				Percent	Numeric
Masonry workers	—	294,200	285,300	-3	-8,900
Brickmasons and blockmasons	47-2021	73,000	73,300	0	300
Stonemasons	47-2022	13,500	12,700	-6	-800
Cement masons and concrete finishers	47-2051	206,200	197,900	-4	-8,300
Terrazzo workers and finishers	47-2053	1,600	1,400	-12	-200

Contacts for More Information

Apprenticeship information is available from the U.S. Department of Labor's Apprenticeship program online or by phone at 877-872-5627. Visit Apprenticeship.gov to search for apprenticeship opportunities.

For more information, visit

- Associated Builders and Contractors, Inc.
- Bricklayers and Allied Craftworkers International Union
- Home Builders Institute
- International Masonry Institute
- Mason Contractors Association of America
- National Association of Home Builders
- NCCER
- Operative Plasterers' and Cement Masons' International Association
- The Associated General Contractors of America
- The National Terrazzo and Mosaic Association

Painters, Construction and Maintenance

Summary

Quick Facts: Construction and Maintenance Painters

2022 Median Pay	$46,090 per year $22.16 per hour
Typical Entry-Level Education	No formal educational credential
Work Experience in a Related Occupation	None
On-the-job Training	Moderate-term on-the-job training
Number of Jobs, 2022	372,400
Job Outlook, 2022-32	1% (Little or no change)
Employment Change, 2022-32	5,500

What Construction and Maintenance Painters Do

Painters apply paint, stain, and coatings to walls and ceilings, buildings, large machinery and equipment, and bridges and other structures.

Work Environment

Painters work indoors and outdoors. Painting is physically demanding and requires a lot of bending, kneeling, reaching, and climbing. Those who paint bridges or buildings may work at extreme heights or in uncomfortable positions.

How to Become a Construction and Maintenance Painter

Painters typically learn their trade on the job. No formal education is typically required to enter the occupation.

Pay

The median annual wage for painters, construction and maintenance was $46,090 in May 2022.

Painters cover trim and molding before applying paint.

Job Outlook

Employment of painters, construction and maintenance is projected to show little or no change from 2022 to 2032.

Despite limited employment growth, about 29,300 openings for painters, construction and maintenance are projected each year, on average, over the decade. Most of those openings are expected to result from the need to replace workers who transfer to different occupations or exit the labor force, such as to retire.

What Construction and Maintenance Painters Do

Painters apply paint, stain, and coatings to walls and ceilings, buildings, large machinery and equipment, and bridges and other structures.

Duties

Painters typically do the following:

- Protect floors, furniture, and trim by covering surfaces with drop cloths and tarps and securing with tape
- Install scaffolding and raise ladders
- Fill holes and cracks with putty or plaster
- Prepare surfaces by removing outlet and switch covers and by scraping, wire brushing, or sanding to a smooth finish

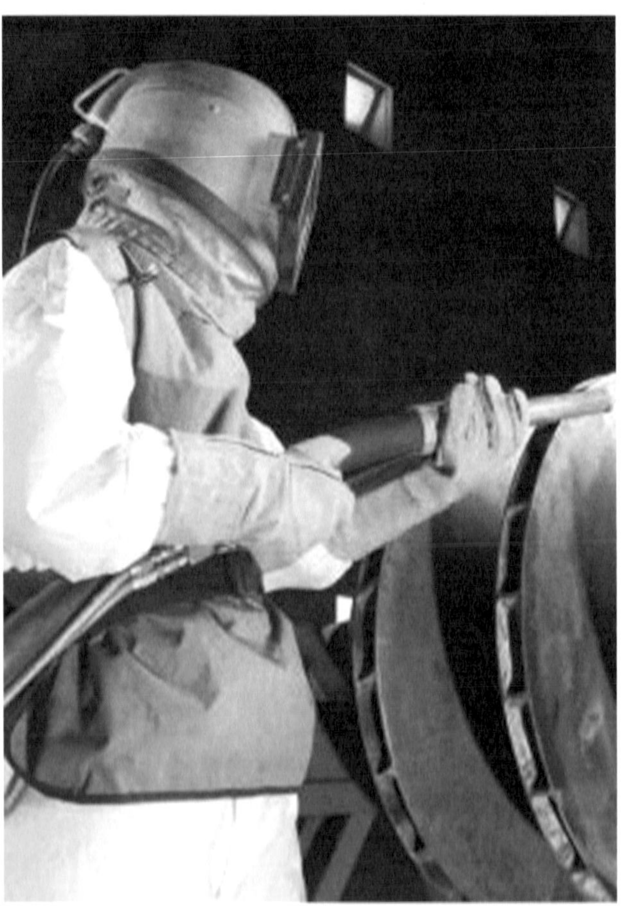

Painters sometimes wear self-contained suits for protection.

- Calculate the size of the area to be painted and the amount of paint needed for the area
- Apply primers or sealers so the paint will stick to the surface
- Apply paint, coatings, or other finishes, using hand brushes, rollers, or sprayers

Painters apply liquid coatings and other sealers that dry into solids to add texture or color to interiors and to protect exterior surfaces from damage caused by weather, sunlight, and pollution.

For each job, painters must choose the correct tool, such as a roller, power sprayer, or brush. There are several ways to apply paint, and deciding on which tool to use typically depends on both the type of surface to be painted and the characteristics of the paint. Some employers require painters to provide their own tools

The following are types of painters:

Commercial painters prepare and paint the interiors and exteriors of offices, businesses, and other nonresidential buildings. Commercial painters may work with and be responsible for large areas due to the size of buildings involved in nonresidential projects.

Industrial painters prepare and paint large machinery, such as industrial or manufacturing equipment; vehicles, such as cars and ships; and structures, such as bridges and water towers. Industrial painters may also apply special coating materials to structure or equipment surfaces to protect them from corrosion or deterioration.

Industrial painters must contain the area in which they are working to prevent hazardous materials from contaminating the environment and exposing the public to risks. Industrial and commercial painters also must perform quality control and quality assurance to ensure that they find mistakes, meet technical specifications, and use materials appropriately.

Residential painters prepare and paint the interiors and exteriors of homes and multifamily residential buildings. Residential painters may interact with customers living in the home while painting is in progress. As a result, residential painters may need to adjust their hours or work plans to accommodate customer needs or schedules.

Work Environment

Painters, construction and maintenance held about 372,400 jobs in 2022. The largest employers of painters, construction and maintenance were as follows:

Self-employed workers	41%
Painting and wall covering contractors	37
Residential building construction	4
Government	2
Nonresidential building construction	2

Painters work on a variety of structures, including bridges, machinery, and the interiors and exteriors of buildings. Painting requires a lot of bending, kneeling, reaching, and climbing.

Many painters work outdoors.

Some specialty painters may need certification.

Those who paint bridges or buildings may work at extreme heights or in uncomfortable positions; some painters are suspended by ropes or cables as they work.

Painters typically work both indoors and outdoors. When working outside or in confined spaces, painters may be exposed to extreme temperatures.

Painters may need to wear special safety equipment for a job. For example, painters working in confined spaces, such as the inside of a large storage tank, must wear self-contained suits to avoid inhaling toxic fumes. Some painters wear additional clothing and protective eyewear when operating abrasive blasters to remove old coatings. When painting bridges, ships, tall buildings, or oil rigs, painters may work from scaffolding or harnesses.

Injuries and Illnesses

Painters risk injury on the job. Common hazards include falls from ladders, muscle strains from lifting, and exposure to drywall dust and other irritants.

Work Schedules

Most painters work full time. Self-employed painters may be able to set their own schedules. Industrial painters may be required to travel for work. Painting jobs that are outdoors may be seasonal.

How to Become a Construction and Maintenance Painter

Painters typically learn their trade on the job. No formal education is typically required to enter the occupation.

Education

There are no formal education requirements to become a painter. Some technical schools offer optional certificates in painting.

Training

Painters typically learn on the job: how to prepare surfaces, apply coating, hang wall covering, and match colors. Painters may have to complete additional safety training in order to work with scaffolding and harnesses.

Although less common, painting apprenticeships lasting 3 or 4 years may be available for candidates who have a high school diploma or equivalent and who are at least 18 years old. For example, the International Union of Painters and Allied Trades, in conjunction with the Finishing Trades Institute, offers a 3-year apprenticeship for painters. For each year of a typical program, apprentices must complete a predetermined number of hours of technical training and paid on-the-job training before becoming journey workers. Apprenticeship program requirements differ based on the type of program and by region.

Although most painters learn their trade on the job or through an apprenticeship, some new workers enter training programs offered by the hiring contractor.

Licenses, Certifications, and Registrations

Those interested in industrial painting can earn several certifications from NACE International Institute or from the Society for Protective Coatings. Courses range from 1 day to several weeks, depending on the certification program and specialty. Applicants also must meet work experience requirements.

The U.S. Environmental Protection Agency provides certification for lead paint abatement.

Some states require licensing for lead paint removal. Contact your state's licensing board for more information.

Employers may require workers to have a driver's license to commute to jobsites.

Advancement

After gaining experience, painters may advance to supervisors, superintendents, or managers, directing other painters and the jobsite. Painters may also work as estimators or start their own business.

Painters who work in a union may have advancement opportunities within the organization as a union official, training instructor, or business manager.

Important Qualities

Ability to work at heights. Painters must be able to work at heights on scaffolding, lifts, and ladders.

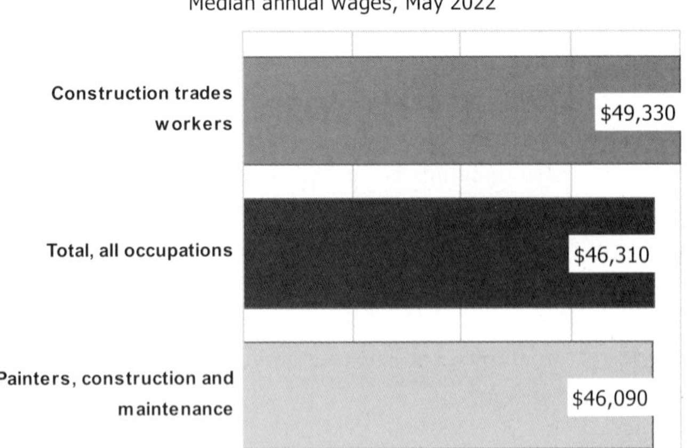

Note: All Occupations includes all occupations in the U.S. Economy.
Source: U.S. Bureau of Labor Statistics, Occupational Employment and Wage Statistics.

Communication skills. Painters interact with clients and must be able to convey information in order to ensure accuracy of color selection and application techniques. Painters must also communicate with coworkers.

Detail oriented. Painters must be precise when creating or painting edges for overall quality of appearance.

Physical stamina. Painters should be able to stay physically active for many hours and spend much of the workday standing or climbing ladders.

Physical strength. Painters must be able to lift at least 50 pounds and move heavy items during the course of a job.

Pay

The median annual wage for painters, construction and maintenance was $46,090 in May 2022. The median wage is the wage at which half the workers in an occupation earned more than that amount and half earned less. The lowest 10 percent earned less than $32,510, and the highest 10 percent earned more than $72,160.

In May 2022, the median annual wages for painters, construction and maintenance in the top industries in which they worked were as follows:

Government	$61,480
Nonresidential building construction	48,970
Residential building construction	46,850
Painting and wall covering contractors	45,540

Apprentices make less than fully trained painters, but they receive increases as they learn to do more.

Most painters work full time. Self-employed workers may be able to set their own schedule.

Job Outlook

Employment of painters, construction and maintenance is projected to show little or no change from 2022 to 2032.

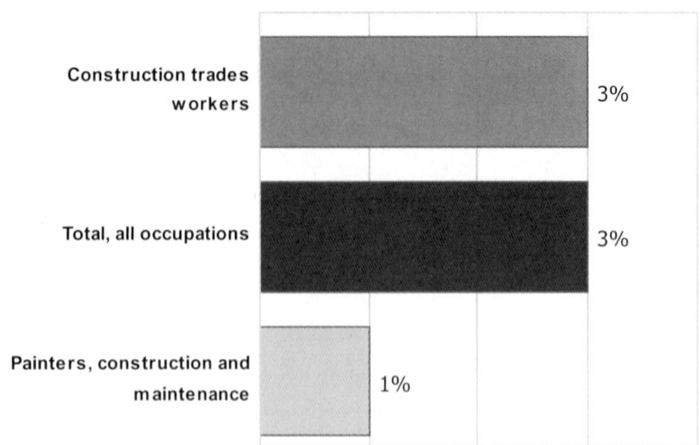

Note: All Occupations includes all occupations in the U.S. Economy.
Source: U.S. Bureau of Labor Statistics, Employment Projections program.

Despite limited employment growth, about 29,300 openings for painters, construction and maintenance are projected each year, on average, over the decade. Most of those openings are expected to result from the need to replace workers who transfer to different occupations or exit the labor force, such as to retire.

Employment

The expected increase in new construction will continue to create a need for painters. Investors who sell or lease properties also will require painters' services. However, many homeowners choose to do painting themselves rather than hire workers for it, which will temper employment growth for painters.

Occupational Title	SOC Code	Employment, 2022	Projected Employment, 2032	Change, 2022-32	
				Percent	Numeric
Painters, construction and maintenance	47-2141	372,400	377,900	1	5,500

Contacts for More Information

Apprenticeship information is available from the U.S. Department of Labor's Apprenticeship program online or by phone at 877-872-5627.

For more information about painters and training opportunities, visit

- Associated Builders and Contractors
- International Union of Painters and Allied Trades
- Home Builders Institute
- NCCER
- Painting and Decorating Contractors of America
- Home Builders Institute
- NACE International Institute
- Society of Protective Coatings
- Helmets to Hardhats

Plumbers, Pipefitters, and Steamfitters

Summary

Quick Facts: Plumbers, Pipefitters, and Steamfitters	
2022 Median Pay	$60,090 per year $28.89 per hour
Typical Entry-Level Education	High school diploma or equivalent
Work Experience in a Related Occupation	None
On-the-job Training	Apprenticeship
Number of Jobs, 2022	482,700
Job Outlook, 2022-32	2% (As fast as average)
Employment Change, 2022-32	10,900

What Plumbers, Pipefitters, and Steamfitters Do

Plumbers, pipefitters, and steamfitters install and repair piping fixtures and systems.

Work Environment

Plumbers, pipefitters, and steamfitters work in factories, homes, businesses, and other places where there are pipes and related systems. Plumbers are often on call for emergencies, so evening and weekend work is common.

How to Become a Plumber, Pipefitter, or Steamfitter

Most plumbers, pipefitters, and steamfitters learn on the job through an apprenticeship. Some attend a vocational-technical school before receiving on-the-job training. Most states require plumbers to be licensed.

Pay

The median annual wage for plumbers, pipefitters, and steamfitters was $60,090 in May 2022.

Plumbers inspect pipes for damage.

Job Outlook

Employment of plumbers, pipefitters, and steamfitters is projected to grow 2 percent from 2022 to 2032, about as fast as the average for all occupations.

About 42,600 openings for plumbers, pipefitters, and steamfitters are projected each year, on average, over the decade. Many of those openings are expected to result from the need to replace workers who transfer to different occupations or exit the labor force, such as to retire.

What Plumbers, Pipefitters, and Steamfitters Do

Plumbers, pipefitters, and steamfitters install and repair piping fixtures and systems.

Duties

Plumbers, pipefitters, and steamfitters typically do the following:

- Prepare cost estimates for clients
- Read blueprints and follow state and local building codes
- Determine the materials and equipment needed for a job
- Install pipes and fixtures
- Inspect and test installed pipe systems and pipelines
- Troubleshoot malfunctioning systems
- Maintain and repair plumbing sysems

Pipefitters install a variety of pipes to move liquids and gasses.

Although plumbers, pipefitters, and steamfitters have distinct responsibilities, they often have similar duties. For example, they all install pipes and fittings that carry water, gas, and other fluids and substances. They determine the necessary materials for a job, connect pipes, and test pressure to ensure that a pipe system is airtight and watertight. Their tools include drills, saws, welding torches, press fitting tools, and drain cleaning tools.

Plumbers, pipefitters, and steamfitters may use different materials and construction techniques, depending on the project. For example, residential water systems use copper, steel, and plastic pipe that one or two plumbers install. Industrial plant water systems, in contrast, are made of large steel pipes that usually take a crew of pipefitters to install.

Journey- and master-level plumbers, pipefitters, and steamfitters frequently direct apprentices and helpers.

Master plumbers on construction jobs may help develop blueprints that show the placement of pipes and fixtures. Their input ensures that a structure's plumbing meets building codes, stays within budget, and works well with the location of other features, such as electric wires. Many diagrams are created digitally with Building Information Modeling (BIM), which allows workers in several occupations to collaborate in planning a building's physical systems.

Some of the specific tasks performed by these workers are as follows:

Plumbers install and repair water, gas, and other piping systems in homes, businesses, and factories. They install plumbing fixtures, such as bathtubs and toilets, and appliances, such as dishwashers and water heaters. They clean drains, remove obstructions, and repair or replace broken pipes and fixtures. Plumbers also help maintain septic systems—large, underground holding tanks that collect waste from houses that are not connected to a sewer system.

Pipefitters and steamfitters, sometimes simply called *fitters*, install and maintain pipes that may carry chemicals, acids, and gases. These pipes are mostly in manufacturing, commercial, and industrial settings. Fitters install and repair pipe systems in power plants, as well as heating and cooling systems in large office buildings. *Steamfitters* specialize in systems that are designed for the flow of liquids or gases at high pressure. Other fitters may specialize as gasfitters or sprinklerfitters.

Work Environment

Plumbers, pipefitters, and steamfitters held about 482,700 jobs in 2022. The largest employers of plumbers, pipefitters, and steamfitters were as follows:

Plumbing, heating, and air-conditioning contractors	64%
Self-employed workers	10
Heavy and civil engineering construction	4
Government	4
Manufacturing	3

Plumbers risk getting burned as they solder pipes.

Plumbers, pipefitters, and steamfitters work in factories, homes, businesses, and other places where there are pipes and related systems. Plumbers and fitters lift heavy materials, climb ladders, and work in tight spaces. Some plumbers travel to worksites every day. Outdoor work, in all types of weather, may be required.

Injuries and Illnesses

Plumbers, pipefitters, and steamfitters sometimes get injured on the job. Common injuries include cuts from sharp tools, burns from hot pipes and soldering equipment, and falls from ladders.

Work Schedules

Most plumbers, pipefitters, and steamfitters work full time, including nights and weekends. They are often on call to handle emergencies. Self-employed plumbers may be able to set their own schedules.

How to Become a Plumber, Pipefitter, or Steamfitter

Most plumbers, pipefitters, and steamfitters learn on the job through an apprenticeship. Some also attend vocational-technical school. Most states and some localities require plumbers to be licensed.

Education

A high school diploma or equivalent is typically required to become a plumber, pipefitter, or steamfitter. Vocational-technical schools offer courses in pipe system design, safety, and tool use. They also offer welding courses that are required by some pipefitter and steamfitter apprenticeship training programs.

Training

Most plumbers, pipefitters, and steamfitters learn their trade through a 4- or 5-year apprenticeship. Apprentices typically receive 2,000 hours of paid on-the-job training, as well as some technical instruction, each year. Technical instruction includes

Most plumbers, pipefitters, and steamfitters learn their jobs through an apprenticeship.

safety, local plumbing codes and regulations, and blueprint reading. Apprentices also study mathematics, applied physics, and chemistry. Apprenticeship programs are sponsored by unions, trade associations, and businesses. Most apprentices enter a program directly, but some start out as helpers or complete a pre-apprenticeship training programs in plumbing and other trades.

Plumbers, pipefitters, and steamfitters complete an apprenticeship program and pass the required licensing exam to become journey-level workers. Journey-level plumbers, pipefitters, and steamfitters are qualified to perform tasks independently. Plumbers with several years of plumbing experience who pass another exam earn master status. Some states require master plumber status in order to obtain a plumbing contractor's license.

Licenses, Certifications, and Registrations

Most states and some localities require plumbers to be licensed. Although licensing requirements vary, states and localities often require workers to have 2 to 5 years of experience and to pass an exam that shows their knowledge of the trade before allowing plumbers to work independently.

Plumbers may also obtain optional certification, such as in plumbing design, to broaden career opportunities. In addition, most employers require plumbers to have a driver's license.

Some states require pipefitters and steamfitters to be licensed; they may also require a special license to work on gas lines. Licensing typically requires an exam or work experience or both. Contact your state's licensing board for more information.

Advancement

After completing an apprenticeship and becoming licensed at the journey level, plumbers may advance to become a master plumber, supervisor, or project manager. Some plumbers choose to start their own business as an independent contractor, which may require additional licensing.

Important Qualities

Communication skills. Plumbers must be able to direct workers, bid on jobs, and plan work schedules. Plumbers also talk to customers regularly.

Dexterity. Plumbers must be able to maneuver parts and tools precisely, often in tight spaces.

Mechanical skills. Plumbers, pipefitters, and steamfitters choose from a variety of tools to assemble, maintain, and repair pipe systems.

Physical strength. Plumbers, pipefitters, and steamfitters must be able to lift and move heavy tools and materials.

Troubleshooting skills. Plumbers, pipefitters, and steamfitters find, diagnose, and repair problems. They also help with setting up and testing new plumbing and piping systems.

The median annual wage for plumbers, pipefitters, and steamfitters was $60,090 in May 2022. The median wage is the wage at which half the workers in an occupation earned more than that amount and half earned less. The lowest 10 percent earned less than $37,250, and the highest 10 percent earned more than $101,190.

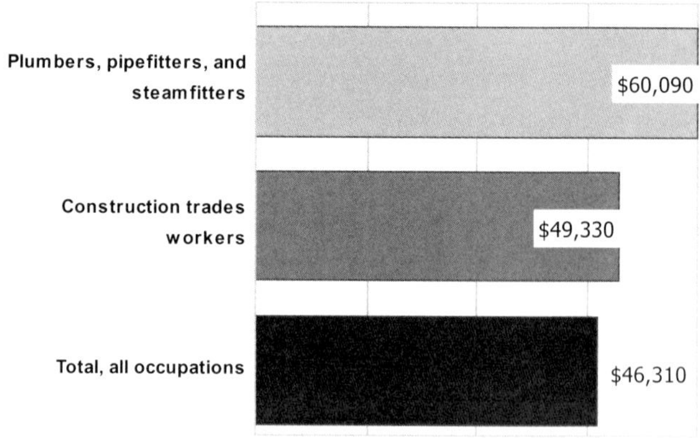

Note: All Occupations includes all occupations in the U.S. Economy.
Source: U.S. Bureau of Labor Statistics, Occupational Employment and Wage Statistics.

In May 2022, the median annual wages for plumbers, pipefitters, and steamfitters in the top industries in which they worked were as follows:

Manufacturing	$62,300
Heavy and civil engineering construction	60,450
Plumbing, heating, and air-conditioning contractors	60,010
Government	59,950

Apprentices earn less than fully trained plumbers, pipefitters, and steamfitters. However, their pay increases as they learn to do more.

Most plumbers, pipefitters, and steamfitters work full time, including nights and weekends. Plumbers are often on call to handle emergencies. Self-employed plumbers may be able to set their own schedules.

Job Outlook

Employment of plumbers, pipefitters, and steamfitters is projected to grow 2 percent from 2022 to 2032, about as fast as the average for all occupations.

About 42,600 openings for plumbers, pipefitters, and steamfitters are projected each year, on average, over the decade. Many of those openings are expected to result from the need to replace workers who transfer to different occupations or exit the labor force, such as to retire.

Employment

Demand for plumbers will stem from new construction and from the need to maintain and repair plumbing systems in existing residences and other buildings. Employment of sprinklerfitters is expected to increase as states continue to adopt changes to building codes that require the use of fire suppression systems.

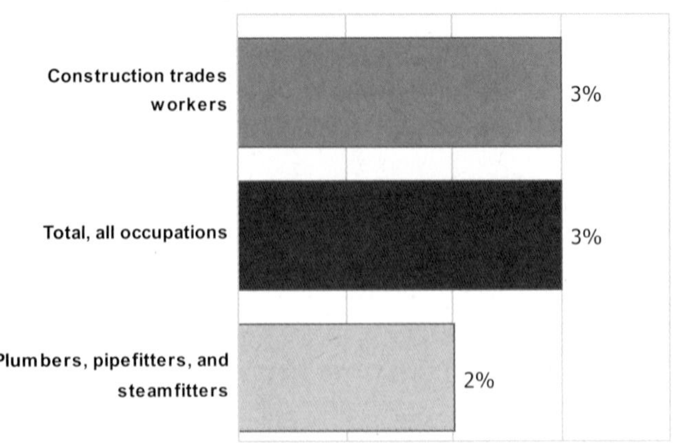

Note: All Occupations includes all occupations in the U.S. Economy.
Source: U.S. Bureau of Labor Statistics, Employment Projections program.

Occupational Title	SOC Code	Employment, 2022	Projected Employment, 2032	Change, 2022-32	
				Percent	Numeric
Plumbers, pipefitters, and steamfitters	47-2152	482,700	493,600	2	10,900

Contacts for More Information

For more information, visit

- Mechanical Contractors Association of America
- NCCER
- Plumbing-Heating-Cooling Contractors Association
- American Fire Sprinkler Association
- National Fire Sprinkler Association
- United Association: Union of Plumbers, Fitters, Welders, and Service Techs
- Home Builders Institute
- Plumbing Heating Cooling Contractors Association
- National Building Trades Union

Roofers

Summary

Quick Facts: Roofers	
2022 Median Pay	$47,920 per year $23.04 per hour
Typical Entry-Level Education	No formal educational credential
Work Experience in a Related Occupation	None
On-the-job Training	Moderate-term on-the-job training
Number of Jobs, 2022	154,500
Job Outlook, 2022-32	2% (As fast as average)
Employment Change, 2022-32	3,100

What Roofers Do

Roofers replace, repair, and install the roofs of buildings.

Work Environment

Roofing work is physically demanding because it involves climbing, bending, kneeling, and heavy lifting. Roofers may work overtime in order to finish a particular job, especially during busy summer months.

How to Become a Roofer

There are typically no formal education requirements for roofers. Although most roofers learn on the job, some enter the occupation through an apprenticeship.

Pay

The median annual wage for roofers was $47,920 in May 2022.

Job Outlook

Employment of roofers is projected to grow 2 percent from 2022 to 2032, about as fast as the average for all occupations.

Roofers use a variety of tools when working on roofs depending on the type of roof being installed.

About 12,200 openings for roofers are projected each year, on average, over the decade. Many of those openings are expected to result from the need to replace workers who transfer to different occupations or exit the labor force, such as to retire.

What Roofers Do

Roofers replace, repair, and install the roofs of buildings, using a variety of materials, including shingles, bitumen, and metal.

Duties

Roofers typically do the following:

- Inspect problem roofs to determine the best way to repair them
- Measure roofs to calculate the quantities of materials needed
- Replace damaged or rotting joists or plywood
- Remove existing roof systems
- Install vapor barriers or layers of insulation
- Install roof ventilation
- Install shingles, asphalt, metal, or other materials to make the roof weatherproof
- Align roofing materials with edges of the roof
- Cut roofing materials to fit around walls or vents
- Cover exposed nail or screw heads with roofing cement or caulk to prevent leakage

Roofers install shingles, asphalt, metal, or other materials to make the roof weatherproof.

Properly installing and repairing roofs keeps water from leaking into buildings and damaging the interior, including equipment and furnishings. Roofers install or repair two basic types of roofs: low slope and steep slope.

Low-slope roofs are the most common, as they are typical on commercial, industrial, and apartment buildings. The complexity of installing low-slope roofs varies with the type of building. Roofers may install these roofs in layers, building up piles of felt set in hot bitumen over insulation boards to form a waterproof membrane. They also may install a single-ply membrane of waterproof rubber or thermoplastic compound over roof insulation boards.

Steep-slope roofs are typical on single-family homes. Roofers commonly install asphalt shingles, although they may also lay tile, solar shingles, metal shingles, slate, or shakes (rough wooden shingles) on steep-slope roofs.

Roofers also install green technology rooftop applications. These include vegetative roofs, rainwater harvesting systems, and photovoltaic products, such as solar shingles and solar tiles; however, solar photovoltaic (PV) installers typically install PV panels. Plumbers and heating, air conditioning, and refrigeration mechanics also may install solar thermal systems.

Roofers use a variety of tools when installing or repairing roofs. Their tools include roofing shovels, roof cutters, and pry bars to remove old roofing systems and hammers, nail guns, and framing squares to install new ones.

Most roofers learn their trade on the job working with experienced coworkers.

Work Environment

Roofers held about 154,500 jobs in 2022. The largest employers of roofers were as follows:

Roofing contractors	76%
Self-employed workers	14
Construction of buildings	4

Roofing work is physically demanding because it involves climbing, bending, kneeling, and heavy lifting. Roofers work outdoors in extreme temperatures, but they usually do not work during inclement weather.

Although some roofers work alone, many work as part of a crew.

Injuries and Illnesses

Roofers have one of the highest rates of injuries and illnesses of all occupations, as well as one of the highest rates of occupational fatalities.

Workers may slip or fall from scaffolds, ladders, or roofs. They may also be burned by hot bitumen. Roofs can become extremely hot during the summer, causing heat-related illnesses. Roofers must wear proper safety equipment to reduce the risk of injuries.

Work Schedules

Most roofers work full time. In northern states, roofing work may be limited during the winter months. During the busy summer months, roofers may work overtime to complete jobs.

How to Become a Roofer

There are no specific education requirements for roofers. Although most learn on the job, some roofers enter the occupation through an apprenticeship.

Education

No formal educational credential is typically required for roofers.

Training

Roofers typically receive on-the-job training to become competent in the occupation. In most on-the-job training programs, experienced roofers teach new workers how to use roofing tools, equipment, machines, and materials. Trainees begin with tasks such as carrying equipment and material and erecting scaffolds and hoists. Within a few months, they learn to measure, cut, and fit roofing materials. Later, they lay asphalt or fiberglass shingles. Because some roofing materials, such as solar tiles,

Most roofers learn their trade on the job working with experienced coworkers.

are used infrequently, it may take several years to gain experience for all types of roofing.

A few groups, including the United Union of Roofers, Waterproofers & Allied Workers and some contractor associations, sponsor apprenticeship programs for roofers. Apprenticeships combine on-the-job training with technical instruction, usually requiring a predetermined number of hours for both.

Licenses, Certifications, and Registrations

Roofers may obtain specific certification to qualify for additional work opportunities or greater pay.

The National Roofing Contractors Association offers certification for experienced roofers. Experienced roofers may become certified in various roofing systems, such as thermoplastic systems or asphalt shingles. Certification as a roofing foreman is also available for experienced roofers.

Most employers require that roofers complete safety certification that meets Occupational Safety and Health Administration (OSHA) guidelines, either before or after being hired.

Some employers require roofers to have a driver's license to enable commuting to different jobsites.

Advancement

After gaining experience in the occupation, roofers may have opportunities to advance to become a supervisor, job superintendent, or estimator or to start their own business. Roofers working in a union may advance within their local union to become a business manager or apprenticeship instructor or to other positions of union leadership.

Important Qualities

Ability to work at heights. Roofers must be comfortable working at great heights.

Attention to detail. Roofing materials must be installed to precisely match design patterns and to ensure that the roof is waterproof.

Balance. Roofers should have excellent balance to avoid falling, because they often work on steep slopes at great heights.

Manual dexterity. Roofers need to be precise in handling and installing roofing materials in order to prevent damage to the roof and building.

Math skills. Roofers use math to measure and calculate roofing areas.

Physical stamina. Roofers must be able to endure spending hours on their feet or bending and stooping, often in hot weather.

Physical strength. Roofers often lift and carry heavy materials, such as bundles of shingles that weigh 60 pounds or more.

Pay

The median annual wage for roofers was $47,920 in May 2022. The median wage is the wage at which half the workers in an occupation earned more than that amount and half earned less. The lowest 10 percent earned less than $31,470, and the highest 10 percent earned more than $75,930.

In May 2022, the median annual wages for roofers in the top industries in which they worked were as follows:

Construction of buildings	$49,090
Roofing contractors	47,950

Most roofers work full time. In northern states, roofing work may be limited during the winter months. During the busy summer months, roofers may work overtime to complete jobs.

The starting pay for apprentices is usually 50 percent of what journey workers receive. Apprentices get pay increases as they advance through the apprenticeship program.

Job Outlook

Employment of roofers is projected to grow 2 percent from 2022 to 2032, about as fast as the average for all occupations.

Roofers

Median annual wages, May 2022

Construction trades workers $49,330
Roofers $47,920
Total, all occupations $46,310

Note: All Occupations includes all occupations in the U.S. Economy.
Source: U.S. Bureau of Labor Statistics, Occupational Employment and Wage Statistics.

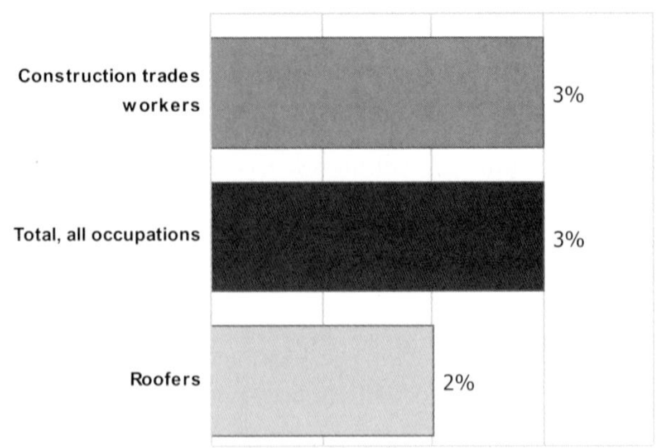

Note: All Occupations includes all occupations in the U.S. Economy.
Source: U.S. Bureau of Labor Statistics, Employment Projections program.

About 12,200 openings for roofers are projected each year, on average, over the decade. Many of those openings are expected to result from the need to replace workers who transfer to different occupations or exit the labor force, such as to retire.

Employment

Replacement and repair of roofs, as well as the installation of new roofs, will create demand for roofers. Some of this demand may come from the installation of solar photovoltaic panels on building rooftops.

Occupational Title	SOC Code	Employment, 2022	Projected Employment, 2032	Change, 2022-32	
				Percent	Numeric
Roofers	47-2181	154,500	157,600	2	3,100

Contacts for More Information

Apprenticeship information is available from the U.S. Department of Labor's Apprenticeship program online, or by phone at 877-872-5627. Visit Apprenticeship.gov to search for apprenticeship opportunities.

For more information about the work of roofers, visit

- National Roofing Contractors Association
- United Union of Roofers, Waterproofers & Allied Workers
- Occupational Safety and Health Administration

Sheet Metal Workers

Summary

Quick Facts: Sheet Metal Workers	
2022 Median Pay	$55,350 per year $26.61 per hour
Typical Entry-Level Education	High school diploma or equivalent
Work Experience in a Related Occupation	None
On-the-job Training	Apprenticeship
Number of Jobs, 2022	126,200
Job Outlook, 2022-32	0% (Little or no change)
Employment Change, 2022-32	-200

What Sheet Metal Workers Do

Sheet metal workers fabricate or install products that are made from thin metal sheets.

Work Environment

Sheet metal workers often lift heavy materials and stand for long periods of time. Those who install sheet metal must often bend, climb, and squat. Most work full time.

How to Become a Sheet Metal Worker

Sheet metal workers employed in construction typically learn their trade through an apprenticeship. Those employed in manufacturing typically learn on the job or at a technical school.

Pay

The median annual wage for sheet metal workers was $55,350 in May 2022.

Job Outlook

Employment of sheet metal workers is projected to show little or no change from 2022 to 2032.

Despite limited employment growth, about 11,400 openings for sheet metal workers are projected each year, on average, over the decade. Most of those openings are expected to result

Sheet metal workers carefully place sheet metal so that it can be bent evenly.

from the need to replace workers who transfer to different occupations or exit the labor force, such as to retire.

What Sheet Metal Workers Do

Sheet metal workers fabricate or install products that are made from thin metal sheets, such as ducts used in heating and air conditioning systems.

Duties

Sheet metal workers typically do the following:

- Select types of sheet metal according to building or design plans
- Measure and mark dimensions and reference lines on metal sheets
- Drill holes in metal for screws, bolts, and rivets
- Install metal sheets with supportive frameworks
- Fabricate or alter parts at construction sites
- Maneuver and anchor large sheet metal parts
- Fasten seams or joints by welding, bolting, riveting, or soldering

Sheet metal workers use pieces of thin steel, aluminum, or other alloyed metal in both manufacturing and construction. Sheet metal products include heating and air conditioning ducts, rain gutters, outdoor signs, and siding.

The following are examples of types of sheet metal workers:

Fabrication sheet metal workers, sometimes called *precision sheet metal workers*, make precision sheet metal parts for a variety of industries, including power generation and medical device manufacturing. They often work in shops and factories, operating tools and equipment. In large-scale manufacturing, their tasks may be highly automated and repetitive. Some fabrication shops have automated machinery, such as computer-controlled saws, lasers, shears, and presses, which measure, cut, bend, and fasten pieces of sheet metal. Workers may use computer-aided drafting and design (CADD) systems to make products. Some of these workers are responsible for limited programming of the computers controlling their equipment. Workers who primarily program computerized equipment are called metal and plastic machine workers.

Installation sheet metal workers put in heating, ventilation, and air conditioning (HVAC) ducts. They also install other sheet metal products, such as metal roofs, siding, and gutters. They typically work on new construction and on renovation projects. In addition to installing sheet metal, some workers install nonmetallic materials such as fiberglass and plastic board. Information about workers who install or repair roofing systems is in the profile on roofers.

Maintenance sheet metal workers repair and clean ventilation systems so the systems use less energy. Workers remove dust and moisture and fix leaks or breaks in the sheet metal that makes up the ductwork.

Testing and balancing sheet metal specialists ensure that HVAC systems heat and cool rooms properly by adjusting sheet metal ducts to achieve proper airflow. Information on workers who install or repair HVAC systems is in the profile on heating, air conditioning, and refrigeration mechanics and installers.

Work Environment

Sheet metal workers held about 126,200 jobs in 2022. The largest employers of sheet metal workers were as follows:

Specialty trade contractors	59%
Manufacturing	23
Government	5
Construction of buildings	4
Employment services	2

Sheet metal fabricators usually work in manufacturing plants and small shops, where they often lift heavy materials and stand for long periods of time.

Workers who install sheet metal at construction sites must bend, climb, and squat, sometimes in close quarters, in awkward positions, or at great heights. Sheet metal installers who work

Sheet metal workers mark metal before drilling holes.

Some sheet metal workers install sheet metal at construction sites, which requires climbing and working at great heights.

outdoors are exposed to all types of weather. The work environment may be noisy or dusty, and job tasks may create vibrations.

Injuries and Illnesses

Sheet metal workers risk injury on the job. Common injuries include cuts from sharp metal, burns from soldering or welding, and falls from ladders or scaffolding.

Some sheet metal fabricators work around high-speed machines, which may be dangerous and also may carry risks of loud noise, dust particles, and vibrations. To reduce injuries resulting from these hazards, workers often must wear safety glasses, ear protection, and dust masks and must not wear jewelry or loose-fitting clothing that could easily get caught in a machine. To avoid repetitive strain injuries, sheet metal workers may rotate through different production stations.

Work Schedules

Most sheet metal workers work full time.

How to Become a Sheet Metal Worker

Sheet metal workers who work in construction typically learn their trade through an apprenticeship. Those who work in manufacturing often learn on the job or at a technical school.

Education

Sheet metal workers typically need a high school diploma or equivalent. Those interested in becoming a sheet metal worker should take high school classes in algebra and geometry. Vocational-education courses such as blueprint reading, mechanical drawing, and welding are also helpful.

Technical schools may have programs that teach welding and metalworking. These programs help provide the basic welding and sheet metal fabrication knowledge that sheet metal workers need to do their job.

Some manufacturers have partnerships with local technical schools to develop training programs specific to their factories.

Training

Most construction sheet metal workers learn their trade through 4- or 5-year apprenticeships, which include both paid on-the-job training and related technical instruction. Apprentices learn construction basics such as blueprint reading, math, building code requirements, and safety and first aid practices. Welding may be included as part of the training.

Some workers start out as helpers before entering apprenticeships.

Apprenticeship programs are sponsored by unions and businesses. The basic qualifications for entering an apprenticeship program are being 18 years old and having a high school diploma or the equivalent.

After completing an apprenticeship program, sheet metal workers are considered journey workers who are qualified to perform tasks on their own.

Sheet metal workers learn their trade through an apprenticeship or on-the-job training, or at a technical school.

Licenses, Certifications, and Registrations

Some states require licenses for sheet metal workers. Check with your state for more information.

Although not required, sheet metal workers may earn certifications for several tasks that they perform. For example, some sheet metal workers become certified in welding from the American Welding Society. In addition, the International Certification Board offers certification in testing and balancing, HVAC fire life safety, and other related activities for eligible sheet metal workers. The Fabricators & Manufacturers Association, International, offers a certification in precision sheet metal work.

Important Qualities

Detail oriented. Sheet metal workers must precisely measure and cut, follow detailed directions, and monitor their surroundings for safety risks.

Dexterity. Sheet metal workers need good hand–eye coordination and motor control to make precise cuts and bends in metal pieces.

Math skills. Sheet metal workers must calculate the proper sizes and angles of fabricated sheet metal to ensure the alignment and fit of ductwork.

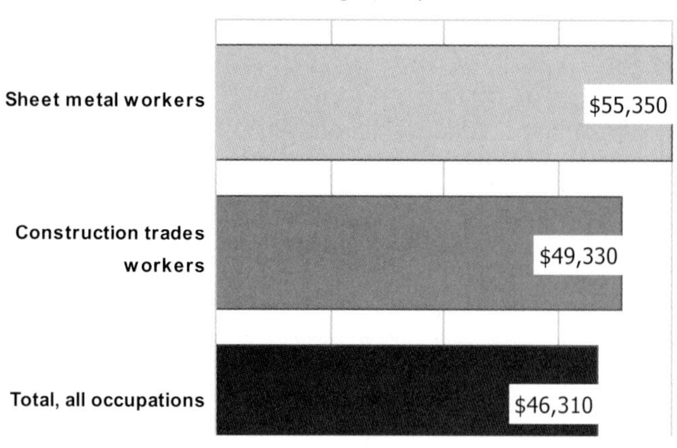

Note: All Occupations includes all occupations in the U.S. Economy.
Source: U.S. Bureau of Labor Statistics, Occupational Employment and Wage Statistics.

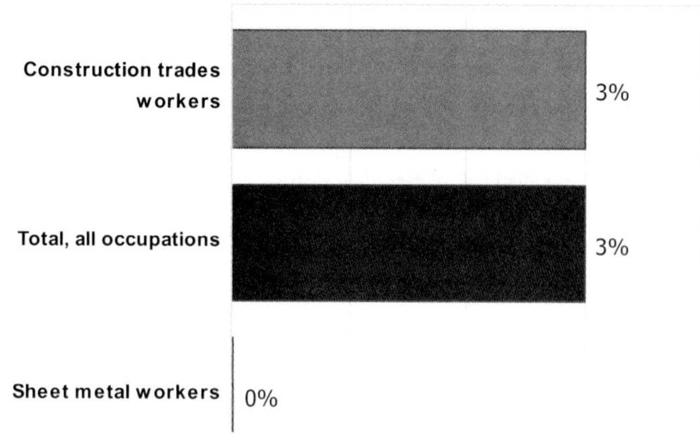

Note: All Occupations includes all occupations in the U.S. Economy.
Source: U.S. Bureau of Labor Statistics, Employment Projections program.

Mechanical skills. Sheet metal workers use saws, lasers, shears, and presses. They should have good mechanical skills in order to operate and maintain equipment.

Physical stamina. Sheet metal workers in factories may spend many hours standing at their workstation.

Physical strength. Sheet metal workers must be able to lift and move ductwork that is heavy and cumbersome. Some jobs require workers to push, pull, or lift 50 pounds or more.

Pay

The median annual wage for sheet metal workers was $55,350 in May 2022. The median wage is the wage at which half the workers in an occupation earned more than that amount and half earned less. The lowest 10 percent earned less than $35,570, and the highest 10 percent earned more than $99,560.

In May 2022, the median annual wages for sheet metal workers in the top industries in which they worked were as follows:

Government	$62,250
Specialty trade contractors	58,550
Construction of buildings	48,950
Manufacturing	48,110
Employment services	37,200

The starting pay for apprentices is usually less than what fully trained sheet metal workers make. As apprentices learn more skills, their pay increases.

Most sheet metal workers work full time.

Job Outlook

Employment of sheet metal workers is projected to show little or no change from 2022 to 2032.

Despite limited employment growth, about 11,400 openings for sheet metal workers are projected each year, on average, over the decade. Most of those openings are expected to result from the need to replace workers who transfer to different occupations or exit the labor force, such as to retire.

Employment

There will be continuing need to install and maintain energy-efficient HVAC systems in new and existing buildings over the projected decade. However, the use of prefabricated duct systems will limit the need for sheet metal workers on residential construction sites. Some sheet metal fabrication equipment is automated, further reducing the need for workers outside of construction.

Occupational Title	SOC Code	Employment, 2022	Projected Employment, 2032	Change, 2022-32	
				Percent	Numeric
Sheet metal workers	47-2211	126,200	126,000	0	-200

Contacts for More Information

Apprenticeship information is available from the U.S. Department of Labor's Apprenticeship program online or by phone at 877-872-5627. Visit Apprenticeship.gov to search for apprenticeship opportunities.

For more information, visit

- International Association of Sheet Metal, Air, Rail and Transportation Workers (SMART)
- International Training Institute for the Sheet Metal and Air Conditioning Industry
- NCCER
- Sheet Metal and Air Conditioning Contractors' National Association
- American Welding Society
- Fabricators & Manufacturers Association, International
- International Certification Board
- Helmet to Hardhats

Solar Photovoltaic Installers

Summary

Quick Facts: Solar Photovoltaic Installers	
2022 Median Pay	$45,230 per year $21.75 per hour
Typical Entry-Level Education	High school diploma or equivalent
Work Experience in a Related Occupation	None
On-the-job Training	Moderate-term on-the-job training
Number of Jobs, 2022	29,400
Job Outlook, 2022-32	22% (Much faster than average)
Employment Change, 2022-32	6,600

What Solar Photovoltaic Installers Do
Solar photovoltaic (PV) installers assemble, set up, and maintain rooftop or other systems that convert sunlight into energy.

Work Environment
Most solar panel installations are done outdoors, but PV installers sometimes work in attics and crawl spaces to connect panels to the electrical grid. Installers also must travel to jobsites.

How to Become a Solar Photovoltaic Installer
Although installers typically need a high school diploma, some take courses at a technical school or community college. Installers typically receive on-the-job training lasting up to 1 year.

Pay
The median annual wage for solar photovoltaic installers was $45,230 in May 2022.

PV panels are placed on specially built framework.

Job Outlook
Employment of solar photovoltaic installers is projected to grow 22 percent from 2022 to 2032, much faster than the average for all occupations.

About 3,500 openings for solar photovoltaic installers are projected each year, on average, over the decade. Many of those openings are expected to result from the need to replace workers who transfer to different occupations or exit the labor force, such as to retire.

What Solar Photovoltaic Installers Do
Solar photovoltaic (PV) installers, also known as *PV installers*, assemble, set up, and maintain rooftop or other systems that convert sunlight into energy.

Duties
PV installers typically do the following:

- Plan PV system configurations based on customer needs and site conditions
- Measure, cut, and assemble the support structure for solar PV panels
- Install solar modules, panels, and support structures according to building codes and standards
- Connect PV panels to the electrical system
- Apply weather sealant to equipment being installed
- Activate and test PV systems
- Perform routine PV system maintenance

At the jobsite, PV installers verify the measurements and design of the structure on which the PV system is being set up. For PV systems on flat roofs, PV installers must first add a structure that allows the PV system to be mounted at an angle. PV installers set up new systems on support structures and place PV panels or PV shingles on top of them. Once the panels are in place, they sometimes connect the panels to electrical components. After the system is in place, PV installers must test the system and its components.

PV installers use a variety of handtools and power tools, including drills, wrenches, saws, and screwdrivers, to set up

Solar photovoltaic installers usually work as part of a team.

Some photovoltaic installers place thin solar film on rooftops.

PV panels and connect them to frames, wires, and support structures.

Depending on the job and state laws, PV installers may connect the solar panels to the electrical grid, although electricians sometimes do this task. Once the panels are set up, workers check the electrical systems for proper wiring, polarity, and grounding, and they also perform maintenance as needed.

Work Environment

Solar photovoltaic installers held about 29,400 jobs in 2022. The largest employers of solar photovoltaic installers were as follows:

Electrical contractors and other wiring installation contractors	37%
Plumbing, heating, and air-conditioning contractors	10
Self-employed workers	5
Power and communication line and related structures construction	5
Utilities	5

Because photovoltaic (PV) panels convert sunlight into electricity, most PV installation is done outdoors. Residential installers work on rooftops but also sometimes work in attics and crawl spaces to connect panels to the electrical grid. PV installers who build solar farms work at ground level.

PV installers may work alone or as part of a team. Installation of solar panels may require the help of roofers and electricians.

Injuries and Illnesses

Solar photovoltaic installers risk falls from ladders and roofs, shocks from electricity, and burns from hot equipment and materials while installing and maintaining PV systems. To reduce the risk of injury, PV installers must wear safety equipment, such as harnesses, gloves, and hard hats.

How to Become a Solar Photovoltaic Installer

There are multiple paths to becoming a solar photovoltaic (PV) installer, or *PV installer*. These workers typically need a high school diploma, but some take courses at a technical school or community college; they also receive on-the-job training lasting up to 1 year. Some PV installers learn to install panels as part of an apprenticeship.

Most photovoltaic installers learn on the job working with experienced installers.

Education

PV installers typically need a high school diploma. Some PV installers take courses at local community colleges or technical schools to learn about solar panel installation. Courses range from basic safety and PV knowledge to system design. Although course length varies, most usually last a few days to several months.

Some candidates, especially those with construction experience, enter the field by taking online training courses.

Training

Some PV installers learn their trade on the job by working with experienced installers. On-the-job training usually lasts between 1 month and 1 year. During training, PV installers learn about safety, tools, and PV system installation techniques.

Electrician and roofing apprentices and journey workers may complete photovoltaic-specific training modules through apprenticeships.

Solar PV system manufacturers may also provide training on specific products. Such training usually includes a system overview and proper installation techniques for the manufacturer's products.

Military veterans may benefit from the Solar Ready Vets program, which is funded by the U.S Department of Energy and prepares veterans to connect with training and jobs in the solar industry.

Work Experience in a Related Occupation

Experience in construction may shorten a new employee's training time. For example, workers with experience as an electrician, roofer, carpenter, or laborer typically already understand and can perform basic construction duties.

Licenses, Certifications, and Registrations

Some states require a license for PV installers. Contact your state's licensing board for more information.

PV installers must travel to jobsites, so employers may require them to have a driver's license.

Although not required for employment, certification demonstrates competency in solar panel installation. The Electronics Technicians Association, International (ETA) and the North American Board of Certified Energy Practitioners offer certification for PV installers. Some states require that for projects to qualify for solar-related subsidies, all PV installers working on the projects must have certification.

Advancement

PV installers may advance to become a project supervisor or project manager after gaining experience in the trade. PV installers may also transition to sales roles within the industry, given their knowledge of and experience with PV installation. They also may choose to start their own PV installation business.

Important Qualities

Ability to work at heights. PV installers often must work on roofs, ladders, or lifts that are far above the ground.

Communication skills. PV installers need to convey information effectively to clients, team members, and other workers.

Detail oriented. PV installers must carefully follow instructions to ensure that the system works properly.

Math skills. PV installers use algebra, geometry, and trigonometry to calculate angles, measurements, and areas.

Mechanical skills. PV installers work with complex electrical and mechanical equipment in order to build support structures for solar panels, connect the panels to the electrical system, and troubleshoot problems.

Physical stamina. PV installers are often on their feet carrying panels and other heavy equipment. Especially when installing rooftop panels, workers may need to climb ladders many times throughout the day.

Physical strength. PV installers must lift heavy equipment and materials weighing up to 60 pounds.

Pay

The median annual wage for solar photovoltaic installers was $45,230 in May 2022. The median wage is the wage at which half the workers in an occupation earned more than that amount and half earned less. The lowest 10 percent earned less than $35,520, and the highest 10 percent earned more than $63,330.

In May 2022, the median annual wages for solar photovoltaic installers in the top industries in which they worked were as follows:

Plumbing, heating, and air-conditioning contractors	$48,320
Electrical contractors and other wiring installation contractors	48,130
Power and communication line and related structures construction	47,960
Utilities	45,280

Job Outlook

Employment of solar photovoltaic installers is projected to grow 22 percent from 2022 to 2032, much faster than the average for all occupations.

About 3,500 openings for solar photovoltaic installers are projected each year, on average, over the decade. Many of those openings are expected to result from the need to replace workers who transfer to different occupations or exit the labor force, such as to retire.

Employment

The continued expansion and adoption of solar PV systems is expected to create jobs for their installation and upkeep.

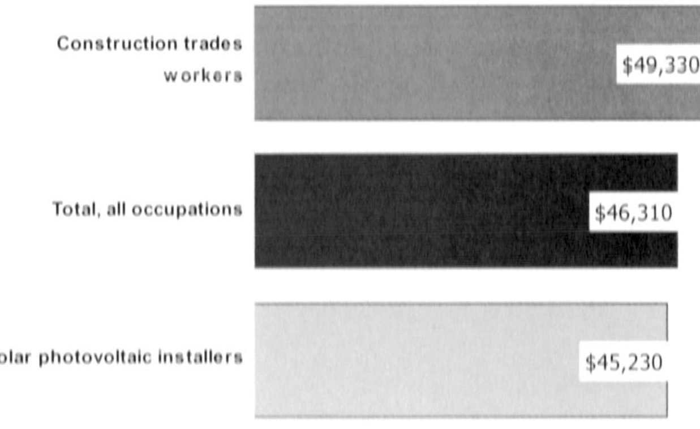

Note: All Occupations includes all occupations in the U.S. Economy.
Source: U.S. Bureau of Labor Statistics, Occupational Employment and Wage Statistics.

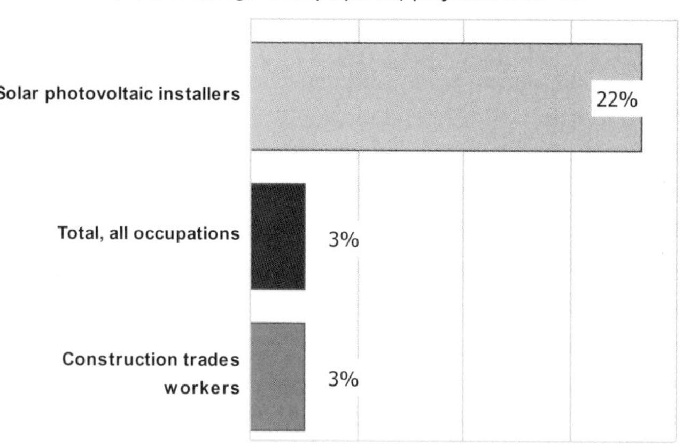

Note: All Occupations includes all occupations in the U.S. Economy.
Source: U.S. Bureau of Labor Statistics, Employment Projections program.

As the cost of PV panels and shingles continues to decrease, more households are expected to take advantage of these systems, resulting in greater demand for the workers who install and maintain them. The increasing popularity of solar leasing plans—in which homeowners lease, rather than purchase, systems—should create additional demand, because homeowners no longer bear the upfront costs of installation.

Demand may be greatest in states and localities that provide incentives to reduce the cost of PV systems.

Occupational Title	SOC Code	Employment, 2022	Projected Employment, 2032	Change, 2022-32	
				Percent	Numeric
Solar photovoltaic installers	47-2231	29,400	35,900	22	6,600

Contacts for More Information

Apprenticeship information is available from the U.S. Department of Labor's Apprenticeship program online or by phone at 877-872-5627. Visit Apprenticeship.gov to search for apprenticeship opportunities.

For more information about accredited training programs, visit

- American Solar Workforce
- Electronics Technicians Association, International (ETA)
- Interstate Renewable Energy Council, Inc.
- North American Board of Certified Energy Practitioners
- NCCER
- IBEW–NECA Electrical Training Alliance
- The Solar Foundation

Education, Training, and Library

Adult Basic and Secondary Education and ESL Teachers

Summary

Quick Facts: Adult Basic and Secondary Education and ESL Teachers	
2022 Median Pay	$58,590 per year $28.17 per hour
Typical Entry-Level Education	Bachelor's degree
Work Experience in a Related Occupation	None
On-the-job Training	None
Number of Jobs, 2022	42,200
Job Outlook, 2022-32	-13% (Decline)
Employment Change, 2022-32	-5,300

What Adult Basic and Secondary Education and ESL Teachers Do

Adult basic and secondary education and ESL (English as a Second Language) teachers instruct adults in fundamental skills, such as reading and speaking English. They also help students earn their high school equivalency credential.

Work Environment

Adult basic and secondary education and ESL teachers are often employed by community colleges, community-based organizations, and public schools. Part-time work is common.

How to Become an Adult Basic or Secondary Education or ESL Teacher

Adult basic and secondary education and ESL teachers who work in public schools typically need at least a bachelor's degree and a license or certification.

Adult literacy and high school equivalency diploma teachers instruct adults in basic skills.

Pay

The median annual wage for adult basic and secondary education and ESL teachers was $58,590 in May 2022.

Job Outlook

Employment of adult basic and secondary education and ESL teachers is projected to decline 13 percent from 2022 to 2032.

Despite declining employment, about 4,200 openings for adult basic and secondary education and ESL teachers are projected each year, on average, over the decade. All of those openings are expected to result from the need to replace workers who transfer to other occupations or exit the labor force, such as to retire.

What Adult Basic and Secondary Education and ESL Teachers Do

Adult basic and secondary education and ESL (English as a Second Language) teachers instruct adults in fundamental skills, such as reading, writing, and speaking English. They also help students earn their high school equivalency credential.

Duties

Adult basic and secondary education and ESL teachers typically do the following:

- Plan and teach lessons to help students gain the knowledge and skills needed to earn their high school equivalency credential
- Adapt teaching methods based on students' strengths and weaknesses
- Emphasize skills that will help students find jobs, such as learning English words and common phrases used in the workplace
- Assess students for learning disabilities
- Monitor students' progress
- Help students develop study skills
- Connect students to other resources in their community, such as job placement services

Students' educational level and skills are assessed before they enter these programs. Teachers may conduct the assessments; however, sometimes another staff member assesses students. Based on the results of the assessment and the student's goals, teachers develop an education plan.

Teachers must formally evaluate their students periodically to determine their progress and potential to go on to the next level of classes. However, teachers may informally evaluate their students' progress continually.

Adult education and ESL teachers use different teaching strategies to meet their students' needs.

Adult basic and secondary education and ESL teachers often have students of various ability levels in their classes. As a result, these teachers need to use different strategies to meet the needs of all of their students. They may work with students in classes or teach them one-on-one.

There are three types of education that adult basic and secondary education and ESL teachers provide:

Adult basic education (ABE) classes teach students the basics of reading, writing, and math. The students generally are age 16 or older and need to gain proficiency in these skills to improve their job situation. Teachers prepare students for further education and help them to develop skills that they will need in the workplace. For example, they may teach students how to write a resume.

Adult secondary education classes prepare students to take the test to earn a high school equivalency credential. Some programs are combined with career preparation programs so that students can earn a high school equivalency and a career-related credential at the same time.

The high school equivalency exam is composed of four subjects: language arts, math, science, and social studies. In addition to teaching these subjects, teachers also help their students improve their skills in communicating, critical thinking, and problem solving—skills they will need in preparing for further education and successful careers.

English as a Second Language (ESL), also called *English for Speakers of Other Languages (ESOL)*, classes teach students to read, write, and speak English. Students in these classes are immigrants to the United States or those whose native language is not English. ESL teachers may have students from many different countries and cultures in their classroom. Because the ESL teacher and the students may not share a common native language, ESL teachers must be creative with their communication in the classroom.

ESL teachers often focus on helping their students with practical vocabulary for jobs and daily living. They also may focus on preparing their students to take the citizenship exam.

Work Environment

Adult basic and secondary education and ESL teachers held about 42,200 jobs in 2022. The largest employers of adult basic and secondary education and ESL teachers were as follows:

Elementary and secondary schools; state, local, and private	33%
Junior colleges; state, local, and private	23
Other schools and instruction; state, local, and private	10
Self-employed workers	7
Colleges, universities, and professional schools; state, local, and private	3

Students in adult education and ESL programs attend classes by choice. As a result, they are often highly motivated, which may make teaching them rewarding and satisfying.

Adult basic and secondary education and ESL teachers often work in community colleges, community-based organizations, and public schools.

Work Schedules

These teachers often work in the mornings and evenings, because classes are held at times when students are not at work. Part-time work is common.

How to Become an Adult Basic or Secondary Education or ESL Teacher

Adult basic and secondary education and ESL teachers who work in public schools typically need at least a bachelor's degree and a license or certification.

Education

Adult basic and secondary education and ESL teachers in public schools typically need at least a bachelor's degree. Some community colleges prefer to hire those with a master's degree or graduate coursework in adult education or English as a Second Language (ESL).

Programs in adult education prepare prospective teachers to use effective strategies for adult learners, work with students from a variety of cultures and backgrounds, and teach adults with learning disabilities. Some programs allow these prospective teachers to specialize in adult basic education, secondary education, or ESL.

Prospective ESL teachers should take courses or training in linguistics and theories of how people learn second languages. Knowledge of a second language is not necessary to teach ESL, but it can be helpful.

Teacher education programs instruct prospective teachers in how to present information to students and how to work with students of varying abilities and backgrounds. Programs typically include an opportunity for student-teachers to work with a mentor and get experience in a classroom. For information about teacher preparation programs in your state, visit Teach.org.

Working with students of different abilities and backgrounds can be difficult and teachers must respond with patience when students struggle with material.

Adult basic and secondary education and ESL teachers may take professional development classes to improve their teaching skills and ensure that they keep up with research about teaching adults.

Licenses, Certifications, and Registrations

Adult basic and secondary education and ESL teachers who work in public schools must have a teaching certificate. Some states have certificates specifically for adult education. Other states require teachers to have a certificate in elementary or secondary education.

To obtain a license, adult basic and secondary education and ESL teachers typically need a bachelor's degree and must complete a student-teaching program. For more information, contact the director of adult education for your state. Contact information is available from the U.S. Department of Education.

Important Qualities

Communication skills. Adult basic and secondary education and ESL teachers must collaborate with other teachers and program administrators. In addition, they must explain concepts in terms that students can understand.

Cultural sensitivity. Teachers work with students from a variety of cultural, educational, and economic backgrounds. They must be respectful of their students' backgrounds and be understanding of their concerns.

Patience. Working with students of different abilities and backgrounds can be difficult. Teachers must be patient when students struggle to understand the material.

Resourcefulness. Teachers must be able to think on their feet and find ways to keep students engaged in learning. They may have to change their methods of instruction to address the different needs of their students.

Pay

The median annual wage for adult basic and secondary education and ESL teachers was $58,590 in May 2022. The median wage is the wage at which half the workers in an occupation earned more than that amount and half earned less. The lowest 10 percent earned less than $36,970, and the highest 10 percent earned more than $97,010.

In May 2022, the median annual wages for adult basic and secondary education and ESL teachers in the top industries in which they worked were as follows:

Elementary and secondary schools; state, local, and private	$62,340
Other schools and instruction; state, local, and private	56,260
Colleges, universities, and professional schools; state, local, and private	53,660
Junior colleges; state, local, and private	52,920

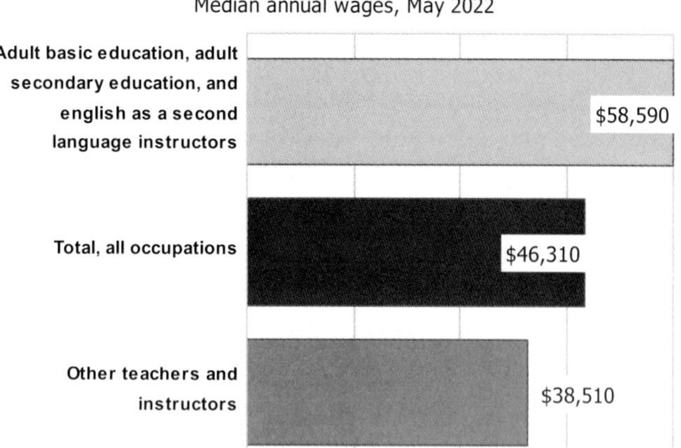

Note: All Occupations includes all occupations in the U.S. Economy. Source: U.S. Bureau of Labor Statistics, Occupational Employment and Wage Statistics.

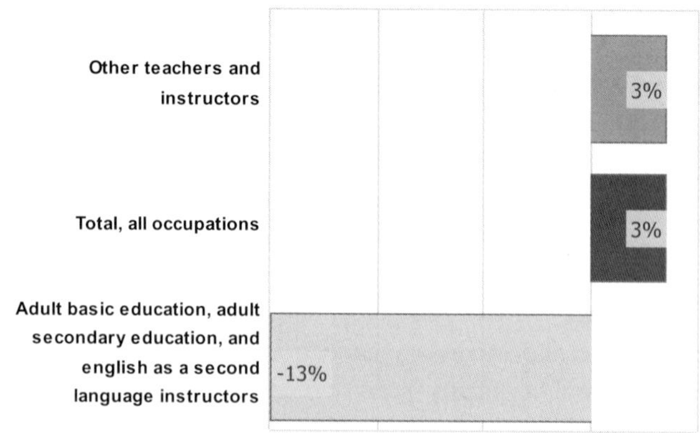

Note: All Occupations includes all occupations in the U.S. Economy. Source: U.S. Bureau of Labor Statistics, Employment Projections program.

Teachers often work in the mornings and evenings, because classes are held at times when students are not at work. Part-time work is common.

Job Outlook

Employment of adult basic and secondary education and ESL teachers is projected to decline 13 percent from 2022 to 2032.

Despite declining employment, about 4,200 openings for adult basic and secondary education and ESL teachers are projected each year, on average, over the decade. All of those openings are expected to result from the need to replace workers who transfer to other occupations or exit the labor force, such as to retire.

Employment

Enrollment in adult education and ESL programs has declined in recent years. At the same time, high school graduation rates have increased, reducing the number of adults seeking to obtain high school equivalency credentials. As these trends continue, the demand for adult basic and secondary education and ESL teachers may decline.

Changes in government funding for adult education and ESL programs also may impact the demand for these workers.

Occupational Title	SOC Code	Employment, 2022	Projected Employment, 2032	Change, 2022-32	
				Percent	Numeric
Adult basic education, adult secondary education, and english as a second language instructors	25-3011	42,200	36,900	-13	-5,300

Contacts for More Information

For more information about adult education in your state, visit

- U.S. Department of Education
- Teach.org

Archivists, Curators, and Museum Workers

Summary

Quick Facts: Archivists, Curators, and Museum Workers	
2022 Median Pay	$53,420 per year $25.68 per hour
Typical Entry-Level Education	See How to Become One
Work Experience in a Related Occupation	None
On-the-job Training	None
Number of Jobs, 2022	37,700
Job Outlook, 2022-32	10% (Much faster than average)
Employment Change, 2022-32	3,700

What Archivists, Curators, and Museum Workers Do

Archivists and curators oversee institutions' collections, such as of historical items or of artwork. Museum technicians and conservators prepare and restore items in those collections.

Work Environment

Archivists, curators, museum technicians, and conservators work in museums, historical sites, governments, colleges and universities, corporations, and other institutions. Most work full time.

How to Become an Archivist, Curator, or Museum Worker

Archivists, curators, and conservators typically need a master's degree in a field related to their position. Museum technicians typically need a bachelor's degree. Experience gained through an internship or by volunteering in archives or museums is helpful.

Pay

The median annual wage for archivists, curators, and museum workers was $53,420 in May 2022.

Job Outlook

Overall employment of archivists, curators, and museum workers is projected to grow 10 percent from 2022 to 2032, much faster than the average for all occupations.

About 5,000 openings for archivists, curators, and museum workers are projected each year, on average, over the decade. Many of those openings are expected to result from the need to replace workers who transfer to different occupations or exit the labor force, such as to retire.

What Archivists, Curators, and Museum Workers Do

Archivists appraise, process, catalog, and preserve permanent records and historically valuable documents. Curators oversee collections of artwork and historical items and may conduct public service activities for an institution. Museum technicians and conservators prepare and restore objects and documents in museum collections and exhibits.

Duties

Archivists typically do the following:

- Authenticate and appraise historical documents and archival materials
- Preserve and maintain documents and objects
- Create and manage a system to maintain and preserve electronic records
- Organize and classify archival materials
- Safeguard records by creating film and digital copies
- Direct workers to help arrange, exhibit, and maintain collections
- Set and administer policy guidelines concerning public access to materials

Archivists, curators, and museum workers maintain and display art.

Museum technicians often prepare materials for display.

- Find and acquire new materials for their archives

Curators, museum technicians, and conservators typically do the following:

- Acquire, store, and exhibit collections
- Select the theme and design of exhibits
- Design, organize, and conduct tours and workshops for the public
- Attend meetings and civic events to promote their institution
- Clean objects such as ancient tools, coins, and statues
- Direct and supervise curatorial, technical, and student staff
- Plan and conduct special research projects

Archivists preserve important or historically significant documents and records. They coordinate educational and public outreach programs, such as tours, lectures, and classes. They also may work with researchers on topics and items relevant to their collections.

Some archivists specialize in a particular era of history so that they can have a better understanding of the records from that period. Archivists typically work with specific forms of documentation, such as manuscripts, electronic records, websites, photographs, maps, motion pictures, or sound recordings.

Curators, who also may be *museum directors,* lead the acquisition, storage, and exhibition of collections. They negotiate and authorize the purchase, sale, exchange, and loan of collections. They also may research, authenticate, evaluate, and categorize the items in a collection.

Curators often perform administrative tasks and help manage their institution's research projects and related educational programs. They may represent their institution in the media, at public events, and at professional conferences.

In large institutions, some curators may specialize in a particular field, such as botany, art, or history. For example, a large natural history museum might employ separate curators for its collections of birds, fish, and mammals.

In small institutions, one curator may be responsible for many tasks, from taking care of collections to directing the affairs of the museum.

Museum technicians, who may be known as *preparators, registrars,* or *collections specialists,* care for and safeguard objects in museum collections and exhibitions.

Preparators focus on readying items in museum collections for display or storage. For example, they might make frames and mats for artwork or fit mounts to support objects. They also help to create exhibits, such as by building exhibit cases, installing items, and ensuring proper lighting. And they transport items and prepare them for shipping.

Registrars and collections specialists oversee the logistics of acquisitions, insurance policies, risk management, and loaning of objects to and from the museum for exhibition or research. They keep detailed records of the conditions and locations of the objects that are on display, in storage, or being transported to another museum. They also maintain and store any documentation associated with the objects.

These workers also may answer questions from the public and help curators and outside scholars use the museum's collections.

Conservators handle, preserve, treat, and keep records of artifacts, specimens, and works of art. They may perform substantial historical, scientific, and archeological research. They document their findings and treat items in order to minimize deterioration or restore them to their original state. Conservators usually specialize in a particular material or group of objects, such as documents and books, paintings, or textiles.

Some conservators use x rays, chemical testing, microscopes, special lights, and other laboratory equipment and techniques to examine objects, determine their condition, and decide on the best way to preserve them. They also may participate in outreach programs, research topics in their specialty, and write articles for scholarly journals.

Work Environment

Archivists, curators, and museum workers held about 37,700 jobs in 2022. Employment in the detailed occupations that make up archivists, curators, and museum workers was distributed as follows:

Museum technicians and conservators	14,400
Curators	13,900
Archivists	9,400

The largest employers of archivists, curators, and museum workers were as follows:

Museums, historical sites, and similar institutions	37%
Government	22
Educational services; state, local, and private	16
Self-employed workers	9
Religious, grantmaking, civic, professional, and similar organizations	5

Depending on the size of the institution and the position archivists, curators, and museum workers hold, these workers may spend time either at a desk or with the public, providing reference assistance and educational services. Museum workers who restore and set up exhibits or work with bulky, heavy record containers may have to lift objects, climb ladders and scaffolding, and stretch to reach items.

Work Schedules

Most archivists, curators, museum technicians, and conservators work full time.

Some archivists coordinate educational and public outreach programs.

Archivists in government agencies and corporations generally work during regular business hours. Curators in large institutions may travel extensively to evaluate potential additions to the collection, organize exhibits, and conduct research. For curators in small institutions, however, travel may be rare. Museum technicians may need to work evenings and weekends if their institutions are open to the public during those times.

How to Become an Archivist, Curator, or Museum Worker

Archivists, curators, and conservators typically need a master's degree; museum technicians typically need a bachelor's degree. Fields of degree may include fine and performing arts, history, or social science. Experience gained through an internship or by volunteering in archives or museums is helpful.

Education

Archivists. Archivists typically need a master's degree in history, library science, archival studies, political science, or public administration. Students may gain valuable archiving experience through volunteer or internship opportunities.

Prior experience through an internship or by volunteering in archives and museums is helpful in getting a position as an archivist, curator, museum technician, or conservator.

Curators. Curators typically need a master's degree in art history, history, archaeology, or museum studies. In small museums, curator positions may be available to applicants with a bachelor's degree. Because curators have administrative and managerial responsibilities, courses in business administration, public relations, marketing, and fundraising are recommended.

Museum technicians. Museum technicians typically need a bachelor's degree in museum studies or a related field, such as archaeology, art history, or history. Some jobs require candidates to have a master's degree in museum studies. In addition, museum employers may prefer candidates who have knowledge of the museum's specialty or have experience working in museums.

Conservators. Conservators typically need a master's degree in conservation or a related field. Graduate programs last 2 to 4 years, the latter part of which includes an internship. To qualify for entry into these programs, a student must have a background in archaeology, art history, chemistry, or studio art. Completing a conservation internship as an undergraduate may enhance an applicant's prospects into a graduate program.

Licenses, Certifications, and Registrations

Although most employers do not require certification, some archivists may choose to earn voluntary certification because it allows them to demonstrate expertise in a particular area.

The Academy of Certified Archivists offers the Certified Archivist credential. To earn certification, candidates usually must have a master's degree, have professional archival experience, and pass an exam. They must renew their certification periodically by retaking the exam or fulfilling continuing education credits.

Other Experience

To gain experience, candidates may have to work part time, as an intern or as a volunteer, during or after completing their education. Substantial experience in collection management, research, exhibit design, or restoration, as well as database management skills, is necessary for full-time positions.

Advancement

Continuing education is available through meetings, conferences, and workshops sponsored by archival, historical, and museum associations. Some large organizations, such as the U.S. National Archives and Records Administration in Washington, DC, offer in-house training.

Top museum positions are highly sought after. Performing unique research and producing published work are important for advancement in large institutions. In addition, a doctoral degree may be needed for some advanced positions.

Museum workers employed in small institutions may have limited opportunities for promotion. They typically advance by transferring to a larger institution that has supervisory positions.

Important Qualities

Analytical skills. Archivists, curators, museum technicians, and conservators must explore minutiae to determine the origin, history, and importance of the objects they work with.

Customer-service skills. Archivists, curators, museum technicians, and conservators work regularly with the general public. They must be courteous, friendly, and able to help users find materials.

Detail oriented. Archivists and museum technicians must be able to focus on specifics because they use and develop complex databases related to the materials they store and access.

Organizational skills. Archivists, curators, museum technicians, and conservators store and easily retrieve records and documents. They must also develop logical systems of storage for the public to use.

Pay

The median annual wage for archivists, curators, and museum workers was $53,420 in May 2022. The median wage is the wage at which half the workers in an occupation earned more than that amount and half earned less. The lowest 10 percent earned less than $31,820, and the highest 10 percent earned more than $98,500.

Median annual wages for archivists, curators, and museum workers in May 2022 were as follows:

Curators	$60,380
Archivists	58,640
Museum technicians and conservators	47,270

In May 2022, the median annual wages for archivists, curators, and museum workers in the top industries in which they worked were as follows:

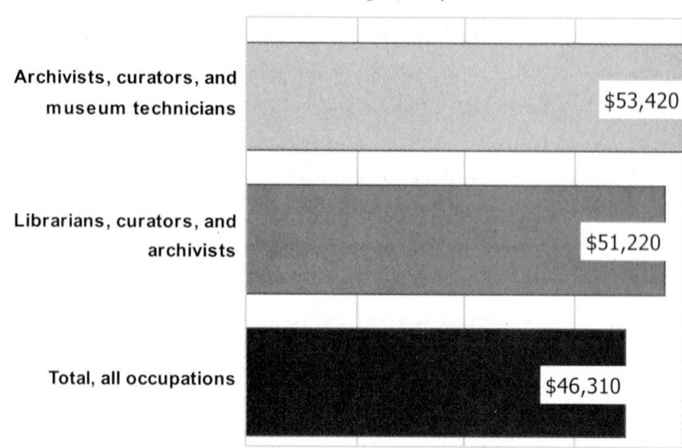

Note: All Occupations includes all occupations in the U.S. Economy.
Source: U.S. Bureau of Labor Statistics, Occupational Employment and Wage Statistics.

Educational services; state, local, and private	$59,860
Government	55,700
Museums, historical sites, and similar institutions	49,710
Religious, grantmaking, civic, professional, and similar organizations	49,240

Most archivists, curators, museum technicians, and conservators work full time.

Archivists in government agencies and corporations generally work during regular business hours. Curators in large institutions may travel extensively to evaluate potential additions to the collection, organize exhibits, and conduct research. However, for curators in small institutions, travel may be rare. Museum technicians may need to work evenings and weekends if their institutions are open to the public during those times.

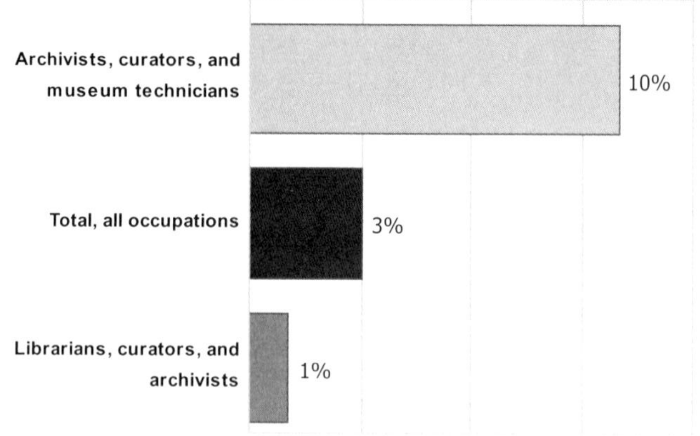

Note: All Occupations includes all occupations in the U.S. Economy.
Source: U.S. Bureau of Labor Statistics, Employment Projections program.

Job Outlook

Overall employment of archivists, curators, and museum workers is projected to grow 10 percent from 2022 to 2032, much faster than the average for all occupations.

About 5,000 openings for archivists, curators, and museum workers are projected each year, on average, over the decade. Many of those openings are expected to result from the need to replace workers who transfer to different occupations or exit the labor force, such as to retire.

Employment

Demand for archivists is expected to increase as public and private organizations have more information and records that need to be organized and made accessible. In particular, the growing use of electronic records may create jobs for archivists.

Continued public interest in museums and other cultural centers is expected to increase the demand for curators, museum technicians, and conservators.

Archives and museums that receive federal funds may be affected by changes to the federal budget, which in turn might impact employment of archivists, curators, museum technicians, and conservators.

Occupational Title	SOC Code	Employment, 2022	Projected Employment, 2032	Change, 2022-32	
				Percent	Numeric
Archivists, curators, and museum technicians	25-4010	37,700	41,500	10	3,700
Archivists	25-4011	9,400	10,200	8	800
Curators	25-4012	13,900	15,400	11	1,500
Museum technicians and conservators	25-4013	14,400	15,900	10	1,400

Contacts for More Information

For information about archivists and about schools offering courses in archival studies, visit

- Society of American Archivists
- Academy of Certified Archivists
- Council of State Archivists
- U.S. National Archives and Records Administration
- Association of Registrars and Collections Specialists
- American Alliance of Museums
- American Institute for Conservation
- USAJobs

Career and Technical Education Teachers

Summary

Quick Facts: Career and Technical Education Teachers

2022 Median Pay	$61,450 per year
Typical Entry-Level Education	Bachelor's degree
Work Experience in a Related Occupation	Less than 5 years
On-the-job Training	None
Number of Jobs, 2022	212,100
Job Outlook, 2022-32	0% (Little or no change)
Employment Change, 2022-32	-800

What Career and Technical Education Teachers Do

Career and technical education teachers instruct students in various technical and vocational subjects, such as auto repair, healthcare, and culinary arts.

Work Environment

Most career and technical education teachers work in middle, high, and postsecondary schools, such as 2-year colleges. Others work in technical, trade, and business schools. Although they generally work during school hours, some teach evening or weekend classes.

How to Become a Career or Technical Education Teacher

Career and technical education teachers typically need at least a bachelor's degree and work experience in the subject that they teach. Public school teachers may be required to have a state-issued teaching certification or license.

Career and technical education teachers teach academic and technical content to provide students with the skills and knowledge necessary to enter an occupation.

Pay

The median annual wage for career and technical education teachers was $61,450 in May 2022.

Job Outlook

Overall employment of career and technical education teachers is projected to show little or no change from 2022 to 2032.

Despite limited employment growth, about 14,800 openings for career and technical education teachers are projected each year, on average, over the decade. Most of those openings are expected to result from the need to replace workers who transfer to different occupations or exit the labor force, such as to retire.

What Career and Technical Education Teachers Do

Career and technical education (CTE) teachers provide training in subjects such as auto repair, cosmetology, and culinary arts. They teach vocational and technical content to give students the skills and knowledge necessary to enter an occupation.

Duties

Career and technical education teachers typically do the following:

- Create lesson plans and assignments
- Instruct students on how to develop certain skills
- Show students how to apply classroom knowledge through hands-on activities
- Demonstrate and supervise safe and proper use of tools and equipment
- Monitor students' progress, assign tasks, and grade assignments
- Discuss students' progress with parents, students, and counselors

Technical education teachers often work in classrooms and help students.

- Develop and enforce classroom rules and safety procedures

CTE teachers help students explore and prepare to enter a career or technical occupation. They use a variety of teaching methods to help students learn and develop skills related to a specific occupation or career field. They demonstrate tasks, techniques, and tools used in an occupation. They may assign hands-on tasks, such as replacing brakes on cars, taking blood pressure, or applying makeup. Teachers typically oversee these activities in workshops and laboratories in the school.

Some teachers work with local businesses and nonprofit organizations to provide practical work experience for students. They also serve as advisers to students participating in career and technical student organizations.

The specific duties of CTE teachers vary by the grade and subject they teach. In middle schools and high schools, they teach general concepts in a classroom and practical exercises in workshops and laboratories.

In postsecondary schools, they teach specific career skills that help students earn a certificate, a diploma, or an associate's degree and prepare them for a specific job. For example, welding instructors teach students welding techniques and safety practices. They also monitor the use of tools and equipment and have students practice procedures until they meet the standards required by the trade.

In most states, teachers in middle and high schools teach one subject within major career fields. CTE teachers combine academic instruction with experiential learning in their subject of expertise.

For example, teachers of courses in ***agricultural, food, and natural resources*** teach topics such as agricultural production; agriculture-related business; veterinary science; and plant, animal, and food systems. They may have students plant and care for crops and animals to apply what they have learned in the classroom.

For information about the programs for major career fields, visit Advance CTE.

Work Environment

Career and technical education teachers held about 212,100 jobs in 2022. Employment in the detailed occupations that make up career and technical education teachers was distributed as follows:

Career/technical education teachers, postsecondary	113,000
Career/technical education teachers, secondary school	88,000
Career/technical education teachers, middle school	11,100

The largest employers of career and technical education teachers were as follows:

Technical education teachers demonstrate the theories and techniques of their field.

Employer	Percent
Elementary and secondary schools; state, local, and private	45%
Junior colleges; state, local, and private	20
Technical and trade schools; state, local, and private...	20
Colleges, universities, and professional schools; state, local, and private	7
State government, excluding education and hospitals	4

Career and technical education teachers typically work in middle, high, and postsecondary schools, such as 2-year colleges. Others work in technical, trade, and business schools.

Work Schedules

Career and technical education teachers in middle and high schools generally work during school hours. They may meet with parents, students, and school staff before and after classes.

Some career and technical education teachers, especially those in postsecondary schools, teach courses and develop lesson plans during evening hours and on weekends.

Teachers usually work the traditional 10-month school year and have a 2-month break during the summer. They also have a short midwinter break. Some teachers work for summer programs.

Teachers in districts with a year-round schedule typically work 9 weeks in a row and then have a break for 3 weeks before starting a new school session.

How to Become a Career or Technical Education Teacher

Career and technical education teachers typically need at least a bachelor's degree and work experience in the subject they teach. Public schools may require a state-issued teaching certification or license.

Education

Career and technical education teachers generally need a bachelor's degree in the field they teach, such as agriculture, engineering, or computer and information technology.

Teachers need years of experience in their field of expertise.

All states require prospective career and technical education teachers in public schools to complete a period of fieldwork, called a student-teaching program, in which they work with a mentor teacher and get experience teaching students in a classroom. For information about teacher preparation programs in your state, visit Teach.org.

Work Experience in a Related Occupation

Many career and technical education teachers need work experience in the field they teach. For example, automotive mechanics, chefs, and nurses typically spend years in their career before moving into teaching.

Licenses, Certifications, and Registrations

States may require career and technical education teachers in public schools to be licensed or certified. Requirements for certification or licensure vary by state, but generally involve the following:

- A bachelor's degree with a minimum grade point average
- Completion of a student-teaching program
- Passing a background check
- Passing a general teaching certification test, as well as a test that demonstrates their knowledge of the subject they will teach.

For information on certification requirements in your state, visit Teach.org.

Career and technical education teachers who prepare students for an occupation that requires a license or certification may need to have and maintain the same credential. For example, career and technical education teachers who teach welding may need to have certification in welding. In addition, teachers may be required to complete annual professional development courses to maintain their license or certification.

Some states offer an alternative route to certification or licensure for prospective teachers who have a bachelor's degree or work experience in their field but lack the education courses required for certification. Alternative programs typically cover teaching methods, development of lesson plans, and classroom management.

Advancement

Experienced teachers may advance to become mentors or lead teachers, helping less experienced teachers to improve their teaching skills.

Teachers may become school counselors, instructional coordinators, or principals. These positions generally require additional education, an advanced degree, or certification. An advanced degree in education administration or leadership may be helpful.

Important Qualities

Communication skills. Career and technical education teachers must explain concepts in terms that students can understand.

Organizational skills. Career and technical education teachers must coordinate their time and teaching materials.

Patience. Working with students of different abilities and backgrounds can be difficult. Teachers must be even-tempered with students to develop a positive learning environment.

Resourcefulness. Teachers need to create different ways of presenting information and demonstrating tasks so that all students learn the material.

Pay

The median annual wage for career and technical education teachers was $61,450 in May 2022. The median wage is the wage at which half the workers in an occupation earned more than that amount and half earned less. The lowest 10 percent earned less than $40,300, and the highest 10 percent earned more than $100,120.

Median annual wages for career and technical education teachers in May 2022 were as follows:

Career/technical education teachers, middle school	$62,630
Career/technical education teachers, secondary school	62,500
Career/technical education teachers, postsecondary	59,840

In May 2022, the median annual wages for career and technical education teachers in the top industries in which they worked were as follows:

Colleges, universities, and professional schools; state, local, and private	$65,490
Elementary and secondary schools; state, local, and private	62,620
Junior colleges; state, local, and private	61,050
State government, excluding education and hospitals	56,600
Technical and trade schools; state, local, and private	56,200

Career and technical education teachers in middle and high schools generally work during school hours. They may meet with parents, students, and school staff before and after classes.

Some career and technical education teachers, especially those in postsecondary schools, teach courses and develop lesson plans during evening hours and on weekends.

Teachers usually work the traditional 10-month school year and have a 2-month break during the summer. They also have a short midwinter break. Some teachers work for summer programs.

Career and Technical Education Teachers

Median annual wages, May 2022

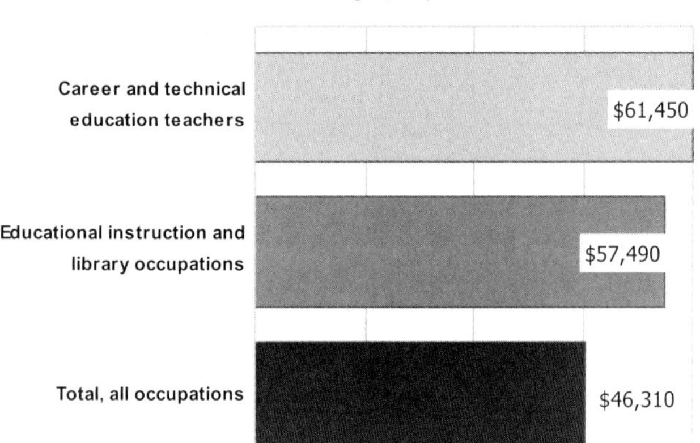

Note: All Occupations includes all occupations in the U.S. Economy.
Source: U.S. Bureau of Labor Statistics, Occupational Employment and Wage Statistics.

Career and Technical Education Teachers

Percent change in employment, projected 2022-32

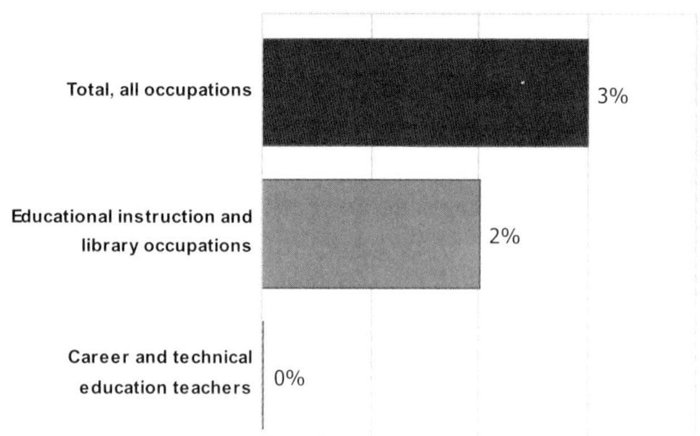

Note: All Occupations includes all occupations in the U.S. Economy.
Source: U.S. Bureau of Labor Statistics, Employment Projections program.

Teachers in districts with a year-round schedule typically work 9 weeks in a row and then have a break for 3 weeks before starting a new school session.

Job Outlook

Overall employment of career and technical education teachers is projected to show little or no change from 2022 to 2032.

Despite limited employment growth, about 14,800 openings for career and technical education teachers are projected each year, on average, over the decade. Most of those openings are expected to result from the need to replace workers who transfer to different occupations or exit the labor force, such as to retire.

Employment

Some demand for these workers is expected over the projections decade due to continued interest in career and technical education programs in middle schools, high schools, and postsecondary institutions. However, this demand is likely to be tempered as schools continue to require students to take more academic classes.

In addition, public schools often depend on government funding for career and technical education programs. When budgets for these programs are reduced, employment growth for career and technical education teachers may be limited.

Occupational Title	SOC Code	Employment, 2022	Projected Employment, 2032	Change, 2022-32	
				Percent	Numeric
Career and technical education teachers	—	212,100	211,300	0	-800
Career/technical education teachers, postsecondary	25-1194	113,000	112,500	0	-600
Career/technical education teachers, middle school	25-2023	11,100	11,100	0	0
Career/technical education teachers, secondary school	25-2032	88,000	87,700	0	-200

Contacts for More Information

For more information about career and technical education teachers, visit

- Association for Career and Technical Education
- Advance CTE
- Teach.org

High School Teachers

Summary

Quick Facts: High School Teachers

2022 Median Pay	$62,360 per year
Typical Entry-Level Education	Bachelor's degree
Work Experience in a Related Occupation	None
On-the-job Training	None
Number of Jobs, 2022	1,072,300
Job Outlook, 2022-32	1% (Little or no change)
Employment Change, 2022-32	11,100

What High School Teachers Do

High school teachers teach academic lessons and various skills that students will need to attend college and to enter the job market.

Work Environment

High school teachers work in schools. They work during school hours but may also work evenings and weekends to prepare lessons and grade papers. Most do not teach during the summer.

How to Become a High School Teacher

High school teachers typically have at least a bachelor's degree. In addition, public school teachers must have a state-issued certification or license, which may require an academic background in the subject(s) they will be certified to teach.

Pay

The median annual wage for high school teachers was $62,360 in May 2022.

High school teachers prepare students for life after graduation by teaching lessons and skills students will need to attend college or enter the job market.

Job Outlook

Employment of high school teachers is projected to show little or no change from 2022 to 2032.

Despite limited employment growth, about 67,100 openings for high school teachers are projected each year, on average, over the decade. Most of those openings are expected to result from the need to replace workers who transfer to different occupations or exit the labor force, such as to retire.

What High School Teachers Do

High school teachers help prepare students for life after graduation. They teach academic lessons and various skills that students will need to attend college or to enter the job market.

Duties

High school teachers typically do the following:

- Plan lessons and instruct their students in the subject they teach
- Assess students' abilities, strengths, and weaknesses
- Adapt lessons to changes in class size
- Grade students' assignments and exams
- Communicate with parents about students' progress
- Work with individual students to challenge them and to improve their abilities
- Prepare students for standardized tests required by the state
- Develop and enforce classroom rules and administrative policies
- Supervise students outside of the classroom—for example, during lunchtime or detention

High school teachers generally teach students from the 9th through 12th grades. They usually specialize in one area. Some teach core subjects, such as math, science, or history. Others specialize in elective courses, such as art, music, or physical education. They may teach several different classes within their subject area. For example, a high school math teacher may teach algebra, calculus, and/or geometry.

High school teachers generally specialize in a subject, such as English, math, or science.

High school teachers who specialize in science class may spend some of their day working in a lab.

High school teachers may instruct students from different grades throughout the day. For example, one class may have mostly students from the 9th grade, and another may have 12th-grade students. In many schools, students are divided into classes on the basis of their abilities, so teachers need to adapt their lessons based on students' skills.

Outside of their instructional time, teachers plan lessons, grade assignments, and meet with other teachers and staff.

Teachers of English as a second language (ESL) or English for speakers of other languages (ESOL) work exclusively with students who are learning the English language. These teachers work with students individually or in groups to help them improve their English language skills and help them with assignments for other classes.

Students with learning disabilities and emotional or behavioral disorders are often taught in traditional classes. High school teachers work with special education teachers to adapt lessons to these students' needs and to monitor the students' progress.

Teachers must be comfortable with using and learning new technology. With parents, they may use text-messaging applications to communicate about students' assignments and upcoming events. With students, teachers may create websites or discussion boards to present information and to expand a lesson taught in class.

Some high school teachers take on additional responsibilities, such as coaching sports or advising academic clubs, activities that frequently take place before or after school.

Work Environment

High school teachers held about 1.1 million jobs in 2022. The largest employers of high school teachers were as follows:

Elementary and secondary schools; local	81%
Elementary and secondary schools; private	16

Most states have tenure laws, which provide job security after a certain number of years of satisfactory classroom teaching.

Teachers may find it rewarding to watch students develop new skills and gain an appreciation for knowledge.

However, teaching may be stressful. Some schools have large classes and lack important teaching tools, such as current technology and up-to-date textbooks. Occasionally, teachers must cope with unmotivated or disrespectful students. Some states are developing teacher mentoring programs and teacher development courses to help with the challenges of being a teacher.

Work Schedules

High school teachers generally work during school hours when students are present. They may meet with parents, students, and other teachers before and after school. They often spend time in the evenings and on weekends grading papers and preparing lessons. Teachers who coach sports or advise clubs generally do so before or after school.

Many teachers work a traditional 10-month school year and have a 2-month break during the summer. They also have a short midwinter break. Some teachers work during the summer.

Teachers in districts with a year-round schedule typically work 9 weeks in a row and then have a break for 3 weeks before starting a new school session.

How to Become a High School Teacher

High school teachers typically must have at least a bachelor's degree. In addition, public school teachers must have a state-issued certification or license.

Education

All states require public high school teachers to have at least a bachelor's degree, which may be in education. Many states require high school teachers to have majored in a content area, such as mathematics or science.

High school teachers need to explain difficult concepts in terms students can understand.

Teacher education programs typically provide instruction on presenting information to students of different abilities and backgrounds. Programs typically include a student-teaching program, in which prospective teachers work with a mentor teacher and get experience instructing students in a classroom. For information about teacher preparation programs in your state, visit Teach.org.

Some states require high school teachers to earn a master's degree after earning their teaching certification and obtaining a job.

Teachers in private schools do not need to meet state requirements. However, private schools typically seek high school teachers who have a bachelor's degree and a major in a subject area.

Licenses, Certifications, and Registrations

All states require teachers in public schools to be licensed or certified in the specific grade level they will teach. Those who teach in private schools typically are not required to be licensed.

High school teachers typically are awarded a secondary or high school certification, which allows them to teach the 7th through the 12th grades.

Requirements for certification or licensure vary by state but generally involve the following:

- A bachelor's degree with a minimum grade point average
- Completion of a student-teaching program
- Passing a background check
- Passing a general teaching certification test, as well as a test that demonstrates their knowledge in the subject they will teach.

For information on certification requirements in your state, visit Teach.org.

Teachers often are required to complete professional development classes to keep their license or certification. Some states require teachers to complete a master's degree after receiving their certification and obtaining a job.

All states offer an alternative route to certification or licensure for people who already have a bachelor's degree but lack the education courses required for certification. Some alternative certification programs allow candidates to begin teaching immediately with supervision by an experienced teacher. These programs cover teaching methods and other topics, such as resource management. After they complete the program, candidates are awarded full certification. Other programs require students to take classes in education before they can teach.

Important Qualities

Communication skills. Teachers must share ideas with their students, other teachers, and school administrators and staff.

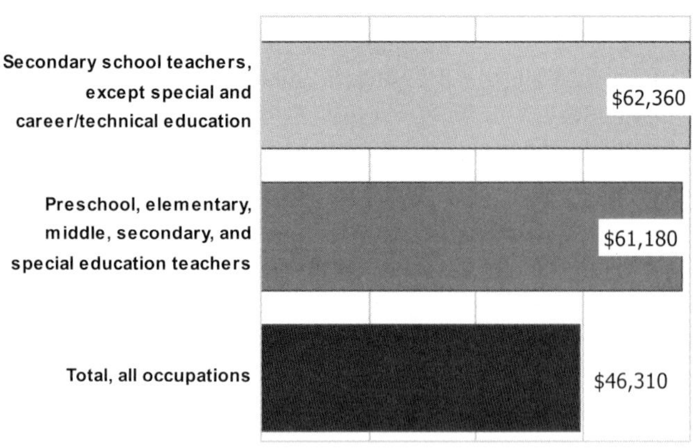

Note: All Occupations includes all occupations in the U.S. Economy.
Source: U.S. Bureau of Labor Statistics, Occupational Employment and Wage Statistics.

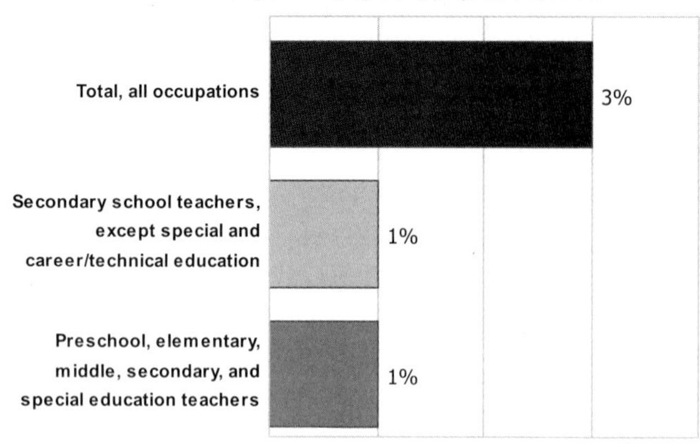

Note: All Occupations includes all occupations in the U.S. Economy.
Source: U.S. Bureau of Labor Statistics, Employment Projections program.

In addition, they need to discuss students' progress with parents.

Patience. High school teachers must stay calm in difficult situations, such as when students struggle with material.

Resourcefulness. High school teachers need to engage students in learning and adapt lessons to each student's needs.

Advancement

Experienced teachers may advance to serve as mentors to new teachers; they may also become a lead teacher. In these positions, they help less experienced teachers improve their teaching skills.

With additional education or certification, teachers may become school counselors, school librarians, or instructional coordinators. Some become assistant principals or principals. Becoming a principal usually requires additional instruction in education administration or leadership. For more information, see the profiles on school and career counselors, librarians, instructional coordinators, and elementary, middle, and high school principals.

Pay

The median annual wage for high school teachers was $62,360 in May 2022. The median wage is the wage at which half the workers in an occupation earned more than that amount and half earned less. The lowest 10 percent earned less than $46,480, and the highest 10 percent earned more than $101,710.

In May 2022, the median annual wages for high school teachers in the top industries in which they worked were as follows:

Elementary and secondary schools; local	$62,930
Elementary and secondary schools; private	58,640

High school teachers generally work during school hours when students are present. They may meet with parents, students, and other teachers before and after school. They often spend time in the evenings and on weekends grading papers and preparing lessons. Teachers who coach sports or advise clubs generally do so before or after school.

Many teachers work a traditional 10-month school year and have a 2-month break during the summer. They also have a short midwinter break. Although most do not teach during the summer, some teach in summer school programs for which they are paid.

Teachers in districts with a year-round schedule typically work 9 weeks in a row and then have a break for 3 weeks before starting a new school session.

Job Outlook

Employment of high school teachers is projected to show little or no change from 2022 to 2032.

Despite limited employment growth, about 67,100 openings for high school teachers are projected each year, on average, over the decade. Most of those openings are expected to result from the need to replace workers who transfer to different occupations or exit the labor force, such as to retire.

Employment

Employment growth for public high school teachers may depend on state and local government budgets. If state and local governments experience budget deficits, school boards may lay off employees, including teachers. As a result, these budget deficits may limit the employment growth projected for high school teachers. Conversely, budget surpluses at the state and local level could lead to additional employment growth for high school teachers.

Projected declines over the decade in both the school-aged demographic and student enrollment should constrain demand for high school teachers.

Occupational Title	SOC Code	Employment, 2022	Projected Employment, 2032	Change, 2022-32	
				Percent	Numeric
Secondary school teachers, except special and career/technical education	25-2031	1,072,300	1,083,400	1	11,100

Contacts for More Information

For more information about teaching and becoming a teacher, visit

- Teach.org
- American Federation of Teachers
- National Education Association
- Council for the Accreditation of Educator Preparation

Instructional Coordinators

Summary

Quick Facts: Instructional Coordinators	
2022 Median Pay	$66,490 per year $31.97 per hour
Typical Entry-Level Education	Master's degree
Work Experience in a Related Occupation	5 years or more
On-the-job Training	None
Number of Jobs, 2022	216,600
Job Outlook, 2022-32	2% (As fast as average)
Employment Change, 2022-32	5,300

What Instructional Coordinators Do

Instructional coordinators oversee school curriculums and teaching standards. They develop instructional material, implement it, and assess its effectiveness.

Work Environment

Most instructional coordinators work in elementary and secondary schools, colleges, professional schools, or educational support services or for state and local governments. They typically work year round.

Instructional coordinators work with teachers and school administrators to implement curriculums.

How to Become an Instructional Coordinator

Instructional coordinators typically need a master's degree and related work experience, such as in teaching or school administration, to enter the occupation. Coordinators in public schools may be required to have a state-issued license.

Pay

The median annual wage for instructional coordinators was $66,490 in May 2022.

Job Outlook

Employment of instructional coordinators is projected to grow 2 percent from 2022 to 2032, about as fast as the average for all occupations.

About 19,200 openings for instructional coordinators are projected each year, on average, over the decade. Many of those openings are expected to result from the need to replace workers who transfer to different occupations or exit the labor force, such as to retire.

What Instructional Coordinators Do

Instructional coordinators oversee school curriculums and teaching standards. They develop educational material, implement it with teachers and principals, and assess its effectiveness.

Duties

Instructional coordinators typically do the following:

- Develop and implement the curriculums
- Plan, organize, and conduct teacher training, conferences, or workshops
- Analyze students' test data
- Assess and discuss the curriculum standards with school staff
- Review and suggest textbooks and other educational materials
- Recommend teaching techniques and the use of different or new technologies
- Develop procedures for teachers to implement a curriculum
- Train teachers and other instructional staff in new content or programs
- Mentor or coach teachers to improve their skills

Instructional coordinators need a master's degree and related work experience.

Instructional coordinators, also known as *curriculum specialists*, evaluate the effectiveness of curriculums and teaching techniques established by school boards, states, or federal regulations. They observe teachers in the classroom, review student test data, and discuss the curriculum with the school staff. Based on their research, they may recommend changes in curriculums to the school board.

Instructional coordinators may conduct training for teachers related to teaching or technology. For example, instructional coordinators explain new learning standards to teachers and demonstrate effective teaching methods to achieve them.

Instructional coordinators may specialize in particular grade levels or specific subjects. Those in elementary and secondary schools may focus on programs such as special education or English as a second language.

Work Environment

Instructional coordinators held about 216,600 jobs in 2022. The largest employers of instructional coordinators were as follows:

Elementary and secondary schools; state, local, and private	43%
Colleges, universities, and professional schools; state, local, and private	18
Educational support services; state, local, and private	8
Government	7

Most instructional coordinators work in an office but they may also spend time traveling to schools within their school district.

Most instructional coordinators work in elementary and secondary schools, colleges, professional schools, or educational support services or for state and local governments. They typically work year round.

Work Schedules

Instructional coordinators generally work full time. They typically work year round and do not have summer breaks. Coordinators may meet with teachers and other administrators outside of classroom hours.

How to Become an Instructional Coordinator

Instructional coordinators typically need a master's degree and related work experience, such as in teaching or school administration, to enter the occupation. Coordinators in public schools may be required to have a state-issued license.

Education

Instructional coordinators in public schools are required to have a master's degree in education or curriculum and instruction. Some instructional coordinators need a degree in a specialized field, such as math or history.

Master's degree programs in curriculum and instruction teach about curriculum design, instructional theory, and collecting and analyzing data. To enter these programs, candidates usually need a bachelor's degree in education.

Licenses, Certifications, and Registrations

Instructional coordinators in public schools may be required to have a license, such as a teaching license or an education administrator license. For information about teaching licenses, see the profiles on kindergarten and elementary

Instructional coordinators need to be able to train teachers on the newest teaching techniques and tools.

school teachers, middle school teachers, and high school teachers. For information about education administrator licenses, see the profile on elementary, middle, and high school principals. Check with your state's Board of Education for specific license requirements.

Work Experience in a Related Occupation

Most instructional coordinators need several years of related work experience as a teacher or an instructional leader. For some positions, experience teaching a specific subject or grade level is required.

Advancement

With enough experience and more education, instructional coordinators may become superintendents.

Important Qualities

Analytical skills. Instructional coordinators evaluate student test data and teaching strategies. Based on their analysis, they recommend improvements in curriculums and teaching.

Communication skills. Instructional coordinators need to clearly explain changes in the curriculum and teaching standards to school staff.

Decision-making skills. Instructional coordinators must be decisive when recommending changes to curriculums, teaching methods, and textbooks.

Interpersonal skills. Instructional coordinators need to be able to establish and maintain positive working relationships with teachers, principals, and other administrators.

Leadership skills. Instructional coordinators serve as mentors to teachers. They train teachers in developing useful and effective teaching techniques.

Pay

The median annual wage for instructional coordinators was $66,490 in May 2022. The median wage is the wage at which half the workers in an occupation earned more than that

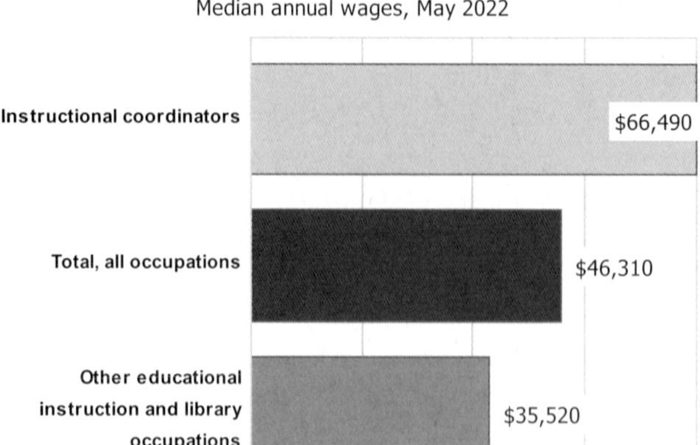

Note: All Occupations includes all occupations in the U.S. Economy.
Source: U.S. Bureau of Labor Statistics, Occupational Employment and Wage Statistics.

amount and half earned less. The lowest 10 percent earned less than $42,000, and the highest 10 percent earned more than $105,210.

In May 2022, the median annual wages for instructional coordinators in the top industries in which they worked were as follows:

Government	$79,810
Elementary and secondary schools; state, local, and private	75,290
Educational support services; state, local, and private	63,600
Colleges, universities, and professional schools; state, local, and private	62,300

Instructional coordinators generally work full time. They typically work year round and do not have summer breaks. Coordinators may meet with teachers and other administrators outside of classroom hours.

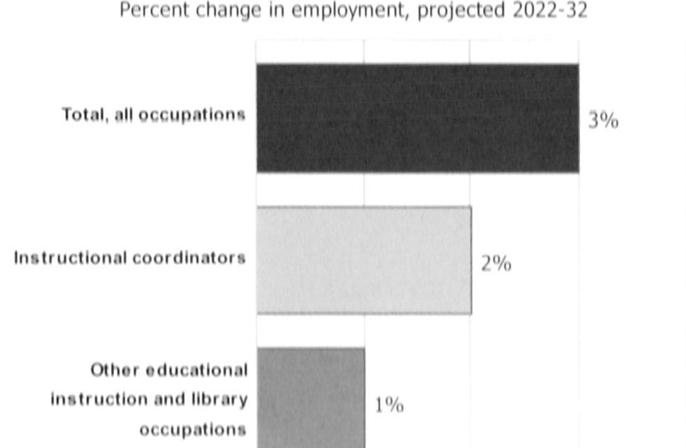

Note: All Occupations includes all occupations in the U.S. Economy.
Source: U.S. Bureau of Labor Statistics, Employment Projections program.

Job Outlook

Employment of instructional coordinators is projected to grow 2 percent from 2022 to 2032, about as fast as the average for all occupations.

About 19,200 openings for instructional coordinators are projected each year, on average, over the decade. Many of those openings are expected to result from the need to replace workers who transfer to different occupations or exit the labor force, such as to retire.

Employment

States and school districts will continue to be held accountable for test scores and graduation rates, putting more of an emphasis on student achievement data. Schools may increasingly turn to instructional coordinators to develop better curriculums and improve teachers' effectiveness. The training that instructional coordinators provide for teachers in curriculum changes and teaching techniques should help schools meet their standards in student achievement. As schools seek additional training for teachers, demand for instructional coordinators is projected to grow.

Occupational Title	SOC Code	Employment, 2022	Projected Employment, 2032	Change, 2022-32	
				Percent	Numeric
Instructional coordinators	25-9031	216,600	222,000	2	5,300

Contacts for More Information

For more information about instructional coordinators, visit

- ➤ Learning Forward
- ➤ ASCD (formerly the Association for Supervision and Curriculum Development)

Kindergarten and Elementary School Teachers

Summary

Quick Facts: Kindergarten and Elementary School Teachers	
2022 Median Pay	$61,620 per year
Typical Entry-Level Education	Bachelor's degree
Work Experience in a Related Occupation	None
On-the-job Training	None
Number of Jobs, 2022	1,548,400
Job Outlook, 2022-32	1% (Little or no change)
Employment Change, 2022-32	10,700

Kindergarten and elementary school teachers teach basic subjects.

What Kindergarten and Elementary School Teachers Do

Kindergarten and elementary school teachers instruct young students in basic subjects in order to prepare them for future schooling.

Work Environment

Kindergarten and elementary school teachers work in public and private schools. They generally work during school hours when students are present and use nights and weekends to prepare lessons and grade papers. Most kindergarten and elementary school teachers do not work during the summer.

How to Become a Kindergarten or Elementary School Teacher

Kindergarten and elementary school teachers usually must have at least a bachelor's degree. In addition, public school teachers must have a state-issued certification or license.

Pay

The median annual wage for elementary school teachers, except special education was $61,690 in May 2022.

The median annual wage for kindergarten teachers, except special education was $60,490 in May 2022.

Job Outlook

Overall employment of kindergarten and elementary school teachers is projected to show little or no change from 2022 to 2032.

Despite limited employment growth, about 109,000 openings for kindergarten and elementary school teachers

Kindergarten and elementary school teachers use a variety of tools, such as computers, to present information to students.

are projected each year, on average, over the decade. Most of those openings are expected to result from the need to replace workers who transfer to different occupations or exit the labor force, such as to retire.

What Kindergarten and Elementary School Teachers Do

Kindergarten and elementary school teachers instruct young students in basic subjects, such as math and reading, in order to prepare them for middle school.

Duties

Kindergarten and elementary school teachers typically do the following:

- Create lesson plans to teach students subjects, such as reading, science, and math
- Teach students how to interact with others
- Observe students to evaluate their abilities, strengths, and weaknesses
- Instruct an entire class or smaller groups of students
- Grade students' assignments
- Communicate with parents or guardian about their child's progress
- Work with students individually to help them overcome specific learning challenges
- Prepare students for standardized tests required by the state
- Develop and enforce classroom rules to teach children proper behavior
- Supervise children outside of the classroom—for example, during lunchtime or recess

Kindergarten and elementary school teachers help students learn and apply important concepts. Many teachers use a hands-on approach to help students understand abstract concepts, solve problems, and develop critical-thinking skills. For example, they may demonstrate how to do a science experiment and then have the students conduct the experiment themselves. They may have students work together to solve problems.

Elementary school typically goes from first through fifth or sixth grades. However, in some schools, elementary school continues through eighth grade.

Kindergarten and elementary school teachers typically instruct students in several subjects throughout the day. Teachers may escort students to assemblies, recess, or classes taught by other teachers, such as art or music. While students are away from the classroom, teachers plan lessons, grade assignments, or meet with other teachers and staff.

In some schools, teachers may work on subject specialization teams in which they teach one or two specific subjects, typically either English and social studies or math and science. Generally, students spend half their time with one teacher and half their time with the other.

There are kindergarten and elementary school teachers who specialize in subjects such as art, music, or physical education.

Some schools employ *English as a second language (ESL)* or *English for speakers of other languages (ESOL) teachers* who work exclusively with students learning the English language. These teachers work with students individually or in groups to help them improve their English language skills and to help them with class assignments.

Students with learning disabilities or emotional or behavioral disorders are often taught in traditional classes. Kindergarten and elementary teachers work with special education teachers to adapt lesson plans to these students' needs and monitor the students' progress. In some cases, kindergarten and elementary school teachers may co-teach lessons with special education teachers.

Some teachers use technology in their classroom as a teaching aide. They must be comfortable with using and learning new technology. Teachers also may maintain websites to communicate with parents about students' assignments, upcoming events, and grades. For students in higher grades, teachers may create websites or discussion boards to present information or to expand on a lesson taught in class.

Work Environment

Elementary school teachers, except special education held about 1.4 million jobs in 2022. The largest employers of elementary school teachers, except special education were as follows:

Elementary and secondary schools; local	85%
Elementary and secondary schools; private	13

Kindergarten teachers, except special education held about 123,400 jobs in 2022. The largest employers of kindergarten teachers, except special education were as follows:

Kindergarten and elementary school teachers may meet with parents, students, and other teachers before and after school.

Elementary and secondary schools; local	81%
Elementary and secondary schools; private	15
Child day care services	1

Most states have tenure laws, which provide job security after a certain number of years of satisfactory teaching.

Kindergarten and elementary school teachers may find it rewarding to watch students develop new skills and learn information. However, teaching may be stressful. Some schools have large classes and lack important teaching tools, such as computers and up-to-date textbooks. Some states are developing teacher mentoring programs and teacher development courses to help with the challenges of being a teacher.

Work Schedules

Kindergarten and elementary school teachers generally work during school hours when students are present. They may meet with parents, students, and other teachers before and after school. They often spend time in the evenings and on weekends grading papers and preparing lessons.

Many kindergarten and elementary school teachers work the traditional 10-month school year and have a 2-month break during the summer. They also have a short midwinter break. Some teachers work during the summer.

Teachers in districts with a year-round schedule typically work 9 weeks in a row, and then have a break for 3 weeks before starting a new schooling session.

How to Become a Kindergarten or Elementary School Teacher

Kindergarten and elementary school teachers usually must have a bachelor's degree. In addition, public school teachers must have a state-issued certification or license.

Education

Public kindergarten and elementary school teachers typically need a bachelor's degree in elementary education. Private schools typically have the same requirement. In some states, public schools also require these teachers to major in a content area, such as mathematics.

Kindergarten and elementary school teachers need to be able to explain concepts in terms young students can understand.

Those with a bachelor's degree in another subject can still become elementary education teachers. They must complete a teacher education program to obtain certification to teach. Requirements vary by state.

In teacher education programs, future teachers learn how to present information to young students and how to work with young students of varying abilities and backgrounds. Programs typically include a student-teaching program, in which they work with a mentor teacher and get experience teaching students in a classroom setting. For information about teacher preparation programs in your state, visit Teach.org.

Some states require teachers to earn a master's degree after receiving their teaching certification and obtaining a job.

Licenses, Certifications, and Registrations

All states require teachers in public schools to be licensed or certified in the specific grade level that they will teach. Those who teach in private schools typically do not need a license. Requirements for certification or licensure vary by state but generally involve the following:

- A bachelor's degree with a minimum grade point average
- Completion of a student teaching program
- Passing a background check
- Passing a general teaching certification test, as well as a test that demonstrates their knowledge of the subject they will teach.

For information on certification requirements in your state, visit Teach.org.

Teachers are frequently required to complete professional development classes to keep their license or certification. Some states require teachers to complete a master's degree after receiving their certification and obtaining a job.

All states offer an alternative route to certification or licensure for people who already have a bachelor's degree but lack the education courses required for certification. Some alternative certification programs allow candidates to begin teaching immediately after graduation, under the supervision of an experienced teacher. These programs cover teaching methods and child development. After they complete the program, candidates are awarded full certification. Other programs require students to take classes in education before they can teach.

Important Qualities

Communication skills. Teachers need to discuss students' needs with parents and administrators. They also need to be able to communicate the subject content to students in a manner in which they will understand.

Patience. Kindergarten and elementary school teachers must respond with patience when students struggle with material. Working with students of different abilities and backgrounds can be difficult.

Physical stamina. Working with kindergarten- and elementary-age students can be tiring. Teachers need to be able to physically, mentally, and emotionally keep up with the students.

Resourcefulness. Kindergarten and elementary school teachers must be able to get students engaged in learning. They also should be prepared to adapt their lessons to meet students' needs.

Advancement

Experienced teachers may advance to serve as mentors to new teachers or become lead teachers. In these roles, they help less-experienced teachers to improve their teaching skills.

With additional education or certification, teachers may become school counselors, school librarians, or instructional coordinators. Some become assistant principals or principals, both of which generally require additional schooling in education administration or leadership.

Pay

Kindergarten and Elementary School Teachers

Median annual wages, May 2022

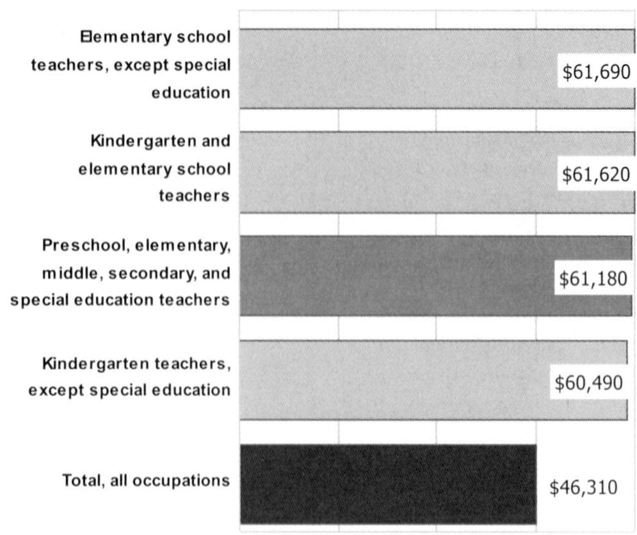

Note: All Occupations includes all occupations in the U.S. Economy.
Source: U.S. Bureau of Labor Statistics, Occupational Employment and Wage Statistics.

The median annual wage for elementary school teachers, except special education was $61,690 in May 2022. The median wage is the wage at which half the workers in an occupation earned more than that amount and half earned less. The lowest 10 percent earned less than $45,470, and the highest 10 percent earned more than $101,310.

The median annual wage for kindergarten teachers, except special education was $60,490 in May 2022. The lowest 10 percent earned less than $40,620, and the highest 10 percent earned more than $100,020.

In May 2022, the median annual wages for elementary school teachers, except special education in the top industries in which they worked were as follows:

Elementary and secondary schools; local	$62,190
Elementary and secondary schools; private	48,380

In May 2022, the median annual wages for kindergarten teachers, except special education in the top industries in which they worked were as follows:

Elementary and secondary schools; local	$61,780
Elementary and secondary schools; private	46,970
Child day care services	35,940

Kindergarten and elementary school teachers generally work during school hours when students are present. They may meet with parents, students, and other teachers before and after school. They often spend time in the evenings and on weekends grading papers and preparing lessons.

Many kindergarten and elementary school teachers work the traditional 10-month school year and have a 2-month break during the summer. They also have a short midwinter break. Some teachers work during the summer.

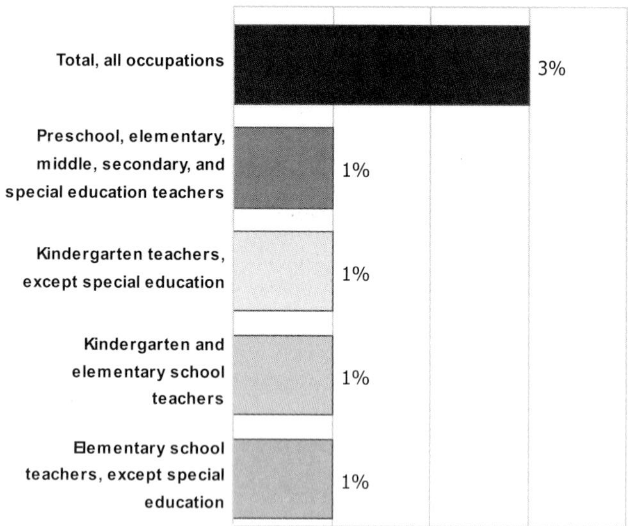

Note: All Occupations includes all occupations in the U.S. Economy.
Source: U.S. Bureau of Labor Statistics, Employment Projections program.

Teachers in districts with a year-round schedule typically work 9 weeks in a row and then have a break for 3 weeks before starting a new school session.

Job Outlook

Overall employment of kindergarten and elementary school teachers is projected to show little or no change from 2022 to 2032.

Despite limited employment growth, about 109,000 openings for kindergarten and elementary school teachers are projected each year, on average, over the decade. Most of those openings are expected to result from the need to replace workers who transfer to different occupations or exit the labor force, such as to retire.

Employment

The number of students enrolling in public kindergarten and elementary schools is expected to decrease over the projections decade. However, as parents and teachers support smaller class sizes, the number of classes should remain stable and result in a need for more teachers of students in these schools.

Employment growth for kindergarten and elementary school teachers also will depend on state and local government budgets. If state and local governments experience budget deficits, they may lay off employees, including teachers.

Occupational Title	SOC Code	Employment, 2022	Projected Employment, 2032	Change, 2022-32	
				Percent	Numeric
Kindergarten and elementary school teachers	—	1,548,400	1,559,000	1	10,700
Kindergarten teachers, except special education	25-2012	123,400	124,100	1	700
Elementary school teachers, except special education	25-2021	1,425,000	1,435,000	1	10,000

Contacts for More Information

For more information about teaching and becoming a teacher, visit

- American Federation of Teachers
- National Education Association
- Teach.org
- Council for the Accreditation of Educator Preparation

Librarians and Library Media Specialists

Summary

Quick Facts: Librarians and Library Media Specialists	
2022 Median Pay	$61,660 per year $29.65 per hour
Typical Entry-Level Education	Master's degree
Work Experience in a Related Occupation	None
On-the-job Training	None
Number of Jobs, 2022	141,200
Job Outlook, 2022-32	3% (As fast as average)
Employment Change, 2022-32	4,300

What Librarians and Library Media Specialists Do

Librarians and library media specialists help people find information and conduct research for personal and professional use.

Work Environment

Librarians and library media specialists work for local governments, schools, and other organizations. Most work full time, although part-time work is common.

How to Become a Librarian or Library Media Specialist

Librarians typically need a master's degree in library science (MLS). School librarians and library media specialists

Librarians help people find information and conduct research for personal and professional use.

typically need a bachelor's or master's degree in a related field, along with a teaching certificate; requirements vary by state.

Pay

The median annual wage for librarians and library media specialists was $61,660 in May 2022.

Job Outlook

Employment of librarians and library media specialists is projected to grow 3 percent from 2022 to 2032, about as fast as the average for all occupations.

About 13,700 openings for librarians and library media specialists are projected each year, on average, over the decade. Many of those openings are expected to result from the need to replace workers who transfer to different occupations or exit the labor force, such as to retire.

What Librarians and Library Media Specialists Do

Librarians and library media specialists help people find information and conduct research for personal and professional use. Their job duties may change based on the type of setting they work in, such as public, school, or medical libraries.

Duties

Librarians and library media specialists typically do the following:

- Create and use databases of library materials
- Organize library materials so they are easy to find
- Help library patrons to conduct research to evaluate search results and reference materials
- Research new books and materials by reading book reviews, publishers' announcements, and catalogs
- Maintain existing collections and choose new books, videos, and other materials for purchase
- Plan programs for different audiences, such as story time for children

Librarian's job duties vary based on the type of library they work in, such as a public, school, or medical library.

- Teach classes about information resources
- Research computers and other equipment for purchase, as needed
- Train and supervise library technicians, assistants, other support staff, and volunteers
- Prepare library budgets

In small libraries, these workers are often responsible for many or all aspects of library operations. In large libraries, they usually focus on one aspect of the library, such as user services, technical services, or administrative services.

The following are examples of types of librarians and library media specialists:

Academic librarians assist students, faculty, and staff in postsecondary institutions. They help students research topics related to their coursework and teach students how to access information. They also assist faculty and staff in locating resources related to their research projects or studies. Some campuses have multiple libraries, and librarians may specialize in a particular subject.

Administrative services librarians manage libraries, prepare budgets, and negotiate contracts for library materials and equipment. Some conduct public relations or fundraising activities for the library.

Public librarians work in their communities to serve all members of the public. They help patrons find books to read for pleasure; conduct research for schoolwork, business, or personal interest; and learn how to access the library's resources. Many public librarians plan programs for patrons, such as story time for children, book clubs, or educational activities.

School librarians, sometimes called *school library media specialists*, typically work in elementary, middle, and high school libraries. They teach students how to use library resources, including technology. They also help teachers develop lesson plans and find materials for classroom instruction.

Special librarians work in settings other than school or public libraries. They are sometimes called *information professionals*. Businesses, museums, government agencies, and many other groups have their own libraries that use special librarians. The main purpose of these libraries and information centers is to serve the information needs of the organization that houses the library. Therefore, special librarians collect and organize materials focused on those subjects. Special librarians may need an additional degree in the subject that they specialize in. The following are examples of special librarians:

- *Corporate librarians* assist employees of private businesses in conducting research and finding information. They work for a wide range of organizations, including insurance companies, consulting firms, and publishers.
- *Law librarians* conduct research or help lawyers, judges, law clerks, and law students locate and analyze legal resources. They often work in law firms and law school libraries.
- *Medical librarians*, also called *health science librarians*, help health professionals, patients, and researchers find health and science information. They may provide information about new clinical trials and medical treatments and procedures, teach medical students how to locate medical information, or answer consumers' health questions.

Technical services librarians obtain, prepare, and organize print and electronic library materials. They arrange materials for patrons' ease in finding information. They are also responsible for ordering new library materials and archiving to preserve older items.

User services librarians help patrons conduct research using both electronic and print resources. They teach patrons how to use library resources to find information on their own. This may include familiarizing patrons with catalogs of print materials, helping them access and search digital libraries, or educating them on Internet search techniques. Some user services librarians work with a particular audience, such as children or young adults.

Work Environment

Librarians and library media specialists held about 141,200 jobs in 2022. The largest employers of librarians and library media specialists were as follows:

Librarians plan outreach programs targeted toward different groups, such as story time for children.

Elementary and secondary schools; state, local, and private	35%
Local government, excluding education and hospitals	31
Colleges, universities, and professional schools; state, local, and private	18
Information	6

Most librarians and library media specialists typically work on the floor with patrons, behind the circulation desk, or in offices. Some have private offices, but those in small libraries usually share work space with others.

Work Schedules

Most librarians and library media specialists work full time, although part-time work is common. Public and academic librarians often work on weekends and evenings and may work holidays. School librarians and library media specialists usually have the same work and vacation schedules as teachers, including summers off. Special librarians, such as corporate librarians, typically work normal business hours but may need to work more than 40 hours per week to help meet deadlines.

How to Become a Librarian or Library Media Specialist

Librarians typically need a master's degree in library science (MLS). School librarians and library media specialists typically need a bachelor's or master's degree in a related field, along with a teaching certificate; requirements vary by state.

Education

Librarians typically need a master's degree in library science. Some colleges and universities have other names for their library science programs, such as Master of Information Studies or Master of Library and Information Studies.

Some librarians assist patrons with research.

Students need a bachelor's degree in any major to enter MLS or similar programs.

MLS programs usually take 1 to 2 years to complete. Coursework typically covers information such as learning different research methods and strategies, online reference systems, and Internet search techniques. The American Library Association accredits master's degree programs in library and information studies.

Requirements for public school librarians and library media specialists vary by state. Most states require an MLS or a bachelor's or master's degree in education, often with a specialization related to library media.

Special librarians, such as those in a corporate, law, or medical library, usually supplement a master's degree in library science with knowledge of their specialized field. Some employers require special librarians to have a master's degree, a professional degree, or a Ph.D. in that subject. For example, a law librarian may be required to have a law degree.

Licenses, Certifications, and Registrations

Public school librarians and library media specialists typically need a teacher's certification. Some states require school librarians to pass a standardized test, such as the PRAXIS II Library Media Specialist test. Contact your state department of education for details about requirements in your state.

Some states also require certification for librarians in public libraries. Contact your state's licensing board for specific requirements.

Important Qualities

Communication skills. Librarians and library media specialists need to be able to explain ideas and information in ways that patrons understand.

Initiative. New information, technology, and resources constantly change librarians' and library media specialists' duties. Workers must be able and willing to continually update their knowledge of these changes to be effective at their jobs.

Interpersonal skills. Librarians and library media specialists must be able to work both as part of a team and with the public or with researchers.

Organizational skills. Librarians and library media specialists help patrons research topics efficiently. They should be able to direct the logical use of resources, databases, and other materials.

Problem-solving skills. These workers need to be able to identify a problem, figure out where to find information to solve the problem, and draw conclusions based on the information found.

Reading skills. Librarians and library media specialists must be excellent readers. Those working in special libraries are expected to read the latest literature in their field of specialization.

Pay

The median annual wage for librarians and library media specialists was $61,660 in May 2022. The median wage is the wage at which half the workers in an occupation earned more than that amount and half earned less. The lowest 10 percent earned less than $36,260, and the highest 10 percent earned more than $98,650.

In May 2022, the median annual wages for librarians and library media specialists in the top industries in which they worked were as follows:

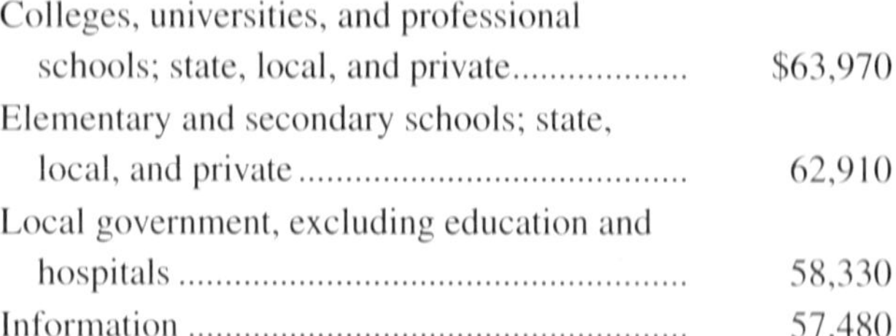

Colleges, universities, and professional schools; state, local, and private	$63,970
Elementary and secondary schools; state, local, and private	62,910
Local government, excluding education and hospitals	58,330
Information	57,480

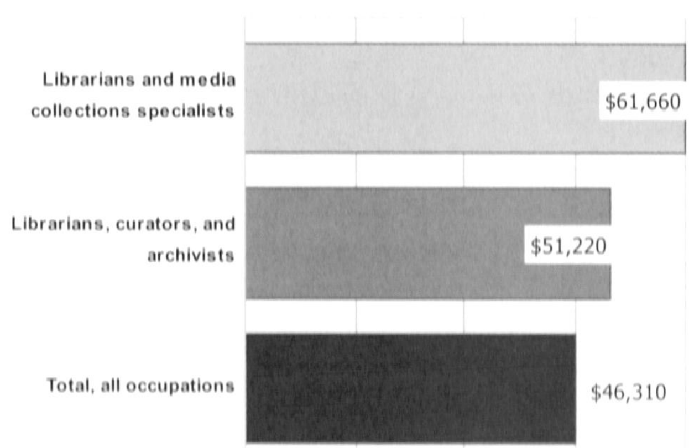

Note: All Occupations includes all occupations in the U.S. Economy.
Source: U.S. Bureau of Labor Statistics, Occupational Employment and Wage Statistics.

Most librarians and library media specialists work full time, although part-time work is common. Public and academic librarians often work on weekends and evenings, and may work holidays. School librarians and library media specialists usually have the same work and vacation schedules as teachers, including summers off. Special librarians, such as corporate librarians, typically work normal business hours but may need to work more than 40 hours per week to help meet deadlines.

Job Outlook

Employment of librarians and library media specialists is projected to grow 3 percent from 2022 to 2032, about as fast as the average for all occupations.

About 13,700 openings for librarians and library media specialists are projected each year, on average, over the decade. Many of those openings are expected to result from the need to replace workers who transfer to different occupations or exit the labor force, such as to retire.

Employment

Despite a decline by the public in traditional borrowing of materials, libraries still need librarians to host a variety of services and activities. Therefore, there will be a need for librarians to manage libraries and to help patrons find information. Parents value the learning opportunities that libraries present for children because libraries have information and learning materials that children often cannot access from home. Library patrons are expected to continue attending events and using other library services, such as child-focused activities and employment assistance.

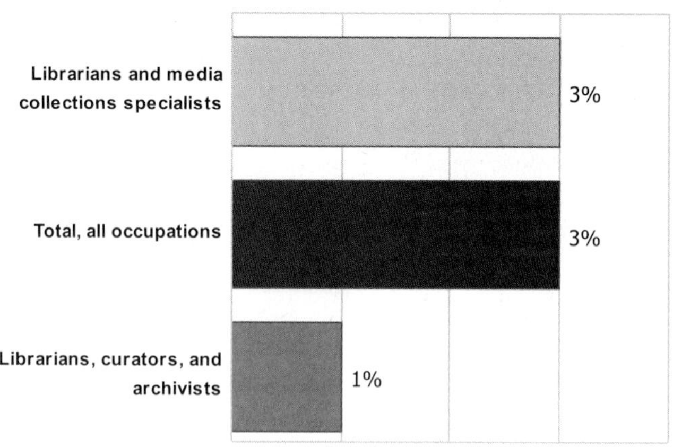

Note: All Occupations includes all occupations in the U.S. Economy.
Source: U.S. Bureau of Labor Statistics, Employment Projections program.

Occupational Title	SOC Code	Employment, 2022	Projected Employment, 2032	Change, 2022-32	
				Percent	Numeric
Librarians and media collections specialists	25-4022	141,200	145,500	3	4,300

Contacts for More Information

- For more information, visit
- American Library Association
- Medical Library Association
- American Association of Law Libraries
- Special Libraries Association

Library Technicians and Assistants

Summary

Quick Facts: Library Technicians and Assistants

2022 Median Pay	$35,280 per year $16.96 per hour
Typical Entry-Level Education	See How to Become One
Work Experience in a Related Occupation	None
On-the-job Training	See How to Become One
Number of Jobs, 2022	161,500
Job Outlook, 2022-32	-6% (Decline)
Employment Change, 2022-32	-9,600

What Library Technicians and Assistants Do

Library technicians and assistants help librarians with all aspects of running a library.

Work Environment

Library technicians and assistants work in local public libraries, corporate and specialty libraries, and school and university libraries.

How to Become a Library Technician or Assistant

Library technicians typically need a postsecondary certificate. Library assistants typically need a high school diploma or its equivalent, combined with short-term on-the-job training.

Pay

The median hourly wage for library assistants, clerical was $14.98 in May 2022.

The median hourly wage for library technicians was $18.08 in May 2022.

Job Outlook

Overall employment of library technicians and assistants is projected to decline 6 percent from 2022 to 2032.

Library technicians and assistants help patrons find library resources.

Despite declining employment, about 25,700 openings for library technicians and assistants are projected each year, on average, over the decade. All of those openings are expected to result from the need to replace workers who transfer to other occupations or exit the labor force, such as to retire.

What Library Technicians and Assistants Do

Library technicians and assistants help librarians with all aspects of running a library. They assist patrons, organize library materials and information, and do clerical and administrative tasks.

Duties

Library technicians and assistants typically do the following:

- Loan library materials to patrons and collect returned materials
- Sort and reshelve returned books, periodicals, and other materials
- Catalogue and maintain library materials
- Handle interlibrary loans
- Register new patrons and issue library cards
- Answer routine reference questions from patrons
- Teach patrons how to use library resources
- Maintain computer databases used to locate library materials
- Perform routine clerical tasks such as answering phones and organizing files
- Help plan and participate in special programs, such as used-book sales, story times, or outreach programs

A librarian usually supervises library technicians and assistants. Both technicians and assistants help patrons find information and organize library materials. However, library technicians typically have more responsibilities than library assistants.

Library technicians and assistants in small libraries have a broad range of duties. In large libraries, they tend to specialize in a particular area, such as user services or technical services. Those specializing in user services assist library patrons with locating resources and information. Those specializing in technical services research, acquire, catalog, and process materials to be added to the library's collections.

The following are examples of types of library technicians and assistants:

Academic library technicians and assistants help students, faculties, and staff in colleges and universities access resources and information related to coursework or research projects. Some teach students how to access and use library resources. They may work at service desks for reserve materials, special collections, or computer labs.

Public library technicians and assistants work in community libraries to serve members of the public. They help patrons find books to read for pleasure, assist patrons with their research, or teach patrons how to access the library's resources. Some technicians in public libraries may help plan programs for users, such as story time for children or book clubs for teens or adults.

School library technicians and assistants show students how to find and use library resources, maintain textbook collections, and help teachers develop curriculum materials.

Special library technicians and assistants work in settings other than school or public libraries, including government agencies, corporations, museums, law firms, and medical centers. They assist users, search library resources, compile bibliographies, and provide information on subjects of interest to the organization.

Work Environment

Library assistants, clerical held about 82,900 jobs in 2022. The largest employers of library assistants, clerical were as follows:

Library technicians and assistants help shelve and organize materials.

Local government, excluding education and hospitals	63%
Elementary and secondary schools; local	11
Colleges, universities, and professional schools; state, local, and private	11

Library technicians held about 78,600 jobs in 2022. The largest employers of library technicians were as follows:

Local government, excluding education and hospitals	53%
Colleges, universities, and professional schools; state, local, and private	17
Elementary and secondary schools; state, local, and private	16
Junior colleges; state, local, and private	3

Library technicians and assistants generally work indoors. They spend much of their time at public service desks or at computer terminals. They may spend time in the library stacks reshelving books, a task that may require bending or stretching to reach the shelves.

Work Schedules

Many library technicians and assistants work part time. Library technicians and assistants in school libraries work during school hours. Those in public or college libraries may work weekends, evenings, and some holidays. In special libraries, technicians and assistants typically work during normal business hours but may have to work evenings and weekends.

How to Become a Library Technician or Assistant

Library technicians typically need a postsecondary certificate. Library assistants typically need a high school diploma or its equivalent, combined with short-term on-the-job training.

Education

Library technicians typically need a postsecondary certificate in library technology, which may include coursework in acquisitions, cataloguing, circulation, reference, and automated library systems. The American Library Association has information about certificate programs available by state.

Most library assistants typically need a high school diploma or equivalent.

Training

Library assistants usually receive short-term on-the-job training to learn about libraries and library resources.

Cataloguing or reshelving books may require bending or stretching to reach shelves.

Library technicians and assistants provide customer service to library patrons.

Important Qualities

Communication skills. Library technicians and assistants must be able to answer patrons' questions clearly and explain use of library resources.

Detail oriented. Library technicians and assistants must pay close attention to ensure that library materials and information are organized correctly and according to the library's organizational system.

Interpersonal skills. Library technicians and assistants need to work with library patrons, librarians, teachers, or researchers.

Listening skills. Library technicians and assistants need to listen to patrons to help them with research topics or with finding materials.

Advancement

Library technicians and assistants may advance to become supervisors and oversee daily library operations. To become a librarian, technicians and assistants need to earn a master's degree in library science.

Pay

The median hourly wage for library assistants, clerical was $14.98 in May 2022. The median wage is the wage at which half the workers in an occupation earned more than that amount and half earned less. The lowest 10 percent earned less than $10.60, and the highest 10 percent earned more than $23.44.

The median hourly wage for library technicians was $18.08 in May 2022. The lowest 10 percent earned less than $12.37, and the highest 10 percent earned more than $28.64.

In May 2022, the median hourly wages for library assistants, clerical in the top industries in which they worked were as follows:

Colleges, universities, and professional schools; state, local, and private	$16.82
Elementary and secondary schools; local	15.13
Local government, excluding education and hospitals	14.84

In May 2022, the median hourly wages for library technicians in the top industries in which they worked were as follows:

Colleges, universities, and professional schools; state, local, and private	$21.17
Junior colleges; state, local, and private	19.20
Elementary and secondary schools; state, local, and private	18.71
Local government, excluding education and hospitals	17.61

Many library technicians and assistants work part time. Library technicians and assistants in school libraries work during regular school hours. Those in public or college libraries may work weekends, evenings, and some holidays. In corporate libraries, library technicians and assistants work normal business hours but may have to work evenings and weekends.

Job Outlook

Overall employment of library technicians and assistants is projected to decline 6 percent from 2022 to 2032.

Despite declining employment, about 25,700 openings for library technicians and assistants are projected each year, on average, over the decade. All of those openings are expected to result from the need to replace workers who transfer to other occupations or exit the labor force, such as to retire.

Library Technicians and Assistants

Percent change in employment, projected 2022-32

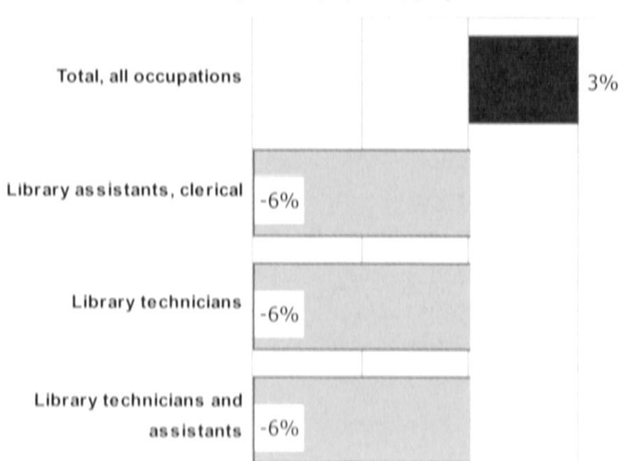

Note: All Occupations includes all occupations in the U.S. Economy.
Source: U.S. Bureau of Labor Statistics, Occupational Employment and Wage Statistics.

Library Technicians and Assistants

Median hourly wages, May 2022

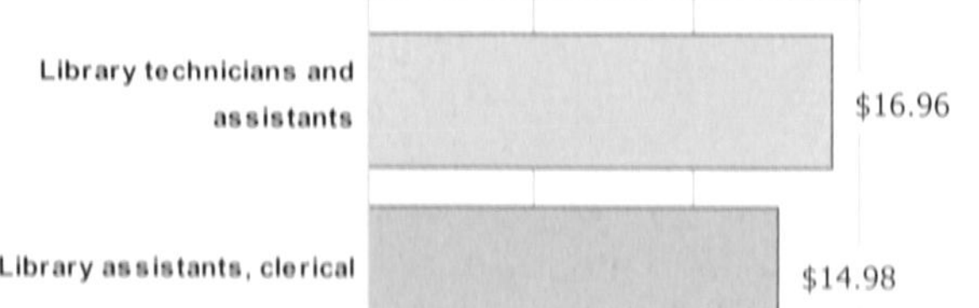

Note: All Occupations includes all occupations in the U.S. Economy.
Source: U.S. Bureau of Labor Statistics, Employment Projections program.

Employment

Library use has decreased despite community efforts to rebrand libraries for a variety of services and activities. This decrease in use reduces the need for library workers to help patrons find information and to operate libraries. Additionally, budget constraints may limit the number of library technicians and assistants in local government and education services.

Occupational Title	SOC Code	Employment, 2022	Projected Employment, 2032	Change, 2022-32	
				Percent	Numeric
Library technicians and assistants	—	161,500	151,900	-6	-9,600

Occupational Title	SOC Code	Employment, 2022	Projected Employment, 2032	Change, 2022-32	
				Percent	Numeric
Library technicians	25-4031	78,600	73,800	-6	-4,800
Library assistants, clerical	43-4121	82,900	78,200	-6	-4,800

Contacts for More Information

For more information about library technicians and assistants careers, visit

- American Library Association
- Medical Library Association
- American Association of Law Libraries
- Special Libraries Association

Middle School Teachers

Summary

Quick Facts: Middle School Teachers

2022 Median Pay	$61,810 per year
Typical Entry-Level Education	Bachelor's degree
Work Experience in a Related Occupation	None
On-the-job Training	None
Number of Jobs, 2022	625,500
Job Outlook, 2022-32	1% (Little or no change)
Employment Change, 2022-32	5,100

What Middle School Teachers Do

Middle school teachers educate students, typically in sixth through eighth grades.

Middle school teachers help students build on the fundamentals they learned in elementary schools to prepare them for the more difficult subjects and lessons in high school.

Work Environment

Middle school teachers work in public and private schools. They generally work during school hours when students are present and use nights and weekends to prepare lessons and grade papers. Most do not work during the summer.

How to Become a Middle School Teacher

Middle school teachers typically need at least a bachelor's degree. In addition, public school teachers must have a state-issued certification or license.

Pay

The median annual wage for middle school teachers was $61,810 in May 2022.

Job Outlook

Employment of middle school teachers is projected to show little or no change from 2022 to 2032.

Despite limited employment growth, about 42,200 openings for middle school teachers are projected each year, on average, over the decade. Most of those openings are expected to result from the need to replace workers who transfer to different occupations or exit the labor force, such as to retire.

What Middle School Teachers Do

Middle school teachers educate students, typically in sixth through eighth grade. Middle school teachers help students build on the fundamentals taught in elementary school and prepare students for high school.

Duties

Middle school teachers typically do the following:

- Create lesson plans to teach students a subject
- Assess students to evaluate their abilities, strengths, and weaknesses

Some middle school teachers specialize in teaching a particular subject, such as science or math.

- Teach lessons they have planned to an entire class or to smaller groups
- Grade students' assignments and exams
- Communicate with parents or guardians about their child's progress
- Work with students individually to help them overcome specific learning challenges
- Prepare students for standardized tests required by the state
- Develop and enforce classroom rules
- Supervise students outside of the classroom—for example, during lunchtime or detention

Middle school typically goes from sixth to eighth grades. However, in some school districts, middle school may begin in fourth grade or extend through ninth grade.

In many schools, middle school teachers are responsible for certain subjects. For example, one teacher may teach math to several different classes of students throughout the day. However, other middle school teachers instruct on every subject to a single class.

Teachers use time during the day when they do not have classes to plan lessons, grade assignments, or meet with other teachers and staff.

Some middle schools have *English as a second language (ESL)* or *English for speakers of other languages (ESOL) teachers* who work with students learning the English language. ESL and ESOL teachers work with students individually or in groups to help them improve their English language skills and to help the students with assignments for their classes.

Middle school teachers may also work with special education teachers to adapt lessons. In some cases, middle school teachers may co-teach lessons with special education teachers.

Teachers must be comfortable using and learning new technology. With parents, teachers may use text-messaging applications to communicate about students' assignments and upcoming events. With their students, teachers may create websites or discussion boards to present information or to expand on a lesson taught in class.

Some middle school teachers coach sports teams and advise student clubs and groups, whose practices and meetings frequently take place before or after school.

Work Environment

Middle school teachers held about 625,500 jobs in 2022. The largest employers of middle school teachers were as follows:

Elementary and secondary schools; local	85%

Most states have tenure laws, which provide job security after a certain number of years of satisfactory teaching.

Middle school teachers may find it rewarding to watch students develop new skills and gain an appreciation for knowledge and learning. However, teaching may be stressful. Schools may have large classes and lack important teaching tools, such as current technology and textbooks. Some states are developing teacher mentoring programs and teacher development courses to help with the challenges of being a teacher.

Working with middle school students as they become adolescents also can be challenging. Teachers need to be aware of and understand what their students are going through outside of the classroom.

Work Schedules

Middle school teachers generally work during school hours when students are present. They may meet with parents, students, and other teachers before and after school. Teachers who coach sports or advise clubs generally do so before or after school. They often spend time in the evenings and on weekends grading papers and preparing lessons.

Middle school teachers may advise clubs or meet with students and parents before or after school.

Many teachers work a traditional 10-month school year and have a 2-month break during the summer. They also have a short midwinter break. Some teachers work during the summer.

Teachers in districts with a year-round schedule typically work 9 weeks in a row and then have a break for 3 weeks before starting a new school session.

How to Become a Middle School Teacher

Middle school teachers typically need a bachelor's degree. In addition, public school teachers must have a state-issued certification or license.

Education

All states require public middle school teachers to have at least a bachelor's degree. Many states require middle school teachers to major in a content area, such as mathematics or history. Other states require middle school teachers to major in elementary education.

Middle school teachers typically enroll in their college's teacher education program, which instructs them on presenting information to students of different abilities and backgrounds. Programs typically include a student-teaching program, in which they work with a mentor teacher and get experience teaching students in a classroom setting. For information about teacher preparation programs in your state, visit Teach.org.

Middle school teachers need good communication skills in order to discuss students' needs with parents and administrators.

Some states require middle school teachers to earn a master's degree after receiving their teaching certification and obtaining a job.

Teachers in private schools do not need to meet state requirements. However, private schools typically seek middle school teachers who have a bachelor's degree and a major in elementary education or a content area.

Licenses, Certifications, and Registrations

All states require teachers in public schools to be licensed or certified in the specific grade level that they will teach. Those who teach in private schools typically do not need a license. Requirements for certification or licensure vary by state but generally involve the following:

- A bachelor's degree with a minimum grade point average
- Completion of a student-teaching program
- Passing a background check
- Passing a general teaching certification test, as well as a test that demonstrates their knowledge of the subject they will teach.

For information about certification requirements in your state, visit Teach.org. Teachers are often required to complete professional development classes to keep their license or certification. Some states require teachers to complete a master's degree after receiving their certification and obtaining a job.

All states offer an alternative route to certification or licensure for people who already have a bachelor's degree but lack the education courses required for certification. Some alternative certification programs allow candidates to begin teaching immediately under the supervision of an experienced teacher. These programs cover teaching methods and child development. After they complete the program, candidates are awarded full certification. Other programs require students to take classes in education before they can teach.

Important Qualities

Communication skills. Teachers must share ideas with their students, other teachers, and school administrators and staff. In addition, they need to discuss student progress with parents.

Patience. Middle school teachers must stay calm in challenging situations, such as when students struggle with material or create disturbances in class.

Physical stamina. Working with middle school students can be tiring. Teachers need to keep up with the students physically, mentally, and emotionally.

Resourcefulness. Middle school teachers need to get students engaged in learning and adapt lessons to each student's needs.

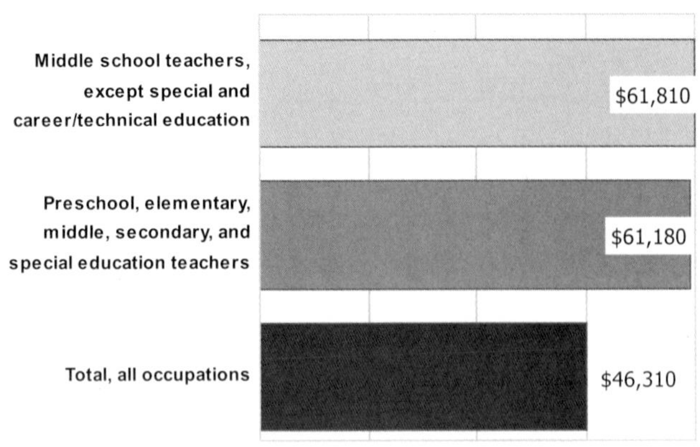

Note: All Occupations includes all occupations in the U.S. Economy.
Source: U.S. Bureau of Labor Statistics, Occupational Employment and Wage Statistics.

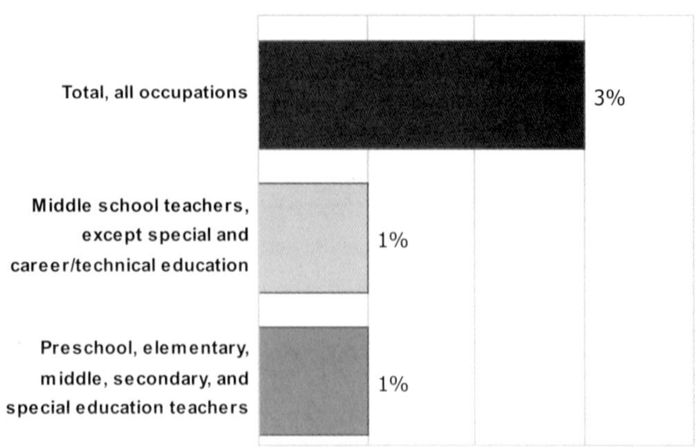

Note: All Occupations includes all occupations in the U.S. Economy.
Source: U.S. Bureau of Labor Statistics, Employment Projections program.

Advancement

Experienced teachers may advance to serve as mentors to new teachers; they may also become lead teachers. In these positions, they help less experienced teachers to improve teaching skills.

With additional education or certification, teachers may become school counselors, school librarians, or instructional coordinators. Some become assistant principals or principals, both of which generally require additional education in education administration or leadership. For more information, see the profiles on school and career counselors, librarians, instructional coordinators, and elementary, middle, and high school principals.

Pay

The median annual wage for middle school teachers was $61,810 in May 2022. The median wage is the wage at which half the workers in an occupation earned more than that amount and half earned less. The lowest 10 percent earned less than $45,910, and the highest 10 percent earned more than $100,570.

In May 2022, the median annual wages for middle school teachers in the top industries in which they worked were as follows:

Elementary and secondary schools; local $62,310

Middle school teachers generally work school hours when students are present. They may meet with parents, students, and other teachers before and after school. Teachers who coach sports or advise clubs generally do so before or after school. Teachers often spend time in the evenings and on weekends grading papers and preparing lessons.

Many teachers work the traditional 10-month school year and have a 2-month break during the summer. They also have a short midwinter break. Some teachers work during the summer.

Teachers in districts with a year-round schedule typically work 9 weeks in a row and then have a break for 3 weeks before starting a new school session.

Job Outlook

Employment of middle school teachers is projected to show little or no change from 2022 to 2032.

Despite limited employment growth, about 42,200 openings for middle school teachers are projected each year, on average, over the decade. Most of those openings are expected to result from the need to replace workers who transfer to different occupations or exit the labor force, such as to retire.

Employment

The number of students in public middle schools is expected to decrease over the projections decade. The number of classes needed to accommodate these students will depend on class size, with larger classes requiring fewer teachers than smaller ones.

Employment growth for middle school teachers also will depend on state and local government budgets. If state and local governments experience budget deficits, they may increase class size while maintaining or reducing teaching staff levels. Conversely, budget surpluses at the state and local level could lead to additional employment growth for middle school teachers.

Occupational Title	SOC Code	Employment, 2022	Projected Employment, 2032	Change, 2022-32	
				Percent	Numeric
Middle school teachers, except special and career/ technical education	25-2022	625,500	630,600	1	5,100

Contacts for More Information

For more information about teaching and becoming a teacher, visit

- Teach.org
- American Federation of Teachers
- National Education Association
- Council for the Accreditation of Educator Preparation

Postsecondary Teachers

Summary

Quick Facts: Postsecondary Teachers	
2022 Median Pay	$80,840 per year
Typical Entry-Level Education	See How to Become One
Work Experience in a Related Occupation	See How to Become One
On-the-job Training	None
Number of Jobs, 2022	1,333,900
Job Outlook, 2022-32	8% (Faster than average)
Employment Change, 2022-32	108,100

What Postsecondary Teachers Do

Postsecondary teachers instruct students in a variety of academic subjects beyond the high school level.

Work Environment

Most postsecondary teachers work in public and private colleges and universities, professional schools, and junior or community colleges. Most work full time, although part-time work is common.

How to Become a Postsecondary Teacher

Educational requirements vary by subject and the type of educational institution. Typically, postsecondary teachers must have a Ph.D. However, a master's degree may be enough for some postsecondary teachers at community colleges, and others may need work experience in their field of expertise.

Pay

The median annual wage for postsecondary teachers was $80,840 in May 2022.

Job Outlook

Overall employment of postsecondary teachers is projected to grow 8 percent from 2022 to 2032, faster than the average for all occupations.

About 118,800 openings for postsecondary teachers are projected each year, on average, over the decade. Many of those openings are expected to result from the need to replace workers who transfer to different occupations or exit the labor force, such as to retire.

What Postsecondary Teachers Do

Postsecondary teachers instruct students in a variety of academic subjects beyond the high school level. They may also conduct research and publish scholarly papers and books.

Postsecondary teachers instruct students in a variety of academic subjects beyond the high school level.

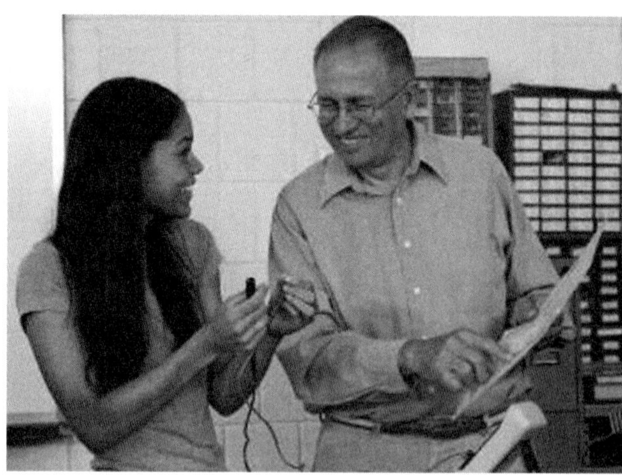

Professors may teach a variety of subjects, such as history, science, or business.

Duties

Postsecondary teachers typically do the following:

- Develop an instructional plan (known as a course outline or syllabus) for the course(s) they teach and ensure that it meets college and department standards
- Plan lessons and assignments
- Teach courses in their subject area
- Assess students' progress by grading assignments, papers, exams, and other work
- Advise students about which courses to take and how to achieve their goals
- Work with colleagues to develop or modify the curriculum for a degree or certificate program involving in-person, online, or hybrid delivery of course material
- Stay informed about changes and innovations in their field
- Serve on academic or administrative committees, as needed

Postsecondary teachers, often referred to as *professors* or *faculty*, specialize in a variety of subjects and fields. At colleges and universities, professors are organized into departments by degree field, such as history, science, or business. A professor may teach one or more courses within that department. For example, a mathematics professor may teach calculus, statistics, and a graduate seminar on a topic related to polynomials.

Postsecondary teachers' duties vary, often based on the size of their employing institution. In large colleges or universities, they may teach courses, conduct research or experiments, publish original research, apply for grants to fund their research, or supervise graduate teaching assistants. In small colleges and universities or in community colleges, they may spend most of their time teaching courses and working with students.

Full-time professors, particularly those who have tenure (that is, they cannot be fired without just cause), often are expected to devote a great deal of time on original research. Tenured professors must document their analyses or critical reviews and publish their research findings. They also may be expected to serve on college and university committees.

Part-time professors, often known as *adjunct professors*, usually spend most of their time teaching students.

Professors may teach large classes of several hundred students (often with the help of graduate teaching assistants), smaller classes of about 40 to 50 students, seminars with a few students, or laboratories in which students practice the subject matter. Some teach online, either exclusively or in addition to providing live instruction.

Professors' tasks also may include collaborating with their colleagues and attending conferences to keep up with developments in their field.

Information about postsecondary teachers who provide vocational training in subjects such as repair, transportation, and cosmetology is available in the profile on career and technical education teachers.

Work Environment

Postsecondary teachers held about 1.3 million jobs in 2022. Employment in the detailed occupations that make up postsecondary teachers was distributed as follows:

Health specialties teachers, postsecondary	262,800
Art, drama, and music teachers, postsecondary	123,900
Business teachers, postsecondary	99,900
Nursing instructors and teachers, postsecondary	85,900
Education teachers, postsecondary	74,300
English language and literature teachers, postsecondary	70,100
Biological science teachers, postsecondary	62,400
Mathematical science teachers, postsecondary	55,900
Psychology teachers, postsecondary	50,900
Engineering teachers, postsecondary	45,500
Computer science teachers, postsecondary	42,000
Communications teachers, postsecondary	33,600
Philosophy and religion teachers, postsecondary	29,100
Chemistry teachers, postsecondary	25,900
Foreign language and literature teachers, postsecondary	24,700
History teachers, postsecondary	22,800
Law teachers, postsecondary	19,800
Political science teachers, postsecondary	19,300
Social sciences teachers, postsecondary, all other	19,200
Criminal justice and law enforcement teachers, postsecondary	16,500
Recreation and fitness studies teachers, postsecondary	16,300
Physics teachers, postsecondary	16,200
Social work teachers, postsecondary	15,500

Most classes are held during the day, but some are held on nights and weekends.

Sociology teachers, postsecondary	15,000
Economics teachers, postsecondary	14,800
Atmospheric, earth, marine, and space sciences teachers, postsecondary	13,600
Area, ethnic, and cultural studies teachers, postsecondary	11,900
Agricultural sciences teachers, postsecondary	10,100
Architecture teachers, postsecondary	8,200
Environmental science teachers, postsecondary	7,900
Anthropology and archeology teachers, postsecondary	6,200
Library science teachers, postsecondary	5,400
Geography teachers, postsecondary	4,100
Family and consumer sciences teachers, postsecondary	2,900
Forestry and conservation science teachers, postsecondary	1,500

The largest employers of postsecondary teachers were as follows:

Colleges, universities, and professional schools; private	41%
Colleges, universities, and professional schools; state	39
Junior colleges; local	10
Junior colleges; state	6

Postsecondary teachers often find it rewarding to share their expertise with students and colleagues. However, it may be stressful, especially for beginning teachers seeking advancement, to balance teaching duties with an emphasis on research and publication. At the community college level, professors are more likely to focus on teaching students.

Work Schedules

Most postsecondary teachers work full time, although part-time work is common. Postsecondary teachers who work part time may offer instruction at several colleges or universities. Some have a full-time job in their field of expertise in addition to a part-time teaching position. For example, an active lawyer or judge might teach an evening course at a law school.

College and university courses are generally during the day, although some are offered in the evenings or on weekends to accommodate students who have jobs or other obligations.

Academic calendars typically include breaks, such as between terms. The availability and type of course offerings during the summer vary by institution. Although some postsecondary teachers provide instruction in summer courses, others use the time to conduct research or engage in professional development.

Postsecondary teachers' schedules generally are flexible. Full-time teachers typically need to be on campus to teach classes and have office hours but otherwise are free to set their own schedules.

How to Become a Postsecondary Teacher

Educational requirements vary with the subject taught and the type of educational institution. Typically, postsecondary teachers must have a Ph.D. or other doctoral degree in their field. However, a master's degree may be enough for some postsecondary teachers at community colleges. Other postsecondary teachers may need work experience in their field of expertise.

Education

Postsecondary teachers who work for 4-year colleges and universities typically need a Ph.D. or other doctorate in their field of degree. For some specialties or for part-time positions, schools may hire those with a master's degree or who are doctoral degree candidates.

Doctoral programs usually take several years to complete, and students typically need a bachelor's or master's degree to enroll. Most Ph.D. programs require students to write a doctoral dissertation, a paper presenting original research in

Institutions may prefer to hire those with teaching or other work experience.

their field of study, which they then defend in questioning from experts. Candidates usually specialize in a subfield, such as organic chemistry or European history.

Community colleges may hire those with a master's degree. However, some institutions prefer that applicants have a Ph.D.

Work Experience in a Related Occupation

Institutions may prefer to hire those with teaching or other work experience.

In some fields, such as health specialties, art, law, and education, hands-on work experience is especially important. Postsecondary teachers in these fields often gain experience by working in an occupation related to their field of study.

In other fields, such as biological science, physics, and chemistry, some postsecondary teachers have postdoctoral research experience. Sometimes called a "post-doc," this experience takes the form of a job that usually involves working for 2 to 3 years as a research associate or in a similar position, often at a college or university.

Some postsecondary teachers gain teaching experience by working as graduate teaching assistants—students who are enrolled in a graduate program and teach classes at the institution in which they are enrolled.

Licenses, Certifications, and Registrations

Postsecondary teachers who prepare students for an occupation that requires a license, certification, or registration, may need to have—or may benefit from having—the same credential. For example, a postsecondary nursing teacher might need a nursing license or a postsecondary education teacher might need a teaching license.

Advancement

Postsecondary teachers with a doctoral degree often seek tenure—a guarantee that a professor cannot be fired without just cause. Attaining tenure may take up to 7 years of progressing through the positions by rank: assistant professor, associate professor, and professor. The decision to grant tenure is based on a candidate's research, contribution to the institution, and teaching.

Some professors advance to high-level administrative positions, such as dean or president. For information on deans and other administrative positions, see the profile on postsecondary education administrators. For more information about college and university presidents, see the profile on top executives.

Important Qualities

Critical-thinking skills. To conduct original research and design experiments, postsecondary teachers need to analyze information logically.

Interpersonal skills. Postsecondary teachers need to work well with others for tasks such as instructing students and serving on committees.

Resourcefulness. Postsecondary teachers must be able to present information in a way that students will understand. They need to adapt to the different learning styles of their students and be able to use technology for lessons or assignments.

Speaking skills. Postsecondary teachers need good communication skills to present lectures and provide feedback to students.

Writing skills. Postsecondary teachers need strong writing ability to publish original research and analysis.

Pay

The median annual wage for postsecondary teachers was $80,840 in May 2022. The median wage is the wage at which half the workers in an occupation earned more than that amount and half earned less. The lowest 10 percent earned less than $47,370, and the highest 10 percent earned more than $173,730.

Median annual wages for postsecondary teachers in May 2022 were as follows:

Law teachers, postsecondary	$108,860
Economics teachers, postsecondary	103,930
Engineering teachers, postsecondary	103,550
Health specialties teachers, postsecondary	100,300
Atmospheric, earth, marine, and space sciences teachers, postsecondary	97,770
Forestry and conservation science teachers, postsecondary	96,500
Architecture teachers, postsecondary	93,220
Business teachers, postsecondary	88,790
Physics teachers, postsecondary	86,550
Agricultural sciences teachers, postsecondary	85,860
Anthropology and archeology teachers, postsecondary	85,000
Computer science teachers, postsecondary	84,760

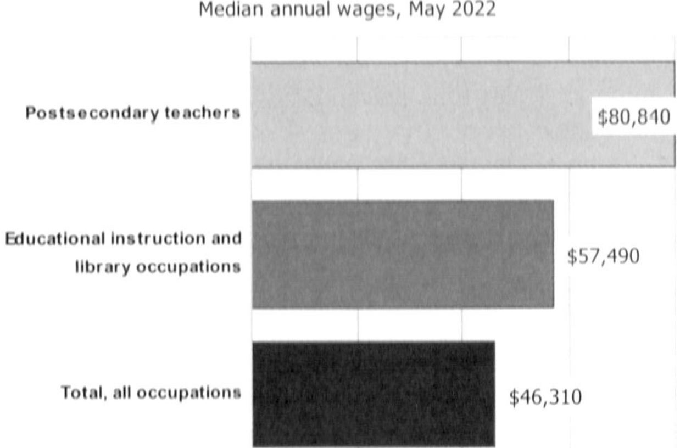

Note: All Occupations includes all occupations in the U.S. Economy.
Source: U.S. Bureau of Labor Statistics, Occupational Employment and Wage Statistics.

Political science teachers, postsecondary	83,770
Environmental science teachers, postsecondary	83,040
Geography teachers, postsecondary	81,920
Biological science teachers, postsecondary	81,650
Area, ethnic, and cultural studies teachers, postsecondary	80,910
Chemistry teachers, postsecondary	80,720
History teachers, postsecondary	79,400
Sociology teachers, postsecondary	78,970
Psychology teachers, postsecondary	78,810
Philosophy and religion teachers, postsecondary	78,780
Nursing instructors and teachers, postsecondary	78,580
Mathematical science teachers, postsecondary	77,420
Art, drama, and music teachers, postsecondary	77,280
Family and consumer sciences teachers, postsecondary	76,440
Library science teachers, postsecondary	76,370
Communications teachers, postsecondary	76,250
Foreign language and literature teachers, postsecondary	76,030
Social sciences teachers, postsecondary, all other	75,390
English language and literature teachers, postsecondary	74,280
Recreation and fitness studies teachers, postsecondary	72,650
Education teachers, postsecondary	66,930
Social work teachers, postsecondary	66,510
Criminal justice and law enforcement teachers, postsecondary	64,990

In May 2022, the median annual wages for postsecondary teachers in the top industries in which they worked were as follows:

Junior colleges; local	$82,940
Colleges, universities, and professional schools; private	81,880
Colleges, universities, and professional schools; state	81,710
Junior colleges; state	62,670

Wages vary by institution type. Postsecondary teachers typically have higher wages in colleges, universities, and professional schools than they do in community colleges or other types of schools.

Most postsecondary teachers work full time, although part-time work is common. Postsecondary teachers who work part time may offer instruction at several colleges or universities. Some have a full-time job in their field of expertise in addition to a part-time teaching position. For example, an active lawyer or judge might teach an evening course at a law school.

College and university courses are generally during the day, although some are offered in the evenings or on weekends to accommodate students who have jobs or other obligations.

Academic calendars typically include breaks, such as between terms. The availability and type of course offerings during the summer vary by institution. Although some postsecondary teachers provide instruction in summer courses, others use the time to conduct research or engage in professional development.

Postsecondary teachers' schedules generally are flexible. Full-time teachers typically need to be on campus to teach classes and have office hours but otherwise are free to set their own schedules.

Job Outlook

Overall employment of postsecondary teachers is projected to grow 8 percent from 2022 to 2032, faster than the average for all occupations.

About 118,800 openings for postsecondary teachers are projected each year, on average, over the decade. Many of those openings are expected to result from the need to replace workers who transfer to different occupations or exit the labor force, such as to retire.

Employment

Projected employment of postsecondary teachers varies by occupation (see table). Both part-time and full-time postsecondary teachers are included in these projections.

Postsecondary Teachers

Percent change in employment, projected 2022-32

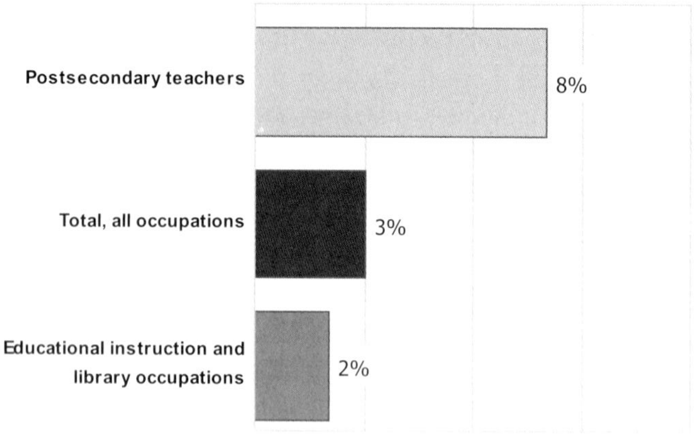

Note: All Occupations includes all occupations in the U.S. Economy.
Source: U.S. Bureau of Labor Statistics, Employment Projections program.

The number of people attending postsecondary institutions is expected to grow over the projections decade. Students will continue to seek higher education to gain the knowledge and skills necessary to meet their career goals. As more people enter colleges and universities, more postsecondary teachers will be needed to serve these additional students. Colleges and universities are likely to hire more part-time teachers to meet this demand. In all disciplines, there is expected to be a limited number of full-time nontenure and full-time tenure positions.

A growing number of older people, who are more likely than young people to need medical care, will create increased demand for healthcare. More postsecondary teachers are expected to be needed to help educate workers who provide healthcare services.

However, despite expected increases in enrollment, employment growth in public colleges and universities will depend on state and local government budgets. If budgets for higher education are reduced, employment growth may be limited.

Occupational Title	SOC Code	Employment, 2022	Projected Employment, 2032	Change, 2022-32	
				Percent	Numeric
Postsecondary teachers	—	1,333,900	1,442,000	8	108,100
Business teachers, postsecondary	25-1011	99,900	106,900	7	6,900
Computer science teachers, postsecondary	25-1021	42,000	44,300	5	2,200
Mathematical science teachers, postsecondary	25-1022	55,900	57,700	3	1,800
Architecture teachers, postsecondary	25-1031	8,200	8,500	4	300
Engineering teachers, postsecondary	25-1032	45,500	49,700	9	4,200
Agricultural sciences teachers, postsecondary	25-1041	10,100	10,500	5	500
Biological science teachers, postsecondary	25-1042	62,400	67,700	9	5,300
Forestry and conservation science teachers, postsecondary	25-1043	1,500	1,600	5	100
Atmospheric, earth, marine, and space sciences teachers, postsecondary	25-1051	13,600	14,100	4	500
Chemistry teachers, postsecondary	25-1052	25,900	26,800	4	900
Environmental science teachers, postsecondary	25-1053	7,900	8,200	4	300
Physics teachers, postsecondary	25-1054	16,200	16,800	4	600
Anthropology and archeology teachers, postsecondary	25-1061	6,200	6,400	4	200
Area, ethnic, and cultural studies teachers, postsecondary	25-1062	11,900	12,400	4	500
Economics teachers, postsecondary	25-1063	14,800	15,400	4	600
Geography teachers, postsecondary	25-1064	4,100	4,300	4	200
Political science teachers, postsecondary	25-1065	19,300	20,000	4	700
Psychology teachers, postsecondary	25-1066	50,900	53,600	5	2,700
Sociology teachers, postsecondary	25-1067	15,000	15,500	4	600
Social sciences teachers, postsecondary, all other	25-1069	19,200	19,700	3	500
Health specialties teachers, postsecondary	25-1071	262,800	313,000	19	50,200
Nursing instructors and teachers, postsecondary	25-1072	85,900	101,500	18	15,600
Education teachers, postsecondary	25-1081	74,300	77,100	4	2,800
Library science teachers, postsecondary	25-1082	5,400	5,600	4	200
Criminal justice and law enforcement teachers, postsecondary	25-1111	16,500	16,900	3	400
Law teachers, postsecondary	25-1112	19,800	20,400	3	600
Social work teachers, postsecondary	25-1113	15,500	16,100	4	600
Art, drama, and music teachers, postsecondary	25-1121	123,900	127,800	3	3,900
Communications teachers, postsecondary	25-1122	33,600	34,800	3	1,200
English language and literature teachers, postsecondary	25-1123	70,100	70,900	1	900
Foreign language and literature teachers, postsecondary	25-1124	24,700	25,000	1	300
History teachers, postsecondary	25-1125	22,800	23,100	1	300
Philosophy and religion teachers, postsecondary	25-1126	29,100	29,900	3	800
Family and consumer sciences teachers, postsecondary	25-1192	2,900	3,000	4	100
Recreation and fitness studies teachers, postsecondary	25-1193	16,300	16,800	3	500

Contacts for More Information

For more information about postsecondary teachers, visit

- American Association of University Professors
- Council of Graduate Schools

Preschool Teachers

Summary

Quick Facts: Preschool Teachers	
2022 Median Pay	$35,330 per year $16.99 per hour
Typical Entry-Level Education	Associate's degree
Work Experience in a Related Occupation	None
On-the-job Training	None
Number of Jobs, 2022	512,300
Job Outlook, 2022-32	3% (As fast as average)
Employment Change, 2022-32	17,200

What Preschool Teachers Do

Preschool teachers educate and care for children younger than age 5 who have not yet entered kindergarten.

Work Environment

Preschool teachers typically work in public and private schools or childcare centers. Many work the traditional 10-month school year, but some work year-round.

How to Become a Preschool Teacher

Education and training requirements vary based on settings and state regulations. Preschool teachers typically need at least an associate's degree.

Pay

The median annual wage for preschool teachers was $35,330 in May 2022.

Job Outlook

Employment of preschool teachers is projected to grow 3 percent from 2022 to 2032, about as fast as the average for all occupations.

Preschool teachers educate and care for children, younger than the age of 5, who have not yet entered kindergarten.

About 56,300 openings for preschool teachers are projected each year, on average, over the decade. Many of those openings are expected to result from the need to replace workers who transfer to different occupations or exit the labor force, such as to retire.

What Preschool Teachers Do

Preschool teachers educate and care for children younger than age 5 who have not yet entered kindergarten. They teach language, motor, and social skills to young children.

Duties

Preschool teachers typically do the following:

- Teach children basic skills such as identifying colors, shapes, numbers, and letters
- Work with children in groups or one on one, depending on the needs of children and on the subject matter
- Plan and carry out a curriculum that focuses on different areas of child development
- Organize activities so children can learn about the world, explore interests, and develop skills
- Develop schedules and routines to ensure children have enough physical activity and rest

Preschool teachers use play to teach children about the world.

- Watch for signs of emotional or developmental problems in each child and bring them to the attention of the child's parents
- Keep records of the children's progress, routines, and interests, and inform parents about their child's development

Young children learn from playing, problem solving, and experimenting. Preschool teachers use play and other instructional techniques to teach children. For example, they use storytelling and rhyming games to teach language and vocabulary. They may help improve children's social skills by having them work together to build a neighborhood in a sandbox or teach math by having children count when building with blocks.

Preschool teachers work with children from different ethnic, racial, and religious backgrounds. Teachers include topics in their lessons that teach children how to respect people of different backgrounds and cultures.

Work Environment

Preschool teachers held about 512,300 jobs in 2022. The largest employers of preschool teachers were as follows:

Child day care services	62%
Elementary and secondary schools; state, local, and private	16
Religious, grantmaking, civic, professional, and similar organizations	14
Individual and family services	2

It may be rewarding to see children develop new skills and gain an appreciation of knowledge and learning. However, it can also be tiring to work with young, active children all day.

Work Schedules

Preschool teachers in public schools generally work during school hours. Many work the traditional 10-month school year and have a 2-month break during the summer. Some preschool teachers may teach in summer programs.

Teachers in districts with a year-round schedule typically work 9 weeks in a row and then have a break for 3 weeks before starting a new school session.

Those working in daycare settings may work year-round with longer hours.

How to Become a Preschool Teacher

Education and training requirements vary based on settings and state regulations. Preschool teachers typically need at least an associate's degree.

Education

Preschool teachers typically need at least an associate's degree.

Preschool teachers in center-based Head Start programs are required to have at least an associate's degree. However, at least 50 percent of all preschool teachers in Head Start programs nationwide must have a bachelor's degree in early childhood education or a related field. Those with a degree in a related field, such as psychology, must have experience teaching preschool-age children.

In public schools, preschool teachers are generally required to have at least a bachelor's degree in early childhood education or a related field. Bachelor's degree programs include instruction on children's development, teaching young children, and observing and documenting children's progress.

Licenses, Certifications, and Registrations

Some states require preschool teachers to obtain the Child Development Associate (CDA) credential offered by the Council for Professional Recognition. Obtaining the CDA credential requires coursework, experience in the field, a written exam, and observation of the candidate working

Preschool teachers usually work in public schools, private schools, and childcare centers that have preschool programs.

Preschool teachers must plan lessons that engage young students and must also adapt their lessons to suit different learning styles.

with children. The CDA credential must be renewed every 3 years.

In public schools, preschool teachers must be licensed to teach early childhood education, which covers preschool through third grade. Requirements vary by state, but they generally require a bachelor's degree and passing an exam to demonstrate competency. Most states require teachers to complete continuing education credits in order to maintain their license.

Other Experience

A few states require preschool teachers to have some work experience in a childcare setting. In these states, preschool teachers often start out as childcare workers or teacher assistants. The amount of experience needed varies by state.

Important Qualities

Communication skills. Preschool teachers need good writing and speaking skills to talk to parents and colleagues about children's progress. They must also be able to communicate well with small children.

Creativity. Preschool teachers must plan lessons that engage young children. In addition, they need to adapt their lessons to suit different learning styles.

Interpersonal skills. Preschool teachers must understand children's emotional needs and be able to develop relationships with parents, children, and coworkers.

Organizational skills. Teachers need to be organized to plan lessons and keep records of the children.

Patience. Working with children may be stressful. Preschool teachers should be able to respond calmly to overwhelming and difficult situations.

Physical stamina. Preschool teachers should have a lot of energy, because working with children can be physically demanding.

Advancement

Experienced preschool teachers may advance to become the director of a preschool or childcare center or a lead teacher. Those with a bachelor's degree in early childhood education frequently are qualified to teach kindergarten through grade 3, in addition to preschool. Teaching positions at these higher grades typically pay more. For more information, see the profiles on preschool and childcare center directors and kindergarten and elementary school teachers.

Pay

The median annual wage for preschool teachers was $35,330 in May 2022. The median wage is the wage at which half the workers in an occupation earned more than that amount and half earned less. The lowest 10 percent earned less than $23,920, and the highest 10 percent earned more than $58,580.

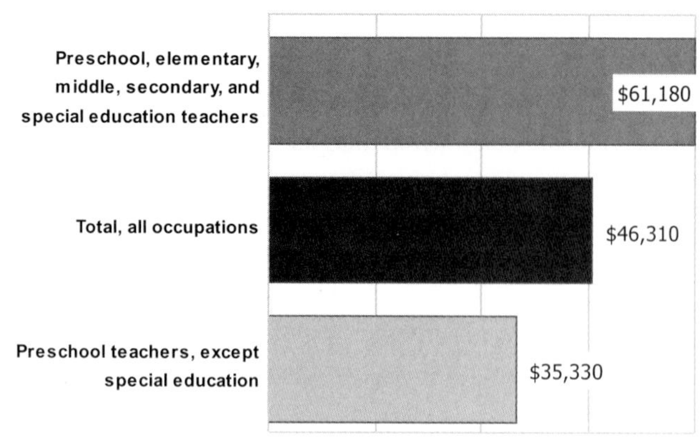

Note: All Occupations includes all occupations in the U.S. Economy.
Source: U.S. Bureau of Labor Statistics, Occupational Employment and Wage Statistics.

In May 2022, the median annual wages for preschool teachers in the top industries in which they worked were as follows:

Elementary and secondary schools; state, local, and private	$49,670
Individual and family services	37,550
Religious, grantmaking, civic, professional, and similar organizations	37,500
Child day care services	31,010

Preschool teachers in public schools generally work during school hours. Many work the traditional 10-month school year and a 2-month break during the summer. Some preschool teachers may teach in summer programs.

Teachers in districts with a year-round schedule typically work 8 weeks in a row and then have a break for 1 week before starting a new school session. They also have a 5-week midwinter break.

Those working in daycare settings may work year-round and have longer hours.

Job Outlook

Employment of preschool teachers is projected to grow 3 percent from 2022 to 2032, about as fast as the average for all occupations.

About 56,300 openings for preschool teachers are projected each year, on average, over the decade. Many of those openings are expected to result from the need to replace workers who transfer to different occupations or exit the labor force, such as to retire.

Employment

Early childhood education is important for a child's intellectual and social development. More preschool teachers

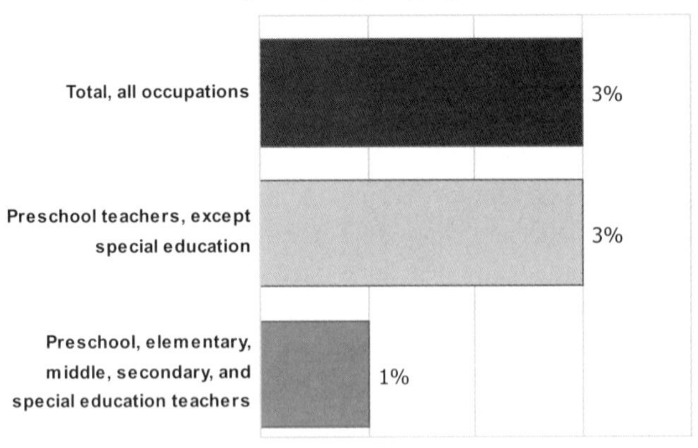

Note: All Occupations includes all occupations in the U.S. Economy.
Source: U.S. Bureau of Labor Statistics, Employment Projections program.

should be needed to meet the demand for early childhood education.

Occupational Title	SOC Code	Employment, 2022	Projected Employment, 2032	Change, 2022-32	
				Percent	Numeric
Preschool teachers, except special education	25-2011	512,300	529,600	3	17,200

Contacts for More Information

For more information about early childhood education, visit

- National Association for the Education of Young Children

For more information about professional credentials, visit

- Council for Professional Recognition

Special Education Teachers

Summary

Quick Facts: Special Education Teachers	
2022 Median Pay	$62,950 per year
Typical Entry-Level Education	Bachelor's degree
Work Experience in a Related Occupation	None
On-the-job Training	None
Number of Jobs, 2022	498,400
Job Outlook, 2022-32	0% (Little or no change)
Employment Change, 2022-32	2,200

What Special Education Teachers Do

Special education teachers work with students who have a wide range of learning, mental, emotional, and physical disabilities.

Work Environment

Most special education teachers work in public schools, teaching students from preschool to high school. Many work the traditional 10-month school year, but some work year round.

How to Become a Special Education Teacher

Special education teachers in public schools are required to have a bachelor's degree and a state-issued certification or license. Teachers in private schools typically need a bachelor's degree but may not be required to have a state license or certification.

Pay

The median annual wage for special education teachers was $62,950 in May 2022.

Job Outlook

Overall employment of special education teachers is projected to show little or no change from 2022 to 2032.

Despite limited employment growth, about 33,500 openings for special education teachers are projected each year, on average, over the decade. Most of those openings are expected to result from the need to replace workers who transfer to different occupations or exit the labor force, such as to retire.

Special education teachers work with students who have a wide range of learning disabilities.

What Special Education Teachers Do

Special education teachers work with students who have learning, mental, emotional, or physical disabilities. They adapt general education lessons and teach various subjects to students with mild to moderate disabilities. They also teach basic skills to students with severe disabilities.

Duties

Special education teachers typically do the following:

- Assess students' skills and determine their educational needs
- Adapt general lessons to meet students' needs
- Develop Individualized Education Programs (IEPs) for each student
- Plan activities that are specific to each student's abilities
- Teach and mentor students as a class, in small groups, and one-on-one
- Implement IEPs, assess students' performance, and track their progress
- Update IEPs throughout the school year to reflect students' progress and goals
- Discuss students' progress with parents, other teachers, counselors, and administrators
- Supervise and mentor teacher assistants who work with students with disabilities
- Prepare and help students transition from grade to grade and from school to life outside of school

Special education teachers work with students from preschool to high school. They instruct students who have mental, emotional, physical, or learning disabilities. For example, some help students develop study skills, such as highlighting text and using flashcards. Others work with students who have physical disabilities and may use a wheelchair or other adaptive devices. Still others work with students who have sensory disabilities, such as visual or hearing impairments. They also may work with those who have autism spectrum disorders or emotional disorders, such as anxiety and depression.

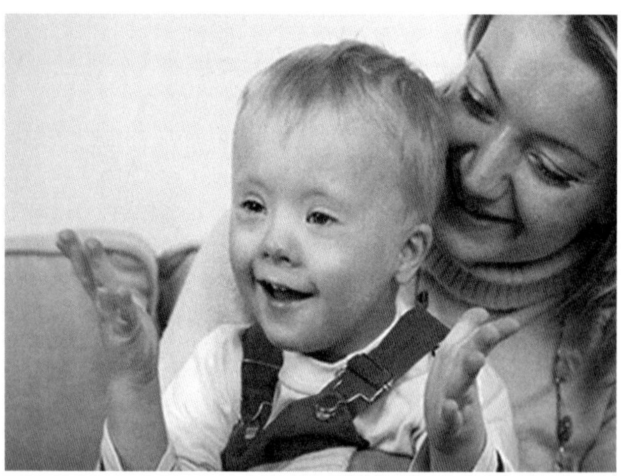

Special education teachers may teach students in small groups or on a one-on-one basis.

Special education teachers work with general education teachers, specialists, administrators, and parents to develop IEPs. Students' IEPs outline their goals, including academic or behavioral milestones, and services they are to receive, such as speech therapy. Educators and parents also meet to discuss updates and changes to IEPs.

Special education teachers must be comfortable using and learning new technology. Most use computers to keep records of their students' performance, prepare lesson plans, and update IEPs. Some teachers also use assistive technology aids, such as Braille writers and computer software, that help them communicate with their students.

Special education teachers' duties vary by their work setting, students' disabilities, and specialties.

Some special education teachers work in classrooms or resource centers that include only students with disabilities. In these settings, teachers plan, adapt, and present lessons to meet each student's needs. They teach students individually or in small groups.

In inclusive classrooms, special education teachers instruct students with disabilities who are in general education classrooms. They work with general education teachers to adapt lessons so that students with disabilities can more easily understand them.

Some special education teachers work with students who have moderate to severe disabilities. These teachers help students, who may be eligible for services until age 21, develop basic life skills. Some teach the skills necessary for students with moderate disabilities to live independently, find a job, and manage money and their time. For more information about other workers who help individuals with disabilities develop skills necessary to live independently, see the profiles on occupational therapists and occupational therapy assistants and aides.

Work Environment

Special education teachers held about 498,400 jobs in 2022. Employment in the detailed occupations that make up special education teachers was distributed as follows:

Special education teachers, kindergarten and elementary school	194,700
Special education teachers, secondary school	153,200
Special education teachers, middle school	82,800
Special education teachers, all other	43,900
Special education teachers, preschool	23,800

The largest employers of special education teachers were as follows:

Special education teachers work with students from preschool to high school.

Elementary and secondary schools; local	85%
Elementary and secondary schools; private	8

A small number of special education teachers work with students in residential facilities, hospitals, and the students' homes. They may travel to these locations. Some teachers work with infants and toddlers at the child's home. They teach the child's parents ways to help the child develop skills.

Helping students with disabilities may be rewarding. It also can be stressful, emotionally demanding, and physically draining.

Work Schedules

Special education teachers typically work during school hours. In addition to providing instruction during this time, they grade papers, update students' records, and prepare lessons. They may meet with parents, students, and other teachers or specialists before and after classes.

Many work the traditional 10-month school year and have a 2-month break during the summer. They also have a short midwinter break. Some teachers work in summer programs.

Teachers in districts with a year-round schedule typically work 9 weeks in a row and then are on break for 3 weeks.

How to Become a Special Education Teacher

Special education teachers in public schools are required to have at least a bachelor's degree and a state-issued certification or license. Private schools typically require teachers to have a bachelor's degree, but the teachers are not required to be licensed or certified.

Education

All states require special education teachers in public schools to have at least a bachelor's degree. Some require teachers to earn a degree specifically in special education. Others allow them to major in education or a content area,

Special education teachers need to be able to explain concepts in terms students with learning disabilities can understand.

such as mathematics or science, and pursue a minor in special education.

In a program leading to a bachelor's degree in special education, prospective teachers learn about the different types of disabilities and how to present information so that students will understand. Programs typically include a student-teaching program, in which prospective teachers work with a mentor and get experience instructing students in a classroom setting. To become fully certified, states may require special education teachers to complete a master's degree in special education after obtaining a job.

Private schools typically require teachers to have at least a bachelor's degree in special education.

Licenses, Certifications, and Registrations

All states require teachers in public schools to be licensed in the specific grade level that they teach. A license frequently is referred to as a certification. Those who teach in private schools typically do not need to be licensed.

Requirements for certification or licensure can vary by state but generally involve the following:

- A bachelor's degree with a minimum grade point average
- Completion of a student-teaching program
- Passing a background check
- Passing a general teaching certification test, as well as a test that demonstrates knowledge of the subject the candidate will teach

For information about teacher preparation programs and certification requirements, visit Teach.org or contact your state's board of education.

All states offer an alternative route to certification or licensure for people who already have a bachelor's degree. These alternative programs cover teaching methods and child development. Candidates are awarded full certification after they complete the program. Other alternative programs require prospective teachers to take classes in education before they can start to teach. Teachers may be awarded a master's degree after completing either type of program.

Advancement

Experienced teachers may advance to become mentors who help less experienced teachers improve their instructional skills. They also may become lead teachers.

Teachers may become school counselors, instructional coordinators, and elementary, middle, and high school principals. These positions generally require additional education, an advanced degree, or certification. An advanced degree in education administration or leadership may be helpful.

Important Qualities

Communication skills. Special education teachers need to explain concepts in terms that students with learning disabilities can understand. They also must write Individualized Education Programs (IEPs) and share students' progress with general education teachers, counselors and other specialists, administrators, and parents.

Critical-thinking skills. Special education teachers must be able to assess students' progress and use the information to adapt lessons.

Interpersonal skills. Special education teachers work regularly with a team of educators and the student's parents to develop IEPs. As a result, they need to be able to build positive working relationships.

Patience. Special education teachers must be able to stay calm instructing students with disabilities, who may lack basic skills, present behavioral or other challenges, or require repeated efforts to understand material.

Resourcefulness. Special education teachers must develop different ways to present information that meet their students' needs. They also help general education teachers adapt their lessons to the needs of students with disabilities.

Pay

The median annual wage for special education teachers was $62,950 in May 2022. The median wage is the wage at which half the workers in an occupation earned more than that amount and half earned less. The lowest 10 percent earned less than $45,780, and the highest 10 percent earned more than $102,450.

Median annual wages for special education teachers in May 2022 were as follows:

Special education teachers, all other	$63,950
Special education teachers, secondary school	63,560
Special education teachers, middle school	62,990
Special education teachers, kindergarten and elementary school	62,390
Special education teachers, preschool	62,240

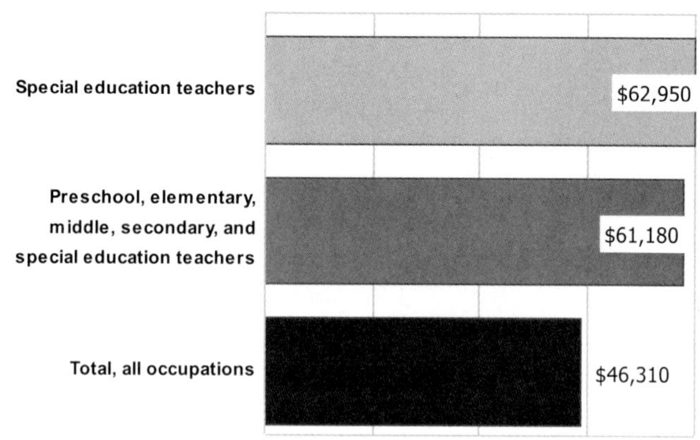

Note: All Occupations includes all occupations in the U.S. Economy.
Source: U.S. Bureau of Labor Statistics, Occupational Employment and Wage Statistics.

In May 2022, the median annual wages for special education teachers in the top industries in which they worked were as follows:

Elementary and secondary schools; local	$63,290
Elementary and secondary schools; private	55,690

Special education teachers typically work during school hours. In addition to providing instruction during this time, they grade papers, update students' records, and prepare lessons. They may meet with parents, students, and other teachers or specialists before and after classes.

Many work the traditional 10-month school year and have a 2-month break during the summer. They also have a short midwinter break. Some teachers work in summer programs.

Teachers in districts with a year-round schedule typically work 9 weeks in a row and then are on break for 3 weeks.

Job Outlook

Overall employment of special education teachers is projected to show little or no change from 2022 to 2032.

Despite limited employment growth, about 33,500 openings for special education teachers are projected each year, on average, over the decade. Most of those openings are expected to result from the need to replace workers who transfer to different occupations or exit the labor force, such as to retire.

Employment

Demand for special education teachers will be driven by school enrollments and the need for special education services.

These teachers and services will continue to be needed as children with disabilities are identified earlier and are enrolled into special education programs.

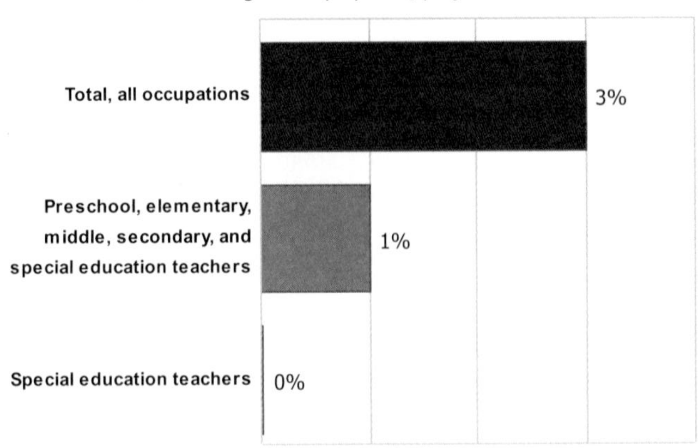

Note: All Occupations includes all occupations in the U.S. Economy.
Source: U.S. Bureau of Labor Statistics, Employment Projections program.

Federal law requires that every state maintain the same level of financial support for special education every year. However, employment growth of special education teachers may depend on funding availability.

Occupational Title	SOC Code	Employment, 2022	Projected Employment, 2032	Change, 2022-32	
				Percent	Numeric
Special education teachers	25-2050	498,400	500,700	0	2,200

Occupational Title	SOC Code	Employment, 2022	Projected Employment, 2032	Change, 2022-32	
				Percent	Numeric
Special education teachers, preschool	25-2051	23,800	24,300	2	500
Special education teachers, kindergarten and elementary school	25-2052	194,700	194,600	0	-100
Special education teachers, middle school	25-2057	82,800	82,600	0	-100
Special education teachers, secondary school	25-2058	153,200	154,000	0	700
Special education teachers, all other	25-2059	43,900	45,200	3	1,300

Contacts for More Information

For more information about special education teachers, visit

- Council for Exceptional Children
- Personnel Improvement Center
- National Association of Special Education Teachers
- Teach.org
- American Federation of Teachers
- National Education Association

Teacher Assistants

Summary

Quick Facts: Teacher Assistants	
2022 Median Pay	$30,920 per year
Typical Entry-Level Education	Some college, no degree
Work Experience in a Related Occupation	None
On-the-job Training	None
Number of Jobs, 2022	1,298,900
Job Outlook, 2022-32	0% (Little or no change)
Employment Change, 2022-32	900

What Teacher Assistants Do

Teacher assistants work with a licensed teacher to give students additional attention and instruction.

Work Environment

Teacher assistants typically work in schools, at childcare centers, and for religious organizations. Most work full time, although part-time work is common. They generally do not work during the summer.

How to Become a Teacher Assistant

To enter the occupation, teacher assistants typically need to have completed at least 2 years of college coursework.

Teacher assistants work under the supervision of a teacher and provide additional attention and instruction to students.

Pay
The median annual wage for teacher assistants was $30,920 in May 2022.

Job Outlook
Employment of teacher assistants is projected to show little or no change from 2022 to 2032.

Despite limited employment growth, about 151,000 openings for teacher assistants are projected each year, on average, over the decade. Most of those openings are expected to result from the need to replace workers who transfer to different occupations or exit the labor force, such as to retire.

What Teacher Assistants Do
Teacher assistants work with a licensed teacher to give students additional attention and instruction.

Duties
Teacher assistants typically do the following:

- Reinforce lessons by reviewing material with students one-on-one or in small groups
- Follow school and class rules to teach students proper behavior
- Help teachers with recordkeeping, such as taking attendance and calculating grades
- Get equipment or materials ready to help teachers prepare for lessons
- Supervise students outside of the classroom, such as between classes, during lunch and recess, and on field trips

Teacher assistants also are called *teacher aides*, *instructional aides*, *paraprofessionals*, *education assistants*, and *paraeducators*.

Teacher assistants work with or under the guidance of a licensed teacher. Reviewing with students individually or in small groups, teacher assistants help reinforce the lessons that teachers introduce.

Some teacher assistants work exclusively with special education students who attend traditional classes.

Teacher assistants may provide feedback to teachers for monitoring student progress. Some teacher assistants meet regularly with teachers to discuss lesson plans and students' development.

Some teacher assistants work only with special education students. When special education students attend regular classes, these teacher assistants help them understand the material and adapt the information to their learning style. Teacher assistants may also work with students who have severe disabilities in separate classrooms. They help these students with basic needs, such as eating or personal hygiene. Teacher assistants may help young adults with disabilities to learn skills necessary for finding a job or living independently after graduation.

Some teacher assistants help in specific areas. For example, they may work in a computer laboratory, helping students use programs or software. Others may work as cafeteria attendants, supervising students during lunchtime.

Teacher assistants in childcare centers work with a lead teacher to provide individualized attention that young children need. They help with educational activities, supervise the children at play, and help with feeding and other basic care.

Work Environment
Teacher assistants held about 1.3 million jobs in 2022. The largest employers of teacher assistants were as follows:

Elementary and secondary schools; local	73%
Child day care services	10
Elementary and secondary schools; private	9

Teacher assistants may spend some time outside, when students are at recess or getting on and off the bus. They may need to lift the students at certain times.

Injuries and Illnesses
Teacher assistants sometimes get injured on the job. They actively work with students, including lifting and otherwise assisting special education students, which can place them at risk for injuries such as strains.

Work Schedules
Most teacher assistants work full time, although part-time work is common. Some monitor students on school buses before and after school. Many teacher assistants do not work during the summer; however, some work in year-round schools or assist teachers in summer school.

How to Become a Teacher Assistant
To enter the occupation, teacher assistants typically need to have completed at least 2 years of college coursework.

Some teacher assistants work in specific locations within schools, such as libraries.

Education

Teacher assistants in public schools need at least 2 years of college coursework or an associate's degree. Those who work in schools with a Title 1 program (a federal program for schools that have a large proportion of students from low-income households) must have at least a 2-year degree, 2 years of college, or pass a state or local assessment.

Teacher assistants reinforce lessons presented in class by reviewing material with students one-on-one or in small groups.

Associate's degree programs for teacher assistants prepare participants to develop educational materials, observe students, and understand the role of teaching assistants in working with classroom teachers.

Some teacher assistants have a bachelor's degree in fields such as education and psychology.

Most states require teacher assistants who work with special-needs students to pass a skills test.

Licenses, Certifications, and Registrations

Some jobs may require staff to have certifications in cardiopulmonary resuscitation (CPR) and first aid.

Important Qualities

Communication skills. Teacher assistants need to be clear and concise in discussing student progress with teachers and parents.

Interpersonal skills. Teacher assistants must be able to develop relationships with a variety of people, including teachers, students, parents, and administrators.

Patience. Working with students of different abilities and backgrounds may be difficult. Teacher assistants must be understanding with students.

Resourcefulness. Teacher assistants must find ways to explain information to students who have different learning styles.

Advancement

Teacher assistants may become a kindergarten and elementary school teacher, middle school teacher, high school teacher, or special education teacher upon obtaining additional education, training, and a license or certification.

Pay

The median annual wage for teacher assistants was $30,920 in May 2022. The median wage is the wage at which half

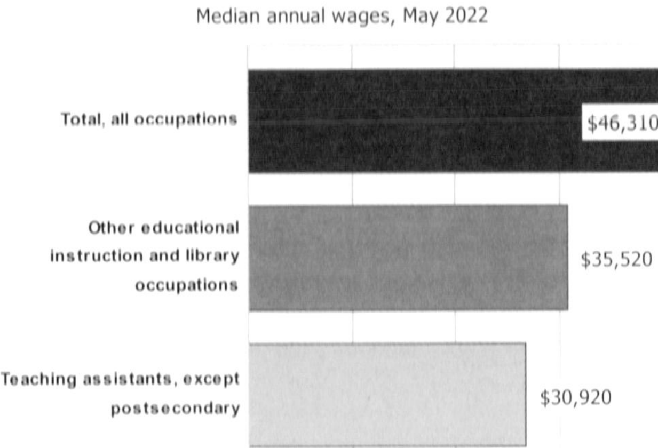

Note: All Occupations includes all occupations in the U.S. Economy.
Source: U.S. Bureau of Labor Statistics, Occupational Employment and Wage Statistics.

the workers in an occupation earned more than that amount and half earned less. The lowest 10 percent earned less than $22,720, and the highest 10 percent earned more than $46,840.

In May 2022, the median annual wages for teacher assistants in the top industries in which they worked were as follows:

Elementary and secondary schools; local	$31,530
Elementary and secondary schools; private	30,900
Child day care services	28,780

Most teacher assistants work full time, although part-time work is common. Some monitor students on school buses before and after school. Many teacher assistants do not work during the summer; however, some work in year-round schools or assist teachers in summer school.

Job Outlook

Employment of teacher assistants is projected to show little or no change from 2022 to 2032.

Despite limited employment growth, about 151,000 openings for teacher assistants are projected each year, on average, over the decade. Most of those openings are expected to result from the need to replace workers who transfer to different occupations or exit the labor force, such as to retire.

Employment

Teacher assistants' employment opportunities may depend on school districts' budgets. Schools may be more likely to eliminate positions for teacher assistants when there is a budget shortfall, and they may be more likely to hire teacher assistants when there is a budget surplus.

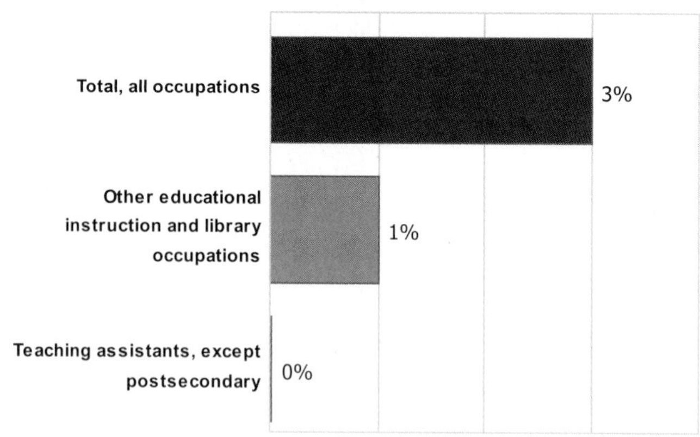

Note: All Occupations includes all occupations in the U.S. Economy.
Source: U.S. Bureau of Labor Statistics, Employment Projections program.

Occupational Title	SOC Code	Employment, 2022	Projected Employment, 2032	Change, 2022-32 Percent	Change, 2022-32 Numeric
Teaching assistants, except postsecondary	25-9045	1,298,900	1,299,800	0	900

Contacts for More Information

For more information about teacher assistants, visit

- National Education Association
- American Federation of Teachers
- National Resource Center for Paraeducators

Tutors

Summary

Quick Facts: Tutors

2022 Median Pay	$36,680 per year
Typical Entry-Level Education	Some college, no degree
Work Experience in a Related Occupation	None
On-the-job Training	None
Number of Jobs, 2022	223,700
Job Outlook, 2022-32	3% (As fast as average)
Employment Change, 2022-32	7,400

What Tutors Do

Tutors instruct students individually or in small groups to support formal class instruction or improve academic performance. Some tutors prepare students for standardized tests.

Work Environment

Most tutors work part time, and their schedules may vary. For example, they may work evenings and weekends and may have more hours during the school year or leading up to standardized test dates.

How to Become a Tutor

Tutors typically need to have completed some college courses, specifically in subjects they want to teach. However, education requirements vary. Some employers do not require credentials; others prefer to hire tutors who have a bachelor's degree.

Pay

The median annual wage for tutors was $36,680 in May 2022.

Job Outlook

Employment of tutors is projected to grow 3 percent from 2022 to 2032, about as fast as the average for all occupations.

Tutors review learning material with students.

About 39,100 openings for tutors are projected each year, on average, over the decade. Many of those openings are expected to result from the need to replace workers who transfer to different occupations or exit the labor force, such as to retire.

What Tutors Do

Tutors instruct students individually or in small groups to support formal class instruction or improve academic performance. Some tutors prepare students for standardized or admissions tests.

Duties

Tutors typically do the following:

- Set goals with students
- Assist students with homework or practice problems
- Teach students organizational and study skills
- Provide feedback to students
- Review learning materials with students
- Prepare session materials or practice questions
- Monitor student progress to discuss with students, parents, or teachers

Tutors work with students one-on-one or in groups to help them learn or to reinforce subject material. For example, they may help students with homework assignments or review worksheets, drills, or other academic exercises. They may create tools and activities, such as educational games, or find resources in textbooks or online.

Tutors structure their lessons based on a variety of factors, including their students' needs and age. For example, some students may respond well to rapid-response or high-energy activities while other students, such as those with disabilities, may require a slower pace or less sensory stimulation.

Tutors also may help students improve their study and organizational skills. They may help students develop good habits through the use of tools, such as flash cards, and strategies, including note-taking systems or calendars for managing time.

The following are examples of types of tutors:

Language and ESL tutors assist students who are learning a foreign language or English as a second language (ESL). They may help students develop fluency or literacy by focusing on grammar, pronunciation, reading, and writing in the target language.

Special education tutors work with students who have physical, mental, emotional, or behavioral disabilities. These tutors develop lesson plans and teaching methods based on the specific needs of each student. Special education tutors may help with life skills and social skills in addition to academic subjects.

Subject tutors typically help with homework or other coursework and with reteaching concepts. These tutors typically have a background in the subject that they tutor. For example, a math tutor may have a degree in mathematics or have completed numerous mathematics or related courses.

Test preparation tutors help students prepare for standardized examinations that measure knowledge or skills in a consistent, or "standard," manner. These tutors may work with students on developing test-taking strategies, such as time management and question analysis, specific to their standardized test.

Work Environment

Tutors held about 223,700 jobs in 2022. The largest employers of tutors were as follows:

Other schools and instruction; private	28%
Self-employed workers	15
Elementary and secondary schools; local	13
Colleges, universities, and professional schools; state	12
Educational support services; state, local, and private	6

Tutors work in a variety of settings, such as schools and tutoring centers. Some tutors travel to students' homes.

Tutors work in a variety of settings, such as schools and tutoring centers.

Work Schedules

Most tutors work part time, and their schedules may vary. For example, they may work evenings and weekends and may have more hours during the school year or leading up to standardized test dates. Because such schedules are common, many of these workers hold other jobs or attend school outside of their tutoring hours.

How to Become a Tutor

Tutors typically need to have completed some college courses, specifically in the subjects that they want to teach. However, education requirements vary. Some employers do not require credentials; others prefer to hire tutors who have a bachelor's degree.

Education and Training

Tutors typically need to have some college education, specifically in subjects that they want to teach. Some tutors, such as those still in high school, may not have completed college courses but have a strong knowledge or background in a specific subject.

Some employers require that tutors have a bachelor's degree in a field such as education. Other employers may prefer to hire tutors whose degree relates closely to their tutoring subject, such as mathematics or a foreign language.

Depending on the position, tutors may receive training on the job.

Other Experience

Test preparation tutors usually need to have scored highly on the standardized tests for which they help students prepare. Student tutors, such as those in college, may need a minimum grade point average (GPA) or must have high grades in the subjects that they tutor.

Some employers prefer to hire tutors who have teaching experience or who have a state-issued teaching certification or license.

Tutors must find creative ways to keep students engaged in learning.

Important Qualities

Communication skills. Tutors must explain concepts in terms that students can understand. They may need to discuss student progress with parents or teachers.

Creativity. Tutors must be able to keep students engaged in learning. They may have to change their methods of instruction to address the needs of different students.

Instructional skills. Tutors must understand the fundamentals of teaching and lesson planning. They must adjust their teaching style and lessons to meet the needs of each student.

Organizational skills. Tutors must coordinate schedules with students, parents, or employers. They must prepare lesson plans and instructional materials for tutoring sessions.

Patience. Working with students of different abilities and backgrounds can be difficult. Tutors must be patient, especially with students who may become distracted or who struggle to master the material.

Pay

The median annual wage for tutors was $36,680 in May 2022. The median wage is the wage at which half the workers in an occupation earned more than that amount and half earned less. The lowest 10 percent earned less than $26,040, and the highest 10 percent earned more than $73,400.

In May 2022, the median annual wages for tutors in the top industries in which they worked were as follows:

Elementary and secondary schools; local	$45,930
Educational support services; state, local, and private	38,490
Other schools and instruction; private	37,070
Colleges, universities, and professional schools; state	32,520

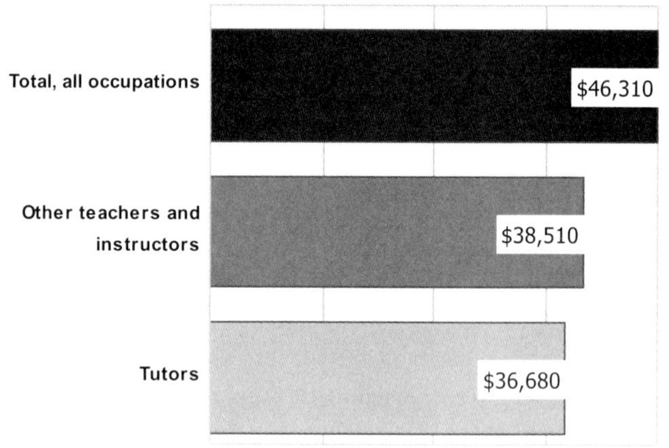

Note: All Occupations includes all occupations in the U.S. Economy.
Source: U.S. Bureau of Labor Statistics, Occupational Employment and Wage Statistics.

Tutors

Percent change in employment, projected 2022-32

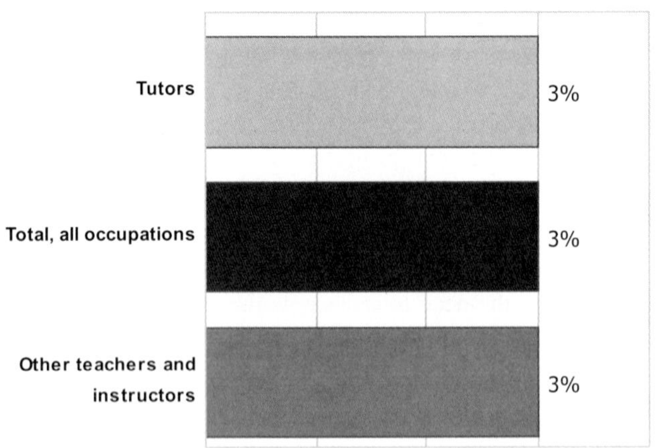

Note: All Occupations includes all occupations in the U.S. Economy.
Source: U.S. Bureau of Labor Statistics, Employment Projections program.

Most tutors work part time, and their schedules may vary. For example, they may work evenings and weekends and may have more hours during the school year or leading up to standardized test dates.

Job Outlook

Employment of tutors is projected to grow 3 percent from 2022 to 2032, about as fast as the average for all occupations.

About 39,100 openings for tutors are projected each year, on average, over the decade. Many of those openings are expected to result from the need to replace workers who transfer to different occupations or exit the labor force, such as to retire.

Employment

Employment growth for tutors will depend on the size of the student population requiring additional academic assistance. Demand for private tutoring services will continue as students preparing for college strive to differentiate themselves from other applicants through academic achievement. Also, some applicants to graduate school programs will hire tutors to help them prepare for entrance exams. The ability of schools, students, and families to pay for tutoring services will impact future demand for these workers.

Occupational Title	SOC Code	Employment, 2022	Projected Employment, 2032	Change, 2022-32	
				Percent	Numeric
Tutors	25-3041	223,700	231,100	3	7,400

Contacts for More Information

For more information about tutors or educational resources, visit

- City Year
- Learning Disabilities Association of America
- National College Learning Center Association
- National Organization for Student Success

Entertainment and Sports

Actors

Summary

Quick Facts: Actors	
2022 Median Pay	$17.94 per hour
Typical Entry-Level Education	Some college, no degree
Work Experience in a Related Occupation	None
On-the-job Training	Long-term on-the-job training
Number of Jobs, 2022	78,100
Job Outlook, 2022-32	3% (As fast as average)
Employment Change, 2022-32	2,500

What Actors Do
Actors express ideas and portray characters in theater, film, television, and other performing arts media.

Work Environment
Actors work in various settings, including production studios, theaters, and theme parks, or on location. Work assignments are usually short, ranging from 1 day to a few months.

How to Become an Actor
Actors typically enhance their skills through formal education, and long-term training is common.

Pay
The median hourly wage for actors was $17.94 in May 2022.

Actors interpret a writer's script to entertain or inform an audience.

Job Outlook
Employment of actors is projected to grow 3 percent from 2022 to 2032, about as fast as the average for all occupations.

About 9,300 openings for actors are projected each year, on average, over the decade. Many of those openings are expected to result from the need to replace workers who transfer to different occupations or exit the labor force, such as to retire.

What Actors Do
Actors express ideas and portray characters in theater, film, television, and other performing arts media. They interpret a writer's script to entertain or inform an audience.

Duties
Actors typically do the following:

- Read scripts and meet with agents and other professionals before accepting a role
- Audition in front of directors, producers, and casting directors
- Research their character's personal traits and circumstances to portray the characters more authentically to an audience

Actors must memorize and rehearse their lines.

- Memorize their lines
- Rehearse their lines and performance, including on stage or in front of the camera, with other actors
- Discuss their role with the director, producer, and other actors to improve the overall performance of the show
- Perform the role, following the director's directions

Most actors struggle to find steady work, and few achieve recognition as stars. Some work as "extras"—actors who have no lines to deliver but are included in scenes to give a more realistic setting. Some actors do voiceover or narration work for animated features, audiobooks, or other electronic media.

In some stage or film productions, actors sing, dance, or play a musical instrument. For some roles, an actor must learn a new skill, such as horseback riding or stage fighting.

Most actors have long periods of unemployment between roles and often hold other jobs in order to make a living. Some actors teach acting classes as a second job.

Work Environment

Actors held about 78,100 jobs in 2022. The largest employers of actors were as follows:

Self-employed workers	26%
Motion picture and video industries	25
Accounting, tax preparation, bookkeeping, and payroll services	22
Amusement parks and arcades	8
Theater companies and dinner theaters	6

Work assignments are usually short, ranging from 1 day to a few months, and actors often hold another job in order to make a living. They are frequently under the stress of having to find their next job. Some actors in touring companies may be employed for several years.

Actors may perform in unpleasant conditions, such as outdoors in bad weather, under hot stage lights, or while wearing an uncomfortable costume or makeup.

Some actors wear elaborate makeup and costumes.

Work Schedules

Work hours for actors are extensive and irregular. Early morning, evening, weekend, and holiday work is common. Some actors work part time. Few actors work full time, and many have variable schedules. Those who work in theater may travel with a touring show across the country. Film and television actors may also travel to work on location.

How to Become an Actor

Actors typically enhance their skills through formal education, and long-term training is common.

Education

Actors typically enhance their skills through formal education. Those who specialize in theater may have a bachelor's degree in a field such as performing arts, but a degree is not required.

Although some people succeed in acting without getting a formal education, most actors acquire some formal preparation through a theater company's acting conservatory or a university drama or theater arts program. Students can take college classes in drama or filmmaking to prepare for a career as an actor. Classes in dance or music may help as well.

Actors who do not have a college degree may take acting or film classes to learn their craft. Community colleges, acting

Actors may audition for many roles before getting a job.

conservatories, and private film schools typically offer these classes. Many theater companies also have education programs.

Important Qualities

Creativity. Actors interpret their characters' feelings and motives in order to portray the characters in the most compelling way.

Memorization skills. Actors memorize many lines before filming begins or a show opens. Television actors often appear on camera with little time to memorize scripts, and scripts frequently may be revised or even written just moments before filming.

Persistence. Actors may audition for many roles before getting a job. They must be able to accept rejection and keep going.

Physical stamina. Actors should be in good enough physical condition to endure the heat from stage or studio lights and the weight of heavy costumes or makeup. They may work many hours, including acting in more than one performance a day, and they must do so without getting overly tired.

Reading skills. Actors must read scripts and be able to interpret how a writer has developed their character.

Speaking skills. Actors—particularly stage actors—must say their lines clearly, project their voice, and pronounce words so that audiences understand them.

In addition to these qualities, actors usually must be physically coordinated to perform predetermined, sometimes complex movements with other actors, such as dancing or stage fighting, in order to complete a scene.

Training

It takes many years of practice to develop the skills needed to be a successful actor, and actors never truly finish training. They work to improve their acting skills throughout their career. Many actors continue to train through workshops, rehearsals, or mentoring by a drama coach.

Every role is different, and an actor may need to learn something new for each one. For example, a role may require learning how to sing or dance, or an actor may have to learn to speak with an accent or to play a musical instrument or sport.

Many aspiring actors begin by participating in school plays or local theater productions. In television and film, actors usually start out in smaller roles or independent movies and work their way up to bigger productions.

Advancement

As an actor's reputation grows, he or she may work on bigger projects or in more prestigious venues. Some actors become producers and directors.

Pay

The median hourly wage for actors was $17.94 in May 2022. The median wage is the wage at which half the workers in an occupation earned more than that amount and half earned less.

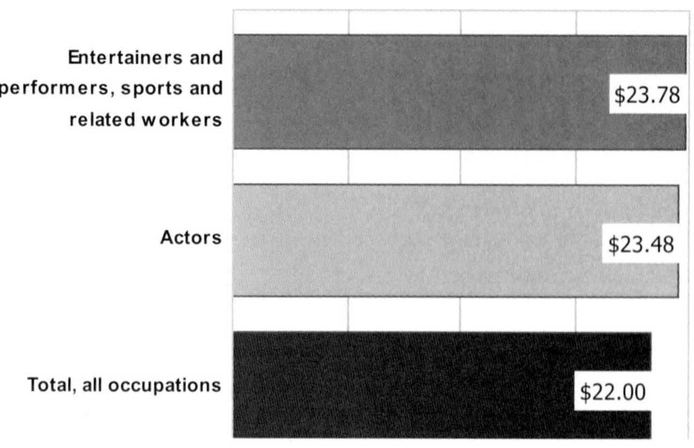

Note: All Occupations includes all occupations in the U.S. Economy.
Source: U.S. Bureau of Labor Statistics, Occupational Employment and Wage Statistics.

The lowest 10 percent earned less than $13.20, and the highest 10 percent earned more than $109.46.

In May 2022, the median hourly wages for actors in the top industries in which they worked were as follows:

Theater companies and dinner theaters	$23.14
Amusement parks and arcades	17.94
Motion picture and video industries	16.70
Accounting, tax preparation, bookkeeping, and payroll services	15.79

Work hours for actors are extensive and irregular. Early morning, evening, weekend, and holiday work is common. Some actors work part time. Few actors work full time, and many have variable schedules. Those who work in theater may travel with a touring show across the country. Actors in movies may also travel to work on location.

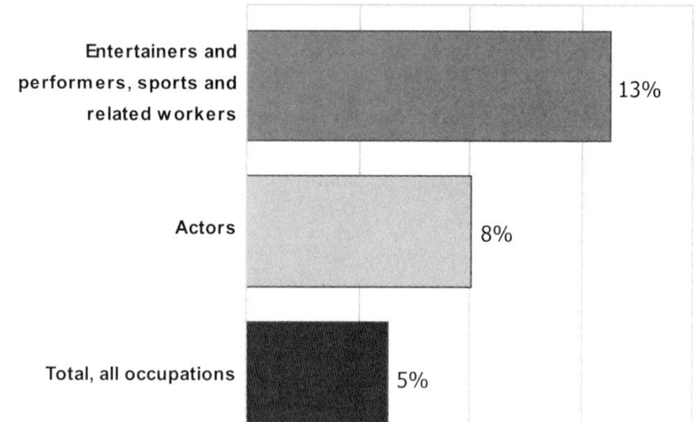

Note: All Occupations includes all occupations in the U.S. Economy.
Source: U.S. Bureau of Labor Statistics, Employment Projections program.

Job Outlook

Employment of actors is projected to grow 3 percent from 2022 to 2032, about as fast as the average for all occupations.

About 9,300 openings for actors are projected each year, on average, over the decade. Many of those openings are expected to result from the need to replace workers who transfer to different occupations or exit the labor force, such as to retire.

Employment

Streaming services and other online-only platforms are expected to drive employment demand for actors as the number of shows produced and the volume of content increase.

However, lack of funding may reduce the number of performances held at theaters, which would impact employment of actors in these establishments. Theaters with more stable sources of funding and well-known plays and musicals may be less susceptible to fluctuations in employment demand.

Occupational Title	SOC Code	Employment, 2022	Projected Employment, 2032	Change, 2022-32	
				Percent	Numeric
Actors	27-2011	78,100	80,600	3	2,500

Contacts for More Information

For more information about actors, visit

- Actors' Equity Association
- National Endowment for the Arts
- SAG-AFTRA

Athletes and Sports Competitors

Summary

Quick Facts: Athletes and Sports Competitors	
2022 Median Pay	$94,270 per year
Typical Entry-Level Education	No formal educational credential
Work Experience in a Related Occupation	None
On-the-job Training	Long-term on-the-job training
Number of Jobs, 2022	14,000
Job Outlook, 2022-32	9% (Much faster than average)
Employment Change, 2022-32	1,300

What Athletes and Sports Competitors Do

Athletes and sports competitors participate in organized, officiated sporting events to entertain spectators.

Athletes and sports competitors participate in officiated sports events to entertain spectators.

Work Environment

Athletes and sports competitors may work irregular schedules, including evenings, weekends, and holidays. They typically work more than 40 hours per week for several months during their particular sports season. They frequently work outside, so they may be exposed to all weather conditions.

How to Become an Athlete or Sports Competitor

No formal educational credential is typically required to become an athlete or sports competitor. Athletes must have athletic talent and an extensive knowledge of their sport. They typically get such knowledge through years of practice and experience at lower levels of competition.

Pay

The median annual wage for athletes and sports competitors was $94,270 in May 2022.

Job Outlook

Employment of athletes and sports competitors is projected to grow 9 percent from 2022 to 2032, much faster than the average for all occupations.

About 1,900 openings for athletes and sports competitors are projected each year, on average, over the decade. Many of those openings are expected to result from the need to replace workers who transfer to different occupations or exit the labor force, such as to retire.

What Athletes and Sports Competitors Do

Athletes and sports competitors participate in organized, officiated sporting events to entertain spectators.

Duties

Athletes and sports competitors typically do the following:

- Practice to develop and improve their skills
- Keep their sports equipment in good condition

Athletes and sports competitors practice under the direction of coaches and sports instructors.

Athletes and sports competitors are often exposed to all types of weather conditions.

- Exercise, train, and follow special diets to stay in the best physical condition
- Take instructions regarding strategy and tactics from coaches and other sports staff during practices and competitions
- Follow the rules of the sport during competitions
- Assess performance after each event and identify their strengths and weaknesses

Many people dream of becoming a professional athlete. Few people, however, make a full-time living from professional athletics—and when they do, professional athletes often have short careers with little job security.

When performing, athletes and sports competitors must understand the strategies involved in their sport while following its rules and regulations. The events in which athletes compete include team sports, such as baseball, football, hockey, and soccer, and individual sports, such as golf, racecar driver, and tennis. The level of play varies. Some athletes compete in regional events; others compete in national or international events.

Being an athlete involves more than competing in athletic events. Athletes spend most days practicing and improving their skills under the guidance of a coach or a sports instructor. They review videos to critique and improve their performance and technique. To gain a competitive advantage, athletes also study their opponents' tendencies and weaknesses.

Because of the physical demands required by many sports, career-ending injuries are always a risk. Some athletes work regularly with fitness trainers and instructors to gain muscle and stamina and to prevent injury. They also may work with athletic trainers or exercise physiologists to recover and rebuild from injuries, even minor ones.

Sports competition at the professional level is intense, and job security is always in question. Therefore, many pro athletes train throughout the year to maintain or improve their form and technique to remain in peak physical condition. Little downtime from the sport exists at the professional level.

Work Environment

Athletes and sports competitors held about 14,000 jobs in 2022. The largest employers of athletes and sports competitors were as follows:

Performing arts, spectator sports, and related industries	75%
Self-employed workers	8
Fitness and recreational sports centers	2

Athletes and sports competitors who participate in outdoor competitions may be exposed to weather conditions of the season in which they play their sport. In addition, many athletes must travel to sporting events. Such travel may include long bus rides or plane trips, and, in some cases, international travel.

Injuries and Illnesses

Athletes and sports competitors have one of the highest rates of injuries and illnesses of all occupations. Many of these workers wear gloves, helmets, pads, and other protective gear to guard against injury. And although fatalities are uncommon, athletes and sports competitors experience one of the highest rates of occupational fatalities of all occupations.

Work Schedules

Athletes and sports competitors may work irregular schedules, including evenings, weekends, and holidays; part-time work is also common. During the sports season, they typically work more than 40 hours per week for several months as they practice, train, travel, and compete.

How to Become an Athlete or Sports Competitor

No formal educational credential is typically required to become an athlete or sports competitor. Athletes must have athletic talent and extensive knowledge of their sport. They typically get such knowledge through years of experience at lower levels of competition.

Athletes and sports competitors gain experience by competing in high school, college, or club teams.

Education

Although no formal educational credential is typically required to enter the occupation, most athletes and sports competitors have at least a high school diploma or equivalent. Some play their sport in college, where they take courses that may lead to a degree. They must have extensive knowledge of the way the sport is played—especially its rules, regulations, and strategies.

Other Experience

Athletes typically learn the rules of the game and develop their skills by playing the sport at lower levels of competition. They often begin training at a young age and may compete on club teams or in high school and collegiate athletics. In addition, athletes may improve their skills by taking private or group lessons or attending sports camps.

Training

It typically takes many years of practice and experience to become an athlete or sports competitor.

Licenses, Certifications, and Registrations

Some sports and states require athletes and sports competitors to be licensed or certified to practice. For example, racecar drivers need a driver's license issued by their state and a certification or license from an automobile racing organization to compete in some races. State licensing boards and professional athletics associations, which serve as governing bodies of various sports, may revoke licenses and suspend participants who do not meet the required performance or training. In addition, athletes may have their licenses or certification suspended for inappropriate activity.

Advancement

Turning professional is often the biggest advancement that aspiring athletes make in their careers. They may begin to compete immediately, although some also may spend more time on the bench (as a reserve) to gain experience. In some sports, such as baseball, athletes may begin their professional career on a minor league team before moving up to the major leagues. Professional athletes generally advance in their sport by displaying superior performance and receiving accolades; in turn, they typically earn a higher salary. They also may receive endorsements from companies and brands.

Important Qualities

Athleticism. Athletes and sports competitors need athletic ability to compete against opponents.

Concentration. Athletes and sports competitors must focus when competing, which includes being able to block out distractions from fans and opponents.

Decision-making skills. Athletes and sports competitors often must make split-second decisions that affect the outcome of a play or the entire competition.

Dedication. Athletes and sports competitors must practice regularly to develop their skills and improve or maintain their physical conditioning.

Hand–eye coordination. Athletes and sports competitors must be able to gauge depth and distance to react and maneuver quickly during competition, such as to strike a fast-moving ball or guide a jumping horse.

Stamina. Endurance is important for helping athletes and sports competitors manage stress during events and ensure that their bodies remain in peak performance condition.

Teamwork. The ability to work toward a shared goal with others, including teammates and coaches, is essential for athletes' and sports competitors' success.

Professional athletes also may be required to pass drug tests.

Pay

The median annual wage for athletes and sports competitors was $94,270 in May 2022. The median wage is the wage at which half the workers in an occupation earned more than that amount

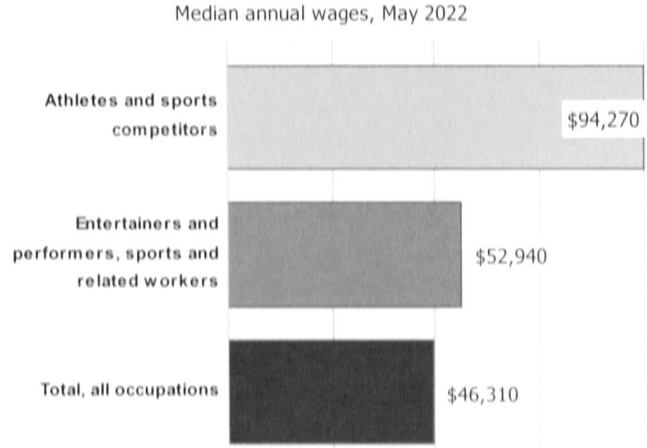

Note: All Occupations includes all occupations in the U.S. Economy.
Source: U.S. Bureau of Labor Statistics, Occupational Employment and Wage Statistics.

and half earned less. The lowest 10 percent earned less than $28,510, and the highest 10 percent earned more than $239,200.

In May 2022, the median annual wages for athletes and sports competitors in the top industries in which they worked were as follows:

Performing arts, spectator sports, and related industries	$110,030
Fitness and recreational sports centers	61,590

Athletes and sports competitors may work irregular schedules, including evenings, weekends, and holidays; part-time work is also common. During the sports season, they typically work more than 40 hours per week for several months as they practice, train, travel, and compete.

Job Outlook

Employment of athletes and sports competitors is projected to grow 9 percent from 2022 to 2032, much faster than the average for all occupations.

About 1,900 openings for athletes and sports competitors are projected each year, on average, over the decade. Many of those openings are expected to result from the need to replace workers who transfer to different occupations or exit the labor force, such as to retire.

Employment

Employment growth is expected to stem from an increased public interest in professional sports. Expansion is rare in professional sports leagues because forming new teams is costly and risky. However, several leagues discussing future expansion plans could affect the demand for athletes and sports competitors over the projections decade.

An interim rule change in college sports and legislation for a Name, Image and Likeness (NIL) policy in many states will allow student-athletes to sign endorsements. As a result, there should be an increase in self-employment for athletes and sports competitors over the decade.

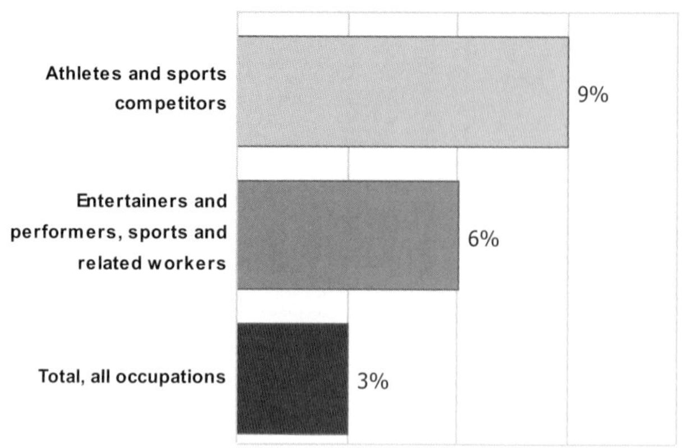

Note: All Occupations includes all occupations in the U.S. Economy.
Source: U.S. Bureau of Labor Statistics, Employment Projections program.

Occupational Title	SOC Code	Employment, 2022	Projected Employment, 2032	Change, 2022-32	
				Percent	Numeric
Athletes and sports competitors	27-2021	14,000	15,200	9	1,300

Contacts for More Information

For more information about team and individual sports, visit

- National Collegiate Athletic Association
- National Council of Youth Sports
- National Federation of State High School Associations

For more information related to individual sports, refer to the organization that represents the sport.

Coaches and Scouts

Summary

Quick Facts: Coaches and Scouts	
2022 Median Pay	$44,890 per year
Typical Entry-Level Education	Bachelor's degree
Work Experience in a Related Occupation	None
On-the-job Training	None
Number of Jobs, 2022	275,200
Job Outlook, 2022-32	9% (Much faster than average)
Employment Change, 2022-32	25,300

What Coaches and Scouts Do

Coaches teach amateur or professional athletes the skills they need to succeed at their sport. Scouts evaluate athletes as possible recruits.

Work Environment

Part-time work is common for coaches and scouts. Full-time coaches may work more than 40 hours a week for several months during the sports season. Work schedules for coaches and scouts vary and may involve irregular hours, including evenings, weekends, and holidays. They may need to travel frequently.

How to Become a Coach or Scout

Coaches and scouts typically need a bachelor's degree. However, educational requirements may vary from no formal educational credential to a bachelor's or higher degree. These workers also need extensive knowledge of the sport. Coaches typically gain this knowledge through their own experiences playing the sport at some level. Although previous playing experience may be beneficial, it is typically not required for most scouting jobs.

Coaches instruct amateur and professional athletes, teaching them the fundamental skills of sports.

Pay

The median annual wage for coaches and scouts was $44,890 in May 2022.

Job Outlook

Employment of coaches and scouts is projected to grow 9 percent from 2022 to 2032, much faster than the average for all occupations.

About 38,400 openings for coaches and scouts are projected each year, on average, over the decade. Many of those openings are expected to result from the need to replace workers who transfer to different occupations or exit the labor force, such as to retire.

What Coaches and Scouts Do

Coaches teach amateur and professional athletes the skills they need to succeed at their sport. Scouts look for new players, evaluating their skills and likelihood for success at the amateur, college, or professional level. Many coaches also are involved in scouting potential athletes for their team.

Duties

Coaches typically do the following:

- Plan, organize, and conduct practice sessions

Coaches and scouts analyze the strengths and weaknesses of individual athletes and opposing teams.

- Analyze the strengths and weaknesses of individual athletes and opposing teams
- Plan strategies and choose team members for each competition
- Direct, encourage, and motivate athletes to prepare them for competitions
- Call plays and make decisions about strategy and athlete substitutions during competitions
- Plan and direct physical conditioning programs that enable athletes to reach maximum performance
- Instruct athletes on proper techniques, strategies, sportsmanship, and the rules of the sport
- Keep records of athletes' and opponents' performances
- Identify and recruit potential athletes
- Arrange for and offer incentives to prospective players

Coaches teach amateur and professional athletes the fundamental skills of individual and team sports. They hold practice and training sessions to improve the athletes' form, skills, and stamina. Along with refining athletes' individual skills, coaches are responsible for instilling the importance of good sportsmanship, a competitive spirit, and teamwork.

Many coaches evaluate their opponents to determine strategies and to establish particular plays to practice. During competition, coaches call specific plays intended to defeat, surprise, or overpower the opponent, and they also may substitute players to get optimum team chemistry and success.

Some high school coaches are teachers or school administrators who supplement their income by coaching part time.

Coaches may assign specific drills and correct athletes' techniques. They may spend their time working one-on-one with athletes, designing customized training programs. Coaches also may specialize in teaching the skills of an individual sport, such as golf, ice skating, or tennis. Some coaches, such as baseball coaches, may teach individual athletes involved in team sports.

Scouts typically do the following:

- Research news media and other sources to find athletes to consider
- Attend competitions, view videos of the athletes' performances, and study data about the athletes to determine their talent and potential
- Talk to the athlete and the coaches to gauge whether the athlete is likely to be successful
- Report to the coach, manager, or owner of the team for which he or she is scouting
- Arrange for and offer incentives to prospective players

Scouts assess the skills of both amateur and professional athletes. Scouts seek out top athletic candidates for colleges or professional teams and evaluate their likelihood of success at a higher competitive level.

Work Environment

Coaches and scouts held about 275,200 jobs in 2022. The largest employers of coaches and scouts were as follows:

Coaches provide direction, encouragement, and motivation to athletes.

Colleges, universities, and professional schools; state, local, and private	24%
Arts, entertainment, and recreation	21
Elementary and secondary schools; state, local, and private	18
Self-employed workers	11

Some scouts work for organizations that deal directly with high school athletes. These scouts collect information on the athlete and help sell his or her talents to potential colleges.

At the college level, scouts typically work for scouting organizations or are self-employed. In either case, they help colleges recruit the best high school athletes.

Scouts who work at the professional level are typically employed by the team or organization directly.

Those who coach and scout for outdoor sports may be exposed to all weather conditions of the season. In addition, they travel often to attend sporting events. This is particularly true for those in professional sports.

Work Schedules

Part-time work is common for coaches and scouts. Their work schedules vary and may involve irregular hours, including evenings, weekends, and holidays. Full-time coaches may work more than 40 hours a week for several months during the sports

Coaches and scouts must have overall knowledge of the game or sport.

season. High school coaches may work part time and have other jobs aside from coaching.

How to Become a Coach or Scout

Coaches and scouts typically need a bachelor's degree. However, educational requirements for coaches and scouts may vary from no formal educational credential to a bachelor's or higher degree. These workers also need extensive knowledge of the sport. Coaches typically gain this knowledge through their own experiences playing the sport at some level. Although previous playing experience may be beneficial, it is not required for most scouting jobs.

Education

Many coaches and scouts have a bachelor's degree, but educational requirements vary. Part-time workers and those in smaller facilities or youth leagues may be less likely to need formal education.

Coaches and scouts who attend college may study a recreation and fitness field, such as kinesiology, physical education, or sports medicine. Others major in a business field, such as marketing or sports management.

High schools typically hire teachers or administrators at the school for most coaching jobs. If no suitable teacher is found, schools hire a qualified candidate from outside the school. For more information on education requirements for teachers, see the profile on high school teachers.

Other Experience

College and professional coaching jobs typically require experience playing the sport at some level.

Scouting jobs may not require experience playing a sport at the college or professional level, but doing so can be beneficial. Employers look for applicants who have a passion for sports and an ability to spot players who have exceptional athletic ability and skills.

Licenses, Certifications, and Registrations

Certification often requires that coaches be at least 18 years old and be trained in cardiopulmonary resuscitation (CPR) and first aid. Coaches also may need to attend classes related to sports safety and coaching fundamentals.

Public high school coaches may need to be certified or complete mandatory education courses. Coaches who are also teachers must meet state licensing requirements, including a background check. For information about specific requirements, contact the state's high school athletic association or visit the National Federation of State High School Associations.

College and university coaches may need to meet certification or training requirements as outlined by college athletic associations, such as the National Collegiate Athletic Association (NCAA) or the National Association of Intercollegiate Athletics (NAIA).

Organizations specific to various sports, such as golf or tennis, may offer certification for coaches. Check with the sport's national governing body for information on approved programs.

Advancement

To reach the rank of a professional coach, a candidate typically needs years of coaching experience and a winning record at a college. Coaches who do not have coaching experience may still be hired at the professional level if they were successful as an athlete in their sport.

Some college coaches begin their careers as graduate assistants or assistant coaches to gain the experience and knowledge needed to become a head coach. Large schools and colleges that compete at the highest levels require a head coach who has had substantial experience at another school or as an assistant coach.

Other college coaches may begin out as high school coaches before moving up to the collegiate level.

Scouts may begin working as talent spotters in a particular area or region. They typically advance to become supervising scouts responsible for a whole territory or region.

Important Qualities

Communication skills. Because coaches instruct, organize, and motivate athletes, they must be able to convey information clearly. They must communicate proper techniques, strategies, and rules of the sport effectively enough for every player on the team to understand.

Decision-making skills. Coaches must choose the appropriate players to use during a game and the proper time to use game-managing tools, such as timeouts. Coaches and scouts also must be selective when recruiting players.

Dedication. Coaches must attend daily practices and assist their team and individual athletes in improving their skills and physical conditioning. Coaches must be dedicated to their sport, as it often takes years to become successful.

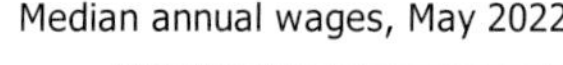

Median annual wages, May 2022

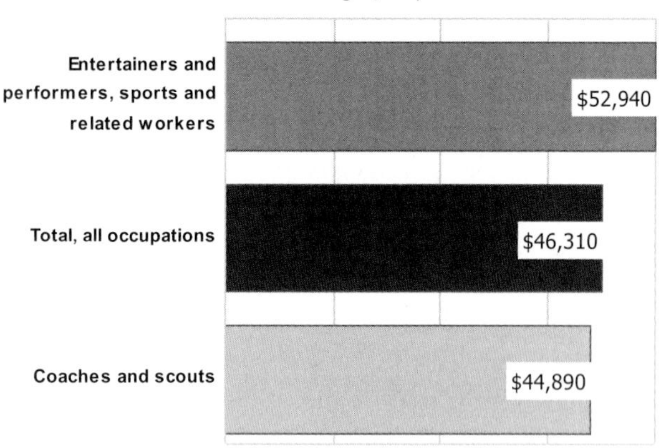

Note: All Occupations includes all occupations in the U.S. Economy.
Source: U.S. Bureau of Labor Statistics, Occupational Employment and Wage Statistics.

Coaches and Scouts

Percent change in employment, projected 2022-32

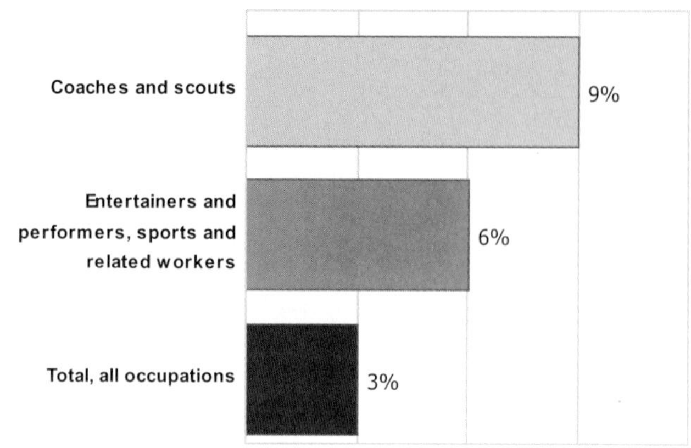

Note: All Occupations includes all occupations in the U.S. Economy.
Source: U.S. Bureau of Labor Statistics, Employment Projections program.

Interpersonal skills. Being able to relate to athletes helps coaches and scouts foster positive relationships with their current players and in recruiting potential players.

Leadership skills. Coaches must motivate, develop, and direct athletes to help them reach their potential.

Resourcefulness. Coaches must find and develop a strategy that yields the best chances for winning a competition. Coaches often need to create original plays or formations that provide a competitive advantage and confuse opponents.

Pay

The median annual wage for coaches and scouts was $44,890 in May 2022. The median wage is the wage at which half the workers in an occupation earned more than that amount and half earned less. The lowest 10 percent earned less than $24,910, and the highest 10 percent earned more than $93,590.

In May 2022, the median annual wages for coaches and scouts in the top industries in which they worked were as follows:

Colleges, universities, and professional schools; state, local, and private	$51,110
Arts, entertainment, and recreation	46,600
Elementary and secondary schools; state, local, and private	44,880

Part-time work is common for coaches and scouts. Their work schedules vary and may involve irregular hours, including evenings, weekends, and holidays. Full-time coaches may work more than 40 hours a week for several months during the sports season. High school coaches may work part time and have other jobs aside from coaching.

Job Outlook

Employment of coaches and scouts is projected to grow 9 percent from 2022 to 2032, much faster than the average for all occupations.

About 38,400 openings for coaches and scouts are projected each year, on average, over the decade. Many of those openings are expected to result from the need to replace workers who transfer to different occupations or exit the labor force, such as to retire.

Employment

The growing interest in college sports, professional sports, and sports recreation instruction will increase demand for coaches and scouts. To remain competitive, colleges often seek the best athletes for their sports teams. Successful teams help colleges enhance their reputation, recruit future students, and raise donations from alumni. Therefore, colleges will rely on scouts to recruit the best high school athletes.

Growth in the demand for sports instruction is expected to rise, as concerns about lack of physical activity continue to be a focus for the public.

Occupational Title	SOC Code	Employment, 2022	Projected Employment, 2032	Change, 2022-32	
				Percent	Numeric
Coaches and scouts	27-2022	275,200	300,500	9	25,300

Contacts for More Information

For more information about coaching and scouting for team and individual sports, visit

- National Association of Intercollegiate Athletics (NAIA)
- National Collegiate Athletic Association (NCAA)
- National Collegiate Scouting Association (NCSA)
- National Federation of State High School Associations (NFHS)
- National High School Coaches Association (NHSCA)

For more information related to individual sports, contact the sport's national governing body or coaches' association.

Dancers and Choreographers

Summary

Quick Facts: Dancers and Choreographers	
2022 Median Pay	$22.62 per hour
Typical Entry-Level Education	See How to Become One
Work Experience in a Related Occupation	See How to Become One
On-the-job Training	Long-term on-the-job training
Number of Jobs, 2022	18,400
Job Outlook, 2022-32	5% (Faster than average)
Employment Change, 2022-32	1,000

What Dancers and Choreographers Do

Dancers and choreographers use dance performances to express ideas and stories.

Work Environment

Some dancers work in performing arts companies, or are self-employed. Choreographers may work in dance schools, and others may work as self-employed choreographers.

How to Become a Dancer or Choreographer

Education and training requirements vary with the type of dancer; however, all dancers need many years of formal training. Nearly all choreographers began their careers as dancers.

Pay

The median hourly wage for choreographers was $24.52 in May 2022.

The median hourly wage for dancers was $21.64 in May 2022.

There are many different types of dance, such as ballet, tango, modern dance, tap, and jazz.

Job Outlook

Overall employment of dancers and choreographers is projected to grow 5 percent from 2022 to 2032, faster than the average for all occupations.

About 3,000 openings for dancers and choreographers are projected each year, on average, over the decade. Many of those openings are expected to result from the need to replace workers who transfer to different occupations or exit the labor force, such as to retire.

What Dancers and Choreographers Do

Dancers and choreographers use dance performances to express ideas and stories. There are many types of dance, such as ballet, tango, modern dance, tap, and jazz.

Duties

Dancers typically do the following:

- Audition for a part in a show or for a job within a dance company
- Learn complex dance movements that entertain an audience
- Rehearse several hours each day to prepare for their performance
- Study new and emerging types of dance
- Work closely with instructors, choreographers, or other dancers to interpret or modify their routines

Some dancers perform in theater productions.

- Attend promotional events, such as photography sessions, for the production in which they are appearing

Dancers spend years learning dances and perfecting their skills. They usually perform as part of a group and know a variety of dance styles, including ballet, tap, and modern dance. In addition to traditional performances in front of a live audience, many perform on TV, in videos on the Internet, and in music videos, in which they also may sing or act. Many dancers perform in shows at casinos, in theme parks, and on cruise ships.

Choreographers typically do the following:

- Put together moves in a sequence to create new dances or interpretations of existing dances
- Choose the music that will accompany a dance routine
- Audition dancers for a role in a show or within a dance company
- Assist with costume design, lighting, and other artistic aspects of a show
- Teach complex dance movements
- Study new and emerging types of dance to design more creative dance routines
- Help with the administrative duties of a dance company, such as budgeting

Choreographers create original dances and develop new interpretations of existing dances. They work in dance schools, theaters, dance companies, and movie studios. During rehearsals, they typically demonstrate dance moves, to instruct dancers in the proper technique. Many choreographers also perform the dance routines they create. Some choreographers work with performers who are not trained dancers. For example, the complex martial arts scenes performed by actors in movies are arranged by choreographers who specialize in martial arts.

Some dancers and choreographers hold other jobs between roles to make a living.

Work Environment

Choreographers held about 6,900 jobs in 2022. The largest employers of choreographers were as follows:

Educational services; state, local, and private	51%
Self-employed workers	19
Performing arts companies	18

Dancers held about 11,500 jobs in 2022. The largest employers of dancers were as follows:

Performing arts companies	30%
Amusement, gambling, and recreation industries	29
Self-employed workers	19
Drinking places (alcoholic beverages)	13
Spectator sports	2

Dancers may rehearse several hours each day to prepare for their performance.

Injuries and Illnesses

Dance takes a toll on a person's body, so on-the-job injuries are common in dancers. In fact, dancers have one of the highest rates of injuries and illnesses of all occupations.

Many dancers stop performing by the time they reach their late thirties because of the physical demands of their work. Nonperforming dancers may continue to work as choreographers, directors, or dance teachers.

Work Schedules

Schedules for dancers and choreographers vary with where they work. During tours, dancers and choreographers have long workdays, rehearsing most of the day and performing at night.

Choreographers who work in dance schools may have a standard workweek when they are instructing students. They also spend hours working independently to create new dance routines.

How to Become a Dancer or Choreographer

Education and training requirements vary with the type of dancer; however, all dancers need many years of formal training. Nearly all choreographers began their careers as dancers.

Most dancers begin training at a young age.

Education and Training

Many dancers begin training when they are young and continue to learn throughout their careers. Ballet dancers begin training the earliest, usually between the ages of 5 and 8 for girls and a few years later for boys. Their training becomes more serious as they enter their teens, and most ballet dancers begin their professional careers by the time they are 18.

Leading professional dance companies sometimes have intensive summer training programs from which they might select candidates for admission to their regular full-time training programs.

Modern dancers normally begin formal training while they are in high school. They attend afterschool dance programs and summer training programs to prepare for their career or for a college dance program.

Some dancers and choreographers pursue postsecondary education. Many colleges and universities offer bachelor's and/or master's degrees in dance, typically through departments of theater or fine arts. As of March 2016, there were about 75 dance programs accredited by the National Association of Schools of Dance. Most programs include coursework in a variety of dance styles, including modern dance, jazz, ballet, and hip-hop. Most entrants into college dance programs have previous formal training.

Some choreographers work as dance teachers. Teaching dance in a college, high school, or elementary school requires a college degree. Some dance studios and conservatories prefer instructors who have a degree; however, they may accept previous work in lieu of a degree.

Work Experience in a Related Occupation

Nearly all choreographers begin their careers as dancers. While working as dancers, they study different types of dance and learn how to choreograph routines.

Advancement

Some dancers take on more responsibility if they are promoted to dance captain in musical theater companies. They lead rehearsals or work with less experienced dancers when the choreographer is not present.

Some dancers become choreographers. Dancers and choreographers also may become theater, film, or television producers and directors.

Important Qualities

Athleticism. Successful dancers must have excellent balance, physical strength, and physical dexterity so that they can move their bodies without falling or losing their sense of rhythm.

Creativity. Dancers need artistic ability and creativity to express ideas through movement. Choreographers also must have artistic ability and innovative ideas, to create new and interesting dance routines.

Leadership skills. Choreographers must be able to direct a group of dancers to perform the routines that they have created.

Persistence. Dancers must commit to years of intense practice. They need to be able to accept rejection after auditions and to continue to practice for future performances. Choreographers must keep studying and creating new routines.

Physical stamina. Dancers are often physically active for long periods, so they must be able to rehearse for many hours without getting tired.

Teamwork. Most dance routines involve a group or pairs, so dancers must be able to work together to be successful.

Pay

The median hourly wage for choreographers was $24.52 in May 2022. The median wage is the wage at which half the workers in an occupation earned more than that amount and half earned less. The lowest 10 percent earned less than $13.95, and the highest 10 percent earned more than $48.28.

The median hourly wage for dancers was $21.64 in May 2022. The lowest 10 percent earned less than $13.20, and the highest 10 percent earned more than $39.03.

In May 2022, the median hourly wages for choreographers in the top industries in which they worked were as follows:

Performing arts companies	$30.19
Educational services; state, local, and private	21.28

In May 2022, the median hourly wages for dancers in the top industries in which they worked were as follows:

Performing arts companies	$23.53
Amusement, gambling, and recreation industries	18.16
Drinking places (alcoholic beverages)	15.56
Spectator sports	12.18

Schedules for dancers and choreographers vary with where they work. During tours, dancers and choreographers have long workdays, rehearsing most of the day and performing at night.

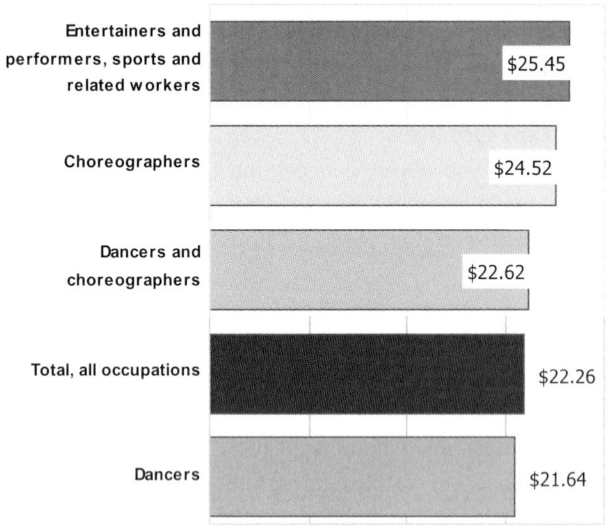

Note: All Occupations includes all occupations in the U.S. Economy.
Source: U.S. Bureau of Labor Statistics, Occupational Employment and Wage Statistics.

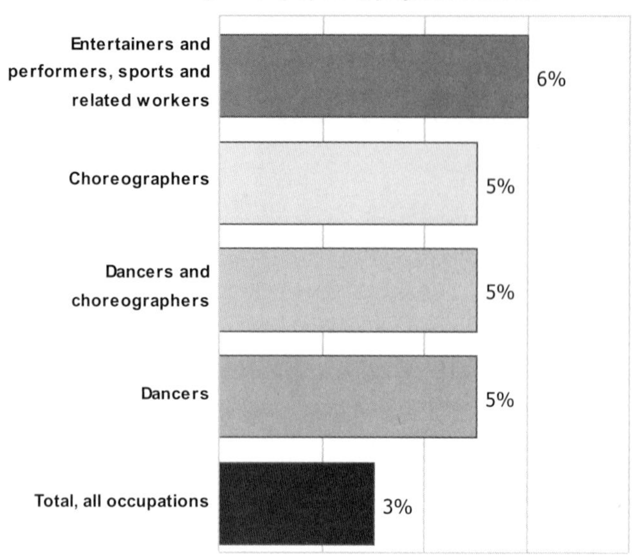

Note: All Occupations includes all occupations in the U.S. Economy.
Source: U.S. Bureau of Labor Statistics, Employment Projections program.

Choreographers who work in dance schools may have a standard workweek when they are instructing students. They also spend hours working independently to create new dance routines.

Job Outlook

Overall employment of dancers and choreographers is projected to grow 5 percent from 2022 to 2032, faster than the average for all occupations.

About 3,000 openings for dancers and choreographers are projected each year, on average, over the decade. Many of those openings are expected to result from the need to replace workers who transfer to different occupations or exit the labor force, such as to retire.

Employment

Employment growth in these relatively small occupations is closely tied to the demand for performing arts. Social media, which allows dancers and choreographers to reach a larger and more diverse audience, is expected to generate some interest in dance performances. New jobs may be concentrated in specific markets, such as cities with strong arts culture, or with certain employers, such as private dance studios. However, funding constraints may offset demand for these workers.

Occupational Title	SOC Code	Employment, 2022	Projected Employment, 2032	Change, 2022-32	
				Percent	Numeric
Dancers and choreographers	27-2030	18,400	19,400	5	1,000
Dancers	27-2031	11,500	12,200	5	600
Choreographers	27-2032	6,900	7,300	5	300

Contacts for More Information

For more information about dancers and choreographers, visit

- Dance/USA
- National Endowment for the Arts
- National Association of Schools of Dance
- USA Dance

Music Directors and Composers

Summary

Quick Facts: Music Directors and Composers	
2022 Median Pay	$62,940 per year $30.26 per hour
Typical Entry-Level Education	Bachelor's degree
Work Experience in a Related Occupation	Less than 5 years
On-the-job Training	None
Number of Jobs, 2022	51,800
Job Outlook, 2022-32	1% (Little or no change)
Employment Change, 2022-32	600

What Music Directors and Composers Do

Music directors lead musical groups during performances and recording sessions. Composers write and arrange original music in a variety of musical styles.

Work Environment

Most music directors work for religious organizations and schools, or are self-employed. Music directors may spend a lot of time traveling to different performances. Composers can work in offices, recording studios, or their own homes.

How to Become a Music Director or Composer

Educational and training requirements for music directors and composers vary, although most positions require related work experience. A music director or conductor for a symphony orchestra typically needs a master's degree; a choir director may need a bachelor's degree. There are no formal educational requirements for those interested in writing popular music.

Pay

The median annual wage for music directors and composers was $62,940 in May 2022.

Job Outlook

Employment of music directors and composers is projected to show little or no change from 2022 to 2032.

Despite limited employment growth, about 5,100 openings for music directors and composers are projected each year, on average, over the decade. Most of those openings are expected to result from the need to replace workers who transfer to different occupations or exit the labor force, such as to retire.

What Music Directors and Composers Do

Music directors, also called *conductors*, lead orchestras and other musical groups during performances and recording sessions. Composers write and arrange original music in a variety of musical styles.

Duties

Music directors typically do the following:

- Select musical arrangements and compositions to be performed for live audiences or recordings
- Prepare for performances by reviewing and interpreting musical scores
- Direct rehearsals to prepare for performances and recordings
- Choose guest performers and soloists
- Audition new performers or assist section leaders with auditions
- Practice conducting to improve their technique
- Meet with potential donors and attend fundraisers

Music directors lead orchestras, choirs, and other musical groups. They ensure that musicians play with one coherent sound, balancing the melody, timing, rhythm, and volume. They also give feedback to musicians and section leaders on sound and style.

Music directors may work with a variety of musical groups, including church choirs, youth orchestras, and high school or college bands, choirs, or orchestras. Some work with orchestras that accompany dance and opera companies.

Composers typically do the following:

Music directors lead choirs and other musical groups during performance sessions.

Composers write and arrange original music in a variety of musical styles.

- Write original music that orchestras, bands, and other musical groups perform
- Arrange existing music into new compositions
- Write lyrics for music or work with a lyricist
- Meet with orchestras, musical groups, and others who are interested in commissioning a piece of music
- Study and listen to music of various styles for inspiration
- Work with musicians to record their music

Composers write music for a variety of types of musical groups and users. Some work in a particular style of music, such as classical or jazz. They also may write for musicals, operas, or other types of theatrical productions.

Some composers write scores for movies or television; others write jingles for commercials. Many songwriters focus on composing music for audiences of popular music.

Some composers use instruments to help them as they write music. Others use software that allows them to hear a piece without musicians.

Some music directors and composers give private music lessons to children and adults. Others teach music in elementary, middle, or high schools. For more information, see the profiles on kindergarten and elementary school teachers, middle school teachers, and high school teachers.

For more information about careers in music, see the profile on musicians and singers.

Work Environment

Music directors and composers held about 51,800 jobs in 2022. The largest employers of music directors and composers were as follows:

Religious, grantmaking, civic, professional, and similar organizations	62%
Self-employed workers	22
Performing arts companies	7
Elementary and secondary schools; state, local, and private	2

Music directors ensure that musicians play with one coherent sound, balancing the melody, timing, rhythm, and volume.

Music directors commonly work in concert halls and recording studios, and they may spend a lot of time traveling to different performances. Composers can work in offices, recording studios, or their own homes.

Jobs for music directors and composers are found all over the country. However, many jobs are located in cities in which entertainment activities are concentrated, such as New York, Los Angeles, Nashville, and Chicago.

Work Schedules

Rehearsals and recording sessions are commonly held during business hours, but performances take place most often on nights and weekends. Because music writing is done primarily independently, composers may be able to set their own schedules.

How to Become a Music Director or Composer

Educational and training requirements for music directors and composers vary, although most positions require related work experience. A conductor for a symphony orchestra typically needs a master's degree; a choir director may need a bachelor's degree. There are no formal educational requirements for those interested in writing popular music.

Education

For positions as a conductor or classical composer, employers generally prefer to hire candidates who have a master's degree in music theory, music composition, or conducting.

Applicants to postsecondary programs in music typically are required to submit recordings, audition in person, or both. These programs teach students about music history and styles, along with instruction in composing and conducting techniques. Information on degree programs is available from the National Association of Schools of Music.

Choir directors typically need a bachelor's degree. Common fields of degree include fine and performing arts and education. Those who work in public schools may need a teaching

In order to become a music director or composer, one must have the talent to play, write, and conduct music.

license or certification. For more information, see the profiles on teachers.

There are no specific educational requirements for those interested in writing popular music. These composers usually find employment by submitting recordings of their compositions to bands, singers, record companies, and movie studios. Composers may promote themselves through personal websites, social media, or online video or audio of their musical work.

Important Qualities

Discipline. Talent is not enough for most music directors and composers to find employment in this field. They must constantly practice and seek to improve their technique and style.

Interpersonal skills. Music directors and composers need to work with agents, musicians, and recording studio personnel. Being friendly, respectful, and open to criticism as well as praise, while enjoying being with others, can help music directors and composers work well with a variety of people.

Leadership. Music directors and composers must guide musicians and singers by preparing musical arrangements and helping them achieve the best possible sound.

Musical talent. To become a music director or composer, one must have musical talent.

Perseverance. Music directors and composers need determination to continue submitting their compositions after receiving rejections. Also, reviewing auditions can be frustrating because it may take many different auditions to find the best musicians.

Promotional skills. Music directors and composers need to promote their performances through local communities, word of mouth, and social media platforms. Good self-promotional skills are helpful in building a fan base and getting more work opportunities.

Training

Music directors and composers typically begin their musical training at a young age by learning to play an instrument or singing, and perhaps performing as a musician or singer. Music directors and composers who are interested in classical music may seek additional training through music camps and fellowships. These programs provide participants with classes, lessons, and performance opportunities.

Work Experience in a Related Occupation

Music directors and composers often work as musicians or singers in a group, a choir, or an orchestra before they take on a leadership role. They use this time to master their instrument and gain an understanding of how the group functions. For more information, see the profile on musicians and singers.

Pay

The median annual wage for music directors and composers was $62,940 in May 2022. The median wage is the wage at which half the workers in an occupation earned more than that amount and half earned less. The lowest 10 percent earned less than $31,750, and the highest 10 percent earned more than $165,760.

In May 2022, the median annual wages for music directors and composers in the top industries in which they worked were as follows:

Performing arts companies	$66,820
Elementary and secondary schools; state, local, and private	60,550
Religious, grantmaking, civic, professional, and similar organizations	59,700

Rehearsals and recording sessions are commonly held during business hours, but performances take place most often on nights and weekends. Because music writing is done primarily independently, composers may be able to set their own schedules.

Job Outlook

Employment of music directors and composers is projected to show little or no change from 2022 to 2032.

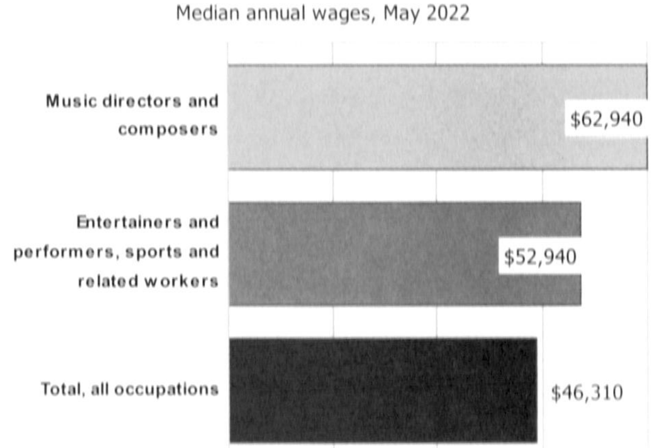

Note: All Occupations includes all occupations in the U.S. Economy.
Source: U.S. Bureau of Labor Statistics, Occupational Employment and Wage Statistics.

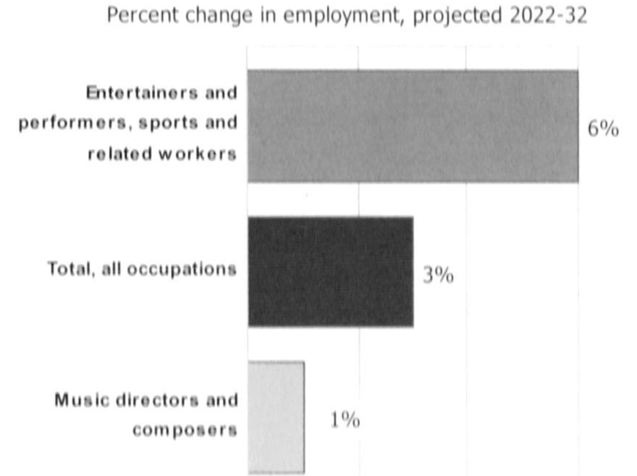

Note: All Occupations includes all occupations in the U.S. Economy.
Source: U.S. Bureau of Labor Statistics, Employment Projections program.

Despite limited employment growth, about 5,100 openings for music directors and composers are projected each year, on average, over the decade. Most of those openings are expected to result from the need to replace workers who transfer to different occupations or exit the labor force, such as to retire.

Employment

Music directors will be needed to lead orchestras for concerts and musical theater performances. They also will conduct the music that accompanies ballet troupes and opera companies.

In addition, there will likely be a need for composers to write original music and arrange known works for performances. Composers will be needed as well to write film scores and music for television and commercials.

However, orchestras, opera companies, and other musical groups can have difficulty getting funds. Some music groups are nonprofit organizations that rely on donations and corporate sponsorships, in addition to ticket sales, to fund their work. These organizations often have difficulty finding enough money to cover their expenses. In addition, growth may be limited for music directors in schools due to struggles with school funding, and music programs may be cut.

Occupational Title	SOC Code	Employment, 2022	Projected Employment, 2032	Change, 2022-32	
				Percent	Numeric
Music directors and composers	27-2041	51,800	52,400	1	600

Contacts for More Information

For more information about music degree programs, visit

➤ National Association of Schools of Music

For more information about careers in music, visit

➤ Future of Music Coalition

Musicians and Singers

Summary

Quick Facts: Musicians and Singers

2022 Median Pay	$39.14 per hour
Typical Entry-Level Education	No formal educational credential
Work Experience in a Related Occupation	None
On-the-job Training	Long-term on-the-job training
Number of Jobs, 2022	173,500
Job Outlook, 2022-32	1% (Little or no change)
Employment Change, 2022-32	2,100

What Musicians and Singers Do

Musicians and singers play instruments or sing for live audiences and in recording studios.

Musicians must practice playing instruments to improve their technique.

Work Environment

Musicians and singers often perform in settings such as concert halls, churches, and clubs. Part-time work is common, and work schedules may vary and include mornings, nights, or weekends.

How to Become a Musician or Singer

Musicians and singers typically do not need formal postsecondary education to enter the occupation. However, those pursuing careers in some genres, such as classical or opera, may choose to earn a bachelor's or higher degree. Musicians and singers need extensive training and regular practice to acquire their skills.

Pay

The median hourly wage for musicians and singers was $39.14 in May 2022.

Job Outlook

Employment of musicians and singers is projected to show little or no change from 2022 to 2032.

Despite limited employment growth, about 22,600 openings for musicians and singers are projected each year, on average, over the decade. Most of those openings are expected to result from the need to replace workers who transfer to different occupations or exit the labor force, such as to retire.

What Musicians and Singers Do

Musicians and singers play instruments or sing for live audiences and in recording studios. They perform a variety of genres, such as classical, jazz, and rock.

Duties

Musicians and singers typically do the following:

Musicians in bands may play clubs and bars while they try to build enough fans to get a recording contract or representation by an agent.

- Perform music for live audiences and recordings
- Audition for positions in orchestras, choirs, bands, and other types of music groups
- Practice playing instruments or singing to improve their technique
- Rehearse music and parts to prepare for performances
- Find and book locations for performances or concerts
- Promote their careers by maintaining a website or social media presence or by doing photo shoots and interviews

Musicians play one or more instruments. To make themselves more marketable, many become proficient in multiple musical instruments or styles. Some diversify by both singing and playing instruments.

Musicians play solo or in orchestras, bands, or limited-size groups, such as trios. Those in bands or groups may play at small venues, such as private parties or bars, sometimes building enough of a fan base to get a recording contract or representation by an agent. Musicians who work in orchestras perform in venues with a stage large enough to accommodate all the musicians and their instruments. A few orchestra musicians become section leaders, who may be responsible for assigning parts to other musicians or for leading rehearsals.

Singers perform vocal music in a variety of genres. Some specialize in a particular vocal style, such as opera or jazz. Singers may perform in different languages, such as French or Italian, particularly if they specialize in classical music or opera. In addition to singing, those in opera and musical theater productions must act during their performances.

Musicians who specialize in playing backup for a singer or band leader during recording sessions and live performances are known as session musicians. Singers who provide background vocals to harmonize with or support a lead singer are known as backup singers or backing vocalists.

Sometimes, musicians and singers write their own music to record and perform. For more information about careers in songwriting, see the profile on music directors and composers.

Some musicians and singers give private music lessons to children and adults. Others with a background in music may teach music in elementary, middle, and high schools, which typically requires a bachelor's degree and a teaching license. For more information, see the profiles on kindergarten and elementary school teachers, middle school teachers, and high school teachers.

Work Environment

Musicians and singers held about 173,500 jobs in 2022. The largest employers of musicians and singers were as follows:

Self-employed workers	48%
Religious, grantmaking, civic, professional, and similar organizations	37
Performing arts, spectator sports, and related industries	11
Educational services; state, local, and private	3

Musicians and singers perform in settings such as concert halls, churches, and clubs. Musicians and singers travel frequently for performances, either locally, nationally, or internationally. When recording music, they may spend time in a studio.

Some musicians and singers spend time in recording studios.

Work Schedules
Musicians and singers often have irregular work schedules. This includes rehearsing and performing during the day or night on weekdays and weekends.

Many musicians and singers find only part-time or intermittent work and may have long periods of unemployment between jobs. The stress of constantly looking for work may require them to accept full-time jobs in other occupations while working part time as a musician or singer.

How to Become a Musician or Singer
Musicians and singers typically do not need formal postsecondary education to enter the occupation. However, those pursuing careers in some genres, such as classical or opera, may choose to earn a bachelor's or higher degree. Musicians and singers need extensive training and regular practice to acquire their skills.

Education
Musicians and singers typically need no postsecondary education to enter the occupation. Musicians and singers of some genres, such as classical music and opera, may pursue training that leads to a bachelor's degree in a field such as music theory or performance. To be accepted into one of these programs, applicants typically are required to submit recordings or to audition in person and sometimes must do both.

Undergraduate music programs teach students about music history and styles. In addition, they teach methods for improving instrumental and vocal techniques and musical expression. Undergraduate voice programs also may include courses in diction. Courses in a foreign language may benefit students who intend to perform in that language. Some business courses, such as marketing, may be helpful for learning about the self-promotion often required for professional musicians and singers.

Some musicians and singers choose to continue their education by pursuing a master's degree in fine arts or music.

To work as a classical musician or singer, a bachelor's degree in music theory or music performance is generally required.

Training
Musicians and singers need extensive training and regular practice to acquire the skills and knowledge necessary to perform music professionally. They typically begin singing or learning to play an instrument at a young age by taking private lessons and school classes. As they advance, they may participate in music camps, festivals, or fellowships.

Advancement
As with other occupations in which people perform, advancement for musicians and singers means becoming better known, finding work more easily, and earning more money for each performance. Successful musicians and singers often rely on agents or managers to find them jobs, negotiate contracts, and develop their careers. Some musicians and singers advance to leading musical groups or becoming section leaders in an orchestra. Others may advance to become music directors and composers.

Important Qualities
Dedication. Auditioning for jobs can be a frustrating process because it may take many different auditions to get hired. Musicians and singers must be determined to continue auditioning after receiving rejections.

Discipline. Talent is not enough for most musicians and singers to find employment in this field. They must practice and rehearse consistently to improve their technique, style, and performance.

Interpersonal skills. Musicians and singers need to work well with a variety of people, such as agents, producers, and conductors. They must be able to build connections and create good working relationships.

Musical talent. Professional musicians or singers must have superior musical abilities.

Physical stamina. Musicians and singers who perform on stage or go on tour for weeks or months must be able to endure frequent travel and irregular performance schedules.

Promotional skills. To build a fan base, musicians and singers need to promote their music and performances through local communities, word of mouth, and social media.

Pay
The median hourly wage for musicians and singers was $39.14 in May 2022. The median wage is the wage at which half the workers in an occupation earned more than that amount and half earned less. The lowest 10 percent earned less than $14.42, and the highest 10 percent earned more than $100.22.

In May 2022, the median hourly wages for musicians and singers in the top industries in which they worked were as follows:

Performing arts, spectator sports, and related industries	$45.17

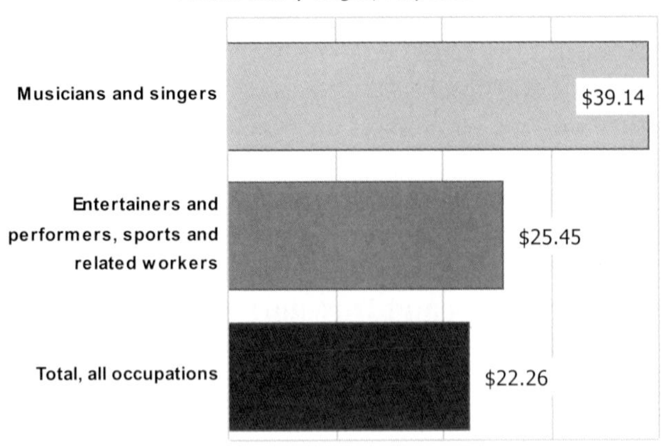

Note: All Occupations includes all occupations in the U.S. Economy.
Source: U.S. Bureau of Labor Statistics, Occupational Employment and Wage Statistics.

Religious, grantmaking, civic, professional, and similar organizations	39.38
Educational services; state, local, and private	28.64

Musicians and singers often have irregular work schedules. This includes rehearsing and performing during the day or night on weekdays and weekends.

Many musicians and singers find only part-time or intermittent work and may have long periods of unemployment between jobs. The stress of constantly looking for work may require them to accept full-time jobs in other occupations while working part time as a musician or singer.

Job Outlook

Employment of musicians and singers is projected to show little or no change from 2022 to 2032.

Despite limited employment growth, about 22,600 openings for musicians and singers are projected each year, on average, over the decade. Most of those openings are expected to result from the need to replace workers who transfer to different occupations or exit the labor force, such as to retire.

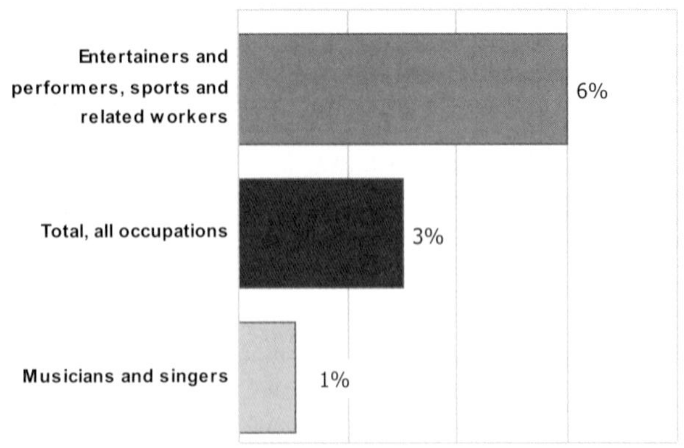

Note: All Occupations includes all occupations in the U.S. Economy.
Source: U.S. Bureau of Labor Statistics, Employment Projections program.

Employment

Interest in live music is expected to support demand across the performing arts. However, the expected decline in public attendance of classical music performances and reduced participation in church activities may slow overall employment growth for musicians and singers.

Occupational Title	SOC Code	Employment, 2022	Projected Employment, 2032	Change, 2022-32	
				Percent	Numeric
Musicians and singers	27-2042	173,500	175,600	1	2,100

Contacts for More Information

For more information about music careers and compensation, visit

➤ Future of Music Coalition

For more information about music degree programs, visit

➤ National Association of Schools of Music

Producers and Directors

Summary

Quick Facts: Producers and Directors	
2022 Median Pay	$85,320 per year $41.02 per hour
Typical Entry-Level Education	Bachelor's degree
Work Experience in a Related Occupation	Less than 5 years
On-the-job Training	None
Number of Jobs, 2022	175,300
Job Outlook, 2022-32	7% (Faster than average)
Employment Change, 2022-32	11,700

What Producers and Directors Do

Producers and directors make business and creative decisions about film, television, stage, and other productions.

Work Environment

Producers and directors are often under pressure to finish their work on time. Most producers and directors work full time, and some work more than 40 hours per week. Their schedules may vary.

How to Become a Producer or Director

Producers and directors typically need a bachelor's degree. They also typically need several years of experience working on set in film, TV, stage, or other productions in positions such as actors, film and video editors, or cinematographers or in related occupations, such as theater managers.

Pay

The median annual wage for producers and directors was $85,320 in May 2022.

Job Outlook

Employment of producers and directors is projected to grow 7 percent from 2022 to 2032, faster than the average for all occupations.

About 16,000 openings for producers and directors are projected each year, on average, over the decade. Many of those openings are expected to result from the need to replace workers who transfer to different occupations or exit the labor force, such as to retire.

What Producers and Directors Do

Producers and directors make business and creative decisions about, film, television, stage, and other productions. They interpret a writer's script to entertain, inform, or instruct an audience.

Duties

Producers and directors typically do the following:

- Select scripts or topics for a film, television, video, stage, or radio production
- Audition and select cast members and the film or stage crew
- Approve the design and financial aspects of a production
- Oversee the production process, including sound, lighting, and performances
- Oversee the postproduction process, including editing, music selection, special effects, and a performance's overall tone
- Ensure that a project stays on schedule and within budget
- Promote finished productions or works through advertisements, film festivals, and interviews

Although producers and directors have distinct roles in a production, their work may overlap. For example, directors ultimately answer to producers, but some directors share producing duties for their own films.

Producers and directors create motion pictures, television shows, live theater, and other performing arts productions.

Stage directors make sure the cast and crew give a consistently strong live performance.

Producers make the business and financial decisions for a film, stage production, or TV show. They raise money for the project and hire the director and crew, which may include designers, editors, and other workers. Some producers also assist in the selection of cast members. Producers set the budget and approve any major changes to the project. They make sure that the production is completed on time, and they are ultimately responsible for the final product.

Various producers often share responsibilities on large productions. For example, on a large movie set, an *executive producer* is in charge of the entire production and a *line producer* runs the day-to-day operations. A TV show may employ several *assistant producers* to whom the head or executive producer gives certain duties, such as supervising the costume and makeup teams.

Directors are responsible for the creative decisions of a production. They select cast members, conduct rehearsals, and direct the work of the cast and crew. During rehearsals, they work with the actors to help them portray their characters accurately. For nonfiction video, such as documentaries or live broadcasts, directors choose topics or subjects to film. They research the topic and may interview experts or relevant participants on camera. Directors also work with cinematographers and other crew members to ensure that the final product matches the overall vision.

Directors work with set designers, location scouts, and art directors to build a project's set. They also work with costume designers to ensure that clothing suits the overall look of the production. During a film's postproduction phase, they work closely with film editors and music supervisors to make sure that the final product meets the producer's and director's vision. *Stage directors*, unlike *television or film directors*, who document their product with cameras, make sure that the cast and crew give consistently strong live performances.

As with assistant producers, several *assistant directors* may work on large productions. Assistant directors help the director with small production tasks, such as making set changes or notifying the performers when it is their time to go onstage. Their specific responsibilities vary with the size and type of production they work on.

For more information about occupations related to producers and directors, see the profiles on actors, writers and authors, film and video editors and camera operators, dancers and choreographers, and multimedia artists and animators.

Work Environment

Producers and directors held about 175,300 jobs in 2022. The largest employers of producers and directors were as follows:

Motion picture and video industries	35%
Media streaming distribution services, social networks, and other media networks and content providers	13
Performing arts, spectator sports, and related industries	9
Self-employed workers	8
Television broadcasting stations	7

Producers and directors audition and select cast members.

Producers and directors are often under pressure to finish their work on time. Work assignments may be short, ranging from 1 day to a few months. They sometimes must work in unpleasant conditions, such as bad weather.

Theater directors and producers may travel with a touring show across the country, while those in film and television may work on location (a site away from the studio and where all or part of the filming occurs).

Work Schedules

Workdays for producers and directors may be long and irregular. Many do not have a standard workweek, because their schedules may change with each assignment or project. Evening, weekend, and holiday work is common. Most producers and directors work full time, and some work more than 40 hours per week.

How to Become a Producer or Director

Producers and directors typically have a bachelor's degree. They also typically need several years of experience working

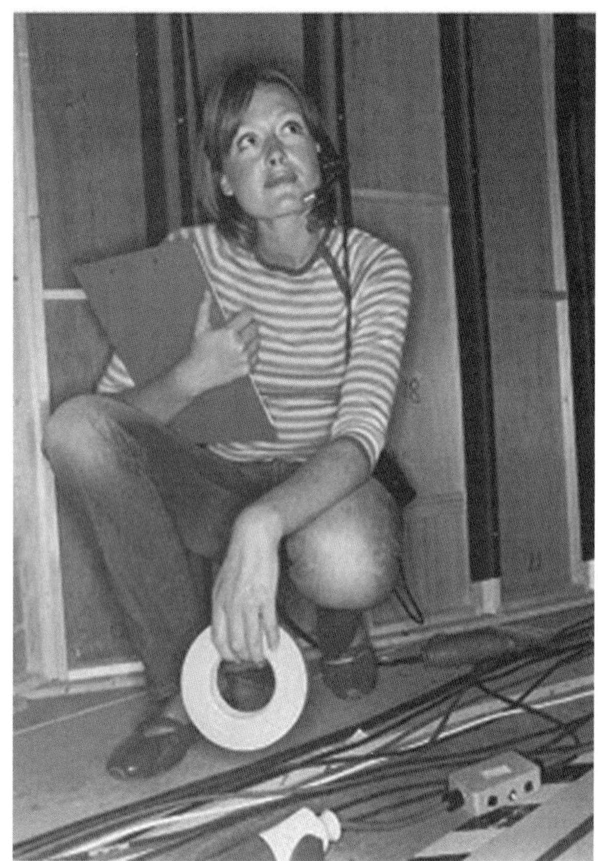

Producers and directors ensure that a project stays on schedule and within budget.

on set in film, TV, stage, or other productions in positions such as actors, cinematographers, or film and video editors or in related occupations, such as theater managers.

Education

Producers and directors typically need a bachelor's degree in film or cinema studies or a related field, such as arts management, business, communications technology, or theater. In film or cinema studies programs, students learn about film history, editing, screenwriting, cinematography, and the filmmaking process.

Stage directors may complete a degree in theater, and some go on to earn a Master of Fine Arts (MFA) degree. Courses may include directing, playwriting, set design, and acting.

Work Experience in a Related Occupation

Producers and directors might start out working in theatrical management offices as business or company managers. In television or film, they may begin as assistants or in other low-profile studio jobs. They may also participate in internships that provide opportunities to work alongside producers and directors. For more information, see the profile on film and video editors and camera operators.

Advancement

As a producer's or director's reputation grows, he or she may work on increasingly large, challenging, and expensive projects that attract publicity.

Important Qualities

Communication skills. Producers and directors must convey information and ideas clearly in order to coordinate many people to finish a production on time and within budget.

Creativity. Because a script may be interpreted in different ways, directors must decide on their approach and on how to represent the script's ideas for the production.

Decision-making skills. Producers must find and hire, within budget, the best director and crew for the production. Directors must make choices that affect the look and feel of the production.

Leadership skills. Directors instruct actors and help them portray their characters in a believable manner. They also supervise the crew, which is responsible for behind-the-scenes work.

Pay

The median annual wage for producers and directors was $85,320 in May 2022. The median wage is the wage at which half the workers in an occupation earned more than that amount and half earned less. The lowest 10 percent earned less than $42,140, and the highest 10 percent earned more than $179,930.

In May 2022, the median annual wages for producers and directors in the top industries in which they worked were as follows:

Motion picture and video industries	$101,030
Media streaming distribution services, social networks, and other media networks and content providers	84,700
Performing arts, spectator sports, and related industries	73,690
Television broadcasting stations	58,780

Some producers and directors earn a percentage of ticket sales. A few of the most successful producers and directors have extraordinarily high earnings, but most do not.

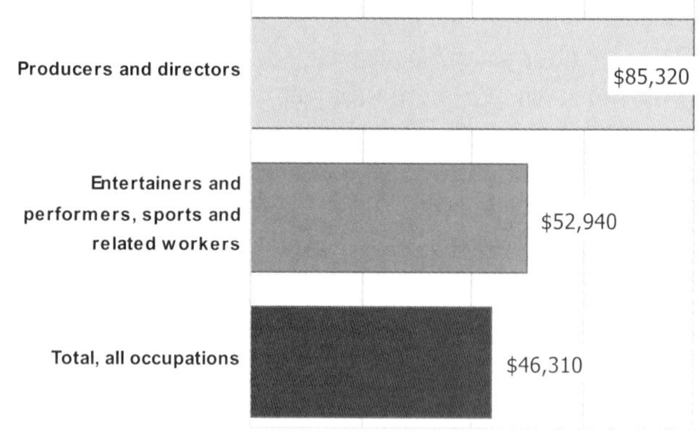

Note: All Occupations includes all occupations in the U.S. Economy.
Source: U.S. Bureau of Labor Statistics, Occupational Employment and Wage Statistics.

Workdays for producers and directors may be long and irregular. Many do not have a standard workweek, because their schedules may change with each assignment or project. Evening, weekend, and holiday work is common. Most producers and directors work full time, and some work more than 40 hours per week.

Job Outlook

Employment of producers and directors is projected to grow 7 percent from 2022 to 2032, faster than the average for all occupations.

About 16,000 openings for producers and directors are projected each year, on average, over the decade. Many of those openings are expected to result from the need to replace workers who transfer to different occupations or exit the labor force, such as to retire.

Employment

The volume of TV shows is expected to grow as the number of online-only platforms, such as streaming services, increases along with the number of shows produced for these platforms. This growth should lead to more opportunities for producers and directors.

Demand for theater producers and directors will depend on funding availability. If there is a steady revenue stream, these workers may be in high demand. However, opportunities for theater producers and directors may be limited in theaters with funding challenges.

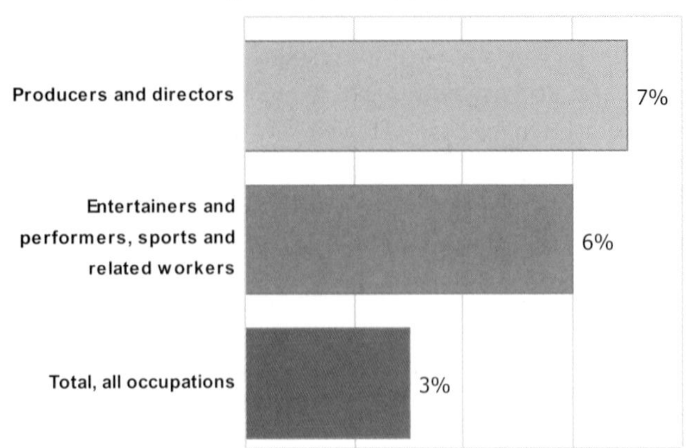

Note: All Occupations includes all occupations in the U.S. Economy.
Source: U.S. Bureau of Labor Statistics, Employment Projections program.

Occupational Title	SOC Code	Employment, 2022	Projected Employment, 2032	Change, 2022-32	
				Percent	Numeric
Producers and directors	27-2012	175,300	187,000	7	11,700

Contacts for More Information

For more information about producers and directors, visit

- Directors Guild of America
- Producers Guild of America
- National Association of Schools of Theatre
- National Endowment for the Arts

Umpires, Referees, and Other Sports Officials

Summary

Quick Facts: Umpires, Referees, and Other Sports Officials	
2022 Median Pay	$36,010 per year
Typical Entry-Level Education	High school diploma or equivalent
Work Experience in a Related Occupation	None
On-the-job Training	Moderate-term on-the-job training
Number of Jobs, 2022	20,400
Job Outlook, 2022-32	10% (Much faster than average)
Employment Change, 2022-32	2,000

What Umpires, Referees, and Other Sports Officials Do

Umpires, referees, and other sports officials preside over competitive athletic or sporting events to help maintain standards of play.

Work Environment

Part-time, seasonal work is common for umpires, referees, and other sports officials. Schedules may vary, and they often work irregular hours that including evenings, weekends, and holidays. Officials working outdoors are exposed to all types of weather conditions.

Umpires, referees, and other sports officials preside over competitive athletic or sporting events.

How to Become an Umpire, Referee, or Other Sports Official

Requirements for umpires, referees, and other sports officials typically vary by state and local sports association. Although some positions have no formal education requirements, others may require a high school diploma.

Pay

The median annual wage for umpires, referees, and other sports officials was $36,010 in May 2022.

Job Outlook

Employment of umpires, referees, and other sports officials is projected to grow 10 percent from 2022 to 2032, much faster than the average for all occupations.

About 5,000 openings for umpires, referees, and other sports officials are projected each year, on average, over the decade. Many of those openings are expected to result from the need to replace workers who transfer to different occupations or exit the labor force, such as to retire.

What Umpires, Referees, and Other Sports Officials Do

Umpires, referees, and other sports officials preside over competitive athletic or sporting events to help maintain standards of play. They detect infractions and decide penalties according to the rules of the game.

Duties

Umpires, referees, and other sports officials typically do the following:

- Officiate sporting competitions
- Judge performances in sporting competitions to determine a winner
- Inspect sports equipment and observe all participants to ensure safety
- Keep track of event times, starting or stopping play when necessary
- Signal participants and other officials when infractions occur or to regulate play or competition
- Settle claims of infractions or complaints by participants
- Enforce the rules of the game and assess penalties when necessary

Umpires, referees, and other sports officials regulate play by signaling participants and other officials.

While officiating at sporting competitions, umpires, referees, and other sports officials must anticipate play and position themselves where they can best see the action, assess the situation, and identify any violations of the rules.

Sports officials typically rely on their judgment to make split-second rulings on infractions and penalties. Officials in some sports may use video replay to help make the correct call.

Some sports officials, such as boxing referees, may work independently. Others, such as baseball or softball umpires, work in groups. Each official working in a group may have different responsibilities. For example, in baseball, one umpire is responsible for signaling balls and strikes while others are responsible for signaling fair and foul balls out in the field.

Work Environment

Umpires, referees, and other sports officials held about 20,400 jobs in 2022. The largest employers of umpires, referees, and other sports officials were as follows:

Umpires, referees and other sports officials work indoors and out, in all types of weather.

Self-employed workers	34%
Amusement, gambling, and recreation industries	17
Performing arts, spectator sports, and related industries	16
Educational services; state, local, and private	7
Civic and social organizations	3

Umpires, referees, and other sports officials work indoors and outdoors. Those working outdoors will be exposed to all types of weather conditions. Some officials travel by bus to sporting events. Others, especially officials in professional sports, may travel by air.

Some sports require officials to stand, squat, walk, or run for extended periods.

Regardless of the sport, the job is stressful because officials often must make split-second rulings. These rulings may result in strong disagreement from coaches, players, and spectators.

Work Schedules

Seasonal work is common for umpires, referees, and other sports officials. Schedules may vary, and they often work irregular hours that include evenings, weekends, and holidays.

Many umpires, referees, and other sports officials are employed primarily in other occupations and supplement their income by officiating part time.

How to Become an Umpire, Referee, or Other Sports Official

Requirements for umpires, referees, and other sports officials typically vary by state and local sports association. Although some positions have no formal education requirements, others may require a high school diploma. Officiating sports requires extensive knowledge of the rules of the game.

Education

Umpires, referees, and other sports officials typically need a high school diploma, although requirements may vary. Each state and sport association has its own education requirements for umpires, referees, and other sports officials. Some do not require formal education, while others may require umpires, referees, and sports officials to have a high school diploma.

Some sports, such as baseball, have their own professional training schools that prepare aspiring umpires and officials for a career at the minor and major league levels.

For more information on educational requirements, refer to the specific state athletic or activity association.

Training

To attain competency in the occupation, umpires, referees, and other sports officials typically need up to 1 year of on-the-job training. This training may include informational sessions covering topics such as positioning, signaling, and other responsibilities or shadowing an experienced official to help manage competitions.

Education and training requirements for umpires, referees, and other sports officials vary by the level and type of sport.

Umpires, referees, and other sports officials may be required to attend training camps, classes, and seminars before, during, and after the season. These sessions allow officials to learn about rule updates, review and evaluate their own performances, and improve their officiating.

Licenses, Certifications, and Registrations

Credentialing requirements vary by competition level. For example, to officiate high school athletic events, umpires, referees, and other officials must typically register with the state or local agency that oversees high school athletics. They also typically need to pass an exam on the rules of the particular sport. Some states and associations require applicants to attend umpiring or refereeing classes before taking the exam or joining the association. Other associations require officials to attend annual training workshops before renewing their officiating credential.

For more information, visit your state's athletic association website or the National Association of Sports Officials.

Advancement

Most new umpires, referees, and other sports officials begin by officiating youth sports. After a few years, they may advance to the high school level. Those who wish to advance to the collegiate level must typically officiate at the high school level for many years.

Some umpires, referees, and other officials may advance through the high school and collegiate levels to reach the professional level. Advancement may continue within the professional ranks. For example, baseball umpires begin their professional careers officiating in the minor leagues and typically need 7 to 10 years of experience there before advancing on to the major leagues.

Standards for umpires and other officials become more stringent as the level of competition increases.

Other Experience

Umpires, referees, and other sports officials must have an extensive knowledge of the rules of the sport they are officiating.

Some officials may have gained much of their knowledge through years of playing the sport at some level. However, playing experience is not a requirement for becoming an umpire, referee, or other sports official.

Important Qualities

Communication skills. Umpires, referees, and other sports officials must have good communication skills because they inform athletes on a sport's rules, discuss infractions, and settle disputes.

Decision-making skills. Umpires, referees, and other sports officials must observe play, assess situations, and make split-second rulings.

Good vision. Umpires, referees, and other sports officials must have good vision to identify violations during play. In some sports, such as diving or gymnastics, sports officials also must be able to observe an athlete's form for imperfections.

Physical stamina. Many umpires, referees, and other sports officials are required to run, squat, stand, or walk for long periods during competitions.

Teamwork. Because umpires, referees, and other sports officials may work in groups to officiate a game, they must be able to cooperate and come to a mutual decision.

Pay

The median annual wage for umpires, referees, and other sports officials was $36,010 in May 2022. The median wage is the wage at which half the workers in an occupation earned more than that amount and half earned less. The lowest 10 percent earned less than $22,090, and the highest 10 percent earned more than $69,010.

In May 2022, the median annual wages for umpires, referees, and other sports officials in the top industries in which they worked were as follows:

Performing arts, spectator sports, and related industries	$44,500
Educational services; state, local, and private	32,990
Amusement, gambling, and recreation industries	32,830
Civic and social organizations	27,250

Most umpires, referees, and other sports officials are paid on a per-game basis. Pay typically rises as the level of competition increases.

Seasonal work is common for umpires, referees, and other sports officials. Schedules may vary and often include evenings, weekends, and holidays.

Many umpires, referees, and other sports officials are employed primarily in other occupations and supplement their income by officiating part time.

Job Outlook

Employment of umpires, referees, and other sports officials is projected to grow 10 percent from 2022 to 2032, much faster than the average for all occupations.

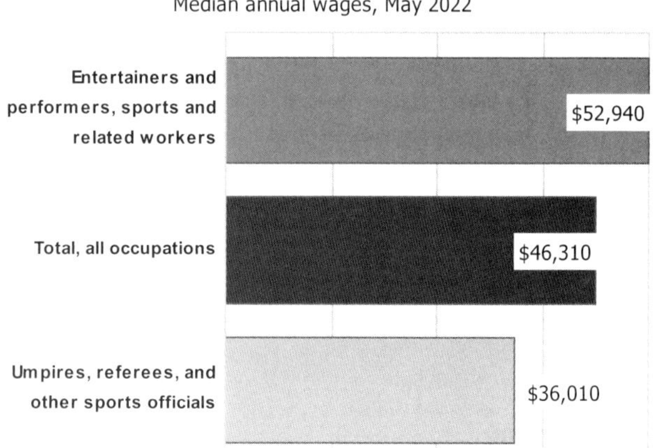

Note: All Occupations includes all occupations in the U.S. Economy. Source: U.S. Bureau of Labor Statistics, Occupational Employment and Wage Statistics.

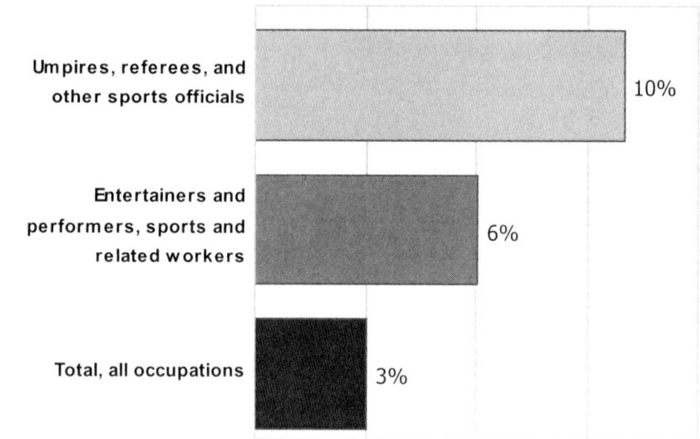

Note: All Occupations includes all occupations in the U.S. Economy. Source: U.S. Bureau of Labor Statistics, Employment Projections program.

About 5,000 openings for umpires, referees, and other sports officials are projected each year, on average, over the decade. Many of those openings are expected to result from the need to replace workers who transfer to different occupations or exit the labor force, such as to retire.

Employment

The demand for umpires, referees, and other sports officials may increase with a growing interest in college sports, professional sports, and sports recreation and with more athletes participating in sports. While funding for school athletic programs may be cut when budgets become tight, the popularity of interscholastic sports sometimes enables shortfalls to be offset with assistance from fundraisers, booster clubs, and parents.

Occupational Title	SOC Code	Employment, 2022	Projected Employment, 2032	Change, 2022-32	
				Percent	Numeric
Umpires, referees, and other sports officials	27-2023	20,400	22,400	10	2,000

Contacts for More Information

For more information about umpires, referees, and other sports officials, visit

- National Association of Sports Officials (NASO)
- National Federation of State High School Associations (NFHS)

For more information on umpires, referees, and other sports officials, refer to the organization that represents the sport and the locality.

Farming, Fishing, and Forestry

Agricultural Workers

Summary

Quick Facts: Agricultural Workers	
2022 Median Pay	$33,290 per year $16.01 per hour
Typical Entry-Level Education	See How to Become One
Work Experience in a Related Occupation	None
On-the-job Training	See How to Become One
Number of Jobs, 2022	804,600
Job Outlook, 2022-32	-2% (Decline)
Employment Change, 2022-32	-16,000

What Agricultural Workers Do
Agricultural workers maintain crops and tend livestock.

Work Environment
Agricultural workers usually do their tasks outdoors in all kinds of weather. Most work full time, and some work more than 40 hours per week.

How to Become an Agricultural Worker
Most agricultural workers do not need a formal educational credential to enter these occupations; however, animal breeders typically need a high school diploma. Agricultural workers typically receive on-the-job training.

Pay
The median annual wage for agricultural workers was $33,290 in May 2022.

Job Outlook
Overall employment of agricultural workers is projected to decline 2 percent from 2022 to 2032.

Despite declining employment, about 115,700 openings for agricultural workers are projected each year, on average, over the decade. All of those openings are expected to result from the need to replace workers who transfer to other occupations or exit the labor force, such as to retire.

What Agricultural Workers Do
Agricultural workers maintain crops and tend livestock. They perform physical labor and operate machinery under the supervision of farmers, ranchers, and other agricultural managers.

Duties
Agricultural workers typically do the following:

- Plant, inspect, and harvest crops
- Irrigate farm soil and maintain ditches or pipes and pumps
- Operate and service farm machinery and tools
- Apply fertilizer or pesticide solutions to control insects, fungi, and weeds
- Move plants, shrubs, and trees with wheelbarrows or tractors
- Feed livestock and clean and disinfect their cages, pens, and yards
- Examine animals to detect symptoms of illnesses or injuries and administer vaccines to protect animals from diseases
- Use brands, tags, or tattoos to mark livestock ownership and grade
- Herd livestock to pastures for grazing or to scales, trucks, or other enclosures

The following are examples of types of agricultural workers:

Agricultural workers maintain crops and tend to livestock.

Agricultural workers operate farm machinery.

Agricultural equipment operators use a variety of farm equipment to plow and sow seeds, as well as to maintain and harvest crops. They may use machines such as tractors, balers, conveyor belts, fertilizer spreaders, and threshers. Workers also may adjust and make minor repairs to the machines and equipment.

Animal breeders select animals that will mate and produce offspring with desired traits and characteristics. For example, they breed chickens that lay more eggs, pigs that produce leaner meat, and sheep with more desirable wool. Others breed and raise cats, dogs, and other household pets.

To know which animals to breed and when to breed them, animal breeders keep detailed records. Breeders note an animal's health, size, and weight, as well as the amount and quality of its product or byproduct. Animal breeders also track the traits of animals' offspring.

Some animal breeders consult with farmers, ranchers, and other agricultural managers about their livestock.

Crop, nursery, and greenhouse farmworkers and laborers perform numerous tasks related to growing and harvesting grains, fruits, vegetables, nuts, and other crops. They plant, seed, prune, irrigate, and harvest crops, and pack and load them for shipment.

Farmworkers also apply fertilizers, herbicides, and pesticides to crops. They repair fences and some farm equipment.

Nursery and greenhouse workers prepare land or greenhouse beds for growing horticultural products, such as trees, plants, flowers, and sod. They also plant, water, prune, weed, and spray the plants. They may cut, roll, and stack sod; stake trees; tie, wrap, and pack plants to fill orders; and dig up or move field-grown shrubs and trees.

Farm and ranch animal farmworkers care for live animals, including cattle, sheep, pigs, goats, horses, poultry, finfish, shellfish, and bees. These animals usually are raised to supply meat, skins, feathers, eggs, milk, or honey.

Farmworkers may feed, herd, brand, weigh, and load animals. They also keep records on animals; examine animals to detect diseases and injuries; and administer medications, vaccinations, or insecticides.

Many workers clean and maintain animal housing areas every day. On dairy farms, animal farmworkers operate milking machines.

Work Environment

Agricultural workers held about 804,600 jobs in 2022. Employment in the detailed occupations that make up agricultural workers was distributed as follows:

Farmworkers and laborers, crop, nursery, and greenhouse	523,500
Farmworkers, farm, ranch, and aquacultural animals	199,400
Agricultural equipment operators	64,000
Agricultural workers, all other	11,200
Animal breeders	6,500

Many agricultural workers have seasonal work schedules.

The largest employers of agricultural workers were as follows:

Industry	Percent
Crop production	54%
Animal production and aquaculture	24
Wholesale trade	5
Support activities for agriculture and forestry	3

Agricultural workers usually do their tasks outdoors in all kinds of weather.

Agricultural workers' jobs may be difficult. To harvest fruits and vegetables by hand, workers frequently bend and crouch. They also lift and carry crops and tools that may be heavy.

Injuries and Illnesses

Agricultural work may be dangerous. Although agricultural workers may be exposed to pesticides applied on crops or plants, the risk is minimized if workers follow safety procedures. Tractors and other farm machinery may cause serious injuries, so workers must stay alert. Additionally, agricultural workers who deal directly with animals risk being bitten, kicked, or stung.

Work Schedules

Most work full time, and some work more than 40 hours per week. Because living crops and animals need constant care, workers' schedules may vary to include early mornings, weekends, and holidays.

Many agricultural workers have seasonal schedules. Seasonal schedules typically include longer periods of work during planting or harvesting or when animals must be sheltered and fed.

Some agricultural workers, called *migrant farmworkers*, move from location to location as crops ripen. Their unsettled lifestyles and periods of unemployment between jobs may cause stress.

How to Become an Agricultural Worker

Most agricultural workers do not need a formal educational credential to enter these occupations; however, animal breeders typically need at least a high school diploma. Agricultural workers typically receive on-the-job training.

Education

Agricultural workers typically need no formal educational credential. However, animal breeders typically need a high school diploma, and some jobs require postsecondary education.

Training

Many agricultural workers receive short-term on-the-job training of up to 1 month. Employers instruct them on how to use simple farming tools and complex machinery while following safety procedures. Agricultural equipment operators may need more extensive training before being allowed to operate expensive farming equipment.

Licenses, Certifications, and Registrations

Some agricultural workers, especially those who operate equipment, need a valid driver's license. Agricultural workers who handle pesticides might need a pesticide applicator license. And in a few states, certain types of animal breeders must be licensed. Check with your state licensing boards for more information.

Agricultural workers typically receive on-the-job training once they are hired.

Important Qualities

Dexterity. Agricultural workers need excellent hand-eye coordination to harvest crops and operate farm machinery.

Listening skills. Agricultural workers must listen carefully to ensure that they understand instructions from farmers and other agricultural managers and supervisors.

Mechanical skills. Agricultural workers must be able to operate complex farm machinery. They also occasionally do routine maintenance on the equipment.

Physical stamina. Agricultural workers must have physical endurance because they do laborious tasks repeatedly.

Physical strength. Agricultural workers must be strong enough to lift heavy objects, including tools and crops.

Other Experience

Animal breeders sometimes need work experience interacting with livestock. Ranch workers may transition into animal breeding after they become more familiar with animals and learn how to handle them.

Some agricultural equipment operators might need work experience on a farm or operating heavy equipment.

Advancement

Agricultural workers may advance to crew leader or other supervisory positions. The ability to speak both English and Spanish is helpful for agricultural supervisors.

Some agricultural workers aspire to become farmers, ranchers, or agricultural managers or to own their own farms and ranches. Knowledge of produce and livestock may provide an excellent background for becoming buyers or purchasing agents of farm products. Those who earn a college degree in agricultural science could become agricultural or food scientists.

Pay

The median annual wage for agricultural workers was $33,290 in May 2022. The median wage is the wage at which half the workers in an occupation earned more than that amount and half earned less. The lowest 10 percent earned less than $28,450, and the highest 10 percent earned more than $45,200.

Median annual wages for agricultural workers in May 2022 were as follows:

Animal breeders	$45,320
Agricultural equipment operators	37,780
Agricultural workers, all other	35,720
Farmworkers, farm, ranch, and aquacultural animals	34,150
Farmworkers and laborers, crop, nursery, and greenhouse	33,000

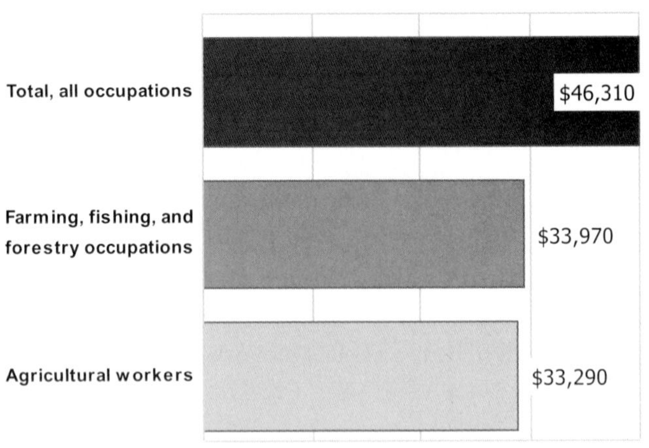

Note: All Occupations includes all occupations in the U.S. Economy.
Source: U.S. Bureau of Labor Statistics, Occupational Employment and Wage Statistics.

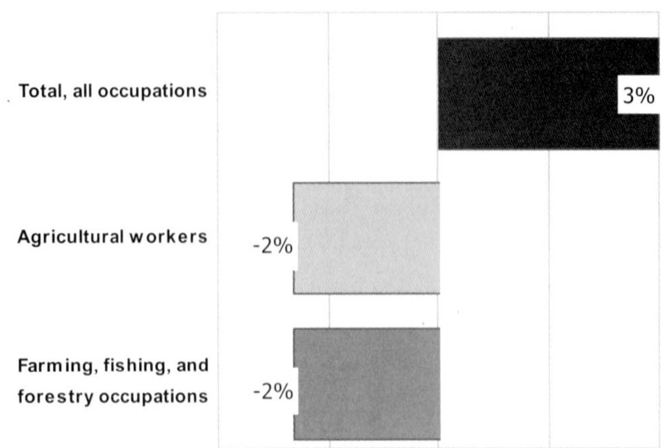

Note: All Occupations includes all occupations in the U.S. Economy.
Source: U.S. Bureau of Labor Statistics, Employment Projections program.

In May 2022, the median annual wages for agricultural workers in the top industries in which they worked were as follows:

Wholesale trade.. $34,840

Most work full time, and some work more than 40 hours per week. Because living plants and animals need constant care, workers' schedules may vary to include early mornings, weekends, and holidays.

Many agricultural workers have seasonal work schedules. Seasonal schedules typically include longer periods of work during planting or harvesting or when animals must be sheltered and fed.

Some agricultural workers, called *migrant farmworkers*, move from location to location as crops ripen. Their unsettled lifestyles and periods of unemployment between jobs can cause stress.

Job Outlook

Overall employment of agricultural workers is projected to decline 2 percent from 2022 to 2032.

Despite declining employment, about 115,700 openings for agricultural workers are projected each year, on average, over the decade. All of those openings are expected to result from the need to replace workers who transfer to other occupations or exit the labor force, such as to retire.

Employment

Projected employment of agricultural workers varies by occupation (see table). Despite increased demand for crops and other agricultural products, demand for some types of farmworkers and agricultural workers is expected to be limited as agricultural establishments continue to use technologies that increase farmworkers' productivity.

Employment of agricultural equipment operators is projected to grow much faster than the average for all occupations and faster than any other type of agricultural worker over the projections decade. Increased use of mechanization on farms is expected to lead to more jobs for agricultural equipment operators relative to farmworkers and laborers.

Small farms that sell their products directly to consumers through venues such as farmers' markets might create opportunities for some agricultural workers.

Occupational Title	SOC Code	Employment, 2022	Projected Employment, 2032	Change, 2022-32	
				Percent	Numeric
Agricultural workers	—	804,600	788,700	-2	-16,000
Animal breeders	45-2021	6,500	6,600	2	100
Agricultural equipment operators	45-2091	64,000	69,500	9	5,500
Farmworkers and laborers, crop, nursery, and greenhouse	45-2092	523,500	512,200	-2	-11,300
Farmworkers, farm, ranch, and aquacultural animals	45-2093	199,400	188,900	-5	-10,500
Agricultural workers, all other	45-2099	11,200	11,400	2	200

Contacts for More Information

For more information about agricultural workers, visit

- Association of Farmworker Opportunity Programs

For more information about careers in agriculture, visit

- AgExplorer, National FFA Organization
- New Farmers, U.S. Department of Agriculture

Fishing and Hunting Workers

Summary

Quick Facts: Fishing and Hunting Workers	
2022 Median Pay	
Typical Entry-Level Education	No formal educational credential
Work Experience in a Related Occupation	None
On-the-job Training	Moderate-term on-the-job training
Number of Jobs, 2022	27,300
Job Outlook, 2022-32	0% (Little or no change)
Employment Change, 2022-32	-100

What Fishing and Hunting Workers Do

Fishing and hunting workers catch and trap various types of animal life.

Work Environment

The work environment for fishing and hunting operations varies with the region, body of water or land, and kinds of animals sought. Fishing and hunting workers often work under hazardous conditions that can lead to injuries or fatalities.

How to Become a Fishing or Hunting Worker

Fishing and hunting workers usually learn on the job. No formal education is required.

Pay

Wage data reported for this occupation were updated most recently in May 2017.

The median annual wage for fishing and hunting workers was $28,530 in May 2017.

Job Outlook

Employment of fishing and hunting workers is projected to show little or no change from 2022 to 2032.

Despite limited employment growth, about 3,500 openings for fishing and hunting workers are projected each year, on average, over the decade. Most of those openings are expected to result from the need to replace workers who transfer to different occupations or exit the labor force, such as to retire.

What Fishing and Hunting Workers Do

Fishing and hunting workers catch and trap various types of animal life. The fish and wild animals they catch are for human food, animal feed, bait, and other uses.

Duties

Fishers and related fishing workers typically do the following:

- Locate fish with the use of fish-finding equipment
- Steer vessels and operate navigational instruments
- Maintain engines, fishing gear, and other onboard equipment by making minor repairs
- Sort, pack, and store the catch in holds with ice and other freezing methods
- Measure fish to ensure that they are of legal size
- Return undesirable or illegal catches to the water
- Guide nets, traps, and lines onto vessels by hand or with hoisting equipment
- Signal other workers to move, hoist, and position loads of the catch

Hunters and trappers typically do the following:

- Locate wild animals with the use of animal-finding equipment
- Catch wild animals with weapons, such as rifles or bows, or with traps, such as snares

Fishers use nets to catch fish.

The fish and wild animals that fishers and hunting workers catch and trap are used for food, bait, and other purposes.

- Sort, pack, and store the catch with ice and other freezing methods
- Follow hunting regulations, which vary by state and always include a safety component
- Sell what they catch for food and decorative purposes

Fishers and related fishing workers work in deep or shallow water. In deep water, they typically perform their duties on large fishing boats that are equipped for long stays at sea. Some process the catch on board and prepare the fish for sale.

Other fishers work in shallow water on small boats that often have a crew of only one or two. They might put nets across the mouths of rivers or inlets; use pots and traps to catch fish or shellfish, such as lobsters and crabs; or use dredges to gather other shellfish, such as oysters and scallops.

Some fishers harvest marine vegetation rather than fish. They use rakes and hoes to gather Irish moss and kelp.

The following are types of fishers and related fishing workers:

- *Fishing boat captains* plan and oversee the fishing operation including the species of fish to be caught, the location of the best fishing grounds, the method of capture, trip length, and sale of the catch. They also supervise the crew and record daily activities in the ship's log.To plot a ship's course, fishing boat captains use electronic navigational equipment, including Global Positioning System (GPS) instruments. They also use radar and sonar to avoid obstacles above and below the water and to find fish.
- *Fishing deckhands* perform the everyday tasks of baiting; setting lines or traps; hauling in and sorting the catch; and maintaining the boat and fishing gear. Deckhands also secure and remove mooring lines when docking or undocking the boat.

Fishers work in commercial fishing, which does not include recreational fishing. For more information on workers on boats that handle fishing charters, see the profile on water transportation workers.

Aquaculture—raising and harvesting fish and other aquatic life under controlled conditions in ponds or confined bodies of water—is a different field. For more information, see the profile on farmers, ranchers, and other agricultural managers.

Hunters and trappers locate wild animals with GPS instruments, compasses, charts, and whistles. They then catch or kill them with traps or weapons. Hunters and trappers sell the wild animals they catch, for either food, fur, or decorative purposes.

Work Environment

Fishing and hunting workers held about 27,300 jobs in 2022. The largest employers of fishing and hunting workers were as follows:

Fishing, hunting and trapping	61%
Self-employed workers	36

Fishing and hunting workers work under various environmental conditions, depending on the region, body of water, and the kind of species sought.

Fishing and hunting operations are conducted under various environmental conditions, depending on the geographic region, body of water or land, and kinds of animals sought. Storms, fog, and wind may hamper fishing vessels or cause them to suspend fishing operations and return to port.

Although fishing gear has improved and operations have become more mechanized, netting and processing fish are nonetheless strenuous activities. Newer vessels have improved living quarters and amenities, but crews still experience the aggravations of confined quarters and the absence of family.

Injuries and Illnesses

Commercial fishing and hunting can be dangerous and can lead to workplace injuries or fatalities. Fishing and hunting workers often work under hazardous conditions. Transportation to a hospital or doctor is often not readily available for these workers because they can be out at sea or in a remote area.

And although fatalities are uncommon, fishing and hunting workers experience one of the highest rates of occupational fatalities of all occupations.

Most fatalities that happen to fishers and related fishing workers are from drowning. The crew must guard against the danger of injury from malfunctioning fishing gear, entanglement in fishing nets and gear, slippery decks, ice formation, or large waves washing over the deck. Malfunctioning navigation and communication equipment and other factors may lead to collisions, shipwrecks, or other dangerous situations, such as vessels becoming caught in storms.

Hunting accidents can occur because of the weapons and traps these workers use. Hunters and trappers minimize injury by wearing the appropriate gear and following detailed safety procedures. Specific safety guidelines vary by state.

Work Schedules

Fishing and hunting workers often endure long shifts and irregular work schedules. Commercial fishing trips may require workers to be away from their home port for several weeks or months.

Many fishers are seasonal workers, and those jobs are usually filled by students and by people from other occupations who are available for seasonal work, such as teachers. For example, employment of fishers in Alaska increases significantly during the summer months, which constitute the salmon season. During these times, fishers can expect to work long hours. Additionally, states may only allow hunters and trappers to hunt or trap during certain times of the year depending on the type of wild animals sought.

How to Become a Fishing or Hunting Worker

Fishing and hunting workers usually learn on the job. A formal educational credential is not required.

Education

A formal educational credential is not required for one to become fishing or hunting worker. However, fishers may improve their chances of getting a job by enrolling in a 2-year vocational–technical program. Some community colleges and universities offer fishery technology and related programs that include courses in seamanship, vessel operations, marine safety, navigation, vessel repair, and fishing gear technology.

Fishers and hunting workers usually acquire their occupational skills on the job.

These programs are typically located near coastal areas and include hands-on experience.

Training

Most fishing and hunting workers learn on the job. They first learn how to sort and clean the animals they catch. Fishers would go on to learn how to operate the boat and fishing equipment.

Other Experience

Many prospective fishers start by finding work through family or friends, or simply by walking around the docks and asking for employment. Aspiring fishers also can look online for employment. Some larger trawlers and processing ships are run by big fishing companies with human resources departments to which new workers can apply. Operators of large commercial fishing vessels must complete a training course approved by the U.S. Coast Guard.

Most hunters and trappers have previous recreational hunting experience.

Licenses, Certifications, and Registrations

Captains of fishing boats and hunters and trappers must be licensed.

Crewmembers on certain fish-processing vessels may need a merchant mariner's document. The U.S. Coast Guard issues these documents, as well as licenses, to people who meet specific health, physical, and academic requirements.

States set licensing requirements for boats operating in state waters, defined as inland waters and waters within 3 miles of the coast.

Fishers need a permit to fish in almost any water. Permits are distributed by states for state waters and by regional fishing councils for federal waters. The permits specify the fishing season, the type and amount of fish that may be caught, and, sometimes, the type of permissible fishing gear.

Hunters and trappers need a state license to hunt in any land or forest. Licenses specify the hunting season, the type and amount of wild animals that may be caught, and the type of weapons or traps that can be used.

Advancement

Experienced, reliable fishing boat deckhands can become boatswains, then second mates, first mates, and, finally, captains. Those who are interested in ship engineering may gain experience with maintaining and repairing ship engines to become licensed chief engineers on large commercial boats. In doing so, they must meet the Coast Guard's licensing requirements as well. For more information, see the profile on water transportation workers.

Almost all captains are self-employed, and most eventually own, or partially own, one or more fishing boats.

Important Qualities

Critical-thinking skills. Fishing and hunting workers must reach conclusions through sound reasoning and judgment. They determine how to improve their catch and must react appropriately to weather conditions.

Detail oriented. Fishing and hunting workers must be precise and accurate when measuring the quality of their catch or prey. They must also pay attention to detail when working with various fishing and hunting gear to guard against injury.

Listening skills. Because they take instructions from captains and other crewmembers or hunters, fishing and hunting workers need to communicate well and listen effectively.

Machine operation skills. Fishing and hunting workers must be able to operate and perform routine maintenance on complex fishing and navigation machinery, as well as weapons and traps.

Physical stamina. Fishing and hunting workers need endurance. They must be able to work long hours, often under strenuous conditions.

Physical strength. Fishing and hunting workers must use physical strength, along with hand dexterity and coordination, to perform difficult tasks repeatedly.

Pay

Wage data reported for this occupation were updated most recently in May 2017.

The median annual wage for fishing and hunting workers was $28,530 in May 2017. The median wage is the wage at which half the workers in an occupation earned more than that amount and half earned less. The lowest 10 percent earned less than $18,710, and the highest 10 percent earned more than $48,170.

Fishers are typically paid a percentage of the boat's overall catch, commonly referred to as a crew share. The more fish that are caught, the greater the crew share becomes. This can lead to unpredictable swings in pay from one season to another, as the overall catch can vary. More experienced crewmembers often receive a greater share compared to entry-level workers.

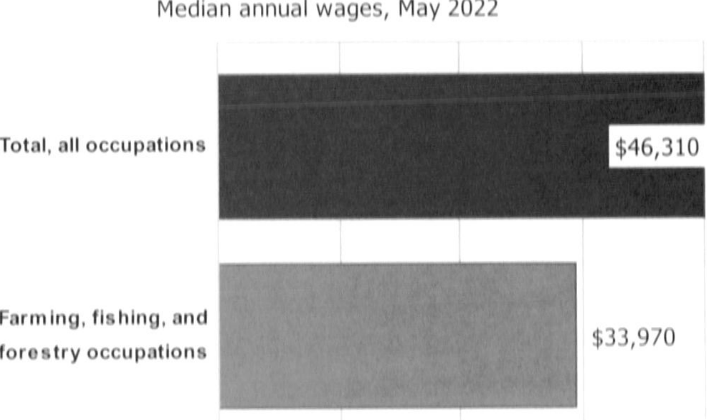

Note: All Occupations includes all occupations in the U.S. Economy.
Source: U.S. Bureau of Labor Statistics, Occupational Employment and Wage Statistics.

Trappers are typically paid per pelt, and the amount received can vary depending on the species and the quality of the fur. For example, trappers typically receive more for coyote pelts than for smaller species, such as muskrats.

Fishing and hunting workers endure strenuous outdoor work and long hours. Commercial fishing trips may require workers to be away from their home port for several weeks or months.

Many fishers are seasonal workers, and those jobs are usually filled by students and by people from other occupations who are available for seasonal work, such as teachers. For example, employment of fishers in Alaska increases significantly during the summer months, which constitute the salmon season. During these times, fishers can expect to work long hours. Additionally, states may only allow hunters and trappers to hunt or trap during certain times of the year.

Job Outlook

Employment of fishing and hunting workers is projected to show little or no change from 2022 to 2032.

Despite limited employment growth, about 3,500 openings for fishing and hunting workers are projected each year, on average, over the decade. Most of those openings are expected to result from the need to replace workers who transfer to different occupations or exit the labor force, such as to retire.

Employment

Employment of fishing and hunting workers depends on the availability of fish stocks and wild animals.

Governmental efforts to reduce overfishing and replenish fish stocks have led to some species being regulated under fishing quotas or catch shares. Quotas dictate how many fish each fisher may catch and keep. These programs may limit demand for fishers over the projections decade.

For hunting workers, an expected decline in recreational hunting will limit demand for guided hunts. Animal pelts will

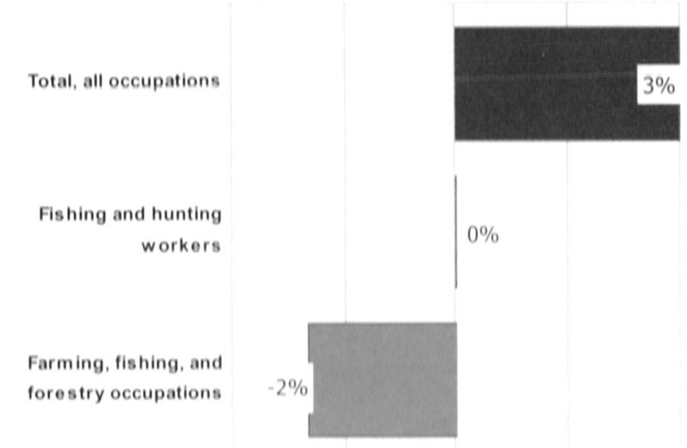

Note: All Occupations includes all occupations in the U.S. Economy.
Source: U.S. Bureau of Labor Statistics, Employment Projections program.

continue to be used to manufacture fur coats, hats, and gloves, which may increase demand for trappers. However, most of the fur used in clothing comes from ranches or farms that breed, maintain, and harvest desirable species, such as mink.

Occupational Title	SOC Code	Employment, 2022	Projected Employment, 2032	Change, 2022-32	
				Percent	Numeric
Fishing and hunting workers	45-3031	27,300	27,200	0	-100

Contacts for More Information

For more information, visit

- National Maritime Center, U.S. Coast Guard Headquarters
- Where to Hunt

Forest and Conservation Workers

Summary

Quick Facts: Forest and Conservation Workers	
2022 Median Pay	$32,270 per year $15.51 per hour
Typical Entry-Level Education	High school diploma or equivalent
Work Experience in a Related Occupation	None
On-the-job Training	Moderate-term on-the-job training
Number of Jobs, 2022	11,300
Job Outlook, 2022-32	-9% (Decline)
Employment Change, 2022-32	-1,000

What Forest and Conservation Workers Do

Forest and conservation workers perform physical labor to improve the quality of natural areas such as forests, rangelands, and wetlands.

Work Environment

Forest and conservation workers often work outdoors, sometimes in remote locations and in all types of weather. Most forest and conservation workers are employed full time, although part-time or seasonal work is common.

Forest and conservation workers measure and improve the quality of forests.

How to Become a Forest and Conservation Worker

Forest and conservation workers typically need a high school diploma to enter the occupation and receive on-the-job training to attain competency.

Pay

The median annual wage for forest and conservation workers was $32,270 in May 2022.

Job Outlook

Employment of forest and conservation workers is projected to decline 9 percent from 2022 to 2032.

Despite declining employment, about 1,800 openings for forest and conservation workers are projected each year, on average, over the decade. All of those openings are expected to result from the need to replace workers who transfer to other occupations or exit the labor force, such as to retire.

What Forest and Conservation Workers Do

Forest and conservation workers improve the quality of forests, rangelands, and wetlands. Under the supervision of conservation scientists and foresters, they develop, maintain, and protect forests.

Duties

Forest and conservation workers typically do the following:

- Plant seedlings to reforest land
- Clear brush and debris from trails, roadsides, and camping areas
- Count and measure trees during tree-measuring efforts
- Select or cut trees according to markings, sizes, types, or grades
- Protect plants from disease by spraying trees or injecting vegetation with insecticides, fungicides, or herbicides
- Identify and remove diseased or undesirable plant life or trees
- Help prevent and suppress forest fires
- Maintain equipment to ensure that it operates properly

Forest and conservation workers count trees during tree-measuring efforts.

Forest and conservation workers do physical tasks to maintain and improve the quality of a forest. They use a variety of equipment, including digging and planting tools to plant seedlings and power saws to cut down diseased trees.

Some work on tree farms or orchards, where their duties include planting and cultivating many kinds of trees. Their duties vary with the type of farm and may include planting seedlings or spraying to control weeds and insects.

Some forest and conservation workers are employed by forest nurseries, where they sort through tree seedlings, discarding the ones that do not meet standards. Others gather woodland products, such as decorative greenery, tree cones, moss, and other wild plant life. Still others tap trees to make syrup or chemicals.

Forest and conservation workers who are employed by or are under contract with government agencies may clear brush and debris from trails, roadsides, and camping areas. They may clean restrooms and other public facilities at recreational sites and campgrounds.

These workers also may help to suppress forest fires. For example, they may construct firebreaks, which are gaps in vegetation that can help slow or stop the progress of a fire. They also sometimes respond to forest emergencies.

Forest and conservation workers are supervised by conservation scientists and foresters, who direct their work and evaluate progress.

Work Environment

Forest and conservation workers held about 11,300 jobs in 2022. The largest employers of forest and conservation workers were as follows:

State government, excluding education and hospitals	26%
Forestry	23
Support activities for agriculture and forestry	10
Self-employed workers	9
Crop production	2

Forest and conservation workers work outdoors, sometimes in remote locations and in all types of weather. Workers may wear personal protective equipment (PPE), such as hardhats, safety glasses, and coveralls.

Their work is often physically demanding. In addition, forest and conservation workers may have to walk long distances through dense woods while carrying heavy equipment.

Injuries and Illnesses

Forest and conservation workers have one of the highest rates of injuries and illnesses of all occupations. The work may be especially dangerous for those whose primary duties involve fire suppression. To protect against injury, forest

Forest and conservation workers work outdoors, sometimes in remote locations and in all types of weather.

and conservation workers must wear PPE and follow safety procedures.

Work Schedules

Most forest and conservation workers are employed full time, although part-time or seasonal work is common. Responding to an emergency may require workers to work additional hours at any time of day.

How to Become a Forest and Conservation Worker

Forest and conservation workers typically need a high school diploma to enter the occupation and receive on-the-job training to attain competency.

Education

Forest and conservation workers typically need a high school diploma to enter the occupation and a valid driver's license before they begin working. Some students take postsecondary courses in forestry and conservation topics, such as forest ecology, wildlife management, or resource conservation.

Training

After they are hired, forest and conservation workers typically get on-the-job training. They help experienced workers with labor-intensive tasks, such as planting or thinning trees. They also learn how to operate and maintain equipment safely.

In addition, some states may require that crews and individuals receive training, and sometimes a license, in the use of commercial pesticides. For more information, consult states' agriculture department.

Advancement

To advance their careers and become forest and conservation technicians or conservation scientists or foresters, forest and conservation workers typically need an associate's or bachelor's degree in forestry, natural resources, or a related field.

Forest and conservation workers typically need a high school diploma before they begin working.

Important Qualities

Communication skills. Forest and conservation workers must convey information to foresters and conservation scientists and other workers.

Decision-making skills. Forest and conservation workers must make judgments and act quickly, especially when conditions are dangerous.

Detail oriented. Forest and conservation workers must observe gauges, dials, and other indicators to ensure that equipment works properly. They also must be precise in following safety procedures.

Listening skills. Forest and conservation workers must understand the instructions they receive before performing tasks.

Physical stamina. Forest and conservation workers perform a variety of strenuous tasks. They also must be able to walk long distances through dense woods, often while carrying heavy equipment.

Pay

The median annual wage for forest and conservation workers was $32,270 in May 2022. The median wage is the wage at which half the workers in an occupation earned more than that amount and half earned less. The lowest 10 percent earned less than $26,690, and the highest 10 percent earned more than $48,270.

In May 2022, the median annual wages for forest and conservation workers in the top industries in which they worked were as follows:

State government, excluding education and hospitals	$31,200

Most forest and conservation workers are employed full time, although part-time or seasonal work is common. Responding to an emergency may require workers to work additional hours at any time of day.

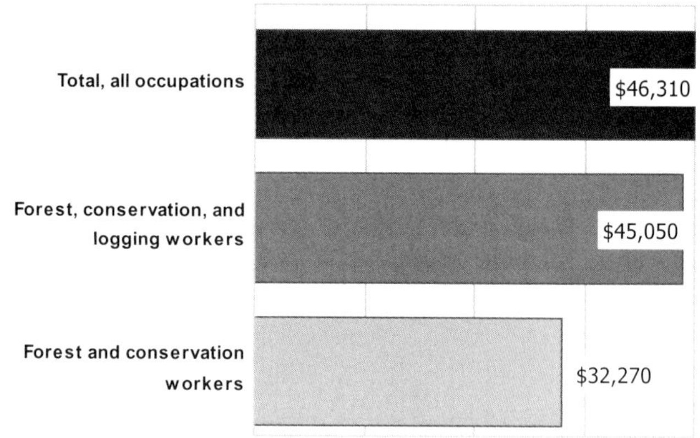

Note: All Occupations includes all occupations in the U.S. Economy.
Source: U.S. Bureau of Labor Statistics, Occupational Employment and Wage Statistics.

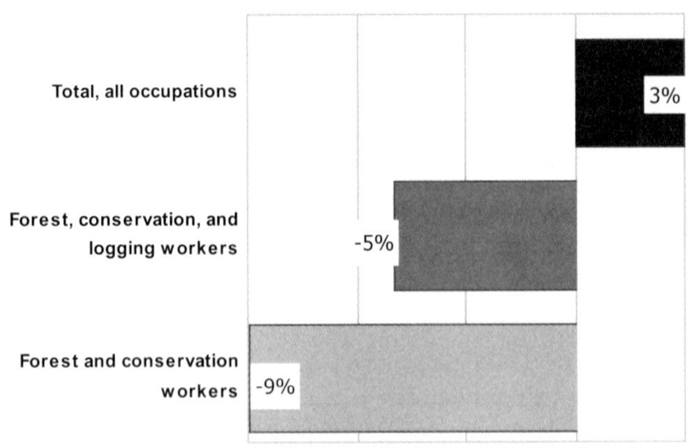

Note: All Occupations includes all occupations in the U.S. Economy.
Source: U.S. Bureau of Labor Statistics, Employment Projections program.

Job Outlook

Employment of forest and conservation workers is projected to decline 9 percent from 2022 to 2032.

Despite declining employment, about 1,800 openings for forest and conservation workers are projected each year, on average, over the decade. All of those openings are expected to result from the need to replace workers who transfer to other occupations or exit the labor force, such as to retire.

Employment

Automation of forest and conservation workers' tasks is expected to reduce employment demand over the projections decade.

Despite heightened demand for U.S. timber and wood pellets, improved technology will lessen the need for forest and conservation workers to do certain tasks. For example, remote sensing allows fewer workers to count and identify trees. As automation of manual forestry tasks continues, fewer of these workers will be needed to do the same amount of work.

However, a rise in the number of wildfires may create some demand for the fire suppression activities of forest and conservation workers, especially in state-owned forest lands. As more people continue to build homes in western forests, there will be a need for workers to protect those areas from fires.

Occupational Title	SOC Code	Employment, 2022	Projected Employment, 2032	Change, 2022-32	
				Percent	Numeric
Forest and conservation workers	45-4011	11,300	10,300	-9	-1,000

Contacts for More Information

For information, visit

- Society of American Foresters (SAF)
- Student Conservation Association (SCA)
- The Wildlife Society (TWS)
- Forest Stewards Guild
- National Association of State Departments of Agriculture
- Society for Range Management (SRM)
- U.S. Forest Service

Logging Workers

Summary

Quick Facts: Logging Workers

2022 Median Pay	$46,580 per year $22.40 per hour
Typical Entry-Level Education	High school diploma or equivalent
Work Experience in a Related Occupation	None
On-the-job Training	Moderate-term on-the-job training
Number of Jobs, 2022	52,300
Job Outlook, 2022-32	-5% (Decline)
Employment Change, 2022-32	-2,400

What Logging Workers Do

Logging workers harvest forests to provide the raw material for many consumer goods and industrial products.

Work Environment

Logging is physically demanding and can be dangerous. Workers spend all their time outdoors, sometimes in poor weather and often in isolated areas.

How to Become a Logging Worker

Most logging workers have a high school diploma. They get on-the-job training to become familiar with forest environments and to learn how to operate logging machinery.

Pay

The median annual wage for logging workers was $46,580 in May 2022.

Job Outlook

Overall employment of logging workers is projected to decline 5 percent from 2022 to 2032.

Logging workers harvest thousands of acres of forests each year.

Despite declining employment, about 7,100 openings for logging workers are projected each year, on average, over the decade. All of those openings are expected to result from the need to replace workers who transfer to other occupations or exit the labor force, such as to retire.

What Logging Workers Do

Logging workers harvest thousands of acres of forests each year. The timber they harvest provides the raw material for countless consumer and industrial products.

Duties

Logging workers typically do the following:

- Cut down trees
- Fasten cables around logs to be dragged by tractors
- Operate machinery that drag logs to the landing or deck area
- Separate logs by species and type of wood and load them onto trucks

Loggers cut trees with hand-held power chain saws or mobile felling machines.

- Drive and maneuver feller–buncher tree harvesters to shear trees and cut logs into desired lengths
- Grade logs according to characteristics such as knot size and straightness
- Inspect equipment for safety, and perform necessary basic maintenance tasks, before using the equipment

The cutting and logging of timber is done by a logging crew. The following are examples of types of logging workers:

Fallers cut down trees with hand-held power chain saws.

Buckers work alongside fallers, trimming the tops and branches of felled trees and bucking (cutting) the logs into specific lengths.

Tree climbers use special equipment to scale tall trees and remove their limbs. They carry heavy tools and safety gear as they climb the trees, and are kept safe by a harness attached to a rope.

Choke setters fasten steel cables or chains, known as chokers, around logs to be skidded (dragged) by tractors or forwarded by the cable-yarding system to the landing or deck area, where the logs are separated by species and type of product.

Rigging slingers and chasers set up and dismantle the cables and guy wires of the yarding system.

Log sorters, markers, movers, and chippers sort, mark, and move logs on the basis of their species, size, and ownership. They also tend machines that chip up logs.

Logging equipment operators use tree harvesters to fell trees, shear off tree limbs, and cut trees into desired lengths. They drive tractors and operate self-propelled machines called skidders or forwarders, which drag or otherwise transport logs to a loading area.

Log graders and scalers inspect logs for defects and measure the logs to determine their volume. They estimate the value of logs or pulpwood. These workers often use hand-held data collection devices into which they enter data about trees.

A logging crew might consist of the following members:

- one or two tree fallers or one or two logging equipment operators with a tree harvester to cut down trees
- one bucker to cut logs
- two choke setters with tractors to drag felled trees to the loading deck
- one logging equipment operator to delimb, cut logs to length, and load the logs onto trucks

Work Environment

Logging workers held about 52,300 jobs in 2022. Employment in the detailed occupations that make up logging workers was distributed as follows:

Logging equipment operators	35,300
Fallers	6,500
Log graders and scalers	5,600
Logging workers, all other	4,900

Workers spend their time outdoors, sometimes in poor weather and often in isolated areas.

The largest employers of logging workers were as follows:

Logging	46%
Self-employed workers	28
Sawmills and wood preservation	11
Landscaping services	6
Forestry	3

Logging is physically demanding and can be dangerous. Workers spend all their time outdoors, sometimes in poor weather and often in isolated areas. The increased use of enclosed machines has decreased some of the discomforts caused by bad weather and has generally made logging much safer.

Most logging work involves lifting, climbing, and other strenuous activities, although machinery has eliminated some heavy labor. Falling branches, vines, and rough terrain are constant hazards, as are dangers associated with felling trees and handling logs.

Chain saws and other power equipment can be dangerous; therefore, workers must be careful and must use proper safety measures and equipment, such as hardhats, safety clothing, hearing protection devices, and boots.

Injuries and Illnesses

Despite the industry's strong emphasis on safety, logging workers sometimes get injured on the job. And although fatalities are uncommon, fallers experience one of the highest rates of occupational fatalities of all occupations. Most fatalities occur through contact with a machine or an object, such as a log.

Work Schedules

Workers sometimes commute long distances between their homes and logging sites. In more densely populated states, commuting distances are shorter. Logging work is often seasonal, and workers can find more employment opportunities during the warmer months because snow and cold weather adversely affect working conditions.

Most logging workers have a high school diploma.

How to Become a Logging Worker

Most logging workers have a high school diploma. They get on-the-job training to become familiar with forest environments and to learn how to operate logging machinery.

Education

A high school diploma is enough for most logging worker jobs. Some vocational or technical schools and community colleges offer associate's degrees or certificates in forest technology. This additional education may help workers get a job. Programs may include field trips to observe or participate in logging activities.

A few community colleges offer education programs for logging equipment operators.

Training

Many states have training programs for loggers. Although specific coursework may vary by state, programs usually include technical instruction or field training in a number of areas, including best management practices, environmental compliance, and reforestation.

Safety training is a vital part of logging workers' instruction. Many state forestry or logging associations provide training sessions for logging equipment operators, whose jobs require more technical skill than other logging positions. Sessions take place in the field, where trainees have the opportunity to practice various logging techniques and use particular equipment.

Logging companies and trade associations offer training programs for workers who operate large, expensive machinery and equipment. These programs often culminate in a state-recognized safety certification from the logging company.

Important Qualities

Communication skills. Logging workers must communicate with other crew members so that they can cut and delimb trees efficiently and safely.

Decision-making skills. Logging workers must make quick, intelligent decisions when hazards arise.

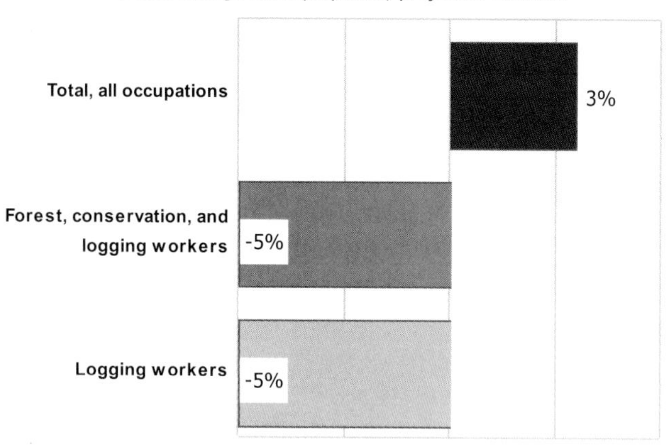

Note: All Occupations includes all occupations in the U.S. Economy.
Source: U.S. Bureau of Labor Statistics, Occupational Employment and Wage Statistics.

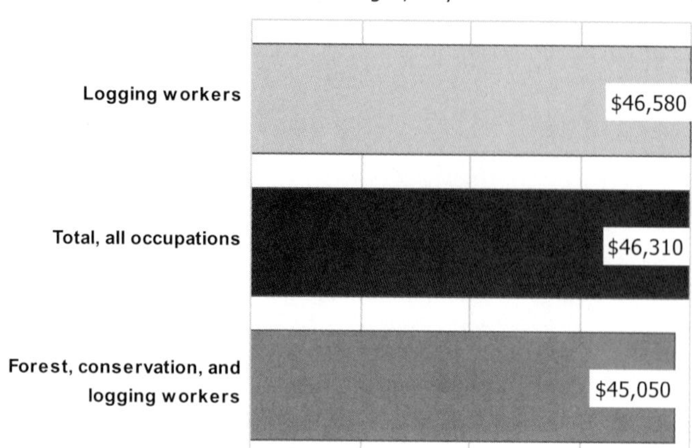

Note: All Occupations includes all occupations in the U.S. Economy.
Source: U.S. Bureau of Labor Statistics, Employment Projections program.

Detail oriented. Logging workers must watch gauges, dials, and other indicators to determine whether their equipment and tools are working properly.

Physical stamina. Logging workers need to be able to perform laborious tasks repeatedly.

Physical strength. Logging workers must be able to handle heavy equipment.

Pay

The median annual wage for logging workers was $46,580 in May 2022. The median wage is the wage at which half the workers in an occupation earned more than that amount and half earned less. The lowest 10 percent earned less than $29,440, and the highest 10 percent earned more than $65,150.

Median annual wages for logging workers in May 2022 were as follows:

Fallers	$49,160
Logging workers, all other	47,110
Logging equipment operators	46,400
Log graders and scalers	42,370

In May 2022, the median annual wages for logging workers in the top industries in which they worked were as follows:

Logging	$47,740
Landscaping services	46,520
Sawmills and wood preservation	38,910

Workers sometimes commute long distances between their homes and logging sites. In more densely populated states, commuting distances are shorter. Logging work is often seasonal, and workers can find more employment opportunities during the warmer months because snow and cold weather adversely affect working conditions.

Job Outlook

Overall employment of logging workers is projected to decline 5 percent from 2022 to 2032.

Despite declining employment, about 7,100 openings for logging workers are projected each year, on average, over the decade. All of those openings are expected to result from the need to replace workers who transfer to other occupations or exit the labor force, such as to retire.

Employment

The mechanization of logging operations and improvements in logging equipment have increased productivity, which is expected to reduce demand for logging workers. However, the need to prevent destructive wildfires by thinning susceptible forests is expected to support some employment.

Occupational Title	SOC Code	Employment, 2022	Projected Employment, 2032	Change, 2022-32	
				Percent	Numeric
Logging workers	45-4020	52,300	49,900	-5	-2,400
Fallers	45-4021	6,500	5,900	-9	-600
Logging equipment operators	45-4022	35,300	34,000	-4	-1,300
Log graders and scalers	45-4023	5,600	5,500	-2	-100
Logging workers, all other	45-4029	4,900	4,600	-7	-300

Contacts for More Information

For information about timber-cutting and logging careers, visit

➤ Forest Resources Association

Food Preparation and Serving

Bartenders

Summary

Quick Facts: Bartenders	
2022 Median Pay	$29,380 per year $14.12 per hour
Typical Entry-Level Education	No formal educational credential
Work Experience in a Related Occupation	None
On-the-job Training	Short-term on-the-job training
Number of Jobs, 2022	641,300
Job Outlook, 2022-32	3% (As fast as average)
Employment Change, 2022-32	21,300

What Bartenders Do

Bartenders mix drinks and serve them directly to customers or through wait staff.

Work Environment

Bartenders work at restaurants, hotels, and other food service and drinking establishments. During busy hours, they are under pressure to serve customers quickly and efficiently. They often work late evenings, on weekends, and on holidays. Part-time work is common, and schedules may vary.

How to Become a Bartender

Bartenders typically do not need formal education credentials to enter the occupation. Most states require workers who serve alcoholic beverages to be at least 18 years old. They typically learn their skills on the job.

Pay

The median hourly wage for bartenders was $14.12 in May 2022.

Job Outlook

Employment of bartenders is projected to grow 3 percent from 2022 to 2032, about as fast as the average for all occupations.

About 113,500 openings for bartenders are projected each year, on average, over the decade. Many of those openings are expected to result from the need to replace workers who transfer to different occupations or exit the labor force, such as to retire.

What Bartenders Do

Bartenders mix drinks and serve them directly to customers or through wait staff.

Duties

Bartenders typically do the following:

- Greet customers, offer menus, and inform them of specials
- Take customers' food and drink orders
- Pour and serve wine, beer, and other drinks
- Mix drinks according to recipes
- Check customers' identification to ensure that they are of legal drinking age
- Clean bars, tables, and work areas
- Collect payment from customers and return change
- Engage with customers
- Manage the operation of the bar and restock liquor and bar supplies
- Monitor the level of intoxication of customers

Bartenders mix drinks and serve them to customers.

Bartenders mix drinks according to recipes.

Bartenders fill drink orders for customers either directly at the bar or through waiters and waitresses serving the dining room. Bartenders must know a wide range of drink recipes and be able to mix drinks quickly. When measuring and pouring beverages, they must avoid spillage or overpouring. They should be personable with customers at the bar and also work well with waiters and waitresses and kitchen staff to ensure prompt service.

In addition to mixing and serving drinks, bartenders stock and prepare beverage garnishes and maintain ice, glasses, and other bar supplies. They also wash glassware and utensils and serve food to customers who eat at the bar. Bartenders usually are responsible for stocking and maintaining an inventory of liquor, mixers, and other bar supplies.

Bartenders may collect payment from customers after each drink is served or open a tab for a customer and collect payment when closing it at the end of service. They also must monitor customers for intoxication, determine when to deny service and, in some cases, arrange for safe transportation.

Work Environment

Bartenders held about 641,300 jobs in 2022. The largest employers of bartenders were as follows:

Restaurants and other eating places	43%
Drinking places (alcoholic beverages)	28
Traveler accommodation	6
Amusement, gambling, and recreation industries	6
Civic and social organizations	5

Bartenders typically work indoors, some work outdoors at pool or beach bars or at catered events.

During busy hours, bartenders are under pressure to serve customers quickly and efficiently while ensuring that no alcohol is served to minors or to overly intoxicated customers.

Bartenders do repetitive tasks, and sometimes they lift heavy kegs of beer and cases of liquor. In addition, the work may be stressful, particularly when they deal with intoxicated customers.

Work Schedules

Bartenders often work late evenings, on weekends, and on holidays. Part-time work is common, and schedules may vary.

How to Become a Bartender

Bartenders typically do not need formal education credentials to enter the occupation, although some employers require or prefer for candidates to have a high school diploma. They typically learn their skills through on-the-job training that lasts a few weeks. Some bartenders gain experience in other jobs or occupations.

Most states require workers who serve alcoholic beverages to be at least 18 years old. Bartenders must be familiar with state and local laws concerning the sale of alcoholic beverages.

Education

Bartenders typically need no formal education to enter the occupation, although employers may prefer or require candidates to have a high school diploma. Some aspiring bartenders acquire their skills by attending a school for bartending or taking courses at a community college. These programs usually include instruction on mixing cocktails, serving customers, and setting up a bar. Some schools help their graduates find jobs.

Training

Bartenders typically receive on-the-job training that lasts a few weeks. Under the guidance of an experienced bartender, trainees learn cocktail recipes, bar-setup procedures, and customer service, including how to handle unruly customers and other challenging situations. In establishments where bartenders serve food, training may cover teamwork and proper food-handling procedures.

Bartenders usually work evenings and weekends.

Bartenders should be friendly, tactful, and attentive when dealing with customers.

Some employers teach bartending skills to new workers by providing self-study programs, which may include videos and instructional booklets, that explain service skills.

License and Certification

Depending on the state and locality, a server, owner, manager, or business may be required to maintain a license to sell alcohol. Most states require that bartenders be at least 18 years old.

Many states and localities require bartenders to complete a responsible-server course. This course typically covers topics such as laws related to the sale of alcoholic beverages, responsible serving practices, and conflict management.

Although optional, professional certification may demonstrate basic knowledge or competency in bartending practices. Certification is available upon successful completion of some courses or programs.

Work Experience in a Related Occupation

Bartenders typically do not need related work experience to enter the occupation. However, some employers prefer or require candidates to have food-service experience in occupations such as waiters and waitresses or food and beverage serving and related workers. Others start as bartender helpers and progress to become bartenders as they learn basic mixing procedures and recipes.

Important Qualities

Communication skills. Bartenders must listen carefully to their customers' orders, explain drink and food items, and make menu recommendations. They also should be able to converse with customers on a variety of subjects.

Customer-service skills. By creating a friendly and welcoming environment, bartenders help to ensure repeat business.

Decision-making skills. Bartenders must observe customers, identify those who are intoxicated or underage, and deny them service.

Multitasking skills. Bartenders must make drinks for and take orders from multiple customers, monitor customers at the bar, and receive payments in a fast, efficient manner.

Physical stamina. Bartenders spend hours walking or standing while preparing drinks and serving customers.

Physical strength. Bartenders should be able to lift and carry cases of liquor, beer, and other bar supplies that may weigh up to 50 pounds.

Pay

The median hourly wage for bartenders was $14.12 in May 2022. The median wage is the wage at which half the workers in an occupation earned more than that amount and half earned less. The lowest 10 percent earned less than $9.18, and the highest 10 percent earned more than $27.51.

In May 2022, the median hourly wages for bartenders in the top industries in which they worked were as follows:

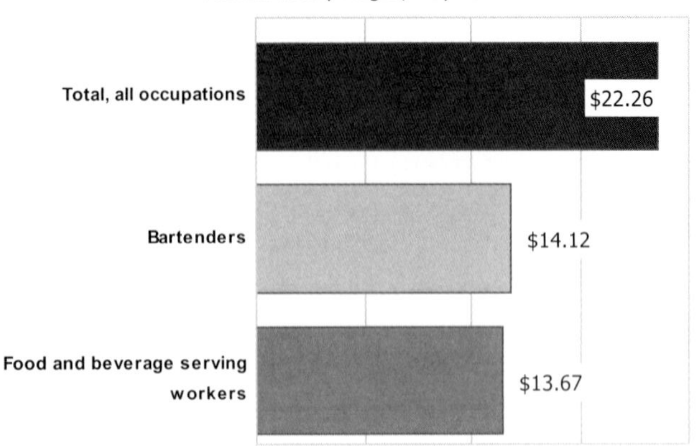

Note: All Occupations includes all occupations in the U.S. Economy.
Source: U.S. Bureau of Labor Statistics, Occupational Employment and Wage Statistics.

Traveler accommodation	$14.73
Restaurants and other eating places	14.61
Drinking places (alcoholic beverages)	13.73
Amusement, gambling, and recreation industries	13.43
Civic and social organizations	11.39

These wage data include tips. Tipped employees earn at least the federal minimum wage, which may be paid as a combination of direct wages and tips, depending on the state. The Wage and Hour Division of the U.S. Department of Labor maintains a website listing minimum wages for tipped employees, by state, although some localities have enacted minimum wages higher than their state requires.

Bartenders often work late evenings, on weekends, and on holidays. Part-time work is common, and schedules may vary.

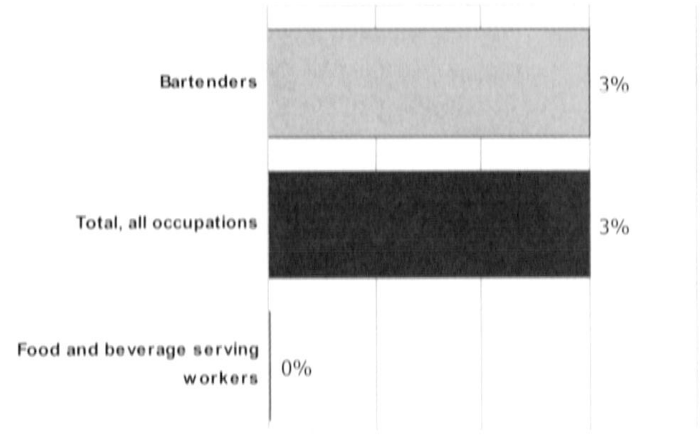

Note: All Occupations includes all occupations in the U.S. Economy.
Source: U.S. Bureau of Labor Statistics, Employment Projections program.

Job Outlook

Employment of bartenders is projected to grow 3 percent from 2022 to 2032, about as fast as the average for all occupations.

About 113,500 openings for bartenders are projected each year, on average, over the decade. Many of those openings are expected to result from the need to replace workers who transfer to different occupations or exit the labor force, such as to retire.

Employment

Population and income growth are expected to result in increased demand for food, drinks, and entertainment. More bartenders will be needed to meet this demand, especially in full-service restaurants and breweries. Bartenders also will be needed in some entertainment venues as services expand.

Occupational Title	SOC Code	Employment, 2022	Projected Employment, 2032	Change, 2022-32	
				Percent	Numeric
Bartenders	35-3011	641,300	662,600	3	21,300

Contacts for More Information

For more information about bartenders, visit

➤ United States Bartenders Guild

Chefs and Head Cooks

Summary

Quick Facts: Chefs and Head Cooks	
2022 Median Pay	$56,520 per year $27.17 per hour
Typical Entry-Level Education	High school diploma or equivalent
Work Experience in a Related Occupation	5 years or more
On-the-job Training	None
Number of Jobs, 2022	174,400
Job Outlook, 2022-32	5% (Faster than average)
Employment Change, 2022-32	9,200

What Chefs and Head Cooks Do

Chefs and head cooks oversee the daily food preparation at restaurants and other places where food is served.

Chefs direct kitchen staff in restaurants.

Work Environment

Chefs and head cooks work in restaurants, hotels, and other food service establishments. They often work early mornings, late evenings, weekends, and holidays. The work can be hectic and fast-paced. Most chefs and head cooks work full time.

How to Become a Chef or Head Cook

Chefs and head cooks typically need a high school diploma and work experience to enter the occupation. Some attend a culinary program at a community college, technical school, culinary arts school, or 4-year college. Others learn through apprenticeship programs.

Pay

The median annual wage for chefs and head cooks was $56,520 in May 2022.

Job Outlook

Employment of chefs and head cooks is projected to grow 5 percent from 2022 to 2032, faster than the average for all occupations.

About 22,000 openings for chefs and head cooks are projected each year, on average, over the decade. Many of those openings are expected to result from the need to replace workers who transfer to different occupations or exit the labor force, such as to retire.

What Chefs and Head Cooks Do

Chefs and head cooks oversee the daily food preparation at restaurants and other places where food is served. They direct kitchen staff and handle any food-related concerns.

Duties

Chefs and head cooks typically do the following:

- Check the freshness of food and ingredients
- Supervise and coordinate activities of cooks and other food preparation workers

Chefs plan menus and order supplies.

- Develop recipes and determine how to present dishes
- Plan menus and ensure the quality of meals
- Inspect supplies, equipment, and work areas for cleanliness and functionality
- Hire, train, and supervise cooks and other food preparation workers
- Order and maintain an inventory of food and supplies
- Monitor sanitation practices and follow kitchen safety standards

Chefs and head cooks use a variety of kitchen and cooking equipment, including step-in coolers, high-quality knives, meat slicers, and grinders. They also have access to large quantities of meats, spices, and produce. Some chefs use scheduling and purchasing software to help them in their administrative tasks.

Chefs who run their own restaurant or catering business are often busy with kitchen and office work. Some chefs use social media to promote their business by advertising new menu items or addressing patrons' reviews.

The following are examples of types of chefs and head cooks:

Executive chefs, head cooks, and chefs de cuisine are responsible primarily for overseeing the operation of a kitchen. They coordinate the work of sous chefs and other cooks, who prepare most of the meals. Executive chefs also have many duties beyond the kitchen. They design the menu, review food and beverage purchases, and often train cooks and other food preparation workers. Some executive chefs primarily handle administrative tasks and may spend less time in the kitchen.

Sous chefs are a kitchen's second-in-command. They supervise the restaurant's cooks, prepare meals, and report results to the head chefs. In the absence of the head chef, sous chefs run the kitchen.

Work Environment

Chefs and head cooks held about 174,400 jobs in 2022. The largest employers of chefs and head cooks were as follows:

Restaurants and other eating places	51%
Special food services	11
Traveler accommodation	9
Amusement, gambling, and recreation industries	6
Self-employed workers	4

Chefs and head cooks work in restaurants, hotels, and other food service establishments. All of the cooking and food preparation areas in these facilities must be kept clean and sanitary. Chefs and head cooks usually stand for long periods and work in a fast-paced environment.

Some self-employed chefs run their own restaurants or catering businesses, and their work may be more stressful. For example, outside the kitchen, they often spend many hours managing all aspects of the business to ensure that bills and salaries are paid and that the business is profitable.

Injuries and Illnesses

Chefs and head cooks risk injury in kitchens, which are usually crowded and potentially dangerous. Common hazards include burns from hot ovens, falls on slippery floors, and cuts from knives and other sharp objects, but these injuries are seldom serious. To reduce the risk of harm, workers often wear long-sleeve shirts and nonslip shoes.

Chefs and head cooks must stand for long periods.

Most chefs and head cooks learn their skills through work experience.

Work Schedules

Most chefs and head cooks work full time, including early mornings, late evenings, weekends, and holidays. Some work more than 40 hours per week.

How to Become a Chef or Head Cook

To enter the occupation, chefs and head cooks typically need a high school diploma plus experience. Some attend a culinary program at a community college, technical school, culinary arts school, or 4-year college. Others learn through apprenticeship programs or in the Armed Forces.

Education

Chefs and head cooks are typically required to have a high school diploma or equivalent to enter the occupation. Although they are not always required to have postsecondary education, many attend programs at community colleges, technical schools, culinary arts schools, and 4-year colleges.

Students in culinary programs spend most of their time in kitchens, practicing their cooking skills. Programs cover all aspects of kitchen work, including menu planning, food sanitation procedures, and purchasing and inventory methods. Most programs also require students to gain experience in a commercial kitchen through an internship or apprenticeship program.

Work Experience in a Related Occupation

Chefs and head cooks often start by working in other positions, such as line cooks, learning cooking skills from the chefs they work for. Many spend years working in kitchens before gaining enough experience to be promoted to chef or head cook positions.

Training

Some chefs and head cooks train on the job, where they learn the same skills as in a formal education program. Some train in mentorship programs, where they work under the direction of an experienced chef. Executive chefs, head cooks, and sous chefs who work in upscale restaurants often have many years of training and experience.

Chefs and head cooks also may learn through apprenticeship programs sponsored by professional culinary institutes, industry associations, or trade unions. The American Culinary Federation accredits many training programs and sponsors apprenticeships through these programs. Some of the apprenticeship programs are registered with the U.S. Department of Labor.

Apprenticeship programs generally combine instruction and on-the-job training. Apprentices typically receive both instruction and paid on-the-job training. Instruction usually covers food sanitation and safety, basic knife skills, and equipment operation. Apprentices spend the rest of their training learning practical skills in a commercial kitchen under a chef's supervision.

Licenses, Certifications, and Registrations

Some states and localities require chefs and head cooks to have a food handler's certification. For more information, contact your state or local licensing board.

Although not required, other types of certification may lead to advancement and higher pay. The American Culinary Federation certifies various levels of chefs, such as certified sous chefs and certified executive chefs. Certification standards are based primarily on work experience and formal training.

Important Qualities

Business skills. Executive chefs and chefs who run their own restaurant need to know how to budget for supplies, set prices, and manage workers so that the restaurant is profitable.

Communication skills. Chefs must convey their instructions clearly and effectively to staff so that patrons' orders are prepared correctly.

Creativity. Chefs and head cooks need to develop and prepare interesting and innovative recipes.

Dexterity. Chefs and head cooks need agility to handle knives properly for cutting, chopping, and dicing.

Leadership skills. Chefs and head cooks must be able to motivate kitchen staff and to develop constructive and cooperative working relationships.

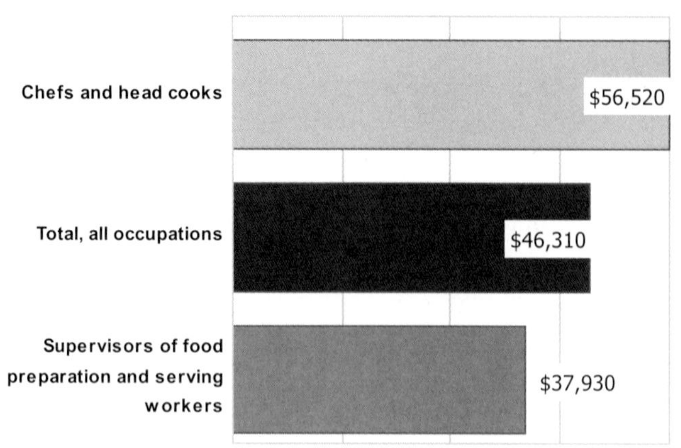

Note: All Occupations includes all occupations in the U.S. Economy.
Source: U.S. Bureau of Labor Statistics, Occupational Employment and Wage Statistics.

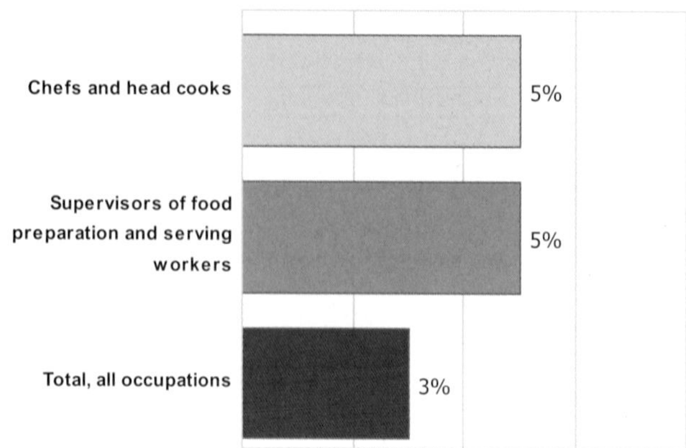

Note: All Occupations includes all occupations in the U.S. Economy.
Source: U.S. Bureau of Labor Statistics, Employment Projections program.

Physical stamina. Chefs and head cooks often work long shifts and sometimes spend entire evenings on their feet, overseeing the preparation and serving of meals.

Sense of taste and smell. Chefs and head cooks must have a keen sense of taste and smell in order to inspect food quality and to design meals that their patrons will enjoy.

Time-management skills. Chefs and head cooks must ensure efficiency in meal preparation and service, especially during busy hours.

Pay

The median annual wage for chefs and head cooks was $56,520 in May 2022. The median wage is the wage at which half the workers in an occupation earned more than that amount and half earned less. The lowest 10 percent earned less than $33,750, and the highest 10 percent earned more than $91,520.

In May 2022, the median annual wages for chefs and head cooks in the top industries in which they worked were as follows:

Amusement, gambling, and recreation industries	$62,930
Traveler accommodation	61,630
Special food services	61,210
Restaurants and other eating places	52,830

The level of pay for chefs and head cooks varies by region and employer. Pay is usually highest in upscale restaurants and hotels, where many executive chefs work, as well as in major metropolitan and resort areas.

Most chefs and head cooks work full time and often work early mornings, late evenings, weekends, and holidays. Some work more than 40 hours per week.

Job Outlook

Employment of chefs and head cooks is projected to grow 5 percent from 2022 to 2032, faster than the average for all occupations.

About 22,000 openings for chefs and head cooks are projected each year, on average, over the decade. Many of those openings are expected to result from the need to replace workers who transfer to different occupations or exit the labor force, such as to retire.

Employment

Income growth is expected to result in greater demand for high-quality dishes at a variety of dining venues. As a result, more restaurants and other dining places are expected to open to satisfy consumer desire for dining out.

Consumers are continuing to demand healthier meals made from scratch in restaurants, cafeterias, grocery stores, and other places that sell food. To ensure high-quality dishes, these establishments hire experienced chefs to oversee food preparation.

Occupational Title	SOC Code	Employment, 2022	Projected Employment, 2032	Change, 2022-32	
				Percent	Numeric
Chefs and head cooks	35-1011	174,400	183,600	5	9,200

Contacts for More Information

Visit Apprenticeship.gov to search for information about apprenticeship opportunities.

For information about certification, contact your state or local licensing board or a professional association.

For more information, visit

- American Culinary Federation
- National Restaurant Association

Cooks

Summary

Quick Facts: Cooks	
2022 Median Pay	$30,910 per year $14.86 per hour
Typical Entry-Level Education	See How to Become One
Work Experience in a Related Occupation	See How to Become One
On-the-job Training	See How to Become One
Number of Jobs, 2022	2,729,300
Job Outlook, 2022-32	6% (Faster than average)
Employment Change, 2022-32	175,300

What Cooks Do

Cooks season and prepare foods, including soups, salads, entrees, and desserts.

Work Environment

Cooks work in restaurants, schools, hospitals, private households, and other places where food is prepared and served. Their work hours may include early mornings, late evenings, holidays, and weekends. Most cooks work full time, although part-time work is common.

How to Become a Cook

Cooks typically learn their skills through on-the-job training and related work experience. Although no formal education is required, some cooks attend culinary school.

Pay

The median hourly wage for cooks was $14.86 in May 2022.

Job Outlook

Overall employment of cooks is projected to grow 6 percent from 2022 to 2032, faster than the average for all occupations.

About 439,300 openings for cooks are projected each year, on average, over the decade. Many of those openings are expected to result from the need to replace workers who transfer to different occupations or exit the labor force, such as to retire.

What Cooks Do

Cooks season and prepare foods, including soups, salads, entrees, and desserts.

Duties

Cooks typically do the following:

- Ensure the freshness of ingredients
- Weigh, measure, and mix ingredients according to recipes
- Bake, grill, or fry meats, fish, vegetables, and other foods
- Boil and steam meats, fish, vegetables, and other foods
- Arrange and garnish food on serving dishes
- Clean work areas, equipment, utensils, and dishes
- Cook, handle, and store food or ingredients

Cooks usually work under the direction of chefs, head cooks, or food service managers. Large restaurants and food service establishments often have multiple menus and large kitchen staffs. Teams of restaurant cooks, sometimes called *assistant cooks* or *line cooks*, work at assigned stations equipped with the stoves, grills, pans, and ingredients they need to prepare food.

Job titles often reflect the principal ingredient cooks prepare or the type of cooking they do, such as *fry cook* or *grill cook*.

Cooks use a variety of kitchen equipment, including broilers, grills, slicers, grinders, and blenders.

Cooks' responsibilities vary depending on the type of food service establishment, the size of the facility, and the level of service offered. However, in all establishments, they follow sanitation procedures when handling food. For example, they

Cooks prepare a wide range of dishes.

Cooks may prepare fresh vegetables.

store food and ingredients at the correct temperatures to prevent bacterial growth.

The following are examples of types of cooks:

Fast food cooks prepare a limited selection of menu items in fast-food restaurants. They cook and package food, such as hamburgers and fried chicken, to be kept warm until served. For more information about workers who prepare and serve items in fast-food restaurants, see the profiles on food preparation workers and food and beverage serving and related workers.

Institution and cafeteria cooks work in the kitchens of schools, cafeterias, businesses, hospitals, and other establishments. They typically prepare a large quantity of entrees, vegetables, and desserts according to preset menus. However, they sometimes customize meals, such as for diners' dietary considerations.

Private household cooks, sometimes called *personal chefs,* plan and prepare meals in private homes, according to the client's tastes and dietary needs. They pick up groceries and supplies, clean the kitchen, and wash dishes and utensils. They also may cater parties, holiday meals, luncheons, and other events. Private household cooks typically work full-time for one client, although many are self-employed or employed by an agency, regularly preparing meals for multiple clients.

Restaurant cooks prepare a variety of dishes, usually by individual order, in eating establishments. Some restaurant cooks order supplies and help maintain the stock room.

Short order cooks prepare and sometimes serve foods in restaurants and coffee shops that emphasize fast service. For example, they might make sandwiches, fry eggs, and cook french fries, often working on several orders at the same time.

Work Environment

Cooks held about 2.7 million jobs in 2022. Employment in the detailed occupations that make up cooks was distributed as follows:

Cooks, restaurant	1,361,200
Cooks, fast food	742,000
Cooks, institution and cafeteria	434,500
Cooks, short order	137,400
Cooks, private household	34,000
Cooks, all other	20,200

Cooks often work in restaurants.

The largest employers of cooks were as follows:

Restaurants and other eating places	72%
Healthcare and social assistance	6
Educational services; state, local, and private	6

Cooks work in restaurants, schools, hospitals, hotels, and other establishments where food is prepared and served. They often prepare only part of a dish and coordinate with other cooks and kitchen workers to complete meals on time. Some work in private homes.

Cooks stand for long periods and work under pressure in a fast-paced environment. Although most cooks work indoors in kitchens, some may work outdoors at food stands, at catered events, or in mobile food trucks.

Injuries and Illnesses

Kitchens are usually crowded and filled with potential dangers, such as hot ovens or slippery floors. Cooks, all other, in particular, have one of the highest rates of injuries and illnesses of all occupations. ("All other" titles represent occupations with a wide range of characteristics that do not fit into any of the other detailed occupations.)

The most common hazards are slips, falls, cuts, and burns, although injuries are seldom serious. To reduce the risks, cooks wear gloves, long-sleeve shirts, aprons, and nonslip shoes.

Work Schedules

Most cooks work full time, although part-time work is common. Work schedules vary and may include early mornings, late evenings, weekends, and holidays. In school cafeterias and some institutional cafeterias, cooks usually have more regular hours.

Cooks who are employed in schools may work only during the school year, typically for 9 or 10 months. Similarly, cooks who are employed in some resort establishments work only for seasonal operation.

How to Become a Cook

Most cooks learn their skills through on-the-job training and work-related experience. Although no formal education is typically required, some cooks attend culinary schools. Others attend vocational or apprenticeship programs.

Education

Cooks typically do not need formal education. However, employers may require or prefer that applicants have a high school diploma.

Cooks typically learn their skills on the job from an experienced chef.

Vocational cooking schools, professional culinary institutes, and some colleges offer programs and courses on topics such as cooking techniques and international cuisines. Programs generally last from a few months to 2 years, and applicants may be required to have a high school diploma or equivalent. Depending on the type and length of the program, graduates generally qualify for entry-level positions as a restaurant cook.

Training

Cooks typically learn their skills on the job. The length of on-the-job training varies for different types of cooks. Trainees generally first learn kitchen basics and workplace safety and then learn how to handle and cook food.

Some cooks learn through an apprenticeship program. Culinary institutes, industry associations, and trade unions may sponsor such programs for cooks. Apprentices complete courses in food sanitation and safety, basic knife skills, and equipment operation. They also learn practical cooking skills under the supervision of an experienced chef. The length of apprenticeship programs vary but typically last about 1 year.

The American Culinary Federation accredits many academic training programs and sponsors apprenticeships through these programs around the country. Minimum qualifications for entering an apprenticeship program typically include being at least 17 years old and having a high school diploma or equivalent.

Some hotels and restaurants offer their own training programs.

Licenses, Certifications, and Registrations

Many states do not require certification for cooks. Some states and localities require cooks to have a food handler's certification. For more information, contact your state or local licensing board.

Work Experience in a Related Occupation

Many cooks, particularly those who work in restaurants and private households, learn their skills through work-related experience. Starting as a kitchen helper or food preparation worker allows cooks to learn basic skills, which may lead to opportunities to gain experience in assistant cook or line cook positions. Some work under the guidance of more experienced cooks.

Advancement

The American Culinary Federation certifies chefs, personal chefs, pastry chefs, and culinary administrators, among others. Professional certification may lead to higher level or higher paying positions.

Advancement opportunities for cooks often depend on training, work experience, and the ability to prepare complex dishes. Those interested in advancing should learn new cooking skills and take on increasing responsibility, such as supervising kitchen staff in the absence of a chef. Some cooks train or supervise kitchen staff, and some become head cooks, chefs, or food service managers.

Important Qualities

Attention to detail. Cooks need to listen carefully to orders and follow recipes to prepare dishes correctly.

Dexterity. Cooks should have excellent hand–eye coordination. For example, they need to use proper knife techniques for cutting, chopping, and dicing.

Physical stamina. Cooks spend a lot of time standing in one place, cooking food over hot stoves, and cleaning work areas.

Sense of taste and smell. Cooks must have a keen sense of taste and smell to prepare meals that customers enjoy.

Pay

The median hourly wage for cooks was $14.86 in May 2022. The median wage is the wage at which half the workers in an occupation earned more than that amount and half earned less. The lowest 10 percent earned less than $10.57, and the highest 10 percent earned more than $20.56.

Median hourly wages for cooks in May 2022 were as follows:

Cooks, private household	$18.54
Cooks, restaurant	16.40
Cooks, all other	16.06
Cooks, institution and cafeteria	15.63

Cooks

Median hourly wages, May 2022

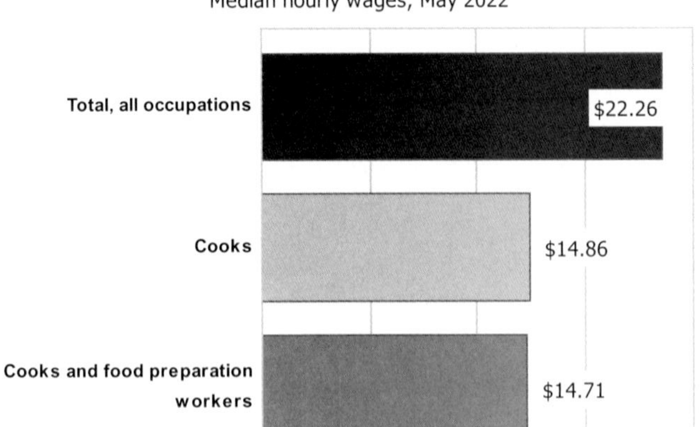

Note: All Occupations includes all occupations in the U.S. Economy.
Source: U.S. Bureau of Labor Statistics, Occupational Employment and Wage Statistics.

Cooks, short order	14.60
Cooks, fast food	13.29

In May 2022, the median hourly wages for cooks in the top industries in which they worked were as follows:

Healthcare and social assistance	$16.36
Restaurants and other eating places	14.58
Educational services; state, local, and private	14.30

Pay for cooks varies greatly by region and type of employer. Pay is usually highest in upscale hotels and restaurants, as well as in major metropolitan and resort areas.

Most cooks work full time, although part-time work is common. Work schedules may vary and may include early mornings, late evenings, weekends, and holidays. In school cafeterias and some institutional cafeterias, cooks usually have more regular hours.

Cooks employed in schools may work only during the school year, typically for 9 or 10 months. Similarly, cooks employed in some resort establishments work only for seasonal operation.

Job Outlook

Overall employment of cooks is projected to grow 6 percent from 2022 to 2032, faster than the average for all occupations.

About 439,300 openings for cooks are projected each year, on average, over the decade. Many of those openings are expected to result from the need to replace workers who transfer to different occupations or exit the labor force, such as to retire.

Employment

Projected employment of cooks varies by occupation (see table).

Population and income growth are expected to result in greater consumer demand for food at a variety of dining places.

Cooks

Percent change in employment, projected 2022-32

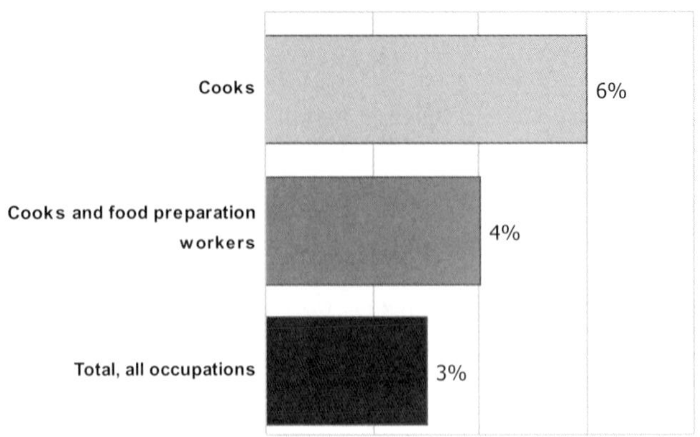

Note: All Occupations includes all occupations in the U.S. Economy.
Source: U.S. Bureau of Labor Statistics, Employment Projections program.

People will continue to eat out, buy takeout meals, or have food delivered. New restaurants, cafeterias, and catering services are expected to open, requiring more cooks to prepare meals for this increased consumer demand.

In addition, consumers continue to prefer healthy foods in restaurants, grocery stores, and other dining venues. To prepare high-quality meals at these places, many managers and chefs will require experienced cooks.

Employment of some cooks is projected to decline, however. For example, reduced demand for fast food cooks is expected because of automated systems, employment of workers who both prepare and serve food, and other efforts to streamline operations.

Occupational Title	SOC Code	Employment, 2022	Projected Employment, 2032	Change, 2022-32	
				Percent	Numeric
Cooks	35-2010	2,729,300	2,904,500	6	175,300
Cooks, fast food	35-2011	742,000	640,400	-14	-101,600
Cooks, institution and cafeteria	35-2012	434,500	443,400	2	8,900
Cooks, private household	35-2013	34,000	32,100	-6	-1,900
Cooks, restaurant	35-2014	1,361,200	1,638,900	20	277,600
Cooks, short order	35-2015	137,400	128,900	-6	-8,400
Cooks, all other	35-2019	20,200	20,800	3	600

Contacts for More Information

Visit Apprenticeship.gov to search for information about apprenticeship opportunities.

For information about certification, contact your state or local licensing board or a professional association.

For more information about cooking careers, visit

- American Culinary Federation
- National Restaurant Association
- United States Personal Chef Association

Food and Beverage Serving and Related Workers

Summary

Quick Facts: Food and Beverage Serving and Related Workers	
2022 Median Pay	$28,130 per year $13.52 per hour
Typical Entry-Level Education	No formal educational credential
Work Experience in a Related Occupation	None
On-the-job Training	Short-term on-the-job training
Number of Jobs, 2022	4,540,700
Job Outlook, 2022-32	2% (As fast as average)
Employment Change, 2022-32	79,700

What Food and Beverage Serving and Related Workers Do

Food and beverage serving and related workers take and prepare orders, clear tables, and do other tasks associated with providing food and drink to customers.

Work Environment

Food and beverage serving and related workers are employed in restaurants, schools, and other dining places. Work shifts often include early mornings, late evenings, weekends, and holidays. Part-time work is common.

How to Become a Food and Beverage Serving or Related Worker

Food and beverage serving and related workers typically have no requirements for formal education or work experience to enter the occupation. They learn their skills on the job.

Pay

The median hourly wage for food and beverage serving and related workers was $13.52 in May 2022.

Job Outlook

Overall employment of food and beverage serving and related workers is projected to grow 2 percent from 2022 to 2032, about as fast as the average for all occupations.

About 1,026,200 openings for food and beverage serving and related workers are projected each year, on average, over the decade. Many of those openings are expected to result from the need to replace workers who transfer to different occupations or exit the labor force, such as to retire.

What Food and Beverage Serving and Related Workers Do

Food and beverage serving and related workers take and prepare orders, clear tables, and do other tasks associated with providing food and drink to customers.

Duties

Food and beverage serving and related workers typically do the following:

- Greet customers and answer their questions about menu items and specials
- Take food and drink orders from customers
- Prepare food and drink orders, such as sandwiches and coffee
- Relay customers' orders to other kitchen staff
- Serve food and drinks to customers at a counter, at a stand, or in a hotel room
- Accept payment and provide customers with receipts
- Clean assigned work areas, such as dining tables or serving counters
- Stock service stations, cabinets, and tables
- Set tables or prepare food stations for new customers

Food and beverage serving workers serve coffee, soda, and other beverages.

Food and beverage workers may work directly with customers.

Food and beverage serving and related workers are the front line of customer service in restaurants, cafeterias, and other food service establishments. They seat customers, take or prepare food and drink orders, clear and set tables, and serve food and beverages. Depending on the establishment, they may do some or all of these tasks during their shift.

Most work as part of a team, although their responsibilities and job titles vary.

The following are examples of types of food and beverage serving and related workers:

Dining room and cafeteria attendants and bartender helpers—sometimes collectively referred to as bus staff—help waiters, waitresses, and bartenders by cleaning and setting tables, removing dirty dishes, and stocking serving areas with supplies. They also may help waiters and waitresses by bringing meals from the kitchen, distributing dishes to diners, filling water glasses, and delivering condiments.

Fast food and counter workers are employed primarily by limited-service restaurants, cafeterias, and snack bars at which customers generally order and pay before eating. These workers take food and beverage orders, prepare or retrieve items, and accept payment. They also heat food items and make salads and sandwiches.

Hosts and hostesses greet customers, seat guests, and manage reservations and waiting lists. They also may provide menus, take and prepare to-go orders, and assist with maintaining cleanliness of the dining area.

Nonrestaurant food servers provide food to customers outside a restaurant environment. For example, they may deliver room-service orders in hotels or meals to hospital rooms. Some work as carhops at venues such as drive-in movie theaters, bringing orders to customers in parked cars.

Work Environment

Food and beverage serving and related workers held about 4.5 million jobs in 2022. Employment in the detailed occupations that make up food and beverage serving and related workers was distributed as follows:

Fast food and counter workers	3,410,100
Dining room and cafeteria attendants and bartender helpers	459,200
Hosts and hostesses, restaurant, lounge, and coffee shop	412,800
Food servers, nonrestaurant	258,600

The largest employers of food and beverage serving and related workers were as follows:

Restaurants and other eating places	77%
Retail trade	4
Healthcare and social assistance	4
Special food services	4
Educational services; state, local, and private	3

Food servers bring meals to customers outside a restaurant.

Food and beverage serving and related workers spend most of their shift on their feet. They carry trays of food, dishes, or glassware, which are often heavy. During busy dining periods, they are under pressure to serve customers quickly and efficiently.

Injuries and Illnesses

Food preparation and serving areas in restaurants often have potential safety hazards, such as hot ovens and slippery floors. Common injuries include slips, cuts, and burns. To reduce these risks, workers may wear gloves, aprons, or nonslip shoes.

Work Schedules

Part-time work is common for food and beverage serving and related workers. Because restaurants and other eating places typically have extended dining hours, work shifts often include early mornings, late evenings, weekends, and holidays.

Work may be seasonal. Food and beverage serving and related workers may not work or may have limited hours during certain times of the year. For example, those in school cafeterias may work only during the school year, usually 9 to 10 months.

In addition, business hours in restaurants allow for flexible schedules that appeal to teenagers. Food and beverage serving

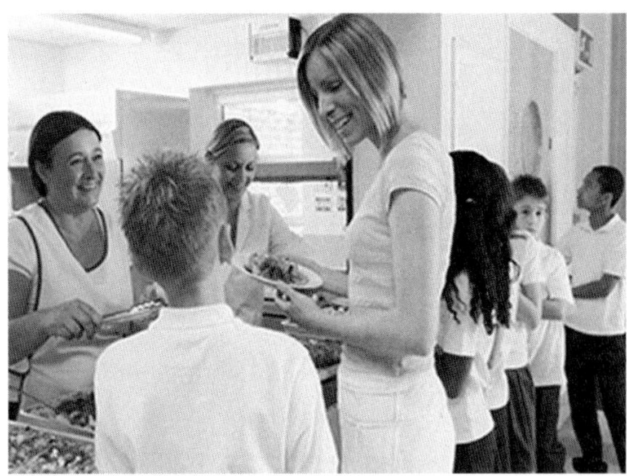

Food and beverage and related workers need customer service skills.

and related workers employs more 16- to 19-year-olds than any other occupation.

How to Become a Food and Beverage Serving or Related Worker

Food and beverage serving and related workers typically have no requirements for education to enter the occupation. They receive short-term on-the-job training.

Most states require workers who serve alcoholic beverages, even as an accompaniment to meals, to be at least 18 years old.

Education

There typically are no formal education requirements for becoming a food and beverage serving worker.

Training

Workers typically learn through on-the-job training, which may last from few days to several weeks. Training includes basic customer service, kitchen safety, safe food-handling procedures, and sanitation guidelines.

Food and beverage serving and related workers typically learn their duties by watching and working with experienced staff. Some employers, particularly those in fast-food restaurants, have specific training programs for new workers.

Bartender helpers and other workers in establishments where alcohol is served may need training on state and local laws concerning the sale of alcoholic beverages. Some states, counties, and cities mandate such training, which typically lasts a few hours.

Advancement

Some food and beverage serving and related workers advance to waiter, waitress, or bartender positions as they learn the basics of serving food or preparing drinks. Kitchen staff may advance to become food preparation workers or cooks. Still others may move up to supervisory or food service manager positions.

Important Qualities

Communication skills. Food and beverage serving and related workers must listen to customers' orders and relay them correctly to the kitchen staff so that the orders are prepared as requested.

Customer-service skills. Food service establishments rely on good food and customer service to keep customers and succeed in a competitive industry. As a result, workers should be courteous and be able to attend to customers' requests.

Physical stamina. Food and beverage serving and related workers spend most of their shift doing physical tasks such as standing, carrying trays, and cleaning work areas.

Physical strength. Food and beverage serving and related workers need to be able to lift and carry stock and equipment that can weigh up to 50 pounds.

Pay

The median hourly wage for food and beverage serving and related workers was $13.52 in May 2022. The median wage is the wage at which half the workers in an occupation earned more than that amount and half earned less. The lowest 10 percent earned less than $10.14, and the highest 10 percent earned more than $17.26.

Median hourly wages for food and beverage serving and related workers in May 2022 were as follows:

Food servers, nonrestaurant	$14.57
Dining room and cafeteria attendants and bartender helpers	14.00
Fast food and counter workers	13.43
Hosts and hostesses, restaurant, lounge, and coffee shop	13.33

In May 2022, the median hourly wages for food and beverage serving and related workers in the top industries in which they worked were as follows:

Food and Beverage Serving and Related Workers

Median hourly wages, May 2022

Occupation	Median hourly wage
Total, all occupations	$22.26
Food preparation and serving related occupations	$14.25
Food and beverage serving and related workers	$13.52

Note: All Occupations includes all occupations in the U.S. Economy.
Source: U.S. Bureau of Labor Statistics, Occupational Employment and Wage Statistics.

Educational services; state, local, and private	$15.17
Healthcare and social assistance	14.94
Retail trade	14.52
Special food services	14.10
Restaurants and other eating places	13.31

Although some workers in these occupations earn tips, most get their earnings from hourly wages alone.

In some restaurants, workers may contribute all or a portion of their tips to a tip pool, which is distributed among qualifying workers. Tip pools allow workers who do not usually receive tips directly from customers, such as dining room attendants, to be part of a team and to share in the rewards for good service.

Employers may provide meals and uniforms but may deduct those costs from the worker's wages.

Part-time work is common for food and beverage serving and related workers. Because restaurants and other eating places typically have extended dining hours, work shifts often include early mornings, late evenings, weekends, and holidays.

Work may be seasonal. Food and beverage serving and related workers may not work or may have limited hours during certain times of the year. For example, those in school cafeterias may work only during the school year, usually 9 to 10 months.

In addition, business hours in restaurants allow for flexible schedules that appeal to teenagers. Food and beverage serving and related workers employs more 16- to 19-year-olds than any other occupation.

Job Outlook

Overall employment of food and beverage serving and related workers is projected to grow 2 percent from 2022 to 2032, about as fast as the average for all occupations.

About 1,026,200 openings for food and beverage serving and related workers are projected each year, on average, over the decade. Many of those openings are expected to result from the need to replace workers who transfer to different occupations or exit the labor force, such as to retire.

Employment

Projected employment of food and beverage serving and related workers varies by occupation (see table).

As a growing population continues to dine out, purchase takeout meals, or have food delivered, more restaurants, particularly

Food and Beverage Serving and Related Workers

Percent change in employment, projected 2022-32

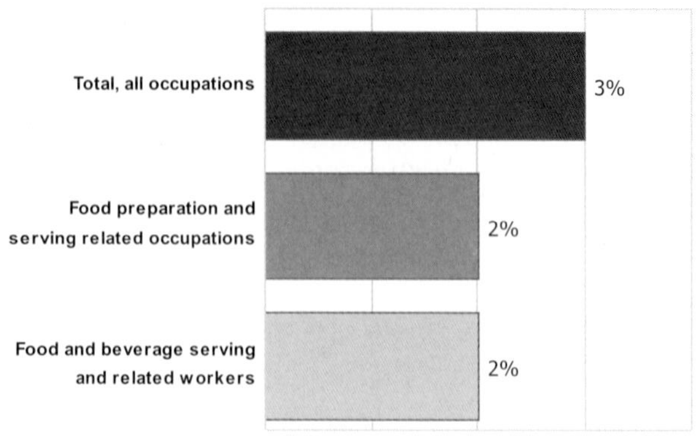

Note: All Occupations includes all occupations in the U.S. Economy.
Source: U.S. Bureau of Labor Statistics, Employment Projections program.

fast-food and casual dining restaurants, are expected to open. In response, more food and beverage serving and related workers are expected to be needed.

In addition, nontraditional food service operations, such as those inside grocery stores and cafeterias in hospitals and residential care facilities, are expected to serve more prepared meals. Because these workers are essential to the operation of a food-serving establishment, they should continue to be in demand.

Occupational Title	SOC Code	Employment, 2022	Projected Employment, 2032	Change, 2022-32	
				Percent	Numeric
Food and beverage serving and related workers	—	4,540,700	4,620,500	2	79,700
Fast food and counter workers	35-3023	3,410,100	3,460,500	1	50,400
Food servers, nonrestaurant	35-3041	258,600	266,600	3	8,100
Dining room and cafeteria attendants and bartender helpers	35-9011	459,200	478,400	4	19,200
Hosts and hostesses, restaurant, lounge, and coffee shop	35-9031	412,800	414,900	0	2,000

Contacts for More Information

For more information on food and beverage serving careers, visit

➤ National Restaurant Association

Food Preparation Workers

Summary

Quick Facts: Food Preparation Workers	
2022 Median Pay	$29,790 per year $14.32 per hour
Typical Entry-Level Education	No formal educational credential
Work Experience in a Related Occupation	None
On-the-job Training	Short-term on-the-job training
Number of Jobs, 2022	931,800
Job Outlook, 2022-32	-5% (Decline)
Employment Change, 2022-32	-44,800

What Food Preparation Workers Do

Food preparation workers perform a variety of tasks other than cooking, such as slicing meat and brewing coffee.

Work Environment

Food preparation workers are employed in places where food is made or served, such as cafeterias, grocery stores, hospitals, and schools. Part-time work is common. Work schedules may vary to include early mornings, late evenings, weekends, or holidays.

How to Become a Food Preparation Worker

Food preparation workers typically do not need a formal educational credential or previous work experience to enter the occupation. They learn through on-the-job training that usually lasts several weeks.

Pay

The median hourly wage for food preparation workers was $14.32 in May 2022.

Food preparation workers prepare ingredients for dishes.

Job Outlook

Employment of food preparation workers is projected to decline 5 percent from 2022 to 2032.

Despite declining employment, about 157,100 openings for food preparation workers are projected each year, on average, over the decade. All of those openings are expected to result from the need to replace workers who transfer to other occupations or exit the labor force, such as to retire.

What Food Preparation Workers Do

Food preparation workers perform a variety of tasks other than cooking. Their duties include preparing cold foods, slicing meat, peeling and cutting vegetables, brewing coffee or tea, and doing many other food service tasks.

Duties

Food preparation workers typically do the following:

- Clean and sanitize work areas, equipment, utensils, and dishes
- Weigh or measure ingredients, such as meats and liquids
- Prepare fruit and vegetables for cooking
- Cut meats, poultry, and seafood and prepare them for cooking
- Mix ingredients for salads
- Keep food in suitable containers and storage areas to prevent spoilage
- Take and record the temperature of food and food storage areas
- Place food trays over food warmers for immediate service

Food preparation workers help cooks and other kitchen staff by preparing ingredients for dishes. Common duties include slicing and dicing fruits, vegetables, and meat; making salads, sandwiches, and other cold food items; and keeping salad bars and buffet tables stocked and clean. They usually work under the direction of cooks, chefs, or food service managers.

Food preparation workers also retrieve pots and pans, clean and store kitchen equipment, and unload and store food supplies. When needed, they retrieve food and equipment for

Food preparation workers clean and sanitize work areas.

cooks and chefs. In some kitchens, food preparation workers use a variety of commercial kitchen equipment, such as commercial dishwashers, blenders, slicers, or grinders.

In addition, these workers may stock and use soda machines, tea brewers, and coffeemakers to prepare beverages for customers.

Work Environment

Food preparation workers held about 931,800 jobs in 2022. The largest employers of food preparation workers were as follows:

Restaurants and other eating places	54%
Grocery and specialty food retailers	19
Healthcare and social assistance	6
Special food services	5
Educational services; state, local, and private	3

Food preparation workers held about 886,700 jobs in 2019. The largest employers of food preparation workers were as follows:

The work is often strenuous. Food preparation workers may stand for hours at a time while cleaning or preparing ingredients. Some are required to move heavy pots or food supplies.

The fast-paced environment in kitchens may be hectic, especially during peak dining hours. Ensuring that dishes are prepared properly and on time may be stressful.

Food preparation workers wear gloves for safe food handling.

Injuries and Illnesses

Food preparation areas in kitchens have potential safety hazards, such as hot ovens and slippery floors. As a result, food preparation workers have one of the highest rates of injuries and illnesses of all occupations. The most common risks include minor slips, falls, cuts, and burns. To reduce these risks, workers often wear gloves, aprons, and nonslip shoes.

Work Schedules

Part-time work is common for food preparation workers. Work schedules may vary to include early mornings, late evenings, weekends, or holidays.

Those in school cafeterias may have more regular schedules and may work only during the academic year, usually 9 or 10 months. In establishments that offer seasonal employment, food preparation workers may be hired for only a few months each year.

How to Become a Food Preparation Worker

Food preparation workers typically do not need a formal educational credential or previous work experience to enter the occupation. They learn their job tasks through on-the-job training.

Education

There typically are no formal education requirements for becoming a food preparation worker. However, employers may require or prefer that candidates have some high school education or a diploma.

Training

Food preparation workers typically get short-term on-the-job training, which usually lasts several weeks. Trainees typically learn basic kitchen duties from an experienced worker. Their training also may include basic sanitation and workplace safety regulations, as well as instructions on how to handle and prepare food.

Advancement

Opportunities for food preparation workers to advance depend on their training and work experience. Food preparation

Food preparation workers typically learn their skills on the job from an experienced worker.

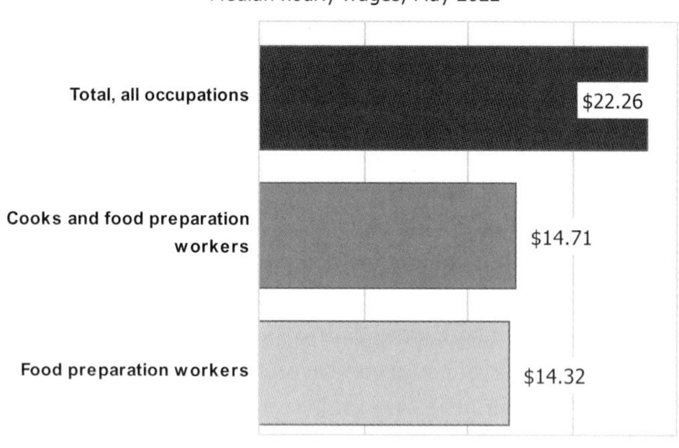

Note: All Occupations includes all occupations in the U.S. Economy.
Source: U.S. Bureau of Labor Statistics, Occupational Employment and Wage Statistics.

workers may advance to become assistant cooks or line cooks as they learn basic cooking skills.

Important Qualities

Dexterity. Food preparation workers must be able to quickly and safely chop vegetables, cut meat, and perform other tasks with sharp knives.

Interpersonal skills. Food preparation workers must work well with kitchen staff to ensure that dishes are prepared properly and on time.

Listening skills. Food preparation workers must understand customers' orders and follow directions from cooks, chefs, or food service managers.

Physical stamina. Food preparation workers stand on their feet for long periods while they prepare food, clean work areas, or lift pots from the stove.

Physical strength. Food preparation workers may need to move heavy food supply items and kitchen equipment.

Pay

The median hourly wage for food preparation workers was $14.32 in May 2022. The median wage is the wage at which half the workers in an occupation earned more than that amount and half earned less. The lowest 10 percent earned less than $10.47, and the highest 10 percent earned more than $18.65.

In May 2022, the median hourly wages for food preparation workers in the top industries in which they worked were as follows:

Educational services; state, local, and private	$15.87
Special food services	14.83
Grocery and specialty food retailers	14.81
Healthcare and social assistance	14.08
Restaurants and other eating places	13.91

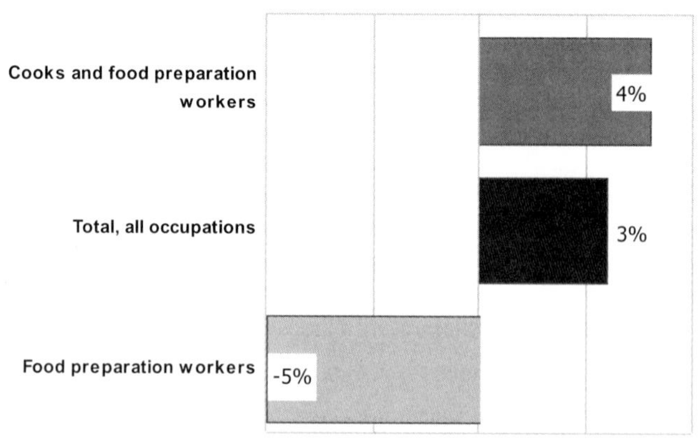

Note: All Occupations includes all occupations in the U.S. Economy.
Source: U.S. Bureau of Labor Statistics, Employment Projections program.

Part-time work is common for food preparation workers. Work schedules may vary to include early mornings, late evenings, weekends, or holidays.

Those in school cafeterias may have more regular hours and may work only during the academic year, usually 9 or 10 months. In establishments that offer seasonal employment, food preparation workers may be hired for only a few months each year.

Job Outlook

Employment of food preparation workers is projected to decline 5 percent from 2022 to 2032.

Despite declining employment, about 157,100 openings for food preparation workers are projected each year, on average, over the decade. All of those openings are expected to result from the need to replace workers who transfer to other occupations or exit the labor force, such as to retire.

Employment

Restaurants and cafeterias may customize their food orders from wholesalers and distributors in an effort to lower costs. For example, they may order prewashed, precut, or preseasoned ingredients, which is expected to reduce the need for food preparation workers. Additionally, some establishments prefer to employ fast food and counter workers, who both prepare and serve food to customers, which also may reduce the need for food preparation workers.

Occupational Title	SOC Code	Employment, 2022	Projected Employment, 2032	Change, 2022-32	
				Percent	Numeric
Food preparation workers	35-2021	931,800	887,000	-5	-44,800

Contacts for More Information

For more information about job opportunities, contact local employers and local offices of the state employment service.

For more information about food preparation workers, visit

➤ National Restaurant Association

Waiters and Waitresses

Summary

Quick Facts: Waiters and Waitresses	
2022 Median Pay	$29,120 per year $14.00 per hour
Typical Entry-Level Education	No formal educational credential
Work Experience in a Related Occupation	None
On-the-job Training	Short-term on-the-job training
Number of Jobs, 2022	2,194,100
Job Outlook, 2022-32	-3% (Decline)
Employment Change, 2022-32	-68,600

What Waiters and Waitresses Do

Waiters and waitresses take orders and serve food and beverages to customers in dining establishments.

Work Environment

Waiters and waitresses work in restaurants, bars, hotels, and other food-serving and drinking establishments. Part-time work is common, and schedules may vary to include early mornings, late evenings, weekends, and holidays.

How to Become a Waiter or Waitress

Waiters and waitresses typically do not need formal education to enter the occupation. They are typically trained on the job.

Pay

The median hourly wage for waiters and waitresses was $14.00 in May 2022.

Job Outlook

Employment of waiters and waitresses is projected to decline 3 percent from 2022 to 2032.

Waiters and waitresses serve food and beverages to customers.

Despite declining employment, about 440,000 openings for waiters and waitresses are projected each year, on average, over the decade. All of those openings are expected to result from the need to replace workers who transfer to other occupations or exit the labor force, such as to retire.

What Waiters and Waitresses Do

Waiters and waitresses take orders and serve food and beverages to customers in dining establishments.

Duties

Waiters and waitresses typically do the following:

- Greet customers, explain daily specials, and answer questions related to the menu
- Take orders from customers for food and beverages
- Relay food and beverage orders to the kitchen, such as via a point-of-sale system
- Prepare certain menu items, such as assembling garnishes or brewing coffee
- Carry trays of food or drinks from the kitchen to the dining tables
- Check on customers to confirm satisfaction and assist with other requests
- Clear tables after customers finish dining, or as needed

Some states require workers who serve alcohol to be at least 18 years old.

- Prepare customers' itemized checks, take payment, and return change
- Set up dining areas and stock service areas

Waiters and waitresses, also called *servers*, ensure that customers have a satisfying dining experience. Specific duties vary with the establishment in which they work.

Before and between waiting on customers, servers usually prepare tables and work stations. Tasks may include refilling containers, such as napkin holders, salt and pepper shakers, and condiment dispensers; keeping tables from becoming overcrowded; and tidying the serving area and dining room. Servers also may prepare some foods and nonalcoholic drinks, such as assembling salads, brewing coffee, and portioning desserts. In fine-dining restaurants, they may set tables with linens, eating utensils, and glassware.

Food service duties include taking customers' orders, placing those orders with the kitchen, and delivering food and drinks to the table. Servers attend to customers throughout the meal and collect payment at the end. In restaurants that do not employ bus staff, servers often are responsible for cleaning tables after customers finish dining.

In establishments that sell alcohol, servers verify that customers meet the age requirement for its purchase.

Servers may meet with managers and chefs before each shift to discuss topics such as the menu or specials, ingredients for potential food allergies, and coordination between the kitchen and dining room. They may have cleaning duties, such as vacuuming carpet and emptying trash, at the end of the shift.

Work Environment

Waiters and waitresses held about 2.2 million jobs in 2022. The largest employers of waiters and waitresses were as follows:

Restaurants and other eating places	82%
Traveler accommodation	5
Arts, entertainment, and recreation	4

Waiters and waitresses stand most of their shift and often carry heavy trays of food, dishes, and drinks. The work may be hectic and fast-paced. During busy dining periods, they may be under pressure to serve customers quickly and efficiently. They must be able to work as part of a team with kitchen staff to ensure that customers receive prompt service.

Waiters and waitresses may be required to wear a uniform or to comply with a specific dress code.

Work Schedules

Part time work is common, and schedules may vary to include early mornings, late evenings, weekends, and holidays.

In establishments that offer seasonal employment, waiters and waitresses may be employed for only a few months each year.

How to Become a Waiter or Waitress

Waiters and waitresses typically do not need formal education or related work experience to enter the occupation. They typically learn through on-the-job training that lasts 1 month or less.

Most states require workers who serve alcoholic beverages to be at least 18 years old, but some states require servers to be older. Waiters and waitresses who serve alcohol must be familiar with state and local laws concerning the sale of alcoholic beverages.

Education

Typically, no formal education is required to become a waiter or waitress. However, some employers require or prefer that workers have a high school diploma.

Training

Waiters and waitresses typically learn through short-term on-the-job-training, usually lasting from several days to a few weeks. Trainees typically work with an experienced waiter or waitress, who teaches them basic serving techniques.

Waiters and waitresses mostly work in full-service restaurants.

Waiters and waitresses typically learn on the job.

On-the-job training helps new workers learn serving techniques and use of the restaurant's order-placement, payment, and other systems. Training also prepares waiters and waitresses to properly handle difficult situations and unpleasant or unruly customers.

Training for waiters and waitresses in establishments that serve alcohol typically involves learning state and local laws concerning the sale of alcoholic beverages. Some states, counties, and cities mandate the training, which typically lasts a few hours and may be offered online or in-house.

Some states require that servers take training related to the safe handling of food.

Advancement

Waiters and waitresses who have experience may advance to work in fine-dining restaurants. Advancement may offer improved conditions, such as preferred schedules or higher tips.

Important Qualities

Communication skills. Waiters and waitresses must listen to customers, ask questions as needed, and relay information to the kitchen staff so that orders are prepared to the customers' satisfaction.

Customer-service skills. Waiters and waitresses are frontline workers for their restaurant. They should be friendly and polite and be able to develop a rapport with customers.

Detail oriented. Waiters and waitresses must record customers' orders accurately. They should be able to recall the details of each order and match the food or drink orders to the correct customers.

Physical stamina. Waiters and waitresses spend most of their work hours standing or walking and carrying trays, dishes, and drinks.

Physical strength. Waiters and waitresses need to be able to lift and carry trays of food or other items.

Pay

The median hourly wage for waiters and waitresses was $14.00 in May 2022. The median wage is the wage at which half the workers in an occupation earned more than that amount and half earned less. The lowest 10 percent earned less than $8.77, and the highest 10 percent earned more than $26.62.

In May 2022, the median hourly wages for waiters and waitresses in the top industries in which they worked were as follows:

Arts, entertainment, and recreation	$14.32
Traveler accommodation	14.26
Restaurants and other eating places	13.91

These wage data include tips. Tipped employees earn at least the federal minimum wage, which may be paid as a combination of direct wages and tips, depending on the state. The Wage and Hour Division of the U.S. Department of Labor maintains a website listing minimum wages for tipped employees, by state, although some localities have enacted minimum wages higher than their state requires.

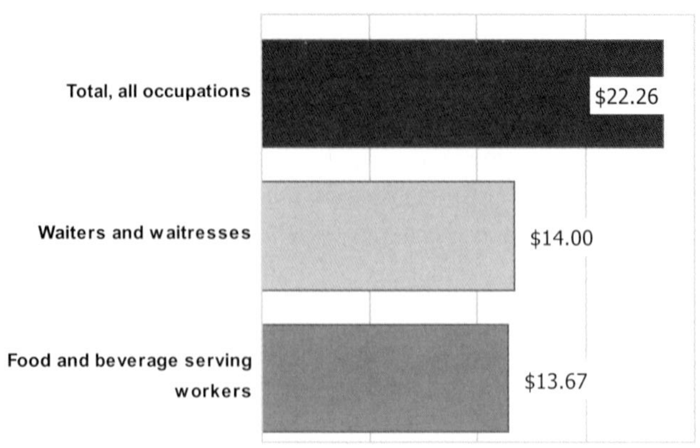

Note: All Occupations includes all occupations in the U.S. Economy.
Source: U.S. Bureau of Labor Statistics, Occupational Employment and Wage Statistics.

Part-time work is common for waiters and waitresses. Schedules may vary to include early mornings, late evenings, weekends, and holidays.

In establishments that offer seasonal employment, waiters and waitresses may be employed for only a few months each year.

Job Outlook

Employment of waiters and waitresses is projected to decline 3 percent from 2022 to 2032.

Despite declining employment, about 440,000 openings for waiters and waitresses are projected each year, on average, over the decade. All of those openings are expected to result from

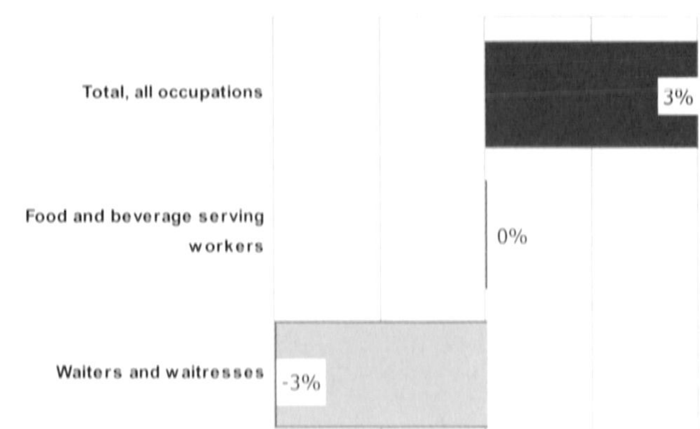

Note: All Occupations includes all occupations in the U.S. Economy.
Source: U.S. Bureau of Labor Statistics, Employment Projections program.

the need to replace workers who transfer to other occupations or exit the labor force, such as to retire.

Employment

Many establishments will continue to use waiters and waitresses to serve food and beverages and to provide customer service. However, reduced need for these workers is expected due to increases in the use of self-service technology, such as kiosks that allow customers to order and pay for food, and in carryout.

Occupational Title	SOC Code	Employment, 2022	Projected Employment, 2032	Change, 2022-32	
				Percent	Numeric
Waiters and waitresses	35-3031	2,194,100	2,125,500	-3	-68,600

Contacts for More Information

For more information on careers as a waiter or waitress, visit

➤ Choose Restaurants

Healthcare

Athletic Trainers

Summary

Quick Facts: Athletic Trainers	
2022 Median Pay	$53,840 per year
Typical Entry-Level Education	Master's degree
Work Experience in a Related Occupation	None
On-the-job Training	None
Number of Jobs, 2022	33,800
Job Outlook, 2022-32	14% (Much faster than average)
Employment Change, 2022-32	4,800

What Athletic Trainers Do

Athletic trainers specialize in preventing, diagnosing, and treating muscle and bone injuries and illnesses.

Work Environment

Many athletic trainers work in educational settings, such as colleges, universities, elementary schools, and secondary schools. Others work in hospitals, fitness centers, or physicians' offices, or for professional sports teams.

How to Become an Athletic Trainer

Athletic trainers typically need at least a bachelor's degree, and master's degrees are common. Nearly all states require athletic trainers to have a license or certification; requirements vary by state.

Pay

The median annual wage for athletic trainers was $53,840 in May 2022.

Job Outlook

Employment of athletic trainers is projected to grow 14 percent from 2022 to 2032, much faster than the average for all occupations.

About 2,700 openings for athletic trainers are projected each year, on average, over the decade. Many of those openings are expected to result from the need to replace workers who transfer to different occupations or exit the labor force, such as to retire.

What Athletic Trainers Do

Athletic trainers specialize in preventing, diagnosing, and treating muscle and bone injuries and illnesses.

Duties

Athletic trainers typically do the following:

- Apply protective or injury-preventive devices, such as tape, bandages, and braces
- Recognize and evaluate injuries
- Provide first aid or emergency care
- Develop and carry out rehabilitation programs for injured athletes
- Plan and implement comprehensive programs to prevent injury and illness among athletes
- Perform administrative tasks, such as keeping records and writing reports on injuries and treatment programs

Athletic trainers specialize in preventing, diagnosing, and treating muscle and bone injuries and illnesses.

Athletic trainers carry out rehabilitation programs for injured athletes.

Athletic trainers work with people of all ages and all skill levels, from young children to soldiers and professional athletes. Athletic trainers are usually one of the first healthcare providers on the scene when injuries occur on the field. They work under the direction of a licensed physician and with other healthcare providers, often discussing specific injuries and treatment options or evaluating and treating patients, as directed by a physician. Some athletic trainers meet with a team physician or consulting physician regularly.

An athletic trainer's administrative responsibilities may include regular meetings with an athletic director or another administrative officer to deal with budgets, purchasing, policy implementation, and other business-related issues. Athletic trainers plan athletic programs that are compliant with federal and state regulations; for example, they may ensure a football program adheres to laws related to athlete concussions.

Athletic trainers should not be confused with fitness trainers and instructors, which include *personal trainers*.

Work Environment

Athletic trainers held about 33,800 jobs in 2022. The largest employers of athletic trainers were as follows:

Educational services; state, local, and private	40%
Hospitals; state, local, and private	18
Offices of physical, occupational and speech therapists, and audiologists	15
Fitness and recreational sports centers	3
Self-employed workers	3

Athletic trainers also may work with military, with law enforcement, with professional sports teams, or with performing artists.

Athletic trainers may spend their time working outdoors on sports fields in all types of weather.

Work Schedules

Most athletic trainers work full time. Athletic trainers who work with teams during sporting events may work evenings or weekends and travel often.

How to Become an Athletic Trainer

Athletic trainers typically need at least a bachelor's degree, and master's degrees are common. Nearly all states require athletic trainers to have a license or certification; requirements vary by state.

Education

To enter the occupation, athletic trainers typically need a degree from a program accredited by the Commission on Accreditation of Athletic Training Education (CAATE). Although some jobs are available for workers with a bachelor's degree, many athletic trainers have a master's degree.

Admission into athletic trainer master's programs generally requires a bachelor's degree with completion of coursework in science and health. Master's degree programs have classroom and clinical components and include instruction in areas such as injury prevention, therapeutic modalities, and nutrition.

High school students interested in postsecondary athletic training programs should take courses in anatomy, physiology, and physics.

Licenses, Certifications, and Registrations

Nearly all states require athletic trainers to be licensed or certified; requirements vary by state. For specific requirements, contact the particular state's licensing board.

The Board of Certification for the Athletic Trainer (BOC) offers the standard certification examination that most states use for licensing athletic trainers. Certification requires graduating from a CAATE-accredited program and passing the BOC exam. To maintain certification, athletic trainers must adhere to the BOC Standards of Professional Practice and take continuing education courses.

Athletic trainers may travel to games with athletes.

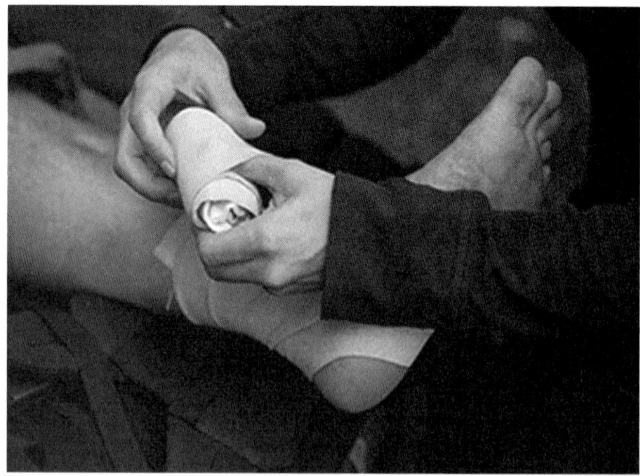

Athletic trainers must be licensed or certified in nearly all states.

Important Qualities

Compassion. Athletic trainers work with athletes and patients who may be in considerable pain or discomfort. The trainers must be sympathetic while providing treatments.

Decision-making skills. Athletic trainers must make informed clinical decisions that could affect the health or livelihood of patients.

Detail oriented. Athletic trainers must record patients' progress accurately and ensure that they are receiving the appropriate treatments or practicing the correct fitness regimen.

Interpersonal skills. Athletic trainers must have strong interpersonal skills in order to manage difficult situations. They must communicate well with others, including physicians, patients, athletes, coaches, and parents.

Advancement

Assistant athletic trainers may become head athletic trainers, athletic directors, or physician, hospital, or clinic practice administrators. In any of these positions, they will assume a management role. Athletic trainers working in colleges and universities may pursue an advanced degree to increase their advancement opportunities.

Pay

The median annual wage for athletic trainers was $53,840 in May 2022. The median wage is the wage at which half the workers in an occupation earned more than that amount and half earned less. The lowest 10 percent earned less than $39,670, and the highest 10 percent earned more than $78,000.

In May 2022, the median annual wages for athletic trainers in the top industries in which they worked were as follows:

Educational services; state, local, and private...	$56,930
Hospitals; state, local, and private.....................	53,440
Fitness and recreational sports centers.............	51,960
Offices of physical, occupational and speech therapists, and audiologists	49,960

Most athletic trainers work full time. Athletic trainers who work with teams during sporting events may work evenings or weekends and travel often.

Job Outlook

Employment of athletic trainers is projected to grow 14 percent from 2022 to 2032, much faster than the average for all occupations.

About 2,700 openings for athletic trainers are projected each year, on average, over the decade. Many of those openings are expected to result from the need to replace workers who transfer to different occupations or exit the labor force, such as to retire.

Employment

Sports programs at all ages and for all experience levels will continue to create demand for athletic trainers. With high levels of participation by children and youth in individual and team sports, athletic trainers will be needed to manage emergency and non-emergency situations that arise. The popularity of college sports and continued participation by student athletes will increase demand for these workers to help athletes prevent and recover from injuries and perform at their highest level.

Meanwhile, growing numbers of middle-aged and older people are remaining physically active. Their continued

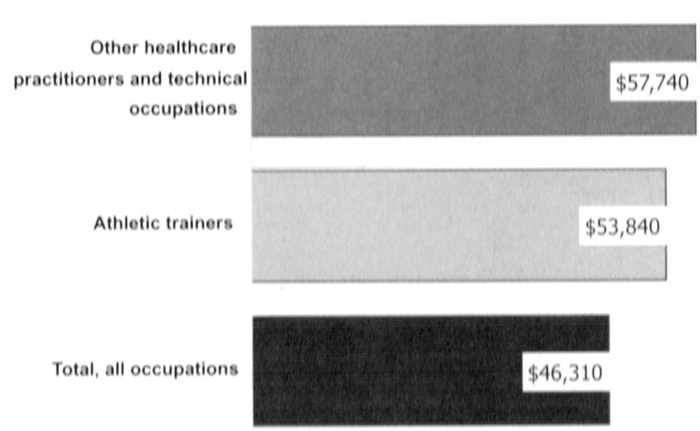

Note: All Occupations includes all occupations in the U.S. Economy.
Source: U.S. Bureau of Labor Statistics, Occupational Employment and Wage Statistics.

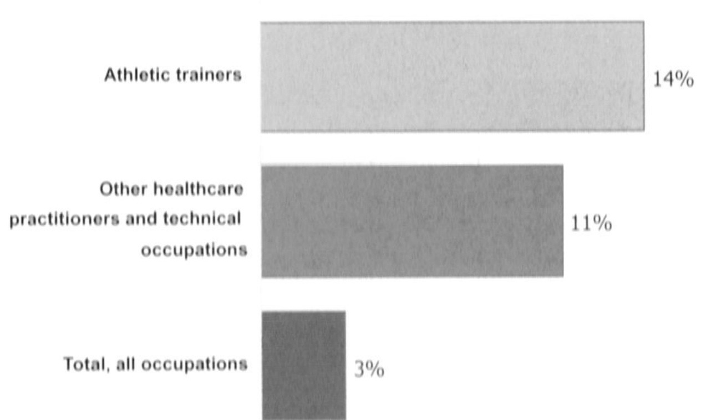

Note: All Occupations includes all occupations in the U.S. Economy.
Source: U.S. Bureau of Labor Statistics, Employment Projections program.

activity will likely lead to an increase in athletics-related injuries, such as sprains. Athletic trainers will be needed to provide sophisticated treatments in injury prevention and detection.

Occupational Title	SOC Code	Employment, 2022	Projected Employment, 2032	Change, 2022-32	
				Percent	Numeric
Athletic trainers	29-9091	33,800	38,500	14	4,800

Contacts for More Information

For more information about athletic trainers, visit

- National Athletic Trainers' Association
- Commission on Accreditation of Athletic Training Education
- Board of Certification for the Athletic Trainer

Audiologists

Summary

Quick Facts: Audiologists

2022 Median Pay	$82,680 per year $39.75 per hour
Typical Entry-Level Education	Doctoral or professional degree
Work Experience in a Related Occupation	None
On-the-job Training	None
Number of Jobs, 2022	14,400
Job Outlook, 2022-32	11% (Much faster than average)
Employment Change, 2022-32	1,500

What Audiologists Do

Audiologists diagnose, manage, and treat patients who have hearing, balance, or related problems.

Work Environment

Most audiologists work in healthcare facilities, such as physicians' offices, audiology clinics, and hospitals. Some work in schools or for school districts and travel between facilities.

How to Become an Audiologist

Audiologists typically need a doctor of audiology degree (Au.D.) to enter the occupation. All states require audiologists to be licensed.

Pay

The median annual wage for audiologists was $82,680 in May 2022.

Job Outlook

Employment of audiologists is projected to grow 11 percent from 2022 to 2032, much faster than the average for all occupations.

About 900 openings for audiologists are projected each year, on average, over the decade. Many of those openings are expected to result from the need to replace workers who transfer to different occupations or exit the labor force, such as to retire.

What Audiologists Do

Audiologists diagnose, manage, and treat patients who have hearing, balance, or related problems.

Duties

Audiologists typically do the following:

Audiologists fit and dispense hearing aids.

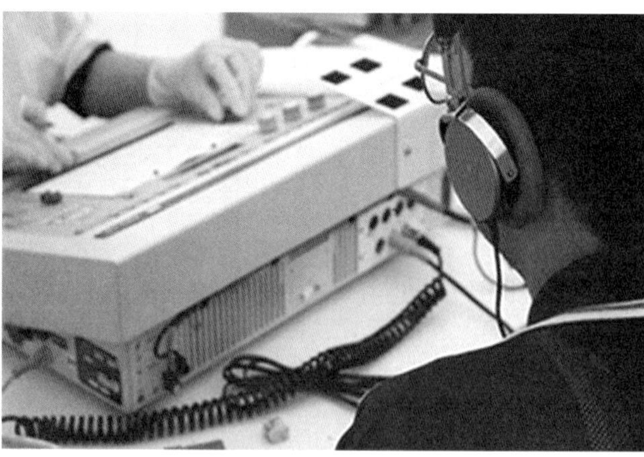

Audiologists diagnose, manage, and treat patients who have hearing, balance, or related problems.

- Examine patients who have conditions related to the outer, middle, or inner ear
- Assess the results of the examination and diagnose problems
- Create treatment plans to meet patients' goals
- Provide care for routine procedures, such as testing
- Fit and dispense hearing aids and other assistive listening devices
- Counsel patients and their families on ways to listen and communicate, such as by lip reading or through technology
- Evaluate patients regularly to monitor their condition and modify treatment plans, as needed
- Record patient progress
- Research the causes and treatment of hearing and balance disorders
- Educate patients on ways to prevent hearing loss

Audiologists diagnose conditions such as hearing loss and tinnitus (ringing in the ear). They use a variety of devices to identify the extent and underlying cause of hearing loss. For example, with audiometers they measure the volume and frequency at which a person hears.

Treatment depends on the type and severity of a patient's hearing loss and may range from cleaning wax out of ear canals to fitting and checking hearing aids. (Audiologists' ability to diagnose as well as treat patients distinguishes their work from that of hearing aid specialists.) Audiologists work with physicians and surgeons treating patients whose hearing may be improved with cochlear implants, small devices that are surgically embedded near the ear to deliver electrical impulses to the auditory nerve.

Audiologists also counsel patients and their families on adapting to hearing loss, such as through use of technology, and may refer them to resources and other support.

In addition to their work related to hearing conditions, audiologists help patients who have vertigo or other balance problems. For example, they may demonstrate exercises involving head movement or positioning to relieve some symptoms.

Some audiologists work with specific age groups, such as older adults or children. Other audiologists may fit patients for products that help protect their hearing on the job.

Work Environment

Audiologists held about 14,400 jobs in 2022. The largest employers of audiologists were as follows:

Employer	Percent
Offices of physical, occupational and speech therapists, and audiologists	27%
Offices of physicians	25
Hospitals; state, local, and private	14
Educational services; state, local, and private	11

Some audiologists, such as those contracted by a school system, travel between multiple facilities. Audiologists may work closely with other healthcare specialists, including audiology assistants (a type of medical assistant), physicians and surgeons, registered nurses, and speech-language pathologists.

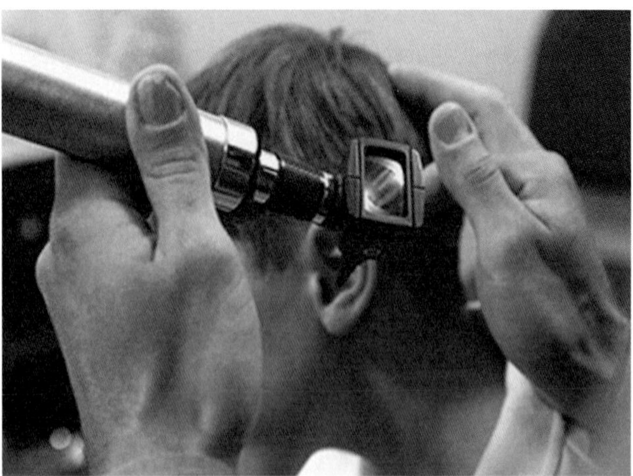

Audiologists identify symptoms of hearing loss and other auditory, balance, and related sensory and neural disorders.

Work Schedules

Most audiologists work full time. Some work weekends and evenings to meet patients' needs.

How to Become an Audiologist

Audiologists typically need a doctor of audiology (Au.D.) degree to enter the occupation. All states require audiologists to be licensed.

Education

Audiologists need a doctor of audiology (Au.D.) degree, which typically takes 4 years to complete. To enter an Au.D. program, students need a bachelor's degree.

Au.D. coursework includes anatomy and physiology, diagnosis and treatment, and statistics. Students also complete supervised clinical practice.

Licenses, Certifications, and Registrations

Audiologists must be licensed in all states. Requirements vary by state but typically include having earned an Au.D. from an accredited program. For specific requirements, contact your state's licensing board for audiologists.

Audiologists may earn other credentials, such as certificates or certifications offered by the American Speech-Language-Hearing Association and the American Board of Audiology. These credentials usually require completion of an accredited doctor of audiology program and passing an exam. Some employers may require or prefer that candidates have certification or a certificate, and in some states having the credential can help to meet licensure requirements.

Important Qualities

Communication skills. Audiologists need to convey information, including test results and proposed treatments, so that patients understand their diagnosis and options.

Compassion. Audiologists should be empathetic and supportive of their patients, who may be frustrated because of their hearing or balance problems.

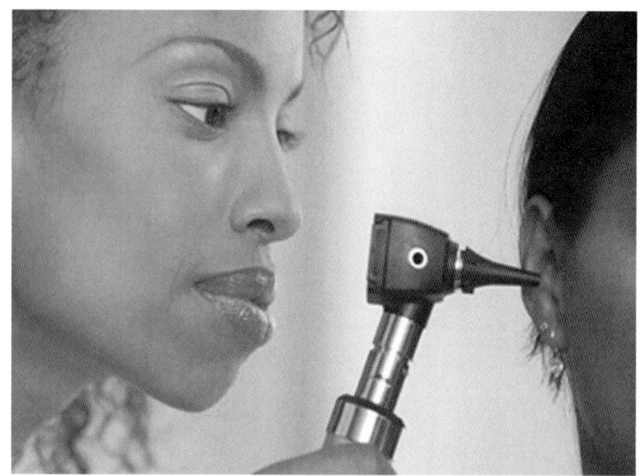

Audiologists must be licensed in all states.

Critical-thinking skills. In order to propose the best treatment options, audiologists must concentrate when testing a patient's hearing and in analyzing the results.

Interpersonal skills. Audiologists often collaborate with other healthcare providers regarding patient care.

Patience. Audiologists work with patients who may have communication difficulties and need extra time or attention.

Problem-solving skills. Audiologists must figure out the causes of hearing or balance problems and determine appropriate treatment options. They also must be able to propose alternatives if patients do not respond to initial treatment.

Pay

The median annual wage for audiologists was $82,680 in May 2022. The median wage is the wage at which half the workers in an occupation earned more than that amount and half earned less. The lowest 10 percent earned less than $56,990, and the highest 10 percent earned more than $120,380.

In May 2022, the median annual wages for audiologists in the top industries in which they worked were as follows:

Hospitals; state, local, and private	$95,300
Educational services; state, local, and private	86,040
Offices of physicians	83,140
Offices of physical, occupational and speech therapists, and audiologists	76,440

Most audiologists work full time. Some may work weekends and evenings to meet patients' needs. Those who work on a contract basis may spend time traveling between facilities.

Job Outlook

Employment of audiologists is projected to grow 11 percent from 2022 to 2032, much faster than the average for all occupations.

About 900 openings for audiologists are projected each year, on average, over the decade. Many of those openings are expected to result from the need to replace workers who transfer to different occupations or exit the labor force, such as to retire.

Audiologists

Median annual wages, May 2022

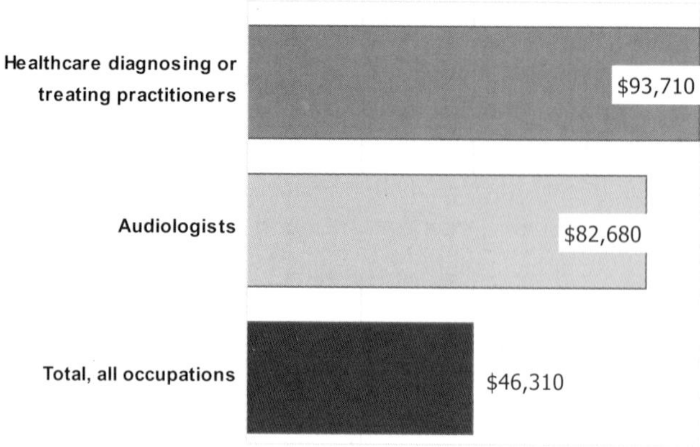

Note: All Occupations includes all occupations in the U.S. Economy.
Source: U.S. Bureau of Labor Statistics, Occupational Employment and Wage Statistics.

Employment

Because health problems are prevalent in older age groups, an aging baby-boom population will continue to increase the demand for most healthcare services. This includes hearing loss and balance disorders, with larger numbers of older people creating increased demand for audiologists.

The early identification and diagnosis of hearing disorders in infants also may support employment growth. Growing awareness regarding advances in hearing aid technology, such as smaller size and reduced feedback, may make such devices more appealing as a means to treat auditory loss. This may lead to more demand for audiologists.

Audiologists

Percent change in employment, projected 2022-32

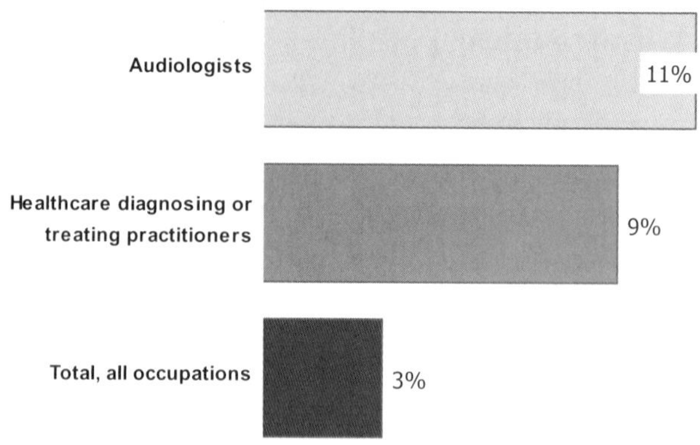

Note: All Occupations includes all occupations in the U.S. Economy.
Source: U.S. Bureau of Labor Statistics, Employment Projections program.

Occupational Title	SOC Code	Employment, 2022	Projected Employment, 2032	Change, 2022-32	
				Percent	Numeric
Audiologists	29-1181	14,400	15,900	11	1,500

Contacts for More Information

For more information on state-specific licensing requirements, contact the state's licensing board.

For more information about audiologists, including requirements for certification and state licensure, visit

- American Speech-Language-Hearing Association (ASHA)
- American Academy of Audiology
- Accreditation Commission for Audiology Education (ACAE)
- Council on Academic Accreditation

Chiropractors

Summary

Quick Facts: Chiropractors

2022 Median Pay	$75,380 per year $36.24 per hour
Typical Entry-Level Education	Doctoral or professional degree
Work Experience in a Related Occupation	None
On-the-job Training	None
Number of Jobs, 2022	55,000
Job Outlook, 2022-32	9% (Much faster than average)
Employment Change, 2022-32	4,900

What Chiropractors Do

Chiropractors evaluate and treat patients' neuromusculoskeletal system, which includes nerves, bones, muscles, ligaments, and tendons.

Work Environment

Most chiropractors work in a solo or group chiropractic practice. Some are self-employed. Chiropractors usually work full time, but part-time work is common.

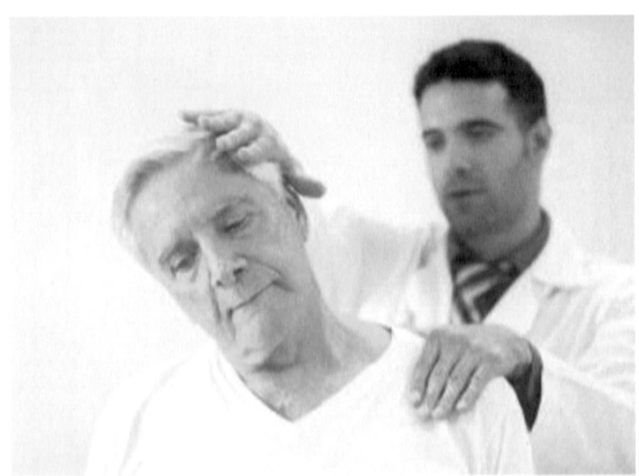

Chiropractors treat patients with health problems of the neuromusculoskeletal system.

How to Become a Chiropractor

Chiropractors typically need a Doctor of Chiropractic (D.C.) degree. Completing a D.C. program typically takes about 4 years, in addition to at least 3 years of undergraduate study. Every state requires chiropractors to be licensed.

Pay

The median annual wage for chiropractors was $75,380 in May 2022.

Job Outlook

Employment of chiropractors is projected to grow 9 percent from 2022 to 2032, much faster than the average for all occupations.

About 2,600 openings for chiropractors are projected each year, on average, over the decade. Many of those openings are expected to result from the need to replace workers who transfer to different occupations or exit the labor force, such as to retire.

What Chiropractors Do

Chiropractors evaluate and treat patients' neuromusculoskeletal system, which includes nerves, bones, muscles, ligaments, and tendons. They use spinal adjustments and manipulation, as well as other clinical interventions, to manage patients' health concerns, such as back and neck pain.

Duties

Chiropractors typically do the following:

- Review a patient's medical history and listen to their concerns
- Perform a physical examination to analyze the patient's posture, spine, and reflexes
- Provide neuromusculoskeletal therapy, which involves adjusting a patient's spinal column and other joints
- Give additional treatments, such as applying heat or cold to a patient's injured areas
- Advise patients on health and lifestyle issues, such as exercise and nutrition
- Refer patients to other healthcare professionals if needed

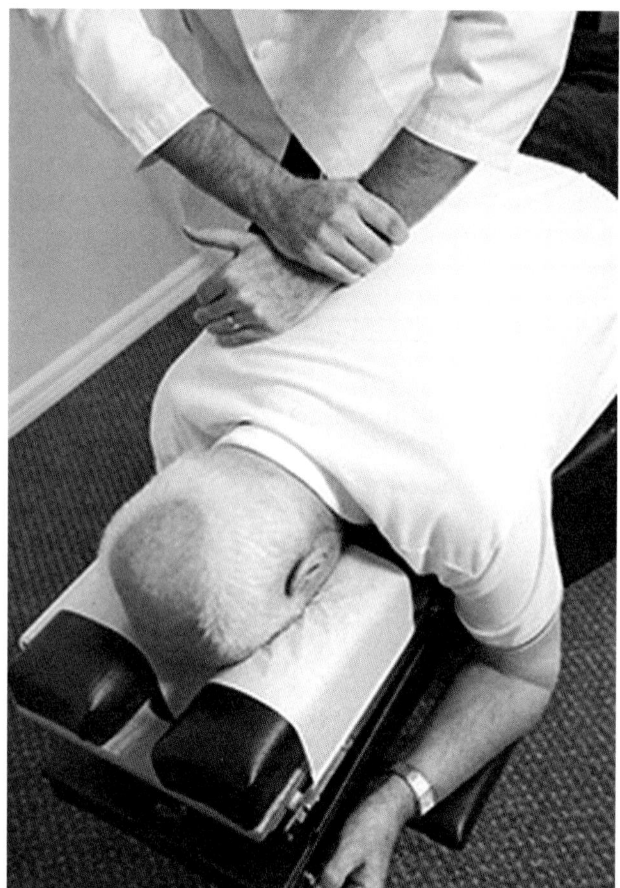

Chiropractors perform manual therapy to help patients with back and neck pain.

Chiropractors treat a variety of problems related to the neuromusculoskeletal system. They focus on pain in the back, neck, and joints and how relieving this pain can improve patients' overall health. The goal is to improve the body's motion and function.

In diagnosing a patient's condition, chiropractors often use both external and internal assessments. For example, a chiropractor may observe the patient's range of motion related to shoulder pain and then follow up with x rays to provide more detailed information.

Some chiropractors treat patients using procedures such as massage therapy, rehabilitative exercise, and electrical muscle stimulation in addition to spinal adjustments and manipulation. They also may apply supports, such as braces or tape, to treat patients and relieve pain.

In addition to operating a general chiropractic practice, chiropractors may specialize in areas such as sports, neurology, or nutrition. Chiropractors who are self-employed or work in private practice may have additional responsibilities that include marketing their business, hiring staff, and keeping records.

Work Environment

Chiropractors held about 55,000 jobs in 2022. The largest employers of chiropractors were as follows:

Offices of chiropractors	63%
Self-employed workers	31

Chiropractors typically work in office settings. They may need to stand for long periods and lift or turn patients.

Work Schedules

Most chiropractors work full time, but part-time work is common. Work schedules may vary and include evenings or weekends to accommodate patients. Self-employed chiropractors may have the flexibility to set their own hours.

How to Become a Chiropractor

Chiropractors typically need a Doctor of Chiropractic (D.C.) degree. Completing a D.C. program typically takes about 4 years, in addition to at least 3 years of undergraduate study. Every state requires chiropractors to be licensed.

Education

Chiropractors must have a Doctor of Chiropractic (D.C.) degree from an accredited chiropractic college. A D.C. degree usually takes 4 years to complete. Chiropractic colleges are accredited by The Council on Chiropractic Education.

Admission to D.C. programs requires at least 3 years of undergraduate education, although applicants commonly have a bachelor's degree. Typical bachelor's degrees for prospective D.C. students include biology, healthcare and related fields, or kinesiology, exercise physiology, or other subjects focusing on physical movement. Chiropractic programs generally require applicants to have completed coursework in sciences such as physics, chemistry, and biology, as well as general education studies.

A D.C. program includes coursework in anatomy, physiology, biology, and similar subjects. Courses in business management, such as marketing and finance, also may be included. Chiropractic students gain supervised clinical experience in areas such as diagnosis, spinal assessment, and adjustment

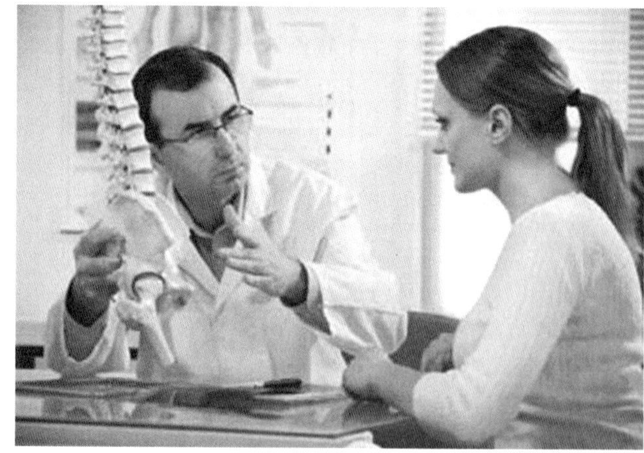

Chiropractors assess a patient's medical condition and explain treatment options.

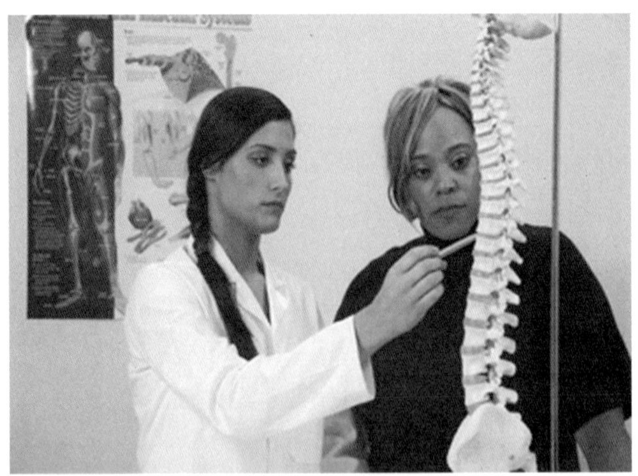

Chiropractors must earn a Doctor of Chiropractic (D.C.) degree and get a state license.

techniques. D.C. programs may offer a dual-degree option, in which students earn either a bachelor's or a master's degree in another field while completing their D.C.

Some chiropractors complete postgraduate programs that lead to diplomate credentials. These programs provide additional training in specialty areas, such as orthopedics, acupuncture, and pediatrics.

Licenses, Certifications, and Registrations

All states require chiropractors to be licensed, although requirements vary by state. At a minimum, all require the completion of an accredited Doctor of Chiropractic (D.C.) degree program and passing all four parts of the National Board of Chiropractic Examiners (NBCE) exam. States also may require candidates to pass a background check and state-specific law exams, called jurisprudence exams.

All states require practicing chiropractors to earn a specified number of hours of continuing education credits to maintain a chiropractic license. Contact your state's board of chiropractic examiners or health department for more specific information about licensure.

Important Qualities

Communication skills. Chiropractors must listen to patients and explain procedures clearly both orally and in written reports.

Decision-making skills. Chiropractors must evaluate each patient's needs and recommend treatment based on those needs. They must also decide when to refer patients to other healthcare professionals.

Detail oriented. Chiropractors must pay attention when diagnosing and treating patients to avoid mistakes that could harm them.

Dexterity. Chiropractors must have good coordination when performing manual adjustments to a patient's spine and other joints.

Empathy. Chiropractors often care for people who are in pain. They must be understanding and sympathetic to their patients' problems and needs.

Interpersonal skills. Chiropractors must be personable in order to put patients at ease and expand their practice.

Pay

The median annual wage for chiropractors was $75,380 in May 2022. The median wage is the wage at which half the workers in an occupation earned more than that amount and half earned less. The lowest 10 percent earned less than $38,170, and the highest 10 percent earned more than $132,630.

In May 2022, the median annual wages for chiropractors in the top industries in which they worked were as follows:

Offices of chiropractors	$73,070

Wage data do not cover self-employed workers or owners and partners of unincorporated businesses.

Earnings vary with the chiropractor's number of years in practice, geographic region of practice, and hours worked. Chiropractors tend to earn more as they build a client base and become owners of, or partners in, a practice.

Most chiropractors work full time, but part-time work is common. Work schedules may vary and include evenings or weekends to accommodate patients. Self-employed chiropractors may have the flexibility to set their own hours.

Job Outlook

Employment of chiropractors is projected to grow 9 percent from 2022 to 2032, much faster than the average for all occupations.

About 2,600 openings for chiropractors are projected each year, on average, over the decade. Many of those openings are expected to result from the need to replace workers who transfer to different occupations or exit the labor force, such as to retire.

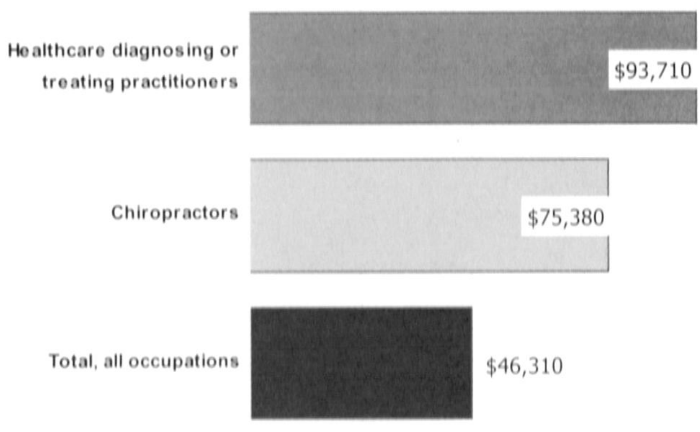

Employment

Demand is expected to increase for chiropractic services as a nonsurgical, drug-free way to treat pain and improve overall wellness. Rising interest in integrative or complementary healthcare has led to more acceptance of chiropractic treatment of the back, neck, limbs, and involved joints. As a result, chiropractors are increasingly working with other healthcare workers, such as physicians and physical therapists, through referrals and complementary care.

Opportunities for chiropractors also will be created by the continued aging of the large baby-boom generation. Older adults are more likely than younger people to have neuromusculoskeletal and joint problems, and they will continue to seek chiropractic care and other types of treatment for these conditions.

Occupational Title	SOC Code	Employment, 2022	Projected Employment, 2032	Change, 2022-32	
				Percent	Numeric
Chiropractors	29-1011	55,000	59,800	9	4,900

Chiropractors

Percent change in employment, projected 2022-32

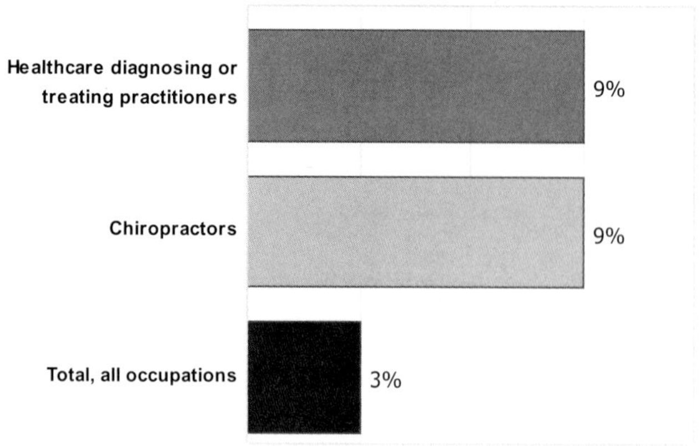

Note: All Occupations includes all occupations in the U.S. Economy.
Source: U.S. Bureau of Labor Statistics, Employment Projections program.

Contacts for More Information

For more information on a career as a chiropractor, visit

- American Chiropractic Association
- International Chiropractors Association
- Discover Chiropractic
- Association of Chiropractic Colleges
- The Council on Chiropractic Education
- Federation of Chiropractic Licensing Boards
- For information about licensing exams, visit
- National Board of Chiropractic Examiners

Clinical Laboratory Technologists and Technicians

Summary

Quick Facts: Clinical Laboratory Technologists and Technicians

2022 Median Pay	$57,380 per year $27.59 per hour
Typical Entry-Level Education	Bachelor's degree
Work Experience in a Related Occupation	None
On-the-job Training	None
Number of Jobs, 2022	342,900
Job Outlook, 2022-32	5% (Faster than average)
Employment Change, 2022-32	16,800

What Clinical Laboratory Technologists and Technicians Do

Clinical laboratory technologists and technicians perform medical laboratory tests for the diagnosis, treatment, and prevention of disease.

Work Environment

Most clinical laboratory technologists and technicians work in healthcare settings such as hospitals, medical and diagnostic laboratories, and doctor's offices. Most work full time.

Clinical laboratory personnel examine and test body fluids and cells.

How to Become a Clinical Laboratory Technologist or Technician

Clinical laboratory technologists and technicians typically need a bachelor's degree to enter the occupation. Technicians sometimes qualify for jobs with an associate's degree. Some states require technologists and technicians to be licensed.

Pay

The median annual wage for clinical laboratory technologists and technicians was $57,380 in May 2022.

Job Outlook

Employment of clinical laboratory technologists and technicians is projected to grow 5 percent from 2022 to 2032, faster than the average for all occupations.

About 24,000 openings for clinical laboratory technologists and technicians are projected each year, on average, over the decade. Many of those openings are expected to result from the need to replace workers who transfer to different occupations or exit the labor force, such as to retire.

What Clinical Laboratory Technologists and Technicians Do

Clinical laboratory technologists (also known as *medical laboratory technologists*) and clinical laboratory technicians (also known as *medical laboratory technicians*) perform medical laboratory tests for the diagnosis, treatment, and prevention of disease.

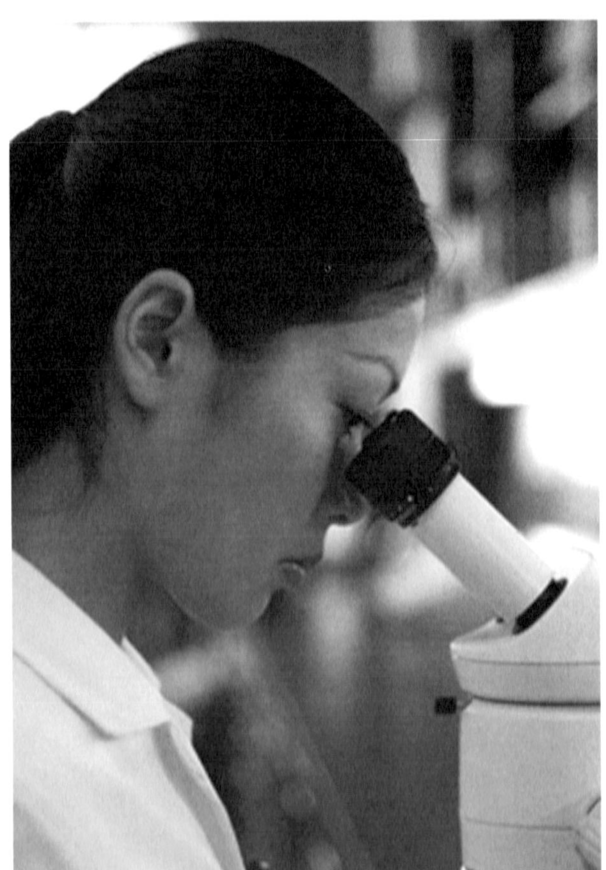

Clinical laboratory technologists operate sophisticated laboratory equipment, such as microscopes and cell counters.

Duties

Clinical laboratory technologists and technicians typically do the following:

- Test and analyze body fluids, such as blood, urine, and tissue samples
- Operate laboratory equipment, such as microscopes and automated cell counters
- Use automated equipment that analyzes multiple samples at the same time
- Record data from medical tests and enter results into a patient's medical record
- Discuss results and findings of laboratory tests and procedures with physicians

Both technicians and technologists perform tests and procedures that physicians and surgeons or other healthcare practitioners order. However, technologists perform more complex tests and laboratory procedures than technicians do. For example, technologists may prepare specimens and perform detailed manual tests, whereas technicians perform routine tests that may be more automated. Clinical laboratory technicians usually work under the general supervision of clinical laboratory technologists or laboratory managers.

Clinical laboratory technologists and technicians set up, calibrate, and maintain the microscopes, cell counters, and other equipment they use. Maintenance includes troubleshooting, cleaning, and testing sterility to ensure quality control. Technologists have more responsibilities related to overall quality assurance in laboratories than do technicians.

Some technologists specialize in a certain type of test. The following are examples of types of specialized clinical laboratory technologists:

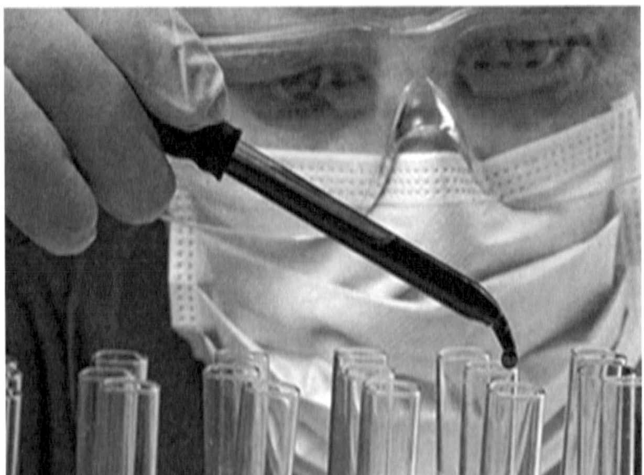

Laboratory personnel wear protective masks, gloves, and goggles to ensure their safety.

Blood bank technologists collect blood, classify it by type, and prepare blood and its components for transfusions.

Clinical chemistry technologists prepare specimens and analyze the chemical and hormonal contents of body fluids.

Cytotechnologists prepare and examine slides of body cells under a microscope. They look for abnormalities that may signal the beginning of a cancerous growth.

Hematology technologists examine blood to identify conditions or diseases, such as blood clots or cancer.

Histotechnologists perform tests on human tissue to identify diseases.

Microbiology technologists examine and identify bacteria and other microorganisms.

Molecular biology technologists perform protein and nucleic acid tests, such as gene sequencing, on cell samples.

Like technologists, clinical laboratory technicians may work in several areas or specialize in one area. For example, *histotechnicians* are a type of clinical laboratory technician who cut and stain tissue specimens for pathologists—doctors who study the cause and development of diseases.

Work Environment

Clinical laboratory technologists and technicians held about 342,900 jobs in 2022. The largest employers of clinical laboratory technologists and technicians were as follows:

General medical and surgical hospitals; state, local, and private	44%
Medical and diagnostic laboratories	21
Offices of physicians	9
Junior colleges, colleges, universities, and professional schools; state, local, and private	5
Outpatient care centers	3

Clinical laboratory technologists and technicians work with infectious specimens and other biohazardous substances.

Technologists and technicians may need to stand for long periods.

Injuries and Illnesses

Clinical laboratory technologists and technicians may incur injury or illness on the job. For example, they may be subject to repetitive motion injuries because they do the same tasks repeatedly or to illness from working with biohazardous material. To reduce the risk of infection, they follow laboratory safety protocol and wear protective masks, gloves, and goggles.

Work Schedules

Most clinical laboratory technologists and technicians work full time. Because they may work in medical facilities that are always open, such as hospitals, they may have shifts that include nights, weekends, or holidays.

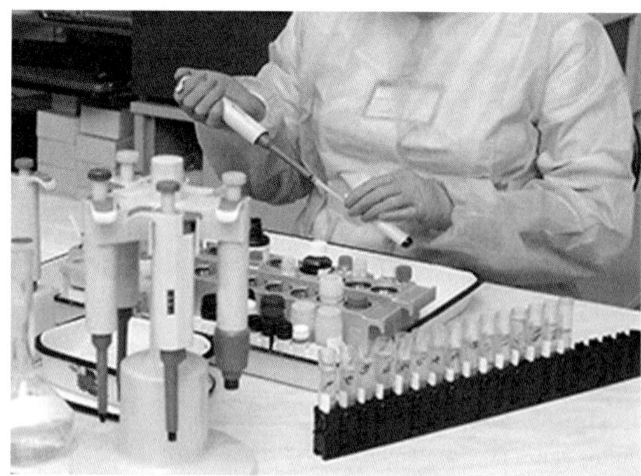

Clinical laboratory technologists typically need a bachelor's degree.

How to Become a Clinical Laboratory Technologist or Technician

Clinical laboratory technologists and technicians typically need a bachelor's degree to enter the occupation. Technicians sometimes qualify for jobs with an associate's degree. Some states require technologists and technicians to be licensed. Employers may prefer to hire candidates who have certification.

Education

High school students who are interested in becoming a clinical laboratory technologist or technician should take classes in chemistry, biology, and math.

Clinical laboratory technologists typically earn a bachelor's degree in medical technology or a related life sciences field, such as biology or chemistry.

Bachelor's degree programs in medical laboratory technology, also known as a medical laboratory scientist degree, include courses in chemistry, biology, and hematology. Accredited programs typically include instruction in laboratory skills, such as safety procedures and lab management, as well as hands-on training in a hospital or other clinical setting. Some laboratory science programs can be completed in 2 years or less and require prior college coursework or a bachelor's degree.

Clinical laboratory technicians typically complete an associate's degree program in clinical laboratory science. The Armed Forces and vocational or technical schools also may offer postsecondary certificate programs for medical laboratory technicians. Accredited technician programs provide skills in basic laboratory testing and, like medical laboratory scientist degree programs, may offer clinical experience.

Certain types of technologists, such as cytotechnologists, must attend specialized education programs.

For a list of accredited bachelor's and associate's degree programs, visit organizations such as the National Accrediting Agency for Clinical Laboratory Sciences (NAACLS).

Licenses, Certifications, and Registrations

Some states require laboratory personnel to be licensed or registered. Requirements vary by state and specialty. For specific requirements, contact your state department of health or state board of occupational licensing.

In some states, licensure requires certification. Although certification is not always required to enter the occupation, employers may prefer to hire certified technologists and technicians.

Individuals may earn certification as a medical laboratory scientist or medical laboratory technician. Completion of an accredited education program is typically required to sit for a certification exam. A number of organizations offer certification, including the American Association of Bioanalysts, American Medical Technologists, and the American Society for Clinical Pathology.

Specialty certification is available in areas such as histology and clinical chemistry for those who meet requirements for additional education and work experience.

Advancement

Some clinical laboratory technicians advance to technologist positions after gaining experience and additional education.

Important Qualities

Analytical skills. Clinical laboratory technologists and technicians must examine the specimens they test to determine whether there are abnormalities.

Detail oriented. Clinical laboratory technologists and technicians must follow instructions and laboratory procedures when performing tests.

Dexterity. Clinical laboratory technologists and technicians must work carefully when handling needles, specimens, and laboratory equipment.

Interpersonal skills. Clinical laboratory technologists and technicians may collect blood or tissue samples from patients who feel stressed. They must be supportive and sympathetic in their interactions with patients.

Physical stamina. Clinical laboratory technologists and technicians may stand for long periods while collecting samples. They may need to lift or turn patients to collect samples for testing.

Pay

The median annual wage for clinical laboratory technologists and technicians was $57,380 in May 2022. The median wage is the wage at which half the workers in an occupation earned more than that amount and half earned less. The lowest 10 percent earned less than $35,220, and the highest 10 percent earned more than $84,670.

In May 2022, the median annual wages for clinical laboratory technologists and technicians in the top industries in which they worked were as follows:

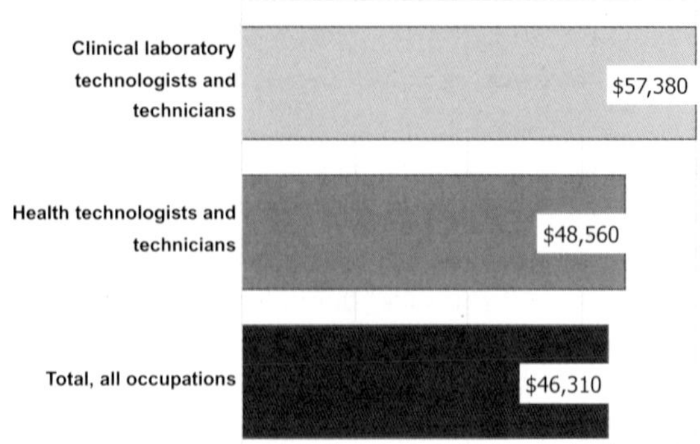

Note: All Occupations includes all occupations in the U.S. Economy.
Source: U.S. Bureau of Labor Statistics, Occupational Employment and Wage Statistics.

Outpatient care centers	$62,870
General medical and surgical hospitals; state, local, and private	62,470
Junior colleges, colleges, universities, and professional schools; state, local, and private	51,460
Medical and diagnostic laboratories	50,670
Offices of physicians	49,530

Most clinical laboratory technologists and technicians work full time. Because technologists and technicians may work in facilities that are always open, such as hospitals, they may have shifts that include nights, weekends, or holidays.

Job Outlook

Employment of clinical laboratory technologists and technicians is projected to grow 5 percent from 2022 to 2032, faster than the average for all occupations.

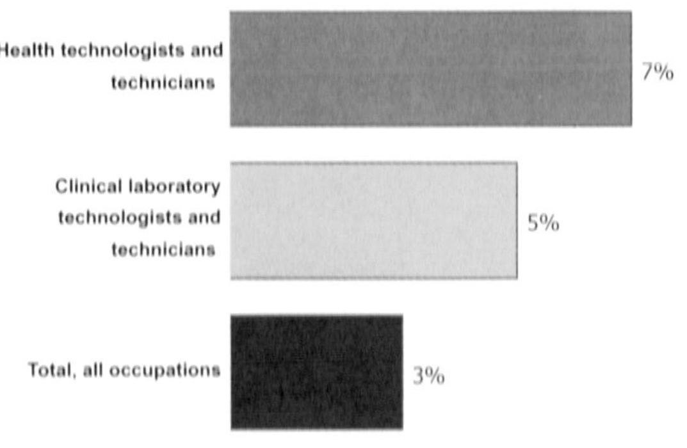

Note: All Occupations includes all occupations in the U.S. Economy.
Source: U.S. Bureau of Labor Statistics, Employment Projections program.

About 24,000 openings for clinical laboratory technologists and technicians are projected each year, on average, over the decade. Many of those openings are expected to result from the need to replace workers who transfer to different occupations or exit the labor force, such as to retire.

Employment

An increase in the population of older adults is expected to lead to a greater need for diagnosing medical conditions, such as cancer or type 2 diabetes, through laboratory procedures. Prenatal testing for various types of genetic conditions also is increasingly common. Clinical laboratory technologists and technicians will be in demand to use and maintain the equipment needed for diagnosis and treatment.

Occupational Title	SOC Code	Employment, 2022	Projected Employment, 2032	Change, 2022-32	
				Percent	Numeric
Clinical laboratory technologists and technicians	29-2010	342,900	359,700	5	16,800

Contacts for More Information

For more information about clinical laboratory technologists and technicians, visit

- The American Society for Clinical Laboratory Science
- American Society of Cytopathology
- National Accrediting Agency for Clinical Laboratory Sciences
- American Association of Bioanalysts
- American Medical Technologists
- American Society for Clinical Pathology

Dental Assistants

Summary

Quick Facts: Dental Assistants

2022 Median Pay	$44,820 per year $21.55 per hour
Typical Entry-Level Education	Postsecondary nondegree award
Work Experience in a Related Occupation	None
On-the-job Training	None
Number of Jobs, 2022	371,000
Job Outlook, 2022-32	7% (Faster than average)
Employment Change, 2022-32	25,700

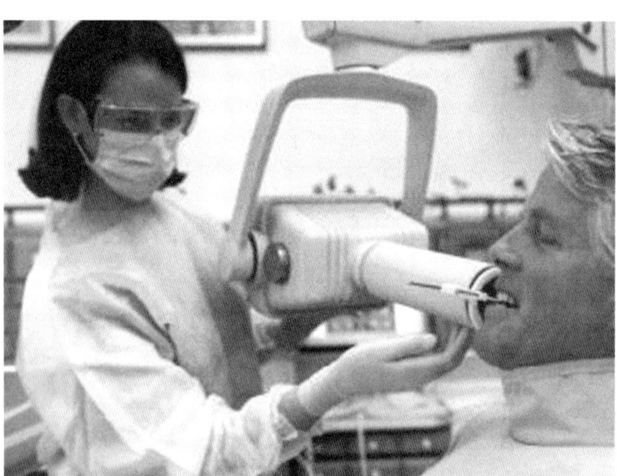

Dental assistants perform many tasks, ranging from providing patient care and taking x rays to recordkeeping and scheduling appointments.

What Dental Assistants Do

Dental assistants provide patient care, take x rays, keep records, and schedule appointments.

Work Environment

Almost all dental assistants work in dentists' offices. Most work full time.

How to Become a Dental Assistant

There are several possible paths to becoming a dental assistant. Some states require assistants to graduate from an accredited program and pass an exam. In other states, there are no formal educational requirements, and dental assistants learn through on-the-job training.

Pay

The median annual wage for dental assistants was $44,820 in May 2022.

Job Outlook

Employment of dental assistants is projected to grow 7 percent from 2022 to 2032, faster than the average for all occupations.

About 55,100 openings for dental assistants are projected each year, on average, over the decade. Many of those openings are expected to result from the need to replace workers who transfer to different occupations or exit the labor force, such as to retire.

What Dental Assistants Do

Dental assistants have many tasks, including patient care, recordkeeping, and appointment scheduling. Their duties vary by state and by the dentists' offices in which they work.

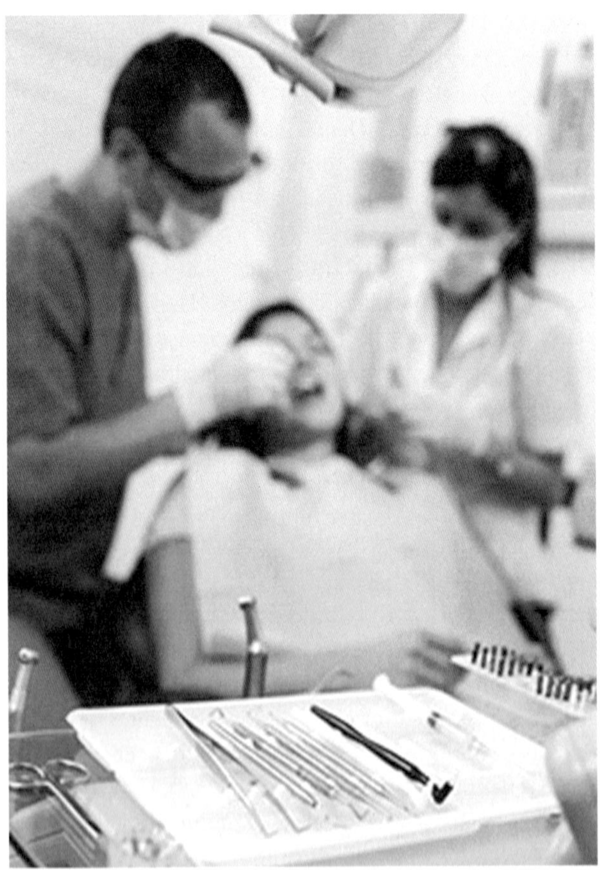

Assistants prepare and organize tools needed by dentists to work on a patient.

Duties

Dental assistants typically do the following:

- Ensure that patients are comfortable in the dental chair
- Prepare patients and the work area for treatments and procedures
- Sterilize dental instruments
- Hand instruments to dentists during procedures
- Dry patients' mouths using suction hoses and other equipment
- Instruct patients in proper oral hygiene
- Process x rays and complete lab tasks, under the direction of a dentist
- Keep records of dental treatments
- Schedule patient appointments
- Work with patients on billing and payment

Dental assistants often spend much of their day working closely with patients and dentists. For example, dental assistants might take a patient's medical history, blood pressure, and pulse before a procedure; explain what will be done; and talk to patients about oral care. They help dentists during a procedure by passing instruments and holding equipment such as suction hoses, matrix bands, and dental curing lights. Other tasks include preparing the treatment room and making sure that instruments and equipment are sterile. Dental assistants also may document the procedure that is done and schedule followup appointments.

Some dental assistants are specially trained to take x rays of teeth and the surrounding areas. They place a protective apron over patients' chest and lap, position the x-ray machine, place the x-ray sensor or film in patients' mouths, and take the x rays. Afterward, dental assistants ensure that the images are clear.

Assistants who perform lab tasks, such as taking impressions of a patient's teeth, work under the direction of a dentist. They may prepare materials for dental impressions or temporary crowns.

Each state regulates the scope of practice for dental assistants. Some states let dental assistants polish teeth to remove stains and plaque from the enamel or apply sealants, fluoride, or topical anesthetic.

Work Environment

Dental assistants held about 371,000 jobs in 2022. The largest employers of dental assistants were as follows:

Offices of dentists	90%
Offices of physicians	2
Government	2

Dental assistants work under the supervision of dentists and work closely with dental hygienists in their day-to-day activities.

Dental assistants wear safety glasses, surgical masks, protective clothing, and gloves to protect themselves and patients from infectious diseases. They also must follow safety procedures to minimize risks associated with x-ray machines.

Work Schedules

Most dental assistants work full time. Some work evenings or weekends.

How to Become a Dental Assistant

There are several possible paths to becoming a dental assistant. Some states require assistants to graduate from an accredited

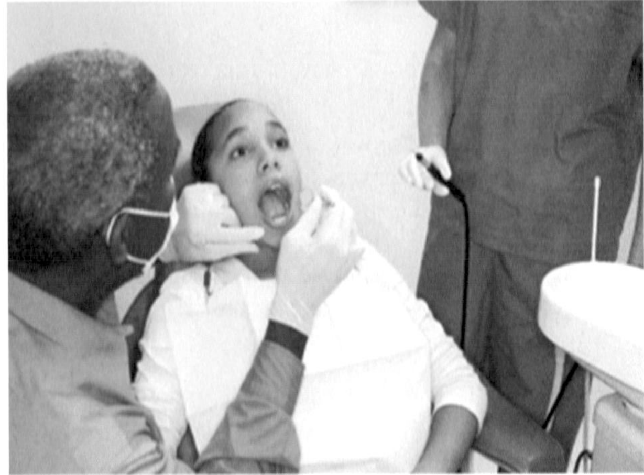

Dental assistants provide support to dentists as they work on patients.

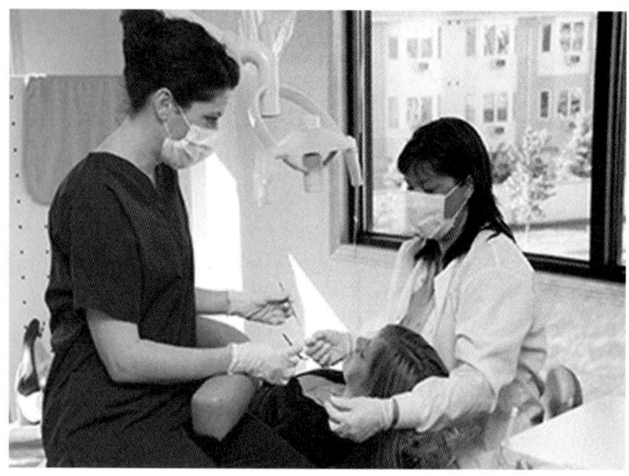

Sometimes, patients are in extreme pain and/or mental distress, so the assistant should be sensitive to their emotions.

program and pass an exam. In other states, there are no formal educational requirements, and dental assistants learn through on-the-job training.

Education

Some states require dental assistants to graduate from an accredited program and pass an exam. Most programs are offered by community colleges, although they also may be offered by vocational or technical schools.

Many dental assisting programs take about 1 year to complete and lead to a certificate or diploma. Programs that last 2 years are less common and lead to an associate's degree. The Commission on Dental Accreditation (CODA), part of the American Dental Association, accredits about 250 dental assisting training programs.

Accredited programs include classroom and laboratory work. Students learn about teeth, gums, jaws, and other areas that dentists work on and the instruments that dentists use. These programs also include supervised practical experience.

High school students interested in a career as a dental assistant should take courses in anatomy, biology, and chemistry.

Training

Dental assistants who do not have formal education in dental assisting may learn their duties through on-the-job training. In the office, a dental hygienist, dentist, or experienced dental assistant teaches the new assistant dental terminology, the names of the instruments, how to complete daily tasks, how to interact with patients, and other activities necessary to help keep the dental office running smoothly.

Important Qualities

Detail oriented. Dental assistants must follow specific rules and protocols, such as infection control procedures, when helping dentists treat patients.

Dexterity. Dental assistants must be good at working with their hands. They generally work in tight spaces on a small part of the body, using precise tools and instruments.

Interpersonal skills. Dental assistants work closely with dentists. They also must be considerate in working with patients who are sensitive to pain or have a fear of undergoing dental treatment.

Listening skills. Dental assistants must pay attention to patients and other healthcare workers. They need to follow directions from a dentist or dental hygienist so they can help treat patients and do tasks, such as taking x rays.

Organizational skills. Dental assistants should have excellent organizational skills. They need to have the correct tools in place for a dentist or dental hygienist to use when treating a patient, and they need to maintain patient schedules and office records.

Licenses, Certifications, and Registrations

States typically do not require licenses for entry-level dental assistants. Some states require dental assistants to be licensed, registered, or certified for entry or advancement. For example, states may require assistants to meet specific licensing requirements in order to work in radiography (x ray), infection control, or other specialties. For specific requirements, contact your state's Board of Dental Examiners.

States that allow assistants to perform expanded duties, such as coronal polishing, require that they be licensed, registered, or hold certifications from the Dental Assisting National Board (DANB). To earn certification from DANB, applicants must pass an exam. The educational requirements for DANB certification are that dental assistants must either have graduated from an accredited program or have a high school diploma and complete the required amount of work experience. Applicants also must have current certification in CPR (cardiopulmonary resuscitation).

Pay

The median annual wage for dental assistants was $44,820 in May 2022. The median wage is the wage at which half the workers in an occupation earned more than that amount and half earned less. The lowest 10 percent earned less than $31,450, and the highest 10 percent earned more than $59,200.

In May 2022, the median annual wages for dental assistants in the top industries in which they worked were as follows:

Government	$47,390
Offices of dentists	44,860
Offices of physicians	40,080

Most dental assistants work full time. Some work evenings or weekends.

Dental Assistants

Median annual wages, May 2022

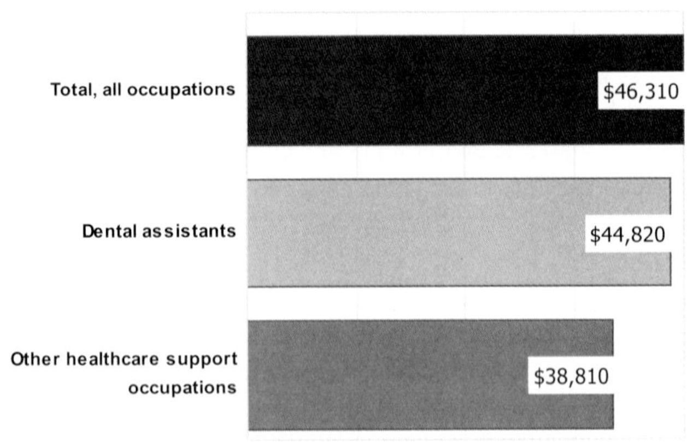

Note: All Occupations includes all occupations in the U.S. Economy.
Source: U.S. Bureau of Labor Statistics, Occupational Employment and Wage Statistics.

Dental Assistants

Percent change in employment, projected 2022-32

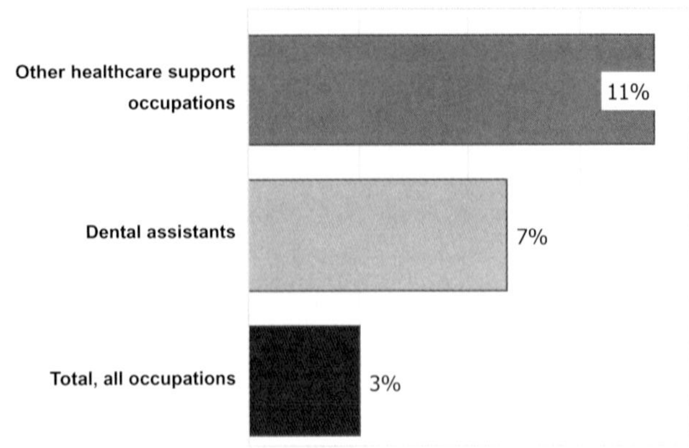

Note: All Occupations includes all occupations in the U.S. Economy.
Source: U.S. Bureau of Labor Statistics, Employment Projections program.

Job Outlook

Employment of dental assistants is projected to grow 7 percent from 2022 to 2032, faster than the average for all occupations.

About 55,100 openings for dental assistants are projected each year, on average, over the decade. Many of those openings are expected to result from the need to replace workers who transfer to different occupations or exit the labor force, such as to retire.

Employment

Ongoing research linking oral health and general health will continue to increase demand for preventive dental services. Dentists will continue to hire dental assistants to complete routine tasks, allowing dentists to work more efficiently. As dental practices grow, more dental assistants will be needed.

The large baby-boom population continues to enter older age groups, which typically have more problems related to oral health than younger people do. In addition, people keep more of their original teeth now than in previous generations, leading to continued increases in the need for dental care to maintain and treat teeth.

Occupational Title	SOC Code	Employment, 2022	Projected Employment, 2032	Change, 2022-32	
				Percent	Numeric
Dental assistants	31-9091	371,000	396,700	7	25,700

Contacts for More Information

For more information, visit

- American Dental Assistants Association
- Commission on Dental Accreditation, American Dental Association
- Dental Assisting National Board, Inc.

Dental Hygienists

Summary

Quick Facts: Dental Hygienists	
2022 Median Pay	$81,400 per year $39.14 per hour
Typical Entry-Level Education	Associate's degree
Work Experience in a Related Occupation	None
On-the-job Training	None
Number of Jobs, 2022	219,400
Job Outlook, 2022-32	7% (Faster than average)
Employment Change, 2022-32	16,300

What Dental Hygienists Do

Dental hygienists examine patients for signs of oral diseases, such as gingivitis, and provide preventive care, including oral hygiene.

Work Environment

Nearly all dental hygienists work in dentists' offices, and many work part time.

How to Become a Dental Hygienist

Dental hygienists typically need an associate's degree in dental hygiene. Programs usually take 3 years to complete. All states require dental hygienists to be licensed; requirements vary by state.

Pay

The median annual wage for dental hygienists was $81,400 in May 2022.

Job Outlook

Employment of dental hygienists is projected to grow 7 percent from 2022 to 2032, faster than the average for all occupations.

About 16,400 openings for dental hygienists are projected each year, on average, over the decade. Many of those openings are expected to result from the need to replace workers who transfer to different occupations or exit the labor force, such as to retire.

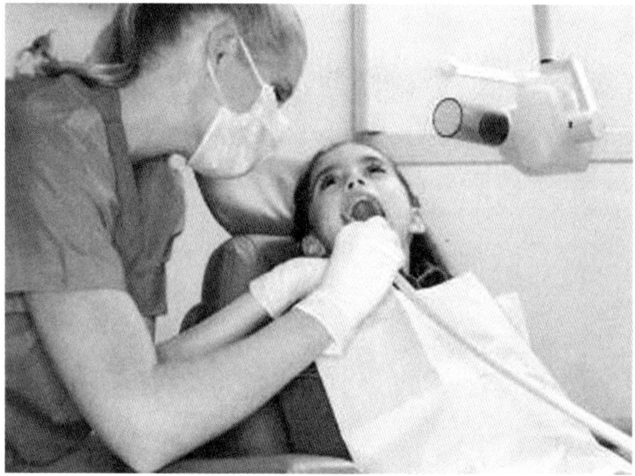

Dental hygienists examine patients' teeth and gums for signs of oral diseases or abnormalities.

What Dental Hygienists Do

Dental hygienists examine patients for signs of oral diseases, such as gingivitis, and provide preventive care, including oral hygiene. They also educate patients about oral health.

Duties

Dental hygienists typically do the following:

- Remove tartar, stains, and plaque from teeth
- Apply sealants and fluorides to help protect teeth
- Take and develop dental x rays
- Assess patients' oral health and report findings to dentists
- Document patient care and treatment plans
- Educate patients about oral hygiene techniques, such as how to brush and floss correctly

Dental hygienists use many types of tools—including hand, power, and ultrasonic tools—in their work. In some cases, they use lasers. Hygienists remove stains with an air-polishing device, which sprays a combination of air, water, and baking soda. They polish teeth with a power tool that works like an automatic toothbrush. Hygienists also use x-ray machines to take pictures to check for tooth or jaw problems.

Dental hygienists talk to patients about ways to keep their teeth and gums healthy. For example, they may explain the relationship between diet and oral health. They may also advise patients on how to select toothbrushes and other oral care devices.

The tasks hygienists may perform, and the extent to which they must be supervised by a dentist, vary by state and by the setting in which the dental hygienist works. A few states allow hygienists with additional training, sometimes called *dental therapists*, to provide some restorative services, such as extracting primary teeth and placing temporary crowns.

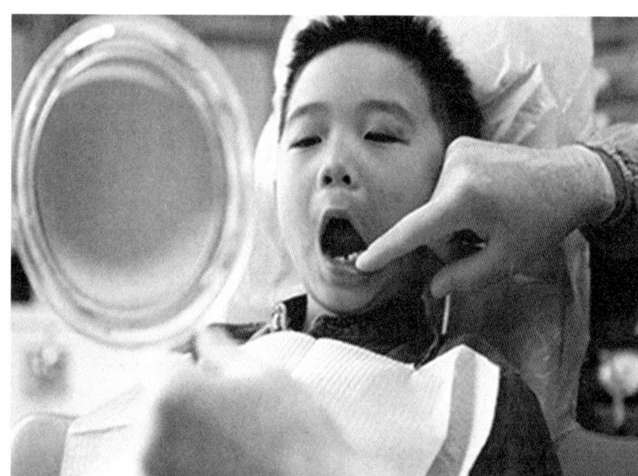

Dental hygienists wear safety glasses, surgical masks, and gloves to protect themselves and their patients from diseases.

Work Environment

Dental hygienists held about 219,400 jobs in 2022. The largest employers of dental hygienists were as follows:

Offices of dentists	93%
Offices of physicians	1
Government	1

Dental hygienists wear safety glasses, surgical masks, and gloves to protect themselves and patients from infectious diseases. When taking x rays, they follow procedures to protect themselves and patients from radiation.

Work Schedules

Many dental hygienists work part time. Dentists may hire hygienists to work only a few days a week, so some hygienists work for more than one dentist.

How to Become a Dental Hygienist

Dental hygienists typically need an associate's degree in dental hygiene. Programs usually take 3 years to complete. All states require dental hygienists to be licensed; requirements vary by state.

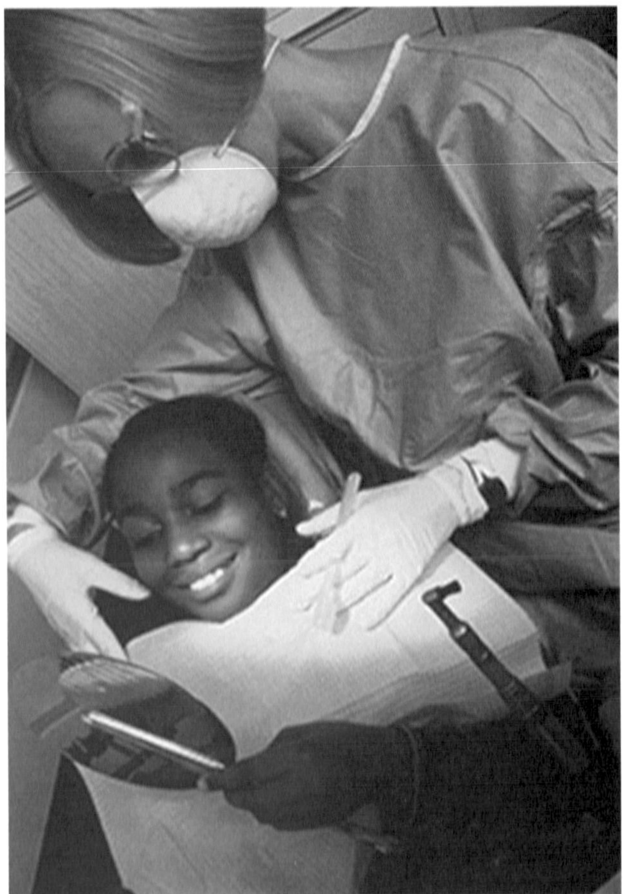

Dental hygienists discuss diet and other topics that affect a patient's dental health.

Education

Dental hygienists typically need an associate's degree in dental hygiene; they may also get a bachelor's degree. Master's degree programs in dental hygiene are available but are relatively uncommon. A bachelor's or master's degree usually is required for research, teaching, or clinical practice in public or school health programs.

Dental hygiene programs are often found in community colleges, technical schools, and universities. The Commission on Dental Accreditation, part of the American Dental Association, accredits more than 300 dental hygiene programs.

Programs typically take 3 years to complete and offer laboratory, clinical, and classroom instruction. Areas of study include anatomy, medical ethics, and periodontics, which is the study of gum disease.

High school students interested in becoming dental hygienists should take courses in biology, chemistry, and math. Most dental hygiene programs also require applicants to complete prerequisites, which often include college-level courses. Specific requirements vary by school.

Important Qualities

Critical thinking. Dental hygienists must be able to assess and evaluate patients and to develop oral hygiene care plans.

Communication skills. Dental hygienists must share information with dentists and patients about oral health status, oral hygiene care plans, and, if necessary, lifestyle counseling.

Detail oriented. Dental hygienists must follow specific rules and protocols to help dentists diagnose and treat a patient. Depending on the state in which they work and/or the treatment provided, dental hygienists may work without the direct supervision of a dentist.

Dexterity. Dental hygienists must be good at working with their hands. They generally work in tight spaces on a small part of the body, which requires fine motor skills using precise tools and instruments.

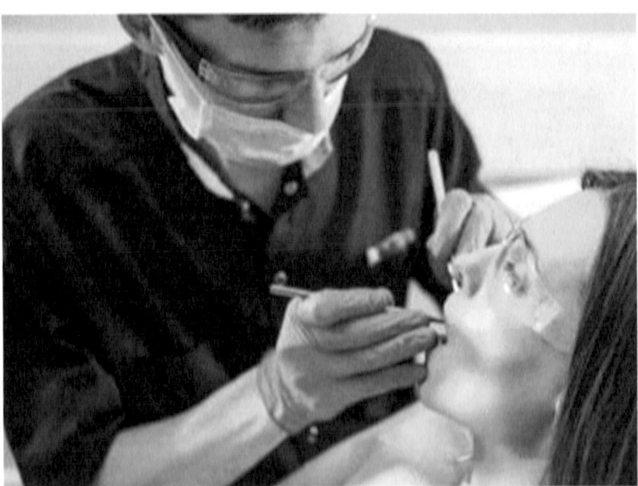

Dental hygienists remove tartar and plaque from teeth.

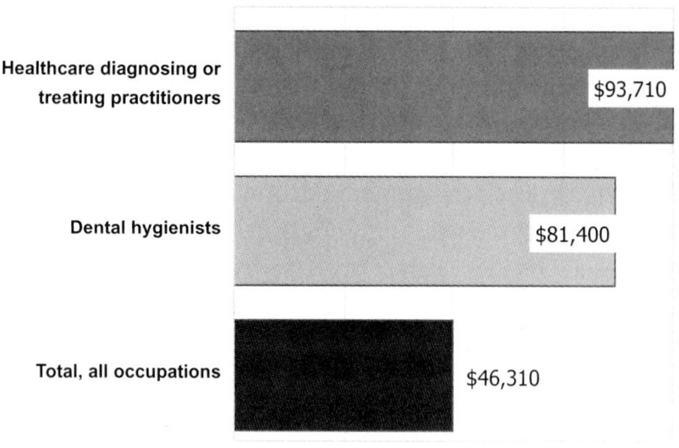

Note: All Occupations includes all occupations in the U.S. Economy.
Source: U.S. Bureau of Labor Statistics, Occupational Employment and Wage Statistics.

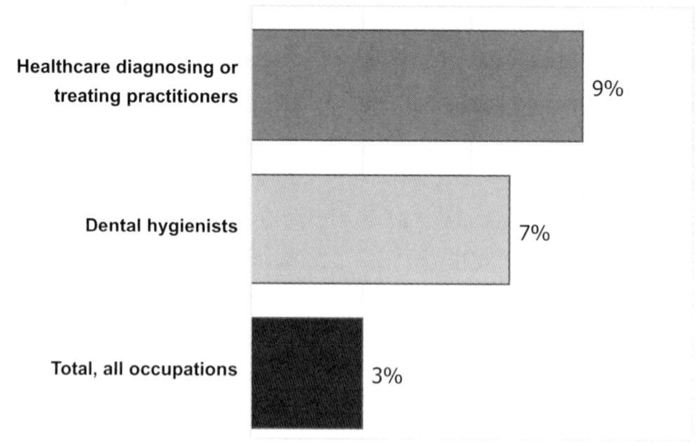

Note: All Occupations includes all occupations in the U.S. Economy.
Source: U.S. Bureau of Labor Statistics, Employment Projections program.

Interpersonal skills. Dental hygienists work closely with dentists. They also must be considerate in working with patients, especially with those who are sensitive to pain or who have fears about undergoing dental treatment.

Problem-solving skills. Dental hygienists develop and implement oral hygiene care plans to maintain or improve patients' oral health.

Licenses, Certifications, and Registrations

Every state requires dental hygienists to be licensed; requirements vary by state. In most states, a degree from an accredited dental hygiene program and passing written and clinical examinations are required for licensure. To maintain licensure, hygienists must complete continuing education requirements. For specific requirements, contact your state's Board of Dental Examiners.

Many jobs also require cardiopulmonary resuscitation (CPR) certification.

Pay

The median annual wage for dental hygienists was $81,400 in May 2022. The median wage is the wage at which half the workers in an occupation earned more than that amount and half earned less. The lowest 10 percent earned less than $61,510, and the highest 10 percent earned more than $107,640.

In May 2022, the median annual wages for dental hygienists in the top industries in which they worked were as follows:

Offices of dentists	$81,460
Offices of physicians	75,730
Government	67,700

Benefits, such as vacation, sick leave, and retirement contributions, vary by employer and may be available only to full-time workers.

Many dental hygienists work part time. Dentists may hire hygienists to work only a few days a week, so some hygienists work for more than one dentist.

Job Outlook

Employment of dental hygienists is projected to grow 7 percent from 2022 to 2032, faster than the average for all occupations.

About 16,400 openings for dental hygienists are projected each year, on average, over the decade. Many of those openings are expected to result from the need to replace workers who transfer to different occupations or exit the labor force, such as to retire.

Employment

Demand for dental services is expected to increase as the large baby-boom population ages and as people keep more of their original teeth than in previous generations.

Studies linking oral health and general health, along with efforts to expand access to oral hygiene services, should continue to drive demand for preventive dental services, including those performed by hygienists. In addition, demand for dental hygienists is expected to grow as state laws increasingly allow dental hygienists to work at the top of their training.

Occupational Title	SOC Code	Employment, 2022	Projected Employment, 2032	Change, 2022-32	
				Percent	Numeric
Dental hygienists	29-1292	219,400	235,700	7	16,300

Contacts for More Information

For more information, visit

- American Dental Hygienists' Association
- Commission on Dental Accreditation, American Dental Association

Dentists

Summary

Quick Facts: Dentists	
2022 Median Pay	$159,530 per year $76.70 per hour
Typical Entry-Level Education	Doctoral or professional degree
Work Experience in a Related Occupation	None
On-the-job Training	See How to Become One
Number of Jobs, 2022	155,000
Job Outlook, 2022-32	4% (As fast as average)
Employment Change, 2022-32	6,800

What Dentists Do

Dentists diagnose and treat problems with patients' teeth, gums, and related parts of the mouth.

Work Environment

Some dentists have their own business and work alone or with a small staff. Other dentists have partners in their practice. Still others work as associate dentists for established dental practices.

How to Become a Dentist

Dentists must be licensed in the state in which they work. Licensure requirements vary by state, although candidates usually must graduate from an accredited dental program and pass written and clinical exams.

Pay

The median annual wage for dentists was $159,530 in May 2022.

Job Outlook

Overall employment of dentists is projected to grow 4 percent from 2022 to 2032, about as fast as the average for all occupations.

About 5,100 openings for dentists are projected each year, on average, over the decade. Many of those openings are expected to result from the need to replace workers who transfer to different occupations or exit the labor force, such as to retire.

What Dentists Do

Dentists diagnose and treat problems with patients' teeth, gums, and related parts of the mouth. They provide advice and instruction on taking care of the teeth and gums and on diet choices that affect oral health.

Duties

Dentists typically do the following:

- Remove decay from teeth and fill cavities
- Repair or remove damaged teeth
- Place sealants or whitening agents on teeth
- Administer anesthetics to keep patients from feeling pain during procedures
- Prescribe antibiotics or other medications
- Examine x rays of teeth, gums, the jaw, and nearby areas in order to diagnose problems
- Make models and measurements for dental appliances, such as dentures
- Teach patients about diets, flossing, the use of fluoride, and other aspects of dental care

Dentists use a variety of equipment, including x-ray machines, drills, mouth mirrors, probes, forceps, brushes, and scalpels. They also use lasers, digital scanners, and other technologies.

In addition, dentists in private practice oversee a variety of administrative tasks, including bookkeeping and buying

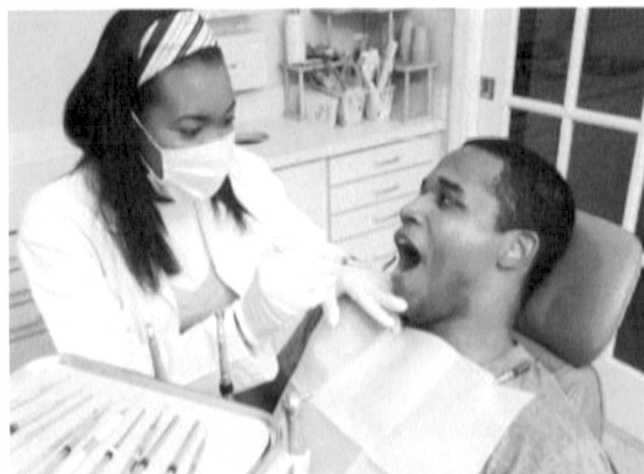

Dentists diagnose and treat problems with a patient's teeth, gums, and related parts of the mouth.

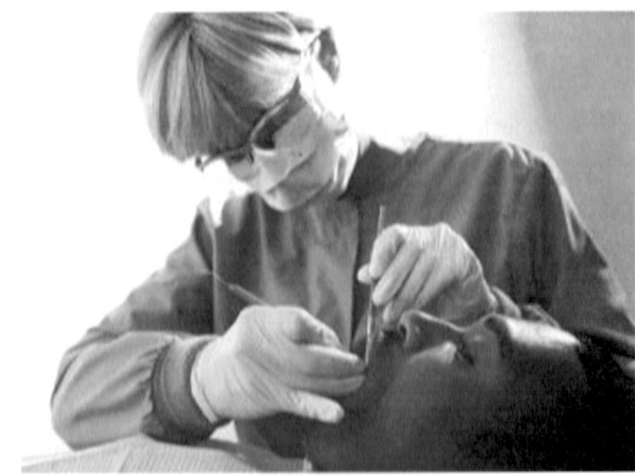

Dentists remove tooth decay, fill cavities, and repair fractured teeth.

equipment and supplies. They employ and supervise dental hygienists, dental assistants, dental laboratory technicians, and receptionists.

Most dentists are general practitioners and handle a variety of dental needs. Other dentists practice in a specialty area, such as one of the following:

Dental anesthesiologists administer drugs (anesthetics) to reduce or eliminate pain during a dental procedure, monitor sedated patients to keep them safe, and help patients manage pain afterward.

Dental public health specialists promote good dental health and the prevention of dental diseases in specific communities.

Endodontists perform root canal therapy, removing the nerves and blood supply from injured or infected teeth.

Oral and maxillofacial radiologists diagnose diseases in the head and neck through the use of imaging technologies.

Oral and maxillofacial surgeons operate on the mouth, jaws, teeth, gums, neck, and head, performing procedures such as surgically repairing a cleft lip and palate or removing impacted teeth.

Oral pathologists diagnose conditions in the mouth, such as bumps or ulcers, and oral diseases, such as cancer.

Orthodontists straighten teeth by applying pressure to the teeth with braces or other appliances.

Pediatric dentists focus on dentistry for children and special-needs patients.

Periodontists treat the gums and bones supporting the teeth.

Dentists also may do research. Or, they may teach part time, including supervising students in dental school clinics. For more information, see the profiles on medical scientists and postsecondary teachers.

Work Environment

Dentists held about 155,000 jobs in 2022. Employment in the detailed occupations that make up dentists was distributed as follows:

Occupation	Employment
Dentists, general	136,700
Orthodontists	7,200
Dentists, all other specialists	5,800
Oral and maxillofacial surgeons	4,900
Prosthodontists	400

The largest employers of dentists were as follows:

Employer	Percent
Offices of dentists	78%
Self-employed workers	11
Government	3
Offices of physicians	2
Outpatient care centers	2

Some dentists have their own business and work alone or with a small staff. Other dentists have partners in their practice. Still others work as associate dentists for established dental practices.

Dentists wear masks, gloves, and safety glasses to protect themselves and their patients from infectious diseases.

Work Schedules

Dentists' work schedules vary. Some work evenings and weekends to meet their patients' needs. Many dentists work less than 40 hours a week, although some work considerably more.

How to Become a Dentist

Dentists must be licensed in the state in which they work. Licensure requirements vary by state, although candidates usually must have a Doctor of Dental Surgery (DDS) or Doctor of Medicine in Dentistry/Doctor of Dental Medicine (DMD) degree from an accredited dental program and pass written and clinical exams. Dentists who practice in a specialty area must complete postdoctoral training.

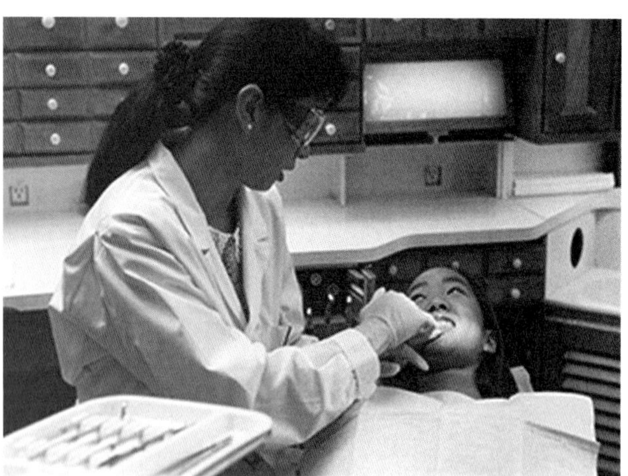

Dentists provide instruction on diet, brushing, flossing, the use of fluorides, and other areas of dental care.

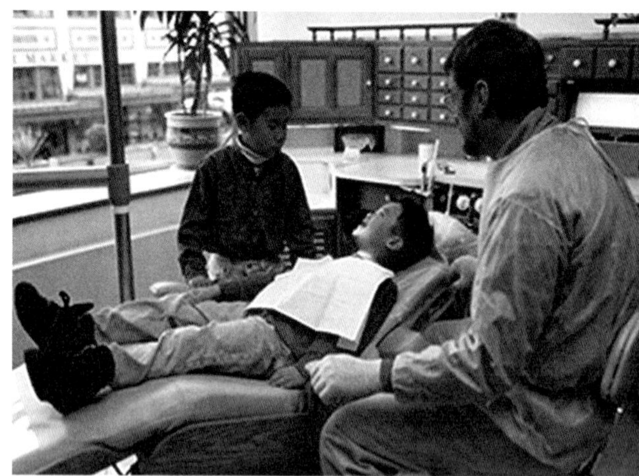

Dentists must be licensed in all states; requirements vary by state.

Education

Dentists typically need a DDS or DMD degree from a dental program that has been accredited by the Commission on Dental Accreditation (CODA). Most programs require that applicants have at least a bachelor's degree and have completed certain science courses, such as biology or chemistry. Although no specific undergraduate major is required, programs may prefer applicants who have a bachelor's degree in a science, such as biology.

Applicants to dental schools usually take the Dental Admission Test (DAT). Dental schools use this test along with other factors, such as grade point average, interviews, and recommendations, to admit students into their programs.

Dental school programs typically include coursework in subjects such as local anesthesia, anatomy, periodontics (the study of oral disease and health), and radiology. All programs at dental schools include clinical experience in which students work directly with patients under the supervision of a licensed dentist.

As early as high school, students interested in becoming dentists can take courses in subjects such as biology, chemistry, and math.

Training

All dental specialties require dentists to complete additional training before practicing that specialty. This training is usually a 2- to 4-year residency in a CODA-accredited program related to the specialty, which often culminates in a postdoctoral certificate or master's degree. Oral and maxillofacial surgery programs typically take 4 to 6 years and may result in candidates earning a joint Medical Doctor (M.D.) degree.

General dentists do not need additional training after dental school.

Dentists who want to teach or do research full time may need advanced dental training, such as in a postdoctoral program in general dentistry.

Licenses, Certifications, and Registrations

Dentists must be licensed in the state in which they work. All states require dentists to be licensed; requirements vary by state. Most states require a dentist to have a DDS or DMD degree from an accredited dental program, pass the written National Board Dental Examination, and pass a state or regional clinical examination.

In addition, a dentist who wants to practice in a dental specialty must have a license in that specialty. Licensure requires the completion of a residency after dental school and, in some cases, the completion of a special state exam.

Important Qualities

Communication skills. Dentists must communicate effectively with patients, dental hygienists, dental assistants, and receptionists.

Detail oriented. Dentists must pay attention to the shape and color of teeth and to the space between them. For example, they may need to closely match a false tooth with a patient's other teeth.

Dexterity. Dentists must be good with their hands. They must work carefully with tools in small spaces to ensure the safety of their patients.

Leadership skills. Dentists, especially those with their own practices, may need to manage staff or mentor other dentists.

Organizational skills. Keeping accurate records of patient care is critical in both medical and business settings.

Patience. Dentists may work for long periods with patients who need special attention, including children and those with a fear of dental work.

Problem-solving skills. Dentists must evaluate patients' symptoms and choose the appropriate treatment.

Pay

The median annual wage for dentists was $159,530 in May 2022. The median wage is the wage at which half the workers in an occupation earned more than that amount and half earned less. The lowest 10 percent earned less than $71,460, and the highest 10 percent earned more than $239,200.

Median annual wages for dentists in May 2022 were as follows:

Oral and maxillofacial surgeons	$239,200 or more
Dentists, all other specialists	212,740
Orthodontists	174,360
Dentists, general	155,040

In May 2022, the median annual wages for dentists in the top industries in which they worked were as follows:

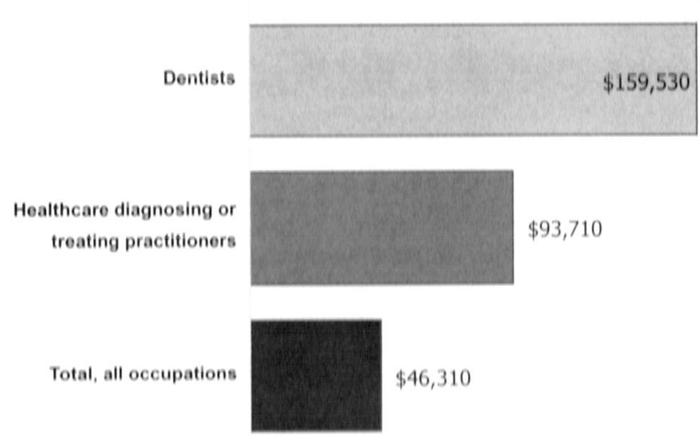

Note: All Occupations includes all occupations in the U.S. Economy.
Source: U.S. Bureau of Labor Statistics, Occupational Employment and Wage Statistics.

Government	$190,400
Outpatient care centers	166,170
Offices of physicians	163,800
Offices of dentists	159,530

Wages vary with the dentist's location, number of hours worked, specialty, and number of years in practice.

Dentists' work schedules vary. Some work evenings and weekends to meet their patients' needs. Many dentists work less than 40 hours a week, although some may work considerably more.

Job Outlook

Overall employment of dentists is projected to grow 4 percent from 2022 to 2032, about as fast as the average for all occupations.

About 5,100 openings for dentists are projected each year, on average, over the decade. Many of those openings are expected to result from the need to replace workers who transfer to different occupations or exit the labor force, such as to retire.

Employment

Demand for dentists is expected to increase as larger numbers of older people require dental services. Because each generation is more likely to keep their teeth than the previous generation, more dental care is expected to be needed in the years to come. In addition, dentists will be needed to treat dentofacial injuries and other conditions as well as to perform restorative procedures to treat complications from oral disease, such as gum disease and oral cancer. The growing popularity of cosmetic dentistry also is expected to support demand for dentists.

Occupational Title	SOC Code	Employment, 2022	Projected Employment, 2032	Change, 2022-32	
				Percent	Numeric
Dentists	29-1020	155,000	161,800	4	6,800
Dentists, general	29-1021	136,700	142,700	4	6,000
Oral and maxillofacial surgeons	29-1022	4,900	5,100	5	200
Orthodontists	29-1023	7,200	7,500	4	300
Prosthodontists	29-1024	400	500	6	0
Dentists, all other specialists	29-1029	5,800	6,000	3	200

Dentists

Percent change in employment, projected 2022-32

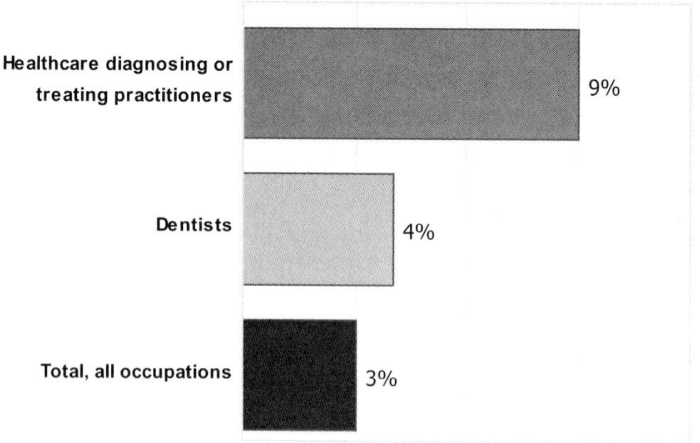

Note: All Occupations includes all occupations in the U.S. Economy.
Source: U.S. Bureau of Labor Statistics, Employment Projections program.

Contacts for More Information

For more information, visit

- American Dental Association, Commission on Dental Accreditation

For information about admission to dental schools, visit

- American Dental Education Association
- Academy of General Dentistry
- American Academy of Oral and Maxillofacial Pathology
- American Academy of Oral and Maxillofacial Radiology
- American Association of Oral and Maxillofacial Surgeons
- American Academy of Pediatric Dentistry
- American Academy of Periodontology
- American Association of Endodontists
- American Association of Orthodontists
- American Association of Public Health Dentistry
- American College of Prosthodontists
- American Society of Dentist Anesthesiologists

Diagnostic Medical Sonographers and Cardiovascular Technologists and Technicians

Summary

Quick Facts: Diagnostic Medical Sonographers and Cardiovascular Technologists and Technicians	
2022 Median Pay	$78,210 per year $37.60 per hour
Typical Entry-Level Education	Associate's degree
Work Experience in a Related Occupation	None
On-the-job Training	None
Number of Jobs, 2022	142,800
Job Outlook, 2022-32	10% (Much faster than average)
Employment Change, 2022-32	14,200

What Diagnostic Medical Sonographers and Cardiovascular Technologists and Technicians Do

Diagnostic medical sonographers and cardiovascular technologists and technicians operate special equipment to create images or to conduct tests.

Work Environment

Most diagnostic medical sonographers and cardiovascular technologists and technicians work in healthcare settings, such as hospitals and offices of physicians. Although most are full time, part-time work is common.

How to Become a Diagnostic Medical Sonographer or Cardiovascular Technologist and Technician

Diagnostic medical sonographers and cardiovascular technologists and technicians typically need formal education, such as an associate's degree or a postsecondary certificate. Employers may require or prefer that workers have certification.

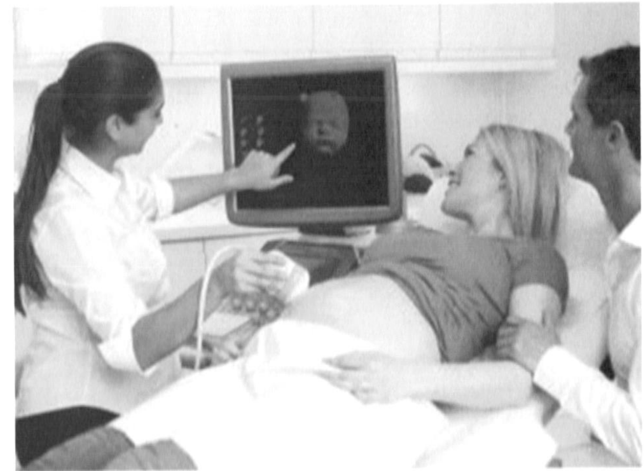

Diagnostic medical sonographers operate special equipment to create images.

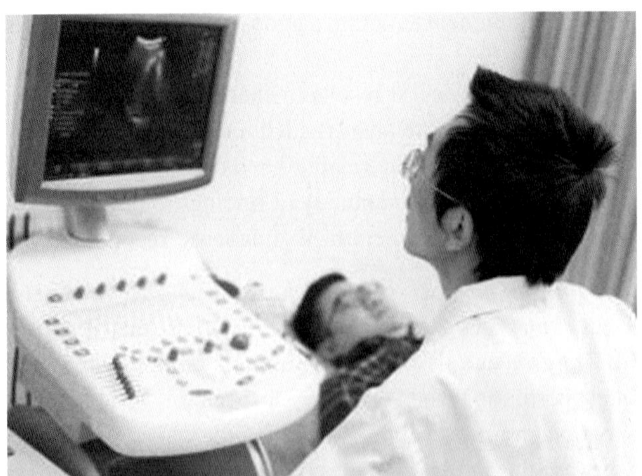

Diagnostic sonographers use high-frequency sound waves to produce images of the inside of the body.

Pay

The median annual wage for cardiovascular technologists and technicians was $63,020 in May 2022.

The median annual wage for diagnostic medical sonographers was $81,350 in May 2022.

Job Outlook

Overall employment of diagnostic medical sonographers and cardiovascular technologists and technicians is projected to grow 10 percent from 2022 to 2032, much faster than the average for all occupations.

About 9,600 openings for diagnostic medical sonographers and cardiovascular technologists and technicians are projected each year, on average, over the decade. Many of those openings are expected to result from the need to replace workers who transfer to different occupations or exit the labor force, such as to retire.

What Diagnostic Medical Sonographers and Cardiovascular Technologists and Technicians Do

Diagnostic medical sonographers and cardiovascular technologists and technicians operate special equipment to create images or conduct tests. They work closely with physicians and surgeons, who view the images and test results to assess and diagnose medical conditions.

Duties

Diagnostic medical sonographers and cardiovascular technologists and technicians typically do the following:

- Prepare patients by explaining the procedure to them and answering their questions
- Prepare exam rooms and maintain diagnostic imaging equipment
- Properly situate patients for imaging

- Operate equipment to obtain diagnostic images or to conduct tests
- Review images or test results to check for quality and adequate coverage of the areas needed for diagnoses
- Analyze results for abnormalities and other diagnostic information and provide a summary of findings to physicians
- Record findings and keep track of patients' records

Diagnostic medical sonographers specialize in creating images, known as sonograms or ultrasounds, that depict the body's organs and tissues. Sonography is often the first imaging test performed when disease is suspected.

Sonography uses high-energy sound waves to produce images of the inside of the body. The sonographer uses an instrument called a transducer to scan parts of the patient's body that are being examined. The transducer emits pulses of sound that bounce back, causing echoes. The echoes form an image on a computer that physicians use for diagnosis.

The following are examples of types of medical sonographers:

- *Abdominal sonographers* specialize in imaging a patient's abdominal cavity and nearby organs, such as the kidney, liver, gallbladder, pancreas, and spleen. Abdominal sonographers may assist with biopsies or other examinations requiring ultrasound guidance.
- *Breast sonographers* specialize in imaging a patient's breast tissue. Sonography can confirm the presence of cysts and tumors that may have been detected by the patient, the physician, or a mammogram. Breast sonographers assist with procedures that track tumors and help to provide information that will aid physicians in making decisions about treatment options for breast cancer patients.
- *Cardiac sonographers (echocardiographers)* specialize in imaging a patient's heart. They use ultrasound equipment to examine the heart's chambers, valves, and vessels. An echocardiogram may be performed either while the patient is resting or after the patient has been physically active. Cardiac sonographers also may take echocardiograms of fetal hearts so that physicians can diagnose cardiac conditions during pregnancy.
- *Musculoskeletal sonographers* specialize in imaging muscles, ligaments, tendons, and joints. These sonographers may assist with ultrasound guidance for injections, or during surgical procedures, that deliver medication or treatment directly to affected tissues.
- *Pediatric sonographers* specialize in imaging of children and infants. Many of the medical conditions they image are associated with premature births or birth defects. Pediatric sonographers may work closely with pediatricians and other caregivers.
- *Obstetric and gynecologic sonographers* specialize in imaging the female reproductive system. For example, many pregnant women receive sonograms to track the baby's growth and health.
- *Vascular technologists (vascular sonographers)* create images of blood vessels and collect data that help physicians diagnose disorders affecting blood flow. Vascular technologists often evaluate blood flow and identify blocked arteries or blood clots.

Cardiovascular technologists and technicians create images and conduct tests involving the heart and lungs. The following are examples of types of cardiovascular technologists and technicians:

- *Cardiovascular invasive specialists*, also known as *cardiac catheterization technologists* or *cardiovascular technologists*, monitor patients' heart rates and help physicians in diagnosing and treating heart problems. They assist with cardiac catheterization, which involves threading a catheter through a patient's artery to the heart. They also prepare and monitor patients during open-heart surgery and during insertion of pacemakers, defibrillators, and stents. Technologists may prepare patients for procedures by shaving and cleansing the area into which the catheter will be inserted and by administering topical anesthesia. During the procedure, they monitor the patient's blood pressure and heart rate.
- *Cardiographic or electrocardiogram (EKG) technicians* specialize in EKG testing. EKG machines monitor the heart's performance through electrodes attached to a patient's chest, arms, and legs. Tests record heart metrics while the patient is at rest or is physically active, such as walking on a treadmill.
- *Pulmonary function technologists* monitor and test patients' lungs and breathing. For example, they use a spirometer to measure how much and how fast patients can inhale or exhale. These technologists help physicians in diagnosing and treating problems of the pulmonary system.

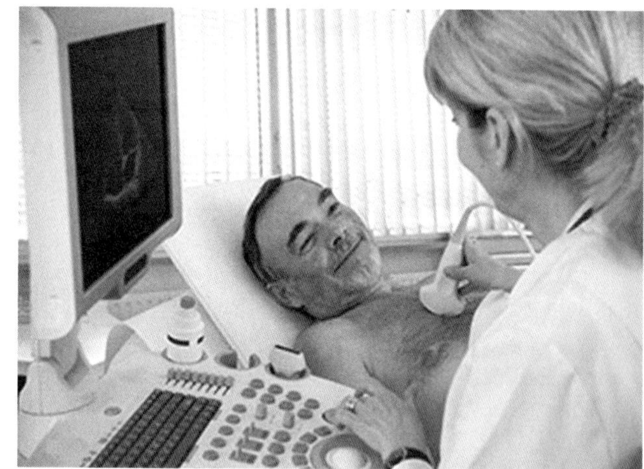

Diagnostic imaging workers may perform procedures at patient's bedsides.

Work Environment

Cardiovascular technologists and technicians held about 58,900 jobs in 2022. The largest employers of cardiovascular technologists and technicians were as follows:

Hospitals; state, local, and private	76%
Offices of physicians	12
Self-employed workers	4
Outpatient care centers	3
Medical and diagnostic laboratories	1

Diagnostic medical sonographers held about 83,800 jobs in 2022. The largest employers of diagnostic medical sonographers were as follows:

Hospitals; state, local, and private	56%
Offices of physicians	24
Medical and diagnostic laboratories	10
Outpatient care centers	4
Self-employed workers	2

Diagnostic medical sonographers and cardiovascular technologists and technicians complete most of their work at diagnostic imaging machines in dimly lit rooms. They may need to stand for long periods and to lift or turn patients who are ill or disabled.

Diagnostic medical sonographers and cardiovascular technologists and technicians work as part of a healthcare team that includes physicians and surgeons, registered nurses, and respiratory therapists.

Work Schedules

Most diagnostic medical sonographers and cardiovascular technologists and technicians are full time, although part-time work is common. Because they may work in medical facilities that are always open, they may have shifts that include evenings, weekends, or overnights.

How to Become a Diagnostic Medical Sonographer or Cardiovascular Technologist and Technician

Diagnostic medical sonographers and cardiovascular technologists and technicians typically need formal education, such as an associate's degree or a postsecondary certificate. Employers may require or prefer that workers have certification.

Education

High school students who are interested in medical sonography or cardiovascular technology should take classes in anatomy, physiology, physics, and math. EKG technicians may qualify for entry-level jobs with a high school diploma or the equivalent.

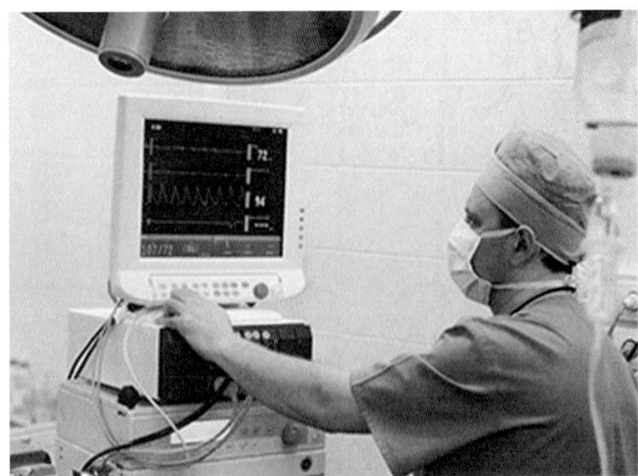

Cardiovascular technologists monitor patients' heart rates and perform and assist in the diagnosis and treatment of problems having to do with the patient's heart.

Colleges and universities offer both associate's and bachelor's degree programs in sonography and in cardiovascular technology. One-year certificate programs also are available from colleges and some hospitals.

Sonography and cardiovascular education programs usually include courses in anatomy, medical terminology, and applied sciences. Instruction in sonography programs generally corresponds to the relevant certification field, such as abdominal sonography or breast sonography. Cardiovascular programs include coursework in either invasive or noninvasive procedures. Programs also typically include a clinical component in which students earn credit while working under the direction of an experienced technologist in a hospital, a physician's office, or an imaging laboratory.

Licenses, Certifications, and Registrations

Employers may prefer to hire diagnostic medical sonographers and cardiovascular technologists and technicians who have professional certification, or they may expect applicants to earn certification shortly after being hired. For payment purposes, insurance providers and Medicare may stipulate that a certified sonographer, technologist, or technician perform certain procedures. Certification is available from several organizations, such as the American Registry for Diagnostic Medical Sonographers, American Registry of Radiologic Technologists, Cardiovascular Credentialing International, and National Healthcareer Association.

All diagnostic medical sonographers and cardiovascular technologists and technicians must pass an exam to earn certification. To sit for the exam, eligibility requirements vary and may include graduating from an accredited program or a combination of education and experience. Certifications are typically for specialties in diagnostic imaging; for example, a sonographer may earn a certification in areas such as abdominal, breast, or pediatric sonography.

In addition, employers may prefer to hire candidates who have basic life support (BLS) or cardiopulmonary resuscitation (CPR) certification.

States may require diagnostic medical sonographers and cardiovascular technologists and technicians to be licensed. Typically, certification is required for licensure; other requirements vary by state. Contact state medical boards for more information.

Important Qualities

Communication skills. Diagnostic medical sonographers and cardiovascular technologists and technicians work closely with patients, including those who may be in pain, and must be able to explain the procedure in an understandable way. They also must convey information clearly when discussing images with physicians and other members of the healthcare team.

Detail oriented. Diagnostic medical sonographers and cardiovascular technologists and technicians must follow precise instructions to obtain the images needed to diagnose and treat patients. They also must pay attention to the images they produce, because healthy and unhealthy areas may be subtle.

Hand–eye coordination. To get quality images, diagnostic medical sonographers and cardiovascular technologists and technicians must accurately move equipment on the patient's body in response to what they see on the screen.

Physical stamina. Diagnostic medical sonographers and cardiovascular technologists and technicians stand for long periods and must be able to lift and move patients who need assistance.

Technical skills. Diagnostic medical sonographers and cardiovascular technologists and technicians must understand how to operate complex machinery and computerized instruments.

Pay

The median annual wage for cardiovascular technologists and technicians was $63,020 in May 2022. The median wage is the wage at which half the workers in an occupation earned more than that amount and half earned less. The lowest 10 percent earned less than $33,950, and the highest 10 percent earned more than $102,000.

The median annual wage for diagnostic medical sonographers was $81,350 in May 2022. The lowest 10 percent earned less than $61,430, and the highest 10 percent earned more than $107,730.

In May 2022, the median annual wages for cardiovascular technologists and technicians in the top industries in which they worked were as follows:

Outpatient care centers	$83,890
Medical and diagnostic laboratories	72,990
Offices of physicians	66,470
Hospitals; state, local, and private	62,060

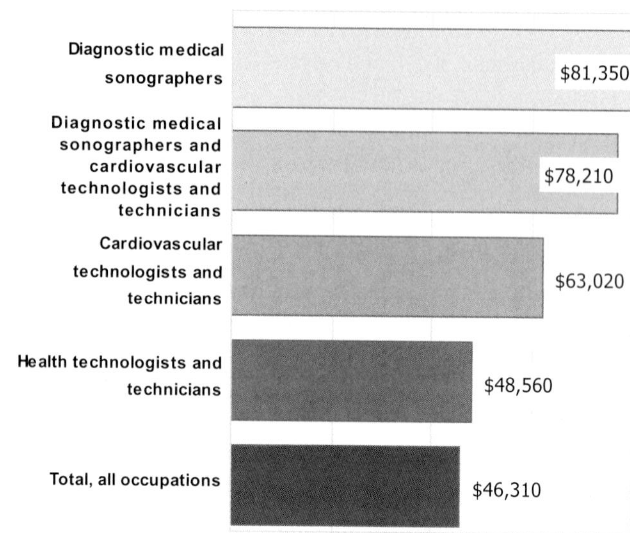

Note: All Occupations includes all occupations in the U.S. Economy.
Source: U.S. Bureau of Labor Statistics, Occupational Employment and Wage Statistics.

In May 2022, the median annual wages for diagnostic medical sonographers in the top industries in which they worked were as follows:

Outpatient care centers	$107,970
Offices of physicians	82,110
Hospitals; state, local, and private	81,420
Medical and diagnostic laboratories	79,070

Most diagnostic medical sonographers and cardiovascular technologists and technicians are full time, although part-time work is common. Because they may work in medical facilities that are always open, they may have shifts that include evenings, weekends, or overnights.

Job Outlook

Overall employment of diagnostic medical sonographers and cardiovascular technologists and technicians is projected to grow 10 percent from 2022 to 2032, much faster than the average for all occupations.

About 9,600 openings for diagnostic medical sonographers and cardiovascular technologists and technicians are projected each year, on average, over the decade. Many of those openings are expected to result from the need to replace workers who transfer to different occupations or exit the labor force, such as to retire.

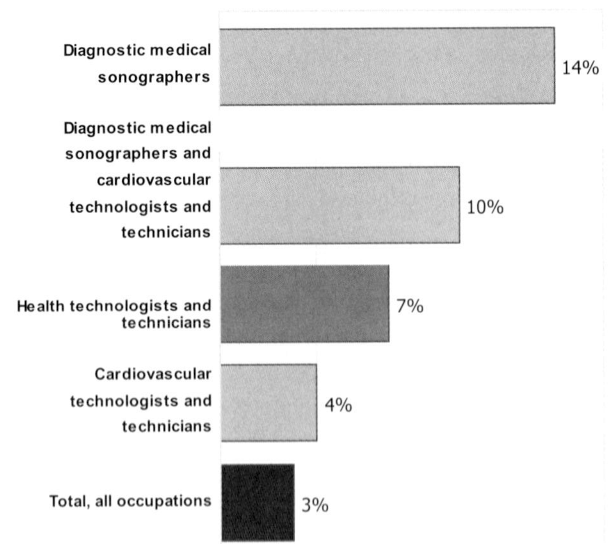

Note: All Occupations includes all occupations in the U.S. Economy.
Source: U.S. Bureau of Labor Statistics, Employment Projections program.

Employment

Projected employment of diagnostic imaging workers varies by occupation (see table). As the large baby-boom population continues to age, the need to diagnose medical conditions that affect older adults—such as blood clots and heart disease—will likely increase. Diagnostic medical sonographers and cardiovascular technologists and technicians use imaging technology as a tool to help physicians diagnose these conditions. Moreover, these workers will continue to be needed in healthcare settings to provide an alternative to imaging techniques that involve radiation.

Occupational Title	SOC Code	Employment, 2022	Projected Employment, 2032	Change, 2022-32 Percent	Change, 2022-32 Numeric
Diagnostic medical sonographers and cardiovascular technologists and technicians	—	142,800	156,900	10	14,200
Cardiovascular technologists and technicians	29-2031	58,900	61,100	4	2,200
Diagnostic medical sonographers	29-2032	83,800	95,800	14	12,000

Contacts for More Information

For more information, visit

- Alliance of Cardiovascular Professionals
- American Society of Echocardiography
- Society for Vascular Ultrasound
- Society of Diagnostic Medical Sonography
- For more information about certification, visit
- American Registry for Diagnostic Medical Sonography
- American Registry of Radiologic Technologists
- Cardiovascular Credentialing International
- National Healthcareer Association
- Commission on Accreditation of Allied Health Education Programs

---

Dietitians and Nutritionists

Summary

Quick Facts: Dietitians and Nutritionists

2022 Median Pay	$66,450 per year $31.95 per hour
Typical Entry-Level Education	Bachelor's degree
Work Experience in a Related Occupation	None
On-the-job Training	Internship/residency
Number of Jobs, 2022	78,600
Job Outlook, 2022-32	7% (Faster than average)
Employment Change, 2022-32	5,200

What Dietitians and Nutritionists Do

Dietitians and nutritionists plan and conduct food service or nutritional programs to help people lead healthy lives.

Work Environment

Dietitians and nutritionists work in many settings, including hospitals, nursing homes, clinics, cafeterias, and for state and local governments.

How to Become a Dietitian or Nutritionist

To enter the occupation, dietitians and nutritionists typically need at least a bachelor's degree. They also typically are required to have supervised training through an internship. Many states require dietitians and nutritionists to be licensed.

Pay

The median annual wage for dietitians and nutritionists was $66,450 in May 2022.

Job Outlook

Employment of dietitians and nutritionists is projected to grow 7 percent from 2022 to 2032, faster than the average for all occupations.

Dietitians and nutritionists may help clients maintain a healthy weight.

About 5,600 openings for dietitians and nutritionists are projected each year, on average, over the decade. Many of those openings are expected to result from the need to replace workers who transfer to different occupations or exit the labor force, such as to retire.

What Dietitians and Nutritionists Do

Dietitians and nutritionists are experts in the use of food and nutrition to promote health and manage disease. They plan and conduct food service or nutritional programs to help people lead healthy lives.

Duties

Dietitians and nutritionists typically do the following:

- Assess clients' nutritional and health needs
- Counsel clients on nutrition issues and healthy eating habits
- Develop meal and nutrition plans, taking clients' preferences and budgets into account
- Evaluate and monitor the effects of nutrition plans and practices and make changes as needed

Dietitians and nutritionists counsel clients on nutrition issues and healthy eating habits.

- Promote healthy lifestyles by speaking to groups about diet, nutrition, and the relationship between good eating habits and preventing or managing specific diseases
- Create educational materials about healthy food choices and lifestyle
- Keep up with or contribute to the latest food and nutritional science research
- Document clients' progress

Dietitians and nutritionists evaluate the health of their clients through nutrition assessment and diagnostic laboratory testing. Based on their findings, dietitians and nutritionists advise clients on behavior modifications and intervention plans, including which foods to eat—and which to avoid—to improve their health.

Dietitians and nutritionists help prevent or support treatment of health conditions such as heart disease, autoimmune disease, and obesity. Many dietitians and nutritionists provide personalized information for individuals. For example, a dietitian or nutritionist might teach a client with diabetes how to plan meals to improve and balance the person's blood sugar. Other dietitians and nutritionists work with groups of people who have similar needs. For example, a dietitian or nutritionist might plan a diet with healthy fat and limited sugar to help clients who are at risk for heart disease. Dietitians and nutritionists may work as part of a team with other healthcare staff to coordinate client care.

Dietitians and nutritionists who are self-employed may meet with clients, or they may work as consultants for a variety of organizations. Self-employed workers may need to spend time on marketing and other business-related tasks, such as scheduling appointments and keeping records.

Although many dietitians and nutritionists do similar tasks, there are several specialties within the occupations. The following are examples of types of dietitians and nutritionists:

Clinical dietitians and clinical nutritionists provide medical nutrition therapy. They create customized nutritional programs based on the health needs of clients and counsel clients on how to improve their health through nutrition. Clinical dietitians and clinical nutritionists may further specialize, such as by working only with people who have kidney disease, diabetes, digestive disorders, or other specific conditions. They work in institutions such as hospitals, long-term care facilities, and clinics, as well as in private practice.

Community dietitians and community nutritionists develop programs and counsel the public on topics related to food, health, and nutrition. They often work with specific groups of people, such as adolescents or the elderly. They work in public health clinics, government and nonprofit agencies, health maintenance organizations (HMOs), and other settings.

Management dietitians plan food programs. They may be responsible for buying food and for carrying out other business-related tasks, such as budgeting. Management dietitians may

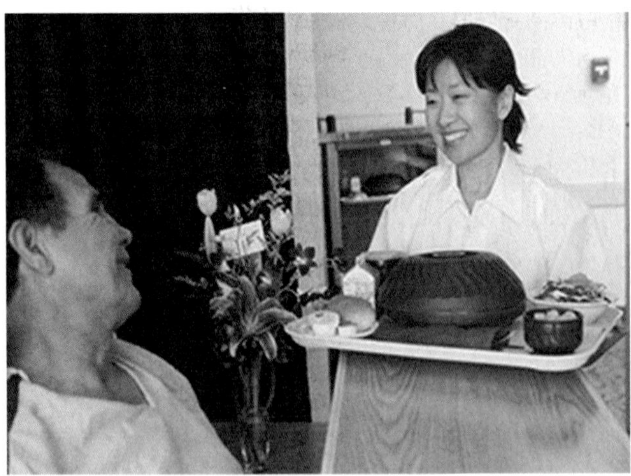

Dietitians and nutritionists develop meal and nutrition plans to meet the health needs of clients.

Dietitians and nutritionists must clearly explain nutrition plans to other healthcare workers.

oversee kitchen staff or other dietitians. They work in food service settings such as cafeterias, hospitals, prisons, and schools.

Work Environment

Dietitians and nutritionists held about 78,600 jobs in 2022. The largest employers of dietitians and nutritionists were as follows:

Hospitals; state, local, and private	27%
Government	11
Outpatient care centers	9
Nursing and residential care facilities	8
Self-employed workers	8

Work Schedules

Most dietitians and nutritionists work full time. They may work evenings and weekends to meet with clients who are unavailable at other times.

How to Become a Dietitian or Nutritionist

To enter the occupation, dietitians and nutritionists typically need at least a bachelor's degree. They also typically are required to have supervised training through an internship. Many states require dietitians and nutritionists to be licensed.

Education

Dietitians and nutritionists typically need a bachelor's or higher degree in dietetics, food and nutrition, or a related field to enter the occupation. Many dietitians and nutritionists have an advanced degree.

Training

Dietitians and nutritionists typically receive supervised training, usually in the form of an internship following graduation from college. Some schools offer coordinated programs in dietetics that allow students to complete supervised training as part of their undergraduate- or graduate-level coursework.

Licenses, Certifications, and Registrations

Many states require dietitians and nutritionists to be licensed in order to practice. Other states require only state registration or certification to use certain titles, and a few states have no regulations for this occupation.

The requirements for state licensure and state certification vary by state, but most include having a bachelor's or an advanced degree in food and nutrition or a related area, completing supervised practice, and passing an exam.

Employers may prefer to hire candidates who have a professional credential, such as the Registered Dietitian (RD)/ Registered Dietitian Nutritionist (RDN) or the Certified Nutrition Specialist (CNS) designation. Although these credentials are not always required, the qualifications may be the same as those necessary for becoming a licensed dietitian or nutritionist in states that require a license.

The RD/RDN designation is administered by the Commission on Dietetic Registration, the credentialing agency for the Academy of Nutrition and Dietetics. It requires completion of a minimum of a bachelor's degree and a Dietetic Internship (DI), which includes supervised experience. Students may complete both criteria at once through a coordinated program, or they may finish their degree before applying for an internship. In order to maintain the RDN credential, dietitians and nutritionists must complete continuing professional education credits within a designated number of years. Beginning in 2024, education requirements will increase to a master's degree.

The Certified Nutrition Specialist (CNS) designation is administered by the Board for Certification of Nutrition Specialists, the certifying arm of the American Nutrition Association. Many states accept the CNS credential or exam for licensure purposes. To qualify for the credential, applicants must have a master's or doctoral degree, complete supervised experience, and pass an exam. To maintain the CNS credential, nutritionists must complete continuing education credits within a designated number of years.

Dietitians and nutritionists may seek additional certifications in an area of specialty, such as diabetes education, oncology nutrition, or sports dietetics.

Important Qualities

Analytical skills. Dietitians and nutritionists must keep up with food and nutrition research. They should be able to interpret scientific studies and translate nutrition science into practical guidance.

Compassion. Dietitians and nutritionists must be caring and empathetic when helping clients address health and dietary issues and any related emotions.

Listening skills. Dietitians and nutritionists must listen carefully to understand clients' goals and concerns. They may work with other healthcare workers as part of a team to improve the health of a client, and they need to listen to team members when creating nutrition plans.

Organizational skills. Dietitians and nutritionists must prepare and maintain many types of records for multiple clients. Self-employed dietitians and nutritionists may need to schedule appointments, manage employees, and bill insurance companies in addition to maintaining client files.

Problem-solving skills. Dietitians and nutritionists must evaluate the health status of clients and determine appropriate food choices to improve overall health or manage disease.

Speaking skills. Dietitians and nutritionists must explain complicated topics in a way that people can understand. They must clearly explain eating plans to clients and to other healthcare workers involved in a patient's care.

Pay

The median annual wage for dietitians and nutritionists was $66,450 in May 2022. The median wage is the wage at which half the workers in an occupation earned more than that amount and half earned less. The lowest 10 percent earned less than $44,140, and the highest 10 percent earned more than $95,130.

In May 2022, the median annual wages for dietitians and nutritionists in the top industries in which they worked were as follows:

Outpatient care centers	$75,860
Government	66,370
Hospitals; state, local, and private	66,170
Nursing and residential care facilities	64,310

Most dietitians and nutritionists work full time. They may work evenings and weekends to meet with clients who are unavailable at other times.

Job Outlook

Employment of dietitians and nutritionists is projected to grow 7 percent from 2022 to 2032, faster than the average for all occupations.

About 5,600 openings for dietitians and nutritionists are projected each year, on average, over the decade. Many of those openings are expected to result from the need to replace workers who transfer to different occupations or exit the labor force, such as to retire.

Employment

Interest in the role of food and nutrition in promoting wellness and preventive care, particularly in medical settings, continues to increase.

The importance of diet in preventing and controlling certain illnesses, such as diabetes and heart disease, is well established. More dietitians and nutritionists will be needed to provide care for people who have, or are at risk of developing, these conditions.

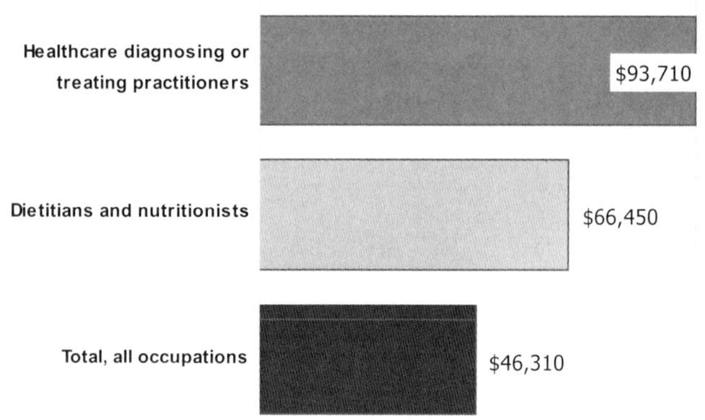

Note: All Occupations includes all occupations in the U.S. Economy.
Source: U.S. Bureau of Labor Statistics, Occupational Employment and Wage Statistics.

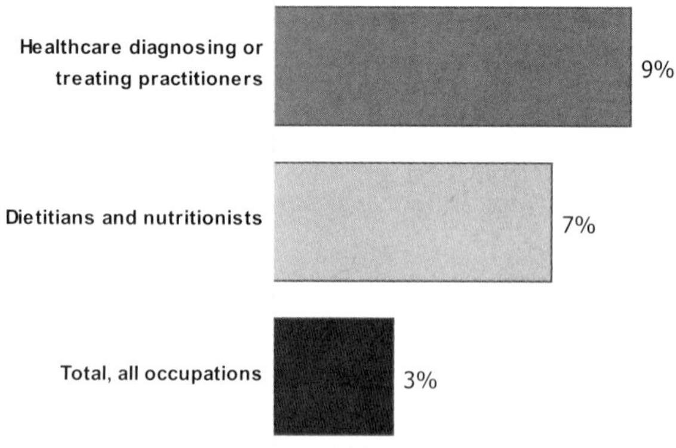

Note: All Occupations includes all occupations in the U.S. Economy.
Source: U.S. Bureau of Labor Statistics, Employment Projections program.

Moreover, as the population ages and looks for ways to stay healthy, there will be more demand for dietetic and nutrition services.

Occupational Title	SOC Code	Employment, 2022	Projected Employment, 2032	Change, 2022-32	
				Percent	Numeric
Dietitians and nutritionists	29-1031	78,600	83,800	7	5,200

Contacts for More Information

For more information about dietitians and nutritionists, visit

- Academy of Nutrition and Dietetics
- Accreditation Council for Education in Nutrition and Dietetics
- Commission on Dietetic Registration
- Board for Certification of Nutrition Specialists
- Clinical Nutrition Certification Board

EMTs and Paramedics

Summary

Quick Facts: EMTs and Paramedics

2022 Median Pay	$39,410 per year $18.95 per hour
Typical Entry-Level Education	Postsecondary nondegree award
Work Experience in a Related Occupation	See How to Become One
On-the-job Training	None
Number of Jobs, 2022	269,000
Job Outlook, 2022-32	5% (Faster than average)
Employment Change, 2022-32	14,600

What EMTs and Paramedics Do

Emergency medical technicians (EMTs) and paramedics assess injuries and illnesses, provide emergency medical care, and may transport patients to medical facilities.

Work Environment

Most EMTs and paramedics work full time, and some work more than 40 hours per week. Schedules may vary to include nights, weekends, and holidays. Their work may be physically strenuous and stressful, sometimes involving life-or-death situations.

How to Become an EMT or Paramedic

Emergency medical technicians (EMTs) and paramedics typically complete a postsecondary educational program. All states require EMTs and paramedics to be licensed in the state in which they work; requirements vary by state.

Pay

The median annual wage for emergency medical technicians was $36,680 in May 2022.

The median annual wage for paramedics was $49,090 in May 2022.

Job Outlook

Overall employment of EMTs and paramedics is projected to grow 5 percent from 2022 to 2032, faster than the average for all occupations.

About 18,100 openings for EMTs and paramedics are projected each year, on average, over the decade. Many of those openings are expected to result from the need to replace workers who transfer to different occupations or exit the labor force, such as to retire.

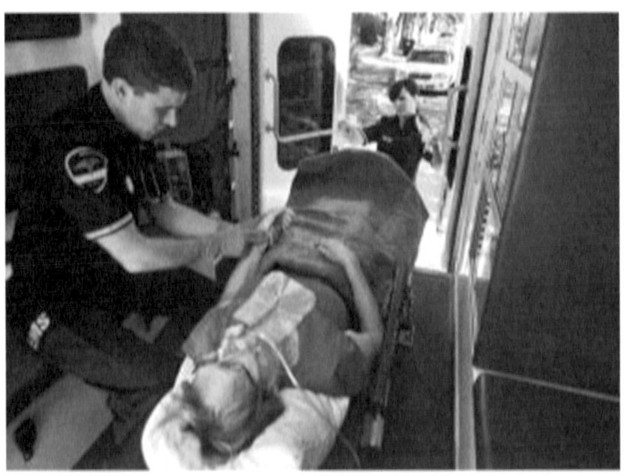

EMTs and paramedics transport patients to medical facilities.

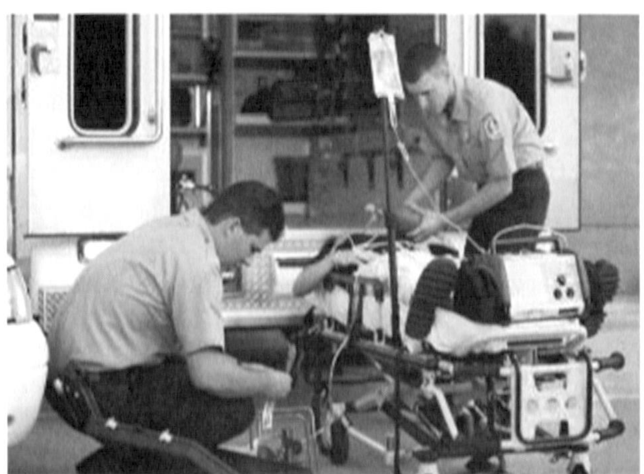

EMTs and paramedics assess a patient's condition and administer emergency medical care.

What EMTs and Paramedics Do

Emergency medical technicians (EMTs) and paramedics assess injuries and illnesses, provide emergency medical care, and may transport patients to medical facilities.

Duties

EMTs and paramedics typically do the following:

- Respond to calls for medical assistance, such as at the scene of a car accident in which someone is injured
- Assess people's condition and determine what treatment, if any, is needed
- Provide treatment, such as first aid or life support care, to sick or injured patients
- Prepare patients for and safely transport them to the emergency department of a hospital or other healthcare facility
- Document and report observations and any treatment provided, to physicians, nurses, or other healthcare staff
- Inventory and replace medical supplies and clean equipment after use

When transporting a patient in an ambulance, one EMT or paramedic may drive the ambulance while another monitors the patient's vital signs and provides emergency medical care. Some paramedics work as part of a helicopter's or an airplane's flight crew to transport critically ill or injured patients to a hospital.

In addition to transporting patients from the scene of an emergency, EMTs and paramedics transfer patients from one medical facility to another. Some patients may need to be transferred to a hospital that specializes in treating their particular injury or illness or to a facility that provides long-term care, such as a nursing home.

EMTs and paramedics must decontaminate the interior of an ambulance after treating a patient who has a contagious disease. They also may need to report the case to the proper authorities.

The specific responsibilities of EMTs and paramedics depend on their level of certification and the state in which they work. EMTs and paramedics sometimes begin with emergency medical responder (EMR) certification and advance to other levels of certification as they gain competency. The following are some of the duties at each of these EMT or paramedic certification levels.

An ***EMT***, also known as an *EMT-Basic*, cares for patients at the scene of an incident and while taking patients by ambulance to a hospital. An EMT has the skills to assess a patient's condition and to manage emergencies such as those related to respiratory, cardiac, or trauma incidents.

An ***Advanced EMT***, also known as an *EMT-Intermediate,* has completed both requirements for the EMT-Basic level and instruction that allows them to perform more advanced medical procedures, such as administering intravenous fluids and some medications.

Paramedics provide more extensive prehospital care than do EMTs. In addition to doing the tasks of EMTs, they are able to administer a wider range of medications, such as through intravenous methods. Paramedics also perform advanced airflow management and interpret electrocardiograms (EKGs)—which monitor heart function—and other types of equipment.

EMTs and paramedics typically interact with other public safety and support personnel. For example, a 911 operator sends EMTs and paramedics to the scene of an emergency, where they often work with police and firefighters.

Work Environment

Emergency medical technicians held about 170,700 jobs in 2022. The largest employers of emergency medical technicians were as follows:

Ambulance services	46%
Local government, excluding education and hospitals	26
General medical and surgical hospitals; private	15
General medical and surgical hospitals; local	3
Outpatient care centers	2

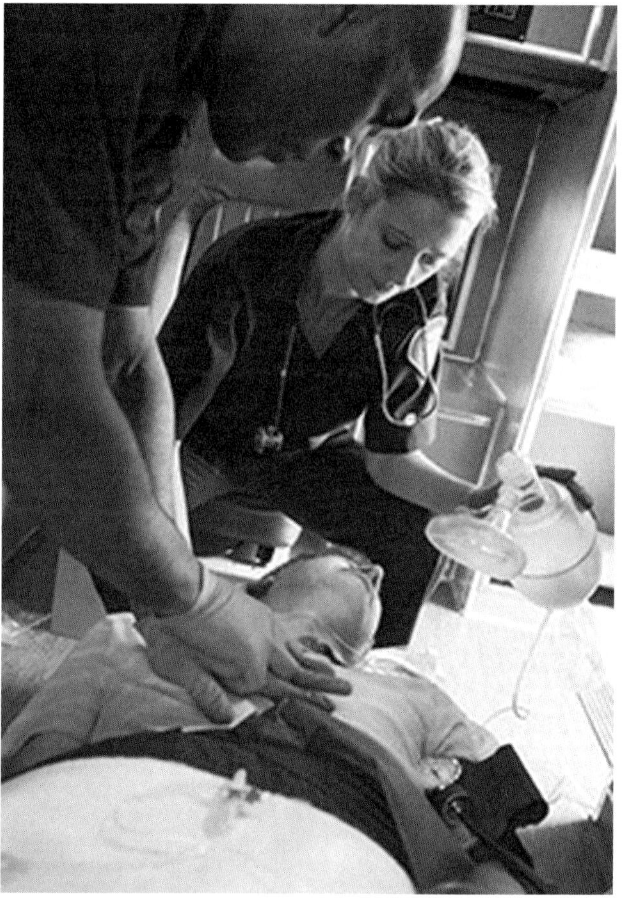

EMTs and paramedics care for sick or injured patients in a prehospital setting.

Paramedics held about 98,300 jobs in 2022. The largest employers of paramedics were as follows:

Ambulance services	39%
Local government, excluding education and hospitals	37
General medical and surgical hospitals; private	13
General medical and surgical hospitals; local	4
Offices of physicians	1

These employment data exclude volunteer EMTs and paramedics, who share many of the same duties as paid EMTs and paramedics.

EMTs and paramedics work both indoors and outdoors, in all types of weather. Their work is physically strenuous, and they spend much of their time standing or moving. Their work also may be stressful, especially when it involves life-or-death situations. Some paramedics must fly on helicopters or airplanes as part of an air ambulance flight crew.

Injuries and Illnesses

EMTs and paramedics spend considerable time kneeling, bending, and lifting while caring for and moving patients. They may be exposed to serious diseases and viruses, such as HIV. EMTs and paramedics may reduce the risk of injury and illness by following proper safety procedures, such as waiting for police to clear an area in violent situations or wearing a mask and gloves while working with a patient.

Work Schedules

Most EMTs and paramedics work full time. Some work more than 40 hours per week. Because EMTs and paramedics must be available to work in emergencies, their schedules may vary to include nights, weekends, and holidays. Some EMTs and paramedics work extended shifts, such as ones lasting 12, 18, or 24 hours.

How to Become an EMT or Paramedic

Emergency medical technicians (EMTs) and paramedics typically complete a postsecondary educational program. All states require EMTs and paramedics to be licensed in the state in which they work; requirements vary by state.

Education

High school students interested in becoming EMTs or paramedics should take courses in life sciences and consider becoming certified in cardiopulmonary resuscitation (CPR). Some high schools offer EMT training through vocational or technical education programs.

EMTs typically need to complete a postsecondary education program to enter the occupation. Program applicants usually need a high school diploma or equivalent and certification in

EMTs and paramedics need to be physically fit as their job requires bending, lifting, and kneeling.

CPR and basic life support (BLS). However, program entry requirements vary by state.

Most EMT programs lead to a nondegree award. They vary in length but typically take less than 1 year for EMT-Basic certification and up to 2 years for EMT-Intermediate certification. Programs are offered by technical institutes, community colleges, universities, and facilities that specialize in emergency care training. Some instruction may take place in a hospital or ambulance setting.

EMT-Basic programs cover topics such as assessing patients' conditions, handling emergencies, and using field equipment. Programs that do not require BLS and CPR certification prior to admission include instruction that leads to those certifications as part of the program. EMT-Intermediate programs require additional instruction for advanced skills, such as using complex airway devices, intravenous fluids, and some medications.

Paramedic postsecondary programs require applicants to have EMT-Intermediate certification. Most programs at community colleges typically lead to a nondegree award or an associate's degree. Some programs are offered by 4-year universities and lead to a bachelor's degree. Paramedic programs include courses such as anatomy and physiology, EKG interpretation, and maintaining airflow. They typically include supervised field experience.

The Commission on Accreditation of Allied Health Education Programs offers a list of accredited programs for paramedics.

Licenses, Certifications, and Registrations

The National Registry of Emergency Medical Technicians (NREMT) certifies EMTs and paramedics at the national level. All levels of NREMT certification—including EMT-Basic, EMT-Intermediate, and paramedics—require completing an approved education program and passing the written national exam. EMT-Intermediates and paramedics have a higher level of skill and must complete an additional hands-on component to complete their certifications.

All states require EMTs and paramedics to be licensed; requirements vary by state. Most states require candidates to have NREMT certification, but others require passage of an equivalent state exam. States also may have other requirements for licensing, such as a minimum age and passing a background check.

Employers typically require job candidates to have a driver's license and may prefer that they have ambulance driver certification.

Other Work Experience

Paramedics typically need work experience as an EMT prior to entering a paramedic education program.

Working as a volunteer EMT or paramedic may be helpful in getting experience for employment in these occupations.

Advancement

With additional education, paramedics may transfer into other healthcare occupations. For example, paramedic-to-RN programs offer an accelerated pathway to becoming a registered nurse.

Important Qualities

Communication skills. EMTs and paramedics must listen to patients describe their injuries and illnesses and to dispatchers and others conveying information. They also need to provide clear instruction and explain procedures.

Compassion. EMTs and paramedics must be able to provide care and emotional support to patients who may be in life-threatening situations or under extreme mental distress.

Interpersonal skills. EMTs and paramedics must be able to coordinate activities with other members of their team. They also interact with a variety of people when responding to calls for assistance.

Physical strength. EMTs and paramedics must be comfortable bending, lifting, and kneeling over the course of their shift.

Problem-solving skills. EMTs and paramedics must evaluate patients' symptoms and determine the appropriate treatment.

Pay

The median annual wage for emergency medical technicians was $36,680 in May 2022. The median wage is the wage at which half the workers in an occupation earned more than that amount and half earned less. The lowest 10 percent earned less than $28,270, and the highest 10 percent earned more than $56,890.

The median annual wage for paramedics was $49,090 in May 2022. The lowest 10 percent earned less than $36,490, and the highest 10 percent earned more than $76,630.

In May 2022, the median annual wages for emergency medical technicians in the top industries in which they worked were as follows:

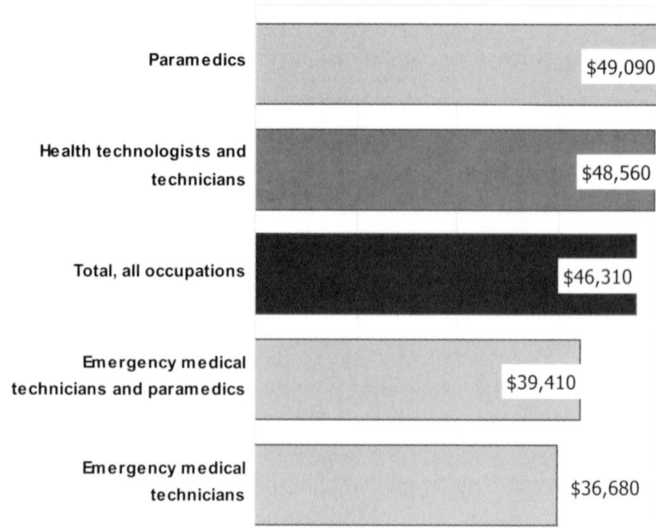

Note: All Occupations includes all occupations in the U.S. Economy.
Source: U.S. Bureau of Labor Statistics, Occupational Employment and Wage Statistics.

Outpatient care centers	$62,340
General medical and surgical hospitals; private	38,320
Local government, excluding education and hospitals	37,440
General medical and surgical hospitals; local	36,330
Ambulance services	35,350

In May 2022, the median annual wages for paramedics in the top industries in which they worked were as follows:

General medical and surgical hospitals; private	$50,050
Offices of physicians	49,690
Local government, excluding education and hospitals	49,030
Ambulance services	48,790
General medical and surgical hospitals; local	47,840

Most EMTs and paramedics work full time. Some work more than 40 hours per week. Because EMTs and paramedics must be available to work in emergencies, their schedules may vary to include nights, weekends, and holidays. Some EMTs and paramedics work extended shifts, such as ones lasting 12, 18, or 24 hours.

Job Outlook

Overall employment of EMTs and paramedics is projected to grow 5 percent from 2022 to 2032, faster than the average for all occupations.

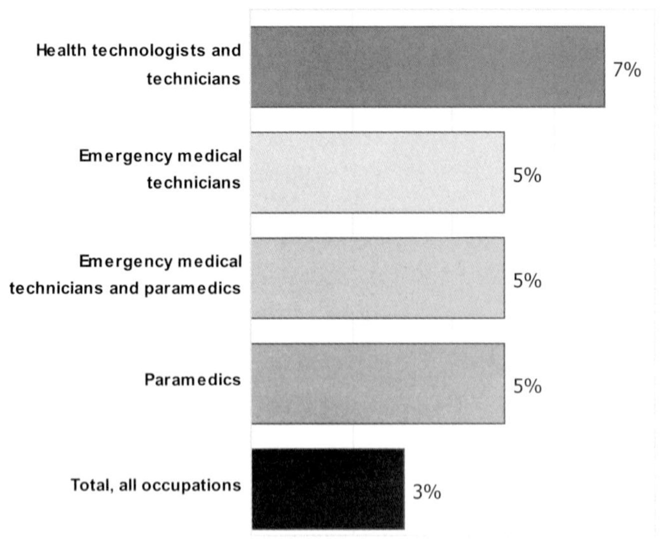

Note: All Occupations includes all occupations in the U.S. Economy.
Source: U.S. Bureau of Labor Statistics, Employment Projections program.

About 18,100 openings for EMTs and paramedics are projected each year, on average, over the decade. Many of those openings are expected to result from the need to replace workers who transfer to different occupations or exit the labor force, such as to retire.

Employment

Emergencies, such as car crashes, natural disasters, drug abuse incidents, and acts of violence, will continue to require the skills of EMTs and paramedics.

Growth in the middle-aged and older population will lead to an increase in age-related health emergencies, such as falls, heart attacks, and strokes. This increase, in turn, will support demand for EMT and paramedic services.

Occupational Title	SOC Code	Employment, 2022	Projected Employment, 2032	Change, 2022-32	
				Percent	Numeric
Emergency medical technicians and paramedics	29-2040	269,000	283,600	5	14,600
Emergency medical technicians	29-2042	170,700	180,000	5	9,300
Paramedics	29-2043	98,300	103,600	5	5,300

Contacts for More Information

For more information, visit

- National Association of Emergency Medical Technicians
- National Association of State EMS Officials
- National Highway Traffic Safety Administration, Office of Emergency Medical Services
- National Registry of Emergency Medical Technicians
- Commission on Accreditation of Allied Health Education Programs

Exercise Physiologists

Summary

Quick Facts: Exercise Physiologists	
2022 Median Pay	$51,350 per year $24.69 per hour
Typical Entry-Level Education	Bachelor's degree
Work Experience in a Related Occupation	None
On-the-job Training	None
Number of Jobs, 2022	16,500
Job Outlook, 2022-32	10% (Much faster than average)
Employment Change, 2022-32	1,700

What Exercise Physiologists Do

Exercise physiologists develop fitness and exercise programs that help injured or sick patients recover.

Work Environment

About half of exercise physiologists are self-employed. Most others work for hospitals and other healthcare providers. Most exercise physiologists work full time.

How to Become an Exercise Physiologist

Exercise physiologists typically need at least a bachelor's degree to enter the occupation. Degree programs include science and health-related courses, such as biology, anatomy, kinesiology, and nutrition, as well as clinical work.

Pay

The median annual wage for exercise physiologists was $51,350 in May 2022.

Job Outlook

Employment of exercise physiologists is projected to grow 10 percent from 2022 to 2032, much faster than the average for all occupations.

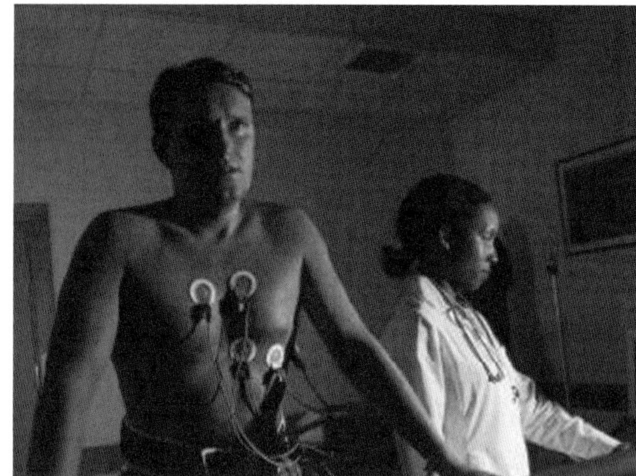

Exercise physiologists develop fitness and exercise programs that help patients recover from chronic diseases.

About 1,200 openings for exercise physiologists are projected each year, on average, over the decade. Many of those openings are expected to result from the need to replace workers who transfer to different occupations or exit the labor force, such as to retire.

What Exercise Physiologists Do

Exercise physiologists develop fitness and exercise programs that help patients recover from chronic diseases and improve cardiovascular function, body composition, and flexibility.

Duties

Exercise physiologists typically do the following:

- Analyze a patient's medical history to assess their risk during exercise and to determine the best possible exercise and fitness regimen for the patient
- Perform fitness and stress tests with medical equipment and analyze the resulting patient data
- Measure blood pressure, oxygen usage, heart rhythm, and other key patient health indicators
- Develop exercise programs to improve patients' health

Exercise physiologists work to improve overall patient health. Many of their patients suffer from health problems such as cardiovascular disease or pulmonary (lung) disease. Exercise physiologists provide health education and exercise plans to improve key health indicators.

Some physiologists work closely with primary care physicians, who may prescribe exercise regimens for their patients and refer them to exercise physiologists. The physiologists then work with patients to develop individualized treatment plans that will help the patients meet their health and fitness goals.

Exercise physiologists should not be confused with fitness trainers and instructors (including personal trainers) or athletic trainers.

Exercise physiologists analyze a patient's medical history to determine the best possible exercise and fitness regimen.

Work Environment

Exercise physiologists held about 16,500 jobs in 2022. The largest employers of exercise physiologists were as follows:

Employer	Percent
Self-employed workers	59%
Hospitals; state, local, and private	26
Offices of physical, occupational and speech therapists, and audiologists	4
Offices of physicians	3
Government	2

Work Schedules

Most exercise physiologists work full time.

How to Become an Exercise Physiologist

Exercise physiologists typically need at least a bachelor's degree to enter the occupation. Degree programs include

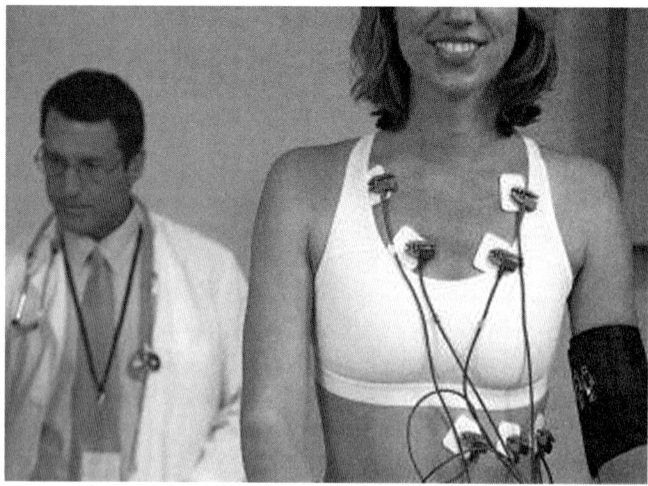

Exercise physiologists perform fitness and stress tests with medical equipment and analyze the subsequent patient data.

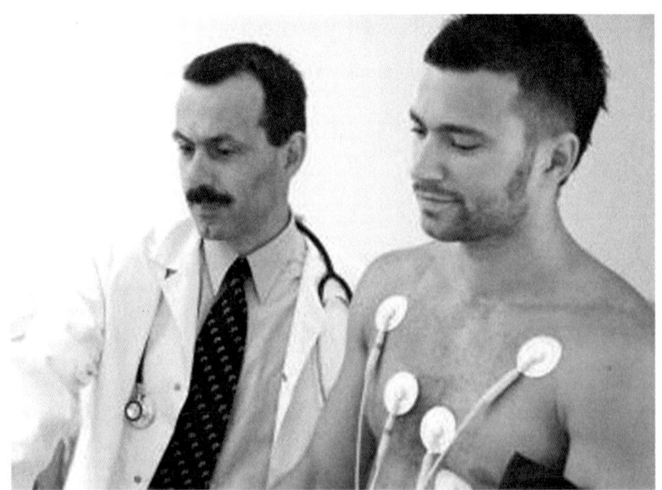

Exercise physiologists typically need at least a bachelor's degree.

science and health-related courses, such as biology, anatomy, kinesiology, and nutrition, as well as clinical work.

Education

Exercise physiologists typically need at least a bachelor's degree in exercise physiology, exercise science, kinesiology, or another healthcare and related field. Master's degree programs also are available. Degree programs in exercise physiology, exercise science, and kinesiology are accredited by the Commission on Accreditation of Allied Health Education Programs (CAAHEP). These programs usually include courses in science and health-related subjects, such as biology, anatomy, statistics, kinesiology, and nutrition, as well as clinical work.

Licenses, Certifications, and Registrations

Louisiana is the only state that requires exercise physiologists to be licensed, although some states have pending legislation to create licensure requirements.

Employers typically require exercise physiologists to have Basic Life Support (BLS) certification or Advanced Life Support (ACLS) certification, both of which include training in cardiopulmonary resuscitation (CPR).

The American Society of Exercise Physiologists (ASEP) offers the Exercise Physiologist Certified (EPC) certification, which physiologists can use to demonstrate their qualifications. To be eligible for certification, candidates must pass the ASEP exam and hold ASEP membership. In addition, candidates must have either a bachelor's degree in exercise physiology or a bachelor's degree in a related field, and they must have completed specific coursework requirements. To maintain certification, candidates must complete continuing education courses every 5 years.

The American College of Sports Medicine (ACSM) also offers certifications for exercise physiologists: the Certified Exercise Physiologist (EP-C) and the Certified Clinical Exercise Physiologist (CEP) credentials for candidates with a bachelor's degree, as well as the Registered Clinical Exercise Physiologist (RCEP) for candidates with a master's or higher degree. All three ACSM credentials require CPR certification and passing an exam. Candidates for the CEP and the RCEP also must have at least 400 and 600 hours of supervised clinical experience, respectively. All three ACSM certifications require candidates to complete continuing education courses every 3 years, and keep their CPR certification up to date.

Important Qualities

Compassion. Because exercise physiologists work with patients who may be in considerable pain or discomfort, they must be sympathetic while working with patients.

Decision-making skills. Exercise physiologists must make informed clinical decisions because those decisions could affect the health or livelihood of patients.

Detail oriented. Exercise physiologists must record detailed, accurate information about their patients' conditions and about any progress the patients make. For example, they must ensure that patients are completing the appropriate stress tests or practicing the correct fitness regimen.

Interpersonal skills. Exercise physiologists must have strong interpersonal skills and manage difficult situations. They must communicate clearly with others, including physicians, patients, and patients' families.

Pay

The median annual wage for exercise physiologists was $51,350 in May 2022. The median wage is the wage at which half the workers in an occupation earned more than that amount and half earned less. The lowest 10 percent earned less than $39,250, and the highest 10 percent earned more than $77,980.

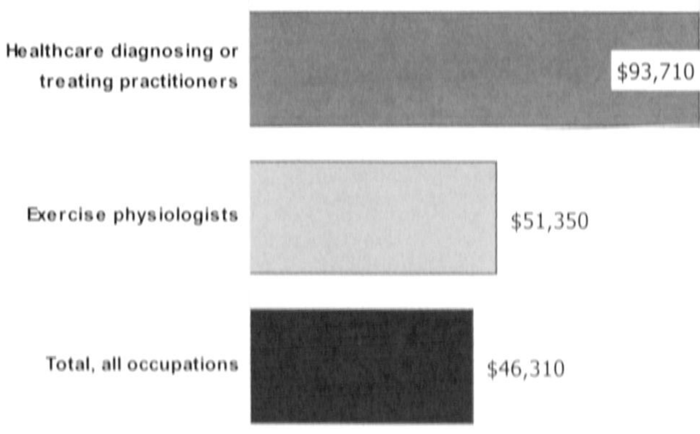

Note: All Occupations includes all occupations in the U.S. Economy.
Source: U.S. Bureau of Labor Statistics, Occupational Employment and Wage Statistics.

In May 2022, the median annual wages for exercise physiologists in the top industries in which they worked were as follows:

Government	$83,870
Hospitals; state, local, and private	51,730
Offices of physical, occupational and speech therapists, and audiologists	51,100
Offices of physicians	50,040

Most exercise physiologists work full time.

Job Outlook

Employment of exercise physiologists is projected to grow 10 percent from 2022 to 2032, much faster than the average for all occupations.

About 1,200 openings for exercise physiologists are projected each year, on average, over the decade. Many of those openings are expected to result from the need to replace workers who transfer to different occupations or exit the labor force, such as to retire.

Employment

As the prevalence of chronic conditions grows, more exercise physiologists will be needed to help patients manage their symptoms and improve their overall health through personalized exercise programs. Some employment growth is expected in settings such as hospitals, in which exercise physiologists play a central role in rehabilitating patients with cardiac, pulmonary, or other conditions.

Occupational Title	SOC Code	Employment, 2022	Projected Employment, 2032	Change, 2022-32	
				Percent	Numeric
Exercise physiologists	29-1128	16,500	18,200	10	1,700

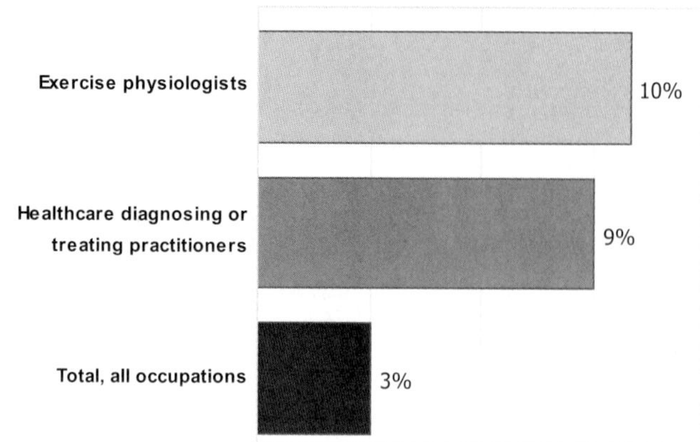

Note: All Occupations includes all occupations in the U.S. Economy.
Source: U.S. Bureau of Labor Statistics, Employment Projections program.

Contacts for More Information

For more information about exercise physiologists and certifications, visit

- American Society of Exercise Physiologists
- American College of Sports Medicine
- Committee on Accreditation for the Exercise Sciences
- Clinical Exercise Physiology Association
- Commission on Accreditation of Allied Health Education Programs

Genetic Counselors

Summary

Quick Facts: Genetic Counselors	
2022 Median Pay	$89,990 per year $43.26 per hour
Typical Entry-Level Education	Master's degree
Work Experience in a Related Occupation	None
On-the-job Training	None
Number of Jobs, 2022	3,500
Job Outlook, 2022-32	16% (Much faster than average)
Employment Change, 2022-32	600

What Genetic Counselors Do

Genetic counselors assess clients' risk for a variety of inherited conditions, such as birth defects.

Work Environment

Genetic counselors work primarily in hospitals, physicians' offices, outpatient care centers, university medical centers, and diagnostic laboratories. Most work full time.

How to Become a Genetic Counselor

Genetic counselors typically need a master's degree in genetic counseling. Nearly all states require genetic counselors to be licensed, and licensure typically requires board certification.

Genetic counselors assess individual or family risk for a variety of inherited conditions, such as genetic disorders and birth defects.

Pay

The median annual wage for genetic counselors was $89,990 in May 2022.

Job Outlook

Employment of genetic counselors is projected to grow 16 percent from 2022 to 2032, much faster than the average for all occupations.

About 300 openings for genetic counselors are projected each year, on average, over the decade. Many of those openings are expected to result from the need to replace workers who transfer to different occupations or exit the labor force, such as to retire.

What Genetic Counselors Do

Genetic counselors assess clients' risk for a variety of inherited conditions, such as birth defects. They review genetic test results with individuals and families and support them in making decisions based on those results. They also offer information to other healthcare providers.

Duties

Genetic counselors typically do the following:

- Collect comprehensive family and medical histories through means such as interviews, discussions with physicians, and reviewing medical records
- Evaluate genetic information to identify clients at risk for specific hereditary disorders
- Document information from counseling sessions to send to clients or to referring physicians
- Discuss testing options and the associated risks, benefits, and limitations with clients and other healthcare providers
- Educate clients and provide information about genetic risks and inherited conditions
- Provide psychological, emotional, or other support to clients distressed by test results
- Research hereditary disorders and developments in the field of genetics

Genetic counselors identify hereditary risks through the study of genetics. Specifically, they study genetic disorders or syndromes that are inherited from one's family. Prospective parents may consult genetic counselors to assess the risk of having children with hereditary disorders, such as cystic fibrosis. Genetic counselors also assess the risk for an individual to develop a disease, such as certain forms of cancer.

Counselors use DNA testing to identify clients' inherited conditions. Clinical laboratory technologists and technicians perform lab tests, which genetic counselors then evaluate and use for counseling clients. They share this information with other healthcare providers, such as physicians.

Genetic counselors may focus on a particular area of genetic counseling, such as prenatal, cancer, or pediatric. They also may work in one or more specialty fields, such as cardiovascular health, genomic medicine, or psychiatry.

Genetic counselors provide information and advice to other healthcare providers, or to individuals and families concerned with the risk of inherited conditions.

Genetic counselors work in university medical centers, private and public hospitals, and physicians' offices.

Genetic counselors must be sensitive and compassionate when communicating their findings.

Work Environment

Genetic counselors held about 3,500 jobs in 2022. The largest employers of genetic counselors were as follows:

Hospitals; state, local, and private	42%
Offices of physicians	18
Medical and diagnostic laboratories	9
Outpatient care centers	8
Colleges, universities, and professional schools; state, local, and private	7

Genetic counselors work with individuals, families, and other healthcare providers.

Work Schedules

Most genetic counselors work full time.

How to Become a Genetic Counselor

Genetic counselors typically need a master's degree in genetic counseling. Nearly all states require genetic counselors to be licensed, and licensure usually requires board certification.

Education

Genetic counselors typically need a master's degree in genetic counseling. Admission to master's degree programs varies. Some schools require a bachelor's degree in a science-related field, such as biology. Other programs require coursework in subjects such as biology, genetics, or statistics. Prospective students should check with an individual school regarding its requirements.

Genetic counseling programs typically take 2 years of post-baccalaureate study. A list of accredited programs is available from the Accreditation Council for Genetic Counseling.

In addition to medical topics, coursework in genetic counseling focuses on client interaction and research. Students typically complete supervised clinical rotations that provide students an opportunity to work with clients in different clinical environments.

Licenses, Certifications, and Registrations

Most states require genetic counselors to be licensed. Although requirements vary by state, licensure typically requires certification. For specific information, contact your state's medical board.

The American Board of Genetic Counseling offers certification for genetic counselors. To become certified, candidates must complete an accredited master's degree program and pass an exam. Counselors must complete continuing education courses to maintain board certification.

Even in states that do not require certification, employers may require or prefer that job candidates be certified or receive certification within a specified time after being hired.

Important Qualities

Communication skills. Genetic counselors must be able to explain complex information in a way that their clients understand.

Compassion. Genetic counselors must be sensitive and empathetic when discussing clients' options regarding potentially upsetting test results.

Critical-thinking skills. Genetic counselors recommend the proper test and analyze findings for each client.

Interpersonal skills. Genetic counselors must be able to relate well with clients and their families, as well as to work with other healthcare providers offering services to clients.

Organizational skills. Genetic counselors manage multiple clients and must keep accurate, complete records on each of them.

Pay

The median annual wage for genetic counselors was $89,990 in May 2022. The median wage is the wage at which half the

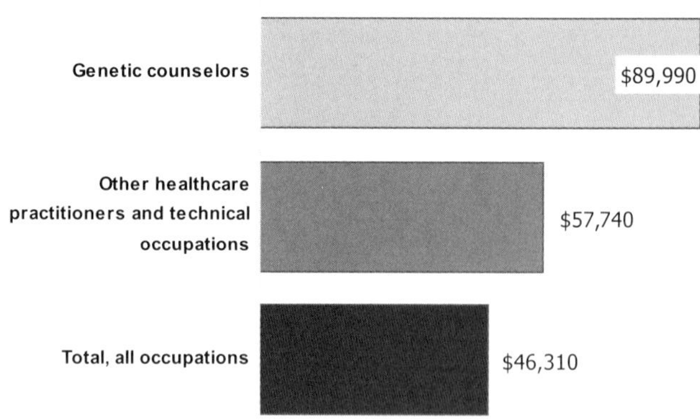

Note: All Occupations includes all occupations in the U.S. Economy.
Source: U.S. Bureau of Labor Statistics, Occupational Employment and Wage Statistics.

workers in an occupation earned more than that amount and half earned less. The lowest 10 percent earned less than $64,360, and the highest 10 percent earned more than $128,380.

In May 2022, the median annual wages for genetic counselors in the top industries in which they worked were as follows:

Outpatient care centers	$110,630
Medical and diagnostic laboratories	101,560
Hospitals; state, local, and private	87,340
Colleges, universities, and professional schools; state, local, and private	84,520
Offices of physicians	82,820

Most genetic counselors work full time.

Job Outlook

Employment of genetic counselors is projected to grow 16 percent from 2022 to 2032, much faster than the average for all occupations.

About 300 openings for genetic counselors are projected each year, on average, over the decade. Many of those openings are expected to result from the need to replace workers who transfer to different occupations or exit the labor force, such as to retire.

Employment

Employment growth is expected as ongoing technological innovations are giving genetic counselors opportunities to conduct more types of analyses. Developments in cancer genomics, for example, increasingly allow these counselors to determine a patient's risk for specific types of cancer. In addition, the number and types of lab tests that genetic counselors can evaluate have increased over the past few years. Many of these tests are covered by health insurance providers, which should further strengthen the demand for genetic counseling services.

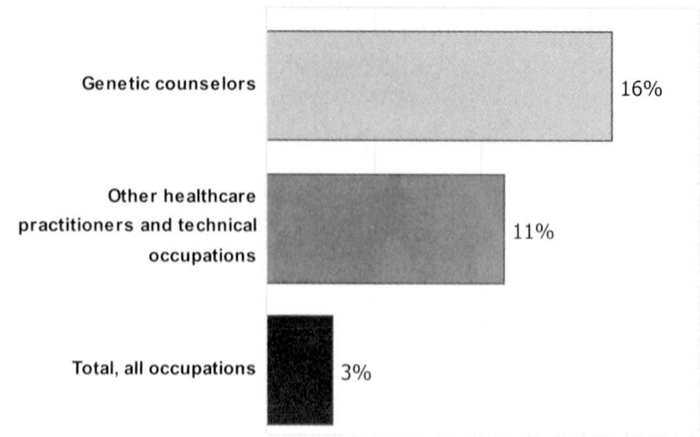

Note: All Occupations includes all occupations in the U.S. Economy.
Source: U.S. Bureau of Labor Statistics, Employment Projections program.

Occupational Title	SOC Code	Employment, 2022	Projected Employment, 2032	Change, 2022-32	
				Percent	Numeric
Genetic counselors	29-9092	3,500	4,000	16	600

Contacts for More Information

For more information, visit

- American Board of Genetic Counseling
- National Society of Genetic Counselors
- Accreditation Council for Genetic Counseling

Health Information Technologists and Medical Registrars

Summary

Quick Facts: Health Information Technologists and Medical Registrars

2022 Median Pay	$58,250 per year $28.01 per hour
Typical Entry-Level Education	Associate's degree
Work Experience in a Related Occupation	None
On-the-job Training	None
Number of Jobs, 2022	37,900
Job Outlook, 2022-32	16% (Much faster than average)
Employment Change, 2022-32	6,200

What Health Information Technologists and Medical Registrars Do

Health information technologists and medical registrars advise organizations on computerized healthcare systems and analyze clinical data.

Work Environment

Health information technologists and medical registrars usually work in an office setting and may spend many hours at a computer. Most work full time.

How to Become a Health Information Technologist or Medical Registrar

Education requirements for health information technologists and medical registrars vary. Some workers typically need an associate's degree; others need a bachelor's or higher degree. Certification may be required or preferred.

Health information technologists and medical registrars work with computerized healthcare systems.

Pay

The median annual wage for health information technologists and medical registrars was $58,250 in May 2022.

Job Outlook

Employment of health information technologists and medical registrars is projected to grow 16 percent from 2022 to 2032, much faster than the average for all occupations.

About 3,100 openings for health information technologists and medical registrars are projected each year, on average, over the decade. Many of those openings are expected to result from the need to replace workers who transfer to different occupations or exit the labor force, such as to retire.

What Health Information Technologists and Medical Registrars Do

Health information technologists and medical registrars advise organizations on computerized healthcare systems and analyze clinical data.

Duties

Health information technologists and medical registrars typically do the following:

- Help to determine requirements for computerized healthcare systems
- Evaluate and support implementation of health information systems
- Organize and update information in clinical databases or registries
- Compile data and generate reports, such as for disease registry or treatment
- Track patient outcomes for quality assessment
- Validate the integrity of patient data
- Ensure privacy, security, and confidentiality of patients' health information

Health information technologists and medical registrars help to design and develop electronic healthcare systems.

Health information technologists and medical registrars help to design and develop electronic healthcare systems. They abstract, collect, and analyze clinical data related to medical treatment, followup, and results. Their work supports the delivery and improvement of patient care.

Health information technologists apply their knowledge of information technology (IT) and healthcare concepts in a variety of ways. Some specialize in the electronic health records systems used for storing and retrieving patient data, which may include implementing the systems and educating staff on their use. Others analyze healthcare data for a range of purposes, such as for research or to evaluate programs and services.

Medical registrars create and maintain databases of information, such as those used to track a particular disease or condition. For example, *cancer registrars* collect and analyze information for facility, regional, and national databases of cancer patients. They review patients' records and pathology reports to verify completeness and accuracy; assign classification codes to represent the diagnosis and treatment of cancers and benign tumors; and track treatment, survival, and recovery.

For information about workers who compile, process, and maintain patient files, see the profile for medical records specialists.

Work Environment

Health information technologists and medical registrars held about 37,900 jobs in 2022. The largest employers of health information technologists and medical registrars were as follows:

Hospitals; state, local, and private	50%
Offices of physicians	7
Management of companies and enterprises	7
Professional, scientific, and technical services	7
Administrative and support services	5

Health information technologists and medical registrars may spend many hours at a computer.

Health information technologists and medical registrars usually work in an office setting and may spend many hours at a computer.

Work Schedules

Most health information technologists and medical registrars work full time.

How to Become a Health Information Technologist or Medical Registrar

Education requirements for health information technologists and medical registrars vary. Some workers typically need an associate's degree; others may need a bachelor's or higher degree. Certification may be required or preferred.

Education

Health information technologists and medical registrars typically need at least an associate's degree to enter the occupation. Some positions require a bachelor's or master's degree.

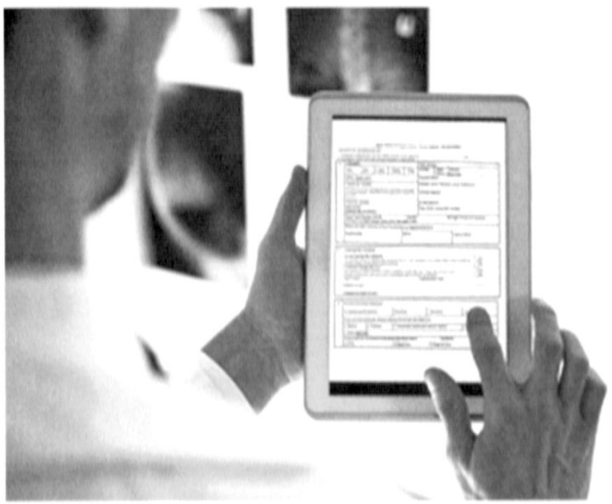

Health information technologists and medical registrars typically need at least an associate's degree.

High school students interested in becoming a health information technologist or medical registrar may benefit from taking classes that include anatomy and physiology, biology, computer science, and math.

A degree may be in health information management or another healthcare and related field or in nonmedical subjects, such as computer and information technology.

The Commission on Accreditation for Health Informatics and Information Management accredits programs at the associate's, bachelor's, and master's degree level. The National Cancer Registrars Association accredits programs in cancer registry management. Programs may include courses in medical terminology, health data requirements, medical ethics, and classification and coding systems.

Licenses, Certifications, and Registrations

Employers may prefer to hire health information technologists and medical registrars who have certification, or they may expect applicants to earn certification after being hired.

Credentials for a variety of specializations are available from professional organizations. For example, certifications from the American Health Information Management Association include the Registered Health Information Technician (RHIT), the Certified Documentation Improvement Practitioner (CDIP), and the Certified Health Data Analyst (CHDA). Individuals may hold multiple certifications.

Cancer registrars may need the Certified Tumor Registrar (CTR) credential. This certification requires completion of a formal education program and experience, along with passing an exam.

Advancement

Health information technologists and medical registrars sometimes advance to become medical and health services managers. Employers may require that workers seeking to advance have a higher level certification or a bachelor's or master's degree in health information management or a related field.

Important Qualities

Analytical skills. Health information technologists and medical registrars must be able to interpret data and use their findings to suggest improvements.

Detail oriented. To ensure accuracy, health information technologists and medical registrars need to be precise when working with clinical data.

Integrity. Health information technologists and medical registrars must exercise discretion and act ethically when working with patient data to protect patient confidentiality, as required by law.

Interpersonal skills. Health information technologists and medical registrars must collaborate with other members of the healthcare team.

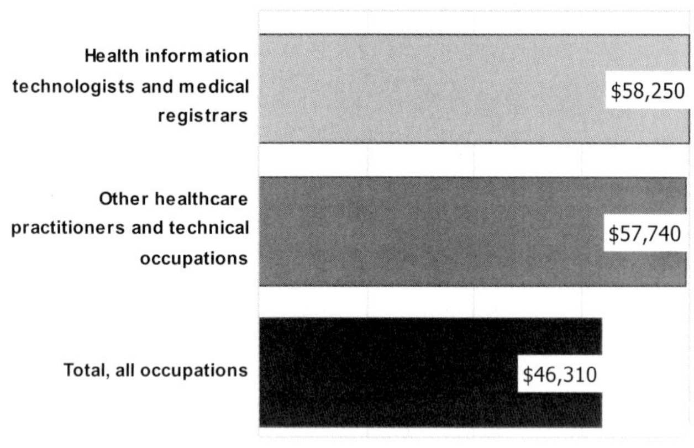

Note: All Occupations includes all occupations in the U.S. Economy.
Source: U.S. Bureau of Labor Statistics, Occupational Employment and Wage Statistics.

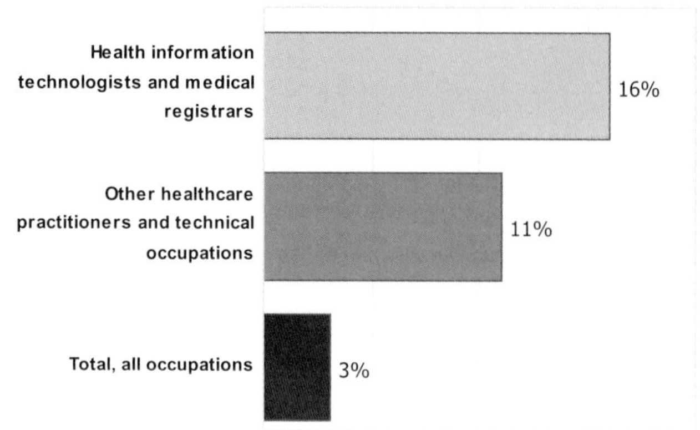

Note: All Occupations includes all occupations in the U.S. Economy.
Source: U.S. Bureau of Labor Statistics, Employment Projections program

Problem-solving skills. These workers must be able to identify and address issues related to the use of healthcare information systems.

Pay

The median annual wage for health information technologists and medical registrars was $58,250 in May 2022. The median wage is the wage at which half the workers in an occupation earned more than that amount and half earned less. The lowest 10 percent earned less than $34,970, and the highest 10 percent earned more than $103,380.

In May 2022, the median annual wages for health information technologists and medical registrars in the top industries in which they worked were as follows:

Management of companies and enterprises	$73,150
Professional, scientific, and technical services	65,150
Administrative and support services	59,760
Hospitals; state, local, and private	57,920
Offices of physicians	48,630

Most health information technologists and medical registrars work full time.

Job Outlook

Employment of health information technologists and medical registrars is projected to grow 16 percent from 2022 to 2032, much faster than the average for all occupations.

About 3,100 openings for health information technologists and medical registrars are projected each year, on average, over the decade. Many of those openings are expected to result from the need to replace workers who transfer to different occupations or exit the labor force, such as to retire.

Employment

The volume of electronic health information generated by healthcare providers and patients continues to grow. As a result, more health information technologists will be needed to analyze these vast quantities of data and offer insight to help make informed decisions.

Similarly, the increasing availability of medical data will contribute to more demand for medical registrars to update clinical registries, abstract relevant details, and convert data into meaningful information. Organizations continue to rely on these workers for insight into improving the quality of care, to control costs, and for other purposes.

Occupational Title	SOC Code	Employment, 2022	Projected Employment, 2032	Change, 2022-32	
				Percent	Numeric
Health information technologists and medical registrars	29-9021	37,900	44,100	16	6,200

Contacts for More Information

For more information, visit

- American Health Information Management Association
- Commission on Accreditation for Health Informatics and Information Management Education
- National Cancer Registrars Association

Home Health and Personal Care Aides

Summary

Quick Facts: Home Health and Personal Care Aides	
2022 Median Pay	$30,180 per year $14.51 per hour
Typical Entry-Level Education	High school diploma or equivalent
Work Experience in a Related Occupation	None
On-the-job Training	Short-term on-the-job training
Number of Jobs, 2022	3,715,500
Job Outlook, 2022-32	22% (Much faster than average)
Employment Change, 2022-32	804,600

What Home Health and Personal Care Aides Do

Home health and personal care aides monitor the condition of people with disabilities or chronic illnesses and help them with daily living activities.

Work Environment

Home health and personal care aides work in a variety of settings, including clients' homes, group homes, and day services programs. Most aides work full time, although part-time work is common. Work schedules may vary.

How to Become a Home Health or Personal Care Aide

Home health and personal care aides typically need a high school diploma or equivalent, but some positions do not require it. Those working in certified home health or hospice agencies may need to complete formal training or pass a standardized test.

Home health aides may provide some basic health-related services, such as checking a client's blood pressure.

Pay

The median annual wage for home health and personal care aides was $30,180 in May 2022.

Job Outlook

Employment of home health and personal care aides is projected to grow 22 percent from 2022 to 2032, much faster than the average for all occupations.

About 684,600 openings for home health and personal care aides are projected each year, on average, over the decade. Many of those openings are expected to result from the need to replace workers who transfer to different occupations or exit the labor force, such as to retire.

What Home Health and Personal Care Aides Do

Home health and personal care aides monitor the condition of people with disabilities or chronic illnesses and help them with daily living activities. They often help older adults who need assistance. Under the direction of a nurse or other healthcare practitioner, home health aides may be allowed to give a client medication or to check the client's vital signs.

Duties

Home health and personal care aides typically do the following:

- Assist clients in their daily personal tasks, such as bathing or dressing
- Perform housekeeping tasks, such as laundry, washing dishes, and vacuuming
- Help to organize a client's schedule and plan appointments
- Arrange transportation to doctors' offices or other outings
- Shop for groceries and prepare meals to meet a client's dietary specifications
- Keep clients engaged in their social networks and communities

Home health aides may provide some basic health-related services—such as checking a client's pulse, temperature, and

Personal care aides assist clients in everyday tasks.

respiration rate—depending on the state in which they work. They also may help with simple prescribed exercises and with giving medications. Occasionally, they change bandages or dressings, give massages, care for skin, or help with braces and artificial limbs. With special training, experienced home health aides also may help with medical equipment, such as ventilators to help clients breathe.

Home health aides are supervised by medical practitioners, usually nurses, and may work with therapists and other medical staff. These aides keep records on the client, such as services received, condition, and progress. They report changes in the client's condition to a supervisor or case manager.

Personal care aides, sometimes called caregivers or personal attendants, are generally limited to providing nonmedical services, including companionship, cleaning, cooking, and driving. Some of these aides work specifically with people who have developmental or intellectual disabilities to help create a behavior plan and teach self-care skills, such as doing laundry or cooking meals.

Work Environment

Home health and personal care aides held about 3.7 million jobs in 2022. The largest employers of home health and personal care aides were as follows:

Individual and family services	49%
Home healthcare services	24
Residential intellectual and developmental disability facilities	7
Continuing care retirement communities and assisted living facilities for the elderly	7

Many home health and personal care aides work in clients' homes; others work in group homes or care communities. Some aides work with only one client, while others work with groups of clients. They sometimes stay with one client on a long-term basis or for a specific purpose, such as hospice care. They may work with other aides in shifts so that the client always has an aide.

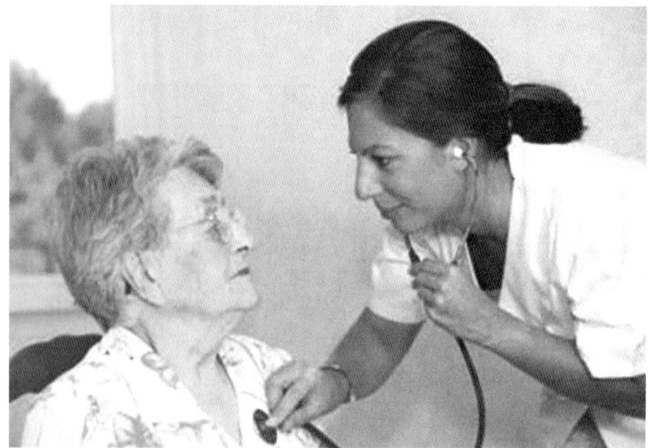

Many aides work in clients' homes; others work in group homes or care communities.

Aides may travel as they help people with disabilities go to work and stay engaged in their communities.

Injuries and Illnesses

Work as a home health or personal care aide can be physically and emotionally demanding. Because they often move clients into and out of bed or help with standing or walking, aides must use proper lifting techniques to guard against back injury.

In addition, aides may work with clients who have cognitive impairments or mental health issues and who may display difficult or violent behaviors. Aides also face hazards from minor infections and exposure to communicable diseases but can lessen their chance of infection by following proper procedures.

Work Schedules

Most aides work full time, although part-time work is common. They may work evening and weekend hours, depending on their clients' needs. Work schedules may vary.

How to Become a Home Health or Personal Care Aide

Home health and personal care aides typically need a high school diploma or equivalent, but some positions do not require it. Those working in certified home health or hospice agencies must complete formal training and pass a standardized test.

Education

Home health and personal care aides typically need a high school diploma or equivalent, although some positions do not require a formal educational credential. Postsecondary nondegree award programs are available at community colleges and vocational schools.

Training

Home health and personal care aides may be trained in housekeeping tasks, such as cooking for clients who have special dietary needs. Aides may learn basic safety techniques, including how to respond in an emergency. If state certification is required, specific training may be needed.

Training may be completed on the job or through programs. Training typically includes learning about personal hygiene, reading and recording vital signs, infection control, and basic nutrition.

In addition, individual clients may have preferences that aides need time to learn.

Licenses, Certifications, and Registrations

Home health and personal care aides may need to meet requirements specific to the state in which they work. For example, some states require home health aides to have a license or certification, which may involve completing training and passing a

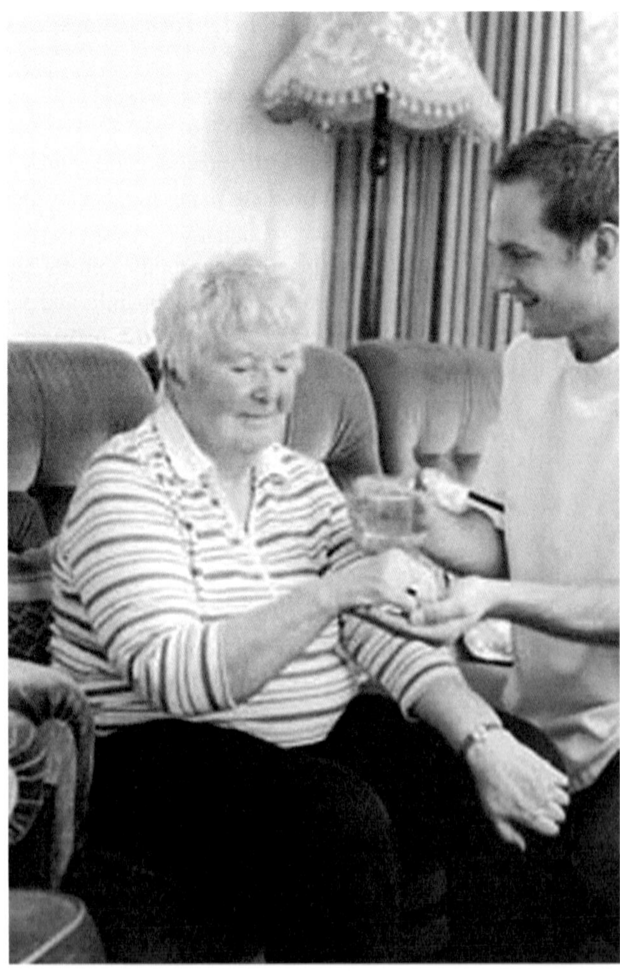

Under the direction of a nurse or other healthcare practitioner, home health aides may be allowed to give a client medication.

background check and a competency exam. For more information, check with your state board of health.

Certified home health or hospice agencies that receive payments from federally funded programs, such as Medicare, must comply with regulations regarding aides' employment. Private care agencies that do not receive federal funds may have other employment requirements that vary by state.

Aides also may be required to obtain certification in first aid and cardiopulmonary resuscitation (CPR).

Important Qualities

Detail oriented. Home health and personal care aides must adhere to specific rules and protocols to help care for clients. They must carefully follow instructions, such as how to care for wounds, that they receive from other healthcare workers.

Emotional skills. Home health and personal care aides must be sensitive to clients' needs, especially while in extreme pain or distress. Aides must be compassionate and enjoy helping people.

Integrity. Home health and personal care aides must be dependable and trustworthy so that clients and their families can rely on them. They also should be respectful when tending to personal activities, such as helping clients bathe.

Interpersonal skills. Home health and personal care aides must be able to communicate with clients and other healthcare workers. They need to listen closely to what they are being told and convey information clearly.

Physical stamina. Home health and personal care aides should be comfortable doing physical tasks. They might need to be on their feet for many hours or do strenuous tasks, such as lifting or turning clients.

Pay

The median annual wage for home health and personal care aides was $30,180 in May 2022. The median wage is the wage at which half the workers in an occupation earned more than that amount and half earned less. The lowest 10 percent earned less than $22,500, and the highest 10 percent earned more than $38,350.

In May 2022, the median annual wages for home health and personal care aides in the top industries in which they worked were as follows:

Residential intellectual and developmental disability facilities	$31,350
Continuing care retirement communities and assisted living facilities for the elderly	31,230
Individual and family services	29,930
Home healthcare services	29,730

Most aides work full-time, although part-time work is common. They may work evening and weekend hours, depending on their clients' needs. Work schedules may vary.

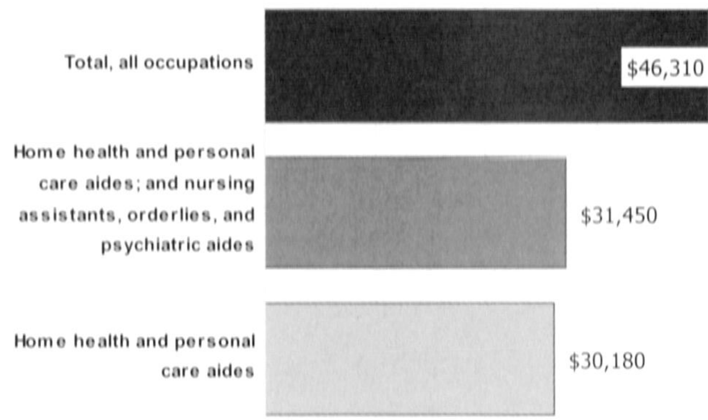

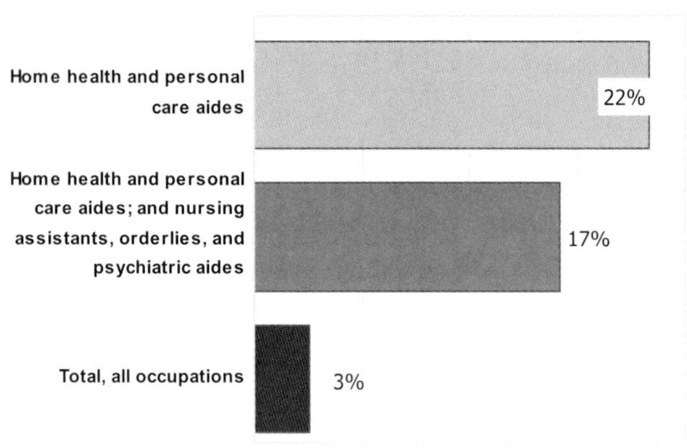

Note: All Occupations includes all occupations in the U.S. Economy.
Source: U.S. Bureau of Labor Statistics, Employment Projections program.

Job Outlook

Employment of home health and personal care aides is projected to grow 22 percent from 2022 to 2032, much faster than the average for all occupations.

About 684,600 openings for home health and personal care aides are projected each year, on average, over the decade. Many of those openings are expected to result from the need to replace workers who transfer to different occupations or exit the labor force, such as to retire.

Employment

The services that home health and personal care aides provide will be in high demand to care for the rising number of older people.

The locations in which care is offered are affected by both policy changes and lifestyle preferences of older adults and people with disabilities. Long-term care services are increasingly shifting from institutional settings, such as nursing homes, to home- and community-based settings. This shift is expected to create many new jobs for home health and personal care aides.

Occupational Title	SOC Code	Employment, 2022	Projected Employment, 2032	Change, 2022-32	
				Percent	Numeric
Home health and personal care aides	31-1120	3,715,500	4,520,100	22	804,600

Contacts for More Information

For more information about home health and personal care aides, visit

- American Society on Aging
- National Association for Home Care & Hospice
- PHI

Licensed Practical and Licensed Vocational Nurses

Summary

Quick Facts: Licensed Practical and Licensed Vocational Nurses

2022 Median Pay	$54,620 per year $26.26 per hour
Typical Entry-Level Education	Postsecondary nondegree award
Work Experience in a Related Occupation	None
On-the-job Training	None
Number of Jobs, 2022	655,000
Job Outlook, 2022-32	5% (Faster than average)
Employment Change, 2022-32	34,900

What Licensed Practical and Licensed Vocational Nurses Do

Licensed practical nurses (LPNs) and licensed vocational nurses (LVNs) provide basic medical care.

Work Environment

Licensed practical and licensed vocational nurses work in a variety of settings, including nursing and residential care facilities, hospitals, physicians' offices, and private homes. Most work full time.

How to Become a Licensed Practical or Licensed Vocational Nurse

Licensed practical and licensed vocational nurses must complete a state-approved educational program, which typically takes about 1 year. They must be licensed.

Licensed practical and licensed vocational nurses discuss the care they are providing with patients.

Pay

The median annual wage for licensed practical and licensed vocational nurses was $54,620 in May 2022.

Job Outlook

Employment of licensed practical and licensed vocational nurses is projected to grow 5 percent from 2022 to 2032, faster than the average for all occupations.

About 54,400 openings for licensed practical and licensed vocational nurses are projected each year, on average, over the decade. Many of those openings are expected to result from the need to replace workers who transfer to different occupations or exit the labor force, such as to retire.

What Licensed Practical and Licensed Vocational Nurses Do

Licensed practical nurses (LPNs) and licensed vocational nurses (LVNs) provide basic medical care to ill, injured, or convalescing patients or to persons with disabilities. Responsibilities for LPNs and LVNs are nearly identical; their title depends on the state in which they work.

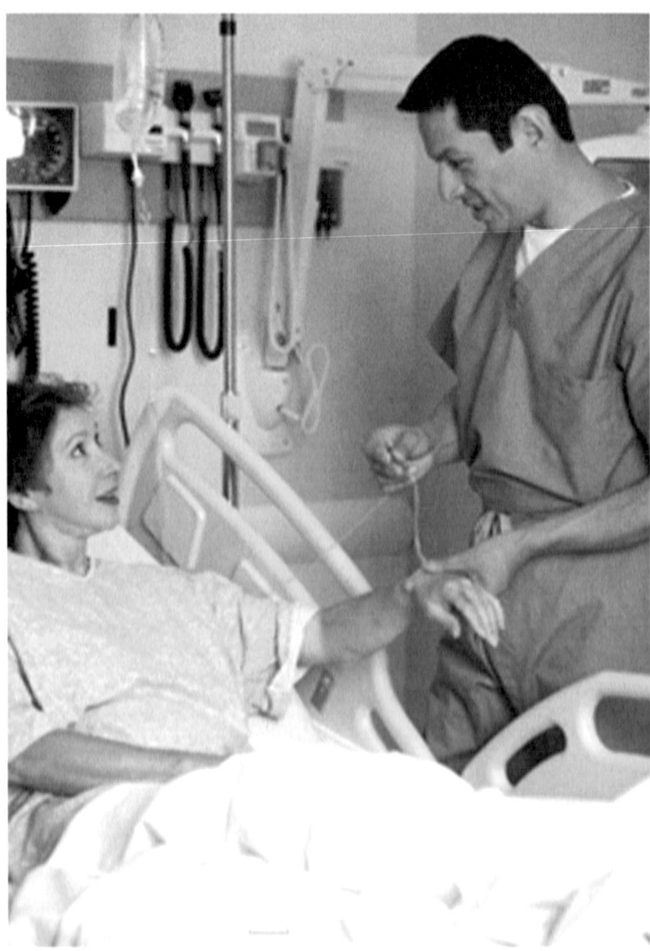

In some states, licensed practical and vocational nurses can give medication or start intravenous (IV) drips.

Duties

Licensed practical and licensed vocational nurses typically do the following:

- Monitor patients' health by checking their blood pressure, body temperature, and other vital signs
- Provide basic patient care and comfort, including changing bandages and helping with bathing or dressing
- Discuss care with patients and listen to their concerns
- Report patients' status and concerns to registered nurses, advanced practice nurses, or physicians
- Document patient care and maintain health records

Responsibilities of LPNs and LVNs vary by work setting. For example, in private homes, they may reinforce registered nurses' instruction regarding how family members should care for a relative. In hospitals, they might collect samples for testing and do routine laboratory tests. In nursing and residential care facilities, they may feed patients who need help eating.

LPN and LVN duties also may depend on the state in which they work. For example, in some states, LPNs with proper training may give medication or start intravenous (IV) drips.

LPNs and LVNs typically work under the supervision of registered nurses and doctors. States determine the extent to which LPNs and LVNs must be directly supervised. Some states allow experienced LPNs and LVNs to oversee other LPNs and LVNs or unlicensed medical staff.

Work Environment

Licensed practical and licensed vocational nurses held about 655,000 jobs in 2022. The largest employers of licensed practical and licensed vocational nurses were as follows:

Nursing and residential care facilities	35%
Hospitals; state, local, and private	15
Home healthcare services	13
Offices of physicians	12
Government	6

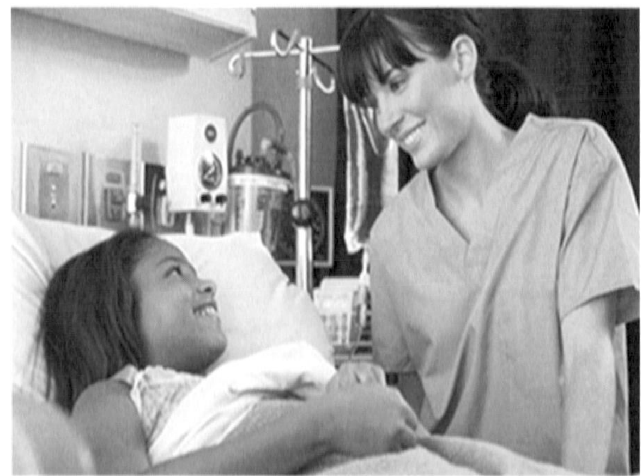

Licensed practical and vocational nurses must be empathetic and caring toward the people they serve.

Licensed practical nurses (LPNs) and licensed vocational nurses (LVNs) may spend a lot of time walking, bending, stretching, and standing. Because they often move or lift patients, LPNs and LVNs must use proper lifting techniques to guard against back injury.

The work of LPNs and LVNs may put them in close contact with people who have infectious diseases, and they frequently come into contact with potentially harmful and hazardous drugs and other substances. Therefore, LPNs and LVNs must follow strict guidelines to guard against diseases and other dangers, such as accidental needle sticks and exposure to radiation or to chemicals used in creating a sterile environment.

Work Schedules

Most licensed practical and licensed vocational nurses (LPNs and LVNs) work full time. Some work nights, weekends, and holidays, because medical care takes place at all hours. They may be required to work shifts of longer than 8 hours.

How to Become a Licensed Practical or Licensed Vocational Nurse

Licensed practical nurses (LPNs) and licensed vocational nurses (LVNs) must complete a state-approved educational program, which typically takes about 1 year. They also must have a license.

Education

LPNs and LVNs must complete an approved educational program. Certificate and diploma programs are commonly found in community colleges and technical schools, including some high schools, and typically take about 1 year to complete.

Practical nursing programs include subjects such as nursing fundamentals, anatomy and physiology, and pharmacology. All programs also include supervised clinical experience.

For a list of approved programs, contact your state board of nursing.

Licensed practical and vocational nurses provide basic medical care, such as checking a patient's blood pressure.

Licenses, Certifications, and Registrations

After completing a state-approved educational program, prospective LPNs and LVNs must pass the National Council Licensure Examination (NCLEX-PN). For more information on the NCLEX-PN, visit the National Council of State Boards of Nursing.

Optional certifications for LPNs and LVNs are available through professional associations in areas such as gerontology, wound care, and intravenous (IV) therapy. Certifications show that an LPN or LVN has an advanced level of knowledge about a specific subject.

Some employers require or prefer that candidates have cardiopulmonary resuscitation (CPR) or basic life support (BLS) certification.

Advancement

With experience, licensed practical and licensed vocational nurses may advance to supervisory positions. Some LPNs and LVNs transfer into other healthcare occupations. For example, an LPN may complete an LPN-to-RN education program to become a registered nurse.

Important Qualities

Compassion. LPNs and LVNs must be empathetic and caring toward the people they serve.

Communication skills. LPNs and LVNs must be able to convey information effectively. For example, they may need to relay a patient's test results to a registered nurse.

Detail oriented. LPNs and LVNs need to pay attention to minutiae because they must ensure that patients get the correct care at the right time.

Interpersonal skills. LPNs and LVNs must be able to build a rapport to interact with patients and other healthcare providers.

Multitasking skills. LPNs and LVNs often work with multiple patients who have a variety of health needs. They must ensure that each patient receives appropriate care and attention.

Physical stamina. LPNs and LVNs should be able to perform physical tasks, such as bending over patients for a long time.

Pay

The median annual wage for licensed practical and licensed vocational nurses was $54,620 in May 2022. The median wage is the wage at which half the workers in an occupation earned more than that amount and half earned less. The lowest 10 percent earned less than $40,490, and the highest 10 percent earned more than $72,650.

In May 2022, the median annual wages for licensed practical and licensed vocational nurses in the top industries in which they worked were as follows:

Nursing and residential care facilities	$58,140
Government	57,200
Home healthcare services	54,080

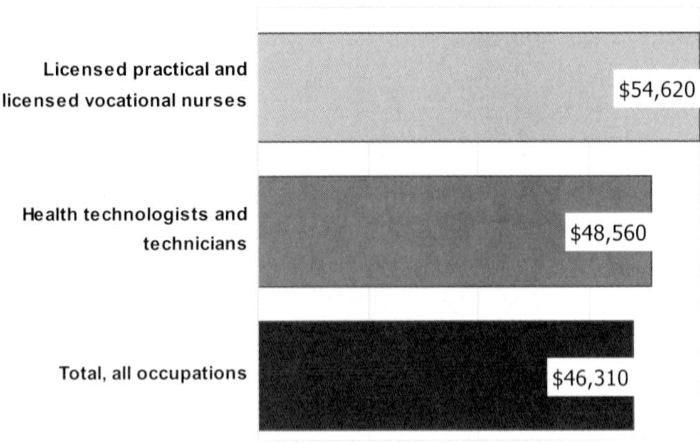

Note: All Occupations includes all occupations in the U.S. Economy. Source: U.S. Bureau of Labor Statistics, Occupational Employment and Wage Statistics.

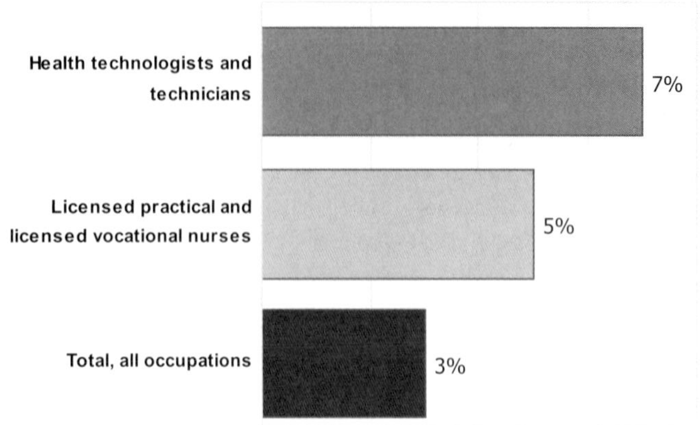

Note: All Occupations includes all occupations in the U.S. Economy. Source: U.S. Bureau of Labor Statistics, Employment Projections program.

Hospitals; state, local, and private	49,760
Offices of physicians	48,300

Most licensed practical and licensed vocational nurses (LPNs and LVNs) work full time. Some work nights, weekends, and holidays, because medical care takes place at all hours. They may be required to work shifts of longer than 8 hours.

Job Outlook

Employment of licensed practical and licensed vocational nurses is projected to grow 5 percent from 2022 to 2032, faster than the average for all occupations.

About 54,400 openings for licensed practical and licensed vocational nurses are projected each year, on average, over the decade. Many of those openings are expected to result from the need to replace workers who transfer to different occupations or exit the labor force, such as to retire.

Employment

As the baby-boom population ages, the overall need for healthcare services is expected to increase. LPNs and LVNs will be needed in residential care facilities and in home health environments to care for older patients.

A number of chronic conditions, such as diabetes and obesity, have become more prevalent in recent years. LPNs and LVNs will be needed to assist and care for patients with these and other conditions. In addition, many procedures that once could be done only in hospitals are now being done outside of hospitals, creating demand in other settings, such as outpatient care centers.

Occupational Title	SOC Code	Employment, 2022	Projected Employment, 2032	Change, 2022-32	
				Percent	Numeric
Licensed practical and licensed vocational nurses	29-2061	655,000	689,900	5	34,900

Contacts for More Information

For more information, visit

- National Association of Licensed Practical Nurses
- National Council of State Boards of Nursing

Massage Therapists

Summary

Quick Facts: Massage Therapists	
2022 Median Pay	$49,860 per year $23.97 per hour
Typical Entry-Level Education	Postsecondary nondegree award
Work Experience in a Related Occupation	None
On-the-job Training	None
Number of Jobs, 2022	134,300
Job Outlook, 2022-32	18% (Much faster than average)
Employment Change, 2022-32	24,600

What Massage Therapists Do

Massage therapists treat clients by applying pressure to manipulate the body's soft tissues and joints.

Work Environment

Massage therapists work in an array of settings, such as spas and offices of other health practitioners. Some also travel to local events, clients' homes, or other sites. Part-time work is common, and work schedules may vary. Many massage therapists are self-employed.

How to Become a Massage Therapist

Massage therapists typically complete a postsecondary education that combines study and experience, although standards and requirements vary by state. Most states regulate massage therapy and require massage therapists to have a license or certification.

Pay

The median annual wage for massage therapists was $49,860 in May 2022.

Job Outlook

Employment of massage therapists is projected to grow 18 percent from 2022 to 2032, much faster than the average for all occupations.

About 22,000 openings for massage therapists are projected each year, on average, over the decade. Many of those openings are expected to result from the need to replace workers who transfer to different occupations or exit the labor force, such as to retire.

What Massage Therapists Do

Massage therapists treat clients by applying pressure to manipulate the body's soft tissues and joints. This treatment may help to relieve pain, heal injuries, relieve stress, and aid in the general wellness of clients.

Duties

Massage therapists typically do the following:

- Talk with clients about their symptoms, medical history, and treatment goals
- Evaluate clients prior to and during the massage to locate painful or tense areas of the body
- Manipulate muscles, tendons, ligaments, and other soft tissues of the body
- Increase range of motion through joint mobilization techniques
- Provide guidance on stretching, strengthening, overall relaxation, and improving their posture
- Document clients' conditions and progress
- Clean their workspace and sanitize equipment

Massage therapists manipulate clients' soft tissues and joints to treat injuries and promote general wellness. They may use their hands, fingers, forearms, elbows, and feet as tools during the session.

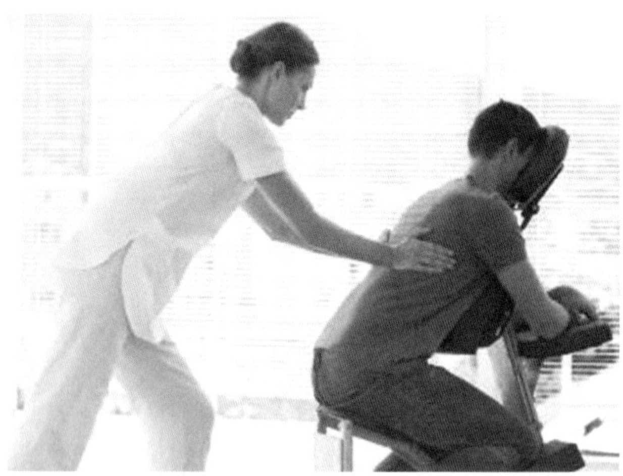

Massage therapists use touch to manipulate a client's muscles and other soft tissues.

Massage therapists knead muscles and other soft tissues of the body to provide treatment for injuries and to promote general wellness.

Massage therapists may use lotions and oils and massage tables or chairs when treating a client. The length of a session varies based on type of massage. For example, a chair massage may be as short as 5 to 10 minutes, whereas a table massage typically lasts between 30 and 90 minutes.

Massage therapists talk with clients about what the desired outcome of massage. They may suggest personalized treatment plans for the client, including information about additional relaxation techniques to practice between sessions.

Massage therapists may specialize in different massage modalities, or specialties, such as Swedish massage, deep-tissue massage, and sports massage. Massage therapists may specialize in several modalities.

The type of massage given typically depends on the client's needs and physical condition. Different populations, such as athletes or pregnant women, require different techniques for their massages.

In addition to giving massages, therapists, especially those who are self-employed, may spend time recording notes on clients, marketing, booking clients, and conducting other business tasks.

Work Environment

Massage therapists held about 134,300 jobs in 2022. The largest employers of massage therapists were as follows:

Self-employed workers	35%
Personal care services	33
Offices of all other health practitioners	12
Offices of chiropractors	7
Accommodation	6

Some massage therapists travel to local events, clients' homes or other sites. Others work out of their own homes. Massage therapists, especially those who are self-employed, may provide their own table or chair, sheets, pillows, and body lotions or oils.

Massage therapists' working conditions vary. For example, some therapists provide relaxing massages in dimly lit settings and use candles, incense, and soothing music. Others offer rehabilitative massages in brightly lit clinical settings or at outdoor events.

Injuries and Illnesses

Because giving massages is physically demanding, massage therapists may injure themselves if they do not use proper technique. Repetitive-motion problems and fatigue from standing for extended periods are most common.

Therapists can limit these risks by using good body mechanics, spacing sessions properly, exercising, and receiving a massage regularly themselves.

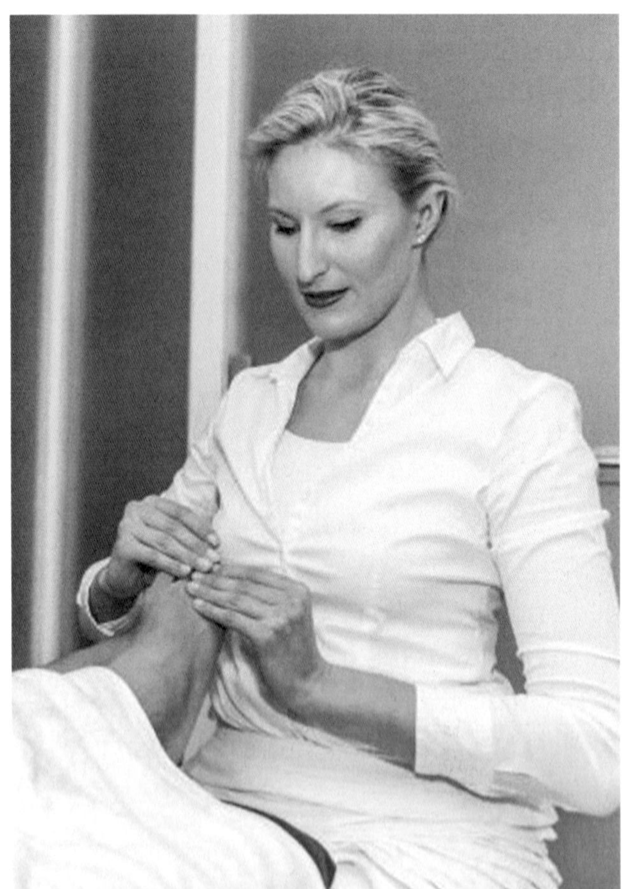

Massage therapists create an environment intended to make clients feel relaxed.

Work Schedules

Part-time work is common for massage therapists. Because therapists usually work by appointment, their schedules and the number of hours worked each week vary considerably. Moreover, because of the strength and endurance needed to give a massage, many therapists cannot perform massage services 8 hours per day, 5 days per week.

How to Become a Massage Therapist

Massage therapists typically complete a postsecondary education program that combines study and experience, although standards and requirements vary by state. Most states regulate massage therapy and require massage therapists to have a license or certification.

Education

Massage therapy education programs are typically in private, independent schools or in community colleges or other public postsecondary institutions. Depending on the program, earning a diploma or certificate requires several months or years to complete.

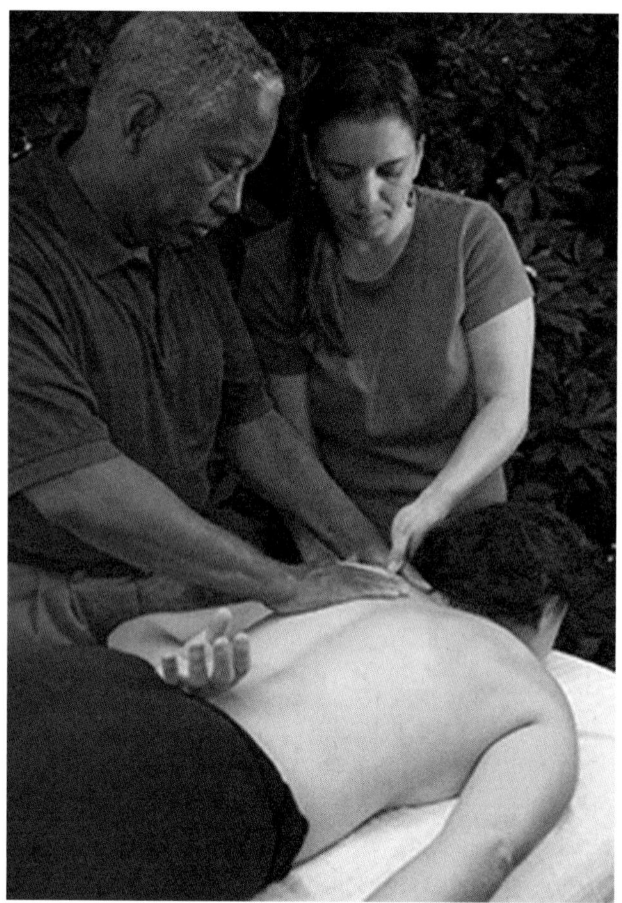

Massage therapists typically complete a postsecondary education program of 500 or more hours of study and experience.

Applicants to massage therapy programs typically need at least a high school diploma or equivalent. The curriculum generally includes both classroom study and hands-on practice of massage techniques. Required coursework includes sciences, such as anatomy, physiology, kinesiology, and pathology, as well as subjects such as business and ethics.

Some programs concentrate on certain modalities, or specialties, such as sports, rehabilitative, or oncology massage.

Licenses, Certifications, and Registrations

Massage therapists typically need a state-issued license or must register with the state. Requirements vary but typically include graduation from an approved massage therapy program and passing an exam. The Massage and Bodywork Licensing Examination (MBLEx) licensing exam is administered by the Federation of State Massage Therapy Boards.

Other requirements for massage therapists may include passing a background check, having liability insurance, and being certified in cardiopulmonary resuscitation (CPR). Many states require massage therapists to complete continuing education credits and to renew their license periodically. For more information, contact the licensing board for the state in which you intend to practice.

Important Qualities

Communication skills. Massage therapists must listen carefully and convey information clearly in order to ensure that clients achieve desired results through massage sessions.

Decision-making skills. Massage therapists must evaluate each client's needs and recommend the best treatment based on that person's needs.

Empathy. Massage therapists often treat clients who are in pain. They must be compassionate and sympathetic to their clients' problems and needs.

Integrity. Massage therapists often have access to clients' medical histories and other privacy information. Therefore, they must be trustworthy and protect client confidentiality.

Interpersonal skills. Massage therapists must give clients a positive experience. Building trust and making clients feel comfortable are necessary for therapists to expand their client base.

Physical stamina. Massage therapists may give several treatments during a workday and must be able to stand throughout massage appointments.

Physical strength and dexterity. Massage therapists must be strong and able to exert pressure through a variety of movements when manipulating a client's muscles.

Time-management skills. Massage therapists must be effective in using the time allocated for appointments to help each client accomplish his or her goals.

Pay

The median annual wage for massage therapists was $49,860 in May 2022. The median wage is the wage at which half the workers in an occupation earned more than that amount and half earned less. The lowest 10 percent earned less than $29,040, and the highest 10 percent earned more than $90,530.

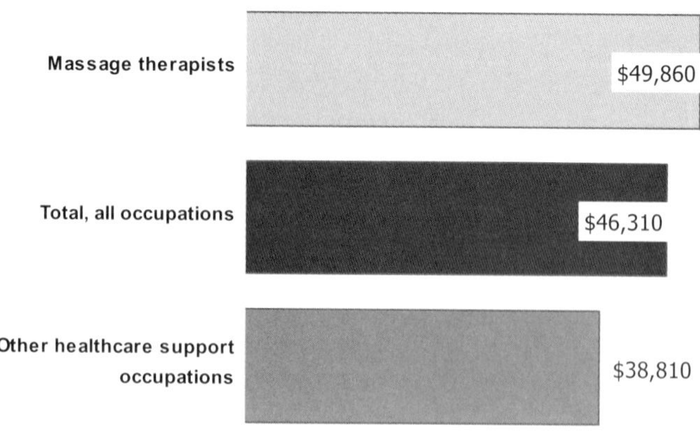

Note: All Occupations includes all occupations in the U.S. Economy.
Source: U.S. Bureau of Labor Statistics, Occupational Employment and Wage Statistics.

In May 2022, the median annual wages for massage therapists in the top industries in which they worked were as follows:

Offices of chiropractors	$61,180
Offices of all other health practitioners	51,980
Personal care services	49,020
Accommodation	33,680

Part-time work is common for massage therapists. Because therapists usually work by appointment, their schedules and the number of hours worked each week vary considerably. Moreover, because of the strength and endurance needed to give a massage, many therapists cannot perform massage services 8 hours per day, 5 days a week.

Job Outlook

Employment of massage therapists is projected to grow 18 percent from 2022 to 2032, much faster than the average for all occupations.

About 22,000 openings for massage therapists are projected each year, on average, over the decade. Many of those openings are expected to result from the need to replace workers who transfer to different occupations or exit the labor force, such as to retire.

Employment

Continued growth in the demand for massage services will lead to new jobs for massage therapists. Not only does massage help relieve stress and increase relaxation, but it is also becoming more accepted as a natural and safe treatment method for managing pain. Demand for massage therapists is expected to increase as more people look to massage to maintain overall health and well-being.

Massage Therapists

Percent change in employment, projected 2022-32

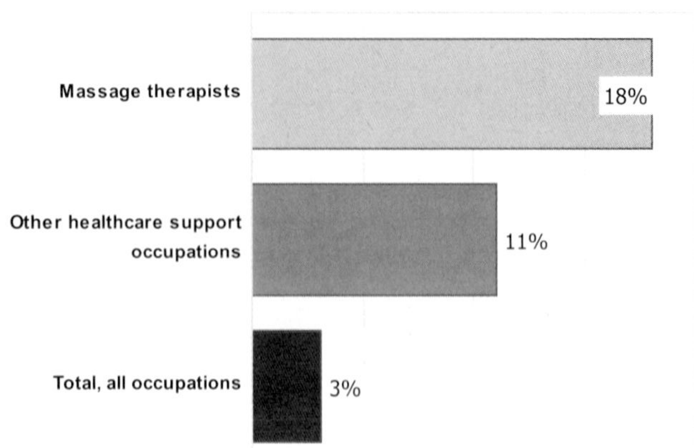

Note: All Occupations includes all occupations in the U.S. Economy.
Source: U.S. Bureau of Labor Statistics, Employment Projections program.

Occupational Title	SOC Code	Employment, 2022	Projected Employment, 2032	Change, 2022-32	
				Percent	Numeric
Massage therapists	31-9011	134,300	158,900	18	24,600

Contacts for More Information

For more information, visit

- Associated Bodywork & Massage Professionals
- American Massage Therapy Association
- National Certification Board for Therapeutic Massage & Bodywork
- Federation of State Massage Therapy Boards
- Commission on Massage Therapy Accreditation

Medical Assistants

Summary

Quick Facts: Medical Assistants	
2022 Median Pay	$38,270 per year $18.40 per hour
Typical Entry-Level Education	Postsecondary nondegree award
Work Experience in a Related Occupation	None
On-the-job Training	None
Number of Jobs, 2022	764,400
Job Outlook, 2022-32	14% (Much faster than average)
Employment Change, 2022-32	105,900

What Medical Assistants Do

Medical assistants complete administrative and clinical tasks, such as scheduling appointments and taking patients' vital signs.

Work Environment

Most medical assistants work full time. They are employed in physicians' offices, hospitals, outpatient clinics, and other healthcare facilities.

How to Become a Medical Assistant

Medical assistants typically need postsecondary education, such as a certificate. Some enter the occupation with a high school diploma and learn through on-the-job training.

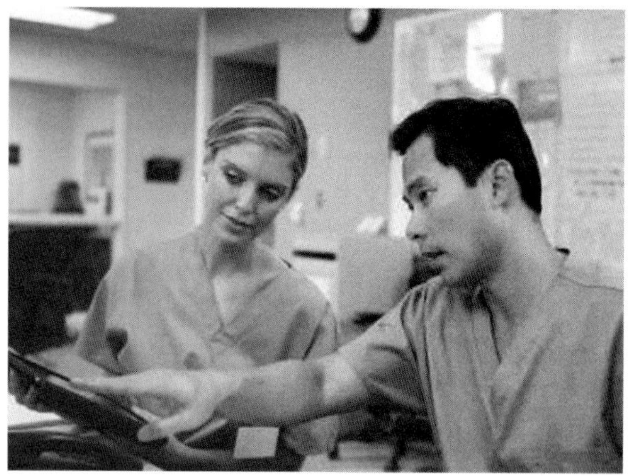

Medical assistants complete administrative and clinical tasks in the offices of physicians, hospitals, and other healthcare facilities.

Pay

The median annual wage for medical assistants was $38,270 in May 2022.

Job Outlook

Employment of medical assistants is projected to grow 14 percent from 2022 to 2032, much faster than the average for all occupations.

About 114,600 openings for medical assistants are projected each year, on average, over the decade. Many of those openings are expected to result from the need to replace workers who transfer to different occupations or exit the labor force, such as to retire.

What Medical Assistants Do

Medical assistants complete administrative and clinical tasks, such as scheduling appointments and taking patients' vital signs. Their duties vary by location, specialty, and employer.

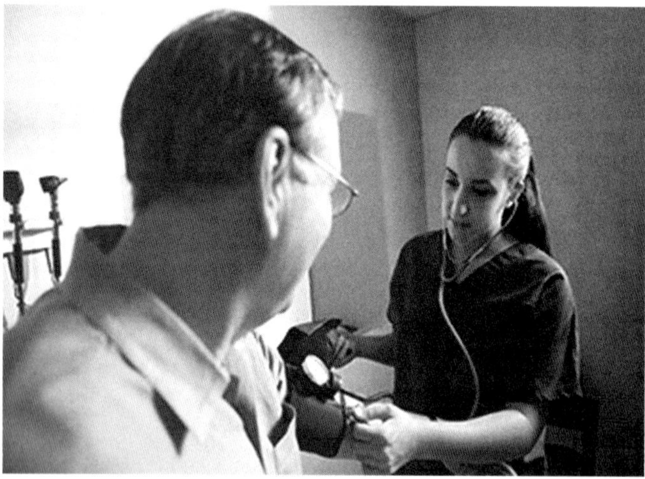

Medical assistants often take medical histories and record vital signs of patients.

Duties

Medical assistants typically do the following:

- Interview patients and record their medical history
- Measure patients' vital signs, such as their blood pressure and weight
- Help physicians with patient examinations
- Give patients injections or medications as directed by physicians and as permitted by state law
- Schedule patient appointments
- Collect and prepare samples of blood and other specimens for laboratory tests
- Enter patient information, such as their vital signs and test results, into medical records
- Maintain inventory of medical and office supplies

Medical assistants often focus on either clinical or administrative tasks, although some do both. Their primary clinical tasks involve taking and recording patients' personal information and medical history. Other tasks that assistants are allowed to do vary by state and may include performing basic laboratory tests, disposing of contaminated supplies, and sterilizing medical instruments. Some assistants have additional responsibilities, such as instructing patients about medications or drawing blood.

Medical assistants may have a range of administrative tasks. They help patients understand and receive their insurance coverage, such as by completing forms, coding information, and contacting companies about billing. They also inventory, order, and restock medical and office supplies; answer telephones; and schedule appointments.

Some medical assistants specialize according to the type of medical practice in which they work. For example, medical assistants who help ophthalmologists and optometrists show patients how to insert, remove, and care for contact lenses.

Medical assistants must adhere to confidentiality standards when working with patients and patient information.

Medical assistants should not be confused with other healthcare occupations that may have similar titles or duties. For example, both medical assistants and physician assistants work under the direction of physicians; however, physician assistants practice medicine and can prescribe medication under a physician's supervision.

Work Environment

Medical assistants held about 764,400 jobs in 2022. The largest employers of medical assistants were as follows:

Offices of physicians	56%
Hospitals; state, local, and private	15
Outpatient care centers	9
Offices of other health practitioners	8

Medical assistants perform administrative and clinical tasks to keep the offices of health practitioners running smoothly.

Some medical assistants spend a lot of time standing or walking as they visit patients. Others sit at a computer for much of the day to work on administrative tasks.

Work Schedules

Most medical assistants work full time. Some work evening, weekend, or holiday shifts in medical facilities that are open around the clock.

How to Become a Medical Assistant

Medical assistants typically need postsecondary education, such as a certificate. Some workers enter the occupation with a high school diploma and learn through on-the-job training.

Education

High school students interested in a career as a medical assistant should take science classes, including biology and chemistry. Although employers often prefer to hire candidates with more education, some medical assistants have a high school diploma and learn their duties on the job.

Medical assistant programs typically include supervised experience, such as a practicum.

Medical assistants typically complete a postsecondary program, such as for a medical assistant certificate or an associate's degree. Programs are available in community colleges, vocational schools, technical schools, and universities and take about 1 or 2 years to complete. Medical assistant programs include courses such as medical terminology, anatomy, and pharmacology. They also typically include supervised experience, such as a practicum or an internship.

Training

Medical assistants who do not have postsecondary education may learn their skills through on-the-job training or an apprenticeship. Physicians or other medical assistants may teach a new assistant tasks such as how to take vital signs and how to interact with patients It may take several months for an assistant to complete training, depending on the facility.

Licenses, Certifications, and Registrations

Some states require that medical assistants graduate from an accredited program, be licensed or certified, or meet other prerequisites in order to practice. Contact your state licensing agency for more information.

Although most states do not require it, employers may prefer or require that medical assistants be certified. certification is available from a number of organizations, including the American Association of Medical Assistants, the American Medical Certification Association, National Center for Competency Testing, and the National Healthcareer Association.

Some employers may require medical assistants to meet other qualifications, such as Basic Life Support (BLS) certification.

Important Qualities

Analytical skills. Medical assistants must be able to understand medical charts and diagnoses.

Communication skills. Medical assistants need to convey important information to patients, such as when scheduling appointments or explaining medical information.

Compassion. Medical assistants interact with patients who are sick or injured and who may be in extreme pain or distress. They must be empathetic toward patients and their families.

Detail oriented. Medical assistants must be precise when taking vital signs or recording patient information. Physicians, patients, and insurance companies rely on accurate records.

Interpersonal skills. Medical assistants work with other healthcare professionals, such as physicians, and need to be able to discuss patient information with them. They also interact with patients and must be courteous.

Pay

The median annual wage for medical assistants was $38,270 in May 2022. The median wage is the wage at which half the workers in an occupation earned more than that amount

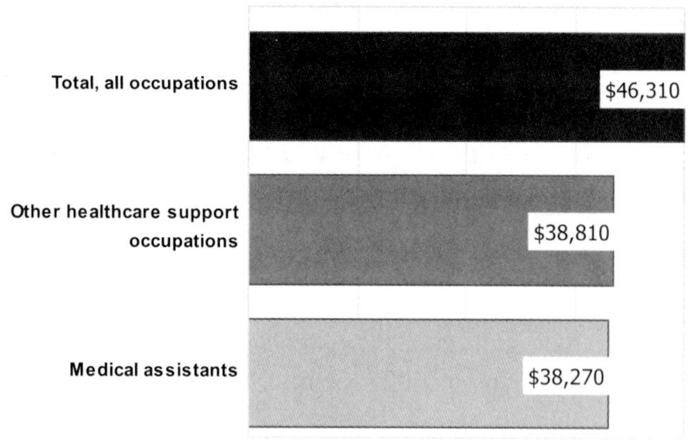

Note: All Occupations includes all occupations in the U.S. Economy.
Source: U.S. Bureau of Labor Statistics, Occupational Employment and Wage Statistics.

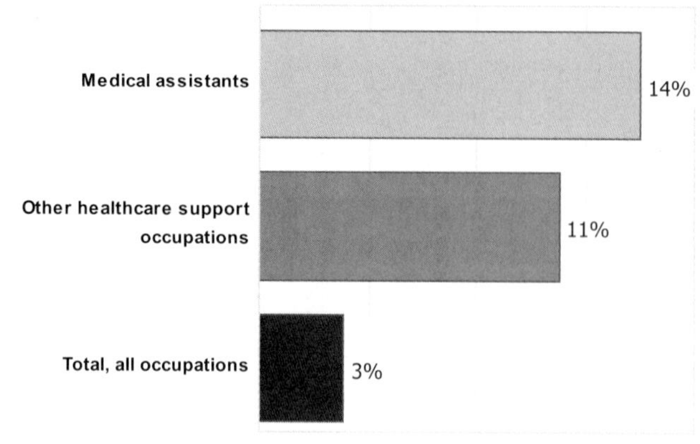

Note: All Occupations includes all occupations in the U.S. Economy.
Source: U.S. Bureau of Labor Statistics, Employment Projections program.

and half earned less. The lowest 10 percent earned less than $30,390, and the highest 10 percent earned more than $51,710.

In May 2022, the median annual wages for medical assistants in the top industries in which they worked were as follows:

Outpatient care centers	$42,820
Hospitals; state, local, and private	40,060
Offices of physicians	37,970
Offices of other health practitioners	35,070

Most medical assistants work full time. Some work evening, weekend, or holiday shifts in medical facilities that are open around the clock.

Job Outlook

Employment of medical assistants is projected to grow 14 percent from 2022 to 2032, much faster than the average for all occupations.

About 114,600 openings for medical assistants are projected each year, on average, over the decade. Many of those openings are expected to result from the need to replace workers who transfer to different occupations or exit the labor force, such as to retire.

Employment

The large baby-boom population continues to enter older age groups, which typically have more healthcare concerns than younger age groups and will continue to increase demand for medical services. As a result, more medical assistants will be needed to perform routine administrative and clinical duties in physicians' offices and other primary care settings.

Occupational Title	SOC Code	Employment, 2022	Projected Employment, 2032	Change, 2022-32	
				Percent	Numeric
Medical assistants	31-9092	764,400	870,200	14	105,900

Contacts for More Information

For more information, visit

- American Association of Medical Assistants
- American Medical Certification Association
- American Medical Technologists
- Institute for Credentialing Excellence
- National Center for Competency Testing
- National Healthcareer Association

Medical Dosimetrists

Summary

Quick Facts: Medical Dosimetrists	
2022 Median Pay	$128,970 per year $62.01 per hour
Typical Entry-Level Education	Bachelor's degree
Work Experience in a Related Occupation	None
On-the-job Training	None
Number of Jobs, 2022	3,500
Job Outlook, 2022-32	3% (As fast as average)
Employment Change, 2022-32	100

What Medical Dosimetrists Do

Medical dosimetrists calculate doses of radiation and design and oversee treatment plans for patients with cancer and other serious diseases.

Work Environment

Most medical dosimetrists work in healthcare settings, such as hospitals and physicians' offices. They may spend much of their time working at a computer.

How to Become a Medical Dosimetrist

To enter the occupation, medical dosimetrists typically need a bachelor's degree and must complete an accredited medical dosimetry program. Employers usually require workers to have certification.

Pay

The median annual wage for medical dosimetrists was $128,970 in May 2022.

Job Outlook

Employment of medical dosimetrists is projected to grow 3 percent from 2022 to 2032, about as fast as the average for all occupations.

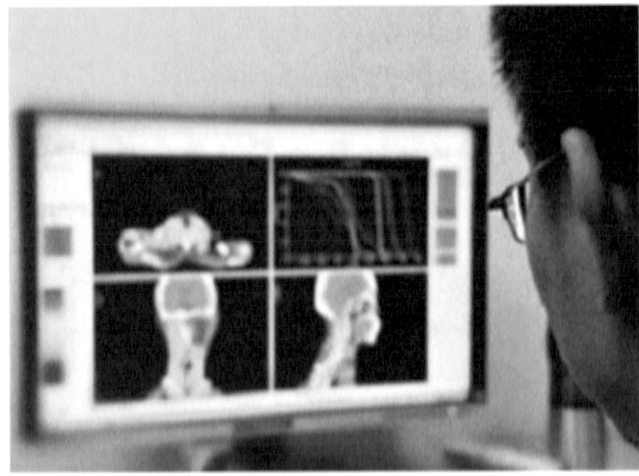

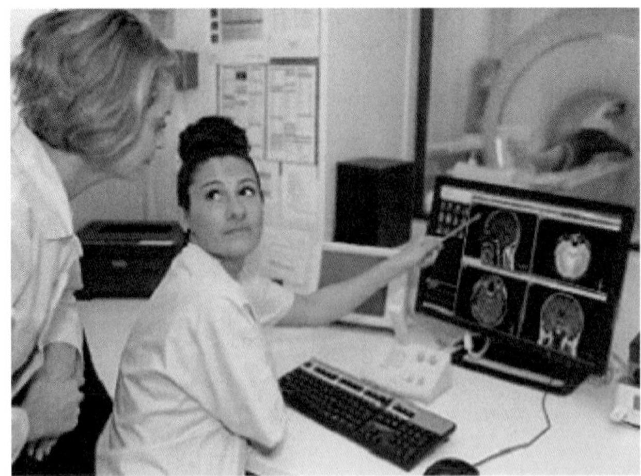

Medical dosimetrists consult with other members of the oncology team to create patient treatment plans.

About 200 openings for medical dosimetrists are projected each year, on average, over the decade. Many of those openings are expected to result from the need to replace workers who transfer to different occupations or exit the labor force, such as to retire.

What Medical Dosimetrists Do

Medical dosimetrists calculate doses of radiation and design and oversee treatment plans for patients with cancer and other serious diseases.

Duties

Medical dosimetrists typically do the following:

- Review a patient's documents, such as their CT and MRI scans
- Calculate the proper dose of radiation to be administered to a patient
- Consult with other members of the radiation oncology team and design the radiation-delivery plan for patients
- May assist in designing molds, casts, and other immobilization devices to position patients during treatment
- Document treatment provided to a patient
- Perform quality assurance checks of treatment equipment

Medical dosimetrists develop and manage the radiation plans for patients receiving treatment for cancer or other diseases. They may begin by reviewing patient records, such as computer tomography (CT) and magnetic resonance imaging (MRI) scans. Then, based on a dosage range prescribed by the physician, medical dosimetrists calculate the exact dose and angle of radiation to be administered. They make these calculations both manually and with computers.

Medical dosimetrists' calculations may vary based on the type of radiation treatment a physician prescribes. For example, external beam radiation angled at a tumor from outside the body may be administered at a higher dose than brachytherapy,

Medical dosimetrists spend much of their time working at a computer.

which involves placing a radioactive device near the tumor inside the body.

In addition to overseeing radiation treatment, medical dosimetrists' other responsibilities include helping to design immobilization devices that ensure patients remain motionless during procedures. They also keep records of each patient's treatment, load or receive shipments, use radiation monitoring devices to measure radioactivity levels in patients, and calibrate equipment to ensure accuracy.

Dosimetrists are part of a radiation oncology team that usually includes medical physicists, oncology nurses, radiation oncologists and other physicians, and radiation therapists.

Work Environment

Medical dosimetrists held about 3,500 jobs in 2022. The largest employers of medical dosimetrists were as follows:

Hospitals; state, local, and private	48%
Offices of physicians	23
Self-employed workers	5
Outpatient care centers	4
Colleges, universities, and professional schools; state, local, and private	3

Medical dosimetrists spend much of their time at the computer when calculating doses of radiation and designing treatment plans. Dosimetrists typically have less direct contact with patients compared with other members of the radiation oncology team. However, they occasionally interact with patients, such as to reposition them for procedures.

Injuries and Illnesses

Medical dosimetrists work with radiation and radioactive material, so they must follow procedures for safe handling. Safety protocol includes wearing a film badge dosimeter to track radiation exposure.

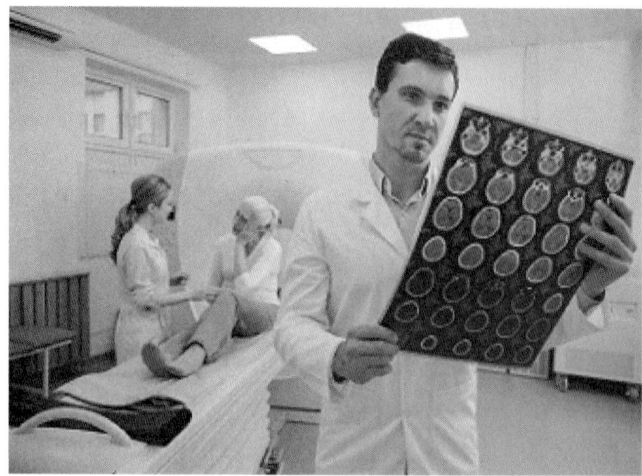

Medical dosimetrists must complete an accredited medical dosimetry program.

Work Schedules

Most medical dosimetrists work full time. They usually have a regular work schedule because radiation therapy procedures are often planned in advance.

How to Become a Medical Dosimetrist

To enter the occupation, medical dosimetrists typically need a bachelor's degree and must complete an accredited medical dosimetry program. Employers usually require workers to have certification.

Education

Medical dosimetrists typically need a bachelor's degree in medical dosimetry or a related field, such as biology or physical science. Prospective dosimetrists whose degree is not in medical dosimetry may complete a certificate or master's degree program in medical dosimetry. These programs usually last 1 to 2 years. A list of accredited medical dosimetry programs is available from the Joint Review Committee on Education in Radiologic Technology (JRCERT).

Admission to medical dosimetry programs is often competitive. Applicants may be required to be a registered radiation therapist or have a bachelor's degree that includes coursework in specific subjects, such as biology, medical terminology, and calculus.

Medical dosimetry programs include courses such as physics, anatomy, and radiology. Programs also include supervised clinical experience in which students work onsite with practicing dosimetrists.

Licenses, Certifications, and Registrations

Employers usually prefer to hire medical dosimetrists who have earned the Certified Medical Dosimetrist (CMD) credential from the Medical Dosimetrist Certification Board (MDCB). Certification requires that candidates have a bachelor's degree, graduate from an accredited medical dosimetry program, and pass an exam. Maintaining certification requires completion of a specified number of hours of continuing education.

Work Experience in a Related Occupation

Some medical dosimetrists work as radiation therapists before earning the credentials to become dosimetrists.

Important Qualities

Communication skills. To ensure proper treatment, medical dosimetrists must convey important information about a patient's radiation dosage both orally and in writing.

Critical-thinking skills. Medical dosimetrists analyze a patient's needs and health-related data, along with other factors, to determine treatment plans.

Detail oriented. Medical dosimetrists must be precise when calculating the amount and location of radiation that a patient will receive.

Interpersonal skills. Medical dosimetrists collaborate with other members of the radiation oncology team throughout a patient's treatment.

Math skills. Medical dosimetrists need a strong background in mathematics in order to calculate and verify the proper doses of radiation.

Technical skills. Medical dosimetrists use computers and must be comfortable working with a variety of specialized medical equipment.

Pay

The median annual wage for medical dosimetrists was $128,970 in May 2022. The median wage is the wage at which half the workers in an occupation earned more than that amount and half earned less. The lowest 10 percent earned less than $90,970, and the highest 10 percent earned more than $163,040.

In May 2022, the median annual wages for medical dosimetrists in the top industries in which they worked were as follows:

Offices of physicians	$131,510
Hospitals; state, local, and private	129,540
Outpatient care centers	123,000
Colleges, universities, and professional schools; state, local, and private	106,560

Most medical dosimetrists work full time. They usually have a regular work schedule because radiation therapy procedures are often planned in advance.

Job Outlook

Employment of medical dosimetrists is projected to grow 3 percent from 2022 to 2032, about as fast as the average for all occupations.

About 200 openings for medical dosimetrists are projected each year, on average, over the decade. Many of those openings are expected to result from the need to replace workers who transfer to different occupations or exit the labor force, such as to retire.

Employment

As adults get older, their likelihood of being diagnosed with cancer rises. The expected increase in the number of older people will therefore increase the demand for cancer care. Because radiotherapy plays a vital role in treating this disease, medical dosimetrists will be needed to help develop treatment plans for patients.

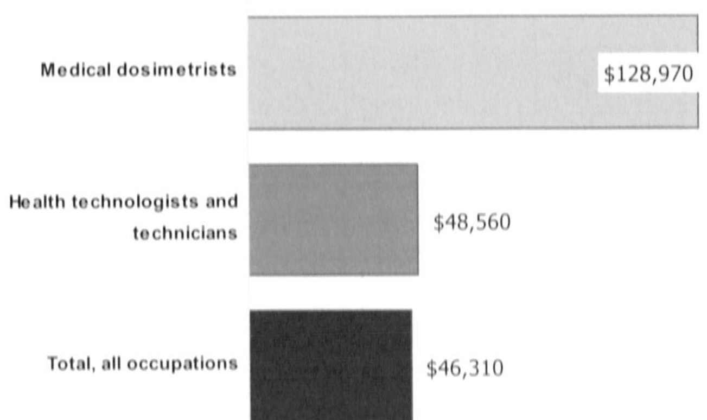

Note: All Occupations includes all occupations in the U.S. Economy.
Source: U.S. Bureau of Labor Statistics, Occupational Employment and Wage Statistics.

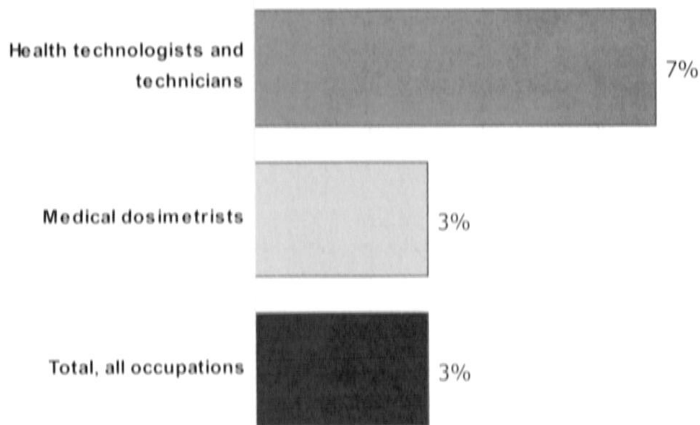

Note: All Occupations includes all occupations in the U.S. Economy.
Source: U.S. Bureau of Labor Statistics, Employment Projections program.

Occupational Title	SOC Code	Employment, 2022	Projected Employment, 2032	Change, 2022-32	
				Percent	Numeric
Medical dosimetrists	29-2036	3,500	3,600	3	100

Contacts for More Information

For more information, visit

- ➤ American Association of Medical Dosimetrists (AAMD)
- ➤ Joint Review Committee on Education in Radiologic Technology (JRCERT)
- ➤ Medical Dosimetrist Certification Board (MDCB)

Medical Records Specialists

Summary

Quick Facts: Medical Records Specialists

2022 Median Pay	$47,180 per year $22.69 per hour
Typical Entry-Level Education	Postsecondary nondegree award
Work Experience in a Related Occupation	None
On-the-job Training	None
Number of Jobs, 2022	194,300
Job Outlook, 2022-32	8% (Faster than average)
Employment Change, 2022-32	16,500

What Medical Records Specialists Do

Medical records specialists compile, process, and maintain patient files.

Work Environment

Medical records specialists typically spend many hours at a computer. Most work full time.

How to Become a Medical Records Specialist

Medical records specialists typically need a postsecondary certificate to enter the occupation, although some qualify with a high school diploma. Others might need an associate's or bachelor's degree. Certification may be required or preferred.

Medical records and health information specialists meet with other healthcare workers to clarify diagnoses or to get additional information.

Pay

The median annual wage for medical records specialists was $47,180 in May 2022.

Job Outlook

Employment of medical records specialists is projected to grow 8 percent from 2022 to 2032, faster than the average for all occupations.

About 15,000 openings for medical records specialists are projected each year, on average, over the decade. Many of those openings are expected to result from the need to replace workers who transfer to different occupations or exit the labor force, such as to retire.

What Medical Records Specialists Do

Medical records specialists compile, process, and maintain patient files. They also may classify and enter patients' medical information into the healthcare industry's numerical coding system.

Duties

Medical records specialists typically do the following:

- Review patients' records for timeliness, completeness, and accuracy

Medical records specialists validate and enter patient's health information into electronic health records systems.

- Use classification systems to assign clinical codes for patients' diagnoses, procedures, medical services, and related information
- Maintain and retrieve records for insurance reimbursement and data analysis
- Electronically record data for collection, storage, analysis, retrieval, and reporting
- Ensure confidentiality of patients' records

Medical records specialists have a variety of data entry and recordkeeping tasks. They may gather patients' medical histories, symptoms, test results, treatments, and other health information and enter the details into electronic health records (EHR) systems. Some workers categorize medical information for purposes such as insurance reimbursement and providing data to clinicians.

When handling medical records, these workers follow administrative, ethical, and legal requirements for safeguarding patient privacy. Medical records specialists also may serve as gatekeepers for access to patient files. They ensure access only to authorized people and retrieve, scan, and transmit files according to established protocols.

Medical coders assign the diagnosis and procedure codes for patient care, population health statistics, and billing purposes. For example, they might review patient information for preexisting conditions, such as diabetes, to ensure proper coding of patient data. They also work as the liaison between healthcare providers and billing offices.

Although medical records specialists do not provide direct patient care, they work regularly with registered nurses and other healthcare workers. They meet with these workers to clarify diagnoses or to get additional information.

For information about other workers who deal with healthcare records, see the profile for health information technologists and medical registrars.

Work Environment

Medical records specialists held about 194,300 jobs in 2022. The largest employers of medical records specialists were as follows:

Hospitals; state, local, and private	27%
Offices of physicians	19
Professional, scientific, and technical services	9
Management of companies and enterprises	9
Administrative and support services	8

Medical records specialists typically work at a computer.

Work Schedules

Most medical records specialists work full time. In healthcare facilities that are always open, such as hospitals, specialists may work shifts, including nights or weekends.

This is one of the few health-related occupations in which there is no direct hands-on patient care.

How to Become a Medical Records Specialist

Medical records specialists typically need a postsecondary certificate to enter the occupation, although some qualify with a high school diploma. Others might need an associate's degree. Certification may be required or preferred.

Education

A high school diploma or equivalent and experience in a healthcare setting are enough to qualify for some positions, but others may require a postsecondary certificate or an associate's or bachelor's degree.

High school students may benefit from taking classes in subjects such as biology, computer science, and anatomy.

Community colleges and technical schools offer certificate and associate's degree programs for medical records specialists. These programs typically include courses in medical terminology, health data requirements and standards, and classification and coding systems.

Employers may prefer to hire medical records specialists who have acquired certification.

Licenses, Certifications, and Registrations

Employers may prefer to hire medical records specialists who have certification, or they may expect applicants to earn certification shortly after being hired. For example, some medical records specialists earn the Registered Health Information Technician (RHIT) credential; certifications for medical coders include the Certified Billing & Coding Specialists (CBCS), Certified Coding Associate (CCA), Certified Coding Specialist (CCS), and Certified Professional Coder (CPC).

Certifications usually require candidates to pass an exam and might require previous experience or education. Certificate, associate's, or bachelor's degree programs may help students to meet these requirements.

Advancement

Medical records specialists may advance to become health information technologists or medical registrars or medical or health services managers after completing a higher certification program or earning a degree in health information technology. Requirements vary by facility.

Important Qualities

Analytical skills. Medical records specialists must interpret medical documentation to assess diagnoses, which they then code into a patient's medical record.

Detail oriented. Medical records specialists must be precise about verifying and coding patient information.

Integrity. Medical records specialists must exercise discretion and act ethically when working with patient data to protect patient confidentiality, as required by law.

Interpersonal skills. Medical records specialists need to discuss patient information, discrepancies, and data requirements with physicians, finance personnel, and other workers involved in patient care and recordkeeping.

Pay

The median annual wage for medical records specialists was $47,180 in May 2022. The median wage is the wage at which half the workers in an occupation earned more than that amount and half earned less. The lowest 10 percent earned less than $31,710, and the highest 10 percent earned more than $75,460.

In May 2022, the median annual wages for medical records specialists in the top industries in which they worked were as follows:

Management of companies and enterprises	$50,370
Hospitals; state, local, and private	49,660
Administrative and support services	49,470
Professional, scientific, and technical services	47,520
Offices of physicians	39,350

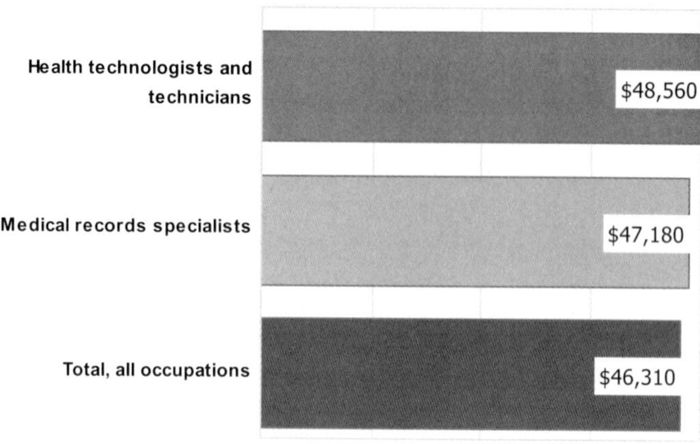

Note: All Occupations includes all occupations in the U.S. Economy.
Source: U.S. Bureau of Labor Statistics, Occupational Employment and Wage Statistics.

Most medical records specialists work full time. In healthcare facilities that are always open, such as hospitals, specialists may work shifts, including nights or weekends.

Job Outlook

Employment of medical records specialists is projected to grow 8 percent from 2022 to 2032, faster than the average for all occupations.

About 15,000 openings for medical records specialists are projected each year, on average, over the decade. Many of those openings are expected to result from the need to replace

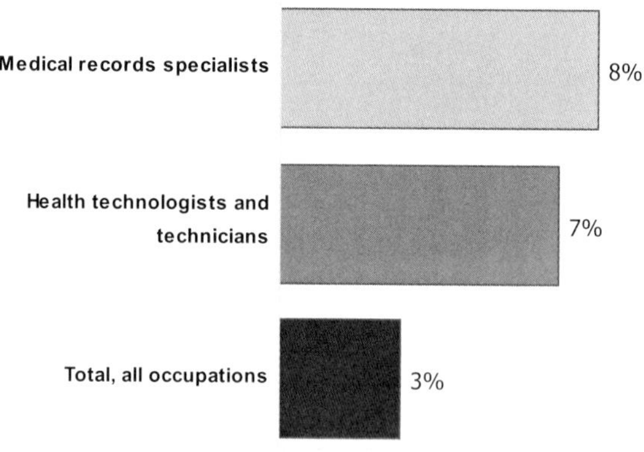

Note: All Occupations includes all occupations in the U.S. Economy.
Source: U.S. Bureau of Labor Statistics, Employment Projections program.

workers who transfer to different occupations or exit the labor force, such as to retire.

Employment

An increasing share of the population is entering older age groups, which typically require more medical services. In addition, there is a growing prevalence of heart disease, diabetes, and other chronic conditions. As a result, more medical records specialists will be needed to translate patient information and services delivered into standardized codes to be used for insurance reimbursement and other purposes.

However, the increase in adoption of Artificial Intelligence (AI)-powered solutions that make the medical coding process more efficient may affect the demand for these workers.

Occupational Title	SOC Code	Employment, 2022	Projected Employment, 2032	Change, 2022-32	
				Percent	Numeric
Medical records specialists	29-2072	194,300	210,900	8	16,500

Contacts for More Information

For more information, visit

- American Health Information Management Association
- American Academy of Professional Coders
- National Healthcareer Association
- Commission on Accreditation for Health Informatics and Information Management Education

Medical Transcriptionists

Summary

Quick Facts: Medical Transcriptionists	
2022 Median Pay	$34,730 per year $16.70 per hour
Typical Entry-Level Education	Postsecondary nondegree award
Work Experience in a Related Occupation	None
On-the-job Training	None
Number of Jobs, 2022	49,000
Job Outlook, 2022-32	-4% (Decline)
Employment Change, 2022-32	-1,800

What Medical Transcriptionists Do

Medical transcriptionists use electronic devices to convert voice recordings from physicians and other healthcare workers into formal reports.

Work Environment

Many medical transcriptionists work for hospitals, physicians' offices, and third-party transcription companies that provide services to healthcare establishments. Most are full time, but part-time work is common.

How to Become a Medical Transcriptionist

Medical transcriptionists typically need postsecondary education that leads to a certificate. Prospective medical transcriptionists must know basic medical terminology, anatomy and physiology, and rules of grammar.

Pay

The median annual wage for medical transcriptionists was $34,730 in May 2022.

Medical transcriptionists listen to recorded dictation from a physician.

Job Outlook

Employment of medical transcriptionists is projected to decline 4 percent from 2022 to 2032.

Despite declining employment, about 8,100 openings for medical transcriptionists are projected each year, on average, over the decade. All of those openings are expected to result from the need to replace workers who transfer to other occupations or exit the labor force, such as to retire.

What Medical Transcriptionists Do

Medical transcriptionists, sometimes referred to as *healthcare documentation specialists*, use electronic devices to convert voice recordings from physicians and other healthcare workers into formal reports. Transcriptionists also may edit medical records for accuracy and return documents for review and approval.

Duties

Medical transcriptionists typically do the following:

Medical transcriptionists review medical reports for accuracy.

- Listen to the recorded dictation of a physician or other healthcare worker
- Interpret and transcribe the dictation for medical reports, such as patient histories, discharge summaries, and physical examinations
- Review and edit drafts prepared by speech recognition software, making sure that the transcription is accurate, complete, and consistent in style
- Translate medical abbreviations and jargon into the appropriate long form
- Identify inconsistencies, errors, and missing information in a report that could compromise patient care
- Submit reports to physicians and other healthcare providers for review and approval
- Follow patient confidentiality guidelines and legal documentation requirements
- Enter medical reports into electronic health records (EHR) systems

Medical transcriptionists use a variety of equipment to produce reports. The most common is speech recognition technology, which involves specialized software that automatically prepares an initial draft of a report. The transcriptionist then listens to the voice file and reviews the draft for accuracy, identifying any errors and editing the report, as necessary. A less common technology requires these workers to use audio-playback equipment for listening to and transcribing dictation. Transcriptionists also use word-processing and other software to prepare the transcripts, as well as medical reference materials when needed.

Medical transcriptionists must be familiar with medical terminology, anatomy, and physiology. Additionally, they must have knowledge of English grammar in order to ensure that their transcriptions are correct. Transcriptionists' ability to understand the healthcare worker's recording, to correctly transcribe that information, and to identify inaccuracies in the transcript is critical to preventing ineffective or even harmful treatment.

Medical transcriptionists who work in physicians' offices may have other duties, such as answering phones and greeting patients.

Work Environment

Medical transcriptionists held about 49,000 jobs in 2022. The largest employers of medical transcriptionists were as follows:

Administrative and support services	37%
Offices of physicians	34
Hospitals; state, local, and private	12
Management, scientific, and technical consulting services	2

Administrative and support services includes companies that provide transcription services and temporary help firms.

Medical transcriptionists may work from home, receiving dictation and submitting drafts electronically. Their work may be stressful because they need to ensure that reports are accurate and completed within a quick turnaround time.

Work Schedules

Most medical transcriptionists are full time, but part-time work is common. Medical transcriptionists who work from home

Medical transcriptions must understand what the healthcare worker has recorded and correctly transcribe that information.

Transcriptionists listen to dictated recordings made by physicians and other healthcare professionals and transcribe them into medical reports, correspondence, and other administrative material.

may work outside typical business hours and may have flexibility in determining their schedules.

How to Become a Medical Transcriptionist

Medical transcriptionists typically need postsecondary education that leads to a certificate. Prospective medical transcriptionists must know basic medical terminology, anatomy and physiology, and rules of grammar. Some choose to become certified.

Education

Employers may prefer to hire transcriptionists who have completed postsecondary education in medical transcription. Medical transcription programs may be offered online as well as in person by vocational schools, community colleges, and career institutes. They vary in length but typically may be completed in less than 1 year; programs that lead to an associate's degree may take longer.

Programs typically include coursework in anatomy and physiology, medical terminology, laws relating to healthcare documentation, and English grammar and punctuation. These programs may include the opportunity to gain experience through supervised transcription. Prospective transcriptionists who are familiar with medical terminology from working in other healthcare occupations, such as nursing assistants or medical secretaries, may become proficient through refresher courses and training.

Licenses, Certifications, and Registrations

Although certification is not required, some medical transcriptionists choose to become certified. For example, the Association for Healthcare Documentation Integrity offers the Registered Healthcare Documentation Specialist (RHDS) and the Certified Healthcare Documentation Specialist (CHDS) certifications. Both certifications require passing an exam and are valid for a specified number of years. In order to recertify, individuals must earn continuing education credits.

The RHDS certification is for recent graduates with little experience who work in a single specialty environment, such as a clinic or a physician's office. The CHDS certification is for transcriptionists who currently hold the RHDS designation. In addition, CHDS candidates must have a specified number of years of experience in acute care, including experience handling dictation in various medical specialties.

Important Qualities

Computer skills. Medical transcriptionists must know how to operate electronic health records (EHR) systems and should be comfortable using software to prepare reports.

Critical-thinking skills. Medical transcriptionists must assess medical reports and correct any inaccuracies and inconsistencies in finished drafts.

Listening skills. Medical transcriptionists must pay attention to hear and interpret the intended meaning of dictations.

Time-management skills. Medical transcriptionists must organize their schedules well because they may need to produce transcriptions under tight deadlines.

Writing skills. Medical transcriptionists need a good understanding of English grammar in order to ensure that transcribed reports are correct.

Pay

The median annual wage for medical transcriptionists was $34,730 in May 2022. The median wage is the wage at which half the workers in an occupation earned more than that amount and half earned less. The lowest 10 percent earned less than $24,340, and the highest 10 percent earned more than $51,280.

In May 2022, the median annual wages for medical transcriptionists in the top industries in which they worked were as follows:

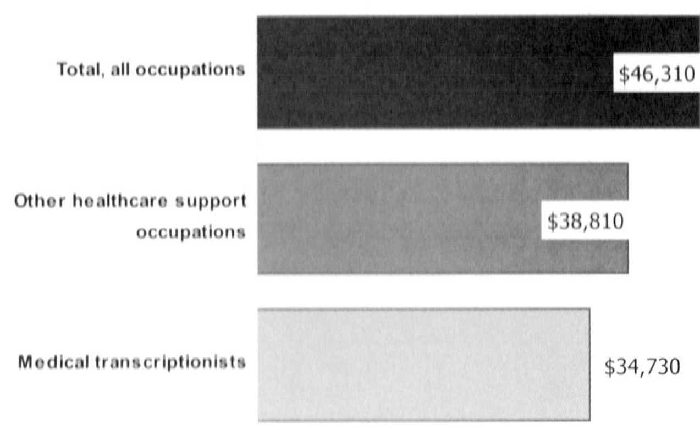

Note: All Occupations includes all occupations in the U.S. Economy.
Source: U.S. Bureau of Labor Statistics, Occupational Employment and Wage Statistics.

Hospitals; state, local, and private	$43,130
Offices of physicians	37,460
Management, scientific, and technical consulting services	30,440
Administrative and support services	29,330

Some medical transcriptionists are paid based on the volume of transcription they produce. Others are paid an hourly rate or an annual salary.

Most medical transcriptionists are full time, but part-time work is common. Medical transcriptionists who work from home may work outside typical business hours and have some flexibility in determining their schedules.

Job Outlook

Employment of medical transcriptionists is projected to decline 4 percent from 2022 to 2032.

Despite declining employment, about 8,100 openings for medical transcriptionists are projected each year, on average, over the decade. All of those openings are expected to result from the need to replace workers who transfer to other occupations or exit the labor force, such as to retire.

Employment

Technological advances in speech recognition and electronic health records (EHR) software allow physicians to document some information in the moment, reducing the need for medical transcriptionists. In addition, these technologies increase medical transcriptionists' productivity, allowing more transcription by fewer workers.

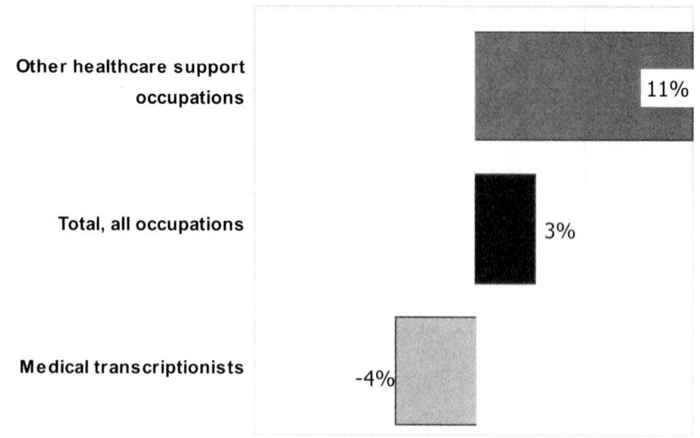

Note: All Occupations includes all occupations in the U.S. Economy.
Source: U.S. Bureau of Labor Statistics, Employment Projections program.

Meanwhile, as healthcare providers seek to cut costs, some will contract out transcription services and not do in-house transcription.

Occupational Title	SOC Code	Employment, 2022	Projected Employment, 2032	Change, 2022-32	
				Percent	Numeric
Medical transcriptionists	31-9094	49,000	47,200	-4	-1,800

Contacts for More Information

For more information, visit

- Association for Healthcare Documentation Integrity

Nuclear Medicine Technologists

Summary

Quick Facts: Nuclear Medicine Technologists

2022 Median Pay	$85,300 per year $41.01 per hour
Typical Entry-Level Education	Associate's degree
Work Experience in a Related Occupation	None
On-the-job Training	None
Number of Jobs, 2022	18,100
Job Outlook, 2022-32	0% (Little or no change)
Employment Change, 2022-32	100

What Nuclear Medicine Technologists Do

Nuclear medicine technologists prepare and administer radioactive drugs for imaging or treatment.

Work Environment

Most nuclear medicine technologists work in hospitals. Some work in physicians' offices, diagnostic laboratories, or imaging clinics. Most nuclear medicine technologists work full time.

How to Become a Nuclear Medicine Technologist

Nuclear medicine technologists typically need an associate's degree from an accredited nuclear medicine technology program. Formal education programs in nuclear medicine technology or a related healthcare field lead to a certificate, an associate's degree, or a bachelor's degree. Most nuclear medicine technologists become certified, and some must be licensed.

Pay

The median annual wage for nuclear medicine technologists was $85,300 in May 2022.

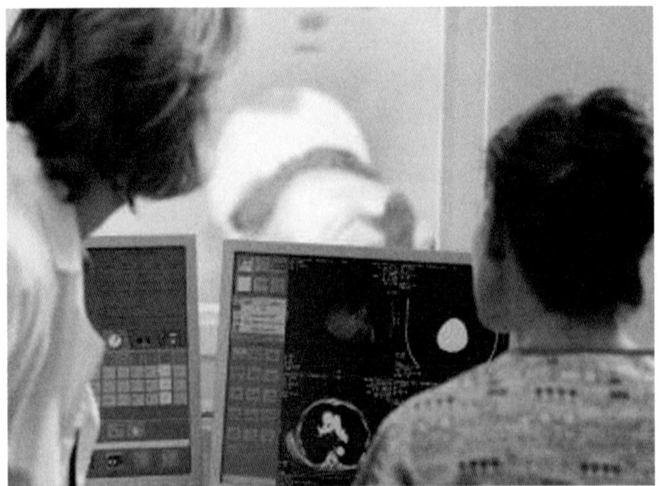

Nuclear medicine technologists operate equipment that creates images of areas of a patient's body.

Job Outlook

Employment of nuclear medicine technologists is projected to show little or no change from 2022 to 2032.

Despite limited employment growth, about 800 openings for nuclear medicine technologists are projected each year, on average, over the decade. Most of those openings are expected to result from the need to replace workers who transfer to different occupations or exit the labor force, such as to retire.

What Nuclear Medicine Technologists Do

Nuclear medicine technologists prepare radioactive drugs and administer them to patients for imaging or treatment. They provide technical support to physicians or others who diagnose, care for, and treat patients and to researchers who investigate uses of radioactive drugs. They also may act as emergency responders in the event of a nuclear disaster.

Duties

Nuclear medicine technologists typically do the following:

- Explain medical procedures to the patient and answer questions

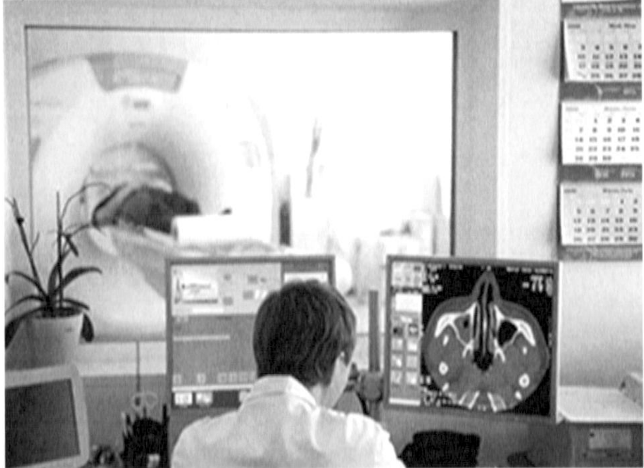

Most nuclear medicine technologists work in hospitals.

- Follow safety procedures to protect themselves and the patient from unnecessary radiation exposure
- Prepare radioactive drugs and administer them to the patient
- Maintain and operate imaging equipment
- Keep detailed records of procedures
- Follow procedures for radiation disposal

Nuclear medicine technologists work with radioactive drugs, known as radiopharmaceuticals, to help physicians and surgeons diagnose a patient's condition. For example, they may inject radiopharmaceuticals into the bloodstream of a patient with foot pain and then use special scanning equipment that captures images of the bones; a radiologist interprets the scan results, based on the concentration of radioactivity appearing in the image, to identify the source of the patient's pain.

Nuclear medicine technologists also deliver radiopharmaceuticals in prescribed doses to specific areas, such as tumors, to treat medical conditions. Internal radiation treatment may be used in conjunction with, or as an alternative to, surgery.

In the event of a radioactive incident or nuclear disaster, some nuclear medicine technologists may be involved in emergency response efforts. These workers' experience with radiation detection and monitoring equipment may be useful during a response to events that involve radiological materials.

The following are types of nuclear medicine technologists:

Nuclear cardiology technologists use radioactive drugs to obtain images of the heart. Patients may exercise during the imaging process while the technologist creates images of the heart and blood flow.

Nuclear medicine computed tomography (CT) technologists use radioactive isotopes in combination with x-ray imaging to create two-dimensional or three-dimensional pictures of the inside of the body.

Positron emission tomography (PET) technologists use a machine that creates a three-dimensional image of a part of the body, such as the brain. They also use radiopharmaceuticals to measure body functions, such as metabolism.

Some nuclear medicine technologists support researchers in developing nuclear medicine applications for imagery or treatment.

Work Environment

Nuclear medicine technologists held about 18,100 jobs in 2022. The largest employers of nuclear medicine technologists were as follows:

Hospitals; state, local, and private	69%
Offices of physicians	14
Medical and diagnostic laboratories	7
Outpatient care centers	2

Technologists are on their feet for long periods and may need to lift or turn patients who are ill or injured.

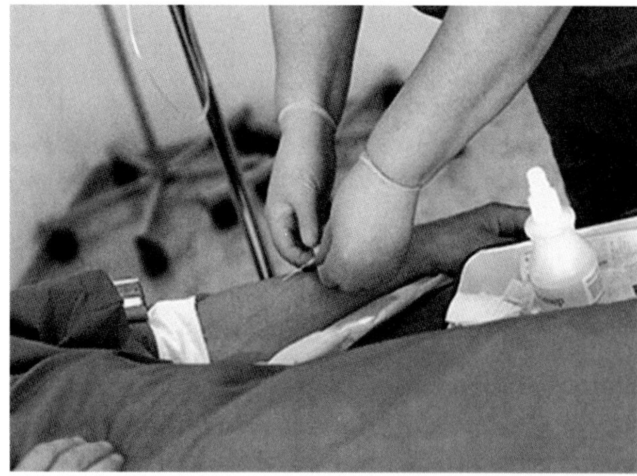

Some radiopharmaceuticals are given intravenously to treat cancers, blood diseases, or other illnesses.

Injuries and Illnesses

Although radiation hazards exist in this occupation, they are minimized by the use of gloves and other shielding devices. Nuclear medicine technologists wear badges that measure radiation levels in the radiation area. Instruments monitor their radiation exposure and detailed records are kept on how much radiation they get over their lifetime. When preparing radioactive drugs, technologists use safety procedures to minimize radiation exposure to patients, other healthcare workers, and themselves.

Like other healthcare workers, nuclear medicine technologists may be exposed to infectious diseases.

Work Schedules

Most nuclear medicine technologists work full time. Some nuclear medicine technologists work irregular hours, such as evenings or weekends. They also may be on call, especially if they work in hospitals.

How to Become a Nuclear Medicine Technologist

Nuclear medicine technologists typically need an associate's degree from an accredited nuclear medicine technology program. Formal education programs in nuclear medicine technology or a related healthcare field lead to a certificate, an associate's degree, or a bachelor's degree. Most nuclear medicine technologists become certified, and some must be licensed.

Education

High school students interested in nuclear medicine technology should take courses in math and sciences, including biology, chemistry, anatomy, and physics.

Nuclear medicine technologists typically need an associate's degree in nuclear medicine technology to enter the occupation. Bachelor's degrees also are common. Some technologists complete an associate's or a bachelor's degree program in a related health field, such as radiologic technology or nursing, followed by a 12-month certificate program in nuclear medicine technology.

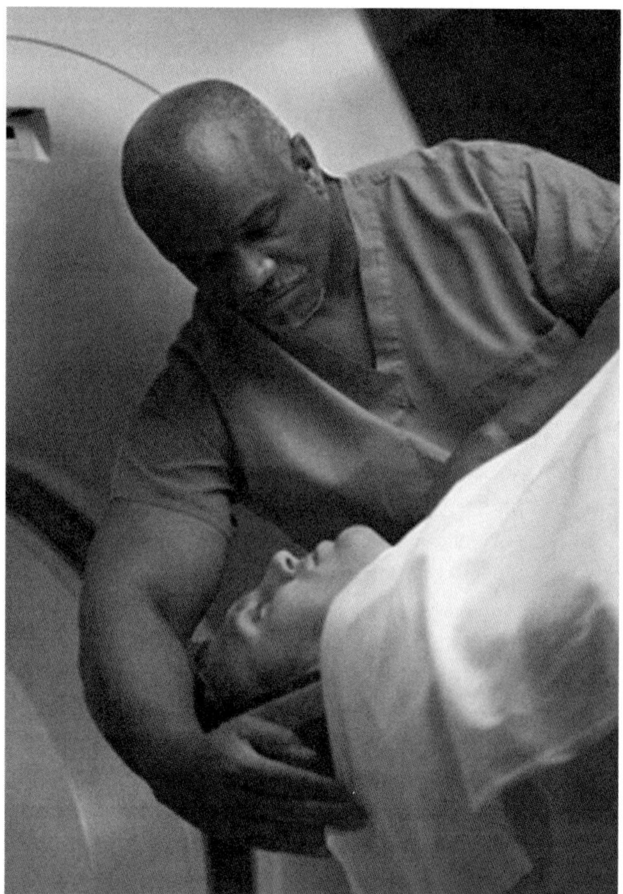

Nuclear medicine technologists can earn specialty certifications that show their proficiency in specific procedures or equipment.

Nuclear medicine technology programs often include courses in human anatomy and physiology, physics, chemistry, radioactive drugs, and computer science. In addition, these programs include clinical experience—practice under the supervision of a certified nuclear medicine technologist and a physician or surgeon who specializes in nuclear medicine.

Graduating from a nuclear medicine program accredited by the Joint Review Committee on Educational Programs in Nuclear Medicine Technology may be required for licensure or by an employer.

Licenses, Certifications, and Registrations

Most nuclear medicine technologists become certified. Although certification is not required for a license, it fulfills most of the requirements for state licensure. Licensing requirements vary by state. For specific requirements, contact the state's health board.

Some employers require certification, regardless of state regulations. Certification usually involves graduating from an accredited nuclear medicine technology program. Certification is available from the American Registry of Radiologic

Technologists (ARRT) and the Nuclear Medicine Technology Certification Board (NMTCB).

In addition to receiving general certification, technologists may earn specialty certifications that show their proficiency in procedures or equipment. A technologist must pass an exam offered by the NMTCB to earn certification in positron emission tomography (PET), nuclear cardiology (NCT), or computed tomography (CT).

Technologists also may be required to have one or more other certifications, such as in basic life support (BLS), advanced cardiovascular life support (ACLS), or cardiopulmonary resuscitation (CPR).

Important Qualities

Ability to use technology. Nuclear medicine technologists work with computers and large pieces of electronic equipment and must be comfortable operating them.

Analytical skills. Nuclear medicine technologists must understand anatomy, physiology, and other sciences to assess whether dosage is accurate.

Compassion. Nuclear medicine technologists must be able to reassure patients who are stressed or upset.

Detail oriented. Nuclear medicine technologists must follow instructions precisely to ensure correct dosage and prevent overexposure to radiation.

Interpersonal skills. Nuclear medicine technologists interact with patients and often work as part of a team. They must be able to communicate effectively with their supervising physician.

Physical stamina. Nuclear medicine technologists must stand for long periods and be able to lift and move patients who need help.

Pay

The median annual wage for nuclear medicine technologists was $85,300 in May 2022. The median wage is the wage at which half the workers in an occupation earned more than that amount and half earned less. The lowest 10 percent earned less than $64,680, and the highest 10 percent earned more than $114,100.

In May 2022, the median annual wages for nuclear medicine technologists in the top industries in which they worked were as follows:

Outpatient care centers	$133,650
Offices of physicians	85,640
Medical and diagnostic laboratories	85,060
Hospitals; state, local, and private	84,900

Most nuclear medicine technologists work full time. Some nuclear medicine technologists work irregular hours, such as evenings or weekends. They also may be on call, especially if they work in hospitals.

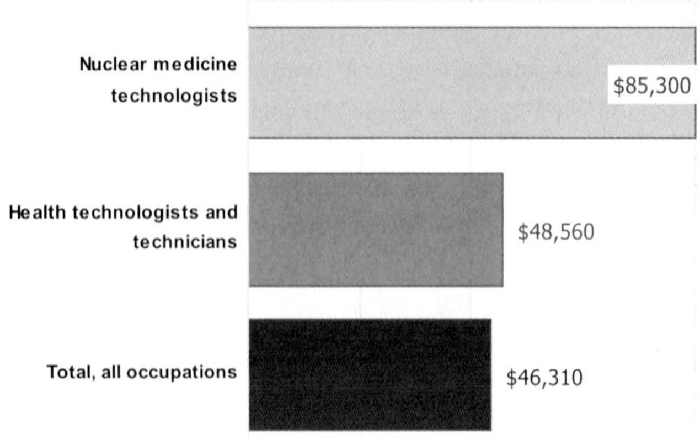

Note: All Occupations includes all occupations in the U.S. Economy.
Source: U.S. Bureau of Labor Statistics, Occupational Employment and Wage Statistics.

Job Outlook

Employment of nuclear medicine technologists is projected to show little or no change from 2022 to 2032.

Despite limited employment growth, about 800 openings for nuclear medicine technologists are projected each year, on average, over the decade. Most of those openings are expected to result from the need to replace workers who transfer to different occupations or exit the labor force, such as to retire.

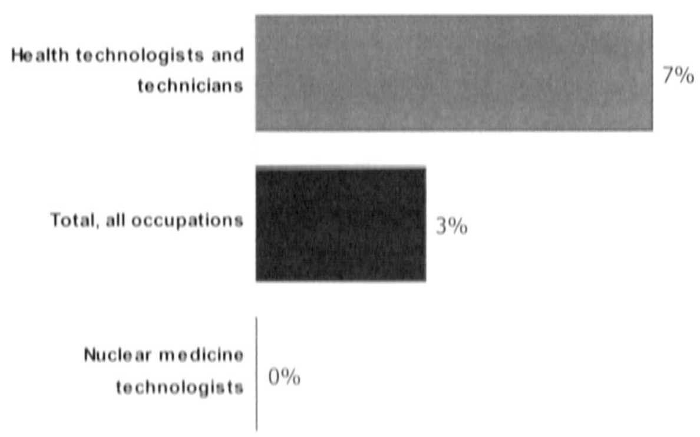

Note: All Occupations includes all occupations in the U.S. Economy.
Source: U.S. Bureau of Labor Statistics, Employment Projections program.

Employment

Among other medical uses, nuclear imaging is common in detecting, staging, and evaluating treatment for different types of cancers. Nuclear medicine technologists will continue to be needed to administer these tests due to the growing number of people entering older age groups, in which cancer is more prevalent.

However, declining use of nuclear imaging may dampen employment demand for technologists over the decade.

Occupational Title	SOC Code	Employment, 2022	Projected Employment, 2032	Change, 2022-32	
				Percent	Numeric
Nuclear medicine technologists	29-2033	18,100	18,200	0	100

Contacts for More Information

For more information about nuclear and radiologic medicine, visit

- American Board of Nuclear Medicine
- American Board of Radiology
- American College of Nuclear Medicine
- Society of Nuclear Medicine and Molecular Imaging
- Joint Review Committee on Educational Programs in Nuclear Medicine Technology
- Nuclear Medicine Technology Certification Board
- American Registry of Radiologic Technologists

Nurse Anesthetists, Nurse Midwives, and Nurse Practitioners

Summary

Quick Facts: Nurse Anesthetists, Nurse Midwives, and Nurse Practitioners

2022 Median Pay	$125,900 per year $60.53 per hour
Typical Entry-Level Education	Master's degree
Work Experience in a Related Occupation	None
On-the-job Training	None
Number of Jobs, 2022	323,900
Job Outlook, 2022-32	38% (Much faster than average)
Employment Change, 2022-32	123,600

What Nurse Anesthetists, Nurse Midwives, and Nurse Practitioners Do

Nurse anesthetists, nurse midwives, and nurse practitioners coordinate patient care and may provide primary and specialty healthcare.

Work Environment

Nurse anesthetists, nurse midwives, and nurse practitioners work in a variety of healthcare settings, including hospitals, physicians' offices, and clinics. Most advanced practice registered nurses (APRNs) work full time.

How to Become a Nurse Anesthetist, Nurse Midwife, or Nurse Practitioner

Nurse anesthetists, nurse midwives, and nurse practitioners must earn at least a master's degree in one of the APRN roles. They must also be licensed in their state and pass a national certification exam.

Pay

The median annual wage for nurse anesthetists, nurse midwives, and nurse practitioners was $125,900 in May 2022.

Job Outlook

Overall employment of nurse anesthetists, nurse midwives, and nurse practitioners is projected to grow 38 percent from 2022 to 2032, much faster than the average for all occupations.

About 29,200 openings for nurse anesthetists, nurse midwives, and nurse practitioners are projected each year, on average, over the decade. Many of those openings are expected to result from the need to replace workers who transfer to different occupations or exit the labor force, such as to retire.

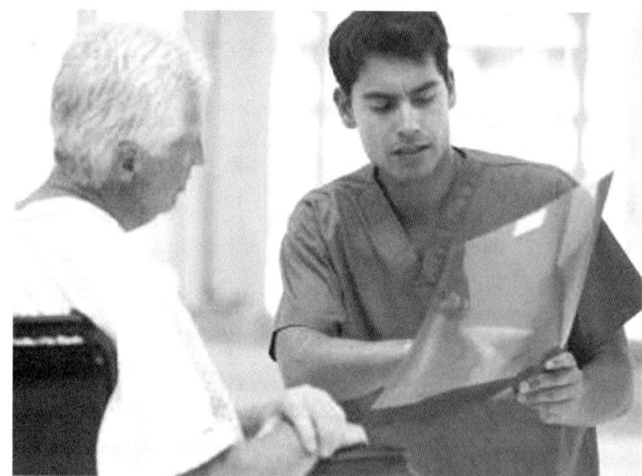

APRNs focus on patient-centered care, which means understanding a patient's concerns and lifestyle before choosing a course of action.

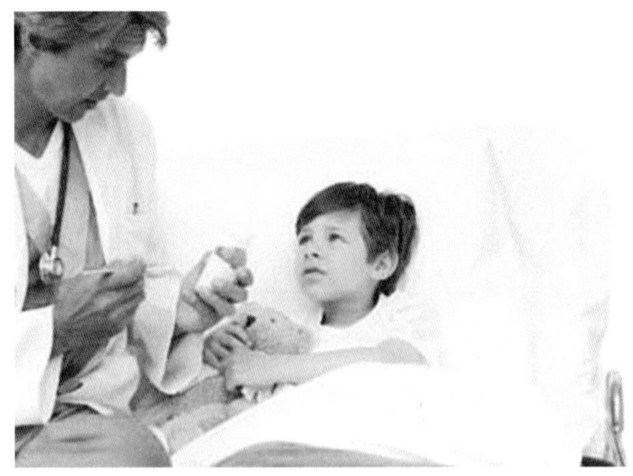

APRNs give patients medicines and treatments.

What Nurse Anesthetists, Nurse Midwives, and Nurse Practitioners Do

Nurse anesthetists, nurse midwives, and nurse practitioners, also referred to as *advanced practice registered nurses (APRNs)*, coordinate patient care and may provide primary and specialty healthcare. The scope of practice varies from state to state.

Duties

Advanced practice registered nurses typically do the following:

- Take and record patients' medical histories and symptoms
- Perform physical exams and observe patients
- Create patient care plans or contribute to existing plans
- Perform and order diagnostic tests
- Operate and monitor medical equipment
- Diagnose various health problems
- Analyze test results or changes in a patient's condition and alter treatment plans, as needed
- Give patients medicines and treatments
- Evaluate a patient's response to medicines and treatments
- Consult with doctors and other healthcare professionals, as needed
- Counsel and teach patients and their families how to stay healthy or manage their illnesses or injuries
- Conduct research

APRNs work independently or in collaboration with physicians. In most states, they can prescribe medications, order medical tests, and diagnose health problems. APRNs may provide primary and preventive care and may specialize in care for certain groups of people, such as children, pregnant women, or patients with mental health disorders.

APRNs have some of the same duties as registered nurses, including gathering information about a patient's condition and taking action to treat or manage the patient's health. However, APRNs are trained to do other tasks, including ordering and evaluating test results, referring patients to specialists, and diagnosing and treating ailments. APRNs focus on patient-centered care, which means understanding a patient's concerns and lifestyle before choosing a course of action.

Some APRNs also conduct research or teach staff about new policies or procedures. Others may provide consultation services based on a specific field of knowledge, such as oncology, which is the study of cancer.

The following are types of APRNs:

Nurse anesthetists (CRNAs) administer anesthesia and provide care before, during, and after surgical, therapeutic, diagnostic, and obstetrical procedures. They also provide pain management and some emergency services. Before a procedure begins, nurse anesthetists discuss with a patient any medications the patient is taking as well as any allergies or illnesses the patient may have, so that anesthesia can be safely administered. Nurse anesthetists then give a patient general anesthesia to put the patient to sleep so they feel no pain during surgery or administer a regional or local anesthesia to numb an area of the body. During the procedure, they monitor the patient's vital signs and adjust the anesthesia as necessary.

Nurse midwives (CNMs) provide care to women, including gynecological exams, family planning services, and prenatal care. They deliver babies, manage emergency situations during labor, repair lacerations, and may provide surgical assistance to physicians during cesarean births. Nurse midwives may act as primary maternity care providers for women. They also provide wellness care, educating their patients on how to lead healthy lives by discussing topics such as nutrition and disease prevention. Nurse midwives also provide care to their patients' partners for sexual or reproductive health issues.

Nurse practitioners (NPs) serve as primary and specialty care providers, delivering advanced nursing services to patients and their families. They assess patients, determine how to improve or manage a patient's health, and discuss ways to integrate health promotion strategies into a patient's life. Nurse practitioners typically care for a certain population of people. For instance, NPs may work in adult and geriatric health, pediatric health, or psychiatric and mental health.

Although the scope of their duties varies by state, many nurse practitioners work independently, prescribe medications, and order laboratory tests. Nurse practitioners consult with physicians and other health professionals when needed.

See the profile on registered nurses for more information about ***clinical nurse specialists*** (CNSs), also considered to be a type of APRN.

Work Environment

Nurse anesthetists, nurse midwives, and nurse practitioners held about 323,900 jobs in 2022. Employment in the detailed occupations that make up nurse anesthetists, nurse midwives, and nurse practitioners was distributed as follows:

Nurse practitioners	266,300
Nurse anesthetists	49,400
Nurse midwives	8,200

APRNs work in a variety of healthcare settings, including hospitals.

The largest employers of nurse anesthetists, nurse midwives, and nurse practitioners were as follows:

Offices of physicians	47%
Hospitals; state, local, and private	25
Outpatient care centers	9
Offices of other health practitioners	4
Educational services; state, local, and private	3

Some advanced practice registered nurses (APRNs) provide care in patients' homes. Some nurse midwives work in birthing centers, which are a type of outpatient care center.

APRNs may travel long distances to help care for patients in places where there are not enough healthcare workers.

Injuries and Illnesses

APRN work can be both physically and emotionally demanding. Some APRNs spend much of their day on their feet. They are vulnerable to back injuries because they must lift and move patients. APRN work can also be stressful because they make critical decisions that affect a patient's health.

Because of the environments in which they work, APRNs may come in close contact with infectious diseases. Therefore, they must follow strict guidelines to guard against diseases and other dangers, such as accidental needle sticks or patient outbursts.

Work Schedules

Most APRNs work full time. In physicians' offices, APRNs typically work during normal business hours. In hospitals and other healthcare facilities, they may work in shifts—including nights, weekends, and holidays—to provide round-the-clock patient care. Some APRNs, especially those who work in critical care or those who deliver babies, also may need to be on call.

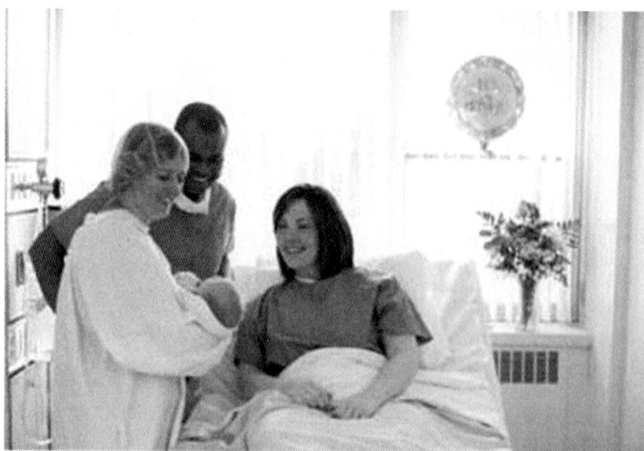

APRNs must earn a master's degree which typically includes clinical experience.

How to Become a Nurse Anesthetist, Nurse Midwife, or Nurse Practitioner

Nurse anesthetists, nurse midwives, and nurse practitioners, also referred to as *advanced practice registered nurses (APRNs)*, must have at least a master's degree in their specialty role. APRNs also must be licensed registered nurses in their state, pass a national certification exam, and have a state APRN license.

Education

Nurse anesthetists, nurse midwives, and nurse practitioners typically need at least a master's degree in an advanced practice nursing field. Accredited healthcare and related programs in these specialties typically include classroom education and clinical experience. Courses in subjects such as advanced health assessment, pathophysiology, and pharmacology are common as well as coursework specific to the chosen APRN role.

An APRN must have a registered nursing (RN) license before pursuing education in one of the advanced practice roles, and a strong background in science is helpful.

Most APRN programs prefer candidates who have a bachelor's degree in nursing. However, some schools offer bridge programs for registered nurses with an associate's degree or diploma in nursing. Graduate-level programs are also available for individuals who did not obtain a bachelor's degree in nursing but in a related health science field. These programs prepare the student for the RN licensure exam in addition to offering the APRN curriculum.

Although a master's degree is the most common form of entry-level education, APRNs may choose to earn a Doctor of Nursing Practice (DNP) or a Ph.D. The specific educational requirements and qualifications for each of the roles are available on professional organizations' websites.

Prospective nurse anesthetists must have 1 year of experience working as registered nurse in a critical care setting as a prerequisite for admission to an accredited nurse anesthetist program.

Licenses, Certifications, and Registrations

States' requirements for APRNs vary. In general, APRNs must have a registered nursing license, complete an accredited graduate-level program, pass a national certification exam, and have an APRN license. Details are available from each state's board of nursing.

To become licensed and use an APRN title, most states require national certification.

The National Board of Certification and Recertification for Nurse Anesthetists (NBCRNA) offers the National Certification Examination (NCE). Certified registered nurse anesthetists (CRNAs) must maintain their certification through the Continued Professional Certification (CPC) Program.

The American Midwifery Certification Board offers the Certified Nurse-Midwife (CNM). Individuals with this designation must recertify via the Certificate Maintenance Program.

There are several different certifications for nurse practitioners, including those available from the American Academy of Nurse Practitioners Certification Board (AANPCB), the American Nurses Credentialing Center (ANCC), and the Pediatric Nursing Certification Board (PNCB). Each of these certifications requires periodic renewal.

In addition, APRN positions may require cardiopulmonary resuscitation (CPR), basic life support (BLS), or advanced cardiac life support (ACLS) certification.

Important Qualities

Communication skills. Advanced practice registered nurses have to be able to communicate with patients and other healthcare professionals to ensure the appropriate course of action.

Critical-thinking skills. APRNs must be able to assess changes in a patient's health, quickly determine the most appropriate course of action, and decide if a consultation with another healthcare professional is needed.

Compassion. APRNs should be caring and sympathetic when treating patients.

Detail oriented. APRNs need to be thorough in providing treatments and medications that affect their patients' health. During an evaluation, they must notice even small changes in a patient's condition.

Interpersonal skills. APRNs must work with patients and families as well as with other healthcare providers and staff. They work as part of a team to determine and execute healthcare options for the patients they treat.

Leadership skills. APRNs often work in positions of seniority. They must effectively direct and sometimes manage other nurses on staff when providing patient care.

Resourcefulness. APRNs should know where to find the answers that they need.

Advancement

Some APRNs take on managerial or administrative roles; others go into academia. APRNs who earn a doctoral degree may conduct independent research or work on an interprofessional research team.

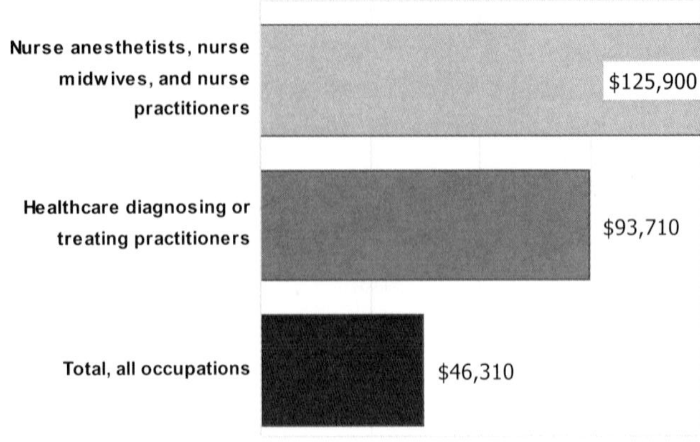

Note: All Occupations includes all occupations in the U.S. Economy.
Source: U.S. Bureau of Labor Statistics, Occupational Employment and Wage Statistics.

Pay

The median annual wage for nurse anesthetists, nurse midwives, and nurse practitioners was $125,900 in May 2022. The median wage is the wage at which half the workers in an occupation earned more than that amount and half earned less. The lowest 10 percent earned less than $91,250, and the highest 10 percent earned more than $208,080.

Median annual wages for nurse anesthetists, nurse midwives, and nurse practitioners in May 2022 were as follows:

Nurse anesthetists	$203,090
Nurse practitioners	121,610
Nurse midwives	120,880

In May 2022, the median annual wages for nurse anesthetists, nurse midwives, and nurse practitioners in the top industries in which they worked were as follows:

Hospitals; state, local, and private	$133,030
Outpatient care centers	131,200
Offices of physicians	122,560
Educational services; state, local, and private	110,260
Offices of other health practitioners	107,220

Most advanced practice registered nurses (APRNs) work full time. In physicians' offices, APRNs typically work during normal business hours. In hospitals and other healthcare facilities, they may work in shifts—including nights, weekends, and holidays—to provide round-the-clock patient care. Some APRNs, especially those who work in critical care or those who deliver babies, also may need to be on call.

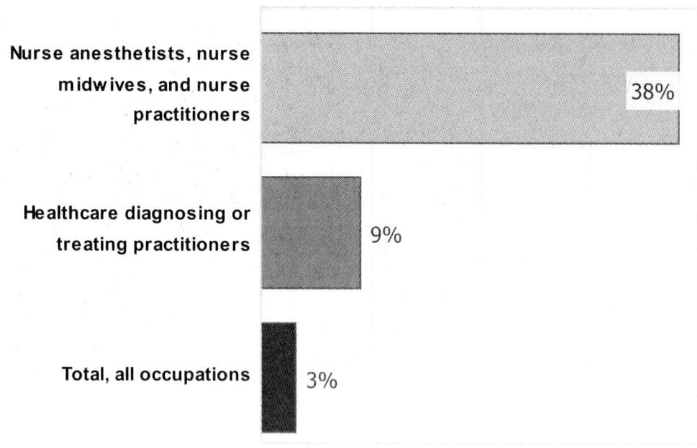

Note: All Occupations includes all occupations in the U.S. Economy.
Source: U.S. Bureau of Labor Statistics, Employment Projections program.

Job Outlook

Overall employment of nurse anesthetists, nurse midwives, and nurse practitioners is projected to grow 38 percent from 2022 to 2032, much faster than the average for all occupations.

About 29,200 openings for nurse anesthetists, nurse midwives, and nurse practitioners are projected each year, on average, over the decade. Many of those openings are expected to result from the need to replace workers who transfer to different occupations or exit the labor force, such as to retire.

Employment

Projected employment of nurse anesthetists, nurse midwives, and nurse practitioners varies by occupation (see table). Growth will occur because of an increase in the demand for healthcare services. Several factors will contribute to this demand, including an increased emphasis on preventive care and demand for healthcare services from the aging population.

Advanced practice registered nurses (APRNs) perform many of the same services as physicians. APRNs will be increasingly used in team-based models of care, particularly in hospitals, offices of physicians, clinics, and other ambulatory care settings, where they will be needed to provide preventive and primary care.

APRNs will also be needed to care for the large baby-boom population. As baby boomers age, they will experience ailments and complex conditions that require medical care. APRNs will be needed to keep these patients healthy and to treat the growing number of patients with chronic and acute conditions.

As states change their laws governing APRN practice authority, APRNs are being allowed to perform more services. APRNs also are being recognized more widely by the public as a source for primary healthcare.

Occupational Title	SOC Code	Employment, 2022	Projected Employment, 2032	Change, 2022-32	
				Percent	Numeric
Nurse anesthetists, nurse midwives, and nurse practitioners	—	323,900	447,400	38	123,600
Nurse anesthetists	29-1151	49,400	53,800	9	4,500
Nurse midwives	29-1161	8,200	8,700	6	500
Nurse practitioners	29-1171	266,300	384,900	45	118,600

Contacts for More Information

For more information, visit

- American Association of Nurse Anesthetists
- American College of Nurse-Midwives
- American Association of Nurse Practitioners
- American Nurses Association
- National League for Nursing
- American Association of Colleges of Nursing
- National Council of State Boards of Nursing
- American Academy of Nurse Practitioners Certification Board
- American Association of Critical-Care Nurses
- American Midwifery Certification Board
- American Nurses Credentialing Center
- National Certification Corporation
- National Board of Certification and Recertification for Nurse Anesthetists
- Pediatric Nursing Certification Board

Nursing Assistants and Orderlies

Summary

Quick Facts: Nursing Assistants and Orderlies	
2022 Median Pay	$35,740 per year $17.18 per hour
Typical Entry-Level Education	See How to Become One
Work Experience in a Related Occupation	None
On-the-job Training	See How to Become One
Number of Jobs, 2022	1,406,800
Job Outlook, 2022-32	4% (As fast as average)
Employment Change, 2022-32	58,400

What Nursing Assistants and Orderlies Do

Nursing assistants provide basic care and help patients with activities of daily living. Orderlies transport patients and clean treatment areas.

Work Environment

Most nursing assistants and orderlies work in nursing and residential care facilities and in hospitals. They are physically active and may need to help lift or move patients.

How to Become a Nursing Assistant or Orderly

Nursing assistants often need to complete a state-approved education program and pass their state's competency exam to become licensed or certified. Orderlies typically have at least a high school diploma.

Pay

The median annual wage for nursing assistants was $35,760 in May 2022.

The median annual wage for orderlies was $34,520 in May 2022.

Job Outlook

Overall employment of nursing assistants and orderlies is projected to grow 4 percent from 2022 to 2032, about as fast as the average for all occupations.

About 209,400 openings for nursing assistants and orderlies are projected each year, on average, over the decade. Many of those openings are expected to result from the need to replace workers who transfer to different occupations or exit the labor force, such as to retire.

What Nursing Assistants and Orderlies Do

Nursing assistants, sometimes called *nursing aides*, provide basic care and help patients with activities of daily living. Orderlies transport patients and clean treatment areas.

Duties

Nursing assistants and orderlies work as part of a healthcare team under the supervision of licensed practical or licensed vocational nurses and registered nurses.

Nursing assistants provide basic care and help with activities of daily living. They typically do the following:

- Clean and bathe patients
- Help patients use the toilet and dress
- Turn, reposition, and transfer patients between beds and wheelchairs
- Listen to and record patients' health concerns and report that information to nurses
- Measure patients' vital signs, such as blood pressure and temperature
- Serve meals and help patients eat

Depending on their training level and the state in which they work, nursing assistants also may dispense medication.

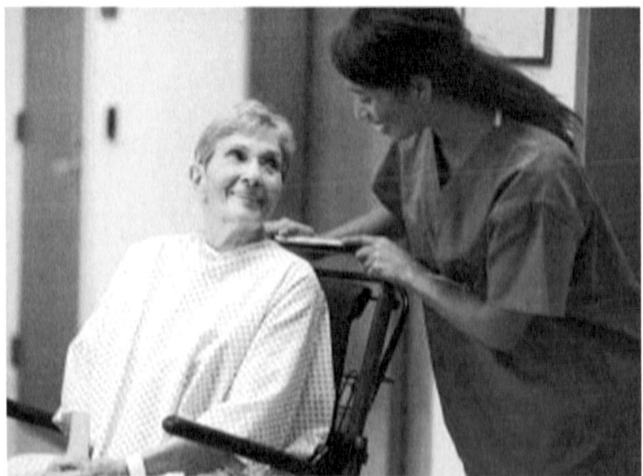

Orderlies help transport patients in hospitals or residents in nursing homes.

Nursing assistants help patients with activities of daily living like eating and bathing.

Nursing assistants are often the principal caregivers in nursing and residential care facilities. Nursing assistants often develop relationships with their patients because some patients stay in these facilities for months or years.

Orderlies typically do the following:

- Help patients to move around the facility, such as by pushing their wheelchairs
- Clean equipment and facilities
- Change linens
- Stock supplies

Work Environment

Nursing assistants held about 1.4 million jobs in 2022. The largest employers of nursing assistants were as follows:

Nursing care facilities (skilled nursing facilities)	33%
Hospitals; state, local, and private	33
Continuing care retirement communities and assisted living facilities for the elderly	11
Home healthcare services	6
Government	4

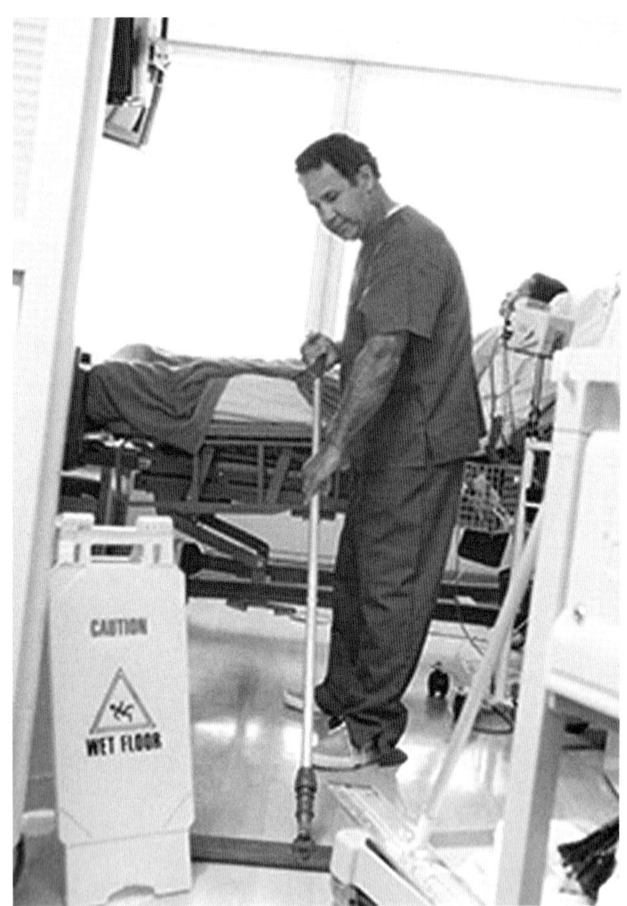

Orderlies are responsible for keeping hospitals and other facilities clean and tidy.

Orderlies held about 45,500 jobs in 2022. The largest employers of orderlies were as follows:

Hospitals; state, local, and private	85%
Ambulatory healthcare services	6
Government	1

The work of nursing assistants and orderlies may be strenuous. They spend much of their time on their feet as they care for patients.

Injuries and Illnesses

Nursing assistants and orderlies have one of the highest rates of injuries and illnesses of all occupations. These workers frequently move patients and have other physically demanding tasks. They typically get training in how to properly lift people, which can reduce the risk of injuries.

Work Schedules

Although most nursing assistants and orderlies work full time, some work part time. Because nursing and residential care facilities and hospitals provide care at all hours, nursing assistants and orderlies may need to work nights, weekends, and holidays.

How to Become a Nursing Assistant or Orderly

Nursing assistants typically must complete a state-approved education program and pass their state's competency exam. Orderlies typically have at least a high school diploma or equivalent.

Education and Training

Nursing assistants often need to complete a state-approved education program that includes both instruction on the principles of nursing and supervised clinical work. These programs are available in high schools, community colleges, vocational and technical schools, hospitals, and nursing homes.

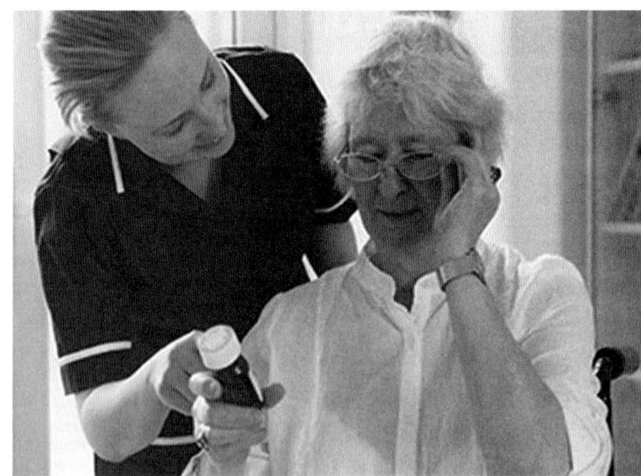
Nursing assistants must be able to communicate effectively to address patients' or residents' concerns.

In addition, nursing assistants typically complete a brief period of on-the-job training to learn about their specific employer's policies and procedures.

Orderlies typically have at least a high school diploma or equivalent and receive a short period of on-the-job training.

Licenses, Certifications, and Registrations

Specific requirements for nursing assistants vary by state. Nursing assistants often need a state-issued license or certification. After completing an approved education program, nursing assistants often must pass a competency exam, which allows them to use state-specific titles. In some states, a nursing assistant is called a Certified Nursing Assistant (CNA), but titles vary by state.

Nursing assistants who have passed the competency exam are placed on a state registry. They must be on the state registry to work in a nursing home.

Some states have other requirements as well, such as continuing education and a criminal background check. Check with state certifying agencies for more information.

In some states, nursing assistants may earn additional credentials, such as Certified Medication Assistant (CMA). As a CMA, they may dispense medications.

Orderlies do not need a license; however, jobs might require certification in cardiopulmonary resuscitation (CPR) or basic life support (BLS).

Important Qualities

Communication skills. Nursing assistants and orderlies must listen and respond to patients' concerns. They also need to share information with other healthcare workers.

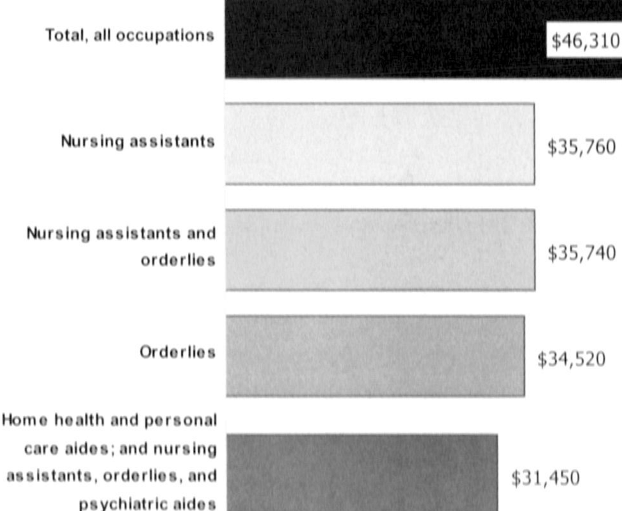

Note: All Occupations includes all occupations in the U.S. Economy.
Source: U.S. Bureau of Labor Statistics, Occupational Employment and Wage Statistics.

Compassion. Nursing assistants and orderlies help and care for people who are sick, injured, or need aid for other reasons. They need an empathetic attitude to do their work.

Patience. The routine tasks of cleaning, feeding, and bathing patients may be stressful. Nursing assistants and orderlies must be able to complete these tasks with professionalism.

Physical stamina. Nursing assistants and orderlies spend much of their time on their feet. They must be able to perform tasks such as lifting or moving patients.

Pay

The median annual wage for nursing assistants was $35,760 in May 2022. The median wage is the wage at which half the workers in an occupation earned more than that amount and half earned less. The lowest 10 percent earned less than $28,030, and the highest 10 percent earned more than $45,940.

The median annual wage for orderlies was $34,520 in May 2022. The lowest 10 percent earned less than $27,630, and the highest 10 percent earned more than $46,700.

In May 2022, the median annual wages for nursing assistants in the top industries in which they worked were as follows:

Government	$39,250
Hospitals; state, local, and private	36,480
Nursing care facilities (skilled nursing facilities)	35,480
Continuing care retirement communities and assisted living facilities for the elderly	34,600
Home healthcare services	31,280

In May 2022, the median annual wages for orderlies in the top industries in which they worked were as follows:

Government	$37,050
Hospitals; state, local, and private	34,660
Ambulatory healthcare services	33,220

Although most nursing assistants and orderlies work full time, some work part time. Because nursing and residential care facilities and hospitals provide care at all hours, nursing aides and orderlies may need to work nights, weekends, and holidays.

Job Outlook

Overall employment of nursing assistants and orderlies is projected to grow 4 percent from 2022 to 2032, about as fast as the average for all occupations.

About 209,400 openings for nursing assistants and orderlies are projected each year, on average, over the decade. Many of those openings are expected to result from the need to replace workers who transfer to different occupations or exit the labor force, such as to retire.

Employment

As the baby-boom population ages, nursing assistants and orderlies will be needed to help care for an increasing number

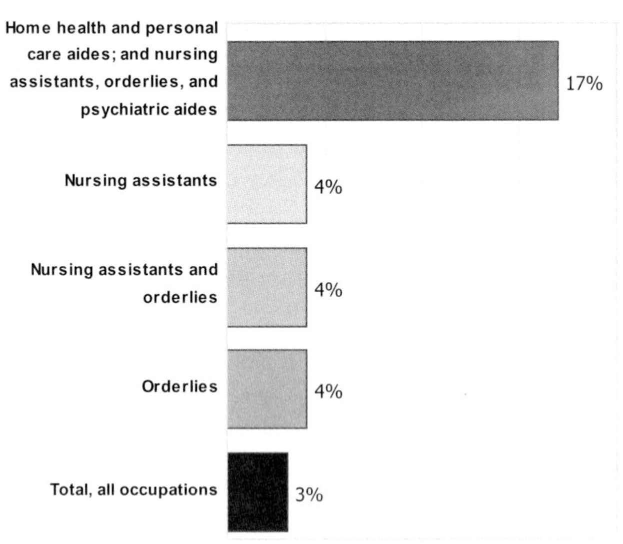

Note: All Occupations includes all occupations in the U.S. Economy. Source: U.S. Bureau of Labor Statistics, Employment Projections program.

of older people who have chronic or progressive diseases, such as heart disease and diabetes.

Demand for nursing assistants may be constrained by financial pressures on nursing homes, which might lead some facilities to close or reduce staff. However, increased opportunities are expected in home- and community-based settings as patient preferences and shifts in federal and state funding generate demand for care in these settings.

Occupational Title	SOC Code	Employment, 2022	Projected Employment, 2032	Change, 2022-32	
				Percent	Numeric
Nursing assistants and orderlies	—	1,406,800	1,465,200	4	58,400
Nursing assistants	31-1131	1,361,300	1,417,800	4	56,500
Orderlies	31-1132	45,500	47,400	4	1,900

Contacts for More Information

For information about healthcare assistants, visit

- National Association of Health Care Assistants (NAHCA)
- National Council of State Boards of Nursing

Occupational Health and Safety Specialists and Technicians

Summary

Quick Facts: Occupational Health and Safety Specialists and Technicians

2022 Median Pay	$75,240 per year $36.17 per hour
Typical Entry-Level Education	See How to Become One
Work Experience in a Related Occupation	None
On-the-job Training	See How to Become One
Number of Jobs, 2022	138,400
Job Outlook, 2022-32	13% (Much faster than average)
Employment Change, 2022-32	17,700

What Occupational Health and Safety Specialists and Technicians Do

Occupational health and safety specialists and technicians collect data on, analyze, and design improvements to work environments and procedures.

Work Environment

Occupational health and safety specialists and technicians work in a variety of indoor or outdoor settings, such as offices and factories or construction sites. Their jobs may involve considerable travel and fieldwork. Most work full time, and some work more than 40 hours per week.

How to Become an Occupational Health and Safety Specialist or Technician

Occupational health and safety specialists typically need a bachelor's degree in occupational health and safety or a related field. Occupational health and safety technicians typically need at least a high school diploma to enter the occupation, and they receive training on the job.

Pay

The median annual wage for occupational health and safety specialists was $78,570 in May 2022.

Occupational health and safety specialists and technicians collect data on and analyze many types of work environments and work procedures.

The median annual wage for occupational health and safety technicians was $57,970 in May 2022.

Job Outlook

Overall employment of occupational health and safety specialists and technicians is projected to grow 13 percent from 2022 to 2032, much faster than the average for all occupations.

About 17,200 openings for occupational health and safety specialists and technicians are projected each year, on average, over the decade. Many of those openings are expected to result from the need to replace workers who transfer to different occupations or exit the labor force, such as to retire.

What Occupational Health and Safety Specialists and Technicians Do

Occupational health and safety specialists and technicians collect data on, analyze, and design improvements to many types of work environments and procedures. Specialists inspect workplaces and enforce adherence to regulations on safety, health, and the environment. Technicians work with specialists to implement and evaluate programs aimed at mitigating risks to workers, property, the environment, and the public.

Duties

Occupational health and safety specialists and technicians typically do the following:

- Inspect, test, and evaluate workplace environments, programs, equipment, and practices to ensure that they follow government safety regulations
- Design and implement workplace programs and procedures that control or prevent chemical, physical, or other risks to workers
- Educate employers and workers about maintaining workplace safety
- Demonstrate use of safety equipment and ensure proper use by workers
- Investigate incidents to determine the cause and possible prevention
- Prepare written reports of their findings

Occupational health and safety specialists examine worksites for environmental or physical factors that could harm employee health, safety, comfort, or performance. They then find ways to improve potential risk factors. For example, they may notice potentially hazardous conditions inside a chemical plant and suggest changes to lighting, equipment, materials, or ventilation.

Occupational health and safety technicians assist specialists by collecting data on work environments and implementing the worksite improvements that specialists plan. Technicians also may check to make sure that workers are using required protective gear, such as masks and hardhats.

Occupational health and safety specialists and technicians may develop and conduct employee training programs. These programs cover a range of topics, such as how to use safety equipment correctly and how to respond in an emergency.

In the event of a workplace safety incident, specialists and technicians investigate its cause. They then analyze data from the incident, such as the number of people impacted, and look for trends in occurrence. This evaluation helps them to recommend improvements to prevent future incidents.

Work Environment

Occupational health and safety specialists held about 113,800 jobs in 2022. The largest employers of occupational health and safety specialists were as follows:

Government	20%
Manufacturing	17
Construction	14
Management, scientific, and technical consulting services	7
Hospitals; state, local, and private	3

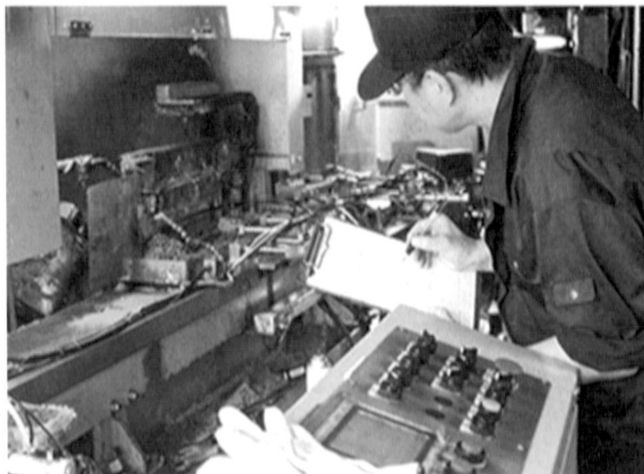

Occupational health and safety specialists inspect workplaces for adherence to regulations on safety, health, and the environment.

Occupational health and safety technicians often work with complex equipment to test and evaluate workplace environments and equipment.

Occupational health and safety technicians held about 24,700 jobs in 2022. The largest employers of occupational health and safety technicians were as follows:

Manufacturing	24%
Construction	9
Management, scientific, and technical consulting services	9
Government	9
Hospitals; state, local, and private	3

Occupational health and safety specialists and technicians work in a variety of indoor or outdoor settings, such as offices and factories or construction sites. Their jobs may involve considerable travel and fieldwork.

The work of these specialists may be strenuous and involve a lot of standing, squatting, and lifting. It also may be stressful, such as in cases of emergency, falling debris, or other hazardous situations. To minimize the risk of illness or injury, they use gloves, helmets, respirators, and other personal protective and safety equipment.

Work Schedules

Most occupational health and safety specialists and technicians work full time, and some work more than 40 hours per week. Technicians may be on call to work weekends or irregular schedules in emergencies.

How to Become an Occupational Health and Safety Specialist or Technician

Occupational health and safety specialists typically need a bachelor's degree in occupational health and safety or a related field. Technicians typically need at least a high school diploma to enter the occupation, and they receive training on the job. Some pursue professional certification.

Specialists and technicians carry out and evaluate programs on workplace safety and health.

Education

Occupational health and safety specialists typically need a bachelor's degree in occupational health and safety or a related field, such as biology or healthcare and related majors. For some positions, a master's degree is required. In addition to science, coursework should include topics such as ergonomics, safety management, and industrial hygiene.

Occupational health and safety technicians typically need at least a high school diploma to enter the occupation. High school students interested in this occupation should take classes in chemistry, biology, and physics. Some technicians earn an associate's degree or certificate from a community college or university. These programs typically take 2 years or less and include courses in hazardous materials, fire prevention, and safety regulations.

Licenses, Certifications, and Registrations

Employers may prefer or require occupational health and safety specialists and technicians to have professional certification. This certification is available through several organizations, such as the Board for Global EHS Credentialing, Board of Certified Safety Professions, and National Association of Safety Professionals.

Obtaining certification typically requires graduating from an accredited educational program, completing work experience, and passing an examination. Maintaining certification usually requires completing a specified number of hours of continuing education.

Training

Occupational health and safety technicians usually receive some on-the-job training. They may learn about specific laws and regulations, how to perform inspections, and how to conduct tests. The length of training varies with the employee's level of experience, education, and industry in which he or she works.

Occupational health and safety specialists sometimes receive on-the-job training. However, training is less common for specialists than it is for technicians.

Work Experience in a Related Occupation

Some employers prefer to hire occupational health and safety specialists who have prior experience in the industry. Specialists may gain this experience by working in a related occupation, such as health and safety engineer.

Important Qualities

Communication skills. Occupational health and safety specialists and technicians deliver safety trainings and instruction to employees and managers. They also write reports that effectively convey their findings.

Detail oriented. Occupational health and safety specialists and technicians must be meticulous when checking work environments. They need to ensure that sites follow safety standards and government regulations.

Physical stamina. Occupational health and safety specialists and technicians must be able to stand for long periods and may have to squat or kneel. Some work in uncomfortable environments, such as tunnels or mines.

Problem-solving skills. Occupational health and safety specialists and technicians determine proper design and implementation of workplace processes or procedures to help protect workers from hazardous conditions.

Technology skills. Occupational health and safety specialists and technicians use a variety of digital tools and testing equipment, such as devices that measure air quality.

Pay

The median annual wage for occupational health and safety specialists was $78,570 in May 2022. The median wage is the wage at which half the workers in an occupation earned more than that amount and half earned less. The lowest 10 percent earned less than $47,160, and the highest 10 percent earned more than $121,510.

The median annual wage for occupational health and safety technicians was $57,970 in May 2022. The lowest 10 percent earned less than $36,180, and the highest 10 percent earned more than $94,830.

In May 2022, the median annual wages for occupational health and safety specialists in the top industries in which they worked were as follows:

Hospitals; state, local, and private	$86,980
Manufacturing	80,000
Government	79,170
Construction	78,060
Management, scientific, and technical consulting services	75,750

In May 2022, the median annual wages for occupational health and safety technicians in the top industries in which they worked were as follows:

Construction	$67,900
Manufacturing	59,610
Hospitals; state, local, and private	58,590
Government	57,680
Management, scientific, and technical consulting services	48,770

Most occupational health and safety specialists and technicians work full time, and some work more than 40 hours per week. Some may be on call and work weekends or irregular hours in emergencies.

Job Outlook

Overall employment of occupational health and safety specialists and technicians is projected to grow 13 percent from 2022 to 2032, much faster than the average for all occupations.

About 17,200 openings for occupational health and safety specialists and technicians are projected each year, on average, over the decade. Many of those openings are expected to result from the need to replace workers who transfer to different occupations or exit the labor force, such as to retire.

Occupational Health and Safety Specialists and Technicians

Median annual wages, May 2022

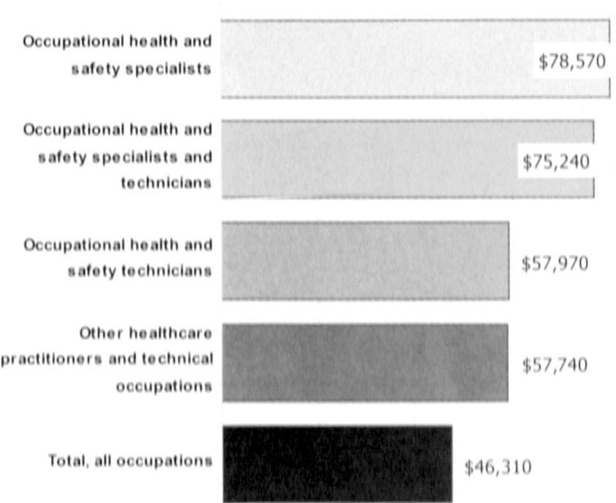

Note: All Occupations includes all occupations in the U.S. Economy.
Source: U.S. Bureau of Labor Statistics, Occupational Employment and Wage Statistics.

Occupational Health and Safety Specialists and Technicians

Percent change in employment, projected 2022-32

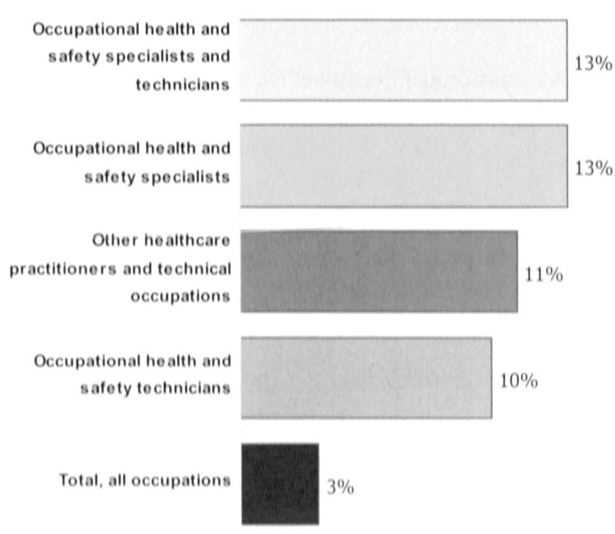

Note: All Occupations includes all occupations in the U.S. Economy.
Source: U.S. Bureau of Labor Statistics, Employment Projections program.

Employment

Occupational health and safety specialists and technicians will be needed in a variety of industries and government agencies to ensure safe working conditions that comply with regulations.

In recent years, employers have emphasized worker health, safety, and wellness. This trend is expected to continue, which should contribute to increased demand for occupational health and safety specialists and technicians.

Among the factors contributing to this demand are the adoption of new technologies, such as robotics, that require updated safety practices and the need to protect workers from climate-related hazards, such as excessive heat.

Occupational Title	SOC Code	Employment, 2022	Projected Employment, 2032	Change, 2022-32	
				Percent	Numeric
Occupational health and safety specialists and technicians	19-5000	138,400	156,100	13	17,700

Occupational Title	SOC Code	Employment, 2022	Projected Employment, 2032	Change, 2022-32	
				Percent	Numeric
Occupational health and safety specialists	19-5011	113,800	128,900	13	15,200
Occupational health and safety technicians	19-5012	24,700	27,200	10	2,500

Contacts for More Information

For more information, visit

- Board for Global EHS Credentialing (BGC)
- Board of Certified Safety Professionals (BCSP)
- National Association of Safety Professionals (NASP)
- U.S. Department of Labor, Occupational Safety and Health Administration (OSHA)
- Centers for Disease Control and Prevention, National Institute for Occupational Safety and Health (NIOSH)
- USAJOBS

Occupational Therapists

Summary

Quick Facts: Occupational Therapists

2022 Median Pay	$93,180 per year $44.80 per hour
Typical Entry-Level Education	Master's degree
Work Experience in a Related Occupation	None
On-the-job Training	None
Number of Jobs, 2022	139,600
Job Outlook, 2022-32	12% (Much faster than average)
Employment Change, 2022-32	16,100

What Occupational Therapists Do

Occupational therapists evaluate and treat people who have injuries, illnesses, or disabilities to help them with vocational, daily living, and other skills that promote independence.

Work Environment

Occupational therapists work in a variety of settings, such as hospitals, schools, and outpatient clinics. They stand for long periods and may need to lift or move clients.

How to Become an Occupational Therapist

To enter the occupation, occupational therapists typically need a master's degree in occupational therapy. All states require occupational therapists to be licensed.

Pay

The median annual wage for occupational therapists was $93,180 in May 2022.

Job Outlook

Employment of occupational therapists is projected to grow 12 percent from 2022 to 2032, much faster than the average for all occupations.

About 9,600 openings for occupational therapists are projected each year, on average, over the decade. Many of those openings are expected to result from the need to replace workers who transfer to different occupations or exit the labor force, such as to retire.

Occupational therapists develop a treatment plan for patients.

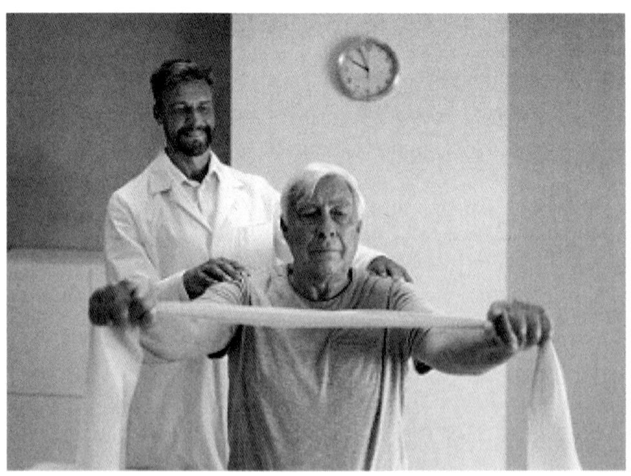

Occupational therapists help people, such as those with disabilities, live independently.

What Occupational Therapists Do

Occupational therapists evaluate and treat people who have injuries, illnesses, or disabilities. They help clients meet goals to develop, recover, improve, and maintain skills needed for daily living and working.

Duties

Occupational therapists typically do the following:

- Evaluate clients' conditions by reviewing their medical history, interviewing them, and observing them perform various tasks
- Develop and implement treatment plans that have specific activities to help clients work toward their goals
- Help clients relearn and perform daily living tasks, such as teaching a person who has had a stroke how to get dressed
- Demonstrate exercises—for example, stretching the joints for arthritis relief—to help relieve clients' pain
- Evaluate a client's home, school, or workplace to identify potential accessibility improvements, such as labeling kitchen cabinets for an older person with poor memory
- Educate a client's family about how to accommodate and care for them
- Recommend special equipment, such as mobility aids and eating aids, and instruct clients and families on how to use it
- Assess and record clients' activities and progress for client evaluations, billing, and other purposes

Occupational therapists work with people who have permanent disabilities, such as cerebral palsy, and may need help with daily tasks. They recommend options and show clients how to use appropriate adaptive equipment, such as leg braces, wheelchairs, and eating aids. These devices help clients live their lives more independently.

Some occupational therapists work with children in inpatient, outpatient, or educational settings. They may provide early intervention therapy to infants and toddlers or work with school-aged children to encourage engagement, such as participating in academic activities.

Therapists who work with older adults help clients live independently and improve their quality of life. They assess clients' abilities and environment and make recommendations to improve the clients' everyday lives. For example, therapists may identify potential fall hazards in a client's home and recommend their removal or help clients attend social outings.

Occupational therapists help clients create functional work environments. They evaluate the workspace, recommend modifications, and meet with the client's employer to collaborate on changes to the client's work environment or schedule.

Occupational therapists also may work in mental health settings, where they help clients who have developmental disabilities or mental health conditions. Therapists assist and educate clients on improving skills such as managing time, using public transportation, and doing household chores. In addition, therapists may work with individuals who have problems related to drug or alcohol abuse, depression, or trauma.

Some occupational therapists, such as those employed in hospitals, work as part of a healthcare team along with doctors, registered nurses, and other types of therapists, including physical therapists. They may work with patients who have chronic conditions, such as diabetes or arthritis, or help rehabilitate a patient recovering from a stroke or spinal cord injury. Occupational therapists also oversee the work of occupational therapy assistants and aides.

Work Environment

Occupational therapists held about 139,600 jobs in 2022. The largest employers of occupational therapists were as follows:

Hospitals; state, local, and private	29%
Offices of physical, occupational and speech therapists, and audiologists	28
Elementary and secondary schools; state, local, and private	12
Home healthcare services	8
Nursing care facilities (skilled nursing facilities)	7

Occupational therapists may spend a lot of time on their feet working with clients.

Occupational therapists must be sympathetic to clients' needs and concerns.

Occupational therapists may spend a lot of time standing while working with clients. They may be required to lift and move clients or heavy equipment, which can cause injuries. To limit the risk of injury, occupational therapists must use proper body mechanics and lifting techniques.

Therapists sometimes travel between multiple locations, such as between a hospital and a client's home.

Work Schedules

Most occupational therapists work full time, but part-time work is common. They may work nights or weekends, as needed, to accommodate clients' schedules.

How to Become an Occupational Therapist

To enter the occupation, occupational therapists typically need a master's degree in occupational therapy. All states require occupational therapists to be licensed.

Education

Occupational therapists typically need a master's degree in occupational therapy to enter the occupation. Occupational therapy programs are accredited by the Accreditation Council for Occupational Therapy Education.

Admission to graduate programs in occupational therapy requires a bachelor's degree, although it may not need to be in a particular subject. However, master's degree programs frequently require applicants to have completed coursework in biology, psychology, and other sciences. Some programs also require applicants to have volunteered or worked in an occupational therapy setting. To learn about specific requirements, applicants should contact the program in which they are interested in enrolling.

Master's degree programs usually take 2 to 3 years to complete and typically include courses such as kinesiology, neuroscience, and anatomy. Additionally, these programs require a specified number of hours of supervised fieldwork during which prospective occupational therapists gain clinical experience.

Some schools offer a dual-degree program in which the student earns a bachelor's degree and a master's degree upon completion.

Licenses, Certifications, and Registrations

All states require occupational therapists to be licensed. Licensing requirements vary by state, but at a minimum, candidates must pass the national certification examination administered by the National Board for Certification in Occupational Therapy (NBCOT). To sit for the NBCOT exam, candidates must have earned a degree from an accredited occupational therapy program that includes fieldwork.

Therapists must pass the NBCOT exam to use the title "Occupational Therapist Registered" (OTR). They also must complete a specified number of hours of continuing education to maintain state licensure and NBCOT certification.

The American Occupational Therapy Association offers board and specialty certifications in a number of areas, such as gerontology, pediatrics, and physical rehabilitation.

Some employers require candidates to have cardiopulmonary resuscitation (CPR) or basic life support (BLS) certification.

Important Qualities

Adaptability. Occupational therapists must be accommodating when working with clients. They must be able to change treatment plans based on clients' needs.

Communication skills. Occupational therapists must listen closely to clients. They also must be able to explain treatment plans and goals to clients, clients' families, and other members of the healthcare team.

Compassion. Occupational therapists work with patients who may struggle with life's daily activities. Because of this, they must be empathetic and sensitive to a client's needs and concerns.

Interpersonal skills. Occupational therapists spend much of their time interacting with clients and explaining treatment. They must be able to develop a rapport with clients.

Patience. Occupational therapists work with clients who have problems with everyday activities. Therapists must remain calm in order to provide quality care.

Pay

The median annual wage for occupational therapists was $93,180 in May 2022. The median wage is the wage at which half the workers in an occupation earned more than that amount and half earned less. The lowest 10 percent earned less than $63,320, and the highest 10 percent earned more than $123,870.

In May 2022, the median annual wages for occupational therapists in the top industries in which they worked were as follows:

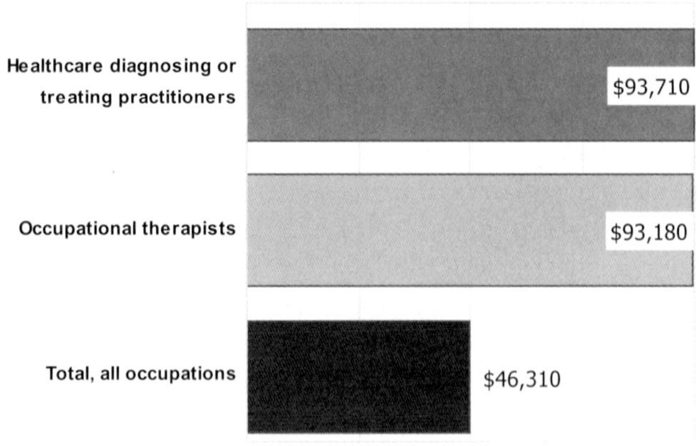

Note: All Occupations includes all occupations in the U.S. Economy.
Source: U.S. Bureau of Labor Statistics, Occupational Employment and Wage Statistics.

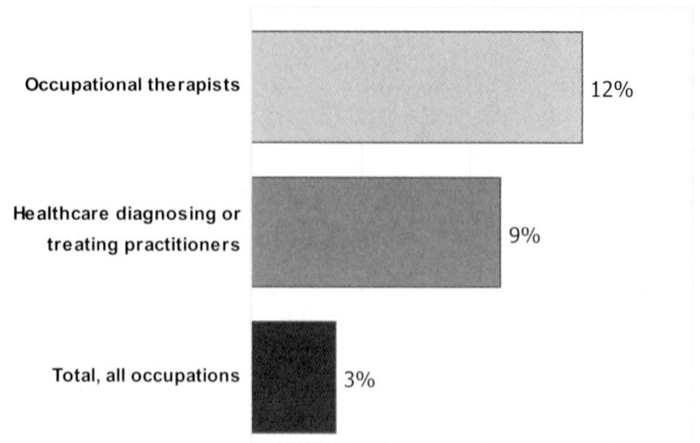

Note: All Occupations includes all occupations in the U.S. Economy.
Source: U.S. Bureau of Labor Statistics, Employment Projections program.

Home healthcare services	$101,500
Nursing care facilities (skilled nursing facilities)	99,560
Hospitals; state, local, and private	97,400
Offices of physical, occupational and speech therapists, and audiologists	91,420
Elementary and secondary schools; state, local, and private	79,660

Most occupational therapists work full time. They may work nights or weekends, as needed, to accommodate clients' schedules.

Job Outlook

Employment of occupational therapists is projected to grow 12 percent from 2022 to 2032, much faster than the average for all occupations.

About 9,600 openings for occupational therapists are projected each year, on average, over the decade. Many of those openings are expected to result from the need to replace workers who transfer to different occupations or exit the labor force, such as to retire.

Employment

Occupational therapy will continue to be an important part of treatment for people with various illnesses and disabilities, such as Alzheimer's disease, cerebral palsy, autism, or the loss of a limb.

The need for occupational therapists is expected to increase as the large baby-boom generation ages and people remain active later in life. Occupational therapists help older adults maintain their independence by recommending home modifications and strategies that make daily activities easier.

People will continue to seek noninvasive outpatient treatment for long-term disabilities and illnesses, and they may need occupational therapy to become more independent. Therapists will continue to be needed to assist people with autism spectrum disorder in improving their social skills and accomplishing a variety of daily tasks.

Occupational Title	SOC Code	Employment, 2022	Projected Employment, 2032	Change, 2022-32	
				Percent	Numeric
Occupational therapists	29-1122	139,600	155,600	12	16,100

Contacts for More Information

For more information about occupational therapists, visit

- American Occupational Therapy Association, Inc.
- National Board for Certification in Occupational Therapy

Occupational Therapy Assistants and Aides

Summary

Quick Facts: Occupational Therapy Assistants and Aides

2022 Median Pay	$63,450 per year $30.51 per hour
Typical Entry-Level Education	See How to Become One
Work Experience in a Related Occupation	None
On-the-job Training	See How to Become One
Number of Jobs, 2022	49,000
Job Outlook, 2022-32	23% (Much faster than average)
Employment Change, 2022-32	11,000

What Occupational Therapy Assistants and Aides Do

Occupational therapy assistants and aides help patients develop, recover, improve, as well as maintain the skills needed for daily living and working.

Work Environment

Occupational therapy assistants and aides work primarily in occupational therapists' offices, in hospitals, and in nursing care facilities. Occupational therapy assistants and aides spend much of their time on their feet while setting up equipment and, in the case of assistants, providing therapy to patients.

How to Become an Occupational Therapy Assistant or Aide

Occupational therapy assistants need an associate's degree from an accredited occupational therapy assistant program. All states regulate the practice of occupational therapy assistants. Occupational therapy aides typically need a high school diploma or equivalent and receive training on the job.

Pay

The median annual wage for occupational therapy aides was $37,060 in May 2022.

The median annual wage for occupational therapy assistants was $64,250 in May 2022.

Job Outlook

Overall employment of occupational therapy assistants and aides is projected to grow 23 percent from 2022 to 2032, much faster than the average for all occupations.

About 8,600 openings for occupational therapy assistants and aides are projected each year, on average, over the decade. Many of those openings are expected to result from the need to replace workers who transfer to different occupations or exit the labor force, such as to retire.

What Occupational Therapy Assistants and Aides Do

Occupational therapy assistants and aides help patients develop, recover, improve, as well as maintain the skills needed for daily living and working. Occupational therapy assistants are directly involved in providing therapy to patients; occupational therapy aides typically perform support activities. Both assistants and aides work under the direction of occupational therapists.

Duties

Occupational therapy assistants typically do the following:

- Help patients do therapeutic activities, such as stretches and other exercises
- Lead children who have developmental disabilities in play activities that promote coordination and socialization
- Encourage patients to complete activities and tasks
- Teach patients how to use special equipment—for example, showing a patient with Parkinson's disease how to use devices that make eating easier

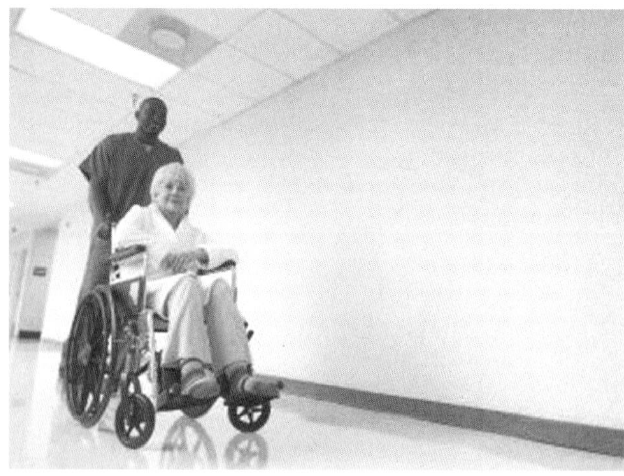

Occupational therapy aides transport patients to and from treatment areas.

Occupational therapy aides may handle some clerical tasks, like answering calls from patients and scheduling appointments.

- Record patients' progress, report to occupational therapists, and do other administrative tasks

Occupational therapy aides typically do the following:

- Prepare treatment areas, such as setting up therapy equipment
- Transport patients
- Clean treatment areas and equipment
- Help patients with billing and insurance forms
- Perform clerical tasks, including scheduling appointments and answering telephones

Occupational therapy assistants collaborate with occupational therapists to develop and carry out a treatment plan for each patient. Plans include diverse activities such as teaching the proper way for patients to move from a bed into a wheelchair and advising patients on the best way to stretch their muscles. For example, an occupational therapy assistant might work with injured workers to help them get back into the workforce by teaching them how to work around lost motor skills. Occupational therapy assistants also may work with people who have learning disabilities, teaching them skills that allow them to be more independent.

Assistants monitor activities to make sure that patients are doing them correctly. They record the patient's progress and provide feedback to the occupational therapist so that the therapist can change the treatment plan if the patient is not getting the desired results.

Occupational therapy aides typically prepare materials and assemble equipment used during treatment. They may assist patients with moving to and from treatment areas. After a therapy session, aides clean the treatment area, put away equipment, and gather laundry.

Occupational therapy aides fill out insurance forms and other paperwork and are responsible for a range of clerical tasks, such as scheduling appointments, answering the telephone, and monitoring inventory levels.

Work Environment

Occupational therapy aides held about 3,800 jobs in 2022. The largest employers of occupational therapy aides were as follows:

Offices of other health practitioners	40%
Hospitals; state, local, and private	28
Nursing care facilities (skilled nursing facilities)	10

Occupational therapy assistants held about 45,100 jobs in 2022. The largest employers of occupational therapy assistants were as follows:

Offices of physical, occupational and speech therapists, and audiologists	45%
Hospitals; state, local, and private	18
Nursing care facilities (skilled nursing facilities)	15
Home healthcare services	7
Educational services; state, local, and private	6

Occupational therapy assistants may work with children who have developmental disabilities.

Occupational therapy assistants and aides spend much of their time on their feet while setting up equipment and, in the case of assistants, providing therapy to patients. Constant kneeling and stooping are part of the job, as is the occasional need to lift patients.

Injuries and Illnesses

Occupational therapy aides have one of the highest rates of injuries and illnesses of all occupations. Their work may require physically demanding tasks, such as lifting patients, which can cause injuries.

Work Schedules

Most occupational therapy assistants and aides work full time. Occupational therapy assistants and aides may work during evenings or on weekends to accommodate patients' schedules.

How to Become an Occupational Therapy Assistant or Aide

Occupational therapy assistants need an associate's degree from an accredited occupational therapy assistant program. All states regulate the practice of occupational therapy assistants. Occupational therapy aides typically need a high school diploma or equivalent and are trained on the job.

Education and Training

Occupational therapy assistants typically need an associate's degree from an accredited program. Occupational therapy assistant programs are commonly found in community colleges and technical schools. In 2017, there were more than 200 occupational therapy assistant programs accredited by the Accreditation Council for Occupational Therapy Education, a part of the American Occupational Therapy Association.

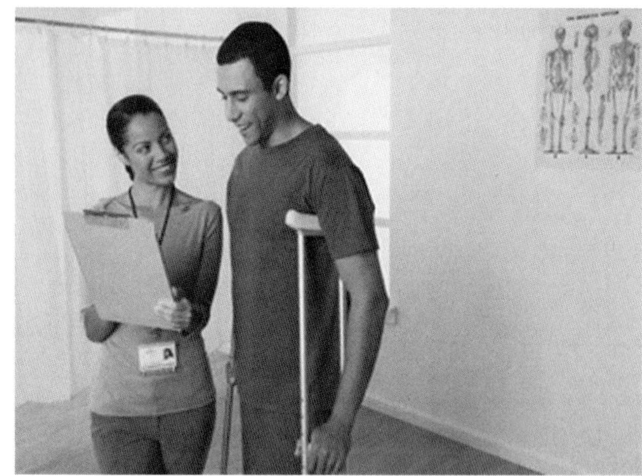

Occupational therapy aides help patients with billing and insurance forms.

These programs generally require 2 years of full-time study and include instruction in subjects such as psychology, biology, and pediatric health. In addition to taking coursework, occupational therapy assistants must complete at least 16 weeks of fieldwork to gain hands-on work experience.

People interested in becoming an occupational therapy assistant should take high school courses in biology and health education. They also can increase their chances of getting into a community college or technical school program by doing volunteer work in a healthcare setting, such as a nursing care facility, an occupational therapist's office, or a physical therapist's office.

Occupational therapy aides typically need a high school diploma or equivalent. They are trained on the job under the supervision of more experienced assistants or aides. Training can last from several days to a few weeks and covers a number of topics, including the setting up of therapy equipment and infection control procedures, among others. Previous work experience in healthcare may be helpful in getting a job.

Both occupational therapy assistants and aides often need certifications in cardiopulmonary resuscitation (CPR) and basic life support (BLS).

Important Qualities

Adaptability. Assistants must be flexible when treating patients. Because not every type of therapy will work for each patient, assistants may need to be creative when working with occupational therapists to determine the best therapy to achieve a patient's goals.

Compassion. Occupational therapy assistants and aides frequently work with patients who struggle with many of life's basic activities. As a result, they should be compassionate and have the ability to encourage others.

Detail oriented. Occupational therapy assistants and aides must quickly and accurately follow the instructions, both written and spoken, of an occupational therapist. In addition, aides must pay attention to detail when performing clerical tasks, such as helping a patient fill out an insurance form.

Interpersonal skills. Occupational therapy assistants and aides spend much of their time interacting with patients and therefore should be friendly and courteous. They also should communicate clearly with patients and with patients' families to the extent of their training.

Physical strength. Assistants and aides need to have a moderate degree of strength because of the physical exertion required to assist patients. Constant kneeling, stooping, and standing for long periods also are part of the job.

Licenses, Certifications, and Registrations

All states regulate the practice of occupational therapy assistants, with most requiring licensure. Licensure typically requires the completion of an accredited occupational therapy assistant education program, completion of all fieldwork requirements, and passing the National Board for Certification in Occupational Therapy (NBCOT) exam. Some states have additional requirements.

Occupational therapy assistants must pass the NBCOT exam to use the title "Certified Occupational Therapy Assistant" (COTA). They must also take continuing education classes to maintain their certification.

The American Occupational Therapy Association also offers a number of specialty certifications for occupational therapy assistants who want to demonstrate their specialized level of knowledge, skills, and abilities in specialized areas of practice such as low vision or feeding, eating, and swallowing.

Occupational therapy aides are not regulated by state law.

Advancement

Some occupational therapy assistants and aides advance by gaining additional education and becoming occupational therapists. A small number of occupational therapist "bridge" education programs are designed to qualify occupational therapy assistants to advance and become therapists.

Pay

The median annual wage for occupational therapy aides was $37,060 in May 2022. The median wage is the wage at which half the workers in an occupation earned more than that amount and half earned less. The lowest 10 percent earned less than $25,100, and the highest 10 percent earned more than $68,070.

The median annual wage for occupational therapy assistants was $64,250 in May 2022. The lowest 10 percent earned less than $47,940, and the highest 10 percent earned more than $85,580.

In May 2022, the median annual wages for occupational therapy aides in the top industries in which they worked were as follows:

Occupational Therapy Assistants and Aides

Median annual wages, May 2022

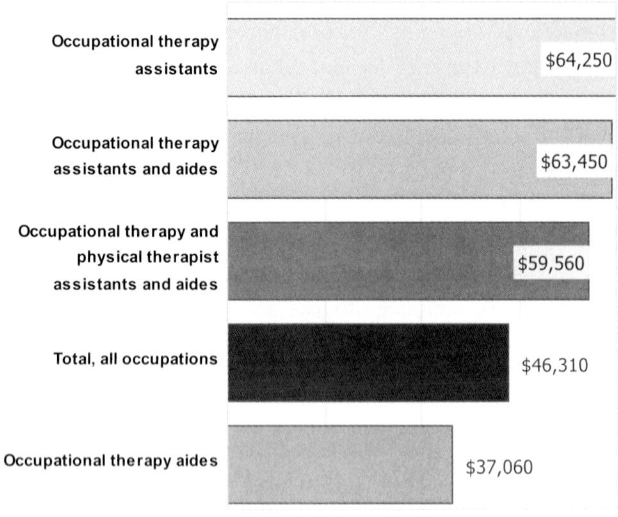

Note: All Occupations includes all occupations in the U.S. Economy.
Source: U.S. Bureau of Labor Statistics, Occupational Employment and Wage Statistics.

Occupational Therapy Assistants and Aides

Percent change in employment, projected 2022-32

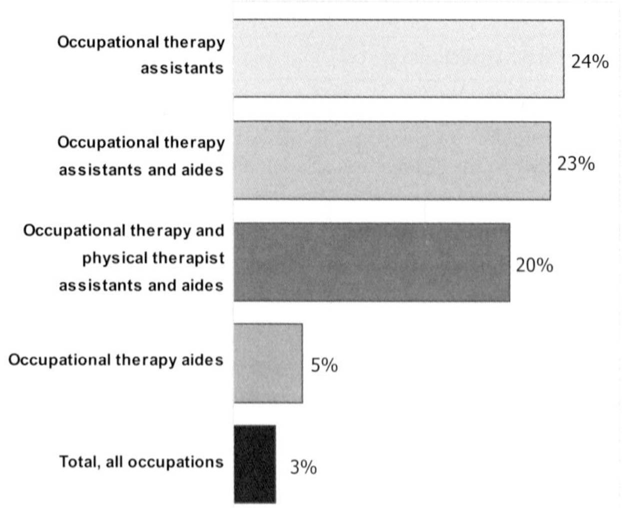

Note: All Occupations includes all occupations in the U.S. Economy.
Source: U.S. Bureau of Labor Statistics, Employment Projections program.

Nursing care facilities (skilled nursing facilities)	$58,510
Hospitals; state, local, and private	36,480
Offices of other health practitioners	31,650

In May 2022, the median annual wages for occupational therapy assistants in the top industries in which they worked were as follows:

Home healthcare services	$75,990
Nursing care facilities (skilled nursing facilities)	71,460
Offices of physical, occupational and speech therapists, and audiologists	63,370
Hospitals; state, local, and private	63,140
Educational services; state, local, and private	58,640

Most occupational therapy assistants and aides work full time. Occupational therapy assistants and aides may work during evenings or on weekends to accommodate patients' schedules.

Job Outlook

Overall employment of occupational therapy assistants and aides is projected to grow 23 percent from 2022 to 2032, much faster than the average for all occupations.

About 8,600 openings for occupational therapy assistants and aides are projected each year, on average, over the decade. Many of those openings are expected to result from the need to replace workers who transfer to different occupations or exit the labor force, such as to retire.

Employment

Demand for occupational therapy is likely to grow over the decade in response to the healthcare needs of an aging population.

Older adults are more prone than young people to conditions and ailments, such as arthritis and strokes, that may affect the ability to do everyday activities. Occupational therapy assistants and aides will be needed to help occupational therapists in caring for these patients. Occupational therapy also will continue to be used in treating children and young adults with developmental disorders, such as autism.

Healthcare providers, especially those specializing in long-term care, will continue to employ occupational therapy assistants to reduce the cost of occupational therapy services. However, restrictions in insurance reimbursement for services provided by occupational therapy aides may constrain demand for this occupation.

Occupational Title	SOC Code	Employment, 2022	Projected Employment, 2032	Change, 2022-32	
				Percent	Numeric
Occupational therapy assistants and aides	31-2010	49,000	60,000	23	11,000
Occupational therapy assistants	31-2011	45,100	56,000	24	10,800
Occupational therapy aides	31-2012	3,800	4,000	5	200

Contacts for More Information

For more information about occupational therapy assistants or aides, visit

- American Occupational Therapy Association, Inc.
- National Board for Certification in Occupational Therapy

Opticians

Summary

Quick Facts: Opticians	
2022 Median Pay	$39,610 per year $19.04 per hour
Typical Entry-Level Education	High school diploma or equivalent
Work Experience in a Related Occupation	None
On-the-job Training	Long-term on-the-job training
Number of Jobs, 2022	73,300
Job Outlook, 2022-32	3% (As fast as average)
Employment Change, 2022-32	2,000

What Opticians Do
Opticians help fit eyeglasses and contact lenses, following prescriptions from ophthalmologists and optometrists.

Work Environment
About half of opticians work in offices of optometrists or offices of physicians. Other opticians worked in stores that sell eyeglasses, contact lenses, visual aids, and other optical goods. These stores may be stand-alone businesses or parts of larger retail establishments, such as department stores.

How to Become an Optician
Opticians typically have a high school diploma or equivalent and some form of on-the-job training. Some opticians enter the occupation with an associate's degree or a certificate from a community college or technical school. About half of the states require opticians to be licensed.

Pay
The median annual wage for opticians was $39,610 in May 2022.

Job Outlook
Employment of opticians is projected to grow 3 percent from 2022 to 2032, about as fast as the average for all occupations.

About 6,400 openings for opticians are projected each year, on average, over the decade. Many of those openings are expected to result from the need to replace workers who transfer to different occupations or exit the labor force, such as to retire.

What Opticians Do
Opticians help fit eyeglasses and contact lenses, following prescriptions from ophthalmologists and optometrists. They also help customers decide which eyeglass frames or contact lenses to buy.

Duties
Opticians typically do the following:

- Receive customers' prescriptions for eyeglasses or contact lenses
- Measure customers' eyes and faces, such as the distance between their pupils
- Help customers choose eyeglass frames and lens treatments, such as eyewear for occupational use or sports, tints, or anti-reflective coatings, based on their vision needs and style preferences
- Create work orders for ophthalmic laboratory technicians, providing information about the lenses needed
- Adjust eyewear to ensure a good fit
- Repair or replace broken eyeglass frames
- Educate customers about eyewear—for example, show them how to care for their contact lenses
- Perform business tasks, such as maintaining sales records, keeping track of customers' prescriptions, and ordering and maintaining inventory

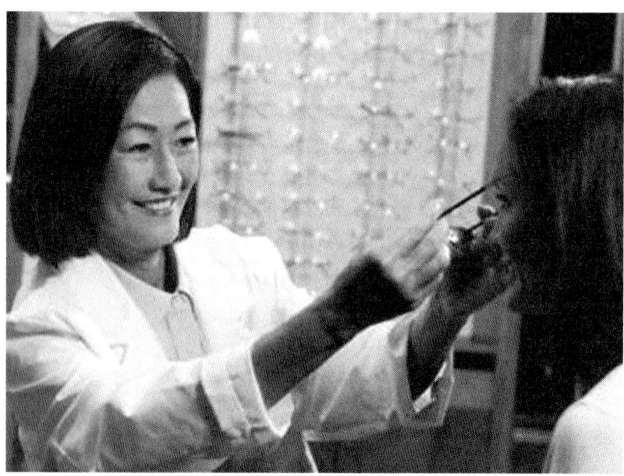

Opticians help customers choose eyeglass frames and lens treatments.

Opticians advise customers on styles of eyewear that suit their needs.

Opticians who work in small shops or prepare custom orders may cut lenses and insert them into frames—tasks usually performed by ophthalmic laboratory technicians.

Work Environment

Opticians held about 73,300 jobs in 2022. The largest employers of opticians were as follows:

Offices of optometrists	43%
Health and personal care retailers	23
Offices of physicians	11
Self-employed workers	0

Opticians who work as part of a group optometry or medical practice work with optometrists and ophthalmologists to provide eye-related medical care to patients.

Work Schedules

Opticians who work in large retail establishments, such as department stores, may have to work evenings and weekends. Most opticians work full time, although part-time opportunities also are available.

How to Become an Optician

Opticians typically have a high school diploma or equivalent and receive some form of on-the-job training. Some opticians enter the occupation with an associate's degree or a certificate from a community college or technical school. About half of the states require opticians to be licensed.

Education and Training

Opticians typically have a high school diploma or equivalent and learn job skills through on-the-job training. Training includes technical instruction in which, for example, a new optician measures a customer's eyes or adjusts frames under the supervision of an experienced optician. Trainees also learn sales and office management practices. Some opticians complete an apprenticeship, which typically takes at least 2 years.

Opticians may work in retail stores that sell eyeglasses and other optical goods.

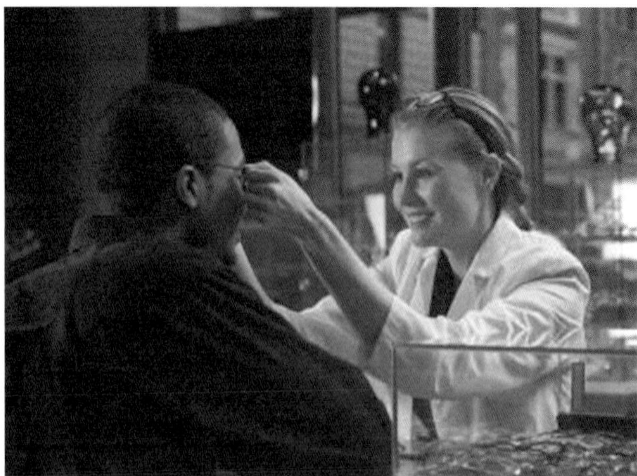

Opticians learn to adjust eyeglass frames during training.

Other opticians complete a postsecondary education program at a community college or technical school. These programs award a 2-year associate's degree or a 1-year certificate. As of 2017, the Commission on Opticianry Accreditation accredited 19 programs in 11 states.

Education programs typically include both classroom instruction and clinical experience. Coursework includes classes in optics, eye physiology, math, and business management, among other topics. Students also do supervised clinical work that gives them hands-on experience working as opticians and learning optical math, optical physics, and the use of precision measuring instruments. Some programs have distance-learning options.

The National Academy of Opticianry offers the Ophthalmic Career Progression Program (OCPP), a program designed for individuals who are already working in the field. The OCPP offers opticians another way to prepare for licensure exams or certifications.

Licenses, Certifications, and Registrations

About half of the states require opticians to be licensed. Licensure usually requires completing formal education through an approved program or completing an apprenticeship. In addition, opticians must pass one or more exams to be licensed. The opticianry licensing board in each state can supply information on licensing requirements.

Opticians may choose to become certified in eyeglass dispensing or contact lens dispensing or both. Certification requires passing exams from the American Board of Opticianry (ABO) and National Contact Lens Examiners (NCLE). Nearly all state licensing boards use the ABO and NCLE exams as the basis for state licensing. Some states also require opticians to pass state-specific practical exams.

In most states that require licensure, opticians must renew their license every 1 to 3 years and must complete continuing education requirements.

Important Qualities

Business skills. Opticians are often responsible for the business aspects of running an optical store. They should be comfortable

Opticians

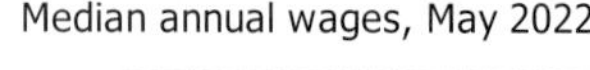

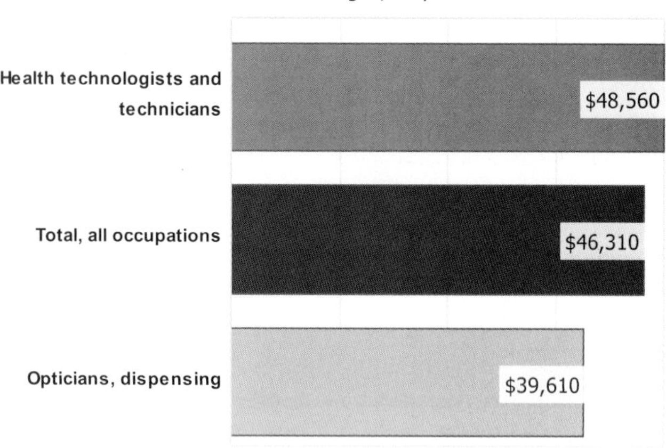

Note: All Occupations includes all occupations in the U.S. Economy.
Source: U.S. Bureau of Labor Statistics, Occupational Employment and Wage Statistics.

Opticians

Percent change in employment, projected 2022-32

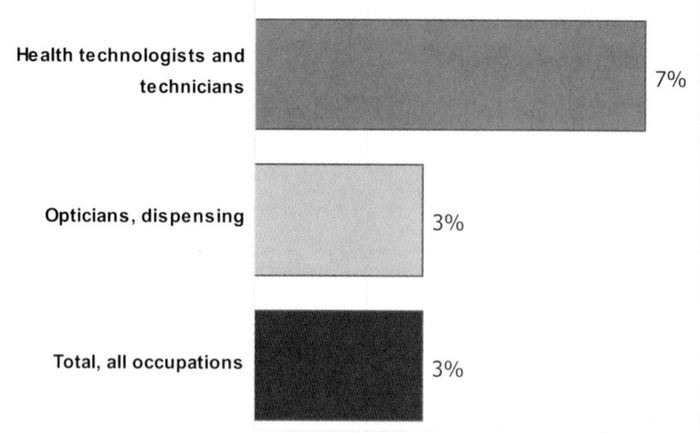

Note: All Occupations includes all occupations in the U.S. Economy.
Source: U.S. Bureau of Labor Statistics, Employment Projections program.

making decisions and have some knowledge of sales and inventory management.

Communication skills. Opticians must listen closely to what customers want. They must clearly explain options and instructions for care in ways that customers understand.

Customer-service skills. Because some opticians work in stores, they must answer questions and know about the products they sell. They interact with customers on a personal level, fitting eyeglasses or contact lenses. To succeed, they must be friendly, courteous, patient, and helpful to customers.

Decision-making skills. Opticians must determine what adjustments need to be made to eyeglasses and contact lenses. They must decide which materials and styles are most appropriate for each customer on the basis of their preferences and lifestyle.

Dexterity. Opticians frequently use special tools to make final adjustments and repairs to eyeglasses. They must have good hand-eye coordination to do that work quickly and accurately.

Pay

The median annual wage for opticians was $39,610 in May 2022. The median wage is the wage at which half the workers in an occupation earned more than that amount and half earned less. The lowest 10 percent earned less than $29,540, and the highest 10 percent earned more than $64,760.

In May 2022, the median annual wages for opticians in the top industries in which they worked were as follows:

Offices of physicians	$44,320
Health and personal care retailers	43,540
Offices of optometrists	37,130

Opticians employed in retail settings may work evenings and weekends. Most opticians work full time, although part-time opportunities also are available.

Job Outlook

Employment of opticians is projected to grow 3 percent from 2022 to 2032, about as fast as the average for all occupations.

About 6,400 openings for opticians are projected each year, on average, over the decade. Many of those openings are expected to result from the need to replace workers who transfer to different occupations or exit the labor force, such as to retire.

Employment

Greater demand for eye-care services is expected because of growth in the number of older people, who usually have more eye problems than younger people.

Increasing rates of chronic diseases also may increase demand for opticianry services because some diseases, such as diabetes, cause vision problems. In addition, opticians will be needed to fill prescriptions for corrective eyewear for people who have eye refraction problems such as myopia and astigmatism.

However, growing consumer interest in purchasing eyewear online may temper employment demand somewhat.

Occupational Title	SOC Code	Employment, 2022	Projected Employment, 2032	Change, 2022-32	
				Percent	Numeric
Opticians, dispensing	29-2081	73,300	75,200	3	2,000

Contacts for More Information

For more information, visit

- American Board of Opticianry and National Contact Lens Examiners
- Commission on Opticianry Accreditation
- National Academy of Opticianry
- National Federation of Opticianry Schools
- Opticians Association of America

Optometrists

Summary

Quick Facts: Optometrists

2022 Median Pay	$125,590 per year $60.38 per hour
Typical Entry-Level Education	Doctoral or professional degree
Work Experience in a Related Occupation	None
On-the-job Training	None
Number of Jobs, 2022	43,400
Job Outlook, 2022-32	9% (Much faster than average)
Employment Change, 2022-32	3,800

What Optometrists Do
Optometrists diagnose, manage, and treat conditions and diseases of the human eye and visual system, including examining eyes and prescribing corrective lenses.

Work Environment
Most optometrists work in offices or in optical goods stores. Optometrists usually work full time, but part-time work is common. Schedules may vary to include evenings and weekends.

How to Become an Optometrist
Optometrists typically need a Doctor of Optometry (O.D.) degree, which take 4 years of graduate-level study to complete. Every state requires optometrists to be licensed.

Pay
The median annual wage for optometrists was $125,590 in May 2022.

Job Outlook
Employment of optometrists is projected to grow 9 percent from 2022 to 2032, much faster than the average for all occupations.

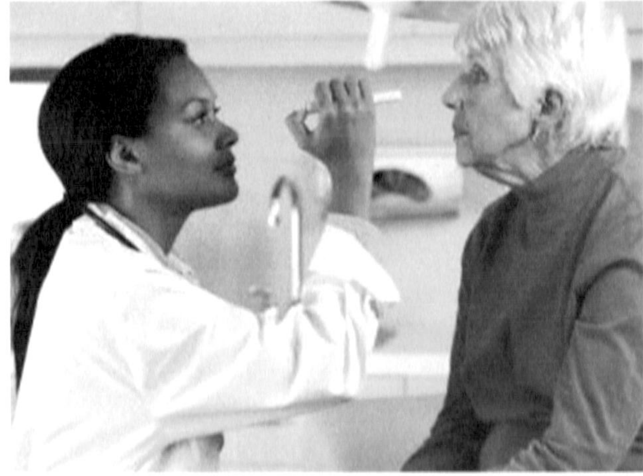

Optometrists diagnose and treat eye problems in children and adults.

About 1,700 openings for optometrists are projected each year, on average, over the decade. Many of those openings are expected to result from the need to replace workers who transfer to different occupations or exit the labor force, such as to retire.

What Optometrists Do
Optometrists diagnose, manage, and treat conditions and diseases of the human eye and visual system, including examining eyes and prescribing corrective lenses.

Duties
Optometrists typically do the following:

- Perform vision tests and analyze results
- Diagnose vision problems, such as nearsightedness or farsightedness, and eye diseases, such as glaucoma
- Prescribe eyeglasses, contact lenses, and other visual aids
- As permitted by state law, perform minor surgical procedures and prescribe medications to correct or treat visual or eye issues
- Provide treatments such as vision therapy or low-vision rehabilitation
- Provide pre- and postoperative care to patients undergoing eye surgery
- Evaluate patients for the presence of other diseases and conditions, such as diabetes or high blood pressure, and refer patients to other healthcare providers as needed
- Promote eye and general health by counseling patients

Optometrists are doctors who focus on eyes and vision. Their tasks range from offering preventive care through routine checkups to providing referrals to other specialists for treatment of health conditions, such as autoimmune diseases, that may lead to serious eye problems.

Some optometrists provide specialized care in addition to general eye care. For example, some optometrists focus on

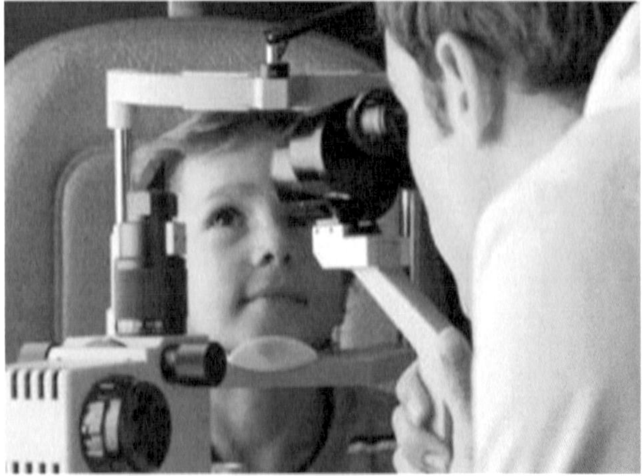

Optometrists check patients for common vision problems, like astigmatism.

treating patients who have partial sight, a condition known as low vision. Others may specialize in treating a certain population, such as infants and children.

Optometrists promote eye health by counseling patients on how general health can affect eyesight. For example, they may counsel patients on how quitting smoking lowers the risk of developing cataracts.

All states allow optometrists to prescribe medication, but states vary in the type of medication they allow optometrists to prescribe. States also vary in whether optometrists may perform surgery or other procedures, such as providing vaccinations.

Optometrists should not be confused with ophthalmologists or opticians. Ophthalmologists are physicians who, like optometrists, treat eye diseases, perform eye exams, and prescribe eyeglasses and contact lenses. However, ophthalmologists perform a wider range of surgeries than optometrists do. For more information about ophthalmologists, see the physicians and surgeons profile. Opticians fit and adjust eyeglasses and, in some states, fill contact lens prescriptions that an optometrist or ophthalmologist has written. For more information, see the opticians profile.

Work Environment

Optometrists held about 43,400 jobs in 2022. The largest employers of optometrists were as follows:

Offices of optometrists	56%
Offices of physicians	17
Self-employed workers	7
Outpatient care centers	4

Optometrists typically work in office settings. This includes offices of optometry and offices of physicians. They also may work in retail settings, such as stores that sell eyeglasses.

Work Schedules

Most optometrists work full time, but part-time work is common. Schedules may vary to include evenings and weekends.

How to Become an Optometrist

Optometrists typically need a Doctor of Optometry (O.D.) degree. O.D. programs take 4 years to complete, and applicants typically have bachelor's degree before entering a program. Every state requires optometrist to be licensed.

Education

Optometrists typically need a Doctor of Optometry (O.D.) degree from a program accredited by the Accreditation Council on Optometric Education. Applicants to these graduate programs must have completed at least 3 years of undergraduate education. However, applicants to O.D. programs typically have a bachelor's degree in a field such as biology or physical science. Programs that do not require a specific field of degree for admissions might require that applicants have completed courses in subjects such as chemistry, physics, and calculus.

Applicants to O.D. programs also must take the Optometry Admission Test (OAT), which covers four subject areas: natural sciences, reading comprehension, physics, and quantitative reasoning.

O.D. programs take 4 years to complete. They include both academic coursework and supervised clinical experience. Coursework includes anatomy, visual science, and the diagnosis and treatment of diseases and disorders of the visual system. During clinical training, students gain experience treating patients in a variety of settings, such as hospitals and private practice.

After finishing an O.D. degree, optometrists may choose to get 1 year of advanced clinical training in the area in which they wish to specialize. Areas of specialization include primary care, cornea and contact lenses, and ocular disease.

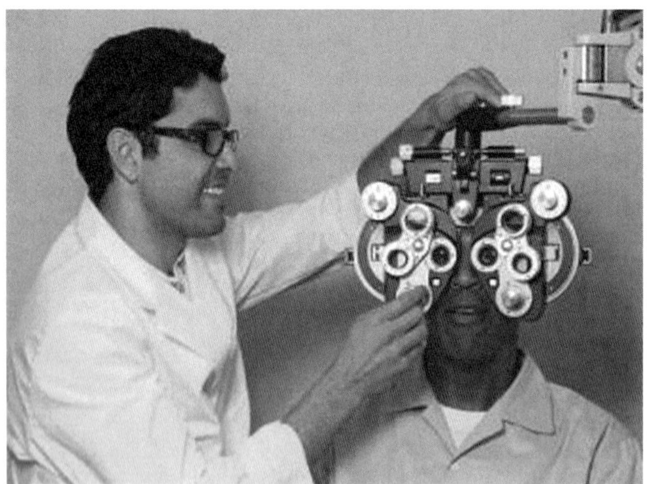

Optometrists work in exam rooms where they use tools to determine patient's prescriptions.

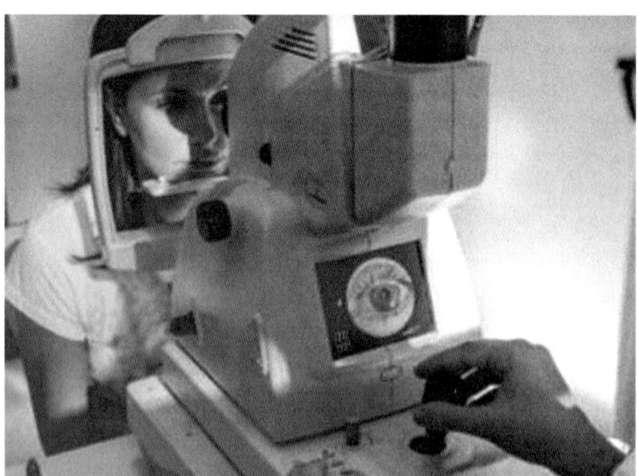

Doctor of Optometry programs combine classroom learning and clinical experience.

Licenses, Certifications, and Registrations

All states require optometrists to be licensed. Prospective optometrist must have an O.D. degree from an accredited optometry school and must complete all sections of the National Board of Examiners in Optometry exam. Some states require candidates to pass an additional exam, such as on clinical skills or on laws relating to optometry.

All states require optometrists to take continuing education classes and to renew their license periodically. For more information, contact the licensing board for the state in which you plan to practice.

Optometrists may obtain an optional credential to become board certified by the American Board of Optometry. This certification requires passing an examination.

Important Qualities

Decision-making skills. Optometrists must evaluate the results of diagnostic tests and decide on the best course of treatment for a patient.

Communication skills. Optometrists must explain diagnosis, treatment, and eye care in a way that patients can understand.

Compassion. Optometrists treat a variety of patients, including those who are frustrated by visual problems. They must be understanding of and sympathetic to their patients' concerns.

Detail oriented. Optometrists must take care to provide appropriate treatment, including accurate prescriptions. They also must monitor and record specific information related to patient care.

Pay

The median annual wage for optometrists was $125,590 in May 2022. The median wage is the wage at which half the workers in an occupation earned more than that amount and half earned less. The lowest 10 percent earned less than $62,150, and the highest 10 percent earned more than $191,430.

In May 2022, the median annual wages for optometrists in the top industries in which they worked were as follows:

Outpatient care centers	$176,400
Offices of physicians	136,510
Offices of optometrists	110,800

Most optometrists work full time, but part-time work is common. Schedules may vary to include evenings and weekends.

Job Outlook

Employment of optometrists is projected to grow 9 percent from 2022 to 2032, much faster than the average for all occupations. About 1,700 openings for optometrists are projected each year, on average, over the decade. Many of those openings are expected to result from the need to replace workers who transfer to different occupations or exit the labor force, such as to retire.

Employment

Because vision problems tend to occur more frequently later in life, an aging population will lead to demand for optometrists. As people age, they become more susceptible to developing diseases that impair vision, such as cataracts and macular degeneration, and will need vision care.

The increasing prevalence of refractive errors, particularly myopia, among the general population is another key source of demand for optometrists as they will be needed to diagnose and treat these common eye problems. Moreover, the growing use of electronic devices has translated into an increasing number of individuals experiencing digital eye strain, which may lead to more demand for eye care services. Meanwhile, diabetes has been linked to increased rates of diabetic retinopathy, a condition that affects the blood vessels in the eye and may lead to

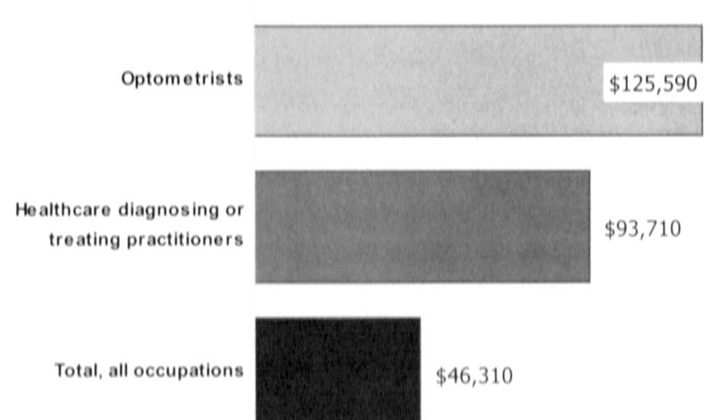

Note: All Occupations includes all occupations in the U.S. Economy.
Source: U.S. Bureau of Labor Statistics, Occupational Employment and Wage Statistics.

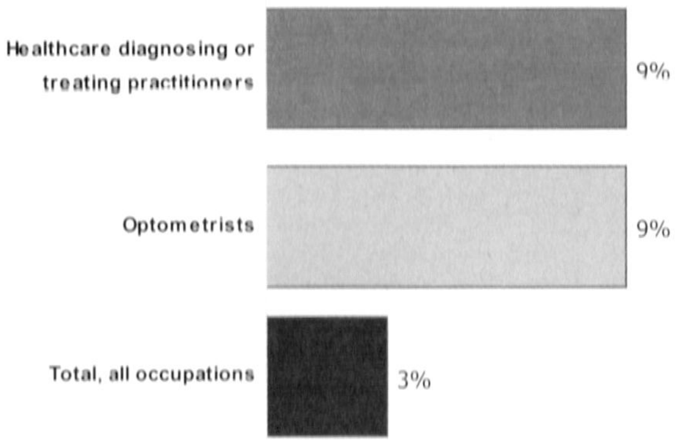

Note: All Occupations includes all occupations in the U.S. Economy.
Source: U.S. Bureau of Labor Statistics, Employment Projections program.

loss of vision. With diabetes on the rise, optometrists will be needed to monitor, treat, and refer these patients.

Occupational Title	SOC Code	Employment, 2022	Projected Employment, 2032	Change, 2022-32	
				Percent	Numeric
Optometrists	29-1041	43,400	47,300	9	3,800

Contacts for More Information

For more information about optometry, visit

- American Optometric Association
- Association of Schools and Colleges of Optometry
- National Boards of Examiners in Optometry
- American Board of Optometry

Orthotists and Prosthetists

Summary

Quick Facts: Orthotists and Prosthetists

2022 Median Pay	$77,070 per year $37.05 per hour
Typical Entry-Level Education	Master's degree
Work Experience in a Related Occupation	None
On-the-job Training	Internship/residency
Number of Jobs, 2022	9,500
Job Outlook, 2022-32	15% (Much faster than average)
Employment Change, 2022-32	1,500

What Orthotists and Prosthetists Do

Orthotists and prosthetists design and fabricate medical supportive devices and measure and fit patients for them.

Work Environment

Orthotists and prosthetists work in various industries, including manufacturing, health and personal care stores, doctors' offices, and hospitals. Most work full time.

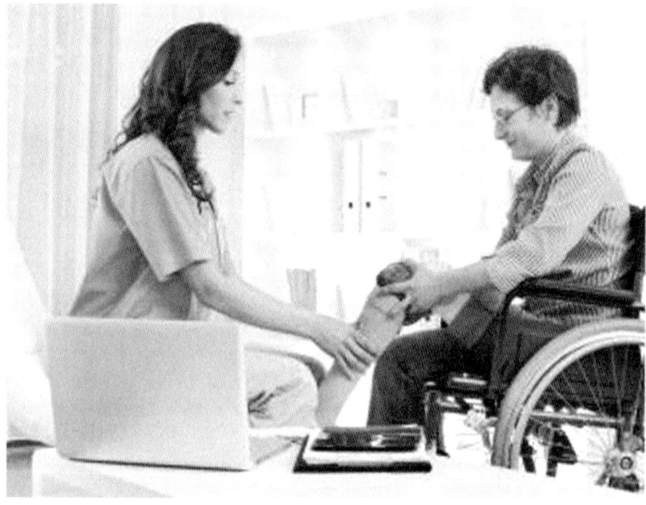

Orthotists and prosthetists fit, test, and adjust orthotic and prosthetic devices.

How to Become an Orthotist and Prosthetist

Orthotists and prosthetists typically need a master's degree and certification to enter the occupation. Both orthotists and prosthetists must complete a residency before they can be certified.

Pay

The median annual wage for orthotists and prosthetists was $77,070 in May 2022.

Job Outlook

Employment of orthotists and prosthetists is projected to grow 15 percent from 2022 to 2032, much faster than the average for all occupations.

Orthotists and prosthetists create devices that allow patients to regain or improve mobility and functionality.

About 800 openings for orthotists and prosthetists are projected each year, on average, over the decade. Many of those openings are expected to result from the need to replace workers who transfer to different occupations or exit the labor force, such as to retire.

What Orthotists and Prosthetists Do

Orthotists and prosthetists design and fabricate medical supportive devices and measure and fit patients for them. These devices include artificial limbs (arms, hands, legs, and feet), braces, and other medical or surgical devices.

Duties

Orthotists and prosthetists typically do the following:

- Evaluate and interview patients to determine their needs
- Take measurements or impressions of the part of a patient's body that will be fitted with a brace or artificial limb
- Design and fabricate orthopedic and prosthetic devices based on physicians' prescriptions
- Select materials to be used for the orthotic or prosthetic device
- Instruct patients in how to use and care for their devices
- Adjust, repair, or replace prosthetic and orthotic devices
- Document care in patients' records

Orthotists and prosthetists evaluate and interview patients to determine their needs.

Orthotists and prosthetists may work in both orthotics and prosthetics, or they may choose to specialize in one area. Orthotists are specifically trained to work with medical supportive devices, such as spinal or knee braces. Prosthetists are specifically trained to work with prostheses, such as artificial limbs and other body parts.

Some orthotists and prosthetists construct devices for their patients. Others supervise the construction of the orthotic or prosthetic devices by medical appliance technicians.

Work Environment

Orthotists and prosthetists held about 9,500 jobs in 2022. The largest employers of orthotists and prosthetists were as follows:

Medical equipment and supplies manufacturing	33%
Ambulatory healthcare services	29
Health and personal care retailers	13
Federal government, excluding postal service	10
Hospitals; state, local, and private	9

Orthotists and prosthetists who fabricate orthotics and prosthetics may be exposed to health or safety hazards when handling certain materials, but there is little risk of injury if workers follow proper procedures, such as wearing goggles, gloves, and masks.

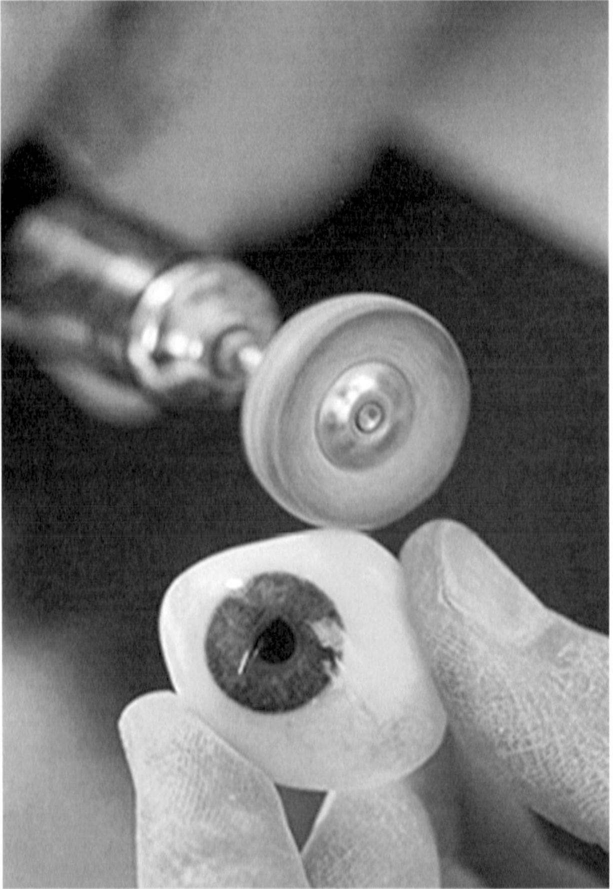

Orthotists and prosthetists must be precise to ensure that devices are fabricated and fit properly.

Work Schedules

Most orthotists and prosthetists work full time.

How to Become an Orthotist and Prosthetist

Orthotists and prosthetists typically need a master's degree and certification to enter the occupation. Both orthotists and prosthetists must complete a residency before they can be certified.

Education

All orthotists and prosthetists must complete a master's degree in orthotics and prosthetics. These programs include courses in upper and lower extremity orthotics and prosthetics, spinal orthotics, and plastics and other materials used for fabrication. In addition, orthotics and prosthetics programs have a clinical component in which the student works under the direction of an orthotist or prosthetist.

Master's programs usually take 2 years to complete. Prospective students seeking a master's degree may have a bachelor's degree in any discipline if they have fulfilled prerequisite courses in science and math. Requirements vary by program.

Orthotics and prosthetics programs are accredited by the Commission on Accreditation of Allied Health Education Programs (CAAHEP).

Training

Following graduation from a master's degree program, candidates must complete a residency that has been accredited by the National Commission on Orthotic and Prosthetic Education (NCOPE). Candidates typically complete a 1-year residency program in either orthotics or prosthetics. Individuals who want to become certified in both orthotics and prosthetics need to complete 1 year of residency training for each specialty or an 18-month residency in both orthotics and prosthetics.

Licenses, Certifications, and Registrations

Some states require orthotists and prosthetists to be licensed. States that license orthotists and prosthetists often require certification in order for them to practice, although requirements vary by state. Many orthotists and prosthetists become certified regardless of state requirements, because certification demonstrates competence.

The American Board for Certification in Orthotics, Prosthetics & Pedorthics (ABC) offers certification for orthotists and prosthetists. To earn certification, a candidate must complete a CAAHEP-accredited master's program, an NCOPE-accredited residency program, and pass a series of three exams.

Important Qualities

Communication skills. Orthotists and prosthetists must be able to communicate effectively with the technicians who often fabricate the medical devices. They must also be able to explain to patients how to use and care for the devices.

Orthotists and Prosthetists

Median annual wages, May 2022

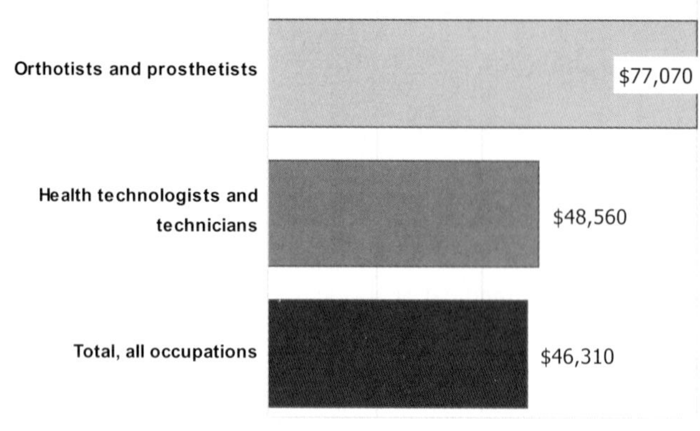

Note: All Occupations includes all occupations in the U.S. Economy.
Source: U.S. Bureau of Labor Statistics, Occupational Employment and Wage Statistics.

Detail oriented. Orthotists and prosthetists must be precise when recording measurements to ensure that devices are fabricated and fit properly.

Patience. Orthotists and prosthetists may work for long periods with patients who need special attention.

Physical dexterity. Orthotists and prosthetists must be good at working with their hands. They may fabricate orthotics or prosthetics with intricate mechanical parts.

Physical stamina. Orthotists and prosthetists should be comfortable performing physical tasks, such as working with shop equipment and hand tools. They may spend a lot of time bending over or crouching to examine or measure patients.

Problem-solving skills. Orthotists and prosthetists must evaluate their patients' situations and often look for creative solutions to their rehabilitation needs.

Pay

The median annual wage for orthotists and prosthetists was $77,070 in May 2022. The median wage is the wage at which half the workers in an occupation earned more than that amount and half earned less. The lowest 10 percent earned less than $40,360, and the highest 10 percent earned more than $110,120.

In May 2022, the median annual wages for orthotists and prosthetists in the top industries in which they worked were as follows:

Ambulatory healthcare services	$79,870
Medical equipment and supplies manufacturing	79,750
Federal government, excluding postal service	79,440
Health and personal care retailers	64,100
Hospitals; state, local, and private	58,740

Most orthotists and prosthetists work full time.

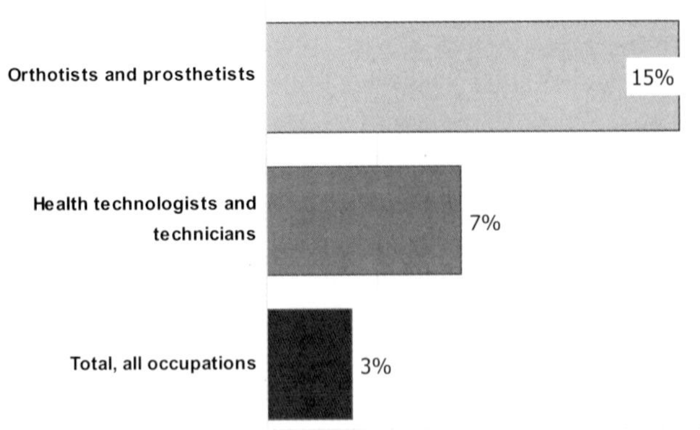

Note: All Occupations includes all occupations in the U.S. Economy. Source: U.S. Bureau of Labor Statistics, Employment Projections program.

Job Outlook

Employment of orthotists and prosthetists is projected to grow 15 percent from 2022 to 2032, much faster than the average for all occupations.

About 800 openings for orthotists and prosthetists are projected each year, on average, over the decade. Many of those openings are expected to result from the need to replace workers who transfer to different occupations or exit the labor force, such as to retire.

Employment

Demand for orthotists and prosthetists is projected to rise due to the aging population, the growing prevalence of obesity and diabetes, and the continued occurrence of trauma events.

The growing size of the older population and the consequent rise in age-related health issues, such as osteoarthritis and injuries from falls, will increase the need for devices that help improve bodily function and relieve pain. In addition, rising obesity rates will place greater demand on orthoses to alleviate foot and heel pain, and prosthetic care will be needed to address amputations and other complications from diabetes.

Trauma event survivors, such as those who have experienced industrial or car accidents, will need orthotic and prosthetic care to regain or improve mobility.

Occupational Title	SOC Code	Employment, 2022	Projected Employment, 2032	Change, 2022-32	
				Percent	Numeric
Orthotists and prosthetists	29-2091	9,500	10,900	15	1,500

Contacts for More Information

For more information about orthotists and prosthetists, visit

- American Academy of Orthotists & Prosthetists
- Board of Certification/Accreditation
- Commission on Accreditation of Allied Health Education Programs
- National Commission on Orthotic and Prosthetic Education
- American Board for Certification in Orthotics, Prosthetics & Pedorthics

Pharmacists

Summary

Quick Facts: Pharmacists	
2022 Median Pay	$132,750 per year $63.82 per hour
Typical Entry-Level Education	Doctoral or professional degree
Work Experience in a Related Occupation	None
On-the-job Training	None
Number of Jobs, 2022	334,200
Job Outlook, 2022-32	3% (As fast as average)
Employment Change, 2022-32	8,700

What Pharmacists Do

Pharmacists dispense prescription medications and provide information to patients about the drugs and their use.

Work Environment

Pharmacists work in pharmacies, including those in drug, general merchandise, and grocery stores. They also work in hospitals and other healthcare facilities that are open 24 hours. Most pharmacists work full time, and some work nights, weekends, and holidays.

How to Become a Pharmacist

Pharmacists typically need a Doctor of Pharmacy (Pharm.D.) degree. Every state requires pharmacists to be licensed.

Pharmacists fill prescriptions and instruct customers on the safe use of medications.

Pay

The median annual wage for pharmacists was $132,750 in May 2022.

Job Outlook

Employment of pharmacists is projected to grow 3 percent from 2022 to 2032, about as fast as the average for all occupations.

About 13,400 openings for pharmacists are projected each year, on average, over the decade. Many of those openings are expected to result from the need to replace workers who transfer to different occupations or exit the labor force, such as to retire.

What Pharmacists Do

Pharmacists dispense prescription medications and provide information to patients about the drugs and their use. They also advise physicians and other healthcare workers on the selection, dosage, interactions, and side effects of medications to treat health problems. They may help patients with their overall health through activities such as providing immunizations.

Duties

Pharmacists typically do the following:

- Fill prescriptions to the proper amount based on physicians' instructions
- Check patients' allergies, medical conditions, and other drugs they are taking to ensure that the newly prescribed medication does not cause adverse reaction
- Instruct patients on proper use, side effects, and storage of prescribed medicine
- Administer vaccinations, such as flu shots
- Advise patients about general health topics, such as exercise and managing stress, and on other issues, such as what equipment or supplies would be best to treat a health problem
- Work with insurance companies to resolve billing issues
- Supervise the work of pharmacy technicians and pharmacists in training (interns)

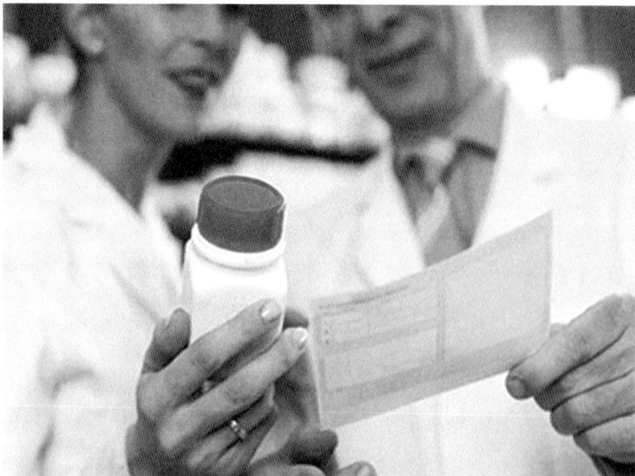

Pharmacists review the accuracy of each filled prescription before it is given to the customer.

- Maintain patient and pharmacy records
- Educate other healthcare workers about proper medication therapies for patients

Pharmacists verify instructions from physicians to fill and dispense prescription medications. For many drugs, pharmacists use standard dosages from pharmaceutical companies. However, pharmacists also may create customized medications by mixing ingredients themselves, a process known as compounding.

Pharmacists usually have a variety of other duties. In addition to answering patients' questions about their prescriptions, for example, pharmacists may advise about or assist with topics of general health or the use of over-the-counter medications. Pharmacists also may have administrative responsibilities, including keeping records and managing inventory.

The following are examples of types of pharmacists:

Community pharmacists work in retail settings such as chain drug stores or independently owned pharmacies. They dispense medications to patients and answer any questions that patients may have about prescriptions, over-the-counter medications, or health concerns. They also may provide some primary care services such as giving flu shots and performing health screenings.

Clinical pharmacists work in hospitals, clinics, and other healthcare settings where they provide direct patient care. They may go on rounds in a hospital with a physician or healthcare team. Additionally, they recommend medications to patients and oversee the dosage and timing of the delivery of those medications. They also evaluate the effectiveness of drugs and a patient's progress. Clinical pharmacists may conduct certain medical tests and offer advice to patients. For example, pharmacists may earn credentials to work in a diabetes clinic, where they counsel patients on how and when to take medications, suggest healthy food choices, and monitor patients' blood sugar.

Consultant pharmacists advise healthcare facilities or insurance providers on patient medication use. They may give advice directly to patients, such as helping seniors manage their prescriptions. Consultant pharmacists also advise facilities on improving services to ensure compliance with state and federal regulations.

Pharmaceutical industry pharmacists work in areas such as marketing, sales, or research and development. Their work includes designing or conducting clinical trials of new drugs. They may also help to establish safety regulations and ensure quality control for drugs.

Work Environment

Pharmacists held about 334,200 jobs in 2022. The largest employers of pharmacists were as follows:

Pharmacies and drug retailers	42%
Hospitals; state, local, and private	27
General merchandise retailers	6
Ambulatory healthcare services	6

Pharmacists may consult with physicians if they have questions concerning a patient's prescription.

Pharmacists must pay attention to detail, ensuring the accuracy of the prescriptions they fill.

Pharmacists collaborate on patient care with other healthcare workers, including physicians and surgeons, physician assistants, and nurse practitioners.

Pharmacists spend much of their workday standing. Their work may expose them to harmful substances, but following safety protocol and wearing lab coats, gloves, and other protective gear reduces the risk of injury or illness.

Work Schedules

Most pharmacists work full time. In hospitals and other facilities that are open 24 hours, pharmacists may work nights, weekends, and holidays.

How to Become a Pharmacist

Pharmacists typically need a Doctor of Pharmacy (Pharm.D.) degree from an accredited pharmacy program. Every state requires pharmacists to be licensed.

Education

Pharmacists typically need a Doctor of Pharmacy (Pharm.D.) degree from an accredited pharmacy program. (A list of accredited programs is available from the Accreditation Council for Pharmacy Education (ACPE).)

Admission requirements vary; however, Pharm.D. programs typically require applicants to have at least 2 years of prerequisite undergraduate courses in subjects such as anatomy and physiology, physics, and statistics. Some Pharm.D. programs require or prefer that applicants have a bachelor's degree in biology, a healthcare and related, or a physical science field, such as chemistry.

Pharm.D. programs usually take 4 years to finish, although some programs offer a 3-year option. Others admit high school graduates into a 6-year program. Pharm.D. programs include courses in sciences, pharmacology, and pharmacy law. Students also complete supervised work experiences, sometimes referred to as internships, in settings such as hospitals and retail pharmacies.

Some pharmacy programs offer a dual-degree option. These programs allow students to get another graduate degree, such as a master's degree in business administration (MBA) or a master's degree in public health (MPH), along with their Pharm.D. degree.

Training

Following graduation from a Pharm.D. program, pharmacists seeking a clinical or other advanced position may opt to complete a residency or fellowship. These program typically last 1 to 2 years and provide additional training and research opportunities. Pharmacists who choose a 2-year residency program train in a specialty area such as cardiology, internal medicine, or pediatric care.

Licenses, Certifications, and Registrations

All states require pharmacists to be licensed, although licensure requirements vary. After completing their degree, prospective pharmacists typically must pass two exams to get a license. The North American Pharmacist Licensure Exam (NAPLEX) tests pharmacy skills and knowledge and is required in all states.

The Multistate Pharmacy Jurisprudence Exam (MPJE) or state-specific test on pharmacy law is also required. Applicants also must complete a state-specified number of hours as an intern. To maintain licensure, pharmacists must complete continuing education.

In most states, pharmacists must be certified to administer vaccinations. For information about certification, see the American Pharmacists Association's Pharmacy-Based Immunization Delivery program.

Pharmacists may choose to earn a certification to show advanced knowledge in a specific field. For example, a pharmacist may become a Certified Diabetes Care and Education Specialist, a credential offered by the Certification Board for Diabetes Care and Education, or earn certification in a specialty area, such as emergency care or oncology, from the Board of Pharmacy Specialties. Certifications from both organizations generally require applicants to have work experience and pass an exam.

Important Qualities

Analytical skills. Pharmacists must evaluate the contents and side effects of prescribed medication to ensure that the patient may safely take it.

Communication skills. Pharmacists frequently must explain to patients about how to take medication and what its potential side effects are. They also may need to convey information to pharmacy technicians, interns, and other healthcare staff.

Compassion. Pharmacists often work with people who have health issues. They must be sympathetic to patients' problems and needs.

Detail oriented. Pharmacists are responsible for accurately providing the appropriate medication for each patient.

Interpersonal skills. Pharmacists spend much of their time interacting with patients and as part of a healthcare team coordinating patient care.

Managerial skills. Pharmacists, particularly those who run a retail pharmacy, must have good leadership skills. These skills include ability to oversee inventory and direct staff.

Pay

The median annual wage for pharmacists was $132,750 in May 2022. The median wage is the wage at which half the workers in an occupation earned more than that amount and half earned less. The lowest 10 percent earned less than $79,950, and the highest 10 percent earned more than $164,230.

In May 2022, the median annual wages for pharmacists in the top industries in which they worked were as follows:

General merchandise retailers	$139,680
Ambulatory healthcare services	138,720
Hospitals; state, local, and private	137,440
Pharmacies and drug retailers	129,920

Most pharmacists work full time. In hospitals and other facilities that are open 24 hours, pharmacists may work nights, weekends, and holidays.

Job Outlook

Employment of pharmacists is projected to grow 3 percent from 2022 to 2032, about as fast as the average for all occupations.

About 13,400 openings for pharmacists are projected each year, on average, over the decade. Many of those openings are expected to result from the need to replace workers who

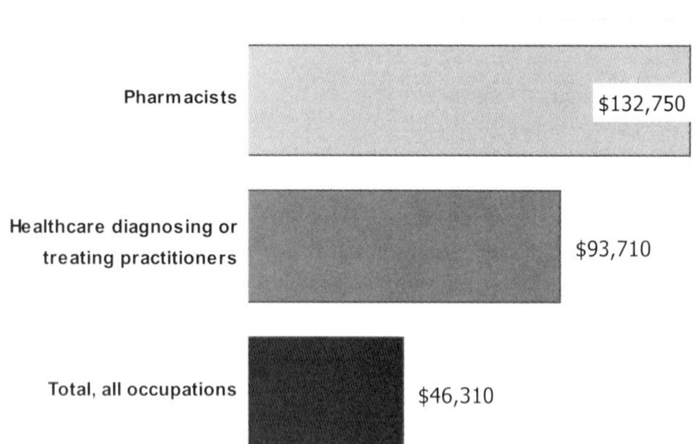

Note: All Occupations includes all occupations in the U.S. Economy.
Source: U.S. Bureau of Labor Statistics, Occupational Employment and Wage Statistics.

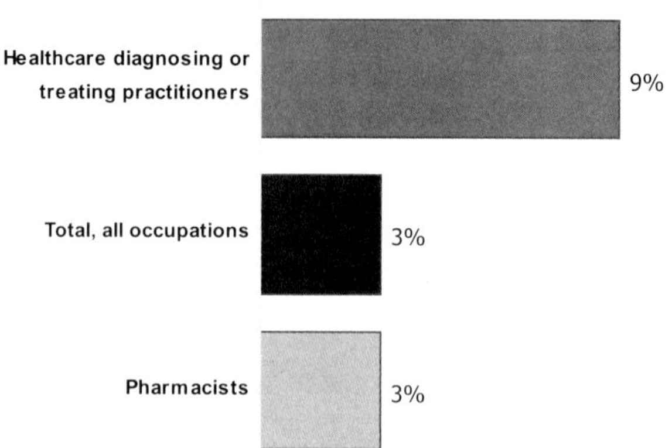

Note: All Occupations includes all occupations in the U.S. Economy.
Source: U.S. Bureau of Labor Statistics, Employment Projections program.

transfer to different occupations or exit the labor force, such as to retire.

Employment

Demand is projected to increase for pharmacists in some healthcare settings, such as in hospitals and clinics. As the roles of pharmacists expand beyond traditional drug-dispensing duties, these workers increasingly will be integrated into healthcare teams to provide medication management and other patient care services in these facilities.

Meanwhile, many pharmacists work in retail pharmacies, which includes independent and chain drug stores as well as supermarket and mass merchandiser pharmacies. Fewer pharmacist jobs are expected in these settings as the industry consolidates and more people fill their prescriptions online or by mail.

Occupational Title	SOC Code	Employment, 2022	Projected Employment, 2032	Change, 2022-32	
				Percent	Numeric
Pharmacists	29-1051	334,200	342,900	3	8,700

Contacts for More Information

For more information about pharmacists, visit

- American College of Clinical Pharmacy
- American Pharmacists Association
- American Society of Health-System Pharmacists
- National Association of Chain Drug Stores
- American Association of Colleges of Pharmacy
- Accreditation Council for Pharmacy Education
- Board of Pharmacy Specialties
- Certification Board for Diabetes Care and Education

Pharmacy Technicians

Summary

Quick Facts: Pharmacy Technicians	
2022 Median Pay	$37,790 per year $18.17 per hour
Typical Entry-Level Education	High school diploma or equivalent
Work Experience in a Related Occupation	None
On-the-job Training	Moderate-term on-the-job training
Number of Jobs, 2022	459,600
Job Outlook, 2022-32	6% (Faster than average)
Employment Change, 2022-32	25,900

What Pharmacy Technicians Do

Pharmacy technicians help pharmacists dispense prescription medication to customers or health professionals.

Pharmacy technicians measure amounts of medication for prescriptions.

Work Environment

Pharmacy technicians work in pharmacies, including those found in drug, general merchandise, and grocery stores, and in hospitals. Most work full time, but many work part time.

How to Become a Pharmacy Technician

Pharmacy technicians usually need a high school diploma or equivalent and learn their duties through on-the-job training, or they may complete a postsecondary education program in pharmacy technology. Most states regulate pharmacy technicians, which is a process that may require passing an exam or completing a formal education or training program.

Pay

The median annual wage for pharmacy technicians was $37,790 in May 2022.

Job Outlook

Employment of pharmacy technicians is projected to grow 6 percent from 2022 to 2032, faster than the average for all occupations.

Pharmacy technicians fill prescriptions and check inventory.

About 44,900 openings for pharmacy technicians are projected each year, on average, over the decade. Many of those openings are expected to result from the need to replace workers who transfer to different occupations or exit the labor force, such as to retire.

What Pharmacy Technicians Do

Pharmacy technicians help pharmacists dispense prescription medication to customers or health professionals. They mainly work in retail pharmacies and hospitals.

Duties

Pharmacy technicians typically do the following:

- Collect information needed to fill a prescription from customers or health professionals
- Measure amounts of medication for prescriptions
- Package and label prescriptions
- Organize inventory and alert pharmacists to any shortages of medications or supplies
- Accept payment for prescriptions and process insurance claims
- Enter customer or patient information, including any prescriptions taken, into a computer system
- Answer phone calls from customers
- Arrange for customers to speak with pharmacists if customers have questions about medications or health matters

Pharmacy technicians work primarily in pharmacies, including those found in grocery and drug stores, and in hospitals.

Pharmacy technicians work under the supervision of pharmacists, who must review prescriptions before they are given to patients. In most states, technicians can compound or mix some medications and call physicians for prescription refill authorizations. Technicians also may need to operate automated dispensing equipment when filling prescription orders.

Pharmacy technicians working in hospitals and other medical facilities prepare a greater variety of medications, such as intravenous medications. They may make rounds in the hospital, giving medications to patients.

Work Environment

Pharmacy technicians held about 459,600 jobs in 2022. The largest employers of pharmacy technicians were as follows:

Pharmacies and drug retailers	52%
Hospitals; state, local, and private	16

Pharmacy technicians spend most of the workday on their feet.

Work Schedules

Most pharmacy technicians work full time. Pharmacies may be open at all hours. Therefore, pharmacy technicians may have to work nights or weekends.

How to Become a Pharmacy Technician

Pharmacy technicians usually need a high school diploma or equivalent and learn their duties through on-the-job training, or they may complete a postsecondary education program in pharmacy technology. Most states regulate pharmacy technicians, which is a process that may require passing an exam or completing a formal education or training program.

Education and Training

Pharmacy technicians usually need a high school diploma or equivalent and typically learn their duties through on-the-job training. The training periods vary in length and subject matter according to the employer's requirements.

Pharmacy technicians spend much of their time interacting with customers.

Other pharmacy technicians enter the occupation after completing postsecondary education programs in pharmacy technology. These programs are usually offered by vocational schools or community colleges. Most programs award a certificate after 1 year or less, although some programs last longer and lead to an associate's degree. They cover a variety of subjects, such as arithmetic used in pharmacies, recordkeeping, ways of dispensing medications, and pharmacy law and ethics. Technicians also learn the names, uses, and doses of medications. Most programs also include clinical experience opportunities, in which students gain hands-on experience in a pharmacy.

The American Society of Health-System Pharmacists (ASHP) accredits pharmacy technician programs that include at least 600 hours of instruction over a minimum of 15 weeks. In 2017, there were 309 fully accredited programs, including a few in retail drugstore chains.

Licenses, Certifications, and Registrations

Most states regulate pharmacy technicians in some way. Consult state Boards of Pharmacy for particular regulations. Requirements for pharmacy technicians in the states that regulate them typically include some or all of the following:

- High school diploma or GED
- Formal education or training program
- Exam
- Fees
- Continuing education
- Criminal background check

Some states and employers require pharmacy technicians to be certified. Even where it is not required, certification may make it easier to get a job. Many employers of pharmacy technicians will pay for employees to take the certification exam.

Two organizations offer certification. The Pharmacy Technician Certification Board (PTCB) certification requires a high school diploma and the passing of an exam. Applicants for the National Healthcareer Association (NHA) certification must be at least 18 years old, have a high school diploma, and have completed a training program or have 1 year of work experience. Technicians must recertify every 2 years by completing 20 hours of continuing education courses.

Important Qualities

Customer-service skills. Pharmacy technicians spend much of their time interacting with customers, so being helpful and polite is required of pharmacy technicians in a retail setting.

Detail oriented. Serious health problems can result from mistakes in filling prescriptions. Although the pharmacist is responsible for ensuring the safety of all medications dispensed, pharmacy technicians should pay attention to detail so that complications are avoided.

Listening skills. Pharmacy technicians must communicate clearly with pharmacists and doctors when taking prescription orders. When speaking with customers, technicians must listen carefully to understand customers' needs and determine if they need to speak with a pharmacist.

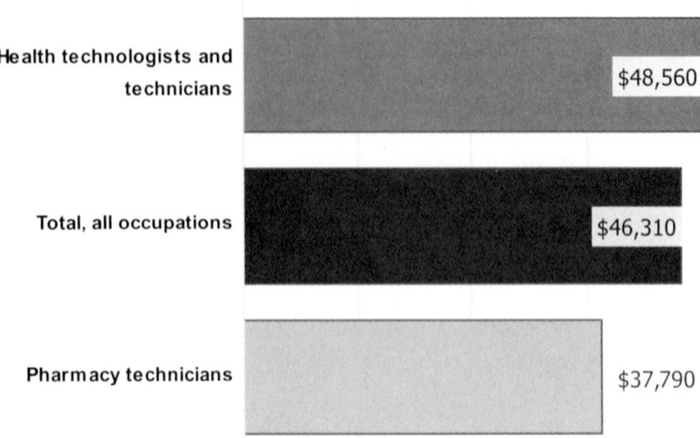

Note: All Occupations includes all occupations in the U.S. Economy.
Source: U.S. Bureau of Labor Statistics, Occupational Employment and Wage Statistics.

Math skills. Pharmacy technicians need to have an understanding of the math concepts used in pharmacies when counting pills and compounding medications.

Organizational skills. Working as a pharmacy technician involves balancing a variety of responsibilities. Pharmacy technicians need good organizational skills to complete the work delegated by pharmacists while at the same time providing service to customers or patients.

Pay

The median annual wage for pharmacy technicians was $37,790 in May 2022. The median wage is the wage at which half the workers in an occupation earned more than that amount and half earned less. The lowest 10 percent earned less than $29,640, and the highest 10 percent earned more than $50,640.

In May 2022, the median annual wages for pharmacy technicians in the top industries in which they worked were as follows:

Hospitals; state, local, and private	$45,300
Pharmacies and drug retailers	36,360

Most pharmacy technicians work full time. Pharmacies may be open at all hours. Therefore, pharmacy technicians may have to work nights or weekends.

Job Outlook

Employment of pharmacy technicians is projected to grow 6 percent from 2022 to 2032, faster than the average for all occupations.

About 44,900 openings for pharmacy technicians are projected each year, on average, over the decade. Many of those openings

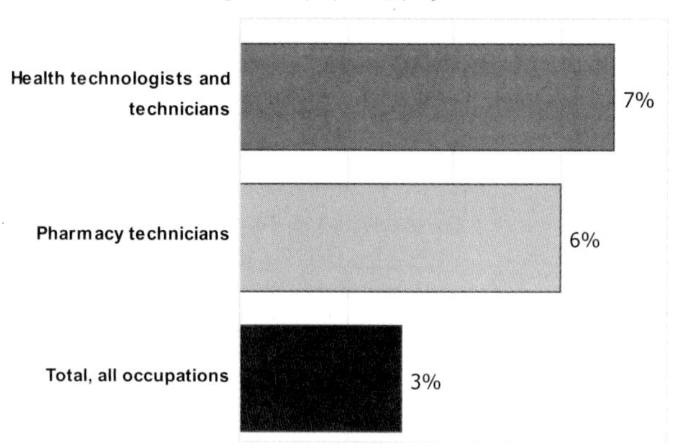

Note: All Occupations includes all occupations in the U.S. Economy.
Source: U.S. Bureau of Labor Statistics, Employment Projections program.

are expected to result from the need to replace workers who transfer to different occupations or exit the labor force, such as to retire.

Employment

Demand for pharmacy services is expected to increase because of the large number of older people, who typically use more prescription medicines than younger people. Higher rates of chronic diseases, such as diabetes, among all age groups also will lead to increased demand for prescription medications.

In addition, pharmacy technicians will be needed to take on a greater role in pharmacy operations because pharmacists are increasingly performing more patient care activities. Technicians will need to perform tasks—such as collecting patient information, handling prescription transfers, and verifying the work of other technicians—that were previously done by pharmacists.

Occupational Title	SOC Code	Employment, 2022	Projected Employment, 2032	Change, 2022-32	
				Percent	Numeric
Pharmacy technicians	29-2052	459,600	485,500	6	25,900

Contacts for More Information

For more information about accredited pharmacy technician programs, visit

- American Society of Health-System Pharmacists
- National Association of Boards of Pharmacy
- For more information about certification, visit
- Pharmacy Technician Certification Board
- National Healthcareer Association

Phlebotomists

Summary

Quick Facts: Phlebotomists	
2022 Median Pay	$38,530 per year $18.53 per hour
Typical Entry-Level Education	Postsecondary nondegree award
Work Experience in a Related Occupation	None
On-the-job Training	None
Number of Jobs, 2022	139,400
Job Outlook, 2022-32	8% (Faster than average)
Employment Change, 2022-32	10,800

What Phlebotomists Do

Phlebotomists draw blood for tests, transfusions, research, or blood donations.

Work Environment

Phlebotomists are employed in a variety of settings, including hospitals, medical and diagnostic laboratories, blood donor centers, and doctors' offices.

How to Become a Phlebotomist

Phlebotomists typically enter the occupation with a certificate from a postsecondary phlebotomy program, but some qualify with a high school diploma and on-the-job training. Employers may prefer to hire candidates who have earned professional certification.

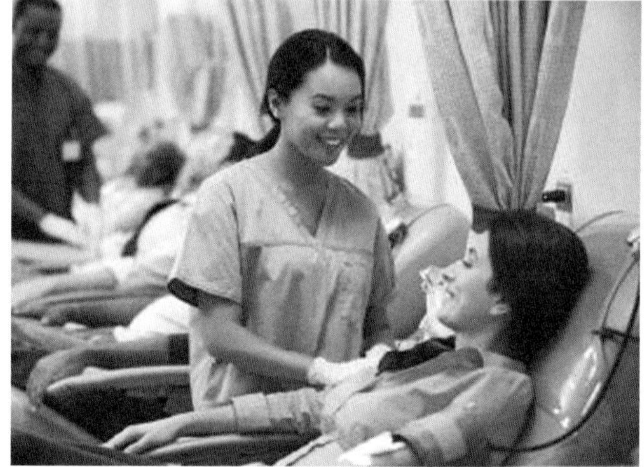

Phlebotomists draw blood for tests, transfusions, research, or blood donations.

Pay

The median annual wage for phlebotomists was $38,530 in May 2022.

Job Outlook

Employment of phlebotomists is projected to grow 8 percent from 2022 to 2032, faster than the average for all occupations.

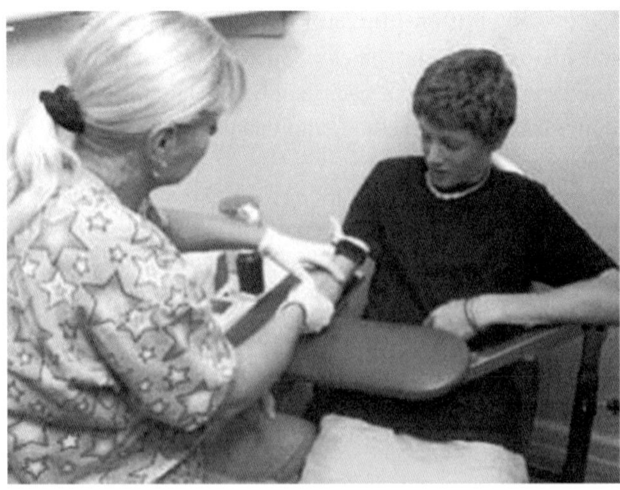

Phlebotomists talk with patients and donors so they are less nervous about having their blood drawn.

About 19,500 openings for phlebotomists are projected each year, on average, over the decade. Many of those openings are expected to result from the need to replace workers who transfer to different occupations or exit the labor force, such as to retire.

What Phlebotomists Do

Phlebotomists draw blood for purposes such as tests, research, or donations. They help patients or donors who are anxious before or have an adverse reaction after the blood draw.

Duties

Phlebotomists typically do the following:

- Draw blood from patients or blood donors
- Explain their work to help relax patients or donors who feel nervous about having blood drawn
- Verify a patient's or donor's identity
- Label the collected blood for testing or processing
- Label sterile containers for other samples, such as urine, and instruct patients on proper collection procedures.
- Enter sample information into a database
- Assemble, maintain, and dispose of medical instruments such as needles, test tubes, and blood vials
- Keep work areas and equipment clean and sanitary

Phlebotomists primarily draw blood, which is then used for different kinds of medical laboratory testing or for procedures, such as transfusions. In medical and diagnostic laboratories, patients sometimes interact only with the phlebotomist. In donation centers or locations that have blood drives, phlebotomists draw blood from donors. Because all blood looks the same, phlebotomists must carefully identify and label the blood they have collected and enter the information into a database.

In addition to drawing blood, phlebotomists also may collect urine or other samples. They instruct patients on procedures for proper collection and ensure that the sample is acceptable and clearly labeled in its container.

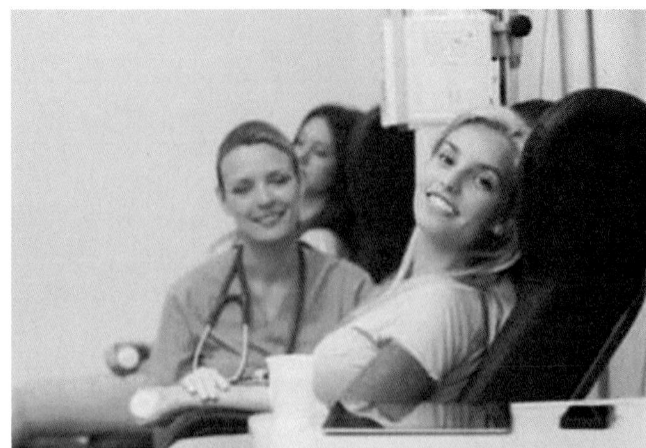

Phlebotomists work mainly in hospitals, medical and diagnostic laboratories, and doctor's offices.

Phlebotomists must keep their work area and instruments clean and sanitary to avoid causing infections or other complications. Some phlebotomists also ship or transport blood or other samples to different locations.

Work Environment

Phlebotomists held about 139,400 jobs in 2022. The largest employers of phlebotomists were as follows:

Hospitals; state, local, and private	34%
Medical and diagnostic laboratories	34
All other ambulatory healthcare services	15
Offices of physicians	7
Outpatient care centers	2

Phlebotomists who collect blood donations sometimes travel to different offices or sites in order to set up mobile donation centers. Some phlebotomists travel to long-term care centers or patients' homes.

Phlebotomists may be required to stand for long periods of time.

Injuries and Illnesses

Phlebotomists must be careful when handling blood, needles, and other medical supplies. Injuries may occur if they are not careful with medical equipment.

Work Schedules

Most phlebotomists work full time. Phlebotomists who work in hospitals and labs may need to work nights, weekends, and holidays.

How to Become a Phlebotomist

Phlebotomists typically enter the occupation with a certificate from a postsecondary phlebotomy program, but some qualify with a high school diploma and on-the-job training. Employers

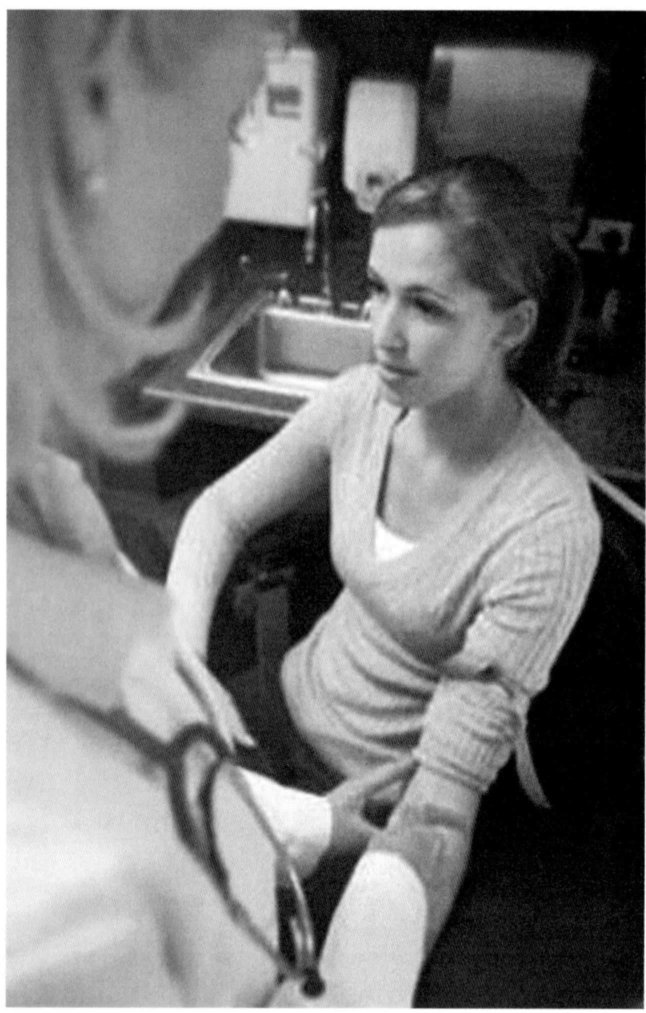

Many employers look for phlebotomists who have completed some kind of professional certification.

may prefer to hire candidates who have earned professional certification.

Education and Training

Phlebotomists typically enter the occupation with a postsecondary nondegree award from a phlebotomy program. These programs are available from community colleges, vocational schools, or technical schools and usually take less than 1 year to complete. They involve instruction in anatomy, physiology, and medical terminology and laboratory work and lead to a certificate.

The National Accrediting Agency for Clinical Laboratory Sciences (NAACLS) and the American Society for Clinical Pathology (ASCP) are among the organizations that accredit phlebotomy education programs.

Some employers hire candidates with a high school diploma and train them on the job. Whether through formal education or employer-provided training, the training that all phlebotomists receive includes instruction on how to identify, label, and track blood samples.

Licenses, Certifications, and Registrations

States may require that phlebotomists complete an accredited training program, have a license or certification, or meet other requirements. For specific requirements, contact your state licensing agency.

Some employers prefer to hire phlebotomists who have earned professional certification, such as those offered by professional organizations. Requirements vary by organization but may include education and clinical experience, passing an exam, and practical components, such as drawing blood.

Phlebotomists also may need to have Basic Life Support certification. Those who transport samples may need a driver's license.

Important Qualities

Communication skills. Phlebotomists must be able to clearly explain procedures and provide instruction to patients.

Compassion. Some patients become anxious about having blood drawn, so phlebotomists should be considerate in performing their duties.

Detail oriented. Phlebotomists must draw the correct amount of blood for the tests ordered, carefully label the vials collected, and enter information into a database to avoid misplacing samples or injuring patients.

Dexterity. Phlebotomists must be able to use their equipment efficiently to minimize patients' discomfort.

Interpersonal skills. Phlebotomists work with other members of the medical staff and must interact with them cooperatively.

Physical stamina. Phlebotomists stand for long periods and are often on the move throughout the workday.

Pay

The median annual wage for phlebotomists was $38,530 in May 2022. The median wage is the wage at which half the workers

Phlebotomists

Median annual wages, May 2022

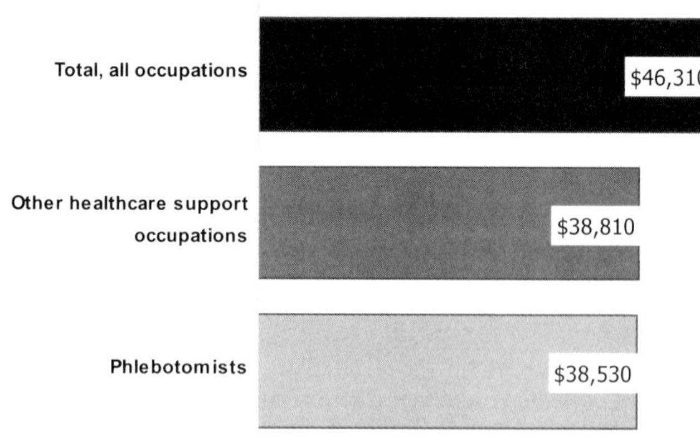

Note: All Occupations includes all occupations in the U.S. Economy.
Source: U.S. Bureau of Labor Statistics, Occupational Employment and Wage Statistics.

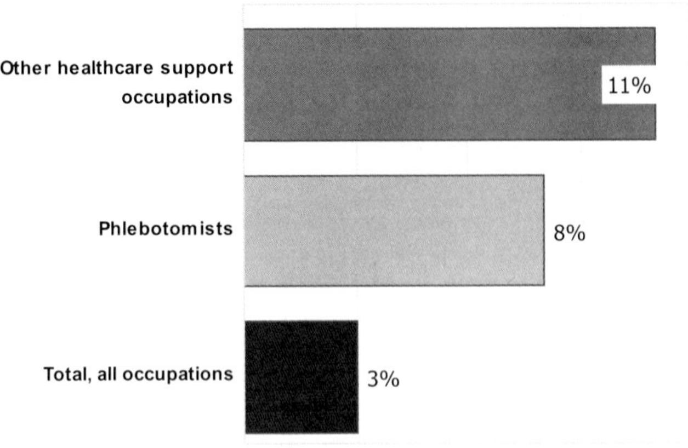

Note: All Occupations includes all occupations in the U.S. Economy.
Source: U.S. Bureau of Labor Statistics, Employment Projections program.

in an occupation earned more than that amount and half earned less. The lowest 10 percent earned less than $30,250, and the highest 10 percent earned more than $51,610.

In May 2022, the median annual wages for phlebotomists in the top industries in which they worked were as follows:

Outpatient care centers	$42,750
Medical and diagnostic laboratories	41,580
Hospitals; state, local, and private	37,400
Offices of physicians	36,970
All other ambulatory healthcare services	36,190

Most phlebotomists work full time. Phlebotomists who work in hospitals and labs may need to work nights, weekends, and holidays.

Job Outlook

Employment of phlebotomists is projected to grow 8 percent from 2022 to 2032, faster than the average for all occupations.

About 19,500 openings for phlebotomists are projected each year, on average, over the decade. Many of those openings are expected to result from the need to replace workers who transfer to different occupations or exit the labor force, such as to retire.

Employment

The growing population, with its rising share of older people, will continue to increase demand for medical services, including blood testing.

Blood analysis remains an essential part of medical care, as it is used to check for a wide range of issues. Therefore, demand for phlebotomists will remain high as doctors and other healthcare professionals require bloodwork for analysis and diagnosis.

Occupational Title	SOC Code	Employment, 2022	Projected Employment, 2032	Change, 2022-32	
				Percent	Numeric
Phlebotomists	31-9097	139,400	150,200	8	10,800

Contacts for More Information

For more information about phlebotomy careers, including professional certification, visit

- American Medical Technologists (AMT)
- American Society of Phlebotomy Technicians, Inc.
- American Society for Clinical Pathology
- National Center for Competency Testing
- National Certification Medical Association
- National Healthcareer Association
- National Phlebotomy Association
- National Phlebotomy Certification Examination

Physical Therapist Assistants and Aides

Summary

Quick Facts: Physical Therapist Assistants and Aides

2022 Median Pay	$57,240 per year $27.52 per hour
Typical Entry-Level Education	See How to Become One
Work Experience in a Related Occupation	None
On-the-job Training	See How to Become One
Number of Jobs, 2022	145,100
Job Outlook, 2022-32	19% (Much faster than average)
Employment Change, 2022-32	27,600

What Physical Therapist Assistants and Aides Do

Physical therapist assistants and aides are supervised by physical therapists to help patients regain movement and manage pain after injuries and illnesses.

Work Environment

Most physical therapist assistants and aides work in physical therapists' offices or in hospitals. They are frequently on their feet as they set up equipment and help care for patients.

How to Become a Physical Therapist Assistant or Aide

Physical therapist assistants entering the occupation typically need an associate's degree from an accredited program and a

Physical therapist aides do a variety of clerical tasks, such as scheduling patients and recording insurance information.

license or certification. Physical therapist aides usually need a high school diploma or equivalent and on-the-job training.

Pay

The median annual wage for physical therapist aides was $31,410 in May 2022.

The median annual wage for physical therapist assistants was $62,770 in May 2022.

Job Outlook

Overall employment of physical therapist assistants and aides is projected to grow 19 percent from 2022 to 2032, much faster than the average for all occupations.

About 24,300 openings for physical therapist assistants and aides are projected each year, on average, over the decade. Many of those openings are expected to result from the need to replace workers who transfer to different occupations or exit the labor force, such as to retire.

What Physical Therapist Assistants and Aides Do

Physical therapist assistants, sometimes called *PTAs*, and physical therapist aides work under the direction and supervision of physical therapists. They help patients who are recovering from injuries and illnesses to regain movement and manage pain.

Physical therapist assistants are involved in the direct care of patients.

Physical therapist aides often have tasks that are indirectly related to patient care, such as cleaning and setting up the treatment area, moving patients, and doing clerical duties.

Duties

Physical therapist assistants typically do the following:

- Observe patients before, during, and after therapy, noting the patient's status and reporting it to a physical therapist
- Help patients do specific exercises as part of the plan of care
- Treat patients using a variety of techniques, such as massage and stretching
- Use devices and equipment, such as walkers, to help patients
- Educate patients and family members about what to do after treatment

Under the direction and supervision of physical therapists, physical therapist assistants treat patients through exercise, massage, gait and balance training, and other therapeutic interventions. They record patients' progress and report the results of each treatment to the physical therapist.

Physical therapist aides typically do the following:

- Clean treatment areas and set up therapy equipment
- Wash linens
- Help patients move to or from a therapy area
- Do clerical tasks, such as answering phones and scheduling patients

Physical therapist aides are supervised by physical therapists or physical therapist assistants. The tasks that physical therapist

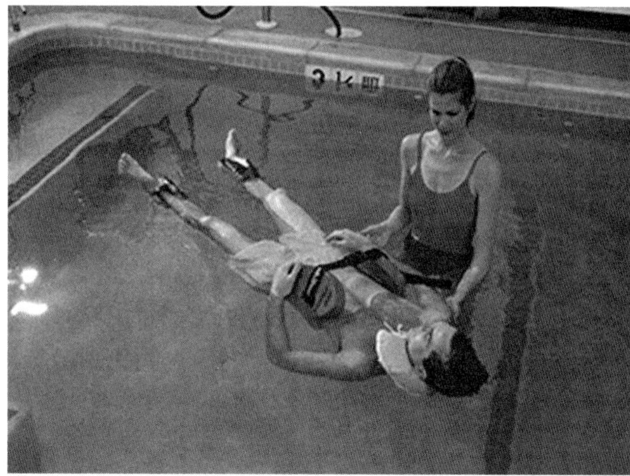

Physical therapist assistants help patients do specific exercises as part of the plan of care.

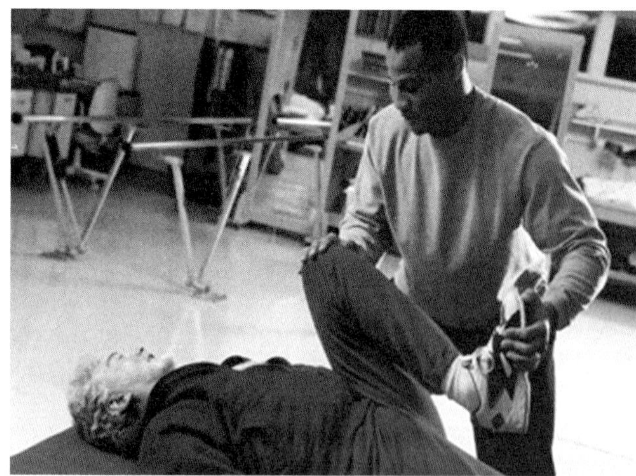

Physical therapist assistants give therapy through exercise, stretching, and other interventions.

aides are allowed to do vary by state. They usually are responsible for keeping the treatment area clean and organized, preparing for each patient's therapy, and helping patients as needed in moving to or from a treatment area. In addition, aides do a variety of clerical tasks, such as ordering supplies, scheduling treatment sessions, and completing insurance forms.

Work Environment

Physical therapist aides held about 44,500 jobs in 2022. The largest employers of physical therapist aides were as follows:

Offices of physical, occupational and speech therapists, and audiologists	64%
Hospitals; state, local, and private	18
Offices of physicians	10
Nursing care facilities (skilled nursing facilities)	2
Government	2

Physical therapist assistants held about 100,700 jobs in 2022. The largest employers of physical therapist assistants were as follows:

Offices of physical, occupational and speech therapists, and audiologists	45%
Hospitals; state, local, and private	22
Home healthcare services	12
Nursing care facilities (skilled nursing facilities)	9
Offices of physicians	5

Physical therapist assistants and aides are frequently on their feet and moving as they set up equipment and help and treat patients. Because they must often lift and move patients, they are vulnerable to back injuries. Assistants and aides can limit these risks by using proper techniques when they work with patients.

Work Schedules

Most physical therapist assistants and aides work full time, although part time work is common. Some work nights and weekends because many physical therapy offices and clinics have extended hours to accommodate patients' schedules.

How to Become a Physical Therapist Assistant or Aide

Physical therapist assistants entering the occupation typically need an associate's degree from an accredited program and a license or certification. Physical therapist aides usually need a high school diploma or equivalent and on-the-job training.

Education and Training

All states require physical therapist assistants to have an associate's degree from a program accredited by the Commission on Accreditation in Physical Therapy Education. Programs

Physical therapist assistants gain hands-on experience during supervised clinical work.

typically last about 2 years and include coursework in subjects such as anatomy, physiology, and kinesiology. Assistants also gain hands-on experience during supervised clinical work.

Physical therapist aides typically need a high school diploma or equivalent. They also usually need on-the-job training that can last from about one week to one month.

Licenses, Certifications, and Registrations

All states require physical therapist assistants to be licensed or certified. Licensure typically requires graduation from an accredited physical therapist assistant program and passing the National Physical Therapy Exam for physical therapist assistants. The exam is administered by the Federation of State Boards of Physical Therapy. Some states require that applicants pass an exam on the state's laws regulating the practice of physical therapy assistants, undergo a criminal background check, and be at least 18 years old. Physical therapist assistants also may need to take continuing education courses to keep their license. Check with your state board for specific licensing requirements.

Additionally, physical therapy assistants may earn certifications in cardiopulmonary resuscitation (CPR), basic life support (BLS), or other first-aid skills.

States do not require physical therapist aides to be licensed.

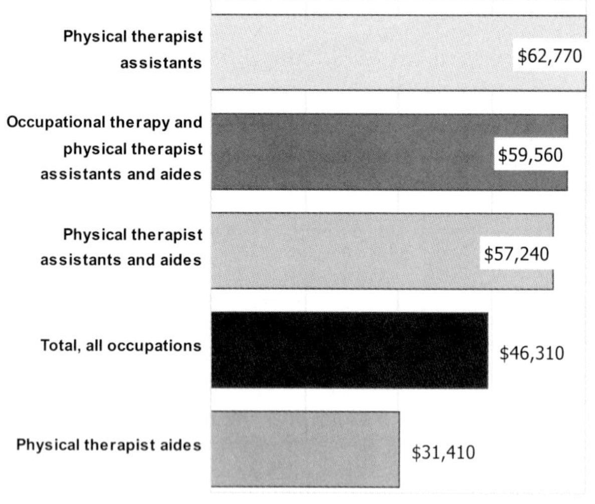

Note: All Occupations includes all occupations in the U.S. Economy. Source: U.S. Bureau of Labor Statistics, Occupational Employment and Wage Statistics.

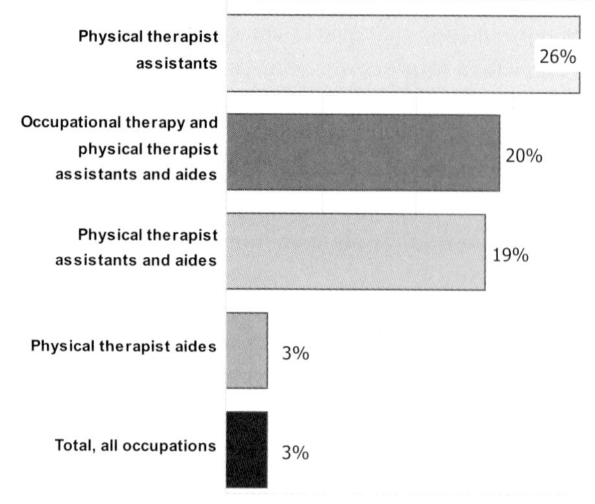

Note: All Occupations includes all occupations in the U.S. Economy. Source: U.S. Bureau of Labor Statistics, Employment Projections program.

Important Qualities

Compassion. Physical therapist assistants and aides should enjoy helping people. They work with people who are in pain and must have empathy to help their patients.

Detail oriented. Physical therapist assistants and aides should be organized, keep accurate records, and follow written and verbal instructions carefully to ensure quality care.

Dexterity. Physical therapist assistants should be comfortable using their hands to provide manual therapy and therapeutic exercises. Aides should also be comfortable working with their hands to set up equipment and prepare treatment areas.

Interpersonal skills. Physical therapist assistants and aides spend much of their time interacting with patients, their families, and other healthcare practitioners; therefore, they should be courteous and friendly.

Physical stamina. Physical therapist assistants and aides are frequently on their feet and moving as they work with their patients. They must often kneel, stoop, bend, and stand for long periods.

Pay

The median annual wage for physical therapist aides was $31,410 in May 2022. The median wage is the wage at which half the workers in an occupation earned more than that amount and half earned less. The lowest 10 percent earned less than $22,380, and the highest 10 percent earned more than $41,320.

The median annual wage for physical therapist assistants was $62,770 in May 2022. The lowest 10 percent earned less than $43,340, and the highest 10 percent earned more than $85,230.

In May 2022, the median annual wages for physical therapist aides in the top industries in which they worked were as follows:

Nursing care facilities (skilled nursing facilities)	$36,920
Hospitals; state, local, and private	34,500
Offices of physicians	33,650
Offices of physical, occupational and speech therapists, and audiologists	29,800
Government	28,040

In May 2022, the median annual wages for physical therapist assistants in the top industries in which they worked were as follows:

Home healthcare services	$76,210
Nursing care facilities (skilled nursing facilities)	74,070
Hospitals; state, local, and private	63,330
Offices of physical, occupational and speech therapists, and audiologists	60,090
Offices of physicians	59,650

Most physical therapist assistants and aides work full time, although part time work is common. Some work nights and weekends because many physical therapy offices and clinics have extended hours to accommodate patients' schedules.

Job Outlook

Overall employment of physical therapist assistants and aides is projected to grow 19 percent from 2022 to 2032, much faster than the average for all occupations.

About 24,300 openings for physical therapist assistants and aides are projected each year, on average, over the decade. Many of those openings are expected to result from the need to replace workers who transfer to different occupations or exit the labor force, such as to retire.

Employment

Demand for physical therapy is expected to increase in response to the health needs of an aging population, particularly the large baby-boom generation. This group is staying more active later in life than previous generations did. However, many baby boomers also are entering the prime age for heart attacks, strokes, and mobility-related injuries, increasing the demand for physical therapy in rehabilitation.

In addition, more physical therapist assistants and aides will be needed to help patients maintain their mobility and manage the effects of chronic conditions, such as diabetes and obesity.

Physical therapists are expected to rely on physical therapist assistants, particularly in long-term care environments, in order to reduce the cost of physical therapy services. This should contribute to employment growth of physical therapist assistants. However, restrictions in insurance reimbursement for services provided by physical therapist aides may constrain demand for this occupation.

Occupational Title	SOC Code	Employment, 2022	Projected Employment, 2032	Change, 2022-32	
				Percent	Numeric
Physical therapist assistants and aides	31-2020	145,100	172,700	19	27,600
Physical therapist assistants	31-2021	100,700	126,900	26	26,300
Physical therapist aides	31-2022	44,500	45,800	3	1,300

Contacts for More Information

For more information about physical therapist assistants, visit

- American Physical Therapy Association
- Commission on Accreditation in Physical Therapy Education
- Federation of State Boards of Physical Therapy

Physical Therapists

Summary

Quick Facts: Physical Therapists	
2022 Median Pay	$97,720 per year $46.98 per hour
Typical Entry-Level Education	Doctoral or professional degree
Work Experience in a Related Occupation	None
On-the-job Training	None
Number of Jobs, 2022	246,800
Job Outlook, 2022-32	15% (Much faster than average)
Employment Change, 2022-32	37,300

Physical therapists develop individualized plans of care for patients.

What Physical Therapists Do

Physical therapists help injured or ill people improve movement and manage pain.

Work Environment

Physical therapists typically work in private offices and clinics, hospitals, patients' homes, and nursing homes. They spend much of their time on their feet, actively working with patients.

How to Become a Physical Therapist

Physical therapists entering the occupation need a Doctor of Physical Therapy (DPT) degree. All states require physical therapists to be licensed.

Pay

The median annual wage for physical therapists was $97,720 in May 2022.

Physical therapists evaluate and record a patient's progress.

Job Outlook

Employment of physical therapists is projected to grow 15 percent from 2022 to 2032, much faster than the average for all occupations.

About 13,900 openings for physical therapists are projected each year, on average, over the decade. Many of those openings are expected to result from the need to replace workers who transfer to different occupations or exit the labor force, such as to retire.

What Physical Therapists Do

Physical therapists help injured or ill people improve movement and manage pain. They are often an important part of preventive care, rehabilitation, and treatment for patients with chronic conditions, illnesses, or injuries.

Duties

Physical therapists typically do the following:

- Review patients' medical history and referrals or notes from doctors, surgeons, or other healthcare workers
- Diagnose patients' functions and movements by observing them stand or walk and by listening to their concerns
- Develop individualized plans of care for patients, outlining the patients' goals and the expected outcomes of the plans
- Use exercises, stretching maneuvers, hands-on therapy, and equipment to ease patients' pain, help them increase their mobility, prevent further pain or injury, and facilitate health and wellness
- Evaluate and record a patients' progress, modifying the plan of care and trying new treatments as needed
- Educate patients and their families about what to expect from the recovery process and how to cope with challenges throughout the process

Physical therapists, sometimes called *PTs*, care for people of all ages who have functional problems resulting from back and neck injuries; sprains, strains, and fractures; arthritis; amputations; neurological disorders, such as stroke or cerebral palsy; injuries related to work and sports; and other conditions.

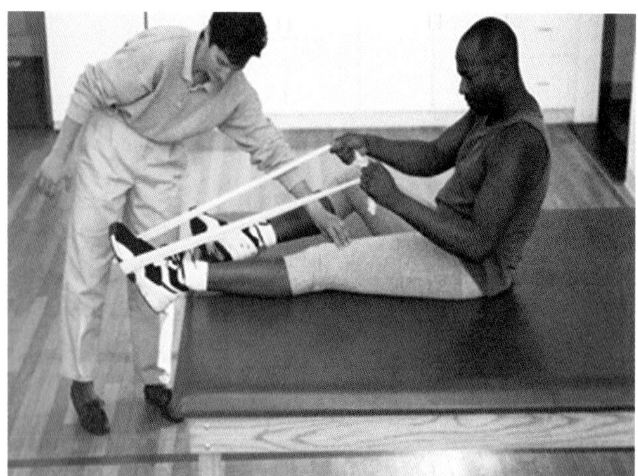

Physical therapists use exercises and stretching maneuvers to ease patient's pain.

Physical therapists use a variety of techniques to care for their patients. These techniques include exercises; training in functional movement, which may include the use of equipment such as canes, crutches, wheelchairs, and walkers; and special movements of joints, muscles, and other soft tissue to improve mobility and decrease pain.

The work of physical therapists varies by type of patient. For example, a patient working to recover mobility lost after a stroke needs care different from that of a patient recovering from a sports injury. Some physical therapists specialize in one type of care, such as orthopedics or geriatrics. Many physical therapists also help patients maintain or improve mobility by developing fitness and wellness programs that encourage healthy, active lifestyles.

Physical therapists work as part of a healthcare team, overseeing the work of physical therapist assistants and aides and consulting with physicians and surgeons and other specialists.

Work Environment

Physical therapists held about 246,800 jobs in 2022. The largest employers of physical therapists were as follows:

Offices of physical, occupational and speech therapists, and audiologists	35%
Hospitals; state, local, and private	28
Home healthcare services	10
Nursing and residential care facilities	5
Self-employed workers	4

Physical therapists spend much of their time on their feet, working with patients. Because they must often lift and move patients, they are vulnerable to back injuries. Physical therapists can limit these risks by using proper body mechanics and lifting techniques when assisting patients.

Work Schedules

Most physical therapists work full time, although part time work is common. They usually work during normal business hours, but some work evenings or weekends.

How to Become a Physical Therapist

Physical therapists entering the occupation need a Doctor of Physical Therapy (DPT) degree. All states require physical therapists to be licensed.

Education

Physical therapists need a Doctor of Physical Therapy (DPT) degree from a program accredited by the Commission on Accreditation in Physical Therapy Education (CAPTE).

DPT programs typically last 3 years. Physical therapy programs typically require a bachelor's degree, which may be in

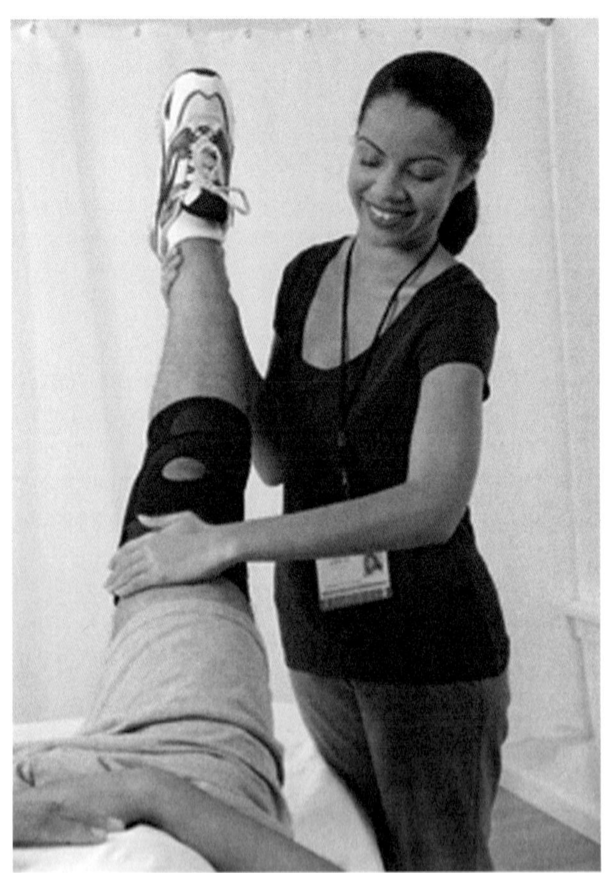

Physical therapists use a variety of techniques, such as massage and stretching, to treat patients.

recreation and fitness or healthcare and related fields, and prerequisite courses such as anatomy, chemistry, and physics.

Most DPT programs require candidates to apply through the Physical Therapist Centralized Application Service (PTCAS).

Physical therapist programs often include courses in biomechanics, neuroscience, and pharmacology. Physical therapist students also complete clinical work, during which they gain supervised experience in areas such as acute care and orthopedic care.

Physical therapists may apply to a clinical residency program after graduation. Residencies typically last about 1 year and provide additional training and experience in specialty areas of care. Physical therapists who have completed a residency program may choose to specialize further by participating in a fellowship in an advanced clinical area. The American Board of Physical Therapy Residency and Fellowship Education has directories of physical therapist residency and fellowship programs.

Licenses, Certifications, and Registrations

All states require physical therapists to be licensed, which includes passing the National Physical Therapy Examination administered by the Federation of State Boards of Physical Therapy. Other requirements vary by state. For example, some states also require a law exam and a criminal background check. Continuing education is typically required for physical therapists to keep their license. Check with your state board for specific licensing requirements.

After gaining work experience, some physical therapists choose to become a board-certified specialist. The American Board of Physical Therapy Specialties offers certification in clinical specialty areas of physical therapy, such as orthopedics, sports, and geriatrics. Board specialist certification requires passing an exam and completing clinical work in the specialty area.

Important Qualities

Communication skills. Physical therapists must clearly explain treatment programs, motivate patients, and listen to patients' concerns in order to provide effective therapy.

Compassion. Physical therapists spend a lot of time interacting with patients, so they should have a desire to help people. They work with people who are in pain and must have empathy for their patients.

Detail oriented. Like other healthcare providers, physical therapists should have strong analytic and observational skills to diagnose a patient's problem, evaluate treatments, and provide safe, effective care.

Dexterity. Physical therapists must use their hands to provide manual therapy and therapeutic exercises. They should feel comfortable massaging and otherwise physically assisting patients.

Physical stamina. Physical therapists spend much of their time on their feet, moving to demonstrate proper techniques and to help patients perform exercises. They should enjoy physical activity.

Resourcefulness. Physical therapists customize treatment plans for patients. They must be flexible and adapt plans of care to meet the needs of each patient.

Physical Therapists

Median annual wages, May 2022

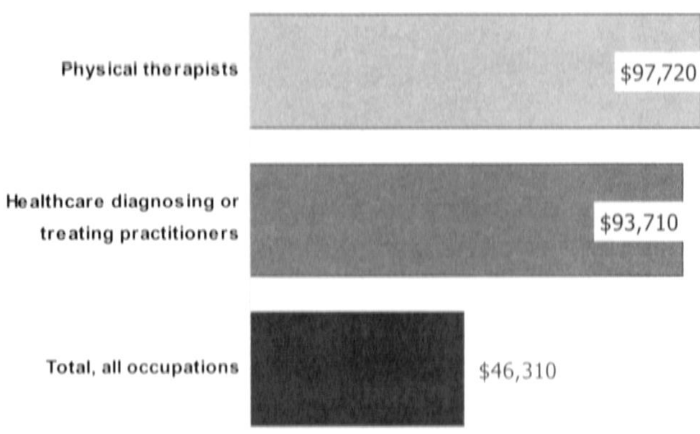

Note: All Occupations includes all occupations in the U.S. Economy.
Source: U.S. Bureau of Labor Statistics, Occupational Employment and Wage Statistics.

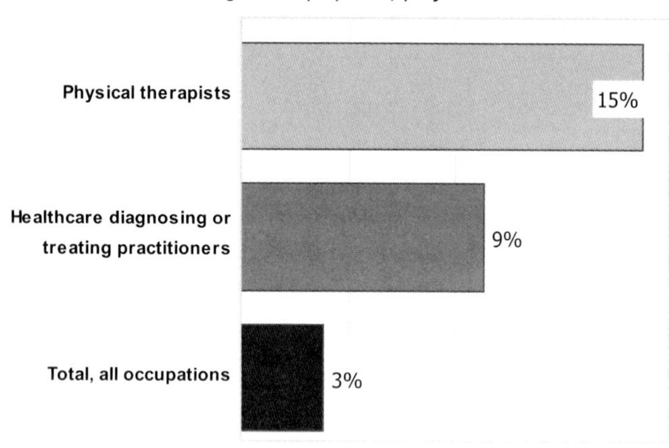

Note: All Occupations includes all occupations in the U.S. Economy.
Source: U.S. Bureau of Labor Statistics, Employment Projections program.

Time-management skills. Physical therapists typically treat several patients each day. They must be able to provide appropriate care to patients as well as complete administrative tasks, such as documenting patient progress.

Pay

The median annual wage for physical therapists was $97,720 in May 2022. The median wage is the wage at which half the workers in an occupation earned more than that amount and half earned less. The lowest 10 percent earned less than $67,910, and the highest 10 percent earned more than $128,830.

In May 2022, the median annual wages for physical therapists in the top industries in which they worked were as follows:

Home healthcare services	$105,130
Nursing and residential care facilities	101,910
Hospitals; state, local, and private	101,440
Offices of physical, occupational and speech therapists, and audiologists	86,610

Most physical therapists work full time. Although most therapists work during normal business hours, some work evenings or weekends.

Job Outlook

Employment of physical therapists is projected to grow 15 percent from 2022 to 2032, much faster than the average for all occupations.

About 13,900 openings for physical therapists are projected each year, on average, over the decade. Many of those openings are expected to result from the need to replace workers who transfer to different occupations or exit the labor force, such as to retire.

Employment

Demand for physical therapy will come, in part, from the large number of aging baby boomers, who are staying more active later in life than their counterparts of previous generations. Older people are more likely to experience heart attacks, strokes, and mobility-related injuries that require physical therapy for rehabilitation.

In addition, a number of chronic conditions, such as diabetes and obesity, have become prevalent. More physical therapists will be needed to help people with these conditions maintain their mobility and manage their disease or illness.

A greater emphasis on non-opioid approaches to manage pain also is expected to support employment growth.

Occupational Title	SOC Code	Employment, 2022	Projected Employment, 2032	Change, 2022-32	
				Percent	Numeric
Physical therapists	29-1123	246,800	284,100	15	37,300

Contacts for More Information

For more information about physical therapists, visit

- American Physical Therapy Association
- Commission on Accreditation in Physical Therapy Education
- Federation of State Boards of Physical Therapy
- American Board of Physical Therapy Specialties
- American Board of Physical Therapy Residency and Fellowship Education
- Physical Therapist Centralized Application Service (PTCAS)

Physician Assistants

Summary

Quick Facts: Physician Assistants	
2022 Median Pay	$126,010 per year $60.58 per hour
Typical Entry-Level Education	Master's degree
Work Experience in a Related Occupation	None
On-the-job Training	None
Number of Jobs, 2022	148,000
Job Outlook, 2022-32	27% (Much faster than average)
Employment Change, 2022-32	39,300

What Physician Assistants Do

Physician assistants examine, diagnose, and treat patients under the supervision of a physician.

Work Environment

Physician assistants work in physicians' offices, hospitals, outpatient clinics, and other healthcare settings. Most work full time.

How to Become a Physician Assistant

To enter the occupation, physician assistants typically need a master's degree from an accredited program. All states require physician assistants to be licensed.

Pay

The median annual wage for physician assistants was $126,010 in May 2022.

Job Outlook

Employment of physician assistants is projected to grow 27 percent from 2022 to 2032, much faster than the average for all occupations.

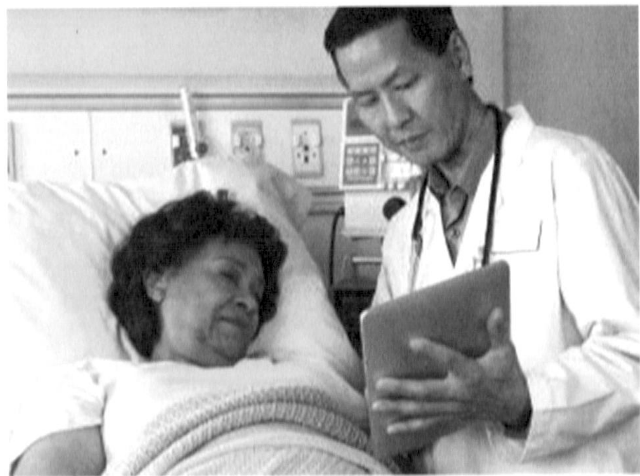

Physician assistants practice medicine on a team with physicians and surgeons and other healthcare workers.

About 12,200 openings for physician assistants are projected each year, on average, over the decade. Many of those openings are expected to result from the need to replace workers who transfer to different occupations or exit the labor force, such as to retire.

What Physician Assistants Do

Physician assistants, also known as *PAs*, examine, diagnose, and treat patients under the supervision of a physician.

Duties

Physician assistants typically do the following:

- Obtain and review patients' medical histories
- Examine patients
- Order and interpret diagnostic tests, such as x rays or blood tests
- Diagnose a patient's injury or illness
- Provide treatment, such as setting broken bones, stitching wounds, and immunizing patients
- Educate and counsel patients and their families on a variety of issues, such as treatment and self-care for asthma
- Prescribe medication
- Assess and record a patient's progress
- Research the latest treatments to ensure quality of patient care

Physician assistants are on teams with physicians or surgeons and other healthcare workers. The amount of collaboration and the extent to which they must be supervised by physicians or surgeons differ by state.

Physician assistants work in a variety of healthcare specialties, including primary care and family medicine, emergency medicine, and psychiatry. The work of physician assistants depends, in large part, on their specialty or the type of medical practice in which they work. For example, a physician assistant

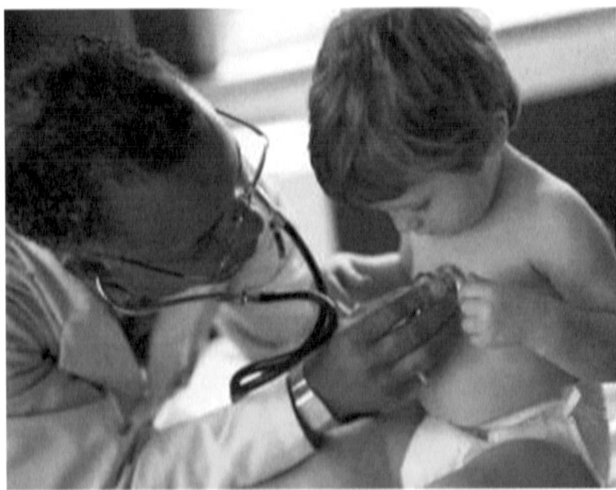

Physician assistants work in all areas of medicine, including primary care and family medicine, emergency medicine, and psychiatry.

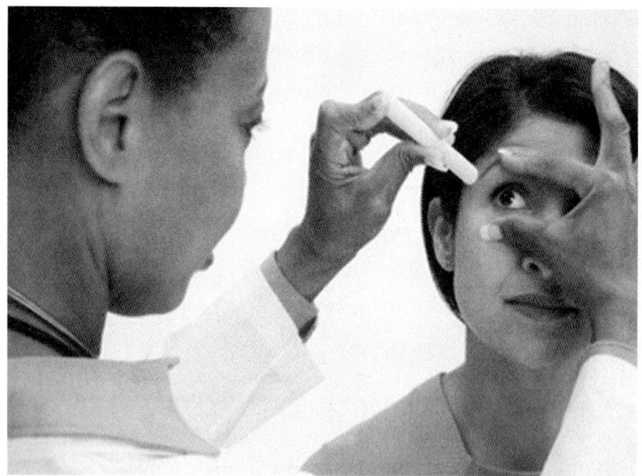

Many physician assistants work in primary care specialties, such as general internal medicine, pediatrics, and family medicine.

working in surgery may close incisions and provide care before, during, and after an operation. A physician assistant working in pediatrics may examine a child and give routine vaccinations.

In some areas, especially rural and medically underserved communities, physician assistants may be the primary care providers at clinics where a physician is present only 1 or 2 days per week. In these locations, physician assistants collaborate with the physician as needed and as required by law.

Some physician assistants make house calls or visit nursing homes to treat patients.

Physician assistants differ from nurse practitioners in their training and the level of care they provide; for example, nurse practitioners cannot provide surgical care, whereas physician assistants can. They also differ from medical assistants, who do routine clinical and clerical tasks but do not practice medicine.

Work Environment

Physician assistants held about 148,000 jobs in 2022. The largest employers of physician assistants were as follows:

Offices of physicians	52%
Hospitals; state, local, and private	24
Outpatient care centers	9
Educational services; state, local, and private	4
Government	2

Working with patients can be both physically and emotionally demanding. Physician assistants spend much of their time standing or walking to make rounds and evaluate patients. Physician assistants who work in operating rooms often stand for extended periods.

Work Schedules

Most physician assistants work full time. Work schedules vary and may include nights, weekends, or holidays. Physician assistants also may be on call, meaning that they must be ready to respond to a work request with little notice.

Physician assistants often treat minor injuries, instruct and counsel patients, and order or carry out therapy.

How to Become a Physician Assistant

Physician assistants typically need a master's degree from an accredited educational program. Applicants to these programs typically have a bachelor's degree and experience caring directly for patients. All states require physician assistants to be licensed.

Education

Applicants to physician assistant education programs typically have a bachelor's degree and some experience with patient care. Although programs vary, most require applicants to have taken undergraduate coursework with a focus in science. Bachelor's degrees are often in healthcare or a related field, such as biology. Programs also may require that applicants have experience as a medical assistant, EMT or paramedic, or another occupation that involves patient care.

Physician assistant education programs usually take at least 2 years of postbaccalaureate study. A list of accredited physician assistant programs is available from the Accreditation Review Commission on Education for the Physician Assistant, Inc. (ARC-PA).

Physician assistant education includes classroom and laboratory instruction in subjects such as human anatomy, clinical medicine, and pharmacology. The programs also include supervised clinical training in several specialties, such as family medicine, internal medicine, and emergency medicine.

Licenses, Certifications, and Registrations

All states and the District of Columbia require physician assistants to be licensed. To become licensed, candidates must pass the Physician Assistant National Certifying Examination (PANCE) administered by the National Commission on Certification of Physician Assistants (NCCPA). A physician assistant who passes the exam may use the credential "Physician Assistant-Certified (PA-C)."

To maintain their PA-C certification, physician assistants must complete continuing education and pass a recertification exam within a specified number of years.

In most states, laws require physician assistants to hold an agreement with a supervising physician. Although the physician does not need to be onsite at all times, collaboration between physicians and physician assistants is required for practice.

Physician assistant positions may require basic life support (BLS) certification.

Advancement

Some physician assistants pursue additional education in a specialty. Postgraduate programs are available in specialties such as emergency medicine and psychiatry. To enter one of these programs, a physician assistant must be a graduate of an accredited program and have their PA-C. Additional certification in specialty areas is offered by the NCCPA.

Important Qualities

Communication skills. Physician assistants must explain complex medical issues in a way that patients can understand.

Compassion. Physician assistants deal with patients who are sick or injured and who may be in extreme pain or distress. They must be sympathetic toward and understanding of patients and their families.

Detail oriented. Physician assistants should be observant and have a strong ability to focus when evaluating and treating patients.

Emotional stability. Physician assistants, particularly those working in surgery or emergency medicine, should work well under pressure. They must remain calm in stressful situations in order to provide quality care.

Interpersonal skills. Physician assistants must work well as part of a team of other healthcare professionals to ensure proper patient care.

Problem-solving skills. Physician assistants need to evaluate patients' symptoms and administer the appropriate treatments. They must be diligent when investigating complicated medical issues so they can determine the best course of treatment for each patient.

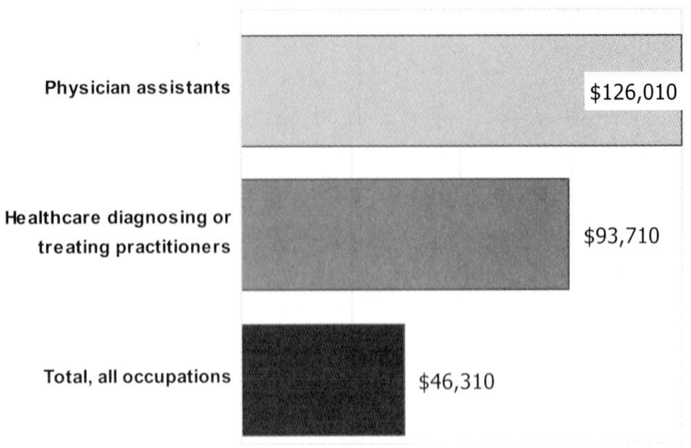

Note: All Occupations includes all occupations in the U.S. Economy.
Source: U.S. Bureau of Labor Statistics, Occupational Employment and Wage Statistics.

Pay

The median annual wage for physician assistants was $126,010 in May 2022. The median wage is the wage at which half the workers in an occupation earned more than that amount and half earned less. The lowest 10 percent earned less than $83,820, and the highest 10 percent earned more than $168,120.

In May 2022, the median annual wages for physician assistants in the top industries in which they worked were as follows:

Outpatient care centers	$134,180
Hospitals; state, local, and private	129,690
Offices of physicians	123,430
Government	113,900
Educational services; state, local, and private	107,410

Most physician assistants work full time. Work schedules vary and may include nights, weekends, or holidays. Physician

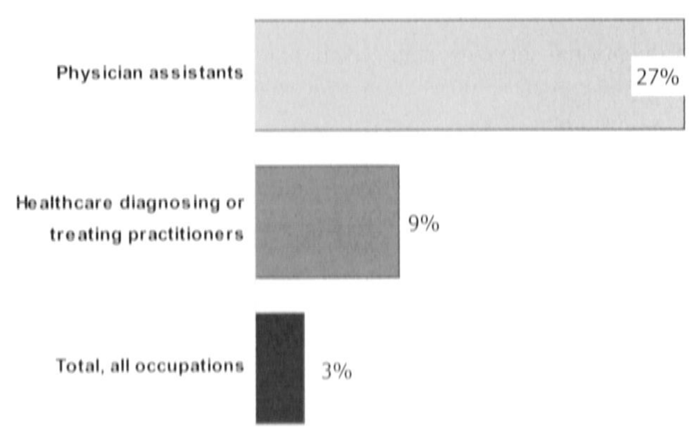

Note: All Occupations includes all occupations in the U.S. Economy.
Source: U.S. Bureau of Labor Statistics, Employment Projections program.

assistants also may be on call, meaning that they must be ready to respond to a work request with little notice.

Job Outlook

Employment of physician assistants is projected to grow 27 percent from 2022 to 2032, much faster than the average for all occupations.

About 12,200 openings for physician assistants are projected each year, on average, over the decade. Many of those openings are expected to result from the need to replace workers who transfer to different occupations or exit the labor force, such as to retire.

Employment

The growing population will continue to increase demand for healthcare services. A rise in the number of older people, who are more likely than young people to require medical care, and of patients with chronic diseases, such as diabetes, will also increase healthcare demand. These increases, in turn, drive the need for healthcare providers such as physician assistants (PAs), who often provide preventive care and treat the sick.

PAs, who can provide many of the same services as physicians, are expected to continue to expand their role in providing healthcare services for a number of reasons. They can be trained more quickly than physicians, and team-based healthcare provision models will continue to evolve and become more common. Furthermore, states continue to expand allowable procedures and autonomy, and insurance companies are extending coverage to physician assistant services.

Occupational Title	SOC Code	Employment, 2022	Projected Employment, 2032	Change, 2022-32	
				Percent	Numeric
Physician assistants	29-1071	148,000	187,300	27	39,300

Contacts for More Information

For more information about physician assistants, visit

- American Academy of PAs
- Physician Assistant Education Association
- Accreditation Review Commission on Education for the Physician Assistant, Inc. (ARC-PA)
- Association of Postgraduate Physician Assistant Programs
- National Commission on Certification of Physician Assistants

Physicians and Surgeons

Summary

Quick Facts: Physicians and Surgeons	
2022 Median Pay	$229,300 per year $110.24 per hour
Typical Entry-Level Education	Doctoral or professional degree
Work Experience in a Related Occupation	None
On-the-job Training	Internship/residency
Number of Jobs, 2022	816,900
Job Outlook, 2022-32	3% (As fast as average)
Employment Change, 2022-32	24,600

What Physicians and Surgeons Do

Physicians and surgeons diagnose and treat injuries or illnesses and address health maintenance.

Work Environment

Physicians and surgeons work in both clinical and nonclinical settings. Clinical settings include physicians' offices and hospitals; nonclinical settings include government agencies, nonprofit organizations, and insurance companies.

How to Become a Physician or Surgeon

Physicians and surgeons typically need a bachelor's degree as well as a medical degree, which takes an additional 4 years to complete. Depending on their specialty, they also need 3 to 9 years in internship and residency programs. Subspecialization includes additional training in a fellowship of 1 to 3 years.

Pay

The median annual wage for physicians and surgeons was $229,300 in May 2022.

Job Outlook

Overall employment of physicians and surgeons is projected to grow 3 percent from 2022 to 2032, about as fast as the average for all occupations.

Physicians examine patients; obtain medical histories; and order, perform, and interpret diagnostic tests.

About 24,200 openings for physicians and surgeons are projected each year, on average, over the decade. Many of those openings are expected to result from the need to replace workers who transfer to different occupations or exit the labor force, such as to retire.

What Physicians and Surgeons Do

Physicians and surgeons diagnose and treat injuries or illnesses and address health maintenance. Physicians examine patients; take medical histories; prescribe medications; and order, perform, and interpret diagnostic tests. They often counsel patients on diet, hygiene, and preventive healthcare. Surgeons operate on patients to treat injuries, such as broken bones; diseases, such as cancerous tumors; and deformities, such as cleft palates.

There are two types of physicians, with similar degrees: M.D. (Medical Doctor) and D.O. (Doctor of Osteopathic Medicine). Both use the same methods of treatment, including drugs and surgery, but D.O.s place additional emphasis on the body's musculoskeletal system, preventive medicine, and holistic (whole-person) patient care. D.O.s are most likely to be primary care physicians, although they work in all specialties.

Duties

Physicians and surgeons typically do the following:

- Take a patient's medical history and perform a physical exam
- Document and update charts and patient information to show findings and treatments
- Order tests and consultations for other physicians or healthcare staff to perform
- Review test results to identify abnormal findings
- Recommend, design, and implement a treatment plan
- Address concerns or answer questions that patients have about their health and well-being
- Help patients take care of their health by discussing topics such as proper nutrition and hygiene

Physicians often work closely with other healthcare staff including physician assistants, registered nurses, and medical records and health information technicians.

Physicians and surgeons focus on a particular type of practice. Within their area of focus, they also may specialize or subspecialize. The following are examples of types of physicians and surgeons:

Anesthesiologists focus on the care of surgical patients and on pain relief. They administer drugs (anesthetics) that reduce or eliminate the sensation of pain during an operation or another medical procedure. During surgery, they adjust the amount of anesthetic as needed and monitor the patient's heart rate, body temperature, blood pressure, and breathing. They also provide pain relief for patients in intensive care, for women in labor, and for patients suffering from chronic pain.

Cardiologists diagnose and treat diseases or conditions of the heart and blood vessels, such as valve problems, high blood pressure, and heart attacks. Cardiologists may work with adults or specialize in pediatrics (typically newborns through age 21). Although they treat many of the same disorders in either population, cardiologists in pediatric care focus on conditions that patients are born with rather than on those that develop later in life.

Dermatologists provide care for diseases relating to the skin, hair, and nails. They treat patients who may have melanoma or other skin cancers. They may offer both medical and surgical dermatology services.

Emergency medicine physicians treat patients in urgent medical situations. These physicians evaluate, care for, and stabilize patients whose illness or injury requires immediate attention. Unlike many other physicians, who often choose to specialize, most emergency medical physicians are generalists.

Family medicine physicians are generalists who address health maintenance and assess and treat conditions that occur in everyday life. These conditions include sinus and respiratory infections, intestinal ailments, and broken bones. Family medicine physicians typically have regular, long-term patients, who may include all members of the same household.

General internal medicine physicians diagnose and provide nonsurgical treatment for a range of problems that affect internal organs and systems such as the stomach, kidneys, liver, and digestive tract. Internists use a variety of diagnostic techniques to treat patients through medication or hospitalization. Their patients are mostly adults. They may specialize, such as in gastroenterology or endocrinology.

Neurologists diagnose and treat those with disorders of the brain and nervous system, such as Alzheimer's disease, amyotrophic lateral sclerosis (ALS), and epilepsy. These physicians may specialize in one or more conditions, or they may work as pediatric neurologists to diagnose and manage the care of children with autism, behavioral disorders, or other neurological conditions.

Obstetricians and gynecologists (OB/GYNs) provide care and counsel to women regarding pregnancy, childbirth, and the female reproductive system. They also diagnose and treat health issues specific to women, such as cervical cancer, ovarian cysts, and symptoms related to menopause.

Ophthalmologists diagnose and treat conditions of the eye. Treatment may include surgery to correct vision problems or to prevent vision loss from glaucoma and other diseases. Ophthalmologists also may fit eyeglasses, prescribe contact lenses, and provide other vision services.

Orthopedic surgeons diagnose and treat conditions of or injuries to the musculoskeletal system, which includes bones, muscles, ligaments, and tendons. They may specialize in certain areas of the body, such as the foot and ankle, or in a particular type of practice, such as sports medicine.

Pathologists test body tissue, fluids, and organs and review test results to diagnose diseases. These physicians may choose specializations that include clinical pathology, which focuses on laboratory analysis of bodily fluids, and anatomical pathology, which focuses on examinations of tissue and other samples acquired through autopsy or surgery.

Pediatricians provide care for infants, children, teenagers, and young adults. They specialize in diagnosing and treating problems specific to younger people. Most pediatricians administer vaccinations and treat common illnesses, minor injuries, and infectious diseases. Some pediatricians specialize in serious medical conditions that commonly affect younger patients, such as autoimmune disorders.

Pediatric surgeons diagnose, treat, and manage a variety of disorders and diseases in fetuses, infants, children, and adolescents. These surgeons collaborate with physicians involved in a child's medical care—including neonatologists, pediatricians, and family medicine physicians—to determine the best treatment options for the child.

Psychiatrists are primary mental health physicians. They diagnose and treat mental illnesses through a combination of personal counseling (psychotherapy), psychoanalysis, hospitalization, and medication. Psychotherapy involves psychiatrists helping their clients change behavioral patterns and explore past experiences. Psychoanalysis involves long-term psychotherapy and counseling. Psychiatrists may prescribe medications to correct chemical imbalances that cause some mental illnesses.

Radiologists review and interpret x rays and other medical images, such as ultrasounds, to diagnose injuries or diseases. They may specialize, such as in diagnostic radiology, which involves reviewing images and recommending treatment or additional testing, or in interventional radiology, which includes diagnosing patients and treating them with minimally invasive techniques.

Physicians in healthcare establishments work daily with other healthcare staff, such as registered nurses, other physicians, medical assistants, and medical records and health information technicians.

Some physicians choose to work in fields that do not involve patient care, such as medical research or public policy.

Work Environment

Physicians and surgeons held about 816,900 jobs in 2022. Employment in the detailed occupations that make up physicians and surgeons was distributed as follows:

Physicians, all other	330,900
Family medicine physicians	108,000
General internal medicine physicians	72,600
Anesthesiologists	40,000
Pediatricians, general	35,900
Emergency medicine physicians	31,300
Radiologists	31,200
Psychiatrists	28,600
Surgeons, all other	26,500
Obstetricians and gynecologists	22,900
Orthopedic surgeons, except pediatric	19,400
Cardiologists	18,000
Physicians, pathologists	13,200
Ophthalmologists, except pediatric	12,800
Dermatologists	12,400
Neurologists	12,200

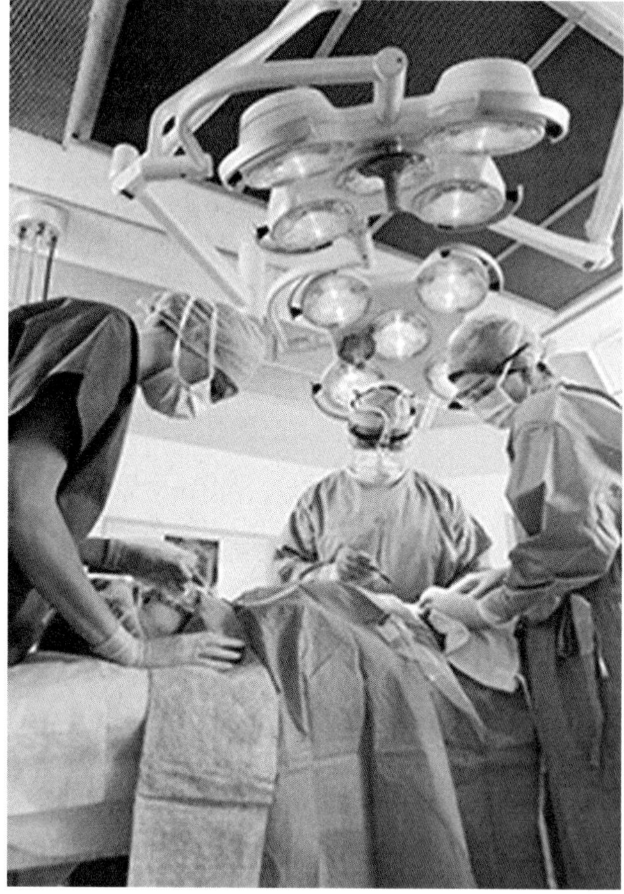

Surgeons and anesthesiologists usually work in a sterile environment and must follow protocol to maintain it during procedures.

Pediatric surgeons 800

Physicians and surgeons work in both clinical and nonclinical settings. Some examples of clinical settings are physicians' offices and hospitals, including academic hospitals associated with residency programs or schools of medicine. Nonclinical settings include government agencies, nonprofit organizations, and insurance companies.

In clinical settings, physicians may work as part of a group practice or healthcare organization. These arrangements allow them to coordinate patient care but give them less independence than solo practitioners have.

Physicians and surgeons may stand for long periods throughout the day. Other working conditions may vary by specialty. For example, surgeons and anesthesiologists usually work in a sterile environment and must follow protocol to maintain it during procedures.

Work Schedules

Most physicians and surgeons work full time. Some work more than 40 hours per week. Many physicians and surgeons work long shifts, which may include irregular and overnight hours or being on call. Physicians and surgeons may travel between their offices and the hospital to care for patients. While on call, a physician may need to address a patient's concerns over the phone or make an emergency visit to another location, such as a nursing home.

How to Become a Physician or Surgeon

Physicians and surgeons typically need a bachelor's degree as well as a degree from a medical school, which takes an additional 4 years to complete. Depending on their specialty, they also need 3 to 9 years in internship and residency programs. Subspecialization includes additional training in a fellowship of 1 to 3 years.

Education

In addition to requiring a bachelor's degree, physicians and surgeons typically need either a Medical Doctor (M.D.) or a Doctor of Osteopathic Medicine (D.O.) degree. No specific undergraduate degree is required to enter an M.D. or D.O. program, but applicants to medical school usually have studied subjects such as biology, physical science, or healthcare and related fields.

Medical schools are highly competitive. Applicants usually must submit transcripts, scores from the Medical College Admission Test (MCAT), and letters of recommendation. Medical schools also consider an applicant's personality, leadership qualities, and participation in extracurricular activities. Most schools require applicants to interview with members of the admissions committee.

Some medical schools offer combined undergraduate and medical school programs that last 6 to 8 years. Schools may also offer combined graduate degrees, such as M.D.-Ph.D., M.D.-MBA, and M.D.-MPH.

Students spend the first phase of medical school in classrooms, small groups, and laboratories, taking courses such as anatomy, biochemistry, pharmacology, psychology, medical ethics, and in the laws governing medicine. They also gain practical skills: learning to take medical histories, examine patients, and diagnose illnesses.

During their second phase of medical school, students work with patients under the supervision of experienced physicians in hospitals and clinics. They gain experience in diagnosing and treating illnesses through clerkships, or rotations, in a variety of areas, including internal medicine, pediatrics, and surgery.

Training

After medical school, almost all graduates enter a residency program in their specialty of interest. A residency usually takes place in a hospital or clinic and varies in duration, typically lasting from 3 to 9 years, depending on the specialty. Subspecialization, such as infectious diseases or hand surgery, includes additional training in a fellowship of 1 to 3 years.

Licenses, Certifications, and Registrations

All states require physicians and surgeons to be licensed; requirements vary by state. To qualify for a license, candidates must graduate from an accredited medical school and complete residency training in their specialty.

Licensure requirements include passing standardized national exams. M.D.s take the U.S. Medical Licensing Examination (USMLE). D.O.s take the Comprehensive Osteopathic Medical Licensing Examination (COMLEX-USA). For specific state information about licensing, contact your state's medical board.

Board certification in a specialty is not required for physicians and surgeons; however, it may increase their employment opportunities. M.D.s and D.O.s seeking board certification in

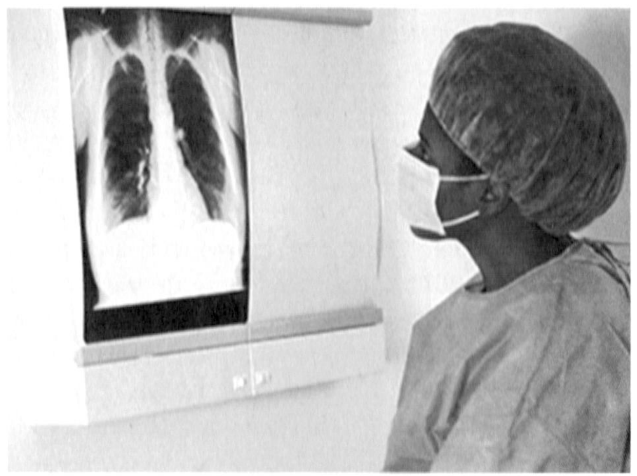

Physicians and surgeons may work in a medical specialty, such as cardiology, dermatology, pathology, or radiology.

a specialty may spend up to 9 years in residency training; the length of time varies with the specialty. To become board certified, candidates must complete a residency program and pass a specialty certification exam from a medical certifying board. Examples of certifying boards include the American Board of Medical Specialties (ABMS), the American Osteopathic Association (AOA), and the American Board of Physician Specialties (ABPS).

Important Qualities

Communication skills. Physicians and surgeons need to convey information effectively to their patients and to other healthcare workers. They also must be able to dictate or write reports that clearly describe a patient's medical condition or procedure outcome.

Compassion. Patients who are sick or injured may be in extreme pain or distress. Physicians and surgeons must treat patients and their families with understanding.

Detail oriented. To ensure that patients receive appropriate treatment, including medication, physicians and surgeons must be precise in monitoring them and recording information related to their care.

Dexterity. Physicians and surgeons must be agile and sure handed, especially when working with extremely sharp medical instruments.

Leadership skills. Physicians and surgeons must coordinate with a team of other healthcare workers to manage patient care or direct medical procedures.

Organizational skills. Good recordkeeping and other administrative skills are critical for physicians and surgeons in both medical and business settings.

Patience. Physicians and surgeons must remain calm and tolerant when working with patients who need special attention, such as those who fear or ignore medical treatment.

Physical stamina. Physicians and surgeons may spend many hours on their feet, including walking between patient visits or procedures. Surgeons may spend a great deal of time bending over patients during surgery.

Problem-solving skills. Physicians and surgeons need to evaluate patients' symptoms to determine appropriate treatment. In some situations, such as emergencies, they may need to analyze and resolve crises quickly.

Pay

The median annual wage for physicians and surgeons was $229,300 in May 2022. The median wage is the wage at which half the workers in an occupation earned more than that amount and half earned less. The lowest 10 percent earned less than $65,620, and the highest 10 percent earned more than $239,200.

Median annual wages for physicians and surgeons in May 2022 were as follows:

Anesthesiologists	$239,200 or more
Surgeons, all other	239,200 or more
Pediatric surgeons	239,200 or more
Orthopedic surgeons, except pediatric	239,200 or more
Radiologists	239,200 or more
Physicians, pathologists	239,200 or more
Obstetricians and gynecologists	239,200 or more
Cardiologists	239,200 or more
Dermatologists	239,200 or more
Emergency medicine physicians	239,200 or more
Psychiatrists	226,880
Neurologists	224,260
Physicians, all other	223,410
Ophthalmologists, except pediatric	219,810
General internal medicine physicians	214,460
Family medicine physicians	211,300
Pediatricians, general	190,350

Because BLS does not publish median annual wages above $239,200, the previous table does not show variations in pay for some physicians and surgeons. Mean (average) annual wages for physicians and surgeons in May 2022 were as follows:

Cardiologists	$421,330
Orthopedic surgeons, except pediatric	371,400
Pediatric surgeons	362,970
Surgeons, all other	347,870
Radiologists	329,080
Dermatologists	327,650
Emergency medicine physicians	316,600

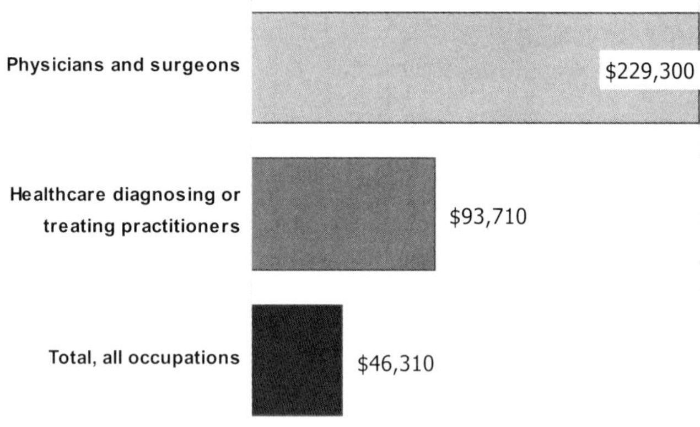

Note: All Occupations includes all occupations in the U.S. Economy.
Source: U.S. Bureau of Labor Statistics, Occupational Employment and Wage Statistics.

Anesthesiologists	302,970
Obstetricians and gynecologists	277,320
Ophthalmologists, except pediatric	265,450
Neurologists	255,510
Physicians, pathologists	252,850
Psychiatrists	247,350
Physicians, all other	238,700
General internal medicine physicians	225,270
Family medicine physicians	224,460
Pediatricians, general	203,240

Most physicians and surgeons work full time. Some work more than 40 hours per week. Many physicians and surgeons work long shifts, which may include irregular and overnight hours or being on call. Physicians and surgeons may travel between their offices and the hospital to care for patients. While on call, a physician may need to address a patient's concerns over the phone or make an emergency visit to another location, such as a nursing home.

Job Outlook

Overall employment of physicians and surgeons is projected to grow 3 percent from 2022 to 2032, about as fast as the average for all occupations.

About 24,200 openings for physicians and surgeons are projected each year, on average, over the decade. Many of those openings are expected to result from the need to replace workers who transfer to different occupations or exit the labor force, such as to retire.

Employment

Projected employment of physicians and surgeons varies by occupation (see table). Population growth and an increasing number of older adults, who have a higher likelihood than young people of experiencing health problems and of needing complex care, are expected to drive overall employment growth for physician and surgeons.

Growing demand for psychiatric care and improved access to mental health services will contribute to a need for psychiatrists.

Increasing rates of chronic illnesses—such as diabetes, cancer, and heart disease—will result in continued reliance on physicians and surgeons by large numbers of people seeking medical care.

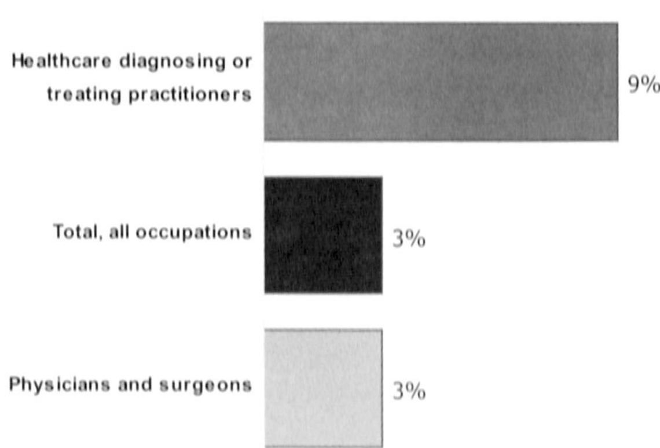

Note: All Occupations includes all occupations in the U.S. Economy.
Source: U.S. Bureau of Labor Statistics, Employment Projections program.

Occupational Title	SOC Code	Employment, 2022	Projected Employment, 2032	Change, 2022-32	
				Percent	Numeric
Physicians and surgeons	—	816,900	841,500	3	24,600
Physicians	29-1210	757,400	780,900	3	23,600
Anesthesiologists	29-1211	40,000	41,100	3	1,000
Cardiologists	29-1212	18,000	18,600	3	600
Dermatologists	29-1213	12,400	12,800	3	400
Emergency medicine physicians	29-1214	31,300	32,200	3	900
Family medicine physicians	29-1215	108,000	112,000	4	4,000
General internal medicine physicians	29-1216	72,600	74,400	2	1,800
Neurologists	29-1217	12,200	12,500	3	400
Obstetricians and gynecologists	29-1218	22,900	23,400	2	500
Pediatricians, general	29-1221	35,900	36,200	1	300
Physicians, pathologists	29-1222	13,200	13,900	5	600
Psychiatrists	29-1223	28,600	30,500	7	1,900
Radiologists	29-1224	31,200	32,400	4	1,100
Physicians, all other	29-1229	330,900	341,000	3	10,000
Surgeons	29-1240	59,600	60,600	2	1,000
Ophthalmologists, except pediatric	29-1241	12,800	13,300	4	500
Orthopedic surgeons, except pediatric	29-1242	19,400	19,700	2	300
Pediatric surgeons	29-1243	800	800	1	0
Surgeons, all other	29-1249	26,500	26,800	1	200

Contacts for More Information

For more information about physicians and surgeons, visit

- American Medical Association
- American Osteopathic Association
- American Academy of Family Physicians
- American Board of Medical Specialties
- American Board of Physician Specialties
- American College of Obstetricians and Gynecologists
- American College of Physicians
- American College of Surgeons
- Association of American Medical Colleges
- American Association of Colleges of Osteopathic Medicine
- Federation of State Medical Boards
- National Board of Medical Examiners
- National Board of Osteopathic Medical Examiners
- United States Medical Licensing Examination

Podiatrists

Summary

Quick Facts: Podiatrists	
2022 Median Pay	$148,720 per year $71.50 per hour
Typical Entry-Level Education	Doctoral or professional degree
Work Experience in a Related Occupation	None
On-the-job Training	Internship/residency
Number of Jobs, 2022	10,600
Job Outlook, 2022-32	1% (Little or no change)
Employment Change, 2022-32	100

What Podiatrists Do
Podiatrists provide medical and surgical care for people with foot, ankle, and lower leg problems.

Work Environment
Podiatrists usually work in offices of podiatry, other medical offices, or hospitals. Most work full time, and some need to be on call for emergencies.

How to Become a Podiatrist
Podiatrists must earn a Doctor of Podiatric Medicine (DPM) degree and complete a 3-year residency program. Every state requires podiatrists to be licensed.

Pay
The median annual wage for podiatrists was $148,720 in May 2022.

Job Outlook
Employment of podiatrists is projected to show little or no change from 2022 to 2032.

Podiatrists may diagnose foot, ankle, and lower leg problems through x rays.

Despite limited employment growth, about 300 openings for podiatrists are projected each year, on average, over the decade. Most of those openings are expected to result from the need to replace workers who transfer to different occupations or exit the labor force, such as to retire.

What Podiatrists Do
Podiatrists diagnose illnesses, treat injuries, and perform surgery for people with foot, ankle, and lower leg problems.

Duties
Podiatrists typically do the following:

- Diagnose and assess patients' conditions by reviewing medical histories, performing physical exams, and reviewing x rays and medical laboratory tests.
- Provide nonsurgical treatment for foot, ankle, and lower leg ailments, such as prescribing special shoe inserts (orthotics) to improve a patient's mobility
- Perform foot and ankle surgeries, such as removing bone spurs, repairing fractures, and correcting other foot and ankle problems
- Advise and instruct patients about foot and ankle care and wellness
- Prescribe medications

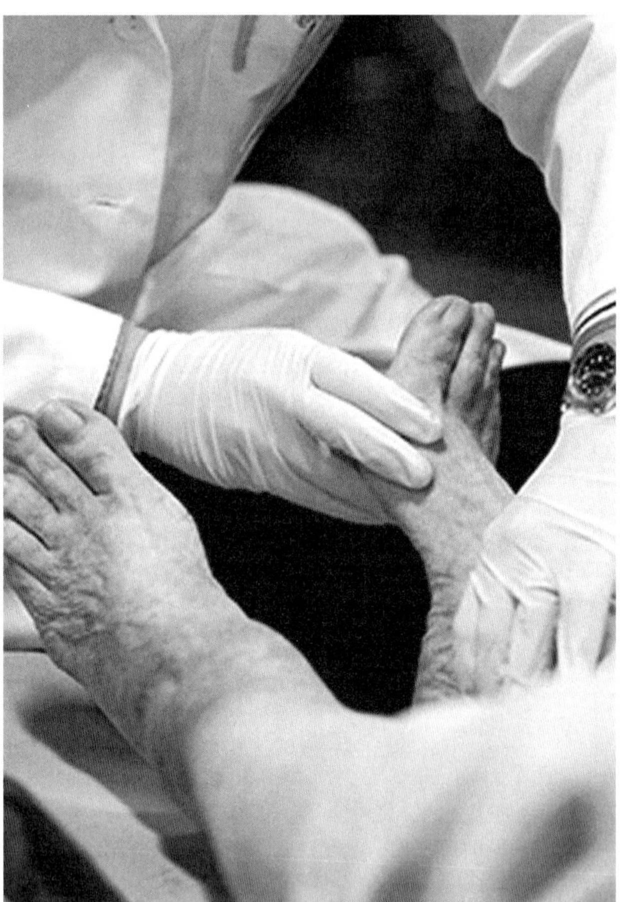

Podiatrists treat injuries involving the lower extremities.

- Refer patients to other physicians or specialists if they detect other health problems, such as diabetes or vascular disease
- Conduct research, read journals, and attend conferences to keep up with advances in podiatric medicine and surgery

Podiatrists treat a variety of foot and ankle ailments, including calluses, ingrown toenails, heel spurs, arthritis, and arch problems. They also treat foot and leg problems associated with diabetes, obesity, and other health conditions. Some podiatrists spend most of their time performing surgery, such as foot and ankle reconstruction. Others may choose a specialty such as sports medicine, pediatrics, or diabetic foot care.

Podiatrists who own their practice may spend time on business-related activities, such as hiring employees and managing inventory.

Work Environment

Podiatrists held about 10,600 jobs in 2022. The largest employers of podiatrists were as follows:

Offices of other health practitioners	52%
Offices of physicians	20
Self-employed workers	10
Federal government, excluding postal service	8
Hospitals; state, local, and private	7

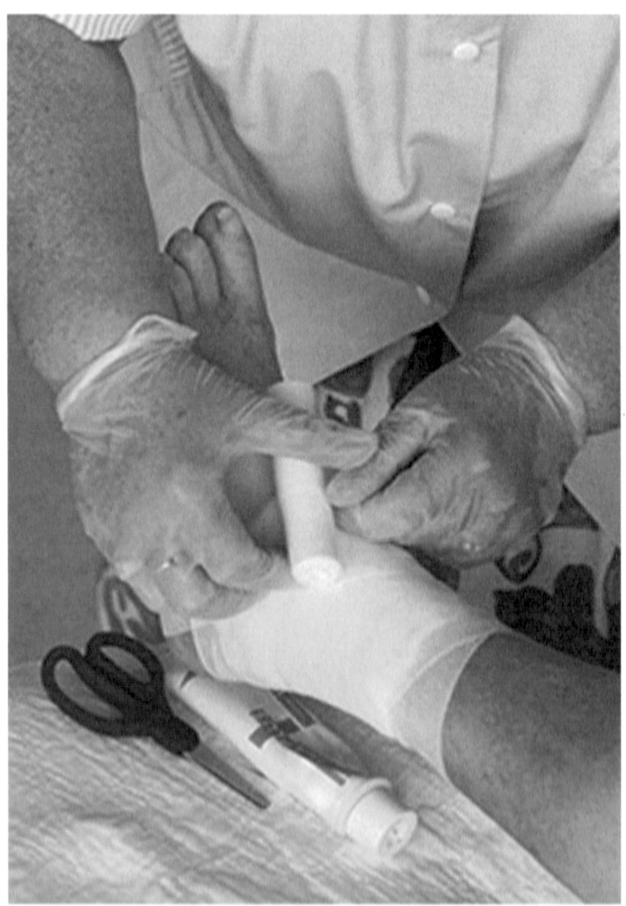

Patients with diabetes may develop foot problems that require the care of a podiatrist.

Offices of podiatry are counted among offices of other healthcare practitioners.

Some podiatrists work in group practices with other physicians or specialists. Podiatrists may work closely with physicians and surgeons, physician assistants, nurse practitioners, registered nurses, medical assistants, and dietitians and nutritionists.

Work Schedules

Most podiatrists work full time, and some work more than 40 hours per week. Work schedules may vary and include evenings or weekends to accommodate patients. Some podiatrists, such as those who work in urgent-care facilities, may need to be on call for emergencies. Self-employed podiatrists or those who own their practice may have flexibility in setting their own hours.

How to Become a Podiatrist

Podiatrists must earn a Doctor of Podiatric Medicine (DPM) degree and complete a 3-year residency program. Every state requires podiatrists to be licensed.

Education

Podiatrists must have a Doctor of Podiatric Medicine (DPM) degree from an accredited college of podiatric medicine. A DPM degree program takes 4 years to complete. Colleges of podiatric medicine are accredited by the Council on Podiatric Medical Education, which provides a list online of accredited programs.

Admission to podiatric medicine programs requires at least 3 years of undergraduate education, but nearly all prospective students have a bachelor's degree in healthcare, biology, or physical science. Although programs might not specify the undergraduate degree required for admission, applicants must have completed courses in laboratory sciences such as biology, chemistry, and physics, as well as general coursework in subjects such as English. Applicants to DPM schools usually submit scores from the Medical College Admission Test (MCAT) and letters of recommendation. They also may indicate that they shadowed a podiatrist.

Courses for a DPM degree are similar to those for other medical degrees. They include anatomy, physiology, pharmacology, and pathology. Podiatric medical students gain supervised experience by completing clinical rotations while in school.

Training

After earning a DPM, podiatrists must apply to and complete a podiatric medicine and surgery residency (PMSR) program. Residency programs, which last several years, take place in

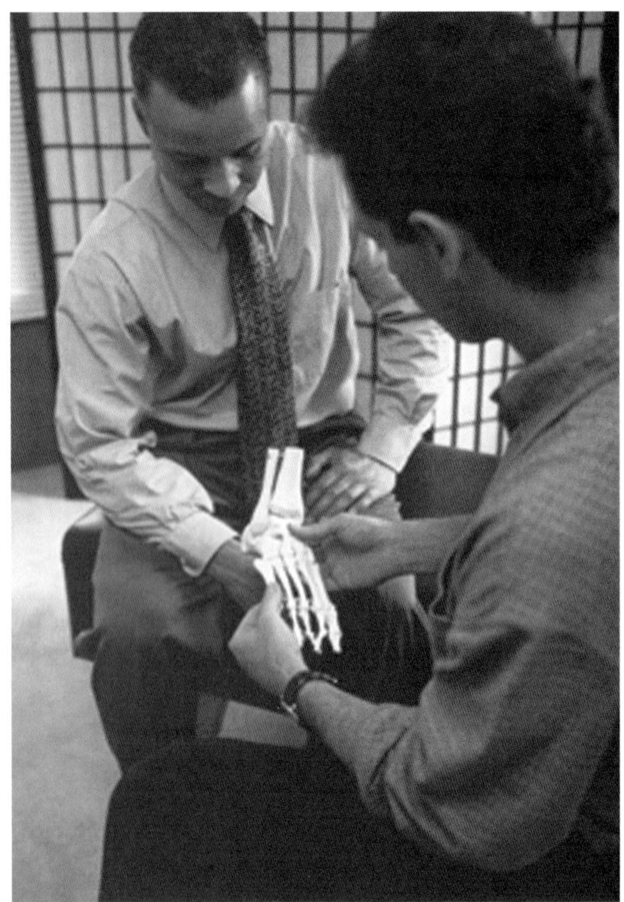

Podiatrists listen to patients' concerns about their feet, ankles, or lower legs.

hospitals and allow podiatrists to gain experience providing medical and surgical care to patients.

Podiatrists may complete additional training in specific fellowship areas, such as podiatric wound care, diabetic foot care, or limb preservation.

Licenses, Certifications, and Registrations

Podiatrists in every state must be licensed. Podiatrists must pay a fee and pass all parts of the American Podiatric Medical Licensing Exam (APMLE), offered by the National Board of Podiatric Medical Examiners. Some states have additional requirements. A full list of requirements for each state is available from the Federation of Podiatric Medical Boards.

Many podiatrists choose to become board certified. Certification generally requires a combination of work experience and passing an exam. Board certification is offered by the American Board of Foot and Ankle Surgery, the American Board of Lower Extremity Surgery, the American Board of Podiatric Medicine, and the American Board of Multiple Specialties in Podiatry.

Important Qualities

Communication skills. Podiatrists must be able to listen and convey information to patients, such as about the diagnosis and ways to improve their condition.

Compassion. Because podiatrists provide care for patients who may be in pain, they must treat patients with understanding.

Critical-thinking skills. Podiatrists must be analytical to correctly diagnose a patient and determine the best course of treatment.

Detail oriented. When diagnosing a problem, podiatrists must pay attention to details, such as those about the patient's medical history and current conditions.

Interpersonal skills. Podiatrists spend much of their time interacting with patients and also must work well as part of a medical team coordinating patient care.

Pay

The median annual wage for podiatrists was $148,720 in May 2022. The median wage is the wage at which half the workers in an occupation earned more than that amount and half earned less. The lowest 10 percent earned less than $60,280, and the highest 10 percent earned more than $239,200.

In May 2022, the median annual wages for podiatrists in the top industries in which they worked were as follows:

Offices of physicians	$191,450
Federal government, excluding postal service	183,840
Offices of other health practitioners	123,180
Hospitals; state, local, and private	92,940

Most podiatrists work full time, and some work more than 40 hours per week. Work schedules may vary and include evenings or weekends to accommodate patients. Some podiatrists, such as those who work in urgent-care facilities, may need to be on call for emergencies. Self-employed podiatrists or those who own their practice may have flexibility in setting their own hours.

Job Outlook

Employment of podiatrists is projected to show little or no change from 2022 to 2032.

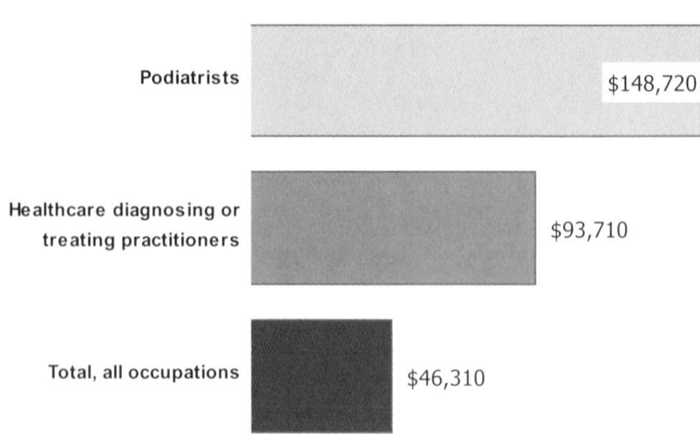

Note: All Occupations includes all occupations in the U.S. Economy.
Source: U.S. Bureau of Labor Statistics, Occupational Employment and Wage Statistics.

Podiatrists

Percent change in employment, projected 2022-32

Healthcare diagnosing or treating practitioners 9%

Total, all occupations 3%

Podiatrists 1%

Note: All Occupations includes all occupations in the U.S. Economy.
Source: U.S. Bureau of Labor Statistics, Employment Projections program.

Despite limited employment growth, about 300 openings for podiatrists are projected each year, on average, over the decade. Most of those openings are expected to result from the need to replace workers who transfer to different occupations or exit the labor force, such as to retire.

Employment

The U.S. population continues to age and to see an associated increase in its rates of chronic diseases, such as diabetes and obesity. As a result, people will continue to have mobility and foot-related problems, and podiatrists will be needed to treat many of these conditions. However, demand for podiatrists is expected to be limited because many patients may acquire services from a non-podiatrist physician or other appropriate caregiver.

Occupational Title	SOC Code	Employment, 2022	Projected Employment, 2032	Change, 2022-32	
				Percent	Numeric
Podiatrists	29-1081	10,600	10,700	1	100

Contacts for More Information

For more information about podiatrists, visit

- American Podiatric Medical Association
- American Association of Colleges of Podiatric Medicine
- Council on Podiatric Medical Education
- National Board of Podiatric Medical Examiners
- American Board of Foot and Ankle Surgery
- American Board of Lower Extremity Surgery
- American Board of Podiatric Medicine
- American Board of Multiple Specialties in Podiatry

Psychiatric Technicians and Aides

Summary

Quick Facts: Psychiatric Technicians and Aides

2022 Median Pay	$37,330 per year $17.95 per hour
Typical Entry-Level Education	See How to Become One
Work Experience in a Related Occupation	See How to Become One
On-the-job Training	Short-term on-the-job training
Number of Jobs, 2022	139,600
Job Outlook, 2022-32	9% (Much faster than average)
Employment Change, 2022-32	12,000

What Psychiatric Technicians and Aides Do

Psychiatric technicians and aides care for people who have mental conditions or developmental disabilities.

Work Environment

Psychiatric technicians and aides work primarily in healthcare settings, such as psychiatric hospitals and residential mental health facilities. The work may be physically demanding, and technicians and aides risk injury on the job. Most are full time, but part-time work is common; schedules may include nights, weekends, or holidays in facilities that are open 24 hours.

How to Become a Psychiatric Technician or Aide

To enter the occupation, psychiatric technicians typically need a postsecondary certificate, and aides need at least a high school diploma or equivalent. Some states require technicians to be licensed. Both technicians and aides get on-the-job training.

Psychiatric technicians and aides care for people who have mental illness and developmental disabilities.

Pay

The median annual wage for psychiatric aides was $37,160 in May 2022.

The median annual wage for psychiatric technicians was $37,380 in May 2022.

Job Outlook

Overall employment of psychiatric technicians and aides is projected to grow 9 percent from 2022 to 2032, much faster than the average for all occupations.

About 15,200 openings for psychiatric technicians and aides are projected each year, on average, over the decade. Many of those openings are expected to result from the need to replace workers who transfer to different occupations or exit the labor force, such as to retire.

What Psychiatric Technicians and Aides Do

Psychiatric technicians and aides care for people who have mental or emotional conditions or developmental disabilities. Technicians typically monitor patients' conditions and provide therapeutic care, such as overseeing their medications. Aides help patients in their daily activities and ensure a safe and clean environment.

Duties

Psychiatric technicians, sometimes called mental health technicians, typically do the following:

- Listen to patients' concerns, observe their behavior, and record their condition
- Report changes in patient health or behavior to medical staff
- Lead patients in therapeutic and recreational activities
- Provide medications and other treatments to patients, following instructions from doctors and other medical professionals
- Help with patient intake and discharge
- Monitor patients' vital signs, such as their blood pressure and body temperature
- Help patients with daily living activities, including eating and bathing
- Restrain patients who are or may become physically violent

Psychiatric aides typically do the following:

- Monitor patients' behavior and location in a mental healthcare facility
- Escort patients within a facility
- Help patients with daily living activities, such as bathing and dressing
- Serve meals and help patients eat
- Keep facilities clean by doing tasks such as changing bed linens
- Participate in or accompany patients to group activities, such as recreational sports or field trips
- Restrain patients who are or may become physically violent

Psychiatric technicians may monitor patients' vital signs, such as taking their blood pressure.

Some psychiatric technicians and aides provide care to patients who have severe developmental disabilities or mental health issues. Others work with patients undergoing rehabilitation for drug and alcohol addiction. Their work varies based on the types of patients they work with.

Psychiatric technicians and aides work as part of a medical team under the direction of physicians or registered nurses. Other team members may include psychiatrists, psychologists, social workers, counselors, and therapists. For more information about the counselors and therapists they may work with, see the profiles on substance abuse, behavioral disorder, and mental health counselors, rehabilitation counselors, and marriage and family therapists.

Work Environment

Psychiatric aides held about 32,400 jobs in 2022. The largest employers of psychiatric aides were as follows:

Psychiatric and substance abuse hospitals; state, local, and private	45%
State government, excluding education and hospitals	21
General medical and surgical hospitals; state, local, and private	11

Psychiatric aides and technicians work as part of a medical team, under the direction of physicians.

Residential mental health and substance abuse facilities	5
Outpatient mental health and substance abuse centers	2

Psychiatric technicians held about 107,100 jobs in 2022. The largest employers of psychiatric technicians were as follows:

Psychiatric and substance abuse hospitals; state, local, and private	31%
General medical and surgical hospitals; state, local, and private	14
Offices of mental health practitioners (except physicians)	10
Residential mental health and substance abuse facilities	9
Outpatient mental health and substance abuse centers	8

Psychiatric technicians and aides may need to stand for long periods, and the work can be physically demanding. Some of their tasks are unpleasant, and it can be challenging to care for patients who are disoriented, uncooperative, or violent.

Despite their work's challenges, however, psychiatric technicians and aides may find it rewarding. For example, their close contact with patients allows technicians and aides to have a positive influence on patients' outlook and treatment.

Injuries and Illnesses

Psychiatric technicians and aides have some of the highest rates of injuries and illnesses of all occupations. Common injuries may include sprains and strains, such as from lifting and turning patients. Injuries also may result from working with patients who are physically uncooperative.

Psychiatric technicians and aides learn proper lifting techniques to minimize their risk of injury. In addition, these workers receive safety training to help with handling patients who may be a danger to themselves or others.

Work Schedule

Most psychiatric technicians and aides work full time, but part-time work is common. Because hospitals and residential facilities operate 24 hours a day, psychiatric technicians and aides may work nights, weekends, and holidays.

How to Become a Psychiatric Technician or Aide

To enter the occupation, psychiatric technicians typically need a postsecondary certificate, and aides need at least a high school diploma or equivalent. Some states require technicians to be licensed. Both technicians and aides get on-the-job training.

Education

Psychiatric technicians typically need a postsecondary certificate for psychiatric technicians, behavioral health technicians, or similar titles. Programs for these certificates or associate's degrees, available at community colleges and technical schools, train students in basic nursing skills. They include courses in psychology, anatomy, and pharmacology and also may include supervised clinical work experience. Some employers prefer to hire candidates who have a bachelor's degree.

Psychiatric aides typically need a high school diploma or equivalent.

Training

Psychiatric technicians and aides may have a short period of on-the-job training. This training may include working with patients while under the supervision of an experienced technician or aide.

Other Experience

Employers may prefer that psychiatric technicians and aides have experience in a related occupation, such as having worked with

Psychiatric technicians observe patients' behavior and listen to their concerns.

people who have developmental disabilities or mental health conditions. Technician experience also may include a clinical component, which they can gain in occupations such as nursing assistant or licensed practical or licensed vocational nurse.

Licenses, Certifications, and Registrations

Some states require psychiatric technicians to have a license. Requirements may include completing an accredited education program and passing an exam. Contact your state licensing board for additional information.

Psychiatric technicians may choose to earn optional certification. For example, the American Association of Psychiatric Technicians offers four levels of certification for psychiatric technicians. Requirements vary based on education and work experience.

Employers may require candidates to have certification in cardiopulmonary resuscitation (CPR) or basic life support (BLS).

Important Qualities

Compassion. Psychiatric technicians and aides spend much of their time interacting with patients who have mental, emotional, or developmental conditions. They must be caring and understanding of their patients.

Interpersonal skills. Psychiatric technicians and aides may want to develop a rapport with patients in order to properly care for them. They also must be able to work well as part of a medical team.

Observational skills. Psychiatric technicians and aides must watch patients closely and be sensitive to changes in behavior. For their safety and that of their patients, they must recognize signs of discomfort or trouble among patients.

Patience. Working with people who have mental, emotional, or developmental conditions may be challenging. Psychiatric technicians and aides must be able to stay calm in stressful situations.

Physical stamina. Psychiatric technicians and aides must lift, move, and sometimes restrain patients. They also spend much of their time standing.

Pay

The median annual wage for psychiatric aides was $37,160 in May 2022. The median wage is the wage at which half the workers in an occupation earned more than that amount and half earned less. The lowest 10 percent earned less than $25,900, and the highest 10 percent earned more than $52,050.

The median annual wage for psychiatric technicians was $37,380 in May 2022. The lowest 10 percent earned less than $28,660, and the highest 10 percent earned more than $58,880.

In May 2022, the median annual wages for psychiatric aides in the top industries in which they worked were as follows:

Psychiatric and substance abuse hospitals; state, local, and private	$38,810
General medical and surgical hospitals; state, local, and private	37,460
State government, excluding education and hospitals	33,280
Residential mental health and substance abuse facilities	29,060
Outpatient mental health and substance abuse centers	27,860

In May 2022, the median annual wages for psychiatric technicians in the top industries in which they worked were as follows:

General medical and surgical hospitals; state, local, and private	$38,240

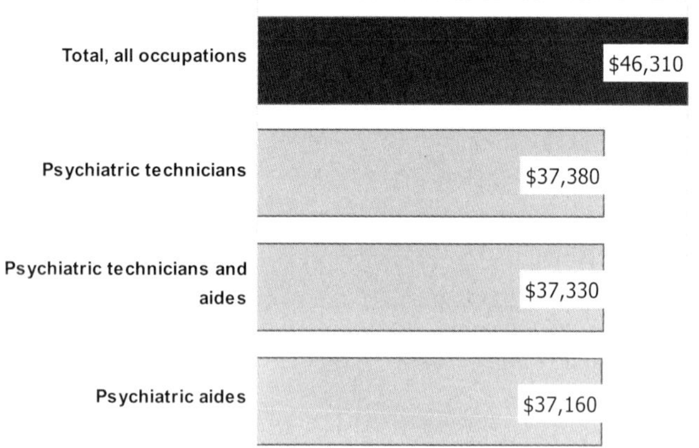

Note: All Occupations includes all occupations in the U.S. Economy.
Source: U.S. Bureau of Labor Statistics, Occupational Employment and Wage Statistics.

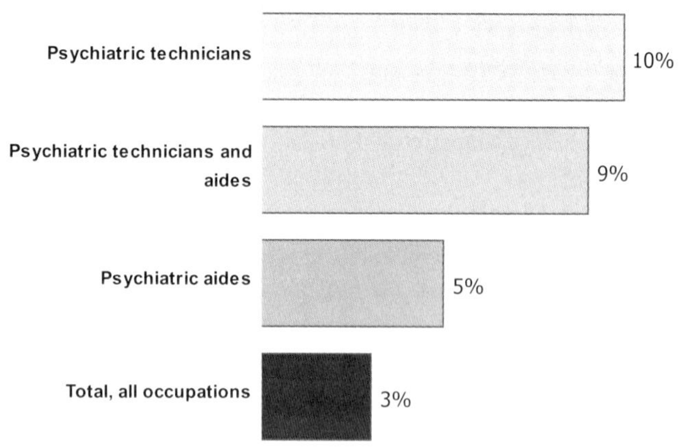

Note: All Occupations includes all occupations in the U.S. Economy.
Source: U.S. Bureau of Labor Statistics, Employment Projections program.

Offices of mental health practitioners (except physicians)	37,360
Psychiatric and substance abuse hospitals; state, local, and private	37,330
Outpatient mental health and substance abuse centers	35,660
Residential mental health and substance abuse facilities	34,060

Most psychiatric technicians and aides work full time, but part-time work is common. Because hospitals and residential facilities operate 24 hours a day, psychiatric technicians and aides may work nights, weekends, and holidays.

Job Outlook

Overall employment of psychiatric technicians and aides is projected to grow 9 percent from 2022 to 2032, much faster than the average for all occupations.

About 15,200 openings for psychiatric technicians and aides are projected each year, on average, over the decade. Many of those openings are expected to result from the need to replace workers who transfer to different occupations or exit the labor force, such as to retire.

Employment

Projected employment of psychiatric technicians and aides varies by occupation (see table). Cognitive disorders, such as Alzheimer's disease and dementia, are more likely to occur in older people. As the nation's population of older people grows, demand is expected to increase for psychiatric technicians and aides who care for patients affected by such disorders.

Psychiatric technicians and aides also will be needed to care for people who have mental health and substance abuse issues.

Occupational Title	SOC Code	Employment, 2022	Projected Employment, 2032	Change, 2022-32	
				Percent	Numeric
Psychiatric technicians and aides	—	139,600	151,500	9	12,000
Psychiatric technicians	29-2053	107,100	117,500	10	10,400
Psychiatric aides	31-1133	32,400	34,000	5	1,600

Contacts for More Information

For more information about psychiatric technicians and aides, visit

➤ American Association of Psychiatric Technicians

Radiation Therapists

Summary

Quick Facts: Radiation Therapists	
2022 Median Pay	$89,530 per year $43.04 per hour
Typical Entry-Level Education	Associate's degree
Work Experience in a Related Occupation	None
On-the-job Training	None
Number of Jobs, 2022	15,900
Job Outlook, 2022-32	2% (As fast as average)
Employment Change, 2022-32	400

What Radiation Therapists Do

Radiation therapists administer doses of radiation to patients who have cancer or other serious diseases.

Work Environment

Radiation therapists work in hospitals, offices of physicians, and outpatient centers. Most radiation therapists work full time.

How to Become a Radiation Therapist

Radiation therapists typically need an associate's or bachelor's degree in radiation therapy. Most states require radiation therapists to be licensed or certified, which often includes passing a national certification exam.

Pay

The median annual wage for radiation therapists was $89,530 in May 2022.

Job Outlook

Employment of radiation therapists is projected to grow 2 percent from 2022 to 2032, about as fast as the average for all occupations.

About 700 openings for radiation therapists are projected each year, on average, over the decade. Many of those openings are expected to result from the need to replace workers who transfer to different occupations or exit the labor force, such as to retire.

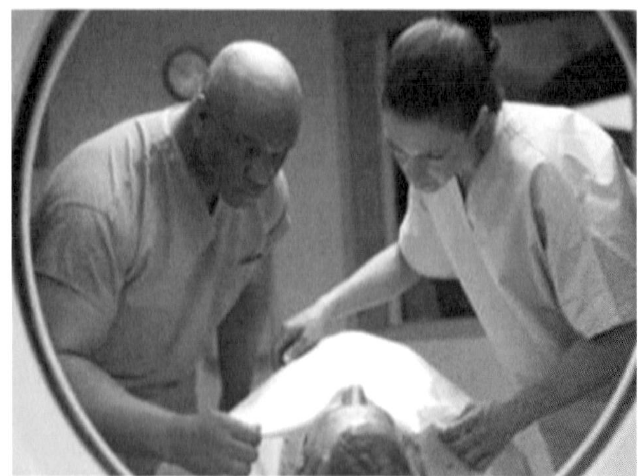

Radiation therapists treat cancer and other diseases in patients by administering radiation treatments.

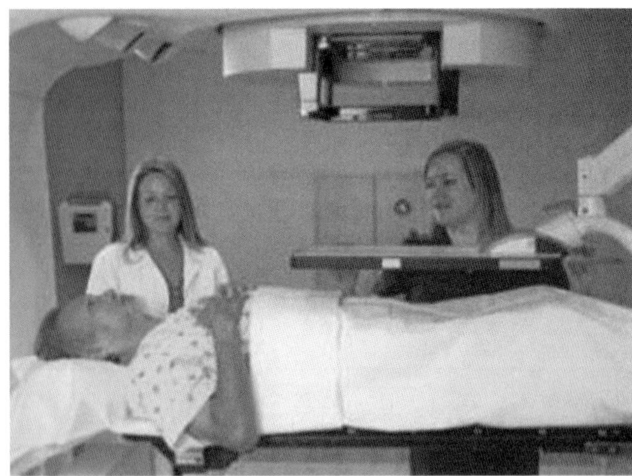

Radiation therapists are part of the oncology teams that treat patients with cancer.

What Radiation Therapists Do

Radiation therapists administer doses of radiation to patients who have cancer or other serious diseases.

Duties

Radiation therapists typically do the following:

- Explain treatment plans to the patient and answer questions about treatment
- Protect the patients and themselves from improper exposure to radiation
- Determine the location of tumors to ensure correct positioning of patients for administering each treatment
- Calibrate and operate the machine to treat the patient with radiation
- Monitor the patient to check for unusual reactions to the treatment
- Keep detailed records of treatment

Radiation therapists operate machines, such as linear accelerators, to deliver concentrated radiation therapy to the region of a patient's tumor. Radiation treatment may shrink or eliminate cancers and tumors.

Radiation therapists are part of the oncology teams that treat patients with cancer. They often work with the following specialists:

- Medical dosimetrists calculate the correct dose of radiation for cancer treatment
- Medical physicists help in planning radiation treatments, develop better and safer radiation therapies, and check that radiation output is accurate
- Oncology nurses specialize in caring for patients with cancer
- Radiation oncologists are physicians who specialize in radiation therapy

Work Environment

Radiation therapists held about 15,900 jobs in 2022. The largest employers of radiation therapists were as follows:

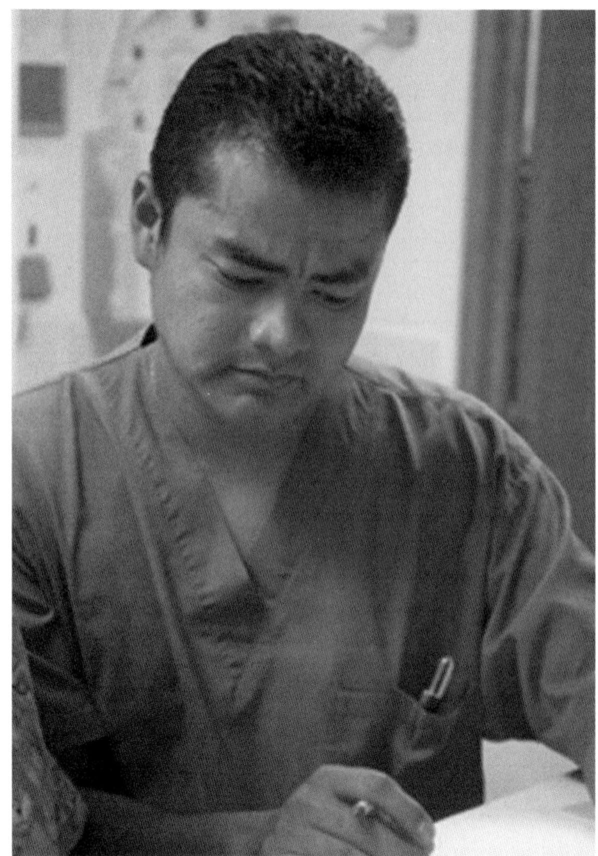

Radiation therapists work in hospitals, offices of physicians, and outpatient centers.

Hospitals; state, local, and private	66%
Offices of physicians	24
Outpatient care centers	3

Radiation therapists stand for long periods and may need to lift or turn patients.

Injuries and illnesses

Because radiation therapists work with radiation and radioactive materials, they should be aware of the risks involved and must follow safety procedures. These procedures require therapists to be in a different room while administering radiation to a patient and to wear a film badge dosimeter to track their exposure.

Work Schedules

Most radiation therapists work full time. They have a regular work schedule because radiation therapy procedures are usually planned in advance.

How to Become a Radiation Therapist

Radiation therapists typically need an associate's or bachelor's degree in radiation therapy. Most states require radiation therapists to be licensed or certified, which often includes passing a national certification exam.

Education

Employers usually prefer to hire applicants who have an associate's degree or a bachelor's degree in a healthcare and related

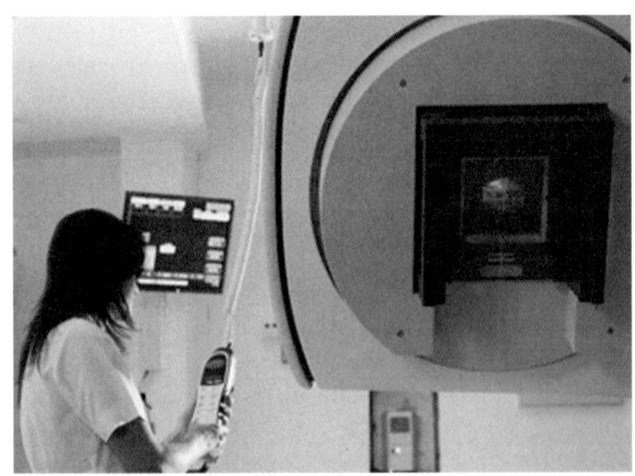

Radiation therapists must be licensed or certified in most states.

field, such as radiation therapy, or in science technologies or biology. However, candidates may qualify for some positions by completing a certificate program.

Radiation therapy programs include courses in radiation therapy procedures and the scientific theories behind them. These programs often include experience in a clinical setting and courses such as human anatomy and physiology, physics, and algebra. A list of accredited radiation therapy programs is available from the Joint Review Committee on Education in Radiologic Technology (JRCERT).

Important Qualities

Compassion. Radiation therapists work with patients who are suffering from cancer or another serious disease. They must display empathy while helping patients through the experience.

Detail oriented. Radiation therapists must follow precise instructions and input exact measurements to make sure the patient is exposed to the correct amount of radiation.

Interpersonal skills. Radiation therapists work closely with patients over multiple weeks and must be able to explain the treatment. Radiation therapists also must work well with other members of the oncology team to effectively coordinate care.

Technical skills. Radiation therapists work with computers and large pieces of technological equipment, so they must be comfortable operating those devices.

Licenses, Certifications, and Registrations

In most states, radiation therapists must be licensed or certified. Requirements vary by state but may include graduating from an accredited radiation therapy program and passing an exam or earning certification from the American Registry of Radiologic Technologists (ARRT).

To become ARRT certified, an applicant must earn an associate's or higher degree from an approved radiation therapy program, adhere to ARRT ethical standards, and pass the certification exam. The exam covers topics such as radiation protection, treatment planning, and patient care and education.

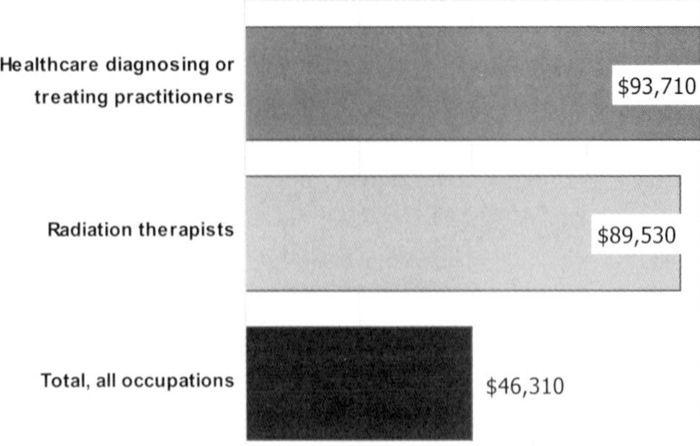

Note: All Occupations includes all occupations in the U.S. Economy.
Source: U.S. Bureau of Labor Statistics, Occupational Employment and Wage Statistics.

Many jobs also require cardiopulmonary resuscitation (CPR) or basic life support (BLS) certification.

Advancement

With additional education and certification, therapists may become *medical dosimetrists*. Dosimetrists are responsible for calculating the correct dose of radiation that is used in the treatment of cancer patients.

Pay

The median annual wage for radiation therapists was $89,530 in May 2022. The median wage is the wage at which half the workers in an occupation earned more than that amount and half earned less. The lowest 10 percent earned less than $65,760, and the highest 10 percent earned more than $133,260.

In May 2022, the median annual wages for radiation therapists in the top industries in which they worked were as follows:

Outpatient care centers	$116,750
Offices of physicians	88,700
Hospitals; state, local, and private	88,040

Most radiation therapists work full time. They have a regular work schedule because radiation therapy procedures are usually planned in advance.

Job Outlook

Employment of radiation therapists is projected to grow 2 percent from 2022 to 2032, about as fast as the average for all occupations.

About 700 openings for radiation therapists are projected each year, on average, over the decade. Many of those openings are expected to result from the need to replace workers who

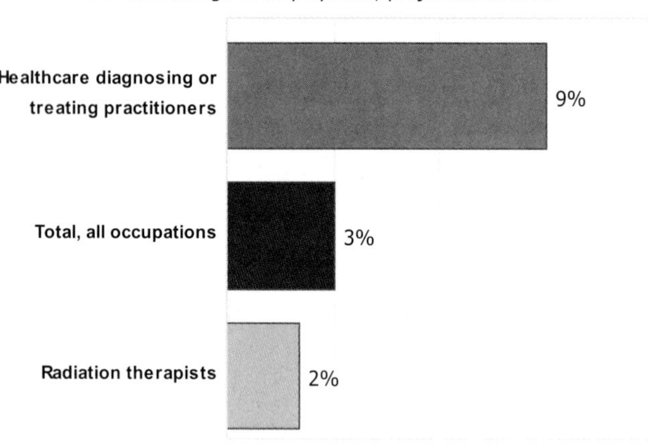

Note: All Occupations includes all occupations in the U.S. Economy.
Source: U.S. Bureau of Labor Statistics, Employment Projections program.

transfer to different occupations or exit the labor force, such as to retire.

Employment

Radiotherapy plays a central role in cancer treatment, with around half of cancer patients requiring radiation at some point during their care. Because the incidence of cancer increases as people age, a rise in the number of older people is likely to increase demand for radiation therapists. However, growing adoption of more efficient radiotherapy techniques, which allow patients to finish their treatment in fewer visits, may limit employment demand.

Occupational Title	SOC Code	Employment, 2022	Projected Employment, 2032	Change, 2022-32	
				Percent	Numeric
Radiation therapists	29-1124	15,900	16,300	2	400

Contacts for More Information

For more information about radiation therapists, visit

- American Society of Radiologic Technologists
- The American Registry of Radiologic Technologists
- For a list of accredited programs in radiation therapy, visit
- The Joint Review Committee on Education in Radiologic Technology

Radiologic and MRI Technologists

Summary

Quick Facts: Radiologic and MRI Technologists	
2022 Median Pay	$67,180 per year $32.30 per hour
Typical Entry-Level Education	Associate's degree
Work Experience in a Related Occupation	See How to Become One
On-the-job Training	None
Number of Jobs, 2022	264,100
Job Outlook, 2022-32	6% (Faster than average)
Employment Change, 2022-32	15,400

What Radiologic and MRI Technologists Do

Radiologic technologists perform diagnostic imaging examinations on patients. MRI technologists operate magnetic resonance imaging (MRI) scanners to create diagnostic images.

Work Environment

Radiologic and MRI technologists work in healthcare facilities, and more than half work in hospitals. Most radiologic and MRI technologists work full time.

How to Become a Radiologic or MRI Technologist

Radiologic technologists and MRI technologists typically need an associate's degree. MRI technologists also typically need several years of related work experience. Most states require radiologic technologists to be licensed or certified, but few states require licensure for MRI technologists. Regardless of state requirements, employers typically require or prefer to hire technologists who are certified.

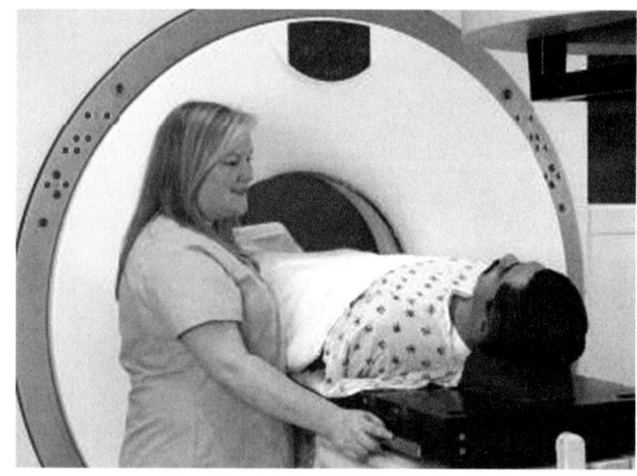

Radiologic and MRI technologists perform diagnostic imaging examinations, such as magnetic resonance, on patients.

Pay

The median annual wage for magnetic resonance imaging technologists was $80,090 in May 2022.

The median annual wage for radiologic technologists and technicians was $65,140 in May 2022.

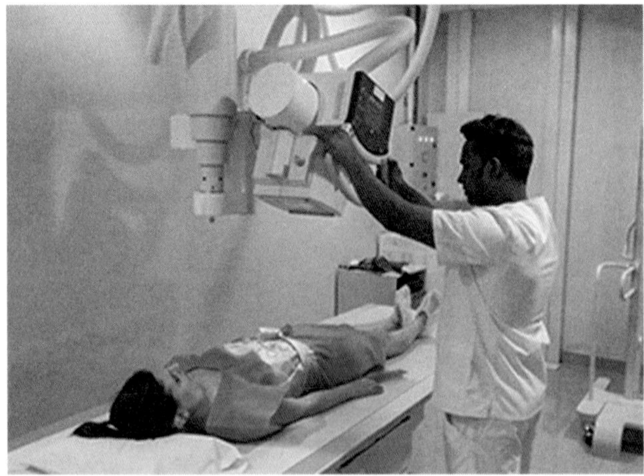

Radiologic technologists specialize in x-ray and computed tomography (CT) imaging.

Job Outlook

Overall employment of radiologic and MRI technologists is projected to grow 6 percent from 2022 to 2032, faster than the average for all occupations.

About 15,700 openings for radiologic and MRI technologists are projected each year, on average, over the decade. Many of those openings are expected to result from the need to replace workers who transfer to different occupations or exit the labor force, such as to retire.

What Radiologic and MRI Technologists Do

Radiologic technologists, also known as *radiographers*, perform x rays and other diagnostic imaging examinations on patients. MRI technologists operate magnetic resonance imaging (MRI) scanners to create diagnostic images.

Duties

Radiologic and MRI technologists typically do the following:

- Adjust and maintain imaging equipment
- Follow precise orders from physicians on what areas of the body to image
- Prepare patients for procedures, including taking a medical history and shielding exposed areas that do not need to be imaged
- Position the patient and the equipment in order to get the correct image
- Operate the computerized equipment to take the images
- Work with physicians to evaluate the images and to determine whether additional images need to be taken
- Keep detailed patient records

Radiologic technologists are trained in the use of different types of medical diagnostic equipment. They may choose to specialize, such as in x-ray, mammography, or computed tomography (CT) imaging. Some radiologic technologists provide a mixture for the patient to drink that allows soft tissue to be viewed on the images that the radiologist reviews.

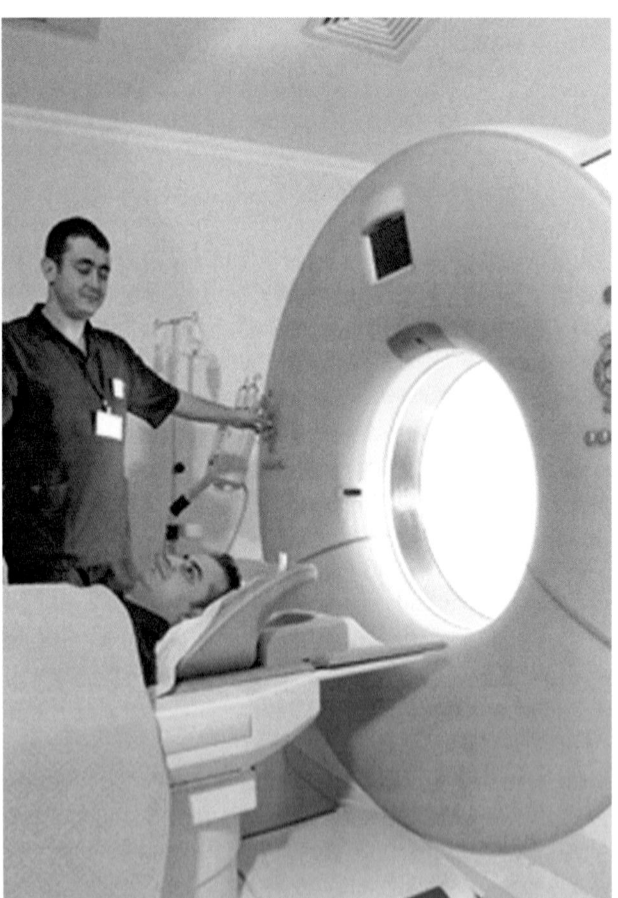

Radiologic and MRI technologists work in hospitals and other healthcare facilities.

MRI technologists specialize in magnetic resonance imaging scanners. They inject patients with contrast media, such as a dye, so that the images will show up on the scanner. The scanners use magnetic fields in combination with the contrast agent to produce images that a physician can use to diagnose medical problems.

For information about healthcare workers who specialize in other diagnostic equipment, see the profiles for nuclear medicine technologists and diagnostic medical sonographers, and cardiovascular technologists and technicians, including vascular technologists.

Work Environment

Magnetic resonance imaging technologists held about 41,400 jobs in 2022. The largest employers of magnetic resonance imaging technologists were as follows:

Hospitals; state, local, and private	56%
Medical and diagnostic laboratories	18
Offices of physicians	14
Outpatient care centers	3

Radiologic technologists and technicians held about 222,800 jobs in 2022. The largest employers of radiologic technologists and technicians were as follows:

Hospitals; state, local, and private	58%
Offices of physicians	18
Medical and diagnostic laboratories	7
Outpatient care centers	7
Federal government, excluding postal service	3

Radiologic and MRI technologists are often on their feet for long periods and may need to lift or turn patients, such as to help those who are injured.

Injuries and Illnesses

Like other healthcare workers, radiologic and MRI technologists may be exposed to infectious diseases. In addition, because radiologic technologists work with imaging equipment that uses radiation, they must wear badges that measure radiation levels in the radiation area. Detailed records are kept on their cumulative lifetime dose. Although radiation hazards exist in this occupation, they are minimized by the use of protective lead aprons, gloves, and other shielding devices and by the badges that monitor exposure to radiation.

Work Schedules

Most radiologic and MRI technologists work full time. Because imaging is sometimes needed in emergency situations, some technologists work evenings, weekends, or overnight.

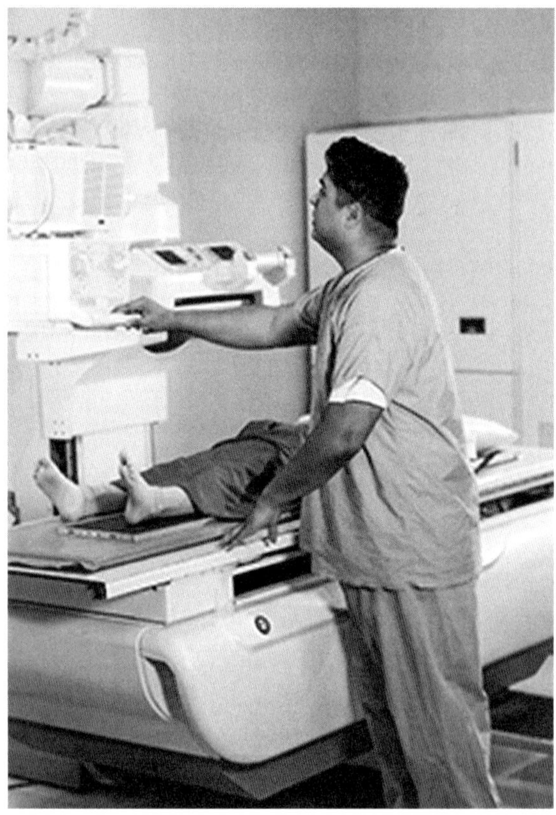

Radiologic technologists must follow instructions exactly to get the images needed for diagnoses.

How to Become a Radiologic or MRI Technologist

Radiologic technologists and MRI technologists typically need an associate's degree. MRI technologists may start out as radiologic technologists. Most states require radiologic technologists to be licensed or certified, but few states require licensure for MRI technologists. Regardless of state requirements, employers typically require or prefer to hire technologists who are certified.

Education

High school students who are interested in radiologic or MRI technology should take courses that focus on math and science, such as anatomy, biology, chemistry, and physics.

An associate's degree is the education typically required for radiologic and MRI technologists. There also are postsecondary education programs that lead to graduate certificates or bachelor's degrees in healthcare and related fields and science technologies. Depending on the field of degree, education programs may include both academic study and clinical work. Coursework includes anatomy, pathology, patient care, radiation physics and protection, and image evaluation.

The Joint Review Committee on Education in Radiologic Technology (JRCERT) accredits programs in radiography and magnetic resonance, and the American Registry of Magnetic Resonance Imaging Technologists (ARMRIT) accredits MRI programs. Some states require candidates for licensure to complete an accredited program.

Work Experience in a Related Occupation

MRI technologists typically need less than 5 years of experience in a related occupation, most often from working as a radiologic technologist.

Licenses, Certifications, and Registrations

Most states require radiologic technologists to be licensed or certified. Few states require licensure for MRI technologists. Requirements vary by state.

To become licensed, technologists usually must graduate from an accredited program and either pass a certification exam from the state or obtain certification from a credentialing organization. Technologists may be certified in multiple specialties. Certifications for radiologic technologists are available from the American Registry of Radiologic Technologists (ARRT). Certification for MRI technologists is available from the ARRT and from the American Registry of Magnetic Resonance Imaging Technologists (ARMRIT). For specific licensure requirements for radiologic technologists and MRI technologists, contact the state's health board.

Employers typically require or prefer prospective technologists to be certified even if the state does not require it. Employers also may require or prefer that prospective technologists have certification in cardiopulmonary resuscitation (CPR) or basic life support (BLS).

Important Qualities

Detail oriented. Radiologic and MRI technologists must follow instructions exactly to get the images needed for diagnoses.

Interpersonal skills. Radiologic and MRI technologists work closely with patients who may be stressed or in pain. They must put patients at ease to get usable images.

Math skills. Radiologic and MRI technologists may need to calculate the proper amount of radiation or magnetic resonance emitted in imaging procedures.

Physical stamina. Radiologic and MRI technologists often work on their feet for long periods during their shift and must be able to lift and move patients who need help.

Technical skills. Radiologic and MRI technologists must understand how to operate complex machinery.

Pay

The median annual wage for magnetic resonance imaging technologists was $80,090 in May 2022. The median wage is the wage at which half the workers in an occupation earned more than that amount and half earned less. The lowest 10 percent earned less than $60,530, and the highest 10 percent earned more than $104,850.

The median annual wage for radiologic technologists and technicians was $65,140 in May 2022. The lowest 10 percent earned less than $47,760, and the highest 10 percent earned more than $97,940.

In May 2022, the median annual wages for magnetic resonance imaging technologists in the top industries in which they worked were as follows:

Outpatient care centers	$111,290
Hospitals; state, local, and private	80,370
Medical and diagnostic laboratories	79,110
Offices of physicians	79,020

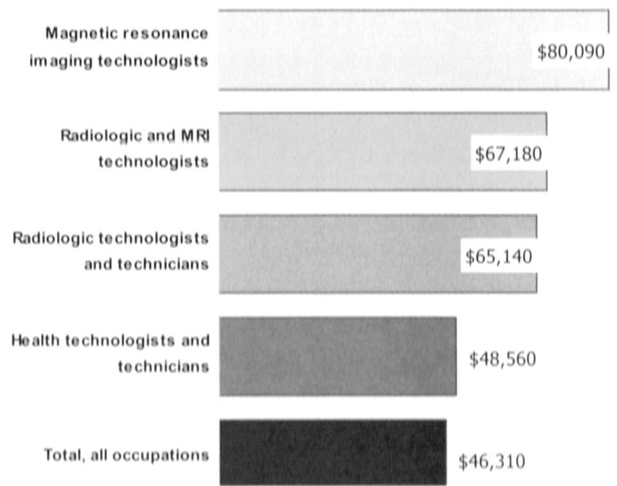

Note: All Occupations includes all occupations in the U.S. Economy.
Source: U.S. Bureau of Labor Statistics, Occupational Employment and Wage Statistics.

In May 2022, the median annual wages for radiologic technologists and technicians in the top industries in which they worked were as follows:

Federal government, excluding postal service	$76,070
Outpatient care centers	74,030
Medical and diagnostic laboratories	72,220
Hospitals; state, local, and private	66,060
Offices of physicians	60,550

Most radiologic and MRI technologists work full time. Because imaging is sometimes needed in emergency situations, some technologists work evenings, weekends, or overnight.

Job Outlook

Overall employment of radiologic and MRI technologists is projected to grow 6 percent from 2022 to 2032, faster than the average for all occupations.

About 15,700 openings for radiologic and MRI technologists are projected each year, on average, over the decade. Many of those openings are expected to result from the need to replace workers who transfer to different occupations or exit the labor force, such as to retire.

Employment

The growing size of the older population and the rising prevalence of chronic disease will lead to greater demand for healthcare services, including diagnostic procedures. More radiologic and MRI technologists will be needed to perform the imaging exams that are essential for making diagnoses and creating treatment plans.

Falls and associated injuries, such as broken bones or head trauma, are common in older people and require x rays or computed tomography (CT) scans to assess the extent of harm. In

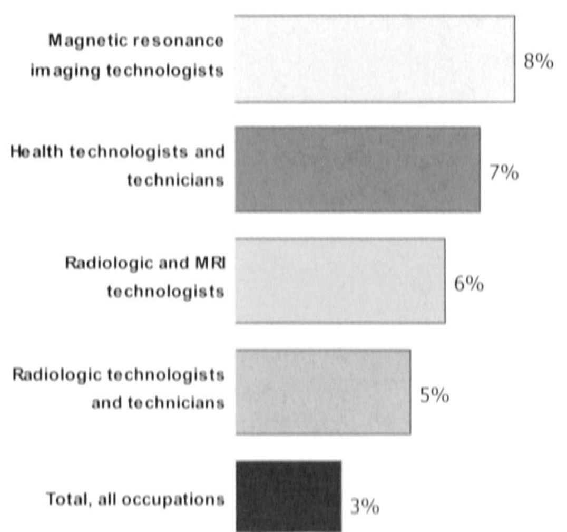

Note: All Occupations includes all occupations in the U.S. Economy.
Source: U.S. Bureau of Labor Statistics, Employment Projections program.

addition, MRI scans are useful for imaging various types of cancers, including of the brain, spine, and liver. As the number of falls and cancer cases rises, these technologists and technicians will be needed to operate the equipment that helps detect, assess, and diagnose these injuries and diseases.

Occupational Title	SOC Code	Employment, 2022	Projected Employment, 2032	Change, 2022-32	
				Percent	Numeric
Radiologic and MRI technologists	—	264,100	279,600	6	15,400
Radiologic technologists and technicians	29-2034	222,800	235,000	5	12,200
Magnetic resonance imaging technologists	29-2035	41,400	44,600	8	3,200

Contacts for More Information

For more information about radiologic and MRI technology, visit

- American Society of Radiologic Technologists
- Joint Review Committee on Education in Radiologic Technology
- American Registry of Radiologic Technologists
- American Registry of Magnetic Resonance Imaging Technologists

Recreational Therapists

Summary

Quick Facts: Recreational Therapists

2022 Median Pay	$51,330 per year $24.68 per hour
Typical Entry-Level Education	Bachelor's degree
Work Experience in a Related Occupation	None
On-the-job Training	None
Number of Jobs, 2022	16,800
Job Outlook, 2022-32	4% (As fast as average)
Employment Change, 2022-32	600

What Recreational Therapists Do

Recreational therapists plan, direct, and coordinate recreation-based medical treatment programs for people with disabilities, injuries, or illnesses.

Work Environment

Recreational therapists work in a variety of settings, including hospitals, nursing homes, and government parks and recreation departments. Most work full time.

How to Become a Recreational Therapist

Recreational therapists typically need a bachelor's degree to enter the occupation. Many employers require them to be certified.

Pay

The median annual wage for recreational therapists was $51,330 in May 2022.

Job Outlook

Employment of recreational therapists is projected to grow 4 percent from 2022 to 2032, about as fast as the average for all occupations.

Recreational therapists engage patients in therapeutic activities, such as swimming.

About 1,300 openings for recreational therapists are projected each year, on average, over the decade. Many of those openings are expected to result from the need to replace workers who transfer to different occupations or exit the labor force, such as to retire.

What Recreational Therapists Do

Recreational therapists plan, direct, and coordinate recreation-based medical treatment programs to help maintain or improve patients' physical, social, and emotional well-being. These therapists use a variety of techniques, including art expression; drama, music, and dance; sports and games; aquatics; and community outings.

Duties

Recreational therapists typically do the following:

- Assess patients' needs through observation, medical records, tests, and discussions with other healthcare workers and patients and their families
- Develop and implement treatment plans that meet patients' goals and interests
- Engage patients in therapeutic activities, such as exercise, games, and community outings
- Help patients learn social skills needed to become or remain independent
- Help patients to reduce and cope with stress, anxiety, or depression
- Document and analyze a patient's progress to ensure that their goals are met and to modify treatment as needed

Recreational therapists use recreation-based medical treatment to help people reduce depression, stress, and anxiety; recover basic physical and mental abilities; build confidence; and socialize effectively.

Recreational therapists are trained to use interventions to help patients of all ages. For example, they may help people with physical disabilities by teaching them adaptive sports. Therapists also may inform people about how to use community resources and participate in recreational activities.

These therapists also help people improve their mental health. They may provide interventions to help patients develop social and coping skills for managing their depression or anxiety.

Therapists may work with physicians or surgeons, registered nurses, psychologists, social workers, physical therapists, teachers, or occupational therapists. Recreational therapists are different from recreation workers, who organize recreational activities primarily for enjoyment.

Work Environment

Recreational therapists held about 16,800 jobs in 2022. The largest employers of recreational therapists were as follows:

Hospitals; state, local, and private	40%
Nursing and residential care facilities	27
Government	20
Ambulatory healthcare services	6
Social assistance	5

Recreational therapists work in an office setting for planning or other administrative activities, such as patient assessment, but they also may travel when working with patients. Therapy may be provided in a clinical or community setting. For example, therapists may take their patients to recreation centers or parks for sports and other activities.

Some therapists spend a lot of time standing when actively working with patients. They also may need to physically assist patients or lift heavy objects, such as wheelchairs.

Work Schedules

Most recreational therapists work full time. Some recreational therapists work evenings and weekends to meet the needs of their patients.

Therapy may be provided in a clinical setting or out in a community.

Most recreational therapists need a bachelor's degree in recreational therapy or a related field.

How to Become a Recreational Therapist

Recreational therapists typically need a bachelor's degree to enter the occupation. Employers may require or prefer therapists to be certified.

Education

Recreational therapists typically need a bachelor's degree in a healthcare field, such as recreational therapy, or in recreation and fitness.

Recreational therapy programs include courses in physiology, human anatomy, and psychology. Bachelor's degree programs usually include an internship.

Licenses, Certifications, and Registrations

Employers may require or prefer recreational therapists to be certified. The National Council for Therapeutic Recreation Certification (NCTRC) offers the Certified Therapeutic Recreation Specialist (CTRS) credential. Candidates may qualify for certification in more than one way. For example, one option requires a bachelor's degree in recreational therapy, completing a supervised internship, and passing an exam. Another option also requires passing an exam but allows candidates with a bachelor's degree in an unrelated subject to qualify with a combination of education and work experience. In order to maintain certification, therapists must either pass an exam or complete work experience and continuing education requirements after a specified number of years.

The NCTRC also offers certification in specialization area designations, including adaptive sports and recreation, behavioral health, and developmental disabilities. Therapists also may earn certificates from other organizations to show proficiency in specific therapy techniques, such as aquatic therapy or aromatherapy.

A small number of states require recreational therapists to be licensed or certified. For specific requirements, contact a state's licensing board.

Some employers prefer to hire recreational therapists who have basic life support (BLS) or cardiopulmonary resuscitation (CPR) certification.

Important Qualities

Communication skills. Recreational therapists need to give clear instructions during activities or for healthy coping techniques. They also must write clearly in documenting patient progress.

Compassion. Recreational therapists may deal with people who are in pain, so they should be empathetic when providing support to patients and their families.

Leadership skills. Recreational therapists must be engaging and able to motivate patients to participate in a variety of therapeutic activities.

Listening skills. Recreational therapists must pay attention to patients' concerns in order to determine an appropriate course of treatment.

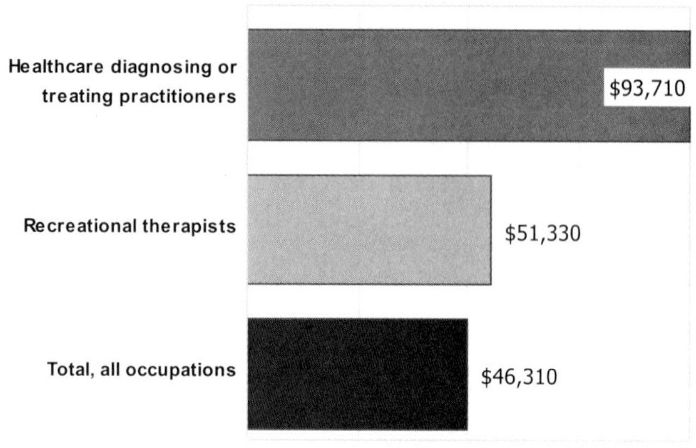

Note: All Occupations includes all occupations in the U.S. Economy.
Source: U.S. Bureau of Labor Statistics, Occupational Employment and Wage Statistics.

Patience. Recreational therapists may work with patients who require more time and special attention than do others.

Resourcefulness. Recreational therapists must be both creative and flexible when customizing treatment plans and adapting activities or programs to meet patients' needs.

Pay

The median annual wage for recreational therapists was $51,330 in May 2022. The median wage is the wage at which half the workers in an occupation earned more than that amount and half earned less. The lowest 10 percent earned less than $33,930, and the highest 10 percent earned more than $84,410.

In May 2022, the median annual wages for recreational therapists in the top industries in which they worked were as follows:

Government	$67,610
Ambulatory healthcare services	58,440
Hospitals; state, local, and private	54,430
Social assistance	44,730
Nursing and residential care facilities	44,180

Most recreational therapists work full time. Some recreational therapists work evenings and weekends to meet the needs of their patients.

Job Outlook

Employment of recreational therapists is projected to grow 4 percent from 2022 to 2032, about as fast as the average for all occupations.

About 1,300 openings for recreational therapists are projected each year, on average, over the decade. Many of those openings are expected to result from the need to replace workers who transfer to different occupations or exit the labor force, such as to retire.

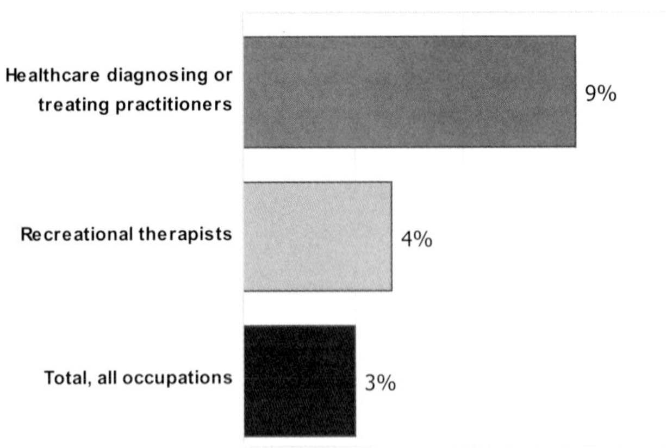

Note: All Occupations includes all occupations in the U.S. Economy.
Source: U.S. Bureau of Labor Statistics, Employment Projections program.

Employment

Demand for recreational therapists is expected to increase in some industries. For example, psychiatric facilities use recreational therapy as a key component of treatment for people struggling with mental illness or addiction. Recreational therapists will be needed to help these patients regain their physical and mental health and to support them in their recovery.

In addition, as large numbers of the U.S. population move into older age groups, more people will need recreational therapists to help them maintain and improve their functional abilities. Therapists also will be needed to help healthy seniors remain social, active, and independent in their communities as they age. However, funding challenges around the provision of recreational therapy services in some settings, such as nursing homes, may dampen demand for the occupation.

Occupational Title	SOC Code	Employment, 2022	Projected Employment, 2032	Change, 2022-32	
				Percent	Numeric
Recreational therapists	29-1125	16,800	17,400	4	600

Contacts for More Information

For more information on careers and academic programs in recreational therapy, visit

- American Therapeutic Recreation Association

For more information about certification, visit

- National Council for Therapeutic Recreation Certification

Registered Nurses

Summary

Quick Facts: Registered Nurses	
2022 Median Pay	$81,220 per year $39.05 per hour
Typical Entry-Level Education	Bachelor's degree
Work Experience in a Related Occupation	None
On-the-job Training	None
Number of Jobs, 2022	3,172,500
Job Outlook, 2022-32	6% (Faster than average)
Employment Change, 2022-32	177,400

What Registered Nurses Do

Registered nurses (RNs) provide and coordinate patient care and educate patients and the public about various health conditions.

Work Environment

Registered nurses work in hospitals, physicians' offices, home healthcare services, and nursing care facilities. Others work in outpatient clinics and schools.

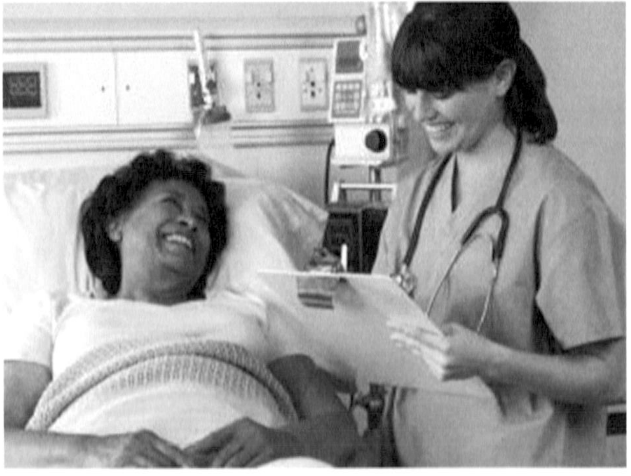

Registered nurses teach patients how to manage their illnesses or injuries.

How to Become a Registered Nurse

Registered nurses usually take one of three education paths: a bachelor's degree in nursing, an associate's degree in nursing, or a diploma from an approved nursing program. Registered nurses must be licensed.

Pay

The median annual wage for registered nurses was $81,220 in May 2022.

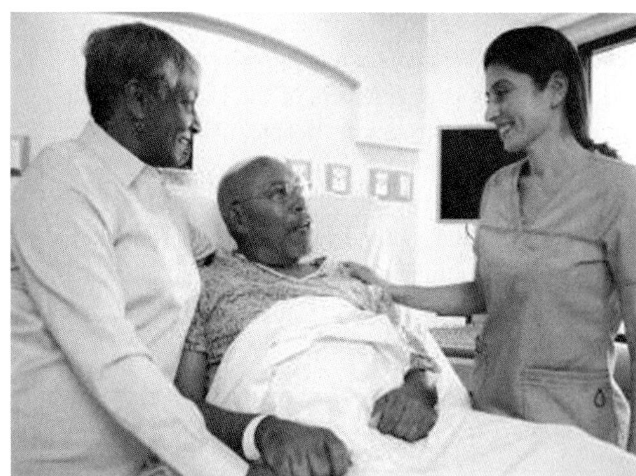

Registered nurses set up plans for patient care.

Job Outlook

Employment of registered nurses is projected to grow 6 percent from 2022 to 2032, faster than the average for all occupations.

About 193,100 openings for registered nurses are projected each year, on average, over the decade. Many of those openings are expected to result from the need to replace workers who transfer to different occupations or exit the labor force, such as to retire.

What Registered Nurses Do

Registered nurses (RNs) provide and coordinate patient care, educate patients and the public about various health conditions, and provide advice and emotional support to patients and their families.

Duties

Registered nurses typically do the following:

- Assess patients' conditions
- Record patients' medical histories and symptoms
- Observe patients and record the observations
- Administer patients' medicines and treatments
- Set up plans for patients' care or contribute information to existing plans
- Consult and collaborate with doctors and other healthcare professionals
- Operate and monitor medical equipment
- Help perform diagnostic tests and analyze the results
- Teach patients and their families how to manage illnesses or injuries
- Explain what to do at home after treatment

Most registered nurses work as part of a team with physicians and other healthcare specialists. Some registered nurses oversee licensed practical nurses, nursing assistants, and home health aides.

Registered nurses' duties and titles often depend on where they work and the patients they work with. For example, an oncology nurse works with cancer patients and a geriatric nurse works with elderly patients. Some registered nurses combine one or more areas of practice. For example, a pediatric oncology nurse works with children and teens who have cancer.

Many possibilities exist for working with specific patient groups. The following list includes some examples:

Addiction nurses care for patients who need help to overcome addictions to alcohol, drugs, and other substances.

Cardiovascular nurses care for patients who have heart disease or heart conditions and people who have had heart surgery.

Critical care nurses work in intensive-care units in hospitals, providing care to patients with serious, complex, and acute illnesses and injuries that need close monitoring and treatment.

Genetics nurses provide screening, counseling, and treatment for patients with genetic disorders, such as cystic fibrosis.

Neonatal nurses take care of newborn babies who have health issues.

Nephrology nurses care for patients who have kidney-related health issues stemming from diabetes, high blood pressure, substance abuse, or other causes.

Public health nurses promote public health by educating people on warning signs and symptoms of disease or managing chronic health conditions. They may also run health screenings, immunization clinics, blood drives, or other community outreach programs.

Rehabilitation nurses care for patients who have temporary or permanent disabilities or have chronic illnesses.

Some nurses do not work directly with patients, but they must still have an active registered nurse license. For example, they may work as nurse educators, healthcare consultants, or hospital administrators.

Clinical nurse specialists **(CNSs)** are a type of advanced practice registered nurse (APRN). They provide direct patient care in one of many nursing specialties, such as psychiatric-mental health or pediatrics. CNSs also provide indirect care by working with other nurses and medical staff to improve the quality of care that patients receive. They often serve in leadership roles and may educate and advise other nursing staff. CNSs also may conduct research and may advocate for certain policies.

Work Environment

Registered nurses held about 3.2 million jobs in 2022. The largest employers of registered nurses were as follows:

Hospitals; state, local, and private	59%
Ambulatory healthcare services	18
Nursing and residential care facilities	6
Government	5
Educational services; state, local, and private	3

Ambulatory healthcare services includes industries such as physicians' offices, home healthcare, and outpatient care centers. Nurses who work in home health travel to patients' homes;

Registered nurses work in many settings, from schools to doctor's offices.

public health nurses may travel to community centers, schools, and other sites.

Some nurses travel frequently in the United States and throughout the world to help care for patients in places where there are not enough healthcare workers.

Injuries and Illnesses

Registered nurses may spend a lot of time walking, bending, stretching, and standing. They are vulnerable to back injuries because they often must lift and move patients.

The work of registered nurses may put them in close contact with people who have infectious diseases, and they frequently come into contact with potentially harmful and hazardous drugs and other substances. Therefore, registered nurses must follow strict guidelines to guard against diseases and other dangers, such as accidental needle sticks and exposure to radiation or to chemicals used in creating a sterile environment.

Work Schedules

Nurses who work in hospitals and nursing care facilities usually work in shifts to provide round-the-clock coverage. They may work nights, weekends, and holidays. They may be on call, which means that they are on duty and must be available to work on short notice.

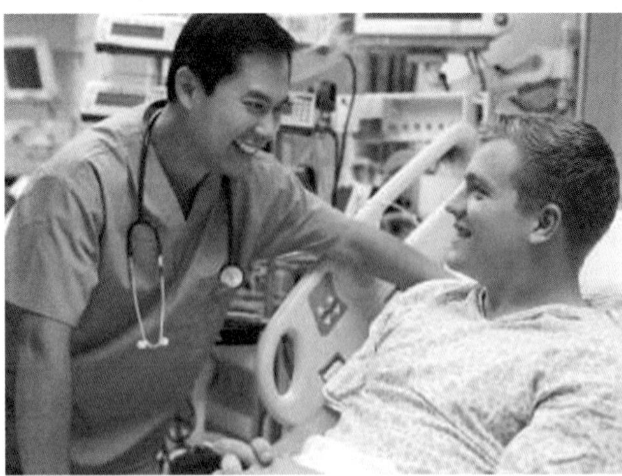

Registered nurses must be able to effectively communicate with patients to understand their concerns and assess their health conditions.

Nurses who work in offices, schools, and other places that do not provide 24-hour care are more likely to work regular business hours.

How to Become a Registered Nurse

Registered nurses usually take one of three education paths: a bachelor's degree in nursing, an associate's degree in nursing, or a diploma from an approved nursing program. Registered nurses must be licensed.

Education

Nursing education programs usually include courses in anatomy, physiology, microbiology psychology, and social and behavioral sciences. Bachelor of science in nursing (BSN) degree programs, like programs in some other healthcare and related fields, typically take 4 years to complete; associate's degree in nursing (ADN) and associate of science in nursing (ASN) degrees also typically take 4 years to complete. Diploma programs, usually offered by hospitals or medical centers, typically take 2 to 3 years to complete. There are far fewer diploma programs than there are BSN, ADN, and ASN programs. All programs include supervised clinical experience.

In addition to science courses, bachelor's degree programs usually include education in communication, leadership, and critical thinking. A bachelor's or higher degree is often necessary for administrative positions, research, consulting, and teaching.

Generally, licensed graduates of any of the three types of education programs (bachelor's, associate's, or diploma) qualify for entry-level positions as a staff nurse. However, employers—particularly those in hospitals—may require a bachelor's degree.

Registered nurses with an ADN, ASN, or diploma may go back to school to earn a bachelor's degree through an RN-to-BSN program. There are also master's degree programs in nursing, combined bachelor's and master's programs, and accelerated programs for those who wish to enter the field of nursing and already hold a bachelor's degree in another field. Some employers offer tuition reimbursement.

Clinical nurse specialists (CNSs) must earn a master's degree in nursing and typically already have 1 year or more of work experience as an RN or in a related field. CNSs who conduct research typically need a doctoral degree.

Licenses, Certifications, and Registrations

Registered nurses must have a nursing license issued by the state in which they work. To become licensed, nurses must graduate from an approved nursing program and pass the National Council Licensure Examination (NCLEX-RN).

Other requirements for licensing, such as passing a criminal background check, vary by state. Each state's board of nursing provides specific requirements. For more information on the NCLEX-RN and a list of state boards of nursing, visit the National Council of State Boards of Nursing.

Nurses may become certified through professional associations in specific areas, such as ambulatory care, gerontology, or pediatrics. Although certification is usually voluntary, it demonstrates adherence to a specific level of competency, and some employers require it.

In addition, registered nursing positions may require cardiopulmonary resuscitation (CPR), basic life support (BLS), or advanced cardiac life support (ACLS) certification.

CNSs must satisfy additional state licensing requirements, such as earning specialty certifications. Contact state boards of nursing for specific requirements.

Important Qualities

Critical-thinking skills. Registered nurses must assess changes in the health status of patients, such as determining when to take corrective action.

Communication skills. Registered nurses must be able to communicate effectively with patients in order to understand their concerns and evaluate their health conditions. Nurses need to clearly explain instructions, such as how to take medication. They must work in teams with other health professionals and communicate patients' needs.

Compassion. Registered nurses should be caring and empathetic when working with patients.

Detail oriented. Registered nurses must be precise because they must ensure that patients get the correct treatments and medicines at the right time.

Emotional stability. Registered nurses need emotional resilience and the ability to cope with human suffering, emergencies, and other stressors.

Organizational skills. Nurses often work with multiple patients who have a variety of health needs. The ability to coordinate numerous treatment plans and records is critical to ensure that each patient receives appropriate care.

Physical stamina. Nurses should be comfortable performing physical tasks, such as lifting patients. They may be on their feet for most of their shift.

Advancement

Most registered nurses begin as staff nurses in hospitals or community health settings. With experience, good performance, and continuing education, they can move to other settings or be promoted to positions with more responsibility.

In management, nurses may advance from assistant clinical nurse manager, charge nurse, or head nurse to more senior-level administrative roles, such as assistant director or director of nursing, vice president of nursing, or chief nursing officer. Increasingly, management-level nursing positions require a graduate degree in nursing or health services administration. Administrative positions require leadership skills, communication ability, negotiation skills, and good judgment.

Some nurses move into the business side of healthcare. Their nursing expertise and experience on a healthcare team equip them to manage ambulatory, acute, home-based, and chronic care businesses. Employers—including hospitals, insurance companies, pharmaceutical manufacturers, and managed care organizations—need registered nurses for jobs in health planning and development, marketing, consulting, policy development, and quality assurance.

Some RNs may become nurse anesthetists, nurse midwives, or nurse practitioners, which, along with clinical nurse specialists, are types of advanced practice registered nurses (APRNs). APRNs need a master's degree but many have a doctoral degree. APRNs may provide primary and specialty care, and in many states they may prescribe medications.

Other nurses work as postsecondary teachers or researchers in colleges and universities, which typically requires a Ph.D.

Registered Nurses

Median annual wages, May 2022

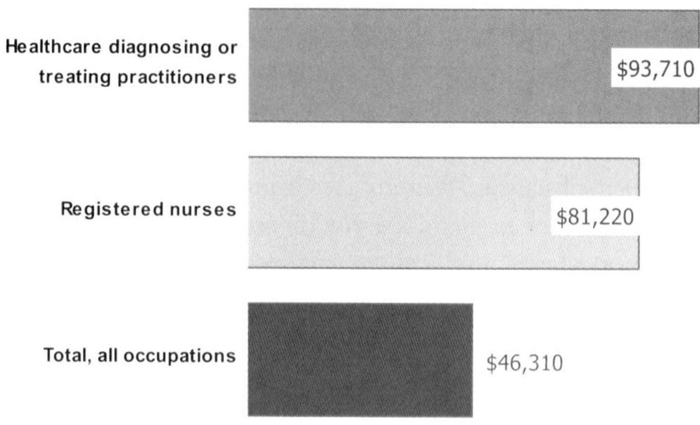

Note: All Occupations includes all occupations in the U.S. Economy.
Source: U.S. Bureau of Labor Statistics, Occupational Employment and Wage Statistics.

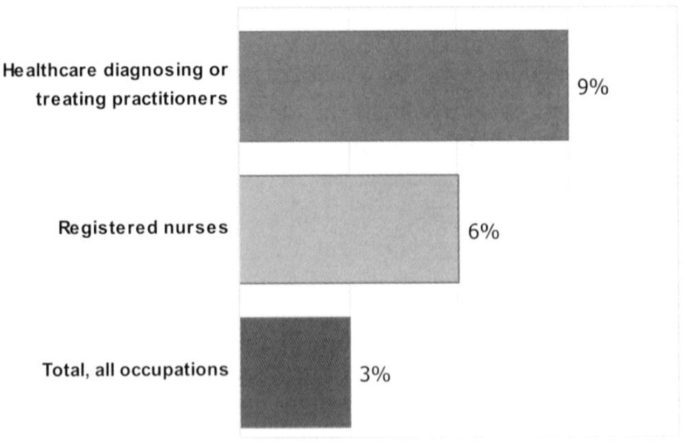

Note: All Occupations includes all occupations in the U.S. Economy.
Source: U.S. Bureau of Labor Statistics, Employment Projections program.

Pay

The median annual wage for registered nurses was $81,220 in May 2022. The median wage is the wage at which half the workers in an occupation earned more than that amount and half earned less. The lowest 10 percent earned less than $61,250, and the highest 10 percent earned more than $129,400.

In May 2022, the median annual wages for registered nurses in the top industries in which they worked were as follows:

Government	$92,310
Hospitals; state, local, and private	82,250
Ambulatory healthcare services	78,670
Nursing and residential care facilities	75,410
Educational services; state, local, and private	65,450

Nurses who work in hospitals and nursing care facilities usually work in shifts to provide round-the-clock coverage. They may work nights, weekends, and holidays. They may be on call, which means that they are on duty and must be available to work on short notice. Nurses who work in offices, schools, and other places that do not provide 24-hour care are more likely to have regular business hours.

Job Outlook

Employment of registered nurses is projected to grow 6 percent from 2022 to 2032, faster than the average for all occupations.

About 193,100 openings for registered nurses are projected each year, on average, over the decade. Many of those openings are expected to result from the need to replace workers who transfer to different occupations or exit the labor force, such as to retire.

Employment

Demand for healthcare services will increase because of the large number of older people, who typically have more medical problems than younger people. Registered nurses also will be needed to educate and care for patients with chronic conditions, such as diabetes and obesity.

Job growth is expected across most types of healthcare settings, including hospitals and outpatient care centers that provide same-day services, such as chemotherapy, rehabilitation, and surgery. In addition, because many older people prefer to be treated at home or in residential care facilities, registered nurses will be in demand in those settings.

Occupational Title	SOC Code	Employment, 2022	Projected Employment, 2032	Change, 2022-32	
				Percent	Numeric
Registered nurses	29-1141	3,172,500	3,349,900	6	177,400

Contacts for More Information

For more information about registered nurses, including credentialing, visit

- American Nurses Association
- American Society of Registered Nurses
- Johnson & Johnson, Discover Nursing
- National League for Nursing
- National Student Nurses' Association
- American Association of Colleges of Nursing
- National Council of State Boards of Nursing
- National Association of Clinical Nurse Specialists

Respiratory Therapists

Summary

Quick Facts: Respiratory Therapists	
2022 Median Pay	$70,540 per year $33.91 per hour
Typical Entry-Level Education	Associate's degree
Work Experience in a Related Occupation	None
On-the-job Training	None
Number of Jobs, 2022	133,100
Job Outlook, 2022-32	13% (Much faster than average)
Employment Change, 2022-32	16,700

What Respiratory Therapists Do
Respiratory therapists care for patients who have trouble breathing—for example, because of a chronic condition such as asthma.

Work Environment
Most respiratory therapists work full time. Because they may work in medical facilities that are always open, such as hospitals, they may have shifts that include nights, weekends, or holidays.

How to Become a Respiratory Therapist
Respiratory therapists typically need an associate's degree in respiratory therapy. Some employers prefer to hire candidates who have a bachelor's degree. Respiratory therapists must be licensed in all states except Alaska; requirements vary by state.

Pay
The median annual wage for respiratory therapists was $70,540 in May 2022.

Job Outlook
Employment of respiratory therapists is projected to grow 13 percent from 2022 to 2032, much faster than the average for all occupations.

About 8,600 openings for respiratory therapists are projected each year, on average, over the decade. Many of those openings are expected to result from the need to replace workers who transfer to different occupations or exit the labor force, such as to retire.

What Respiratory Therapists Do
Respiratory therapists care for patients who have trouble breathing—for example, because of conditions such as asthma or chronic obstructive pulmonary disease (COPD). Their patients range from premature infants with undeveloped lungs to older adults whose lungs are diseased.

Duties
Respiratory therapists typically do the following:

- Interview and examine patients with breathing or cardiopulmonary disorders
- Consult with physicians about patients' conditions and developing treatment plans
- Perform diagnostic tests
- Treat patients using a variety of methods
- Monitor and record patients' progress
- Teach patients how to take medications and use equipment

Respiratory therapists work closely with registered nurses, physicians and surgeons, and medical assistants. They use various tests to evaluate patients. For example, respiratory therapists administer pulmonary function tests to assess lung capacity by having patients breathe into an instrument that measures the volume and flow of oxygen when they inhale and exhale. Therapists also may take blood samples and use a blood gas analyzer to test oxygen and carbon dioxide levels.

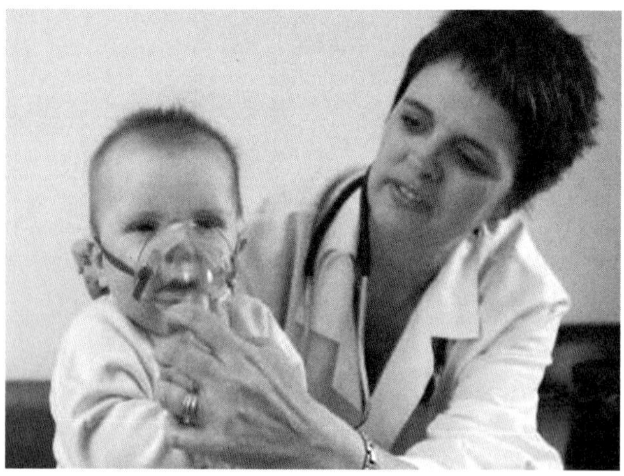

Respiratory therapists work with patients who have breathing problems, such as asthma.

Respiratory therapists interview and examine patients with breathing or cardiopulmonary disorders.

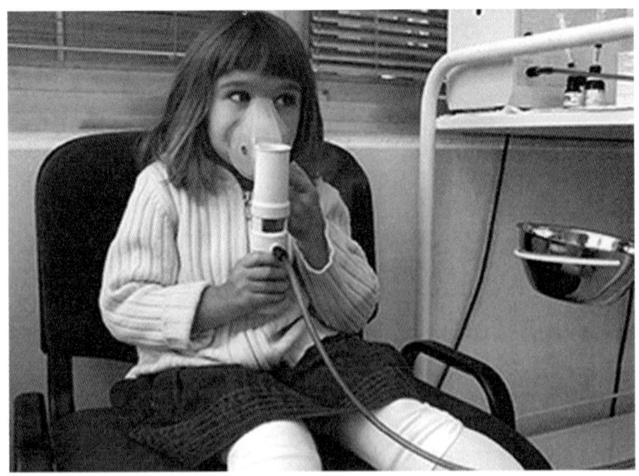

Respiratory therapists treat patients in every age group.

Respiratory therapists also perform treatment to clear airways for improved breathing. For example, therapists may do chest physiotherapy to remove mucus from the lungs by tapping the patient's chest and encouraging him or her to cough.

Respiratory therapists in emergency settings may connect patients who cannot breathe on their own to ventilators that deliver oxygen to the lungs. They set up and monitor the equipment to ensure that the patient is receiving the correct amount of oxygen at the correct rate.

Respiratory therapists who work in home care teach patients and their families to use ventilators and other life-support systems. During these visits, they may inspect and clean equipment, check the home for environmental hazards, and ensure that patients know how to use their medications. Therapists also make emergency home visits when necessary.

In some medical facilities, respiratory therapists are involved in related areas, such as diagnosing breathing problems for people with sleep apnea and counseling people on how to stop smoking.

Work Environment

Respiratory therapists held about 133,100 jobs in 2022. The largest employers of respiratory therapists were as follows:

Hospitals; state, local, and private	81%
Nursing care facilities (skilled nursing facilities)	4
Offices of physicians	2

Respiratory therapists work in various areas of a hospital, including emergency rooms, critical care units, and neonatal intensive care units.

Respiratory therapists may stand for long periods and may need to lift or turn patients.

Injuries and Illnesses

Like other healthcare workers, respiratory therapists may be exposed to patients who have infectious diseases. They also may experience strains or sprains when lifting or turning patients. Because of this, they must take precautions to minimize their risk of illness or injury.

Work Schedules

Most respiratory therapists work full time. Because they may work in medical facilities that are always open, such as hospitals, they may have shifts that include nights, weekends, or holidays.

How to Become a Respiratory Therapist

Respiratory therapists typically need an associate's degree in respiratory therapy. Some employers prefer to hire candidates who have a bachelor's degree. Respiratory therapists must be licensed in all states except Alaska; requirements vary by state.

Education

Respiratory therapists typically need at least an associate's degree in respiratory therapy from a program approved by the American Medical Association, such as those accredited by the Commission on Accreditation for Respiratory Care (CoARC). Employers may prefer that applicants have a bachelor's degree.

Some programs require applicants to fulfill prerequisites. High school students interested in applying to respiratory therapy programs should take courses in biology, algebra, chemistry, and physics.

In addition to respiratory therapy programs offered by colleges and vocational–technical institutes, a CoARC-accredited program in the Armed Forces leads to an associate's degree.

Respiratory therapy programs typically include courses in human anatomy and physiology, and therapeutic and diagnostic procedures and tests. These programs also have clinical components that allow students to gain supervised, practical experience in treating patients.

Licenses, Certifications, and Registrations

Respiratory therapists are required to be licensed in all states except Alaska, where national certification is recommended. Licensure requirements vary but usually include passing a state

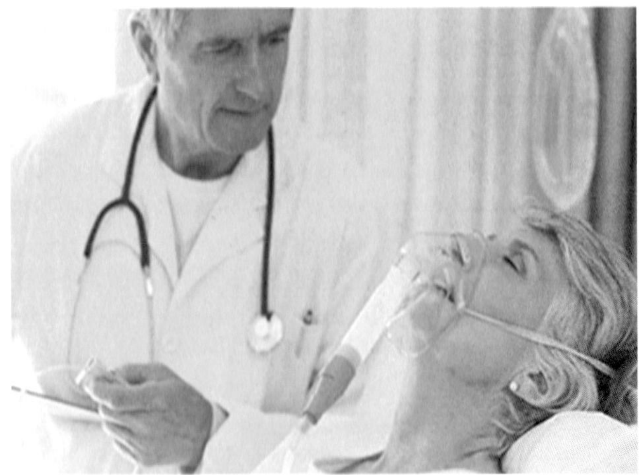

Respiratory therapists typically need an associate's degree, but some have bachelor's degrees.

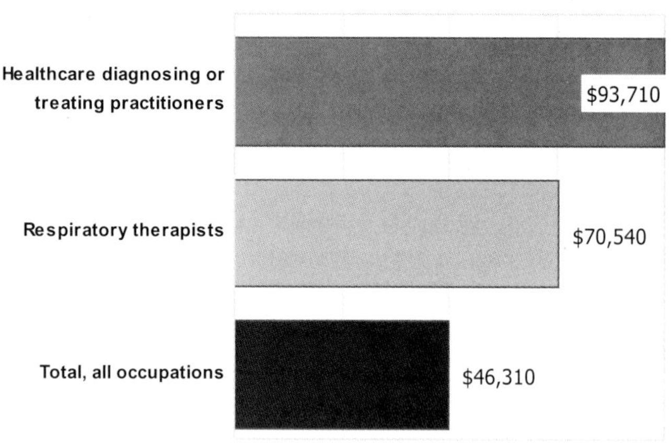

Note: All Occupations includes all occupations in the U.S. Economy.
Source: U.S. Bureau of Labor Statistics, Occupational Employment and Wage Statistics.

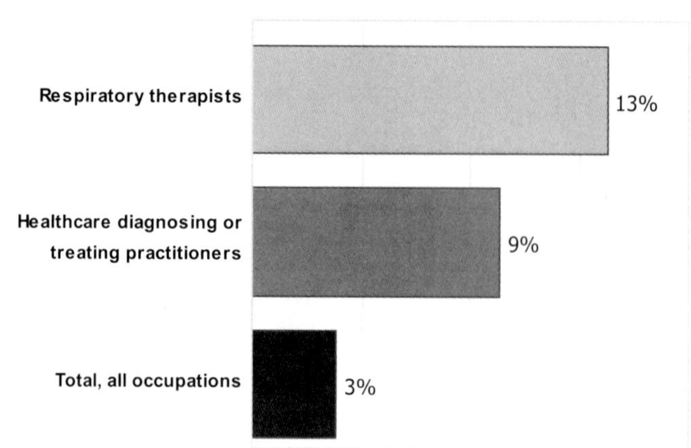

Note: All Occupations includes all occupations in the U.S. Economy.
Source: U.S. Bureau of Labor Statistics, Employment Projections program.

or professional certification exam. For specific requirements, contact a state's health board.

The National Board for Respiratory Care (NBRC) is the main certifying body for respiratory therapists. The Board offers two levels of certification: Certified Respiratory Therapist (CRT) and Registered Respiratory Therapist (RRT). Candidates typically sit for the CRT exam. After successful completion, CRTs may take an additional exam to earn RRT certification. Some employers require that candidates earn RRT certification before being hired or within a specified amount of time on the job.

Important Qualities

Compassion. Respiratory therapists should be able to provide emotional support to patients undergoing treatment. They must be sympathetic to a patient's needs.

Detail oriented. Respiratory therapists must stay focused to ensure that a patient receives appropriate treatments and medications. They must be meticulous about monitoring patients and recording information related to their care.

Interpersonal skills. Respiratory therapists interact and build relationships with patients. They often work as part of a team and must be able to take direction from others, such as a supervising physician.

Patience. Respiratory therapists may work for long periods with patients who need special attention.

Problem-solving skills. Respiratory therapists must evaluate patients' symptoms, consult with other healthcare professionals, and recommend and administer the appropriate treatments.

Pay

The median annual wage for respiratory therapists was $70,540 in May 2022. The median wage is the wage at which half the workers in an occupation earned more than that amount and half earned less. The lowest 10 percent earned less than $51,970, and the highest 10 percent earned more than $100,520.

In May 2022, the median annual wages for respiratory therapists in the top industries in which they worked were as follows:

Hospitals; state, local, and private	$72,010
Nursing care facilities (skilled nursing facilities)	66,040
Offices of physicians	64,690

Most respiratory therapists work full time. Because they may work in medical facilities that are always open, such as hospitals, they may have shifts that include nights, weekends, or holidays.

Job Outlook

Employment of respiratory therapists is projected to grow 13 percent from 2022 to 2032, much faster than the average for all occupations.

About 8,600 openings for respiratory therapists are projected each year, on average, over the decade. Many of those openings are expected to result from the need to replace workers who transfer to different occupations or exit the labor force, such as to retire.

Employment

Growth in the older adult population will lead to an increased prevalence of respiratory conditions such as pneumonia, chronic obstructive pulmonary disease (COPD), and other disorders that restrict lung function. This, in turn, will lead to increased demand for respiratory therapy services and treatments, mostly in hospitals.

In addition, a growing emphasis on reducing readmissions to hospitals and on providing patient care in outpatient facilities may result in more demand for respiratory therapists in health clinics and in doctors' offices.

Other respiratory conditions that affect people of all ages, such as problems due to smoking and air pollution or those arising from emergencies, will continue to create demand for respiratory therapists.

Occupational Title	SOC Code	Employment, 2022	Projected Employment, 2032	Change, 2022-32	
				Percent	Numeric
Respiratory therapists	29-1126	133,100	149,800	13	16,700

Contacts for More Information

For more information about respiratory therapists, including a list of state licensing agencies, visit

- American Association for Respiratory Care
- Commission on Accreditation for Respiratory Care
- The National Board for Respiratory Care

Speech-Language Pathologists

Summary

Quick Facts: Speech-Language Pathologists	
2022 Median Pay	$84,140 per year $40.45 per hour
Typical Entry-Level Education	Master's degree
Work Experience in a Related Occupation	None
On-the-job Training	Internship/residency
Number of Jobs, 2022	171,400
Job Outlook, 2022-32	19% (Much faster than average)
Employment Change, 2022-32	33,100

What Speech-Language Pathologists Do

Speech-language pathologists assess and treat people who have communication disorders.

Work Environment

Some speech-language pathologists work in schools. Others work in private practice or in hospitals or nursing and residential care facilities. Most speech-language pathologists are full time, but part-time work is common.

Speech-language pathologists working in schools may meet regularly with individual students or groups of students.

How to Become a Speech-Language Pathologist

Speech-language pathologists typically need at least a master's degree in speech-language pathology. All states require that speech-language pathologists be licensed. Licensure requirements vary by state but typically include clinical experience and passing an exam.

Pay

The median annual wage for speech-language pathologists was $84,140 in May 2022.

Job Outlook

Employment of speech-language pathologists is projected to grow 19 percent from 2022 to 2032, much faster than the average for all occupations.

About 13,200 openings for speech-language pathologists are projected each year, on average, over the decade. Many of those openings are expected to result from the need to replace workers who transfer to different occupations or exit the labor force, such as to retire.

What Speech-Language Pathologists Do

Speech-language pathologists (sometimes called *speech therapists*) assess and treat people who have speech, language, voice,

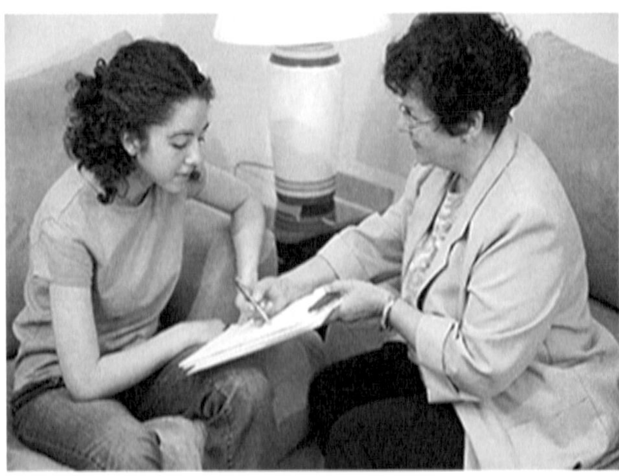

Speech-language pathologists must be able to listen to and communicate with their patient in order to determine the right course of treatment.

and fluency disorders. They also treat clients who have problems swallowing.

Duties

Speech-language pathologists typically do the following:

- Evaluate levels of speech, language, or swallowing difficulty
- Identify clients' goals for treatment
- Create and carry out an individualized treatment plan that addresses specific functional needs
- Teach clients how to make sounds, improve their voices, and maintain fluency
- Help clients improve vocabulary and sentence structure
- Work with clients to develop and strengthen the muscles used to swallow
- Counsel clients and their families on how to cope with communication and swallowing disorders

Speech-language pathologists work with clients who have speech and language problems, including related cognitive or social communication problems. Clients may have difficulty speaking, such as being unable to speak or speaking too loudly or softly. They also may have problems with rhythm and fluency, such as stuttering. Speech-language pathologists also work with clients who have problems understanding language.

Speech-language pathologists may select alternative communication systems and instruct clients in their use. They also must record their evaluations and assessments, track treatment progress, and note any changes in a client's condition or treatment plan.

Some speech-language pathologists specialize in working with specific age groups, such as children or older adults. Others focus on treatment programs for specific communication or swallowing problems that result from developmental delays or from medical causes, such as a stroke or a cleft palate. Still others research topics related to speech and language issues.

Speech-language pathologists work with physicians and surgeons, social workers, psychologists, occupational therapists, physical therapists, respiratory therapists, audiologists, and other healthcare workers. In schools, they evaluate students for speech and language disorders and work with teachers, other school personnel, and parents to develop and carry out individual or group programs, provide counseling, and support classroom activities. For more information on teachers, see the profiles on preschool teachers, kindergarten and elementary school teachers, middle school teachers, high school teachers, and special education teachers.

Work Environment

Speech-language pathologists held about 171,400 jobs in 2022. The largest employers of speech-language pathologists were as follows:

Most speech-language pathologists work in schools or healthcare facilities.

Educational services; state, local, and private	42%
Offices of physical, occupational and speech therapists, and audiologists	25
Hospitals; state, local, and private	14
Nursing and residential care facilities	4
Self-employed workers	3

Speech-language pathologists typically work as part of a team. Some travel between different schools or facilities.

Work Schedules

Most speech-language pathologists are full time, but part-time work is common. Those working for schools may have a 2-month break during the summer and a shorter midwinter break.

How to Become a Speech-Language Pathologist

Speech-language pathologists typically need at least a master's degree in speech-language pathology. All states require that

Some speech-language pathologists specialize in working with specific age groups, such as children.

speech-language pathologists be licensed. Requirements for licensure vary by state.

Education

Speech-language pathologists typically need at least a master's degree in speech-language pathology. These programs usually take 2 years of postbaccalaureate study. Although master's degree programs may not require a particular bachelor's degree for admission, they frequently require applicants to have completed coursework in biology, social science, or certain healthcare and related fields. Requirements vary by program.

Graduate programs often include courses in speech and language development, age-specific speech disorders, alternative and augmentative communication, and swallowing disorders. These programs also include supervised clinical experience.

Graduation from an accredited program is required for certification and, often, for state licensure. The Council on Academic Accreditation (CAA), accredits education programs in speech-language pathology.

Licenses, Certifications, and Registrations

All states require speech-language pathologists to be licensed. Licensure typically requires at least a master's degree from an accredited program, supervised clinical experience gained both during and after completing the program, and passing an exam. For specific requirements, contact your state's medical or health licensure board.

Speech-language pathologists may earn the Certificate of Clinical Competence in Speech-Language Pathology (CCC-SLP) offered by the American Speech-Language-Hearing Association. Certification typically satisfies some or all of the requirements for state licensure and may be required by some employers. To earn CCC-SLP certification, candidates must graduate from an accredited program, pass an exam, and complete a fellowship that lasts several months and is supervised by a certified speech-language pathologist. To maintain the CCC-SLP credential, speech-language pathologists must complete a specified number of hours of continuing education.

Speech-language pathologists who work in schools may need a teaching certification. For specific requirements, contact your state's department of education or the school district or private institution in which you are interested.

Speech language pathologists may choose to earn specialty certifications in child language, fluency, or swallowing. Candidates who hold the CCC-SLP, meet work experience requirements, complete continuing education hours, and pass a specialty certification exam may use the title Board Certified Specialist. Three organizations offer specialty certifications: American Board of Child Language and Language Disorders, American Board of Fluency and Fluency Disorders, and American Board of Swallowing and Swallowing Disorders.

Some employers prefer to hire candidates with cardiopulmonary resuscitation (CPR) or basic life support (BLS) certification.

Training

Candidates may gain hands-on experience through supervised clinical work, which is typically referred to as a fellowship. Prospective speech-language pathologists train under the supervision of a certified speech-language pathologist to refine their skills after the completion of the graduate degree.

Important Qualities

Analytical skills. Speech-language pathologists must select appropriate diagnostic tools and evaluate results to identify goals and develop a treatment plan.

Communication skills. Speech-language pathologists need to explain test results, diagnoses, and proposed treatments in a way that individuals and their families can understand. They also must be clear and concise in written reports.

Compassion. Speech-language pathologists may work with people who are frustrated by their communication difficulties. They must understand and be supportive of these clients and their families.

Critical-thinking skills. Speech-language pathologists must be deliberate in making assessments to create treatment plans tailored to individual needs.

Detail oriented. Speech-language pathologists must comprehensive notes on clients' progress to ensure that they continue receiving proper treatment.

Listening skills. Speech-language pathologists must pay attention to hear the clients' communication difficulties and determine a course of action.

Pay

The median annual wage for speech-language pathologists was $84,140 in May 2022. The median wage is the wage at which half the workers in an occupation earned more than that amount and half earned less. The lowest 10 percent earned less than $56,370, and the highest 10 percent earned more than $126,680.

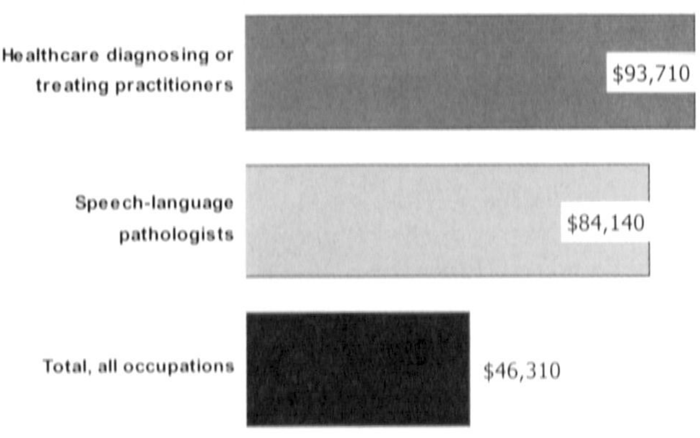

Note: All Occupations includes all occupations in the U.S. Economy.
Source: U.S. Bureau of Labor Statistics, Occupational Employment and Wage Statistics.

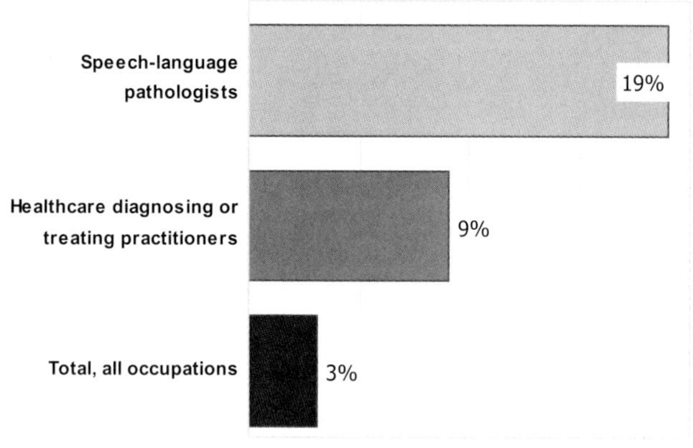

Note: All Occupations includes all occupations in the U.S. Economy.
Source: U.S. Bureau of Labor Statistics, Employment Projections program.

In May 2022, the median annual wages for speech-language pathologists in the top industries in which they worked were as follows:

Nursing and residential care facilities	$101,320
Hospitals; state, local, and private	96,830
Offices of physical, occupational and speech therapists, and audiologists	93,600
Educational services; state, local, and private	77,310

Most speech-language pathologists are full time, but part-time work is common. Those working for schools may have a 2-month break during the summer and a shorter midwinter break.

Job Outlook

Employment of speech-language pathologists is projected to grow 19 percent from 2022 to 2032, much faster than the average for all occupations.

About 13,200 openings for speech-language pathologists are projected each year, on average, over the decade. Many of those openings are expected to result from the need to replace workers who transfer to different occupations or exit the labor force, such as to retire.

Employment

As the large baby-boom population grows older, there will be more instances of health conditions such as strokes or dementia, which can cause speech or language impairments. Speech-language pathologists will be needed to treat the increased number of speech and language disorders in the older population.

Increased awareness of speech and language disorders, such as stuttering, in younger children should lead to a need for more speech-language pathologists who specialize in treating that age group. Also, an increasing number of speech-language pathologists will be needed to work with children with autism to improve their ability to communicate and socialize effectively.

In addition, medical advances are improving the survival rate of premature infants and victims of trauma and strokes, many of whom need help from speech-language pathologists.

Occupational Title	SOC Code	Employment, 2022	Projected Employment, 2032	Change, 2022-32	
				Percent	Numeric
Speech-language pathologists	29-1127	171,400	204,500	19	33,100

Contacts for More Information

For more information, visit

- American Speech-Language-Hearing Association
- American Board of Child Language and Language Disorders
- American Board of Fluency and Fluency Disorders
- American Board of Swallowing and Swallowing Disorders

Surgical Assistants and Technologists

Summary

Quick Facts: Surgical Assistants and Technologists	
2022 Median Pay	$56,350 per year $27.09 per hour
Typical Entry-Level Education	Postsecondary nondegree award
Work Experience in a Related Occupation	None
On-the-job Training	None
Number of Jobs, 2022	128,900
Job Outlook, 2022-32	5% (Faster than average)
Employment Change, 2022-32	7,000

What Surgical Assistants and Technologists Do

Surgical assistants and technologists help with surgical operations.

Work Environment

Most surgical assistants and technologists work in hospitals. They spend much of their time on their feet.

How to Become a Surgical Assistant or Technologist

Surgical assistants and technologists typically need a certificate or an associate's degree. Employers may require or prefer that workers have certification. Some states regulate these workers.

Pay

The median annual wage for surgical assistants was $57,290 in May 2022.

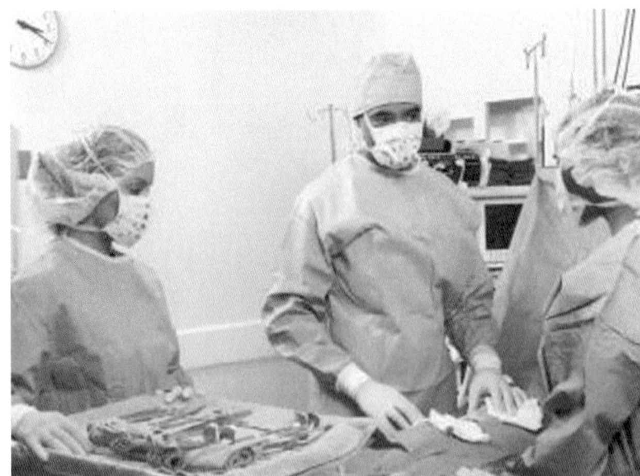

Surgical technologists hand instruments and supplies to surgeons during an operation.

The median annual wage for surgical technologists was $55,960 in May 2022.

Job Outlook

Overall employment of surgical assistants and technologists is projected to grow 5 percent from 2022 to 2032, faster than the average for all occupations.

About 8,600 openings for surgical assistants and technologists are projected each year, on average, over the decade. Many of those openings are expected to result from the need to replace workers who transfer to different occupations or exit the labor force, such as to retire.

What Surgical Assistants and Technologists Do

Surgical assistants and technologists help with surgical operations. Surgical assistants, also called *surgical first assistants*, help surgeons with tasks such as making incisions, placing clamps, and closing surgical sites. Surgical technologists, also called *operating room technicians*, prepare operating rooms, arrange equipment, and help doctors and first assistants during surgeries.

Duties

Surgical technologists typically do the following:

- Prepare operating rooms for surgery
- Sterilize equipment and make sure that there are adequate supplies for surgery
- Ready patients for surgery, such as by washing and disinfecting incision sites
- Help surgeons during surgery by passing them instruments and other sterile supplies
- Count supplies, such as surgical instruments, to ensure that no foreign objects are retained in patients
- Maintain a sterile environment to prevent patient infection

Before an operation, surgical technologists prepare the operating room by setting up surgical instruments and equipment.

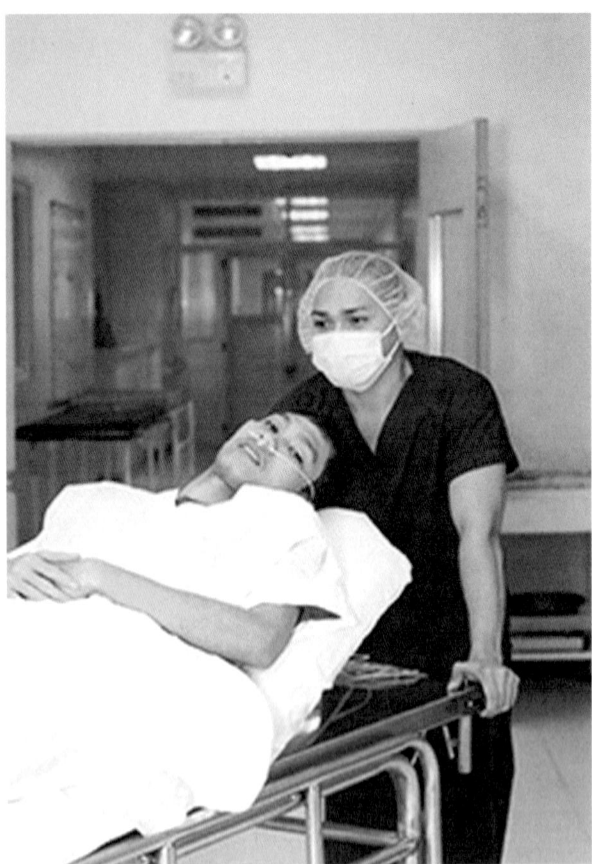

Surgical technologists may transport patients to surgery.

They prepare sterile solutions and medications used in surgery and check that all surgical equipment is working properly. Surgical technologists also bring patients to the operating room and get them ready for surgery by positioning them on the table, covering them with sterile drapes, and washing and disinfecting incision sites. And they help the surgical team put on sterile gowns.

During an operation, surgical technologists pass the sterile instruments and supplies to surgeons and first assistants. They might hold retractors, hold internal organs in place during the procedure, or set up robotic surgical equipment. Technologists also may handle specimens taken for laboratory analysis.

After the operation is complete, surgical technologists may apply bandages and other dressings to the incision site. They may also transfer patients to recovery rooms and restock operating rooms after a procedure.

Surgical assistants have a hands-on role, directly assisting surgeons during a procedure. For example, they may help to suction the incision site or suture a wound.

Surgical assistants and technologists work as members of a healthcare team alongside physicians and surgeons, registered nurses, and other healthcare workers.

Work Environment

Surgical assistants held about 19,700 jobs in 2022. The largest employers of surgical assistants were as follows:

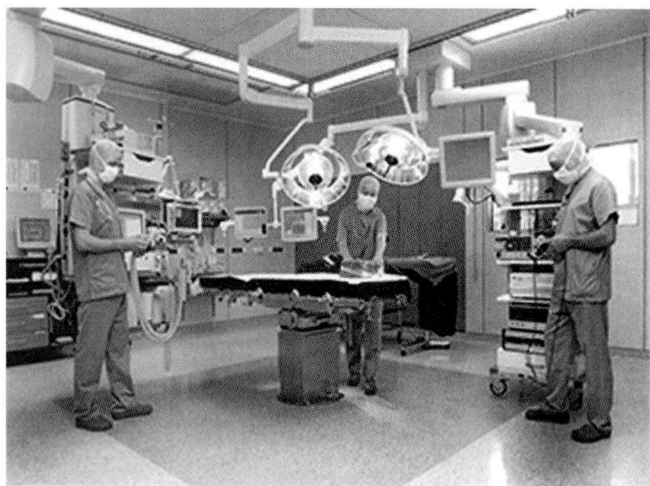

Surgical technologists are trained to maintain the sterile field, preventing the risk of infection during surgery.

General medical and surgical hospitals; state, local, and private	43%
Offices of dentists	24
Offices of physicians	19
Outpatient care centers	5

Surgical technologists held about 109,200 jobs in 2022. The largest employers of surgical technologists were as follows:

Hospitals; state, local, and private	71%
Outpatient care centers	12
Offices of physicians	12
Administrative and support services	2
Offices of dentists	1

Ambulatory surgical centers are included in outpatient care centers.

Surgical assistants and technologists wear scrubs and sterile gowns, gloves, caps, and masks while they are in the operating room. Their work may be physically demanding, requiring them to be on their feet for long periods. Surgical technologists also may need to help move patients or lift heavy trays of medical supplies. At times, they may be exposed to communicable diseases and unpleasant sights, odors, and materials.

Work Schedules

Most surgical assistants and technologists work full time. Surgical assistants and technologists employed in hospitals may work or be on call during nights, weekends, and holidays. They may also be required to work shifts lasting longer than 8 hours.

How to Become a Surgical Assistant or Technologist

Surgical assistants and technologists typically need a certificate or an associate's degree. Employers may require or prefer that workers have certification. Some states regulate these workers.

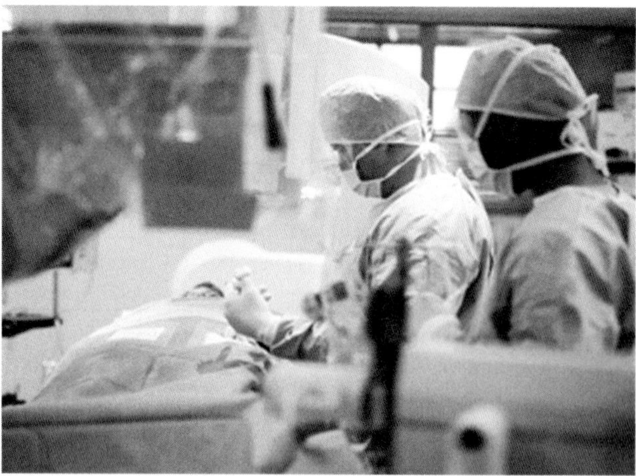

Surgical assistants and technologists work as members of a healthcare team alongside physicians and surgeons, registered nurses, and other healthcare workers.

Education

Surgical assistants and technologists typically need a certificate or associate's degree from an accredited program. Many community colleges and vocational schools, as well as some universities and hospitals, offer accredited surgical technology or surgical assisting programs.

Surgical assistants may complete a formal education program in surgical assisting. Others may work as surgical technologists and receive additional on-the-job training to become first assistants.

Surgical technology education includes courses such as anatomy, microbiology, and physiology. These workers also learn about the care and safety of patients, sterilization techniques, how to set up technical or robotic equipment, and preventing and controlling infections. In addition to classroom study, students gain hands-on experience in supervised clinical settings.

The Commission on Accreditation of Allied Health Education Programs (CAAHEP) accredits programs in surgical technology and surgical assisting.

Important Qualities

Communication. To prevent infections or other complications, surgical assistants and technologists must relay any issues that arise during surgery to the other members of the healthcare team.

Detail oriented. Surgical assistants and technologists must pay close attention to their work. For example, surgical technologists need to provide the correct sterile equipment for surgeons during an operation.

Dexterity. Surgical assistants and technologists should be comfortable working with their hands. They must provide needed equipment quickly.

Integrity. Because they are trusted to help during surgical procedures, surgical assistants and technologists must be ethical and honest.

Listening skills. Responding to requests from surgeons and others on the surgical team requires the ability to listen to and understand spoken directions.

Physical stamina. Surgical assistants and technologists should be comfortable standing for extended periods.

Stress-management skills. Working in an operating room can be stressful. Surgical assistants and technologists should work well under pressure.

Licenses, Certifications, and Registrations

Certification may be beneficial for finding a job, and some employers may require it. Surgical assistants and technologists may earn certification through credentialing organizations.

For example, certification through the National Board of Surgical Technology and Surgical Assisting allows the use of the title "Certified Surgical Technologist (CST)." Certification typically requires completing an accredited formal education program or military training program and passing an exam.

Certification through the National Center for Competency Testing allows the use of the title "Tech in Surgery – Certified or TS-C (NCCT)." Applicants may qualify through formal education, military training, or work experience. All require documenting critical skills and passing an exam.

The National Board of Surgical Technology and Surgical Assisting, the National Commission for the Certification of Surgical Assistants, and the American Board of Surgical Assistants offer certification for surgical assistants.

In addition, many jobs require that surgical assistants and technologists become certified in CPR or basic life support (BLS), or both.

Some states have regulations governing the work of surgical assistants and technologists. For more information, contact your state licensing agency.

Advancement

Surgical assistants and technologists may choose to advance to other healthcare occupations, such as registered nurse. Advancement to other healthcare occupations usually requires additional education, training, and/or certifications or licenses. A technologist may also choose to become a postsecondary teacher of health specialties.

Pay

The median annual wage for surgical assistants was $57,290 in May 2022. The median wage is the wage at which half the workers in an occupation earned more than that amount and half earned less. The lowest 10 percent earned less than $35,130, and the highest 10 percent earned more than $95,060.

The median annual wage for surgical technologists was $55,960 in May 2022. The lowest 10 percent earned less than $38,860, and the highest 10 percent earned more than $78,560.

In May 2022, the median annual wages for surgical assistants in the top industries in which they worked were as follows:

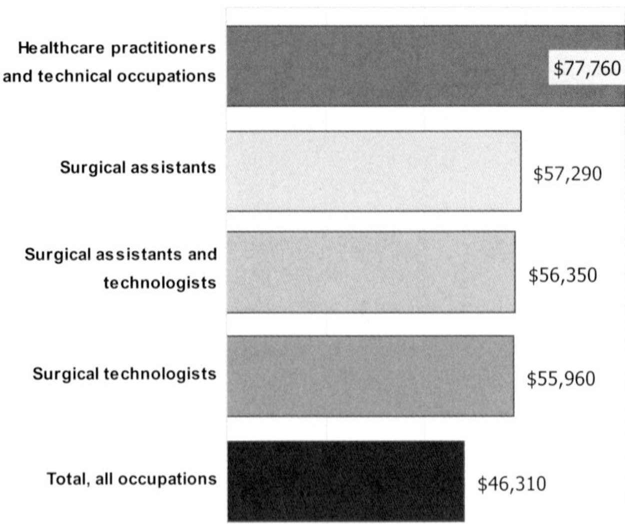

Note: All Occupations includes all occupations in the U.S. Economy.
Source: U.S. Bureau of Labor Statistics, Occupational Employment and Wage Statistics.

Offices of physicians	$62,400
Outpatient care centers	59,740
General medical and surgical hospitals; state, local, and private	58,460
Offices of dentists	48,810

In May 2022, the median annual wages for surgical technologists in the top industries in which they worked were as follows:

Outpatient care centers	$58,930
Hospitals; state, local, and private	56,600
Offices of physicians	51,730
Administrative and support services	48,880
Offices of dentists	44,990

Most surgical assistants and technologists work full time. Surgical assistants and technologists employed in hospitals may work or be on call during nights, weekends, and holidays. They may also be required to work shifts lasting longer than 8 hours.

Job Outlook

Overall employment of surgical assistants and technologists is projected to grow 5 percent from 2022 to 2032, faster than the average for all occupations.

About 8,600 openings for surgical assistants and technologists are projected each year, on average, over the decade. Many of those openings are expected to result from the need to replace workers who transfer to different occupations or exit the labor force, such as to retire.

Surgical Assistants and Technologists

Percent change in employment, projected 2022-32

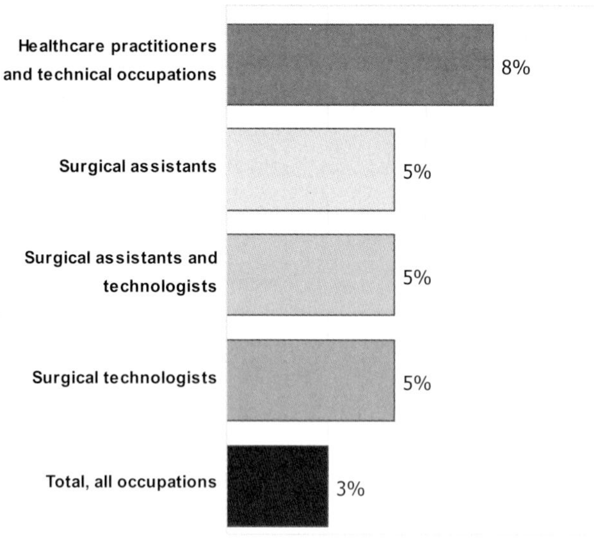

Note: All Occupations includes all occupations in the U.S. Economy.
Source: U.S. Bureau of Labor Statistics, Employment Projections program.

Employment

The aging of the large baby-boom generation is expected to increase the demand for surgical procedures, which should result in a greater need for surgical assistants and technologists. A rise in the number of surgeries among all age groups also is expected to support job growth.

Heightened demand for these workers is expected in outpatient settings, such as ambulatory surgery centers. These facilities are seeing an increase in the number of surgeries because of advances in medical technology and changes in insurers' policies.

Occupational Title	SOC Code	Employment, 2022	Projected Employment, 2032	Change, 2022-32	
				Percent	Numeric
Surgical assistants and technologists	—	128,900	135,900	5	7,000
Surgical assistants	29-9093	19,700	20,700	5	1,000
Surgical technologists	29-2055	109,200	115,200	5	5,900

Contacts for More Information

For more information about surgical technologists, visit

- Association of Surgical Technologists
- Commission on Accreditation of Allied Health Education Programs
- The National Board of Surgical Technology and Surgical Assisting
- National Center for Competency Testing
- National Commission for the Certification of Surgical Assistants
- American Board of Surgical Assistants

Veterinarians

Summary

Quick Facts: Veterinarians

2022 Median Pay	$103,260 per year $49.64 per hour
Typical Entry-Level Education	Doctoral or professional degree
Work Experience in a Related Occupation	None
On-the-job Training	None
Number of Jobs, 2022	89,500
Job Outlook, 2022-32	20% (Much faster than average)
Employment Change, 2022-32	17,700

What Veterinarians Do

Veterinarians care for the health of animals and work to protect public health.

Work Environment

Most veterinarians work in private clinics and hospitals. Others travel to farms or work in settings such as laboratories, classrooms, or zoos.

How to Become a Veterinarian

Veterinarians must have a Doctor of Veterinary Medicine degree from an accredited veterinary college, as well as a state license.

Pay

The median annual wage for veterinarians was $103,260 in May 2022.

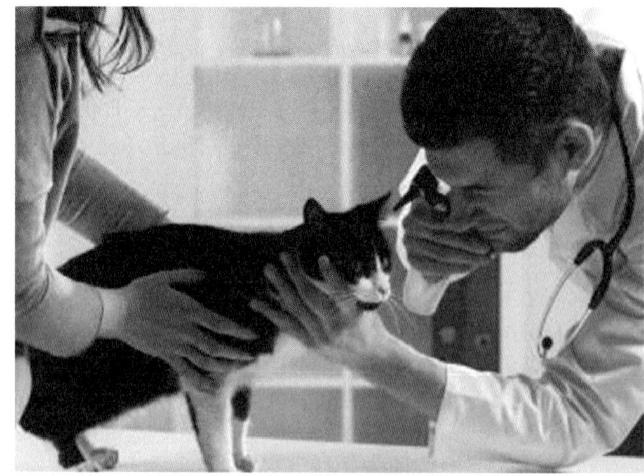

Veterinarians check for symptoms of illnesses in pets.

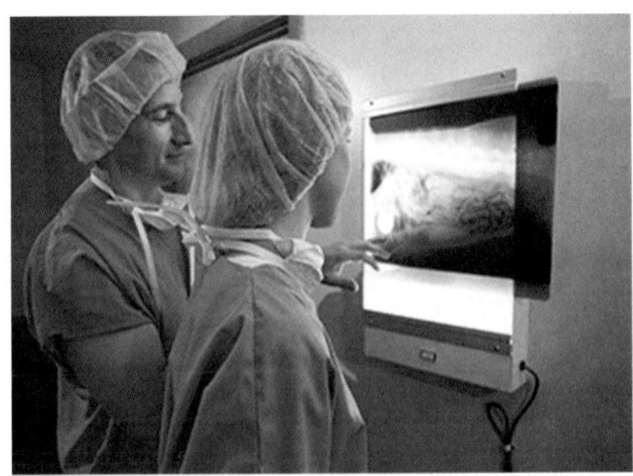

Veterinarians use x rays to diagnose animals.

Job Outlook

Employment of veterinarians is projected to grow 20 percent from 2022 to 2032, much faster than the average for all occupations.

About 5,000 openings for veterinarians are projected each year, on average, over the decade. Many of those openings are expected to result from the need to replace workers who transfer to different occupations or exit the labor force, such as to retire.

What Veterinarians Do

Veterinarians care for the health of animals and work to protect public health. They diagnose, treat, and research medical conditions and diseases of pets, livestock, and other animals.

Duties

Veterinarians typically do the following:

- Examine animals to assess their health and diagnose problems
- Treat and dress wounds
- Perform surgery on animals
- Test for and vaccinate against diseases
- Operate medical equipment, such as x-ray machines
- Advise animal owners about general care, medical conditions, and treatments
- Prescribe medication
- Euthanize animals

Veterinarians treat the injuries and illnesses of pets and other animals with a variety of medical equipment, including surgical tools and x-ray and ultrasound machines. They provide treatment for animals that is similar to the services a physician provides to humans.

The following are examples of types of veterinarians:

Companion animal veterinarians treat pets and generally work in private clinics and hospitals. They most often care for cats and dogs, but they also treat other pets, such as birds, ferrets, and rabbits. These veterinarians diagnose and provide treatment for animal health problems; consult with animal owners about preventive healthcare; and carry out medical and surgical procedures, such as vaccinations, dental work, and setting fractures.

Food animal veterinarians work with farm animals such as pigs, cattle, and sheep, which are raised to be food sources. They spend their time visiting farms and ranches to treat ill and injured animals and to test for and vaccinate against disease. They may advise farm owners or managers about feeding, housing, and general health practices.

Food safety and inspection veterinarians inspect and test livestock and animal products for major animal diseases. They also provide vaccines to treat animals, enhance animal welfare, conduct research to improve animal health, and enforce government food safety regulations. They design and administer animal and public health programs to prevent and control diseases transmissible among animals and between animals and people.

Work Environment

Veterinarians held about 89,500 jobs in 2022. The largest employers of veterinarians were as follows:

Veterinary services	83%
Self-employed workers	10
Government	2
Social advocacy organizations	1
Educational services; state, local, and private	1

Most veterinarians work in private clinics and hospitals. Others travel to farms or work in settings such as laboratories, classrooms, or zoos.

Veterinarians who treat horses or food animals travel between their offices and farms and ranches. They work outdoors in all kinds of weather and may have to perform surgery, often in remote locations.

Most veterinarians work in veterinary clinics.

Veterinarians who work in food safety and inspection travel to farms, slaughterhouses, and food-processing plants to inspect the health of animals and to ensure that the facility follows safety protocols.

The work can be emotionally stressful, as veterinarians care for abused animals, euthanize sick ones, and offer support to the animals' anxious owners. Working on farms and ranches, in slaughterhouses, or with wildlife can also be physically demanding.

Injuries and Illnesses

When working with animals that are frightened or in pain, veterinarians risk being bitten, kicked, and scratched. In addition, veterinarians working with diseased animals risk being infected by the disease.

Work Schedules

Most veterinarians work full time, often working more than 40 hours per week. Some work nights or weekends, and they may have to respond to emergencies outside of scheduled work hours.

How to Become a Veterinarian

Veterinarians must have a Doctor of Veterinary Medicine degree from an accredited veterinary college, as well as a state license.

Education

Veterinarians must complete a Doctor of Veterinary Medicine (DVM or VMD) degree at an accredited college of veterinary medicine. A veterinary medicine program generally takes 4 years to complete and includes classroom, laboratory, and clinical components.

Admission to veterinary programs is competitive. Applicants to veterinary school typically have a bachelor's degree in a field such as biology. Veterinary medical colleges typically require applicants to have taken many science classes, including biology, chemistry, and animal science. Most programs also require math, humanities, and social science courses.

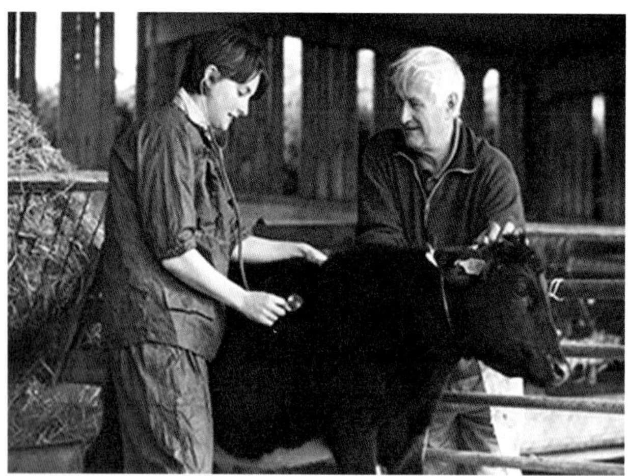

A veterinary medicine program generally takes 4 years to complete and includes classroom, laboratory, and clinical components.

Some veterinary medical colleges prefer candidates who have studied agriculture or have experience working with animals on a farm, at a stable, or in an animal shelter.

In veterinary medicine programs, students take courses on animal anatomy and physiology, as well as disease prevention, diagnosis, and treatment. Most programs include 3 years of classroom, laboratory, and clinical work. Students typically spend the final year of the 4-year program doing clinical rotations in a veterinary medical center or hospital.

Licenses, Certifications, and Registrations

Veterinarians must be licensed in order to practice in the United States. Licensing requirements vary by state, but prospective veterinarians in all states must complete an accredited veterinary program and pass the North American Veterinary Licensing Examination.

In addition to passing the national exam, most states require that veterinarians pass a state licensing exam. However, veterinarians employed by state or federal government may not need a state license, because government agencies differ in what they require.

Each state's exam covers its laws and regulations. Few states accept licenses from other states, so veterinarians usually must take exams for the states in which they want to be licensed.

The American Veterinary Medical Association has an Educational Commission for Foreign Veterinary Graduates (ECFVG) certification program, which allows foreign graduates to fulfill the educational prerequisites for licensure.

Important Qualities

Communication skills. Strong communication skills are essential for veterinarians, who must be able to discuss their recommendations and explain treatment options to animal owners and give instructions to their staff.

Compassion. Veterinarians must be compassionate when working with animals and their owners. They must treat animals with kindness and respect, and they must be sensitive when dealing with the animal owners.

Decision-making skills. Veterinarians must decide the correct method for treating the injuries and illnesses of animals.

Manual dexterity. Veterinarians must control their hand movements and be precise when treating injuries and performing surgery.

Problem-solving skills. Veterinarians need strong problem-solving skills because they must figure out what is ailing animals. Those who test animals to determine the effects of drug therapies also need excellent diagnostic skills.

Pay

The median annual wage for veterinarians was $103,260 in May 2022. The median wage is the wage at which half the workers

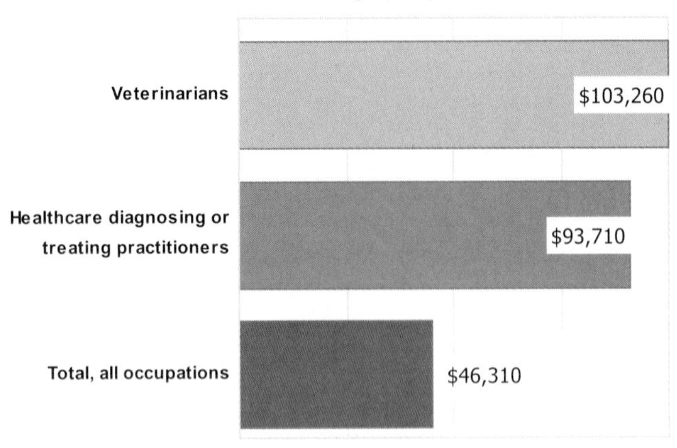

Note: All Occupations includes all occupations in the U.S. Economy.
Source: U.S. Bureau of Labor Statistics, Occupational Employment and Wage Statistics.

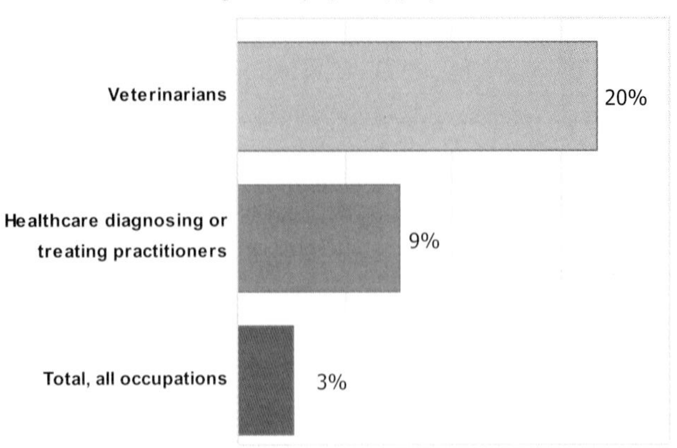

Note: All Occupations includes all occupations in the U.S. Economy.
Source: U.S. Bureau of Labor Statistics, Employment Projections program.

in an occupation earned more than that amount and half earned less. The lowest 10 percent earned less than $62,350, and the highest 10 percent earned more than $174,500.

In May 2022, the median annual wages for veterinarians in the top industries in which they worked were as follows:

Social advocacy organizations	$104,030
Educational services; state, local, and private	103,550
Veterinary services	103,210
Government	99,800

Most veterinarians work full time, often working more than 40 hours per week. Some work nights or weekends, and they may have to respond to emergencies outside of scheduled work hours.

Job Outlook

Employment of veterinarians is projected to grow 20 percent from 2022 to 2032, much faster than the average for all occupations.

About 5,000 openings for veterinarians are projected each year, on average, over the decade. Many of those openings are expected to result from the need to replace workers who transfer to different occupations or exit the labor force, such as to retire.

Employment

Increases in consumers' pet-related spending, expanding treatment options, and a growing, aging pet population are expected to drive employment growth of veterinarians.

Veterinary medicine has advanced considerably. Today's veterinarians are able to offer many services that are comparable to healthcare for humans, including more complicated procedures such as cancer treatments and kidney transplants.

Occupational Title	SOC Code	Employment, 2022	Projected Employment, 2032	Change, 2022-32	
				Percent	Numeric
Veterinarians	29-1131	89,500	107,200	20	17,700

Contacts for More Information

For more information, visit

- American Veterinary Medical Association
- Association of American Veterinary Medical Colleges
- International Council for Veterinary Assessment

Veterinary Assistants and Laboratory Animal Caretakers

Summary

Quick Facts: Veterinary Assistants and Laboratory Animal Caretakers

2022 Median Pay	$34,740 per year $16.70 per hour
Typical Entry-Level Education	High school diploma or equivalent
Work Experience in a Related Occupation	None
On-the-job Training	Short-term on-the-job training
Number of Jobs, 2022	114,800
Job Outlook, 2022-32	20% (Much faster than average)
Employment Change, 2022-32	23,500

What Veterinary Assistants and Laboratory Animal Caretakers Do

Veterinary assistants and laboratory animal caretakers handle routine animal care and help scientists, veterinarians, and others with their daily tasks.

Work Environment

Veterinary assistants and laboratory animal caretakers work mainly in clinics, animal hospitals, and research laboratories. Their work may be physically and emotionally demanding.

How to Become a Veterinary Assistant or Laboratory Animal Caretaker

Most veterinary assistants and laboratory animal caretakers have a high school diploma or equivalent and learn the occupation on the job.

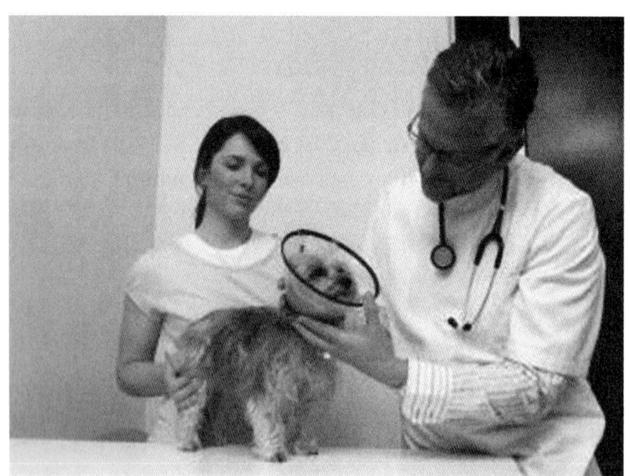

Veterinary assistants care for animals under the supervision of veterinarians and veterinary technicians.

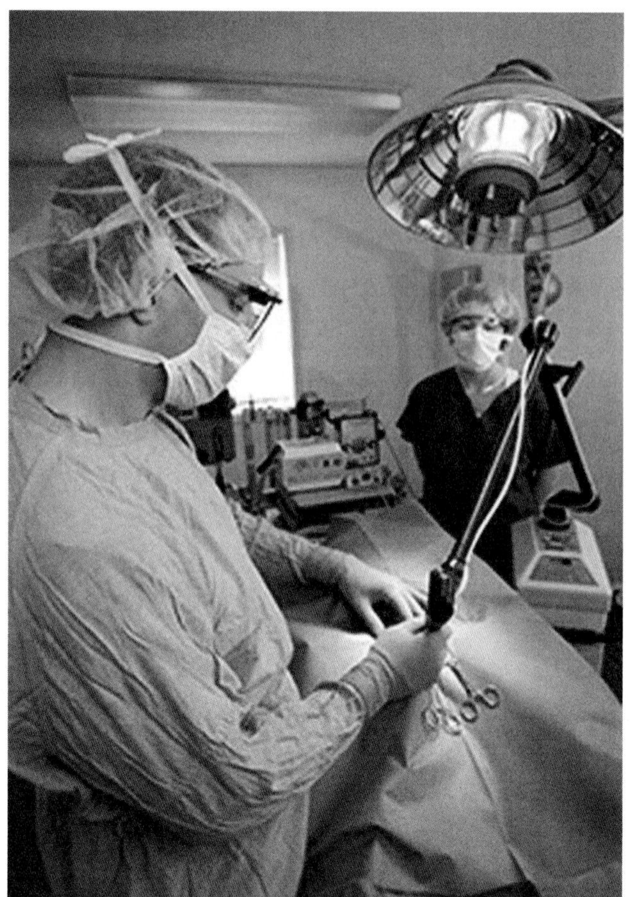

Veterinary assistants may maintain and sterilize surgical instruments and equipment.

Pay

The median annual wage for veterinary assistants and laboratory animal caretakers was $34,740 in May 2022.

Job Outlook

Employment of veterinary assistants and laboratory animal caretakers is projected to grow 20 percent from 2022 to 2032, much faster than the average for all occupations.

About 26,800 openings for veterinary assistants and laboratory animal caretakers are projected each year, on average, over the decade. Many of those openings are expected to result from the need to replace workers who transfer to different occupations or exit the labor force, such as to retire.

What Veterinary Assistants and Laboratory Animal Caretakers Do

Veterinary assistants and laboratory animal caretakers handle routine animal care and help scientists, veterinarians, and veterinary technologists and technicians with their daily tasks.

Duties

Veterinary assistants and laboratory animal caretakers typically do the following:

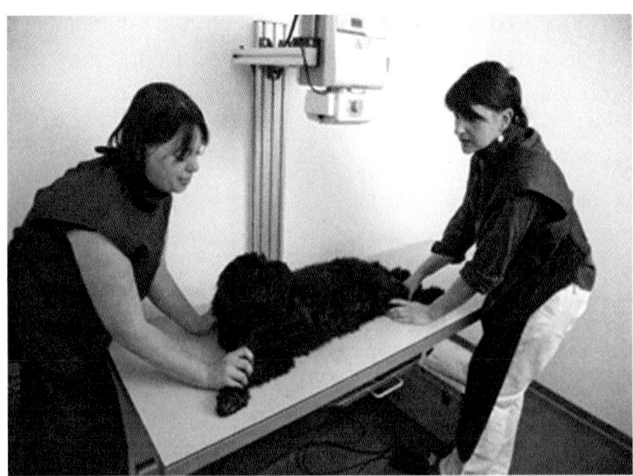

Veterinary assistants move animals and prepare equipment before procedures.

- Feed, bathe, and exercise animals
- Clean and disinfect cages, kennels, and examination and operating rooms
- Restrain animals during examination and laboratory procedures
- Maintain and sterilize surgical instruments and equipment
- Monitor and care for animals after surgery
- Help provide emergency first aid to sick and injured animals
- Give medication or immunizations that veterinarians prescribe
- Assist in collecting blood, urine, and tissue samples

Veterinary assistants and laboratory animal caretakers also provide nursing care before surgery and other medical procedures.

They may prepare equipment and pass surgical instruments and materials to veterinarians during surgery. They also move animals during testing and other procedures.

Veterinary assistants typically help veterinarians and veterinary technologists and technicians treat injuries and illnesses of animals.

Laboratory animal caretakers' daily tasks include feeding animals, cleaning kennels, and monitoring animals.

Work Environment

Veterinary assistants and laboratory animal caretakers held about 114,800 jobs in 2022. The largest employers of veterinary assistants and laboratory animal caretakers were as follows:

Veterinary services	91%
Junior colleges, colleges, universities, and professional schools; state, local, and private	3
Scientific research and development services	2

Veterinary assistants and laboratory animal caretakers work primarily in clinics and animal hospitals, colleges and universities, and research laboratories.

The work of veterinary assistants and laboratory animal caretakers may be physically and emotionally demanding. Workers may handle sick or abused animals and may assist in euthanizing animals.

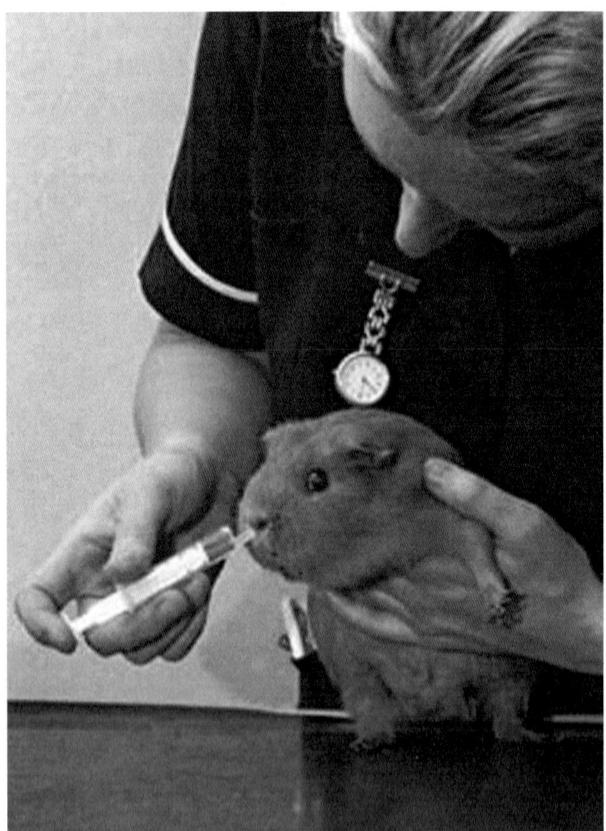

Veterinary assistants learn through on-the-job training.

Injuries and Illnesses

Veterinary assistants and laboratory animal caretakers have one of the highest rates of injuries and illnesses of all occupations. When working with scared and aggressive animals, workers may be bitten, scratched, or kicked. Workers may also be injured while holding, bathing, or restraining an animal.

Work Schedules

Some veterinary assistants and laboratory animal caretakers work part time. Veterinary assistants and laboratory animal caretakers may work nights, weekends, or holidays.

How to Become a Veterinary Assistant or Laboratory Animal Caretaker

Most veterinary assistants and laboratory animal caretakers have a high school diploma or equivalent and learn the occupation on the job. Experience working with or being around animals may be helpful for jobseekers.

Education

Most workers entering the occupation have a high school diploma or equivalent.

Training

Most veterinary assistants and laboratory animal caretakers receive short-term on-the-job training.

Licenses, Certifications, and Registrations

Although certification is not mandatory, it allows workers to demonstrate competency in animal husbandry, health and welfare, and facility administration.

The National Association of Veterinary Technicians in America (NAVTA) offers the Approved Veterinary Assistant (AVA) designation for veterinary assistants. To qualify for the designation, candidates must graduate from a NAVTA-approved program and pass an exam.

Laboratory animal caretakers become certified through the American Association for Laboratory Animal Science (AALAS). AALAS offers three levels of certification: Assistant Laboratory Animal Technician (ALAT), Laboratory Animal Technician (LAT), and Laboratory Animal Technologist (LATG). For AALAS certification, candidates must have experience working in a laboratory animal facility and pass an exam.

Important Qualities

Communication skills. Veterinary assistants and laboratory animal caretakers communicate with pet owners, veterinarians, veterinary technologists and technicians, and other assistants. They need to be able to explain instructions, procedures, and other information clearly and effectively.

Compassion. Veterinary assistants and laboratory animal caretakers must treat animals with kindness and show compassion to both the animals and their owners.

Detail oriented. Veterinary assistants and laboratory animal caretakers must follow instructions exactly as directed. For example, they must be precise when sterilizing surgical equipment, monitoring animals, and giving medication.

Manual dexterity. Veterinary assistants and laboratory animal caretakers must be adept in both handling animals and using medical instruments and laboratory equipment.

Physical strength. Veterinary assistants and laboratory animal caretakers must be strong enough to handle, move, and restrain animals.

Pay

The median annual wage for veterinary assistants and laboratory animal caretakers was $34,740 in May 2022. The median wage is the wage at which half the workers in an occupation earned more than that amount and half earned less. The lowest 10 percent earned less than $25,270, and the highest 10 percent earned more than $44,920.

In May 2022, the median annual wages for veterinary assistants and laboratory animal caretakers in the top industries in which they worked were as follows:

Scientific research and development services	$43,780
Junior colleges, colleges, universities, and professional schools; state, local, and private	41,090
Veterinary services	34,380

Some veterinary assistants and laboratory animal caretakers work part time. Veterinary assistants and laboratory animal caretakers may work nights, weekends, or holidays.

Job Outlook

Employment of veterinary assistants and laboratory animal caretakers is projected to grow 20 percent from 2022 to 2032, much faster than the average for all occupations.

About 26,800 openings for veterinary assistants and laboratory animal caretakers are projected each year, on average, over the decade. Many of those openings are expected to result from the need to replace workers who transfer to different occupations or exit the labor force, such as to retire.

Veterinary Assistants and Laboratory Animal Caretakers

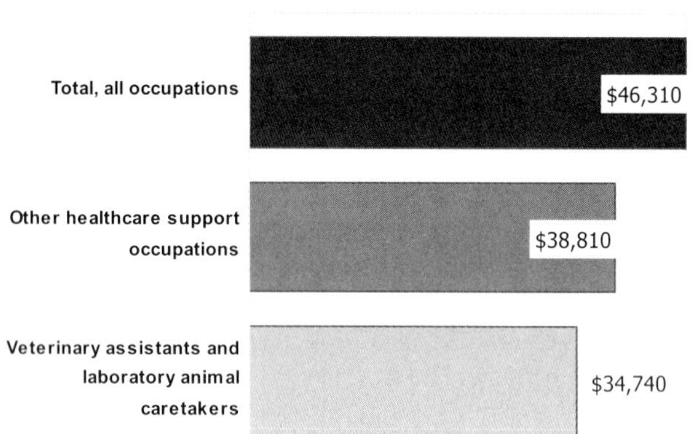

Note: All Occupations includes all occupations in the U.S. Economy.
Source: U.S. Bureau of Labor Statistics, Occupational Employment and Wage Statistics.

Veterinary Assistants and Laboratory Animal Caretakers

Percent change in employment, projected 2022-32

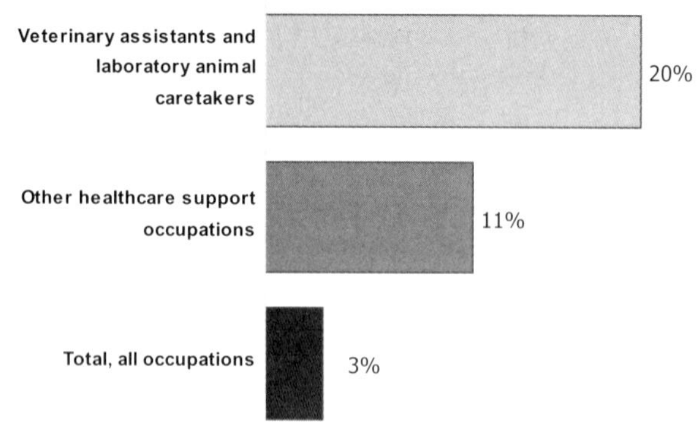

Note: All Occupations includes all occupations in the U.S. Economy.
Source: U.S. Bureau of Labor Statistics, Employment Projections program.

Employment

Increases in consumers' pet-related spending are expected to drive employment in the veterinary services industry, which employs most veterinary assistants and laboratory animal caretakers. In clinics and other veterinary service establishments, assistants help veterinarians and veterinary technicians and technologists with various procedures. Demand for veterinary assistants will continue as the demand for these procedures increases.

Occupational Title	SOC Code	Employment, 2022	Projected Employment, 2032	Change, 2022-32	
				Percent	Numeric
Veterinary assistants and laboratory animal caretakers	31-9096	114,800	138,300	20	23,500

Contacts for More Information

For more information about certification as a laboratory animal caretaker, visit

- American Association for Laboratory Animal Science

For more information about certification as a veterinary assistant, visit

- National Association of Veterinary Technicians in America

For more information about becoming a veterinary assistant, including career opportunities, visit

- American Animal Hospital Association

Veterinary Technologists and Technicians

Summary

Quick Facts: Veterinary Technologists and Technicians

2022 Median Pay	$38,240 per year $18.38 per hour
Typical Entry-Level Education	Associate's degree
Work Experience in a Related Occupation	None
On-the-job Training	None
Number of Jobs, 2022	122,900
Job Outlook, 2022-32	21% (Much faster than average)
Employment Change, 2022-32	25,200

What Veterinary Technologists and Technicians Do

Veterinary technologists and technicians do medical tests that help diagnose animals' injuries and illnesses.

Veterinary technologists and technicians perform medical tests under the supervision of a licensed veterinarian to assist in diagnosing the injuries and illnesses of animals.

Work Environment

Veterinary technologists and technicians work in private clinics, laboratories, and animal hospitals. Their jobs may be physically or emotionally demanding. Many work evenings, weekends, or holidays.

How to Become a Veterinary Technologist or Technician

Veterinary technologists and technicians must complete a postsecondary program in veterinary technology. Technologists usually need a 4-year bachelor's degree, and technicians need a 2-year associate's degree. Typically, both technologists and technicians must take a credentialing exam and become registered, licensed, or certified, depending on the requirements of the state in which they work.

Pay

The median annual wage for veterinary technologists and technicians was $38,240 in May 2022.

Veterinary technologists and technicians are responsible for the careful and humane handling of laboratory animals.

Job Outlook

Employment of veterinary technologists and technicians is projected to grow 21 percent from 2022 to 2032, much faster than the average for all occupations.

About 14,800 openings for veterinary technologists and technicians are projected each year, on average, over the decade. Many of those openings are expected to result from the need to replace workers who transfer to different occupations or exit the labor force, such as to retire.

Learn more about veterinary technologists and technicians by visiting additional resources, including O*NET, a source on key characteristics of workers and occupations.

What Veterinary Technologists and Technicians Do

Veterinary technologists and technicians, supervised by licensed veterinarians, do medical tests that help diagnose animals' injuries and illnesses.

Duties

Veterinary technologists and technicians typically do the following:

- Observe the behavior and condition of animals
- Provide nursing care or emergency first aid to recovering or injured animals
- Bathe animals, clip nails or claws, and brush or cut animals' hair
- Restrain animals during exams or procedures
- Administer anesthesia to animals and monitor their responses
- Take x rays and collect and perform laboratory tests, such as urinalyses and blood counts
- Prepare animals and instruments for surgery
- Administer medications, vaccines, and treatments prescribed by a veterinarian
- Collect and record animals' case histories

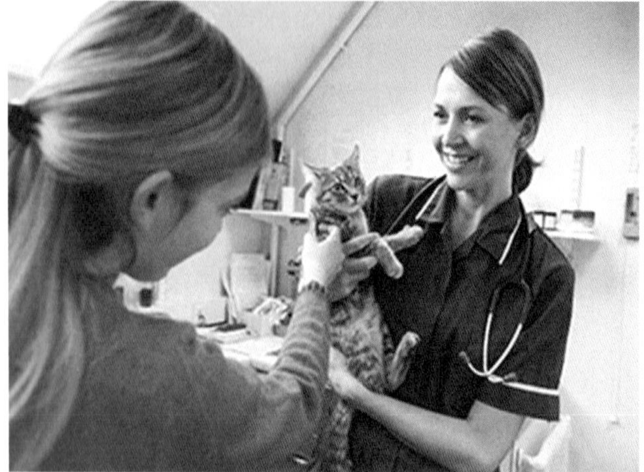

Veterinary technologists and technicians typically work in private clinics and animal hospitals.

In addition to helping veterinarians during animal exams, veterinary technologists and technicians do a variety of clinical, care, and laboratory tasks.

Veterinary technologists and technicians who work in research-related jobs ensure that animals are handled carefully and are treated humanely. They may help veterinarians or scientists on research projects in areas such as biomedical research, disaster preparedness, and food safety.

Typically working with small-animal practitioners who care for cats and dogs, veterinary technologists and technicians also may have tasks that involve mice, cattle, or other animals.

Veterinary technologists and technicians may specialize in a particular discipline, such as dentistry, anesthesia, emergency and critical care, and zoological medicine.

Veterinary technologists typically work in more advanced research-related jobs, usually under the guidance of a scientist or veterinarian. Some technologists work in private clinical practices. Working primarily in a laboratory setting, they may administer medications; prepare tissue samples for examination; or record an animal's genealogy, weight, diet, and signs of pain.

Veterinary technicians generally work in private clinical practices under the guidance of a licensed veterinarian. Technicians may do laboratory tests, such as a urinalysis, and help veterinarians conduct a variety of other diagnostic tests. Although they do some of their work in a laboratory, technicians also talk with animal owners. For example, they explain a pet's condition or how to administer medication prescribed by a veterinarian.

Work Environment

Veterinary technologists and technicians held about 122,900 jobs in 2022. The largest employers of veterinary technologists and technicians were as follows:

Veterinary services	90%
Junior colleges, colleges, universities, and professional schools; state, local, and private	3
Social advocacy organizations	2

Veterinary technologists and technicians typically work in private clinics and animal hospitals. They also may work in laboratories, colleges and universities, and humane societies.

Their jobs may be physically or emotionally demanding. For example, they may witness abused animals or may need to help euthanize sick, injured, or unwanted animals.

Injuries and Illnesses

Veterinary technologists and technicians risk injury on the job. They may be bitten, scratched, or kicked while working with scared or aggressive animals. Injuries may happen while the technologist or technician is holding, cleaning, or restraining an animal.

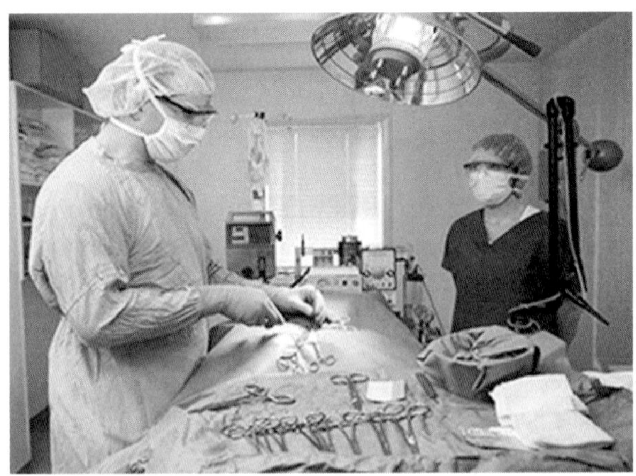

Typically, both technologists and technicians must pass a credentialing exam and must become registered, licensed, or certified, depending on the state in which they work.

Work Schedules

Veterinary technologists and technicians may have to work evenings, weekends, or holidays.

How to Become a Veterinary Technologist or Technician

Veterinary technologists and technicians must complete a postsecondary program in veterinary technology. Technologists usually need a 4-year bachelor's degree, and technicians need a 2-year associate's degree. Typically, both technologists and technicians must pass a credentialing exam to become registered, licensed, or certified, depending on the requirements of the state in which they work.

Education

Veterinary technologists usually have a 4-year bachelor's degree in veterinary technology. Veterinary technicians usually have a 2-year associate's degree in a veterinary technology program. The American Veterinary Medical Association (AVMA) accredits veterinary technology programs. Most of these programs offer a 2-year associate's degree for veterinary technicians; others offer a 4-year bachelor's degree for veterinary technologists

People interested in becoming a veterinary technologist or technician can prepare by taking biology and other science courses in high school.

Licenses, Certifications, and Registrations

Although each state regulates veterinary technologists and technicians differently, most candidates must pass a credentialing exam. Most states require technologists and technicians to pass the Veterinary Technician National Examination (VTNE), offered by the American Association of Veterinary State Boards.

Important Qualities

Communication skills. Veterinary technologists and technicians communicate with supervisors, other staff, and animal owners. A growing number of technicians counsel pet owners on animal behavior and nutrition.

Compassion. Veterinary technologists and technicians must treat animals with kindness and must be sensitive when dealing with the owners of sick pets.

Detail oriented. Veterinary technologists and technicians must pay attention to detail. They must be precise when recording information, performing diagnostic tests, and administering medication.

Manual dexterity. Veterinary technologists and technicians must handle animals, medical instruments, and laboratory equipment with care. They need a steady hand for intricate tasks such as doing dental work, giving anesthesia, and taking x rays.

Physical strength. Veterinary technologists and technicians need to be able to manage and lift animals.

Pay

The median annual wage for veterinary technologists and technicians was $38,240 in May 2022. The median wage is the wage at which half the workers in an occupation earned more than that amount and half earned less. The lowest 10 percent earned less than $29,000, and the highest 10 percent earned more than $54,680.

In May 2022, the median annual wages for veterinary technologists and technicians in the top industries in which they worked were as follows:

Junior colleges, colleges, universities, and professional schools; state, local, and private	$49,050
Veterinary services	37,960
Social advocacy organizations	37,480

Veterinary technologists and technicians working in research positions often earn more than those in other fields.

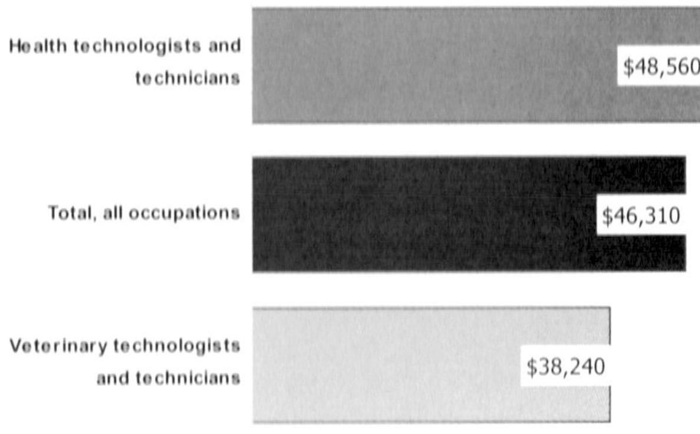

Note: All Occupations includes all occupations in the U.S. Economy. Source: U.S. Bureau of Labor Statistics, Occupational Employment and Wage Statistics.

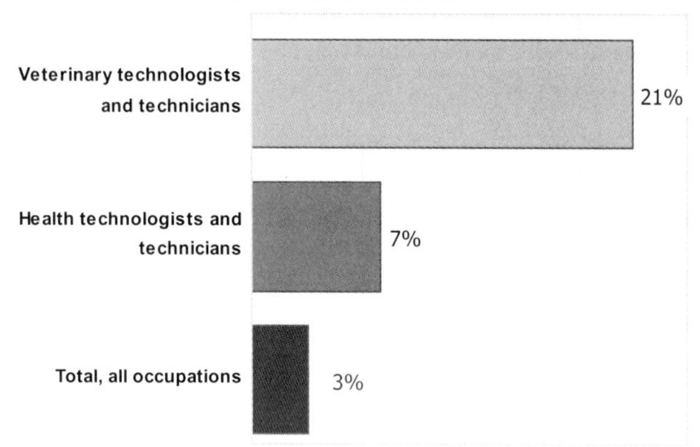

Note: All Occupations includes all occupations in the U.S. Economy.
Source: U.S. Bureau of Labor Statistics, Employment Projections program.

Veterinary technologists and technicians may have to work evenings, weekends, or holidays.

Job Outlook

Employment of veterinary technologists and technicians is projected to grow 21 percent from 2022 to 2032, much faster than the average for all occupations.

About 14,800 openings for veterinary technologists and technicians are projected each year, on average, over the decade. Many of those openings are expected to result from the need to replace workers who transfer to different occupations or exit the labor force, such as to retire.

Employment

As the number of households with pets and spending on pets continue to rise, strong demand is expected for veterinary technologists and technicians. Increased treatment options also will contribute to rising demand for these workers over the projections decade.

Employment projections data for veterinary technologists and technicians, 2022-32

Occupational Title	SOC Code	Employment, 2022	Projected Employment, 2032	Change, 2022-32		Employment by Industry
				Percent	Numeric	
SOURCE: U.S. Bureau of Labor Statistics, Employment Projections program						
Veterinary technologists and technicians	29-2056	122,900	148,100	21	25,200	Get data

Contacts for More Information

For information, visit

- American Veterinary Medical Association
- National Association of Veterinary Technicians in America
- American Association for Laboratory Animal Science
- American Association of Veterinary State Boards

Installation, Maintenance, and Repair

Aircraft and Avionics Equipment Mechanics and Technicians

Summary

Quick Facts: Aircraft and Avionics Equipment Mechanics and Technicians	
2022 Median Pay	$70,740 per year $34.01 per hour
Typical Entry-Level Education	See How to Become One
Work Experience in a Related Occupation	None
On-the-job Training	None
Number of Jobs, 2022	161,000
Job Outlook, 2022-32	4% (As fast as average)
Employment Change, 2022-32	7,000

What Aircraft and Avionics Equipment Mechanics and Technicians Do

Aircraft and avionics equipment mechanics and technicians repair and perform scheduled maintenance on aircraft.

Work Environment

Aircraft and avionics equipment mechanics and technicians work in hangars, in repair stations, or on airfields. The environment can be loud because of aircraft engines and equipment.

Aircraft and avionics equipment mechanics and technicians perform scheduled maintenance, make repairs, and complete inspections.

How to Become an Aircraft and Avionics Equipment Mechanic or Technician

Most aircraft and avionics equipment mechanics and technicians learn their trade at an Federal Aviation Administration (FAA)-approved aviation maintenance technician school or on the job. Some learn through training received in the military.

Pay

The median annual wage for aircraft mechanics and service technicians was $70,010 in May 2022.

The median annual wage for avionics technicians was $75,450 in May 2022.

Job Outlook

Overall employment of aircraft and avionics equipment mechanics and technicians is projected to grow 4 percent from 2022 to 2032, about as fast as the average for all occupations.

About 12,800 openings for aircraft and avionics equipment mechanics and technicians are projected each year, on average, over the decade. Many of those openings are expected to result from the need to replace workers who transfer to different occupations or exit the labor force, such as to retire.

What Aircraft and Avionics Equipment Mechanics and Technicians Do

Aircraft and avionics equipment mechanics and technicians repair and perform scheduled maintenance on aircraft.

Duties

Aircraft mechanics typically do the following:

- Diagnose mechanical or electrical problems
- Repair wings, brakes, electrical systems, and other aircraft components
- Replace defective parts, using hand tools or power tools
- Examine replacement aircraft parts for defects
- Read maintenance manuals to identify repair procedures
- Test aircraft parts with gauges and other diagnostic equipment
- Inspect completed work to ensure that it meets performance standards
- Keep records of maintenance and repair work

Avionics technicians typically do the following:

Aircraft mechanics diagnose mechanical or electrical problems.

- Test electronic instruments, using circuit testers, oscilloscopes, and voltmeters
- Interpret flight test data to diagnose malfunctions and performance problems
- Assemble components, such as electrical controls and junction boxes, and install software
- Install instrument panels, using hand tools, power tools, and soldering irons
- Repair or replace malfunctioning components
- Keep records of maintenance and repair work

Airplanes require reliable parts and maintenance in order to fly safely. To keep an airplane in operating condition, aircraft and avionics equipment mechanics and technicians perform scheduled maintenance, make repairs, and complete inspections. They must follow detailed regulations set by the Federal Aviation Administration (FAA) that dictate maintenance schedules for different operations.

Many mechanics are generalists and work on many different types of aircraft, such as jets, piston-driven airplanes, and helicopters. Others specialize in one section, such as the engine, hydraulic system, or electrical system, of a particular type of aircraft. In independent repair shops, mechanics usually inspect and repair many types of aircraft.

The following are examples of types of aircraft and avionics equipment mechanics and technicians:

Airframe and Powerplant (A&P) mechanics are certified generalist mechanics who can independently perform many maintenance and alteration tasks on aircraft. A&P mechanics repair and maintain most parts of an aircraft, including the engines, landing gear, brakes, and air-conditioning system. Some specialized activities require additional experience and certification.

Maintenance schedules for aircraft may be based on hours flown, days since the last inspection, trips flown, or a combination of these factors. Maintenance also may need to be done at other times to address specific issues recognized by mechanics or manufacturers.

Mechanics use precision instruments to measure wear and identify defects. They may use x rays or magnetic or ultrasonic inspection equipment to discover cracks that cannot be seen on a plane's exterior. They check for corrosion, distortion, and cracks in the aircraft's main body, wings, and tail. They then repair the metal, fabric, wood, or composite materials that make up the airframe and skin.

After completing all repairs, mechanics test the equipment to ensure that it works properly and record all maintenance completed on an aircraft.

Avionics technicians are specialists who repair and maintain a plane's electronic instruments, such as radio communication devices and equipment, radar systems, and navigation aids. As the use of digital technology increases, more time is spent maintaining computer systems. The ability to repair and maintain many avionics and flight instrument systems is granted through the Airframe rating, but other licenses or certifications may be needed as well.

Designated airworthiness representatives (DARs) examine, inspect, and test aircraft for airworthiness. They issue airworthiness certificates, which aircraft must have to fly. There are two types of DARs: manufacturing DARs and maintenance DARs.

Inspection authorized (IA) mechanics are mechanics who have both Airframe and Powerplant certification and may perform inspections on aircraft and return them to service. IA mechanics are able to do a wider variety of maintenance activities and alterations than any other type of maintenance personnel. They can do comprehensive annual inspections or return aircraft to service after a major repair.

Repairmen certificate holders may or may not have the A&P certificate or other certificates. Repairmen certificates are issued by certified repair stations to aviation maintenance personnel, and the certificates allow them to do specific duties. Repairmen certificates are valid only while the mechanic works at the issuing repair center and are not transferable to other employers.

Work Environment

Aircraft mechanics and service technicians held about 140,200 jobs in 2022. The largest employers of aircraft mechanics and service technicians were as follows:

Support activities for air transportation	29%
Scheduled air transportation	18
Aerospace product and parts manufacturing	16
Federal government, excluding postal service	10
Nonscheduled air transportation	5

Avionics technicians held about 20,800 jobs in 2022. The largest employers of avionics technicians were as follows:

Support activities for air transportation	34%
Aerospace product and parts manufacturing	32

Aircraft mechanics climb, reach, and balance on a plane's exterior.

Professional, scientific, and technical services	13
Federal government	7

Aircraft and avionics equipment mechanics and technicians work in hangars, in repair stations, or on airfields. They must meet strict deadlines while following safety standards.

Most of these mechanics and technicians work near major airports. They may work outside on the airfield, or in climate-controlled shops and hangars. Civilian aircraft and avionics equipment mechanics and technicians employed by the U.S. Armed Forces work on military installations.

Injuries and Illnesses

Aircraft and avionics equipment mechanics and technicians often lift heavy objects, handle dangerous chemicals, or operate large power tools. They may work on scaffolds or ladders, and noise and vibrations are common, especially when engines are being tested. Workers must take precautions against injuries, such as wearing ear protection and brightly colored vests to ensure that they are seen when working around large aircraft.

Work Schedules

Aircraft and avionics equipment mechanics and technicians usually work full time on rotating 8-hour shifts. Overtime and weekend work are common.

How to Become an Aircraft and Avionics Equipment Mechanic or Technician

Some aircraft and avionics equipment mechanics and technicians learn their trade at an Federal Aviation Administration (FAA)-approved aviation maintenance technician school. Others are trained on the job or learn through training in the military. Aircraft mechanics and avionics technicians typically are certified by the FAA. (See Title 14 of the Code of Federal Regulations (14 CFR), part 65, subparts D and E, for the most current requirements for becoming a certified mechanic.)

Some aircraft and avionics equipment mechanics and technicians learn their trade on the job.

Education

Aircraft mechanics and service technicians typically enter the occupation after attending a Part 147 FAA-approved aviation maintenance technician school. These schools award a certificate of completion that the FAA recognizes as an alternative to the experience requirements stated in regulations. The schools also grant holders the right to take the relevant FAA exams.

Avionics technicians typically earn an associate's degree before entering the occupation. Aircraft controls, systems, and flight instruments have become increasingly digital and computerized. Workers who have the proper background in aviation flight instruments or computer repair are needed to maintain these complex systems.

Although not required, bachelor's degree study in engineering or a related field, such as transportation, may provide useful background knowledge.

Training

Some aircraft mechanics and service technicians enter the occupation with a high school diploma or equivalent and receive on-the-job training to learn their skills and to be able to pass the FAA exams. Aviation maintenance personnel who are not certified by the FAA work under supervision until they have enough experience and knowledge and become certified.

Licenses, Certifications, and Registrations

The FAA requires that aircraft maintenance be done either by a certified mechanic with the appropriate ratings or authorizations or under the supervision of such a mechanic.

The FAA offers separate certifications for bodywork (Airframe mechanics, or "A") and engine work (Powerplant mechanics, or "P"), but employers may prefer to hire mechanics who have both Airframe and Powerplant (A&P) ratings. The A&P ratings generally certify that aviation mechanics meet basic knowledge and ability standards.

Mechanics must be at least 18 years of age, be fluent in English, and have 30 months of experience to qualify for either the A or the P rating or both (the A&P rating). Completion of a program at a Part 147 FAA-approved aviation maintenance technician school can substitute for the experience requirement and shorten the time requirements for becoming eligible to take the FAA exams.

Applicants must pass written, oral, and practical exams that demonstrate the required skills within a timeframe of 2 years.

To keep their certification, mechanics must have completed relevant repair or maintenance work within the previous 24 months. To fulfill this requirement, mechanics may take classes from their employer, a school, or an aircraft manufacturer.

The Inspection Authorization (IA) is available to mechanics who have had their A&P ratings for at least 3 years and meet other requirements. These mechanics are able to review and approve many major repairs and alterations.

Avionics technicians typically are certified through a repair station for the specific work they perform on aircraft, or they hold the Airframe rating to work on an aircraft's electronic and flight instrument systems. An Aircraft Electronics Technician (AET) certification is available through the American Society for Testing and Materials (ASTM). It certifies that aviation mechanics have a basic level of knowledge in the subject area, but it is not required by the FAA for any specific tasks. Avionics technicians who work on communications equipment may need to have the proper radiotelephone operator certification issued by the Federal Communications Commission (FCC).

Work Experience in a Related Occupation

Some avionics technicians begin their careers as aircraft mechanics and service technicians. As aircraft mechanics and service technicians gain experience, they may attend classes or otherwise choose to pursue additional certifications that grant privileges to work on specialized flight instruments. Eventually, they may become avionics technicians who work exclusively on flight instruments.

Advancement

As aircraft mechanics gain experience, they may advance to lead mechanic, lead inspector, or shop supervisor. Opportunities to advance may be best for those who have an inspection authorization (IA). Mechanics with broad experience in maintenance and repair may become inspectors or examiners for the FAA.

Important Qualities

Detail oriented. Mechanics and technicians need to adjust airplane parts to exact specifications. For example, they often use precision tools to tighten wheel bolts to a specified tension.

Dexterity. Mechanics and technicians need to coordinate the movement of their fingers and hands in order to grasp, manipulate, or assemble parts.

Observational skills. Mechanics and technicians must recognize engine noises, read gauges, and collect other information to determine whether an aircraft's systems are working properly.

Strength. Mechanics and technicians may carry or move heavy equipment or aircraft parts, climb on airplanes, balance, and reach without falling.

Pay

The median annual wage for aircraft mechanics and service technicians was $70,010 in May 2022. The median wage is the wage at which half the workers in an occupation earned more than that amount and half earned less. The lowest 10 percent earned less than $41,020, and the highest 10 percent earned more than $108,200.

The median annual wage for avionics technicians was $75,450 in May 2022. The lowest 10 percent earned less than $40,980, and the highest 10 percent earned more than $109,160.

In May 2022, the median annual wages for aircraft mechanics and service technicians in the top industries in which they worked were as follows:

Scheduled air transportation	$100,260
Nonscheduled air transportation	73,140
Aerospace product and parts manufacturing	72,850
Federal government, excluding postal service	67,040
Support activities for air transportation	61,070

In May 2022, the median annual wages for avionics technicians in the top industries in which they worked were as follows:

Professional, scientific, and technical services	$93,070
Aerospace product and parts manufacturing	81,850
Federal government	64,420
Support activities for air transportation	60,320

Aircraft and Avionics Equipment Mechanics and Technicians

Median annual wages, May 2022

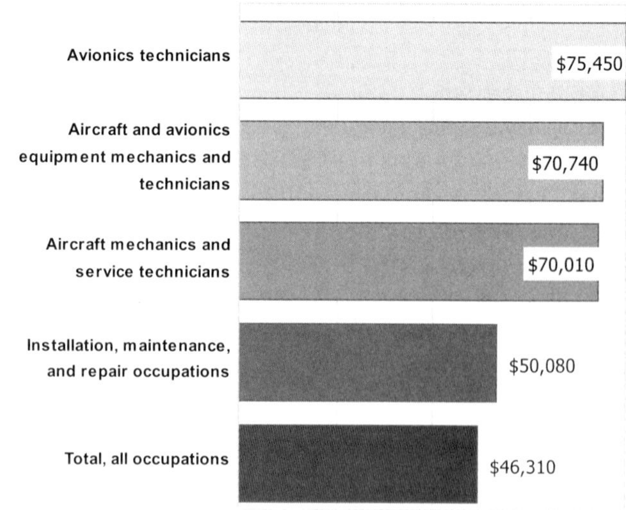

Note: All Occupations includes all occupations in the U.S. Economy. Source: U.S. Bureau of Labor Statistics, Occupational Employment and Wage Statistics.

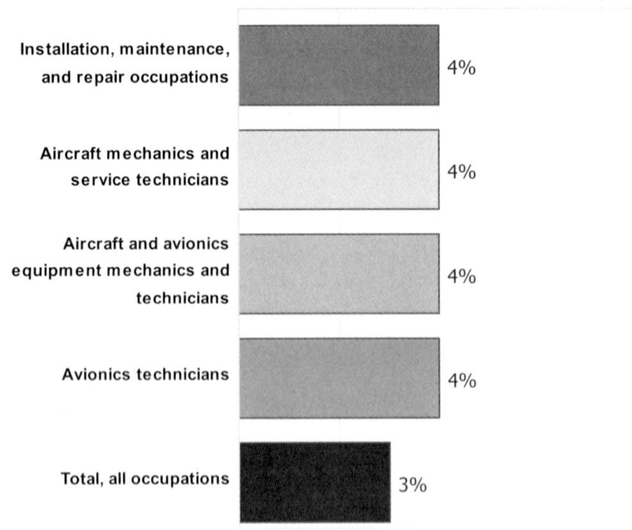

Note: All Occupations includes all occupations in the U.S. Economy.
Source: U.S. Bureau of Labor Statistics, Employment Projections program.

Mechanics and technicians usually work full time on rotating 8-hour shifts. Overtime and weekend work are common.

Job Outlook

Overall employment of aircraft and avionics equipment mechanics and technicians is projected to grow 4 percent from 2022 to 2032, about as fast as the average for all occupations.

About 12,800 openings for aircraft and avionics equipment mechanics and technicians are projected each year, on average, over the decade. Many of those openings are expected to result from the need to replace workers who transfer to different occupations or exit the labor force, such as to retire.

Employment

As air traffic increases, more workers are expected to be needed to maintain a growing number of aircraft.

Occupational Title	SOC Code	Employment, 2022	Projected Employment, 2032	Change, 2022-32	
				Percent	Numeric
Aircraft and avionics equipment mechanics and technicians	—	161,000	168,000	4	7,000
Avionics technicians	49-2091	20,800	21,700	4	900
Aircraft mechanics and service technicians	49-3011	140,200	146,200	4	6,100

Contacts for More Information

For more information, visit

- Aircraft Mechanics Fraternal Association
- Aviation Maintenance Magazine
- Federal Aviation Administration
- National Business Aviation Association
- American Society for Testing and Materials
- Professional Aviation Maintenance Association

Automotive Body and Glass Repairers

Summary

Quick Facts: Automotive Body and Glass Repairers

2022 Median Pay	$47,270 per year $22.73 per hour
Typical Entry-Level Education	High school diploma or equivalent
Work Experience in a Related Occupation	None
On-the-job Training	See How to Become One
Number of Jobs, 2022	175,200
Job Outlook, 2022-32	1% (Little or no change)
Employment Change, 2022-32	2,300

What Automotive Body and Glass Repairers Do

Automotive body and glass repairers restore, refinish, and replace vehicle bodies and frames, windshields, and window glass.

Work Environment

Automotive body repairers work indoors in body shops, which are often noisy. Shops are typically well ventilated, so that dust and paint fumes can be dispersed. Repairers sometimes work in awkward and cramped positions, and their work can be physically demanding.

Automotive glass installers and repairers often travel to the customer's location to repair damaged windshields and window glass.

How to Become an Automotive Body or Glass Repairer

Most employers prefer to hire automotive body and glass repairers who have completed a training program in automotive body or glass repair. Still, many new automotive body and glass repairers begin work without previous training. Industry certification is becoming increasingly important.

Pay

The median annual wage for automotive body and related repairers was $47,670 in May 2022.

Automotive body repairers restore automobile frames to factory specifications.

The median annual wage for automotive glass installers and repairers was $43,700 in May 2022.

Job Outlook

Overall employment of automotive body and glass repairers is projected to show little or no change from 2022 to 2032.

Despite limited employment growth, about 15,100 openings for automotive body and glass repairers are projected each year, on average, over the decade. Most of those openings are expected to result from the need to replace workers who transfer to different occupations or exit the labor force, such as to retire.

What Automotive Body and Glass Repairers Do

Automotive body and glass repairers restore, refinish, and replace vehicle bodies and frames, windshields, and window glass.

Duties

Automotive body repairers typically do the following:

- Review damage reports, prepare cost estimates, and plan work
- Inspect cars for structural damage
- Remove damaged body parts, including bumpers, fenders, hoods, grilles, and trim
- Realign car frames and chassis to repair structural damage
- Hammer out or patch dents, dimples, and other minor body damage
- Fit, attach, and weld replacement parts into place
- Sand, buff, and prime refurbished and repaired surfaces
- Apply new finish to restored body parts

Automotive glass installers and repairers typically do the following:

- Examine damaged glass or windshields and assess repairability

Automotive body and glass repairers inspect car frames for structural damage.

- Clean damaged areas and prepare the surfaces for repair
- Stabilize chips and cracks with clear resin
- Remove glass that cannot be repaired
- Check windshield frames for rust
- Clean windshield frames and prepare them for installation
- Apply urethane sealant to the windshield frames
- Install replacement glass
- Replace any parts removed prior to repairs

Automotive body and glass repairers can repair most damage from vehicle collisions and make vehicles look and drive like new. Repairs may be minor, such as replacing a cracked windshield, or major, such as replacing an entire door panel. After a major collision, the underlying frame of a car can become weakened or compromised. Body repairers restore the structural integrity of car frames to manufacturer specifications.

Body repairers use pneumatic tools and plasma cutters to remove damaged parts, such as bumpers and door panels. They also often use heavy-duty hydraulic jacks and hammers for major structural repairs, such as aligning the body. For some work, they use common hand tools, such as metal files, pliers, wrenches, hammers, and screwdrivers.

In some cases, body repairers complete an entire job by themselves. In other cases, especially in large shops, they use an assembly line approach in which they work as a team with each individual performing a specialized task.

Although body repairers sometimes prime and paint repaired parts, painting and coating workers generally perform these tasks.

Glass installers and repairers often travel to the customer's location and perform their work in the field. They commonly use specialized tools such as vacuum pumps to fill windshield cracks and chips with a stabilizing resin. When windshields are badly damaged, they use knives to remove the damaged windshield, and then they secure the new windshield using a special urethane adhesive.

Work Environment

Automotive body and related repairers held about 153,300 jobs in 2022. The largest employers of automotive body and related repairers were as follows:

Automotive body, paint, interior, and glass repair	61%
Automobile dealers	16
Self-employed workers	8
Automotive mechanical and electrical repair and maintenance	7

Automotive glass installers and repairers held about 21,900 jobs in 2022. The largest employers of automotive glass installers and repairers were as follows:

Automotive body, paint, interior, and glass repair	66%
Self-employed workers	19
Construction	3

Body repairers typically work indoors in body shops, which are often noisy. Most shops are well ventilated, so that dust and paint fumes can be dispersed. Glass installers and repairers often travel to the customer's location to repair damaged windshields and window glass.

Automotive body and glass repairers sometimes work in awkward and cramped positions, and their work can be physically demanding.

Work Schedules

Most automotive body and glass repairers work full time. When shops have to complete a backlog of work, overtime is common. This often includes working evenings and weekends.

How to Become an Automotive Body or Glass Repairer

Most employers prefer to hire automotive body and glass repairers who have completed a training program in automotive body or glass repair. Still, many new body and glass repairers begin work without previous training. Industry certification is increasingly important.

Education

High school, trade and technical school, and community college programs in collision repair combine hands-on practice and technical instruction. Topics usually include electronics, repair cost estimation, and welding, all of which provide a strong educational foundation for a career as a body repairer.

Trade and technical school programs typically award certificates after 6 months to 1 year of study. Some community colleges offer 2-year programs in collision repair. Many of these schools also offer certificates for individual courses, so students can take classes part time or as needed.

Training

New workers typically begin their on-the-job training by helping an experienced body repairer with basic tasks, such as fixing minor dents. As they gain experience, they move on to more complex work, such as aligning car frames. Some body repairers may become trained in as little as 1 year, but they generally need 2 or 3 years of hands-on training to become fully independent body repairers.

Basic automotive glass installation and repair can be learned in as little as 6 months, but becoming fully independent can take up to a year of training.

Workers who complete programs in collision repair often require significantly less on-the-job training. They typically advance to independent work more quickly than those who do not have the same level of education.

Throughout their careers, body repairers need to continue their training to keep up with rapidly changing automotive technology and materials. Body repairers are expected to develop their skills by reading technical manuals and by attending classes and seminars. Many employers regularly send workers to advanced training programs, such as those offered by the Inter-Industry Conference on Auto Collision Repair (I-CAR).

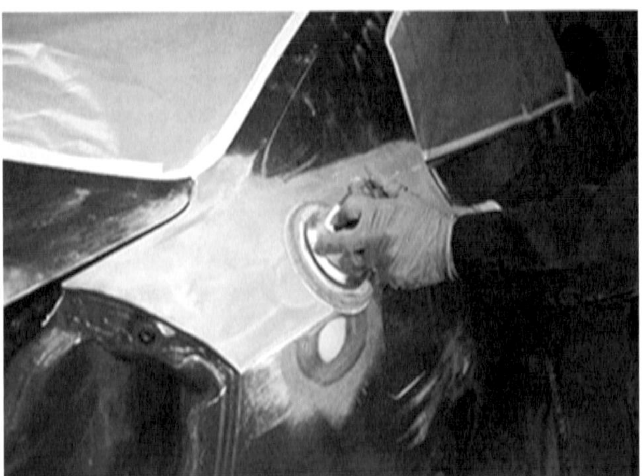

Automotive body repairers typically work indoors in body shops.

Automotive glass repairers receive hands-on practice while attending programs in collision repair.

Licenses, Certifications, and Registrations

Although not required, certification is recommended because it shows competence and usually brings higher pay. In some instances it is required for advancement beyond entry-level work.

Certification from the National Institute for Automotive Service Excellence (ASE) is a standard credential for body repairers. In addition, many vehicle and paint manufacturers have product certification programs that are used to train body repairers in specific technologies and repair methods.

A few states require a license to perform automotive glass installation and repair. Check with your state for more information.

Advancement

Automotive body and glass repairers earn more money as they gain experience, and some may advance into management positions within body shops, especially those workers with 2- or 4-year degrees.

Important Qualities

Critical-thinking skills. Automotive body and glass repairers evaluate vehicle damage and determine necessary repair strategies. In some cases, they must decide if a vehicle is "totaled," or too damaged to justify the cost of repair.

Customer-service skills. Automotive body and glass repairers discuss auto body and glass problems, along with options to fix them, with customers. Workers must be courteous, good listeners, and ready to answer customers' questions.

Detail oriented. Automotive body and glass repairers must pay close attention to detail. Restoring a damaged auto body or windshield requires workers to have a keen eye for even the smallest imperfection.

Dexterity. Automotive body repairers' tasks, such as removing door panels, hammering out dents, and using hand tools to install parts, require a steady hand and good hand–eye coordination.

Mechanical skills. Automotive body repairers must know which diagnostic, hydraulic, pneumatic, and other power equipment and tools are appropriate for certain procedures and repairs. They must know how to apply the correct techniques and methods necessary to repair automobiles.

Physical strength. Automotive body and glass repairers must sometimes lift heavy parts, such as door panels and windshields.

Time-management skills. Automotive body and glass repairers must be timely in their repairs. For many people, their automobile is their primary mode of transportation.

Pay

The median annual wage for automotive body and related repairers was $47,670 in May 2022. The median wage is the wage at which half the workers in an occupation earned more than that amount and half earned less. The lowest 10 percent earned less than $32,370, and the highest 10 percent earned more than $78,460.

The median annual wage for automotive glass installers and repairers was $43,700 in May 2022. The lowest 10 percent earned less than $29,650, and the highest 10 percent earned more than $59,900.

In May 2022, the median annual wages for automotive body and related repairers in the top industries in which they worked were as follows:

Automotive body, paint, interior, and glass repair	$47,890
Automotive mechanical and electrical repair and maintenance	47,170
Automobile dealers	46,410

In May 2022, the median annual wages for automotive glass installers and repairers in the top industries in which they worked were as follows:

Automotive body, paint, interior, and glass repair	$44,840
Construction	39,520

The majority of repair shops and auto dealers pay automotive body and glass repairers on an incentive basis. In addition to receiving a guaranteed base salary, employers pay workers a set amount for completing various tasks. Their earnings depend on both the amount of work assigned and how fast they complete it.

Most automotive body and glass repairers work full time. When shops have to complete a backlog of work, overtime is common. This often includes working evenings and weekends.

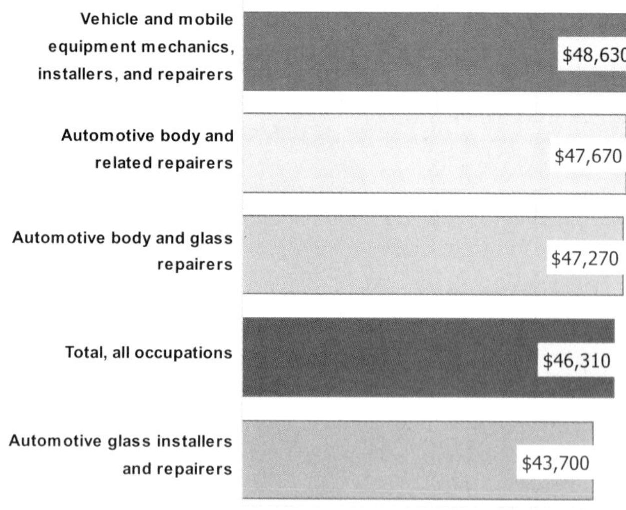

Note: All Occupations includes all occupations in the U.S. Economy.
Source: U.S. Bureau of Labor Statistics, Occupational Employment and Wage Statistics.

Job Outlook

Overall employment of automotive body and glass repairers is projected to show little or no change from 2022 to 2032.

Despite limited employment growth, about 15,100 openings for automotive body and glass repairers are projected each year, on average, over the decade. Most of those openings are expected to result from the need to replace workers who transfer to different occupations or exit the labor force, such as to retire.

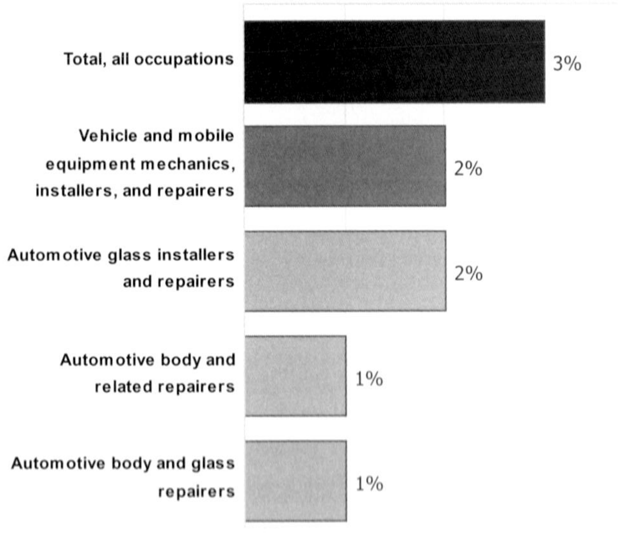

Note: All Occupations includes all occupations in the U.S. Economy.
Source: U.S. Bureau of Labor Statistics, Employment Projections program.

Employment

New vehicles are getting safer, which will help reduce car accidents and, in turn, the need for repairs. Older vehicles, which may have fewer modern safety features, will continue to need repairs and create demand for these workers.

Occupational Title	SOC Code	Employment, 2022	Projected Employment, 2032	Change, 2022-32	
				Percent	Numeric
Automotive body and glass repairers	—	175,200	177,400	1	2,300
Automotive body and related repairers	49-3021	153,300	155,200	1	1,900
Automotive glass installers and repairers	49-3022	21,900	22,200	2	400

Contacts for More Information

For more information, visit

- Accrediting Commission of Career Schools and Colleges
- Inter-Industry Conference on Auto Collision Repair
- National Automotive Technicians Education Foundation
- National Glass Association
- National Institute for Automotive Service Excellence
- Society of Collision Repair Specialists

Automotive Service Technicians and Mechanics

Summary

Quick Facts: Automotive Service Technicians and Mechanics	
2022 Median Pay	$46,970 per year $22.58 per hour
Typical Entry-Level Education	Postsecondary nondegree award
Work Experience in a Related Occupation	None
On-the-job Training	Short-term on-the-job training
Number of Jobs, 2022	782,200
Job Outlook, 2022-32	2% (As fast as average)
Employment Change, 2022-32	12,800

What Automotive Service Technicians and Mechanics Do

Automotive service technicians and mechanics inspect, maintain, and repair cars and light trucks.

Work Environment

Most automotive service technicians and mechanics work in well-ventilated and well-lit repair shops. Although technicians often identify and fix automotive problems with computers, they commonly work with greasy parts and tools, sometimes in uncomfortable positions.

How to Become an Automotive Service Technician or Mechanic

Employers prefer that automotive service technicians and mechanics complete a program at a postsecondary institution.

Automotive service technicians and mechanics use a variety of tools throughout their day.

Industry certification is usually required once the person is employed.

Pay

The median annual wage for automotive service technicians and mechanics was $46,970 in May 2022.

Job Outlook

Employment of automotive service technicians and mechanics is projected to grow 2 percent from 2022 to 2032, about as fast as the average for all occupations.

About 67,700 openings for automotive service technicians and mechanics are projected each year, on average, over the decade. Many of those openings are expected to result from the need to replace workers who transfer to different occupations or exit the labor force, such as to retire.

What Automotive Service Technicians and Mechanics Do

Automotive service technicians and mechanics, often called *service technicians* or *service techs*, inspect, maintain, and repair cars and light trucks.

Duties

Automotive service technicians and mechanics typically do the following:

- Identify problems, often by using computerized diagnostic equipment
- Plan work procedures, using charts, technical manuals, and experience
- Test parts and systems to ensure that they work properly
- Follow checklists to ensure that all critical parts are examined
- Perform basic care and maintenance, including changing oil, checking fluid levels, and rotating tires

Automotive service technicians and mechanics perform oil changes on vehicles.

- Repair or replace worn parts, such as brake pads, wheel bearings, and sensors
- Perform repairs to manufacturer and customer specifications
- Explain automotive problems and repairs to clients

Although service technicians work on traditional mechanical systems, such as engines, transmissions, and drivebelts, they also must be familiar with a growing number of electronic systems. Braking, transmission, and steering systems, for example, are controlled primarily by computers and electronic components.

Other integrated electronic systems, such as accident-avoidance sensors, are becoming common as well. In addition, a growing number of technicians are required to work on vehicles that use electricity or alternative fuels, such as ethanol.

Service technicians use many different tools, including computerized diagnostic tools and power tools such as pneumatic wrenches, lathes, welding torches, and jacks and hoists. These tools usually are owned by their employers.

Service technicians also use many common hand tools, such as wrenches, pliers, and sockets and ratchets. Service technicians generally own these tools themselves. In fact, experienced workers often have thousands of dollars invested in their personal tool collection. For example, some invest in their own set of pneumatic tools—such as impact wrenches—powered by compressed air.

The following are examples of types of service technicians:

Automotive air-conditioning technicians install and repair air-conditioners and parts, such as compressors, condensers, and controls. These workers must be trained and certified in handling refrigerants.

Brake technicians diagnose brake system problems, adjust brakes, replace brake rotors and pads, and make other repairs on brake systems. Some technicians specialize in both brake and front-end work. (See "Front-end technicians.")

Drivability technicians, also known as *diagnostic technicians*, use their extensive knowledge of engine management and fuel, electrical, ignition, and emissions systems to diagnose issues that prevent engines from performing efficiently. They often use the onboard diagnostic system of a car and electronic testing equipment such as scan tools and multimeters to find the malfunction.

Front-end technicians diagnose ride, handling, and tire wear problems. To correct these problems, they frequently use special alignment equipment and wheel-balancing machines.

Transmission technicians and rebuilders work on gear trains, couplings, hydraulic pumps, and other parts of transmissions. An extensive knowledge of computer controls and the ability to diagnose electrical and hydraulic problems are needed to work on these complex components.

Technicians who work on large trucks and buses are described in the diesel service technicians and mechanics profile.

Technicians who work on farm equipment, construction vehicles, and railcars are described in the heavy vehicle and mobile equipment service technicians profile.

Technicians who repair and service motorcycles, motorboats, and small all-terrain vehicles are described in the profile on small engine mechanics.

Work Environment

Automotive service technicians and mechanics held about 782,200 jobs in 2022. The largest employers of automotive service technicians and mechanics were as follows:

Automobile dealers	32%
Automotive mechanical and electrical repair and maintenance	25
Self-employed workers	14

Service technicians stand for most of the day, and they typically work in well-ventilated and well-lit repair shops. Although technicians often identify and fix automotive problems with computers, they commonly work with greasy parts and tools, sometimes in uncomfortable positions.

Work Schedules

Most service technicians work full time, and many work evenings or weekends. Overtime is common.

Injuries and Illnesses

Automotive service technicians and mechanics frequently work with heavy parts and tools. As a result, workplace injuries, such as small cuts, sprains, and bruises, are common.

How to Become an Automotive Service Technician or Mechanic

Employers prefer that automotive service technicians and mechanics complete a program at a postsecondary institution. Industry certification is usually required once the person is employed.

Education

High school courses in automotive repair, electronics, computers, and mathematics provide a good background for prospective service technicians. However, high school graduates typically need further training to become fully qualified.

Completing a vocational or other postsecondary education program in automotive service technology is considered the best preparation for entry-level positions. Programs usually last 6 months to a year and provide intensive career preparation through classroom instruction and hands-on practice. Short-term certificate programs in a particular subject, such as brake maintenance or engine performance, are also available.

Some service technicians get an associate's degree. Courses usually include mathematics, electronics, and automotive repair. Some programs add classes in customer service and other necessary skills.

Various automobile manufacturers and dealers sponsor associate's degree programs. Students in these programs typically spend alternating periods attending classes full time and working full time in service shops under the guidance of an experienced technician.

Automotive service technicians and mechanics keep records of diagnostic tests and repairs.

Automotive service technicians and mechanics learn from more experienced workers.

Training

Service technicians who have graduated from postsecondary programs in automotive service technology generally require little on-the-job training.

Those who have not completed postsecondary education, however, generally start as trainee technicians, technicians' helpers, or lubrication workers. They gradually acquire more knowledge and experience by working with experienced mechanics and technicians.

Licenses, Certifications, and Registrations

The U.S. Environmental Protection Agency (EPA) requires all technicians who buy or work with refrigerants to be certified in proper refrigerant handling. No formal test preparation is required, but many trade schools, unions, and employer associations offer training programs designed for the EPA exam.

Certification from the National Institute for Automotive Service Excellence (ASE) is the standard credential for service technicians. Certification demonstrates competence and usually brings higher pay. Many employers require their service technicians to become certified.

ASE certification is available in nine different automobile specialty areas: automatic transmission/transaxle, brakes, light vehicle diesel engines, electrical/electronic systems, engine performance, engine repair, heating and air-conditioning, manual drive train and axles, and suspension and steering.

To become certified, technicians must have at least 2 years of experience (or relevant schooling and 1 year of experience) and pass an exam. Technicians who achieve certification in all of the foregoing areas (light vehicle diesel engine certification is not required) may earn ASE Master Technician status.

Important Qualities

Customer-service skills. Service technicians discuss automotive problems—along with options to fix them—with their customers. Because workers may depend on repeat clients for business, they must be courteous, good listeners, and ready to answer customers' questions.

Detail oriented. Service technicians must be aware of small details when inspecting or repairing vehicle systems, because mechanical and electronic malfunctions are often due to misalignments or other easy-to-miss causes.

Dexterity. Service technicians perform many tasks that require steady hands and good hand–eye coordination, such as assembling or attaching components and subassemblies.

Mechanical skills. Service technicians must be familiar with engine components and systems and know how they interact with each other. They often must take apart major parts for repairs and be able to put them back together properly.

Organizational skills. Service technicians must keep workspaces clean and organized in order to maintain safety and ensure accountability of parts.

Physical strength. Service technicians must sometimes lift and maneuver heavy parts such as engines and body panels.

Troubleshooting skills. Service technicians use diagnostic equipment on engine systems and components in order to identify and fix problems in increasingly complicated mechanical and electronic systems. They must be familiar with electronic control systems and the appropriate tools needed to fix and maintain them.

Pay

Automotive Service Technicians and Mechanics

The median annual wage for automotive service technicians and mechanics was $46,970 in May 2022. The median wage is the wage at which half the workers in an occupation earned more than that amount and half earned less. The lowest 10 percent earned less than $29,270, and the highest 10 percent earned more than $75,360.

In May 2022, the median annual wages for automotive service technicians and mechanics in the top industries in which they worked were as follows:

Automobile dealers	$49,260
Automotive mechanical and electrical repair and maintenance	46,480

Many experienced technicians working for automobile dealers and independent repair shops receive a commission related to the labor cost charged to the customer. Under this system, which is commonly known as "flat rate" or "flag rate," weekly earnings depend on the amount of work completed. Some repair shops pay technicians on an hourly basis instead.

Most service technicians work full time, and many work evenings or weekends. Overtime is common.

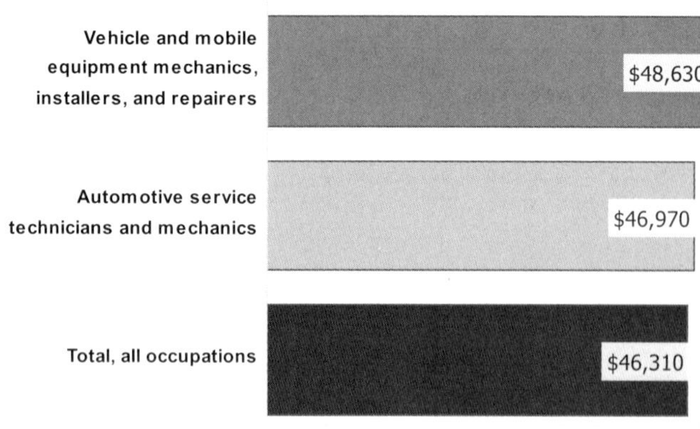

Note: All Occupations includes all occupations in the U.S. Economy.
Source: U.S. Bureau of Labor Statistics, Occupational Employment and Wage Statistics.

Automotive Service Technicians and Mechanics

Percent change in employment, projected 2022-32

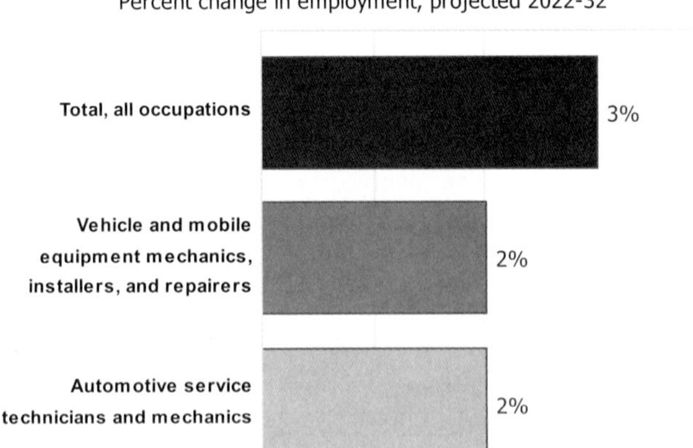

Note: All Occupations includes all occupations in the U.S. Economy.
Source: U.S. Bureau of Labor Statistics, Employment Projections program.

Job Outlook

Employment of automotive service technicians and mechanics is projected to grow 2 percent from 2022 to 2032, about as fast as the average for all occupations.

About 67,700 openings for automotive service technicians and mechanics are projected each year, on average, over the decade. Many of those openings are expected to result from the need to replace workers who transfer to different occupations or exit the labor force, such as to retire.

Employment

The number of vehicles in use is expected to continue rising over the projections decade, and some service technicians will be needed to maintain and repair them. Many owners are keeping their vehicles longer, which should support demand for these workers to provide the servicing that older vehicles often require.

However, the increasing prevalence of electric vehicles, which require less maintenance and repair, may limit future demand for these workers.

Occupational Title	SOC Code	Employment, 2022	Projected Employment, 2032	Change, 2022-32	
				Percent	Numeric
Automotive service technicians and mechanics	49-3023	782,200	795,000	2	12,800

Contacts for More Information

For more information, see

- Automotive Youth Educational Systems
- National Automotive Technicians Education Foundation
- National Institute for Automotive Service Excellence

Calibration Technologists and Technicians

Summary

Quick Facts: Calibration Technologists and Technicians

2022 Median Pay	$62,050 per year $29.83 per hour
Typical Entry-Level Education	Associate's degree
Work Experience in a Related Occupation	None
On-the-job Training	None
Number of Jobs, 2022	11,300
Job Outlook, 2022-32	4% (As fast as average)
Employment Change, 2022-32	500

What Calibration Technologists and Technicians Do

Calibration technologists and technicians inspect, adjust, and test measurement devices against standards, such as those used in manufacturing, healthcare, and other industries.

Work Environment

Calibration technologists and technicians work in a variety of settings. Most work full time.

How to Become a Calibration Technologist or Technician

Calibration technologists and technicians typically need an associate's degree or other postsecondary training in a technical or scientific field. Some enter the occupation with a high school diploma and learn their skills on the job.

Pay

The median annual wage for calibration technologists and technicians was $62,050 in May 2022.

Job Outlook

Employment of calibration technologists and technicians is projected to grow 4 percent from 2022 to 2032, about as fast as the average for all occupations.

About 1,100 openings for calibration technologists and technicians are projected each year, on average, over the decade. Many of those openings are expected to result from the need to replace workers who transfer to different occupations or exit the labor force, such as to retire.

What Calibration Technologists and Technicians Do

Calibration technologists and technicians inspect, adjust, and test measurement devices against standards, such as those used in manufacturing, healthcare, and other industries.

Duties

- Inspect equipment for defects
- Compare readings of measurement devices with established standards to ensure proper output
- Adjust, if necessary, and test devices to check that calibration was successful and readings are accurate
- Perform preventive maintenance on equipment
- Record test results and maintenance performed
- Coordinate schedules for servicing devices

Calibration technologists and technicians ensure precision across an industry by applying the principles of measurement science to processes, systems, and products. They work with a variety of instruments, meters, gauges, and other measurement devices.

The devices that these workers calibrate are used in a range of industries. For example, they may evaluate and adjust pressure gauges used in automotive manufacturing to verify that assembly equipment is functioning properly or develop anemometer tests for measuring output from wind turbines to confirm efficiency.

Calibration technologists and technicians ensure that measurement devices produce the proper output.

Some measurement devices are calibrated to industry standards, such as those set by the National Institute of Standards and Technology. For other devices, calibration technologists and technicians may be involved in helping to establish standards by developing tests and guidelines.

Work Environment

Calibration technologists and technicians held about 11,300 jobs in 2022. The largest employers of calibration technologists and technicians were as follows:

Industry	Percent
Manufacturing	29%
Testing laboratories	20
Electronic and precision equipment repair and maintenance	10
Merchant wholesalers, durable goods	4
Research and development in the physical, engineering, and life sciences	3

Calibration technologists and technicians work in a variety of settings, depending on the industry in which the tools they calibrate are used. For example, in manufacturing they may work in a plant that produces chemicals, computers and electronics, machinery, or other products. Research and development might require working in a testing laboratory.

Some workers are required to travel between sites.

Injuries and Illnesses

Calibration technologists and technicians may encounter health and safety hazards in the workplace, such as exposure to loud or dangerous machinery in manufacturing facilities or to toxic materials in laboratories. To minimize their risk of injury or illness, they may wear hearing protection, gloves, a mask, or other personal protective equipment.

Work Schedules

Most calibration technologists and technicians work full time. Some work shifts that may include early mornings, nights, or weekends.

How to Become a Calibration Technologist or Technician

Calibration technologists and technicians typically need an associate's degree or other postsecondary training in a technical or scientific field. Some workers enter the occupation with a high school diploma and learn their skills on the job.

Education and Training

High school students interested in this occupation should take classes in math and science. Some calibration technologists and technicians qualify for positions with a high school diploma or

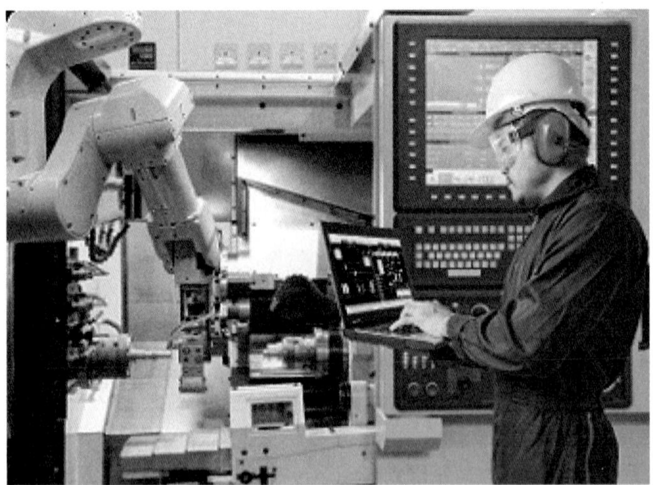

Calibration technologists and technicians work in a variety of settings, such as manufacturing plants.

equivalent. To become fully competent, they receive training on the job, which may include guidance or supervision from an experienced calibration technician.

Calibration technologists and technicians typically need an associate's degree in a field such as electronics engineering technology. These programs are usually offered at community colleges and technical schools and may include coursework in topics such as circuitry, metrology, and engineering.

Other Experience

Calibration technologists and technicians sometimes enter the occupation after gaining experience in the same industry for which a particular measurement device is used. For example, in the healthcare industry, a cardiovascular technician may become a calibration technician who works on pacemakers.

Licenses, Certification, and Registrations

Some calibration technologists and technicians earn optional certification, such as the Calibration Technician Certification from the American Society for Quality. Certification may require a certain level of education, a specified amount of work experience, and passing an examination.

Important Qualities

Communication skills. Calibration technologists and technicians must be able to convey information both orally and in writing, such as explaining results and writing reports about calibration tests.

Critical-thinking skills. Calibration technologists and technicians may need to create new methods for adjusting measurement devices based on calibration requirements.

Detail oriented. Calibration technologists and technicians must ensure that measurement devices are adjusted to precise outputs.

Calibration technologists and technicians must have dexterity when using the tools to calibrate and test measurement devices.

Dexterity. Calibration technologists and technicians must be agile and steady-handed when using tools to calibrate and test measurement devices.

Physical strength. Calibration technologists and technicians may have to lift heavy equipment or machinery.

Technical skills. Calibration technologists and technicians must know how to operate and fix manufacturing, laboratory, and other machinery or equipment.

Pay

The median annual wage for calibration technologists and technicians was $62,050 in May 2022. The median wage is the wage at which half the workers in an occupation earned more than that amount and half earned less. The lowest 10 percent earned less than $39,760, and the highest 10 percent earned more than $99,300.

In May 2022, the median annual wages for calibration technologists and technicians in the top industries in which they worked were as follows:

Research and development in the physical, engineering, and life sciences	$69,200
Manufacturing	61,960
Electronic and precision equipment repair and maintenance	58,980
Merchant wholesalers, durable goods	56,600
Testing laboratories	54,670

Most calibration technologists and technicians work full time. Some work shifts that may include early mornings, nights, or weekends.

Job Outlook

Employment of calibration technologists and technicians is projected to grow 4 percent from 2022 to 2032, about as fast as the average for all occupations.

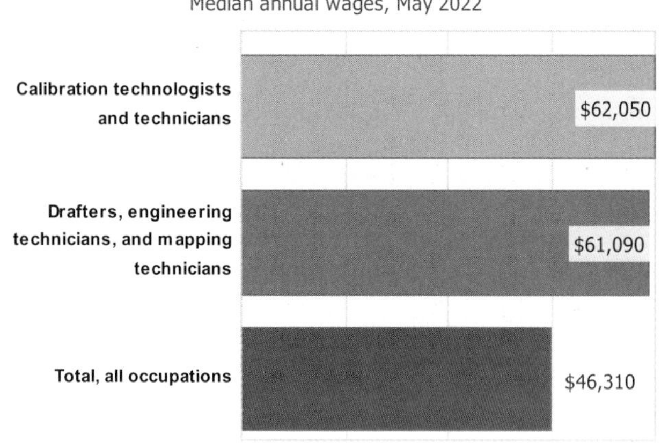

Note: All Occupations includes all occupations in the U.S. Economy.
Source: U.S. Bureau of Labor Statistics, Occupational Employment and Wage Statistics.

About 1,100 openings for calibration technologists and technicians are projected each year, on average, over the decade. Many of those openings are expected to result from the need to replace workers who transfer to different occupations or exit the labor force, such as to retire.

Employment

As automation increases the complexity of measurement devices, calibration technologists and technicians will be needed to apply their knowledge of measurement science to evaluate and adjust a variety of equipment. However, improved technology may slightly offset employment growth as self-calibrating devices are expected to increase worker productivity.

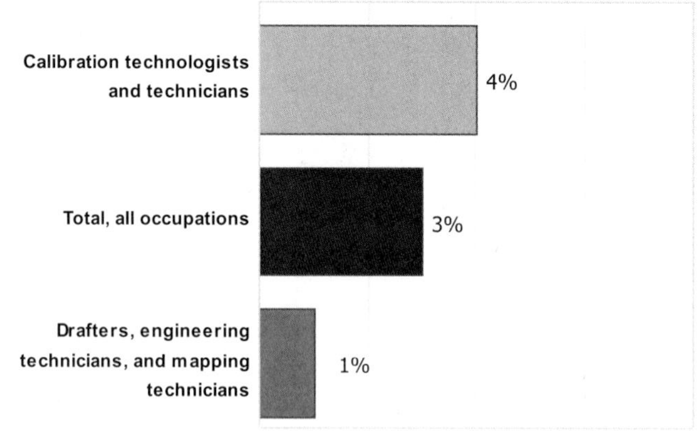

Note: All Occupations includes all occupations in the U.S. Economy.
Source: U.S. Bureau of Labor Statistics, Employment Projections program.

Occupational Title	SOC Code	Employment, 2022	Projected Employment, 2032	Change, 2022-32	
				Percent	Numeric
Calibration technologists and technicians	17-3028	11,300	11,800	4	500

Contacts for More Information

For more information, see

- ➤ National Institute of Standards and Technology
- ➤ NCSL International
- ➤ ABET
- ➤ American Society for Quality

Diesel Service Technicians and Mechanics

Summary

Quick Facts: Diesel Service Technicians and Mechanics	
2022 Median Pay	$54,360 per year $26.14 per hour
Typical Entry-Level Education	High school diploma or equivalent
Work Experience in a Related Occupation	None
On-the-job Training	Long-term on-the-job training
Number of Jobs, 2022	291,600
Job Outlook, 2022-32	1% (Little or no change)
Employment Change, 2022-32	2,500

What Diesel Service Technicians and Mechanics Do

Diesel service technicians and mechanics inspect, repair, and overhaul buses, trucks, or any vehicle with a diesel engine.

Work Environment

Diesel service technicians and mechanics usually work in well-ventilated and sometimes noisy repair shops. They occasionally repair vehicles on roadsides or at worksites. Most diesel technicians work full time, and overtime and evening shifts are common.

How to Become a Diesel Service Technician or Mechanic

Although most diesel service technicians and mechanics learn on the job after a high school education, employers are increasingly preferring applicants who have completed postsecondary

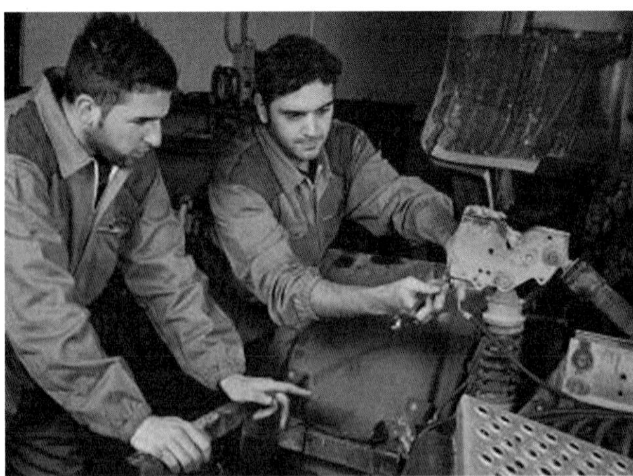

Diesel service technicians and mechanics repair diesel engine vehicles, such as buses and trucks.

training programs in diesel engine repair. In addition, industry certification may be important.

Pay

The median annual wage for diesel service technicians and mechanics was $54,360 in May 2022.

Job Outlook

Employment of diesel service technicians and mechanics is projected to show little or no change from 2022 to 2032.

Despite limited employment growth, about 24,300 openings for diesel service technicians and mechanics are projected each year, on average, over the decade. Most of those openings are expected to result from the need to replace workers who transfer to different occupations or exit the labor force, such as to retire.

What Diesel Service Technicians and Mechanics Do

Diesel service technicians and mechanics (also known as *diesel technicians*) inspect, repair, or overhaul buses and trucks, or maintain and repair any type of diesel engine.

Duties

Diesel service technicians and mechanics typically do the following:

- Consult with customers, read work orders, and determine work required
- Plan work procedures, using technical charts and manuals
- Inspect brake systems, steering mechanisms, transmissions, engines, and other parts of vehicles
- Follow checklists to ensure that all critical parts are examined
- Read and interpret diagnostic test results to identify mechanical problems
- Repair or replace malfunctioning components, parts, and other mechanical or electrical equipment

Diesel service technicians and mechanics may work on a vehicle's electrical system, make major engine repairs, or retrofit engines with emission control systems to comply with pollution regulations.

- Perform basic care and maintenance, including changing oil, checking fluid levels, and rotating tires
- Test-drive vehicles to ensure that they run smoothly

Because of their efficiency and durability, diesel engines have become the standard in powering trucks and buses. Other heavy vehicles and mobile equipment, including bulldozers and cranes, also are powered by diesel engines, as are many commercial boats and some passenger vehicles and pickups.

Diesel technicians make major and minor engine repairs, and work on a vehicle's electrical and exhaust systems to comply with pollution regulations.

Diesel engine maintenance and repair is becoming more complex as engines and other components use more electronic systems to control their operation. For example, fuel injection and engine timing systems rely on microprocessors to maximize fuel efficiency and minimize harmful emissions. In most shops, workers often use hand-held or laptop computers to diagnose problems and adjust engine functions.

Diesel technicians also use a variety of power and machine tools, such as pneumatic wrenches, lathes, grinding machines, and welding equipment. Hand tools, including pliers, sockets and ratchets, and screwdrivers, are commonly used.

Employers typically provide expensive power tools and computerized equipment, but workers generally acquire their own hand tools over time.

Technicians and mechanics who work primarily on automobiles are described in the profile on automotive service technicians and mechanics.

Technicians and mechanics who work primarily on farm equipment, construction vehicles, and railcars, are described in the profile on heavy vehicle and mobile equipment service technicians.

Technicians and mechanics who work primarily on motorboats, motorcycles, and small all-terrain vehicles are described in the small engine mechanics profile.

Diesel technicians usually work in well-ventilated and sometimes noisy repair shops.

Work Environment

Diesel service technicians and mechanics held about 291,600 jobs in 2022. The largest employers of diesel service technicians and mechanics were as follows:

Truck transportation	20%
Wholesale trade	15
Automotive repair and maintenance	9
Local government, excluding education and hospitals	9
Rental and leasing services	6

Diesel technicians usually work in well-ventilated and sometimes noisy repair shops. They occasionally repair vehicles on roadsides or at worksites.

Injuries and Illnesses

Diesel service technicians and mechanics often lift heavy parts and tools, handle greasy or dirty equipment, and work in uncomfortable positions. Sprains and cuts are common among these workers. Diesel technicians need to follow some safety precautions when in the workplace.

Diesel technicians initially learn to perform routine maintenance and repair tasks.

Work Schedules

Most diesel technicians work full time. Overtime is common, as many repair shops extend their service hours during evenings and weekends. In addition, some truck and bus repair shops provide 24-hour maintenance and repair services.

How to Become a Diesel Service Technician or Mechanic

Although most diesel technicians learn on the job after a high school education, employers are increasingly preferring applicants who have completed postsecondary training programs in diesel engine repair. In addition, obtaining industry certification may be helpful because certification demonstrates a diesel technician's competence and experience.

Education

Most employers require a high school diploma or equivalent. High school or postsecondary courses in automotive repair, electronics, and mathematics provide a strong educational background for a career as a diesel technician.

Some employers prefer to hire workers with postsecondary education in diesel engine repair. Many community colleges and trade and vocational schools offer certificate or degree programs in diesel engine repair.

These degree programs mix classroom instruction with hands-on training and include learning the basics of diesel technology, repair techniques and equipment, and practical exercises. Students also learn how to interpret technical manuals and electronic diagnostic reports.

Training

Diesel technicians who begin working without any postsecondary education are trained extensively on the job. Trainees are assigned basic tasks, such as cleaning parts, checking fuel and oil levels, and driving vehicles in and out of the shop.

After they learn routine maintenance and repair tasks and demonstrate competence, trainees move on to more complicated subjects, such as vehicle diagnostics. This process can take from 3 to 4 years, at which point a trainee is usually considered a journey-level diesel technician.

Over the course of their careers, diesel technicians must learn to use new techniques and equipment. Employers often send experienced technicians to special training classes conducted by manufacturers and vendors to learn about the latest diesel technology.

Licenses, Certifications, and Registrations

Certification from the National Institute for Automotive Service Excellence (ASE) is the standard credential for diesel and other automotive service technicians and mechanics. Although not required, this certification demonstrates a diesel technician's competence and experience to potential employers and clients, and often brings higher pay.

Diesel technicians may be certified in specific repair areas, such as drivetrains, electronic systems, and preventative maintenance and inspection. To earn certification, technicians must have 2 years of work experience and pass one or more ASE exams. To remain certified, diesel technicians must pass a recertification exam every 5 years.

Many diesel technicians are required to have a commercial driver's license so that they may test-drive buses and large trucks.

Important Qualities

Customer-service skills. Diesel technicians frequently discuss automotive problems and necessary repairs with their customers. They must be courteous, good listeners, and ready to answer customers' questions.

Detail oriented. Diesel technicians must be aware of small details when inspecting or repairing engines and components, because mechanical and electronic malfunctions are often due to misalignments and other easy-to-miss causes.

Dexterity. Mechanics need a steady hand and good hand–eye coordination for many tasks, such as disassembling engine parts, connecting or attaching components, and using hand tools.

Mechanical skills. Diesel technicians must be familiar with engine components and systems and know how they interact with each other. They often disassemble major parts for repairs, and they must be able to put them back together properly.

Organizational skills. Diesel technicians must keep workspaces clean and organized in order to maintain safety and accountability for parts.

Physical strength. Diesel technicians often lift heavy parts and tools, such as exhaust system components and pneumatic wrenches.

Troubleshooting skills. Diesel technicians use diagnostic equipment on engine systems and components in order to identify and fix problems in mechanical and electronic systems.

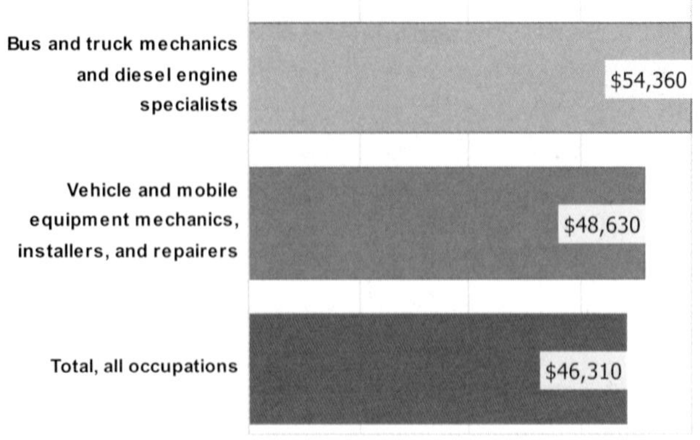

Note: All Occupations includes all occupations in the U.S. Economy.
Source: U.S. Bureau of Labor Statistics, Occupational Employment and Wage Statistics.

They must be familiar with electronic control systems and the appropriate tools needed to fix and maintain them.

Pay

The median annual wage for diesel service technicians and mechanics was $54,360 in May 2022. The median wage is the wage at which half the workers in an occupation earned more than that amount and half earned less. The lowest 10 percent earned less than $37,030, and the highest 10 percent earned more than $78,340.

In May 2022, the median annual wages for diesel service technicians and mechanics in the top industries in which they worked were as follows:

Local government, excluding education and hospitals	$62,940
Wholesale trade	58,750
Automotive repair and maintenance	52,800
Rental and leasing services	50,390
Truck transportation	48,940

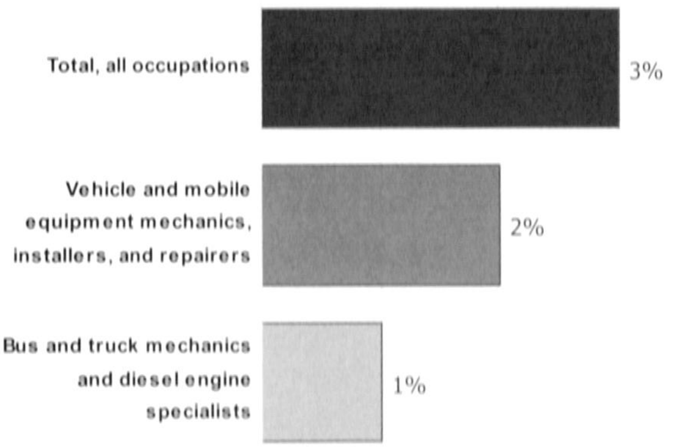

Note: All Occupations includes all occupations in the U.S. Economy.
Source: U.S. Bureau of Labor Statistics, Employment Projections program.

Many diesel technicians, especially those employed by truck fleet dealers and repair shops, receive a commission in addition to their base salary.

Most diesel technicians work full time. Overtime is common, as many repair shops extend their service hours during evenings and weekends. In addition, some truck and bus repair shops provide 24-hour maintenance and repair services.

Job Outlook

Employment of diesel service technicians and mechanics is projected to show little or no change from 2022 to 2032.

Despite limited employment growth, about 24,300 openings for diesel service technicians and mechanics are projected each year, on average, over the decade. Most of those openings are expected to result from the need to replace workers who transfer to different occupations or exit the labor force, such as to retire.

Employment

As more freight is shipped across the country, additional diesel-powered trucks will be needed to carry freight wherever trains and pipelines are neither available nor economical. In addition, aging vehicles with diesel engines are likely to require more maintenance and repair, supporting the need for diesel technicians.

However, demand for these workers may be reduced as more firms turn away from diesel-powered trucks in favor of electric ones, which require less maintenance and repair. For example, trucks used for short-haul transportation, such as local delivery services, are expected to increasingly be electric.

Occupational Title	SOC Code	Employment, 2022	Projected Employment, 2032	Change, 2022-32	
				Percent	Numeric
Bus and truck mechanics and diesel engine specialists	49-3031	291,600	294,100	1	2,500

Contacts for More Information

For more information, visit

- Association of Diesel Specialists
- National Automotive Technicians Education Foundation
- National Institute for Automotive Service Excellence

Electrical and Electronics Installers and Repairers

Summary

Quick Facts: Electrical and Electronics Installers and Repairers	
2022 Median Pay	$64,190 per year $30.86 per hour
Typical Entry-Level Education	See How to Become One
Work Experience in a Related Occupation	See How to Become One
On-the-job Training	See How to Become One
Number of Jobs, 2022	113,300
Job Outlook, 2022-32	-2% (Decline)
Employment Change, 2022-32	-2,100

What Electrical and Electronics Installers and Repairers Do

Electrical and electronics installers and repairers install or repair a variety of electrical equipment.

Work Environment

Many electrical and electronics installers and repairers work in repair shops or in factories. Installers and repairers may have to lift heavy equipment and work in awkward positions. The majority work full time.

How to Become an Electrical or Electronics Installer and Repairer

Electrical and electronics installers and repairers need at least a high school education, but most specializations require further preparation through advanced education, apprenticeship training, or work experience.

Pay

The median annual wage for electrical and electronics installers and repairers was $64,190 in May 2022.

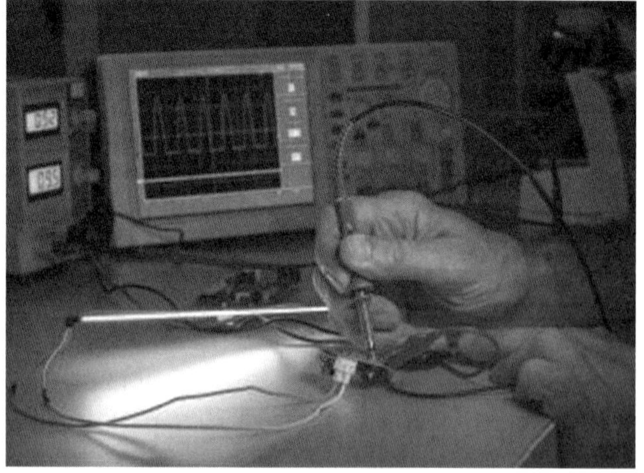

Electrical and electronics installers and repairers use special testing equipment to determine problems.

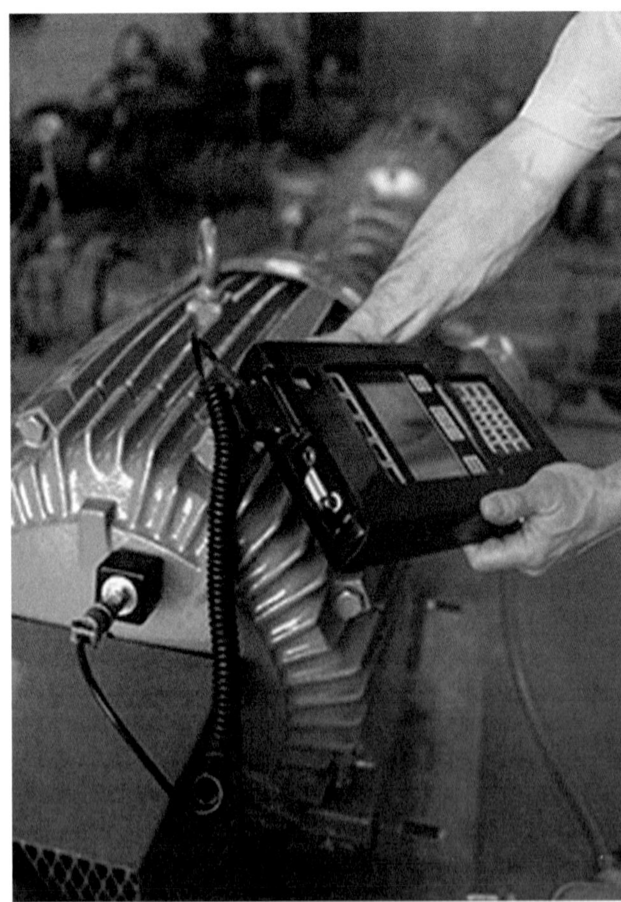

Electrical and electronics installers and repairers use diagnostic equipment to troubleshoot electric motors.

Job Outlook

Overall employment of electrical and electronics installers and repairers is projected to decline 2 percent from 2022 to 2032.

Despite declining employment, about 9,100 openings for electrical and electronics installers and repairers are projected each year, on average, over the decade. All of those openings are expected to result from the need to replace workers who transfer to other occupations or exit the labor force, such as to retire.

What Electrical and Electronics Installers and Repairers Do

Electrical and electronics installers and repairers install or repair a variety of electrical equipment in transportation, utilities, and other industries.

Duties

Electrical and electronics installers and repairers typically do the following:

- Discuss problems and requirements with customers
- Inspect and test equipment
- Reproduce, isolate, and diagnose problems
- Disassemble equipment as necessary to access problematic components
- Clean, repair, and replace components
- Reassemble and test equipment after repairs
- Keep records of repairs, tests, parts, and labor hours

Modern manufacturing plants and transportation systems use a large amount of electrical and electronics equipment, from assembly line motors to sonar systems. Electrical and electronics installers and repairers fix and maintain these complex pieces of equipment.

Because automated electronic control systems are becoming more complex, repairers use software programs and testing equipment to diagnose malfunctions. Among their diagnostic tools are multimeters—which measure voltage, current, and resistance—and advanced multimeters, which measure the capacitance, inductance, and current gain of transistors.

Repairers also use signal generators, which provide test signals, and oscilloscopes, which display signals graphically. In addition, repairers often use hand tools such as pliers, screwdrivers, and wrenches to replace faulty parts and adjust equipment.

The following are examples of types of electrical and electronics installers and repairers:

Commercial and industrial electrical and electronics equipment repairers adjust, test, repair, or install electronic equipment, such as industrial controls, transmitters, and antennas.

Electric motor, power tool, and related repairers—such as *armature winders, generator mechanics,* and *electric golf cart repairers*—specialize in installing, maintaining, and repairing electric motors, wiring, or switches.

Electrical and electronics installers and repairers of transportation equipment install, adjust, or maintain mobile communication equipment, including sound, sonar, security, navigation, and surveillance systems on trains, watercraft, or other vehicles.

Electronic equipment installers and repairers of motor vehicles install, diagnose, and repair sound, security, and navigation equipment in motor vehicles. These installers and repairers work with a range of complex electronic equipment,

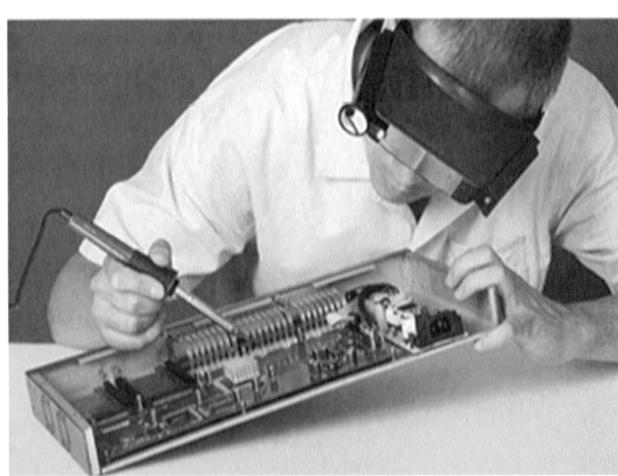

Electrical and electronics installers and repairers usually work in a clean shop.

including digital audio and video players, navigation systems, and passive and active security systems.

Powerhouse, substation, and relay electrical and electronics repairers inspect, test, maintain, or repair electrical equipment used in generating stations, substations, and in-service relays. These workers also may be known as *powerhouse electricians, relay technicians*, or *power transformer repairers.*

Work Environment

Electrical and electronics installers and repairers held about 113,300 jobs in 2022. Employment in the detailed occupations that make up electrical and electronics installers and repairers was distributed as follows:

Electrical and electronics repairers, commercial and industrial equipment	53,600
Electrical and electronics repairers, powerhouse, substation, and relay	26,100
Electric motor, power tool, and related repairers	16,100
Electronic equipment installers and repairers, motor vehicles	9,700
Electrical and electronics installers and repairers, transportation equipment	7,900

The largest employers of electrical and electronics installers and repairers were as follows:

Manufacturing	16%
Utilities	15
Wholesale trade	10
Repair and maintenance	9
Federal government, excluding postal service	8

Many electrical and electronics installers and repairers work in repair shops or in factories, and some may work outside when they travel to job sites.

Installers and repairers may have to lift heavy equipment and work in awkward positions. They spend most of their day walking, standing, or kneeling.

Many technical colleges have basic electronics programs that include practical experience labs.

Work Schedules

The majority of electrical and electronics installers and repairers work full time.

How to Become an Electrical or Electronics Installer and Repairer

Electrical and electronics installers and repairers need at least a high school education, but most specializations require further preparation through advanced education, work experience, or both.

Education

Electrical and electronics installers and repairers must understand electrical equipment and electronics. As a result, employers often prefer applicants who have taken courses in electronics at a community college or technical school. Courses usually cover AC and DC electronics, electronic devices, and microcontrollers. It is important for prospects to choose schools that include hands-on training in order to gain practical experience.

Training

In addition to technical education, workers usually receive training on specific types of equipment. This may involve manufacturer-specific training for repairers who will perform warranty work.

Before working independently, entry-level repairers usually develop their skills while working with experienced technicians who provide technical guidance.

Work Experience in a Related Occupation

Some electrical and electronics installers and repairers need prior work experience. Electric motor, power tool, and related repairers typically begin by helping in machine or electrical workshops, where they gain experience with tools and motors.

Powerhouse, substation, and relay electrical and electronics repairers often gain experience by first working as electricians.

Licenses, Certifications, and Registrations

While certification is not required, a number of organizations offer it, and it can be useful in getting a job. For example, the Electronics Technicians Association International (ETA International) offers more than 50 certification programs in numerous electronics specialties for various levels of competency. The International Society of Certified Electronics Technicians (ISCET) also offers certification for several levels of competence. The ISCET focuses on a broad range of topics, including basic electronics, electronic systems, and appliance service. To become certified, applicants must meet prerequisites and pass a comprehensive exam.

Important Qualities

Color vision. Electrical and electronics installers and repairers must be able to identify the color-coded components that are often used in electronic equipment.

Communication skills. Electrical and electronics installers and repairers work closely with customers, so they must listen to and understand customers' descriptions of problems and explain solutions in a simple, clear manner.

Physical stamina. Some electrical and electronics installers and repairers must stand at their station for their full shift, which can be tiring.

Physical strength. Electrical and electronics installers and repairers may need to lift heavy parts during the repair process. Some components weigh over 50 pounds.

Technical skills. Electrical and electronics installers and repairers use a variety of mechanical and diagnostic tools to install or repair equipment.

Troubleshooting skills. Electrical and electronics installers and repairers must be able to identify problems with equipment and systems and make the necessary repairs.

Pay

The median annual wage for electrical and electronics installers and repairers was $64,190 in May 2022. The median wage is the wage at which half the workers in an occupation earned more than that amount and half earned less. The lowest 10 percent earned less than $37,620, and the highest 10 percent earned more than $104,030.

Median annual wages for electrical and electronics installers and repairers in May 2022 were as follows:

Electrical and electronics repairers, powerhouse, substation, and relay	$93,720
Electrical and electronics installers and repairers, transportation equipment	73,630
Electrical and electronics repairers, commercial and industrial equipment	64,030
Electric motor, power tool, and related repairers	48,260
Electronic equipment installers and repairers, motor vehicles	41,600

Electrical and Electronics Installers and Repairers

Median annual wages, May 2022

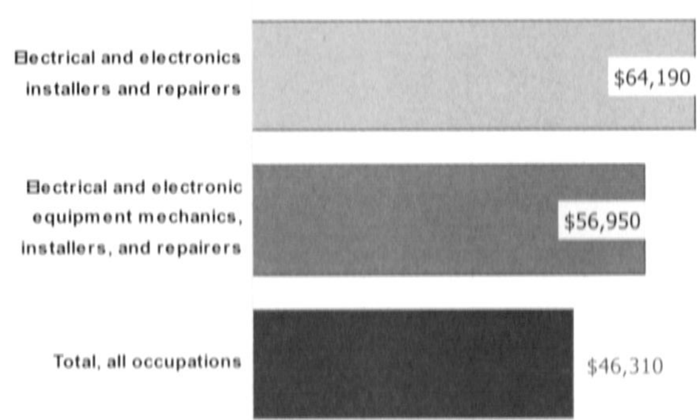

Note: All Occupations includes all occupations in the U.S. Economy.
Source: U.S. Bureau of Labor Statistics, Occupational Employment and Wage Statistics.

Electrical and Electronics Installers and Repairers

Percent change in employment, projected 2022-32

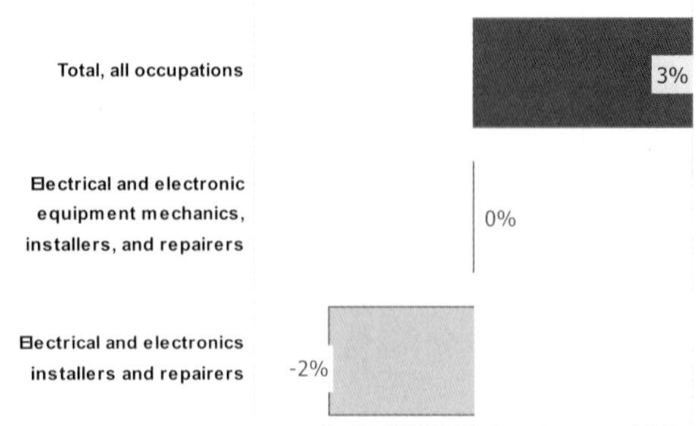

Note: All Occupations includes all occupations in the U.S. Economy.
Source: U.S. Bureau of Labor Statistics, Employment Projections program.

In May 2022, the median annual wages for electrical and electronics installers and repairers in the top industries in which they worked were as follows:

Utilities	$98,610
Federal government, excluding postal service	68,330
Manufacturing	62,990
Wholesale trade	50,090
Repair and maintenance	49,990

The majority of electrical and electronics installers and repairers work full time.

Job Outlook

Overall employment of electrical and electronics installers and repairers is projected to decline 2 percent from 2022 to 2032.

Despite declining employment, about 9,100 openings for electrical and electronics installers and repairers are projected each year, on average, over the decade. All of those openings are expected to result from the need to replace workers who transfer to other occupations or exit the labor force, such as to retire.

Employment

Projected employment of electrical and electronics installers and repairers varies by occupation (see table).

Over the projections decade, improvements in electrical and electronics equipment design and increased use of disposable tool parts are expected to dampen the need for electrical and electronics equipment installers and repairers.

Upgrades to transportation electronics systems, such as those on trains, buses, and ships, will support some demand for installers and repairers of this equipment.

Motor vehicle manufacturers continue to install and integrate high-quality sound, security, entertainment, and navigation systems in new vehicles. In addition, smartphones offer many features previously installed directly in vehicles. These consumer offerings reduce demand for installing aftermarket products and for repairing high-quality systems, which is expected to limit the need for electrical and electronics installers and repairers.

Occupational Title	SOC Code	Employment, 2022	Projected Employment, 2032	Change, 2022-32	
				Percent	Numeric
Electrical and electronics installers and repairers	—	113,300	111,200	-2	-2,100
Electric motor, power tool, and related repairers	49-2092	16,100	16,500	3	400
Electrical and electronics installers and repairers, transportation equipment	49-2093	7,900	8,300	5	400
Electrical and electronics repairers, commercial and industrial equipment	49-2094	53,600	53,200	-1	-400
Electrical and electronics repairers, powerhouse, substation, and relay	49-2095	26,100	25,400	-3	-700
Electronic equipment installers and repairers, motor vehicles	49-2096	9,700	7,900	-18	-1,700

Contacts for More Information

For more information, visit

- Electronics Technicians Association International
- International Society of Certified Electronics Technicians

Electrical Power-Line Installers and Repairers

Summary

Quick Facts: Electrical Power-Line Installers and Repairers

2022 Median Pay	$82,340 per year $39.59 per hour
Typical Entry-Level Education	High school diploma or equivalent
Work Experience in a Related Occupation	None
On-the-job Training	Long-term on-the-job training
Number of Jobs, 2022	122,400
Job Outlook, 2022-32	3% (As fast as average)
Employment Change, 2022-32	3,500

What Electrical Power-Line Installers and Repairers Do

Electrical power-line installers and repairers install or repair cables or wires used in electrical power or distribution systems.

Work Environment

Electrical power-line installers and repairers encounter serious hazards on the job, including working with high-voltage electricity, often at great heights. The work also can be physically demanding. Most electrical power-line installers and repairers work full time, and some work more than 40 hours per week.

How to Become an Electrical Power-Line Installer and Repairer

To enter the occupation, electrical power-line installers and repairers typically need a high school diploma or equivalent. To become proficient, they typically require technical instruction and on-the-job training. Apprenticeships are common.

Pay

The median annual wage for electrical power-line installers and repairers was $82,340 in May 2022.

Line installers and repairers often work in teams to install and fix cables and wires.

Electrical power-line installers and repairers use a truck-mounted bucket to access equipment.

Job Outlook

Employment of electrical power-line installers and repairers is projected to grow 3 percent from 2022 to 2032, about as fast as the average for all occupations.

About 9,700 openings for electrical power-line installers and repairers are projected each year, on average, over the decade. Many of those openings are expected to result from the need to replace workers who transfer to different occupations or exit the labor force, such as to retire.

What Electrical Power-Line Installers and Repairers Do

Electrical power-line installers and repairers install or repair cables or wires used in electrical power or distribution systems. They also may erect poles or transmission towers.

Duties

Electrical power-line installers and repairers typically do the following:

- Install, maintain, or repair the power lines that move electricity
- String electrical cable and wires between poles, towers, and buildings
- Identify defective devices, voltage regulators, transformers, and switches
- Inspect and test electrical power lines and auxiliary equipment
- Climb poles and transmission towers and use truck-mounted buckets to reach equipment
- Operate power equipment when installing and repairing poles, towers, and lines

Electrical power-line installers and repairers install and maintain the power grid: the network of cables and wires that moves electricity from generating plants to consumers. They routinely work with high-voltage electricity, which requires extreme caution.

Electrical power-line installers and repairers who maintain the interstate power grid work on crews that travel throughout a region to service transmission lines and towers. Those who are employed by local utilities maintain equipment such as transformers, voltage regulators, and switches. They also may work on traffic lights and street lights.

Workers generally start a new project by digging underground trenches or erecting utility poles and towers to carry the wires and cables. They use a variety of construction equipment, including trucks equipped with augers and cranes to dig holes and set poles in place.

To identify maintenance needs, electrical power-line installers and repairers check for outage reports from remote monitoring, aerial inspections, and customers.

To fix an electrical power-line problem, workers must first identify the cause through diagnostic testing with specialized equipment. To work on poles, electrical power-line installers usually use bucket trucks to raise themselves to the top of the structure. They sometimes need to climb poles and towers, using special safety equipment to keep from falling.

Work Environment

Electrical power-line installers and repairers held about 122,400 jobs in 2022. The largest employers of electrical power-line installers and repairers were as follows:

Electrical power-line installers and repairers may be required to work at great heights.

Utilities	50%
Utility system construction	31
Local government, excluding education and hospitals	11
Specialty trade contractors	4
Professional, scientific, and technical services	1

The work of electrical power-line installers and repairers can be physically demanding. They must be comfortable working at great heights and in confined spaces. They must be able to climb utility poles and transmission towers, as well as to balance while working on them.

Electrical power-line installers and repairers work outdoors in all types of weather, such as rain or wind when storms and other natural disasters damage power lines, to restore electricity. They often drive utility vehicles, and those who are part of a crew working on interstate power grids may need to travel long distances.

Injuries and Illnesses

Electrical power-line installers and repairers encounter serious hazards in their jobs and must follow safety procedures to minimize danger.

These workers may be electrocuted if they come in contact with a live cable on a high-voltage power line. When workers engage live wires, they use electrically insulated protective devices and tools to minimize their risk.

Most electrical power-line installers and repairers have a high school diploma and receive long-term on-the-job training.

To prevent injuries when working on poles or towers, electrical power-line installers and repairers use fall-protection equipment. Safety procedures and training have reduced the danger for electrical power-line installers and repairers.

Work Schedules

Most electrical power-line installers and repairers work full time, and some work more than 40 hours per week. In emergencies or after storms and other natural disasters, they may have to travel to impacted areas and work long hours for several days in a row.

How to Become an Electrical Power-Line Installer and Repairer

To enter the occupation, electrical power-line installers and repairers typically need a high school diploma or equivalent. To become proficient, they typically need technical instruction and on-the-job training. Apprenticeships are common.

Education

Electrical line installers and repairers typically need a high school diploma or equivalent. Employers may prefer to hire candidates who have basic knowledge of algebra and trigonometry. In addition, technical knowledge of electricity or electronics obtained through military service, vocational programs, or community colleges may be helpful.

Some community colleges offer programs for electrical power-line installers and repairers that lead to a 1-year certificate or 2-year associate's degree. These programs cover topics such as electrical distribution, line construction, and pole top and bucket rescue. The programs also may include an internship or hands-on fieldwork.

Training

Electrical power-line installers and repairers typically complete apprenticeships or other employer-sponsored training programs. These programs, which may last up to 3 years, combine on-the-job training with technical instruction and are sometimes administered jointly by the employer and the union representing the workers.

Qualifications to enter an apprenticeship program may include a high school diploma or equivalent, 1 year of high school algebra or the college-level equivalent, a qualifying score on an aptitude test, and passing a substance abuse screening. Apprentices also may have to meet physical requirements, including passing a fitness test.

Licenses, Certifications, and Registrations

Although not mandatory, certification is available for electrical power-line installers and repairers. For example, the Electrical Training Alliance offers certification for electrical power-line installation as part of its apprenticeship program.

Workers who drive heavy vehicles usually need a state-issued commercial driver's license (CDL). Workers who drive crews that cross state lines need an interstate CDL, which may have additional requirements regulated by the Federal Motor Carrier Safety Administration.

Other requirements, such as medical or other certifications and minimum age, vary by state. Check with your state for more details.

Advancement

After 3 or 4 years of working, qualified electrical power-line apprentices reach the journey level. A journey-level worker is no longer considered an apprentice and can perform most tasks without supervision.

Experienced electrical power-line installers and repairers may become supervisors or trainers.

Important Qualities

Ability to work at heights. Electrical power-line installers and repairers must be comfortable working at great heights. They may work from ladders or bucket lifts and climb utility poles.

Color vision. Workers who handle electrical wires and cables must be able to distinguish colors because the wires and cables are often color coded.

Interpersonal skills. Because these workers rely on their fellow crew members for safety, they must be able to collaborate as part of a team.

Physical stamina. Electrical power-line installers and repairers often must climb poles with heavy tools and equipment.

Physical strength. Electrical power-line installers and repairers must be able to lift heavy tools, cables, and equipment on the job.

Problem-solving skills. Electrical power-line installers and repairers must diagnose problems in electrical systems and lines and be able to repair or replace faulty equipment.

Technical skills. Electrical power-line installers use diagnostic equipment on circuit breakers, switches, and transformers. They must be familiar with electrical systems and the appropriate tools needed to fix and maintain them.

Pay

The median annual wage for electrical power-line installers and repairers was $82,340 in May 2022. The median wage is the wage at which half the workers in an occupation earned more than that amount and half earned less. The lowest 10 percent earned less than $47,070, and the highest 10 percent earned more than $114,590.

In May 2022, the median annual wages for electrical power-line installers and repairers in the top industries in which they worked were as follows:

Utilities	$95,450
Local government, excluding education and hospitals	79,180
Specialty trade contractors	67,580
Utility system construction	65,630
Professional, scientific, and technical services	56,240

Electrical Power-Line Installers and Repairers

Median annual wages, May 2022

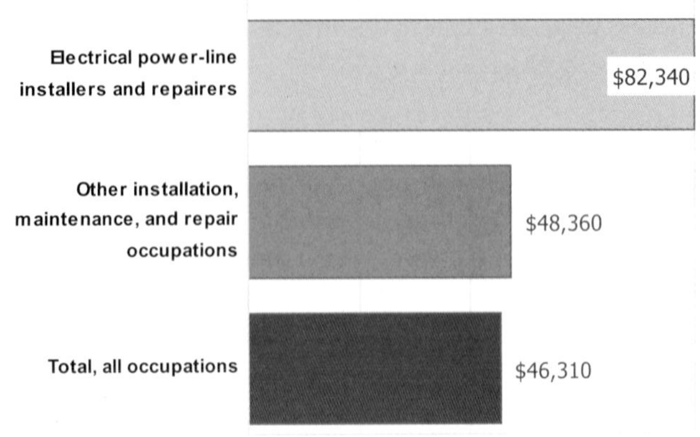

Note: All Occupations includes all occupations in the U.S. Economy.
Source: U.S. Bureau of Labor Statistics, Occupational Employment and Wage Statistics.

Most electrical power-line installers and repairers work full time, and some work more than 40 hours per week. In emergencies or after storms and other natural disasters, they may have to travel to impacted areas and work long hours for several days in a row.

Job Outlook

Employment of electrical power-line installers and repairers is projected to grow 3 percent from 2022 to 2032, about as fast as the average for all occupations.

Electrical Power-Line Installers and Repairers

Percent change in employment, projected 2022-32

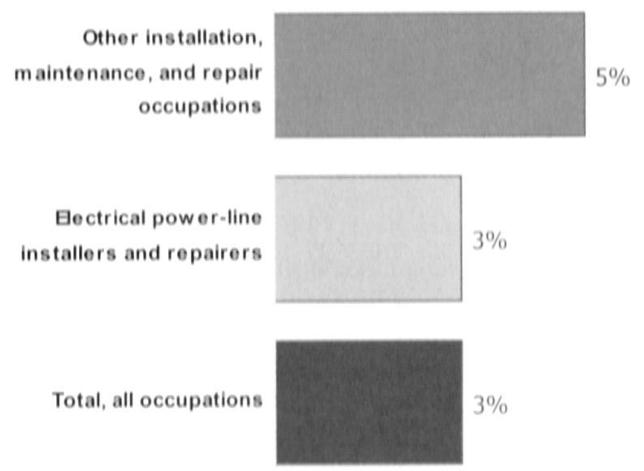

Note: All Occupations includes all occupations in the U.S. Economy.
Source: U.S. Bureau of Labor Statistics, Employment Projections program.

About 9,700 openings for electrical power-line installers and repairers are projected each year, on average, over the decade. Many of those openings are expected to result from the need to replace workers who transfer to different occupations or exit the labor force, such as to retire.

Employment

Employment of electrical power-line installers and repairers is expected to grow, largely due to increasing electrical grid needs. With each new housing development or business complex, new electric power lines are installed and will require maintenance. The increasing prevalence of electric vehicles will also require more of these workers to install new grid connections. In addition, the interstate power grid will continue to become more complex to ensure reliability.

Occupational Title	SOC Code	Employment, 2022	Projected Employment, 2032	Change, 2022-32	
				Percent	Numeric
Electrical power-line installers and repairers	49-9051	122,400	125,800	3	3,500

Contacts for More Information

Apprenticeship information is available from the U.S. Department of Labor's Apprenticeship program online or by phone at 1 (877) 872-5627. Visit Apprenticeship.gov to search for apprenticeship opportunities.

For more information about line installers and repairers, visit

- American Public Power Association
- Center for Energy Workforce Development
- Electrical Training ALLIANCE
- International Brotherhood of Electrical Workers

General Maintenance and Repair Workers

Summary

Quick Facts: General Maintenance and Repair Workers	
2022 Median Pay	$44,980 per year $21.62 per hour
Typical Entry-Level Education	High school diploma or equivalent
Work Experience in a Related Occupation	None
On-the-job Training	Moderate-term on-the-job training
Number of Jobs, 2022	1,607,200
Job Outlook, 2022-32	4% (As fast as average)
Employment Change, 2022-32	57,200

What General Maintenance and Repair Workers Do

General maintenance and repair workers fix and maintain machines, mechanical equipment, and buildings.

Work Environment

General maintenance and repair workers often carry out many different tasks in a single day. They could work at any number of indoor or outdoor locations. They may work inside a single building, such as a hotel or hospital, or be responsible for the maintenance of many buildings, such as those in an apartment complex or on a college campus.

How to Become a General Maintenance and Repair Worker

Jobs in this occupation typically require a high school diploma or equivalent. General maintenance and repair workers often learn their skills on the job for several years. They start out performing simple tasks while watching and learning from skilled maintenance workers.

Pay

The median annual wage for general maintenance and repair workers was $44,980 in May 2022.

Workers use hand tools and power tools to fix appliances and equipment.

Workers are responsible for the upkeep of many homes and apartment buildings.

Job Outlook

Employment of general maintenance and repair workers is projected to grow 4 percent from 2022 to 2032, about as fast as the average for all occupations.

About 152,400 openings for general maintenance and repair workers are projected each year, on average, over the decade. Many of those openings are expected to result from the need to replace workers who transfer to different occupations or exit the labor force, such as to retire.

What General Maintenance and Repair Workers Do

General maintenance and repair workers fix and maintain machines, mechanical equipment, and buildings. They paint, repair flooring, and work on plumbing, electrical, and air-conditioning and heating systems.

Duties

General maintenance and repair workers typically do the following:

- Maintain and repair machines, mechanical equipment, and buildings
- Fix or replace faulty electrical switches, outlets, and circuit breakers
- Inspect and diagnose problems and figure out the best way to correct them
- Perform routine preventive maintenance to ensure that machines continue to run smoothly
- Assemble and set up machinery or equipment
- Plan repair work using blueprints or diagrams
- Do general cleaning and upkeep of buildings and properties
- Order supplies from catalogs and storerooms
- Meet with clients to estimate repairs and costs
- Keep detailed records of their work

General maintenance and repair workers are hired for maintenance and repair tasks that are not complex enough to need the specialized training of a licensed tradesperson, such as a plumber or electrician.

These workers are also responsible for recognizing when a job is above their skill level and requires the expertise of an electrician; a carpenter; a heating, air-conditioning, and refrigeration mechanic or installer; or a plumber, pipefitter, or steamfitter.

General maintenance and repair workers may fix or paint roofs, windows, doors, floors, woodwork, walls, and other parts of buildings.

They also maintain and repair specialized equipment and machinery in cafeterias, laundries, hospitals, stores, offices, and factories.

General maintenance and repair workers get supplies and parts from distributors or storerooms to fix problems. They use common hand and power tools, such as screwdrivers, saws, drills, wrenches, and hammers to fix, replace, or repair equipment and parts of buildings.

Work Environment

General maintenance and repair workers held about 1.6 million jobs in 2022. The largest employers of general maintenance and repair workers were as follows:

Many workers need safety gear when working with certain tools and equipment.

Real estate and rental and leasing	20%
Manufacturing	12
Government	11
Accommodation and food services	9
Educational services; state, local, and private	8

General maintenance and repair workers often carry out many different tasks in a single day at any number of locations. They may work inside a single building, such as a hotel or hospital, or be responsible for the maintenance of many buildings, such as those in an apartment complex or on a college campus.

General maintenance and repair workers may have to stand for long periods or lift heavy objects. These workers may work in uncomfortably hot or cold environments, in uncomfortable or cramped positions, or on ladders. The work involves a lot of walking, climbing, and reaching.

Injuries and Illnesses

General maintenance and repair workers have one of the highest rates of injuries and illnesses of all occupations. Common injuries include electrical shocks, falls, cuts, and bruises.

Work Schedules

Most general maintenance and repair workers work full time, including evenings or weekends. Some are on call for emergency repairs.

How to Become a General Maintenance and Repair Worker

Jobs in this field typically do not require any formal education beyond high school. General maintenance and repair workers often learn their skills on the job. They start by doing simple tasks and watching and learning from skilled maintenance workers.

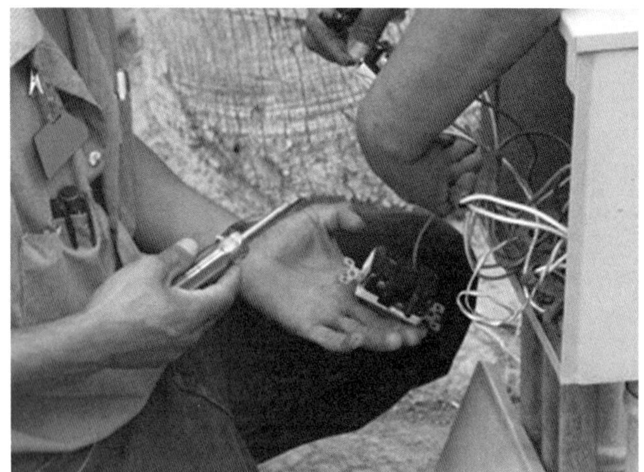

Beginners often work under the supervision of more experienced workers.

Education

Many maintenance and repair workers learn some basic skills in high school shop or technical education classes, postsecondary trade or vocational schools, or community colleges.

Courses in mechanical drawing, electricity, woodworking, blueprint reading, mathematics, and computers are useful. Maintenance and repair workers often do work that involves electrical, plumbing, heating, and air-conditioning systems or painting and roofing tasks. Workers need a good working knowledge of many repair and maintenance tasks.

Practical training, available at many adult education centers and community colleges, is another option for workers to learn tasks such as drywall repair and basic plumbing.

Training

General maintenance and repair workers usually start by watching and learning from skilled maintenance workers. They begin by doing simple tasks, such as fixing leaky faucets and replacing lightbulbs. After gaining experience, general maintenance and repair workers move on to more difficult tasks, such as overhauling machinery or building walls.

Some general maintenance and repair workers learn their skills by assisting other types of repair or construction workers, including machinery repairers, carpenters, or electricians.

Licenses, Certifications, and Registrations

Licensing requirements vary by state and locality. For more complex tasks, workers may need to be licensed in a particular specialty, such as electrical or plumbing work.

Advancement

Some maintenance and repair workers decide to train in one specific craft and become craftworkers, such as electricians, heating and air-conditioning mechanics, or plumbers.

Other maintenance workers eventually open their own repair or contracting business. However, those who want to become a project manager or own their own business may need some postsecondary education or a degree in construction management. For more information, see the profile on construction managers.

Within small organizations, promotion opportunities may be limited.

Important Qualities

Customer-service skills. These workers interact with customers on a regular basis. They need to be friendly and able to address customers' questions.

Dexterity. Many repair and maintenance tasks, such as repairing small devices, connecting or attaching components, and using hand tools, require a steady hand and good hand–eye coordination.

General Maintenance and Repair Workers

Median annual wages, May 2022

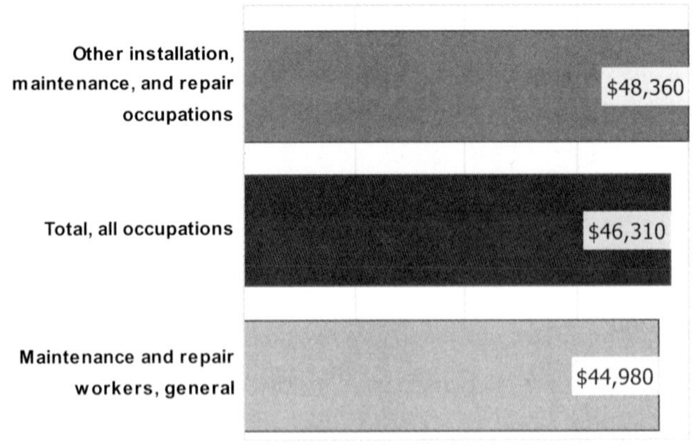

Note: All Occupations includes all occupations in the U.S. Economy.
Source: U.S. Bureau of Labor Statistics, Occupational Employment and Wage Statistics.

General Maintenance and Repair Workers

Percent change in employment, projected 2022-32

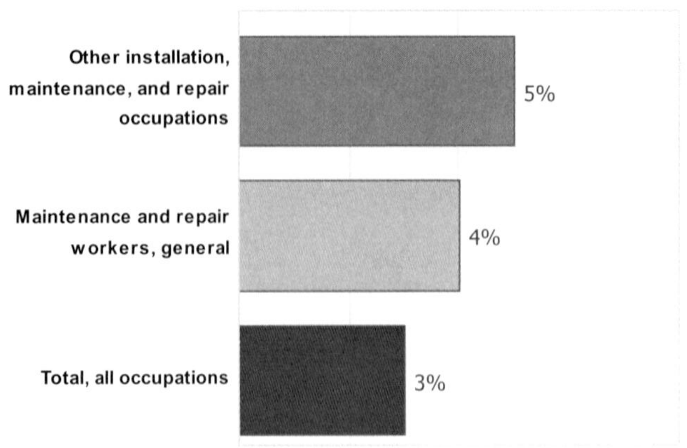

Note: All Occupations includes all occupations in the U.S. Economy.
Source: U.S. Bureau of Labor Statistics, Employment Projections program.

Troubleshooting skills. Workers find, diagnose, and repair problems. They perform tests to figure out the cause of problems before fixing equipment.

Pay

The median annual wage for general maintenance and repair workers was $44,980 in May 2022. The median wage is the wage at which half the workers in an occupation earned more than that amount and half earned less. The lowest 10 percent earned less than $29,220, and the highest 10 percent earned more than $68,930.

In May 2022, the median annual wages for general maintenance and repair workers in the top industries in which they worked were as follows:

Manufacturing	$53,100
Government	47,630
Educational services; state, local, and private	46,780
Real estate and rental and leasing	43,290
Accommodation and food services	35,590

Most general maintenance and repair workers work full time, including evenings or weekends. Some are on call for emergency repairs.

Job Outlook

Employment of general maintenance and repair workers is projected to grow 4 percent from 2022 to 2032, about as fast as the average for all occupations.

About 152,400 openings for general maintenance and repair workers are projected each year, on average, over the decade. Many of those openings are expected to result from the need to replace workers who transfer to different occupations or exit the labor force, such as to retire.

Employment

Maintenance and repair work is closely related to the demand for home and building maintenance. Maintenance and repair workers will continue to be needed to upgrade and renovate older homes. Homeowners may invest in projects to accommodate their future living needs, allowing them to remain in their homes after retirement or to sell their property.

In addition to the work required for residential properties, maintenance and repair is also needed for nonresidential properties. For example, maintenance and repair workers will be needed to work on older commercial and public buildings. Older homes and buildings typically require more maintenance or repair, especially for pipes, insulation, electrical, and air-conditioning and heating systems.

Occupational Title	SOC Code	Employment, 2022	Projected Employment, 2032	Change, 2022-32	
				Percent	Numeric
Maintenance and repair workers, general	49-9071	1,607,200	1,664,400	4	57,200

Contacts for More Information

For more information, visit

➤ United Handyman Association

Heating, Air Conditioning, and Refrigeration Mechanics and Installers

Summary

Quick Facts: Heating, Air Conditioning, and Refrigeration Mechanics and Installers

2022 Median Pay	$51,390 per year $24.71 per hour
Typical Entry-Level Education	Postsecondary nondegree award
Work Experience in a Related Occupation	None
On-the-job Training	Long-term on-the-job training
Number of Jobs, 2022	415,800
Job Outlook, 2022-32	6% (Faster than average)
Employment Change, 2022-32	23,000

What Heating, Air Conditioning, and Refrigeration Mechanics and Installers Do

Heating, air conditioning, and refrigeration mechanics and installers work on heating, ventilation, cooling, and refrigeration systems.

Work Environment

HVACR technicians work mostly in homes, schools, hospitals, office buildings, or factories. Their worksites may be very hot or cold because the heating and cooling systems they must repair may not be working properly and because some parts of these systems are located outdoors. Working in cramped spaces and during irregular hours is common.

How to Become a Heating, Air Conditioning, or Refrigeration Mechanic and Installer

Because HVACR systems have become increasingly complex, employers generally prefer applicants with postsecondary education or those who have completed an apprenticeship. Some states and localities may require technicians to be licensed.

Pay

The median annual wage for heating, air conditioning, and refrigeration mechanics and installers was $51,390 in May 2022.

Job Outlook

Employment of heating, air conditioning, and refrigeration mechanics and installers is projected to grow 6 percent from 2022 to 2032, faster than the average for all occupations.

About 37,700 openings for heating, air conditioning, and refrigeration mechanics and installers are projected each year, on average, over the decade. Many of those openings are expected to result from the need to replace workers who transfer to different occupations or exit the labor force, such as to retire.

What Heating, Air Conditioning, and Refrigeration Mechanics and Installers Do

Heating, air conditioning, and refrigeration mechanics and installers—often called *HVACR technicians*—work on heating, ventilation, cooling, and refrigeration systems that control the temperature and air quality in buildings.

Duties

Heating, air conditioning, and refrigeration mechanics and installers typically do the following:

- Install, clean, and maintain HVACR systems
- Install electrical components and wiring
- Inspect and test HVACR systems and components
- Discuss system malfunctions with customers
- Repair or replace worn or defective parts
- Recommend maintenance to improve system performance
- Keep records of work performed

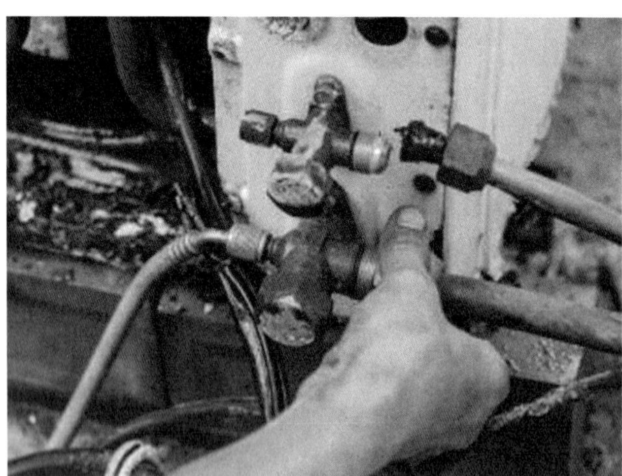

HVACR technicians must follow EPA rules when they work with gases and refrigerants.

HVACR technicians install, maintain, and repair heating, cooling, and refrigeration systems.

Heating and air conditioning systems control the temperature, humidity, and overall air quality in homes, businesses, and other buildings. By providing a climate-controlled environment, refrigeration systems make it possible to store and transport food, medicine, and other perishable items.

Some HVACR technicians specialize in one or more specific aspects of HVACR, such as radiant heating systems, solar panels, testing and balancing, or commercial refrigeration.

When installing or repairing air conditioning and refrigeration systems, technicians must follow government regulations regarding the conservation, recovery, and recycling of refrigerants. The regulations include those concerning the proper handling and disposal of fluids and pressurized gases.

Some HVACR technicians sell service contracts to their clients, providing periodic maintenance of heating and cooling systems. The service usually includes inspecting the system, cleaning ducts, replacing filters, and checking refrigerant levels.

Other workers sometimes help HVACR technicians install or repair cooling and heating systems. For example, on a large air conditioning installation job, especially one in which workers are covered by union contracts, ductwork may be installed by sheet metal workers, electrical work by electricians, and pipework by plumbers, pipefitters, and steamfitters. Boiler systems are sometimes installed by a boilermaker.

Home appliance repairers usually service window air conditioners and household refrigerators.

HVACR technicians work indoors and outdoors.

Work Environment

Heating, air conditioning, and refrigeration mechanics and installers held about 415,800 jobs in 2022. The largest employers of heating, air conditioning, and refrigeration mechanics and installers were as follows:

Plumbing, heating, and air-conditioning contractors	67%
Self-employed workers	8
Wholesale trade	3
Educational services; state, local, and private	3
Retail trade	3

HVACR technicians work mostly in homes, schools, stores, hospitals, office buildings, or factories. Some technicians are assigned to specific jobsites at the beginning of each day. Others travel to several different locations, making service calls.

Although most technicians work indoors, some may have to work on outdoor heat exchangers, even in bad weather. Technicians often work in awkward or cramped spaces, and some work in buildings that are uncomfortable because the air conditioning or heating system is not working properly.

Injuries and Illnesses

HVACR technicians have one of the highest rates of injuries and illnesses of all occupations. Potential hazards include electrical shock, burns, muscle strains, and injuries from handling heavy equipment.

Appropriate safety equipment is necessary in handling refrigerants, because they are hazardous and contact can cause skin damage, frostbite, or blindness. When working in tight spaces, inhalation of refrigerants is also a potential hazard. Several refrigerants are highly flammable and require additional care.

Work Schedules

The majority of HVACR technicians work full time. Evening or weekend shifts may be required, and HVACR technicians often work overtime or irregular hours during peak heating and cooling seasons.

How to Become a Heating, Air Conditioning, or Refrigeration Mechanic and Installer

Because HVACR systems have become increasingly complex, employers generally prefer applicants with postsecondary education or those who have completed an apprenticeship. Some states and localities may require technicians to be licensed. Workers may need to pass a background check prior to being hired.

Education

Many HVACR technicians receive postsecondary instruction from technical and trade schools or community colleges that offer programs in heating, air conditioning, and refrigeration. These programs generally last from 6 months to 2 years and lead to a certificate or an associate's degree.

New HVACR technicians typically begin by working alongside experienced technicians.

High school students interested in becoming an HVACR technician should take courses in vocational education, math, and physics. Knowledge of plumbing or electrical work and a basic understanding of electronics is also helpful.

Training

New HVACR technicians typically begin by working alongside experienced technicians. At first, they perform basic tasks such as insulating refrigerant lines or cleaning furnaces. In time, they move on to more difficult tasks, including cutting and soldering pipes or checking electrical circuits.

Some technicians receive their training through an apprenticeship. Apprenticeship programs usually last 3 to 5 years. Over the course of the apprenticeship, technicians learn safety practices, blueprint reading, and how to use tools. They also learn about the numerous systems that heat and cool buildings.

Several groups, including unions and contractor associations, sponsor apprenticeship programs. Apprenticeship requirements vary by state and locality.

Licenses, Certifications, and Registrations

The U.S. Environmental Protection Agency (EPA) requires all technicians who buy, handle, or work with refrigerants to be certified in proper refrigerant handling. Many trade schools, unions, and employer associations offer training programs designed to prepare students for the EPA certification exam.

In addition, some states and localities require HVACR technicians to be licensed; check with your state and locality for more information.

Important Qualities

Customer-service skills. HVACR technicians often work in customers' homes or business offices, so it is important that they be friendly, polite, and punctual. Repair technicians sometimes deal with unhappy customers whose heating or air conditioning is not working.

Detail oriented. HVACR technicians must carefully maintain records of all work performed. The records must include the nature of the work performed and the time it took, as well as a list of specific parts and equipment that were used.

Math skills. HVACR technicians need to calculate the correct load requirements to ensure that the HVACR equipment properly heats or cools the space required.

Mechanical skills. HVACR technicians install and work on complicated climate-control systems, so they must understand the HVAC components and be able to properly assemble, disassemble, and, if needed, program them.

Physical stamina. HVACR technicians may spend many hours walking and standing. The constant physical activity can be tiring.

Physical strength. HVACR technicians may have to lift and support heavy equipment and components, often without help.

Time-management skills. HVACR technicians frequently have a set number of daily maintenance calls. They should be able to keep a schedule and complete all necessary repairs or tasks.

Troubleshooting skills. HVACR technicians must be able to identify problems on malfunctioning heating, air conditioning, and refrigeration systems and then determine the best way to repair them.

Pay

The median annual wage for heating, air conditioning, and refrigeration mechanics and installers was $51,390 in May 2022. The median wage is the wage at which half the workers in an occupation earned more than that amount and half earned less. The lowest 10 percent earned less than $36,170, and the highest 10 percent earned more than $82,630.

In May 2022, the median annual wages for heating, air conditioning, and refrigeration mechanics and installers in the top industries in which they worked were as follows:

Wholesale trade	$57,760
Educational services; state, local, and private	54,950
Retail trade	54,760
Plumbing, heating, and air-conditioning contractors	49,630

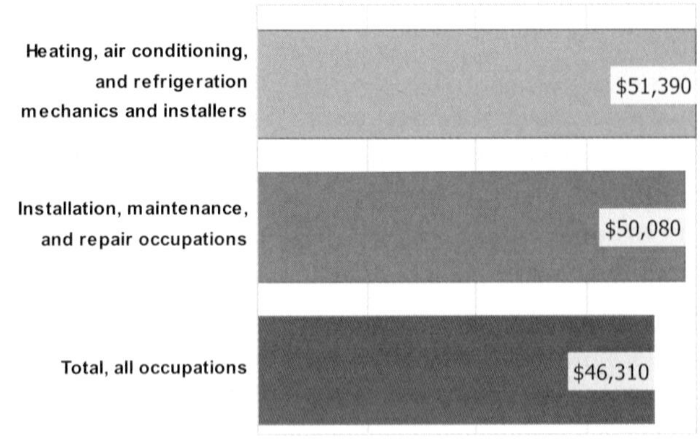

Note: All Occupations includes all occupations in the U.S. Economy.
Source: U.S. Bureau of Labor Statistics, Occupational Employment and Wage Statistics.

Apprentices usually earn about half of the wage paid to experienced workers. As they learn to do more, their pay increases.

Most HVACR technicians work full time. Evening or weekend shifts may be required, and HVACR technicians often work overtime or irregular hours during peak heating and cooling seasons.

Job Outlook

Employment of heating, air conditioning, and refrigeration mechanics and installers is projected to grow 6 percent from 2022 to 2032, faster than the average for all occupations.

About 37,700 openings for heating, air conditioning, and refrigeration mechanics and installers are projected each year, on average, over the decade. Many of those openings are expected to result from the need to replace workers who transfer to different occupations or exit the labor force, such as to retire.

Employment

Commercial and residential building construction is expected to drive employment growth. The growing number of sophisticated climate-control systems is also expected to increase demand for qualified heating, air conditioning, and refrigeration (HVACR) technicians.

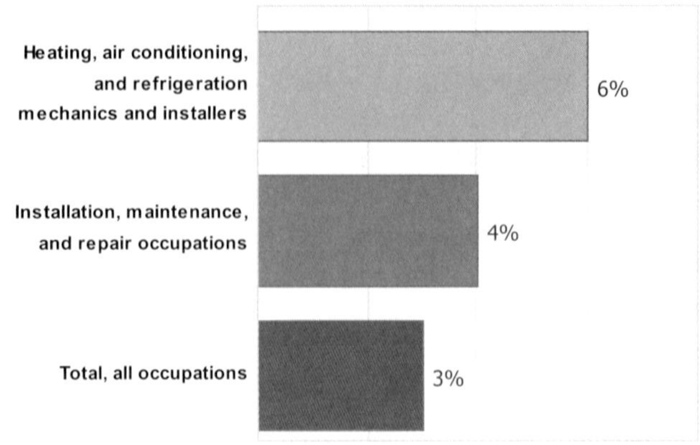

Note: All Occupations includes all occupations in the U.S. Economy.
Source: U.S. Bureau of Labor Statistics, Employment Projections program.

Repair and replacement of HVACR systems is a large part of what technicians do. The growing emphasis on energy efficiency and pollution reduction is likely to increase the demand for HVACR technicians as climate-control systems are retrofitted, upgraded, or replaced entirely.

Occupational Title	SOC Code	Employment, 2022	Projected Employment, 2032	Change, 2022-32	
				Percent	Numeric
Heating, air conditioning, and refrigeration mechanics and installers	49-9021	415,800	438,800	6	23,000

Contacts for More Information

For Apprenticeship information is available from the U.S. Department of Labor's Apprenticeship program online or by phone at 877-872-5627.

For more information, visit

- Associated Builders and Contractors
- North American Technician Excellence
- Plumbing-Heating-Cooling Contractors Association
- Refrigerating Engineers and Technicians Association
- Refrigeration Service Engineers Society (RSES)
- United Association Union of Plumbers, Fitters, Welders, and Service Techs

Heavy Vehicle and Mobile Equipment Service Technicians

Summary

Quick Facts: Heavy Vehicle and Mobile Equipment Service Technicians	
2022 Median Pay	$58,350 per year $28.06 per hour
Typical Entry-Level Education	High school diploma or equivalent
Work Experience in a Related Occupation	None
On-the-job Training	Long-term on-the-job training
Number of Jobs, 2022	234,800
Job Outlook, 2022-32	6% (Faster than average)
Employment Change, 2022-32	13,000

What Heavy Vehicle and Mobile Equipment Service Technicians Do

Heavy vehicle and mobile equipment service technicians inspect, maintain, and repair vehicles and machinery used in construction, farming, and other industries.

Work Environment

Service technicians usually work indoors in noisy repair shops. They often lift heavy parts and tools, handle greasy and dirty equipment, and stand or lie in uncomfortable positions. Most service technicians work full time, and many work evenings and weekends.

How to Become a Heavy Vehicle or Mobile Equipment Service Technician

Most heavy vehicle and mobile equipment service technicians have a high school diploma or equivalent. Because vehicle and equipment technology is increasingly sophisticated and computerized, some employers prefer to hire service technicians who have completed a training program at a postsecondary institution.

Pay

The median annual wage for heavy vehicle and mobile equipment service technicians was $58,350 in May 2022.

Job Outlook

Overall employment of heavy vehicle and mobile equipment service technicians is projected to grow 6 percent from 2022 to 2032, faster than the average for all occupations.

About 21,100 openings for heavy vehicle and mobile equipment service technicians are projected each year, on average, over the decade. Many of those openings are expected to result from the need to replace workers who transfer to different occupations or exit the labor force, such as to retire.

What Heavy Vehicle and Mobile Equipment Service Technicians Do

Heavy vehicle and mobile equipment service technicians, also called *mechanics*, inspect, maintain, and repair vehicles and machinery used in construction, farming, rail transportation, and other industries.

Duties

Heavy vehicle and mobile equipment service technicians typically do the following:

- Consult equipment operating manuals, blueprints, and drawings
- Perform scheduled maintenance, such as cleaning and lubricating parts
- Diagnose and identify malfunctions, using computerized tools and equipment

Heavy vehicle and mobile equipment service technicians repair vehicles such as bulldozers and tractors.

Mechanics inspect, repair, and replace defective or worn parts.

- Inspect, repair, and replace defective or worn parts, such as bearings, pistons, and gears
- Overhaul and test major components, such as engines, hydraulic systems, and electrical systems
- Disassemble and reassemble heavy equipment and components
- Travel to worksites to repair large equipment, such as cranes
- Maintain logs of equipment condition and work performed

Heavy vehicles and mobile equipment are critical to many industrial activities, including construction and railroad transportation. Various types of equipment, such as tractors, cranes, and bulldozers, are used to haul materials, till land, lift beams, and dig earth to pave the way for development and construction.

Heavy vehicle and mobile equipment service technicians repair and maintain engines, hydraulic systems, transmissions, and electrical systems of agricultural, industrial, construction, and rail equipment. They ensure the performance and safety of fuel lines, brakes, and other systems.

These service technicians use diagnostic computers and equipment to identify problems and make adjustments or repairs. For example, they may use an oscilloscope to observe the signals produced by electronic components. Service technicians also use many different power and machine tools, including pneumatic wrenches, lathes, and welding equipment. A pneumatic tool, such as an impact wrench, is a tool powered by compressed air.

Service technicians also use many different hand tools, such as screwdrivers, pliers, and wrenches, to work on small parts and in hard-to-reach areas. They generally purchase these tools over the course of their careers, often investing thousands of dollars in their inventory.

After identifying malfunctioning equipment, service technicians repair, replace, and recalibrate components such as hydraulic pumps and spark plugs. Doing this may involve disassembling and reassembling major equipment or making adjustments through an onboard computer program.

The following are examples of types of heavy vehicle and mobile equipment service technicians:

Farm equipment mechanics and service technicians service and repair farm equipment, such as tractors and harvesters. They also work on smaller consumer-grade lawn and garden tractors. Most work for dealer repair shops, where farmers increasingly send their equipment for maintenance.

Mobile heavy equipment mechanics repair and maintain construction and surface mining equipment, such as bulldozers, cranes, graders, and excavators. Most work for governments, equipment rental and leasing shops, and large construction and mining companies.

Rail car repairers specialize in servicing railroad locomotives, subway cars, and other rolling stock. They usually work for railroads, public and private transit companies, and railcar manufacturers.

Mechanics who work primarily on automobiles are described in the profile on automotive service technicians and mechanics.

Mechanics who work primarily on large trucks and buses are described in the profile on diesel service technicians and mechanics.

Mechanics who work primarily on motorboats, motorcycles, and small all-terrain vehicles are described in the profile on small engine mechanics.

Work Environment

Heavy vehicle and mobile equipment service technicians held about 234,800 jobs in 2022. Employment in the detailed occupations that make up heavy vehicle and mobile equipment service technicians was distributed as follows:

Mobile heavy equipment mechanics, except engines	169,100
Farm equipment mechanics and service technicians	45,600
Rail car repairers	20,100

The largest employers of heavy vehicle and mobile equipment service technicians were as follows:

Some service technicians travel to worksites to make repairs.

Farm and garden machinery and equipment merchant wholesalers	10%
Transportation and warehousing	9
Government	8
Heavy and civil engineering construction	8
Rental and leasing services	7

Although many service technicians work indoors in repair shops, some service technicians travel to worksites to make repairs because it is often too expensive to transport heavy or mobile equipment to a shop. Generally, more experienced service technicians specialize in field service. These workers drive trucks that are specially equipped with replacement parts and tools, and they spend considerable time outdoors and often drive long distances.

Heavy vehicle and mobile equipment service technicians frequently lift heavy parts and tools, handle greasy and dirty equipment, and stand or lie in awkward positions.

Injuries and Illnesses

Farm equipment mechanics and service technicians have one of the highest rates of injuries and illnesses of all occupations. Farm equipment mechanics and service techs frequently work with heavy parts and tools. Common workplace injuries include small cuts, sprains, and bruises.

Work Schedules

Most heavy vehicle and mobile equipment service technicians work full time, and many work evenings or weekends. Overtime is common.

Farm equipment mechanics' work varies by time of the year. During busy planting and harvesting seasons, for example, mechanics often work six or seven 12-hour days per week. In the winter months, however, they may work less than full time.

How to Become a Heavy Vehicle or Mobile Equipment Service Technician

Most heavy vehicle and mobile equipment service technicians have a high school diploma or equivalent. Because vehicle and equipment technology is increasingly sophisticated and computerized, some employers prefer to hire service technicians who have completed a formal training program at a postsecondary institution.

Education

Most heavy vehicle and mobile equipment service technicians have a high school diploma or equivalent. High school courses in automotive repair, electronics, physics, and welding provide a strong foundation for a service technician's career. However, high school graduates often need further training to become fully qualified.

Completing a vocational or other postsecondary training program in diesel technology or heavy equipment mechanics is increasingly considered the best preparation for some entry-level positions. Offered by vocational schools and community colleges, these programs cover the basics of diagnostic techniques, electronics, and other related subjects. Each program may last 1 to 2 years and lead to a certificate of completion. Other programs, which lead to associate's degrees, generally take 2 years to complete.

Heavy vehicle and mobile equipment service technicians must be familiar with engine components and systems.

Training

Entry-level workers with no formal background in heavy vehicle repair often receive a few months of on-the-job training before they begin performing routine service tasks and making minor repairs. Trainees advance to more complex work as they show competence, and they usually become fully qualified after 3 to 4 years of work.

Service technicians who have completed a postsecondary training program in diesel technology or heavy equipment mechanics typically require less on-the-job training.

Many employers send new service technicians to training sessions conducted by equipment manufacturers. Training sessions may focus on particular components and technologies or particular types of equipment.

Licenses, Certifications, and Registrations

Some manufacturers offer certification in specific repair methods or equipment. Although not required, certification can demonstrate a service technician's competence and usually commands higher pay.

Important Qualities

Dexterity. Heavy vehicle and mobile equipment service technicians must perform many tasks, such as disassembling engine parts, connecting or attaching components, and using hand tools, with a steady hand and good hand-eye coordination.

Mechanical skills. Heavy vehicle and mobile equipment service technicians must be familiar with engine components and systems and know how they interact with each other. They must often disassemble major parts for repairs and be able to reassemble them.

Organizational skills. Heavy vehicle and mobile equipment service technicians must maintain accurate service records and parts inventories.

Physical strength. Heavy vehicle and mobile equipment service technicians must be able to lift and move heavy equipment, tools, and parts without risking injury.

Troubleshooting skills. Heavy vehicle and mobile equipment service technicians must be familiar with diagnostic equipment to find the source of malfunctions.

Pay

The median annual wage for heavy vehicle and mobile equipment service technicians was $58,350 in May 2022. The median wage is the wage at which half the workers in an occupation earned more than that amount and half earned less. The lowest 10 percent earned less than $37,650, and the highest 10 percent earned more than $79,570.

Median annual wages for heavy vehicle and mobile equipment service technicians in May 2022 were as follows:

Rail car repairers	$62,510
Mobile heavy equipment mechanics, except engines	59,440
Farm equipment mechanics and service technicians	48,010

In May 2022, the median annual wages for heavy vehicle and mobile equipment service technicians in the top industries in which they worked were as follows:

Government	$63,170
Transportation and warehousing	59,900
Heavy and civil engineering construction	57,930

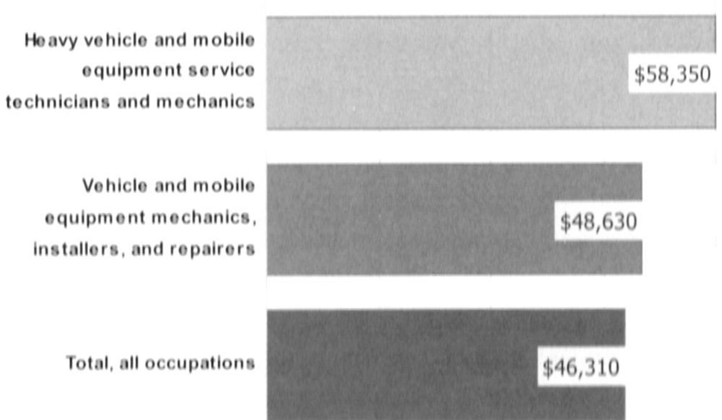

Note: All Occupations includes all occupations in the U.S. Economy.
Source: U.S. Bureau of Labor Statistics, Occupational Employment and Wage Statistics.

Rental and leasing services	54,760
Farm and garden machinery and equipment merchant wholesalers	48,330

Most heavy vehicle and mobile equipment service technicians work full time, and many work evenings or weekends. Overtime is common.

Farm equipment mechanics' work varies by time of the year. During busy planting and harvesting seasons, for example, mechanics often work six or seven 12-hour days per week. In the winter months, however, they may work less than full time.

Job Outlook

Overall employment of heavy vehicle and mobile equipment service technicians is projected to grow 6 percent from 2022 to 2032, faster than the average for all occupations.

About 21,100 openings for heavy vehicle and mobile equipment service technicians are projected each year, on average, over the decade. Many of those openings are expected to result from the need to replace workers who transfer to different occupations or exit the labor force, such as to retire.

Employment

As the stock of heavy vehicles and mobile equipment continues to increase, more service technicians will be needed to maintain it. Projected employment of heavy vehicle and mobile equipment service technicians varies by occupation (see table).

Agricultural production requires the use of increasingly complex software-driven farm equipment, which is expected to create demand for farm equipment mechanics and service technicians to maintain and to train customers in its use.

Population and business growth should result in greater demand for new houses, commercial real estate, bridges, and other structures, which in turn may require more mobile heavy equipment mechanics in the construction industry.

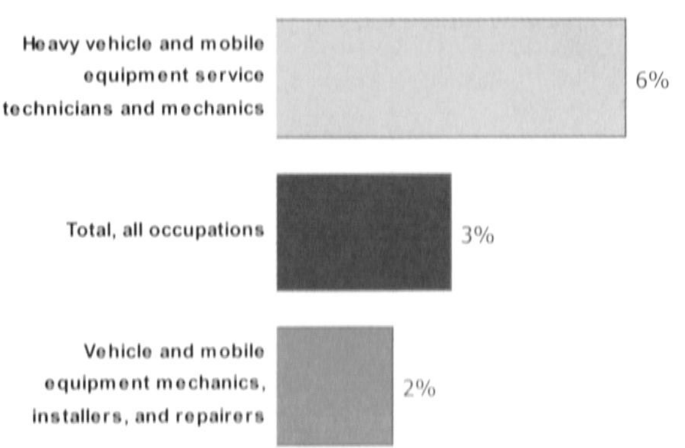

Note: All Occupations includes all occupations in the U.S. Economy.
Source: U.S. Bureau of Labor Statistics, Employment Projections program.

Rail car repairers will continue to be needed to service trains used for freight transportation. In addition, public transit agencies will rely on these workers to maintain their rail fleets.

Occupational Title	SOC Code	Employment, 2022	Projected Employment, 2032	Change, 2022-32	
				Percent	Numeric
Heavy vehicle and mobile equipment service technicians and mechanics	49-3040	234,800	247,800	6	13,000
Farm equipment mechanics and service technicians	49-3041	45,600	49,300	8	3,700
Mobile heavy equipment mechanics, except engines	49-3042	169,100	177,600	5	8,600
Rail car repairers	49-3043	20,100	20,800	4	700

Contacts for More Information

For more information, visit

- Associated Equipment Distributors
- National Automotive Technicians Education Foundation
- National Institute for Automotive Service Excellence

Industrial Machinery Mechanics, Machinery Maintenance Workers, and Millwrights

Summary

Quick Facts: Industrial Machinery Mechanics, Machinery Maintenance Workers, and Millwrights

2022 Median Pay	$59,470 per year $28.59 per hour
Typical Entry-Level Education	High school diploma or equivalent
Work Experience in a Related Occupation	None
On-the-job Training	See How to Become One
Number of Jobs, 2022	507,900
Job Outlook, 2022-32	13% (Much faster than average)
Employment Change, 2022-32	64,700

Industrial machinery mechanics, machinery maintenance workers, and millwrights all repair manufacturing equipment.

What Industrial Machinery Mechanics, Machinery Maintenance Workers, and Millwrights Do

Industrial machinery mechanics, machinery maintenance workers, and millwrights install, maintain, and repair factory equipment and other industrial machinery.

Work Environment

Workers in this occupation must follow safety precautions and use protective equipment, such as hardhats, safety glasses, and hearing protectors. Most work full time in manufacturing facilities. However, they may be on call and work night or weekend shifts. Overtime is common.

How to Become an Industrial Machinery Mechanic, Machinery Maintenance Worker, or Millwright

Industrial machinery mechanics, machinery maintenance workers, and millwrights typically need a high school diploma. Industrial machinery mechanics and machinery maintenance workers also usually need at least a year of on-the-job training. Most millwrights go through an apprenticeship program that may last up to 4 years.

Pay

The median annual wage for industrial machinery mechanics, machinery maintenance workers, and millwrights was $59,470 in May 2022.

Job Outlook

Overall employment of industrial machinery mechanics, machinery maintenance workers, and millwrights is projected to grow 13 percent from 2022 to 2032, much faster than the average for all occupations.

About 49,100 openings for industrial machinery mechanics, machinery maintenance workers, and millwrights are projected each year, on average, over the decade. Many of those openings are expected to result from the need to replace workers who transfer to different occupations or exit the labor force, such as to retire.

Industrial machinery mechanics and machinery maintenance workers adjust and calibrate equipment.

What Industrial Machinery Mechanics, Machinery Maintenance Workers, and Millwrights Do

Industrial machinery mechanics and machinery maintenance workers maintain and repair factory equipment and other industrial machinery, such as conveying systems, production machinery, and packaging equipment. Millwrights install, dismantle, repair, reassemble, and move machinery in factories, power plants, and construction sites.

Duties

Industrial machinery mechanics, machinery maintenance workers, and millwrights typically do the following:

- Read technical manuals to understand equipment and controls
- Disassemble machinery and equipment when there is a problem
- Repair or replace broken or malfunctioning components
- Perform tests and run initial batches to make sure that the machine is running smoothly
- Detect minor problems by performing basic diagnostic tests
- Test malfunctioning machinery to determine whether major repairs are needed
- Adjust and calibrate equipment and machinery to optimal specifications
- Clean and lubricate equipment or machinery
- Move machinery and equipment

Industrial machinery mechanics, also called *maintenance machinists*, keep machines in working order by detecting and correcting errors before the machine or the products it produces are damaged. Many of these machines are increasingly run by computers. Industrial machinery mechanics use technical manuals, their understanding of industrial equipment, and observation to determine the cause of a problem. For example, after detecting a vibration from a machine, they must decide whether it is the result of worn belts, weak motor bearings, or some other problem. They may use computerized diagnostic systems and vibration analysis techniques to help figure out the source of problems. Examples of machines they may work with are robotic welding arms, automobile assembly line conveyor belts, and hydraulic lifts.

After diagnosing a problem, the industrial machinery mechanic may take the equipment apart to repair or replace the necessary parts. Once a repair is made, mechanics test a machine to ensure that it is operating correctly.

In addition to working with hand tools, mechanics commonly use lathes, grinders, and drill presses. Many also are required to weld.

Machinery maintenance workers do basic maintenance and repairs on machines. They clean and lubricate machinery, perform basic diagnostic tests, check the performance of the machine, and test damaged machine parts to determine whether major repairs are necessary.

Machinery maintenance workers must follow machine specifications and adhere to maintenance schedules. They perform minor repairs, generally leaving major repairs to industrial machinery mechanics.

Maintenance workers use a variety of tools to do repairs and preventive maintenance. For example, they may use a screwdriver or socket wrenches to adjust a motor's alignment, or they might use a hoist to lift a heavy printing press off the ground.

Millwrights install, maintain, and disassemble industrial machines. Putting together a machine can take a few days or several weeks.

Millwrights perform repairs that include replacing worn or defective parts of machines. They also may be involved in taking apart the entire machine, a common situation when a manufacturing plant needs to clear floor space for new machinery. In taking apart a machine, millwrights carefully disassemble, categorize, and package each part of the machine.

Millwrights use a variety of hand tools, such as hammers and levels, as well as equipment for welding, brazing, and cutting. They also use measuring tools, such as micrometers, measuring tapes, lasers, and other precision-measuring devices. On large projects, they commonly use cranes and trucks. When millwrights and managers determine the best place for a machine, millwrights use forklifts, hoists, winches, cranes, and other equipment to bring the parts to the desired location.

Work Environment

Industrial machinery mechanics, machinery maintenance workers, and millwrights held about 507,900 jobs in 2022. Employment in the detailed occupations that make up industrial machinery mechanics, machinery maintenance workers, and millwrights was distributed as follows:

Industrial machinery mechanics	402,200
Maintenance workers, machinery	63,600
Millwrights	42,100

Industrial machinery mechanics, machinery maintenance workers, and millwrights usually work in manufacturing facilities.

The largest employers of industrial machinery mechanics, machinery maintenance workers, and millwrights were as follows:

Manufacturing	53%
Wholesale trade	12
Commercial and industrial machinery and equipment (except automotive and electronic) repair and maintenance	9
Construction	5

Injuries and Illnesses

Working with industrial machinery can be dangerous. To avoid injury, workers must follow safety precautions and use protective equipment, such as hardhats, safety glasses, steel-toed shoes, gloves, and earplugs.

Work Schedules

Most industrial machinery mechanics and machinery maintenance workers are employed full time during regular business hours. However, mechanics may be on call and work night or weekend shifts. Overtime is common, particularly for mechanics.

How to Become an Industrial Machinery Mechanic, Machinery Maintenance Worker, or Millwright

Industrial machinery mechanics, machinery maintenance workers, and millwrights typically need a high school diploma. Industrial machinery mechanics and machinery maintenance workers also usually need a year or more of training after high school.

Most millwrights go through an apprenticeship program that lasts about 4 years.

Education

Industrial machinery mechanics, machinery maintenance workers, and millwrights generally need at least a high school diploma or equivalent. Some mechanics and millwrights complete a 2-year associate's degree program in industrial maintenance. Industrial maintenance programs may include courses such as welding, mathematics, hydraulics, and pneumatics.

Industrial machinery mechanics may receive more than a year of on-the-job training, while machinery maintenance workers typically receive training that lasts a few months to a year.

Training

Industrial machinery mechanics and machinery maintenance workers typically receive more than a year of on-the-job training. Industrial machinery mechanics and machinery maintenance workers learn how to perform routine tasks, such as setting up, cleaning, lubricating, and starting machinery. They also may be instructed in subjects such as shop mathematics, blueprint reading, proper hand tool use, welding, electronics, and computer programming. This training may be offered on the job by professional trainers hired by the employer or by representatives of equipment manufacturers.

Most millwrights learn their trade through a 3- or 4-year apprenticeship. For each year of the program, apprentices must have at least 144 hours of relevant technical instruction and up to 2,000 hours of paid on-the-job training. On the job, apprentices learn to set up, clean, lubricate, repair, and start machinery. During technical instruction, they are taught welding, mathematics, how to read blueprints, and machinery troubleshooting. Many also receive computer training.

After completing an apprenticeship program, millwrights are considered fully qualified and can usually perform tasks with less guidance.

Employers, local unions, contractor associations, and the state labor department often sponsor apprenticeship programs. The basic qualifications for entering an apprenticeship program are as follows:

- Minimum age of 18
- High school diploma or equivalent
- Physically able to do the work

Important Qualities

Manual dexterity. Industrial machinery mechanics, machinery maintenance workers, and millwrights must have a steady hand and good hand–eye coordination when handling very small parts.

Mechanical skills. Industrial machinery mechanics, machinery maintenance workers, and millwrights use technical manuals and sophisticated diagnostic equipment to figure out why machines are not working. Workers must be able to reassemble large, complex machines after finishing a repair.

Troubleshooting skills. Industrial machinery mechanics, machinery maintenance workers, and millwrights must observe, diagnose, and fix problems that a machine may be having.

Pay

The median annual wage for industrial machinery mechanics, machinery maintenance workers, and millwrights was $59,470 in May 2022. The median wage is the wage at which half the workers in an occupation earned more than that amount and half earned less. The lowest 10 percent earned less than $38,440, and the highest 10 percent earned more than $82,070.

Median annual wages for industrial machinery mechanics, machinery maintenance workers, and millwrights in May 2022 were as follows:

Millwrights	$60,930
Industrial machinery mechanics	59,830
Maintenance workers, machinery	53,310

In May 2022, the median annual wages for industrial machinery mechanics, machinery maintenance workers, and millwrights in the top industries in which they worked were as follows:

Manufacturing	$60,400
Construction	58,790
Wholesale trade	57,940
Commercial and industrial machinery and equipment (except automotive and electronic) repair and maintenance	51,800

Most industrial machinery mechanics and machinery maintenance workers are employed full time during regular business hours. However, mechanics may be on call or assigned to work night or weekend shifts. Overtime is common, particularly for mechanics.

Job Outlook

Overall employment of industrial machinery mechanics, machinery maintenance workers, and millwrights is projected to grow 13 percent from 2022 to 2032, much faster than the average for all occupations.

About 49,100 openings for industrial machinery mechanics, machinery maintenance workers, and millwrights are projected each year, on average, over the decade. Many of those openings are expected to result from the need to replace workers who transfer to different occupations or exit the labor force, such as to retire.

Employment

Projected employment of industrial machinery mechanics, machinery maintenance workers, and millwrights varies by occupation (see table).

The continued adoption of automated manufacturing machinery is expected to create jobs for these workers, as they will be needed to help keep machines in good working order. The use of automated conveyors to move products and materials in

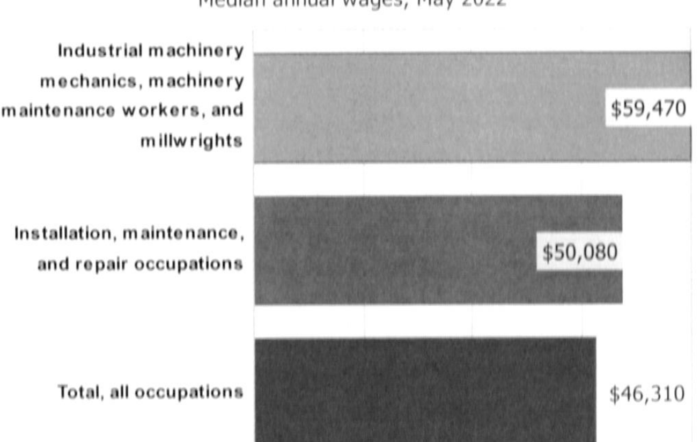

Note: All Occupations includes all occupations in the U.S. Economy.
Source: U.S. Bureau of Labor Statistics, Occupational Employment and Wage Statistics.

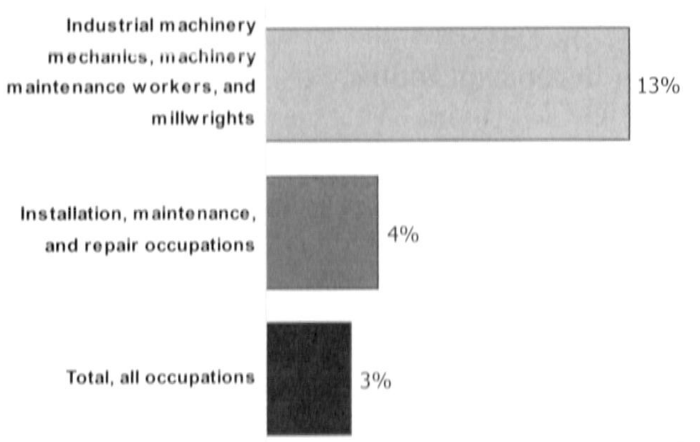

Note: All Occupations includes all occupations in the U.S. Economy.
Source: U.S. Bureau of Labor Statistics, Employment Projections program.

factories is likely to be an area of high demand for these workers, because the conveyor belts, motors, and rollers need regular care and maintenance.

Occupational Title	SOC Code	Employment, 2022	Projected Employment, 2032	Change, 2022-32	
				Percent	Numeric
Industrial machinery mechanics, machinery maintenance workers, and millwrights	—	507,900	572,600	13	64,700
Industrial machinery mechanics	49-9041	402,200	462,100	15	59,900
Maintenance workers, machinery	49-9043	63,600	67,100	6	3,500
Millwrights	49-9044	42,100	43,400	3	1,300

Contacts for More Information

Apprenticeship information is also available from the U.S. Department of Labor's Apprenticeship program online or by phone at 877-872-5627.

For information, visit

- National Association of Manufacturers
- Society for Maintenance & Reliability Professionals
- Precision Machined Products Association

Medical Equipment Repairers

Summary

Quick Facts: Medical Equipment Repairers

2022 Median Pay	$57,860 per year $27.82 per hour
Typical Entry-Level Education	Associate's degree
Work Experience in a Related Occupation	None
On-the-job Training	Moderate-term on-the-job training
Number of Jobs, 2022	66,400
Job Outlook, 2022-32	13% (Much faster than average)
Employment Change, 2022-32	8,800

What Medical Equipment Repairers Do

Medical equipment repairers install, maintain, and repair patient care equipment.

Work Environment

Although medical equipment repairers usually work during the day, they are sometimes expected to be on call, including evenings and weekends. Because repairing vital medical equipment is urgent, the work is sometimes stressful. Those who work in a patient-caring environment are potentially exposed to germs, diseases, and other health risks.

How to Become a Medical Equipment Repairer

Employers generally prefer candidates who have an associate's degree in biomedical technology or engineering. Depending on the area of specialization, repairers may need a bachelor's degree, especially for advancement.

Pay

The median annual wage for medical equipment repairers was $57,860 in May 2022.

Job Outlook

Employment of medical equipment repairers is projected to grow 13 percent from 2022 to 2032, much faster than the average for all occupations.

About 7,300 openings for medical equipment repairers are projected each year, on average, over the decade. Many of those openings are expected to result from the need to replace workers who transfer to different occupations or exit the labor force, such as to retire.

What Medical Equipment Repairers Do

Medical equipment repairers install, maintain, and repair patient care equipment.

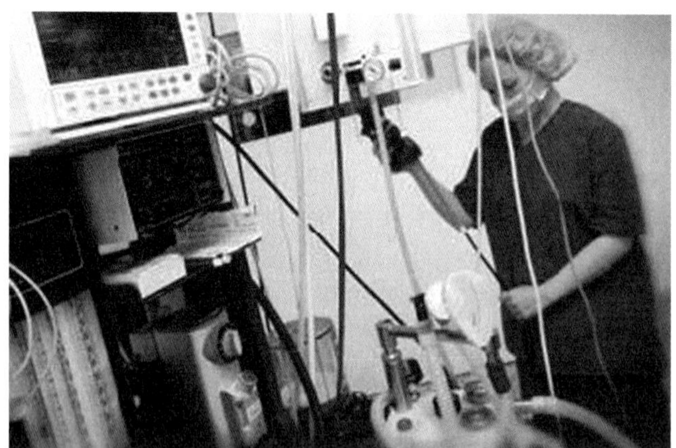

Medical equipment repairers adjust and repair medical equipment.

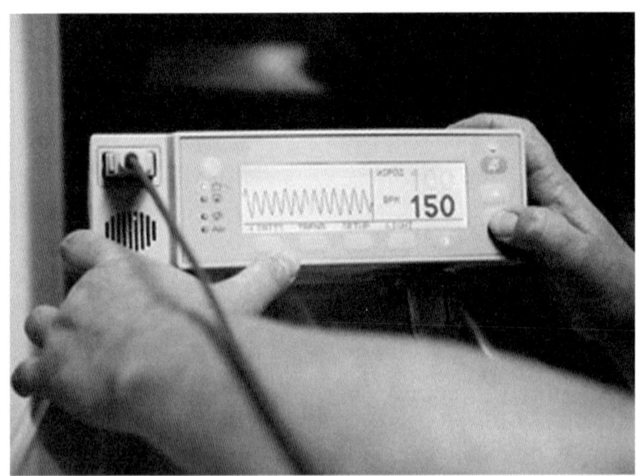

Medical equipment repairers often test and calibrate equipment.

Duties

Medical equipment repairers typically do the following:

- Install medical equipment
- Test and calibrate parts and equipment
- Repair and replace parts
- Perform preventive maintenance and service
- Keep records of maintenance and repairs
- Review technical manuals and regularly attend training sessions
- Explain and demonstrate how to operate medical equipment
- Manage replacement of medical equipment

Medical equipment repairers, also known as *biomedical equipment technicians* (BMETs), repair a wide range of electronic, electromechanical, and hydraulic equipment used in hospitals and health practitioners' offices. They may work on patient monitors, defibrillators, ventilators, anesthesia machines, and other life-supporting equipment. They also may work on medical imaging equipment (x rays, CAT scanners, and ultrasound equipment), voice-controlled operating tables, and electric wheelchairs. In addition, they repair medical equipment that dentists and eye doctors use.

If a machine has problems or is not functioning to its potential, repairers first diagnose the problem. They then adjust the mechanical, electronic, or hydraulic parts or modify the software in order to recalibrate the equipment and fix the issue.

Medical equipment repairers use a variety of tools. Most use hand tools, such as screwdrivers, wrenches, and soldering irons. Others use electronic tools, such as multimeters (an electronic measuring device that combines several measures) and computers. Much of the equipment that they maintain and repair uses specialized test-equipment software. Repairers use this software to calibrate the machines.

Many doctors, particularly specialty practitioners, rely on complex medical devices to run tests and diagnose patients, and they must be confident that the readings are accurate. Therefore, medical equipment repairers sometimes perform routine scheduled maintenance to ensure that sophisticated equipment, such as x-ray machines and CAT scanners, are in good working order. For less complicated equipment, such as electric hospital beds, workers make repairs as needed.

In a hospital setting, medical equipment repairers must be comfortable working around patients because repairs occasionally must take place while equipment is being used. When this is the case, the repairer must take great care to ensure that their work activities do not disturb patients.

Although some medical equipment repairers are trained to fix a variety of equipment, others specialize in repairing one or a small number of machines.

Work Environment

Medical equipment repairers held about 66,400 jobs in 2022. The largest employers of medical equipment repairers were as follows:

Employer	%
Professional and commercial equipment and supplies merchant wholesalers	37%
Hospitals; state, local, and private	10
Ambulatory healthcare services	8
Rental and leasing services	6
Health and personal care retailers	4

Medical equipment repairers who work as contractors often have to travel—sometimes long distances—to perform needed repairs. Repairers often must work in a patient-caring environment, which has the potential to expose them to germs, diseases and other health risks.

Because repairing vital medical equipment is urgent, the work can be stressful. In addition, installing and repairing medical equipment often involves lifting and carrying heavy objects as well as working in tight spaces.

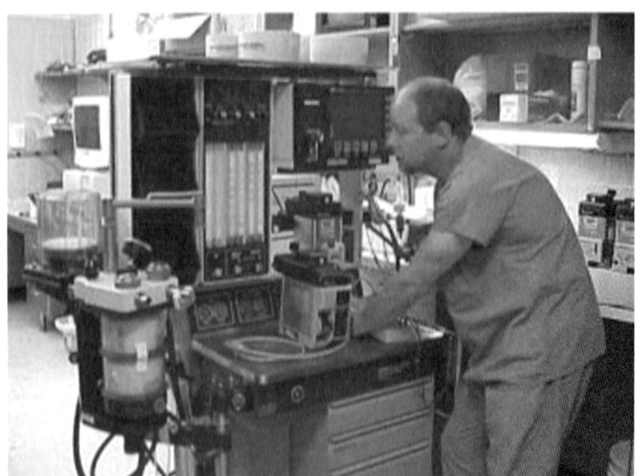

Medical equipment repairers often must work in a patient-caring environment.

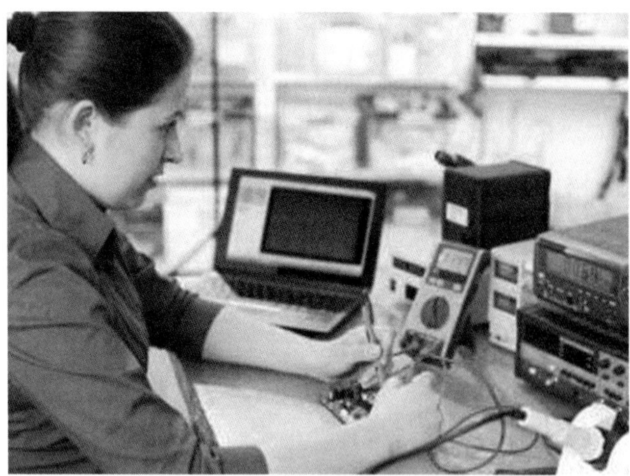

Medical equipment repairers need good technical skills in order to diagnose problems and fix equipment.

Work Schedules

Although medical equipment repairers usually work during the day, they are sometimes expected to be on call, including evenings and weekends. Most medical equipment repairers work full time, but some repairers have variable schedules.

How to Become a Medical Equipment Repairer

Employers generally prefer candidates who have an associate's degree in biomedical technology or engineering. Depending on the area of specialization, repairers may need a bachelor's degree, especially for advancement.

Education

Education requirements for medical equipment repairers vary, depending on a worker's experience and area of specialization. However, the most common education is an associate's degree in biomedical equipment technology or engineering. Those who repair less-complicated equipment, such as hospital beds and electric wheelchairs, may learn entirely through on-the-job training, sometimes lasting up to 1 year. Repairers who work on more sophisticated equipment, such as CAT scanners and defibrillators, may need a bachelor's degree.

Training

New workers generally observe and help experienced repairers for 3 to 6 months to start. As they learn, workers gradually become more independent while still under supervision.

Each piece of equipment is different, so medical equipment repairers must learn each one separately. In some cases, this requires studying a machine's technical specifications and operating manual. Medical device manufacturers also may provide technical training.

Medical equipment technology is rapidly evolving, and new devices are frequently introduced. Repairers must continually update their skills and knowledge of new technologies and equipment through seminars and self-study. The original equipment manufacturers (OEMs) may also offer training.

Licenses, Certifications, and Registrations

Although not mandatory, certification can demonstrate competence and professionalism, making candidates more attractive to employers. It can also increase a repairer's opportunities for advancement. Most manufacturers and employers, particularly those in hospitals, often pay for their in-house medical repairers to become certified.

Some associations offer certifications for medical equipment repairers. For example, the Association for the Advancement of Medical Instrumentation (AAMI) offers certification in three specialty areas—Certified Biomedical Equipment Technician (CBET), Certified Radiology Equipment Specialists (CRES), and Certified Laboratory Equipment Specialist (CLES).

Important Qualities

Communication skills. Medical equipment repairers must effectively communicate technical information by telephone, in writing, and in person when speaking to clients, supervisors, and co-workers.

Dexterity. Many tasks, such as connecting or attaching parts and using hand tools, require a steady hand and good hand-eye coordination.

Mechanical skills. Medical equipment repairers must be familiar with medical components and systems and how they interact. Often, repairers must disassemble and reassemble major parts for repair.

Physical stamina. Standing, crouching, and bending in awkward positions are common when making repairs to equipment. Therefore, workers should be physically fit.

Technical skills. Technicians use sophisticated diagnostic tools when working on complex medical equipment. They must be familiar with both the equipment's internal parts and the appropriate tools needed to fix them.

Time-management skills. Because repairing vital medical equipment is urgent, workers must make good use of their time and perform repairs quickly.

Troubleshooting skills. As medical equipment becomes more intricate, problems become more difficult to identify. Therefore, repairers must be able to find and solve problems that are not immediately apparent.

Pay

The median annual wage for medical equipment repairers was $57,860 in May 2022. The median wage is the wage at which half the workers in an occupation earned more than that amount and half earned less. The lowest 10 percent earned less than $35,530, and the highest 10 percent earned more than $94,310. In May 2022, the median annual wages for medical equipment repairers in the top industries in which they worked were as follows:

Hospitals; state, local, and private	$66,450
Professional and commercial equipment and supplies merchant wholesalers	60,750

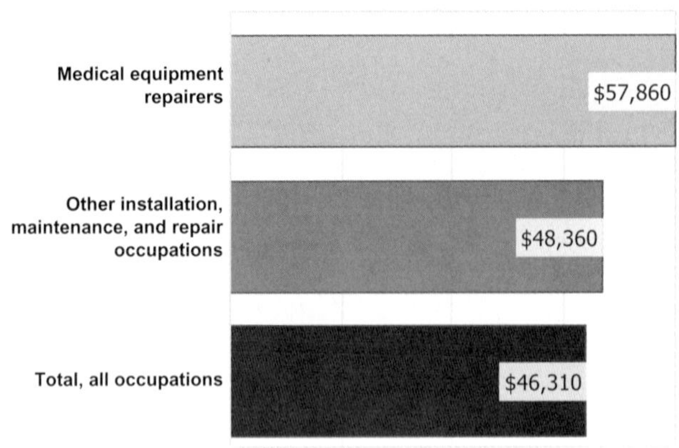

Note: All Occupations includes all occupations in the U.S. Economy.
Source: U.S. Bureau of Labor Statistics, Occupational Employment and Wage Statistics.

Ambulatory healthcare services	53,650
Health and personal care retailers	39,960
Rental and leasing services	38,300

Although medical equipment repairers usually work during the day, they are sometimes expected to be on call, including evenings and weekends. Most work full time, but some repairers have variable schedules.

Job Outlook

Employment of medical equipment repairers is projected to grow 13 percent from 2022 to 2032, much faster than the average for all occupations.

About 7,300 openings for medical equipment repairers are projected each year, on average, over the decade. Many of those openings are expected to result from the need to replace workers who transfer to different occupations or exit the labor force, such as to retire.

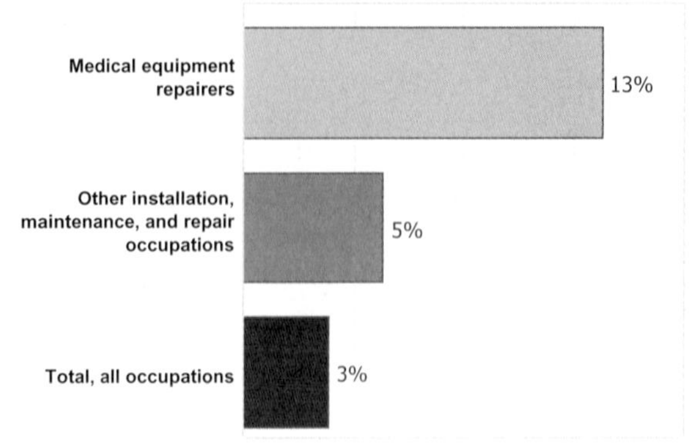

Note: All Occupations includes all occupations in the U.S. Economy.
Source: U.S. Bureau of Labor Statistics, Employment Projections program.

Employment

Medical equipment repairers will be needed to fix and maintain the medical equipment used in healthcare facilities. With the expected increase in the number of older adults and the prevalence of chronic diseases among them, demand for medical care and the equipment used to diagnose, monitor, and treat diseases will grow. Thus, more medical equipment repairers will be needed to ensure that these machines work properly.

Occupational Title	SOC Code	Employment, 2022	Projected Employment, 2032	Change, 2022-32	
				Percent	Numeric
Medical equipment repairers	49-9062	66,400	75,100	13	8,800

Contacts for More Information

For more information, visit

- Association for the Advancement of Medical Instrumentation

Small Engine Mechanics

Summary

Quick Facts: Small Engine Mechanics

2022 Median Pay	$44,080 per year $21.19 per hour
Typical Entry-Level Education	See How to Become One
Work Experience in a Related Occupation	None
On-the-job Training	See How to Become One
Number of Jobs, 2022	88,000
Job Outlook, 2022-32	3% (As fast as average)
Employment Change, 2022-32	2,500

What Small Engine Mechanics Do

Small engine mechanics inspect, service, and repair motorized power equipment.

Work Environment

Small engine mechanics generally work in well-ventilated but noisy repair shops. They sometimes make onsite repair calls, which may require working in poor weather conditions. Although most work full time, seasonal workers often see their hours fluctuate. Workers frequently are busiest during the spring and summer, when equipment use is the highest.

Small engine mechanics test and inspect engines for malfunctioning parts.

Motorcycle mechanics specialize in working on motorcycles, scooters, mopeds, dirt bikes, and all-terrain vehicles.

How to Become a Small Engine Mechanic

Small engine mechanics typically enter the occupation with a high school diploma or postsecondary nondegree award and learn their trade through on-the-job training.

Pay

The median annual wage for small engine mechanics was $44,080 in May 2022.

Job Outlook

Overall employment of small engine mechanics is projected to grow 3 percent from 2022 to 2032, about as fast as the average for all occupations.

About 9,000 openings for small engine mechanics are projected each year, on average, over the decade. Many of those openings are expected to result from the need to replace workers who transfer to different occupations or exit the labor force, such as to retire.

What Small Engine Mechanics Do

Small engine mechanics inspect, service, and repair motorized power equipment. Mechanics often specialize in one type of equipment, such as motorcycles, motorboats, or outdoor power equipment.

Duties

Small engine mechanics typically do the following:

- Discuss equipment issues, maintenance plans, and work performed with customers
- Perform routine engine maintenance, such as lubricating parts and replacing spark plugs
- Test and inspect engines for malfunctioning parts
- Adjust components according to specifications
- Repair or replace worn, defective, or broken parts
- Reassemble and reinstall components and engines following repairs
- Keep records of inspections, test results, work performed, and parts used

Small engine mechanics work on power equipment ranging from snowmobiles to chain saws. When equipment breaks down, mechanics use many strategies to diagnose the source and extent of the problem. Small engine mechanics identify mechanical, electrical, and fuel system problems and make necessary repairs.

Mechanics' tasks vary in complexity and difficulty. Maintenance inspections and repairs, for example, involve minor adjustments or the replacement of a single part. Hand calibration, piston calibration, and spark plug replacement, however, may require taking an engine apart completely. Some mechanics use computerized equipment to tune racing motorcycles and motorboats.

Mechanics use a variety of hand tools, including screwdrivers, wrenches, and pliers, for many common tasks. Some mechanics also may use compression gauges, ammeters, and voltmeters to test engine performance. For more complicated procedures, they commonly use pneumatic tools, which are powered by compressed air, or diagnostic equipment.

Although employers usually provide the more expensive tools and testing equipment, some mechanics may be required to use their own hand tools. Some mechanics have thousands of dollars invested in their tool collections.

The following are examples of types of small engine mechanics:

Motorboat mechanics and service technicians maintain and repair the mechanical and electrical components of boat engines. Most of their work, whether on small outboard engines or large diesel-powered inboard motors, is performed at docks and marinas where the repair shop is located. Motorboat mechanics also may work on propellers, steering mechanisms, marine plumbing, and other boat equipment.

Motorcycle mechanics specialize in working on motorcycles, scooters, mopeds, dirt bikes, and all-terrain vehicles. They service engines, transmissions, brakes, and ignition systems and make minor body repairs, among other tasks. Most work for dealerships, servicing and repairing specific makes and models.

Outdoor power equipment and other small engine mechanics service and repair outdoor power equipment, such as lawnmowers, edge trimmers, garden tractors, and portable generators. Some mechanics may work on snowblowers and snowmobiles, but this work is highly seasonal and regional.

Technicians and mechanics who work primarily on automobiles are described in the profile on automotive service technicians and mechanics.

Technicians who work primarily on large trucks and buses are described in the profile on diesel service technicians and mechanics.

Technicians and mechanics who work primarily on farm equipment, construction vehicles, and rail cars are described in the profile on heavy vehicle and mobile equipment service technicians.

Work Environment

Small engine mechanics held about 88,000 jobs in 2022. Employment in the detailed occupations that make up small engine mechanics was distributed as follows:

Outdoor power equipment and other small engine mechanics	41,600
Motorboat mechanics and service technicians	29,300
Motorcycle mechanics	17,100

The largest employers of small engine mechanics were as follows:

Other motor vehicle dealers	27%
Building material and garden equipment and supplies dealers	14
Self-employed workers	13
Repair and maintenance	12
Amusement, gambling, and recreation industries	10

Small engine mechanics generally work in well-ventilated but noisy repair shops. They sometimes make onsite repair calls, which may require working in poor weather conditions. When repairing onboard engines, motorboat mechanics may work in cramped and uncomfortable positions.

Work Schedules

Most small engine mechanics work full time, although seasonal workers often see their work hours fluctuate.

Most mechanics are busiest during the spring and summer, when demand for work on equipment from lawnmowers to motorboats is the highest. During the peak seasons, some mechanics work many overtime hours. In contrast, some may work only part time during the winter, when demand for small engine work is lowest.

Many employers try to keep work more consistent by scheduling major repair work, such as rebuilding engines, during the off-season.

How to Become a Small Engine Mechanic

Small engine mechanics typically enter the occupation with a high school diploma or postsecondary nondegree award and learn their trade through on-the-job training.

Education

Motorboat and outdoor power equipment mechanics typically begin work with a high school diploma and learn on the job, although some of them seek postsecondary education. High school or vocational school courses in small engine repair and automobile mechanics are often beneficial.

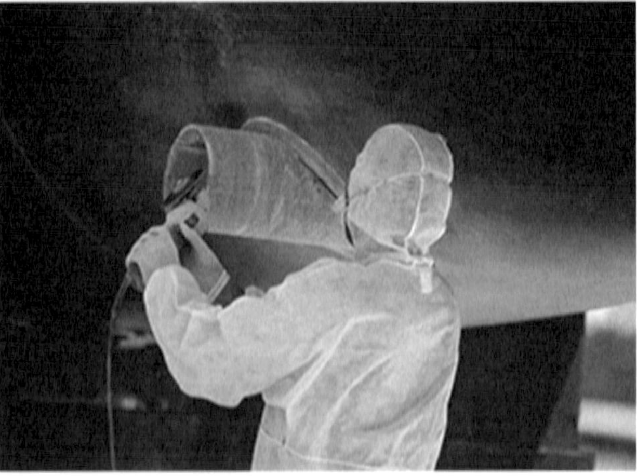

Motorboat mechanics and service technicians maintain and repair the mechanical and electrical components of boat engines.

Many tasks, such as disassembling engine parts, connecting or attaching components, and using hand tools, require a steady hand and good hand-eye coordination.

Motorcycle mechanics typically complete postsecondary education programs in motorcycle repair, and employers prefer to hire these workers because they usually require less on-the-job training.

Training

Trainees work closely with experienced mechanics while learning basic tasks, such as replacing spark plugs or disassembling engine components. As they gain experience, trainees move on to more difficult tasks, such as advanced computerized diagnosis and engine overhauls. Achieving competency may take anywhere from several months to 3 years, depending on a mechanic's specialization and ability.

Because of the increased complexity of boat and motorcycle engines, motorcycle and motorboat mechanics who do not complete postsecondary education often need more on-the-job training than that needed by outdoor power equipment mechanics.

Employers frequently send mechanics to training courses run by motorcycle, motorboat, and outdoor power equipment manufacturers and dealers. These courses teach mechanics the most up-to-date technology and techniques. Often, such courses are a prerequisite to performing warranty and manufacturer-specific work.

Licenses, Certifications, and Registrations

Many motorboat and motorcycle manufacturers offer certification specific to their own models, and certification from the Equipment & Engine Training Council is the recognized industry credential for outdoor power equipment mechanics. Although not required, certification can demonstrate a mechanic's competence and usually brings higher pay.

Motorcycle mechanics usually need a driver's license with a motorcycle endorsement.

Important Qualities

Customer-service skills. Small engine mechanics frequently discuss problems and necessary repairs with their customers. They must be courteous, be good listeners, and always remain ready to answer customers' questions.

Detail oriented. Small engine mechanics must be aware of small details when inspecting or repairing engines and components, because mechanical and electronic malfunctions are often due to misalignments and other easy-to-miss causes.

Dexterity. Small engine mechanics need a steady hand and good hand–eye coordination for many tasks, such as disassembling engine parts, connecting or attaching components, and using hand tools.

Mechanical skills. Small engine mechanics must be familiar with engine components and systems and know how they interact with each other. They often disassemble major parts for repairs, and they must be able to put them back together properly.

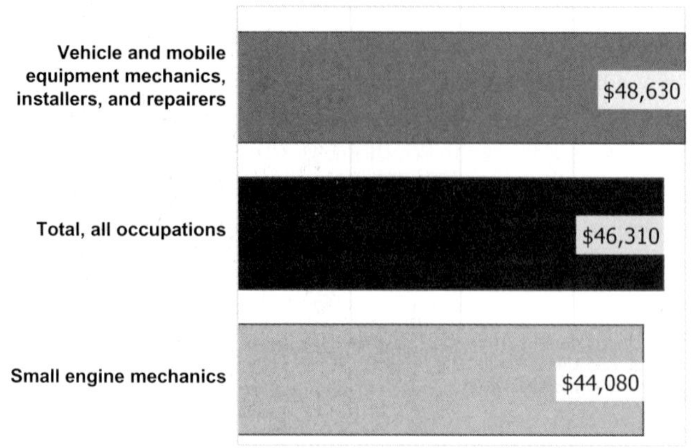

Note: All Occupations includes all occupations in the U.S. Economy.
Source: U.S. Bureau of Labor Statistics, Occupational Employment and Wage Statistics.

Organizational skills. Small engine mechanics keep workspaces clean and organized in order to maintain safety and ensure accountability for parts.

Troubleshooting skills. Small engine mechanics use diagnostic equipment on engine systems and components to identify and fix problems. They must be familiar with electronic control systems and the appropriate tools needed to fix and maintain them.

Pay

The median annual wage for small engine mechanics was $44,080 in May 2022. The median wage is the wage at which half the workers in an occupation earned more than that amount and half earned less. The lowest 10 percent earned less than $29,820, and the highest 10 percent earned more than $63,240.

Median annual wages for small engine mechanics in May 2022 were as follows:

Motorboat mechanics and service technicians	$48,280
Motorcycle mechanics	43,370
Outdoor power equipment and other small engine mechanics	40,030

In May 2022, the median annual wages for small engine mechanics in the top industries in which they worked were as follows:

Amusement, gambling, and recreation industries	$46,890
Repair and maintenance	44,930
Other motor vehicle dealers	44,750
Building material and garden equipment and supplies dealers	37,920

Most small engine mechanics work full time, although seasonal workers often see their work hours fluctuate.

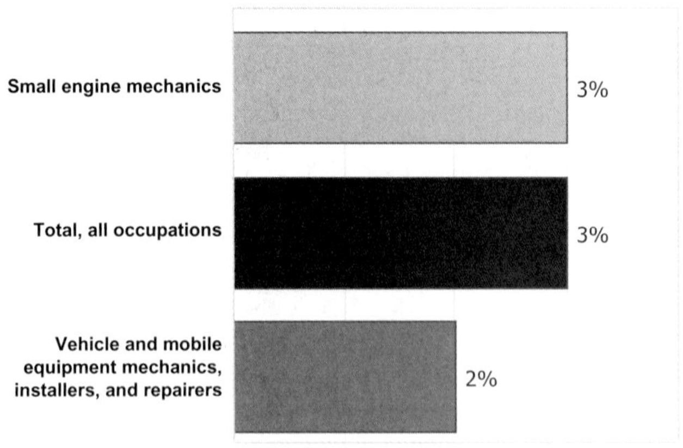

Note: All Occupations includes all occupations in the U.S. Economy.
Source: U.S. Bureau of Labor Statistics, Employment Projections program.

Most mechanics are busiest during the spring and summer, when demand for work on equipment from lawnmowers to boats is the highest. During the peak seasons, some mechanics work many overtime hours. In contrast, some mechanics may work only part time during the winter, when demand for small engine work is lowest.

Many employers try to keep work more consistent by scheduling major repair work, such as rebuilding engines, during the off-season.

Job Outlook

Overall employment of small engine mechanics is projected to grow 3 percent from 2022 to 2032, about as fast as the average for all occupations.

About 9,000 openings for small engine mechanics are projected each year, on average, over the decade. Many of those openings are expected to result from the need to replace workers who transfer to different occupations or exit the labor force, such as to retire.

Employment

Projected employment of small engine mechanics varies by occupation (see table).

Increased demand for motorboats and motorcycles, as well as for outdoor power equipment, is expected to create jobs for small engine mechanics over the projections decade. In addition, boat and motorcycle engines, as well as engines and parts for outdoor power equipment, have become more sophisticated, which should create demand for small engine mechanics who can fix and maintain them.

However, electric-powered small engines, such as those in lawn mowers and chain saws, may require less routine maintenance and repair services than traditional engines, which might reduce demand for some of these workers.

Occupational Title	SOC Code	Employment, 2022	Projected Employment, 2032	Change, 2022-32	
				Percent	Numeric
Small engine mechanics	49-3050	88,000	90,500	3	2,500
Motorboat mechanics and service technicians	49-3051	29,300	31,000	6	1,700
Motorcycle mechanics	49-3052	17,100	17,400	2	300
Outdoor power equipment and other small engine mechanics	49-3053	41,600	42,100	1	500

Contacts for More Information

For more information, visit

➤ Equipment & Engine Training Council

Telecommunications Technicians

Summary

Quick Facts: Telecommunications Technicians

2022 Median Pay	$60,190 per year $28.94 per hour
Typical Entry-Level Education	See How to Become One
Work Experience in a Related Occupation	None
On-the-job Training	See How to Become One
Number of Jobs, 2022	299,300
Job Outlook, 2022-32	6% (Faster than average)
Employment Change, 2022-32	18,900

What Telecommunications Technicians Do

Telecommunications technicians install, maintain, and repair radio, internet, and other telecommunications infrastructure.

Work Environment

Most telecommunications technicians work full time. They may have to work night or weekend shifts to maintain or repair telecommunications networks. Technicians travel frequently to installation and repair sites.

How to Become a Telecommunications Technician

Telecommunications technicians typically need at least a high school diploma or equivalent to enter the occupation. Employers

Telecom technicians install and repair telecommunications equipment.

may prefer to hire candidates who have a certificate or associate's degree. These workers also receive on-the-job training.

Pay

The median annual wage for telecommunications technicians was $60,190 in May 2022.

Job Outlook

Overall employment of telecommunications technicians is projected to grow 6 percent from 2022 to 2032, faster than the average for all occupations.

About 31,500 openings for telecommunications technicians are projected each year, on average, over the decade. Many of those openings are expected to result from the need to replace workers who transfer to different occupations or exit the labor force, such as to retire.

What Telecommunications Technicians Do

Telecommunications technicians, also known as *telecom technicians*, install and maintain telecommunications infrastructure.

Telecom technicians inspect and service equipment and wiring.

They set up and fix different types of devices or equipment that carry communications signals, such as internet routers and fiber optic lines.

Duties

Telecommunications technicians typically do the following:

- Install telecommunications lines or equipment
- Operate, maintain, or repair damaged or malfunctioning telecommunications lines or equipment
- Test telecommunications lines or devices to ensure that they work properly
- Keep records of maintenance, repairs, and installations
- Explain the use and maintenance of equipment to customers

Telecommunications technicians construct and maintain the infrastructure that transmits information electronically, often across great distances. They install and repair telecommunications lines and fiber optic cables. They also set up and maintain equipment that carries communications signals.

The specific tasks of telecom technicians vary with their specialization and where they work. The following are examples of types of telecommunications technicians:

Radio, cellular, and tower equipment installers and repairers install, repair, or maintain radio transmitting, broadcasting, and receiving equipment and two-way radio communications systems. These systems are used in cellular telecommunications, mobile broadband, and radio equipment in service and emergency vehicles. Radio, cellular, and tower equipment installers and repairers may test and analyze network coverage and troubleshoot solutions during network outages.

Telecommunications equipment installers and repairers set up and maintain various types of devices or equipment that carry communications signals, such as telephone lines and internet routers. *Central office technicians* set up and maintain switches, fiber optic cables, and other equipment at switching hubs, called central offices. These hubs send, process, and amplify data from thousands of telephone, internet, and cable connections. Central office technicians receive alerts about equipment malfunctions from automonitoring switches and are able to correct the problems remotely. Technicians who work at distribution centers for cable and television companies may be called *headend technicians*. Headends are control centers in which technicians monitor signals for local cable networks. *Residential and business installers and repairers* set up and repair telecommunications equipment, such as modems for internet and cable television services, in customers' homes and businesses. They also may need to install aerial and underground wiring.

Telecommunications line installers and repairers install and maintain the cables used by network communications companies. Depending on the service provided—local and long-distance telephone, cable television, or internet—telecommunications companies use fiber optic and other types of

Some telecom technicians provide in-home installation and repair services, while others work in central offices or electronic service centers.

cables. Telecommunications line installers and repairers use specialized tools to test and troubleshoot cables and networking equipment. Those who work with fiber optic cables must be able to splice and terminate optical cables.

Work Environment

Telecommunications technicians held about 299,300 jobs in 2022. Employment in the detailed occupations that make up telecommunications technicians was distributed as follows:

Telecommunications equipment installers and repairers, except line installers	173,700
Telecommunications line installers and repairers	112,100
Radio, cellular, and tower equipment installers and repairers	13,500

The largest employers of telecommunications technicians were as follows:

Industry	Percent
Telecommunications	59%
Specialty trade contractors	14
Heavy and civil engineering construction	6
Professional, scientific, and technical services	4
Administrative and support and waste management and remediation services	3

Some telecom technicians provide installation and repair services indoors, such as in homes, businesses, or central offices. Others work outdoors to install telecommunications cables and equipment.

Telecom technicians' work may require them to climb onto rooftops; into attics; and up ladders, telephone poles, and telecommunications towers. They occasionally work in cramped spaces and in awkward positions, including stooping, crouching, or crawling. Other times they must reach high or lift and move heavy equipment and parts.

Postsecondary education in electronics, telecommunications, or computer networking is typically needed to become a telecom technician.

Injuries and Illnesses

The work of telecom technicians can be dangerous. Telecommunications equipment installers and repairers and telecommunications line installers and repairers have some of the highest rates of injuries and illnesses of all occupations. Common injuries include falls and strains.

To reduce the risk of injury, workers wear hardhats and harnesses when working on ladders or on elevated equipment. To prevent electrical shock, technicians may switch off power to equipment that is under repair.

Work Schedules

Most telecom technicians work full time. Telecom technicians may be required to work night or weekend shifts to maintain or upgrade telecommunications equipment. Some are on call around the clock in case of emergency.

How to Become a Telecommunications Technician

Telecommunications technicians typically need at least a high school diploma or equivalent to enter the occupation. Employers may prefer to hire candidates who have a certificate or associate's degree. These workers also receive on-the-job training.

Education

Telecommunications technicians typically need at least a high school diploma or equivalent. Employers of telecommunications equipment installers and repairers and radio, cellular, and tower equipment installers and repairers may prefer to hire candidates who have some postsecondary education in electronics, telecommunications, or computer networking. Some employers prefer to hire candidates who have an associate's degree.

Community colleges and technical schools offer courses in subjects such as data transmission systems, data communication, AC/DC electrical circuits, and computer programming. These courses typically are included in programs that lead to a certificate or an associate's degree in telecommunications or related subjects.

Training

Once hired, telecommunications technicians typically receive on-the-job training that lasts from several months to several years. Training involves a combination of formal instruction and hands-on work with an experienced technician. In these settings, workers learn about the equipment's internal parts and the tools needed for repair.

Training length and topics vary by position and employer. For example, central office technicians typically receive electrical training. Telecommunications line installers and repairers who work for telecommunications companies may benefit from additional training provided by equipment manufacturers, schools, unions, or industry organizations. Radio, cellular, and tower equipment installers and repairers typically learn subjects such as tower climbing and rescue, electrical skills and concepts, and radio frequency fundamentals.

Licenses, Certifications, and Registrations

Manufacturer or employer-provided certification may be helpful for some telecom technicians. For example, the Society of Cable Telecommunications Engineers offers the Broadband Telecom Center Specialist (BTCS) certification, and the Fiber Optic Association offers multiple fiber optic certifications for telecommunications line installers and repairers.

Telecom technicians may need a driver's license to travel to jobsites, and workers who drive heavy vehicles usually need a commercial driver's license (CDL). Some employers prefer or require that candidates have certification in first aid or in cardiopulmonary resuscitation (CPR).

Important Qualities

Ability to work at heights. Telecom technicians must be comfortable working at heights on lifts, telecommunications towers, and other elevated surfaces.

Color vision. Telecom technicians work with color-coded wires, and they must be able to tell them apart.

Customer-service skills. Telecom technicians who work in customers' homes and offices should be friendly and polite. They must be able to explain to customers about maintaining and operating communications equipment.

Dexterity. Telecom technicians' tasks, such as connecting components and using handtools, require good hand–eye coordination to avoid injuring themselves and damaging materials.

Mechanical skills. Telecom technicians must be familiar with the devices they work on and with the tools they need to install or fix those devices. They must also be able to understand manufacturers' instructions when installing or repairing equipment.

Physical stamina. Telecom technicians must be able to climb ladders or towers with heavy tools or equipment, work on their feet for extended periods, and dig trenches for telecommunications cables.

Physical strength. Telecom technicians must be able to lift heavy tools, cables, and equipment on a regular basis.

Problem-solving skills. Telecom technicians must be able to troubleshoot and devise solutions to problems that arise when installing or repairing equipment or devices.

Pay

The median annual wage for telecommunications technicians was $60,190 in May 2022. The median wage is the wage at which half the workers in an occupation earned more than that amount and half earned less. The lowest 10 percent earned less than $37,060, and the highest 10 percent earned more than $93,300.

Median annual wages for telecommunications technicians in May 2022 were as follows:

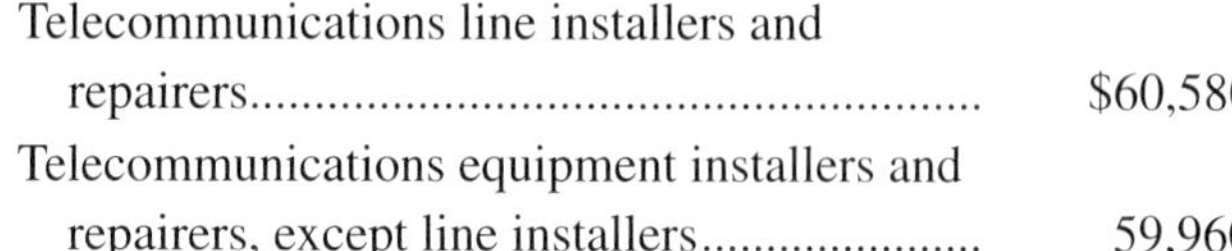

Telecommunications line installers and repairers	$60,580
Telecommunications equipment installers and repairers, except line installers	59,960

Telecommunications Technicians

Median annual wages, May 2022

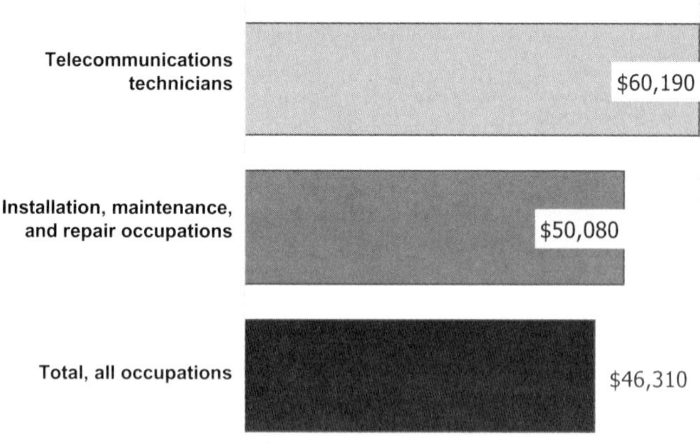

Note: All Occupations includes all occupations in the U.S. Economy.
Source: U.S. Bureau of Labor Statistics, Employment Projections program.

Radio, cellular, and tower equipment installers and repairers.. 59,720

In May 2022, the median annual wages for telecommunications technicians in the top industries in which they worked were as follows:

Telecommunications $64,600
Specialty trade contractors............................ 48,470
Professional, scientific, and technical services... 47,920
Administrative and support and waste management and remediation services 47,580
Heavy and civil engineering construction..... 47,190

Most telecom technicians work full time. Telecom technicians may be required to work night or weekend shifts to maintain or upgrade telecommunications equipment. Some are on call around the clock in case of emergency.

Job Outlook

Overall employment of telecommunications technicians is projected to grow 6 percent from 2022 to 2032, faster than the average for all occupations.

About 31,500 openings for telecommunications technicians are projected each year, on average, over the decade. Many of those openings are expected to result from the need to replace workers who transfer to different occupations or exit the labor force, such as to retire.

Employment

Employment of telecommunications technicians is expected to grow as telecommunications providers construct new infrastructure where it did not exist previously and as existing wired telecommunications equipment is upgraded to fiber optic cable with improved capabilities. Telecom line installers will be needed to install cables, and telecom equipment installers will be needed to install devices and to connect customers' homes and businesses.

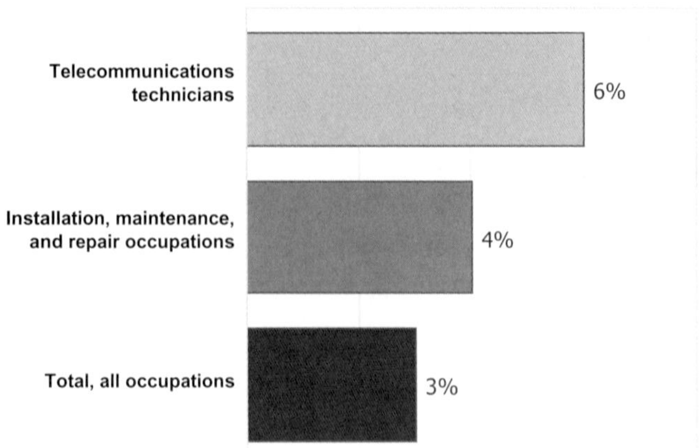

Note: All Occupations includes all occupations in the U.S. Economy.
Source: U.S. Bureau of Labor Statistics, Occupational Employment and Wage Statistics.

Occupational Title	SOC Code	Employment, 2022	Projected Employment, 2032	Change, 2022-32	
				Percent	Numeric
Telecommunications technicians	—	299,300	318,200	6	18,900
Radio, cellular, and tower equipment installers and repairers	49-2021	13,500	13,900	3	500
Telecommunications equipment installers and repairers, except line installers	49-2022	173,700	184,700	6	11,000
Telecommunications line installers and repairers	49-9052	112,100	119,600	7	7,500

Contacts for More Information

For information, visit

- The Fiber Optic Association
- National Coalition for Telecommunications Education and Learning
- Society of Cable Telecommunications Engineers
- Telecommunications Industry Association

Wind Turbine Technicians

Summary

Quick Facts: Wind Turbine Technicians	
2022 Median Pay	$57,320 per year $27.56 per hour
Typical Entry-Level Education	Postsecondary nondegree award
Work Experience in a Related Occupation	None
On-the-job Training	Long-term on-the-job training
Number of Jobs, 2022	11,200
Job Outlook, 2022-32	45% (Much faster than average)
Employment Change, 2022-32	5,000

What Wind Turbine Technicians Do

Wind turbine service technicians maintain and repair wind turbines.

Work Environment

Wind turbine service technicians generally work outdoors, in confined spaces, and often at great heights. Most windtechs work full time, and they also may be on call in the evening or on weekends.

How to Become a Wind Turbine Technician

Wind turbine service technicians typically need a postsecondary nondegree award to enter the occupation. They also typically receive on-the-job training.

Pay

The median annual wage for wind turbine technicians was $57,320 in May 2022.

Job Outlook

Employment of wind turbine technicians is projected to grow 45 percent from 2022 to 2032, much faster than the average for all occupations.

About 1,800 openings for wind turbine technicians are projected each year, on average, over the decade. Many of those openings are expected to result from the need to replace workers who transfer to different occupations or exit the labor force, such as to retire.

What Wind Turbine Technicians Do

Wind turbine service technicians, also known as *windtechs*, maintain and repair wind turbines.

Duties

Wind turbine service technicians typically do the following:

- Assist engineers and ironworkers in installing new wind turbines
- Inspect the exterior and physical integrity of wind turbine towers
- Climb wind turbine towers to inspect or repair wind turbine equipment
- Perform routine maintenance on wind turbines
- Test and troubleshoot electrical, mechanical, and hydraulic components and systems
- Replace worn or malfunctioning components
- Collect turbine data for testing or research and analysis
- Service underground transmission systems, wind field substations, or fiber optic sensing and control systems

Windtechs maintain and fix the components of wind turbines, large mechanical structures that convert wind energy into electricity. The three major components of each turbine are a tower; a nacelle, which contains the equipment that generates electricity; and three blades attached to the nacelle. Most of a windtech's work focuses on maintaining the nacelle.

Wind turbine technicians visually inspect wind turbines for damage.

Wind turbine technicians often monitor turbines from the ground.

Windtechs typically maintain turbines by inspecting components and lubricating parts. Maintenance schedules are largely determined by the hours a turbine operates but also may vary by manufacturer. For turbines that operate year round, windtechs may do routine maintenance one to three times a year.

Turbines have electronic monitoring equipment, usually located in the nacelle, that provides an alert when a problem is detected. Although windtechs may access monitoring equipment both onsite and off, they must travel to the worksite to make repairs to turbine components.

Windtechs use a safety harness when climbing the tower, which may be 200 feet or higher, to reach the nacelle. They use a variety of handtools and power tools to make adjustments or repairs, and they use computers to diagnose electrical malfunctions.

Work Environment

Wind turbine technicians held about 11,200 jobs in 2022. The largest employers of wind turbine technicians were as follows:

Wind electric power generation	29%
Commercial and industrial machinery and equipment (except automotive and electronic) repair and maintenance	25
Power and communication line and related structures construction	16
Self-employed workers	11
Machinery, equipment, and supplies merchant wholesalers	2

Wind turbine technicians often work at great heights.

Wind turbine service technicians, also known as *windtechs*, generally work outdoors, including in extreme temperatures, on rural or offshore wind farms. They must be physically able to work at great heights. For example, workers must climb ladders to reach the nacelle—which is mounted on towers that are more than 200 feet tall—while wearing a fall-protection harness and carrying tools. When repairing blades, windtechs rappel, or descend by sliding down a rope, from the nacelle to the section of the blade that needs servicing.

When maintaining mechanical systems, windtechs work in the confined space of the nacelle.

Windtechs sometimes work with another windtech or with other specialists, such as electricians, when doing major service or repairs.

Injuries and Illnesses

Wind turbine service technicians have one of the highest rates of injuries and illnesses of all occupations.

To reduce their risk of falls, windtechs follow safety protocols such as using a harness and other safety equipment during climbs. To guard against injury, they wear hard hats, gloves, and other protective gear.

Work Schedules

Most windtechs work full time, and they also may be on call in the evening or on weekends.

Windtechs may travel to wind farms in rural areas or on offshore wind farms. Working on offshore farms may require being away from home for several days or weeks at a time.

Wind turbine technicians receive on-the-job training from experienced workers.

How to Become a Wind Turbine Technician

Wind turbine service technicians, also known as *windtechs*, typically need a postsecondary nondegree award to enter the occupation. They also typically receive on-the-job training from their employer.

Education

Windtechs typically attend technical schools or community colleges, where they may complete a postsecondary certificate in wind energy technology or choose to earn an associate's degree.

Many technical schools have onsite wind turbines that students service as part of their studies. In addition to hands-on learning, windtech coursework includes maintenance instruction for electrical and hydraulic systems, braking and mechanical systems, and programmable logic control systems. Students also receive instruction in tower climbing, along with training for rescues, safety, first aid, and CPR.

Training

Once hired, windtechs typically receive employer- or manufacturer-provided on-the-job training that is related to the specific wind turbines they will maintain and repair.

Licenses, Certifications, and Registrations

Although not mandatory, professional certification allows workers to demonstrate a certain level of knowledge and competence. Certification subjects for windtechs include workplace electrical safety, tower climbing, and self-rescue. Employers often direct workers to the certifications they need.

Important Qualities

Ability to work at heights. Windtechs must be comfortable working at heights to maintain or repair turbines. Tower ladders are usually at least 200 feet high.

Communication skills. Windtechs must exchange information with windtechs or specialists, such as electricians, in order to work safely and effectively.

Detail oriented. Windtechs must maintain records of all of the services they perform. Turbine maintenance requires precise measurements, a strict order of operations, and numerous safety procedures.

Mechanical skills. Windtechs must understand and be able to maintain and repair a turbine's various technical systems.

Physical stamina. Windtechs must be able to climb turbine towers, often with tools and equipment.

Physical strength. Windtechs must lift heavy equipment, parts, and tools, some of which weigh 50 pounds or more.

Problem-solving skills. Windtechs must diagnose and repair turbine problems. When a malfunction or other issue arises, technicians must determine the cause and make the necessary repairs.

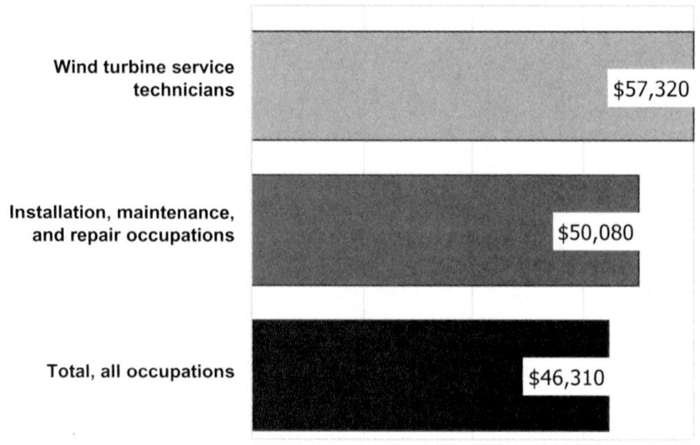

Note: All Occupations includes all occupations in the U.S. Economy.
Source: U.S. Bureau of Labor Statistics, Occupational Employment and Wage Statistics.

Pay

The median annual wage for wind turbine technicians was $57,320 in May 2022. The median wage is the wage at which half the workers in an occupation earned more than that amount and half earned less. The lowest 10 percent earned less than $45,150, and the highest 10 percent earned more than $80,170.

In May 2022, the median annual wages for wind turbine technicians in the top industries in which they worked were as follows:

Wind electric power generation	$59,890
Commercial and industrial machinery and equipment (except automotive and electronic) repair and maintenance	56,660
Power and communication line and related structures construction	54,480
Machinery, equipment, and supplies merchant wholesalers	53,890

Most wind turbine service technicians, also known as *windtechs*, work full time, and they also may be on call in the evening or on weekends.

Job Outlook

Employment of wind turbine technicians is projected to grow 45 percent from 2022 to 2032, much faster than the average for all occupations.

About 1,800 openings for wind turbine technicians are projected each year, on average, over the decade. Many of those openings are expected to result from the need to replace workers who transfer to different occupations or exit the labor force, such as to retire.

Wind Turbine Technicians

Percent change in employment, projected 2022-32

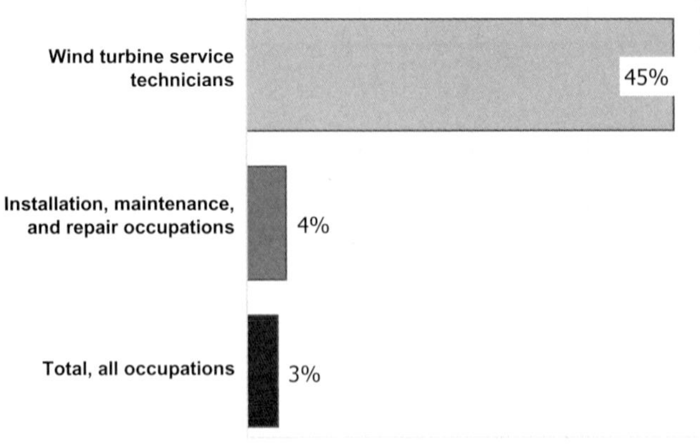

Note: All Occupations includes all occupations in the U.S. Economy.
Source: U.S. Bureau of Labor Statistics, Employment Projections program.

Employment

Development of taller towers with larger blades has reduced the cost of wind power generation, making it more competitive with coal, natural gas, and other forms of power generation. As additional wind turbines are erected, more windtechs will be needed to install and maintain turbines.

Occupational Title	SOC Code	Employment, 2022	Projected Employment, 2032	Change, 2022-32	
				Percent	Numeric
Wind turbine service technicians	49-9081	11,200	16,200	45	5,000

Contacts for More Information

For more information about educational opportunities and career paths, visit

- U.S. Department of Energy, Office of Energy Efficiency & Renewable Energy
- WindExchange

Legal

Arbitrators, Mediators, and Conciliators

Summary

Quick Facts: Arbitrators, Mediators, and Conciliators	
2022 Median Pay	$64,030 per year $30.78 per hour
Typical Entry-Level Education	Bachelor's degree
Work Experience in a Related Occupation	Less than 5 years
On-the-job Training	Moderate-term on-the-job training
Number of Jobs, 2022	9,100
Job Outlook, 2022-32	5% (Faster than average)
Employment Change, 2022-32	500

What Arbitrators, Mediators, and Conciliators Do

Arbitrators, mediators, and conciliators facilitate negotiation and dialogue between disputing parties to help resolve conflicts outside of the court system.

Work Environment

Many arbitrators, mediators, and conciliators work for state or local governments or in the legal services industry.

How to Become an Arbitrator, Mediator, or Conciliator

Arbitrators, mediators, and conciliators typically need at least a bachelor's degree at the entry level. They learn their skills through a combination of education, training, and work experience.

Arbitrators, mediators, and conciliators help disputing parties resolve their conflict by facilitating dialogue and negotiations.

Pay

The median annual wage for arbitrators, mediators, and conciliators was $64,030 in May 2022.

Job Outlook

Employment of arbitrators, mediators, and conciliators is projected to grow 5 percent from 2022 to 2032, faster than the average for all occupations.

About 400 openings for arbitrators, mediators, and conciliators are projected each year, on average, over the decade. Many of those openings are expected to result from the need to replace workers who transfer to different occupations or exit the labor force, such as to retire.

What Arbitrators, Mediators, and Conciliators Do

Arbitrators, mediators, and conciliators facilitate negotiation and dialogue between disputing parties to help resolve conflicts outside of the court system.

Duties

Arbitrators, mediators, and conciliators typically do the following:

- Facilitate communication between disputants to guide parties toward mutual agreement
- Clarify issues, concerns, needs, and interests of all parties involved
- Conduct initial meetings with disputants to outline the arbitration process
- Settle procedural matters such as fees, or determine details such as witness numbers and time requirements

Arbitrators, mediators, and conciliators help parties come to mutually acceptable agreements.

- Set up appointments for parties to meet for mediation or arbitration
- Interview claimants, agents, or witnesses to obtain information about disputed issues
- Prepare settlement agreements for disputants to sign
- Apply relevant laws, regulations, policies, or precedents to reach conclusions
- Evaluate information from documents such as claim applications, birth or death certificates, and physician or employer records

Arbitrators, mediators, and conciliators help opposing parties settle disputes outside of court. They hold private, confidential hearings, which are less formal than a court trial.

Arbitrators are usually attorneys, business professionals, or retired judges with expertise in a particular field. As impartial third parties, they hear and decide disputes between opposing parties. Arbitrators may work alone or in a panel with other arbitrators. In some cases, arbitrators may decide procedural issues, such as what evidence may be submitted and when hearings will be held.

Arbitration may be required by law for some claims and disputes. When it is not required, the parties in dispute sometimes voluntarily agree to arbitration rather than proceed with litigation or a trial. In some cases, parties may appeal the arbitrator's decision.

Mediators are neutral parties who help people resolve their disputes. However, unlike arbitrators, they do not render binding decisions. Rather, mediators help facilitate discussion and guide the parties toward a mutually acceptable agreement. If the opposing sides cannot reach a settlement with the mediator's help, they are free to pursue other options.

Conciliators are similar to mediators. Although their role is to help guide opposing sides to a settlement, they typically meet with the parties separately. The opposing sides must decide in advance if they will be bound by the conciliator's recommendations.

Arbitrators, mediators, and conciliators usually work in private offices or meeting rooms.

Work Environment

Arbitrators, mediators, and conciliators held about 9,100 jobs in 2022. The largest employers of arbitrators, mediators, and conciliators were as follows:

Employer	Percent
State government, excluding education and hospitals	14%
Local government, excluding education and hospitals	13
Self-employed workers	11
Insurance carriers and related activities	8
Other professional, scientific, and technical services	7

Arbitrators, mediators, and conciliators usually work in private offices or meeting rooms. They may travel to a neutral site chosen for negotiations.

The work may be stressful because arbitrators, mediators, and conciliators sometimes work with difficult or confrontational individuals or with highly charged and emotional situations, such as injury settlements or family disputes.

How to Become an Arbitrator, Mediator, or Conciliator

Arbitrators, mediators, and conciliators typically need at least a bachelor's degree at the entry level. They learn their skills through a combination of education, training, and work experience.

Arbitrators, mediators, and conciliators are usually lawyers or business professionals with expertise in a particular field.

Education

Few candidates for these jobs receive a degree specific to the field of arbitration, mediation, or conflict resolution. Rather, many positions require education appropriate to the applicant's field of expertise. A bachelor's degree is often sufficient, but some positions require candidates to have a law degree, a master's in business administration, or another type of advanced degree.

Work Experience in a Related Occupation

Arbitrators, mediators, and conciliators are usually lawyers, retired judges, or business professionals with expertise in a particular field, such as construction, finance, or insurance. They need to have knowledge of that industry and be able to relate well to people from different cultures and backgrounds.

Training

Mediators typically work under the supervision of an experienced mediator for a certain number of cases before working independently.

Training for arbitrators, mediators, and conciliators is available through independent mediation programs, national and local mediation membership organizations, and postsecondary schools. Training is also available by volunteering at a community mediation center.

Licenses, Certifications, and Registrations

There is no national license for arbitrators, mediators, and conciliators. However, some states require arbitrators and mediators to become certified to work on certain types of cases. Qualifications, standards, and the number of training hours required vary by state or by court. Most states require mediators to complete 20 to 40 hours of training courses to become certified. Some states require additional hours of training in a specialty area.

Some states require licenses appropriate to the applicant's field of expertise. For example, some courts may require applicants to be licensed attorneys or certified public accountants.

Important Qualities

Critical-thinking skills. Arbitrators, mediators, and conciliators must apply rules of law. They must remain neutral and not let their own personal assumptions interfere with the proceedings.

Decision-making skills. Arbitrators, mediators, and conciliators must be able to weigh facts, apply the law or rules, and make a decision relatively quickly.

Interpersonal skills. Arbitrators, mediators, and conciliators deal with disputing parties and must be able to facilitate discussion in a calm and respectful way.

Listening skills. Arbitrators, mediators, and conciliators must pay close attention to what is being said in order for them to evaluate information.

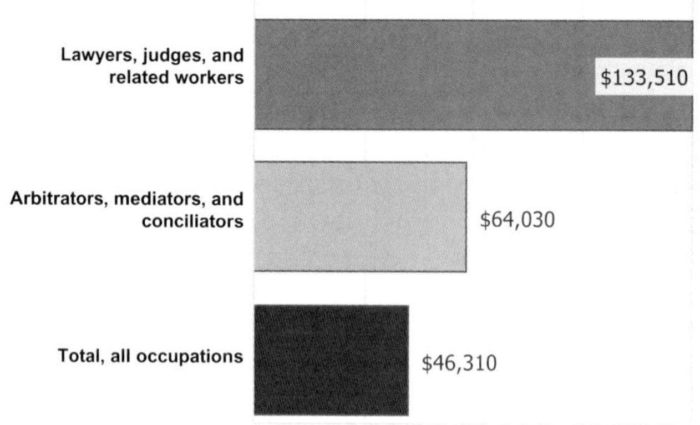

Note: All Occupations includes all occupations in the U.S. Economy.
Source: U.S. Bureau of Labor Statistics, Occupational Employment and Wage Statistics.

Reading skills. Arbitrators, mediators, and conciliators must be able to evaluate and distinguish important facts from large amounts of complex information.

Writing skills. Arbitrators, mediators, and conciliators write recommendations or decisions relating to appeals or disputes. They must be able to write their decisions clearly so that all sides understand the decision.

Pay

The median annual wage for arbitrators, mediators, and conciliators was $64,030 in May 2022. The median wage is the wage at which half the workers in an occupation earned more than that amount and half earned less. The lowest 10 percent earned less than $33,980, and the highest 10 percent earned more than $194,630.

In May 2022, the median annual wages for arbitrators, mediators, and conciliators in the top industries in which they worked were as follows:

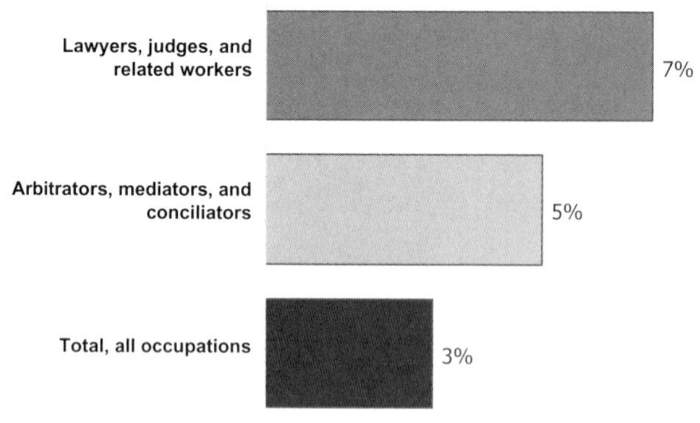

Note: All Occupations includes all occupations in the U.S. Economy.
Source: U.S. Bureau of Labor Statistics, Employment Projections program.

Local government, excluding education and hospitals $83,300
State government, excluding education and hospitals 67,160
Other professional, scientific, and technical services........ 60,980
Insurance carriers and related activities........ 51,570

Job Outlook

Employment of arbitrators, mediators, and conciliators is projected to grow 5 percent from 2022 to 2032, faster than the average for all occupations.

About 400 openings for arbitrators, mediators, and conciliators are projected each year, on average, over the decade. Many of those openings are expected to result from the need to replace workers who transfer to different occupations or exit the labor force, such as to retire.

Employment

The alternative methods of resolving disputes that these workers provide often are quicker and less expensive than trials and litigation. In addition, many contracts, such as those for employment and real estate, include clauses requiring mediation or arbitration to resolve complaints and disputes. These factors should help to support demand for arbitrators, mediators, and conciliators.

However, because alternative dispute resolution in government is contingent on available funds, state and local government budgets may affect public sector employment of arbitrators, mediators, and conciliators.

Occupational Title	SOC Code	Employment, 2022	Projected Employment, 2032	Change, 2022-32	
				Percent	Numeric
Arbitrators, mediators, and conciliators	23-1022	9,100	9,600	5	500

Contacts for More Information

For more information, visit

- American Arbitration Association
- Association for Conflict Resolution

Court Reporters and Simultaneous Captioners

Summary

Quick Facts: Court Reporters and Simultaneous Captioners	
2022 Median Pay	$63,560 per year $30.56 per hour
Typical Entry-Level Education	Postsecondary nondegree award
Work Experience in a Related Occupation	None
On-the-job Training	Short-term on-the-job training
Number of Jobs, 2022	21,300
Job Outlook, 2022-32	3% (As fast as average)
Employment Change, 2022-32	600

What Court Reporters and Simultaneous Captioners Do

Court reporters create word-for-word transcriptions at trials, depositions, and other legal proceedings. Simultaneous captioners provide similar transcriptions for television or for presentations in other settings, such as press conferences and business meetings, for people who are deaf or hard of hearing.

Work Environment

Most court reporters work in courts or legislatures; simultaneous captioners may work from their home or a central office. Some court reporters and simultaneous captioners travel to other locations, such as meeting sites or public events.

How to Become a Court Reporter or Simultaneous Captioner

Many community colleges and technical institutes offer postsecondary certificate programs for court reporters and simultaneous captioners. These workers typically receive on-the-job training that varies by type of reporting or captioning. Many states require court reporters and simultaneous captioners who work in legal settings to have a state license or a certification from a professional association.

Pay

The median annual wage for court reporters and simultaneous captioners was $63,560 in May 2022.

Court reporters attend legal proceedings to create word-for-word transcriptions.

Job Outlook

Employment of court reporters and simultaneous captioners is projected to grow 3 percent from 2022 to 2032, about as fast as the average for all occupations.

About 2,100 openings for court reporters and simultaneous captioners are projected each year, on average, over the decade. Many of those openings are expected to result from the need to replace workers who transfer to different occupations or exit the labor force, such as to retire.

What Court Reporters and Simultaneous Captioners Do

Court reporters create word-for-word transcriptions at trials, depositions, administrative hearings, and other legal proceedings. Simultaneous captioners provide similar transcriptions for television or for presentations in other settings, such as press conferences and business meetings, for people who are deaf or hard of hearing.

Duties

Court reporters and simultaneous captioners typically do the following:

- Attend depositions, hearings, proceedings, and other events that require verbatim transcripts

Court reporters provide an accurate description of court proceedings.

- Capture spoken dialogue with special equipment, such as stenography machines and digital recording devices
- Report speakers' identification, gestures, and actions
- Read or play back portions of events or legal proceedings upon request
- Ask speakers to clarify inaudible statements or testimony
- Review notes they have taken, including the spelling of names and technical terminology
- Provide copies of transcripts and recordings to the parties involved
- Transcribe television or movie dialogue for the benefit of viewers
- Provide real-time transcription of presentations in public forums for people who are deaf or hard of hearing

Court reporters have a critical role in legal proceedings, which require an exact record of what occurred. These workers are responsible for producing a complete, accurate, and secure transcript of depositions, trials, and other legal proceedings. The official record allows judges and lawyers to efficiently search for important information contained in the transcript. Court reporters also index and catalog exhibits used during legal proceedings.

Simultaneous captioners primarily serve people who are deaf or hard of hearing by transcribing speech to text as the speech occurs. They typically work in settings other than courtrooms or law offices.

The following are examples of types of simultaneous captioners:

Broadcast captioners provide transcriptions for television programs (called closed captions). They capture dialogue for displaying to television viewers, primarily those who are deaf or hard of hearing. Some broadcast captioners may transcribe dialogue in real time during broadcasts; others caption during the program's postproduction.

Communication access real-time translation (CART) providers work primarily with people who are deaf or hard of hearing during meetings, doctors' appointments, and other situations requiring real-time transcription. For example, CART providers may caption the dialogue of college classes and present an immediate transcript to students who are learning English as a second language.

Although some simultaneous captioners accompany their clients to events, many broadcast captioners and CART providers do not. Establishing remote access allows these workers to hear and type dialogue without having to be physically present in the room.

Court reporters and simultaneous captioners turn dialogue into text for a variety of audiences. For information about workers who convey dialogue through sign language, cued speech, or other means to people who are deaf or hard of hearing, see the profile on interpreters and translators.

Court reporters and simultaneous captioners use different methods for recording speech, such as stenotype machines, steno masks, and digital recording devices.

Stenotype machines work like keyboards but create words through key combinations rather than single characters, allowing court reporters to keep up with fast-moving dialogue.

With steno masks, court reporters and simultaneous captioners speak directly into a covered microphone to record dialogue and to describe gestures and actions. Because the microphone is covered, others cannot hear what the reporter or captioner is saying.

Digital recording devices create an audio or video file rather than a written transcript. In addition to recording dialogue, court reporters and simultaneous captioners who use this equipment also take notes to identify the speakers and provide context for the recording. In some cases, they use the audio recording to create a written transcript.

Work Environment

Court reporters and simultaneous captioners held about 21,300 jobs in 2022. The largest employers of court reporters and simultaneous captioners were as follows:

Self-employed workers	31%
Business support services	23
Local government, excluding education and hospitals	22
State government, excluding education and hospitals	19

Most court reporters work in courts or legislatures. Many are self-employed (freelance) reporters who are hired by law firms or corporations for pretrial depositions and other events on an as-needed basis.

Some court reporters and simultaneous captioners travel to other locations, such as meeting sites or public events. Simultaneous captioners may work remotely from either their home or a central office.

Because of the speed and accuracy required to capture a verbatim record and the time-sensitive nature of legal proceedings, court reporting positions may be stressful.

Work Schedules

Court reporters and simultaneous captioners who work in a legal setting or office typically work full time recording events and preparing transcripts. Freelance reporters often have more flexibility in their work schedules.

How to Become a Court Reporter or Simultaneous Captioner

Many community colleges and technical institutes offer postsecondary certificate programs for court reporters and simultaneous captioners. These workers typically on-the-job training; the length of training varies by type of reporting or captioning. Many states require court reporters and simultaneous captioners to have a state license or a certification from a professional association.

Education

Many court reporters and simultaneous captioners attend programs at community colleges or technical institutes that lead to either a certificate or an associate's degree. Either credential qualifies applicants for many entry-level positions. Certification programs prepare students to pass the licensing exams and typing-speed tests required by most states and employers.

Most court reporting programs include courses in English grammar and phonetics, legal procedures, and legal terminology. Students also practice preparing transcripts to improve the speed and accuracy of their work.

Some schools also offer training in the use of different transcription equipment, such as stenotype machines or steno masks.

Completing a court reporting program typically takes 2 or 3 years.

Court reporters may work in courtrooms or office buildings.

Court reporters must give their full attention to the speaker and capture every word that is said.

Licenses, Certifications, and Registrations

Many states require court reporters and simultaneous captioners to be licensed or certified by a professional association. Licensing requirements vary by state and by method of reporting or captioning.

The National Court Reporters Association (NCRA) offers certification for court reporters and simultaneous captioners. Currently, about half of states accept or use the Registered Professional Reporter (RPR) certification in place of a state certification or licensing exam.

Digital and voice reporters may obtain certification through the American Association of Electronic Reporters and Transcribers (AAERT), which offers the Certified Electronic Reporter (CER) and Certified Electronic Transcriber (CET) designations.

Voice reporters also may obtain certification through the National Verbatim Reporters Association (NVRA). As with the RPR designation, some states with certification or licensing requirements accept the NVRA designation in place of a state license.

Certification through the NCRA, AAERT, and NVRA all require the successful completion of a written test, as well as a skills test in which applicants must type, record, or transcribe a minimum number of words per minute with a high level of accuracy.

In addition, all associations require court reporters and simultaneous captioners to obtain a certain amount of continuing education credits in order to renew their certification.

For more information on certification, exams, and continuing education requirements, visit the specific association's website. State licensing and continuing education requirements are available on the state association's or state judicial agency's website.

Training

After completing their formal program, court reporters and simultaneous captioners must undergo on-the-job training. The length of training varies by type of reporting or captioning but typically includes training on the specific equipment and technical terminology that may be used during complex medical or legal proceedings.

Important Qualities

Concentration. Court reporters and simultaneous captioners must be able to focus for long periods so that they remain attentive to the dialogue they are recording.

Detail oriented. Court reporters and simultaneous captioners must produce error-free work because they create transcripts that serve as legal records.

Listening skills. Court reporters and simultaneous captioners must give their full attention to speakers and capture every word that is said.

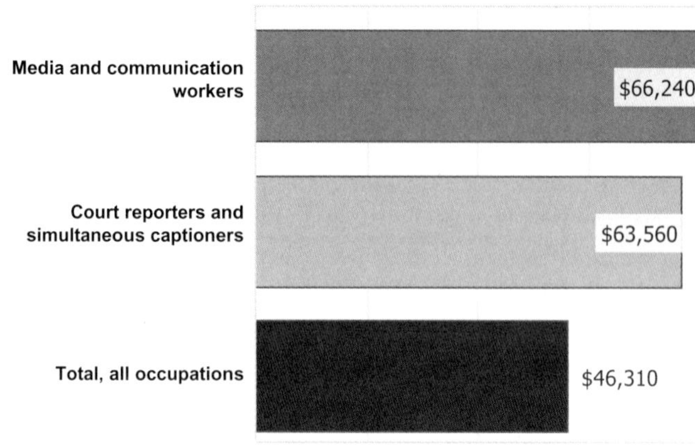

Note: All Occupations includes all occupations in the U.S. Economy.
Source: U.S. Bureau of Labor Statistics, Occupational Employment and Wage Statistics.

Writing skills. Court reporters and simultaneous captioners need a good command of grammar, vocabulary, and punctuation.

Pay

The median annual wage for court reporters and simultaneous captioners was $63,560 in May 2022. The median wage is the wage at which half the workers in an occupation earned more than that amount and half earned less. The lowest 10 percent earned less than $33,030, and the highest 10 percent earned more than $116,380.

In May 2022, the median annual wages for court reporters and simultaneous captioners in the top industries in which they worked were as follows:

Local government, excluding education and hospitals	$70,290
State government, excluding education and hospitals	67,230
Business support services	44,840

Freelance court reporters and simultaneous captioners typically charge an hourly rate; court reporters may also sell additional copies of the transcript, usually charging a set price per page.

Court reporters and simultaneous captioners who work in a legal setting or office typically work full time recording events and preparing transcripts. Freelance reporters often have more flexibility in their work schedules.

Job Outlook

Employment of court reporters and simultaneous captioners is projected to grow 3 percent from 2022 to 2032, about as fast as the average for all occupations.

About 2,100 openings for court reporters and simultaneous captioners are projected each year, on average, over the decade.

Court Reporters and Simultaneous Captioners

Percent change in employment, projected 2022-32

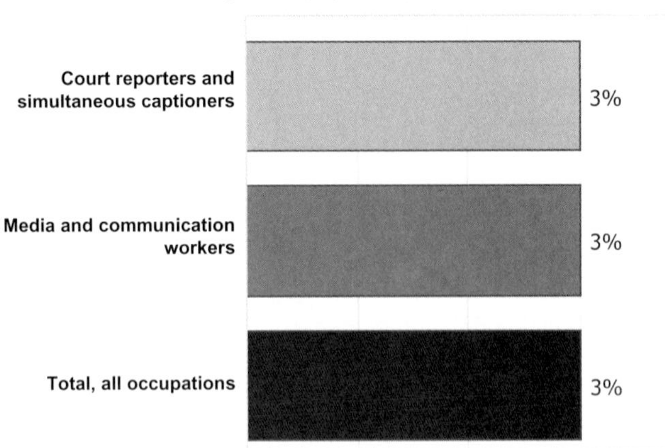

Note: All Occupations includes all occupations in the U.S. Economy.
Source: U.S. Bureau of Labor Statistics, Employment Projections program

Many of those openings are expected to result from the need to replace workers who transfer to different occupations or exit the labor force, such as to retire.

Employment

Court reporters will continue to be needed to create detailed, accurate records of legal proceedings. However, state and local government budgets may affect the employment of court reporters because judicial budgets are contingent on available funds.

Demand for simultaneous captioners will be influenced by federal regulations requiring an expanded use of captioning for television, the internet, and other technologies. New television programming will continue to need closed captioning, and networks will likely expand their use of broadcast captioners to comply with federal regulations.

An increase in the number of older people, a group that may experience hearing loss, also will spur demand for simultaneous captioners who provide communication access real-time translation (CART) or who accompany clients to proceedings such as doctor appointments, town hall meetings, or religious services. In addition, movie theaters and sports stadiums will provide closed captioning for attendees who are deaf or hard of hearing.

Employment projections data for court reporters and simultaneous captioners, 2022-32

Occupational Title	SOC Code	Employment, 2022	Projected Employment, 2032	Change, 2022-32		Employment by Industry
				Percent	Numeric	
SOURCE: U.S. Bureau of Labor Statistics, Employment Projections program						
Court reporters and simultaneous captioners	27-3092	21,300	21,900	3	600	Get data

Contacts for More Information

For more information, visit

- National Court Reporters Association
- American Association of Electronic Reporters and Transcribers
- National Verbatim Reporters Association

Judges and Hearing Officers

Summary

Quick Facts: Judges and Hearing Officers

2022 Median Pay	$128,610 per year $61.83 per hour
Typical Entry-Level Education	Doctoral or professional degree
Work Experience in a Related Occupation	5 years or more
On-the-job Training	Short-term on-the-job training
Number of Jobs, 2022	42,800
Job Outlook, 2022-32	2% (As fast as average)
Employment Change, 2022-32	800

What Judges and Hearing Officers Do

Judges and hearing officers apply the law by overseeing the legal process in courts.

Work Environment

All judges and hearing officers are employed by the federal government or by local and state governments. Most work in courts.

How to Become a Judge or Hearing Officer

Judges typically have law degrees and work experience as lawyers. However, some administrative law judge, hearing officer, and magistrate positions require only a bachelor's degree.

Pay

The median annual wage for administrative law judges, adjudicators, and hearing officers was $94,990 in May 2022.

The median annual wage for judges, magistrate judges, and magistrates was $151,030 in May 2022.

Job Outlook

Overall employment of judges and hearing officers is projected to grow 2 percent from 2022 to 2032, about as fast as the average for all occupations.

Judges and hearing officers research and apply laws to reach judgments or resolve disputes between parties.

About 1,700 openings for judges and hearing officers are projected each year, on average, over the decade. Many of those openings are expected to result from the need to replace workers who transfer to different occupations or exit the labor force, such as to retire.

What Judges and Hearing Officers Do

Judges and hearing officers apply the law by overseeing the legal process in courts. They also conduct pretrial hearings, resolve administrative disputes, facilitate negotiations between opposing parties, and issue legal decisions.

Judges preside over hearings and listen to the arguments of opposing parties.

Duties

Judges and hearing officers typically do the following:

- Research legal issues
- Read and evaluate information from documents, such as motions, claim applications, and records
- Preside over hearings and listen to and read arguments by opposing parties
- Determine if the information presented supports the charge, claim, or dispute
- Decide if the procedure is being conducted according to the rules and law
- Apply laws or precedents to reach judgments and to resolve disputes between parties
- Write opinions, decisions, and instructions regarding cases, claims, and disputes

Judges commonly preside over trials and hearings of cases regarding nearly every aspect of society, from individual traffic offenses to issues concerning the rights of large corporations. Judges listen to arguments and determine if the evidence presented deserves a trial. In criminal cases, judges may decide that people charged with crimes should be held in jail until the trial, or they may set conditions for their release. They also approve search warrants and arrest warrants.

Judges interpret the law to determine how a trial will proceed, which is particularly important when unusual circumstances arise for which standard procedures have not been established. They ensure that hearings and trials are conducted fairly and that the legal rights of all involved parties are protected.

In trials in which juries are selected to decide the case, judges instruct jurors on applicable laws and direct them to consider the facts from the evidence. For other trials, judges decide the case. A judge who determines guilt in criminal cases may impose a sentence or penalty on the guilty party. In civil cases, the judge may award relief, such as compensation for damages, to the parties who win lawsuits.

Judges use various forms of technology, such as electronic databases and software, to manage cases and to prepare for trials. In some cases, a judge may manage the court's administrative and clerical staff.

The following are examples of types of judges and hearing officers:

Judges, magistrate judges, and magistrates preside over trials and hearings. They typically work in local, state, and federal courts.

In local and state court systems, they have a variety of titles, such as *municipal court judge*, *county court judge*, and *justice of the peace*. Traffic violations, misdemeanors, small-claims cases, and pretrial hearings make up the bulk of these judges' work.

In federal and state court systems, *district court judges* and *general trial court judges* have authority over any case in their system. *Appellate court judges* rule on a small number of cases,

Judges do some of their work in courtrooms.

by reviewing decisions of the lower courts and lawyers' written and oral arguments.

Administrative law judges, adjudicators, and hearing officers usually work for local, state, and federal government agencies. They decide many issues, such as whether a person is eligible for workers' compensation benefits or whether employment discrimination occurred.

Work Environment

Administrative law judges, adjudicators, and hearing officers held about 13,200 jobs in 2022. The largest employers of administrative law judges, adjudicators, and hearing officers were as follows:

State government, excluding education and hospitals	58%
Federal government	25
Local government, excluding education and hospitals	17

Judges, magistrate judges, and magistrates held about 29,600 jobs in 2022. The largest employers of judges, magistrate judges, and magistrates were as follows:

State government, excluding education and hospitals	57%
Local government, excluding education and hospitals	43

Judges and hearing officers do most of their work in offices and courtrooms. Their jobs can be demanding, because they must sit in the same position in the court or hearing room for long periods and give undivided attention to the process.

Some judges and hearing officers may be required to travel to different counties and courthouses throughout their state.

The work may be stressful as judges and hearing officers sometimes work with difficult or confrontational individuals.

Work Schedules

Some courthouses have evening and weekend hours. In addition, judges may have to be on call during nights or weekends to issue emergency orders, such as search warrants and restraining orders.

How to Become a Judge or Hearing Officer

Judges and hearing officers typically need a law degree and work experience as a lawyer.

Education

Although there may be a few positions available for those with a bachelor's degree, a Juris Doctor (J.D.) degree is typically required for most jobs as a local, state, or federal judge or hearing officer.

In addition to earning a law degree, federal administrative law judges must pass a competitive exam from the U.S. Office of Personnel Management.

Earning a law degree usually takes 7 years of full-time study after high school: 4 years of undergraduate study in any field, followed by 3 years of law school. Law degree programs include courses such as constitutional law, contracts, property law, civil procedure, and legal writing.

Most judges and magistrates must be appointed or elected into their positions, a procedure that often requires political support. Many local and state judges are appointed to serve fixed renewable terms, ranging from 4 to 14 years. A few judges, such as appellate court judges, are appointed for life. Judicial

Judges must be able to listen well to the facts provided by opposing parties.

nominating commissions screen candidates for judgeships in many states and for some federal judgeships.

For specific state information, including information on the number of judgeships by state, term lengths, and requirements for qualification, visit the National Center for State Courts.

Work Experience in a Related Occupation

Most judges and hearing officers learn their skills through years of experience as practicing lawyers. Some states allow those who are not lawyers to hold limited-jurisdiction judgeships, but opportunities are better for those with law experience.

Training

All states have some type of orientation and training requirements for newly elected or appointed judges. The Federal Judicial Center, American Bar Association, National Judicial College, and National Center for State Courts provide judicial education and training for judges and other judicial branch personnel.

More than half of all states, as well as Puerto Rico, require judges to take continuing education courses while serving on the bench. General and continuing education courses usually last from a few days to 3 weeks.

Licenses, Certifications, and Registrations

Most judges and hearing officers are required to have a law license. In addition, they typically must maintain their law license and good standing with their state bar association while working as a judge or hearing officer.

Advancement

Advancement for some judicial workers means moving to courts with a broader jurisdiction. Advancement for various hearing officers includes taking on more complex cases, practicing law, and becoming district court judges.

Important Qualities

Critical-thinking skills. Judges and hearing officers must apply rules of law. They cannot let their own personal assumptions interfere with the proceedings. For example, they must base their decisions on specific meanings of the law when evaluating and deciding whether a person is a threat to others and must be sent to jail.

Decision-making skills. Judges and hearing officers must be able to weigh the facts, to apply the law and rules, and to make a decision relatively quickly.

Listening skills. Judges and hearing officers evaluate information, so they must pay close attention to what is being said.

Reading skills. Judges and hearing officers must be able to distinguish important facts from large amounts of sometimes complex information and then evaluate the facts objectively.

Writing skills. Judges and hearing officers write recommendations and decisions on appeals and disputes. They must be able to write their decisions clearly so that all sides understand the decision.

Pay

The median annual wage for administrative law judges, adjudicators, and hearing officers was $94,990 in May 2022. The median wage is the wage at which half the workers in an occupation earned more than that amount and half earned less. The lowest 10 percent earned less than $46,070, and the highest 10 percent earned more than $151,470.

The median annual wage for judges, magistrate judges, and magistrates was $151,030 in May 2022. The lowest 10 percent earned less than $46,470, and the highest 10 percent earned more than $227,850.

In May 2022, the median annual wages for administrative law judges, adjudicators, and hearing officers in the top industries in which they worked were as follows:

Federal government	$114,340
Local government, excluding education and hospitals	90,460
State government, excluding education and hospitals	83,390

In May 2022, the median annual wages for judges, magistrate judges, and magistrates in the top industries in which they worked were as follows:

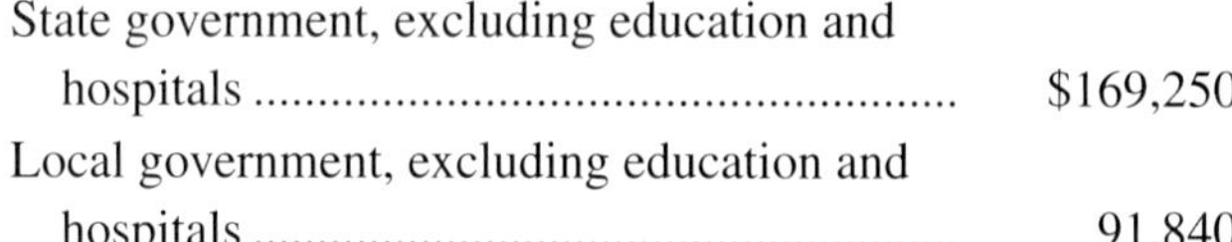

State government, excluding education and hospitals	$169,250
Local government, excluding education and hospitals	91,840

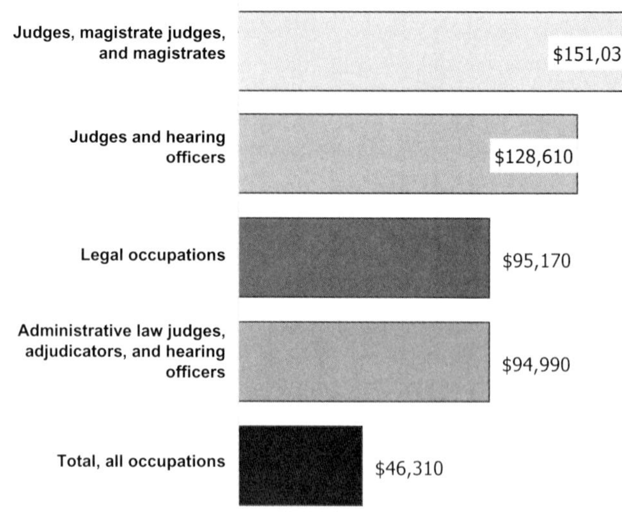

Note: All Occupations includes all occupations in the U.S. Economy.
Source: U.S. Bureau of Labor Statistics, Occupational Employment and Wage Statistics

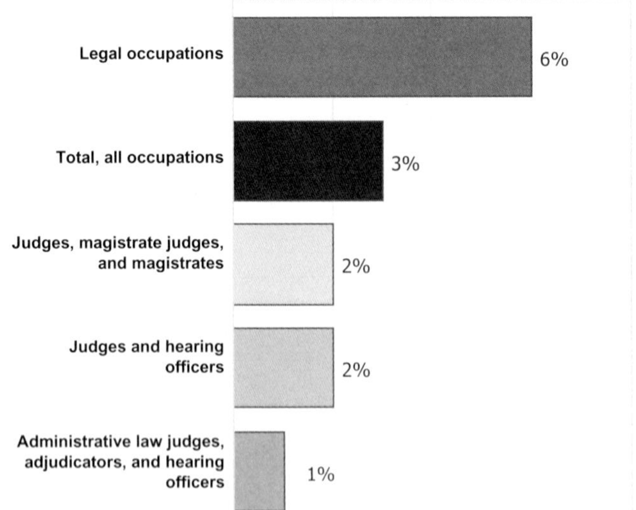

Note: All Occupations includes all occupations in the U.S. Economy.
Source: U.S. Bureau of Labor Statistics, Employment Projections program

Some courthouses have evening and weekend hours. In addition, judges have to be on call during nights or weekends to issue emergency orders, such as search warrants and restraining orders.

Job Outlook

Overall employment of judges and hearing officers is projected to grow 2 percent from 2022 to 2032, about as fast as the average for all occupations.

About 1,700 openings for judges and hearing officers are projected each year, on average, over the decade. Many of those openings are expected to result from the need to replace workers who transfer to different occupations or exit the labor force, such as to retire.

Employment

These workers play an essential role in the legal system, and their services will continue to be needed into the future. However, budgetary constraints in federal, state, and local governments may limit the ability of these governments to fill vacant judge and hearing officer positions or authorize new ones. If there are governmental budget concerns, this could limit the employment growth opportunities of hearing officers and administrative law judges working for local, state, and federal government agencies, despite the continued need for these workers to settle disputes.

Employment projections data for judges and hearing officers, 2022-32

Occupational Title	SOC Code	Employment, 2022	Projected Employment, 2032	Change, 2022-32		Employment by Industry
				Percent	Numeric	
SOURCE: U.S. Bureau of Labor Statistics, Employment Projections program						
Judges and hearing officers	—	42,800	43,600	2	800	
Administrative law judges, adjudicators, and hearing officers	23-1021	13,200	13,400	1	100	Get data
Judges, magistrate judges, and magistrates	23-1023	29,600	30,200	2	700	Get data

Contacts for More Information

For more information, visit

- National Center for State Courts
- Administrative Office of the United States Courts
- U.S. Office of Personnel Management
- American Bar Association
- Federal Judicial Center
- The National Judicial College

Lawyers

Summary

Quick Facts: Lawyers	
2022 Median Pay	$135,740 per year $65.26 per hour
Typical Entry-Level Education	Doctoral or professional degree
Work Experience in a Related Occupation	None
On-the-job Training	None
Number of Jobs, 2022	826,300
Job Outlook, 2022-32	8% (Faster than average)
Employment Change, 2022-32	62,400

What Lawyers Do
Lawyers advise and represent clients on legal proceedings or transactions.

Work Environment
Lawyers work for a variety of organizations, usually in office settings. Some work for federal, local, or state governments. Most work full time, and some work more than 40 hours per week.

How to Become a Lawyer
Lawyers typically need a law degree and a state license, which usually requires passing a bar examination.

Pay
The median annual wage for lawyers was $135,740 in May 2022.

Job Outlook
Employment of lawyers is projected to grow 8 percent from 2022 to 2032, faster than the average for all occupations.

About 39,100 openings for lawyers are projected each year, on average, over the decade. Many of those openings are expected to result from the need to replace workers who transfer to different occupations or exit the labor force, such as to retire.

What Lawyers Do
Lawyers advise and represent clients on legal proceedings or transactions.

Duties
Lawyers typically do the following:

- Advise and represent clients in criminal or civil proceedings and in other legal matters
- Communicate with clients, colleagues, judges, and others involved in a case
- Conduct research and analysis of legal issues
- Interpret laws, rulings, and regulations for individuals and businesses
- Present facts and findings relevant to a case on behalf of their clients
- Prepare and file legal documents, such as lawsuits, contracts, and wills

Lawyers, also called *attorneys*, research the intent of laws and judicial decisions and determine whether they apply to the specific circumstances of their client's case. They act as both advocates and advisors for one party in a criminal (offense against the state or the nation) or civil (matters between individuals or organizations) proceeding.

As advocates, they may present evidence and argue in support of their client for settlements outside of court, such as through plea bargaining or arbitration, or during court appearances, such as in hearings and trials. As advisors, they counsel clients about their legal rights, obligations, and options and suggest courses of action.

Lawyers advise and represent individuals, businesses, or government agencies on legal issues or disputes.

Lawyers represent clients in criminal or civil proceedings, including trials.

Lawyers may have different titles and duties, depending on where they work.

For example, in law firms, lawyers perform legal work for individuals or businesses. Those who represent clients accused of wrongdoing or carelessness may be called *criminal law attorneys* or *defense attorneys*. Those whose expertise includes representing clients in trials are sometimes called *litigators* or *trial lawyers*.

Corporate counsels, also called *in-house counsels*, are lawyers who work for a single organization. They advise the organization's executives about legal issues related to its business activities, such as patents, contracts with other companies, taxes, and collective-bargaining agreements with unions.

Attorneys in federal, state, and local governments may have a variety of titles, including prosecutor, public defender, or general counsel. *Prosecutors* typically pursue the government's charges against an individual or organization accused of violating the law. *Public defense attorneys* represent criminal defendants who cannot afford to hire a private attorney. *Government counsels* help write regulations, interpret laws, and set up enforcement procedures, and they may argue cases on behalf of the government.

Public-interest lawyers work for organizations that provide legal services to disadvantaged people or to others who otherwise might not be able to afford legal representation. They often handle cases involving issues related to social justice or individual liberty, such as housing discrimination or consumer rights.

Lawyers may oversee the work of support staff, such as paralegals and legal assistants and legal secretaries.

In addition to working in different industries, lawyers may specialize in particular legal fields, including the following:

Environmental lawyers deal with issues and regulations that are related to the natural world. They may work for advocacy groups, waste disposal companies, or corporations. In government agencies, such as the U.S. Environmental Protection Agency, they help to ensure compliance with relevant laws.

Family lawyers handle a variety of legal issues that pertain to spousal, parent-child, and other familial relationships. They may advise and advocate for clients in proceedings on topics such as divorce, child custody, and adoption. Family lawyers also may work for local, state, or federal agencies to ensure compliance with relevant government regulations.

Intellectual property lawyers deal with the laws related to inventions, patents, trademarks, and creative works, such as music, books, and movies. For example, an intellectual property lawyer may advise clients about whether they may use published material in a forthcoming book. Some intellectual property lawyers work for the U.S. Patent and Trademark Office.

Personal injury lawyers represent clients in civil proceedings who have been harmed by the actions or lack of action by another party.

Lawyers typically work in law offices.

Securities lawyers work on legal issues arising from the buying and selling of financial instruments. They may advise corporations that are interested in listing on a stock exchange through an initial public offering (IPO) or in buying shares in another corporation. In government, they may work for their state's securities regulator or for a federal regulatory agency, such as the U.S. Securities and Exchange Commission.

Tax lawyers handle a variety of tax-related issues for individuals and organizations. They may help clients navigate complex tax regulations, handle tax disputes, and represent clients in court on tax-related matters. Tax lawyers also may work for government agencies, such as the Internal Revenue Service (IRS).

Those who handle a range of legal issues without specializing in a particular area of law are known as *general practice lawyers*. These lawyers may handle criminal and civil matters related to common legal matters, such as traffic violations, wills and estate planning, and real estate negotiations.

Work Environment

Lawyers held about 826,300 jobs in 2022. The largest employers of lawyers were as follows:

Legal services	52%
Self-employed workers	13
Local government, excluding education and hospitals	8
State government, excluding education and hospitals	6
Federal government	5

Lawyers work mostly in office settings. They may travel to meet with current or prospective clients at various locations, such as homes or prisons, and to appear in court.

Lawyers' work may be stressful, such as during trials or when meeting deadlines.

All lawyers must have a law degree and must also typically pass a state's written bar examination.

Work Schedules

Most lawyers work full time, and some work more than 40 hours per week. Lawyers who are self-employed may have flexibility in setting their own schedules.

How to Become a Lawyer

Lawyers typically need a law degree and a state license, which usually requires passing a bar examination.

Education

Becoming a lawyer usually takes 7 years of full-time study after high school: 4 years of undergraduate study followed by 3 years of law school. Although most law schools do not require a specific bachelor's degree for entry, common undergraduate fields of study include law and legal studies, history, and social science.

Most states and jurisdictions require lawyers to earn a Juris Doctor (J.D.) degree from a law school accredited by the American Bar Association (ABA). ABA-accredited programs include courses such as constitutional law, contracts, property law, civil procedure, and legal writing.

As part of their admissions process, law schools may consider an applicant's score on the Law School Admission Test (LSAT). LSAT questions cover reasoning, writing, and other aptitudes needed for the study of law.

Those interested in pursuing a career in some legal fields may need to meet additional requirements. For example, patent lawyers typically need a degree, specific credits, or a background in science or engineering and must pass an exam administered by the U.S. Patent and Trademark Office (commonly known as the patent bar exam). Tax lawyers may choose to earn a Master of Laws (LL.M) degree in tax after completing a J.D. program.

Licenses, Certifications, and Registrations

Prospective lawyers take a licensing exam, called the "bar exam." Most states have adopted the Uniform Bar Exam, which is coordinated by the National Conference of Bar Examiners (NCBE). A score from the uniform exam is transferable across jurisdictions that accept it.

Lawyers who receive a license to practice law are "admitted to the bar." Each state's highest court establishes its rules for bar admission. Rules for federal courts differ, and requirements vary by state and jurisdiction. For more details on individual state and jurisdiction requirements, visit the NCBE.

Most states require that applicants graduate from an ABA-accredited law school, pass the written bar exam, and be found by an admitting board to have the character to represent and advise others. Prior felony convictions, academic misconduct, and a history of substance abuse are examples of factors that may disqualify an applicant from being admitted to the bar.

Lawyers who want to practice in more than one state usually must meet licensing requirements for each state in which they wish to work. Most states have reciprocity agreements that streamline the process for lawyers licensed in one state to get licensed in another state.

After bar admission, lawyers must keep informed about legal developments that affect their practice. States may require lawyers to participate in continuing legal education to maintain licensure.

Other Experience

Law students who have completed their first or second year of law school may be eligible for part-time jobs or summer internships in law firms, government agencies, and organizations' legal departments. Gaining experience in these summer positions may help law students decide on an area of legal focus for their careers. As for students in many fields, successful completion of a summer job or internship may result in an offer of employment after graduation.

Some law school graduates pursue a judicial clerkship prior to working as a lawyer. Clerkships are typically a specified length of time, such as 1- or 2-year terms, and help law school graduates develop skills required for a legal career. Judges may prefer to hire clerks who have passed the bar exam, but clerks may work without a law license because they have limited duties and are not yet practicing lawyers.

Advancement

Newly hired attorneys usually start as associates and work on teams with more experienced lawyers. Some lawyers advance to become partners, which means that they are partial owners of the firm.

After gaining experience, some lawyers go into practice for themselves. Others may move to a large organization, either working in its legal department or as in-house counsel.

Some experienced lawyers become judges. Most judges must be appointed or elected to their positions, a procedure that often requires political support.

Important Qualities

Analytical skills. Lawyers interpret the law as it applies to their client's case. They must be able to evaluate large amounts of information, interpret relevant findings, and apply them to facts.

Communication skills. Lawyers must be able to clearly present and explain information to clients, opposing parties, and other members of the legal community. They also need to be precise when preparing documents, such as court filings and wills.

Interpersonal skills. Lawyers must build relationships with current and prospective clients, as well as with their colleagues and other members of the legal community.

Persuasion. Lawyers work to convince others that particular laws or findings apply to their client's case in a way that is most favorable to their client.

Problem-solving skills. Lawyers must evaluate information to propose viable solutions, mediate disputes, and reach agreements or settlements for their clients.

Research skills. Lawyers need to find laws and regulations that apply to a specific matter in order to provide appropriate legal advice for their clients.

Pay

The median annual wage for lawyers was $135,740 in May 2022. The median wage is the wage at which half the workers in an occupation earned more than that amount and half earned less. The lowest 10 percent earned less than $66,470, and the highest 10 percent earned more than $239,200.

In May 2022, the median annual wages for lawyers in the top industries in which they worked were as follows:

Federal government	$158,370
Legal services	132,120
Local government, excluding education and hospitals	109,140
State government, excluding education and hospitals	97,640

These wage data do not cover self-employed workers or owners and partners of unincorporated businesses.

Most lawyers work full time, and some work more than 40 hours per week. Lawyers who are self-employed may have flexibility in setting their own schedules.

Job Outlook

Employment of lawyers is projected to grow 8 percent from 2022 to 2032, faster than the average for all occupations.

About 39,100 openings for lawyers are projected each year, on average, over the decade. Many of those openings are expected to result from the need to replace workers who

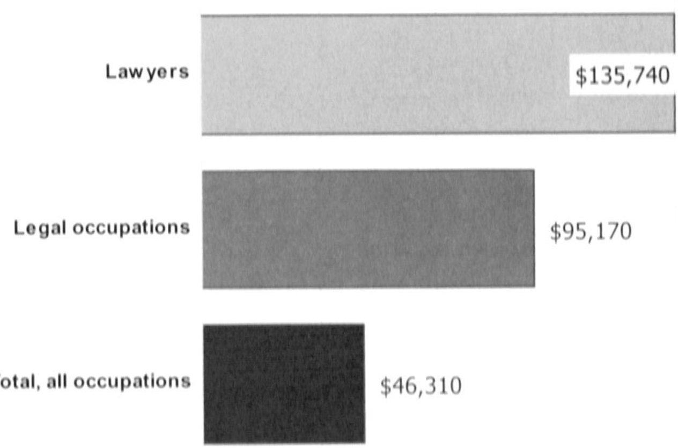

Note: All Occupations includes all occupations in the U.S. Economy.
Source: U.S. Bureau of Labor Statistics, Occupational Employment and Wage Statistics
Source: U.S. Bureau of Labor Statistics, Occupational Employment and Wage Statistics.

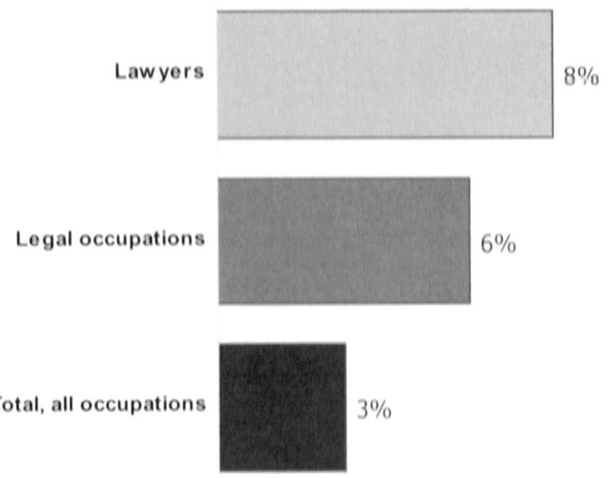

Note: All Occupations includes all occupations in the U.S. Economy.
Source: U.S. Bureau of Labor Statistics, Employment Projections program

transfer to different occupations or exit the labor force, such as to retire.

Employment

Demand for legal work is expected to continue as individuals, businesses, and all levels of government require legal services in many areas.

Despite this need for legal services, more price competition over the projections decade may lead law firms to rethink project staffing to reduce costs to clients. Clients are expected to cut back on legal expenses by negotiating rates and scrutinizing invoices. Some routine legal work may be outsourced to lower cost legal providers located overseas.

Although law firms will continue to be among the largest employers of lawyers, many large corporations are increasing their in-house legal departments to cut costs.

Employment projections data for lawyers, 2022-32

Occupational Title	SOC Code	Employment, 2022	Projected Employment, 2032	Change, 2022-32		Employment by Industry
				Percent	Numeric	
Lawyers	23-1011	826,300	888,700	8	62,400	Get data

SOURCE: U.S. Bureau of Labor Statistics, Employment Projections program

Contacts for More Information

For more information about law schools and a career in law, visit

- American Bar Association
- National Association for Law Placement
- Law School Admission Council
- National Conference of Bar Examiners
- USAJobs

Paralegals and Legal Assistants

Summary

Quick Facts: Paralegals and Legal Assistants

2022 Median Pay	$59,200 per year $28.46 per hour
Typical Entry-Level Education	Associate's degree
Work Experience in a Related Occupation	None
On-the-job Training	None
Number of Jobs, 2022	354,300
Job Outlook, 2022-32	4% (As fast as average)
Employment Change, 2022-32	14,800

What Paralegals and Legal Assistants Do

Paralegals and legal assistants perform a variety of tasks to support lawyers.

Paralegals and legal assistants help lawyers prepare for hearings, trials, and corporate meetings.

Work Environment

Paralegals and legal assistants are found in all types of organizations, but most work for law firms, corporate legal departments, and government agencies. They usually work full time, and some may have to work more than 40 hours a week to meet deadlines.

How to Become a Paralegal or Legal Assistant

Most paralegals and legal assistants have at least an associate's degree or a certificate in paralegal studies. In some cases, employers may hire college graduates with a bachelor's degree but no legal experience or specialized education and train them on the job.

Pay

The median annual wage for paralegals and legal assistants was $59,200 in May 2022.

Job Outlook

Employment of paralegals and legal assistants is projected to grow 4 percent from 2022 to 2032, about as fast as the average for all occupations.

About 38,000 openings for paralegals and legal assistants are projected each year, on average, over the decade. Many of those openings are expected to result from the need to replace workers who transfer to different occupations or exit the labor force, such as to retire.

What Paralegals and Legal Assistants Do

Paralegals and legal assistants perform a variety of tasks to support lawyers, including maintaining and organizing files, conducting legal research, and drafting documents.

Paralegals and legal assistants may conduct legal research.

Duties

Paralegals and legal assistants typically do the following:

- Investigate and gather the facts of a case
- Conduct research on relevant laws, regulations, and legal articles
- Organize and maintain documents in paper or electronic filing systems
- Gather and arrange evidence and other legal documents for attorney review and case preparation
- Write or summarize reports to help lawyers prepare for trials
- Draft correspondence and legal documents, such as contracts and mortgages
- Get affidavits and other formal statements that may be used as evidence in court
- Help lawyers during trials by handling exhibits, taking notes, or reviewing trial transcripts
- File exhibits, briefs, appeals and other legal documents with the court or opposing counsel
- Call clients, witnesses, lawyers, and outside vendors to schedule interviews, meetings, and depositions

Paralegals and legal assistants help lawyers prepare for hearings, trials, and corporate meetings.

Paralegals use technology and computer software for managing and organizing the increasing amount of documents and data collected during a case. Many paralegals use computer software to catalog documents, and to review documents for specific keywords or subjects. Because of these responsibilities, paralegals must be familiar with electronic database management and be current on the latest software used for electronic discovery. Electronic discovery refers to all electronic materials obtained by the parties during the litigation or investigation. These materials may be emails, data, documents, accounting databases, and websites.

Paralegals' specific duties often vary depending on the area of law in which they work. The following are examples of types of paralegals and legal assistants:

Corporate paralegals, for example, often help lawyers prepare employee contracts, shareholder agreements, stock-option plans, and companies' annual financial reports. Corporate paralegals may monitor and review government regulations to ensure that the corporation is aware of new legal requirements.

Litigation paralegals maintain documents received from clients, conduct research for lawyers, retrieve and organize evidence for use at depositions and trials, and draft settlement agreements. Some litigation paralegals may also help coordinate the logistics of attending a trial, including reserving office space, transporting exhibits and documents to the courtroom, and setting up computers and other equipment.

Paralegals may also specialize in other legal areas, such as personal injury, criminal law, employee benefits, intellectual property, bankruptcy, immigration, family law, and real estate.

Specific job duties may also vary by the size of the law firm.

In small firms, paralegals' duties tend to vary more. In addition to reviewing and organizing documents, paralegals may prepare written reports that help lawyers determine how to handle their cases. If lawyers decide to file lawsuits on behalf of clients, paralegals may help draft documents to be filed with the court.

In large organizations, paralegals may work on a particular phase of a case, rather than handling a case from beginning to end. For example, paralegals may only review legal material

Most paralegals and legal assistants work in law offices.

for internal use, maintain reference files, conduct research for lawyers, or collect and organize evidence for hearings. After gaining experience, a paralegal may become responsible for more complicated tasks.

Unlike the work of other administrative and legal support staff employed in a law firm, the paralegal's work is often billed to the client.

Paralegals may have frequent interactions with clients and third-party vendors. In addition, experienced paralegals may assume supervisory responsibilities, such as overseeing team projects or delegating work to other paralegals.

Work Environment

Paralegals and legal assistants held about 354,300 jobs in 2022. The largest employers of paralegals and legal assistants were as follows:

Legal services	74%
Local government, excluding education and hospitals	5
Federal government	5
Finance and insurance	4
State government, excluding education and hospitals	3

Paralegals and legal assistants often work in teams with attorneys, fellow paralegals, and other legal support staff.

Paralegals do most of their work in offices. Occasionally, they may travel to gather information, collect and review documents, accompany attorneys to depositions or trials, and do other tasks.

Some of the work can be fast-paced, and paralegals must be able to work on multiple projects under tight deadlines.

Work Schedules

Most paralegals and legal assistants work full time. Some may work more than 40 hours per week in order to meet deadlines.

How to Become a Paralegal or Legal Assistant

Most paralegals and legal assistants have an associate's degree in paralegal studies, or a bachelor's degree in another field and a certificate in paralegal studies.

Education

There are several paths a person can take to become a paralegal. A common path is for candidates to earn an associate's degree in paralegal studies from a postsecondary institution.

However, many employers may prefer, or even require, applicants to have a bachelor's degree. Because only a small number of schools offer bachelor's degrees in paralegal studies, applicants typically have a bachelor's degree in another subject and earn a certificate in paralegal studies from a paralegal education program approved by the American Bar Association.

Many paralegals and legal assistants have an associate's degree or a certificate in paralegal studies.

Common fields of degree include social science, business, and security and protective service.

Associate's and bachelor's degree programs in paralegal studies or law and legal studies usually offer paralegal training courses in legal research, legal writing, and the legal applications of computers, along with courses in other academic subjects, such as corporate law and international law. Most certificate programs provide intensive paralegal training for people who already hold college degrees.

Employers sometimes hire college graduates with no legal experience or legal education and train them on the job.

Licenses, Certifications, and Registrations

Although not required, some employers may prefer to hire applicants who have completed a paralegal certification program.

Some national and local paralegal organizations offer voluntary paralegal certifications to students able to pass an exam. Other organizations offer voluntary paralegal certifications for paralegals who meet certain experience and education criteria.

Important Qualities

Communication skills. Paralegals must be able to document and present their research and related information to their supervising attorney.

Computer skills. Paralegals need to be familiar with using computers for legal research and litigation support. They also use computer programs for organizing and maintaining important documents.

Interpersonal skills. Paralegals spend most of their time working with clients and other professionals and must be able to develop good relationships. They must make clients feel comfortable sharing personal information related to their cases.

Organizational skills. Paralegals may be responsible for many cases at one time. They must adapt quickly to changing deadlines.

Research skills. Paralegals gather facts of the case and research information on relevant laws and regulations to

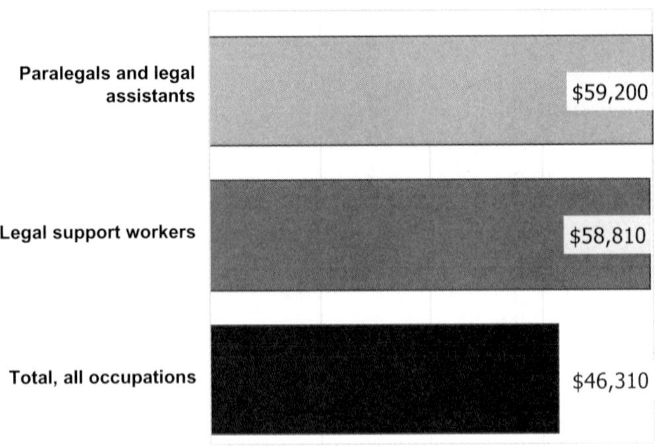

Note: All Occupations includes all occupations in the U.S. Economy.
Source: U.S. Bureau of Labor Statistics, Occupational Employment and Wage Statistics

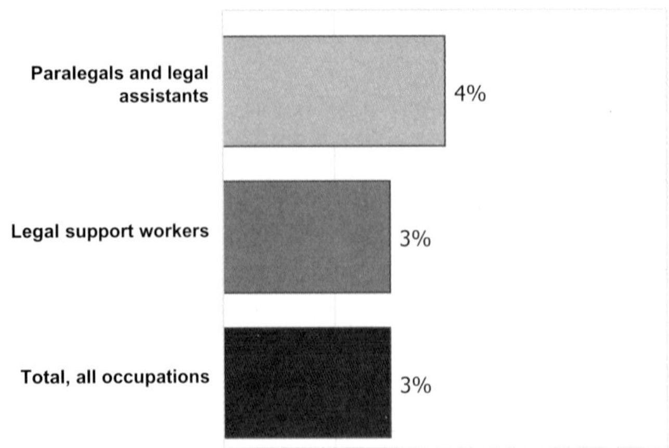

Note: All Occupations includes all occupations in the U.S. Economy.
Source: U.S. Bureau of Labor Statistics, Employment Projections program

prepare drafts of legal documents for attorneys and help them prepare for a case.

Pay

The median annual wage for paralegals and legal assistants was $59,200 in May 2022. The median wage is the wage at which half the workers in an occupation earned more than that amount and half earned less. The lowest 10 percent earned less than $37,690, and the highest 10 percent earned more than $94,960.

In May 2022, the median annual wages for paralegals and legal assistants in the top industries in which they worked were as follows:

Finance and insurance	$73,050
Federal government	72,320
Local government, excluding education and hospitals	58,000
Legal services	57,250
State government, excluding education and hospitals	50,310

Most paralegals and legal assistants work full time. Some may work more than 40 hours per week in order to meet deadlines.

Job Outlook

Employment of paralegals and legal assistants is projected to grow 4 percent from 2022 to 2032, about as fast as the average for all occupations.

About 38,000 openings for paralegals and legal assistants are projected each year, on average, over the decade. Many of those openings are expected to result from the need to replace workers who transfer to different occupations or exit the labor force, such as to retire.

Employment

Law firms will continue to be the largest employer of paralegals, as these workers are needed to help prepare and organize legal documents. However, many large corporations are increasing their in-house legal departments to cut costs. This should lead to an increase in the demand for legal workers in a variety of settings.

Occupational Title	SOC Code	Employment, 2022	Projected Employment, 2032	Change, 2022-32	
				Percent	Numeric
Paralegals and legal assistants	23-2011	354,300	369,100	4	14,800

Contacts for More Information

For more information, visit

- NALA – The National Association of Legal Assistants
- NALS – The Association for Legal Professionals
- National Federation of Paralegal Associations
- American Bar Association

Life, Physical, and Social Science

Agricultural and Food Science Technicians

Summary

Quick Facts: Agricultural and Food Science Technicians	
2022 Median Pay	$46,140 per year $22.18 per hour
Typical Entry-Level Education	Associate's degree
Work Experience in a Related Occupation	None
On-the-job Training	Moderate-term on-the-job training
Number of Jobs, 2022	38,800
Job Outlook, 2022-32	5% (Faster than average)
Employment Change, 2022-32	1,900

What Agricultural and Food Science Technicians Do

Agricultural and food science technicians assist agricultural and food scientists.

Work Environment

Agricultural and food science technicians work in laboratories, processing plants, farms and ranches, greenhouses, and offices.

How to Become an Agricultural or Food Science Technician

Agricultural and food science technicians typically need an associate's degree in biology, chemistry, crop or animal science, or a related field. Some positions require candidates to have a bachelor's degree, and others a high school diploma or equivalent plus related work experience.

Pay

The median annual wage for agricultural technicians was $41,760 in May 2022.

The median annual wage for food science technicians was $47,860 in May 2022.

Job Outlook

Overall employment of agricultural and food science technicians is projected to grow 5 percent from 2022 to 2032, faster than the average for all occupations.

About 5,500 openings for agricultural and food science technicians are projected each year, on average, over the decade. Many of those openings are expected to result from the need to replace workers who transfer to different occupations or exit the labor force, such as to retire.

What Agricultural and Food Science Technicians Do

Agricultural and food science technicians assist agricultural and food scientists by performing duties such as measuring and analyzing the quality of food and agricultural products. Duties range from performing agricultural labor with added record-keeping duties to laboratory testing with significant amounts of office work, depending on the particular field the technician works in.

Agricultural and food science technicians may apply new agricultural chemicals to plants and perform tests to verify their effects.

Agricultural and food science technicians may keep detailed records and collect samples for analyses.

Duties

Specific duties of these technicians vary with their specialty.

Agricultural science technicians typically do the following:

- Follow protocols to collect, prepare, analyze, and properly store crop or animal samples
- Operate farm equipment and maintain agricultural production areas to conform to scientific testing parameters
- Examine animal and crop specimens to determine the presence of diseases or other problems
- Measure ingredients used in animal feed and other inputs
- Prepare and operate laboratory testing equipment
- Compile and analyze test results
- Prepare charts, presentations, and reports describing test results

Food science technicians typically do the following:

- Collect and prepare samples in accordance with established procedures
- Test food, food additives, and food containers to ensure that they comply with established safety standards
- Help food scientists with food research, development, and quality control
- Analyze chemical properties of food to determine ingredients and formulas
- Compile and analyze test results
- Prepare charts, presentations, and reports describing test results
- Prepare and maintain quantities of chemicals needed to perform laboratory tests
- Maintain a safe, sterile laboratory environment

Agricultural and food science technicians often specialize by subject area, which includes animal health, farm machinery, fertilizers, agricultural chemicals, or processing technology. Duties can vary considerably by specialization.

Agricultural science technicians typically study ways to increase the productivity of crops and animals. These workers may keep detailed records, collect samples for analyses, ensure that samples meet proper safety and quality standards, and test crops and animals for disease or to confirm the results of scientific experiments.

Food science technicians who work in manufacturing investigate new production or processing techniques. They also ensure that products will be fit for distribution or are produced as efficiently as expected. Many food science technicians spend time inspecting foodstuffs, chemicals, and additives to determine whether they are safe and have the proper combination of ingredients.

Work Environment

Agricultural technicians held about 17,600 jobs in 2022. The largest employers of agricultural technicians were as follows:

Agricultural and food science technicians work on farms and ranches, in greenhouses, offices, laboratories, and processing plants.

Colleges, universities, and professional schools; state, local, and private	16%
Wholesale trade	12
Animal production and aquaculture	11
Research and development in the physical, engineering, and life sciences	10
Crop production	6

Food science technicians held about 21,200 jobs in 2022. The largest employers of food science technicians were as follows:

Food manufacturing	40%
Animal production and aquaculture	13
Crop production	7
Beverage and tobacco product manufacturing	6
Professional, scientific, and technical services	6

Technicians work in a variety of settings, including laboratories, processing plants, farms and ranches, greenhouses, and offices. Technicians who work in processing plants and agricultural settings may face noise from processing and farming machinery, extreme temperatures, and odors from chemicals or animals. They may need to lift and carry objects, and be physically active for long periods of time.

Work Schedules

Agricultural and food science technicians typically work full time and have standard work schedules. Technicians may need to travel, including international travel.

How to Become an Agricultural or Food Science Technician

Agricultural and food science technicians typically need an associate's degree in biology, chemistry, crop or animal science, or a related field. Some positions require candidates to have a bachelor's degree, and others a high school diploma or equivalent plus related work experience.

Education

Students interested in a career as an agricultural or food science technician should take as many high school science and math classes as possible. A solid background in applied chemistry, biology, physics, math, and statistics is important. Knowledge of how to use spreadsheets and databases also may be necessary.

Agricultural and food science technicians typically need an associate's degree in biology, chemistry, crop or animal science, or a related field from an accredited college or university. Some agricultural and food science technician positions require a bachelor's degree.

Students may take courses in biology, chemistry, plant or animal science, and agricultural engineering as part of their programs. Programs include technical instruction and hands-on experience. Many schools offer internships, cooperative-education, and other programs designed to provide practical experience and enhance employment prospects.

Some agricultural and food science technicians successfully enter the occupation with a high school diploma or equivalent, but they typically need related work experience and on-the-job training that may last a year or more.

Agricultural and food science technicians conduct a variety of observations and on-site measurements.

Training

Agricultural and food science technicians typically undergo on-the-job training. Various federal government regulations outline the types of training needed for technicians, which varies by work environment and specific job requirements. Training may cover topics such as production techniques, personal hygiene, and sanitation procedures.

Important Qualities

Analytical skills. Agricultural and food science technicians must conduct a variety of observations and on-site measurements, all of which require precision, accuracy, and math skills.

Communication skills. Agricultural and food science technicians must understand and give clear instructions, keep detailed records, and, occasionally, write reports.

Critical-thinking skills. Agricultural and food science technicians reach conclusions through sound reasoning and judgment. They determine how to improve food quality and must test products for a variety of safety standards.

Interpersonal skills. Agricultural and food science technicians need to work well with others. They may supervise agricultural and food processing workers and receive instruction from scientists or specialists, so effective communication is critical.

Physical stamina. Agricultural and food science technicians who work in manufacturing or agricultural settings may need to stand for long periods, lift objects, and generally perform physical labor.

Work Experience in a Related Occupation

Workers who enter the occupation with only a high school diploma or equivalent often must have experience in a related occupation during which they develop their knowledge of agriculture or manufacturing processes. These related occupations include food and tobacco processing workers and agricultural workers.

Pay

The median annual wage for agricultural technicians was $41,760 in May 2022. The median wage is the wage at which half the workers in an occupation earned more than that amount and half earned less. The lowest 10 percent earned less than $29,900, and the highest 10 percent earned more than $63,720.

The median annual wage for food science technicians was $47,860 in May 2022. The lowest 10 percent earned less than $36,050, and the highest 10 percent earned more than $71,370.

In May 2022, the median annual wages for agricultural technicians in the top industries in which they worked were as follows:

Wholesale trade	$51,030
Colleges, universities, and professional schools; state, local, and private	47,650
Research and development in the physical, engineering, and life sciences	43,980

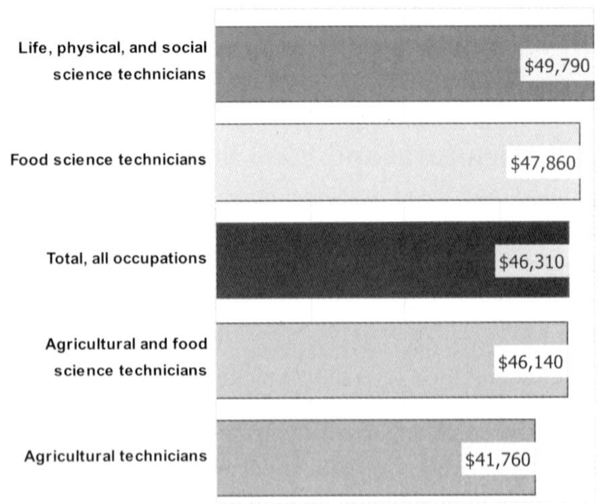

Note: All Occupations includes all occupations in the U.S. Economy.
Source: U.S. Bureau of Labor Statistics, Occupational Employment and Wage Statistics

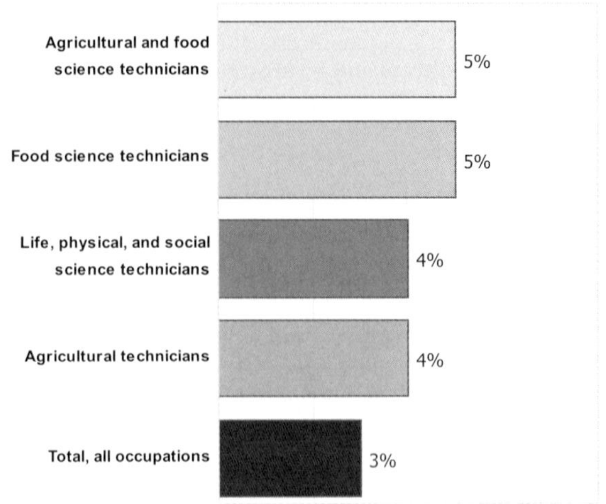

Note: All Occupations includes all occupations in the U.S. Economy.
Source: U.S. Bureau of Labor Statistics, Employment Projections program

In May 2022, the median annual wages for food science technicians in the top industries in which they worked were as follows:

Beverage and tobacco product manufacturing	$54,780
Professional, scientific, and technical services	47,810
Food manufacturing	46,580

Agricultural and food science technicians typically work full time and have standard work schedules. Technicians may need to travel, including international travel.

Job Outlook

Overall employment of agricultural and food science technicians is projected to grow 5 percent from 2022 to 2032, faster than the average for all occupations.

About 5,500 openings for agricultural and food science technicians are projected each year, on average, over the decade. Many of those openings are expected to result from the need to replace workers who transfer to different occupations or exit the labor force, such as to retire.

Employment

Demand will continue for agricultural research into topics such as water resources, pests and pathogens, climate and weather patterns, and biofuels and other agricultural products.

Agricultural science technicians will be needed to assist agricultural and food scientists in investigating and improving the diets, living conditions, and genetic makeup of livestock. Food science technicians will help scientists improve food-processing techniques, ensuring that products are safe, waste is limited, and food is shipped efficiently. Technicians also will continue to be needed to help analyze soil composition and soil improvement techniques, find uses for agricultural byproducts, and selectively breed crops to resist pests and disease or to improve taste.

Occupational Title	SOC Code	Employment, 2022	Projected Employment, 2032	Change, 2022-32	
				Percent	Numeric
Agricultural and food science technicians	19-4010	38,800	40,700	5	1,900
Agricultural technicians	19-4012	17,600	18,400	4	800
Food science technicians	19-4013	21,200	22,300	5	1,100

Contacts for More Information

For more information, visit

- American Society of Agronomy
- Future Farmers of America
- Soil Science Society of America
- American Registry of Professional Animal Scientists
- American Society of Animal Science
- Institute of Food Technologists
- U.S. Department of Agriculture
- U.S. Food and Drug Administration
- Smithsonian Institution

Agricultural and Food Scientists

Summary

Quick Facts: Agricultural and Food Scientists	
2022 Median Pay	$74,940 per year $36.03 per hour
Typical Entry-Level Education	Bachelor's degree
Work Experience in a Related Occupation	None
On-the-job Training	None
Number of Jobs, 2022	35,400
Job Outlook, 2022-32	6% (Faster than average)
Employment Change, 2022-32	2,100

What Agricultural and Food Scientists Do

Agricultural and food scientists research ways to improve the efficiency and safety of agricultural establishments and products.

Work Environment

Agricultural and food scientists work in laboratories, in offices, and in the field. Most agricultural and food scientists work full time.

How to Become an Agricultural or Food Scientist

Agricultural and food scientists need at least a bachelor's degree from an accredited postsecondary institution, although many get advanced degrees.

Pay

The median annual wage for agricultural and food scientists was $74,940 in May 2022.

Job Outlook

Overall employment of agricultural and food scientists is projected to grow 6 percent from 2022 to 2032, faster than the average for all occupations.

Soil scientists examine the composition of soil and how it affects plant or crop growth.

About 3,000 openings for agricultural and food scientists are projected each year, on average, over the decade. Many of those openings are expected to result from the need to replace workers who transfer to different occupations or exit the labor force, such as to retire.

What Agricultural and Food Scientists Do

Agricultural and food scientists research ways to improve the efficiency and safety of agricultural establishments and products.

Duties

Agricultural and food scientists typically do the following:

- Conduct research and experiments to improve the productivity and sustainability of field crops and farm animals
- Create new food products and develop new and better ways to process, package, and deliver them
- Study the composition of soil as it relates to plant growth, and research ways to improve it
- Communicate research findings to the scientific community, food producers, and the public
- Travel between facilities to oversee the implementation of new projects

Agricultural and food scientists play an important role in maintaining and expanding the nation's food supply. Many work in basic or applied research and development. Basic research seeks to understand the biological and chemical processes by which crops and livestock grow. Applied research seeks to discover ways to improve the quality, quantity, and safety of agricultural products.

Many agricultural and food scientists work with little supervision, forming their own hypotheses and developing their research methods. In addition, they often lead teams of technicians or students who help in their research. Agricultural and

Agricultural and food scientists may observe the production of field crops and farm animals so that they can research solutions to problems.

food scientists who are employed in private industry may need to travel between different worksites.

The following are types of agricultural and food scientists:

Animal scientists typically conduct research on domestic farm animals. With a focus on food production, they explore animal genetics, nutrition, reproduction, diseases, growth, and development. They work to develop efficient ways to produce and process meat, poultry, eggs, and milk. Animal scientists may crossbreed animals to make them more productive or improve other characteristics. They advise farmers on how to upgrade housing for animals, lower animal death rates, increase growth rates, or otherwise increase the quality and efficiency of livestock.

Food scientists and technologists use chemistry, biology, and other sciences to study the basic elements of food. They analyze the nutritional content of food, discover new food sources, and research ways to make processed foods safe and healthy. Food technologists generally work in product development, applying findings from food science research to develop new or better ways of selecting, preserving, processing, packaging, and distributing food. Some food scientists use problem-solving techniques from nanotechnology—the science of manipulating matter on an atomic scale—to develop sensors that can detect contaminants in food. Other food scientists enforce government regulations, inspecting food-processing areas to ensure that they are sanitary and meet waste management standards.

Plant scientists work to improve crop yields and advise food and crop developers about techniques that could enhance production. They may develop ways to control pests and weeds.

Soil scientists examine the composition of soil, how it affects plant or crop growth, and how alternative soil treatments affect crop productivity. They develop methods of conserving and managing soil that farmers and forestry companies can use. Because soil science is closely related to environmental science, people trained in soil science also work to ensure environmental quality and effective land use.

Agricultural and food scientists in private industry commonly work for food production companies, farms, and processing plants. They may improve inspection standards or overall food quality. They spend their time in a laboratory, where they do tests and experiments, or in the field, where they take samples or assess overall conditions. Other agricultural and food scientists work for pharmaceutical companies, where they use biotechnology processes to develop drugs or other medical products. Some look for ways to process agricultural products into fuels, such as ethanol produced from corn.

At universities, agricultural and food scientists do research and investigate new methods of improving animal or soil health, nutrition, and other facets of food quality. They also write grants to organizations, such as the United States Department of Agriculture (USDA) or the National Institutes of Health (NIH), to get funding for their research. For more information on professors who teach agricultural and food science at universities, see the profile on postsecondary teachers.

In the federal government, agricultural and food scientists conduct research on animal safety and on methods of improving food and crop production. They spend most of their time conducting clinical trials or developing experiments on animal and plant subjects.

Agricultural and food scientists may eventually present their findings in peer-reviewed journals or other publications.

Work Environment

Agricultural and food scientists held about 35,400 jobs in 2022. Employment in the detailed occupations that make up agricultural and food scientists was distributed as follows:

Soil and plant scientists	17,200
Food scientists and technologists	15,300
Animal scientists	2,800

The largest employers of agricultural and food scientists were as follows:

Employer	Percent
Food manufacturing	19%
Research and development in the physical, engineering, and life sciences	13
Colleges, universities, and professional schools; state, local, and private	11
Government	10

Agricultural and food scientists work in laboratories, in offices, and in the field. They spend most of their time studying data and reports in a laboratory or an office. Fieldwork includes visits to farms or processing plants.

When visiting a food or animal production facility, agricultural and food scientists must follow biosecurity measures, wear suitable clothing, and tolerate the environment associated with food production processes. This environment may include

Agricultural and food scientists spend most of their time in laboratories and offices.

noise associated with large production machinery, cold temperatures associated with food production or storage, and close proximity to animal byproducts.

Certain positions may require travel, either domestic, international, or both. The amount of travel can vary widely.

Work Schedules

Agricultural and food scientists typically work full time.

How to Become an Agricultural or Food Scientist

Agricultural and food scientists need at least a bachelor's degree from an accredited postsecondary institution, although many earn advanced degrees. Some animal scientists earn a doctor of veterinary medicine (DVM) degree.

Education

Every state has at least one land-grant college that offers agricultural science degrees. Many other colleges and universities also offer agricultural science degrees or related courses. Soil and plant scientists typically need a bachelor's degree in agriculture or a related field, such as biology or chemistry.

Undergraduate coursework for food scientists and technologists and for soil and plant scientists typically includes biology, chemistry, botany, and plant conservation. Students preparing to be food scientists take courses such as food chemistry, food analysis, food microbiology, food engineering, and food-processing operations. Students preparing to be soil and plant scientists take courses in plant pathology, soil chemistry, entomology (the study of insects), plant physiology, and biochemistry.

Undergraduate students in agricultural and food sciences typically gain a strong foundation in their specialty, with an emphasis on teamwork through internships and research opportunities. Students also are encouraged to take humanities courses, which can help them develop good communication skills, and computer courses, which can familiarize them with common programs and databases.

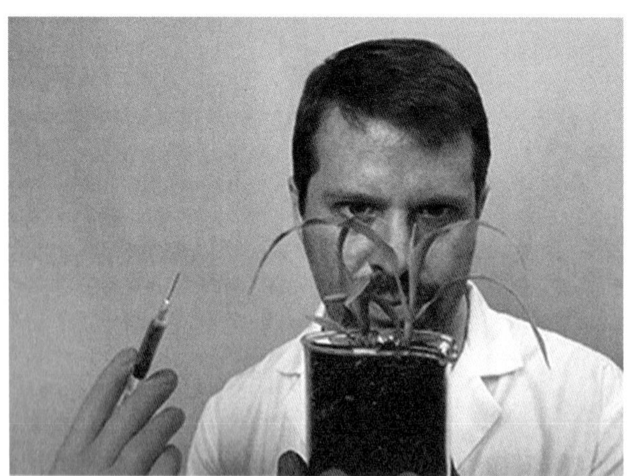

Agricultural and food scientists need at least a bachelor's degree.

Many people with bachelor's degrees in agricultural sciences find work in related jobs rather than becoming an agricultural or food scientist. For example, a bachelor's degree in agricultural science is a useful background for farming, ranching, agricultural inspection, farm credit institutions, or companies that make or sell feed, fertilizer, seed, or farm equipment. Combined with coursework in business, agricultural and food science could be a good background for managerial jobs in farm-related or ranch-related businesses. For more information, see the profile on farmers, ranchers, and other agricultural managers.

Many students with bachelors' degrees in application-focused food sciences or agricultural sciences earn advanced degrees in applied topics such as toxicology or dietetics. Students who major in a more basic field, such as biology or chemistry, may be better suited for getting their Ph.D. and doing research within the agricultural and food sciences. During graduate school, there is additional emphasis on lab work and original research, in which prospective animal scientists have the opportunity to do experiments and sometimes supervise undergraduates.

Advanced research topics include genetics, animal reproduction, agronomy, and biotechnology, among others. Advanced coursework also emphasizes statistical analysis and experiment design, which are important as Ph.D. candidates begin their research.

Some agricultural and food scientists receive a doctor of veterinary medicine (DVM). Like Ph.D. candidates in animal science, DVM candidates must first have a bachelor's degree to attend veterinary school.

Important Qualities

Communication skills. Communication skills are critical for agricultural and food scientists. They must explain their studies: what they were trying to learn, the methods they used, what they found, and what they think the implications of their findings are. They must also communicate well when working with others, including technicians and student assistants.

Critical-thinking skills. Agricultural and food scientists must use their expertise to determine the best way to answer a specific research question.

Data-analysis skills. Agricultural and food scientists, like other researchers, collect data using a variety of methods, including quantitative surveys. They must then apply standard data analysis techniques to understand the data and get the answers to the questions they are studying.

Math skills. Agricultural and food scientists, like many other scientists, must have a sound grasp of mathematical concepts.

Observation skills. Agricultural and food scientists conduct experiments that require precise observation of samples and other data. Any mistake could lead to inconclusive or inaccurate results.

Licenses, Certifications, and Registrations

Some states require soil scientists to be licensed to practice. Licensing requirements vary by state, but generally include holding a bachelor's degree with a certain number of credit hours in soil science, working under a licensed scientist for a certain number of years, and passing an exam.

Otherwise, certifications are generally not required for agriculture and food scientists, but they can be useful in advancing one's career. Agricultural and food scientists can get certifications from organizations such as the American Society of Agronomy, the American Registry of Professional Animal Scientists (ARPAS), the Institute of Food Technologists (IFT), or the Soil Science Society of America (SSSA), and others. These certifications recognize expertise in agricultural and food science, and enhance the status of those who are certified.

Qualification for certification is generally based on education, previous professional experience, and passing a comprehensive exam. Scientists may need to take continuing education courses to keep their certification, and they must follow the organization's code of ethics.

Other Experience

Internships are highly recommended for prospective food scientists and technologists. Many entry-level jobs in this occupation are related to food manufacturing, and firsthand experience is often valued in that environment.

Pay

The median annual wage for agricultural and food scientists was $74,940 in May 2022. The median wage is the wage at which half the workers in an occupation earned more than that amount and half earned less. The lowest 10 percent earned less than $43,060, and the highest 10 percent earned more than $129,490.

Median annual wages for agricultural and food scientists in May 2022 were as follows:

Food scientists and technologists	$79,860
Animal scientists	69,390
Soil and plant scientists	65,730

In May 2022, the median annual wages for agricultural and food scientists in the top industries in which they worked were as follows:

Research and development in the physical, engineering, and life sciences	$82,840
Food manufacturing	78,860
Government	71,140
Colleges, universities, and professional schools; state, local, and private	59,610

Agricultural and food scientists typically work full time.

Job Outlook

Overall employment of agricultural and food scientists is projected to grow 6 percent from 2022 to 2032, faster than the average for all occupations.

About 3,000 openings for agricultural and food scientists are projected each year, on average, over the decade. Many of those openings are expected to result from the need to replace workers who transfer to different occupations or exit the labor force, such as to retire.

Employment

Employment of agricultural and food scientists is projected to grow as research into agricultural production methods and

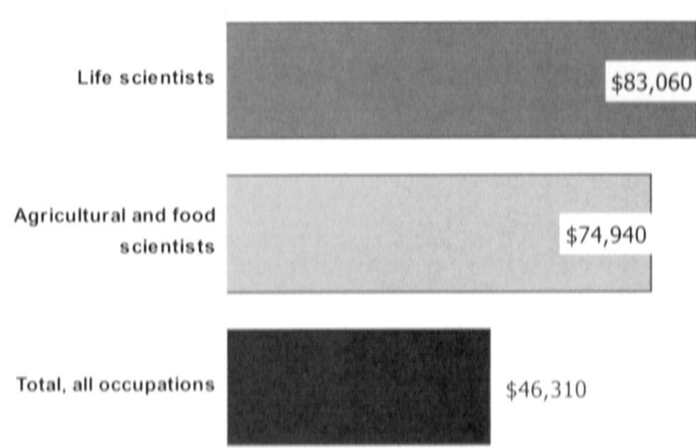

Note: All Occupations includes all occupations in the U.S. Economy.
Source: U.S. Bureau of Labor Statistics, Occupational Employment and Wage Statistics

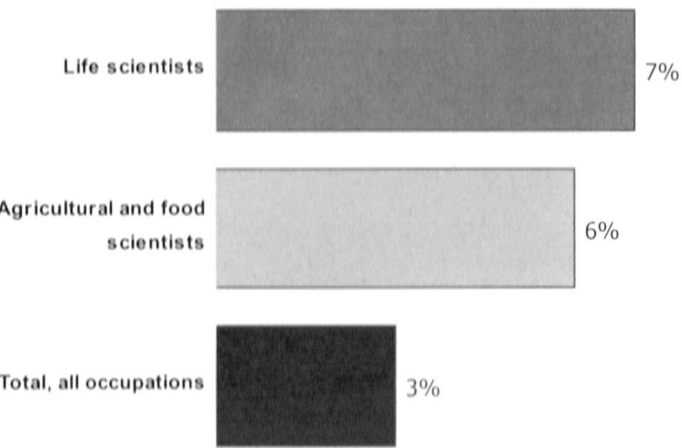

Note: All Occupations includes all occupations in the U.S. Economy.
Source: U.S. Bureau of Labor Statistics, Employment Projections program

techniques continues. The need to address challenges such as increased demand for water resources, combating pests and pathogens, and changes in climate and weather patterns is expected to create jobs for these workers. Demand for agricultural products, including biofuels, also is expected to contribute to employment growth.

Occupational Title	SOC Code	Employment, 2022	Projected Employment, 2032	Change, 2022-32	
				Percent	Numeric
Agricultural and food scientists	19-1010	35,400	37,500	6	2,100
Animal scientists	19-1011	2,800	2,900	6	200
Food scientists and technologists	19-1012	15,300	16,500	7	1,100
Soil and plant scientists	19-1013	17,200	18,100	5	800

Contacts for More Information

For more information about food and animal scientists, including certifications, visit

- American Society of Agronomy
- American Society of Animal Science
- American Registry of Professional Animal Scientists
- Future Farmers of America
- Institute of Food Technologists
- Soil Science Society of America
- U.S. Food and Drug Administration
- Smithsonian Institution
- U.S. Department of Agriculture
- National Institutes of Health

Anthropologists and Archeologists

Summary

Quick Facts: Anthropologists and Archeologists

2022 Median Pay	$63,940 per year $30.74 per hour
Typical Entry-Level Education	Master's degree
Work Experience in a Related Occupation	None
On-the-job Training	None
Number of Jobs, 2022	8,000
Job Outlook, 2022-32	4% (As fast as average)
Employment Change, 2022-32	300

What Anthropologists and Archeologists Do

Anthropologists and archeologists study the origin, development, and behavior of humans.

Work Environment

Anthropologists and archeologists typically work in research organizations, government, and consulting firms. Although most work in offices, some analyze samples in laboratories or do fieldwork. Fieldwork may require travel for extended periods.

How to Become an Anthropologist or Archeologist

To enter the occupation, anthropologists and archeologists typically need at least a master's degree in anthropology or archeology. Experience doing fieldwork in either discipline is also important. Bachelor's degree holders may find work as assistants or fieldworkers.

Pay

The median annual wage for anthropologists and archeologists was $63,940 in May 2022.

Job Outlook

Employment of anthropologists and archeologists is projected to grow 4 percent from 2022 to 2032, about as fast as the average for all occupations.

About 700 openings for anthropologists and archeologists are projected each year, on average, over the decade. Many of those openings are expected to result from the need to replace workers who transfer to different occupations or exit the labor force, such as to retire.

What Anthropologists and Archeologists Do

Anthropologists and archeologists study the origin, development, and behavior of humans. They examine the cultures, languages, archeological remains, and physical characteristics of people in various parts of the world.

Duties

Anthropologists and archeologists typically do the following:

- Plan cultural research
- Customize data collection methods according to a particular region, specialty, or project

Anthropologists and archeologists often do fieldwork.

- Collect information from observations, interviews, and documents
- Record and manage records of observations taken in the field
- Analyze data, laboratory samples, and other sources of information to uncover patterns about human life, culture, and origins
- Prepare reports and present research findings
- Advise organizations on the cultural impact of policies, programs, and products

By drawing and building on knowledge from the humanities and the social, physical, and biological sciences, anthropologists and archeologists examine the ways of life, languages, archeological remains, and physical characteristics of people in various parts of the world. They also examine the customs, values, and social patterns of different cultures.

Although the equipment used by anthropologists and archeologists varies by task and specialty, it often includes excavation and measurement tools, laboratory and recording equipment, statistical and database software, and Geographic Information Systems (GIS).

Archeologists examine, recover, and preserve evidence of human activity from past cultures. They analyze human remains and artifacts, such as tools, pottery, cave paintings, and ruins of buildings. They connect their findings with information about past environments to learn about the history, customs, and living habits of people in earlier eras.

Archeologists also manage and protect archeological sites. Some work in national parks or at historical sites, providing site protection and educating the public. Others assess building sites to ensure that construction plans comply with federal regulations related to site preservation. Archeologists often specialize in a particular geographic area, period, or object of study, such as animal remains or underwater sites.

Anthropology is divided into three primary fields: biological or physical anthropology, cultural or social anthropology, and linguistic anthropology. Biological and physical anthropologists study the changing nature of the biology of humans and closely related primates. Cultural anthropologists study the social and cultural consequences of various human-related issues, such as overpopulation, natural disasters, warfare, and poverty. Linguistic anthropology studies the history and development of languages.

Some anthropologists and archeologists excavate artifacts.

A growing number of anthropologists perform market research for businesses, studying the demand for products by a particular culture or social group. Using their anthropological background and a variety of techniques—including interviews, surveys, and observations—they may collect data on how a product is used by specific demographic groups.

Many people with a Ph.D. in anthropology or archeology become professors or museum curators. For more information, see the profiles on postsecondary teachers, and archivists, curators, and museum technicians.

Work Environment

Anthropologists and archeologists held about 8,000 jobs in 2022. The largest employers of anthropologists and archeologists were as follows:

Research and development in the social sciences and humanities	31%
Federal government, excluding postal service	21
Management, scientific, and technical consulting services	18
Engineering services	7
Self-employed workers	2

The work of anthropologists varies according to the specific job. Although most anthropologists work in offices, some analyze samples in laboratories or work in the field.

Archeologists often work for cultural resource management (CRM) firms. These firms identify, assess, and preserve archeological sites and ensure that developers and builders comply with regulations regarding those sites. Archeologists also work in museums, at historical sites, and for government agencies, such as the U.S. Department of the Interior's National Park Service.

Anthropologists and archeologists often do fieldwork, either in the United States or in foreign countries. Fieldwork may involve learning foreign languages, living in remote areas, and examining and excavating archeological sites. Fieldwork usually requires travel for extended periods—about 4 to 8 weeks per year. Those doing fieldwork often will have to return to the field for several years to complete their research.

During fieldwork, anthropologists and archeologists must live with the people they study to learn about their culture. The work can involve rugged living conditions and strenuous physical exertion. While in the field, anthropologists and archeologists often work many hours to meet research deadlines. They also may work with limited funding for their projects.

Anthropologists often travel to and live with the people they are studying.

Students assist in the surveying of proposed building sites for artifacts.

Work Schedules

Many anthropologists and archeologists work full time during regular business hours. When doing fieldwork, however, anthropologists and archeologists may be required to travel and to work many and irregular hours, including evenings and weekends.

How to Become an Anthropologist or Archeologist

To enter the occupation, anthropologists and archeologists typically need at least a master's degree in anthropology or archeology. Experience doing fieldwork in either discipline is also important. Those with a bachelor's degree may find work as assistants or fieldworkers.

Education

Anthropologists and archeologists typically qualify for positions with a master's degree in anthropology or archeology. Master's degree programs usually take 2 years to complete and include field or laboratory research.

In graduate programs, anthropology and archeology students typically conduct field research in a local community or working abroad. Students also may attend archeological field schools, which teach them how to excavate historical and archeological sites and how to record and interpret their findings and data.

Although a master's degree is sufficient for many positions, a Ph.D. may be needed for jobs that require leadership skills and advanced knowledge. Anthropologists and archeologists typically need a Ph.D. to work internationally in order to comply with the requirements of foreign governments. A Ph.D. takes additional years of study beyond a master's degree. Also, Ph.D. students must complete a doctoral dissertation, which typically includes between 18 and 30 months of field research and knowledge of a foreign language.

Those with a bachelor's degree in anthropology or archeology and experience gained through an internship or field school may work as field or laboratory technicians or research assistants.

Other Experience

Graduates of anthropology and archeology programs usually need experience in their respective fields and training in quantitative and qualitative research methods. Many students gain this experience through field training or internships with museums, historical societies, or nonprofit organizations while still in school.

Important Qualities

Analytical skills. Anthropologists and archeologists must possess knowledge of scientific methods and data, which are often used in their research.

Critical-thinking skills. Anthropologists and archeologists must be able to draw conclusions from observations, laboratory experiments, and other methods of research. They must be able to combine various sources of information to try to solve problems and to answer research questions.

Communication skills. Anthropologists and archeologists often have to write reports or papers in academic journals and present their research and findings to their peers and to general audiences. These activities require strong writing, speaking, and listening skills.

Physical stamina. Anthropologists and archeologists working in the field may need to hike or walk several miles while carrying equipment to a research site.

Pay

The median annual wage for anthropologists and archeologists was $63,940 in May 2022. The median wage is the wage at which half the workers in an occupation earned more than that amount and half earned less. The lowest 10 percent earned less than $40,260, and the highest 10 percent earned more than $100,560.

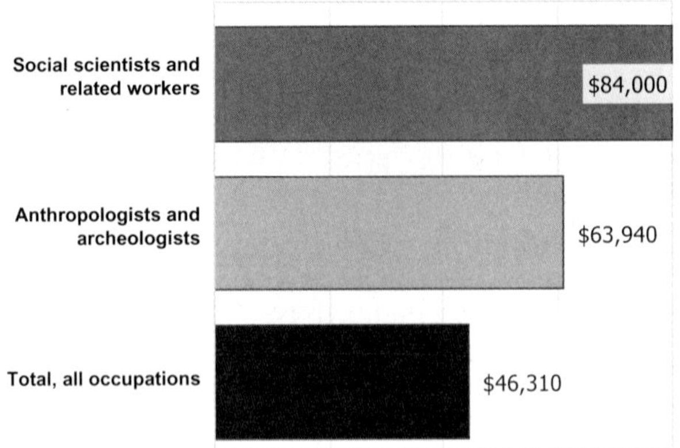

Note: All Occupations includes all occupations in the U.S. Economy.
Source: U.S. Bureau of Labor Statistics, Occupational Employment and Wage Statistics

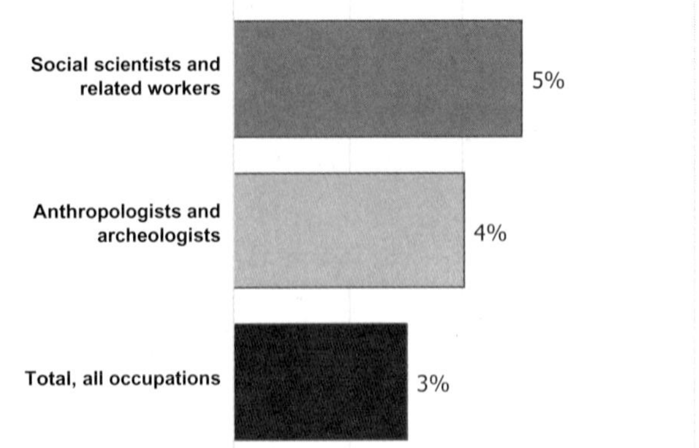

Note: All Occupations includes all occupations in the U.S. Economy.
Source: U.S. Bureau of Labor Statistics, Employment Projections program

In May 2022, the median annual wages for anthropologists and archeologists in the top industries in which they worked were as follows:

Federal government, excluding postal service	$83,870
Engineering services	70,100
Management, scientific, and technical consulting services	59,420
Research and development in the social sciences and humanities	57,690

Many anthropologists and archeologists work full time during regular business hours. When doing fieldwork, however, anthropologists and archeologists may be required to travel and to work many and irregular hours, including evenings and weekends.

Job Outlook

Employment of anthropologists and archeologists is projected to grow 4 percent from 2022 to 2032, about as fast as the average for all occupations.

About 700 openings for anthropologists and archeologists are projected each year, on average, over the decade. Many of those openings are expected to result from the need to replace workers who transfer to different occupations or exit the labor force, such as to retire.

Employment

Corporations will continue to use anthropological research to gain a better understanding of consumer demand within specific cultures or social groups. Anthropologists also will be needed to analyze markets, allowing businesses to serve their clients better or to target new customers or demographic groups.

Archeologists will be needed to ensure that builders, museums, and other organizations comply with federal regulations pertaining to the preservation and handling of archeological and historical artifacts.

Because anthropological and archeological research may depend on research funding, federal budgetary decisions can affect the rate of employment growth in research.

Employment projections data for anthropologists and archeologists, 2022-32

Occupational Title	SOC Code	Employment, 2022	Projected Employment, 2032	Change, 2022-32 Percent	Change, 2022-32 Numeric	Employment by Industry
SOURCE: U.S. Bureau of Labor Statistics, Employment Projections program						
Anthropologists and archeologists	19-3091	8,000	8,300	4	300	Get data

Contacts for More Information

For more information, visit

- American Anthropological Association
- Archaeological Institute of America
- Society for American Archaeology
- American Association of Physical Anthropologists

Atmospheric Scientists, Including Meteorologists

Summary

Quick Facts: Atmospheric Scientists, Including Meteorologists	
2022 Median Pay	$83,780 per year $40.28 per hour
Typical Entry-Level Education	Bachelor's degree
Work Experience in a Related Occupation	None
On-the-job Training	None
Number of Jobs, 2022	10,500
Job Outlook, 2022-32	4% (As fast as average)
Employment Change, 2022-32	500

What Atmospheric Scientists, Including Meteorologists Do

Atmospheric scientists study, report on, and forecast the weather and climate.

Work Environment

Most atmospheric scientists work indoors in weather stations, offices, or laboratories. They may work outdoors to observe the weather. Most atmospheric scientists are full time and may work extended hours during weather emergencies.

How to Become an Atmospheric Scientist

Atmospheric scientists typically need a bachelor's degree in meteorology or a related field to enter the occupation. Those who work in research typically need a master's degree or a Ph.D.

Pay

The median annual wage for atmospheric scientists, including meteorologists was $83,780 in May 2022.

Job Outlook

Employment of atmospheric scientists, including meteorologists is projected to grow 4 percent from 2022 to 2032, about as fast as the average for all occupations.

About 900 openings for atmospheric scientists, including meteorologists are projected each year, on average, over the decade. Many of those openings are expected to result from the need to replace workers who transfer to different occupations or exit the labor force, such as to retire.

What Atmospheric Scientists, Including Meteorologists Do

Atmospheric scientists study the weather and climate. They may compile data, prepare reports and forecasts, and assist in developing new data collection instruments.

Duties

Atmospheric scientists typically do the following:

- Measure atmospheric properties, such as temperature, dewpoint, humidity, and windspeed
- Use computer models that analyze atmospheric data (also called meteorological data)
- Write computer programs to support their modeling efforts
- Conduct research to improve understanding of weather phenomena
- Generate weather graphics for users
- Report current weather conditions
- Prepare long- and short-term weather forecasts using computers, mathematical models, satellites, radar, and local station data
- Plan, organize, and participate in outreach programs to educate the public about weather
- Issue warnings to protect life and property threatened by severe weather, such as hurricanes and tornadoes

Atmospheric scientists use instruments such as radar systems, satellites, and weather balloons to monitor the weather and to

Research meteorologists prepare to test hurricane resiliency of homes and warehouses in their lab.

Research meteorologists study atmospheric phenomena such as lightning.

collect data. They also use graphics software to illustrate data in forecasts and reports for their clients or the public.

The data that atmospheric scientists collect and analyze are critical to understanding issues related to weather and climate. Atmospheric scientists may work with geoscientists, hydrologists, or other scientists to help solve problems in areas such as agriculture, commerce, energy, the environment, and transportation. For example, atmospheric scientists may work with hydrologists and government organizations to study how rainfall and temperatures impact the water supply and its management.

The following are examples of types of atmospheric scientists:

Broadcast meteorologists give forecasts to the public through television, radio, and digital media, such as streaming videos. They use graphics software to develop maps and charts that explain their forecasts. Not all weather broadcasters appearing on television are meteorologists or atmospheric scientists; reporters, correspondents, and broadcast news analysts may present weather conditions and forecasts but do not have specific training in meteorology.

Climatologists study how climate changes over time so that they can interpret long-term weather patterns or shifts in climate. They may examine data from remote sensing imagery, either analyzing the images by software or combining them into color composites to highlight details not visible to the naked eye.

Forensic meteorologists use historical weather data to reconstruct weather conditions for a specific location and time. They investigate whether the weather was a factor in events such as traffic accidents and fires. Forensic meteorologists may be called as experts to testify in court.

Research meteorologists develop new methods of data collection, observation, and forecasting. They also conduct studies to improve understanding of climate, weather, and other aspects of the atmosphere. For example, they may study severe weather patterns to understand why cyclones form and to develop better ways of predicting hurricanes and tornadoes. Others focus on environmental problems, such as air pollution.

Weather forecasters use computer and mathematical models to produce weather reports and short-term forecasts ranging from a few minutes to more than a week. In addition to developing forecasts for the public, their forecasts for business clients—including airports, utility companies, or grocery stores—help these clients plan for weather events that may affect demand for products or services. They also issue warnings for potentially severe weather, such as blizzards and hurricanes. Some forecasters prepare long-range outlooks to predict whether temperatures and precipitation levels will be above or below average in a particular month or season.

Work Environment

Atmospheric scientists, including meteorologists held about 10,500 jobs in 2022. The largest employers of atmospheric scientists, including meteorologists were as follows:

Many atmospheric scientists work at weather stations located throughout the country.

Federal government, excluding postal service	29%
Other professional, scientific, and technical services	23
Television broadcasting stations	10
Research and development in the physical, engineering, and life sciences	10

In the federal government, most atmospheric scientists work as weather forecasters with the National Weather Service of the National Oceanic and Atmospheric Administration (NOAA) in weather stations throughout the United States: at airports, in or near cities, and in isolated and remote areas. In small stations, they often work alone; in larger ones, they work as part of a team.

Atmospheric scientists involved in professional, scientific, and technical services or research often work in offices and laboratories. Some travel frequently to collect data and to observe weather events, such as tornadoes, up close. They also may observe weather conditions from aircraft.

Broadcast meteorologists present their reports to the public from television and radio studios. They also may broadcast from outdoor locations to highlight current weather conditions, such as near the ocean before a tropical storm.

Atmospheric scientists who work in private industry may have to travel to meet with clients or to gather information in the field. For example, forensic meteorologists may need to collect information from the scene of an accident as part of their investigation.

Work Schedules

Most atmospheric scientists work full time. Weather may change quickly, so weather forecasters need to continually monitor conditions. Schedules vary by position and employer. For example, some meteorologists work shifts to ensure 24-hour coverage. While some atmospheric scientists may have a standard workweek, broadcast meteorologists may work evenings and weekends. In addition, they may work extended hours during severe weather, such as hurricanes.

How to Become an Atmospheric Scientist

Atmospheric scientists typically need a bachelor's degree in meteorology or a related field to enter the occupation. For research positions, these scientists typically need a master's degree or a Ph.D. In addition, experience gained through an internship or by volunteering while in college may be helpful.

Education

Atmospheric scientists typically need a bachelor's degree in meteorology or a related physical science. In addition to meteorology and atmospheric science, course requirements may include physics, mathematics, and computer programming.

Atmospheric scientists who work in research typically need at least a master's degree or a Ph.D. in atmospheric science or a related field. Graduate programs may not require program applicants to have a bachelor's degree in atmospheric science; a bachelor's degree in mathematics, physics, or engineering is usually acceptable.

Training

Atmospheric scientists and meteorologists may need training after they are hired, depending on where they work. For example, new employees of the National Weather Service (NWS) need training on the use of equipment for issuing warnings about severe weather.

Atmospheric scientists issue warnings for severe weather.

Other Experience

Experience gained in the military or through opportunities during college, such as internships or volunteering, may be helpful for prospective atmospheric scientists. For example, the National Weather Service offers opportunities for students through internship, fellowship, volunteer, and scholarship programs.

Licenses and Certifications

Although not required, professional certification may benefit atmospheric scientists in some fields. For example, forensic meteorologists may enhance their credibility for testimony if they have the American Meteorological Society's (AMS) Certified Consulting Meteorologist credential.

Certification demonstrates a level of knowledge that employers often value. For example, employers of broadcast meteorologists may prefer to hire candidates who have the AMS designation of Certified Broadcast Meteorologist.

Important Qualities

Analytical skills. Atmospheric scientists need to evaluate large amounts of data produced by computer models.

Communication skills. Atmospheric scientists must be able to write and speak clearly so that their weather information is useful to the public or business clients.

Critical-thinking skills. Atmospheric scientists need to interpret data and information to create forecasts or reports.

Math skills. Atmospheric scientists must understand the mathematics used to develop models for weather forecasts and to calculate relationships between atmospheric properties, such as how changes in air pressure may affect air temperature.

Pay

The median annual wage for atmospheric scientists, including meteorologists was $83,780 in May 2022. The median wage is the wage at which half the workers in an occupation earned more than that amount and half earned less. The lowest 10 percent earned less than $50,490, and the highest 10 percent earned more than $141,520.

In May 2022, the median annual wages for atmospheric scientists, including meteorologists in the top industries in which they worked were as follows:

Federal government, excluding postal service	$110,090
Research and development in the physical, engineering, and life sciences	99,320
Television broadcasting stations	75,130
Other professional, scientific, and technical services	68,820

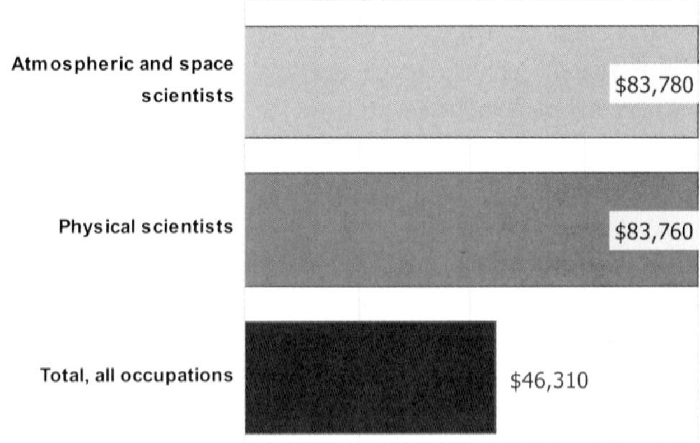

Note: All Occupations includes all occupations in the U.S. Economy.
Source: U.S. Bureau of Labor Statistics, Occupational Employment and Wage Statistics

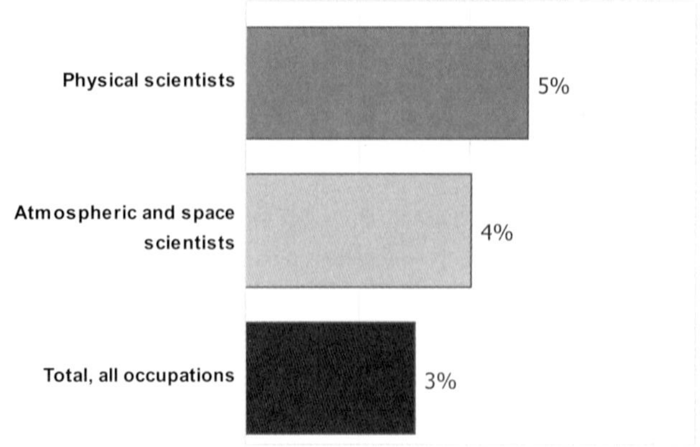

Note: All Occupations includes all occupations in the U.S. Economy.
Source: U.S. Bureau of Labor Statistics, Employment Projections program

Most atmospheric scientists work full time. Weather may change quickly, so weather forecasters need to continually monitor conditions. Schedules vary by position and employer. For example, some meteorologists work shifts to ensure 24-hour coverage. While some atmospheric scientists may have a standard workweek, broadcast meteorologists may work nights and weekends. In addition, they may work extended hours during severe weather, such as hurricanes.

Job Outlook

Employment of atmospheric scientists, including meteorologists is projected to grow 4 percent from 2022 to 2032, about as fast as the average for all occupations.

About 900 openings for atmospheric scientists, including meteorologists are projected each year, on average, over the decade. Many of those openings are expected to result from the need to replace workers who transfer to different occupations or exit the labor force, such as to retire.

Employment

New types of computer models have vastly improved the accuracy of forecasts, allowing atmospheric scientists to tailor forecasts to specific purposes. This should support demand for atmospheric scientists as businesses require more specialized weather information.

Businesses increasingly rely on just-in-time delivery to avoid the expenses incurred by traditional inventory management methods. Severe weather can interrupt ground or air transportation and delay inventory delivery. Businesses have begun to maintain forecasting teams around the clock to advise delivery personnel, and this availability helps them stay on schedule. In addition, severe weather patterns have become widely recognizable, and industries have become increasingly concerned about their impact, which will create demand for work in atmospheric science.

As utility companies continue to adopt wind and solar power, they depend more heavily on weather forecasting to arrange for buying and selling power.

Occupational Title	SOC Code	Employment, 2022	Projected Employment, 2032	Change, 2022-32	
				Percent	Numeric
Atmospheric and space scientists	19-2021	10,500	11,000	4	500

Contacts for More Information

For more information, visit

- American Meteorological Society (AMS)
- American Geosciences Institute (AGI)
- University Corporation for Atmospheric Research (UCAR)
- U.S. Office of Personnel Management (OPM)
- MetEd
- USAJOBS
- National Weather Service (NWS)

Biochemists and Biophysicists

Summary

Quick Facts: Biochemists and Biophysicists	
2022 Median Pay	$103,810 per year $49.91 per hour
Typical Entry-Level Education	Doctoral or professional degree
Work Experience in a Related Occupation	None
On-the-job Training	None
Number of Jobs, 2022	34,500
Job Outlook, 2022-32	7% (Faster than average)
Employment Change, 2022-32	2,300

What Biochemists and Biophysicists Do
Biochemists and biophysicists study the chemical and physical principles of living things and of biological processes.

Work Environment
Biochemists and biophysicists typically work in laboratories and offices to conduct experiments and analyze the results. Most work full time.

How to Become a Biochemist or Biophysicist
Biochemists and biophysicists need a Ph.D. to work in independent research and development. Many Ph.D. holders begin their careers in temporary postdoctoral research positions. Bachelor's and master's degree holders qualify for some entry-level positions in biochemistry and biophysics.

Pay
The median annual wage for biochemists and biophysicists was $103,810 in May 2022.

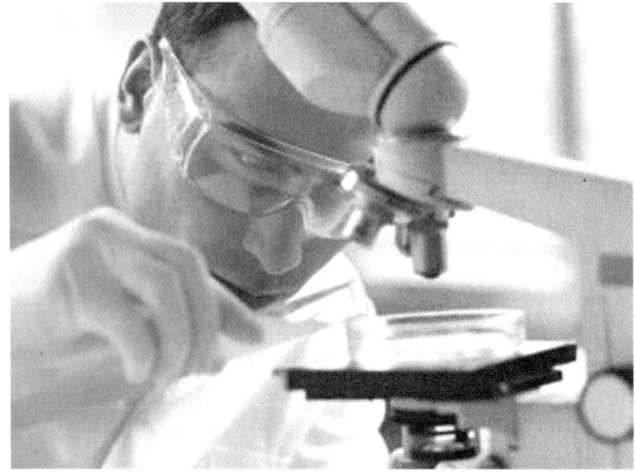

Biochemists and biophysicists study the chemical and physical properties of cells.

Job Outlook
Employment of biochemists and biophysicists is projected to grow 7 percent from 2022 to 2032, faster than the average for all occupations.

About 2,800 openings for biochemists and biophysicists are projected each year, on average, over the decade. Many of those openings are expected to result from the need to replace workers who transfer to different occupations or exit the labor force, such as to retire.

What Biochemists and Biophysicists Do
Biochemists and biophysicists study the chemical and physical principles of living things and of biological processes, such as cell development, growth, heredity, and disease.

Duties
Biochemists and biophysicists typically do the following:

- Plan and conduct complex projects in basic and applied research
- Manage laboratory teams and monitor the quality of their work
- Isolate, analyze, and synthesize proteins, fats, DNA, and other molecules

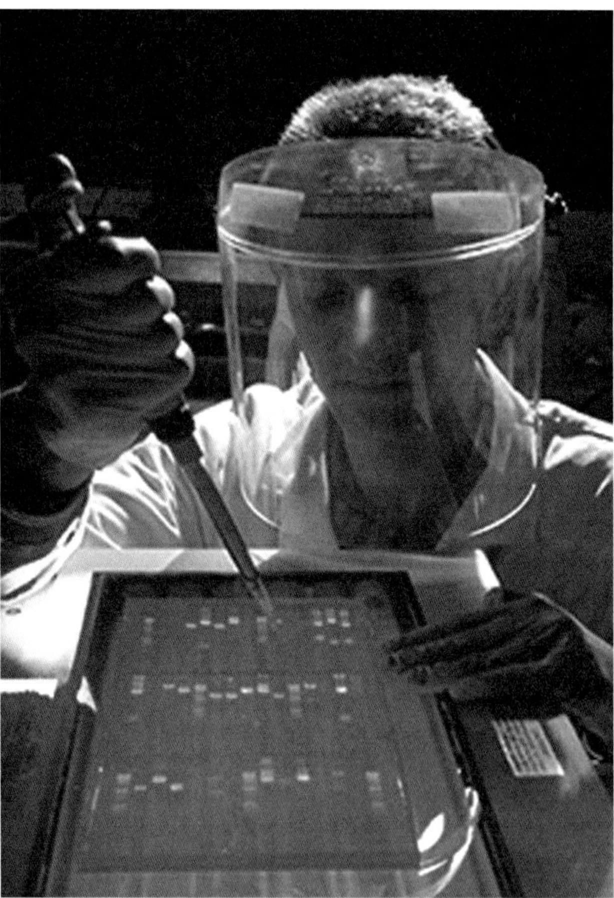

Biochemists and biophysicists play a key role in developing new medicines to fight diseases such as cancer.

- Research the effects of substances such as drugs, hormones, and nutrients on tissues and biological processes
- Review literature and the findings of other researchers and attend conferences
- Prepare technical reports, research papers, and recommendations based on their research findings
- Present research findings to scientists, engineers, and other colleagues
- Secure funding and write grant applications

Biochemists and biophysicists use advanced technologies, such as lasers and fluorescent microscopes, to conduct scientific experiments and analyses. They also use x rays and computer modeling software to determine the three-dimensional structures of proteins and other molecules. Biochemists and biophysicists involved in biotechnology research use chemical enzymes to synthesize recombinant DNA.

Biochemists and biophysicists work in basic and applied research. Basic research is conducted without any immediately known application; the goal is to expand human knowledge. Applied research is directed toward solving a particular problem.

Biochemists, sometimes called *molecular biologists* or *cellular biologists*, may study the molecular mechanisms by which cells feed, divide, and grow. Others study the evolution of plants and animals, to understand how genetic traits are carried through successive generations.

Biophysicists may conduct basic research to learn how nerve cells communicate or how proteins work. Biochemists and biophysicists who conduct basic research typically must submit written grant proposals to colleges and universities, private foundations, and the federal government to get the money they need for their research.

Biochemists and biophysicists who conduct applied research attempt to develop products and processes that improve people's lives. For example, in medicine, biochemists and biophysicists develop tests used to detect infections, genetic disorders, and other diseases. They also develop new drugs and medications, such as those used to treat cancer or Alzheimer's disease.

Applied research in biochemistry and biophysics has many uses outside of medicine. In agriculture, biochemists and biophysicists research ways to genetically engineer crops so that they will be resistant to drought, disease, insects, and other afflictions. Biochemists and biophysicists also investigate alternative fuels, such as biofuels—renewable energy sources from plants. In addition, they develop ways to protect the environment and clean up pollution.

Many people with a biochemistry background become professors and teachers. For more information, see the profile on postsecondary teachers.

Work Environment

Biochemists and biophysicists held about 34,500 jobs in 2022. The largest employers of biochemists and biophysicists were as follows:

Most biochemists and biophysicists work in laboratories.

Scientific research and development services	58%
Pharmaceutical and medicine manufacturing	18
Colleges, universities, and professional schools; state, local, and private	7
Wholesale trade	3

Biochemists and biophysicists typically work in laboratories and offices, to conduct experiments and analyze the results. Those who work with dangerous organisms or toxic substances in the laboratory must follow safety procedures to avoid contamination.

Most biochemists and biophysicists work on teams. Research projects are often interdisciplinary, and biochemists and biophysicists frequently work with experts in other fields, such as physics, chemistry, computer science, and engineering. Those working in biological research generate large amounts of data. They collaborate with specialists called ***bioinformaticians***, who use their knowledge of statistics, math, engineering, and computer science to mine datasets for correlations that might explain biological phenomena.

Some biotech companies need researchers to help sell their products. These products often rely on very complex technologies, and having an expert explain them to potential customers might be necessary. This role for researchers may be more common in smaller companies, where workers often fulfill multiple roles, such as working in research and in sales. Working in sales may require a substantial amount of travel. For more information on sales representatives, see the profile on wholesale and manufacturing sales representatives.

Work Schedules

Most biochemists and biophysicists work full time and keep regular hours. They may have to work additional hours to meet project deadlines or to perform time-sensitive laboratory experiments.

How to Become a Biochemist or Biophysicist

Biochemists and biophysicists need a Ph.D. to work in independent research-and-development positions. Most Ph.D. holders begin their careers in temporary postdoctoral research positions. Bachelor's and master's degree holders are qualified for some entry-level positions in biochemistry and biophysics.

Education

High school students interested in becoming a biochemist or biophysicist should take classes in natural and physical sciences, as well as in math.

Ph.D. holders in biochemistry and biophysics typically have a bachelor's degree in biochemistry or a related field, such as biology, physical science, or engineering. Students in these programs usually take courses in math and physics in addition to courses in biological and chemical sciences. Most programs also require laboratory work. Students may gain lab experience working in a university's laboratories or through internships with prospective employers, such as pharmaceutical and medicine manufacturers.

Ph.D. programs typically include advanced coursework in topics such as toxicology, genetics, and proteomics (the study of proteins). Several graduate programs include courses in bioinformatics, which involves using computers to study and analyze large amounts of biological data. Graduate students also spend a lot of time conducting laboratory research. Study at the master's level is generally considered good preparation for those interested in doing hands-on laboratory work. Ph.D.-level studies provide additional training in the planning and execution of research projects.

Training

Many biochemistry and biophysics Ph.D. holders begin their careers in temporary postdoctoral research positions. During their postdoctoral appointments, they work with experienced scientists as they continue to learn about their specialties or develop a broader understanding of related areas of research.

Postdoctoral positions frequently offer the opportunity to publish research findings. A solid record of published research is essential to getting a permanent college or university faculty position.

Biochemists and biophysicists need a Ph.D. to work in independent research and development positions.

Important Qualities

Analytical skills. Biochemists and biophysicists must be able to conduct scientific experiments and analyses with accuracy and precision.

Communication skills. Biochemists and biophysicists have to write and publish reports and research papers, give presentations of their findings, and communicate clearly with team members.

Critical-thinking skills. Biochemists and biophysicists draw conclusions from experimental results through sound reasoning and judgment.

Interpersonal skills. Biochemists and biophysicists typically work on interdisciplinary research teams and need to work well with others toward a common goal. Many serve as team leaders and must be able to motivate and direct other team members.

Math skills. Biochemists and biophysicists use complex equations and formulas regularly in their work. They need a broad understanding of math, including calculus and statistics.

Perseverance. Biochemists and biophysicists need to be thorough in their research and in their approach to problems. Scientific research involves substantial trial and error, and biochemists and biophysicists must not become discouraged in their work.

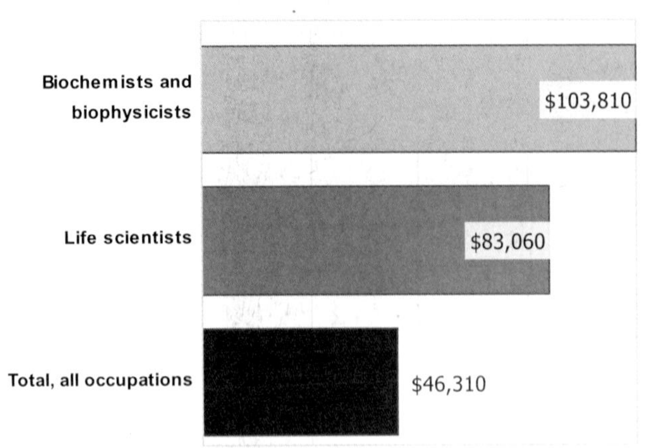

Note: All Occupations includes all occupations in the U.S. Economy.
Source: U.S. Bureau of Labor Statistics, Occupational Employment and Wage Statistics

Problem-solving skills. Biochemists and biophysicists use scientific experiments and analysis to find solutions to complex scientific problems.

Time-management skills. Biochemists and biophysicists usually need to meet deadlines when conducting research. They must be able to manage time and prioritize tasks efficiently while maintaining their quality of work.

Advancement

Some biochemists and biophysicists become natural sciences managers. Those who pursue management careers spend much of their time on administrative tasks, such as preparing budgets and schedules.

Pay

The median annual wage for biochemists and biophysicists was $103,810 in May 2022. The median wage is the wage at which half the workers in an occupation earned more than that amount and half earned less. The lowest 10 percent earned less than $61,540, and the highest 10 percent earned more than $171,010.

In May 2022, the median annual wages for biochemists and biophysicists in the top industries in which they worked were as follows:

Wholesale trade	$138,220
Scientific research and development services	108,660
Pharmaceutical and medicine manufacturing	99,870
Colleges, universities, and professional schools; state, local, and private	63,220

Most biochemists and biophysicists work full time and keep regular hours. They may have to work additional hours to meet project deadlines or to perform time-sensitive laboratory experiments.

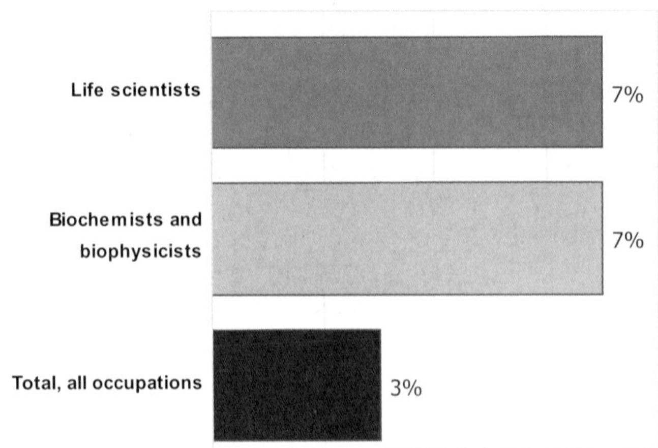

Note: All Occupations includes all occupations in the U.S. Economy.
Source: U.S. Bureau of Labor Statistics, Employment Projections program

Job Outlook

Employment of biochemists and biophysicists is projected to grow 7 percent from 2022 to 2032, faster than the average for all occupations.

About 2,800 openings for biochemists and biophysicists are projected each year, on average, over the decade. Many of those openings are expected to result from the need to replace workers who transfer to different occupations or exit the labor force, such as to retire.

Employment

Biochemists and biophysicists will continue to be needed to do basic research that increases scientific knowledge and to research and develop biological products and processes that improve people's lives. Techniques, tools, and applications of biochemistry and biophysics are expanding as technology and knowledge progress.

The aging population will drive demand for new drugs and procedures to prevent, cure, or manage disease. This increased demand is, in turn, likely to create demand for biochemists and biophysicists involved in biomedical research. For example, biochemists and biophysicists will be needed to conduct genetic research and to develop new medicines and treatments that are used to fight genetic disorders and diseases, such as cancer. They also will be needed to develop new tests used to detect diseases and other illnesses.

Areas of research and development in biotechnology other than health also are expected to provide employment growth for biochemists and biophysicists. These workers will continue to be needed to study topics that advance our capabilities related to clean energy, efficient food production, and environmental protection.

Occupational Title	SOC Code	Employment, 2022	Projected Employment, 2032	Change, 2022-32	
				Percent	Numeric
Biochemists and biophysicists	19-1021	34,500	36,800	7	2,300

Contacts for More Information

For more information about biochemists, visit

- American Chemical Society
- American Chemical Society, Division of Biological Chemistry
- American Society for Biochemistry and Molecular Biology
- International Union of Biochemistry and Molecular Biology
- Biophysical Society
- International Union for Pure and Applied Biophysics
- American Institute of Biological Sciences
- Federation of American Societies for Experimental Biology
- National Institutes of Health

Biological Technicians

Summary

Quick Facts: Biological Technicians	
2022 Median Pay	$49,650 per year $23.87 per hour
Typical Entry-Level Education	Bachelor's degree
Work Experience in a Related Occupation	None
On-the-job Training	None
Number of Jobs, 2022	81,400
Job Outlook, 2022-32	5% (Faster than average)
Employment Change, 2022-32	3,900

What Biological Technicians Do

Biological technicians help biological and medical scientists conduct laboratory tests and experiments.

Work Environment

Biological technicians typically work in laboratories. Most biological technicians work full time.

How to Become a Biological Technician

To enter the occupation, biological technicians typically need a bachelor's degree in biology or a related field.

Pay

The median annual wage for biological technicians was $49,650 in May 2022.

Job Outlook

Employment of biological technicians is projected to grow 5 percent from 2022 to 2032, faster than the average for all occupations.

About 10,600 openings for biological technicians are projected each year, on average, over the decade. Many of those openings are expected to result from the need to replace workers who transfer to different occupations or exit the labor force, such as to retire.

Biological technicians gather and prepare biological samples for laboratory analysis.

What Biological Technicians Do

Biological technicians help biological and medical scientists conduct laboratory tests and experiments.

Duties

Biological technicians typically do the following:

- Set up, maintain, and clean laboratory instruments and equipment, such as microscopes, scales, pipets, and test tubes
- Gather and prepare biological samples, such as blood, food, and bacteria cultures, for laboratory analysis
- Conduct biological tests and experiments
- Document their work, including procedures, observations, and results
- Analyze experimental data and interpret results
- Write reports that summarize their findings

Biological technicians, sometimes called *laboratory assistants*, typically are responsible for doing scientific tests, experiments,

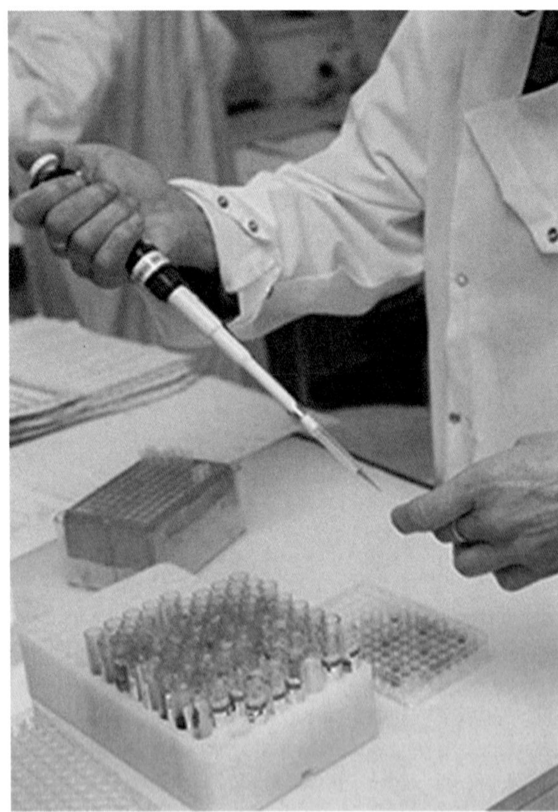

Biological technicians prepare samples for further testing.

Most biological technicians work in laboratories.

and analyses under the supervision of biologists (such as microbiologists) or medical scientists who direct and evaluate their work. Biological technicians use traditional laboratory instruments, advanced robotics, and automated equipment to conduct experiments. They use specialized computer software to collect, analyze, and model experimental data. Some biological technicians, such as those who assist the work of zoologists and wildlife biologists, may collect samples in the field, so they may need the ability to hike rugged terrain or otherwise travel through wilderness areas.

Biological technicians work in many research areas. They may assist medical researchers by administering new medicines and treatments to laboratory animals. They may separate proteins from other cell material, and analyze data from an experiment.

Biological technicians working in a microbiological context typically study living microbes and perform techniques specific to microbiology, such as staining specimens to aid identification.

Biological technicians also may work in private industry and assist in the study of a wide range of topics concerning industrial production. They may test samples in environmental impact studies, or monitor production processes to help ensure that products are not contaminated.

Work Environment

Biological technicians held about 81,400 jobs in 2022. The largest employers of biological technicians were as follows:

Scientific research and development services	28%
Colleges, universities, and professional schools; state, local, and private	24
Federal government, excluding postal service	11
Pharmaceutical and medicine manufacturing	10
Hospitals; state, local, and private	8

Biological technicians typically work in laboratories and offices, where they conduct experiments and analyze the results under the supervision of biological scientists and medical scientists. Some biological technicians who do fieldwork may be exposed to weather events and wildlife, such as mosquitoes.

Biological technicians must follow strict procedures to avoid contaminating the experiment, themselves, or the environment. Some experiments may involve dangerous organisms or toxic substances.

Biological technicians work together on teams under the direction of biologists or other scientists.

Work Schedules

Most biological technicians work full time and keep regular hours.

How to Become a Biological Technician

To enter the occupation, biological technicians typically need a bachelor's degree in biology or a related field. Although less

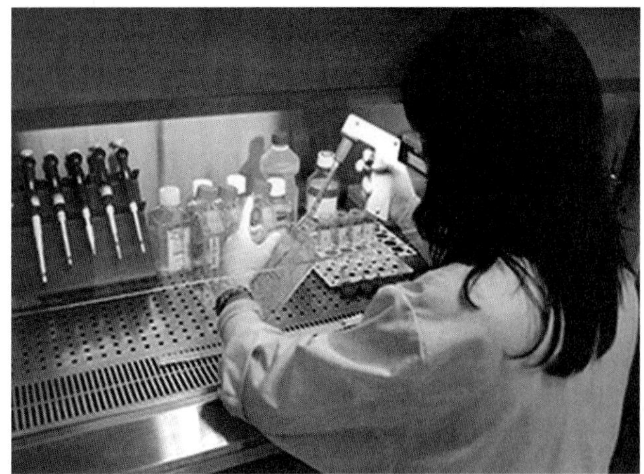

Most biological technicians gain laboratory experience while in school.

common, some positions are available to candidates who have less than a bachelor's degree.

Education

Biological technicians typically need a bachelor's degree in biology or a related field, such as physical science or natural resources. Positions are sometimes open to candidates who have less education than a bachelor's degree but have laboratory experience.

Biology programs typically include subfields such as ecology, microbiology, and physiology. In addition to studying biological sciences, students may need to take courses in math and physics, as well as in other sciences. Students need laboratory experience, so science coursework should include a lab component.

Other Experience

Prospective biological technicians should have laboratory experience. In addition to coursework, students may gain laboratory experience during summer internships with prospective employers, such as pharmaceutical and medicine manufacturers, or in university laboratories.

Advancement

Biological technicians may advance to scientist positions, such as microbiologist or biochemist and biophysicist, after a few years of experience working as a technician or after earning a master's degree or Ph.D. Gaining more experience and higher levels of education often allows biological technicians to move into positions such as natural sciences managers or postsecondary teachers.

Important Qualities

Analytical skills. Biological technicians need to conduct scientific experiments and analyses with accuracy and precision.

Communication skills. Biological technicians must understand and follow the instructions of their managing scientists. They also need to communicate their processes and findings clearly in written reports.

Critical-thinking skills. Biological technicians draw conclusions from experimental results through sound reasoning and judgment.

Observational skills. Biological technicians must constantly monitor their experiments. They need to keep a complete, accurate record of their work, including the conditions under which the experiment was carried out, the procedures they followed, and the results they obtained.

Technical skills. Biological technicians need to set up and operate sophisticated equipment and instruments. They also may need to adjust equipment to ensure that experiments are conducted properly.

Pay

The median annual wage for biological technicians was $49,650 in May 2022. The median wage is the wage at which half the workers in an occupation earned more than that amount and half earned less. The lowest 10 percent earned less than $33,480, and the highest 10 percent earned more than $79,110.

In May 2022, the median annual wages for biological technicians in the top industries in which they worked were as follows:

Pharmaceutical and medicine manufacturing	$63,980
Scientific research and development services	52,200
Hospitals; state, local, and private	50,100
Colleges, universities, and professional schools; state, local, and private	48,830
Federal government, excluding postal service	43,470

Most biological technicians work full time and keep regular hours.

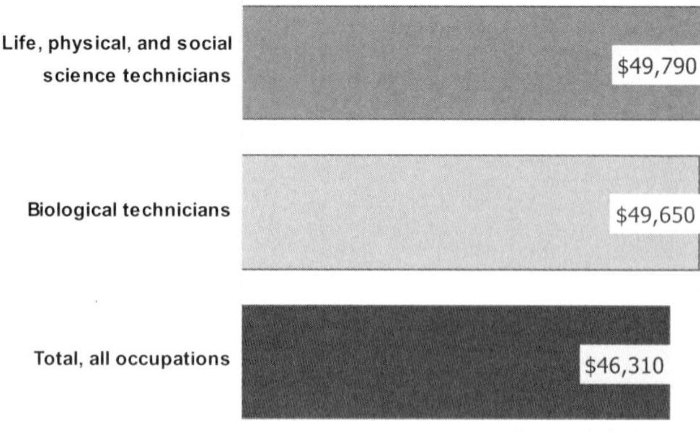

Note: All Occupations includes all occupations in the U.S. Economy.
Source: U.S. Bureau of Labor Statistics, Occupational Employment and Wage Statistics

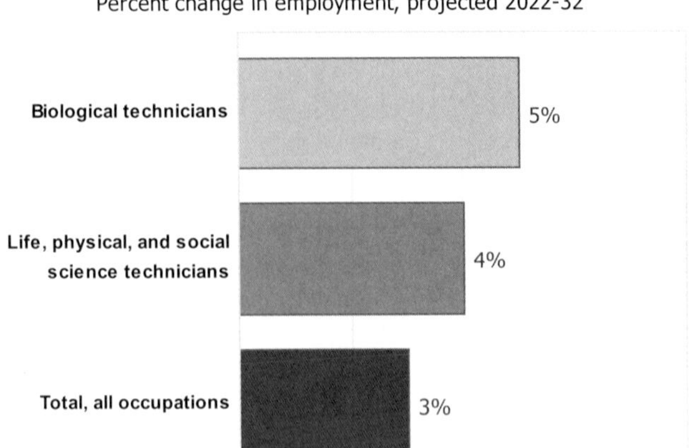

Note: All Occupations includes all occupations in the U.S. Economy.
Source: U.S. Bureau of Labor Statistics, Employment Projections program

Job Outlook

Employment of biological technicians is projected to grow 5 percent from 2022 to 2032, faster than the average for all occupations.

About 10,600 openings for biological technicians are projected each year, on average, over the decade. Many of those openings are expected to result from the need to replace workers who transfer to different occupations or exit the labor force, such as to retire.

Employment

Demand for biological and medical research is expected to increase the need for biological technicians. Synthetic biology, a relatively new area of biotechnology, will employ biological technicians to redesign biological systems or living organisms for medical, manufacturing, and agriculture applications. Continued growth in biotechnology research and development projects, such as using cells to deliver drugs within the human body, is expected to support demand for biological technicians.

Employment projections data for biological technicians, 2022-32

Occupational Title	SOC Code	Employment, 2022	Projected Employment, 2032	Change, 2022-32		Employment by Industry
				Percent	Numeric	
SOURCE: U.S. Bureau of Labor Statistics, Employment Projections program						
Biological technicians	19-4021	81,400	85,300	5	3,900	Get data

Contacts for More Information

For more information about career opportunities in the biological sciences, visit

- American Institute of Biological Sciences
- American Society for Cell Biology
- American Society for Microbiology
- DIYbio
- Federation of American Societies for Experimental Biology
- USAJOBS

Chemical Technicians

Summary

Quick Facts: Chemical Technicians

2022 Median Pay	$50,840 per year $24.44 per hour
Typical Entry-Level Education	Associate's degree
Work Experience in a Related Occupation	None
On-the-job Training	Moderate-term on-the-job training
Number of Jobs, 2022	58,800
Job Outlook, 2022-32	3% (As fast as average)
Employment Change, 2022-32	1,900

What Chemical Technicians Do

Chemical technicians conduct laboratory tests to help scientists analyze the properties of materials.

Work Environment

Chemical technicians often work in laboratories or in manufacturing facilities, such as chemical manufacturing plants. Most technicians work full time.

How to Become a Chemical Technician

To enter the occupation, chemical technicians typically need an associate's degree or 2 years of postsecondary education. Some positions require candidates to have a bachelor's degree; others require a high school diploma. Most chemical technicians receive on-the-job training.

Pay

The median annual wage for chemical technicians was $50,840 in May 2022.

Job Outlook

Employment of chemical technicians is projected to grow 3 percent from 2022 to 2032, about as fast as the average for all occupations.

About 7,100 openings for chemical technicians are projected each year, on average, over the decade. Many of those openings are expected to result from the need to replace workers who transfer to different occupations or exit the labor force, such as to retire.

What Chemical Technicians Do

Chemical technicians use laboratory instruments and techniques to help scientists analyze the properties of materials.

Chemical technicians often use laboratory equipment to help chemists and chemical engineers test chemical products.

Duties

Chemical technicians typically do the following:

- Monitor chemical processes and test product quality to make sure that they meet standards and specifications
- Set up, operate, and maintain laboratory instruments and equipment
- Maintain production equipment and troubleshoot problems
- Prepare chemical solutions
- Conduct, compile, and interpret results of chemical and physical experiments, tests, and analyses for a variety of purposes, including research and development
- Prepare and present reports, graphs, and charts that summarize their results

Technicians who work in laboratories may help conduct experiments that contribute to research and development. For example, some chemical technicians help chemists and other scientists develop new medicines.

Other chemical technicians work in manufacturing, where they may assist in monitoring quality, maintaining equipment, and improving production processes.

Typically, chemists or chemical engineers direct chemical technicians' work and evaluate their results. Most technicians work on teams, but they also may be required to work independently on projects. Experienced technicians may serve as mentors to technicians who are new to a lab or to a specific area of research.

Work Environment

Chemical technicians held about 58,800 jobs in 2022. The largest employers of chemical technicians were as follows:

Chemical manufacturing	30%
Testing laboratories	18
Research and development in the physical, engineering, and life sciences	10
Wholesale trade	4
Educational services; state, local, and private	3

Chemical technicians often work in laboratories or in manufacturing facilities. Chemical manufacturing plants make a variety of products, such as fertilizers, medicines, and soaps.

Injuries and Illnesses

Chemical technicians may be exposed to health or safety hazards when handling certain chemicals and manufacturing equipment, but there is little risk if proper procedures are followed.

Work Schedules

Most technicians work full time. Occasionally, they may have to work additional hours to meet project deadlines or troubleshoot problems with manufacturing processes. Some work irregular schedules to monitor laboratory experiments or manufacturing operations.

Chemical technicians monitor and adjust processing equipment at manufacturing facilities.

Chemical technicians typically work in laboratories or in industrial facilities.

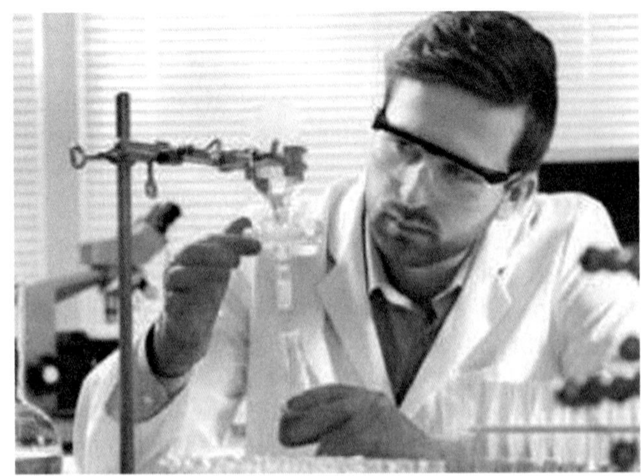

Laboratory experience provides students with hands-on experience in using various instruments and techniques properly.

How to Become a Chemical Technician

To enter the occupation, chemical technicians typically need an associate's degree or 2 years of postsecondary education. Some positions require candidates to have a bachelor's degree; others require a high school diploma. Most chemical technicians receive on-the-job training.

Education

Chemical technicians typically need an associate's degree or 2 years of postsecondary education in applied science or chemical technology. Some employers prefer to hire candidates who have a bachelor's degree in those or related fields, such as biology or physical science. Other employers may consider candidates who have a high school diploma.

Technical and community college programs in applied sciences or chemical technology typically include courses in math, physics, and biology in addition to chemistry. Coursework in statistics and computer science is also useful for learning data analysis and modeling.

Courses that include a laboratory component provide students with hands-on practice in conducting experiments and proper use of instruments and techniques. Participating in internships and cooperative-education programs while attending school helps students gain experience.

Important Qualities

Analytical skills. Chemical technicians must be methodical in conducting scientific experiments and interpreting data.

Communication skills. Chemical technicians must explain their work to scientists and engineers or to workers who may not have a technical background. They often write reports to summarize their results.

Detail oriented. Chemical technicians need to set up, operate, and maintain precision laboratory equipment and instruments. They also must keep meticulous records of their experiments, observations, and results.

Interpersonal skills. Chemical technicians must work well as part of a team that often includes scientists, engineers, and other technicians.

Training

Chemical technicians typically receive on-the-job training from experienced technicians, who explain proper methods and procedures for conducting experiments and operating equipment. The length of training varies with the new employee's level of experience and education and by industry.

Advancement

Technicians who have a bachelor's degree may advance to become chemical engineers or chemists.

Pay

The median annual wage for chemical technicians was $50,840 in May 2022. The median wage is the wage at which half the workers in an occupation earned more than that amount and half earned less. The lowest 10 percent earned less than $35,770, and the highest 10 percent earned more than $81,610.

In May 2022, the median annual wages for chemical technicians in the top industries in which they worked were as follows:

Research and development in the physical, engineering, and life sciences	$62,150
Chemical manufacturing	55,900
Wholesale trade	51,220
Educational services; state, local, and private	49,110
Testing laboratories	45,460

Most technicians work full time. Occasionally, they may have to work additional hours to meet project deadlines or troubleshoot problems with manufacturing processes. Some work

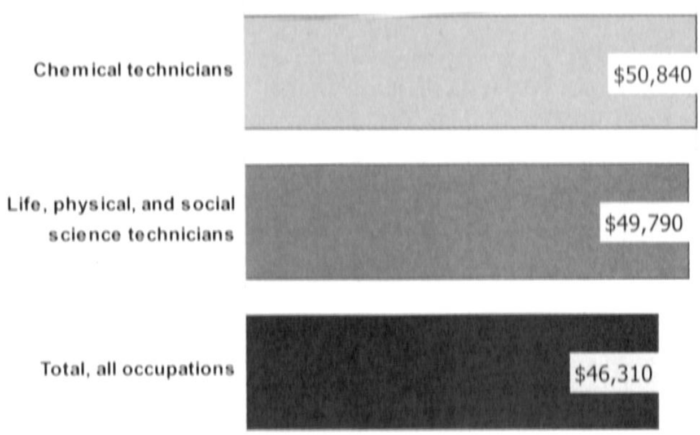

Note: All Occupations includes all occupations in the U.S. Economy.
Source: U.S. Bureau of Labor Statistics, Occupational Employment and Wage Statistics

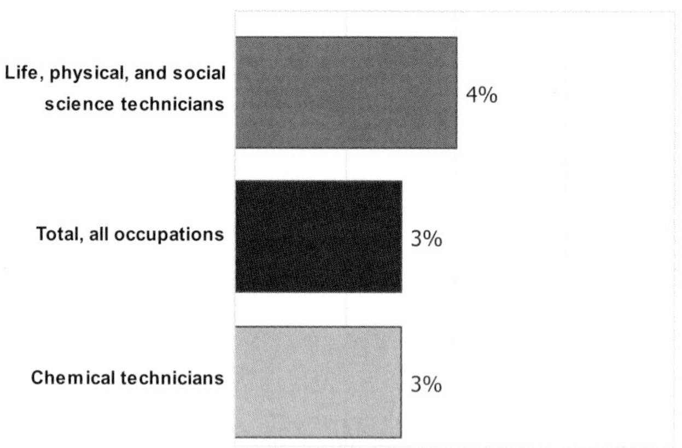

Note: All Occupations includes all occupations in the U.S. Economy.
Source: U.S. Bureau of Labor Statistics, Employment Projections program

irregular schedules to monitor laboratory experiments or manufacturing operations.

Job Outlook

Employment of chemical technicians is projected to grow 3 percent from 2022 to 2032, about as fast as the average for all occupations.

About 7,100 openings for chemical technicians are projected each year, on average, over the decade. Many of those openings are expected to result from the need to replace workers who transfer to different occupations or exit the labor force, such as to retire.

Employment

Chemical technicians will continue to be in demand to test new materials and products developed by chemists and chemical engineers. They also will be needed to monitor the quality of chemical products and processes. In addition, increased demand for these technicians is expected due to greater interest in environmental issues such as pollution control, clean energy, and sustainability.

Occupational Title	SOC Code	Employment, 2022	Projected Employment, 2032	Change, 2022-32	
				Percent	Numeric
Chemical technicians	19-4031	58,800	60,700	3	1,900

Contacts for More Information

For more information about chemical technicians, visit

- American Chemical Society
- American Chemistry Council

Chemists and Materials Scientists

Summary

Quick Facts: Chemists and Materials Scientists	
2022 Median Pay	$81,810 per year $39.33 per hour
Typical Entry-Level Education	Bachelor's degree
Work Experience in a Related Occupation	None
On-the-job Training	None
Number of Jobs, 2022	95,000
Job Outlook, 2022-32	6% (Faster than average)
Employment Change, 2022-32	5,800

What Chemists and Materials Scientists Do

Chemists and materials scientists research and analyze the chemical properties of substances to develop new materials, products, or knowledge.

Work Environment

Chemists and materials scientists work in laboratories, offices, and manufacturing facilities. Most work full time.

How to Become a Chemist or Materials Scientist

To enter the occupation, chemists and materials scientists typically need at least a bachelor's degree in chemistry or a related field. However, they may need a master's degree or Ph.D. for some jobs, such as research positions.

Pay

The median annual wage for chemists was $80,670 in May 2022.

The median annual wage for materials scientists was $104,380 in May 2022.

Job Outlook

Overall employment of chemists and materials scientists is projected to grow 6 percent from 2022 to 2032, faster than the average for all occupations.

About 7,200 openings for chemists and materials scientists are projected each year, on average, over the decade. Many of those openings are expected to result from the need to replace workers who transfer to different occupations or exit the labor force, such as to retire.

Chemists and materials scientists perform experiments that require creative problem solving and detailed recordkeeping.

What Chemists and Materials Scientists Do

Chemists and materials scientists research and analyze the chemical properties of substances to develop new materials, products, or knowledge.

Duties

Chemists and materials scientists typically do the following:

- Plan and carry out research projects, such as development of products and of testing methods
- Direct technicians and other staff in chemical processing and testing, including for ingredients, mixing times, and operating temperatures
- Collaborate with engineers and other scientists on experiments, product development, and production processes
- Prepare solutions, compounds, and reagents used in laboratory procedures
- Analyze substances to determine their composition and concentration of elements
- Conduct tests on materials and other substances to ensure that safety and quality standards are met

Most chemists and materials scientists work as part of a team.

- Write technical reports that detail methods and findings
- Present research findings to scientists, engineers, and other colleagues

Chemists and materials scientists work usually work in either basic or applied research. In basic research, chemists and materials scientists investigate the properties, composition, and structure of matter. They also experiment with combinations of elements and the ways in which they interact. In applied research, chemists and materials scientists investigate developing new products or improving existing ones, such as medications, batteries, and cleaners.

Chemists and materials scientists use computers and other laboratory equipment for modeling, simulation, and analysis. For example, chemists may use three-dimensional modeling software to study the structure and properties of complex molecules.

Most chemists and materials scientists work as part of a team that may include physicists, microbiologists, and engineers. For example, chemists in pharmaceutical research may work with biochemists and biophysicists or chemical engineers to develop new drugs and with industrial engineers to design ways to mass-produce the drugs.

Chemists may work in interdisciplinary fields, such as biochemistry or geochemistry. They also may specialize in a particular field. The following are examples of types of chemists:

Analytical chemists identify elements and compounds in a substance to determine its structure, composition, and nature. They also study the interactions between parts of compounds. Some analytical chemists specialize in developing new methods of evaluation. Their research has a range of applications, including food safety and pollution control.

Forensic chemists aid in criminal investigations by testing and analyzing evidence, such as DNA. These chemists work primarily in laboratories but may testify in court as expert witnesses to explain the results of their analyses.

Inorganic chemists study the structure, properties, and reactions of substances that do not contain carbon, such as metals. They work to understand the behavior and the characteristics of inorganic substances, such as ceramics and superconductors, for modifying, separating, or using in products or for other purposes.

Medicinal chemists research and develop chemical compounds to create and test new drug products. They also help develop and improve manufacturing processes to effectively produce new drugs on a large scale.

Organic chemists study the structure, properties, and reactions of molecules that contain carbon. They also design and make organic substances for use in developing new commercial products, such as medicine and plastics.

Physical chemists study how matter behaves and how chemical reactions occur. From their analyses, physical chemists may develop theories, such as how complex structures are formed, and research potential uses for new materials.

Theoretical chemists investigate abstract methods that predict the outcomes of chemical experiments. Their specializations may incorporate different branches of computer science, such as artificial intelligence. Some examples of *theoretical chemists* are *computational chemists*, *mathematical chemists*, and *chemical informaticians*.

Materials scientists typically specialize in the material they work with most often. Examples include ceramics, metals, polymers, and semiconductors.

Work Environment

Chemists held about 87,100 jobs in 2022. The largest employers of chemists were as follows:

Chemical manufacturing	30%
Research and development in the physical, engineering, and life sciences	21
Testing laboratories	9
Federal government, excluding postal service	7
Administrative and support and waste management and remediation services	4

Materials scientists held about 7,900 jobs in 2022. The largest employers of materials scientists were as follows:

Research and development in the physical, engineering, and life sciences	36%
Architectural, engineering, and related services	12
Chemical manufacturing	11
Colleges, universities, and professional schools; state, local, and private	8
Computer and electronic product manufacturing	5

Chemists and materials scientists typically work in laboratories and offices, where they conduct experiments and analyze their results. Some chemists and materials scientists work in industrial manufacturing facilities.

Chemists and materials scientists who work for manufacturing companies, especially ones with multiple facilities, may travel occasionally.

Injuries and Illnesses

Chemists and materials scientists may be exposed to health or safety hazards when handling certain chemicals. They wear protective clothing, such as goggles and masks, and follow safety procedures to reduce the risk of injury or illness.

Work Schedules

Most chemists and materials scientists work full time. Occasionally, they may have to work additional hours to meet project deadlines or perform time-sensitive laboratory experiments during off-hours.

How to Become a Chemist or Materials Scientist

To enter the occupation, chemists and materials scientists typically need at least a bachelor's degree in chemistry or a related field. However, they may need a master's degree or Ph.D. for some jobs, such as research positions.

Education

Chemists and materials scientists typically need a bachelor's degree in chemistry or a related physical science field. Some jobs require a master's degree or Ph.D. and work experience. Chemists and materials scientists with a Ph.D. and postdoctoral experience may lead research teams.

Undergraduate chemistry programs typically require a number of courses in chemistry, most of which include a laboratory component. They also require courses in a variety of other subjects, including math, biological sciences, and physics.

Some chemistry programs offer materials science as a specialization, and some engineering programs offer a joint degree in materials science and engineering.

Graduate programs in chemistry commonly include specialization in a subfield, such as analytical chemistry or inorganic

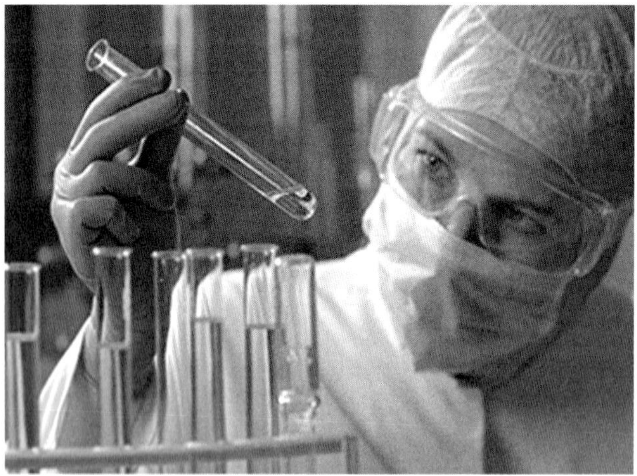

Chemists must wear protective clothing such as gloves and goggles when handling hazardous chemicals.

Laboratory experience through internships, fellowships, or work–study programs in industry is useful.

chemistry. For example, those interested in doing pharmaceutical research may choose to develop a strong background in medicinal or organic chemistry.

Combined programs, which offer an accelerated bachelor's and master's degree in chemistry, also are available.

Training

Laboratory equipment in the workplace is expensive and may differ from the equipment available in university laboratories. As a result, chemists and materials scientists may receive training after they are hired, with experienced chemists and materials scientists demonstrating proper use of their employers' laboratory equipment.

Laboratory experience gained through internships, fellowships, or cooperative programs in industry is also useful.

Advancement

Chemists may advance as they gain experience, typically by receiving greater responsibility and independence in their work.

Another path to advancement is through further education. For example, Ph.D. chemists may lead research teams and take on larger, more complicated projects as they progress.

Some chemists and materials scientists advance to become natural sciences managers.

Important Qualities

Analytical skills. Chemists and materials scientists need to evaluate the results of experiments to ensure accuracy in their research.

Communication skills. Chemists and materials scientists must be able to convey information clearly in reports and presentations for both technical and nontechnical audiences.

Interpersonal skills. Chemists and materials scientists typically work on teams and need to be cooperative. Chemists and material scientists who serve as team leaders must be able to motivate and direct others.

Math skills. Chemists and materials scientists regularly use calculus, algebra, statistics, and other math for calculations.

Organizational skills. Chemists and materials scientists must document processes carefully when conducting experiments, tracking outcomes, and analyzing results.

Perseverance. Chemists and materials scientists must persist in the trial-and-error demands of research. They must be self-motivated to avoid becoming discouraged.

Problem-solving skills. Chemists' and materials scientists' work involves posing questions during research and finding answers through results.

Time-management skills. Chemists and materials scientists usually need to meet deadlines and must be able to prioritize tasks while maintaining quality.

Chemists and Materials Scientists

Median annual wages, May 2022

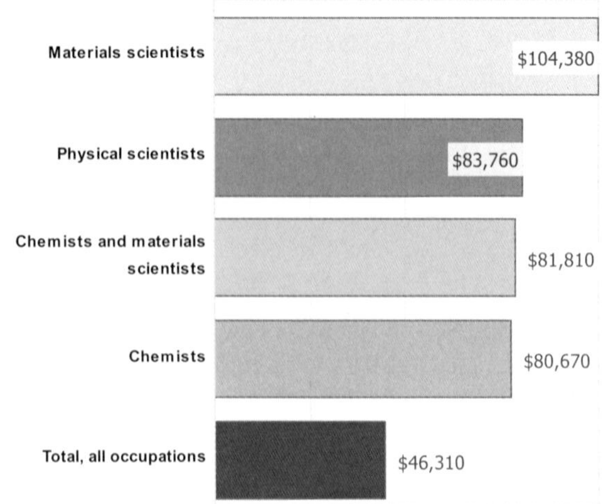

Note: All Occupations includes all occupations in the U.S. Economy.
Source: U.S. Bureau of Labor Statistics, Occupational Employment and Wage Statistics

Pay

The median annual wage for chemists was $80,670 in May 2022. The median wage is the wage at which half the workers in an occupation earned more than that amount and half earned less. The lowest 10 percent earned less than $49,050, and the highest 10 percent earned more than $139,200.

The median annual wage for materials scientists was $104,380 in May 2022. The lowest 10 percent earned less than $61,730, and the highest 10 percent earned more than $165,840.

In May 2022, the median annual wages for chemists in the top industries in which they worked were as follows:

Federal government, excluding postal service	$121,060
Research and development in the physical, engineering, and life sciences	100,120
Chemical manufacturing	78,430
Testing laboratories	60,780
Administrative and support and waste management and remediation services	58,180

In May 2022, the median annual wages for materials scientists in the top industries in which they worked were as follows:

Computer and electronic product manufacturing	$133,040
Research and development in the physical, engineering, and life sciences	115,970
Chemical manufacturing	107,470
Architectural, engineering, and related services	85,060
Colleges, universities, and professional schools; state, local, and private	81,690

Most chemists and materials scientists work full time. Occasionally, they may have to work additional hours to meet project

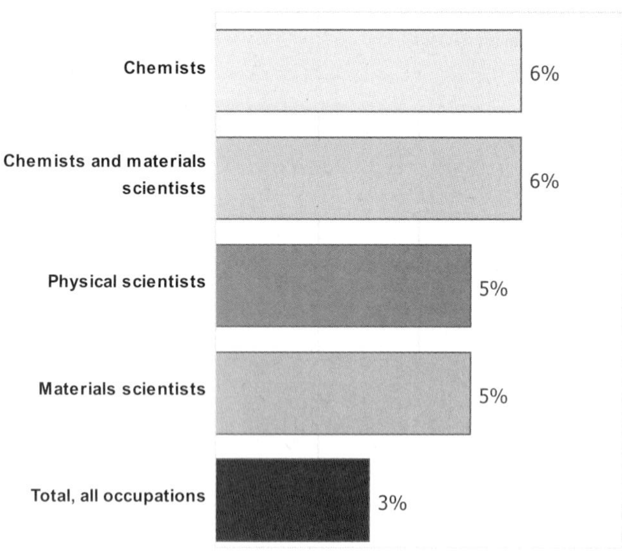

Note: All Occupations includes all occupations in the U.S. Economy.
Source: U.S. Bureau of Labor Statistics, Employment Projections program

deadlines or perform time-sensitive laboratory experiments during off-hours.

Job Outlook

Overall employment of chemists and materials scientists is projected to grow 6 percent from 2022 to 2032, faster than the average for all occupations.

About 7,200 openings for chemists and materials scientists are projected each year, on average, over the decade. Many of those openings are expected to result from the need to replace workers who transfer to different occupations or exit the labor force, such as to retire.

Employment

Demand for chemists and materials scientists is expected to stem from innovations in a variety of research areas, including nanotechnology and biomaterials.

Chemists will be needed to develop improved products and processes, such as new medicines and methods for ensuring food safety. Materials scientists will be needed to research and develop affordable, safe, high-quality materials for electronics, energy, transportation, and other uses.

Occupational Title	SOC Code	Employment, 2022	Projected Employment, 2032	Change, 2022-32	
				Percent	Numeric
Chemists and materials scientists	19-2030	95,000	100,800	6	5,800
Chemists	19-2031	87,100	92,500	6	5,400
Materials scientists	19-2032	7,900	8,300	5	400

Contacts for More Information

For more information, visit

- American Chemical Society
- American Chemistry Council
- ASM International
- Materials Research Society
- American Chemical Society Committee on Professional Training
- American Chemical Society Green Chemistry Academic Programs
- USAJOBS

Conservation Scientists and Foresters

Summary

Quick Facts: Conservation Scientists and Foresters	
2022 Median Pay	$64,420 per year $30.97 per hour
Typical Entry-Level Education	Bachelor's degree
Work Experience in a Related Occupation	None
On-the-job Training	None
Number of Jobs, 2022	36,000
Job Outlook, 2022-32	4% (As fast as average)
Employment Change, 2022-32	1,300

What Conservation Scientists and Foresters Do

Conservation scientists and foresters manage the land quality of forests, parks, rangelands, and other natural resources.

Work Environment

Conservation scientists and foresters work for federal, state, and local governments; on privately owned lands; or in social advocacy organizations. Most conservation scientists and foresters work full time, and schedules may vary.

How to Become a Conservation Scientist or Forester

Conservation scientists and foresters typically need a bachelor's degree in forestry, natural resources, or a related field.

Pay

The median annual wage for conservation scientists was $64,460 in May 2022.

The median annual wage for foresters was $64,220 in May 2022.

Job Outlook

Overall employment of conservation scientists and foresters is projected to grow 4 percent from 2022 to 2032, about as fast as the average for all occupations.

Conservation scientists and foresters manage and monitor overall land quality of forests, parks, rangelands, and other natural resources.

About 3,000 openings for conservation scientists and foresters are projected each year, on average, over the decade. Many of those openings are expected to result from the need to replace workers who transfer to different occupations or exit the labor force, such as to retire.

What Conservation Scientists and Foresters Do

Conservation scientists and foresters manage the land quality of forests, parks, rangelands, and other natural resources.

Duties

Conservation scientists and foresters typically do the following:

- Oversee conservation and forestry activities to ensure compliance with government regulations and protection of habitats
- Negotiate terms and conditions for contracts related to forest harvesting or land use
- Establish plans for managing forest lands and resources
- Choose and prepare sites for new trees, using controlled burning, bulldozers, or herbicides to clear land
- Monitor forest-cleared lands and forest regeneration
- Direct and participate in forest fire suppression
- Work with private landowners, governments, farmers, and others to remove timber or improve land with minimal environmental damage

Conservation scientists and foresters evaluate data on forest and soil quality, assessing damage to trees and forest lands caused by fires and logging activities. In addition, they lead activities such as suppressing fires and planting seedlings. Fire-suppression activities include measuring the speed at which fires spread and the success of planned suppression.

Conservation scientists and foresters use a variety of tools and equipment. For example, they use clinometers to measure tree height, diameter tapes to measure tree circumference, and

Conservation scientists and foresters study forest and soil quality.

increment borers and bark gauges to measure tree growth for calculating timber volume and estimating growth rates. They also may use drones, aerial photographs, satellite images, and Geographic Information System (GIS) data to map large forest or range areas.

Conservation scientists manage, improve, and protect natural resources. They work with private landowners and federal, state, and local governments to find ways to use and improve the land while safeguarding the environment. They also advise farmers, ranchers, and other agricultural managers on ways to improve land while safeguarding the environment.

The following are examples of types of conservation scientists:

Conservation land managers work for land trusts or other conservation organizations to protect the wildlife habitats, biodiversity, scenic value, and other specific attributes of preserves and conservation lands.

Range managers, also called *range conservationists*, protect grazing lands to maximize their use without harming the environment. Rangelands contain many natural resources and cover millions of acres in the United States. Range managers may catalog animals, plants, and soils; develop resource management plans; help to restore ecosystems; or help oversee a ranch. They also maintain soil stability and vegetation for wildlife habitats, outdoor recreation, and other uses. Like foresters, range managers work to prevent and reduce wildfires and invasive species.

Soil and water conservationists give technical help in managing concerns related to soil and water. They develop programs to help landowners make their land productive without causing damage. They also help landowners and governments by advising on water quality, preserving water supplies, and handling erosion.

Foresters' responsibilities vary by employer. Their duties may include creating plans to regenerate forested lands, monitoring the progress of reforested lands, and supervising tree harvests. They also design plans to keep forests free from disease, harmful insects, and damaging wildfires. Foresters may direct the work of forest and conservation workers and technicians.

The following are examples of types of foresters:

Procurement foresters contact, negotiate with, and buy timber from local forest owners. Procurement typically requires taking inventory on the type, amount, and location of a property's standing timber. Procurement foresters then appraise the timber's worth, negotiate its purchase, and draw up a contract for purchase and removal. After the contract is in place, these foresters usually subcontract with loggers or pulpwood cutters to fell trees and to help lay out roads for removing the timber.

Urban foresters live and work in cities and manage the trees. These workers focus on issues related to urban wellbeing, including air quality, shade, and storm water runoff.

Conservation education foresters train teachers and students about issues facing forest lands.

Conservation scientists and foresters typically work in offices, in laboratories, and outdoors, sometimes in remote locations performing fieldwork.

Work Environment

Conservation scientists held about 24,700 jobs in 2022. The largest employers of conservation scientists were as follows:

Employer	Percent
Federal government, excluding postal service	31%
State government, excluding education and hospitals	22
Local government, excluding education and hospitals	18
Social advocacy organizations	14
Professional, scientific, and technical services	6

Foresters held about 11,300 jobs in 2022. The largest employers of foresters were as follows:

Employer	Percent
State government, excluding education and hospitals	27%
Federal government, excluding postal service	12
Local government, excluding education and hospitals	12
Support activities for agriculture and forestry	11
Forestry and logging	5

Conservation scientists and foresters typically work in offices, in laboratories, and outdoors, sometimes traveling to remote locations. When visiting or working near logging operations or wood yards, they wear a hardhat and other protective gear to guard against injury. They also wear protective gear for activities related to fire suppression, which may include prevention or emergency response. Insect bites, poisonous plants, and other natural hazards also present some risk.

The work can be physically demanding. Some conservation scientists and foresters work outdoors in all types of weather. They may need to walk long distances through dense trees or plant growth.

Work Schedules

Most conservation scientists and foresters work full time, and schedules may vary to include weekends. Some work more than 40 hours per week, such as when traveling to remote locations.

How to Become a Conservation Scientist or Forester

Conservation scientists and foresters typically need a bachelor's degree in forestry, natural resources, or a related field.

Education

To enter their occupation, conservation scientists and foresters typically need a bachelor's degree in forestry, natural resources, or a related subject, such as agriculture or biology.

Conservation scientists and foresters typically need a bachelor's degree in forestry or a related field.

Bachelor's degree programs in forestry and related fields typically include courses in biology, ecology, and forest measurement. Conservation scientists and foresters also typically have a background in Geographic Information System (GIS) technology, remote sensing, and other forms of computer modeling.

The Society of American Foresters accredits academic programs in forestry, urban forestry, and natural resources and ecosystem management.

Licenses, Certifications, and Registrations

Several states may require some type of credentialing process for conservation scientists and foresters. In some of these states, conservation scientists and foresters must be licensed; check with your state licensing board for more information.

Some conservation scientists and foresters earn optional certification related to their area of work. For example, the Society of American Foresters (SAF) offers forester certification to candidates who have at least a bachelor's degree from a SAF-accredited or equivalent forestry program, professional experience, and passed an exam.

The Society for Range Management offers certification in rangeland management or as a range management consultant to candidates who have a bachelor's degree in range management of a related field, related work experience, and passed an exam.

Important Qualities

Analytical skills. Conservation scientists and foresters must be able to evaluate results from field tests and experiments to determine potential impacts on soil, forest lands, and the spread of fires.

Communication skills. Conservation scientists and foresters must convey information to firefighters, forest and conservation workers, landowners, and, sometimes, the public.

Critical-thinking skills. Conservation scientists and foresters use reasoning to reach conclusions and to determine improvements for forest conditions.

Management skills. Conservation scientists and foresters must be able to lead the forest and conservation workers and technicians they supervise.

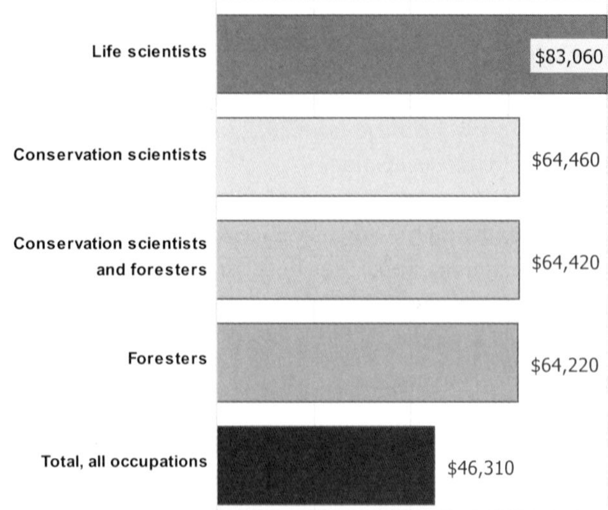

Note: All Occupations includes all occupations in the U.S. Economy.
Source: U.S. Bureau of Labor Statistics, Occupational Employment and Wage Statistics

Physical stamina. Conservation scientists and foresters may walk long distances in challenging terrain, such as steep or wooded areas, and may work in all kinds of weather conditions.

Pay

The median annual wage for conservation scientists was $64,460 in May 2022. The median wage is the wage at which half the workers in an occupation earned more than that amount and half earned less. The lowest 10 percent earned less than $41,360, and the highest 10 percent earned more than $102,670.

The median annual wage for foresters was $64,220 in May 2022. The lowest 10 percent earned less than $45,260, and the highest 10 percent earned more than $97,460.

In May 2022, the median annual wages for conservation scientists in the top industries in which they worked were as follows:

Federal government, excluding postal service	$79,350
Professional, scientific, and technical services	77,190
Social advocacy organizations	61,080
State government, excluding education and hospitals	59,720
Local government, excluding education and hospitals	58,100

In May 2022, the median annual wages for foresters in the top industries in which they worked were as follows:

Federal government, excluding postal service	$70,620
Local government, excluding education and hospitals	64,460
State government, excluding education and hospitals	61,210

Most conservation scientists and foresters work full time, and schedules may vary to include weekends. Some work more than 40 hours per week, such as when traveling to remote locations.

Job Outlook

Overall employment of conservation scientists and foresters is projected to grow 4 percent from 2022 to 2032, about as fast as the average for all occupations.

About 3,000 openings for conservation scientists and foresters are projected each year, on average, over the decade. Many of those openings are expected to result from the need to replace workers who transfer to different occupations or exit the labor force, such as to retire.

Employment

Changing weather conditions and the development of unused land have contributed to a rise in wildfires. Preventing and suppressing these fires have become the primary concerns for managing forests and rangelands. In addition, with the increasing numbers of forest fires and of people who live on or near forest lands, foresters and conservation scientists will be needed to mitigate growing humanitarian and environmental impacts of forest fires.

Occupational Title	SOC Code	Employment, 2022	Projected Employment, 2032	Change, 2022-32	
				Percent	Numeric
Conservation scientists and foresters	19-1030	36,000	37,300	4	1,300
Conservation scientists	19-1031	24,700	25,700	4	1,000
Foresters	19-1032	11,300	11,600	2	300

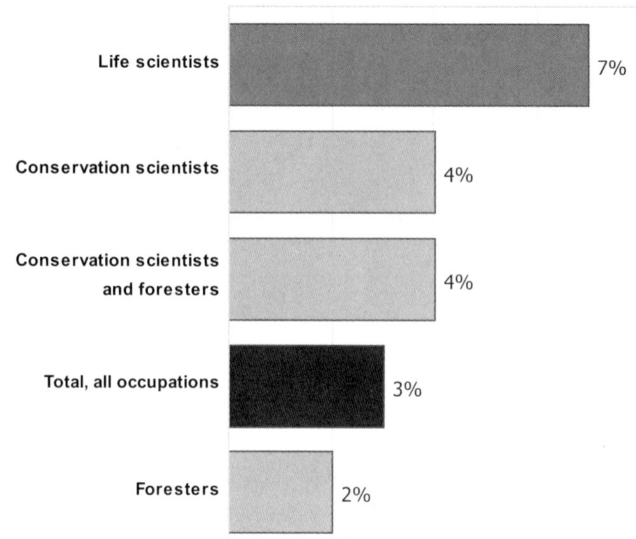

Note: All Occupations includes all occupations in the U.S. Economy.
Source: U.S. Bureau of Labor Statistics, Employment Projections program

Contacts for More Information

For more information, visit

- Society of American Foresters (SAF)
- Forest Stewards Guild
- Society for Range Management (SRM)
- U.S. Forest Service

Economists

Summary

Quick Facts: Economists

2022 Median Pay	$113,940 per year $54.78 per hour
Typical Entry-Level Education	Master's degree
Work Experience in a Related Occupation	None
On-the-job Training	None
Number of Jobs, 2022	17,600
Job Outlook, 2022-32	6% (Faster than average)
Employment Change, 2022-32	1,100

What Economists Do

Economists conduct research, prepare reports, and evaluate issues related to monetary and fiscal policy. They also may collect and analyze statistical data.

Work Environment

Economists typically work in an office setting, either independently or collaborating with a variety of other workers. Most economists work full time, and some work more than 40 hours per week.

How to Become an Economist

Economists typically need at least a master's degree to enter the occupation. However, some economists—primarily in government—qualify for entry-level positions with a bachelor's degree. Others need a Ph.D.

Pay

The median annual wage for economists was $113,940 in May 2022.

Job Outlook

Employment of economists is projected to grow 6 percent from 2022 to 2032, faster than the average for all occupations.

Economists interpret and forecast market trends.

About 1,200 openings for economists are projected each year, on average, over the decade. Many of those openings are expected to result from the need to replace workers who transfer to different occupations or exit the labor force, such as to retire.

What Economists Do

Economists conduct research, prepare reports, and evaluate issues related to monetary and fiscal policy. They also may collect and analyze statistical data.

Duties

Economists typically do the following:

- Research economic issues related to education, the labor force, international trade, and other topics
- Conduct surveys and collect data
- Analyze data using mathematical models, statistical tools, and other software
- Interpret and forecast trends, such as of financial markets
- Advise businesses, governments, and individuals on problems related to fiscal policy or other economic topics
- Present research in tables, graphs, and articles for academic journals, government publications, and other media

Economists analyze topics related to the production, distribution, and use (consumption) of goods and services. They work in or across a variety of fields, such as business, health, and the environment. For example, some economists study the cost of products, healthcare, or energy, while others examine employment levels and trends, business cycles, inflation, or interest rates.

Economists study historical trends and make forecasts, using software to analyze data. The focus of their research may vary, depending on their employer

Economists who work in federal, state, and local government may collect and analyze data about the economy, including employment, prices, productivity, and wages. For example,

Economists prepare reports, tables, and charts.

they may evaluate various economic policies or proposals to inform policymakers about the impact of laws and regulations.

Business economists help managers understand the economy to inform their decision making. For example, economists may analyze consumer demand and sales to help a company maximize its profits.

Economists also work for international organizations, research firms, and consulting firms. They may present their findings to a variety of audiences or publish their analyses and forecasts in newspapers, journals, or other media.

Work Environment

Economists held about 17,600 jobs in 2022. The largest employers of economists were as follows:

Federal government, excluding postal service	27%
Management, scientific, and technical consulting services	20
Scientific research and development services	11
State government, excluding education and hospitals	10
Local government, excluding education and hospitals	7

Economists typically work in an office setting. They often work independently, but they also may collaborate with data scientists, statisticians, or other specialists. Some economists may be required to travel, such as to attend conferences.

Work Schedules

Most economists work full time, and some work more than 40 hours per week.

How to Become an Economist

Economists typically need at least a master's degree to enter the occupation. However, some economists—primarily in government—qualify for positions with a bachelor's degree. Others need a Ph.D.

Economists typically work with computers.

Education

Economists typically need a master's degree. Positions in business, research, or international organizations may require a master's degree or Ph.D. and work experience.

To pursue an advanced degree in economics, program applicants may need to have completed undergraduate coursework in subjects such as economics or mathematics.

Candidates who have a bachelor's degree with sufficient course credits in economics, statistics, or mathematics may qualify for some entry-level economist positions, including jobs with the federal government. Courses that introduce students to statistical analysis software also may be helpful. An advanced degree is sometimes required or preferred for higher level positions.

Important Qualities

Analytical skills. Economists must be able to review data and observe patterns to draw logical conclusions.

Communication skills. Economists must be able to explain their work through presentations and in written reports. Their audiences may vary from colleagues and other economists to those who do not have a background in economics.

Computer skills. Economists often use statistical analysis and other software to analyze data.

Critical-thinking skills. Economists must use sound reasoning to solve complex problems.

Math skills. Economists use mathematics, including calculus and linear algebra, to develop models and analyses.

Pay

The median annual wage for economists was $113,940 in May 2022. The median wage is the wage at which half the workers in an occupation earned more than that amount and half earned less. The lowest 10 percent earned less than $62,480, and the highest 10 percent earned more than $207,230.

In May 2022, the median annual wages for economists in the top industries in which they worked were as follows:

Communication skills are important for economists, since they sometimes present research to colleagues.

Management, scientific, and technical consulting services	$130,160
Federal government, excluding postal service	130,100
Scientific research and development services	106,720
Local government, excluding education and hospitals	86,910
State government, excluding education and hospitals	80,520

Most economists work full time, and some work more than 40 hours per week.

Job Outlook

Employment of economists is projected to grow 6 percent from 2022 to 2032, faster than the average for all occupations.

About 1,200 openings for economists are projected each year, on average, over the decade. Many of those openings are expected to result from the need to replace workers who transfer to different occupations or exit the labor force, such as to retire.

Economists

Median annual wages, May 2022

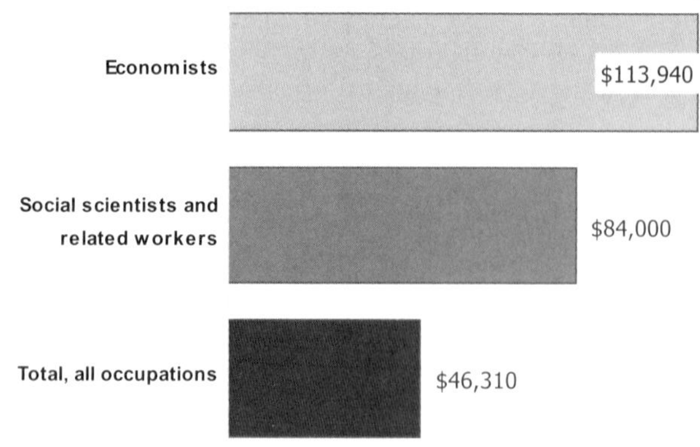

Note: All Occupations includes all occupations in the U.S. Economy.
Source: U.S. Bureau of Labor Statistics, Occupational Employment and Wage Statistics

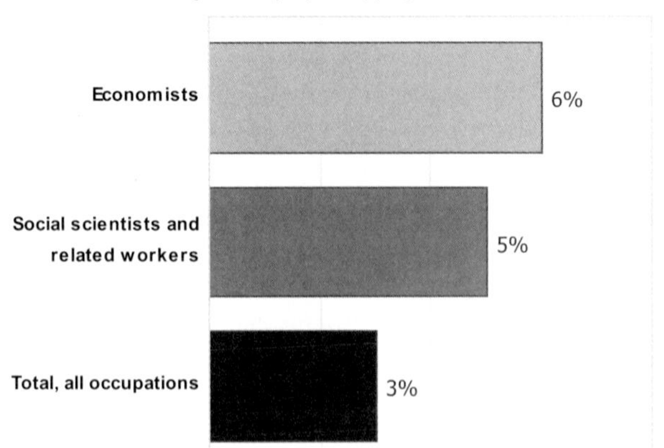

Note: All Occupations includes all occupations in the U.S. Economy.
Source: U.S. Bureau of Labor Statistics, Employment Projections program

Employment

Organizations across many industries use economic analysis and quantitative methods to study and forecast business, sales, and other market trends. Employment demand is expected to be strong for these workers, as organizations increasingly turn to economists to apply analysis of big data to pricing, advertising, and other areas. The increasing complexity of the global economy also is expected to support demand for economists.

Occupational Title	SOC Code	Employment, 2022	Projected Employment, 2032	Change, 2022-32	
				Percent	Numeric
Economists	19-3011	17,600	18,700	6	1,100

Contacts for More Information

For more information about economists, visit

- American Economic Association
- National Association for Business Economics
- USAJOBS

Environmental Science and Protection Technicians

Summary

Quick Facts: Environmental Science and Protection Technicians	
2022 Median Pay	$48,380 per year $23.26 per hour
Typical Entry-Level Education	Associate's degree
Work Experience in a Related Occupation	None
On-the-job Training	None
Number of Jobs, 2022	35,000
Job Outlook, 2022-32	6% (Faster than average)
Employment Change, 2022-32	2,000

What Environmental Science and Protection Technicians Do

Environmental science and protection technicians monitor the environment and investigate sources of pollution and contamination.

Work Environment

Environmental science and protection technicians work in offices, laboratories, and the field.

How to Become an Environmental Science and Protection Technician

Environmental science and protection technicians typically need an associate's degree or 2 years of postsecondary education, although some positions require a bachelor's degree.

Environmental science and protection technicians must carry out a wide range of field tests.

Pay

The median annual wage for environmental science and protection technicians was $48,380 in May 2022.

Job Outlook

Employment of environmental science and protection technicians is projected to grow 6 percent from 2022 to 2032, faster than the average for all occupations.

About 3,800 openings for environmental science and protection technicians are projected each year, on average, over the decade. Many of those openings are expected to result from the need to replace workers who transfer to different occupations or exit the labor force, such as to retire.

What Environmental Science and Protection Technicians Do

Environmental science and protection technicians monitor the environment and investigate sources of pollution and contamination, including those affecting public health.

Duties

Environmental science and protection technicians typically do the following:

- Inspect establishments, including public places and businesses, to ensure that there are no environmental, health, or safety hazards
- Set up and maintain equipment used to monitor pollution levels, such as remote sensors that measure emissions from smokestacks
- Collect samples of air, soil, water, and other materials for laboratory analysis
- Clearly label, track, and ensure the integrity of samples being transported to the laboratory
- Use equipment, such as microscopes, to evaluate and analyze samples for the presence of pollutants or other contaminants
- Prepare charts and reports that summarize test results
- Discuss test results and analyses with clients
- Verify compliance with regulations that help prevent pollution

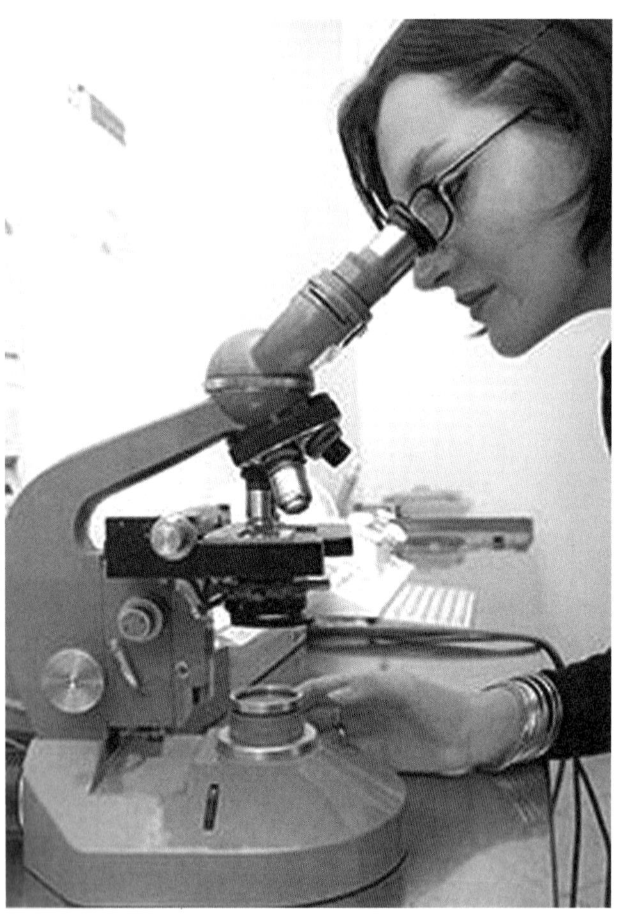

Environmental science and protection technicians use laboratory equipment, such as microscopes, to analyze samples collected in the field.

Many environmental science and protection technicians work under the supervision of environmental scientists and specialists, who direct the technicians' work and evaluate their results. In addition, technicians often work on teams with scientists, engineers, and technicians in other fields to solve complex problems related to environmental degradation and public health. For example, they may work on teams with geoscientists and hydrologists to manage the cleanup of contaminated soils and ground water around an abandoned bomb-manufacturing site.

Most environmental science and protection technicians work for consulting firms, state or local governments, or testing laboratories.

In **consulting firms**, environmental science and protection technicians help clients monitor and manage the environment and comply with regulations. For example, they help businesses develop cleanup plans for contaminated sites, and they recommend ways to reduce, control, or eliminate pollution. Also, environmental science and protection technicians conduct feasibility studies for, and monitor the environmental impact of, new construction projects.

In **state and local governments**, environmental science and protection technicians inspect businesses and public places, and investigate complaints related to air quality, water quality, and food safety. They may be involved with the enforcement of environmental regulations. They also may help protect the environment and people's health by performing environmental impact studies of new construction. Or they may evaluate the environmental health of sites that may contaminate the environment, such as abandoned industrial sites.

In **testing laboratories**, environmental science and protection technicians collect and track samples, and perform tests that are often similar to those carried out by chemical technicians, biological technicians, or microbiologists. However, in contrast to the work done by these science workers, that done by environmental science and protection technicians focuses on topics that are directly related to the environment and how it affects human health.

Environmental science and protection technicians typically specialize either in laboratory testing or in fieldwork and sample collection. However, it is common for laboratory technicians to occasionally collect samples from the field and for fieldworkers to do some work in a laboratory.

Work Environment

Environmental science and protection technicians held about 35,000 jobs in 2022. The largest employers of environmental science and protection technicians were as follows:

Management, scientific, and technical consulting services	23%
Local government, excluding education and hospitals	21
Testing laboratories	15
Engineering services	9
State government, excluding education and hospitals	7

Environmental science and protection technicians work in laboratories, offices, and the field. Fieldwork offers a variety of settings.

Environmental science and protection technicians monitor levels of pollution.

Environmental science and protection technicians need an associate's degree or comparable postsecondary training.

For example, technicians may investigate an abandoned manufacturing plant, or work outdoors to test the water quality of lakes and rivers. They may work near streams and rivers, monitoring the levels of pollution caused by runoff from cities and landfills, or they may have to use the crawl spaces under a house in order to neutralize natural health risks such as radon. While working outdoors, they may be exposed to adverse weather conditions.

In the field, environmental science and protection technicians spend most of their time on their feet, which can be physically demanding. They also may need to carry and set up testing equipment, which can involve some heavy lifting and frequent bending and crouching. Fieldwork may be seasonal, depending on the location, since low temperatures in the winter could inhibit taking samples from water sources or soil.

Depending on the type of work and fieldwork they do, technicians may need to wear protective gear such as hardhats, masks, and coveralls to protect them from hazards.

Work Schedules

Environmental science and protection technicians typically work full time. Working in the field exposes them to all types of weather. Also, technicians may need to travel to meet with clients or to perform fieldwork, either of which may require technicians to work additional or irregular hours.

How to Become an Environmental Science and Protection Technician

Environmental science and protection technicians typically need an associate's degree or 2 years of postsecondary education, although some positions require a bachelor's degree.

Education

Environmental science and protection technicians typically need an associate's degree in environmental science, environmental health, or public health, or a related degree. Because of the wide range of tasks, environments, and industries in which these technicians work, there are jobs that do not require postsecondary education and others that require a bachelor's degree.

A background in natural sciences is important for environmental science and protection technicians. Students should take courses in chemistry, biology, geology, and physics. Coursework in math, statistics, and computer science also is useful, because technicians routinely do data analysis and modeling.

Many technical and community colleges offer programs in environmental studies or a related technology, such as remote sensing or geographic information systems (GISs). While in college, students should include coursework that provides laboratory experience.

Associate's degree programs at community colleges often are designed to allow students to easily transfer to bachelor's degree programs at public colleges and universities.

Training

Technicians whose jobs involve handling hazardous waste typically need to complete training in accordance with Occupational Safety & Health Administration (OSHA) standards. The length of training depends on the type of hazardous material that workers handle. The training covers health hazards, personal protective equipment and clothing, site safety, recognizing and identifying hazards, and decontamination.

Important Qualities

Analytical skills. Environmental science and protection technicians must carry out a wide range of laboratory and field tests, and their results must be accurate and precise.

Communication skills. Environmental science and protection technicians must have good listening and writing skills, because they must follow precise directions for sample collection and communicate their results effectively in written reports. They also need to discuss their results with colleagues, clients, and, sometimes, public audiences.

Critical-thinking skills. Environmental science and protection technicians reach their conclusions through sound reasoning and judgment. They have to determine the best way to address environmental hazards.

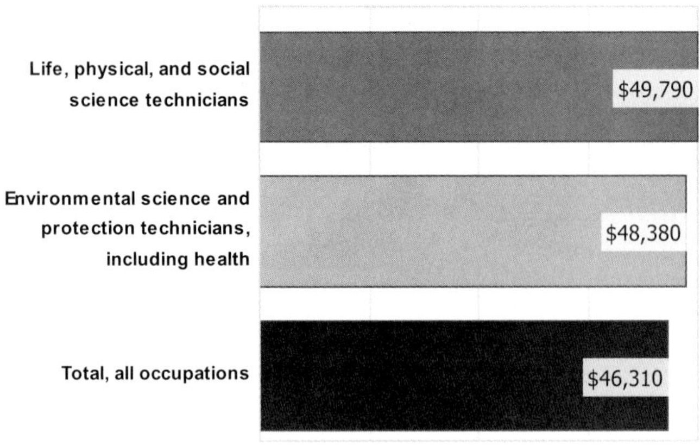

Note: All Occupations includes all occupations in the U.S. Economy.
Source: U.S. Bureau of Labor Statistics, Occupational Employment and Wage Statistics

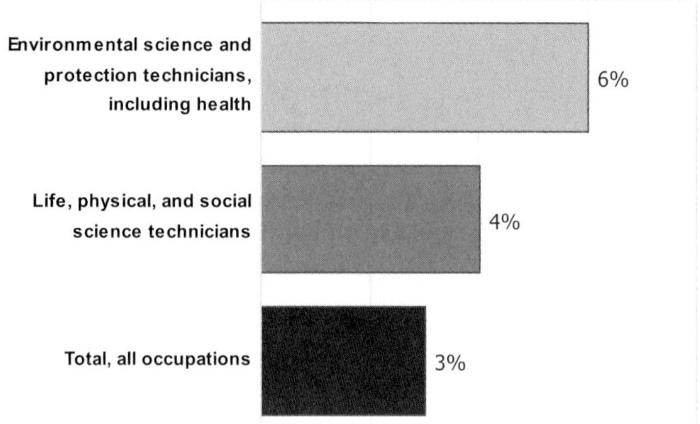

Note: All Occupations includes all occupations in the U.S. Economy.
Source: U.S. Bureau of Labor Statistics, Employment Projections program

Interpersonal skills. Environmental science and protection technicians need to work well and collaborate with others, because they often work with scientists and other technicians.

Licenses, Certifications, and Registrations

In some states, environmental science and protection technicians can benefit from obtaining certification to conduct certain types of environmental and health inspections. For example, certification for technicians who test buildings for radon is offered through the National Radon Safety Board (NRSB).

The Registered Environmental Health Specialist/Registered Sanitarian (REHS/RS) credential is offered through the National Environmental Health Association (NEHA).

Pay

The median annual wage for environmental science and protection technicians was $48,380 in May 2022. The median wage is the wage at which half the workers in an occupation earned more than that amount and half earned less. The lowest 10 percent earned less than $32,180, and the highest 10 percent earned more than $82,690.

In May 2022, the median annual wages for environmental science and protection technicians in the top industries in which they worked were as follows:

Local government, excluding education and hospitals	$58,710
State government, excluding education and hospitals	50,590
Engineering services	48,940
Management, scientific, and technical consulting services	46,640
Testing laboratories	44,090

Environmental science and protection technicians typically work full time. Working in the field exposes them to all types of weather. Also, technicians may need to travel to meet with clients or to perform fieldwork, either of which may require technicians to work additional or irregular hours.

Job Outlook

Employment of environmental science and protection technicians is projected to grow 6 percent from 2022 to 2032, faster than the average for all occupations.

About 3,800 openings for environmental science and protection technicians are projected each year, on average, over the decade. Many of those openings are expected to result from the need to replace workers who transfer to different occupations or exit the labor force, such as to retire.

Employment

Heightened public interest in issues involving the environment, such as fracking, and the increasing demands placed on the environment by population growth should lead to more jobs for environmental science and protection technicians as businesses and governments rely on these workers to help monitor the environment and comply with regulations.

Occupational Title	SOC Code	Employment, 2022	Projected Employment, 2032	Change, 2022-32	
				Percent	Numeric
Environmental science and protection technicians, including health	19-4042	35,000	37,100	6	2,000

Contacts for More Information

For more information about environmental health technicians and related occupations, visit

- National Environmental Health Association
- UCAR
- Occupational Safety and Health Administration
- National Radon Safety Board

Environmental Scientists and Specialists

Summary

Quick Facts: Environmental Scientists and Specialists	
2022 Median Pay	$76,480 per year $36.77 per hour
Typical Entry-Level Education	Bachelor's degree
Work Experience in a Related Occupation	None
On-the-job Training	None
Number of Jobs, 2022	80,500
Job Outlook, 2022-32	6% (Faster than average)
Employment Change, 2022-32	4,900

What Environmental Scientists and Specialists Do

Environmental scientists and specialists use their knowledge of the natural sciences to protect the environment and human health.

Work Environment

Environmental scientists and specialists work in offices and laboratories. Some may spend time in the field gathering data and monitoring environmental conditions firsthand. Most environmental scientists and specialists work full time.

How to Become an Environmental Scientist or Specialist

Environmental scientists and specialists need at least a bachelor's degree in a natural science or science-related field for most entry-level jobs.

Pay

The median annual wage for environmental scientists and specialists was $76,480 in May 2022.

Environmental scientists and specialists analyze environmental problems and develop solutions.

Job Outlook

Employment of environmental scientists and specialists is projected to grow 6 percent from 2022 to 2032, faster than the average for all occupations.

About 6,900 openings for environmental scientists and specialists are projected each year, on average, over the decade. Many of those openings are expected to result from the need to replace workers who transfer to different occupations or exit the labor force, such as to retire.

What Environmental Scientists and Specialists Do

Environmental scientists and specialists use their knowledge of the natural sciences to protect the environment and human health. They may clean up polluted areas, advise policymakers, or work with industry to reduce waste.

Duties

Environmental scientists and specialists typically do the following:

- Determine data collection methods for research projects, investigations, and surveys

Environmental scientists use their knowledge of the natural sciences to protect the environment.

- Collect and compile environmental data from samples of air, soil, water, food, and other materials for scientific analysis
- Analyze samples, surveys, and other information to identify and assess threats to the environment
- Develop plans to prevent, control, or fix environmental problems, such as land or water pollution
- Provide information and guidance to government officials, businesses, and the general public on possible environmental hazards and health risks
- Prepare technical reports and presentations that explain their research and findings

Environmental scientists and specialists analyze environmental problems and develop solutions to them. For example, many environmental scientists and specialists work to reclaim lands and waters that have been contaminated by pollution. Others assess the risks that new construction projects pose to the environment and make recommendations to governments and businesses on how to minimize the environmental impact of these projects. Environmental scientists and specialists may do research and provide advice on manufacturing practices, such as advising against the use of chemicals that are known to harm the environment.

The federal government and many state and local governments have regulations to ensure that there is clean air to breathe and safe water to drink, and that there are no hazardous materials in the soil. The regulations also place limits on development, particularly near sensitive ecosystems, such as wetlands. Environmental scientists and specialists who work for governments ensure that the regulations are followed. Other environmental scientists and specialists work for consulting firms that help companies comply with regulations and policies.

Some environmental scientists and specialists focus on environmental regulations that are designed to protect people's health, while others focus on regulations designed to minimize society's impact on the ecosystem. The following are examples of types of specialists:

Climate change analysts study effects on ecosystems caused by the changing climate. They may do outreach education activities and grant writing typical of scientists.

Environmental health and safety specialists study how environmental factors affect human health. They investigate potential environmental health risks. For example, they may investigate and address issues arising from soil and water contamination caused by nuclear weapons manufacturing. They also educate the public about health risks that may be present in the environment.

Environmental restoration planners assess polluted sites and determine the cost and activities necessary to clean up the area.

Industrial ecologists work with industry to increase the efficiency of their operations and thereby limit the impacts these activities have on the environment. They analyze costs and benefits of various programs, as well as their impacts on ecosystems.

Other environmental scientists and specialists perform work and receive training similar to that of other physical or life scientists, but they focus on environmental issues. For example, ***environmental chemists*** study the effects that various chemicals have on ecosystems. To illustrate, they may study how acids affect plants, animals, and people. Some areas in which they work include waste management and the remediation of contaminated soils, water, and air.

Many people with backgrounds in environmental science become postsecondary teachers or high school teachers.

Work Environment

Environmental scientists and specialists held about 80,500 jobs in 2022. The largest employers of environmental scientists and specialists were as follows:

State government, excluding education and hospitals	26%
Management, scientific, and technical consulting services	21
Local government, excluding education and hospitals	14
Engineering services	10
Federal government, excluding postal service	7

Environmental scientists and specialists work in offices and laboratories. Some may spend time in the field gathering data and monitoring environmental conditions firsthand, but this work is much more likely to be done by environmental science and protection technicians. Fieldwork can be physically demanding, and environmental scientists and specialists may work in all types of weather. Environmental scientists and specialists may have to travel to meet with clients or present research at conferences.

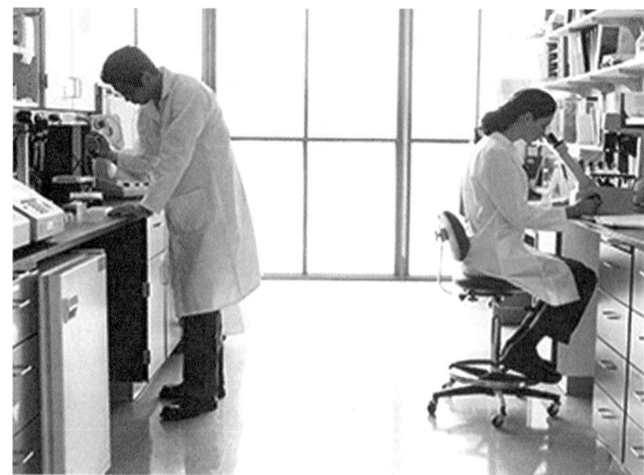

Many environmental scientists and specialists work in laboratories.

For most jobs, environmental scientists and specialists need at least a bachelor's degree in environmental science or a related field.

Work Schedules

Most environmental scientists and specialists work full time. They may have to work more than 40 hours a week when working in the field.

How to Become an Environmental Scientist or Specialist

For most jobs, environmental scientists and specialists need at least a bachelor's degree in a natural science.

Education and Training

Environmental scientists and specialists typically need a bachelor's degree in environmental science or a related natural resources field. However, a master's degree may be needed for advancement. Environmental scientists and specialists who have a doctoral degree make up a small percentage of the occupation, and this level of training typically is needed only for the relatively few postsecondary teaching and basic research positions.

A bachelor's degree in environmental science offers a broad approach to the natural sciences. Students typically take courses in biology, chemistry, geology, and physics. Students often take specialized courses in hydrology or waste management as part of their degree as well. Classes in environmental policy and regulation are also beneficial. Students who want to reach the Ph.D. level may find it advantageous to major in a more specific natural science, such as chemistry, biology, physics, or geology, rather than earn a broader environmental science degree.

Many environmental science programs include an internship, which allows students to gain practical experience. Prospective scientists also may volunteer for or participate in internships after graduation to develop skills needed for the occupation.

Students should look for classes and internships that include work in computer modeling, data analysis, and Geographic Information Systems (GISs). Students with experience in these programs will be the best prepared to enter the job market. The University Corporation for Atmospheric Research (UCAR) offers several programs to help students broaden their understanding of environmental sciences.

Important Qualities

Analytical skills. Environmental scientists and specialists base their conclusions on careful analysis of scientific data. They must consider all possible methods and solutions in their analyses.

Communication skills. Environmental scientists and specialists may need to present and explain their findings to audiences of varying backgrounds and write technical reports.

Interpersonal skills. Environmental scientists and specialists typically work on teams along with scientists, engineers, and technicians. Team members must be able to work together effectively to achieve their goals.

Problem-solving skills. Environmental scientists and specialists try to find the best possible solution to problems that affect the environment and people's health.

Self-discipline. Environmental scientists and specialists may spend a lot of time working alone. They need to stay motivated and get their work done without supervision.

Advancement

As environmental scientists and specialists gain experience, they earn more responsibilities and autonomy, and may supervise the work of technicians or other scientists. Eventually, they may be promoted to project leader, program manager, or some other management or research position.

Other environmental scientists and specialists go on to work as researchers or faculty at colleges and universities. For more information, see the profile on postsecondary teachers.

Licenses, Certifications, and Registrations

Environmental scientists and specialists can become Certified Hazardous Materials Managers through the Institute of Hazardous Materials Management (IHMM). This certification, which must be renewed every 5 years, shows that an environmental scientist or specialist is staying current with developments relevant to the occupation's work. In addition, the Ecological Society of America (ESA) offers several levels of certification for environmental scientists who wish to demonstrate their proficiency in ecology.

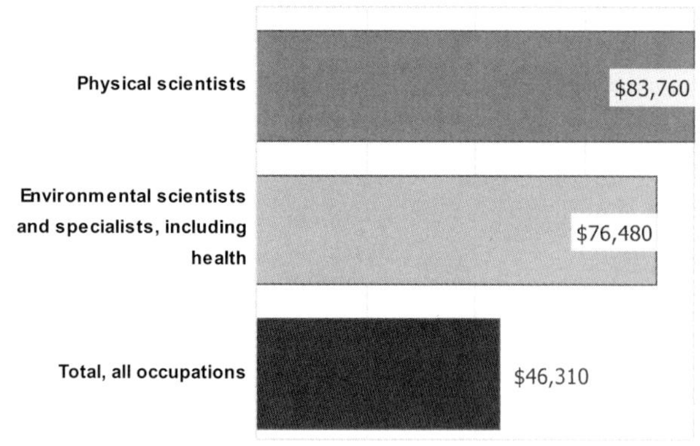

Note: All Occupations includes all occupations in the U.S. Economy.
Source: U.S. Bureau of Labor Statistics, Occupational Employment and Wage Statistics.

Work Experience in a Related Occupation

Environmental scientists and specialists often begin their careers as field analysts, research assistants, or environmental science and protection technicians in laboratories and offices.

Some environmental scientists and specialists begin their careers as scientists in related occupations, such as hydrology or engineering, and then move into the more interdisciplinary field of environmental science.

Pay

The median annual wage for environmental scientists and specialists was $76,480 in May 2022. The median wage is the wage at which half the workers in an occupation earned more than that amount and half earned less. The lowest 10 percent earned less than $46,920, and the highest 10 percent earned more than $130,770.

In May 2022, the median annual wages for environmental scientists and specialists in the top industries in which they worked were as follows:

Federal government, excluding postal service	$104,640
Management, scientific, and technical consulting services	76,870
Engineering services	76,480
Local government, excluding education and hospitals	76,300
State government, excluding education and hospitals	70,080

Most environmental scientists and specialists work full time. They may have to work more than 40 hours a week if they work in the field.

Job Outlook

Employment of environmental scientists and specialists is projected to grow 6 percent from 2022 to 2032, faster than the average for all occupations.

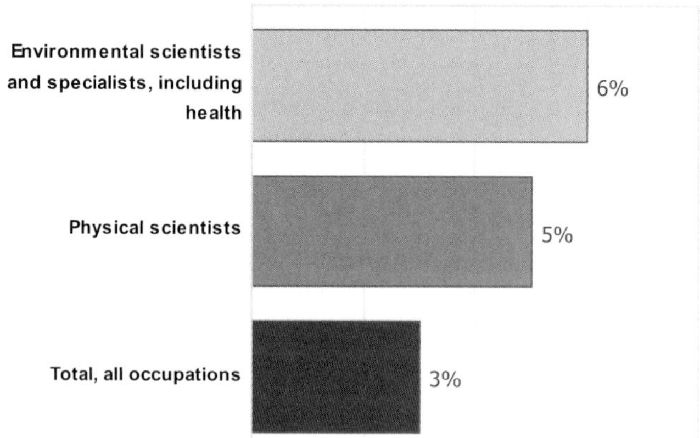

Note: All Occupations includes all occupations in the U.S. Economy.
Source: U.S. Bureau of Labor Statistics, Employment Projections program.

About 6,900 openings for environmental scientists and specialists are projected each year, on average, over the decade. Many of those openings are expected to result from the need to replace workers who transfer to different occupations or exit the labor force, such as to retire.

Employment

Heightened public interest in hazards facing the environment is projected to create demand for environmental scientists and specialists. These workers will continue to be needed to analyze environmental problems and develop solutions that ensure communities' health.

Businesses are expected to continue consulting with environmental scientists and specialists to help reduce the impact of their operations on the environment. For example, environmental consultants help businesses to develop practices that minimize waste, prevent pollution, and conserve resources. Other environmental scientists and specialists will be needed to help planners develop and construct buildings, utilities, and transportation systems that protect natural resources and limit damage to the land.

Occupational Title	SOC Code	Employment, 2022	Projected Employment, 2032	Change, 2022-32	
				Percent	Numeric
Environmental scientists and specialists, including health	19-2041	80,500	85,300	6	4,900

Contacts for More Information

For more information about environmental scientists and specialists, including training, visit

- American Geosciences Institute (AGI)
- University Corporation for Atmospheric Research (UCAR)
- Institute of Hazardous Materials Management (IHMM)
- Ecological Society of America (ESA)
- National Environmental Health Association (NEHA)

Epidemiologists

Summary

Quick Facts: Epidemiologists	
2022 Median Pay	$78,520 per year $37.75 per hour
Typical Entry-Level Education	Master's degree
Work Experience in a Related Occupation	None
On-the-job Training	None
Number of Jobs, 2022	10,000
Job Outlook, 2022-32	27% (Much faster than average)
Employment Change, 2022-32	2,700

What Epidemiologists Do
Epidemiologists are public health workers who investigate patterns and causes of disease and injury.

Work Environment
Epidemiologists work in offices and laboratories, usually at health departments for state and local governments, in hospitals, and at colleges and universities.

How to Become an Epidemiologist
Epidemiologists typically need at least a master's degree to enter the occupation. They may have a master's degree in public health (MPH) or a related field, and some have completed a doctoral degree in epidemiology or medicine.

Pay
The median annual wage for epidemiologists was $78,520 in May 2022.

Epidemiologists collect and analyze data, sometimes through interviews, to find the causes of diseases or other health problems.

Job Outlook
Employment of epidemiologists is projected to grow 27 percent from 2022 to 2032, much faster than the average for all occupations.

About 800 openings for epidemiologists are projected each year, on average, over the decade. Many of those openings are expected to result from the need to replace workers who transfer to different occupations or exit the labor force, such as to retire.

What Epidemiologists Do
Epidemiologists are public health workers who investigate patterns and causes of disease and injury. They seek to reduce the risk and occurrence of negative health outcomes through research, community education and health policy.

Duties
Epidemiologists typically do the following:

- Plan and direct studies of public health problems to find ways to prevent them or to treat them if they arise
- Collect and analyze information—including data from observations, interviews, surveys, and samples of blood or other bodily fluids—to find the causes of diseases or other health problems
- Communicate findings to health practitioners, policymakers, and the public
- Manage programs through planning, monitoring progress, and seeking ways to improve
- Supervise professional, technical, and clerical personnel
- Write grant proposals to fund research

Epidemiologists collect and analyze data to investigate health issues. For example, an epidemiologist might study demographic data to determine groups at high risk for a particular disease. They also may research trends in populations of survivors of certain diseases, such as cancer, to identify effective treatments.

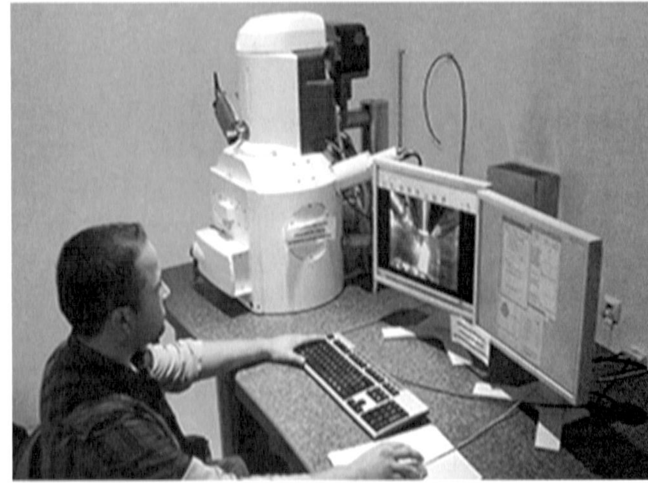

Epidemiologists monitor infectious diseases, bioterrorism threats, and other problem areas for public health agencies.

Epidemiologists typically work in applied public health or in research. Applied epidemiologists work for state and local governments, often addressing public health problems through education outreach and survey efforts in communities. Research epidemiologists typically work for universities or in affiliation with federal agencies, such as the Centers for Disease Control and Prevention (CDC) or the National Institutes of Health (NIH).

Epidemiologists who work in private industry may conduct research for health insurance providers or pharmaceutical companies. Those in nonprofit companies often focus on public health advocacy instead of research, which is expected to be unbiased.

Epidemiologists typically specialize in one or more public health areas, including the following:

- Chronic diseases
- Environmental health
- Genetic and molecular epidemiology
- Infectious diseases
- Injury
- Maternal and child health
- Mental health
- Public health preparedness and emergency response
- Veterinary epidemiology

For more information on occupations that concentrate on the biology or effects of disease, see the profiles for biochemists and biophysicists, medical scientists, microbiologists, and physicians and surgeons.

Work Environment

Epidemiologists held about 10,000 jobs in 2022. The largest employers of epidemiologists were as follows:

Employer	Percent
State government, excluding education and hospitals	36%
Local government, excluding education and hospitals	21
Hospitals; state, local, and private	12
Colleges, universities, and professional schools; state, local, and private	9
Scientific research and development services	7

Work environments vary because of the diverse nature of epidemiological specializations. Epidemiologists typically work in offices and laboratories to study data and prepare reports. They also may work in clinical settings or the field, supporting emergency actions.

Epidemiologists working in the field may need to be active in the community, including traveling to support education efforts or to administer studies and surveys. Because modern science has reduced the prevalence of infectious disease in developed countries, infectious disease epidemiologists often travel to remote areas and developing nations in order to carry out their studies.

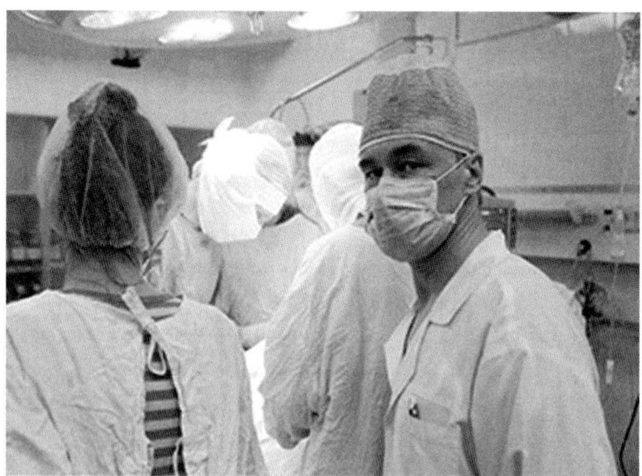

Field work may require interaction with sick patients, yet safety precautions ensure that the likelihood of exposure to disease is minimal.

Epidemiologists encounter minimal risk when working in laboratories or in the field, because they have received appropriate training and take precautions before interacting with samples or patients.

Work Schedules

Epidemiologists who work full time and typically have a standard schedule. Occasionally, epidemiologists may have to work irregular schedules in order to complete fieldwork or attend to duties during public health emergencies.

How to Become an Epidemiologist

Epidemiologists typically need at least a master's degree to enter the occupation. They may have a master's degree in public health (MPH) or a related field, and some have completed a doctoral degree in epidemiology or medicine.

Education

Epidemiologists typically need at least a master's degree. The degree may be in a range of fields or specializations, although a master's degree in public health with an emphasis in epidemiology is common. Epidemiologists who direct research projects—including those who work as postsecondary teachers in colleges and universities—often have a Ph.D. or medical degree in their chosen field.

To enter graduate programs in epidemiology, applicants typically need a bachelor's degree in a field such as biology, public policy and social services, or social science. Epidemiology programs include coursework in public health, biological and physical sciences, and math and statistics. Topics of study may include comparative healthcare systems, medical informatics, and survey and study design.

Master's degree programs in public health, as well as other programs that are specific to epidemiology, may require students to complete an internship or practicum that typically ranges in length from a semester to a year. Internships and other

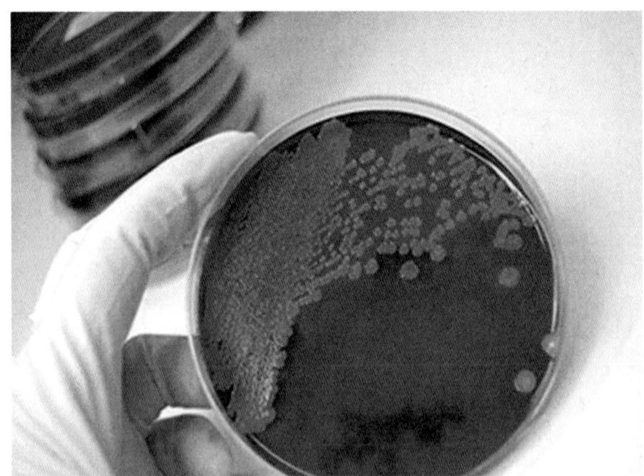

Epidemiologists typically need at least a master's degree to enter the occupation.

training opportunities are available at federal agencies such as the Centers for Disease Control and Prevention (CDC) and the National Institutes of Health (NIH).

Some epidemiologists have degrees in both epidemiology and medicine. These scientists often focus on clinical work. In medical school, students spend most of their first 2 years in laboratories and classrooms, taking courses such as anatomy, microbiology, and pathology. Medical students also learn to take medical histories, examine patients, and diagnose illnesses.

Important Qualities

Communication skills. Epidemiologists use speaking and writing skills to inform officials and the public, such as for community outreach activities to explain health risks. They also must be able to convey information effectively to other health workers.

Critical-thinking skills. Epidemiologists must be able to consider a variety of resources in responding to a public health problem or health-related emergency.

Detail oriented. Epidemiologists must be precise and accurate in moving from observation and interview to conclusions.

Leadership skills. Epidemiologists may direct staff in research or in investigating a disease. They also may need to assign work and evaluate staff performances.

Math and statistical skills. Epidemiologists may need to analyze data when reviewing results from studies and surveys. Skill in using large databases and statistical computer programs is critical.

Pay

The median annual wage for epidemiologists was $78,520 in May 2022. The median wage is the wage at which half the workers in an occupation earned more than that amount and half earned less. The lowest 10 percent earned less than $51,170, and the highest 10 percent earned more than $123,430.

In May 2022, the median annual wages for epidemiologists in the top industries in which they worked were as follows:

Scientific research and development services	$103,650
Hospitals; state, local, and private	95,240
Colleges, universities, and professional schools; state, local, and private	80,180
Local government, excluding education and hospitals	70,910
State government, excluding education and hospitals	69,510

Epidemiologists who work full time typically have a standard schedule. Occasionally, epidemiologists may have to work irregular schedules in order to complete fieldwork or attend to duties during public health emergencies.

Job Outlook

Employment of epidemiologists is projected to grow 27 percent from 2022 to 2032, much faster than the average for all occupations.

About 800 openings for epidemiologists are projected each year, on average, over the decade. Many of those openings are expected to result from the need to replace workers who transfer to different occupations or exit the labor force, such as to retire.

Employment

Demand for epidemiologists is expected to increase as enhancements in healthcare technology permit the discovery of new and emerging diseases. These discoveries require research to understand the diseases and to develop methods for mitigating adverse health consequences.

Many jobs for these workers are in state and local governments, where epidemiologists are needed to help provide public health services and respond to emergencies. However, because epidemiological and public health programs largely depend

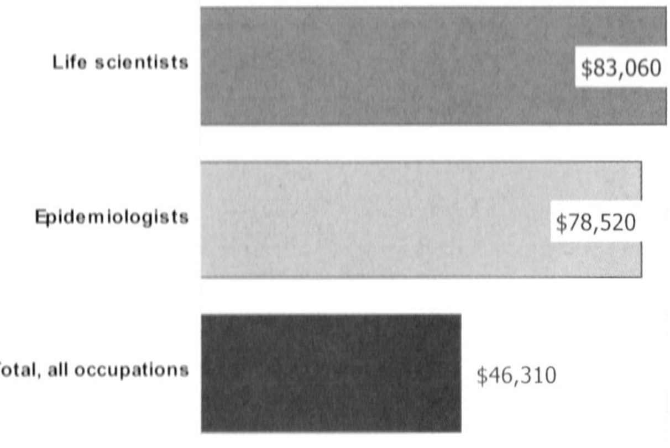

Note: All Occupations includes all occupations in the U.S. Economy.
Source: U.S. Bureau of Labor Statistics, Occupational Employment and Wage Statistics.

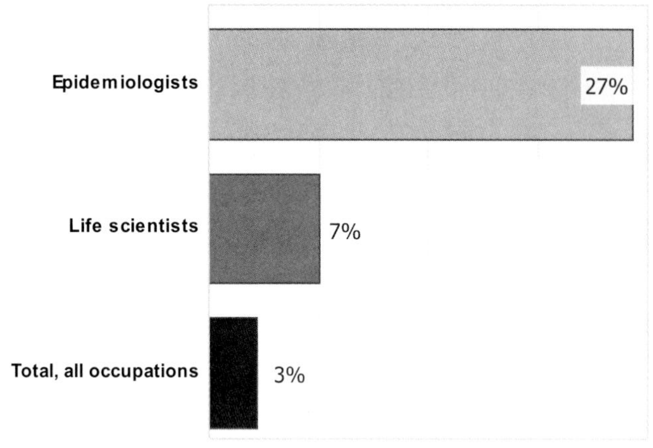

Note: All Occupations includes all occupations in the U.S. Economy.
Source: U.S. Bureau of Labor Statistics, Employment Projections program.

on public funding, budgetary constraints may directly impact employment growth.

Demand for epidemiologists also is expected to increase as more hospitals join programs such as the National Healthcare Safety Network and realize the benefits of strengthened infection control programs.

Occupational Title	SOC Code	Employment, 2022	Projected Employment, 2032	Change, 2022-32	
				Percent	Numeric
Epidemiologists	19-1041	10,000	12,700	27	2,700

Contacts for More Information

For more information about epidemiologists, visit

- American College of Epidemiology
- Council of State and Territorial Epidemiologists
- The Society for Healthcare Epidemiology of America
- Centers for Disease Control and Prevention
- National Institutes of Health
- American Epidemiological Society
- American Public Health Association
- Association of State and Territorial Health Officials
- National Academy for State Health Policy
- Public Health Foundation

Forensic Science Technicians

Summary

Quick Facts: Forensic Science Technicians

2022 Median Pay	$63,740 per year $30.64 per hour
Typical Entry-Level Education	Bachelor's degree
Work Experience in a Related Occupation	None
On-the-job Training	Moderate-term on-the-job training
Number of Jobs, 2022	18,500
Job Outlook, 2022-32	13% (Much faster than average)
Employment Change, 2022-32	2,300

What Forensic Science Technicians Do

Forensic science technicians aid criminal investigations by collecting and analyzing evidence.

Work Environment

Most laboratory forensic science technicians work during regular business hours. Crime scene investigators may work extended or unusual hours and travel to crime scenes within their jurisdiction.

How to Become a Forensic Science Technician

Forensic science technicians typically need at least a bachelor's degree. On-the-job training is typically required, both for both those who investigate crime scenes and for those who work in labs.

Pay

The median annual wage for forensic science technicians was $63,740 in May 2022.

Job Outlook

Employment of forensic science technicians is projected to grow 13 percent from 2022 to 2032, much faster than the average for all occupations.

About 2,600 openings for forensic science technicians are projected each year, on average, over the decade. Many of those openings are expected to result from the need to replace workers who transfer to different occupations or exit the labor force, such as to retire.

What Forensic Science Technicians Do

Forensic science technicians aid criminal investigations by collecting and analyzing evidence. Many technicians specialize in either crime scene investigation or laboratory analysis.

Forensic science technicians perform chemical, biological, and physical analysis on evidence taken from crime scenes.

Duties

Forensic science technicians work in laboratories and on crime scenes. At crime scenes, forensic science technicians typically do the following:

- Analyze crime scenes to determine what evidence should be collected and how
- Take photographs of the crime scene and evidence
- Make sketches of the crime scene
- Record observations and findings, such as the location and position of evidence
- Collect evidence, including weapons, fingerprints, and bodily fluids
- Catalog and preserve evidence for transfer to crime labs
- Reconstruct crime scenes

In laboratories, forensic science technicians typically do the following:

- Perform chemical, biological, and microscopic analyses on evidence taken from crime scenes

Crime scene investigators collect evidence from crime scenes.

- Explore possible links between suspects and criminal activity, using the results of DNA or other scientific analyses
- Consult with experts in specialized fields, such as toxicology (the study of poisons and their effect on the body) and odontology (a branch of forensic medicine that concentrates on teeth)

Forensic science technicians may be generalists who perform many or all of the duties listed above or they may specialize in certain techniques and sciences. Generalist forensic science technicians, sometimes called ***criminalists*** or ***crime scene investigators***, collect evidence at the scene of a crime and perform scientific and technical analysis in laboratories or offices.

Forensic science technicians who work primarily in laboratories may specialize in the natural sciences or engineering. These workers, such as ***forensic biologists*** and ***forensic chemists***, typically use chemicals and laboratory equipment such as microscopes when analyzing evidence. They also may use computers to examine DNA, substances, and other evidence collected at crime scenes. They often work to match evidence to people or other known elements, such as vehicles or weapons. Most forensic science technicians who perform laboratory analysis specialize in a specific type of evidence, such as DNA or ballistics.

Some forensic science technicians, called ***forensic computer examiners*** or ***digital forensics analysts,*** specialize in computer-based crimes. They collect and analyze data to uncover and prosecute electronic fraud, scams, and identity theft. The abundance of digital data helps them solve crimes in the physical world as well. Computer forensics technicians must adhere to the same strict standards of evidence gathering found in general forensic science because legal cases depend on the integrity of evidence.

All forensic science technicians prepare written reports that detail their findings and investigative methods. They must be able to explain their reports to lawyers, detectives, and other law enforcement officials. In addition, forensic science technicians may be called to testify in court about their findings and methods.

Work Environment

Forensic science technicians held about 18,500 jobs in 2022. The largest employers of forensic science technicians were as follows:

Local government, excluding education and hospitals	60%
State government, excluding education and hospitals	26
Testing laboratories	3
Medical and diagnostic laboratories	2

Forensic science technicians may have to work outside in all types of weather, spend many hours in laboratories and offices,

Forensic science technicians often work in crime labs.

or do some combination of both. They often work with specialists and other law enforcement personnel. Many specialist forensic science technicians work only in laboratories.

Crime scene investigators may travel throughout their jurisdictions, which may be cities, counties, or states.

Work Schedules

Crime scene investigators may work staggered day, evening, or night shifts and may have to work overtime because they must always be available to collect or analyze evidence. Technicians working in laboratories usually work a standard workweek, although they may have to be on call outside of normal business hours if they are needed to work immediately on a case.

How to Become a Forensic Science Technician

Forensic science technicians typically need at least a bachelor's degree. On-the-job training is usually required both for those who investigate crime scenes and for those who work in labs.

Forensic science technicians usually have a background in natural sciences.

Education

Forensic science technicians typically need at least a bachelor's degree in a field such as physical science, biology, or forensic science. Forensic science programs may specialize in a specific area of study, such as toxicology, pathology, or DNA. Students who enroll in general natural science programs should make an effort to take classes related to forensic science. A list of schools that offer degrees in forensic science is available from the American Academy of Forensic Sciences. Many of those who seek to become forensic science technicians will have an undergraduate degree in the natural sciences and a master's degree in forensic science.

Many crime scene investigators who work for police departments are sworn police officers and have met educational requirements necessary for admittance into a police academy. Applicants for civilian crime scene investigator jobs should have a bachelor's degree in either forensic science, with a strong basic science background, or the natural sciences. For more information on police officers, see the profile on police and detectives.

Training

Forensic science technicians receive on-the-job training before they are ready to work on cases independently.

Newly hired crime scene investigators may work under experienced investigators while they learn proper procedures and methods for collecting and documenting evidence.

Forensic science technicians learn laboratory specialties on the job. The length of this training varies by specialty, but is usually less than a year. Technicians may need to pass a proficiency exam or otherwise be approved by a laboratory or accrediting body before they are allowed to perform independent casework.

Throughout their careers, forensic science technicians need to keep up with advances in technology and science that improve the collection or analysis of evidence.

Licenses, Certifications, and Registrations

A range of licenses and certifications is available to help credential, and aid in the professional development of, many types of forensic science technicians. Certifications and licenses are not typically necessary for entry into the occupation. Credentials can vary widely because standards and regulations vary considerably from one jurisdiction to another.

Important Qualities

Communication skills. Forensic science technicians write reports and testify in court. They often work with other law enforcement officials and specialists.

Critical-thinking skills. Forensic science technicians use their best judgment when matching physical evidence, such as fingerprints and DNA, to suspects.

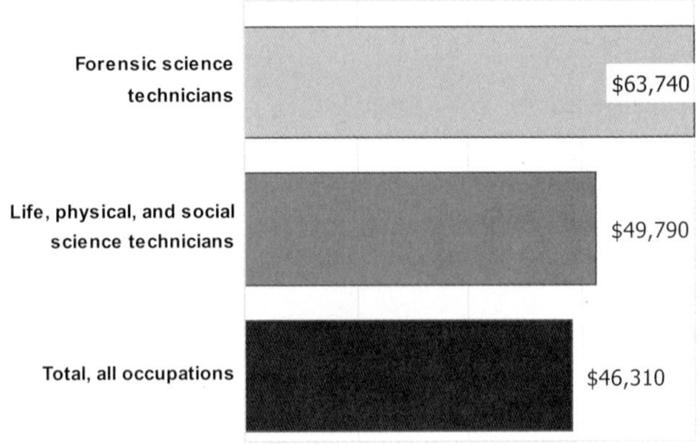

Note: All Occupations includes all occupations in the U.S. Economy. Source: U.S. Bureau of Labor Statistics, Occupational Employment and Wage Statistics.

Detail oriented. Forensic science technicians must be able to notice small changes in mundane objects to be good at collecting and analyzing evidence.

Math and science skills. Forensic science technicians need a solid understanding of statistics and natural sciences to be able to analyze evidence.

Problem-solving skills. Forensic science technicians use scientific tests and methods to help law enforcement officials solve crimes.

Pay

The median annual wage for forensic science technicians was $63,740 in May 2022. The median wage is the wage at which half the workers in an occupation earned more than that amount and half earned less. The lowest 10 percent earned less than $39,710, and the highest 10 percent earned more than $104,330.

In May 2022, the median annual wages for forensic science technicians in the top industries in which they worked were as follows:

State government, excluding education and hospitals	$64,500
Local government, excluding education and hospitals	63,760
Testing laboratories	63,730
Medical and diagnostic laboratories	42,600

Crime scene investigators may work staggered day, evening, or night shifts and may have to work overtime because they must always be available to collect or analyze evidence. Technicians working in laboratories usually work a standard workweek, although they may have to be on call outside of normal business hours if they are needed to work immediately on a case.

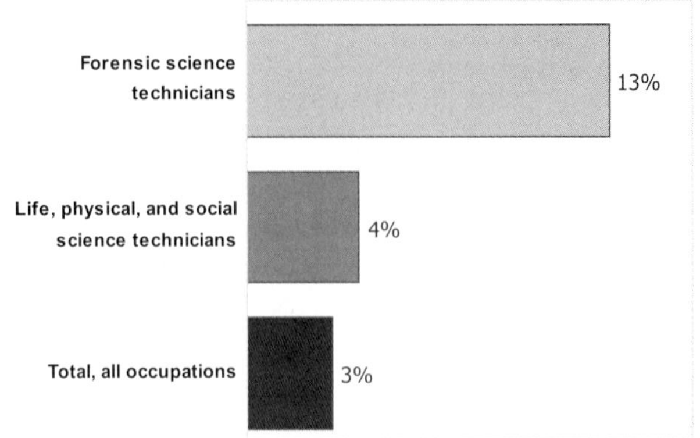

Note: All Occupations includes all occupations in the U.S. Economy. Source: U.S. Bureau of Labor Statistics, Employment Projections program.

Job Outlook

Employment of forensic science technicians is projected to grow 13 percent from 2022 to 2032, much faster than the average for all occupations.

About 2,600 openings for forensic science technicians are projected each year, on average, over the decade. Many of those openings are expected to result from the need to replace workers who transfer to different occupations or exit the labor force, such as to retire.

Employment

State and local governments are expected to continue to hire forensic science technicians to process their high caseloads. Additionally, scientific and technological advances are expected to increase the availability, reliability, and usefulness of objective forensic information used as evidence in trials. As a result, more forensic science technicians will be needed to provide forensics information to law enforcement agencies and courts.

Occupational Title	SOC Code	Employment, 2022	Projected Employment, 2032	Change, 2022-32	
				Percent	Numeric
Forensic science technicians	19-4092	18,500	20,800	13	2,300

Contacts for More Information

For more information, visit

- American Academy of Forensic Sciences
- American Board of Criminalistics
- American Board of Medicolegal Death Investigators
- Association of Firearm and Tool Mark Examiners
- International Crime Scene Investigators Association

Geographers

Summary

Quick Facts: Geographers	
2022 Median Pay	$88,900 per year $42.74 per hour
Typical Entry-Level Education	Bachelor's degree
Work Experience in a Related Occupation	None
On-the-job Training	None
Number of Jobs, 2022	1,500
Job Outlook, 2022-32	1% (Little or no change)
Employment Change, 2022-32	0

What Geographers Do

Geographers study the Earth and the distribution of its land, features, and inhabitants.

Work Environment

Most geographers work full time. Geographers who do field-work may travel to foreign countries or remote locations.

How to Become a Geographer

Geographers typically need at least a bachelor's degree to enter the occupation. Some jobs require a master's or doctoral degree.

Pay

The median annual wage for geographers was $88,900 in May 2022.

Job Outlook

Employment of geographers is projected to show little or no change from 2022 to 2032.

Despite limited employment growth, about 100 openings for geographers are projected each year, on average, over the decade. Most of those openings are expected to result from the need to replace workers who transfer to different occupations or exit the labor force, such as to retire.

Geographers use Geographic Information Systems (GIS) equipment to create maps.

Geographers use maps and global positioning systems in their work.

What Geographers Do

Geographers study the Earth and the distribution of its land, features, and inhabitants. They research the interactions between the physical aspects of a region and the human activities within it.

Duties

Geographers typically do the following:

- Gather geographic data through field observations, maps, photographs, satellite imagery, and censuses
- Conduct research via surveys, interviews, and focus groups
- Create and modify maps or other visual representations of geographic data
- Analyze the geographic distribution of physical and cultural characteristics and occurrences
- Collect, analyze, and display geographic data with Geographic Information Systems (GIS)
- Write reports and present research findings
- Assist, advise, or lead others in using GIS and geographic data
- Link geographic data with economic, health, or other data

Some geographers travel to do fieldwork.

Geographers use several technologies in their work, such as GIS, remote sensing, and global positioning systems (GPS), to find relationships and trends in geographic data. They then present the data visually as maps, reports, and charts. For example, geographers may overlay aerial or satellite images with GIS data, such as population density in a given region, and create digital maps. They then use the maps to inform governments, businesses, and the public on a variety of topics, including urban planning and disaster response.

The following are examples of types of geographers:

Physical geographers study features of the natural environment, such as landforms, climate, soils, natural hazards, water, and plants. For example, physical geographers may map where a natural resource occurs in a country or study the implications of proposed economic development on the surrounding natural environment.

Human geographers often combine other disciplines with their research, which may include economic, environmental, medical, cultural, social, or political topics. Some human geographers rely primarily on quantitative research methods; others rely more heavily on qualitative methods, such as field observations and interviews.

Geographers often work on projects with people in related fields. For example, geographers may work with urban planners, civil engineers, legislators, or real estate agents to determine the best location for new public transportation infrastructure.

People who study geography and who use GIS in their work also may be employed as surveyors, cartographers and photogrammetrists, surveying and mapping technicians, urban and regional planners, geoscientists, or hydrologists. People who earn a Ph.D. in geography may become postsecondary teachers.

Work Environment

Geographers held about 1,500 jobs in 2022. The largest employers of geographers were as follows:

Federal government, excluding postal service	65%
Educational services; state, local, and private	11
State government, excluding education and hospitals	9
Professional, scientific, and technical services	6

Geographers who do fieldwork may travel to foreign countries or remote locations to gather data and observe geographic features, such as the landscape and environment.

Work Schedules

Most geographers work full time.

How to Become a Geographer

Geographers typically need at least a bachelor's degree to enter the occupation. Some jobs require a master's or doctoral degree.

Education

High school students interested in becoming geographers should take classes in physical sciences, computer programming, and geography.

Geographers with a bachelor's degree may qualify for entry-level jobs and for positions with the federal government. Geographers working outside of the federal government may need a master's degree in geography or in Geographic Information Systems (GIS). Some employers allow candidates to substitute work experience or GIS proficiency for an advanced degree. Research positions may require a Ph.D. or a master's degree and several years of relevant experience.

Geography programs may include courses in physical and human geography, statistics or math, remote sensing, and GIS. Because geography is an interdisciplinary field, courses in a variety of areas, such as business, economics, or real estate, may be helpful.

College students may benefit from participating in internships that put geography principles into practice.

Licenses, Certifications, and Registrations

Although not required, certification may indicate professional expertise. For example, the GIS Certification Institute and the

Geographers may perform fieldwork as part of their education.

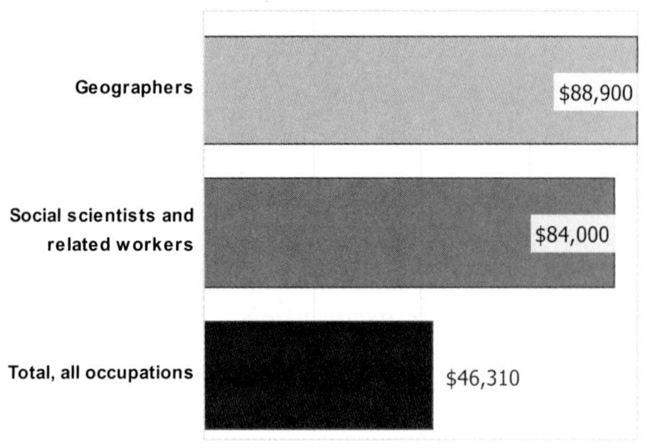

Note: All Occupations includes all occupations in the U.S. Economy.
Source: U.S. Bureau of Labor Statistics, Occupational Employment and Wage Statistics.

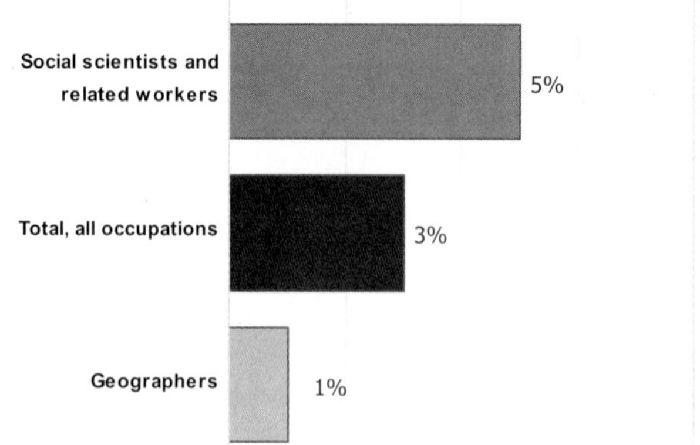

Note: All Occupations includes all occupations in the U.S. Economy.
Source: U.S. Bureau of Labor Statistics, Employment Projections program.

American Society for Photogrammetry and Remote Sensing both offer certification in GIS. Candidates may qualify for certification by passing an exam and meeting other requirements, such as for education or experience.

Important Qualities

Analytical skills. Geographers study data and information from a variety of sources and must be able to draw conclusions about their usefulness and meaning.

Computer skills. Geographers must be proficient in GIS programming, database management, and data visualization techniques and should be comfortable creating and manipulating digital images with GIS software.

Communication skills. Geographers often need to write reports and funding proposals. They also present their research and findings to their peers and nontechnical audiences and must be able to convey the meaning of data in understandable ways.

Critical-thinking skills. Geographers must be able to choose the appropriate data, methods, and scale of analysis for projects.

Pay

The median annual wage for geographers was $88,900 in May 2022. The median wage is the wage at which half the workers in an occupation earned more than that amount and half earned less. The lowest 10 percent earned less than $57,430, and the highest 10 percent earned more than $121,060.

In May 2022, the median annual wages for geographers in the top industries in which they worked were as follows:

Federal government, excluding postal service	$97,880
Professional, scientific, and technical services	71,510
Educational services; state, local, and private	65,840
State government, excluding education and hospitals	63,950

Most geographers work full time.

Job Outlook

Employment of geographers is projected to show little or no change from 2022 to 2032.

Despite limited employment growth, about 100 openings for geographers are projected each year, on average, over the decade. Most of those openings are expected to result from the need to replace workers who transfer to different occupations or exit the labor force, such as to retire.

Employment

Budget constraints are expected to reduce employment for geographers in federal government. However, governments and businesses will still need geographers to research topics such as natural hazards and the use of resources. For example, geographers' analyses on population distribution and land use are important for infrastructure planning and development by both governments and businesses.

Occupational Title	SOC Code	Employment, 2022	Projected Employment, 2032	Change, 2022-32	
				Percent	Numeric
Geographers	19-3092	1,500	1,500	1	0

Contacts for More Information

For more information, visit

- Association of American Geographers
- American Society for Photogrammetry and Remote Sensing
- GIS Certification Institute
- USAJobs

Geological and Hydrologic Technicians

Summary

Quick Facts: Geological and Hydrologic Technicians	
2022 Median Pay	$49,590 per year $23.84 per hour
Typical Entry-Level Education	Associate's degree
Work Experience in a Related Occupation	None
On-the-job Training	Moderate-term on-the-job training
Number of Jobs, 2022	12,500
Job Outlook, 2022-32	2% (As fast as average)
Employment Change, 2022-32	300

What Geological and Hydrologic Technicians Do

Geological and hydrologic technicians support scientists and engineers in exploring, extracting, and monitoring natural resources.

Work Environment

Geological and hydrologic technicians work in offices, laboratories, and the field. Most geological and hydrologic technicians work full time.

How to Become a Geological or Hydrologic Technician

Geological and hydrologic technicians typically need an associate's degree or 2 years of postsecondary training in applied science or a science-related technology. Some jobs may require a bachelor's degree. Geological and hydrologic technicians also receive on-the-job training.

Pay

The median annual wage for geological technicians, except hydrologic technicians was $48,490 in May 2022.

Geological and petroleum technicians monitor well exploration activities, and record data such as well temperatures and pressures.

The median annual wage for hydrologic technicians was $58,360 in May 2022.

Job Outlook

Overall employment of geological and hydrologic technicians is projected to grow 2 percent from 2022 to 2032, about as fast as the average for all occupations.

About 1,300 openings for geological and hydrologic technicians are projected each year, on average, over the decade. Many of those openings are expected to result from the need to replace workers who transfer to different occupations or exit the labor force, such as to retire.

What Geological and Hydrologic Technicians Do

Geological and hydrologic technicians support scientists and engineers in exploring, extracting, and monitoring natural resources, such as soil, natural gas, and water.

Duties

Geological and hydrologic technicians typically do the following:

- Install and maintain laboratory and field equipment
- Gather samples in the field, such as mud and water, and prepare them for analysis in the laboratory
- Conduct scientific tests on samples to determine their content and characteristics
- Record data from tests and compile information from reports, databases, and other sources
- Prepare reports and maps to identify geological characteristics of areas that may have valuable natural resources

Geological and hydrologic technicians typically specialize either in fieldwork and laboratory study or in analyzing data. However, technicians may have duties that overlap into multiple areas.

Geological and hydrologic technicians help identify locations that are suitable for oil and gas wells.

In the field, geological and hydrologic technicians use equipment, such as seismic instruments and depth sensors, to gather data. They also use tools, such as shovels and gauges, to collect samples for analysis. In laboratories, these technicians use microscopes, computers, and other equipment to analyze samples for problem-solving and other purposes.

Geological and hydrologic technicians work on teams under the supervision of scientists and engineers. Geological technicians help with tasks such as exploring and developing prospective sites or monitoring the productivity of existing ones. Hydrologic technicians assist with a variety of projects, such as providing information for negotiating water rights.

Geologic and hydrologic technicians also might work with scientists and technicians of other disciplines. For example, these technicians may work with environmental scientists and technicians to identify the potential impacts of drilling on an area's soil and water quality.

Work Environment

Geological technicians, except hydrologic technicians held about 9,400 jobs in 2022. The largest employers of geological technicians, except hydrologic technicians were as follows:

Architectural, engineering, and related services	53%
Mining, quarrying, and oil and gas extraction	17
Management, scientific, and technical consulting services	6
Transportation and warehousing	4
Management of companies and enterprises	3

Fieldwork requires technicians to work outdoors, sometimes in remote locations, where they are exposed to all types of weather.

Hydrologic technicians held about 3,100 jobs in 2022. The largest employers of hydrologic technicians were as follows:

Federal government	59%
Professional, scientific, and technical services	9
Local government, excluding education and hospitals	7
Chemical manufacturing	4

Geological and hydrologic technicians work either in fields and laboratories or in offices. Fieldwork requires technicians to be outdoors, sometimes in remote locations, where they are exposed to all types of weather. In addition, technicians may need to stay on location for days or weeks to collect data and monitor equipment. Geological and hydrologic technicians who work in offices spend most of their time on computers to organize and analyze data, write reports, and produce maps.

Work Schedules

Most geological and hydrologic technicians work full time. Technicians generally work standard hours in laboratories and offices but may have irregular schedules in the field.

How to Become a Geological or Hydrologic Technician

Geological and hydrologic technicians typically need at least an associate's degree in applied science or science-related technology to enter the occupation. Some employers require a bachelor's degree. Geological and hydrologic technicians also receive on-the-job training.

Geological and hydrologic technicians use laboratory equipment such as microscopes to analyze samples collected in the field.

Education

Although entry-level positions typically require an associate's degree in applied science or a science-related technology, employers may prefer to hire applicants who have a bachelor's degree. Geological and hydrologic technician jobs that are data intensive or highly technical may require a bachelor's degree.

Community colleges and technical institutes may offer programs in geosciences, mining, or a related subject, such as geographic information systems (GIS). Regardless of the program, most students take courses in geology, mathematics, computer science, chemistry, and physics. Schools also may offer internships and cooperative-education programs in which students gain experience while attending school.

Licenses, Certifications, and Registrations

Some geological and hydrologic technicians may be required to have the Occupational Safety & Health Administration (OSHA) Hazardous Waste Operations and Emergency Response Standard (HAZWOPER) certification. HAZWOPER certification includes training in health hazards, personal protective equipment, site safety, recognizing and identifying hazards, and decontamination. Refresher training may be required to maintain certification.

The American Institute of Hydrology (AIH) offers different levels of voluntary certification for hydrologic technicians. Each level requires different amounts of education and experience. Recertification is required periodically.

Important Qualities

Analytical skills. Geological and hydrologic technicians evaluate data and samples using a variety of techniques, including laboratory experimentation and computer modeling.

Communication skills. Geological and hydrologic technicians explain their methods and findings through oral and written reports to scientists, engineers, managers, and other technicians.

Critical-thinking skills. Geological and hydrologic technicians must use their judgment when interpreting scientific data and determining what is relevant to their work.

Interpersonal skills. Geological and hydrologic technicians need to be able to work well with others as part of a team.

Physical stamina. To do fieldwork, geological and hydrologic technicians must be able to reach remote locations while carrying testing and sampling equipment.

Training

Geological and hydrologic technicians typically receive on-the-job training to attain competency. Under the supervision of experienced technicians, new technicians gain hands-on experience using field and laboratory equipment and computer software. The length of training may vary from 1 to 12 months.

Geological and Hydrologic Technicians

Median annual wages, May 2022

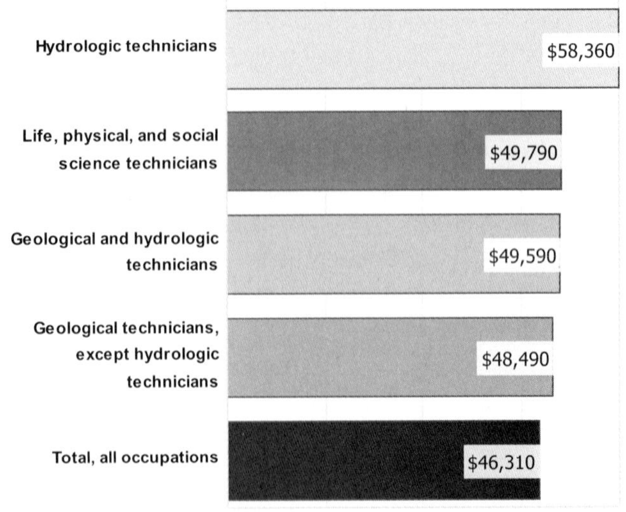

Note: All Occupations includes all occupations in the U.S. Economy.
Source: U.S. Bureau of Labor Statistics, Occupational Employment and Wage Statistics.

Pay

The median annual wage for geological technicians, except hydrologic technicians was $48,490 in May 2022. The median wage is the wage at which half the workers in an occupation earned more than that amount and half earned less. The lowest 10 percent earned less than $34,740, and the highest 10 percent earned more than $102,190.

The median annual wage for hydrologic technicians was $58,360 in May 2022. The lowest 10 percent earned less than $36,880, and the highest 10 percent earned more than $108,990.

In May 2022, the median annual wages for geological technicians, except hydrologic technicians in the top industries in which they worked were as follows:

Management of companies and enterprises	$92,920
Mining, quarrying, and oil and gas extraction	65,730
Management, scientific, and technical consulting services	50,960
Architectural, engineering, and related services	46,860
Transportation and warehousing	44,560

In May 2022, the median annual wages for hydrologic technicians in the top industries in which they worked were as follows:

Chemical manufacturing	$135,410
Federal government	58,360
Local government, excluding education and hospitals	54,970
Professional, scientific, and technical services	48,480

Most geological and hydrologic technicians work full time. Technicians generally work standard hours in laboratories and offices but may have irregular schedules in the field.

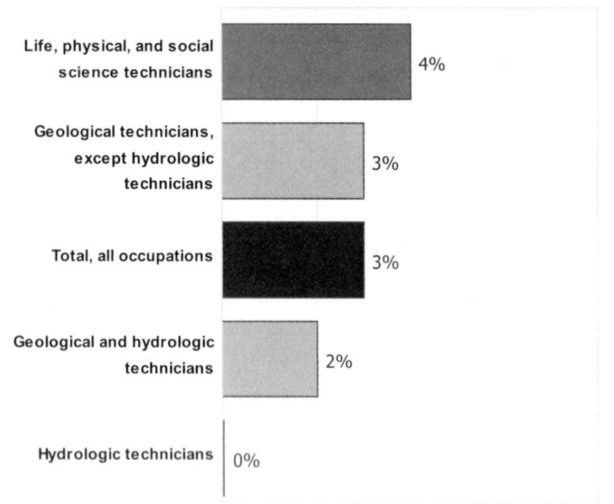

Note: All Occupations includes all occupations in the U.S. Economy.
Source: U.S. Bureau of Labor Statistics, Employment Projections program.

Job Outlook

Overall employment of geological and hydrologic technicians is projected to grow 2 percent from 2022 to 2032, about as fast as the average for all occupations.

About 1,300 openings for geological and hydrologic technicians are projected each year, on average, over the decade. Many of those openings are expected to result from the need to replace workers who transfer to different occupations or exit the labor force, such as to retire.

Employment

Projected employment of geological and hydrologic technicians varies by occupation (see table). Demand for natural gas, along with exploration and management of resources such as minerals and water, is expected to increase demand for geological exploration and extraction.

Occupational Title	SOC Code	Employment, 2022	Projected Employment, 2032	Change, 2022-32	
				Percent	Numeric
Geological and hydrologic technicians	—	12,500	12,800	2	300
Geological technicians, except hydrologic technicians	19-4043	9,400	9,600	3	300
Hydrologic technicians	19-4044	3,100	3,100	0	0

Contacts for More Information

For more information about careers in geology, visit

- American Geosciences Institute
- National Ground Water Association (NGWA)
- The American Institute of Hydrology (AIH)
- American Association of Petroleum Geologists
- Society of Petroleum Engineers
- National Mining Association

Geoscientists

Summary

Quick Facts: Geoscientists

2022 Median Pay	$87,480 per year $42.06 per hour
Typical Entry-Level Education	Bachelor's degree
Work Experience in a Related Occupation	None
On-the-job Training	None
Number of Jobs, 2022	26,300
Job Outlook, 2022-32	5% (Faster than average)
Employment Change, 2022-32	1,300

What Geoscientists Do

Geoscientists study the physical aspects of the Earth.

Work Environment

Geoscientists usually split their time between work in an office setting, in laboratories, and outdoors. Most geoscientists work full time, and some work more than 40 hours per week. Schedules vary to include irregular hours when doing fieldwork.

How to Become a Geoscientist

Geoscientists typically need a bachelor's degree to enter the occupation. For some positions, employers prefer to hire candidates who have a master's degree. Most geoscientists need a state-issued license.

Pay

The median annual wage for geoscientists was $87,480 in May 2022.

Job Outlook

Employment of geoscientists is projected to grow 5 percent from 2022 to 2032, faster than the average for all occupations.

About 2,200 openings for geoscientists are projected each year, on average, over the decade. Many of those openings are expected to result from the need to replace workers who transfer to different occupations or exit the labor force, such as to retire.

What Geoscientists Do

Geoscientists study the physical aspects of the Earth, such as its composition, structure, and processes, to learn about its past and present and to predict future events.

Geoscientists often work outdoors, sometimes in remote areas and in both warm and cold climates.

Duties

Geoscientists typically do the following:

- Plan and carry out field studies, in which they visit locations to collect samples and conduct surveys
- Analyze aerial photographs, rock samples, and other data sources to locate deposits of natural resources and estimate their size
- Conduct laboratory tests on samples collected in the field
- Make geologic maps and charts
- Prepare written reports
- Present their findings to varied audiences, including clients and colleagues

Geoscientists study the Earth's composition, or layers; its structure, which focuses on the properties of rocks; and its processes, such as erosion and volcanic activity. By analyzing rocks, fossils, and other clues, geoscientists are able to create timelines of events in the Earth's geologic history. They also research changes in its resources to provide guidance in meeting human demands, such as for water, and to predict geological risks and hazards.

Petroleum geologists (a type of geoscientist) search for oil and gas deposits that are suitable for commercial extraction.

Geoscientists use a variety of tools in their work. In the field, they may use a hammer and chisel to collect rock samples or ground-penetrating radar equipment to search for minerals. In laboratories, they may use x-rays and electron microscopes to determine the chemical and physical composition of rock samples. They also may use remote sensing equipment to collect data, as well as geographic information systems (GIS) and modeling software to analyze the data collected.

Geoscientists may supervise the work of technicians and coordinate work with other scientists, both in the field and in the lab.

As geological challenges increase, geoscientists may opt to work as generalists. However, some choose to specialize in a particular aspect of the Earth. The following are examples of types of geoscientists:

Environmental geologists study how consequences of human activity, such as pollution and waste management, affect the quality of the Earth's air, soil, and water. They also may work to solve problems associated with natural threats, such as flooding and erosion.

Geologists study the materials, processes, and history of the Earth. They investigate how rocks were formed and what has happened to them since their formation. There are subgroups of geologists as well, such as *stratigraphers*, who study stratified rock, and mineralogists, who study the structure and composition of minerals.

Oceanographers study the motion and circulation of ocean waters; the physical and chemical properties of the oceans; and the ways these properties affect coastal areas, climate, and weather.

Paleontologists study fossils found in geological formations in order to trace the evolution of plant and animal life and the geologic history of the Earth.

Petroleum geologists collect rock and sediment samples from sites through drilling and other methods and test the samples for the presence of oil and gas. They also estimate the size of oil and gas deposits and work to develop extraction sites.

Seismologists study earthquakes and related phenomena, such as tsunamis. They use seismographs and other instruments to collect data on these events.

For a more extensive list of geoscientist specialties, visit the American Geosciences Institute (AGI).

Work Environment

Geoscientists held about 26,300 jobs in 2022. The largest employers of geoscientists were as follows:

Architectural, engineering, and related services	28%
Management, scientific, and technical consulting services	19

Geoscientists frequently work outdoors so they can study geological aspects of the Earth, such as geysers, up close.

Mining, quarrying, and oil and gas extraction	15
Federal government, excluding postal service	9
State government, excluding education and hospitals	8

Geoscientists may work as part of a team with other scientists and engineers. For example, they may work closely in natural resource extraction fields with petroleum engineers to find new sources of oil and gas.

Geoscientists usually split their time between work in the field, in laboratories, and in office settings. Fieldwork may require geoscientists to be outdoors frequently or to travel all over the world, including to remote locations, for extended periods. For example, oceanographers may spend months at sea on a research ship, and paleontologists may spend long periods in remote areas during expeditions.

Extensive travel, especially for long periods away from home, may be stressful.

Work Schedules

Most geoscientists work full time, and some work more than 40 hours per week. Schedules may vary to include irregular hours when doing fieldwork. Geoscientists travel frequently to meet with clients and to conduct fieldwork.

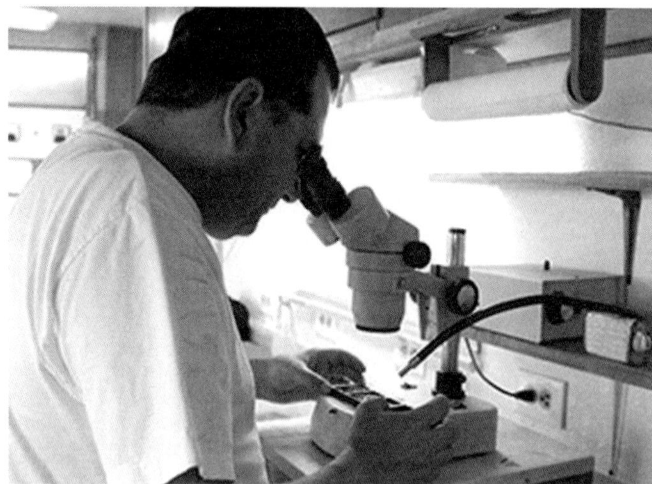

Laboratory experience is important for prospective geoscientists.

How to Become a Geoscientist

Geoscientists typically need a bachelor's degree to enter the occupation. For some positions, employers prefer to hire candidates who have a master's or doctoral degree. Most geoscientists need a state-issued license.

Education

Geoscientists typically need a bachelor's degree in geoscience or a related field, such as physical science or natural resources.

Geoscience programs include courses in mineralogy, geology, and other sciences, along with subjects such as mathematics and engineering. Some programs focus on a particular area of geoscience, such as environmental geology, while others prepare students to become generalists.

Programs also usually involve geology fieldwork that provides students with practical experience. Students may gain additional experience by completing a geosciences internship while in college. Interns usually work under the supervision of a senior geoscientist on tasks such as preparing for field visits, collecting samples, and writing reports.

Master's and doctoral degree programs in geoscience typically involve more specialization, research, and technical experience than bachelor's programs do. Having a graduate degree may make candidates more competitive for certain entry-level positions or for advancement.

Licenses, Certifications, and Registrations

Most states require licensing for geologists who offer services to the public. Public service activities include those associated with civil engineering projects, environmental protection, and regulatory compliance.

Licensure requirements vary by state, but applicants typically must meet minimum education and experience requirements and earn a passing score on an exam. Examining authorities also vary by state. For example, some states use exams by the National Association of State Boards of Geology (ASBOG) or the American Institute of Professional Geologists (AIPG).

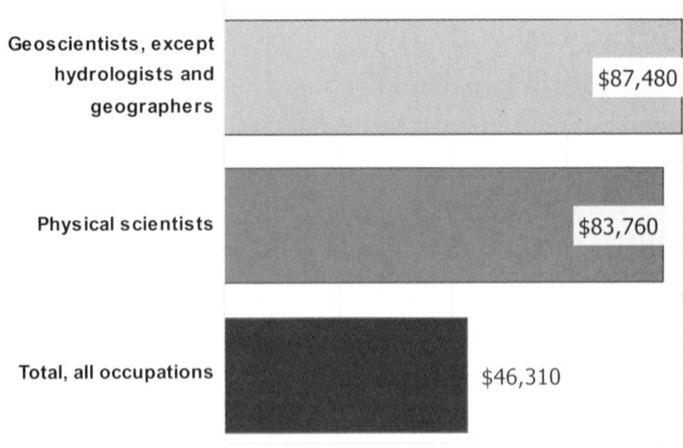

Note: All Occupations includes all occupations in the U.S. Economy.
Source: U.S. Bureau of Labor Statistics, Occupational Employment and Wage Statistics.

Contact your state licensing board for more information.

Important Qualities

Communication skills. Geoscientists must be able to present their research findings clearly to a variety of audiences, including both scientists and those who do not have a background in geoscience.

Critical-thinking skills. Geoscientists conduct research through observation and testing, then evaluate data to explain their findings.

Outdoor skills. Geoscientists may spend significant time outdoors performing fieldwork. They must be comfortable being outside for long periods, which may include overnight camping.

Physical stamina. Geoscientists need to be physically fit because they may need to hike, sometimes to remote locations, while carrying equipment for fieldwork.

Problem-solving skills. Geoscientists must be able to analyze statistical DATA and other information in order to address problems.

Pay

The median annual wage for geoscientists was $87,480 in May 2022. The median wage is the wage at which half the workers in an occupation earned more than that amount and half earned less. The lowest 10 percent earned less than $49,150, and the highest 10 percent earned more than $173,620.

In May 2022, the median annual wages for geoscientists in the top industries in which they worked were as follows:

Federal government, excluding postal service	$106,450
Mining, quarrying, and oil and gas extraction	105,170
Architectural, engineering, and related services	80,240
State government, excluding education and hospitals	78,500
Management, scientific, and technical consulting services	77,260

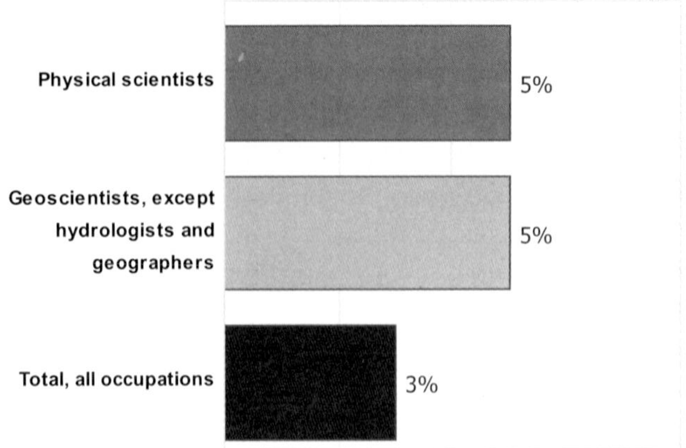

Note: All Occupations includes all occupations in the U.S. Economy.
Source: U.S. Bureau of Labor Statistics, Employment Projections program.

Most geoscientists work full time, and some work more than 40 hours per week. Schedules may vary to include irregular hours when doing fieldwork. Geoscientists travel frequently to meet with clients and to conduct fieldwork.

Job Outlook

Employment of geoscientists is projected to grow 5 percent from 2022 to 2032, faster than the average for all occupations.

About 2,200 openings for geoscientists are projected each year, on average, over the decade. Many of those openings are expected to result from the need to replace workers who transfer to different occupations or exit the labor force, such as to retire.

Employment

The need for energy, environmental protection, and responsible land and resource management is expected to spur demand for geoscientists.

Geoscientists will be involved in discovering and developing sites for traditional and alternative energy sources. For example, geoscientists study wind speeds and patterns to determine sites that are suitable for wind turbines. The increased use of and demand for alternative energy should lead to more jobs for these workers.

Occupational Title	SOC Code	Employment, 2022	Projected Employment, 2032	Change, 2022-32	
				Percent	Numeric
Geoscientists, except hydrologists and geographers	19-2042	26,300	27,600	5	1,300

Contacts for More Information

For more information about geoscientists, visit

- American Geophysical Union (AGU)
- American Geosciences Institute (AGI)
- Geological Society of America (GSA)
- U.S. National Committee for Geological Sciences
- American Institute of Professional Geologists (AIPG)
- National Association of State Boards of Geology (ASBOG)
- USAJOBS

Historians

Summary

Quick Facts: Historians	
2022 Median Pay	$64,540 per year $31.03 per hour
Typical Entry-Level Education	Master's degree
Work Experience in a Related Occupation	None
On-the-job Training	None
Number of Jobs, 2022	3,500
Job Outlook, 2022-32	3% (As fast as average)
Employment Change, 2022-32	100

What Historians Do
Historians research, analyze, interpret, and write about the past by studying historical documents and sources.

Work Environment
Historians must travel to carry out research. Most work full time.

How to Become a Historian
Historians typically need at least a master's degree to enter the occupation. Those with a bachelor's degree in history may qualify for some entry-level positions, but most will find jobs in different fields.

Pay
The median annual wage for historians was $64,540 in May 2022.

Job Outlook
Employment of historians is projected to grow 3 percent from 2022 to 2032, about as fast as the average for all occupations.

About 300 openings for historians are projected each year, on average, over the decade. Many of those openings are expected to result from the need to replace workers who transfer to different occupations or exit the labor force, such as to retire.

What Historians Do
Historians research, analyze, interpret, and write about the past by studying historical documents and sources.

Duties
Historians typically do the following:

- Gather historical data from various sources, including archives, books, and artifacts
- Analyze and interpret historical information to determine its authenticity and significance
- Trace historical developments in a particular field
- Engage with the public through educational programs and presentations
- Archive or preserve materials and artifacts in museums, visitor centers, and historic sites
- Provide advice or guidance on historical topics and preservation issues
- Write reports, articles, and books on findings and theories

Historians conduct research and analysis for governments, businesses, individuals, nonprofits, historical associations, and other organizations. They use a variety of sources in their work, including government and institutional records, newspapers, photographs, interviews, films, and unpublished manuscripts, such as personal diaries, letters, and other primary source documents. They also may process, catalog, and archive these documents and artifacts.

Many historians present and interpret history in order to inform or build upon public knowledge of past events. They often trace and build a historical profile of a particular person, area, idea, organization, or event. Once their research is

Historians may engage with the public through educational programs and presentations.

Historians often study and preserve archival materials.

complete, they present their findings through articles, books, reports, exhibits, websites, and educational programs.

In government, some historians conduct research to provide information on specific events or groups. Many write about the history of a particular government agency, activity, or program, such as a military operation or space missions. For example, they may research the people and events related to Operation Desert Storm.

In historical associations, historians may work with archivists, curators, and museum workers to preserve artifacts and explain the historical significance of a wide variety of subjects, such as historic buildings, religious groups, and battlegrounds. Workers with a background in history also may go into one of these occupations.

Many people with a degree in history also become high school teachers or postsecondary teachers.

Work Environment

Historians held about 3,500 jobs in 2022. The largest employers of historians were as follows:

Federal government, excluding postal service	22%
Professional, scientific, and technical services	21
Local government, excluding education and hospitals	18
State government, excluding education and hospitals	14

Historians work in museums, archives, historical societies, and research organizations. Some work as consultants for these organizations while being employed by consulting firms, and some work as independent consultants.

Work Schedules

Most historians work full time during regular business hours. Some work independently and are able to set their own schedules. Historians who work in museums or other institutions open to the public may work evenings or weekends. Some historians may travel to collect artifacts, conduct interviews, or visit an area to better understand its culture and environment.

Historians may spend much of their time researching and writing reports.

How to Become a Historian

Historians typically need at least a master's degree to enter the occupation. Those with a bachelor's degree in history may qualify for some entry-level positions, but most will find jobs in different fields.

Education

Historians typically need a master's degree or Ph.D. to enter the occupation. Many historians have a master's degree in history or public history. Others complete degrees in related fields, such as museum studies, historical preservation, or archival management.

In addition to coursework, most master's programs in public history and similar fields require an internship as part of the curriculum.

Research positions in the federal government and positions in academia typically require a Ph.D. Students in history Ph.D. programs usually concentrate in a specific area of history. Possible specializations include a particular country or region, period, or field, such as social, political, or cultural history.

Candidates with a bachelor's degree in history may qualify for entry-level positions at museums, historical associations, or other small organizations. However, most bachelor's degree holders usually work outside of traditional historian jobs—for example, jobs in education, communications, law, business, publishing, or journalism.

Historians learn to use primary sources, such as letters and photographs, in their research.

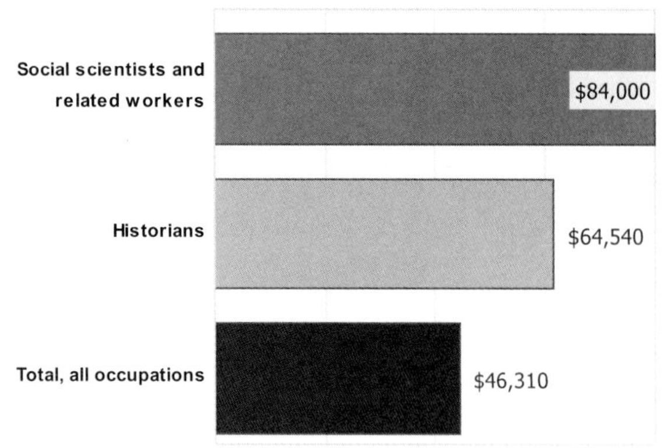

Note: All Occupations includes all occupations in the U.S. Economy.
Source: U.S. Bureau of Labor Statistics, Occupational Employment and Wage Statistics.

Other Experience

Many employers recommend that prospective historians complete an internship during their formal educational studies. Internships offer an opportunity for students to learn practical skills, such as handling and preserving artifacts and creating exhibits. They also give students an opportunity to apply their academic knowledge in a hands-on setting.

Important Qualities

Analytical skills. Historians must be able to examine various types of historical resources and draw clear and logical conclusions based on their findings.

Communication skills. Historians must communicate effectively when collecting information, collaborating with colleagues, and presenting their research to the public through written documents and presentations.

Foreign language skills. Historians may need to review primary source materials that are not in English. This makes knowledge of the other language useful during research.

Problem-solving skills. Historians try to answer questions about the past. They may investigate something unknown about a past idea, event, or person; decipher historical information; or identify how the past has affected the present.

Research skills. Historians must be able to examine and process information from a large number of historical resources, including documents, images, and material artifacts.

Pay

The median annual wage for historians was $64,540 in May 2022. The median wage is the wage at which half the workers in an occupation earned more than that amount and half earned less. The lowest 10 percent earned less than $37,280, and the highest 10 percent earned more than $123,260.

In May 2022, the median annual wages for historians in the top industries in which they worked were as follows:

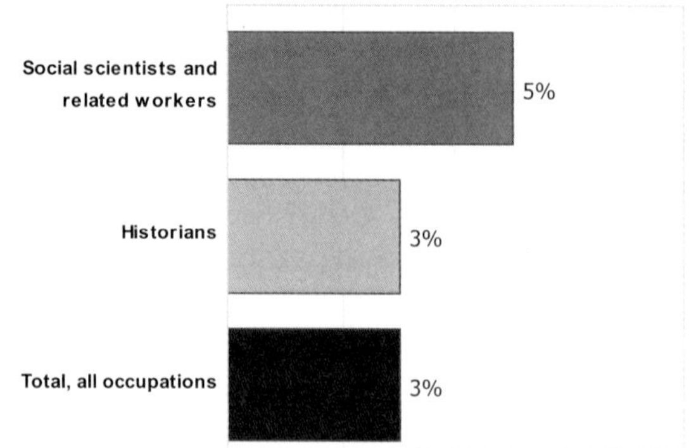

Note: All Occupations includes all occupations in the U.S. Economy.
Source: U.S. Bureau of Labor Statistics, Employment Projections program.

Federal government, excluding postal service....	$104,670
Professional, scientific, and technical services...	64,720
State government, excluding education and hospitals	53,870
Local government, excluding education and hospitals	45,050

Most historians work full time during standard business hours. Some work independently and are able to set their own schedules. Historians who work in museums or other institutions open to the public may work evenings or weekends. Some historians may travel to collect artifacts, conduct interviews, or visit an area to better understand its culture and environment.

Job Outlook

Employment of historians is projected to grow 3 percent from 2022 to 2032, about as fast as the average for all occupations.

About 300 openings for historians are projected each year, on average, over the decade. Many of those openings are expected to result from the need to replace workers who transfer to different occupations or exit the labor force, such as to retire.

Employment

Organizations that employ historians, such as historical societies and government agencies, often depend on donations or public funding. Thus, employment growth will depend largely on the amount of funding available.

Occupational Title	SOC Code	Employment, 2022	Projected Employment, 2032	Change, 2022-32	
				Percent	Numeric
Historians	19-3093	3,500	3,600	3	100

Contacts for More Information

For more information about historians, visit

- ➤ American Association for State and Local History
- ➤ American Historical Association
- ➤ National Council on Public History
- ➤ Organization of American Historians

Hydrologists

Summary

Quick Facts: Hydrologists	
2022 Median Pay	$85,990 per year $41.34 per hour
Typical Entry-Level Education	Bachelor's degree
Work Experience in a Related Occupation	None
On-the-job Training	None
Number of Jobs, 2022	6,600
Job Outlook, 2022-32	1% (Little or no change)
Employment Change, 2022-32	100

What Hydrologists Do

Hydrologists study how water moves across and through the Earth's crust.

Work Environment

Hydrologists work in offices and in the field. In offices, hydrologists spend much of their time using computers to analyze data and model their findings. In the field, hydrologists may have to wade into lakes and streams to collect samples or to read and inspect monitoring equipment.

How to Become a Hydrologist

Hydrologists typically need a bachelor's degree for entry-level jobs; however, some employers prefer to hire candidates who have a master's degree.

Pay

The median annual wage for hydrologists was $85,990 in May 2022.

Hydrologists work closely with engineers, scientists, and public officials to study and manage the water supply.

Job Outlook

Employment of hydrologists is projected to show little or no change from 2022 to 2032.

Despite limited employment growth, about 500 openings for hydrologists are projected each year, on average, over the decade. Most of those openings are expected to result from the need to replace workers who transfer to different occupations or exit the labor force, such as to retire.

What Hydrologists Do

Hydrologists study how water moves across and through the Earth's crust. They study how rain, snow, and other forms of precipitation impact river flows or groundwater levels, and how surface water and groundwater evaporate back into the atmosphere or eventually reach the oceans. Hydrologists analyze how water influences the surrounding environment and how changes to the environment influence the quality and quantity of water. They use their expertise to solve problems concerning water quality and availability.

Duties

Hydrologists typically do the following:

- Measure the properties of bodies of water, such as volume and stream flow

Hydrologists collect water samples in the field.

- Collect water and soil samples to test for certain properties, such as the pH or pollution levels
- Analyze data on the environmental impacts of pollution, erosion, drought, and other problems
- Research ways to minimize the negative impacts of erosion, sedimentation, or pollution on the environment
- Use computer models to forecast future water supplies, the spread of pollution, floods, and other events
- Evaluate the feasibility of water-related projects, such as hydroelectric power plants, irrigation systems, and wastewater treatment facilities
- Prepare written reports and presentations of their findings

Hydrologists may use remote sensing equipment to collect data. They, or technicians whom they supervise, usually install and maintain this equipment. Hydrologists also use sophisticated computer programs to analyze the data collected. Computer models are often developed by hydrologists to help them understand complex datasets.

Hydrologists work closely with engineers, scientists, and public officials to study and manage the water supply. For example, they work with policymakers to develop water conservation plans and with biologists to monitor wildlife in order to allow for their water needs.

Most hydrologists specialize in a particular water source or a certain aspect of the water cycle, such as the evaporation of water from lakes and streams. The following are examples of types of hydrologists:

Groundwater hydrologists study the water below the Earth's surface. Some groundwater hydrologists focus on water supply and decide the best locations for wells and the amount of water available for pumping. Other groundwater hydrologists focus on the cleanup of groundwater contaminated by spilled chemicals at a factory, an airport, or a gas station. These hydrologists often give advice about the best places to build waste disposal sites to ensure that groundwater is not contaminated.

Surface water hydrologists study water from aboveground sources such as streams, lakes, and snowpacks. They may predict future water levels by tracking usage and precipitation data to help reservoir managers decide when to release or store water. They also produce flood forecasts and help develop flood management plans.

Work done by hydrologists can sometimes include topics typically associated with atmospheric scientists, including meteorologists. Scientists with an education in hydrology and a concentration in water quality are environmental scientists and specialists. Some people with a hydrology background become high school teachers or postsecondary teachers.

Work Environment

Hydrologists held about 6,600 jobs in 2022. The largest employers of hydrologists were as follows:

Hydrologists solve problems concerning water quality and availability.

Employer	Percent
Federal government, excluding postal service	27%
Management, scientific, and technical consulting services	22
State government, excluding education and hospitals	21
Engineering services	14
Local government, excluding education and hospitals	9

Hydrologists work in offices and in the field. In offices, hydrologists spend much their time using computers to analyze data and model their findings. In the field, hydrologists may have to wade into lakes and streams to collect samples or to read and inspect monitoring equipment. Hydrologists also need to write reports detailing the status of surface water and groundwater in specific regions. Many jobs require significant travel. Jobs in the private sector may require international travel.

Work Schedules

Most hydrologists work full time. However, the length of daily shifts may vary when hydrologists work in the field.

How to Become a Hydrologist

Hydrologists typically need a bachelor's degree for entry-level jobs; however, some employers prefer to hire candidates who have a master's degree.

Education

Hydrologists typically need a bachelor's degree in physical science or a related field, such as natural resources. Employers sometimes prefer to hire candidates who have a master's degree. Hydrologists conducting research or teaching at the postsecondary level typically need a Ph.D.

Few universities offer undergraduate degrees in hydrology; instead, universities may offer hydrology concentrations in their geosciences, engineering, or earth science programs.

Hydrologists may be involved in ensuring waste water and other waste disposal sites do not leak contaminates into the groundwater.

Coursework requirements may include math, statistics, and life sciences.

Important Qualities

Analytical skills. Hydrologists need to analyze data collected in the field and examine the results of laboratory tests.

Communication skills. Hydrologists prepare detailed reports that document their research methods and findings. They may have to present their findings to people who do not have a technical background, such as government officials or the general public.

Critical-thinking skills. Hydrologists develop and use models to assess the potential risks to the water supply by pollution, floods, droughts, and other threats. They develop water management plans to handle these threats.

Interpersonal skills. Most hydrologists work as part of a diverse team with engineers, technicians, and other scientists.

Physical stamina. When they are in the field, hydrologists may need to hike to remote locations while carrying testing and sampling equipment.

Pay

The median annual wage for hydrologists was $85,990 in May 2022. The median wage is the wage at which half the workers in an occupation earned more than that amount and half earned less. The lowest 10 percent earned less than $54,590, and the highest 10 percent earned more than $150,490.

In May 2022, the median annual wages for hydrologists in the top industries in which they worked were as follows:

Management, scientific, and technical consulting services	$96,790
Federal government, excluding postal service	94,290
Local government, excluding education and hospitals	84,730

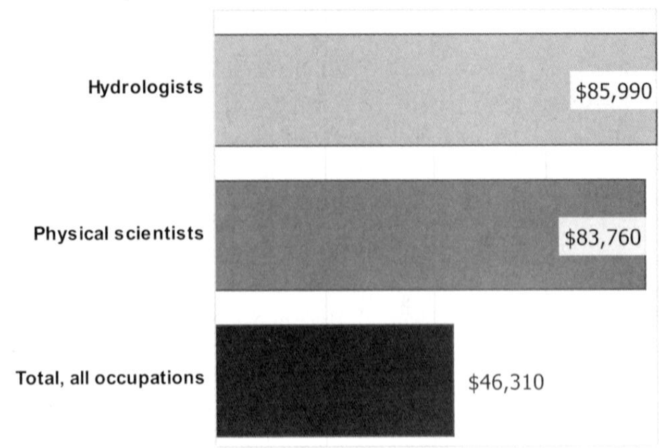

Note: All Occupations includes all occupations in the U.S. Economy.
Source: U.S. Bureau of Labor Statistics, Occupational Employment and Wage Statistics.

Engineering services	82,700
State government, excluding education and hospitals	73,020

Most hydrologists work full time. However, the length of daily shifts may vary when hydrologists work in the field.

Job Outlook

Employment of hydrologists is projected to show little or no change from 2022 to 2032.

Despite limited employment growth, about 500 openings for hydrologists are projected each year, on average, over the decade. Most of those openings are expected to result from the need to replace workers who transfer to different occupations or exit the labor force, such as to retire.

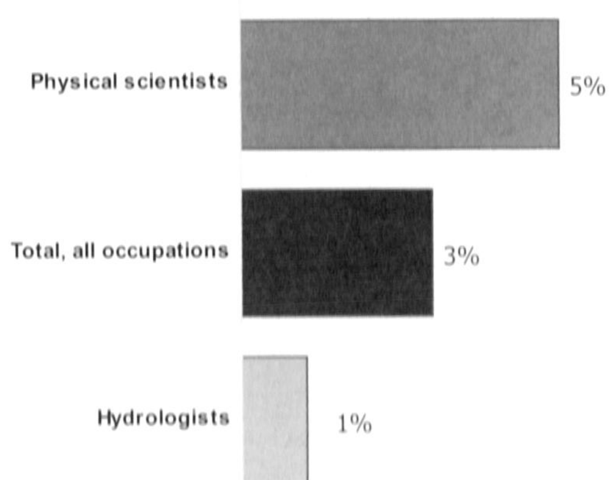

Note: All Occupations includes all occupations in the U.S. Economy.
Source: U.S. Bureau of Labor Statistics, Employment Projections program.

Employment

Demand for the services of hydrologists will stem from ongoing human activities such as mining, construction, and hydraulic fracturing. Environmental concerns, especially global climate change that may contribute to flooding and drought, are likely to increase demand for these scientists. Hydrologists will be needed to assess threats to local, state, and national water supplies and to develop comprehensive water management plans. However, the development and use of integrated technology and review systems may limit the need for some hydrologists.

Population expansion into areas that were previously uninhabited also may increase the risk of flooding, and new communities may encounter water availability issues. Although governments value hydrologists' expertise in finding sustainable solutions to managing water resources, budget constraints will limit hiring and impact growth.

Occupational Title	SOC Code	Employment, 2022	Projected Employment, 2032	Change, 2022-32	
				Percent	Numeric
Hydrologists	19-2043	6,600	6,700	1	100

Contacts for More Information

For more information about hydrology and the work of hydrologists in the federal government, visit

- U.S. Geological Survey
- U.S. Office of Personnel Management
- USAJOBS
- American Geophysical Union
- American Geosciences Institute
- American Institute of Hydrology
- American Water Resources Association
- Consortium of Universities for the Advancement of Hydrologic Science, INC. (CUAHSI)
- MetEd

Medical Scientists

Summary

Quick Facts: Medical Scientists	
2022 Median Pay	$99,930 per year $48.04 per hour
Typical Entry-Level Education	Doctoral or professional degree
Work Experience in a Related Occupation	None
On-the-job Training	None
Number of Jobs, 2022	119,000
Job Outlook, 2022-32	10% (Much faster than average)
Employment Change, 2022-32	11,600

What Medical Scientists Do

Medical scientists conduct research aimed at improving overall human health.

Work Environment

Medical scientists typically work in offices and laboratories. Most work full time, and some work more than 40 hours per week.

How to Become a Medical Scientist

Medical scientists typically have a Ph.D., usually in biology or a related life science. Some get a medical degree instead of, or in addition to, a Ph.D.

Pay

The median annual wage for medical scientists was $99,930 in May 2022.

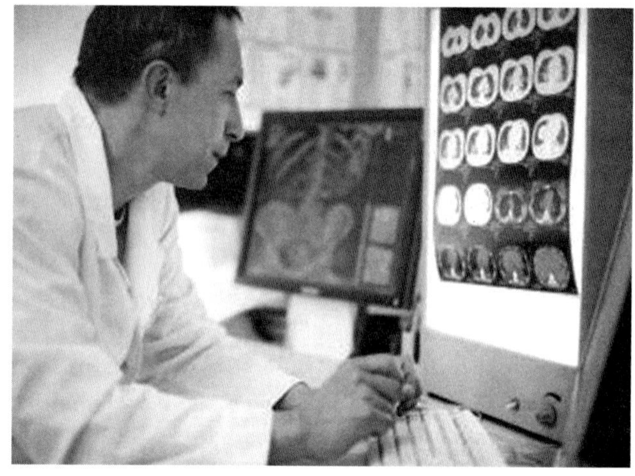

Medical scientists usually specialize in a area of research, such as neuroscience.

Job Outlook

Employment of medical scientists is projected to grow 10 percent from 2022 to 2032, much faster than the average for all occupations.

About 7,500 openings for medical scientists are projected each year, on average, over the decade. Many of those openings are expected to result from the need to replace workers who transfer to different occupations or exit the labor force, such as to retire.

What Medical Scientists Do

Medical scientists conduct research aimed at improving overall human health. They often use clinical trials and other investigative methods to reach their findings.

Medical scientists design and conduct studies to investigate human diseases, and methods to prevent and treat them.

Duties

Medical scientists typically do the following:

- Design and conduct studies to investigate human diseases and methods to prevent and treat diseases
- Prepare and analyze data from medical samples and investigate causes and treatment of toxicity, pathogens, or chronic diseases
- Standardize drugs' potency, doses, and methods of administering to allow for their mass manufacturing and distribution
- Create and test medical devices
- Follow safety procedures, such as decontaminating workspaces
- Write research grant proposals and apply for funding from government agencies, private funding, and other sources
- Write articles for publication and present research findings

Medical scientists form hypotheses and develop experiments. They study the causes of diseases and other health problems in a variety of ways. For example, they may conduct clinical trials, working with licensed physicians to test treatments on patients who have agreed to participate in the study. They analyze data from the trial to evaluate the effectiveness of the treatment.

Some medical scientists choose to write about and publish their findings in scientific journals after completion of the clinical trial. They also may have to present their findings in ways that nonscientist audiences understand.

Medical scientists often lead teams of technicians or students who perform support tasks. For example, a medical scientist may have assistants take measurements and make observations for the scientist's research.

Medical scientists usually specialize in an area of research, with the goal of understanding and improving human health outcomes. The following are examples of types of medical scientists:

Clinical pharmacologists research new drug therapies for health problems, such as seizure disorders and Alzheimer's disease.

Medical scientists usually work in offices and laboratories.

Medical pathologists research the human body and tissues, such as how cancer progresses or how certain issues relate to genetics.

Toxicologists study the negative impacts of chemicals and pollutants on human health.

Medical scientists conduct research to better understand disease or to develop breakthroughs in treatment. For information about an occupation that tracks and develops methods to prevent the spread of diseases, see the profile on epidemiologists.

Work Environment

Medical scientists held about 119,000 jobs in 2022. The largest employers of medical scientists were as follows:

Employer	Percent
Research and development in the physical, engineering, and life sciences	36%
Hospitals; state, local, and private	19
Colleges, universities, and professional schools; state, local, and private	19
Medical and diagnostic laboratories	5
Pharmaceutical and medicine manufacturing	4

Medical scientists typically work in offices and laboratories. In the lab, they sometimes work with dangerous biological samples and chemicals. They must take precautions in the lab to ensure safety, such as by wearing protective gloves, knowing the location of safety equipment, and keeping work areas neat.

Work Schedules

Most medical scientists work full time, and some work more than 40 hours per week.

How to Become a Medical Scientist

Medical scientists typically have a Ph.D., usually in biology or a related life science. Some get a medical degree instead of, or in addition to, a Ph.D.

Education

Medical scientists typically need a Ph.D. or medical degree. Candidates sometimes qualify for positions with a master's

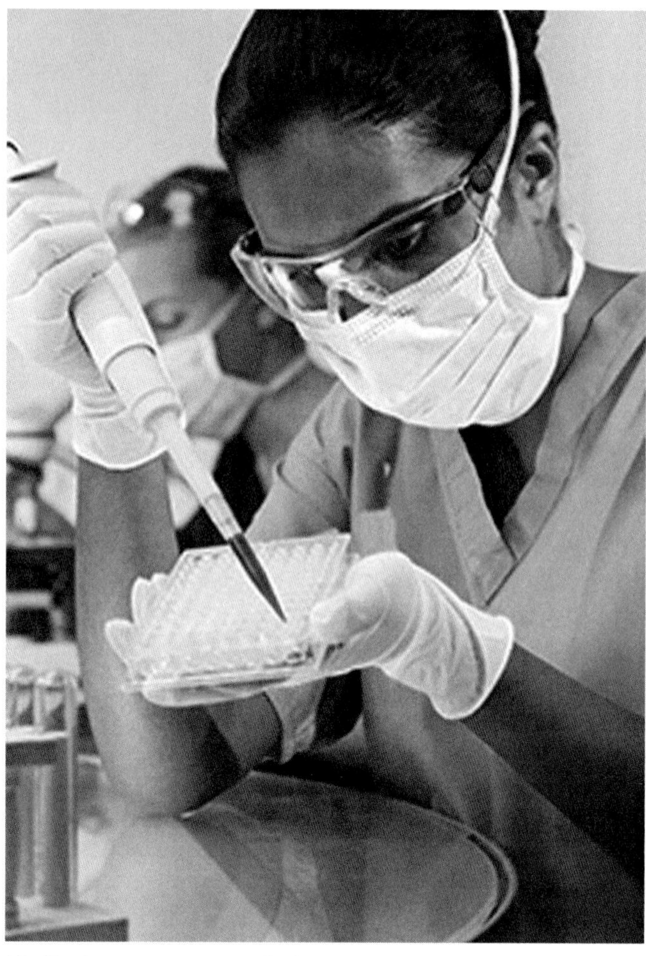

Medical scientists typically have a Ph.D. and sometimes are certified medical doctors as well.

degree and experience. Applicants to master's or doctoral programs typically have a bachelor's degree in biology or a related physical science field, such as chemistry.

Ph.D. programs for medical scientists typically focus on research in a particular field, such as immunology, neurology, or cancer. Through laboratory work, Ph.D. students develop experiments related to their research.

Medical degree programs include Medical Doctor (M.D.), Doctor of Dental Surgery (D.D.S.), Doctor of Dental Medicine (D.M.D.), Doctor of Osteopathic Medicine (D.O.), Doctor of Pharmacy (Pharm.D.), and advanced nursing degrees. In medical school, students usually spend the first phase of their education in labs and classrooms, taking courses such as anatomy, biochemistry, and medical ethics. During their second phase, medical students typically participate in residency programs.

Some medical scientist training programs offer dual degrees that pair a Ph.D. with a medical degree. Students in dual-degree programs learn both the research skills needed to be a scientist and the clinical skills needed to be a healthcare practitioner.

Licenses, Certifications, and Registrations

Medical scientists primarily conduct research and typically do not need licenses or certifications. However, those who practice medicine, such as by treating patients in clinical trials or in private practice, must be licensed as physicians or other healthcare practitioners.

Training

Medical scientists with a Ph.D. may begin their careers in postdoctoral research positions; those with a medical degree often complete a residency. During postdoctoral appointments, Ph.D.s work with experienced scientists to learn more about their specialty area and improve their research skills. Medical school graduates who enter a residency program in their specialty generally spend several years working in a hospital or doctor's office.

Important Qualities

Communication skills. Medical scientists must be able to explain their research in nontechnical ways. In addition, they may write grant proposals in order to get funding for their research.

Critical-thinking skills. Medical scientists must use their expertise to determine the best method for approaching research questions.

Data-analysis skills. Medical scientists use statistics to evaluate research questions and information from clinical trials.

Decision-making skills. Medical scientists must determine what research questions to ask, how to investigate the questions, and which data answer the questions.

Observation skills. Medical scientists conduct experiments that require monitoring samples and other health-related data.

Pay

The median annual wage for medical scientists was $99,930 in May 2022. The median wage is the wage at which half the workers in an occupation earned more than that amount and half

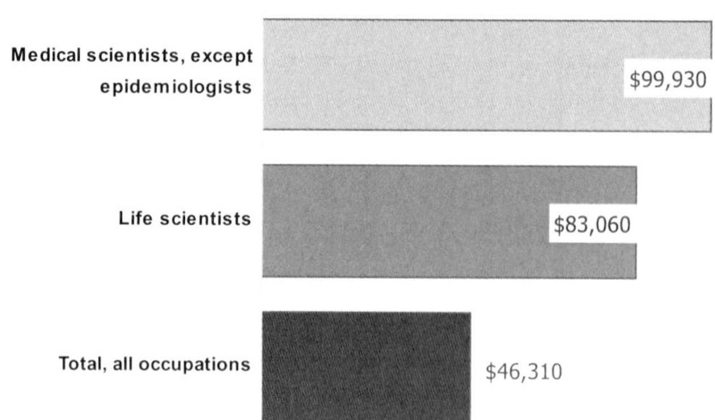

earned less. The lowest 10 percent earned less than $58,190, and the highest 10 percent earned more than $170,260.

In May 2022, the median annual wages for medical scientists in the top industries in which they worked were as follows:

Research and development in the physical, engineering, and life sciences	$109,560
Pharmaceutical and medicine manufacturing	105,210
Medical and diagnostic laboratories	97,420
Hospitals; state, local, and private	81,180
Colleges, universities, and professional schools; state, local, and private	65,380

Most medical scientists work full time, and some work more than 40 hours per week.

Job Outlook

Employment of medical scientists is projected to grow 10 percent from 2022 to 2032, much faster than the average for all occupations.

About 7,500 openings for medical scientists are projected each year, on average, over the decade. Many of those openings are expected to result from the need to replace workers who transfer to different occupations or exit the labor force, such as to retire.

Employment

Demand for medical scientists will stem from greater demand for a variety of healthcare services as the population continues to age and rates of chronic disease continue to increase. These scientists will be needed for research into treating diseases, such as Alzheimer's disease and cancer, and problems related to treatment, such as resistance to antibiotics. In addition, medical scientists will continue to be needed for medical research as a growing population travels globally and facilitates the spread of diseases.

The availability of federal funds for medical research grants also may affect opportunities for these scientists.

Medical Scientists

Percent change in employment, projected 2022-32

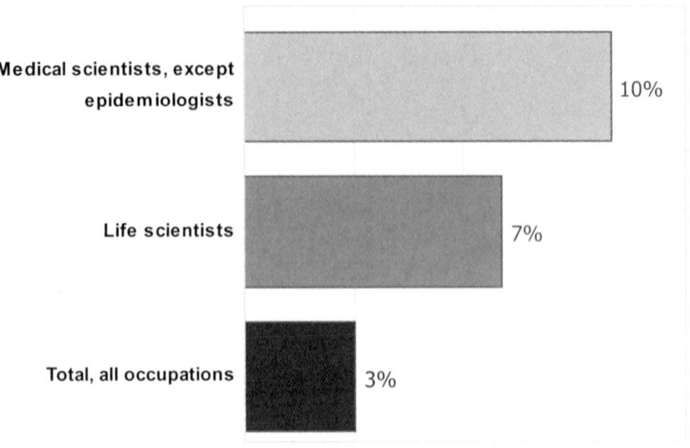

Note: All Occupations includes all occupations in the U.S. Economy.
Source: U.S. Bureau of Labor Statistics, Employment Projections program.

Occupational Title	SOC Code	Employment, 2022	Projected Employment, 2032	Change, 2022-32	
				Percent	Numeric
Medical scientists, except epidemiologists	19-1042	119,000	130,700	10	11,600

Contacts for More Information

For more information, visit

- American Association for Cancer Research
- American Physician Scientists Association
- American Society for Biochemistry and Molecular Biology
- The American Society for Clinical Laboratory Science
- American Society for Clinical Pathology
- American Society for Clinical Pharmacology and Therapeutics
- The American Society for Pharmacology and Experimental Therapeutics
- The Gerontological Society of America
- Infectious Diseases Society of America
- National Institute of General Medical Sciences
- Society for Neuroscience
- Society of Toxicology

Microbiologists

Summary

Quick Facts: Microbiologists	
2022 Median Pay	$81,990 per year $39.42 per hour
Typical Entry-Level Education	Bachelor's degree
Work Experience in a Related Occupation	None
On-the-job Training	None
Number of Jobs, 2022	20,900
Job Outlook, 2022-32	5% (Faster than average)
Employment Change, 2022-32	1,100

What Microbiologists Do

Microbiologists study microorganisms such as bacteria, viruses, algae, fungi, and some types of parasites.

Work Environment

Microbiologists work in laboratories and offices, where they conduct scientific experiments and analyze the results. Most microbiologists work full time and keep regular hours.

How to Become a Microbiologist

Microbiologists typically need a bachelor's degree in microbiology or a related field for entry-level jobs. They typically need a Ph.D. to work in research or in colleges and universities.

Pay

The median annual wage for microbiologists was $81,990 in May 2022.

Job Outlook

Employment of microbiologists is projected to grow 5 percent from 2022 to 2032, faster than the average for all occupations.

About 1,700 openings for microbiologists are projected each year, on average, over the decade. Many of those openings are expected to result from the need to replace workers who transfer to different occupations or exit the labor force, such as to retire.

What Microbiologists Do

Microbiologists study microorganisms such as bacteria, viruses, algae, fungi, and some types of parasites. They try to understand how these organisms live, grow, and interact with their environments.

Duties

Microbiologists typically do the following:

- Plan and conduct complex research projects, such as improving sterilization procedures or developing new drugs to combat infectious diseases
- Perform laboratory experiments that are used in the diagnosis and treatment of illnesses
- Supervise the work of biological technicians and other workers and evaluate the accuracy of their results
- Isolate and maintain cultures of bacteria or other microorganisms for study
- Identify and classify microorganisms found in specimens collected from humans, plants, animals, or the environment
- Monitor the effect of microorganisms on plants, animals, other microorganisms, or the environment
- Review literature and the findings of other researchers and attend conferences
- Prepare technical reports, publish research papers, and make recommendations based on their research findings
- Present research findings to scientists, nonscientist executives, engineers, other colleagues, and the public

Many microbiologists work in research and development conducting basic research or applied research. The aim of basic research is to increase scientific knowledge. An example is

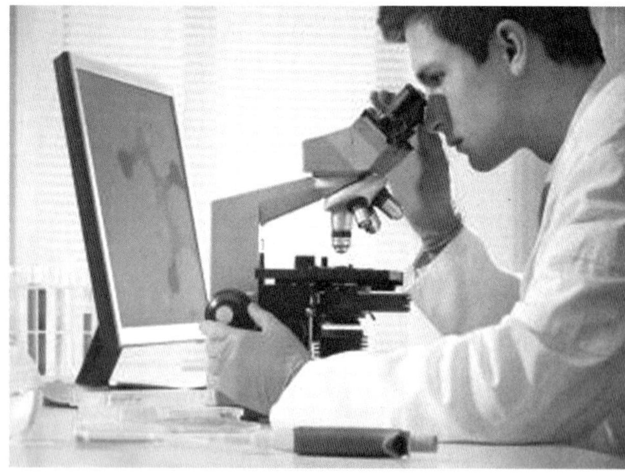

Microbiologists use laboratory equipment such as microscopes to study microorganisms.

Most microbiologists work on research teams with other scientists and technicians.

growing strains of bacteria in various conditions to learn how they react to those conditions. Other microbiologists conduct applied research and develop new products to solve particular problems. For example, microbiologists may aid in the development of genetically engineered crops, better biofuels, or new vaccines.

Microbiologists use computers and a wide variety of sophisticated laboratory instruments to do their experiments. Electron microscopes are used to study bacteria, and advanced computer software is used to analyze the growth of microorganisms found in samples.

It is increasingly common for microbiologists to work on teams with technicians and scientists in other fields, because many scientific research projects involve multiple disciplines. Microbiologists may work with medical scientists or molecular biologists while researching new drugs, or they may work in medical diagnostic laboratories alongside physicians and nurses to help prevent, treat, and cure diseases.

The following are examples of types of microbiologists:

Bacteriologists study the growth, development, and other properties of bacteria, including the positive and negative effects that bacteria have on plants, animals, and humans.

Clinical microbiologists perform a wide range of clinical laboratory tests on specimens collected from plants, humans, and animals to aid in detection of disease. Clinical and medical microbiologists whose work involves directly researching human health may be classified as medical scientists.

Environmental microbiologists study how microorganisms interact with the environment and each other. They may study the use of microbes to clean up areas contaminated by heavy metals or study how microbes could aid crop growth.

Industrial microbiologists study and solve problems related to industrial production processes. They may examine microbial growth found in the pipes of a chemical factory, monitor the impact industrial waste has on the local ecosystem, or oversee the microbial activities used in cheese production to ensure quality.

Mycologists study the properties of fungi such as yeast and mold. They also study the ways fungi can be used to benefit society (for example, in food or the environment) and the risks fungi may pose.

Parasitologists study the life cycle of parasites, the parasite-host relationship, and how parasites adapt to different environments. They may investigate the outbreak and control of parasitic diseases such as malaria.

Public health microbiologists examine specimens to track, control, and prevent communicable diseases and other health hazards. They typically provide laboratory services for local health departments and community health programs.

Virologists study the structure, development, and other properties of viruses and any effects viruses have on infected organisms.

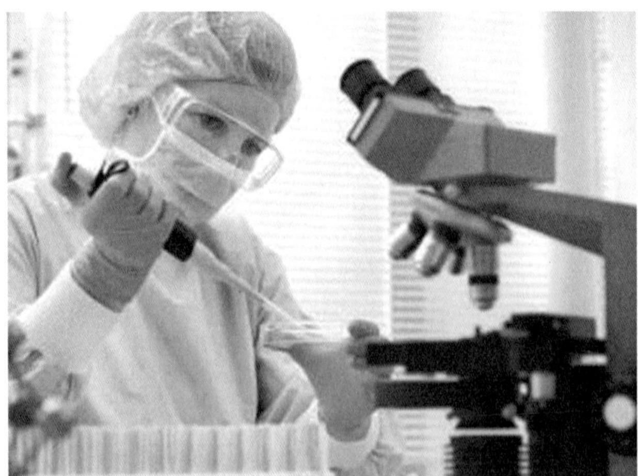

Microbiologists who work with dangerous organisms must follow strict safety procedures to avoid contamination.

Many people with a microbiology background become high school teachers or postsecondary teachers.

Work Environment

Microbiologists held about 20,900 jobs in 2022. The largest employers of microbiologists were as follows:

Research and development in the physical, engineering, and life sciences	28%
Pharmaceutical and medicine manufacturing	15
Federal government, excluding postal service	11
State government, excluding education and hospitals	6
Colleges, universities, and professional schools; state, local, and private	6

Microbiologists typically work in laboratories, offices, and industrial settings where they conduct experiments and analyze the results. Microbiologists who work with dangerous

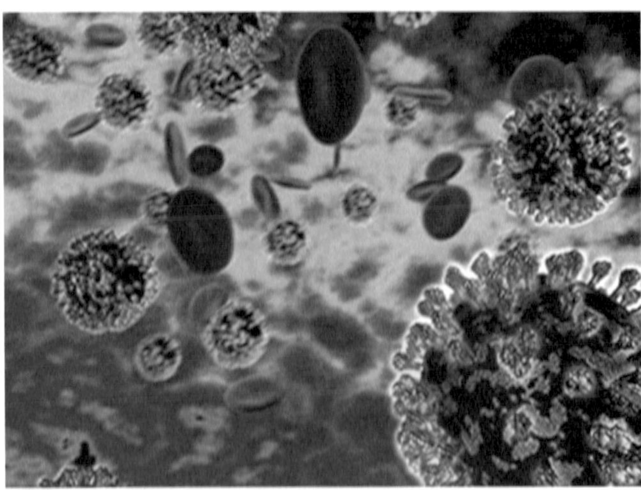

Microbiologists study the growth and characteristics of microscopic organisms such as viruses.

organisms must follow strict safety procedures to avoid contamination. Some microbiologists may conduct onsite visits or collect samples from the environment or worksites, and, as a result, may travel occasionally and spend some time outside.

Basic researchers who work in academia usually choose the focus of their research and run their own laboratories. Applied researchers who work for companies study the products that the company will sell or suggest modifications to the production process so that the company can become more efficient. Basic researchers often need to fund their research by winning grants. These grants often put pressure on researchers to meet deadlines and other specifications. Research grants are generally awarded through a competitive selection process.

Work Schedules

Most microbiologists work full time and keep regular hours.

How to Become a Microbiologist

Microbiologists typically need a bachelor's degree in microbiology or a related field for entry-level jobs. They typically need a Ph.D. to work in research or in colleges and universities.

Education

Microbiologists typically need at least a bachelor's degree in microbiology or a related field, such as biology or natural resources, that provides substantial coursework in microbiology.

Microbiology study usually includes courses in microbial genetics, microbial physiology, environmental microbiology, and virology. Students also may benefit from taking courses in other sciences, such as biochemistry, chemistry, and physics; in statistics and mathematics; and in computer science.

Prospective microbiologists also need to work in a laboratory, which is required in most undergraduate microbiology programs. Students may gain additional laboratory experience through internships with companies, such as drug manufacturers, in which microbiologists are employed.

Microbiologists typically need a Ph.D. to work on independent research or in colleges and universities. Graduate students studying microbiology commonly specialize in a subfield, such as bacteriology or immunology. Ph.D. programs usually include class work, laboratory research, and completing a thesis or dissertation.

Training

Many microbiology Ph.D. holders begin their careers in temporary postdoctoral research positions. During their postdoctoral appointment, they work with experienced scientists as they continue to learn about their specialties and develop a broader understanding of related areas of research.

Postdoctoral positions typically offer the opportunity to publish research findings. A solid record of published research is essential to getting a permanent college or university faculty position.

Important Qualities

Communication skills. Microbiologists should be able to effectively communicate their research processes and findings so that knowledge may be applied correctly.

Detail oriented. Microbiologists must be able to conduct scientific experiments and analyses with accuracy and precision.

Interpersonal skills. Microbiologists typically work on research teams and thus must work well with others toward a common goal. Many also lead research teams and must be able to motivate and direct other team members.

Logical-thinking skills. Microbiologists draw conclusions from experimental results through sound reasoning and judgment.

Math skills. Microbiologists regularly use complex mathematical equations and formulas in their work. Therefore, they need a broad understanding of math, including calculus and statistics.

Observation skills. Microbiologists must constantly monitor their experiments. They need to keep a complete, accurate record of their work, noting conditions, procedures, and results.

Perseverance. Microbiological research involves substantial trial and error, and microbiologists must not become discouraged in their work.

Problem-solving skills. Microbiologists use scientific experiments and analysis to find solutions to complex scientific problems.

Time-management skills. Microbiologists usually need to meet deadlines when conducting research and laboratory tests. They must be able to manage time and prioritize tasks efficiently while maintaining their quality of work.

Advancement

Microbiologists typically receive greater responsibility and independence in their work as they gain experience. They also gain greater responsibility through certification and higher education. Ph.D. microbiologists usually lead research teams and control the direction and content of projects.

Some microbiologists move into managerial positions, often as natural sciences managers. Those who pursue management careers spend much of their time on administrative tasks, such as preparing budgets and schedules.

Licenses, Certifications, and Registrations

Certifications are not mandatory for the majority of work done by microbiologists. However, certifications are available for clinical microbiologists and for those who specialize in the fields of food safety and quality and pharmaceuticals and medical devices. Certification may help workers gain employment in the occupation or advance to new positions of responsibility.

Pay

The median annual wage for microbiologists was $81,990 in May 2022. The median wage is the wage at which half the

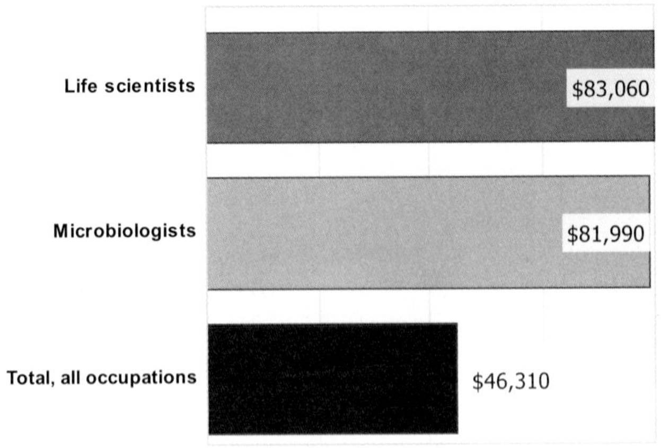

Note: All Occupations includes all occupations in the U.S. Economy.
Source: U.S. Bureau of Labor Statistics, Occupational Employment and Wage Statistics.

workers in an occupation earned more than that amount and half earned less. The lowest 10 percent earned less than $46,270, and the highest 10 percent earned more than $136,630.

In May 2022, the median annual wages for microbiologists in the top industries in which they worked were as follows:

Federal government, excluding postal service	$119,500
Research and development in the physical, engineering, and life sciences	103,540
Pharmaceutical and medicine manufacturing	72,930
State government, excluding education and hospitals	63,500
Colleges, universities, and professional schools; state, local, and private	61,030

Most microbiologists work full time and keep regular hours.

Job Outlook

Employment of microbiologists is projected to grow 5 percent from 2022 to 2032, faster than the average for all occupations.

About 1,700 openings for microbiologists are projected each year, on average, over the decade. Many of those openings are expected to result from the need to replace workers who transfer to different occupations or exit the labor force, such as to retire.

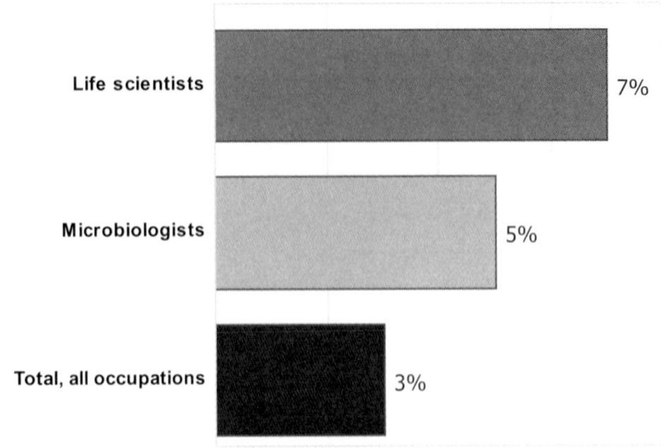

Note: All Occupations includes all occupations in the U.S. Economy.
Source: U.S. Bureau of Labor Statistics, Employment Projections program.

Employment

Microbiologists are expected to be needed to help pharmaceutical and biotechnology companies develop new drugs that are produced with the aid of microorganisms. In addition, demand for biofuels production is expected to increase the need for microbiologists to conduct advanced research and development in these areas. Efforts to discover new and improved ways to preserve the environment and safeguard public health also are expected to support demand for these workers.

Occupational Title	SOC Code	Employment, 2022	Projected Employment, 2032	Change, 2022-32	
				Percent	Numeric
Microbiologists	19-1022	20,900	22,000	5	1,100

Contacts for More Information

For more information about microbiologists, visit

- American Society for Microbiology
- International Union of Microbiological Societies
- Society for Industrial Microbiology and Biotechnology
- USAJOBS
- American Institute of Biological Sciences
- The American Society for Cell Biology
- American Society for Clinical Pathology
- Federation of American Societies for Experimental Biology
- Microbiological Garden
- Tree of Life Web Project

Nuclear Technicians

Summary

Quick Facts: Nuclear Technicians	
2022 Median Pay	$100,420 per year $48.28 per hour
Typical Entry-Level Education	Associate's degree
Work Experience in a Related Occupation	None
On-the-job Training	Moderate-term on-the-job training
Number of Jobs, 2022	5,900
Job Outlook, 2022-32	-1% (Little or no change)
Employment Change, 2022-32	-100

What Nuclear Technicians Do

Nuclear technicians assist physicists, engineers, and other professionals in nuclear research and nuclear energy production.

Work Environment

In nuclear power plants, nuclear technicians typically work in offices and control rooms where they use computers and other equipment to monitor and help operate nuclear reactors. Most nuclear technicians work full-time, variable schedules in the nuclear power industry. Their schedules may include working nights, holidays, and weekends. Nuclear technicians must take safety precautions to avoid exposure to radiation.

How to Become a Nuclear Technician

Nuclear technicians typically need an associate's degree in nuclear science or a nuclear-related technology. Nuclear technicians also go through extensive on-the-job training.

Pay

The median annual wage for nuclear technicians was $100,420 in May 2022.

Nuclear technicians working for nuclear power plants use computers and other equipment to monitor and help operate nuclear reactors.

Nuclear technicians use instruments, such as geiger counters, to monitor radiation levels.

Job Outlook

Employment of nuclear technicians is projected to show little or no change from 2022 to 2032.

Despite limited employment growth, about 600 openings for nuclear technicians are projected each year, on average, over the decade. Most of those openings are expected to result from the need to replace workers who transfer to different occupations or exit the labor force, such as to retire.

What Nuclear Technicians Do

Nuclear technicians typically work in nuclear energy production or assist physicists, engineers, and other professionals in nuclear research. They operate special equipment used in these activities and monitor the levels of radiation that are produced.

Duties

Nuclear technicians typically do the following:

- Monitor the performance of equipment used in nuclear experiments and power generation
- Measure the levels and types of radiation produced by nuclear experiments, power generation, and other activities
- Collect samples of air, water, and soil, and test for radioactive contamination
- Instruct personnel on radiation safety procedures and warn them of hazardous conditions
- Operate and maintain radiation monitoring equipment

Job duties and titles of nuclear technicians often depend on where they work and what purpose the facility serves. Most nuclear technicians work in nuclear power plants, where they ensure that reactors and other equipment are operated safely and efficiently. The following are types of nuclear technicians who work in the power generation industry:

Operating technicians monitor the performance of systems in nuclear power plants. They measure levels of radiation and other contaminants in water systems. The levels they find could indicate a leak or could decrease the efficiency of the turbines

Nuclear technicians may monitor radiation levels at nuclear power plants.

Most employers prefer applicants who have at least an associate's degree in nuclear science or a nuclear-related technology.

in the power plants. They measure efficiency and ensure safety by making calculations based on factors such as temperature, pressure, and radiation intensity. Operating technicians must make adjustments and repairs to maintain or improve the performance of reactors and other equipment.

Radiation protection technicians monitor levels of radiation contamination to protect personnel in nuclear power facilities and the surrounding environment. They use radiation detectors to measure levels in and around facilities, and they use dosimeters to measure the levels present in people and objects. Technicians map radiation levels throughout the plant and the surrounding environment and recommend radioactive decontamination plans and safety procedures for personnel. They also monitor worker activity from a control room and alert personnel who may be entering a dangerous area or working in an unsafe way.

Nuclear technicians also work in waste management and treatment facilities, where they monitor the disposal, recycling, and storage of nuclear waste. They perform duties similar to those of radiation protection technicians at nuclear power plants.

Some nuclear technicians work in laboratories. They help nuclear physicists, nuclear engineers, and other scientists conduct research and develop new types of nuclear reactors, fuels, medicines, and other technologies. They use equipment such as radiation detectors, spectrometers (utilized to measure gamma ray and x-ray radiation), and particle accelerators to conduct experiments and gather data. They also may use remote-controlled equipment to manipulate radioactive materials or materials exposed to radiation.

Work Environment

Nuclear technicians held about 5,900 jobs in 2022. The largest employers of nuclear technicians were as follows:

Electric power generation, transmission and distribution	61%
Professional, scientific, and technical services	20
Manufacturing	7

Most nuclear technicians work in nuclear power plants, where they typically work in offices and control rooms. The technicians use computers and other equipment to monitor and help operate nuclear reactors. Nuclear technicians also need to measure radiation levels onsite, requiring them to visit several areas in and around the plant throughout the workday. This task may sometimes require them to work outside, regardless of weather conditions. Working around nuclear reactors may involve exposure to high temperatures. Nuclear technicians who conduct scientific tests for scientists and engineers typically work in laboratories.

Nuclear technicians must take precautions when working with or around nuclear materials. They often have to wear protective gear and special badges that indicate whether they have been exposed to radiation. Protective gear may include hardhats, hearing and eye protection, plastic suits, and respirators.

Work Schedules

Most nuclear technicians work full time. In power plants, which operate 24 hours a day, technicians may work variable schedules that include nights, holidays, and weekends. Occasionally, plants stop operations for maintenance and upgrades. Workers may need to work overtime during these periods. In laboratories, technicians typically work during normal business hours.

How to Become a Nuclear Technician

Nuclear technicians typically need an associate's degree in nuclear science or a nuclear-related technology. Some may have gained equivalent experience from serving in the military. Nuclear technicians also go through extensive on-the-job training. For safety and security reasons, nuclear technicians usually must undergo a background check and receive some type of security clearance after they are hired.

Education

Nuclear technicians typically need an associate's degree, or they may have equivalent experience from serving in the military—specifically, the U.S. Navy. Many community colleges and technical institutes offer associate's degree programs in nuclear science, nuclear technology, or related fields. Students study nuclear energy, radiation, and the equipment and components used in nuclear power plants and laboratories. Other coursework includes mathematics, physics, and chemistry.

Training

In nuclear power plants, nuclear technicians start out as trainees under the supervision of more experienced technicians. During their training, they are taught the proper ways to use operating and monitoring equipment. They are also taught safety procedures, regulations, and plant policies. Workers who do not have the appropriate associate's degree or its equivalent usually have a substantial period of onsite technical training provided by their employer before they begin full duties and a normal training schedule.

Training varies with the technician's previous experience and education. Most training programs last between 6 months and 2 years. Nuclear technicians go through additional training and education throughout their careers to keep up with advances in nuclear science and technology.

Licenses, Certifications, and Registrations

The Nuclear Energy Institute offers a certificate through its Nuclear Uniform Curriculum Program. The American Society for Nondestructive Testing offers Industrial Radiography and Radiation Safety Personnel certification. The National Registry of Radiation Protection Technologists offers certification as a Registered Radiation Protection Technologist.

Important Qualities

Communication skills. Nuclear technicians receive complex instructions from scientists and engineers that they must follow exactly. They have to ask questions to clarify anything they do not understand. Nuclear technicians must explain their work to scientists, engineers, and reactor operators. They must also instruct others on safety procedures and warn them of hazardous conditions. Many of the daily procedures and work processes must be thoroughly documented because of the risky nature of the work.

Computer skills. Nuclear technicians must use computers for plant operations and for normal office work, such as documenting their activities.

Critical-thinking skills. Nuclear technicians must carefully evaluate all available information before deciding on a course of action. For example, radiation protection technicians must evaluate data from radiation detectors to determine if areas are safe and must develop decontamination plans if they are not safe.

Math skills. Nuclear technicians use scientific and mathematical formulas to analyze experimental and production data, such as reaction rates and radiation exposures.

Mechanical skills. Nuclear technicians need to have strong mechanical aptitude. Nuclear power facilities are complex, and workers need to understand how the facilities work in order to make adjustments and repairs to equipment and to maintain a safe working environment. Employers hiring nuclear technicians in nuclear power plants often conduct mechanical aptitude tests as part of the hiring process.

Monitoring skills. Nuclear technicians must assess data from sensors, gauges, and other instruments to make sure that equipment and experiments are functioning properly and that radiation levels are controlled.

Advancement

With additional training and experience, technicians may become nuclear power reactor operators at nuclear power plants. Technicians can become nuclear engineers by earning a bachelor's degree in nuclear engineering. Nuclear physicists need a Ph.D. in physics. For more information, see the profiles on power plant operators, distributors, and dispatchers; nuclear engineers; and physicists and astronomers.

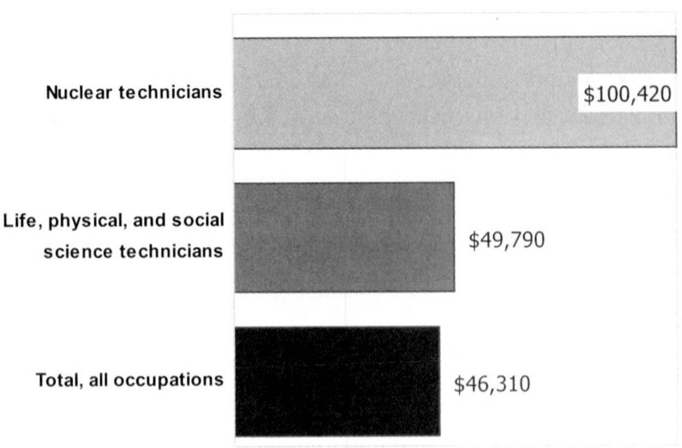

Note: All Occupations includes all occupations in the U.S. Economy.
Source: U.S. Bureau of Labor Statistics, Occupational Employment and Wage Statistics.

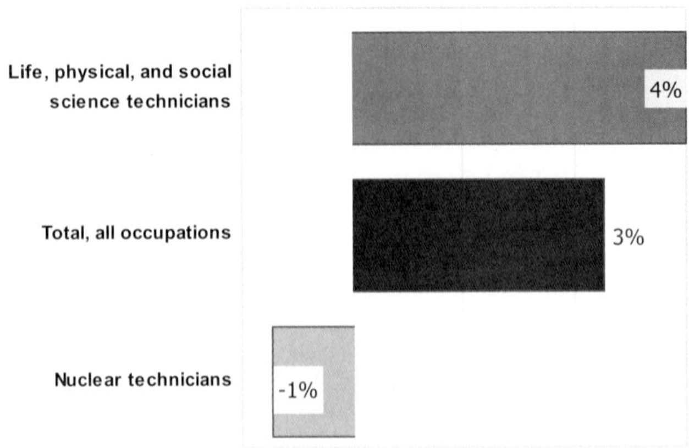

Note: All Occupations includes all occupations in the U.S. Economy.
Source: U.S. Bureau of Labor Statistics, Employment Projections program.

Pay

The median annual wage for nuclear technicians was $100,420 in May 2022. The median wage is the wage at which half the workers in an occupation earned more than that amount and half earned less. The lowest 10 percent earned less than $63,500, and the highest 10 percent earned more than $126,050.

In May 2022, the median annual wages for nuclear technicians in the top industries in which they worked were as follows:

Electric power generation, transmission and distribution	$104,540
Professional, scientific, and technical services	90,010
Manufacturing	84,100

Most nuclear technicians work full time. In power plants, which operate 24 hours a day, technicians may work variable schedules that include nights, holidays, and weekends. Occasionally, plants stop operations for maintenance and upgrades. Workers may need to work overtime during these periods. In laboratories, technicians typically work during normal business hours.

Job Outlook

Employment of nuclear technicians is projected to show little or no change from 2022 to 2032.

Despite limited employment growth, about 600 openings for nuclear technicians are projected each year, on average, over the decade. Most of those openings are expected to result from the need to replace workers who transfer to different occupations or exit the labor force, such as to retire.

Employment

Traditionally, utilities that own or build nuclear power plants have employed the greatest number of nuclear technicians. However, both the increasing viability of renewable energy and limited construction of new nuclear power plants put economic pressure on traditional nuclear power generation and reduce demand for these technicians. Even with this pressure, there will still be a need for some technicians to help maintain and upgrade existing nuclear power plants.

Occupational Title	SOC Code	Employment, 2022	Projected Employment, 2032	Change, 2022-32	
				Percent	Numeric
Nuclear technicians	19-4051	5,900	5,800	-1	-100

Contacts for More Information

For more information about nuclear technicians, visit

- Center for Energy Workforce Development
- Get Into Energy
- Nuclear Energy Institute
- For information about certification, visit
- American Society for Nondestructive Testing
- National Registry of Radiation Protection Technologists

Physicists and Astronomers

Summary

Quick Facts: Physicists and Astronomers	
2022 Median Pay	$139,220 per year $66.93 per hour
Typical Entry-Level Education	Doctoral or professional degree
Work Experience in a Related Occupation	None
On-the-job Training	None
Number of Jobs, 2022	23,600
Job Outlook, 2022-32	5% (Faster than average)
Employment Change, 2022-32	1,100

What Physicists and Astronomers Do

Physicists and astronomers study the interactions of matter and energy.

Work Environment

Physicists and astronomers may work in offices, research laboratories, and observatories. Most physicists and astronomers work full time, and some work more than 40 hours per week.

How to Become a Physicist or Astronomer

Physicists and astronomers typically need a Ph.D. for jobs in research and academia. However, entry-level physicist jobs in the federal government typically require a bachelor's degree in physics.

Pay

The median annual wage for astronomers was $128,330 in May 2022.

The median annual wage for physicists was $142,850 in May 2022.

Some physicists study theoretical areas, while others design and perform experiments.

Job Outlook

Overall employment of physicists and astronomers is projected to grow 5 percent from 2022 to 2032, faster than the average for all occupations.

About 1,500 openings for physicists and astronomers are projected each year, on average, over the decade. Many of those openings are expected to result from the need to replace workers who transfer to different occupations or exit the labor force, such as to retire.

What Physicists and Astronomers Do

Physicists and astronomers study the interactions of matter and energy. Theoretical physicists and astronomers may study the nature of time or the origin of the universe. Some physicists design and perform experiments with sophisticated equipment such as particle accelerators, electron microscopes, and lasers.

Duties

Physicists and astronomers typically do the following:

- Develop scientific theories and models to explain the properties of the natural world, such as the force of gravity or the formation of subatomic particles
- Plan and conduct scientific experiments and studies to test theories and discover properties of matter and energy
- Write proposals and apply for research funding
- Do mathematical calculations to analyze physical and astronomical data, such as for new material properties or the existence of planets in distant solar systems
- Design new scientific equipment, such as telescopes and lasers
- Develop computer software to analyze and model data
- Write scientific papers for publication
- Present research findings at conferences and lectures

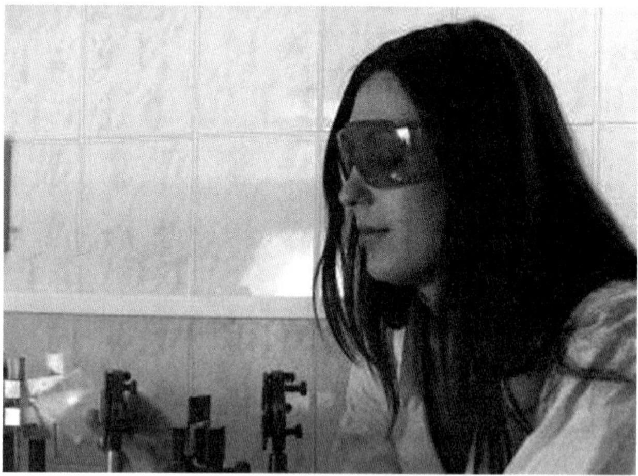

Physicists plan and conduct scientific experiments and studies to test theories and to discover properties of matter and energy.

Physicists explore the fundamental properties and laws that govern space, time, energy, and matter. They may study theory, design and perform experiments, or apply their knowledge in developing materials or equipment.

Astronomers study planets, stars, and other celestial bodies. They use ground-based equipment, such as optical telescopes, and space-based equipment, such as the Hubble Space Telescope. Some astronomers study distant galaxies and phenomena such as black holes and neutron stars. Others monitor space debris that could interfere with satellite operations.

Many physicists and astronomers work in applied research. They use their knowledge to develop technology or solve problems in areas such as energy storage, electronics, communications, and navigation. Others work in basic research to develop theories that explain concepts such as what gravity is or how the universe was formed.

Astronomers and physicists typically work on research teams with engineers, technicians, and other scientists. Senior astronomers and physicists may assign tasks to other team members and monitor their progress. They also may need to find and apply for research funding.

Experimental physicists develop equipment or sensors to study properties of matter, create theories, and test theories through experiments. *Theoretical and computational physicists* develop concepts that predict properties of materials or describe unexplained results. Although all of physics involves the same fundamental principles, physicists generally specialize in one of many subfields. The following are examples of physicist job titles:

Atomic, molecular, and optical physicists study atoms, simple molecules, electrons, and light and the interactions among them. Some look for ways to control the states of individual atoms, because such control might allow for further miniaturization or might contribute toward developing new materials or technology.

Computational physicists study the use of algorithms, numerical analysis, and datasets to explore the interaction between theoretical and experimental physics. They explore complex phenomena in atoms, molecules, plasmas, and high-energy particles; problems in astrophysics; and applied phenomena, such as traffic, the behavior of oceans, and biological dynamics.

Condensed matter and materials physicists study the physical properties of matter in molecules, nanostructures, or novel compounds. They study a wide range of phenomena, such as superconductivity, liquid crystals, sensors, and nanomachines.

Health physicists study the effects of radiation on people, communities, and the environment. They manage the beneficial use of radiation while protecting workers and the public from potential hazards posed by radiation.

Medical physicists work in healthcare and use their knowledge of physics to develop new medical technologies and radiation-based treatments. For example, some develop safer radiation therapies for cancer patients. Others develop improved imaging technologies for radiant energy, such as magnetic resonance imaging (MRI) and ultrasound imaging.

Particle and nuclear physicists study the properties of atomic and subatomic particles, such as quarks, electrons, and nuclei and the forces that cause their interactions.

Plasma physicists study plasmas, a distinct state of matter that occur naturally in stars and interplanetary space and artificially in products such as neon signs and fluorescent lights. These physicists may study ways to create fusion reactors as a potential energy source.

Quantum information physicists study ways to use quantum objects, such as atoms and photons, to probe information processing, computing, and cryptography. They focus on ways to use the fundamental nature of quantum mechanics and its associated uncertainties.

Unlike physicists, astronomers cannot experiment on their subjects, which are so far away that they cannot be touched or interacted with. Therefore, astronomers generally make observations or work on theory. *Observational astronomers* view celestial objects and collect data on them. *Theoretical astronomers* analyze, model, and speculate about systems and how they work and evolve. The following are examples of astronomer job titles:

Cosmologists and extragalactic/galactic, planetary, and stellar astronomers study the creation, evolution, and possible futures of the universe and its galaxies, stars, planets, and solar systems. These astronomers develop and test concepts, such as string theory and dark-matter and dark-energy theories, and study models of galactic and stellar evolution, planetary formation, and interactions between stars.

Optical and radio astronomers use optical, radio, and gravitational-wave telescopes to study the motions and evolution of stars, galaxies, and the larger scale structure of the universe.

Physicists also may work in interdisciplinary fields, such as biophysics, chemical physics, and geophysics. For more information, see the profiles on biochemists and biophysicists and geoscientists.

People who have a background in physics or astronomy also may become professors or teachers. For more information, see the profiles on high school teachers and postsecondary teachers.

Work Environment

Astronomers held about 2,400 jobs in 2022. The largest employers of astronomers were as follows:

Research and development in the physical, engineering, and life sciences	48%
Federal government, excluding postal service	21
Colleges, universities, and professional schools; state, local, and private	20

Physicists held about 21,100 jobs in 2022. The largest employers of physicists were as follows:

Some astronomers work away from home temporarily at national or international facilities that have unique equipment.

Scientific research and development services	41%
Federal government, excluding postal service	16
Colleges, universities, and professional schools; state, local, and private	14
Ambulatory healthcare services	3

The scientific research and development services industry includes both private and federally funded national laboratories, such as those overseen by the U.S. Department of Energy, the National Aeronautics and Space Administration (NASA), and the U.S. Department of Homeland Security. In addition to NASA, other federal agencies that employ physicists and astronomers include the U.S. Department of Defense.

Although physics research often requires working in laboratories, physicists also spend time outside of the lab to plan, analyze, fundraise, and report on research.

Most astronomers work in offices and occasionally visit observatories, buildings that house ground-based telescopes used to observe natural phenomenon and gather data. Some astronomers work full time in observatories.

Some physicists and astronomers work temporarily at national or international facilities that have unique equipment, such as particle accelerators and gamma ray telescopes. They also travel to meetings to present research results and learn about developments in their field.

Astronomers study planets, stars, galaxies, and other celestial bodies.

Work Schedules

Most physicists and astronomers work full time, and some work more than 40 hours per week. Astronomers may need to do observation work at night. However, astronomers typically visit observatories only a few times per year.

How to Become a Physicist or Astronomer

Physicists and astronomers typically need a Ph.D. for jobs in research and academia. However, physicist jobs in the federal government typically require a bachelor's degree in physics.

Education

A Ph.D. in physics, astronomy, or a related field is typically required for jobs in research or academia.

Graduate students may concentrate in a subfield of physics or astronomy, such as condensed matter physics or cosmology. In addition to coursework in physics or astronomy, Ph.D. students need to take courses in math, such as calculus, linear algebra, and statistics. Computer science also may be useful for developing programs to gather, analyze, and model data.

A bachelor's degree in physical science or a related field, such as engineering, usually is required to enter a graduate program in physics or astronomy. Undergraduate physics programs typically include courses such as quantum mechanics, thermodynamics, and electromagnetism.

Undergraduate students may choose to complete an internship to gain hands-on experience. The American Astronomical Society has a directory of internships for astronomy students, and the American Physical Society lists internships for physics students.

Jobseekers with a bachelor's degree in physics usually are qualified to work as technicians and research assistants in related fields, such as engineering and computer science. Those with a bachelor's degree in astronomy also may qualify to work as an assistant at an observatory. Students who do not want to continue their studies to the doctoral level may want to take courses in instrument building and computer science.

Master's degree and bachelor's degree holders may be eligible for jobs in the federal government. Others may become science teachers in middle schools or high schools.

Training

Physics and astronomy Ph.D. holders who seek employment as researchers may begin their careers in a postdoctoral research position, typically for 2 to 3 years. Senior scientists supervise these researchers as they gain experience and independence doing increasingly complex tasks.

Important Qualities

Analytical skills. Physicists and astronomers must evaluate their work and the work of others to avoid errors that could invalidate their research.

Communication skills. Physicists and astronomers present their research at conferences, to the public, and to others. They also write technical reports for publication and write proposals for research funding.

Critical-thinking skills. Physicists and astronomers need to think logically in carrying out scientific experiments and studies. They must determine whether results and conclusions are accurate.

Interpersonal skills. Physicists and astronomers must collaborate with others and therefore need to work well with team members and colleagues.

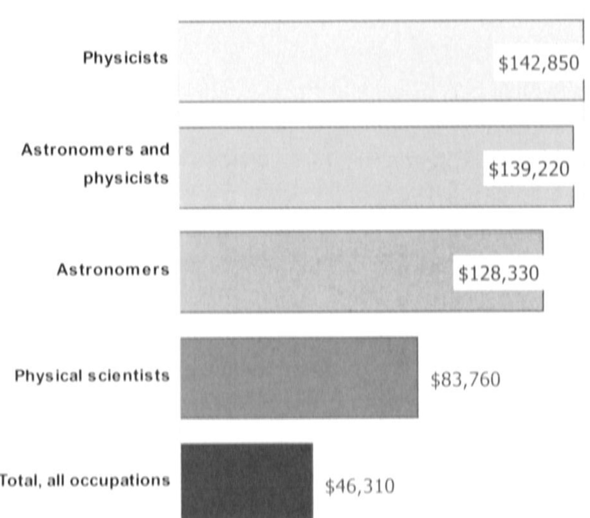

Note: All Occupations includes all occupations in the U.S. Economy.
Source: U.S. Bureau of Labor Statistics, Occupational Employment and Wage Statistics.

Math skills. Physicists and astronomers do calculations involving calculus, geometry, algebra, and other areas of math. They must express their research in mathematical terms.

Problem-solving skills. Physicists and astronomers use scientific observation and analysis, as well as creative thinking, to solve problems. For example, they may need to redesign their approach and find alternatives when an experiment or theory fails to produce the desired result.

Self-discipline. Physicists and astronomers need to be motivated, since their work may require them to focus on large datasets for long periods.

Licenses, Certifications, and Registrations

Some positions with the federal government, such as those involving nuclear energy, may require applicants to be U.S. citizens and hold a security clearance.

Advancement

With experience, physicists and astronomers may gain greater independence in their work and advance to senior positions. Experience also may lead to tenure for those in university positions. Some physicists and astronomers advance to become natural sciences managers.

Pay

The median annual wage for astronomers was $128,330 in May 2022. The median wage is the wage at which half the workers in an occupation earned more than that amount and half earned less. The lowest 10 percent earned less than $63,390, and the highest 10 percent earned more than $181,510.

The median annual wage for physicists was $142,850 in May 2022. The lowest 10 percent earned less than $74,760, and the highest 10 percent earned more than $219,760.

In May 2022, the median annual wages for astronomers in the top industries in which they worked were as follows:

Federal government, excluding postal service	$158,370
Research and development in the physical, engineering, and life sciences	129,570
Colleges, universities, and professional schools; state, local, and private	81,920

In May 2022, the median annual wages for physicists in the top industries in which they worked were as follows:

Ambulatory healthcare services	$212,880
Scientific research and development services	167,590
Federal government, excluding postal service	129,240
Colleges, universities, and professional schools; state, local, and private	87,620

Most physicists and astronomers work full time, and some work more than 40 hours per week. Astronomers may need to do observation work at night. However, astronomers typically visit observatories only a few times per year.

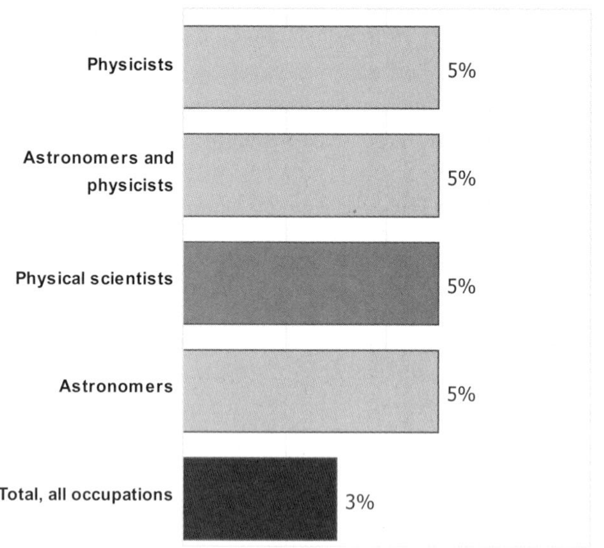

Note: All Occupations includes all occupations in the U.S. Economy.
Source: U.S. Bureau of Labor Statistics, Employment Projections program.

Job Outlook

Overall employment of physicists and astronomers is projected to grow 5 percent from 2022 to 2032, faster than the average for all occupations.

About 1,500 openings for physicists and astronomers are projected each year, on average, over the decade. Many of those openings are expected to result from the need to replace workers who transfer to different occupations or exit the labor force, such as to retire.

Employment

Deep space telescope operations and special off-planet missions may require additional astronomers and physicists over the projections decade. However, federal spending is the primary source of physics- and astronomy-related research funds, especially for basic research. Therefore, budgetary concerns may limit access by these workers to funding for basic research.

Occupational Title	SOC Code	Employment, 2022	Projected Employment, 2032	Change, 2022-32	
				Percent	Numeric
Astronomers and physicists	19-2010	23,600	24,700	5	1,100
Astronomers	19-2011	2,400	2,600	5	100
Physicists	19-2012	21,100	22,100	5	1,000

Contacts for More Information

For more information, visit

- American Astronomical Society
- Physics Careers Resource
- American Institute of Physics
- American Physical Society
- American Astronomical Society
- American Physical Society

Political Scientists

Summary

Quick Facts: Political Scientists

2022 Median Pay	$128,020 per year $61.55 per hour
Typical Entry-Level Education	Master's degree
Work Experience in a Related Occupation	None
On-the-job Training	None
Number of Jobs, 2022	6,200
Job Outlook, 2022-32	7% (Faster than average)
Employment Change, 2022-32	400

What Political Scientists Do

Political scientists study the origin, development, and operation of political systems.

Work Environment

Political scientists typically work full time in an office. They sometimes work additional hours to finish reports and meet deadlines.

How to Become a Political Scientist

To enter the occupation, political scientists typically need at least a master's degree in political science, public administration, or a related field.

Pay

The median annual wage for political scientists was $128,020 in May 2022.

Job Outlook

Employment of political scientists is projected to grow 7 percent from 2022 to 2032, faster than the average for all occupations.

About 600 openings for political scientists are projected each year, on average, over the decade. Many of those openings are expected to result from the need to replace workers who transfer to different occupations or exit the labor force, such as to retire.

What Political Scientists Do

Political scientists study the origin, development, and operation of political systems. They research political ideas and analyze governments, policies, political trends, and related issues.

Political scientists research policies, trends, and issues.

Duties

Political scientists typically do the following:

- Research political subjects, such as the U.S. political system and foreign relations
- Collect and analyze data from sources such as public opinion surveys
- Develop and test political theories
- Evaluate the effects of policies and laws on government, businesses, and people
- Monitor current events, policy decisions, and other related issues
- Forecast political, economic, and social trends
- Submit research results by giving presentations and publishing articles

Political scientists usually conduct research in one of the following areas: national politics, comparative politics, international relations, or political theory.

Often, political scientists use qualitative methods in their research, gathering information from numerous sources. For example, they may use historical documents to analyze past government structures and policies. Political scientists also rely on quantitative methods to develop and research theories. For example, they may analyze voter registration data to identify voting patterns. Political scientists study a wide range of topics such as U.S. political parties, how political structures differ among countries, globalization, and the history of political thought.

Political scientists often present their findings.

Political scientists also work as *policy analysts* for organizations that have a stake in policy, such as government, labor unions, and political groups. They evaluate current policies and events using public opinion surveys, economic data, and election results. From these sources, they try to anticipate the effects of new policies.

Political scientists often research the effects of government policies on a particular region or population, both domestically and internationally. As a result, they provide information and analysis that help in planning, developing, or carrying out policies.

Many people with a political science background become postsecondary teachers and high school teachers.

Work Environment

Political scientists held about 6,200 jobs in 2022. The largest employers of political scientists were as follows:

Employer	Percent
Federal government, excluding postal service	61%
Professional, scientific, and technical services	18
Religious, grantmaking, civic, professional, and similar organizations	10
Educational services; state, local, and private	5

Work Schedules

Political scientists typically work full time in an office. They may work additional hours to finish reports and meet deadlines.

Political scientists work in a variety of organizations that have a stake in policy, such as government, labor, and political organizations.

Political scientists learn to analyze quantitative and qualitative data.

How to Become a Political Scientist

To enter the occupation, political scientists typically need at least a master's degree in political science, public administration, or a related field.

Education

Political scientists typically need to complete either a master's or Ph.D. program to enter the occupation. Applicants to a graduate program should have completed undergraduate courses in political science, writing, and statistics. They also may benefit from having related work or internship experience.

Political scientists often complete a master of public administration (MPA), master of public policy (MPP), or master of public affairs degree. These programs usually combine several disciplines, and students can choose to concentrate in a specific area of interest. Most offer core courses in research methods, policy formation, program evaluation, and statistics. Some colleges and universities also offer master's degrees in political science, international relations, or other applied political science specialties.

Some political scientists also complete a Ph.D. program, which requires several years of coursework followed by independent research for a dissertation. Most Ph.D. candidates choose to specialize in one of four primary subfields of political science: national politics, comparative politics, international relations, or political theory.

Jobseekers with a bachelor's degree in political science usually qualify for entry-level positions in a related occupation, such as assistants in research organizations, political campaigns, or nonprofit organizations. They may also qualify for some government positions. Others work outside of politics and policymaking, such as in business or law.

Other Experience

Entry-level jobseekers can benefit from internships or volunteer work through clubs and political organizations. These activities can give students a chance to apply their academic knowledge in a professional setting and to develop the analytic, research, and writing skills needed for the field.

Important Qualities

Analytical skills. Political scientists often use qualitative and quantitative research methods. They require analytical skills to collect, evaluate, and interpret data.

Communication skills. Political scientists often collaborate with other researchers when writing reports or giving presentations. They must communicate their findings to a wide variety of audiences.

Creativity. Political scientists must continually explore new ideas and information to produce original papers and research. They must stay current on political subjects and come up with new ways to think about and address issues.

Critical-thinking skills. Political scientists must be able to examine and process available information and draw logical conclusions from their findings.

Pay

The median annual wage for political scientists was $128,020 in May 2022. The median wage is the wage at which half the workers in an occupation earned more than that amount and half earned less. The lowest 10 percent earned less than $65,200, and the highest 10 percent earned more than $176,280.

In May 2022, the median annual wages for political scientists in the top industries in which they worked were as follows:

Federal government, excluding postal service	$138,840
Professional, scientific, and technical services	124,020
Religious, grantmaking, civic, professional, and similar organizations	81,350
Educational services; state, local, and private	78,140

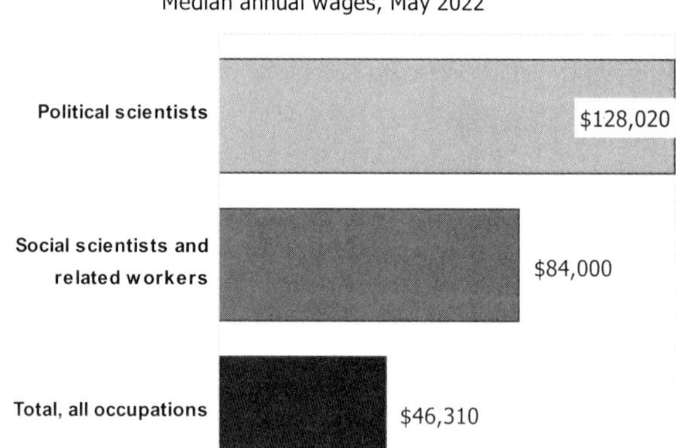

Note: All Occupations includes all occupations in the U.S. Economy.
Source: U.S. Bureau of Labor Statistics, Occupational Employment and Wage Statistics.

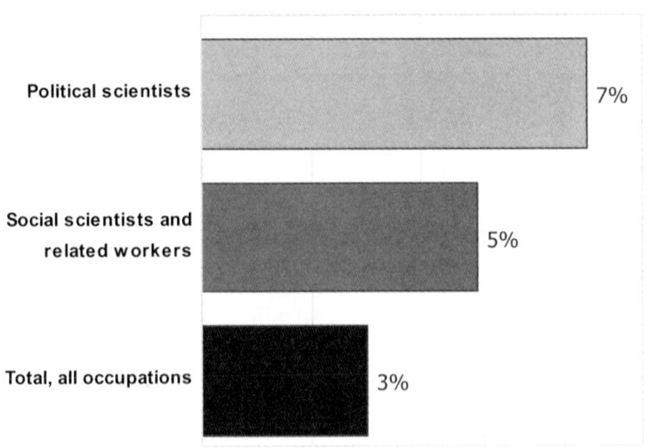

Note: All Occupations includes all occupations in the U.S. Economy.
Source: U.S. Bureau of Labor Statistics, Employment Projections program.

Political scientists typically work full time in an office. They may work additional hours to finish reports and meet deadlines.

Job Outlook

Employment of political scientists is projected to grow 7 percent from 2022 to 2032, faster than the average for all occupations.

About 600 openings for political scientists are projected each year, on average, over the decade. Many of those openings are expected to result from the need to replace workers who transfer to different occupations or exit the labor force, such as to retire.

Employment

Increased demand for public policy analysis will support employment growth for these workers. Political scientists will continue to be needed in government to assess the impact of public policy and proposals, such as service efficiencies, budget changes, and other improvements.

Political organizations, lobbying firms, and labor unions rely on political scientists' knowledge to manage complex regulations. Political scientists will be needed at research and policy institutes to focus on politics and political theory. Organizations that research or advocate for specific causes, such as healthcare or the environment, need political scientists to analyze policies relating to their field.

Occupational Title	SOC Code	Employment, 2022	Projected Employment, 2032	Change, 2022-32	
				Percent	Numeric
Political scientists	19-3094	6,200	6,600	7	400

Contacts for More Information

For more information about political scientists and political science careers, visit

- American Political Science Association
- American Association of Political Consultants
- Network of Schools of Public Policy, Affairs, and Administration

Psychologists

Summary

Quick Facts: Psychologists	
2022 Median Pay	$85,330 per year $41.02 per hour
Typical Entry-Level Education	See How to Become One
Work Experience in a Related Occupation	None
On-the-Job Training	Internship/residency
Number of Jobs, 2022	196,000
Job Outlook, 2022-32	6% (Faster than average)
Employment Change, 2022-32	12,000

What Psychologists Do

Psychologists study cognitive, emotional, and social processes and behavior by observing, interpreting, and recording how individuals relate to one another and to their environments.

Work Environment

Some psychologists work independently, conducting research, consulting with clients, or working with patients. Others work as part of a healthcare team, collaborating with physicians and social workers, or in school settings, working with students, teachers, parents, and other educators. Those in private practice often work evenings and weekends to accommodate clients.

How to Become a Psychologist

Although psychologists typically need a doctoral degree in psychology, a master's degree is sufficient for some positions. Most psychologists also need a license.

Pay

The median annual wage for psychologists was $85,330 in May 2022.

Psychologists study cognitive, emotional, and social processes and behavior.

Job Outlook

Overall employment of psychologists is projected to grow 6 percent from 2022 to 2032, faster than the average for all occupations.

About 12,800 openings for psychologists are projected each year, on average, over the decade. Many of those openings are expected to result from the need to replace workers who transfer to different occupations or exit the labor force, such as to retire.

What Psychologists Do

Psychologists study cognitive, emotional, and social processes and behavior by observing, interpreting, and recording how people relate to one another and to their environments. They use their findings to help improve processes and behaviors.

Duties

Psychologists typically do the following:

- Conduct scientific studies of behavior and brain function
- Observe, interview, and survey individuals

Industrial-organizational psychologists apply psychological research and methods to workplace issues.

- Identify psychological, emotional, behavioral, or organizational issues and diagnose disorders
- Research and identify behavioral or emotional patterns
- Test for patterns that will help them better understand and predict behavior
- Discuss the treatment of problems with clients
- Write articles, research papers, and reports to share findings and educate others
- Supervise interns, clinicians, and counseling professionals

Psychologists seek to understand and explain thoughts, emotions, feelings, and behavior. They use techniques such as observation, assessment, and experimentation to develop theories about the beliefs and feelings that influence individuals.

Psychologists often gather information and evaluate behavior through controlled laboratory experiments, psychoanalysis, or psychotherapy. They also may administer personality, performance, aptitude, or intelligence tests. They look for patterns of behavior or relationships between events, and they use this information when testing theories in their research or when treating patients.

The following are examples of types of psychologists:

Clinical psychologists assess, diagnose, and treat mental, emotional, and behavioral disorders. Clinical psychologists help people deal with problems ranging from short-term personal issues to severe, chronic conditions.

Clinical psychologists are trained to use a variety of approaches to help individuals. Although strategies generally differ by specialty, clinical psychologists often interview patients, give diagnostic tests, and provide individual, family, or group psychotherapy. They also design behavior modification programs and help patients implement their particular program. Some clinical psychologists focus on specific populations, such as children or the elderly, or on certain specialties, such as neuropsychology.

Clinical psychologists often consult with other health professionals regarding the best treatment for patients, especially treatment that includes medication. Currently, only Idaho, Illinois, Iowa, Louisiana, and New Mexico allow clinical psychologists to prescribe medication to patients.

Counseling psychologists help patients deal with and understand problems, including issues at home, at the workplace, or in their community. Through counseling, these psychologists work with patients to identify their strengths or resources they can use to manage problems. For information on other counseling occupations, see the profiles on marriage and family therapists, substance abuse, behavioral disorder, and mental health counselors, and social workers.

Developmental psychologists study the psychological progress and development that take place throughout life. Many developmental psychologists focus on children and adolescents, but they also may study aging and problems facing older adults.

Counseling psychologists often have their own practices.

Forensic psychologists use psychological principles in the legal and criminal justice system to help judges, attorneys, and other legal specialists understand the psychological aspects of a particular case. They often testify in court as expert witnesses. They typically specialize in family, civil, or criminal casework.

Industrial–organizational psychologists apply psychology to the workplace by using psychological principles and research methods to solve problems and improve the quality of worklife. They study issues such as workplace productivity, management or employee working styles, and employee morale. They also help top executives, training and development managers, and training and development specialists with policy planning, employee screening or training, and organizational development.

Rehabilitation psychologists work with physically or developmentally disabled individuals. They help improve quality of life or help individuals adjust after a major illness or accident. They may work with physical therapists and teachers to improve health and learning outcomes.

School psychologists apply psychological principles and techniques to education disorders and developmental disorders. They may address student learning and behavioral problems; design and implement performance plans, and evaluate performances; and counsel students and families. They also may consult with other school-based professionals to suggest improvements to teaching, learning, and administrative strategies.

Some psychologists become postsecondary teachers or high school teachers.

Work Environment

Psychologists held about 196,000 jobs in 2022. Employment in the detailed occupations that make up psychologists was distributed as follows:

Clinical and counseling psychologists	67,500
School psychologists	62,200
Psychologists, all other	56,300
Industrial-organizational psychologists	10,100

In most states, practicing psychology or using the title of "psychologist" requires licensure.

The largest employers of psychologists were as follows:

Employer	Percent
Self-employed workers	28%
Elementary and secondary schools; state, local, and private	27
Ambulatory healthcare services	21
Government	8
Hospitals; state, local, and private	4

Some psychologists work alone, doing independent research, consulting with clients, or counseling patients. Others work as part of a healthcare team, collaborating with physicians, social workers, and others to treat illness and promote overall wellness.

Work Schedules

Psychologists in private practice often set their own hours, and many work part time as independent consultants. They may work evenings or weekends to accommodate clients. Those employed in hospitals or other healthcare facilities may also have evening or weekend shifts. Most psychologists in clinics, government, industry, or schools work full-time schedules during regular business hours.

How to Become a Psychologist

Although psychologists typically need a doctoral degree in psychology, a master's degree may be sufficient for school and industrial organizational positions. Psychologists in clinical practice need a license.

Education

Most clinical, counseling, and research psychologists need a doctoral degree. Students can complete a Ph.D. in psychology or a Doctor of Psychology (Psy.D.) degree. A Ph.D. in psychology is a research degree that is obtained after taking a comprehensive exam and writing a dissertation based on original research. Ph.D. programs typically include courses on statistics and experimental procedures. The Psy.D. is a clinical degree often based on practical work and examinations rather than a dissertation. In clinical, counseling, school, or health service settings, students usually complete a 1-year internship as part of the doctoral program.

School psychologists need an advanced degree and either certification or licensure to work. Common advanced degrees include education specialist degrees (Ed.S.) and doctoral degrees (Ph.D. or Psy.D.). School psychologist programs include coursework in education and psychology because their work addresses both education and mental health components of students' development.

Industrial–organizational psychologists typically need a master's degree, usually including courses in industrial–organizational psychology, statistics, and research design.

When working under the supervision of a doctoral psychologist, other master's degree graduates can also work as psychological assistants in clinical, counseling, or research settings.

At the bachelor's degree level, common fields of degree include psychology, education, and social science.

Licenses, Certifications, and Registrations

In most states, practicing psychology or using the title "psychologist" requires licensure. In all states and the District of Columbia, psychologists who practice independently must be licensed where they work.

Licensing laws vary by state and by type of position. Most clinical and counseling psychologists need a doctorate in psychology, an internship, and at least 1 to 2 years of supervised professional experience. They also must pass the Examination for Professional Practice in Psychology. Information on specific state requirements can be obtained from the Association of State and Provincial Psychology Boards. In many states, licensed psychologists must complete continuing education courses to keep their licenses.

The American Board of Professional Psychology awards specialty certification in 15 areas of psychology, such as clinical health psychology, couple and family psychology, and rehabilitation psychology. The American Board of Clinical Neuropsychology offers certification in neuropsychology. Board certification can demonstrate professional expertise in a specialty area. Certification is not required for most psychologists, but some hospitals and clinics do require certification. In those cases, candidates must have a doctoral degree in psychology, a state license or certification, and any additional criteria required by the specialty field.

Training

Most prospective psychologists must have pre- or postdoctoral supervised experience, including an internship. Internships allow students to gain experience in an applied setting. Candidates must complete an internship before they can qualify for state licensure. The required number of hours of the internship varies by state.

Important Qualities

Analytical skills. Psychologists must examine the information they collect and draw logical conclusions.

Communication skills. Psychologists must have strong communication skills because they spend much of their time listening to and speaking with patients or describing their research.

Integrity. Psychologists must keep patients' problems in confidence, and patients must be able to trust psychologists' expertise in treating sensitive problems.

Interpersonal skills. Psychologists study and help individuals, so they must be able to work well with clients, patients, and other professionals.

Observational skills. Psychologists study attitude and behavior. They must understand the possible meanings of facial expressions, body positions, actions, and interactions.

Patience. Psychologists must demonstrate patience, because conducting research or treating patients may take a long time.

Problem-solving skills. Psychologists need problem-solving skills to collect information, design research, evaluate programs, and find treatments or solutions to mental and behavioral problems.

Pay

The median annual wage for psychologists was $85,330 in May 2022. The median wage is the wage at which half the workers in an occupation earned more than that amount and half earned less. The lowest 10 percent earned less than $48,010, and the highest 10 percent earned more than $141,910.

Median annual wages for psychologists in May 2022 were as follows:

Industrial-organizational psychologists	$139,280

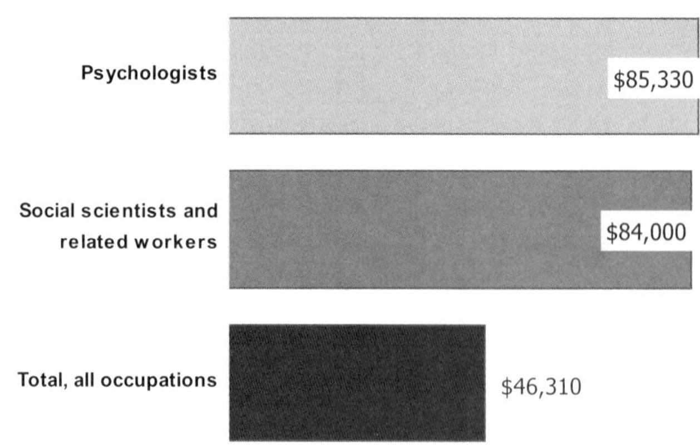

Note: All Occupations includes all occupations in the U.S. Economy.
Source: U.S. Bureau of Labor Statistics, Occupational Employment and Wage Statistics.

Psychologists

Percent change in employment, projected 2022-32

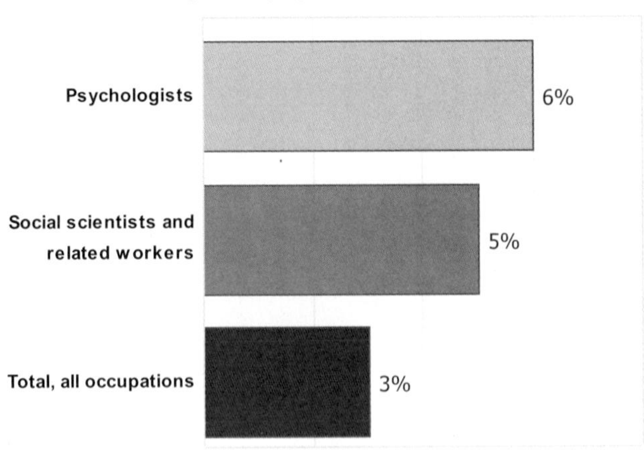

Note: All Occupations includes all occupations in the U.S. Economy.
Source: U.S. Bureau of Labor Statistics, Employment Projections program.

Psychologists, all other	106,420
Clinical and counseling psychologists	90,130
School psychologists	81,500

In May 2022, the median annual wages for psychologists in the top industries in which they worked were as follows:

Government	$106,690
Hospitals; state, local, and private	101,030
Ambulatory healthcare services	92,170
Elementary and secondary schools; state, local, and private	81,620

Psychologists in private practice often set their own hours, and many work part time as independent consultants. They may work evenings or weekends to accommodate clients. Those employed in hospitals or other healthcare facilities also may have evening or weekend shifts. Most psychologists in clinics, government, industry, or schools work full-time schedules during regular business hours.

Job Outlook

Overall employment of psychologists is projected to grow 6 percent from 2022 to 2032, faster than the average for all occupations.

About 12,800 openings for psychologists are projected each year, on average, over the decade. Many of those openings are expected to result from the need to replace workers who transfer to different occupations or exit the labor force, such as to retire.

Employment

Employment of clinical, counseling, and school psychologists is projected to grow due to demand for psychological services in schools, hospitals, mental health centers, and social service agencies.

Demand for clinical and counseling psychologists will increase as more people turn to psychologists for help with their problems.

Employment of school psychologists will continue to grow because of an increased awareness of the connection between mental health and learning. These workers also will be needed to help students whose educational, behavioral, or developmental issues impact their ability to learn.

Organizations will continue to employ industrial–organizational psychologists to help with tasks such as selecting and retaining employees, implementing trainings, and improving office morale.

Occupational Title	SOC Code	Employment, 2022	Projected Employment, 2032	Change, 2022-32	
				Percent	Numeric
Psychologists	19-3030	196,000	208,000	6	12,000
Industrial-organizational psychologists	19-3032	10,100	10,600	6	600
Clinical and counseling psychologists	19-3033	67,500	75,200	11	7,700
School psychologists	19-3034	62,200	63,000	1	800
Psychologists, all other	19-3039	56,300	59,100	5	2,900

Contacts for More Information

For more information about careers in all fields of psychology, visit

- American Psychological Association
- National Association of School Psychologists
- Association of State and Provincial Psychology Boards
- American Board of Professional Psychology
- Society for Industrial and Organizational Psychology
- American Board of Professional Neuropsychology

Sociologists

Summary

Quick Facts: Sociologists	
2022 Median Pay	$98,590 per year $47.40 per hour
Typical Entry-Level Education	Master's degree
Work Experience in a Related Occupation	None
On-the-job Training	None
Number of Jobs, 2022	3,300
Job Outlook, 2022-32	5% (Faster than average)
Employment Change, 2022-32	100

What Sociologists Do

Sociologists study society and social behavior.

Work Environment

Sociologists typically work full time during regular business hours.

How to Become a Sociologist

Sociologists typically need at least a master's degree to enter the occupation.

Pay

The median annual wage for sociologists was $98,590 in May 2022.

Job Outlook

Employment of sociologists is projected to grow 5 percent from 2022 to 2032, faster than the average for all occupations.

About 300 openings for sociologists are projected each year, on average, over the decade. Many of those openings are expected to result from the need to replace workers who transfer to different occupations or exit the labor force, such as to retire.

Sociologists design research projects to test theories about social issues.

Some sociologists conduct interviews for their research.

What Sociologists Do

Sociologists study society and social behavior by examining the groups, cultures, organizations, social institutions, and processes that develop when people interact and work together.

Duties

Sociologists typically do the following:

- Design research projects to test theories about social issues
- Collect data through surveys, observations, interviews, and other sources
- Analyze and draw conclusions from data
- Prepare reports, articles, or presentations detailing their research findings
- Collaborate with and advise other social scientists, policymakers, or other groups on research findings and sociological issues

Sociologists study human behavior, interaction, and organization. They observe the activity of social, religious, political, and economic groups, organizations, and institutions. They examine the effect of social influences, including organizations and institutions, on different individuals and groups. They also trace the origin and growth of these groups and interactions. For example, they may research the impact of a new law or policy on a specific demographic.

Sociologists often use both quantitative and qualitative methods when conducting research, and they frequently use statistical analysis programs during the research process.

Their research may help administrators, educators, lawmakers, and social workers to solve social problems and formulate public policy. Sociologists may specialize in a wide range of social topics, including, but not limited to:

- education and health;
- crime and poverty;
- families and population;
- and gender, racial, and ethnic relations.

Sociologists who specialize in crime may be called *criminologists* or *penologists*. These workers apply their sociological knowledge to conduct research and analyze penal systems and populations and to study the causes and effects of crime.

Many people with a sociology background become postsecondary teachers and high school teachers. Most others find work in related jobs outside the sociologist profession such as policy analysts, demographers, survey researchers, and statisticians.

Work Environment

Sociologists held about 3,300 jobs in 2022. The largest employers of sociologists were as follows:

Employer	Percent
Scientific research and development services	37%
State government, excluding education and hospitals	20
Educational services; state, local, and private	14
Local government, excluding education and hospitals	6
Self-employed workers	2

Sociologists typically work in an office. They may work outside of an office setting when conducting research through interviews or observations or presenting research results.

Sociologists may work outside of an office setting when conducting research through interviews or observations or presenting research results.

Many sociology programs offer opportunities to gain experience through internships or by preparing reports.

Work Schedules

Most sociologists work full time during regular business hours.

How to Become a Sociologist

Sociologists typically need at least a master's degree to enter the occupation. Bachelor's degree holders may find positions in related fields, such as social services, education, or public policy.

Education

Sociologists typically need a master's degree or Ph.D. to enter the occupation. There are two types of sociology master's degree programs: traditional programs and applied, clinical, and professional programs. Traditional programs prepare students to enter a Ph.D. program. Applied, clinical, and professional programs prepare students to enter the workplace, teaching them the necessary analytical skills to perform sociological research in a professional setting.

Courses in research methods and statistics are important for candidates in both master's and Ph.D. programs. Many programs also offer opportunities to gain experience through internships or by preparing reports for clients.

Jobseekers who have a bachelor's degree in sociology may find entry-level positions in related fields, such as social services, education, or public policy.

Other Experience

Candidates with a bachelor's degree may benefit from internships or volunteer work when looking for entry-level positions in sociology or a related field. These types of opportunities give students a chance to apply their academic knowledge in a professional setting and develop skills needed for the field.

Important Qualities

Analytical skills. Sociologists must be able to examine data and other information, often using statistical methods to test their theories.

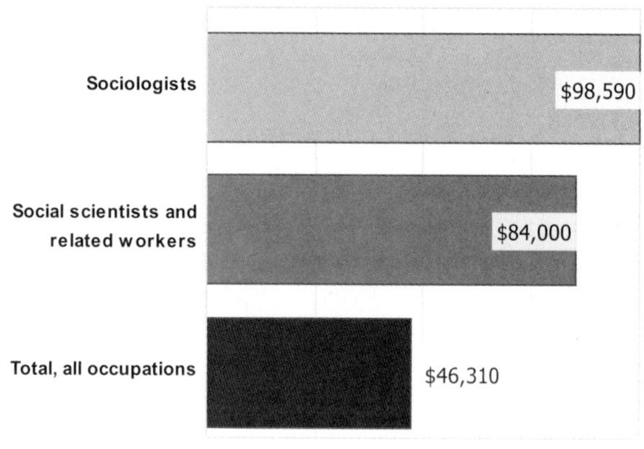

Note: All Occupations includes all occupations in the U.S. Economy.
Source: U.S. Bureau of Labor Statistics, Occupational Employment and Wage Statistics.

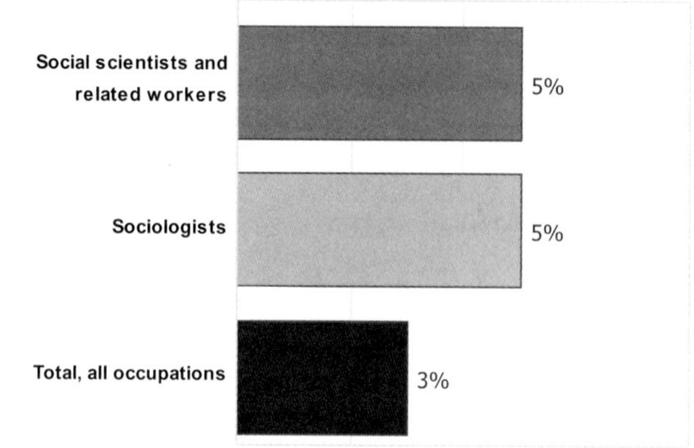

Note: All Occupations includes all occupations in the U.S. Economy.
Source: U.S. Bureau of Labor Statistics, Employment Projections program.

Communication skills. Sociologists need strong communication skills when they conduct interviews, collaborate with colleagues, and write and present research results.

Critical-thinking skills. Sociologists design research projects and collect, process, and analyze information to draw logical conclusions about society and various groups of people.

Pay

The median annual wage for sociologists was $98,590 in May 2022. The median wage is the wage at which half the workers in an occupation earned more than that amount and half earned less. The lowest 10 percent earned less than $57,490, and the highest 10 percent earned more than $166,040.

In May 2022, the median annual wages for sociologists in the top industries in which they worked were as follows:

Scientific research and development services	$99,600
State government, excluding education and hospitals	91,250
Local government, excluding education and hospitals	84,320
Educational services; state, local, and private	72,120

Most sociologists work full time during regular business hours.

Job Outlook

Employment of sociologists is projected to grow 5 percent from 2022 to 2032, faster than the average for all occupations.

About 300 openings for sociologists are projected each year, on average, over the decade. Many of those openings are expected to result from the need to replace workers who transfer to different occupations or exit the labor force, such as to retire.

Employment

Sociologists will continue to be needed to apply sociological research to other disciplines. For example, sociologists may collaborate with researchers in other social sciences, such as economists, psychologists, and survey researchers, to study how social structures or groups influence policy decisions about health, education, politics, criminal justice, business, or economics.

Occupational Title	SOC Code	Employment, 2022	Projected Employment, 2032	Change, 2022-32	
				Percent	Numeric
Sociologists	19-3041	3,300	3,400	5	100

Contacts for More Information

For more information about careers in sociology, visit

➤ American Sociological Association

Survey Researchers

Summary

Quick Facts: Survey Researchers	
2022 Median Pay	$60,410 per year $29.04 per hour
Typical Entry-Level Education	Master's degree
Work Experience in a Related Occupation	None
On-the-job Training	None
Number of Jobs, 2022	8,800
Job Outlook, 2022-32	-4% (Decline)
Employment Change, 2022-32	-300

What Survey Researchers Do

Survey researchers design and conduct surveys and analyze data.

Work Environment

Most survey researchers work in research firms, polling organizations, nonprofits, corporations, colleges and universities, and government agencies. The majority work full time during regular business hours.

How to Become a Survey Researcher

Survey researchers typically need at least a master's degree to enter the occupation. However, a bachelor's degree may be sufficient for some entry-level positions.

Pay

The median annual wage for survey researchers was $60,410 in May 2022.

Job Outlook

Employment of survey researchers is projected to decline 4 percent from 2022 to 2032.

Survey researchers meet with clients to determine appropriate survey methods.

Survey researchers often present their findings.

Despite declining employment, about 700 openings for survey researchers are projected each year, on average, over the decade. All of those openings are expected to result from the need to replace workers who transfer to other occupations or exit the labor force, such as to retire.

What Survey Researchers Do

Survey researchers design surveys and analyze data. Surveys are used to collect factual data, such as employment and salary information, or to ask questions in order to understand people's opinions, preferences, beliefs, or desires.

Duties

Survey researchers typically do the following:

- Conduct background research on survey topics
- Plan and design surveys, and determine appropriate survey methods
- Test surveys to make sure that people will understand the questions being asked
- Coordinate the work of survey interviewers and data collectors
- Account for and solve problems caused by nonresponse or other sampling issues

Survey researchers often work alone, compiling results and analyzing data.

- Analyze data, using statistical software and techniques
- Summarize survey data, using tables, graphs, and fact sheets
- Evaluate surveys, the methods underlying them, and their performance to improve future surveys

Survey researchers design and conduct surveys for different research purposes. Surveys for scientific research cover various topics, including government, health, social sciences, and education. For example, a survey researcher may try to capture information about the prevalence of drug use or disease.

Some survey researchers design public opinion surveys, which are intended to gather information about the attitudes and opinions of society or of a certain group. Surveys can cover a wide variety of topics, including politics, culture, the economy, or health.

Other survey researchers design marketing surveys which examine products or services that consumers want, need, or prefer. Researchers who collect and analyze market research data are known as market research analysts.

Survey researchers may conduct surveys in many different formats, such as interviews, questionnaires, and focus groups (in-person, small group sessions led by a facilitator). They use different methods to collect data, including the Internet, mail, and telephone and in-person interviews.

Some researchers use surveys to solicit the opinions of an entire population. The decennial census is an example of such a survey. Others use surveys to target a smaller group, such as a specific demographic group, residents of a particular state, or members of a political party.

Researchers survey a sample of the population and use statistics to make sure that the sample accurately represents the target population group. Researchers use a variety of statistical techniques and analytical software to plan surveys, adjust for errors in the data, and analyze the results.

Survey researchers sometimes supervise interviewers who collect survey data through in-person interviews or by telephone.

Many research positions require a master's degree or Ph.D., though a bachelor's degree may be sufficient for some entry-level positions.

Work Environment

Survey researchers held about 8,800 jobs in 2022. The largest employers of survey researchers were as follows:

Other professional, scientific, and technical services ...	34%
Scientific research and development services	23
Educational services; state, local, and private	17
Religious, grantmaking, civic, professional, and similar organizations	5
Self-employed workers	2

Survey researchers work in research firms, polling organizations, nonprofits, and corporations.

Survey researchers who conduct interviews have frequent contact with the public. Some may work outside the office, traveling to meet with clients or conducting in-person interviews and focus group sessions. When designing surveys and analyzing data, they usually work alone in an office setting, although some work on teams with other researchers.

How to Become a Survey Researcher

Survey researchers typically need at least a master's degree to enter the occupation. However, a bachelor's degree may be sufficient for some entry-level positions.

Education

Survey researchers typically need a master's degree or Ph.D. The master's degree may be in a variety of fields, including marketing or survey research, statistics, or social sciences. A bachelor's degree is sufficient for some entry-level positions.

To prepare to enter this occupation, students should take courses in research methods, survey methodology, computer science, mathematics, and statistics. Many also may benefit from taking business courses, such as marketing and consumer behavior, and social science courses, such as psychology, sociology, and economics.

Other Experience

Prospective survey researchers can gain experience through internships or fellowships. Many businesses, research and polling firms, and marketing companies offer internships for college students or recent graduates who want to work in market and survey research. These opportunities, which provide valuable experience, can be very helpful toward getting a job.

Licenses, Certifications, and Registrations

Although survey researchers are not required by law to be licensed or certified, certification can show a level of professional competence.

The Insights Association offers the Professional Researcher Certification for survey researchers. To qualify, candidates must have at least 3 years of experience working in opinion and marketing research, pass an exam, and be a member of a professional organization. Researchers must complete continuing education courses and apply for renewal every 2 years to maintain their certification.

Important Qualities

Analytical skills. Survey researchers must be able to apply statistical techniques to large amounts of data and interpret the results correctly. They also should be proficient in the statistical software used to analyze data.

Communication skills. Survey researchers need strong communication skills when conducting surveys and interpreting and presenting results to clients.

Critical-thinking skills. Survey researchers must design or choose a survey and a survey method that together best capture the information needed. They must also be able to look at the data and draw reasonable conclusions from the results of the survey.

Detail oriented. Survey researchers must pay attention to details, because survey results depend on collecting, analyzing, and reporting the data accurately.

Problem-solving skills. Survey researchers need problem-solving skills when identifying survey design issues, adjusting survey questions, and interpreting survey results.

Pay

The median annual wage for survey researchers was $60,410 in May 2022. The median wage is the wage at which half the workers in an occupation earned more than that amount and half earned less. The lowest 10 percent earned less than $30,770, and the highest 10 percent earned more than $104,890.

In May 2022, the median annual wages for survey researchers in the top industries in which they worked were as follows:

Religious, grantmaking, civic, professional, and similar organizations	$62,590
Scientific research and development services	62,280
Other professional, scientific, and technical services	61,300
Educational services; state, local, and private	49,960

Job Outlook

Employment of survey researchers is projected to decline 4 percent from 2022 to 2032.

Despite declining employment, about 700 openings for survey researchers are projected each year, on average, over the decade. All of those openings are expected to result from the need to replace workers who transfer to other occupations or exit the labor force, such as to retire.

Employment

Survey researchers will continue to be employed in marketing, research, and polling establishments to plan and design surveys and to analyze data. However, ongoing adoption of data mining—finding trends in large sets of existing data—and collecting information from social media sites are expected to lessen the need for some traditional survey methods, such as telephone and in-person

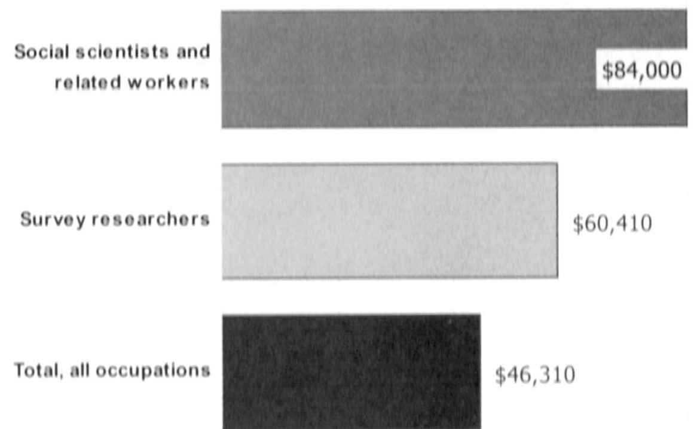

Note: All Occupations includes all occupations in the U.S. Economy.
Source: U.S. Bureau of Labor Statistics, Occupational Employment and Wage Statistics.

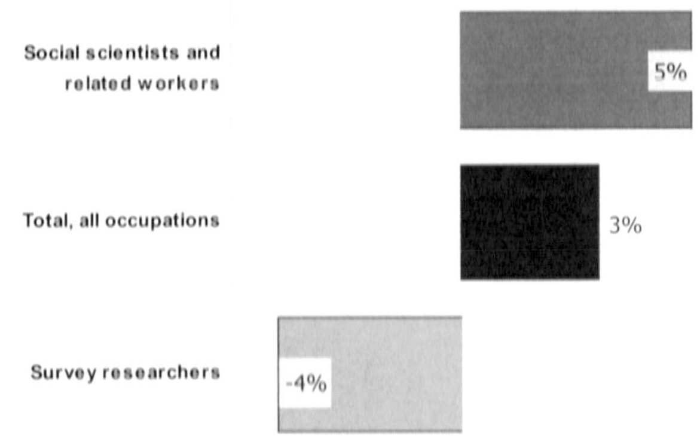

Note: All Occupations includes all occupations in the U.S. Economy.
Source: U.S. Bureau of Labor Statistics, Employment Projections program.

interviews. The use of big data in market research will reduce the demand for survey researchers to gather survey information.

Occupational Title	SOC Code	Employment, 2022	Projected Employment, 2032	Change, 2022-32	
				Percent	Numeric
Survey researchers	19-3022	8,800	8,400	-4	-300

Contacts for More Information

For more information about careers in survey research, visit

- American Association for Public Opinion Research
- Insights Association

Urban and Regional Planners

Summary

Quick Facts: Urban and Regional Planners

2022 Median Pay	$79,540 per year $38.24 per hour
Typical Entry-Level Education	Master's degree
Work Experience in a Related Occupation	None
On-the-job Training	None
Number of Jobs, 2022	44,700
Job Outlook, 2022-32	4% (As fast as average)
Employment Change, 2022-32	1,700

What Urban and Regional Planners Do

Urban and regional planners develop land use plans and programs that help create communities, accommodate population growth, and revitalize physical facilities.

Work Environment

Most urban and regional planners work full time during normal business hours, and some may work evenings or weekends to attend meetings with officials, planning commissions, and neighborhood groups.

How to Become an Urban or Regional Planner

Urban and regional planners need a master's degree from an accredited planning program to qualify for most positions.

Urban and regional planners often present projects to communities and planning officials.

Pay

The median annual wage for urban and regional planners was $79,540 in May 2022.

Job Outlook

Employment of urban and regional planners is projected to grow 4 percent from 2022 to 2032, about as fast as the average for all occupations.

About 3,700 openings for urban and regional planners are projected each year, on average, over the decade. Many of those openings are expected to result from the need to replace workers who transfer to different occupations or exit the labor force, such as to retire.

Urban and regional planners review site plans submitted by developers.

What Urban and Regional Planners Do

Urban and regional planners develop land use plans and programs that help create communities, accommodate population growth, and revitalize physical facilities in towns, cities, counties, and metropolitan areas.

Duties

Urban and regional planners typically do the following:

- Meet with public officials, developers, and the public regarding development plans and land use
- Administer government plans or policies affecting land use
- Gather and analyze data from market research, censuses, and economic and environmental studies
- Conduct field investigations to analyze factors affecting community development and decline, including land use
- Review site plans submitted by developers
- Assess the feasibility of proposals and identify needed changes
- Recommend whether proposals should be approved or denied
- Present projects to communities, planning officials, and planning commissions
- Stay current on zoning and building codes, environmental regulations, and other legal issues

Urban and regional planners identify community needs and develop short- and long-term solutions to improve and revitalize communities and areas. As an area grows or changes, planners help communities manage the related economic, social, and environmental issues, such as planning new parks, sheltering the homeless, and making the region more attractive to businesses.

When beginning a project, planners often work with public officials, community members, and other groups to identify community issues and goals. Through research, data analysis, and collaboration with interest groups, they formulate strategies to address issues and to meet goals. Planners may also help carry out community plans by overseeing projects, enforcing zoning regulations, and organizing the work of the groups involved.

Urban and regional planners use a variety of tools and technology in their work. They commonly use statistical software, data visualization and presentation programs, financial spreadsheets, and other database and software programs. Geographic Information System (GIS) software is used to integrate data, such as for population density, with digital maps.

Urban and regional planners may specialize in areas such as transportation planning, community development, historic preservation, or urban design, among other fields of interest.

Planners often collaborate with public officials, civil engineers, environmental engineers, architects, lawyers, and real estate developers.

Work Environment

Urban and regional planners held about 44,700 jobs in 2022. The largest employers of urban and regional planners were as follows:

Local government, excluding education and hospitals	65%
Architectural, engineering, and related services	8
Management, scientific, and technical consulting services	3
Federal government	2

Planners work throughout the country, but most work in large metropolitan areas.

Urban and regional planners may travel to inspect proposed changes and their impacts on land conditions, the environment, and land use.

Work Schedules

Most urban and regional planners work full time during normal business hours, and some may work evenings or weekends

Urban and regional planners may travel to development sites.

Urban and regional planners must be effective communicators when they meet with public officials, developers, and the public regarding development plans and land use.

to attend meetings with officials, planning commissions, and neighborhood groups. Some planners work more than 40 hours per week.

How to Become an Urban or Regional Planner

Urban and regional planners need a master's degree from an accredited planning program to qualify for most positions.

Education

Urban and regional planners typically need a master's degree from an urban or regional planning program accredited by an organization such as the Planning Accreditation Board (PAB). Master's degree programs accept students with a wide range of undergraduate backgrounds, including economics, geography, political science, or a related field, such as architecture.

Most master's programs have students spending considerable time in seminars, workshops, and laboratory courses, in which they learn to analyze and solve planning problems. Although most master's programs have a similar core curriculum, there is some variability in the courses they offer and the issues they focus on. For example, programs located in agricultural states may focus on rural planning, and programs located in larger cities may focus on urban revitalization.

Bachelor's degree holders may qualify for jobs as assistant or junior planners.

Other Experience

Although not necessary for all positions, some entry-level positions require 1 to 2 years of work experience in a related field, such as architecture, public policy, or economic development. Many students gain experience through real planning projects or part-time internships while enrolled in a master's planning program. Others enroll in full-time internships after completing their degree.

Licenses, Certifications, and Registrations

As of 2016, New Jersey was the only state that required urban and regional planners to be licensed. More information is available from the regulatory board of New Jersey.

The American Institute of Certified Planners (AICP) offers the AICP certification for planners. To become certified, candidates must meet certain education and experience requirements and pass an exam.

Important Qualities

Analytical skills. Urban and regional planners analyze information and data from a variety of sources, such as market research studies, censuses, and environmental impact studies. They use statistical techniques and technologies such as Geographic Information Systems (GIS) in their analyses to determine the significance of the data.

Communication skills. Urban and regional planners must be able to communicate clearly and effectively because they interact with colleagues and stakeholders, prepare research

Urban and Regional Planners

Median annual wages, May 2022

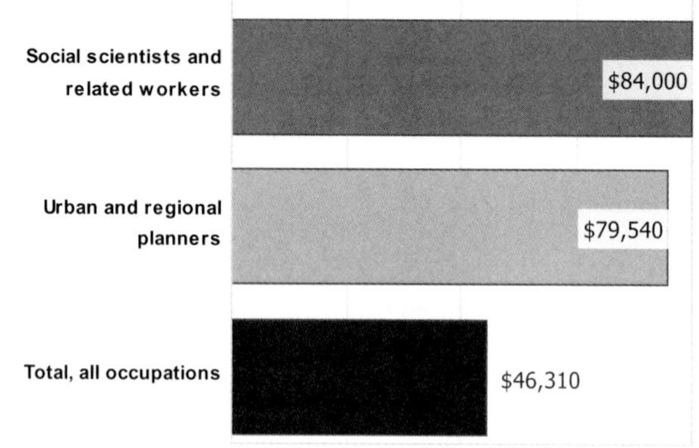

Note: All Occupations includes all occupations in the U.S. Economy.
Source: U.S. Bureau of Labor Statistics, Occupational Employment and Wage Statistics.

reports, give presentations, and meet with a wide variety of audiences, including public officials, interest groups, and community members.

Decision-making skills. Urban and regional planners must weigh all possible planning options and combine analysis, creativity, and realism to choose the appropriate action or plan.

Leadership skills. Urban and regional planners must be able to manage projects, which may include overseeing tasks and planning assignments.

Pay

The median annual wage for urban and regional planners was $79,540 in May 2022. The median wage is the wage at which half the workers in an occupation earned more than that amount and half earned less. The lowest 10 percent earned less than $49,960, and the highest 10 percent earned more than $121,460.

In May 2022, the median annual wages for urban and regional planners in the top industries in which they worked were as follows:

Federal government	$105,620
Management, scientific, and technical consulting services	80,890
Architectural, engineering, and related services	80,740
Local government, excluding education and hospitals	78,660

Most urban and regional planners work full time during normal business hours, and some may work evenings or weekends to attend meetings with officials, planning commissions, and neighborhood groups. Some planners work more than 40 hours per week.

Job Outlook

Employment of urban and regional planners is projected to grow 4 percent from 2022 to 2032, about as fast as the average for all occupations.

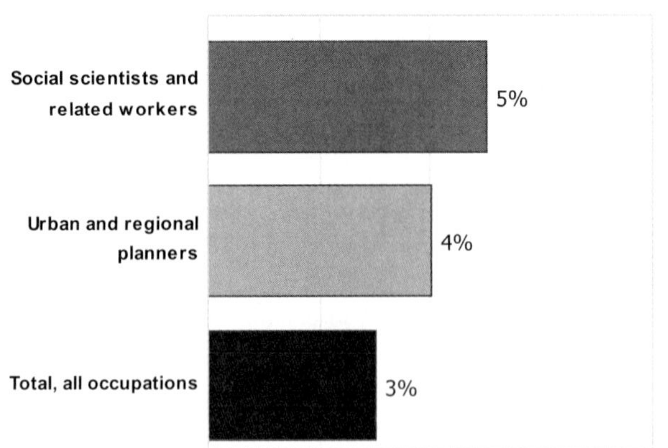

Note: All Occupations includes all occupations in the U.S. Economy.
Source: U.S. Bureau of Labor Statistics, Employment Projections program.

About 3,700 openings for urban and regional planners are projected each year, on average, over the decade. Many of those openings are expected to result from the need to replace workers who transfer to different occupations or exit the labor force, such as to retire.

Employment

Demographic, transportation, and environmental changes will drive employment growth for planners.

Within cities, urban planners will be needed to develop revitalization projects and address issues associated with population growth, environmental degradation, the movement of people and goods, and resource scarcity. Similarly, suburban areas and municipalities will need planners to address the challenges associated with population changes, including housing needs and transportation systems covering larger areas with less population density.

Planners will also be needed as new and existing communities require extensive development and improved infrastructure, including housing, roads, sewer systems, parks, and schools.

However, federal, state, and local government budgets may affect the employment of planners in government, because development projects are contingent on available funds.

Occupational Title	SOC Code	Employment, 2022	Projected Employment, 2032	Change, 2022-32	
				Percent	Numeric
Urban and regional planners	19-3051	44,700	46,400	4	1,700

Contacts for More Information

For more information about careers in urban and regional planning, visit

- American Planning Association
- American Institute of Certified Planners
- New Jersey State Board of Professional Planners
- Planning Accreditation Board

Zoologists and Wildlife Biologists

Summary

Quick Facts: Zoologists and Wildlife Biologists	
2022 Median Pay	$67,430 per year $32.42 per hour
Typical Entry-Level Education	Bachelor's degree
Work Experience in a Related Occupation	None
On-the-job Training	None
Number of Jobs, 2022	19,100
Job Outlook, 2022-32	3% (As fast as average)
Employment Change, 2022-32	600

What Zoologists and Wildlife Biologists Do

Zoologists and wildlife biologists study animals, those both in captivity and in the wild, and how they interact with their ecosystems.

Work Environment

Most zoologists and wildlife biologists work full time. Zoologists and wildlife biologists work in a variety of settings, including offices and laboratories. Depending on their job, they also may spend time outdoors, gathering data and studying animals in their natural habitats.

How to Become a Zoologist or Wildlife Biologist

Zoologists and wildlife biologists typically need a bachelor's degree for entry-level positions and may need a master's degree for higher level jobs. They typically need a Ph.D. to lead research projects.

Pay

The median annual wage for zoologists and wildlife biologists was $67,430 in May 2022.

Job Outlook

Employment of zoologists and wildlife biologists is projected to grow 3 percent from 2022 to 2032, about as fast as the average for all occupations.

About 1,500 openings for zoologists and wildlife biologists are projected each year, on average, over the decade. Many of those openings are expected to result from the need to replace

Zoologists and wildlife biologists often work outdoors in the field gathering data and studying animals in their natural habitats.

workers who transfer to different occupations or exit the labor force, such as to retire.

What Zoologists and Wildlife Biologists Do

Zoologists and wildlife biologists study animals, those both in captivity and in the wild, and how they interact with their ecosystems. They focus primarily on undomesticated animals and their behavior, as well as on the impact humans have on wildlife and natural habitats.

Duties

Zoologists and wildlife biologists typically do the following:

- Develop and conduct experimental studies with animals in controlled or natural surroundings
- Collect and analyze specimens and other biological data
- Study the characteristics of animals, such as their reproduction, interactions with other species, diseases, and movement patterns

Marine biologists study fish and other wildlife that inhabit the oceans.

- Research, initiate, and maintain breeding programs that support game animals, endangered species, or other terrestrial or aquatic wildlife
- Estimate, monitor, and manage wildlife populations and invasive species
- Analyze how human activity influences wildlife and their natural habitats
- Develop and implement programs to prevent harm to wildlife from human activities, including farming and aircraft operations
- Write research papers, reports, and other documents that explain their findings
- Present research findings to academics, policymakers, and the public
- Develop conservation plans and recommend action related to wildlife conservation and management

Zoologists' and wildlife biologists' study of animals includes conducting scientific tests and experiments, such as taking blood samples to assess an animal's health, and researching their habitats. Although the roles of zoologists and wildlife biologists often overlap, zoologists typically research certain types of animals, such as birds, whereas wildlife biologists study specific ecosystems or animal populations, such as an at-risk species.

Zoologists and wildlife biologists use geographic information systems (GIS), modeling software, and other technology for a variety of purposes. For example, they may use technology to estimate wildlife populations, track animal movement, forecast the spread of invasive species or diseases, and assess potential threats to habitats.

Zoologists generally specialize in either vertebrates or invertebrates for an individual species. Following are some examples of specialization by species:

- Cetologists study marine mammals, such as whales and dolphins.
- Entomologists study insects, such as beetles and butterflies.
- Herpetologists study reptiles and amphibians, such as snakes and frogs.
- Ichthyologists study wild fish, such as sharks and lungfish.
- Malacologists study mollusks, such as snails and clams.
- Mammalogists study mammals, such as monkeys and bears.
- Ornithologists study birds, such as hawks and penguins.
- Teuthologists study cephalopods, such as octopuses and cuttlefish.

Other zoologists and wildlife biologists specialize in a particular field of study, such as evolution or animal behavior. Following are some examples of specialization by field of study:

- Anatomy is the study of structure of organisms and their parts.
- Embryology is the study of the development of embryos and fetuses.

Fieldwork can require zoologists and wildlife biologists to travel to remote locations anywhere in the world.

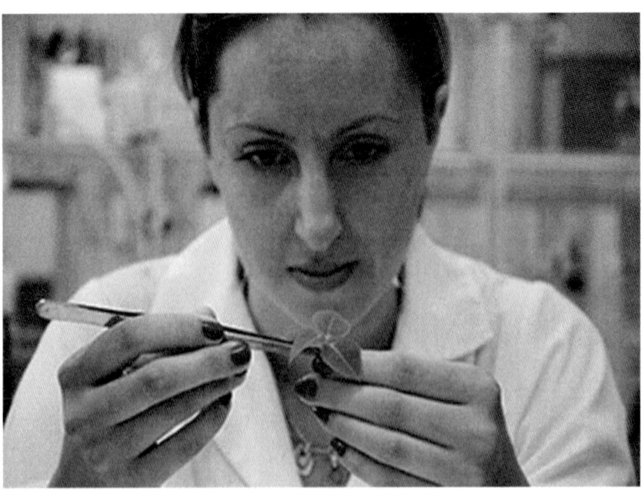

Zoologists and wildlife biologists study specimens collected in the field.

- Ethology, sometimes called behavioral ecology, is the study of animal behaviors as natural or adaptive traits.
- Histology, or microscopic anatomy, is the study of cells and tissues in plants and animals.
- Physiology is the study of the normal function of living systems.
- Soil zoology is the study of animals which live fully or partially in the soil.
- Teratology is the study of abnormal physiological development.
- Zoography is the study of descriptive zoology and describes plants and animals.

Zoologists and wildlife biologists are often part of a team of scientists and technicians working on conservation efforts. For example, zoologists and wildlife biologists may work with environmental scientists and hydrologists to monitor water pollution and its effects on fish populations.

Work Environment

Zoologists and wildlife biologists held about 19,100 jobs in 2022. The largest employers of zoologists and wildlife biologists were as follows:

Government	65%
Management, scientific, and technical consulting services	8
Social advocacy organizations	7
Research and development in the physical, engineering, and life sciences	5
Colleges, universities, and professional schools; state, local, and private	4

Zoologists and wildlife biologists work in a variety of settings, including offices and laboratories. Depending on their job, they may spend time outdoors, gathering data and studying animals in their natural habitats.

Fieldwork may require zoologists and wildlife biologists to travel to remote locations for long periods. For example, cetologists studying whale populations may spend months at sea; herpetologists researching snakes may spend significant time in deserts or forests.

Fieldwork can be physically demanding, especially for zoologists and wildlife biologists whose research involves working outdoors in all types of weather.

Injuries and Illnesses

Some zoologists and wildlife biologists handle wild animals or spend significant time outdoors in difficult terrain or in extreme temperatures. To avoid injury or illness, they must use caution when handling wildlife or working under challenging circumstances.

Work Schedules

Most zoologists and wildlife biologists work full time. They may have irregular schedules, especially when doing fieldwork. Zoologists and wildlife biologists who work with nocturnal animals may need to work at night.

How to Become a Zoologist or Wildlife Biologist

Zoologists and wildlife biologists typically need a bachelor's degree for entry-level positions and may need a master's degree for higher level jobs. They typically need a Ph.D. to lead research projects.

Education

Zoologists and wildlife biologists typically need a bachelor's degree to enter the occupation. Students may pursue a degree in zoology, wildlife biology, or a related field, such as natural resources. Some students major in biology and take coursework in zoology and wildlife biology.

Zoologists and wildlife biologists typically need at least a master's degree for higher level positions and a Ph.D. for independent research positions.

Coursework in undergraduate and graduate-level science programs often includes academic, laboratory, and field work. In addition, students may need to take mathematics and statistics to learn data analysis.

Zoology and wildlife biology students may gain practical experience through internships, volunteer work, or other employment during college.

Other Experience

Some zoologists and wildlife biologists need outdoor skills to work in remote locations. For example, they may need to be comfortable driving a tractor, boat, or all-terrain vehicle (ATV); using a generator; or providing for themselves.

Advancement

Zoologists and wildlife biologists typically take on greater responsibility and independence in their work as they gain experience or have more education. For example, zoologists and wildlife biologists with a Ph.D. may lead independent research and control the direction and content of projects.

Important Qualities

Attention to detail. Zoologists and wildlife biologists must be able to notice changes in an animal's behavior or appearance.

Communication skills. Zoologists and wildlife biologists write about and present their research to the public, policymakers, and academic audiences.

Critical-thinking skills. Zoologists and wildlife biologists need sound reasoning and judgment to draw conclusions from their experiments and observations.

Interpersonal skills. Zoologists and wildlife biologists typically work on teams and must be able to work effectively with others.

Outdoor skills. Zoologists and wildlife biologists may need to navigate rough terrain, carry heavy equipment for long distances, or perform other activities associated with living in remote areas.

Problem-solving skills. Zoologists and wildlife biologists try to find solutions to wildlife threats, such as disease and habitat loss.

Pay

The median annual wage for zoologists and wildlife biologists was $67,430 in May 2022. The median wage is the wage at which half the workers in an occupation earned more than that amount and half earned less. The lowest 10 percent earned less than $44,610, and the highest 10 percent earned more than $104,750.

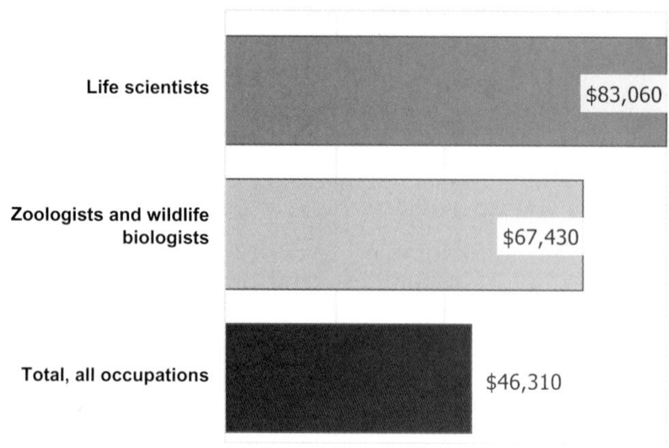

Note: All Occupations includes all occupations in the U.S. Economy.
Source: U.S. Bureau of Labor Statistics, Occupational Employment and Wage Statistics.

In May 2022, the median annual wages for zoologists and wildlife biologists in the top industries in which they worked were as follows:

Government	$69,490
Management, scientific, and technical consulting services	67,840
Research and development in the physical, engineering, and life sciences	65,160
Colleges, universities, and professional schools; state, local, and private	62,490
Social advocacy organizations	54,240

Most zoologists and wildlife biologists work full time. They may have irregular schedules, especially when doing fieldwork.

Job Outlook

Employment of zoologists and wildlife biologists is projected to grow 3 percent from 2022 to 2032, about as fast as the average for all occupations.

About 1,500 openings for zoologists and wildlife biologists are projected each year, on average, over the decade. Many of those openings are expected to result from the need to replace workers who transfer to different occupations or exit the labor force, such as to retire.

Employment

Some zoologists and wildlife biologists are expected to be needed to help combat the loss of biodiversity caused by human activities, as well as to research climate-driven ecosystem changes. These workers also may be needed to develop and implement conservation plans to reduce threats to animals and protect natural resources. However, demand for zoologists and

Zoologists and Wildlife Biologists

Percent change in employment, projected 2022-32

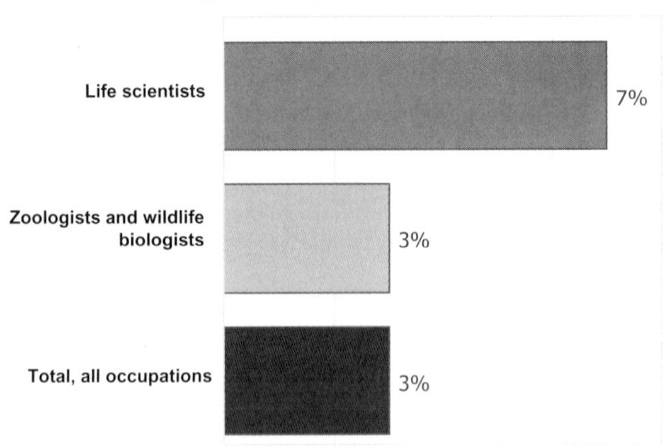

Note: All Occupations includes all occupations in the U.S. Economy.
Source: U.S. Bureau of Labor Statistics, Employment Projections program.

wildlife biologists may be limited by budgetary constraints, as jobs and funding for these workers often come from state, federal, and local governments.

Employment projections data for zoologists and wildlife biologists, 2022-32

Occupational Title	SOC Code	Employ-ment, 2022	Projected Employment, 2032	Change, 2022-32 Percent	Change, 2022-32 Numeric	Employment by Industry
SOURCE: U.S. Bureau of Labor Statistics, Employment Projections program						
Zoologists and wildlife biologists	19-1023	19,100	19,700	3	600	Get data

Contacts for More Information

For more information about zoologists and wildlife biologists, visit

- American Ornithological Society (AOS)
- American Society of Ichthyologists and Herpetologists (ASIH)
- American Society of Mammalogists (ASM)
- Association of Zoos and Aquariums (AZA)
- MarineBio
- The Wildlife Society (TWS)
- Zoological Association of America (ZAA)
- National Park Service
- U.S. Fish and Wildlife Service
- USAJOBS

Management

Administrative Services and Facilities Managers

Summary

Quick Facts: Administrative Services and Facilities Managers	
2022 Median Pay	$101,870 per year $48.98 per hour
Typical Entry-Level Education	Bachelor's degree
Work Experience in a Related Occupation	Less than 5 years
On-the-job Training	None
Number of Jobs, 2022	377,800
Job Outlook, 2022-32	5% (Faster than average)
Employment Change, 2022-32	19,900

What Administrative Services and Facilities Managers Do

Administrative services and facilities managers plan, direct, and coordinate activities that help an organization run efficiently.

Work Environment

Most administrative services and facilities managers work full time, and some work more than 40 hours per week.

How to Become an Administrative Services or Facilities Manager

Although administrative services and facilities managers' educational requirements vary by organization and the work they do, these workers typically need a bachelor's degree and related work experience.

Pay

The median annual wage for administrative services managers was $103,330 in May 2022.

The median annual wage for facilities managers was $99,030 in May 2022.

Job Outlook

Overall employment of administrative services and facilities managers is projected to grow 5 percent from 2022 to 2032, faster than the average for all occupations.

About 31,400 openings for administrative services and facilities managers are projected each year, on average, over the decade. Many of those openings are expected to result from the need to replace workers who transfer to different occupations or exit the labor force, such as to retire.

What Administrative Services and Facilities Managers Do

Administrative services and facilities managers plan, direct, and coordinate activities that help an organization run efficiently.

Duties

Administrative services and facilities managers typically do the following:

- Supervise staff
- Set goals and deadlines for their department or facility
- Recommend changes to policies or procedures in order to improve operations, such as reassessing supplies or recordkeeping

Administrative services managers keep records, distribute supplies, and maintain facilities.

Administrative services managers plan, coordinate, and direct a broad range of services that allow organizations to operate efficiently.

- Monitor facilities to make sure that they remain safe, secure, and well maintained
- Oversee the maintenance and repair of machinery, equipment, and electrical and mechanical systems
- Make sure that facilities meet environmental, health, and security standards and comply with regulations

Administrative services managers oversee one or more office support services for an organization. In a large organization, these workers may specialize in an area such as recordkeeping or mail distribution. In a small organization, they may direct all support services and may be called the *business office manager*.

Specific tasks for administrative services managers may vary. For example, these workers might be responsible for ensuring that an organization has the supplies and services it needs. Other tasks might include examining energy consumption patterns, technology use, and office equipment and planning for future upgrades.

Records and information managers develop, monitor, and manage an organization's records. They provide information to chief executives and ensure that employees follow records and information management guidelines. They may direct the operations of onsite or offsite records facilities. These managers also work closely with an organization's attorneys and its technology and business operations staff. Records and information managers do not handle medical records, which are administered by medical and health services managers.

Facilities managers oversee buildings, grounds, equipment, and supplies. Their responsibilities cover several categories, including operations, maintenance, and planning and managing projects. For example, facilities managers may oversee renovation projects to improve efficiency or to meet regulations and environmental, health, and security standards. In addition, they continually monitor facilities to ensure that the premises are safe, secure, and well maintained.

Facilities managers also direct staff, including grounds maintenance workers, janitors and building cleaners, and general maintenance and repair workers.

Work Environment

Administrative services managers held about 250,800 jobs in 2022. The largest employers of administrative services managers were as follows:

Professional, scientific, and technical services	14%
Healthcare and social assistance	12
Educational services; state, local, and private	12
Finance and insurance	9
Local government, excluding education and hospitals	8

Facilities managers held about 127,000 jobs in 2022. The largest employers of facilities managers were as follows:

Administrative services managers spend much of their day in an office.

Educational services; state, local, and private	13%
Manufacturing	11
Healthcare and social assistance	10
Local government, excluding education and hospitals	7
Administrative and support and waste management and remediation services	7

Administrative services and facilities managers spend much of their day in an office. They may observe workers throughout the building, go outdoors to supervise groundskeeping activities, or visit other facilities they direct.

Work Schedules

Most administrative services and facilities managers work full time, and some work more than 40 hours per week. Facilities managers often are on call to address problems that arise at all hours.

How to Become an Administrative Services or Facilities Manager

Educational requirements for administrative services and facilities managers vary by organization and the work they do. But these workers typically need a bachelor's degree and related work experience.

Education

Administrative services and facilities managers typically need a bachelor's degree, often in business or a related field. However, some people enter the occupation with a high school diploma.

Work Experience

Administrative services and facilities managers must have related work experience that reflects managerial and leadership abilities. Facilities managers should have experience in business operations, project management, and building maintenance, such as from having worked as a general maintenance and repair worker or a cost estimator. Records and information managers should have administrative or business operations experience involving recordkeeping. Records and information managers in the legal field often must have experience as a paralegal or legal assistant.

Licenses, Certifications, and Registrations

Although it is not required, professional certification may give candidates an advantage when applying for jobs.

Several professional associations for administrative services and facilities managers offer certifications. Some associations, including the International Facility Management Association (IFMA), offer certification that specializes in facility management. Others offering certification include the Institute of Certified Records Managers (ICRM), for records and information managers, and the ARMA International for those specializing in information governance.

In managing workers and coordinating administrative duties, administrative services managers must show leadership ability.

Important Qualities

Analytical skills. Administrative services and facilities managers must be able to review an organization's procedures for ways to improve efficiency.

Communication skills. Administrative services and facilities managers often work with others. They must be able to convey ideas clearly, both orally and in writing.

Detail oriented. Administrative services and facilities managers must pay attention to details across a range of tasks, such as ensuring that the organization complies with building codes and managing the process of buying equipment.

Leadership skills. In directing workers and coordinating organizational duties, administrative services and facilities managers must be able to motivate employees and handle problems that arise.

Pay

The median annual wage for administrative services managers was $103,330 in May 2022. The median wage is the wage at which half the workers in an occupation earned more than that amount and half earned less. The lowest 10 percent earned less than $59,070, and the highest 10 percent earned more than $178,870.

The median annual wage for facilities managers was $99,030 in May 2022. The lowest 10 percent earned less than $59,280, and the highest 10 percent earned more than $164,080.

In May 2022, the median annual wages for administrative services managers in the top industries in which they worked were as follows:

Finance and insurance	$122,060

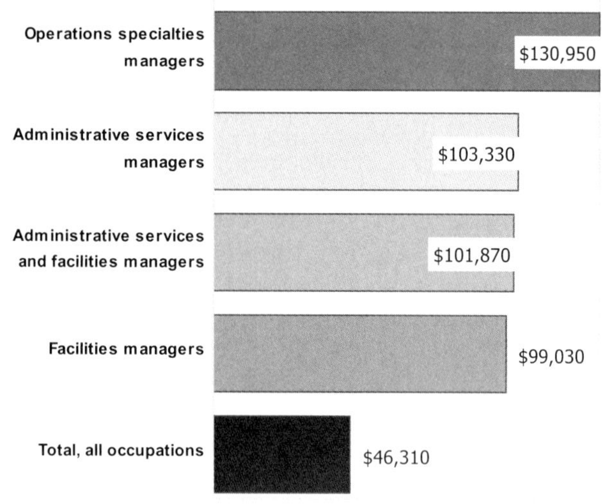

Professional, scientific, and technical services	114,680
Local government, excluding education and hospitals	105,180
Educational services; state, local, and private	97,450
Healthcare and social assistance	93,170

In May 2022, the median annual wages for facilities managers in the top industries in which they worked were as follows:

Manufacturing	$115,990
Local government, excluding education and hospitals	99,670
Educational services; state, local, and private	96,720
Administrative and support and waste management and remediation services	95,780
Healthcare and social assistance	88,760

Most administrative services and facilities managers work full time, and some work more than 40 hours per week. Facilities managers often are on call to address problems that arise at all hours.

Job Outlook

Overall employment of administrative services and facilities managers is projected to grow 5 percent from 2022 to 2032, faster than the average for all occupations.

About 31,400 openings for administrative services and facilities managers are projected each year, on average, over the decade. Many of those openings are expected to result from the need to replace workers who transfer to different occupations or exit the labor force, such as to retire.

Employment

A continuing focus on the environmental impact and energy efficiency of buildings will keep facilities managers in demand. Improving energy efficiency can reduce costs and often is required by regulation. For example, building codes typically ensure that buildings meet environmental standards. Facilities managers will be needed to oversee these improvements in a wide range of areas, from heating and air-conditioning systems to roofing. In addition, facilities managers will be needed to plan for natural disasters, ensuring that any damage to a building will be minimal and that the organization can get back to work quickly.

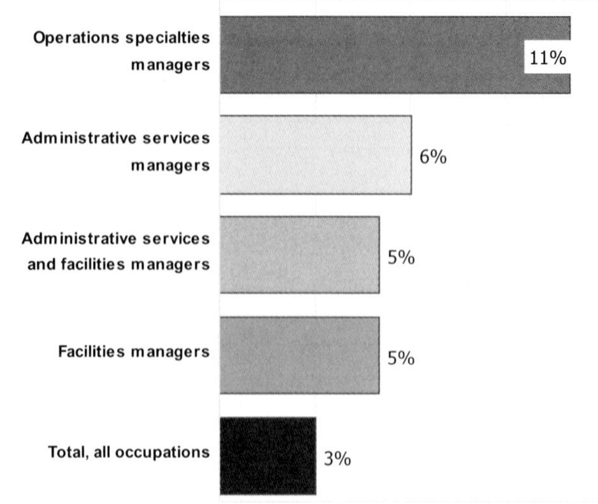

Note: All Occupations includes all occupations in the U.S. Economy.
Source: U.S. Bureau of Labor Statistics, Employment Projections program

Demand for administrative services managers is expected to be particularly strong for those working in records and information management. As cloud computing continues to expand, these workers will have a critical role in helping organizations develop new records and information management practices and in maintaining data security.

Occupational Title	SOC Code	Employment, 2022	Projected Employment, 2032	Change, 2022-32	
				Percent	Numeric
Administrative services and facilities managers	11-3010	377,800	397,700	5	19,900
Administrative services managers	11-3012	250,800	264,900	6	14,000
Facilities managers	11-3013	127,000	132,800	5	5,800

Contacts for More Information

For more information, visit

- International Facility Management Association
- ARMA International
- Institute of Certified Records Managers

Advertising, Promotions, and Marketing Managers

Summary

Quick Facts: Advertising, Promotions, and Marketing Managers	
2022 Median Pay	$138,730 per year $66.70 per hour
Typical Entry-Level Education	Bachelor's degree
Work Experience in a Related Occupation	See How to Become One
On-the-job Training	None
Number of Jobs, 2022	389,000
Job Outlook, 2022-32	6% (Faster than average)
Employment Change, 2022-32	24,300

What Advertising, Promotions, and Marketing Managers Do

Advertising, promotions, and marketing managers plan programs to generate interest in products or services.

Work Environment

Advertising, promotions, and marketing managers typically work in an office setting. They may travel to meet with clients or media representatives. Most of these managers work full time, and some work more than 40 hours per week.

How to Become an Advertising, Promotions, or Marketing Manager

Advertising, promotions, and marketing managers typically need a bachelor's degree. They also typically need work experience in a related occupation.

Pay

The median annual wage for advertising and promotions managers was $127,830 in May 2022.

Advertising, promotions, and marketing managers inspect layouts, which are sketches or plans for an advertisement.

The median annual wage for marketing managers was $140,040 in May 2022.

Job Outlook

Overall employment of advertising, promotions, and marketing managers is projected to grow 6 percent from 2022 to 2032, faster than the average for all occupations.

About 34,000 openings for advertising, promotions, and marketing managers are projected each year, on average, over the decade. Many of those openings are expected to result from the need to replace workers who transfer to different occupations or exit the labor force, such as to retire.

What Advertising, Promotions, and Marketing Managers Do

Advertising, promotions, and marketing managers plan programs to generate interest in products or services. They work with art directors, advertising sales agents, financial staff, and others to develop strategies and materials.

Duties

Advertising, promotions, and marketing managers typically do the following:

Advertising managers can be found in advertising agencies that put together advertising campaigns for clients, in media firms that sell advertising space or time, and in companies that advertise heavily.

- Work with department heads or staff to discuss topics such as budgets and contracts, creative vision, marketing plans, and media buying
- Plan promotional campaigns, such as contests or giveaways, to boost brand loyalty and reach new customers
- Plan advertising campaigns, including in which media—such as radio, television, or email—to advertise
- Negotiate advertising contracts with clients and partners
- Evaluate the look and feel of displays or websites in advertising or marketing campaigns
- Initiate market research studies and analyze their findings to understand customer and market opportunities for businesses
- Develop pricing and other strategies, such as how to acquire and retain customers and manage their data, for marketing products or services
- Meet and strategize with clients to provide marketing or related advice
- Direct the hiring and daily activities of advertising, promotions, and marketing staff

Advertising managers create interest among potential buyers of a product or service. They do this for a department, an entire organization, or individual projects (referred to as an account).

Advertising managers work with sales staff and others to generate ideas for an advertising campaign. They oversee the staff that develops the advertising. They work with the finance department to prepare a budget and cost estimates for the campaign. Often, advertising managers serve as liaisons between the client and the advertising or promotion agency that develops and places the ads.

Some advertising managers specialize in a particular field or type of advertising. For example, *media directors* determine the way in which an advertising campaign reaches customers, whether through radio, television, or various other media. *Account executives* have a different focus: they oversee client accounts but do not develop or supervise advertising projects themselves.

Promotions managers direct programs that combine advertising with purchasing incentives and target them to customers in media, in displays, or at events to increase sales. Purchasing incentives may include discounts, rebates, contests, and other programs to strengthen brand loyalty. Promotions managers also contribute to developing brand loyalty programs.

Marketing managers estimate demand and identify potential markets for products and services that an organization and its competitors offer. They may develop pricing and other strategies, such as ways to acquire and retain customers. They work with product development, public relations, and sales staff to help organizations maximize their profits and market share while ensuring customer satisfaction.

Work Environment

Advertising and promotions managers held about 30,900 jobs in 2022. The largest employers of advertising and promotions managers were as follows:

Advertising, public relations, and related services	29%
Self-employed workers	27
Information	14
Management of companies and enterprises	7
Wholesale trade	2

Marketing managers held about 358,200 jobs in 2022. The largest employers of marketing managers were as follows:

Professional, scientific, and technical services	25%
Management of companies and enterprises	12
Finance and insurance	10
Wholesale trade	9
Manufacturing	7

Advertising, promotions, and marketing managers work with art directors, advertising sales agents, financial staff, and others to develop strategies and materials. Because their work affects a firm's revenue, these managers also collaborate with top executives.

Advertising, promotions, and marketing managers typically work in an office setting. They may travel to meet with clients or media representatives. Their work may be stressful, particularly near deadlines.

Work Schedules

Most advertising, promotions, and marketing managers work full time. Some work more than 40 hours per week.

How to Become an Advertising, Promotions, or Marketing Manager

Advertising, promotions, and marketing managers typically need a bachelor's degree. They also typically need work experience in a related occupation.

Education

Advertising, promotions, and marketing managers typically need a bachelor's degree in a business field, such as marketing,

Advertising, promotions, and marketing managers may travel to meet with clients or representatives of communications media.

or in a related field, such as communications. Relevant courses might include consumer behavior, market research, and art history.

Some employers prefer to hire candidates who have a master's degree.

Advertising and marketing managers may begin as trainees or participate in mentoring or shadowing opportunities. In addition, completing an internship while in school may make candidates more attractive to prospective employers.

Work Experience in a Related Occupation

These managers typically need work experience in a related advertising, marketing, promotions, or sales occupation. For example, they may have worked as sales representatives, market research analysts, or public relations specialists.

Important Qualities

Analytical skills. Advertising, promotions, and marketing managers must be able to evaluate industry trends and determine the best strategies for their clients.

Communication skills. These workers must be able to collaborate with other managers and staff. They also must be persuasive in communicating with the public.

Creativity. Advertising, promotions, and marketing managers must be able to generate new and imaginative ideas.

Decision-making skills. These workers often must choose between competing advertising and marketing strategies put forward by staff.

Interpersonal skills. Managers must deal with a range of people and personalities in different roles, both inside and outside their organization.

Organizational skills. Advertising, promotions, and marketing managers must manage their time and budget efficiently while directing and motivating staff.

These managers typically have previous work experience in advertising, marketing, promotions, or sales.

Pay

The median annual wage for advertising and promotions managers was $127,830 in May 2022. The median wage is the wage at which half the workers in an occupation earned more than that amount and half earned less. The lowest 10 percent earned less than $60,380, and the highest 10 percent earned more than $239,200.

The median annual wage for marketing managers was $140,040 in May 2022. The lowest 10 percent earned less than $76,790, and the highest 10 percent earned more than $239,200.

In May 2022, the median annual wages for advertising and promotions managers in the top industries in which they worked were as follows:

Information	$146,900
Management of companies and enterprises	133,110
Advertising, public relations, and related services	131,190
Wholesale trade	107,860

In May 2022, the median annual wages for marketing managers in the top industries in which they worked were as follows:

Management of companies and enterprises	$162,870
Finance and insurance	161,040
Professional, scientific, and technical services	148,810
Manufacturing	147,940
Wholesale trade	135,540

Most advertising, promotions, and marketing managers work full time. Some work more than 40 hours per week.

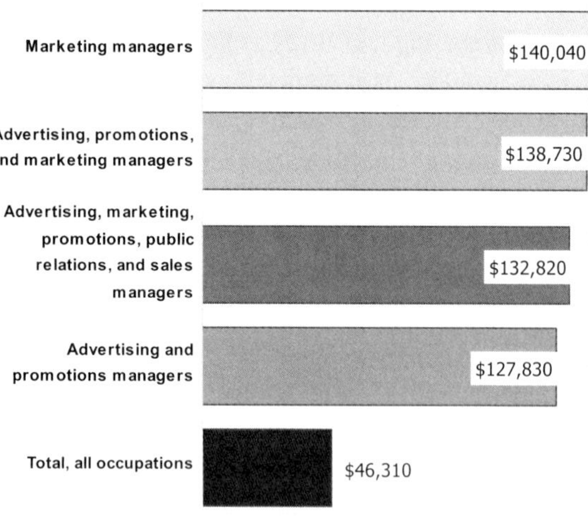

Note: All Occupations includes all occupations in the U.S. Economy.
Source: U.S. Bureau of Labor Statistics, Occupational Employment and Wage Statistics

Job Outlook

Overall employment of advertising, promotions, and marketing managers is projected to grow 6 percent from 2022 to 2032, faster than the average for all occupations.

About 34,000 openings for advertising, promotions, and marketing managers are projected each year, on average, over the decade. Many of those openings are expected to result from the need to replace workers who transfer to different occupations or exit the labor force, such as to retire.

Employment

Marketing managers will continue to be in demand as organizations use marketing campaigns to maintain and expand their market share. These managers will be sought after for their advice on crafting pricing strategies and finding new ways to reach customers.

The continued rise of electronic media will result in decreasing demand for print advertisements. However, the demand for advertising and promotions managers is expected to be concentrated in industries that rely on these workers to create digital media campaigns that target customers through the use of websites, social media, or live chats.

Occupational Title	SOC Code	Employment, 2022	Projected Employment, 2032	Change, 2022-32	
				Percent	Numeric
Advertising, promotions, and marketing managers	—	389,000	413,300	6	24,300
Advertising and promotions managers	11-2011	30,900	31,400	2	600

Advertising, Promotions, and Marketing Managers

Percent change in employment, projected 2022-32

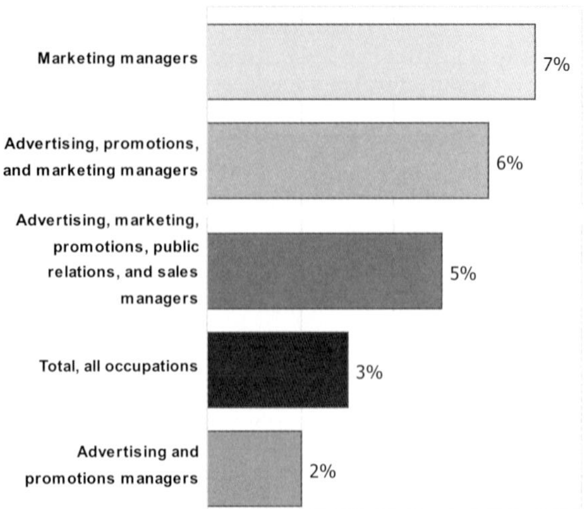

Note: All Occupations includes all occupations in the U.S. Economy.
Source: U.S. Bureau of Labor Statistics, Employment Projections program

Occupational Title	SOC Code	Employment, 2022	Projected Employment, 2032	Change, 2022-32	
				Percent	Numeric
Marketing managers	11-2021	358,200	381,900	7	23,700

Contacts for More Information

For more information about advertising managers, visit:

- American Association of Advertising Agencies (4 A's)
- American Marketing Association (AMA)

Architectural and Engineering Managers

Summary

Quick Facts: Architectural and Engineering Managers	
2022 Median Pay	$159,920 per year $76.88 per hour
Typical Entry-Level Education	Bachelor's degree
Work Experience in a Related Occupation	5 years or more
On-the-job Training	None
Number of Jobs, 2022	201,500
Job Outlook, 2022-32	4% (As fast as average)
Employment Change, 2022-32	8,200

What Architectural and Engineering Managers Do

Architectural and engineering managers plan, direct, and coordinate activities in the fields of architecture and engineering.

Work Environment

Architectural and engineering managers typically work in offices, although some work in other settings, such as research laboratories or industrial production plants. Most work full time, and some work more than 40 hours a week.

How to Become an Architectural or Engineering Manager

To enter the occupation, architectural and engineering managers typically need at least a bachelor's degree and considerable work experience as an architect or engineer.

Pay

The median annual wage for architectural and engineering managers was $159,920 in May 2022.

Job Outlook

Employment of architectural and engineering managers is projected to grow 4 percent from 2022 to 2032, about as fast as the average for all occupations.

About 13,600 openings for architectural and engineering managers are projected each year, on average, over the decade. Many of those openings are expected to result from the need to replace workers who transfer to different occupations or exit the labor force, such as to retire.

What Architectural and Engineering Managers Do

Architectural and engineering managers plan, direct, and coordinate activities in the fields of architecture and engineering.

Duties

Architectural and engineering managers typically do the following:

- Make detailed plans to research and develop products, processes, or designs
- Determine staff, training, and equipment needs
- Propose budgets for projects and programs
- Hire and supervise staff
- Oversee research and development projects, including directing staff output and quality
- Coordinate work and collaborate with other staff and managers

Architectural and engineering managers use their knowledge of architecture or engineering to oversee a variety of activities. They may direct and coordinate construction or manufacturing related to production, operations, quality assurance, testing, or maintenance.

As part of their oversight responsibilities, architectural and engineering managers set goals and develop detailed plans,

Architectural and engineering managers plan activities in architectural and engineering companies.

Architectural and engineering managers assign workers specific parts of a project to carry out.

including production schedules. They also prepare budgets for projects, staff, and equipment needs. In this way, managers anticipate problems that may arise and which might otherwise hinder a project's completion.

Architectural and engineering managers hire staff and assign them to carry out specific parts of a project. They also supervise employees' work, which may include collaborating with other organizations, to monitor the project's quality and progress through completion.

Work Environment

Architectural and engineering managers held about 201,500 jobs in 2022. The largest employers of architectural and engineering managers were as follows:

Manufacturing	36%
Architectural, engineering, and related services	27
Government	8
Scientific research and development services	6
Management of companies and enterprises	5

Most architectural and engineering managers work in offices. Some work in settings such as research laboratories or industrial production plants. These managers may work in groups and supervise other staff members, such as architects and engineers. They are often under pressure to meet deadlines and budgets.

Work Schedules

Most architectural and engineering managers work full time. Working more than 40 hours a week is common, especially when meeting deadlines.

How to Become an Architectural or Engineering Manager

To enter the occupation, architectural and engineering managers typically need at least a bachelor's degree and considerable work experience as an architect or engineer.

Education

Architectural and engineering managers typically need at least a bachelor's degree in engineering or architecture.

Bachelor's degree programs in architecture and engineering usually include coursework in mathematics and physical sciences. In addition, architecture programs may include courses such as architectural history and theory, computer-aided design and drafting (CADD), and construction methods; these programs take about 5 years to complete. Engineering programs vary by concentration and often take about 4 years of classroom, laboratory, and field studies in engineering principles and systems.

Architectural and engineering managers or prospective managers may complete a master's degree in engineering management (MEM or MsEM), technology management (MSTM), or business administration (MBA). Some earn their master's degree before entering a management position; others earn it while working as a manager. Typically, those who prefer to manage in technical areas pursue an MsEM or MSTM, and those interested in general management skills earn an MBA.

Engineering and technology management programs include courses such as accounting, marketing, and finance that focus on the particular field. Programs in engineering management also include coursework in supply chain management and product development. Programs in technology management include courses in information security and systems development.

Architectural and engineering managers frequently work in groups.

Architectural and engineering managers advance to their positions after years of employment as an architect or engineer.

Licenses, Certifications, and Registrations

Architectural and engineering managers typically do not need a license. However, these managers may advance from other occupations that do require licensure. For example, all states require architects to be licensed, and some engineers obtain a professional engineering (PE) license. Contact your state licensing board for more information.

Some managers choose to earn certification. For example, certification in technology management is available from the Association of Technology, Management, and Applied Engineering.

Work Experience in a Related Occupation

Architectural and engineering managers typically advance to their positions after years of experience as an architect or engineer. In those positions, they may have worked on complex projects, developed designs, solved problems, and led teams.

Important Qualities

Analytical skills. Architectural and engineering managers evaluate information to solve problems.

Communication skills. Architectural and engineering managers must effectively convey information and expectations related to projects.

Interpersonal skills. Architectural and engineering managers must be able to collaborate with other staff to meet deadlines and achieve goals.

Leadership skills. Architectural and engineering managers lead teams, which requires an ability to organize, direct, and motivate others.

Math skills. Architectural and engineering managers use calculus and other mathematics to develop new products and processes.

Organizational skills. Architectural and engineering managers keep track of many workers, schedules, and budgets simultaneously.

Pay

The median annual wage for architectural and engineering managers was $159,920 in May 2022. The median wage is the wage at which half the workers in an occupation earned more than that amount and half earned less. The lowest 10 percent earned less than $102,450, and the highest 10 percent earned more than $221,550.

In May 2022, the median annual wages for architectural and engineering managers in the top industries in which they worked were as follows:

Scientific research and development services..	$175,670
Management of companies and enterprises.....	169,140
Manufacturing..........	159,700
Architectural, engineering, and related services..........	157,100
Government..........	141,040

Most architectural and engineering managers work full time. Working more than 40 hours a week is common, especially when meeting deadlines.

Job Outlook

Employment of architectural and engineering managers is projected to grow 4 percent from 2022 to 2032, about as fast as the average for all occupations.

About 13,600 openings for architectural and engineering managers are projected each year, on average, over the decade. Many of those openings are expected to result from the need to replace workers who transfer to different occupations or exit the labor force, such as to retire.

Employment

Employment growth will largely reflect the growth of the industries in which these managers are employed. Demand for civil engineering services is expected to continue as the nation's

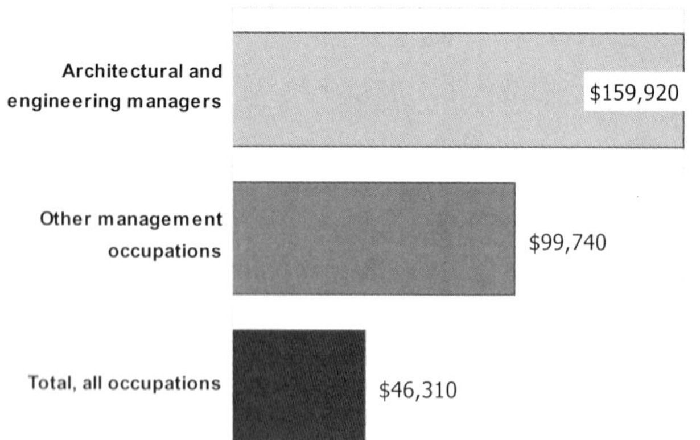

Note: All Occupations includes all occupations in the U.S. Economy.
Source: U.S. Bureau of Labor Statistics, Occupational Employment and Wage Statistics.

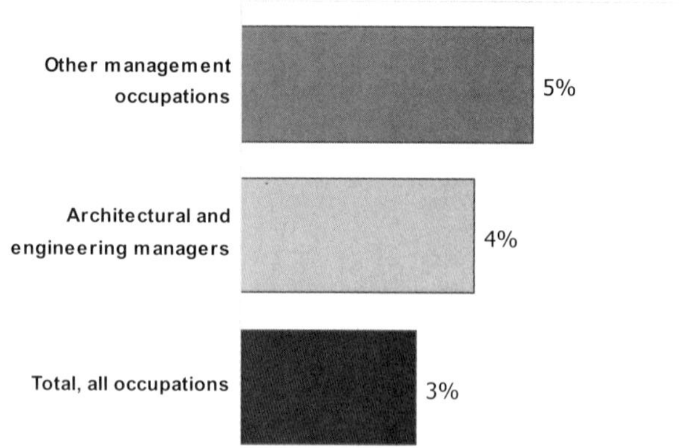

Note: All Occupations includes all occupations in the U.S. Economy.
Source: U.S. Bureau of Labor Statistics, Employment Projections program.

aging infrastructure requires expansion and repair. These managers also should be needed for projects such as wind turbine farms and other renewable energy construction and design.

Occupational Title	SOC Code	Employment, 2022	Projected Employment, 2032	Change, 2022-32	
				Percent	Numeric
Architectural and engineering managers	11-9041	201,500	209,700	4	8,200

Contacts for More Information

For information on architecture and engineering management programs, visit

- ABET
- American Institute of Architects
- Association of Technology, Management, and Applied Engineering

Compensation and Benefits Managers

Summary

Quick Facts: Compensation and Benefits Managers	
2022 Median Pay	$131,280 per year $63.11 per hour
Typical Entry-Level Education	Bachelor's degree
Work Experience in a Related Occupation	5 years or more
On-the-job Training	None
Number of Jobs, 2022	17,500
Job Outlook, 2022-32	2% (As fast as average)
Employment Change, 2022-32	400

What Compensation and Benefits Managers Do

Compensation and benefits managers plan, develop, and oversee programs to pay employees.

Work Environment

Compensation and benefits managers work in nearly every industry. Some work more than 40 hours per week.

How to Become a Compensation or Benefits Manager

Compensation and benefits managers typically need a bachelor's degree and related work experience.

Compensation and benefits managers work in nearly every industry.

Pay

The median annual wage for compensation and benefits managers was $131,280 in May 2022.

Job Outlook

Employment of compensation and benefits managers is projected to grow 2 percent from 2022 to 2032, about as fast as the average for all occupations.

About 1,100 openings for compensation and benefits managers are projected each year, on average, over the decade. Many of those openings are expected to result from the need to replace workers who transfer to different occupations or exit the labor force, such as to retire.

What Compensation and Benefits Managers Do

Compensation and benefits managers plan, develop, and oversee programs to pay employees.

Duties

Compensation and benefits managers typically do the following:

- Coordinate and supervise the work activities of staff
- Set the organization's pay and benefits structure

Managers ensure that pay plans comply with federal regulations.

- Monitor competitive wage rates to develop or modify compensation plans
- Choose and manage outside partners, such as benefits vendors, insurance brokers, and investment managers
- Oversee the distribution of pay and benefits information to the organization's employees
- Ensure that pay and benefits plans comply with federal and state regulations
- Prepare a program budget and operate within that budget

Although some managers administer both the compensation and benefits programs in an organization, other managers—particularly at large organizations—specialize and oversee one or the other. However, all compensation and benefits managers routinely meet with senior staff, managers of other human resources departments, and the financial officers of their organization. They use their expertise to recommend compensation and benefits policies, programs, and plans.

Compensation and benefits managers may analyze data to determine the best pay and benefits plans for an organization. They may also monitor trends affecting pay and benefits and assess ways for their organization to improve practices or policies. Using analytical, database, and presentation software, managers draw conclusions, present their findings, and make recommendations to other managers in the organization.

Compensation managers direct an organization's pay structure. They monitor market conditions and government regulations to ensure that their organization's pay rates are current and competitive. They analyze data on wages and salaries, and they evaluate how their organization's pay structure compares with that of other organizations. Compensation managers use this information to maintain or develop pay levels for an organization.

Some also design pay-for-performance plans, which include guidelines for bonuses and incentive pay. They also may help determine commission rates and other incentives for sales staff.

Benefits managers administer an organization's employee benefits program, which may include retirement plans, leave policies, wellness programs, and insurance policies such as health, life, and disability. They select benefits vendors and oversee enrollment, renewal, and delivery of benefits to the organization's employees. They frequently monitor government regulations and market trends to ensure that their programs are current, competitive, and legal.

Work Environment

Compensation and benefits managers held about 17,500 jobs in 2022. The largest employers of compensation and benefits managers were as follows:

Management of companies and enterprises	22%
Professional, scientific, and technical services	16
Insurance carriers and related activities	12
Government	7
Healthcare and social assistance	6

Compensation and benefits managers coordinate the work activities of specialists in offices.

Compensation and benefits managers work in nearly every industry. Most of these managers work in offices.

Work Schedules

Most compensation and benefits managers work full time. Some work more than 40 hours per week. They may work more hours during peak times to meet deadlines, especially during the benefits enrollment period of their organization.

How to Become a Compensation or Benefits Manager

Compensation and benefits managers typically need a combination of education and related work experience.

Compensation and benefits managers often start out as compensation, benefits, and job analysis specialists.

Education

For most positions, compensation and benefits managers typically need a bachelor's degree in business, human resources, or a related field, such as social science or psychology.

Work Experience in a Related Occupation

Work experience is essential for compensation and benefits managers. Managers often specialize in either compensation or benefits, depending on the experience they gain in previous jobs. Managers often start out as compensation, benefits, and job analysis specialists. Work experience in other human resource fields, in finance, or in management is also helpful.

Licenses, Certifications, and Registrations

Although not required, certification gives compensation and benefits managers credibility because it shows that they have expertise. Employers may prefer to hire candidates with certification, and some positions require it.

Certification often requires several years of related work experience and passing an exam. Professional associations, including the Society for Human Resource Management, the International Foundation of Employee Benefit Plans and WorldatWork, offer certification programs that may be helpful for compensation and benefits managers.

Important Qualities

Analytical skills. Compensation and benefits managers analyze data on wages and salaries and the cost of benefits, and they assess and devise programs that best fit an organization and its employees.

Business skills. These managers oversee a budget, build a case for their recommendations, and understand how compensation and benefits plans affect an organization's finances.

Communication skills. Compensation and benefits managers direct staff, give presentations, and work with colleagues. With each of these groups, they must be able to clearly explain concepts and respond to concerns.

Decision-making skills. These managers weigh the strengths and weaknesses of different pay structures and benefits plans and choose the best options for an organization.

Leadership skills. Compensation and benefits managers coordinate the activities of their staff and administer compensation and benefits programs, ensuring that the work is completed accurately and on schedule.

Pay

The median annual wage for compensation and benefits managers was $131,280 in May 2022. The median wage is the wage at which half the workers in an occupation earned more than that amount and half earned less. The lowest 10 percent earned less than $77,230, and the highest 10 percent earned more than $217,650.

In May 2022, the median annual wages for compensation and benefits managers in the top industries in which they worked were as follows:

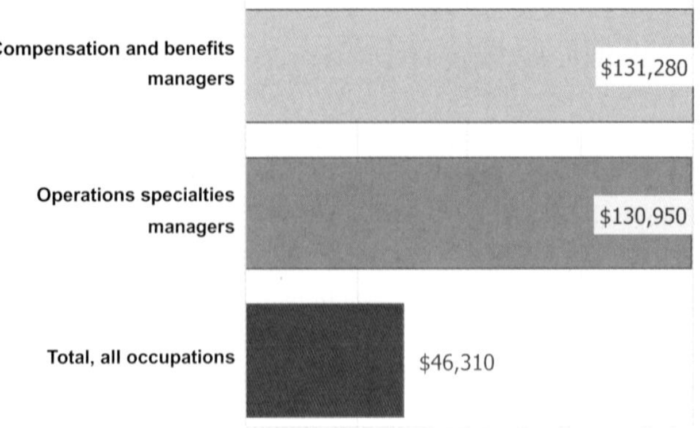

Note: All Occupations includes all occupations in the U.S. Economy.
Source: U.S. Bureau of Labor Statistics, Occupational Employment and Wage Statistics.

Management of companies and enterprises	$154,110
Professional, scientific, and technical services	142,570
Insurance carriers and related activities	126,220
Healthcare and social assistance	121,780
Government	104,310

Most compensation and benefits managers work full time. Some work more than 40 hours per week. They may work more hours during peak times to meet deadlines, especially during the benefits enrollment period of their organization.

Job Outlook

Employment of compensation and benefits managers is projected to grow 2 percent from 2022 to 2032, about as fast as the average for all occupations.

About 1,100 openings for compensation and benefits managers are projected each year, on average, over the decade. Many of those openings are expected to result from the need

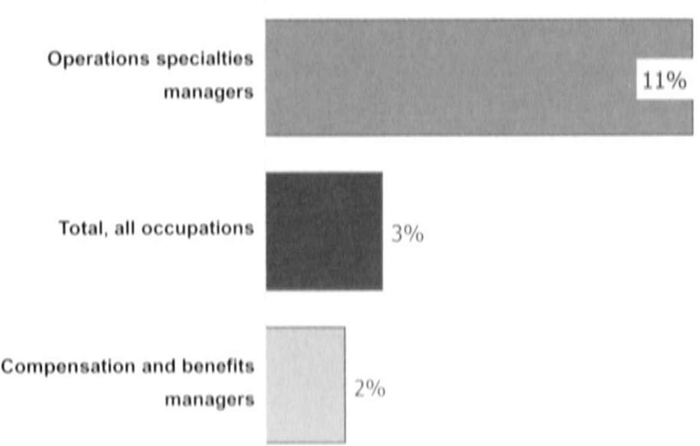

Note: All Occupations includes all occupations in the U.S. Economy.
Source: U.S. Bureau of Labor Statistics, Employment Projections program.

to replace workers who transfer to different occupations or exit the labor force, such as to retire.

Employment

Organizations continue to focus on reducing compensation and benefits costs, such as by introducing pay-for-performance and health and wellness programs. Organizations will need managers to evaluate and direct these compensation and benefits policies and plans.

However, organizations may contract out a portion of their compensation and benefits functions to human resources consulting firms in order to reduce costs and gain access to technical expertise. For example, to reduce administrative costs, organizations commonly use an outside vendor for processing payroll and insurance claims. These consulting firms automate tasks and operate call centers to handle employee questions, thereby reducing the need for compensation and benefits managers.

Occupational Title	SOC Code	Employment, 2022	Projected Employment, 2032	Change, 2022-32	
				Percent	Numeric
Compensation and benefits managers	11-3111	17,500	17,800	2	400

Contacts for More Information

For more information about compensation and benefits managers, including certification, visit

- International Foundation of Employee Benefit Plans
- WorldatWork
- Society for Human Resource Management

Computer and Information Systems Managers

Summary

Quick Facts: Computer and Information Systems Managers

2022 Median Pay	$164,070 per year $78.88 per hour
Typical Entry-Level Education	Bachelor's degree
Work Experience in a Related Occupation	5 years or more
On-the-job Training	None
Number of Jobs, 2022	557,400
Job Outlook, 2022-32	15% (Much faster than average)
Employment Change, 2022-32	86,000

Computer and information systems managers learn about new technology and look for ways to upgrade their organization's computer systems.

What Computer and Information Systems Managers Do

Computer and information systems managers plan, coordinate, and direct computer-related activities in an organization.

Work Environment

Most computer and information systems managers work full time. Some work more than 40 hours per week.

How to Become a Computer and Information Systems Manager

Typically, candidates need a bachelor's degree in computer or information science and related work experience. Many computer and information systems managers also have a graduate degree.

Pay

The median annual wage for computer and information systems managers was $164,070 in May 2022.

Job Outlook

Employment of computer and information systems managers is projected to grow 15 percent from 2022 to 2032, much faster than the average for all occupations.

About 46,900 openings for computer and information systems managers are projected each year, on average, over the decade. Many of those openings are expected to result from the need to replace workers who transfer to different occupations or exit the labor force, such as to retire.

What Computer and Information Systems Managers Do

Computer and information systems managers, often called information technology (IT) managers or IT project managers, plan, coordinate, and direct computer-related activities in an organization. They help determine the information technology goals of an organization and are responsible for implementing computer systems to meet those goals.

Duties

Computer and information systems managers typically do the following:

- Analyze their organization's computer needs and recommend possible upgrades for top executives to consider
- Plan and direct the installation and maintenance of computer hardware and software
- Ensure the security of an organization's network and electronic documents
- Assess the costs and benefits of new projects and justify funding on projects to top executives
- Learn about new technology and look for ways to upgrade their organization's computer systems
- Determine short- and long-term personnel needs for their department
- Plan and direct the work of other IT professionals, including computer systems analysts, software developers, information security analysts, and computer support specialists
- Negotiate with vendors to get the highest level of service for the organization's technology

Few managers carry out all of these duties. There are various types of computer and information systems managers, and the specific duties of each are determined by the size and structure of the firm. Smaller firms may not employ every type of manager.

The following are examples of types of computer and information systems managers:

IT directors sometimes present new ideas to a firm's top executives.

Chief information officers (CIOs) determine the technology or information goals of an organization and then oversee implementation of technology to meet those goals.

CIOs may focus on a specific area, such as electronic data processing or information systems, but CIOs tend to focus more on long-term or big picture issues. At small organizations a CIO has more direct control over the IT department, and at larger organizations other managers under the CIO may handle the day-to-day activities of the IT department.

CIOs who do not have technical expertise and who focus solely on a company's business aspects are included in top executives.

Chief technology officers (CTOs) evaluate new technology and determine how it can help their organization. When both CIOs and CTOs are present, the CTO usually has more technical expertise.

The CTO usually reports directly to the CIO and is responsible for designing and recommending the appropriate technology solutions to support the CIO's policies and directives. CTOs also work with different departments to implement the organization's technology plans.

When a company does not have a CIO, the CTO determines the overall technology strategy for the firm and presents it to top executives.

IT directors, including management information systems (MIS) directors, are in charge of their organizations' information technology (IT) departments, and they directly supervise other employees. IT directors help to determine the business requirements for IT systems, and they implement the policies that have been chosen by top executives. IT directors often have a direct role in hiring members of the IT department. It is their job to ensure the availability of data and network services by coordinating IT activities. IT directors also oversee the financial aspects of their department, such as budgeting.

IT security managers oversee their organizations' network and data security. They work with top executives to plan security policies and promote a culture of information security throughout the organization. They develop programs to keep employees aware of security threats. These managers must keep up to date on IT security measures. They also supervise investigations if there is a security violation.

Work Environment

Computer and information systems managers held about 557,400 jobs in 2022. The largest employers of computer and information systems managers were as follows:

Computer systems design and related services	21%
Information	14
Finance and insurance	11
Management of companies and enterprises	9
Manufacturing	7

Computer and information systems managers plan and direct the work of other information technology (IT) professionals.

Work Schedules

Most computer and information systems managers work full time. If problems arise, managers may need to work more than 40 hours a week to come up with solutions.

How to Become a Computer and Information Systems Manager

Typically, a bachelor's degree in computer or information science, plus related work experience, is required. Many computer and information systems managers also have a graduate degree.

Education

Computer and information systems managers typically need a bachelor's degree in computer and information technology or a related field, such as engineering technologies. These degrees include courses in computer programming, software development, and mathematics. Management information systems (MIS) programs usually include business classes as well as computer-related ones.

Many organizations require their computer and information systems managers to have a graduate degree as well. A Master of Business Administration (MBA) is common and takes 2 years beyond the undergraduate level to complete. Many people pursuing an MBA take classes while working, an option that can increase the time required to complete that degree.

Work Experience in a Related Occupation

Most jobs for computer and information systems managers require several years of experience in a related information technology (IT) job. Lower-level management positions may require only a few years of experience. Directors are more likely to need 5 to 10 years of related work experience. A chief technology officer (CTO), who oversees the technology plan for a large organization, may need more than 15 years of experience in the IT field before being considered for a job.

The number of years of experience required varies with the organization. Generally, smaller or newer companies do not require as much experience as larger or more established ones.

Most jobs for computer and information systems managers require several years of experience in a related information technology (IT) job.

Computer systems are used throughout the economy, and IT employees may gain experience in a variety of industries. However, an applicant's work experience should be in the same industry they are applying to work in. For example, an IT security manager should have previously worked in information security. A hospital IT director should have experience in the healthcare field.

Advancement

Most computer and information systems managers start out as lower-level managers and advance to higher positions within the IT department. IT directors or project managers can advance to become CTOs. A CTO or other manager who is especially business-minded can advance to become a chief information officer (CIO), the person in charge of all IT-related decisions in an organization. CIOs can advance to become top executives in an organization.

Important Qualities

Analytical skills. IT managers must analyze problems and consider and select the best ways to solve them.

Business skills. IT managers must develop and implement strategic plans to reach the goals of their organizations.

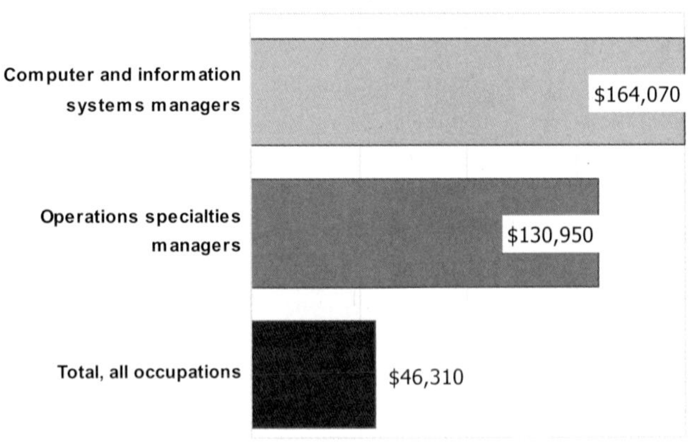

Note: All Occupations includes all occupations in the U.S. Economy.
Source: U.S. Bureau of Labor Statistics, Occupational Employment and Wage Statistics.

Communication skills. IT managers must explain their work to top executives and give clear instructions to their subordinates.

Decision-making skills. Some IT managers must make important decisions about how to allocate resources in order to reach their organizations' goals.

Leadership skills. IT managers must lead and motivate IT teams or departments so that workers are efficient and effective.

Organizational skills. Some IT managers must coordinate the work of several different IT departments to make the organization run efficiently.

Pay

The median annual wage for computer and information systems managers was $164,070 in May 2022. The median wage is the wage at which half the workers in an occupation earned more than that amount and half earned less. The lowest 10 percent earned less than $97,430, and the highest 10 percent earned more than $239,200.

In May 2022, the median annual wages for computer and information systems managers in the top industries in which they worked were as follows:

Information	$173,540
Manufacturing	167,690
Finance and insurance	166,640
Management of companies and enterprises	166,070
Computer systems design and related services	165,740

Most computer and information systems managers work full time. If problems arise, managers may need to work more than 40 hours a week to come up with solutions.

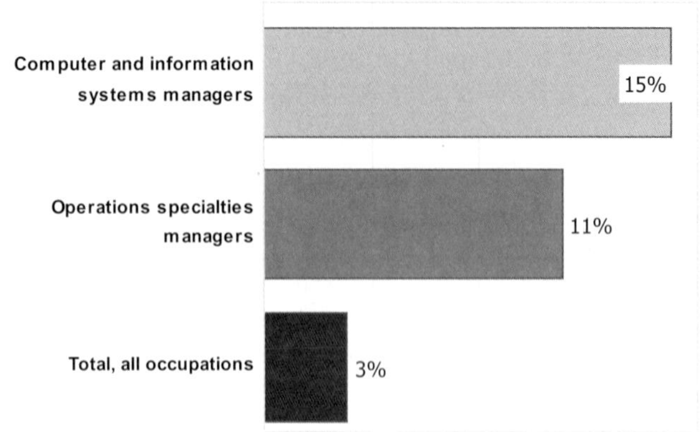

Note: All Occupations includes all occupations in the U.S. Economy.
Source: U.S. Bureau of Labor Statistics, Employment Projections program

Job Outlook

Employment of computer and information systems managers is projected to grow 15 percent from 2022 to 2032, much faster than the average for all occupations.

About 46,900 openings for computer and information systems managers are projected each year, on average, over the decade. Many of those openings are expected to result from the need to replace workers who transfer to different occupations or exit the labor force, such as to retire.

Employment

Demand for computer and information systems managers will grow as organizations increasingly rely on information technology (IT) services and require these workers to plan and oversee computer hardware and software needs.

Employment growth is projected to result from the need to bolster cybersecurity in computer and information systems that businesses use. As cybersecurity threats increase, implementing more robust security policies will be especially critical for organizations that manage sensitive information.

Occupational Title	SOC Code	Employment, 2022	Projected Employment, 2032	Change, 2022-32	
				Percent	Numeric
Computer and information systems managers	11-3021	557,400	643,300	15	86,000

Contacts for More Information

For more information about computer careers, visit:

- Association for Computing Machinery
- CompTIA
- Computing Research Association
- IEEE Computer Society
- National Center for Women & Information Technology

Construction Managers

Summary

Quick Facts: Construction Managers	
2022 Median Pay	$101,480 per year $48.79 per hour
Typical Entry-Level Education	Bachelor's degree
Work Experience in a Related Occupation	None
On-the-job Training	Moderate-term on-the-job training
Number of Jobs, 2022	505,800
Job Outlook, 2022-32	5% (Faster than average)
Employment Change, 2022-32	22,900

What Construction Managers Do
Construction managers plan, coordinate, budget, and supervise construction projects from start to finish.

Work Environment
Construction managers may have a main office but spend most of their time in a field office onsite, where they monitor projects and make decisions about construction activities. Their schedules may vary.

How to Become a Construction Manager
Construction managers typically need a bachelor's degree, and they learn management techniques through on-the-job training. Large construction firms may prefer to hire candidates who have both construction experience and a bachelor's degree in a construction-related field.

Pay
The median annual wage for construction managers was $101,480 in May 2022.

Job Outlook
Employment of construction managers is projected to grow 5 percent from 2022 to 2032, faster than the average for all occupations.

About 38,700 openings for construction managers are projected each year, on average, over the decade. Many of those openings are expected to result from the need to replace workers who transfer to different occupations or exit the labor force, such as to retire.

What Construction Managers Do
Construction managers plan, coordinate, budget, and supervise construction projects from start to finish.

Duties
Construction managers typically do the following:

- Prepare cost estimates, budgets, and work timetables
- Interpret and explain contracts and technical information to other professionals
- Collaborate with architects, engineers, and other construction specialists
- Select subcontractors and schedule and coordinate their activities
- Monitor projects and report progress and budget matters to the construction firm and clients
- Respond to work delays, emergencies, and other problems with the project
- Ensure that the project complies with legal requirements, such building and safety codes

Construction managers, often called *general contractors* or *project managers*, coordinate and supervise a variety of projects, including building public, residential, commercial, and industrial structures as well as roads and bridges. Either a general contractor or a construction manager oversees the construction phase of a project, including personnel, but a construction

Construction managers need to coordinate activities on large projects.

Construction managers often collaborate with engineers and architects.

manager may also consult with the client during the design phase to help refine construction plans and control costs.

These managers coordinate construction processes so that projects meet design specifications and are completed on time within budget. Some construction managers are responsible for several projects—for example, building multiple homes—at once.

Construction managers work closely with other building specialists, such as architects, civil engineers, and tradesworkers, including stonemasons, electricians, and carpenters. Depending on the project, construction managers may interact with lawyers or government officials. For example, when installing municipal sidewalks, construction managers may confer with city inspectors to ensure that the project meets required material specifications.

For large building projects, such as industrial complexes, a top-level construction manager may hire other managers for different aspects of the project. Each construction manager then oversees completion of a specific phase, such as structural foundation or electrical work, and the top-level manager coordinates with the managers to complete the entire project.

To maximize efficiency, construction managers often perform the tasks of a cost estimator. They use cost-estimating and planning software to allocate time and money for scheduling project deadlines.

Work Environment

Construction managers held about 505,800 jobs in 2022. The largest employers of construction managers were as follows:

Self-employed workers	39%
Specialty trade contractors	16
Nonresidential building construction	15
Residential building construction	11
Heavy and civil engineering construction	7

Construction managers supervise on-site activity.

Construction managers may have a main office but spend most of their time in a field office onsite, where they monitor projects and make decisions about construction activities. Those who manage multiple projects must visit the different worksites, which may require travelling out of state or being away from home for extended periods.

Work Schedules

Most construction managers work full time, and some work more than 40 hours per week. Construction managers' work schedules may vary. They may need to work extra hours to meet deadlines, and they may have to be on call 24 hours a day to respond to project emergencies.

How to Become a Construction Manager

Construction managers typically need a bachelor's degree, and they learn management techniques through on-the-job training. Large construction firms may prefer to hire candidates who have both construction experience and a bachelor's degree in a construction-related field. Firms might hire as managers those who have a high school diploma and many years of experience in a construction trade; however, these people may be more likely to work as self-employed general contractors than to be hired as construction managers.

Education

Construction managers typically need a bachelor's degree in construction, business, engineering, or a related field.

Bachelor's degree programs in construction-related majors often include courses in project control and management, design, construction methods and materials, and cost estimation. Courses in business, communications, and mathematics are also helpful.

Some construction managers earn an associate's degree in construction management or construction technology. An associate's degree combined with work experience may be typical for managers who supervise small projects.

New construction managers are typically hired as assistants and work under the guidance of an experienced manager.

Candidates who have a high school diploma and several years of relevant work experience may qualify to become construction managers. However, these people may be more likely to work as self-employed general contractors than to be hired as construction managers.

Training

Newly hired construction managers typically work under the guidance of an experienced manager for up to 1 year. Depending on the firm, however, this on-the-job training may last for several years.

Work Experience in a Related Occupation

Construction experience is important for these managers, especially for ones who do not have a bachelor's degree. For construction managers to qualify for jobs solely through experience, they must have worked many years in carpentry, masonry, or other construction specialties.

College students who participate in internships and cooperative education programs may gain experience through such programs.

Licenses, Certifications, and Registrations

Some states require construction managers to be licensed. For more information, contact your state licensing board.

Professional certification, although not required, demonstrates a particular level of knowledge and experience.

The Construction Management Association of America awards the Certified Construction Manager (CCM) credential to workers who have the required experience and who pass a technical exam. Candidates complete a self-study course that covers topics related to construction managers, including the manager's role, legal issues, and risk allocation.

The American Institute of Constructors awards the Associate Constructor (AC) and Certified Professional Constructor (CPC) credential to candidates who meet its requirements, which include passing construction exams.

Important Qualities

Analytical skills. Construction managers must be able to plan strategies, investigate project cost variances, and solve problems over the course of a project.

Business skills. Construction managers need to prepare and follow project budgets, hire and manage staff, and coordinate with other workers and managers. Self-employed construction managers must generate their own business opportunities and be proactive in finding new clients.

Communication skills. Construction managers must be able to clearly convey information orally and in writing. In addition to talking with owners and clients, managers must give clear orders and explain complex information to construction workers and discuss technical details with inspectors and other specialists, such as engineers.

Decision-making skills. Construction managers need to choose personnel and subcontractors for specific tasks and jobs. They also must make myriad judgment calls about projects to ensure that they adhere to deadlines and budgets.

Leadership skills. Construction managers must effectively delegate tasks to construction workers, subcontractors, and other lower level managers to ensure that projects are completed accurately and on time.

Technical skills. Construction managers must have an applied knowledge of concepts and practices common in the industry, such as construction technologies, contracts, and technical drawings.

Pay

The median annual wage for construction managers was \$101,480 in May 2022. The median wage is the wage at which half the workers in an occupation earned more than that amount and half earned less. The lowest 10 percent earned less than \$62,210, and the highest 10 percent earned more than \$168,390.

In May 2022, the median annual wages for construction managers in the top industries in which they worked were as follows:

Heavy and civil engineering construction	$104,600
Nonresidential building construction	103,770
Specialty trade contractors	98,730
Residential building construction	82,860

Construction Managers

Median annual wages, May 2022

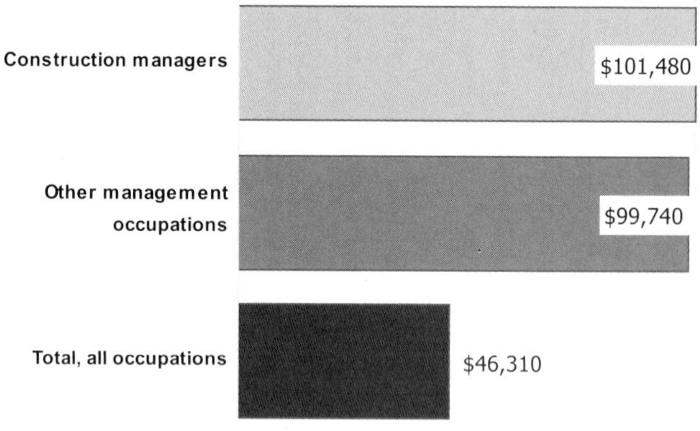

Note: All Occupations includes all occupations in the U.S. Economy.
Source: U.S. Bureau of Labor Statistics, Occupational Employment and Wage Statistics.

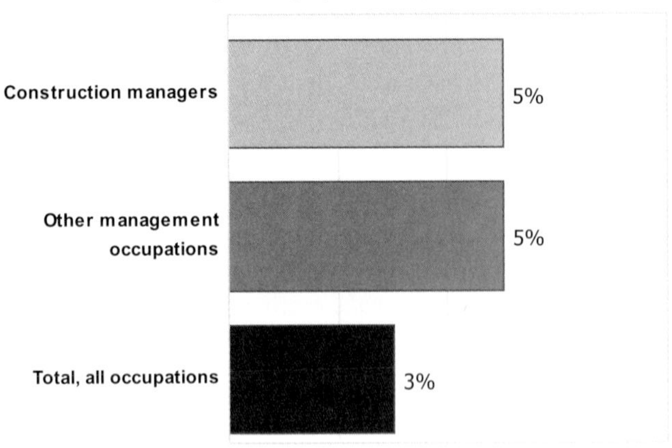

Note: All Occupations includes all occupations in the U.S. Economy.
Source: U.S. Bureau of Labor Statistics, Employment Projections program.

In addition to salary, construction managers may also earn bonuses. Their earnings depend on the amount of business they generate.

Most construction managers work full time, and some work more than 40 hours per week. Construction managers' work schedules may vary. They may need to work extra hours to meet deadlines, and they may have to be on call 24 hours a day to respond to project emergencies.

Job Outlook

Employment of construction managers is projected to grow 5 percent from 2022 to 2032, faster than the average for all occupations.

About 38,700 openings for construction managers are projected each year, on average, over the decade. Many of those openings are expected to result from the need to replace workers who transfer to different occupations or exit the labor force, such as to retire.

Employment

Construction managers are expected to be needed as overall construction activity expands. Over the projections decade, population and business growth will result in the construction of new residences, office buildings, retail outlets, hospitals, schools, restaurants, and other structures. Also, the need to improve portions of the national infrastructure may spur employment growth as roads, bridges, and sewer pipe systems are upgraded or replaced.

In addition, a continuing emphasis on retrofitting buildings to make them more energy efficient should create jobs for general contractors, who are more likely to manage the renovation and upgrading of buildings than to oversee new large-scale construction projects.

Construction processes and building technology are becoming more complex, requiring greater oversight and spurring demand for specialized management personnel even as technology makes construction managers more productive.

Occupational Title	SOC Code	Employment, 2022	Projected Employment, 2032	Change, 2022-32	
				Percent	Numeric
Construction managers	11-9021	505,800	528,700	5	22,900

Contacts for More Information

For more information about construction manager certification, visit

- American Institute of Constructors
- Construction Management Association of America
- ABET
- American Council for Construction Education
- NCCER
- Helmets to Hardhats

Elementary, Middle, and High School Principals

Summary

Quick Facts: Elementary, Middle, and High School Principals	
2022 Median Pay	$101,320 per year
Typical Entry-Level Education	Master's degree
Work Experience in a Related Occupation	5 years or more
On-the-job Training	None
Number of Jobs, 2022	300,400
Job Outlook, 2022-32	1% (Little or no change)
Employment Change, 2022-32	3,300

What Elementary, Middle, and High School Principals Do

Elementary, middle, and high school principals oversee all school operations, including daily school activities.

Work Environment

Principals work in public and private elementary, middle, and high schools. Typically, principals work year round.

How to Become an Elementary, Middle, or High School Principal

Principals typically need a master's degree in education administration or leadership. In addition, they need teaching experience.

Pay

The median annual wage for elementary, middle, and high school principals was $101,320 in May 2022.

Job Outlook

Employment of elementary, middle, and high school principals is projected to show little or no change from 2022 to 2032.

Despite limited employment growth, about 20,200 openings for elementary, middle, and high school principals are projected each year, on average, over the decade. Most of those openings are expected to result from the need to replace workers who transfer to different occupations or exit the labor force, such as to retire.

What Elementary, Middle, and High School Principals Do

Elementary, middle, and high school principals oversee all school operations, including daily school activities. They coordinate curriculums, manage staff, and provide a safe and productive learning environment for students.

Duties

Elementary, middle, and high school principals typically do the following:

- Manage school activities and staff, including teachers and support personnel
- Establish and oversee class schedules
- Develop, implement, and maintain curriculum standards
- Counsel and discipline students
- Observe teachers and evaluate their performance
- Meet with parents and teachers to discuss students' progress and behavior
- Assess and prepare reports on test scores and other student achievement data
- Organize professional development programs and workshops for staff
- Manage the school's budget, order school supplies, and schedule maintenance
- Establish and coordinate security procedures for students, staff, and visitors

Elementary, middle, and high school principals direct the overall operation of schools. They set and oversee academic goals

Elementary, middle, and high school principals manage the day-to-day operations of schools.

Principals counsel students.

and ensure that teachers have the equipment and resources to meet those goals. Principals may establish and supervise additional programs in their school, such as counseling, extracurricular activities, and before- and after-school childcare.

In public schools, principals also implement standards and programs set by the school district, state, and federal regulations. They evaluate and prepare reports based on these standards by assessing student achievement and teacher performance at their school.

Principals serve as the public representative of their school. They listen to, and try to address, the concerns of parents and the community.

The duties of principals vary by the size of the school and district. In large schools and districts, principals may have additional resources and staff to help them achieve goals. For example, large school districts often have instructional coordinators who help with data analysis and with teachers' professional development. Principals also may have staff who help with hiring school personnel. In smaller school districts, principals may need to assume these and other duties themselves.

Many schools have assistant principals who help principals with school administration. Principals typically assign specific duties to their assistant principals. In some school districts, assistant principals handle a subject area, such as literacy or math. Assistants may handle student safety, provide student academic counseling, or enforce disciplinary or attendance rules. They may also coordinate buses or supervise building and grounds maintenance.

Work Environment

Elementary, middle, and high school principals held about 300,400 jobs in 2022. The largest employers of elementary, middle, and high school principals were as follows:

Elementary and secondary schools; local	75%
Elementary and secondary schools; private	20

Elementary, middle, and high school principals may find it rewarding to work with students. However, coordinating and interacting with faculty, parents, students, and community members may be demanding. Principals' work is sometimes stressful because they are accountable for their school meeting state and federal standards for student performance and teacher qualification.

Work Schedules

Most principals work full time, and some work more than 40 hours per week. They may work evenings or weekends to meet with parents and other members of the community and to attend school functions, such as concerts and athletic events.

Typically, principals work year round and do not have summers off, even if students are not in school. During the summer, principals schedule building maintenance, order school supplies, and hire new teachers and other staff in preparation for the upcoming school year.

How to Become an Elementary, Middle, or High School Principal

Most schools require elementary, middle, and high school principals to have a master's degree in education administration or leadership. Principals also need teaching experience.

Education

Principals typically need a master's degree in education leadership or education administration. These master's degree programs teach prospective principals how to manage staff, create budgets, set goals, and work with parents and the community. To enter a master's degree program, candidates typically need a bachelor's degree in education, counseling, or a related field.

Work Experience in a Related Occupation

Principals need several years of teaching experience. For more information on how to become a teacher, see the profiles on

Principals meet with parents and teachers to discuss students' progress.

Principals must communicate effectively with students, teachers, and parents.

kindergarten and elementary school teachers, middle school teachers, and high school teachers.

Licenses, Certifications, and Registrations

Most states require public school principals to be licensed as school administrators. Licensure requirements vary by state, but most require a master's degree. Some states have alternative programs for candidates who do not have a master's degree in education administration or leadership. Most states also require candidates to pass an exam and a background check.

Principals in private schools are not required to have a state-issued license.

Advancement

An assistant principal can advance to become a principal. Some principals advance to become superintendents or other types of education administrators, which may require additional education. Others become instructional coordinators.

Important Qualities

Communication skills. Principals must communicate effectively with students, teachers, and parents. For example, when dealing with academic issues, they must listen to students and teachers in order to restate their understanding of the problem.

Critical-thinking skills. Principals analyze student test results and testing procedures to determine if improvements are needed. They must assess available options to help students achieve the best results.

Decision-making skills. Because principals are responsible for students, staff, and the overall operation of the school, they consider many factors when making decisions.

Interpersonal skills. Principals work with teachers, parents, and superintendents and must develop positive working relationships with them.

Leadership skills. Principals set educational goals and establish policies and procedures for the school. They need to be able to motivate staff to achieve these goals.

Problem-solving skills. Teachers, students, and other staff report problems to the principal. Principals need to be able to analyze problems and find appropriate solutions.

Pay

The median annual wage for elementary, middle, and high school principals was $101,320 in May 2022. The median wage is the wage at which half the workers in an occupation earned more than that amount and half earned less. The lowest 10 percent earned less than $64,690, and the highest 10 percent earned more than $158,770.

In May 2022, the median annual wages for elementary, middle, and high school principals in the top industries in which they worked were as follows:

Elementary and secondary schools; local	$102,400
Elementary and secondary schools; private	82,990

Elementary, Middle, and High School Principals

Median annual wages, May 2022

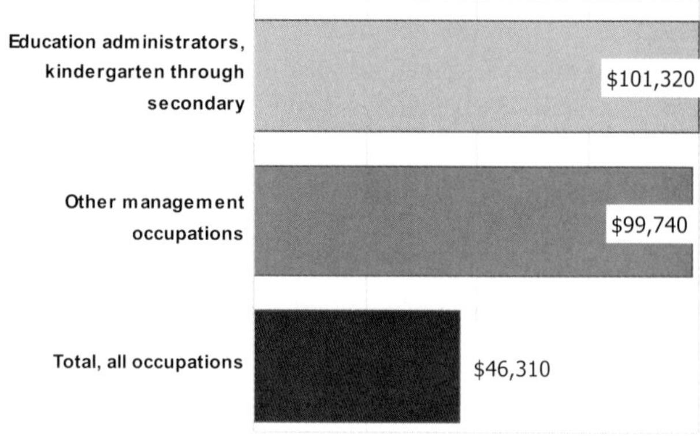

Note: All Occupations includes all occupations in the U.S. Economy.
Source: U.S. Bureau of Labor Statistics, Occupational Employment and Wage Statistics.

Most principals work full time, and some work more than 40 hours per week. They may work evenings or weekends to meet with parents and other members of the community and to attend school functions, such as concerts and athletic events.

Typically, principals work year round and do not have summers off, even if students are not in school. During the summer, principals prepare for the upcoming school year, schedule building maintenance, order school supplies, and hire teachers and other staff.

Job Outlook

Employment of elementary, middle, and high school principals is projected to show little or no change from 2022 to 2032.

Despite limited employment growth, about 20,200 openings for elementary, middle, and high school principals are projected each year, on average, over the decade. Most of those

Elementary, Middle, and High School Principals

Percent change in employment, projected 2022-32

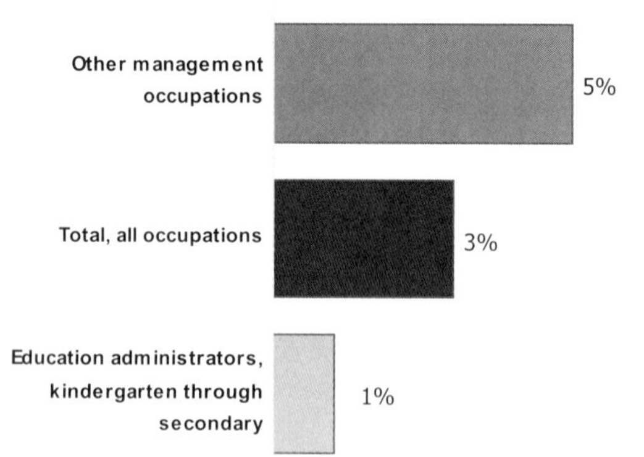

Note: All Occupations includes all occupations in the U.S. Economy.
Source: U.S. Bureau of Labor Statistics, Employment Projections program.

openings are expected to result from the need to replace workers who transfer to different occupations or exit the labor force, such as to retire.

Employment

Employment growth will be affected by student enrollment and the number of educational institutions.

There are a limited number of principal positions available per school. If student enrollment increases, more schools will open, which could increase demand. Conversely, stagnant or decreasing student enrollment may reduce the demand for principals.

Employment growth of school principals also will depend on state and local budgets. Budget constraints may delay the building or opening of new schools. In addition, some school districts may consolidate and close some schools within their districts, thereby limiting employment growth. If there is a budget surplus, however, school districts may open more schools, which could lead to employment growth.

Occupational Title	SOC Code	Employment, 2022	Projected Employment, 2032	Change, 2022-32	
				Percent	Numeric
Education administrators, kindergarten through secondary	11-9032	300,400	303,700	1	3,300

Contacts for More Information

For more information on elementary, middle, and high school principals, visit

- National Association of Elementary School Principals
- National Association of Secondary School Principals

Emergency Management Directors

Summary

Quick Facts: Emergency Management Directors

2022 Median Pay	$79,180 per year $38.07 per hour
Typical Entry-Level Education	Bachelor's degree
Work Experience in a Related Occupation	5 years or more
On-the-job Training	None
Number of Jobs, 2022	11,800
Job Outlook, 2022-32	3% (As fast as average)
Employment Change, 2022-32	400

Emergency management directors work with government officials, private companies, and the general public to design emergency response plans.

What Emergency Management Directors Do

Emergency management directors prepare plans and procedures for responding to natural disasters or other emergencies. They also help lead the response during and after emergencies.

Work Environment

Most emergency management directors work for local or state governments. Others work for organizations such as hospitals, colleges and universities, or private companies.

How to Become an Emergency Management Director

Emergency management directors typically need a bachelor's degree and many years of work experience in emergency response, disaster planning, or public administration.

Pay

The median annual wage for emergency management directors was $79,180 in May 2022.

Job Outlook

Employment of emergency management directors is projected to grow 3 percent from 2022 to 2032, about as fast as the average for all occupations.

About 900 openings for emergency management directors are projected each year, on average, over the decade. Many of those openings are expected to result from the need to replace workers who transfer to different occupations or exit the labor force, such as to retire.

What Emergency Management Directors Do

Emergency management directors prepare plans and procedures for responding to natural disasters and other emergencies. They

Emergency management directors may help train volunteers and first responders in emergency procedures.

also help lead the response during and after emergencies, often in coordination with public safety officials, elected officials, nonprofit organizations, and government agencies.

Duties

Emergency management directors typically do the following:

- Assess hazards and prepare plans to respond to emergencies and disasters in order to minimize risk to people and property
- Meet with public safety officials, private companies, and the public regarding emergency response plans
- Organize emergency response training for staff, volunteers, and other responders
- Coordinate the sharing of resources and equipment within and across communities to assist in responding to an emergency
- Analyze and prepare damage assessments following disasters or emergencies
- Review emergency plans of individual organizations, such as medical facilities, to ensure their adequacy
- Apply for federal funding for emergency management planning, responses, and recovery, and report on the use of funds allocated
- Review local emergency operations plans and revise them if necessary
- Maintain facilities used during emergency operations

Emergency management directors are responsible for planning and leading the responses to natural disasters and other emergencies. Directors work with government agencies, nonprofits, private companies, and the public to develop effective plans that minimize damage and disruptions during an emergency.

To develop emergency response plans, directors typically research "best practices" from around the country and from other emergency management agencies. Directors also must prepare plans and procedures that meet local, state, and federal regulations.

Directors must analyze the resources, equipment, and staff available to respond to emergencies. If resources are limited or equipment is lacking, directors must either revise their plans or get what they need from another community or state. Many directors coordinate with fire, emergency medical service, police departments, and public works agencies in other communities to locate and share equipment during an emergency. Directors must be in contact with other agencies to collect and share information regarding the scope of the emergency, the potential costs, and the resources or staff needed.

After they develop plans, emergency management directors typically ensure that individuals and groups become familiar with the emergency procedures. Directors often use social media to disseminate plans and warnings to the public.

Emergency management directors oversee training courses and disaster exercises for staff, volunteers, and local agencies to help ensure an effective and coordinated response to an emergency. Directors also may visit schools, hospitals, or other community groups to provide updates on plans for emergencies.

During an emergency, directors typically maintain a command center at which staff monitor and manage the emergency operations. Directors help lead the response, prioritizing certain actions if necessary. These actions may include ordering evacuations, conducting rescue missions, or opening public shelters for those displaced by the emergency. Emergency management directors also may need to conduct press conferences or other outreach activities to keep the public informed about the emergency.

Following an emergency, directors must assess the damage to their community and coordinate getting any needed assistance and supplies into the community. Directors may need to request state or federal assistance to help execute their emergency response plan and provide support to affected citizens, organizations, and communities. Directors may also revise their plans and procedures to prepare for future emergencies or disasters.

Emergency management directors working for hospitals, universities, or private companies may be called ***business continuity managers***. Similar to their counterparts in local and state government, business continuity managers prepare plans and procedures to help businesses maintain operations and minimize losses during and after an emergency.

Work Environment

Emergency management directors held about 11,800 jobs in 2022. The largest employers of emergency management directors were as follows:

Local government, excluding education and hospitals	56%
State government, excluding education and hospitals	15
Hospitals; state, local, and private	5
Colleges, universities, and professional schools; state, local, and private	3
Professional, scientific, and technical services	3

Most emergency management directors must be on call at all times to assist in emergency response.

Although most emergency management directors work in an office, they also typically travel to meet with various government agencies, community groups, and private companies.

During disasters and emergencies, directors often work in stressful situations.

Work Schedules

Most emergency management directors work full time. In addition, most are on call at all times and may need to work overtime to respond to emergencies and to support emergency management operations. Others may work evenings and weekends to meet with various community groups in preparing their emergency response plans.

How to Become an Emergency Management Director

Emergency management directors typically need a bachelor's degree and many years of work experience in emergency response, disaster planning, or public administration.

Education

Emergency management directors typically need a bachelor's degree in security and protective service, business, or emergency management. Some directors working in the private sector in business continuity management may need a degree in computer science, information systems administration, or another computer and information technology (IT) field.

Small municipalities or local governments may hire applicants whose highest level of educational attainment is a high school diploma. However, these applicants usually must have extensive work experience in emergency management if they are to be hired.

Work Experience in a Related Occupation

Candidates typically need many years of work experience before they can be hired as an emergency management director. Their experience usually must be with the military, law enforcement, fire safety, or in another emergency management

Applicants need years of work experience in law enforcement, fire safety, or an emergency management field.

field. Work experience in these areas enables candidates to make difficult decisions in stressful and time-sensitive situations. Such experience also prepares them to coordinate with various agencies to ensure that proper resources are used to respond to emergencies.

For more information, see the profiles on police and detectives, firefighters, police, fire, and ambulance dispatchers, and EMTs and paramedics.

Licenses, Certifications, and Registrations

Some states require directors to obtain certification within a certain timeframe after being hired in the position.

Many agencies and states offer voluntary certification programs to help emergency management directors obtain additional skills. Some employers may prefer or even require a Certified Emergency Manager (CEM), Certified Business Continuity Professional (CBCP), or equivalent designation. Emergency management directors can attain the CEM designation through the International Association of Emergency Managers (IAEM); the CBCP designation is given by the Disaster Recovery Institute International (DRI).

Certification must be renewed after a specified number of years. Both organizations require candidates to complete certain continuing education courses prior to recertification.

Important Qualities

Communication skills. Emergency management directors must be able to clearly convey their emergency preparedness plans, both orally and in writing, to a variety of audiences.

Critical-thinking skills. Emergency management directors must anticipate hazards and problems that may arise from an emergency in order to respond effectively.

Decision-making skills. Emergency management directors must analyze and choose among options, often in stressful situations. They must identify the strengths and weaknesses, costs and benefits, and other variables of each approach.

Interpersonal skills. Emergency management directors must work with other government agencies, law enforcement and fire officials, and the public to coordinate emergency responses.

Leadership skills. To ensure effective responses to emergencies, emergency management directors need to organize and train a variety of people.

Pay

The median annual wage for emergency management directors was $79,180 in May 2022. The median wage is the wage at which half the workers in an occupation earned more than that amount and half earned less. The lowest 10 percent earned less than $46,920, and the highest 10 percent earned more than $147,870.

In May 2022, the median annual wages for emergency management directors in the top industries in which they worked were as follows:

Professional, scientific, and technical services	$106,000
Hospitals; state, local, and private	93,540
Colleges, universities, and professional schools; state, local, and private	85,780
Local government, excluding education and hospitals	75,050
State government, excluding education and hospitals	66,750

Most emergency management directors work full time. In addition, most are on call at all times and may need to work overtime to respond to emergencies and to support emergency management operations. Others may work evenings and weekends to meet with various community groups in preparing their emergency response plans.

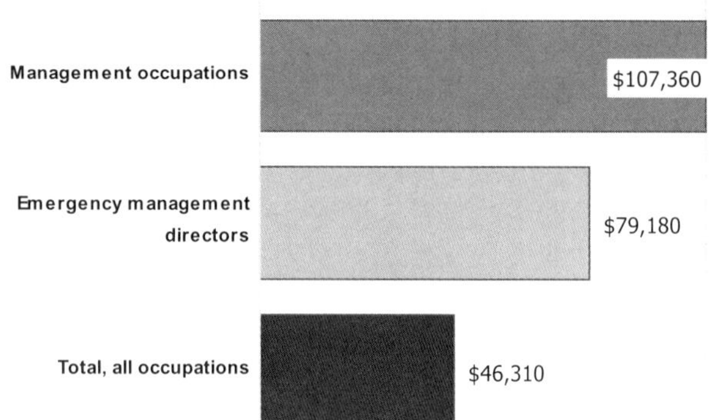

Note: All Occupations includes all occupations in the U.S. Economy.
Source: U.S. Bureau of Labor Statistics, Occupational Employment and Wage Statistics.

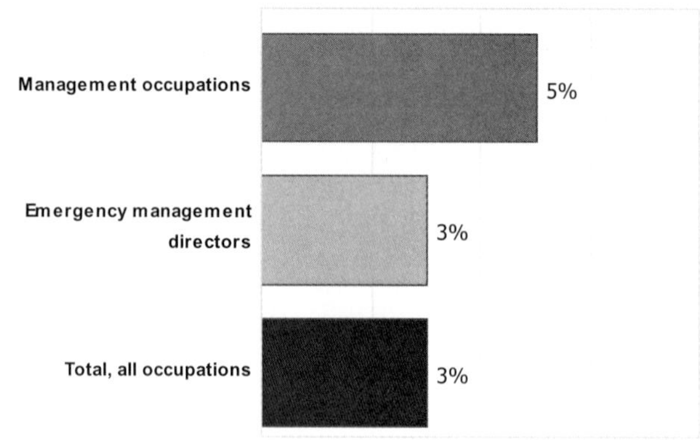

Note: All Occupations includes all occupations in the U.S. Economy.
Source: U.S. Bureau of Labor Statistics, Employment Projections program.

Job Outlook

Employment of emergency management directors is projected to grow 3 percent from 2022 to 2032, about as fast as the average for all occupations.

About 900 openings for emergency management directors are projected each year, on average, over the decade. Many of those openings are expected to result from the need to replace workers who transfer to different occupations or exit the labor force, such as to retire.

Employment

The importance of preparing for and minimizing the risks from emergencies will help sustain demand and employment opportunities for emergency management directors. These workers will be needed to help businesses and organizations continue to provide essential services during and after emergencies.

The outlook for public-sector employment of these managers is often related to budget constraints. Some local and state governments rely on federal financial assistance to fund their emergency management agencies. Counties may not hire full-time, stand-alone emergency management directors, choosing instead to shift the job responsibilities to the fire chief, police chief, or other government employees.

Occupational Title	SOC Code	Employment, 2022	Projected Employment, 2032	Change, 2022-32	
				Percent	Numeric
Emergency management directors	11-9161	11,800	12,200	3	400

Contacts for More Information

For more information, visit

- Disaster Recovery Institute International
- National Emergency Management Association
- International Association of Emergency Managers

Entertainment and Recreation Managers

Summary

Quick Facts: Entertainment and Recreation Managers

2022 Median Pay	$67,220 per year $32.32 per hour
Typical Entry-Level Education	Bachelor's degree
Work Experience in a Related Occupation	Less than 5 years
On-the-job Training	None
Number of Jobs, 2022	26,400
Job Outlook, 2022-32	8% (Faster than average)
Employment Change, 2022-32	2,200

What Entertainment and Recreation Managers Do

Entertainment and recreation managers plan, direct, and coordinate activities and operations related to fitness and leisure.

Work Environment

Entertainment and recreation managers typically work in various office settings, such as in recreational facilities or on cruise ships. However, many also spend time at event sites or outdoors, such as in parks. Most work full time. Work schedules may vary and can include nights, weekends, and holidays.

How to Become an Entertainment or Recreation Manager

Requirements vary for becoming an entertainment or recreation manager. Some workers typically need a bachelor's degree, while others enter the occupation with a high school diploma. Work experience is also important.

Pay

The median annual wage for entertainment and recreation managers was $67,220 in May 2022.

Job Outlook

Employment of entertainment and recreation managers is projected to grow 8 percent from 2022 to 2032, faster than the average for all occupations.

About 3,100 openings for entertainment and recreation managers are projected each year, on average, over the decade. Many of those openings are expected to result from the need to replace workers who transfer to different occupations or exit the labor force, such as to retire.

What Entertainment and Recreation Managers Do

Entertainment and recreation managers plan, direct, or coordinate activities and operations related to fitness and leisure.

Duties

Entertainment and recreation managers typically do the following:

- Plan programs of events or schedules of activities
- Write, present, and manage strategies and budgets for events or activities
- Manage the daily operation of an event, activity, facility, or program
- Engage with customers to convey information about events and activities or to resolve complaints
- Explain rules and regulations of facilities and programs
- Ensure that facilities and programs are safe and accessible for participants
- Hire, train, and direct staff

Entertainment and recreation managers organize and lead a variety of leisure, wellness, or social activities. The types of programs they plan and guide may differ by setting, participants, and other factors. For example, on a cruise ship, they may organize arts and crafts activities for children and yoga classes for seniors; for a community center, they may conduct nature hikes based on ability levels from beginner to advanced.

Entertainment and recreation managers organize and le ad a variety of leisure, wellness, or social activities.

Entertainment and recreation managers often are tasked with creating a positive experience for participants. They ensure that supplies are in stock and inspect equipment, ordering materials or arranging for maintenance as needed. In addition, they evaluate facility services and programs to create or improve offerings, which may involve soliciting input or analyzing customer feedback.

Entertainment and recreation managers also oversee staff orientation and development. Their responsibilities may include recruiting, interviewing, and hiring candidates; training and scheduling workers; monitoring and appraising work; and reassigning staff to meet facility or program needs.

Work Environment

Entertainment and recreation managers held about 26,400 jobs in 2022. The largest employers of entertainment and recreation managers were as follows:

Fitness and recreational sports centers	18%
Local government, excluding education and hospitals	17
Self-employed workers	8
Performing arts, spectator sports, and related industries	6
Accommodation and food services	6

Entertainment and recreation managers typically work in an office setting. However, they also may spend time outside their office, performing duties such as checking equipment or interacting with customers. Some managers are required to work outdoors or travel to entertainment or recreation sites.

Work Schedules

Most entertainment and recreation managers work full time. Work schedules may vary and can include nights, weekends, and holidays. Managers may need to work extra hours during peak season, such as for summer vacations at a resort. Some entertainment and recreation managers must be on call in case of emergencies, such as power outages during severe weather.

How to Become an Entertainment or Recreation Manager

Requirements vary for becoming an entertainment or recreation manager. Some workers typically need a bachelor's degree, while others enter the occupation with a high school diploma. Work experience is also important.

Education

Entertainment and recreation managers have a variety of academic backgrounds, ranging from a high school diploma to a bachelor's or higher degree. Requirements vary by organization and the specific work that managers do. For example, a recreation manager might need a bachelor's degree in park management, recreation and fitness, or leisure studies. An entertainment manager might need a degree in theater, music, or a related visual or performing arts field.

Some college students participate in internships. Through internships, students gain practical experience in their field of study while completing their education.

Licenses and Certifications

Some states may require a license for certain types of entertainment and recreation managers. For more information, contact your state licensing board.

Safety certifications may be required, but professional certification is usually optional. For example, some employers require entertainment and recreation managers to have first aid or CPR certification. Optional credentials, such as the Certified Park and Recreation Professional (CPRP) certification available for recreation managers, may demonstrate a particular level of knowledge and experience.

Work Experience in a Related Occupation

Experience in a related occupation is important for entertainment and recreation managers. Employers often prefer to hire managers who have experience in supervising others, planning programs or events, or providing customer service in a leisure or hospitality setting.

The type of experience needed may vary by position. For example, some workers benefit from experience with recreation programs or fitness center operations. Other managers might need entertainment, theater, music, or cruise industry experience.

Employers may consider students' internships as part of the work experience they need for entry-level positions.

Entertainment and recreation managers typically work in an office setting and oversee staff.

Important Qualities

Business skills. Entertainment and recreation managers create, present, and oversee budgets and strategies, such as for a facility's quarterly activities schedule.

Communication skills. Entertainment and recreation managers must be able to clearly convey information both orally and in writing to customers, suppliers, and staff.

Interpersonal skills. Entertainment and recreation managers interact with customers, staff, and vendors. They must be able to establish and maintain positive relationships with a variety of people.

Leadership skills. Entertainment and recreation managers direct workers and oversee facilities. They must be able to motivate staff and be decisive in handling operations.

Organizational skills. Entertainment and recreation managers oversee many responsibilities at once, so they must be able to multitask and pay attention to details.

Problem-solving skills. Entertainment and recreation managers must be able to anticipate potential issues and prepare solutions so that customers have a positive experience.

Pay

The median annual wage for entertainment and recreation managers was $67,220 in May 2022. The median wage is the wage at which half the workers in an occupation earned more than that amount and half earned less. The lowest 10 percent earned less than $38,350, and the highest 10 percent earned more than $130,040.

In May 2022, the median annual wages for entertainment and recreation managers in the top industries in which they worked were as follows:

Local government, excluding education and hospitals	$84,660
Accommodation and food services	77,660
Performing arts, spectator sports, and related industries	77,060
Fitness and recreational sports centers	59,970

Entertainment and recreation managers may benefit from having work experience in fitness center operations.

Most entertainment and recreation managers work full time. Work schedules may vary and can include nights, weekends, and holidays. Managers may need to work extra hours during peak season, such as for summer vacations at a resort. Some entertainment and recreation managers must be on call in case of emergencies, such as power outages during severe weather.

Job Outlook

Employment of entertainment and recreation managers is projected to grow 8 percent from 2022 to 2032, faster than the average for all occupations.

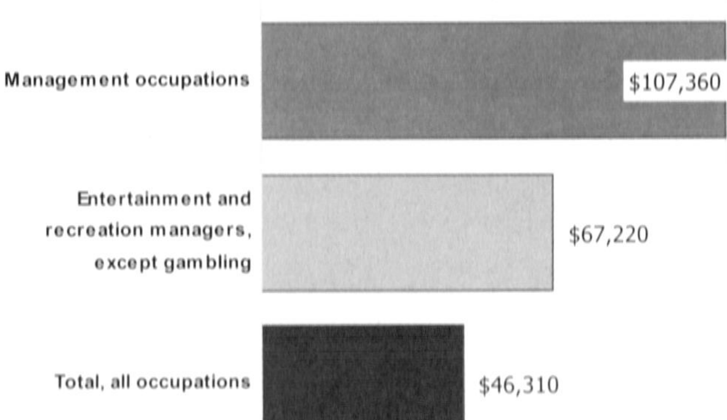

Note: All Occupations includes all occupations in the U.S. Economy.
Source: U.S. Bureau of Labor Statistics, Occupational Employment and Wage Statistics.

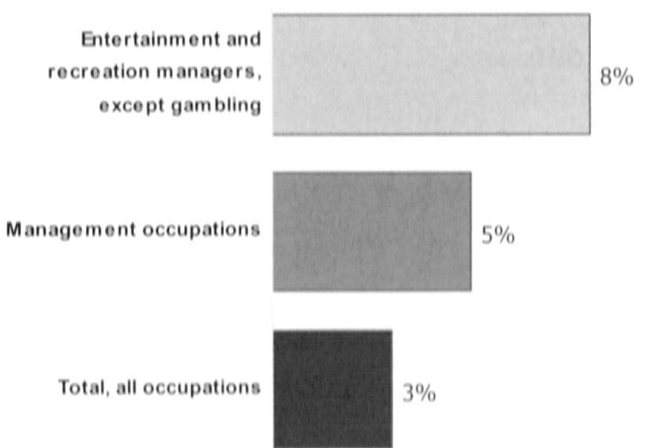

Note: All Occupations includes all occupations in the U.S. Economy.
Source: U.S. Bureau of Labor Statistics, Employment Projections program.

About 3,100 openings for entertainment and recreation managers are projected each year, on average, over the decade. Many of those openings are expected to result from the need to replace workers who transfer to different occupations or exit the labor force, such as to retire.

Employment

Employment growth will stem from public interest in recreational activities, such as golf and tennis. In addition, an increased emphasis on the importance of lifelong well-being is expected to create demand for entertainment and recreation managers in a variety of settings, including country clubs, fitness centers, and parks.

Occupational Title	SOC Code	Employment, 2022	Projected Employment, 2032	Change, 2022-32	
				Percent	Numeric
Entertainment and recreation managers, except gambling	11-9072	26,400	28,600	8	2,200

Contacts for More Information

For more information, visit

- American Academy for Park and Recreation Administration (AAPRA)
- National Recreation and Park Association (NRPA)
- Resort and Commercial Recreation Association (RCRA)

Farmers, Ranchers, and Other Agricultural Managers

Summary

Quick Facts: Farmers, Ranchers, and Other Agricultural Managers	
2022 Median Pay	$75,760 per year $36.42 per hour
Typical Entry-Level Education	High school diploma or equivalent
Work Experience in a Related Occupation	5 years or more
On-the-job Training	None
Number of Jobs, 2022	922,900
Job Outlook, 2022-32	-5% (Decline)
Employment Change, 2022-32	-42,300

Farmers, ranchers, and other agricultural managers operate establishments that produce crops, livestock, and dairy products.

What Farmers, Ranchers, and Other Agricultural Managers Do

Farmers, ranchers, and other agricultural managers run establishments that produce crops, livestock, and dairy products.

Work Environment

Farmers, ranchers, and other agricultural managers typically work outdoors but also may spend time in an office. Their work is often physically demanding.

How to Become a Farmer, Rancher, or Other Agricultural Manager

Farmers, ranchers, and other agricultural managers typically need at least a high school diploma and work experience in a related occupation.

Pay

The median annual wage for farmers, ranchers, and other agricultural managers was $75,760 in May 2022.

Job Outlook

Employment of farmers, ranchers, and other agricultural managers is projected to decline 5 percent from 2022 to 2032.

Despite declining employment, about 88,800 openings for farmers, ranchers, and other agricultural managers are projected each year, on average, over the decade. All of those openings are expected to result from the need to replace workers who transfer to other occupations or exit the labor force, such as to retire.

What Farmers, Ranchers, and Other Agricultural Managers Do

Farmers, ranchers, and other agricultural managers run establishments that produce crops, livestock, and dairy products.

Some farmers work primarily with crops and vegetables, whereas other farmers and ranchers handle livestock.

Duties

Farmers, ranchers, and other agricultural managers typically do the following:

- Supervise all steps of crop production or ranging, including planting, fertilizing, harvesting, and herding
- Make decisions about crops or livestock by evaluating factors such as market conditions, disease, soil conditions, and the availability of federal programs
- Choose and buy supplies, such as seed, fertilizer, and farm machinery
- Maintain farming equipment
- Maintain farm facilities, such as water pipes, fences, and animal shelters
- Serve as the sales agent for crops, livestock, and dairy products
- Record financial, tax, production, and employee information

Farmers, ranchers, and other agricultural managers monitor the prices for their products. They use different strategies to protect themselves financially from unpredictable changes in the markets. For example, some farmers carefully plan the combination of crops they grow, so that if the price of one crop drops, they have enough income from another crop to make up for the loss. Farmers and ranchers also track disease and weather conditions, either or both of which may negatively impact crop yields or animal health. By planning ahead, farmers and ranchers may be able to store their crops or keep their livestock in order to take advantage of higher prices later in the year.

Some farmers choose to sell a portion of their goods directly to consumers through farmer's markets or cooperatives to reduce their financial risk and to gain a larger share of the final price of their goods.

Farmers, ranchers, and other agricultural managers negotiate with banks and other credit lenders to get financing, because they must buy seed, livestock, and equipment before they have products to sell.

Farmers, ranchers, and other agricultural managers typically work outdoors, but they may spend some time in offices.

Farmers and ranchers run farms that are primarily family owned. Those who do not own the land themselves may lease it from a landowner to operate as a working farm.

The size of the farm or range determines which tasks farmers and ranchers handle. Those who run small farms or ranges may do all tasks, including harvesting and inspecting the land, growing crops, and raising animals. In addition, they keep records, service machinery, and maintain buildings.

By contrast, farmers and ranchers who run large farms generally hire others—including agricultural workers—to help with physical work. Some of the workers on large farms are in nonfarm occupations, such as truck drivers, sales representatives, bookkeepers, and information technology specialists.

Farmers and ranchers follow improvements in animal breeding methods and seed science, choosing products that may increase output. Livestock and dairy farmers monitor and attend to the health of their herds, which may include assisting in births.

Agricultural managers take care of the day-to-day operations of one or more farms, ranches, nurseries, timber tracts, greenhouses, and other agricultural establishments for corporations, farmers, and owners who do not live and work on their farm or ranch.

Agricultural managers usually do not participate directly in production activities. Instead, they hire and supervise farm and livestock workers to do most of the daily production tasks.

Managers may determine budgets and decide how to store, transport, and sell crops. They also may oversee the maintenance of equipment and property.

The following are examples of types of farmers, ranchers, and other agricultural managers:

Crop farmers and managers are responsible for all stages of plant growth, including planting, fertilizing, watering, and harvesting crops. These farmers may grow grain, fruits, vegetables, and other crops. After a harvest, they make sure that the crops are properly packaged and stored.

Livestock, dairy, and poultry farmers, ranchers, and managers feed and care for animals, such as cows or chickens, in order to harvest meat, milk, or eggs. They keep livestock and poultry in barns, pens, and other farm buildings. These workers also may oversee animal breeding in order to maintain appropriate herd or flock size.

Nursery and greenhouse managers oversee the production of trees, shrubs, flowers, and plants (including turf) used for landscaping. In addition to applying pesticides and fertilizers to help plants grow, they often are responsible for keeping track of marketing activity and inventory.

Aquaculture farmers and managers raise fish and shellfish in ponds, floating net pens, raceways, and recirculating systems. They stock, feed, and maintain aquatic life used for food and recreational fishing.

Work Environment

Farmers, ranchers, and other agricultural managers held about 922,900 jobs in 2022. The largest employers of farmers, ranchers, and other agricultural managers were as follows:

Self-employed workers	67%
Crop production	19
Animal production and aquaculture	12

Farmers, ranchers, and other agricultural managers typically work outdoors but also may spend time in an office. Their work is often physically demanding.

Some farmers work primarily with crops. Other farmers and ranchers handle livestock.

Injuries and Illnesses

The work environment for farmers, ranchers, and other agricultural managers can be hazardous. Tractors, tools, and other farm machinery and equipment can cause serious injury, and exposure to substances in pesticides and fertilizers may be harmful. These workers must operate equipment and handle chemicals properly to avoid accidents and safeguard themselves and the environment.

Farmers and ranchers that care for animals keep livestock in pens, barns, and other farm buildings.

Work Schedules

Most farmers, ranchers, and other agricultural managers work full time, and many work more than 40 hours per week. Farm work is often seasonal, and the number of hours worked may change according to the season. Farmers and farm managers on crop farms usually work from sunrise to sunset during the planting and harvesting seasons. During the rest of the year, they plan the next season's crops, market their output, and repair and maintain machinery. Managers of greenhouses, nurseries, or farms that operate in mild or temperate climates may work year round.

On livestock-producing farms and ranches, work goes on throughout the year. Animals must be fed and cared for every day.

On large farms, farmers and farm managers meet with farm supervisors. Managers who oversee several farms may divide their time between traveling to meet farmers and landowners and working in offices to plan farm operations.

How to Become a Farmer, Rancher, or Other Agricultural Manager

Farmers, ranchers, and other agricultural managers typically need at least a high school diploma and work experience in a related occupation.

Education

Farmers, ranchers, and other agricultural managers typically need at least a high school diploma to enter the occupation. As farm and land management has grown more complex, farmers, ranchers, and other agricultural managers may benefit from postsecondary education. Associate's degree or bachelor's degree fields of study commonly include agriculture, natural resources, or business.

Most state university systems have at least one land-grant college or university with a school of agriculture. Programs of study include agricultural economics and business, animal science, and plant science.

There are a number of government programs that help farmers connect with farming services. The United States Department of Agriculture (USDA) has service centers across the country that assist new farmers in accessing USDA programs. These service centers connect farmers with programs such as those that provide financing for land and capital, help with creating a business plan, and input on conservation practices.

Work Experience in a Related Occupation

Prospective farmers, ranchers, and agricultural managers typically work as agricultural workers for several years to gain the knowledge and experience needed to run their own farm. Some gain experience while growing up on a family farm. The amount of experience needed varies with the complexity of the work and the size of the farm. Those with postsecondary education in agriculture may not need additional work experience.

Licenses, Certifications, and Registrations

To show competency in farm management, agricultural managers may choose to complete certification programs. The American Society of Farm Managers and Rural Appraisers (ASFMRA) offers the Accredited Farm Manager (AFM) credential. AFM requirements include ASFMRA coursework, a bachelor's degree, experience in farmland management, and passing an exam. A complete list of requirements is available from ASFMRA.

Important Qualities

Analytical skills. Farmers, ranchers, and other agricultural managers monitor and assess the quality of their land or livestock.

Critical-thinking skills. Farmers, ranchers, and other agricultural managers determine how to improve their harvest and livestock while reacting to conditions that may affect their short- or long-term plans.

Initiative. Many farmers, ranchers, and other agricultural managers are self-employed. They must be self-motivated in order to maximize crop or livestock production.

Interpersonal skills. Farmers, ranchers, and other agricultural managers supervise laborers and other workers, so they must be able to communicate and interact with a variety of people.

Mechanical skills. Farmers, ranchers, and other agricultural managers operate complex machinery and occasionally perform routine maintenance.

Physical stamina. Farmers, ranchers, and other agricultural managers—particularly those who work on small farms—must be able to do physically strenuous, repetitive tasks, such as bending, stooping, and lifting.

Pay

The median annual wage for farmers, ranchers, and other agricultural managers was $75,760 in May 2022. The median wage is the wage at which half the workers in an occupation earned more than that amount and half earned less. The lowest 10 percent earned less than $37,440, and the highest 10 percent earned more than $139,040.

Farmers, Ranchers, and Other Agricultural Managers

Median annual wages, May 2022

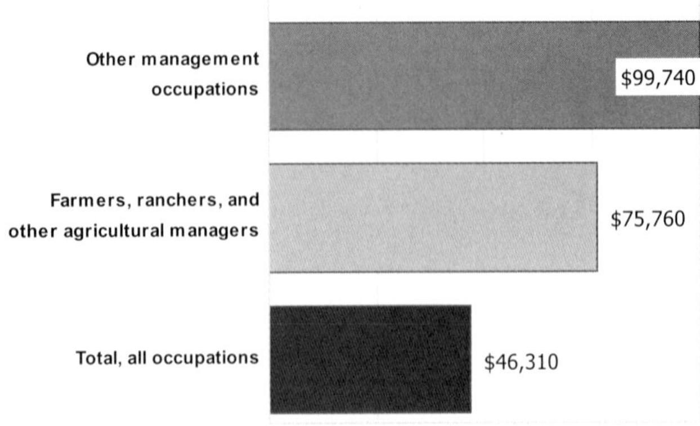

Note: All Occupations includes all occupations in the U.S. Economy.
Source: U.S. Bureau of Labor Statistics, Occupational Employment and Wage Statistics.

Incomes of farmers and ranchers vary from year to year because prices of farm products fluctuate with weather conditions and other factors. In addition to earning income from their farm business, farmers may receive government subsidies or other payments that reduce some of the risks of farming.

Most farmers, ranchers, and other agricultural managers work full time, and many work more than 40 hours per week. Farm work is often seasonal, and the number of hours worked may change according to the season. Farmers and farm managers on crop farms usually work from sunrise to sunset during the planting and harvesting seasons. During the rest of the year, they plan the next season's crops, market their output, and repair and maintain machinery. Managers of greenhouses, nurseries, or farms that operate in mild or temperate climates may work year round.

On livestock-producing farms and ranches, work goes on throughout the year. Animals must be fed and cared for daily.

Job Outlook

Employment of farmers, ranchers, and other agricultural managers is projected to decline 5 percent from 2022 to 2032.

Despite declining employment, about 88,800 openings for farmers, ranchers, and other agricultural managers are projected each year, on average, over the decade. All of those openings are expected to result from the need to replace workers who transfer to other occupations or exit the labor force, such as to retire.

Employment

Over the past several decades, increased efficiencies in crop production have led to consolidation and fewer, but larger,

Farmers, Ranchers, and Other Agricultural Managers

Percent change in employment, projected 2022-32

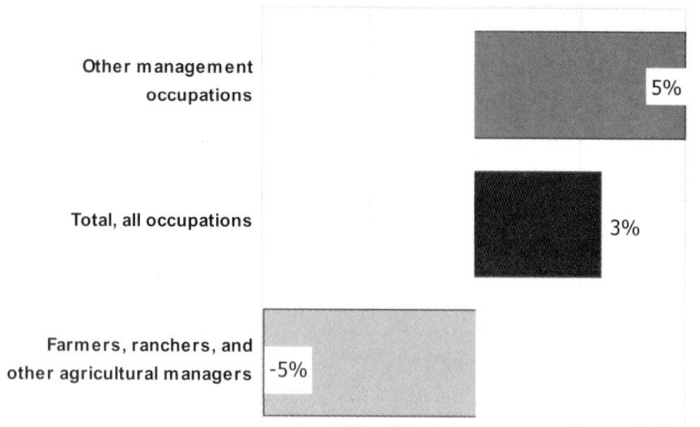

Note: All Occupations includes all occupations in the U.S. Economy.
Source: U.S. Bureau of Labor Statistics, Employment Projections program.

farms. This means that fewer farmers are needed to produce the same agricultural output. In addition, as farms become larger, they invest more in productivity-enhancing technologies, reinforcing this effect.

Despite steady demand for agricultural products, many small farms operate with slim profit margins and are vulnerable to poor market conditions. As in the past, operators of small farms will likely continue to exit the business over the decade.

Occupational Title	SOC Code	Employment, 2022	Projected Employment, 2032	Change, 2022-32	
				Percent	Numeric
Farmers, ranchers, and other agricultural managers	11-9013	922,900	880,600	-5	-42,300

Contacts for More Information

For more information, visit

- Center for Rural Affairs
- New Farmers
- Farm Service Agency
- For more information on farm manager certification, visit
- American Society of Farm Managers and Rural Appraisers

Financial Managers

Summary

Quick Facts: Financial Managers

2022 Median Pay	$139,790 per year $67.21 per hour
Typical Entry-Level Education	Bachelor's degree
Work Experience in a Related Occupation	5 years or more
On-the-job Training	None
Number of Jobs, 2022	792,600
Job Outlook, 2022-32	16% (Much faster than average)
Employment Change, 2022-32	126,600

What Financial Managers Do

Financial managers create financial reports, direct investment activities, and develop plans for the long-term financial goals of their organization.

Work Environment

Financial managers work in many industries, including banks, investment firms, and insurance companies. Most financial managers work full time, and some work more than 40 hours per week.

How to Become a Financial Manager

Financial managers typically need a bachelor's degree and 5 years or more of experience in another business or financial occupation, such as accountant, securities sales agent, or financial analyst.

Pay

The median annual wage for financial managers was $139,790 in May 2022.

Job Outlook

Employment of financial managers is projected to grow 16 percent from 2022 to 2032, much faster than the average for all occupations.

About 69,600 openings for financial managers are projected each year, on average, over the decade. Many of those openings are expected to result from the need to replace workers who transfer to different occupations or exit the labor force, such as to retire.

What Financial Managers Do

Financial managers are responsible for the financial health of an organization. They create financial reports, direct investment activities, and develop plans for the long-term financial goals of their organization.

Duties

Financial managers typically do the following:

- Prepare financial statements, business activity reports, and forecasts
- Monitor financial details to ensure that legal requirements are met
- Supervise employees who do financial reporting and budgeting
- Review financial reports and seek ways to reduce costs

Financial managers are responsible for the financial health of an organization.

- Analyze market trends to maximize profits and find expansion opportunities
- Help management make financial decisions

Financial managers spend much of their time analyzing data and advising senior managers on ways to maximize profits. They often work on teams, acting as advisors to top executives.

Financial managers must have knowledge of the topics, tax laws, and regulations that are specific to their organization or industry. For example, government financial managers must be experts on appropriations and budgeting processes; healthcare financial managers must understand billing, reimbursement, and other business matters related to healthcare.

The following are examples of types of financial managers:

Controllers direct the preparation of financial reports that summarize and forecast an organization's financial position. These reports may include income statements, balance sheets, and analyses of future earnings or expenses. Controllers also are in charge of preparing reports required by governmental agencies that regulate businesses. Often, controllers oversee the accounting, audit, and budget departments of their organization.

Treasurers and ***finance officers*** direct an organization's budgets to meet its financial goals. They oversee investments and other plans to raise capital, such as issuing stocks or bonds, to support their organization's growth. They also develop financial plans for mergers (two companies joining together) and acquisitions (one company buying another).

Credit managers oversee an organization's credit business. They set credit-rating standards, determine credit limits, and monitor the collections of past-due accounts.

Cash managers monitor and control the flow of money into and out of an organization to meet business and investment needs. For example, they must project whether the organization will have a shortage or surplus of cash.

Risk managers use strategies to limit or offset an organization's chance of financial loss or exposure to financial uncertainty. Among the risks they try to limit are those arising from currency or commodity price changes.

Insurance managers decide how to limit an organization's losses by protecting against risks, such as for disability payments to an employee who gets hurt on the job or for costs imposed by a lawsuit against the organization.

Work Environment

Financial managers held about 792,600 jobs in 2022. The largest employers of financial managers were as follows:

Finance and insurance	30%
Professional, scientific, and technical services	14
Management of companies and enterprises	10
Government	6
Manufacturing	6

Financial managers work closely with top executives and with departments that develop data needed for analysis.

Financial managers perform data analysis and advise senior managers on profit-maximizing ideas.

Financial managers work closely with top managers and with departments that develop the data that financial managers need.

Financial managers usually have experience in another business or financial occupation such as a loan officer, accountant, auditor, securities sales agent, or financial analyst.

Work Schedules

Most financial managers work full time, and some work more than 40 hours per week.

How to Become a Financial Manager

Financial managers typically need a bachelor's degree and 5 years or more of experience in another business or financial occupation, such as an accountant, securities sales agent, or financial analyst.

Education

Financial managers typically need at least a bachelor's degree in business, economics, or a related field. These disciplines help students learn analytical skills and methods.

Licenses, Certifications, and Registrations

Although it is not required, professional certification indicates competence for financial managers who have it. The Association of Government Accountants (AGA) offers the Certified Government Financial Manager (CGFM) designation to financial managers working with federal, state, or local government. To earn this certification, candidates must have a bachelor's degree from an accredited college or university, pass examinations, and have professional-level experience in government financial management. To keep the certification, CGFMs must complete continuing professional education.

The CFA Institute confers the Chartered Financial Analyst (CFA) certification to investment professionals who have at least a bachelor's degree or 4 years of work experience, or a combination of experience and education, and who pass three exams. The Association for Financial Professionals confers the Certified Treasury Professional (CTP) credential to those who have at least 2 years of relevant experience or 1 year of experience and a graduate degree in business, finance, or a related field. This association also confers the Certified Corporate Financial Planning Analysis Professional (FP&A) credential to those who have a bachelor's degree or who are currently enrolled in an undergraduate program with a finance-related major and will graduate within 2 years. Both credentials require passing an exam.

Certified public accountants (CPAs) are licensed by their state's board of accountancy and must pass an exam administered by the American Institute of Certified Public Accountants (AICPA).

Work Experience in a Related Occupation

Financial managers usually have experience in another business or financial occupation. For example, they may have worked as a loan officer, accountant, securities sales agent, or financial analyst.

In some cases, companies provide management training to help prepare motivated, skilled financial workers to become managers.

Advancement

Experienced financial managers may advance to become chief financial officers (CFOs). These executives are responsible for the accuracy of an organization's financial reporting.

Important Qualities

Analytical skills. To assist executives in making decisions, financial managers need to evaluate data and information that affects their organization.

Communication skills. Financial managers must be able to explain and justify complex financial transactions.

Detail oriented. In preparing and analyzing reports, such as balance sheets and income statements, financial managers must be precise and attentive to their work in order to avoid errors.

Math skills. Financial managers need strong skills in certain branches of mathematics, including algebra. Ability to

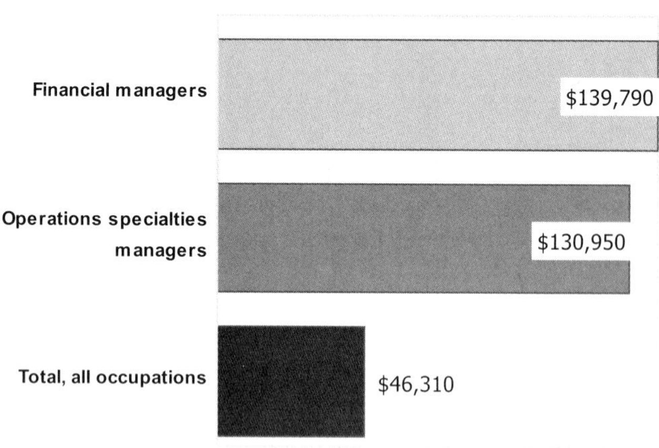

Note: All Occupations includes all occupations in the U.S. Economy.
Source: U.S. Bureau of Labor Statistics, Occupational Employment and Wage Statistics.

understand international finance and complex financial documents also is important.

Organizational skills. Because financial managers deal with a range of information and documents, they must have structures in place to be effective in their work.

Pay

The median annual wage for financial managers was $139,790 in May 2022. The median wage is the wage at which half the workers in an occupation earned more than that amount and half earned less. The lowest 10 percent earned less than $79,050, and the highest 10 percent earned more than $239,200.

In May 2022, the median annual wages for financial managers in the top industries in which they worked were as follows:

Management of companies and enterprises	$164,660
Professional, scientific, and technical services	164,490
Manufacturing	142,120
Finance and insurance	139,980
Government	124,400

Most financial managers work full time, and some work more than 40 hours per week.

Job Outlook

Employment of financial managers is projected to grow 16 percent from 2022 to 2032, much faster than the average for all occupations.

About 69,600 openings for financial managers are projected each year, on average, over the decade. Many of those openings are expected to result from the need to replace workers who transfer to different occupations or exit the labor force, such as to retire.

Employment

Services provided by financial managers, such as planning, directing, and coordinating investments, are likely to stay in demand as the economy grows. In addition, several specialties within financial management, particularly cash management and risk management, are expected to be in high demand over the decade.

Companies, particularly those with operations in foreign countries, have accumulated more cash on their balance sheets in recent years. As globalization continues, this trend is likely to persist. This practice should lead to demand for financial managers, as companies will need expertise in managing cash.

There has been an increased emphasis on risk management within the financial industry, and this trend is expected to continue. Banking institutions are expected to emphasize stability and managing risk over profits. This emphasis is expected to lead to employment growth for risk managers.

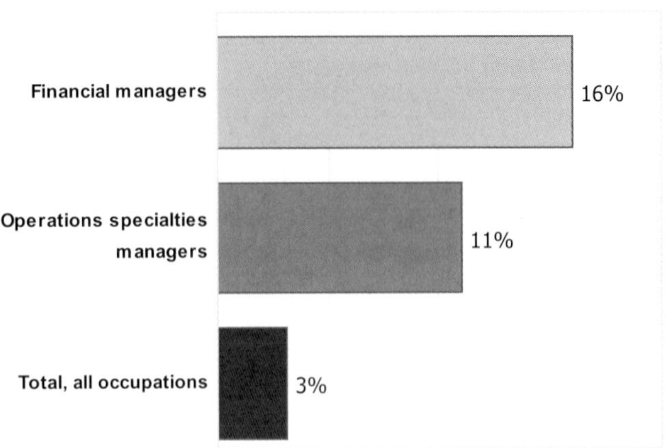

Note: All Occupations includes all occupations in the U.S. Economy.
Source: U.S. Bureau of Labor Statistics, Employment Projections program.

Employment projections data for financial managers, 2022-32

Occupational Title	SOC Code	Employment, 2022	Projected Employment, 2032	Change, 2022-32 Percent	Change, 2022-32 Numeric	Employment by Industry
SOURCE: U.S. Bureau of Labor Statistics, Employment Projections program						
Financial managers	11-3031	792,600	919,200	16	126,600	Get data

Contacts for More Information

For more information, visit

- Global Academy of Finance and Management
- Association of Government Accountants
- Association for Financial Professionals
- CFA Institute
- American Institute of Certified Public Accountants (AICPA)

Food Service Managers

Summary

Quick Facts: Food Service Managers

2022 Median Pay	$61,310 per year $29.48 per hour
Typical Entry-Level Education	High school diploma or equivalent
Work Experience in a Related Occupation	Less than 5 years
On-the-job Training	Short-term on-the-job training
Number of Jobs, 2022	357,500
Job Outlook, 2022-32	0% (Little or no change)
Employment Change, 2022-32	1,600

What Food Service Managers Do

Food service managers are responsible for the daily operation of restaurants or other establishments that prepare and serve food and beverages.

Work Environment

Food service managers work in restaurants, hotels, school cafeterias, and other establishments where food is prepared and served. They often work evenings, weekends, and holidays. The work is often hectic, and dealing with dissatisfied customers may be stressful.

How to Become a Food Service Manager

Food service managers typically need a high school diploma and several years of work experience in the food service industry. Some receive additional training at community colleges, technical or vocational schools, culinary schools, or 4-year colleges.

Pay

The median annual wage for food service managers was $61,310 in May 2022.

Job Outlook

Employment of food service managers is projected to show little or no change from 2022 to 2032.

Despite limited employment growth, about 39,600 openings for food service managers are projected each year, on average, over the decade. Most of those openings are expected to result from the need to replace workers who transfer to different occupations or exit the labor force, such as to retire.

What Food Service Managers Do

Food service managers are responsible for the daily operation of restaurants or other establishments that prepare and serve food and beverages. They direct staff to ensure that customers are satisfied with their dining experience, and they manage the business to ensure that it runs efficiently.

Duties

Food service managers typically do the following:

- Hire, train, discipline, and sometimes fire employees
- Order food and beverages, equipment, and supplies
- Oversee food preparation and other kitchen operations
- Inspect supplies, equipment, and work areas
- Ensure that employees comply with health and food safety standards
- Address complaints regarding food quality or service
- Schedule staff hours and assign duties
- Manage budgets and payroll records
- Establish standards for personnel performance and customer service

Managers coordinate activities of the kitchen and dining room staff to ensure that customers are served properly and in a timely manner. They oversee orders in the kitchen, and, if needed, they work with the chef to remedy service delays.

Food service managers are responsible for all functions of the business related to employees, including overseeing staffing and scheduling workers for each shift. During busy periods,

Food service managers are responsible for the daily operation of a restaurant.

Food service managers ensure that customers are satisfied with their dining experience.

managers may expedite service by helping to serve customers, process payments, or clean tables.

Managers also arrange for cleaning and maintenance of the equipment and facility in order to comply with health and sanitary regulations. For example, they may arrange for trash removal, pest control, and heavy cleaning when the dining room and kitchen are not in use.

In addition, managers have financial responsibilities that include budgeting, ensuring cash flow, and monitoring operational costs. They may set sales goals and determine promotional items.

Most managers prepare the payroll and manage employee records. They also may review or complete paperwork related to licensing, taxes and wages, and unemployment compensation. Although they sometimes assign these tasks to an assistant manager or a bookkeeper, most managers are responsible for the accuracy of business records.

Some managers add up the cash and charge slips and secure them in a safe place. They also may check that ovens, grills, and other equipment are properly cleaned and secured and that the establishment is locked at the close of business.

Work Environment

Food service managers held about 357,500 jobs in 2022. The largest employers of food service managers were as follows:

Restaurants and other eating places	49%
Self-employed workers	33
Special food services	5
Accommodation	2

Full-service restaurants (those with table service) may have a management team that includes a general manager, one or more assistant managers, and an executive chef.

Food service managers' work is often hectic, and dealing with dissatisfied customers may be stressful.

Injuries and illnesses

Kitchens are usually crowded and filled with dangerous objects and areas, such as hot ovens and slippery floors. As a result, injuries are a risk for food service managers, who may spend some of their time helping in the kitchen. Common hazards include slips, falls, and cuts. To reduce these risks, managers often wear nonslip shoes while in the kitchen.

Work Schedules

Most food service managers work full time, and some work more than 40 hours per week. Work schedules vary and may include early mornings, nights, weekends, and holidays. They may be called in at short notice.

Managers of food service facilities or cafeterias in schools, factories, or office buildings may be more likely to work traditional business hours.

Food service managers' schedules vary and may include nights, weekends, and holidays.

How to Become a Food Service Manager

Food service managers typically need a high school diploma and several years of experience in the food service industry working as a cook, waiter or waitress, or supervisor of food preparation and serving workers. Some receive additional training at a community college, technical or vocational school, culinary school, or 4-year college.

Education

Food service managers typically need a high school diploma, but education requirements for individual positions may vary from no formal educational credential to a college degree.

Employers may prefer to hire candidates who have postsecondary education, especially for jobs at upscale restaurants and hotels. Some food service companies, hotels, and restaurant chains recruit management trainees from college hospitality or food service management programs. These programs may require the participants to work in internships and to have food-industry–related experiences in order to graduate.

Many colleges and universities offer a bachelor's degree in restaurant and hospitality management or institutional food service management, both of which may be part of a personal and culinary services program. Another field of degree that

Some food service managers start working in industry-related jobs, such as cooks.

may be helpful for managers is business. In addition, numerous community colleges, technical institutes, and other institutions offer associate's degree programs. Some culinary schools offer programs in restaurant management with courses designed for those who want to start and run their own restaurant.

Most programs provide instruction in nutrition, sanitation, and food preparation, as well as courses in accounting, business law, and management. Some programs combine classroom and practical study with internships.

Work Experience in a Related Occupation

Most food service managers start working in related jobs, such as cooks, waiters and waitresses, or supervisors of food preparation and serving workers. They often spend years working in the food service industry, gaining experience and learning the necessary skills before they are promoted to manager positions.

Training

Food service managers typically receive on-the-job training of at least 1 month. Topics covered during this training may include food preparation, sanitation, security, company policies, personnel management, and recordkeeping.

Licenses, Certifications, and Registrations

Some states and localities require that food service managers have food safety certification. For more information, contact your state or local health department.

Although certification is not always required, managers may obtain the Food Protection Manager Certification (FPMC) by passing a food safety exam. The American National Standards Institute accredits institutions that offer the FPMC.

Important Qualities

Business skills. Food service managers must understand all aspects of the restaurant business, including how to budget for supplies, comply with regulations, and manage workers.

Communication skills. Food service managers must give clear orders to staff and be able to convey information effectively to employees and customers.

Customer-service skills. Food service managers must be courteous and attentive when dealing with patrons.

Leadership skills. Managers must establish good relationships with staff to maintain a productive work environment.

Organizational skills. Managers have many different responsibilities, including scheduling and overseeing staff, budgeting, and maintaining financial records. The larger the establishment, the more complex their job is.

Physical stamina. Managers often work long shifts and sometimes spend entire evenings actively helping to serve customers.

Problem-solving skills. Managers need to be able to resolve personnel issues and customer-related problems.

Pay

The median annual wage for food service managers was $61,310 in May 2022. The median wage is the wage at which half the workers in an occupation earned more than that amount and half earned less. The lowest 10 percent earned less than $38,740, and the highest 10 percent earned more than $100,520.

In May 2022, the median annual wages for food service managers in the top industries in which they worked were as follows:

Accommodation	$76,560
Special food services	73,350
Restaurants and other eating places	59,600

Most food service managers work full time, and some work more than 40 hours per week. Work schedules vary and may include early mornings, nights, weekends, and holidays. They may be called in at short notice.

Job Outlook

Food Service Managers

Employment of food service managers is projected to show little or no change from 2022 to 2032.

Despite limited employment growth, about 39,600 openings for food service managers are projected each year, on average, over the decade. Most of those openings are expected to result from the need to replace workers who transfer to different occupations or exit the labor force, such as to retire.

Employment

Food service managers will be needed to oversee food preparation and service as people continue to dine out, purchase takeout meals, and have food delivered to their homes or workplaces. However, more dining establishments are expected to

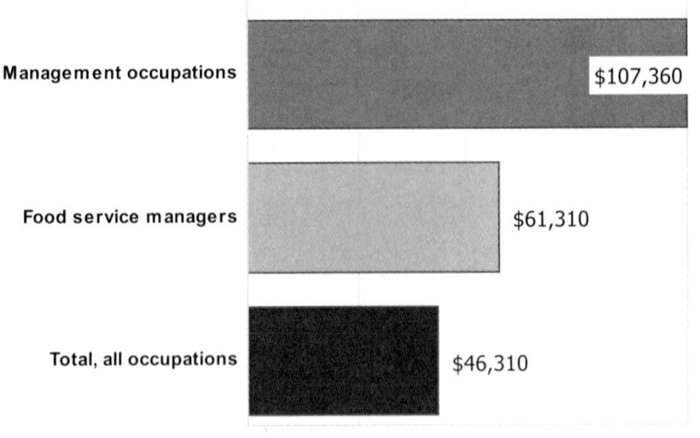

Note: All Occupations includes all occupations in the U.S. Economy.
Source: U.S. Bureau of Labor Statistics, Occupational Employment and Wage Statistics.

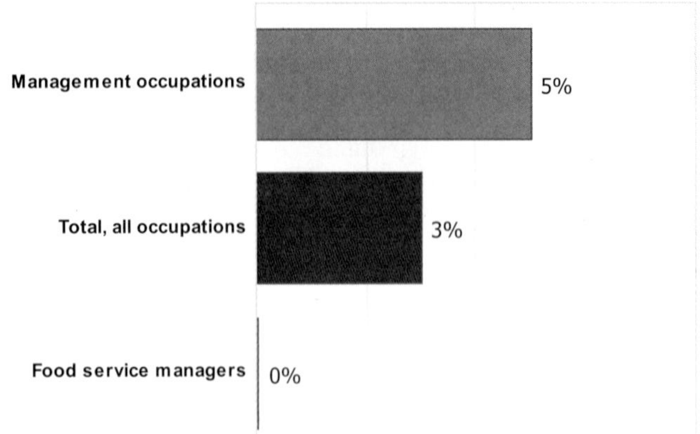

Note: All Occupations includes all occupations in the U.S. Economy.
Source: U.S. Bureau of Labor Statistics, Employment Projections program.

rely on chefs and head cooks instead of hiring additional food service managers, which should limit employment growth in this occupation.

Occupational Title	SOC Code	Employment, 2022	Projected Employment, 2032	Change, 2022-32	
				Percent	Numeric
Food service managers	11-9051	357,500	359,200	0	1,600

Contacts for More Information

For more information about the Food Protection Manager Certification, visit

- American National Standards Institute
- National Restaurant Association
- Society for Hospitality and Foodservice Management

Human Resources Managers

Summary

Quick Facts: Human Resources Managers

2022 Median Pay	$130,000 per year $62.50 per hour
Typical Entry-Level Education	Bachelor's degree
Work Experience in a Related Occupation	5 years or more
On-the-job Training	None
Number of Jobs, 2022	191,600
Job Outlook, 2022-32	5% (Faster than average)
Employment Change, 2022-32	10,000

What Human Resources Managers Do

Human resources managers plan, coordinate, and direct the administrative functions of an organization.

Work Environment

Human resources managers are employed in nearly every industry. They work in offices, and most work full time during regular business hours. Some travel to attend professional meetings or to recruit employees.

How to Become a Human Resources Manager

Candidates typically need a combination of education and several years of related work experience to become a human

Human resources managers oversee an organization's recruitment, interview, selection, and hiring processes.

Human resources managers often coordinate the work of a team of specialists.

resources manager. Although positions typically require a bachelor's degree, some require a master's degree.

Pay

The median annual wage for human resources managers was $130,000 in May 2022.

Job Outlook

Employment of human resources managers is projected to grow 5 percent from 2022 to 2032, faster than the average for all occupations.

About 15,500 openings for human resources managers are projected each year, on average, over the decade. Many of those openings are expected to result from the need to replace workers who transfer to different occupations or exit the labor force, such as to retire.

What Human Resources Managers Do

Human resources managers plan, coordinate, and direct the administrative functions of an organization. They oversee the recruiting, interviewing, and hiring of new staff; consult with top executives on strategic planning; and serve as a link between an organization's management and its employees.

Duties

Human resources managers typically do the following:

- Plan and coordinate an organization's workforce to best use employees' talents
- Link an organization's management with its employees
- Plan and oversee employee benefit programs
- Serve as a consultant to advise other managers on human resources issues, such as equal employment opportunity and sexual harassment
- Coordinate and supervise the work of specialists and support staff
- Oversee an organization's recruitment, interview, selection, and hiring processes
- Handle staffing issues, such as mediating disputes and directing disciplinary procedures

Organizations want to attract, motivate, and keep qualified employees and match them to jobs for which they are well-suited. Human resources managers accomplish this aim by directing the administrative functions of human resources departments. Their work involves overseeing employee relations, securing regulatory compliance, and administering employee-related services such as payroll, training, and benefits. They supervise the department's specialists and support staff and make sure that tasks are completed accurately and on time.

Human resources managers also consult with top executives regarding strategic planning and talent management. They identify ways to maximize the value of the organization's employees and ensure that they are used efficiently. For example, they might assess worker productivity and recommend changes to help the organization meet budgetary goals.

Some human resources managers oversee all aspects of an organization's human resources department, including the compensation and benefits program and the training and development program. In many larger organizations, these programs are directed by specialized managers, such as compensation and benefits managers and training and development managers.

The following are examples of types of human resources managers:

Labor relations directors, also called ***employee relations managers***, oversee employment policies in union and nonunion settings. They negotiate, draft, and administer labor contracts that cover issues such as wages, benefits, and union and management practices. They also handle labor complaints between employees and management, and they coordinate grievance procedures.

Payroll managers supervise an organization's payroll department. They ensure that all aspects of payroll are processed correctly and on time. They administer payroll procedures, prepare reports for the accounting department, and resolve payroll problems.

Recruiting managers, sometimes called ***staffing managers***, oversee the recruiting and hiring responsibilities of the human resources department. They often supervise a team of recruiters, and some take on recruiting duties for filling high-level positions. They must develop a recruiting strategy that helps them meet the staffing needs of their organization and compete effectively to attract the best employees.

Work Environment

Human resources managers held about 191,600 jobs in 2022. The largest employers of human resources managers were as follows:

Professional, scientific, and technical services	15%
Management of companies and enterprises	13
Manufacturing	10
Healthcare and social assistance	8
Government	8

Human resources managers work in offices. Some managers, especially those working for organizations that have offices nationwide, travel to visit other branches, attend professional meetings, or recruit employees.

Work Schedules

Most human resources managers work full time during regular business hours. Some human resources managers work more than 40 hours per week.

How to Become a Human Resources Manager

Candidates typically need a combination of education and several years of related work experience to become a human resources manager. Although most positions require a bachelor's degree, some require a master's degree.

Education

Human resources managers typically need a bachelor's degree to enter the occupation. The degree may be in human resources or another field, such as business, communications, or psychology. Courses in subjects such as conflict management may be helpful.

Some jobs may require a master's degree in human resources, labor relations, or business administration (MBA).

Human resources managers typically need a combination of a bachelor's degree and work experience.

Work Experience in a Related Occupation

To demonstrate abilities in organizing, directing, and leading others, human resources managers must have related work experience. Some managers start out as human resources specialists or labor relations specialists.

Management positions typically require an understanding of human resources programs, such as compensation and benefits plans; human resources software; and federal, state, and local employment laws.

Licenses, Certifications, and Registrations

Although certification is voluntary, it shows professional expertise and credibility, and it may enhance job opportunities. Employers may prefer to hire candidates with certification, and some positions may require it. The Society for Human Resource Management (SHRM), HR Certification Institute (HRCI), WorldatWork, and International Foundation of Employee Benefit Plans are among many professional associations that offer certification programs.

Important Qualities

Communication skills. Human resources managers need strong speaking, writing, and listening skills to give presentations and direct their staff.

Decision-making skills. Human resources managers must be able to balance the strengths and weaknesses of different options and decide the best course of action.

Interpersonal skills. Human resources managers regularly interact with people, such as to collaborate on teams, and must develop working relationships with their colleagues.

Leadership skills. Human resources managers must coordinate work activities and ensure that staff complete the duties and responsibilities of their department.

Organizational skills. Human resources managers must be able to prioritize tasks and manage several projects at once.

Pay

The median annual wage for human resources managers was $130,000 in May 2022. The median wage is the wage at which half the workers in an occupation earned more than that amount and half earned less. The lowest 10 percent earned less than $76,610, and the highest 10 percent earned more than $224,360.

In May 2022, the median annual wages for human resources managers in the top industries in which they worked were as follows:

Professional, scientific, and technical services	$153,830
Management of companies and enterprises	144,640

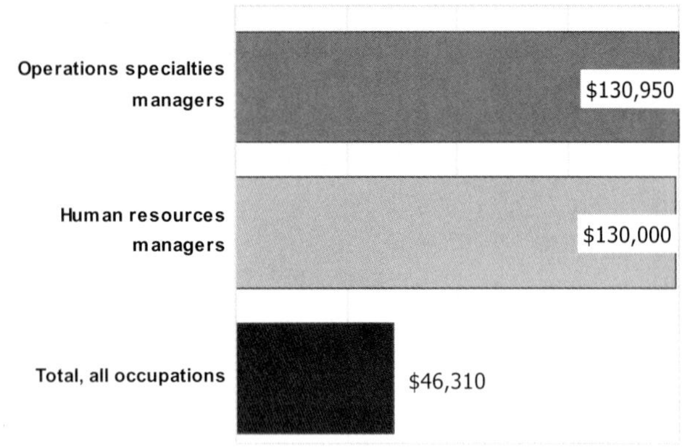

Note: All Occupations includes all occupations in the U.S. Economy.
Source: U.S. Bureau of Labor Statistics, Occupational Employment and Wage Statistics.

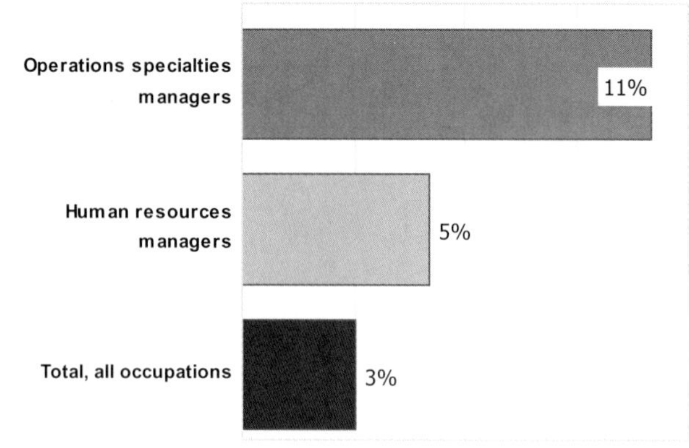

Note: All Occupations includes all occupations in the U.S. Economy.
Source: U.S. Bureau of Labor Statistics, Employment Projections program.

Manufacturing	128,620
Government	109,990
Healthcare and social assistance	107,120

Most human resources managers work full time during regular business hours. Some human resources managers work more than 40 hours per week.

Job Outlook

Employment of human resources managers is projected to grow 5 percent from 2022 to 2032, faster than the average for all occupations.

About 15,500 openings for human resources managers are projected each year, on average, over the decade. Many of those openings are expected to result from the need to replace workers who transfer to different occupations or exit the labor force, such as to retire.

Employment

Employment growth depends largely on the performance and growth of individual companies. As new companies form and organizations expand their operations, they will need more human resources managers to administer and monitor their programs.

Human resources managers also will be needed to ensure that firms adhere to changing and complex employment laws regarding topics such as equal employment opportunity, healthcare, and retirement plans.

Employment projections data for human resources managers, 2022-32

Occupational Title	SOC Code	Employment, 2022	Projected Employment, 2032	Change, 2022-32 Percent	Change, 2022-32 Numeric	Employment by Industry
SOURCE: U.S. Bureau of Labor Statistics, Employment Projections program						
Human resources managers	11-3121	191,600	201,600	5	10,000	Get data

Contacts for More Information

For more information about human resources managers, including certification, visit

- Society for Human Resource Management
- HR Certification Institute
- International Public Management Association for Human Resources
- International Foundation of Employee Benefit Plans
- WorldatWork
- Association for Talent Development
- International Society for Performance Improvement

Industrial Production Managers

Summary

Quick Facts: Industrial Production Managers	
2022 Median Pay	$107,560 per year $51.71 per hour
Typical Entry-Level Education	Bachelor's degree
Work Experience in a Related Occupation	5 years or more
On-the-job Training	None
Number of Jobs, 2022	222,100
Job Outlook, 2022-32	2% (As fast as average)
Employment Change, 2022-32	3,600

What Industrial Production Managers Do

Industrial production managers oversee the operations of manufacturing and related plants.

Work Environment

Most industrial production managers work full time, and some work more than 40 hours per week.

How to Become an Industrial Production Manager

Industrial production managers typically need a bachelor's degree and several years of related work experience.

Pay

The median annual wage for industrial production managers was $107,560 in May 2022.

Job Outlook

Employment of industrial production managers is projected to grow 2 percent from 2022 to 2032, about as fast as the average for all occupations.

About 15,300 openings for industrial production managers are projected each year, on average, over the decade. Many of those openings are expected to result from the need to replace workers who transfer to different occupations or exit the labor force, such as to retire.

Industrial production managers develop the manufacturing plan and establish procedures for manufacturing plants.

What Industrial Production Managers Do

Industrial production managers oversee the operations of manufacturing and related plants. They coordinate, plan, and direct activities involved in creating a range of goods, such as cars, computer equipment, and paper products.

Duties

Industrial production managers typically do the following:

- Decide how best to use a plant's workers and equipment to meet production goals
- Ensure that production stays on schedule and within budget
- Communicate with sales staff, customers, and suppliers
- Hire, train, and evaluate workers
- Analyze production data
- Review production reports
- Monitor a plant's workers and programs to ensure they meet performance and safety requirements
- Streamline the production process
- Assess whether production needs, such as for equipment upgrades or overtime work, are within budget
- Lead staff in resolving problems or improving production

Industrial production managers, also called *plant managers*, may oversee an entire manufacturing plant or a specific area of production.

Some industrial production managers are responsible for carrying out quality control programs to make sure the finished product meets standards for quality. Often called *quality control systems managers*, their work helps to identify a defect in products, identify the cause of the defect, and solve the problem that created it. For example, a manager may determine that a defect is being caused by parts from an outside supplier. The manager can then work with the supplier to improve the quality of the parts.

Industrial production managers who oversee an entire plant often work closely with managers from other departments, such as sales, warehousing, and research and design. For example, they might coordinate with a manager for the procurement (buying) department about orders for supplies that the production department needs.

Work Environment

Industrial production managers held about 222,100 jobs in 2022. The largest employers of industrial production managers were as follows:

Transportation equipment manufacturing	11%
Fabricated metal product manufacturing	9
Chemical manufacturing	9

Industrial production managers monitor a plant's workers to ensure they meet safety standards.

Food manufacturing	7
Machinery manufacturing	7

Industrial production managers spend some of their time in an office and some of it in the production area. When they are in the production area, they may need to wear protective equipment, such as a helmet, hearing protection, or safety goggles.

Work Schedules

Most industrial production managers work full time, and some work more than 40 hours per week. They may need to be on call to deal with emergencies at any time. Some industrial production managers work night or weekend shifts.

How to Become an Industrial Production Manager

Industrial production managers typically need a bachelor's degree and several years of related work experience.

Education

Employers typically require or prefer that industrial production managers have a bachelor's degree. However, some workers qualify for jobs if they have a high school diploma and extensive production experience.

For workers who have a degree, common majors include business and engineering. Some employers prefer to hire industrial production managers who have a Master of Business Administration (MBA) or a graduate degree in industrial management.

Work Experience in a Related Occupation

Industrial production managers usually need years of work experience in supervisory or other leadership positions. Some begin as production workers and move up through the ranks.

Industrial production workers usually advance to supervisory or other leadership positions before eventually becoming industrial production managers. Some take company-sponsored management classes to increase their chances of a promotion.

Those with a college degree might begin as a supervisor or lower-level manager. Other college graduates may be hired as an industrial production manager and complete training programs. Some begin working as an industrial production manager directly after college or graduate school. They may spend their first few months in training programs, becoming familiar with the production process, company policies, and safety regulations. In large companies, they may spend short periods of time working in other departments, such as purchasing or accounting, to learn more about the company.

Licenses, Certifications, and Registrations

Although they are not required to do so, industrial production managers may earn certifications to demonstrate competency in quality or management systems. The American Society of Quality (ASQ) offers credentials in quality control and various levels of Six Sigma certifications. Because these credentials often require specific work experience, they typically are not available prior to entering the occupation.

Important Qualities

Business skills. Industrial production managers handle budgets for production facilities, hire and manage staff, and coordinate work between different departments.

Interpersonal skills. Industrial production managers must have excellent communication skills to work well other

Industrial production managers work in a variety of manufacturing industries.

Industrial production managers need leadership and interpersonal skills to supervise manufacturing employees.

managers and with staff. Some industrial production managers oversee customer relationships.

Leadership skills. To keep the production process running smoothly, industrial production managers must motivate and direct employees.

Organizational skills. Industrial production managers must keep track of many details to efficiently manage the operations of a production facility.

Problem-solving skills. Production managers must identify and address problems that arise. For example, if a product has a defect, the manager determines whether it is a one-time problem or the result of the production process.

Pay

The median annual wage for industrial production managers was $107,560 in May 2022. The median wage is the wage at which half the workers in an occupation earned more than that amount and half earned less. The lowest 10 percent earned less than $67,720, and the highest 10 percent earned more than $178,470.

In May 2022, the median annual wages for industrial production managers in the top industries in which they worked were as follows:

Chemical manufacturing	$127,140
Transportation equipment manufacturing	120,130
Machinery manufacturing	103,610
Food manufacturing	101,580
Fabricated metal product manufacturing	99,140

Most industrial production managers work full time, and some work more than 40 hours per week. They may need to be on call to deal with emergencies at any time. Some industrial production managers work night or weekend shifts.

Job Outlook

Employment of industrial production managers is projected to grow 2 percent from 2022 to 2032, about as fast as the average for all occupations.

About 15,300 openings for industrial production managers are projected each year, on average, over the decade. Many of those openings are expected to result from the need to replace workers who transfer to different occupations or exit the labor force, such as to retire.

Employment

Most of these managers are employed in manufacturing industries, some of which are expected to have declining employment due to greater productivity. However, because industrial production managers are responsible for coordinating work activities with the goal of increasing productivity, they will continue to be needed in this capacity.

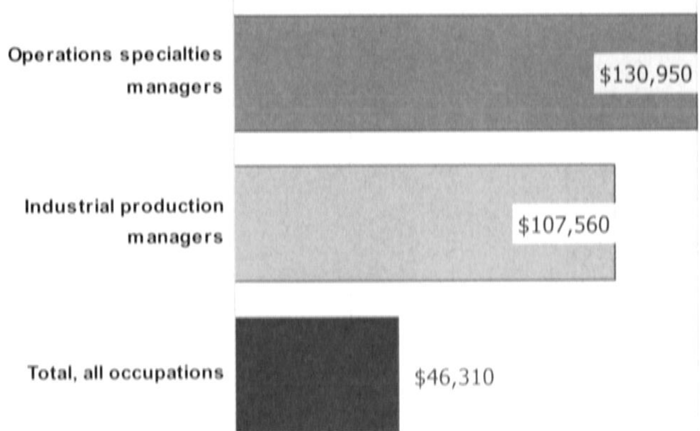

Note: All Occupations includes all occupations in the U.S. Economy. Source: U.S. Bureau of Labor Statistics, Occupational Employment and Wage Statistics.

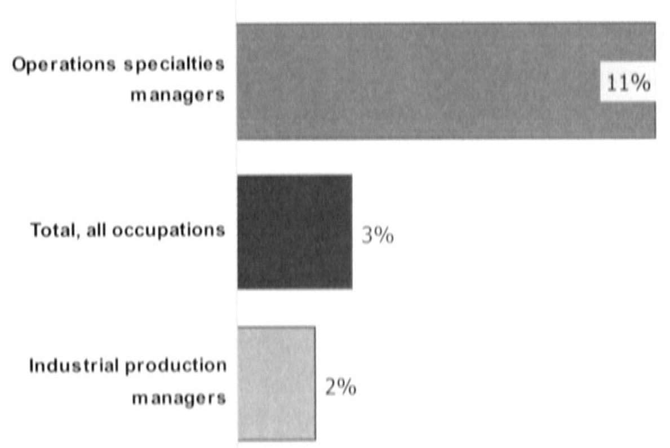

Note: All Occupations includes all occupations in the U.S. Economy. Source: U.S. Bureau of Labor Statistics, Employment Projections program.

Employment projections data for industrial production managers, 2022-32

Occupational Title	SOC Code	Employment, 2022	Projected Employment, 2032	Change, 2022-32 Percent	Change, 2022-32 Numeric	Employment by Industry
Industrial production managers	11-3051	222,100	225,700	2	3,600	Get data

SOURCE: U.S. Bureau of Labor Statistics, Employment Projections program

Contacts for More Information

For more information about quality management and certification, visit

- American Society for Quality
- National Association of Manufacturers

Lodging Managers

Summary

Quick Facts: Lodging Managers

2022 Median Pay	\$61,910 per year \$29.76 per hour
Typical Entry-Level Education	High school diploma or equivalent
Work Experience in a Related Occupation	Less than 5 years
On-the-job Training	None
Number of Jobs, 2022	50,800
Job Outlook, 2022-32	7% (Faster than average)
Employment Change, 2022-32	3,400

What Lodging Managers Do

Lodging managers ensure that guests have a pleasant experience at an accommodations facility. They also plan, direct, or coordinate activities to ensure that the facility is efficient and profitable.

Work Environment

Most lodging managers work full time. Work schedules may vary and often include evenings, weekends, and holidays. Because these facilities are open around the clock, some managers are on call 24 hours a day.

How to Become a Lodging Manager

To enter the occupation, lodging managers typically take one of three paths: a high school diploma combined with several years of experience working in a lodging facility, a bachelor's degree in hospitality or hotel management, or an associate's degree or certificate in hotel management.

Pay

The median annual wage for lodging managers was \$61,910 in May 2022.

Job Outlook

Employment of lodging managers is projected to grow 7 percent from 2022 to 2032, faster than the average for all occupations.

About 5,400 openings for lodging managers are projected each year, on average, over the decade. Many of those openings are expected to result from the need to replace workers who transfer to different occupations or exit the labor force, such as to retire.

Lodging managers greet and register guests.

Lodging managers ensure that company standards for guest services are met.

What Lodging Managers Do

Lodging managers ensure that guests have a pleasant experience at a hotel, motel, or other type of facility with accommodations. Lodging managers also plan, direct, or coordinate activities to ensure that the facility is efficient and profitable.

Duties

Lodging managers typically do the following:

- Inspect guest rooms, public areas, and grounds for cleanliness and appearance
- Ensure that company standards for guest services, décor, and housekeeping are met
- Answer questions from guests about the lodging facility's policies and services
- Interview, hire, train, and sometimes fire staff members
- Monitor staff performance to ensure that guests are happy and that the facility is well run
- Coordinate the facility's front-desk activities and resolve problems
- Set budgets, approve expenditures, and allocate funds to various departments
- Keep track of how much money the facility is making

A comfortable room and a helpful staff can make being away from home an enjoyable experience for guests. Lodging managers, who occasionally greet and register guests, try to make sure that guests have a good experience.

Lodging establishments vary in size, from bed and breakfasts with just a few rooms to resorts with thousands of rooms. Facilities are sometimes identified according to the level of amenities they offer, such as limited service or full service. The larger the number of amenities a facility provides—for example, a swimming pool, a casino, and a restaurant—the greater the range of duties for lodging managers who oversee them.

The following are examples of types of lodging managers:

Convention service managers coordinate the activities of various departments, to accommodate meetings, conventions, and special events. They meet with representatives of groups to plan the number of conference rooms to be reserved, design the configuration of the meeting space, and determine what other services the groups will need, such as catering or audiovisual requirements. During a meeting or event, they resolve unexpected problems and ensure that facility operations meet a group's expectations.

Front-desk managers coordinate reservations and room assignments and train and direct the facility's front-desk staff. They ensure that guests are treated courteously, that complaints and problems are resolved, and that requests for special services are carried out. Most front-desk managers are also responsible for adjusting bills.

General managers oversee all lodging operations at a facility. At large establishments with several departments and multiple layers of management, the general manager and several

The majority of lodging managers work in traditional hotels and motels.

assistant managers coordinate the activities of separate departments. These departments may include human resources, marketing and sales, recreational facilities, and others. For more information, see the profiles on human resources managers; public relations and fundraising managers; financial managers; advertising, promotions, and marketing managers; and food service managers.

Revenue managers direct a property's finances. Their responsibilities include monitoring room sales and reservations, overseeing accounting and cash-flow matters, projecting occupancy levels, and deciding which rooms to discount and when to offer special rates.

Work Environment

Lodging managers held about 50,800 jobs in 2022. The largest employers of lodging managers were as follows:

Traveler accommodation	69%
Self-employed workers	17
RV (recreational vehicle) parks and recreational camps	4

The pressures of coordinating a wide range of activities, turning a profit for investors, and dealing with dissatisfied guests may be stressful.

Work Schedules

Most lodging managers work full time. Work schedules may vary and often include evenings, weekends, and holidays. Because these facilities are open around the clock, some managers are on call 24 hours a day.

How to Become a Lodging Manager

To enter the occupation, lodging managers typically take one of three paths: a high school diploma combined with several years of experience working in a lodging facility, a bachelor's degree in hospitality or hotel management, or an associate's degree or certificate in hotel management.

Most full-service hotel chains prefer candidates with a degree in hospitality or hotel management.

Education

Lodging managers typically need at least a high school diploma to enter the occupation. High school students interested in becoming a lodging manger may benefit from taking classes in hospitality management, which may be offered at some high schools.

Full-service facilities may prefer to hire candidates who have a bachelor's degree in hospitality or hotel management. Hotel management programs typically include instruction in hotel administration, housekeeping, food service management, and hotel maintenance, as well as in business subjects such as accounting, marketing, and sales. Systems training is also an integral part of many degree programs, because lodging facilities use hospitality-specific software in reservations, billing, and housekeeping management. Employers may seek candidates whose degree is from an accredited hospitality management program.

At limited-service facilities, candidates with an associate's degree or a certificate in hotel, restaurant, or hospitality management may qualify for lodging manager positions. Technical institutes and vocational or trade schools also may offer courses that are recognized by the hospitality industry.

Work Experience in a Related Occupation

To enter the occupation, lodging managers with a high school diploma or its equivalent typically need experience working in guest services, at the front desk, or in related positions. Candidates with a degree often have experience too, which they gain through internships or by working as a management trainee.

Licenses, Certifications, and Registrations

Professional certification may be beneficial. For example, the American Hotel & Lodging Educational Institute (AHLEI) offers the Certified Hospitality and Tourism Management Program (CHTMP) for high school students, which requires passing exams and completing industry work experience. College students and working professionals can obtain the Certification in Hotel Industry Analytics (CHIA) through AHLEI.

Advancement

Lodging facility employees who show leadership potential and have several years of experience may qualify for assistant manager positions.

Large facilities, including well-established chains, may offer better advancement opportunities than small, independently owned ones. For example, opportunities may include advancing from assistant manager to manager or from managing one facility to managing several in a region.

Important Qualities

Business skills. Lodging managers need to operate a facility that is profitable. To do so, they must be able to address budget matters and coordinate and supervise workers.

Customer-service skills. Lodging managers must have excellent customer-service skills. Satisfying guests is critical to a facility's success and helps to ensure their loyalty.

Interpersonal skills. Lodging managers interact regularly with many different people. They must be effective communicators and be able to have positive interactions with guests and staff, even in stressful situations.

Leadership skills. Lodging managers must establish a productive work environment, which may involve motivating personnel, resolving conflicts, and handling guests' complaints.

Listening skills. Lodging managers must have excellent listening skills for attending to the needs of guests and maintaining a good working relationship with staff.

Organizational skills. Lodging managers need to keep track of many different schedules, budgets, and people at once.

Problem-solving skills. Lodging managers must be able to resolve personnel issues and guest complaints.

Pay

The median annual wage for lodging managers was $61,910 in May 2022. The median wage is the wage at which half the workers in an occupation earned more than that amount and half earned less. The lowest 10 percent earned less than $36,860, and the highest 10 percent earned more than $122,440.

In May 2022, the median annual wages for lodging managers in the top industries in which they worked were as follows:

Traveler accommodation	$61,760
RV (recreational vehicle) parks and recreational camps	58,880

Most lodging managers work full time. Work schedules may vary and often include evenings, weekends, and holidays. Because these facilities are open around the clock, some managers are on call 24 hours a day.

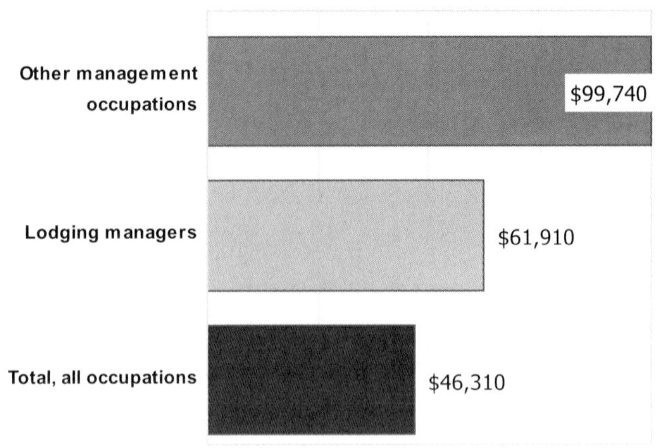

Note: All Occupations includes all occupations in the U.S. Economy. Source: U.S. Bureau of Labor Statistics, Occupational Employment and Wage Statistics.

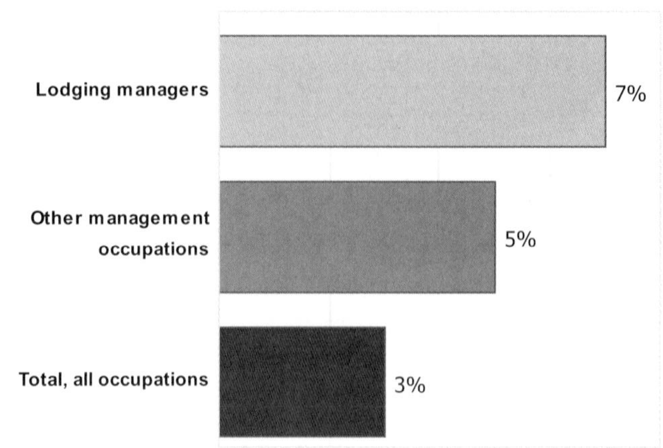

Note: All Occupations includes all occupations in the U.S. Economy. Source: U.S. Bureau of Labor Statistics, Employment Projections program.

Job Outlook

Employment of lodging managers is projected to grow 7 percent from 2022 to 2032, faster than the average for all occupations.

About 5,400 openings for lodging managers are projected each year, on average, over the decade. Many of those openings are expected to result from the need to replace workers who transfer to different occupations or exit the labor force, such as to retire.

Employment

Overall travel spending patterns will translate to strong demand for lodging managers in hotels and other lodging establishments. However, the growth of short-term rentals has offered competition for traditional hotels, which may limit demand for these workers.

Employment projections data for lodging managers, 2022-32

Occupational Title	SOC Code	Employ-ment, 2022	Projected Employment, 2032	Change, 2022-32		Employment by Industry
				Percent	Numeric	
SOURCE: U.S. Bureau of Labor Statistics, Employment Projections program						
Lodging managers	11-9081	50,800	54,200	7	3,400	Get data

Contacts for More Information

For information, visit

- American Hotel & Lodging Educational Institute (AHLEI)
- Association of Lodging Professionals (ALP)
- Accreditation Commission for Programs in Hospitality Administration (ACPHA)
- International Council on Hotel, Restaurant, and Institutional Education (CHRIE)

Medical and Health Services Managers

Summary

Quick Facts: Medical and Health Services Managers	
2022 Median Pay	$104,830 per year $50.40 per hour
Typical Entry-Level Education	Bachelor's degree
Work Experience in a Related Occupation	Less than 5 years
On-the-job Training	None
Number of Jobs, 2022	509,500
Job Outlook, 2022-32	28% (Much faster than average)
Employment Change, 2022-32	144,700

What Medical and Health Services Managers Do

Medical and health services managers plan, direct, and coordinate the business activities of healthcare providers.

Work Environment

Most medical and health services managers work in healthcare facilities, including hospitals and nursing homes, and group medical practices. Most work full time, and some work more than 40 hours per week.

How to Become a Medical or Health Services Manager

Medical and health services managers typically need a bachelor's degree to enter the occupation; however, education requirements may vary. Prospective managers also typically need work experience in an administrative or clinical role in a hospital or other healthcare facility.

Pay

The median annual wage for medical and health services managers was $104,830 in May 2022.

Medical and health services managers plan, direct, and coordinate the delivery of healthcare.

Job Outlook

Employment of medical and health services managers is projected to grow 28 percent from 2022 to 2032, much faster than the average for all occupations.

About 54,700 openings for medical and health services managers are projected each year, on average, over the decade. Many of those openings are expected to result from the need to replace workers who transfer to different occupations or exit the labor force, such as to retire.

What Medical and Health Services Managers Do

Medical and health services managers, also called *healthcare executives* or *healthcare administrators*, plan, direct, and coordinate medical and health services. They may manage an entire facility, a specific clinical area or department, or a medical practice for a group of physicians. Medical and health services managers must adapt to changes in healthcare laws, regulations, and technology.

Duties

Medical and health services managers typically do the following:

In group medical practices, medical and health services managers work closely with physicians.

- Develop goals and objectives related to efficiency and quality of healthcare services
- Ensure that the facility in which they work complies with laws and regulations
- Prepare and monitor budgets and manage finances, including patient fees and billing
- Recruit, train, and supervise staff members
- Create work schedules
- Represent the facility or department at investor meetings or on governing boards
- Keep and organize records of facility services, such as the number of inpatient beds used

Medical and health services managers set and carry out policies, goals, and procedures for their departments or facilities. Their duties include hiring, scheduling, and evaluating staff; monitoring compliance with state and federal guidelines; and developing reports and budgets. Responsibilities may vary by employer. For example, managers of large facilities may focus on broad oversight, while tasks for those in small departments might include ordering medical supplies and materials.

Medical and health services managers work with physicians and surgeons, registered nurses, medical records specialists, and other healthcare personnel. They also may interact with patients or insurance agents.

Medical and health services managers' titles depend on their facility or area of expertise.

The following are examples of types of medical and health services managers:

Nursing home administrators manage all aspects of a facility, including admissions and building maintenance, as well as care of its residents.

Clinical managers oversee a department, such as intensive care or physical therapy, and have responsibilities based on that specialty.

Health information managers ensure that databases of patient records are complete, accurate, and accessible only to authorized personnel.

Some medical and health services managers oversee the activities of a number of facilities.

Work Environment

Medical and health services managers held about 509,500 jobs in 2022. The largest employers of medical and health services managers were as follows:

Hospitals; state, local, and private	30%
Offices of physicians	12
Nursing and residential care facilities	9
Government	7
Outpatient care centers	7

Medical and health services managers may work on a team with other healthcare providers, such as licensed practical nurses and medical assistants.

Work Schedules

Most medical and health services managers work full time, and some work more than 40 hours per week. Evening or weekend work may be required in healthcare settings that operate around the clock, such as hospitals and nursing homes. Medical and health services managers may need to be on call in case of emergencies.

How to Become a Medical or Health Services Manager

Medical and health services managers typically need a bachelor's degree to enter the occupation; however, educational requirements vary by facility and specific function. Prospective managers also typically need work experience in an administrative or clinical role in a hospital or other healthcare facility.

Education

Medical and health services managers typically need a bachelor's degree to enter the occupation, although requirements may vary. For example, some employers hire candidates with

Medical and health services managers must effectively communicate policies and procedures with other health professionals.

an associate's degree; others prefer to hire those with a master's degree. Work experience sometimes may substitute for education.

Common majors for medical and health services managers include healthcare and related fields, such as health administration or nursing, or other relevant fields, such as business. Degrees that focus on both management and healthcare combine business-related topics with those such as medical terminology, hospital organization, and health information systems. For example, a degree in health administration or health information management may include courses in health services management, accounting and budgeting, and health informatics.

Work Experience in a Related Occupation

Employers may require prospective medical and health services managers to have work experience in either an administrative or a clinical role in a hospital or other healthcare facility. For example, nursing home administrators may have years of experience working as a registered nurse.

Other managers may begin their careers as medical records specialists, administrative assistants, or financial clerks in a healthcare office.

Licenses, Certifications, and Registrations

Some medical and health services managers need a state-issued license. For example, all states require licensure for nursing home administrators; requirements vary by state. For more information, contact your local or state licensing board.

Some positions may require candidates to be licensed as a registered nurse or social worker.

Although certification is not required, some managers choose to earn a professional credential. For example, the American Health Information Management Association and the Project Management Institute offer certification specific to their areas of focus.

Advancement

Some health information managers advance by taking on additional responsibilities, such as for an entire hospital's information systems. Other managers may advance to top executive positions within an organization. Advancement to top level executive positions may require a master's degree.

Important Qualities

Analytical skills. Medical and health services managers review and evaluate healthcare metrics for ways to improve efficiency and meet goals.

Communication skills. Medical and health services managers must convey information to their staff, other healthcare workers, and, sometimes, patients and insurance agents.

Detail oriented. Medical and health services managers must pay attention to detail. They might be required to organize and

Medical and Health Services Managers

Median annual wages, May 2022

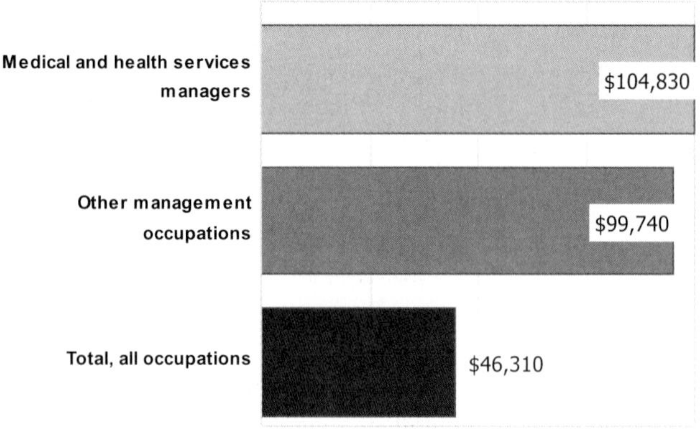

Note: All Occupations includes all occupations in the U.S. Economy.
Source: U.S. Bureau of Labor Statistics, Occupational Employment and Wage Statistics.

maintain scheduling and billing information for very large facilities, such as hospitals.

Leadership skills. Medical and health services managers hire, train, and direct staff. They must be able to motivate others and create an environment in which workers can succeed.

Technical skills. Medical and health services managers must stay up to date with advances in healthcare technology, such as the coding and electronic health record (EHR) systems their facility adopts.

Pay

The median annual wage for medical and health services managers was $104,830 in May 2022. The median wage is the wage at which half the workers in an occupation earned more than that amount and half earned less. The lowest 10 percent earned less than $64,100, and the highest 10 percent earned more than $209,990.

In May 2022, the median annual wages for medical and health services managers in the top industries in which they worked were as follows:

Hospitals; state, local, and private	$125,280
Government	119,100
Outpatient care centers	101,890
Offices of physicians	99,440
Nursing and residential care facilities	93,610

Most medical and health services managers work full time, and some work more than 40 hours per week. Evening or weekend work may be required in healthcare settings that operate around the clock, such as hospitals and nursing homes. Medical and health services managers may need to be on call in case of emergencies.

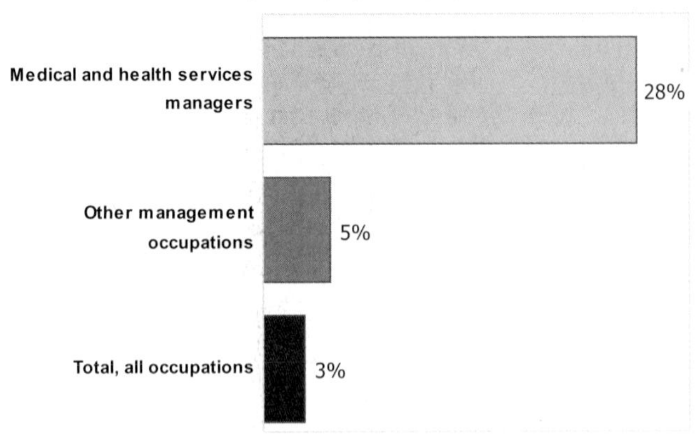

Note: All Occupations includes all occupations in the U.S. Economy.
Source: U.S. Bureau of Labor Statistics, Employment Projections program.

Job Outlook

Employment of medical and health services managers is projected to grow 28 percent from 2022 to 2032, much faster than the average for all occupations.

About 54,700 openings for medical and health services managers are projected each year, on average, over the decade. Many of those openings are expected to result from the need to replace workers who transfer to different occupations or exit the labor force, such as to retire.

Employment

As the large baby-boom population enters older age groups, which typically experience more health problems, there should be increased demand for healthcare services. This means there will be greater need for physicians and other healthcare workers, medical procedures, and healthcare facilities, and therefore greater need for managers to organize and oversee medical information and healthcare staff. These managers are important for improving care coordination, which is key in team-based care.

In addition, widespread use of electronic health records (EHRs) will continue to create demand for managers with knowledge of health information technology (IT) and informatics systems. Medical and health services managers will be needed to organize, oversee, and integrate these records across areas of the healthcare industry.

Employment projections data for medical and health services managers, 2022-32

Occupational Title	SOC Code	Employment, 2022	Projected Employment, 2032	Change, 2022-32		Employment by Industry
				Percent	Numeric	
SOURCE: U.S. Bureau of Labor Statistics, Employment Projections program						
Medical and health services managers	11-9111	509,500	654,200	28	144,700	Get data

Contacts for More Information

For more information about medical and healthcare management, visit

- Professional Association of Health Care Office Management
- American Health Information Management Association
- American College of Health Care Administrators
- Association of University Programs in Health Administration
- Commission on Accreditation of Healthcare Management Education
- American College of Healthcare Executives
- Medical Group Management Association
- National Association of Long Term Care Administrator Boards
- Project Management Institute

Natural Sciences Managers

Summary

Quick Facts: Natural Sciences Managers	
2022 Median Pay	$144,440 per year $69.44 per hour
Typical Entry-Level Education	Bachelor's degree
Work Experience in a Related Occupation	5 years or more
On-the-job Training	None
Number of Jobs, 2022	86,300
Job Outlook, 2022-32	5% (Faster than average)
Employment Change, 2022-32	4,200

What Natural Sciences Managers Do
Natural sciences managers supervise the work of scientists, including chemists, physicists, and biologists.

Work Environment
Natural sciences managers spend most of their time in offices, but they also may spend time in laboratories. Most natural sciences managers work full time.

How to Become a Natural Sciences Manager
Natural sciences managers typically need at least a bachelor's degree in a natural science or a related field. Most natural sciences managers work as scientists before becoming managers.

Pay
The median annual wage for natural sciences managers was $144,440 in May 2022.

Job Outlook
Employment of natural sciences managers is projected to grow 5 percent from 2022 to 2032, faster than the average for all occupations.

About 6,500 openings for natural sciences managers are projected each year, on average, over the decade. Many of those openings are expected to result from the need to replace workers who transfer to different occupations or exit the labor force, such as to retire.

Laboratory managers review staff members' methodology and the accuracy of their research results.

What Natural Sciences Managers Do

Natural sciences managers supervise the work of scientists, including chemists, physicists, and biologists. They direct activities related to research and development, and coordinate activities such as testing, quality control, and production.

Duties

Natural sciences managers typically do the following:

- Work with top executives to develop goals and strategies for researchers and developers
- Budget resources for projects and programs by determining staffing, training, and equipment needs
- Hire, supervise, and evaluate scientists, technicians, and other staff members
- Review staff members' methodology and the accuracy of their research results
- Monitor the progress of projects, review research performed, and draft operational reports
- Ensure that laboratories are stocked with equipment and supplies
- Provide technical assistance to scientists, technicians, and support staff
- Establish and follow administrative procedures, policies, and standards
- Communicate project proposals, research findings, and the status of projects to clients and top management

Natural sciences managers direct scientific research activities and direct and coordinate product development projects and production activities. The duties of natural sciences managers

Natural sciences managers direct research and development projects.

vary with the field of science (such as biology or chemistry) or the industry they work in. Research projects may be aimed at improving manufacturing processes, advancing basic scientific knowledge, or developing new products.

Some natural sciences managers are former scientists and, after becoming managers, may continue to conduct their own research as well as oversee the work of others. These managers are sometimes called ***working managers*** and usually have smaller staffs, allowing them to do research in addition to carrying out their administrative duties.

Managers who are responsible for larger staffs may not have time to contribute to research and may spend all their time performing administrative duties.

Laboratory managers need to ensure that laboratories are fully supplied so that scientists can run their tests and experiments. Some specialize in the management of laboratory animals.

During all stages of a project, natural sciences managers coordinate the activities of their unit with those of other units or organizations. They work with higher levels of management; with financial, production, and marketing specialists; and with equipment and materials suppliers.

Work Environment

Natural sciences managers held about 86,300 jobs in 2022. The largest employers of natural sciences managers were as follows:

Employer	Percent
Research and development in the physical, engineering, and life sciences	38%
Federal government, excluding postal service	14
Manufacturing	8
Healthcare and social assistance	8
State government, excluding education and hospitals	5

Most of the time, they work in offices, but they also may spend time in laboratories. Like managers in other fields, natural sciences managers may spend a large portion of their time using computers and talking to other members of their organization.

Natural sciences managers often present their research findings to other managers, top executives, and clients.

Natural sciences managers have different requirements based on the size of their staff. Managers with larger staffs spend their time primarily in offices performing administrative duties and spend little time doing research or working in the field or in laboratories. Working managers who have research responsibilities and smaller staffs may need to work in laboratories or in the field, which may require traveling, sometimes to remote locations.

Work Schedules

Most natural sciences managers work full time. Some work more than 40 hours per week.

How to Become a Natural Sciences Manager

Natural sciences managers usually advance to management positions after years of employment as scientists. Natural sciences managers typically have a bachelor's degree, master's degree, or Ph.D. in a scientific discipline or a related field, such as engineering. Some managers may find it helpful to have an advanced management degree—for example, a Professional Science Master's (PSM) degree.

Natural sciences managers typically begin their careers as scientists.

Education

Natural sciences managers typically begin their careers as scientists; therefore, most have a bachelor's degree, master's degree, or Ph.D. in a science field, such as biology or healthcare, or a related field, such as engineering. Scientific and technical knowledge is essential for managers because they must be able to understand the work of their subordinates and provide technical assistance when needed.

Natural sciences managers who are interested in acquiring postsecondary education in management should be able to find master's degree or Ph.D. programs in a natural science that incorporate business management courses. Professional Science Master's (PSM) degree programs blend advanced training in a particular science field, such as biotechnology or environmental science, with business skills, such as communications and program management, and policy. Those interested in acquiring general management skills may pursue a Master of Business Administration (MBA) or a Master of Public Administration (MPA). Some natural sciences managers will have studied psychology or some other management-related field to enter this occupation.

Sciences managers must continually upgrade their knowledge because of the rapid growth of scientific developments.

Work Experience in a Related Occupation

Natural sciences managers usually work several years in the sciences before advancing to management positions. While employed as scientists, they typically are given more responsibility and independence in their work as they gain experience. Eventually, they may lead research teams and have control over the direction and content of projects before being promoted to an managerial position.

Licenses, Certifications, and Registrations

Although certification is not typically required to become a natural sciences manager, many relevant certifications are available. These certifications range from those related to specific scientific areas of study or practice, such as laboratory animal management, to general management topics, such as project management.

Important Qualities

Communication skills. Natural sciences managers must be able to communicate clearly with a variety of audiences, such as scientists, policymakers, and the public. Both written and oral communication are important.

Critical-thinking skills. Natural sciences managers must carefully evaluate the work of others. They must determine if their staff's methods and results are based on sound science.

Interpersonal skills. Natural sciences managers lead research teams and therefore need to work well with others in order to reach common goals. Managers routinely deal with conflict, which they must be able to turn into positive outcomes for their organization.

Leadership skills. Natural sciences managers must be able to organize, direct, and motivate others. They need to identify the strengths and weaknesses of their workers and create an environment in which the workers can succeed.

Problem-solving skills. Natural sciences managers use scientific observation and analysis to find answers to complex technical questions.

Time-management skills. Natural sciences managers must be able to perform multiple administrative, supervisory, and technical tasks while ensuring that projects remain on schedule.

Pay

The median annual wage for natural sciences managers was $144,440 in May 2022. The median wage is the wage at which half the workers in an occupation earned more than that amount and half earned less. The lowest 10 percent earned less than $73,730, and the highest 10 percent earned more than $239,200.

In May 2022, the median annual wages for natural sciences managers in the top industries in which they worked were as follows:

Research and development in the physical, engineering, and life sciences	$178,830
Manufacturing	170,220
Federal government, excluding postal service	126,380
Healthcare and social assistance	98,270
State government, excluding education and hospitals	89,150

Most natural sciences managers work full time. Some work more than 40 hours per week.

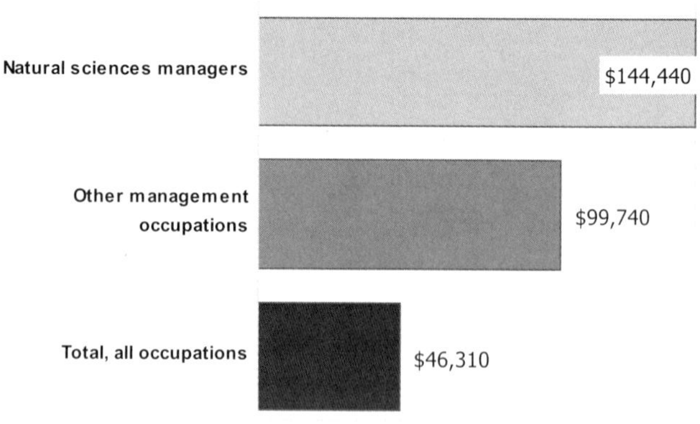

Note: All Occupations includes all occupations in the U.S. Economy.
Source: U.S. Bureau of Labor Statistics, Occupational Employment and Wage Statistics.

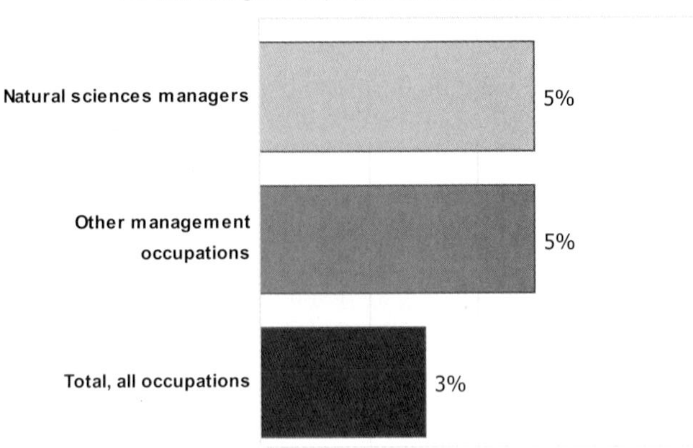

Note: All Occupations includes all occupations in the U.S. Economy.
Source: U.S. Bureau of Labor Statistics, Employment Projections program.

Job Outlook

Employment of natural sciences managers is projected to grow 5 percent from 2022 to 2032, faster than the average for all occupations.

About 6,500 openings for natural sciences managers are projected each year, on average, over the decade. Many of those openings are expected to result from the need to replace workers who transfer to different occupations or exit the labor force, such as to retire.

Employment

Employment growth should be affected by many of the same factors that affect employment growth for the scientists whom these managers supervise. For example, when organizations hire more hydrologists for water conservation, they also may need to hire more natural sciences managers to oversee them. However, managers often are flexible in the number of workers they supervise, which may reduce demand in organizations looking to cut costs.

Employment projections data for natural sciences managers, 2022-32

Occupational Title	SOC Code	Employment, 2022	Projected Employment, 2032	Change, 2022-32		Employment by Industry
				Percent	Numeric	
SOURCE: U.S. Bureau of Labor Statistics, Employment Projections program						
Natural sciences managers	11-9121	86,300	90,500	5	4,200	Get data

Contacts for More Information

For more information, visit

- Professional Science Master's
- American Association for the Advancement of Science
- USAJOBS

Postsecondary Education Administrators

Summary

Quick Facts: Postsecondary Education Administrators

2022 Median Pay	$99,940 per year $48.05 per hour
Typical Entry-Level Education	Master's degree
Work Experience in a Related Occupation	Less than 5 years
On-the-job Training	None
Number of Jobs, 2022	218,200
Job Outlook, 2022-32	4% (As fast as average)
Employment Change, 2022-32	7,700

What Postsecondary Education Administrators Do

Postsecondary education administrators oversee student services, academics, and faculty research at colleges and universities.

Work Environment

Postsecondary education administrators work for public and private schools. Most work full time.

How to Become a Postsecondary Education Administrator

Postsecondary education administrators typically need a master's degree. However, there will be some opportunities for those with a bachelor's degree. Employers typically prefer to hire candidates who have experience working in a postsecondary

Postsecondary education administrators oversee student services, academics, and faculty research at colleges and universities.

education administrative office, especially for occupations such as registrars and academic deans.

Pay

The median annual wage for postsecondary education administrators was $99,940 in May 2022.

Job Outlook

Employment of postsecondary education administrators is projected to grow 4 percent from 2022 to 2032, about as fast as the average for all occupations.

About 15,300 openings for postsecondary education administrators are projected each year, on average, over the decade. Many of those openings are expected to result from the need to replace workers who transfer to different occupations or exit the labor force, such as to retire.

What Postsecondary Education Administrators Do

Postsecondary education administrators oversee student services, academics, and faculty research at colleges and universities. Their job duties vary depending on the department in which they work, such as admissions, student affairs, or the registrar's office.

Duties

Education administrators' duties depend on the size of their college or university. Small schools often have small staffs that take on many different responsibilities, but larger schools may have different offices for each of these functions. For example, at a small college, the Office of Student Life may oversee student athletics and other activities, whereas a large university may have an Athletics Department.

Postsecondary education administrators who work in ***admissions*** decide which applicants should be admitted to the school. They typically do the following:

Postsecondary education administrators assist students with a variety of tasks, such as registering for classes and completing admissions applications.

- Determine how many students to admit to the school
- Meet with prospective students and encourage them to apply
- Review applications to determine which students should be admitted
- Analyze data about applicants and admitted students

Admissions officers also prepare promotional materials about the school. They often are assigned a region of the country to which they travel and speak to high school counselors and students.

Admissions officers who work with the financial aid department offer packages of federal and institutional financial aid to prospective students.

Postsecondary education administrators may be ***provosts*** or ***academic deans***. Provosts, also called *chief academic officers*, help college presidents develop academic policies, participate in making faculty appointments and tenure decisions, and manage budgets. They also oversee faculty research at colleges and universities. Academic deans coordinate the activities of the individual colleges or schools. For example, a large university may have a separate dean for business, law, and medical schools.

Postsecondary education administrators who work in the ***registrar's office***, sometimes called *registrars*, maintain student and course records. They typically do the following:

- Schedule course offerings, including space and times for classes
- Oversee student registration for classes
- Ensure that students meet graduation requirements
- Plan commencement ceremonies
- Prepare transcripts and diplomas for students
- Produce data about students and classes
- Maintain the academic records of the institution

Registrars' duties vary throughout the school year. During registration and at the beginning of the academic term, for example, they help students sign up for, drop, and add courses. Registrars need computer skills to create and maintain databases.

Postsecondary education administrators who work in ***student affairs*** are responsible for a variety of cocurricular school functions. They typically do the following:

- Advise students on topics such as housing, personal problems, or academics
- Communicate with parents or guardians
- Create, support, and assess nonacademic programs for students
- Schedule programs and services, such as athletic events or recreational activities

Postsecondary education administrators in student affairs may specialize in areas such as student activities, housing and residential life, or multicultural affairs. In student activities, they plan events and advise student clubs and organizations. In housing and

Postsecondary education administrators work in colleges, universities, community colleges, and technical and trade schools.

residential life, they assign students to rooms and match them with roommates, ensure that residential facilities are well maintained, and train residential advisers. In multicultural affairs, they plan events to celebrate different cultures and diverse backgrounds. Sometimes, they manage multicultural centers on campus.

Work Environment

Postsecondary education administrators held about 218,200 jobs in 2022. The largest employers of postsecondary education administrators were as follows:

Colleges, universities, and professional schools; state, local, and private	81%
Junior colleges; state, local, and private	12

Work Schedules

Postsecondary education administrators generally work full time. Most work year-round, but some administrators may reduce their hours during the summer.

How to Become a Postsecondary Education Administrator

Postsecondary education administrators typically need a master's degree. However, there will be some opportunities for those with a bachelor's degree. Employers typically prefer candidates who have experience working in a postsecondary academic administrative office, particularly for occupations such as registrars and academic deans.

Education

Postsecondary education administrators typically need a master's degree. However, a bachelor's degree may be sufficient for positions at small colleges and universities. Degrees may be in a variety of fields, such as education, business, or social science.

Postsecondary education administrators need to build good relationships with colleagues, students, and parents.

Provosts and deans often must have a Ph.D. Some begin their careers as professors and later move into administration. They have a doctorate in the field in which they taught or in higher education.

Work Experience in a Related Occupation

Employers typically prefer to hire candidates who have several years of experience in a college administrative setting. Some postsecondary education administrators work in the registrar's office or as a resident assistant while in college to gain the necessary experience. For other positions, such as those in admissions and student affairs, experience may not be necessary.

Important Qualities

Computer skills. Postsecondary education administrators need to be comfortable working with computers so they can use software to manage student and school records.

Interpersonal skills. Postsecondary education administrators need to build good relationships with colleagues, students, and parents. For example, those in admissions need to be outgoing so they can encourage prospective students to apply to the school.

Organizational skills. Administrators need to be organized so they can manage records, prioritize tasks, and coordinate activities with their staff.

Problem-solving skills. Administrators need to react calmly when a difficult situation arises and develop creative solutions.

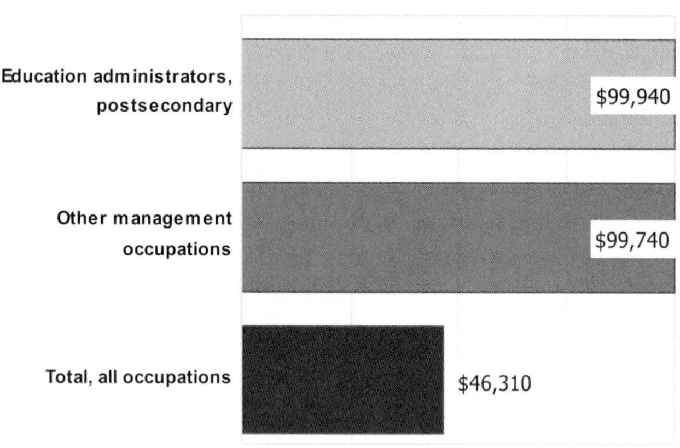

Note: All Occupations includes all occupations in the U.S. Economy.
Source: U.S. Bureau of Labor Statistics, Occupational Employment and Wage Statistics.

Advancement

Education administrators with advanced degrees may be promoted to higher level positions within their department or the college. Some become college presidents, an occupation discussed in the profile on top executives.

Pay

The median annual wage for postsecondary education administrators was $99,940 in May 2022. The median wage is the wage at which half the workers in an occupation earned more than that amount and half earned less. The lowest 10 percent earned less than $61,000, and the highest 10 percent earned more than $196,420.

In May 2022, the median annual wages for postsecondary education administrators in the top industries in which they worked were as follows:

Colleges, universities, and professional schools; state, local, and private	$100,720
Junior colleges; state, local, and private	94,990

As part of their employee benefits plan, many colleges and universities allow full-time employees to attend classes at a discount or for free.

Postsecondary education administrators generally work full time. Most work year-round, but some schools may reduce their hours during the summer.

Job Outlook

Employment of postsecondary education administrators is projected to grow 4 percent from 2022 to 2032, about as fast as the average for all occupations.

About 15,300 openings for postsecondary education administrators are projected each year, on average, over the decade. Many of those openings are expected to result from the need to replace workers who transfer to different occupations or exit the labor force, such as to retire.

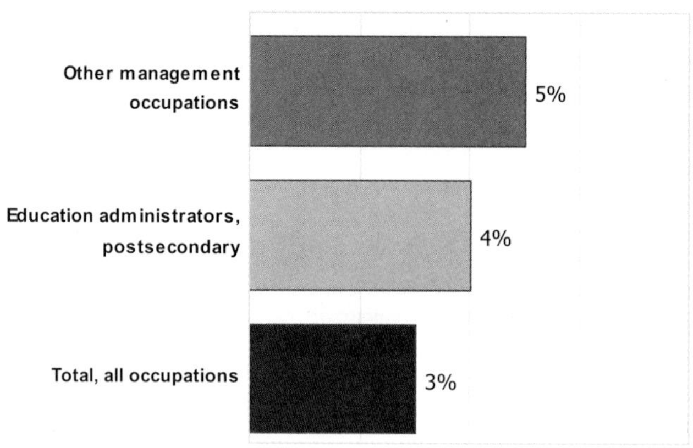

Note: All Occupations includes all occupations in the U.S. Economy.
Source: U.S. Bureau of Labor Statistics, Employment Projections program.

Employment

Employment growth in the occupation is tied to student enrollments at colleges and universities.

People will continue to seek postsecondary education to accomplish their career goals. As more people enter colleges and universities, more postsecondary education administrators will be needed to serve the needs of these additional students.

Additional admissions officers will be needed to process students' applications. Registrars will be needed to direct student registration for classes and ensure that they meet graduation requirements. Student affairs workers will be needed to make housing assignments and plan events for students.

Provosts and academic dean positions will be limited, since there is typically a set number of these positions per institution.

Despite expected increases in enrollment, employment growth in public colleges and universities will depend on state and local government budgets. If there is a budget deficit, postsecondary institutions may lay off employees, including administrators. If there is a budget surplus, postsecondary institutions may hire more employees.

Employment projections data for postsecondary education administrators, 2022-32

Occupational Title	SOC Code	Employment, 2022	Projected Employment, 2032	Change, 2022-32		Employment by Industry
				Percent	Numeric	
Education administrators, postsecondary	11-9033	218,200	225,900	4	7,700	Get data

SOURCE: U.S. Bureau of Labor Statistics, Employment Projections program

Contacts for More Information

For more information about registrars or admissions counselors, visit

- American Association of Collegiate Registrars and Admissions Officers
- NASPA - Student Affairs Administrators in Higher Education

Preschool and Childcare Center Directors

Summary

Quick Facts: Preschool and Childcare Center Directors	
2022 Median Pay	$49,690 per year $23.89 per hour
Typical Entry-Level Education	Bachelor's degree
Work Experience in a Related Occupation	Less than 5 years
On-the-job Training	None
Number of Jobs, 2022	74,800
Job Outlook, 2022-32	-3% (Decline)
Employment Change, 2022-32	-2,200

What Preschool and Childcare Center Directors Do

Preschool and childcare center directors supervise and lead their staffs, design program plans, oversee daily activities, and prepare budgets.

Work Environment

Preschool and childcare center directors work primarily in child daycare services. Most work full time, and some work more than 40 hours per week.

How to Become a Preschool or Childcare Center Director

A bachelor's degree and experience in early childhood education are typically required to become a preschool and childcare center director. However, educational requirements vary. Additionally, some employers require these directors to have a nationally recognized credential, such as the Child Development Associate (CDA) credential.

Pay

The median annual wage for preschool and childcare center directors was $49,690 in May 2022.

Job Outlook

Employment of preschool and childcare center directors is projected to decline 3 percent from 2022 to 2032.

Despite declining employment, about 4,600 openings for preschool and childcare center directors are projected each year, on average, over the decade. All of those openings are expected to result from the need to replace workers who transfer to other occupations or exit the labor force, such as to retire.

What Preschool and Childcare Center Directors Do

Preschool and childcare center directors supervise and lead staffs, design program plans, oversee daily activities, and prepare budgets. They are responsible for all aspects of their center's program, which may include before- and after-school care.

Duties

Preschool and childcare center directors typically do the following:

- Supervise preschool teachers and childcare workers
- Hire and train new staff members
- Provide professional development opportunities for staff
- Establish policies and communicate them to staff and parents
- Develop educational programs and standards
- Maintain instructional excellence
- Assist staff in communicating with parents and children
- Meet with parents and staff to discuss students' progress
- Prepare budgets and allocate program funds
- Ensure that facilities are maintained and cleaned according to state regulations

Some preschools and childcare centers are independently owned and operated. In these facilities, directors must follow the instructions and guidelines of the owner. Sometimes, the directors are the owners, so they decide how to operate them.

Other preschools and childcare centers are part of a national chain or franchise. The director of a chain or franchise must

Preschool and childcare center directors lead staff, design program plans, oversee daily activities, and prepare plans and budgets.

Preschool and childcare center directors assist staff with caring for and teaching children.

ensure that the facility meets the parent organization's standards and regulations.

In addition, some preschools and childcare centers, such as Head Start programs, receive state and federal funding. Directors need to follow the requirements set by Department of Health and Human Services for program, staff, and facilities.

Work Environment

Preschool and childcare center directors held about 74,800 jobs in 2022. The largest employers of preschool and childcare center directors were as follows:

Child day care services	71%
Religious, grantmaking, civic, professional, and similar organizations	8
Self-employed workers	7
Elementary and secondary schools; state, local, and private	6

Although preschool and childcare center directors work in schools and childcare centers, they spend most of their day in an office. They also visit classrooms to check on students, speak to preschool teachers or childcare workers, and meet with parents.

Preschool and childcare center directors may find working in an early childhood educational environment rewarding, but they also have significant responsibilities. Coordinating and interacting with staff, parents, and children may be fast paced and stimulating but also stressful.

Most preschool and childcare center directors work in childcare facilities.

Work Schedules

Most preschool and childcare center directors work full time, and some work more than 40 hours per week. They are on the job while the childcare center is open and may work early in the morning and late in the evening, particularly in centers that provide before- and after-school care. In large facilities, the director and assistant directors may stagger their schedules to ensure that someone is always onsite.

How to Become a Preschool or Childcare Center Director

A bachelor's degree and experience in early childhood education are typically required to become a preschool or childcare center director. However, educational requirements vary. Additionally, some employers require these directors to have a nationally recognized credential, such as the Child Development Associate (CDA) credential.

Education

Most states require preschool and childcare center directors to have at least a bachelor's degree, but educational requirements vary by state. Employers may prefer candidates who have a degree, or at least some postsecondary coursework, in early childhood education. These programs teach child development, provide strategies for instructing young children, and show how to observe and document children's progress.

Work Experience in a Related Occupation

Most positions for preschool and childcare center directors require several years of experience in early childhood education. The length of experience required varies by job.

Licenses, Certifications, and Registrations

States may require childcare centers, including those in private homes, to be licensed. To qualify for licensure, staff must pass a background check and meet a minimum training requirement.

Preschool and childcare center directors need to be able to interact with children, staff, and parents.

Some states have more requirements, such as requiring staff to have certifications in cardiopulmonary resuscitation (CPR) and first aid.

Some employers have additional requirements, such as the CDA credential offered by the Council for Professional Recognition. Candidates need to pay a fee, take coursework, obtain experience in the field, and be observed while working with children. This credential needs to be renewed every 3 years.

Important Qualities

Business skills. Preschool and childcare center directors manage childcare centers and need to be able to operate the business effectively.

Communication skills. Directors inform parents and staff about the children's progress. They need good writing and speaking skills to convey this information.

Interpersonal skills. Preschool and childcare center directors must be able to develop relationships with parents, children, and staff.

Leadership skills. Preschool and childcare center directors need leadership skills to supervise staff and inspire diligence. They also must enforce rules and regulations.

Organizational skills. Directors need to maintain clear records about children and staff. In addition, they must be able to multitask when several people or situations require their attention.

Pay

The median annual wage for preschool and childcare center directors was $49,690 in May 2022. The median wage is the wage at which half the workers in an occupation earned more than that amount and half earned less. The lowest 10 percent earned less than $35,190, and the highest 10 percent earned more than $85,390.

In May 2022, the median annual wages for preschool and childcare center directors in the top industries in which they worked were as follows:

Elementary and secondary schools; state, local, and private	$65,130
Religious, grantmaking, civic, professional, and similar organizations	53,320
Child day care services	48,420

Most preschool and childcare center directors work full time, and some work more than 40 hours per week. They are on the job while the childcare center is open and may work early in the morning and late in the evening, particularly in centers that provide before- and after-school care. In large facilities, the director and assistant directors may stagger their schedules to ensure that someone is always onsite.

Job Outlook

Employment of preschool and childcare center directors is projected to decline 3 percent from 2022 to 2032.

Despite declining employment, about 4,600 openings for preschool and childcare center directors are projected each year, on average, over the decade. All of those openings are expected to result from the need to replace workers who transfer to other occupations or exit the labor force, such as to retire.

Employment

Early childhood education is widely recognized as important for a child's intellectual and emotional development. However, the rising cost of childcare may limit the demand for preschool and childcare center directors over the projections decade.

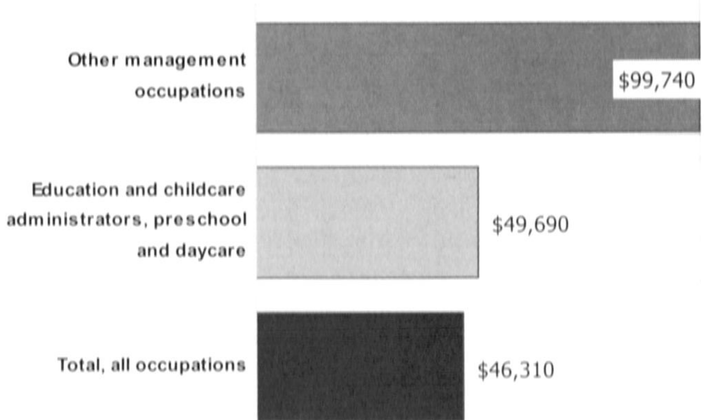

Note: All Occupations includes all occupations in the U.S. Economy.
Source: U.S. Bureau of Labor Statistics, Occupational Employment and Wage Statistics.

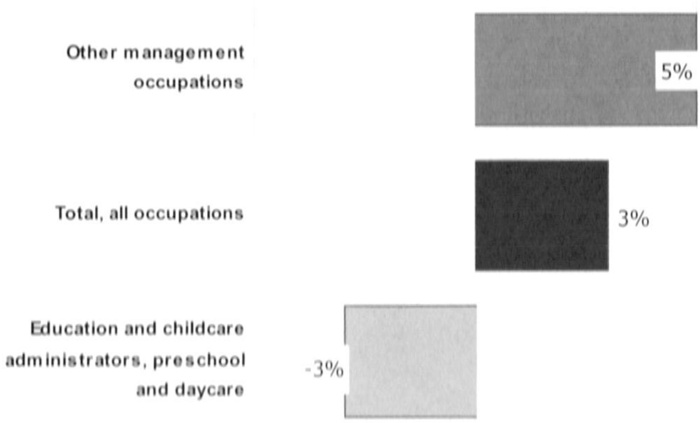

Note: All Occupations includes all occupations in the U.S. Economy.
Source: U.S. Bureau of Labor Statistics, Employment Projections program.

Employment projections data for preschool and childcare center directors, 2022-32						
Occupational Title	SOC Code	Employment, 2022	Projected Employment, 2032	Change, 2022-32 Percent	Change, 2022-32 Numeric	Employment by Industry
SOURCE: U.S. Bureau of Labor Statistics, Employment Projections program						
Education and childcare administrators, preschool and daycare	11-9031	74,800	72,600	-3	-2,200	Get data

Contacts for More Information

For more information on childcare centers, visit

- Child Care Aware
- National Association for the Education of Young Children
- Council for Professional Recognition
- National Early Childhood Program Accreditation

Property, Real Estate, and Community Association Managers

Summary

Quick Facts: Property, Real Estate, and Community Association Managers	
2022 Median Pay	$60,670 per year $29.17 per hour
Typical Entry-Level Education	High school diploma or equivalent
Work Experience in a Related Occupation	Less than 5 years
On-the-job Training	Short-term on-the-job training
Number of Jobs, 2022	429,600
Job Outlook, 2022-32	5% (Faster than average)
Employment Change, 2022-32	23,400

What Property, Real Estate, and Community Association Managers Do

Property, real estate, and community association managers oversee many aspects of residential, commercial, or industrial properties.

Licensed real estate managers may show, lease, or sell properties to clients.

Work Environment

Most property, real estate, and community association managers work full time. They usually work in an office setting but may spend part of their workday on tasks away from the office, such as showing apartments, inspecting the grounds, or meeting with owners.

How to Become a Property, Real Estate, or Community Association Manager

Property, real estate, and community association managers typically need a high school diploma combined with several years of related work experience for entry-level positions, although employers may prefer to hire college graduates. Some managers also must have a state-issued license.

Pay

The median annual wage for property, real estate, and community association managers was $60,670 in May 2022.

Job Outlook

Employment of property, real estate, and community association managers is projected to grow 5 percent from 2022 to 2032, faster than the average for all occupations.

About 35,900 openings for property, real estate, and community association managers are projected each year, on average, over the decade. Many of those openings are expected to result from the need to replace workers who transfer to different occupations or exit the labor force, such as to retire.

What Property, Real Estate, and Community Association Managers Do

Property, real estate, and community association managers oversee many aspects of residential, commercial, or industrial properties. They ensure that the property is well maintained, has a nice appearance, operates smoothly, and preserves its resale value.

Duties

Property, real estate, and community association managers typically do the following:

- Meet with prospective tenants or owners and show them properties

Onsite managers often show apartments.

- Discuss the lease and explain the terms of occupancy or ownership
- Collect monthly fees from tenants or individual owners
- Inspect building facilities, including the grounds and equipment
- Arrange for new equipment or repairs as needed
- Pay bills or delegate bill payment for such expenditures as insurance, maintenance, payroll, and taxes
- Contract for landscaping, maintenance, trash removal, and other services
- Investigate and settle complaints, disturbances, and violations
- Keep records of rental activity and owner requests
- Prepare budgets and financial reports
- Comply with anti-discrimination laws, such as the Americans with Disabilities Act and the Federal Fair Housing Amendment Act, when advertising or leasing properties

Real estate proprietors who lack the time or expertise needed for the day-to-day management of their properties often hire a property or real estate manager or a community association manager. These managers are employed either directly by the proprietor or indirectly through a contract with a property management firm.

Property and real estate managers oversee the operation of income-producing commercial or residential properties and ensure that real estate investments achieve their expected revenues. They handle the financial operations of the property, making certain that rent is collected and that mortgages, taxes, insurance premiums, payroll, and maintenance bills are paid on time. They may oversee financial statements, and they periodically report to the proprietors on the status of the property, occupancy rates, expiration dates of leases, and other matters. When vacancies occur, these managers may advertise the property or hire a leasing agent to find a tenant. They may also suggest to the proprietors how much to charge for rent.

Community association managers work on behalf of property members in a geographic group, such as homeowners in a subdivision, to manage common areas and services of condominiums, cooperatives, and planned communities. Usually hired by a community association's volunteer board of directors, these managers supervise the daily affairs and maintenance of its property and facilities. Like property managers, community association managers collect monthly fees, prepare financial statements and budgets, negotiate with contractors, and help to resolve complaints. Community association managers also help homeowners and non-owner residents comply with the association's rules and regulations.

The following are examples of types of property, real estate, and community association managers:

Onsite property managers are responsible for the day-to-day operation of a single property, such as an apartment complex or a shopping center. To ensure that the property is well maintained, onsite managers routinely inspect the grounds, facilities, and equipment. They meet with current residents or tenants to handle requests for repairs or to resolve complaints. They also meet with prospective residents or tenants to show vacant units. In addition, onsite managers enforce the terms of the lease and an association's governing rules. For example, they make sure that tenants pay their rent, follow restrictions on parking or pets, and follow the correct procedures when the lease is up. Other important duties of onsite managers include keeping accurate, up-to-date records of income and expenditures from property operations and submitting regular expense reports to the senior-level property manager or proprietor.

Real estate asset managers plan and direct the purchase, sale, and development of real estate properties on behalf of businesses and investors. They focus on long-term strategic financial planning, rather than on day-to-day operations of the property. In deciding to acquire property, real estate asset managers consider several factors, such as property value, zoning, and traffic volume. After a site is selected, they negotiate contracts to buy or lease the property. Real estate asset managers review their company's real estate holdings periodically and identify properties that are no longer financially profitable. They then negotiate the sale of the properties or arrange for the end of leases.

Work Environment

Property, real estate, and community association managers held about 429,600 jobs in 2022. The largest employers of property, real estate, and community association managers were as follows:

Real estate	50%
Self-employed workers	38
Religious, grantmaking, civic, professional, and similar organizations	2

Most property, real estate, and community association managers work in an office setting. However, managers may

Property, real estate, and community association managers must interact with clients every day.

spend much of their time away from their desks. Onsite managers, in particular, may spend a large part of their workday showing units, checking on the maintenance staff, or investigating problems reported by residents. Real estate asset managers may spend time away from home while traveling to company real estate holdings or searching for properties to buy.

Work Schedules

Most property, real estate, and community association managers work full time. Work schedules may vary; for example, they may need to respond to emergencies during off-duty hours or attend evening meetings with residents, property owners, or community association board members. Some managers are required to live onsite at the properties they manage.

How to Become a Property, Real Estate, or Community Association Manager

Property, real estate, and community association managers typically need a high school diploma combined with several years of related work experience for entry-level positions. Some managers also must have a state-issued license.

Education

A high school diploma or equivalent is typically required for onsite property management positions. Employers may prefer to hire college graduates for positions in commercial management positions related to overseeing a property's finances or contracts. Fields of degree for bachelor's or master's study may include business administration, accounting, finance, real estate, or public administration.

Work Experience in a Related Occupation

Property, real estate, and community association managers typically need several years of work experience in a related occupation. For example, real estate brokers and sales agents also show commercial properties to prospective tenants or buyers, and customer service representatives gain experience dealing with many types of people.

A high school diploma combined with several years of related work experience is typically required for entry-level positions.

Licenses, Certifications, and Registrations

Property, real estate, and community association managers may need a license issued by the state in which they work. In most states, property managers must have a property management license or real estate broker's license. Real estate managers who buy or sell property must have a real estate license in the state in which they practice. In some states, community association managers also need a real estate license. Managers of public housing subsidized by the federal government must hold certifications.

Many states require property, real estate, and community association managers to obtain professional credentials or licensure. Requirements vary by state, but managers working in states without requirements may still obtain designations to show competence and professionalism. For example, BOMI International, the Community Associations Institute, the Institute of Real Estate Management (IREM), the National Association of Residential Property Managers (NARPM), and the Community Association Managers International Certification Board (CAMICB) offer various designations, certifications, and professional development courses. Most states require recertification. For more information, contact your state licensing agency.

Training

Employers typically require managers to attend formal training programs available through professional and trade real estate associations. These programs may help to develop managerial skills and expand knowledge of specialized fields, such as insurance and risk management, tenant relations, and accounting and financial concepts. With related job experience, completing these programs and receiving a satisfactory score on a written exam may lead to certification or professional designation by the sponsoring association.

Advancement

Property, real estate, and community association managers who participate in professional training programs may prepare themselves for positions of increased responsibility. People may start as onsite managers of properties, such as apartment buildings, office complexes, or community associations. As they gain experience, they may advance to assistant property manager positions in which they handle a broad range of duties.

People also might begin as assistant managers, working closely with a property manager, and advance to property manager positions over time.

Property, real estate, and community association managers' responsibilities increase as they manage more and larger properties. Property managers may oversee several properties at a time. Experienced managers may open their own property management firms.

Important Qualities

Communication skills. Property, real estate, and community association managers must understand contracts and must be able to clearly explain the materials and answer questions raised by residents, board members, or service providers.

Customer-service skills. Property, real estate, and community association managers must provide excellent support to keep existing clients and expand their business with new ones.

Interpersonal skills. Property, real estate, and community association managers interact with different types of people every day. They must be empathetic, respectful, and patient in their dealings with others.

Listening skills. Property, real estate, and community association managers pay attention to residents and proprietors in order to understand and meet their needs.

Organizational skills. Property, real estate, and community association managers must be able to plan, coordinate, and direct multiple contractors at the same time, often for multiple properties.

Problem-solving skills. Property, real estate, and community association managers must be able to mediate disputes or legal issues between different groups of people, such as residents and board members.

Property, Real Estate, and Community Association Managers

Median annual wages, May 2022

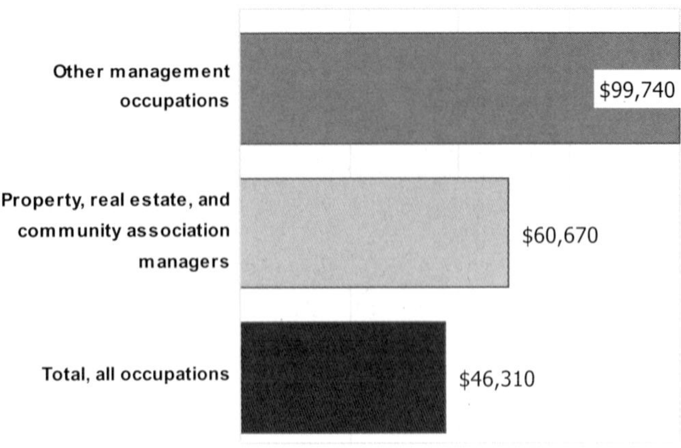

Note: All Occupations includes all occupations in the U.S. Economy.
Source: U.S. Bureau of Labor Statistics, Occupational Employment and Wage Statistics.

Pay

The median annual wage for property, real estate, and community association managers was $60,670 in May 2022. The median wage is the wage at which half the workers in an occupation earned more than that amount and half earned less. The lowest 10 percent earned less than $35,210, and the highest 10 percent earned more than $129,900.

In May 2022, the median annual wages for property, real estate, and community association managers in the top industries in which they worked were as follows:

Religious, grantmaking, civic, professional, and similar organizations	$60,800
Real estate	59,330

Most property, real estate, and community association managers work full time. Work schedules may vary; for example, they may need to respond to emergencies during off-duty hours or attend evening meetings with residents, property owners, or community association board members. Some managers are required to live onsite at the properties they manage.

Job Outlook

Employment of property, real estate, and community association managers is projected to grow 5 percent from 2022 to 2032, faster than the average for all occupations.

About 35,900 openings for property, real estate, and community association managers are projected each year, on average, over the decade. Many of those openings are expected to result from the need to replace workers who transfer to different occupations or exit the labor force, such as to retire.

Employment

Employment demand will be driven by the number people living in buildings that property management companies operate,

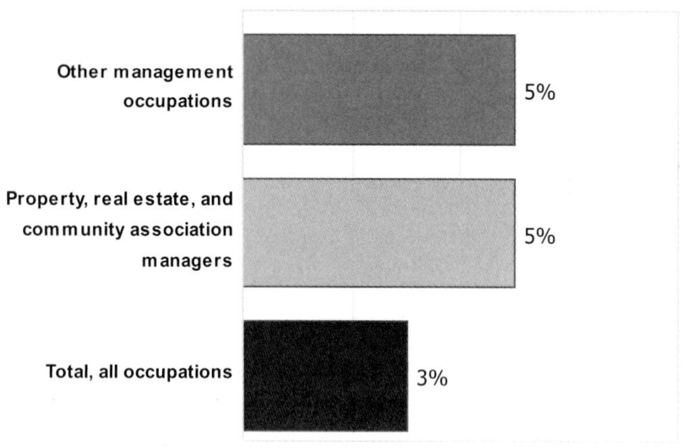

Note: All Occupations includes all occupations in the U.S. Economy.
Source: U.S. Bureau of Labor Statistics, Employment Projections program.

such as apartment buildings, condominiums, cooperatives, planned communities, and senior housing.

Growth in the single-family housing market may have a positive influence on demand, as some new housing developments will require property managers to oversee jointly owned common areas, such as pools, gyms, and business centers and to enforce homeowner association laws. However, the automation of some property management tasks, such as posting vacancies and assigning maintenance requests, may slow employment growth.

Employment projections data for property, real estate, and community association managers, 2022-32

Occupational Title	SOC Code	Employment, 2022	Projected Employment, 2032	Change, 2022-32 Percent	Change, 2022-32 Numeric	Employment by Industry
SOURCE: U.S. Bureau of Labor Statistics, Employment Projections program						
Property, real estate, and community association managers	11-9141	429,600	453,000	5	23,400	Get data

Contacts for More Information

For more information, visit

- BOMI International
- Community Associations Institute
- Community Association Managers International Certification Board (CAMICB)
- Institute of Real Estate Management (IREM)
- National Association of Residential Property Managers (NARPM)

Public Relations and Fundraising Managers

Summary

Quick Facts: Public Relations and Fundraising Managers

2022 Median Pay	$125,620 per year $60.40 per hour
Typical Entry-Level Education	Bachelor's degree
Work Experience in a Related Occupation	5 years or more
On-the-job Training	None
Number of Jobs, 2022	105,700
Job Outlook, 2022-32	6% (Faster than average)
Employment Change, 2022-32	6,000

What Public Relations and Fundraising Managers Do

Public relations managers direct the creation of materials that will enhance the public image of their employer or client. Fundraising managers coordinate campaigns that bring in donations for their organization.

Work Environment

Public relations and fundraising managers generally work in offices during regular business hours. However, many of these managers travel to give speeches and to attend meetings and community activities. Some work more than 40 hours per week.

How to Become a Public Relations or Fundraising Manager

Public relations and fundraising managers typically need at least a bachelor's degree, and some positions may require a

Public relations and fundraising managers plan campaigns to raise donations or improve the public image of their clients.

master's degree. Many years of related work experience are also necessary.

Pay

The median annual wage for fundraising managers was $107,390 in May 2022.

The median annual wage for public relations managers was $129,430 in May 2022.

Job Outlook

Overall employment of public relations and fundraising managers is projected to grow 6 percent from 2022 to 2032, faster than the average for all occupations.

About 7,800 openings for public relations and fundraising managers are projected each year, on average, over the decade. Many of those openings are expected to result from the need to replace workers who transfer to different occupations or exit the labor force, such as to retire.

What Public Relations and Fundraising Managers Do

Public relations managers plan and direct the creation of material that will enhance the public image of their employer or client. Fundraising managers coordinate campaigns that bring in donations for their organization.

Duties

Public relations managers typically do the following:

- Develop their organization's or client's corporate image and identity
- Identify audiences and determine the best way to reach them
- Designate an appropriate spokesperson or information source for media inquiries
- Help clients communicate effectively with the public

Public relations and fundraising managers plan an organization's communication with the public, including consumers, investors, and media outlets.

- Write press releases and prepare information for the media
- Assist and inform an organization's executives and spokespeople
- Devise advertising and promotion programs
- Assign, supervise, and review the activities of staff

Fundraising managers typically do the following:

- Develop and carry out fundraising strategies
- Identify and contact potential donors
- Create and plan different events that can generate donations
- Meet face-to-face with donors
- Apply for grants
- Manage progress toward achieving an organization's fundraising goals
- Assign, supervise, and review the activities of staff

Public relations managers review press releases and sponsor corporate events to help maintain and improve the image of their organization or client.

Public relations managers help clarify their organization's point of view to its main audience through media releases and interviews. They monitor social, economic, and political trends that might affect their organization, and they recommend ways to enhance the firm's image on the basis of those trends. For example, in response to concern about damage to the environment, the public relations manager for an oil company may create a campaign to publicize its efforts to develop cleaner fuels.

In large organizations, public relations managers often supervise a staff of public relations specialists. They also work with advertising, promotions, and marketing managers to ensure that advertising campaigns are compatible with the image the company or client is trying to portray. For example, if a firm decides to emphasize its appeal to a certain group, such as young people, the public relations manager needs to make sure that current advertisements are well received by that group.

In addition, public relations managers may handle internal communications, such as company newsletters, and may help financial managers produce an organization's reports. They may also draft speeches, arrange interviews, and maintain other forms of public contact to help the organization's top executives.

Public relations managers must be able to work well with many types of specialists. In some cases, the information they write has legal consequences. As a result, they must work with the company's or client's lawyers to be sure that the information they release is both legally accurate and clear to the public.

Fundraising managers oversee campaigns and events intended to bring in donations for their organization. Many organizations that hire fundraising workers rely heavily on the donations they gather in order to run their operations.

Fundraising managers usually decide which fundraising techniques are necessary in a certain situation. Common techniques include annual campaigns, capital campaigns, planned giving, and soliciting for major gifts. Social media has created another avenue for fundraising managers to connect with potential donors and to spread their organization's message.

Those who work on annual campaigns focus heavily on contacting donors who have given in the past to request that they give again. Finding new contacts for future donations is also part of a successful annual campaign.

In contrast, fundraising managers who work on capital campaigns generally focus on raising money over a short time period for a specific project, such as the construction of a new building at a university.

Fundraising managers who spend most of their time on planned giving must have specialized training in taxes related to gifts of stocks, bonds, charitable annuities, and real estate bequests in a will. Major gifts are a feature of many fundraising efforts, and fundraising managers generally request these gifts in person, given the large value of the potential donation.

Work Environment

Fundraising managers held about 33,700 jobs in 2022. The largest employers of fundraising managers were as follows:

Religious, grantmaking, civic, professional, and similar organizations	36%
Educational services; state, local, and private	30
Social assistance	7
Arts, entertainment, and recreation	6
Hospitals; state, local, and private	5

Public relations managers held about 72,000 jobs in 2022. The largest employers of public relations managers were as follows:

Professional, scientific, and technical services	20%
Religious, grantmaking, civic, professional, and similar organizations	18
Educational services; state, local, and private	13
Management of companies and enterprises	8
Government	6

Public relations and fundraising managers usually work in offices during regular business hours. However, many must travel to deliver speeches and attend meetings and community activities.

They work in high-stress environments, often managing and organizing several events at the same time.

Work Schedules

Most public relations and fundraising managers work full time, which often includes long workdays. Some managers work more than 40 hours per week.

How to Become a Public Relations or Fundraising Manager

Public relations and fundraising managers typically need at least a bachelor's degree, and some positions may require a master's degree. Many years of related work experience are also necessary.

Education

For public relations and fundraising management positions, a bachelor's degree in a field such as public relations, communications, or business typically is required. However, some employers prefer to hire candidates who have a master's degree, particularly in public relations, journalism, fundraising, or nonprofit management.

Courses in advertising, business administration, public affairs, public speaking, and creative and technical writing can be helpful.

Licenses, Certifications, and Registrations

Although not mandatory, public relations managers can become certified through the Public Relations Society of America. Candidates qualify based on a combination of experience and education and must pass an exam to become certified.

Public relations managers and specialists work in fairly high-stress environments, often managing and organizing several events at the same time.

A bachelor's degree and years of work experience are typically needed for public relations or fundraising manager positions.

The Certified Fund Raising Executive program, offered by CFRE International, is also voluntary, but fundraisers who are awarded certification demonstrate a level of professional competency to prospective employers. To become certified, candidates must meet certain education, professional practice, and professional performance requirements, as well as pass an exam. Fundraisers must apply for renewal every 3 years to keep their certification valid.

The International Association of Business Communicators offers two credentials that allow communications specialists to demonstrate higher levels of knowledge and expertise. Public relations and fundraising managers may apply to take the certification exams when they have 6 to 8 years of experience in the communications field.

Work Experience in a Related Occupation

Public relations and fundraising managers must have several years of experience in a related occupation, such as public relations specialist or fundraiser.

Important Qualities

Interpersonal skills. Public relations and fundraising managers deal with the public regularly; therefore, they must be friendly enough to build a rapport with, and receive support from, their media contacts and donors.

Leadership skills. Managers often lead large teams of specialists or fundraisers and must be able to guide their activities.

Organizational skills. Public relations and fundraising managers are often in charge of running several events at the same time, requiring superior organizational skills.

Problem-solving skills. Managers sometimes must explain how the company or client is handling sensitive issues. They must use good judgment in what they report and how they report it.

Speaking skills. Public relations and fundraising managers regularly speak for their organization. When doing so, they must be able to explain the organization's position clearly.

Writing skills. Managers must be able to write well-organized and clear press releases and speeches. They must be able to succinctly present the key messages they want to get across in order to keep the attention of busy readers or listeners.

Pay

The median annual wage for fundraising managers was $107,390 in May 2022. The median wage is the wage at which half the workers in an occupation earned more than that amount and half earned less. The lowest 10 percent earned less than $63,320, and the highest 10 percent earned more than $205,230.

The median annual wage for public relations managers was $129,430 in May 2022. The lowest 10 percent earned less than $71,710, and the highest 10 percent earned more than $239,200.

In May 2022, the median annual wages for fundraising managers in the top industries in which they worked were as follows:

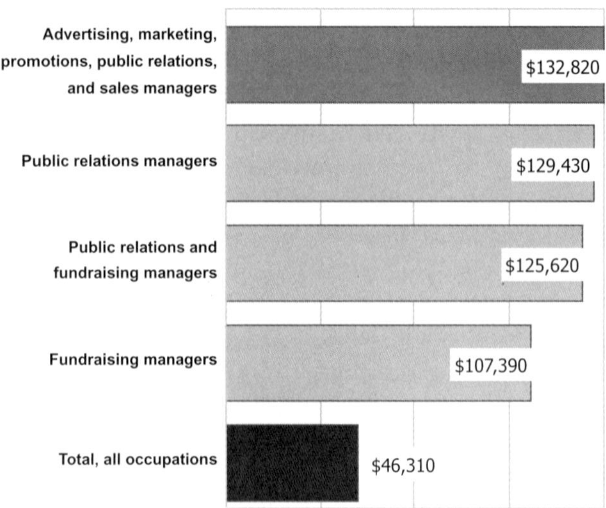

Note: All Occupations includes all occupations in the U.S. Economy.
Source: U.S. Bureau of Labor Statistics, Occupational Employment and Wage Statistics.

Hospitals; state, local, and private	$131,100
Religious, grantmaking, civic, professional, and similar organizations	112,680
Educational services; state, local, and private	108,150
Arts, entertainment, and recreation	97,310
Social assistance	85,600

In May 2022, the median annual wages for public relations managers in the top industries in which they worked were as follows:

Management of companies and enterprises	$160,610
Professional, scientific, and technical services	150,060
Religious, grantmaking, civic, professional, and similar organizations	126,610
Government	107,040
Educational services; state, local, and private	102,770

Most public relations and fundraising managers work full time, which often includes long workdays. Some managers work more than 40 hours per week.

Job Outlook

Overall employment of public relations and fundraising managers is projected to grow 6 percent from 2022 to 2032, faster than the average for all occupations.

About 7,800 openings for public relations and fundraising managers are projected each year, on average, over the decade. Many of those openings are expected to result from the need to replace workers who transfer to different occupations or exit the labor force, such as to retire.

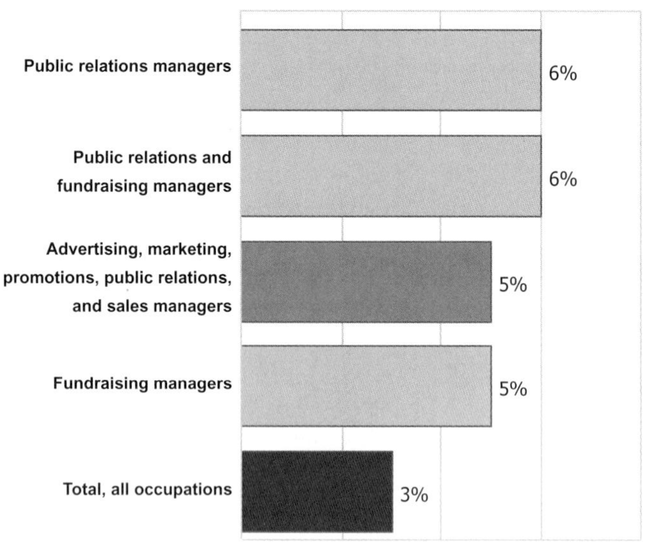

Note: All Occupations includes all occupations in the U.S. Economy. Source: U.S. Bureau of Labor Statistics, Employment Projections program.

Employment

Organizations continue to emphasize community outreach and customer relations as a way to enhance their reputation and visibility. Public opinion can change quickly, particularly as social media increases the speed at which news travels. Consequently, public relations managers will be needed to coordinate and help respond to news developments to maintain their organization's reputation.

Fundraising managers are expected to become increasingly important for organizations, such as colleges and universities, that depend heavily on donations. More nonprofit organizations are focusing on cultivating an online presence and are increasingly using social media for fundraising activities.

Employment projections data for public relations and fundraising managers, 2022-32

Occupational Title	SOC Code	Employment, 2022	Projected Employment, 2032	Change, 2022-32 Percent	Change, 2022-32 Numeric	Employment by Industry
SOURCE: U.S. Bureau of Labor Statistics, Employment Projections program						
Public relations and fundraising managers	—	105,700	111,700	6	6,000	
Fundraising managers	11-2033	33,700	35,400	5	1,700	Get data
Public relations managers	11-2032	72,000	76,300	6	4,300	Get data

Contacts for More Information

For more information, visit

- CFRE International
- International Association of Business Communicators
- Public Relations Society of America

Sales Managers

Summary

Quick Facts: Sales Managers

2022 Median Pay	$130,600 per year $62.79 per hour
Typical Entry-Level Education	Bachelor's degree
Work Experience in a Related Occupation	Less than 5 years
On-the-job Training	None
Number of Jobs, 2022	554,700
Job Outlook, 2022-32	4% (As fast as average)
Employment Change, 2022-32	22,500

What Sales Managers Do

Sales managers direct organizations' sales teams.

Work Environment

Sales managers often are required to travel. Most sales managers work full time, and they often have to work additional hours on evenings and weekends.

How to Become a Sales Manager

Most sales managers have a bachelor's degree and work experience as a sales representative.

Sales managers set sales goals, analyze data, and develop training programs for organizations' sales representatives.

Pay

The median annual wage for sales managers was $130,600 in May 2022.

Job Outlook

Employment of sales managers is projected to grow 4 percent from 2022 to 2032, about as fast as the average for all occupations.

About 43,200 openings for sales managers are projected each year, on average, over the decade. Many of those openings are expected to result from the need to replace workers who transfer to different occupations or exit the labor force, such as to retire.

What Sales Managers Do

Sales managers direct organizations' sales teams. They set sales goals, analyze data, and develop training programs for organizations' sales representatives.

Duties

Sales managers typically do the following:

- Resolve customer complaints regarding sales and service
- Prepare budgets and approve expenditures
- Monitor customer preferences to determine the focus of sales efforts

Sales managers recruit, hire, and train new members of the sales staff.

- Analyze sales statistics
- Project sales and determine the profitability of products and services
- Determine discount rates or special pricing plans
- Develop plans to acquire new customers or clients through direct sales techniques, cold calling, and business-to-business marketing visits
- Assign sales territories and set sales quotas
- Plan and coordinate training programs for sales staff

Sales managers' responsibilities vary with the size of their organizations. However, most sales managers direct the distribution of goods and services by assigning sales territories, setting sales goals, and establishing training programs for the organization's sales representatives.

Sales managers recruit, hire, and train new members of the sales staff, including retail sales workers and wholesale and manufacturing sales representatives.

Sales managers advise sales representatives on ways to improve their sales performance. In large multiproduct organizations, they oversee regional and local sales managers and their staffs.

Sales managers also stay in contact with dealers and distributors. They analyze sales statistics generated from their staff to determine the sales potential and inventory requirements of products and stores and to monitor customers' preferences.

Sales managers work closely with managers from other departments in the organization. For example, the marketing department identifies new customers that the sales department can target. The relationship between these two departments is critical to helping an organization expand its client base. Sales managers also work closely with research and design departments because they know customers' preferences, and with warehousing departments because they know inventory needs.

Sales managers are increasingly using data on customer shopping habits to identify potential customers more effectively. This allows them more time to facilitate sales through customized sales pitches to individual customers.

The following are examples of types of sales managers:

Business to business (B2B) sales managers oversee sales from one business to another. These managers may work for a manufacturer selling to a wholesaler, or a wholesaler selling to a retailer. Examples of these workers include sales managers overseeing sales of software to business firms, and sales managers overseeing wholesale food sales to grocery stores.

Business to consumer (B2C) sales managers oversee direct sales between businesses and individual consumers. These managers typically work in retail settings. Examples of these workers include sales managers of automobile dealerships and department stores.

Work Environment

Sales managers held about 554,700 jobs in 2022. The largest employers of sales managers were as follows:

Sales managers have a lot of responsibility, and the position can be stressful.

Wholesale trade	20%
Retail trade	18
Professional, scientific, and technical services	13
Manufacturing	10
Finance and insurance	10

Sales managers have a lot of responsibility, and the position can be stressful. Many sales managers travel to national, regional, and local offices and to dealers' and distributors' offices.

Work Schedules

Most sales managers work full time, and they often have to work additional hours on evenings and weekends.

How to Become a Sales Manager

Most sales managers have a bachelor's degree and work experience as a sales representative.

Education

Sales managers are typically required to have a bachelor's degree, although some positions may only require a high school diploma. Courses in business law, management, economics, accounting, finance, mathematics, marketing, and statistics are advantageous.

Most sales managers have a bachelor's degree and previous work experience as a sales representative.

Work Experience in a Related Occupation

Work experience is typically required for someone to become a sales manager. The preferred duration varies, but employers usually seek candidates who have at least 1 to 5 years of experience in sales.

Sales managers typically enter the occupation from other sales and related occupations, such as retail sales workers, wholesale and manufacturing sales representatives, or purchasing agents. In small organizations, the number of sales manager positions often is limited, so advancement for sales workers usually comes slowly. In large organizations, promotion may occur more quickly.

Important Qualities

Analytical skills. Sales managers must collect and interpret complex data to target the most promising geographic areas and demographic groups, and determine the most effective sales strategies.

Communication skills. Sales managers need to work with colleagues and customers, so they must be able to communicate clearly.

Customer-service skills. When helping to make a sale, sales managers must listen and respond to the customer's needs.

Leadership skills. Sales managers must be able to evaluate how their sales staff performs and must develop strategies for meeting sales goals.

Pay

The median annual wage for sales managers was $130,600 in May 2022. The median wage is the wage at which half the workers in an occupation earned more than that amount and half earned less. The lowest 10 percent earned less than $61,040, and the highest 10 percent earned more than $239,200.

In May 2022, the median annual wages for sales managers in the top industries in which they worked were as follows:

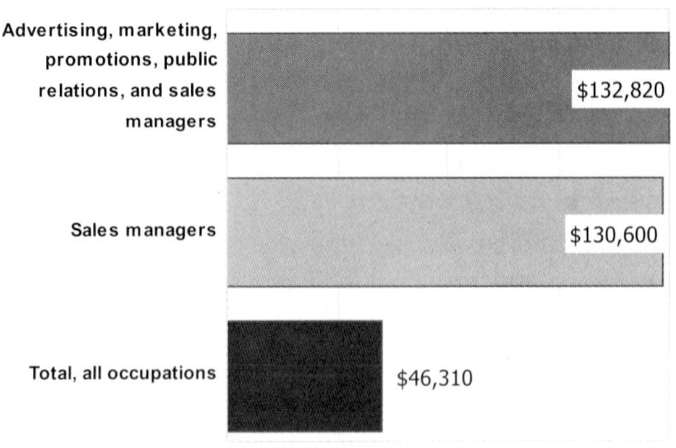

Note: All Occupations includes all occupations in the U.S. Economy.
Source: U.S. Bureau of Labor Statistics, Occupational Employment and Wage Statistics.

Finance and insurance	$161,040
Professional, scientific, and technical services	160,590
Manufacturing	138,400
Wholesale trade	129,800
Retail trade	82,540

Compensation methods for sales managers vary significantly with the type of organization and the product sold. Most employers use a combination of salary and commissions or salary plus bonuses. Commissions usually are a percentage of the value of sales, whereas bonuses may depend on individual performance, on the performance of all sales workers in the group or district, or on the organization's performance.

Most sales managers work full time, and they often have to work additional hours on evenings and weekends.

Job Outlook

Employment of sales managers is projected to grow 4 percent from 2022 to 2032, about as fast as the average for all occupations.

About 43,200 openings for sales managers are projected each year, on average, over the decade. Many of those openings are expected to result from the need to replace workers who transfer to different occupations or exit the labor force, such as to retire.

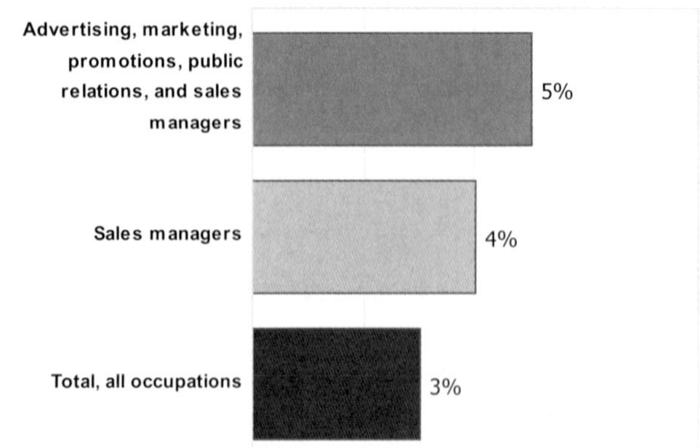

Note: All Occupations includes all occupations in the U.S. Economy.
Source: U.S. Bureau of Labor Statistics, Employment Projections program.

Employment

Employment growth of these managers will depend primarily on growth or contraction in the industries that employ them.

An effective sales team remains crucial for profitability. As the economy grows, organizations will focus on generating new sales and will look to their sales strategy as a way to increase competitiveness.

Online shopping is expected to continue to increase, meaning more sales will be completed without a sales worker involved in the transaction. However, brick-and-mortar retail stores also are expected to increase their emphasis on customer service as a way to compete with online sellers. Because sales managers will be needed to direct and navigate this mix between online and brick-and-mortar sales, sustained demand is expected for these workers.

Employment projections data for sales managers, 2022-32

Occupational Title	SOC Code	Employment, 2022	Projected Employment, 2032	Change, 2022-32		Employment by Industry
				Percent	Numeric	
Sales managers	11-2022	554,700	577,200	4	22,500	Get data

SOURCE: U.S. Bureau of Labor Statistics, Employment Projections program

Contacts for More Information

For more information about sales managers, visit

➤ Sales Management Association

Social and Community Service Managers

Summary

Quick Facts: Social and Community Service Managers	
2022 Median Pay	$74,240 per year $35.69 per hour
Typical Entry-Level Education	Bachelor's degree
Work Experience in a Related Occupation	Less than 5 years
On-the-job Training	None
Number of Jobs, 2022	178,400
Job Outlook, 2022-32	9% (Much faster than average)
Employment Change, 2022-32	16,200

What Social and Community Service Managers Do

Social and community service managers coordinate and supervise programs and organizations that support public well-being.

Work Environment

Social and community service managers work for nonprofit organizations, for-profit social service companies, and government agencies. Most work full time.

How to Become a Social and Community Service Manager

Social and community service managers typically need at least a bachelor's degree and work experience.

Pay

The median annual wage for social and community service managers was $74,240 in May 2022.

Job Outlook

Employment of social and community service managers is projected to grow 9 percent from 2022 to 2032, much faster than the average for all occupations.

Social and community service managers suggest and implement improvements to programs and services.

About 16,000 openings for social and community service managers are projected each year, on average, over the decade. Many of those openings are expected to result from the need to replace workers who transfer to different occupations or exit the labor force, such as to retire.

What Social and Community Service Managers Do

Social and community service managers coordinate and supervise programs and organizations that support public well-being. They direct workers who provide these services to the public.

Duties

Social and community service managers typically do the following:

- Work with community members and other stakeholders to identify necessary programs and services
- Oversee administrative aspects of programs to meet the objectives of the stakeholders
- Analyze data to determine the effectiveness of programs
- Suggest and implement improvements to programs and services
- Plan and manage outreach activities for increased awareness of programs
- Write proposals for social services funding

Social and community service managers work for a variety of organizations. Some of these organizations focus on working with a particular demographic, such as children, people who are homeless, older adults, or veterans. Others focus on helping people with particular challenges, such as substance abuse, mental health needs, and chronic hunger.

A routine part of social and community service managers' job is to show that their programs and services are effective. They collect statistics and other information to evaluate the impact their programs have on the community or their target audience. They are usually required to report this information to administrators or funders. They may also use evaluations to

Social and community service managers meet with community members and funding providers to discuss their programs.

identify opportunities to improve their programs, such as providing mentorship and assessments for their staff.

Although the specific job duties of social and community service managers may vary with the size of the organization, most managers recruit, hire, and train new staff members. They also supervise staff, such as social workers, who provide services directly to clients. Additionally, they may perform some of the services of the workers they oversee.

In large agencies, social and community service managers tend to have specialized duties. They may be responsible for running only one program in an organization and reporting to the agency's upper management. They usually do not design programs but instead supervise and implement programs set up by administrators, elected officials, or other stakeholders.

In small organizations, social and community managers often have many roles. They represent their organization through public speaking engagements or in communitywide committees; oversee programs and execute their implementations; spend time on administrative tasks, such as managing budgets; and help with raising funds and meeting with potential donors.

Work Environment

Social and community service managers held about 178,400 jobs in 2022. The largest employers of social and community service managers were as follows:

Individual and family services	27%
Nursing and residential care facilities	12
Local government, excluding education and hospitals	10
Religious, grantmaking, civic, professional, and similar organizations	10
Community and vocational rehabilitation services	9

Social and community service managers work for nonprofit organizations, for-profit social service companies, and government agencies. They also work in a variety of settings, including offices, clinics, hospitals, and shelters.

Work Schedules

Most social and community service managers work full time. Some work more than 40 hours per week.

How to Become a Social and Community Service Manager

Social and community service managers typically need at least a bachelor's degree and work experience. However, some positions also require a master's degree.

Education

Social and community service managers typically need a bachelor's degree in social work or a related public policy and social services field. However, some positions also require a master's degree.

Work Experience

Workers usually need experience in order to become a social and community service manager, and it is essential for those with a bachelor's degree. Candidates can get this experience by working as a social worker, substance abuse counselor, or in a similar occupation.

Important Qualities

Analytical skills. Social and community service managers need to understand and evaluate data in order to provide strategic guidance to their organization. They must be able to monitor and assess current programs as well as determine new initiatives.

Communication skills. Social and community service managers must be able to speak and write clearly. Public speaking experience is also helpful because these managers often participate in community outreach.

Social and community service managers work in a variety of settings, including offices, clinics, hospitals, and shelters.

Social and community service managers typically need at least a bachelor's degree and work experience in a related occupation.

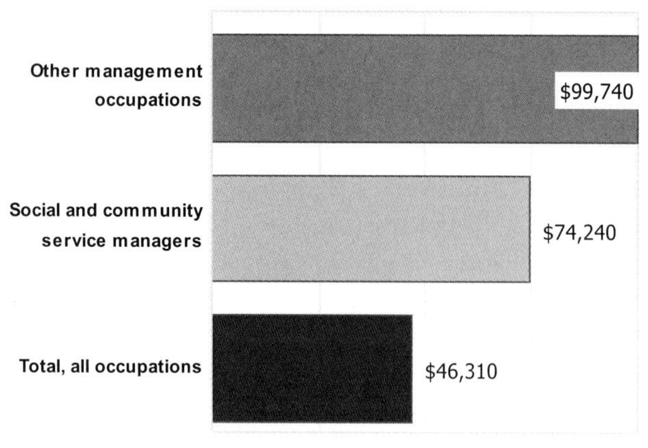

Note: All Occupations includes all occupations in the U.S. Economy.
Source: U.S. Bureau of Labor Statistics, Occupational Employment and Wage Statistics.

Managerial skills. Social and community service managers spend much of their time administering budgets and responding to a variety of issues.

Problem-solving skills. Social and community service managers must be able to address client, staff, and agency-related issues.

Time-management skills. Social and community service managers must prioritize and handle numerous tasks, often in a short timeframe.

Pay

The median annual wage for social and community service managers was $74,240 in May 2022. The median wage is the wage at which half the workers in an occupation earned more than that amount and half earned less. The lowest 10 percent earned less than $46,770, and the highest 10 percent earned more than $123,320.

In May 2022, the median annual wages for social and community service managers in the top industries in which they worked were as follows:

Local government, excluding education and hospitals	$96,050
Religious, grantmaking, civic, professional, and similar organizations	72,110
Individual and family services	65,170
Nursing and residential care facilities	64,030
Community and vocational rehabilitation services	63,370

Most social and community service managers work full time. Some work more than 40 hours per week.

Job Outlook

Employment of social and community service managers is projected to grow 9 percent from 2022 to 2032, much faster than the average for all occupations.

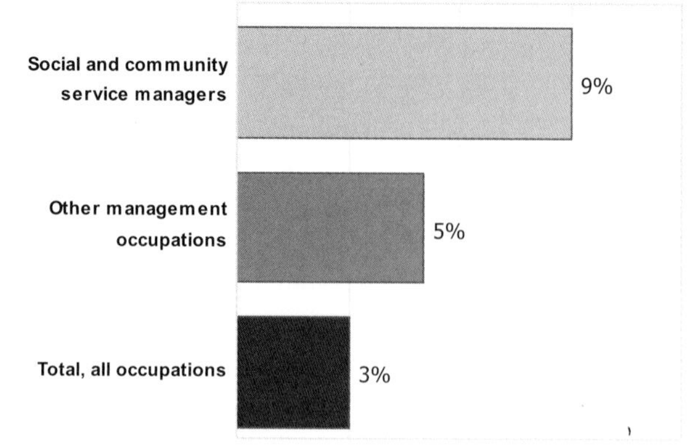

Note: All Occupations includes all occupations in the U.S. Economy.
Source: U.S. Bureau of Labor Statistics, Employment Projections program.

About 16,000 openings for social and community service managers are projected each year, on average, over the decade. Many of those openings are expected to result from the need to replace workers who transfer to different occupations or exit the labor force, such as to retire.

Employment

Much of the job growth in this occupation is the result of a population increasing its number of older adults. This age group has a greater need for social services, such as adult daycare, creating demand for social and community service managers.

In addition, employment growth is projected as people continue to seek treatment for their addictions and as people with substance abuse disorders are increasingly being directed to treatment programs rather than sent to jail. As a result, managers who direct treatment programs will be needed.

Employment projections data for social and community service managers, 2022-32

Occupational Title	SOC Code	Employment, 2022	Projected Employment, 2032	Change, 2022-32 Percent	Change, 2022-32 Numeric	Employment by Industry
SOURCE: U.S. Bureau of Labor Statistics, Employment Projections program						
Social and community service managers	11-9151	178,400	194,600	9	16,200	Get data

Contacts for More Information

For more information, visit

- The Network for Social Work Management
- Council on Social Work Education
- National Association of Social Workers

Top Executives

Summary

Quick Facts: Top Executives	
2022 Median Pay	$100,090 per year $48.12 per hour
Typical Entry-Level Education	Bachelor's degree
Work Experience in a Related Occupation	5 years or more
On-the-job Training	None
Number of Jobs, 2022	3,787,800
Job Outlook, 2022-32	3% (As fast as average)
Employment Change, 2022-32	124,200

What Top Executives Do

Top executives plan strategies and policies to ensure that an organization meets its goals.

Work Environment

Top executives work in nearly every industry, for both small and large organizations. They often have irregular schedules, which may include working evenings and weekends. Travel is common, particularly for chief executives.

How to Become a Top Executive

Top executives typically need at least a bachelor's degree and considerable work experience to enter the occupation.

Pay

The median annual wage for chief executives was $189,520 in May 2022.

The median annual wage for general and operations managers was $98,100 in May 2022.

Top executives are the highest level of management at an organization and often work closely with other executives and managers.

Job Outlook

Overall employment of top executives is projected to grow 3 percent from 2022 to 2032, about as fast as the average for all occupations.

About 311,600 openings for top executives are projected each year, on average, over the decade. Many of those openings are expected to result from the need to replace workers who transfer to different occupations or exit the labor force, such as to retire.

What Top Executives Do

Top executives plan strategies and policies to ensure that an organization meets its goals. They coordinate and direct work activities of companies and organizations.

Duties

Top executives typically do the following:

- Establish and carry out departmental or organizational goals, policies, and procedures
- Direct and oversee an organization's financial and budgetary activities
- Manage general activities related to making products and providing services
- Consult with other executives, staff, and board members about general operations
- Negotiate or approve contracts and agreements
- Appoint department heads and managers
- Analyze financial statements, sales reports, and other performance indicators
- Identify places to cut costs and to improve performance, policies, and programs

The responsibilities of top executives largely depend on an organization's size. In small organizations, such as an independent retail store, an owner or manager often is responsible for hiring, training, quality control, and day-to-day supervisory duties. In large organizations, chief executives typically focus

Top executives often report to a board of directors.

on formulating policies and planning strategies, while general and operations managers direct day-to-day operations.

The following are examples of types of top executives:

Chief executive officers (CEOs), who are also known by titles such as *executive director*, *managing director*, or *president*, provide overall direction for companies and organizations. CEOs manage company operations, formulate and implement policies, and ensure that goals are met. They collaborate with and direct the work of other top executives and typically report to a board of directors.

There may be other types of chief executives—such as *chief operating officers* (COOs), *chief financial officers* (CFOs), or *chief human resources officers*—who manage a specific part of the organization. The knowledge, skills, and job duties that these executives have differ, depending on which department they oversee.

General and operations managers oversee activities that are too diverse to be classified into one area of management or administration. Responsibilities may include formulating policies, directing daily operations, and planning the use of materials and human resources. These managers make staff schedules, assign work, and ensure that projects are completed. In some organizations, the tasks of chief executive officers may overlap with those of general and operations managers.

Mayors, ***city managers***, ***county administrators***, and ***governors*** are chief executive officers of governments. They usually oversee budgets, programs, and the use of resources. Mayors and governors must be elected to office, whereas managers and administrators are typically appointed.

School superintendents and ***college*** or ***university presidents*** are chief executive officers of school districts and postsecondary schools. They manage issues such as student achievement, budgets and resources, general operations, and relations with government agencies and other stakeholders.

Work Environment

Chief executives held about 280,000 jobs in 2022. The largest employers of chief executives were as follows:

Self-employed workers	21%
Professional, scientific, and technical services	13
Government	9
Healthcare and social assistance	6
Manufacturing	5

General and operations managers held about 3.5 million jobs in 2022. The largest employers of general and operations managers were as follows:

Retail trade	13%
Professional, scientific, and technical services	12
Wholesale trade	8
Manufacturing	8
Construction	7

Top executives often work many hours, including evenings and weekends.

Top executives work in nearly every industry. They work for both small and large organizations, ranging from businesses in which they are the sole employee to firms with hundreds or thousands of employees.

Because top executives often are held responsible for their organization's success, their work may be stressful.

Top executives frequently travel to attend meetings and conferences or to visit local, regional, national, or international offices of interest.

Top executives often interact with other high-level executives, such as financial managers, human resource managers, or chief technology officers.

Work Schedules

Most top executives work full time, and many work more than 40 hours per week, including evenings and weekends.

How to Become a Top Executive

Top executives typically need at least a bachelor's degree and considerable work experience to enter the occupation.

Education

Top executives typically need a bachelor's or master's degree in an area related to their field of work, such as business or engineering. Top executives in the public sector may have a degree in business administration, public administration, law, or the liberal arts. Top executives of large corporations may have a master's degree in business administration (MBA).

College presidents and school superintendents are typically required to have a master's degree, although a doctorate is often preferred.

Although many mayors, governors, and other public sector executives have at least a bachelor's degree, these positions typically do not have any specific education requirements.

Top executives typically need many years of previous work experience.

Work Experience in a Related Occupation

Many top executives advance within their own organizations, moving up from lower level management occupations or supervisory positions. However, some companies may prefer to hire qualified candidates from outside their organization. Top executives who are promoted from lower level positions may be able to substitute experience for education to move up in the organization.

Chief executives typically need extensive managerial experience, and this experience is expected to be in the organization's area of specialty. Most general and operations managers hired from outside an organization need lower level supervisory or management experience in a related field.

Some general managers move into higher level managerial or executive positions. Executive training programs and development programs often benefit managers or executives.

Licenses, Certifications, and Registrations

Some top executive positions may require the applicant to have a license or certification relevant to their area of management. For example, some employers may require their chief executive officer to be a certified public accountant (CPA).

Important Qualities

Communication skills. Top executives must be able to convey information clearly and persuasively. They must discuss issues and negotiate with others, direct staff, and explain policies and decisions to people within and outside the organization.

Decision-making skills. When setting policies and managing an organization, top executives must be able to assess different options and choose the best course of action.

Leadership skills. Top executives must be able to shape and direct an organization by coordinating policies, people, and resources.

Problem-solving skills. Top executives need to identify and resolve issues within an organization. They must be able to recognize shortcomings and carry out solutions.

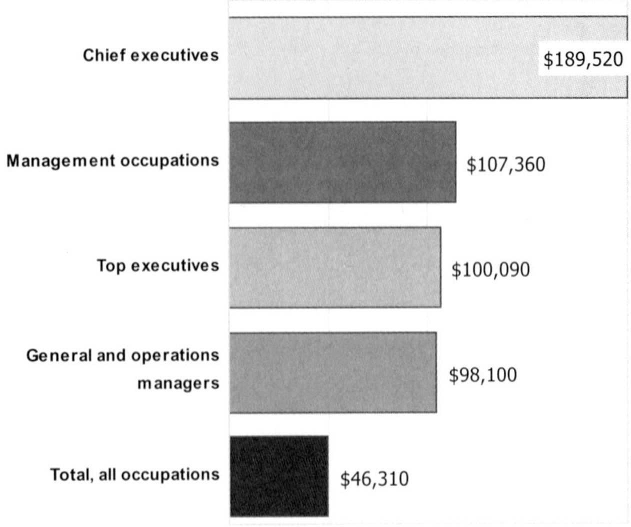

Note: All Occupations includes all occupations in the U.S. Economy.
Source: U.S. Bureau of Labor Statistics, Occupational Employment and Wage Statistics.

Time-management skills. Top executives do many tasks concurrently to ensure that their work gets done and that the organization meets its goals.

Pay

The median annual wage for chief executives was $189,520 in May 2022. The median wage is the wage at which half the workers in an occupation earned more than that amount and half earned less. The lowest 10 percent earned less than $74,920, and the highest 10 percent earned more than $239,200.

The median annual wage for general and operations managers was $98,100 in May 2022. The lowest 10 percent earned less than $43,470, and the highest 10 percent earned more than $221,270.

In May 2022, the median annual wages for chief executives in the top industries in which they worked were as follows:

Manufacturing	$231,640
Professional, scientific, and technical services	211,600
Healthcare and social assistance	169,440
Government	124,090

In May 2022, the median annual wages for general and operations managers in the top industries in which they worked were as follows:

Professional, scientific, and technical services	$131,970
Manufacturing	120,050
Wholesale trade	102,680
Construction	99,390
Retail trade	72,100

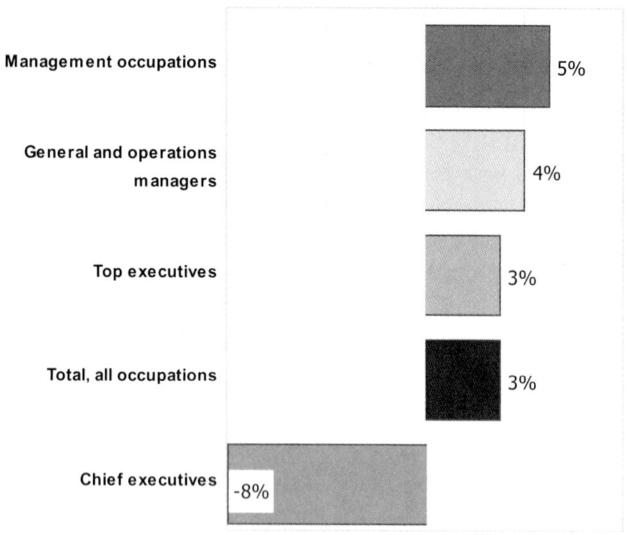

Note: All Occupations includes all occupations in the U.S. Economy.
Source: U.S. Bureau of Labor Statistics, Employment Projections program.

Top executives are among the highest paid workers in the United States. However, salary levels vary substantially. For example, a top manager in a large corporation may earn significantly more than the mayor of a small town.

Similarly, earnings for general and operations managers differ across industries because their responsibilities also vary by industry.

In addition to salaries, total compensation for corporate executives often includes stock options and other performance bonuses. These executives also may enjoy benefits such as access to expense allowances, use of company-owned aircraft and cars, and membership to exclusive clubs. Nonprofit and government executives usually receive fewer of these types of benefits.

Top executives often work many hours and have irregular schedules, which may include evenings and weekends.

Job Outlook

Overall employment of top executives is projected to grow 3 percent from 2022 to 2032, about as fast as the average for all occupations.

About 311,600 openings for top executives are projected each year, on average, over the decade. Many of those openings are expected to result from the need to replace workers who transfer to different occupations or exit the labor force, such as to retire.

Employment

Projected employment of top executives varies by occupation (see table).

Demand for general and operations managers will grow as organizations increasingly rely on these workers for help in functioning smoothly.

Employment of chief executives is projected to decline as office technology improves, increasing the ability of these workers to perform tasks previously done by multiple chief executives. In addition, changing organizational structures may lead to fewer new jobs for these workers as more companies adopt a workplace structure with fewer chief executive positions.

Employment projections data for top executives, 2022-32

Occupational Title	SOC Code	Employment, 2022	Projected Employment, 2032	Change, 2022-32 Percent	Change, 2022-32 Numeric	Employment by Industry
SOURCE: U.S. Bureau of Labor Statistics, Employment Projections program						
Top executives	—	3,787,800	3,912,000	3	124,200	
Chief executives	11-1011	280,000	257,000	-8	-23,000	Get data
General and operations managers	11-1021	3,507,800	3,655,100	4	147,300	Get data

Contacts for More Information

For more information, visit

- American Management Association
- National Management Association
- Financial Executives International
- Financial Management Association International

Training and Development Managers

Summary

Quick Facts: Training and Development Managers

2022 Median Pay	$120,000 per year $57.69 per hour
Typical Entry-Level Education	Bachelor's degree
Work Experience in a Related Occupation	5 years or more
On-the-job Training	None
Number of Jobs, 2022	41,300
Job Outlook, 2022-32	6% (Faster than average)
Employment Change, 2022-32	2,700

What Training and Development Managers Do

Training and development managers plan, coordinate, and direct skills- and knowledge-enhancement programs for an organization's staff.

Work Environment

Training and development managers work in nearly every industry. They typically work full time, spending much of their day with people. Some work more than 40 hours per week.

How to Become a Training and Development Manager

Training and development managers typically need a bachelor's or master's degree and related work experience.

Pay

The median annual wage for training and development managers was $120,000 in May 2022.

Job Outlook

Employment of training and development managers is projected to grow 6 percent from 2022 to 2032, faster than the average for all occupations.

About 3,500 openings for training and development managers are projected each year, on average, over the decade. Many of those openings are expected to result from the need to replace workers who transfer to different occupations or exit the labor force, such as to retire.

What Training and Development Managers Do

Training and development managers plan, coordinate, and direct skills- and knowledge-enhancement programs for an organization's staff.

Duties

Training and development managers typically do the following:

- Oversee training and development staff
- Assess employees' needs for training
- Align training with the organization's goals
- Create and manage training budgets
- Develop and implement training programs
- Review and select training materials from a variety of vendors
- Update training programs to ensure that they are relevant
- Teach training methods and skills to instructors and supervisors
- Evaluate the effectiveness of training programs and instructors

Training and development managers oversee training programs, staff, and budgets. They are responsible for creating or selecting course content and materials for training programs. Training may be in the form of a video, self-guided instructional manual, or online application and delivered in person or through a computer or other hand-held electronic device. Training also may be collaborative, with employees informally connecting with experts, mentors, and colleagues, often through social media or other online medium. Managers must ensure that training methods, content, software, systems, and equipment are appropriate.

Training and development managers work with specialists to design curriculums.

Training and development managers teach training methods to specialists.

Training and development managers typically supervise a staff of training and development specialists, such as instructional designers, program developers, and instructors. Managers teach training methods to specialists who, in turn, instruct the organization's employees—both new and experienced. Managers direct the daily activities of specialists and evaluate their effectiveness. Although training and development managers primarily oversee specialists and program operations, some also conduct training courses.

Training and development managers often confer with managers of other departments to identify training needs. They may work with top executives and financial managers to identify and match training priorities with overall business goals. They may also prepare training budgets and ensure that expenses stay within budget.

Work Environment

Training and development managers held about 41,300 jobs in 2022. The largest employers of training and development managers were as follows:

Training and development managers may meet with training vendors to choose training materials.

Professional, scientific, and technical services	13%
Management of companies and enterprises	13
Educational services; state, local, and private	12
Finance and insurance	10
Healthcare and social assistance	9

Training and development managers typically work in offices. Some travel between a main office and regional offices or training facilities. They spend much of their time working with people and overseeing training activities.

Work Schedules

Most training and development managers work full time during regular business hours. Some work more than 40 hours per week.

How to Become a Training and Development Manager

Candidates typically need a combination of education and related work experience to become a training and development manager. Although many positions require a bachelor's degree, some jobs require a master's degree.

Education

Many positions require training and development managers to have a bachelor's degree, but some jobs require a master's degree. Although training and development managers come from a variety of educational backgrounds, these workers commonly have a bachelor's degree in business, communications, social science, or a related field.

Some employers prefer or require training and development managers to have a master's degree with a concentration in training and development, human resources management, organizational development, or business administration (MBA).

Most candidates need a combination of education and related work experience to become a training and development manager.

Training and development managers may also benefit from studying instructional design, behavioral psychology, or educational psychology.

Work Experience in a Related Occupation

Related work experience is essential for training and development managers. Many positions require work experience in management, teaching, or training and development or another human resources field. For example, some training and development managers start out as training and development specialists. Some employers also prefer experience in the industry in which the company operates.

Licenses, Certifications, and Registrations

Although it is not required for training and development managers, certification may show professional expertise. Some employers prefer to hire candidates who have certification, and some positions require it.

Many professional associations for human resources professionals offer classes to enhance the skills of their members. Some associations, including the Association for Talent Development and the International Society for Performance Improvement, specialize in training and development and offer certification programs. The Society for Human Resource Management offers general human resources certification.

Important Qualities

Business skills. Training and development managers must understand business operations in order to match training with business goals. They also need to be able to plan and adhere to budgets.

Collaboration skills. Training and development managers need strong interpersonal skills for working with staff, trainees, subject matter experts, and organization leaders. They accomplish much of their work through teams.

Communication skills. Training and development managers must clearly convey information to diverse audiences. They also must be able to effectively instruct their staff.

Critical-thinking skills. Training and development managers use critical-thinking skills when assessing classes, materials, and programs. They must identify the training needs of an organization and make changes and improvements as required.

Decision-making skills. Training and development managers must select or create the best training programs to meet the needs of an organization. For example, they must review available training methods and materials and choose those that best fit each program.

Collaboration skills. Training and development managers need strong interpersonal skills because delivering training programs requires working in concert with staff, trainees, subject matter experts, and the organization's leaders. They also accomplish much of their work through teams.

Instructional skills. Training and development managers need to understand the fundamentals of teaching and lesson

Training and Development Managers

Median annual wages, May 2022

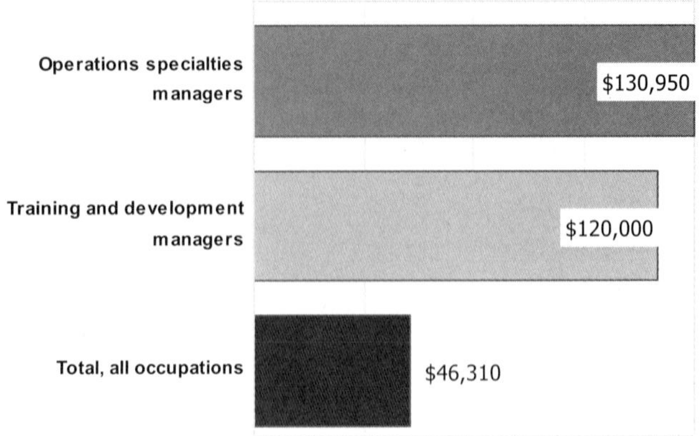

Note: All Occupations includes all occupations in the U.S. Economy.
Source: U.S. Bureau of Labor Statistics, Occupational Employment and Wage Statistics.

planning. In addition to developing training, they may lead courses or seminars.

Leadership skills. Managers are often in charge of a staff and programs. They must be able to organize, motivate, and instruct those working for them.

Pay

The median annual wage for training and development managers was $120,000 in May 2022. The median wage is the wage at which half the workers in an occupation earned more than that amount and half earned less. The lowest 10 percent earned less than $68,450, and the highest 10 percent earned more than $210,470.

In May 2022, the median annual wages for training and development managers in the top industries in which they worked were as follows:

Professional, scientific, and technical services	$143,670
Management of companies and enterprises....	130,310
Finance and insurance..................................	121,590
Healthcare and social assistance	104,480
Educational services; state, local, and private.	103,550

Most training and development managers work full time during regular business hours. Some work more than 40 hours per week.

Job Outlook

Employment of training and development managers is projected to grow 6 percent from 2022 to 2032, faster than the average for all occupations.

About 3,500 openings for training and development managers are projected each year, on average, over the decade. Many of those openings are expected to result from the need

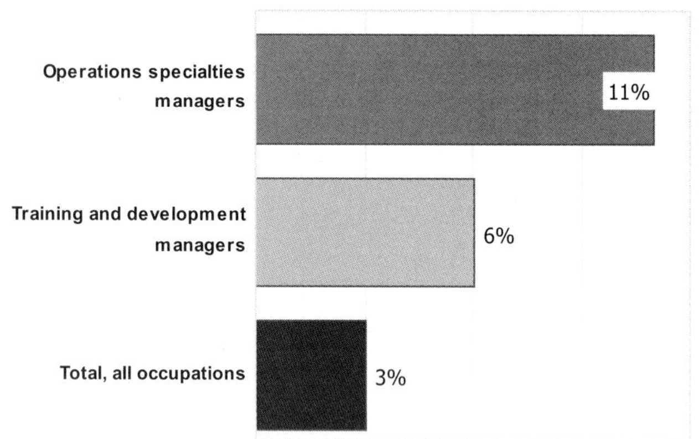

Note: All Occupations includes all occupations in the U.S. Economy.
Source: U.S. Bureau of Labor Statistics, Employment Projections program.

to replace workers who transfer to different occupations or exit the labor force, such as to retire.

Employment

In many occupations, employees are required to take continuing education and skill development courses throughout their careers, creating demand for workers who develop and provide training materials.

Innovations in training methods and learning technology are expected to continue throughout the decade, particularly for organizations with remote workers. Organizations use social media, visual simulations, mobile learning, and social networks in their training programs. Training and development managers need to continue modifying training programs, allocating budgets, and integrating these features into training programs and curriculums.

In addition, as companies seek to reduce costs, training and development managers may be required to structure programs to enlist available experts, take advantage of existing resources, and facilitate positive relationships among staff. Training and development managers may use informal collaborative learning and social media to engage and train employees in the most cost-effective way.

Employment projections data for training and development managers, 2022-32

Occupational Title	SOC Code	Employment, 2022	Projected Employment, 2032	Change, 2022-32		Employment by Industry
				Percent	Numeric	
SOURCE: U.S. Bureau of Labor Statistics, Employment Projections program						
Training and development managers	11-3131	41,300	44,000	6	2,700	Get data

Contacts for More Information

For more information, visit

- Association for Talent Development
- International Society for Performance Improvement
- Society for Human Resource Management

Math

Actuaries

Summary

Quick Facts: Actuaries	
2022 Median Pay	$113,990 per year $54.80 per hour
Typical Entry-Level Education	Bachelor's degree
Work Experience in a Related Occupation	None
On-the-job Training	Long-term on-the-job training
Number of Jobs, 2022	30,000
Job Outlook, 2022-32	23% (Much faster than average)
Employment Change, 2022-32	7,000

What Actuaries Do

Actuaries use mathematics, statistics, and financial theory to analyze the economic costs of risk and uncertainty.

Work Environment

Most actuaries work for insurance companies. Although most work full time in an office setting, some actuaries who work as consultants travel to meet with clients.

How to Become an Actuary

Actuaries typically need a bachelor's degree to enter the occupation and must pass a series of exams to become certified. They must have a strong background in mathematics, statistics, and business.

Pay

The median annual wage for actuaries was $113,990 in May 2022.

Job Outlook

Employment of actuaries is projected to grow 23 percent from 2022 to 2032, much faster than the average for all occupations.

About 2,300 openings for actuaries are projected each year, on average, over the decade. Many of those openings are expected to result from the need to replace workers who transfer to different occupations or exit the labor force, such as to retire.

What Actuaries Do

Actuaries analyze the financial costs of risk and uncertainty. They use mathematics, statistics, and financial theory to assess the risk of potential events, and they help businesses and clients develop policies that minimize the cost of that risk. Actuaries' work is essential to the insurance industry.

Duties

Actuaries typically do the following:

- Compile and analyze statistical data and other information
- Estimate the probability and likely economic cost of an event such as death, sickness, an accident, or a natural disaster
- Design and test insurance policies, investments, and other business strategies to minimize risk and maximize profitability
- Calculate cash reserves needed, based on existing policies and liabilities, in case of payout or claims
- Produce charts, tables, and reports that explain calculations and proposals
- Explain their findings and proposals to company executives, government officials, shareholders, and clients

Actuaries use database software to compile information. They use statistical and modeling software to forecast the

Actuaries use advanced statistics and modeling software to forecast the cost and probability of an event.

Actuaries produce charts, tables, and reports to explain their calculations.

probability of an event occurring, the potential costs of the event if it does occur, and whether the insurance company has enough money to pay future claims.

Actuaries typically work on teams that often include managers and workers from other fields, such as accounting, underwriting, and finance. For example, some actuaries work with accountants and financial analysts to set the price for security offerings or with data scientists to forecast demand for new products.

Most actuaries work for insurance companies, where they help design policies and determine the premiums that should be charged for each policy. They must ensure that the premiums are profitable yet competitive with other insurance companies.

Some actuaries work as consultants and provide advice to clients on a contract basis. Many consulting actuaries audit the work of internal actuaries at insurance companies or handle actuarial duties for insurance companies that are not large enough to keep their own actuaries on staff.

Actuaries in the insurance industry typically specialize in one field of insurance, such as the following:

Health insurance actuaries help develop long-term care and health insurance policies by predicting expected costs of providing care under the terms of an insurance contract. Their predictions are based on numerous factors, including family history, geographic location, and occupation.

Life insurance actuaries help develop annuity and life insurance policies for individuals and groups by creating estimates of how long someone will live. These estimates are based on risk factors, such as age and tobacco use.

Property and casualty insurance actuaries help develop policies that insure policyholders against property loss and liability resulting from accidents, natural disasters, fires, and other events. For example, they calculate the expected number of claims resulting from automobile accidents, which varies with the insured person's age, driving history, type of car, and other factors.

Some actuaries apply their expertise to financial matters outside of the insurance industry. For example, they develop investment strategies that manage risks and maximize returns for companies or individuals. Actuaries outside of the insurance industry include the following:

Enterprise risk management actuaries identify risks, including economic, financial, and geopolitical risks that may affect a company's short-term or long-term objectives. They help top executives determine how much risk the business is willing to take, and they develop strategies to mitigate the financial impact of those risks.

Pension and retirement benefits actuaries design, test, and evaluate company pension plans to determine if funds available in the future will be enough to ensure payment of benefits. They must report the results of their evaluations to the federal government. Pension actuaries also help businesses develop other types of retirement benefits, such as 401(k)s and healthcare plans for retirees. In addition, they provide retirement planning advice to individuals.

Public sector actuaries have different duties, based on the level of government in which they work. In the federal government, actuaries may evaluate proposed changes to Social Security or Medicare or conduct economic and demographic studies to project benefit obligations. At the state level, actuaries may examine and regulate the rates charged by insurance companies.

Work Environment

Actuaries held about 30,000 jobs in 2022. The largest employers of actuaries were as follows:

Finance and insurance	80%
Professional, scientific, and technical services	12
Management of companies and enterprises	4
Government	3

Actuaries typically work on teams that often include managers and professionals in other fields, such as accounting, underwriting, and finance.

Although actuaries usually work in an office setting, those who work for consulting firms may need to travel to meet with clients.

Work Schedules

Most actuaries work full time, and some work more than 40 hours per week.

How to Become an Actuary

To enter the occupation, actuaries typically need a bachelor's degree in mathematics, actuarial science, statistics, or some other analytical field. Students must complete coursework in subjects such as economics, applied statistics, and corporate finance and must pass a series of exams to become certified.

Actuaries typically work on teams that often include managers and professionals in other fields, such as accounting, underwriting, and finance.

Actuaries need a bachelor's degree and must pass a series of exams to become certified professionals.

Education

Actuaries need a strong background in mathematics, statistics, and business. Typically, actuaries have an undergraduate degree in mathematics, business, actuarial science, or some other analytical field.

To become certified, students must complete coursework in subjects such as economics, statistics, and corporate finance. Coursework in computer science, especially programming languages, and the ability to use and develop spreadsheets, databases, and statistical analysis tools also is important.

Because the different types of practice areas include health, life, pension, and casualty, internships may be helpful for students deciding on which actuarial track to pursue.

Licenses, Certification, and Registrations

Two professional organizations—the Casualty Actuarial Society (CAS) and the Society of Actuaries (SOA)—offer two levels of certification: associate and fellow.

The CAS certifies actuaries who work in the property and casualty field, which includes automobile, homeowners, commercial, and workers' compensation insurance.

The SOA certifies actuaries who work in life insurance, health insurance, retirement benefits, investments, and finance.

Both credentials require candidates to complete coursework in economics, finance, and mathematical statistics while in college. Candidates also must pass a series of exams and take seminars on professionalism.

Many employers expect prospective hires to have passed at least one or two of these certification exams before graduation.

It may take up to 7 years for an actuary to earn the associate-level certification because of the lengthy preparation required. After becoming associates, actuaries typically take several more years to earn fellowship status. Both the CAS and the SOA have a continuing education requirement.

The SOA offers fellowship certification in five separate tracks: life and annuities, group and health benefits, retirement benefits, quantitative finance and investments, and corporate finance/enterprise risk management. Unlike the SOA, the CAS does not offer specialized study tracks for fellowship certification.

Pension actuaries typically must be licensed by the U.S. Department of Labor and U.S. Department of the Treasury's Joint Board for the Enrollment of Actuaries. Licensed pension actuaries, known as enrolled actuaries, must meet certain experience requirements and pass exams administered through the SOA.

Training

Entry-level actuaries typically start out as trainees. They are usually on teams with experienced actuaries who serve as mentors. Trainees begin work on basic tasks, such as compiling data, and take on more complex duties, such as conducting research and writing reports, as they gain experience. Trainees also may work in other departments, such as marketing, underwriting, and product development, to learn how actuaries fit into all aspects of a company.

Most employers support their actuaries throughout the certification process. For example, employers may pay the cost of exams and study materials or provide paid time to study. Employees may receive raises or bonuses for each exam that they pass.

Advancement

Advancement usually depends on job performance and the number of actuarial exams passed. For example, actuaries who achieve fellowship status often supervise the work of other actuaries and provide input to senior management. Actuaries with a broad knowledge of risk management and how it applies to business may advance to become top executives, such as chief risk officers or chief financial officers.

Important Qualities

Analytical skills. Actuaries identify patterns and trends in complex sets of data to determine the factors that affect certain types of events.

Communication skills. Actuaries must be able to explain complex technical matters to those without an actuarial background. They also must describe their work and recommendations clearly in written reports and memos.

Computer skills. Actuaries must know programming languages and be able to use and develop spreadsheets, databases, and statistical analysis tools.

Actuaries

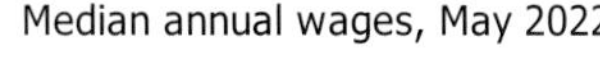

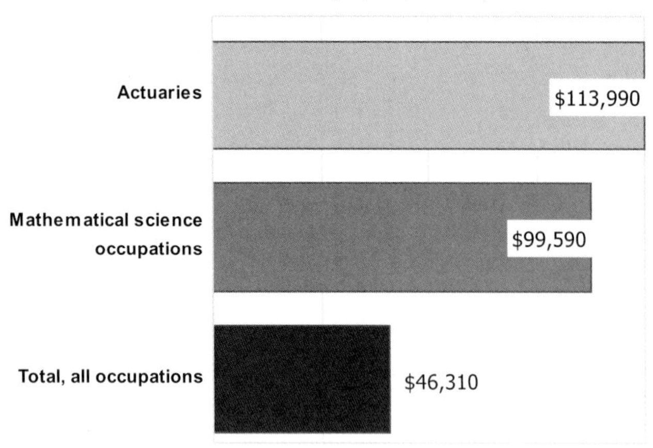

Note: All Occupations includes all occupations in the U.S. Economy.
Source: U.S. Bureau of Labor Statistics, Occupational Employment and Wage Statistics.

Actuaries

Percent change in employment, projected 2022-32

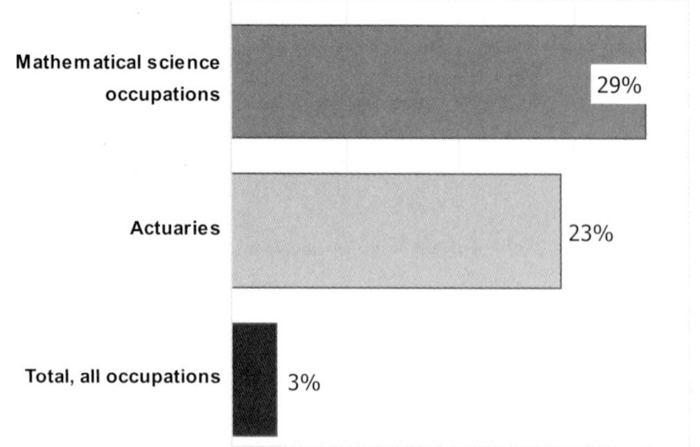

Note: All Occupations includes all occupations in the U.S. Economy.
Source: U.S. Bureau of Labor Statistics, Employment Projections program.

Interpersonal skills. Actuaries serve as leaders and members of teams, so they must be able to listen to and collaborate with others.

Math skills. Actuaries quantify risk by using the principles of calculus, statistics, and probability.

Problem-solving skills. Actuaries identify risks and develop ways for businesses to manage those risks.

Pay

The median annual wage for actuaries was $113,990 in May 2022. The median wage is the wage at which half the workers in an occupation earned more than that amount and half earned less. The lowest 10 percent earned less than $71,760, and the highest 10 percent earned more than $199,300.

In May 2022, the median annual wages for actuaries in the top industries in which they worked were as follows:

Finance and insurance	$115,910
Government	115,860
Professional, scientific, and technical services	107,990
Management of companies and enterprises	101,570

Most actuaries work full time, and some work more than 40 hours per week.

Job Outlook

Employment of actuaries is projected to grow 23 percent from 2022 to 2032, much faster than the average for all occupations.

About 2,300 openings for actuaries are projected each year, on average, over the decade. Many of those openings are expected to result from the need to replace workers who transfer to different occupations or exit the labor force, such as to retire.

Employment

Actuaries will be needed to develop, price, and evaluate a variety of insurance products and calculate the costs of new risks.

More actuaries also will be needed to help companies manage their own risk, a practice known as enterprise risk management. These actuaries help companies adjust their business or investment strategies across all areas of operation.

Insurance companies will need actuaries to analyze the large amount of information, such as medical or property data, collected from consumers. These data will allow insurance companies to develop new products, set competitive prices, predict consumer behavior, and improve projections of future risks and costs.

In addition, health insurance companies will require actuaries to help evaluate the effects of changing healthcare regulations and guidelines, expand into new insurance markets, and offer products to new customers.

Employment projections data for actuaries, 2022-32

Occupational Title	SOC Code	Employment, 2022	Projected Employment, 2032	Change, 2022-32		Employment by Industry
				Percent	Numeric	
Actuaries	15-2011	30,000	36,900	23	7,000	Get data

SOURCE: U.S. Bureau of Labor Statistics, Employment Projections program

Contacts for More Information

For more information about actuaries, visit

- American Academy of Actuaries
- Casualty Actuarial Society
- Society of Actuaries
- Be an Actuary
- American Society of Pension Professionals and Actuaries
- U.S. Department of Labor and U.S. Department of the Treasury's Joint Board for the Enrollment of Actuaries

Data Scientists

Summary

Quick Facts: Data Scientists	
2022 Median Pay	$103,500 per year $49.76 per hour
Typical Entry-Level Education	Bachelor's degree
Work Experience in a Related Occupation	None
On-the-job Training	None
Number of Jobs, 2022	168,900
Job Outlook, 2022-32	35% (Much faster than average)
Employment Change, 2022-32	59,400

What Data Scientists Do

Data scientists use analytical tools and techniques to extract meaningful insights from data.

Work Environment

Data scientists spend much of their time in an office setting. Most work full time.

How to Become a Data Scientist

Data scientists typically need at least a bachelor's degree in mathematics, statistics, computer science, or a related field to enter the occupation. Some employers require or prefer that applicants have a master's or doctoral degree.

Pay

The median annual wage for data scientists was $103,500 in May 2022.

Job Outlook

Employment of data scientists is projected to grow 35 percent from 2022 to 2032, much faster than the average for all occupations.

About 17,700 openings for data scientists are projected each year, on average, over the decade. Many of those openings are expected to result from the need to replace workers who transfer to different occupations or exit the labor force, such as to retire.

What Data Scientists Do

Data scientists use analytical tools and techniques to extract meaningful insights from data.

Duties

Data scientists typically do the following:

- Determine which data are available and useful for the project
- Collect, categorize, and analyze data
- Create, validate, test, and update algorithms and models
- Use data visualization software to present findings
- Make business recommendations to stakeholders based on data analysis

Data scientists often begin a project by gathering or identifying relevant data sources, such as surveys. They may use a variety of methods to obtain data, including through access to other organizations' databases or by using web-scraping tools (software that extracts specific information from websites). They may start with large, unstructured datasets, commonly referred to as raw data. To properly analyze the data, these scientists must "clean" the raw data, a process by which they structure the data to make them readable by software programs.

Data scientists develop algorithms (sets of instructions that tell computers what to do) and models to support programs for machine learning. They use machine learning to classify or categorize data or to make predictions related to the models. Scientists also must test the algorithms and models for accuracy, including for updates with newly collected data.

Data scientists often use data visualization software to present their findings as charts, maps, and other graphics. Visualization

Data scientists use machine learning to classify data.

To present their findings, these scientists often make use of data visualization.

techniques allow data scientists to clearly communicate their analyses to technical and nontechnical audiences, including colleagues, managers, and clients. Ensuring that audiences understand the information helps data scientists make recommendations for business decisions or process changes based on the results of their analysis.

Some data scientists choose to focus on a particular area of work. For example, data scientists who have a strong coding or engineering background may develop or recommend systems, build machine learning algorithms, and devise ways to enhance web-browsing functions. Others conduct research for reports or academic journals. Still others focus on improving business strategy for activities such as marketing, sales, and user engagement.

Work Environment

Data scientists held about 168,900 jobs in 2022. The largest employers of data scientists were as follows:

Computer systems design and related services	13%
Insurance carriers and related activities	9
Management of companies and enterprises	8
Management, scientific, and technical consulting services	7
Scientific research and development services	5

Data scientists spend much of their time in an office setting.

Work Schedules

Most data scientists work full time.

How to Become a Data Scientist

Data scientists typically need at least a bachelor's degree in mathematics, statistics, computer science, or a related field to enter the occupation. However, some employers require or prefer that candidates have a master's or doctoral degree.

Education

Data scientists typically need at least a bachelor's degree, but some jobs require a master's or doctoral degree. Common fields of degree include mathematics, statistics, computer science, business, and engineering.

Because data science involves the use of algorithms and statistical techniques, students need extensive study in mathematics and statistics. High school students interested in becoming data scientists should take classes in subjects such as linear algebra, calculus, and probability and statistics.

At the college level, courses in computer science are important in addition to math and statistics. Students must learn data-oriented programming languages as well as statistical, database, and other software for presenting analyses.

Other Experience

Some employers require industry-related experience or education. For example, data scientists seeking work in an asset management company may need to have experience in the finance industry or to have completed coursework that demonstrates an understanding of investments, banking, or related subjects.

Important Qualities

Analytical skills. Data scientists must be adept at researching and at examining and interpreting findings.

Computer skills. Data scientists must be able to write code, analyze data, develop or improve algorithms, and use data visualization tools.

Communication skills. Data scientists must be able to convey the results of their analysis to technical and nontechnical audiences to make business recommendations.

Logical-thinking skills. Data scientists must understand and be able to design and develop statistical models and to analyze data.

Math skills. Data scientists use statistical methods to collect and organize data.

Data scientists typically work in an office setting.

Data scientists need strong computer skills.

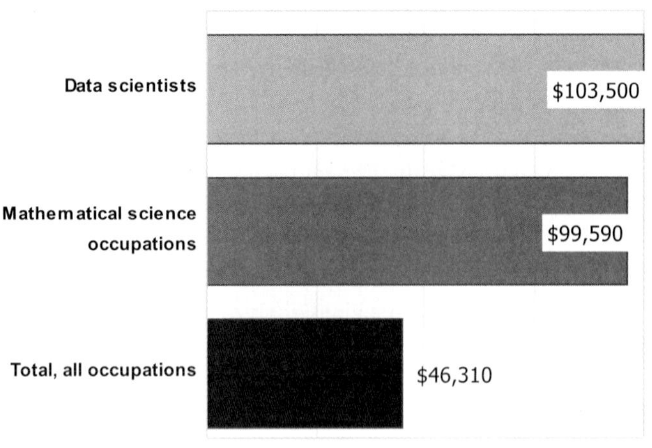

Note: All Occupations includes all occupations in the U.S. Economy.
Source: U.S. Bureau of Labor Statistics, Occupational Employment and Wage Statistics

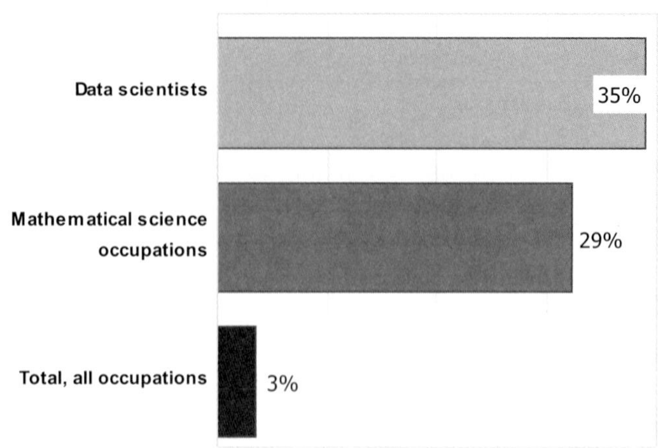

Note: All Occupations includes all occupations in the U.S. Economy.
Source: U.S. Bureau of Labor Statistics, Employment Projections program

Problem-solving skills. Data scientists must devise solutions to the problems they encounter in data collection and cleaning and in developing statistical models and algorithms.

Pay

The median annual wage for data scientists was $103,500 in May 2022. The median wage is the wage at which half the workers in an occupation earned more than that amount and half earned less. The lowest 10 percent earned less than $58,510, and the highest 10 percent earned more than $174,790.

In May 2022, the median annual wages for data scientists in the top industries in which they worked were as follows:

Scientific research and development services...	$118,620
Management of companies and enterprises......	106,510
Computer systems design and related services.	106,180
Insurance carriers and related activities...........	102,700
Management, scientific, and technical consulting services.......................................	101,760

Most data scientists work full time.

Job Outlook

Employment of data scientists is projected to grow 35 percent from 2022 to 2032, much faster than the average for all occupations.

About 17,700 openings for data scientists are projected each year, on average, over the decade. Many of those openings are expected to result from the need to replace workers who transfer to different occupations or exit the labor force, such as to retire.

Employment

Employment growth for data scientists is expected to stem from an increased demand for data-driven decisions. The volume of data available and the potential uses for that data will increase over the projections decade. As a result, organizations will likely need more data scientists to mine and analyze the large amounts of information and data collected. Data scientists' analysis will help organizations to make informed decisions and improve their business processes, to design and develop new products, and to better market their products.

Occupational Title	SOC Code	Employment, 2022	Projected Employment, 2032	Change, 2022-32	
				Percent	Numeric
Data scientists	15-2051	168,900	228,200	35	59,400

Contacts for More Information

For more information about data scientists, visit

- Academic Data Science Alliance
- Institute for Operations Research and the Management Sciences

Mathematicians and Statisticians

Summary

Quick Facts: Mathematicians and Statisticians	
2022 Median Pay	$99,960 per year $48.06 per hour
Typical Entry-Level Education	Master's degree
Work Experience in a Related Occupation	None
On-the-job Training	None
Number of Jobs, 2022	35,600
Job Outlook, 2022-32	30% (Much faster than average)
Employment Change, 2022-32	10,600

What Mathematicians and Statisticians Do
Mathematicians and statisticians analyze data and apply computational techniques to solve problems.

Work Environment
The top employers of mathematicians and statisticians are the federal government and scientific research and development companies. Mathematicians and statisticians may work on teams with engineers, scientists, and other specialists.

How to Become a Mathematician or Statistician
Mathematicians and statisticians typically need at least a master's degree in mathematics or statistics. However, some positions are available to those with a bachelor's degree.

Pay
The median annual wage for mathematicians was $112,110 in May 2022.

The median annual wage for statisticians was $98,920 in May 2022.

Job Outlook
Overall employment of mathematicians and statisticians is projected to grow 30 percent from 2022 to 2032, much faster than the average for all occupations.

About 3,500 openings for mathematicians and statisticians are projected each year, on average, over the decade. Many of those openings are expected to result from the need to replace workers who transfer to different occupations or exit the labor force, such as to retire.

What Mathematicians and Statisticians Do
Mathematicians and statisticians analyze data and apply computational techniques to solve problems.

Duties
Mathematicians and statisticians typically do the following:

- Decide what data are needed to answer specific questions or problems
- Apply mathematical theories and techniques to solve practical problems in business, engineering, the sciences, and other fields
- Design surveys, experiments, or opinion polls to collect data
- Develop mathematical or statistical models to analyze data
- Interpret data and communicate analyses to technical and nontechnical audiences
- Use statistical software to analyze data and create visualizations to aid decision making in business

To solve problems, mathematicians rely on statisticians to design surveys, questionnaires, experiments, and opinion polls for collecting the data they need. For most surveys and opinion polls, statisticians gather data from some people in a particular group. Statisticians determine the type and size of this sample for collecting data in the survey or poll.

Mathematicians and statisticians solve practical problems in fields such as business, government, engineering, and the sciences.

Mathematicians and statisticians work with formulas and data to help solve problems in industry, academia, and government.

Following data collection is analysis, which involves mathematicians and statisticians using specialized statistical software. In their analyses, mathematicians and statisticians identify trends and relationships within the data. They also conduct tests to determine the data's validity and to account for possible errors. Some help write software code to analyze data more accurately and efficiently.

Mathematicians and statisticians present findings from their analyses and discuss the data's limitations in order to ensure accurate interpretation. They may present written reports, tables, and charts to team members, clients, and other users.

Mathematicians and statisticians work in any field that benefits from data analysis, including education, government, healthcare, and research and development.

Colleges and universities. Mathematicians and statisticians working in postsecondary schools may study theoretical or abstract concepts in these fields. They identify, research, and work to resolve unexplained issues in mathematics and explore mathematical or statistical theories to increase knowledge and understanding about the field.

Government. Mathematicians and statisticians working in government develop surveys and collect and analyze data on a variety of topics, including employment, crop production, and energy use. At all levels of government, these data help to inform policy proposals and decisions that affect the public.

Healthcare. Statisticians known as biostatisticians or biometricians work in pharmaceutical companies, public health agencies, or hospitals. They may design studies to test whether drugs successfully treat diseases or medical conditions. They may also help identify the sources of outbreaks of illnesses in humans and animals.

Research and development. Mathematicians and statisticians design experiments for product testing and development. For example, they may help design experiments to see how car engines perform when exposed to extreme weather or analyze consumer data for use in developing marketing strategies.

Typically, mathematicians and statisticians work on teams with other specialists to solve problems. For example, they may work with chemists, materials scientists, and chemical engineers to analyze the effectiveness of a new drug or help data scientists develop statistical models.

Work Environment

Mathematicians held about 2,300 jobs in 2022. The largest employers of mathematicians were as follows:

Employer	Percent
Federal government	54%
Professional, scientific, and technical services	19
Colleges, universities, and professional schools; state, local, and private	16

Statisticians held about 33,300 jobs in 2022. The largest employers of statisticians were as follows:

Mathematicians and statisticians may work on teams with engineers and scientists.

Employer	Percent
Research and development in the physical, engineering, and life sciences	16%
Federal government	16
Colleges, universities, and professional schools; state, local, and private	11
Healthcare and social assistance	7
Computer systems design and related services	6

Mathematicians and statisticians typically work in offices. They also may work on teams with engineers, scientists, and other specialists.

Work Schedules

Most mathematicians and statisticians work full time. Deadlines and last-minute requests for data or analysis may require overtime. In addition, these workers may travel to attend seminars and conferences.

How to Become a Mathematician or Statistician

Mathematicians and statisticians typically need at least a master's degree in mathematics or statistics. However, some positions are available to those with a bachelor's degree.

Education

Students who are interested in becoming mathematicians or statisticians should take as many math courses as possible in high school.

For jobs with the federal government, candidates need at least a bachelor's degree or significant coursework in mathematics. In private industry, mathematicians typically need either a master's or a doctoral degree; statisticians typically need a master's degree, but some entry-level positions may accept candidates with a bachelor's degree.

Most colleges and universities have bachelor's degree programs in mathematics. Courses usually include calculus, differential equations, and linear and abstract algebra. Mathematics students also commonly take courses in a related field, such as computer science, physics, or statistics.

Years of study are required to become a mathematician or statistician.

Many universities offer master's and doctoral degrees in theoretical or applied mathematics. Students who get a doctoral degree may work as professors of mathematics in a college or university.

Statisticians typically need a master's degree, but some entry-level positions may accept candidates with a bachelor's degree.

Students majoring in statistics also may take courses in another field, such as computer science, life sciences, or physical sciences. These courses may help prepare students to work in a variety of industries. For example, coursework in biology, chemistry, or health sciences is useful for testing pharmaceutical or agricultural products. Physics may be useful for statisticians working in manufacturing on quality improvement.

Advancement

Mathematicians and statisticians may advance to become senior mathematicians or statisticians or to work in other managerial roles. A master's or doctoral degree may be required for some advancement opportunities.

Important Qualities

Analytical skills. Mathematicians and statisticians use mathematical techniques and models to evaluate large amounts of data.

Communication skills. Mathematicians and statisticians must be able to explain technical concepts and solutions in nontechnical ways.

Logical-thinking skills. Mathematicians and statisticians must understand and be able to use computer programming languages to design and develop models and to analyze data.

Math skills. Mathematicians and statisticians use statistics, calculus, and linear algebra to develop their models and analyses.

Problem-solving skills. Mathematicians and statisticians must devise solutions to problems encountered in science, engineering, and other fields.

Pay

The median annual wage for mathematicians was $112,110 in May 2022. The median wage is the wage at which half the workers in an occupation earned more than that amount and half earned less. The lowest 10 percent earned less than $57,680, and the highest 10 percent earned more than $171,540.

The median annual wage for statisticians was $98,920 in May 2022. The lowest 10 percent earned less than $58,090, and the highest 10 percent earned more than $161,300.

In May 2022, the median annual wages for mathematicians in the top industries in which they worked were as follows:

Professional, scientific, and technical services .	$134,220
Federal government	119,100
Colleges, universities, and professional schools; state, local, and private	53,680

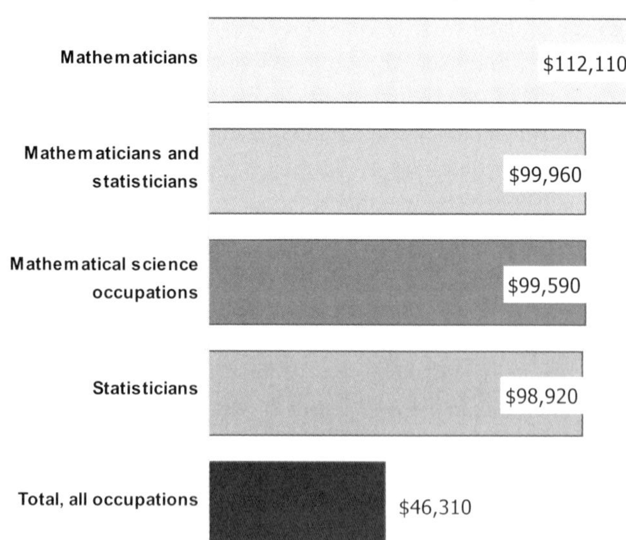

Note: All Occupations includes all occupations in the U.S. Economy.
Source: U.S. Bureau of Labor Statistics, Occupational Employment and Wage Statistics.

In May 2022, the median annual wages for statisticians in the top industries in which they worked were as follows:

Research and development in the physical, engineering, and life sciences	$125,700
Federal government	117,500
Computer systems design and related services	107,740
Healthcare and social assistance	84,930
Colleges, universities, and professional schools; state, local, and private	82,930

Most mathematicians and statisticians work full time. Deadlines and last-minute requests for data or analysis may require overtime. In addition, these workers may travel to attend seminars and conferences.

Job Outlook

Overall employment of mathematicians and statisticians is projected to grow 30 percent from 2022 to 2032, much faster than the average for all occupations.

About 3,500 openings for mathematicians and statisticians are projected each year, on average, over the decade. Many of those openings are expected to result from the need to replace workers who transfer to different occupations or exit the labor force, such as to retire.

Employment

Projected employment of mathematicians and statisticians varies by occupation (see table). Employment growth for statisticians is expected to result from more widespread use of statistical analysis to inform business, healthcare, and policy decisions. The amount of digitally stored data will increase over the projections decade as people and companies continue to conduct business online and use social media, smartphones, and other mobile devices. As a result, businesses will increasingly need statisticians to analyze the large amount of information and data collected. Statistical analyses will help companies improve their business processes, design and develop new products, and advertise products to potential customers.

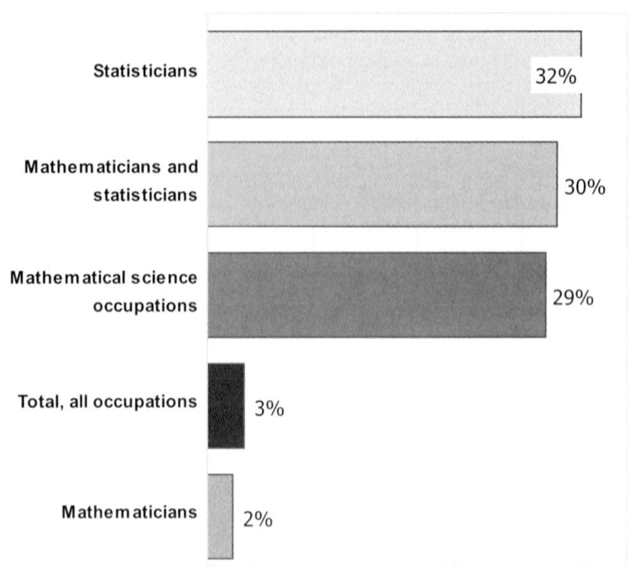

Note: All Occupations includes all occupations in the U.S. Economy.
Source: U.S. Bureau of Labor Statistics, Employment Projections program.

Occupational Title	SOC Code	Employment, 2022	Projected Employment, 2032	Change, 2022-32	
				Percent	Numeric
Mathematicians and statisticians	—	35,600	46,200	30	10,600
Mathematicians	15-2021	2,300	2,300	2	100
Statisticians	15-2041	33,300	43,900	32	10,500

Contacts for More Information

For more information about mathematicians, including training, especially for doctoral-level employment, visit

- American Mathematical Society

For more information about statisticians, visit

- American Statistical Association
- This is Statistics
- Society for Industrial and Applied Mathematics
- U.S. Office of Personnel Management

Operations Research Analysts

Summary

Quick Facts: Operations Research Analysts	
2022 Median Pay	$85,720 per year $41.21 per hour
Typical Entry-Level Education	Bachelor's degree
Work Experience in a Related Occupation	None
On-the-job Training	None
Number of Jobs, 2022	109,900
Job Outlook, 2022-32	23% (Much faster than average)
Employment Change, 2022-32	24,700

What Operations Research Analysts Do
Operations research analysts use mathematics and logic to help solve complex issues.

Work Environment
Operations research analysts spend much of their time in office settings, although travel may be necessary to meet with clients. Most operations research analysts work full time.

How to Become an Operations Research Analyst
Operations research analysts typically need at least a bachelor's degree to enter the occupation. Some employers require or prefer that applicants have a master's degree. Analysts may need a degree in operations research or a related field, such as applied mathematics.

Pay
The median annual wage for operations research analysts was $85,720 in May 2022.

Job Outlook
Employment of operations research analysts is projected to grow 23 percent from 2022 to 2032, much faster than the average for all occupations.

About 9,800 openings for operations research analysts are projected each year, on average, over the decade. Many of those openings are expected to result from the need to replace workers who transfer to different occupations or exit the labor force, such as to retire.

What Operations Research Analysts Do
Operations research analysts use mathematics and logic to help organizations make informed decisions and solve problems.

Duties
Operations research analysts typically do the following:

- Identify problems in areas such as business, logistics, healthcare, or other fields
- Collect and organize information from a variety of sources, such as databases, sales histories, and customer feedback
- Gather input from workers or subject-matter experts
- Analyze collected data and extract information relevant to the problem being addressed
- Develop and test quantitative models, support software, and analytical tools
- Write memos, reports, and other documents explaining their findings and recommendations for managers, executives, and other officials

Operations research analysts may be involved in many aspects of an organization. For example, they may help managers decide how to allocate resources, develop production schedules, oversee the supply chain, and set prices.

To begin a project, analysts first identify the problem to be solved or the processes to be improved. They typically collect data and interview clients, workers, or others involved in the business processes being examined.

Analysts then break down the problem into its various parts using statistical and database software and analytical techniques, such as forecasting and data mining. They also study the effect that different changes and circumstances would have

Operations research analysts use statistical analysis and simulations to analyze and solve business problems.

Operations research analysts advise managers and other decision makers on the appropriate course of action to solve a problem.

on each of these parts. For example, to help an airline schedule flights and set ticket prices, analysts may take into account the cities involved, the amount and cost of fuel required, the expected number of passengers, the pilots' schedules, and the maintenance costs.

Operations research analysts provide alternatives to pursuing different actions and may assist in achieving a consensus on how to proceed. They weigh the costs and benefits of alternative solutions or approaches in their recommendations to managers.

Work Environment

Operations research analysts held about 109,900 jobs in 2022. The largest employers of operations research analysts were as follows:

Professional, scientific, and technical services	25%
Finance and insurance	24
Management of companies and enterprises	9
Federal government	5
Manufacturing	5

Some operations research analysts in the federal government work for the Department of Defense, which also employs analysts through private consulting firms.

Operations research analysts spend much of their time in office settings. They may travel to gather information, observe business processes, work with clients, or attend conferences.

Work Schedules

Most operations research analysts work full time.

How to Become an Operations Research Analyst

Operations research analysts typically need at least a bachelor's degree to enter the occupation. Some employers require or prefer that applicants have a master's degree. Analysts may need a degree in operations research or a related field, such as applied mathematics.

Operations research analysts typically work in an office setting.

Operations research analysts typically need at least a bachelor's degree to enter the occupation.

Education

Operations research analysts typically need at least a bachelor's degree, but some jobs require a master's degree. Fields of degree may include operations research or a related field, such as business, mathematics, engineering, or computer science.

Because operations research is based on quantitative analysis, students need extensive coursework in mathematics. Coursework in computer science is important because analysts rely on statistical and database software to assess and model data.

Other Experience

Some operations research analysts are veterans of the U.S. Armed Forces. Certain positions may require applicants to undergo a background check in order to obtain a security clearance.

Important Qualities

Analytical skills. Operations research analysts use a range of methods, including forecasting and data mining, to examine and interpret data.

Communication skills. Operations research analysts write memos, reports, and other documents and often present their data and conclusions to managers and other executives. They must be able to convey technical information in a way that is understandable to nontechnical audiences.

Critical-thinking skills. Operations research analysts must be able to organize information and make connections between ideas and facts.

Interpersonal skills. Operations research analysts typically work on teams. They also need to be able to persuade managers and executives to accept their recommendations.

Math skills. The models and methods used by operations research analysts are rooted in statistics, calculus, linear algebra, and other mathematics disciplines.

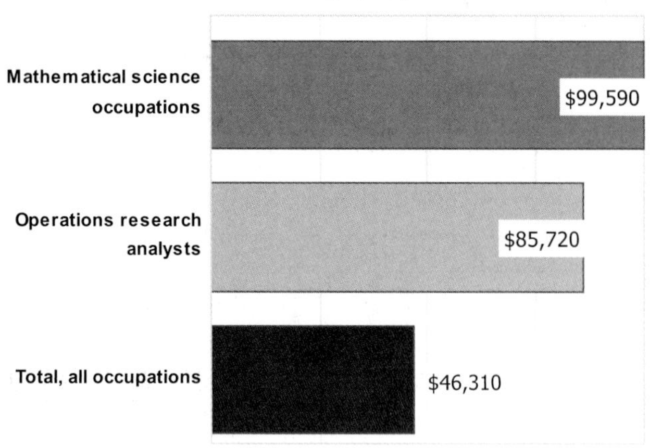

Note: All Occupations includes all occupations in the U.S. Economy.
Source: U.S. Bureau of Labor Statistics, Occupational Employment and Wage Statistics.

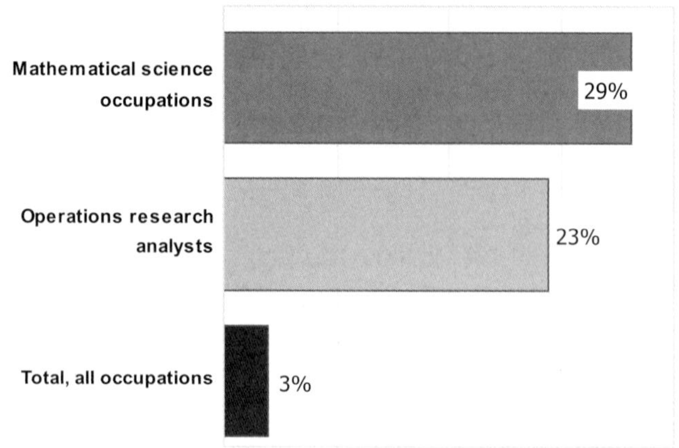

Note: All Occupations includes all occupations in the U.S. Economy.
Source: U.S. Bureau of Labor Statistics, Occupational Employment and Wage Statistics.

Problem-solving skills. Operations research analysts need to be able to diagnose problems and study relevant information to solve them.

Pay

The median annual wage for operations research analysts was $85,720 in May 2022. The median wage is the wage at which half the workers in an occupation earned more than that amount and half earned less. The lowest 10 percent earned less than $50,440, and the highest 10 percent earned more than $149,640.

In May 2022, the median annual wages for operations research analysts in the top industries in which they worked were as follows:

Federal government	$124,610
Manufacturing	106,280
Professional, scientific, and technical services	96,210
Management of companies and enterprises	90,600
Finance and insurance	81,470

Most operations research analysts work full time.

Job Outlook

Employment of operations research analysts is projected to grow 23 percent from 2022 to 2032, much faster than the average for all occupations.

About 9,800 openings for operations research analysts are projected each year, on average, over the decade. Many of those openings are expected to result from the need to replace workers who transfer to different occupations or exit the labor force, such as to retire.

Employment

As technology advances and companies and government agencies seek efficiency and cost savings, demand for operations research analysis should continue to grow. In addition, increasing demand should occur for these workers in the field of analytics to improve business planning and decision making.

Technological advances have made it faster and easier for organizations to get data. Operations research analysts manage and evaluate data to improve business operations, supply chains, pricing models, and marketing. In addition, improvements in analytical software have made operations research more affordable and applicable to a wider range of areas. More companies are expected to employ operations research analysts to help them turn data into information that managers use to make decisions about all aspects of their business.

Occupational Title	SOC Code	Employment, 2022	Projected Employment, 2032	Change, 2022-32	
				Percent	Numeric
Operations research analysts	15-2031	109,900	134,700	23	24,700

Contacts for More Information

For more information, visit

- Institute for Operations Research and the Management Sciences
- Military Operations Research Society

Media and Communication

Announcers and DJs

Summary

Quick Facts: Announcers and DJs	
2022 Median Pay	$20.46 per hour
Typical Entry-Level Education	See How to Become One
Work Experience in a Related Occupation	None
On-the-job Training	See How to Become One
Number of Jobs, 2022	51,800
Job Outlook, 2022-32	-4% (Decline)
Employment Change, 2022-32	-2,200

What Announcers and DJs Do

Announcers present news and sports or may interview guests on media such as radio and television. Disc jockeys (DJs) act as masters of ceremonies (emcees) or play recorded music at weddings, parties, or clubs.

Work Environment

Many announcers and DJs work in radio and television studios or are self-employed. Some work part time, and schedules might include early mornings, nights, weekends, and holidays.

How to Become an Announcer or DJ

Entry requirements for announcers and DJs vary. Broadcast announcers and radio DJs typically need a bachelor's degree in journalism, broadcasting, or communications; experience gained from internships or working at a school radio or television station is helpful. Other types of DJs typically need a high school diploma and some on-the-job training.

Pay

The median hourly wage for broadcast announcers and radio disc jockeys was $20.07 in May 2022.

The median hourly wage for disc jockeys, except radio was $21.34 in May 2022.

Job Outlook

Overall employment of announcers and DJs is projected to decline 4 percent from 2022 to 2032.

Despite declining employment, about 4,400 openings for announcers and DJs are projected each year, on average, over the decade. All of those openings are expected to result from the need to replace workers who transfer to other occupations or exit the labor force, such as to retire.

What Announcers and DJs Do

Announcers present news and sports or may interview guests on media such as radio and television. Disc jockeys (DJs) act as masters of ceremonies (emcees) or play recorded music at weddings, parties, or clubs.

Duties

Announcers and DJs typically do the following:

- Present music and information on radio or television shows or at venues
- Interview guests on their shows
- Research topics for comment and discussion during shows
- Read prepared scripts on radio or television shows or at venues
- Provide commentary for the audience during events
- Select program content

Announcers present music, sports, and news to audiences.

Radio and television announcers present news and opinions and take calls from listeners.

- Introduce upcoming acts and guide the audience through the entertainment
- Make promotional appearances at public or private events

Broadcast announcers and radio DJs present music or the news, sports, traffic, and weather. Announcers are expected to be up to date with current events or a specific field, such as politics or sports, so that they can comment on these issues during their programs. In addition, they schedule guests on their shows and work with producers to develop other creative content. Radio DJs typically specialize in one kind of music genre and announce selections as they air them. They may take requests from listeners, manage radio contests, or announce traffic conditions.

Broadcast announcers and radio DJs also may be responsible for other aspects of television or radio programming. They may operate studio equipment, sell commercial time to advertisers, or develop advertisements and other recorded material. At many radio stations, they do much of the work traditionally done by editors and broadcast technicians, such as broadcasting program schedules, commercials, and public service announcements.

Many broadcast announcers and DJs maintain a presence on social media sites. Establishing a presence allows them to promote their stations and engage with their audiences, especially through listener feedback, music requests, or program contests. They also make promotional appearances at charity functions or other community events.

The following are examples of types of broadcast announcers and radio DJs:

- *Podcasters* stream live or record shows that can be downloaded for listening at any time. Like traditional talk radio, podcasts typically focus on a specific subject, such as sports, politics, or movies. Podcasters may interview guests and experts on the specific program topic. Listeners may subscribe to a podcast to have new episodes automatically downloaded to their computer or mobile devices.
- *Talk show hosts* may work in radio or television and specialize in an area of interest, such as politics, personal finance, sports, or health. They contribute to the preparation of program content, interview guests, and discuss issues with viewers, listeners, or the studio audience.

DJs, except radio play prerecorded music for live audiences at a variety of venues or events, including clubs, parties, and wedding receptions. The following are examples of types of DJs, except radio:

- *Emcees* host planned events. They introduce speakers or performers to the audience. They may tell jokes or provide commentary to transition from one speaker to the next.
- *Party DJs* are hired to provide music and commentary at an event, such as a wedding, a birthday party, or a corporate party.

Radio and television announcers work with a variety of studio equipment.

Work Environment

Broadcast announcers and radio disc jockeys held about 28,000 jobs in 2022. The largest employers of broadcast announcers and radio disc jockeys were as follows:

Broadcasting and content providers	84%
Performing arts, spectator sports, and related industries	6
Self-employed workers	3
Educational services; state, local, and private	3

Disc jockeys, except radio held about 23,800 jobs in 2022. The largest employers of disc jockeys, except radio were as follows:

Self-employed workers	76%
Performing arts, spectator sports, and related industries	9
Food services and drinking places	8
Amusement, gambling, and recreation industries	2
Other personal services	2

Broadcast announcers and radio DJs usually work in well-lit, temperature-controlled, soundproof studios. Some radio DJs produce and record their shows while working from home.

DJs, except radio work in a variety of settings, either indoors or outdoors or both. They travel to the location of the event they are hosting.

The pressure of deadlines and tight work schedules may be stressful.

Work Schedules

Work schedules for announcers and DJs vary and may include early mornings, late nights, weekends, or holidays. Part-time work also may be common.

How to Become an Announcer or DJ

Entry requirements for announcers and DJs vary. Broadcast announcers and radio DJs typically need a bachelor's degree

Many announcers have a bachelor's degree as well as experience working with radio and television equipment.

in journalism, broadcasting, or communications; experience gained from internships or working at a school radio or television station is helpful. Other types of DJs typically need a high school diploma and some on-the-job training.

Education

Broadcast announcers and radio DJs typically need a bachelor's degree in communications, broadcasting, or journalism. However, some jobs may be available for workers who have a high school diploma or equivalent. DJs, except radio typically need a high school diploma and some on-the-job training.

Employers may prefer to hire candidates who have hands-on skills or knowledge. High school and college students interested in a career as an announcer or DJ may benefit from taking speech classes and participating in opportunities to practice public speaking. These may include making announcements on their school's public address system, working at their school's radio or television station, or serving as an emcee at events. Internships also may be available, although they are often limited to college students.

Training

Radio and television announcers whose highest level of education is a high school diploma or equivalent also may need some short-term on-the-job training to learn how to operate audio and production equipment.

Advancement

Because radio and television stations in small markets have limited staff, advancement within the same small-market station is unlikely. Rather, many broadcast announcers and radio DJs advance by relocating to a large-market station. These larger markets often offer higher pay and more responsibility and challenges than do small markets.

When making hiring decisions, large-market stations rely on workers' personalities and past performance. Broadcast announcers and radio DJs need to have proven that they can attract, engage, and keep the attention of a sizeable audience.

Important Qualities

Business skills. DJs, except radio who are self-employed must be able to market themselves and identify clients. They also need to manage the details of their business, including billing, budgeting, and other financial matters.

Computer skills. Announcers and DJs, especially those seeking careers in radio or television, should be comfortable using editing software and other broadcast-related devices.

Interpersonal skills. Broadcast announcers and radio DJs interview guests, answer phone calls on air, and may interact with listeners on social media. Party DJs and emcees should be comfortable working with clients to plan entertainment options.

Persistence. Entry into this occupation is very competitive, and candidates may need to audition many times for an opportunity to work on the air. Entry-level broadcast announcers and radio DJs must be willing to work for a small station to secure their first job.

Research skills. Announcers and DJs must research important topics of the day in order to be knowledgeable enough to comment on them during their program.

Speaking skills. Announcers and DJs must have a pleasant and well-controlled voice, good timing, and excellent pronunciation. Party DJs and emcees must be comfortable speaking to large audiences.

Writing skills. Announcers and DJs need strong writing skills because they normally write their own material.

Pay

The median hourly wage for broadcast announcers and radio disc jockeys was $20.07 in May 2022. The median wage is the wage at which half the workers in an occupation earned more than that amount and half earned less. The lowest 10 percent earned less than $11.50, and the highest 10 percent earned more than $82.52.

The median hourly wage for disc jockeys, except radio was $21.34 in May 2022. The lowest 10 percent earned less than $9.87, and the highest 10 percent earned more than $46.84.

In May 2022, the median hourly wages for broadcast announcers and radio disc jockeys in the top industries in which they worked were as follows:

Educational services; state, local, and private	$24.82
Performing arts, spectator sports, and related industries	23.93
Broadcasting and content providers	19.10

In May 2022, the median hourly wages for disc jockeys, except radio in the top industries in which they worked were as follows:

Other personal services	$29.60

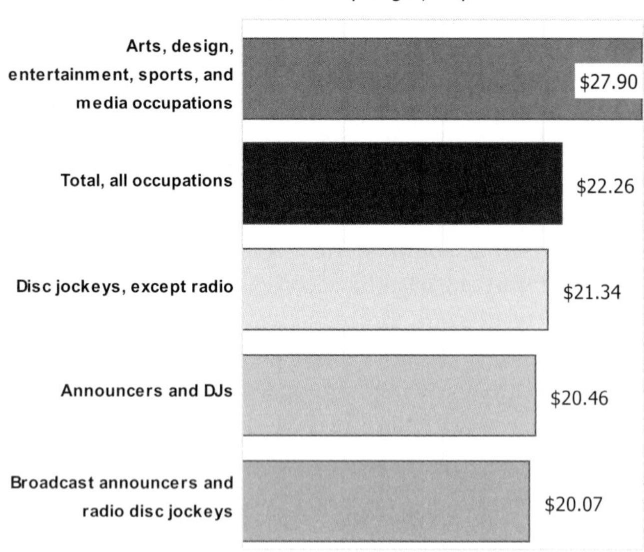

Note: All Occupations includes all occupations in the U.S. Economy.
Source: U.S. Bureau of Labor Statistics, Occupational Employment and Wage Statistics.

Performing arts, spectator sports, and related industries	23.17
Food services and drinking places	15.56
Amusement, gambling, and recreation industries	15.08

Work schedules for announcers and DJs vary and may include early mornings, late nights, weekends, or holidays. Part-time work also may be common.

Job Outlook

Overall employment of announcers and DJs is projected to decline 4 percent from 2022 to 2032.

Despite declining employment, about 4,400 openings for announcers and DJs are projected each year, on average, over the decade. All of those openings are expected to result from the need to replace workers who transfer to other occupations or exit the labor force, such as to retire.

Employment

Projected employment of announcers and DJs varies by occupation (see table).

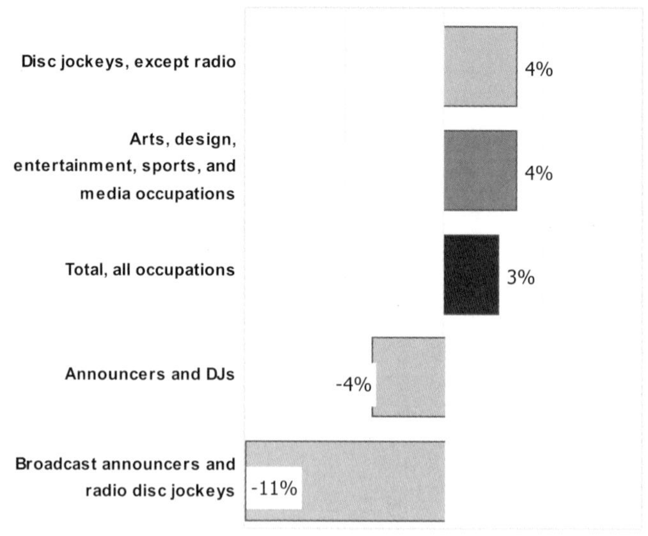

Note: All Occupations includes all occupations in the U.S. Economy.
Source: U.S. Bureau of Labor Statistics, Employment Projections program.

Continuing consolidation of radio and television stations will limit employment growth of broadcast announcers and radio disc jockeys (DJs). In addition, over-the-air radio broadcasts will continue to face competition from an increasing number of online and satellite radio stations. More listeners are tuning in to these stations, which can be personalized, reducing the number of listeners to traditional radio broadcasts and decreasing the demand for radio DJs.

DJs, with the exception of radio DJs, will be in demand to play prerecorded music for live audiences at venues or events such as clubs, parties, and wedding receptions.

Occupational Title	SOC Code	Employment, 2022	Projected Employment, 2032	Change, 2022-32	
				Percent	Numeric
Announcers and DJs	—	51,800	49,600	-4	-2,200
Broadcast announcers and radio disc jockeys	27-3011	28,000	24,800	-11	-3,200
Disc jockeys, except radio	27-2091	23,800	24,800	4	1,000

Contacts for More Information

For more information, visit

➤ National Association of Broadcasters

Broadcast, Sound, and Video Technicians

Summary

Quick Facts: Broadcast, Sound, and Video Technicians	
2022 Median Pay	$53,960 per year $25.94 per hour
Typical Entry-Level Education	See How to Become One
Work Experience in a Related Occupation	None
On-the-job Training	Short-term on-the-job training
Number of Jobs, 2022	142,800
Job Outlook, 2022-32	2% (As fast as average)
Employment Change, 2022-32	2,500

What Broadcast, Sound, and Video Technicians Do
Broadcast, sound, and video technicians set up, operate, and maintain the electrical equipment for media programs.

Work Environment
Broadcast, sound, and video technicians typically work indoors in radio, television, movie, and recording studios. They may also work in hotels, arenas, offices, or schools.

How to Become a Broadcast, Sound, or Video Technician
Broadcast, sound, and video technicians typically need post-secondary education. Depending on the work they do, educational requirements may vary.

Pay
The median annual wage for broadcast, sound, and video technicians was $53,960 in May 2022.

Broadcast and sound engineering technicians operate controls to ensure quality audio and video recordings for radio and television broadcasts.

Job Outlook
Overall employment of broadcast, sound, and video technicians is projected to grow 2 percent from 2022 to 2032, about as fast as the average for all occupations.

About 12,900 openings for broadcast, sound, and video technicians are projected each year, on average, over the decade. Many of those openings are expected to result from the need to replace workers who transfer to different occupations or exit the labor force, such as to retire.

What Broadcast, Sound, and Video Technicians Do
Broadcast, sound, and video technicians set up, operate, and maintain the electrical equipment for radio programs, television broadcasts, concerts, sound recordings, and movies.

Duties
Broadcast, sound, and video technicians typically do the following:

- Operate, monitor, and adjust audio, video, sound, lighting, and broadcast equipment to ensure consistent quality
- Set up and take down equipment for events and live performances

Broadcast, sound, and video technicians operate equipment in schools and office buildings.

- Record speech, music, and other sounds on recording equipment or computers, sometimes using complex software
- Synchronize sounds and dialogue with action taking place on television or in movie productions
- Convert video and audio records to digital formats for editing on computers
- Install audio, video, and lighting equipment in hotels, offices, and schools
- Report any problems that arise with complex equipment and make routine repairs
- Keep records of recordings and equipment used

These workers may be called broadcast or sound engineering *technicians*, *operators*, or *engineers*. They set up and operate audio and video equipment, and the kind of equipment they use may depend on the particular type of technician or industry. At smaller radio and television stations, broadcast, sound, and video technicians may have more responsibilities. At larger stations, they may do more specialized work, although their job assignments may vary from day to day.

Broadcast, sound, and video technicians share many responsibilities, but their duties may vary with their specific area of focus. The following are examples of types of broadcast, sound, and video technicians:

Audio and video technicians, also known as *audio-visual technicians*, set up, maintain, and dismantle audio and video equipment. They also connect wires and cables and set up and operate sound and mixing boards and related electronic equipment.

Audio and video technicians work with microphones, speakers, video screens, projectors, video monitors, and recording equipment. The equipment they operate is used for live or recorded events such as meetings, concerts, sporting events, podcasts, and news conferences.

Broadcast technicians, also known as *broadcast engineers*, set up, operate, and maintain equipment that regulates the signal strength, clarity, and ranges of sounds and colors for radio or television broadcasts. They operate transmitters, either in studios or on location in the field, to broadcast radio or television programs. Broadcast technicians also use computer programs to edit audio and video recordings.

Lighting technicians set up, maintain, and dismantle light fixtures, lighting controls, and associated electrical and rigging equipment used for photography, television, film, video, and live productions. They also may focus or operate light fixtures and attach color filters or other lighting accessories.

Sound engineering technicians, also known as *audio engineers* or *sound mixers*, assemble and operate sound equipment. They use this equipment to record, synchronize, mix, edit, or reproduce music, voices, or sound effects for theater, video, film, television, podcasts, sporting events, and other productions.

Work Environment

Broadcast, sound, and video technicians held about 142,800 jobs in 2022. Employment in the detailed occupations that make up broadcast, sound, and video technicians was distributed as follows:

Audio and video technicians	74,800
Broadcast technicians	39,900
Sound engineering technicians	17,600
Lighting technicians	10,500

The largest employers of broadcast, sound, and video technicians were as follows:

Motion picture and sound recording industries	20%
Broadcasting and content providers	16
Self-employed workers	14
Performing arts, spectator sports, and related industries	8
Educational services; state, local, and private	8

Broadcast, sound, and video technicians typically work indoors in radio, television, movie, or recording studios. However, they may work outdoors in all types of weather in order to broadcast news and other programming on location. Audio and

Broadcast, sound, and video technicians work with a variety of electronic and recording equipment.

video technicians also set up systems in offices, arenas, hotels, schools, hospitals, and homes.

Technicians doing maintenance may climb poles or antenna towers. Those setting up equipment may do heavy lifting.

Work Schedules

Technicians usually work full time. They may occasionally work overtime to meet broadcast deadlines or set up for live events. Evening, weekend, and holiday work is common because most radio and television stations are on the air 24 hours a day.

Technicians who work on motion pictures may be on a tight schedule and may work additional hours to meet contract deadlines with the movie studio.

How to Become a Broadcast, Sound, or Video Technician

Broadcast, sound, and video technicians typically need postsecondary education. Depending on the work they do, educational requirements may vary.

Education

Educational requirements for audio and video, lighting, and sound engineering technicians vary from a high school diploma to a college degree, depending on the position. Broadcast technicians typically need an associate's degree.

Prospective broadcast, sound, and video technicians should complete high school classes in math, physics, and electronics. Employers may prefer to hire candidates who have skills related to audio and video equipment and related technologies.

Postsecondary programs for audio and video, lighting, and sound engineering technicians may take several months to years to complete. These programs, which may lead to either a nondegree award or a college degree, often provide hands-on experience with the equipment used in many entry-level positions.

Broadcast, sound, and video technicians typically need postsecondary education, although some are hired with a high school diploma.

Broadcast technicians typically need an associate's degree. In addition to courses in math and science, coursework for prospective broadcast technicians should emphasize practical skills such as video editing and production management.

Although typically not required, a bachelor's degree in fine and performing arts or a related field, such as communications technology, may be helpful.

Training

Because technology is constantly improving, technicians often enroll in continuing education courses and receive on-the-job training to become skilled in new equipment and hardware. On-the-job training includes setting up cables or automation systems, testing electrical equipment, learning the codes and standards of the industry, and following safety procedures.

Newly hired workers may be trained in a variety of ways, depending on the types of products and services the employer provides. In addition, new workers' level of education may also dictate how much training they need.

Licenses, Certifications, and Registrations

Although it is not required by most employers, voluntary certification may offer advantages in getting a job as a broadcast or sound engineering technician. Certification tells employers that the technician meets certain industry standards and has kept up to date with new technologies.

The Society of Broadcast Engineers offers operator level, engineering level, broadcast networking, and specialist certifications. Most of these certifications require passing an exam.

The Audiovisual and Integrated Experience Association offers the general Certified Technology Specialist (CTS) credential as well as the design CTS and installation CTS. All three credentials require passing an exam and are valid for 3 years.

Other Experience

Gaining practical experience in a high school or college audiovisual department also helps to prepare for work as an audio and video equipment technician.

Advancement

Although many broadcast, sound, and video technicians work first in small markets or at small stations in big markets, they often transfer to larger, better paying radio or television stations after gaining experience and skills. Few large stations hire someone without previous experience, and they value specialized skills.

Experienced workers with strong technical skills may become supervisory broadcast technicians or chief broadcast engineers. To become chief broadcast engineer at large television stations, technicians typically need a bachelor's degree in engineering or computer science.

Important Qualities

Communication skills. Technicians need to communicate with supervisors and coworkers to ensure that clients' needs are met and that equipment is set up properly before broadcasts, live performances, and presentations.

Computer skills. Technicians use computer systems to program equipment and edit audio and video recordings.

Manual dexterity. Some technicians set up audio and video equipment and cables, a job that requires a steady hand and good hand-eye coordination. Others adjust small knobs, dials, and sliders during radio and television broadcasts and live performances.

Problem-solving skills. Technicians need to recognize equipment problems and propose possible solutions to them. Employers typically desire applicants with a variety of skills, such as setting up equipment, maintaining the equipment, and troubleshooting and solving any problems that arise.

Pay

The median annual wage for broadcast, sound, and video technicians was $53,960 in May 2022. The median wage is the wage at which half the workers in an occupation earned more than that amount and half earned less. The lowest 10 percent earned less than $31,010, and the highest 10 percent earned more than $110,260.

Median annual wages for broadcast, sound, and video technicians in May 2022 were as follows:

Lighting technicians	$61,650
Broadcast technicians	60,700
Sound engineering technicians	60,670
Audio and video technicians	50,660

In May 2022, the median annual wages for broadcast, sound, and video technicians in the top industries in which they worked were as follows:

Motion picture and sound recording industries	$82,560
Educational services; state, local, and private	51,960
Performing arts, spectator sports, and related industries	49,510
Broadcasting and content providers	45,930

Technicians working in major cities typically earn more than those working in smaller markets.

Technicians usually work full time. They may occasionally work overtime to meet broadcast deadlines or set up for live events. Evening, weekend, and holiday work is common because most radio and television stations are on the air 24 hours a day.

Technicians who work on motion pictures may be on a tight schedule and may work additional hours to meet contract deadlines with the movie studio.

Job Outlook

Overall employment of broadcast, sound, and video technicians is projected to grow 2 percent from 2022 to 2032, about as fast as the average for all occupations.

About 12,900 openings for broadcast, sound, and video technicians are projected each year, on average, over the decade. Many of those openings are expected to result from the need to replace workers who transfer to different occupations or exit the labor force, such as to retire.

Employment

Projected employment of broadcast, sound, and video technicians varies by occupation (see table).

Companies are continuing to increase their audio and video budgets so they can use video conferencing to reduce travel costs and communicate worldwide with other offices and clients, especially as more people work in a remote or hybrid environment. In addition, an increase in the use of digital signs should lead to higher demand for audio and video technicians.

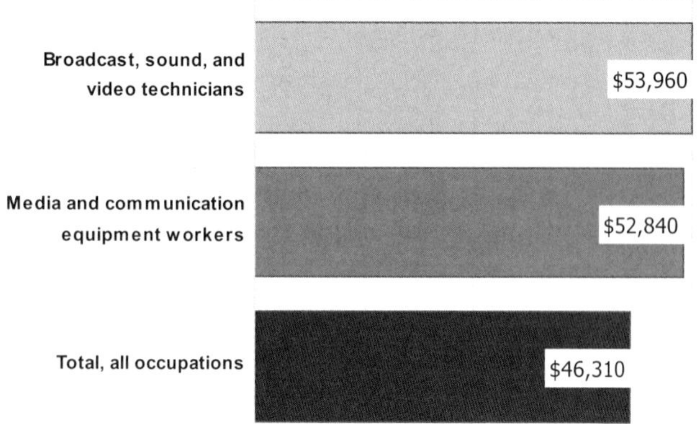

Note: All Occupations includes all occupations in the U.S. Economy.
Source: U.S. Bureau of Labor Statistics, Occupational Employment and Wage Statistics.

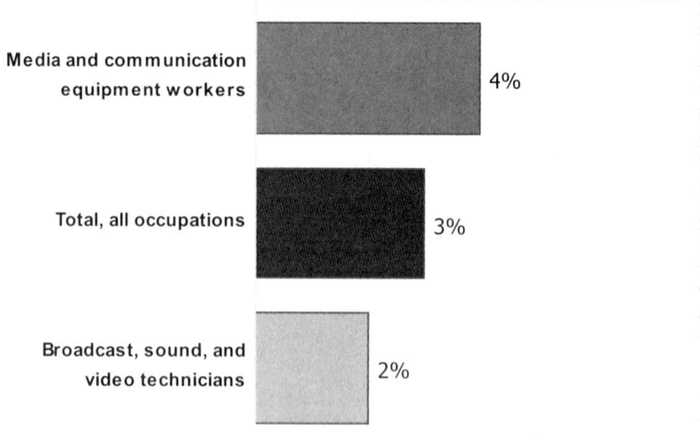

Note: All Occupations includes all occupations in the U.S. Economy.
Source: U.S. Bureau of Labor Statistics, Employment Projections program.

Motion picture and sound recording industries will continue to need broadcast, lighting, and sound engineering technicians to improve the quality of shows and movies. However, advances in technology will allow fewer technicians to set up and operate broadcast, lighting, and sound systems, which is expected to reduce demand for these workers.

Occupational Title	SOC Code	Employment, 2022	Projected Employment, 2032	Change, 2022-32	
				Percent	Numeric
Broadcast, sound, and video technicians	—	142,800	145,300	2	2,500
Audio and video technicians	27-4011	74,800	78,300	5	3,500
Broadcast technicians	27-4012	39,900	39,400	-1	-400
Sound engineering technicians	27-4014	17,600	17,400	-1	-200
Lighting technicians	27-4015	10,500	10,200	-3	-400

Contacts for More Information

For more information, visit

- National Association of Broadcasters
- Audio Engineering Society
- Society of Broadcast Engineers
- Audiovisual and Integrated Experience Association

Editors

Summary

Quick Facts: Editors

2022 Median Pay	$73,080 per year $35.14 per hour
Typical Entry-Level Education	Bachelor's degree
Work Experience in a Related Occupation	Less than 5 years
On-the-job Training	None
Number of Jobs, 2022	122,100
Job Outlook, 2022-32	-4% (Decline)
Employment Change, 2022-32	-4,900

What Editors Do

Editors plan, review, and revise content for publication.

Work Environment

Most editors work in offices, whether onsite with their employer or from a remote location. The work can be stressful because editors often have tight deadlines.

How to Become an Editor

Editors typically need a bachelor's degree in communications, journalism, or English, along with writing and proofreading experience.

Pay

The median annual wage for editors was $73,080 in May 2022.

Job Outlook

Employment of editors is projected to decline 4 percent from 2022 to 2032.

Despite declining employment, about 11,600 openings for editors are projected each year, on average, over the decade. All of those openings are expected to result from the need to replace workers who transfer to other occupations or exit the labor force, such as to retire.

What Editors Do

Editors plan, review, and revise content for publication.

Editors plan, coordinate, and revise material for publication.

Editors constantly work under pressure to meet deadlines.

Duties

Editors typically do the following:

- Read content and correct spelling, punctuation, and grammatical errors
- Rewrite text to make it easier for readers to understand
- Verify facts cited in material for publication
- Evaluate submissions from writers to decide what to publish
- Work with writers to help their ideas and stories succeed
- Develop story and content ideas according to the publication's style and editorial policy
- Allocate space for the text, photos, and illustrations that make up a story or content
- Approve final versions submitted by staff

Editors plan, coordinate, and revise material for publication in books, newspapers, or periodicals or on websites. Editors review story ideas and decide what material will appeal most to readers. During the review process, editors offer comments to improve the product and suggest titles and headlines. In smaller organizations, a single editor may do all the editorial duties or share them with only a few other people.

The following are examples of types of editors:

Assistant editors are responsible for a particular subject, such as local news, international news, feature stories, or sports. Most assistant editors work for newspaper publishers, television broadcasters, magazines, book publishers, or advertising and public relations firms.

Copy editors proofread text for errors in grammar, punctuation, and spelling and check for readability, style, and agreement with editorial policy. They suggest revisions, such as changing words and rearranging sentences and paragraphs to improve clarity or accuracy. They also may carry out research, confirm sources, and verify facts, dates, and statistics. In addition, they may arrange page layouts of articles, photographs, and advertising.

Executive editors oversee assistant editors and generally have the final say about which stories are published and how those stories are covered. Executive editors typically hire writers, reporters, and other employees. They also plan budgets and negotiate contracts with freelance writers, who are sometimes called "stringers" in the news industry. Although many executive editors work for newspaper publishers, some work for television broadcasters, magazines, or advertising and public relations firms.

Managing editors typically work for magazines, newspaper publishers, and television broadcasters and are responsible for the daily operations of a news department.

Publication assistants who work for book-publishing houses may read and evaluate manuscripts, proofread uncorrected drafts, and answer questions about published material. Assistants on small newspapers or in smaller media markets may compile articles available from wire services or the Internet, answer phones, and proofread articles.

Work Environment

Editors held about 122,100 jobs in 2022. The largest employers of editors were as follows:

Self-employed workers	13%
Newspaper publishers	12
Professional, scientific, and technical services	12
Motion picture and video industries	9
Media streaming distribution services, social networks, and other media networks and content providers	7

Most editors work in offices, whether onsite with their employer or from a remote location. They often use desktop or electronic publishing software, scanners, and other electronic communications equipment.

Jobs are somewhat concentrated in major media and entertainment markets—Boston, Chicago, Los Angeles, New York, and Washington, DC—but improved communications and Internet capabilities are allowing editors to work from a greater variety of locations.

Overseeing and coordinating multiple writing projects simultaneously is common among editors and may lead to stress or fatigue.

Self-employed editors face the added pressures of finding work on an ongoing basis and continually adjusting to new work environments.

Editors usually work full time in offices.

Work Schedules

Most editors work full time, and their schedules are generally determined by production deadlines and type of editorial position. Editors typically work in busy offices and have to deal with production deadline pressures and the stresses of ensuring that the information they publish is correct. As a result, editors often work many hours, especially at those times leading up to a publication deadline. These work hours can be even more frequent when an editor is working on digital material for the Internet or for a live broadcast.

How to Become an Editor

A bachelor's degree in communications, journalism, or English, combined with previous writing and proofreading experience, is typically required to be an editor.

Education

Editors typically need a bachelor's degree in English or a related field, such as communications or journalism.

Candidates with other backgrounds who can show strong writing skills also may find jobs as editors. Editors who deal with specific subject matter may need related work experience. For example, fashion editors may need expertise in fashion that they gain through formal training or work experience.

Work Experience in a Related Occupation

Many editors start off as editorial assistants, writers, or reporters.

Those who are particularly skilled at identifying good stories, recognizing writing talent, and interacting with writers may be interested in editing jobs.

Other Experience

Editors can gain experience by working on high school and college newspapers and for magazines, radio and television stations, advertising and publishing companies. Magazines and newspapers may have offer student internships. For example, the American Society of Magazine Editors offers a Magazine Internship Program to qualified full-time students in their junior or senior year of college. Interns may write stories, conduct research and interviews, and gain general publishing experience.

Editors need to be proficient in computer use, including electronic publishing, graphics, Web design, social media, and multimedia production.

A college degree is typically required for someone to be an editor.

Advancement

Some editors hold management positions and must make decisions related to running a business. For them, advancement generally means moving up to publications with larger circulation or greater prestige. Copy editors may move into original writing or substantive editing positions or become freelancers.

Important Qualities

Creativity. Editors must be imaginative, curious, and knowledgeable in a broad range of topics. Some editors must regularly come up with interesting content or story ideas and attention-grabbing headlines.

Detail oriented. Editors must be meticulous to ensure that material is error free and matches the style of a publication.

Good judgment. Editors decide whether certain stories are ethical and whether there is enough evidence to publish them.

Interpersonal skills. In working with writers, editors must have tact and the ability to guide and encourage them in their work.

Writing skills. Editors ensure that all written content has correct grammar, punctuation, and syntax. Editors must be able to write clearly and logically.

Pay

The median annual wage for editors was $73,080 in May 2022. The median wage is the wage at which half the workers in an

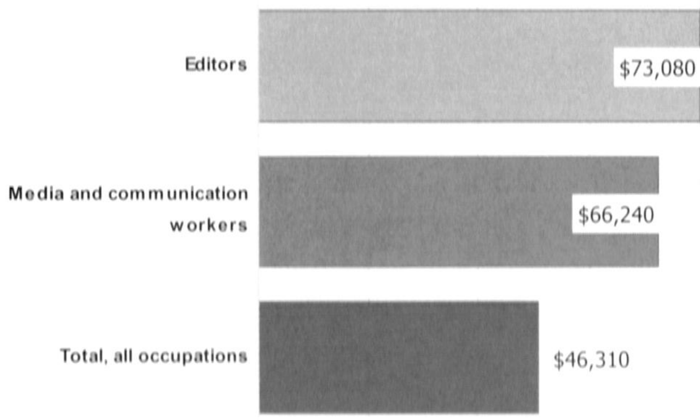

Note: All Occupations includes all occupations in the U.S. Economy.
Source: U.S. Bureau of Labor Statistics, Occupational Employment and Wage Statistics.

occupation earned more than that amount and half earned less. The lowest 10 percent earned less than $38,400, and the highest 10 percent earned more than $145,240.

In May 2022, the median annual wages for editors in the top industries in which they worked were as follows:

Motion picture and video industries	$107,970
Media streaming distribution services, social networks, and other media networks and content providers	80,380
Professional, scientific, and technical services	77,350
Newspaper publishers	57,830

Most editors work full time, and their schedules are generally determined by production deadlines and type of editorial position. Editors typically work in busy offices and have to deal with production deadline pressures and the stresses of ensuring that the information they publish is correct. As a result, editors often work many hours, especially at those times leading up to a publication deadline. These work hours can be even more frequent when an editor is working on digital material for the Internet or for a live broadcast.

Job Outlook

Employment of editors is projected to decline 4 percent from 2022 to 2032.

Despite declining employment, about 11,600 openings for editors are projected each year, on average, over the decade. All of those openings are expected to result from the need to replace workers who transfer to other occupations or exit the labor force, such as to retire.

Employment

As traditional print publications lose ground to other media formats, editors are shifting their focus to online media. Despite

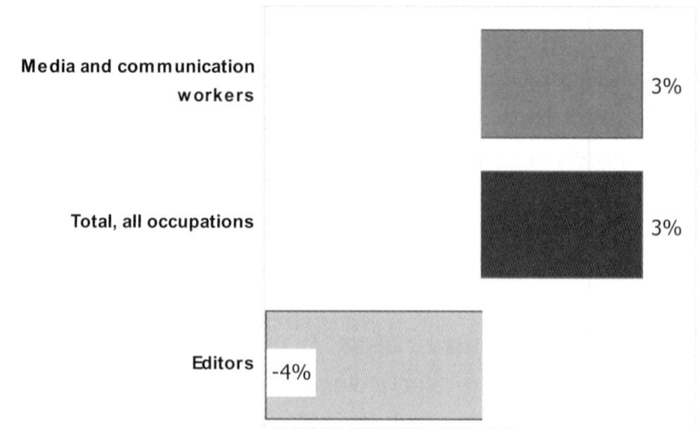

Note: All Occupations includes all occupations in the U.S. Economy.
Source: U.S. Bureau of Labor Statistics, Employment Projections program.

the growth in online media, decreases in traditional print magazine and newspaper readership will cause a decline in overall employment of editors.

Occupational Title	SOC Code	Employment, 2022	Projected Employment, 2032	Change, 2022-32	
				Percent	Numeric
Editors	27-3041	122,100	117,300	-4	-4,900

Contacts for More Information

For more information about editors, visit

- American Copy Editors Society
- American Society of Magazine Editors
- Association of Alternative Newsmedia
- Radio Television Digital News Association

Film and Video Editors and Camera Operators

Summary

Quick Facts: Film and Video Editors and Camera Operators	
2022 Median Pay	$62,420 per year $30.01 per hour
Typical Entry-Level Education	Bachelor's degree
Work Experience in a Related Occupation	None
On-the-job Training	None
Number of Jobs, 2022	87,500
Job Outlook, 2022-32	7% (Faster than average)
Employment Change, 2022-32	5,800

What Film and Video Editors and Camera Operators Do

Film and video editors and camera operators manipulate moving images that entertain or inform an audience.

Work Environment

Film and video editors and camera operators typically work in studios or in offices. Camera operators and videographers often shoot raw footage on location.

How to Become a Film and Video Editor or Camera Operator

Film and video editors and camera operators typically need a bachelor's degree in a field related to film or broadcasting.

Pay

The median annual wage for camera operators, television, video, and film was $58,230 in May 2022.

The median annual wage for film and video editors was $63,520 in May 2022.

Job Outlook

Overall employment of film and video editors and camera operators is projected to grow 7 percent from 2022 to 2032, faster than the average for all occupations.

About 8,200 openings for film and video editors and camera operators are projected each year, on average, over the decade. Many of those openings are expected to result from the need to replace workers who transfer to different occupations or exit the labor force, such as to retire.

What Film and Video Editors and Camera Operators Do

Film and video editors and camera operators manipulate images that entertain or inform an audience. Camera operators capture a wide range of material for television, movies, and other media. Editors arrange footage shot by camera operators and collaborate with producers and directors to create the final content.

Duties

Film and video editors and camera operators typically do the following:

- Shoot and record television programs, films, music videos, documentaries, or news and sporting events
- Organize digital footage with video-editing software
- Collaborate with a director to determine the overall vision of the production
- Discuss filming and editing techniques with a director to improve a scene
- Select the appropriate equipment, such as the type of lens or lighting
- Shoot or edit a scene based on the director's vision

Many camera operators supervise one or more assistants. The assistants set up the camera equipment and may be responsible for its storage and care. Assistants also help the operator

Film and video editors manipulate images that entertain or inform an audience.

Nearly all video editing work is done on a computer.

determine the best shooting angle and make sure that the camera stays in focus.

Likewise, editors often have one or more assistants. The assistants support the editor by keeping track of each shot in a database or loading digital video into an editing bay. Assistants also may do some of the editing tasks.

Most operators prefer using digital cameras because the smaller, more inexpensive instruments give them more flexibility in shooting angles. Digital cameras also have changed the job of some camera assistants: Instead of loading film or choosing lenses, they download digital images or choose a type of software program to use with the camera. In addition, drone cameras give operators an opportunity to film in the air, or in places that are hard to reach.

Nearly all editing work is done on a computer, and editors often are trained in a specific type of editing software.

The following are examples of types of camera operators:

Cinematographers film motion pictures. They usually work with a team of camera operators and assistants. Cinematographers determine the angles and types of equipment that will best capture a shot. They also adjust the lighting in a shot, because that is an important part of how the image looks.

Cinematographers may use stationary cameras that shoot whatever passes in front of them, or they may use a camera mounted on a track and move around the action. Some cinematographers sit on cranes to film an action scene; others carry the camera on their shoulder while they move around the action.

Some cinematographers specialize in filming cartoons or special effects. For information about a career in animation, see special effects artists and animators. Other cinematographers function as a film's artistic director. For information about these workers, see art directors.

Studio camera operators work in a broadcast studio and videotape their subjects from a fixed position. There may be one or several cameras in use at a time. Operators normally follow directions that give the order of the shots. They often have time to practice camera movements before shooting begins. If they are shooting a live event, they must be able to make adjustments at a moment's notice and follow the instructions of the show's director. The use of robotic cameras is common among studio camera operators, and one operator may control several cameras at once.

Videographers film or videotape private ceremonies or special events, such as weddings. They also may work with companies and make corporate documentaries on a variety of topics. Most videographers edit their own material.

Many videographers run their own business or do freelance work. They may submit bids, write contracts, and get permission to shoot on locations that may not be open to the public. They also get copyright protection for their work and keep financial records.

Many editors and camera operators, but particularly videographers, put their creative work online. If it becomes popular, they gain more recognition, which can lead to future employment or freelance opportunities.

Work Environment

Camera operators, television, video, and film held about 36,500 jobs in 2022. The largest employers of camera operators, television, video, and film were as follows:

Self-employed workers	33%
Motion picture and video industries	27
Professional, scientific, and technical services	10
Government	2

Film and video editors held about 51,000 jobs in 2022. The largest employers of film and video editors were as follows:

Motion picture and video industries	37%
Self-employed workers	34
Professional, scientific, and technical services	10

Film and video editors and camera operators typically work in studios or offices. Camera operators and videographers often shoot raw footage on location.

Camera operators work in a variety of conditions and may have to stand for long periods.

Film and video editors work in editing rooms by themselves, or with producers and directors, for many hours at a time. Cinematographers and operators who shoot for movies or television may film on location and be away from home for months at a time. Operators who travel usually must carry heavy equipment to their shooting locations.

Some camera operators work in uncomfortable or even dangerous conditions, such as severe weather, military conflicts, and natural disasters. They may have to stand for long periods waiting for an event to take place. They may carry heavy equipment while on shooting assignment.

Work Schedules

Most film and video editors and camera operators work full time, although part-time work is common. Work hours often vary with the type of operator or editor. Those who work in broadcasting may put in additional hours to meet a deadline. Those who work in the motion picture industry may have busy schedules while filming, but they go through a period of looking for work once a film is complete and before they are hired for their next job.

How to Become a Film and Video Editor or Camera Operator

Film and video editors and camera operators typically need a bachelor's degree in a field related to film or broadcasting.

Education

Film and video editors and camera operators typically need a bachelor's degree to enter the occupation. The degree is often in film, broadcasting, or a related fine and performing arts or communications field. Many colleges offer courses in cinematography or video-editing software. Coursework involves a mix of film theory with practical training.

Film and video editors and camera operators must have an understanding of digital cameras and editing software because both are now used on film sets.

Most editor and camera operator positions require a bachelor's degree in a field related to film or broadcasting.

Training

Employers may offer new employees training in the type of specialized editing software those employers use. Most editors eventually specialize in one type of software, but beginners should be familiar with as many types as possible.

Licenses, Certifications, and Registrations

Editors may demonstrate competence in various types of editing software by earning certification, which is generally offered by software vendors. Certification requires passing a comprehensive exam, and candidates can prepare for the exam on their own, through online tutorials, or through classroom instruction.

Advancement

Experienced film and video editors and camera operators with creativity and leadership skills can advance to overseeing their own projects. For more information, see the profile on producers and directors.

Important Qualities

Communication skills. Film and video editors and camera operators must communicate with other members of a production team, including producers and directors, to ensure that the project goes smoothly.

Computer skills. Film and video editors must use sophisticated editing software.

Creativity. Film and video editors and camera operators should be able to imagine what the result of their filming or editing will look like to an audience.

Detail oriented. Editors look at every frame of film and decide what should be kept or cut in order to maintain the best content.

Hand–eye coordination. Camera operators need to be able to move about the action while holding a camera steady.

Physical stamina. Camera operators may need to carry heavy equipment for long periods, particularly when they are filming on location.

Visual skills. Film and video editors and camera operators must see clearly what they are filming or editing in the postproduction process.

Pay

The median annual wage for camera operators, television, video, and film was $58,230 in May 2022. The median wage is the wage at which half the workers in an occupation earned more than that amount and half earned less. The lowest 10 percent earned less than $33,190, and the highest 10 percent earned more than $116,770.

The median annual wage for film and video editors was $63,520 in May 2022. The lowest 10 percent earned less than $36,930, and the highest 10 percent earned more than $166,730.

In May 2022, the median annual wages for camera operators, television, video, and film in the top industries in which they worked were as follows:

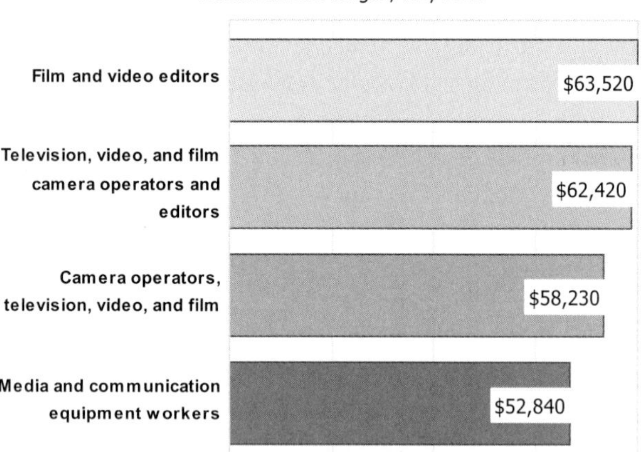

Note: All Occupations includes all occupations in the U.S. Economy.
Source: U.S. Bureau of Labor Statistics, Occupational Employment and Wage Statistics.

Motion picture and video industries	$66,750
Government	56,730
Professional, scientific, and technical services	52,000

In May 2022, the median annual wages for film and video editors in the top industries in which they worked were as follows:

Professional, scientific, and technical services	$65,330
Motion picture and video industries	65,200

Most film and video editors and camera operators work full time, although part-time work is common. Work hours often vary with the type of operator or editor. Those who work in broadcasting may put in additional hours to meet a deadline. Those who work in the motion picture industry may have busy schedules while filming, but they go through a period of looking for work once a film is complete and before they are hired for their next job.

Job Outlook

Overall employment of film and video editors and camera operators is projected to grow 7 percent from 2022 to 2032, faster than the average for all occupations.

About 8,200 openings for film and video editors and camera operators are projected each year, on average, over the decade. Many of those openings are expected to result from the need to replace workers who transfer to different occupations or exit the labor force, such as to retire.

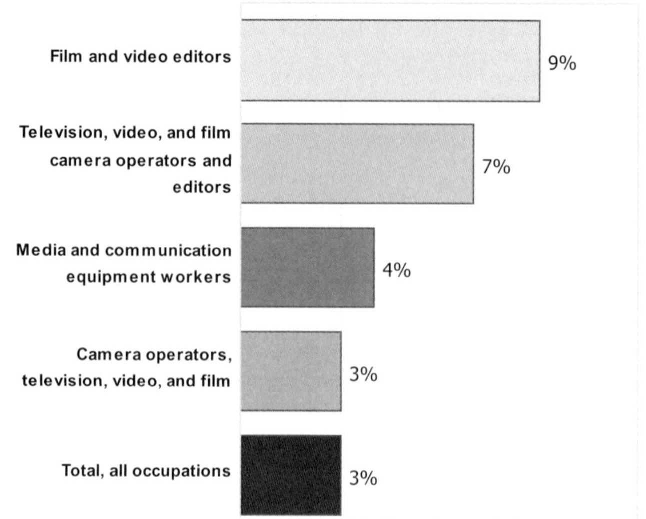

Note: All Occupations includes all occupations in the U.S. Economy.
Source: U.S. Bureau of Labor Statistics, Employment Projections program.

Employment

Projected employment of film and video editors and camera operators varies by occupation (see table).

The number of online-only platforms, such as streaming services, is likely to increase, along with the number of shows produced for these platforms. This growth may lead to more work for film and video editors and camera operators.

The consolidation of roles—such as editors who determine the best angles for a shoot, the use of robotic cameras, and the increasing reliance on amateur film footage—may lead to fewer jobs for camera operators. However, more film and video editors are expected to be needed because of an increase in special effects and overall available content.

Occupational Title	SOC Code	Employment, 2022	Projected Employment, 2032	Change, 2022-32	
				Percent	Numeric
Television, video, and film camera operators and editors	27-4030	87,500	93,300	7	5,800
Camera operators, television, video, and film	27-4031	36,500	37,500	3	1,000
Film and video editors	27-4032	51,000	55,800	9	4,800

Contacts for More Information

For more information about film and video editors and camera operators, visit

➤ Motion Picture Editors Guild

Interpreters and Translators

Summary

Quick Facts: Interpreters and Translators	
2022 Median Pay	$53,640 per year $25.79 per hour
Typical Entry-Level Education	Bachelor's degree
Work Experience in a Related Occupation	None
On-the-job Training	None
Number of Jobs, 2022	68,700
Job Outlook, 2022-32	4% (As fast as average)
Employment Change, 2022-32	3,000

What Interpreters and Translators Do

Interpreters and translators convert information from one language into another language.

Work Environment

Interpreters and translators work in settings such as schools, hospitals, courtrooms, meeting rooms, and conference centers. Part-time work is common, and work schedules may vary.

How to Become an Interpreter or Translator

Interpreters and translators typically need at least a bachelor's degree to enter the occupation. They also must be proficient in English and at least one other language, as well as in the interpretation or translation service they intend to provide.

Pay

The median annual wage for interpreters and translators was $53,640 in May 2022.

Job Outlook

Employment of interpreters and translators is projected to grow 4 percent from 2022 to 2032, about as fast as the average for all occupations.

Interpreters and translators convert information from one language into another.

About 7,200 openings for interpreters and translators are projected each year, on average, over the decade. Many of those openings are expected to result from the need to replace workers who transfer to different occupations or exit the labor force, such as to retire.

What Interpreters and Translators Do

Interpreters and translators convert information from one language into another language. Interpreters work in spoken or sign language; translators work in written language.

Duties

Interpreters and translators typically do the following:

- Convert concepts, style, and tone in the source language to equivalent concepts, style, and tone of the target language
- Compile information and technical terms into glossaries and terminology databases for use in their oral renditions and translations
- Speak, read, and write fluently in at least two languages, one of which is usually English
- Render spoken messages accurately, quickly, and clearly

Interpreters and translators aid communication by converting messages or text from one language (typically called the source language) into another language (the target language).

Interpreters and translators speak, read, and write in at least two languages fluently.

Although some people do both, interpreting and translating are different skills: interpreters work with spoken communication, and translators work with written communication.

Interpreters convert information from one spoken language into another—or, in the case of sign language interpreters, between spoken language and sign language. The interpreter's goal is for people to experience the target language as seamlessly as if it were the source language. Interpreters typically must be fluent speakers or signers of both languages, because they communicate between people who do not share a common language. Interpreters may provide their services remotely as well as in person.

The three common modes of interpreting are:

- **Simultaneous interpreters** convey a spoken or signed message into another language at the same time someone is speaking or signing. Simultaneous interpreters must be familiar with the subject matter and maintain a high level of concentration to convey the message accurately and completely. Due to the mental fatigue involved, simultaneous interpreters may work in pairs or small teams if they are interpreting for long periods of time, such as in a court or conference setting.
- **Consecutive interpreters** convey the speaker's or signer's message in another language after the person has stopped to allow for interpretation. Note taking is generally an essential part of consecutive interpreting.
- **Sight translation interpreters** provide translation of a written document directly into a spoken language for immediate understanding, not for the purposes of producing a translated document in writing.

Translators convert written materials from one language into another language. The translator's goal is for people to read the target language as if it were the source language of the written material. To do that, the translator must be able to maintain or duplicate the written structure and style of the source text while also keeping the ideas and facts accurate. Translators must properly transmit cultural references, including slang, and other expressions that do not translate literally.

Translators must read the source language fluently. The target language into which they translate is usually their native language. They adapt a range of products, including websites, marketing materials, and user documentation.

Nearly all translators use software in their work. Computer-assisted translation (CAT) tools, which use a computer database of previously translated sentences or segments (called a "translation memory") to translate new text, allow translators to be efficient and consistent. Machine translation software automatically generates text from the source language into the target language, which translators then review in a process called post-editing. Translations often go through several revisions before becoming final.

Although most interpreters and translators specialize in a particular field or industry, many have more than one area of specialization.

The following are examples of types of interpreters and translators:

Community interpreters work in a variety of public settings to provide language interpretation one-on-one or for groups. Community interpreters often are needed at parent-teacher conferences, community events, business and public meetings, social and government agencies, new-home purchases, and in many other work and community settings.

Conference interpreters work at events that have non-English-speaking attendees. The work is often in the field of international business or diplomacy, although conference interpreters may provide services for any organization that works with speakers of foreign languages. Employers generally prefer experienced interpreters who can convert two languages into one native language—for example, the ability to interpret from Spanish and French into English. For some positions, such as those with the United Nations, this qualification is required.

Conference interpreters often do simultaneous interpreting. Attendees at a conference or meeting who do not understand the language of the speaker wear earphones tuned to the interpreter who speaks the language they want to hear.

Healthcare or medical interpreters and translators typically work in healthcare settings and help patients communicate with doctors, nurses, technicians, and other medical staff. Interpreters and translators must have knowledge of medical terminology in both languages. They may translate patient consent documents, patients' records, pharmaceutical and informational brochures, regulatory information, and research material from one language into another.

Healthcare or medical interpreters must be sensitive to patients' personal circumstances and must maintain confidentiality and ethical standards.

Liaison or escort interpreters accompany either U.S. visitors abroad or foreign visitors in the United States who have limited English proficiency. Interpreting in both formal and informal settings, these specialists ensure that the visitors are able to communicate during their stay.

Legal or judicial interpreters and translators typically work in courts and other judicial settings. At arraignments, depositions, hearings, and trials, they help people who have limited English proficiency. Accordingly, they must understand legal terminology. Court interpreters must sometimes read source documents aloud in a target language, a task known as sight translation.

Literary translators convert books, poetry, and other published works from the source language into a target language. Whenever possible, literary translators work closely with authors to capture the intended meaning, as well as the literary and cultural references, of the original publication.

Localizers engage in a comprehensive process of adapting text and graphics from a source language into the target language. The goal of localizers' translation is to make a product or service appear to have originated in the country where it will be sold. They must not only know both languages, but also understand the technical information they are working with and the culture of the people who will be using the product or service. Localizers generally work in teams.

Sign language interpreters facilitate communication between people who are deaf or hard of hearing and people who can hear. Sign language interpreters must be fluent in English and in American Sign Language (ASL), which combines signing, finger spelling, and specific body language. ASL is a separate language from English and has its own grammar.

Some interpreters specialize in other forms of interpreting for people who are deaf or hard of hearing.

Some people who are deaf or hard of hearing lip-read English instead of, or in addition to, signing in ASL. Interpreters who work with these people do "oral interpretation," mouthing speech silently and carefully. They also may use facial expressions and gestures to help the lip-reader understand.

Other modes of interpreting include cued speech, which uses hand shapes placed near the mouth to give lip-readers more information; signing exact English; and tactile signing, which is interpreting for people who are blind as well as deaf by making hand signs into the person's hand.

Trilingual interpreters facilitate communication among an English speaker, a speaker of another language, and an ASL user. They must have the versatility and cultural understanding necessary to interpret in all three languages without changing the fundamental meaning of the message.

Work Environment

Interpreters and translators held about 68,700 jobs in 2022. The largest employers of interpreters and translators were as follows:

Professional, scientific, and technical services	30%
Self-employed workers	21
Educational services; state, local, and private	20
Hospitals; state, local, and private	8
Government	5

Interpreters work in a variety of settings, including schools, hospitals, courtrooms, detention facilities, and conference centers; they also may work remotely. Some interpreters, such as liaison or escort interpreters, travel frequently. Depending on the setting and type of assignment, interpreting may be stressful.

Translators usually work in offices, which may include remote settings. They usually receive and submit their work electronically and must sometimes deal with the pressure of deadlines and tight schedules.

Legal interpreters must sometimes read documents aloud in a language other than that in which they were written.

Work Schedules

Part-time work is common for interpreters and translators, and work schedules may vary. Interpreters and translators may have periods of limited work and periods of long, irregular hours.

Self-employed interpreters and translators are able to set their own schedules.

How to Become an Interpreter or Translator

Interpreters and translators typically need at least a bachelor's degree to enter the occupation. They also must be proficient in at least two languages (English and one other language), as well as in the interpretation or translation service they intend to provide.

Education

Interpreters and translators typically need a bachelor's degree; common fields of degree include foreign language, business, and communications. Students who study technical subjects, such as engineering or medicine, may be able to provide a higher level of interpreting and translation.

Some interpreters and translators attain a bachelors degree in a specific language or American Sign Language.

Interpreters and translators also need to be proficient in at least two languages, one of which is usually English, and in the translation or interpretation skill they plan to provide.

High school students interested in becoming an interpreter or translator should take a broad range of classes, including in foreign languages and English.

Through community organizations, students interested in sign language interpreting may take introductory classes in American Sign Language (ASL) and seek out volunteer opportunities to work with people who are deaf or hard of hearing.

Internships offer prospective interpreters and translators an opportunity to learn about the work. For example, interns may shadow an experienced interpreter or begin working in industries with particularly high demand for language services, such as court or medical interpreting.

Licenses, Certifications, and Registrations

General certification typically is not required for interpreters and translators. However, workers may show proficiency by passing a variety of optional certification tests. For example, the American Translators Association (ATA) provides certification in many language combinations.

Employers may require or prefer certification for some types of interpreters and translators. For example, most states require certification for court interpreters. Federal courts offer court interpreter certification in several languages, including Spanish, Navajo, and Haitian Creole. At the state level, courts offer certification in multiple languages.

The Certification Commission for Healthcare Interpreters (CCHI) offers two types of certification for healthcare interpreters: Core Certification Healthcare Interpreter (CoreCHI), for interpreters of any language providing services in the United States; and Certified Healthcare Interpreter (CHI), for interpreters of Spanish, Arabic, and Mandarin.

The National Board of Certification for Medical Interpreters (NBCMI) offers two types of certification for medical interpreters: the Hub-CMI credential, a nonlanguage-specific certification available to all interpreters regardless of target language; and the CMI credential for interpreters of Spanish, Cantonese, Mandarin, Russian, Korean, and Vietnamese.

Continuing education is required for most state court and medical interpreter certifications. It is offered by professional interpreter and translator associations, such as the ATA and the National Association of Judiciary Interpreters (NAJIT).

The National Association of the Deaf (NAD) and the Registry of Interpreters for the Deaf (RID) jointly offer certification for general sign language interpreters. In addition, the registry offers specialty tests in legal interpreting, speech reading, and deaf-to-deaf interpreting—which includes interpreting among deaf speakers of different native languages and from ASL to tactile signing.

The U.S. Department of State offers aptitude tests for interpreters and translators at various levels, from basic to advanced. Although these tests are not considered a credential, they are a required step for candidates to be added to a roster for freelance assignments. Other federal agencies may offer similar proficiency tests.

Other Experience

Experience is not typically required to enter the occupation, but it may be especially helpful for interpreters and freelancers pursuing self-employment. Prospective interpreters and translators may benefit from activities such as spending time in a foreign country, interacting directly with foreign cultures, and studying a variety of subjects in English and at least one other language.

Working in-house for a translation company or taking on freelance or volunteer assignments may help people gain firsthand knowledge of the skills that interpreters or translators need. Volunteer opportunities for interpreters may be available through community organizations, hospitals, and sporting events, such as soccer, that involve international competitors.

By developing relationships with experienced workers in the field, interpreters and translators build their skills and confidence and establish a network of contacts. Mentoring may be formal, such as through a professional association; for example, both the American Translators Association (ATA) and the Registry of Interpreters for the Deaf (RID) offer formal mentoring programs. Mentoring also may be informal, such as with a coworker or an acquaintance who has experience interpreting or translating.

Advancement

Experienced interpreters and translators advance by taking on increasingly difficult assignments, gaining certification, and obtaining editorial responsibility.

Some interpreters and translators advance by becoming self-employed. They may submit resumes and samples to different translation and interpreting companies who match their skills to assignments. They may get work based on their reputation or through referrals from clients or colleagues. Those who start their own businesses also may hire translators and interpreters to work for them.

Important Qualities

Business skills. Self-employed interpreters and translators must be able to manage their finances. They need to set prices for their work, bill customers, keep records, and market their services to build their client base.

Communication skills. Interpreters and translators must be able to read, speak clearly, and write effectively in all of the languages in which they are working.

Concentration. Interpreters and translators must be able to focus while others are speaking or moving around them.

Cultural sensitivity. Interpreters and translators must be aware of expectations among the people for whom they are

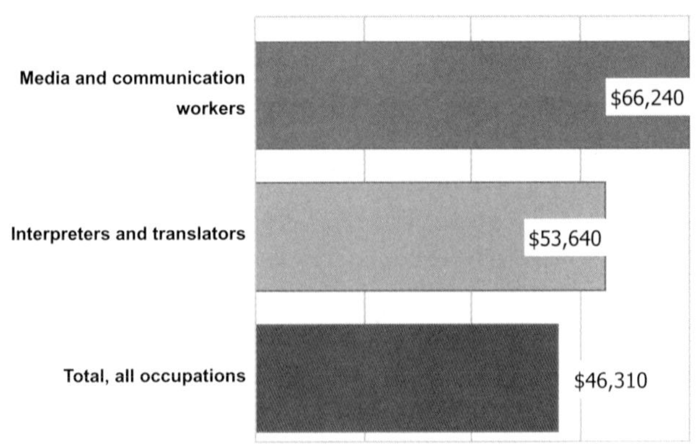

Note: All Occupations includes all occupations in the U.S. Economy.
Source: U.S. Bureau of Labor Statistics, Occupational Employment and Wage Statistics.

helping to facilitate communication. They must understand not only the language but the culture.

Dexterity. Sign language interpreters must be able to make quick and coordinated hand, finger, and arm movements when interpreting.

Interpersonal skills. Interpreters and translators must be able to put clients and others at ease. Interpreters may work on teams and must get along with colleagues to ensure success.

Listening skills. Interpreters must pay attention when interpreting for audiences to ensure that they hear and interpret correctly.

Pay

The median annual wage for interpreters and translators was $53,640 in May 2022. The median wage is the wage at which half the workers in an occupation earned more than that amount and half earned less. The lowest 10 percent earned less than $33,540, and the highest 10 percent earned more than $93,140.

In May 2022, the median annual wages for interpreters and translators in the top industries in which they worked were as follows:

Government	$64,910
Educational services; state, local, and private	56,860
Hospitals; state, local, and private	56,110
Professional, scientific, and technical services	49,710

These wage data exclude self-employed workers. Pay for interpreters and translators may depend on a number of variables, including the language, specialty, experience, education, and certification of the interpreter or translator.

Part-time work is common for interpreters and translators, and work schedules may vary. Interpreters and translators may have periods of limited work and periods of long, irregular hours.

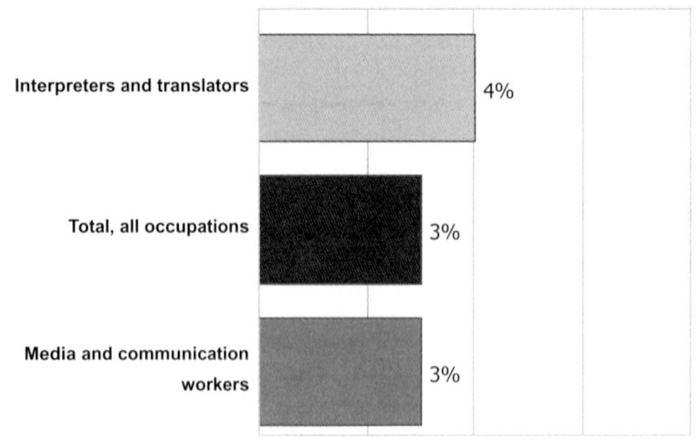

Note: All Occupations includes all occupations in the U.S. Economy.
Source: U.S. Bureau of Labor Statistics, Employment Projections program.

Job Outlook

Employment of interpreters and translators is projected to grow 4 percent from 2022 to 2032, about as fast as the average for all occupations.

About 7,200 openings for interpreters and translators are projected each year, on average, over the decade. Many of those openings are expected to result from the need to replace workers who transfer to different occupations or exit the labor force, such as to retire.

Employment

A more diverse U.S. population and increasing globalization are expected to create demand for interpreters and translators. The ongoing need for military and national security interpreters and translators should result in more jobs as well.

In addition, demand for American Sign Language interpreters is expected to grow due to the increasing use of video relay services, which allow people to conduct online video calls and use a sign language interpreter.

Computers have made the work of translators and localization specialists more efficient. However, many of these jobs cannot be entirely automated because computers cannot yet produce work comparable to what human translators do in most cases.

Occupational Title	SOC Code	Employment, 2022	Projected Employment, 2032	Change, 2022-32	
				Percent	Numeric
Interpreters and translators	27-3091	68,700	71,700	4	3,000

Contacts for More Information

For more information about interpreters, visit

- Discover Interpreting
- American Translators Association (ATA)
- Certification Commission for Healthcare Interpreters (CCHI)

- International Association of Conference Interpreters
- National Association of Judiciary Interpreters and Translators (NAJIT)
- National Association of the Deaf (NAD)
- National Board of Certification for Medical Interpreters
- National Council on Interpreting in Health Care (NCIHC)
- Registry of Interpreters for the Deaf (RID)
- U.S. State Department

News Analysts, Reporters, and Journalists

Summary

Quick Facts: News Analysts, Reporters, and Journalists	
2022 Median Pay	$55,960 per year $26.90 per hour
Typical Entry-Level Education	Bachelor's degree
Work Experience in a Related Occupation	None
On-the-job Training	None
Number of Jobs, 2022	58,500
Job Outlook, 2022-32	-3% (Decline)
Employment Change, 2022-32	-1,900

What News Analysts, Reporters, and Journalists Do

News analysts, reporters, and journalists keep the public updated about current events and noteworthy information.

Work Environment

Most news analysts, reporters, and journalists work for newspaper, website, or magazine publishers or in television or radio broadcasting. Others are self-employed. Most work full time, and their schedules vary.

How to Become a News Analyst, Reporter, or Journalist

News analysts, reporters, and journalists typically need a bachelor's degree to enter the occupation. Internship or work experience on a college newspaper, radio station, or television station also may be helpful.

News analysts, reporters, and journalists keep the public updated about current events and noteworthy information.

Pay

The median annual wage for news analysts, reporters, and journalists was $55,960 in May 2022.

Job Outlook

Employment of news analysts, reporters, and journalists is projected to decline 3 percent from 2022 to 2032.

Despite declining employment, about 6,000 openings for news analysts, reporters, and journalists are projected each year, on average, over the decade. All of those openings are expected to result from the need to replace workers who transfer to other occupations or exit the labor force, such as to retire.

What News Analysts, Reporters, and Journalists Do

News analysts, reporters, and journalists keep the public updated about current events and noteworthy information. They report international, national, and local news for newspapers, magazines, websites, television, and radio.

Duties

News analysts, reporters, and journalists typically do the following:

- Research topics that an editor or news director has assigned to them

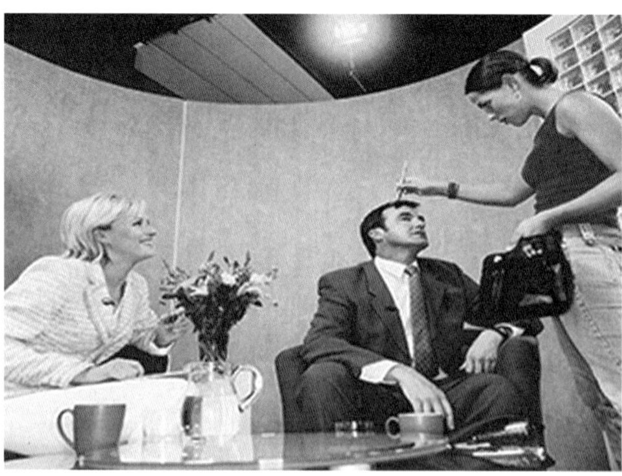

Those who work in television and radio set up and conduct interviews, which can be broadcast live or recorded for future broadcasts.

- Develop relationships with experts and contacts who provide tips and leads on stories or articles
- Interview people who have information, analysis, or opinions about a story or article
- Analyze and interpret information to increase audience understanding of the news
- Write stories or articles for newspapers, magazines, or websites and create scripts to be read on television or radio
- Review stories or articles for accuracy, style, and grammar
- Update stories or articles as new information becomes available
- Investigate new story or article ideas and pitch ideas to editors

News analysts, reporters, and journalists often work for a particular type of media organization, such as a television or radio station, newspaper, or website.

Those who work in television and radio set up and conduct interviews, which can be broadcast live or recorded for future broadcasts. These workers often edit interviews and other recordings to create a cohesive story or report, and they write and record voiceovers to provide the audience with supplementary facts or context. They may create multiple versions of the same story or report for different broadcasts or media platforms.

News analysts, reporters, and journalists for print media conduct interviews and write stories or articles to be used in newspapers, magazines, and online publications. Because most newspapers and magazines have print and online versions, these workers' content typically appears in both versions. As a result, they must stay up to date with developments related to a content item and update the online version with current information, if necessary.

Outlets are increasingly relying on *multimedia journalists* to publish content on a variety of platforms, such as a video content on the website of a daily newspaper. Multimedia journalists typically record, report, write, and edit their own stories or articles. They also gather the audio, video, or graphics that accompany their content.

News analysts, reporters, and journalists may need to maintain a social media presence. Many use social media to cover live events, provide additional information for readers and viewers, promote their stations and newscasts, and engage with their audiences.

Some workers, particularly those in large cities or large news organizations, cover a particular topic, such as sports, medicine, or politics. Those who work in small cities, towns, or organizations may be generalists and cover a wide range of subjects.

Some news analysts, reporters, and journalists are self-employed and accept freelance assignments from news organizations. Because freelancers are paid for individual stories or articles, they may work with many organizations and spend some of their time marketing their content and looking for their next assignment. Self-employed news analysts, reporters, and journalists also may publish news and videos on their own platforms.

The following are examples of types of news analysts, reporters, and journalists:

Columnists write articles offering an opinion or perspective about a particular subject. They submit a piece to a publication, often on a schedule, such as once per week. Their work may be published in a newspaper, magazine, or other outlet or self-published on the columnist's website.

Correspondents report the news to a radio or television network from a remote location. Those who cover international events, called *foreign correspondents*, often live in another country and report about a specific region of the world.

News anchors lead television or radio shows that describe current events. Others are *news commentators* who analyze and interpret reports and offer opinions. They may come from fields outside of journalism and have expertise in a particular subject, such as finance, and are hired on a contract basis to provide their opinion on that subject.

These workers also may collaborate with editors, photographers, videographers, and other reporters and journalists when working on an article or story.

For information about workers with a background in this field who teach journalism or communications at colleges and universities, see the profile on postsecondary teachers.

Work Environment

News analysts, reporters, and journalists held about 58,500 jobs in 2022. The largest employers of news analysts, reporters, and journalists were as follows:

Newspaper publishers	26%
Self-employed workers	25

News analysts, reporters, and journalists spend a lot of time in the field, conducting interviews and investigating stories or articles.

Media streaming distribution services, social networks, and other media networks and content providers	22
Television broadcasting stations	15
Radio broadcasting stations	3

News analysts, reporters, and journalists spend a lot of time in the field, conducting interviews and investigating stories or articles. Reporters spend some time in an office or newsroom, but they often travel to be on location for events or to meet contacts and file stories remotely.

Injuries and Illnesses

Working on news items about some topics or events, such as conflicts and natural disasters, may put news analysts, reporters, and journalists in dangerous situations. In addition, reporters often face pressure or stress when trying to meet a deadline or cover breaking news.

Work Schedules

Most news analysts, reporters, and journalists work full time, and their schedules vary. They may need to work additional hours or change their schedules in order to follow breaking news. Because news can happen at any time, they may need to work nights and weekends. They may also work nights and weekends to lead news programs or provide commentary.

How to Become a News Analyst, Reporter, or Journalist

News analysts, reporters, and journalists typically need a bachelor's degree to enter the occupation. Internship or work experience on a college newspaper, radio station, or television station also may be helpful.

Education

News analysts, reporters, and journalists typically need a bachelor's degree in journalism, communications, or a related field, such as English.

News analysts, reporters, and journalists must be determined when pursuing stories or articles.

Bachelor's degree programs in journalism and communications include courses in journalistic ethics and techniques for researching topics and conducting interviews. Some programs may require students to study liberal arts subjects, such as history and economics, to prepare for covering a range of topics. Students may further specialize in the type of journalism they wish to pursue, such as print or broadcast.

Journalism students may benefit from courses in multimedia design, coding, and programming to be able to develop content that includes video, audio, data, and graphics.

Other Experience

Employers generally prefer to hire candidates who have had an internship or have worked on school newspapers, radio stations, or TV stations. While attending college, students may seek multiple internships with different news organizations. Internships allow students to gain experience and develop samples of their writing or their on-air appearances.

News commentators who come from a field outside of journalism typically have expertise in areas on which they comment.

Advancement

After gaining experience, field reporters at a local news station may become that station's anchor. News analysts, reporters, and journalists may also advance by moving from news organizations in small cities or towns to news organizations in large cities. Large markets may offer opportunities for more responsibility and challenges. Reporters and journalists also may become editors or news directors.

Important Qualities

Communication skills. News analysts, reporters, and journalists must be able to clearly convey information. Strong writing skills also are important.

Interpersonal skills. To develop contacts and conduct interviews, news analysts, reporters, and journalists must be able to build relationships. They also need to work well with other journalists, editors, and news directors.

Persistence. News analysts, reporters, and journalists must be determined when pursuing stories or articles. Investigating topics and gathering facts may be difficult, particularly when those involved refuse to be interviewed or to provide comment.

Stamina. The work of news analysts, reporters, and journalists is often fast paced and exhausting. They must be able to adapt to the irregular hours of work.

Technological skills. News analysts, reporters, and journalists should be able to use editing equipment and other broadcast-related devices. They also should be able to use multimedia and coding software in order to publish stories on websites and mobile devices.

Pay

The median annual wage for news analysts, reporters, and journalists was $55,960 in May 2022. The median wage is the wage

News Analysts, Reporters, and Journalists

Median annual wages, May 2022

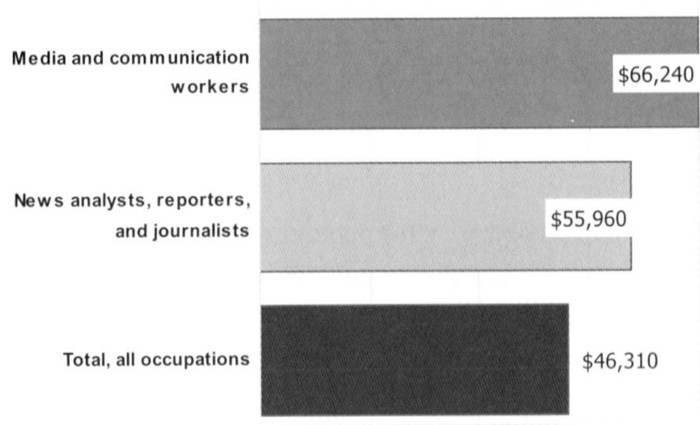

Note: All Occupations includes all occupations in the U.S. Economy.
Source: U.S. Bureau of Labor Statistics, Occupational Employment and Wage Statistics.

News Analysts, Reporters, and Journalists

Percent change in employment, projected 2022-32

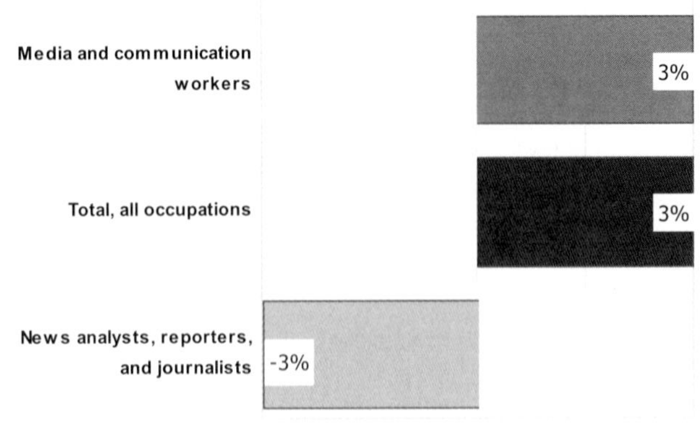

Note: All Occupations includes all occupations in the U.S. Economy.
Source: U.S. Bureau of Labor Statistics, Employment Projections program.

at which half the workers in an occupation earned more than that amount and half earned less. The lowest 10 percent earned less than $30,470, and the highest 10 percent earned more than $136,500.

In May 2022, the median annual wages for news analysts, reporters, and journalists in the top industries in which they worked were as follows:

Media streaming distribution services, social networks, and other media networks and content providers	$79,000
Television broadcasting stations	60,190
Newspaper publishers	40,250
Radio broadcasting stations	40,170

Most news analysts, reporters, and journalists work full time, and schedules vary. They may need to work additional hours or change their schedules in order to follow breaking news. Because news can happen at any time, they may need to work nights and weekends. They may also work nights and weekends to lead news programs or provide commentary.

Job Outlook

Employment of news analysts, reporters, and journalists is projected to decline 3 percent from 2022 to 2032.

Despite declining employment, about 6,000 openings for news analysts, reporters, and journalists are projected each year, on average, over the decade. All of those openings are expected to result from the need to replace workers who transfer to other occupations or exit the labor force, such as to retire.

Employment

Declining advertising revenue in radio, newspapers, and television is expected to impact the long-term demand for these workers. In addition, television and radio stations are continuing to publish content online and on mobile devices. As a result, news organizations may have difficulty selling traditional forms of advertising, which is often their primary source of revenue.

News organizations also continue to consolidate and increasingly share resources, staff, and content with other media outlets. As consolidations, mergers, and news sharing continue, the demand for journalists may decrease as organizations downsize.

In some instances, however, consolidation provides increased funding and resources from the larger organization that helps limit the loss of jobs. In addition, increasing demand for online news may offset some of the impacts from declining advertising revenue and downsizing.

Occupational Title	SOC Code	Employment, 2022	Projected Employment, 2032	Change, 2022-32	
				Percent	Numeric
News analysts, reporters, and journalists	27-3023	58,500	56,600	-3	-1,900

Contacts for More Information

For more information, visit

- National Association of Broadcasters
- Online News Association
- Radio Television Digital News Association
- Society of Professional Journalists
- Dow Jones News Fund

Photographers

Summary

Quick Facts: Photographers	
2022 Median Pay	$40,170 per year $19.31 per hour
Typical Entry-Level Education	High school diploma or equivalent
Work Experience in a Related Occupation	None
On-the-job Training	Moderate-term on-the-job training
Number of Jobs, 2022	148,900
Job Outlook, 2022-32	4% (As fast as average)
Employment Change, 2022-32	6,100

What Photographers Do
Photographers use their technical expertise, creativity, and composition skills to produce and preserve images.

Work Environment
Working conditions for photographers vary by specialty. Some photographers travel for photo shoots, working either indoors or outdoors. Others work in studios; still others work in laboratories and use microscopes to photograph subjects.

How to Become a Photographer
Although portrait photographers are not required to have postsecondary education, many take classes because employers usually seek applicants with creativity and a "good eye," as well as a good technical understanding of photography. Photojournalists and industrial and scientific photographers often need a bachelor's degree.

Pay
The median hourly wage for photographers was $19.31 in May 2022.

Job Outlook
Employment of photographers is projected to grow 4 percent from 2022 to 2032, about as fast as the average for all occupations.

About 13,900 openings for photographers are projected each year, on average, over the decade. Many of those openings are expected to result from the need to replace workers who transfer to different occupations or exit the labor force, such as to retire.

What Photographers Do
Photographers use their technical expertise, creativity, and composition skills to produce and preserve images that tell a story or record an event.

Duties
Photographers typically do the following:

- Market or advertise services to attract clients
- Analyze and plan the composition of photographs
- Use various photographic techniques and lighting equipment
- Capture subjects in professional-quality photographs
- Enhance the subject's appearance with natural or artificial light
- Use photo-enhancing software
- Maintain a digital portfolio to demonstrate their work
- Archive and manage imagery

Nowadays, most photographers use digital cameras instead of traditional film cameras, although some photographers use both. Digital cameras capture images electronically, so the

Some photographers travel for photo shoots, and others work in their own studios.

Photographers capture subjects in commercial-quality photographs.

photographer can edit the image on a computer. Images can be stored on portable memory devices, such as flash drives. Once the raw image has been transferred to a computer, photographers can use image processing software to crop or modify the image and enhance it through color correction and other specialized effects. Photographers who edit their own pictures use computers, editing software, and high-quality printers.

Some photographers use unmanned aerial vehicles, commonly known as drones, to capture shots. The drones are equipped with an integrated camera to capture 360-degree imagery of buildings, landscapes, scenery, or events.

Photographers who work for commercial clients often present photographs in a digital format to the client. Wedding and portrait photographers, who serve primarily noncommercial clients, also may provide framing services and present the photographs they capture in albums.

Many photographers are self-employed. Photographers who own and operate their own business have additional responsibilities. They must advertise, schedule appointments, set up and adjust equipment, buy supplies, keep records, charge customers, pay bills, and—if they have employees—hire, train, and direct their workers.

In addition, some photographers teach photography classes or conduct workshops in schools or in their own studios.

The following are examples of types of photographers:

Aerial photographers travel in planes or helicopters to capture overhead photographs of buildings and landscapes. They often use cameras with gyrostabilizers to counteract the movement of the aircraft and ensure high-quality images.

Commercial and industrial photographers take pictures of subjects such as buildings, models, merchandise, artifacts, and landscapes. They usually go on location to take pictures for magazine covers, engineering projects, or other purposes.

Drone photographers operate unmanned aerial vehicles with an integrated camera to capture 360-degree imagery of buildings, landscapes, scenery, or events.

Fine arts photographers sell their photographs as artwork. In addition to their knowledge of techniques such as lighting and the use of lenses, fine arts photographers need to have creativity and artistic talent.

News photographers, also called *photojournalists*, photograph people, places, and events for newspapers, journals, magazines, or television. In addition to taking still photos, photojournalists often work with digital video.

Portrait photographers take pictures of individuals or groups of people and may work in studios. Photographers who specialize in weddings, religious ceremonies, or school photographs usually work on location.

Scientific photographers capture scientific or medical data or phenomena. Because they focus on accurately representing subjects visually, these photographers limit the use of software to clarify an image. Scientific photographers who take pictures

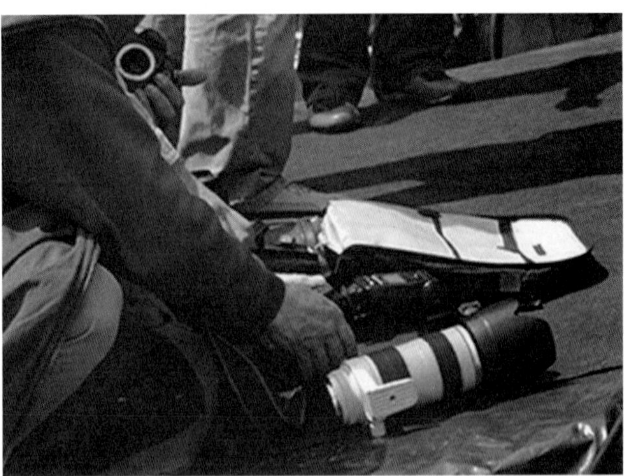

Most photographers stand or walk for long periods while carrying heavy equipment.

of objects too small to be seen with the naked eye use microscopes to photograph their subjects.

Work Environment

Photographers held about 148,900 jobs in 2022. The largest employers of photographers were as follows:

Self-employed workers	69%
Photographic services	16

Working conditions for photographers vary by specialty. Photographers may work indoors or outdoors.

Portrait photographers may work in studios, but they also travel to take photographs at a client's location, such as a school or a home.

News photographers may travel locally or internationally and must be prepared to work in uncomfortable or even dangerous surroundings. For example, a news photographer may be sent to a war zone to capture images. News photographers often work irregular schedules and must be available on short notice.

Aerial photographers work in planes or helicopters to capture a scene, event, or location from an overhead perspective.

Most photographers stand or walk for long periods. They may need to carry heavy equipment.

Work Schedules

Some photographers work part time. Hours often are flexible so that photographers can meet with current and potential clients or visit the sites where they will work. For certain types of photographers, workloads may fluctuate with the season. For example, wedding photographers are typically busiest in the summer and fall.

How to Become a Photographer

Although portrait photographers are not required to have postsecondary education, many take classes because

Portrait photographers take pictures of individuals or groups of people and usually work in their own studios.

employers usually seek applicants with creativity and a "good eye," as well as a good technical understanding of photography. Photojournalists and industrial and scientific photographers often need a bachelor's degree.

Education

Postsecondary education is not required for most photographers. However, many photographers take classes or earn a bachelor's degree to improve their skills and employment prospects.

Many universities, community colleges, vocational–technical institutes, and private trade and technical schools offer classes in photography. Basic photography courses cover equipment, processes, and techniques. Art school training in photographic design and composition also may be useful.

Entry-level positions in photojournalism or in industrial or scientific photography generally require a college degree in photography or in a field related to the industry in which the photographer seeks employment. For example, classes in biology, medicine, or chemistry may be important for scientific photographers.

Business, marketing, and accounting classes may be helpful for self-employed photographers.

Training

Photographers' skill or ability for taking good photos is typically cultivated over years of practice. Photographers often start working as an assistant to a professional photographer, learning on the job. This work provides an opportunity to gain experience, build the photographers' portfolios, and gain exposure to prospective clients. In addition, photographers must learn to use photo-editing software.

For many artists, including photographers, developing a portfolio—a collection of their work that demonstrates their styles and abilities—is essential. Art directors, clients, and others often review portfolios when deciding whether to hire a particular photographer.

Licenses, Certifications, and Registrations

Photographers who commercially operate drones, commonly known as unmanned aerial vehicles, must obtain certification from the Federal Aviation Administration (FAA). They must fulfill the following criteria:

- Be at least 16 years old
- Be able to read, speak, write, and understand English (exceptions may be made if the person is unable to meet one of these requirements for a medical reason, such as a hearing impairment)
- Be in good physical and mental condition to operate a small drone safely
- Pass the initial aeronautical knowledge exam at an FAA-approved knowledge testing center

For specific guidelines and information, visit the FAA website's section on unmanned aircraft systems.

Important Qualities

Artistic ability. Photographers capture their subjects in images, and they must evaluate the artistic quality of a photograph. Photographers need a "good eye": the ability to use colors, shadows, shades, light, and distance to compose aesthetically pleasing photographs.

Business skills. Photographers must plan marketing or advertising strategies, reach out to prospective clients, and anticipate seasonal employment.

Computer skills. Most photographers do their own postproduction work and must be adept at using photo-editing software. They also use computers to maintain a digital portfolio.

Customer-service skills. Photographers must understand the types of shots their clients want and agree on suitable alternatives for ideas that may be unworkable.

Detail oriented. Photographers must focus on details, especially in postproduction. In addition, photographers accumulate many photographs and must maintain them in an orderly fashion.

Interpersonal skills. Photographers often take pictures of people. They must communicate and be flexible when working with clients in order to achieve the desired composition in a photograph.

Pay

The median hourly wage for photographers was $19.31 in May 2022. The median wage is the wage at which half the workers in an occupation earned more than that amount and half earned less. The lowest 10 percent earned less than $12.98, and the highest 10 percent earned more than $39.64.

In May 2022, the median hourly wages for photographers in the top industries in which they worked were as follows:

Photographic services	$17.57

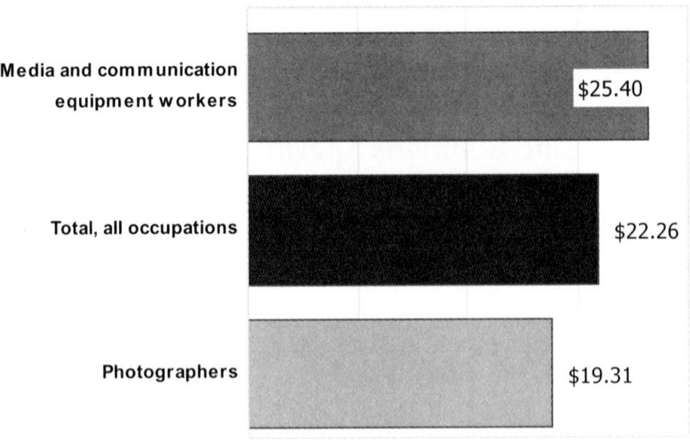

Note: All Occupations includes all occupations in the U.S. Economy.
Source: U.S. Bureau of Labor Statistics, Occupational Employment and Wage Statistics.

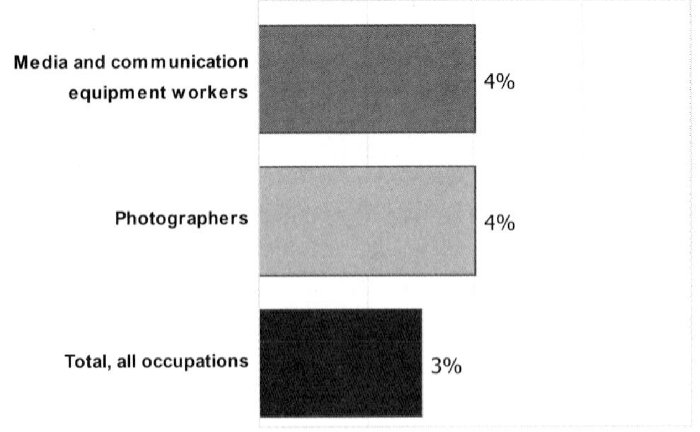

Note: All Occupations includes all occupations in the U.S. Economy.
Source: U.S. Bureau of Labor Statistics, Employment Projections program.

Some photographers work part time. Hours often are flexible so that photographers can meet with current and potential clients or visit the sites where they will work. For certain types of photographers, workloads may fluctuate with the season. For example, wedding photographers are typically busiest in the summer and fall.

Job Outlook

Employment of photographers is projected to grow 4 percent from 2022 to 2032, about as fast as the average for all occupations.

About 13,900 openings for photographers are projected each year, on average, over the decade. Many of those openings are expected to result from the need to replace workers who transfer to different occupations or exit the labor force, such as to retire.

Employment

Employment of self-employed photographers is projected to grow over the projections decade as the number of amateur photographers and hobbyists entering the occupation increases. Demand for portrait photographers will remain as people continue to want new portraits. Corporations also will continue to require commercial photographers' services to develop compelling advertisements to sell products.

However, the ease and quality of photos taken by smartphones may reduce the need for professional photographers. In addition, stock photographic services available online give individuals and businesses access to photographs for a fee or subscription, possibly dampening demand for these workers.

Occupational Title	SOC Code	Employment, 2022	Projected Employment, 2032	Change, 2022-32	
				Percent	Numeric
Photographers	27-4021	148,900	155,000	4	6,100

Contacts for More Information

For more information, visit

- American Society of Media Photographers
- Federal Aviation Administration (FAA)
- University Photographers' Association of America

Public Relations Specialists

Summary

Quick Facts: Public Relations Specialists	
2022 Median Pay	$67,440 per year $32.42 per hour
Typical Entry-Level Education	Bachelor's degree
Work Experience in a Related Occupation	None
On-the-job Training	None
Number of Jobs, 2022	297,100
Job Outlook, 2022-32	6% (Faster than average)
Employment Change, 2022-32	18,000

What Public Relations Specialists Do

Public relations specialists create and maintain a positive public image for the clients they represent.

Work Environment

Public relations specialists work for a variety of organizations, including schools, media buyers, and professional associations. They usually work in offices, but they also deliver speeches, attend meetings and community activities, and occasionally travel.

How to Become a Public Relations Specialist

Public relations specialists typically need a bachelor's degree to enter the occupation.

Pay

The median annual wage for public relations specialists was $67,440 in May 2022.

Job Outlook

Employment of public relations specialists is projected to grow 6 percent from 2022 to 2032, faster than the average for all occupations.

About 25,800 openings for public relations specialists are projected each year, on average, over the decade. Many of those openings are expected to result from the need to replace workers who transfer to different occupations or exit the labor force, such as to retire.

What Public Relations Specialists Do

Public relations specialists create and maintain a positive public image for the individuals, groups, or organizations they represent. They craft media releases and develop social media programs to shape public perception of their clients and to increase awareness of each client's work and goals.

Duties

Public relations specialists typically do the following:

- Write press releases and prepare information for the media
- Respond to information requests from the media
- Help clients communicate effectively with the public
- Draft speeches and arrange interviews for a client's top executives
- Evaluate public opinion of clients through social media
- Evaluate advertising and promotion programs to determine whether they are compatible with their organization's public relations efforts
- Help maintain their organization's image and identity

Public relations specialists, also called *communications specialists*, handle an individual's, group's, or organization's communication with the public, including consumers, investors, reporters, and other media specialists. In government, public relations specialists may be called *press secretaries* and keep the public informed about the activities of government officials and agencies.

Public relations specialists write press releases and contact people in the media who might print or broadcast their material. Many radio or television special reports, newspaper stories, and

Public relations specialists design media releases to shape public perception of their organization.

Public relations specialists evaluate advertising and promotion programs.

magazine articles start at the desks of public relations specialists. For example, a press release might describe a public issue, such as health, energy, or the environment, and what an organization does concerning that issue.

Press releases often are adapted for announcements on social media, in addition to publication through traditional media outlets. Public relations specialists are usually in charge of monitoring and responding to social media questions and concerns.

Public relations specialists are different from advertisers in that they get their stories covered by media instead of purchasing ad space in publications and on television.

Work Environment

Public relations specialists held about 297,100 jobs in 2022. The largest employers of public relations specialists were as follows:

Educational services; state, local, and private	13%
Advertising, public relations, and related services	13
Government	10
Healthcare and social assistance	7
Business, professional, labor, political, and similar organizations	6

Public relations specialists work in many different industries.

Public relations specialists work for a variety of organizations, including schools, media buyers, and professional associations. They usually work in offices, but they also deliver speeches, attend meetings and community activities, and occasionally travel.

Work Schedules

Most public relations specialists work full time. Some work more than 40 hours per week.

How to Become a Public Relations Specialist

Public relations specialists typically need a bachelor's degree to enter the occupation. Employers may prefer to hire candidates who have studied a particular field, such as communications or business.

Education

Public relations specialists typically need a bachelor's degree in public relations or another communications field, social science, or business. Through such programs, students may produce a portfolio of work that demonstrates their ability to prospective employers.

Although it is not typically required to enter the occupation, professional certification is preferred by some employers hiring candidates for public relations specialist jobs.

Other Experience

Internships at public relations firms or in the public relations departments of other businesses may be helpful in getting a job as a public relations specialist.

Some employers prefer candidates who have experience in the field through a school newspaper, social media platforms, or blogs, or through a leadership position in school or in their community.

Important Qualities

Interpersonal skills. Public relations specialists deal with the public and the media regularly. They must be open and friendly in order to maintain a favorable image for their organization.

Public relations specialists typically need a bachelor's degree.

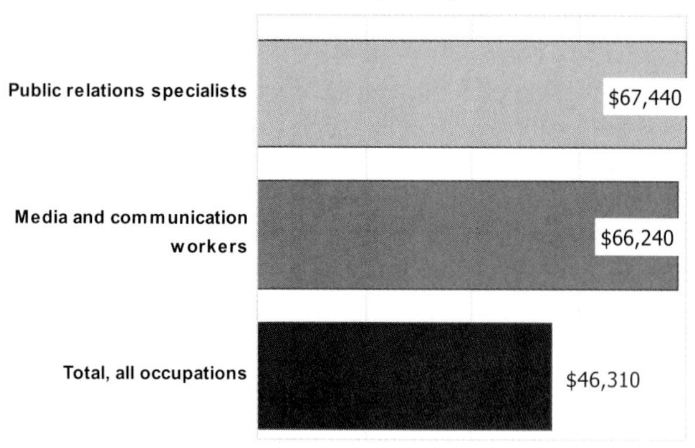

Note: All Occupations includes all occupations in the U.S. Economy.
Source: U.S. Bureau of Labor Statistics, Occupational Employment and Wage Statistics.

Organizational skills. Public relations specialists are often in charge of managing several events or communications at the same time, which requires excellent skills in coordinating arrangements.

Problem-solving skills. Public relations specialists sometimes must explain how a company or client is handling sensitive issues. They must use good judgment in what they report and how they report it.

Speaking skills. Public relations specialists regularly speak on behalf of clients or their organization. When doing so, they must be able to clearly explain the client's or the organization's position.

Writing skills. Public relations specialists must be able to write well-organized and clear press releases, speeches, and social media posts. They must be able to grasp key messages and write them in a succinct but engaging way.

Pay

The median annual wage for public relations specialists was $67,440 in May 2022. The median wage is the wage at which half the workers in an occupation earned more than that amount and half earned less. The lowest 10 percent earned less than $38,630, and the highest 10 percent earned more than $128,450.

In May 2022, the median annual wages for public relations specialists in the top industries in which they worked were as follows:

Advertising, public relations, and related services	$74,980
Government	73,860
Business, professional, labor, political, and similar organizations	73,290
Educational services; state, local, and private.	62,740
Healthcare and social assistance	60,050

Most public relations specialists work full time. Some work more than 40 hours per week.

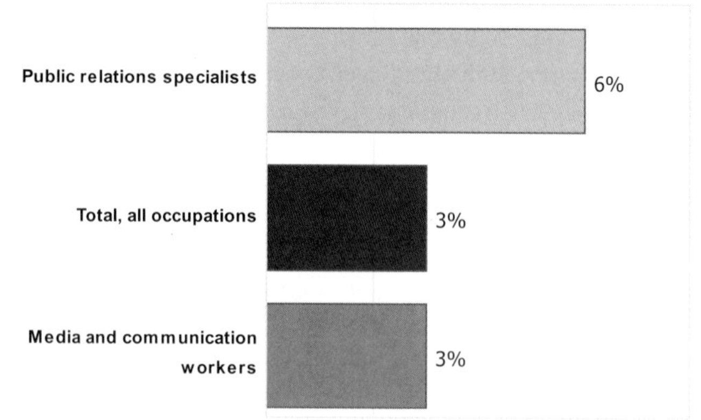

Note: All Occupations includes all occupations in the U.S. Economy.
Source: U.S. Bureau of Labor Statistics, Employment Projections program.

Job Outlook

Employment of public relations specialists is projected to grow 6 percent from 2022 to 2032, faster than the average for all occupations.

About 25,800 openings for public relations specialists are projected each year, on average, over the decade. Many of those openings are expected to result from the need to replace workers who transfer to different occupations or exit the labor force, such as to retire.

Employment

Organizations will continue to emphasize community outreach and customer relations as a way to maintain and enhance their reputation and visibility. Public opinion can change quickly, particularly because both good and bad news spread rapidly through the Internet. Consequently, public relations specialists will be needed to respond to news developments and maintain their organization's reputation.

The use of social media also is expected to create opportunities for public relations specialists as they try to appeal to consumers and the general public in new ways. Public relations specialists will be needed to help their clients use social media effectively.

Occupational Title	SOC Code	Employment, 2022	Projected Employment, 2032	Change, 2022-32	
				Percent	Numeric
Public relations specialists	27-3031	297,100	315,100	6	18,000

Contacts for More Information

For more information about public relations specialists, visit

- Public Relations Society of America
- Public Relations Student Society of America
- International Association of Business Communicators

Technical Writers

Summary

Quick Facts: Technical Writers	
2022 Median Pay	$79,960 per year $38.44 per hour
Typical Entry-Level Education	Bachelor's degree
Work Experience in a Related Occupation	Less than 5 years
On-the-job Training	Short-term on-the-job training
Number of Jobs, 2022	53,300
Job Outlook, 2022-32	7% (Faster than average)
Employment Change, 2022-32	3,700

What Technical Writers Do

Technical writers prepare instruction manuals, how-to guides, journal articles, and other supporting documents to communicate complex and technical information more easily.

Work Environment

Most technical writers work full time. Although technical writers work in a variety of industries, they are concentrated in the computer and management, scientific, and technical industries.

How to Become a Technical Writer

Technical writers typically need a bachelor's degree to enter the occupation. In addition, knowledge of or experience with a technical subject, such as science or engineering, is beneficial.

Pay

The median annual wage for technical writers was $79,960 in May 2022.

Job Outlook

Employment of technical writers is projected to grow 7 percent from 2022 to 2032, faster than the average for all occupations. About 4,800 openings for technical writers are projected each year, on average, over the decade. Many of those openings are expected to result from the need to replace workers who transfer to different occupations or exit the labor force, such as to retire.

What Technical Writers Do

Technical writers, also called *technical communicators*, prepare instruction manuals, how-to guides, journal articles, and other supporting documents to communicate complex and technical information more easily. They also develop, gather, and disseminate technical information through an organization's communications channels.

Duties

Technical writers typically do the following:

- Determine the needs of users of technical documentation
- Study product samples and talk with product designers and developers
- Work with technical staff to make products and instructions easier to use
- Write or revise supporting content for products
- Edit material prepared by other writers or staff
- Incorporate animation, graphs, illustrations, or photographs to increase users' understanding of the material
- Select appropriate medium, such as manuals or videos, for message or audience
- Standardize content across platforms and media
- Collect user feedback to update and improve content

Technical writers routinely work with other technology experts.

Technical writers often create diagrams to show users how a product works.

Technical writers create paper-based and digital operating instructions, how-to manuals, assembly instructions, and "frequently asked questions" pages to help technical support staff, consumers, and other users within a company or an industry. After a product is released, technical writers also may work with product liability specialists and customer-service managers to improve the end-user experience through product design changes.

Technical writers often work with computer hardware engineers, computer support specialists, and software developers to manage the flow of information among project workgroups during development and testing. Therefore, technical writers must be able to understand and discuss complex information with people of diverse occupational backgrounds.

Technical writers may serve on teams that conduct usability studies to improve product design. Technical writers may research topics through visits to libraries and websites, discussions with technical specialists, and observation.

Technical writers are also responsible for managing the consistency of technical content and its use across departments including product development, manufacturing, marketing, and customer relations.

Some technical writers help write grant proposals for research scientists and institutions.

Increasingly, technical information is delivered online and through social media. Technical writers use the interactive technologies of the Web and social media to blend text, graphics, multidimensional images, sound, and video.

Work Environment

Technical writers held about 53,300 jobs in 2022. The largest employers of technical writers were as follows:

Professional, scientific, and technical services	38%
Manufacturing	13
Administrative and support services	9
Publishing industries	6
Self-employed workers	6

Technical writers usually work in offices.

Most technical writers work full time. They routinely work with engineers and other technology experts to manage the flow of information throughout an organization.

Although most technical writers are employed directly by the companies that use their services, some freelance and are paid per assignment. Freelancers are either self-employed or work for a technical consulting firm and are given short-term or recurring assignments, such as writing about a new product.

Technical writing jobs are usually concentrated in locations with a multitude of information technology or scientific and technical research companies, such as ones in California and Texas.

Work Schedules

Technical writers may be expected to work evenings and weekends to meet deadlines.

How to Become a Technical Writer

Technical writers typically need a bachelor's degree to enter the occupation. In addition, knowledge of or experience with a technical subject, such as science or engineering, is beneficial.

Education

Employers generally prefer candidates who have a bachelor's degree in English, communications, journalism, or a related field. Technical writing jobs may require candidates to have knowledge of a technical field, such as engineering or computer and information technology.

Some technical writers work on a freelance basis.

Work Experience in a Related Occupation

Some technical writers begin their careers as specialists or research assistants in a technical field. They eventually develop technical communication skills and assume primary responsibilities for technical writing. In small firms, entry-level technical writers may work on projects right away; in large companies, beginning technical writers may shadow experienced writers and interact with specialists before being assigned projects.

Training

Many technical writers need short-term on-the-job training to adapt their narrative style to a descriptive style of writing.

Licenses, Certifications, and Registrations

Some associations, including the Society for Technical Communication, offer certification for technical writers. In addition, the American Medical Writers Association offers extensive continuing education programs and certificates in medical writing. These certificates are available to professionals in the medical and scientific communication fields.

Although not mandatory, these credentials demonstrate competence and professionalism, making candidates more attractive to employers. A professional credential also may increase a technical writer's opportunities for advancement.

Advancement

Prospects for advancement generally include working on projects that are more complex and leading or training junior staff.

Important Qualities

Critical-thinking skills. Technical writers must be able to simplify complex, technical information for colleagues and consumers who have nontechnical backgrounds.

Detail oriented. Technical writers create instructions for others to follow. As a result, they must be precise about every step.

Imagination. Technical writers must think about a procedure or product as if they are someone who does not have technical knowledge.

Teamwork. Technical writers must be able to work well with other writers, designers, editors, illustrators, and the technical workers whose procedure or product they are explaining.

Technical skills. Technical writers must be able to understand complex information. Technical writers may benefit from a background in fields such as engineering or science.

Writing skills. Technical communicators must have excellent writing skills to be able to explain technical information clearly.

Pay

The median annual wage for technical writers was $79,960 in May 2022. The median wage is the wage at which half the workers in an occupation earned more than that amount and half

Technical Writers

Median annual wages, May 2022

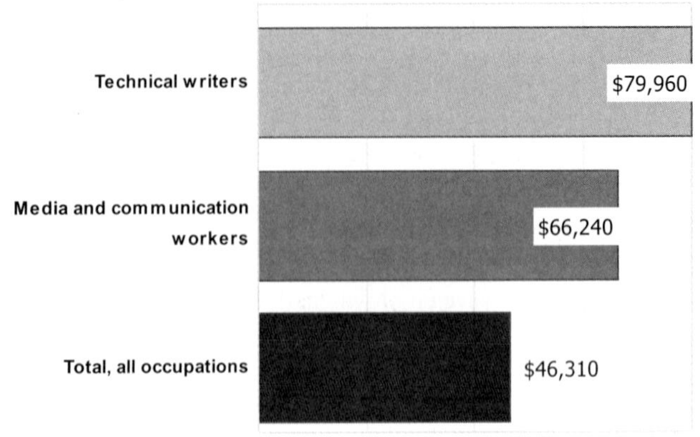

Note: All Occupations includes all occupations in the U.S. Economy.
Source: U.S. Bureau of Labor Statistics, Occupational Employment and Wage Statistics.

earned less. The lowest 10 percent earned less than $47,460, and the highest 10 percent earned more than $128,110.

In May 2022, the median annual wages for technical writers in the top industries in which they worked were as follows:

Administrative and support services	$81,650
Professional, scientific, and technical services	81,420
Manufacturing	79,340
Publishing industries	74,980

Technical writers may be expected to work evenings and weekends to meet deadlines. Most work full time.

Job Outlook

Employment of technical writers is projected to grow 7 percent from 2022 to 2032, faster than the average for all occupations.

Technical Writers

Percent change in employment, projected 2022-32

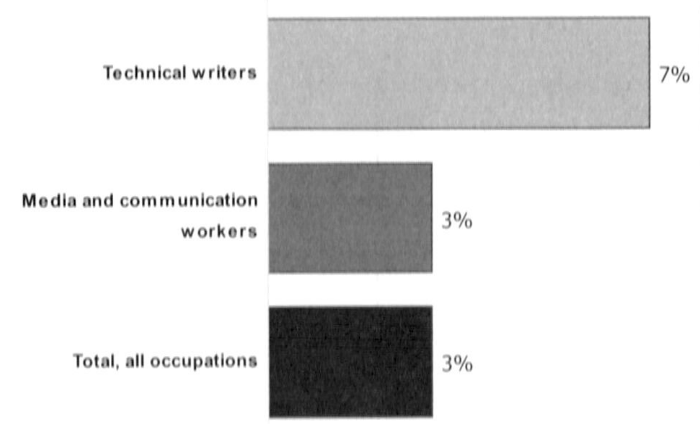

Note: All Occupations includes all occupations in the U.S. Economy.
Source: U.S. Bureau of Labor Statistics, Employment Projections program.

About 4,800 openings for technical writers are projected each year, on average, over the decade. Many of those openings are expected to result from the need to replace workers who transfer to different occupations or exit the labor force, such as to retire.

Employment

As product innovation continues, technical writers will be needed to convert complex information into a format that nontechnical users of these products understand. The continuing expansion of scientific and technical products and growth in digital product support needs will drive employment demand for these writers.

Occupational Title	SOC Code	Employment, 2022	Projected Employment, 2032	Change, 2022-32	
				Percent	Numeric
Technical writers	27-3042	53,300	57,000	7	3,700

Contacts for More Information

For more information about technical writers, visit

- American Medical Writers Association
- National Association of Science Writers
- Society for Technical Communication

Writers and Authors

Summary

Quick Facts: Writers and Authors	
2022 Median Pay	$73,150 per year $35.17 per hour
Typical Entry-Level Education	Bachelor's degree
Work Experience in a Related Occupation	None
On-the-job Training	Long-term on-the-job training
Number of Jobs, 2022	151,200
Job Outlook, 2022-32	4% (As fast as average)
Employment Change, 2022-32	5,600

What Writers and Authors Do

Writers and authors develop written content for various types of media.

Work Environment

Writers and authors may work anywhere they have access to a computer. Many writers and authors are self-employed.

Writers and authors develop written content.

How to Become a Writer or Author

A college degree in English, communications, or journalism is generally required for a full-time position as a writer or author. Experience gained through internships or any writing that improves skill, such as blogging, is beneficial.

Pay

The median annual wage for writers and authors was $73,150 in May 2022.

Job Outlook

Employment of writers and authors is projected to grow 4 percent from 2022 to 2032, about as fast as the average for all occupations.

About 15,500 openings for writers and authors are projected each year, on average, over the decade. Many of those openings are expected to result from the need to replace workers who transfer to different occupations or exit the labor force, such as to retire.

What Writers and Authors Do

Writers and authors develop content for various types of media, including advertisements; blogs; books; magazines; and movie, play, and television scripts.

Duties

Writers and authors typically do the following:

- Choose subjects that interests readers
- Write fiction or nonfiction scripts, biographies, and other formats
- Conduct research to get factual information and authentic detail
- Write advertising copy for newspapers, magazines, broadcasts, and the Internet
- Present drafts to editors and clients for feedback
- Work with editors and clients to shape material for publishing

Writers must establish their credibility with editors and readers through clean prose, strong research, and the use of sources and

Writers and authors perform research in order to give their stories authentic detail.

citations. Writers and authors select the material they want to use and then convey the information to readers. With help from editors, they may revise or rewrite sections, searching for the clearest language and phrasing.

Some writers and authors are self-employed or freelancers. They sell their written content to book and magazine publishers; news organizations; advertising agencies; and movie, theater, and television producers. They may be hired to complete specific short-term or recurring assignments, such as writing a newspaper column, contributing to a series of articles in a magazine, or producing an organization's newsletter.

A number of writers produce material that is published only online, such as for digital news organizations or blogs.

The following are examples of types of writers and authors:

Biographers write a thorough account of a person's life. They gather information from interviews and research about the person to accurately describe important life events.

Bloggers write posts to a Web log (blog) that may pertain to any topic or a specific field, such as fashion, news, or sports.

Content writers write about any topic of interest, unlike writers who usually specialize in a given field.

Copywriters prepare advertisements to promote the sale of a good or service. They often work with a client to produce written content, such as an advertising slogan.

Novelists write books of fiction, creating characters and plots that may be imaginary or based on real events.

Playwrights write scripts for theatrical productions. They come up with a concept, write lines for actors to say, produce stage direction for actors to follow, and suggest ideas for theatrical set design.

Screenwriters create scripts for movies and television. They may produce original stories, characters, and dialogue, or adapt a book into a movie or television script.

Speechwriters compose orations for business leaders, politicians, and others who must speak in front of an audience. Because speeches are often delivered live, speechwriters must think about audience reaction and rhetorical effect.

Work Environment

Writers and authors held about 151,200 jobs in 2022. The largest employers of writers and authors were as follows:

Self-employed workers	62%
Professional, scientific, and technical services	12
Information	10
Educational services; state, local, and private	2
Religious, grantmaking, civic, professional, and similar organizations	2

Writers and authors may work anywhere they have access to a computer.

Jobs are somewhat concentrated in major media and entertainment markets—California, New York, Texas, and Washington, DC—but improved communications and Internet capabilities allow writers and authors to work from almost anywhere. Some writers and authors prefer to work and travel to meet with publishers and clients and to do research or conduct interviews in person.

Work Schedules

Some writers and authors work part time. Most keep regular office hours, either to stay in contact with sources and editors

Writers and authors may work in an office or wherever they have access to a computer.

or to set up a writing routine, but many set their own hours. Others may need to work evenings and weekends to produce something acceptable for an editor or client. Self-employed or freelance writers and authors may face the pressures of juggling multiple projects or continually looking for new work.

How to Become a Writer or Author

A college degree in English, communications, or journalism is generally required for a salaried position as a writer or author. Experience gained through internships or any writing that improves skill, such as blogging, is beneficial.

Education

Writers and authors typically need a bachelor's degree in English or a related field, such as communications or journalism.

Other Work Experience

Writers and authors can get job experience by working for high school and college newspapers, magazines, radio and television stations, advertising and publishing companies, or nonprofit organizations. College theater programs offer playwrights an opportunity to have their work performed. Many magazines and newspapers also have internships for students. Interns may write stories, conduct research and interviews, and gain related experience.

Employers may prefer candidates who are able to create a visual story using tables, charts, infographics, and maps. Knowledge of computer software and editing tools that combine text with graphics, audio, video, and animation may be helpful.

In addition, anyone with Internet access can start a blog and gain writing experience. Some of this writing may lead to paid assignments regardless of education. Writers or authors can come from different backgrounds and experiences.

Training

Writers and authors typically gain writing experience through on-the-job training. They may practice and work with more experienced writers and editors before their writing is ready for publication.

Writers may need formal training or experience related to a particular topic that they want to write about.

Writers and authors may have to manage multiple assignments simultaneously.

Advancement

Writers and authors can get a start by putting their name on their work when writing for small businesses, local newspapers, advertising agencies, and nonprofit organizations. However, opportunities for advancement within these organizations may be limited.

Writers and authors may advance their careers by building a reputation, taking on complex writing assignments, and getting published in prestigious markets and publications. Having published work that has been well received and consistently meeting deadlines are important for advancement.

Many editors begin work as writers. Those who are particularly skilled at identifying stories, correcting writing style, and interacting with writers may be interested in editing jobs.

Important Qualities

Adaptability. Writers and authors need to be able to adapt to updates in software platforms and programs, including various *content management systems* (CMS).

Creativity. Writers and authors must be able to develop interesting plots, characters, or ideas for new stories.

Critical-thinking skills. Writers and authors must be adept at understanding new concepts that they convey through writing.

Determination. Writers and authors must have drive and persevere to meet deadlines.

Persuasion. Writers, especially those in advertising, must be able to convince others to feel a certain way about a good or service.

Social perceptiveness. Writers and authors must understand how readers react to ideas to connect with their audience.

Writing skills. Writers and authors must be able to write clearly and effectively to convey feeling and emotion and to communicate with readers.

Pay

The median annual wage for writers and authors was $73,150 in May 2022. The median wage is the wage at which half the workers in an occupation earned more than that amount and half earned less. The lowest 10 percent earned less than $39,610, and the highest 10 percent earned more than $161,260.

In May 2022, the median annual wages for writers and authors in the top industries in which they worked were as follows:

Information	$83,400
Professional, scientific, and technical services	72,800
Educational services; state, local, and private	67,110
Religious, grantmaking, civic, professional, and similar organizations	65,620

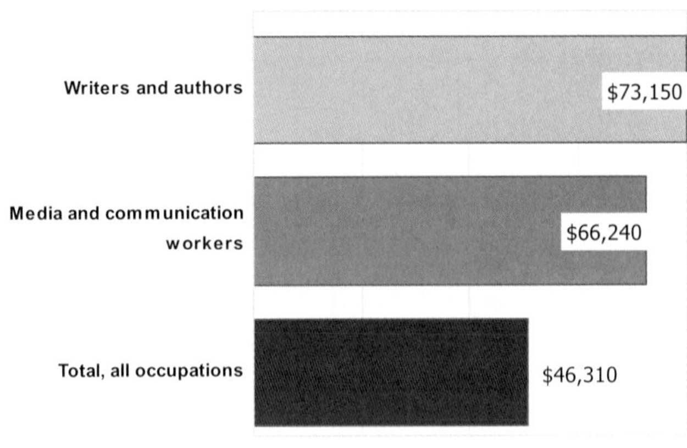

Note: All Occupations includes all occupations in the U.S. Economy.
Source: U.S. Bureau of Labor Statistics, Occupational Employment and Wage Statistics.

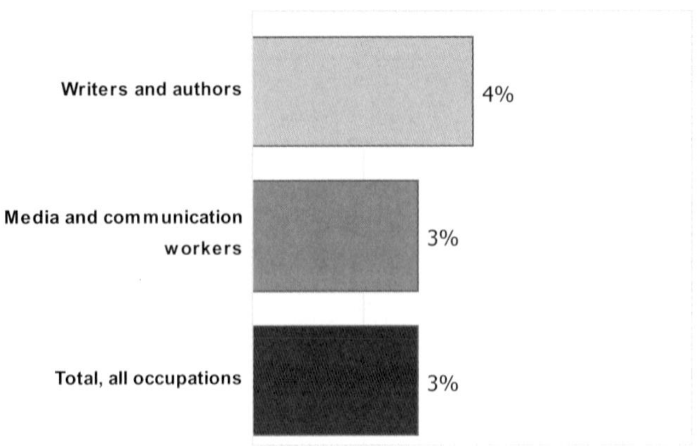

Note: All Occupations includes all occupations in the U.S. Economy.
Source: U.S. Bureau of Labor Statistics, Employment Projections program.

Some writers and authors work part time. Most keep regular office hours, either to stay in contact with sources and editors or to set up a writing routine, but many set their own hours. Others may need to work evenings and weekends to produce something acceptable for an editor or client. Self-employed or freelance writers and authors may face the pressures of juggling multiple projects or continually looking for new work.

Job Outlook

Employment of writers and authors is projected to grow 4 percent from 2022 to 2032, about as fast as the average for all occupations.

About 15,500 openings for writers and authors are projected each year, on average, over the decade. Many of those openings are expected to result from the need to replace workers who transfer to different occupations or exit the labor force, such as to retire.

Employment

As traditional print publications lose ground to other media forms, writers and authors are shifting their focus to online media, which should result in some employment growth for these workers. In addition, the continued rise in self-publishing may lead to increased employment of writers and authors.

Employment projections data for writers and authors, 2022-32

Occupational Title	SOC Code	Employment, 2022	Projected Employment, 2032	Change, 2022-32		Employment by Industry
				Percent	Numeric	
Writers and authors	27-3043	151,200	156,800	4	5,600	Get data

SOURCE: U.S. Bureau of Labor Statistics, Employment Projections program

Contacts for More Information

For more information about writers and authors, visit

- American Society of Journalists and Authors
- Association of Writers & Writing Programs
- National Association of Science Writers
- Society of Professional Journalists
- Writers Guild of America East

Military

Military Careers

What They Do

Members of the U.S. military service maintain the U.S. national defense. Although some service members work in occupations specific to the military, such as fighter pilots or infantrymen, many work in occupations that also exist in the civilian workplace, such as nurses, doctors, and lawyers. Members serve in the Army, Navy, Air Force, Space Force, Marine Corps, or Coast Guard, or in the Reserve components of these branches, and in the Air National Guard and Army National Guard. (The Coast Guard, which is included in this profile, is part of the Department of Homeland Security.)

Duties

The military distinguishes between enlisted and officer careers. Enlisted personnel make up about 82 percent of the Armed Forces and carry out military operations. The remaining 18 percent are officers—military leaders who manage operations and enlisted personnel. About 8 percent of officers are warrant officers, who are technical and tactical experts in a specific area. Army aviators, for example, make up one group of warrant officers.

Enlisted personnel typically do the following:

- Participate in, or support, military operations, such as combat or training operations, or humanitarian or disaster relief
- Operate, maintain, and repair equipment
- Perform technical and support activities
- Supervise junior enlisted personnel

Some members of the military are deployed to other countries or regions to defend U.S. national interests.

Officers typically do the following:

- Plan, organize, and lead troops and activities in military operations
- Manage enlisted personnel
- Operate and command aircraft, ships, or armored vehicles
- Provide medical, legal, engineering, and other services to military personnel

Types of Enlisted Personnel

The following are examples of types of occupations for enlisted personnel:

Administrative personnel maintain information on personnel, equipment, funds, and other military-related activities. They work in support areas, such as finance, accounting, legal affairs, maintenance, supply, and transportation.

Combat specialty personnel train and work in combat units, such as the infantry, artillery, or Special Forces. For example, infantry specialists conduct ground combat operations, armored vehicle specialists operate battle tanks, and seamanship specialists maintain ships. Combat specialty personnel may maneuver against enemy forces and fire artillery, guns, mortars, or missiles to neutralize them. They may also operate various types of combat vehicles, such as amphibious assault vehicles, tanks, or small boats. Members of elite Special Forces teams are trained to perform specialized missions anywhere in the world on a moment's notice.

Construction personnel build or repair buildings, airfields, bridges, and other structures. They also may operate heavy equipment, such as bulldozers or cranes. They work with engineers and other building specialists as part of military construction teams. Some construction personnel specialize in an area such as plumbing, electrical wiring, or water purification.

Electronic and electrical equipment repair personnel maintain and repair electronic equipment used by the military. Repairers specialize in an area such as aircraft electrical systems, computers, optical equipment, communications, or weapons systems. For example, weapons electronic maintenance technicians maintain and repair electronic components and systems that help locate targets and help aim and fire weapons.

Engineering, science, and technical personnel perform a variety of tasks, such as operating technical equipment, solving problems, and collecting and interpreting information. They perform technical tasks in information technology, environmental health and safety, or intelligence:

- Environmental health and safety specialists inspect military facilities and food supplies to ensure that they are safe for use and consumption.

- Information technology specialists manage and maintain computer and network systems.
- Intelligence specialists gather information and prepare reports for military planning and operations.

Healthcare personnel provide medical services to military personnel and their family members. They may work as part of a patient-service team with doctors, nurses, or other healthcare professionals. Some specialize in providing emergency medical treatment in combat or remote areas. Others specialize in laboratory testing of tissue and blood samples; maintaining pharmacy supplies or patients' records; assisting with dental procedures; operating diagnostic tools, such as x-ray and ultrasound machines; or other healthcare tasks.

Human resources development personnel recruit qualified people into the military, place them in suitable occupations, and provide training programs:

- Personnel specialists maintain information about military personnel and their training, job assignments, promotions, and health.
- Recruiting specialists provide information about military careers; explain pay, benefits, and military life; and recruit individuals into the military.
- Training specialists and instructors teach military personnel how to perform their jobs.

Machine operator and repair personnel operate industrial equipment and machinery to make and repair parts for a variety of equipment and structures. They may operate engines, nuclear reactors, or water pumps, usually performing a specific job. Welders and metalworkers, for example, work with various types of metals to repair or form the structural parts of ships, buildings, or equipment. Survival equipment specialists inspect, maintain, and repair survival equipment, such as parachutes and aircraft life-support equipment.

Media and public affairs personnel prepare and present information about military activities to the military and the public. They take photographs, make video programs, present news and music programs, or conduct interviews.

Protective service personnel enforce military laws and regulations and provide emergency responses to disasters:

- Firefighters prevent and extinguish fires in buildings, on aircraft, and aboard ships.
- Military police responsibilities include controlling traffic, preventing crime, and responding to emergencies.
- Other law enforcement and security specialists investigate crimes committed on military property and guard inmates in military correctional facilities.

Support service personnel provide services that support the morale and well-being of military personnel and their families:

- Food service specialists prepare food in dining halls, hospitals, and ships.
- Religious program specialists assist chaplains with religious services, religious education programs, and related administrative duties.

Transportation and material-handling personnel transport military personnel and cargo. Most personnel within this occupational group are classified according to the mode of transportation, such as aircraft, motor vehicle, or ship:

- Aircrew members operate equipment on aircraft.
- Cargo specialists load and unload military supplies, using forklifts and cranes.
- Quartermasters and boat operators navigate and pilot many types of small watercraft, including tugboats, gunboats, and barges.
- Vehicle drivers operate various military vehicles, including fuel or water tank trucks.

Vehicle and machinery mechanical personnel conduct preventive and corrective maintenance on aircraft, automotive and heavy equipment, and powerhouse station equipment. These workers specialize by the type of equipment that they maintain:

- Aircraft mechanics inspect and service various types of aircraft.
- Automotive and heavy-equipment mechanics maintain and repair vehicles, such as Humvees, trucks, tanks, and other combat vehicles. They also repair bulldozers and other construction equipment.
- Heating and cooling mechanics install and repair air-conditioning, refrigeration, and heating equipment.
- Marine engine mechanics repair and maintain engines on ships, boats, and other watercraft.
- Powerhouse mechanics install, maintain, and repair electrical and mechanical equipment in power-generating stations.

Types of Officers

The following are examples of types of officers:

Combat specialty officers plan and direct military operations, oversee combat activities, and serve as combat leaders. They may be in charge of tanks and other armored assault vehicles, artillery systems, special operations, or infantry units. This group also includes naval surface warfare and submarine warfare officers, combat pilots, and aircrews.

Engineering, science, and technical officers' responsibilities depend on their area of expertise. They work in scientific and professional occupations, such as atmospheric scientists, meteorologists, physical scientists, biological scientists, social scientists, attorneys, and other types of scientists or professionals. For example, meteorologists in the military may study the weather to assist in planning flight paths for aircraft.

Executive, administrative, and managerial officers manage administrative functions in the Armed Forces, such as human resources management, training, personnel, information,

Table 1. Active-duty enlisted personnel by broad occupational group and branch of military, and Coast Guard, February 2023

Enlisted	Army[1]	Air Force	Space Force	Coast Guard	Marine Corps	Navy	Total enlisted personnel in each occupational group
Occupational group							
Administrative	4,990	13,252	1	—	11,247	20,250	—
Combat Specialty	106,335	764	—	—	36,545	9,077	—
Construction	14,209	4,959	—	—	5,861	3,772	—
Electronic and Electrical Equipment Repair	20,992	28,201	1	—	14,120	49,520	—
Engineering, Science, and Technical	48,557	55,058	18	—	27,276	46,167	—
Healthcare	25,319	14,682	—	—	—	23,515	—
Human Resource Development	14,853	8,538	3	—	2,333	4,532	—
Machine Operator and Production	4,080	6,502	—	—	2,334	9,267	—
Media and Public Affairs	5,119	6,571	1	—	1,416	3,677	—
Protective Service	19,107	34,098	—	—	4,795	13,160	—
Support Service	8,272	5,510	—	—	1,921	8,805	—
Transportation and Material Handling	45,785	28,552	—	—	23,219	36,110	—
Vehicle and Machinery Mechanic	43,536	46,770	—	—	17,315	47,720	—
Non-occupation or unspecified coded personnel	4,378	4,706	4,018	—	1,684	1,600	—
Total enlisted personnel for each military branch and Coast Guard	365,532	258,163	4,042	30,087	150,066	277,172	1,085,062[2]

[1]Data for Army are estimates.
[2]Data for total enlisted personnel are estimates.
SOURCE: U.S. Department of Defense, Defense Manpower Data Center

police, or other support services. Officers who oversee military bands are included in this category.

Healthcare officers provide medical services to military personnel in order to maintain or improve their health and physical readiness. Officers such as physicians, physician assistants, nurses, and dentists examine, diagnose, and treat patients. Other healthcare officers provide therapy, rehabilitative treatment, and additional healthcare for patients:

- Dentists treat diseases, disorders, and injuries of the mouth.
- Nurses provide and coordinate patient care in military hospitals and clinics.
- Optometrists treat vision problems and prescribe glasses, contact lenses, or medications.
- Pharmacists purchase, store, and dispense drugs and medicines.
- Physical therapists and occupational therapists plan and administer therapy to help patients adjust to injuries, regain independence, and return to work.
- Physicians, surgeons, and physician assistants examine patients, diagnose injuries and illnesses, and provide treatment to military and their families.
- Psychologists provide mental healthcare and also may conduct research on behavior and emotions.

Human resource development officers manage recruitment, placement, and training programs in the military:

- Personnel managers direct and oversee military personnel functions, such as job assignments, staff promotions, and career counseling.
- Recruiting managers direct and oversee recruiting personnel and recruiting activities.
- Training and education directors identify training needs and develop and manage educational programs.

Media and public affairs officers oversee the development, production, and presentation of information or events for the military and the public. They manage the production of videos and television and radio broadcasts that are used for training, news, and entertainment. Some plan, develop, and direct the activities of military bands. Public affairs officers respond to public inquiries about military activities and prepare news releases.

Protective service officers are responsible for the safety and protection of individuals and property on military bases and vessels. Emergency management officers plan and prepare for all types of disasters. They develop warning, evacuation, and response procedures in preparation for disasters. Law enforcement and security officers enforce all applicable laws on military bases and oversee investigations of crimes.

Support services officers manage military activities in key functional areas, such as logistics, transportation, and supply. They may oversee the transportation and distribution of materials by ground vehicles, aircraft, or ships. They also direct food service facilities and other support activities. Purchasing and contracting managers negotiate and monitor contracts for equipment, supplies, and services that the military buys from the private sector.

Transportation officers manage and perform activities related to the safe transport of military personnel and equipment by air, ground, and water. They operate and command an aircraft or a ship:

- Navigators use radar, radio, and other navigation equipment to determine their position and plan their route of travel.

Table 2. Active-duty officer personnel by broad occupational group and branch of military, and Coast Guard, February 2023

Officer	Army[1]	Air Force	Space Force	Coast Guard	Marine Corps	Navy	Total officer personnel in each occupational group
Occupational group							
Combat Specialty	22,021	3,821	57	—	4,254	6,340	—
Engineering, Science, and Technical	24,978	13,285	3,238	—	4,816	11,360	—
Executive, Administrative, and Managerial	13,499	6,825	904	—	2,662	6,770	—
Healthcare	10,934	9,073	—	—	none	6,452	—
Human Resource Development	3,096	1,666	16	—	729	3,397	—
Media and Public Affairs	361	349	1	—	332	270	—
Protective Service	3,248	1,070	1	—	340	1,231	—
Support Service	1,713	838	—	—	31	1,041	—
Transportation	10,620	19,003	5	—	5,067	10,088	—
Non-occupation or unspecified coded personnel	3,124	4,240	23	—	3,225	8,830	—
Total officer personnel for each military branch and Coast Guard	93,594	60,170	4,245	8,659	21,456	55,779	243,903[2]

1 Data for Army are estimates.
2 Data for total enlisted personnel are estimates.
SOURCE: U.S. Department of Defense, Defense Manpower Data Center

- Pilots in the military fly various types of military airplanes and helicopters to carry troops and equipment.
- Ships' engineers direct engineering departments, including engine operations, maintenance, and power generation, aboard ships.

Work Environment

In February 2023, more than 2 million people served in the Armed Forces. More than 1.3 million were on active duty, including the following subtotals:

Army	458,718
Navy	332,773
Air Force	318,090
Marines	170,863

In addition, about 762,270 people served in the Reserves in these branches and in the Air National Guard and Army National Guard. About 38,746 people served in the Coast Guard, which is part of the Department of Homeland Security.

Military members must be physically fit and ready to participate in, or support, combat missions.

The specific work environments and conditions pertaining to military occupations depend on the occupational specialty, unit, branch of service, and other factors. Most active-duty military personnel live and work on or near military bases and facilities throughout the United States and the world. These bases and facilities usually offer housing and amenities, such as stores and recreation centers.

Service members move regularly for training or job assignments, with most rotations lasting 2 to 4 years. Some are deployed internationally to defend U.S. national interests.

Military members must be both physically and mentally fit, and ready to participate in, or support, combat missions that may be difficult and dangerous and involve long periods away from family. Some personnel, however, are rarely deployed near combat areas.

Table 3 shows employment (excluding Coast Guard) for active-duty officers, warrant officers, and enlisted ranks, by grade and branch of service.

Injuries

Members of the military are often placed in dangerous situations with the risk of serious injury or death. Members deployed to combat zones or those who work in dangerous areas, such as the flight deck of an aircraft carrier, face a higher risk of injury or death.

Work Schedules

Military personnel on active duty typically work full time. However, hours vary with the person's occupational specialty, rank, and branch of service, as well as with the needs of the military. Personnel must be prepared to work additional hours to fulfill missions.

Table 3. Military rank and employment for active-duty personnel, March 2022

Grade	Army	Navy	Air Force/ Space Force	Marine Corps	Coast Guard	Active duty personnel (excluding Coast Guard)
Commissioned Officers:						
O-10	General	Admiral	General	General	Admiral	39
O-9	Lieutenant General	Vice Admiral	Lieutenant General	Lieutenant General	Vice Admiral	148
O-8	Major General	Rear Admiral (Upper Half)	Major General	Major General	Rear Admiral (Upper Half)	286
O-7	Brigadier General	Rear Admiral (Lower Half)	Brigadier General	Brigadier General	Rear Admiral (Lower Half)	394
O-6	Colonel	Captain	Colonel	Colonel	Captain	11,204
O-5	Lieutenant Colonel	Commander	Lieutenant Colonel	Lieutenant Colonel	Commander	27,586
O-4	Major	Lieutenant Commander	Major	Major	Lieutenant Commander	45,667
O-3	Captain	Lieutenant	Captain	Captain	Lieutenant	71,308
O-2	1st Lieutenant	Lieutenant Junior Grade	1st Lieutenant	1st Lieutenant	Lieutenant Junior Grade	34,776
O-1	2nd Lieutenant	Ensign	2nd Lieutenant	2nd Lieutenant	Ensign	24,381
Warrant Officers:						
W-5	Chief Warrant Officer 5	Chief Warrant Officer 5	—	Chief Warrant Officer 5		759
W-4	Chief Warrant Officer 4	Chief Warrant Officer 4	—	Chief Warrant Officer 4	Chief Warrant Officer 4	2,701
W-3	Chief Warrant Officer 3	Chief Warrant Officer 3	—	Chief Warrant Officer 3	Chief Warrant Officer 3	4,758
W-2	Chief Warrant Officer 2	Chief Warrant Officer 2	—	Chief Warrant Officer 2	Chief Warrant Officer 2	7,548
W-1	Warrant Officer 1		—	Warrant Officer 1		3,369
Enlisted Personnel:						
E-9	Sergeant Major	Master Chief Petty Officer	Chief Master Sergeant	Sergeant Major/Master Gunnery Sergeant	Master Chief Petty Officer	10,464
E-8	First Sergeant/Master Sergeant	Senior Chief Petty Officer	Senior Master Sergeant	First Sergeant/Master Sergeant	Senior Chief Petty Officer	27,405
E-7	Sergeant First Class	Chief Petty Officer	Master Sergeant	Gunnery Sergeant	Chief Petty Officer	93,769
E-6	Staff Sergeant	Petty Officer First Class	Technical Sergeant	Staff Sergeant	Petty Officer First Class	170,541
E-5	Sergeant	Petty Officer Second Class	Staff Sergeant	Sergeant	Petty Officer Second Class	223,483
E-4	Corporal/Specialist	Petty Officer Third Class	Senior Airman	Corporal	Petty Officer Third Class	266,159
E-3	Private First Class	Seaman	Airman First Class	Lance Corporal	Seaman	189,892
E-2	Private	Seaman Apprentice	Airman	Private First Class	Seaman Apprentice	61,284
E-1	Private	Seaman Recruit	Airman Basic	Private	Seaman Recruit	34,155

SOURCE: U.S. Department of Defense, Defense Manpower Data Center

After basic training, military members attend additional training at technical schools that prepare them for a particular military occupational specialty.

How to Become a Member of the Armed Forces

To join the military, applicants must meet age, education, aptitude, physical, and character requirements. These requirements vary by branch of service and for officers and enlisted members.

Although entry requirements for each service vary, certain qualifications for enlistment are common to all branches:

- Minimum of 17 years of age
- U.S. citizenship or permanent resident status
- Have a high school diploma or equivalent
- Never convicted of a felony
- Able to pass a medical exam

Applicants who are 17 years old must have the consent of a parent or legal guardian before entering the military.

Age limits for entering active-duty service as an enlisted member are as follows:

- In the Army, the maximum age is 35.
- In the Navy, the maximum age is 41.
- In the Marine Corps, the maximum age is 28.
- In the Air Force, the maximum age is 39.
- In the Space Force, the maximum age is 39.
- In the Coast Guard, the maximum age is 42.

Age limits for commissioned officers differ by branch but may be lower than those for enlisted members. A recruiter can help prospective service members determine whether they qualify as an officer or for enlistment. A recruiter can also explain the various enlistment options and describe the military occupational specialties.

All applicants must meet certain physical requirements for height, weight, vision, and overall health. Officers must be U.S. citizens. Officers and some enlisted members must be able to obtain a security clearance. Candidates interested in becoming officers through training in the federal service academies must be unmarried and without dependents.

Service members are assigned an occupational specialty based on their aptitude, previous training, and the needs of their branch of service. All members must sign a contract and commit to a minimum term of service.

Women are eligible to enter all military specialties.

Become an enlisted member

Prospective recruits who wish to enlist must take a placement exam called the Armed Forces Vocational Aptitude Battery (ASVAB), which is used to determine an applicant's suitability for military occupational specialties.

A recruiter can schedule applicants to take the ASVAB without any obligation to join the military. Many high schools offer the exam as a way for students to explore the possibility of a military career. The selection for a certain job specialty is based on ASVAB test results, the physical requirements for the job, and the needs of the service.

Applicants who decide to join the military must pass the physical examination before signing an enlistment contract. The contract involves a number of enlistment options, such as the length of active-duty or reserve-duty time, the length and kind of job training, and the amount of bonuses that may be earned, if any. Most active-duty programs have first-term enlistments of 4 years, although there are some 2-, 3-, and 6-year programs.

All branches of the Armed Services offer a delayed-entry program allowing candidates to postpone entry to active duty for up to one year after enlisting. High school students can enlist during their senior year and enter service after graduation. Others may delay entry because their desired job training is not immediately available or because they need time to arrange their personal affairs.

Become an officer

To become an officer, candidates typically need to have at least a bachelor's degree, be a U.S. citizen, pass a background check, and meet physical and age requirements. Candidates for officer positions do not need to take the ASVAB. Some achieve officer candidacy by completing a degree and training through the federal service academies (Army, Navy, Air Force, Coast Guard, and Merchant Marine) or through the Reserve Officers' Training Corps (ROTC) programs offered at many colleges and universities.

Education

All branches of the Armed Forces require their members to be high school graduates or have equivalent credentials. Officers usually need a bachelor's degree in any field. Some officers entering the service may need to have education beyond a bachelor's degree. For example, officers entering as military lawyers need a law degree.

Those who want to become an officer have several options to meet the education requirements, including the aforementioned federal service academies (Army, Navy, Air Force, Coast Guard, and Merchant Marine), the Reserve Officers' Training Corps (ROTC) programs, Officer Candidate School (OCS), and other programs.

Important Qualities

Leadership skills. Members of the Armed Forces work together to achieve their missions. Those who want to advance ranks need to be able lead others in the completion of assigned duties or missions.

Mental preparedness. Members of the Armed Forces must be mentally fit and able to handle stressful situations that can occur during military operations.

Physical fitness. Members of the Armed Forces must be physically fit to participate in, or support, combat missions that may be difficult or dangerous.

Readiness. Members of the Armed Forces must be ready and able to report for military assignments on short notice.

Training

Training for enlisted personnel. Newly enlisted members of the Armed Forces undergo initial-entry training, better known as *basic training* or *boot camp*. Basic training includes courses in military skills and protocols and lasts 7 to 13 weeks, including a week of orientation and introduction to military life. Basic training also includes weapons training, team building, and rigorous physical exercise designed to improve strength and endurance.

Following basic training, enlisted members attend technical schools for additional training that prepares them for a particular military occupational specialty. This formal training period generally lasts from 10 to 20 weeks. Training for certain occupations—nuclear power plant operator, for example—may take as long as a year. In addition to getting technical instruction, military members receive on-the-job training at their first duty assignment.

Training for warrant officers. All services except the U.S. Air Force have warrant officer programs. Selection to attend Warrant Officer Candidate School is highly competitive and is restricted to those who meet rank and length-of-service requirements. The only exception is the selection process for Army aviator warrant officers, a process that has no requirement of previous military service. Training may last several weeks.

Training for officers. Officer training in the Armed Forces is provided through the federal service academies (Army, Navy, Air Force, Coast Guard, and Merchant Marine), the Reserve Officers' Training Corps (ROTC) program, Officer Candidate School (OCS) or Officer Training School (OTS), the National Guard (State Officer Candidate School programs), and the Uniformed Services University of the Health Sciences.

- *Training for officers in the federal service academies.* The federal service academies provide a Bachelor of Science (B.S.) degree. Midshipmen and cadets receive free room and board, free tuition, free medical and dental care, and a monthly allowance. Graduates receive regular or reserve commissions and typically have a 5-year active-duty obligation, which may be longer for some specialties, such as medicine or aviation. Service academy cadet or midshipman candidates must be nominated by an authorized source, usually a member of Congress. In addition, nominees must submit their academic record, college aptitude test scores, and recommendations from teachers or other school officials. They must also pass a medical examination and have no dependents. Academies make appointments from the list of eligible nominees. Appointments to the Coast Guard Academy, however, are based on merit and do not require a nomination.
- *Training for officers in ROTC programs.* Participants in ROTC programs take regular college courses along with 3 to 5 hours of military instruction per week. After graduation, they may serve as officers on active duty or in the Reserves or National Guard. In the last 2 years of an ROTC program, students receive a monthly allowance while attending school, as well as additional pay for summer training. ROTC scholarships for 2, 3, and 4 years of school are available on a competitive basis.
- *Training for officers through OCS or OTS.* College graduates can earn a commission in the Armed Forces through OCS or OTS training programs in the Army, Navy, Air Force, Marine Corps, Coast Guard, Air National Guard, and Army National Guard. These programs consist of several weeks of academic, physical, and leadership training. Those who complete the programs as officers must usually complete their service obligation on active duty.
- *Training for officers through the Uniformed Services University of the Health Sciences.* Personnel with training in certain health occupations may qualify for direct appointment as officers. For those studying health professions, financial assistance and internship opportunities are available from the military in return for specified periods of military service. Prospective medical students can apply to the Uniformed Services University of the Health Sciences, which offers a salary and free tuition in a program leading to a Doctor of Medicine (M.D.) degree. In return, graduates must serve for at least 7 years in either the military or the U.S. Public Health Service.
- *Training for officers through direct appointments.* Direct appointments are also available for those qualified to serve in other specialty areas, such as the Judge Advocate General's Corps for those in the legal field or the Chaplain Corps for those in religious ministry. All prospective officers who enter the service through a direct appointment attend several weeks of military-related training that typically includes courses in military orientation, academic subjects, and officer leadership and tactics.

Licenses, Certifications, and Registrations

Depending on the occupational specialty, members of the military may need to have and maintain civilian licenses or certifications. For example, officers serving as lawyers, also known as *judge advocates*, may need to have and maintain their state bar licenses to enter and remain in the U.S. military.

Advancement

Each branch of the military has different criteria for determining the promotion of personnel. Criteria for promotion may include time in service and in grade, job performance, a fitness report, and passing scores on written exams. Enlisted personnel can be promoted to higher ranks, which may include serving in a supervisory position and being in charge of junior enlisted members.

Each military service may have other advancement opportunities for its enlisted personnel. For example, enlisted personnel may become warrant officers if they complete a bachelor's degree, have several years of experience in higher enlisted positions, and meet age and physical requirements. The Army offers a direct enlistment option to become a warrant officer aviator.

Officers can also be promoted to higher ranks, which may include the command of a military unit of both enlisted members and officers, or being in charge of an entire military base.

Pay

Basic pay is based on rank and time in service. Pay bands are the same for all branches. Members of the Armed Forces may receive additional pay based on their job assignment or qualifications. For example, they receive additional pay for foreign, hazardous, submarine, or flight duty, or for being medical or dental officers. Retirement pay is generally available after 20 years of service.

Military pay tables and information are available from the U.S. Department of Defense, Defense Finance and Accounting Service.

In addition to receiving basic pay, members of the military are either housed free of charge on base or they receive a housing allowance.

Members who serve for a certain number of years may receive other benefits. These benefits may include educational benefits through the Montgomery GI Bill, which pays for a portion of educational costs at accredited institutions; medical care at military or the U.S. Department of Veterans Affairs hospitals; and guaranteed home loans.

Military personnel on active duty typically work full time. However, hours vary with the person's occupational specialty, rank, and branch of service, as well as with the needs of the military. Personnel must be prepared to work additional hours to fulfill missions.

Job Outlook

Employment

BLS employment projections cover the civilian workforce only.

The goal of the Armed Forces is to maintain a force sufficient to deter, fight, and overcome various threats or conflicts in multiple regions at the same time. Emerging conflicts and global events, however, could lead to changes in the size of the military branches. Consequently, the nation is expected to maintain adequate personnel in the Reserve, Army National Guard, and Air National Guard.

Similar Occupations

The military employs people in numerous occupational specialties, many of which are similar to civilian occupations. To match military occupations with similar civilian occupations, O*Net OnLine offers the Military Crosswalk Search tool.

Contacts for More Information

Each of the military services publishes handbooks, fact sheets, and pamphlets describing its entrance requirements, its training opportunities, and other aspects of military careers.

For more information on the individual services, visit

- U.S. Air Force
- Air National Guard
- U.S. Army
- Army National Guard
- U.S. Coast Guard
- U.S. Marine Corps
- U.S. Navy
- U.S. Space Force

In addition, the Defense Manpower Data Center, an agency of the Department of Defense, maintains a website that provides information and resources for parents, educators, and young adults who are curious about joining military service.

For more information, visit

- Today's Military
- ASVAB
- Working in the Military

Office and Administrative Support

Bill and Account Collectors

Summary

Quick Facts: Bill and Account Collectors	
2022 Median Pay	$39,470 per year $18.98 per hour
Typical Entry-Level Education	High school diploma or equivalent
Work Experience in a Related Occupation	None
On-the-job Training	Moderate-term on-the-job training
Number of Jobs, 2022	209,700
Job Outlook, 2022-32	-10% (Decline)
Employment Change, 2022-32	-20,100

What Bill and Account Collectors Do

Bill and account collectors try to recover payment on overdue bills.

Work Environment

Many bill and account collectors work in a call center for a third-party collection agency rather than the original creditor. Most work full time, and some have flexible schedules.

How to Become a Bill and Account Collector

Collectors usually must have a high school diploma. A few months of on-the-job training is common.

Pay

The median annual wage for bill and account collectors was $39,470 in May 2022.

Job Outlook

Employment of bill and account collectors is projected to decline 10 percent from 2022 to 2032.

Despite declining employment, about 19,200 openings for bill and account collectors are projected each year, on average, over the decade. All of those openings are expected to result from the need to replace workers who transfer to other occupations or exit the labor force, such as to retire.

What Bill and Account Collectors Do

Bill and account collectors try to recover payment on overdue bills. They negotiate repayment plans with debtors and help them find solutions to make paying their overdue bills easier.

Duties

Bill and account collectors typically do the following:

- Find consumers and businesses who have overdue bills
- Track down consumers who have an out-of-date address by using the Internet, post office, credit bureaus, or neighbors—a process called "skip tracing"
- Inform debtors that they have an overdue bill and try to negotiate a payment
- Explain the terms of sale or contract with the debtor, when necessary
- Learn the reasons for the overdue bills, which can help with the negotiations
- Offer credit advice or refer a consumer to a debt counselor, when appropriate

Bill and account collectors generally contact debtors by phone, although sometimes they do so by mail. They use computer systems to update contact information and record past collection

Bill and account collectors try to recover payment on overdue bills.

Collectors look up a person's information on a computer while speaking to them over the phone.

attempts with a particular debtor. Keeping these records can help collectors with future negotiations.

The main job of bill and account collectors is finding a solution that is acceptable to the debtor and maximizes payment to the creditor. Listening to the debtor and paying attention to his or her concerns can help the collector negotiate a solution.

After the collector and debtor agree on a repayment plan, the collector regularly checks to ensure that the debtor pays on time. If the debtor does not pay, the collector submits a statement to the creditor, who can take legal action. In extreme cases, this legal action may include taking back goods or disconnecting service.

Collectors must follow federal and state laws that govern debt collection. These laws require that collectors make sure they are talking with the debtor before announcing that the purpose of the call is to collect a debt. A collector also must give a statement, called "mini-Miranda," which informs the account holder that they are speaking with a bill or debt collector.

Collectors usually have goals they are expected to meet. Typically, these include calls per hour and success rates.

Work Environment

Bill and account collectors held about 209,700 jobs in 2022. The largest employers of bill and account collectors were as follows:

Business support services	26%
Credit intermediation and related activities	19
Healthcare and social assistance	9
Professional, scientific, and technical services	8
Management of companies and enterprises	7

Many collectors work in a call center for a third-party collection agency rather than the original creditor. In all industries, they spend most of their time on the phone tracking down or negotiating with debtors. They also use computers and databases to update information and record the results of their calls.

Collectors' work can be stressful because some people become angry and confrontational when pressed about their debts. Collectors often face resistance while trying to do their job duties. Successful collectors must face regular rejection and still be ready to make the next call in a polite and positive voice. Fortunately, some consumers appreciate help in resolving their outstanding debts and can be quite grateful.

Work Schedules

Most bill and account collectors work full time. Some collectors work flexible schedules, often calling people on weekends or during the evenings as they learn the best times to call.

How to Become a Bill and Account Collector

Collectors usually must have a high school diploma. A few months of on-the-job training is common.

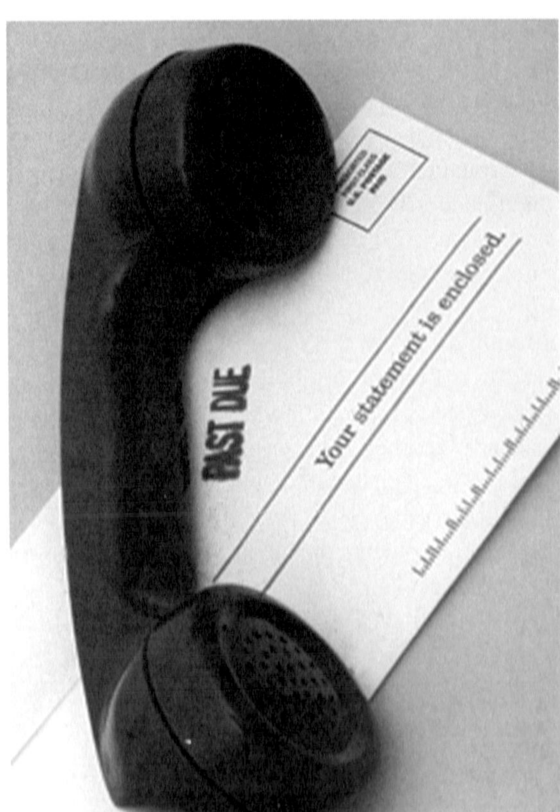

Most bill and account collectors work in call centers for third-party collection agencies.

Collectors are trained on the job.

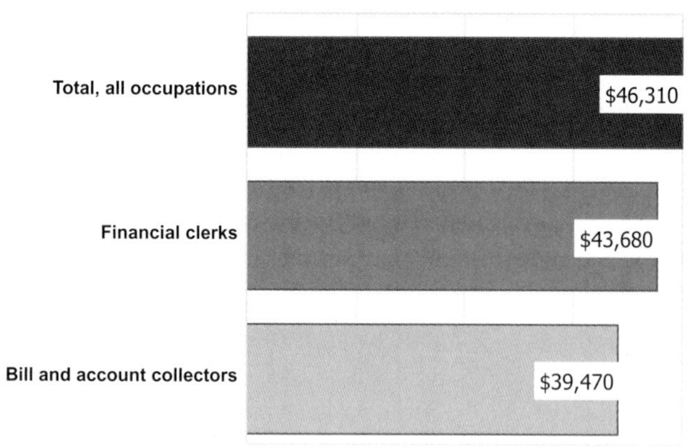

Note: All Occupations includes all occupations in the U.S. Economy.
Source: U.S. Bureau of Labor Statistics, Occupational Employment and Wage Statistics.

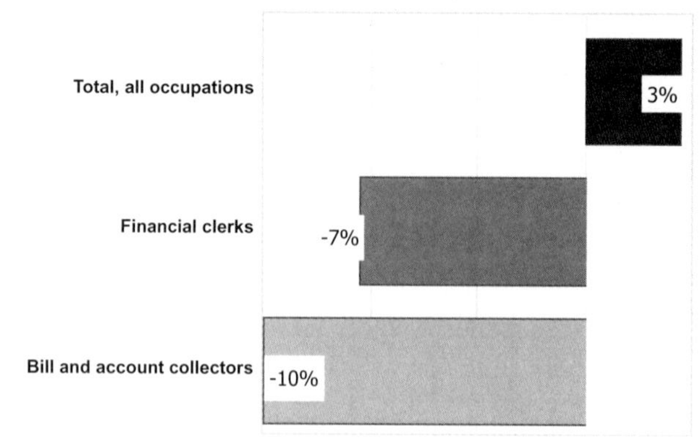

Note: All Occupations includes all occupations in the U.S. Economy.
Source: U.S. Bureau of Labor Statistics, Employment Projections program.

Education

Most bill and account collectors are required to have a high school diploma, although some employers prefer applicants who have taken some college courses. Communications, accounting, and basic computer courses are examples of classes that are helpful for entering this occupation.

Training

Collectors usually receive on-the-job training after being hired. Training includes learning how to use computer software, and instruction on federal debt-collection laws (in the Fair Debt Collection Practices Act) and state debt-collection regulations. Collectors also may be trained in negotiation techniques.

Important Qualities

Listening skills. Collectors must pay attention to what debtors say when trying to negotiate a repayment plan. Learning the particular situation of the debtors and how they fell into debt can help collectors suggest solutions.

Negotiating skills. The main aspects of a collector's job are reconciling the differences between two parties (the debtor and the creditor) and offering a solution that is acceptable to both parties.

Speaking skills. Collectors must be able to speak to debtors to explain their options and ensure that they fully understand what is being said.

Pay

The median annual wage for bill and account collectors was \$39,470 in May 2022. The median wage is the wage at which half the workers in an occupation earned more than that amount and half earned less. The lowest 10 percent earned less than \$29,510, and the highest 10 percent earned more than \$59,610.

In May 2022, the median annual wages for bill and account collectors in the top industries in which they worked were as follows:

Management of companies and enterprises	$46,630
Credit intermediation and related activities	42,230
Professional, scientific, and technical services	40,800
Healthcare and social assistance	40,620
Business support services	35,350

Most bill and account collectors work full time. Some collectors work flexible schedules, often calling people on weekends or during the evenings as they learn the best times to call.

Job Outlook

Employment of bill and account collectors is projected to decline 10 percent from 2022 to 2032.

Despite declining employment, about 19,200 openings for bill and account collectors are projected each year, on average, over the decade. All of those openings are expected to result from the need to replace workers who transfer to other occupations or exit the labor force, such as to retire.

Employment

Continued use of enhanced software and automated calling systems is expected to increase productivity and allow collectors to handle more accounts. This technology will allow more collections work to be done with fewer employees. However, the need to collect various types of debt, including student, credit card, and mortgage debt, should create some demand for bill and account collectors.

Occupational Title	SOC Code	Employment, 2022	Projected Employment, 2032	Change, 2022-32	
				Percent	Numeric
Bill and account collectors	43-3011	209,700	189,600	-10	-20,100

Bookkeeping, Accounting, and Auditing Clerks

Summary

Quick Facts: Bookkeeping, Accounting, and Auditing Clerks

2022 Median Pay	$45,860 per year $22.05 per hour
Typical Entry-Level Education	Some college, no degree
Work Experience in a Related Occupation	None
On-the-job Training	Moderate-term on-the-job training
Number of Jobs, 2022	1,735,800
Job Outlook, 2022-32	-6% (Decline)
Employment Change, 2022-32	-108,300

What Bookkeeping, Accounting, and Auditing Clerks Do

Bookkeeping, accounting, and auditing clerks produce financial records for organizations and check financial records for accuracy.

Work Environment

Bookkeeping, accounting, and auditing clerks work in offices and may do site visits. Some work part time.

How to Become a Bookkeeping, Accounting, or Auditing Clerk

Bookkeeping, accounting, and auditing clerks typically need some postsecondary education to enter the occupation. They also learn some of their skills on the job.

Pay

The median annual wage for bookkeeping, accounting, and auditing clerks was $45,860 in May 2022.

Bookkeeping, accounting, and auditing clerks produce financial records for organizations.

Job Outlook

Employment of bookkeeping, accounting, and auditing clerks is projected to decline 6 percent from 2022 to 2032.

Despite declining employment, about 183,900 openings for bookkeeping, accounting, and auditing clerks are projected each year, on average, over the decade. All of those openings are expected to result from the need to replace workers who transfer to other occupations or exit the labor force, such as to retire.

What Bookkeeping, Accounting, and Auditing Clerks Do

Bookkeeping, accounting, and auditing clerks produce financial records for organizations. They record financial transactions, update statements, and check financial records for accuracy.

Duties

Bookkeeping, accounting, and auditing clerks typically do the following:

- Use bookkeeping software, spreadsheets, and databases
- Enter (post) financial transactions into the appropriate computer software
- Receive and record cash, checks, and vouchers
- Put costs (debits) and income (credits) into the software, assigning each to an appropriate account
- Produce reports, such as balance sheets (costs compared with income), income statements, and totals by account
- Check for accuracy in figures, postings, and reports
- Reconcile or note and report any differences they find in the records

The records that bookkeeping, accounting, and auditing clerks work with include expenditures (money spent), receipts (money that comes in), accounts payable (bills to be paid), accounts

As organizations continue to computerize their financial records, many bookkeeping, accounting, and auditing clerks need to use specialized accounting software, spreadsheets, and databases.

receivable (invoices, or what other people owe the organization), and profit and loss (a report that shows the organization's financial health).

Workers in this occupation engage in a wide range of tasks. Some are full-charge bookkeeping clerks who maintain an entire organization's books. Others are accounting clerks who handle specific tasks.

These clerks use basic mathematics (adding, subtracting) throughout the day.

Bookkeeping, accounting, and auditing clerks use specialized computer accounting software, spreadsheets, and databases to enter information from receipts or bills. They must be comfortable using computers to record and calculate data.

The widespread use of computers also has enabled bookkeeping, accounting, and auditing clerks to take on additional responsibilities, such as payroll, billing, purchasing (buying), and keeping track of overdue bills. Many of these functions require clerks to communicate with clients.

Bookkeeping clerks, also known as *bookkeepers*, often are responsible for some or all of an organization's accounts, known as the general ledger. They record all transactions and post debits (costs) and credits (income).

They also produce financial statements and other reports for supervisors and managers. Bookkeepers prepare bank deposits by compiling data from cashiers, verifying receipts, and sending cash, checks, or other forms of payment to the bank.

In addition, they may handle payroll, make purchases, prepare invoices, and keep track of overdue accounts.

Accounting clerks typically work for larger companies and have more specialized tasks. Their titles, such as accounts payable clerk or accounts receivable clerk, often reflect the type of accounting they do.

The responsibilities of accounting clerks frequently vary by level of experience. Entry-level accounting clerks may post details of transactions (including date, type, and amount), add up accounts, and determine interest charges. They may also monitor loans and accounts to ensure that payments are up to date.

More advanced accounting clerks may add and balance billing vouchers, ensure that account data are complete and accurate, and code documents according to an organization's procedures.

Auditing clerks check figures, postings, and documents to ensure that they are mathematically accurate and properly coded. For smaller errors, such as transcription errors, they may make corrections themselves. In case of major discrepancies, they typically notify senior staff, including accountants and auditors.

Work Environment

Bookkeeping, accounting, and auditing clerks held about 1.7 million jobs in 2022. The largest employers of bookkeeping, accounting, and auditing clerks were as follows:

Professional, scientific, and technical services	13%
Construction	8
Retail trade	8
Wholesale trade	7
Finance and insurance	6

The professional, scientific, and technical services industry includes the accounting, tax preparation, bookkeeping, and payroll services subindustry.

Bookkeeping, accounting, and auditing clerks work in offices. Bookkeepers who work for multiple firms may visit their clients' places of business. They often work alone, but sometimes they collaborate with accountants, managers, and auditing clerks from other departments.

Work Schedules

Most bookkeeping, accounting, and auditing clerks work full time. They may work longer hours to meet deadlines at the end of the fiscal year, during tax time, or when monthly or yearly accounting audits are performed.

How to Become a Bookkeeping, Accounting, or Auditing Clerk

Bookkeeping, accounting, and auditing clerks typically need some postsecondary education to enter the occupation. They also learn some of their skills on the job.

Bookkeeping, accounting, and auditing clerks may work longer hours to meet deadlines at the end of the fiscal year, during tax time, or when monthly or yearly accounting audits are performed.

Most bookkeeping, accounting, and auditing clerks are required to have some postsecondary education.

Education

Employers generally prefer to hire candidates who have a high school diploma and have completed college courses in related subjects, such as accounting.

Although not required, some candidates choose to get a bachelor's degree in a field such as business.

Training

Bookkeeping, accounting, and auditing clerks usually get on-the-job training. Under the guidance of a supervisor or another experienced employee, new clerks learn how to do their tasks, such as double-entry bookkeeping. In double-entry bookkeeping, each transaction is entered twice, once as a debit (cost) and once as a credit (income), to ensure that all accounts are balanced.

Some formal classroom training also may be necessary, such as training in specialized computer software. This on-the-job training typically takes around 6 months.

Licenses, Certifications, and Registrations

Some bookkeeping, accounting, and auditing clerks become certified. For those who do not have postsecondary education, certification is a particularly useful way to gain expertise in the field. The Certified Bookkeeper (CB) designation, awarded by the American Institute of Professional Bookkeepers, shows that those who have earned it have the skills and knowledge needed to carry out all bookkeeping tasks, including overseeing payroll and balancing accounts, according to accepted accounting procedures.

For certification, candidates must have at least 2 years of full-time bookkeeping experience or equivalent part-time work, pass a four-part exam, and adhere to a code of ethics.

The National Association of Certified Public Bookkeepers offers the Certified Public Bookkeeper (CPB) certification. To obtain the certification, candidates must pass the four-part Uniform Bookkeeper Certification Examination.

Advancement

With appropriate experience and additional education, some bookkeeping, accounting, and auditing clerks may become accountants or auditors.

Important Qualities

Computer skills. Bookkeeping, accounting, and auditing clerks need to be comfortable using computer spreadsheets and bookkeeping software.

Detail oriented. Bookkeeping, accounting, and auditing clerks are responsible for producing accurate financial records. They must pay attention to detail in order to avoid making errors and recognize errors that others have made.

Integrity. Bookkeeping, accounting, and auditing clerks have control of an organization's financial documentation, which they must use properly and keep confidential. It is vital that they keep records transparent and guard against misusing an organization's funds.

Math skills. Bookkeeping, accounting, and auditing clerks deal with numbers daily and should be comfortable with basic arithmetic.

Pay

The median annual wage for bookkeeping, accounting, and auditing clerks was $45,860 in May 2022. The median wage is the wage at which half the workers in an occupation earned more than that amount and half earned less. The lowest 10 percent earned less than $30,460, and the highest 10 percent earned more than $65,540.

In May 2022, the median annual wages for bookkeeping, accounting, and auditing clerks in the top industries in which they worked were as follows:

Finance and insurance	$47,410
Construction	47,190

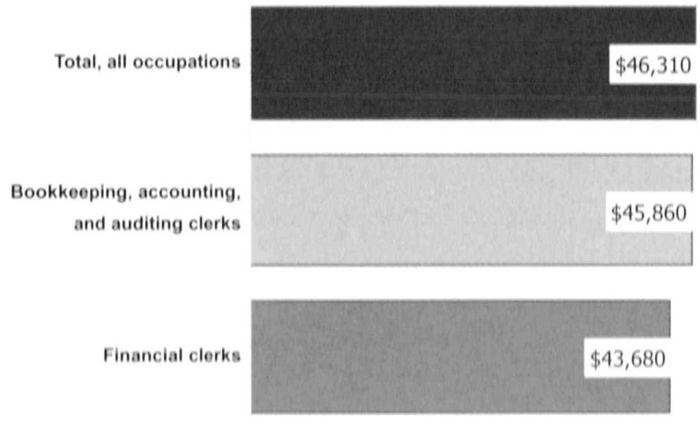

Professional, scientific, and technical services ...	47,000
Wholesale trade	46,220
Retail trade	39,880

Most bookkeeping, accounting, and auditing clerks work full time. They may work longer hours to meet deadlines at the end of the fiscal year, during tax time, or when monthly or yearly accounting audits are performed.

Job Outlook

Employment of bookkeeping, accounting, and auditing clerks is projected to decline 6 percent from 2022 to 2032.

Despite declining employment, about 183,900 openings for bookkeeping, accounting, and auditing clerks are projected each year, on average, over the decade. All of those openings are expected to result from the need to replace workers who transfer to other occupations or exit the labor force, such as to retire.

Employment

Technological change is expected to reduce demand for these workers. Software innovations have automated many of the tasks performed by bookkeeping, accounting, and auditing clerks. As a result, the same amount of work can be done with fewer employees, which is expected to lead to job losses over the projections decade.

With more automation of routine tasks, bookkeeping, accounting, and auditing clerks are expected to take on a more analytical and advisory role over the decade. For example, rather than entering data by hand, these workers may focus on analyzing their clients' books and pointing out potential areas for efficiency gains.

Bookkeeping, Accounting, and Auditing Clerks

Percent change in employment, projected 2022-32

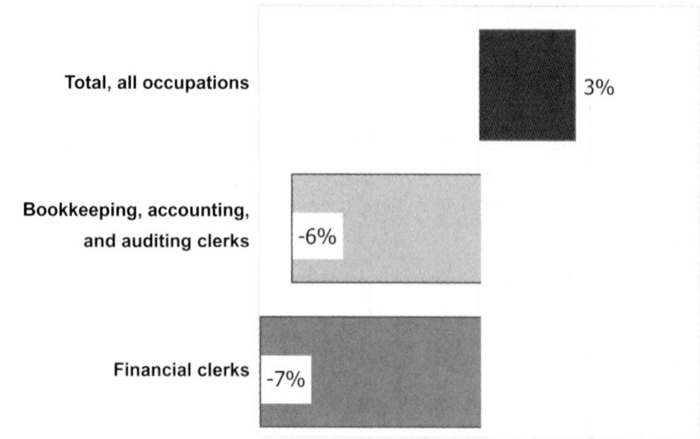

Note: All Occupations includes all occupations in the U.S. Economy.
Source: U.S. Bureau of Labor Statistics, Employment Projections program.

Occupational Title	SOC Code	Employment, 2022	Projected Employment, 2032	Change, 2022-32	
				Percent	Numeric
Bookkeeping, accounting, and auditing clerks	43-3031	1,735,800	1,627,500	-6	-108,300

Contacts for More Information

For more information, visit

- American Institute of Professional Bookkeepers
- National Association of Certified Public Bookkeepers

Customer Service Representatives

Summary

Quick Facts: Customer Service Representatives

2022 Median Pay	$37,780 per year $18.16 per hour
Typical Entry-Level Education	High school diploma or equivalent
Work Experience in a Related Occupation	None
On-the-job Training	Short-term on-the-job training
Number of Jobs, 2022	2,982,900
Job Outlook, 2022-32	-5% (Decline)
Employment Change, 2022-32	-162,700

What Customer Service Representatives Do

Customer service representatives interact with customers to handle complaints, process orders, and answer questions.

Work Environment

Customer service representatives are employed in nearly every industry. Most work full time.

How to Become a Customer Service Representative

Customer service representatives typically need a high school diploma to enter the occupation and are trained on the job. They should be good at communicating and interacting with people.

Pay

The median hourly wage for customer service representatives was $18.16 in May 2022.

Job Outlook

Employment of customer service representatives is projected to decline 5 percent from 2022 to 2032.

Despite declining employment, about 373,400 openings for customer service representatives are projected each year, on average, over the decade. All of those openings are expected

Customer service representatives provide information to customers about products and services.

to result from the need to replace workers who transfer to other occupations or exit the labor force, such as to retire.

What Customer Service Representatives Do

Customer service representatives work with customers to resolve complaints, process orders, and provide information about an organization's products and services.

Duties

Customer service representatives typically do the following:

- Listen to customers' questions and concerns and provide answers or responses
- Provide information about products and services
- Take orders, calculate charges, and process billing or payments
- Review customer accounts and make changes, if necessary
- Handle returns or complaints
- Record details of customer contacts and actions taken
- Refer customers to supervisors or more experienced employees

Customer service representatives listen and respond to customer's questions.

Customer service representatives answer questions or requests from customers or the public. They typically provide services by phone, but some also interact with customers face to face, by email or text, via live chat, and through social media.

The specific duties of customer service representatives vary by industry. For example, representatives who work in banks may answer customers' questions about their accounts. Representatives who work for utility and telecommunications companies may help customers with service problems, such as outages. Those who work in retail stores often handle returns, process refunds, and help customers locate items. Although selling a product or service is not their main job, representatives may help generate sales while providing information.

Customer service representatives typically use a telephone, computer, and other office equipment. For example, representatives who work in call centers answer the phone and use computers to explore solutions for customers.

Work Environment

Customer service representatives held about 3.0 million jobs in 2022. The largest employers of customer service representatives were as follows:

Retail trade	18%
Insurance carriers and related activities	11
Business support services	10
Wholesale trade	6
Professional, scientific, and technical services	6

Customer service representatives are employed in nearly every industry. Representatives in offices may work in a large room alongside other employees, so the area can be noisy. Working from home is also possible in some companies. Representatives may be under pressure to answer a designated number of calls while supervisors monitor them for quality assurance. In addition, the work may be stressful when representatives must interact with dissatisfied customers

Many customer service representatives work in call centers.

In retail stores, representatives may spend hours on their feet assisting customers in person.

Work Schedules

Although most customer service representatives work full time, some work part time. Customer service representatives often need to work during busy times, which may include evenings, weekends, and holidays.

Jobs in call centers may require representatives to work shifts early in the morning or late at night because some call centers are open 24 hours a day.

How to Become a Customer Service Representative

Customer service representatives typically need a high school diploma or equivalent to enter the occupation and receive on-the-job training to learn the specific skills needed for the job. They should be good at communicating and interacting with people.

Education

Customer service representatives typically need a high school diploma or equivalent to enter the occupation. However, some of these workers have postsecondary education that may include a bachelor's degree in fields such as business, communications, and social science.

Training

Customer service representatives usually receive short-term on-the-job training, which typically lasts 2 to 4 weeks. Those who work in finance and insurance may need several months of training to learn complicated financial regulations.

General customer-service training may focus on procedures for answering questions, information about a company's products and services, and computer and telephone use. Trainees often receive guidance from an experienced worker for the first few weeks of employment.

Customer service representatives should be good at communicating and interacting with people and have some experience using computers.

In certain industries, such as finance and insurance, customer service representatives must stay current with changing regulations.

Licenses, Certifications, and Registrations

Customer service representatives who provide information about finance and insurance may need a state license. Although licensing requirements vary by state, they usually include passing an exam. Some employers and organizations provide training for these exams.

Advancement

With experience, customer service representatives may advance to supervisory roles.

Important Qualities

Communication skills. Customer service representatives must be able to provide clear information in writing, by phone, or in person.

Customer-service skills. Representatives help companies retain customers by professionally answering questions and helping to resolve complaints.

Interpersonal skills. Representatives should be able to create positive interactions with customers.

Listening skills. Representatives must listen carefully to ensure that they understand customers in order to assist them.

Patience. Representatives should be patient and polite, especially when interacting with dissatisfied customers.

Problem-solving skills. Representatives must determine solutions to customers' problems. By doing so, representatives contribute to customer loyalty and retention.

Pay

The median hourly wage for customer service representatives was $18.16 in May 2022. The median wage is the wage at which half the workers in an occupation earned more than that amount and half earned less. The lowest 10 percent earned less than $13.46, and the highest 10 percent earned more than $28.67.

In May 2022, the median hourly wages for customer service representatives in the top industries in which they worked were as follows:

Wholesale trade	$21.38
Insurance carriers and related activities	21.06
Professional, scientific, and technical services	18.95
Business support services	16.92
Retail trade	15.75

Although most customer service representatives work full time, some work part time. Customer service representatives often need to work during busy times, which may include evenings, weekends, and holidays.

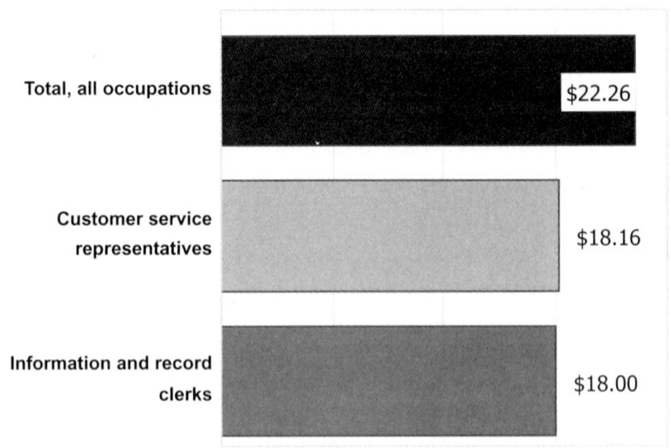

Note: All Occupations includes all occupations in the U.S. Economy.
Source: U.S. Bureau of Labor Statistics, Occupational Employment and Wage Statistics.

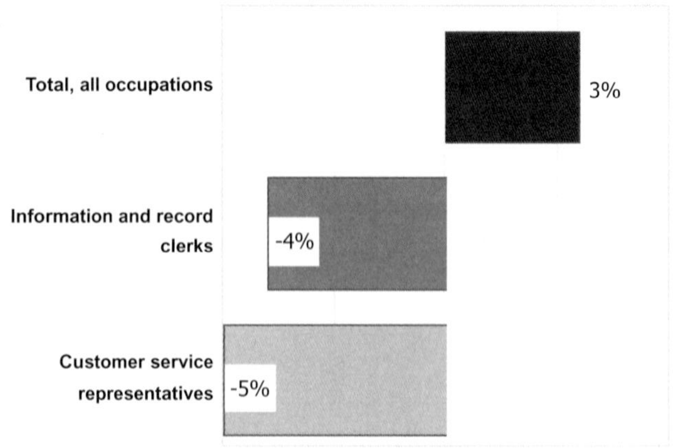

Note: All Occupations includes all occupations in the U.S. Economy.
Source: U.S. Bureau of Labor Statistics, Employment Projections program.

Jobs in call centers may require representatives to work shifts early in the morning or late at night because some call centers are open 24 hours a day.

Job Outlook

Employment of customer service representatives is projected to decline 5 percent from 2022 to 2032.

Despite declining employment, about 373,400 openings for customer service representatives are projected each year, on average, over the decade. All of those openings are expected to result from the need to replace workers who transfer to other occupations or exit the labor force, such as to retire.

Employment

There is expected to be less demand for customer service representatives, especially in retail trade, as their tasks continue to be automated. Self-service systems, social media, and mobile applications enable customers to do simple tasks without interacting with a representative. Advancements in technology will gradually allow these automated systems to do even more tasks. Some companies will continue to use in-house service centers to differentiate themselves from competitors, particularly for complex inquiries such as refunding accounts or confirming insurance coverage.

Occupational Title	SOC Code	Employment, 2022	Projected Employment, 2032	Change, 2022-32	
				Percent	Numeric
Customer service representatives	43-4051	2,982,900	2,820,200	-5	-162,700

Contacts for More Information

The *Handbook* does not have contacts for more information for this occupation.

Desktop Publishers

Summary

Quick Facts: Desktop Publishers	
2022 Median Pay	$47,910 per year $23.04 per hour
Typical Entry-Level Education	Associate's degree
Work Experience in a Related Occupation	None
On-the-job Training	Short-term on-the-job training
Number of Jobs, 2022	8,500
Job Outlook, 2022-32	-13% (Decline)
Employment Change, 2022-32	-1,100

What Desktop Publishers Do

Desktop publishers use computer software to design page layouts for items that are printed or published online.

Work Environment

Many desktop publishers work full time, and they may need to work additional hours to meet publication deadlines.

How to Become a Desktop Publisher

Desktop publishers typically need an associate's degree. They also receive short-term on-the-job training lasting about 1 month.

Pay

The median annual wage for desktop publishers was $47,910 in May 2022.

Job Outlook

Employment of desktop publishers is projected to decline 13 percent from 2022 to 2032.

Despite declining employment, about 700 openings for desktop publishers are projected each year, on average, over the decade. All of those openings are expected to result from the need to replace workers who transfer to other occupations or exit the labor force, such as to retire.

What Desktop Publishers Do

Desktop publishers use computer software to design page layouts for newspapers, books, brochures, and other items that are printed or published online.

Duties

Desktop publishers typically do the following:

- Review text, graphics, or other materials created by writers and designers
- Edit graphics, such as photographs or illustrations
- Import text and graphics into publishing software
- Integrate images and text to create cohesive pages
- Adjust text properties, such as size, column width, and spacing
- Revise layouts and make corrections as necessary
- Submit or upload final files for printing or online publishing

Desktop publishers use publishing software to create page layouts for print or electronic publication. They may edit text by correcting its spelling, punctuation, and grammar.

Desktop publishers often work with other design, media, or marketing workers, including writers, editors, and graphic designers. For example, they work with graphic designers to come up with images that complement the text and fit the available space.

Work Environment

Desktop publishers held about 8,500 jobs in 2022. The largest employers of desktop publishers were as follows:

Publishing industries	29%
Self-employed workers	17

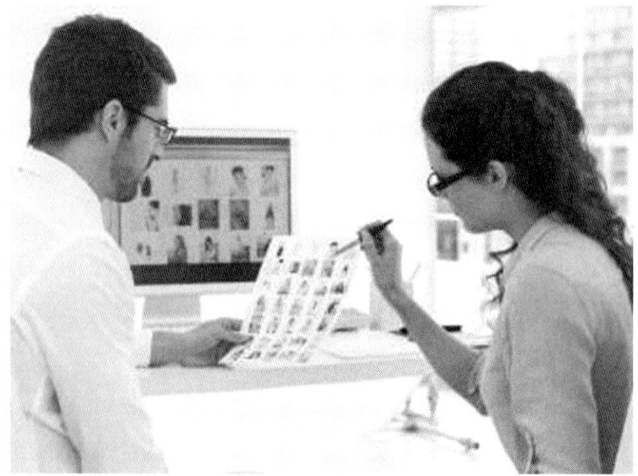

Desktop publishers design layouts for books, newspapers, and other published items.

Desktop publishers edit graphics, such as photographs or illustrations.

Many desktop publishers work in the publishing and printing industries.

Professional, scientific, and technical services	17
Educational services; state, local, and private	4
Printing and related support activities	2

Work Schedules

Many desktop publishers work full time, and they may need to work additional hours to meet publication deadlines.

How to Become a Desktop Publisher

Desktop publishers usually need an associate's degree. They also receive short-term on-the-job training, lasting about 1 month.

Education

Desktop publishers usually need an associate's degree, often in graphic design or graphic communications. Community colleges and technical schools offer desktop-publishing courses, which teach students how to create electronic page layouts and format text and graphics with the use of desktop-publishing software.

Desktop publishers typically learn on the job from an experienced worker.

Training

Desktop publishers typically receive short-term on-the-job training lasting about 1 month. They learn by working closely with more experienced workers or by taking classes that teach them how to use desktop-publishing software. Workers often need to continue training because publishing software changes over time.

Important Qualities

Artistic ability. Desktop publishers must have a good eye for how graphics and text will look, so that they can create pages that are visually appealing and legible.

Communication skills. Desktop publishers must collaborate with others, such as writers, editors, and graphic designers, and communicate ideas effectively.

Detail oriented. Desktop publishers must pay attention to details such as margins, font sizes, and the overall appearance and accuracy of their work.

Organizational skills. Desktop publishers often work under strict deadlines and must be good at scheduling and prioritizing tasks in order to have documents ready in time for publication.

Other Experience

Many employers prefer to hire workers who have experience preparing layouts and using desktop-publishing software. Students may gain experience by working on a publication for a school or other organization.

Pay

The median annual wage for desktop publishers was $47,910 in May 2022. The median wage is the wage at which half the workers in an occupation earned more than that amount and half earned less. The lowest 10 percent earned less than $29,370, and the highest 10 percent earned more than $86,820.

In May 2022, the median annual wages for desktop publishers in the top industries in which they worked were as follows:

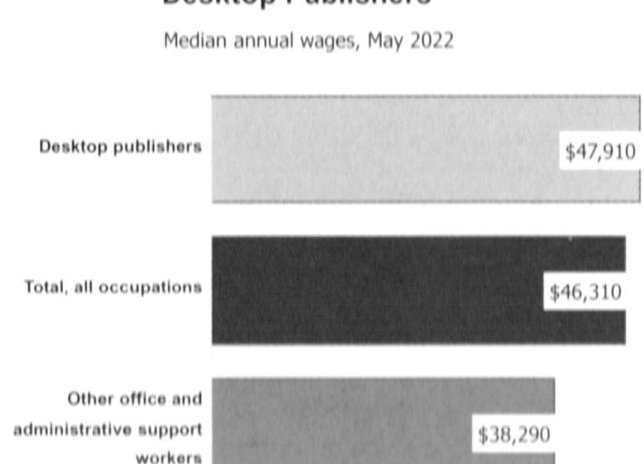

Note: All Occupations includes all occupations in the U.S. Economy.
Source: U.S. Bureau of Labor Statistics, Occupational Employment and Wage Statistics.

Professional, scientific, and technical services	$54,660
Educational services; state, local, and private......	51,660
Printing and related support activities.................	50,050
Publishing industries...	44,000

Many desktop publishers work full time, and they may need to work additional hours to meet publication deadlines.

Job Outlook

Employment of desktop publishers is projected to decline 13 percent from 2022 to 2032.

Despite declining employment, about 700 openings for desktop publishers are projected each year, on average, over the decade. All of those openings are expected to result from the need to replace workers who transfer to other occupations or exit the labor force, such as to retire.

Employment

Companies are expected to hire fewer desktop publishers as desktop-publishing tasks are increasingly performed by other types of workers, such as graphic designers, web designers, and editors. Furthermore, as organizations continue to publish their materials electronically instead of printing them, fewer desktop publishers are expected to be needed.

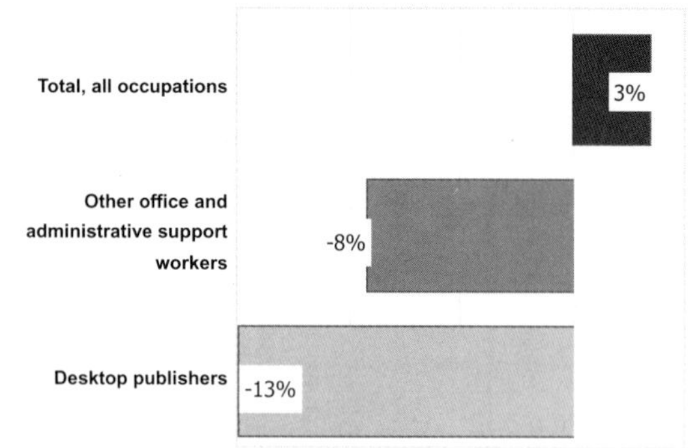

Note: All Occupations includes all occupations in the U.S. Economy.
Source: U.S. Bureau of Labor Statistics, Employment Projections program.

Occupational Title	SOC Code	Employment, 2022	Projected Employment, 2032	Change, 2022-32	
				Percent	Numeric
Desktop publishers	43-9031	8,500	7,400	-13	-1,100

Contacts for More Information

For more information, visit

➤ Printing Industries of America

Financial Clerks

Summary

Quick Facts: Financial Clerks

2022 Median Pay	$45,570 per year $21.91 per hour
Typical Entry-Level Education	High school diploma or equivalent
Work Experience in a Related Occupation	None
On-the-job Training	See How to Become One
Number of Jobs, 2022	1,312,000
Job Outlook, 2022-32	-4% (Decline)
Employment Change, 2022-32	-54,900

What Financial Clerks Do

Financial clerks do administrative work, help customers, and carry out transactions that involve money.

Work Environment

Financial clerks usually work in offices, including bank branches, medical practices, and government agencies. Most work full time.

How to Become a Financial Clerk

A high school diploma is typically required for most financial clerk positions. These workers typically learn their job duties through on-the-job training.

Pay

The median annual wage for financial clerks was $45,570 in May 2022.

Financial clerks provide customer service and maintain financial records.

Job Outlook

Overall employment of financial clerks is projected to decline 4 percent from 2022 to 2032.

Despite declining employment, about 116,600 openings for financial clerks are projected each year, on average, over the decade. All of those openings are expected to result from the need to replace workers who transfer to other occupations or exit the labor force, such as to retire.

What Financial Clerks Do

Financial clerks do administrative work for many types of organizations. They keep records, help customers, and carry out transactions that involve money.

Duties

Financial clerks typically do the following:

- Keep and update financial records
- Calculate bills and charges
- Offer customer assistance
- Carry out financial transactions

Financial clerks' job duties vary by specialty and by setting.

The following are examples of types of financial clerks:

Billing and posting clerks calculate charges and generate bills, which they then prepare to send to customers. They review documents such as purchase orders, sales tickets, charge slips, and hospital records to calculate fees or charges due. They also contact customers to get or give account information.

Brokerage clerks help with tasks associated with securities such as stocks, bonds, commodities, and other kinds of investments. Their duties include writing orders for stock purchases and sales, calculating transfer taxes, verifying stock transactions, accepting and delivering securities, distributing dividends, and recording daily transactions and holdings.

Credit authorizers, checkers, and clerks review the credit history, and get the information needed to determine the creditworthiness, of individuals or businesses applying for credit.

Financial clerks keep and update financial records.

Credit authorizers check customers' credit records and payment histories to decide, based on predetermined standards, whether to approve new credit. Credit checkers contact credit departments of business and service establishments for information about applicants' credit standing.

Gambling cage workers work in casinos and other gambling establishments. The "cage" in which they work is the central depository for money and gambling chips. Gambling cage workers sell gambling chips, tokens, or tickets to patrons. They count funds and reconcile daily summaries of transactions to balance books.

Insurance claims and policy processing clerks process applications for insurance policies. They also handle customers' requests to change or cancel their existing policies. Their duties include interviewing clients and reviewing insurance applications to make sure that all questions have been answered. They also inform insurance agents and accounting departments of policy cancellations or changes.

Loan interviewers, also called *loan processors* or *loan clerks*, interview applicants and others to get and verify personal and financial information needed to complete loan applications. They also prepare the documents that go to the appraiser and are issued at the closing of a loan.

New accounts clerks interview people who want to open accounts in financial institutions. They explain the account services available to prospective customers and help them fill out applications. They also investigate and correct errors in accounts.

Payroll and timekeeping clerks compile and post employee time and payroll data. They verify and record attendance, hours worked, and pay adjustments. They make sure that employees are paid on time and that their paychecks are correct.

Procurement clerks compile requests for materials, prepare purchase orders, keep track of purchases and supplies, and handle questions about orders. They respond to questions from customers and suppliers about the status of orders. Procurement clerks handle requests to change or cancel orders. They make sure that purchases arrive on schedule and that the items meet the buyer's specifications.

Work Environment

Financial clerks held about 1.3 million jobs in 2022. Employment in the detailed occupations that make up financial clerks was distributed as follows:

Billing and posting clerks	456,300
Insurance claims and policy processing clerks	259,000
Loan interviewers and clerks	247,100
Payroll and timekeeping clerks	165,400
Procurement clerks	65,300
New accounts clerks	46,600
Brokerage clerks	43,700

The majority of financial clerks work full time.

Credit authorizers, checkers, and clerks	16,400
Gambling cage workers	12,200

The largest employers of financial clerks were as follows:

Credit intermediation and related activities	21%
Insurance carriers and related activities	19
Healthcare and social assistance	18
Professional, scientific, and technical services	8
Administrative and support services	6

Financial clerks work in a variety of industries, usually in offices.

Work Schedules
Most financial clerks work full time.

How to Become a Financial Clerk
A high school diploma or equivalent is typically required for most financial clerk jobs. These workers typically learn their duties through on-the-job training.

Education
Financial clerks typically need a high school diploma or equivalent to enter the occupation. Employers of brokerage clerks may prefer candidates who have taken some college courses in

A high school diploma is sufficient for most financial clerk positions.

business or economics and, in some cases, have a 2- or 4-year college degree.

Training
Most financial clerks learn how to do their job duties through on-the-job training. Some formal technical training also may be necessary; for example, gambling cage workers may need training in specific gambling regulations and procedures.

Advancement
Financial clerks may advance to related occupations in finance. For example, a loan interviewer or clerk may become a loan officer, and a brokerage clerk may become a securities, commodities, and financial services sales agent, after obtaining the required education and license.

Important Qualities
Communication skills. Financial clerks should be able to explain policies and procedures to colleagues and customers.

Math skills. The job duties of financial clerks includes calculating charges and updating financial records.

Organizational skills. Financial clerks must be able to arrange files so they can find them quickly and efficiently.

Pay
The median annual wage for financial clerks was $45,570 in May 2022. The median wage is the wage at which half the workers in an occupation earned more than that amount and half earned less. The lowest 10 percent earned less than $31,940, and the highest 10 percent earned more than $63,550.

Median annual wages for financial clerks in May 2022 were as follows:

Brokerage clerks	$54,680
Payroll and timekeeping clerks	49,630
Loan interviewers and clerks	46,490

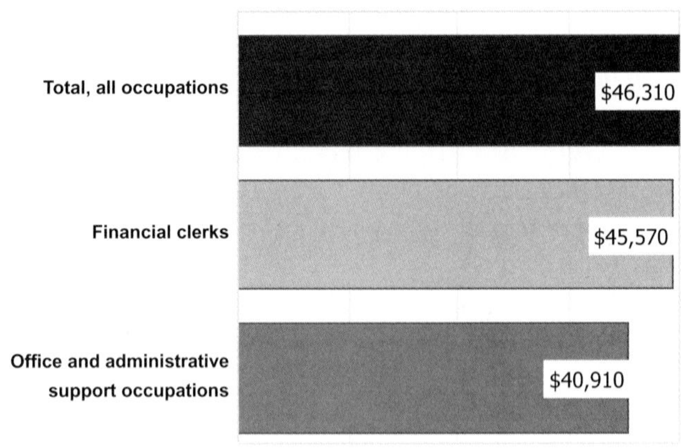

Note: All Occupations includes all occupations in the U.S. Economy.
Source: U.S. Bureau of Labor Statistics, Occupational Employment and Wage Statistics.

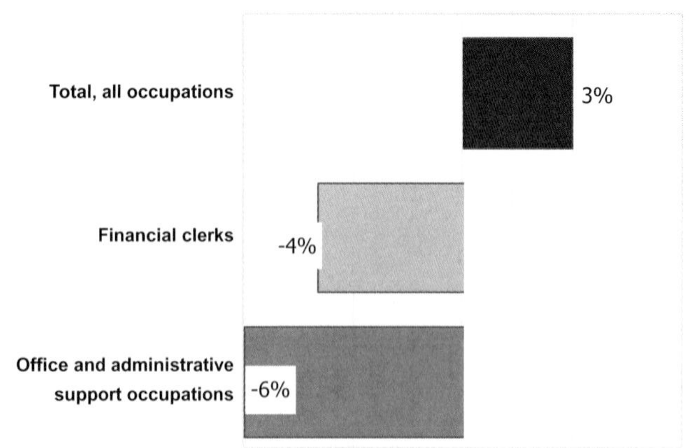

Note: All Occupations includes all occupations in the U.S. Economy.
Source: U.S. Bureau of Labor Statistics, Employment Projections program.

Insurance claims and policy processing clerks	46,080
Procurement clerks	45,240
Credit authorizers, checkers, and clerks	44,830
Billing and posting clerks	42,810
New accounts clerks	40,820
Gambling cage workers	31,720

In May 2022, the median annual wages for financial clerks in the top industries in which they worked were as follows:

Insurance carriers and related activities	$46,550
Credit intermediation and related activities	45,900
Professional, scientific, and technical services	45,060
Administrative and support services	43,420
Healthcare and social assistance	42,640

Most financial clerks work full time.

Job Outlook

Overall employment of financial clerks is projected to decline 4 percent from 2022 to 2032.

Despite declining employment, about 116,600 openings for financial clerks are projected each year, on average, over the decade. All of those openings are expected to result from the need to replace workers who transfer to other occupations or exit the labor force, such as to retire.

Employment

Projected employment of financial clerks varies by occupation (see table). The availability of online tools, which allow financial customers to perform many tasks themselves, is expected to reduce demand for occupations such as new accounts clerks; procurement clerks; and credit authorizers, checkers, and clerks. Similarly, productivity-enhancing technology is expected to limit demand for other clerks, such as payroll and timekeeping clerks, loan interviewers and clerks, brokerage clerks, and insurance claims and policy processing clerks.

Employment of gambling cage workers will be impacted by the adoption of technology in payout processing and online gambling, which limits the need for cage workers.

Employment of billing and posting clerks is expected to rise in fast-growing healthcare industries; however, automated invoice processing software will increase the productivity of these workers and reduce overall employment growth.

Occupational Title	SOC Code	Employment, 2022	Projected Employment, 2032	Change, 2022-32	
				Percent	Numeric
Financial clerks	—	1,312,000	1,257,100	-4	-54,900
Billing and posting clerks	43-3021	456,300	456,400	0	100
Gambling cage workers	43-3041	12,200	11,500	-5	-700
Payroll and timekeeping clerks	43-3051	165,400	138,300	-16	-27,200
Procurement clerks	43-3061	65,300	60,400	-8	-4,900
Brokerage clerks	43-4011	43,700	39,800	-9	-3,900
Credit authorizers, checkers, and clerks	43-4041	16,400	15,500	-6	-1,000
Loan interviewers and clerks	43-4131	247,100	244,600	-1	-2,500
New accounts clerks	43-4141	46,600	39,800	-14	-6,700
Insurance claims and policy processing clerks	43-9041	259,000	250,800	-3	-8,200

Contacts for More Information

For more information, visit

- American Bankers Association
- Mortgage Bankers Association

General Office Clerks

Summary

Quick Facts: General Office Clerks	
2022 Median Pay	$38,040 per year $18.29 per hour
Typical Entry-Level Education	High school diploma or equivalent
Work Experience in a Related Occupation	None
On-the-job Training	Short-term on-the-job training
Number of Jobs, 2022	2,668,200
Job Outlook, 2022-32	-7% (Decline)
Employment Change, 2022-32	-175,400

What General Office Clerks Do

General office clerks perform a variety of clerical tasks, including answering telephones, typing documents, and filing records.

Work Environment

Although general office clerks are employed in nearly every industry, many work in schools, healthcare facilities, and government offices.

How to Become a General Office Clerk

General office clerks typically need a high school diploma or equivalent. Most learn their skills on the job.

Pay

The median hourly wage for general office clerks was $18.29 in May 2022.

Job Outlook

Employment of general office clerks is projected to decline 7 percent from 2022 to 2032.

General office clerks perform a variety of administrative tasks, such as copying and scanning documents.

Despite declining employment, about 290,100 openings for general office clerks are projected each year, on average, over the decade. All of those openings are expected to result from the need to replace workers who transfer to other occupations or exit the labor force, such as to retire.

What General Office Clerks Do

General office clerks perform a variety of clerical tasks, including answering telephones, typing documents, and filing records.

Duties

General office clerks typically do the following:

- Answer and transfer telephone calls or take messages
- Sort and deliver incoming mail and send outgoing mail
- Schedule appointments and receive customers or visitors
- Provide general information to staff, clients, or the public
- Type, format, or edit routine memos or other reports
- Copy, file, and update paper and electronic documents
- Prepare and process bills and other office documents
- Collect information and perform data entry

Rather than performing a single specialized task, general office clerks have responsibilities that often change daily with the current needs of the employer.

Some clerks file documents or answer phones; others enter data into computers or perform other tasks using software applications. They also frequently use photocopiers, scanners, fax machines, and other office equipment.

The specific duties assigned to clerks will depend on the type of office in which they work. For example, a general office clerk at a college or university may process application materials and answer questions from prospective students, while a clerk at a hospital may file and retrieve medical records.

Work Environment

General office clerks held about 2.7 million jobs in 2022. The largest employers of general office clerks were as follows:

General office clerks type, format, or edit routine memos.

General office clerks work in offices.

Healthcare and social assistance	11%
Educational services; state, local, and private	11
Government	10
Construction	9
Professional, scientific, and technical services	8

General office clerks usually work in office settings.

Work Schedules

Most general office clerks work full time.

How to Become a General Office Clerk

General office clerks typically need a high school diploma or equivalent to enter the occupation and learn their skills on the job.

Education

General office clerks usually need a high school diploma or equivalent. Some clerks have a bachelor's degree in fields such as business, social science, and psychology.

Courses in using computer applications, such as word processing and spreadsheet software, may be helpful for those who aren't already familiar with them.

General office clerks usually need a high school diploma or equivalent.

Training

General office clerks usually learn their skills while on the job. Their training typically lasts up to 1 month and may include instructions on office procedures, proper phone etiquette, and the use of office equipment.

Advancement

General office clerks may advance to other administrative positions with more responsibility, such as secretaries and administrative assistants.

Advancement opportunities often depend on work experience.

Important Qualities

Customer-service skills. General office clerks often provide general information to company staff, customers, or the public. They should be courteous and prompt with their responses.

Detail oriented. General office clerks perform many clerical tasks that require attention to detail, such as preparing bills.

Organizational skills. General office clerks file and retrieve records. They need to keep records organized to be able to access them quickly and efficiently.

Pay

The median hourly wage for general office clerks was $18.29 in May 2022. The median wage is the wage at which half the workers in an occupation earned more than that amount and half earned less. The lowest 10 percent earned less than $12.50, and the highest 10 percent earned more than $28.70.

In May 2022, the median hourly wages for general office clerks in the top industries in which they worked were as follows:

Construction	$20.00
Government	19.88

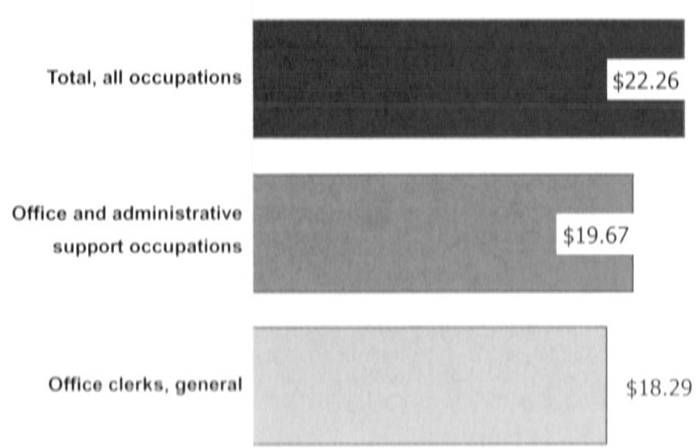

Note: All Occupations includes all occupations in the U.S. Economy.
Source: U.S. Bureau of Labor Statistics, Occupational Employment and Wage Statistics.

Professional, scientific, and technical services	18.70
Healthcare and social assistance	18.01
Educational services; state, local, and private.......	17.71

Most general office clerks work full time.

Job Outlook

Employment of general office clerks is projected to decline 7 percent from 2022 to 2032.

Despite declining employment, about 290,100 openings for general office clerks are projected each year, on average, over the decade. All of those openings are expected to result from the need to replace workers who transfer to other occupations or exit the labor force, such as to retire.

Employment

The continued use of technology that automates document preparation and other clerical tasks, such as automated phone systems, will result in fewer general office clerks needed to perform this work. In addition, electronic filing systems and file sharing software allow other office workers to do the tasks previously done by general office clerks, further decreasing employment of office clerks. However, there will still be some sustained demand for these workers to handle administrative tasks.

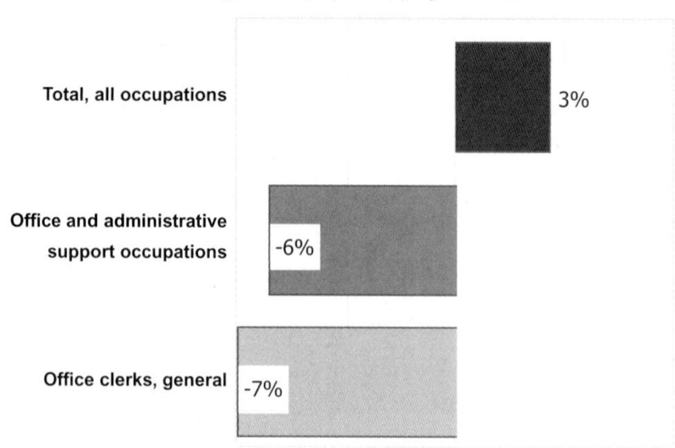

Note: All Occupations includes all occupations in the U.S. Economy.
Source: U.S. Bureau of Labor Statistics, Employment Projections program.

Occupational Title	SOC Code	Employment, 2022	Projected Employment, 2032	Change, 2022-32	
				Percent	Numeric
Office clerks, general	43-9061	2,668,200	2,492,800	-7	-175,400

Contacts for More Information

The *Handbook* does not have contacts for more information for this occupation.

Information Clerks

Summary

Quick Facts: Information Clerks

2022 Median Pay	$38,710 per year $18.61 per hour
Typical Entry-Level Education	See How to Become One
Work Experience in a Related Occupation	None
On-the-job Training	See How to Become One
Number of Jobs, 2022	1,382,600
Job Outlook, 2022-32	-4% (Decline)
Employment Change, 2022-32	-54,000

What Information Clerks Do

Information clerks perform routine clerical duties, maintain records, collect data, and provide information to customers.

Work Environment

Although information clerks are employed in nearly every industry, many work in government agencies, hotels, and healthcare facilities. Most information clerks work full time.

How to Become an Information Clerk

Information clerks typically need a high school diploma and learn their skills on the job. Some employers may prefer to hire candidates with some college education or an associate's degree, depending on the occupation.

Pay

The median annual wage for information clerks was $38,710 in May 2022.

Job Outlook

Overall employment of information clerks is projected to decline 4 percent from 2022 to 2032.

Despite declining employment, about 154,100 openings for information clerks are projected each year, on average, over the decade. All of those openings are expected to result from the need to replace workers who transfer to other occupations or exit the labor force, such as to retire.

What Information Clerks Do

Information clerks do routine clerical tasks such as maintaining records, collecting data, and providing information to customers.

Information clerks maintain records.

Duties

Information clerks typically do the following:

- Prepare routine reports, claims, bills, or orders
- Collect and record data from customers, staff, and the public
- Answer questions from customers and the public about products or services
- File and maintain paper or electronic records

Information clerks do routine clerical tasks in an organization, business, or government. They use telephones, computers, and other office equipment, such as scanners and shredders.

The following are examples of types of information clerks:

Correspondence clerks respond to inquiries from the public or customers. They prepare standard responses to requests for merchandise, damage claims, delinquent accounts, incorrect billings, or complaints about unsatisfactory service. They may also check the organization's records and type response letters for their supervisors to sign.

Court clerks organize and maintain records for courts of law. They prepare the calendar of cases, also known as the docket, and inform attorneys and witnesses about upcoming court appearances. Court clerks also receive, file, and send court documents.

Reservation and transportation ticket agents issue boarding passes to passengers.

Eligibility interviewers ask questions both in person and over the phone to determine whether applicants qualify for government assistance and benefits. They provide information about programs and may refer applicants to other agencies for assistance.

File clerks maintain electronic or paper records. They enter and retrieve data, organize records, and file documents. In organizations with electronic filing systems, file clerks scan and upload documents.

Hotel, motel, and resort desk clerks, also called *front desk clerks*, provide customer service to guests at the establishment's front desk. They check guests in and out, assign rooms, and process payments. They also keep occupancy records; take, confirm, or change room reservations; and provide information about the hotel's policies and services. In addition, front desk clerks answer phone calls, take and deliver messages for guests, and handle guests' requests and complaints.

Human resources assistants provide administrative support to human resources managers. They maintain personnel records on employees, including their addresses, employment history, and performance evaluations. They may post information about job openings and compile candidates' résumé for review.

Interviewers ask questions over the phone, in person, through mail, or online. They use the information to complete forms, applications, or questionnaires for market research surveys, census forms, and medical histories. Interviewers typically follow set procedures and questionnaires to get specific information.

License clerks process applications for licenses and permits, including administering tests and collecting fees. They determine whether applicants are qualified to receive a particular license or must submit additional documentation. They also maintain records of applications received and licenses issued.

Municipal clerks provide administrative support for town or city governments by maintaining government records. They record, file, and distribute minutes of town or city council meetings to local officials and staff and help prepare for elections. They may also answer information requests from local, state, and federal officials and the public.

Order clerks receive requests from customers and process their payments, which may involve entering the customer address and payment method into the order-entry system. They also answer questions about prices and shipping.

Reservation and transportation ticket agents and travel clerks take and confirm passengers' bookings for hotels and transportation. They also sell and issue tickets and answer questions about itineraries, rates, and tours. Ticket agents who work at airports and railroads also check bags and issue boarding passes to passengers.

Work Environment

Information clerks held about 1.4 million jobs in 2022. Employment in the detailed occupations that make up information clerks was distributed as follows:

Hotel desk clerks may work evenings, weekends, and holidays.

Hotel, motel, and resort desk clerks	257,700
Interviewers, except eligibility and loan	175,400
Court, municipal, and license clerks	170,600
Information and record clerks, all other	161,100
Eligibility interviewers, government programs	157,500
Order clerks	132,800
Reservation and transportation ticket agents and travel clerks	123,000
Human resources assistants, except payroll and timekeeping	107,600
File clerks	91,100
Correspondence clerks	6,000

The largest employers of information clerks were as follows:

Traveler accommodation	17%
Healthcare and social assistance	12
State government, excluding education and hospitals	8
Transportation and warehousing	8
Federal government	7

Information clerks work in nearly every industry. Although most clerks work in offices, interviewers may travel to applicants' locations to meet with them.

The work of information clerks who provide customer service can be stressful, particularly when dealing with dissatisfied customers.

Reservation and transportation ticket agents at airports or shipping counters lift and maneuver heavy luggage or packages, which may weigh up to 100 pounds.

Injuries and Illnesses

Reservation and transportation ticket agents and travel clerks have one of the highest rates of injuries and illnesses of all occupations. Lifting and maneuvering heavy luggage or packages may lead to sprains, strains, or overexertion. To avoid injuries, these workers must follow procedures, such as protocols for safe lifting.

Work Schedules

Most information clerks work full time. However, part-time work is common for hotel clerks and file clerks.

Clerks in lodging and transportation establishments that are open around the clock may work evenings, weekends, and holidays.

How to Become an Information Clerk

Information clerks typically need a high school diploma and learn their skills on the job.

Education

Although candidates for most of these positions usually qualify with a high school diploma, human resources assistants generally need an associate's degree. Regardless of whether they pursue a degree, courses in word processing and spreadsheet applications are particularly helpful.

Training

Most information clerks receive short-term on-the-job training, usually lasting a few weeks. Training typically covers clerical procedures and the use of computer applications. Those employed in government receive training that may last several months and includes learning about government programs and regulations.

Information clerks must be comfortable using computers.

Advancement

Some information clerks may advance to other administrative positions with more responsibilities, such as secretaries and administrative assistants. With completion of a bachelor's degree, some human resources assistants may become human resources specialists.

Important Qualities

Communication skills. Information clerks must be able to explain policies and procedures clearly to customers and the public.

Integrity. Information clerks, particularly human resources assistants, have access to confidential information. They must be trusted to adhere to the applicable confidentiality and privacy rules governing the dissemination of this information.

Interpersonal skills. Information clerks who work with the public and customers must understand and communicate information effectively to establish positive relationships.

Organizational skills. Information clerks must be able to retrieve files and other important information quickly and efficiently.

Pay

The median annual wage for information clerks was $38,710 in May 2022. The median wage is the wage at which half the workers in an occupation earned more than that amount and half earned less. The lowest 10 percent earned less than $27,140, and the highest 10 percent earned more than $61,850.

Median annual wages for information clerks in May 2022 were as follows:

Eligibility interviewers, government programs	$49,230
Human resources assistants, except payroll and timekeeping	45,930
Information and record clerks, all other	44,720
Court, municipal, and license clerks	44,140
Reservation and transportation ticket agents and travel clerks	39,160
Correspondence clerks	38,700
Interviewers, except eligibility and loan	38,700
Order clerks	38,060
File clerks	37,290
Hotel, motel, and resort desk clerks	28,910

In May 2022, the median annual wages for information clerks in the top industries in which they worked were as follows:

Federal government	$49,380
State government, excluding education and hospitals	44,740
Transportation and warehousing	39,410
Healthcare and social assistance	39,130
Traveler accommodation	28,900

Most information clerks work full time. However, part-time work is common for hotel clerks and file clerks.

Clerks who work in lodging and transportation establishments that are open around the clock may work evenings, weekends, and holidays.

Job Outlook

Overall employment of information clerks is projected to decline 4 percent from 2022 to 2032.

Despite declining employment, about 154,100 openings for information clerks are projected each year, on average, over the decade. All of those openings are expected to result from the need to replace workers who transfer to other occupations or exit the labor force, such as to retire.

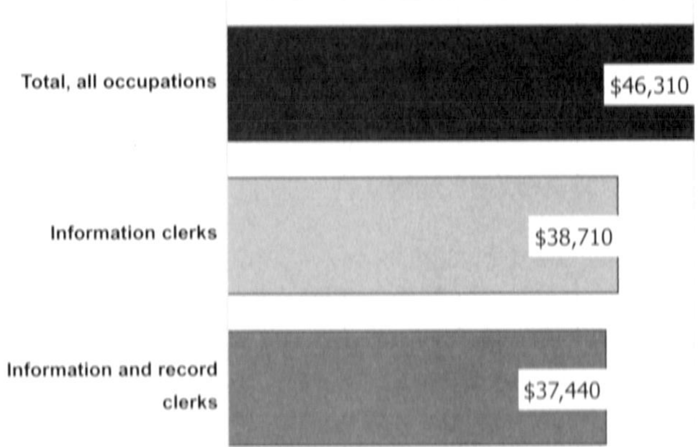

Note: All Occupations includes all occupations in the U.S. Economy.
Source: U.S. Bureau of Labor Statistics, Occupational Employment and Wage Statistics.

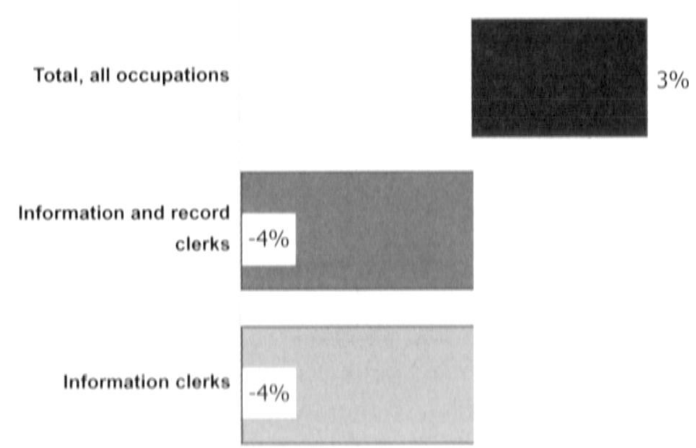

Note: All Occupations includes all occupations in the U.S. Economy.
Source: U.S. Bureau of Labor Statistics, Employment Projections program.

Employment

Projected employment of information clerks varies by occupation (see table). The increased use of online ordering and reservation systems and self-service ticketing kiosks will limit demand for these workers.

Local governments will continue to need court, municipal, and license clerks to do tasks such as prepare case dockets, draft agendas, and issue permits. Eligibility interviewers will continue to be needed to determine whether government assistance, such as unemployment or Social Security benefits, is appropriate for people applying for it. However, the adoption of technology in data collection and document processing, which enables people to submit online responses and documents, will likely limit demand for most other interviewers and clerks.

Occupational Title	SOC Code	Employment, 2022	Projected Employment, 2032	Change, 2022-32	
				Percent	Numeric
Information clerks	—	1,382,600	1,328,600	-4	-54,000
Correspondence clerks	43-4021	6,000	5,600	-6	-400
Court, municipal, and license clerks	43-4031	170,600	175,700	3	5,100
Eligibility interviewers, government programs	43-4061	157,500	161,000	2	3,500
File clerks	43-4071	91,100	76,500	-16	-14,600
Hotel, motel, and resort desk clerks	43-4081	257,700	251,100	-3	-6,600
Interviewers, except eligibility and loan	43-4111	175,400	157,600	-10	-17,700
Order clerks	43-4151	132,800	108,600	-18	-24,200
Human resources assistants, except payroll and timekeeping	43-4161	107,600	102,400	-5	-5,200
Reservation and transportation ticket agents and travel clerks	43-4181	123,000	124,600	1	1,600
Information and record clerks, all other	43-4199	161,100	165,400	3	4,300

Contacts for More Information

For more information, visit

➤ Society for Human Resource Management

Material Recording Clerks

Summary

Quick Facts: Material Recording Clerks	
2022 Median Pay	$40,490 per year $19.47 per hour
Typical Entry-Level Education	High school diploma or equivalent
Work Experience in a Related Occupation	None
On-the-job Training	See How to Become One
Number of Jobs, 2022	1,315,200
Job Outlook, 2022-32	-4% (Decline)
Employment Change, 2022-32	-57,300

What Material Recording Clerks Do

Material recording clerks track product information in order to keep businesses and supply chains on schedule.

Work Environment

Most material recording clerks work full time.

How to Become a Material Recording Clerk

Material recording clerks typically need a high school diploma or equivalent and are trained on the job.

Pay

The median annual wage for material recording clerks was $40,490 in May 2022.

Job Outlook

Overall employment of material recording clerks is projected to decline 4 percent from 2022 to 2032.

Despite declining employment, about 125,300 openings for material recording clerks are projected each year, on average, over the decade. All of those openings are expected to result from the need to replace workers who transfer to other occupations or exit the labor force, such as to retire.

What Material Recording Clerks Do

Material recording clerks track product information in order to keep businesses and supply chains on schedule. They ensure proper scheduling, recordkeeping, and inventory control.

Material recording clerks ensure proper scheduling, recordkeeping, and inventory control.

Shipping, receiving, and inventory clerks track outgoing and incoming shipments.

Duties

Material recording clerks typically do the following:

- Keep records of items shipped, received, or transferred to another location
- Compile reports on various changes in production or inventory
- Organize the assembly, distribution, or delivery of goods to meet production schedules
- Prepare materials for shipping by labeling or checking packages
- Examine products for damage or defects
- Check inventory records for accuracy

Material recording clerks use computers or hand-held devices to keep track of inventory. Sensors and tags enable these electronic tools to automatically detect when and where products are moved, allowing clerks to keep updated reports without manually counting items.

The following are examples of types of material recording clerks:

Production, planning, and expediting clerks manage the flow of information, work, and materials within or among offices in a business. They compile reports on the progress of work and on any production problems that arise. These clerks set workers' schedules, estimate costs, keep track of materials, and write special orders for new materials. They also do general office tasks, such as entering data or distributing mail. Expediting clerks maintain contact with vendors to ensure that supplies and equipment are shipped on time.

Shipping, receiving, and inventory clerks keep track of and record outgoing and incoming shipments. Clerks may scan barcodes with handheld devices or use radio frequency identification (RFID) scanners to keep track of inventory. They check to see whether shipment orders were processed correctly in their company's computer system. They also compute freight costs, prepare invoices, and write inventory reports. Some clerks move goods from the warehouse to the loading dock.

Material and product inspecting clerks weigh, measure, check, sample, and keep records on materials, supplies, and equipment that enters a warehouse. They verify the quantity and quality of items they are assigned to examine, checking for defects and recording what they find. They use scales, counting devices, and calculators. Some decide what to do about a defective product, such as to scrap it or send it back to the factory to be repaired.

Work Environment

Material recording clerks held about 1.3 million jobs in 2022. Employment in the detailed occupations that make up material recording clerks was distributed as follows:

Shipping, receiving, and inventory clerks	862,900
Production, planning, and expediting clerks	396,800
Weighers, measurers, checkers, and samplers, recordkeeping	55,600

The largest employers of material recording clerks were as follows:

Manufacturing	27%
Retail trade	17
Wholesale trade	14
Transportation and warehousing	14
Temporary help services	4

Material recording clerks usually work in an office inside a warehouse or manufacturing plant.

These workers also may spend time on the warehouse or plant floor to handle packages or automatic equipment, such as conveyor systems.

Injuries and Illnesses

Some material recording clerks may need to lift heavy items and to bend frequently, which may lead to injury. Using proper lifting techniques helps to reduce the risk of harm.

Many material recording clerks work in an office inside a warehouse or manufacturing plant.

Work Schedules

Most material recording clerks work full time. Some work nights and weekends or holidays.

How to Become a Material Recording Clerk

Material recording clerks typically need a high school diploma or equivalent and are trained on the job.

Education

Material recording clerks typically need a high school diploma or equivalent.

Some employers prefer to hire production, planning, and expediting clerks who have a college degree.

Training

Material recording clerks usually learn on the job. Training for most material recording clerks lasts up to 1 month. Production, planning, and expediting clerks may train for up to 6 months.

Material recording clerks first may learn to count stock and mark inventory and then move on to more difficult tasks, such as recordkeeping. Production clerks first typically learn how their company operates before they write production and work schedules.

Workers learn safety rules as part of their training. Many of these rules are standardized through the Occupational Safety and Health Administration (OSHA).

Advancement

With additional training or education, material recording clerks may advance to other positions, such as purchasing agent, within their company.

Important Qualities

Communication skills. Material recording clerks are frequently in contact with suppliers, vendors, or managers and need to convey their company's needs effectively.

Material recording clerks learn on the job from an experienced worker.

Customer-service skills. Material recording clerks may interact with customers in order to respond to problems or complaints.

Detail oriented. Material and product inspecting clerks must pay attention to detail when checking items for defects, some of which are small and difficult to spot.

Math skills. Material recording clerks may need to calculate shipping costs or take measurements.

Pay

The median annual wage for material recording clerks was $40,490 in May 2022. The median wage is the wage at which half the workers in an occupation earned more than that amount and half earned less. The lowest 10 percent earned less than $29,930, and the highest 10 percent earned more than $64,540.

Median annual wages for material recording clerks in May 2022 were as follows:

Production, planning, and expediting clerks	$50,630
Weighers, measurers, checkers, and samplers, recordkeeping	39,950
Shipping, receiving, and inventory clerks	37,760

In May 2022, the median annual wages for material recording clerks in the top industries in which they worked were as follows:

Manufacturing	$44,470
Transportation and warehousing	40,960
Wholesale trade	39,330
Retail trade	35,310
Temporary help services	34,150

Most material recording clerks work full time. Some work nights and weekends or holidays.

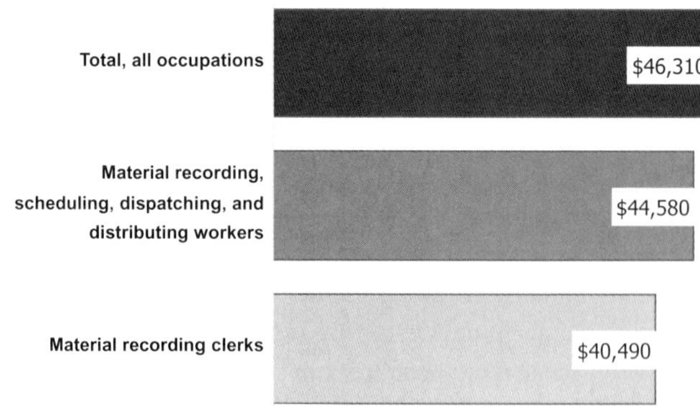

Note: All Occupations includes all occupations in the U.S. Economy.
Source: U.S. Bureau of Labor Statistics, Occupational Employment and Wage Statistics.

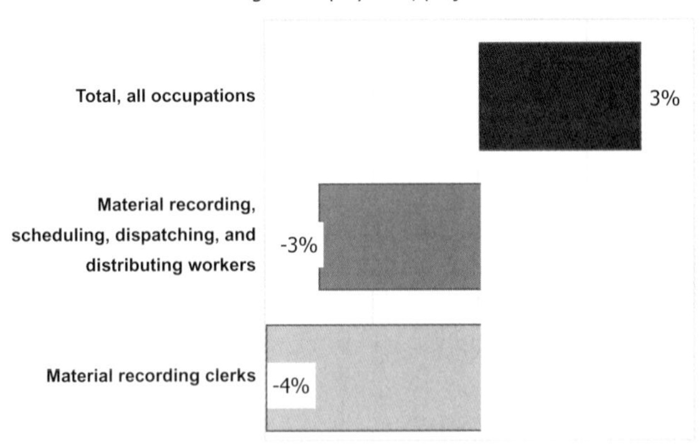

Note: All Occupations includes all occupations in the U.S. Economy.
Source: U.S. Bureau of Labor Statistics, Employment Projections program.

Job Outlook

Overall employment of material recording clerks is projected to decline 4 percent from 2022 to 2032.

Despite declining employment, about 125,300 openings for material recording clerks are projected each year, on average, over the decade. All of those openings are expected to result from the need to replace workers who transfer to other occupations or exit the labor force, such as to retire.

Employment

Projected employment of material recording clerks varies by occupation (see table). As e-commerce continues to grow, companies are expanding their use of automated storage and retrieval tools to meet rising demand for products and for faster delivery. These types of technologies, including radio frequency identification (RFID) tags and collaborative robots, will improve efficiencies of many warehouse operations. Demand for shipping, receiving, and inventory clerks may be limited as use of technology expands and increases productivity of some manual tasks, improving efficiency.

However, employment of production, planning, and expediting clerks is projected to increase because their tasks remain difficult to automate.

Occupational Title	SOC Code	Employment, 2022	Projected Employment, 2032	Change, 2022-32	
				Percent	Numeric
Material recording clerks	—	1,315,200	1,257,900	-4	-57,300
Production, planning, and expediting clerks	43-5061	396,800	413,300	4	16,500
Shipping, receiving, and inventory clerks	43-5071	862,900	790,600	-8	-72,200
Weighers, measurers, checkers, and samplers, recordkeeping	43-5111	55,600	54,000	-3	-1,600

Contacts for More Information

For more information, visit

- MHI
- Warehousing Education and Research Council

Postal Service Workers

Summary

Quick Facts: Postal Service Workers

2022 Median Pay	$53,680 per year $25.81 per hour
Typical Entry-Level Education	No formal educational credential
Work Experience in a Related Occupation	None
On-the-job Training	Short-term on-the-job training
Number of Jobs, 2022	504,300
Job Outlook, 2022-32	-8% (Decline)
Employment Change, 2022-32	-39,000

What Postal Service Workers Do

Postal service workers sell postage and related products and collect, sort, and deliver mail.

Work Environment

Postal service clerks and mail sorters, processors, and processing machine operators work indoors, typically in a post office. Mail carriers mostly work outdoors, delivering mail.

Postal service workers must carefully sort mail

How to Become a Postal Service Worker

Although no formal education is typically required to enter these occupations, most postal service workers have at least a high school diploma. All applicants for these jobs must pass a written exam.

Pay

The median annual wage for postal service workers was $53,680 in May 2022.

Job Outlook

Overall employment of postal service workers is projected to decline 8 percent from 2022 to 2032.

Despite declining employment, about 34,400 openings for postal service workers are projected each year, on average, over the decade. All of those openings are expected to result from the need to replace workers who transfer to other occupations or exit the labor force, such as to retire.

What Postal Service Workers Do

Postal service workers sell postage and related products and collect, sort, and deliver mail.

Duties

Postal service workers typically do the following:

Carriers deliver mail to homes and businesses.

- Collect letters and parcels
- Sort incoming letters and parcels
- Sell stamps and other postal products
- Get customer signatures for registered, certified, and insured mail
- Operate various types of postal equipment
- Distribute letters and parcels

Postal service workers receive and process mail for delivery to homes, businesses, and post office boxes. Workers are classified based on the type of work they do.

The following are examples of types of postal service workers:

Postal service clerks, also called *sales and services distribution associates*, sell stamps, money orders, mailing envelopes and boxes, and other postal products in post offices. These workers register, certify, and insure mail, calculate and collect postage, and answer questions about postal matters. They also may help sort mail.

Postal service mail carriers deliver mail to homes and businesses in cities, towns, and rural areas. Most travel established routes, delivering and collecting mail. Mail carriers cover their routes by foot or vehicle or a combination of both. Some mail carriers collect money for postage due. Others, particularly in rural areas, sell postal products, such as stamps and money orders. Mail carriers also answer customers' questions about postal regulations and services and, upon request, provide change-of-address cards and other postal forms.

Postal service mail sorters, processors, and processing machine operators, also called *mail handlers and processing clerks,* prepare incoming and outgoing mail for distribution at post offices and mail processing centers. They load and unload postal trucks and move mail around processing centers. They also operate and adjust mail processing and sorting machinery.

Work Environment

Postal service workers held about 504,300 jobs in 2022. Employment in the detailed occupations that make up postal service workers was distributed as follows:

Postal service mail carriers	314,500
Postal service mail sorters, processors, and processing machine operators	115,000
Postal service clerks	74,800

The largest employers of postal service workers were as follows:

Postal service	100%

Postal service clerks and mail sorters, processors, and processing machine operators work indoors, typically in a post office. Mail carriers mostly work outdoors, delivering mail in all kinds of weather. Although mail carriers face many natural hazards,

Although mail carriers work outdoors, sorters and processors typically work indoors.

such as extreme temperatures and wet or icy roads and sidewalks, the work is not especially dangerous. However, they may experience repetitive stress injuries from lifting and bending.

Work Schedules

Most postal service workers work full time, and some work more than 40 hours per week. Because mail usually is delivered 6 days a week, many postal service workers must work on Saturdays. Some also work on Sundays.

How to Become a Postal Service Worker

To enter these occupations, postal service workers typically need no formal educational credential. However, job candidates must pass a written exam as part of the application process. The exam covers four areas: address cross comparison, forms completion, memory and coding, and personal characteristics and experience. For more information, contact the post office or mail processing center where you want to work.

Postal service workers must meet certain employment qualifications. For example, they must be at least 18 years old, or 16 years old with a high school diploma; be a U.S. citizen or permanent resident; and pass a criminal background check, a medical assessment, and a drug screening. They also may be asked to show that they can lift and handle heavy mail sacks.

Mail carriers must receive a passing grade on a road test.

Education

Although no formal educational credential is typically required to enter these occupations, most postal service workers have at least a high school diploma or the equivalent.

Training

Newly hired postal service workers receive on-the-job training that usually lasts a few weeks. Beginning carriers may work alongside an experienced carrier.

Licenses, Certifications, and Registrations

Postal service workers who operate a motor vehicle need a driver's license. In addition, mail carriers must have a safe driving record and pass a road test before driving on the job.

Important Qualities

Customer-service skills. Postal service workers, particularly clerks, regularly interact with customers. As a result, they must be courteous and tactful and provide good client service.

Detail oriented. Postal service workers must pay attention to detail to ensure accuracy in sorting and delivering mail.

Physical stamina. Postal service workers may need to stand or walk for long periods.

Physical strength. Postal service workers must be able to lift and carry heavy mail bags and parcels.

Time-management skills. Postal service workers often need to prioritize and handle several tasks at once.

Visual ability. To have a driver's license, postal service workers must be able to pass a state vision test.

Pay

The median annual wage for postal service workers was $53,680 in May 2022. The median wage is the wage at which

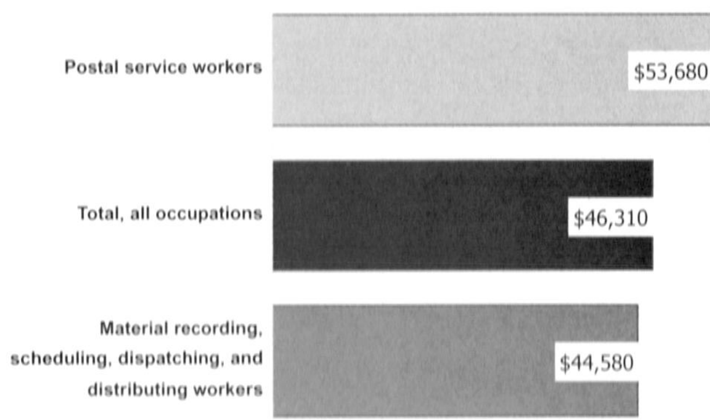

Note: All Occupations includes all occupations in the U.S. Economy.
Source: U.S. Bureau of Labor Statistics, Occupational Employment and Wage Statistics.

half the workers in an occupation earned more than that amount and half earned less. The lowest 10 percent earned less than $39,640, and the highest 10 percent earned more than $71,340.

Median annual wages for postal service workers in May 2022 were as follows:

Postal service clerks	$56,200
Postal service mail carriers	54,250
Postal service mail sorters, processors, and processing machine operators	49,130

In May 2022, the median annual wages for postal service workers in the top industries in which they worked were as follows:

Postal service	$53,680

Most postal service workers work full time, and some work more than 40 hours per week. Because mail usually is delivered 6 days a week, many postal service workers must work on Saturdays. Some also work on Sundays.

Job Outlook

Overall employment of postal service workers is projected to decline 8 percent from 2022 to 2032.

Despite declining employment, about 34,400 openings for postal service workers are projected each year, on average, over the decade. All of those openings are expected to result from the need to replace workers who transfer to other occupations or exit the labor force, such as to retire.

Employment

The postal service likely will need fewer workers because new mail sorting technology can read text and automatically sort, forward, and process mail. The greater use of online services to pay bills and the increased use of online communications should also reduce the need for sorting and processing workers.

Meanwhile, the amount of time carriers save on sorting letter mail and flat mail will allow them to increase the size of their routes, which should reduce the need to hire more carriers. In addition, the postal service is adopting more centralized mail delivery, such as the use of cluster mailboxes, to cut down on the number of door-to-door deliveries.

Postal Service Workers

Percent change in employment, projected 2022-32

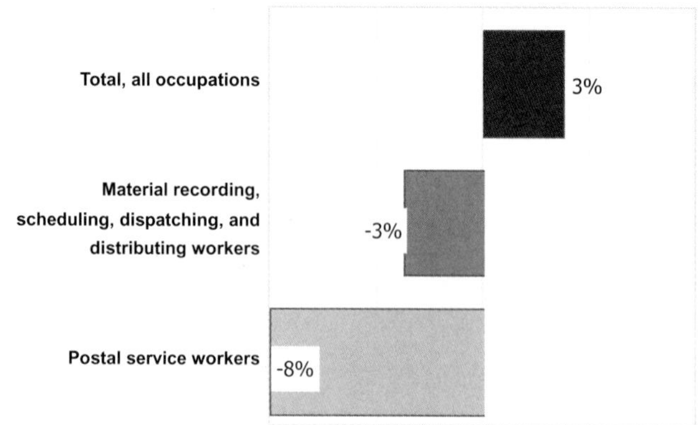

Note: All Occupations includes all occupations in the U.S. Economy.
Source: U.S. Bureau of Labor Statistics, Employment Projections program.

Occupational Title	SOC Code	Employment, 2022	Projected Employment, 2032	Change, 2022-32	
				Percent	Numeric
Postal service workers	43-5050	504,300	465,300	-8	-39,000
Postal service clerks	43-5051	74,800	69,800	-7	-5,000
Postal service mail carriers	43-5052	314,500	293,500	-7	-21,000
Postal service mail sorters, processors, and processing machine operators	43-5053	115,000	102,100	-11	-13,000

Contacts for More Information

For more information, visit

➤ United States Postal Service

Public Safety Telecommunicators

Summary

Quick Facts: Public Safety Telecommunicators	
2022 Median Pay	$46,900 per year $22.55 per hour
Typical Entry-Level Education	High school diploma or equivalent
Work Experience in a Related Occupation	None
On-the-job Training	Moderate-term on-the-job training
Number of Jobs, 2022	99,500
Job Outlook, 2022-32	3% (As fast as average)
Employment Change, 2022-32	3,400

What Public Safety Telecommunicators Do

Public safety telecommunicators, including *911 operators* and *fire dispatchers*, answer emergency and nonemergency calls and provide resources to assist those in need.

Work Environment

Public safety telecommunicators work in emergency communication centers called public safety answering points (PSAPs). These workers usually have shifts that include evenings, weekends, and holidays to provide round-the-clock coverage. The pressure to respond quickly and calmly in alarming situations may be stressful.

How to Become a Public Safety Telecommunicator

Public safety telecommunicators typically need a high school diploma to enter the occupation and then are trained on the job. Many states and localities require these workers to become certified.

Pay

The median annual wage for public safety telecommunicators was $46,900 in May 2022.

Job Outlook

Employment of public safety telecommunicators is projected to grow 3 percent from 2022 to 2032, about as fast as the average for all occupations.

About 10,400 openings for public safety telecommunicators are projected each year, on average, over the decade. Many of those openings are expected to result from the need to replace workers who transfer to different occupations or exit the labor force, such as to retire.

What Public Safety Telecommunicators Do

Public safety telecommunicators, including *911 operators* and *fire dispatchers*, answer emergency and nonemergency calls and provide resources to assist those in need.

Duties

Public safety telecommunicators typically do the following:

- Answer 9-1-1 emergency and nonemergency requests from different sources, such as phone calls, text messages, social media, and alarm systems
- Determine the type of emergency and its location and decide the appropriate response based on agency procedures
- Relay information to the appropriate first-responder agency
- Coordinate the dispatch of emergency response personnel
- Give instructions to the person in need before emergency services arrive
- Monitor and track the status of police, fire, and ambulance units
- Synchronize responses with other area communication centers
- Keep detailed records of calls

Public safety telecommunicators answer requests from people who need help. Depending on the situation, these workers may contact police, firefighters, emergency services, or a

Public safety telecommunicators take emergency and nonemergency requests.

Public safety telecommunicators monitor and track the status of police, fire, and ambulance units.

combination of the three. Telecommunicators take both emergency and nonemergency requests.

Public safety telecommunicators must stay calm while collecting vital information from callers to determine the severity and location of a situation. They also must select and clear a radio channel to establish a stable connection with the appropriate first-responder agency, such as the police or fire department. Telecommunicators then monitor that channel to ensure that resources are provided safely and efficiently.

Public safety telecommunicators use computers to log important facts, such as the nature of the incident and the caller's name. These computer systems screen calls to identify the delivery method, such as phone, text, or video. Telecommunicators then gather information about the location of the person in need.

Public safety telecommunicators are trained to provide instruction over the phone. They often must guide callers on what to do before responders arrive. For example, they might help the caller provide first aid at the scene until emergency medical services arrive. At other times, telecommunicators may advise callers on how to remain safe while waiting for assistance.

Work Environment

Public safety telecommunicators held about 99,500 jobs in 2022. The largest employers of public safety telecommunicators were as follows:

Local government, excluding education and hospitals	82%
State government, excluding education and hospitals	5
Ambulance services	5
Colleges, universities, and professional schools; state, local, and private	3
Hospitals; state, local, and private	2

Public safety telecommunicators typically work in communication centers, often called public safety answering points (PSAPs). Some work for unified communication centers, where they answer calls for all types of emergency services, while others work specifically for police or fire departments.

Work as a public safety telecommunicator may be stressful. These workers often have long shifts, take many calls, and deal with troubling situations. Some calls require them to assist people who are in life-threatening situations, and the pressure to respond quickly and calmly may be demanding.

Work Schedules

Most public safety telecommunicators work full time, often in 8- to 12-hour shifts.

Because emergencies happen at any time, public safety telecommunicators are needed to staff PSAPs around the clock. They may be required to work shifts that are outside standard business hours, such as evenings, weekends, and holidays.

How to Become a Public Safety Telecommunicator

Public safety telecommunicators typically need a high school diploma to enter the occupation and then are trained on the job. Many states and localities require these workers to become certified.

In addition, candidates usually must pass an exam and a typing test. In some instances, candidates may need to pass a background check, lie detector and drug tests, and tests for hearing and vision.

The ability to communicate in another language, such as Spanish or American Sign Language, may be helpful.

Education

Public safety telecommunicators typically need a high school diploma to enter the occupation.

Public safety telecommunicators typically work in communication centers, often called public safety answering points (PSAPs).

Public safety telecommunicators usually must pass a typing test.

Training

Public safety telecommunicators typically receive training on the job. Training requirements and length of training vary by state and locality.

For example, some states require 40 or more hours of training, and others require continuing education every 2 to 3 years. Still other states do not mandate any specific training, leaving individual localities and agencies to structure their own requirements and conduct their own courses.

Training programs typically involve an instructional course and may include on-the-job demonstrations. Training may be followed by a probationary period of about 1 year. However, the period may vary by agency, as there is no national standard governing training or probation.

Training covers a variety of topics, such as local geography, agency protocols, and standard procedures. Public safety telecommunicators learn how to use equipment such as computer-aided dispatch systems, which consist of several monitors that may display call information, maps, and video. They also may receive training to prepare for high-risk incidents, such as child abductions and suicidal callers.

Some agencies have their own training programs for public safety telecommunicators; others use training from separate associations. Agencies often use standards from the Association of Public-Safety Communications Officials (APCO International), the National Emergency Number Association (NENA), and the International Academies of Emergency Dispatch (IAED) as a guideline for their own training programs.

Licenses, Certifications, and Registrations

Many states and localities require public safety telecommunicators to be certified. The Association of Public-Safety Communications Officials (APCO) provides a list of states requiring training and certification. One certification is the Emergency Medical Dispatcher (EMD) certification, which enables dispatchers to give medical assistance over the phone.

Public safety telecommunicators may choose to pursue additional certifications, such as the National Emergency Number Association's Emergency Number Professional (ENP) certification or APCO's Registered Public-Safety Leader (RPL) certification, which demonstrate their leadership skills and knowledge.

Advancement

Training and additional certifications may help public safety telecommunicators become senior dispatchers or supervisors. Additional education and related work experience may be helpful in advancing to management-level positions.

Important Qualities

Ability to multitask. Public safety telecommunicators must stay calm in order to simultaneously answer calls, collect vital information, coordinate responders, monitor multiple displays, and use a variety of equipment.

Communication skills. Public safety telecommunicators work with law enforcement, emergency response teams, and civilians. They must be able to communicate the nature of an emergency effectively and to coordinate the appropriate response.

Decision-making skills. When people call for help, public safety telecommunicators must be able to determine the response dictated by procedures and to work efficiently with the assisting emergency departments.

Empathy. Public safety telecommunicators must be willing to help a range of callers with varying needs. They must be calm, polite, and sympathetic, while also collecting relevant information quickly.

Listening skills. Public safety telecommunicators must listen carefully to collect relevant details, even though some callers might have trouble speaking because of anxiety or stress.

Typing skills. Public safety telecommunicators enter the details of calls into computers; typing speed and accuracy are essential when responding to emergencies.

Pay

The median annual wage for public safety telecommunicators was $46,900 in May 2022. The median wage is the wage at which half the workers in an occupation earned more than that amount and half earned less. The lowest 10 percent earned less than $31,090, and the highest 10 percent earned more than $70,730.

In May 2022, the median annual wages for public safety telecommunicators in the top industries in which they worked were as follows:

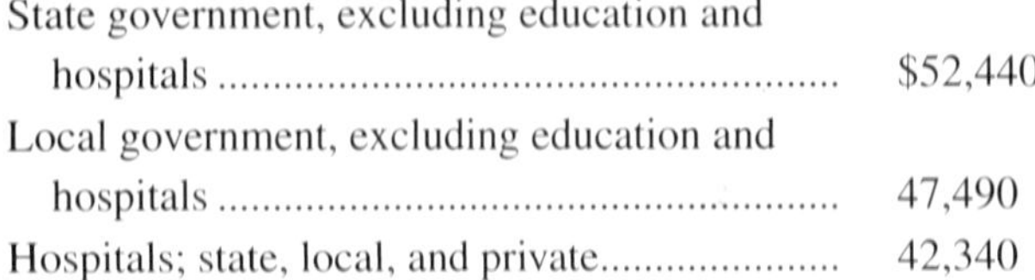

State government, excluding education and hospitals	$52,440
Local government, excluding education and hospitals	47,490
Hospitals; state, local, and private	42,340

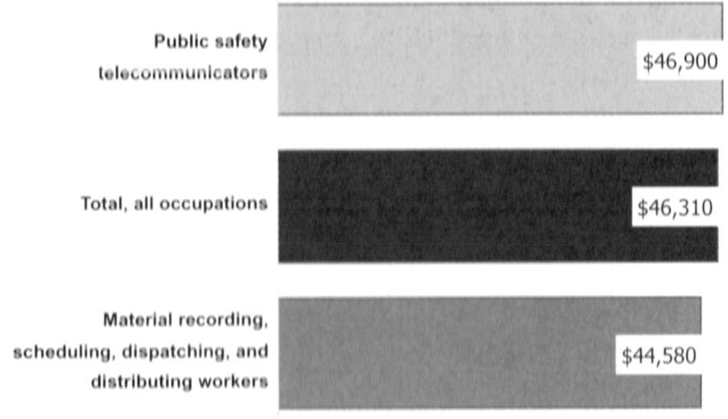

Note: All Occupations includes all occupations in the U.S. Economy.
Source: U.S. Bureau of Labor Statistics, Occupational Employment and Wage Statistics.

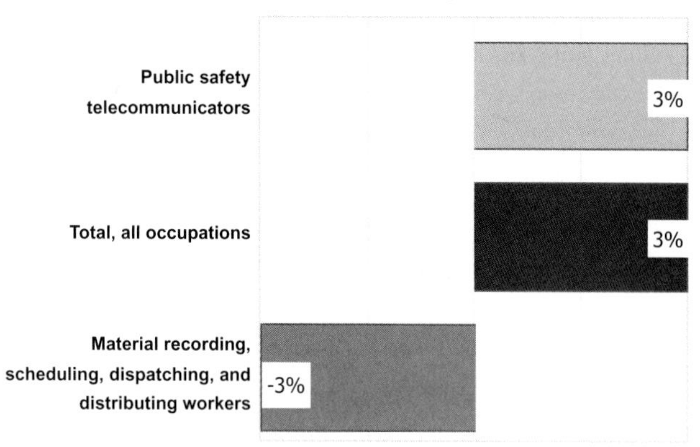

Note: All Occupations includes all occupations in the U.S. Economy.
Source: U.S. Bureau of Labor Statistics, Employment Projections program.

Colleges, universities, and professional schools; state, local, and private	41,080
Ambulance services	38,480

Most public safety telecommunicators work full time, often in 8- to 12-hour shifts.

Because emergencies happen at any time, public safety telecommunicators are needed to staff PSAPs around the clock. They may be required to work shifts that are outside standard business hours, such as evenings, weekends, and holidays.

Job Outlook

Employment of public safety telecommunicators is projected to grow 3 percent from 2022 to 2032, about as fast as the average for all occupations.

About 10,400 openings for public safety telecommunicators are projected each year, on average, over the decade. Many of those openings are expected to result from the need to replace workers who transfer to different occupations or exit the labor force, such as to retire.

Employment

State and local government budget constraints may limit the number of public safety telecommunicators hired over the projections decade. However, population growth and the commensurate increase in 9-1-1 call volume is expected to create demand for these workers.

Occupational Title	SOC Code	Employment, 2022	Projected Employment, 2032	Change, 2022-32	
				Percent	Numeric
Public safety telecommunicators	43-5031	99,500	102,900	3	3,400

Contacts for More Information

For more information, visit

- Association of Public-Safety Communications Officials
- International Academies of Emergency Dispatch
- International Municipal Signal Association
- National Emergency Number Association

Receptionists

Summary

Quick Facts: Receptionists	
2022 Median Pay	$33,960 per year $16.33 per hour
Typical Entry-Level Education	High school diploma or equivalent
Work Experience in a Related Occupation	None
On-the-job Training	Short-term on-the-job training
Number of Jobs, 2022	1,068,800
Job Outlook, 2022-32	0% (Little or no change)
Employment Change, 2022-32	3,900

What Receptionists Do

Receptionists do tasks such as answering phones, receiving visitors, and providing information about their organization to the public.

Work Environment

Receptionists are employed in nearly every industry.

How to Become a Receptionist

Receptionists typically need a high school diploma or equivalent and good communication skills.

Pay

The median hourly wage for receptionists was $16.33 in May 2022.

Job Outlook

Employment of receptionists is projected to show little or no change from 2022 to 2032.

Despite limited employment growth, about 142,600 openings for receptionists are projected each year, on average, over the decade. Most of those openings are expected to result from the need to replace workers who transfer to different occupations or exit the labor force, such as to retire.

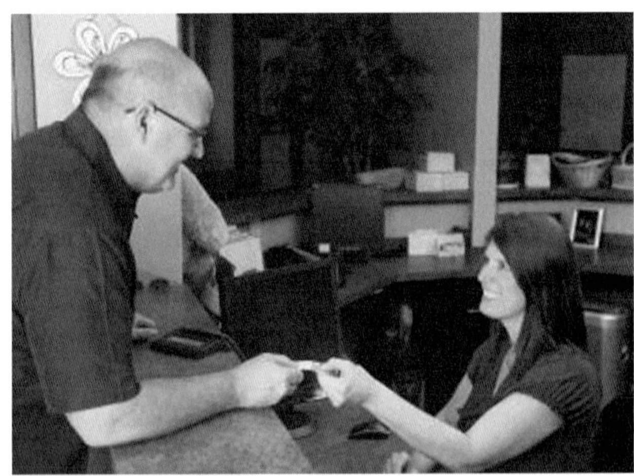

Receptionists provide general information about their organization to visitors.

What Receptionists Do

Receptionists do administrative tasks, such as answering phones, greeting visitors, and providing general information about their organization.

Duties

Receptionists typically do the following:

- Answer the telephone and take messages or forward calls
- Schedule and confirm appointments and maintain calendars
- Greet customers, clients, and other visitors
- Check in visitors and direct or escort them to their destinations
- Inform other employees of visitors' arrivals or cancellations
- Enter customer information into the organization's database
- Copy, file, and maintain paper or electronic documents
- Handle incoming and outgoing correspondence

Receptionists are often the first employee of an organization to have contact with a customer or client. They are responsible for making a good first impression for the organization.

Receptionists' specific responsibilities vary by employer. For example, receptionists in hospitals and doctors' offices may collect patients' personal information and direct patients to the waiting room. Some handle billing and insurance payments.

Receptionists greet patients in hospitals and doctor's offices.

In large corporations and government offices, receptionists may have a security role. For example, they may control access to the organization by issuing visitor passes and escorting visitors to their destination.

Receptionists use telephones, computers, and other office equipment, such as shredders and printers.

Work Environment

Receptionists held about 1.1 million jobs in 2022. The largest employers of receptionists were as follows:

Employer	Percent
Healthcare and social assistance	45%
Professional, scientific, and technical services	11
Personal care services	6
Administrative and support services	4
Religious, grantmaking, civic, professional, and similar organizations	4

Receptionists are employed in nearly every industry.

Receptionists usually work in areas that are visible and accessible to the public and other employees, such as the front desk of a lobby or waiting room.

Some receptionists face stressful situations. They may have to answer numerous phone calls or deal with difficult visitors.

Work Schedules

Most receptionists work full time. Some receptionists, such as those who work in hospitals and nursing homes, work evenings and weekends.

Receptionists are employed in virtually every industry.

Receptionists need to be good at communicating with people.

How to Become a Receptionist

Although hiring requirements vary by industry and employer, receptionists typically need a high school diploma or equivalent and good communication skills.

Education

Receptionists typically need a high school diploma or equivalent, and employers may prefer to hire candidates who have experience with certain computer software. Proficiency in word processing and spreadsheet applications may be particularly helpful.

Training

Most receptionists receive short-term on-the-job training, usually lasting a few days up to a month. Training typically covers procedures for greeting visitors, answering the telephone, and using the computer.

Advancement

Receptionists may advance to other administrative occupations with more responsibilities, such as secretaries and administrative assistants.

Important Qualities

Communication skills. Receptionists must speak and write clearly when providing information and corresponding with customers.

Computer skills. Receptionists should be adept at using computers.

Customer-service skills. Receptionists represent the organization, so they should be courteous, professional, and helpful to customers and the public.

Integrity. Receptionists may handle confidential data, especially in medical and legal offices. They must be trustworthy and protect clients' privacy.

Interpersonal skills. Receptionists should be comfortable interacting with people in different types of situations.

Organizational skills. Receptionists take messages, schedule appointments, and maintain employee files. They need good organizational skills to manage their diverse responsibilities.

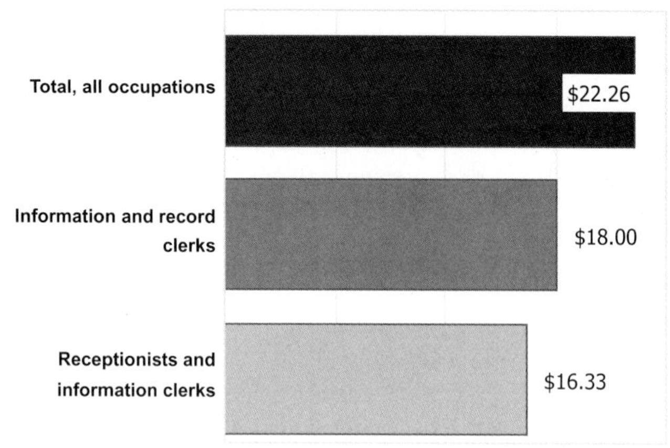

Note: All Occupations includes all occupations in the U.S. Economy.
Source: U.S. Bureau of Labor Statistics, Occupational Employment and Wage Statistics.

Pay

The median hourly wage for receptionists was $16.33 in May 2022. The median wage is the wage at which half the workers in an occupation earned more than that amount and half earned less. The lowest 10 percent earned less than $11.71, and the highest 10 percent earned more than $22.22.

In May 2022, the median hourly wages for receptionists in the top industries in which they worked were as follows:

Healthcare and social assistance	$17.05
Professional, scientific, and technical services	16.69
Administrative and support services	16.19
Religious, grantmaking, civic, professional, and similar organizations	14.98
Personal care services	14.00

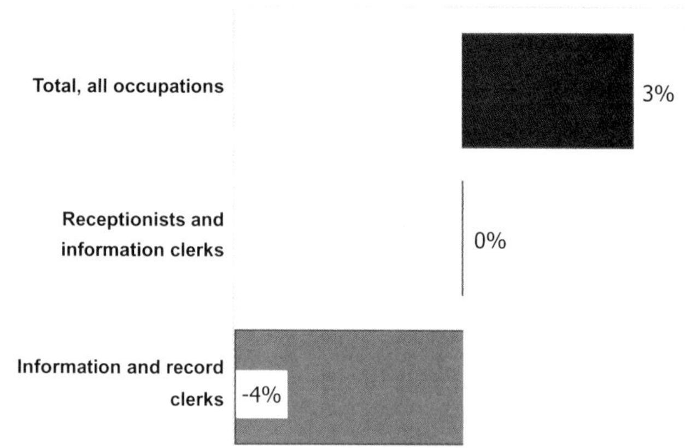

Note: All Occupations includes all occupations in the U.S. Economy.
Source: U.S. Bureau of Labor Statistics, Employment Projections program.

Most receptionists work full time. Receptionists who work in hospitals and nursing homes may work evenings and weekends.

Job Outlook

Employment of receptionists is projected to show little or no change from 2022 to 2032.

Despite limited employment growth, about 142,600 openings for receptionists are projected each year, on average, over the decade. Most of those openings are expected to result from the need to replace workers who transfer to different occupations or exit the labor force, such as to retire.

Employment

Growing healthcare industries are projected to lead demand for receptionists, particularly in physicians' and dentists' offices and in outpatient care centers.

Employment growth of receptionists in other industries is expected to be slower as organizations continue to automate or consolidate administrative functions. For example, many organizations use computer software, websites, mobile applications, or other technology to interact with the public or customers.

Occupational Title	SOC Code	Employment, 2022	Projected Employment, 2032	Change, 2022-32	
				Percent	Numeric
Receptionists and information clerks	43-4171	1,068,800	1,072,700	0	3,900

Contacts for More Information

For more information about training for receptionists and those in other administrative careers, visit

➤ American Society of Administrative Professionals

Secretaries and Administrative Assistants

Summary

Quick Facts: Secretaries and Administrative Assistants	
2022 Median Pay	$44,080 per year $21.19 per hour
Typical Entry-Level Education	High school diploma or equivalent
Work Experience in a Related Occupation	See How to Become One
On-the-job Training	See How to Become One
Number of Jobs, 2022	3,399,200
Job Outlook, 2022-32	-10% (Decline)
Employment Change, 2022-32	-332,600

Secretaries and administrative assistants provide clerical and organizational support.

What Secretaries and Administrative Assistants Do

Secretaries and administrative assistants do routine clerical and organizational tasks.

Work Environment

Although secretaries and administrative assistants work in nearly every industry, about half of all workers in the occupation are employed in healthcare; education; and professional, scientific, and technical services. Most work full time.

How to Become a Secretary or Administrative Assistant

High school graduates who are comfortable using word processing and spreadsheet programs usually qualify for entry-level positions. Although workers typically learn their duties over several weeks on the job, legal and medical secretaries and administrative assistants may need additional training for industry-specific terminology. Executive secretaries and executive administrative assistants typically need several years of related work experience.

Pay

The median annual wage for secretaries and administrative assistants was $44,080 in May 2022.

Job Outlook

Overall employment of secretaries and administrative assistants is projected to decline 10 percent from 2022 to 2032.

Despite declining employment, about 316,000 openings for secretaries and administrative assistants are projected each year, on average, over the decade. All of those openings are expected to result from the need to replace workers who transfer to other occupations or exit the labor force, such as to retire.

Secretaries and administrative assistants maintain databases and filing systems.

What Secretaries and Administrative Assistants Do

Secretaries and administrative assistants do routine clerical and organizational tasks. They arrange files, prepare documents, schedule appointments, and support other staff.

Duties

Secretaries and administrative assistants typically do the following:

- Answer telephones and take messages or transfer calls
- Schedule appointments and update event calendars
- Arrange staff meetings
- Handle incoming and outgoing mail and faxes
- Prepare memos, invoices, or reports
- Edit documents
- Maintain databases and filing systems
- Perform basic bookkeeping

Secretaries and administrative assistants help an organization run efficiently. They use computer software to create spreadsheets; manage databases; and prepare presentations, reports, and documents. They also may negotiate with vendors, buy supplies, and manage stockrooms or corporate libraries. Secretaries and administrative assistants also use videoconferencing and other office equipment. Specific job duties vary by experience, job title, and specialty.

The following are examples of types of secretaries and administrative assistants:

Executive secretaries and executive administrative assistants provide high-level support for an office and for top executives of an organization. They often handle complex responsibilities, such as reviewing incoming documents, conducting research, and preparing reports. Some also supervise clerical staff.

Legal secretaries and administrative assistants must have knowledge of legal terminology and procedures. They prepare summonses, complaints, motions, subpoenas, and other legal documents under the supervision of an attorney or a paralegal. They also review legal journals and help with legal research—for example, by verifying quotes and citations in legal briefs.

Medical secretaries and administrative assistants transcribe dictation and prepare reports or articles for physicians or medical scientists. They also take simple medical histories of patients, arrange for patients to be hospitalized, or process insurance payments. Medical secretaries and administrative assistants need to be familiar with medical terminology and codes, medical records, and hospital or laboratory procedures.

Secretaries and administrative assistants, except legal, medical, and executive form the largest subcategory of secretaries and administrative assistants. They handle administrative activities for offices in almost every sector of the economy, including schools, government, and private corporations. For example, secretaries in schools are often responsible for most of the communications among parents, students, the community, teachers, and school administrators. They schedule appointments, receive visitors, and keep track of student records.

Work Environment

Secretaries and administrative assistants held about 3.4 million jobs in 2022. Employment in the detailed occupations that make up secretaries and administrative assistants was distributed as follows:

Secretaries and administrative assistants, except legal, medical, and executive	2,030,200
Medical secretaries and administrative assistants	696,600
Executive secretaries and executive administrative assistants	511,100
Legal secretaries and administrative assistants	161,400

The largest employers of secretaries and administrative assistants were as follows:

Secretaries and administrative assistants usually work in offices.

Healthcare and social assistance	26%
Educational services; state, local, and private	15
Professional, scientific, and technical services	12
Government	8
Religious, grantmaking, civic, professional, and similar organizations	5

Secretaries and administrative assistants work in nearly every industry.

Most secretaries and administrative assistants work in offices. Some administrative assistants work out of their own homes as *virtual assistants*.

Work Schedules

Most secretaries and administrative assistants work full time.

How to Become a Secretary or Administrative Assistant

High school graduates who are comfortable using word processing and spreadsheet programs typically qualify for entry-level positions. Although workers typically learn their duties over several weeks on the job, legal and medical secretaries and administrative assistants may need additional training to learn industry-specific terminology. Executive secretaries and executive administrative assistants typically need several years of related work experience.

Education

Some community colleges and technical schools offer courses or programs in a variety of secretarial and administrative assistance fields. For example, courses or programs in office procedures focus on working in a business setting; those in industry-specific terminology and practices prepare students for jobs as medical and legal secretaries. Temporary placement agencies also may provide training in word processing, spreadsheet, and database software.

Secretaries and administrative assistants may seek training in word processing, spreadsheet, and database software.

A bachelor's degree typically is not required to become a secretary or administrative assistant. However, some of these workers have a degree in a field such as business, education, or communications. Employers may prefer to hire candidates for executive secretary and executive administrative assistant positions who have taken some college courses or have a bachelor's degree.

Training

Secretaries and administrative assistants typically learn their skills through on-the-job training that lasts a few weeks. During this time, they learn about administrative procedures, including how to prepare documents. Medical and legal secretaries and administrative assistants may train for several months as they learn industry-specific terminology and practices.

Work Experience in a Related Occupation

Executive secretaries and executive administrative assistants typically need several years of work experience in other administrative positions, such as secretaries and general office clerks.

Important Qualities

Decision-making skills. Secretaries and administrative assistants often prioritize tasks and make decisions on their employers' behalf, so good judgment is essential.

Interpersonal skills. Secretaries and administrative assistants interact with clients, customers, or staff. They should communicate effectively and be courteous when interacting with others.

Organizational skills. Secretaries and administrative assistants keep files, folders, and schedules in order so that an office runs efficiently.

Writing skills. Secretaries and administrative assistants write memos and emails when communicating with managers, employees, and customers. Therefore, they must have good grammar, ensure accuracy, and maintain a professional tone.

Pay

The median annual wage for secretaries and administrative assistants was $44,080 in May 2022. The median wage is the wage at which half the workers in an occupation earned more than that amount and half earned less. The lowest 10 percent earned less than $29,930, and the highest 10 percent earned more than $70,380.

Median annual wages for secretaries and administrative assistants in May 2022 were as follows:

Executive secretaries and executive administrative assistants	$65,980
Legal secretaries and administrative assistants	48,780
Secretaries and administrative assistants, except legal, medical, and executive	41,000
Medical secretaries and administrative assistants	38,500

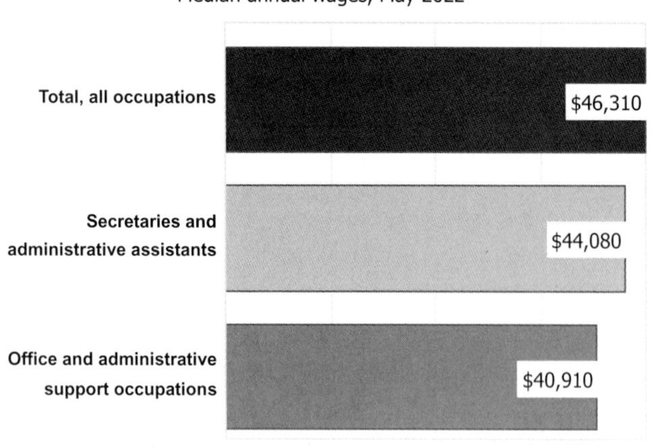

Note: All Occupations includes all occupations in the U.S. Economy. Source: U.S. Bureau of Labor Statistics, Occupational Employment and Wage Statistics.

In May 2022, the median annual wages for secretaries and administrative assistants in the top industries in which they worked were as follows:

Professional, scientific, and technical services ...	$48,190
Government	47,790
Religious, grantmaking, civic, professional, and similar organizations	45,800
Educational services; state, local, and private	45,490
Healthcare and social assistance	39,000

Most secretaries and administrative assistants work full time.

Job Outlook

Overall employment of secretaries and administrative assistants is projected to decline 10 percent from 2022 to 2032.

Despite declining employment, about 316,000 openings for secretaries and administrative assistants are projected each year, on average, over the decade. All of those openings are expected to result from the need to replace workers who transfer to other occupations or exit the labor force, such as to retire.

Employment

Projected employment of secretaries and administrative assistants varies by occupation (see table).

Employment growth is projected for medical secretaries, primarily due to the growth of the healthcare industry. For example, baby boomers will require more medical services as they age. Medical secretaries will be needed to handle administrative tasks related to billing and insurance processing of Medicare and other claims.

Employment is projected to decline for other secretaries and administrative assistants. Technology enables staff in many

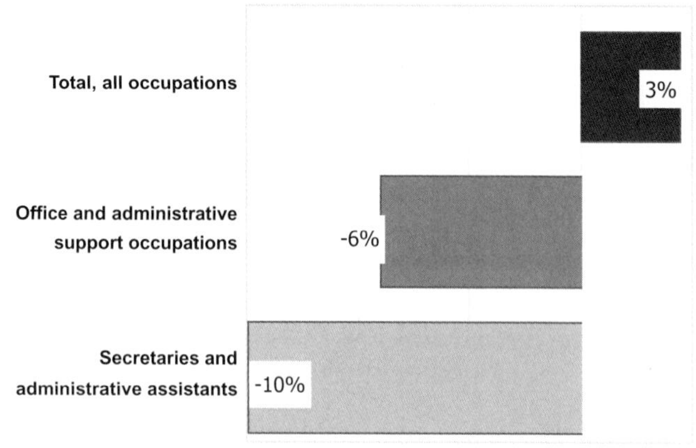

Note: All Occupations includes all occupations in the U.S. Economy. Source: U.S. Bureau of Labor Statistics, Employment Projections program.

organizations to prepare their own documents without the help of secretaries. Additionally, many executive secretaries and executive administrative assistants support more than one manager in an organization, and many managers now do tasks that were previously done by these workers.

Occupational Title	SOC Code	Employment, 2022	Projected Employment, 2032	Change, 2022-32	
				Percent	Numeric
Secretaries and administrative assistants	43-6000	3,399,200	3,066,600	-10	-332,600
Executive secretaries and executive administrative assistants	43-6011	511,100	403,000	-21	-108,100
Legal secretaries and administrative assistants	43-6012	161,400	126,200	-22	-35,300
Medical secretaries and administrative assistants	43-6013	696,600	743,200	7	46,600
Secretaries and administrative assistants, except legal, medical, and executive	43-6014	2,030,200	1,794,300	-12	-235,900

Contacts for More Information

For more information, visit

- American Society of Administrative Professionals
- The Association of Executive and Administrative Professionals
- Executive Support Magazine
- International Association of Administrative Professionals
- NALS
- International Virtual Assistants Association

Tellers

Summary

Quick Facts: Tellers	
2022 Median Pay	$36,380 per year $17.49 per hour
Typical Entry-Level Education	High school diploma or equivalent
Work Experience in a Related Occupation	None
On-the-job Training	Short-term on-the-job training
Number of Jobs, 2022	364,100
Job Outlook, 2022-32	-15% (Decline)
Employment Change, 2022-32	-52,900

What Tellers Do
Tellers are responsible for accurately processing routine transactions at a bank.

Work Environment
Most tellers work in bank branches.

How to Become a Teller
Most tellers have a high school diploma and receive about 1 month of on-the-job training. Some banks do background checks before hiring a new teller.

Pay
The median annual wage for tellers was $36,380 in May 2022.

Job Outlook
Employment of tellers is projected to decline 15 percent from 2022 to 2032.

Despite declining employment, about 29,000 openings for tellers are projected each year, on average, over the decade. All of those openings are expected to result from the need to replace workers who transfer to other occupations or exit the labor force, such as to retire.

What Tellers Do
Tellers are responsible for accurately processing routine transactions at a bank. These transactions include cashing checks, depositing money, and collecting loan payments.

Duties
Tellers typically do the following:

- Count the cash in their drawer at the start of their shift
- Accept checks, cash, and other forms of payment from customers
- Answer questions from customers about their accounts
- Prepare specialized types of funds, such as traveler's checks, savings bonds, and money orders
- Exchange dollars for foreign currency
- Order bank cards and checks for customers
- Record all transactions electronically throughout their shift
- Count the cash in their drawer at the end of their shift and make sure the amounts balance

Tellers are responsible for the safe and accurate handling of the money they process. When cashing a check, they must verify the customer's identity and make sure that the account has enough money to cover the transaction. When counting cash, tellers must be careful not to make errors. If a customer is interested in financial products or services, such as certificates of deposits (CDs) and loans, tellers explain the products and services offered by the bank and refer the customer to the appropriate personnel.

In most banks, tellers record account changes using computers that give them easy access to the customer's financial information. Tellers also can use this information when recommending a new product or service.

Tellers process transactions such as cashing checks, depositing money, and collecting loan payments.

Tellers verify a customer's identity and financial information before processing a transaction.

Head tellers manage teller operations. Besides doing the same tasks as those done by other tellers, they perform some managerial duties, such as setting work schedules or helping less experienced tellers. Because of their experience, head tellers may deal with difficult customer problems, such as errors in customer accounts. Head tellers also go to the vault (where larger amounts of money are kept) and ensure that other tellers have enough cash to cover their shift.

Work Environment

Tellers held about 364,100 jobs in 2022. The largest employers of tellers were as follows:

Credit intermediation and related activities	97%
Management of companies and enterprises	1

The depository credit intermediation industry includes commercial bank branches, where tellers are primarily employed.

Work Schedules

Most tellers work full time.

How to Become a Teller

Most tellers have a high school diploma and receive about 1 month of on-the-job training. Some banks do background checks before hiring a new teller.

Education

Tellers usually need a high school diploma or equivalent. Some tellers may take some college courses, but a degree is rarely required for a job applicant to be hired.

Training

New tellers usually receive brief on-the-job training, typically lasting about 1 month. Normally, a head teller or another experienced teller trains them. During this training, tellers learn how to balance cash drawers and verify signatures. They also learn the computer software that their bank uses and the financial products and services the bank offers.

Most tellers work in bank branches.

Tellers must be friendly, helpful, and patient when interacting with bank customers.

Advancement

Experienced tellers can advance within their bank. They can become head tellers or move to other supervisory positions. Some tellers can advance to other occupations, such as loan officer. They can also move to sales positions.

Important Qualities

Customer-service skills. Tellers spend their day interacting with bank customers. They must be friendly, helpful, and patient. They must be able to understand customer needs and explain service options to their customers.

Detail oriented. Tellers must be sure not to make errors when dealing with customers' money.

Math skills. Because they count and handle large amounts of money, tellers must be good at arithmetic.

Tellers

Median annual wages, May 2022

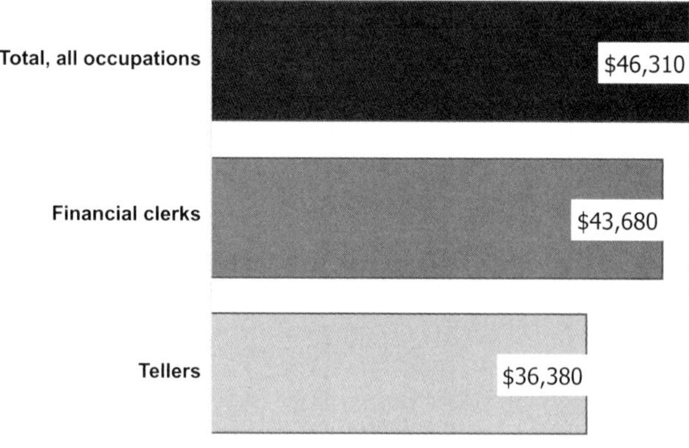

Note: All Occupations includes all occupations in the U.S. Economy.
Source: U.S. Bureau of Labor Statistics, Occupational Employment and Wage Statistics.

Pay

The median annual wage for tellers was $36,380 in May 2022. The median wage is the wage at which half the workers in an occupation earned more than that amount and half earned less. The lowest 10 percent earned less than $28,570, and the highest 10 percent earned more than $46,350.

In May 2022, the median annual wages for tellers in the top industries in which they worked were as follows:

Credit intermediation and related activities	$36,360
Management of companies and enterprises	35,330

Most tellers work full time.

Job Outlook

Employment of tellers is projected to decline 15 percent from 2022 to 2032.

Despite declining employment, about 29,000 openings for tellers are projected each year, on average, over the decade. All of those openings are expected to result from the need to replace workers who transfer to other occupations or exit the labor force, such as to retire.

Employment

Historically, job growth for tellers was driven by the expansion of bank branches, where most tellers work. However, the number of bank branches has been in decline due to technological change. As more people use online banking tools, such as mobile check deposits, fewer bank customers will visit the teller window. This should result in decreased demand for tellers.

In addition, automation is expected to lead to fewer tellers per bank branch. For example, video kiosks that allow customers to interact with tellers through webcams at ATMs will allow tellers to service a greater number of customers from one location, reducing the number of tellers needed for each bank.

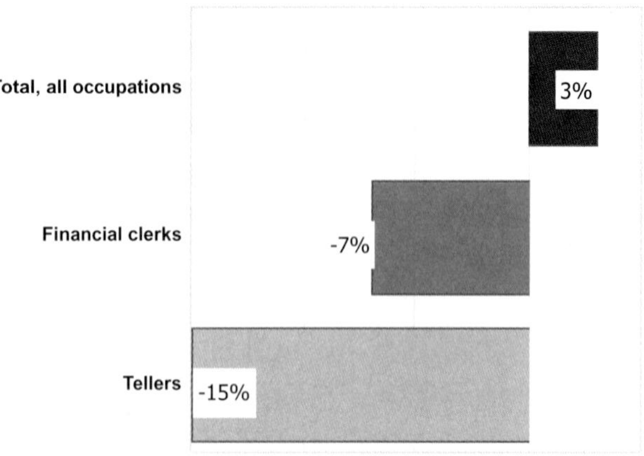

Note: All Occupations includes all occupations in the U.S. Economy.
Source: U.S. Bureau of Labor Statistics, Employment Projections program.

"Enhanced ATMs" are another form of automation technology. These machines are expected to perform an increasing range of customer service and clerical tasks currently done by tellers, such as issuing debit cards or detecting counterfeit currency. The use of these machines will improve teller productivity and allow workers to focus on only the most complex customer service tasks, which in turn is expected to lower demand for these workers.

Occupational Title	SOC Code	Employment, 2022	Projected Employment, 2032	Change, 2022-32	
				Percent	Numeric
Tellers	43-3071	364,100	311,100	-15	-52,900

Contacts for More Information

For more information, visit

➤ American Bankers Association

Personal Care and Service

Animal Care and Service Workers

Summary

Quick Facts: Animal Care and Service Workers	
2022 Median Pay	$29,790 per year $14.32 per hour
Typical Entry-Level Education	High school diploma or equivalent
Work Experience in a Related Occupation	None
On-the-job Training	See How to Become One
Number of Jobs, 2022	393,100
Job Outlook, 2022-32	16% (Much faster than average)
Employment Change, 2022-32	61,200

What Animal Care and Service Workers Do

Animal care and service workers attend to or train animals.

Work Environment

Animal care and service workers are employed in a variety of settings, including kennels, zoos, stables, animal shelters, pet stores, veterinary clinics, and aquariums. Some parts of the job may be physically or emotionally demanding, and workers risk injury when caring for animals.

How to Become an Animal Care and Service Worker

Animal care and service workers typically have a high school diploma or equivalent and learn the occupation on the job. Many employers prefer to hire candidates who have experience working with animals.

Trainers teach animals to respond to commands.

Pay

The median annual wage for animal caretakers was $29,530 in May 2022.

The median annual wage for animal trainers was $35,620 in May 2022.

Job Outlook

Overall employment of animal care and service workers is projected to grow 16 percent from 2022 to 2032, much faster than the average for all occupations.

About 79,900 openings for animal care and service workers are projected each year, on average, over the decade. Many of those openings are expected to result from the need to replace workers who transfer to different occupations or exit the labor force, such as to retire.

What Animal Care and Service Workers Do

Animal care and service workers attend to or train animals. Working with pets and other nonfarm animals, these caretakers and trainers feed, groom, and exercise the animals or teach them to respond to human commands.

Duties

Animal care and service workers typically do the following:

- Give food and water to animals
- Clean equipment and the living spaces of animals
- Monitor animals and record details of their diet, physical condition, and behavior
- Examine animals for signs of illness or injury
- Exercise animals

Pet sitters care for pets while the owner is at work or on vacation.

- Bathe animals, trim nails, clip hair, and attend to other grooming needs
- Train animals to obey or to behave in a specific manner

The following are types of animal care and service workers:

Animal trainers teach animals a variety of skills, such as obedience, performance, riding, security, and assisting people with disabilities. They familiarize animals with human voices and contact, and they teach animals to respond to commands. Most animal trainers work with dogs and horses, but some work with marine mammals, such as dolphins. Trainers teach a variety of skills. For example, some train dogs to guide people with disabilities, or they may train animals for a competition.

Groomers specialize in maintaining a pet's appearance. They typically groom dogs and cats, which may include cutting, trimming, shampooing, and styling fur; clipping nails; and cleaning ears. Groomers also schedule appointments, sell products to pet owners, and identify problems that may require veterinary attention.

Groomers may work in or operate a grooming salon, kennel, veterinary clinic, pet supply store, or mobile grooming service, a self-contained business that travels to clients' homes.

Grooms work at stables, caring for horses and maintaining equipment. Responsibilities include feeding, grooming, and exercising horses; cleaning stalls; polishing saddles; and organizing the tack room, which stores harnesses, saddles, and bridles. Experienced grooms sometimes help train horses.

Kennel attendants care for pets, often overnight, in place of owners. They clean cages and dog runs and feed, exercise, and play with animals. Experienced attendants also may provide basic healthcare, bathe animals, and attend to other basic grooming needs.

Animal shelter attendants typically work with cats and dogs in animal shelters or rescue leagues. These attendants take care of the animals' basic needs and may have administrative duties, such as keeping records, answering questions from the public, educating visitors about pet health, and screening people who want to adopt an animal. Experienced attendants may have more responsibilities, such as helping to vaccinate or euthanize animals alongside a veterinarian.

Pet sitters look after animals while the pet owner is away. Most pet sitters feed, walk, and play with pets daily. They go to the pet owner's home, allowing the pet to stay in its familiar surroundings and follow its routine. Experienced pet sitters also may bathe, groom, or train pets. Pet sitters typically watch over dogs, but some also take care of cats and other pets.

Zookeepers care for animals in zoos. They plan diets, feed animals, and monitor the animals' eating patterns. They also clean the animals' enclosures and monitor behavior for signs of illness or injury. Depending on the size of the zoo, they may work with one species or multiple species of animals.

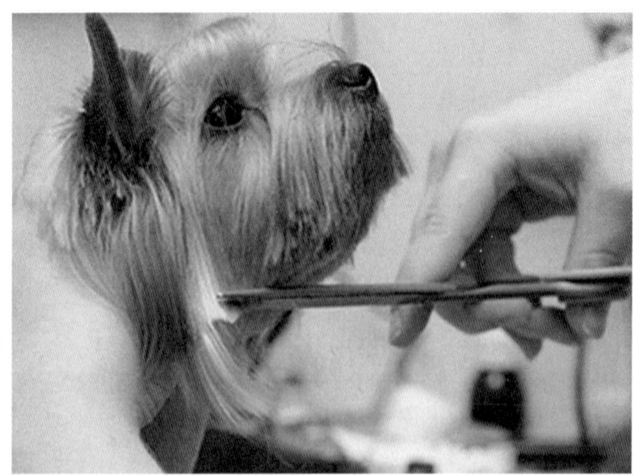

Mobile groomers travel to customers' homes to wash, cut, and brush an animal's coat.

Zookeepers may help raise young animals, and they often spend time answering questions from the public.

For information about workers who care for animals in clinics, animal hospitals, and research laboratories, see the veterinary assistants and laboratory animal caretakers profile. For information about those who attend to farm animals, see the agricultural workers profile.

Work Environment

Animal caretakers held about 339,000 jobs in 2022. The largest employers of animal caretakers were as follows:

Other personal services	38%
Self-employed workers	19
Retail trade	13
Professional, scientific, and technical services	12
Social advocacy organizations	4

Animal trainers held about 54,100 jobs in 2022. The largest employers of animal trainers were as follows:

Self-employed workers	54%
Support activities for agriculture and forestry	11
Retail trade	8
Arts, entertainment, and recreation	5
Animal production and aquaculture	5

Animal care and service workers are employed in a variety of settings. Many work at kennels; others work at zoos, stables, animal shelters, pet stores, veterinary clinics, and aquariums. Their work may involve travel.

Although animal care and service workers may consider their work enjoyable and rewarding, they face unpleasant and emotionally distressing situations at times. For example, those who work in shelters may observe abused, injured, or sick animals. Some caretakers may have to help veterinarians euthanize injured or unwanted animals.

In addition, a lot the work involves physical tasks, such as moving and cleaning cages, lifting bags of food, and exercising animals.

Injuries and Illnesses

Animal caretakers have one of the highest rates of injuries and illnesses of all occupations. Animal care and service workers may be bitten, scratched, or kicked when working with scared or aggressive animals. Injuries may also happen while the caretaker is holding, cleaning, or restraining an animal.

Work Schedules

Although most animal trainers work full time, part-time work is common for both trainers and animal caretakers. Work schedules may vary to include evenings, weekends, and holidays. In facilities that operate 24 hours a day, such as kennels, animal shelters, and stables, animals may need care around the clock.

How to Become an Animal Care and Service Worker

Animal care and service workers typically have a high school diploma or equivalent and learn the occupation on the job. Many employers prefer to hire people who have experience with animals.

Education

Animal care and service workers typically need at least a high school diploma or equivalent.

Although pet groomers typically learn by working under the guidance of an experienced groomer, they can also attend grooming schools.

Animal trainers usually need a high school diploma or equivalent, although some positions may require a bachelor's degree. For example, marine mammal trainers usually need a bachelor's degree in marine biology, animal science, biology, or a related field.

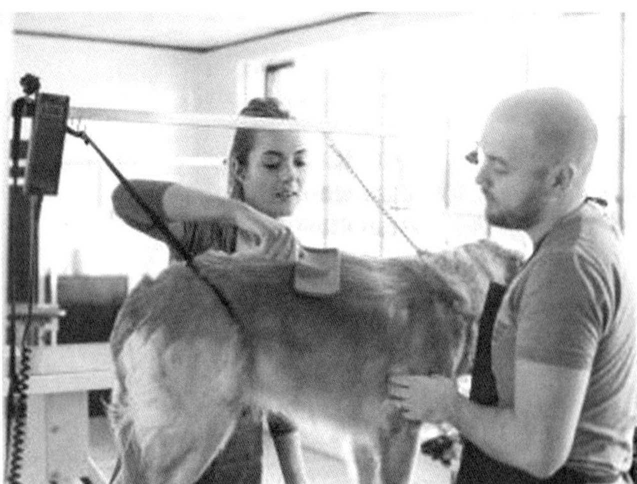

Most animal care and service workers have a high school diploma and learn the occupation on the job.

Dog trainers and horse trainers may take courses at community colleges or vocational and private training schools.

Most zoos require zookeepers to have a bachelor's degree in biology, animal science, or a related field.

Training

Most animal care and service workers learn through on-the-job training.

Animal trainers may learn their skills from an experienced trainer. Pet groomers often learn their trade under the guidance of an experienced groomer.

Licenses, Certifications, and Registrations

Although not required, certifications may help workers establish their credentials and enhance their skills. For example, professional associations and private vocational and state-approved trade schools offer certification for dog trainers.

The National Dog Groomers Association of America offers certification for master status as a groomer. Both the National Association of Professional Pet Sitters and Pet Sitters International offer a home-study certification program for pet sitters. Marine mammal trainers should be certified in scuba diving.

Many states require self-employed animal care and service workers to have a business license.

Other Experience

For many animal care and service workers positions, it helps to have experience working with animals. Volunteering and internships at zoos and aquariums are excellent ways to gain such experience.

Important Qualities

Compassion. Animal care and service workers must be compassionate when dealing with animals and their owners. They should treat animals with kindness.

Customer-service skills. Animal care and service workers should understand pet owners' needs so they can provide excellent customer service. Some workers may need to deal with distraught pet owners. For example, caretakers working in animal shelters may need to reassure owners looking for a lost pet.

Detail oriented. Animal care and service workers are often responsible for maintaining records and monitoring changes in animals' behavior.

Patience. All animal caretakers and animal trainers need to be patient when working with animals.

Physical stamina. Animal care and service workers must be able to kneel, crawl, and lift heavy supplies, such as bags of food.

Problem-solving skills. Animal trainers must be able to assess whether animals are responding to teaching methods and to identify which methods are successful.

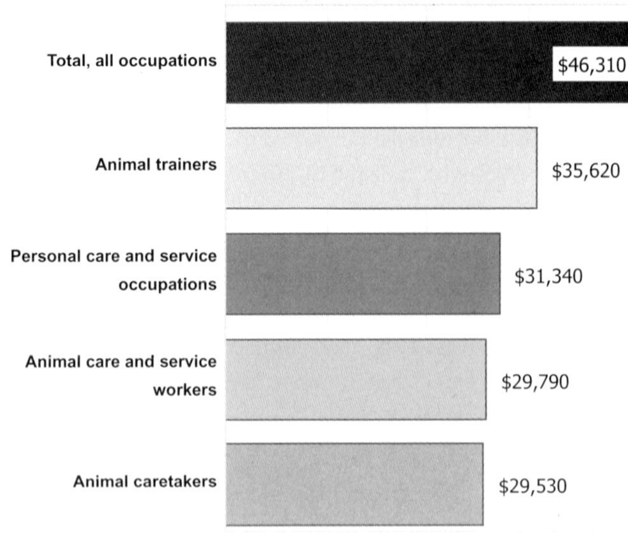

Note: All Occupations includes all occupations in the U.S. Economy.
Source: U.S. Bureau of Labor Statistics, Occupational Employment and Wage Statistics.

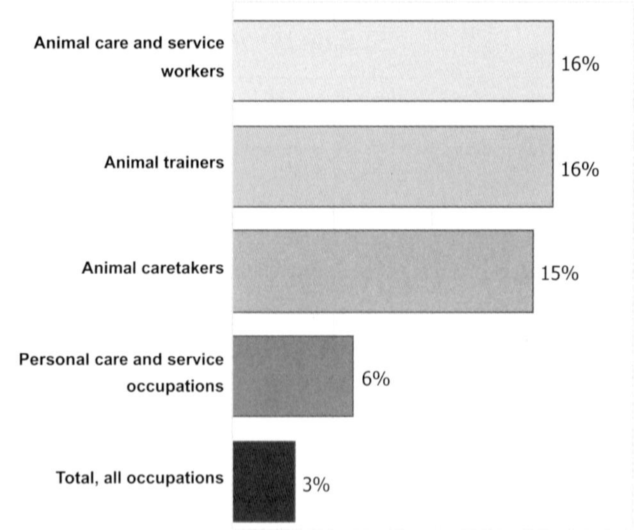

Note: All Occupations includes all occupations in the U.S. Economy.
Source: U.S. Bureau of Labor Statistics, Employment Projections program.

Reliability. Animal care and service workers need to care for animals on schedule and in a timely manner.

Pay

The median annual wage for animal caretakers was $29,530 in May 2022. The median wage is the wage at which half the workers in an occupation earned more than that amount and half earned less. The lowest 10 percent earned less than $22,250, and the highest 10 percent earned more than $44,280.

The median annual wage for animal trainers was $35,620 in May 2022. The lowest 10 percent earned less than $27,050, and the highest 10 percent earned more than $66,850.

In May 2022, the median annual wages for animal caretakers in the top industries in which they worked were as follows:

Retail trade	$29,340
Other personal services	29,160
Professional, scientific, and technical services	28,880
Social advocacy organizations	28,600

In May 2022, the median annual wages for animal trainers in the top industries in which they worked were as follows:

Arts, entertainment, and recreation	$42,390
Retail trade	30,960

Although most animal trainers work full time, part-time work is common for both trainers and animal caretakers. Work schedules may vary to include evenings, weekends, and holidays. In facilities that operate 24 hours a day, such as kennels, animal shelters, and stables, animals may need care around the clock.

Job Outlook

Overall employment of animal care and service workers is projected to grow 16 percent from 2022 to 2032, much faster than the average for all occupations.

About 79,900 openings for animal care and service workers are projected each year, on average, over the decade. Many of those openings are expected to result from the need to replace workers who transfer to different occupations or exit the labor force, such as to retire.

Employment

Many people consider their pets to be a part of their family and are willing to pay more for pet care than pet owners have in the past. As more households include companion pets, employment of animal care and service workers will continue to grow.

Occupational Title	SOC Code	Employment, 2022	Projected Employment, 2032	Change, 2022-32	
				Percent	Numeric
Animal care and service workers	39-2000	393,100	454,300	16	61,200
Animal trainers	39-2011	54,100	62,800	16	8,700
Animal caretakers	39-2021	339,000	391,500	15	52,500

Contacts for More Information

For more information, visit

- National Dog Groomers Association of America, Inc.
- National Association of Professional Pet Sitters
- Pet Sitters International
- The Association of Professional Dog Trainers
- International Marine Animal Trainers' Association
- Association of Zoos & Aquariums
- American Association of Zoo Keepers

Barbers, Hairstylists, and Cosmetologists

Summary

Quick Facts: Barbers, Hairstylists, and Cosmetologists	
2022 Median Pay	$33,400 per year $16.06 per hour
Typical Entry-Level Education	Postsecondary nondegree award
Work Experience in a Related Occupation	None
On-the-job Training	None
Number of Jobs, 2022	618,900
Job Outlook, 2022-32	8% (Faster than average)
Employment Change, 2022-32	47,200

What Barbers, Hairstylists, and Cosmetologists Do

Barbers, hairstylists, and cosmetologists provide haircutting, hairstyling, and other services related to personal appearance.

Work Environment

Barbers, hairstylists, and cosmetologists work mostly in barbershops or salons. Most are full time, although part-time work is common. Work schedules may vary and often include evenings and weekends.

How to Become a Barber, Hairstylist, or Cosmetologist

All states require barbers, hairstylists, and cosmetologists to be licensed. To qualify for a license, candidates typically must graduate from a state-approved barber or cosmetology program and pass an exam.

Pay

The median hourly wage for barbers was $16.82 in May 2022.

The median hourly wage for hairdressers, hairstylists, and cosmetologists was $16.01 in May 2022.

Hairstylists discuss hairstyle options with clients.

Job Outlook

Overall employment of barbers, hairstylists, and cosmetologists is projected to grow 8 percent from 2022 to 2032, faster than the average for all occupations.

About 89,400 openings for barbers, hairstylists, and cosmetologists are projected each year, on average, over the decade. Many of those openings are expected to result from the need to replace workers who transfer to different occupations or exit the labor force, such as to retire.

What Barbers, Hairstylists, and Cosmetologists Do

Barbers, hairstylists, and cosmetologists provide haircutting, hairstyling, and other services related to personal appearance.

Duties

Barbers, hairstylists, and cosmetologists typically do the following:

- Inspect and analyze hair, scalp, and skin to recommend services or treatment
- Discuss hairstyle options
- Shampoo, color, lighten, and condition hair
- Chemically change hair texture
- Cut, dry, and style hair
- Trim facial hair
- Receive payments from client
- Clean and disinfect all tools and work areas

Barbers, hairstylists, and cosmetologists provide hair and other services to enhance clients' appearance. Common tools may include combs and hairbrushes, clippers and scissors, straight razors, blow dryers, and curling and flat irons. They also may keep records of products used and services provided to clients, such as hair color, hair treatment, and clipper setting.

Those who operate their own barbershop or salon have managerial duties that may include hiring, supervising, and firing

Hairstylists provide hair styling and beauty services.

workers. They also may keep business and inventory records, order supplies, and arrange for advertising.

Barbers shampoo, cut, and style hair, mostly for male clients. They also may fit hairpieces, provide facials, trim beards and mustaches, and offer facial and head shaving. Depending on the state in which they work, some barbers are licensed to bleach, color, and highlight hair and to offer permanent-wave services.

Hairstylists and cosmetologists offer a wide range of hair services, such as shampooing, cutting, coloring, and styling. They often provide consultation and advise clients on how to care for their hair at home. Some also clean and style wigs and hairpieces.

Hairstylists and cosmetologists also provide facial and scalp treatments, makeup analysis, and skincare and nail services. In addition, some recommend hair care or skincare products. For more information about workers who specialize in skincare treatment or in fingernail and toenail services, see the profiles for skincare specialists or manicurists and pedicurists, respectively.

Work Environment

Barbers held about 63,100 jobs in 2022. The largest employers of barbers were as follows:

Self-employed workers	79%
Personal care services	20

Barbers usually work in barbershops and must stand for long periods.

Hairdressers, hairstylists, and cosmetologists held about 555,800 jobs in 2022. The largest employers of hairdressers, hairstylists, and cosmetologists were as follows:

Personal care services	48%
Self-employed workers	46
Retail trade	4

Barbers, hairstylists, and cosmetologists work mostly in barbershops or salons, although some work in spas, hotels, or resorts. Some lease booth space from a salon owner. Others manage salons or open their own shop after several years of gaining experience.

Barbers, hairstylists, and cosmetologists usually work in pleasant surroundings with good lighting. Physical stamina is important because they are on their feet for most of their shift. Prolonged exposure to some chemicals may cause skin irritation, so they often wear protective clothing, such as disposable gloves or aprons.

Work Schedules

Most barbers, hairstylists, and cosmetologists are full time, although part-time work is common. Work schedules may vary and often include evenings and weekends—times when barbershops and beauty salons may be busiest. Those who are self-employed and operate their own barbershop or salon may have long workdays, but they usually determine their own schedules.

How to Become a Barber, Hairstylist, or Cosmetologist

All states require barbers, hairstylists, and cosmetologists to be licensed. To qualify for a license, candidates typically must graduate from a state-approved barber or cosmetology program and pass an exam.

Education

Barbers, hairstylists, and cosmetologists usually must complete a state-approved barber or cosmetology program. Admission to these programs varies by state, with some requiring a high school diploma or equivalent. Programs typically involve a mix of classroom studies and hands-on training and lead to a certificate or other postsecondary nondegree award. Some states require health and safety training as part of these programs.

Workers may continue to take advanced courses in hairstyling or in other personal appearance services throughout their careers to keep up with the latest trends. Those who want to open their own business also may benefit from taking courses in sales and marketing.

Licenses, Certifications, and Registrations

Barbers, hairstylists, and cosmetologists must obtain a license in order to work. Qualifications for a license vary by state. Generally, a person must meet state-specified minimum age

Workers must obtain a license through a state-approved barber, hairstyling, or cosmetology program.

requirements, have a high school diploma or equivalent, and have graduated from a state-licensed barber or cosmetology school.

After completing a state-approved training program, graduates take a state licensing exam that includes a written test and, in some cases, a practical test of styling skills or an oral exam.

In many states, cosmetology training may be credited toward a barbering license or vice versa, and a few states combine the two licenses. A fee usually is required to apply for a license, and continuing education units (CEUs) may be required with periodic license renewals.

State reciprocity agreements may allow licensed barbers and cosmetologists to get a license in another state without needing additional formal training or state board testing. Contact your state licensing agency for details.

Important Qualities

Creativity. Barbers, hairstylists, and cosmetologists must keep up with the latest trends and be ready to try new hairstyles for their clients.

Customer-service skills. Workers must be friendly, pleasant, and able to interact with clients to build and retain clientele.

Listening skills. Barbers, hairstylists, and cosmetologists must be attentive when clients describe what they want to ensure satisfaction with the result.

Physical stamina. Barbers, hairstylists, and cosmetologists must be able to stand for long periods.

Tidiness. Workers must keep their work area clean and sanitary for the health and safety of their clients. They also must keep a neat personal appearance so that clients feel comfortable and want to return.

Time-management skills. Barbers, hairstylists, and cosmetologists need to manage their time efficiently when scheduling appointments and providing services. Clients who receive timely hair care are more likely to return, and some services, such as hair coloring, require precise timing.

Pay

The median hourly wage for barbers was $16.82 in May 2022. The median wage is the wage at which half the workers in an occupation earned more than that amount and half earned less. The lowest 10 percent earned less than $11.00, and the highest 10 percent earned more than $29.29.

The median hourly wage for hairdressers, hairstylists, and cosmetologists was $16.01 in May 2022. The lowest 10 percent earned less than $10.48, and the highest 10 percent earned more than $28.88.

Barbers, Hairstylists, and Cosmetologists

Median hourly wages, May 2022

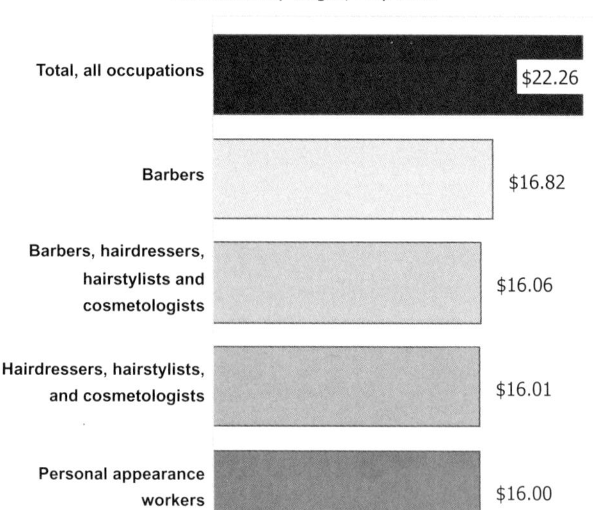

Note: All Occupations includes all occupations in the U.S. Economy.
Source: U.S. Bureau of Labor Statistics, Occupational Employment and Wage Statistics.

In May 2022, the median hourly wages for barbers in the top industries in which they worked were as follows:

Personal care services $16.77

In May 2022, the median hourly wages for hairdressers, hairstylists, and cosmetologists in the top industries in which they worked were as follows:

Personal care services $16.28
Retail trade 12.80

Barbers, hairstylists, and cosmetologists may receive tips from customers. These tips are included in the wage data shown.

Most barbers, hairstylists, and cosmetologists work full time, although part-time work is common. Work schedules may vary and often include evenings and weekends—times when beauty salons and barbershops may be busiest. Those who are self-employed and operate their own barbershop or salon may have long workdays, but they usually determine their own schedules.

Job Outlook

Overall employment of barbers, hairstylists, and cosmetologists is projected to grow 8 percent from 2022 to 2032, faster than the average for all occupations.

About 89,400 openings for barbers, hairstylists, and cosmetologists are projected each year, on average, over the decade. Many of those openings are expected to result from the need to replace workers who transfer to different occupations or exit the labor force, such as to retire.

Employment

The need for barbers and hairdressers will stem primarily from demand for basic hair care services. In addition, an increased demand for hair coloring, hair straightening, and other advanced hair treatments is expected to continue over the projections decade.

Hairdressers, hairstylists, and cosmetologists will continue to compete with providers of specialized services, such as nail and skin care. Consumers often choose manicurists and pedicurists and skincare specialists for these services, rather than to visit hairdressers, hairstylists, and cosmetologists for them. Still, employment is expected to grow to meet increased demand for personal appearance services.

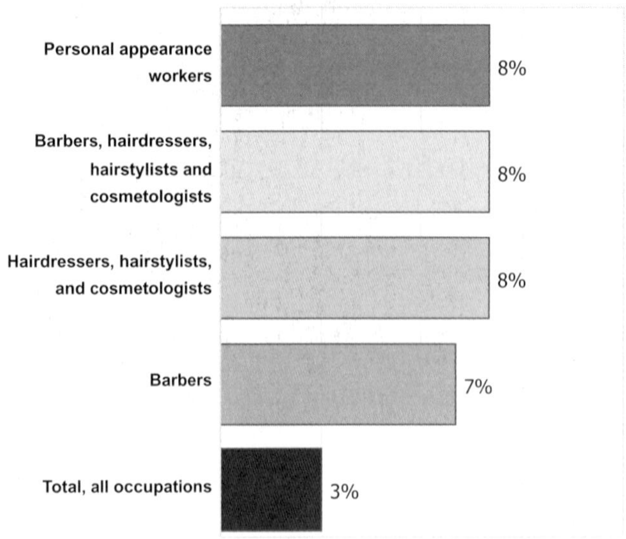

Note: All Occupations includes all occupations in the U.S. Economy.
Source: U.S. Bureau of Labor Statistics, Employment Projections program.

Occupational Title	SOC Code	Employment, 2022	Projected Employment, 2032	Change, 2022-32	
				Percent	Numeric
Barbers, hairdressers, hairstylists and cosmetologists	39-5010	618,900	666,100	8	47,200
Barbers	39-5011	63,100	67,600	7	4,400
Hairdressers, hairstylists, and cosmetologists	39-5012	555,800	598,600	8	42,800

Contacts for More Information

For more information, visit

- American Association of Cosmetology Schools (AACS)
- Beauty Schools Directory
- National Association of Barber Boards of America (NABBA)
- National-Interstate Council of State Boards of Cosmetology (NIC)
- For information about other professional links, visit
- Professional Beauty Association (PBA)

Childcare Workers

Summary

Quick Facts: Childcare Workers	
2022 Median Pay	$28,520 per year $13.71 per hour
Typical Entry-Level Education	High school diploma or equivalent
Work Experience in a Related Occupation	None
On-the-job Training	Short-term on-the-job training
Number of Jobs, 2022	945,900
Job Outlook, 2022-32	-2% (Decline)
Employment Change, 2022-32	-18,500

What Childcare Workers Do
Childcare workers attend to children's needs while helping to foster early development.

Work Environment
Childcare workers typically work in childcare centers, their own home, or private households. Part-time work and irregular hours are common.

How to Become a Childcare Worker
Education and training requirements for childcare workers vary by setting, state, and employer. They range from no formal education to certification in early childhood education.

Pay
The median hourly wage for childcare workers was $13.71 in May 2022.

Job Outlook
Employment of childcare workers is projected to decline 2 percent from 2022 to 2032.

Despite declining employment, about 153,100 openings for childcare workers are projected each year, on average, over the decade. All of those openings are expected to result from the need to replace workers who transfer to other occupations or exit the labor force, such as to retire.

What Childcare Workers Do
Childcare workers attend to children's needs while helping to foster early development. They may help younger children prepare for kindergarten or assist older children with homework.

Duties
Childcare workers typically do the following:

- Supervise and monitor the safety of children
- Prepare and organize mealtimes and snacks for children
- Help children keep good hygiene
- Change the diapers of infants and toddlers
- Organize activities or implement a curriculum that allows children to learn about the world and explore their interests
- Develop schedules and routines to ensure that children have enough physical activity, rest, and playtime
- Watch for signs of emotional or developmental problems in children and bring potential problems to the attention of parents or guardians
- Keep records of children's progress, routines, and interests

Childcare workers read and play with babies and toddlers to introduce basic concepts. For example, they teach them how to share and take turns by playing games with other children.

Childcare workers help preschool-age children prepare for kindergarten. Young children learn from playing, questioning,

Childcare workers attend to the basic needs of children, such as dressing, bathing, feeding, and overseeing play.

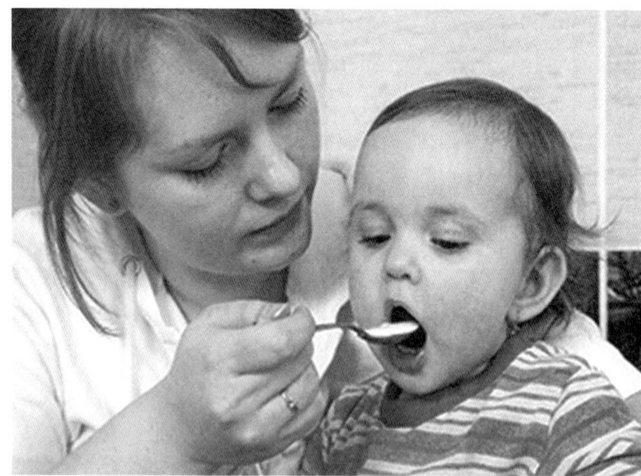

Childcare workers prepare and organize mealtimes and snacks for children.

and experimenting. Childcare workers use play and other instructional techniques to help children's development. For example, they may use storytelling and rhyming games to teach language and vocabulary. They may help improve children's social skills by having them work together to build something in a sandbox. Or they may teach about numbers by having children count when building with blocks. They also involve children in creative activities, such as art, dance, and music.

Childcare workers may also watch school-age children before and after school. They often help these children with their homework and may take them to afterschool activities, such as sports practices and club meetings.

During the summer, when children are out of school, childcare workers may watch older children as well as younger ones while the parents are at work.

The following are examples of types of childcare workers:

Childcare center workers work in facilities that include programs offering Head Start and Early Head Start. They often take a team-based approach and may work with preschool teachers and teacher assistants to teach children through a structured curriculum. They prepare daily and long-term schedules of activities to stimulate and educate the children in their care. They also monitor and keep records of the children's progress.

Family childcare providers run a business out of their own homes to care for children during standard working hours. They need to ensure that their homes and all staff they employ meet the regulations for family childcare providers. They also prepare contracts that set rates of pay, when payment can be expected, and the number of hours children can be in care. Furthermore, they establish policies such as whether sick children can be in their care, who can pick children up, and how behavioral issues will be dealt with. Family childcare providers may market their services to prospective families.

Nannies work in the homes of the families whose children they care for. Most often, they work full time for one family. They may be responsible for driving children to school, appointments, or afterschool activities. Some live in the homes of the families employing them.

Work Environment

Childcare workers held about 945,900 jobs in 2022. The largest employers of childcare workers were as follows:

Child day care services	29%
Self-employed workers	24
Private households	20
Elementary and secondary schools; local	8
Religious, grantmaking, civic, professional, and similar organizations	7

Family childcare workers care for children in their own homes. They may convert a portion of their living space into a dedicated space for the children. Nannies usually work in their employers' homes.

Childcare workers may spend part of their day outdoors.

Many states limit the number of children that each staff member is responsible for by regulating the ratio of staff to children. Ratios vary with the age of the children. Childcare workers are responsible for relatively few babies and toddlers. However, workers may be responsible for greater numbers of older children.

Work Schedules

Childcare workers' schedules vary, and part-time work is common.

Childcare centers usually are open year round, with long hours so that parents or guardians can drop off and pick up their children before and after work. Some centers employ full-time and part-time staff with staggered shifts to cover the entire day.

Family childcare providers may work long or irregular hours to fit parents' work schedules. In some cases, these childcare providers offer evening and overnight care to meet the needs of families. After the children go home, family childcare providers often have more responsibilities, such as shopping for food or supplies, keeping records, and cleaning.

Nannies work either full or part time. Full-time nannies may work more than 40 hours a week to cover parents' time commuting to and from work.

How to Become a Childcare Worker

Education and training requirements vary by setting, state, and employer. They range from no formal education to a certification in early childhood education.

Education

Childcare workers' education requirements vary. Some states require these workers to have a high school diploma or equivalent, but others do not have any education requirements for entry-level positions. Employers often prefer to hire workers who have at least a high school diploma. However, workers with postsecondary education or an early childhood education credential may qualify for higher level positions.

Although it is not required, bachelor's degree study in fields such as education, psychology, or family and consumer sciences may be helpful.

Childcare workers in Head Start and Early Head Start programs must meet specific education and certification requirements, which vary by work setting and job title.

States do not regulate educational requirements for nannies. However, some employers may prefer to hire workers with at least some formal instruction in childhood education or a related field, particularly when they will be hired as full-time nannies.

Licenses, Certifications, and Registrations

Many states require childcare centers, including those in private homes, to be licensed. To qualify for licensure, staff often must pass a background check, have a complete record of immunizations, and meet a minimum training requirement. Some states require staff to have certifications in cardiopulmonary resuscitation (CPR) and first aid.

Childcare workers typically need a high school degree or equivalent.

Some states and employers require childcare workers to have a nationally recognized credential. Most often, states require the Child Development Associate (CDA) credential offered by the Council for Professional Recognition. Obtaining the CDA credential requires coursework, experience in the field, and a period during which the applicant is observed while working with children. The CDA credential must be renewed every 3 years.

Other organizations, such as The National Association for Family Child Care (NAFCC) may also offer optional accreditation.

Training

Many states and employers require providers to complete some training before beginning work. Also, many states require staff in childcare centers to complete a minimum number of training hours annually. Training may include information about topics such as safe sleep practices for infants.

Advancement

With a couple of years of experience and a bachelor's degree, childcare workers may advance to become a preschool or childcare center director.

Important Qualities

Communication skills. Childcare workers need good speaking skills to provide direction or information effectively and good listening skills to understand parents' instructions.

Decision-making skills. Good judgment is necessary for childcare workers so they can respond to emergencies or difficult situations.

Interpersonal skills. Childcare workers need to work well with people in order to develop good relationships with parents, children, and colleagues.

Patience. Childcare workers need to be able to respond calmly to overwhelming and difficult situations.

Physical stamina. Working with children can be physically demanding, so childcare workers should have a lot of energy.

Pay

The median hourly wage for childcare workers was $13.71 in May 2022. The median wage is the wage at which half the workers in an occupation earned more than that amount and half earned less. The lowest 10 percent earned less than $10.22, and the highest 10 percent earned more than $18.79.

In May 2022, the median hourly wages for childcare workers in the top industries in which they worked were as follows:

Elementary and secondary schools; local	$15.25
Religious, grantmaking, civic, professional, and similar organizations	13.63
Child day care services	13.25

Pay varies with the worker's education level and work setting. Those in formal childcare settings and those with more

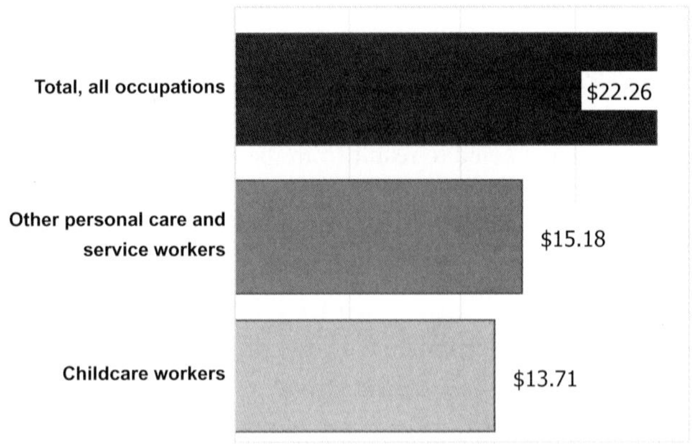

Note: All Occupations includes all occupations in the U.S. Economy. Source: U.S. Bureau of Labor Statistics, Occupational Employment and Wage Statistics.

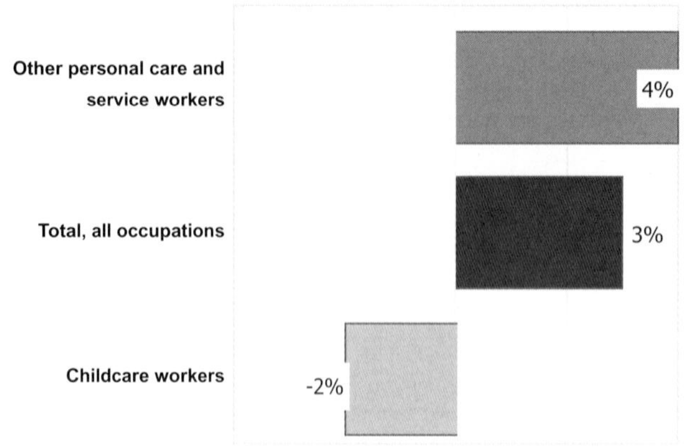

Note: All Occupations includes all occupations in the U.S. Economy. Source: U.S. Bureau of Labor Statistics, Employment Projections program.

education usually earn higher wages. Pay for self-employed workers is based on the number of hours they work and the number and ages of children in their care.

Childcare workers' schedules vary, and part-time work is common.

Childcare centers usually are open year round, with long hours so that parents or guardians can drop off and pick up their children before and after work. Some centers employ full-time and part-time staff with staggered shifts to cover the entire day.

Family childcare providers may work long or irregular hours to fit parents' work schedules. In some cases, these childcare providers may offer evening and overnight care to meet the needs of families. After the children go home, childcare providers often have more responsibilities, such as shopping for food or supplies, keeping records, and cleaning.

Nannies work either full or part time. Full-time nannies may work more than 40 hours a week to cover parents' commuting time to and from work.

Job Outlook

Employment of childcare workers is projected to decline 2 percent from 2022 to 2032.

Despite declining employment, about 153,100 openings for childcare workers are projected each year, on average, over the decade. All of those openings are expected to result from the need to replace workers who transfer to other occupations or exit the labor force, such as to retire.

Employment

Parents or guardians who work will continue to need the assistance of childcare workers. However, the increasing cost of childcare may limit demand for these workers.

Occupational Title	SOC Code	Employment, 2022	Projected Employment, 2032	Change, 2022-32	
				Percent	Numeric
Childcare workers	39-9011	945,900	927,400	-2	-18,500

Contacts for More Information

For more information, visit

- Child Care Aware
- International Nanny Association
- National Association for Family Child Care
- National Association for the Education of Young Children
- Council for Professional Recognition

Fitness Trainers and Instructors

Summary

Quick Facts: Fitness Trainers and Instructors	
2022 Median Pay	$45,380 per year $21.82 per hour
Typical Entry-Level Education	High school diploma or equivalent
Work Experience in a Related Occupation	None
On-the-job Training	Short-term on-the-job training
Number of Jobs, 2022	329,500
Job Outlook, 2022-32	14% (Much faster than average)
Employment Change, 2022-32	45,200

What Fitness Trainers and Instructors Do

Fitness trainers and instructors lead, instruct, and motivate individuals or groups in exercise activities.

Work Environment

Fitness trainers and instructors work in facilities such as recreation centers, health clubs, and yoga studios. Many work variable or part-time schedules that may include nights, weekends, or holidays.

How to Become a Fitness Trainer or Instructor

The education and training typically required for fitness trainers and instructors varies by type of specialty, and employers prefer to hire those with certification.

Pay

The median annual wage for fitness trainers and instructors was $45,380 in May 2022.

Job Outlook

Employment of fitness trainers and instructors is projected to grow 14 percent from 2022 to 2032, much faster than the average for all occupations.

About 69,000 openings for fitness trainers and instructors are projected each year, on average, over the decade. Many of those openings are expected to result from the need to replace workers who transfer to different occupations or exit the labor force, such as to retire.

What Fitness Trainers and Instructors Do

Fitness trainers and instructors lead, instruct, and motivate individuals or groups in exercise activities, including cardiovascular workouts (for the heart and blood circulation), strength training, and stretching. They work with people of all ages and skill levels.

Duties

Fitness trainers and instructors typically do the following:

- Demonstrate or explain how to perform various exercises and routines to minimize injuries and improve fitness
- Watch clients do exercises to ensure that they are using correct technique
- Provide options during workouts to help clients feel successful
- Monitor clients' progress and adapt programs as needed
- Explain and enforce safety rules and regulations on sports, recreational activities, and the use of exercise equipment
- Give clients information or resources about topics such as nutrition and lifestyle
- Give emergency first aid if needed

Fitness trainers and instructors work with individual clients or prepare or choreograph their own group classes. They may do a variety of tasks in addition to their fitness duties, such as

Fitness trainers and instructors lead, instruct, and motivate individuals or groups in exercise activities.

Fitness trainers and instructors work with people of all ages and skill levels.

managing the front desk, signing up new members, giving tours of the facility, or supervising the weight-training and cardiovascular equipment areas. Fitness trainers and instructors also may promote their facilities and instruction through social media, by writing newsletters or blog posts, or by creating posters and flyers.

Exercise trainers, also known as *personal fitness trainers*, work with individual clients or small groups. They may train in a gym or in clients' homes. They evaluate their clients' current fitness level, personal goals, and skills. Then, they develop personalized training programs for their clients to follow and monitor the clients' progress. In gyms or other fitness facilities, these workers often sell training sessions to members.

Group fitness instructors organize and lead group exercise classes, which may include cardiovascular exercises, muscle strengthening, or stretching. Some instructors create a routine or select exercises for participants to follow, and they then choose music that is appropriate to the movement. Others teach prechoreographed routines that were created by fitness companies or organizations. They may lead classes that use specific exercise equipment, such as stationary bicycles; teach a specific conditioning method, such as yoga; or instruct specific age groups, such as seniors or youths.

For information about workers who develop fitness programs to help people recover from illness or injury, see the profile on exercise physiologists.

Work Environment

Fitness trainers and instructors held about 329,500 jobs in 2022. The largest employers of fitness trainers and instructors were as follows:

Fitness and recreational sports centers	54%
Self-employed workers	19
Educational services; state, local, and private	7
Civic and social organizations	7
Government	3

Group instructors may demonstrate how to perform various exercises and routines.

Fitness trainers and instructors may work in standalone fitness centers or centers maintained by other types of establishments for their employees or for members of civic and social organizations. Some work in clients' homes.

Work Schedules

Many fitness trainers and instructors work variable or part-time schedules that may include nights, weekends, or holidays. Some travel to different gyms or to clients' homes to teach classes or conduct personal training sessions. Exercise trainers and group fitness instructors sometimes hold jobs in other fields and conduct training sessions or teach fitness classes at times that accommodate their work schedules.

How to Become a Fitness Trainer or Instructor

The education and training required for fitness trainers and instructors varies by specialty. Employers usually prefer to hire those with certification, but requirements vary by facility.

Education

Fitness trainers and instructors typically need a high school diploma to enter the occupation. Employers may prefer to hire fitness workers, particularly personal trainers, who have an

Personal trainers may work with individual clients or teach group classes.

associate's or bachelor's degree in a field such as recreation and fitness or healthcare and related studies. Programs in exercise science, kinesiology, physical education, or related majors often include courses in nutrition, exercise techniques, biology, and anatomy. Personal trainers also may learn how to develop fitness programs for clients of all ages.

Licenses, Certifications, and Registrations

Most fitness trainers or instructors have certification related to the area of fitness in which they specialize. Personal trainers usually must be certified before they begin working with clients or with members of a gym or health club. Group fitness instructors may begin work without certification, but employers often encourage or require them to get their credentials. Most fitness instructors receive certification for their preferred type of training, such as yoga, kickboxing, or strength training.

Many organizations offer certification. For example the National Commission for Certifying Agencies (NCCA) accredits certifying organizations in the fitness and wellness industry, including several that offer personal trainer or general certification. In addition, some private companies offer certification in the types of classes they offer.

Certification exams that have a written portion measure candidates' knowledge of human physiology, understanding of proper exercise techniques, and ability to assess clients' fitness levels and develop appropriate exercise programs. Certification also may require the candidate to teach a class for a live or video skills demonstration, which is then assessed by the certifying organization.

Most trainers or instructors also need certification in cardiopulmonary resuscitation (CPR) and first aid, as well as in use of automated external defibrillators (AED).

Training

After becoming a certified personal trainer, new trainers may be required to work alongside an experienced trainer before they are allowed to train clients alone.

Training for fitness instructors varies greatly. For example, the Yoga Alliance requires 200 and 500 hours of training, depending on the credential.

Important Qualities

Communication skills. Fitness trainers and instructors must be able to clearly explain exercises that they demonstrate to clients.

Customer-service skills. Many fitness trainers and instructors sell their services, motivating clients to hire them as personal trainers or to sign up for the classes they lead. Fitness trainers and instructors must therefore be encouraging, friendly, and polite to maintain relationships with their clients.

Listening skills. Fitness trainers and instructors must listen carefully to what clients tell them in order to determine the clients' fitness levels and desired fitness goals.

Motivational skills. To keep clients coming back for more classes or to continue personal training, fitness trainers and instructors must keep their clients motivated.

Physical fitness. Fitness trainers and instructors must be able to lead classes and to demonstrate exercises to participants or their clients.

Problem-solving skills. Fitness trainers and instructors must evaluate members' or client's fitness levels and create appropriate fitness plans to meet their needs.

Advancement

Fitness trainers and instructors who are interested in management may need a bachelor's degree in exercise science, physical education, kinesiology, or a related subject. Employers often require that trainers or instructors have experience in order to advance to a management position, such as the *fitness director* who oversees scheduling, workout incentive programs, and selecting exercise equipment in a health club or fitness center.

Personal trainers may advance to a *head trainer* position and become responsible for hiring and overseeing the personal training staff or for bringing in new personal training clients. Fitness trainers and instructors also may go into business for themselves or open their own fitness centers.

Pay

The median annual wage for fitness trainers and instructors was $45,380 in May 2022. The median wage is the wage at which half the workers in an occupation earned more than that amount and half earned less. The lowest 10 percent earned less than $23,920, and the highest 10 percent earned more than $80,330.

In May 2022, the median annual wages for fitness trainers and instructors in the top industries in which they worked were as follows:

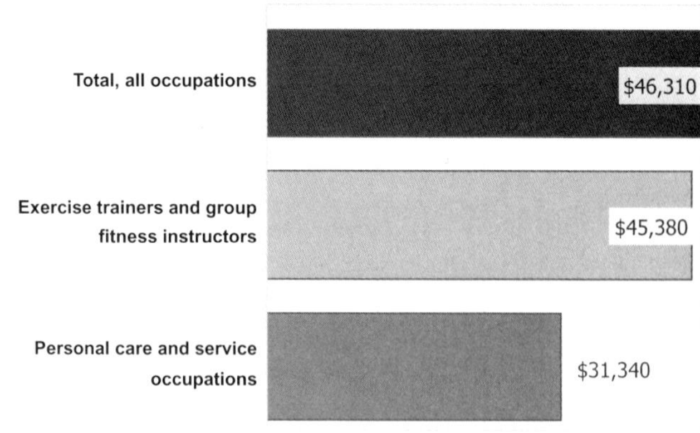

Note: All Occupations includes all occupations in the U.S. Economy.
Source: U.S. Bureau of Labor Statistics, Occupational Employment and Wage Statistics.

Fitness and recreational sports centers..............	$46,840
Government..	41,920
Educational services; state, local, and private....	38,600
Civic and social organizations	34,620

Many fitness trainers and instructors work variable or part-time schedules that may include nights, weekends, or holidays. Some travel to different gyms or to clients' homes to teach classes or conduct personal training sessions. Exercise trainers and group fitness instructors sometimes hold jobs in other fields and conduct training sessions or teach fitness classes at times that accommodate their work schedules.

Job Outlook

Employment of fitness trainers and instructors is projected to grow 14 percent from 2022 to 2032, much faster than the average for all occupations.

About 69,000 openings for fitness trainers and instructors are projected each year, on average, over the decade. Many of those openings are expected to result from the need to replace workers who transfer to different occupations or exit the labor force, such as to retire.

Employment

As employers continue to recognize the benefits of health and fitness programs for their employees, incentives to join gyms or other types of health clubs are expected to increase the need for fitness trainers and instructors. For example, some organizations may open their own exercise facilities onsite to promote employee wellness.

Other employment growth will come from the continuing emphasis on exercise to combat obesity and encourage healthier lifestyles for people of all ages. In particular, the baby-boom generation should continue to remain active to help prevent injuries and illnesses associated with aging.

Participation in yoga and Pilates is expected to continue to increase, driven partly by older adults who want low-impact forms of exercise and relief from arthritis and other ailments.

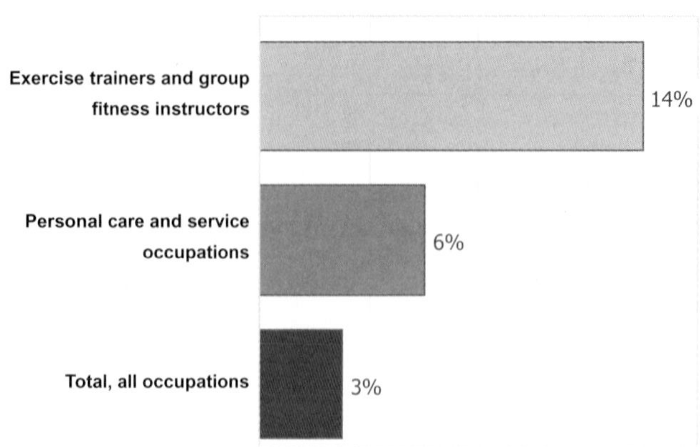

Note: All Occupations includes all occupations in the U.S. Economy.
Source: U.S. Bureau of Labor Statistics, Employment Projections program.

Occupational Title	SOC Code	Employment, 2022	Projected Employment, 2032	Change, 2022-32	
				Percent	Numeric
Exercise trainers and group fitness instructors	39-9031	329,500	374,600	14	45,200

Contacts for More Information

For information, visit

- American College of Sports Medicine
- American Council on Exercise
- National Academy of Sports Medicine
- National Commission for Certifying Agencies (NCCA), part of the Institute for Credentialing Excellence
- National Council on Strength and Fitness
- National Federation of Professional Trainers
- National Pilates Certification Program
- National Strength and Conditioning Association
- US Registry of Exercise Professionals
- Yoga Alliance

For information about health clubs and sports clubs, visit

- International Health, Racquet & Sports Club Association

Funeral Service Workers

Summary

Quick Facts: Funeral Service Workers	
2022 Median Pay	$58,820 per year $28.28 per hour
Typical Entry-Level Education	Associate's degree
Work Experience in a Related Occupation	See How to Become One
On-the-job Training	See How to Become One
Number of Jobs, 2022	60,800
Job Outlook, 2022-32	3% (As fast as average)
Employment Change, 2022-32	1,700

What Funeral Service Workers Do

Funeral service workers organize and manage the details of a ceremony honoring a deceased person.

Work Environment

Funeral service workers are employed in funeral homes and crematories. They are often on call; irregular hours, including evenings and weekends, are common. Most work full time, and some work more than 40 hours per week.

How to Become a Funeral Service Worker

An associate's degree in funeral service or mortuary science is the education typically required to become a funeral service worker. Most employers and state licensing laws require applicants to be 21 years old, have at least 2 years of formal post-secondary education, have supervised training, and pass a state licensing exam.

Pay

The median annual wage for funeral home managers was $72,110 in May 2022.

The median annual wage for morticians, undertakers, and funeral arrangers was $51,570 in May 2022.

Job Outlook

Overall employment of funeral service workers is projected to grow 3 percent from 2022 to 2032, about as fast as the average for all occupations.

About 5,700 openings for funeral service workers are projected each year, on average, over the decade. Many of those openings are expected to result from the need to replace workers who transfer to different occupations or exit the labor force, such as to retire.

What Funeral Service Workers Do

Funeral service workers organize and manage the details of a ceremony honoring a deceased person.

Duties

Funeral service workers typically do the following:

- Offer counsel and comfort to families and friends of the deceased
- Provide information on funeral service options
- Arrange for removal of the deceased's body
- Prepare the remains (the deceased's body) for the funeral
- File death certificates and other legal documents with appropriate authorities

Funeral service workers help to determine the locations, dates, and times of visitations (wakes), funerals or memorial services, burials, and cremations. They handle other details as well, such as helping the family decide whether the body should be buried, entombed, or cremated. This decision is critical because funeral practices vary among cultures and religions.

Most funeral service workers attend to the administrative aspects of a person's death, including submitting papers to state officials to receive a death certificate. They also may help resolve insurance claims, apply for funeral benefits, or notify

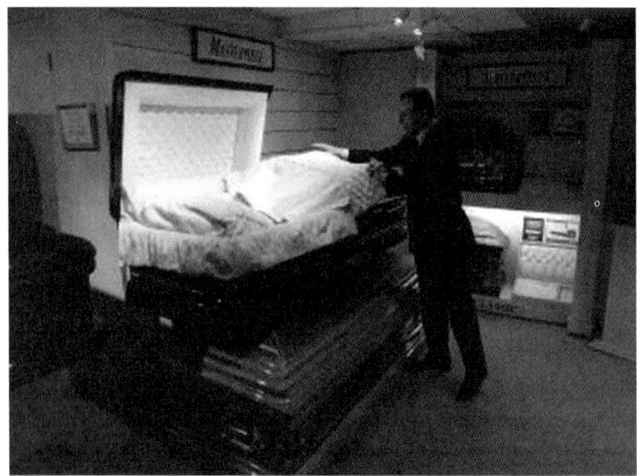

Funeral service workers handle the details of funerals.

Together with the family, funeral directors handle details of the memorial services.

the Social Security Administration or the U.S. Department of Veterans Affairs of the death.

Many funeral service workers help clients who wish to plan their own funerals in advance, to ensure that their needs are met and to ease the planning burden on surviving family members.

Funeral service workers also may provide information and resources, such as support groups, to help grieving friends and family.

The following are examples of types of funeral service workers:

Funeral home managers oversee the general operations of a funeral home business. They perform a variety of duties, such as planning and allocating the resources of the funeral home, managing staff, and handling marketing and public relations.

Morticians and funeral arrangers (also known as *funeral directors* or, historically, *undertakers*) plan the details of a funeral. They often prepare obituaries and arrange for pallbearers and clergy services. If a burial is chosen, they schedule the opening and closing of a grave with a representative of the cemetery. If cremation is chosen, they coordinate the process with the crematory. (Data covering workers who perform cremations are provided in a separate occupation not covered in detail: crematory operators.)

Morticians and funeral arrangers also prepare the sites of all services and provide transportation for the deceased and mourners. In addition, they arrange the shipment of bodies out of state or out of country for final disposition. (Data covering workers who may assist with these tasks are provided in a separate occupation not covered in detail: funeral attendant.)

Finally, these workers handle administrative duties. For example, they often apply for the transfer of any pensions, insurance policies, or annuities on behalf of survivors.

Many morticians and funeral arrangers embalm bodies. Embalming is a cosmetic and temporary preservative process through which the body is prepared for a viewing by family and friends of the deceased. (Data covering those who specialize in this work are provided in a separate occupation not covered in detail: embalmers.)

Work Environment

Funeral home managers held about 36,400 jobs in 2022. The largest employers of funeral home managers were as follows:

Self-employed workers	61%
Death care services	37

Morticians, undertakers, and funeral arrangers held about 24,500 jobs in 2022. The largest employers of morticians, undertakers, and funeral arrangers were as follows:

Death care services	97%
Self-employed workers	1

Funeral directors often have long workdays.

Funeral services traditionally take place in a house of worship, in a funeral home, or at a gravesite or crematory. However, some families prefer to hold the service in their home or in a social center.

Funeral service workers typically perform their duties in a funeral home. Workers also may operate a merchandise display room, crematory, or cemetery, which may be on the funeral home premises. The work is often stressful, because workers must arrange the various details of a funeral within 24 to 72 hours of a death. In addition, they may be responsible for managing multiple funerals on the same day.

Although workers may come into contact with bodies that have contagious diseases, the work is not dangerous if proper safety and health regulations are followed. Those working in crematories are exposed to high temperatures and must wear appropriate protective clothing.

Work Schedules

Most funeral service workers are employed full time, and some work more than 40 hours per week. They are often on call; irregular hours, including evenings and weekends, are common.

How to Become a Funeral Service Worker

An associate's degree in a funeral service or mortuary science education program is the education typically required to become a funeral service worker. Most employers require applicants to be 21 years old, have at least 2 years of formal postsecondary education, have supervised training, and pass a state licensing exam.

Education

An associate's degree in a funeral service or mortuary science education program is typically required for all funeral service workers to enter the occupation. Courses usually cover topics such as ethics, grief counseling, funeral service, and business law. Accredited programs also include courses in embalming and restorative techniques.

Becoming a funeral director requires courses in ethics, grief counseling, and business law.

The American Board of Funeral Service Education (ABFSE) accredits funeral service and mortuary science programs, most of which offer a 2-year associate's degree at community colleges. Some programs offer a bachelor's degree.

Although an associate's degree is typically required, some employers prefer applicants to have a bachelor's degree. Common fields of degree include mortuary science, psychology, and business.

High school students can prepare to become a funeral service worker by taking classes in biology, chemistry, business, and public speaking.

Students may gain relevant experience working part-time or summer jobs in a funeral home.

Training

Those studying to be morticians and funeral arrangers must complete training, usually lasting 1 to 3 years, under the direction of a licensed funeral director or manager. The training, sometimes called an internship or an apprenticeship, may be completed before, during, or after graduating from a funeral service or mortuary science program and passing a national board exam.

Licenses, Certifications, and Registrations

Most states and Washington, DC, require workers to be licensed. An exception is Colorado, which offers a voluntary certification program. Although licensing laws and examinations vary by state, most applicants must meet the following criteria:

- Be 21 years old
- Complete an ABFSE accredited funeral service or mortuary science education program
- Pass a state and/or national board exam
- Serve an internship lasting 1 to 3 years

Working in multiple states requires multiple licenses. For specific requirements, contact each applicable state licensing board.

Most states require funeral directors to earn continuing education credits to keep their licenses.

The Cremation Association of North America (CANA), International Cemetery, Cremation and Funeral Association (ICCFA), and the National Funeral Directors Association (NFDA) offer crematory certification designations. Many states require certification for those who will perform cremations. For specific requirements, contact your state board or the relevant professional organizations.

Work Experience in a Related Occupation

Funeral home managers typically have multiple years of experience working as a funeral director or mortician before becoming managers.

Important Qualities

Business skills. Knowledge of financial statements and the ability to run a funeral home efficiently and profitably are important for funeral directors and managers.

Compassion. Death is a delicate and emotional matter. Funeral service workers must be able to treat clients with care and sympathy in their time of loss.

Interpersonal skills. Funeral service workers should have good interpersonal skills. When speaking with families, for example, they must be tactful and able to explain and discuss all matters about services provided.

Time-management skills. Funeral service workers must be able to handle numerous tasks for multiple customers, often over a short timeframe.

Pay

The median annual wage for funeral home managers was $72,110 in May 2022. The median wage is the wage at which half the workers in an occupation earned more than that amount and half earned less. The lowest 10 percent earned less than $43,910, and the highest 10 percent earned more than $133,010.

The median annual wage for morticians, undertakers, and funeral arrangers was $51,570 in May 2022. The lowest 10 percent earned less than $30,440, and the highest 10 percent earned more than $93,250.

In May 2022, the median annual wages for funeral home managers in the top industries in which they worked were as follows:

Death care services	$72,550

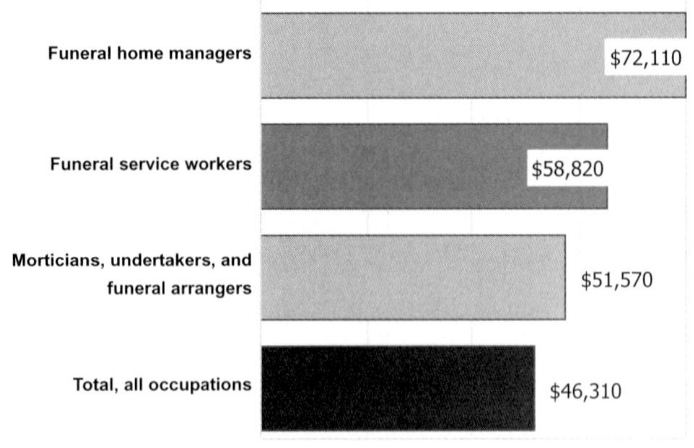

Note: All Occupations includes all occupations in the U.S. Economy.
Source: U.S. Bureau of Labor Statistics, Occupational Employment and Wage Statistics.

In May 2022, the median annual wages for morticians, undertakers, and funeral arrangers in the top industries in which they worked were as follows:

Death care services $50,990

Most funeral service workers are employed full time, and some work more than 40 hours per week. They are often on call; irregular hours, including evenings and weekends are common.

Job Outlook

Overall employment of funeral service workers is projected to grow 3 percent from 2022 to 2032, about as fast as the average for all occupations.

About 5,700 openings for funeral service workers are projected each year, on average, over the decade. Many of those openings are expected to result from the need to replace workers who transfer to different occupations or exit the labor force, such as to retire.

Employment

Funeral service workers will be needed to assist the growing number of people prearranging end-of-life services. This demand will be constrained by consumers increasingly preferring cremation, which costs less and requires fewer workers than do traditional funeral arrangements. However, since most cremations still involve a memorial service or funeral, funeral home managers are expected to be needed to guide families and loved ones through the death care process and to plan end-of-life events.

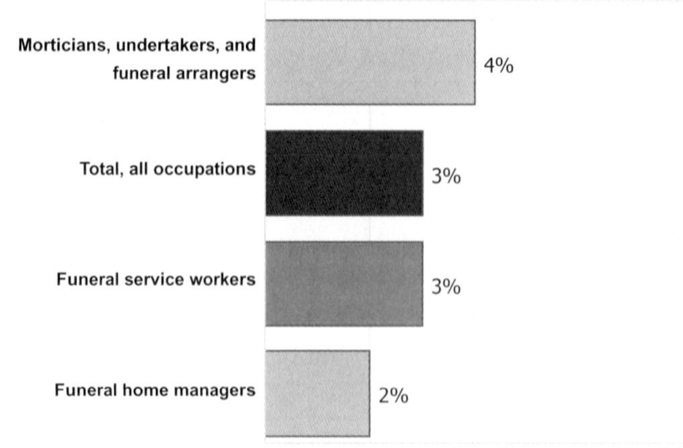

Note: All Occupations includes all occupations in the U.S. Economy.
Source: U.S. Bureau of Labor Statistics, Employment Projections program.

Occupational Title	SOC Code	Employment, 2022	Projected Employment, 2032	Change, 2022-32	
				Percent	Numeric
Funeral service workers	—	60,800	62,500	3	1,700
Funeral home managers	11-9171	36,400	37,200	2	800
Morticians, undertakers, and funeral arrangers	39-4031	24,500	25,400	4	900

Contacts for More Information

For more information, visit

- National Funeral Directors Association
- American Board of Funeral Service Education
- National Funeral Directors & Morticians Association, Inc.
- Cremation Association of North America
- International Cemetery, Cremation and Funeral Association

Gambling Services Workers

Summary

Quick Facts: Gambling Services Workers	
2022 Median Pay	$31,290 per year $15.04 per hour
Typical Entry-Level Education	High school diploma or equivalent
Work Experience in a Related Occupation	See How to Become One
On-the-job Training	See How to Become One
Number of Jobs, 2022	132,100
Job Outlook, 2022-32	1% (Little or no change)
Employment Change, 2022-32	1,700

What Gambling Services Workers Do

Gambling services workers serve customers in gambling establishments, such as casinos or racetracks.

Work Environment

Most gambling services workers are employed in gambling industries. Because most of these establishments are open 24 hours a day, 7 days a week, employees often work nights, weekends, and holidays. Most work full time, although part-time work is common.

How to Become a Gambling Services Worker

Gambling jobs typically require a high school diploma or equivalent to enter. Some employers require gambling managers to have a college degree. In addition, all gambling services workers must have excellent customer-service skills.

Pay

The median annual wage for gambling services workers was $31,290 in May 2022.

Many gaming services workers are employed by casinos.

Job Outlook

Overall employment of gambling services workers is projected to show little or no change from 2022 to 2032.

Despite limited employment growth, about 19,400 openings for gambling services workers are projected each year, on average, over the decade. Most of those openings are expected to result from the need to replace workers who transfer to different occupations or exit the labor force, such as to retire.

What Gambling Services Workers Do

Gambling services workers serve customers in gambling establishments, such as casinos or racetracks. Some workers tend slot machines or deal cards. Others take bets or pay out winnings. Still others supervise or manage gambling workers and operations.

Duties

Gambling services workers typically do the following:

- Interact with customers and make sure that they have a pleasant experience
- Monitor customers for violations of gambling rules or the establishment's policies
- Inform their supervisor or a security employee of any irregularities they see
- Enforce safety rules and report hazards
- Explain to customers how to play the games

Many gambling dealers specialize in one type of game.

The following are examples of types of gambling services workers:

First-line supervisors of gambling services workers directly monitor and coordinate the activities of workers in assigned gambling areas. They move within their assigned areas make sure that everything is running smoothly and that all areas are properly staffed. ***Table games supervisors*** (also called floor supervisors) oversee gambling dealers, table games, and players. ***Slot supervisors*** oversee activities of the slot department.

Gambling and sports book writers and runners handle bets on sporting events and take and record bets for customers. In addition, they help run games such as bingo and keno. They verify tickets and pay out winning tickets, and some runners collect winning tickets from customers.

Gambling dealers operate table games such as blackjack, craps, and roulette. They control the pace and action of the game, announcing each player's move to the rest of the table and letting players know when it is their turn. They inspect cards or dice, pay off winning bets, and collect on winning bets. Dealers are often required to work at least two games, usually blackjack or craps.

Gambling managers, who also may be *casino managers*, plan, coordinate, or direct operations in a gambling establishment. They may create house rules, such as for betting limits, and address customer complaints about service. Gambling managers also hire and train new employees.

For information on *gambling cage workers*, see the profile on financial clerks. For information on *gambling surveillance officers and gambling investigators*, see the profile on security guards and gambling surveillance officers.

Work Environment

Gambling services workers held about 132,100 jobs in 2022. Employment in the detailed occupations that make up gambling services workers was distributed as follows:

Gambling dealers	75,600
First-line supervisors of gambling services workers	29,700
Gambling service workers, all other	13,100
Gambling and sports book writers and runners	8,400
Gambling managers	5,300

Slot supervisors are in charge of the slot department.

The largest employers of gambling services workers were as follows:

Casino hotels	33%
Government	26
Gambling industries (except casino hotels)	25
Self-employed workers	8
Spectator sports	2

Gambling dealers spend most of their shift standing or sitting behind a table. Although managers and supervisors may spend limited time working in an office, they frequently monitor activities by circulating among areas on the floor of the establishment.

Casinos in some states are exempt from laws prohibiting smoking indoors. The atmosphere in these facilities may expose gambling services workers to hazards such as secondhand smoke from cigarettes, cigars, or pipes.

Noise from slot machines, gambling tables, and loud customers may be distracting, although workers may wear protective headgear in areas where machinery is used to count money.

Work Schedules

Most casinos are open 24 hours a day, 7 days a week. Employees are often scheduled to work nights, weekends, and holidays, which are typically the busiest times for casinos. Most work full time, although part-time work is common.

How to Become a Gambling Services Worker

Gambling jobs typically require a high school diploma or equivalent to enter. Some employers require gambling managers to have a college degree.

Education

Gambling dealers, gambling supervisors, and gambling and sports book writers and runners typically need a high school diploma or equivalent. Educational requirements for gambling managers differ by establishment. Some require a high school diploma or equivalent, while others require gambling managers to have some college or a degree. Those who pursue a degree may choose to study casino management, hotel management, or hospitality, in addition to taking courses in business.

Training

Individual casinos or other gambling establishments have their own training requirements. New gambling dealers may be sent to gambling school for a few weeks to learn a table game, such as blackjack or craps. These schools teach the game's rules

Dealers should have good customer-service skills.

and procedures, as well as state and local laws and regulations related to it.

Although gambling school is primarily for new employees, some experienced dealers go to gambling school if they want to be trained in a new game.

Completing gambling school before being hired may increase a prospective dealer's chances of being hired, but it does not guarantee a job. Employers usually audition prospective dealers for open positions to assess their personal qualities.

Gambling and sports book writers and runners usually do not have to go to gambling school. They typically are trained in less than 1 month. The employer provides instruction on state and local laws and regulations related to the game, as well the particulars of their job, such as keno calling.

Licenses, Certifications, and Registrations

Gambling services workers must be licensed by a state regulatory agency, such as a state casino control board or gambling commission. Licensing requirements for supervisory or managerial positions may differ from those for gambling dealers, gambling and sports book writers and runners, and all other gambling workers. However, all candidates for a license must provide photo identification and pay a fee. Typically, they also must pass an extensive background check and drug test. Failure to pass the background check may prevent candidates from getting a job or a gambling license.

Age requirements also vary by state. For specific licensing requirements, visit the state's gambling commission website.

Work Experience in a Related Occupation

Gambling supervisors and gambling managers usually have several years of experience working in a casino or other gambling establishment. Gambling managers often have experience as a dealer or in the customer outreach department. Slot supervisors and table games supervisors usually have experience working in the activities of their respective areas. Some also have worked in entry-level marketing or customer-service positions.

Advancement

Often, gambling managers are promoted from positions as slot supervisors or table games supervisors. They also may be moved from a management job in another part of the establishment, such as hospitality, after learning about the establishment's operations through an internship or on-the-job training.

Gambling dealers may advance to become gambling supervisors and, eventually, managers. A slot supervisor or table games supervisor may also advance to become a gambling manager.

Important Qualities

Communication skills. Gambling services workers must explain the rules of the game to customers and answer their questions. Misunderstandings can cost a customer money and damage the establishment's reputation.

Customer-service skills. Gambling jobs involve interaction with customers. The success or failure of a gambling establishment depends on how customers view the experience, making customer service important for all of these occupations.

Leadership skills. Gambling managers and supervisors oversee other gambling services workers and must guide them in doing their jobs and developing their skills.

Math skills. Because they may deal with large amounts of money, gambling services workers must be good at math.

Organizational skills. Gambling managers and supervisors should have an orderly system in place to handle administrative and other tasks for overseeing gambling services workers.

Patience. All gambling services workers must stay composed when they encounter a customer who becomes upset or breaks a rule. They also must stay calm when dealing with equipment failures or malfunctions.

Pay

The median annual wage for gambling services workers was $31,290 in May 2022. The median wage is the wage at which half the workers in an occupation earned more than that amount and half earned less. The lowest 10 percent earned less than $20,710, and the highest 10 percent earned more than $73,070.

Median annual wages for gambling services workers in May 2022 were as follows:

Gambling managers	$80,710
First-line supervisors of gambling services workers	56,290
Gambling service workers, all other	30,350
Gambling dealers	29,120
Gambling and sports book writers and runners	28,940

In May 2022, the median annual wages for gambling services workers in the top industries in which they worked were as follows:

Government	$34,490

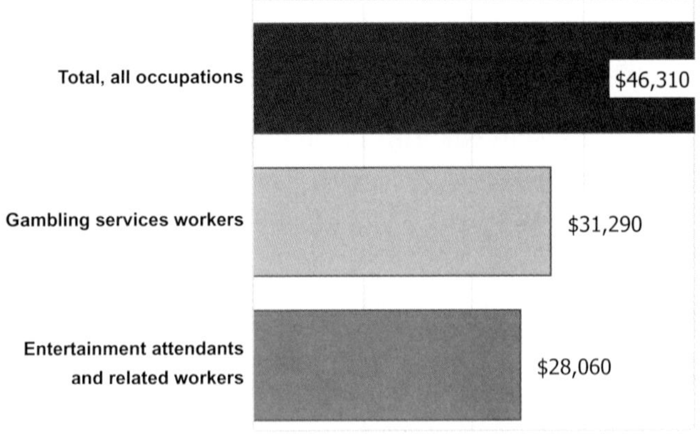

Note: All Occupations includes all occupations in the U.S. Economy. Source: U.S. Bureau of Labor Statistics, Occupational Employment and Wage Statistics.

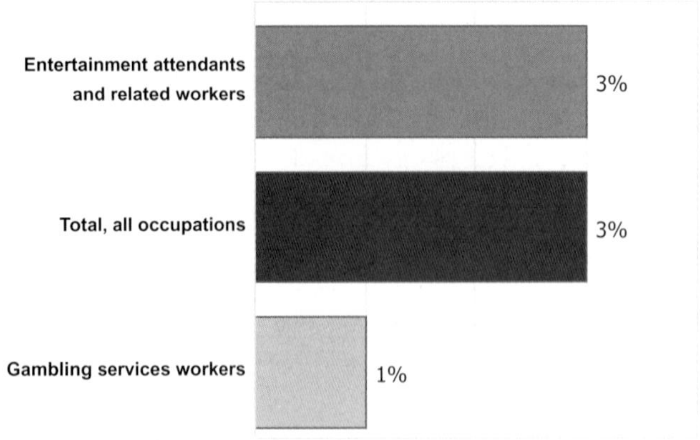

Note: All Occupations includes all occupations in the U.S. Economy. Source: U.S. Bureau of Labor Statistics, Employment Projections program.

Gambling industries (except casino hotels)	31,690
Spectator sports	28,800
Casino hotels	27,040

Most casinos are open 24 hours a day, 7 days a week. Employees are often scheduled to work nights, weekends, and holidays, which are typically the busiest times for casinos. Most work full time, although part-time work is common.

Job Outlook

Overall employment of gambling services workers is projected to show little or no change from 2022 to 2032.

Despite limited employment growth, about 19,400 openings for gambling services workers are projected each year, on average, over the decade. Most of those openings are expected to result from the need to replace workers who transfer to different occupations or exit the labor force, such as to retire.

Employment

Projected employment of gambling services workers varies by occupation (see table).

Demand is expected to be driven by the increasing popularity of gambling establishments. Additional states currently without commercial gambling establishments may allow new casinos to be built over the next decade in an effort to bring in more tax revenue.

The growth of online gambling may limit employment for some of these workers, including gambling and sports book writers and runners. Although some online gambling is linked to physical locations, online-only gambling sites do not require the same mix of employees.

Also, as more states approve expansions in the number of physical and online gambling establishments, the competition for customers will increase. Establishments that fail to keep or attract customers may close, thereby negating some of the jobs created.

Occupational Title	SOC Code	Employment, 2022	Projected Employment, 2032	Change, 2022-32	
				Percent	Numeric
Gambling services workers	—	132,100	133,700	1	1,700
Gambling managers	11-9071	5,300	5,400	3	100
First-line supervisors of gambling services workers	39-1013	29,700	30,600	3	1,000
Gambling dealers	39-3011	75,600	76,400	1	800
Gambling and sports book writers and runners	39-3012	8,400	8,100	-4	-300
Gambling service workers, all other	39-3019	13,100	13,200	1	100

Contacts for More Information

For more information, visit

- American Gaming Association
- Casino Careers

Manicurists and Pedicurists

Summary

Quick Facts: Manicurists and Pedicurists	
2022 Median Pay	$31,130 per year $14.97 per hour
Typical Entry-Level Education	Postsecondary non-degree award
Work Experience in a Related Occupation	None
On-the-job Training	None
Number of Jobs, 2022	196,900
Job Outlook, 2022-32	9% (Much faster than average)
Employment Change, 2022-32	17,100

What Manicurists and Pedicurists Do

Manicurists and pedicurists clean, shape, and beautify fingernails and toenails.

Work Environment

Manicurists and pedicurists usually work in a nail salon, spa, or hair salon. Most manicurists and pedicurists work full time, although part-time work is common. Work schedules may vary and often include evenings and weekends.

How to Become a Manicurist or Pedicurist

Manicurists and pedicurists must complete a state-approved cosmetology or nail technician program and then pass a state exam for licensure.

Pay

The median hourly wage for manicurists and pedicurists was $14.97 in May 2022.

Job Outlook

Employment of manicurists and pedicurists is projected to grow 9 percent from 2022 to 2032, much faster than the average for all occupations.

About 25,500 openings for manicurists and pedicurists are projected each year, on average, over the decade. Many of those openings are expected to result from the need to replace workers who transfer to different occupations or exit the labor force, such as to retire.

What Manicurists and Pedicurists Do

Manicurists and pedicurists clean, shape, and beautify fingernails and toenails.

Duties

Manicurists and pedicurists typically do the following:

- Discuss nail treatments and services available
- Remove clients' nail polish, if any
- Clean, trim, and file nails
- Soften calluses and remove rough skin
- Massage and moisturize hands (for a manicure) and feet (for a pedicure)
- Polish or buff nails
- Apply or remove artificial nails and nail art
- Advise clients about nail and skin care for hands and feet
- Clean and disinfect their work area and tools

Manicurists and pedicurists, sometimes called *nail technicians*, work exclusively on the hands and feet to groom fingernails and toenails. A typical service involves soaking the clients' hands or feet to soften the skin in order to remove dead skin cells and artificial nails. Manicurists and pedicurists apply lotion to the hands and feet to moisturize the skin. They also may shape and apply polish to natural fingernails or toenails or apply and decorate artificial fingernails.

Manicurists and pedicurists use equipment that includes nail clippers, nail files, and cuticle tools. They must be focused while they perform their duties, because most of the tools they use are sharp. They keep their tools clean and sanitary and follow health regulations to protect consumer safety.

Manicurists and pedicurists clean, shape, and beautify fingernails and toenails.

Manicurists and pedicurists polish or buff nails.

Some manicurists and pedicurists operate their own nail salon, which requires performing business tasks such as keeping inventory and ordering supplies. They also hire and supervise workers and may sell nail care products, such as nail polish and hand or foot cream.

Work Environment

Manicurists and pedicurists held about 196,900 jobs in 2022. The largest employers of manicurists and pedicurists were as follows:

Personal care services	70%
Self-employed workers	29

Manicurists and pedicurists usually work in a nail salon, spa, or hair salon. The job involves a lot of sitting. A small number of manicurists and pedicurists make house calls, traveling to their clients' locations to provide mobile services. However, mobile services may not be widely available.

Manicurists and pedicurists use chemicals when working on fingernails and toenails, so they often wear protective clothing such as gloves and masks.

Work Schedules

Most manicurists and pedicurists work full time, although part-time work is common. Schedules may vary and often include evenings and weekends. Some manicurists and pedicurists work more than 40 hours per week. Self-employed workers often set their own schedules.

How to Become a Manicurist or Pedicurist

Manicurists and pedicurists must complete a state-approved cosmetology or nail technician program and then pass a state exam for licensure.

Education

Manicurists and pedicurists must complete a state-approved cosmetology or nail technician program. These programs usually involve classroom and hands-on training. For a list of approved programs, contact your state licensing agency.

Licenses, Certifications, and Registrations

State licensing requirements vary but usually include completing a state-approved cosmetology or nail technician program and passing a state exam. Applicants also may need to be at least 16 or 18 years old and have a high school diploma or the equivalent. Check with your state licensing agency for details.

Under state reciprocity agreements, licensed manicurists and pedicurists may be able to get a license in another state without needing to complete an additional program or to pass that state's exam.

Important Qualities

Business skills. Manicurists and pedicurist who run their own nail salon must understand business principles. For example, they should be skilled at administrative tasks, such as

Manicurists and pedicurists work in spas or nail salons, and often sit for long periods.

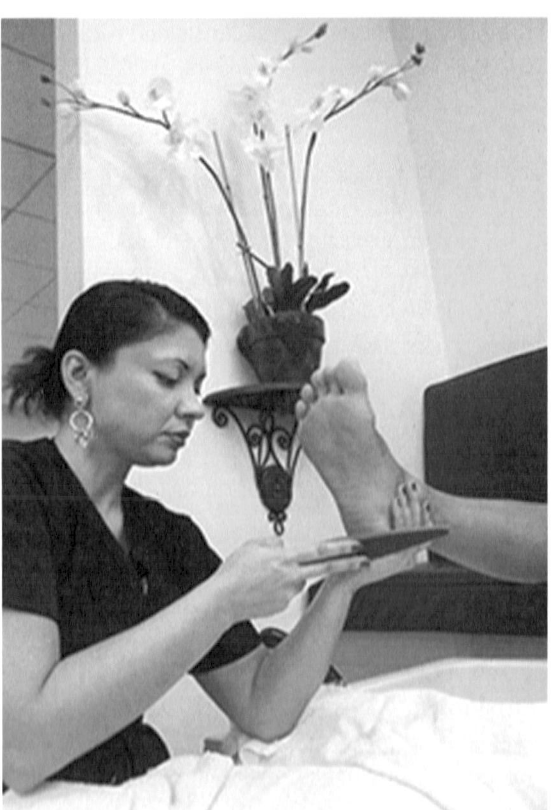

Manicurists and pedicurists must pass a state-approved cosmetology program before licensure.

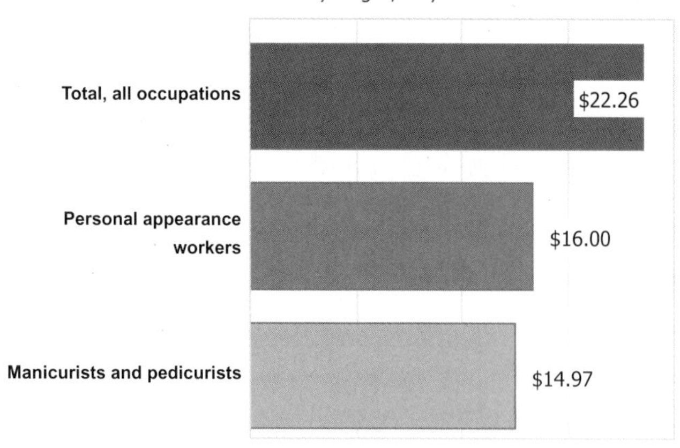

Note: All Occupations includes all occupations in the U.S. Economy.
Source: U.S. Bureau of Labor Statistics, Occupational Employment and Wage Statistics.

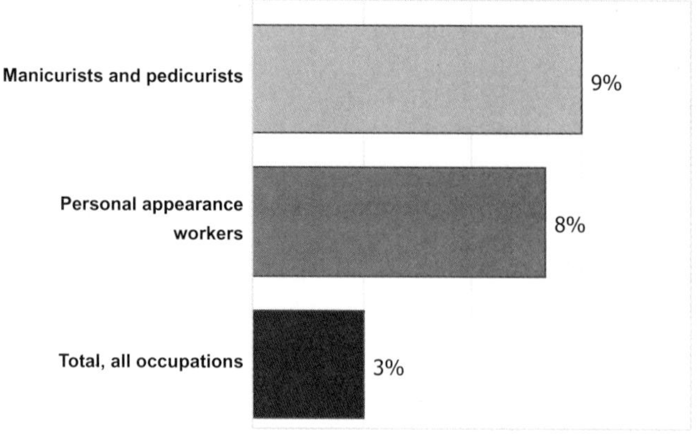

Note: All Occupations includes all occupations in the U.S. Economy.
Source: U.S. Bureau of Labor Statistics, Employment Projections program.

accounting, and be able to manage a salon and its personnel efficiently and profitably.

Creativity. Manicurists and pedicurists must be able to neatly finish small, intricate nail designs, as well as to suggest designs and match them to individual tastes.

Customer-service skills. Manicurists and pedicurists must have good listening and interpersonal skills to meet clients' needs. Interacting with clients while doing a manicure or pedicure encourages repeat business.

Dexterity. A steady hand is essential in achieving precise nail design. In addition, because manicurists and pedicurists often use sharp tools, they must have good finger dexterity.

Pay

The median hourly wage for manicurists and pedicurists was $14.97 in May 2022. The median wage is the wage at which half the workers in an occupation earned more than that amount and half earned less. The lowest 10 percent earned less than $11.22, and the highest 10 percent earned more than $21.72.

In May 2022, the median hourly wages for manicurists and pedicurists in the top industries in which they worked were as follows:

Personal care services $14.97

Most manicurists and pedicurists work full time, although part-time work is common. Schedules may vary and often include evenings and weekends. Some manicurists and pedicurists work more than 40 hours per week. Self-employed workers often set their own schedules.

Job Outlook

Employment of manicurists and pedicurists is projected to grow 9 percent from 2022 to 2032, much faster than the average for all occupations.

About 25,500 openings for manicurists and pedicurists are projected each year, on average, over the decade. Many of those openings are expected to result from the need to replace workers who transfer to different occupations or exit the labor force, such as to retire.

Employment

The projected increase in employment reflects demand for nail services, such as mini-sessions (quick manicures at a low cost) and mobile manicures and pedicures (nail services offered outside of the salon).

The desire among many women and a growing number of men to lead a healthier lifestyle through better grooming and wellness is expected to result in higher employment for manicurists and pedicurists.

Considered a low-cost luxury service, manicures and pedicures will continue to be in demand by individuals at all income levels.

Occupational Title	SOC Code	Employment, 2022	Projected Employment, 2032	Change, 2022-32	
				Percent	Numeric
Manicurists and pedicurists	39-5092	196,900	214,000	9	17,100

Contacts for More Information

For more information, visit

- American Association of Cosmetology Schools (AACS)
- Beauty Schools Directory
- National–Interstate Council of State Boards of Cosmetology (NIC)
- Professional Beauty Association (PBA)

Recreation Workers

Summary

Quick Facts: Recreation Workers	
2022 Median Pay	$31,680 per year $15.23 per hour
Typical Entry-Level Education	High school diploma or equivalent
Work Experience in a Related Occupation	None
On-the-job Training	Short-term on-the-job training
Number of Jobs, 2022	289,400
Job Outlook, 2022-32	5% (Faster than average)
Employment Change, 2022-32	13,400

What Recreation Workers Do

Recreation workers design and lead activities to help people stay active, improve fitness, and have fun.

Work Environment

Recreation workers are employed in a variety of settings, including recreation centers, parks, summer camps, and nursing and residential care facilities. Many workers spend much of their time being physically active in the outdoors.

How to Become a Recreation Worker

Education and training requirements for recreation workers vary with the type of job, but workers typically need at least a high school diploma or the equivalent and a few weeks of on-the-job training.

Pay

The median annual wage for recreation workers was $31,680 in May 2022.

Job Outlook

Employment of recreation workers is projected to grow 5 percent from 2022 to 2032, faster than the average for all occupations.

About 61,700 openings for recreation workers are projected each year, on average, over the decade. Many of those openings are expected to result from the need to replace workers who transfer to different occupations or exit the labor force, such as to retire.

What Recreation Workers Do

Recreation workers design and lead activities to help people stay active, improve fitness, and have fun. They work with groups in summer camps, fitness and recreational sports centers, nursing care facilities, nature parks, and other settings. They may lead such activities as arts and crafts, sports, music, dramatics, or games.

Duties

Recreation workers typically do the following:

- Plan, organize, and lead activities for groups or recreation centers
- Explain the rules of activities and instruct participants at a variety of skill levels
- Enforce safety rules to prevent injury
- Modify activities to suit the needs of specific groups, such as seniors
- Administer basic first aid if needed
- Organize and set up the equipment that is used in recreational activities

The specific responsibilities of recreation workers vary greatly with their job title, their level of training, and the state they work in.

The following are examples of types of recreation workers:

Activity specialists provide instruction and coaching primarily in one activity, such as dance, swimming, or tennis. These

Recreation workers may lead children in nature study activities at a day camp.

Recreation workers lead groups in activities such as arts and crafts.

workers may work in camps, aquatic centers, or anywhere else where there is interest in a single activity.

Recreation leaders are responsible for a recreation program's daily operation. They primarily organize and direct participants, schedule the use of facilities, set up and keep records of equipment use, and ensure that recreation facilities and equipment are used and maintained properly. They may lead classes and provide instruction in a recreational activity, such as kayaking or golf.

Camp counselors work directly with youths in residential (overnight) or day camps. They often lead and instruct children and teenagers in a variety of outdoor activities, such as swimming, hiking, horseback riding, or nature study. Counselors also provide guidance and supervise daily living and socialization. Some counselors may specialize in a specific activity, such as archery, boating, music, drama, or gymnastics.

Work Environment

Recreation workers held about 289,400 jobs in 2022. The largest employers of recreation workers were as follows:

Local government, excluding education and hospitals	30%
Nursing and residential care facilities	20
Religious, grantmaking, civic, professional, and similar organizations	12
Social assistance	6

Many workers spend much of their time outdoors. Others provide instruction indoors, for activities such as dance or karate. Still others typically spend most of their time in an office, planning programs and special events.

Recreation workers may face some injury risk while participating in physical activities.

Work Schedules

Many recreation workers, such as camp counselors or activity specialists, work weekends or part-time or irregular hours, or may be seasonally employed. Seasonal workers may work as few as 90 days or as long as 9 months during a season, depending on where they are employed and the type of activity they lead. For example, in areas of the United States that have warm winters, outdoor swimming pools may employ related recreation workers for a majority of the year. In other areas of the country, they may work only during the summer.

Activity specialists who teach dance usually provide instruction indoors.

How to Become a Recreation Worker

Education and training requirements for recreation workers vary with the type of job, but workers typically need at least a high school diploma or the equivalent and receive on-the-job training.

Education and Training

Recreation workers typically need at least a high school diploma or the equivalent. Many receive on-the-job training that typically lasts less than a month.

Entry-level educational requirements vary with the type of position. For example, an activity leader position working with the elderly will have different requirements than a position as a summer camp counselor working with children.

Some positions may require a bachelor's degree or college coursework. In 2017, the Council on Accreditation of Parks, Recreation, Tourism, and Related Professions, a branch of the National Recreation and Park Association (NRPA), accredited more than 70 bachelor's degree programs in recreation or leisure studies. A bachelor's degree in other subjects, such as liberal arts or public administration, may also qualify applicants for some positions.

Important Qualities

Communication skills. Recreation workers must be able to communicate well. They often work with large groups of people and need to give clear instructions, motivate participants, and maintain order and safety.

Flexibility. Recreation workers must be flexible when planning activities. They must be able to adapt plans to suit changing environmental conditions and participants' needs.

Recreation workers maintain order and safety.

Leadership skills. Recreation workers should be able to lead both large and small groups. They often lead activities for people of all ages and abilities.

Physical strength. Most recreation workers should be physically fit. Their job may require a considerable amount of movement because they often demonstrate activities while explaining them.

Problem-solving skills. Recreation workers need strong problem-solving skills. They must be able to create and reinvent activities and programs for all types of participants.

For recreation workers who generally work part time, such as camp counselors and activity specialists, certain qualities may be more important than education. These qualities include a worker's experience leading activities, the ability to work well with children or the elderly, and the ability to ensure the safety of participants.

Licenses, Certifications, and Registrations

The NRPA offers four certifications for recreation workers:

- Certified Parks and Recreation Professional (CPRP)
- Certified Parks and Recreation Executive (CPRE)
- Aquatic Facility Operator (AFO)
- Certified Playground Safety Inspector (CPSI)

Applicants may qualify for certification with different combinations of education and work experience. They also must take continuing education classes to maintain their certification.

The American Camp Association offers certificates for various levels of camp staff, including Entry-Level Program Staff Certificate and Camp Director Certificate. Individuals who complete online courses may show their advanced level of knowledge of core competencies.

Some recreation jobs require other kinds of certification. For example, first aid and CPR (cardiopulmonary resuscitation) certifications may be required for leading camp or sports activities. These certifications are available from organizations such as the American Heart Association or the American Red Cross.

Jobs for recreation workers may also require a valid driver's license and the ability to pass a background check.

Specific requirements vary by job and employer.

Advancement

As workers gain experience, they may be promoted to positions with greater responsibilities. Recreation workers with experience and managerial skills may advance to supervisory or managerial positions. Eventually, they may become directors of a recreation department or may start their own recreation company.

Pay

The median annual wage for recreation workers was $31,680 in May 2022. The median wage is the wage at which half the workers in an occupation earned more than that amount

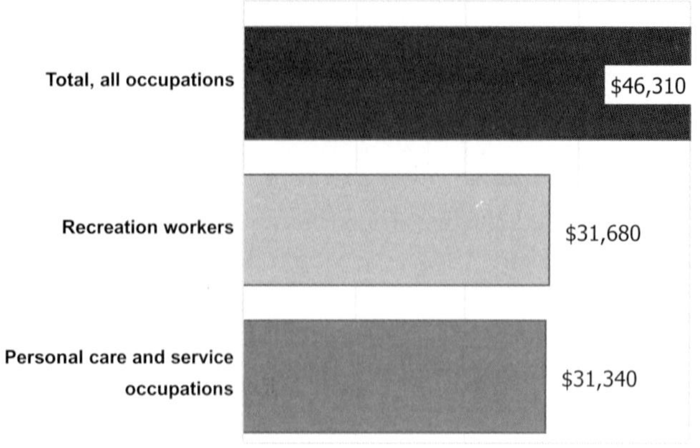

Note: All Occupations includes all occupations in the U.S. Economy.
Source: U.S. Bureau of Labor Statistics, Occupational Employment and Wage Statistics.

and half earned less. The lowest 10 percent earned less than $22,580, and the highest 10 percent earned more than $48,270.

In May 2022, the median annual wages for recreation workers in the top industries in which they worked were as follows:

Nursing and residential care facilities	$33,660
Local government, excluding education and hospitals	32,030
Social assistance	32,000
Religious, grantmaking, civic, professional, and similar organizations	31,210

Many recreation workers, such as camp counselors or activity specialists, work weekends or part-time or irregular hours, or may be seasonally employed. Seasonal workers may work as few as 90 days or as long as 9 months during a season, depending on where they are employed and the type of activity they lead. For example, in areas of the United States that have warm

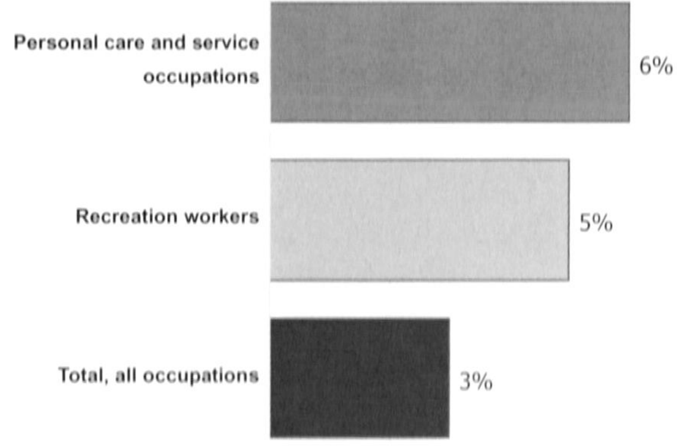

Note: All Occupations includes all occupations in the U.S. Economy.
Source: U.S. Bureau of Labor Statistics, Employment Projections program.

winters, outdoor swimming pools may employ related recreation workers for a majority of the year. In other areas of the country, they may work only during the summer.

Job Outlook

Employment of recreation workers is projected to grow 5 percent from 2022 to 2032, faster than the average for all occupations.

About 61,700 openings for recreation workers are projected each year, on average, over the decade. Many of those openings are expected to result from the need to replace workers who transfer to different occupations or exit the labor force, such as to retire.

Employment

An increased emphasis on the importance of lifelong well-being is expected to create demand for recreation workers in a variety of settings, including fitness and recreational sports centers, country clubs, and other organizations. Parks and recreation departments may contract out the services of activity specialists.

In addition, there will be more demand for recreation workers to work with older clients, especially in continuing care retirement communities and assisted living facilities.

Occupational Title	SOC Code	Employment, 2022	Projected Employment, 2032	Change, 2022-32	
				Percent	Numeric
Recreation workers	39-9032	289,400	302,700	5	13,400

Contacts for More Information

For more information, visit

- National Recreation and Park Association
- American Camp Association
- American Heart Association
- American Red Cross

Skincare Specialists

Summary

Quick Facts: Skincare Specialists

2022 Median Pay	$38,060 per year $18.30 per hour
Typical Entry-Level Education	Postsecondary nondegree award
Work Experience in a Related Occupation	None
On-the-job Training	None
Number of Jobs, 2022	82,000
Job Outlook, 2022-32	9% (Much faster than average)
Employment Change, 2022-32	7,500

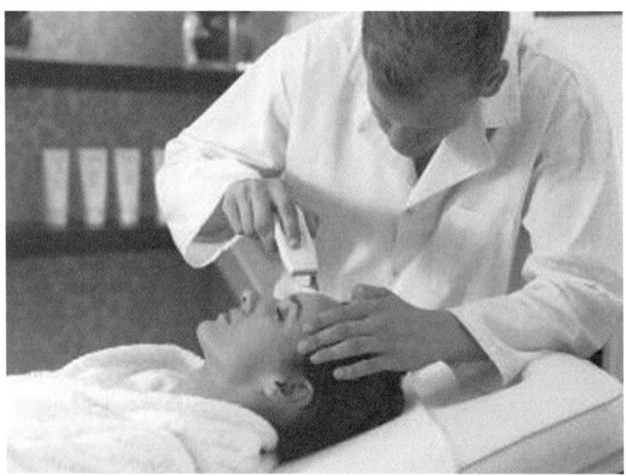

Skincare specialists provide treatments, such as peels, masks, or scrubs, to remove dead or dry skin.

What Skincare Specialists Do

Skincare specialists provide cleansing and other face and body treatments to enhance a person's appearance.

Work Environment

Skincare specialists usually work in salons and beauty and health spas, and some are self-employed. Part-time work is common, and work schedules may vary and include evenings and weekends.

How to Become a Skincare Specialist

Skincare specialists must complete a state-approved cosmetology or esthetician program and then pass a state exam for licensure.

Pay

The median hourly wage for skincare specialists was $18.30 in May 2022.

Job Outlook

Employment of skincare specialists is projected to grow 9 percent from 2022 to 2032, much faster than the average for all occupations.

About 12,400 openings for skincare specialists are projected each year, on average, over the decade. Many of those openings are expected to result from the need to replace workers who transfer to different occupations or exit the labor force, such as to retire.

What Skincare Specialists Do

Skincare specialists, also known as *estheticians*, provide cleansing and other face and body treatments to enhance a person's appearance.

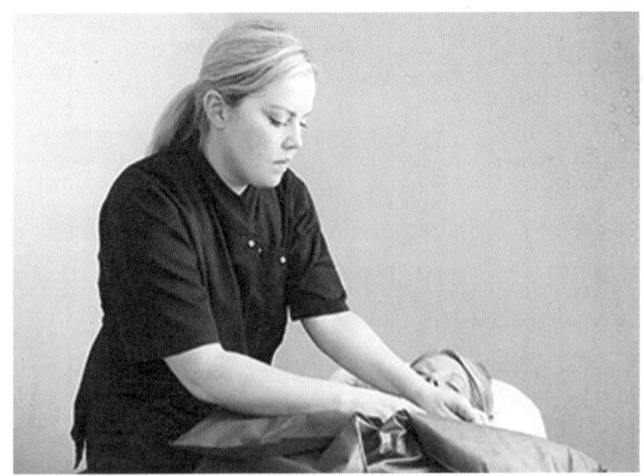

Skincare specialists remove unwanted hair using wax or laser treatment.

Duties

Skincare specialists typically do the following:

- Disinfect equipment and clean work areas before and after procedures
- Evaluate clients' skin condition and appearance
- Discuss available treatments and determine which products will improve clients' skin quality
- Remove unwanted hair, using wax, lasers, or other approved treatments
- Clean the skin before applying makeup
- Recommend skincare products, such as cleansers, creams, or lotions
- Teach and advise clients on how to apply makeup and how to care for their skin
- Refer clients to another skincare specialist, such as a dermatologist, for serious skin problems

Skincare specialists give facials, full-body treatments, and head and neck massages to improve the health and appearance of the skin. Some provide other skincare treatments to remove dead or dry skin, such as masks, peels, and scrubs. They also may provide eyelash services, makeup application, and hair removal.

In addition, these specialists create daily skincare routines for clients based on skin analysis and help them understand which products will work best for them.

Those who operate their own salons have managerial duties that include hiring, firing, and supervising workers, as well as keeping business and inventory records, ordering supplies, and arranging for advertising.

Work Environment

Skincare specialists held about 82,000 jobs in 2022. The largest employers of skincare specialists were as follows:

Personal care services	53%
Self-employed workers	24
Offices of physicians	9
Health and personal care retailers	5
Traveler accommodation	3

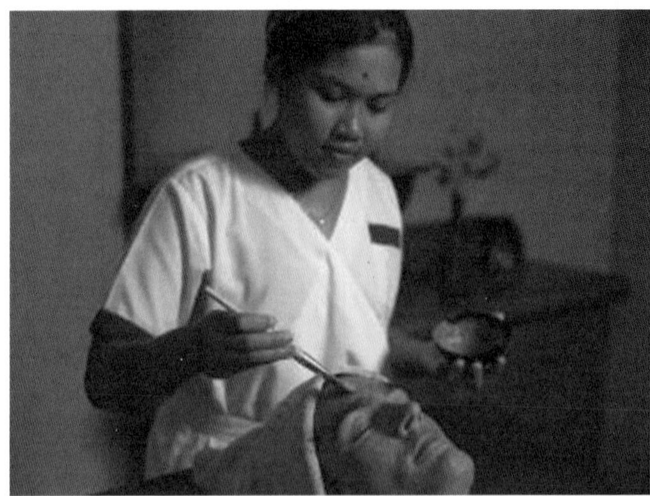

Skincare specialists work in salons, beauty spas, and sometimes in medical offices.

Skincare specialists usually work in salons and beauty and health spas. Some work in medical offices. Skincare specialists may have to stand for extended periods of time.

Because skincare specialists must evaluate the condition of the skin, good lighting and clean surroundings are important. Protective clothing and good ventilation also may be necessary, because skincare specialists often use chemicals on the face and body.

Work Schedules

Part-time work is common for skincare specialists. Work schedules may vary and include evenings and weekends.

How to Become a Skincare Specialist

Skincare specialists must complete a state-approved cosmetology or esthetician program and then pass a state exam for licensure.

Education

To enter the occupation, skincare specialists typically must complete a state-approved cosmetology or esthetician program. Although some high schools may offer vocational training, most people receive their training from a postsecondary vocational school. The Associated Skin Care Professionals organization offers a State Regulation Guide, downloadable as a PDF, on its Requirements by State page.

Licenses, Certifications, and Registrations

After completing an approved cosmetology or esthetician program, skincare specialists take a written and practical exam to get a state license. Licensing requirements vary by state, so those interested should contact their state board.

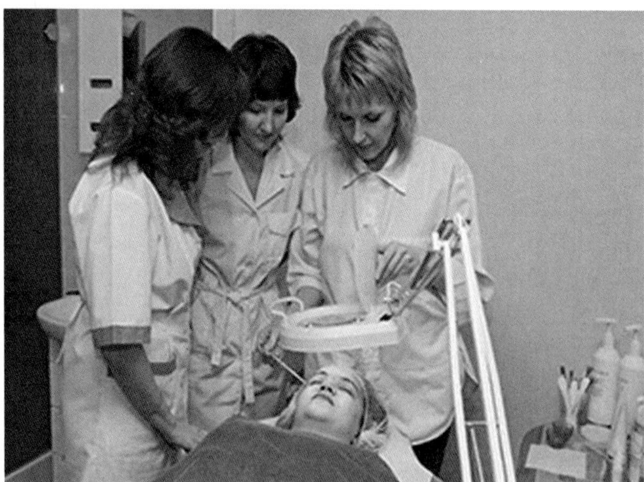

Skincare specialists must pass a state-approved cosmetology program before getting licensed.

The National-Interstate Council of State Boards of Cosmetology and American Association of Cosmetology Schools provide contact information for state licensing boards. Resources about exam and licensing requirements include sample exam questions.

Many states offer continuing education seminars and programs designed to keep skincare specialists current on new techniques and products. Post-licensing training is also available through manufacturers, associations, and at trade shows.

State reciprocity agreements may allow licensed skincare specialists to get a license in another state without needing additional formal training or state board testing. Contact your state licensing agency for details.

Important Qualities

Business skills. Skincare specialists who run their own salon must understand business principles, such as accounting, to manage a salon efficiently and profitably.

Customer-service skills. Skincare specialists should be friendly and courteous to their clients to encourage repeat business.

Initiative. Self-employed skincare specialists generate their own business opportunities and must be proactive in finding new clients.

Physical stamina. Skincare specialists spend most of their day standing.

Tidiness. Workers must keep their work area clean and sanitary for the health and safety of their clients. They also must keep a neat personal appearance to increase the likelihood that clients will return.

Time-management skills. Skincare specialists need to manage their time efficiently for scheduling appointments and providing services.

Pay

The median hourly wage for skincare specialists was $18.30 in May 2022. The median wage is the wage at which half the workers in an occupation earned more than that amount and half earned less. The lowest 10 percent earned less than $12.28, and the highest 10 percent earned more than $38.13.

In May 2022, the median hourly wages for skincare specialists in the top industries in which they worked were as follows:

Offices of physicians	$20.62
Personal care services	18.14
Health and personal care retailers	16.78
Traveler accommodation	16.46

Part-time work is common for skincare specialists. Work schedules may vary and include evenings and weekends.

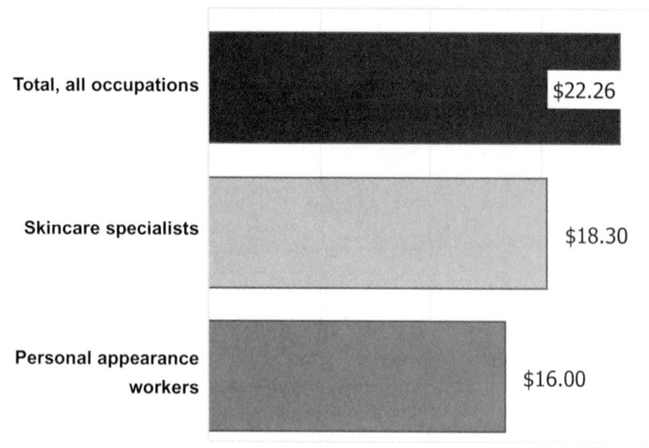

Note: All Occupations includes all occupations in the U.S. Economy.
Source: U.S. Bureau of Labor Statistics, Occupational Employment and Wage Statistics.

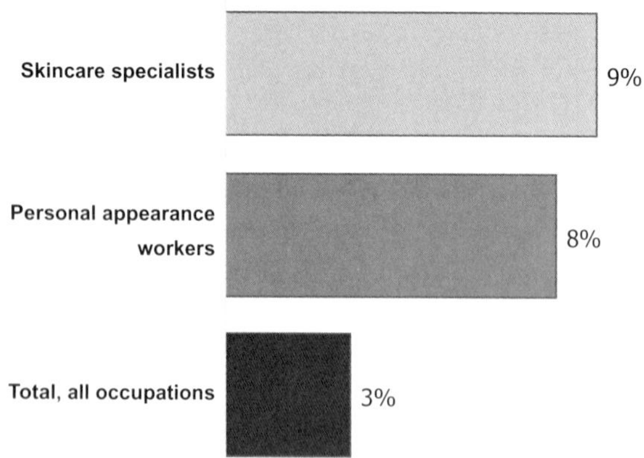

Note: All Occupations includes all occupations in the U.S. Economy.
Source: U.S. Bureau of Labor Statistics, Employment Projections program.

Job Outlook

Employment of skincare specialists is projected to grow 9 percent from 2022 to 2032, much faster than the average for all occupations.

About 12,400 openings for skincare specialists are projected each year, on average, over the decade. Many of those openings are expected to result from the need to replace workers who transfer to different occupations or exit the labor force, such as to retire.

Employment

The projected increase in employment reflects demand for services being offered, such as mini-sessions (quick facials at a lower cost) and mobile facials (making house calls) directly from skincare specialists rather than hairdressers, hairstylists, and cosmetologists. Employment growth also should result from the desire among many women and a growing number of men who seek out skincare services to reduce the effects of aging, to look good on social media platforms, and to lead a healthier lifestyle through better grooming.

Occupational Title	SOC Code	Employment, 2022	Projected Employment, 2032	Change, 2022-32	
				Percent	Numeric
Skincare specialists	39-5094	82,000	89,400	9	7,500

Contacts for More Information

For more information, visit

- Associated Skin Care Professionals (ASCP)
- Beauty Schools Directory
- International Spa Association (ISPA)
- American Association of Cosmetology Schools (AACS)
- National-Interstate Council of State Boards of Cosmetology (NIC)
- Professional Beauty Association (PBA)

Production

Assemblers and Fabricators

Summary

Quick Facts: Assemblers and Fabricators	
2022 Median Pay	$37,930 per year $18.24 per hour
Typical Entry-Level Education	High school diploma or equivalent
Work Experience in a Related Occupation	None
On-the-job Training	Moderate-term on-the-job training
Number of Jobs, 2022	1,961,900
Job Outlook, 2022-32	-6% (Decline)
Employment Change, 2022-32	-125,700

What Assemblers and Fabricators Do

Assemblers and fabricators build finished products and the parts that go into them.

Work Environment

Most assemblers and fabricators work in manufacturing plants. Their duties may involve long periods of standing or sitting. Most work full time, including some evenings and weekends.

How to Become an Assembler or Fabricator

The education and qualifications typically needed to enter these occupations vary by industry and employer. Although a high school diploma is enough for most jobs, experience and training are needed for advanced assembly work.

Pay

The median annual wage for assemblers and fabricators was $37,930 in May 2022.

Job Outlook

Overall employment of assemblers and fabricators is projected to decline 6 percent from 2022 to 2032.

Despite declining employment, about 188,600 openings for assemblers and fabricators are projected each year, on average, over the decade. All of those openings are expected to result from the need to replace workers who transfer to other occupations or exit the labor force, such as to retire.

What Assemblers and Fabricators Do

Assemblers and fabricators build finished products and the parts that go into them. They use handtools and machines to make vehicles, toys, electronic devices, and more.

Duties

Assemblers and fabricators typically do the following:

- Read and understand schematics and blueprints
- Position or align components and parts either manually or with hoists
- Use handtools or machines to assemble parts
- Conduct quality control checks
- Clean and maintain work area and equipment, including tools

Assemblers and fabricators need a range of knowledge and skills. For example, assemblers putting together complex

Assemblers and fabricators assemble both finished products and the parts that go into them.

Assemblers and fabricators conduct quality checks for faulty components or mistakes in the assembly process.

machines must be able to read detailed schematics. After determining how parts should connect, they use handtools or power tools to trim, cut, and make other adjustments to fit components together. When the parts are properly aligned, they connect them with bolts and screws, or they weld or solder pieces together.

Assemblers look for faulty components and mistakes throughout the assembly process. Such assessments help to ensure quality by allowing assemblers to fix problems before defective products are made.

Modern manufacturing systems use robots, computers, and other technologies. These systems use teams of workers to produce entire products or components.

Assemblers and fabricators may also be involved in product development. Designers and engineers may consult manufacturing workers during the design stage to improve product reliability and manufacturing efficiency. Some experienced assemblers work with designers and engineers to build prototypes or test products.

Although most assemblers and fabricators are classified as team assemblers, others specialize in producing one type of product or in doing the same or similar tasks throughout the manufacturing process.

The following are examples of types of assemblers and fabricators:

Aircraft structure, surfaces, rigging, and systems assemblers fit, fasten, and install parts of airplanes, missiles, or space vehicles. These parts include the wings, landing gear, and heating and ventilating systems.

Coil winders, tapers, and finishers roll wire curs of electrical components used in electric and electronic products, including resistors, transformers, and electric motors. Using handtools, these workers also attach and trim coils or insulation.

Electrical and electronic equipment assemblers build products such as computers, electric motors, and sensing equipment. Unlike in industries with automated systems, much of the small-scale production of electronic devices for aircraft, military systems, and medical equipment must be done by hand. These workers use devices such as soldering irons.

Electromechanical equipment assemblers make and modify mechanical devices that run on electricity, such as household appliances, computer tomography scanners, and vending machines. These workers use tools such as rulers, rivet guns, and soldering irons.

Engine and machine assemblers construct and rebuild motors, turbines, and machines used in automobiles, construction and mining equipment, and power generators.

Fiberglass laminators and fabricators overlay fiberglass onto molds, forming protective surfaces for boat decks and hulls, golf cart bodies, and other products.

Structural metal fabricators and fitters cut, align, and fit together structural metal parts and may help weld or rivet the parts together.

Team assemblers rotate through different tasks on an assembly line, rather than specializing in a single task. Team members may decide how work is assigned and tasks are completed.

Timing device assemblers, adjusters, and calibrators manufacture or modify instruments that require precise measurement of time, such as clocks, watches, and chronometers.

Work Environment

Assemblers and fabricators held about 2.0 million jobs in 2022. Employment in the detailed occupations that make up assemblers and fabricators was distributed as follows:

Miscellaneous assemblers and fabricators	1,500,400
Electrical, electronic, and electromechanical assemblers, except coil winders, tapers, and finishers	282,900
Structural metal fabricators and fitters	59,600
Engine and other machine assemblers	50,900
Aircraft structure, surfaces, rigging, and systems assemblers	33,900
Fiberglass laminators and fabricators	22,600
Coil winders, tapers, and finishers	11,100
Timing device assemblers and adjusters	400

The largest employers of assemblers and fabricators were as follows:

Industry	Percent
Transportation equipment manufacturing	25%
Temporary help services	12
Machinery manufacturing	9
Computer and electronic product manufacturing	8
Fabricated metal product manufacturing	8

Most assemblers and fabricators work in manufacturing plants, and working conditions vary by plant and by industry. Many physically difficult tasks, such as tightening massive bolts or moving heavy parts into position, have been automated or made easier through the use of power tools. Assembly work,

Assemblers and fabricators work in plants and factories.

however, may still involve long periods of standing, sitting, or working on ladders.

Injuries and Illnesses

Some assemblers come into contact with potentially dangerous chemicals or fumes, but ventilation systems usually minimize any harmful effects. Other assemblers come into contact with oil and grease, and their work areas may be noisy. Fiberglass laminators and fabricators are exposed to fiberglass, which may irritate the skin; these workers must wear protective gear, such as gloves and long sleeves, and must use respirators for safety.

Work Schedules

Most assemblers and fabricators work full time. Some assemblers and fabricators work in shifts, which may require evening, weekend, and night work.

How to Become an Assembler or Fabricator

The education and qualifications typically needed to enter these occupations vary by industry and employer. Although a high school diploma is enough for most jobs, experience and training are needed for advanced assembly work.

Education

Assemblers and fabricators typically need a high school diploma or equivalent to enter the occupation.

Training

Workers typically receive several months of on-the-job training, sometimes including employer-sponsored technical instruction.

Skilled assemblers and fabricators may need special training or an associate's degree, depending on the employer. For example, workers in electrical, electronic, and aircraft and motor vehicle products manufacturing typically need postsecondary education. Apprenticeship programs are also available.

Assemblers and fabricators usually receive training in a specialty area.

Licenses, Certifications, and Registrations

The Fabricators & Manufacturers Association, International (FMA) offers certificates and training programs in fabrication, coil processing, and other related topics. Although not required, these credentials demonstrate competence and professionalism and may help a candidate advance in the occupation.

In addition, many employers, especially those in the aerospace and defense industries, require electrical and electronic assembly workers to have certifications in soldering. The Association Connecting Electronics Industries, also known as IPC, offers a number of certification programs related to electronic assembly and soldering.

Advancement

Experienced assemblers and fabricators may advance to become a supervisor or manager.

Important Qualities

Color vision. Assemblers and fabricators who make electrical and electronic products must distinguish different colors, because the wires they often work with are color coded.

Dexterity. Assemblers and fabricators should have a steady hand and good hand–eye coordination, as they must grasp, manipulate, and assemble parts and components that are often very small.

Mechanical skills. Assemblers and fabricators must have a working knowledge of basic machinery to use programmable motion-control devices, computers, and robots on the factory floor.

Physical stamina. Assemblers and fabricators must be able to stand for long periods and do repetitive tasks. Some assemblers, such as those in the aerospace industry, must frequently bend or climb ladders when assembling parts.

Physical strength. Assemblers and fabricators must be able to lift heavy components or pieces of machinery.

Technical skills. Assemblers and fabricators must understand technical manuals, blueprints, and schematics for manufacturing a range of products and machines.

Pay

The median annual wage for assemblers and fabricators was $37,930 in May 2022. The median wage is the wage at which half the workers in an occupation earned more than that amount and half earned less. The lowest 10 percent earned less than $28,980, and the highest 10 percent earned more than $61,050.

Median annual wages for assemblers and fabricators in May 2022 were as follows:

Aircraft structure, surfaces, rigging, and systems assemblers	$58,430
Engine and other machine assemblers	50,850
Structural metal fabricators and fitters	47,200
Coil winders, tapers, and finishers	43,160

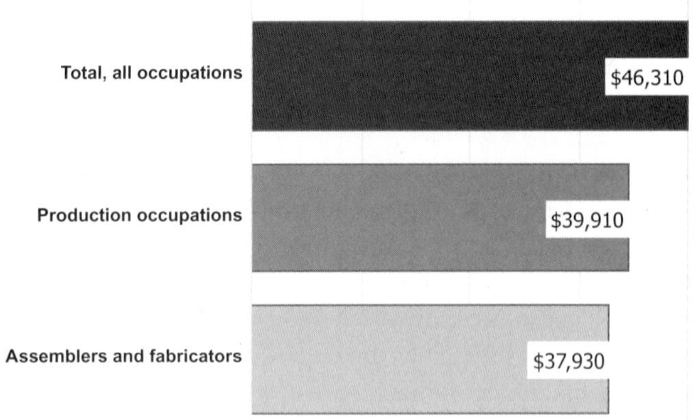

Note: All Occupations includes all occupations in the U.S. Economy.
Source: U.S. Bureau of Labor Statistics, Occupational Employment and Wage Statistics.

Timing device assemblers and adjusters	42,290
Electrical, electronic, and electromechanical assemblers, except coil winders, tapers, and finishers	38,580
Fiberglass laminators and fabricators	38,110
Miscellaneous assemblers and fabricators	37,280

In May 2022, the median annual wages for assemblers and fabricators in the top industries in which they worked were as follows:

Transportation equipment manufacturing	$45,960
Machinery manufacturing	40,860
Fabricated metal product manufacturing	38,880
Computer and electronic product manufacturing	38,110
Temporary help services	32,180

Wages vary by industry, geographic region, skill, education level, and complexity of the machinery operated.

Most assemblers and fabricators work full time, and some work evenings and weekends.

Job Outlook

Overall employment of assemblers and fabricators is projected to decline 6 percent from 2022 to 2032.

Despite declining employment, about 188,600 openings for assemblers and fabricators are projected each year, on average, over the decade. All of those openings are expected to result from the need to replace workers who transfer to other occupations or exit the labor force, such as to retire.

Employment

Projected employment of assemblers and fabricators varies by occupation (see table).

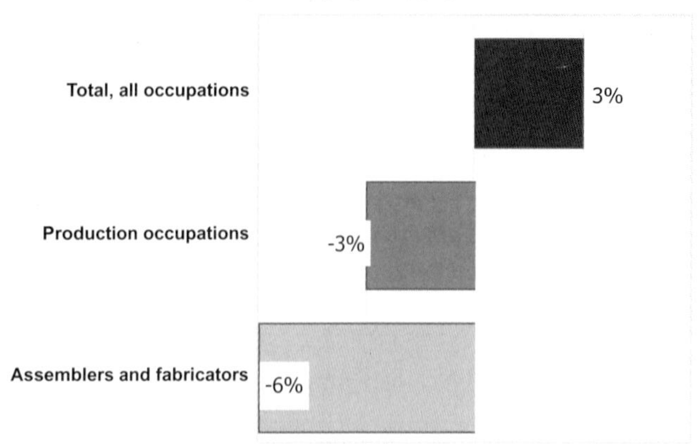

Note: All Occupations includes all occupations in the U.S. Economy.
Source: U.S. Bureau of Labor Statistics, Employment Projections program.

In general, employment of assemblers and fabricators is projected to decline or have limited growth because many manufacturing sectors are expected to become more efficient and able to produce more with fewer workers.

In most manufacturing industries, improved processes, tools, and automation will reduce job growth. Increasingly, new advances in robotics have enabled machinery to perform more complex and delicate tasks previously performed by workers. In addition, assemblers and fabricators are increasing efficiency by working alongside robots, also known as "collaborative robotics," which may reduce the demand for some assemblers and fabricators.

Changes in the cost of operations both in the United States and abroad may encourage some manufacturers to bring back production that was previously sent offshore. However, because new facilities in the United States likely will incorporate more automation technologies, they may require less labor overall and may require workers to have high-level skills.

Occupational Title	SOC Code	Employment, 2022	Projected Employment, 2032	Change, 2022-32	
				Percent	Numeric
Assemblers and fabricators	—	1,961,900	1,836,200	-6	-125,700
Aircraft structure, surfaces, rigging, and systems assemblers	51-2011	33,900	28,800	-15	-5,100
Coil winders, tapers, and finishers	51-2021	11,100	9,300	-17	-1,800
Electrical, electronic, and electromechanical assemblers, except coil winders, tapers, and finishers	51-2028	282,900	295,600	4	12,700
Engine and other machine assemblers	51-2031	50,900	41,300	-19	-9,600
Structural metal fabricators and fitters	51-2041	59,600	49,800	-16	-9,800
Fiberglass laminators and fabricators	51-2051	22,600	22,500	0	-100

Occupational Title	SOC Code	Employment, 2022	Projected Employment, 2032	Change, 2022-32 Percent	Change, 2022-32 Numeric
Timing device assemblers and adjusters	51-2061	400	300	-19	-100
Miscellaneous assemblers and fabricators	51-2090	1,500,400	1,388,600	-7	-111,800

Contacts for More Information

For more information, visit

- Fabricators & Manufacturers Association, International
- Nuts, Bolts & Thingamajigs
- Association Connecting Electronics Industries

Bakers

Summary

Quick Facts: Bakers

2022 Median Pay	$32,780 per year $15.76 per hour
Typical Entry-Level Education	No formal educational credential
Work Experience in a Related Occupation	None
On-the-job Training	Moderate-term on-the-job training
Number of Jobs, 2022	218,800
Job Outlook, 2022-32	5% (Faster than average)
Employment Change, 2022-32	10,800

What Bakers Do

Bakers mix ingredients according to recipes in order to make breads, pastries, and other baked goods.

Work Environment

Most bakers work in retail or commercial bakeries (manufacturing facilities), grocery stores or wholesale club stores, and restaurants. Work shifts often include early mornings, nights, weekends, and holidays.

Bakers make a variety of breads and baked goods.

How to Become a Baker

Although bakers typically need no formal educational credential, employers may prefer or require that candidates have a high school diploma. Some choose to attend a technical or culinary school. They typically learn their skills through on-the-job training, which may include participating in an apprenticeship program.

Pay

The median annual wage for bakers was $32,780 in May 2022.

Job Outlook

Employment of bakers is projected to grow 5 percent from 2022 to 2032, faster than the average for all occupations.

About 33,800 openings for bakers are projected each year, on average, over the decade. Many of those openings are expected to result from the need to replace workers who transfer to different occupations or exit the labor force, such as to retire.

What Bakers Do

Bakers mix ingredients according to recipes in order to make breads, pastries, and other baked goods.

Duties

Bakers typically do the following:

- Prepare workstation for baking
- Measure and weigh ingredients
- Combine measured ingredients in mixers or blenders
- Knead, roll, cut, and shape dough
- Prepare and fill pans, molds, or baking sheets
- Set oven temperatures and place items into ovens
- Monitor baking process and adjust oven temperature or item positioning as needed

Bakers produce breads, pastries, and other baked goods sold by grocers, wholesalers, restaurants, and institutional food services. Standard procedure for each batch includes checking the condition of ingredients, following instructions for recipes, and examining the quality of the final product.

The following are examples of types of bakers:

Commercial bakers, also called *production bakers,* work in manufacturing facilities that produce breads, pastries, and other baked products. In these facilities, bakers use high-volume

Bakers prepare various types of baked goods.

Bakers stand for extended periods while they prepare dough.

mixing machines, ovens, and other equipment, which may be automated, to mass-produce standardized baked goods. They often work with other production workers, such as helpers and maintenance staff, to keep equipment cleaned and ready.

Retail bakers work primarily in grocery stores and specialty shops, including bakeries. In these settings, they produce small quantities of baked goods for people to eat in the shop or for sale as specialty items. Retail bakers may take orders from customers, prepare baked products to order, and occasionally serve customers. Most retail bakers are also responsible for cleaning their work area and equipment and unloading supplies.

Some retail bakers own bakery shops where they make and sell breads, pastries, pies, and other baked goods. In addition to preparing the baked goods and overseeing the entire baking process, they are also responsible for hiring, training, and supervising their staff. They must budget for and order supplies, set prices, and decide how much to produce each day.

Work Environment

Bakers held about 218,800 jobs in 2022. The largest employers of bakers were as follows:

Bakeries and tortilla manufacturing	32%
Restaurants and other eating places	26
Grocery and specialty food retailers	25
Self-employed workers	4
Special food services	2

The work can be stressful because bakers must maintain consistent quality while following time-sensitive baking procedures, often under deadline.

Bakers are exposed to high temperatures when working around hot ovens. They stand for long periods while observing the baking process, making the dough, or cleaning the equipment.

Injuries and Illnesses

Bakeries, especially large manufacturing facilities, have potential dangers such as hot ovens, mixing machines, and dough cutters. Although their work is generally safe, bakers may experience back strain from lifting heavy items, as well as cuts, scrapes, and burns. To reduce risk of injury, bakers often wear back supports and heat-resistant aprons and gloves.

Work Schedules

Most bakers work full time, although part-time work is common. Schedules may vary and often include early morning, night, weekend, or holiday shifts. Some facilities operate around the clock.

How to Become a Baker

Bakers typically need no formal educational credential to enter the occupation; however, employers may prefer or require that candidates have a high school diploma, and some candidates choose to attend a technical or culinary school. Bakers typically learn their skills through on-the-job training, which may include participating in an apprenticeship program.

Education

High school students interested in becoming a baker may benefit from enrolling in culinary classes, if available, at their school.

Postsecondary options include attending a technical, culinary arts, or baking program that covers topics such as nutrition, food safety, and pastry techniques. Enrollees may be required to have a high school diploma or equivalent to enter these programs, which typically last 1 to 2 years.

Training

Most bakers learn their skills through on-the-job training. The length of training varies but may last up to 1 year. Some employers provide apprenticeship programs for aspiring bakers, which may take months or years to complete.

Training or apprenticeship programs cover topics such as baking and decorating techniques, production processes, and food safety.

Other Experience

Some bakers learn their skills through work experience related to baking. For example, they may start as a baker's assistant and progress to becoming a baker as they take on more responsibility and refine their technique.

Licenses, Certifications, and Registrations

Employers may require candidates to obtain certification in food safety procedures. Check with your state or local health department for certification information.

On-the-job training is the most common method of learning for bakers.

Optional certification may demonstrate a level of competence and experience that makes candidates more attractive to employers.

For example, Retail Bakers of America offers certification for several levels of competence, with a focus on topics such as baking sanitation, management, retail sales, and staff training. Those who wish to become certified must satisfy requirements for education and experience before taking an exam. Other organizations may offer credentials for specific skills, such as the American Culinary Federation's pastry chef certifications.

Important Qualities

Communication skills. Bakers must be able to convey information effectively to other workers or to customers.

Detail oriented. Bakers must follow recipes and instructions precisely. They also should have an eye for detail because many pastries and cakes require intricate decorations.

Math skills. Bakers need basic math skills, especially knowledge of fractions, in order to mix recipes, weigh ingredients, or adjust mixes.

Physical stamina. Bakers stand for extended periods while they prepare dough, monitor baking, or package baked goods.

Physical strength. Bakers should be able to move heavy items, such as bulk-sized bags of flour, from storage to a work area.

Pay

The median annual wage for bakers was $32,780 in May 2022. The median wage is the wage at which half the workers in an occupation earned more than that amount and half earned less. The lowest 10 percent earned less than $24,060, and the highest 10 percent earned more than $45,650.

In May 2022, the median annual wages for bakers in the top industries in which they worked were as follows:

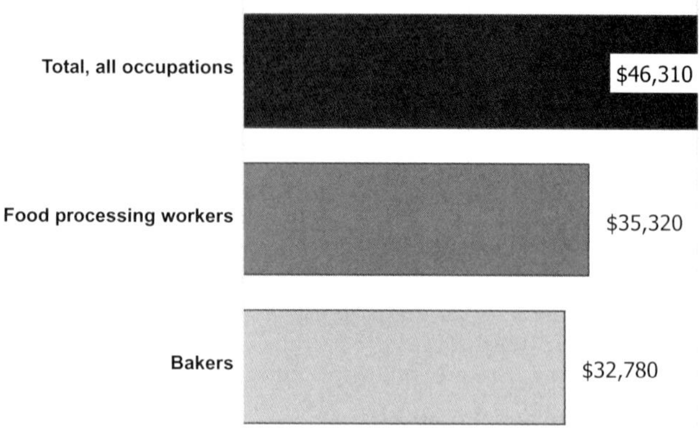

Note: All Occupations includes all occupations in the U.S. Economy. Source: U.S. Bureau of Labor Statistics, Occupational Employment and Wage Statistics.

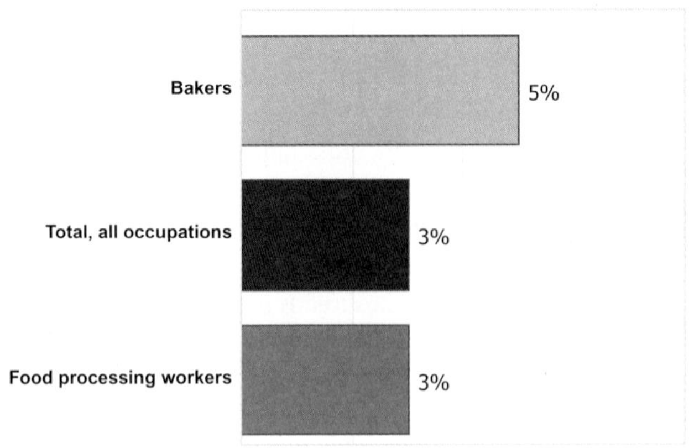

Note: All Occupations includes all occupations in the U.S. Economy.
Source: U.S. Bureau of Labor Statistics, Employment Projections program.

Special food services	$34,310
Grocery and specialty food retailers	33,920
Bakeries and tortilla manufacturing	33,700
Restaurants and other eating places	30,770

Most bakers work full time, although part-time work is common. Schedules may vary and often include early morning, night, weekend, or holiday shifts. Some facilities operate around the clock.

Job Outlook

Employment of bakers is projected to grow 5 percent from 2022 to 2032, faster than the average for all occupations.

About 33,800 openings for bakers are projected each year, on average, over the decade. Many of those openings are expected to result from the need to replace workers who transfer to different occupations or exit the labor force, such as to retire.

Employment

Baked goods, including cereals, breads, and snacks, remain a major part of the daily diet for many people and are often valued for their convenience. Population and income growth are expected to result in greater demand for a variety of commercial and retail specialty baked goods, including cupcakes, pies, and cakes.

As a result, more bakers are expected to be needed in food manufacturing and retail establishments that make and sell baked goods.

Occupational Title	SOC Code	Employment, 2022	Projected Employment, 2032	Change, 2022-32	
				Percent	Numeric
Bakers	51-3011	218,800	229,600	5	10,800

Contacts for More Information

Apprenticeship information is available from the U.S. Department of Labor's Apprenticeship program online or by phone at 877-872-5627. Visit Apprenticeship.gov to search for apprenticeship opportunities.

For more information, visit

- AIB International
- American Culinary Federation
- Retail Bakers of America

Butchers

Summary

Quick Facts: Butchers	
2022 Median Pay	$36,930 per year $17.76 per hour
Typical Entry-Level Education	No formal educational credential
Work Experience in a Related Occupation	None
On-the-job Training	Long-term on-the-job training
Number of Jobs, 2022	131,600
Job Outlook, 2022-32	-1% (Little or no change)
Employment Change, 2022-32	-1,600

What Butchers Do

Butchers cut, trim, and package meat for retail sale.

Work Environment

Most butchers work in grocery stores and specialty meat shops. The work can be physically demanding and may include exposure to repetitive motions, dangerous equipment, and cold temperatures.

How to Become a Butcher

Butchers typically need no formal educational credential. They learn their skills on the job.

Pay

The median annual wage for butchers was $36,930 in May 2022.

Job Outlook

Employment of butchers is projected to show little or no change from 2022 to 2032.

Despite limited employment growth, about 15,300 openings for butchers are projected each year, on average, over the

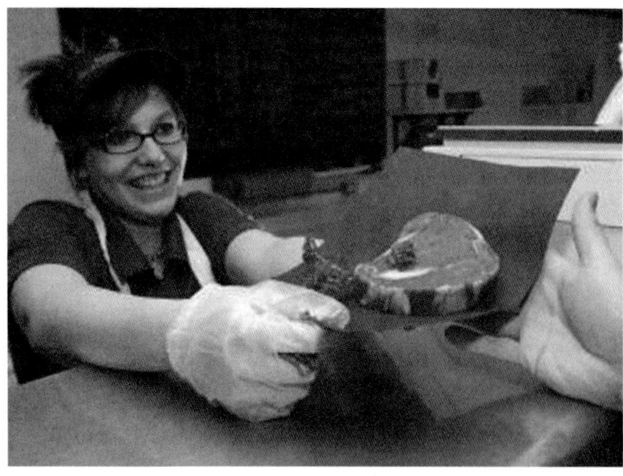

Butchers cut meat to customers' orders.

decade. Most of those openings are expected to result from the need to replace workers who transfer to different occupations or exit the labor force, such as to retire.

What Butchers Do

Butchers cut, trim, and package meat for retail sale.

Duties

Butchers typically do the following:

Butchers cut meat for display and retail sale.

- Receive, inspect, and store meat upon delivery
- Sharpen knives and adjust cutting equipment
- Cut, debone, or grind pieces of meat, including preparing orders to customers' specifications
- Weigh and wrap meat or meat products for display or to fulfill customers' orders
- Clean equipment and work areas to maintain health and sanitation standards
- Store meats in refrigerators or freezers at the required temperature
- Monitor inventory and sales trends and order meat

Butchers cut and trim meat from larger, wholesale portions into steaks, chops, roasts, and other cuts. They then prepare meat for sale by doing various tasks, such as weighing meat, wrapping it, and putting it out for display. In retail stores, they also wait on customers and prepare special cuts of meat upon request.

Butchers use equipment such as knives, grinders, and meat saws. They follow sanitation standards while working and when cleaning equipment, countertops, and working areas in order to prevent meat contamination.

Butchers also keep track of inventory and determine what to stock, especially in anticipation of seasonal demands such as grilling meats for summer and turkeys for Thanksgiving. Butchers must also track inventory and sales to limit waste by determining which items have not sold well. They also order supplies and have other duties, including maintaining records for purposes of federal safety and inspection.

Work Environment

Butchers held about 131,600 jobs in 2022. The largest employers of butchers were as follows:

Grocery and specialty food retailers	77%
General merchandise retailers	9
Animal slaughtering and processing	7
Merchant wholesalers, nondurable goods	3
Restaurants and other eating places	1

The work may be physically demanding, particularly for butchers who make repetitive cuts. Butchers typically stand while cutting meat and often lift and move heavy carcasses or boxes of meat supplies.

Because meat must be kept at cool temperatures, butchers commonly work in cold rooms—typically around 40 degrees Fahrenheit—for extended periods.

Butchers must keep their hands and working areas clean to prevent contamination, and those working in retail settings must remain presentable to customers.

Injuries and Illnesses

Butchers have one of the highest rates of injuries and illnesses of all occupations. These workers use dangerous tools, such as

Butchers often lift and move heavy carcasses.

sharp knives and meat saws, and work in areas with slippery floors and surfaces. To reduce the risk of cuts and falls, workers wear protective clothing, such as cut-resistant gloves, heavy aprons, and nonslip footwear.

Work Schedules

Most butchers work full time. Some work early mornings, late evenings, weekends, and holidays.

How to Become a Butcher

Butchers typically need no formal educational credential to enter the occupation. They learn their skills through on-the-job training.

Education

No formal education credential is typically required for becoming a butcher, although some employers may prefer to hire workers who have a high school diploma.

Training

Butchers typically learn their skills on the job, and the length of training varies considerably. Training for simple meat cutting, such as for prepared food items, may take about a week. However, more complicated cutting tasks, such as for specialty cuts of meat from a large animal, generally require training that may last from several months to more than a year.

Training for entry-level workers often begins by having the worker learn less difficult tasks, such as making simple cuts, removing bones, or dividing wholesale cuts into retail portions. Under the guidance of more experienced workers, trainees learn the proper use and care of tools. For example, they learn how to sharpen knives and clean working areas and equipment.

Trainees also may learn how to shape, roll, and tie roasts; make sausage; and cure meat. Employees also receive training in food safety to minimize the risk of foodborne pathogens in meats.

Workers typically enter the occupation as a meat clerk or meat cutter. After gaining experience as a meat cutter and demonstrating proficiency, they may become a butcher.

Some employers or unions may offer apprenticeship programs for butchers.

Butchers typically learn their skills on the job.

Licenses, Certifications, and Registrations

Some states and localities require butchers to have a food handler's certification. Requirements vary. For more information, contact your state or local licensing board.

Butchers who follow religious dietary guidelines for food preparation may be required to undergo more specialized training that leads to certification before becoming endorsed by a religious organization to prepare meat.

Important Qualities

Customer-service skills. Butchers who work in retail stores should be courteous, be able to answer customers' questions, and fill orders to customers' satisfaction.

Dexterity. Butchers use sharp knives and meatcutting equipment as part of their duties. They must have good hand control in order to make proper cuts of meat that are the right size.

Physical stamina. Butchers spend hours on their feet while cutting, packaging, or storing meat.

Physical strength. Butchers should be able to lift and carry heavy boxes of meat, which may weigh more than 50 pounds.

Pay

The median annual wage for butchers was $36,930 in May 2022. The median wage is the wage at which half the workers in an occupation earned more than that amount and half earned less. The lowest 10 percent earned less than $26,030, and the highest 10 percent earned more than $51,180.

In May 2022, the median annual wages for butchers in the top industries in which they worked were as follows:

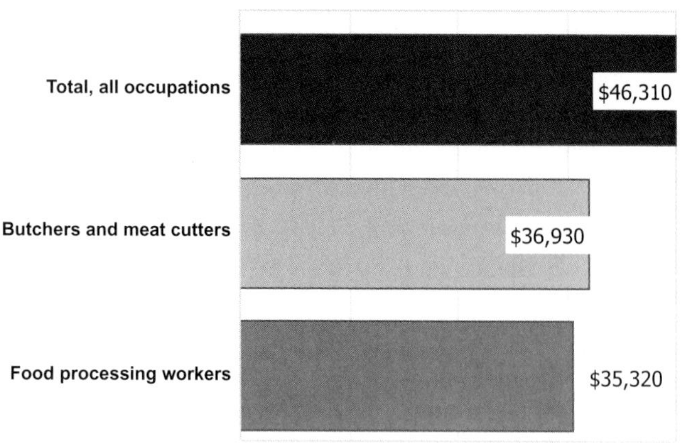

Note: All Occupations includes all occupations in the U.S. Economy. Source: U.S. Bureau of Labor Statistics, Occupational Employment and Wage Statistics.

Restaurants and other eating places	$41,600
General merchandise retailers	41,600
Merchant wholesalers, nondurable goods	39,560
Animal slaughtering and processing	37,710
Grocery and specialty food retailers	36,210

Most butchers work full time. Some work early mornings, late evenings, weekends, and holidays.

Job Outlook

Employment of butchers is projected to show little or no change from 2022 to 2032.

Despite limited employment growth, about 15,300 openings for butchers are projected each year, on average, over the decade. Most of those openings are expected to result from the need to replace workers who transfer to different occupations or exit the labor force, such as to retire.

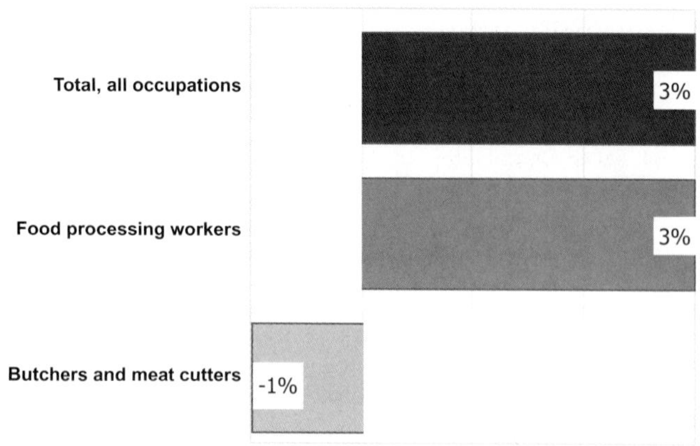

Note: All Occupations includes all occupations in the U.S. Economy. Source: U.S. Bureau of Labor Statistics, Employment Projections program.

Employment

Long-term food purchasing patterns have trended towards more pre-made and pre-packaged meat products and cuts. This trend is expected to continue over the decade, which may limit employment demand for butchers and meat cutters.

Occupational Title	SOC Code	Employment, 2022	Projected Employment, 2032	Change, 2022-32	
				Percent	Numeric
Butchers and meat cutters	51-3021	131,600	130,100	-1	-1,600

Contacts for More Information

Apprenticeship information is available from the U.S. Department of Labor's Apprenticeship program online or by phone at 877-872-5627. Visit Apprenticeship.gov to search for apprenticeship opportunities.

For more information, visit

➤ North American Meat Institute

Dental and Ophthalmic Laboratory Technicians and Medical Appliance Technicians

Summary

Quick Facts: Dental and Ophthalmic Laboratory Technicians and Medical Appliance Technicians

2022 Median Pay	$41,180 per year $19.80 per hour
Typical Entry-Level Education	High school diploma or equivalent
Work Experience in a Related Occupation	None
On-the-job Training	Moderate-term on-the-job training
Number of Jobs, 2022	73,400
Job Outlook, 2022-32	-1% (Little or no change)
Employment Change, 2022-32	-1,000

What Dental and Ophthalmic Laboratory Technicians and Medical Appliance Technicians Do

Dental and ophthalmic laboratory technicians and medical appliance technicians make or repair dentures, eyeglasses, prosthetics, and related products.

Work Environment

Dental and ophthalmic laboratory technicians and medical appliance technicians usually work in clean, well-lighted spaces and may spend time standing or bending. Most work full time, and schedules may vary.

How to Become a Dental or Ophthalmic Laboratory Technician or Medical Appliance Technician

To enter the occupation, dental or ophthalmic laboratory technicians or medical appliance technicians typically need at least a high school diploma or equivalent. They typically receive on-the-job training to attain competency.

Pay

The median annual wage for dental and ophthalmic laboratory technicians and medical appliance technicians was $41,180 in May 2022.

Job Outlook

Overall employment of dental and ophthalmic laboratory technicians and medical appliance technicians is projected to show little or no change from 2022 to 2032.

Despite limited employment growth, about 8,300 openings for dental and ophthalmic laboratory technicians and medical appliance technicians are projected each year, on average, over the decade. Most of those openings are expected to result from the need to replace workers who transfer to different occupations or exit the labor force, such as to retire.

What Dental and Ophthalmic Laboratory Technicians and Medical Appliance Technicians Do

Dental and ophthalmic laboratory technicians and medical appliance technicians make or repair dentures, eyeglasses, prosthetics, and related products.

Duties

Dental and ophthalmic laboratory technicians and medical appliance technicians typically do the following:

- Read and follow detailed work orders and prescriptions
- Bend, form, and shape material for appliances or devices
- Polish and shape appliances and devices, using handtools or power tools
- Adjust appliances or devices to allow for a natural look or to improve function
- Inspect the final product for quality and accuracy
- Repair damaged appliances and devices

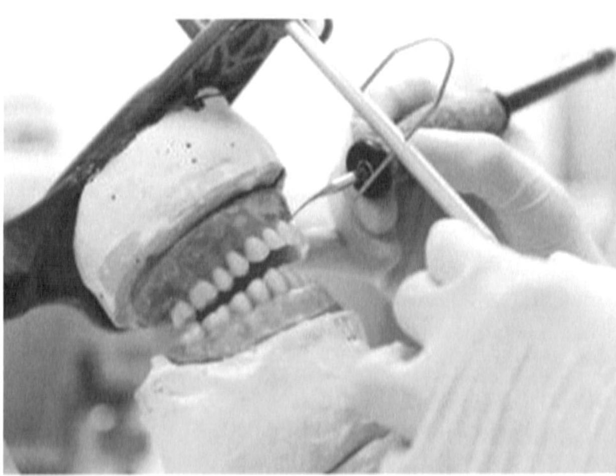

Dental laboratory technicians create crowns, bridges, dentures, and other dental prosthetics.

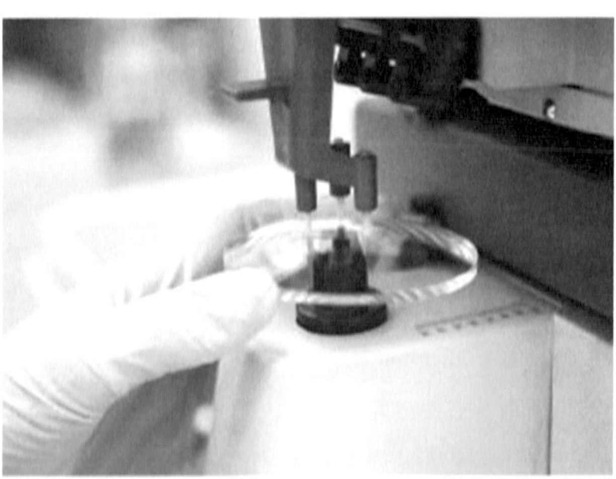

Ophthalmic laboratory technicians often use automated equipment to make lenses.

Technicians' duties vary, depending on their employer. In small offices and retail establishments, technicians may handle every phase of production. In large manufacturing and wholesale facilities, technicians may be responsible for only one phase of production, such as polishing, measuring, or testing.

Dental laboratory technicians use impressions or molds of a patient's teeth to create crowns, bridges, dentures, and other dental appliances. They work closely with dentists but have limited contact with patients.

Dental laboratory technicians work with small handtools, such as files and polishers, and with many different materials, including wax, alloy, ceramic, plastic, and porcelain. Technicians also use computer programs and three-dimensional printers to create dental appliances and restorations.

Dental laboratory technicians may specialize in one or more of the following: orthodontic appliances, crowns and bridges, complete dentures, partial dentures, implants, or ceramics. Technicians may have different job titles, depending on their specialty. For example, technicians who make ceramic restorations such as veneers and bridges, are called *ceramists*.

Ophthalmic laboratory technicians make prescription eyeglasses and contact lenses. They are also commonly known as *optical laboratory technicians*.

Ophthalmic laboratory technicians typically use automated equipment to make lenses. Some technicians manufacture lenses for optical instruments, such as telescopes and binoculars. Ophthalmic laboratory technicians should not be confused with dispensing opticians, who work with customers to select eyewear and may prepare work orders for ophthalmic laboratory technicians.

Medical appliance technicians construct and repair medical supportive devices, such as hearing aids or leg braces. They use many different types of materials, such as metal, plastic, and leather.

Medical appliance technicians who create orthoses (braces, supports, and other devices) and prostheses (replacement limbs and facial parts) are sometimes referred to as *orthotic and prosthetic technicians* or *O&P technicians*.

Medical appliance technicians should not be confused with hearing aid specialists or orthotists and prosthetists, who work directly with patients. However, technicians may work closely with these other specialists to ensure proper fit or to repair devices.

Work Environment

Dental and ophthalmic laboratory technicians and medical appliance technicians held about 73,400 jobs in 2022. Employment in the detailed occupations that make up dental and ophthalmic laboratory technicians and medical appliance technicians was distributed as follows:

Dental laboratory technicians	35,400
Ophthalmic laboratory technicians	21,300
Medical appliance technicians	16,600

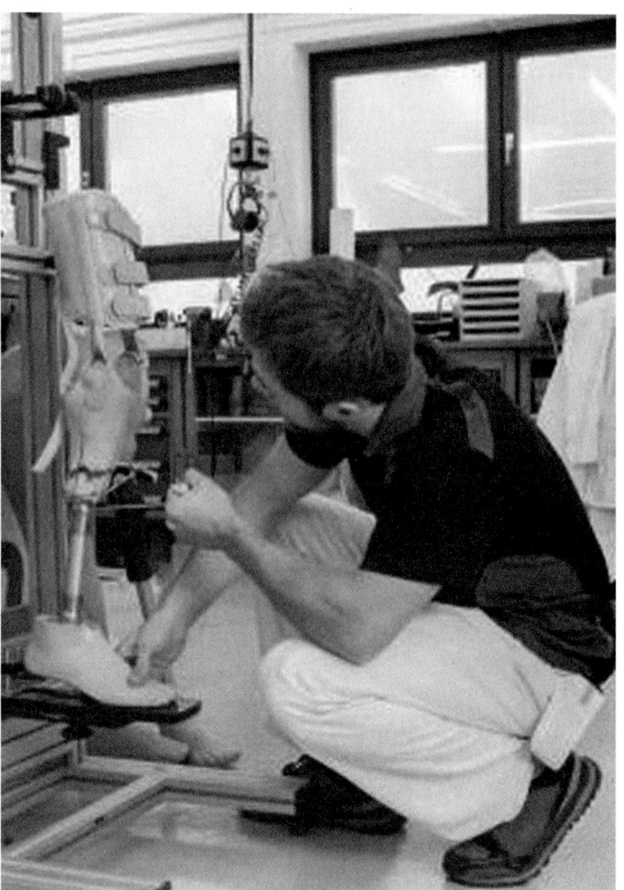

Medical appliance technicians construct and repair medical supportive devices, including prosthetic limbs.

The largest employers of dental and ophthalmic laboratory technicians and medical appliance technicians were as follows:

Employer	Percent
Medical equipment and supplies manufacturing	60%
Health and personal care retailers	6
Professional and commercial equipment and supplies merchant wholesalers	5
Offices of dentists	5
Offices of optometrists	4

Technicians may be exposed to health and safety hazards when handling certain materials. Workers typically wear protective equipment, such as goggles, gloves, or masks, to protect themselves from injury. They may spend a great deal of time standing or bending.

Work Schedules

Most dental and ophthalmic laboratory technicians and medical appliance technicians work full time, and schedules may vary.

How to Become a Dental or Ophthalmic Laboratory Technician or Medical Appliance Technician

To enter the occupation, dental and ophthalmic laboratory technicians and medical appliance technicians typically need at least a high school diploma or equivalent. They typically receive on-the-job training to attain competency.

Education

Dental and ophthalmic laboratory technicians and medical appliance technicians typically need at least a high school diploma or equivalent. High school students interested in becoming a dental or ophthalmic laboratory technician or medical appliance technician may benefit from taking classes in science, mathematics, and art.

Employers may prefer to hire candidates who have a postsecondary certificate or associate's degree. Some community colleges and technical schools offer programs in dental or ophthalmic laboratory technology in which students gain experience completing specific tasks, such as surfacing and finishing prescription eyewear. Community colleges and technical schools also may offer programs in medical appliance technology fields, such as orthotics and prosthetics technology.

Most dental and ophthalmic laboratory technicians and medical appliance technicians learn their skills through on-the-job training. They may begin as helpers and learn more advanced skills as they gain experience. For example, dental laboratory technicians may start out making models from impressions and progress to designing and fabricating crowns and bridges.

Licenses, Certifications, and Registrations

Although optional, certification may demonstrate a level of competence and professionalism that makes candidates more attractive to employers. It also may increase opportunities for advancement.

The National Board for Certification in Dental Laboratory Technology offers certification as a Certified Dental Technician (CDT). Certification is available in six specialty areas: orthodontics, crown and bridge, complete dentures, partial dentures, implants, and ceramics. To qualify for the CDT, technicians must pass several exams and meet education, training, or experience requirements.

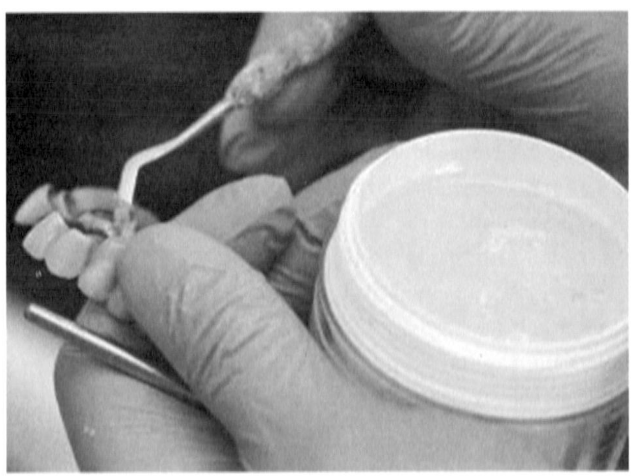

Dental laboratory technicians need dexterity to work with precision instruments.

The American Board for Certification in Orthotics, Prosthetics & Pedorthics offers certification for orthotic and/or prosthetic technicians. Technicians are eligible for the certification exam after completing an accredited program or if they have experience as a technician under the direct supervision of a certified orthotist or prosthetist or O&P technician.

Some employers prefer that ophthalmic laboratory technicians obtain certification from the American Board of Opticianry and National Contact Lens Examiners (ABO-NCLE) prior to hiring or after completing on-the-job training. Basic certification is earned after passing an exam.

Advancement

In large facilities, dental and ophthalmic laboratory technicians and medical appliance technicians may work their way up to a supervisory level and train new technicians. Some go on to own their own laboratory.

Important Qualities

Detail oriented. Dental and ophthalmic laboratory technicians and medical appliance technicians must follow work orders and prescriptions precisely. They also need to be able to recognize and correct any imperfections in their work.

Dexterity. Dental and ophthalmic laboratory technicians and medical appliance technicians must work well with their hands to use precision instruments.

Interpersonal skills. Dental and ophthalmic laboratory technicians and medical appliance technicians must be able to work effectively with others. They may be part of a team of technicians working on a single project.

Problem-solving skills. Dental and ophthalmic laboratory technicians and medical appliance technicians may encounter challenges when constructing or repairing medical devices. They need to be resourceful in finding solutions.

Technical skills. Dental and ophthalmic laboratory technicians and medical appliance technicians need to understand how different tools and materials work. They also must know how to operate automated machinery and may need proficiency in design software.

Pay

The median annual wage for dental and ophthalmic laboratory technicians and medical appliance technicians was $41,180 in May 2022. The median wage is the wage at which half the workers in an occupation earned more than that amount and half earned less. The lowest 10 percent earned less than $29,900, and the highest 10 percent earned more than $66,070.

Median annual wages for dental and ophthalmic laboratory technicians and medical appliance technicians in May 2022 were as follows:

Dental laboratory technicians	$46,050
Medical appliance technicians	42,160
Ophthalmic laboratory technicians	36,810

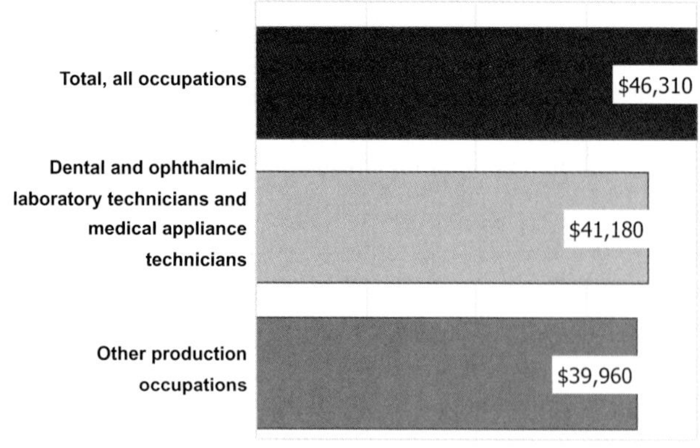

Note: All Occupations includes all occupations in the U.S. Economy.
Source: U.S. Bureau of Labor Statistics, Occupational Employment and Wage Statistics.

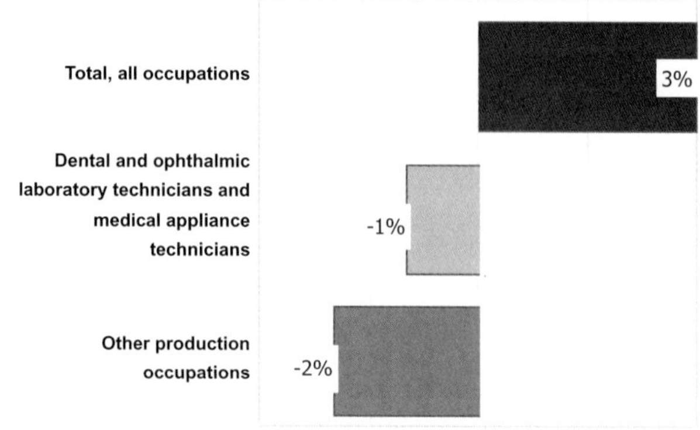

Note: All Occupations includes all occupations in the U.S. Economy.
Source: U.S. Bureau of Labor Statistics, Employment Projections program.

In May 2022, the median annual wages for dental and ophthalmic laboratory technicians and medical appliance technicians in the top industries in which they worked were as follows:

Offices of dentists	$44,700
Medical equipment and supplies manufacturing	43,370
Professional and commercial equipment and supplies merchant wholesalers	39,240
Health and personal care retailers	35,820
Offices of optometrists	34,230

Most dental and ophthalmic laboratory technicians and medical appliance technicians work full time, and schedules may vary.

Job Outlook

Overall employment of dental and ophthalmic laboratory technicians and medical appliance technicians is projected to show little or no change from 2022 to 2032.

Despite limited employment growth, about 8,300 openings for dental and ophthalmic laboratory technicians and medical appliance technicians are projected each year, on average, over the decade. Most of those openings are expected to result from the need to replace workers who transfer to different occupations or exit the labor force, such as to retire.

Employment

Projected employment of dental and ophthalmic laboratory technicians and medical appliance technicians varies by occupation (see table).

Demand for dental laboratory technicians is expected to decline as 3D printing and other laborsaving technologies are increasingly used to produce dental parts and appliances.

The increasing number of older adults and an associated rise in age-related ailments will drive demand for medical appliance technicians. For example, these workers will be needed to produce supportive devices to help reduce pain and improve function for people with osteoporosis and osteoarthritis. Rising obesity rates in the general population will also translate into a greater need for orthoses, such as those for foot and ankle support. Meanwhile, the growing prevalence of diabetes, which may lead to limb loss, will spur demand for prosthetic care.

Ophthalmic laboratory technicians will be needed to make eyewear, such as glasses and contact lenses, as a growing population continues to require vision correction. However, automation in lens manufacturing will limit opportunities for these technicians.

Occupational Title	SOC Code	Employment, 2022	Projected Employment, 2032	Change, 2022-32	
				Percent	Numeric
Dental and ophthalmic laboratory technicians and medical appliance technicians	51-9080	73,400	72,400	-1	-1,000
Dental laboratory technicians	51-9081	35,400	33,800	-5	-1,600
Medical appliance technicians	51-9082	16,600	17,100	2	400
Ophthalmic laboratory technicians	51-9083	21,300	21,600	1	200

Contacts for More Information

For more information, visit

- National Board for Certification in Dental Laboratory Technology
- National Association of Dental Laboratories
- International Council of Accreditation
- American Academy of Orthotists & Prosthetists
- National Commission on Orthotic and Prosthetic Education
- American Board for Certification in Orthotics, Prosthetics & Pedorthics
- American Board of Opticianry and National Contact Lens Examiners

Food Processing Equipment Workers

Summary

Quick Facts: Food Processing Equipment Workers	
2022 Median Pay	$36,190 per year $17.40 per hour
Typical Entry-Level Education	See How to Become One
Work Experience in a Related Occupation	None
On-the-job Training	Moderate-term on-the-job training
Number of Jobs, 2022	269,200
Job Outlook, 2022-32	6% (Faster than average)
Employment Change, 2022-32	16,400

What Food Processing Equipment Workers Do

Food processing equipment workers operate machinery that mixes, cooks, or processes ingredients for manufacturing food products.

Work Environment

Most food processing equipment workers are employed in manufacturing facilities. Because of production schedules, shift work is common and may include early mornings, evenings, or nights. Most food processing equipment workers are employed full time.

How to Become a Food Processing Equipment Worker

Education requirements vary for food processing equipment workers. Some typically need no formal education credential; however, others typically need a high school diploma or equivalent.

Pay

The median annual wage for food and tobacco processing workers was $36,190 in May 2022.

Job Outlook

Overall employment of food processing equipment workers is projected to grow 6 percent from 2022 to 2032, faster than the average for all occupations.

About 39,900 openings for food processing equipment workers are projected each year, on average, over the decade. Many of those openings are expected to result from the need to replace workers who transfer to different occupations or exit the labor force, such as to retire.

Food and tobacco processing workers use machines to mix ingredients.

What Food Processing Equipment Workers Do

Food processing equipment workers operate machinery that mixes, cooks, or processes ingredients for manufacturing food products.

Duties

Food processing equipment workers typically do the following:

- Set up, start, or load food processing equipment
- Check, weigh, and mix ingredients according to recipes
- Set and control temperatures, flow rates, and pressures of machinery
- Monitor and adjust ingredient mixes during production processes
- Observe and regulate equipment gauges and controls
- Record batch production data
- Clean workspaces and equipment according to health and safety standards
- Check final products to ensure quality

Food processing equipment workers often have different duties depending on the type of machinery they use or the goods they process. Job titles may be specific to the type of food workers produce.

Food and tobacco roasting, baking, and drying machine operators and tenders run equipment that uses dry heat to make food or tobacco products. For example, *coffee roasters* follow recipes and tend machines to produce standard or specialty

A food batchmaker stirs curd to make cheese.

coffees; *dryers of fruits and vegetables* operate machines that produce raisins, prunes, and other dehydrated foods.

Food batchmakers operate equipment that mixes or blends ingredients to produce shelf-stable, refrigerated, or frozen foods. For example, *cheese makers* load raw ingredients into machinery, monitoring the temperature and consistency throughout the production process; *candy makers* may operate machinery to shape, stretch, or mold lollipops, gumdrops, and other sweets.

Food cooking machine operators and tenders oversee equipment that makes steamed, fried, boiled, or related food products. For example, *dumpling machine operators* set up and monitor commercial steamers and *potato chip manufacturing workers* may operate frying equipment.

Other food processing equipment workers operate machines that mix spices, mill grains, or extract oil from seeds.

Work Environment

Food and tobacco processing workers held about 269,200 jobs in 2022. Employment in the detailed occupations that make up food and tobacco processing workers was distributed as follows:

Food batchmakers	171,500
Food processing workers, all other	48,800
Food cooking machine operators and tenders	27,300
Food and tobacco roasting, baking, and drying machine operators and tenders	21,500

The largest employers of food and tobacco processing workers were as follows:

Food manufacturing	76%
Employment services	6

Food manufacturing facilities are typically large, open-floor areas with loud machinery. When operating cooking equipment, workers are frequently exposed to high temperatures. When working with goods that need to be refrigerated or frozen, they may be exposed to cold temperatures for long periods.

Depending on the type of food being processed, workers may be required to wear ear protection to guard against hearing loss in noisy facilities. They also may wear masks, hairnets, or gloves to prevent product contamination.

Workers usually stand during their shifts while tending machines or observing the production process. Loading, unloading, or cleaning equipment may require lifting, bending, and reaching.

Injuries and Illnesses

Food processing workers, all other, have one of the highest rates of injuries and illnesses of all occupations. ("All other" titles represent occupations with a wide range of characteristics that do not fit into any of the other detailed occupations.) Working around hot liquids or machinery that cuts or presses can be dangerous. Common injuries include cuts or result from slips and falls.. To reduce the risks of injuries, workers are required to wear protective clothing and nonslip shoes.

Work Schedules

Most food processing equipment workers are employed full time; part-time work may be common for food cooking machine operators and tenders. Because of production schedules, shift work is common and may include early mornings, evenings, or nights.

Some food processing positions are seasonal.

How to Become a Food Processing Equipment Worker

Education requirements vary for food processing equipment workers. Some typically need no formal education credential; however, others typically need a high school diploma or equivalent. Food processing equipment workers usually learn their skills through on-the-job training.

Food processing workers often work on a production line and stand most of the time.

Experienced workers show trainees how to properly use equipment.

Education

Employers may require or prefer that applicants to food processing equipment jobs have a high school diploma or equivalent.

Because these workers often adjust the quantity of ingredients that go into a mix, math and reading skills are helpful.

Training

Food processing equipment workers learn on the job. Training may last from a few weeks to a few months. During training, workers learn health and safety rules related to the type of food that they process, as well as how to operate specific equipment and detect malfunctions.

Experienced workers typically teach trainees how to properly use and care for equipment.

Important Qualities

Detail oriented. Workers must be able to detect small changes in the quality or quantity of food products. They must also follow health and safety standards to avoid injury and prevent food contamination.

Physical stamina. Workers stand for long periods as they tend machines and monitor the production process.

Physical strength. Food processing equipment workers must be able to lift or move heavy boxes of ingredients, which may weigh up to 50 pounds.

Math skills. Workers may need math skills in order to accurately mix specific quantities of ingredients.

Pay

The median annual wage for food processing equipment workers was $36,190 in May 2022. The median wage is the wage at which half the workers in an occupation earned more than that amount and half earned less. The lowest 10 percent earned less than $27,080, and the highest 10 percent earned more than $51,420.

Median annual wages for food processing equipment workers in May 2022 were as follows:

Food and tobacco roasting, baking, and drying machine operators and tenders	$37,790
Food cooking machine operators and tenders	36,700
Food batchmakers	36,580
Food processing workers, all other	34,710

In May 2022, the median annual wages for food and tobacco processing workers in the top industries in which they worked were as follows:

Food manufacturing	$36,850
Employment services	31,730

Most food processing equipment workers are employed full time; part-time work may be common for food cooking machine operators and tenders. Because of production schedules, shift work is common and may include early mornings, evenings, or nights.

Some food processing positions are seasonal.

Job Outlook

Overall employment of food processing equipment workers is projected to grow 6 percent from 2022 to 2032, faster than the average for all occupations.

About 39,900 openings for food processing equipment workers are projected each year, on average, over the decade. Many of those openings are expected to result from the need to replace workers who transfer to different occupations or exit the labor force, such as to retire.

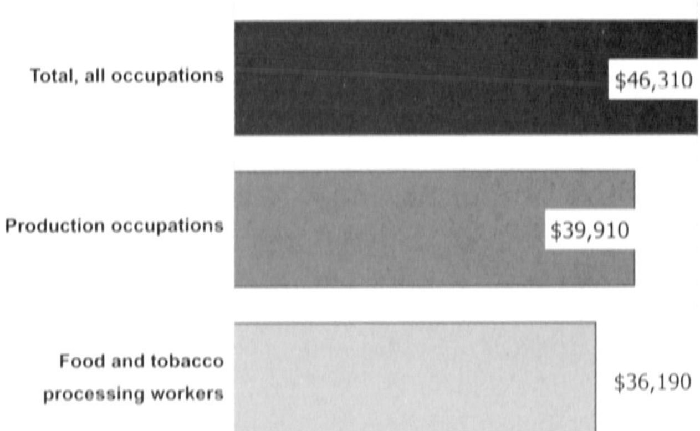

Note: All Occupations includes all occupations in the U.S. Economy.
Source: U.S. Bureau of Labor Statistics, Occupational Employment and Wage Statistics.

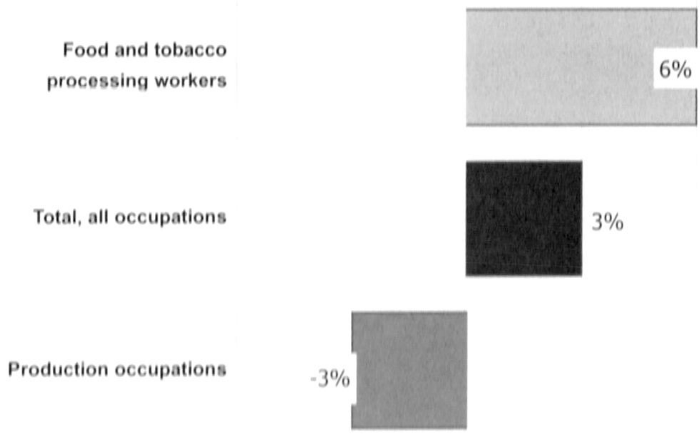

Note: All Occupations includes all occupations in the U.S. Economy.
Source: U.S. Bureau of Labor Statistics, Employment Projections program.

Employment

Projected employment of food processing equipment workers varies by occupation (see table). Population growth and continuing consumer preference for convenience foods are expected to drive the demand for food, which will in turn require more food processing workers to produce it. Some food manufacturing companies use equipment that automatically weighs and mixes ingredients, which requires fewer workers to operate machines.

Occupational Title	SOC Code	Employment, 2022	Projected Employment, 2032	Change, 2022-32	
				Percent	Numeric
Food and tobacco processing workers	—	269,200	285,600	6	16,400
Food and tobacco roasting, baking, and drying machine operators and tenders	51-3091	21,500	22,200	3	700
Food batchmakers	51-3092	171,500	185,000	8	13,400
Food cooking machine operators and tenders	51-3093	27,300	27,700	2	400
Food processing workers, all other	51-3099	48,800	50,700	4	1,900

Contacts for More Information

For more information, visit

- Bakery, Confectionary, Tobacco Workers, and Grain Millers International (BCTGM)
- International Brotherhood of Teamsters
- The United Food and Commercial Workers International Union

Jewelers and Precious Stone and Metal Workers

Summary

Quick Facts: Jewelers and Precious Stone and Metal Workers

2022 Median Pay	$47,140 per year $22.66 per hour
Typical Entry-Level Education	High school diploma or equivalent
Work Experience in a Related Occupation	None
On-the-job Training	Long-term on-the-job training
Number of Jobs, 2022	47,200
Job Outlook, 2022-32	-3% (Decline)
Employment Change, 2022-32	-1,400

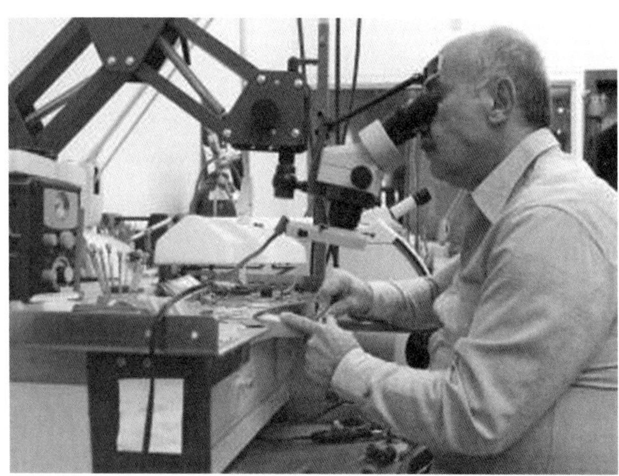

Jewelers and precious stone and metal workers typically work at a jeweler's bench.

What Jewelers and Precious Stone and Metal Workers Do

Jewelers and precious stone and metal workers design, construct, adjust, repair, appraise and sell jewelry.

Work Environment

Jewelers and precious stone and metal workers spend much of their time at a workbench or polishing station, using tools and chemicals.

How to Become a Jeweler or Precious Stone and Metal Worker

Jewelers and precious stone and metal workers typically need a high school diploma to enter the occupation, and they learn the skills of the trade through on-the-job training.

Pay

The median annual wage for jewelers and precious stone and metal workers was $47,140 in May 2022.

Job Outlook

Employment of jewelers and precious stone and metal workers is projected to decline 3 percent from 2022 to 2032.

Despite declining employment, about 6,100 openings for jewelers and precious stone and metal workers are projected each year, on average, over the decade. All of those openings are expected to result from the need to replace workers who transfer to other occupations or exit the labor force, such as to retire.

What Jewelers and Precious Stone and Metal Workers Do

Jewelers and precious stone and metal workers design, construct, adjust, repair, appraise and sell jewelry.

Jeweler's torches are used to resize and repair jewelry.

Duties

Jewelers and precious stone and metal workers typically do the following:

- Design and create jewelry from precious metals and stones
- Examine and grade diamonds and other gems
- Clean and polish jewelry using polishing wheels and chemical baths
- Repair jewelry by replacing broken clasps, altering ring sizes, or resetting stones
- Smooth joints and rough spots and polish smoothed areas
- Compute the costs of labor and material for new pieces and repairs
- Model new pieces with carved wax or computer-aided design, and then cast them in metal
- Shape metal to hold the gems in pieces of jewelry
- Solder pieces together and insert stones

Technology is helping to produce high-quality jewelry at a reduced cost and in less time than traditional methods allow. For example, lasers are often used for cutting and improving the quality of stones, for intricate engraving or design work, and for inscribing personal messages on jewelry. Jewelers also use lasers to weld metals together without seams or blemishes, improving the quality and appearance of jewelry.

Some manufacturing firms use computer-aided design and computer-aided manufacturing (CAD/CAM) to make product design easier and to automate some steps. With CAD, jewelers can create a model of a piece of jewelry on a computer and then view the effect of changing different aspects—for example, the design, the stone, or the setting—before cutting a stone or taking other costly steps. With CAM, they can then create a mold of the piece, which makes producing many copies easy.

Some jewelers also use CAD software to design custom jewelry. They let the customer review the design on a computer and see the effect of changes, so that the customer is satisfied before committing to the expense of a customized piece of jewelry.

The following are examples of types of jewelers and precious stone and metal workers:

Bench jewelers, also known as metalsmiths, silversmiths, goldsmiths, and platinumsmiths, are the most common type of jewelers. They possess a wide array of skills. They usually do tasks ranging from simple jewelry cleaning and repair to making molds and pieces from scratch. Some specialize in particular tasks such as repairs, hand engraving, stringing, wax carving/model making, enameling, stone cutting, soldering, stone setting, and hand building.

Gemologists analyze, describe, and certify the quality and characteristics of gemstones. After using microscopes, computerized tools, and other grading instruments to examine gemstones or finished pieces of jewelry, they write reports certifying that the items are of a particular quality. Most gemologists have completed the Graduate Gemologist program through the Gemological Institute of America.

Jewelry appraisers carefully examine jewelry to determine its value and then write appraisal documents. They determine value by researching the jewelry market and by using reference books, auction catalogs, price lists, and the Internet. They may work for jewelry stores, appraisal firms, auction houses, pawnbrokers, or insurance companies. Many gemologists also become appraisers.

Jewelry designers create design concepts and manage the prototype and model-making process.

Production jewelers fabricate and assemble pieces in a manufacturing setting and typically work on one aspect of the manufacturing process.

Work Environment

Jewelers and precious stone and metal workers held about 47,200 jobs in 2022. The largest employers of jewelers and precious stone and metal workers were as follows:

Self-employed workers	46%
Jewelry, luggage, and leather goods retailers	26
Jewelry and silverware manufacturing	13
Merchant wholesalers, durable goods	8
Personal and household goods repair and maintenance	2

Some jewelers and precious stone and metal workers work from home and sell their products at trade and craft shows. Online sales are also a growing source of sales for jewelers.

Jewelers and precious stone and metal workers use various tools and chemicals.

Jewelers and precious stone and metal workers spend much of their time sitting at a workbench or standing at a polishing station. Computer-aided design (CAD) is also an important tool in the jewelry industry.

There is exposure to machines, fumes, and toxic or caustic chemicals, and risk of radiation. Many tools, such as jeweler's torches and lasers, must be handled carefully to avoid injury. Polishing processes such as chemical baths also must be performed in a safe manner.

Self-employed workers usually work at home in their workshop or studio. In retail stores, jewelers may talk with customers about repairs, perform custom design work, and sell items to customers. Because many of their materials are valuable, jewelers must follow security procedures, including making use of burglar alarms and, in larger jewelry stores, working in the presence of security guards.

Work Schedules

Most jewelers and precious stone and metal workers work full time.

Many self-employed workers show and sell their products at trade and craft shows during weekends. Retail store workers might also work nonstandard hours because they must be available when customers are not working, such as on holidays and weekends.

How to Become a Jeweler or Precious Stone and Metal Worker

Jewelers and precious stone and metal workers typically need a high school diploma to enter the occupation, and they learn the skills of the trade through on-the-job training.

Education

Although most jewelers and precious stone and metal workers have a high school diploma, many trade schools offer courses for workers who seek additional education. Course topics can include introduction to gems and metals, resizing, repair, and computer-aided design (CAD). Programs vary from 3 months to 1 year, and many teach students how to design, cast, set, and polish jewelry and gems, as well as how to use and care for a jeweler's tools and equipment. Graduates of these programs may be more attractive to employers because they require less on-the-job training. Many gemologists graduate from the Gemological Institute of America. Trade programs usually require applicants to have a high school diploma or equivalent.

Although most jewelers and precious stone and metal workers have a high school diploma, many trade schools offer courses for workers who seek additional education.

Training

Many jewelers learn and develop their skills on the job. The length of training required to become proficient depends on the difficulty of the specialty, but often lasts at least a year. Training usually focuses on casting, setting stones, making models, or engraving.

Other Experience

Some workers gain their skills through related work experience. This may include working alongside a bench jeweler or gemologist while performing the duties of a salesperson in a retail jewelry store. Time spent in a store with a bench jeweler or gemologist can provide valuable experience.

Advancement

In manufacturing, some jewelers advance to supervisory jobs, such as master jeweler or head jeweler. Jewelers who work in jewelry stores or repair shops may become managers.

Important Qualities

Artistic ability. Jewelers must have the ability to create designs that are unique and beautiful.

Detail oriented. Jewelers and precious stone and metal workers must pay attention to large and small details on the pieces they make.

Dexterity. Jewelers and precious stone and metal workers must precisely move their fingers and tools in order to grasp, manipulate, and assemble very small objects.

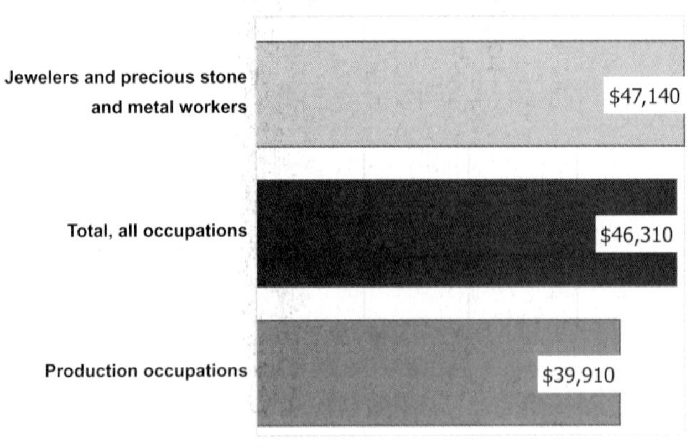

Note: All Occupations includes all occupations in the U.S. Economy.
Source: U.S. Bureau of Labor Statistics, Occupational Employment and Wage Statistics.

Fashion sense. Jewelry designers must know what is stylish and attractive and presently in demand by consumers.

Interpersonal skills. Jewelers and precious stone and metal workers interact with customers, whether they sell products in stores or at craft shows.

Near vision. Jewelers and precious stone and metal workers need the ability to see details at close range (within a few feet of the observer).

Visualization skills. Jewelers and precious stone and metal workers must imagine how something might look after its shape is altered or when its parts are rearranged.

Pay

The median annual wage for jewelers and precious stone and metal workers was $47,140 in May 2022. The median wage is the wage at which half the workers in an occupation earned more than that amount and half earned less. The lowest 10 percent earned less than $30,150, and the highest 10 percent earned more than $76,130.

In May 2022, the median annual wages for jewelers and precious stone and metal workers in the top industries in which they worked were as follows:

Jewelry, luggage, and leather goods retailers	$49,600
Merchant wholesalers, durable goods	48,470
Personal and household goods repair and maintenance	45,110
Jewelry and silverware manufacturing	38,460

Jewelers who work in retail stores may earn commissions for jewelry sold.

Most jewelers and precious stone and metal workers work full time.

Many self-employed workers show and sell their products at trade and craft shows during weekends. Retail store workers might also work nonstandard hours because they must be available when customers are not working, such as on holidays and weekends.

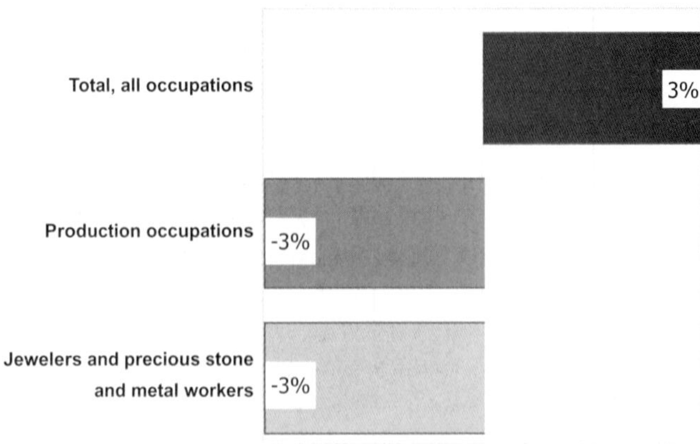

Note: All Occupations includes all occupations in the U.S. Economy.
Source: U.S. Bureau of Labor Statistics, Employment Projections program.

Job Outlook

Employment of jewelers and precious stone and metal workers is projected to decline 3 percent from 2022 to 2032.

Despite declining employment, about 6,100 openings for jewelers and precious stone and metal workers are projected each year, on average, over the decade. All of those openings are expected to result from the need to replace workers who transfer to other occupations or exit the labor force, such as to retire.

Employment

Declining employment in jewelry and silverware manufacturing is expected due to increasing imports of jewelry and rising productivity. Additionally, traditional jewelry stores may continue to lose some of their customers to nontraditional sellers, such as department stores and online retailers. This shift is also likely to reduce employment for jewelers and precious stone and metal workers.

Occupational Title	SOC Code	Employment, 2022	Projected Employment, 2032	Change, 2022-32	
				Percent	Numeric
Jewelers and precious stone and metal workers	51-9071	47,200	45,800	-3	-1,400

Contacts for More Information

For more information about jewelers, precious stone and metal workers, and gemologists, including job opportunities and training programs, visit

- Gemological Institute of America Inc.
- Jewelers of America
- Manufacturing Jewelers & Suppliers of America

Machinists and Tool and Die Makers

Summary

Quick Facts: Machinists and Tool and Die Makers	
2022 Median Pay	$49,560 per year $23.83 per hour
Typical Entry-Level Education	See How to Become One
Work Experience in a Related Occupation	None
On-the-job Training	Long-term on-the-job training
Number of Jobs, 2022	389,700
Job Outlook, 2022-32	0% (Little or no change)
Employment Change, 2022-32	1,000

What Machinists and Tool and Die Makers Do

Machinists and tool and die makers set up and operate equipment to produce precision metal parts, instruments, and tools.

Work Environment

Machinists and tool and die makers work in machine shops and factories. Many work full time during regular business hours. However, working overtime, as well as nights and weekends, may be common.

How to Become a Machinist or Tool and Die Maker

Although machinists typically need a high school diploma to enter the occupation, tool and die makers also may need to complete postsecondary courses. Machinists and tool and die makers typically are trained on the job. Some learn through training or apprenticeship programs, vocational schools, or community and technical colleges.

Pay

The median annual wage for machinists was $48,510 in May 2022.

Machinists and tool and die makers set up and operate many different machines.

The median annual wage for tool and die makers was $59,800 in May 2022.

Job Outlook

Overall employment of machinists and tool and die makers is projected to show little or no change from 2022 to 2032.

Despite limited employment growth, about 38,200 openings for machinists and tool and die makers are projected each year, on average, over the decade. Most of those openings are expected to result from the need to replace workers who transfer to different occupations or exit the labor force, such as to retire.

What Machinists and Tool and Die Makers Do

Machinists and tool and die makers set up and operate a variety of computer-controlled and mechanically controlled equipment to produce precision metal parts, instruments, and tools.

Duties

Machinists typically do the following:

- Read detailed drawings or files, such as blueprints, sketches, and those for computer-aided design (CAD) and computer-aided manufacturing (CAM)
- Set up, operate, and disassemble manual, automatic, and computer numerically controlled (CNC) machine tools
- Align, secure, and adjust cutting tools and workpieces
- Monitor the feed and speed of machines
- Turn, mill, drill, shape, and grind machine parts to specifications
- Verify that completed products meet requirements

Tool and die makers typically do the following:

- Read detailed drawings or files—such as blueprints, sketches, specifications, and those for CAD and CAM—to make tools, molds, and dies
- Compute and verify dimensions, sizes, shapes, and tolerances of workpieces
- Set up, operate, and disassemble conventional, manual, and CNC machine tools
- File, grind, and adjust parts so that they fit together
- Test completed tools and dies to ensure that they meet specifications
- Smooth and polish the surfaces of tools and dies

Machinists use lathes, milling machines, grinders, and other machine tools to produce precision metal parts. Many machinists must be able to use both manual and CNC machinery. CNC machines control the cutting tool speed and do all necessary cuts to create a part. The machinist programs instructions into the CNC machine to determine the cutting path, cutting speed, and feed rate.

Although workers may produce large quantities of one part, precision machinists often produce small batches or single items. The parts that machinists make include steel bolts, titanium bone screws, and automobile pistons.

Some machinists repair broken parts or make new parts that an industrial machinery mechanic discovers in a machine. The machinist refers to engineering drawings to create the replacement.

Some manufacturing processes use lasers, water jets, and electrified wires to cut the workpiece. As engineers design and build new types of machine tools, machinists must learn new machining properties and techniques.

Tool and die makers construct precision tools or metal forms, called dies, that are used to cut, shape, and mold metal, plastics, and other materials.

Tool and die makers use CAD to develop products and parts. They enter designs into computer programs that produce blueprints for the required tools and dies. CNC programmers, described in the metal and plastic machine workers profile, convert CAD designs into CAM programs that contain instructions for a sequence of cutting-tool operations. Machinists normally operate CNC machines, but tool and die makers often are trained to both operate CNC machines and write CNC programs and thus may do either task.

Work Environment

Machinists held about 327,000 jobs in 2022. The largest employers of machinists were as follows:

Fabricated metal product manufacturing	33%
Machinery manufacturing	20
Transportation equipment manufacturing	13
Employment services	4
Wholesale trade	4

Tool and die makers held about 62,700 jobs in 2022. The largest employers of tool and die makers were as follows:

Transportation equipment manufacturing	26%
Machinery manufacturing	23
Fabricated metal product manufacturing	21
Primary metal manufacturing	6
Plastics product manufacturing	6

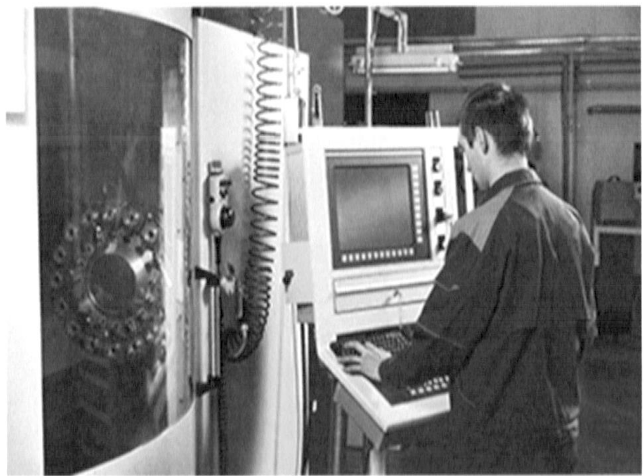

Some machinists and tool and die makers work evenings and weekends because facilities may operate around the clock.

Injuries and Illnesses

Because machinists and tool and die makers may work with machine tools that present hazards, these workers must take precautions to avoid injuries. For example, workers must wear protective equipment, such as safety glasses to shield against bits of flying metal and earplugs to dampen the noise produced by machinery.

Work Schedules

Many machinists and tool and die makers work full time during regular business hours. However, some work nights and weekends in facilities that operate around the clock. Some work more than 40 hours a week.

How to Become a Machinist or Tool and Die Maker

Although machinists typically need a high school diploma to enter the occupation, tool and die makers also may need to

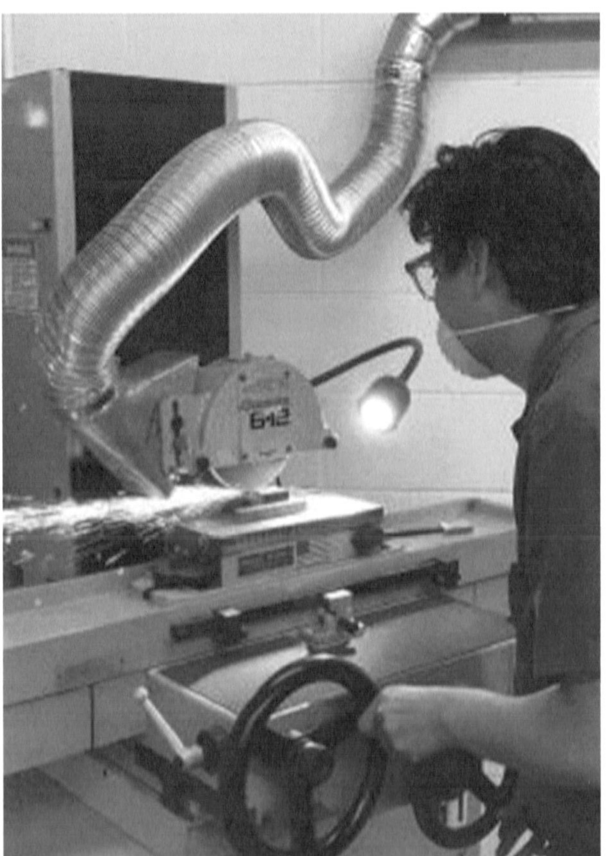

Machinists and tool and die makers typically are trained on the job.

complete postsecondary courses. Machinists and tool and die makers typically are trained on the job. Some learn through training or apprenticeship programs, vocational schools, or community and technical colleges.

Education

Machinists typically need a high school diploma or equivalent; tool and die makers also may need to complete postsecondary courses. High school courses in math, blueprint reading, metalworking, and CAD/CAM are considered useful.

Some community colleges and technical schools have 2-year degree programs or shorter nondegree certificate programs that train students to become machinists or tool and die makers. These programs usually teach design and how to read engineering drawings, the use of a variety of welding and cutting tools, and the programming and function of CNC machines.

Training

Machinists and tool and die makers typically gain competency through on-the-job training or an apprenticeship.

Trainees usually learn on the job, which may include technical instruction outside of typical work hours. Trainees often begin as machine operators and gradually take on more difficult assignments. Machinists and tool and die makers must be comfortable using computers to work with CAD/CAM technology, CNC machine tools, and computerized measuring machines. Some machinists become tool and die makers.

Some new workers enter apprenticeship programs, which are typically sponsored by an employer. Apprenticeship programs often consist of paid training on the job and related technical instruction lasting several years. The technical instruction may be provided in cooperation with local community colleges and vocational–technical schools. Workers typically need a high school diploma or equivalent to enter an apprenticeship.

Licenses, Certifications, and Registrations

Completing a certification program, though optional, allows machinists and tool and die makers to demonstrate competency and may be helpful for advancement. Colleges and organizations, such as the National Institute for Metalworking Skills (NIMS), offer certifications and credentials in CNC machine operation, CAD/CAM technology, and other relevant competencies.

Important Qualities

Analytical skills. Machinists and tool and die makers must be able to interpret technical blueprints, models, and specifications so that they can craft precision tools and metal parts.

Manual dexterity. Machinists' and tool and die makers' work demands accuracy, sometimes to within .0001 of an inch. This level of accuracy requires both concentration and agility.

Mechanical skills. Machinists and tool and die makers may operate milling machines, lathes, grinders, laser and water jetting machines, wire electrical discharge machines, and other machine tools.

Physical stamina. Machinist and tool and die makers must stand for extended periods and perform repetitious movements.

Technical skills. Machinists and tool and die makers must understand metalworking processes. They must be able to work with CAD/CAM technology, CNC machine tools, and manual and computerized measuring machines.

Pay

The median annual wage for machinists was $48,510 in May 2022. The median wage is the wage at which half the workers in an occupation earned more than that amount and half earned less. The lowest 10 percent earned less than $33,720, and the highest 10 percent earned more than $71,820.

The median annual wage for tool and die makers was $59,800 in May 2022. The lowest 10 percent earned less than $38,470, and the highest 10 percent earned more than $79,540.

In May 2022, the median annual wages for machinists in the top industries in which they worked were as follows:

Transportation equipment manufacturing	$52,360
Wholesale trade	48,420
Machinery manufacturing	48,400
Fabricated metal product manufacturing	47,390
Employment services	35,610

In May 2022, the median annual wages for tool and die makers in the top industries in which they worked were as follows:

Transportation equipment manufacturing	$66,050

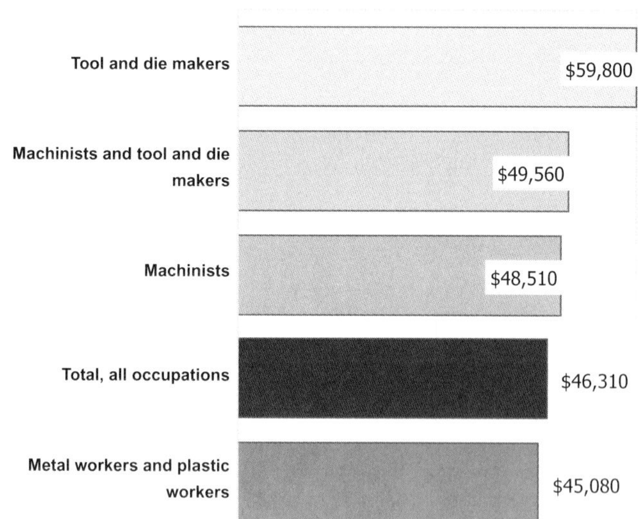

Note: All Occupations includes all occupations in the U.S. Economy.
Source: U.S. Bureau of Labor Statistics, Occupational Employment and Wage Statistics.

Fabricated metal product manufacturing	60,040
Machinery manufacturing	58,990
Plastics product manufacturing	58,450
Primary metal manufacturing	47,640

The pay of apprentices is tied to their skill level. As they reach specific levels of performance and experience, their pay increases.

Many machinists and tool and die makers work full time during regular business hours. However, some work nights and weekends in facilities that operate around the clock. Some work more than 40 hours a week.

Job Outlook

Overall employment of machinists and tool and die makers is projected to show little or no change from 2022 to 2032.

Despite limited employment growth, about 38,200 openings for machinists and tool and die makers are projected each year, on average, over the decade. Most of those openings are expected to result from the need to replace workers who transfer to different occupations or exit the labor force, such as to retire.

Employment

Projected employment of machinists and tool and die makers varies by occupation (see table).

Although machinists will be required to set up, monitor, and maintain systems, such as computer numerically controlled (CNC) machine tools, autoloaders, and high-speed machining, their employment growth is expected to be limited as improvements in these technologies increase these workers' efficiency over the projections decade.

Employment of tool and die makers is expected to decline as advances in automation, including CNC machine tools, reduce demand for certain tasks that these workers do, such as programming how parts fit together.

Occupational Title	SOC Code	Employment, 2022	Projected Employment, 2032	Change, 2022-32	
				Percent	Numeric
Machinists and tool and die makers	—	389,700	390,700	0	1,000
Machinists	51-4041	327,000	333,300	2	6,300
Tool and die makers	51-4111	62,700	57,400	-8	-5,300

Machinists and Tool and Die Makers

Percent change in employment, projected 2022-32

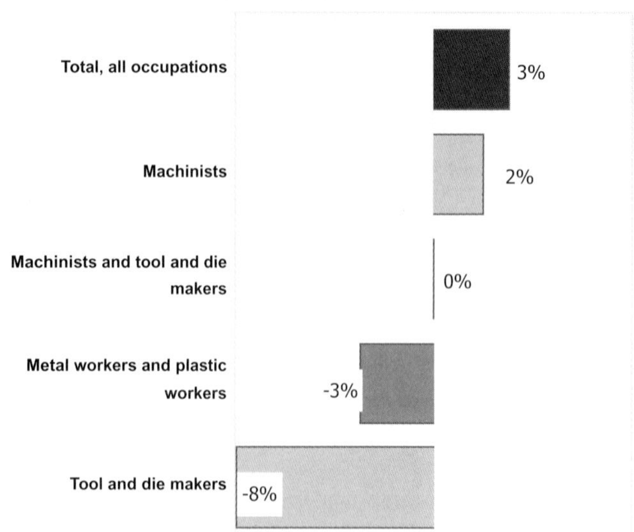

Note: All Occupations includes all occupations in the U.S. Economy.
Source: U.S. Bureau of Labor Statistics, Employment Projections program.

Contacts for More Information

Apprenticeship information is available from the U.S. Department of Labor's Apprenticeship program online or by phone at 877-872-5627. Visit Apprenticeship.gov to search for apprenticeship opportunities.

For more information, visit

- Fabricators & Manufacturers Association, International (FMA)
- Manufacturing Institute (MI)
- National Institute for Metalworking Skills (NIMS)
- American Mold Builders Association (AMBA)
- Association for Manufacturing Technology (AMT)
- National Tooling and Machining Association (NTMA)
- Precision Machined Products Association (PMPA)
- Precision Metalforming Association (PMA)

Metal and Plastic Machine Workers

Summary

Quick Facts: Metal and Plastic Machine Workers	
2022 Median Pay	$41,060 per year $19.74 per hour
Typical Entry-Level Education	See How to Become One
Work Experience in a Related Occupation	None
On-the-job Training	Moderate-term on-the-job training
Number of Jobs, 2022	1,048,200
Job Outlook, 2022-32	-6% (Decline)
Employment Change, 2022-32	-67,200

What Metal and Plastic Machine Workers Do

Metal and plastic machine workers set up and operate equipment that cuts, shapes, and forms metal and plastic materials or pieces.

Work Environment

Metal and plastic machine workers are employed mainly in factories. Workers must adhere to safety standards to protect themselves from workplace hazards. Most work full time, which for some includes evenings and weekends.

How to Become a Metal or Plastic Machine Worker

Metal and plastic workers typically need a high school diploma to enter the occupation and receive 1 year of on-the-job training. Computer numerically controlled (CNC) tool programmers typically need postsecondary training.

Pay

The median annual wage for metal and plastic machine workers was $41,060 in May 2022.

Job Outlook

Overall employment of metal and plastic machine workers is projected to decline 6 percent from 2022 to 2032.

Despite declining employment, about 90,800 openings for metal and plastic machine workers are projected each year, on average, over the decade. All of those openings are expected to result from the need to replace workers who transfer to other occupations or exit the labor force, such as to retire.

What Metal and Plastic Machine Workers Do

Metal and plastic machine workers set up and operate equipment that cuts, shapes, and forms metal and plastic materials or pieces.

Duties

Metal and plastic machine workers typically do the following:

- Set up and adjust machines according to blueprints
- Monitor machines status to ensure proper functioning
- Insert material into machines, either manually or using material handling equipment
- Operate shaping and forming equipment, such as metal or plastic molding, casting, or coremaking machines
- Operate stock removal metalworking machines, such as lathes or mills
- Adjust machine settings for temperature, cycle times, and speed and feed rates
- Remove finished products and document output in a database
- Measure, test, and inspect finished workpieces according to blueprints
- Observe and adjust or replace dull or damaged cutting tools

Metal and plastic machine workers operate equipment that creates the parts for consumer products. In general, these workers are separated into two groups: those who set up machines for operation and those who operate machines during production. However, many workers perform both tasks.

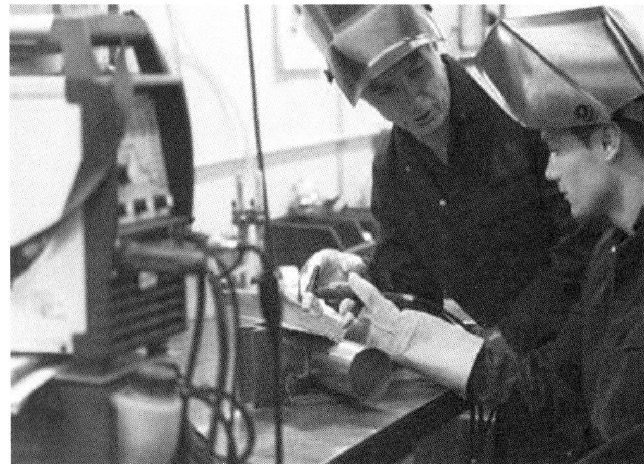

Metal and plastic machine workers set up and operate automated and computer-controlled machinery.

Metal and plastic machine workers monitor and adjust machines during operation.

Although many workers both set up and operate machines, some specialize in being either a machine setter or a machine operator and tender.

Machine setters, or setup workers, prepare the machines before production, do test runs, and, if necessary, adjust and make minor repairs to the machinery before and during operation. Computer numerically controlled (CNC) setters upload computer control programs.

After installing the tools into a machine, setup workers often produce the initial batch of goods, inspect the products, and turn over the machine to an operator.

Machine operators and tenders monitor the machinery during production.

After a setter prepares a machine for production, an operator observes the machine and the products it makes. Operators may have to load the machine with materials for production or adjust machine speeds during production. They must periodically inspect the parts that a machine produces to ensure everything works properly, repairing equipment as needed. For example, the parts a machine produces may show defects if the cutting tool inside a machine becomes dull or damaged after extended use. When that happens, it is common for an operator to remove the worn tool and replace it with a new one produced by tool and die makers. Operators may fix minor problems themselves but may have an industrial machinery mechanic fix more serious problems.

Setters, operators, and tenders are usually identified by the type of machine they work with. Job duties generally vary with the size of the manufacturer and the type of machine being operated. Although some workers specialize in one or two types of machines, others are trained to set up or operate a variety of them. Automation often allows machine operators to control multiple machines at the same time.

In addition, production techniques, such as team-oriented "lean" manufacturing, require machine operators to rotate between different machines. Rotating assignments results in more varied work but also requires workers to have a range of skills.

The following are examples of types of metal and plastic machine workers:

Computer numerically controlled tool operators operate CNC equipment or robots to perform functions on metal or plastic workpieces.

Computer numerically controlled tool programmers develop computer programs to control the machining or processing of metal or plastic parts by automatic machine tools, equipment, or systems.

Cutting, punching, and press machine setters, operators, and tenders set up or operate machines to saw, cut, shear, notch, bend, or straighten metal or plastic materials.

Drilling and boring machine tool setters, operators, and tenders set up or operate drilling machines to drill, bore, mill, or countersink metal or plastic workpieces.

Extruding and drawing machine setters, operators, and tenders set up or operate machines to extrude (pull out) thermoplastic or metal materials in the form of tubes, rods, hoses, wire, bars, or structural shapes.

Forging machine setters, operators, and tenders set up or operate machines that shape or form metal or plastic into parts.

Foundry mold and coremakers make or form wax or sand cores or molds used in the production of metal castings in foundries.

Grinding, lapping, polishing, and buffing machine tool setters, operators, and tenders set up or operate grinding and related machine tools that remove excess material from surfaces, sharpen edges or corners, or buff or polish metal or plastic workpieces.

Heat-treating equipment setters, operators, and tenders set up or operate heating equipment, such as heat-treating furnaces, flame-hardening machines, induction machines, soaking pits, or vacuum equipment, to temper, harden, anneal, or heat treat metal or plastic objects.

Lathe and turning machine tool setters, operators, and tenders set up or operate lathe and turning machines to turn, bore, thread, or form metal or plastic materials, such as bars, rods, and castings.

Metal-refining furnace operators and tenders operate or tend furnaces, such as gas, oil, coal, electric-arc or electric-induction, and oxygen furnaces. These furnaces may be used to melt and refine metal before casting.

Milling and planing machine setters, operators, and tenders set up or operate milling or planing machines to shape, groove, or profile metal or plastic workpieces.

Model makers set up and operate machines, such as milling and engraving machines, to make working models of metal or plastic objects. They may also use 3D printing technology.

Molding, coremaking, and casting machine setters, operators, and tenders set up or operate metal or plastic molding, casting, or coremaking machines to mold or cast metal or thermoplastic parts or products.

Multiple machine tool setters, operators, and tenders set up or operate two or more types of cutting or forming machine tool or robot.

Patternmakers lay out, machine, fit, and assemble castings and parts to metal or plastic foundry patterns and core molds.

Plating machine setters, operators, and tenders set up or operate plating machines and perform chemical checks for coating metal or plastic products with zinc, copper, nickel, or some other metal to protect or decorate surfaces.

Pourers and casters operate computer- or hand-controlled machines to pour and regulate the flow of molten metal into molds to produce castings or ingots.

Rolling machine setters, operators, and tenders set up or operate machines to roll steel or plastic or to flatten, temper, or reduce the thickness of materials.

Welding, soldering, and brazing machine setters, operators, and tenders (including workers who operate laser cutters

Metal and plastic machine workers usually wear protective equipment, such as safety glasses.

or laser-beam machines) set up or operate welding, soldering, or brazing machines or robots that weld, braze, solder, or heat treat metal products, components, or assemblies.

Work Environment

Metal and plastic machine workers held about 1.0 million jobs in 2022. Employment in the detailed occupations that make up metal and plastic machine workers was distributed as follows:

Occupation	Employment
Cutting, punching, and press machine setters, operators, and tenders, metal and plastic	184,800
Computer numerically controlled tool operators	181,800
Molding, coremaking, and casting machine setters, operators, and tenders, metal and plastic	167,900
Multiple machine tool setters, operators, and tenders, metal and plastic	139,900
Grinding, lapping, polishing, and buffing machine tool setters, operators, and tenders, metal and plastic	75,000
Extruding and drawing machine setters, operators, and tenders, metal and plastic	64,300
Plating machine setters, operators, and tenders, metal and plastic	32,900
Welding, soldering, and brazing machine setters, operators, and tenders	32,900
Computer numerically controlled tool programmers	28,500
Rolling machine setters, operators, and tenders, metal and plastic	28,200
Metal-refining furnace operators and tenders	19,700
Lathe and turning machine tool setters, operators, and tenders, metal and plastic	19,700
Heat treating equipment setters, operators, and tenders, metal and plastic	16,000
Milling and planing machine setters, operators, and tenders, metal and plastic	15,700
Foundry mold and coremakers	11,500
Forging machine setters, operators, and tenders, metal and plastic	10,900
Drilling and boring machine tool setters, operators, and tenders, metal and plastic	6,600
Pourers and casters, metal	6,200
Model makers, metal and plastic	3,400
Patternmakers, metal and plastic	2,300

The largest employers of metal and plastic machine workers were as follows:

Industry	Percent
Fabricated metal product manufacturing	25%
Plastics and rubber products manufacturing	16
Transportation equipment manufacturing	13
Primary metal manufacturing	11
Machinery manufacturing	11

Injuries and Illnesses

These workers often operate powerful, high-speed machines that can be dangerous and must observe safety rules. Operators usually wear protective equipment, such as safety glasses, earplugs, and steel-toed boots, to guard against flying particles of metal or plastic, machine noise, and heavy objects, respectively.

Other required safety equipment varies by work setting and machine. For example, respirators are common for those in the plastics industry who work near materials that emit dangerous fumes or dust.

Welding, soldering, and brazing machine setters, operators, and tenders have one of the highest rates of injuries and illnesses of all occupations.

Work Schedules

Most metal and plastic machine workers are employed full time. Some work more than 40 hours per week. Because many manufacturers run their machinery for extended periods, evening and weekend work is also common.

How to Become a Metal or Plastic Machine Worker

Metal and plastic workers typically need a high school diploma to enter the occupation and receive 1 year of on-the-job training. Computer numerically controlled (CNC) tool programmers typically need postsecondary education.

Education

Although metal and plastic machine workers typically need a high school diploma, CNC tool programmers usually need coursework beyond high school. Some community colleges and other schools offer courses and certificate programs in operating metal and plastics machines including CNC programming.

For metal and plastic machine workers, high school classes in computer programming, math, and vocational technology may be useful.

Metal and plastic machine workers must be able to stand for long periods and perform repetitive work.

Training

Machine operator trainees usually begin by watching and helping experienced workers on the job. Under supervision, they may supply materials, start and stop the machines, or remove finished products. Then, they advance to operators' more difficult tasks, such as adjusting feeds and speeds, replacing tools, and measuring finished products for conformance. Eventually, some operators develop the skills and experience to set up machines.

The complexity of the equipment usually determines the time required to become an operator. Some operators and tenders are trained on basic machine operations and functions in a few months. Others, such as CNC tool operators, may need training for up to 1 year.

Because of the prevalence of computerized machines in manufacturing, training on computer-aided design (CAD), computer-aided manufacturing (CAM), and CNC equipment may be helpful.

Licenses, Certifications, and Registrations

Certification can show competence and can be helpful for advancement. The National Institute for Metalworking Skills (NIMS) offers certification in numerous metalworking specializations.

Advancement

With skill and experience, workers may advance to positions that offer higher pay and more responsibility. It is common for machine operators to move into setup or machinery maintenance positions. Setup workers may become industrial machinery mechanics and maintenance workers, machinists, or tool and die makers.

Experienced workers with good communication and analytical skills may advance to supervisory positions.

Important Qualities

Computer skills. Metal and plastic machine workers must be able to use programmable devices, computers, and robots on the factory floor.

Mechanical skills. These workers must be comfortable with machines and have a good understanding of how all the parts work.

Physical stamina. Metal and plastic machine workers must be able to stand for long periods and do repetitive tasks.

Physical strength. Metal and plastic machine workers must be able to secure and tighten heavy fixtures into place.

Pay

The median annual wage for metal and plastic machine workers was $41,060 in May 2022. The median wage is the wage at which half the workers in an occupation earned more than that amount and half earned less. The lowest 10 percent earned less than $30,350, and the highest 10 percent earned more than $61,840.

Median annual wages for metal and plastic machine workers in May 2022 were as follows:

Computer numerically controlled tool programmers	$60,800
Model makers, metal and plastic	57,620
Patternmakers, metal and plastic	54,970
Metal-refining furnace operators and tenders	50,280
Lathe and turning machine tool setters, operators, and tenders, metal and plastic	47,020
Milling and planing machine setters, operators, and tenders, metal and plastic	46,870
Computer numerically controlled tool operators	46,760
Forging machine setters, operators, and tenders, metal and plastic	46,540
Rolling machine setters, operators, and tenders, metal and plastic	46,310
Pourers and casters, metal	45,070
Welding, soldering, and brazing machine setters, operators, and tenders	44,920

Metal and Plastic Machine Workers

Median annual wages, May 2022

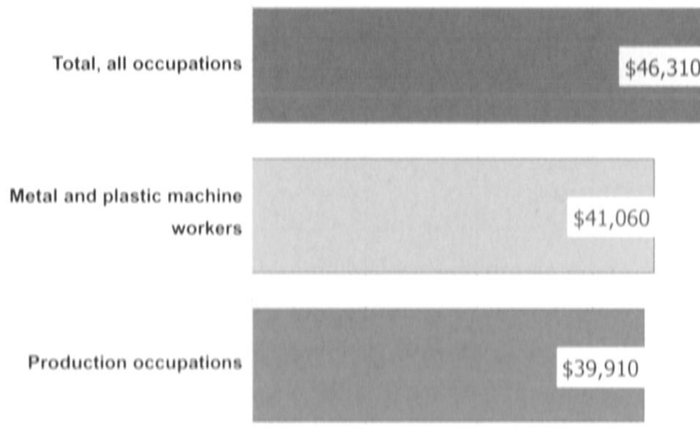

Note: All Occupations includes all occupations in the U.S. Economy.
Source: U.S. Bureau of Labor Statistics, Occupational Employment and Wage Statistics.

Drilling and boring machine tool setters, operators, and tenders, metal and plastic	42,450
Heat treating equipment setters, operators, and tenders, metal and plastic	40,900
Foundry mold and coremakers	40,120
Extruding and drawing machine setters, operators, and tenders, metal and plastic	39,970
Cutting, punching, and press machine setters, operators, and tenders, metal and plastic	39,340
Multiple machine tool setters, operators, and tenders, metal and plastic	39,210
Grinding, lapping, polishing, and buffing machine tool setters, operators, and tenders, metal and plastic	38,910
Plating machine setters, operators, and tenders, metal and plastic	37,900
Molding, coremaking, and casting machine setters, operators, and tenders, metal and plastic	37,050

In May 2022, the median annual wages for metal and plastic machine workers in the top industries in which they worked were as follows:

Machinery manufacturing	$46,960
Transportation equipment manufacturing	45,520
Primary metal manufacturing	44,730
Fabricated metal product manufacturing	42,460
Plastics and rubber products manufacturing	37,150

Most metal and plastic machine workers are employed full time. Some work more than 40 hours per week. Because many manufacturers run their machinery for extended periods, evening and weekend work also is common.

Job Outlook

Overall employment of metal and plastic machine workers is projected to decline 6 percent from 2022 to 2032.

Despite declining employment, about 90,800 openings for metal and plastic machine workers are projected each year, on average, over the decade. All of those openings are expected to result from the need to replace workers who transfer to other occupations or exit the labor force, such as to retire.

Employment

Projected employment of metal and plastic machine workers varies by occupation (see table).

One of the most important factors influencing employment of these workers is the use of laborsaving machinery. Many firms are continuing to expand the use of technologies, such as computer numerically controlled (CNC) tools and robots, to improve quality and lower production costs. The use of CNC equipment requires CNC tool programmers instead of machine

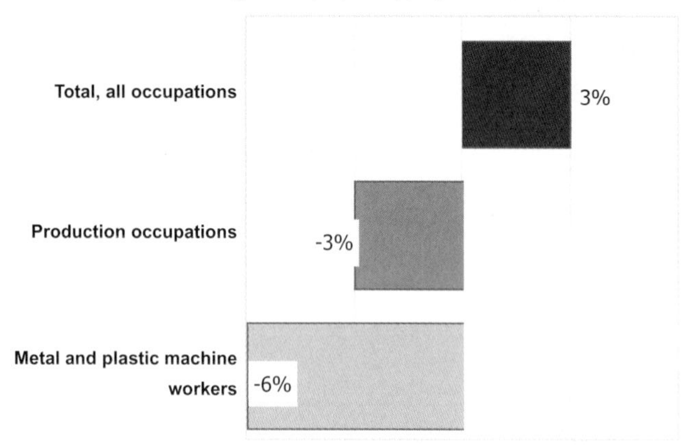

Note: All Occupations includes all occupations in the U.S. Economy.
Source: U.S. Bureau of Labor Statistics, Employment Projections program.

setters, operators, and tenders. Therefore, demand for most manual tool operators and tenders is likely to be reduced, while demand for CNC tool programmers is expected to be strong.

Additionally, the use of software to create digital and 3D-print prototypes may reduce the need for some of these workers, including patternmakers and model makers.

Employment of metal and plastic machine workers also is affected by the demand for the parts they produce. Both plastic and metal manufacturing industries face foreign competition that limits the orders for parts produced in this country. Changes in the cost of operations in the United States and abroad may encourage some manufacturers to bring back production that was previously sent offshore. However, new facilities in the United States will likely incorporate more automation technologies, requiring less labor overall.

Occupational Title	SOC Code	Employment, 2022	Projected Employment, 2032	Change, 2022-32	
				Percent	Numeric
Metal and plastic machine workers	—	1,048,200	981,000	-6	-67,200
Extruding and drawing machine setters, operators, and tenders, metal and plastic	51-4021	64,300	63,100	-2	-1,200
Forging machine setters, operators, and tenders, metal and plastic	51-4022	10,900	9,300	-15	-1,600
Rolling machine setters, operators, and tenders, metal and plastic	51-4023	28,200	25,100	-11	-3,100
Cutting, punching, and press machine setters, operators, and tenders, metal and plastic	51-4031	184,800	164,700	-11	-20,100
Drilling and boring machine tool setters, operators, and tenders, metal and plastic	51-4032	6,600	5,400	-18	-1,200

Occupational Title	SOC Code	Employment, 2022	Projected Employment, 2032	Change, 2022-32	
				Percent	Numeric
Grinding, lapping, polishing, and buffing machine tool setters, operators, and tenders, metal and plastic	51-4033	75,000	67,900	-9	-7,100
Lathe and turning machine tool setters, operators, and tenders, metal and plastic	51-4034	19,700	17,800	-9	-1,900
Milling and planing machine setters, operators, and tenders, metal and plastic	51-4035	15,700	13,500	-14	-2,200
Metal-refining furnace operators and tenders	51-4051	19,700	18,100	-8	-1,600
Pourers and casters, metal	51-4052	6,200	5,600	-9	-600
Model makers, metal and plastic	51-4061	3,400	2,800	-19	-600
Patternmakers, metal and plastic	51-4062	2,300	1,800	-22	-500
Foundry mold and coremakers	51-4071	11,500	8,800	-24	-2,700
Molding, coremaking, and casting machine setters, operators, and tenders, metal and plastic	51-4072	167,900	161,700	-4	-6,200
Multiple machine tool setters, operators, and tenders, metal and plastic	51-4081	139,900	140,700	1	800
Welding, soldering, and brazing machine setters, operators, and tenders	51-4122	32,900	30,100	-8	-2,800
Heat treating equipment setters, operators, and tenders, metal and plastic	51-4191	16,000	14,600	-9	-1,500
Plating machine setters, operators, and tenders, metal and plastic	51-4193	32,900	29,800	-9	-3,100
Computer numerically controlled tool operators	51-9161	181,800	167,200	-8	-14,600
Computer numerically controlled tool programmers	51-9162	28,500	33,000	16	4,600

Contacts for More Information

For more information, visit

- Fabricators & Manufacturers Association, International (FMA)
- National Institute for Metalworking Skills (NIMS)
- Association for Manufacturing Technology (AMT)
- National Tooling and Machining Association (NTMA)
- Precision Machined Products Association (PMPA)
- Precision Metalforming Association (PMA)

Painting and Coating Workers

Summary

Quick Facts: Painting and Coating Workers

2022 Median Pay	$43,370 per year $20.85 per hour
Typical Entry-Level Education	See How to Become One
Work Experience in a Related Occupation	None
On-the-job Training	Moderate-term on-the-job training
Number of Jobs, 2022	185,900
Job Outlook, 2022-32	1% (Little or no change)
Employment Change, 2022-32	1,000

What Painting and Coating Workers Do

Painting and coating workers apply finishes, often using machines, to a range of products.

Work Environment

Most painting and coating workers are employed full time. They frequently stand for long periods in specially ventilated areas.

How to Become a Painting and Coating Worker

Painting and coating workers typically need a high school diploma or equivalent to enter the occupation. New workers usually train on the job for several months.

Pay

The median annual wage for coating, painting, and spraying machine setters, operators, and tenders was $43,960 in May 2022.

Painting and coating workers paint many different surfaces.

The median annual wage for painting, coating, and decorating workers was $38,270 in May 2022.

Job Outlook

Overall employment of painting and coating workers is projected to show little or no change from 2022 to 2032.

Despite limited employment growth, about 16,700 openings for painting and coating workers are projected each year, on average, over the decade. Most of those openings are expected to result from the need to replace workers who transfer to different occupations or exit the labor force, such as to retire.

What Painting and Coating Workers Do

Painting and coating workers apply finishes, often using machines, to products such as cars, jewelry, and ceramics.

Duties

Painting and coating workers typically do the following:

- Set up and operate machines that paint or coat products
- Select the paint or coating needed for the job
- Clean and prepare products to be painted or coated
- Determine the required flow of paint and the quality of the coating
- Apply paint or coating
- Measure the thickness of paint or coating material applied
- Clean and maintain tools, equipment, and work areas

Painting and coating workers apply paint, varnish, rustproofing, or other types of liquid treatments to finish and protect products. They often use machines to spread the liquid over large surfaces but may use handtools on small items or hard-to-reach surfaces.

Before workers apply the paint or other coating, they prepare the surface by sanding or cleaning it to prevent dust from becoming trapped under the paint. They also may cover portions of the product with tape and paper to prevent the paint or coating from touching those areas.

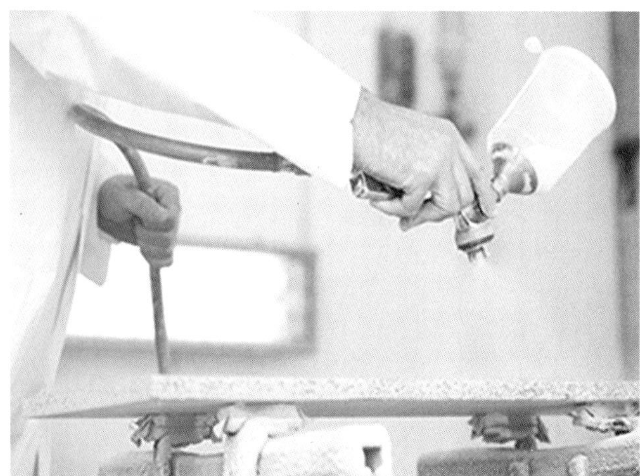

Painters use spray guns to apply paints and coatings in factories.

After the product is prepared, workers may use a number of techniques to apply the paint or coating. Common techniques include spraying products with paint or coating and dipping items in a large vat of paint or other coating. Many factories use automated painting systems. Workers may measure the paint thickness using a coating thickness gauge or painter meter.

The following are examples of types of painting and coating workers:

Coating, painting, and spraying machine setters, operators, and tenders use spraying or rolling machines to apply lacquer, enamel, or other coatings to a variety of products, such as cars, boats, and glassware. These workers position the spray guns, set the nozzles, and synchronize the action of the guns with the speed of the conveyor carrying products through the machine. During the process, they program the machine, tend the equipment, watch gauges on the control panel, and check products to ensure that they are being painted evenly. The operator may use a manual spray gun to touch up flaws.

Painting, coating, and decorating workers use manual spray guns, pens, or brushes to apply various coatings to furniture, glass, pottery, toys, books, and other products. They also may immerse pieces into the liquid and place the coated items into ovens or dryers to harden the finishes. In addition, these workers examine products to be sure that they meet specifications.

For information about workers who paint walls, equipment, buildings, bridges, and other structures, see the profile on construction and maintenance painters.

Work Environment

Coating, painting, and spraying machine setters, operators, and tenders held about 172,400 jobs in 2022. The largest employers of coating, painting, and spraying machine setters, operators, and tenders were as follows:

Fabricated metal product manufacturing	17%
Transportation equipment manufacturing	16
Automotive body, paint, interior, and glass repair	14
Machinery manufacturing	7
Furniture and related product manufacturing	4

Painting, coating, and decorating workers held about 13,500 jobs in 2022. The largest employers of painting, coating, and decorating workers were as follows:

Fabricated metal product manufacturing	12%
Miscellaneous manufacturing	11
Self-employed workers	10
Furniture and related product manufacturing	7
Automotive body, paint, interior, and glass repair	5

Painting and coating is usually done in specially ventilated areas. Workers wear masks or respirators to protect themselves from inhaling microscopic particles or harmful chemicals.

Workers wear masks, gloves, and other protective equipment.

Painting and coating workers can usually become proficient in less than 1 year.

They also may wear gloves and other protective equipment to shield their skin and clothing.

Painting and coating workers often stand for long periods. They also may have to bend, stoop, or crouch in uncomfortable positions to reach different parts of the products they work on.

Injuries and Illnesses

Painting, coating, and decorating workers have one of the highest rates of injuries and illnesses of all occupations. Hazards include muscle strains and exposure to toxic materials. Factories have installed sophisticated paint booths and fresh-air ventilation systems to create a safe work environment.

Work Schedules

Most painting and coating workers are employed full time.

How to Become a Painting and Coating Worker

Painting and coating workers typically need a high school diploma or equivalent to enter the occupation. New workers usually train on the job for several months to attain competency.

Education

Painting and coating workers usually need a high school diploma or equivalent for entry-level positions. However, some employers hire candidates who do not have formal educational credentials.

Some automotive painters attend vocational-technical programs in which they receive practical instruction in mixing and applying different types of paint.

Training

To attain competency, painting and coating workers typically receive on-the-job training. Sometimes this training lasts only a few days, but it usually lasts several months.

Workers who operate computer-controlled equipment may require additional training in computer programming.

Important Qualities

Artistic ability. Some painting and coating workers make elaborate or decorative designs.

Color vision. Workers must be able to blend new paint colors in order to match existing colors on a surface.

Mechanical skills. Workers must be able to operate and maintain sprayers that apply paints and coatings.

Physical stamina. Workers may have to squat or bend frequently and stand for extended periods.

Physical strength. Workers may need to lift heavy objects. Some products that are painted or coated may weigh more than 50 pounds.

Pay

The median annual wage for coating, painting, and spraying machine setters, operators, and tenders was $43,960 in May 2022. The median wage is the wage at which half the workers in an occupation earned more than that amount and half earned less. The lowest 10 percent earned less than $31,200, and the highest 10 percent earned more than $63,430.

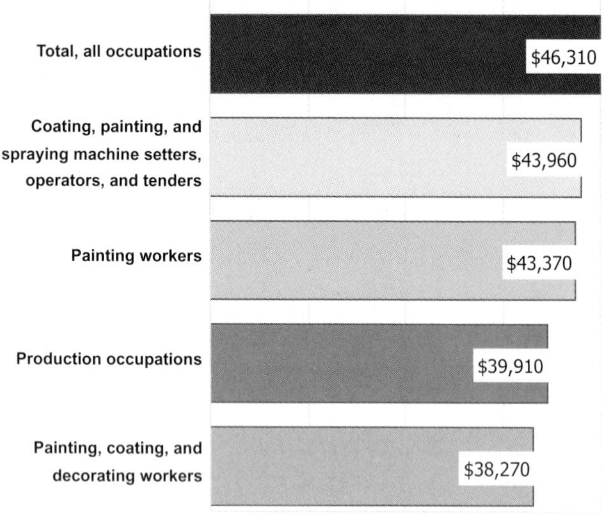

Note: All Occupations includes all occupations in the U.S. Economy.
Source: U.S. Bureau of Labor Statistics, Occupational Employment and Wage Statistics.

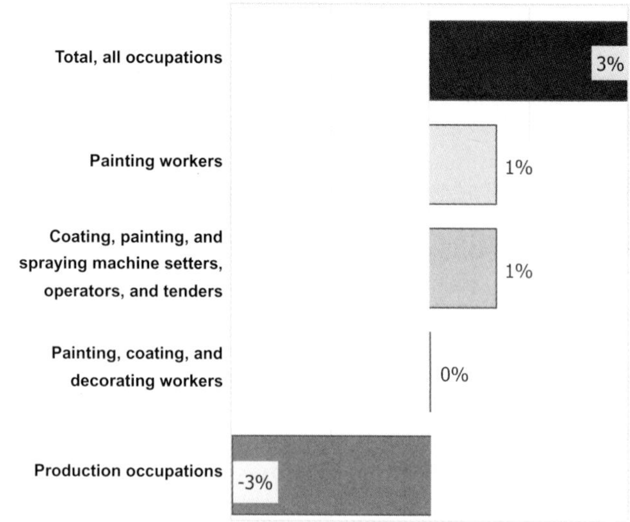

Note: All Occupations includes all occupations in the U.S. Economy.
Source: U.S. Bureau of Labor Statistics, Employment Projections program.

The median annual wage for painting, coating, and decorating workers was $38,270 in May 2022. The lowest 10 percent earned less than $28,850, and the highest 10 percent earned more than $55,120.

In May 2022, the median annual wages for coating, painting, and spraying machine setters, operators, and tenders in the top industries in which they worked were as follows:

Transportation equipment manufacturing	$49,340
Automotive body, paint, interior, and glass repair	48,610
Machinery manufacturing	44,050
Fabricated metal product manufacturing	38,600
Furniture and related product manufacturing	37,250

In May 2022, the median annual wages for painting, coating, and decorating workers in the top industries in which they worked were as follows:

Automotive body, paint, interior, and glass repair	$43,750
Furniture and related product manufacturing	38,030
Miscellaneous manufacturing	37,810
Fabricated metal product manufacturing	35,790

Automotive painters in repair shops may receive a bonus or commission in addition to their wages.

Most painting and coating workers are employed full time.

Job Outlook

Overall employment of painting and coating workers is projected to show little or no change from 2022 to 2032.

Despite limited employment growth, about 16,700 openings for painting and coating workers are projected each year, on average, over the decade. Most of those openings are expected to result from the need to replace workers who transfer to different occupations or exit the labor force, such as to retire.

Employment

Many consumer, commercial, and industrial products require painting and coating services, such as in automotive paint repair or detailing. However, automation is expected to limit opportunities for these workers in some manufacturing establishments.

Occupational Title	SOC Code	Employment, 2022	Projected Employment, 2032	Change, 2022-32	
				Percent	Numeric
Painting workers	51-9120	185,900	186,900	1	1,000
Painting, coating, and decorating workers	51-9123	13,500	13,500	0	0
Coating, painting, and spraying machine setters, operators, and tenders	51-9124	172,400	173,400	1	1,000

Contacts for More Information

For more information about job opportunities for painting and coating workers, visit

- Local manufacturers
- Automotive body repair shops
- Motor vehicle dealers
- Vocational schools
- Local unions representing painting and coating workers
- Local offices of state employment services

For a directory of certified automotive painting programs, visit
➤ National Institute for Automotive Service Excellence

Power Plant Operators, Distributors, and Dispatchers

Summary

Quick Facts: Power Plant Operators, Distributors, and Dispatchers	
2022 Median Pay	$97,570 per year $46.91 per hour
Typical Entry-Level Education	High school diploma or equivalent
Work Experience in a Related Occupation	None
On-the-job Training	Long-term on-the-job training
Number of Jobs, 2022	47,300
Job Outlook, 2022-32	-10% (Decline)
Employment Change, 2022-32	-4,700

What Power Plant Operators, Distributors, and Dispatchers Do

Power plant operators, distributors, and dispatchers control the systems that generate and distribute electric power.

Work Environment

Most power plant operators, distributors, and dispatchers work full time. Many work rotating 8- or 12-hour shifts.

How to Become a Power Plant Operator, Distributor, or Dispatcher

Power plant operators, distributors, and dispatchers typically need a high school diploma or equivalent combined with extensive on-the-job training that may include a combination of classroom and hands-on training. Many jobs require a background check and drug and alcohol screenings. Nuclear power reactor operators also need a license.

Power plant operators monitor power-generating equipment such as nuclear reactors from control rooms.

Pay

The median annual wage for power plant operators, distributors, and dispatchers was $97,570 in May 2022.

Job Outlook

Overall employment of power plant operators, distributors, and dispatchers is projected to decline 10 percent from 2022 to 2032.

Despite declining employment, about 3,200 openings for power plant operators, distributors, and dispatchers are projected each year, on average, over the decade. All of those openings are expected to result from the need to replace workers who transfer to other occupations or exit the labor force, such as to retire.

What Power Plant Operators, Distributors, and Dispatchers Do

Power plant operators, distributors, and dispatchers control the systems that generate and distribute electric power.

Duties

Power plant operators, distributors, and dispatchers typically do the following:

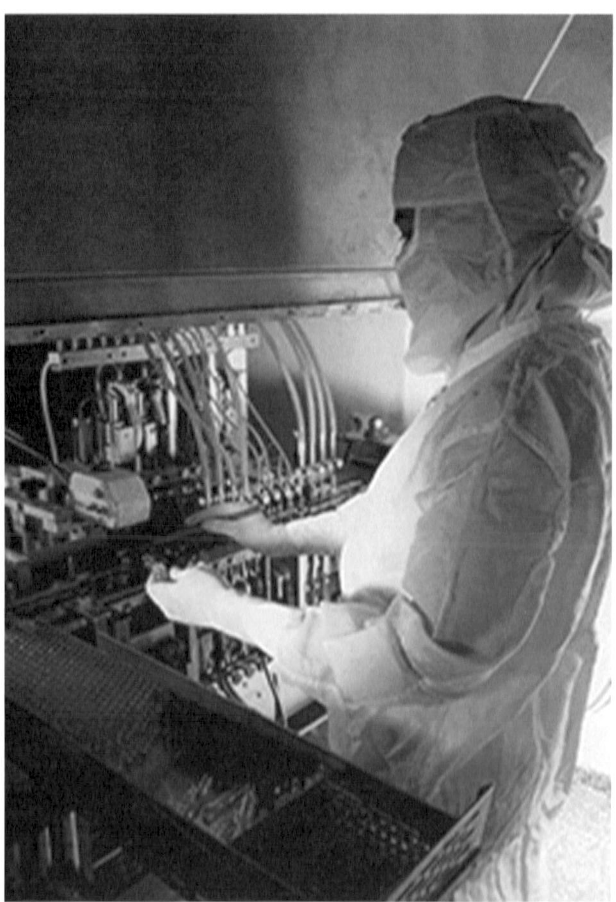

Operators may have to operate or repair complex machinery.

- Control power-generating equipment, which may use any one type of fuel, such as coal, nuclear power, or natural gas
- Read charts, meters, and gauges to monitor voltage and electricity flows
- Check equipment and indicators to detect evidence of operating problems
- Adjust controls to regulate the flow of power
- Start or stop generators, turbines, and other equipment as necessary

Electricity is one of our nation's most vital resources. Power plant operators, distributors, and dispatchers control power plants and the flow of electricity from plants to substations, which distribute electricity to businesses, homes, and factories. Electricity is generated from many sources, including coal, gas, nuclear energy, hydroelectric energy (from water sources), wind, and solar power.

Nuclear power reactor operators control nuclear reactors. They adjust control rods, which affect how much electricity a reactor generates. They monitor reactors, turbines, generators, and cooling systems, adjusting controls as necessary. Operators start and stop equipment and record the data produced. They also respond to abnormalities, determine the causes, and take corrective action.

Power distributors and dispatchers, also known as *systems operators*, control the flow of electricity as it travels from generating stations to substations and users. In exercising such control, they monitor and operate current converters, voltage transformers, and circuit breakers over a network of transmission and distribution lines. They prepare and issue switching orders to route electrical currents around areas that need maintenance or repair. They detect and respond to emergencies, such as transformer or transmission line failures, which can cause cascading power outages over the network. They may work with plant operators to troubleshoot electricity generation issues.

Power plant operators control, operate, and maintain machinery to generate electricity. They use control boards to distribute power among generators and regulate the output of several generators. They monitor instruments to maintain voltage and electricity flows from the plant to meet fluctuating consumer demand throughout the day.

Work Environment

Power plant operators, distributors, and dispatchers held about 47,300 jobs in 2022. Employment in the detailed occupations that make up power plant operators, distributors, and dispatchers was distributed as follows:

Power plant operators	32,200
Power distributors and dispatchers	9,600
Nuclear power reactor operators	5,500

Power plant operators must monitor plant equipment and take action if problems arise.

The largest employers of power plant operators, distributors, and dispatchers were as follows:

Utilities	73%
Government	16

Operators, distributors, and dispatchers who work in control rooms generally sit or stand at a control station. The work requires constant attention. Workers also may do rounds, checking equipment and doing other work outside the control room. Transmission stations and substations where distributors and dispatchers work are typically in locations that are separate from the generating station where power plant operators work.

Because power transmission is both vitally important and sensitive to attack, security is a major concern for utility companies. Nuclear power plants and transmission stations have especially high security, and employees work in secure environments.

Work Schedules

Because electricity is provided around the clock, operators, distributors, and dispatchers usually work rotating 8- or 12-hour shifts. Work on rotating shifts can be stressful and tiring because of the constant changes in living and sleeping patterns.

How to Become a Power Plant Operator, Distributor, or Dispatcher

Power plant operators, distributors, and dispatchers typically need a high school diploma or equivalent combined with extensive on-the-job training, which may include a combination of classroom and hands-on training. Many jobs require a background check and screenings for drugs and alcohol.

Nuclear power reactor operators also need a license.

Many companies require prospective workers to take the Power Plant Maintenance and Plant Operator exams from the Edison Electrical Institute to see if they have the right aptitudes

Most power plant operators work at a control station.

for this work. These tests measure reading comprehension, understanding of mechanical concepts, spatial ability, and mathematical ability.

Education

Power plant operators, distributors, and dispatchers typically need at least a high school diploma or equivalent. However, employers may prefer workers who have a college or vocational school degree.

Employers generally look for people with strong math and science backgrounds for these highly technical jobs. Understanding electricity and math, especially algebra and trigonometry, is important.

Training

Power plant operators and dispatchers undergo rigorous, long-term on-the-job training and technical instruction. Several years of onsite training and experience are necessary for a worker to become fully qualified. Even fully qualified operators and dispatchers must take regular training courses to keep their skills up to date.

Nuclear power reactor operators usually start working as equipment operators or auxiliary operators, helping more experienced workers operate and maintain the equipment while learning the basics of how to operate the power plant.

Along with this extensive on-the-job training, nuclear power plant operators typically receive formal technical training to prepare for the license exam from the U.S. Nuclear Regulatory Commission (NRC). Once licensed, operators are authorized to control equipment that affects the power of the reactor in a nuclear power plant. Operators continue frequent onsite training, which familiarizes them with new monitoring systems that provide operators better real-time information regarding the plant.

Licenses, Certifications, and Registrations

Nuclear power reactor operators must be licensed through the NRC. They typically begin working in nuclear power plants as unlicensed operators, where they gain the required knowledge and experience to start the licensing process. To become licensed, operators must meet training and experience requirements, pass a medical exam, and pass the NRC licensing exam. To keep their license, operators must pass a plant-operating exam each year, pass a medical exam every 2 years, and apply for renewal of their license every 6 years. Licenses cannot be transferred between plants, so an operator must get a new license to work in another facility.

Power plant operators who do not work at a nuclear power reactor may be licensed as engineers or firefighters by state licensing boards. Requirements vary by state and depend on the specific job functions that the operator performs.

Power plant operators, distributors, and dispatchers who are in positions which could affect the power grid may need to be certified through the North American Electric Reliability Corporation's System Operator Certification Program.

Advancement

With sufficient education, training and experience, power plant distributors and dispatchers can become shift supervisors, trainers, or consultants.

Licensed nuclear power plant operators can then advance to senior reactor operators, who supervise the operation of all controls in the control room. Senior reactor operators also may become plant managers or licensed operator instructors.

Important Qualities

Concentration skills. Power plant operators, distributors, and dispatchers must be careful, attentive, and persistent. They must be able to concentrate on a task, such as monitoring the temperature of reactors over a certain length of time, without being distracted.

Detail oriented. Power plant operators, distributors, and dispatchers must monitor complex controls and intricate machinery to ensure that everything is operating properly.

Dexterity. Power plant operators, distributors, and dispatchers must use precise and repeated motions when working in a control room.

Mechanical skills. Power plant operators, distributors, and dispatchers must know how to work with machines and use tools. They must be familiar with how to operate, repair, and maintain equipment.

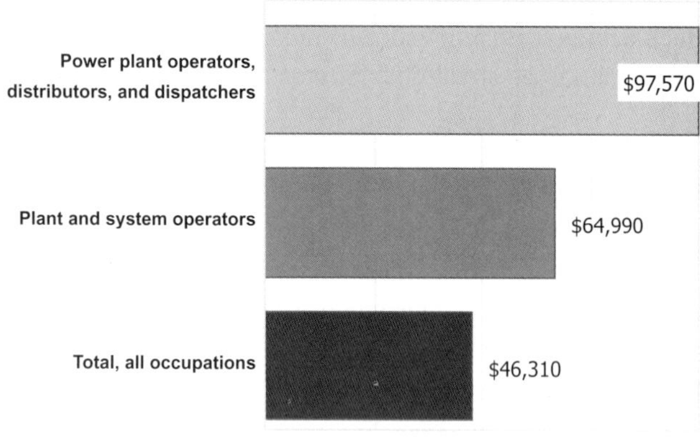

Note: All Occupations includes all occupations in the U.S. Economy.
Source: U.S. Bureau of Labor Statistics, Occupational Employment and Wage Statistics.

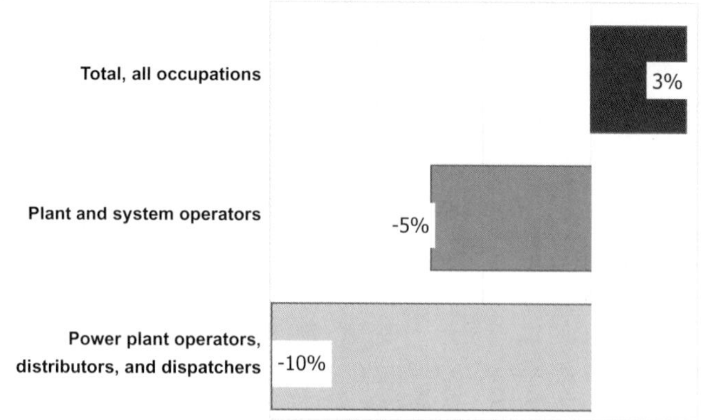

Note: All Occupations includes all occupations in the U.S. Economy.
Source: U.S. Bureau of Labor Statistics, Employment Projections program.

Problem-solving skills. Power plant operators, distributors, and dispatchers must find and quickly solve problems that arise with equipment or controls.

Pay

The median annual wage for power plant operators, distributors, and dispatchers was $97,570 in May 2022. The median wage is the wage at which half the workers in an occupation earned more than that amount and half earned less. The lowest 10 percent earned less than $57,960, and the highest 10 percent earned more than $129,900.

Median annual wages for power plant operators, distributors, and dispatchers in May 2022 were as follows:

Nuclear power reactor operators	$115,870
Power distributors and dispatchers	101,650
Power plant operators	93,060

In May 2022, the median annual wages for power plant operators, distributors, and dispatchers in the top industries in which they worked were as follows:

Utilities	$99,340
Government	93,070

Because electricity is provided around the clock, operators, distributors, and dispatchers usually work rotating 8- or 12-hour shifts. Work on rotating shifts can be stressful and tiring because of the constant changes in living and sleeping patterns.

Job Outlook

Overall employment of power plant operators, distributors, and dispatchers is projected to decline 10 percent from 2022 to 2032.

Despite declining employment, about 3,200 openings for power plant operators, distributors, and dispatchers are projected each year, on average, over the decade. All of those openings are expected to result from the need to replace workers who transfer to other occupations or exit the labor force, such as to retire.

Employment

Although electricity use is expected to increase, technological advances and greater efficiency are expected to reduce employment in these occupations. Projected employment varies by occupation (see table).

Power plants are becoming more efficient and, in many cases, have higher electricity-generating capacity. Modernized control rooms in power plants also will provide workers with more information and will automate some tasks. As a result, power plant operators will be more efficient, which limits the opportunity for new jobs.

Similarly, efficiency gains are expected to impact nuclear power reactor operators' employment. Nuclear power faces steep competition from renewable energy sources, making new, traditional reactors less attractive as many of the existing reactors reach the end of their lifecycles.

Employment of power distributors and dispatchers is projected to decline due to advances in smart-grid technology. Some dispatcher tasks, such as rerouting power during an outage, lend themselves to automation. However, some distributors and dispatchers will still be needed to manage the complex electrical grid.

Occupational Title	SOC Code	Employment, 2022	Projected Employment, 2032	Change, 2022-32	
				Percent	Numeric
Power plant operators, distributors, and dispatchers	51-8010	47,300	42,600	-10	-4,700
Nuclear power reactor operators	51-8011	5,500	5,300	-3	-200

Occupational Title	SOC Code	Employment, 2022	Projected Employment, 2032	Change, 2022-32	
				Percent	Numeric
Power distributors and dispatchers	51-8012	9,600	9,100	-5	-500
Power plant operators	51-8013	32,200	28,200	-13	-4,000

Contacts for More Information

For more information, visit

- American Public Power Association
- Center for Energy Workforce Development
- International Brotherhood of Electrical Workers
- U.S. Nuclear Regulatory Commission
- Nuclear Energy Institute
- North American Electric Reliability Corporation

Quality Control Inspectors

Summary

Quick Facts: Quality Control Inspectors

2022 Median Pay	$43,900 per year $21.11 per hour
Typical Entry-Level Education	High school diploma or equivalent
Work Experience in a Related Occupation	None
On-the-job Training	Moderate-term on-the-job training
Number of Jobs, 2022	595,400
Job Outlook, 2022-32	-4% (Decline)
Employment Change, 2022-32	-23,000

What Quality Control Inspectors Do

Quality control inspectors examine products and materials for defects or deviations from specifications.

Work Environment

Many quality control inspectors work in manufacturing. Most work full time, and overtime may be required to meet production deadlines.

Quality control inspectors monitor production operations, ensuring that specifications are met.

How to Become a Quality Control Inspector

Quality control inspectors typically need a high school diploma to enter the occupation and receive on-the-job training once employed.

Pay

The median annual wage for quality control inspectors was $43,900 in May 2022.

Job Outlook

Employment of quality control inspectors is projected to decline 4 percent from 2022 to 2032.

Despite declining employment, about 64,300 openings for quality control inspectors are projected each year, on average, over the decade. All of those openings are expected to result from the need to replace workers who transfer to other occupations or exit the labor force, such as to retire.

What Quality Control Inspectors Do

Quality control inspectors examine products and materials for defects or deviations from specifications.

Duties

Quality control inspectors typically do the following:

Quality control inspectors remove or discard all products and equipment that fail to meet specifications.

- Read blueprints and specifications
- Monitor operations to ensure that they meet production standards
- Recommend adjustments to the assembly or production process
- Inspect, test, or measure materials
- Measure products with calipers, gauges, or micrometers
- Operate electronic inspection equipment and software
- Accept or reject finished items
- Remove all products and materials that fail to meet specifications
- Report inspection and test data such as weights, temperatures, grades, moisture content, and quantities inspected

Quality control inspectors, also called testers, sorters, samplers, and weighers, monitor nearly all manufactured products to ensure that they meet specified standards. Job duties vary across the manufacturing industries in which most of these inspectors work, which include foods, glassware, motor vehicles, electronic components, and structural steel.

Quality control workers use a variety of tools. Although some still use hand-held measuring devices, such as calipers and alignment gauges, workers more commonly operate electronic inspection equipment, such as coordinate-measuring machines (CMMs) and three-dimensional (3D) scanners. Inspectors testing electrical devices may use voltmeters, ammeters, and ohmmeters to test potential difference, current flow, and resistance, respectively.

Quality control workers record the results of their inspections through test reports. When they find defects, inspectors notify supervisors and help to analyze and correct production problems.

Some manufacturers have automated inspection processes, with advanced vision inspection systems installed at one or several production points. Inspectors monitoring these automated systems check equipment, review output, and conduct random product checks.

The following are examples of types of quality control inspectors:

Materials inspectors check production materials by sight, sound, or feel to locate imperfections such as cuts, scratches, missing pieces, or crooked seams. Materials inspectors also may use devices such as infrared microscopes to analyze plastic, rubber, and other substances and to look for deterioration or defects.

Mechanical inspectors generally verify that parts fit, move correctly, and are properly lubricated. They may check the pressure of gases and the level of liquids, test the flow of electricity, and conduct test runs to ensure that machines run properly.

Work Environment

Quality control inspectors held about 595,400 jobs in 2022. The largest employers of quality control inspectors were as follows:

Quality control inspectors may be required to stand for long periods of time or lift heavy objects.

Manufacturing	64%
Professional, scientific, and technical services	9
Administrative and support services	8
Wholesale trade	6

Inspectors may be required to stand for long periods and may have to lift heavy items.

Injuries and Illnesses

Some quality control inspectors are exposed to loud noises, moving mechanical parts, and hazardous contaminants, such as airborne particles that irritate the eyes and skin. Workers typically wear protective eyewear, ear plugs, and appropriate clothing to help protect themselves from injury.

Work Schedules

Most quality control inspectors work full time. Some inspectors work evenings, overnight, or weekend shifts. Shift assignments may be based on seniority. Overtime may be required to meet production deadlines.

How to Become a Quality Control Inspector

Quality control inspectors typically need a high school diploma to enter the occupation and receive on-the-job training once employed.

Education

Quality control inspectors typically need a high school diploma for entry-level jobs. Postsecondary certificate programs are available for instruction on quality control concepts, such as inspection planning and auditing. Students in these programs also gain familiarity with tools and technologies that quality control inspectors use.

Some employers require or prefer to hire candidates who have an associate's or bachelor's degree in a field such as quality control management or engineering.

Quality control inspectors usually receive up to one year of on-the-job training.

Training

Workers typically receive on-the-job training that lasts more than 1 month and up to 1 year.

In some industries, such as automobile and aerospace manufacturing, inspectors train for the occupation in an apprenticeship program. Apprentices typically receive paid on-the-job training and instruction. Requirements for entering these programs, which are typically sponsored by trade associations or businesses, may include having a high school diploma, related work experience, or relevant licenses.

Training for new inspectors may cover the use of special meters, gauges, computers, and other instruments; quality control techniques such as Six Sigma; blueprint reading; safety; and reporting requirements.

Licenses, Certifications, and Registrations

The American Society for Quality (ASQ) offers various certifications, including a designation for Certified Quality Inspector (CQI), and various levels of Six Sigma certifications. Although optional, certification may demonstrate a level of competence and professionalism that makes candidates more attractive to employers. It also may increase opportunities for advancement. Requirements for certification generally include a certain number of years of experience in the field and passing an exam.

Important Qualities

Detail oriented. Quality control inspectors must be able to focus to notice flaws or deficiencies in finished products or materials.

Math skills. Knowledge of basic math is important for measuring, calibrating, and calculating specifications in quality control testing.

Mechanical skills. Quality control inspectors use tools and machinery when testing products.

Physical stamina. Some quality control inspectors must stand for long periods on the job.

Physical strength. Quality control inspectors may be required to lift or maneuver heavy production materials or finished products.

Technical skills. To ensure that products and parts meet quality standards, inspectors must understand the relevant blueprints, technical documents, and manuals.

Pay

The median annual wage for quality control inspectors was $43,900 in May 2022. The median wage is the wage at which half the workers in an occupation earned more than that amount and half earned less. The lowest 10 percent earned less than $29,950, and the highest 10 percent earned more than $69,100.

In May 2022, the median annual wages for quality control inspectors in the top industries in which they worked were as follows:

Professional, scientific, and technical services	$47,480
Manufacturing	44,900
Wholesale trade	40,560
Administrative and support services	34,190

Most quality control inspectors work full time. Some inspectors work evenings, overnight, or weekend shifts. Shift assignments may be based on seniority. Overtime may be required to meet production deadlines.

Job Outlook

Employment of quality control inspectors is projected to decline 4 percent from 2022 to 2032.

Despite declining employment, about 64,300 openings for quality control inspectors are projected each year, on average, over the decade. All of those openings are expected to result from the need to replace workers who transfer to other occupations or exit the labor force, such as to retire.

Employment

Continued improvements in technology allow manufacturers to automate some inspection tasks, which should increase

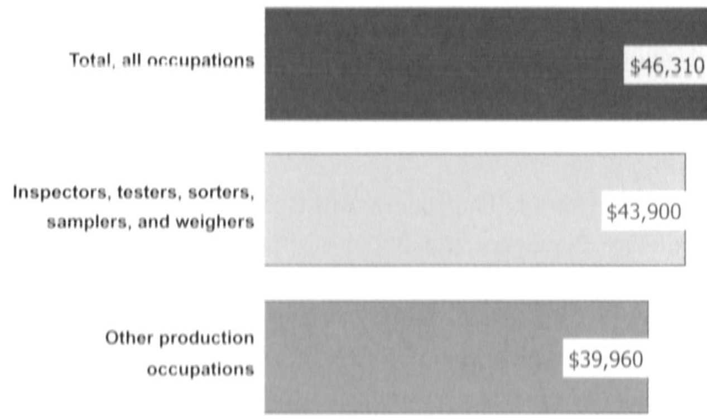

Note: All Occupations includes all occupations in the U.S. Economy.
Source: U.S. Bureau of Labor Statistics, Occupational Employment and Wage Statistics.

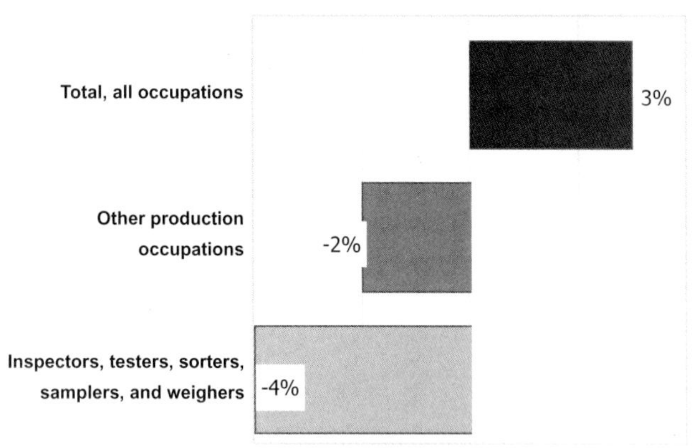

Note: All Occupations includes all occupations in the U.S. Economy.
Source: U.S. Bureau of Labor Statistics, Employment Projections program.

quality control inspectors' productivity. For example, use of three-dimensional (3D) scanners decreases the amount of time required to inspect parts and finished goods for correct measurement. As a result, reduced demand is expected for some quality control inspectors.

Despite technological advances in quality control in many industries, automation cannot replace all tasks that inspectors do. Inspections and testing validation will continue to be needed for many products, including those that require testing for taste, texture, or performance.

Occupational Title	SOC Code	Employment, 2022	Projected Employment, 2032	Change, 2022-32	
				Percent	Numeric
Inspectors, testers, sorters, samplers, and weighers	51-9061	595,400	572,400	-4	-23,000

Contacts for More Information

Apprenticeship information is available from the U.S. Department of Labor's Apprenticeship program online or by phone at 1-877-872-5627. Visit Apprenticeship.gov to search for apprenticeship opportunities.

For more information, visit

- American Society for Quality (ASQ)
- International Society of Automation (ISA)
- Quality Assurance Association (QAA)

Stationary Engineers and Boiler Operators

Summary

Quick Facts: Stationary Engineers and Boiler Operators

2022 Median Pay	$67,120 per year $32.27 per hour
Typical Entry-Level Education	High school diploma or equivalent
Work Experience in a Related Occupation	None
On-the-job Training	Long-term on-the-job training
Number of Jobs, 2022	33,500
Job Outlook, 2022-32	3% (As fast as average)
Employment Change, 2022-32	1,000

What Stationary Engineers and Boiler Operators Do

Stationary engineers and boiler operators control stationary engines, boilers, or other mechanical equipment.

Work Environment

The majority of stationary engineers and boiler operators work in manufacturing, government, educational services, and hospitals. Those who work in facilities that operate around the clock often work evenings and weekends. Shift work also is common.

How to Become a Stationary Engineer or Boiler Operator

Stationary engineers and boiler operators need at least a high school diploma or equivalent and are trained either on the job or through an apprenticeship program. Many employers require stationary engineers and boiler operators to demonstrate competency through licenses or company-specific exams before they are allowed to operate equipment without supervision.

Stationary engineers and boiler operators manage utility or industrial equipment such as boilers, stationary engines, and generators.

Pay

The median annual wage for stationary engineers and boiler operators was $67,120 in May 2022.

Job Outlook

Employment of stationary engineers and boiler operators is projected to grow 3 percent from 2022 to 2032, about as fast as the average for all occupations.

About 3,600 openings for stationary engineers and boiler operators are projected each year, on average, over the decade. Many of those openings are expected to result from the need to replace workers who transfer to different occupations or exit the labor force, such as to retire.

What Stationary Engineers and Boiler Operators Do

Stationary engineers and boiler operators control stationary engines, boilers, or other mechanical equipment to provide utilities for buildings or for industrial purposes.

Duties

Stationary engineers and boiler operators typically do the following:

- Operate engines, boilers, and auxiliary equipment
- Read gauges, meters, and charts to track boiler operations
- Monitor boiler water, chemical, and fuel levels
- Activate valves to change the amount of water, air, and fuel in boilers
- Fire coal furnaces or feed boilers, using gas feeds or oil pumps
- Inspect equipment to ensure that it is operating efficiently
- Check safety devices routinely
- Record data and keep logs of operation, maintenance, and safety activity

Most large commercial facilities have extensive heating, ventilation, and air-conditioning systems that maintain comfortable temperatures all year long. Industrial plants often have additional facilities to provide electrical power, steam, or other services. Stationary engineers and boiler operators control and maintain boilers, air-conditioning and refrigeration equipment, turbines, generators, pumps, and compressors.

Stationary engineers and boiler operators repair malfunctioning equipment.

Stationary engineers and boiler operators start up, regulate, repair, and shut down equipment. They monitor meters, gauges, and computerized controls to ensure that equipment operates safely and within established limits. They use sophisticated electrical and electronic test equipment to service, troubleshoot, repair, and monitor heating, cooling, and ventilation systems.

Stationary engineers and boiler operators also perform routine maintenance. They may completely overhaul or replace defective valves, gaskets, or bearings. In addition, they lubricate moving parts, replace filters, and remove soot and corrosion that can make a boiler less efficient.

Work Environment

Stationary engineers and boiler operators held about 33,500 jobs in 2022. The largest employers of stationary engineers and boiler operators were as follows:

Educational services; state, local, and private	17%
Hospitals; state, local, and private	16
Manufacturing	16
Local government, excluding education and hospitals	11
Traveler accommodation	9

In a large building or industrial plant, a senior stationary engineer or boiler operator may be in charge of all mechanical systems in the building and may supervise a team of assistant stationary engineers, assistant boiler tenders, and other operators or mechanics.

In small buildings, there may be only one stationary engineer or boiler operator who operates and maintains all of the systems.

Some stationary engineers and boiler operators are exposed to high temperatures, dust, dirt, and loud noise from the equipment. Maintenance duties may require contact with oil, grease, and smoke.

Workers spend much of their time on their feet. They also may have to crawl inside boilers and work while crouched, or kneel to inspect, clean, or repair equipment.

Injuries and Illnesses

Stationary engineers and boiler operators risk injury on the job. They must follow procedures to guard against burns, electric shock, noise, dangerous moving parts, and exposure to hazardous materials.

Work Schedules

Most stationary engineers and boiler operators work full time during regular business hours. In facilities that operate around

Stationary engineers and boiler operators typically work in boiler rooms and mechanical rooms.

the clock, engineers and operators may work either one of three 8-hour shifts or one of two 12-hour shifts on a rotating basis. Because buildings such as hospitals are open 365 days a year and depend on the steam generated by boilers and other machines, many of these workers must work weekends and holidays.

How to Become a Stationary Engineer or Boiler Operator

Stationary engineers and boiler operators typically need a high school diploma or equivalent and are trained either on the job or through an apprenticeship program. Many employers require stationary engineers and boiler operators to demonstrate competency through licenses or company-specific exams before they are allowed to operate equipment without supervision.

Education

Stationary engineers and boiler operators need at least a high school diploma. Students should take courses in math, science, and mechanical and technical subjects.

Stationary engineers and boiler operators continue training throughout their career.

With the growing complexity of the work, vocational school or college courses may benefit workers trying to advance in the occupation.

Training

Stationary engineers and boiler operators typically learn their work through long-term on-the-job training under the supervision of an experienced engineer or operator. Trainees are assigned basic tasks, such as monitoring the temperatures and pressures in the heating and cooling systems and low-pressure boilers. After they demonstrate competence in basic tasks, trainees move on to more complicated tasks, such as the repair of cracks or ruptured tubes for high-pressure boilers.

Some stationary engineers and boiler operators complete apprenticeship programs sponsored by the International Union of Operating Engineers. Apprenticeships usually last 4 years, include 8,000 hours of on-the-job training, and require 600 hours of technical instruction. Apprentices learn about operating and maintaining equipment; using controls and balancing heating, ventilation, and air-conditioning (HVAC) systems; safety; electricity; and air quality. Employers may prefer to hire these workers because they usually require considerably less on-the-job training. However, because of the limited number of apprenticeship programs, employers often have difficulty finding workers who have completed one.

Experienced stationary engineers and boiler operators update their skills regularly through training, especially when new equipment is introduced or when regulations change.

Licenses, Certifications, and Registrations

Some state and local governments require licensure for stationary engineers and boiler operators. These governments typically have several classes of stationary engineer and boiler operator licenses. Each class specifies the type and size of equipment the engineer is permitted to operate without supervision. Many employers require stationary engineers and boiler operators to demonstrate competency through licenses or company-specific exams before they are allowed to operate the equipment without supervision.

A top-level engineer or operator is qualified to run a large facility, supervise others, and operate equipment of all types and capacities. Engineers and operators with licenses below this level are limited in the types or capacities of equipment they may operate without supervision.

Applicants for licensure usually must meet experience requirements and pass a written exam. In some cases, employers may require that workers be licensed before starting the job. A stationary engineer or boiler operator who moves from one state or city to another may have to pass an examination for a new license because of regional differences in licensing requirements.

Advancement

Generally, stationary engineers and boiler operators can advance as they become qualified to operate larger, more

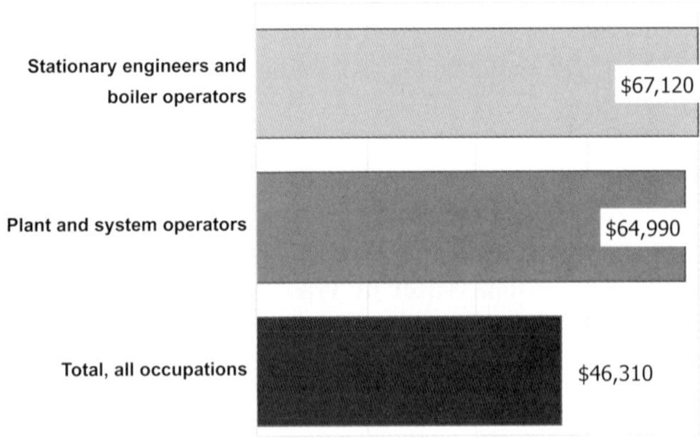

Note: All Occupations includes all occupations in the U.S. Economy.
Source: U.S. Bureau of Labor Statistics, Occupational Employment and Wage Statistics.

powerful, and more varied equipment by obtaining higher class licenses. In jurisdictions where licenses are not required, workers usually advance by taking company-administered exams, ensuring a level of knowledge needed to operate different types of boilers safely.

Important Qualities

Detail oriented. Stationary engineers and boiler operators monitor intricate machinery, gauges, and meters to ensure that everything is operating properly.

Dexterity. Stationary engineers and boiler operators must use precise motions to control or repair machines. They grasp tools and use their hands to perform many tasks.

Mechanical skills. Stationary engineers and boiler operators must know how to use tools and work with machines. They must be able to repair, maintain, and operate equipment.

Problem-solving skills. Stationary engineers and boiler operators must figure out how things work and quickly solve problems that arise with equipment or controls.

Pay

The median annual wage for stationary engineers and boiler operators was $67,120 in May 2022. The median wage is the wage at which half the workers in an occupation earned more than that amount and half earned less. The lowest 10 percent earned less than $40,910, and the highest 10 percent earned more than $108,790.

In May 2022, the median annual wages for stationary engineers and boiler operators in the top industries in which they worked were as follows:

Local government, excluding education and hospitals	$96,580
Hospitals; state, local, and private	72,620
Manufacturing	63,670
Educational services; state, local, and private	59,380
Traveler accommodation	45,240

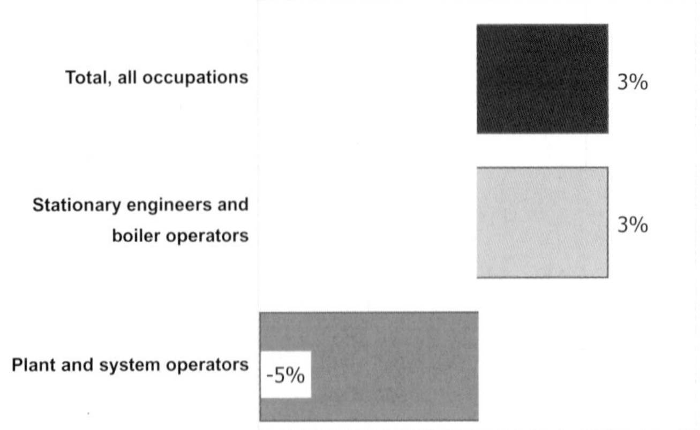

Note: All Occupations includes all occupations in the U.S. Economy.
Source: U.S. Bureau of Labor Statistics, Employment Projections program.

Most stationary engineers and boiler operators work full time. In facilities that operate around the clock, engineers and operators may work either one of three 8-hour shifts or one of two 12-hour shifts on a rotating basis. Because buildings such as hospitals are open 365 days a year and depend on the steam generated by boilers and other machines, many of these workers must work weekends and holidays.

Job Outlook

Employment of stationary engineers and boiler operators is projected to grow 3 percent from 2022 to 2032, about as fast as the average for all occupations.

About 3,600 openings for stationary engineers and boiler operators are projected each year, on average, over the decade. Many of those openings are expected to result from the need to replace workers who transfer to different occupations or exit the labor force, such as to retire.

Employment

Steam is an important and cost-effective way to fuel machinery and to provide utilities in large facilities. Workers will be needed for routine maintenance and to ensure that the equipment is working properly.

Occupational Title	SOC Code	Employment, 2022	Projected Employment, 2032	Change, 2022-32	
				Percent	Numeric
Stationary engineers and boiler operators	51-8021	33,500	34,400	3	1,000

Contacts for More Information

For more information, visit

- National Association of Power Engineers, Inc.
- State employment service offices
- Local chapters of the International Union of Operating Engineers
- Vocational schools
- State and local licensing agencies
- Information about apprenticeships is also available from the U.S. Department of Labor's toll-free help line, (877) 872-5627; or the Employment and Training Administration.

Water and Wastewater Treatment Plant and System Operators

Summary

Quick Facts: Water and Wastewater Treatment Plant and System Operators

2022 Median Pay	$51,600 per year $24.81 per hour
Typical Entry-Level Education	High school diploma or equivalent
Work Experience in a Related Occupation	None
On-the-job Training	Long-term on-the-job training
Number of Jobs, 2022	124,800
Job Outlook, 2022-32	-6% (Decline)
Employment Change, 2022-32	-7,900

What Water and Wastewater Treatment Plant and System Operators Do

Water and wastewater treatment plant and system operators manage a system of machines to transfer or treat water or wastewater.

Work Environment

Most water and wastewater treatment plant and system operators are employed by local government. Water and wastewater treatment plant and system operators typically work full time.

Operators monitor operating conditions, meters, and gauges.

How to Become a Water or Wastewater Treatment Plant and System Operator

Water and wastewater treatment plant and system operators typically need at least a high school diploma or equivalent and a license to work. They also complete on-the-job training.

Pay

The median annual wage for water and wastewater treatment plant and system operators was $51,600 in May 2022.

Job Outlook

Employment of water and wastewater treatment plant and system operators is projected to decline 6 percent from 2022 to 2032.

Despite declining employment, about 10,500 openings for water and wastewater treatment plant and system operators are projected each year, on average, over the decade. All of those openings are expected to result from the need to replace workers who transfer to other occupations or exit the labor force, such as to retire.

What Water and Wastewater Treatment Plant and System Operators Do

Water and wastewater treatment plant and system operators manage a system of machines, often through the use of control boards, to transfer or treat water or wastewater.

Duties

Water and wastewater treatment plant and system operators typically do the following:

- Add chemicals, such as ammonia or chlorine, to disinfect water or other liquids
- Inspect equipment on a regular basis
- Monitor operating conditions, meters, and gauges
- Collect and test water and sewage samples
- Record meter and gauge readings and operational data
- Document and report test results to regulatory agencies
- Operate equipment to purify and clarify water or to process or dispose of sewage
- Clean and maintain equipment, tanks, filter beds, and other work areas
- Follow U.S. Environmental Protection Agency (EPA) regulations
- Ensure safety standards are met

Water and wastewater treatment plant operators collect and test water and sewage samples.

It takes many steps to get water from natural sources—reservoirs, streams, and groundwater—into people's houses. Similarly, it is a complicated process to convert the wastewater from drains and sewers into a form that is safe to release into the environment.

The specific duties of plant operators depend on the type and size of the plant. In a small plant, one operator may be responsible for maintaining all of the systems. In large plants, multiple operators work the same shifts and are more specialized in their duties, often relying on computerized systems to help them monitor plant processes.

Water and wastewater treatment plant and system operators must be able to manually operate the equipment if there is a plant malfunction due to power outages or electrical issues.

Water treatment plant and system operators work in water treatment plants. Fresh water is pumped from wells, rivers, streams, or reservoirs to water treatment plants, where it is treated and distributed to customers. Water treatment plant and system operators run the equipment, control the processes, and monitor the plants that treat water to make it safe to drink.

Wastewater treatment plant and system operators remove pollutants from domestic and industrial waste. Used water, also known as wastewater, travels through sewer pipes to treatment plants where it is treated and either returned to streams, rivers, and oceans, or used for irrigation.

Work Environment

Water and wastewater treatment plant and system operators held about 124,800 jobs in 2022. The largest employers of water and wastewater treatment plant and system operators were as follows:

Local government, excluding education and hospitals	74%
Utilities	12
Manufacturing	4

Water and wastewater treatment plant and system operators work both indoors and outdoors. Their work is physically demanding and usually is performed in locations that are unclean or difficult to access. Operators may be exposed to noise from machinery and are often exposed to unpleasant odors.

Injuries and Illnesses

Water and wastewater treatment plant and system operators sometimes get injured on the job. They must pay close attention to safety procedures because of hazardous conditions, such as slippery walkways, the presence of dangerous gases, and malfunctioning equipment.

Operators are trained in emergency management procedures and use safety equipment to protect their health, as well as that of the public.

Water and wastewater treatment plant and system operators often perform physically demanding tasks.

Work Schedules

Water and waste treatment plant and system operators typically work full time. Plants operate 24 hours a day, 7 days a week. In small plants, operators are likely to work during the day and be on call nights and weekends. In medium- and large-size plants that require constant monitoring, operators work in shifts to control the plant at all hours.

Occasionally, operators must work during emergencies. For example, they may need to work during weather conditions that cause large amounts of storm water or wastewater to flow into sewers, exceeding a plant's capacity. Emergencies also may be caused by malfunctions within a plant, such as chemical leaks or oxygen deficiencies.

How to Become a Water or Wastewater Treatment Plant and System Operator

Water and wastewater treatment plant and system operators typically need at least a high school diploma or equivalent and a license to work. They also complete on-the-job training.

Education

Water and wastewater treatment plant and system operators typically need a high school diploma or equivalent to become operators. Employers may prefer applicants who have completed a certificate, an associate's, or a bachelor's degree program in a related field such as environmental science or wastewater treatment technology.

Training

Water and wastewater treatment plant and system operators need long-term on-the-job training to become fully qualified. Water and wastewater treatment is a complex process. Trainees learn their skills on the job under the direction of an experienced operator. The trainees learn by observing and doing routine tasks, such as recording meter readings, taking samples of wastewater and sludge, and performing simple maintenance and repair work on plant equipment. They also learn about industrial safety and how to use personal protective equipment.

Water and wastewater treatment plant and system operators need long-term on-the-job training to become fully qualified.

Larger treatment plants usually combine this on-the-job training with formal classroom or self-paced study programs. As plants get larger and more complicated, operators need more skills before they are allowed to work without supervision.

Licenses, Certifications, and Registrations

Water and wastewater treatment plant and system operators must be licensed by the state in which they work. Requirements and standards vary widely depending on the state.

State licenses typically have multiple levels, which indicate the operator's experience and training. Although some states will honor licenses from other states, operators who move from one state to another may need to take a new set of exams to become licensed in their new state.

Advancement

Most states have multiple levels of licenses for water and wastewater treatment plant and system operators. Each increase in license level allows the operator to perform more complicated processes without supervision.

At the largest plants, operators who have the highest license level work as shift supervisors and may be in charge of large teams of operators.

Important Qualities

Analytical skills. Water and wastewater treatment plant and system operators must conduct tests and inspections on water or wastewater and evaluate the results.

Detail oriented. Water and wastewater treatment plant and system operators must monitor machinery, gauges, dials, and controls to ensure everything is operating properly. Because tap water and wastewater are highly regulated by the U.S. Environmental Protection Agency, operators must be careful and thorough in completing these tasks.

Math skills. Water and wastewater treatment plant and system operators must have the ability to apply data to formulas that determine treatment requirements, flow levels, and concentration levels.

Mechanical skills. Water and wastewater treatment plant and system operators must know how to work with machines and use tools. They must be familiar with how to operate, repair, and maintain equipment.

Pay

The median annual wage for water and wastewater treatment plant and system operators was $51,600 in May 2022. The median wage is the wage at which half the workers in an occupation earned more than that amount and half earned less. The lowest 10 percent earned less than $34,100, and the highest 10 percent earned more than $81,210.

Water and Wastewater Treatment Plant and System Operators

Median annual wages, May 2022

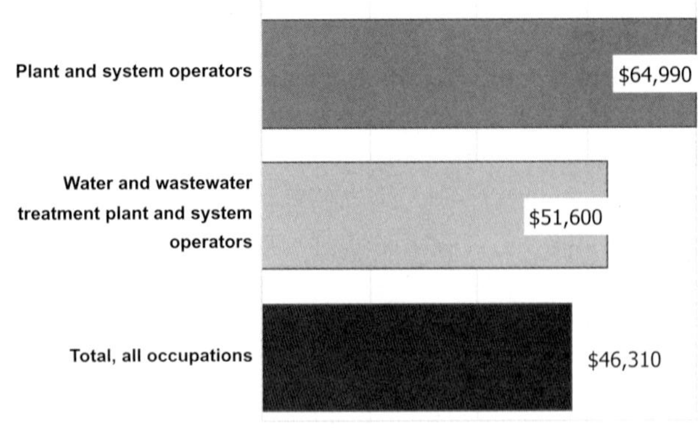

Note: All Occupations includes all occupations in the U.S. Economy. Source: U.S. Bureau of Labor Statistics, Occupational Employment and Wage Statistics.

In May 2022, the median annual wages for water and wastewater treatment plant and system operators in the top industries in which they worked were as follows:

Local government, excluding education and hospitals	$51,590
Manufacturing	50,620
Utilities	49,110

Water and waste treatment plant and system operators work full time. Plants operate 24 hours a day, 7 days a week. In small plants, operators are likely to work during the day and be on call nights and weekends. In medium- and large-size plants that require constant monitoring, operators work in shifts to control the plant at all hours.

Occasionally, operators must work during emergencies. For example, they may need to work during weather conditions that cause large amounts of storm water or wastewater to flow into sewers, exceeding a plant's capacity. Emergencies also may be caused by malfunctions within a plant, such as chemical leaks or oxygen deficiencies.

Job Outlook

Employment of water and wastewater treatment plant and system operators is projected to decline 6 percent from 2022 to 2032.

Despite declining employment, about 10,500 openings for water and wastewater treatment plant and system operators are projected each year, on average, over the decade. All of those openings are expected to result from the need to replace workers who transfer to other occupations or exit the labor force, such as to retire.

Water and Wastewater Treatment Plant and System Operators

Percent change in employment, projected 2022-32

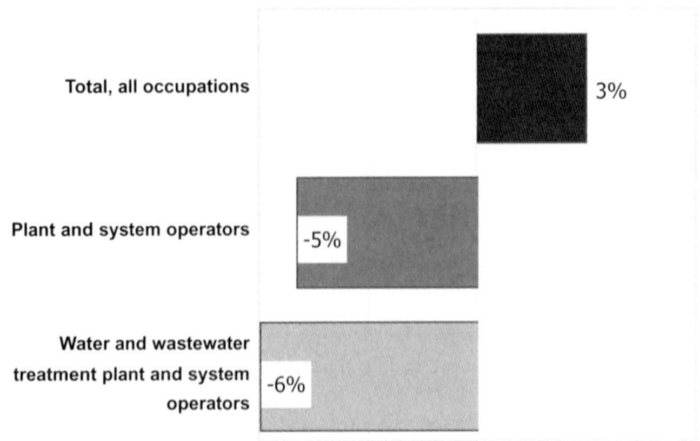

Note: All Occupations includes all occupations in the U.S. Economy. Source: U.S. Bureau of Labor Statistics, Employment Projections program.

Employment

As water and wastewater treatment plants become more advanced with automated systems to manage treatment processes, fewer workers may be needed. Although some work can be automated, plants will still need skilled workers to operate increasingly complex controls and water and wastewater systems.

Occupational Title	SOC Code	Employment, 2022	Projected Employment, 2032	Change, 2022-32	
				Percent	Numeric
Water and wastewater treatment plant and system operators	51-8031	124,800	116,900	-6	-7,900

Contacts for More Information

For more information, visit

- American Water Works Association
- The National Rural Water Association
- Water Environment Federation
- Work for Water
- Association of Boards of Certification

Welders, Cutters, Solderers, and Brazers

Summary

Quick Facts: Welders, Cutters, Solderers, and Brazers	
2022 Median Pay	$47,540 per year $22.86 per hour
Typical Entry-Level Education	High school diploma or equivalent
Work Experience in a Related Occupation	None
On-the-job Training	Moderate-term on-the-job training
Number of Jobs, 2022	431,800
Job Outlook, 2022-32	1% (Little or no change)
Employment Change, 2022-32	6,200

What Welders, Cutters, Solderers, and Brazers Do

Welders, cutters, solderers, and brazers use hand-held or remotely controlled equipment to join, repair, or cut metal parts and products.

Work Environment

Welders, cutters, solderers, and brazers may work outdoors in all types of weather, or they may work indoors, sometimes in a confined area. Most work full time, and some work more than 40 hours per week.

How to Become a Welder, Cutter, Solderer, or Brazer

Welders, cutters, solderers, and brazers typically need a high school diploma or equivalent, combined with technical and on-the-job training, to enter the occupation.

Pay

The median annual wage for welders, cutters, solderers, and brazers was $47,540 in May 2022.

Job Outlook

Employment of welders, cutters, solderers, and brazers is projected to show little or no change from 2022 to 2032.

Despite limited employment growth, about 42,600 openings for welders, cutters, solderers, and brazers are projected each year, on average, over the decade. Most of those openings are expected to result from the need to replace workers who transfer to different occupations or exit the labor force, such as to retire.

What Welders, Cutters, Solderers, and Brazers Do

Welders, cutters, solderers, and brazers use hand-held or remotely controlled equipment to join or cut metal parts. They also fill holes, indentations, or seams in metal products.

Duties

Welders, cutters, solderers, and brazers typically do the following:

- Read and interpret blueprints, sketches, and specifications
- Calculate and measure the dimensions of parts to be welded
- Inspect structures or materials to be welded
- Weld materials according to blueprint specifications
- Monitor the welding process and adjust heat as necessary
- Maintain equipment and machinery

Welders, cutters, solderers, and brazers use welding torches and other equipment to apply heat to metal pieces, melting and fusing them to form a permanent bond. Some workers specialize in welding; others perform all disciplines or a combination of them.

Welders, cutters, solderers, and brazers occasionally must work in awkward positions using hand-held welding, flame-cutting, and soldering tools.

Welders, cutters, solderers, and brazers use hand-held or remotely controlled equipment to join or cut metal parts.

Welders join metals using a variety of techniques and processes. For example, in arc welding they use machinery that produces electrical currents to create heat and bond metals together. Welders usually choose a welding process based on a number of factors, such as the types of metals being joined.

Cutters use heat from an electric arc, a stream of ionized gas called plasma, or burning gases to cut and trim metal objects to specific dimensions. They also dismantle large objects, such as ships, railroad cars, and buildings.

Solderers and ***brazers*** use equipment to heat molten metal and join two or more metal objects. Soldering and brazing are similar, except that the temperature used to melt the filler metal is lower in soldering. Solderers commonly work with small pieces that must be positioned precisely, such as to make computer chips. Brazers connect dissimilar metals through the application of a filler material, which creates strong joints in products created with multiple metals; they also may apply coatings to parts in order to reduce wear and protect against corrosion.

For information on workers who operate welding, soldering, and brazing machines, see the profile on metal and plastic machine workers.

Work Environment

Welders, cutters, solderers, and brazers held about 431,800 jobs in 2022. The largest employers of welders, cutters, solderers, and brazers were as follows:

Manufacturing	65%
Specialty trade contractors	7
Repair and maintenance	4
Self-employed workers	4

Welders and cutters may work outdoors in all types of weather, or indoors, sometimes in a confined area designed to contain sparks and glare. They may work on a scaffold or platform high off the ground.

In addition, they may have to lift heavy objects and work in awkward positions, such as overhead, while bending, stooping, or standing.

Injuries and Illnesses

Welders, cutters, solderers, and brazers risk injury on the job. They may be exposed to a number of hazards, including fumes, very hot materials, and intense light created by the arc. Workers avoid injuries by following safety procedures and using personal protective equipment, such as welding helmets, hearing protection, and heat-resistant gloves.

Work Schedules

Most welders, cutters, solderers, and brazers work full time, and some work more than 40 hours per week. Many manufacturing firms have two or three 8- to 12-hour shifts each day, allowing the firm to continue production around the clock if needed. As a result, welders, cutters, solderers, and brazers may work evenings and weekends.

Welders, cutters, solderers, and brazers wear protective clothing and welding helmets for safety.

How to Become a Welder, Cutter, Solderer, or Brazer

Welders, cutters, solderers, and brazers typically need a high school diploma or equivalent, combined with technical and on-the-job training, to enter the occupation.

Education & Training

Employers often prefer or require candidates to have a high school diploma or equivalent and technical training. This training may be available through high school technical education classes or programs at vocational–technical institutes, community colleges, and private welding, soldering, and brazing schools. In addition, the U.S. Armed Forces offer welding-related training.

Courses in blueprint reading, shop mathematics, and mechanical drawing may be helpful. An understanding of electricity also is useful.

Workers also may enter the occupation through an employer-based apprenticeship program. Some apprenticeships are available for entry-level workers who have no prior experience or training, while others are targeted toward those who have completed a vocational–technical school welding program.

Welders, cutters, solderers, and brazers must have a steady hand to hold a torch in place.

Although some employers hire inexperienced entry-level workers and train them on the job, many prefer to hire workers who have completed training or credentialing programs. Entry-level workers with formal technical training still receive several months of on-the-job training.

Licenses, Certifications, and Registrations

Welders must be licensed in some states and localities; requirements vary. Contact individual state or local government licensing agencies for more information.

Professional organizations offer courses leading to general certification. For example, the American Welding Society offers the Certified Welder designation.

The American Society of Mechanical Engineers (ASME) offers certification in practical welding technology for workers seeking to enhance core competencies, and the Institute for Printed Circuits offers certification and training in soldering.

The Occupational Safety and Health Administration (OSHA) requires that welders complete training on electrical safety. Other types of OSHA training are available but generally are not required.

Some employers require general or specific certification for particular jobs. They may pay the cost of training and testing for employees.

Important Qualities

Detail oriented. Welders, cutters, solderers, and brazers perform precision work, often with straight edges. The ability to see characteristics of the joint and detect changes in molten metal flows requires attention to detail.

Manual dexterity. Welders, cutters, solderers, and brazers must have a steady hand to hold a torch in place. They also need good hand–eye coordination.

Physical stamina. These workers must be able to endure long periods in awkward positions while bending, stooping, or standing.

Welders, Cutters, Solderers, and Brazers

Median annual wages, May 2022

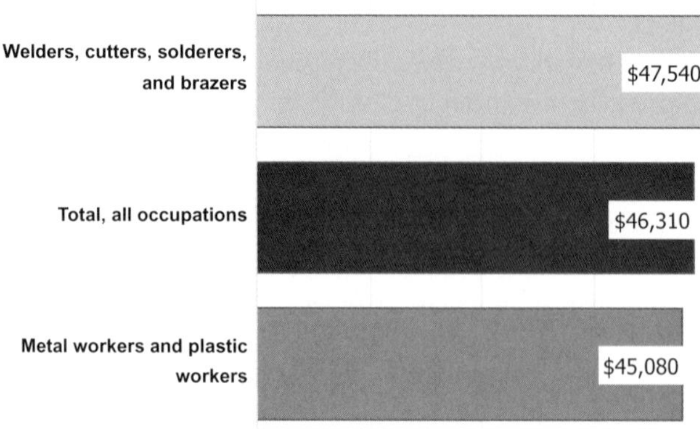

Note: All Occupations includes all occupations in the U.S. Economy.
Source: U.S. Bureau of Labor Statistics, Occupational Employment and Wage Statistics.

Physical strength. Welders, cutters, solderers, and brazers must be able to lift heavy pieces of metal and move welding or cutting equipment.

Spatial-orientation skills. Welders, cutters, solderers, and brazers must be able to read and interpret two- and three-dimensional diagrams in order to fit metal products correctly.

Pay

The median annual wage for welders, cutters, solderers, and brazers was $47,540 in May 2022. The median wage is the wage at which half the workers in an occupation earned more than that amount and half earned less. The lowest 10 percent earned less than $35,380, and the highest 10 percent earned more than $68,750.

In May 2022, the median annual wages for welders, cutters, solderers, and brazers in the top industries in which they worked were as follows:

Specialty trade contractors	$49,630
Repair and maintenance	48,430
Manufacturing	46,880

Wages for welders, cutters, solderers, and brazers vary with the worker's experience and skill level, the industry, and the size of the company.

Most welders, cutters, solderers, and brazers work full time, and some work more than 40 hours per week. Many manufacturing firms have two or three 8- to 12-hour shifts each day, allowing the firm to continue production around the clock if needed. As a result, welders, cutters, solderers, and brazers may work evenings and weekends.

Job Outlook

Welders, Cutters, Solderers, and Brazers

Employment of welders, cutters, solderers, and brazers is projected to show little or no change from 2022 to 2032.

Welders, Cutters, Solderers, and Brazers

Percent change in employment, projected 2022-32

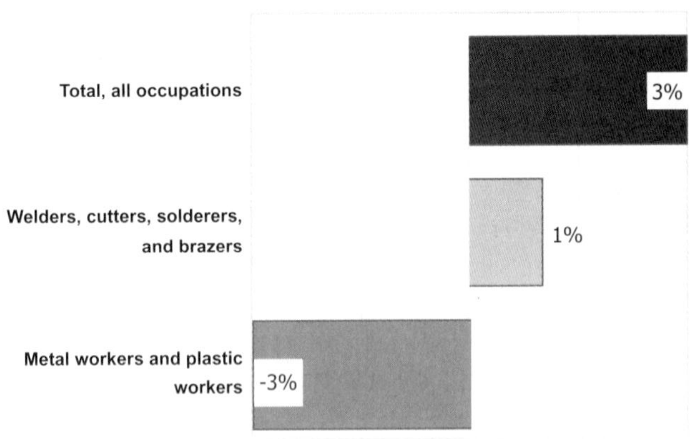

Note: All Occupations includes all occupations in the U.S. Economy.
Source: U.S. Bureau of Labor Statistics, Employment Projections program.

Despite limited employment growth, about 42,600 openings for welders, cutters, solderers, and brazers are projected each year, on average, over the decade. Most of those openings are expected to result from the need to replace workers who transfer to different occupations or exit the labor force, such as to retire.

Employment

The nation's aging infrastructure will require the expertise of welders, cutters, solderers, and brazers to help rebuild bridges, highways, and buildings. These workers also will be needed in manufacturing plants, such as those that produce metal products and machinery. However, automation in manufacturing may limit overall demand for these workers.

Occupational Title	SOC Code	Employment, 2022	Projected Employment, 2032	Change, 2022-32	
				Percent	Numeric
Welders, cutters, solderers, and brazers	51-4121	431,800	438,000	1	6,200

Contacts for More Information

Apprenticeship information is available from the U.S. Department of Labor's Apprenticeship program online or by phone at 877-872-5627. Visit Apprenticeship.gov to search for apprenticeship opportunities.

For more information, visit

- American Society of Mechanical Engineers
- American Welding Society
- Fabricators & Manufacturers Association, International
- Institute for Printed Circuits
- Precision Machined Products Association

Woodworkers

Summary

Quick Facts: Woodworkers

2022 Median Pay	$37,590 per year $18.07 per hour
Typical Entry-Level Education	High school diploma or equivalent
Work Experience in a Related Occupation	None
On-the-job Training	See How to Become One
Number of Jobs, 2022	238,900
Job Outlook, 2022-32	-1% (Little or no change)
Employment Change, 2022-32	-2,700

What Woodworkers Do

Woodworkers manufacture a variety of products, such as cabinets and furniture, using wood, veneers, and laminates.

Work Environment

Most woodworkers are employed in manufacturing industries. Although their working conditions vary, woodworkers may encounter machinery noise and wood dust.

How to Become a Woodworker

A high school diploma or equivalent is typically required to become a woodworker. Although some entry-level jobs may be learned in 1 month or less, becoming proficient typically requires several months to more than a year of on-the-job training. The ability to use computer-controlled machinery also is important.

Pay

The median annual wage for woodworkers was $37,590 in May 2022.

Workers use automated machinery, such as computerized numerical control (CNC) machines, to do much of the work.

Job Outlook

Overall employment of woodworkers is projected to show little or no change from 2022 to 2032.

Despite limited employment growth, about 23,400 openings for woodworkers are projected each year, on average, over the decade. Most of those openings are expected to result from the need to replace workers who transfer to different occupations or exit the labor force, such as to retire.

What Woodworkers Do

Woodworkers manufacture a variety of products, such as cabinets and furniture, using wood, veneers, and laminates. They often combine and incorporate different materials into wood.

Duties

Woodworkers typically do the following:

- Read detailed architectural drawings, schematics, shop drawings, and blueprints
- Prepare and set up machines and tooling for woodwork manufacturing
- Lift wood pieces onto machines, either by hand or with hoists
- Operate woodworking machines, including saws and milling and sanding machines
- Listen for unusual sounds and watch for excessive vibration in machinery
- Ensure that products meet industry standards and project specifications, adjusting as necessary
- Select the proper cutting, milling, boring, and sanding tools for completing a job
- Use handtools to trim pieces or assemble products
- Maintain machines, such as by cleaning and oiling them or replacing worn blades

Woodworkers ensure that products meet industry standards and project specifications.

Woodworkers make products from lumber and synthetic wood materials. Many of these products, including most furniture, kitchen cabinets, and musical instruments, are mass produced. Other products are custom made from architectural designs and drawings.

Modern woodworking is highly technical. Skilled operators use automated machinery, such as computerized numerical control (CNC) machines, to ensure accuracy in all phases of their work. Woodworkers do many of their tasks on an assembly line, but some customized work must be done by hand.

Woodworkers set up, operate, and tend all types of woodworking machines, such as saws, milling machines, drill presses, sanders, and wood-fastening machines. Operators use equipment to cut and shape wooden parts and to verify dimensions, using a template, caliper, and rule. Woodworkers add fasteners and adhesives and connect the parts to form an assembled unit. They also install hardware, such as pulls and drawer slides, and fit specialty products for glass, metal trims, electrical components, and stone. Finally, workers sand, stain, and, if necessary, coat the wood product with a sealer or topcoats, such as a lacquer or varnish.

The following are examples of types of woodworkers:

Cabinetmakers and ***bench carpenters*** cut, shape, and assemble parts for wood products. They often design and create sets of customized cabinets, sometimes seeing a project all the way through to installation.

Furniture finishers shape, finish, and refinish damaged and worn furniture. They may work with antiques and must judge how to preserve and repair them. They also do the staining, sealing, and top coating at the end of the production process.

Woodworking machine setters, operators, and tenders use band saws, circular saws, hack saws, or other equipment to cut wood. They also use drill presses, lathes, sanders, and other types of woodworking equipment to smooth and shape wood.

Work Environment

Woodworkers held about 238,900 jobs in 2022. Employment in the detailed occupations that make up woodworkers was distributed as follows:

Cabinetmakers and bench carpenters	105,700
Woodworking machine setters, operators, and tenders, except sawing	64,600
Sawing machine setters, operators, and tenders, wood	49,400
Furniture finishers	19,200

Woodworkers make wood products from lumber and synthetic wood materials.

The largest employers of woodworkers were as follows:

Furniture and related product manufacturing	40%
Wood product manufacturing	36
Self-employed workers	7
Specialty trade contractors	3

Working conditions vary. At times, woodworkers handle heavy, bulky materials and may encounter noise and dust. As a result, they regularly wear hearing protection, safety glasses, and respirators or masks.

Injuries and Illnesses

Wood sawing machine setters, operators, and tenders have one of the highest rates of injuries and illnesses of all occupations. These workers use saws and other tools and equipment that may be dangerous and can cause cuts or lacerations. Workers must wear safety equipment and be mindful of their surroundings to avoid injury.

Woodworkers are exposed to hazards such as harmful dust, chemicals, or fumes, and often wear a respirator or mask. Others may be exposed to excessive noise and wear hearing protection.

Most injuries involve sprains, back pain, carpal tunnel syndrome, and hernias. These injuries come from awkward bending, reaching, or twisting and overexertion or repetition.

Work Schedules

Most woodworkers work full time during regular business hours. Work schedules vary for some woodworkers.

How to Become a Woodworker

A high school diploma or equivalent is typically required to become a woodworker. Although some entry-level jobs may be learned in 1 month or less, becoming fully proficient may take several months to more than a year of on-the-job training. Woodworkers also must be able to use computer-controlled machinery.

Education

A high school diploma is typically required to enter the occupation. Training in computer applications and math may enhance employment prospects.

For woodworking production jobs, employers may prefer to hire candidates who have taken some vocational-technical or college courses.

Training

Typically, entry-level woodworkers train on the job, learning their skills from experienced workers. Beginning workers do basic tasks, such as feeding a piece of wood through a machine and stacking the finished product at the end of the process. As they gain experience, woodworkers do more complex tasks with less supervision.

Becoming a skilled woodworker often takes several months or years. Skilled woodworkers read blueprints, set up machines, and plan work sequences.

Some workers also receive training through apprenticeships offered by employers or unions.

Licenses, Certifications, and Registrations

Although not required, credentials often demonstrate competence and professionalism. They also may help a candidate advance in the occupation.

After high school, most woodworkers are trained on the job, learning from more experienced workers.

The Woodwork Career Alliance of North America offers a national certificate program, with five progressive credentials.

Because of the prevalence of CNC machines in production, workers also may benefit from obtaining CNC machine certification. Certification is offered by community colleges and CNC machine manufacturers.

Advancement

With experience, skilled woodworkers may advance to other positions that offer greater responsibility. For example, they may be promoted to team lead or floor supervisor, positions in which they help to oversee the work of other woodworkers.

Important Qualities

Detail oriented. Woodworkers must pay attention to details in order to meet specifications and to keep themselves safe.

Dexterity. Woodworkers must make precise cuts with a variety of handtools and power tools, so they need good hand-eye coordination.

Math skills. Woodworkers need to understand basic geometry in order to visualize how a three-dimensional wooden object, such as a cabinet or piece of furniture, will fit together.

Mechanical skills. The use of handtools, such as screwdrivers and wrenches, is required to set up, adjust, and calibrate machines. These automated systems also require woodworkers to use computers and other programmable devices.

Physical stamina. Woodworkers often stand for long periods performing many of the same functions.

Physical strength. Woodworkers must be able to lift bulky, heavy pieces of wood.

Technical skills. Woodworkers must be able to interpret design drawings and technical manuals for a range of products and machines. They also should be able to troubleshoot issues as they arise.

Pay

The median annual wage for woodworkers was $37,590 in May 2022. The median wage is the wage at which half the workers in an occupation earned more than that amount and half earned less. The lowest 10 percent earned less than $28,160, and the highest 10 percent earned more than $53,530.

Median annual wages for woodworkers in May 2022 were as follows:

Cabinetmakers and bench carpenters	$38,810
Furniture finishers	37,960
Woodworking machine setters, operators, and tenders, except sawing	36,830
Sawing machine setters, operators, and tenders, wood	36,270

In May 2022, the median annual wages for woodworkers in the top industries in which they worked were as follows:

Specialty trade contractors	$40,680
Furniture and related product manufacturing	38,050
Wood product manufacturing	36,630

Most woodworkers work full time during regular business hours.

Job Outlook

Overall employment of woodworkers is projected to show little or no change from 2022 to 2032.

Despite limited employment growth, about 23,400 openings for woodworkers are projected each year, on average, over the decade. Most of those openings are expected to result from the need to replace workers who transfer to different occupations or exit the labor force, such as to retire.

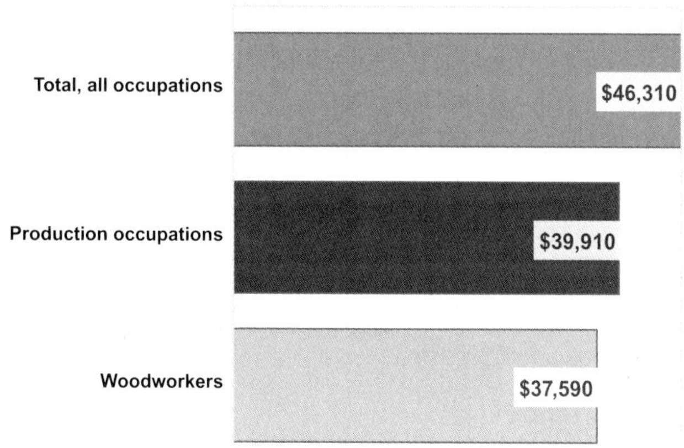

Note: All Occupations includes all occupations in the U.S. Economy.
Source: U.S. Bureau of Labor Statistics, Occupational Employment and Wage Statistics.

Note: All Occupations includes all occupations in the U.S. Economy.
Source: U.S. Bureau of Labor Statistics, Employment Projections program.

Employment

Overall demand for woodworkers is expected to be limited by automation, especially the use of computer numerically controlled (CNC) machines in wood product manufacturing. However, demand for some wood products, such as those used in home renovation projects and outdoor structures for restaurants and other businesses, may sustain demand for some woodworkers.

Occupational Title	SOC Code	Employment, 2022	Projected Employment, 2032	Change, 2022-32	
				Percent	Numeric
Woodworkers	—	238,900	236,200	-1	-2,700
Cabinetmakers and bench carpenters	51-7011	105,700	103,700	-2	-2,000
Furniture finishers	51-7021	19,200	19,100	-1	-100
Sawing machine setters, operators, and tenders, wood	51-7041	49,400	49,500	0	100
Woodworking machine setters, operators, and tenders, except sawing	51-7042	64,600	63,900	-1	-600

Contacts for More Information

Apprenticeship information is available from the U.S. Department of Labor's Apprenticeship program online or by phone at 877-872-5627. Visit Apprenticeship.gov to search for apprenticeship opportunities.

For more information about woodworkers, visit

- Architectural Woodwork Institute
- Association for Manufacturing Technology
- Fabricators & Manufacturers Association, International
- National Tooling and Machining Association
- Woodwork Career Alliance of North America
- Wood Industry Resource Collaborative
- Woodworking Machinery Industry Association

Protective Service

Correctional Officers and Bailiffs

Summary

Quick Facts: Correctional Officers and Bailiffs	
2022 Median Pay	$49,610 per year $23.85 per hour
Typical Entry-Level Education	High school diploma or equivalent
Work Experience in a Related Occupation	None
On-the-job Training	Moderate-term on-the-job training
Number of Jobs, 2022	395,700
Job Outlook, 2022-32	-7% (Decline)
Employment Change, 2022-32	-29,000

What Correctional Officers and Bailiffs Do

Correctional officers guard people in penal institutions and guard those in transit between jail, courtroom, prison, or other point. Bailiffs are law enforcement officers who maintain order in courtrooms.

Work Environment

Working in a correctional institution can be stressful and dangerous. Correctional officers work in shifts that cover all hours of the day and night, including weekends and holidays. Bailiffs usually work when court is in session.

How to Become a Correctional Officer or Bailiff

Correctional officers and bailiffs typically need a high school diploma to enter their occupation. They typically go to a training academy and then are assigned to a facility, where they receive on-the-job training. Although qualifications vary by state and agency, many agencies have an age requirement for correctional officers. Some federal agencies also require officers to have a bachelor's degree or related work experience.

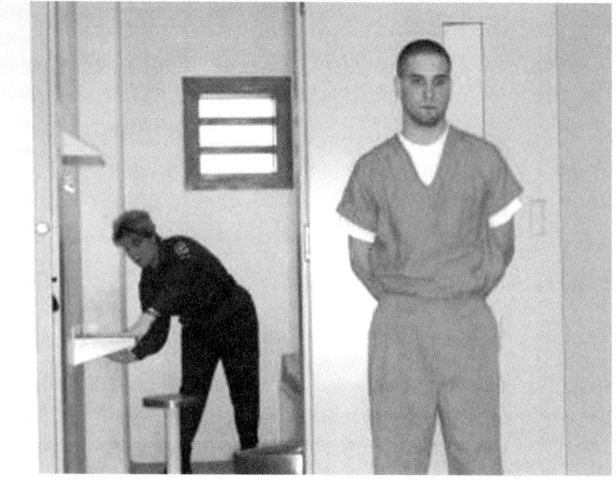

Correctional officers inspect inmates' living quarters.

Pay

The median annual wage for bailiffs was $49,100 in May 2022.

The median annual wage for correctional officers and jailers was $49,610 in May 2022.

Job Outlook

Overall employment of correctional officers and bailiffs is projected to decline 7 percent from 2022 to 2032.

Despite declining employment, about 30,900 openings for correctional officers and bailiffs are projected each year, on average, over the decade. All of those openings are expected to result from the need to replace workers who transfer to other occupations or exit the labor force, such as to retire.

What Correctional Officers and Bailiffs Do

Correctional officers guard people in penal institutions and guard those in transit between jail, courtroom, prison, or other point. Bailiffs, also known as *marshals* or *court officers*, are law enforcement officers who maintain order in courtrooms.

Duties

Correctional officers typically do the following:

- Enforce rules and keep order within jails or prisons
- Supervise activities of people in custody
- Inspect facilities to ensure that they meet security and safety standards

Correctional officers must follow procedures to maintain their personal safety as well as the safety of the inmates they oversee.

- Conduct searches in the facility, such as of persons and property, for rule violations
- Report on the conduct of people in custody
- Escort and transport people in custody between jail, courtroom, prison, or other point

Bailiffs typically do the following:

- Ensure the security of the courtroom
- Enforce courtroom rules
- Follow court procedures
- Escort judges, jurors, witnesses, and people in custody into and out of the courtroom
- Handle evidence and deliver court documents

Inside the prison or jail, correctional officers enforce rules and regulations. They maintain security by preventing disturbances, assaults, and escapes and by inspecting facilities. They check cells and other areas for unsanitary conditions, contraband, signs of a security breach (such as tampering with window bars and doors), and other rule violations. Officers also inspect mail and visitors for prohibited items. They conduct regular counts of people in custody to ensure that everyone is present. They write reports and fill out daily logs detailing anything of note that occurred during their shift.

Correctional officers may have to restrain people in custody, such as by using handcuffs and leg irons to escort them to and from cells. Officers also escort people in custody to courtrooms, medical facilities, and other destinations.

Bailiffs' specific duties vary by court, but their primary duty is to maintain order and security in courts of law. They enforce courtroom procedures that protect the integrity of the legal process. For example, they ensure that attorneys and witnesses do not influence juries outside of the courtroom, and they also may isolate juries from the public in some circumstances. As a neutral party, they may handle evidence during court hearings to ensure that only permitted evidence is displayed.

Work Environment

Bailiffs held about 17,100 jobs in 2022. The largest employers of bailiffs were as follows:

Local government, excluding education and hospitals	64%
State government, excluding education and hospitals	34

Correctional officers and jailers held about 378,500 jobs in 2022. The largest employers of correctional officers and jailers were as follows:

State government, excluding education and hospitals	51%
Local government, excluding education and hospitals	41
Federal government	4
Facilities support services	4

Because jail and prison security must be provided 24 hours a day, officers work in shifts that cover all hours of the day and night, including weekends and holidays.

Correctional officers may work both indoors and outdoors at penal institutions. For example, their shift may include patrolling the facility inside and supervising outdoor recreational activities of people in custody. Bailiffs generally work in courtrooms.

Both correctional officers and bailiffs may be required to stand for long periods. They must be alert and ready to react throughout their entire shift.

Injuries and Illnesses

Working in a correctional institution can be stressful and dangerous. Correctional officers and jailers may become injured in confrontations with people in custody, leading to their having one of the highest rates of injuries and illnesses of all occupations. They may wear safety gear, such as gloves and helmets, to protect against injury.

Work Schedules

Most correctional officers and bailiffs work full time. Because jail and prison security must be provided around the clock, correctional officers work in shifts that cover all hours of the day and night, including weekends and holidays. Correctional officers may be required to work overtime. Bailiffs usually work when court is in session.

How to Become a Correctional Officer or Bailiff

Correctional officers and bailiffs typically need a high school diploma to enter their occupation. They typically attend a training academy.

Although qualifications vary by state and agency, many agencies set a minimum age for correctional officers that is usually between 18 and 21. Federal agencies also may require officers to have a bachelor's degree or work experience and may have a maximum age for entry.

Correctional officers typically attend training at an academy before being assigned to a facility.

Education

Correctional officers and bailiffs typically must have at least a high school diploma or equivalent.

For employment in federal prisons, the Federal Bureau of Prisons requires entry-level correctional officers to have a bachelor's degree or several years of experience in a field providing counseling, assistance, or supervision. Bachelor's degree fields vary but commonly include security and protective service or a related field, such as social science.

Training

Correctional officers and bailiffs complete training at an academy. Training varies by state. The International Association of Directors of Law Enforcement Standards and Training maintains links to states' Peace Officer Standards and Training (POST) programs. Academy trainees receive instruction in a number of subjects, including self-defense, institutional policies, regulations, operations, and security procedures.

Correctional officers and bailiffs may shadow experienced officers after graduating from a training academy.

Licenses, Certifications, and Registrations

Some states require correctional officers to complete state certification. For more information, check with your state's public safety, corrections, or other agency that establishes this certification.

Advancement

Correctional officers may advance to supervisory positions such as sergeant, lieutenant, or captain. They also may move into specialized units, such as gang task force or hostage negotiation.

Bailiffs may advance to senior bailiff or other supervisory positions.

Important Qualities

Decision-making skills. Correctional officers and bailiffs must determine the best course of action to maintain order and discipline, often in stressful situations.

Detail oriented. Correctional officers and bailiffs follow and enforce procedures in correctional facilities and courts to ensure safety.

Interpersonal skills. Correctional officers and bailiffs must be able to interact and communicate effectively with people in custody, visitors, and other officers of penal institutions and the court to maintain order.

Negotiating skills. Correctional officers must be able to assist in resolving conflict in order to ensure safety.

Physical strength. Correctional officers and bailiffs must be able to physically subdue people as necessary, including those in or visiting penal institutions and those attending court proceedings.

Self-discipline. Correctional officers must be able to control their emotions in hostile situations.

Pay

The median annual wage for bailiffs was $49,100 in May 2022. The median wage is the wage at which half the workers in an occupation earned more than that amount and half earned less. The lowest 10 percent earned less than $28,290, and the highest 10 percent earned more than $82,530.

The median annual wage for correctional officers and jailers was $49,610 in May 2022. The lowest 10 percent earned less than $35,510, and the highest 10 percent earned more than $82,600.

In May 2022, the median annual wages for bailiffs in the top industries in which they worked were as follows:

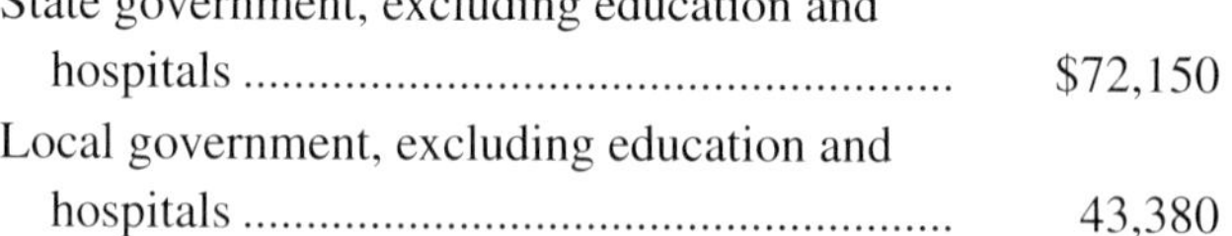

Industry	Median annual wage
State government, excluding education and hospitals	$72,150
Local government, excluding education and hospitals	43,380

Correctional Officers and Bailiffs

Median annual wages, May 2022

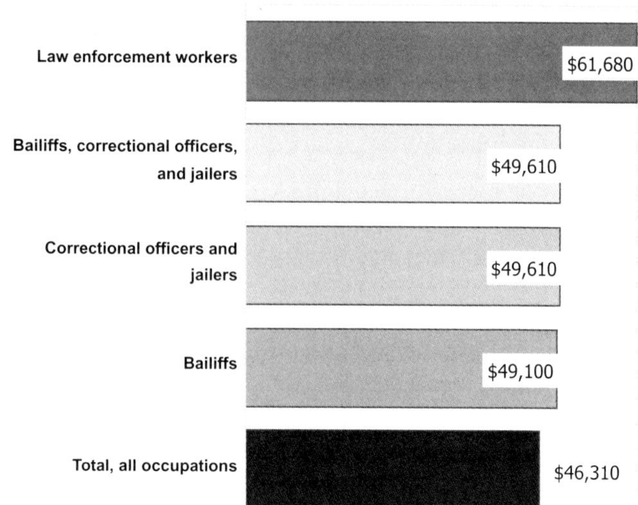

Note: All Occupations includes all occupations in the U.S. Economy.
Source: U.S. Bureau of Labor Statistics, Occupational Employment and Wage Statistics.

In May 2022, the median annual wages for correctional officers and jailers in the top industries in which they worked were as follows:

Federal government	$62,750
State government, excluding education and hospitals	51,750
Local government, excluding education and hospitals	48,730
Facilities support services	40,020

Most correctional officers and bailiffs work full time. Because jail and prison security must be provided around the clock, correctional officers work in shifts that cover all hours of the day and night, including weekends and holidays. Correctional officers may be required to work overtime. Bailiffs usually work when court is in session.

Job Outlook

Overall employment of correctional officers and bailiffs is projected to decline 7 percent from 2022 to 2032.

Despite declining employment, about 30,900 openings for correctional officers and bailiffs are projected each year, on average, over the decade. All of those openings are expected to result from the need to replace workers who transfer to other occupations or exit the labor force, such as to retire.

Employment

Lower incarceration rates and prison population levels are expected to reduce demand for these workers.

Although correctional officers and bailiffs will continue to be needed, changes to criminal laws have a large effect on how many people are arrested and incarcerated each year. Faced with high costs for keeping people in prison, many state governments have moved toward laws requiring shorter prison terms and alternatives to prison. While keeping the public safe, community-based programs that are designed to rehabilitate prisoners and limit their risk of repeated offenses also may reduce prisoner counts.

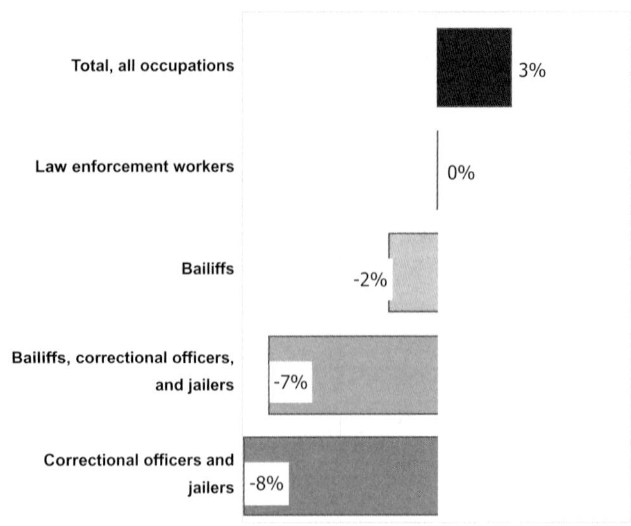

Note: All Occupations includes all occupations in the U.S. Economy.
Source: U.S. Bureau of Labor Statistics, Employment Projections program.

Occupational Title	SOC Code	Employment, 2022	Projected Employment, 2032	Change, 2022-32	
				Percent	Numeric
Bailiffs, correctional officers, and jailers	33-3010	395,700	366,700	-7	-29,000
Bailiffs	33-3011	17,100	16,800	-2	-400
Correctional officers and jailers	33-3012	378,500	349,900	-8	-28,600

Contacts for More Information

For more information, visit

- International Association of Directors of Law Enforcement Standards and Training
- Federal Bureau of Prisons
- U.S. Office of Personnel Management

Firefighters

Summary

Quick Facts: Firefighters	
2022 Median Pay	$51,680 per year $24.85 per hour
Typical Entry-Level Education	Postsecondary nondegree award
Work Experience in a Related Occupation	None
On-the-job Training	Long-term on-the-job training
Number of Jobs, 2022	334,200
Job Outlook, 2022-32	4% (As fast as average)
Employment Change, 2022-32	12,000

What Firefighters Do

Firefighters control and put out fires and respond to emergencies involving life, property, or the environment.

Work Environment

On the scene of a fire or other emergency, firefighters' work may be dangerous. On call at fire stations, firefighters sleep, eat, and perform other duties during shifts that often last 24 hours. Most paid firefighters work full time.

How to Become a Firefighter

Firefighters typically need a high school diploma and training in emergency medical services. Most firefighters receive training at a fire academy. Other credential requirements, such as emergency medical technician (EMT) certification, vary by state or locality.

Pay

The median annual wage for firefighters was $51,680 in May 2022.

Firefighters control fires and respond to other emergencies.

Job Outlook

Employment of firefighters is projected to grow 4 percent from 2022 to 2032, about as fast as the average for all occupations.

About 26,400 openings for firefighters are projected each year, on average, over the decade. Many of those openings are expected to result from the need to replace workers who transfer to different occupations or exit the labor force, such as to retire.

What Firefighters Do

Firefighters control and put out fires and respond to emergencies involving life, property, or the environment.

Duties

Firefighters typically do the following:

- Respond to emergencies
- Drive firetrucks and other emergency vehicles
- Put out fires using water hoses, fire extinguishers, and water pumps
- Find and rescue occupants of burning buildings or other emergency situations
- Treat sick or injured people
- Prepare written reports about emergency incidents
- Clean and maintain equipment
- Conduct and participate in drills related to rescue tactics, equipment use, and treatment of victims in emergency medical situations

When responding to a fire, firefighters are responsible for connecting hoses to hydrants, operating the pumps that power the hoses, climbing ladders, and using other tools to break through debris. Firefighters also enter burning buildings to extinguish fires, rescue any occupants inside, and give medical treatment as needed.

Firefighters provide medical attention in a variety of situations. In fact, most calls to firefighters are for medical emergencies, not fires, according to the National Fire Protection

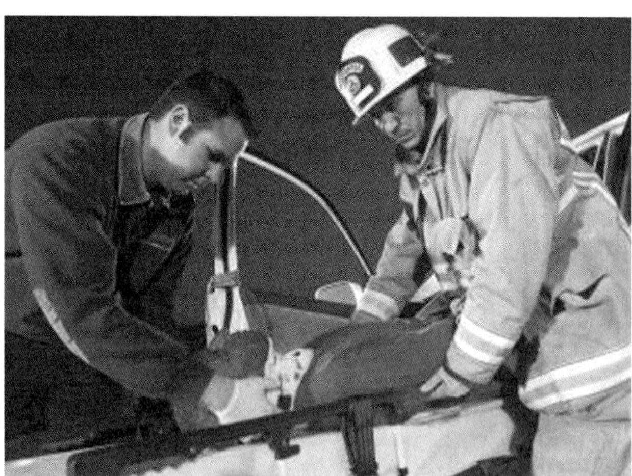

Many firefighters are responsible for providing medical attention.

Association. Other types of emergency calls that firefighters respond to include disaster aid, search-and-rescue operations, and traffic accidents.

Some firefighters also work in hazardous materials (hazmat) units and are specially trained in controlling and cleaning up oil spills, chemical accidents, and other potentially harmful substances. They work with hazardous materials removal workers in these cases.

When firefighters are not responding to an emergency, they often participate in other activities related to their work. For example, they must maintain a high level of physical fitness. On call at a fire station, firefighters regularly inspect equipment and practice drills. They also eat and sleep at the station, as their shifts usually last 24 hours. Some firefighters make presentations about fire safety to educate the public, such as at a school.

Wildland firefighters are specially trained to control forest fires. Wildland firefighters frequently create fire lines—a swath of cut-down trees and dug-up grass in the path of a fire—to deprive a fire of fuel. They also use prescribed fires to burn potential fire fuel under controlled conditions. Some wildland firefighters, known as *smoke jumpers*, parachute from airplanes to reach otherwise inaccessible areas.

Work Environment

Firefighters held about 334,200 jobs in 2022. The largest employers of firefighters were as follows:

Local government, excluding education and hospitals	86%
State government, excluding education and hospitals	4
Federal government, excluding postal service	2

These employment numbers exclude volunteer firefighters, who share the same duties as paid firefighters.

Volunteer firefighters account for the largest share of firefighters nationwide, especially in communities of fewer than 25,000, according to the National Fire Protection Association.

When responding to an emergency, firefighters often wear protective gear, which can be very heavy and hot. On call at fire stations, firefighters sleep, eat, and do other nonemergency tasks, such as work on equipment.

Injuries and Illnesses

Firefighters have one of the highest rates of injuries and illnesses of all occupations. They often encounter dangerous situations, including collapsing floors and walls and overexposure to flames and smoke. Workers must wear protective gear to help lower these risks.

Work Schedules

Firefighters typically work long periods; overtime is common, and their hours vary. For example, firefighters may work 24-hour shifts on duty, followed by 48 or 72 hours off duty.

When combating forest and wildland fires, firefighters may work for extended periods. For example, wildland firefighters may have to stay in a fire camp, a temporary site set up to provide shelter and support for days or weeks when a wildland fire breaks out.

Work for wildland firefighters may be seasonal. During certain times of the year, wildland firefighters might not work or might have limited hours.

How to Become a Firefighter

Firefighters typically need a high school diploma and training in emergency medical services. Prospective firefighters must pass written and physical tests, complete interviews, and train at a fire academy. Additionally, fire departments may require firefighters to have other credentials, such as emergency medical technician (EMT) certification. Firefighters must complete continuing education to obtain or maintain these credentials.

Applicants for firefighter jobs typically must be at least 18 years old and have a valid driver's license. They must also pass a medical exam and drug screening to be hired. After being

Firefighters respond to emergencies such as car accidents.

Firefighters begin their careers by attending fire academy training.

hired, firefighters may be subject to random drug tests and also need to complete routine physical fitness assessments.

Education

The entry-level education typically required to become a firefighter is a high school diploma or equivalent. However, some postsecondary instruction, such as in assessing patients' conditions, dealing with trauma, and clearing obstructed airways, is usually needed to obtain the emergency medical technician (EMT) certification. EMT requirements vary by city and state.

Training

Entry-level firefighters receive a few months of training at fire academies run by the fire department or by the state. Recruits learn firefighting and fire-prevention techniques, local building codes, and emergency medical procedures. They also learn how to fight fires with standard equipment, including axes, chain saws, fire extinguishers, and ladders. After attending a fire academy, firefighters usually must complete a probationary period.

Those wishing to become wildland firefighters may attend apprenticeship programs that last up to 4 years. These programs combine instruction with on-the-job-training under the supervision of experienced firefighters.

In addition to participating in training programs conducted by local or state fire departments and agencies, some firefighters attend federal training sessions sponsored by the National Fire Academy. These sessions cover topics including anti-arson techniques, disaster preparedness, hazardous materials control, and public fire safety and education.

Licenses, Certifications, and Registrations

Requirements for licensure or certification vary by state or locality. Check with your local state licensing agency or local fire department for more information.

Firefighters may need certain credentials, such as emergency medical technician (EMT) and paramedic certifications. The National Registry of Emergency Medical Technicians (NREMT) certifies EMTs and paramedics who have completed a formal program and passed the national exam. More information about EMTs and paramedics is available in a separate profile.

Continuing education is required to maintain these credentials.

Depending on the state or locality, some firefighters are required to have a commercial driver's license (CDL) or driver's license with firefighter endorsement to operate a firetruck.

Other Experience

Working as a volunteer firefighter may be helpful in getting a job as a career firefighter.

Advancement

Firefighters may be promoted to engineer, then to lieutenant, captain, battalion chief, assistant chief, deputy chief, and chief. For promotion to positions beyond battalion chief, many fire departments require candidates to have a bachelor's degree, preferably in fire science, public administration, or a related field. Some firefighters eventually become fire inspectors or investigators after gaining enough experience.

Important Qualities

Communication skills. Firefighters must be able to explain conditions at an emergency scene to other firefighters and to emergency-response crews.

Compassion. Firefighters, like EMTs and paramedics, need to provide emotional support to those in emergency situations.

Decision-making skills. Firefighters must be able to make difficult choices quickly, sometimes in life-or-death situations.

Mental preparedness. Firefighters must be able to handle the stressfulness of their work, which may involve entering a burning building or treating medical emergencies.

Physical stamina. Firefighters may have to stay at disaster scenes for long periods of time to rescue and treat victims.

Physical strength. Firefighters must be strong enough to carry heavy equipment and move debris at an emergency site. They also carry victims who cannot walk.

Pay

The median annual wage for firefighters was $51,680 in May 2022. The median wage is the wage at which half the workers in an occupation earned more than that amount and half earned less. The lowest 10 percent earned less than $29,150, and the highest 10 percent earned more than $84,750.

In May 2022, the median annual wages for firefighters in the top industries in which they worked were as follows:

Federal government, excluding postal service...	$56,660
Local government, excluding education and hospitals	55,700

Firefighters

Median annual wages, May 2022

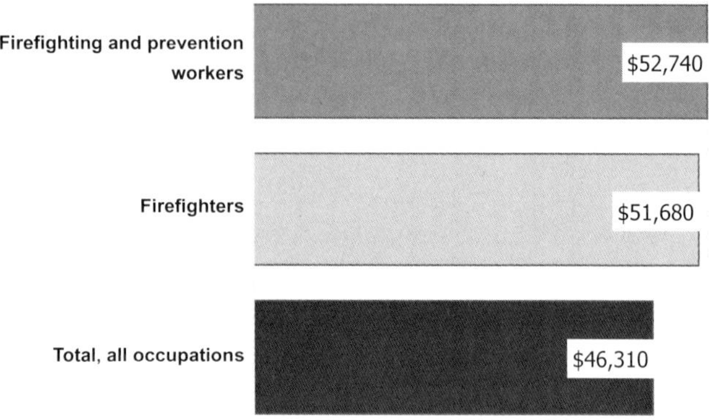

Note: All Occupations includes all occupations in the U.S. Economy.
Source: U.S. Bureau of Labor Statistics, Occupational Employment and Wage Statistics.

Firefighters

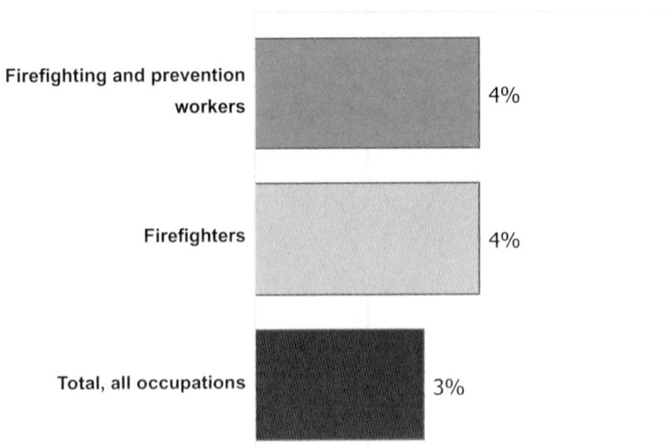

Note: All Occupations includes all occupations in the U.S. Economy.
Source: U.S. Bureau of Labor Statistics, Employment Projections program.

State government, excluding education and hospitals	50,880

Firefighters typically work long periods; overtime is common, and their hours vary. For example, firefighters may work 24-hour shifts on duty, followed by 48 or 72 hours off duty.

When combating forest and wildland fires, firefighters may work for extended periods. For example, wildland firefighters may have to stay for days or weeks when a wildland fire breaks out.

Job Outlook

Employment of firefighters is projected to grow 4 percent from 2022 to 2032, about as fast as the average for all occupations.

About 26,400 openings for firefighters are projected each year, on average, over the decade. Many of those openings are expected to result from the need to replace workers who transfer to different occupations or exit the labor force, such as to retire.

Employment

Although improved building materials and building codes have resulted in a long-term decrease in fires and fire fatalities, firefighters will still be needed to respond to fires. Wildland firefighters will still be needed to combat active fires and manage the environment to reduce the impact of fires. Firefighters will also continue to respond to medical emergencies.

Occupational Title	SOC Code	Employment, 2022	Projected Employment, 2032	Change, 2022-32	
				Percent	Numeric
Firefighters	33-2011	334,200	346,200	4	12,000

Contacts for More Information

For more information, visit

- International Association of Fire Fighters
- International Association of Women in Fire & Emergency Services
- U.S. Fire Administration
- National Fire Protection Association
- National Wildfire Coordinating Group
- National Fire Academy, U.S. Fire Administration
- National Registry of Emergency Medical Technicians

Fire Inspectors

Summary

Quick Facts: Fire Inspectors	
2022 Median Pay	$65,800 per year $31.63 per hour
Typical Entry-Level Education	See How to Become One
Work Experience in a Related Occupation	See How to Become One
On-the-job Training	Moderate-term on-the-job training
Number of Jobs, 2022	17,400
Job Outlook, 2022-32	5% (Faster than average)
Employment Change, 2022-32	900

What Fire Inspectors Do

Fire inspectors detect fire hazards, recommend prevention measures, ensure compliance with state and local fire regulations, and investigate causes of fires.

Work Environment

Fire inspectors work in office settings and onsite, including outdoors. Most work full time, and some work more than 40 hours per week. Their schedules may include evenings, weekends, and holidays because they must be ready to respond when fires occur.

How to Become a Fire Inspector

To enter the occupation, fire inspectors typically need at least a high school diploma or equivalent and work experience as a firefighter or in a related occupation. Once hired, they typically receive on-the-job-training in inspection and investigation. They also may need certification.

Fire investigators work at the scene of a fire to determine its cause.

Pay

The median annual wage for fire inspectors and investigators was $69,450 in May 2022.

The median annual wage for forest fire inspectors and prevention specialists was $48,110 in May 2022.

Job Outlook

Overall employment of fire inspectors is projected to grow 5 percent from 2022 to 2032, faster than the average for all occupations.

About 1,600 openings for fire inspectors are projected each year, on average, over the decade. Many of those openings are expected to result from the need to replace workers who transfer to different occupations or exit the labor force, such as to retire.

What Fire Inspectors Do

Fire inspectors detect fire hazards, recommend prevention measures, ensure compliance with state and local fire codes, and investigate causes of fires.

Duties

Fire inspectors and investigators examine buildings and scenes of fires; forest fire inspectors and prevention specialists assess conditions for outdoor fire risks.

Fire inspectors and investigators typically do the following:

- Search buildings for fire hazards
- Review building blueprints with developers
- Ensure that existing buildings and designs comply with fire codes
- Conduct fire and safety education programs and review emergency evacuation plans
- Collect and analyze evidence from scenes of fires and explosions
- Testify in civil and criminal legal proceedings
- Work with law enforcement or exercise police powers, such as the power of arrest, and carry a weapon

Fire inspectors inspect building plans to ensure that they meet fire codes.

Forest fire inspectors and prevention specialists typically do the following:

- Patrol assigned areas to look for forest fires, hazardous conditions, and weather phenomena that pose wildfire risk
- Assist in wildfire suppression
- Operate, maintain, and repair firefighting equipment
- Review development proposals and inspect areas for nonconforming properties or structures
- Create and administer programs to educate the public about forest fire risks and prevention

Fire inspectors and investigators examine buildings to look for fire hazards and study fire scenes to determine the cause of a fire. Inspectors visit homes, offices, hazardous materials storage facilities, or other buildings to enforce local ordinances and state laws. They may test fire alarms, sprinklers, and fire prevention equipment as part of their inspections. Investigators may have to clear and sort through debris at the scene of a fire or explosion for evidence such as glass, metal fragments, and accelerant residue. They analyze the evidence they collect and may interview witnesses as part of their investigation.

In some areas, inspectors also work as investigators.

Forest fire inspectors and prevention specialists assess outdoor fire hazards in public and residential areas. Similar to fire inspectors who visit buildings, forest fire inspectors and prevention specialists look for fire code violations and for conditions that pose a fire risk. They also recommend ways to reduce fire hazards. During patrols, they enforce fire regulations, report fire conditions to their central command center, and extinguish small fires they encounter. For large fires, they may direct the efforts of wildland firefighters.

Fire inspectors, investigators, and prevention specialists keep detailed records of their inspections and investigations. Inspectors and prevention specialists identify infractions, document corrective action required, and conduct followup inspections to ensure compliance with instructions. Investigators document all the evidence from a fire scene to help determine

Fire investigators often work in the field when determining the origin and cause of a fire.

the cause and may need to refer to their notes and files during legal proceedings.

Work Environment

Fire inspectors and investigators held about 15,000 jobs in 2022. The largest employers of fire inspectors and investigators were as follows:

Local government, excluding education and hospitals	75%
State government, excluding education and hospitals	8
Administrative and support services	8
Specialty trade contractors	2
Educational services; state, local, and private	2

Forest fire inspectors and prevention specialists held about 2,400 jobs in 2022. The largest employers of forest fire inspectors and prevention specialists were as follows:

State government, excluding education and hospitals	51%
Local government, excluding education and hospitals	43

Fire inspectors work both in office settings and onsite, including outdoors. Fire inspectors and investigators visit buildings, such as apartment complexes and industrial plants. Forest fire inspectors and prevention specialists travel to natural environments, such as forests and fields.

During onsite visits, fire inspectors may work in poorly ventilated areas and be exposed to smoke, fumes, and other hazardous agents. They may wear personal protective equipment (PPE)—including coveralls, gloves, shoe covers, and safety glasses or goggles—to reduce exposure to harmful materials. Some must wear fully enclosed protective suits, often for several hours, which may make their work physically demanding and strenuous.

Forest fire inspectors and prevention specialists spend much of their time outdoors.

Injuries and Illnesses

Forest fire inspectors and prevention specialists have one of the highest rates of injuries and illnesses of all occupations. Working at the scene of a fire can be dangerous. Injuries may occur when workers are patrolling in remote areas with rugged terrain.

To reduce their risk of injury and illness, workers often wear PPE during patrols or investigations.

Work Schedules

Most fire inspectors work full time, and some work more than 40 hours per week. Their schedules may include evenings, weekends, and holidays because they must be ready to respond when fires occur.

How to Become a Fire Inspector

To enter the occupation, fire inspectors typically need at least a high school diploma or the equivalent and work experience as a firefighter or in a related occupation. Once hired, they typically receive on-the-job-training in inspection and investigation.

Fire inspectors usually must pass a background check, which may include a drug test. Employers also typically require that candidates have a valid driver's license. Because of their police powers, investigators and inspectors may need to be U.S. citizens. They also may need certification.

Education

Fire inspectors' education requirements vary, but most need at least a high school diploma or the equivalent. Some need postsecondary instruction, such as that required for emergency medical technician (EMT) certification.

Employers may prefer to hire candidates who have a 2- or 4-year degree in fire science or a field related to the position. For example, fire investigators might have a degree in criminal

Many fire inspectors and investigators have a firefighter background.

justice, and forest fire inspectors and prevention specialists might have a degree in forestry or forest management. In some cases, postsecondary education may substitute for work experience.

Training

Training requirements for fire inspectors vary. Programs are available through employers, federal agencies, and professional organizations and usually include both technical instruction and on-the-job training.

Technical instruction often takes place over several months at a fire or police academy. Topics covered include inspection or investigation processes, legal codes, courtroom procedures, hazardous and explosive materials handling protocol, and proper use of equipment.

After inspectors and investigators complete technical instruction, they typically also receive on-the-job training, during which they work with an experienced inspector or investigator.

Work Experience in a Related Occupation

Fire inspectors typically need several years of work experience as a firefighter or in a related occupation. For example, experience in building inspection or law enforcement may be helpful for fire inspectors and investigators, respectively, and experience in forestry or land management may be helpful for forest fire inspectors and prevention specialists.

Licenses, Certifications, and Registrations

Requirements for licensure or certification vary by state or locality. Check with your state licensing agency or local fire department for more information.

The International Code Council and The National Fire Protection Association offer additional certification for fire inspectors.

Fire investigators also may choose to pursue more certification from a nationally recognized professional association. Among these are the Certified Fire Investigator (CFI) certification from the International Association of Arson Investigators and the Certified Fire and Explosion Investigator (CFEI) certification from the National Association of Fire Investigators (NAFI).

The National Fire Protection Association also offers Certified Wildfire Mitigation Specialist certification for forest fire inspectors and prevention specialists.

Important Qualities

Communication skills. Fire inspectors must clearly explain fire code violations to building and property managers. Fire investigators must thoroughly interview witnesses, including those who may be distressed or uncooperative, as part of their fact-finding mission.

Critical-thinking skills. Fire investigators must be able to analyze evidence from a fire and come to a reasonable conclusion.

Detail oriented. Fire inspectors must notice minutiae when inspecting sites for code violations or fire risks or for investigating the cause of a fire.

Physical stamina. Fire investigators may be required to sort through debris at the scene of a fire for long periods, often while wearing heavy or uncomfortable protective gear.

Physical strength. Fire investigators may have to move debris at the site of a fire in order to get a more accurate understanding of the scene.

Problem-solving skills. Fire inspectors must be able to recognize code violations and fire risks and recommend a way to fix them.

Pay

The median annual wage for fire inspectors and investigators was $69,450 in May 2022. The median wage is the wage at which half the workers in an occupation earned more than that amount and half earned less. The lowest 10 percent earned less than $42,930, and the highest 10 percent earned more than $125,610.

The median annual wage for forest fire inspectors and prevention specialists was $48,110 in May 2022. The lowest 10 percent earned less than $30,000, and the highest 10 percent earned more than $90,120.

In May 2022, the median annual wages for fire inspectors and investigators in the top industries in which they worked were as follows:

Local government, excluding education and hospitals	$73,630
State government, excluding education and hospitals	63,400
Administrative and support services	58,480
Educational services; state, local, and private	57,760
Specialty trade contractors	49,810

In May 2022, the median annual wages for forest fire inspectors and prevention specialists in the top industries in which they worked were as follows:

Local government, excluding education and hospitals	$68,750
State government, excluding education and hospitals	38,660

Most fire inspectors work full time, and some work more than 40 hours per week. Their schedules may include evenings, weekends, and holidays because they must be ready to respond when fires occur.

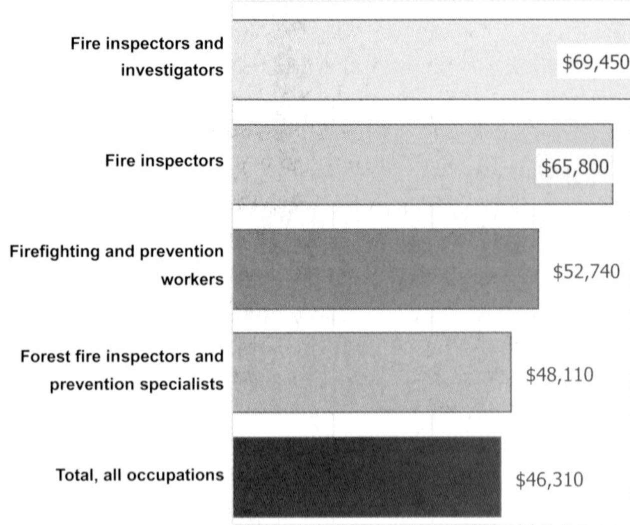

Note: All Occupations includes all occupations in the U.S. Economy. Source: U.S. Bureau of Labor Statistics, Occupational Employment and Wage Statistics.

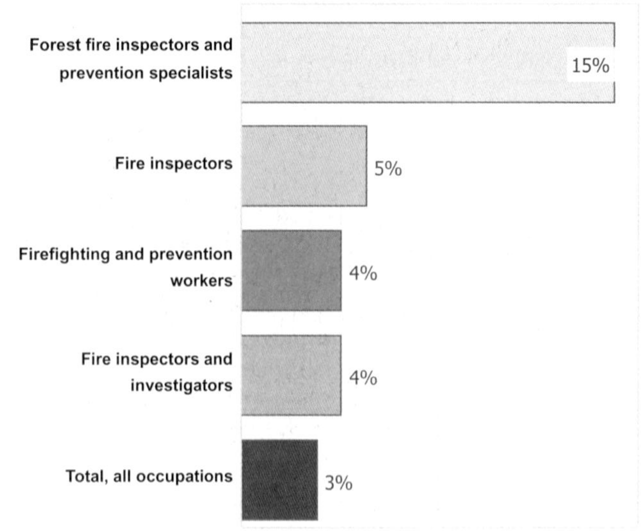

Note: All Occupations includes all occupations in the U.S. Economy. Source: U.S. Bureau of Labor Statistics, Employment Projections program.

Job Outlook

Overall employment of fire inspectors is projected to grow 5 percent from 2022 to 2032, faster than the average for all occupations.

About 1,600 openings for fire inspectors are projected each year, on average, over the decade. Many of those openings are expected to result from the need to replace workers who transfer to different occupations or exit the labor force, such as to retire.

Employment

Projected employment of fire inspectors varies by occupation (see table).

Fire inspectors will be needed to assess potential fire hazards in newly constructed residential, commercial, public, and other buildings. Fire inspectors also will be needed to ensure that existing buildings meet updated federal, state, and local fire codes. Although the number of structural fires occurring across the country has been falling for some time, fire investigators will still be needed to determine the cause of fires and explosions.

Forest fire inspectors and prevention specialists are expected to be needed to help prevent and control increasingly destructive wildfires.

Occupational Title	SOC Code	Employment, 2022	Projected Employment, 2032	Change, 2022-32	
				Percent	Numeric
Fire inspectors	33-2020	17,400	18,400	5	900
Fire inspectors and investigators	33-2021	15,000	15,600	4	600
Forest fire inspectors and prevention specialists	33-2022	2,400	2,800	15	400

Contacts for More Information

For more information, visit

- Bureau of Alcohol, Tobacco, Firearms and Explosives
- National Fire Academy
- Wildland Fire Training | US Forest Service
- International Association of Arson Investigators
- International Code Council
- National Association of Fire Investigators
- National Fire Protection Association

Police and Detectives

Summary

Quick Facts: Police and Detectives	
2022 Median Pay	$69,160 per year $33.25 per hour
Typical Entry-Level Education	See How to Become One
Work Experience in a Related Occupation	See How to Become One
On-the-job Training	Moderate-term on-the-job training
Number of Jobs, 2022	808,700
Job Outlook, 2022-32	3% (As fast as average)
Employment Change, 2022-32	23,800

What Police and Detectives Do

Police officers protect lives and property. Detectives and criminal investigators gather facts and collect evidence of possible crimes.

Work Environment

Police and detective work can be physically demanding, stressful, and dangerous. Police and sheriff's patrol officers and transit and railroad police have some of the highest rates of injuries and illnesses of all occupations. Working around the clock in shifts is common.

How to Become a Police Officer or Detective

The education typically required to enter the occupation ranges from a high school diploma to a college degree. Most police and detectives must graduate from their agency's training academy before completing on-the-job training. Other requirements vary, but candidates usually must be at least 21 years old and able to meet rigorous physical and personal qualifications.

Police officers, detectives, and game wardens enforce laws to protect people and their property.

Pay

The median annual wage for police and detectives was $69,160 in May 2022.

Job Outlook

Overall employment of police and detectives is projected to grow 3 percent from 2022 to 2032, about as fast as the average for all occupations.

About 64,500 openings for police and detectives are projected each year, on average, over the decade. Many of those openings are expected to result from the need to replace workers who transfer to different occupations or exit the labor force, such as to retire.

What Police and Detectives Do

Police officers protect lives and property. Detectives and criminal investigators, who are sometimes called *agents* or *special agents*, gather facts and collect evidence of crimes.

Duties

Police officers, detectives, and criminal investigators typically do the following:

- Respond to emergency and nonemergency calls
- Patrol assigned areas, observing people and activities
- Conduct traffic stops and issue citations
- Search restricted-access databases for vehicle or other records and warrants
- Obtain and serve warrants for arrests, searches, and other purposes
- Arrest people suspected of committing crimes
- Collect and secure evidence from crime scenes
- Observe the activities of suspects
- Write detailed reports and fill out forms
- Prepare cases for legal proceedings and testify in court

Job duties differ by employer and function, but police and detectives are required by law to write detailed reports and

Police officers use computers to check license information.

keep meticulous records. Most carry law enforcement equipment such as radios, handcuffs, and guns.

The following are examples of types of police and detectives:

Detectives and criminal investigators are uniformed or plainclothes officers who gather facts and collect evidence related to criminal cases. They conduct interviews, examine records, monitor suspects, and participate in raids and arrests. Detectives typically investigate serious crimes, such as assaults, robberies, and homicides. In large police departments, detectives usually specialize in investigating one type of crime, such as homicide or fraud. They are typically assigned cases on a rotating basis and work on them until an arrest and trial are completed or until the case is dropped.

Federal Bureau of Investigation (FBI) agents, sometimes called *special agents*, investigate and pursue criminal cases that violate federal law. FBI agents are responsible for crimes against public agencies, such as Medicare fraud, or that cross state lines. In addition, federal agents may join or take over investigations of certain types of state cases, such as those related to prescription drugs or large sums of money.

Fish and game wardens enforce fishing, hunting, and boating laws. They patrol fishing and hunting areas, conduct search and rescue operations, investigate complaints and accidents, and educate the public about laws pertaining to the outdoors. Federal fish and game wardens are often referred to as Federal Wildlife Officers.

Police and sheriff's patrol officers are the most common type of police and detectives, and they have general law enforcement duties. They wear uniforms that allow the public to easily recognize them as police officers. They have regular patrols and also respond to emergency and nonemergency calls. During patrols, officers observe people and activities to ensure order and safety.

Some police officers work only on a specific type of crime, such as narcotics. Officers, especially those working in large departments, may work in special units, such as mounted (horseback), motorcycle, or special weapons and tactics (SWAT). Typically, officers must work as patrol officers for a certain number of years before they are appointed to a special unit.

Transit and railroad police patrol train yards and transportation hubs, such as subway stations. They protect property, employees, and passengers from crimes such as thefts and robberies. They remove trespassers from railroad and transit properties and check IDs of people who try to enter secure areas.

Work Environment

Police and detectives held about 808,700 jobs in 2022. Employment in the detailed occupations that make up police and detectives was distributed as follows:

Police and sheriff's patrol officers	684,000
Detectives and criminal investigators	114,400
Fish and game wardens	6,900
Transit and railroad police	3,400

Police and detectives regularly work at crime and accident scenes.

The largest employers of police and detectives were as follows:

Government	96%
Educational services; state, local, and private	4

Police and detective work can be physically demanding, stressful, and dangerous. Officers must be alert and ready to react throughout their entire shift. Officers regularly work at crime and accident scenes and encounter suffering and the results of violence. Although a career in law enforcement may be stressful, many officers find it rewarding to help members of their communities.

Some federal agencies, such as the Federal Bureau of Investigation and U.S. Secret Service, require extensive travel, often on short notice. These agents may relocate a number of times over the course of their careers. Other agencies, such as U.S. Border Patrol, may require work outdoors in rugged terrain and in all kinds of weather.

Injuries and Illnesses

Police and sheriff's patrol officers and transit and railroad police have some of the highest rates of injuries and illnesses of all occupations. They may face physical injuries during conflicts with criminals and other high-risk situations.

Work Schedules

Most police and detectives work full time. Paid overtime is common, and shift work is necessary to protect the public at all times.

FBI special agents must work at least 50 hours a week and are on call 24 hours a day, 7 days a week.

How to Become a Police Officer or Detective

The education typically required to enter the occupation ranges from a high school diploma to a college degree. Most police and detectives must graduate from their agency's training academy before completing a period of on-the-job training. Other requirements vary, but candidates usually must be at least 21 years old and able to meet rigorous physical and personal qualifications. A felony conviction or drug use may disqualify a candidate.

Education

Police and detective applicants must have at least a high school diploma or equivalent, although some federal agencies and police departments may require that applicants have completed college coursework or a college degree. Many community colleges and 4-year colleges and universities offer programs in law enforcement and criminal justice. Knowledge of a foreign language is an asset in many federal agencies and geographical regions.

Police and detectives must use good judgment and have strong communication skills when gathering facts about a crime.

Fish and game wardens typically need a bachelor's degree; desirable fields of study include wildlife science, biology, or natural resources. Federal Wildlife Officers and some state-level fish and game wardens typically do not need a bachelor's degree.

Federal agencies such as the Federal Bureau of Investigation may require prospective detectives and investigators to have a bachelor's degree.

Many applicants for entry-level police jobs have completed some college coursework, and a significant number are college graduates. Common fields of degree include security and protective service and social science.

Training

Candidates for law enforcement appointment usually attend a training academy before becoming an officer. Training includes classroom instruction in state and local laws and constitutional law, civil rights, and police ethics. Recruits also receive training and supervised experience in subjects such as patrol, traffic control, firearm use, self-defense, first aid, and emergency response.

Federal law enforcement agents undergo extensive training, usually at the U.S. Marine Corps base in Quantico, Virginia, or at a Federal Law Enforcement Training Center.

Work Experience in a Related Occupation

Because they need experience in law enforcement, detectives typically begin their careers as police officers.

FBI special agent applicants must have at least 2 years of full-time work experience, or 1 year of experience plus an advanced degree (master's or higher).

Other Experience

Some police departments have cadet programs for people interested in a career in law enforcement who do not yet meet age requirements for becoming an officer. These cadets do clerical work and attend classes until they reach the minimum age requirement and can apply for a position with the regular force. Military or police experience may be considered beneficial for prospective cadets.

Cadet candidates usually must be at least 18 years old, have a driver's license, and meet specific physical qualifications. Applicants may have to pass physical exams of vision, hearing, strength, and agility, as well as written exams. Candidates typically go through a series of interviews and may be asked to take polygraph (lie detector) and drug tests. A felony conviction may disqualify a candidate.

Most states and local jurisdictions require candidates to be U.S. citizens, but some do not. Federal officers must be U.S. citizens.

Advancement

Police officers usually become eligible for promotion after a probationary period. Promotions to corporal, sergeant, lieutenant, and captain usually are made according to scores on a written examination and on-the-job performance. In large departments, an officer may be promoted to detective or to specialize in one type of police work, such as working with juveniles.

Along with exam and performance scores, a bachelor's degree may be required for advancement to positions of lieutenant or higher rank.

Important Qualities

Communication skills. Police and detectives must be able to speak with people and to express details in writing about an incident.

Empathy. Police officers need to understand the perspectives of a variety of people in their jurisdiction and be willing to help the public.

Good judgment. Police and detectives must be able to determine the best way to solve an array of problems.

Leadership skills. Police officers must be comfortable with being a highly visible member of their community, as the public looks to them for help in emergencies.

Perceptiveness. Officers, detectives, and fish and game wardens must be able to anticipate people's reactions and understand why they act a certain way.

Physical stamina. Officers and detectives must be in good physical shape, both to pass required tests for entry into the field and to keep up with the daily rigors of the job.

Physical strength. Police officers must be strong enough to physically apprehend suspects and to assist people in precarious situations.

Pay

The median annual wage for police and detectives was $69,160 in May 2022. The median wage is the wage at which half the workers in an occupation earned more than that amount and half earned less. The lowest 10 percent earned less than $41,660, and the highest 10 percent earned more than $109,580.

Median annual wages for police and detectives in May 2022 were as follows:

Detectives and criminal investigators	$86,280
Transit and railroad police	69,150
Police and sheriff's patrol officers	65,790
Fish and game wardens	59,500

In May 2022, the median annual wages for police and detectives in the top industries in which they worked were as follows:

Government	$70,910
Educational services; state, local, and private	56,060

Most police and detectives work full time. Paid overtime is common, and shift work is necessary to protect the public at all times.

Other Compensation and Benefits

Many law enforcement agencies provide officers with an allowance for uniforms, as well as extensive benefits and the option to retire at an age that is younger than the typical retirement age. Some police departments offer additional pay for bilingual officers or those with college degrees.

Job Outlook

Overall employment of police and detectives is projected to grow 3 percent from 2022 to 2032, about as fast as the average for all occupations.

About 64,500 openings for police and detectives are projected each year, on average, over the decade. Many of those openings are expected to result from the need to replace

Median annual wages, May 2022

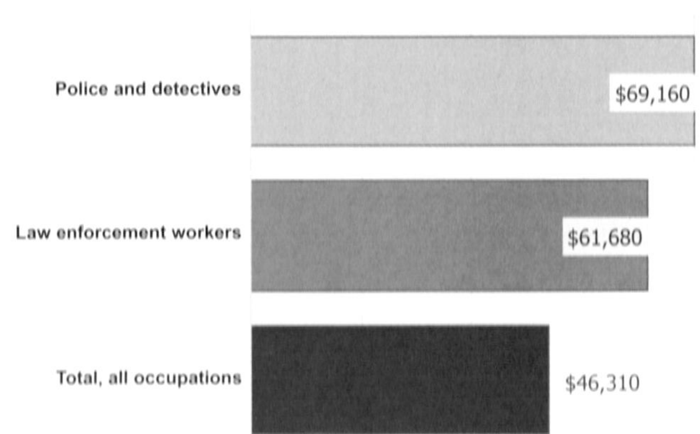

Note: All Occupations includes all occupations in the U.S. Economy.
Source: U.S. Bureau of Labor Statistics, Occupational Employment and Wage Statistics.

Police and Detectives

Percent change in employment, projected 2022-32

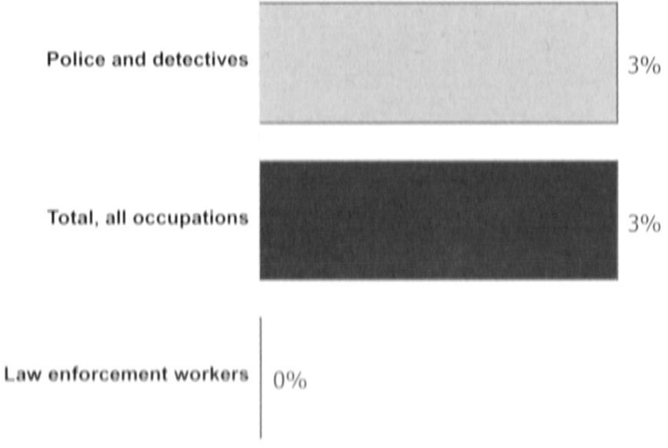

Note: All Occupations includes all occupations in the U.S. Economy.
Source: U.S. Bureau of Labor Statistics, Employment Projections program.

workers who transfer to different occupations or exit the labor force, such as to retire.

Employment

Projected employment of police and detectives varies by occupation (see table).

A desire for public safety may result in a need for more officers. However, demand for employment is expected to vary by location, driven largely by local and state budgets. Even when crime rates fall, demand for police services to maintain public safety is expected to continue.

Occupational Title	SOC Code	Employment, 2022	Projected Employment, 2032	Change, 2022-32	
				Percent	Numeric
Police and detectives	—	808,700	832,500	3	23,800
Detectives and criminal investigators	33-3021	114,400	116,100	1	1,700
Fish and game wardens	33-3031	6,900	6,500	-6	-400
Police and sheriff's patrol officers	33-3051	684,000	706,500	3	22,500
Transit and railroad police	33-3052	3,400	3,500	3	100

Contacts for More Information

For more information, visit

- Bureau of Alcohol, Tobacco, Firearms and Explosives
- Drug Enforcement Administration
- Federal Bureau of Investigation
- U.S. Customs and Border Protection
- U.S. Department of Homeland Security
- U.S. Fish & Wildlife Service
- U.S. Marshals Service
- U.S. Secret Service

Private Detectives and Investigators

Summary

Quick Facts: Private Detectives and Investigators

2022 Median Pay	$52,120 per year $25.06 per hour
Typical Entry-Level Education	High school diploma or equivalent
Work Experience in a Related Occupation	Less than 5 years
On-the-job Training	Moderate-term on-the-job training
Number of Jobs, 2022	38,300
Job Outlook, 2022-32	6% (Faster than average)
Employment Change, 2022-32	2,300

What Private Detectives and Investigators Do

Private detectives and investigators search for information about legal, financial, and personal matters.

Work Environment

Private detectives and investigators work in many places, depending on their assignment or case. Some spend more time in offices, researching cases on computers, while others spend more time in the field, conducting interviews and performing surveillance. Private detectives and investigators often work irregular hours.

How to Become a Private Detective or Investigator

Most private detectives and investigators need several years of work experience and a high school diploma. In addition, the vast majority of states require private detectives and investigators to have a license.

Pay

The median annual wage for private detectives and investigators was $52,120 in May 2022.

Job Outlook

Employment of private detectives and investigators is projected to grow 6 percent from 2022 to 2032, faster than the average for all occupations.

About 3,800 openings for private detectives and investigators are projected each year, on average, over the decade. Many of those openings are expected to result from the need to replace workers who transfer to different occupations or exit the labor force, such as to retire.

Private detectives and investigators obtain information for clients.

Private detectives and investigators must properly collect and document evidence so that it may be used in a court of law.

What Private Detectives and Investigators Do

Private detectives and investigators search for information about legal, financial, and personal matters. They offer many services, such as verifying people's backgrounds and statements, finding missing persons, and investigating computer crimes.

Duties

Private detectives and investigators typically do the following:

- Interview people to gather information
- Search online, public, and court records to uncover clues
- Conduct surveillance
- Collect evidence for clients
- Check for civil judgments and criminal history

Private detectives and investigators offer many services for individuals, attorneys, and businesses. Examples include performing background checks, investigating employees for possible theft from a company, proving or disproving infidelity in a divorce case, and helping to locate a missing person.

Private detectives and investigators use a variety of tools when researching the facts in a case. Much of their work is done with a computer, allowing them to obtain information such as telephone numbers, details about social networks, descriptions of online activities, and records of a person's prior arrests. They make phone calls to verify facts and interview people when conducting a background investigation.

Detectives also conduct surveillance when investigating a case. They may watch locations, such as a person's home or office, often from a hidden position. Using cameras and binoculars, detectives gather information on people of interest.

Detectives and investigators must be mindful of the law when conducting investigations. Because they lack police authority, their work must be done with the same authority as a private citizen. As a result, detectives and investigators must have a good understanding of federal, state, and local laws, such as privacy laws, and other legal issues affecting their work. Otherwise, evidence they collect may not be useable in court and they could face prosecution.

Skip tracers specialize in locating people whose whereabouts are unknown. For example, debt collectors may employ them to locate people who have unpaid bills.

Work Environment

Private detectives and investigators held about 38,300 jobs in 2022. The largest employers of private detectives and investigators were as follows:

Investigation, guard, and armored car services	19%
Retail trade	17
Self-employed workers	15
Professional, scientific, and technical services	14
Government	10

Private detectives and investigators work in many environments, depending on the case. Some spend more time in offices, researching cases on computers and making phone calls. Others spend more time in the field, conducting interviews or performing surveillance. In addition, private detectives and investigators may have to work outdoors or from a vehicle, in all kinds of weather, in order to obtain the information their client needs.

Although investigators often work alone, some work with others while conducting surveillance or carrying out large, complicated assignments.

Work Schedules

Private detectives and investigators often work irregular hours because they conduct surveillance and contact people outside of normal work hours. They may work early mornings, evenings, weekends, and holidays.

How to Become a Private Detective or Investigator

Private detectives and investigators typically need several years of work experience and a high school diploma. In addition, the

Many private detectives and investigators spend time away from their desks while conducting surveillance in the field.

vast majority of states require private detectives and investigators to have a license.

Education

Education requirements vary greatly with the job, but most jobs require a high school diploma. Some, though, may require a 2- or 4-year degree in a field such as criminal justice.

Training

Most private detectives and investigators learn through on-the-job training, typically lasting between several months and a year.

Although new investigators must learn how to gather information, additional training depends on the type of firm that hires them. For example, investigators may learn to conduct remote surveillance, reconstruct accident scenes, or investigate insurance fraud. Corporate investigators hired by large companies may receive formal training in business practices, management structure, and various finance-related topics.

Work Experience in a Related Occupation

Private detectives and investigators must typically have previous work experience, usually in law enforcement, the military, or federal intelligence. Those in such jobs, who are frequently able to retire after 20 or 25 years of service, may become private detectives or investigators in a second career.

Although most learn on the job, many private detectives and investigators have a law enforcement background.

Other private detectives and investigators may have previously worked as bill and account collectors, claims adjusters, paralegals, or process servers.

Licenses, Certifications, and Registrations

Most states require private detectives and investigators to have a license. Check with your state for more information; Professional Investigator Magazine has links to most states' licensing requirements. Because laws often change, jobseekers should verify the licensing laws related to private investigators with the state and locality in which they want to work.

Candidates may also obtain certification, although it is not required for employment. Still, becoming certified through professional organizations can demonstrate competence and may help candidates advance in their careers.

For investigators who specialize in negligence or criminal defense investigation, the National Association of Legal Investigators offers the Certified Legal Investigator certification. For other investigators, ASIS International offers the Professional Certified Investigator certification.

Important Qualities

Communication skills. Private detectives and investigators must listen carefully and ask appropriate questions when interviewing a person of interest.

Decision-making skills. Private detectives and investigators must be able to think on their feet and make quick decisions, based on the limited information that they have at a given time.

Inquisitiveness. Private detectives and investigators must want to ask questions and search for the truth.

Patience. Private detectives and investigators may have to spend long periods conducting surveillance while waiting for an event to occur. Investigations may take a long time, and they may not provide a resolution quickly—or at all.

Resourcefulness. Private detectives and investigators must work persistently with whatever leads they have, no matter how limited, to determine the next step toward their goal. They sometimes need to anticipate what a person of interest will do next.

Pay

The median annual wage for private detectives and investigators was $52,120 in May 2022. The median wage is the wage at which half the workers in an occupation earned more than that amount and half earned less. The lowest 10 percent earned less than $33,710, and the highest 10 percent earned more than $92,660.

In May 2022, the median annual wages for private detectives and investigators in the top industries in which they worked were as follows:

Government	$64,220
Professional, scientific, and technical services	61,280

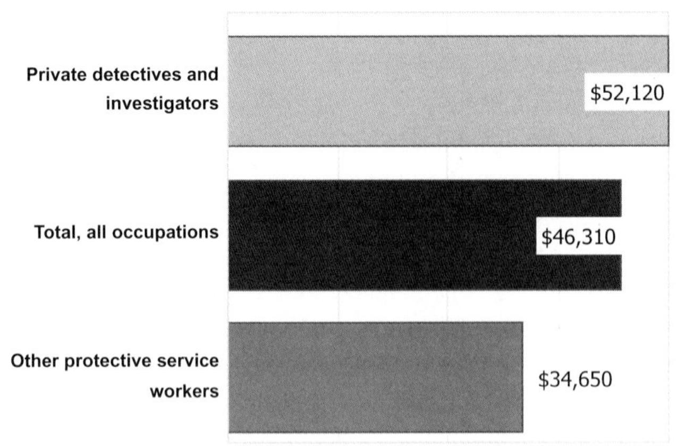

Note: All Occupations includes all occupations in the U.S. Economy.
Source: U.S. Bureau of Labor Statistics, Occupational Employment and Wage Statistics.

Investigation, guard, and armored car services..	47,280
Retail trade	37,290

Private detectives and investigators often work irregular hours because they conduct surveillance and contact people outside of normal work hours. They may work early mornings, evenings, weekends, and holidays.

Job Outlook

Employment of private detectives and investigators is projected to grow 6 percent from 2022 to 2032, faster than the average for all occupations.

About 3,800 openings for private detectives and investigators are projected each year, on average, over the decade. Many of those openings are expected to result from the need to replace workers who transfer to different occupations or exit the labor force, such as to retire.

Employment

Continued lawsuits, fraud and other crimes, and interpersonal mistrust are expected to create demand for investigative services. In addition, background checks will continue to be a source of work for some investigators, as online investigations are not always sufficient.

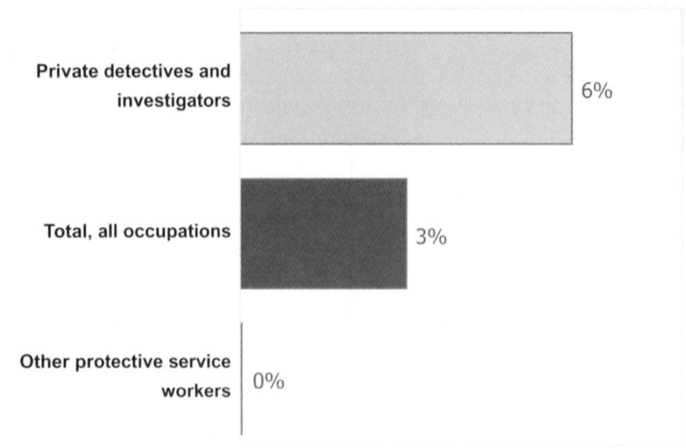

Note: All Occupations includes all occupations in the U.S. Economy.
Source: U.S. Bureau of Labor Statistics, Employment Projections program.

Occupational Title	SOC Code	Employment, 2022	Projected Employment, 2032	Change, 2022-32	
				Percent	Numeric
Private detectives and investigators	33-9021	38,300	40,600	6	2,300

Contacts for More Information

For more information about private detectives and investigators, including information on certification, visit

- National Association of Legal Investigators
- ASIS International

For more information about state licensing requirements, visit

- Professional Investigator Magazine

Security Guards and Gambling Surveillance Officers

Summary

Quick Facts: Security Guards and Gambling Surveillance Officers	
2022 Median Pay	$34,770 per year $16.71 per hour
Typical Entry-Level Education	High school diploma or equivalent
Work Experience in a Related Occupation	See How to Become One
On-the-job Training	See How to Become One
Number of Jobs, 2022	1,166,700
Job Outlook, 2022-32	-1% (Little or no change)
Employment Change, 2022-32	-14,800

What Security Guards and Gambling Surveillance Officers Do

Security guards and gambling surveillance officers protect property from illegal activity.

Work Environment

Security guards work in a variety of places, including industrial settings, retail stores, and office buildings. Gambling surveillance officers work mostly in casinos. Because many buildings and casinos are open 24 hours a day, security guards and officers often must work around the clock.

How to Become a Security Guard or Gambling Surveillance Officer

Security guards and gambling surveillance officers typically need a high school diploma. Gambling surveillance officers may also need experience with security and video surveillance, depending on their work assignment. Most states require guards to be licensed by the state, especially if they carry a firearm.

Pay

The median annual wage for gambling surveillance officers and gambling investigators was $35,970 in May 2022.

The median annual wage for security guards was $34,750 in May 2022.

Job Outlook

Overall employment of security guards and gambling surveillance officers is projected to show little or no change from 2022 to 2032.

Despite limited employment growth, about 151,700 openings for security guards and gambling surveillance officers are projected each year, on average, over the decade. Most of those openings are expected to result from the need to replace workers who transfer to different occupations or exit the labor force, such as to retire.

What Security Guards and Gambling Surveillance Officers Do

Security guards and gambling surveillance officers protect property against theft, vandalism, and other illegal activity.

Duties

Security guards and gaming surveillance officers typically do the following:

- Patrol property
- Enforce rules and regulations of an employer's property
- Monitor alarms and video-surveillance systems
- Respond to emergencies
- Deter criminal activity
- Control building access by employees and visitors
- Conduct security checks over a specified area
- Write reports on what they observed while on duty

Security guards conduct security checks over their assigned patrol area.

Security guards control building access for employees and visitors.

Guards and officers must stay alert, watching for anything unusual. In an emergency, they are required to contact police, fire, or ambulance services. Some security guards carry firearms.

Security guards work wherever people and assets need to be protected. Responsibilities vary by employer. In offices and factories, for example, security guards protect workers and equipment and check the credentials of people and vehicles entering and leaving the premises. In retail stores, guards protect people, merchandise, money, and equipment. They may work with undercover store detectives to prevent theft by customers and employees, detain shoplifting suspects until the police arrive, and patrol parking lots.

Gambling surveillance officers work in freestanding casinos and other facilities that have designated areas for gambling, such as hotels, video gaming terminals, and riverboats. They typically work from an observation room within the gaming facility.

Security guards, also called *security officers*, protect property, enforce rules on the property, and deter criminal activity. Some guards are assigned a stationary position from which they monitor alarms or surveillance cameras. Other guards are assigned a patrol area where they conduct security checks.

Gambling surveillance officers and gambling investigators act as security agents for casinos. Using audio and video equipment, they watch casino operations for suspicious activities, such as cheating and theft, and monitor compliance with rules, regulations, and laws. They maintain and organize recordings from security cameras, which are sometimes used as evidence in police investigations.

Work Environment

Gambling surveillance officers and gambling investigators held about 10,800 jobs in 2022. The largest employers of gambling surveillance officers and gambling investigators were as follows:

Local government, excluding education and hospitals	50%
Gambling industries (except casino hotels)	21
Casino hotels	18
State government, excluding education and hospitals	5
Spectator sports	1

Security guards held about 1.2 million jobs in 2022. The largest employers of security guards were as follows:

Investigation, guard, and armored car services	60%
Educational services; state, local, and private	6
Healthcare and social assistance	6
Accommodation and food services	5
Government	4

Security guards and gambling surveillance officers may need to monitor activity on multiple cameras.

Security guards work in a variety of places, including industrial settings, stores, and office buildings. Gambling surveillance officers and investigators are employed in casinos and other gaming facilities only in locations where gambling is legal.

Guards may spend considerable time on their feet patrolling buildings and grounds or may sit for long periods at a single post, such as in a guardhouse at the entrance to a gated facility or community. Others may spend periods of time in a vehicle, patrolling the property and grounds.

Both security guards and gambling surveillance officers may spend much of their shift sitting at a desk or counter in a dark room, observing customers on video surveillance equipment. They may have to monitor activity on multiple screens for long periods of time without distraction.

Work Schedules

Security guards and gambling surveillance officers usually work in shifts of about 8 hours, with rotating schedules. Night shifts are common. Most security guards and gambling surveillance officers work full time. Seasonal work may be available during the holidays and during the warmer summer months in some states.

How to Become a Security Guard or Gambling Surveillance Officer

Security guards and gambling surveillance officers typically require a high school diploma and on-the-job training. Gambling surveillance officers sometimes need experience with security and video surveillance. Most states require security guards to be licensed by the state, especially if they carry a firearm.

Education

Security guards typically need a high school diploma or equivalent, although some jobs may not require formal educational credentials. Gambling surveillance officers also need a high school diploma or equivalent.

A bachelor's degree is not required to enter the occupation. However, some security guards and gambling surveillance

Most states require that guards be registered with the state in which they work.

officers study in degree fields such as security and protective service or social science.

Training

Although most employers provide instruction for newly hired security guards and surveillance officers, the amount of training varies. Most security guards learn their job in a few weeks, but gambling surveillance officers and investigators may need several months. Employer-provided training typically covers emergency procedures, crime prevention, and proper communication.

Many states recommend that security guards receive about 8 hours of pre-assignment training, 8 to 16 hours of on-the-job training, and 8 hours of annual training. Instruction may include protection, public relations, report writing, deterring crises, first aid, and other specialized training related to the security guard's assignment.

Training is more rigorous for armed guards because they require weapons training. Armed guards may be tested periodically in the use of firearms.

Gambling surveillance officers and investigators receive training in topics such as the rules of casino games, gaming regulations, identifying cheating techniques, and the proper use of video and radio equipment.

Drug testing may be required both as a condition of employment and randomly during employment.

Work experience in a related occupation

To enter the occupation, gambling surveillance officers and investigators typically need work experience in casinos or with video monitoring technology. Candidates sometimes gain video monitoring experience by working as a security guard.

Licenses, Certifications, and Registrations

Most states require that security guards be licensed by the state in which they work. Although licensing requirements vary by state, basic qualifications for candidates are as follows:

- Be at least 18 years old
- Pass a background check
- Complete training

Guards who carry weapons usually must be licensed by the appropriate government authority. Positions for armed guards have more stringent background checks and entry requirements than do those for unarmed guards. Most states require rigorous hiring and screening programs, including background, criminal record, and fingerprint checks, for armed guards.

Some states and gaming facilities require a minimum age of 21 to work in a casino.

Some jobs may also require a driver's license.

Important Qualities

Communication skills. Security guards and surveillance officers must communicate effectively with others, even in stressful situations.

Interpersonal skills. Security guards often regularly interact with the public; in addition, they must be able to handle and deescalate confrontational situations.

Observation skills. Security guards and surveillance officers must be alert and aware of their surroundings, and be able to quickly recognize anything out of the ordinary.

Problem-solving skills. Security guards and surveillance officers must be able to quickly determine the best course of action when a dangerous situation arises.

Pay

The median annual wage for gambling surveillance officers and gambling investigators was $35,970 in May 2022. The median wage is the wage at which half the workers in an occupation earned more than that amount and half earned less. The lowest 10 percent earned less than $27,400, and the highest 10 percent earned more than $57,190.

The median annual wage for security guards was $34,750 in May 2022. The lowest 10 percent earned less than $24,020, and the highest 10 percent earned more than $51,350.

In May 2022, the median annual wages for gambling surveillance officers and gambling investigators in the top industries in which they worked were as follows:

State government, excluding education and hospitals	$72,490
Casino hotels	36,280
Local government, excluding education and hospitals	35,880
Gambling industries (except casino hotels)	34,720
Spectator sports	34,020

In May 2022, the median annual wages for security guards in the top industries in which they worked were as follows:

Educational services; state, local, and private	$38,480
Healthcare and social assistance	37,380

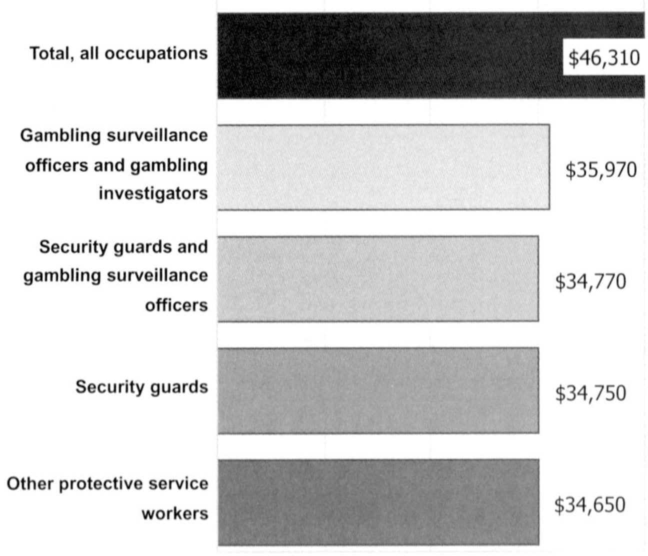

Note: All Occupations includes all occupations in the U.S. Economy.
Source: U.S. Bureau of Labor Statistics, Occupational Employment and Wage Statistics.

Government	37,320
Investigation, guard, and armored car services	33,770
Accommodation and food services	32,140

Security guards and gambling surveillance officers usually work in shifts of about 8 hours, with rotating schedules. Night shifts are common.

Job Outlook

Overall employment of security guards and gambling surveillance officers is projected to show little or no change from 2022 to 2032.

Despite limited employment growth, about 151,700 openings for security guards and gambling surveillance officers are projected each year, on average, over the decade. Most of those openings are expected to result from the need to replace workers who transfer to different occupations or exit the labor force, such as to retire.

Employment

Security guards will continue to be needed to protect both people and property because of concerns about crime and vandalism.

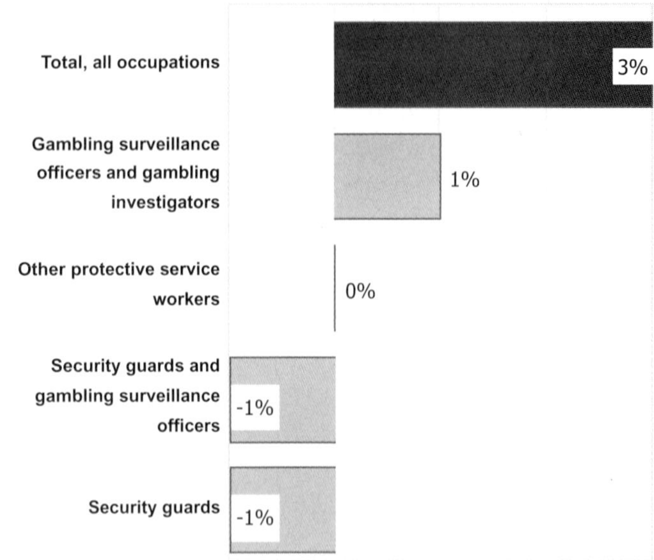

Note: All Occupations includes all occupations in the U.S. Economy.
Source: U.S. Bureau of Labor Statistics, Employment Projections program.

States continue to legalize gambling and casinos continue to grow in number, resulting in the need for gambling surveillance officers and investigators.

Advances in remote monitoring technology, such as robots and drones, to prevent cheating may limit the employment of some security guards and gambling surveillance officers and investigators.

Occupational Title	SOC Code	Employment, 2022	Projected Employment, 2032	Change, 2022-32	
				Percent	Numeric
Security guards and gambling surveillance officers	33-9030	1,166,700	1,151,900	-1	-14,800
Gambling surveillance officers and gambling investigators	33-9031	10,800	10,900	1	100
Security guards	33-9032	1,155,900	1,141,000	-1	-14,900

Contacts for More Information

For more information, visit

- The International Union, Security, Police and Fire Professionals of America

Sales

Advertising Sales Agents

Summary

Quick Facts: Advertising Sales Agents	
2022 Median Pay	$58,450 per year $28.10 per hour
Typical Entry-Level Education	High school diploma or equivalent
Work Experience in a Related Occupation	None
On-the-job Training	Moderate-term on-the-job training
Number of Jobs, 2022	111,400
Job Outlook, 2022-32	-7% (Decline)
Employment Change, 2022-32	-8,000

What Advertising Sales Agents Do

Advertising sales agents sell advertising space to businesses and individuals.

Work Environment

Advertising sales agents work under pressure to meet sales quotas. They work in a range of industries, including advertising agencies, radio, television, and Internet publishing.

How to Become an Advertising Sales Agent

Although a high school diploma is typically enough for an entry-level advertising sales position, some employers prefer applicants who have a bachelor's degree. Sales and communication skills are essential.

Pay

The median annual wage for advertising sales agents was $58,450 in May 2022.

Job Outlook

Employment of advertising sales agents is projected to decline 7 percent from 2022 to 2032.

Despite declining employment, about 10,500 openings for advertising sales agents are projected each year, on average, over the decade. All of those openings are expected to result from the need to replace workers who transfer to other occupations or exit the labor force, such as to retire.

What Advertising Sales Agents Do

Advertising sales agents, also called *advertising sales representatives*, sell advertising space to businesses and individuals. They contact potential clients, make sales presentations, and maintain client accounts.

Duties

Advertising sales agents typically do the following:

- Locate and contact potential clients to offer their firm's advertising services
- Explain to clients how specific types of advertising will help promote their products or services in the most effective way
- Provide clients with estimates of the costs of advertising products or services
- Process all correspondence and paperwork related to accounts

Advertising sales agents contact potential clients, make sales presentations, and maintain customer accounts.

Agents may spend much of their time visiting prospective advertisers and maintaining business with current clients.

- Prepare and deliver sales presentations to new and existing clients
- Inform clients of available options for advertising art, formats, or features and provide samples of previous work for other clients
- Deliver advertising or illustration proofs to clients for approval
- Prepare promotional plans, sales literature, media kits, and sales contracts
- Recommend appropriate sizes and formats for advertising

Advertising sales agents work outside the office occasionally, meeting with clients and prospective clients at their places of business. Some may make telephone sales calls as well—calling prospects, attempting to sell the media firm's advertising space or time, and arranging followup appointments with interested prospects.

A critical part of building relationships with clients is learning about their needs. Before the first meeting with a client, a sales agent gathers background information on the client's products, current clients, prospective clients, and the geographic area of the target market.

The sales agent then meets with the client to explain how specific types of advertising will help promote the client's products or services most effectively. If a client wishes to proceed, the advertising sales agent prepares and presents an advertising proposal to the client. The proposal may include an overview of the advertising medium to be used, sample advertisements, and cost estimates for the project.

Because of consolidation among media industries, agents are increasingly selling several types of ads in one package. For example, agents may sell ads that would be found in print editions, as well as online editions, of a particular publication, such as a newspaper.

In addition to maintaining sales and overseeing their accounts, advertising sales agents analyze sales statistics and prepare reports about clients' accounts. They keep up to date on industry trends by reading about both current and new products, and they monitor the sales, prices, and products of their competitors.

In many firms, the advertising sales agent drafts contracts, which specify the cost and the advertising work to be done. Agents also may continue to help the client, answering questions or addressing problems the client may have with the proposal.

In addition, sales agents may be responsible for developing sales tools, promotional plans, and media kits, all of which they use to help make a sale. In other cases, firms may have a marketing team that sales agents work with to develop these sales tools.

Work Environment

Advertising sales agents held about 111,400 jobs in 2022. The largest employers of advertising sales agents were as follows:

Companies generally set monthly sales quotas and place considerable pressure on advertising sales agents to meet those quotas.

Advertising, public relations, and related services	41%
Newspaper publishers	11
Self-employed workers	4

Selling can be stressful because income and job security depend directly on agents' ability to keep and expand their client base. Companies generally set monthly sales quotas and place considerable pressure on advertising sales agents to meet those quotas.

Getting new accounts is an important part of the job, and agents may spend much of their time traveling to and visiting prospective advertisers and maintaining relationships with current clients. Sales agents also may work in their employer's offices and handle sales for walk-in clients or for those who call or email the firm to ask about advertising.

Work Schedules

Most advertising sales agents work full time. Some advertising sales agents work more than 40 hours a week. Some work irregular hours and on weekends and holidays.

How to Become an Advertising Sales Agent

Although a high school diploma is typically enough education for an entry-level advertising sales position, some employers prefer applicants with a bachelor's degree. Sales and communication skills are essential. Most training for advertising sales agents takes place on the job.

Education

Although a high school diploma is typically the minimum education requirement for an entry-level advertising sales position, some employers prefer applicants with a college degree. Publishing companies with large circulations and broadcasting stations with a large audience typically prefer workers with a college degree. Courses in marketing, communications,

Advertising sales agents must actively seek new clients and initiate communication with current clients in order to meet sales quotas.

business, and advertising are helpful. For those who have a proven record of successfully selling other products, educational requirements are not likely to be strict.

Training

Most training takes place on the job and can be either formal or informal. In the majority of cases, an experienced sales manager instructs a newly hired advertising sales agent who lacks sales experience. In this one-on-one environment, supervisors typically coach new hires and observe them as they make sales calls and contact clients. Supervisors then advise the new hires on ways to improve their interaction with clients. Employers may bring in consultants to lead formal training sessions when agents sell to a specialized market segment, such as automotive dealers or real estate professionals.

Advancement

Agents with proven leadership ability and a strong sales record may advance to supervisory and managerial positions, such as sales manager, account executive, and vice president of sales. Successful advertising sales agents may also advance to positions in other industries, such as corporate sales.

Important Qualities

Communication skills. Advertising sales agents must be persuasive during sales calls. In addition, they should listen to the client's desires and concerns, and recommend an appropriate advertising package.

Initiative. Advertising sales agents must actively seek new clients, keep in touch with current clients, and expand their client base, in order to meet sales quotas.

Organizational skills. Agents work with many clients, each of whom may be at a different stage in the sales process. Agents must be well organized to keep track of their clients and potential clients.

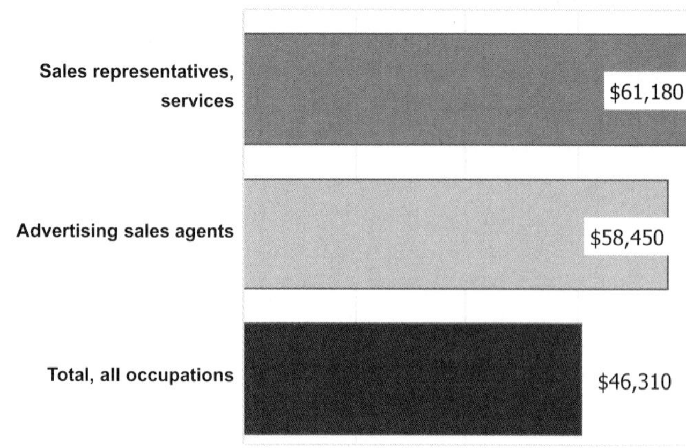

Note: All Occupations includes all occupations in the U.S. Economy.
Source: U.S. Bureau of Labor Statistics, Occupational Employment and Wage Statistics.

Self-confidence. Advertising sales agents should be confident when calling potential clients (making cold calls). Because potential clients are often unwilling to commit on a first call, agents frequently must continue making sales calls, even if rejected at first.

Pay

The median annual wage for advertising sales agents was $58,450 in May 2022. The median wage is the wage at which half the workers in an occupation earned more than that amount and half earned less. The lowest 10 percent earned less than $30,510, and the highest 10 percent earned more than $132,640.

In May 2022, the median annual wages for advertising sales agents in the top industries in which they worked were as follows:

Advertising, public relations, and related services	$64,130
Newspaper publishers	38,710

Performance-based pay, including bonuses and commissions, can make up a large portion of an advertising sales agent's earnings. Most employers pay some combination of salaries, commissions, and bonuses. Commissions usually are based on individual sales numbers. Bonuses may depend on individual performance, the performance of all sales workers in a group, or the performance of the entire firm.

Most advertising sales agents work full time. Some advertising sales agents work more than 40 hours a week. Some work irregular hours and on weekends and holidays.

Job Outlook

Employment of advertising sales agents is projected to decline 7 percent from 2022 to 2032.

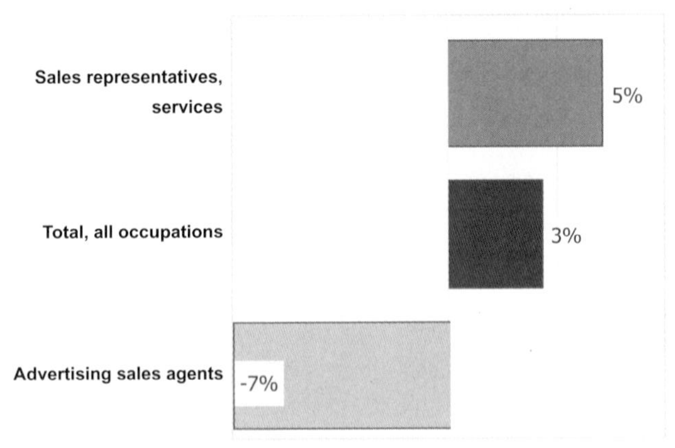

Note: All Occupations includes all occupations in the U.S. Economy.
Source: U.S. Bureau of Labor Statistics, Employment Projections program.

Despite declining employment, about 10,500 openings for advertising sales agents are projected each year, on average, over the decade. All of those openings are expected to result from the need to replace workers who transfer to other occupations or exit the labor force, such as to retire.

Employment

Newspapers and magazines are expected to continue to experience circulation declines. With fewer consumers viewing advertisements in print media, fewer advertising sales agents are expected to be needed.

Advertising will continue to grow in digital media, including online video ads, search engine ads, and other digital ads intended for cell phones or tablet-style computers. Although advertising sales agents are still needed in digital media, the ability to automate digital ad placement and the use of ad blockers by digital users will limit employment demand for advertising sales agents along these channels.

Occupational Title	SOC Code	Employment, 2022	Projected Employment, 2032	Change, 2022-32	
				Percent	Numeric
Advertising sales agents	41-3011	111,400	103,400	-7	-8,000

Contacts for More Information

For information, visit

- News Media Alliance
- Radio Advertising Bureau

Cashiers

Summary

Quick Facts: Cashiers

2022 Median Pay	$28,240 per year $13.58 per hour
Typical Entry-Level Education	No formal educational credential
Work Experience in a Related Occupation	None
On-the-job Training	Short-term on-the-job training
Number of Jobs, 2022	3,345,800
Job Outlook, 2022-32	-10% (Decline)
Employment Change, 2022-32	-348,100

What Cashiers Do

Cashiers process payments from customers purchasing goods and services.

Work Environment

Most cashiers work in retail establishments, such as grocery stores, gasoline stations, and other general merchandise stores.

How to Become a Cashier

Cashiers are trained on the job. There are no formal education requirements to become a cashier.

Pay

The median hourly wage for cashiers was $13.58 in May 2022.

Job Outlook

Employment of cashiers is projected to decline 10 percent from 2022 to 2032.

Despite declining employment, about 577,600 openings for cashiers are projected each year, on average, over the decade. All of those openings are expected to result from the need to replace workers who transfer to other occupations or exit the labor force, such as to retire.

Cashiers process customers' payments.

Cashiers process returns and exchanges of merchandise.

What Cashiers Do

Cashiers process payments from customers purchasing goods and services.

Duties

Cashiers typically do the following:

- Greet customers
- Scan or register customers' purchases
- Accept payments from customers and give change and receipts
- Bag or wrap customers' purchases
- Process returns and exchanges of merchandise
- Answer customers' questions and provide information about store policies
- Help customers sign up for store rewards programs or credit cards
- Count the money in their register at the beginning and end of each shift

In some establishments, cashiers have to check the age of their customers when selling age-restricted products, such as alcohol and tobacco. Some cashiers may have duties not directly related to sales and customer service, such as mopping floors, taking out the trash, and other custodial tasks. Others may stock shelves or mark prices on items.

Cashiers use scanners, registers, or calculators to process payments and returns or exchanges of merchandise.

Work Environment

Cashiers held about 3.3 million jobs in 2022. The largest employers of cashiers were as follows:

Gasoline stations	19%
General merchandise retailers	17
Restaurants and other eating places	10
Pharmacies and drug retailers	5

The work is often repetitive, and cashiers spend most of their time standing behind counters or checkout stands. Dealing with dissatisfied customers can be stressful.

Cashiers spend most of their time on their feet.

Work Schedules

Cashiers' work hours vary by employer. Cashiers often work during weekends and holidays. Some cashiers employed in establishments that operate 24 hours a day, such as gasoline stations, work overnight shifts. Part-time work is common.

Employers may restrict the use of time off from Thanksgiving through early January because that is the busiest time of the year for most retailers.

How to Become a Cashier

Cashiers are trained on the job. There are no formal education requirements to become a cashier.

Education

Although most jobs for cashiers have no specific education requirements, some employers prefer applicants with a high school diploma or equivalent. Cashiers should have a basic knowledge of mathematics, because they need to be able to make change and count the money in their registers.

Training

Cashiers receive on-the-job training, which may last a few weeks. An experienced worker typically helps new cashiers learn how to operate equipment such as scanners or registers.

Advancement

Working as a cashier is often a means to advance to other careers in retail. For example, with experience, cashiers may become customer service representatives or retail sales workers.

Important Qualities

Communication skills. Cashiers must pay attention to customers' questions and explain pricing.

Customer-service skills. Cashiers must be courteous and friendly when helping customers.

Dexterity. Cashiers use their hands to operate registers and scan purchases.

Cashiers need to have good customer service skills.

Near vision. Cashiers need to see well enough to scan items and process transactions accurately.

Patience. Cashiers must be able to remain calm when interacting with customers.

Physical stamina. Cashiers stand for long periods.

Pay

The median hourly wage for cashiers was $13.58 in May 2022. The median wage is the wage at which half the workers in an occupation earned more than that amount and half earned less. The lowest 10 percent earned less than $10.31, and the highest 10 percent earned more than $17.26.

In May 2022, the median hourly wages for cashiers in the top industries in which they worked were as follows:

Pharmacies and drug retailers	$14.27
Gasoline stations	13.23
General merchandise retailers	13.08
Restaurants and other eating places	12.82

Cashiers' work hours vary by employer. Cashiers often work during weekends and holidays. Some cashiers employed in establishments that operate 24 hours a day, such as gasoline stations, work overnight shifts. Part-time work is common.

Employers may restrict the use of time off from Thanksgiving through early January because that is the busiest time of the year for most retailers.

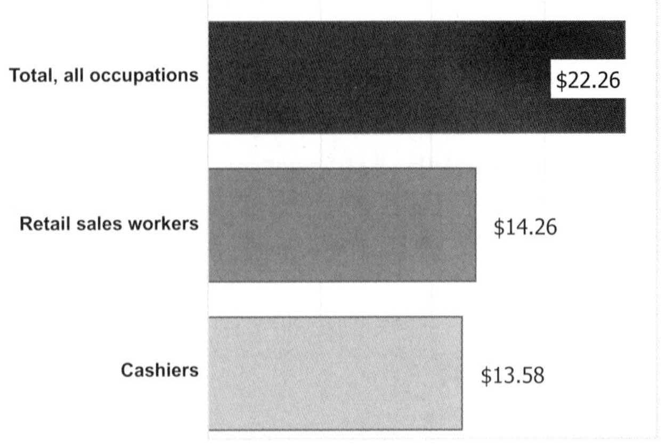

Note: All Occupations includes all occupations in the U.S. Economy.
Source: U.S. Bureau of Labor Statistics, Occupational Employment and Wage Statistics.

Job Outlook

Employment of cashiers is projected to decline 10 percent from 2022 to 2032.

Despite declining employment, about 577,600 openings for cashiers are projected each year, on average, over the decade. All of those openings are expected to result from the need to replace workers who transfer to other occupations or exit the labor force, such as to retire.

Employment

Although retail sales are expected to increase over the projections decade, employment of cashiers is expected to decline because of advances in technology, such as the use of self-service checkout stands in retail stores and increasing online sales.

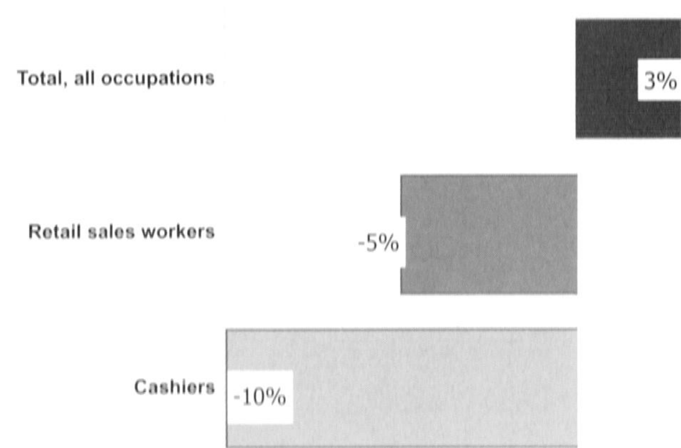

Note: All Occupations includes all occupations in the U.S. Economy.
Source: U.S. Bureau of Labor Statistics, Employment Projections program.

Occupational Title	SOC Code	Employment, 2022	Projected Employment, 2032	Change, 2022-32	
				Percent	Numeric
Cashiers	41-2011	3,345,800	2,997,700	-10	-348,100

Contacts for More Information

The *Handbook* does not have contacts for more information for this occupation.

Insurance Sales Agents

Summary

Quick Facts: Insurance Sales Agents	
2022 Median Pay	$57,860 per year $27.82 per hour
Typical Entry-Level Education	High school diploma or equivalent
Work Experience in a Related Occupation	None
On-the-job Training	Moderate-term on-the-job training
Number of Jobs, 2022	536,800
Job Outlook, 2022-32	8% (Faster than average)
Employment Change, 2022-32	42,500

What Insurance Sales Agents Do

Insurance sales agents contact potential customers and sell one or more types of insurance.

Work Environment

Most insurance sales agents work in office settings, although they may spend time traveling to meet with clients.

How to Become an Insurance Sales Agent

Although employers typically require that agents have a high school diploma, they may prefer to hire agents who have a bachelor's degree. Agents must be licensed in the states where they work.

Insurance sales agents explain various insurance policies and help clients choose plans that suit them.

Pay

The median annual wage for insurance sales agents was $57,860 in May 2022.

Job Outlook

Employment of insurance sales agents is projected to grow 8 percent from 2022 to 2032, faster than the average for all occupations.

About 48,300 openings for insurance sales agents are projected each year, on average, over the decade. Many of those openings are expected to result from the need to replace workers who transfer to different occupations or exit the labor force, such as to retire.

What Insurance Sales Agents Do

Insurance sales agents contact potential customers and sell one or more types of insurance. These agents explain various

Insurance sales agents commonly sell one or more types of insurance, such as property and casualty, life, health, and long-term care.

insurance policies and help clients choose the plans that suit them.

Duties

Insurance sales agents typically do the following:

- Contact potential clients to expand their own customer base
- Interview prospective clients to get information about their financial situation and discuss existing coverage
- Explain the features of various insurance policies
- Analyze clients' current policies and suggest additions or other changes
- Customize insurance programs to suit individual clients
- Handle policy sales and renewals
- Assist clients with the insurance claims process
- Maintain client records

Insurance sales agents commonly sell one or more types of insurance, such as property and casualty, life, health, and long-term care.

Property and casualty insurance agents sell policies that protect people and businesses from financial loss resulting from automobile accidents or from fire, theft, and other events that damage property. For businesses, property and casualty insurance also covers claims related to workers' compensation, product liability, and medical malpractice.

Life insurance agents specialize in selling policies that pay beneficiaries when a policyholder dies. Life insurance agents also sell annuities, which require the policyholder to make a single deposit or a series of payments in exchange for regular disbursements over time.

Health and long-term care insurance agents sell policies that cover some or all of the costs of medical care and of assisted-living services for older adults. They also may sell insurance for dental care and for short- and long-term disability.

Agents may specialize in selling any one of these products or function as generalists providing multiple products.

In addition to offering insurance, these agents may become licensed to sell mutual funds, variable annuities, and other securities. This practice is most common with life insurance agents who already sell annuities, but many property and casualty agents also sell financial products.

Many agents market their services to create or expand their own client base. For example, they may make sales calls to people who are not current clients, often through referrals from current clients.

Insurance agents may work for either a single company or several companies.

Captive agents are insurance sales agents who work exclusively for one company. They sell policies provided only by the company that employs them.

Independent insurance agents may sell the policies of several companies to match their clients' needs with the company that offers the best rate and coverage.

Most insurance sales agents work in offices, although some may spend much of their time traveling to meet with clients.

Insurance brokers work for insurance brokerage firms. They represent their clients, rather than insurers, and may offer advice about competing companies' rates, coverage, and reputation. Like agents, brokers may be either captive or independent; however, because independent brokers are not associated with insurance companies, they must involve an insurer or insurance agent to complete a sale.

Work Environment

Insurance sales agents held about 536,800 jobs in 2022. The largest employers of insurance sales agents were as follows:

Insurance agencies and brokerages	61%
Self-employed workers	11
Direct insurance (except life, health, and medical) carriers	9
Direct health and medical insurance carriers	5

Most insurance sales agents work in office settings, although they may spend time traveling to meet with clients.

Work Schedules

Most insurance sales agents work full time.

How to Become an Insurance Sales Agent

Insurance sales agents typically need a high school diploma to enter the occupation. However, employers may prefer to hire candidates who have a bachelor's degree. Agents must be licensed in the states where they work.

Education

A high school diploma is typically required for insurance sales agents. However, some employers prefer to hire candidates who have a bachelor's degree in a field such as business.

Training

Insurance sales agents learn many of their duties on the job, such as by shadowing an experienced agent. New agents learn

Agents must be licensed in the states where they plan to work.

about insurance products, the sales process, and how to interact with clients.

Employers often expect agents to stay abreast of changes in tax laws, government benefits programs, and other state and federal regulations that may affect clients' insurance needs and the way in which agents conduct business. Agents may take continuing education to meet employer expectations.

Licenses, Certifications, and Registrations

Insurance sales agents must have a license in the states where they work. Separate licenses are required for agents to sell life and health insurance and property and casualty insurance. In most states, licenses are issued only to applicants who complete specified courses and who pass state exams covering insurance fundamentals and state insurance laws. Most state licensing authorities also require agents to take continuing education courses focusing on topics such as insurance laws, consumer protection, ethics, and the technical details of various insurance policies.

Some insurance sales agents also sell securities and other financial products. To do so, they must become licensed by the Financial Industry Regulatory Authority (FINRA). FINRA's Series 6 exam is for agents who want to sell financial products, such as municipal fund securities, mutual funds, and variable annuities. Its Series 7 exam is the main FINRA series license, which qualifies agents as general securities sales representatives.

A number of organizations offer certifications that show an agent's expertise in insurance specialties. These certifications are not required for employment, but they may give job candidates an advantage over other applicants. For details on specific designations, contact The Institutes and The American College of Financial Services.

Important Qualities

Analytical skills. Insurance sales agents must evaluate the needs of each client to determine the appropriate insurance policy.

Communication skills. Insurance sales agents must listen to clients and be able to clearly explain suitable policies.

Initiative. Insurance sales agents need to actively seek out new clients in order to increase business.

Interpersonal skills. Insurance sales agents must be able to establish trust in networking for prospective clients and in interactions with existing clients, including to handle claims.

Self-confidence. Insurance sales agents should be confident when contacting prospective clients. They must be persuasive and able to maintain composure if rejected.

Pay

The median annual wage for insurance sales agents was $57,860 in May 2022. The median wage is the wage at which half the workers in an occupation earned more than that amount and half earned less. The lowest 10 percent earned less than $31,530, and the highest 10 percent earned more than $130,350.

In May 2022, the median annual wages for insurance sales agents in the top industries in which they worked were as follows:

Direct health and medical insurance carriers	$68,460
Insurance agencies and brokerages	56,620
Direct insurance (except life, health, and medical) carriers	55,740

Wage data are from nonfarm establishments. The data exclude self-employed workers and owners and partners in unincorporated businesses. Tips, sales commissions, and bonuses for meeting production targets are included in wages; premium pay, such as overtime and shift differentials, is not.

Independent agents may be paid by commission only. Sales workers who are employees of an agency or an insurance carrier may be paid in one of three ways: salary only, salary plus commission, or salary plus bonus.

In general, commissions are the most common form of compensation, especially for experienced agents. The amount of the commission depends on the type and amount of insurance sold and on whether the transaction is a new policy or a renewal. When agents meet their sales goals or when an agency meets its profit goals, agents usually get bonuses. Some agents involved with financial planning receive a fee for their services rather than a commission.

Most insurance sales agents work full time.

Job Outlook

Employment of insurance sales agents is projected to grow 8 percent from 2022 to 2032, faster than the average for all occupations.

About 48,300 openings for insurance sales agents are projected each year, on average, over the decade. Many of those openings are expected to result from the need to replace workers who transfer to different occupations or exit the labor force, such as to retire.

Insurance Sales Agents

Median annual wages, May 2022

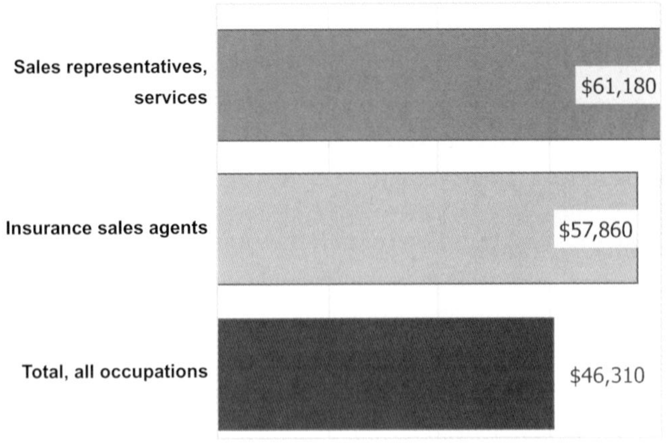

Note: All Occupations includes all occupations in the U.S. Economy.
Source: U.S. Bureau of Labor Statistics, Occupational Employment and Wage Statistics.

Insurance Sales Agents

Percent change in employment, projected 2022-32

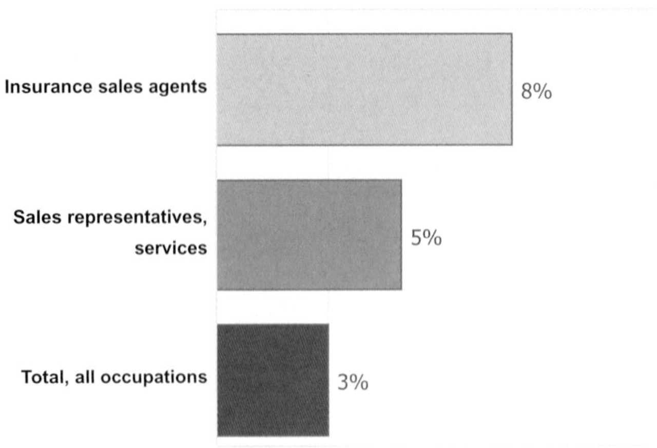

Note: All Occupations includes all occupations in the U.S. Economy.
Source: U.S. Bureau of Labor Statistics, Employment Projections program.

Employment

Because the profitability of insurance companies depends on a steady stream of new customers, the demand for insurance sales agents is expected to continue. Employment growth will likely be strongest for independent sales agents as insurance companies rely more on brokerages and less on captive agents in an effort to control costs.

Many clients do their own research and purchase insurance online, which reduces demand for an insurance sales agent's services. However, agents will still be needed to help clients understand their options and choose a policy that is right for them. Many customers lack the time or expertise to study the different types of insurance to decide what they need and so they will continue to rely on advice from insurance sales agents.

Occupational Title	SOC Code	Employment, 2022	Projected Employment, 2032	Change, 2022-32	
				Percent	Numeric
Insurance sales agents	41-3021	536,800	579,300	8	42,500

Contacts for More Information

For more information, visit

- National Association of Professional Insurance Agents
- Insurance Information Institute
- National Association of Health Underwriters
- The Institutes
- The American College of Financial Services
- Financial Industry Regulatory Authority (FINRA)

Models

Summary

Quick Facts: Models	
2022 Median Pay	$43,130 per year $20.73 per hour
Typical Entry-Level Education	No formal educational credential
Work Experience in a Related Occupation	None
On-the-job Training	None
Number of Jobs, 2022	2,200
Job Outlook, 2022-32	0% (Little or no change)
Employment Change, 2022-32	0

What Models Do
Models pose for artists, photographers, and other clients to help advertise products.

Work Environment
Models work in a variety of conditions, from comfortable indoor studios and runway fashion shows to outdoors in all weather conditions. Most models work part time and have unpredictable work schedules. Many also experience periods of unemployment.

How to Become a Model
No formal educational credential is required and training is limited. Specific requirements depend on the client. However, most models must be within certain ranges for height, weight, and clothing size to meet the needs of fashion designers, photographers, and advertisers.

Pay
The median hourly wage for models was $20.73 in May 2022.

Job Outlook
Employment of models is projected to show little or no change from 2022 to 2032.

Despite limited employment growth, about 400 openings for models are projected each year, on average, over the decade. Most of those openings are expected to result from the need to replace workers who transfer to different occupations or exit the labor force, such as to retire.

What Models Do
Models pose for artists, photographers, or customers to help advertise a variety of products, including clothing, cosmetics, food, and appliances. Models also work as a fit or fitting model, enabling the manufacturer or fashion designer to achieve the best fit for new styles.

Duties
Models typically do the following:

- Display clothing and merchandise in print and online advertisements
- Promote products and services in television commercials
- Wear designers' clothing for runway fashion shows
- Represent companies and brands at conventions, trade shows, and other events
- Pose for photos, paintings, or sculptures
- Work closely with photographers, hair and clothing stylists, makeup artists, and clients to produce a desired look
- Create and maintain a portfolio of their work
- Travel to meet and interview with potential clients
- Conduct research on the product being promoted—for example, the designer or type of clothing fabric
- Answer questions from consumers about the products

Almost all models sign with modeling agencies. Agencies represent and promote a model to clients in return for a portion of the model's earnings. Models typically apply for a position with an agency by submitting their photographs through its

Models pose for artists and photographers.

Models make changes to their expressions in order to capture a look desired by the photographer.

website or by attending open casting calls and meeting with agents directly.

Models must research an agency before signing, in order to ensure that the agency has a good reputation in the modeling industry. For information on agencies, models should contact a local consumer affairs organization, such as the Better Business Bureau.

Some freelance models do not sign with agencies. Instead, they market themselves to potential clients and apply for modeling jobs directly. However, because most clients prefer to work with agents, it is difficult for new models to pursue a freelance career.

Models must put together and maintain up-to-date portfolios and composite cards. A portfolio is a collection of a model's previous work. A composite card contains the best photographs from a model's portfolio, along with his or her body measurements. Both portfolios and composite cards are typically taken to all casting calls and client auditions.

Because advertisers often need to target specific segments of the population, models may specialize in a certain area. For example, petite and plus-size fashions are modeled by women whose sizes are respectively smaller and larger than that worn by the typical model. Models who are disabled may be used to model fashions or products for consumers with disabilities. "Parts" models have a body part, such as a hand or foot, particularly well suited to model products such as nail polish or shoes.

Models appear in different types of media to promote a product or service. Models advertise products and merchandise in magazine or newspaper advertisements, department store catalogs, or television commercials. Increasingly, models are appearing in online ads or on retail websites. Models also pose for sketch artists, painters, and sculptors.

Models often participate in photo shoots and pose for photographers to show off the features of clothing and other products. Models change their posture and facial expressions to capture the look the client wants. The photographer usually takes many pictures of the model in different poses and expressions during the photo shoot.

Models also display clothes and merchandise live in different situations. At fashion shows, models stand, turn, and walk to show off clothing to an audience of photographers, journalists, designers, and garment buyers. Other clients may require models to interact directly with customers. In retail establishments and department stores, models display clothing directly to shoppers and describe the features and prices of the merchandise. At trade shows or conventions, models show off a business' products and provide information to consumers. These models may work alongside demonstrators and product promoters to help advertise and sell merchandise.

Models often prepare for photo shoots or fashion shows by having their hair and makeup done by professionals in those industries. The hairstylists and makeup artists may touch up the model's hair and makeup and change the model's look throughout the event. However, models are sometimes responsible for applying their own makeup and bringing their own clothing.

Models may work in studios with photographers and stylists.

Work Environment

Models held about 2,200 jobs in 2022. The largest employers of models were as follows:

Professional, scientific, and technical services	16%
Colleges, universities, and professional schools; state, local, and private	12
Junior colleges; state, local, and private	8
Temporary help services	7

Models work in a variety of conditions, from comfortable photography studios and runway fashion shows to outdoors in all weather conditions.

Models also may need to travel for photo shoots or to meet clients in different cities.

Work Schedules

Models' schedules can be demanding and stressful. Many models work part time and have unpredictable work schedules. They must be ready to work for a show or attend a photo shoot on short notice. The number of hours worked varies with the job. Many models experience periods of unemployment.

How to Become a Model

No formal education credential is required to become a model. Specific requirements depend on the client, with different jobs requiring different physical characteristics. However, most models must be within certain ranges for height, weight, and clothing size.

Education

There are no formal educational credentials required to become a model. Most modeling agencies allow applicants to email photos directly to the agency. The agency will then contact and

Specific requirements depend on the client, but most models must be within certain ranges for height, weight, and clothing size.

interview prospective models who show potential. Many agencies also have "open calls," whereby aspiring models can walk into an agency during a specified time and meet directly with agents and clients.

Some aspiring models may attend modeling schools that provide training in posing, walking, applying makeup, and other basic tasks. Although some models are discovered when agents scout for "fresh faces" at modeling schools, attending such schools does not necessarily lead to job opportunities.

Advancement

Models advance by working more regularly and being selected for assignments that offer higher pay. They may appear in magazines, print advertising campaigns, commercials, or runway shows that have higher profiles and provide more widespread exposure.

Because advancement depends on a model's previous work, maintaining a good portfolio of high-quality, up-to-date photographs is important in getting assignments. In addition, actively participating in social media and building a large number of followers increases exposure.

A model's selection of an agency is also important for advancement: the better the reputation and skill of the agency, the more assignments a model is likely to get.

Important Qualities

Specific requirements depend on the client, but most models must be within certain ranges for height, weight, and clothing size. Requirements may change slightly over time as perceptions of physical beauty change.

Discipline. A model's career depends on the person's maintaining his or her physical characteristics. Models must control their diet, exercise regularly, and get enough sleep to stay healthy and photogenic. Haircuts, pedicures, and manicures are necessary work-related expenses.

Interpersonal skills. Models must interact with a large number of people, such as agents, photographers, and customers. It is important to be polite, professional, prompt, and respectful.

Listening skills. Models must take direction from photographers and clients during photo shoots and commercials.

Organizational skills. Models must manage their portfolios and their work and travel schedules.

Persistence. Competition for jobs is strong, and most clients have specific needs for each job, so patience and persistence are essential.

Photogenic. Models spend most of their time being photographed. They must be comfortable in front of a camera in order for photographers to capture the desired look.

Style. Models must have a basic knowledge of hair styling, makeup, and clothing. For photographic and runway work, models must move gracefully and confidently.

Pay

The median hourly wage for models was $20.73 in May 2022. The median wage is the wage at which half the workers in an occupation earned more than that amount and half earned less. The lowest 10 percent earned less than $13.06, and the highest 10 percent earned more than $75.00.

In May 2022, the median hourly wages for models in the top industries in which they worked were as follows:

Models

Median hourly wages, May 2022

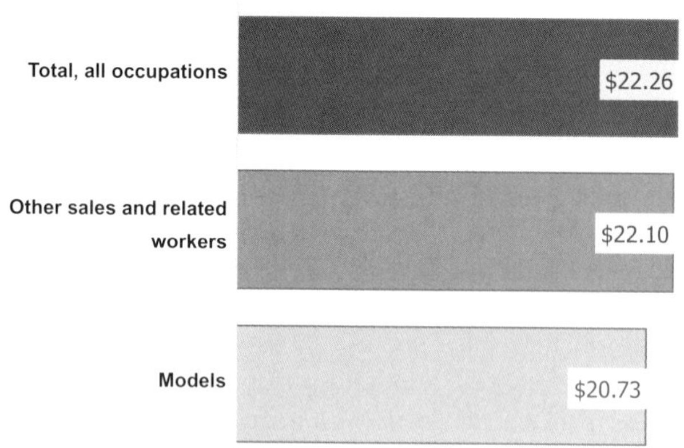

Note: All Occupations includes all occupations in the U.S. Economy.
Source: U.S. Bureau of Labor Statistics, Occupational Employment and Wage Statistics.

Temporary help services	$50.67
Junior colleges; state, local, and private	25.31
Professional, scientific, and technical services	22.47
Colleges, universities, and professional schools; state, local, and private	18.56

Models' schedules can be demanding and stressful. Many models work part time and have unpredictable work schedules. They must be ready to work for a show or attend a photo shoot on short notice. The number of hours worked varies with the job. Many models experience periods of unemployment.

Job Outlook

Employment of models is projected to show little or no change from 2022 to 2032.

Despite limited employment growth, about 400 openings for models are projected each year, on average, over the decade. Most of those openings are expected to result from the need to replace workers who transfer to different occupations or exit the labor force, such as to retire.

Employment

Rising retail sales, particularly online and in e-commerce, will encourage businesses to increase their digital advertising and marketing budgets. Demand for models to appear in digital advertisements is expected to lead to employment opportunities for these workers. However, less expensive digital and social media options are allowing companies to promote their products and brands directly to consumers, which may moderate employment demand for models.

Models

Percent change in employment, projected 2022-32

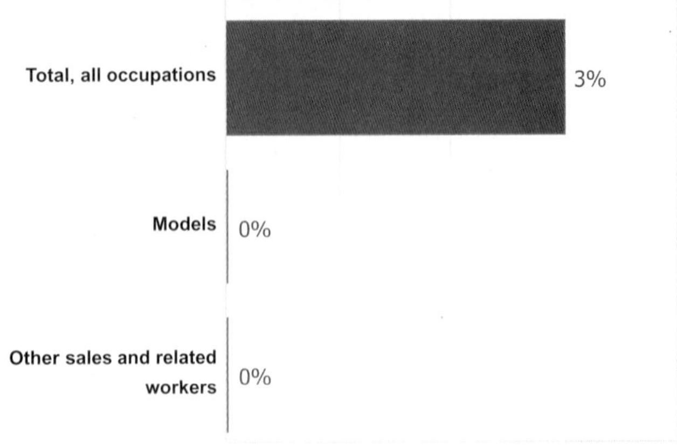

Note: All Occupations includes all occupations in the U.S. Economy.
Source: U.S. Bureau of Labor Statistics, Employment Projections program.

Occupational Title	SOC Code	Employment, 2022	Projected Employment, 2032	Change, 2022-32	
				Percent	Numeric
Models	41-9012	2,200	2,200	0	0

Contacts for More Information

For more information about modeling schools and agencies in your area, contact a local consumer affairs organization, such as the Better Business Bureau.

Real Estate Brokers and Sales Agents

Summary

Quick Facts: Real Estate Brokers and Sales Agents

2022 Median Pay	$52,030 per year $25.02 per hour
Typical Entry-Level Education	High school diploma or equivalent
Work Experience in a Related Occupation	See How to Become One
On-the-job Training	See How to Become One
Number of Jobs, 2022	589,800
Job Outlook, 2022-32	3% (As fast as average)
Employment Change, 2022-32	19,400

What Real Estate Brokers and Sales Agents Do

Real estate brokers and sales agents help clients buy, sell, and rent properties.

Work Environment

Most real estate brokers and sales agents are self-employed. Although they often work irregular hours, many are able to set their own schedules.

How to Become a Real Estate Broker or Sales Agent

Real estate brokers and sales agents typically need a high school diploma or equivalent to enter the occupation. Every state requires real estate brokers and agents to be licensed.

Pay

The median annual wage for real estate brokers was $62,190 in May 2022.

The median annual wage for real estate sales agents was $49,980 in May 2022.

Job Outlook

Overall employment of real estate brokers and sales agents is projected to grow 3 percent from 2022 to 2032, about as fast as the average for all occupations.

Real estate brokers and sales agents help clients buy or sell real estate.

About 51,600 openings for real estate brokers and sales agents are projected each year, on average, over the decade. Many of those openings are expected to result from the need to replace workers who transfer to different occupations or exit the labor force, such as to retire.

What Real Estate Brokers and Sales Agents Do

Real estate brokers and sales agents help clients buy, sell, and rent properties. Although brokers and agents do similar work, brokers are licensed to manage their own real estate businesses. Sales agents must work with a real estate broker.

Duties

Real estate brokers and sales agents typically do the following:

- Solicit potential clients to buy, sell, and rent properties
- Advise clients on prices, mortgages, market conditions, and related information
- Compare properties to determine a competitive market price
- Generate lists of properties for sale or rent, including details such as location and features
- Promote properties through advertisements, open houses, and listing services
- Take prospective buyers or renters to see properties
- Present purchase offers to sellers for consideration
- Mediate negotiations between buyer and seller
- Ensure that terms of purchase contracts are met
- Prepare documents, such as closing statements, purchase agreements, and leases

Real estate brokers and sales agents help clients find a home that meets their needs.

Because of the complexity of buying or selling a residential or commercial property, people often seek help from real estate brokers and sales agents.

Most real estate brokers and sales agents sell residential property. Others sell commercial property, and a small number sell industrial, agricultural, or other types of real estate.

Real estate brokers and sales agents also may list and show commercial and residential properties for rent. They help clients seeking to rent a property find a property that best suits their needs.

Brokers and agents may represent either the buyer or the seller in a transaction. Buyers' brokers and agents meet with clients to determine what they are looking for in a property and how much they can afford. Sellers' brokers and agents meet with clients to help them decide how much to ask for and to assure them that the agent or broker can find them a qualified buyer.

Real estate brokers and sales agents must be knowledgeable about the real estate market in their area. To match properties to clients' needs, they should be familiar with local communities, including knowing the crime information and the proximity to schools and shopping. Brokers and agents also must stay current on financing options; government programs; types of available mortgages; and real estate, zoning, and fair housing laws.

Some brokers and agents become active in community organizations and local real estate organizations to broaden their contacts and increase their sales.

The following are examples of types of real estate brokers and sales agents:

Real estate brokers are licensed to manage their own businesses. As independent businesspeople, brokers often sell real estate owned by others. In addition to helping clients buy and sell properties, they may help rent or manage properties for a fee. Many operate a real estate office, handling business details and overseeing the work of sales agents.

Real estate sales agents must work with a broker. Sales agents often work for brokers on a contract basis, earning a portion of the commission from each property they sell.

Work Environment

Real estate brokers held about 127,200 jobs in 2022. The largest employers of real estate brokers were as follows:

Real estate brokers and sales agents show properties to prospective buyers.

Real estate brokers and sales agents often find new clients through referrals.

Self-employed workers	58%
Real estate and rental and leasing	39

Real estate sales agents held about 462,600 jobs in 2022. The largest employers of real estate sales agents were as follows:

Self-employed workers	57%
Real estate and rental and leasing	35
Construction	3

Workplace size for real estate brokers and sales agents ranges from a one-person business to a large firm with numerous branch offices. Many brokers have franchise agreements with national or regional real estate companies. Under this arrangement, the broker pays a fee to be affiliated with a widely known real estate organization.

Real estate brokers and sales agents typically work in an office setting. However, they spend much of their time away from their desks to show properties, see properties, and meet with current or prospective clients.

Work Schedules

Most real estate brokers and sales agents work full time, and some work more than 40 hours per week. Work schedules may vary and often include evenings and weekends to accommodate clients' schedules. Many brokers and sales agents spend a significant amount of time networking and attending community events to meet potential clients. Although they frequently work irregular hours, many are able to set their own schedules.

Some brokers and sales agents work part time.

How to Become a Real Estate Broker or Sales Agent

Real estate brokers and sales agents typically need a high school diploma or equivalent to enter the occupation. They also must complete a number of real estate courses and pass a licensing exam. States typically require licensed agents to have experience before obtaining a broker's license.

Education

In addition to having a high school diploma, real estate brokers and sales agents must complete some real estate courses to be eligible for licensure. Although most brokers and agents must take state-accredited prelicensing courses to become licensed, some states waive this requirement if the candidate has taken college courses in real estate.

Some community colleges and 4-year universities offer courses, degree programs, or certificate programs in real estate. These postsecondary credentials typically are not required, but many real estate brokers and sales agents have a bachelor's degree. Courses in finance, business administration, economics, and law also may be useful.

Prospective brokers who plan to open their own company may find it helpful to take business courses, such as marketing and accounting.

In addition to offering prelicensing courses, many real estate associations have courses and professional development programs for both beginners and experienced agents. These courses cover a variety of topics, such as real estate fundamentals, real estate law, and mortgage financing.

Licenses, Certifications, and Registrations

All states require real estate brokers and sales agents to be licensed. Minimum requirements for candidate licensure vary by state but typically include being at least age 18, having a high school diploma or equivalent, completing prelicensing courses, and passing an exam.

Some states have additional requirements, such as passing a background check. Licenses typically are not transferable between states. However, some states have reciprocity agreements that streamline the process for brokers and agents licensed in one state to get a license in another state.

For a broker's license, states typically require that candidates have a specified number of years of experience as a licensed sales agent and take additional formal training. In some states, a bachelor's degree may be substituted for some experience or training requirements.

State licenses typically must be renewed every 2 to 4 years. In most states, brokers and agents must complete continuing education courses to renew their license. Prospective brokers and agents should verify requirements with the real estate licensing commission of the state in which they wish to work.

Work Experience in a Related Occupation

Most states require that candidates for a broker's license have experience working as a licensed real estate sales agent. Requirements vary by state, but most require at least 2 years of experience.

Training

Real estate sales agents improve their skills through practice and repetition. Training varies depending on the real estate company. Some provide formal training, while others allow their agents to enter the field immediately after obtaining their license. In some states, agents must be sponsored by a broker while they are working to get their license.

Because of the sales environment and the complexity of real estate deals, new agents may observe and work closely with more senior agents. Larger real estate companies may provide formal classroom training for new agents as a way to gain knowledge and experience, while others provide training to employees studying for their real estate licensing exam.

The length of training also may vary, depending on the number of real estate transactions in which the agent takes part. Agents involved in a large number of home sales may have a shorter period of on-the-job training than agents involved in few transactions.

Advancement

Sales agents may advance by getting a broker's license. Brokers may open their own business or work as associate brokers to manage an independent office within a real estate company. Their responsibilities might include hiring, training, and assisting sales agents.

Important Qualities

Business skills. Because most real estate brokers and sales agents are self-employed, they must be able to manage every aspect of their business, including billing and advertising.

Interpersonal skills. Real estate brokers and sales agents spend much of their time interacting with others, such as clients and contractors. They must be pleasant, respectful, and dependable.

Organizational skills. Real estate brokers and sales agents must be able to manage their own time for planning and prioritizing their work.

Problem-solving skills. Real estate brokers and sales agents must be able to address concerns relating to a property. They also mediate negotiations between a seller and a buyer.

Self-motivated. Because they often have little or no supervision, real estate brokers and sales agents must be able to work independently.

Pay

The median annual wage for real estate brokers was $62,190 in May 2022. The median wage is the wage at which half the workers in an occupation earned more than that amount and half earned less. The lowest 10 percent earned less than $36,360, and the highest 10 percent earned more than $173,000.

The median annual wage for real estate sales agents was $49,980 in May 2022. The lowest 10 percent earned less than $29,130, and the highest 10 percent earned more than $113,320.

In May 2022, the median annual wages for real estate brokers in the top industries in which they worked were as follows:

Real estate and rental and leasing	$60,590

In May 2022, the median annual wages for real estate sales agents in the top industries in which they worked were as follows:

Construction	$56,200
Real estate and rental and leasing	47,930

Brokers and sales agents earn most of their income from commissions on sales. The commission varies by the type of property and its value. Commissions often are divided among the buying agent, selling agent, brokers, and firms.

An agent's income often depends on economic conditions, the agent's individual motivation, and the types of property available. Income usually increases as agents become more

Real Estate Brokers and Sales Agents

Median annual wages, May 2022

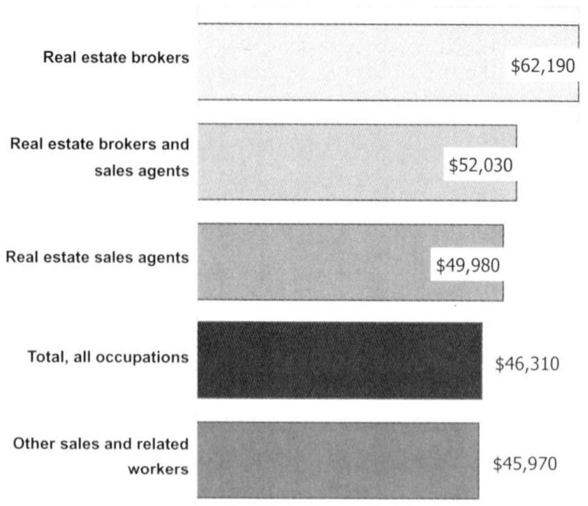

Real estate brokers $62,190
Real estate brokers and sales agents $52,030
Real estate sales agents $49,980
Total, all occupations $46,310
Other sales and related workers $45,970

Note: All Occupations includes all occupations in the U.S. Economy.
Source: U.S. Bureau of Labor Statistics, Occupational Employment and Wage Statistics.

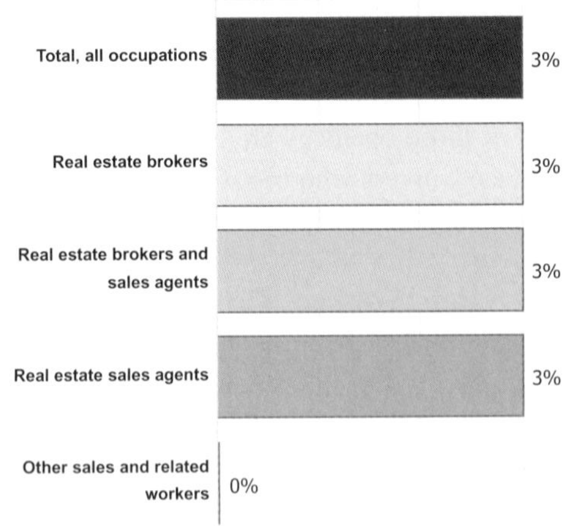

Note: All Occupations includes all occupations in the U.S. Economy.
Source: U.S. Bureau of Labor Statistics, Employment Projections program.

experienced at sales. Earnings may be irregular, especially for beginners, and agents sometimes go weeks or months without a sale.

Most real estate brokers and sales agents work full time, and some work more than 40 hours per week. Work schedules may vary and often include evenings and weekends to accommodate clients' schedules. Many brokers and sales agents spend a significant amount of time networking and attending community events to meet potential clients. Although they frequently work irregular hours, many are able to set their own schedules.

Some brokers and sales agents work part time.

Job Outlook

Overall employment of real estate brokers and sales agents is projected to grow 3 percent from 2022 to 2032, about as fast as the average for all occupations.

About 51,600 openings for real estate brokers and sales agents are projected each year, on average, over the decade. Many of those openings are expected to result from the need to replace workers who transfer to different occupations or exit the labor force, such as to retire.

Employment

There will be a continued demand for real estate brokers and sales agents because people turn to these workers when looking for a new home, relocating, or purchasing property for a business, among other reasons. Employment is projected to grow along with the real estate market.

Tighter credit regulations and increasing real estate prices may force some people to continue renting as opposed to entering the housing market, which may result in fewer new jobs for real estate brokers and sales agents.

The real estate market is highly sensitive to fluctuations in the economy, and projected employment of real estate brokers and agents varies accordingly. In periods of economic growth or stability, employment should grow to accommodate people looking to buy homes and commercial or retail space. Alternatively, during periods of declining economic activity or rising interest rates, the amount of work for brokers and agents often slows and employment may decline.

Occupational Title	SOC Code	Employment, 2022	Projected Employment, 2032	Change, 2022-32	
				Percent	Numeric
Real estate brokers and sales agents	41-9020	589,800	609,200	3	19,400
Real estate brokers	41-9021	127,200	131,600	3	4,400
Real estate sales agents	41-9022	462,600	477,600	3	14,900

Contacts for More Information

For more information, visit

- National Association of Real Estate Brokers
- National Association of Realtors

Retail Sales Workers

Summary

Quick Facts: Retail Sales Workers	
2022 Median Pay	$30,750 per year $14.79 per hour
Typical Entry-Level Education	No formal educational credential
Work Experience in a Related Occupation	None
On-the-job Training	See How to Become One
Number of Jobs, 2022	4,031,700
Job Outlook, 2022-32	-2% (Decline)
Employment Change, 2022-32	-76,600

What Retail Sales Workers Do
Retail sales workers help customers find products they want and process customers' payments.

Work Environment
Most retail sales workers work in clean, well-lit stores. Many sales workers work evenings and weekends. Some retail salespersons work part time.

How to Become a Retail Sales Worker
Typically, there are no formal education requirements for retail sales workers. Most receive on-the-job training, which usually lasts a few days to a few months.

Pay
The median hourly wage for parts salespersons was $17.21 in May 2022.

The median hourly wage for retail salespersons was $14.71 in May 2022.

Job Outlook
Overall employment of retail sales workers is projected to decline 2 percent from 2022 to 2032.

Despite declining employment, about 563,000 openings for retail sales workers are projected each year, on average, over the decade. All of those openings are expected to result from the need to replace workers who transfer to other occupations or exit the labor force, such as to retire.

What Retail Sales Workers Do
Retail sales workers help customers find products they want and process customers' payments. There are two types of retail sales workers: retail salespersons, who sell retail merchandise, such as clothing, furniture, and automobiles; and parts salespersons, who sell spare and replacement parts and equipment, especially car parts.

Duties
Retail sales workers typically do the following:

- Greet customers and offer them assistance
- Recommend merchandise based on customers' wants and needs
- Explain the use and benefit of merchandise to customers
- Answer customers' questions
- Show how merchandise works, if applicable
- Add up customers' total purchases and accept payment
- Inform customers about current sales, promotions, and policies about payments and exchanges

The following are examples of types of retail sales workers:

Retail salespersons work in stores where they sell goods, such as books, cars, clothing, cosmetics, electronics, furniture, lumber, plants, shoes, and many other types of merchandise.

In addition to helping customers find and select items to buy, many retail salespersons process the payment for the sale, which typically involves operating cash registers.

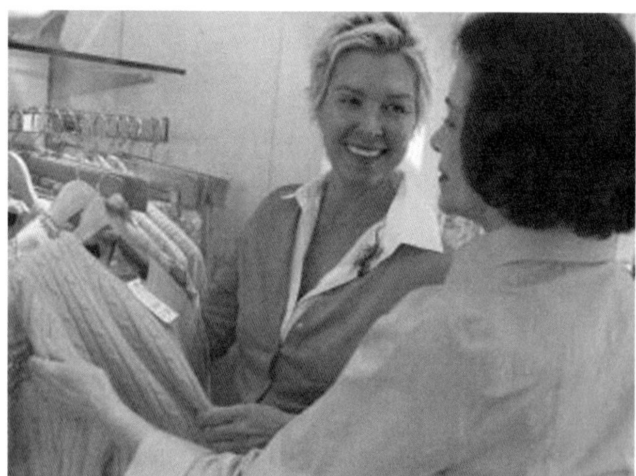

Retail sales workers help customers find the products they want and process customers' payments.

Retail sales workers maintain knowledge of current sales and promotions.

After taking payment for the purchases, retail salespersons may bag or package the purchases.

Depending on the hours they work, retail salespersons may have to open or close cash registers. This includes counting the money in the register and separating charge slips, coupons, and exchange vouchers. They may also make deposits at a cash office.

For information about other workers who receive and disburse money, see the profile on cashiers.

In addition, retail salespersons may help stock shelves or racks, arrange for mailing or delivery of purchases, mark price tags, take inventory, and prepare displays.

For some retail sales jobs, particularly those involving expensive and complex items, retail sales workers need special knowledge or skills. For example, those who sell cars must be able to explain the features of various models, manufacturers' specifications, different types of options on the car, financing available, and the details of associated warranties.

In addition, retail sales workers must recognize security risks and thefts and understand their organization's procedures for handling thefts, which may include notifying security guards or calling police.

Parts salespersons sell spare and replacement parts and equipment, especially car parts. Most work in either automotive parts stores or automobile dealerships. They take customers' orders, inform customers of part availability and price, and take inventory.

Retail sales workers often stand for long periods and may need supervisory approval to leave the sales floor.

Work Environment

Parts salespersons held about 266,100 jobs in 2022. The largest employers of parts salespersons were as follows:

Automotive parts, accessories, and tire retailers	44%
Automobile dealers	21
Wholesale trade	20
Repair and maintenance	5
Other motor vehicle dealers	4

Retail salespersons held about 3.8 million jobs in 2022. The largest employers of retail salespersons were as follows:

Clothing, clothing accessories, shoe, and jewelry retailers	17%
General merchandise retailers	17
Sporting goods, hobby, musical instrument, book, and miscellaneous retailers	15
Building material and garden equipment and supplies dealers	13
Furniture, home furnishings, electronics, and appliance retailers	8

Most retail sales work is performed in clean, well-lit stores. Retail sales workers spend most of their time interacting with customers, answering questions, and assisting them with purchases.

Workers often stand for long periods and may need permission from a supervisor to leave the sales floor. If they sell items such as cars, plants, or lumberyard materials, they may work outdoors.

Work Schedules

Many sales workers work evenings and weekends, particularly during holidays and other peak sales periods. Because the end-of-year holiday season is often the busiest time for retail stores, many employers limit retail sales workers' use of vacation time between November and the beginning of January.

Some retail salespersons work part time.

How to Become a Retail Sales Worker

Typically, there are no formal education requirements for retail sales workers. Most receive on-the-job training, which usually lasts a few days to a few months.

Education

Although retail or parts sales positions usually have no formal education requirements, some employers prefer applicants who have a high school diploma or equivalent, especially employers who sell technical products or "big-ticket" items, such as electronics or cars.

A friendly and outgoing personality is important for these workers, as the job requires almost constant interaction with people.

Training

Most retail sales workers receive on-the-job training, which usually lasts a few days to a few months. In small stores, an experienced employee often trains newly hired workers. In large stores, training programs are more formal and usually conducted over several days.

During training sessions, topics often include customer service, security, the store's policies and procedures, and how to operate the cash register.

Depending on the type of product they are selling, employees may be given additional specialized training. For example, salespersons working in cosmetics get instruction on the types of products the store offers and for whom the cosmetics would be most beneficial. Likewise, those who sell auto parts may be instructed on the technical functions of various parts, in addition to sales technique.

Because providing exceptional service to customers is a priority for many employers, employees often get periodic training to update and refine their skills.

Advancement

Retail sales workers typically have opportunities to advance to supervisory or managerial positions. Some employers want candidates for managerial positions to have a college degree.

As sales workers gain experience and seniority, they often move into positions that have greater responsibility and may be given their choice of departments in which to work. This opportunity often means moving to positions with higher potential earnings and commissions. The highest earnings potential usually involves selling "big-ticket" items, such as cars, jewelry, furniture, and electronics. These positions often require workers with extensive knowledge of the product and excellent sales skills.

Important Qualities

Customer-service skills. Retail sales workers must be responsive to the wants and needs of customers. They should explain the product options available to customers and make appropriate recommendations.

Interpersonal skills. A friendly and outgoing personality is important for these workers because the job requires almost constant interaction with people.

Math skills. Retail sales workers must have the ability to calculate price totals, discounts, and change owed to customers.

Persistence. A large number of attempted sales may not be successful, so sales workers should not be discouraged easily. They must start each new sales attempt with a positive attitude.

Selling skills. Retail sales workers must be persuasive when interacting with customers. They must clearly and effectively explain the benefits of the merchandise.

Pay

The median hourly wage for parts salespersons was $17.21 in May 2022. The median wage is the wage at which half the workers in an occupation earned more than that amount and half earned less. The lowest 10 percent earned less than $11.31, and the highest 10 percent earned more than $28.40.

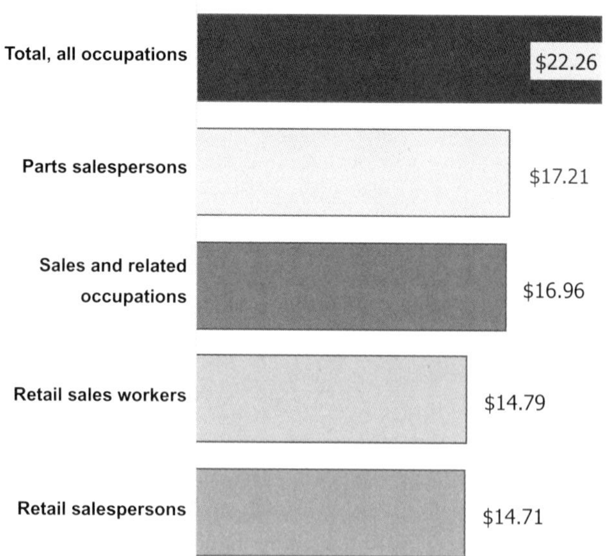

The median hourly wage for retail salespersons was $14.71 in May 2022. The lowest 10 percent earned less than $10.86, and the highest 10 percent earned more than $22.69.

In May 2022, the median hourly wages for parts salespersons in the top industries in which they worked were as follows:

Wholesale trade	$21.79
Repair and maintenance	20.73
Automobile dealers	18.59
Other motor vehicle dealers	17.57
Automotive parts, accessories, and tire retailers	14.31

In May 2022, the median hourly wages for retail salespersons in the top industries in which they worked were as follows:

Furniture, home furnishings, electronics, and appliance retailers	$16.47
Building material and garden equipment and supplies dealers	15.36
General merchandise retailers	14.79
Sporting goods, hobby, musical instrument, book, and miscellaneous retailers	14.06
Clothing, clothing accessories, shoe, and jewelry retailers	13.63

Compensation systems vary by type of establishment and merchandise sold. Retail sales workers get hourly wages, commissions, or a combination of the two. Under a commission system, they get a percentage of the sales they make. This system offers sales workers the opportunity to increase their earnings considerably, but they may find that their earnings depend strongly on their ability to sell their product and on the ups and downs of the economy. Commissions are most common for retail sales workers selling "big-ticket" items, such as cars or electronics.

Many retail sales workers work evenings and weekends, particularly during holidays and other peak sales periods. Because the end-of-year holiday season is often the busiest time for retail stores, many employers limit sales workers' use of vacation time between November and the beginning of January.

Some retail salespersons work part time.

Job Outlook

Overall employment of retail sales workers is projected to decline 2 percent from 2022 to 2032.

Despite declining employment, about 563,000 openings for retail sales workers are projected each year, on average, over the decade. All of those openings are expected to result from the need to replace workers who transfer to other occupations or exit the labor force, such as to retire.

Employment

The increase in online sales is expected to continue over the projections decade, limiting growth in the number of physical retail stores and reducing demand for retail sales workers. Projected employment of retail sales workers varies by occupation (see table).

Retail Sales Workers

Percent change in employment, projected 2022-32

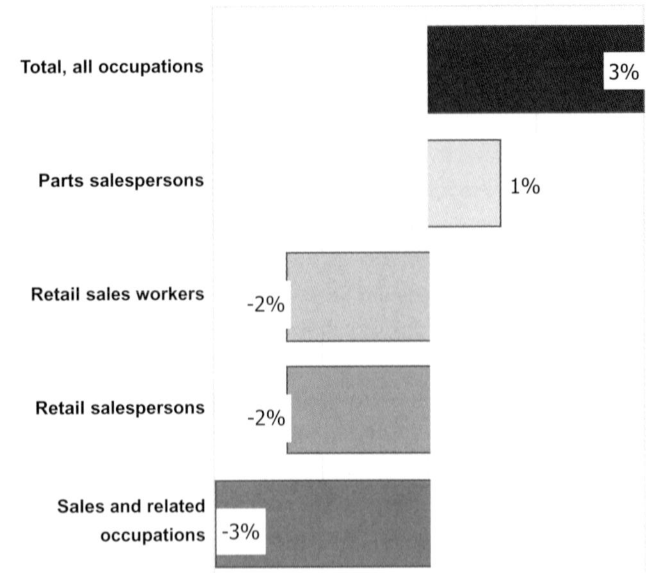

Note: All Occupations includes all occupations in the U.S. Economy.
Source: U.S. Bureau of Labor Statistics, Employment Projections program.

Competition from e-commerce is expected to reduce demand for retail salespersons. However, brick-and-mortar retail stores may increase their emphasis on customer service as a way to compete with online sellers. And cost pressures may lead retailers to hire workers who can perform a broad range of tasks, such as helping customers find items, operating a cash register, and restocking shelves. Because retail salespersons provide this versatile range of services, and because many consumers are still expected to visit physical stores, retail salespersons should continue to be needed to help customers and to complete sales.

Demand for car parts and parts salespersons is expected to continue as growing numbers of older cars require repairs. Moreover, demand for ride-hailing services has shifted some public transportation use back to automobiles services, further adding to the need for car parts in upkeep and maintenance, which should support demand for parts salespersons.

Occupational Title	SOC Code	Employment, 2022	Projected Employment, 2032	Change, 2022-32	
				Percent	Numeric
Retail sales workers	—	4,031,700	3,955,100	-2	-76,600
Parts salespersons	41-2022	266,100	268,700	1	2,600
Retail salespersons	41-2031	3,765,600	3,686,400	-2	-79,100

Contacts for More Information

For more information, visit

- National Retail Federation
- Retail Industry Leaders Association
- National Automobile Dealers Association

Sales Engineers

Summary

Quick Facts: Sales Engineers	
2021 Median Pay	$103,710 per year $49.86 per hour
Typical Entry-Level Education	Bachelor's degree
Work Experience in a Related Occupation	None
On-the-job Training	Moderate-term on-the-job training
Number of Jobs, 2021	60,700
Job Outlook, 2021-31	6% (As fast as average)
Employment Change, 2021-31	3,400

What Sales Engineers Do
Sales engineers sell complex scientific and technological products or services to businesses.

Work Environment
Sales engineers often work under stressful conditions because their income and job security depend on commission from successfully completing sales. Some sales engineers may work additional and irregular hours to meet sales goals and client needs.

How to Become a Sales Engineer
To enter the occupation, sales engineers typically need a bachelor's degree in engineering or a related field. Successful sales engineers combine technical knowledge of the products or services they are selling with strong interpersonal skills.

Pay
The median annual wage for sales engineers was $103,710 in May 2021.

Job Outlook
Employment of sales engineers is projected to grow 6 percent from 2021 to 2031, about as fast as the average for all occupations.

About 6,900 openings for sales engineers are projected each year, on average, over the decade. Many of those openings are expected to result from the need to replace workers who transfer to different occupations or exit the labor force, such as to retire.

What Sales Engineers Do
Sales engineers sell complex scientific and technological products or services to businesses. They must have extensive knowledge of the products' parts and functions and must understand the scientific processes that make these products work.

Duties
Sales engineers typically do the following:

- Prepare and deliver technical presentations explaining products or services to existing and prospective customers
- Talk with customers and engineers to assess equipment needs and to determine system requirements
- Collaborate with sales teams to understand customer requirements and provide sales support
- Secure and renew orders and arrange delivery
- Plan and modify products to meet customer needs
- Help clients solve problems with installed equipment
- Recommend improved materials or machinery to customers, showing how changes will lower costs or increase production
- Help in researching and developing new products

Sales engineers specialize in technologically and scientifically advanced products. They use their technical skills to explain the benefits of their products or services to potential customers and to show how their products or services are better than their competitors'. Some sales engineers work for the companies that design and build technical products. Others work for independent sales firms.

Many of the duties of sales engineers are similar to those of other salespersons. They must interest the client in buying their products or services, negotiate a price, and complete the sale. To do this, sales engineers give technical presentations during

Sales engineers sell complex scientific and technological products or services to businesses.

Sales engineers specialize in technologically and scientifically advanced products.

which they explain the technical aspects of the product and how it will solve a specific customer problem.

Some sales engineers team with other salespersons, such as wholesale and manufacturing sales representatives, who concentrate on marketing and selling the product, which lets the sales engineer concentrate on the technical aspects of the job. By working as part of a sales team, each member is able to focus on his or her strengths and expertise.

In addition to giving technical presentations, sales engineers are increasingly doing other tasks related to sales, such as market research. They also may ask for technical requirements from customers and modify and adjust products to meet customers' specific needs. Some sales engineers work with research and development (R&D) departments to help identify and develop new products.

Work Environment

Sales engineers held about 60,700 jobs in 2021. The largest employers of sales engineers were as follows:

Manufacturing	23%
Merchant wholesalers, durable goods	20
Computer systems design and related services	19
Wholesale electronic markets and agents and brokers	5
Telecommunications	5

Some sales engineers have large territories and travel extensively. Because sales regions may cover several states, sales engineers may be away from home for several days or even weeks at a time. Other sales engineers cover a smaller region and spend only a few nights away from home.

Sales engineers may encounter stress because their income and job security often depend directly on their success in sales and customer service.

Work Schedules

Most sales engineers work full time. Some may work additional and irregular hours to meet sales goals and client needs.

Sales engineers often give presentations in which they describe the technical aspects of a product and explain how it will solve a specific customer problem.

How to Become a Sales Engineer

To enter the occupation, sales engineers typically need a bachelor's degree. Successful sales engineers combine technical knowledge of the products or services they are selling with strong interpersonal skills.

Education

Sales engineers typically need a bachelor's degree in engineering or a related field, such as business. However, candidates who do not have a degree sometimes meet qualifications if they have sales experience and technical experience or training.

College engineering programs generally require 4 years of study. They vary in content, but all programs include courses in math and the physical sciences. In addition, most programs require developing strong computer skills.

Most engineering programs require students to choose an area of specialization. The most common majors are electrical, mechanical, or civil engineering, but some engineering departments offer additional majors, such as chemical, biomedical, or computer hardware engineering. However, some undergraduate programs offer a general engineering curriculum; students then specialize in a particular area either on the job or in graduate school.

Training

New graduates with engineering degrees typically need sales experience and training before they can work independently as sales engineers. Training covers general sales techniques and may involve teaming with a sales mentor who is familiar with the employer's business practices, customers, procedures, and company culture. After the training period, sales engineers may continue to partner with someone who lacks technical skills yet excels in the art of sales.

It is important for sales engineers to continue their engineering and sales education throughout their careers. Much of their value to their employers depends on their knowledge of, and ability to sell, the latest technologies. Sales engineers

Successful sales engineers will have a combination of technical knowledge of the products they are selling and strong interpersonal skills.

in high-technology fields, such as information technology and advanced electronics, may find that their technical knowledge rapidly becomes obsolete, requiring frequent retraining.

Advancement

Promotions may include a higher commission rate, a larger sales territory, or elevation to the position of supervisor or sales manager.

Important Qualities

Interpersonal skills. Strong interpersonal skills are a valuable characteristic for sales engineers, both for building relationships with clients and effectively communicating with other members of the sales team.

Problem-solving skills. Sales engineers must be able to listen to the customer's desires and concerns, and then recommend solutions, such as customizing a product for the customer.

Self-confidence. Sales engineers should be confident and persuasive when making sales presentations.

Technological skills. Sales engineers must have extensive knowledge of the technologically sophisticated products they sell in order to explain their advantages and answer questions.

Pay

The median annual wage for sales engineers was $103,710 in May 2021. The median wage is the wage at which half the workers in an occupation earned more than that amount and half earned less. The lowest 10 percent earned less than $62,300, and the highest 10 percent earned more than $182,850.

In May 2021, the median annual wages for sales engineers in the top industries in which they worked were as follows:

Computer systems design and related services	$127,180
Telecommunications	116,480
Wholesale electronic markets and agents and brokers	103,840
Merchant wholesalers, durable goods	102,130
Manufacturing	101,590

How much a sales engineer earns varies considerably by the type of firm and the product sold. Most employers offer a combination of salary and commission payments or salary plus a bonus. Some sales engineers who work for independent sales companies earn only commissions.

Commissions are usually based on the value of sales. Bonuses may depend on individual performance, on the performance of all workers in the group or district, or on the company's performance. Earnings from commissions and bonuses may vary from year to year depending on sales ability, the demand for the company's products or services, and the overall economy.

In addition to their earnings, sales engineers who work for manufacturers are usually reimbursed for expenses such as transportation, meals, hotels, and customer entertainment.

Most sales engineers work full time. Some may work additional and irregular hours to meet sales goals and client needs.

Job Outlook

Employment of sales engineers is projected to grow 6 percent from 2021 to 2031, about as fast as the average for all occupations.

About 6,900 openings for sales engineers are projected each year, on average, over the decade. Many of those openings are expected to result from the need to replace workers who transfer to different occupations or exit the labor force, such as to retire.

Employment

Sales engineers are expected to be in demand to help promote an increasing number of technologically sophisticated products and services.

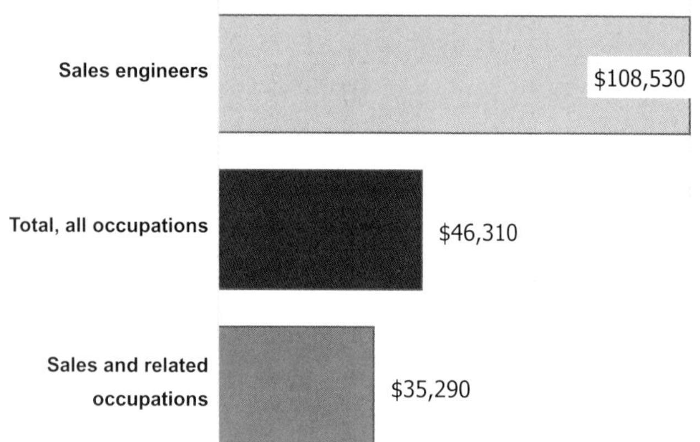

Note: All Occupations includes all occupations in the U.S. Economy.
Source: U.S. Bureau of Labor Statistics, Employment Projections program.

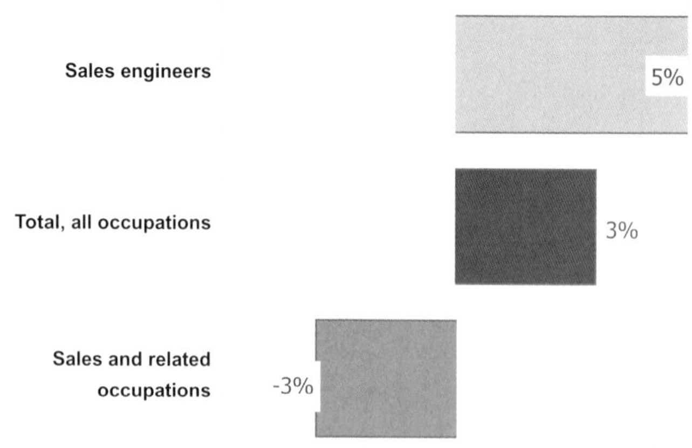

Note: All Occupations includes all occupations in the U.S. Economy.
Source: U.S. Bureau of Labor Statistics, Occupational Employment and Wage Statistics.

Employment growth is likely to be strong for sales engineers selling computer software and hardware. Strong industry growth is expected in computer systems design and related services, contributing to employment growth in the occupation.

Occupational Title	SOC Code	Employment, 2021	Projected Employment, 2031	Change, 2021-31	
				Percent	Numeric
Sales engineers	41-9031	60,700	64,100	6	3,400

Contacts for More Information

For more information, visit

- Manufacturers' Agents National Association (MANA)
- Manufacturers' Representatives Educational Research Foundation (MRERF)

Securities, Commodities, and Financial Services Sales Agents

Summary

Quick Facts: Securities, Commodities, and Financial Services Sales Agents

2022 Median Pay	$67,480 per year $32.44 per hour
Typical Entry-Level Education	Bachelor's degree
Work Experience in a Related Occupation	None
On-the-job Training	Moderate-term on-the-job training
Number of Jobs, 2022	482,200
Job Outlook, 2022-32	7% (Faster than average)
Employment Change, 2022-32	35,600

What Securities, Commodities, and Financial Services Sales Agents Do

Securities, commodities, and financial services sales agents connect buyers and sellers in financial markets.

Work Environment

Securities, commodities, and financial services sales agents work in high-stress environments and often work more than 40 hours per week.

Securities, commodities, and financial services sales agents connect buyers and sellers in financial markets.

How to Become a Securities, Commodities, or Financial Services Sales Agent

Securities, commodities, and financial services sales agents typically need a bachelor's degree for entry-level jobs. A master's degree in business administration (MBA) is useful for advancement.

Pay

The median annual wage for securities, commodities, and financial services sales agents was $67,480 in May 2022.

Job Outlook

Employment of securities, commodities, and financial services sales agents is projected to grow 7 percent from 2022 to 2032, faster than the average for all occupations.

About 40,100 openings for securities, commodities, and financial services sales agents are projected each year, on average, over the decade. Many of those openings are expected to result from the need to replace workers who transfer to different occupations or exit the labor force, such as to retire.

What Securities, Commodities, and Financial Services Sales Agents Do

Securities, commodities, and financial services sales agents connect buyers and sellers in financial markets. They sell

Securities, commodities, and financial services sales agents spend much of the day interacting with people, whether selling stock to an individual or discussing the status of a merger deal with a company executive.

securities to individuals, advise companies in search of investors, and conduct trades.

Duties

Securities, commodities, and financial services sales agents typically do the following:

- Contact prospective clients to present information and explain available services
- Offer advice on the purchase or sale of particular securities
- Buy and sell securities, such as stocks and bonds
- Buy and sell commodities, such as corn, oil, and gold
- Monitor financial markets and the performance of individual securities
- Analyze company finances to provide recommendations for public offerings, mergers, and acquisitions
- Evaluate cost and revenue of agreements

Securities, commodities, and financial services sales agents deal with a wide range of products and clients. Agents spend much of the day interacting with people, whether selling stock to an individual or discussing the status of a merger deal with a company executive. The work is usually stressful because agents deal with large amounts of money and have time constraints.

A security or commodity can be traded in two ways: electronically or in an auction-style setting on the floor of an exchange market. Markets such as the National Association of Securities Dealers Automated Quotation system (NASDAQ) use vast computer networks rather than human traders to match buyers and sellers. Others, such as the New York Stock Exchange (NYSE), rely on floor brokers to complete transactions.

The following are examples of types of securities, commodities, and financial services sales agents:

Brokers sell securities and commodities directly to individual clients. They advise people on appropriate investments based on the client's needs and financial ability. The people they advise may have very different levels of expertise in financial matters.

Finding clients is a large part of a broker's job. They must create their own client base by calling from a list of potential clients. Some agents network by joining social groups, and others may rely on referrals from satisfied clients.

Investment bankers connect businesses that need money to finance their operations or expansion plans with investors who are interested in providing that funding. This process is called underwriting, and it is the main function of investment banks. The banks first sell their advisory services to help companies issue new stocks or bonds, and then the banks sell the issued securities to investors.

Some of the most important services that investment bankers provide are initial public offerings (IPOs), and mergers and acquisitions. An IPO is the process by which a company becomes open for public investment by issuing its first stock. Investment bankers must estimate how much the company is worth and ensure that it meets the legal requirements to become publicly traded.

Investment bankers also connect companies in mergers (when two companies join together) and acquisitions (when one company buys another). Investment bankers provide advice throughout the process to ensure that the transaction goes smoothly.

Investment banking sales agents and traders carry out buy and sell orders for stocks, bonds, and commodities from clients and make trades on behalf of the firm itself. Investment banks primarily employ these workers, although some work for commercial banks, hedge funds, and private equity groups. Because markets fluctuate so much, trading is a split-second decisionmaking process. Slight changes in the price of a trade can greatly affect its profitability, making the trader's decision extremely important.

Floor brokers work directly on the floor—a large room where trading is done—of a securities or commodities exchange. After a trader places an order for a security, floor brokers negotiate the price, make the sale, and forward the purchase price to the trader.

Financial services sales agents consult on a wide variety of banking, securities, insurance, and related services to individuals and businesses, often catering the services to meet the client's financial needs. They contact potential clients to explain their services, which may include the handling of checking accounts, loans, certificates of deposit, individual retirement accounts, credit cards, and estate and retirement planning.

Work Environment

Securities, commodities, and financial services sales agents held about 482,200 jobs in 2022. The largest employers of securities, commodities, and financial services sales agents were as follows:

Credit intermediation and related activities	54%
Securities, commodity contracts, and other financial investments and related activities	33

Electronic trading is changing the exchange floor environment, with more traders carrying out orders behind a desk and fewer working on the exchange floor.

Self-employed workers	6
Management of companies and enterprises	3

Most securities, commodities, and financial services sales agents work many hours under stressful conditions. The pace of work is fast, and managers are usually demanding of their workers, because both commissions and advancements are tied to sales.

Investment bankers travel extensively because they frequently work with companies in other countries.

Because computers can conduct trades faster than people can, electronic trading is quickly replacing verbal auction-style trades on exchange floors. The environment of the stock exchange is changing as a result, with more traders carrying out orders behind a desk and fewer working on the exchange floor.

Because most of the major investment banks are in New York City, employment of securities, commodities, and financial services sales agents is concentrated in that metropolitan area.

Work Schedules

Securities, commodities, and financial services sales agents usually work full time and some work more than 40 hours per week. In addition, they may work evenings and weekends because many of their clients work during the day.

How to Become a Securities, Commodities, or Financial Services Sales Agent

Securities, commodities, and financial services sales agents typically need a bachelor's degree for entry-level jobs. A master's degree in business administration (MBA) is useful for advancement.

Education

Securities, commodities, and financial services sales agents typically need a bachelor's degree to enter the occupation. A common field of degree is business, which usually includes coursework in topics such as finance, accounting, and economics. Summer internships often provide useful experience, and employers may prefer to hire candidates who have worked as interns.

Numerous agents eventually get a master's degree in business administration (MBA), which is often a requirement for high-level positions in the securities industry. Because the MBA exposes students to real-world business practices, it can be a major asset for jobseekers. Employers often reward MBA holders with higher level positions, better compensation, and large signing bonuses.

Brokers and investment bankers must register as representatives of their firm with the Financial Industry Regulatory Authority (FINRA).

Training

Most employers provide intensive on-the-job training, teaching employees the specifics of the job, such as the products and services offered. Trainees in large firms may receive technical instruction in securities analysis and selling strategies. Firms often rotate their trainees among various departments to give them a broad understanding of the securities business.

Securities, commodities, and financial services sales agents must keep up with new products and services and other developments. They attend conferences and training seminars regularly.

Licenses, Certifications, and Registrations

Brokers and investment bankers must register as representatives of their firm with the Financial Industry Regulatory Authority (FINRA). To obtain the license, potential agents must pass a series of exams.

Many other licenses are available, each of which gives the holder the right to sell different investment products and services. Traders and some other sales representatives also need licenses, although these vary by firm and specialization. Financial services sales agents may need to be licensed, especially if they sell securities or insurance. Most firms offer training to help their employees pass the licensing exams.

Agents who are registered with FINRA must attend continuing education classes to keep their licenses. Courses consist of computer-based training on legal requirements or new financial products or services.

Although not always required, certification enhances professional standing and is recommended by employers. Brokers, investment bankers, and financial services sales agents can earn the Chartered Financial Analyst (CFA) certification, sponsored by the CFA Institute. To qualify for this certification, applicants need a bachelor's degree or 4 years of related work experience and must pass three exams, which require several hundred hours of independent study. Applicants also must have an international passport. Exams cover subjects in accounting, economics, securities analysis, financial markets and instruments, corporate finance, asset valuation, and portfolio management. Applicants can take the exams while they are getting the required work experience.

Advancement

Securities, commodities, and financial services sales agents usually advance to senior positions in a firm by accumulating a greater number of accounts. Although beginners often service the accounts of individual investors, they may eventually service large institutional accounts, such as those of banks and retirement funds. Getting an MBA may also help advancement opportunities.

After taking a series of tests, some brokers become portfolio managers and have greater authority to make investment decisions regarding an account.

Some experienced sales agents become branch office managers and supervise other sales agents while continuing to provide services for their own clients. A few agents advance to top management positions or become partners in their firms.

Many investment banks use an "up or out" policy, in which entry-level investment bankers are either promoted or terminated after 2 or 3 years. Investment banks use this policy to ensure that entry-level positions are not occupied long term, allowing the bank to bring in new workers.

Important Qualities

Analytical skills. To judge the profitability of potential deals, securities, commodities, and financial services sales agents must have strong analytical skills. This includes computer programming skills which they use to analyze financial products.

Customer-service skills. Securities, commodities, and financial services sales agents must be persuasive and make clients feel comfortable with the agent's recommendations.

Decision-making skills. Investment banking traders must make split-second decisions, with large sums of money at stake.

Detail oriented. Investment bankers must pay close attention to the details of initial public offerings and mergers and acquisitions because small changes can have large consequences.

Initiative. Securities, commodities, and financial services sales agents must create their own client base by making "cold" sales calls to people to whom they have not been referred and to people not expecting the call.

Math skills. Securities, commodities, and financial services sales agents need to be familiar with mathematical tools, including investment formulas.

Pay

The median annual wage for securities, commodities, and financial services sales agents was $67,480 in May 2022. The median wage is the wage at which half the workers in an occupation earned more than that amount and half earned less. The lowest 10 percent earned less than $40,200, and the highest 10 percent earned more than $189,620.

In May 2022, the median annual wages for securities, commodities, and financial services sales agents in the top industries in which they worked were as follows:

Securities, Commodities, and Financial Services Sales Agents

Median annual wages, May 2022

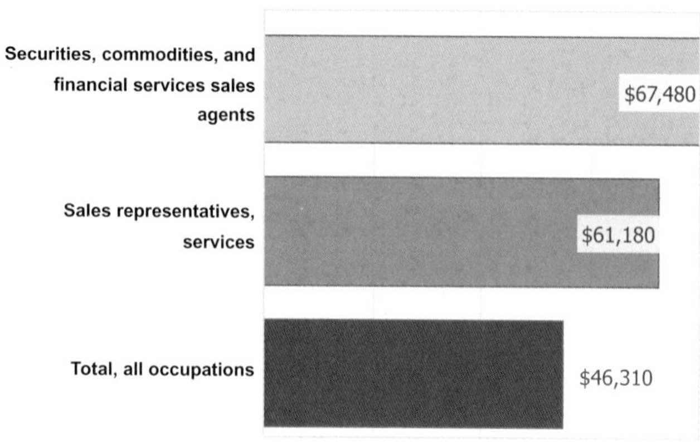

Note: All Occupations includes all occupations in the U.S. Economy.
Source: U.S. Bureau of Labor Statistics, Occupational Employment and Wage Statistics.

Securities, commodity contracts, and other financial investments and related activities	$91,420
Management of companies and enterprises	84,380
Credit intermediation and related activities	57,940

Many securities and commodities brokers earn a commission based on the monetary value of the products they sell. Most firms pay brokers a minimum salary in addition to commissions.

Trainee brokers usually earn a salary until they develop a client base. The salary gradually decreases in favor of commissions as the broker gains clients.

Investment bankers in corporate finance and mergers and acquisitions generally earn a base salary with the opportunity to earn a substantial bonus. At higher levels, bonuses far exceed base salary.

Securities, commodities, and financial services sales agents usually work full time and some work more than 40 hours per week. In addition, they may work evenings and weekends because many of their clients work during the day.

Job Outlook

Employment of securities, commodities, and financial services sales agents is projected to grow 7 percent from 2022 to 2032, faster than the average for all occupations.

About 40,100 openings for securities, commodities, and financial services sales agents are projected each year, on average, over the decade. Many of those openings are expected to result from the need to replace workers who transfer to different occupations or exit the labor force, such as to retire.

Employment

Services that investment bankers provide, such as helping with initial public offerings and mergers and acquisitions, will continue to be in demand as the economy grows. The United States

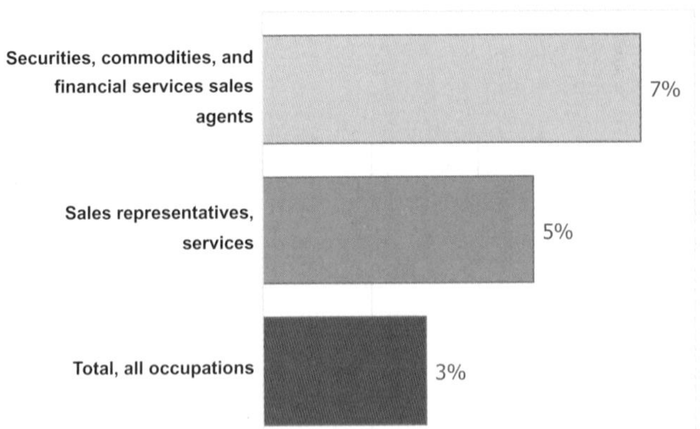

Note: All Occupations includes all occupations in the U.S. Economy.
Source: U.S. Bureau of Labor Statistics, Employment Projections program.

remains an international financial center, meaning that the economic growth of countries around the world will contribute to employment growth in the U.S. financial industry. An aging population and the decline of traditional pensions may boost demand for these workers, as individuals approaching retirement seek brokers to facilitate securities purchases.

However, automated trading systems have reduced demand for securities traders. Because simpler stock purchases can be made online without a broker, financial firms will focus on hiring sales agents with specialized areas of expertise and strong customer-service skills.

Occupational Title	SOC Code	Employment, 2022	Projected Employment, 2032	Change, 2022-32	
				Percent	Numeric
Securities, commodities, and financial services sales agents	41-3031	482,200	517,700	7	35,600

Contacts for More Information

For more information, visit

- Securities Industry and Financial Markets Association (SIFMA)
- Financial Industry Regulatory Authority (FINRA)
- CFA Institute

Travel Agents

Summary

Quick Facts: Travel Agents	
2022 Median Pay	$46,400 per year $22.31 per hour
Typical Entry-Level Education	High school diploma or equivalent
Work Experience in a Related Occupation	None
On-the-job Training	Moderate-term on-the-job training
Number of Jobs, 2022	66,300
Job Outlook, 2022-32	3% (As fast as average)
Employment Change, 2022-32	2,300

What Travel Agents Do

Travel agents sell transportation, lodging, and entertainment activities to individuals and groups planning trips.

Work Environment

Travel agents typically spend much of their day sitting, working on the phone and on the computer. Most travel agents work for travel agencies; many are self-employed.

How to Become a Travel Agent

A high school diploma typically is required for someone to become a travel agent. However, employers may prefer to hire candidates who have sales experience or relevant certification or education. Good communication and customer service skills are essential.

Pay

The median annual wage for travel agents was $46,400 in May 2022.

Job Outlook

Employment of travel agents is projected to grow 3 percent from 2022 to 2032, about as fast as the average for all occupations.

Travel agents sell transportation, lodging, and admission to activities to those planning trips.

About 8,600 openings for travel agents are projected each year, on average, over the decade. Many of those openings are expected to result from the need to replace workers who transfer to different occupations or exit the labor force, such as to retire.

What Travel Agents Do

Travel agents sell transportation, lodging, and admission to entertainment activities to individuals and groups planning trips. They offer advice on destinations, plan trip itineraries, and make travel arrangements for clients.

Duties

Travel agents typically do the following:

- Arrange travel for business and vacation clients
- Determine clients' needs and preferences, such as schedules and costs
- Plan and arrange tour packages, excursions, and day trips
- Find fare and schedule information
- Calculate total travel costs
- Book reservations for travel, hotels, rental cars, and special events, such as tours and excursions
- Describe trips to clients and advise about local customs and attractions
- Give details on required documents, such as passports and visas, and on complying with cross-border entry requirements, such as health and safety protocols
- Make alternative booking arrangements if changes arise before or during the trip

Travel agents sort through vast amounts of information to find and arrange the best trip options for travelers. In addition, resorts and specialty groups use travel agents to promote vacation packages to their clients.

Travel agents may visit destinations to get firsthand experience so that they can make recommendations to clients. They visit hotels, resorts, and restaurants to evaluate the comfort, cleanliness, and quality of establishments. Self-employed travel agents may have additional responsibilities related to running their business, such as recordkeeping, managing staff, and marketing. However, travel agents most of their time talking with clients, promoting tours, and contacting airlines and hotels to make travel accommodations.

The following are examples of types of travel agents:

Leisure travel agents sell vacation packages to the public. They are responsible for arranging trip itineraries based on clients' interests and budget. Leisure travel agents often focus on a specific geographic area or type of travel, such as adventure tours. Some cater to a specific group, such as students or single people.

Corporate travel agents, also called travel coordinators, primarily make travel arrangements for businesses. They book transportation and accommodations for an organization's employees who are traveling to conduct business or attend conferences.

Work Environment

Travel agents held about 66,300 jobs in 2022. The largest employers of travel agents were as follows:

Travel arrangement and reservation services	62%
Self-employed workers	18

Travel agents typically spend much of their day sitting, working on the phone and on the computer. Agents may face stress during travel emergencies or unanticipated schedule changes.

Work Schedules

Most travel agents work full time, although part-time work is common. Some work additional hours during peak travel times or when they must accommodate clients' schedule changes and last-minute needs.

Travel agents offer advice on destinations, plan trip itineraries, and make travel arrangements for clients.

Travel agents work in an office environment where they spend much of their time on the phone.

Good communication and computer skills are essential for travel agents.

How to Become a Travel Agent

A high school diploma typically is required to become a travel agent. However, employers may prefer to hire candidates who have sales experience or relevant certification or education. Communication and customer service skills are essential.

Education

Travel agents typically need at least a high school diploma to enter the occupation, but employers may prefer to hire candidates who have a college degree or who have taken courses related to the travel industry.

Community colleges, vocational schools, and industry associations may offer technical training, certificates, or continuing education in professional travel planning. In addition, some 4-year colleges offer degrees in travel and tourism. Courses usually focus on reservations systems, marketing, and regulations regarding international travel.

Training

Employers in the travel industry typically provide on-the-job training that lasts at least 1 month. This training covers topics such as how to operate computer systems that are used in the industry. For example, a travel agent could be trained to work with a reservation system used by several airlines.

Licenses, Certifications, and Registrations

High school graduates with limited experience may demonstrate competence by taking the Travel Agent Proficiency (TAP) test. The test has no eligibility requirements, but study and preparation may be required. The test is administered by The Travel Institute.

The Travel Institute also provides training and professional credentials for travel agents at three different experience levels. These credentialing programs are the Certified Travel Associate (CTA), Certified Travel Counselor (CTC), and Certified Travel Industry Executive (CTIE). To maintain the credential, each program requires continuing education annually.

The American Society of Travel Advisors (ASTA) offers credentialing and educational programs for those seeking to become a travel agent. ASTA offers the Verified Travel Advisor (VTA) program and the ASTA Roadmap to Becoming a Travel Advisor.

The Cruise Lines International Association (CLIA) offers four levels of certification: Certified (CCC), Accredited (ACC), Master (MCC), and Elite Cruise Counselor (ECC). Each level requires a certain amount of training and product knowledge.

Some states require travel agents to have a business license, to register with the state, or to meet other conditions. Requirements vary by state. Contact individual state licensing agencies for more information.

Other Experience

Some agencies prefer to hire travel agents who have extensive traveling experience. These agencies especially prefer travel agents who focus on particular destinations or types of travelers, such as groups with a special interest or corporate travelers. Agencies also may prefer to hire travel agents who have sales experience.

Important Qualities

Communication skills. Travel agents must listen to clients' travel needs and offer travel advice and information that meet those needs.

Customer-service skills. Travel agents must be able to interact with clients and respond to questions and complaints in a friendly, professional manner.

Detail oriented. Travel agents must ensure that the reservations they make are for the dates, times, and locations that match travelers' schedules.

Organizational skills. Travel agents often work on itineraries for many clients at once. Ability to keep information in order and to ensure that bills and receipts are processed in a timely manner is essential.

Sales skills. Travel agents must be able to persuade clients to buy transportation, lodging, or tours.

Pay

The median annual wage for travel agents was $46,400 in May 2022. The median wage is the wage at which half the workers in an occupation earned more than that amount and half earned less. The lowest 10 percent earned less than $29,650, and the highest 10 percent earned more than $64,100.

In May 2022, the median annual wages for travel agents in the top industries in which they worked were as follows:

Travel arrangement and reservation services.....	$45,370

These wage data include money earned from commissions. Earnings for many travel agents depend on commissions and service fees.

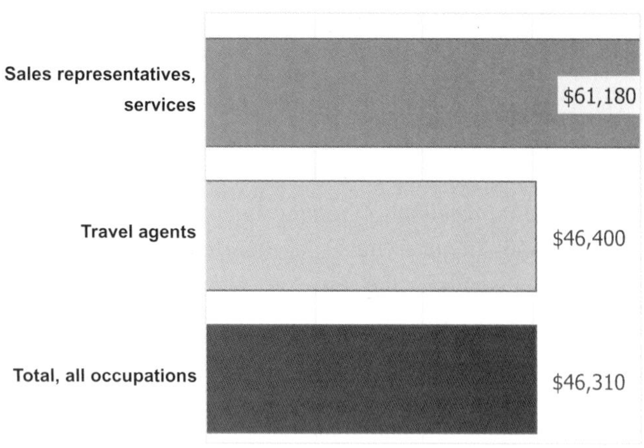

Note: All Occupations includes all occupations in the U.S. Economy.
Source: U.S. Bureau of Labor Statistics, Occupational Employment and Wage Statistics.

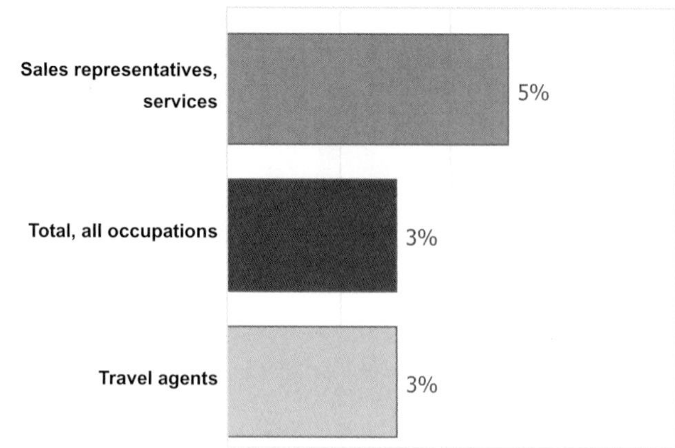

Note: All Occupations includes all occupations in the U.S. Economy.
Source: U.S. Bureau of Labor Statistics, Employment Projections program.

Most travel agents work full time, although part-time work is common. Some work additional hours during peak travel times or when they must accommodate clients' schedule changes and last-minute needs.

Job Outlook

Employment of travel agents is projected to grow 3 percent from 2022 to 2032, about as fast as the average for all occupations.

About 8,600 openings for travel agents are projected each year, on average, over the decade. Many of those openings are expected to result from the need to replace workers who transfer to different occupations or exit the labor force, such as to retire.

Employment

Demand is projected to increase for travel agents' expertise in recommending options to clients seeking personalized travel experiences. People are expected to continue relying on travel agents for their advice on popular or unique destinations and for their ability to handle travel issues.

However, the ability of travelers to use online resources to research vacations and book their own trips may limit demand for travel agents.

Employment projections data for travel agents, 2022-32

Occupational Title	SOC Code	Employment, 2022	Projected Employment, 2032	Change, 2022-32		Employment by Industry
				Percent	Numeric	
SOURCE: U.S. Bureau of Labor Statistics, Employment Projections program						
Travel agents	41-3041	66,300	68,600	3	2,300	Get data

Contacts for More Information

For more information, visit

- American Society of Travel Agents
- Cruise Lines International Association (CLIA)
- The Travel Institute

Wholesale and Manufacturing Sales Representatives

Summary

Quick Facts: Wholesale and Manufacturing Sales Representatives

2022 Median Pay	$67,750 per year $32.57 per hour
Typical Entry-Level Education	See How to Become One
Work Experience in a Related Occupation	None
On-the-job Training	Moderate-term on-the-job training
Number of Jobs, 2022	1,649,900
Job Outlook, 2022-32	1% (Little or no change)
Employment Change, 2022-32	20,500

What Wholesale and Manufacturing Sales Representatives Do

Wholesale and manufacturing sales representatives sell goods for wholesalers or manufacturers to businesses, government agencies, and other organizations.

Work Environment

Wholesale and manufacturing sales representatives work under pressure because their income and job security depend on the amount of merchandise they sell. Some sales representatives travel frequently.

How to Become a Wholesale or Manufacturing Sales Representative

Educational requirements vary for sales representatives and depend on the type of products sold. If the products are not scientific or technical, a high school diploma is generally sufficient for entry into the occupation. If the products are scientific or technical, sales representatives typically need at least a bachelor's degree.

Wholesale and manufacturing sales representatives sell goods for wholesalers or manufacturers to businesses, government agencies, and other organizations.

Pay

The median annual wage for sales representatives, wholesale and manufacturing, except technical and scientific products was $63,230 in May 2022.

The median annual wage for sales representatives, wholesale and manufacturing, technical and scientific products was $97,710 in May 2022.

Job Outlook

Overall employment of wholesale and manufacturing sales representatives is projected to show little or no change from 2022 to 2032.

Despite limited employment growth, about 148,000 openings for wholesale and manufacturing sales representatives are projected each year, on average, over the decade. Most of those openings are expected to result from the need to replace workers who transfer to different occupations or exit the labor force, such as to retire.

What Wholesale and Manufacturing Sales Representatives Do

Wholesale and manufacturing sales representatives sell goods for wholesalers or manufacturers to businesses, government agencies, and other organizations. They contact customers, explain the features of the products they are selling, negotiate prices, and answer any questions that their customers may have about the products.

Duties

Wholesale and manufacturing sales representatives typically do the following:

- Identify prospective customers by using business directories, following leads from existing clients, and attending trade shows and conferences
- Contact new and existing customers to discuss their needs and explain how specific products and services can meet these needs
- Help customers select products to meet customers' needs, product specifications, and regulations
- Emphasize product features that will meet customers' needs, and exhibit the capabilities and limitations of their products
- Answer customers' questions about the prices, availability, and uses of the products they are selling
- Negotiate prices and terms of sales and service agreements
- Prepare sales contracts and submit orders for processing
- Collaborate with colleagues to exchange information, such as information on selling strategies and marketing information

Some wholesale and manufacturing sales representatives specialize in technical and scientific products, ranging from agricultural and mechanical equipment to computer and pharmaceutical goods.

- Follow up with customers to make sure that they are satisfied with their purchases and to answer any questions or concerns they might have

Wholesale and manufacturing sales representatives—sometimes called *manufacturers' representatives* or *manufacturers' agents*—generally work for manufacturers or wholesalers. Some work for a single organization, while others represent several companies and sell a range of products.

Unlike retail sales workers, who sell goods directly to consumers, wholesale and manufacturing sales representatives deal with businesses, government agencies, and other organizations.

Some wholesale and manufacturing sales representatives work with nonscientific products, such as food, office supplies, and clothing. Other representatives specialize in technical and scientific products, ranging from agricultural and mechanical equipment to computer and pharmaceutical goods.

Wholesale and manufacturing sales representatives who lack expertise about a given product frequently team with a technical expert. In this arrangement, the technical expert—sometimes a sales engineer—attends the sales presentation to explain the product and answer questions or concerns. The sales representative makes the initial contact with customers, introduces the company's product, and obtains final agreement from the potential buyer.

By working with a technical expert, the representative is able to spend more time maintaining and soliciting accounts and less time seeking technical knowledge.

After the sale, representatives may make followup visits to ensure that equipment is functioning properly and may even help train customers' employees to operate and maintain new equipment.

Those selling consumer goods often suggest how and where merchandise should be displayed. When working with retailers, they may help arrange promotional programs, store displays, and advertising.

In addition to selling products, wholesale and manufacturing sales representatives analyze sales statistics, prepare reports, and handle administrative duties such as filing expense accounts, scheduling appointments, and making travel plans.

Staying up to date on new products and the changing needs of customers is important. Sales representatives accomplish this aim in a variety of ways, including attending trade shows at which new products and technologies are showcased. They attend conferences and conventions to meet other sales representatives and clients and to discuss new product developments. They also read about new and existing products and monitor the sales, prices, and products of their competitors.

The following are examples of types of wholesale and manufacturing sales representatives:

Inside sales representatives work mostly in offices while making sales. Frequently, they are responsible for getting new clients by "cold-calling" various organizations, meaning that they call potential customers who are not expecting to be contacted. That way, a representative can establish an initial contact. They also take incoming calls from customers who are interested in their product, and they process paperwork to complete the sale.

Outside sales representatives spend much of their time traveling to and visiting with current clients and prospective buyers. During a sales call, they discuss the client's needs and suggest how they can meet those needs with merchandise or services. They may show samples or catalogs that describe items their company provides, and they may inform customers about the prices and availability of the products they are selling and the ways in which their products can save money and boost productivity.

Work Environment

Sales representatives, wholesale and manufacturing, except technical and scientific products held about 1.3 million jobs in 2022. The largest employers of sales representatives, wholesale and manufacturing, except technical and scientific products were as follows:

Merchant wholesalers, durable goods	32%

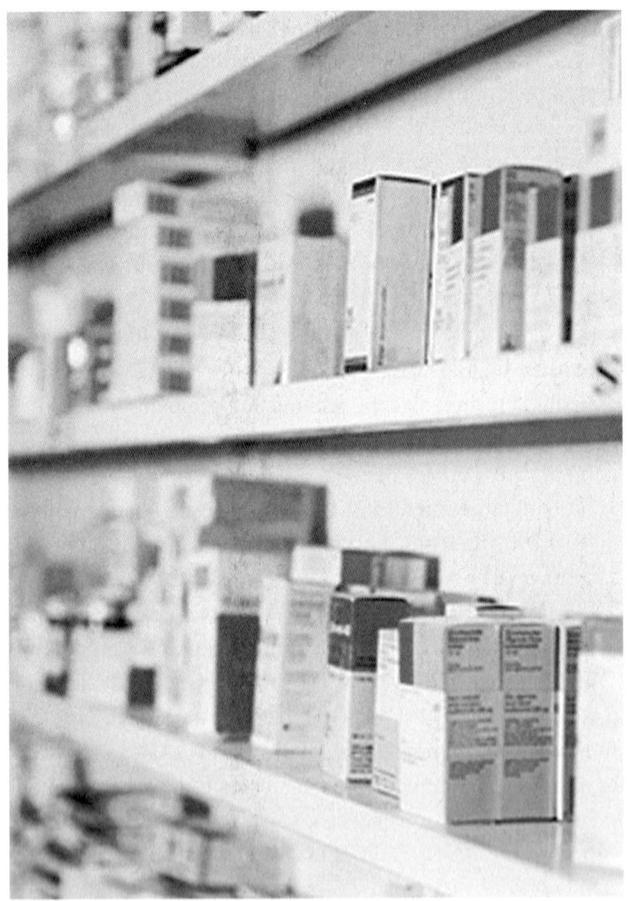

Some wholesale and manufacturing sales representatives have large territories and travel considerably.

Merchant wholesalers, nondurable goods	19
Manufacturing	18
Wholesale trade agents and brokers	11
Retail trade	5

Sales representatives, wholesale and manufacturing, technical and scientific products held about 305,600 jobs in 2022. The largest employers of sales representatives, wholesale and manufacturing, technical and scientific products were as follows:

Professional and commercial equipment and supplies merchant wholesalers	23%
Merchant wholesalers, nondurable goods	17
Manufacturing	12
Professional, scientific, and technical services	12
Wholesale trade agents and brokers	6

Some wholesale and manufacturing sales representatives have large territories and travel considerably. Because a sales region may cover several states, representatives may be away from home for several days or weeks at a time. Sales representatives who cover a smaller region may not spend much time away from home.

Other wholesale and manufacturing sales representatives spend a lot of their time on the phone, selling goods, taking orders, and resolving problems or complaints about the merchandise. They also use Web technology, including chats, email, and video conferencing, to contact clients.

Workers in this occupation can be under considerable stress because their income and job security often depend directly on the amount of merchandise they sell and their companies usually set goals or quotas that they are expected to meet.

Work Schedules

Most wholesale and manufacturing sales representatives work full time and many work more than 40 hours per week.

How to Become a Wholesale or Manufacturing Sales Representative

Educational requirements vary with the type of product sold. If the products are not scientific or technical, a high school diploma is generally enough for entry into the occupation. If the products are scientific or technical, sales representatives typically need at least a bachelor's degree.

Sales representatives of scientific or technical products, such as pharmaceuticals or medical instruments, typically need a degree in a field related to the product sold.

Education

A high school diploma is typically sufficient for many positions, primarily those selling nontechnical or nonscientific products. However, representatives selling scientific and technical products usually must have a bachelor's degree. Scientific and technical products include pharmaceuticals, medical instruments, and industrial equipment. A field of degree related to the product sold, such as agriculture or biology, is sometimes required.

Many sales representatives attend seminars in sales techniques or take courses in marketing, economics, communication, or even a foreign language to improve their ability to make sales.

Training

Many companies have formal training programs for beginning wholesale and manufacturing sales representatives. These programs may last up to 1 year. In some, trainees rotate among jobs in plants and offices in order to learn all phases of producing, installing, and distributing the product. In others, trainees receive formal technical instruction at the plant, followed by on-the-job training under the supervision of a field sales manager.

New employees may be trained by going along with experienced workers on their sales calls. As they gain familiarity with the firm's products and clients, the new workers gain more responsibility until they eventually get their own territory.

Licenses, Certifications, and Registrations

The Certified Professional Manufacturers' Representative (CPMR) certification and the Certified Sales Professional (CSP) certification are both offered by the Manufacturers' Representatives Educational Research Foundation (MRERF). Certification typically involves completing formal technical training and passing an exam. In addition, the CPMR requires 10 hours of continuing education every year in order to maintain certification.

Advancement

Frequently, promotion takes the form of an assignment to a larger account or territory, for which commissions are likely to be greater. Those who have good sales records and leadership ability may advance to higher level positions, such as sales manager, sales supervisor, district manager, or vice president of sales.

Important Qualities

Customer-service skills. Wholesale and manufacturing sales representatives must be able to listen to the customer's needs and concerns before and after the sale.

Interpersonal skills. Wholesale and manufacturing sales representatives must be able to work well with many types of people. They must be able to build good relationships with clients and with other members of the sales team.

Physical stamina. Wholesale and manufacturing sales representatives are often on their feet for a long time and may carry heavy sample products.

Self-confidence. Wholesale and manufacturing sales representatives must be confident and persuasive when making sales presentations. In addition, making a call to a potential customer who is not expecting to be contacted, or "cold-calling," requires confidence and composure.

Pay

The median annual wage for sales representatives, wholesale and manufacturing, except technical and scientific products was $63,230 in May 2022. The median wage is the wage at which half the workers in an occupation earned more than that amount and half earned less. The lowest 10 percent earned less than $35,790, and the highest 10 percent earned more than $129,450.

The median annual wage for sales representatives, wholesale and manufacturing, technical and scientific products was $97,710 in May 2022. The lowest 10 percent earned less than $46,160, and the highest 10 percent earned more than $182,610.

In May 2022, the median annual wages for sales representatives, wholesale and manufacturing, except technical and scientific products in the top industries in which they worked were as follows:

Wholesale trade agents and brokers	$74,870
Manufacturing	71,880
Merchant wholesalers, durable goods	61,470

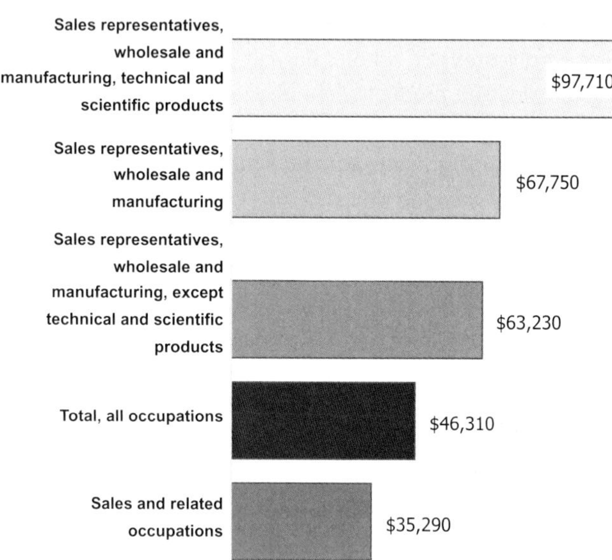

Note: All Occupations includes all occupations in the U.S. Economy.
Source: U.S. Bureau of Labor Statistics, Occupational Employment and Wage Statistics.

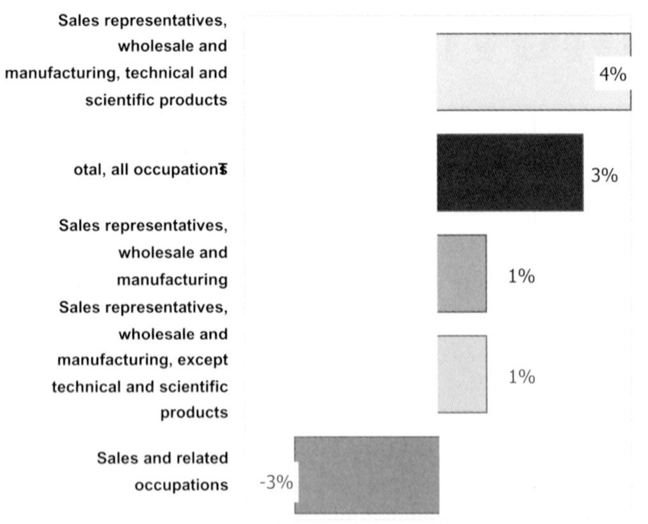

Note: All Occupations includes all occupations in the U.S. Economy.
Source: U.S. Bureau of Labor Statistics, Employment Projections program.

Merchant wholesalers, nondurable goods	61,390
Retail trade	55,240

In May 2022, the median annual wages for sales representatives, wholesale and manufacturing, technical and scientific products in the top industries in which they worked were as follows:

Merchant wholesalers, nondurable goods	$121,010
Professional, scientific, and technical services	108,570
Manufacturing	101,790
Wholesale trade agents and brokers	99,990
Professional and commercial equipment and supplies merchant wholesalers	82,530

Compensation for representatives varies considerably with the type of firm and the product sold. Most employers use a combination of salary and commissions or salary plus bonuses. Commissions usually are based on a percentage of sales. Bonuses may depend on the individual's performance, on the performance of all sales workers in the group or district, or on the company's performance.

Most wholesale and manufacturing sales representatives work full time and many work more than 40 hours per week.

Job Outlook

Overall employment of wholesale and manufacturing sales representatives is projected to show little or no change from 2022 to 2032.

Despite limited employment growth, about 148,000 openings for wholesale and manufacturing sales representatives are projected each year, on average, over the decade. Most of those openings are expected to result from the need to replace workers who transfer to different occupations or exit the labor force, such as to retire.

Employment

Projected employment of wholesale and manufacturing sales representatives varies by occupation (see table).

A rising total volume of sales, as well as a wider range of products and technologies, will create demand for sales representatives. Wholesale sales are increasingly being conducted online. However, these online sales are expected to complement, rather than replace, face-to-face selling.

Occupational Title	SOC Code	Employment, 2022	Projected Employment, 2032	Change, 2022-32	
				Percent	Numeric
Sales representatives, wholesale and manufacturing	41-4000	1,649,900	1,670,400	1	20,500
Sales representatives, wholesale and manufacturing, technical and scientific products	41-4011	305,600	317,100	4	11,400
Sales representatives, wholesale and manufacturing, except technical and scientific products	41-4012	1,344,300	1,353,400	1	9,100

Contacts for More Information

For more information, visit

- Manufacturers' Agents National Association (MANA)
- Manufacturers' Representatives Educational Research Foundation (MRERF)

Transportation and Material Moving

Airline and Commercial Pilots

Summary

Quick Facts: Airline and Commercial Pilots	
2022 Median Pay	$148,900 per year
Typical Entry-Level Education	See below
Work Experience in a Related Occupation	See below
On-the-job Training	Moderate-term on-the-job training
Number of Jobs, 2022	142,600
Job Outlook, 2022-32	4% (As fast as average)
Employment Change, 2022-32	5,600

What Airline and Commercial Pilots Do

Airline and commercial pilots fly and navigate airplanes, helicopters, and other aircraft.

Work Environment

Pilots usually have variable work schedules, with overnight layovers that are more common for airline pilots.

How to Become an Airline or Commercial Pilot

Airline pilots typically need a bachelor's degree and experience as a commercial or military pilot. Commercial pilots typically need flight training. Both also must meet Federal Aviation Administration (FAA) requirements.

Airline and commercial pilots fly and navigate airplanes, helicopters, and other aircraft.

Pay

The median annual wage for airline pilots, copilots, and flight engineers was $211,790 in May 2022.

The median annual wage for commercial pilots was $103,910 in May 2022.

Job Outlook

Overall employment of airline and commercial pilots is projected to grow 4 percent from 2022 to 2032, about as fast as the average for all occupations.

About 16,800 openings for airline and commercial pilots are projected each year, on average, over the decade. Many of those openings are expected to result from the need to replace workers who transfer to different occupations or exit the labor force, such as to retire.

State & Area Data

Explore resources for employment and wages by state and area for airline and commercial pilots.

Similar Occupations

Compare the job duties, education, job growth, and pay of airline and commercial pilots with similar occupations.

More Information, Including Links to O*NET

Learn more about airline and commercial pilots by visiting additional resources, including O*NET, a source on key characteristics of workers and occupations.

What Airline and Commercial Pilots Do

Airline and commercial pilots fly and navigate airplanes, helicopters, and other aircraft.

Duties

Pilots typically do the following:

- Check the overall condition of the aircraft before and after every flight
- Ensure that the aircraft is balanced and below its weight limit
- Verify that the fuel supply is adequate and that weather conditions are acceptable
- Prepare and submit flight plans to air traffic control
- Communicate with air traffic control over the aircraft's radio system

Commercial pilots are involved in activities such as firefighting and crop dusting.

- Operate and control aircraft along planned routes and during takeoffs and landings
- Monitor engines, fuel consumption, and other aircraft systems during flight
- Respond to changing conditions, such as weather events and emergencies (for example, a mechanical malfunction)
- Navigate the aircraft by using cockpit instruments and visual references

Pilots plan their flights by checking that the aircraft is operable and safe, that the cargo has been loaded correctly, and that weather conditions are acceptable. They file flight plans with air traffic control and may modify the plans in flight because of changing weather conditions or other factors.

Takeoff and landing can be the most demanding parts of a flight. They require close coordination among the pilot; copilot; flight engineer, if present; air traffic controllers; and ground personnel. Once in the air, the captain may have the first officer, if present, fly the aircraft, but the captain remains responsible for the aircraft. After landing, pilots fill out records that document their flight and the status of the aircraft.

Some pilots are also instructors using simulators and dual-controlled aircraft to teach students how to fly.

The following are examples of types of pilots:

Airline pilots work primarily for airlines that transport passengers and cargo on a fixed schedule. The captain or pilot in command, usually the most experienced pilot, supervises all other crew members and has primary responsibility for the flight. The copilot, often called the first officer or second in command, shares flight duties with the captain. Some older planes require a third pilot known as a flight engineer, who monitors instruments and operates controls. Technology has automated many of these tasks, and new aircraft do not require flight engineers.

Commercial pilots are involved in unscheduled flight activities, such as aerial application, charter flights, and aerial tours. Commercial pilots may have additional nonflight duties. Some commercial pilots schedule flights, arrange for maintenance of the aircraft, and load luggage themselves. Pilots who transport company executives, also known as corporate pilots, greet their passengers before embarking on the flight.

Agricultural pilots typically handle agricultural chemicals, such as pesticides, and may be involved in other agricultural practices in addition to flying. Pilots, such as helicopter pilots, who fly at low levels must constantly look for trees, bridges, power lines, transmission towers, and other obstacles.

With proper training, airline pilots also may be deputized as federal law enforcement officers and be issued firearms to protect the cockpit.

Work Environment

Airline pilots, copilots, and flight engineers held about 91,700 jobs in 2022. The largest employers of airline pilots, copilots, and flight engineers were as follows:

Industry	Percent
Scheduled air transportation	85%
Couriers and express delivery services	5
Federal government, excluding postal service	4
Support activities for transportation	2
Nonscheduled air transportation	1

Pilots have variable work schedules, which may include overnight layovers.

Commercial pilots held about 50,900 jobs in 2022. The largest employers of commercial pilots were as follows:

Nonscheduled air transportation	38%
Support activities for air transportation	10
Ambulance services	8
Scheduled air transportation	7
Technical and trade schools; private	7

Pilots assigned to long-distance routes may experience fatigue and jetlag. Weather conditions may result in turbulence, requiring pilots to change the flying altitude. Flights can be long and flight decks are often sealed, so pilots work in small teams for long periods in close proximity to one another.

Aerial applicators, also known as crop dusters, may be exposed to toxic chemicals, typically use unimproved landing strips, such as grass, dirt, or gravel surface, and may be at risk of collision with power lines. Helicopter pilots involved in rescue operations may fly at low levels during bad weather or at night, and land in areas surrounded by power lines, highways, and other obstacles. Pilots use hearing protection devices to prevent their exposure to engine noise.

The high level of concentration required to fly an aircraft and the mental stress of being responsible for the safety of passengers can be fatiguing. Pilots must be alert and quick to react if something goes wrong. Federal law requires pilots to retire at age 65.

Most pilots are based near large airports.

Injuries and Illnesses

Although fatalities are uncommon, commercial pilots experience one of the highest rates of occupational fatalities of all occupations.

Work Schedules

Federal regulations set the maximum work hours and minimum requirements for rest between flights for most pilots. Airline pilots fly an average of 75 hours per month and work an additional 150 hours per month performing other duties, such as checking weather conditions and preparing flight plans. Pilots have variable work schedules that may include some days of work followed by some days off. Flight assignments are based on seniority. Seniority enables pilots who have worked at a company for a long time to get preferred routes and schedules.

Airline pilots may spend several nights a week away from home because flight assignments often involve overnight layovers. When pilots are away from home, the airlines typically provide hotel accommodations, transportation to the airport, and an allowance for meals and other expenses.

Commercial pilots also may have irregular schedules. Although most commercial pilots remain near their home overnight, some may still work nonstandard hours.

Airline and commercial pilots who are newly hired by airlines or on-demand air services companies must undergo on-the-job training.

How to Become an Airline or Commercial Pilot

Airline pilots typically need a bachelor's degree and experience as a commercial or military pilot. Commercial pilots typically need flight training, and some employers may require or prefer them to have a degree.

Airline and commercial pilots also must have specific certificates and ratings from the Federal Aviation Administration (FAA).

Education

Airline pilots typically need a bachelor's degree in any field, including transportation, engineering, or business. They also complete flight training with independent FAA-certified flight instructors or at schools that offer flight training.

Commercial pilots typically complete flight training, and some employers require or prefer that they have a degree.

The FAA certifies hundreds of civilian flight schools, which range from small fixed base operators (FBO) to state universities. Some colleges and universities offer pilot training as part of a 2- or 4-year aviation degree.

Training

Airline and commercial pilots who are newly hired by airlines or on-demand air services companies undergo on-the-job training in accordance with federal regulations. This training usually includes several weeks of ground school and flight training. Various types of ratings for specific aircraft, such as the Boeing 737 or Cessna Citation, typically are acquired through employer-based training and generally are earned by pilots who have at least a commercial pilot certificate.

Pilots also must maintain their experience in performing certain maneuvers. This requirement means that pilots must perform specific maneuvers and procedures a given number of times within a specified amount of time. Pilots also must undergo periodic training and medical examinations, generally every year or every other year.

Work Experience in a Related Occupation

Airline pilots typically need work experience as a commercial or military pilot.

To get a job with a major or regional airline, pilots need extensive flight experience. Some pilots work as flight instructors or on-demand charter pilots, positions that usually require less experience than airline jobs require, to help build enough flying hours so that they can apply to the airlines.

Military pilots may transfer to civilian aviation and apply directly to airlines to become airline pilots.

Licenses, Certifications, and Registrations

Those who are seeking a career as a professional pilot must meet FAA requirements. Pilots typically get their FAA-issued certificates and ratings in the following order:

- Student pilot certificate
- Private pilot certificate
- Instrument rating
- Commercial pilot certificate
- Multi-engine rating
- Airline transport pilot certificate

Each certificate and rating requires that pilots pass a knowledge test on the ground and a practical flying exam, usually called a check ride, in an appropriate aircraft. In addition to earning these credentials, many pilots get a flight instructor certificate after they get their commercial pilot certificate. The flight instructor certificate helps them build flight time and experience quickly and at less personal expense.

Commercial pilot certificate. To qualify for a commercial pilot certificate, applicants must meet age and flight-hour requirements. Student pilots use a logbook and keep detailed records of their flight time, which must be endorsed by a flight instructor. Federal regulations specify the types and quantities of flight experience and knowledge needed.

Applicants must pass the appropriate medical exam, meet all of the detailed flight experience and knowledge requirements, and pass a written exam and a practical flight exam in order to get a commercial pilot certificate. The medical exam confirms that the pilot's vision is correctable to 20/20 and that no physical or mental conditions exist that could impair the pilot's performance.

Commercial pilots must hold an instrument rating if they want to carry passengers for pay more than 50 miles from the point of origin of their flight, or at night.

Instrument rating. Pilots who earn an instrument rating can fly during periods of low visibility, also known as instrument meteorological conditions, or IMC. They may qualify for this rating by having at least 40 hours of instrument flight experience and 50 hours of cross-country flight time as pilot in command, and by meeting other requirements detailed in the federal regulations.

Airline transport pilot (ATP) certificate. All pilot crews of a scheduled commercial airliner must have ATP certificates. To earn the ATP certificate, applicants must meet certain federal requirements, such as for age, hours of flight, and written and practical exams. A commercial pilot certificate is a prerequisite for the ATP. Airline pilots usually maintain one or more aircraft-type ratings, which allow them to fly aircraft that require specific training, depending on the requirements of their particular airline.

Pilots must pass periodic physical and practical flight examinations to be able to perform the duties granted by their certificate.

Advancement

Commercial pilots may advance to airline pilots after completing a degree, accruing required flight time, and obtaining an ATP certificate.

Advancement for airline pilots depends on a system of seniority outlined in collective bargaining contracts.

Important Qualities

Communication skills. Pilots must speak clearly when conveying information to air traffic controllers and other crew members. They must also listen carefully for instructions.

Observational skills. Pilots regularly watch over screens, gauges, and dials to make sure that all systems are in working order. They also need to maintain situational awareness by looking for other aircraft or obstacles. Pilots must be able to see clearly, be able to judge the distance between objects, and possess good color vision.

Problem-solving skills. Pilots must be able to identify complex problems and figure out appropriate solutions. When a plane encounters turbulence, for example, pilots assess the weather conditions and request a change in route or altitude from air traffic control.

Quick reaction time. Pilots must respond quickly, and with good judgment, to any impending danger.

Pay

The median annual wage for airline pilots, copilots, and flight engineers was $211,790 in May 2022. The median wage is the wage at which half the workers in an occupation earned more than that amount and half earned less. The lowest 10 percent earned less than $98,680, and the highest 10 percent earned more than $239,200.

The median annual wage for commercial pilots was $103,910 in May 2022. The lowest 10 percent earned less than $54,100, and the highest 10 percent earned more than $217,530.

In May 2022, the median annual wages for airline pilots, copilots, and flight engineers in the top industries in which they worked were as follows:

Couriers and express delivery services	$239,200 or more
Scheduled air transportation	221,160

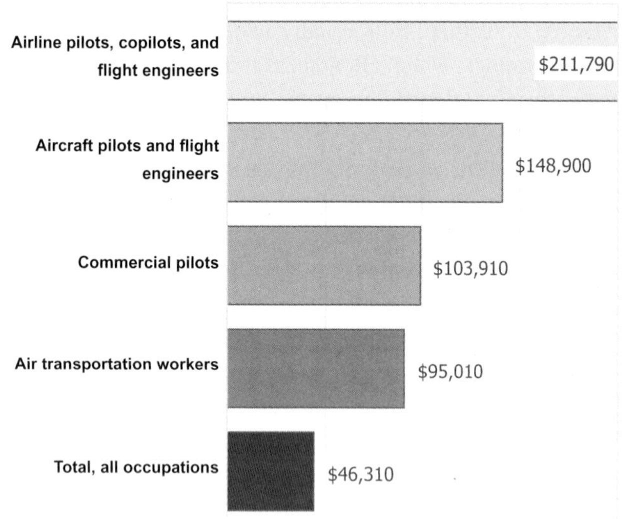

Note: All Occupations includes all occupations in the U.S. Economy.
Source: U.S. Bureau of Labor Statistics, Occupational Employment and Wage Statistics.

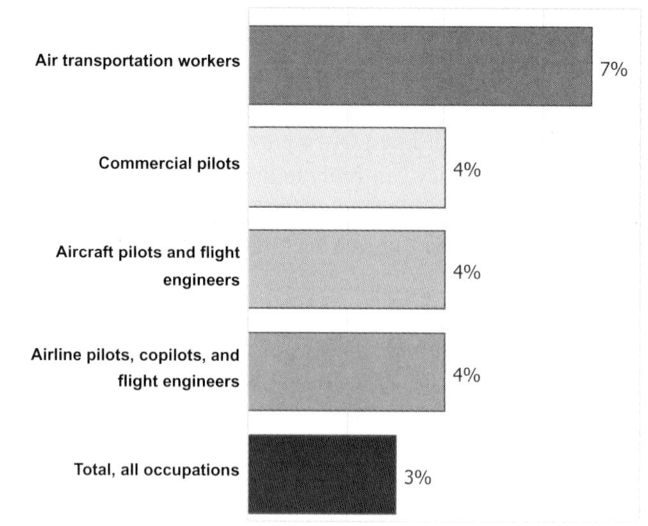

Note: All Occupations includes all occupations in the U.S. Economy.
Source: U.S. Bureau of Labor Statistics, Employment Projections program.

Federal government, excluding postal service	116,380
Support activities for transportation	110,030
Nonscheduled air transportation	106,710

In May 2022, the median annual wages for commercial pilots in the top industries in which they worked were as follows:

Scheduled air transportation	$155,650
Support activities for air transportation	109,210
Nonscheduled air transportation	107,080
Ambulance services	84,800
Technical and trade schools; private	77,570

Airline pilots usually begin their careers as first officers and receive wage increases as they accumulate experience and seniority.

In addition, airline pilots receive an expense allowance, or "per diem," for every hour they are away from home, and they may earn extra pay for international flights. Airline pilots and their immediate families usually are entitled to free or reduced-fare flights.

Federal regulations set the maximum work hours and minimum requirements for rest between flights for most pilots. Airline pilots fly an average of 75 hours per month and work an additional 150 hours per month performing other duties, such as checking weather conditions and preparing flight plans. Pilots have variable work schedules that may include several days of work followed by some days off.

Airline pilots may spend several nights a week away from home because flight assignments often involve overnight layovers. When pilots are away from home, the airlines typically provide hotel accommodations, transportation to the airport, and an allowance for meals and other expenses.

Commercial pilots also may have irregular schedules. Although most commercial pilots remain near their home overnight, they may still work nonstandard hours.

Job Outlook

Overall employment of airline and commercial pilots is projected to grow 4 percent from 2022 to 2032, about as fast as the average for all occupations.

About 16,800 openings for airline and commercial pilots are projected each year, on average, over the decade. Many of those openings are expected to result from the need to replace workers who transfer to different occupations or exit the labor force, such as to retire.

Employment

Employment of airline and commercial pilots is projected to grow as the demand for air travel increases. The post-pandemic expansion of hybrid and remote work arrangements is likely to increase demand for trips that combine business and personal travel, also known as "bleisure" travel, supporting employment demand for pilots.

Continued demand for private chartered flights is expected to sustain job growth for commercial pilots.

Occupational Title	SOC Code	Employment, 2022	Projected Employment, 2032	Change, 2022-32	
				Percent	Numeric
Aircraft pilots and flight engineers	53-2010	142,600	148,100	4	5,600
Airline pilots, copilots, and flight engineers	53-2011	91,700	95,200	4	3,500

Occupational Title	SOC Code	Employment, 2022	Projected Employment, 2032	Change, 2022-32	
				Percent	Numeric
Commercial pilots	53-2012	50,900	52,900	4	2,100

Contacts for More Information

For more information, visit

- Code of Federal Regulations, Title 14
- Aircraft Owners and Pilots Association
- Air Line Pilots Association, International
- Coalition of Airline Pilots Associations
- Federal Aviation Administration
- Helicopter Association International
- National Agricultural Aviation Association

Air Traffic Controllers

Summary

Quick Facts: Air Traffic Controllers	
2022 Median Pay	$132,250 per year $63.58 per hour
Typical Entry-Level Education	Associate's degree
Work Experience in a Related Occupation	None
On-the-job Training	Long-term on-the-job training
Number of Jobs, 2022	23,000
Job Outlook, 2022-32	1% (Little or no change)
Employment Change, 2022-32	300

What Air Traffic Controllers Do

Air traffic controllers coordinate the movement of aircraft to maintain safe distances between them.

Work Environment

Air traffic controllers work in control towers, approach control facilities, or en route centers. Their work can be stressful because maximum concentration is required at all times. Night, weekend, and rotating shifts are common.

Air traffic controllers coordinate the movement of air traffic.

How to Become an Air Traffic Controller

There are several paths to becoming an air traffic controller. Candidates typically need an associate's or a bachelor's degree from the Air Traffic Collegiate Training Initiative program, several years of progressively responsible work experience, or a combination of education and experience. They also must be a U.S. citizen, submit to medical and background checks, and complete training at Federal Aviation Administration (FAA) academy.

Pay

The median annual wage for air traffic controllers was $132,250 in May 2022.

Job Outlook

Employment of air traffic controllers is projected to show little or no change from 2022 to 2032.

Despite limited employment growth, about 2,000 openings for air traffic controllers are projected each year, on average, over the decade. Most of those openings are expected to result from the need to replace workers who transfer to different occupations or exit the labor force, such as to retire.

What Air Traffic Controllers Do

Air traffic controllers coordinate the movement of aircraft, including within the vicinity of airports and between altitude sectors and control centers, so that they maintain safe distances.

Air traffic controllers authorize flight path changes.

Duties

Air traffic controllers typically do the following:

- Monitor and direct the movement of aircraft on the ground and in the air
- Control all ground traffic at airport runways and taxiways
- Issue takeoff and landing instructions to pilots
- Transfer control of departing flights to other traffic control centers and accept control of arriving flights
- Inform pilots about weather, runway closures, and other critical information
- Alert airport response staff in the event of an aircraft emergency

Air traffic controllers' primary concern is safety, but they also must direct aircraft efficiently to minimize delays. They manage the flow of aircraft into and out of the airport airspace, guide pilots during takeoff and landing, and monitor aircraft as they travel through the skies. Air traffic controllers use radio equipment to communicate with pilots. They also use radar, computers, and other visual references to monitor and direct aircraft movement in the skies and on airport grounds.

Controllers usually manage multiple aircraft at the same time. For example, a controller might direct one aircraft on its landing approach while providing another aircraft with weather information.

The following are examples of types of air traffic controllers:

Tower controllers direct the movement of aircraft and other vehicles, such as snowplows, on runways and taxiways. They check flight plans, give pilots clearance for takeoff or landing, and direct the flow of aircraft and ground traffic in their area of responsibility. Most observe from control towers, managing traffic from the airport to a radius of 3 to 30 miles out.

Approach and departure controllers ensure that aircraft traveling within an airport's airspace maintain minimum separation for safety. These controllers give pilots clearances to enter controlled airspace and hand off control of aircraft to en route controllers. They also inform pilots about weather conditions and other critical notices. Terminal approach and departure controllers work in buildings known as Terminal Radar Approach Control Centers (TRACONs). They assist an aircraft until it reaches the edge of a facility's airspace, usually about 20 to 50 miles from the airport and up to about 17,000 feet in the air.

En route controllers monitor aircraft that leave an airport's airspace. They work at en route traffic control centers located throughout the country, which typically are not located at airports. Each center is assigned an airspace based on the geography and air traffic in the area in which it is located. As an aircraft approaches and flies through a center's airspace, en route controllers guide it along its route. They may adjust the flight path for safety reasons, such as to avoid collision with another aircraft. En route controllers direct aircraft for the bulk of the flight before handing off oversight to terminal approach controllers.

Some air traffic controllers work at the Air Traffic Control Systems Command Center, where they monitor traffic within the entire national airspace. When they identify a bottleneck, they provide instructions to other controllers to help prevent traffic jams. Their objective is to keep traffic levels manageable for the airports and for en route controllers.

Work Environment

Air traffic controllers held about 23,000 jobs in 2022. The largest employers of air traffic controllers were as follows:

Federal government	91%
Support activities for air transportation	5

Most controllers work for the Federal Aviation Administration (FAA).

Most air traffic controllers work in control towers, approach control facilities, or en route centers. Many tower controllers and approach and departure controllers work near large airports. En route controllers work in secure office buildings across the country, which typically are not located at airports.

Most controllers work in semidark rooms. The aircraft they control appear as points of light moving across their radar screens, and a well-lit room would make it difficult to see the screens properly.

Air traffic controllers must remain focused and react quickly to conditions that change frequently. Being responsible for the safety of aircraft and their passengers may be stressful and exhausting. To prevent burnout, the FAA requires controllers to retire at age 56.

Work Schedules

Most air traffic controllers work full time. The FAA regulates the hours that an air traffic controller may work. Controllers may not work more than 10 straight hours during a shift, which includes required breaks, and must have 9 hours of rest before their next shift.

Air traffic controllers often work in semidark rooms.

As they gain experience, air traffic controllers move to positions in the control room that have more responsibility.

Major airports may operate control towers on a 24-hour basis. Controllers who work at these facilities may work day, evening, or night shifts that include weekends and holidays. Small airports or those that are less busy may have towers that do not operate around the clock. Controllers at these facilities may have standard work schedules.

How to Become an Air Traffic Controller

There are several different paths to becoming an air traffic controller. Candidates typically need an associate's or bachelor's degree through a Federal Aviation Administration (FAA)-approved Air Traffic Collegiate Training Initiative (AT-CTI) program, several years of progressively responsible work experience, or a combination of education and experience.

In addition, prospective air traffic controllers must be U.S. citizens and must pass a medical evaluation, background check, and FAA preemployment tests, including the Air Traffic Controller Specialists Skills Assessment Battery (ATSA). They also must complete a training course at the FAA Academy and apply before the FAA's age cutoff.

Once hired, controllers typically complete on-the-job training that lasts more than 12 months. They also must pass a physical exam each year, a job performance exam twice a year, and periodic drug screenings.

Education

Air traffic controllers typically need an associate's or a bachelor's degree. To qualify with an associate's degree, candidates must complete their studies in an AT-CTI program. A bachelor's degree may be in any field, including transportation, business, or engineering.

The FAA sets guidelines for schools that offer the AT-CTI program. AT-CTI schools offer 2- or 4-year degrees that are designed to prepare students for a career in air traffic control. The curriculum is not standardized, but courses focus on subjects that are fundamental to aviation, including airspace, clearances, chart reading, and federal regulations.

Training

Most newly hired air traffic controllers are trained at the FAA Academy in Oklahoma City. The length of training varies with the candidate's background. Candidates must apply before the FAA's age cutoff.

After graduating from the Academy, trainees are assigned to an air traffic control facility as *developmental controllers* until they complete requirements for becoming a certified air traffic controller. Developmental controllers begin their careers by supplying pilots with basic flight data and airport information. They then may advance to positions within the control room that have more responsibility.

With additional training, controllers may switch from one area of specialization to another. For example, a controller may complete training to transfer from working in an en route center to an airport tower.

Other Experience

Air traffic controllers sometimes qualify through work experience instead of a degree. Candidates either need up to 3 years of progressively responsible generalized work experience that demonstrates the potential for learning and performing air traffic control work or must have specialized work experience in a military or civilian air traffic control facility.

Air traffic controllers who learn their skills in the military are eligible to become civilian air traffic controllers even if their age exceeds the FAA cutoff for applicants.

Licenses, Certifications, and Registrations

All air traffic controllers must hold an Air Traffic Control Tower Operator Certificate or be appropriately qualified and supervised as stated in Title 14 of the Code of Federal Regulations, Part 65.

Important Qualities

Communication skills. Air traffic controllers must be able to give clear, concise instructions, listen carefully to pilots' requests, and respond by speaking clearly in English.

Decision-making skills. Controllers must make quick decisions. For example, when a pilot requests a change of altitude to avoid poor weather, the controller must respond quickly to ensure the aircraft's safety.

Detail oriented. Controllers must be able to concentrate while multiple conversations occur at once. For example, in a large airport tower, several controllers may be speaking with different pilots at the same time.

Math skills. Controllers must be able to do arithmetic accurately and quickly. They often need to compute speeds, times, and distances, and they recommend heading and altitude changes.

Organizational skills. Controllers must be able to coordinate the actions of multiple flights and to prioritize tasks, because they may be required to guide several pilots at the same time.

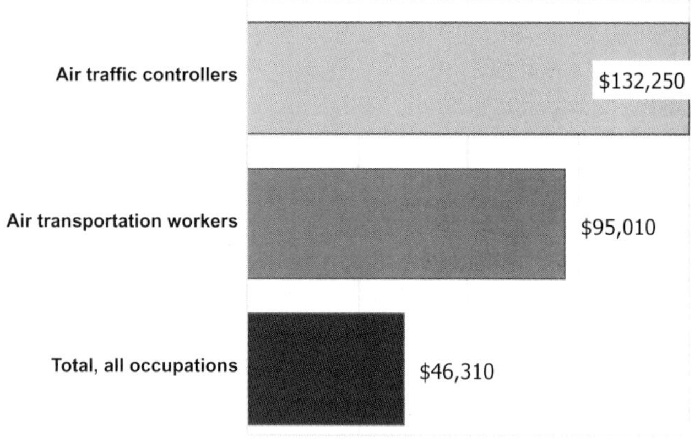

Note: All Occupations includes all occupations in the U.S. Economy.
Source: U.S. Bureau of Labor Statistics, Occupational Employment and Wage Statistics.

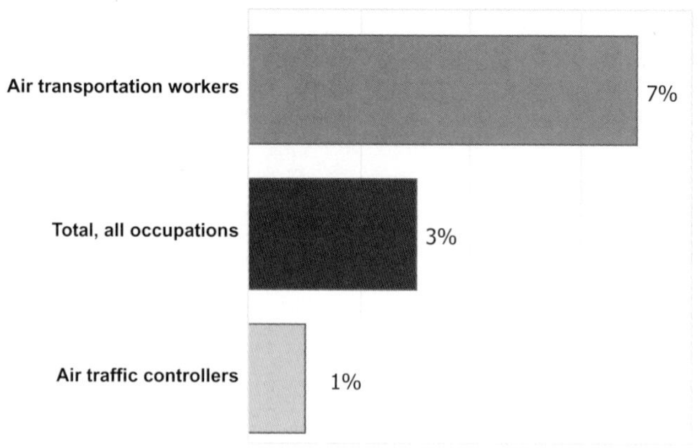

Note: All Occupations includes all occupations in the U.S. Economy.
Source: U.S. Bureau of Labor Statistics, Employment Projections program.

Problem-solving skills. Controllers must be able to understand complex situations, review changing circumstances, and provide pilots with appropriate alternatives.

Teamwork. Controllers must be able to work as members of a team, cooperating with and assisting others in and around their area of responsibility.

Pay

The median annual wage for air traffic controllers was $132,250 in May 2022. The median wage is the wage at which half the workers in an occupation earned more than that amount and half earned less. The lowest 10 percent earned less than $73,590, and the highest 10 percent earned more than $189,800.

In May 2022, the median annual wages for air traffic controllers in the top industries in which they worked were as follows:

Federal government	$140,860
Support activities for air transportation	74,580

The salaries for development controllers increase as they complete successive levels of training. According to the Federal Aviation Administration (FAA), the salaries for more advanced controllers who have completed on-the-job training varies with the location of the facility, the complexity of the flight paths, and other factors. A full explanation of the pay ranges for air traffic controllers can be found on the FAA Pay & Benefits page.

Most air traffic controllers work full time. The FAA regulates the hours that an air traffic controller may work. Controllers may not work more than 10 straight hours during a shift, which includes required breaks, and must have 9 hours of rest before their next shift.

Major airports may operate control towers on a 24-hour basis. Controllers who work at these facilities may work day, evening, or night shifts that include weekends and holiday. Small airports or those that are less busy may have towers that do not operate around the clock. Controllers at these facilities may have standard work schedules.

Job Outlook

Employment of air traffic controllers is projected to show little or no change from 2022 to 2032.

Despite limited employment growth, about 2,000 openings for air traffic controllers are projected each year, on average, over the decade. Most of those openings are expected to result from the need to replace workers who transfer to different occupations or exit the labor force, such as to retire.

Employment

Although air traffic is projected to increase in the coming years, the satellite-based Next Generation Air Transportation System (NextGen) is expected to allow individual controllers to handle more air traffic. As a result, the demand for additional air traffic controllers should be somewhat limited over the projections decade.

Occupational Title	SOC Code	Employment, 2022	Projected Employment, 2032	Change, 2022-32	
				Percent	Numeric
Air traffic controllers	53-2021	23,000	23,300	1	300

Contacts for More Information

For more information, visit

- Air Traffic Control Association
- Federal Aviation Administration
- National Air Traffic Controllers Association
- Professional Women Controllers Inc.
- OPM Classification & Qualifications
- FAA Aviation Careers
- USAJobs

Bus Drivers

Summary

Quick Facts: Bus Drivers	
2022 Median Pay	$44,440 per year $21.36 per hour
Typical Entry-Level Education	High school diploma or equivalent
Work Experience in a Related Occupation	None
On-the-job Training	See How to Become One
Number of Jobs, 2022	515,200
Job Outlook, 2022-32	3% (As fast as average)
Employment Change, 2022-32	13,300

What Bus Drivers Do
Bus drivers transport people between various places.

Work Environment
Part-time work is common for bus drivers. Drivers' schedules may vary and include early mornings, evenings, or weekends. Many bus drivers work for schools, and they work only when schools are in session. Driving through heavy traffic or bad weather and dealing with unruly passengers can be stressful for bus drivers.

How to Become a Bus Driver
Bus drivers must have a commercial driver's license (CDL), which they sometimes earn during on-the-job training. They also need a good driving record and must meet physical, hearing, and vision requirements. In addition, bus drivers typically need a high school diploma or the equivalent and may be required to pass a background check.

Pay
The median annual wage for bus drivers, school was $41,270 in May 2022.

The median annual wage for bus drivers, transit and intercity was $50,890 in May 2022.

Job Outlook
Overall employment of bus drivers is projected to grow 3 percent from 2022 to 2032, about as fast as the average for all occupations.

About 76,400 openings for bus drivers are projected each year, on average, over the decade. Many of those openings are expected to result from the need to replace workers who transfer to different occupations or exit the labor force, such as to retire.

What Bus Drivers Do
Bus drivers transport people between various places—including school, work, and shopping centers—and across state and national borders. Some drive set routes, and others transport passengers on chartered trips or sightseeing tours. They drive a range of vehicles, from 15-passenger buses to 60-foot articulated buses (with two connected sections) that can carry more than 100 passengers.

Duties
Bus drivers typically do the following:

- Pick up and drop off passengers at designated locations
- Follow a planned route according to a time schedule
- Help passengers, including those with disabilities, get on and off the bus
- Obey traffic laws and state and federal transit regulations
- Follow procedures to ensure passenger safety
- Keep passengers informed of possible delays
- Perform basic maintenance (check the bus tires, lights, and oil)
- Keep the bus clean and presentable to the public

Most bus drivers are school bus drivers.

Intercity bus drivers transport passengers between cities or towns.

The following are examples of types of bus drivers:

School bus drivers transport students to and from school and other activities, such as field trips and sporting events, when the academic term is in session. School bus drivers typically do the following:

- Ensure the safety of children getting on and off the bus
- Attend to the needs of children with disabilities
- Keep order and safety on the bus
- Understand and enforce the school system's rules of conduct
- Report disciplinary problems to the school district and parents or guardians

Local transit bus drivers follow a daily schedule while transporting people on set routes along city or suburban streets. They stop frequently, often every few blocks and when a passenger requests a stop. Local transit drivers typically do the following:

- Collect bus fares or manage fare box transactions
- Answer questions about schedules, routes, and transfer points
- Report accidents and other traffic disruptions to a central dispatcher

Intercity bus drivers transport passengers between cities or towns, sometimes crossing state lines. They usually pick up and drop off passengers at bus stations or curbside locations in downtown urban areas. Intercity drivers typically do the following:

- Ensure that all passengers have a valid ticket to ride the bus
- Sell tickets to passengers when there are unsold seats available, if necessary
- Keep track of when passengers get on or off the bus
- Help passengers load and unload baggage

Charter bus drivers, sometimes called *motorcoach drivers*, transport passengers on chartered trips or sightseeing tours. Trip planners generally arrange their schedules and routes based on the convenience of the passengers, who are often on vacation. Charter bus drivers are sometimes away for long periods because they usually stay with the passengers for the length of the trip. Charter bus drivers typically do the following:

- Regulate heating, air-conditioning, and lighting, for passenger comfort
- Ensure that the trip stays on schedule
- Help passengers load and unload baggage
- Account for all passengers before leaving a location
- Act as tour guides for passengers, if necessary

Work Environment

Bus drivers, school held about 358,800 jobs in 2022. The largest employers of bus drivers, school were as follows:

Elementary and secondary schools; local	51%
School and employee bus transportation	32
Local government, excluding education and hospitals	9
Elementary and secondary schools; private	2
Other transit and ground passenger transportation	1

Bus drivers, transit and intercity held about 156,400 jobs in 2022. The largest employers of bus drivers, transit and intercity were as follows:

Local government, excluding education and hospitals	51%
Urban transit systems	15
Charter bus industry	7
Other transit and ground passenger transportation	5
Interurban and rural bus transportation	5

Driving through heavy traffic or bad weather and dealing with unruly passengers can be stressful for bus drivers.

Injuries and Illnesses

Transit and intercity bus drivers have one of the highest rates of injuries and illnesses of all occupations. Most injuries to bus drivers are due to vehicle accidents.

Work Schedules

Part-time work is common for bus drivers. Drivers' schedules may vary and include early mornings, evenings, or weekends.

School bus drivers work only when school is in session, so their work hours are often limited. Some make multiple trips if schools in their district open and close at different times or if students need transportation to other activities.

Intercity and charter bus drivers may make a round trip and go home at the end of each shift. Others spend nights away from home on long-distance routes. The trip or route schedule dictates a driver's hours.

Some school bus drivers make multiple trips if schools in the district open at different times.

All types of bus drivers have to obtain a CDL.

Bus drivers who cross state lines must follow the Federal Motor Carrier Safety Administration's (FMCSA) hours-of-service regulations. Bus drivers are allowed 10 hours of driving time and 15 hours of total on-duty time before they must rest for 8 consecutive hours. Weekly maximum restrictions also apply but may vary by employer schedule.

How to Become a Bus Driver

Bus drivers must have a commercial driver's license (CDL), which they sometimes earn during on-the-job training. They also need a good driving record and must meet physical, hearing, and vision requirements. In addition, bus drivers typically need a high school diploma or the equivalent and may be required to pass a background check.

Education

Bus drivers typically need a high school diploma or equivalent.

Training

Bus drivers typically get on-the-job training. Those who already have a CDL may have a shorter training period. For part of the training, drivers may practice various maneuvers with a bus on a driving course. They then begin to drive in light traffic and eventually make practice runs on the type of route that they expect to drive. New drivers make trips with passengers while accompanied by an experienced driver who gives advice, answers questions, and evaluates the new driver's performance.

Some drivers' training is also spent in the classroom. They learn their company's rules and regulations, state and municipal traffic laws, and safe driving practices. Drivers also learn about schedules and bus routes, fares, and interacting with passengers.

Licenses, Certifications, and Registrations

All bus drivers must have a CDL. Some new bus drivers earn their CDL during on-the-job training. Qualifications vary by state but generally include passing both knowledge and driving tests. States have the right not to issue a license to someone who has had a CDL suspended in another state.

Drivers can get endorsements for a CDL that reflect their ability to drive a special type of vehicle. All bus drivers must have a passenger (P) endorsement, and school bus drivers must also have a school bus (S) endorsement. Getting the P and S endorsements requires additional knowledge and driving tests administered by a certified examiner.

Many states require all bus drivers to be 18 years of age or older and those who drive across state lines to be at least 21 years old. Most bus drivers must pass a background check before they are hired. Check with your state agency for specific licensing requirements.

Federal regulations require interstate bus drivers to pass a physical exam every 2 years and to submit to random drug or alcohol testing. Most states impose similar regulations. Bus drivers may have their CDL suspended if they are convicted of a felony involving the use of a motor vehicle or of driving under the influence of drugs or alcohol. Actions such as excessive speeding or reckless driving also may result in suspension.

Important Qualities

Customer-service skills. Bus drivers regularly interact with passengers and must be courteous and helpful.

Dependability. Passengers rely on bus drivers to pick them up on time and safely transport them to their destination.

Hand-eye coordination. Drivers must watch their surroundings and avoid obstacles and other hazards while operating a bus. Federal regulations require bus drivers to have normal use of their arms and legs.

Hearing ability. Bus drivers need good hearing. Federal regulations require them to be able to hear a forced whisper in one ear at 5 feet, with or without the use of a hearing aid.

Patience. Bus drivers must remain calm and composed when driving through heavy traffic and congestion or when dealing with unruly passengers.

Physical health. Bus drivers must be in good physical condition. Federal and state regulations do not allow people to become bus drivers if they have a medical condition, such as high blood pressure or epilepsy, that may interfere with the safe operation of a bus.

Visual ability. Bus drivers must be able to pass vision tests. Federal regulations require at least 20/40 vision with a 70-degree field of vision in each eye and the ability to distinguish colors on a traffic light.

Pay

The median annual wage for bus drivers, school was $41,270 in May 2022. The median wage is the wage at which half the workers in an occupation earned more than that amount and half earned less. The lowest 10 percent earned less than $25,390, and the highest 10 percent earned more than $58,390.

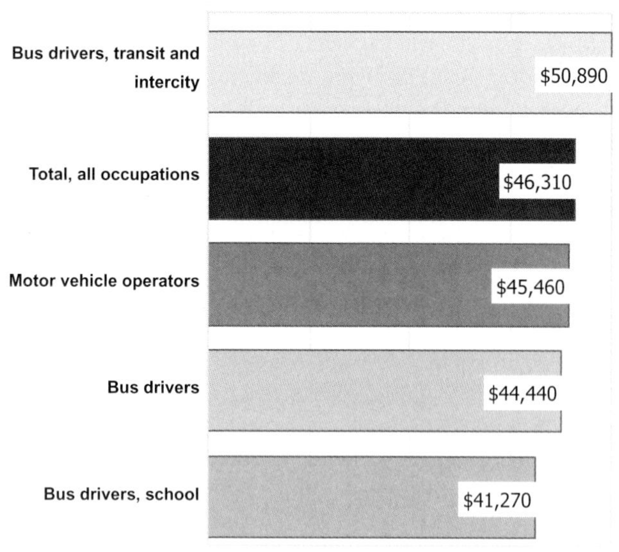

Note: All Occupations includes all occupations in the U.S. Economy. Source: U.S. Bureau of Labor Statistics, Occupational Employment and Wage Statistics.

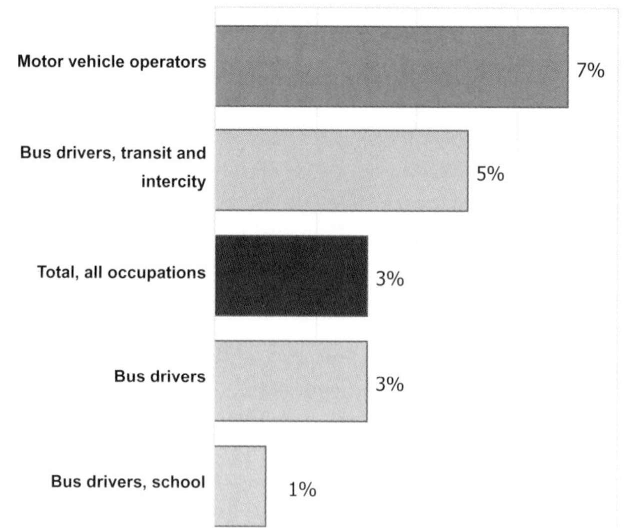

Note: All Occupations includes all occupations in the U.S. Economy. Source: U.S. Bureau of Labor Statistics, Employment Projections program.

The median annual wage for bus drivers, transit and intercity was $50,890 in May 2022. The lowest 10 percent earned less than $33,610, and the highest 10 percent earned more than $80,420.

In May 2022, the median annual wages for bus drivers, school in the top industries in which they worked were as follows:

Local government, excluding education and hospitals	$45,840
School and employee bus transportation	45,630
Elementary and secondary schools; private	39,560
Elementary and secondary schools; local	39,220
Other transit and ground passenger transportation	38,510

In May 2022, the median annual wages for bus drivers, transit and intercity in the top industries in which they worked were as follows:

Local government, excluding education and hospitals	$59,180
Urban transit systems	47,560
Interurban and rural bus transportation	45,540
Other transit and ground passenger transportation	41,410
Charter bus industry	39,950

Part-time work is common for bus drivers. Drivers' schedules may vary and include early mornings, evenings, or weekends.

School bus drivers work only when school is in session, so their work hours are often limited. Some make multiple trips if schools in their district open and close at different times or if students need transportation to other activities.

Intercity and charter bus drivers may make a round trip and go home at the end of each shift. Others spend nights away from home on long-distance routes. The trip or route schedule dictates a driver's hours.

Some passenger vehicle drivers receive tips. Those who provide good customer service are more likely to receive good tips than those whose customer-service skills are poor.

Bus drivers who cross state lines must follow the Federal Motor Carrier Safety Administration's (FMCSA) hours-of-service regulations. Bus drivers are allowed 10 hours of driving time and 15 hours of total on-duty time before they must rest for 8 consecutive hours. Weekly maximum restrictions also apply but may vary by employer schedule.

Job Outlook

Overall employment of bus drivers is projected to grow 3 percent from 2022 to 2032, about as fast as the average for all occupations.

About 76,400 openings for bus drivers are projected each year, on average, over the decade. Many of those openings are expected to result from the need to replace workers who transfer to different occupations or exit the labor force, such as to retire.

Employment

Schools will continue to rely on school bus drivers to transport students. However, declining student enrollments in public and private schools over the decade may constrain demand for these workers.

Employment of transit and intercity bus drivers is expected to increase as public authorities continue to upgrade their public transportation systems, such as by redesigning bus networks, expanding bus services, and rolling out bus rapid transit (BRT) systems. In addition, intercity bus travel should continue to grow because its inexpensive fares and passenger amenities, such as Wi-Fi, are expected to maintain its popularity as a transportation option.

An increasing population of older adults and people with disabilities will place demand on rural transit services, contributing to a need for drivers of these bus routes.

Occupational Title	SOC Code	Employment, 2022	Projected Employment, 2032	Change, 2022-32	
				Percent	Numeric
Bus drivers	—	515,200	528,500	3	13,300
Bus drivers, school	53-3051	358,800	363,700	1	4,900
Bus drivers, transit and intercity	53-3052	156,400	164,800	5	8,400

Contacts for More Information

For more information, visit

- National School Transportation Association
- National Association of State Directors of Pupil Transportation Services
- American Public Transportation Association
- United Motorcoach Association
- Federal Motor Carrier Safety Administration

Delivery Truck Drivers and Driver/Sales Workers

Summary

Quick Facts: Delivery Truck Drivers and Driver/Sales Workers	
2022 Median Pay	$38,220 per year $18.38 per hour
Typical Entry-Level Education	High school diploma or equivalent
Work Experience in a Related Occupation	None
On-the-job Training	Short-term on-the-job training
Number of Jobs, 2022	1,705,600
Job Outlook, 2022-32	10% (Much faster than average)
Employment Change, 2022-32	175,700

What Delivery Truck Drivers and Driver/Sales Workers Do

Delivery truck drivers and driver/sales workers pick up, transport, and drop off packages and small shipments within a local region or urban area.

Work Environment

Delivery truck drivers and driver/sales workers have a physically demanding job. Driving a truck for long periods can be tiring. When loading and unloading cargo, drivers do a lot of lifting, carrying, and walking.

How to Become a Delivery Truck Driver or Driver/Sales Worker

Delivery truck drivers and driver/sales workers typically need a high school diploma or equivalent to enter these occupations. However, some opportunities exist for those without a high school diploma. Workers undergo 1 month or less of on-the-job training. They must have a driver's license from the state in which they work and have a clean driving record.

Pay

The median annual wage for driver/sales workers was $32,690 in May 2022.

The median annual wage for light truck drivers was $40,410 in May 2022.

Job Outlook

Overall employment of delivery truck drivers and driver/sales workers is projected to grow 10 percent from 2022 to 2032, much faster than the average for all occupations.

About 203,800 openings for delivery truck drivers and driver/sales workers are projected each year, on average, over the decade. Many of those openings are expected to result from the need to replace workers who transfer to different occupations or exit the labor force, such as to retire.

Delivery drivers and driver/sales workers transport goods around an urban area or small region.

What Delivery Truck Drivers and Driver/Sales Workers Do

Delivery truck drivers and driver/sales workers pick up, transport, and drop off packages and small shipments within a local region or urban area. They drive trucks weighing less than 26,001 pounds total for vehicle, passengers, and cargo. Delivery truck drivers usually transport merchandise from a distribution center to businesses and households.

Duties

Delivery truck drivers and driver/sales workers typically do the following:

- Load and unload their cargo
- Communicate with customers to determine pickup and delivery needs
- Report any incidents they encounter on the road to a dispatcher
- Follow applicable traffic laws
- Report mechanical problems to the appropriate personnel
- Keep their truck and associated equipment clean and in working order
- Accept payments for delivery
- Handle paperwork, such as receipts or delivery confirmation notices

Most drivers generally receive instructions to go to a delivery location at a particular time, and it is up to them to determine the best route. Other drivers have a regular daily or weekly delivery schedule. All drivers must understand an area's street grid and know which roads allow trucks and which do not.

The following examples are types of delivery truck drivers and driver/sales workers:

Driver/sales workers are delivery drivers who also have sales responsibilities. They recommend products to businesses and solicit new customers. These drivers may have a regular delivery route and may be responsible for adding clients who are located along their route. For example, they may make regular deliveries to a hardware store and encourage the store's manager to offer a new product.

Some driver/sales workers use their own vehicles to deliver goods to customers, such as takeout food, and accept payment for those goods. Freelance or independent driver/sales workers may use smartphone apps to find specific delivery jobs.

Light truck drivers, often called *pickup and delivery* or *P&D drivers,* are the most common type of delivery driver. They drive small trucks or vans from distribution centers to delivery locations. Drivers make deliveries based on a set schedule. Some drivers stop at the distribution center once only, in the morning, and make many stops throughout the day. Others make multiple trips between the distribution center and delivery locations. Some drivers make deliveries from a retail location to customers.

Work Environment

Driver/sales workers held about 541,000 jobs in 2022. The largest employers of driver/sales workers were as follows:

Employer	Percent
Restaurants and other eating places	45%
Wholesale trade	18
Retail trade	11
Self-employed workers	8

Light truck drivers held about 1.2 million jobs in 2022. The largest employers of light truck drivers were as follows:

Employer	Percent
Couriers and messengers	37%
Retail trade	16
Wholesale trade	14
Self-employed workers	8

Delivery truck drivers and driver/sales workers have physically demanding jobs. When loading and unloading cargo, drivers do a lot of lifting, carrying, and walking. Driving in congested traffic or adhering to strict delivery timelines can also be stressful.

Delivery drivers drop off packages with customers.

Delivery truck drivers load and unload packages.

Injuries and Illnesses

Light truck drivers have one of the highest rates of injuries and illnesses of all occupations. Injuries can result from workers lifting and moving heavy objects, as well as from automobile accidents.

Work Schedules

Most drivers work full time, and some work more than 40 hours per week. Those who have regular routes sometimes must begin work very early in the morning or work late at night. For example, a driver who delivers bread to a deli every day must arrive before the deli opens. Drivers often work weekends and holidays, and their schedules may vary.

How to Become a Delivery Truck Driver or Driver/Sales Worker

Delivery truck drivers and driver/sales workers typically need a high school diploma or equivalent to enter these occupations. However, some opportunities exist for those without a high school diploma. Workers undergo 1 month or less of on-the-job training. They must have a driver's license from the state in which they work and have a clean driving record.

Education

Delivery truck drivers and driver/sales workers typically enter the occupation with a high school diploma or equivalent.

Training

Companies train new delivery truck drivers and driver/sales workers on the job. This may include training from a driver-mentor who rides along with a new employee to make sure that the driver is able to operate a truck safely on crowded streets.

New-driver training also covers company policies about package dropoffs and returns, taking payment, and what to do with damaged goods.

Drivers need to maintain a clean driving record and be able to navigate city streets.

Driver/sales workers must learn detailed information about the products they offer. Their company also may teach them proper sales techniques, such as how to approach new customers.

Licenses, Certifications, and Registrations

All delivery drivers need a driver's license.

Other Experience

Some delivery drivers begin as package loaders at warehouse facilities, especially if the driver works for a large company. For more information, see the profile on hand laborers and material movers.

Important Qualities

Customer-service skills. When completing deliveries, drivers often interact with customers and should make a good impression to ensure repeat business.

Hand–eye coordination. Drivers need to observe their surroundings at all times while operating a vehicle.

Math skills. Because delivery truck drivers and driver/sales workers sometimes take payment, they must be able to count cash and make change quickly and accurately.

Patience. When driving through heavy traffic congestion, delivery drivers must remain calm and composed.

Sales skills. Driver/sales workers are expected to persuade customers to purchase new or different products.

Visual ability. To have a driver's license, delivery truck drivers and driver/sales workers must be able to pass a state vision test.

Pay

The median annual wage for driver/sales workers was $32,690 in May 2022. The median wage is the wage at which half the workers in an occupation earned more than that amount and half earned less. The lowest 10 percent earned less than $19,730, and the highest 10 percent earned more than $55,200.

The median annual wage for light truck drivers was $40,410 in May 2022. The lowest 10 percent earned less than $26,740, and the highest 10 percent earned more than $75,780.

In May 2022, the median annual wages for driver/sales workers in the top industries in which they worked were as follows:

Wholesale trade	$44,310
Retail trade	34,680
Restaurants and other eating places	26,450

In May 2022, the median annual wages for light truck drivers in the top industries in which they worked were as follows:

Couriers and messengers	$46,720
Wholesale trade	38,240
Retail trade	30,140

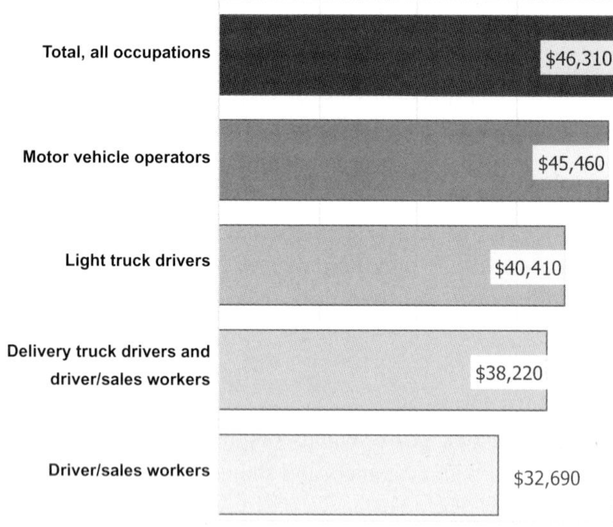

Note: All Occupations includes all occupations in the U.S. Economy.
Source: U.S. Bureau of Labor Statistics, Occupational Employment and Wage Statistics.

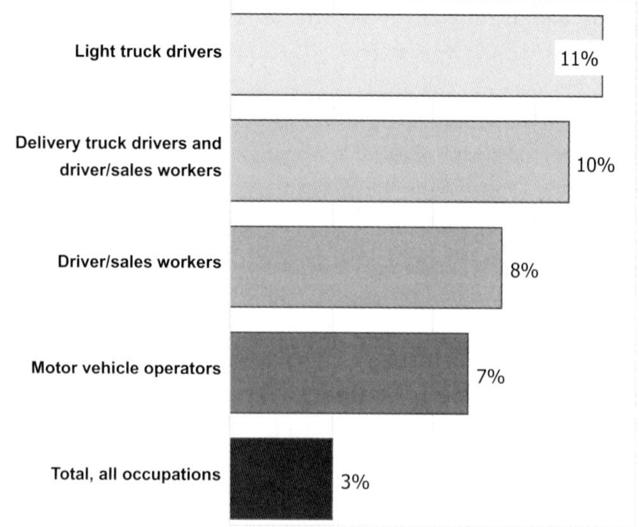

Note: All Occupations includes all occupations in the U.S. Economy.
Source: U.S. Bureau of Labor Statistics, Employment Projections program.

Some drivers/sales workers, such as pizza delivery workers, receive tips in addition to hourly wages. Sales workers can also receive commissions from the products they sell.

Most drivers work full time, and some work more than 40 hour per week. Those who have regular routes sometimes must begin work very early in the morning or work late at night. For example, a driver who delivers bread to a deli every day must arrive before the deli opens. Drivers often work weekends and holidays, and their schedules may vary.

Job Outlook

Overall employment of delivery truck drivers and driver/sales workers is projected to grow 10 percent from 2022 to 2032, much faster than the average for all occupations.

About 203,800 openings for delivery truck drivers and driver/sales workers are projected each year, on average, over the decade. Many of those openings are expected to result from the need to replace workers who transfer to different occupations or exit the labor force, such as to retire.

Employment

Projected employment of delivery truck drivers and driver/sales workers varies by occupation (see table).

Continued growth of e-commerce should increase demand for package delivery services, especially for large and regional shipping companies. More light truck drivers will be needed to fulfill the growing number of e-commerce transactions. Drone delivery services also may be used for some deliveries over the projections decade. However, this technology is expected to complement rather than fully replace these workers, so the downward employment effect is expected to be modest.

The general demand for delivery options is expected to remain strong. Therefore, employment of driver/sales workers is projected to grow as these workers continue to be needed to deliver food, medical supplies, and other items.

Occupational Title	SOC Code	Employment, 2022	Projected Employment, 2032	Change, 2022-32	
				Percent	Numeric
Delivery truck drivers and driver/sales workers	—	1,705,600	1,881,300	10	175,700
Driver/sales workers	53-3031	541,000	582,900	8	41,900
Light truck drivers	53-3033	1,164,600	1,298,400	11	133,800

Contacts for More Information

For more information, visit

➤ American Trucking Associations

Flight Attendants

Summary

Quick Facts: Flight Attendants	
2022 Median Pay	$63,760 per year
Typical Entry-Level Education	High school diploma or equivalent
Work Experience in a Related Occupation	Less than 5 years
On-the-job Training	Moderate-term on-the-job training
Number of Jobs, 2022	111,100
Job Outlook, 2022-32	11% (Much faster than average)
Employment Change, 2022-32	12,600

What Flight Attendants Do

Flight attendants provide routine services and respond to emergencies to ensure the safety and comfort of airline passengers.

Work Environment

Flight attendants have variable work schedules, including evenings, weekends, and holidays, because airlines operate every day, and some offer overnight flights. Attendants work in an aircraft and may be away from home several nights per week.

How to Become a Flight Attendant

Flight attendants typically receive on-the-job training from their employer and must be certified by the Federal Aviation Administration (FAA).

Pay

The median annual wage for flight attendants was $63,760 in May 2022.

Flight attendants provide routine services and respond to emergencies to ensure the safety and comfort of airline passengers.

Job Outlook

Employment of flight attendants is projected to grow 11 percent from 2022 to 2032, much faster than the average for all occupations.

About 16,600 openings for flight attendants are projected each year, on average, over the decade. Many of those openings are expected to result from the need to replace workers who transfer to different occupations or exit the labor force, such as to retire.

What Flight Attendants Do

Flight attendants provide routine services and respond to emergencies to ensure the safety and comfort of airline passengers.

Duties

Flight attendants typically do the following:

- Participate in preflight briefings with pilots to discuss cabin conditions and flight details
- Conduct preflight inspections of emergency equipment
- Demonstrate the location and use of safety equipment and emergency equipment
- Ensure that passengers have their seatbelts fastened when required and that all other safety requirements are observed

Flight attendants demonstrate the use of safety equipment and emergency equipment.

- Serve beverages and snacks
- Sell and serve beverages and meals, if available
- Take care of passengers, particularly those with special needs
- Reassure passengers during the flight, such as when the aircraft hits turbulence
- Administer and coordinate emergency medical care, if needed
- Direct passengers, including for evacuating the aircraft in an emergency

Airlines are required by law to have flight attendants aboard aircraft for the safety and security of passengers. The primary job of flight attendants is to keep passengers safe, ensuring that everyone follows security regulations and that the flight deck is secure. Flight attendants also try to make flights comfortable for passengers. At times, they may deal with passengers who display disruptive behavior.

Before takeoff, the captain (pilot) may conduct a preflight briefing with flight attendants about relevant flight information. Details include the number of hours the flight will take, the route the plane will travel, and weather conditions. Flight attendants check that emergency equipment is working, the cabin is clean, and there is an adequate supply of food and beverages on board. Flight attendants greet passengers as they board the aircraft, direct them to their seats, and help as needed.

Flight attendants demonstrate the location and proper use of safety equipment to all passengers, either in person or through a video recording before the plane takes off. They also check that seatbelts are fastened, seats are locked in the upright position, and all carry-on items are properly stowed in accordance with federal law and company policy. They answer questions about the flight and generally assist all passengers, including those with special needs.

A flight attendant's most important responsibility, however, is to help passengers in the event of an emergency. This responsibility ranges from dealing with unruly passengers to directing evacuations. Flight attendants also are trained to perform first aid, extinguish fires, and protect the flight deck.

Before the plane lands, flight attendants once again ensure that seatbelts are fastened, seats are locked in the upright position, and all carry-on and galley items are properly stowed.

After passengers deplane, flight attendants survey the condition of the cabin. They submit reports on any medical, safety, or security issues that may have occurred during the flight.

Work Environment

Flight attendants held about 111,100 jobs in 2022. The largest employers of flight attendants were as follows:

Scheduled air transportation	96%
Nonscheduled air transportation	1

Flight attendants work primarily in the cabins of passenger aircraft. Dealing directly with passengers and standing for long periods may be stressful and tiring. Occasionally, flights encounter air turbulence, which may make providing service more difficult and cause anxiety in some passengers. Handling emergencies and unruly customers also may be difficult and stressful.

Flight attendants make sure all overhead luggage is properly stored.

Flight attendants may spend many nights away from home. Employers typically provide meal allowances and may arrange sleeping accommodations, such as in hotels or apartments shared by a group of flight attendants.

Injuries and Illnesses

Flight attendants have one of the highest rates of injuries and illnesses of all occupations. Common injuries include sprains, strains, and bruises. To avoid injury, these workers must follow safety procedures. For example, they must ensure that overhead compartments are closed, especially during turbulence, so that carry-on items don't fall and present a risk to everyone in the cabin. Attendants also ensure that carts are properly stowed and latched during emergencies to prevent injuries to passengers and themselves.

Work Schedules

Flight attendants may have variable schedules, and part-time work is common. They often work nights, weekends, and holidays because airlines operate every day and have overnight flights. They may spend several nights per week or per month away from home. In most cases, a contract between the airline and the flight attendant union determines the total daily and monthly workable hours.

On-duty shifts per day may vary from 4 to 18 hours or longer, such as for international flights. The Federal Aviation Administration (FAA) requires specific hours of rest between duty periods based on the duration of a completed duty period. Each month, flight attendants may fly a specified number of hours and generally spend another specified number of hours on the ground preparing flights, writing reports, and waiting for aircraft to arrive.

A flight attendant's assignments of home base and route are based on seniority. New flight attendants must be flexible with their schedule and location. Almost all flight attendants start out working on call, also known as reserve status. Flight attendants on reserve usually live near their home airport, because they may have to report to work on short notice.

As they earn more seniority, flight attendants may have more control over their schedules. For example, some senior flight attendants may choose to live outside their home base and commute to work. Others may choose to work only on regional flights. On small corporate airlines, flight attendants may work on an as-needed basis.

How to Become a Flight Attendant

Flight attendants receive training from their employer and must be certified by the Federal Aviation Administration (FAA). Flight attendants typically need a high school diploma or the equivalent and work experience in customer service.

Applicants must meet minimum age requirements, typically 18 or 21; be eligible to work in the United States; have a valid passport; and pass a background check and drug test. They must have vision that is correctable to at least 20/40 and often need to conform to height requirements set by the airline. Flight attendants also may have to pass a medical evaluation.

Flight attendants should present a professional appearance, which may be defined by the employer.

Education

A high school diploma is typically required to become a flight attendant. Some airlines may prefer to hire applicants who have taken some college courses or who have a college degree.

Those working on international flights may need fluency in a foreign language.

Prospective attendants may enroll in flight attendant academies.

Work Experience in a Related Occupation

Flight attendants typically need 1 or 2 years of work experience in a service occupation before getting their first job as a flight attendant. This experience may include customer service positions in restaurants, hotels, or resorts. Experience in sales or in other positions that require close contact with the public and focus on service to customers also may help develop the skills needed to be a successful flight attendant.

Flight attendants take care of passenger needs.

Training

After a flight attendant is hired, airlines provide initial training that typically lasts for several weeks or a few months. The training usually takes place at the airline's flight training center and is required for FAA certification.

Trainees learn emergency procedures such as evacuating aircraft, operating emergency equipment, and administering first aid. They also receive specific instruction on flight regulations, company operations, and job duties.

Toward the end of the training, students go on practice flights. They must complete the training to keep a job with the airline. Once they have passed initial training, new flight attendants receive the FAA Certificate of Demonstrated Proficiency and continue to receive additional on-the-job training as required by their employer.

Licenses, Certifications, and Registrations

All flight attendants must be certified by the FAA. To become certified, flight attendants must complete their employer's initial training program and pass an exam. Flight attendants are certified for specific types of aircraft and must take new training for each type of aircraft on which they are to work. In addition, attendants receive recurrent training every year to maintain their certification.

Advancement

Career advancement is based on seniority. On international flights, senior attendants frequently oversee the work of other attendants. Senior attendants may be promoted to management positions in which they are responsible for recruiting, instructing, and scheduling.

Important Qualities

Attentiveness. Flight attendants must be aware of security or safety risks during the flight. They also must be attentive to passengers' needs in order to ensure a pleasant travel experience.

Communication skills. Flight attendants should speak clearly and interact effectively with passengers and other crewmembers. They also must be able to write concisely when documenting in-flight issues.

Customer-service skills. Flight attendants need poise, tact, and resourcefulness to handle stressful situations and to address passengers' needs.

Decision-making skills. Flight attendants must be able to act decisively, especially in emergencies.

Physical stamina. Flight attendants push, pull, and carry service items; open and close overhead bins; lift heavy objects; and stand and walk for long periods.

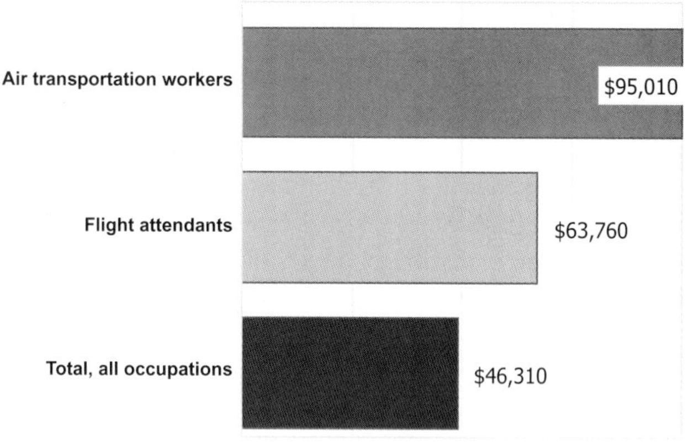

Note: All Occupations includes all occupations in the U.S. Economy.
Source: U.S. Bureau of Labor Statistics, Occupational Employment and Wage Statistics.

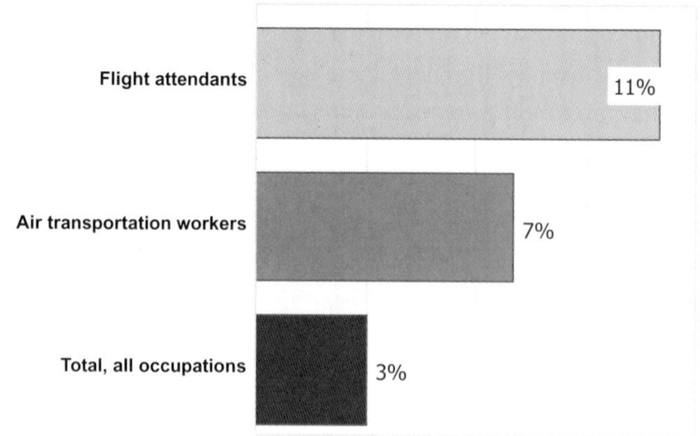

Note: All Occupations includes all occupations in the U.S. Economy.
Source: U.S. Bureau of Labor Statistics, Employment Projections program.

Pay

The median annual wage for flight attendants was $63,760 in May 2022. The median wage is the wage at which half the workers in an occupation earned more than that amount and half earned less. The lowest 10 percent earned less than $37,690, and the highest 10 percent earned more than $97,170.

In May 2022, the median annual wages for flight attendants in the top industries in which they worked were as follows:

Scheduled air transportation	$64,350
Nonscheduled air transportation	61,440

Flight attendants receive an allowance for meals and accommodations while working away from home. Although attendants may be required to purchase an initial set of uniforms and luggage, their employer usually pays for replacements and upkeep. Flight attendants generally are eligible for discounted airfare or free standby seats through their airline.

Flight attendants may have variable schedules, and part-time work is common.

Job Outlook

Employment of flight attendants is projected to grow 11 percent from 2022 to 2032, much faster than the average for all occupations.

About 16,600 openings for flight attendants are projected each year, on average, over the decade. Many of those openings are expected to result from the need to replace workers who transfer to different occupations or exit the labor force, such as to retire.

Employment

Demand for air travel, particularly from leisure travelers, will continue to support employment growth for flight attendants. Federal regulations require a minimum number of attendants per flight. These workers will continue to be needed to ensure the safety and comfort of passengers on flights.

Employment projections data for flight attendants, 2022-32

Occupational Title	SOC Code	Employment, 2022	Projected Employment, 2032	Change, 2022-32		Employment by Industry
				Percent	Numeric	
SOURCE: U.S. Bureau of Labor Statistics, Employment Projections program						
Flight attendants	53-2031	111,100	123,800	11	12,600	Get data

Contacts for More Information

For more information, visit

- Association of Flight Attendants—CWA (AFA-CWA)
- Association of Professional Flight Attendants (APFA)
- Federal Aviation Administration (FAA)

Hand Laborers and Material Movers

Summary

Quick Facts: Hand Laborers and Material Movers	
2022 Median Pay	$34,960 per year $16.81 per hour
Typical Entry-Level Education	See How to Become One
Work Experience in a Related Occupation	None
On-the-job Training	Short-term on-the-job training
Number of Jobs, 2022	7,099,400
Job Outlook, 2022-32	5% (Faster than average)
Employment Change, 2022-32	353,400

What Hand Laborers and Material Movers Do

Hand laborers and material movers manually move freight, stock, or other materials.

Work Environment

Most hand laborers and material movers work full time. Because materials are shipped around the clock, some workers, especially those in warehousing, work overnight shifts.

How to Become a Hand Laborer or Material Mover

There are usually no formal educational requirements to become a hand laborer or material mover. Employers typically require only that applicants be physically able to perform the work.

Pay

The median annual wage for hand laborers and material movers was $34,960 in May 2022.

Many hand laborers pack and transfer materials around a warehouse.

Job Outlook

Overall employment of hand laborers and material movers is projected to grow 5 percent from 2022 to 2032, faster than the average for all occupations.

About 1,075,800 openings for hand laborers and material movers are projected each year, on average, over the decade. Many of those openings are expected to result from the need to replace workers who transfer to different occupations or exit the labor force, such as to retire.

What Hand Laborers and Material Movers Do

Hand laborers and material movers manually move freight, stock, or other materials. Some of these workers feed or remove material to or from machines, clean vehicles, pick up unwanted household goods, and pack materials for moving.

Duties

Hand laborers and material movers typically do the following:

- Manually move material from one place to another
- Pack or wrap products by hand
- Keep a record of the material they move
- Signal machine operators to help move material
- Clean cars, equipment, and workplaces

In warehouses and in wholesale and retail operations, hand laborers and material movers work closely with material moving machine operators and material recording clerks. Some workers are employed in manufacturing industries, loading material onto conveyor belts or other machines.

The following are examples of types of hand laborers and material movers:

Cleaners of vehicles and equipment wash automobiles and other vehicles, as well as storage tanks, pipelines, and related machinery. They use cleaning products, vacuums, hoses, and brushes. Most of these workers clean cars at a carwash, an

Some vehicle and equipment cleaners wash cars.

automobile dealership, or a rental agency. Some clean industrial equipment at manufacturing firms. Some—for example, those who work at a carwash, also known as carwash attendants—interact with customers.

Hand laborers and freight, stock, and material movers move materials to and from storage and production areas, loading docks, delivery trucks, ships, and containers. Although their specific duties may vary, most of these movers, often called *pickers*, work in warehouses. Some workers retrieve products from storage and move them to loading areas. Other workers load and unload cargo from a truck. When moving a package, pickers keep track of the package number, sometimes with a hand-held scanner, to ensure proper delivery. Sometimes they open containers and sort the material.

Hand packers and packagers package a variety of materials by hand. They may label cartons, inspect items for defects, and keep records of items packed. Some of these workers pack materials for shipment and move them to a loading dock. Hand packers in grocery stores, also known as grocery baggers, bag groceries for customers at checkout.

Machine feeders and offbearers process materials by feeding them into equipment or by removing them from equipment. The equipment is generally operated by other workers, such as material moving machine operators. Machine feeders and offbearers help the operator if the machine becomes jammed or needs minor repairs. Machine feeders also track the amount of material they process during a shift.

Refuse and recyclable material collectors gather garbage and recyclables from homes and businesses to transport to a dump, landfill, or recycling center. Many collectors lift garbage cans by hand and empty them into their truck. Some collectors drive the garbage or recycling truck along a scheduled route and may use a hydraulic lift to empty the contents of a dumpster into the truck.

Stockers and order fillers receive, unpack, and track merchandise. Stock clerks move products from a warehouse to store shelves. They keep a record of items that enter or leave the stockroom and inspect for damaged goods. These clerks also use handheld radio frequency identification (RFID) scanners to keep track of merchandise. Order fillers retrieve customer orders and prepare them to be shipped.

Work Environment

Hand laborers and material movers held about 7.1 million jobs in 2022. Employment in the detailed occupations that make up hand laborers and material movers was distributed as follows:

Laborers and freight, stock, and material movers, hand	2,988,500
Stockers and order fillers	2,851,600
Packers and packagers, hand	659,600
Cleaners of vehicles and equipment	401,800
Refuse and recyclable material collectors	146,400
Machine feeders and offbearers	51,500

The largest employers of hand laborers and material movers were as follows:

Retail trade	33%
Transportation and warehousing	22
Administrative and support and waste management and remediation services	14
Wholesale trade	10
Manufacturing	10

Hand laborers and material movers lift and carry heavy objects, and their work is usually repetitive and physically demanding. They bend, kneel, crouch, or crawl in awkward positions.

Injuries and Illnesses

Hand laborers and freight, stock, and material movers and refuse and recyclable material collectors have some of the highest rates of injuries and illnesses of all occupations. Moving heavy objects around warehouses or onto trucks, or bending while cleaning a vehicle, may lead to sprains, strains, or overexertion.

Refuse and recyclable material collectors lift heavy garbage containers.

Work Schedules

Most hand laborers and freight, stock, and material movers work full time.

Shifts longer than 8 hours are common, and sometimes overtime is available. Because materials are shipped around the clock, some workers, especially those in warehousing, work overnight shifts.

How to Become a Hand Laborer or Material Mover

There are usually no formal educational requirements to become a hand laborer or material mover. Employers typically require only that applicants be physically able to perform the work.

Education

There are no formal educational requirements to become a hand laborer or material mover.

Training

Most positions for hand laborers and material movers require less than 1 month of on-the-job training. Some workers need only a few days of training, and most training is done by a supervisor or a more experienced worker who decides when trainees are ready to work on their own.

Workers learn safety rules as part of their training. Many of these rules are standardized through the Occupational Safety and Health Administration (OSHA).

Hand laborers and material movers learn on the job.

Licenses, Certifications, and Registrations

Refuse and recyclable material collectors who drive trucks that exceed a certain capacity—such as vehicles with the combined weight of the vehicle, passengers, and cargo exceeding 26,000 pounds—must have a commercial driver's license (CDL). Obtaining a CDL requires passing written, skill, and vision tests.

Important Qualities

Customer-service skills. Hand laborers and material movers who work with the public, such as grocery baggers or carwash attendants, must be pleasant and courteous to customers.

Hand–eye coordination. Most hand laborers and material movers use their arms and hands to manipulate objects or move objects into specific positions.

Listening skills. Hand laborers and material movers follow instructions that a supervisor gives them.

Physical stamina. Hand laborers and material movers need the endurance to perform strenuous tasks, such as moving or cleaning objects, throughout the day.

Physical strength. Some hand laborers and material movers must be able to lift and carry heavy objects.

Pay

The median annual wage for hand laborers and material movers was $34,960 in May 2022. The median wage is the wage at which half the workers in an occupation earned more than that amount and half earned less. The lowest 10 percent earned less than $26,070, and the highest 10 percent earned more than $47,800.

Median annual wages for hand laborers and material movers in May 2022 were as follows:

Refuse and recyclable material collectors	$43,540
Machine feeders and offbearers	38,040
Laborers and freight, stock, and material movers, hand	36,110
Stockers and order fillers	34,220
Packers and packagers, hand	32,920
Cleaners of vehicles and equipment	31,000

In May 2022, the median annual wages for hand laborers and material movers in the top industries in which they worked were as follows:

Transportation and warehousing	$38,230
Manufacturing	36,920
Wholesale trade	36,840
Administrative and support and waste management and remediation services	32,400
Retail trade	31,310

Some hand laborers and material movers, such as grocery baggers or carwash attendants, may receive tips.

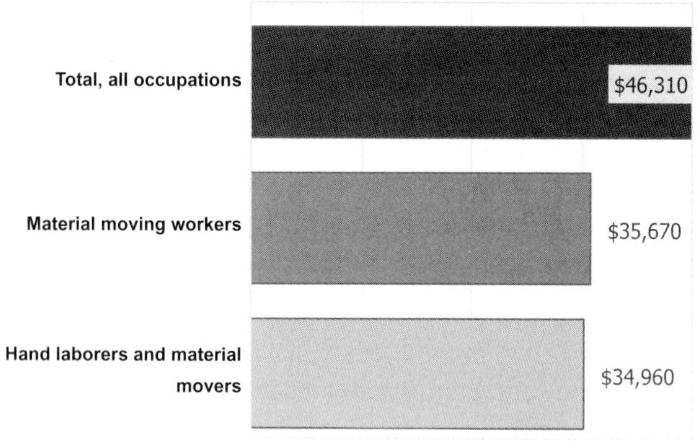

Note: All Occupations includes all occupations in the U.S. Economy.
Source: U.S. Bureau of Labor Statistics, Occupational Employment and Wage Statistics.

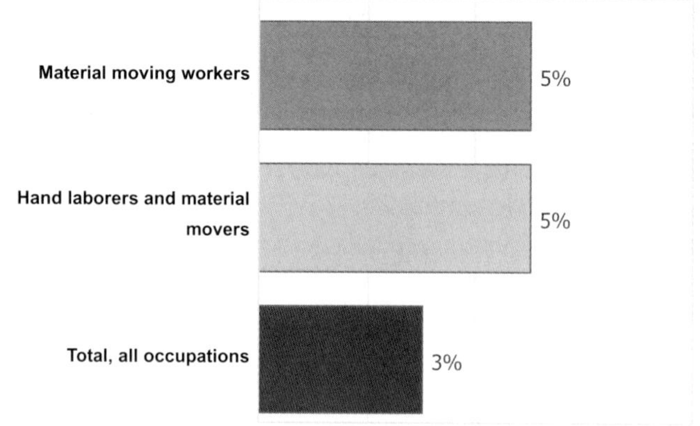

Note: All Occupations includes all occupations in the U.S. Economy.
Source: U.S. Bureau of Labor Statistics, Employment Projections program.

Most hand laborers and freight, stock, and material movers work full time.

Shifts longer than 8 hours are common, and sometimes overtime is available. Because materials are shipped around the clock, some workers, especially those in warehousing, work overnight shifts.

Job Outlook

Overall employment of hand laborers and material movers is projected to grow 5 percent from 2022 to 2032, faster than the average for all occupations.

About 1,075,800 openings for hand laborers and material movers are projected each year, on average, over the decade. Many of those openings are expected to result from the need to replace workers who transfer to different occupations or exit the labor force, such as to retire.

Employment

Projected employment of hand laborers and material movers varies by occupation (see table).

Some warehouses have installed equipment, such as high-speed conveyors and sorting systems, to increase efficiency. However, hand laborers and freight, stock, and material movers will still be needed to move materials in many sectors of the economy. Machine feeders and offbearers will be needed to supply materials into or remove materials from equipment that is automated or tended by other workers.

The continued growth in e-commerce will create an increased demand for packaging activities, supporting the demand for stockers and order fillers to prepare orders for pickup or delivery. In addition, some stores may require more workers to handle orders for pickup. However, companies are expanding the use of automated storage and retrieval tools, such as scanners and radio frequency identification (RFID) tags, in response to rising demand for products. These technologies will increase productivity for some of the manual tasks performed by stockers and order fillers, which may partly offset fast employment growth.

As the population grows, the amount of trash generated also is expected to increase. Refuse and recyclable material collectors will be needed to remove the trash, but efficiencies created by automation and improved routing will constrain employment growth.

Demand for automotive repair and maintenance services is expected to contribute to employment growth of cleaners of vehicles and equipment.

Grocery stores, which employ many hand packers and packagers, may employ fewer baggers as a growing number of stores have self-checkout stands at which customers or existing cashiers bag groceries themselves. Automation is becoming more viable in warehouses, limiting the need for workers there.

Occupational Title	SOC Code	Employment, 2022	Projected Employment, 2032	Change, 2022-32	
				Percent	Numeric
Hand laborers and material movers	—	7,099,400	7,452,800	5	353,400
Cleaners of vehicles and equipment	53-7061	401,800	416,800	4	15,000
Laborers and freight, stock, and material movers, hand	53-7062	2,988,500	3,147,300	5	158,800
Machine feeders and offbearers	53-7063	51,500	54,300	6	2,800
Packers and packagers, hand	53-7064	659,600	652,900	-1	-6,600
Stockers and order fillers	53-7065	2,851,600	3,030,300	6	178,600
Refuse and recyclable material collectors	53-7081	146,400	151,100	3	4,700

Contacts for More Information

For more information, visit

- MHI
- Warehousing Education and Research Council

Heavy and Tractor-trailer Truck Drivers

Summary

Quick Facts: Heavy and Tractor-trailer Truck Drivers	
2022 Median Pay	$49,920 per year $24.00 per hour
Typical Entry-Level Education	Postsecondary non-degree award
Work Experience in a Related Occupation	None
On-the-job Training	Short-term on-the-job training
Number of Jobs, 2022	2,192,300
Job Outlook, 2022-32	4% (As fast as average)
Employment Change, 2022-32	89,300

What Heavy and Tractor-trailer Truck Drivers Do

Heavy and tractor-trailer truck drivers transport goods from one location to another.

Work Environment

Working as a long-haul truck driver is a lifestyle choice because these drivers can be away from home for days or weeks at a time.

How to Become a Heavy or Tractor-trailer Truck Driver

Heavy and tractor-trailer truck drivers usually have a high school diploma and attend a professional truck driving school. They must have a commercial driver's license (CDL).

Pay

The median annual wage for heavy and tractor-trailer truck drivers was $49,920 in May 2022.

Job Outlook

Employment of heavy and tractor-trailer truck drivers is projected to grow 4 percent from 2022 to 2032, about as fast as the average for all occupations.

About 241,200 openings for heavy and tractor-trailer truck drivers are projected each year, on average, over the decade. Many of those openings are expected to result from the need to replace workers who transfer to different occupations or exit the labor force, such as to retire.

State & Area Data

Explore resources for employment and wages by state and area for heavy and tractor-trailer truck drivers.

Similar Occupations

Compare the job duties, education, job growth, and pay of heavy and tractor-trailer truck drivers with similar occupations.

More Information, Including Links to O*NET

Learn more about heavy and tractor-trailer truck drivers by visiting additional resources, including O*NET, a source on key characteristics of workers and occupations.

What Heavy and Tractor-trailer Truck Drivers Do

Heavy and tractor-trailer truck drivers transport goods from one location to another. Most tractor-trailer drivers are long-haul drivers and operate trucks with a total weight exceeding 26,000 pounds for the vehicle, passengers, and cargo. These drivers deliver goods over intercity routes that sometimes span several states.

Duties

Heavy and tractor-trailer truck drivers typically do the following:

- Drive long distances
- Report any incidents encountered on the road to a dispatcher
- Follow all applicable traffic laws
- Secure cargo for transport, using ropes, blocks, chains, or covers
- Inspect their trailers before and after the trip and record any defects they find

Truck drivers transport goods around the country.

Some heavy and tractor-trailer truck drivers plan their own routes.

- Maintain a log of their working hours, following all federal and state regulations
- Report serious mechanical problems to the appropriate people
- Keep their trucks and associated equipment clean and in good working order

Most heavy and tractor-trailer truck drivers' routes are assigned by a dispatcher, but some independent drivers still plan their own routes. When planning routes, drivers must take into account any road restrictions that prohibit large trucks. Drivers also must plan legally required rest periods into their trip.

Some drivers have one or two routes that they drive regularly, and other drivers take many different routes throughout the country. In addition, some drivers have routes that include Mexico or Canada.

Companies sometimes use two drivers, known as teams, on long runs to minimize downtime. On these team runs, one driver sleeps in a berth behind the cab while the other drives.

Certain cargo requires drivers to adhere to additional safety regulations. Some heavy truck drivers who transport hazardous materials, such as chemical waste, must take special precautions when driving and may carry specialized safety equipment in case of an accident. Other drivers, such as those carrying liquids, oversized loads, or cars, must follow rules that apply specifically to them.

Some long-haul truck drivers, also called *owner-operators*, buy or lease trucks and go into business for themselves. In addition to their driving tasks, owner-operators have business tasks, including finding and keeping clients and doing administrative work.

Work Environment

Heavy and tractor-trailer truck drivers held about 2.2 million jobs in 2022. The largest employers of heavy and tractor-trailer truck drivers were as follows:

Truck transportation	42%
Wholesale trade	12
Self-employed workers	8
Manufacturing	7
Construction	6

Working as a long-haul truck driver is a lifestyle choice because these drivers can be away from home for days or weeks at a time. They spend much of this time alone. Driving a truck can be a physically demanding job as well. Driving for many consecutive hours can be tiring, and some drivers must load and unload cargo.

Injuries and Illnesses

Because of the potential for traffic accidents, heavy and tractor-trailer truck drivers have one of the highest rates of injuries and illnesses of all occupations.

Some truck drivers travel far from home and can be on the road for long periods at a time.

Although fatalities are uncommon, heavy and tractor-trailer truck drivers experience one of the highest rates of occupational fatalities of all occupations.

Work Schedules

Most heavy tractor-trailer drivers work full time. The Federal Motor Carrier Safety Administration regulates the hours that a long-haul truck driver may work. Drivers may not work more than 14 hours straight, comprising up to 11 hours driving and the remaining time doing other work, such as unloading cargo. Between working periods, drivers must have at least 10 hours off duty. Drivers also are limited to driving no more than 60 hours within 7 days or 70 hours within 8 days; then drivers must take 34 hours off before starting another 7- or 8-day run. Drivers must record their hours in a logbook. Truck drivers often work nights, weekends, and holidays.

How to Become a Heavy or Tractor-trailer Truck Driver

Heavy and tractor-trailer truck drivers usually have a high school diploma and attend a professional truck driving school. They must have a commercial driver's license (CDL).

Education

Most companies require their truck drivers to have a high school diploma or equivalent.

Many prospective drivers attend professional truck driving schools, where they take training courses to learn how to maneuver large vehicles on highways or through crowded streets. During these classes, drivers also learn the federal laws and regulations governing interstate truck driving. Students may attend either a private truck-driving school or a program at a community college that lasts between 3 and 6 months.

Upon finishing their classes, drivers receive a certificate of completion.

Drivers learn the federal laws and regulations governing interstate trucking.

Licenses, Certifications, and Registrations

All long-haul truck drivers must have a commercial driver's license (CDL). Qualifications for obtaining a CDL vary by state but generally include passing both a knowledge test and a driving test. States have the right to refuse to issue a CDL to anyone who has had a CDL suspended by another state.

Drivers can get endorsements to their CDL that show their ability to drive a specialized type of vehicle. Truck drivers transporting hazardous materials (HAZMAT) must have a hazardous materials endorsement (H). Getting this endorsement requires passing an additional knowledge test and a background check.

Federal regulations require CDL drivers to maintain a clean driving record and pass a physical exam every two years. They are also subject to random testing for drug or alcohol abuse. Truck drivers can have their CDL suspended if they are convicted of driving under the influence of alcohol or drugs or are convicted of a felony involving the use of a motor vehicle.

Other actions can result in a suspension after multiple violations. The Federal Motor Carrier Safety Administration website has a list of these violations. Additionally, some companies have stricter standards than what federal regulations require.

Training

After completing truck-driving school and being hired by a company, drivers normally receive several weeks of on-the-job training. During this time, they drive a truck accompanied by an experienced mentor-driver in the passenger seat. This period of on-the-job training is given so that the new drivers will learn more about the specific type of truck they will drive and material they will transport.

Important Qualities

Hand-eye coordination. Drivers of heavy trucks and tractor-trailers must be able to coordinate their legs, hands, and eyes simultaneously so that they will react appropriately to the situation around them and drive the vehicle safely.

Hearing ability. Truck drivers need good hearing. Federal regulations require that a driver be able to hear a forced whisper in one ear at 5 feet away (with or without the use of a hearing aid).

Physical health. Federal regulations do not allow people to become truck drivers if they have a medical condition, such as high blood pressure or epilepsy, which may interfere with their ability to operate a truck. The Federal Motor Carrier Safety Administration website has a full list of medical conditions that disqualify someone from driving a long-haul truck.

Visual ability. Truck drivers must be able to pass vision tests. Federal regulations require a driver to have at least 20/40 vision with a 70-degree field of vision in each eye and the ability to distinguish the colors on a traffic light.

Pay

The median annual wage for heavy and tractor-trailer truck drivers was $49,920 in May 2022. The median wage is the wage at which half the workers in an occupation earned more than that amount and half earned less. The lowest 10 percent earned less than $35,300, and the highest 10 percent earned more than $75,220.

In May 2022, the median annual wages for heavy and tractor-trailer truck drivers in the top industries in which they worked were as follows:

Truck transportation	$52,800
Wholesale trade	49,440
Manufacturing	48,600
Construction	48,590

Drivers of heavy trucks and tractor-trailers usually are paid by how many miles they have driven, plus bonuses. The per-mile rate varies from employer to employer and may depend on the type of cargo and the experience of the driver. Some long-distance drivers, especially owner-operators, are paid a share of the revenue from shipping.

Most heavy tractor-trailer drivers work full time. The Federal Motor Carrier Safety Administration regulates the hours that a long-haul truck driver may work. Drivers may not work more than 14 hours straight, comprising up to 11 hours driving and the remaining time doing other work, such as unloading cargo.

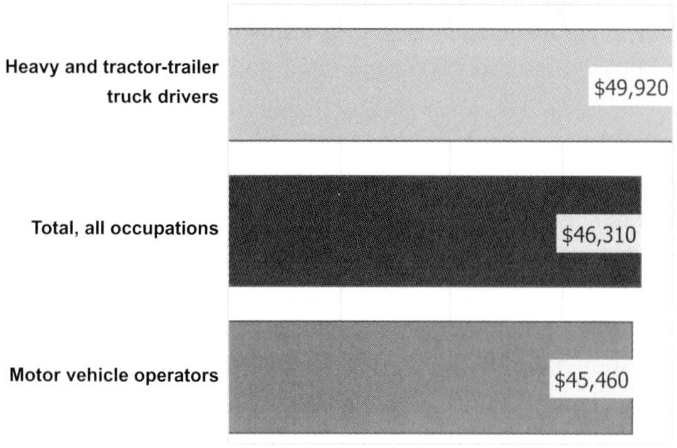

Note: All Occupations includes all occupations in the U.S. Economy.
Source: U.S. Bureau of Labor Statistics, Occupational Employment and Wage Statistics.

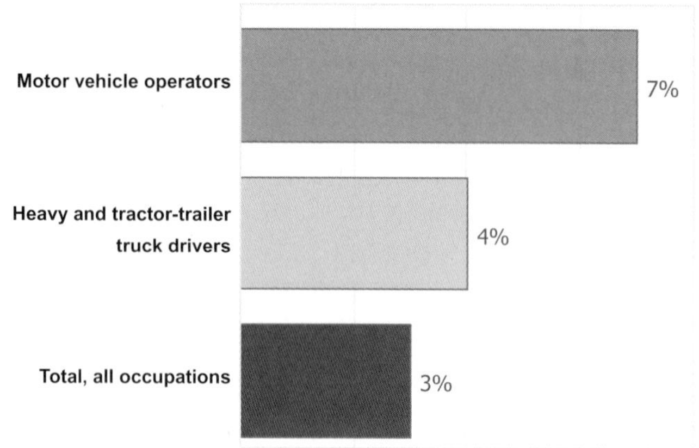

Note: All Occupations includes all occupations in the U.S. Economy.
Source: U.S. Bureau of Labor Statistics, Employment Projections program.

Between working periods, drivers must have at least 10 hours off duty. Drivers also are limited to driving no more than 60 hours within 7 days or 70 hours within 8 days; then drivers must take 34 hours off before starting another 7- or 8-day run. Drivers must record their hours in a logbook. Truck drivers often work nights, weekends, and holidays.

Job Outlook

Employment of heavy and tractor-trailer truck drivers is projected to grow 4 percent from 2022 to 2032, about as fast as the average for all occupations.

About 241,200 openings for heavy and tractor-trailer truck drivers are projected each year, on average, over the decade. Many of those openings are expected to result from the need to replace workers who transfer to different occupations or exit the labor force, such as to retire.

Employment

Trucks transport most of the freight in the United States. The need for truck drivers should rise as households and businesses increase their spending and their demand for goods.

Occupational Title	SOC Code	Employment, 2022	Projected Employment, 2032	Change, 2022-32	
				Percent	Numeric
Heavy and tractor-trailer truck drivers	53-3032	2,192,300	2,281,500	4	89,300

Contacts for More Information

For more information about truck drivers, visit

- American Trucking Associations
- Federal Motor Carrier Safety Administration
- Commercial Vehicle Training Association
- National Association of Publicly Funded Truck Driving Schools

Material Moving Machine Operators

Summary

Quick Facts: Material Moving Machine Operators	
2022 Median Pay	$41,730 per year $20.06 per hour
Typical Entry-Level Education	See How to Become One
Work Experience in a Related Occupation	See How to Become One
On-the-job Training	See How to Become One
Number of Jobs, 2022	879,500
Job Outlook, 2022-32	4% (As fast as average)
Employment Change, 2022-32	31,700

What Material Moving Machine Operators Do

Material moving machine operators use equipment to transport objects.

Work Environment

Most material moving machine operators work full time, and some work more than 40 hours per week. Because materials are shipped around the clock, some operators work overnight shifts.

How to Become a Material Moving Machine Operator

Education requirements vary by occupation. Crane and tower operators typically need work experience in a related occupation.

Pay

The median annual wage for material moving machine operators was $41,730 in May 2022.

Job Outlook

Overall employment of material moving machine operators is projected to grow 4 percent from 2022 to 2032, about as fast as the average for all occupations.

About 88,900 openings for material moving machine operators are projected each year, on average, over the decade. Many of those openings are expected to result from the need to replace workers who transfer to different occupations or exit the labor force, such as to retire.

What Material Moving Machine Operators Do

Material moving machine operators use equipment to transport objects. For example, some operators move goods around factories and storage areas or onto container ships. Others move construction materials around building sites.

Duties

Material moving machine operators typically do the following:

- Set up and inspect material moving equipment
- Control equipment with levers, wheels, or foot pedals
- Move material according to a plan or schedule
- Signal and direct workers to load and unload materials
- Keep a record of the material they move and where they move it to
- Make minor repairs to their equipment

In warehouses and factories, most material moving machine operators use forklifts and conveyor belts. Wireless sensors and tags keep track of merchandise, allowing operators to locate it faster. Some operators also check goods for damage. These operators usually work closely with hand laborers and material movers.

In construction, material moving machine operators transport objects around building sites. Some work on a building site for the entire length of the construction project. For example, certain material moving machine operators help to construct

Material moving machine operators use machinery to move goods around a warehouse or onto container ships.

Crane and tower operators are commonly employed in construction and water transportation.

highrise buildings by transporting materials to workers who are far above ground level. (For information about workers who operate heavy machinery for building, road, and other construction sites, see the profile on construction equipment operators.)

All material moving machine operators are responsible for safely controlling their equipment or vehicle.

The following are examples of types of material moving machine operators:

Conveyor operators and tenders control conveyor systems that move materials on an automatic belt. They monitor sensors to regulate the speed with which the system's conveyor belt moves. They move materials to and from places such as storage areas, vehicles, and building sites. Operators also may check the shipping order and determine the route that materials take along a conveyor.

Crane and tower operators use cable and tower equipment to lift and move materials, machinery, or other heavy objects. From a control station, operators extend and retract horizontal booms, rotate the superstructure, and lower and raise hooks attached to cables at the end of their crane or tower. Operators usually are guided by workers on the ground who use hand signals or transmit voice signals through a radio. Crane and tower operators usually work at construction sites or major ports, where they load and unload cargo. Operators also may work in iron and steel mills.

Dredge operators excavate waterways. They operate equipment on the water to remove sand, gravel, or rock from harbors or lakes. Removing these materials helps to prevent erosion and to maintain navigable waterways, allowing larger ships to use ports. Dredging also is used to help restore wetlands and maintain beaches.

Hoist and winch operators, also called ***derrick operators***, control the movement of platforms, cables, and cages that transport workers or materials in industrial operations, such as constructing a highrise building. Operators regulate the speed of the equipment on the based on the needs of the workers.

Industrial truck and tractor operators drive trucks and tractors that move materials around storage yards, warehouses, or other worksites. These trucks, often called forklifts, have a lifting mechanism and forks, which make them useful for moving heavy and large objects. Some industrial truck and tractor operators drive tractors that pull trailers loaded with material around factories or storage areas.

Work Environment

Material moving machine operators held about 879,500 jobs in 2022. Employment in the detailed occupations that make up material moving machine operators was distributed as follows:

Industrial truck and tractor operators	796,600
Crane and tower operators	48,400
Conveyor operators and tenders	30,600
Hoist and winch operators	2,800
Dredge operators	1,000

Industrial truck and tractor operators use forklifts in warehousing and storage facilities.

The largest employers of material moving machine operators were as follows:

Industry	Percent
Warehousing and storage	37%
Wholesale trade	10
Temporary help services	8
Food manufacturing	5
Construction	3

Material moving machine operators work indoors and outdoors in a variety of industries.

Injuries and Illnesses

Hoist and winch operators have one of the highest rates of injuries and illnesses of all occupations.

Many workers wear personal protective equipment—including gloves, hardhats, and harnesses—to guard against injury.

Work Schedules

Most material moving machine operators work full time, and some work more than 40 hours per week. Because materials are shipped around the clock, some work overnight shifts.

How to Become a Material Moving Machine Operator

Education and training requirements vary by occupation. Crane operators typically have several years of experience in a related occupation.

Education

Although no formal educational credential is typically required, companies may prefer to hire material moving machine operators who have a high school diploma. For crane and tower operators and dredge operators, a high school diploma or equivalent is typically required.

Training

Material moving machine operators typically are trained on the job in less than a month, but the amount of time spent in training varies with the type of machine. Some machines, such as cranes and towers, are complex and may require several months of training. Others, such as industrial trucks and forklifts, may take only a few days to learn how to operate. New workers usually are trained by an experienced employee.

During their training, material moving machine operators learn safety rules, many of which are standardized through the Occupational Safety & Health Administration (OSHA). Employers must certify that each operator has received the proper training. Operators who work with hazardous materials receive additional training.

The International Union of Operating Engineers offers training programs for heavy-equipment operators, such as crane operators.

Material moving machine operators are trained on the job.

Licenses, Certifications, and Registrations

Some states and cities require crane operators to be licensed. Operators typically must complete a skills test in which they show that they can control a crane. They also must pass a written exam that tests their knowledge of safety rules and procedures. Check with your state or city licensing agency for specific requirements.

Employers may require or prefer that workers become certified. For example, the National Commission for the Certification of Crane Operators (NCCCO) offers several certifications for crane operators and related workers.

Work Experience in a Related Occupation

Crane and tower operators typically have several years of experience working as construction equipment operators, hoist and winch operators, or riggers and signalers.

Important Qualities

Communication skills. Material moving machine operators signal and direct workers to load and unload material. They also receive direction from workers on the ground when moving material.

Coordination. Material moving machine operators must have steady hands and feet to guide and control heavy machinery precisely. They use hand controls to maneuver their machines through tight spaces, around large objects, and on uneven surfaces.

Mechanical skills. Material moving machine operators make minor adjustments to their machines and perform basic maintenance on them.

Visual ability. Material moving machine operators must be able to see clearly where they are driving or what they are moving. They must also watch for nearby workers, who may unknowingly be in their path.

Pay

The median annual wage for material moving machine operators was $41,730 in May 2022. The median wage is the wage at which half the workers in an occupation earned more than that amount and half earned less. The lowest 10 percent earned less than $32,070, and the highest 10 percent earned more than $59,610.

Median annual wages for material moving machine operators in May 2022 were as follows:

Crane and tower operators	$61,340
Hoist and winch operators	58,950
Dredge operators	47,090
Industrial truck and tractor operators	41,230
Conveyor operators and tenders	36,890

In May 2022, the median annual wages for material moving machine operators in the top industries in which they worked were as follows:

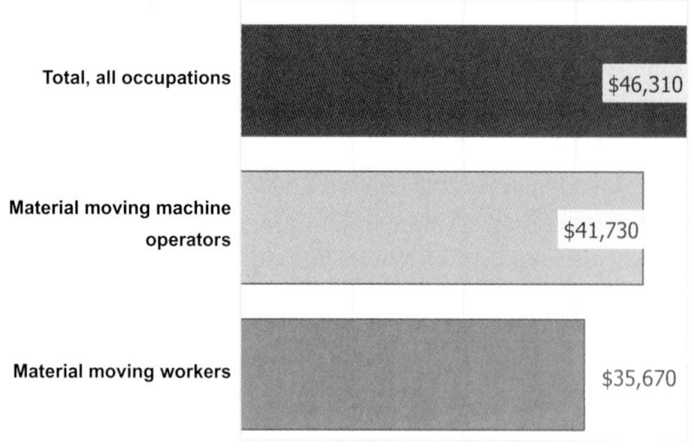

Note: All Occupations includes all occupations in the U.S. Economy.
Source: U.S. Bureau of Labor Statistics, Occupational Employment and Wage Statistics.

Construction	$64,960
Warehousing and storage	44,910
Food manufacturing	40,270
Wholesale trade	39,460
Temporary help services	35,810

Most material moving machine operators work full time, and some work more than 40 hours per week. Because materials are shipped around the clock, some work overnight shifts.

Job Outlook

Overall employment of material moving machine operators is projected to grow 4 percent from 2022 to 2032, about as fast as the average for all occupations.

About 88,900 openings for material moving machine operators are projected each year, on average, over the decade. Many of those openings are expected to result from the need to replace workers who transfer to different occupations or exit the labor force, such as to retire.

Employment

Projected employment of material moving machine operators varies by occupation (see table).

Material moving machine operators will be needed to move materials or products to and from various locations, such as warehouses, stockpiles, or processing stations. The continued growth in e-commerce will increase the amount of materials and products needing to be moved. However, employment demand for these workers may be limited by the expansion of automated machinery and technologies, such as sensors and scanners, that improve operations and increase efficiencies.

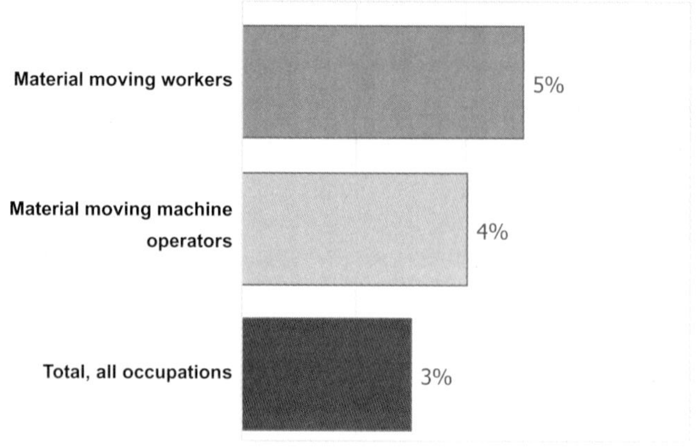

Note: All Occupations includes all occupations in the U.S. Economy.
Source: U.S. Bureau of Labor Statistics, Employment Projections program.

Occupational Title	SOC Code	Employment, 2022	Projected Employment, 2032	Change, 2022-32	
				Percent	Numeric
Material moving machine operators	—	879,500	911,200	4	31,700
Conveyor operators and tenders	53-7011	30,600	32,400	6	1,800
Crane and tower operators	53-7021	48,400	48,500	0	100
Dredge operators	53-7031	1,000	1,100	0	0
Hoist and winch operators	53-7041	2,800	2,700	-2	0
Industrial truck and tractor operators	53-7051	796,600	826,500	4	29,900

Contacts for More Information

For more information, visit

- International Union of Operating Engineers (IUOE)
- MHI
- National Commission for the Certification of Crane Operators (NCCCO)
- Warehousing Education and Research Council (WERC)

Railroad Workers

Summary

Quick Facts: Railroad Workers	
2022 Median Pay	$68,960 per year $33.15 per hour
Typical Entry-Level Education	High school diploma or equivalent
Work Experience in a Related Occupation	See How to Become One
On-the-job Training	Moderate-term on-the-job training
Number of Jobs, 2022	78,600
Job Outlook, 2022-32	1% (Little or no change)
Employment Change, 2022-32	800

What Railroad Workers Do

Railroad workers ensure that passenger and freight trains operate safely. They may drive trains, coordinate the activities of the trains, or control signals and switches in the rail yard.

Work Environment

Nearly all railroad workers are employed in the rail transportation industry. Most work full time, and some work more than 40 hours per week.

How to Become a Railroad Worker

Railroad workers typically need a high school diploma or equivalent and several months of on-the-job training.

Pay

The median annual wage for railroad workers was $68,960 in May 2022.

Job Outlook

Overall employment of railroad workers is projected to show little or no change from 2022 to 2032.

Conductors make sure passengers board safely.

Despite limited employment growth, about 6,500 openings for railroad workers are projected each year, on average, over the decade. Most of those openings are expected to result from the need to replace workers who transfer to different occupations or exit the labor force, such as to retire.

What Railroad Workers Do

Railroad workers ensure that passenger and freight trains run on time and travel safely. Some workers drive trains, some coordinate the activities of the trains, and others operate signals and switches in the rail yard.

Duties

Railroad workers typically do the following:

- Check the mechanical condition of locomotives and make adjustments when necessary
- Document issues with a train that require further inspection
- Operate locomotive engines within or between stations

Freight trains move billions of tons of goods around the country to ports, where the goods are shipped around the world. Passenger trains transport millions of travelers to destinations around the country. Railroad workers are essential to keeping freight and passenger trains running properly.

Workers in railroad occupations frequently collaborate. Locomotive engineers travel with conductors and, sometimes, with brake operators. Locomotive engineers and conductors are in constant contact and keep each other informed of any changes in the train's condition. Signal and switch operators communicate with both locomotive and rail yard engineers to make sure that trains arrive at the correct destination. Workers in all of these occupations are in contact with dispatchers, who direct them on where to go and what to do.

The following are examples of types of railroad workers:

Conductors travel on both freight and passenger trains and coordinate activities of the train crew. On passenger trains,

Locomotive engineers use a variety of controls to operate a train.

they ensure travelers' safety and comfort. They also check passengers' tickets and make announcements to keep passengers informed. On freight trains, they oversee the secure loading and unloading of cargo.

Locomotive engineers drive freight or passenger trains between stations. They drive long-distance trains and commuter trains, but not subway trains. They monitor systems that measure the train's operation, such as speed and air pressure. Locomotive engineers use a variety of controls, such as throttles and airbrakes, to operate the train and ensure that the locomotive runs smoothly. They observe the track for obstructions to ensure safety.

When driving freight trains, engineers must be aware of the goods their train is carrying.

Railroad brake, signal, and switch operators and locomotive firers maintain and monitor equipment to ensure that the trains run safely.

Brake operators help couple and uncouple train cars. Some travel with the train as part of the crew.

Signal operators install and maintain the signals along tracks and in rail yard. Signals are important in preventing accidents because they allow increased communication between trains and dispatchers.

Switch operators monitor the track switches in rail yards. These switches allow trains to move between tracks and ensure trains are heading in the right direction.

Locomotive firers are sometimes part of a train crew and typically monitor tracks and train instruments. They look for equipment that is dragging, obstacles on the tracks, and other potential safety problems. Few trains still use firers, because their work has been automated or is now done by a locomotive engineer or conductor.

Rail yard engineers operate train engines within the rail yard. They move locomotives between tracks to keep the trains organized and on schedule. Sometimes, rail yard engineers are called *hostlers* and drive locomotives to and from maintenance shops or prepare them for the locomotive engineer. Some use remote locomotive technology to move freight cars within the rail yards.

Yardmasters manage schedules and coordinate the activities of workers in the rail yard. They review shipping records of freight trains and ensure that trains are carrying the correct material before leaving the yard. Yardmasters also switch train traffic to a certain section of the line to allow other inbound and outbound trains to get around. They tell yard engineers where to move cars to fit the planned configuration or to load freight.

Not all rail yards use yardmasters. In rail yards that do not have yardmasters, a conductor typically performs yardmaster duties.

Work Environment

Railroad workers held about 78,600 jobs in 2022. Employment in the detailed occupations that make up railroad workers was distributed as follows:

Locomotive engineers who work on long routes are sometimes away from home for long periods at a time.

Railroad conductors and yardmasters	34,200
Locomotive engineers	29,700
Railroad brake, signal, and switch operators and locomotive firers	12,200
Rail yard engineers, dinkey operators, and hostlers	2,600

The largest employers of railroad workers were as follows:

Rail transportation	83%

Conductors on passenger trains generally work in cleaner, more comfortable conditions than conductors on freight trains. However, conductors on passenger trains sometimes must respond to upset or unruly passengers.

Locomotive engineers work in climate-controlled train cabs that are generally large enough to move around in comfortably. However, engineers may need to adjust to the loud noise or frequent vibrations when the train is in motion.

Railroad operators, rail yard engineers, and related workers spend most of their time outside, regardless of the weather.

Injuries and Illnesses

Railroad conductors and yardmasters have one of the highest rates of injuries and illnesses of all occupations. Common injuries include sprains, strains, and bruises.

Work Schedules

Because trains operate 24 hours a day, 7 days a week, railroad workers' schedules may vary to include nights, weekends, and holidays. Most work full time, and some work more than 40 hours per week. Federal regulations require a minimum number of rest hours for train operators.

Locomotive engineers and conductors whose trains travel long routes may be away from home for long periods. Those who work on passenger trains with short routes generally have more predictable schedules. Workers on some freight trains have irregular schedules.

For engineers and conductors, seniority (the number of years on the job) usually dictates who works the most desired shifts. Some engineers and conductors, called *extra-board*, are hired for temporary work only when a railroad needs extra or substitute staff on a certain route.

How to Become a Railroad Worker

Workers in railroad occupations typically need a high school diploma or equivalent and several months of on-the-job training.

Education

Rail companies typically require workers to have at least a high school diploma or equivalent. However, employers may prefer to hire workers who have postsecondary education, such as coursework, a certificate, or an associate's or bachelor's degree.

Training

Locomotive engineers typically receive 3 or more months of on-the-job training before they can operate a train on their own. Typically, this training involves riding with an experienced engineer. In addition, railroad companies provide continuing education so that engineers can maintain their skills.

Most railroad companies have up to 12 months of on-the-job training for conductors and yardmasters. Amtrak (the passenger train company) and some of the larger freight railroad companies operate their own training programs. Small and regional railroads may send conductors to a central training facility or a community college. Yardmasters may be sent to training programs or may be trained by an experienced yardmaster.

Rail yard engineers and signal and switch operators also receive on-the-job training, typically through a company training program. This program may last a few weeks to a few months, depending on the company and the complexity of the job. The program may include both classroom instruction and hands-on training under the direction of an experienced employee.

All train employees need mechanical ability.

Work Experience in a Related Occupation

Most locomotive engineers first work as conductors or yardmasters for several years.

Licenses, Certifications, and Registrations

Locomotive engineers and conductors must be certified by the Federal Railroad Administration (FRA). The certifications, conducted by the railroad that employs them, involve a written knowledge test, a skills test, and a supervisor determination that the engineer or conductor understands all physical aspects of the particular route on which he or she will be operating.

Engineers who change routes must be recertified for the new route. Even engineers and conductors who do not switch routes must be recertified every few years.

At the end of the certification process, the engineer must pass a vision and hearing test.

Conductors who operate on national, regional, or commuter railroads are also required to become certified. To receive certification, new conductors must pass a test that has been designed and administered by the railroad and approved by the FRA.

In addition, railroad workers must be at least 21 years of age and pass a background test. They must also pass random drug and alcohol screenings over the course of their employment.

Advancement

Rail yard engineers, switch operators, and signal operators may advance to become conductors or yardmasters.

Important Qualities

Communication skills. Railroad workers must be able to communicate with other crewmembers, dispatchers, and passengers to ensure safety and keep the trains on schedule.

Customer-service skills. Conductors on passenger trains ensure travelers' comfort, make announcements, and answer questions. They must be courteous and patient, especially when dealing with unruly or upset passengers.

Hand-eye coordination. Locomotive engineers must operate controls based, in part, on their observations of the train's surroundings.

Hearing ability. To ensure safety on the train and in the rail yard, railroad workers must be able to hear warning signals and communicate with other employees.

Leadership skills. On some trains, a conductor directs a crew. In rail yards, yardmasters oversee other workers.

Mechanical skills. Railroad workers should be able to adjust equipment when it does not work properly. Some rail yard engineers spend most of their time fixing broken equipment or conducting mechanical inspections.

Physical strength. Rail yard engineers may have to lift heavy equipment.

Visual ability. To drive a train, locomotive engineers need excellent eyesight, peripheral vision, and color vision.

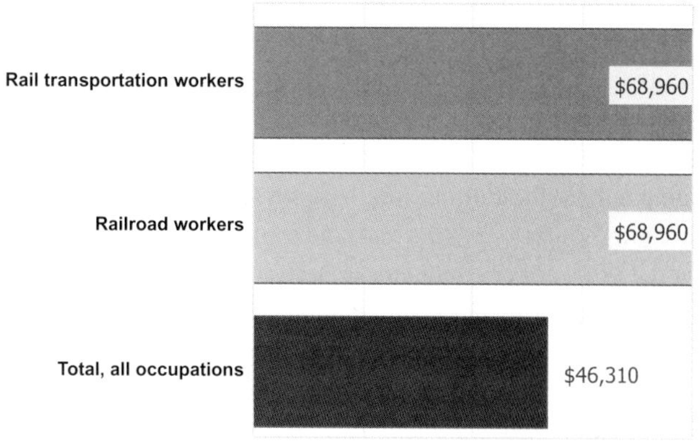

Note: All Occupations includes all occupations in the U.S. Economy.
Source: U.S. Bureau of Labor Statistics, Occupational Employment and Wage Statistics.

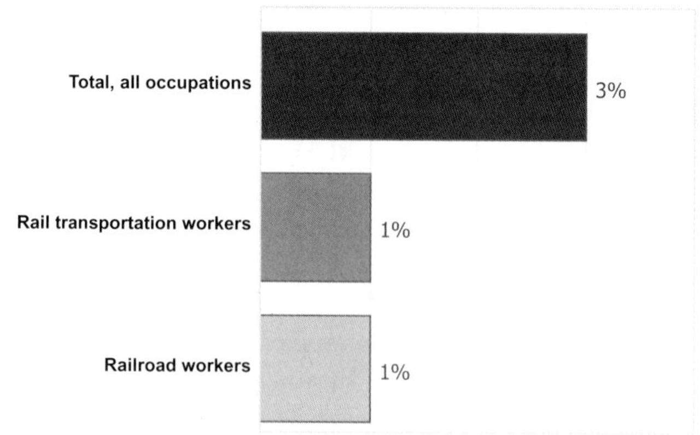

Note: All Occupations includes all occupations in the U.S. Economy.
Source: U.S. Bureau of Labor Statistics, Employment Projections program.

Pay

The median annual wage for railroad workers was $68,960 in May 2022. The median wage is the wage at which half the workers in an occupation earned more than that amount and half earned less. The lowest 10 percent earned less than $48,940, and the highest 10 percent earned more than $87,960.

Median annual wages for railroad workers in May 2022 were as follows:

Locomotive engineers	$74,570
Railroad conductors and yardmasters	68,180
Railroad brake, signal, and switch operators and locomotive firers	67,540
Rail yard engineers, dinkey operators, and hostlers	56,340

In May 2022, the median annual wages for railroad workers in the top industries in which they worked were as follows:

Rail transportation	$70,110

Because trains operate 24 hours a day, 7 days a week, railroad workers' schedules may vary to include nights, weekends, and holidays. Most work full time, and some work more than 40 hours per week. Federal regulations require a minimum number of rest hours for train operators.

Locomotive engineers and conductors whose trains travel long routes can be away from home for long periods of time. Those who work on passenger trains with short routes generally have more predictable schedules. Workers on some freight trains have irregular schedules.

For engineers and conductors, seniority (the number of years on the job) usually dictates who works the most desired shifts. Some engineers and conductors, called *extra-board*, are hired for temporary work only when a railroad needs extra or substitute staff on a certain route.

Job Outlook

Overall employment of railroad workers is projected to show little or no change from 2022 to 2032.

Despite limited employment growth, about 6,500 openings for railroad workers are projected each year, on average, over the decade. Most of those openings are expected to result from the need to replace workers who transfer to different occupations or exit the labor force, such as to retire.

Employment

The expected increase in intermodal freight activity—the shipment of goods through multiple transportation modes—may support demand for railroad workers. However, railroads' efforts to operate more efficiently, such as by deploying automated systems, are likely to limit employment.

Furthermore, a decline in the use of coal, which historically has been the largest commodity moved by rail, may decrease the demand for its transportation by rail.

Occupational Title	SOC Code	Employment, 2022	Projected Employment, 2032	Change, 2022-32	
				Percent	Numeric
Railroad workers	—	78,600	79,500	1	800
Locomotive engineers	53-4011	29,700	29,900	1	200
Rail yard engineers, dinkey operators, and hostlers	53-4013	2,600	2,600	2	100
Railroad brake, signal, and switch operators and locomotive firers	53-4022	12,200	12,300	1	100
Railroad conductors and yardmasters	53-4031	34,200	34,600	1	400

Contacts for More Information

For more information, visit

- National Railroad Passenger Corporation (Amtrak)
- Association of American Railroads (AAR)
- Federal Railroad Administration (FRA)

Taxi Drivers, Shuttle Drivers, and Chauffeurs

Summary

Quick Facts: Taxi Drivers, Shuttle Drivers, and Chauffeurs	
2022 Median Pay	$32,440 per year $15.59 per hour
Typical Entry-Level Education	No formal educational credential
Work Experience in a Related Occupation	None
On-the-job Training	Short-term on-the-job training
Number of Jobs, 2022	395,700
Job Outlook, 2022-32	14% (Much faster than average)
Employment Change, 2022-32	54,000

What Taxi Drivers, Shuttle Drivers, and Chauffeurs Do

Taxi drivers (including ride-hailing drivers), shuttle drivers, and chauffeurs transport people to and from the places they need to go.

Work Environment

Some taxi drivers, shuttle drivers, and chauffeurs work part time. Work schedules vary and may include early mornings, evenings, or weekends.

How to Become a Taxi Driver, Shuttle Driver, or Chauffeur

Taxi drivers, shuttle drivers, and chauffeurs typically have no formal educational requirements. They typically get brief on-the-job training. They also may need a special driver's license, such as a taxi or limousine license.

Taxi drivers charge a fare to transport people to and from the places they need to go.

Pay

The median annual wage for shuttle drivers and chauffeurs was $32,800 in May 2022.

The median annual wage for taxi drivers was $30,670 in May 2022.

Job Outlook

Overall employment of taxi drivers, shuttle drivers, and chauffeurs is projected to grow 14 percent from 2022 to 2032, much faster than the average for all occupations.

About 55,400 openings for taxi drivers, shuttle drivers, and chauffeurs are projected each year, on average, over the decade. Many of those openings are expected to result from the need to replace workers who transfer to different occupations or exit the labor force, such as to retire.

What Taxi Drivers, Shuttle Drivers, and Chauffeurs Do

Taxi drivers (including ride-hailing drivers), shuttle drivers, and chauffeurs drive people to and from the places they need to go, such as homes, workplaces, airports, and shopping centers.

Duties

Taxi drivers, shuttle drivers, and chauffeurs typically do the following:

- Drive taxicabs, vans, limousines, or other motor vehicles to transport passengers
- Pick up passengers and listen to where they want to go
- Help passengers load and unload their luggage, packages, or other belongings
- Check the vehicle for problems and do basic maintenance
- Keep the inside and outside of the vehicle clean
- Operate wheelchair lifts when needed
- Collect fare, if applicable, at passengers' destinations
- Keep a record of miles traveled

Taxi drivers, shuttle drivers, and chauffeurs must stay alert and watch the conditions of the road. They take precautions to ensure their passengers' safety, especially in heavy traffic or bad weather. Taxi drivers and chauffeurs also must follow vehicle-for-hire or livery regulations, such as where they can pick up passengers and how much they can charge.

Drivers are usually familiar with the streets in the areas they serve. They often use Global Positioning System (GPS) navigation to choose efficient routes. They may know on their own how to reach popular destinations, such as airports, train stations, convention centers, hotels, and other points of interest, as well as how to find fire and police stations and hospitals in case of an emergency.

Taxi drivers (including *ride-hailing drivers*) are summoned to pick up passengers and drive them, for a fare, to a destination stated by the passenger. Taxi drivers—also called *cabdrivers* or *cabbies*—typically get requests via a central dispatcher; ride-hailing drivers get requests through a smartphone app. In addition, taxi drivers may pick up passengers who wait at designated sites, such as train stations or hotels, or who signal their need for a ride from public places, such as sidewalks. While taxi drivers use a meter to calculate the fare, ride-hailing drivers pay a fare that is typically specified in the app.

Shuttle drivers and chauffeurs take passengers on planned trips. Shuttle drivers often drive large vans between airports or train stations and hotels or other destinations. Chauffeurs drive limousines, vans, or private vehicles and are hired to transport clients either for single trips or on a regular basis. Some chauffeurs have the duties of executive assistants, acting as driver, secretary, and itinerary planner.

Work Environment

Shuttle drivers and chauffeurs held about 218,400 jobs in 2022. The largest employers of shuttle drivers and chauffeurs were as follows:

Other transit and ground passenger transportation ...	22%
Taxi and limousine service	12
Automobile dealers	6
Local government, excluding education and hospitals	6
Services for the elderly and persons with disabilities	6

Taxi drivers held about 177,300 jobs in 2022. The largest employers of taxi drivers were as follows:

Self-employed workers	91%
Taxi and limousine service	7

Ride-hailing drivers may face stress or anxiety while driving through bad weather or heavy traffic conditions.

Taxi drivers, shuttle drivers, and chauffeurs held about 318,000 jobs in 2021. The largest employers of taxi drivers, shuttle drivers, and chauffeurs were as follows:

Self-employed workers includes those classified as independent contractors. Many taxi drivers, shuttle drivers, and chauffeurs typically work with little or no supervision.

Some taxi drivers own the cab they drive; others lease it from a dispatch company. Regardless of whether they own or lease their vehicle, taxi drivers may contract with a dispatch company to use its passenger-referral service or facilities for a fee. Ride-hailing drivers typically operate their own vehicles. Taxi drivers and ride-hailing drivers usually pay expenses, such as fuel and maintenance, on their vehicle.

Driving through heavy traffic or bad weather may be stressful. Drivers may have to pick up heavy luggage and packages, so they must use proper lifting technique to prevent strain or injury. Most of the injuries they incur result from traffic accidents.

Work Schedules

Work hours vary for taxi drivers, shuttle drivers, and chauffeurs. Some work part time. Evening and weekend work is common. Some drivers work early in the morning or late at night.

Taxi and ride-hailing drivers' work schedules are often flexible.

Shuttle drivers and chauffeurs' work schedules usually are more structured. They may have a set schedule, or they may work hours based on client needs. Some chauffeurs are on call throughout the day and must be ready to drive clients at a moment's notice.

How to Become a Taxi Driver, Shuttle Driver, or Chauffeur

Taxi drivers, shuttle drivers, and chauffeurs typically have no formal educational requirements, although many drivers have a high school diploma or equivalent. They typically get brief on-the-job training. They also may need a special driver's license, such as a taxi or limousine license. Clean driving records and background checks are sometimes required.

Education

Taxi drivers, shuttle drivers, and chauffeurs typically do not need formal educational credentials to enter the occupation. For drivers who are not self-employed, however, companies may prefer to hire drivers who have a high school diploma or postsecondary education.

Training

Companies that hire taxi drivers, shuttle drivers, and chauffeurs typically provide new drivers with a short period of on-the-job training. This training usually takes from 1 day to 2 weeks, depending on the company and the location. Some

Taxi drivers, shuttle drivers, and chauffeurs regularly interact with their passengers and should be courteous and helpful.

cities require the training, which typically covers local traffic laws, driver safety, and street layout. Taxi drivers also get training in operating the taximeter and communications equipment.

Ride-hailing drivers typically receive little to no on-the-job training beyond how to work the electronic hailing app so that they can pick up passengers.

Licenses, Certifications, and Registrations

All taxi drivers, shuttle drivers, and chauffeurs must have a driver's license. States and local municipalities set other requirements; check with your state or local agency for more information.

Taxi drivers and chauffeurs may need a taxi or limousine license. The Federal Motor Carrier Safety Administration requires drivers who transport 16 or more passengers (including the driver) to hold a commercial driver's license (CDL) with a passenger (P) endorsement. Licensure normally requires passing a background check, drug test, driving skills test, and written exam about regulations and local geography.

Regulations for ride-hailing drivers vary by state and city.

Advancement

Some taxi drivers start their own cab service by purchasing a taxi rather than leasing one through a dispatch company. Chauffeurs may advance with increased responsibilities or experiences, such as driving high-profile clients or different types of cars.

Important Qualities

Customer-service skills. Taxi drivers, shuttle drivers, and chauffeurs regularly interact with their passengers and should be courteous and helpful. For ride-hailing drivers, excellent customer-service skills may lead to favorable ratings from passengers.

Dependability. Passengers rely on these drivers to pick them up on time and safely transport them to their destination.

Hand–eye coordination. Drivers must watch their surroundings and avoid obstacles and other hazards while operating a vehicle.

Patience. Drivers must be calm and composed when driving through heavy traffic and congestion or when dealing with rude passengers.

Visual ability. Drivers must be able to pass a state-issued vision test to hold a driver's license.

Pay

The median annual wage for shuttle drivers and chauffeurs was $32,800 in May 2022. The median wage is the wage at which half the workers in an occupation earned more than that amount and half earned less. The lowest 10 percent earned less than $23,680, and the highest 10 percent earned more than $48,070.

The median annual wage for taxi drivers was $30,670 in May 2022. The lowest 10 percent earned less than $22,880, and the highest 10 percent earned more than $41,710.

In May 2022, the median annual wages for shuttle drivers and chauffeurs in the top industries in which they worked were as follows:

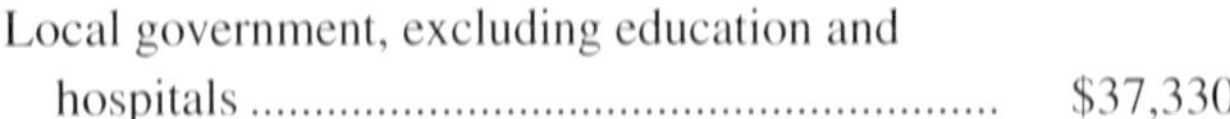

Local government, excluding education and hospitals $37,330

Taxi Drivers, Shuttle Drivers, and Chauffeurs

Median annual wages, May 2022

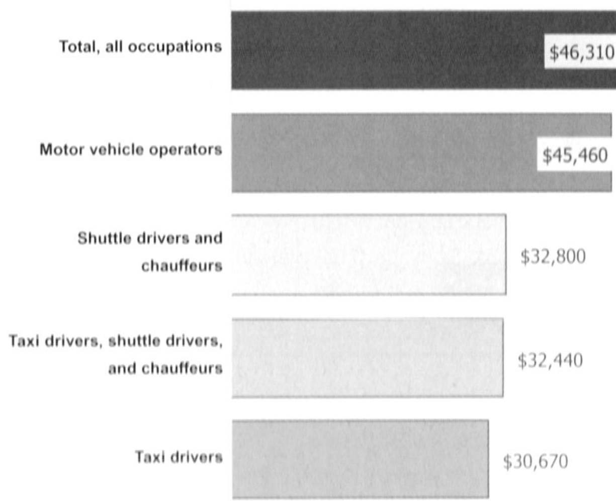

Note: All Occupations includes all occupations in the U.S. Economy.
Source: U.S. Bureau of Labor Statistics, Occupational Employment and Wage Statistics.

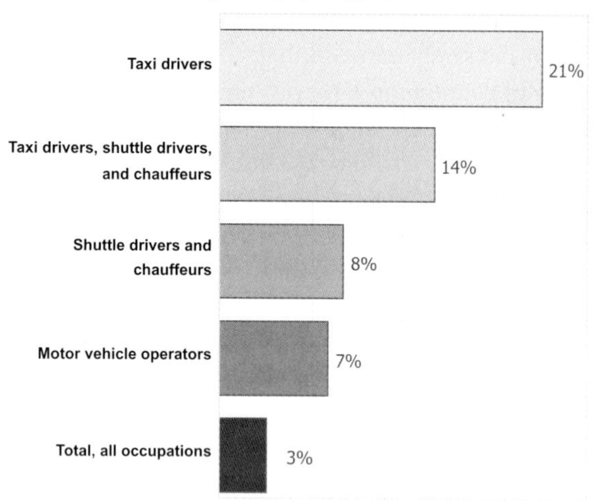

Note: All Occupations includes all occupations in the U.S. Economy.
Source: U.S. Bureau of Labor Statistics, Employment Projections program.

Taxi and limousine service	35,420
Other transit and ground passenger transportation	32,340
Services for the elderly and persons with disabilities	29,490
Automobile dealers	28,370

In May 2022, the median annual wages for taxi drivers in the top industries in which they worked were as follows:

Taxi and limousine service	$30,740

These wage data include money earned from tips. Taxi drivers, shuttle drivers, and chauffeurs who provide good customer service are most likely to receive good tips from their passengers.

Work hours vary for taxi drivers, shuttle drivers, and chauffeurs. Some work part time. Evening and weekend work is common. Some drivers work early in the morning or late at night.

Taxi drivers' work schedules are often flexible.

Shuttle drivers and chauffeurs' work schedules usually are more structured. They may have a set schedule, or they may work hours based on client needs. Some chauffeurs are on call throughout the day and must be ready to drive clients at a moment's notice.

Job Outlook

Overall employment of taxi drivers, shuttle drivers, and chauffeurs is projected to grow 14 percent from 2022 to 2032, much faster than the average for all occupations.

About 55,400 openings for taxi drivers, shuttle drivers, and chauffeurs are projected each year, on average, over the decade. Many of those openings are expected to result from the need to replace workers who transfer to different occupations or exit the labor force, such as to retire.

Employment

Strong employment growth is expected as people continue to rely on these drivers for their transportation needs. Much of the projected growth stems from a greater demand for ride-hailing drivers, who typically work as independent contractors.

Employment of taxi drivers (which includes ride-hailing drivers), shuttle drivers, and chauffeurs may be concentrated in metropolitan areas.

Demand also may arise from an increasing population of older people with chronic conditions who use these services for nonemergency healthcare transportation.

Occupational Title	SOC Code	Employment, 2022	Projected Employment, 2032	Change, 2022-32	
				Percent	Numeric
Taxi drivers, shuttle drivers, and chauffeurs	—	395,700	449,600	14	54,000
Shuttle drivers and chauffeurs	53-3053	218,400	235,900	8	17,500
Taxi drivers	53-3054	177,300	213,700	21	36,400

Contacts for More Information

For more information about taxi drivers and chauffeurs, visit

- The Transportation Alliance (TA)
- National Limousine Association (NLA)
- The Ride Share Guy
- Federal Motor Carrier Safety Administration (FMCSA)

Water Transportation Workers

Summary

Quick Facts: Water Transportation Workers	
2022 Median Pay	$66,100 per year $31.78 per hour
Typical Entry-Level Education	See How to Become One
Work Experience in a Related Occupation	See How to Become One
On-the-job Training	See How to Become One
Number of Jobs, 2022	83,200
Job Outlook, 2022-32	2% (As fast as average)
Employment Change, 2022-32	1,500

What Water Transportation Workers Do

Water transportation workers operate and maintain vessels that take cargo and people over water.

Work Environment

Water transportation workers usually work for long periods and can be exposed to all kinds of weather.

How to Become a Water Transportation Worker

Education and training requirements vary with the type of job. There are no educational requirements for entry-level sailors and marine oilers, but other types of water transportation workers typically complete U.S. Coast Guard-approved training programs.

Pay

The median annual wage for water transportation workers was $66,100 in May 2022.

Job Outlook

Overall employment of water transportation workers is projected to grow 2 percent from 2022 to 2032, about as fast as the average for all occupations.

About 8,800 openings for water transportation workers are projected each year, on average, over the decade. Many of those openings are expected to result from the need to replace workers who transfer to different occupations or exit the labor force, such as to retire.

What Water Transportation Workers Do

Water transportation workers operate and maintain vessels that take cargo and people over water. The vessels travel to and from foreign ports across the ocean and to domestic ports along the coasts, across the Great Lakes, and along the country's many inland waterways.

Duties

Water transportation workers typically do the following:

- Operate and maintain nonmilitary vessels
- Follow their vessel's strict chain of command
- Ensure the safety of all people and cargo on board

These workers, sometimes called *merchant mariners*, work on a variety of ships.

Some operate large deep-sea container ships to transport manufactured goods and refrigerated cargos around the world.

Others work on bulk carriers that move heavy commodities, such as coal or iron ore, across the oceans and over the Great Lakes.

Still others work on both large and small tankers that carry oil and other liquid products around the country and the world. Others work on supply ships that transport equipment and supplies to offshore oil and gas platforms.

Workers on tugboats help barges and other boats maneuver in small harbors and at sea.

Water transportation workers often perform their duties in all types of weather conditions.

Captains and mates supervise other workers.

Salvage vessels that offer emergency services also employ merchant mariners.

Cruise ships also employ water transportation workers, and some merchant mariners work on ferries to transport passengers along shorter distances.

A typical deep-sea merchant ship, large coastal ship, or Great Lakes merchant ship employs a captain and a chief engineer, along with three mates, three assistant engineers, and a number of sailors and marine oilers. Smaller vessels that operate in harbors or rivers may have a smaller crew. The specific complement of mariners is dependent on U.S. Coast Guard regulations.

Also, there are other workers on ships, such as cooks, electricians, and general maintenance and repair workers.

The following are examples of types of water transportation workers:

Captains, sometimes called *masters*, have overall command of a vessel. They have the final responsibility for the safety of the crew, cargo, and passengers. Captains typically do the following:

- Steer and operate vessels
- Direct crew members
- Ensure that proper safety procedures are followed
- Purchase equipment and supplies and arrange for any necessary maintenance and repair Oversee the loading and unloading of cargo or passengers
- Keep logs and other records that track the ship's movements and activities
- Interact with passengers on cruise ships

Mates, or *deck officers*, direct the operation of a vessel while the captain is off duty. Large ships have three officers, called first, second, and third mates. The first mate has the highest authority and takes command of the ship if the captain is incapacitated. Usually, the first mate is in charge of the cargo and/or passengers, the second mate is in charge of navigation, and the third mate is in charge of safety. On smaller vessels, there may be only one mate who handles all of the responsibilities. Deck officers typically do the following:

- Alternate watches with the captain and other officers
- Supervise and coordinate the activities of the deck crew
- Assist with docking the ship
- Monitor the ship's position, using charts and other navigational aides
- Determine the speed and direction of the vessel
- Inspect the cargo hold during loading, to ensure that the cargo is stowed according to specifications
- Make announcements to passengers when needed

Pilots guide ships in harbors, on rivers, and on other confined waterways. They are not part of a ship's crew but go aboard a ship to guide it through a particular waterway that they are familiar with. They work in places where a high degree of familiarity with local tides, currents, and hazards is needed. Some, called *harbor pilots*, work for ports and help many ships that come into the harbor during the day. When coming into a commercial port, a captain will often have to turn control of the vessel over to a pilot, who can safely guide it into the harbor. Pilots typically do the following:

- Board an unfamiliar ship from a small boat in the open water, often using a ladder
- Confer with a ship's captain about the vessel's destination and any special requirements it has
- Establish a positive working relationship with a vessel's captain and deck officers
- Receive mooring instructions from shore dispatchers

Sailors, or *deckhands*, operate and maintain the vessel and deck equipment. They make up the deck crew and keep all parts of a ship, other than areas related to the engine and motor, in good working order. New deckhands are called *ordinary seamen* and do the least complicated tasks. Experienced deckhands are called *able seamen* and usually make up most of a crew. Some large ships have a *boatswain,* who is the chief of the deck crew. Sailors typically do the following:

- Stand watch, looking for other vessels or obstructions in their ship's path and for navigational aids, such as buoys and lighthouses
- Steer the ship under the guidance of an officer and measure water depth in shallow water
- Do routine maintenance, such as painting the deck and chipping away rust
- Keep the inside of the ship clean
- Handle mooring lines when docking or departing
- Tie barges together when they are being towed
- Load and unload cargo
- Help passengers when needed

Ship engineers operate and maintain a vessel's propulsion system, which includes the engine, boilers, generators, pumps, and other machinery. Large vessels usually carry a *chief engineer*, who has command of the engine room and its crew, and a first, second, and third assistant engineer. The assistant engineer oversees the engine and related machinery when the chief engineer is off duty. Small ships might have only one engineer. Engineers typically do the following:

- Maintain a ships' mechanical and electrical equipment and systems
- Start the engine and regulate the vessel's speed, following the captain's orders
- Record information in an engineering log
- Keep an inventory of mechanical parts and supplies
- Do routine maintenance checks throughout the day
- Calculate refueling requirements

Marine oilers work in the engine room, helping the engineers keep the propulsion system in working order. They are the engine room equivalent of sailors. New oilers usually are called *wipers,* or *pumpmen,* on vessels handling liquid cargo. With experience, a wiper can become a Qualified Member of the Engine Department (QMED). Marine oilers typically do the following:

- Lubricate gears, shafts, bearings, and other parts of the engine or motor
- Read pressure and temperature gauges and record data
- Perform daily and periodic maintenance on engine room machinery
- Help engineers with repairs to machinery
- Connect hoses, operate pumps, and clean tanks
- Assist the deck crew with loading or unloading of cargo, if necessary

Motorboat operators run small, motor-driven boats that carry only a few passengers. They provide a variety of services, such as fishing charters, tours, and harbor patrols. Motorboat operators typically do the following:

- Check and change the oil and other fluids on their boat
- Pick up passengers and help them board the boat
- Act as a tour guide, if necessary

Work Environment

Water transportation workers held about 83,200 jobs in 2022. Employment in the detailed occupations that make up water transportation workers was distributed as follows:

Captains, mates, and pilots of water vessels	39,600
Sailors and marine oilers	30,700
Ship engineers	9,300
Motorboat operators	3,600

The largest employers of water transportation workers were as follows:

Industry	Percent
Support activities for water transportation	25%
Inland water transportation	20
Deep sea, coastal, and great lakes water transportation	15
Scenic and sightseeing transportation, water	9
Federal government, excluding postal service	6

Water transportation workers usually work for long periods and can be exposed to all kinds of weather. Many people decide that life at sea is not for them because of difficult conditions onboard ships and long periods away from home.

However, companies try to provide pleasant living conditions aboard their vessels. Most vessels are air-conditioned and include comfortable living quarters. Many also include entertainment systems with satellite TV and Internet connections, and meals may be provided.

Long periods away from home are a reality for some workers.

Work Schedules

Workers on deep-sea ships can spend months at a time away from home.

Workers on supply ships have shorter trips, usually lasting for a few hours or days.

Tugboats and barges travel along the coasts and on inland waterways, and crews are usually away for 2 to 3 weeks at a time.

Those who work on the Great Lakes have longer trips, around 2 months, but often do not work in the winter, when the lakes freeze.

Crews on all vessels often work for long periods, 7 days a week, while aboard.

Ferry workers and motorboat operators usually are away only for a few hours at a time and return home each night. Many ferry and motorboat operators service ships for vacation destinations and have seasonal schedules.

How to Become a Water Transportation Worker

Education and training requirements vary by the type of job. There are no educational requirements for entry-level sailors and marine oilers, but other types of water transportation workers typically complete U.S. Coast Guard-approved training programs. Most water transportation jobs require the Transportation Worker Identification Credential (TWIC) from

Sailors and marine oilers typically receive training on the job.

the Transportation Security Administration and a Merchant Mariner Credential (MMC), plus any related endorsements, from the U.S. Coast Guard.

Education

Sailors and marine oilers usually do not need formal education. Other types of water transportation workers often complete U.S. Coast Guard-approved training programs to help them obtain their required credentials.

Employers may prefer to hire workers who have earned a bachelor's degree from a merchant marine academy. The academy programs offer a bachelor's degree and a Merchant Mariner Credential (MMC) with an endorsement as a third mate or third assistant engineer. Graduates of these programs also can choose to receive a commission as an ensign in the U.S. Naval Reserve, Merchant Marine Reserve, or U.S. Coast Guard Reserve.

Training

Ordinary seamen, wipers, and other entry-level mariners get on-the-job training for 6 months to a year. The length of training depends on the size and type of ship and waterway they work on. For example, workers on deep-sea vessels need more complex training than those whose ships travel on a river.

Licenses, Certifications, and Registrations

All mariners working on ships with U.S. flags must have a Transportation Worker Identification Credential (TWIC) from the Transportation Security Administration. This credential states that a person is a U.S. citizen or permanent resident and has passed a security screening. The TWIC must be renewed every 5 years.

Mariners who work on ships traveling on the open ocean require the Standards of Training, Certification, and Watchkeeping (STWC) endorsement. Regional U.S. Coast Guard offices provide this training, and it includes topics such as first aid and lifeboat safety. The STWC training must be completed every 5 years. Mariners who work on inland waterways and the Great Lakes are excluded from the STWC endorsement.

Most mariners also must have a Merchant Mariner Credential (MMC), which they can apply for at a U.S. Coast Guard regional examination center. Entry-level employees, such as ordinary seamen or wipers, do not have to pass a written exam. However, some have to pass physical, hearing, and vision tests, and all must undergo a drug screening, in order to get their MMC. They also have to take a class on shipboard safety. The MMC must also be renewed every 5 years. More information on MMCs and related endorsements is available from the U.S. Coast Guard National Maritime Center.

Pilots are licensed by the state in which they work. The U.S. Coast Guard licenses pilots on the Great Lakes. The requirements for these licenses vary, depending on where a pilot works.

Work Experience in a Related Occupation

Water transportation workers typically progress from lower level positions to higher level ones, making work experience an important requirement for many jobs. A ship engineer, for example, might need experience as a marine oiler, and mates may have previously worked as sailors. In some cases, workers gain the needed hands-on experience as part of their education program.

Advancement

After obtaining their MMC, crewmembers can apply for endorsements that may allow them to move into more advanced positions.

Wipers can get an endorsement to become a Qualified Member of the Engine Department (QMED) after 6 months of experience by passing a written test.

It takes 3 years of experience and the passing of a written test for an ordinary seaman to become an unlimited able seaman. However, several able seaman endorsements below the level of unlimited are available after 6 months to 1 year of experience, depending on the type of ship the seamen work on.

Able seamen can advance to become third mates after at least 3 years of experience in the deck department. This experience must be on a ship similar to the type they hope to serve on as an officer. They also must take several training courses and pass written and onboard exams to receive the third-mate's endorsement on their MMC. The difficulty of these requirements increases with the complexity and size of the vessel. Similarly,

QMEDs can receive an endorsement as a third assistant engineer after 3 years of experience in the engine room and upon completion of a number of training and testing requirements. Experience and testing requirements increase with the size and complexity of the ship.

Officers who graduate from a maritime academy receive an MMC with an endorsement of a third mate or third assistant engineer, depending on the department in which they are trained.

To move up each step of the occupation ladder, from third mate/third assistant engineer, to second mate, to first mate, and then to captain or chief engineer, requires 365 days of experience at the previous level. A second mate or second assistant engineer who wants to move to first mate/first assistant engineer also must complete a 12-week training course and pass an exam.

Important Qualities

Customer-service skills. Many motorboat operators interact with passengers and must ensure that the passengers have a pleasant experience.

Hand-eye coordination. Officers and pilots who steer ships have to operate various controls while staying aware of their surroundings.

Hearing ability. Mariners must pass a hearing test to get an MMC.

Manual dexterity. Crewmembers need good balance to maneuver through tight spaces and on wet or uneven surfaces.

Mechanical skills. Members of the engine department keep complex machines working properly.

Physical strength. Sailors on freight ships load and unload cargo. While away at sea, most workers have to do some heavy lifting.

Visual ability. Mariners must pass a vision test to get an MMC.

Pay

The median annual wage for water transportation workers was $66,100 in May 2022. The median wage is the wage at which half the workers in an occupation earned more than that amount and half earned less. The lowest 10 percent earned less than $34,770, and the highest 10 percent earned more than $132,340.

Median annual wages for water transportation workers in May 2022 were as follows:

Captains, mates, and pilots of water vessels	$95,210
Ship engineers	87,300
Sailors and marine oilers	47,490
Motorboat operators	41,430

In May 2022, the median annual wages for water transportation workers in the top industries in which they worked were as follows:

Deep sea, coastal, and great lakes water transportation	$78,360
Inland water transportation	76,750
Support activities for water transportation	75,020
Federal government, excluding postal service	53,440
Scenic and sightseeing transportation, water	47,880

Workers on deep-sea ships can spend months at a time away from home.

Workers on supply ships have shorter trips, usually lasting for a few hours to a month.

Tugboats and barges travel along the coasts and on inland waterways and crews are usually away for 2 to 3 weeks at a time.

Those who work on the Great Lakes have longer trips, around 2 months, but often do not work in the winter, when the lakes freeze.

Crews on all vessels often work long hours, 7 days a week.

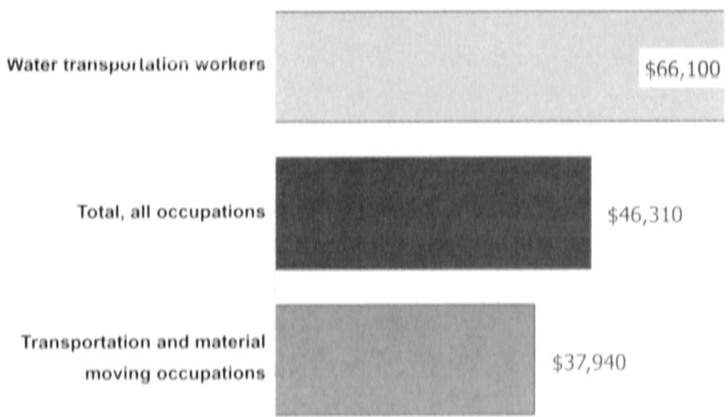

Note: All Occupations includes all occupations in the U.S. Economy. Source: U.S. Bureau of Labor Statistics, Occupational Employment and Wage Statistics.

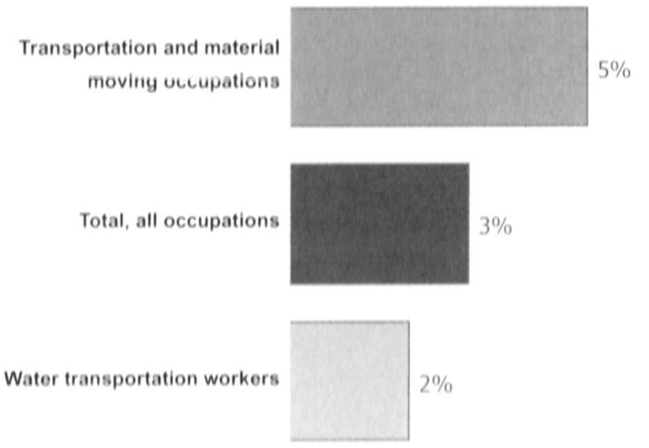

Note: All Occupations includes all occupations in the U.S. Economy. Source: U.S. Bureau of Labor Statistics, Employment Projections program.

Ferry workers and motorboat operators usually are away only for a few hours at a time and return home each night. Many ferry and motorboat operators service ships for vacation destinations and have seasonal schedules.

Job Outlook

Overall employment of water transportation workers is projected to grow 2 percent from 2022 to 2032, about as fast as the average for all occupations.

About 8,800 openings for water transportation workers are projected each year, on average, over the decade. Many of those openings are expected to result from the need to replace workers who transfer to different occupations or exit the labor force, such as to retire.

Employment

Fluctuations in the demand for bulk commodities, such as iron ore and grain, is a key factor influencing employment of water transportation workers. When demand for these commodities is high, the need for these workers increases; when demand slows, so does the need for workers.

Occupational Title	SOC Code	Employment, 2022	Projected Employment, 2032	Change, 2022-32	
				Percent	Numeric
Water transportation workers	53-5000	83,200	84,800	2	1,500
Sailors and marine oilers	53-5011	30,700	31,300	2	600
Captains, mates, and pilots of water vessels	53-5021	39,600	40,300	2	700
Motorboat operators	53-5022	3,600	3,700	3	100
Ship engineers	53-5031	9,300	9,400	1	100

Contacts for More Information

For more information, visit

- Maritime Administration, U.S. Department of Transportation
- For more information about licensing requirements and other credentials, visit
- National Maritime Center, U.S. Coast Guard
- Transportation Security Administration, U.S. Department of Homeland Security
- Lake Carriers' Association
- Passenger Vessel Association
- The American Waterways Operators

Data for Occupations Not Covered in Detail

Although employment for hundreds of occupations is covered in detail in the *Occupational Outlook Handbook*, this page presents summary data on additional occupations for which employment projections are prepared but detailed occupational information is not developed. For each occupation, the Occupational Information Network (O*NET) code, the occupational definition, 2022 employment, the May 2022 median annual wage, the projected employment change and growth rate from 2022 to 2032, and education and training categories are presented.

Management occupations

Legislators

Develop, introduce, or enact laws and statutes at the local, tribal, state, or federal level. Includes only workers in elected positions.

- 2022 employment: **44,400**
- May 2022 median annual wage: **$48,090**
- Projected employment change, 2022–32:
  - Number of new jobs: **1,500**
  - Growth rate: **3 percent (As fast as average)**
- Education and training:
  - Typical entry-level education: **Bachelor's degree**
  - Work experience in a related occupation: **Less than 5 years**
  - Typical on-the-job training: **None**
- O*NET links:
  - 11-1031.00—Legislators
- CareerOneStop videos for this occupation:
  - 11-1031.00—Legislators

Transportation, storage, and distribution managers

Plan, direct, or coordinate transportation, storage, or distribution activities in accordance with organizational policies and applicable government laws or regulations. Includes logistics managers.

- 2022 employment: **177,700**
- May 2022 median annual wage: **$98,560**
- Projected employment change, 2022–32:
  - Number of new jobs: **14,600**
  - Growth rate: **8 percent (Faster than average)**
- Education and training:
  - Typical entry-level education: **High school diploma or equivalent**
  - Work experience in a related occupation: **5 years or more**
  - Typical on-the-job training: **None**
- O*NET links:
  - 11-3071.00—Transportation, Storage, and Distribution Managers
  - 11-3071.04—Supply Chain Managers
- CareerOneStop videos for this occupation:
  - 11-3071.04—Supply Chain Managers

Education administrators, all other

All education administrators not listed separately.

- 2022 employment: **57,600**
- May 2022 median annual wage: **$89,130**
- Projected employment change, 2022–32:
  - Number of new jobs: **1,600**
  - Growth rate: **3 percent (As fast as average)**
- Education and training:
  - Typical entry-level education: **Bachelor's degree**
  - Work experience in a related occupation: **Less than 5 years**
  - Typical on-the-job training: **None**
- O*NET links:
  - 11-9039.00—Education Administrators, All Other

Postmasters and mail superintendents

Plan, direct, or coordinate operational, administrative, management, and support services of a U.S. post office; or coordinate activities of workers engaged in postal and related work in assigned post office.

- 2022 employment: **13,000**
- May 2022 median annual wage: **$82,760**
- Projected employment change, 2022–32:
  - Number of new jobs: **-900**
  - Growth rate: **-7 percent (Decline)**
- Education and training:
  - Typical entry-level education: **High school diploma or equivalent**
  - Work experience in a related occupation: **Less than 5 years**
  - Typical on-the-job training: **Moderate-term on-the-job training**
- O*NET links:
  - 11-9131.00—Postmasters and Mail Superintendents
- CareerOneStop videos for this occupation:
  - 11-9131.00—Postmasters and Mail Superintendents

Personal service managers, all other

All personal service managers not listed separately. Excludes "Financial Specialists" (13-2000). Daycare Managers are included in Education and Childcare Administrators, Preschool and Daycare (11-9031).

- 2022 employment: **23,100**
- May 2022 median annual wage: **$56,090**
- Projected employment change, 2022–32:
  - Number of new jobs: **1,000**
  - Growth rate: **4 percent (As fast as average)**
- Education and training:
  - Typical entry-level education: **High school diploma or equivalent**
  - Work experience in a related occupation: **Less than 5 years**
  - Typical on-the-job training: **None**
- O*NET links:
  - 11-9179.00—Personal Service Managers, All Other
  - 11-9179.01—Fitness and Wellness Coordinators

- 11-9179.02—Spa Managers
- CareerOneStop videos for this occupation:
  - 11-9179.01—Fitness and Wellness Coordinators
  - 11-9179.02—Spa Managers

Managers, all other

All managers not listed separately.

- 2022 employment: **1,228,300**
- May 2022 median annual wage: **$128,620**
- Projected employment change, 2022–32:
  - Number of new jobs: **41,000**
  - Growth rate: **3 percent (As fast as average)**
- Education and training:
  - Typical entry-level education: **Bachelor's degree**
  - Work experience in a related occupation: **Less than 5 years**
  - Typical on-the-job training: **None**
- O*NET links:
  - 11-9199.00—Managers, All Other
  - 11-9199.01—Regulatory Affairs Managers
  - 11-9199.02—Compliance Managers
  - 11-9199.08—Loss Prevention Managers
  - 11-9199.09—Wind Energy Operations Managers
  - 11-9199.10—Wind Energy Development Managers
  - 11-9199.11—Brownfield Redevelopment Specialists and Site Managers
- CareerOneStop videos for this occupation:
  - 11-9199.01—Regulatory Affairs Managers
  - 11-9199.02—Compliance Managers
  - 11-9199.08—Loss Prevention Managers
  - 11-9199.09—Wind Energy Operations Managers
  - 11-9199.10—Wind Energy Development Managers
  - 11-9199.11—Brownfield Redevelopment Specialists and Site Managers

Business and financial operations occupations

Agents and business managers of artists, performers, and athletes

Represent and promote artists, performers, and athletes in dealings with current or prospective employers. May handle contract negotiation and other business matters for clients.

- 2022 employment: **19,900**
- May 2022 median annual wage: **$82,530**
- Projected employment change, 2022–32:
  - Number of new jobs: **1,600**
  - Growth rate: **8 percent (Faster than average)**
- Education and training:
  - Typical entry-level education: **Bachelor's degree**
  - Work experience in a related occupation: **Less than 5 years**
  - Typical on-the-job training: **None**
- O*NET links:
  - 13-1011.00—Agents and Business Managers of Artists, Performers, and Athletes
- CareerOneStop videos for this occupation:
  - 13-1011.00—Agents and Business Managers of Artists, Performers, and Athletes

Compliance officers

Examine, evaluate, and investigate eligibility for or conformity with laws and regulations governing contract compliance of licenses and permits, and perform other compliance and enforcement inspection and analysis activities not classified elsewhere. Excludes "Financial Examiners" (13-2061), "Tax Examiners and Collectors, and Revenue Agents" (13-2081), "Occupational Health and Safety Specialists" (19-5011), "Occupational Health and Safety Technicians" (19-5012), "Transportation Security Screeners" (33-9093), "Agricultural Inspectors" (45-2011), "Construction and Building Inspectors" (47-4011), and "Transportation Inspectors" (53-6051).

- 2022 employment: **377,500**
- May 2022 median annual wage: **$71,690**
- Projected employment change, 2022–32:
  - Number of new jobs: **17,200**
  - Growth rate: **5 percent (Faster than average)**
- Education and training:
  - Typical entry-level education: **Bachelor's degree**
  - Work experience in a related occupation: **None**
  - Typical on-the-job training: **Moderate-term on-the-job training**
- O*NET links:
  - 13-1041.00—Compliance Officers
  - 13-1041.01—Environmental Compliance Inspectors
  - 13-1041.03—Equal Opportunity Representatives and Officers
  - 13-1041.04—Government Property Inspectors and Investigators
  - 13-1041.06—Coroners
  - 13-1041.07—Regulatory Affairs Specialists
  - 13-1041.08—Customs Brokers
- CareerOneStop videos for this occupation:
  - 13-1041.00—Compliance Officers
  - 13-1041.01—Environmental Compliance Inspectors
  - 13-1041.03—Equal Opportunity Representatives and Officers
  - 13-1041.04—Government Property Inspectors and Investigators
  - 13-1041.06—Coroners
  - 13-1041.07—Regulatory Affairs Specialists
  - 13-1041.08—Customs Brokers

Farm labor contractors

Recruit and hire seasonal or temporary agricultural laborers. May transport, house, and provide meals for workers.

- 2022 employment: **1,600**
- May 2022 median annual wage: **$49,330**
- Projected employment change, 2022–32:
  - Number of new jobs: **100**
  - Growth rate: **7 percent (Faster than average)**
- Education and training:
  - Typical entry-level education: **No formal educational credential**
  - Work experience in a related occupation: **Less than 5 years**
  - Typical on-the-job training: **Short-term on-the-job training**
- O*NET links:
  - 13-1074.00—Farm Labor Contractors
- CareerOneStop videos for this occupation:
  - 13-1074.00—Farm Labor Contractors

Business operations specialists, all other

All business operations specialists not listed separately.

- 2022 employment: **1,174,800**
- May 2022 median annual wage: **$75,990**
- Projected employment change, 2022–32:
  - Number of new jobs: **48,700**
  - Growth rate: **4 percent (As fast as average)**
- Education and training:
  - Typical entry-level education: **Bachelor's degree**
  - Work experience in a related occupation: **None**
  - Typical on-the-job training: **None**

- O*NET links:
  - 13-1199.00—Business Operations Specialists, All Other
  - 13-1199.04—Business Continuity Planners
  - 13-1199.05—Sustainability Specialists
  - 13-1199.06—Online Merchants
  - 13-1199.07—Security Management Specialists
- CareerOneStop videos for this occupation:
  - 13-1199.06—Online Merchants
  - 13-1199.07—Security Management Specialists

Credit analysts

Analyze credit data and financial statements of individuals or firms to determine the degree of risk involved in extending credit or lending money. Prepare reports with credit information for use in decision-making. Excludes "Financial Risk Specialists" (13-2054).

- 2022 employment: **73,000**
- May 2022 median annual wage: **$78,850**
- Projected employment change, 2022–32:
  - Number of new jobs: **-3,200**
  - Growth rate: **-4 percent (Decline)**
- Education and training:
  - Typical entry-level education: **Bachelor's degree**
  - Work experience in a related occupation: **None**
  - Typical on-the-job training: **None**
- O*NET links:
  - 13-2041.00—Credit Analysts
- CareerOneStop videos for this occupation:
  - 13-2041.00—Credit Analysts

Credit counselors

Advise and educate individuals or organizations on acquiring and managing debt. May provide guidance in determining the best type of loan and explain loan requirements or restrictions. May help develop debt management plans or student financial aid packages. May advise on credit issues, or provide budget, mortgage, bankruptcy, or student financial aid counseling.

- 2022 employment: **32,800**
- May 2022 median annual wage: **$47,320**
- Projected employment change, 2022–32:
  - Number of new jobs: **1,800**
  - Growth rate: **5 percent (Faster than average)**
- Education and training:
  - Typical entry-level education: **Bachelor's degree**
  - Work experience in a related occupation: **None**
  - Typical on-the-job training: **Moderate-term on-the-job training**
- O*NET links:
  - 13-2071.00—Credit Counselors
- CareerOneStop videos for this occupation:
  - 13-2071.00—Credit Counselors

Tax preparers

Prepare tax returns for individuals or small businesses. Excludes "Accountants and Auditors" (13-2011).

- 2022 employment: **109,500**
- May 2022 median annual wage: **$48,250**
- Projected employment change, 2022–32:
  - Number of new jobs: **1,600**
  - Growth rate: **1 percent (Little or no change)**
- Education and training:
  - Typical entry-level education: **High school diploma or equivalent**
  - Work experience in a related occupation: **None**
  - Typical on-the-job training: **Moderate-term on-the-job training**
- O*NET links:
  - 13-2082.00—Tax Preparers
- CareerOneStop videos for this occupation:
  - 13-2082.00—Tax Preparers

Financial specialists, all other

All financial specialists not listed separately.

- 2022 employment: **136,000**
- May 2022 median annual wage: **$73,810**
- Projected employment change, 2022–32:
  - Number of new jobs: **8,300**
  - Growth rate: **6 percent (Faster than average)**
- Education and training:
  - Typical entry-level education: **Bachelor's degree**
  - Work experience in a related occupation: **None**
  - Typical on-the-job training: **None**
- O*NET links:
  - 13-2099.00—Financial Specialists, All Other
  - 13-2099.01—Financial Quantitative Analysts
  - 13-2099.04—Fraud Examiners, Investigators and Analysts
- CareerOneStop videos for this occupation:
  - 13-2099.01—Financial Quantitative Analysts
  - 13-2099.04—Fraud Examiners, Investigators and Analysts

Computer and mathematical occupations

Computer occupations, all other

All computer occupations not listed separately. Excludes "Computer and Information Systems Managers" (11-3021), "Computer Hardware Engineers" (17-2061), "Electrical and Electronics Engineers" (17-2070), "Computer Science Teachers, Postsecondary" (25-1021), "Special Effects Artists and Animators" (27-1014), "Graphic Designers" (27-1024), "Health Information Technologists and Medical Registrars" (29-9021), and "Computer, Automated Teller, and Office Machine Repairers" (49-2011).

- 2022 employment: **449,400**
- May 2022 median annual wage: **$98,740**
- Projected employment change, 2022–32:
  - Number of new jobs: **43,800**
  - Growth rate: **10 percent (Much faster than average)**
- Education and training:
  - Typical entry-level education: **Bachelor's degree**
  - Work experience in a related occupation: **None**
  - Typical on-the-job training: **None**
- O*NET links:
  - 15-1299.00—Computer Occupations, All Other
  - 15-1299.01—Web Administrators
  - 15-1299.02—Geographic Information Systems Technologists and Technicians
  - 15-1299.03—Document Management Specialists
  - 15-1299.04—Penetration Testers
  - 15-1299.05—Information Security Engineers
  - 15-1299.06—Digital Forensics Analysts
  - 15-1299.07—Blockchain Engineers
  - 15-1299.08—Computer Systems Engineers/Architects
  - 15-1299.09—Information Technology Project Managers
- CareerOneStop videos for this occupation:

- 15-1299.01—Web Administrators
- 15-1299.02—Geographic Information Systems Technologists and Technicians
- 15-1299.03—Document Management Specialists
- 15-1299.04—Penetration Testers
- 15-1299.05—Information Security Engineers
- 15-1299.06—Digital Forensics Analysts
- 15-1299.07—Blockchain Engineers
- 15-1299.08—Computer Systems Engineers/Architects
- 15-1299.09—Information Technology Project Managers

Mathematical science occupations, all other

All mathematical scientists not listed separately.

- 2022 employment: **4,100**
- May 2022 median annual wage: **$71,700**
- Projected employment change, 2022–32:
  - Number of new jobs: **300**
  - Growth rate: **6 percent (Faster than average)**
- Education and training:
  - Typical entry-level education: **Bachelor's degree**
  - Work experience in a related occupation: **None**
  - Typical on-the-job training: **None**
- O*NET links:
  - 15-2099.00—Mathematical Science Occupations, All Other
  - 15-2099.01—Bioinformatics Technicians
- CareerOneStop videos for this occupation:
  - 15-2099.01—Bioinformatics Technicians

Architecture and engineering occupations

Engineers, all other

All engineers not listed separately. Excludes "Sales Engineers" (41-9031), "Locomotive Engineers" (53-4011), and "Ship Engineers" (53-5031).

- 2022 employment: **170,300**
- May 2022 median annual wage: **$104,600**
- Projected employment change, 2022–32:
  - Number of new jobs: **5,700**
  - Growth rate: **3 percent (As fast as average)**
- Education and training:
  - Typical entry-level education: **Bachelor's degree**
  - Work experience in a related occupation: **None**
  - Typical on-the-job training: **None**
- O*NET links:
  - 17-2199.00—Engineers, All Other
  - 17-2199.03—Energy Engineers, Except Wind and Solar
  - 17-2199.05—Mechatronics Engineers
  - 17-2199.06—Microsystems Engineers
  - 17-2199.07—Photonics Engineers
  - 17-2199.08—Robotics Engineers
  - 17-2199.09—Nanosystems Engineers
  - 17-2199.10—Wind Energy Engineers
  - 17-2199.11—Solar Energy Systems Engineers
- CareerOneStop videos for this occupation:
  - 17-2199.03—Energy Engineers, Except Wind and Solar
  - 17-2199.05—Mechatronics Engineers
  - 17-2199.06—Microsystems Engineers
  - 17-2199.07—Photonics Engineers
  - 17-2199.08—Robotics Engineers
  - 17-2199.09—Nanosystems Engineers
  - 17-2199.10—Wind Energy Engineers
  - 17-2199.11—Solar Energy Systems Engineers

Engineering technologists and technicians, except drafters, all other

All engineering technologists and technicians, except drafters, not listed separately.

- 2022 employment: **74,100**
- May 2022 median annual wage: **$65,520**
- Projected employment change, 2022–32:
  - Number of new jobs: **2,300**
  - Growth rate: **3 percent (As fast as average)**
- Education and training:
  - Typical entry-level education: **Associate's degree**
  - Work experience in a related occupation: **None**
  - Typical on-the-job training: **None**
- O*NET links:
  - 17-3029.00—Engineering Technologists and Technicians, Except Drafters, All Other
  - 17-3029.01—Non-Destructive Testing Specialists
  - 17-3029.08—Photonics Technicians

Life, physical, and social science occupations

Biological scientists, all other

All biological scientists not listed separately.

- 2022 employment: **60,400**
- May 2022 median annual wage: **$87,300**
- Projected employment change, 2022–32:
  - Number of new jobs: **2,300**
  - Growth rate: **4 percent (As fast as average)**
- Education and training:
  - Typical entry-level education: **Bachelor's degree**
  - Work experience in a related occupation: **None**
  - Typical on-the-job training: **None**
- O*NET links:
  - 19-1029.00—Biological Scientists, All Other
  - 19-1029.01—Bioinformatics Scientists
  - 19-1029.02—Molecular and Cellular Biologists
  - 19-1029.03—Geneticists
  - 19-1029.04—Biologists
- CareerOneStop videos for this occupation:
  - 19-1029.01—Bioinformatics Scientists
  - 19-1029.02—Molecular and Cellular Biologists
  - 19-1029.03—Geneticists
  - 19-1029.04—Biologists

Life scientists, all other

All life scientists not listed separately.

- 2022 employment: **9,000**
- May 2022 median annual wage: **$83,930**
- Projected employment change, 2022–32:
  - Number of new jobs: **500**
  - Growth rate: **5 percent (Faster than average)**
- Education and training:
  - Typical entry-level education: **Bachelor's degree**
  - Work experience in a related occupation: **None**
  - Typical on-the-job training: **None**
- O*NET links:
  - 19-1099.00—Life Scientists, All Other

Physical scientists, all other

All physical scientists not listed separately.

- 2022 employment: **25,400**
- May 2022 median annual wage: **$107,970**

- Projected employment change, 2022–32:
  - Number of new jobs: **500**
  - Growth rate: **2 percent (As fast as average)**
- Education and training:
  - Typical entry-level education: **Bachelor's degree**
  - Work experience in a related occupation: **None**
  - Typical on-the-job training: **None**
- O*NET links:
  - 19-2099.00—Physical Scientists, All Other
  - 19-2099.01—Remote Sensing Scientists and Technologists
- CareerOneStop videos for this occupation:
  - 19-2099.01—Remote Sensing Scientists and Technologists

Social scientists and related workers, all other

All social scientists and related workers not listed separately.

- 2022 employment: **36,500**
- May 2022 median annual wage: **$88,900**
- Projected employment change, 2022–32:
  - Number of new jobs: **600**
  - Growth rate: **2 percent (As fast as average)**
- Education and training:
  - Typical entry-level education: **Bachelor's degree**
  - Work experience in a related occupation: **None**
  - Typical on-the-job training: **None**
- O*NET links:
  - 19-3099.00—Social Scientists and Related Workers, All Other
  - 19-3099.01—Transportation Planners

Social science research assistants

Assist social scientists in laboratory, survey, and other social science research. May help prepare findings for publication and assist in laboratory analysis, quality control, or data management. Excludes "Teaching Assistants, Postsecondary" (25-9044).

- 2022 employment: **34,400**
- May 2022 median annual wage: **$50,470**
- Projected employment change, 2022–32:
  - Number of new jobs: **1,600**
  - Growth rate: **5 percent (Faster than average)**
- Education and training:
  - Typical entry-level education: **Bachelor's degree**
  - Work experience in a related occupation: **None**
  - Typical on-the-job training: **None**
- O*NET links:
  - 19-4061.00—Social Science Research Assistants
- CareerOneStop videos for this occupation:
  - 19-4061.00—Social Science Research Assistants

Forest and conservation technicians

Provide technical assistance regarding the conservation of soil, water, forests, or related natural resources. May compile data pertaining to size, content, condition, and other characteristics of forest tracts under the direction of foresters, or train and lead forest workers in forest propagation and fire prevention and suppression. May assist conservation scientists in managing, improving, and protecting rangelands and wildlife habitats. Excludes "Conservation Scientists" (19-1031) and "Foresters" (19-1032).

- 2022 employment: **31,500**
- May 2022 median annual wage: **$41,520**
- Projected employment change, 2022–32:
  - Number of new jobs: **200**
  - Growth rate: **1 percent (Little or no change)**
- Education and training:
  - Typical entry-level education: **Associate's degree**
  - Work experience in a related occupation: **None**
  - Typical on-the-job training: **None**
- O*NET links:
  - 19-4071.00—Forest and Conservation Technicians
- CareerOneStop videos for this occupation:
  - 19-4071.00—Forest and Conservation Technicians

Life, physical, and social science technicians, all other

All life, physical, and social science technicians not listed separately.

- 2022 employment: **80,000**
- May 2022 median annual wage: **$50,290**
- Projected employment change, 2022–32:
  - Number of new jobs: **3,000**
  - Growth rate: **4 percent (As fast as average)**
- Education and training:
  - Typical entry-level education: **Associate's degree**
  - Work experience in a related occupation: **None**
  - Typical on-the-job training: **None**
- O*NET links:
  - 19-4099.00—Life, Physical, and Social Science Technicians, All Other
  - 19-4099.01—Quality Control Analysts
  - 19-4099.03—Remote Sensing Technicians
- CareerOneStop videos for this occupation:
  - 19-4099.01—Quality Control Analysts
  - 19-4099.03—Remote Sensing Technicians

Community and social service occupations

Counselors, all other

All counselors not listed separately.

- 2022 employment: **68,200**
- May 2022 median annual wage: **$43,390**
- Projected employment change, 2022–32:
  - Number of new jobs: **11,700**
  - Growth rate: **17 percent (Much faster than average)**
- Education and training:
  - Typical entry-level education: **Master's degree**
  - Work experience in a related occupation: **None**
  - Typical on-the-job training: **None**
- O*NET links:
  - 21-1019.00—Counselors, All Other

Community and social service specialists, all other

All community and social service specialists not listed separately.

- 2022 employment: **103,000**
- May 2022 median annual wage: **$47,290**
- Projected employment change, 2022–32:
  - Number of new jobs: **6,700**
  - Growth rate: **6 percent (Faster than average)**
- Education and training:
  - Typical entry-level education: **Bachelor's degree**
  - Work experience in a related occupation: **None**
  - Typical on-the-job training: **None**
- O*NET links:
  - 21-1099.00—Community and Social Service Specialists, All Other

Clergy

Conduct religious worship and perform other spiritual functions associated with beliefs and practices of religious faith or denomination. Provide spiritual and moral guidance and assistance to members.

- 2022 employment: **266,700**
- May 2022 median annual wage: **$55,550**
- Projected employment change, 2022–32:
  - Number of new jobs: **1,500**
  - Growth rate: **1 percent (Little or no change)**
- Education and training:
  - Typical entry-level education: **Bachelor's degree**
  - Work experience in a related occupation: **None**
  - Typical on-the-job training: **Moderate-term on-the-job training**
- O*NET links:
  - 21-2011.00—Clergy
- CareerOneStop videos for this occupation:
  - 21-2011.00—Clergy

Directors, religious activities and education

Coordinate or design programs and conduct outreach to promote the religious education or activities of a denominational group. May provide counseling, guidance, and leadership relative to marital, health, financial, and religious problems.

- 2022 employment: **171,000**
- May 2022 median annual wage: **$49,380**
- Projected employment change, 2022–32:
  - Number of new jobs: **-400**
  - Growth rate: **0 percent (Little or no change)**
- Education and training:
  - Typical entry-level education: **Bachelor's degree**
  - Work experience in a related occupation: **Less than 5 years**
  - Typical on-the-job training: **None**
- O*NET links:
  - 21-2021.00—Directors, Religious Activities and Education
- CareerOneStop videos for this occupation:
  - 21-2021.00—Directors, Religious Activities and Education

Religious workers, all other

All religious workers not listed separately.

- 2022 employment: **75,800**
- May 2022 median annual wage: **$39,370**
- Projected employment change, 2022–32:
  - Number of new jobs: **400**
  - Growth rate: **1 percent (Little or no change)**
- Education and training:
  - Typical entry-level education: **Bachelor's degree**
  - Work experience in a related occupation: **None**
  - Typical on-the-job training: **None**
- O*NET links:
  - 21-2099.00—Religious Workers, All Other

Legal occupations

Judicial law clerks

Assist judges in court or by conducting research or preparing legal documents. Excludes "Lawyers" (23-1011) and "Paralegals and Legal Assistants" (23-2011).

- 2022 employment: **16,300**
- May 2022 median annual wage: **$57,490**
- Projected employment change, 2022–32:
  - Number of new jobs: **400**
  - Growth rate: **2 percent (As fast as average)**
- Education and training:
  - Typical entry-level education: **Doctoral or professional degree**
  - Work experience in a related occupation: **None**
  - Typical on-the-job training: **None**
- O*NET links:
  - 23-1012.00—Judicial Law Clerks
- CareerOneStop videos for this occupation:
  - 23-1012.00—Judicial Law Clerks

Title examiners, abstractors, and searchers

Search real estate records, examine titles, or summarize pertinent legal or insurance documents or details for a variety of purposes. May compile lists of mortgages, contracts, and other instruments pertaining to titles by searching public and private records for law firms, real estate agencies, or title insurance companies. Excludes "Loan Officers" (13-2072).

- 2022 employment: **62,200**
- May 2022 median annual wage: **$50,490**
- Projected employment change, 2022–32:
  - Number of new jobs: **1,000**
  - Growth rate: **2 percent (As fast as average)**
- Education and training:
  - Typical entry-level education: **High school diploma or equivalent**
  - Work experience in a related occupation: **None**
  - Typical on-the-job training: **Moderate-term on-the-job training**
- O*NET links:
  - 23-2093.00—Title Examiners, Abstractors, and Searchers
- CareerOneStop videos for this occupation:
  - 23-2093.00—Title Examiners, Abstractors, and Searchers

Legal support workers, all other

All legal support workers not listed separately.

- 2022 employment: **51,400**
- May 2022 median annual wage: **$62,340**
- Projected employment change, 2022–32:
  - Number of new jobs: **100**
  - Growth rate: **0 percent (Little or no change)**
- Education and training:
  - Typical entry-level education: **Associate's degree**
  - Work experience in a related occupation: **None**
  - Typical on-the-job training: **None**
- O*NET links:
  - 23-2099.00—Legal Support Workers, All Other

Educational instruction and library occupations

Postsecondary teachers, all other

All postsecondary teachers not listed separately.

- 2022 employment: **262,800**
- May 2022 median annual wage: **$76,920**
- Projected employment change, 2022–32:
  - Number of new jobs: **9,400**
  - Growth rate: **4 percent (As fast as average)**
- Education and training:

 - Typical entry-level education: **Doctoral or professional degree**
 - Work experience in a related occupation: **None**
 - Typical on-the-job training: **None**
- O*NET links:
 - 25-1199.00—Postsecondary Teachers, All Other
- CareerOneStop videos for this occupation:
 - 25-1199.00—Postsecondary Teachers, All Other

Self-enrichment teachers

Teach or instruct individuals or groups for the primary purpose of self-enrichment or recreation, rather than for an occupational objective, educational attainment, competition, or fitness. Excludes "Coaches and Scouts" (27-2022) and "Exercise Trainers and Group Fitness Instructors" (39-9031). Flight instructors are included with "Aircraft Pilots and Flight Engineers" (53-2010).

- 2022 employment: **354,700**
- May 2022 median annual wage: **$44,110**
- Projected employment change, 2022–32:
 - Number of new jobs: **11,400**
 - Growth rate: **3 percent (As fast as average)**
- Education and training:
 - Typical entry-level education: **High school diploma or equivalent**
 - Work experience in a related occupation: **Less than 5 years**
 - Typical on-the-job training: **None**
- O*NET links:
 - 25-3021.00—Self-Enrichment Teachers
- CareerOneStop videos for this occupation:
 - 25-3021.00—Self-Enrichment Teachers

Substitute teachers, short-term

Teach students on a short-term basis as a temporary replacement for a regular classroom teacher, typically using the regular teacher's lesson plan. Excludes long-term substitute teachers who perform all the duties of a regular teacher; these teachers are coded within the 25-1000 or 25-2000 minor groups.

- 2022 employment: **421,600**
- May 2022 median annual wage: **$35,250**
- Projected employment change, 2022–32:
 - Number of new jobs: **17,400**
 - Growth rate: **4 percent (As fast as average)**
- Education and training:
 - Typical entry-level education: **Bachelor's degree**
 - Work experience in a related occupation: **None**
 - Typical on-the-job training: **None**
- O*NET links:
 - 25-3031.00—Substitute Teachers, Short-Term
- CareerOneStop videos for this occupation:
 - 25-3031.00—Substitute Teachers, Short-Term

Teachers and instructors, all other

All teachers and instructors not listed separately.

- 2022 employment: **148,000**
- May 2022 median annual wage: **$61,250**
- Projected employment change, 2022–32:
 - Number of new jobs: **2,900**
 - Growth rate: **2 percent (As fast as average)**
- Education and training:
 - Typical entry-level education: **Bachelor's degree**
 - Work experience in a related occupation: **None**
 - Typical on-the-job training: **None**
- O*NET links:
 - 25-3099.00—Teachers and Instructors, All Other

Farm and home management educators

Instruct and advise individuals and families engaged in agriculture, agricultural-related processes, or home management activities. Demonstrate procedures and apply research findings to advance agricultural and home management activities. May develop educational outreach programs. May instruct on either agricultural issues such as agricultural processes and techniques, pest management, and food safety, or on home management issues such as budgeting, nutrition, and child development. Excludes "Dietitians and Nutritionists" (29-1031).

- 2022 employment: **9,700**
- May 2022 median annual wage: **$53,450**
- Projected employment change, 2022–32:
 - Number of new jobs: **-200**
 - Growth rate: **-2 percent (Decline)**
- Education and training:
 - Typical entry-level education: **Master's degree**
 - Work experience in a related occupation: **None**
 - Typical on-the-job training: **None**
- O*NET links:
 - 25-9021.00—Farm and Home Management Educators
- CareerOneStop videos for this occupation:
 - 25-9021.00—Farm and Home Management Educators

Teaching assistants, postsecondary

Assist faculty or other instructional staff in postsecondary institutions by performing instructional support activities, such as developing teaching materials, leading discussion groups, preparing and giving examinations, and grading examinations or papers. Graduate students who teach one or more full courses should be classified in the 25-1000 minor group.

- 2022 employment: **170,200**
- May 2022 median annual wage: **$38,050**
- Projected employment change, 2022–32:
 - Number of new jobs: **7,100**
 - Growth rate: **4 percent (As fast as average)**
- Education and training:
 - Typical entry-level education: **Bachelor's degree**
 - Work experience in a related occupation: **None**
 - Typical on-the-job training: **None**
- O*NET links:
 - 25-9044.00—Teaching Assistants, Postsecondary
- CareerOneStop videos for this occupation:
 - 25-9044.00—Teaching Assistants, Postsecondary

Educational instruction and library workers, all other

All educational instruction and library workers not listed separately.

- 2022 employment: **145,300**
- May 2022 median annual wage: **$47,650**
- Projected employment change, 2022–32:
 - Number of new jobs: **3,300**
 - Growth rate: **2 percent (As fast as average)**
- Education and training:
 - Typical entry-level education: **Bachelor's degree**
 - Work experience in a related occupation: **None**
 - Typical on-the-job training: **None**
- O*NET links:
 - 25-9099.00—Educational Instruction and Library Workers, All Other

Arts, design, entertainment, sports, and media occupations

Merchandise displayers and window trimmers
Plan and erect commercial displays, such as those in windows and interiors of retail stores and at trade exhibitions.
- 2022 employment: **173,400**
- May 2022 median annual wage: **$35,380**
- Projected employment change, 2022–32:
  - Number of new jobs: **4,100**
  - Growth rate: **2 percent (As fast as average)**
- Education and training:
  - Typical entry-level education: **High school diploma or equivalent**
  - Work experience in a related occupation: **None**
  - Typical on-the-job training: **Short-term on-the-job training**
- O*NET links:
  - 27-1026.00—Merchandise Displayers and Window Trimmers
- CareerOneStop videos for this occupation:
  - 27-1026.00—Merchandise Displayers and Window Trimmers

Set and exhibit designers
Design special exhibits and sets for film, video, television, and theater productions. May study scripts, confer with directors, and conduct research to determine appropriate architectural styles.
- 2022 employment: **27,800**
- May 2022 median annual wage: **$59,990**
- Projected employment change, 2022–32:
  - Number of new jobs: **2,000**
  - Growth rate: **7 percent (Faster than average)**
- Education and training:
  - Typical entry-level education: **Bachelor's degree**
  - Work experience in a related occupation: **None**
  - Typical on-the-job training: **None**
- O*NET links:
  - 27-1027.00—Set and Exhibit Designers
- CareerOneStop videos for this occupation:
  - 27-1027.00—Set and Exhibit Designers

Designers, all other
All designers not listed separately.
- 2022 employment: **33,500**
- May 2022 median annual wage: **$65,390**
- Projected employment change, 2022–32:
  - Number of new jobs: **1,100**
  - Growth rate: **3 percent (As fast as average)**
- Education and training:
  - Typical entry-level education: **Bachelor's degree**
  - Work experience in a related occupation: **None**
  - Typical on-the-job training: **None**
- O*NET links:
  - 27-1029.00—Designers, All Other

Entertainers and performers, sports and related workers, all other
All entertainers and performers, sports and related workers not listed separately.
- 2022 employment: **26,500**
- May 2022 median annual wage: **The annual wage is not available.**
- Projected employment change, 2022–32:
  - Number of new jobs: **2,200**
  - Growth rate: **8 percent (Faster than average)**
- Education and training:
  - Typical entry-level education: **No formal educational credential**
  - Work experience in a related occupation: **None**
  - Typical on-the-job training: **Short-term on-the-job training**
- O*NET links:
  - 27-2099.00—Entertainers and Performers, Sports and Related Workers, All Other

Media and communication workers, all other
All media and communication workers not listed separately.
- 2022 employment: **25,800**
- May 2022 median annual wage: **$65,000**
- Projected employment change, 2022–32:
  - Number of new jobs: **1,100**
  - Growth rate: **4 percent (As fast as average)**
- Education and training:
  - Typical entry-level education: **High school diploma or equivalent**
  - Work experience in a related occupation: **None**
  - Typical on-the-job training: **Short-term on-the-job training**
- O*NET links:
  - 27-3099.00—Media and Communication Workers, All Other

Media and communication equipment workers, all other
All media and communication equipment workers not listed separately.
- 2022 employment: **17,300**
- May 2022 median annual wage: **$69,490**
- Projected employment change, 2022–32:
  - Number of new jobs: **600**
  - Growth rate: **3 percent (As fast as average)**
- Education and training:
  - Typical entry-level education: **High school diploma or equivalent**
  - Work experience in a related occupation: **None**
  - Typical on-the-job training: **Short-term on-the-job training**
- O*NET links:
  - 27-4099.00—Media and Communication Equipment Workers, All Other

Healthcare practitioners and technical occupations

Therapists, all other
All therapists not listed separately.
- 2022 employment: **42,300**
- May 2022 median annual wage: **$60,800**
- Projected employment change, 2022–32:
  - Number of new jobs: **5,200**
  - Growth rate: **12 percent (Much faster than average)**
- Education and training:
  - Typical entry-level education: **Bachelor's degree**
  - Work experience in a related occupation: **None**
  - Typical on-the-job training: **None**
- O*NET links:
  - 29-1129.00—Therapists, All Other
  - 29-1129.01—Art Therapists
  - 29-1129.02—Music Therapists

- CareerOneStop videos for this occupation:
  - 29-1129.01—Art Therapists
  - 29-1129.02—Music Therapists

Acupuncturists

Diagnose, treat, and prevent disorders by stimulating specific acupuncture points within the body using acupuncture needles. May also use cups, nutritional supplements, therapeutic massage, acupressure, and other alternative health therapies. Excludes "Chiropractors" (29-1011).

- 2022 employment: **26,600**
- May 2022 median annual wage: **$72,220**
- Projected employment change, 2022–32:
  - Number of new jobs: **1,400**
  - Growth rate: **5 percent (Faster than average)**
- Education and training:
  - Typical entry-level education: **Master's degree**
  - Work experience in a related occupation: **None**
  - Typical on-the-job training: **None**
- O*NET links:
  - 29-1291.00—Acupuncturists
- CareerOneStop videos for this occupation:
  - 29-1291.00—Acupuncturists

Healthcare diagnosing or treating practitioners, all other

All healthcare diagnosing or treating practitioners not listed separately.

- 2022 employment: **35,200**
- May 2022 median annual wage: **$106,230**
- Projected employment change, 2022–32:
  - Number of new jobs: **700**
  - Growth rate: **2 percent (As fast as average)**
- Education and training:
  - Typical entry-level education: **Master's degree**
  - Work experience in a related occupation: **None**
  - Typical on-the-job training: **None**
- O*NET links:
  - 29-1299.00—Healthcare Diagnosing or Treating Practitioners, All Other
  - 29-1299.01—Naturopathic Physicians
  - 29-1299.02—Orthoptists
- CareerOneStop videos for this occupation:
  - 29-1299.01—Naturopathic Physicians
  - 29-1299.02—Orthoptists

Dietetic technicians

Assist in the provision of food service and nutritional programs, under the supervision of a dietitian. May plan and produce meals based on established guidelines, teach principles of food and nutrition, or counsel individuals.

- 2022 employment: **20,200**
- May 2022 median annual wage: **$33,960**
- Projected employment change, 2022–32:
  - Number of new jobs: **700**
  - Growth rate: **4 percent (As fast as average)**
- Education and training:
  - Typical entry-level education: **Associate's degree**
  - Work experience in a related occupation: **None**
  - Typical on-the-job training: **None**
- O*NET links:
  - 29-2051.00—Dietetic Technicians
- CareerOneStop videos for this occupation:
  - 29-2051.00—Dietetic Technicians

Ophthalmic medical technicians

Assist ophthalmologists by performing ophthalmic clinical functions. May administer eye exams, administer eye medications, and instruct the patient in care and use of corrective lenses.

- 2022 employment: **66,500**
- May 2022 median annual wage: **$38,860**
- Projected employment change, 2022–32:
  - Number of new jobs: **8,400**
  - Growth rate: **13 percent (Much faster than average)**
- Education and training:
  - Typical entry-level education: **Postsecondary nondegree award**
  - Work experience in a related occupation: **None**
  - Typical on-the-job training: **None**
- O*NET links:
  - 29-2057.00—Ophthalmic Medical Technicians
- CareerOneStop videos for this occupation:
  - 29-2057.00—Ophthalmic Medical Technicians

Hearing aid specialists

Select and fit hearing aids for customers. Administer and interpret tests of hearing. Assess hearing instrument efficacy. Take ear impressions and prepare, design, and modify ear molds. Excludes "Audiologists" (29-1181).

- 2022 employment: **10,200**
- May 2022 median annual wage: **$59,020**
- Projected employment change, 2022–32:
  - Number of new jobs: **1,500**
  - Growth rate: **14 percent (Much faster than average)**
- Education and training:
  - Typical entry-level education: **High school diploma or equivalent**
  - Work experience in a related occupation: **None**
  - Typical on-the-job training: **Moderate-term on-the-job training**
- O*NET links:
  - 29-2092.00—Hearing Aid Specialists
- CareerOneStop videos for this occupation:
  - 29-2092.00—Hearing Aid Specialists

Health technologists and technicians, all other

All health technologists and technicians not listed separately.

- 2022 employment: **168,000**
- May 2022 median annual wage: **$44,990**
- Projected employment change, 2022–32:
  - Number of new jobs: **11,100**
  - Growth rate: **7 percent (Faster than average)**
- Education and training:
  - Typical entry-level education: **Postsecondary nondegree award**
  - Work experience in a related occupation: **None**
  - Typical on-the-job training: **None**
- O*NET links:
  - 29-2099.00—Health Technologists and Technicians, All Other
  - 29-2099.01—Neurodiagnostic Technologists
  - 29-2099.05—Ophthalmic Medical Technologists
  - 29-2099.08—Patient Representatives
- CareerOneStop videos for this occupation:
  - 29-2099.01—Neurodiagnostic Technologists
  - 29-2099.05—Ophthalmic Medical Technologists
  - 29-2099.08—Patient Representatives

Healthcare practitioners and technical workers, all other

All healthcare practitioners and technical workers not listed separately.

- 2022 employment: **44,400**
- May 2022 median annual wage: **$60,160**
- Projected employment change, 2022–32:
  - Number of new jobs: **2,300**
  - Growth rate: **5 percent (Faster than average)**
- Education and training:
  - Typical entry-level education: **Postsecondary nondegree award**
  - Work experience in a related occupation: **None**
  - Typical on-the-job training: **None**
- O*NET links:
  - 29-9099.00—Healthcare Practitioners and Technical Workers, All Other
  - 29-9099.01—Midwives
- CareerOneStop videos for this occupation:
  - 29-9099.01—Midwives

Healthcare support occupations

Medical equipment preparers

Prepare, sterilize, install, or clean laboratory or healthcare equipment. May perform routine laboratory tasks and operate or inspect equipment.

- 2022 employment: **66,700**
- May 2022 median annual wage: **$41,480**
- Projected employment change, 2022–32:
  - Number of new jobs: **3,600**
  - Growth rate: **5 percent (Faster than average)**
- Education and training:
  - Typical entry-level education: **High school diploma or equivalent**
  - Work experience in a related occupation: **None**
  - Typical on-the-job training: **Moderate-term on-the-job training**
- O*NET links:
  - 31-9093.00—Medical Equipment Preparers
- CareerOneStop videos for this occupation:
  - 31-9093.00—Medical Equipment Preparers

Pharmacy aides

Record drugs delivered to the pharmacy, store incoming merchandise, and inform the supervisor of stock needs. May operate cash register and accept prescriptions for filling.

- 2022 employment: **43,700**
- May 2022 median annual wage: **$33,270**
- Projected employment change, 2022–32:
  - Number of new jobs: **-1,200**
  - Growth rate: **-3 percent (Decline)**
- Education and training:
  - Typical entry-level education: **High school diploma or equivalent**
  - Work experience in a related occupation: **None**
  - Typical on-the-job training: **Short-term on-the-job training**
- O*NET links:
  - 31-9095.00—Pharmacy Aides
- CareerOneStop videos for this occupation:
  - 31-9095.00—Pharmacy Aides

Healthcare support workers, all other

All healthcare support workers not listed separately.

- 2022 employment: **112,700**
- May 2022 median annual wage: **$40,420**
- Projected employment change, 2022–32:
  - Number of new jobs: **6,400**
  - Growth rate: **6 percent (Faster than average)**
- Education and training:
  - Typical entry-level education: **High school diploma or equivalent**
  - Work experience in a related occupation: **None**
  - Typical on-the-job training: **None**
- O*NET links:
  - 31-9099.00—Healthcare Support Workers, All Other
  - 31-9099.01—Speech-Language Pathology Assistants
  - 31-9099.02—Endoscopy Technicians
- CareerOneStop videos for this occupation:
  - 31-9099.01—Speech-Language Pathology Assistants
  - 31-9099.02—Endoscopy Technicians

Protective service occupations

First-line supervisors of correctional officers

Directly supervise and coordinate activities of correctional officers and jailers.

- 2022 employment: **58,500**
- May 2022 median annual wage: **$63,310**
- Projected employment change, 2022–32:
  - Number of new jobs: **-1,600**
  - Growth rate: **-3 percent (Decline)**
- Education and training:
  - Typical entry-level education: **High school diploma or equivalent**
  - Work experience in a related occupation: **Less than 5 years**
  - Typical on-the-job training: **None**
- O*NET links:
  - 33-1011.00—First-Line Supervisors of Correctional Officers
- CareerOneStop videos for this occupation:
  - 33-1011.00—First-Line Supervisors of Correctional Officers

First-line supervisors of police and detectives

Directly supervise and coordinate activities of members of police force.

- 2022 employment: **137,900**
- May 2022 median annual wage: **$96,290**
- Projected employment change, 2022–32:
  - Number of new jobs: **4,300**
  - Growth rate: **3 percent (As fast as average)**
- Education and training:
  - Typical entry-level education: **High school diploma or equivalent**
  - Work experience in a related occupation: **Less than 5 years**
  - Typical on-the-job training: **Moderate-term on-the-job training**
- O*NET links:
  - 33-1012.00—First-Line Supervisors of Police and Detectives
- CareerOneStop videos for this occupation:
  - 33-1012.00—First-Line Supervisors of Police and Detectives

First-line supervisors of firefighting and prevention workers

Directly supervise and coordinate activities of workers engaged in firefighting and fire prevention and control.

- 2022 employment: **87,100**
- May 2022 median annual wage: **$80,150**
- Projected employment change, 2022–32:

- Number of new jobs: **3,100**
- Growth rate: **4 percent (As fast as average)**
- Education and training:
  - Typical entry-level education: **Postsecondary nondegree award**
  - Work experience in a related occupation: **Less than 5 years**
  - Typical on-the-job training: **Moderate-term on-the-job training**
- O*NET links:
  - 33-1021.00—First-Line Supervisors of Firefighting and Prevention Workers
- CareerOneStop videos for this occupation:
  - 33-1021.00—First-Line Supervisors of Firefighting and Prevention Workers

First-line supervisors of security workers

Directly supervise and coordinate activities of security workers and security guards.

- 2022 employment: **62,200**
- May 2022 median annual wage: **$48,810**
- Projected employment change, 2022–32:
  - Number of new jobs: **-2,400**
  - Growth rate: **-4 percent (Decline)**
- Education and training:
  - Typical entry-level education: **High school diploma or equivalent**
  - Work experience in a related occupation: **Less than 5 years**
  - Typical on-the-job training: **None**
- O*NET links:
  - 33-1091.00—First-Line Supervisors of Security Workers

First-line supervisors of protective service workers, all other

All protective service supervisors not listed separately above.

- 2022 employment: **24,500**
- May 2022 median annual wage: **$61,030**
- Projected employment change, 2022–32:
  - Number of new jobs: **800**
  - Growth rate: **3 percent (As fast as average)**
- Education and training:
  - Typical entry-level education: **High school diploma or equivalent**
  - Work experience in a related occupation: **Less than 5 years**
  - Typical on-the-job training: **None**
- O*NET links:
  - 33-1099.00—First-Line Supervisors of Protective Service Workers, All Other

Parking enforcement workers

Patrol assigned area, such as public parking lot or city streets to issue tickets to overtime parking violators and illegally parked vehicles.

- 2022 employment: **9,000**
- May 2022 median annual wage: **$41,570**
- Projected employment change, 2022–32:
  - Number of new jobs: **-100**
  - Growth rate: **-1 percent (Little or no change)**
- Education and training:
  - Typical entry-level education: **High school diploma or equivalent**
  - Work experience in a related occupation: **None**
  - Typical on-the-job training: **Short-term on-the-job training**
- O*NET links:
  - 33-3041.00—Parking Enforcement Workers

Animal control workers

Handle animals for the purpose of investigations of mistreatment, or control of abandoned, dangerous, or unattended animals.

- 2022 employment: **11,900**
- May 2022 median annual wage: **$39,320**
- Projected employment change, 2022–32:
  - Number of new jobs: **500**
  - Growth rate: **4 percent (As fast as average)**
- Education and training:
  - Typical entry-level education: **High school diploma or equivalent**
  - Work experience in a related occupation: **None**
  - Typical on-the-job training: **Moderate-term on-the-job training**
- O*NET links:
  - 33-9011.00—Animal Control Workers
- CareerOneStop videos for this occupation:
  - 33-9011.00—Animal Control Workers

Crossing guards and flaggers

Guide or control vehicular or pedestrian traffic at such places as streets, schools, railroad crossings, or construction sites.

- 2022 employment: **94,100**
- May 2022 median annual wage: **$33,380**
- Projected employment change, 2022–32:
  - Number of new jobs: **3,800**
  - Growth rate: **4 percent (As fast as average)**
- Education and training:
  - Typical entry-level education: **No formal educational credential**
  - Work experience in a related occupation: **None**
  - Typical on-the-job training: **Short-term on-the-job training**
- O*NET links:
  - 33-9091.00—Crossing Guards and Flaggers
- CareerOneStop videos for this occupation:
  - 33-9091.00—Crossing Guards and Flaggers

Lifeguards, ski patrol, and other recreational protective service workers

Monitor recreational areas, such as pools, beaches, or ski slopes, to provide assistance and protection to participants.

- 2022 employment: **113,500**
- May 2022 median annual wage: **$27,270**
- Projected employment change, 2022–32:
  - Number of new jobs: **7,000**
  - Growth rate: **6 percent (Faster than average)**
- Education and training:
  - Typical entry-level education: **No formal educational credential**
  - Work experience in a related occupation: **None**
  - Typical on-the-job training: **Short-term on-the-job training**
- O*NET links:
  - 33-9092.00—Lifeguards, Ski Patrol, and Other Recreational Protective Service Workers
- CareerOneStop videos for this occupation:
  - 33-9092.00—Lifeguards, Ski Patrol, and Other Recreational Protective Service Workers

Transportation security screeners

Conduct screening of passengers, baggage, or cargo to ensure compliance with Transportation Security Administration (TSA) regulations.

May operate basic security equipment such as x-ray machines and hand wands at screening checkpoints.

- 2022 employment: **51,300**
- May 2022 median annual wage: **$47,710**
- Projected employment change, 2022–32:
  - Number of new jobs: **0**
  - Growth rate: **0 percent (Little or no change)**
- Education and training:
  - Typical entry-level education: **High school diploma or equivalent**
  - Work experience in a related occupation: **None**
  - Typical on-the-job training: **Short-term on-the-job training**
- O*NET links:
  - 33-9093.00—Transportation Security Screeners
- CareerOneStop videos for this occupation:
  - 33-9093.00—Transportation Security Screeners

School bus monitors

Maintain order among students on a school bus. Duties include helping students safely board and exit and communicating behavioral problems. May perform pretrip and posttrip inspections and prepare for and assist in emergency evacuations.

- 2022 employment: **62,400**
- May 2022 median annual wage: **$29,880**
- Projected employment change, 2022–32:
  - Number of new jobs: **-2,200**
  - Growth rate: **-4 percent (Decline)**
- Education and training:
  - Typical entry-level education: **High school diploma or equivalent**
  - Work experience in a related occupation: **None**
  - Typical on-the-job training: **Short-term on-the-job training**
- O*NET links:
  - 33-9094.00—School Bus Monitors
- CareerOneStop videos for this occupation:
  - 33-9094.00—School Bus Monitors

Protective service workers, all other

All protective service workers not listed separately.

- 2022 employment: **95,000**
- May 2022 median annual wage: **$36,460**
- Projected employment change, 2022–32:
  - Number of new jobs: **2,900**
  - Growth rate: **3 percent (As fast as average)**
- Education and training:
  - Typical entry-level education: **High school diploma or equivalent**
  - Work experience in a related occupation: **None**
  - Typical on-the-job training: **Short-term on-the-job training**
- O*NET links:
  - 33-9099.00—Protective Service Workers, All Other
  - 33-9099.02—Retail Loss Prevention Specialists
- CareerOneStop videos for this occupation:
  - 33-9099.02—Retail Loss Prevention Specialists

Food preparation and serving related occupations

First-line supervisors of food preparation and serving workers

Directly supervise and coordinate activities of workers engaged in preparing and serving food.

- 2022 employment: **1,221,700**
- May 2022 median annual wage: **$37,050**
- Projected employment change, 2022–32:
  - Number of new jobs: **60,000**
  - Growth rate: **5 percent (Faster than average)**
- Education and training:
  - Typical entry-level education: **High school diploma or equivalent**
  - Work experience in a related occupation: **Less than 5 years**
  - Typical on-the-job training: **None**
- O*NET links:
  - 35-1012.00—First-Line Supervisors of Food Preparation and Serving Workers
- CareerOneStop videos for this occupation:
  - 35-1012.00—First-Line Supervisors of Food Preparation and Serving Workers

Dishwashers

Clean dishes, kitchen, food preparation equipment, or utensils.

- 2022 employment: **447,100**
- May 2022 median annual wage: **$29,080**
- Projected employment change, 2022–32:
  - Number of new jobs: **-10,200**
  - Growth rate: **-2 percent (Decline)**
- Education and training:
  - Typical entry-level education: **No formal educational credential**
  - Work experience in a related occupation: **None**
  - Typical on-the-job training: **Short-term on-the-job training**
- O*NET links:
  - 35-9021.00—Dishwashers
- CareerOneStop videos for this occupation:
  - 35-9021.00—Dishwashers

Food preparation and serving related workers, all other

All food preparation and serving related workers not listed separately.

- 2022 employment: **85,400**
- May 2022 median annual wage: **$30,840**
- Projected employment change, 2022–32:
  - Number of new jobs: **3,700**
  - Growth rate: **4 percent (As fast as average)**
- Education and training:
  - Typical entry-level education: **No formal educational credential**
  - Work experience in a related occupation: **None**
  - Typical on-the-job training: **Short-term on-the-job training**
- O*NET links:
  - 35-9099.00—Food Preparation and Serving Related Workers, All Other

Building and grounds cleaning and maintenance occupations

First-line supervisors of housekeeping and janitorial workers

Directly supervise and coordinate work activities of cleaning personnel in hotels, hospitals, offices, and other establishments.

- 2022 employment: **254,900**
- May 2022 median annual wage: **$44,440**
- Projected employment change, 2022–32:
  - Number of new jobs: **7,700**
  - Growth rate: **3 percent (As fast as average)**

- Education and training:
  - Typical entry-level education: **High school diploma or equivalent**
  - Work experience in a related occupation: **Less than 5 years**
  - Typical on-the-job training: **None**
- O*NET links:
  - 37-1011.00—First-Line Supervisors of Housekeeping and Janitorial Workers
- CareerOneStop videos for this occupation:
  - 37-1011.00—First-Line Supervisors of Housekeeping and Janitorial Workers

First-line supervisors of landscaping, lawn service, and groundskeeping workers

Directly supervise and coordinate activities of workers engaged in landscaping or groundskeeping activities. Work may involve reviewing contracts to ascertain service, machine, and workforce requirements; answering inquiries from potential customers regarding methods, material, and price ranges; and preparing estimates according to labor, material, and machine costs.

- 2022 employment: **230,900**
- May 2022 median annual wage: **$50,810**
- Projected employment change, 2022–32:
  - Number of new jobs: **6,100**
  - Growth rate: **3 percent (As fast as average)**
- Education and training:
  - Typical entry-level education: **High school diploma or equivalent**
  - Work experience in a related occupation: **Less than 5 years**
  - Typical on-the-job training: **None**
- O*NET links:
  - 37-1012.00—First-Line Supervisors of Landscaping, Lawn Service, and Groundskeeping Workers
- CareerOneStop videos for this occupation:
  - 37-1012.00—First-Line Supervisors of Landscaping, Lawn Service, and Groundskeeping Workers

Maids and housekeeping cleaners

Perform any combination of light cleaning duties to maintain private households or commercial establishments, such as hotels and hospitals, in a clean and orderly manner. Duties may include making beds, replenishing linens, cleaning rooms and halls, and vacuuming.

- 2022 employment: **1,238,800**
- May 2022 median annual wage: **$29,960**
- Projected employment change, 2022–32:
  - Number of new jobs: **1,600**
  - Growth rate: **0 percent (Little or no change)**
- Education and training:
  - Typical entry-level education: **No formal educational credential**
  - Work experience in a related occupation: **None**
  - Typical on-the-job training: **Short-term on-the-job training**
- Occupational Requirements Survey profile for this occupation:
  - Maids and housekeeping cleaners (PDF)
- O*NET links:
  - 37-2012.00—Maids and Housekeeping Cleaners
- CareerOneStop videos for this occupation:
  - 37-2012.00—Maids and Housekeeping Cleaners

Building cleaning workers, all other

All building cleaning workers not listed separately.

- 2022 employment: **17,100**
- May 2022 median annual wage: **$37,200**
- Projected employment change, 2022–32:
  - Number of new jobs: **400**
  - Growth rate: **3 percent (As fast as average)**
- Education and training:
  - Typical entry-level education: **No formal educational credential**
  - Work experience in a related occupation: **None**
  - Typical on-the-job training: **Short-term on-the-job training**
- O*NET links:
  - 37-2019.00—Building Cleaning Workers, All Other

Personal care and service occupations

First-line supervisors of entertainment and recreation workers, except gambling services

Directly supervise and coordinate activities of entertainment and recreation related workers.

- 2022 employment: **114,600**
- May 2022 median annual wage: **$44,660**
- Projected employment change, 2022–32:
  - Number of new jobs: **8,800**
  - Growth rate: **8 percent (Faster than average)**
- Education and training:
  - Typical entry-level education: **High school diploma or equivalent**
  - Work experience in a related occupation: **Less than 5 years**
  - Typical on-the-job training: **None**
- O*NET links:
  - 39-1014.00—First-Line Supervisors of Entertainment and Recreation Workers, Except Gambling Services
- CareerOneStop videos for this occupation:
  - 39-1014.00—First-Line Supervisors of Entertainment and Recreation Workers, Except Gambling Services

First-line supervisors of personal service workers

Supervise and coordinate activities of personal service workers.

- 2022 employment: **159,000**
- May 2022 median annual wage: **$43,680**
- Projected employment change, 2022–32:
  - Number of new jobs: **13,100**
  - Growth rate: **8 percent (Faster than average)**
- Education and training:
  - Typical entry-level education: **High school diploma or equivalent**
  - Work experience in a related occupation: **Less than 5 years**
  - Typical on-the-job training: **None**
- O*NET links:
  - 39-1022.00—First-Line Supervisors of Personal Service Workers
- CareerOneStop videos for this occupation:
  - 39-1022.00—First-Line Supervisors of Personal Service Workers

Motion picture projectionists

Set up and operate motion picture projection and related sound reproduction equipment.

- 2022 employment: **2,100**
- May 2022 median annual wage: **$33,360**
- Projected employment change, 2022–32:
  - Number of new jobs: **-200**
  - Growth rate: **-10 percent (Decline)**

- Education and training:
  - Typical entry-level education: **No formal educational credential**
  - Work experience in a related occupation: **None**
  - Typical on-the-job training: **Short-term on-the-job training**
- O*NET links:
  - 39-3021.00—Motion Picture Projectionists

Ushers, lobby attendants, and ticket takers

Assist patrons at entertainment events by performing duties, such as collecting admission tickets and passes from patrons, assisting in finding seats, searching for lost articles, and helping patrons locate such facilities as restrooms and telephones.

- 2022 employment: **106,600**
- May 2022 median annual wage: **$27,650**
- Projected employment change, 2022–32:
  - Number of new jobs: **1,700**
  - Growth rate: **2 percent (As fast as average)**
- Education and training:
  - Typical entry-level education: **No formal educational credential**
  - Work experience in a related occupation: **None**
  - Typical on-the-job training: **Short-term on-the-job training**
- O*NET links:
  - 39-3031.00—Ushers, Lobby Attendants, and Ticket Takers
- CareerOneStop videos for this occupation:
  - 39-3031.00—Ushers, Lobby Attendants, and Ticket Takers

Amusement and recreation attendants

Perform a variety of attending duties at amusement or recreation facility. May schedule use of recreation facilities, maintain and provide equipment to participants of sporting events or recreational pursuits, or operate amusement concessions and rides.

- 2022 employment: **343,800**
- May 2022 median annual wage: **$27,780**
- Projected employment change, 2022–32:
  - Number of new jobs: **14,400**
  - Growth rate: **4 percent (As fast as average)**
- Education and training:
  - Typical entry-level education: **No formal educational credential**
  - Work experience in a related occupation: **None**
  - Typical on-the-job training: **Short-term on-the-job training**
- O*NET links:
  - 39-3091.00—Amusement and Recreation Attendants
- CareerOneStop videos for this occupation:
  - 39-3091.00—Amusement and Recreation Attendants

Costume attendants

Select, fit, and take care of costumes for cast members, and aid entertainers. May assist with multiple costume changes during performances.

- 2022 employment: **6,100**
- May 2022 median annual wage: **$48,470**
- Projected employment change, 2022–32:
  - Number of new jobs: **300**
  - Growth rate: **5 percent (Faster than average)**
- Education and training:
  - Typical entry-level education: **High school diploma or equivalent**
  - Work experience in a related occupation: **None**
  - Typical on-the-job training: **Short-term on-the-job training**
- O*NET links:
  - 39-3092.00—Costume Attendants

Locker room, coatroom, and dressing room attendants

Provide personal items to patrons or customers in locker rooms, dressing rooms, or coatrooms.

- 2022 employment: **12,900**
- May 2022 median annual wage: **$30,210**
- Projected employment change, 2022–32:
  - Number of new jobs: **900**
  - Growth rate: **7 percent (Faster than average)**
- Education and training:
  - Typical entry-level education: **High school diploma or equivalent**
  - Work experience in a related occupation: **None**
  - Typical on-the-job training: **Short-term on-the-job training**
- O*NET links:
  - 39-3093.00—Locker Room, Coatroom, and Dressing Room Attendants
- CareerOneStop videos for this occupation:
  - 39-3093.00—Locker Room, Coatroom, and Dressing Room Attendants

Entertainment attendants and related workers, all other

All entertainment attendants and related workers not listed separately.

- 2022 employment: **5,200**
- May 2022 median annual wage: **$27,260**
- Projected employment change, 2022–32:
  - Number of new jobs: **300**
  - Growth rate: **5 percent (Faster than average)**
- Education and training:
  - Typical entry-level education: **High school diploma or equivalent**
  - Work experience in a related occupation: **None**
  - Typical on-the-job training: **Short-term on-the-job training**
- O*NET links:
  - 39-3099.00—Entertainment Attendants and Related Workers, All Other

Embalmers

Prepare bodies for interment in conformity with legal requirements.

- 2022 employment: **4,000**
- May 2022 median annual wage: **$49,910**
- Projected employment change, 2022–32:
  - Number of new jobs: **0**
  - Growth rate: **1 percent (Little or no change)**
- Education and training:
  - Typical entry-level education: **Associate's degree**
  - Work experience in a related occupation: **None**
  - Typical on-the-job training: **Long-term on-the-job training**
- O*NET links:
  - 39-4011.00—Embalmers
- CareerOneStop videos for this occupation:
  - 39-4011.00—Embalmers

Crematory operators

Operate crematory equipment to reduce human or animal remains to bone fragments in accordance with state and local regulations. Duties may include preparing the body for cremation and performing general maintenance on crematory equipment. May use traditional flame-based cremation, calcination, or alkaline hydrolysis.

- 2022 employment: **3,000**
- May 2022 median annual wage: **$40,360**
- Projected employment change, 2022–32:
  - Number of new jobs: **100**
  - Growth rate: **4 percent (As fast as average)**
- Education and training:
  - Typical entry-level education: **High school diploma or equivalent**
  - Work experience in a related occupation: **None**
  - Typical on-the-job training: **Short-term on-the-job training**
- O*NET links:
  - 39-4012.00—Crematory Operators
- CareerOneStop videos for this occupation:
  - 39-4012.00—Crematory Operators

Funeral attendants

Perform a variety of tasks during funeral, such as placing casket in parlor or chapel prior to service, arranging floral offerings or lights around casket, directing or escorting mourners, closing casket, and issuing and storing funeral equipment.

- 2022 employment: **33,200**
- May 2022 median annual wage: **$31,160**
- Projected employment change, 2022–32:
  - Number of new jobs: **900**
  - Growth rate: **3 percent (As fast as average)**
- Education and training:
  - Typical entry-level education: **High school diploma or equivalent**
  - Work experience in a related occupation: **None**
  - Typical on-the-job training: **Short-term on-the-job training**
- O*NET links:
  - 39-4021.00—Funeral Attendants
- CareerOneStop videos for this occupation:
  - 39-4021.00—Funeral Attendants

Makeup artists, theatrical and performance

Apply makeup to performers to reflect period, setting, and situation of their role.

- 2022 employment: **4,600**
- May 2022 median annual wage: **$96,370**
- Projected employment change, 2022–32:
  - Number of new jobs: **400**
  - Growth rate: **9 percent (Much faster than average)**
- Education and training:
  - Typical entry-level education: **Postsecondary nondegree award**
  - Work experience in a related occupation: **None**
  - Typical on-the-job training: **None**
- O*NET links:
  - 39-5091.00—Makeup Artists, Theatrical and Performance
- CareerOneStop videos for this occupation:
  - 39-5091.00—Makeup Artists, Theatrical and Performance

Shampooers

Shampoo and rinse customers' hair.

- 2022 employment: **11,300**
- May 2022 median annual wage: **$27,860**
- Projected employment change, 2022–32:
  - Number of new jobs: **1,300**
  - Growth rate: **11 percent (Much faster than average)**
- Education and training:
  - Typical entry-level education: **No formal educational credential**
  - Work experience in a related occupation: **None**
  - Typical on-the-job training: **Short-term on-the-job training**
- O*NET links:
  - 39-5093.00—Shampooers
- CareerOneStop videos for this occupation:
  - 39-5093.00—Shampooers

Baggage porters and bellhops

Handle baggage for travelers at transportation terminals or for guests at hotels or similar establishments.

- 2022 employment: **27,700**
- May 2022 median annual wage: **$31,510**
- Projected employment change, 2022–32:
  - Number of new jobs: **1,700**
  - Growth rate: **6 percent (Faster than average)**
- Education and training:
  - Typical entry-level education: **High school diploma or equivalent**
  - Work experience in a related occupation: **None**
  - Typical on-the-job training: **Short-term on-the-job training**
- O*NET links:
  - 39-6011.00—Baggage Porters and Bellhops
- CareerOneStop videos for this occupation:
  - 39-6011.00—Baggage Porters and Bellhops

Concierges

Assist patrons at hotel, apartment, or office building with personal services. May take messages; arrange or give advice on transportation, business services, or entertainment; or monitor guest requests for housekeeping and maintenance.

- 2022 employment: **38,700**
- May 2022 median annual wage: **$35,560**
- Projected employment change, 2022–32:
  - Number of new jobs: **2,200**
  - Growth rate: **6 percent (Faster than average)**
- Education and training:
  - Typical entry-level education: **High school diploma or equivalent**
  - Work experience in a related occupation: **None**
  - Typical on-the-job training: **Moderate-term on-the-job training**
- O*NET links:
  - 39-6012.00—Concierges
- CareerOneStop videos for this occupation:
  - 39-6012.00—Concierges

Tour and travel guides

The definitions for these occupations are available by following their SOC links.

This occupation includes the following SOC 2018 occupations:

- 39-7011—Tour Guides and Escorts
- 39-7012—Travel Guides
- 2022 employment: **53,600**
- May 2022 median annual wage: **$34,440**
- Projected employment change, 2022–32:
  - Number of new jobs: **4,300**
  - Growth rate: **8 percent (Faster than average)**
- Education and training:
  - Typical entry-level education: **High school diploma or equivalent**
  - Work experience in a related occupation: **None**
  - Typical on-the-job training: **Moderate-term on-the-job training**

- O*NET links:
  - 39-7011.00—Tour Guides and Escorts
  - 39-7012.00—Travel Guides
- CareerOneStop videos for this occupation:
  - 39-7011.00—Tour Guides and Escorts
  - 39-7012.00—Travel Guides

Residential advisors

Coordinate activities in resident facilities in secondary school and college dormitories, group homes, or similar establishments. Order supplies and determine need for maintenance, repairs, and furnishings. May maintain household records and assign rooms. May assist residents with problem solving or refer them to counseling resources.

- 2022 employment: **95,700**
- May 2022 median annual wage: **$35,720**
- Projected employment change, 2022–32:
  - Number of new jobs: **5,700**
  - Growth rate: **6 percent (Faster than average)**
- Education and training:
  - Typical entry-level education: **High school diploma or equivalent**
  - Work experience in a related occupation: **None**
  - Typical on-the-job training: **Short-term on-the-job training**
- O*NET links:
  - 39-9041.00—Residential Advisors
- CareerOneStop videos for this occupation:
  - 39-9041.00—Residential Advisors

Personal care and service workers, all other

All personal care and service workers not listed separately.

- 2022 employment: **87,000**
- May 2022 median annual wage: **$34,670**
- Projected employment change, 2022–32:
  - Number of new jobs: **17,900**
  - Growth rate: **21 percent (Much faster than average)**
- Education and training:
  - Typical entry-level education: **High school diploma or equivalent**
  - Work experience in a related occupation: **None**
  - Typical on-the-job training: **Short-term on-the-job training**
- O*NET links:
  - 39-9099.00—Personal Care and Service Workers, All Other

Sales and related occupations

First-line supervisors of retail sales workers

Directly supervise and coordinate activities of retail sales workers in an establishment or department. Duties may include management functions, such as purchasing, budgeting, accounting, and personnel work, in addition to supervisory duties.

- 2022 employment: **1,405,800**
- May 2022 median annual wage: **$45,250**
- Projected employment change, 2022–32:
  - Number of new jobs: **-94,000**
  - Growth rate: **-7 percent (Decline)**
- Education and training:
  - Typical entry-level education: **High school diploma or equivalent**
  - Work experience in a related occupation: **Less than 5 years**
  - Typical on-the-job training: **None**
- O*NET links:
  - 41-1011.00—First-Line Supervisors of Retail Sales Workers
- CareerOneStop videos for this occupation:
  - 41-1011.00—First-Line Supervisors of Retail Sales Workers

First-line supervisors of non-retail sales workers

Directly supervise and coordinate activities of sales workers other than retail sales workers. May perform duties such as budgeting, accounting, and personnel work, in addition to supervisory duties.

- 2022 employment: **364,400**
- May 2022 median annual wage: **$82,850**
- Projected employment change, 2022–32:
  - Number of new jobs: **-8,000**
  - Growth rate: **-2 percent (Decline)**
- Education and training:
  - Typical entry-level education: **High school diploma or equivalent**
  - Work experience in a related occupation: **Less than 5 years**
  - Typical on-the-job training: **None**
- O*NET links:
  - 41-1012.00—First-Line Supervisors of Non-Retail Sales Workers
- CareerOneStop videos for this occupation:
  - 41-1012.00—First-Line Supervisors of Non-Retail Sales Workers

Gambling change persons and booth cashiers

Exchange coins, tokens, and chips for patrons' money. May issue payoffs and obtain customer's signature on receipt. May operate a booth in the slot machine area and furnish change persons with money bank at the start of the shift, or count and audit money in drawers. Excludes "Cashiers" (41-2011).

- 2022 employment: **19,400**
- May 2022 median annual wage: **$30,010**
- Projected employment change, 2022–32:
  - Number of new jobs: **-1,100**
  - Growth rate: **-6 percent (Decline)**
- Education and training:
  - Typical entry-level education: **No formal educational credential**
  - Work experience in a related occupation: **None**
  - Typical on-the-job training: **Short-term on-the-job training**
- O*NET links:
  - 41-2012.00—Gambling Change Persons and Booth Cashiers
- CareerOneStop videos for this occupation:
  - 41-2012.00—Gambling Change Persons and Booth Cashiers

Counter and rental clerks

Receive orders, generally in person, for repairs, rentals, and services. May describe available options, compute cost, and accept payment. Excludes "Fast Food and Counter Workers" (35-3023), "Hotel, Motel, and Resort Desk Clerks" (43-4081), "Order Clerks" (43-4151), and "Reservation and Transportation Ticket Agents and Travel Clerks" (43-4181).

- 2022 employment: **380,800**
- May 2022 median annual wage: **$35,830**
- Projected employment change, 2022–32:
  - Number of new jobs: **10,400**
  - Growth rate: **3 percent (As fast as average)**
- Education and training:
  - Typical entry-level education: **No formal educational credential**

- Work experience in a related occupation: **None**
- Typical on-the-job training: **Short-term on-the-job training**

- O*NET links:
  - 41-2021.00—Counter and Rental Clerks
- CareerOneStop videos for this occupation:
  - 41-2021.00—Counter and Rental Clerks

Sales representatives of services, except advertising, insurance, financial services, and travel

Sell services to individuals or businesses. May describe options or resolve client problems. Excludes "Advertising Sales Agents" (41-3011), "Insurance Sales Agents" (41-3021), "Securities, Commodities, and Financial Services Sales Agents" (41-3031), "Travel Agents" (41-3041), "Sales Representatives, Wholesale and Manufacturing" (41-4010), and "Telemarketers" (41-9041).

- 2022 employment: **1,113,200**
- May 2022 median annual wage: **$62,400**
- Projected employment change, 2022–32:
  - Number of new jobs: **45,700**
  - Growth rate: **4 percent (As fast as average)**
- Education and training:
  - Typical entry-level education: **High school diploma or equivalent**
  - Work experience in a related occupation: **None**
  - Typical on-the-job training: **Moderate-term on-the-job training**
- O*NET links:
  - 41-3091.00—Sales Representatives of Services, Except Advertising, Insurance, Financial Services, and Travel

Demonstrators and product promoters

Demonstrate merchandise and answer questions for the purpose of creating public interest in buying the product. May sell demonstrated merchandise.

- 2022 employment: **45,000**
- May 2022 median annual wage: **$34,770**
- Projected employment change, 2022–32:
  - Number of new jobs: **1,800**
  - Growth rate: **4 percent (As fast as average)**
- Education and training:
  - Typical entry-level education: **No formal educational credential**
  - Work experience in a related occupation: **None**
  - Typical on-the-job training: **Short-term on-the-job training**
- O*NET links:
  - 41-9011.00—Demonstrators and Product Promoters
- CareerOneStop videos for this occupation:
  - 41-9011.00—Demonstrators and Product Promoters

Telemarketers

Solicit donations or orders for goods or services over the telephone.

- 2022 employment: **97,700**
- May 2022 median annual wage: **$31,030**
- Projected employment change, 2022–32:
  - Number of new jobs: **-20,100**
  - Growth rate: **-21 percent (Decline)**
- Education and training:
  - Typical entry-level education: **No formal educational credential**
  - Work experience in a related occupation: **None**
  - Typical on-the-job training: **Short-term on-the-job training**
- O*NET links:
  - 41-9041.00—Telemarketers
- CareerOneStop videos for this occupation:
  - 41-9041.00—Telemarketers

Door-to-door sales workers, news and street vendors, and related workers

Sell goods or services door-to-door or on the street.

- 2022 employment: **36,400**
- May 2022 median annual wage: **$31,100**
- Projected employment change, 2022–32:
  - Number of new jobs: **-5,800**
  - Growth rate: **-16 percent (Decline)**
- Education and training:
  - Typical entry-level education: **No formal educational credential**
  - Work experience in a related occupation: **None**
  - Typical on-the-job training: **Short-term on-the-job training**
- O*NET links:
  - 41-9091.00—Door-to-Door Sales Workers, News and Street Vendors, and Related Workers

Sales and related workers, all other

All sales and related workers not listed separately.

- 2022 employment: **136,800**
- May 2022 median annual wage: **$44,120**
- Projected employment change, 2022–32:
  - Number of new jobs: **6,100**
  - Growth rate: **4 percent (As fast as average)**
- Education and training:
  - Typical entry-level education: **High school diploma or equivalent**
  - Work experience in a related occupation: **None**
  - Typical on-the-job training: **None**
- O*NET links:
  - 41-9099.00—Sales and Related Workers, All Other

Office and administrative support occupations

First-line supervisors of office and administrative support workers

Directly supervise and coordinate the activities of clerical and administrative support workers.

- 2022 employment: **1,567,200**
- May 2022 median annual wage: **$61,370**
- Projected employment change, 2022–32:
  - Number of new jobs: **-80,700**
  - Growth rate: **-5 percent (Decline)**
- Education and training:
  - Typical entry-level education: **High school diploma or equivalent**
  - Work experience in a related occupation: **Less than 5 years**
  - Typical on-the-job training: **None**
- O*NET links:
  - 43-1011.00—First-Line Supervisors of Office and Administrative Support Workers
- CareerOneStop videos for this occupation:
  - 43-1011.00—First-Line Supervisors of Office and Administrative Support Workers

Switchboard operators, including answering service

Operate telephone business systems equipment or switchboards to relay incoming, outgoing, and interoffice calls. May supply information to callers and record messages.

- 2022 employment: **48,400**
- May 2022 median annual wage: **$34,670**
- Projected employment change, 2022–32:
  - Number of new jobs: **-12,100**
  - Growth rate: **-25 percent (Decline)**
- Education and training:
  - Typical entry-level education: **High school diploma or equivalent**
  - Work experience in a related occupation: **None**
  - Typical on-the-job training: **Short-term on-the-job training**
- O*NET links:
  - 43-2011.00—Switchboard Operators, Including Answering Service

Telephone operators

Provide information by accessing alphabetical, geographical, or other directories. Assist customers with special billing requests, such as charges to a third party and credits or refunds for incorrectly dialed numbers or bad connections. May handle emergency calls and assist children or people with physical disabilities to make telephone calls.

- 2022 employment: **4,100**
- May 2022 median annual wage: **$38,330**
- Projected employment change, 2022–32:
  - Number of new jobs: **-1,100**
  - Growth rate: **-27 percent (Decline)**
- Education and training:
  - Typical entry-level education: **High school diploma or equivalent**
  - Work experience in a related occupation: **None**
  - Typical on-the-job training: **Short-term on-the-job training**
- O*NET links:
  - 43-2021.00—Telephone Operators
- CareerOneStop videos for this occupation:
  - 43-2021.00—Telephone Operators

Communications equipment operators, all other

All communications equipment operators not listed separately.

- 2022 employment: **1,800**
- May 2022 median annual wage: **$46,180**
- Projected employment change, 2022–32:
  - Number of new jobs: **100**
  - Growth rate: **6 percent (Faster than average)**
- Education and training:
  - Typical entry-level education: **High school diploma or equivalent**
  - Work experience in a related occupation: **None**
  - Typical on-the-job training: **Short-term on-the-job training**
- O*NET links:
  - 43-2099.00—Communications Equipment Operators, All Other

Financial clerks, all other

All financial clerks not listed separately.

- 2022 employment: **43,700**
- May 2022 median annual wage: **$47,130**
- Projected employment change, 2022–32:
  - Number of new jobs: **500**
  - Growth rate: **1 percent (Little or no change)**
- Education and training:
  - Typical entry-level education: **High school diploma or equivalent**
  - Work experience in a related occupation: **None**
  - Typical on-the-job training: **Short-term on-the-job training**
- O*NET links:
  - 43-3099.00—Financial Clerks, All Other

Cargo and freight agents

Expedite and route movement of incoming and outgoing cargo and freight shipments in airline, train, and trucking terminals and shipping docks. Take orders from customers and arrange pickup of freight and cargo for delivery to loading platform. Prepare and examine bills of lading to determine shipping charges and tariffs.

- 2022 employment: **95,900**
- May 2022 median annual wage: **$46,860**
- Projected employment change, 2022–32:
  - Number of new jobs: **9,300**
  - Growth rate: **10 percent (Much faster than average)**
- Education and training:
  - Typical entry-level education: **High school diploma or equivalent**
  - Work experience in a related occupation: **None**
  - Typical on-the-job training: **Short-term on-the-job training**
- O*NET links:
  - 43-5011.00—Cargo and Freight Agents
  - 43-5011.01—Freight Forwarders
- CareerOneStop videos for this occupation:
  - 43-5011.00—Cargo and Freight Agents
  - 43-5011.01—Freight Forwarders

Couriers and messengers

Pick up and deliver messages, documents, packages, and other items between offices or departments within an establishment or directly to other business concerns, traveling by foot, bicycle, motorcycle, automobile, or public conveyance. Excludes "Light Truck Drivers" (53-3033).

- 2022 employment: **217,100**
- May 2022 median annual wage: **$35,280**
- Projected employment change, 2022–32:
  - Number of new jobs: **3,500**
  - Growth rate: **2 percent (As fast as average)**
- Education and training:
  - Typical entry-level education: **High school diploma or equivalent**
  - Work experience in a related occupation: **None**
  - Typical on-the-job training: **Short-term on-the-job training**
- O*NET links:
  - 43-5021.00—Couriers and Messengers
- CareerOneStop videos for this occupation:
  - 43-5021.00—Couriers and Messengers

Dispatchers, except police, fire, and ambulance

Schedule and dispatch workers, work crews, equipment, or service vehicles for conveyance of materials, freight, or passengers, or for normal installation, service, or emergency repairs rendered outside the place of business. Duties may include using radio, telephone, or computer to transmit assignments and compiling statistics and reports on work progress.

- 2022 employment: **214,800**
- May 2022 median annual wage: **$44,830**
- Projected employment change, 2022–32:
  - Number of new jobs: **-2,300**

- Growth rate: **-1 percent (Little or no change)**
- Education and training:
  - Typical entry-level education: **High school diploma or equivalent**
  - Work experience in a related occupation: **None**
  - Typical on-the-job training: **Moderate-term on-the-job training**
- O*NET links:
  - 43-5032.00—Dispatchers, Except Police, Fire, and Ambulance
- CareerOneStop videos for this occupation:
  - 43-5032.00—Dispatchers, Except Police, Fire, and Ambulance

Meter readers, utilities

Read meter and record consumption of electricity, gas, water, or steam.

- 2022 employment: **21,100**
- May 2022 median annual wage: **$44,760**
- Projected employment change, 2022–32:
  - Number of new jobs: **-2,600**
  - Growth rate: **-12 percent (Decline)**
- Education and training:
  - Typical entry-level education: **High school diploma or equivalent**
  - Work experience in a related occupation: **None**
  - Typical on-the-job training: **Short-term on-the-job training**
- O*NET links:
  - 43-5041.00—Meter Readers, Utilities
- CareerOneStop videos for this occupation:
  - 43-5041.00—Meter Readers, Utilities

Data entry keyers

Operate data entry device, such as keyboard or photo composing perforator. Duties may include verifying data and preparing materials for printing. Excludes "Word Processors and Typists" (43-9022).

- 2022 employment: **165,600**
- May 2022 median annual wage: **$36,190**
- Projected employment change, 2022–32:
  - Number of new jobs: **-43,100**
  - Growth rate: **-26 percent (Decline)**
- Education and training:
  - Typical entry-level education: **High school diploma or equivalent**
  - Work experience in a related occupation: **None**
  - Typical on-the-job training: **Short-term on-the-job training**
- O*NET links:
  - 43-9021.00—Data Entry Keyers
- CareerOneStop videos for this occupation:
  - 43-9021.00—Data Entry Keyers

Word processors and typists

Use word processor, computer, or typewriter to type letters, reports, forms, or other material from rough draft, corrected copy, or voice recording. May perform other clerical duties as assigned. Excludes "Court Reporters and Simultaneous Captioners" (27-3092), "Medical Transcriptionists" (31-9094), "Secretaries and Administrative Assistants" (43-6010), and "Data Entry Keyers" (43-9021).

- 2022 employment: **44,000**
- May 2022 median annual wage: **$44,330**
- Projected employment change, 2022–32:
  - Number of new jobs: **-17,000**
  - Growth rate: **-39 percent (Decline)**
- Education and training:
  - Typical entry-level education: **High school diploma or equivalent**
  - Work experience in a related occupation: **None**
  - Typical on-the-job training: **Short-term on-the-job training**
- O*NET links:
  - 43-9022.00—Word Processors and Typists
- CareerOneStop videos for this occupation:
  - 43-9022.00—Word Processors and Typists

Mail clerks and mail machine operators, except postal service

Prepare incoming and outgoing mail for distribution. Time-stamp, open, read, sort, and route incoming mail; and address, seal, stamp, fold, stuff, and affix postage to outgoing mail or packages. Duties may also include keeping necessary records and completed forms.

- 2022 employment: **72,800**
- May 2022 median annual wage: **$35,070**
- Projected employment change, 2022–32:
  - Number of new jobs: **-3,400**
  - Growth rate: **-5 percent (Decline)**
- Education and training:
  - Typical entry-level education: **High school diploma or equivalent**
  - Work experience in a related occupation: **None**
  - Typical on-the-job training: **Short-term on-the-job training**
- O*NET links:
  - 43-9051.00—Mail Clerks and Mail Machine Operators, Except Postal Service
- CareerOneStop videos for this occupation:
  - 43-9051.00—Mail Clerks and Mail Machine Operators, Except Postal Service

Office machine operators, except computer

Operate one or more of a variety of office machines, such as photocopying, photographic, and duplicating machines, or other office machines. Excludes "Billing and Posting Clerks" (43-3021) and "Mail Clerks and Mail Machine Operators, Except Postal Service" (43-9051).

- 2022 employment: **31,600**
- May 2022 median annual wage: **$36,710**
- Projected employment change, 2022–32:
  - Number of new jobs: **-4,500**
  - Growth rate: **-14 percent (Decline)**
- Education and training:
  - Typical entry-level education: **High school diploma or equivalent**
  - Work experience in a related occupation: **None**
  - Typical on-the-job training: **Short-term on-the-job training**
- O*NET links:
  - 43-9071.00—Office Machine Operators, Except Computer
- CareerOneStop videos for this occupation:
  - 43-9071.00—Office Machine Operators, Except Computer

Proofreaders and copy markers

Read transcript or proof type setup to detect and mark for correction any grammatical, typographical, or compositional errors. Excludes workers whose primary duty is editing copy. Includes proofreaders of braille.

- 2022 employment: **7,200**
- May 2022 median annual wage: **$45,410**
- Projected employment change, 2022–32:

  - Number of new jobs: **-300**
  - Growth rate: **-4 percent (Decline)**
- Education and training:
  - Typical entry-level education: **Bachelor's degree**
  - Work experience in a related occupation: **None**
  - Typical on-the-job training: **None**
- O*NET links:
  - 43-9081.00—Proofreaders and Copy Markers
- CareerOneStop videos for this occupation:
  - 43-9081.00—Proofreaders and Copy Markers

Statistical assistants

Compile and compute data according to statistical formulas for use in statistical studies. May perform actuarial computations and compile charts and graphs for use by actuaries. Includes actuarial clerks.

- 2022 employment: **7,400**
- May 2022 median annual wage: **$48,880**
- Projected employment change, 2022–32:
  - Number of new jobs: **-100**
  - Growth rate: **-2 percent (Decline)**
- Education and training:
  - Typical entry-level education: **Bachelor's degree**
  - Work experience in a related occupation: **None**
  - Typical on-the-job training: **None**
- O*NET links:
  - 43-9111.00—Statistical Assistants
- CareerOneStop videos for this occupation:
  - 43-9111.00—Statistical Assistants

Office and administrative support workers, all other

All office and administrative support workers not listed separately.

- 2022 employment: **215,100**
- May 2022 median annual wage: **$38,660**
- Projected employment change, 2022–32:
  - Number of new jobs: **-17,800**
  - Growth rate: **-8 percent (Decline)**
- Education and training:
  - Typical entry-level education: **High school diploma or equivalent**
  - Work experience in a related occupation: **None**
  - Typical on-the-job training: **Short-term on-the-job training**
- O*NET links:
  - 43-9199.00—Office and Administrative Support Workers, All Other

Farming, fishing, and forestry occupations

First-line supervisors of farming, fishing, and forestry workers

Directly supervise and coordinate the activities of agricultural, forestry, aquacultural, and related workers. Excludes "First-Line Supervisors of Landscaping, Lawn Service, and Groundskeeping Workers" (37-1012).

- 2022 employment: **56,600**
- May 2022 median annual wage: **$54,490**
- Projected employment change, 2022–32:
  - Number of new jobs: **1,500**
  - Growth rate: **3 percent (As fast as average)**
- Education and training:
  - Typical entry-level education: **High school diploma or equivalent**
  - Work experience in a related occupation: **Less than 5 years**
  - Typical on-the-job training: **None**
- O*NET links:
  - 45-1011.00—First-Line Supervisors of Farming, Fishing, and Forestry Workers
- CareerOneStop videos for this occupation:
  - 45-1011.00—First-Line Supervisors of Farming, Fishing, and Forestry Workers

Agricultural inspectors

Inspect agricultural commodities, processing equipment, and facilities, and fish and logging operations, to ensure compliance with regulations and laws governing health, quality, and safety.

- 2022 employment: **14,100**
- May 2022 median annual wage: **$44,720**
- Projected employment change, 2022–32:
  - Number of new jobs: **300**
  - Growth rate: **2 percent (As fast as average)**
- Education and training:
  - Typical entry-level education: **Bachelor's degree**
  - Work experience in a related occupation: **None**
  - Typical on-the-job training: **Moderate-term on-the-job training**
- O*NET links:
  - 45-2011.00—Agricultural Inspectors
- CareerOneStop videos for this occupation:
  - 45-2011.00—Agricultural Inspectors

Graders and sorters, agricultural products

Grade, sort, or classify unprocessed food and other agricultural products by size, weight, color, or condition. Excludes "Agricultural Inspectors" (45-2011).

- 2022 employment: **30,100**
- May 2022 median annual wage: **$32,550**
- Projected employment change, 2022–32:
  - Number of new jobs: **-1,500**
  - Growth rate: **-5 percent (Decline)**
- Education and training:
  - Typical entry-level education: **No formal educational credential**
  - Work experience in a related occupation: **None**
  - Typical on-the-job training: **Short-term on-the-job training**
- O*NET links:
  - 45-2041.00—Graders and Sorters, Agricultural Products
- CareerOneStop videos for this occupation:
  - 45-2041.00—Graders and Sorters, Agricultural Products

Construction and extraction occupations

First-line supervisors of construction trades and extraction workers

Directly supervise and coordinate activities of construction or extraction workers.

- 2022 employment: **809,900**
- May 2022 median annual wage: **$74,080**
- Projected employment change, 2022–32:
  - Number of new jobs: **20,400**
  - Growth rate: **3 percent (As fast as average)**
- Education and training:
  - Typical entry-level education: **High school diploma or equivalent**

- ◦ Work experience in a related occupation: **5 years or more**
  - ◦ Typical on-the-job training: **None**
- O*NET links:
  - 47-1011.00—First-Line Supervisors of Construction Trades and Extraction Workers
  - 47-1011.03—Solar Energy Installation Managers
- CareerOneStop videos for this occupation:
  - 47-1011.00—First-Line Supervisors of Construction Trades and Extraction Workers
  - 47-1011.03—Solar Energy Installation Managers

Paperhangers

Cover interior walls or ceilings of rooms with decorative wallpaper or fabric, or attach advertising posters on surfaces such as walls and billboards. May remove old materials or prepare surfaces to be papered.

- 2022 employment: **3,900**
- May 2022 median annual wage: **$44,930**
- Projected employment change, 2022–32:
  - Number of new jobs: **100**
  - Growth rate: **4 percent (As fast as average)**
- Education and training:
  - Typical entry-level education: **No formal educational credential**
  - Work experience in a related occupation: **None**
  - Typical on-the-job training: **Long-term on-the-job training**
- O*NET links:
  - 47-2142.00—Paperhangers

Pipelayers

Lay pipe for storm or sanitation sewers, drains, and water mains. Perform any combination of the following tasks: grade trenches or culverts, position pipe, or seal joints. Excludes "Welders, Cutters, Solderers, and Brazers" (51-4121).

- 2022 employment: **38,000**
- May 2022 median annual wage: **$45,990**
- Projected employment change, 2022–32:
  - Number of new jobs: **-1,700**
  - Growth rate: **-4 percent (Decline)**
- Education and training:
  - Typical entry-level education: **No formal educational credential**
  - Work experience in a related occupation: **None**
  - Typical on-the-job training: **Short-term on-the-job training**
- O*NET links:
  - 47-2151.00—Pipelayers
- CareerOneStop videos for this occupation:
  - 47-2151.00—Pipelayers

Plasterers and stucco masons

Apply interior or exterior plaster, cement, stucco, or similar materials. May also set ornamental plaster.

- 2022 employment: **27,300**
- May 2022 median annual wage: **$49,730**
- Projected employment change, 2022–32:
  - Number of new jobs: **600**
  - Growth rate: **2 percent (As fast as average)**
- Education and training:
  - Typical entry-level education: **No formal educational credential**
  - Work experience in a related occupation: **None**
  - Typical on-the-job training: **Long-term on-the-job training**
- O*NET links:
  - 47-2161.00—Plasterers and Stucco Masons
- CareerOneStop videos for this occupation:
  - 47-2161.00—Plasterers and Stucco Masons

Fence erectors

Erect and repair fences and fence gates, using hand and power tools.

- 2022 employment: **35,200**
- May 2022 median annual wage: **$39,840**
- Projected employment change, 2022–32:
  - Number of new jobs: **-300**
  - Growth rate: **-1 percent (Little or no change)**
- Education and training:
  - Typical entry-level education: **No formal educational credential**
  - Work experience in a related occupation: **None**
  - Typical on-the-job training: **Moderate-term on-the-job training**
- O*NET links:
  - 47-4031.00—Fence Erectors
- CareerOneStop videos for this occupation:
  - 47-4031.00—Fence Erectors

Highway maintenance workers

Maintain highways, municipal and rural roads, airport runways, and rights-of-way. Duties include patching broken or eroded pavement and repairing guard rails, highway markers, and snow fences. May also mow or clear brush from along road, or plow snow from roadway. Excludes "Tree Trimmers and Pruners" (37-3013).

- 2022 employment: **151,200**
- May 2022 median annual wage: **$44,930**
- Projected employment change, 2022–32:
  - Number of new jobs: **12,000**
  - Growth rate: **8 percent (Faster than average)**
- Education and training:
  - Typical entry-level education: **High school diploma or equivalent**
  - Work experience in a related occupation: **None**
  - Typical on-the-job training: **Moderate-term on-the-job training**
- O*NET links:
  - 47-4051.00—Highway Maintenance Workers
- CareerOneStop videos for this occupation:
  - 47-4051.00—Highway Maintenance Workers

Rail-track laying and maintenance equipment operators

Lay, repair, and maintain track for standard or narrow-gauge railroad equipment used in regular railroad service or in plant yards, quarries, sand and gravel pits, and mines. Includes ballast cleaning machine operators and railroad bed tamping machine operators.

- 2022 employment: **16,500**
- May 2022 median annual wage: **$63,230**
- Projected employment change, 2022–32:
  - Number of new jobs: **200**
  - Growth rate: **1 percent (Little or no change)**
- Education and training:
  - Typical entry-level education: **High school diploma or equivalent**
  - Work experience in a related occupation: **None**
  - Typical on-the-job training: **Moderate-term on-the-job training**
- O*NET links:
  - 47-4061.00—Rail-Track Laying and Maintenance Equipment Operators

Septic tank servicers and sewer pipe cleaners

Clean and repair septic tanks, sewer lines, or drains. May patch walls and partitions of tank, replace damaged drain tile, or repair breaks in underground piping.

- 2022 employment: **29,500**
- May 2022 median annual wage: **$45,610**
- Projected employment change, 2022–32:
  - Number of new jobs: **2,200**
  - Growth rate: **7 percent (Faster than average)**
- Education and training:
  - Typical entry-level education: **High school diploma or equivalent**
  - Work experience in a related occupation: **None**
  - Typical on-the-job training: **Moderate-term on-the-job training**
- O*NET links:
  - 47-4071.00—Septic Tank Servicers and Sewer Pipe Cleaners
- CareerOneStop videos for this occupation:
  - 47-4071.00—Septic Tank Servicers and Sewer Pipe Cleaners

Miscellaneous construction and related workers

The definitions for these occupations are available by following their SOC links.

This occupation includes the following SOC 2018 occupations:

- 47-4091—Segmental Pavers
- 47-4099—Construction and Related Workers, All Other
- 2022 employment: **32,300**
- May 2022 median annual wage: **$44,890**
- Projected employment change, 2022–32:
  - Number of new jobs: **600**
  - Growth rate: **2 percent (As fast as average)**
- Education and training:
  - Typical entry-level education: **High school diploma or equivalent**
  - Work experience in a related occupation: **None**
  - Typical on-the-job training: **Moderate-term on-the-job training**
- O*NET links:
  - 47-4091.00—Segmental Pavers
  - 47-4099.00—Construction and Related Workers, All Other
  - 47-4099.03—Weatherization Installers and Technicians
- CareerOneStop videos for this occupation:
  - 47-4091.00—Segmental Pavers
  - 47-4099.03—Weatherization Installers and Technicians

Derrick operators, oil and gas

Rig derrick equipment and operate pumps to circulate mud or fluid through drill hole.

- 2022 employment: **11,900**
- May 2022 median annual wage: **$51,220**
- Projected employment change, 2022–32:
  - Number of new jobs: **100**
  - Growth rate: **1 percent (Little or no change)**
- Education and training:
  - Typical entry-level education: **No formal educational credential**
  - Work experience in a related occupation: **None**
  - Typical on-the-job training: **Short-term on-the-job training**
- O*NET links:
  - 47-5011.00—Derrick Operators, Oil and Gas
- CareerOneStop videos for this occupation:
  - 47-5011.00—Derrick Operators, Oil and Gas

Rotary drill operators, oil and gas

Set up or operate a variety of drills to remove underground oil and gas, or remove core samples for testing during oil and gas exploration. Excludes "Earth Drillers, Except Oil and Gas" (47-5023).

- 2022 employment: **13,200**
- May 2022 median annual wage: **$55,260**
- Projected employment change, 2022–32:
  - Number of new jobs: **0**
  - Growth rate: **0 percent (Little or no change)**
- Education and training:
  - Typical entry-level education: **No formal educational credential**
  - Work experience in a related occupation: **None**
  - Typical on-the-job training: **Moderate-term on-the-job training**
- O*NET links:
  - 47-5012.00—Rotary Drill Operators, Oil and Gas
- CareerOneStop videos for this occupation:
  - 47-5012.00—Rotary Drill Operators, Oil and Gas

Service unit operators, oil and gas

Operate equipment to increase oil flow from producing wells or to remove stuck pipe, casing, tools, or other obstructions from drilling wells. Includes fishing-tool technicians.

- 2022 employment: **39,500**
- May 2022 median annual wage: **$50,140**
- Projected employment change, 2022–32:
  - Number of new jobs: **100**
  - Growth rate: **0 percent (Little or no change)**
- Education and training:
  - Typical entry-level education: **No formal educational credential**
  - Work experience in a related occupation: **None**
  - Typical on-the-job training: **Moderate-term on-the-job training**
- O*NET links:
  - 47-5013.00—Service Unit Operators, Oil and Gas
- CareerOneStop videos for this occupation:
  - 47-5013.00—Service Unit Operators, Oil and Gas

Excavating and loading machine and dragline operators, surface mining

Operate or tend machinery at surface mining site, equipped with scoops, shovels, or buckets to excavate and load loose materials.

- 2022 employment: **36,400**
- May 2022 median annual wage: **$48,350**
- Projected employment change, 2022–32:
  - Number of new jobs: **-1,400**
  - Growth rate: **-4 percent (Decline)**
- Education and training:
  - Typical entry-level education: **High school diploma or equivalent**
  - Work experience in a related occupation: **Less than 5 years**
  - Typical on-the-job training: **Moderate-term on-the-job training**
- O*NET links:
  - 47-5022.00—Excavating and Loading Machine and Dragline Operators, Surface Mining
- CareerOneStop videos for this occupation:
  - 47-5022.00—Excavating and Loading Machine and Dragline Operators, Surface Mining

Earth drillers, except oil and gas

Operate a variety of drills such as rotary, churn, and pneumatic to tap subsurface water and salt deposits, to remove core samples during mineral exploration or soil testing, and to facilitate the use of explosives in mining or construction. Includes horizontal and earth boring machine operators.

- 2022 employment: **20,400**
- May 2022 median annual wage: **$51,740**
- Projected employment change, 2022–32:
  - Number of new jobs: **400**
  - Growth rate: **2 percent (As fast as average)**
- Education and training:
  - Typical entry-level education: **High school diploma or equivalent**
  - Work experience in a related occupation: **Less than 5 years**
  - Typical on-the-job training: **Long-term on-the-job training**
- O*NET links:
  - 47-5023.00—Earth Drillers, Except Oil and Gas
- CareerOneStop videos for this occupation:
  - 47-5023.00—Earth Drillers, Except Oil and Gas

Explosives workers, ordnance handling experts, and blasters

Place and detonate explosives to demolish structures or to loosen, remove, or displace earth, rock, or other materials. May perform specialized handling, storage, and accounting procedures.

- 2022 employment: **4,900**
- May 2022 median annual wage: **$56,670**
- Projected employment change, 2022–32:
  - Number of new jobs: **100**
  - Growth rate: **1 percent (Little or no change)**
- Education and training:
  - Typical entry-level education: **High school diploma or equivalent**
  - Work experience in a related occupation: **Less than 5 years**
  - Typical on-the-job training: **Long-term on-the-job training**
- O*NET links:
  - 47-5032.00—Explosives Workers, Ordnance Handling Experts, and Blasters
- CareerOneStop videos for this occupation:
  - 47-5032.00—Explosives Workers, Ordnance Handling Experts, and Blasters

Continuous mining machine operators

Operate self-propelled mining machines that rip coal, metal and nonmetal ores, rock, stone, or sand from the mine face and load it onto conveyors, shuttle cars, or trucks in a continuous operation.

- 2022 employment: **13,900**
- May 2022 median annual wage: **$57,360**
- Projected employment change, 2022–32:
  - Number of new jobs: **-400**
  - Growth rate: **-3 percent (Decline)**
- Education and training:
  - Typical entry-level education: **No formal educational credential**
  - Work experience in a related occupation: **None**
  - Typical on-the-job training: **Moderate-term on-the-job training**
- O*NET links:
  - 47-5041.00—Continuous Mining Machine Operators
- CareerOneStop videos for this occupation:
  - 47-5041.00—Continuous Mining Machine Operators

Roof bolters, mining

Operate machinery to install roof support bolts in underground mine.

- 2022 employment: **1,800**
- May 2022 median annual wage: **$60,210**
- Projected employment change, 2022–32:
  - Number of new jobs: **-500**
  - Growth rate: **-29 percent (Decline)**
- Education and training:
  - Typical entry-level education: **High school diploma or equivalent**
  - Work experience in a related occupation: **None**
  - Typical on-the-job training: **Moderate-term on-the-job training**
- O*NET links:
  - 47-5043.00—Roof Bolters, Mining
- CareerOneStop videos for this occupation:
  - 47-5043.00—Roof Bolters, Mining

Loading and moving machine operators, underground mining

Operate underground loading or moving machine to load or move core, ore, or rock using shuttle or mine car or conveyors. Equipment may include power shovels, hoisting engines equipped with cable-drawn scraper or scoop, or machines equipped with gathering arms and conveyor.

- 2022 employment: **5,400**
- May 2022 median annual wage: **$63,920**
- Projected employment change, 2022–32:
  - Number of new jobs: **-1,000**
  - Growth rate: **-18 percent (Decline)**
- Education and training:
  - Typical entry-level education: **No formal educational credential**
  - Work experience in a related occupation: **None**
  - Typical on-the-job training: **Short-term on-the-job training**
- O*NET links:
  - 47-5044.00—Loading and Moving Machine Operators, Underground Mining
- CareerOneStop videos for this occupation:
  - 47-5044.00—Loading and Moving Machine Operators, Underground Mining

Underground mining machine operators, all other

All underground mining machine operators not listed separately.

- 2022 employment: **2,300**
- May 2022 median annual wage: **$64,180**
- Projected employment change, 2022–32:
  - Number of new jobs: **-300**
  - Growth rate: **-12 percent (Decline)**
- Education and training:
  - Typical entry-level education: **No formal educational credential**
  - Work experience in a related occupation: **None**
  - Typical on-the-job training: **Moderate-term on-the-job training**
- O*NET links:
  - 47-5049.00—Underground Mining Machine Operators, All Other

Rock splitters, quarry

Separate blocks of rough dimension stone from quarry mass using jackhammers, wedges, or chop saws.

- 2022 employment: **4,100**
- May 2022 median annual wage: **$46,010**
- Projected employment change, 2022–32:
  - Number of new jobs: **100**
  - Growth rate: **2 percent (As fast as average)**
- Education and training:
  - Typical entry-level education: **No formal educational credential**
  - Work experience in a related occupation: **None**
  - Typical on-the-job training: **Short-term on-the-job training**
- O*NET links:
  - 47-5051.00—Rock Splitters, Quarry

Roustabouts, oil and gas

Assemble or repair oil field equipment using hand and power tools. Perform other tasks as needed.

- 2022 employment: **42,100**
- May 2022 median annual wage: **$43,590**
- Projected employment change, 2022–32:
  - Number of new jobs: **1,200**
  - Growth rate: **3 percent (As fast as average)**
- Education and training:
  - Typical entry-level education: **No formal educational credential**
  - Work experience in a related occupation: **None**
  - Typical on-the-job training: **Moderate-term on-the-job training**
- O*NET links:
  - 47-5071.00—Roustabouts, Oil and Gas
- CareerOneStop videos for this occupation:
  - 47-5071.00—Roustabouts, Oil and Gas

Helpers--extraction workers

Help extraction craft workers, such as earth drillers, blasters and explosives workers, derrick operators, and mining machine operators, by performing duties requiring less skill. Duties include supplying equipment or cleaning work area. Apprentice workers are classified with the appropriate skilled construction trade occupation (47-2011 through 47-2231).

- 2022 employment: **7,200**
- May 2022 median annual wage: **$43,110**
- Projected employment change, 2022–32:
  - Number of new jobs: **100**
  - Growth rate: **1 percent (Little or no change)**
- Education and training:
  - Typical entry-level education: **High school diploma or equivalent**
  - Work experience in a related occupation: **None**
  - Typical on-the-job training: **Moderate-term on-the-job training**
- O*NET links:
  - 47-5081.00—Helpers--Extraction Workers
- CareerOneStop videos for this occupation:
  - 47-5081.00—Helpers--Extraction Workers

Extraction workers, all other

All extraction workers not listed separately.

- 2022 employment: **6,600**
- May 2022 median annual wage: **$51,600**
- Projected employment change, 2022–32:
  - Number of new jobs: **-100**
  - Growth rate: **-2 percent (Decline)**
- Education and training:
  - Typical entry-level education: **High school diploma or equivalent**
  - Work experience in a related occupation: **None**
  - Typical on-the-job training: **Moderate-term on-the-job training**
- O*NET links:
  - 47-5099.00—Extraction Workers, All Other

Installation, maintenance, and repair occupations

First-line supervisors of mechanics, installers, and repairers

Directly supervise and coordinate the activities of mechanics, installers, and repairers. May also advise customers on recommended services. Excludes team or work leaders.

- 2022 employment: **576,200**
- May 2022 median annual wage: **$73,140**
- Projected employment change, 2022–32:
  - Number of new jobs: **14,000**
  - Growth rate: **2 percent (As fast as average)**
- Education and training:
  - Typical entry-level education: **High school diploma or equivalent**
  - Work experience in a related occupation: **Less than 5 years**
  - Typical on-the-job training: **None**
- O*NET links:
  - 49-1011.00—First-Line Supervisors of Mechanics, Installers, and Repairers
- CareerOneStop videos for this occupation:
  - 49-1011.00—First-Line Supervisors of Mechanics, Installers, and Repairers

Computer, automated teller, and office machine repairers

Repair, maintain, or install computers, word processing systems, automated teller machines, and electronic office machines, such as duplicating and fax machines.

- 2022 employment: **96,400**
- May 2022 median annual wage: **$44,910**
- Projected employment change, 2022–32:
  - Number of new jobs: **-10,400**
  - Growth rate: **-11 percent (Decline)**
- Education and training:
  - Typical entry-level education: **Some college, no degree**
  - Work experience in a related occupation: **None**
  - Typical on-the-job training: **Short-term on-the-job training**
- O*NET links:
  - 49-2011.00—Computer, Automated Teller, and Office Machine Repairers
- CareerOneStop videos for this occupation:
  - 49-2011.00—Computer, Automated Teller, and Office Machine Repairers

Audiovisual equipment installers and repairers

Install, repair, or adjust audio or television receivers, stereo systems, camcorders, video systems, or other electronic entertainment equipment in homes or other venues. May perform routine maintenance. Excludes "Audio and Video Technicians" (27-4011).

- 2022 employment: **26,900**
- May 2022 median annual wage: **$44,960**

- Projected employment change, 2022–32:
  - Number of new jobs: **-1,800**
  - Growth rate: **-7 percent (Decline)**
- Education and training:
  - Typical entry-level education: **Postsecondary nondegree award**
  - Work experience in a related occupation: **None**
  - Typical on-the-job training: **Short-term on-the-job training**
- O*NET links:
  - 49-2097.00—Audiovisual Equipment Installers and Repairers
- CareerOneStop videos for this occupation:
  - 49-2097.00—Audiovisual Equipment Installers and Repairers

Security and fire alarm systems installers

Install, program, maintain, and repair security and fire alarm wiring and equipment. Ensure that work is in accordance with relevant codes. Excludes "Electricians" (47-2111) who do a broad range of electrical wiring.

- 2022 employment: **83,000**
- May 2022 median annual wage: **$50,130**
- Projected employment change, 2022–32:
  - Number of new jobs: **2,300**
  - Growth rate: **3 percent (As fast as average)**
- Education and training:
  - Typical entry-level education: **High school diploma or equivalent**
  - Work experience in a related occupation: **None**
  - Typical on-the-job training: **Moderate-term on-the-job training**
- O*NET links:
  - 49-2098.00—Security and Fire Alarm Systems Installers
- CareerOneStop videos for this occupation:
  - 49-2098.00—Security and Fire Alarm Systems Installers

Bicycle repairers

Repair and service bicycles.

- 2022 employment: **14,400**
- May 2022 median annual wage: **$36,250**
- Projected employment change, 2022–32:
  - Number of new jobs: **500**
  - Growth rate: **4 percent (As fast as average)**
- Education and training:
  - Typical entry-level education: **High school diploma or equivalent**
  - Work experience in a related occupation: **None**
  - Typical on-the-job training: **Moderate-term on-the-job training**
- O*NET links:
  - 49-3091.00—Bicycle Repairers
- CareerOneStop videos for this occupation:
  - 49-3091.00—Bicycle Repairers

Recreational vehicle service technicians

Diagnose, inspect, adjust, repair, or overhaul recreational vehicles including travel trailers. May specialize in maintaining gas, electrical, hydraulic, plumbing, or chassis/towing systems as well as repairing generators, appliances, and interior components. Includes workers who perform customized van conversions. Excludes "Automotive Service Technicians and Mechanics" (49-3023) and "Bus and Truck Mechanics and Diesel Engine Specialists" (49-3031) who also work on recreation vehicles.

- 2022 employment: **17,700**
- May 2022 median annual wage: **$45,030**
- Projected employment change, 2022–32:
  - Number of new jobs: **1,700**
  - Growth rate: **10 percent (Much faster than average)**
- Education and training:
  - Typical entry-level education: **High school diploma or equivalent**
  - Work experience in a related occupation: **None**
  - Typical on-the-job training: **Long-term on-the-job training**
- O*NET links:
  - 49-3092.00—Recreational Vehicle Service Technicians
- CareerOneStop videos for this occupation:
  - 49-3092.00—Recreational Vehicle Service Technicians

Tire repairers and changers

Repair and replace tires.

- 2022 employment: **103,800**
- May 2022 median annual wage: **$34,240**
- Projected employment change, 2022–32:
  - Number of new jobs: **1,200**
  - Growth rate: **1 percent (Little or no change)**
- Education and training:
  - Typical entry-level education: **High school diploma or equivalent**
  - Work experience in a related occupation: **None**
  - Typical on-the-job training: **Short-term on-the-job training**
- O*NET links:
  - 49-3093.00—Tire Repairers and Changers
- CareerOneStop videos for this occupation:
  - 49-3093.00—Tire Repairers and Changers

Mechanical door repairers

Install, service, or repair automatic door mechanisms and hydraulic doors. Includes garage door mechanics.

- 2022 employment: **28,000**
- May 2022 median annual wage: **$47,010**
- Projected employment change, 2022–32:
  - Number of new jobs: **2,700**
  - Growth rate: **10 percent (Much faster than average)**
- Education and training:
  - Typical entry-level education: **High school diploma or equivalent**
  - Work experience in a related occupation: **None**
  - Typical on-the-job training: **Moderate-term on-the-job training**
- O*NET links:
  - 49-9011.00—Mechanical Door Repairers
- CareerOneStop videos for this occupation:
  - 49-9011.00—Mechanical Door Repairers

Control and valve installers and repairers, except mechanical door

Install, repair, and maintain mechanical regulating and controlling devices, such as electric meters, gas regulators, thermostats, safety and flow valves, and other mechanical governors.

- 2022 employment: **47,900**
- May 2022 median annual wage: **$64,810**
- Projected employment change, 2022–32:
  - Number of new jobs: **-300**
  - Growth rate: **-1 percent (Little or no change)**
- Education and training:
  - Typical entry-level education: **High school diploma or equivalent**

  - Work experience in a related occupation: **None**
  - Typical on-the-job training: **Moderate-term on-the-job training**
- O*NET links:
  - 49-9012.00—Control and Valve Installers and Repairers, Except Mechanical Door
- CareerOneStop videos for this occupation:
  - 49-9012.00—Control and Valve Installers and Repairers, Except Mechanical Door

Home appliance repairers

Repair, adjust, or install all types of electric or gas household appliances, such as refrigerators, washers, dryers, and ovens.

- 2022 employment: **36,600**
- May 2022 median annual wage: **$46,000**
- Projected employment change, 2022–32:
  - Number of new jobs: **-1,600**
  - Growth rate: **-4 percent (Decline)**
- Education and training:
  - Typical entry-level education: **High school diploma or equivalent**
  - Work experience in a related occupation: **None**
  - Typical on-the-job training: **Moderate-term on-the-job training**
- O*NET links:
  - 49-9031.00—Home Appliance Repairers
- CareerOneStop videos for this occupation:
  - 49-9031.00—Home Appliance Repairers

Refractory materials repairers, except brickmasons

Build or repair equipment such as furnaces, kilns, cupolas, boilers, converters, ladles, soaking pits, and ovens, using refractory materials.

- 2022 employment: **600**
- May 2022 median annual wage: **$50,550**
- Projected employment change, 2022–32:
  - Number of new jobs: **-100**
  - Growth rate: **-21 percent (Decline)**
- Education and training:
  - Typical entry-level education: **High school diploma or equivalent**
  - Work experience in a related occupation: **None**
  - Typical on-the-job training: **Moderate-term on-the-job training**
- O*NET links:
  - 49-9045.00—Refractory Materials Repairers, Except Brickmasons
- CareerOneStop videos for this occupation:
  - 49-9045.00—Refractory Materials Repairers, Except Brickmasons

Camera and photographic equipment repairers

Repair and adjust cameras and photographic equipment, including commercial video and motion picture camera equipment.

- 2022 employment: **2,400**
- May 2022 median annual wage: **$44,060**
- Projected employment change, 2022–32:
  - Number of new jobs: **0**
  - Growth rate: **1 percent (Little or no change)**
- Education and training:
  - Typical entry-level education: **High school diploma or equivalent**
  - Work experience in a related occupation: **None**
  - Typical on-the-job training: **Long-term on-the-job training**
- O*NET links:
  - 49-9061.00—Camera and Photographic Equipment Repairers

Musical instrument repairers and tuners

Repair percussion, stringed, reed, or wind instruments. May specialize in one area, such as piano tuning. Excludes "Audiovisual Equipment Installers and Repairers" (49-2097) who repair electrical and electronic musical instruments.

- 2022 employment: **7,000**
- May 2022 median annual wage: **$38,150**
- Projected employment change, 2022–32:
  - Number of new jobs: **-700**
  - Growth rate: **-9 percent (Decline)**
- Education and training:
  - Typical entry-level education: **High school diploma or equivalent**
  - Work experience in a related occupation: **None**
  - Typical on-the-job training: **Apprenticeship**
- O*NET links:
  - 49-9063.00—Musical Instrument Repairers and Tuners
- CareerOneStop videos for this occupation:
  - 49-9063.00—Musical Instrument Repairers and Tuners

Watch and clock repairers

Repair, clean, and adjust mechanisms of timing instruments, such as watches and clocks. Includes watchmakers, watch technicians, and mechanical timepiece repairers. Excludes "Timing Device Assemblers and Adjusters" (51-2061).

- 2022 employment: **2,100**
- May 2022 median annual wage: **$48,370**
- Projected employment change, 2022–32:
  - Number of new jobs: **-600**
  - Growth rate: **-30 percent (Decline)**
- Education and training:
  - Typical entry-level education: **High school diploma or equivalent**
  - Work experience in a related occupation: **None**
  - Typical on-the-job training: **Long-term on-the-job training**
- O*NET links:
  - 49-9064.00—Watch and Clock Repairers
- CareerOneStop videos for this occupation:
  - 49-9064.00—Watch and Clock Repairers

Precision instrument and equipment repairers, all other

All precision instrument and equipment repairers not listed separately.

- 2022 employment: **12,100**
- May 2022 median annual wage: **$61,690**
- Projected employment change, 2022–32:
  - Number of new jobs: **0**
  - Growth rate: **0 percent (Little or no change)**
- Education and training:
  - Typical entry-level education: **High school diploma or equivalent**
  - Work experience in a related occupation: **None**
  - Typical on-the-job training: **Long-term on-the-job training**
- O*NET links:
  - 49-9069.00—Precision Instrument and Equipment Repairers, All Other

Coin, vending, and amusement machine servicers and repairers

Install, service, adjust, or repair coin, vending, or amusement machines including video games, juke boxes, pinball machines, or slot machines.

- 2022 employment: **39,200**
- May 2022 median annual wage: **$39,690**
- Projected employment change, 2022–32:
  - Number of new jobs: **-700**
  - Growth rate: **-2 percent (Decline)**
- Education and training:
  - Typical entry-level education: **High school diploma or equivalent**
  - Work experience in a related occupation: **None**
  - Typical on-the-job training: **Short-term on-the-job training**
- O*NET links:
  - 49-9091.00—Coin, Vending, and Amusement Machine Servicers and Repairers

Commercial divers

Work below surface of water, using surface-supplied air or scuba equipment to inspect, repair, remove, or install equipment and structures. May use a variety of power and hand tools, such as drills, sledgehammers, torches, and welding equipment. May conduct tests or experiments, rig explosives, or photograph structures or marine life. Excludes "Athletes and Sports Competitors" (27-2021), "Police and Sheriff's Patrol Officers" (33-3051), and "Fishing and Hunting Workers" (45-3031).

- 2022 employment: **4,400**
- May 2022 median annual wage: **$68,300**
- Projected employment change, 2022–32:
  - Number of new jobs: **300**
  - Growth rate: **6 percent (Faster than average)**
- Education and training:
  - Typical entry-level education: **Postsecondary nondegree award**
  - Work experience in a related occupation: **None**
  - Typical on-the-job training: **Moderate-term on-the-job training**
- O*NET links:
  - 49-9092.00—Commercial Divers
- CareerOneStop videos for this occupation:
  - 49-9092.00—Commercial Divers

Locksmiths and safe repairers

Repair and open locks, make keys, change locks and safe combinations, and install and repair safes.

- 2022 employment: **18,200**
- May 2022 median annual wage: **$47,400**
- Projected employment change, 2022–32:
  - Number of new jobs: **-2,000**
  - Growth rate: **-11 percent (Decline)**
- Education and training:
  - Typical entry-level education: **High school diploma or equivalent**
  - Work experience in a related occupation: **None**
  - Typical on-the-job training: **Long-term on-the-job training**
- O*NET links:
  - 49-9094.00—Locksmiths and Safe Repairers
- CareerOneStop videos for this occupation:
  - 49-9094.00—Locksmiths and Safe Repairers

Manufactured building and mobile home installers

Move or install mobile homes or prefabricated buildings.

- 2022 employment: **4,100**
- May 2022 median annual wage: **$36,820**
- Projected employment change, 2022–32:
  - Number of new jobs: **-900**
  - Growth rate: **-21 percent (Decline)**
- Education and training:
  - Typical entry-level education: **High school diploma or equivalent**
  - Work experience in a related occupation: **None**
  - Typical on-the-job training: **Short-term on-the-job training**
- O*NET links:
  - 49-9095.00—Manufactured Building and Mobile Home Installers

Riggers

Set up or repair rigging for construction projects, manufacturing plants, logging yards, ships and shipyards, or for the entertainment industry.

- 2022 employment: **19,700**
- May 2022 median annual wage: **$54,680**
- Projected employment change, 2022–32:
  - Number of new jobs: **300**
  - Growth rate: **1 percent (Little or no change)**
- Education and training:
  - Typical entry-level education: **High school diploma or equivalent**
  - Work experience in a related occupation: **None**
  - Typical on-the-job training: **Moderate-term on-the-job training**
- O*NET links:
  - 49-9096.00—Riggers
- CareerOneStop videos for this occupation:
  - 49-9096.00—Riggers

Signal and track switch repairers

Install, inspect, test, maintain, or repair electric gate crossings, signals, signal equipment, track switches, section lines, or intercommunications systems within a railroad system.

- 2022 employment: **6,600**
- May 2022 median annual wage: **$81,300**
- Projected employment change, 2022–32:
  - Number of new jobs: **100**
  - Growth rate: **1 percent (Little or no change)**
- Education and training:
  - Typical entry-level education: **High school diploma or equivalent**
  - Work experience in a related occupation: **None**
  - Typical on-the-job training: **Moderate-term on-the-job training**
- O*NET links:
  - 49-9097.00—Signal and Track Switch Repairers

Helpers--installation, maintenance, and repair workers

Help installation, maintenance, and repair workers in maintenance, parts replacement, and repair of vehicles, industrial machinery, and electrical and electronic equipment. Perform duties such as furnishing tools, materials, and supplies to other workers; cleaning work area, machines, and tools; and holding materials or tools for other workers.

- 2022 employment: **96,500**
- May 2022 median annual wage: **$35,100**
- Projected employment change, 2022–32:
  - Number of new jobs: **2,400**
  - Growth rate: **2 percent (As fast as average)**
- Education and training:
  - Typical entry-level education: **High school diploma or equivalent**
  - Work experience in a related occupation: **None**
  - Typical on-the-job training: **Short-term on-the-job training**

- O*NET links:
  - 49-9098.00—Helpers--Installation, Maintenance, and Repair Workers
- CareerOneStop videos for this occupation:
  - 49-9098.00—Helpers--Installation, Maintenance, and Repair Workers

Installation, maintenance, and repair workers, all other

All installation, maintenance, and repair workers not listed separately.

- 2022 employment: **195,400**
- May 2022 median annual wage: **$44,500**
- Projected employment change, 2022–32:
  - Number of new jobs: **2,900**
  - Growth rate: **2 percent (As fast as average)**
- Education and training:
  - Typical entry-level education: **High school diploma or equivalent**
  - Work experience in a related occupation: **None**
  - Typical on-the-job training: **Moderate-term on-the-job training**
- O*NET links:
  - 49-9099.00—Installation, Maintenance, and Repair Workers, All Other
  - 49-9099.01—Geothermal Technicians
- CareerOneStop videos for this occupation:
  - 49-9099.01—Geothermal Technicians

Production occupations

First-line supervisors of production and operating workers

Directly supervise and coordinate the activities of production and operating workers, such as inspectors, precision workers, machine setters and operators, assemblers, fabricators, and plant and system operators. Excludes team or work leaders.

- 2022 employment: **681,700**
- May 2022 median annual wage: **$63,510**
- Projected employment change, 2022–32:
  - Number of new jobs: **1,900**
  - Growth rate: **0 percent (Little or no change)**
- Education and training:
  - Typical entry-level education: **High school diploma or equivalent**
  - Work experience in a related occupation: **Less than 5 years**
  - Typical on-the-job training: **None**
- O*NET links:
  - 51-1011.00—First-Line Supervisors of Production and Operating Workers
- CareerOneStop videos for this occupation:
  - 51-1011.00—First-Line Supervisors of Production and Operating Workers

Meat, poultry, and fish cutters and trimmers

Use hands or hand tools to perform routine cutting and trimming of meat, poultry, and seafood.

- 2022 employment: **141,000**
- May 2022 median annual wage: **$35,070**
- Projected employment change, 2022–32:
  - Number of new jobs: **2,800**
  - Growth rate: **2 percent (As fast as average)**
- Education and training:
  - Typical entry-level education: **No formal educational credential**
  - Work experience in a related occupation: **None**
  - Typical on-the-job training: **Short-term on-the-job training**
- O*NET links:
  - 51-3022.00—Meat, Poultry, and Fish Cutters and Trimmers
- CareerOneStop videos for this occupation:
  - 51-3022.00—Meat, Poultry, and Fish Cutters and Trimmers

Slaughterers and meat packers

Perform nonroutine or precision functions involving the preparation of large portions of meat. Work may include specialized slaughtering tasks, cutting standard or premium cuts of meat for marketing, making sausage, or wrapping meats. Work typically occurs in slaughtering, meat packing, or wholesale establishments. Excludes "Meat, Poultry, and Fish Cutters and Trimmers" (51-3022) who perform routine meat cutting.

- 2022 employment: **81,100**
- May 2022 median annual wage: **$35,240**
- Projected employment change, 2022–32:
  - Number of new jobs: **-800**
  - Growth rate: **-1 percent (Little or no change)**
- Education and training:
  - Typical entry-level education: **No formal educational credential**
  - Work experience in a related occupation: **None**
  - Typical on-the-job training: **Short-term on-the-job training**
- O*NET links:
  - 51-3023.00—Slaughterers and Meat Packers
- CareerOneStop videos for this occupation:
  - 51-3023.00—Slaughterers and Meat Packers

Layout workers, metal and plastic

Lay out reference points and dimensions on metal or plastic stock or workpieces, such as sheets, plates, tubes, structural shapes, castings, or machine parts, for further processing. Includes shipfitters.

- 2022 employment: **7,100**
- May 2022 median annual wage: **$58,260**
- Projected employment change, 2022–32:
  - Number of new jobs: **-700**
  - Growth rate: **-10 percent (Decline)**
- Education and training:
  - Typical entry-level education: **High school diploma or equivalent**
  - Work experience in a related occupation: **None**
  - Typical on-the-job training: **Moderate-term on-the-job training**
- O*NET links:
  - 51-4192.00—Layout Workers, Metal and Plastic
- CareerOneStop videos for this occupation:
  - 51-4192.00—Layout Workers, Metal and Plastic

Tool grinders, filers, and sharpeners

Perform precision smoothing, sharpening, polishing, or grinding of metal objects.

- 2022 employment: **5,500**
- May 2022 median annual wage: **$41,940**
- Projected employment change, 2022–32:
  - Number of new jobs: **-500**
  - Growth rate: **-8 percent (Decline)**
- Education and training:
  - Typical entry-level education: **High school diploma or equivalent**
  - Work experience in a related occupation: **None**
  - Typical on-the-job training: **Moderate-term on-the-job training**

- O*NET links:
  - 51-4194.00—Tool Grinders, Filers, and Sharpeners

Metal workers and plastic workers, all other

All metal workers and plastic workers not listed separately.

- 2022 employment: **21,400**
- May 2022 median annual wage: **$38,340**
- Projected employment change, 2022–32:
  - Number of new jobs: **-1,700**
  - Growth rate: **-8 percent (Decline)**
- Education and training:
  - Typical entry-level education: **High school diploma or equivalent**
  - Work experience in a related occupation: **None**
  - Typical on-the-job training: **Moderate-term on-the-job training**
- O*NET links:
  - 51-4199.00—Metal Workers and Plastic Workers, All Other

Prepress technicians and workers

Format and proof text and images submitted by designers and clients into finished pages that can be printed. Includes digital and photo typesetting. May produce printing plates.

- 2022 employment: **25,700**
- May 2022 median annual wage: **$43,560**
- Projected employment change, 2022–32:
  - Number of new jobs: **-4,400**
  - Growth rate: **-17 percent (Decline)**
- Education and training:
  - Typical entry-level education: **Postsecondary nondegree award**
  - Work experience in a related occupation: **None**
  - Typical on-the-job training: **None**
- O*NET links:
  - 51-5111.00—Prepress Technicians and Workers
- CareerOneStop videos for this occupation:
  - 51-5111.00—Prepress Technicians and Workers

Printing press operators

Set up and operate digital, letterpress, lithographic, flexographic, gravure, or other printing machines. Includes short-run offset printing presses.

- 2022 employment: **155,500**
- May 2022 median annual wage: **$39,350**
- Projected employment change, 2022–32:
  - Number of new jobs: **-13,200**
  - Growth rate: **-8 percent (Decline)**
- Education and training:
  - Typical entry-level education: **High school diploma or equivalent**
  - Work experience in a related occupation: **None**
  - Typical on-the-job training: **Moderate-term on-the-job training**
- O*NET links:
  - 51-5112.00—Printing Press Operators
- CareerOneStop videos for this occupation:
  - 51-5112.00—Printing Press Operators

Print binding and finishing workers

Bind books and other publications or finish printed products by hand or machine. May set up binding and finishing machines.

- 2022 employment: **41,400**
- May 2022 median annual wage: **$36,970**
- Projected employment change, 2022–32:
  - Number of new jobs: **-6,800**
  - Growth rate: **-16 percent (Decline)**
- Education and training:
  - Typical entry-level education: **High school diploma or equivalent**
  - Work experience in a related occupation: **None**
  - Typical on-the-job training: **Moderate-term on-the-job training**
- O*NET links:
  - 51-5113.00—Print Binding and Finishing Workers
- CareerOneStop videos for this occupation:
  - 51-5113.00—Print Binding and Finishing Workers

Laundry and dry-cleaning workers

Operate or tend washing or dry-cleaning machines to wash or dry-clean industrial or household articles, such as cloth garments, suede, leather, furs, blankets, draperies, linens, rugs, and carpets. Includes spotters and dyers of these articles.

- 2022 employment: **184,400**
- May 2022 median annual wage: **$29,060**
- Projected employment change, 2022–32:
  - Number of new jobs: **-2,300**
  - Growth rate: **-1 percent (Little or no change)**
- Education and training:
  - Typical entry-level education: **No formal educational credential**
  - Work experience in a related occupation: **None**
  - Typical on-the-job training: **Short-term on-the-job training**
- O*NET links:
  - 51-6011.00—Laundry and Dry-Cleaning Workers
- CareerOneStop videos for this occupation:
  - 51-6011.00—Laundry and Dry-Cleaning Workers

Pressers, textile, garment, and related materials

Press or shape articles by hand or machine.

- 2022 employment: **29,800**
- May 2022 median annual wage: **$29,690**
- Projected employment change, 2022–32:
  - Number of new jobs: **-6,500**
  - Growth rate: **-22 percent (Decline)**
- Education and training:
  - Typical entry-level education: **No formal educational credential**
  - Work experience in a related occupation: **None**
  - Typical on-the-job training: **Short-term on-the-job training**
- O*NET links:
  - 51-6021.00—Pressers, Textile, Garment, and Related Materials
- CareerOneStop videos for this occupation:
  - 51-6021.00—Pressers, Textile, Garment, and Related Materials

Sewing machine operators

Operate or tend sewing machines to join, reinforce, decorate, or perform related sewing operations in the manufacture of garment or nongarment products.

- 2022 employment: **141,900**
- May 2022 median annual wage: **$31,740**
- Projected employment change, 2022–32:
  - Number of new jobs: **-21,600**
  - Growth rate: **-15 percent (Decline)**
- Education and training:
  - Typical entry-level education: **No formal educational credential**

  - Work experience in a related occupation: **None**
  - Typical on-the-job training: **Short-term on-the-job training**
- O*NET links:
  - 51-6031.00—Sewing Machine Operators
- CareerOneStop videos for this occupation:
  - 51-6031.00—Sewing Machine Operators

Shoe and leather workers and repairers

Construct, decorate, or repair leather and leather-like products, such as luggage, shoes, and saddles. May use hand tools.

- 2022 employment: **9,800**
- May 2022 median annual wage: **$32,460**
- Projected employment change, 2022–32:
  - Number of new jobs: **-1,100**
  - Growth rate: **-11 percent (Decline)**
- Education and training:
  - Typical entry-level education: **High school diploma or equivalent**
  - Work experience in a related occupation: **None**
  - Typical on-the-job training: **Moderate-term on-the-job training**
- O*NET links:
  - 51-6041.00—Shoe and Leather Workers and Repairers
- CareerOneStop videos for this occupation:
  - 51-6041.00—Shoe and Leather Workers and Repairers

Shoe machine operators and tenders

Operate or tend a variety of machines to join, decorate, reinforce, or finish shoes and shoe parts.

- 2022 employment: **3,300**
- May 2022 median annual wage: **$33,060**
- Projected employment change, 2022–32:
  - Number of new jobs: **-400**
  - Growth rate: **-11 percent (Decline)**
- Education and training:
  - Typical entry-level education: **High school diploma or equivalent**
  - Work experience in a related occupation: **None**
  - Typical on-the-job training: **Short-term on-the-job training**
- O*NET links:
  - 51-6042.00—Shoe Machine Operators and Tenders
- CareerOneStop videos for this occupation:
  - 51-6042.00—Shoe Machine Operators and Tenders

Sewers, hand

Sew, join, reinforce, or finish, usually with needle and thread, a variety of manufactured items. Includes weavers and stitchers.

- 2022 employment: **6,900**
- May 2022 median annual wage: **$31,530**
- Projected employment change, 2022–32:
  - Number of new jobs: **-1,100**
  - Growth rate: **-16 percent (Decline)**
- Education and training:
  - Typical entry-level education: **No formal educational credential**
  - Work experience in a related occupation: **None**
  - Typical on-the-job training: **Moderate-term on-the-job training**
- O*NET links:
  - 51-6051.00—Sewers, Hand
- CareerOneStop videos for this occupation:
  - 51-6051.00—Sewers, Hand

Tailors, dressmakers, and custom sewers

Design, make, alter, repair, or fit garments.

- 2022 employment: **33,900**
- May 2022 median annual wage: **$34,280**
- Projected employment change, 2022–32:
  - Number of new jobs: **-4,600**
  - Growth rate: **-14 percent (Decline)**
- Education and training:
  - Typical entry-level education: **No formal educational credential**
  - Work experience in a related occupation: **None**
  - Typical on-the-job training: **Moderate-term on-the-job training**
- O*NET links:
  - 51-6052.00—Tailors, Dressmakers, and Custom Sewers
- CareerOneStop videos for this occupation:
  - 51-6052.00—Tailors, Dressmakers, and Custom Sewers

Textile bleaching and dyeing machine operators and tenders

Operate or tend machines to bleach, shrink, wash, dye, or finish textiles or synthetic or glass fibers.

- 2022 employment: **7,000**
- May 2022 median annual wage: **$32,680**
- Projected employment change, 2022–32:
  - Number of new jobs: **-700**
  - Growth rate: **-10 percent (Decline)**
- Education and training:
  - Typical entry-level education: **High school diploma or equivalent**
  - Work experience in a related occupation: **None**
  - Typical on-the-job training: **Short-term on-the-job training**
- O*NET links:
  - 51-6061.00—Textile Bleaching and Dyeing Machine Operators and Tenders
- CareerOneStop videos for this occupation:
  - 51-6061.00—Textile Bleaching and Dyeing Machine Operators and Tenders

Textile cutting machine setters, operators, and tenders

Set up, operate, or tend machines that cut textiles.

- 2022 employment: **11,100**
- May 2022 median annual wage: **$34,420**
- Projected employment change, 2022–32:
  - Number of new jobs: **-1,200**
  - Growth rate: **-11 percent (Decline)**
- Education and training:
  - Typical entry-level education: **High school diploma or equivalent**
  - Work experience in a related occupation: **None**
  - Typical on-the-job training: **Moderate-term on-the-job training**
- O*NET links:
  - 51-6062.00—Textile Cutting Machine Setters, Operators, and Tenders
- CareerOneStop videos for this occupation:
  - 51-6062.00—Textile Cutting Machine Setters, Operators, and Tenders

Textile knitting and weaving machine setters, operators, and tenders

Set up, operate, or tend machines that knit, loop, weave, or draw in textiles. Excludes "Sewing Machine Operators" (51-6031).

- 2022 employment: **17,800**
- May 2022 median annual wage: **$35,750**
- Projected employment change, 2022–32:
  - Number of new jobs: **-1,900**
  - Growth rate: **-11 percent (Decline)**
- Education and training:
  - Typical entry-level education: **High school diploma or equivalent**
  - Work experience in a related occupation: **None**
  - Typical on-the-job training: **Short-term on-the-job training**
- O*NET links:
  - 51-6063.00—Textile Knitting and Weaving Machine Setters, Operators, and Tenders
- CareerOneStop videos for this occupation:
  - 51-6063.00—Textile Knitting and Weaving Machine Setters, Operators, and Tenders

Textile winding, twisting, and drawing out machine setters, operators, and tenders

Set up, operate, or tend machines that wind or twist textiles; or draw out and combine sliver, such as wool, hemp, or synthetic fibers. Includes slubber machine and drawing frame operators.

- 2022 employment: **25,000**
- May 2022 median annual wage: **$33,720**
- Projected employment change, 2022–32:
  - Number of new jobs: **-2,200**
  - Growth rate: **-9 percent (Decline)**
- Education and training:
  - Typical entry-level education: **High school diploma or equivalent**
  - Work experience in a related occupation: **None**
  - Typical on-the-job training: **Moderate-term on-the-job training**
- O*NET links:
  - 51-6064.00—Textile Winding, Twisting, and Drawing Out Machine Setters, Operators, and Tenders
- CareerOneStop videos for this occupation:
  - 51-6064.00—Textile Winding, Twisting, and Drawing Out Machine Setters, Operators, and Tenders

Extruding and forming machine setters, operators, and tenders, synthetic and glass fibers

Set up, operate, or tend machines that extrude and form continuous filaments from synthetic materials, such as liquid polymer, rayon, and fiberglass.

- 2022 employment: **16,300**
- May 2022 median annual wage: **$39,860**
- Projected employment change, 2022–32:
  - Number of new jobs: **-400**
  - Growth rate: **-2 percent (Decline)**
- Education and training:
  - Typical entry-level education: **High school diploma or equivalent**
  - Work experience in a related occupation: **None**
  - Typical on-the-job training: **Moderate-term on-the-job training**
- O*NET links:
  - 51-6091.00—Extruding and Forming Machine Setters, Operators, and Tenders, Synthetic and Glass Fibers
- CareerOneStop videos for this occupation:
  - 51-6091.00—Extruding and Forming Machine Setters, Operators, and Tenders, Synthetic and Glass Fibers

Fabric and apparel patternmakers

Draw and construct sets of precision master fabric patterns or layouts. May also mark and cut fabrics and apparel.

- 2022 employment: **3,400**
- May 2022 median annual wage: **$60,320**
- Projected employment change, 2022–32:
  - Number of new jobs: **-200**
  - Growth rate: **-7 percent (Decline)**
- Education and training:
  - Typical entry-level education: **High school diploma or equivalent**
  - Work experience in a related occupation: **None**
  - Typical on-the-job training: **Moderate-term on-the-job training**
- O*NET links:
  - 51-6092.00—Fabric and Apparel Patternmakers
- CareerOneStop videos for this occupation:
  - 51-6092.00—Fabric and Apparel Patternmakers

Upholsterers

Make, repair, or replace upholstery for household furniture or transportation vehicles.

- 2022 employment: **31,500**
- May 2022 median annual wage: **$39,600**
- Projected employment change, 2022–32:
  - Number of new jobs: **-800**
  - Growth rate: **-3 percent (Decline)**
- Education and training:
  - Typical entry-level education: **High school diploma or equivalent**
  - Work experience in a related occupation: **None**
  - Typical on-the-job training: **Moderate-term on-the-job training**
- O*NET links:
  - 51-6093.00—Upholsterers
- CareerOneStop videos for this occupation:
  - 51-6093.00—Upholsterers

Textile, apparel, and furnishings workers, all other

All textile, apparel, and furnishings workers not listed separately.

- 2022 employment: **14,300**
- May 2022 median annual wage: **$32,640**
- Projected employment change, 2022–32:
  - Number of new jobs: **-1,100**
  - Growth rate: **-8 percent (Decline)**
- Education and training:
  - Typical entry-level education: **High school diploma or equivalent**
  - Work experience in a related occupation: **None**
  - Typical on-the-job training: **Short-term on-the-job training**
- O*NET links:
  - 51-6099.00—Textile, Apparel, and Furnishings Workers, All Other

Model makers, wood

Construct full-size and scale wooden precision models of products. Includes wood jig builders and loft workers.

- 2022 employment: **1,100**
- May 2022 median annual wage: **$46,940**
- Projected employment change, 2022–32:
  - Number of new jobs: **0**
  - Growth rate: **-4 percent (Decline)**

- Education and training:
  - Typical entry-level education: **High school diploma or equivalent**
  - Work experience in a related occupation: **None**
  - Typical on-the-job training: **Moderate-term on-the-job training**
- O*NET links:
  - 51-7031.00—Model Makers, Wood

Patternmakers, wood

Plan, lay out, and construct wooden unit or sectional patterns used in forming sand molds for castings.

- 2022 employment: **500**
- May 2022 median annual wage: **$44,290**
- Projected employment change, 2022–32:
  - Number of new jobs: **0**
  - Growth rate: **-5 percent (Decline)**
- Education and training:
  - Typical entry-level education: **High school diploma or equivalent**
  - Work experience in a related occupation: **None**
  - Typical on-the-job training: **Moderate-term on-the-job training**
- O*NET links:
  - 51-7032.00—Patternmakers, Wood

Woodworkers, all other

All woodworkers not listed separately.

- 2022 employment: **13,500**
- May 2022 median annual wage: **$35,370**
- Projected employment change, 2022–32:
  - Number of new jobs: **-500**
  - Growth rate: **-4 percent (Decline)**
- Education and training:
  - Typical entry-level education: **High school diploma or equivalent**
  - Work experience in a related occupation: **None**
  - Typical on-the-job training: **Moderate-term on-the-job training**
- O*NET links:
  - 51-7099.00—Woodworkers, All Other

Chemical plant and system operators

Control or operate entire chemical processes or system of machines.

- 2022 employment: **19,300**
- May 2022 median annual wage: **$82,670**
- Projected employment change, 2022–32:
  - Number of new jobs: **-600**
  - Growth rate: **-3 percent (Decline)**
- Education and training:
  - Typical entry-level education: **High school diploma or equivalent**
  - Work experience in a related occupation: **None**
  - Typical on-the-job training: **Moderate-term on-the-job training**
- O*NET links:
  - 51-8091.00—Chemical Plant and System Operators

Gas plant operators

Distribute or process gas for utility companies and others by controlling compressors to maintain specified pressures on main pipelines.

- 2022 employment: **14,800**
- May 2022 median annual wage: **$79,460**
- Projected employment change, 2022–32:
  - Number of new jobs: **-1,700**
  - Growth rate: **-12 percent (Decline)**
- Education and training:
  - Typical entry-level education: **High school diploma or equivalent**
  - Work experience in a related occupation: **None**
  - Typical on-the-job training: **Long-term on-the-job training**
- O*NET links:
  - 51-8092.00—Gas Plant Operators
- CareerOneStop videos for this occupation:
  - 51-8092.00—Gas Plant Operators

Petroleum pump system operators, refinery operators, and gaugers

Operate or control petroleum refining or processing units. May specialize in controlling manifold and pumping systems, gauging or testing oil in storage tanks, or regulating the flow of oil into pipelines.

- 2022 employment: **32,200**
- May 2022 median annual wage: **$85,090**
- Projected employment change, 2022–32:
  - Number of new jobs: **-700**
  - Growth rate: **-2 percent (Decline)**
- Education and training:
  - Typical entry-level education: **High school diploma or equivalent**
  - Work experience in a related occupation: **None**
  - Typical on-the-job training: **Moderate-term on-the-job training**
- O*NET links:
  - 51-8093.00—Petroleum Pump System Operators, Refinery Operators, and Gaugers
- CareerOneStop videos for this occupation:
  - 51-8093.00—Petroleum Pump System Operators, Refinery Operators, and Gaugers

Plant and system operators, all other

All plant and system operators not listed separately.

- 2022 employment: **15,900**
- May 2022 median annual wage: **$57,470**
- Projected employment change, 2022–32:
  - Number of new jobs: **0**
  - Growth rate: **0 percent (Little or no change)**
- Education and training:
  - Typical entry-level education: **High school diploma or equivalent**
  - Work experience in a related occupation: **None**
  - Typical on-the-job training: **Moderate-term on-the-job training**
- O*NET links:
  - 51-8099.00—Plant and System Operators, All Other
  - 51-8099.01—Biofuels Processing Technicians
- CareerOneStop videos for this occupation:
  - 51-8099.01—Biofuels Processing Technicians

Chemical equipment operators and tenders

Operate or tend equipment to control chemical changes or reactions in the processing of industrial or consumer products. Equipment used includes devulcanizers, steam-jacketed kettles, and reactor vessels. Excludes "Chemical Plant and System Operators" (51-8091).

- 2022 employment: **120,200**

- May 2022 median annual wage: **$49,330**
- Projected employment change, 2022–32:
  - Number of new jobs: **-6,600**
  - Growth rate: **-5 percent (Decline)**
- Education and training:
  - Typical entry-level education: **High school diploma or equivalent**
  - Work experience in a related occupation: **None**
  - Typical on-the-job training: **Moderate-term on-the-job training**
- O*NET links:
  - 51-9011.00—Chemical Equipment Operators and Tenders
- CareerOneStop videos for this occupation:
  - 51-9011.00—Chemical Equipment Operators and Tenders

Separating, filtering, clarifying, precipitating, and still machine setters, operators, and tenders

Set up, operate, or tend continuous flow or vat-type equipment; filter presses; shaker screens; centrifuges; condenser tubes; precipitating, fermenting, or evaporating tanks; scrubbing towers; or batch stills. These machines extract, sort, or separate liquids, gases, or solids from other materials to recover a refined product. Includes dairy processing equipment operators. Excludes "Chemical Equipment Operators and Tenders" (51-9011).

- 2022 employment: **55,600**
- May 2022 median annual wage: **$46,250**
- Projected employment change, 2022–32:
  - Number of new jobs: **1,900**
  - Growth rate: **3 percent (As fast as average)**
- Education and training:
  - Typical entry-level education: **High school diploma or equivalent**
  - Work experience in a related occupation: **None**
  - Typical on-the-job training: **Moderate-term on-the-job training**
- O*NET links:
  - 51-9012.00—Separating, Filtering, Clarifying, Precipitating, and Still Machine Setters, Operators, and Tenders
- CareerOneStop videos for this occupation:
  - 51-9012.00—Separating, Filtering, Clarifying, Precipitating, and Still Machine Setters, Operators, and Tenders

Crushing, grinding, and polishing machine setters, operators, and tenders

Set up, operate, or tend machines to crush, grind, or polish materials, such as coal, glass, grain, stone, food, or rubber.

- 2022 employment: **28,800**
- May 2022 median annual wage: **$43,290**
- Projected employment change, 2022–32:
  - Number of new jobs: **-1,000**
  - Growth rate: **-3 percent (Decline)**
- Education and training:
  - Typical entry-level education: **High school diploma or equivalent**
  - Work experience in a related occupation: **None**
  - Typical on-the-job training: **Moderate-term on-the-job training**
- O*NET links:
  - 51-9021.00—Crushing, Grinding, and Polishing Machine Setters, Operators, and Tenders
- CareerOneStop videos for this occupation:
  - 51-9021.00—Crushing, Grinding, and Polishing Machine Setters, Operators, and Tenders

Grinding and polishing workers, hand

Grind, sand, or polish, using hand tools or hand-held power tools, a variety of metal, wood, stone, clay, plastic, or glass objects. Includes chippers, buffers, and finishers.

- 2022 employment: **14,500**
- May 2022 median annual wage: **$36,960**
- Projected employment change, 2022–32:
  - Number of new jobs: **-2,800**
  - Growth rate: **-20 percent (Decline)**
- Education and training:
  - Typical entry-level education: **No formal educational credential**
  - Work experience in a related occupation: **None**
  - Typical on-the-job training: **Moderate-term on-the-job training**
- O*NET links:
  - 51-9022.00—Grinding and Polishing Workers, Hand

Mixing and blending machine setters, operators, and tenders

Set up, operate, or tend machines to mix or blend materials, such as chemicals, tobacco, liquids, color pigments, or explosive ingredients. Excludes "Food Batchmakers" (51-3092).

- 2022 employment: **114,000**
- May 2022 median annual wage: **$43,410**
- Projected employment change, 2022–32:
  - Number of new jobs: **1,700**
  - Growth rate: **2 percent (As fast as average)**
- Education and training:
  - Typical entry-level education: **High school diploma or equivalent**
  - Work experience in a related occupation: **None**
  - Typical on-the-job training: **Moderate-term on-the-job training**
- O*NET links:
  - 51-9023.00—Mixing and Blending Machine Setters, Operators, and Tenders
- CareerOneStop videos for this occupation:
  - 51-9023.00—Mixing and Blending Machine Setters, Operators, and Tenders

Cutters and trimmers, hand

Use hand tools or hand-held power tools to cut and trim a variety of manufactured items, such as carpet, fabric, stone, glass, or rubber.

- 2022 employment: **8,300**
- May 2022 median annual wage: **$36,130**
- Projected employment change, 2022–32:
  - Number of new jobs: **-2,300**
  - Growth rate: **-28 percent (Decline)**
- Education and training:
  - Typical entry-level education: **No formal educational credential**
  - Work experience in a related occupation: **None**
  - Typical on-the-job training: **Short-term on-the-job training**
- O*NET links:
  - 51-9031.00—Cutters and Trimmers, Hand

Cutting and slicing machine setters, operators, and tenders

Set up, operate, or tend machines that cut or slice materials, such as glass, stone, cork, rubber, tobacco, food, paper, or insulating material. Excludes "Cutting, Punching, and Press Machine Setters, Operators, and Tenders, Metal and Plastic" (51-4031), "Textile Cutting Machine

Setters, Operators, and Tenders" (51-6062), and "Woodworking Machine Setters, Operators, and Tenders" (51-7040).

- 2022 employment: **55,800**
- May 2022 median annual wage: **$39,880**
- Projected employment change, 2022–32:
  - Number of new jobs: **-2,300**
  - Growth rate: **-4 percent (Decline)**
- Education and training:
  - Typical entry-level education: **High school diploma or equivalent**
  - Work experience in a related occupation: **None**
  - Typical on-the-job training: **Moderate-term on-the-job training**
- O*NET links:
  - 51-9032.00—Cutting and Slicing Machine Setters, Operators, and Tenders
- CareerOneStop videos for this occupation:
  - 51-9032.00—Cutting and Slicing Machine Setters, Operators, and Tenders

Extruding, forming, pressing, and compacting machine setters, operators, and tenders

Set up, operate, or tend machines, such as glass-forming machines, plodder machines, and tuber machines, to shape and form products such as glassware, food, rubber, soap, brick, tile, clay, wax, tobacco, or cosmetics. Excludes "Shoe Machine Operators and Tenders" (51-6042) and "Paper Goods Machine Setters, Operators, and Tenders" (51-9196).

- 2022 employment: **60,000**
- May 2022 median annual wage: **$39,480**
- Projected employment change, 2022–32:
  - Number of new jobs: **-800**
  - Growth rate: **-1 percent (Little or no change)**
- Education and training:
  - Typical entry-level education: **High school diploma or equivalent**
  - Work experience in a related occupation: **None**
  - Typical on-the-job training: **Moderate-term on-the-job training**
- O*NET links:
  - 51-9041.00—Extruding, Forming, Pressing, and Compacting Machine Setters, Operators, and Tenders
- CareerOneStop videos for this occupation:
  - 51-9041.00—Extruding, Forming, Pressing, and Compacting Machine Setters, Operators, and Tenders

Furnace, kiln, oven, drier, and kettle operators and tenders

Operate or tend heating equipment other than basic metal, plastic, or food processing equipment. Includes activities such as annealing glass, drying lumber, curing rubber, removing moisture from materials, or boiling soap.

- 2022 employment: **16,200**
- May 2022 median annual wage: **$44,530**
- Projected employment change, 2022–32:
  - Number of new jobs: **100**
  - Growth rate: **0 percent (Little or no change)**
- Education and training:
  - Typical entry-level education: **High school diploma or equivalent**
  - Work experience in a related occupation: **None**
  - Typical on-the-job training: **Moderate-term on-the-job training**
- O*NET links:
  - 51-9051.00—Furnace, Kiln, Oven, Drier, and Kettle Operators and Tenders

Packaging and filling machine operators and tenders

Operate or tend machines to prepare industrial or consumer products for storage or shipment. Includes cannery workers who pack food products.

- 2022 employment: **373,200**
- May 2022 median annual wage: **$36,750**
- Projected employment change, 2022–32:
  - Number of new jobs: **17,300**
  - Growth rate: **5 percent (Faster than average)**
- Education and training:
  - Typical entry-level education: **High school diploma or equivalent**
  - Work experience in a related occupation: **None**
  - Typical on-the-job training: **Moderate-term on-the-job training**
- O*NET links:
  - 51-9111.00—Packaging and Filling Machine Operators and Tenders
- CareerOneStop videos for this occupation:
  - 51-9111.00—Packaging and Filling Machine Operators and Tenders

Semiconductor processing technicians

Perform any or all of the following functions in the manufacture of electronic semiconductors: load semiconductor material into furnace; saw formed ingots into segments; load individual segment into crystal growing chamber and monitor controls; locate crystal axis in ingot using x-ray equipment and saw ingots into wafers; and clean, polish, and load wafers into series of special purpose furnaces, chemical baths, and equipment used to form circuitry and change conductive properties.

- 2022 employment: **24,600**
- May 2022 median annual wage: **$44,690**
- Projected employment change, 2022–32:
  - Number of new jobs: **2,000**
  - Growth rate: **8 percent (Faster than average)**
- Education and training:
  - Typical entry-level education: **High school diploma or equivalent**
  - Work experience in a related occupation: **None**
  - Typical on-the-job training: **Moderate-term on-the-job training**
- O*NET links:
  - 51-9141.00—Semiconductor Processing Technicians
- CareerOneStop videos for this occupation:
  - 51-9141.00—Semiconductor Processing Technicians

Photographic process workers and processing machine operators

Perform work involved in developing and processing photographic images from film or digital media. May perform precision tasks such as editing photographic negatives and prints.

- 2022 employment: **6,400**
- May 2022 median annual wage: **$36,280**
- Projected employment change, 2022–32:
  - Number of new jobs: **-800**
  - Growth rate: **-13 percent (Decline)**
- Education and training:

- Typical entry-level education: **High school diploma or equivalent**
- Work experience in a related occupation: **None**
- Typical on-the-job training: **Short-term on-the-job training**

- O*NET links:
  - 51-9151.00—Photographic Process Workers and Processing Machine Operators

Adhesive bonding machine operators and tenders

Operate or tend bonding machines that use adhesives to join items for further processing or to form a completed product. Processes include joining veneer sheets into plywood; gluing paper; or joining rubber and rubberized fabric parts, plastic, simulated leather, or other materials. Excludes "Shoe Machine Operators and Tenders" (51-6042).

- 2022 employment: **11,400**
- May 2022 median annual wage: **$38,780**
- Projected employment change, 2022–32:
  - Number of new jobs: **-300**
  - Growth rate: **-2 percent (Decline)**
- Education and training:
  - Typical entry-level education: **High school diploma or equivalent**
  - Work experience in a related occupation: **None**
  - Typical on-the-job training: **Moderate-term on-the-job training**
- O*NET links:
  - 51-9191.00—Adhesive Bonding Machine Operators and Tenders
- CareerOneStop videos for this occupation:
  - 51-9191.00—Adhesive Bonding Machine Operators and Tenders

Cleaning, washing, and metal pickling equipment operators and tenders

Operate or tend machines to wash or clean products, such as barrels or kegs, glass items, tin plate, food, pulp, coal, plastic, or rubber, to remove impurities.

- 2022 employment: **14,000**
- May 2022 median annual wage: **$37,190**
- Projected employment change, 2022–32:
  - Number of new jobs: **500**
  - Growth rate: **4 percent (As fast as average)**
- Education and training:
  - Typical entry-level education: **High school diploma or equivalent**
  - Work experience in a related occupation: **None**
  - Typical on-the-job training: **Moderate-term on-the-job training**
- O*NET links:
  - 51-9192.00—Cleaning, Washing, and Metal Pickling Equipment Operators and Tenders

Cooling and freezing equipment operators and tenders

Operate or tend equipment such as cooling and freezing units, refrigerators, batch freezers, and freezing tunnels, to cool or freeze products, food, blood plasma, and chemicals.

- 2022 employment: **7,100**
- May 2022 median annual wage: **$42,890**
- Projected employment change, 2022–32:
  - Number of new jobs: **400**
  - Growth rate: **5 percent (Faster than average)**
- Education and training:
  - Typical entry-level education: **High school diploma or equivalent**
  - Work experience in a related occupation: **None**
  - Typical on-the-job training: **Moderate-term on-the-job training**
- O*NET links:
  - 51-9193.00—Cooling and Freezing Equipment Operators and Tenders
- CareerOneStop videos for this occupation:
  - 51-9193.00—Cooling and Freezing Equipment Operators and Tenders

Etchers and engravers

Engrave or etch metal, wood, rubber, or other materials. Includes such workers as etcher-circuit processors, pantograph engravers, and silk screen etchers. Photoengravers are included in "Prepress Technicians and Workers" (51-5111).

- 2022 employment: **8,500**
- May 2022 median annual wage: **$37,980**
- Projected employment change, 2022–32:
  - Number of new jobs: **0**
  - Growth rate: **0 percent (Little or no change)**
- Education and training:
  - Typical entry-level education: **High school diploma or equivalent**
  - Work experience in a related occupation: **None**
  - Typical on-the-job training: **Moderate-term on-the-job training**
- O*NET links:
  - 51-9194.00—Etchers and Engravers
- CareerOneStop videos for this occupation:
  - 51-9194.00—Etchers and Engravers

Molders, shapers, and casters, except metal and plastic

Mold, shape, form, cast, or carve products such as food products, figurines, tile, pipes, and candles consisting of clay, glass, plaster, concrete, stone, or combinations of materials.

- 2022 employment: **44,700**
- May 2022 median annual wage: **$39,590**
- Projected employment change, 2022–32:
  - Number of new jobs: **1,100**
  - Growth rate: **2 percent (As fast as average)**
- Education and training:
  - Typical entry-level education: **High school diploma or equivalent**
  - Work experience in a related occupation: **None**
  - Typical on-the-job training: **Long-term on-the-job training**
- O*NET links:
  - 51-9195.00—Molders, Shapers, and Casters, Except Metal and Plastic
  - 51-9195.03—Stone Cutters and Carvers, Manufacturing
  - 51-9195.04—Glass Blowers, Molders, Benders, and Finishers
  - 51-9195.05—Potters, Manufacturing
- CareerOneStop videos for this occupation:
  - 51-9195.00—Molders, Shapers, and Casters, Except Metal and Plastic
  - 51-9195.03—Stone Cutters and Carvers, Manufacturing
  - 51-9195.04—Glass Blowers, Molders, Benders, and Finishers
  - 51-9195.05—Potters, Manufacturing

Paper goods machine setters, operators, and tenders

Set up, operate, or tend paper goods machines that perform a variety of functions, such as converting, sawing, corrugating, banding, wrapping, boxing, stitching, forming, or sealing paper or paperboard sheets into products.

- 2022 employment: **92,700**
- May 2022 median annual wage: **$45,710**
- Projected employment change, 2022–32:
  - Number of new jobs: **-10,200**
  - Growth rate: **-11 percent (Decline)**
- Education and training:
  - Typical entry-level education: **High school diploma or equivalent**
  - Work experience in a related occupation: **None**
  - Typical on-the-job training: **Moderate-term on-the-job training**
- O*NET links:
  - 51-9196.00—Paper Goods Machine Setters, Operators, and Tenders
- CareerOneStop videos for this occupation:
  - 51-9196.00—Paper Goods Machine Setters, Operators, and Tenders

Tire builders

Operate machines to build tires.

- 2022 employment: **18,900**
- May 2022 median annual wage: **$51,650**
- Projected employment change, 2022–32:
  - Number of new jobs: **-800**
  - Growth rate: **-4 percent (Decline)**
- Education and training:
  - Typical entry-level education: **High school diploma or equivalent**
  - Work experience in a related occupation: **None**
  - Typical on-the-job training: **Moderate-term on-the-job training**
- O*NET links:
  - 51-9197.00—Tire Builders

Helpers--production workers

Help production workers by performing duties requiring less skill. Duties include supplying or holding materials or tools, and cleaning work area and equipment. Apprentice workers are classified in the appropriate production occupations (51-0000).

- 2022 employment: **193,000**
- May 2022 median annual wage: **$34,670**
- Projected employment change, 2022–32:
  - Number of new jobs: **-17,900**
  - Growth rate: **-9 percent (Decline)**
- Education and training:
  - Typical entry-level education: **High school diploma or equivalent**
  - Work experience in a related occupation: **None**
  - Typical on-the-job training: **Short-term on-the-job training**
- O*NET links:
  - 51-9198.00—Helpers--Production Workers
- CareerOneStop videos for this occupation:
  - 51-9198.00—Helpers--Production Workers

Production workers, all other

All production workers not listed separately. Excludes "Packers and Packagers, Hand" (53-7064).

- 2022 employment: **275,300**
- May 2022 median annual wage: **$35,490**
- Projected employment change, 2022–32:
  - Number of new jobs: **3,900**
  - Growth rate: **1 percent (Little or no change)**
- Education and training:
  - Typical entry-level education: **High school diploma or equivalent**
  - Work experience in a related occupation: **None**
  - Typical on-the-job training: **Moderate-term on-the-job training**
- O*NET links:
  - 51-9199.00—Production Workers, All Other

Transportation and material moving occupations

Aircraft cargo handling supervisors

Supervise and coordinate the activities of ground crew in the loading, unloading, securing, and staging of aircraft cargo or baggage. May determine the quantity and orientation of cargo and compute aircraft center of gravity. May accompany aircraft as member of flight crew and monitor and handle cargo in flight, and assist and brief passengers on safety and emergency procedures. Includes loadmasters.

- 2022 employment: **8,000**
- May 2022 median annual wage: **$53,490**
- Projected employment change, 2022–32:
  - Number of new jobs: **700**
  - Growth rate: **9 percent (Much faster than average)**
- Education and training:
  - Typical entry-level education: **High school diploma or equivalent**
  - Work experience in a related occupation: **Less than 5 years**
  - Typical on-the-job training: **None**
- O*NET links:
  - 53-1041.00—Aircraft Cargo Handling Supervisors

First-line supervisors of transportation and material moving workers, except aircraft cargo handling supervisors

The definitions for these occupations are available by following their SOC links.

This occupation includes the following SOC 2018 occupations:

- 53-1042—First-Line Supervisors of Helpers, Laborers, and Material Movers, Hand
- 53-1043—First-Line Supervisors of Material-Moving Machine and Vehicle Operators
- 53-1044—First-Line Supervisors of Passenger Attendants
- 53-1049—First-Line Supervisors of Transportation Workers, All Other
- 2022 employment: **601,100**
- May 2022 median annual wage: **$57,860**
- Projected employment change, 2022–32:
  - Number of new jobs: **28,100**
  - Growth rate: **5 percent (Faster than average)**
- Education and training:
  - Typical entry-level education: **High school diploma or equivalent**
  - Work experience in a related occupation: **Less than 5 years**
  - Typical on-the-job training: **None**
- O*NET links:
  - 53-1042.00—First-Line Supervisors of Helpers, Laborers, and Material Movers, Hand
  - 53-1042.01—Recycling Coordinators
  - 53-1043.00—First-Line Supervisors of Material-Moving Machine and Vehicle Operators

  - 53-1044.00—First-Line Supervisors of Passenger Attendants
  - 53-1049.00—First-Line Supervisors of Transportation Workers, All Other
- CareerOneStop videos for this occupation:
  - 53-1042.00—First-Line Supervisors of Helpers, Laborers, and Material Movers, Hand
  - 53-1042.01—Recycling Coordinators
  - 53-1043.00—First-Line Supervisors of Material-Moving Machine and Vehicle Operators

Airfield operations specialists

Ensure the safe takeoff and landing of commercial and military aircraft. Duties include coordination between air-traffic control and maintenance personnel, dispatching, using airfield landing and navigational aids, implementing airfield safety procedures, monitoring and maintaining flight records, and applying knowledge of weather information.

- 2022 employment: **15,000**
- May 2022 median annual wage: **$49,600**
- Projected employment change, 2022–32:
  - Number of new jobs: **700**
  - Growth rate: **5 percent (Faster than average)**
- Education and training:
  - Typical entry-level education: **High school diploma or equivalent**
  - Work experience in a related occupation: **None**
  - Typical on-the-job training: **Long-term on-the-job training**
- O*NET links:
  - 53-2022.00—Airfield Operations Specialists

Ambulance drivers and attendants, except emergency medical technicians

Drive ambulance or assist ambulance driver in transporting sick, injured, or convalescent persons. Assist in lifting patients.

- 2022 employment: **10,100**
- May 2022 median annual wage: **$30,380**
- Projected employment change, 2022–32:
  - Number of new jobs: **0**
  - Growth rate: **0 percent (Little or no change)**
- Education and training:
  - Typical entry-level education: **High school diploma or equivalent**
  - Work experience in a related occupation: **None**
  - Typical on-the-job training: **Moderate-term on-the-job training**
- O*NET links:
  - 53-3011.00—Ambulance Drivers and Attendants, Except Emergency Medical Technicians
- CareerOneStop videos for this occupation:
  - 53-3011.00—Ambulance Drivers and Attendants, Except Emergency Medical Technicians

Motor vehicle operators, all other

All motor vehicle operators not listed separately.

- 2022 employment: **68,300**
- May 2022 median annual wage: **$33,210**
- Projected employment change, 2022–32:
  - Number of new jobs: **5,400**
  - Growth rate: **8 percent (Faster than average)**
- Education and training:
  - Typical entry-level education: **No formal educational credential**
  - Work experience in a related occupation: **None**
  - Typical on-the-job training: **Short-term on-the-job training**
- O*NET links:
  - 53-3099.00—Motor Vehicle Operators, All Other

Subway and streetcar operators

Operate subway or elevated suburban trains with no separate locomotive, or electric-powered streetcar, to transport passengers. May handle fares.

- 2022 employment: **9,500**
- May 2022 median annual wage: **$88,260**
- Projected employment change, 2022–32:
  - Number of new jobs: **300**
  - Growth rate: **4 percent (As fast as average)**
- Education and training:
  - Typical entry-level education: **High school diploma or equivalent**
  - Work experience in a related occupation: **None**
  - Typical on-the-job training: **Moderate-term on-the-job training**
- O*NET links:
  - 53-4041.00—Subway and Streetcar Operators

Rail transportation workers, all other

All rail transportation workers not listed separately.

- 2022 employment: **2,400**
- May 2022 median annual wage: **$42,280**
- Projected employment change, 2022–32:
  - Number of new jobs: **100**
  - Growth rate: **2 percent (As fast as average)**
- Education and training:
  - Typical entry-level education: **High school diploma or equivalent**
  - Work experience in a related occupation: **None**
  - Typical on-the-job training: **Moderate-term on-the-job training**
- O*NET links:
  - 53-4099.00—Rail Transportation Workers, All Other

Bridge and lock tenders

Operate and tend bridges, canal locks, and lighthouses to permit marine passage on inland waterways, near shores, and at danger points in waterway passages. May supervise such operations. Includes drawbridge operators, lock operators, and slip bridge operators.

- 2022 employment: **3,800**
- May 2022 median annual wage: **$47,280**
- Projected employment change, 2022–32:
  - Number of new jobs: **0**
  - Growth rate: **-1 percent (Little or no change)**
- Education and training:
  - Typical entry-level education: **High school diploma or equivalent**
  - Work experience in a related occupation: **None**
  - Typical on-the-job training: **Short-term on-the-job training**
- O*NET links:
  - 53-6011.00—Bridge and Lock Tenders

Parking attendants

Park vehicles or issue tickets for customers in a parking lot or garage. May park or tend vehicles in environments such as a car dealership or rental car facility. May collect fee.

- 2022 employment: **108,400**
- May 2022 median annual wage: **$30,570**

- Projected employment change, 2022–32:
  - Number of new jobs: **1,600**
  - Growth rate: **1 percent (Little or no change)**
- Education and training:
  - Typical entry-level education: **No formal educational credential**
  - Work experience in a related occupation: **None**
  - Typical on-the-job training: **Short-term on-the-job training**
- O*NET links:
  - 53-6021.00—Parking Attendants
- CareerOneStop videos for this occupation:
  - 53-6021.00—Parking Attendants

Automotive and watercraft service attendants

Service automobiles, buses, trucks, boats, and other automotive or marine vehicles with fuel, lubricants, and accessories. Collect payment for services and supplies. May lubricate vehicle, change motor oil, refill antifreeze, or replace lights or other accessories, such as windshield wiper blades or fan belts. May repair or replace tires. Excludes "Cashiers" (41-2011).

- 2022 employment: **100,700**
- May 2022 median annual wage: **$30,850**
- Projected employment change, 2022–32:
  - Number of new jobs: **200**
  - Growth rate: **0 percent (Little or no change)**
- Education and training:
  - Typical entry-level education: **No formal educational credential**
  - Work experience in a related occupation: **None**
  - Typical on-the-job training: **Short-term on-the-job training**
- O*NET links:
  - 53-6031.00—Automotive and Watercraft Service Attendants
- CareerOneStop videos for this occupation:
  - 53-6031.00—Automotive and Watercraft Service Attendants

Aircraft service attendants

Service aircraft with fuel. May de-ice aircraft, refill water and cooling agents, empty sewage tanks, service air and oxygen systems, or clean and polish exterior.

- 2022 employment: **19,900**
- May 2022 median annual wage: **$37,050**
- Projected employment change, 2022–32:
  - Number of new jobs: **900**
  - Growth rate: **5 percent (Faster than average)**
- Education and training:
  - Typical entry-level education: **High school diploma or equivalent**
  - Work experience in a related occupation: **None**
  - Typical on-the-job training: **Short-term on-the-job training**
- O*NET links:
  - 53-6032.00—Aircraft Service Attendants
- CareerOneStop videos for this occupation:
  - 53-6032.00—Aircraft Service Attendants

Traffic technicians

Conduct field studies to determine traffic volume, speed, effectiveness of signals, adequacy of lighting, and other factors influencing traffic conditions, under direction of traffic engineer.

- 2022 employment: **7,600**
- May 2022 median annual wage: **$50,050**
- Projected employment change, 2022–32:
  - Number of new jobs: **300**
  - Growth rate: **3 percent (As fast as average)**
- Education and training:
  - Typical entry-level education: **High school diploma or equivalent**
  - Work experience in a related occupation: **None**
  - Typical on-the-job training: **Moderate-term on-the-job training**
- O*NET links:
  - 53-6041.00—Traffic Technicians

Transportation inspectors

Inspect equipment or goods in connection with the safe transport of cargo or people. Includes rail transportation inspectors, such as freight inspectors, rail inspectors, and other inspectors of transportation vehicles not elsewhere classified. Excludes "Transportation Security Screeners" (33-9093).

- 2022 employment: **25,700**
- May 2022 median annual wage: **$79,570**
- Projected employment change, 2022–32:
  - Number of new jobs: **700**
  - Growth rate: **3 percent (As fast as average)**
- Education and training:
  - Typical entry-level education: **High school diploma or equivalent**
  - Work experience in a related occupation: **None**
  - Typical on-the-job training: **Moderate-term on-the-job training**
- O*NET links:
  - 53-6051.00—Transportation Inspectors
  - 53-6051.01—Aviation Inspectors
  - 53-6051.07—Transportation Vehicle, Equipment and Systems Inspectors, Except Aviation
- CareerOneStop videos for this occupation:
  - 53-6051.00—Transportation Inspectors
  - 53-6051.01—Aviation Inspectors
  - 53-6051.07—Transportation Vehicle, Equipment and Systems Inspectors, Except Aviation

Passenger attendants

Provide services to ensure the safety of passengers aboard ships, buses, trains, or within the station or terminal. Perform duties such as explaining the use of safety equipment, serving meals or beverages, or answering questions related to travel. Excludes "Baggage Porters and Bellhops" (39-6011) and "Flight Attendants" (53-2031).

- 2022 employment: **13,500**
- May 2022 median annual wage: **$34,630**
- Projected employment change, 2022–32:
  - Number of new jobs: **600**
  - Growth rate: **4 percent (As fast as average)**
- Education and training:
  - Typical entry-level education: **High school diploma or equivalent**
  - Work experience in a related occupation: **None**
  - Typical on-the-job training: **Short-term on-the-job training**
- O*NET links:
  - 53-6061.00—Passenger Attendants

Transportation workers, all other

All transportation workers not listed separately.

- 2022 employment: **12,100**

- May 2022 median annual wage: **$37,430**
- Projected employment change, 2022–32:
  - Number of new jobs: **500**
  - Growth rate: **4 percent (As fast as average)**
- Education and training:
  - Typical entry-level education: **High school diploma or equivalent**
  - Work experience in a related occupation: **None**
  - Typical on-the-job training: **Short-term on-the-job training**
- O*NET links:
  - 53-6099.00—Transportation Workers, All Other

Gas compressor and gas pumping station operators

Operate steam-, gas-, electric motor-, or internal combustion-engine driven compressors. Transmit, compress, or recover gases, such as butane, nitrogen, hydrogen, and natural gas.

- 2022 employment: **3,900**
- May 2022 median annual wage: **$59,990**
- Projected employment change, 2022–32:
  - Number of new jobs: **-100**
  - Growth rate: **-2 percent (Decline)**
- Education and training:
  - Typical entry-level education: **High school diploma or equivalent**
  - Work experience in a related occupation: **None**
  - Typical on-the-job training: **Moderate-term on-the-job training**
- O*NET links:
  - 53-7071.00—Gas Compressor and Gas Pumping Station Operators
- CareerOneStop videos for this occupation:
  - 53-7071.00—Gas Compressor and Gas Pumping Station Operators

Pump operators, except wellhead pumpers

Tend, control, or operate power-driven, stationary, or portable pumps and manifold systems to transfer gases, oil, other liquids, slurries, or powdered materials to and from various vessels and processes.

- 2022 employment: **11,200**
- May 2022 median annual wage: **$55,860**
- Projected employment change, 2022–32:
  - Number of new jobs: **400**
  - Growth rate: **4 percent (As fast as average)**
- Education and training:
  - Typical entry-level education: **High school diploma or equivalent**
  - Work experience in a related occupation: **None**
  - Typical on-the-job training: **Moderate-term on-the-job training**
- O*NET links:
  - 53-7072.00—Pump Operators, Except Wellhead Pumpers
- CareerOneStop videos for this occupation:
  - 53-7072.00—Pump Operators, Except Wellhead Pumpers

Wellhead pumpers

Operate power pumps and auxiliary equipment to produce flow of oil or gas from wells in oil field.

- 2022 employment: **16,200**
- May 2022 median annual wage: **$63,280**
- Projected employment change, 2022–32:
  - Number of new jobs: **-400**
  - Growth rate: **-2 percent (Decline)**
- Education and training:
  - Typical entry-level education: **High school diploma or equivalent**
  - Work experience in a related occupation: **Less than 5 years**
  - Typical on-the-job training: **Moderate-term on-the-job training**
- O*NET links:
  - 53-7073.00—Wellhead Pumpers
- CareerOneStop videos for this occupation:
  - 53-7073.00—Wellhead Pumpers

Tank car, truck, and ship loaders

Load and unload chemicals and bulk solids, such as coal, sand, and grain, into or from tank cars, trucks, or ships, using material moving equipment. May perform a variety of other tasks relating to shipment of products. May gauge or sample shipping tanks and test them for leaks.

- 2022 employment: **13,300**
- May 2022 median annual wage: **$53,930**
- Projected employment change, 2022–32:
  - Number of new jobs: **200**
  - Growth rate: **2 percent (As fast as average)**
- Education and training:
  - Typical entry-level education: **No formal educational credential**
  - Work experience in a related occupation: **None**
  - Typical on-the-job training: **Short-term on-the-job training**
- O*NET links:
  - 53-7121.00—Tank Car, Truck, and Ship Loaders
- CareerOneStop videos for this occupation:
  - 53-7121.00—Tank Car, Truck, and Ship Loaders

Material moving workers, all other

All material moving workers not listed separately.

- 2022 employment: **26,100**
- May 2022 median annual wage: **$38,800**
- Projected employment change, 2022–32:
  - Number of new jobs: **900**
  - Growth rate: **4 percent (As fast as average)**
- Education and training:
  - Typical entry-level education: **No formal educational credential**
  - Work experience in a related occupation: **None**
  - Typical on-the-job training: **Short-term on-the-job training**
- O*NET links:
  - 53-7199.00—Material Moving Workers, All Other

Appendix: Summary of Occupations

Occupation	Job Duties	Entry-Level Education	Median Annual Pay, May 2022
Accountants and Auditors	Accountants and auditors prepare and examine financial records.	Bachelor's degree	$78,000
Actors	Actors express ideas and portray characters in theater, film, television, and other performing arts media.	Some college, no degree	The annual wage is not available.
Actuaries	Actuaries use mathematics, statistics, and financial theory to analyze the economic costs of risk and uncertainty.	Bachelor's degree	$113,990
Administrative Services and Facilities Managers	Administrative services and facilities managers plan, direct, and coordinate activities that help an organization run efficiently.	Bachelor's degree	$101,870
Adult Basic and Secondary Education and ESL Teachers	Adult basic and secondary education and ESL (English as a Second Language) teachers instruct adults in fundamental skills, such as reading and speaking English. They also help students earn their high school equivalency credential.	Bachelor's degree	$58,590
Advertising Sales Agents	Advertising sales agents sell advertising space to businesses and individuals.	High school diploma or equivalent	$58,450
Advertising, Promotions, and Marketing Managers	Advertising, promotions, and marketing managers plan programs to generate interest in products or services.	Bachelor's degree	$138,730
Aerospace Engineering and Operations Technologists and Technicians	Aerospace engineering and operations technologists and technicians run and maintain equipment used to develop, test, produce, and sustain aircraft and spacecraft.	Associate's degree	$74,410
Aerospace Engineers	Aerospace engineers design, develop, and test aircraft, spacecraft, satellites, and missiles.	Bachelor's degree	$126,880
Agricultural and Food Science Technicians	Agricultural and food science technicians assist agricultural and food scientists.	Associate's degree	$46,140
Agricultural and Food Scientists	Agricultural and food scientists research ways to improve the efficiency and safety of agricultural establishments and products.	Bachelor's degree	$74,940
Agricultural Engineers	Agricultural engineers solve problems concerning power supplies, machine efficiency, the use of structures and facilities, pollution and environmental issues, and the storage and processing of agricultural products.	Bachelor's degree	$83,260
Agricultural Workers	Agricultural workers maintain crops and tend livestock.	See entry	$33,290
Air Traffic Controllers	Air traffic controllers coordinate the movement of aircraft to maintain safe distances between them.	Associate's degree	$132,250

Occupation	Job Duties	Entry-Level Education	Median Annual Pay, May 2022
Aircraft and Avionics Equipment Mechanics and Technicians	Aircraft and avionics equipment mechanics and technicians repair and perform scheduled maintenance on aircraft.	See entry	$70,740
Airline and Commercial Pilots	Airline and commercial pilots fly and navigate airplanes, helicopters, and other aircraft.	See entry	$148,900
Animal Care and Service Workers	Animal care and service workers attend to or train animals.	High school diploma or equivalent	$29,790
Announcers and DJs	Announcers present news and sports or may interview guests on media such as radio and television. Disc jockeys (DJs) act as masters of ceremonies (emcees) or play recorded music at weddings, parties, or clubs.	See entry	The annual wage is not available.
Anthropologists and Archeologists	Anthropologists and archeologists study the origin, development, and behavior of humans.	Master's degree	$63,940
Arbitrators, Mediators, and Conciliators	Arbitrators, mediators, and conciliators facilitate negotiation and dialogue between disputing parties to help resolve conflicts outside of the court system.	Bachelor's degree	$64,030
Architects	Architects plan and design houses, factories, office buildings, and other structures.	Bachelor's degree	$82,840
Architectural and Engineering Managers	Architectural and engineering managers plan, direct, and coordinate activities in the fields of architecture and engineering.	Bachelor's degree	$159,920
Archivists, Curators, and Museum Workers	Archivists and curators oversee institutions' collections, such as of historical items or of artwork. Museum technicians and conservators prepare and restore items in those collections.	See entry	$53,420
Art Directors	Art directors are responsible for the visual style and images in magazines, newspapers, product packaging, and movie and television productions.	Bachelor's degree	$105,180
Assemblers and Fabricators	Assemblers and fabricators build finished products and the parts that go into them.	High school diploma or equivalent	$37,930
Athletes and Sports Competitors	Athletes and sports competitors participate in organized, officiated sporting events to entertain spectators.	No formal educational credential	$94,270
Athletic Trainers	Athletic trainers specialize in preventing, diagnosing, and treating muscle and bone injuries and illnesses.	Master's degree	$53,840
Atmospheric Scientists, Including Meteorologists	Atmospheric scientists study, report on, and forecast the weather and climate.	Bachelor's degree	$83,780
Audiologists	Audiologists diagnose, manage, and treat patients who have hearing, balance, or related problems.	Doctoral or professional degree	$82,680
Automotive Body and Glass Repairers	Automotive body and glass repairers restore, refinish, and replace vehicle bodies and frames, windshields, and window glass.	High school diploma or equivalent	$47,270
Automotive Service Technicians and Mechanics	Automotive service technicians and mechanics inspect, maintain, and repair cars and light trucks.	Postsecondary nondegree award	$46,970
Bakers	Bakers mix ingredients according to recipes in order to make breads, pastries, and other baked goods.	No formal educational credential	$32,780

Occupation	Job Duties	Entry-Level Education	Median Annual Pay, May 2022
Barbers, Hairstylists, and Cosmetologists	Barbers, hairstylists, and cosmetologists provide haircutting, hairstyling, and other services related to personal appearance.	Postsecondary nondegree award	$33,400
Bartenders	Bartenders mix drinks and serve them directly to customers or through wait staff.	No formal educational credential	$29,380
Bill and Account Collectors	Bill and account collectors try to recover payment on overdue bills.	High school diploma or equivalent	$39,470
Biochemists and Biophysicists	Biochemists and biophysicists study the chemical and physical principles of living things and of biological processes.	Doctoral or professional degree	$103,810
Bioengineers and Biomedical Engineers	Bioengineers and biomedical engineers combine engineering principles with sciences to design and create equipment, devices, computer systems, and software.	Bachelor's degree	$99,550
Biological Technicians	Biological technicians help biological and medical scientists conduct laboratory tests and experiments.	Bachelor's degree	$49,650
Boilermakers	Boilermakers assemble, install, maintain, and repair boilers, closed vats, and other large vessels or containers that hold liquids and gases.	High school diploma or equivalent	$66,920
Bookkeeping, Accounting, and Auditing Clerks	Bookkeeping, accounting, and auditing clerks produce financial records for organizations and check financial records for accuracy.	Some college, no degree	$45,860
Broadcast, Sound, and Video Technicians	Broadcast, sound, and video technicians set up, operate, and maintain the electrical equipment for media programs.	See entry	$53,960
Budget Analysts	Budget analysts help public and private organizations plan their finances.	Bachelor's degree	$82,260
Bus Drivers	Bus drivers transport people between various places.	High school diploma or equivalent	$44,440
Butchers	Butchers cut, trim, and package meat for retail sale.	No formal educational credential	$36,930
Career and Technical Education Teachers	Career and technical education teachers instruct students in various technical and vocational subjects, such as auto repair, healthcare, and culinary arts.	Bachelor's degree	$61,450
Carpenters	Carpenters construct, repair, and install building frameworks and structures made from wood and other materials.	High school diploma or equivalent	$51,390
Cartographers and Photogrammetrists	Cartographers and photogrammetrists collect, measure, and interpret geographic information in order to create and update maps and charts for regional planning, education, and other purposes.	Bachelor's degree	$71,890
Cashiers	Cashiers process payments from customers purchasing goods and services.	No formal educational credential	$28,240
Chefs and Head Cooks	Chefs and head cooks oversee the daily food preparation at restaurants and other places where food is served.	High school diploma or equivalent	$56,520
Chemical Engineers	Chemical engineers apply the principles of chemistry, physics, and engineering to design equipment and processes for manufacturing products such as gasoline, detergents, and paper.	Bachelor's degree	$106,260

Occupation	Job Duties	Entry-Level Education	Median Annual Pay, May 2022
Chemical Technicians	Chemical technicians conduct laboratory tests to help scientists analyze the properties of materials.	Associate's degree	$50,840
Chemists and Materials Scientists	Chemists and materials scientists research and analyze the chemical properties of substances to develop new materials, products, or knowledge.	Bachelor's degree	$81,810
Childcare Workers	Childcare workers attend to children's needs while helping to foster early development.	High school diploma or equivalent	$28,520
Chiropractors	Chiropractors evaluate and treat patients' neuromusculoskeletal system, which includes nerves, bones, muscles, ligaments, and tendons.	Doctoral or professional degree	$75,380
Civil Engineering Technologists and Technicians	Civil engineering technologists and technicians help civil engineers plan, design, and build infrastructure and development projects.	Associate's degree	$59,630
Civil Engineers	Civil engineers plan, design, and supervise the construction and maintenance of building and infrastructure projects.	Bachelor's degree	$89,940
Claims Adjusters, Appraisers, Examiners, and Investigators	Claims adjusters, appraisers, examiners, and investigators evaluate insurance claims.	See entry	$72,040
Clinical Laboratory Technologists and Technicians	Clinical laboratory technologists and technicians perform medical laboratory tests for the diagnosis, treatment, and prevention of disease.	Bachelor's degree	$57,380
Coaches and Scouts	Coaches teach amateur or professional athletes the skills they need to succeed at their sport. Scouts evaluate athletes as possible recruits.	Bachelor's degree	$44,890
Compensation and Benefits Managers	Compensation and benefits managers plan, develop, and oversee programs to pay employees.	Bachelor's degree	$131,280
Compensation, Benefits, and Job Analysis Specialists	Compensation, benefits, and job analysis specialists oversee wage and nonwage programs that an organization provides to its employees in return for their work. They also evaluate position descriptions to determine details such as classification and salary.	Bachelor's degree	$67,780
Computer and Information Research Scientists	Computer and information research scientists design innovative uses for new and existing computing technology.	Master's degree	$136,620
Computer and Information Systems Managers	Computer and information systems managers plan, coordinate, and direct computer-related activities in an organization.	Bachelor's degree	$164,070
Computer Hardware Engineers	Computer hardware engineers research, design, develop, and test computer systems and components.	Bachelor's degree	$132,360
Computer Network Architects	Computer network architects design and build data communication networks, including local area networks (LANs), wide area networks (WANs), and Intranets.	Bachelor's degree	$126,900
Computer Programmers	Computer programmers write, modify, and test code and scripts that allow computer software and applications to function properly.	Bachelor's degree	$97,800
Computer Support Specialists	Computer support specialists maintain computer networks and provide technical help to computer users.	See entry	$59,660

Occupation	Job Duties	Entry-Level Education	Median Annual Pay, May 2022
Computer Systems Analysts	Computer systems analysts study an organization's current computer systems and design ways to improve efficiency.	Bachelor's degree	$102,240
Conservation Scientists and Foresters	Conservation scientists and foresters manage the land quality of forests, parks, rangelands, and other natural resources.	Bachelor's degree	$64,420
Construction and Building Inspectors	Construction and building inspectors ensure that construction meets building codes and ordinances, zoning regulations, and contract specifications.	High school diploma or equivalent	$64,480
Construction Equipment Operators	Construction equipment operators drive, maneuver, or control the heavy machinery used to construct roads, buildings, and other structures.	High school diploma or equivalent	$51,050
Construction Laborers and Helpers	Construction laborers and helpers perform many tasks that require physical labor on construction sites.	See entry	$39,520
Construction Managers	Construction managers plan, coordinate, budget, and supervise construction projects from start to finish.	Bachelor's degree	$101,480
Cooks	Cooks season and prepare foods, including soups, salads, entrees, and desserts.	See entry	$30,910
Correctional Officers and Bailiffs	Correctional officers guard people in penal institutions and guard those in transit between jail, courtroom, prison, or other point. Bailiffs are law enforcement officers who maintain order in courtrooms.	High school diploma or equivalent	$49,610
Cost Estimators	Cost estimators collect and analyze data in order to assess the time, money, materials, and labor required to make a product or provide a service.	Bachelor's degree	$71,200
Court Reporters and Simultaneous Captioners	Court reporters create word-for-word transcriptions at trials, depositions, and other legal proceedings. Simultaneous captioners provide similar transcriptions for television or for presentations in other settings, such as press conferences and business meetings, for people who are deaf or hard of hearing.	Postsecondary nondegree award	$63,560
Craft and Fine Artists	Craft and fine artists use a variety of materials and techniques to create art for sale and exhibition.	See entry	$53,140
Customer Service Representatives	Customer service representatives interact with customers to handle complaints, process orders, and answer questions.	High school diploma or equivalent	$37,780
Dancers and Choreographers	Dancers and choreographers use dance performances to express ideas and stories.	See entry	The annual wage is not available.
Data Scientists	Data scientists use analytical tools and techniques to extract meaningful insights from data.	Bachelor's degree	$103,500
Database Administrators and Architects	Database administrators and architects create or organize systems to store and secure data.	Bachelor's degree	$112,120
Delivery Truck Drivers and Driver/ Sales Workers	Delivery truck drivers and driver/sales workers pick up, transport, and drop off packages and small shipments within a local region or urban area.	High school diploma or equivalent	$38,220

Occupation	Job Duties	Entry-Level Education	Median Annual Pay, May 2022
Dental and Ophthalmic Laboratory Technicians and Medical Appliance Technicians	Dental and ophthalmic laboratory technicians and medical appliance technicians make or repair dentures, eyeglasses, prosthetics, and related products.	High school diploma or equivalent	$41,180
Dental Assistants	Dental assistants provide patient care, take x rays, keep records, and schedule appointments.	Postsecondary nondegree award	$44,820
Dental Hygienists	Dental hygienists examine patients for signs of oral diseases, such as gingivitis, and provide preventive care, including oral hygiene.	Associate's degree	$81,400
Dentists	Dentists diagnose and treat problems with patients' teeth, gums, and related parts of the mouth.	Doctoral or professional degree	$159,530
Desktop Publishers	Desktop publishers use computer software to design page layouts for items that are printed or published online.	Associate's degree	$47,910
Diagnostic Medical Sonographers and Cardiovascular Technologists and Technicians	Diagnostic medical sonographers and cardiovascular technologists and technicians operate special equipment to create images or to conduct tests.	Associate's degree	$78,210
Diesel Service Technicians and Mechanics	Diesel service technicians and mechanics inspect, repair, and overhaul buses, trucks, or any vehicle with a diesel engine.	High school diploma or equivalent	$54,360
Dietitians and Nutritionists	Dietitians and nutritionists plan and conduct food service or nutritional programs to help people lead healthy lives.	Bachelor's degree	$66,450
Drafters	Drafters use software to convert the designs of engineers and architects into technical drawings.	Associate's degree	$60,400
Drywall Installers, Ceiling Tile Installers, and Tapers	Drywall and ceiling tile installers hang wallboard and install ceiling tile inside buildings. Tapers prepare the wallboard for painting.	No formal educational credential	$51,160
Economists	Economists conduct research, prepare reports, and evaluate issues related to monetary and fiscal policy. They also may collect and analyze statistical data.	Master's degree	$113,940
Editors	Editors plan, review, and revise content for publication.	Bachelor's degree	$73,080
Electrical and Electronic Engineering Technologists and Technicians	Electrical and electronic engineering technologists and technicians help engineers design and develop equipment that is powered by electricity or electric current.	Associate's degree	$66,390
Electrical and Electronics Engineers	Electrical engineers design, develop, test, and supervise the manufacture of electrical equipment.	Bachelor's degree	$104,610
Electrical and Electronics Installers and Repairers	Electrical and electronics installers and repairers install or repair a variety of electrical equipment.	See entry	$64,190
Electrical Power-Line Installers and Repairers	Electrical power-line installers and repairers install or repair cables or wires used in electrical power or distribution systems.	High school diploma or equivalent	$82,340
Electricians	Electricians install, maintain, and repair electrical power, communications, lighting, and control systems.	High school diploma or equivalent	$60,240

Occupation	Job Duties	Entry-Level Education	Median Annual Pay, May 2022
Electro-mechanical and Mechatronics Technologists and Technicians	Electro-mechanical and mechatronics technologists and technicians operate, test, and maintain electromechanical or robotic equipment.	Associate's degree	$60,570
Elementary, Middle, and High School Principals	Elementary, middle, and high school principals oversee all school operations, including daily school activities.	Master's degree	$101,320
Elevator and Escalator Installers and Repairers	Elevator and escalator installers and repairers install, maintain, and fix elevators, escalators, moving walkways, and other lifts.	High school diploma or equivalent	$99,000
Emergency Management Directors	Emergency management directors prepare plans and procedures for responding to natural disasters or other emergencies. They also help lead the response during and after emergencies.	Bachelor's degree	$79,180
EMTs and Paramedics	Emergency medical technicians (EMTs) and paramedics assess injuries and illnesses, provide emergency medical care, and may transport patients to medical facilities.	Postsecondary nondegree award	$39,410
Environmental Engineering Technologists and Technicians	Environmental engineering technologists and technicians implement the plans that environmental engineers develop.	Associate's degree	$50,980
Environmental Engineers	Environmental engineers use engineering disciplines in developing solutions to problems of planetary health.	Bachelor's degree	$96,530
Environmental Science and Protection Technicians	Environmental science and protection technicians monitor the environment and investigate sources of pollution and contamination.	Associate's degree	$48,380
Environmental Scientists and Specialists	Environmental scientists and specialists use their knowledge of the natural sciences to protect the environment and human health.	Bachelor's degree	$76,480
Epidemiologists	Epidemiologists are public health workers who investigate patterns and causes of disease and injury.	Master's degree	$78,520
Exercise Physiologists	Exercise physiologists develop fitness and exercise programs that help injured or sick patients recover.	Bachelor's degree	$51,350
Farmers, Ranchers, and Other Agricultural Managers	Farmers, ranchers, and other agricultural managers run establishments that produce crops, livestock, and dairy products.	High school diploma or equivalent	$75,760
Fashion Designers	Fashion designers create clothing, accessories, and footwear.	Bachelor's degree	$76,700
Film and Video Editors and Camera Operators	Film and video editors and camera operators manipulate moving images that entertain or inform an audience.	Bachelor's degree	$62,420
Financial Analysts	Financial analysts guide businesses and individuals in decisions about expending money to attain profit.	Bachelor's degree	$96,220
Financial Clerks	Financial clerks do administrative work, help customers, and carry out transactions that involve money.	High school diploma or equivalent	$45,570
Financial Examiners	Financial examiners ensure compliance with laws that govern institutions handling monetary transactions.	Bachelor's degree	$82,210

Occupation	Job Duties	Entry-Level Education	Median Annual Pay, May 2022
Financial Managers	Financial managers create financial reports, direct investment activities, and develop plans for the long-term financial goals of their organization.	Bachelor's degree	$139,790
Fire Inspectors	Fire inspectors detect fire hazards, recommend prevention measures, ensure compliance with state and local fire regulations, and investigate causes of fires.	See entry	$65,800
Firefighters	Firefighters control and put out fires and respond to emergencies involving life, property, or the environment.	Postsecondary nondegree award	$51,680
Fishing and Hunting Workers	Fishing and hunting workers catch and trap various types of animal life.	No formal educational credential	The annual wage is not available.
Fitness Trainers and Instructors	Fitness trainers and instructors lead, instruct, and motivate individuals or groups in exercise activities.	High school diploma or equivalent	$45,380
Flight Attendants	Flight attendants provide routine services and respond to emergencies to ensure the safety and comfort of airline passengers.	High school diploma or equivalent	$63,760
Flooring Installers and Tile and Stone Setters	Flooring installers and tile and stone setters lay and finish carpet, wood, vinyl, tile, and other materials.	No formal educational credential	$47,890
Floral Designers	Floral designers arrange live, dried, and silk flowers and greenery to make decorative displays.	High school diploma or equivalent	$33,160
Food and Beverage Serving and Related Workers	Food and beverage serving and related workers take and prepare orders, clear tables, and do other tasks associated with providing food and drink to customers.	No formal educational credential	$28,130
Food Preparation Workers	Food preparation workers perform a variety of tasks other than cooking, such as slicing meat and brewing coffee.	No formal educational credential	$29,790
Food Processing Equipment Workers	Food processing equipment workers operate machinery that mixes, cooks, or processes ingredients for manufacturing food products.	See entry	$36,190
Food Service Managers	Food service managers are responsible for the daily operation of restaurants or other establishments that prepare and serve food and beverages.	High school diploma or equivalent	$61,310
Forensic Science Technicians	Forensic science technicians aid criminal investigations by collecting and analyzing evidence.	Bachelor's degree	$63,740
Forest and Conservation Workers	Forest and conservation workers perform physical labor to improve the quality of natural areas such as forests, rangelands, and wetlands.	High school diploma or equivalent	$32,270
Fundraisers	Fundraisers organize events and campaigns to raise money and other kinds of donations for an organization.	Bachelor's degree	$61,190
Gambling Services Workers	Gambling services workers serve customers in gambling establishments, such as casinos or racetracks.	High school diploma or equivalent	$31,290
General Maintenance and Repair Workers	General maintenance and repair workers fix and maintain machines, mechanical equipment, and buildings.	High school diploma or equivalent	$44,980
General Office Clerks	General office clerks perform a variety of clerical tasks, including answering telephones, typing documents, and filing records.	High school diploma or equivalent	$38,040
Genetic Counselors	Genetic counselors assess clients' risk for a variety of inherited conditions, such as birth defects.	Master's degree	$89,990

Occupation	Job Duties	Entry-Level Education	Median Annual Pay, May 2022
Geographers	Geographers study the Earth and the distribution of its land, features, and inhabitants.	Bachelor's degree	$88,900
Geological and Hydrologic Technicians	Geological and hydrologic technicians support scientists and engineers in exploring, extracting, and monitoring natural resources.	Associate's degree	$49,590
Geoscientists	Geoscientists study the physical aspects of the Earth.	Bachelor's degree	$87,480
Glaziers	Glaziers install glass in windows, skylights, and other fixtures in buildings.	High school diploma or equivalent	$48,720
Graphic Designers	Graphic designers create visual concepts, using computer software or by hand, to communicate ideas that inspire, inform, and captivate consumers.	Bachelor's degree	$57,990
Grounds Maintenance Workers	Grounds maintenance workers install and maintain landscapes, prune trees or shrubs, and do other tasks to ensure that vegetation is attractive, orderly, and safe.	See entry	$36,160
Hand Laborers and Material Movers	Hand laborers and material movers manually move freight, stock, or other materials.	See entry	$34,960
Hazardous Materials Removal Workers	Hazardous materials removal workers identify and dispose of harmful substances such as asbestos, lead, and radioactive waste.	High school diploma or equivalent	$46,690
Health and Safety Engineers	Health and safety engineers combine knowledge of engineering and of health and safety to develop procedures and design systems to protect people from illness and injury and property from damage.	Bachelor's degree	$100,660
Health Education Specialists	Health education specialists develop programs to teach people about conditions affecting well-being.	Bachelor's degree	$59,990
Health Information Technologists and Medical Registrars	Health information technologists and medical registrars advise organizations on computerized healthcare systems and analyze clinical data.	Associate's degree	$58,250
Heating, Air Conditioning, and Refrigeration Mechanics and Installers	Heating, air conditioning, and refrigeration mechanics and installers work on heating, ventilation, cooling, and refrigeration systems.	Postsecondary nondegree award	$51,390
Heavy and Tractor-trailer Truck Drivers	Heavy and tractor-trailer truck drivers transport goods from one location to another.	Postsecondary nondegree award	$49,920
Heavy Vehicle and Mobile Equipment Service Technicians	Heavy vehicle and mobile equipment service technicians inspect, maintain, and repair vehicles and machinery used in construction, farming, and other industries.	High school diploma or equivalent	$58,350
High School Teachers	High school teachers teach academic lessons and various skills that students will need to attend college and to enter the job market.	Bachelor's degree	$62,360
Historians	Historians research, analyze, interpret, and write about the past by studying historical documents and sources.	Master's degree	$64,540
Home Health and Personal Care Aides	Home health and personal care aides monitor the condition of people with disabilities or chronic illnesses and help them with daily living activities.	High school diploma or equivalent	$30,180
Human Resources Managers	Human resources managers plan, coordinate, and direct the administrative functions of an organization.	Bachelor's degree	$130,000

Occupation	Job Duties	Entry-Level Education	Median Annual Pay, May 2022
Human Resources Specialists	Human resources specialists recruit, screen, and interview job applicants and place newly hired workers in jobs. They also may handle compensation and benefits, training, and employee relations.	Bachelor's degree	$64,240
Hydrologists	Hydrologists study how water moves across and through the Earth's crust.	Bachelor's degree	$85,990
Industrial Designers	Industrial designers combine art, business, and engineering to develop the concepts for manufactured products.	Bachelor's degree	$75,910
Industrial Engineering Technologists and Technicians	Industrial engineering technologists and technicians help engineers solve problems affecting manufacturing layout or production.	Associate's degree	$61,210
Industrial Engineers	Industrial engineers devise efficient systems that integrate workers, machines, materials, information, and energy to make a product or provide a service.	Bachelor's degree	$96,350
Industrial Machinery Mechanics, Machinery Maintenance Workers, and Millwrights	Industrial machinery mechanics, machinery maintenance workers, and millwrights install, maintain, and repair factory equipment and other industrial machinery.	High school diploma or equivalent	$59,470
Industrial Production Managers	Industrial production managers oversee the operations of manufacturing and related plants.	Bachelor's degree	$107,560
Information Clerks	Information clerks perform routine clerical duties, maintain records, collect data, and provide information to customers.	See entry	$38,710
Information Security Analysts	Information security analysts plan and carry out security measures to protect an organization's computer networks and systems.	Bachelor's degree	$112,000
Instructional Coordinators	Instructional coordinators oversee school curriculums and teaching standards. They develop instructional material, implement it, and assess its effectiveness.	Master's degree	$66,490
Insulation Workers	Insulation workers install and replace the materials used to insulate buildings or mechanical systems.	See entry	$47,980
Insurance Sales Agents	Insurance sales agents contact potential customers and sell one or more types of insurance.	High school diploma or equivalent	$57,860
Insurance Underwriters	Insurance underwriters evaluate insurance applications and decide whether to approve them.	Bachelor's degree	$76,230
Interior Designers	Interior designers make indoor spaces functional, safe, and beautiful by determining space requirements and selecting essential and decorative items.	Bachelor's degree	$61,590
Interpreters and Translators	Interpreters and translators convert information from one language into another language.	Bachelor's degree	$53,640
Ironworkers	Ironworkers install structural and reinforcing iron and steel to form and support buildings, bridges, and roads.	High school diploma or equivalent	$58,330
Janitors and Building Cleaners	Janitors and building cleaners keep many types of buildings clean, sanitary, orderly, and in good condition.	No formal educational credential	$31,990

Occupation	Job Duties	Entry-Level Education	Median Annual Pay, May 2022
Jewelers and Precious Stone and Metal Workers	Jewelers and precious stone and metal workers design, construct, adjust, repair, appraise and sell jewelry.	High school diploma or equivalent	$47,140
Judges and Hearing Officers	Judges and hearing officers apply the law by overseeing the legal process in courts.	Doctoral or professional degree	$128,610
Kindergarten and Elementary School Teachers	Kindergarten and elementary school teachers instruct young students in basic subjects in order to prepare them for future schooling.	Bachelor's degree	$61,620
Labor Relations Specialists	Labor relations specialists interpret and administer labor contracts.	Bachelor's degree	$82,010
Landscape Architects	Landscape architects design parks and other outdoor spaces.	Bachelor's degree	$73,210
Lawyers	Lawyers advise and represent clients on legal proceedings or transactions.	Doctoral or professional degree	$135,740
Librarians and Library Media Specialists	Librarians and library media specialists help people find information and conduct research for personal and professional use.	Master's degree	$61,660
Library Technicians and Assistants	Library technicians and assistants help librarians with all aspects of running a library.	See entry	$35,280
Licensed Practical and Licensed Vocational Nurses	Licensed practical nurses (LPNs) and licensed vocational nurses (LVNs) provide basic medical care.	Postsecondary nondegree award	$54,620
Loan Officers	Loan officers evaluate, authorize, or recommend approval of loan applications.	Bachelor's degree	$65,740
Lodging Managers	Lodging managers ensure that guests have a pleasant experience at an accommodations facility. They also plan, direct, or coordinate activities to ensure that the facility is efficient and profitable.	High school diploma or equivalent	$61,910
Logging Workers	Logging workers harvest forests to provide the raw material for many consumer goods and industrial products.	High school diploma or equivalent	$46,580
Logisticians	Logisticians analyze and coordinate an organization's supply chain.	Bachelor's degree	$77,520
Machinists and Tool and Die Makers	Machinists and tool and die makers set up and operate equipment to produce precision metal parts, instruments, and tools.	See entry	$49,560
Management Analysts	Management analysts recommend ways to improve an organization's efficiency.	Bachelor's degree	$95,290
Manicurists and Pedicurists	Manicurists and pedicurists clean, shape, and beautify fingernails and toenails.	Postsecondary nondegree award	$31,130
Market Research Analysts	Market research analysts study consumer preferences, business conditions, and other factors to assess potential sales of a product or service.	Bachelor's degree	$68,230
Marriage and Family Therapists	Marriage and family therapists help people manage and overcome problems with family and other relationships.	Master's degree	$56,570
Masonry Workers	Masonry workers use bricks, concrete and concrete blocks, and natural and manmade stones to build structures.	See entry	$49,490

Occupation	Job Duties	Entry-Level Education	Median Annual Pay, May 2022
Massage Therapists	Massage therapists treat clients by applying pressure to manipulate the body's soft tissues and joints.	Postsecondary nondegree award	$49,860
Material Moving Machine Operators	Material moving machine operators use equipment to transport objects.	See entry	$41,730
Material Recording Clerks	Material recording clerks track product information in order to keep businesses and supply chains on schedule.	High school diploma or equivalent	$40,490
Materials Engineers	Materials engineers develop, process, and test materials used to create a wide range of products.	Bachelor's degree	$100,140
Mathematicians and Statisticians	Mathematicians and statisticians analyze data and apply computational techniques to solve problems.	Master's degree	$99,960
Mechanical Engineering Technologists and Technicians	Mechanical engineering technologists and technicians help mechanical engineers design, develop, test, and manufacture machines and other devices.	Associate's degree	$61,990
Mechanical Engineers	Mechanical engineers design, develop, build, and test mechanical and thermal sensors and devices.	Bachelor's degree	$96,310
Medical and Health Services Managers	Medical and health services managers plan, direct, and coordinate the business activities of healthcare providers.	Bachelor's degree	$104,830
Medical Assistants	Medical assistants complete administrative and clinical tasks, such as scheduling appointments and taking patients' vital signs.	Postsecondary nondegree award	$38,270
Medical Dosimetrists	Medical dosimetrists calculate doses of radiation and design and oversee treatment plans for patients with cancer and other serious diseases.	Bachelor's degree	$128,970
Medical Equipment Repairers	Medical equipment repairers install, maintain, and repair patient care equipment.	Associate's degree	$57,860
Medical Records Specialists	Medical records specialists compile, process, and maintain patient files.	Postsecondary nondegree award	$47,180
Medical Scientists	Medical scientists conduct research aimed at improving overall human health.	Doctoral or professional degree	$99,930
Medical Transcriptionists	Medical transcriptionists use electronic devices to convert voice recordings from physicians and other healthcare workers into formal reports.	Postsecondary nondegree award	$34,730
Meeting, Convention, and Event Planners	Meeting, convention, and event planners arrange all aspects of events and professional gatherings.	Bachelor's degree	$52,560
Metal and Plastic Machine Workers	Metal and plastic machine workers set up and operate equipment that cuts, shapes, and forms metal and plastic materials or pieces.	See entry	$41,060
Microbiologists	Microbiologists study microorganisms such as bacteria, viruses, algae, fungi, and some types of parasites.	Bachelor's degree	$81,990
Middle School Teachers	Middle school teachers educate students, typically in sixth through eighth grades.	Bachelor's degree	$61,810
Mining and Geological Engineers	Mining and geological engineers design mines to safely and efficiently remove minerals for use in manufacturing and utilities.	Bachelor's degree	$97,490
Models	Models pose for artists, photographers, and other clients to help advertise products.	No formal educational credential	$43,130

Occupation	Job Duties	Entry-Level Education	Median Annual Pay, May 2022
Music Directors and Composers	Music directors lead musical groups during performances and recording sessions. Composers write and arrange original music in a variety of musical styles.	Bachelor's degree	$62,940
Musicians and Singers	Musicians and singers play instruments or sing for live audiences and in recording studios.	No formal educational credential	The annual wage is not available.
Natural Sciences Managers	Natural sciences managers supervise the work of scientists, including chemists, physicists, and biologists.	Bachelor's degree	$144,440
Network and Computer Systems Administrators	Network and computer systems administrators install, configure, and maintain organizations' computer networks and systems.	Bachelor's degree	$90,520
News Analysts, Reporters, and Journalists	News analysts, reporters, and journalists keep the public updated about current events and noteworthy information.	Bachelor's degree	$55,960
Nuclear Engineers	Nuclear engineers research and develop projects or address problems concerning the release, control, and use of nuclear energy and nuclear waste disposal.	Bachelor's degree	$122,480
Nuclear Medicine Technologists	Nuclear medicine technologists prepare and administer radioactive drugs for imaging or treatment.	Associate's degree	$85,300
Nuclear Technicians	Nuclear technicians assist physicists, engineers, and other professionals in nuclear research and nuclear energy production.	Associate's degree	$100,420
Nurse Anesthetists, Nurse Midwives, and Nurse Practitioners	Nurse anesthetists, nurse midwives, and nurse practitioners coordinate patient care and may provide primary and specialty healthcare.	Master's degree	$125,900
Nursing Assistants and Orderlies	Nursing assistants provide basic care and help patients with activities of daily living. Orderlies transport patients and clean treatment areas.	See entry	$35,740
Occupational Health and Safety Specialists and Technicians	Occupational health and safety specialists and technicians collect data on, analyze, and design improvements to work environments and procedures.	See entry	$75,240
Occupational Therapists	Occupational therapists evaluate and treat people who have injuries, illnesses, or disabilities to help them with vocational, daily living, and other skills that promote independence.	Master's degree	$93,180
Occupational Therapy Assistants and Aides	Occupational therapy assistants and aides help patients develop, recover, improve, as well as maintain the skills needed for daily living and working.	See entry	$63,450
Operations Research Analysts	Operations research analysts use mathematics and logic to help solve complex issues.	Bachelor's degree	$85,720
Opticians	Opticians help fit eyeglasses and contact lenses, following prescriptions from ophthalmologists and optometrists.	High school diploma or equivalent	$39,610
Optometrists	Optometrists diagnose, manage, and treat conditions and diseases of the human eye and visual system, including examining eyes and prescribing corrective lenses.	Doctoral or professional degree	$125,590
Orthotists and Prosthetists	Orthotists and prosthetists design and fabricate medical supportive devices and measure and fit patients for them.	Master's degree	$77,070

Occupation	Job Duties	Entry-Level Education	Median Annual Pay, May 2022
Painters, Construction and Maintenance	Painters apply paint, stain, and coatings to walls and ceilings, buildings, large machinery and equipment, and bridges and other structures.	No formal educational credential	$46,090
Painting and Coating Workers	Painting and coating workers apply finishes, often using machines, to a range of products.	See entry	$43,370
Paralegals and Legal Assistants	Paralegals and legal assistants perform a variety of tasks to support lawyers.	Associate's degree	$59,200
Personal Financial Advisors	Personal financial advisors provide advice to help individuals manage their money and plan for their financial future.	Bachelor's degree	$95,390
Pest Control Workers	Pest control workers remove insects, rodents, and other pests that infest buildings and surrounding areas.	High school diploma or equivalent	$38,310
Petroleum Engineers	Petroleum engineers design and develop methods for extracting oil and gas from deposits below the Earth's surface.	Bachelor's degree	$131,800
Pharmacists	Pharmacists dispense prescription medications and provide information to patients about the drugs and their use.	Doctoral or professional degree	$132,750
Pharmacy Technicians	Pharmacy technicians help pharmacists dispense prescription medication to customers or health professionals.	High school diploma or equivalent	$37,790
Phlebotomists	Phlebotomists draw blood for tests, transfusions, research, or blood donations.	Postsecondary nondegree award	$38,530
Photographers	Photographers use their technical expertise, creativity, and composition skills to produce and preserve images.	High school diploma or equivalent	$40,170
Physical Therapist Assistants and Aides	Physical therapist assistants and aides are supervised by physical therapists to help patients regain movement and manage pain after injuries and illnesses.	See entry	$57,240
Physical Therapists	Physical therapists help injured or ill people improve movement and manage pain.	Doctoral or professional degree	$97,720
Physician Assistants	Physician assistants examine, diagnose, and treat patients under the supervision of a physician.	Master's degree	$126,010
Physicians and Surgeons	Physicians and surgeons diagnose and treat injuries or illnesses and address health maintenance.	Doctoral or professional degree	$229,300
Physicists and Astronomers	Physicists and astronomers study the interactions of matter and energy.	Doctoral or professional degree	$139,220
Plumbers, Pipefitters, and Steamfitters	Plumbers, pipefitters, and steamfitters install and repair piping fixtures and systems.	High school diploma or equivalent	$60,090
Podiatrists	Podiatrists provide medical and surgical care for people with foot, ankle, and lower leg problems.	Doctoral or professional degree	$148,720
Police and Detectives	Police officers protect lives and property. Detectives and criminal investigators gather facts and collect evidence of possible crimes.	See entry	$69,160
Political Scientists	Political scientists study the origin, development, and operation of political systems.	Master's degree	$128,020

Occupation	Job Duties	Entry-Level Education	Median Annual Pay, May 2022
Postal Service Workers	Postal service workers sell postage and related products and collect, sort, and deliver mail.	No formal educational credential	$53,680
Postsecondary Education Administrators	Postsecondary education administrators oversee student services, academics, and faculty research at colleges and universities.	Master's degree	$99,940
Postsecondary Teachers	Postsecondary teachers instruct students in a variety of academic subjects beyond the high school level.	See entry	$80,840
Power Plant Operators, Distributors, and Dispatchers	Power plant operators, distributors, and dispatchers control the systems that generate and distribute electric power.	High school diploma or equivalent	$97,570
Preschool and Childcare Center Directors	Preschool and childcare center directors supervise and lead their staffs, design program plans, oversee daily activities, and prepare budgets.	Bachelor's degree	$49,690
Preschool Teachers	Preschool teachers educate and care for children younger than age 5 who have not yet entered kindergarten.	Associate's degree	$35,330
Private Detectives and Investigators	Private detectives and investigators search for information about legal, financial, and personal matters.	High school diploma or equivalent	$52,120
Probation Officers and Correctional Treatment Specialists	Probation officers and correctional treatment specialists assist in rehabilitating law offenders in custody or on probation or parole.	Bachelor's degree	$59,860
Producers and Directors	Producers and directors make business and creative decisions about film, television, stage, and other productions.	Bachelor's degree	$85,320
Project Management Specialists	Project management specialists coordinate the budget, schedule, staffing, and other details of a project.	Bachelor's degree	$95,370
Property Appraisers and Assessors	Property appraisers and assessors provide a value estimate on real estate and on tangible personal and business property.	Bachelor's degree	$61,560
Property, Real Estate, and Community Association Managers	Property, real estate, and community association managers oversee many aspects of residential, commercial, or industrial properties.	High school diploma or equivalent	$60,670
Psychiatric Technicians and Aides	Psychiatric technicians and aides care for people who have mental conditions or developmental disabilities.	See entry	$37,330
Psychologists	Psychologists study cognitive, emotional, and social processes and behavior by observing, interpreting, and recording how individuals relate to one another and to their environments.	See entry	$85,330
Public Relations and Fundraising Managers	Public relations managers direct the creation of materials that will enhance the public image of their employer or client. Fundraising managers coordinate campaigns that bring in donations for their organization.	Bachelor's degree	$125,620
Public Relations Specialists	Public relations specialists create and maintain a positive public image for the clients they represent.	Bachelor's degree	$67,440
Public Safety Telecommunicators	Public safety telecommunicators, including 911 operators and fire dispatchers, answer emergency and nonemergency calls and provide resources to assist those in need.	High school diploma or equivalent	$46,900

Occupation	Job Duties	Entry-Level Education	Median Annual Pay, May 2022
Purchasing Managers, Buyers, and Purchasing Agents	Buyers and purchasing agents buy products and services for organizations. Purchasing managers oversee the work of buyers and purchasing agents.	Bachelor's degree	$75,120
Quality Control Inspectors	Quality control inspectors examine products and materials for defects or deviations from specifications.	High school diploma or equivalent	$43,900
Radiation Therapists	Radiation therapists administer doses of radiation to patients who have cancer or other serious diseases.	Associate's degree	$89,530
Radiologic and MRI Technologists	Radiologic technologists perform diagnostic imaging examinations on patients. MRI technologists operate magnetic resonance imaging (MRI) scanners to create diagnostic images.	Associate's degree	$67,180
Railroad Workers	Railroad workers ensure that passenger and freight trains operate safely. They may drive trains, coordinate the activities of the trains, or control signals and switches in the rail yard.	High school diploma or equivalent	$68,960
Real Estate Brokers and Sales Agents	Real estate brokers and sales agents help clients buy, sell, and rent properties.	High school diploma or equivalent	$52,030
Receptionists	Receptionists do tasks such as answering phones, receiving visitors, and providing information about their organization to the public.	High school diploma or equivalent	$33,960
Recreation Workers	Recreation workers design and lead activities to help people stay active, improve fitness, and have fun.	High school diploma or equivalent	$31,680
Recreational Therapists	Recreational therapists plan, direct, and coordinate recreation-based medical treatment programs for people with disabilities, injuries, or illnesses.	Bachelor's degree	$51,330
Registered Nurses	Registered nurses (RNs) provide and coordinate patient care and educate patients and the public about various health conditions.	Bachelor's degree	$81,220
Rehabilitation Counselors	Rehabilitation counselors help people with physical, mental, developmental, or emotional disabilities live independently.	Master's degree	$39,990
Respiratory Therapists	Respiratory therapists care for patients who have trouble breathing—for example, because of a chronic condition such as asthma.	Associate's degree	$70,540
Retail Sales Workers	Retail sales workers help customers find products they want and process customers' payments.	No formal educational credential	$30,750
Roofers	Roofers replace, repair, and install the roofs of buildings.	No formal educational credential	$47,920
Sales Engineers	Sales engineers sell complex scientific and technological products or services to businesses.	Bachelor's degree	$108,530
Sales Managers	Sales managers direct organizations' sales teams.	Bachelor's degree	$130,600
School and Career Counselors and Advisors	School counselors help students develop academic and social skills. Career counselors and advisors help people choose a path to employment.	Master's degree	$60,140
Secretaries and Administrative Assistants	Secretaries and administrative assistants do routine clerical and organizational tasks.	High school diploma or equivalent	$44,080

Occupation	Job Duties	Entry-Level Education	Median Annual Pay, May 2022
Securities, Commodities, and Financial Services Sales Agents	Securities, commodities, and financial services sales agents connect buyers and sellers in financial markets.	Bachelor's degree	$67,480
Security Guards and Gambling Surveillance Officers	Security guards and gambling surveillance officers protect property from illegal activity.	High school diploma or equivalent	$34,770
Sheet Metal Workers	Sheet metal workers fabricate or install products that are made from thin metal sheets.	High school diploma or equivalent	$55,350
Skincare Specialists	Skincare specialists provide cleansing and other face and body treatments to enhance a person's appearance.	Postsecondary nondegree award	$38,060
Small Engine Mechanics	Small engine mechanics inspect, service, and repair motorized power equipment.	See entry	$44,080
Social and Community Service Managers	Social and community service managers coordinate and supervise programs and organizations that support public well-being.	Bachelor's degree	$74,240
Social and Human Service Assistants	Social and human service assistants provide client services in a variety of fields, such as psychology, rehabilitation, and social work.	High school diploma or equivalent	$38,520
Social Workers	Social workers help people prevent and cope with problems in their everyday lives.	See entry	$55,350
Sociologists	Sociologists study society and social behavior.	Master's degree	$98,590
Software Developers, Quality Assurance Analysts, and Testers	Software developers design computer applications or programs. Software quality assurance analysts and testers identify problems with applications or programs and report defects.	Bachelor's degree	$124,200
Solar Photovoltaic Installers	Solar photovoltaic (PV) installers assemble, set up, and maintain rooftop or other systems that convert sunlight into energy.	High school diploma or equivalent	$45,230
Special Education Teachers	Special education teachers work with students who have a wide range of learning, mental, emotional, and physical disabilities.	Bachelor's degree	$62,950
Special Effects Artists and Animators	Special effects artists and animators create images that appear to move and visual effects for various forms of media and entertainment.	Bachelor's degree	$98,950
Speech-Language Pathologists	Speech-language pathologists assess and treat people who have communication disorders.	Master's degree	$84,140
Stationary Engineers and Boiler Operators	Stationary engineers and boiler operators control stationary engines, boilers, or other mechanical equipment.	High school diploma or equivalent	$67,120
Substance Abuse, Behavioral Disorder, and Mental Health Counselors	Substance abuse, behavioral disorder, and mental health counselors advise people on a range of issues, such as those relating to alcoholism, addictions, or depression.	Bachelor's degree	$49,710
Surgical Assistants and Technologists	Surgical assistants and technologists help with surgical operations.	Postsecondary nondegree award	$56,350
Survey Researchers	Survey researchers design and conduct surveys and analyze data.	Master's degree	$60,410

Occupation	Job Duties	Entry-Level Education	Median Annual Pay, May 2022
Surveying and Mapping Technicians	Surveying and mapping technicians collect data and make maps of the Earth's surface.	High school diploma or equivalent	$47,180
Surveyors	Surveyors make precise measurements to determine property boundaries.	Bachelor's degree	$63,080
Tax Examiners and Collectors, and Revenue Agents	Tax examiners and collectors, and revenue agents determine how much is owed in taxes and collect tax from individuals and businesses on behalf of the government.	Bachelor's degree	$57,950
Taxi Drivers, Shuttle Drivers, and Chauffeurs	Taxi drivers (including ride-hailing drivers), shuttle drivers, and chauffeurs transport people to and from the places they need to go.	No formal educational credential	$32,440
Teacher Assistants	Teacher assistants work with a licensed teacher to give students additional attention and instruction.	Some college, no degree	$30,920
Technical Writers	Technical writers prepare instruction manuals, how-to guides, journal articles, and other supporting documents to communicate complex and technical information more easily.	Bachelor's degree	$79,960
Telecommunications Technicians	Telecommunications technicians install, maintain, and repair radio, internet, and other telecommunications infrastructure.	See entry	$60,190
Tellers	Tellers are responsible for accurately processing routine transactions at a bank.	High school diploma or equivalent	$36,380
Top Executives	Top executives plan strategies and policies to ensure that an organization meets its goals.	Bachelor's degree	$100,090
Training and Development Managers	Training and development managers plan, coordinate, and direct skills- and knowledge-enhancement programs for an organization's staff.	Bachelor's degree	$120,000
Training and Development Specialists	Training and development specialists plan and administer programs that improve the skills and knowledge of their employees.	Bachelor's degree	$63,080
Travel Agents	Travel agents sell transportation, lodging, and entertainment activities to individuals and groups planning trips.	High school diploma or equivalent	$46,400
Umpires, Referees, and Other Sports Officials	Umpires, referees, and other sports officials preside over competitive athletic or sporting events to help maintain standards of play.	High school diploma or equivalent	$36,010
Urban and Regional Planners	Urban and regional planners develop land use plans and programs that help create communities, accommodate population growth, and revitalize physical facilities.	Master's degree	$79,540
Veterinarians	Veterinarians care for the health of animals and work to protect public health.	Doctoral or professional degree	$103,260
Veterinary Assistants and Laboratory Animal Caretakers	Veterinary assistants and laboratory animal caretakers handle routine animal care and help scientists, veterinarians, and others with their daily tasks.	High school diploma or equivalent	$34,740
Veterinary Technologists and Technicians	Veterinary technologists and technicians do medical tests that help diagnose animals' injuries and illnesses.	Associate's degree	$38,240
Waiters and Waitresses	Waiters and waitresses take orders and serve food and beverages to customers in dining establishments.	No formal educational credential	$29,120

Occupation	Job Duties	Entry-Level Education	Median Annual Pay, May 2022
Water and Wastewater Treatment Plant and System Operators	Water and wastewater treatment plant and system operators manage a system of machines to transfer or treat water or wastewater.	High school diploma or equivalent	$51,600
Water Transportation Workers	Water transportation workers operate and maintain vessels that take cargo and people over water.	See entry	$66,100
Web Developers and Digital Designers	Web developers create and maintain websites. Digital designers develop, create, and test website or interface layout, functions, and navigation for usability.	Bachelor's degree	$80,730
Welders, Cutters, Solderers, and Brazers	Welders, cutters, solderers, and brazers use hand-held or remotely controlled equipment to join, repair, or cut metal parts and products.	High school diploma or equivalent	$47,540
Wholesale and Manufacturing Sales Representatives	Wholesale and manufacturing sales representatives sell goods for wholesalers or manufacturers to businesses, government agencies, and other organizations.	See entry	$67,750
Wind Turbine Technicians	Wind turbine service technicians maintain and repair wind turbines.	Postsecondary nondegree award	$57,320
Woodworkers	Woodworkers manufacture a variety of products, such as cabinets and furniture, using wood, veneers, and laminates.	High school diploma or equivalent	$37,590
Writers and Authors	Writers and authors develop written content for various types of media.	Bachelor's degree	$73,150
Zoologists and Wildlife Biologists	Zoologists and wildlife biologists study animals, those both in captivity and in the wild, and how they interact with their ecosystems.	Bachelor's degree	$67,430

Glossary

A

Annual: recurring, done, or performed every year; yearly

Applicant: a person who formally applies for a job

Apprenticeship: a formal relationship between a worker and a sponsor that consists of a combination of on-the-job training and related occupation-specific instruction in which the worker learns the practical and theoretical aspects of an occupation. Apprenticeship programs are sponsored by individual employers, joint employer–labor groups, and employee associations. Apprenticeship programs usually provide at least 144 hours of occupation-specific technical instruction and 2,000 hours of on-the-job training per year over a 3- to 5-year period. Examples of occupations that utilize apprenticeships include *electricians* and *ironworkers*; see *On-the-job training*

Associate's degree: degree awarded usually for at least 2 years of full-time academic study beyond high school; see *Education*

Average: the quantity calculated by adding together the elements of a set of numbers and dividing the resulting sum by the quantity of numbers summed; see *Mean*

B

Baby-boom generation: individuals born between 1946 and 1964, inclusive

Bachelor's degree: degree awarded usually for at least 4 years of full-time academic study beyond high school; see *Education*

Base year: year used as a reference point for comparison with later years. For example, 2022 is the base year for the 2022–32 employment projections. Employment in the base year is actual 2022 data, whereas employment in the target, or projection, year is projected

Business cycle: the periods of growth and decline in an economy. There are four stages in the cycle: expansion, when the economy grows; peak, the high point of an expansion; contraction, when the economy slows down; and trough, the low point of a contraction

C

Certification: award for demonstrating competency in a skill or a set of skills, typically through work experience, training, and the passage of an examination, or some combination thereof. Some certification programs may require a certain level of educational achievement for eligibility

Consolidation: the merger of two or more commercial interests or corporations

Current Population Survey (CPS): a national survey that samples about 60,000 households on a monthly basis and collects information on labor force characteristics of the U.S. civilian noninstitutional population; the CPS is conducted by the Census Bureau for the Bureau of Labor Statistics

D

Demand for workers: total openings, resulting from employment growth and the need to replace workers who leave their occupation

Doctoral or professional degree: degree awarded usually for at least 3 years of full-time academic work beyond a bachelor's degree; for example, some science and other occupations need a doctoral degree, and all *lawyers, physicians,* and *dentists* need a professional degree for employment; see *Education*

Domestic sourcing: moving jobs to lower cost regions of the United States instead of to other countries

Duties: the major tasks or activities that employees in an occupation usually perform

E

Earnings: pay or wages of a worker or a group of workers for services performed during a specific period—for example, hourly, daily, weekly, or annually. Also see *Pay, Wages*

Education: levels of education typically needed for entry into an occupation are classified as follows:

Doctoral or professional degree: degree awarded usually for at least 3 years of full-time academic work beyond a bachelor's degree; for example, *lawyers, physicians and surgeons,* and *dentists*

Master's degree: degree awarded usually for 1 or 2 years of full-time academic study beyond a bachelor's degree

Bachelor's degree: degree awarded usually for at least 4 years of full-time academic study beyond high school

Associate's degree: degree awarded usually for at least 2 years of full-time academic study beyond high school

Postsecondary nondegree award: usually a certificate or other award that is not a degree and is issued by an educational institution. Certifications issued by professional organizations or certifying bodies are not included in this category. Programs may last only a few weeks to 2 years; for example, *nursing assistants, emergency medical technicians (EMTs) and paramedics,* and *hairstylists*

Some college, no degree: a high school diploma or the equivalent, plus the completion of one or more postsecondary courses that did not result in any degree or award

High school diploma or equivalent: the completion of high school or the equivalent, resulting in the award of a high school diploma or the equivalent

No formal educational credential: signifies that a formal credential issued by an educational institution, such as a high school diploma or a postsecondary certificate, is not typically needed for entry into the occupation; for example, *janitors and cleaners, cashiers,* and *agricultural equipment operators*

Employed: the situation of a person who has an agreement with an employer to work full time, part time, or on a contractual basis for that employer

Employment: the number of jobs in an occupation, including full-time jobs, part-time jobs, and self-employment

Employment growth/decline: increase/decrease in the number of jobs

Entry level: the starting level for workers who are new to an occupation; different occupations may require different levels of education, training, or experience upon entry

F

Fieldwork: an investigation or search for material, data, etc., such that the work is carried out in the field as opposed to the classroom, the laboratory, or official headquarters—for example, the work *archeologists* perform at a dig site in the desert; the work *historians* or *curators* engage in when they find or collect artifacts for museums; and the work *environmental technicians* do when they collect water samples from a pond, a stream, or an ocean

Five years or more (of work experience in a related occupation): the number of years of experience in a related occupation typically needed for entry into a given occupation; see *Work experience in a related occupation*

Fixed work schedules: schedules of employees who work the same hours on an ongoing basis—for example, 9 a.m.–5 p.m.; see *Work schedules*

Flexible work schedules: schedules of employees who set their own hours within specified guidelines and with a fixed number of total hours; see *Work schedules*

Full time: 35 or more hours per week, according to the Current Population Survey; see *Work schedules*

G

GDP (gross domestic product): the market value of all final goods and services produced within a country in a given period; the most commonly used measure of the size of the overall economy; the Bureau of Economic Analysis (BEA) produces estimates of GDP

Greater than full time: more than 40 hours per week; see *Work schedules*

Growth rate: the percent change in the number of jobs added or lost in a U.S. occupation or industry over a given projections decade; growth rate adjectives used in the OOH are defined by the following percent changes for the 2022–32 employment projections:

much faster than the average: increase 9 percent or more
faster than the average: increase 5 percent to 8 percent
as fast as the average: increase 2 percent to 4 percent
little or no change: decrease 1 percent to increase 1 percent
decline: decrease 2 percent or more

H

High school diploma or equivalent: award or credential that is equivalent to a high school diploma; see *Education*

Household: all persons who occupy a housing unit such as an apartment or a single-family home

I

Important qualities: characteristics and personality traits that are likely needed for workers to be successful in given occupations

Industry: a group of establishments that produce similar products or provide similar services; see *North American Industry Classification System (NAICS)*

Injury and illness: in general, a *Handbook* profile will discuss injuries and illnesses only if they are particularly high compared with the rate for all other occupations. Whether they meet this criterion is typically determined with the use of injury and illness data from the BLS Survey of Occupational Injuries and Illnesses (SOII) program. The "**Injuries and Illnesses**" section of each profile is used to discuss potential sources of accidents and injuries in the work environment.

Internship: training under supervision in a professional setting. This category does not include internships that are suggested for advancement; see *On-the-job training*

J

Job: a specific instance of employment; a position of employment to be filled at an establishment; *see Employment*

Job outlook: a statement that conveys the projected rate of growth or decline in employment in an occupation over the next 10 years; also compares the projected growth rate with that projected for all other occupations; see *Growth rate*

L

Labor force: the sum of all persons 16 years and older in the civilian noninstitutional population who are either employed, or unemployed but available for work and actively looking for work

Less than 5 years (of work experience in a related occupation): the number of years of experience in a related occupation typically needed for entry into a given occupation; see *Work experience in a related occupation*

Licenses: permissions granted by government agencies or other accrediting bodies that allow someone to work in a particular occupation or perform certain duties

Long-term on-the-job training: more than 12 months of on-the-job training, or, alternatively, combined work experience and formal classroom instruction (not including apprenticeships), that is needed for the worker to attain competency in the skills needed in the occupation; see *On-the-job training*

M

Master's degree: degree awarded usually for 1 or 2 years of full-time academic study beyond a bachelor's degree; see *Education*

Mean: the mathematical average of a set of numbers, calculated by adding the numbers together and dividing the result by the number of numbers summed; see *Average*

Median: the middle number in an ordered list consisting of an odd number of numbers; the average of the two middle numbers in an ordered list consisting of an even number of numbers

Moderate-term on-the-job training: more than 1 month, and up to 12 months, of combined on-the-job experience and informal training that is needed for the worker to attain competency in the skills needed in the occupation; see *On-the-job training*

N

New job: an addition of a position to an establishment's payroll, usually as a result of economic expansion

No formal educational credential: signifies that a formal credential issued by an educational institution, such as a high school diploma or a postsecondary certificate, is not typically needed for entry into the occupation; for example, *janitors and cleaners, cashiers,* and *agricultural equipment operators*; see *Education*

None (on-the-job training): no additional occupation-specific training or preparation is typically required for the worker to attain competency in an occupation; see *On-the-job training*

None (work experience in a related occupation): no work experience in a related occupation is typically required for the worker to enter a given occupation; see *Work experience in a related occupation*

Nonfixed work schedules: schedules of employees who work different hours on one job; often used to accommodate particular traits of individual workers or because the work required by the employer varies for each individual; see *Work schedules*

North American Industry Classification System (NAICS): industry classification system used by federal statistical agencies in classifying business establishments for the purpose of collecting, analyzing, and publishing statistical data related to the U.S. economy

Number of jobs: number of actual instances of employment, according to the BLS National Employment Matrix; see https://www.bls.gov/emp/documentation/projections-methods.htm for more information about the matrix

Numeric change in employment: a projected change in the number of jobs in an occupation or industry

O

Occupation: a craft, trade, profession, or other means of earning a living. Also, a set of activities or tasks that employees are paid to perform and that, together, go by a certain name. Employees who are in the same occupation perform essentially the same tasks, whether or not they work in the same industry

Occupational openings: opportunities to enter an occupation; openings occur when occupations grow, creating new jobs, and when workers leave an occupation permanently, resulting in the need to replace them

O*NET: an online research source that provides detailed descriptions of occupations for use by jobseekers, workforce development and human resources professionals, students, and researchers. Created for the U.S. Department of Labor, Employment and Training Administration, by the National Center for O*NET Development

On-the-job training: training or preparation that is typically needed for a worker, once employed in an occupation, to attain competency in the occupation. Training is occupation specific rather than job specific; skills learned can be transferred to another job in the same occupation.

Internship/residency: a formal period of training during which individuals work under the supervision of experienced workers in a professional setting, such as a hospital. Internships and residencies occur after the completion of a formal postsecondary degree program and generally are required for state licensure or certification in fields such as medicine, counseling, and architecture. During an internship or residency, trainees may be restricted from independently performing all of the functions of the occupation. Examples of occupations in the internship or residency category include *physicians and surgeons*, and *marriage and family therapists*. This category does not include internships that are suggested for advancement in one's career, such as a marketing internship, or internships that take place as part of a formal degree program.

Apprenticeship: a formal relationship between a worker and a sponsor that consists of a combination of on-the-job training and related occupation-specific instruction in which the worker learns the practical and theoretical aspects of an occupation. Apprenticeship programs are sponsored by individual employers, joint employer-labor groups, and employee associations. Apprenticeship programs usually provide at least 144 hours of occupation-specific technical instruction and 2,000 hours of on-the-job training per year over a 3- to 5-year period. Examples of occupations that utilize apprenticeships include *electricians* and *ironworkers*.

Long-term on-the-job training: more than 12 months of on-the-job training, or, alternatively, combined work experience and formal classroom instruction, that is needed for workers to develop the skills to attain competency in an occupation. This on-the-job training category also includes employer-sponsored training programs, such as those offered by fire academies and schools for *air traffic controllers*. In other occupations—*nuclear power reactor operators*, for example—trainees take formal courses, often provided at the jobsite, to prepare for the required licensing exams. In addition, the category includes occupations in which workers typically need to possess a natural ability or talent—*musicians and singers*, *athletes*, *dancers*, *photographers*, and *actors*, among others—and that ability or talent must be cultivated over several years, sometimes in a nonwork setting. The category excludes apprenticeships.

Moderate-term on-the-job training: more than 1 month, and up to 12 months, of combined on-the-job experience and informal training that is needed for the worker to develop the skills to attain competency in the occupation; this on-the-job training category also includes employer-sponsored training programs.

Short-term on-the-job training: 1 month or less of combined on-the-job experience and informal training that is needed for the worker to develop the skills to attain competency in the occupation; this on-the-job training category also includes employer-sponsored training programs.

None: no additional occupation-specific training or preparation is typically required for the worker to attain competency in the occupation.

P

Part time: less than 35 hours of work per week, according to the Current Population Survey; see *Work schedules*

Pay: earnings or wages of a worker or a group of workers for services performed during a specific period—for example, hourly, daily, weekly, or annually; also see *Earnings*, *Wages*

Percent: one part in a hundred. For example, 62 percent (also written "62%") means 62 parts out of 100

Percent change in employment: employment growth rates expressed as percentages

Percentile wage estimate: the value of a wage below which a certain percentage of workers fall

Personal consumption: total goods and services purchased by individuals in the U.S. economy; the amount of goods and services used or purchased by individuals or households in the U.S. economy; a key statistic in measuring or calculating overall GDP

Population: the total number of inhabitants of the United States; also, the total number of observations under consideration in a statistical study

Postsecondary nondegree award: a certificate or other credential that is awarded by an educational institution upon completion of formal postsecondary schooling. (The postsecondary nondegree certificate is different from certifications issued by professional organizations or certifying bodies.) Postsecondary nondegree award programs may last from just a few weeks to 2 years. Examples of those who need postsecondary nondegree awards are *nursing assistants*, *emergency medical technicians (EMTs) and paramedics*, and *hairstylists*; see *Education*

Q

Qualifications: personality traits, education, training, work experience, or other qualities workers need to enter an occupation

Qualities: characteristics and personality traits that are likely needed for workers to be successful in given occupations

R

Related occupations: occupations that have similar job duties; see *Similar occupations*

Residency: training under supervision in a professional setting; see *On-the-job training*

Rotating work schedules: schedules that have a fixed number of hours and time off, but no set weekly hours, over a period of more than 1 week; see *Work schedules*

S

Salary: earnings of a worker or a group of workers for services performed during a specific period—for example, an hourly straight-time wage rate or, for workers not paid on an hourly basis, straight-time earnings divided by hours worked

Seasonal employment: employment that is not expected to last a full year, but that may reoccur; for example, many *retail sales associates* are hired only for the busy holiday season, and forest *firefighters* are more likely to be employed during the summer months, when vegetation is dryer

Self-employed: those who work for profit or fees in their own business, profession, trade, or farm; only the unincorporated self-employed are included in the self-employed category

Short-term on-the-job training: 1 month or less of on-the-job experience and informal training; see *On-the-job training*

Similar occupations: occupations that tend to share common daily tasks or require similar skills, rather than similar wages or education

Some college, no degree: a high school diploma or the equivalent, plus the completion of one or more postsecondary courses that did not result in any degree or award; see *Education*

Standard Occupational Classification (SOC): the coding system used by all federal statistical agencies to classify workers into occupational categories for the purpose of collecting, calculating, or disseminating data

Supply of workers: the number of people in the labor force; for most occupations, the supply of workers is smaller than the total number in the labor force because the supply is limited to those with particular education or training requirements

T

Training: see *On-the-job training*

U

Union membership: the group of workers who join labor unions, hold union memberships, and enjoy benefits of the organized, coordinated efforts of the union to improve the work environment; also, the status of being a member of a union

V

Vocational school: a secondary school that teaches vocational trades, such as construction trades; vocational schools may or may not award degrees

W

Wages: earnings or pay of a worker or a group of workers for services performed during a specific period—for example, hourly, daily, weekly, or annually; also see *Earnings*, *Pay*

Work experience in a related occupation: the level of work experience in an occupation related to a given occupation; the work experience captures work experience that is commonly considered necessary by employers or is a commonly accepted substitute for other, more formal types of training or education

Five years or more: the number of years of experience in a related occupation typically needed for entry into a given occupation is more than 5 years

Less than 5 years: the number of years of experience in a related occupation typically needed for entry into a given occupation is less than 5 years

None: No work experience in a related occupation is typically needed for entry into a given occupation

Work schedules: the number of daily hours, weekly hours, and annual weeks that employees in an occupation are scheduled to, and do, work. Short-term fluctuations and one-time events are not considered, unless the change becomes permanent

Fixed work schedules: schedules under which employees who work those schedules do so on a continual basis, such as 9 a.m. to 5 p.m.

Flexible work schedules: schedules under which employees set their own hours within guidelines and with a fixed number of total hours

Nonfixed work schedules: schedules of employees who work different hours on one job; often utilized to accommodate particular traits of individual workers or because the work required varies by individual

Rotating work schedules: schedules that have a fixed number of hours and time off, but no set weekly hours, over a period of more than 1 week; see *Work schedules*

Full time: between 35 and 40 hours, inclusive, of work per week

Greater than full time: more than 40 hours of work per week

Part time: Less than 35 hours of work per week

Index